NEW DICTIONARY OF
BIBLICAL THEOLOGY

NEW DICTIONARY OF
BIBLICAL THEOLOGY

Editors:

T. Desmond Alexander
Director of Christian Training, Union Theological College, Belfast;
formerly Lecturer in Semitic Studies, Queen's University of Belfast

Brian S. Rosner
Formerly Lecturer in New Testament, University of Aberdeen; teaches at
Abbotsleigh and lectures at the Macquarie Christian Studies Institute in
Sydney, Australia

Consulting editors:

D. A. Carson
Research Professor of New Testament, Trinity Evangelical Divinity School,
Deerfield, Illinois

Graeme Goldsworthy
Lecturer in Old Testament and Biblical Theology,
Moore Theological College, Sydney

Organizing editor:

Steve Carter
Reference Books Editor, Inter-Varsity Press, Leicester

Inter-Varsity Press
Leicester, England

InterVarsity Press
Downers Grove, Illinois, USA

InterVarsity Press, USA
P.O. Box 1400
Downers Grove, IL 60515-1426, USA
World Wide Web: www.ivpress.com
Email: email@ivpress.com

Inter-Varsity Press, England
Norton Street
Nottingham NG7 3HR, England
Website: www.ivpbooks.com
Email: ivp@ivpbooks.com

©Inter-Varsity Press, 2000

InterVarsity Press®, USA, is the book-publishing division of InterVarsity Christian Fellowship/USA® <www.intervarsity.org> and a member movement of the International Fellowship of Evangelical Students.

Inter-Varsity Press, England, is closely linked with the Universities and Colleges Christian Fellowship, a student movement connecting Christian Unions in universities and colleges throughout Great Britain, and a member movement of the International Fellowship of Evangelical Students. Website: www.uccf.org.uk.

Quotations marked "NIV" are taken from the Holy Bible, New International Version®. NIV® . Copyright © 1973, 1978, 1984 by International Bible Society. Used by permission of Zondervan Publishing House. Distributed in the U.K. by permission of Hodder and Stoughton Ltd. All rights reserved. "NIV" is a registered trademark of International Bible Society. UK trademark number 1448790.

Quotations marked "NRSV" are from the New Revised Standard Version of the Bible, copyright 1989 by the Division of Christian Education of the National Council of the Churches of Christ in the USA. Used by permission. All rights reserved.

USA ISBN 978-0-8308-1438-1
UK ISBN 978-0-85111-976-2

Typeset in Great Britain
Set in Sabon
Printed in the United States of America ∞

Library of Congress Cataloging-in-Publication Data

New dictionary of biblical theology / general editors, T. Desmond Alexander & Brian S. Rosner.
   p. cm.
  Includes bibliographical references and index.
  ISBN 0-8308-1438-8 (cloth: alk. paper)
  1. Bible—Theology—Dictionaries.   I. Alexander, T. Desmond.   II. Rosner, Brian S.

  BS440.N437   2001
  230'.041'03—dc21

            00-047156

British Library Cataloguing in Publication Data

A catalogue record for this book is available from the British Library.

P	24	23	22	21	20	19	18	17	16	15	14	13	12	11	10	9
Y	25	24	23	22	21	20	19	18	17	16	15	14	13	12	11	

Contents

Preface

Throughout most of the 19th and 20th centuries biblical theology has undoubtedly been the Cinderella subject in the academic study of the Bible. Although knowledge of the Hebrew Old Testament and the Greek New Testament has increased remarkably in recent years, this has been, to a large extent, at the expense of our understanding of how these two parts of the Christian Bible relate to each other.

Against this background the Two Testaments Project was launched at the Swanwick Jubilee Conference of the Tyndale Fellowship for Biblical and Theological Research in July 1994. It was to be a co-operative venture involving the Biblical Theology Study Group of the Tyndale Fellowship and Rutherford House, Edinburgh. When a small planning group, consisting of Geoffrey Grogan (chairman), Desmond Alexander (secretary) and David Searle, subsequently presented the idea of a Dictionary of Biblical Theology to Frank Entwistle and David Kingdon of IVP, their enthusiasm for the project led to the appointment of Desmond Alexander and Brian Rosner as main editors, with Steve Carter of IVP as organizing editor and Don Carson and Graeme Goldsworthy as consulting editors.

As main editors our first tasks were to decide upon the format of the Dictionary and to commission authors. We opted for a tripartite arrangement, with Part One providing an introduction to the whole subject of biblical theology. The articles in this section are intended to provide the reader with a clear statement of the basis upon which the rest of the Dictionary is built. Part Two discusses the theology of those books of the OT and NT which are most commonly accepted as canonical within Christianity. The third section focuses on topics which, in our opinion, are of central importance for an understanding of the unity of the Biblical corpus. In the interests of keeping the volume to a manageable size, some sacrifice of detail has had to be made in these two sections. However, we hope that the Dictionary will prove to be a helpful resource for those who want to familiarize themselves with the Bible's theology.

To those who have contributed articles we are most grateful. The nature of this Dictionary sometimes required contributors to work beyond their own area of specialism. Experts in the OT were asked to interact with the NT, and vice versa. To each one who gave so patiently of time and energy in writing we are deeply indebted. We hope that the end result is a volume that not only brings together the best of evangelical scholarship from throughout the world, but also will be a stimulus to further research and writing in the somewhat neglected field of biblical theology.

Our task as editors was eased considerably by the thoughtful and meticulous attention given to this project by Steve Carter. His contribution has been enormous and for this he has our heartfelt thanks. We are also grateful to his many colleagues in IVP who have played a part in bringing this volume to completion, and to its freelance copy editor, Alison Walley. Finally, we have benefited greatly from the expertise of our two consulting editors, Don Carson and Graeme Goldsworthy. When our own abilities were stretched to the limit, they proved invaluable sources of knowledge and wisdom.

Editing this Dictionary has been a mind-expanding and heart-warming experience. We pray that those who use it will likewise find their minds expanded and their hearts warmed as they contemplate both the simplicity and the complexity of God's revelation to humanity. It is our hope that a better understanding of biblical theology, this Cinderella of subjects, will lead each reader to a deeper knowledge of Jesus Christ, the Prince of Life.

DESMOND ALEXANDER
BRIAN ROSNER

How to use this Dictionary

This introduction provides some guidance on how to use the Dictionary to the best advantage.

Arrangement
The Dictionary is arranged in three parts. Part One consists of twelve major articles, arranged thematically, on the fundamental issues of biblical theology. A list of subjects is provided on the Contents page. Part Two begins with seven articles, arranged in (approximately) canonical order, on the most important biblical corpora; these too are listed on the contents page. They are followed by articles, also arranged canonically, on the individual books of the Bible. Part Three consists of articles, arranged alphabetically, on major biblical themes.

Cross-references
It has been editorial policy in the Dictionary to group smaller topics together and treat them in a single larger article. For example, 'apostle' is dealt with in the article on MISSION, and 'predestination' in the article on ELECTION. Some of the major articles in Part One also cover a number of related topics.

Cross-referencing is therefore an important feature of the Dictionary.
1. Numerous one-line entries refer the reader to the title of the article in which the topic is treated, *e.g.* KNOWLEDGE, see WISDOM. All the Part One and Part Two articles have one-line entries, arranged alphabetically, in Part Three.
2. An asterisk before a word or phrase indicates that further relevant information will be found in the article under that title. It is equivalent to the abbreviation *q.v.* Please note that the form of the asterisked word will not always be precisely the same as that of the article to which the asterisk refers. For example, '*eschatological' refers to the article on ESCHATOLOGY, '*baptise' to BAPTISM, and '*kingship' to KINGDOM OF GOD.
3. A reference in brackets in the body of an article, such as '(see *Covenant)', is self-explanatory.
4. Cross-references at the end of an article are headed 'See also'. These refer to the other articles, usually in the same Part, most closely related to the subject-matter.

Abbreviations
A list of abbreviations used in the Dictionary will be found on pp. xi–xv.

Authorship of articles
The author's name is given at the end of each article. A complete list of contributors, in alphabetical order of surname, will be found on pp. xvi–xx. This information was correct at the time of publication.

Bibliographies
Guidance for further study has been provided in most articles, sometimes in the body of the article, but in most cases in the bibliography at the end. The works listed in the bibliography may include studies which take a different position from that of the author of the article.

Bible versions
The first time that the Bible is quoted in any article, the translation is identified in parentheses. All subsequent quotes in the same article are from that translation unless otherwise indicated.

How to use this dictionary

Transliteration
The following systems have been adopted throughout the volume:

Hebrew

א	=	'	ד	=	ḏ	י	=	y	ס	=	s	ר	=	r

אַ = '   ד = ḏ   י = y   ס = s   ר = r
ב = b   ה = h   כ = k   ע = '   שׂ = ś
ב = b   ו = w   כ = ḵ   פ = p   שׁ = š
ג = g   ז = z   ל = l   פ = p̄   ת = t
ג = ḡ   ח = ḥ   מ = m   צ = ṣ   ת = ṯ
ד = d   ט = ṭ   נ = n   ק = q

	Long Vowels			Short Vowels		Very Short Vowels
(ה)ָ = â	ָ = ā	ַ = a	ֲ = ᵃ
ֵ = ê	ֵ = ē	ֶ = e	ֱ = ᵉ
ִ = î		ִ = i	ְ = ᵉ (if vocal)
וֹ = ô	ֹ = ō	ָ = o	ֳ = ᵒ
וּ = û		ֻ = u	

Greek

α	=	a	ι	=	i	ρ	=	r	ῥ	=	rh
β	=	b	κ	=	k	σ, ς	=	s	ʽ	=	h
γ	=	g	λ	=	l	τ	=	t	γξ	=	nx
δ	=	d	μ	=	m	υ	=	y	γγ	=	ng
ε	=	e	ν	=	n	φ	=	ph	αυ	=	au
ζ	=	z	ξ	=	x	χ	=	ch	ευ	=	eu
η	=	ē	ο	=	o	ψ	=	ps	ου	=	ou
θ	=	th	π	=	p	ω	=	ō	υι	=	yι

Abbreviations

1. Books, journals and commentary series

AASF
Annales Academiae Scientarum Fennicae

AB
Anchor Bible

ABD
Anchor Bible Dictionary, ed. D. M. Freedman, 6 vols. (New York, 1992)

ABR
Australian Biblical Review

AJET
African Journal of Evangelical Theology

AJPS
Asian Journal of Pentecostal Studies

ANET
Ancient Near Eastern Texts Relating to the Old Testament, ed. J. B. Pritchard (Princeton, ³1969)

ANTC
Abingdon New Testament Commentaries

AUSS
Andrews University Seminary Studies

AV
Authorized Version

BAGD
Greek-English Lexicon of the New Testament and Other Early Christian Literature, W. Bauer, W. F. Arndt, F. W. Gingrich and F. W. Danker (Chicago, ³1999)

BASR
Biblical Archaeological Society Review

BBR
Bulletin for Biblical Research

BECNT
Baker Exegetical Commentary on the New Testament

BI
Biblical Interpretation

Bib
Biblica

BJRL
Bulletin of the John Rylands Library

BNTC
Black's New Testament Commentary

BR
Bible Review

BRR
Biblical Reformation Review

BS
Bibliotheca Sacra

BST
Bible Speaks Today

BTB
Biblical Theology Bulletin

CBQ
Catholic Biblical Quarterly

CC
Communicator's Commentary

CT
Christianity Today

CTJ
Calvin Theological Journal

CurrTM
Currents in Theology and Mission

DBTE
Dictionary of Biblical Tradition in English, ed. D. L. Jeffrey (Grand Rapids, 1992)

DJG
Dictionary of Jesus and the Gospels, eds. J. B. Green, S. McKnight and I. H. Marshall (Downers Grove and Leicester, 1992)

DLNTD
Dictionary of the Later New Testament and its Developments, eds. R. P. Martin and P. H. Davids (Downers Grove and Leicester, 1997)

DPL
Dictionary of Paul and his Letters, eds. G. F. Hawthorne, R. P. Martin and D. G. Reid (Downers Grove and Leicester, 1994)

DSB
Daily Study Bible

EA
Ex Auditu

EBC
Expositor's Bible Commentary

EDBT
Evangelical Dictionary of Biblical Theology, ed. W. A. Elwell (Grand Rapids and Carlisle, 1996)

EDNT
Exegetical Dictionary of the New Testament, eds. H. Balz and G. Schneider, 3 vols. (ET, Grand Rapids and Edinburgh, 1990–93)

EGGNT
Exegetical Guide to the Greek New Testament

EJ
Encyclopaedia Judaica

EKK
Evangelisch-katholischer Kommentar zum Neuen Testament

EKL
Evangelisches Kirchenlexikon, eds. E. Fahlbusch, J. M. Lochman, J. Mbiti *et. al.* (Göttingen, ³1986–96)

EPC
Epworth Preachers Commentaries

ETL
Ephemerides theologicae lovaniense

EvBC
Everyman's Bible Commentary

EvQ
Evangelical Quarterly

Gratz
Gratz College Annual of Jewish Studies

HAT
Handbuch zum Alten Testament

HBT
Horizons in Biblical Theology

HCOT
Historical Commentary on the Old Testament

HDB
Dictionary of the Bible, ed. J. Hastings, 5 vols. (Edinburgh, 1898–1904)

HS
Hebrew Studies

HTKNT
Herders theologischer Kommentar zum Neuen Testament

HTR
Harvard Theological Review

HWP
Historisches Wörterbuch der Philosophie, eds. J. Ritter and K. Gründer (Basle and Darmstadt, 1971)

ICC
International Critical Commentary

IDB
Interpreter's Dictionary of the Bible, ed. K. R. Crim, 4 vols. (Nashville, ²1993–95)

IDBSup
Interpreter's Dictionary of the Bible, Supplementary Volume, ed. K. R. Crim (Nashville, 1976)

Int
Interpretation

ISBE
International Standard Bible Encyclopedia, ed. G. W. Bromiley, 4 vols. (Grand Rapids, 1979–88)

IVPNTC
IVP New Testament Commentaries

JBL
Journal of Biblical Literature

JBP
J. B. Phillips version

JBR
Journal of Bible and Religion

JETS
Journal of the Evangelical Theological Society

JNES
Journal of Near Eastern Studies

JPSTC
Jewish Publication Society Torah Commentary

JPSV
Jewish Publication Society Version

JSNT
Journal for the Study of the New Testament

JSOT
Journal for the Study of the Old Testament

JSS
Journal of Semitic Studies

JTS
Journal of Theological Studies

Jud
Judaica

KEK
Kritisch-Exegetischer
Kommentar

Louw-Nida
*Greek-English Lexicon of
the New Testament*, eds.
J. P. Louw and E. A.
Nida (New York, ²1989)

LS
Louvain Studies

MeyerK
Meyer Kommentar

MSJ
Master's Seminary
Journal

NASB
New American Standard
Bible

NBD
New Bible Dictionary,
eds. I. H. Marshall, A. R.
Millard, J. I. Packer and
D. J. Wiseman (Leicester
and Downers Grove,
1996)

NCB
New Century Bible

NDCEPT
*New Dictionary of
Christian Ethics and
Pastoral Theology*, eds.
D. J. Atkinson and D. H.
Field (Leicester and
Downers Grove, 1995)

NDT
*New Dictionary of
Theology*, eds. S. B.
Ferguson and D. F.
Wright (Leicester and
Downers Grove, 1988)

NIB
New Interpreter's Bible,
ed. L. E. Keck et al, 12
vols. (Nashville, 1994–)

NIBC
New International
Biblical Commentary

NICNT
New International
Commentary on the New
Testament

NICOT
New International
Commentary on the Old
Testament

NIDNTT
*New International
Dictionary of New
Testament Theology*, ed.
C. Brown, 4 vols.
(Carlisle, 1988)

NIDOTTE
*New International
Dictionary of Old
Testament Theology and
Exegesis*, ed. W. A. Van-
Gemeren, 5 vols. (Grand
Rapids and Carlisle,
1997)

NIGTC
New International Greek
Testament Commentary

NIV
New International
Version

NKJV
New King James Version

NLC
New London
Commentary

NLT
New Living Translation

NovT
Novum Testamentum

NRSV
New Revised Standard
Version

NTS
New Testament Studies

NTT
New Testament Theology

OTG
Old Testament Guides

OTL
Old Testament Library

PNTC
Pillar New Testament
Commentary

PWCJS
*Proceedings of the World
Congress of Jewish
Studies*

RevExp
Review and Expositor

RGG
*Die Religion in
Geschichte und
Gegenwart*, ed. K.
Galling (Tübingen,
³1957–65)

RTR
Reformed Theological
Review

SBET
Scottish Bulletin of
Evangelical Theology

SBLSP
*Society of Biblical
Literature Seminar Papers*

SE
Studia Evangelica

SJOT
*Scandinavian Journal of
the Old Testament*

SJT
Scottish Journal of
Theology

TDNT
*Theological Dictionary of
the New Testament*, ed.
G. W. Bromiley, 10 vols.
(Grand Rapids, 1964–
76), ET of *Theologisches
Wörterbuch zum Neuen
Testament*, eds. G. Kittel
and G. Friedrich
(Stuttgart, 1932–74)

TDOT
*Theological Dictionary of
the Old Testament*, eds.
G. J. Botterweck and H.
Ringgren, 8 vols. (Grand
Rapids, 1978–96), ET of
*Theologisches
Wörterbuch zum Alten
Testament* (Stuttgart,
1970–)

Them
Themelios

ThZ
Theologische Zeitschrift

TJ
Trinity Journal

TLOT
*Theological Lexicon of
the Old Testament*, ed. C.
Spicq, 3 vols. (ET,
Peabody, 1995)

TNTC
Tyndale New Testament
Commentaries

TOTC
Tyndale Old Testament
Commentaries

TPINTC
Trinity Press
International New
Testament Commentaries

TS
Theological Studies

TT
Theology Today

TWAT
See *TDOT*

TynB
Tyndale Bulletin

VE
Vox Evangelica

VT
Vetus Testamentum

WBC
Word Biblical
Commentary

WBT
Word Biblical Themes

WEC
Wycliffe Exegetical
Commentary

WTJ
Westminster Theological
Journal

WW
Word and World

ZAW
Zeitschrift für die
alttestamentliche
Wissenschaft

ZNW
*Zeitschrift für die
neutestamentliche
Wissenschaft*

ZThK
Zeitschrift für Theologie
und Kirche

2. Biblical books

Books of the Old Testament

Gen., Exod., Lev., Num., Deut., Josh., Judg., Ruth, 1,2 Sam., 1,2 Kgs., 1,2 Chr., Ezra,
Neh., Est., Job, Ps.(Pss.), Prov., Eccles., Song, Is., Jer., Lam., Ezek., Dan., Hos., Joel,
Amos, Obad., Jonah, Mic., Nah., Hab., Zeph., Hag., Zech., Mal.

Books of the New Testament

Matt., Mark, Luke, John, Acts, Rom., 1,2 Cor., Gal., Eph., Phil., Col., 1,2 Thess., 1,2
Tim., Titus, Philem., Heb., Jas., 1,2 Pet., 1,2,3 John, Jude, Rev.

3. General abbreviations

ad loc	at the place	Macc.	Maccabees (Apocrypha)
Aram.	Aramaic	mg.	margin
c.	about, approximately	MS(S)	manuscript(s)
cf.	compare	MT	Masoretic Text
ch(s).	chapter(s)	n	note
Ecclus.	Ecclesiasticus (Apocrypha)	n.d.	no date
ed(s).	editor(s)	no.	number
edn	edition	n.s.	new series
e.g.	for example	NT	New Testament
esp.	especially	OT	Old Testament
ET	English translation	p(p).	page(s)
et al.	and others	par.	and parallel
etc.	and so on	pl.	plural
EVV	English versions	repr.	reprinted
f.ff.	and the following	*sic.*	thus
Gk.	Greek	sing.	singular
Heb.	Hebrew	tr.	translated, translation
idem	the same author	v., vv.	verse, verses
i.e.	that is to say	*viz.*	namely
lit.	literally	vol(s).	volume(s)
loc. cit.	in the place already quoted	vss	versions
LXX	Septuagint (Gk. version of OT)		

List of Contributors

P J H Adam, BD, MTh, PhD, Vicar of St Jude's Carlton, Melbourne, Australia

T Desmond Alexander, BA, PhD, Director of Christian Training, Union Theological College, Belfast, formerly Lecturer in Semitic Studies, The Queen's University of Belfast

Carl E Armerding, AB, BD, MA, PhD, Director, Schloss Mittersill Study Centre, Austria

Bill T Arnold, BA, MDiv, PhD, Professor of Old Testament and Semitic Languages, Asbury Theological Seminary, USA

David W Baker, AB, MCS, MPhil, PhD, Professor of Old Testament and Semitic Languages, Ashland Theological Seminary, USA

Peter Balla, MDiv, MTh, PhD, Lecturer and Head of the New Testament Department of the Faculty of Theology of the Károli Gáspár Reformed University, Budapest, Hungary

Robert J Banks, BA, BD, MTh, PhD, Homer L Goddard Professor of the Ministry of the Laity, Fuller Theological Seminary, USA

Craig G Bartholomew, BTh, MA, PhD, Research Fellow in the School of Theology and Religious Studies, Cheltenham and Gloucester College of Higher Education

Gregory K Beale, BA, MA, ThM, PhD, The Kenneth T Wessner Chair of Biblical Studies, Wheaton College Graduate School, USA; formerly Professor of New Testament at Gordon-Conwell Theological Seminary, USA

Roger T Beckwith, MA, BD, DD, former Warden of Latimer House, Oxford

Henri A G Blocher, BD, Diplôme d'Etudes Supérieures de Théologie, DD, Professor of Systematic Theology (and Dean Emeritus), Faculté Libre de Théologie Evangélique, Vaux-sur-Seine, France

Craig L Blomberg, BA, MA, PhD, Professor of New Testament, Denver Seminary, USA

Darrell L Bock, AB, ThM, PhD, Research Professor of New Testament Studies, Dallas Theological Seminary, USA

Gerald L Borchert, PhD, ThM, MDiv, LLB, BA, Professor of New Testament and Director of Doctoral Studies, Northern Baptist Theological Seminary, USA

N E Lennart Boström, MTh, DTh, Lecturer in Old Testament, Örebro Theological Seminary, Sweden

Gerald L Bray, BA, MLitt, DLitt, Anglican Professor of Divinity, Beeson Divinity School, Samford University, USA

Kent E Brower, BSL, MA, PhD, Dean, Nazarene Theological College, Manchester

D A Carson, Research Professor of New Testament, Trinity Evangelical Divinity School, USA

Robert B Chisholm, Jr, BA, MDiv, ThM, ThD, Professor of Old Testament Studies, Dallas Theological Seminary, USA

Roy E Ciampa, BA MDiv, PhD, Lecturer in Biblical Studies, College of Evangelical Theological Education, Portugal

Andrew D Clarke, MA, PhD, Lecturer in New Testament, Department of Divinity with Religious Studies, University of Aberdeen

Edmund P Clowney, AB, ThB, STM, DD, Professor of Practical Theology, Emeritus

F Peter Cotterell, BD, BSc, PhD, DUniv, FRSA, Director, Ethiopian Graduate School of Theology; formerly Principal, London Bible College, Northwood

Peter H Davids, BA, MDiv, PhD, Innsbruck, Austria

Stephen G Dempster, BA, MAR, ThM, MA, PhD, Associate Professor of Religious Studies, Atlantic Baptist University, Canada

John W Drane, MA, PhD, DD, Head of Practical Theology, Department of Divinity with Religious Studies, University of Aberdeen

Iain M Duguid, BSc, MDiv, PhD, Associate Professor of Old Testament, Westminster Theological Seminary in California, USA

Paul Ellingworth, PhD, former Honorary Professor, University of Aberdeen

Mark W Elliott, BA, BD, PhD, Lecturer in Christian Studies, Liverpool Hope University College

Kevin S Ellis, BA, PhD, Anglican Ordinand, The Queen's College, Birmingham

Peter E Enns, PhD, MA, MDiv, BA, Associate Professor of Old Testament, Westminster Theological Seminary, Philadelphia

Craig A Evans, BA, MA, PhD, Professor of Biblical Studies, Trinity Western University, Canada

Mary J Evans, BEd, BA, MPhil, Course Leader for BTh and Lecturer in OT, London Bible College, Northwood

Buist M Fanning, BA, ThM, DPhil, Professor of New Testament Studies, Dallas Theological Seminary, USA

Michael O Fape, BA, STM, PhD, Lecturer in New Testament Studies, Immanuel College of Theology, Nigeria

Richard B Gaffin, Jr, ThD, ThM, BD, AB, Professor of Biblical and Systematic Theology, Westminster Theological Seminary, Philadelphia, USA

Thomas D Gledhill, BA, MA, BD, PhD, Lecturer in Biblical Studies, Evangelical Theological College of Wales

Graeme L Goldsworthy, BA, ThL, BD, MA, ThM, PhD, formerly Lecturer in Old Testament and Biblical Theology, Moore Theological College, Australia

Murray D Gow, MA, BD, ThD, Lecturer, Schloss Mittersill Study Centre, Austria

G L Green, AB, MA, PhD, Associate Professor of New Testament, Wheaton College, USA

Joel B Green, BS, MTh, PhD, Dean of the School of Theology, Director of Greek Studies and Professor of New Testament Interpretation, Asbury Theological Seminary, USA

Geoffrey W Grogan, BD, MTh, DUniv, formerly Principal, Glasgow Bible College

Wayne A Grudem, BA, MDiv, PhD, Professor and Chairman, Department of Biblical and Systematic Theology, Trinity Evangelical Divinity School, USA

Donald A Hagner, BA, BD, ThM, PhD, George Eldon Ladd Professor of New Testament, Fuller Theological Seminary, USA

Victor P Hamilton, BA, BD, ThM, MA, PhD, Professor of Religion, Asbury College, USA

Murray J Harris, MA, Dip Ed, BD, PhD, Professor Emeritus, Trinity Evangelical Divinity School, USA

Ian Hart, BA, BD, MTh, ThD, Minister of Great Victoria Street Presbyterian Church, Belfast

Richard S Hess, BA, MDiv, ThM, PhD, Professor of Old Testament, Denver Seminary, USA

Harold W Hoehner, BA, ThM, ThD, PhD, Chairman and Distinguished Professor of New Testament and Director of PhD Studies, Dallas Theological Seminary, USA

Robert L Hubbard, Jr., AB, BD, MA, PhD, Professor of Biblical Literature, North Park Theological Seminary, USA

Paul E Hughes, BA, MA, PhD, Associate Professor of Religious Studies, Trinity Western University, Canada

David Instone Brewer, BD, PhD, Research Librarian, Tyndale House, Cambridge

D H Johnson, BS, ThM, PhD, Professor of New Testament, Providence Theological Seminary, Canada

Philip S Johnston, BA, BD, MTh, PhD, Tutor, Wycliffe Hall, Oxford

Brian E Kelly, BA, PGCE, BA, PhD, Dean of Chapel, Canterbury Christ Church University College, Canterbury

Gillian Keys, BA, Grad Cert Ed, PhD, Head of Religious Studies, Sullivan Upper School, Co. Down

David P Kingdon, MA, BD, Managing Editor, Bryntirion Press, Bridgend

Nobuyoshi Kiuchi, BA, PhD, Professor of Old Testament, Tokyo Christian University, Japan

Andreas J Köstenberger, PhD, MDiv, Professor of New Testament, Southeastern Baptist Theological Seminary, USA

Colin G Kruse, BD, MPhil, PhD, Lecturer in New Testament, Bible College of Victoria, Australia

Hans Kvalbein, DTh, Professor, The Norwegian Lutheran School of Theology, Norway

Jon C Laansma, BRE, MDiv, PhD, Assistant Professor of Bible, Moody Bible Institute, USA

Tremper Longman III, BA, MDiv, MPhil, PhD, Professor of Old Testament, Westmont College, USA

Ernest C Lucas, BA, MA, PhD, Vice-Principal and Tutor in Biblical Studies, Bristol Baptist College

Jonathan M Lunde, PhD, ThM, MDiv, BS, Assistant Professor of Biblical Studies, The College of Arts and Sciences, Trinity International University, USA

Robert G Maccini, PhD, MDiv, BA, Adjunct Professor of New Testament, Bangor Theological Seminary, USA

Kenneth Magnuson, BA, MDiv, PhD, Assistant Professor of Christian Ethics at Southern Baptist Theological Seminary, USA

Ernest B Manges, BA, MA, MDiv, Lecturer in Theology and Church History, Evangelical Theological College of the Philippines

I Howard Marshall, MA, BD, BA, PhD, DD, Honorary Research Professor of New Testament, University of Aberdeen

Kenneth A Mathews, BA, ThM, MA, PhD, Professor of Divinity, Beeson Divinity School, Samford University, USA

Leslie McFall, BA, MTh, PhD, Researcher, Cambridge

Robert J McKelvey, BA, MTh, DPhil, formerly Principal of Northern College, Manchester

James McKeown, BD, PhD, Vice Principal, Belfast Bible College

Scot McKnight, BA, MA, PhD, Karl A Olsson Professor in Religious Studies, North Park University, Chicago, USA

J Gary Millar, BSc, BD, DPhil, Minister, Howth and Malahide Presbyterian Church, Dublin

Douglas J Moo, BA, MDiv, PhD, Professor, Wheaton Graduate School, USA

Thorsten Moritz, BA, MA, PhD, Senior Lecturer in New Testament, Cheltenham & Gloucester College of Higher Education

J Alec Motyer, MA, BD, DD, Retired Vicar of Christ Church, Westbourne, Bournemouth

Stephen Motyer, BA, MA, MLitt, PhD, Lecturer, London Bible College, Northwood

Raymond C Ortlund, Jr., BA, MA, ThM, PhD, Senior Minister, First Presbyterian Church, Augusta, Georgia, USA

Lawrence H Osborn, BSc, MSc, BD, PhD, Glasgow

William Osborne, BA, MA, MPhil, Lecturer in Hebrew and Old Testament and Co-ordinator for Postgraduate Studies, Bible College of New Zealand, New Zealand

John N Oswalt, AB, BD, ThM, MA, PhD, Research Professor of Old Testament, Wesley Biblical Seminary, USA

J I Packer, MA, DPhil, DD, Board of Governors Professor of Theology, Regent College, Canada

Christine E Palmer, MA, MAR, PhD student, formerly Co-ordinator of Semlink at Gordon-Conwell Theological Seminary, USA

David G Peterson, MA, BD, PhD, Principal, Oak Hill Theological College, London

Christine D Pohl, PhD, MA, BSc, Professor of Social Ethics, Asbury Theological Seminary, USA

Stanley E Porter, BA, MA, PhD, Professor of Theology and Head of the Department of Theology and Religious Studies, University of Surrey, Roehampton

B Ward Powers, BA, BD, Dip RE, BComm, MA, PhD, Director, Tyndale College, Australia

Iain W Provan, MA, BA, PhD, Marshall Sheppard Professor of Biblical Studies, Regent College, Canada

Daniel G Reid, BA, MDiv, PhD, Senior Editor, Inter-Varsity Press, USA

Thomas Renz, PhD, Tutor in Old Testament, Oak Hill College, London

Rainer Riesner, Dr theol. habil., Professor of New Testament, University of Dortmund, Germany

Brian S. Rosner is Senior Lecturer in New Testament and Ethics, Moore Theological College, and Honorary Senior Research Fellow in Ancient History, Macquarie University, both in Sydney; formerly Lecturer in New Testament, University of Aberdeen.

Philip E Satterthwaite, BA, MA, PhD, Lecturer in Old Testament and Hebrew, Biblical Graduate School of Theology, Singapore

Eckhard J Schnabel, PhD, Associate Professor of New Testament, Trinity Evangelical Divinity School, USA

Thomas R Schreiner, BS, MDiv, ThM, PhD, Professor of New Testament, The Southern Baptist Theological Seminary, USA

Richard L Schultz, BA, MDiv, MA, PhD, Professor of Old Testament, Wheaton College, USA

Charles H H Scobie, MA, BD, STM, PhD, DD, Former Cowan Professor of Religious Studies, and Head, Department of Religious Studies, Mount Allison University, Canada

David C Searle, MA, Warden, Rutherford House, Edinburgh

Mark A Seifrid, MDiv, MA, PhD, Associate Professor of New Testament, The Southern Baptist Theological Seminary, USA

Martin J Selman, BA, MA, PhD, Deputy Principal, Spurgeon's College, London

Andrew G Shead, BTh, BSc (Med), MTh, PhD, Lecturer in Old Testament, Moore Theological College, Australia.

Stephen S Smalley, MA, BD, PhD, Dean of Chester

Joel R Soza, MA, Assistant Professor in Biblical Studies, Malone College, USA

Christoph W Stenschke, MDiv, MTh, PhD, Minister, German Baptist Union, Elstal, Germany

Mark L Strauss, PhD, ThM, MDiv, BA, Associate Professor of New Testament, Bethel Seminary, USA

Stephen S Taylor, BA, MA, Associate Professor of New Testament at Westminster Theological Seminary, Philadelphia, USA

List of Contributors

Anthony C Thiselton, BD, MTh, PhD, DD, Professor of Christian Theology and Head of Department of Theology, University of Nottingham; also Canon Theologian of Leicester Cathedral

Derek J Tidball, BA, BD, PhD, Principal, London Bible College

Philip H Towner, BA, MA, PhD, Translation Consultant, United Bible Societies and Adjunct Professor of New Testament, Regent College, Canada

David T Tsumura, BS, MDiv, MA, PhD, Professor of Old Testament, Japan Bible Seminary, Tokyo.

Laurence A Turner, BA, MDiv, ThM, PhD, Senior Lecturer in Old Testament and Head of the Department of Theological Studies, Newbold College, Bracknell

Max Turner, MA, PhD, Professor of New Testament Studies, and Vice Principal for Academic Affairs, London Bible College, Northwood

Graham H Twelftree, BA, MA, PhD, Senior Pastor, North Eastern Vineyard Church, Adelaide, Australia

Gerard Van Groningen, BA, BD, ThM, MA, PhD, President of Trinity Christian College, USA; Retired Adjunct Professor of Old Testament, Covenant Theology Seminary, USA

Kevin J Vanhoozer, BA, MDiv, PhD, Research Professor of Systematic Theology, Trinity International University, USA

Åke Viberg, Dr, Senior Lecturer in Old Testament, Sweden

Peter W L Walker, MA, PhD, Lecturer in New Testament, Wycliffe Hall, Oxford

Rikki E Watts, ARMIT, MA, MDiv, PhD, Associate Professor of New Testament, Regent College, Canada

H H Drake Williams III, PhD, MDiv, BA, BS, Associate Minister, Central Schwenkfelder Church; Adjunct Faculty Member, Biblical Theological Seminary, USA

Stephen N Williams, MA, PhD, Professor of Systematic Theology, Union Theological College, Belfast

Paul R Williamson, BD, PhD, Lecturer in Old Testament, Irish Baptist College, Belfast

Paul D Woodbridge, BA, PhD, Academic Dean and Tutor in New Testament, Oak Hill College, London

Robert W Yarbrough, PhD, MA, BA, Associate Professor of New Testament Studies, Trinity Evangelical Divinity School, USA

PART ONE

Biblical Theology

Biblical theology is integral to the whole process of discerning the meaning of the biblical text and of applying this meaning to the contemporary scene. While we distinguish it from other theological disciplines, such as systematics, historical theology, apologetics and practical theology, its relationship to these disciplines is one of interdependence. Because biblical theology is the fruit of exegesis of the texts of the various biblical corpora it has a logical priority over systematics and the other specialized types of theologizing. However, the mutuality of the disciplines can be seen in our coming to the task of exegesis with certain dogmatic presuppositions about the nature and authority of the Bible. Furthermore, the history of theology and of biblical interpretation means that we engage in our task as biblical theologians from within a living tradition of the Christian church. Biblical theology is principally concerned with the overall theological message of the whole Bible. It seeks to understand the parts in relation to the whole and, to achieve this, it must work with the mutual interaction of the literary, historical, and theological dimensions of the various corpora, and with the interrelationships of these within the whole canon of Scripture. Only in this way do we take proper account of the fact that God has spoken to us in Scripture.

Although arguably the most demanding type of Bible study, ironically biblical theology holds the greatest interest outside the academy, *i.e.* in the Christian church and for ordinary Christians, promoting as it does a high view not only of the Bible, but also of Jesus and the gospel. Most Christians have a genuine interest in the worlds of the Bible, in its language, thought forms, archaeology, geography and history (the subject matter of a conventional Bible dictionary). Most also like to engage in the interpretation of individual passages (the function of a Bible commentary). However, all Christians have an intensely personal interest, or more accurately stake, in the subject of biblical theology, *i.e.* what the Bible teaches about God and his dealings with the human race. And biblical theology of one sort or another, whether acknowledged as such or not, is usually what is going on when the Bible is preached effectively, studied rigorously or read intently by Christian believers.

Of course, not everyone has so positive a view of the discipline. There are some who deny its viability, if not its right to exist. They question its presuppositions, arguing that the the canon was a late decision of the church, that 'orthodoxy' was a late and artificial imposition, and that the books of the Bible present manifold and contradictory theologies. They also believe that literary theory and the social sciences introduce factors that make biblical theology disreputable (see *Challenges to Biblical Theology).

On the other hand, there are doubtless those who may wonder what other sort of theology there could possibly be for Christians if the Bible is supposed to be the foundation of our faith and practice. However, there is no doubt that many theologies are not biblical, just as many studies of the Bible are not theological (see *Systematic Theology and Biblical Theology).

What exactly is biblical theology? It is imperative that we understand what biblical theology is, for the *history of biblical theology shows that confusion ensues and distortions arise when practitioners are not clear about what they are doing. There are in fact a number of valid answers to the question of what biblical theology is, just as there are a number of answers to the question of what civil engineering is, for instance, depending on which way we look at the subject.

To make the comparison clear, civil engineering may be defined as the activity which results from the cooperation of various disciplines including metallurgy, physics, mathematics, sociology and town planning with the goal of producing bridges, sewers, roads, canals, *etc.* It may also be defined as the physical activity of construction in all its vigour and complexity. Similarly, biblical theology may be defined as the cooperation of various disciplines, and with reference to its various processes or methods and its intended product.

The primacy of biblical theology

The Bible is not only the best selling, but also the most studied book of all time. Theologians have pored over its pages for hundreds of years, and most branches of the humanities have brought their expertise to bear on the task of examining it. English departments study it for its aesthetic value, for the way its narratives and poetry enthral and move readers. Sociologists are fascinated by the group dynamics it enshrines, anthropologists by the power of its rites and symbols, and historians by the impact of its movements and ideas on the course of the world at large.

Without questioning the legitimacy of the Bible as an object of academic study for a wide range of disciplines, biblical theology urges that the interpretation of the text cannot be left there. Biblical theology is not just one of a number of ways to read the Bible, as if there is theologically motivated interpretation alongside historically, aesthetically or ideologically motivated interpretation. Not to attend to theological interpretation is to stop short of interpretation, to ignore the interests of the texts themselves. If not to misinterpret, at best it is to engage in incomplete interpretation. Biblical study is incomplete until biblical theology has been done.

The books of the Bible are first and foremost religious texts. To ignore this dimension is forgivable, if one's interests lie elsewhere. No one would dispute the legitimacy of studying Shakespeare's plays for their artistry and language, or to consider the evidence they provide of the social mores or political conventions of their day, or to trace their impact on the history of literature and ideas. But to do only this is by no means to engage in the interpretation of Shakespeare. The same principle applies to the Bible.

Biblical theology as multidisciplinary endeavour

The biblical theologian needs all the help he or she can get from the other areas of biblical and theological study. Indeed, biblical theology must never be thought of as independent of the other disciplines. It presupposes them. In reading the Bible it does not neglect history, for theology is grounded in the revelation of God in history and salvation history is part of real history. Thus biblical theology avoids an atemporal approach and pays close attention to the Bible's overarching 'story'. As well as recognizing the profoundly historical rootedness of the biblical books, it also accepts their occasional nature, literary quality and powerful vitality. And it treats such texts with a due sensitivity to the different genres and literary features represented. Biblical theology is impossible without the contributions of those disciplines which take as their focus the historical and literary dimensions of the Bible.

Strangely enough, within the so-called theological disciplines there has been a neglect of the theological interpretation of Scripture. This is in part due to the explosion of knowledge and the practice of specialization which has led to a compartmentalizing of the disciplines. Biblical scholars, for the purpose of division of labour, divide themselves into OT or NT specialists, and even within these divisions specialize further, in for instance the Pentateuch, wisdom or prophecy, or the Gospels, Paul or Hebrews. Such boundaries become barriers to the extent that no one accepts the responsibility of reading the Bible as a whole. On the contrary, such reading is positively discouraged, as trespassing on someone else's territory and feigning expertise in an area where one is not well versed. Worse still, systematic theologians are discouraged from using Scripture too specifically for the same reason, in order not to seem naive in their exegesis of biblical texts. Without denying the immensity of the intellectual challenge, biblical theology calls for the disciplines to work together towards a common goal. As Francis Watson states, 'biblical theology is an interdisciplinary approach to biblical interpretation which seeks to dismantle the barriers that at present separate biblical scholarship from Christian theology' (*Text and Truth*, p. vii).

Biblical theology as engaged, theological interpretation of Scripture

As noted above, different readers of the Bible treat it differently, depending on the nature of their interest in it. The Bible is everything from ancient artefact to historical testimony to entertaining literature. How the biblical texts are construed distinguishes the different approaches to the Bible. Biblical theology considers the biblical texts to be Christian Scripture and its reading of them is shaped accordingly (see *Scripture). It affirms that

Scripture was written not just for historians and literary critics, but for Christian believers, 'for us' (Rom. 4:24; 1 Cor. 9:10; NIV) and 'for our instruction' (1 Cor. 10:11; RSV).

Indeed the primary location for a theological interpretation of Scripture is the church rather than the university (S. Fowl and L. Jones, *Reading in Communion*). Biblical theology is practised by Christian communities and is intricately linked to their determination to shape their faith, life, worship and service in accordance with Scripture under the guidance of the Spirit (see *Preaching and Biblical Theology). One of the achievements of modern hermeneutics is to lay to rest the fallacy of the dispassionate, disinterested reader. All of us bring to the Bible pre-understandings and pre-dispositions which affect what we make of what we read. Purely objective interpretation is not only a myth but an inappropriate strategy for reading the Bible. For biblical theology, the primary goal of exegesis is not objectivity but to hear Scripture as the word of God.

This is not to say that OT or NT scholars ought not to do biblical theology (contra H. Räisänen). They are in the privileged position of having direct access to the literary and historical study of the Bible upon which biblical theology must build. Rather, it is to say that when Christian biblical scholars read the Bible they ought to read it as Christians, reflecting on their own faith in the light of what they read. Biblical scholars who do not share this faith are of course also able to do biblical theology, in the sense of describing the theology of (say) Paul or even of some theme across the canon. But they do so as outsiders, so to speak, not with sympathy and consent, which is the ideal hermeneutic for biblical theology.

Texts assume a certain kind of audience, someone who is best disposed to make sense of what is written, the person or group for whom the texts are intended (M. Bockmuehl, in *SJT* 51, pp. 298–300). In the case of the Bible the implied or model readers are those who care about what the texts assert and affirm. Such readers believe the apostolic witness to God's work in Jesus Christ, even though they 'have not seen' (1 Pet. 1:8). They have undergone a religious, moral and intellectual conversion to the gospel of which the texts speak. They live their lives as part of a local community of faith. Even texts like Luke-Acts and the Pastoral Epistles, though written to individuals, make clear that their ultimate address is the believing communities to which these individuals belong. And those texts addressed to specific churches often give hints that the author's concern is for an even wider audience (*cf.* 1 Cor. 1:2, 'to ... all those in every place who call on the name of the Lord Jesus'). To do biblical theology, then, is to read the Bible as a Christian, someone who welcomes the witness of Scripture to what God was and is doing in Christ, which is 'according to the Scriptures'. The biblical theologian makes no apology for his or her explicitly theological assumptions about the nature and identity of God.

Peter Stuhlmacher states the matter trenchantly: 'A biblical theology ... must attempt to interpret the Old and New Testament tradition as it wants to be interpreted. For this reason, it cannot read these texts only from a critical distance as historical sources but must, at the same time, take them seriously as testimonies of faith which belong to the Holy Scripture of early Christianity' (*How To Do Biblical Theology*, p. 1).

Biblical theology as construction site

The task of biblical theology is to present the teaching of the Bible about God and his relations to the world in a way that lets the biblical texts set the agenda. This goal is achieved by allowing them to serve as the very stuff of inductive study and by reading the books more or less in their historical sequence. In other words, biblical theology subscribes to the primacy of the text; the interpretive interest of biblical theology corresponds as closely as possible to what the text is about. In this sense biblical theology may be distinguished from philosophical theology, which relies more directly upon reason, natural theology, which looks to the natural world and order for knowledge of God, and systematic theology, which concentrates on the contemporary articulation of Christian faith.

Beyond this fundamental point, the biblical theology which this volume attempts to practise includes five other specifications:

1. the tools of the trade are analysis and synthesis;

2. the building materials consist of both biblical concepts and biblical words;

3. the bridge to be constructed is a single

span across the whole Bible;

4. the building plans follow the blueprint of the Bible's 'storyline'; and

5. the foundation and pinnacle of the structure is Jesus Christ.

Analysis and synthesis

Biblical theology is characterized by two distinct but related activities which may be broadly described as *analysis* and *synthesis*. The first seeks to reconstruct the individual theologies of the writings or collections of writings of the Bible. Exemplary here is G.B. Caird's biblical theology of the NT which hosts an imaginary symposium with the various authors in attendance, such as Luke, Paul, John and the author of Hebrews, a sort of apostolic conference in which each distinctive voice is heard. The accent in such work is on the particular contribution to theology of the book or books in question.

There is a temptation in studying the Bible's theology too quickly to read one part of it in the light of another and thus to miss the individual contours of the terrain and flatten out the whole. In doing biblical theology much is lost if James is read in the light of Paul, or Mark in the light of Matthew. It is more accurate and productive first to let James be James and Mark be Mark and so on, thus appreciating their particular colours and hues, before going on to see how their perspectives look on the larger canonical canvas. Too often one part of the Bible is given undue and oppressive priority over the others (see *Unity and Diversity of Scripture).

Part Two of the present volume employs this method, analysing the distinctive theologies of the various corpora and books of the Bible in their own right. To analyse the theology of a book of the Bible is to read it as articulating a particular vision of the divine–human relationship, to consider its unique part in the progressive unfolding of God's plan of salvation for humanity.

Part Three focuses on the task of synthesis by presenting the theology of particular themes across the whole Bible. This approach, called 'pan-biblical theology' by James Barr, is concerned ultimately to construct one single theology for the Bible in its entirety. It confronts the question: in what sense can the Old and New Testaments be read as a coherent whole (see *Relationship of the Old Testament and New Testament)? This question has

many facets and lies at the heart of not only the method but also the substance of biblical theology.

To return to our analogy with civil engineering, if analysis involves the individual tradespeople working from their own plans on different parts of the project, synthesis recalls the work of the site architect or foreman who is responsible for the overall structure. Both have a necessary function to perform.

Concepts, not just words

A further question of method concerns the extent to which the study of the Bible's theology should be based on word studies. Such an approach admittedly has its attractions; how better to do theology on the Bible's own terms than by undertaking exhaustive investigations of its key terms? A number of major reference works have taken this approach in the past. However, it has been rightly criticized. Word studies alone are a shaky foundation upon which to base theology. A study of the biblical words for *love, for example, does not fairly represent the Bible's teaching on love, since it ignores numerous narratives and parables, such as the Good Samaritan, which do not mention the word 'love' but are nonetheless highly relevant. The word for '*church' is rarely used in the Gospels, but they contain much significant material for a treatment of the topic of the church, including the notion of the kingdom as embodied in the lives of people on earth, the calling of the twelve disciples to be with Jesus, and the frequent use of communal language such as family, fraternity, little flock and city. Sometimes a biblical author will pursue the same concept as another author but with his own vocabulary. Concepts rather than words are a surer footing on which to base thematic study such as that involved in biblical-theological synthesis.

In most cases the concept is in fact far bigger than the words normally used to refer to it, even when the words in question appear frequently. Three examples suffice to make the point, namely, grace, exclusion and gentleness.

A number of biblical words are relevant to an understanding of *grace, including mercy, love, kindness and beneficence. The vocabulary of grace denotes spontaneous kindness and acts of generosity grounded in a disposition of compassion towards those in need. However, the biblical concept includes the notions of loyalty and constancy, often in connection with the covenant. Grace as a characteristic of God grounds divine–human relations in his generous initiative and sustaining faithfulness. Of course, the concept of grace can be present, and often is, even when the related words are absent, especially when God visits people for the purposes of blessing and salvation.

The notion of *exclusion from the believing community (excommunication or church discipline) is captured in a host of terms. In one key passage alone, 1 Corinthians 5, it is expressed in five different ways, using the verbs 'to remove', 'to drive out', '(not) to eat with', 'to deliver (to Satan)' and 'to purge away'. However, the topic raises questions about the motivations for such drastic action which are not communicated simply by the appearance of such words. The fact that people are to be disciplined is less instructive than the reasons for the judgment. In the Bible serious offenders are excluded from the community because of the solidarity of the community, in order to maintain the holiness of the group, due to a breach of covenant, in the hope of restoration and because of the prospect of salvation. Such teaching can be gleaned only from a range of material including both laws and historical examples of exclusion.

*Gentleness is a somewhat ambiguous concept, for it can denote both strength and vulnerability. Usually in the Bible it is a positive quality, a characteristic of peaceable and controlled kindness, the opposite of arrogance or domination. The concept can be expressed using any of the following terms: 'gentleness'; 'graciousness'; 'clemency'; 'kindness'; 'humility'; 'consideration'; 'courtesy'; 'loving-kindness'; and 'meekness'. However, it deserves a coherent treatment which a series of individual word studies does not accomplish, since it is both a defining attribute of God and Jesus and constitutive of Christian character.

If concepts are generally bigger than words, some concepts have a relatively slim lexical base and yet can lay no less a claim to be of central importance. There are many examples, including hospitality, providence, vanity, testimony and revelation.

There is no specific word for *hospitality

in the OT, and yet the practice is evident in the welcome, food, shelter and protection-asylum that guests received in OT times. Commands in the Pentateuch and exhortations in the prophets to care for strangers attest to the importance of hospitality in the OT. Narratives demonstrate that hospitality was closely connected to the recognition of Yahweh's lordship and to covenant loyalty. Stories provide evidence of God's presence and provision in the context of hospitality. And hospitality is at the heart of the gospel and practice of the early church.

One concept which raises issues about the character of God and divine government but does not correspond to one particular term is *providence; the idea is expressed by a cluster of biblical terms. A precise linguistic basis is difficult to identify. The notion of providence, which encapsulates the conviction that God sustains the world that he has created and directs it to its appointed destiny, is scattered throughout and at many points taken for granted in the Bible. Belief in God's providence evokes not only humility and wonder, but also gratitude and trust, for believers know God as Father. The subject simply cannot be treated adequately by doing a few word studies.

The word for *vanity occurs only here and there in the Bible. However, the concept captures much of the human predicament of sin under God's wrath. The whole of salvation history, from creation to the ultimate consummation of all things, illustrates the tension which arises between the wilful desires of human folly and the benevolent purposes of a loving God. The earliest biblical example of this tension is the divine curse on the ground (Gen. 3:17–19), which resulted from the attempt of disobedient humanity to become autonomous, like God. The mutual harmony between God, humanity and the created order was disrupted, and working the land became a toil and burdensome. The removal of vanity, at the other end of salvation history, is a picture of ultimate redemption. The subject is noteworthy in the Bible for both its poignancy and its scant explicit mention.

The technical terms 'witness' and 'testimony', given their infrequent appearance, might seem incidental to the message of the Bible. However, the concept of *testimony is found throughout the canon. Because of the cardinal role played by the law in the formation and life of ancient Israel, the roots of testimony are juridical. But because that life was not divided into discrete legal and religious compartments, those juridical roots blossom throughout the biblical narrative into religious proclamation, confession and martyrdom. This intermingling of legal and religious testimony is entirely natural, for the law was given in order that Israel, by obeying the law, might be a living testimony to its author, the Lord their God (Deut. 4:5–8; 26:16–19). In Scripture heaven, earth, John the Baptist, the apostles and in fact all God's people give testimony. Indeed, the pinnacle of biblical testimony is its proclamation of God's unfolding purpose to bring salvation to the ends of the earth, whereby every tongue will testify that there is but one true God, and that this one true God has made Jesus Christ Lord of all.

The word 'revelation' and its cognates occur fewer than one hundred times in the whole Bible, according to the NIV. However, the ubiquity and centrality of *revelation, as the disclosure by God of truths at which people could not arrive without divine initiative and enabling, is considerably more impressive than this statistic implies. The study of revelation must extend beyond the mere use of the word. The Bible does not so much discuss or reflect on revelation as assume, embody and convey it in a hundred different ways. Revelation is as universal as creation itself, is accomplished by God both speaking and acting, and involves both the miraculous, like dreams, visions and prophecy, and the mundane.

A whole-Bible biblical theology

Over the last couple of centuries there has been a division in the practice of biblical theology into virtually separate consideration of OT and NT theology. Until a few notable exceptions in recent times no one wrote biblical theologies of the whole Bible. The present volume aims to contribute to a whole-Bible biblical theology (see *The Canon of Scripture) in a number of ways. Part Two articles, for instance, are not deaf to such concerns in that while concentrating on analysis, they give some consideration to the place of the distinctive ideas under discussion in the canon, both in terms of OT antecedents (for the NT articles) and NT developments (for the OT articles).

Whereas it might be convenient to treat a book like *Proverbs in isolation, a responsible biblical theological approach goes beyond a summary of its many practical themes and addresses its place in the Bible as a whole. Proverbs displays little interest in the main biblical themes of covenant and salvation-history. How then can it be related to the rest of the Bible when its content seems peripheral? The article in Part Two suggests that the answer may lie partly in the Solomonic narrative, where Solomon's wisdom is connected with the account of the building and dedication of the temple. With Solomon and the temple, God is in the midst of his people in Zion, and rules through his anointed king who is the son of David. In short, the revelation of God's wisdom in his plan of salvation is the only framework within which authentic human wisdom can flourish. The consideration of such questions has a profound effect on how Proverbs is read and distinguishes a whole-Bible biblical theology.

The links between the Testaments in the form of direct quotation of or allusion to the earlier by the later are obvious to every reader familiar with the OT and are of vital importance to biblical theology (see *New Testament use of the Old Testament). Virtually every major doctrine in the NT is supported with some reference to Scripture. The search for the unity of the Bible, however, cannot limit itself to such quotations and even allusions, for even where these explicit links are rare the NT texts can scarcely be understood without reference to the way in which they relate to the OT. In twenty-one chapters the Gospel of *John, for example, quotes the OT only some fifteen times. Yet John's opening phrase, 'in the beginning', recalls the beginning of Genesis, and the Gospel's teaching about Jesus throughout is firmly grounded in OT antecedents, from Jesus as the son sent by the father and the bread descending from heaven, to Jesus as the fulfilment of Jewish feasts (Tabernacles and Passover) and institutions (the Temple), to the seven 'I am' sayings.

Particular biblical themes are investigated in Part Three in a manner which attempts to synthesize the message of the Bible. Obviously the choice of topics in itself has an impact on the results which emerge from the various investigations. As well as subjects which have a basis in a wide range of biblical texts, themes were chosen which span the Testaments and clearly call for some attempt at synthesis. Instead of one article on Passover and another on the Lord's Supper, there is an entry on *Sacred Meals which treats the Passover and the Lord's Supper, along with the peace offering, the last supper and the marriage supper of the Lamb, as part of the one vibrant and purposeful tradition. Similarly, rather than an article on the ascension of Jesus, there is one on *exaltation which sets Jesus' ascension in the context of the frequent presentation of God in the OT as the great king over all the earth, proud humanity's urge to lift itself up in self-sufficiency and disobedience, and Jesus' enthronement in heaven and second coming.

Furthermore, in articles on what might normally be considered specifically NT themes due consideration is given to OT roots. The term '*kingdom of God/heaven', for instance, does not occur in the OT. Nonetheless, the idea of the rule of God over creation, all creatures, the kingdoms of the world and, in a unique and special way, over his chosen and redeemed people, is the very heart of the message of the OT. The 'kingdom' in the NT can be understood only against the backdrop of this rule and dominion, which is characteristically rejected by the human race, and whose final stage is anticipated in the prophets in terms of radical renewal and completion.

The storyline of the Bible

Even though the Bible is strictly speaking a collection of books written over hundreds of years with widely varying contents, it does tell a unified story; the tale of creation, fall, judgment and redemption culminates with the gospel concerning Jesus Christ, which the apostles regarded as attested to by all Scripture (see *Biblical History). As with any other book, a legitimate question to ask when reading the Bible is: what is it about? Even if the Bible's storyline contains numerous subplots, its main story can be told, and often is with reference to major themes of systematic theology such as *sin, *salvation and *worship. Such topics act as centres around which the Bible's basic plot and message can be organized. Thus the Bible is about humankind falling into sin, and God's determination to put things right. It is about salvation, God's rescue plan for human beings under judg-

ment. It is about the worship of the one true God and the rejection of gods that fail.

One goal of biblical theology, however, is, in the words of a famous hymn, to 'tell the old, old story', in fresh and unexpected ways. 'Sin', 'salvation' and 'worship' are not the only one-word answers to the question: what is the Bible about? Others include 'violence', 'peace', 'victory', 'glory' and even 'clothes' and 'cities', to name but a few of the many subjects appearing in part three.

The Bible is about *violence, brutal but sometimes ambiguous. It begins with the foundational premise that the fallen world, and humanity in particular, is violent. An entire episode of human history is sealed with the narrator's judgment that the earth was filled with violence. We first encounter God's own violence in the flood, a divine judgment that destroys the greater part of human and animal life. But God's violence is different in that it is a function of his governance that is ultimately aimed towards the redemption of his creation. The prophets foresaw in Jesus a new and powerful vision of this redemption in which violence is absorbed and transformed.

The Bible is about *peace, the bringing together of warring parties. The OT is full of the language of peace, with which one person wishes peace upon another, or wishes to be and live in peace, free from enemies or other dangers. However, peaceful relations between humans, as important as they might be, are not nearly so important as peace with God, which is achieved through sacrifice, in the end that of Jesus Christ.

The Bible is about *victory, which ultimately belongs to the Lord and is entirely within his gift. Yahweh's military victories, which mark the high points of the national experience of pre- and early monarchical Israel, come about only when the people seek and obey him. Thus it is no surprise when their disobedience leads to ignominious defeat and exile. Confidence that victory still belonged to Yahweh is maintained in some of the Psalms, where it is asserted that Yahweh had conquered the cosmological forces of chaos, and in the prophets, who focus not on a decisive victory in the past, but on the coming decisive demonstration of the victory of God in the future. In the NT, this victory of God is demonstrated supremely in the death and resurrection of the Lord Jesus

Christ. Though the victory has been decisively achieved, its final celebration and realization awaits the day of the Lord which is yet to come.

The Bible is about *glory, radiant and ineffable, lost and regained. God's glorious presence, whether for salvation or destruction, is prominent in the key moments and central institutions of Israel's history and is decisively revealed in Jesus Christ. Through their sinful rebellion, human beings have forfeited the privilege, as image-bearers of God, of reflecting his glory. Yet through Christ believers are restored to glory.

The Bible is about *clothes, used not only to denote community identity, signal social status and enact legal agreements, but also and more significantly to illustrate God's redemptive activity. From the first act of mercy extended to fallen humanity, the covering of Adam and Eve with clothes, to the end of the age, when the community of the redeemed will be clothed with an imperishable, immortal, heavenly dwelling, the exchange and provision of garments portray God's gracious and redemptive provision.

The Bible is about *cities, in particular Jerusalem and Babylon and their fates and associations. Jerusalem as the religious centre of the holy land, both originally and in its final restoration, represents the people of God. The word of God issues forth from Jerusalem, peoples gather in Jerusalem to honour God, and the messianic king will appear there victoriously. Conversely, Babylon serves as a symbol of wickedness. Babylon is the proud and wicked city that will be left uninhabited and in ruins, whose name will be cut off for all time. Christians are citizens of the Jerusalem above. The clash between the city of God and the city of Satan will come to a head in the eschaton, with the fall of Babylon and the arrival of the new Jerusalem.

Thus biblical theology explores the Bible's rich and many-sided presentation of its unified message. It is committed to declaring 'the whole counsel of God ... [in order] to feed the church of God' (Acts 20:27–28).

A Christ-centred structure

Finally, biblical theology maintains a conscious focus on Jesus Christ, not in some naive and implausible sense, where Christ is found in the most unlikely places, but in noting God's faithfulness, wisdom and purpose in the progress of salvation history. It reads not only the NT, but also the OT, as a book about Jesus. Even if in the OT religion was focused on present relationship with God, based on his dealings with and for his people in the past, there is a firm and growing belief in the future coming of God on the day of the Lord for judgment and salvation. Christians believe that this hope culminates in Jesus and read the OT as a book which prepares for and prophesies his coming and the people of God he would renew and call into existence. The books of the NT connect Jesus with the OT in a variety of ways, seeing Jesus as the fulfilment of prophecy, the ideal to which individuals and institutions aspired, or the climax of God's dealings revealed in various types.

Virtually every theme in biblical theology, as may be seen from the examples noted in the previous two sections, leads to Christ as the final and definitive instalment. Not only do we see Christ and his work in a different light by considering themes such as victory, peace and glory; the momentous nature of his appearance means that the reverse is also true. A host of topics, such as *death and resurrection and *sacrifice, and less obviously, but no less profoundly, *humanity, *Israel and *obedience, are seen differently in light of the advent of Christ. The article on *Jesus Christ could be cross-referenced to every article in Part Three, for all the subjects are relevant to him as God's final word and decisive act, and he to them. Even the articles on biblical people, such as *Abraham, *Moses, *David, *Elisha and *Jonah, refer to Christ, in a typological sense and/or as the fulfilment of the promises made to these people. Indeed, the Messiah is the theme which unites the Old and New Testaments (T. D. Alexander, *The Servant King*). If biblical theology seeks to connect text and truth (to use Watson's phrase), it never forgets that Jesus is the truth.

Conclusion

What is biblical theology? To sum up, *biblical theology may be defined as theological interpretation of Scripture in and for the church. It proceeds with historical and literary sensitivity and seeks to analyse and synthesize the Bible's teaching about God and his relations to the world on its own terms, maintaining sight of the Bible's overarching narrative and Christocentric focus.*

Further clarification of the nature and promise of biblical theology is presented in the other articles in Part One. However, in the end, like civil engineering, biblical theology is best judged and understood by examining what it produces. The purists will always want more exact definition. Ultimately the proof that civil engineering and biblical theology are well conceived is in the quality of the things they build. For the latter, this can be inspected in Parts Two and Three.

Bibliography

T. D Alexander, *The Servant King* (Leicester, 1998); J. Barr, *The Concept of Biblical Theology* (London, 1999); M. Bockmuehl, '"To be or not to be": The possible futures of New Testament scholarship', *SJT* 51, 1998, pp. 271–306; G. B. Caird, *New Testament Theology*, compiled and edited by L. D. Hurst (Oxford, 1994); D. A. Carson, 'New Testament theology', in *DLNTD*, pp. 796–814; B. Childs, *Biblical Theology of the Old and New Testaments: Theological Reflection on the Christian Bible* (Minneapolis, 1992); S. Fowl and L. G. Jones, *Reading in Communion: Scripture and Ethics in Christian Life* (Grand Rapids, 1991); R. J. Gibson (ed.), *Interpreting God's Plan: Biblical Theology and the Pastor* (Carlisle, 1998); G. L. Goldsworthy, *According to Plan: The Unfolding Revelation of God in the Bible* (Leicester, 1991); J. B. Green and M. Turner, *Between Two Horizons: Spanning New Testament Studies and Systematic Theology* (Grand Rapids, 1999); H. Räisänen, *Beyond New Testament Theology* (London, 1990); P. Stuhlmacher, *How To Do Biblical Theology* (Allison Park, 1995); W. VanGemeren, *The Progress of Redemption: From Creation to the New Jerusalem* (Carlisle, ²1995); F. Watson, *Text and Truth: Redefining Biblical Theology* (Edinburgh, 1997).

B. S. ROSNER

History of Biblical Theology

Introduction

While some trace the origin of biblical theology to the Protestant Reformation, and others to J. P. Gabler's 1797 address, 'An Oration on the Proper Distinction Between Biblical and Dogmatic Theology and the Specific Objectives of Each', the fact is that the Christian church was concerned from a very early date to articulate a 'biblical theology' in some form. As far as is known, the actual term (*theologia biblica*, *biblische Theologie*) was first used in the early 1600s, but the attempt to discern a unified and consistent theology in the scriptures of the OT and NT is much older.

It might be argued that biblical theology has its origin within the Bible itself. Summaries of 'salvation-history' found in the OT (*e.g.* Deut. 26:5–9; Neh. 9:7–37; Pss. 78, 105, 106) and also in the NT (Acts 7; Heb. 11) trace the continuity of God's dealings with his people. The NT Gospels and epistles interpret the Christ event in the light of the OT, but also reinterpret the OT in the light of the Christ event. Paul, it has been suggested, was the first 'Old Testament theologian', and the same claim could well be made for the writer to the Hebrews.

The early and medieval periods

As soon as the Gospels, the letters of Paul and other Christian writings began to be used alongside the Hebrew Scriptures, and well before the finalizing of what came to be recognized as the NT, these scriptures were employed by the church in formulating its beliefs and in countering what it believed to be false teaching. From the outset it faced the problem of *unity and diversity (a major problem in biblical theology to this day). The church refused to follow Marcion's solution

11

of rejecting the OT altogether, and also set aside proposals to recognize only one Gospel (Marcion) or combine all four in a harmony (Tatian). Instead it opted for the fullness of scriptural witness with the attendant problems of diversity.

Irenaeus (late 2nd century) defended the fourfold Gospel as inspired by the one Spirit, and could well be regarded as the first biblical theologian. In countering the gnostic challenge he sought to develop a Christian understanding of the OT integrated with a consistent interpretation of the Gospels and epistles, an understanding that was in turn integrated with 'the rule of faith' preserved in those churches that claimed direct succession from the apostles.

Following the lead of Origen (c. 185–254), the church made extensive use of allegorization as a method of biblical interpretation. This enabled interpreters to find a uniform theology throughout Scripture, but it frequently bypassed the historical meaning and encouraged the reading of later doctrines back into the text. By medieval times Scripture was supposed to have four senses: literal (or historical); allegorical; moral (or tropological); and anagogical (or spiritual). The allegorizing 'School of Alexandria' was opposed, however, by the 'School of Antioch' which took a more historical approach, anticipating some of the findings of modern scholarship. Despite the popularity of allegory, the historical sense was championed by, for example, the 12th-century Victorines, and its primacy was asserted by Thomas Aquinas (c. 1225–74). For all its faults, medieval interpretation recognized the existence of different levels of meaning in Scripture which could be used to nourish the faith and life of the church.

The Reformation

The Reformers appealed to the teaching of Scripture alone (sola Scriptura) against centuries of church tradition, and consequently practised a form of biblical theology. Martin Luther (1483–1546) scrutinized the church's beliefs and practices in the light of Scripture. In general he rejected allegorization and emphasized the grammatical and literal sense, and he addressed the diversity of the Bible by taking 'justification by faith' as his key hermeneutical concept. He focused on those books that 'show Christ', and questioned the

canonicity of Hebrews, James, Jude and Revelation.

John Calvin (1509–64) regarded Scripture as the supreme authority for Christian belief. Both in his Institutes of the Christian Religion and in his biblical commentaries he sought to ground the faith of the church in the Bible more comprehensively and systematically than Luther did, attempting to do justice to the full range of biblical material. While the supreme revelation is found in the NT, Christ is revealed in the OT also. Faith is essential for the interpretation of Scripture and its truth is conveyed to believers by the 'internal testimony of the Holy Spirit'. Thus while Calvin was, by modern definition, a dogmatic theologian, in many ways he can be seen as the initiator of a truly biblical theology.

The emergence of biblical theology as a separate discipline

The fresh insights and bold discussions of the Reformers were followed by the period of 'Protestant Orthodoxy', which produced rigid dogmatic systems. A notable exception is found in the work of the Reformed theologian Johannes Cocceius (1603–69) who in his major work Summa Doctrina de Foedere et Testamento Dei (1648) sought to interpret the Bible as an organic whole by giving a central place to the concept of 'covenant'. Cocceius laid the basis for the influential 'federal' or 'covenant' theology; he also anticipated later developments in biblical theology through his emphasis on covenant and on God's dealings with his people in the 'history of salvation'.

In the 17th and 18th centuries three major trends led to the emergence of biblical theology as a more separate discipline.

First, the practice developed, especially within Lutheran orthodoxy, of compiling collections of proof texts (dicta probantia) to demonstrate the biblical basis of Protestant doctrine. These collections, sometimes referred to as collegia biblica (collegium = collection) were usually arranged in accordance with the standard topics (loci communes) of dogmatic theology. Beginning around 1560, these collegia flourished for about two centuries, and the earliest works bearing the title 'Biblical Theology' were of this nature. While the shortcomings of a 'proof-texting' approach are obvious, nevertheless these collections did turn attention back to the teaching of the Bible itself.

A second major trend was Pietism which, under the leadership of such figures as P. J. Spener (1635–1705) and A. H. Franke (1663–1727), reacted against dry and rigid orthodoxy and emphasized personal religious experience. Pietists turned to the Bible not for proof texts to support orthodox doctrine (though they did not intend to depart from orthodoxy), but for spiritual and devotional nourishment. Spener contrasted 'biblical theology' (*theologia biblica*) with the prevailing Protestant 'scholastic theology' (*theologia scholastica*), and in the 18th century several Pietists published works with the term 'biblical theology' in their titles.

A third trend was the development in the 17th and 18th centuries of new critical methods of literary and historical research, and of what came to be known as the 'historical-critical' or 'grammatico-historical' approach. Pioneers of the new approach included Richard Simon (1638–1712), Benedict Spinoza (1632–77), and J. S. Semler (1725–91) who argued that the books of the Bible must be studied in their original historical context as one would study any ancient book, and that this study must be separated from the use of the Bible by dogmatic theologians. Eithteenth-century rationalism saw in this new approach an objective method by which to free the church from centuries of dogma and identify the true Christian faith. The rationalists sought to extract from the Bible universal and timeless truths, in accordance with reason, distinguishing them from what was merely historically conditioned and time-bound. This approach is seen in the work of K. F. Bahrdt, and especially in G. T. Zachariä's five volume *Biblische Theologie* (1771–75). W. F. Hufnagel in his *Handbuch der biblischen Theologie* (1785–89) argued that biblical texts must be used to correct theological systems, not vice versa.

Gabler's definition

It was at this point that J. P. Gabler delivered his 1787 inaugural address at the University of Altdorf on 'The Proper Distinction Between Biblical and Dogmatic Theology and the Specific Objectives of Each', an address which most historians see as a significant milestone in the development of biblical theology. Gabler was a professing Christian though strongly influenced by the rationalism

of his day, and saw 'biblical theology' as a historical discipline, separate from 'dogmatic theology' which applies the eternal truths of Christianity to the theologian's own time. Later, however, Gabler drew a distinction within 'biblical theology'. 'True (*wahre*) biblical theology' is the historical study of the OT and the NT, their authors and the contexts in which they were written. This is then to be followed by 'pure (*reine*) biblical theology', which consists of a comparative study of the biblical material with a view to distinguishing what is merely time-conditioned and what is eternal Christian truth; it is the latter that becomes the subject-matter of dogmatic theology. On this view, biblical theology is not merely descriptive but is also part of the hermeneutical process.

Gabler's views were not so much original as typical of his day. As the 19th century progressed, however, the title of his address became more influential than its content. Biblical theology came to be seen as a purely historical, descriptive and objective discipline, separate from the concerns of biblical interpreters. Hence it could increasingly be pursued in an academic setting, in effect divorced from the life and faith of the church.

The rise and fall of biblical theology

In the late 18th and early 19th centuries rationalist scholars made increasing use of the developing historical-critical method to produce 'biblical theologies'. Generally these works were used to criticize orthodox theology. Typical of this approach were the biblical theologies of C. F. von Ammon (*Entwurf einer reinen biblischen Theologie*, 1792) and G. P. C. Kaiser (*Die biblische Theologie*, 1813–21). More significant was the work of W. M. L. de Wette (*Biblische Dogmatik des Alten und Neuen Testaments*, 1813), a more independent scholar who distinguished 'Hebraism' from (post-exilic) 'Judaism', regarding the latter as an inferior form of religion. A more moderate rationalism characterized the *Biblische Theologie* (1836) of D. G. C von Cölln.

Most of these scholars demanded that revelation be subordinated to reason, as they understood it, the result being that the supernatural was largely eliminated from their theology. Diversity within Scripture was addressed by the removal of temporally conditioned ideas (*Zeitideen*), which represented an 'accommodation' to the thought of people in biblical times; what was left was the essence of biblical religion, the timeless rational truths of religion and morality.

Not surprisingly, orthodox and conservative scholars stood aloof from this new movement, though in time they realized that biblical theology could also be written from a more conservative viewpoint. The earliest such work by a conservative scholar was L. F. O. Baumgarten-Crusius' *Grundzüge der Biblischen Theologie* (1828), which adopted a historical approach but emphasized the essential unity of Scripture. The more conservative J. C. K. von Hofman, in reaction to those who sought within Scripture a system of doctrine, stressed that the Bible is rather the record of 'salvation history' (*Heilsgeschichte*), an insight that was to prove influential. J. L. S. Lutz's *Biblische Dogmatik* (1847) and the massive and influential work of H. Ewald (*Die Lehre der Bibel von Gott oder Theologie des Alten und Neuen Bundes*, 1871–76) represent a moderate conservatism.

By the middle of the century, however, historical study of the Bible was revealing ever more clearly the diversity of the biblical material, and above all the difference between the OT and the NT in relation to their original historical settings. The very possibility of a 'biblical' theology was called in question. Ahead of his time in a number of respects, the rationalist scholar G. L. Bauer had written a *Biblische Theologie des Alten Testaments* (1796), followed by a separate *Biblische Theologie des Neuen Testaments* (1800–2). In due course Bauer's procedure came to be accepted as the norm not only by critical scholars but even by conservatives, and a series of 'Theologies of the Old Testament' and 'Theologies of the New Testament' was produced. For approximately a century from around 1870 'biblical theology', in the sense of works on the theology of the OT and NT together, virtually ceased to exist.

OT and NT theology

For the second half of the 19th century and the first half of the 20th, OT and NT theology pursued separate though generally parallel paths frequently reflecting the prevailing theological climate. Thus Hegelian influence was strong in NT theology, especially in the work of F. C. Baur (1792–1860) and the 'Tübingen School'. This approach brought a new awareness of the historical nature of the biblical documents and of historical development in biblical theology.

The application of historical-critical methods altered the consensus on the authorship and dating of the biblical books. Thus, for example, the belief in Mosaic authorship of the Pentateuch was abandoned in favour of source criticism which assigned every verse to J, E, D or P. Mark was deemed to be the earliest Gospel, while the Pastorals were assigned to the 2nd century. As a result new chronological schemes emerged for tracing the theology of both OT and NT; the emphasis was on diversity and development.

Liberal Protestantism tended in this period to downgrade and neglect the OT, so that OT theologies came from conservative scholars such as J. C. F. Steudel (1840), H. A. C. Hävernick (1848) and G. F. Oehler (1873–74). H. Schultz continued to regard religion as divine revelation while being open to more critical views in the later editions of his *Alttestamentliche Theologie* (1869–96). The German monopoly was broken by C. Piepenbring's *Théologie de l'Ancien Testament* (1886) and A. B. Davidson's *The Theology of the Old Testament* (1904).

Despite the shock waves caused by D. F. Strauss' *Life of Jesus* (1835, 1836), liberal scholars generally were confident of rediscovering 'Jesus as he actually was' by means of historical methodology. Harnack found 'the essence of Christianity' in Jesus' teaching on the Fatherhood of God, the brotherhood of humanity and the infinite value of the human soul.

The most influential liberal NT theology was that of H. J. Holtzmann (*Lehrbuch der Neutestamentlichen Theologie*, 1896), while a moderate conservatism, influenced by liberal scholarship, is seen in the NT theologies of B. Weiss (1868–1903) and W. Beyschlag (1891–92). English-speaking scholarship is represented by E. P. Gould (*The Biblical Theology of the New Testament*, 1900) and G. B. Stevens (*The Theology of the New Testament*, 1901). Of major importance was the work of A. Schlatter (1852–1938) who sought to work out a position independent of rationalism and liberalism on the one hand and conservatism on the other; while adopting a historical approach, he emphasized the basic unity of the NT and grounded NT theology in the historical Jesus. Evidence of his stature as a biblical theologian may be seen in the 1973 publication in English of a key methodological essay (in R. Morgan, *The Nature of New Testament Theology*, pp. 117–166), the publication of a biography by Werner Neuer (1996), and the belated translation into English of his *Theologie des Neuen Testaments* (1909–10, ²1921–22) in two volumes, *The History of the Christ: The Foundation of New Testament Theology* (1997) and *The Theology of the Apostles: The Development of New Testament Theology* (1999).

From theology to religion

In the late 19th and early 20th centuries archaeological discoveries (which continue to this day) began to provide information about the ancient Near East and the Greco-Roman world. For many, these discoveries appeared to call in question the uniqueness of biblical faith. Babylonian creation myths and law codes, Jewish apocalypticism, Hellenistic mystery religions and pre-Christian Gnosticism all provided striking parallels to the biblical material, which could no longer be studied in isolation. A comparative approach to biblical religion was strongly favoured. Reacting against both liberals and conservatives who spoke of biblical 'doctrines', the history of religions (*Religionsgeschichte*) approach emphasized that the true subject matter of biblical studies is *religion*. The Bible is not a book of doctrine but the record of the life and religious experience of the communities of Israel and the early church. According to W. Wrede, the true subject matter of 'so-called New Testament Theology' is not in fact theology but early Christian religion, which must be investigated objectively and completely divorced from any system of dogma or systematic theology. The boundaries of the canon should be ignored: the inter-testamental literature and the Apostolic Fathers are just as important for the historian of religion as the canonical books.

An early example of this approach (despite its title) is A. Kaiser's *Die Theologie des Alten Testaments* (1886), while R. Smend's *Lehrbook der alttestamentlichen Religionsgeschichte* (1893) inaugurated a series of works which usually bore the title 'History of Religion' (*Religionsgeschichte*). Representative works from the field of NT studies are H. Weinel's *Biblische Theologie des Neuen Testaments* (1911) and W. Bousset's *Kyrios*

Christos (1913). The influence of this approach in the English-speaking world can be seen in two works with significant titles, S. J. Case's *The Evolution of Early Christianity* (1914) and E. F. Scott's *The Varieties of New Testament Religion* (1943).

The history of religions approach remained dominant until the First World War, and it continues to be a major force in biblical studies, particularly in university 'departments of religious studies'. However legitimate it may be as an academic discipline, from the point of view of the community of faith it raises serious questions. Can an approach which totally ignores the canon really be considered 'biblical', and can an approach that fails to recognize the biblical material as theologically normative be appropriately designated 'theology'? It might appear that the post-Gablerian separation of biblical and dogmatic theology had led not just to the division of biblical theology (into OT and NT theologies) but eventually to its demise.

The revival of theology

The period following the First World War saw a major reaction against liberalism in the theology of Karl Barth. In biblical studies there was a renewed emphasis on biblical 'theology', though still in the form of separate treatments of the OT and NT.

Many see the 1930s as having inaugurated the golden age of OT theology. Particularly influential was W. Eichrodt's *Theologie des Alten Testaments* (1933–39), though the English translation, *Theology of the Old Testament*, did not appear until 1961–67. Other mid-century contributions included OT theologies in German by E. Sellin (1933), L. Köhler (1935) and O. Procksch (1949), in Dutch by T. C. Vriezen (1949) and in French by E. Jacob (1955). The most influential post-Second World War OT theology was that of G. von Rad (1957–60). A notable feature of this period was the entry of Roman Catholic scholars into the field following a 1943 papal encyclical which approved a more modern historical approach to Scripture; a transitional work was the *Theologie des Alten Testaments* (1940) of the Dutch scholar P. Heinisch, and a major contribution was the *Théologie de l'Ancien Testament* (1954–56) of P. van Imschoot. The tradition of writing OT theologies has been continued by such scholars as W. Zimmerli (1972), J. L. McKenzie

(1974), C. Westermann (1978), H. D. Preuss (1991–92) and W. Brueggemann (1997). Another trend has been the entry of conservative-evangelical scholars into the field with contributions by W. C. Kaiser (1978) and W. Dyrness (1979).

The revival of NT theology came somewhat later and was dominated by the brilliant but controversial two-volume work by R. Bultmann (*Theologie des Neuen Testaments*, 1948–53). A sceptical form critic, Bultmann regarded the historical Jesus as a presupposition of NT theology rather than a part of it, and focused largely on Paul and John where he found themes congenial to his existentialist 'demythologizing' of the Christian message. In the Bultmann tradition is H. Conzelmann's *Grundriss der Theologie des Neuen Testaments* (1967), though he adds a section on the Synoptics.

At the opposite pole stand scholars for whom the historical Jesus is the starting point of NT theology. These include A. Richardson (*An Introduction to the Theology of the New Testament*, 1958), and J. Jeremias (*Neutestamentliche Theologie, I: Die Verkündigung Jesu*, 1971: no further volumes were published). Jesus is also the starting point for W. G. Kümmel's *Die Theologie des Neuen Testaments* (1969). Other important works include those by F. C. Grant (1950) and G. B. Caird, whose *New Testament Theology* was published posthumously in 1994. Roman Catholic contributions include NT theologies by M. Meinertz (1950), J. Bonsirven (1951) and the four-volume *Theologie des Neuen Testaments* (1971–78) of K. H. Schelkle. Contributions by conservative-evangelical scholars include New Testament theologies by G. E. Ladd (1974, revised 1993), D. Guthrie (1981) and L. Morris (1986).

Every author who writes a biblical theology of this type has to adopt a structure. The earliest practice was to employ the standard topics of systematic theology ('God', 'Humanity', 'Sin', 'Law', 'Salvation', *etc.*) especially as these had been developed in the *dicta probantia* of Protestant Orthodoxy. Schemes like this were adopted by Pietist and rationalist scholars alike, and they were revived, with some variations, in OT theologies such as those by Köhler (1935), Baab (1949) and van Imschoot (1954). Jacob (1955) attempted to break new ground, but in fact still largely followed a traditional scheme. Twentieth-century NT theologies that have more or less followed traditional theological categories include those of Grant (1950), Richardson (1958) and Schelkle (1968–1976). Though many have adopted this approach it has been widely criticized as imposing an alien scheme on the biblical material, omitting important biblical themes (*e.g.* wisdom, the land), and imposing an artificial unity on the diversity of the biblical books.

With the development of the historical-critical approach in the late 18th and early 19th centuries the Bible began to look less like a textbook of systematic theology and more like a history book. Theologies of both OT and NT generally adopted a chronological structure, tracing the development of religion through the history of Israel and the history of the early church, a common practice to this day. Such schemes generally depend on modern critical reconstructions of the dating of the various books. Some have adopted a hybrid scheme combining the systematic and historical approaches. For example, D. Guthrie's *New Testament Theology* (1981) has a basically systematic structure, but each topic is then traced through the Synoptics, John, Acts, Paul, Hebrews, other epistles and Revelation. Von Rad (1957–60) rejected systematic categories and focused on the biblical testimony to God's continuing activity in the history of Israel (which he saw as something quite different from the history of Israel as reconstructed by modern critical scholarship). A somewhat different approach is adopted by those who follow more or less the canonical order: an OT example is Oehler (1873), and a New Testament one is Ladd (1974).

Dissatisfaction with both systematic and historical approaches has led some scholars to structure their works around themes or topics which they see as arising from the biblical material rather than being imposed upon it. The classic example is Eichrodt, who took the concept of 'covenant' as the organizing principle for his *Theology of the Old Testament*. This stimulated a debate regarding the appropriate 'centre' or 'focal point', initially for OT theology, then for NT theology also. The difficulty of finding any one theme comprehensive enough to embrace all the diverse biblical material led others to adopt a multi-thematic approach. E. A. Martens, for example, in his *Plot and Purpose in the Old*

Testament (1981) identifies four key themes: salvation/deliverance, the covenant community, knowledge/experience of God, and land. W. J. Dumbrell, in a study of Revelation 21 and 22 (1985), traces five basic biblical themes: the new Jerusalem; the new temple; the new covenant; the new Israel; and the new creation. A more recent trend is to emphasize the dialectical nature of biblical theology: Westermann, for example, balances 'The Saving God and History' with a discussion of 'The Blessing God and Creation', while Brueggemann utilizes categories of 'testimony' and 'counter-testimony' in structuring his *Theology of the Old Testament* (1997).

Some have spoken of a 'biblical theology movement' that flourished, especially in the English-speaking world, from around 1945 to 1960. 'Movement' may be too strong a word, but certain trends did characterize this period, including a renewed interest in 'theology' (without the abandonment of the historical-critical approach), and an emphasis on 'the God who acts', on the 'uniqueness' of biblical faith and on the unity of the Bible. O. Cullmann's work on 'salvation-history' was seen by some as a key to understanding the basic unity of the biblical material. Typical also was the 'word-study' approach to biblical theology, evidenced in the production of biblical 'wordbooks'. The 'movement' is generally believed to have collapsed by the early 1960s, partly due to damaging methodological criticisms, and partly due to changing priorities among scholars.

From theology to theologies

One of the dominant trends in the latter part of the 20th century has been a renewed emphasis on diversity and development within the Bible, to the point where not only the concept of 'biblical theology' but even those of OT and NT theology have been radically called in question. This reflects the growing complexity of biblical studies resulting from new discoveries, the proliferation of methodologies and the seemingly endless output of secondary literature. In consequence many no longer consider themselves even OT or NT scholars, but specialize in a narrower area.

Many scholars prefer to speak of OT 'theologies' (Yahwist, Deuteronomic, Priestly, and so on). Similarly, many NT scholars focus on the disparate 'theologies' of Paul, John, Luke, and even of the hypothetical 'Q'

document. Biblical theology appears to have reached an impasse. The post-Gablerian separation of biblical theology from the life and faith of the church, as a discipline to be pursued in an objective, historical, descriptive way, has arrived at the point where many declare that a 'biblical theology' is in fact an impossibility.

New approaches

There has been a wide diversity of approaches to biblical theology in recent decades. One striking feature has been the questioning of the dominance of the historical-critical method. Few would reject it altogether, but many suggest a more thorough questioning of its (often rationalistic) presuppositions, and a willingness to see it as only one among several legitimate approaches to Scripture. Modern hermeneutical theory calls into question whether any approach to an ancient text can be neutral and objective, and scholars such as P. Stuhlmacher have called for 'a hermeneutics of consent to the biblical texts'.

The last third of the 20th century saw an explosion of interest in the literary approach to the Bible. Using diverse methodologies, literary critics focus on the final form of the biblical text. For example, the literary critic N. Frye in his *The Great Code: The Bible and Literature* (1981) sought to understand the Bible as a literary whole, a task for which source analysis and modern theories of authorship are irrelevant. The Bible is undoubtedly the end product of a long and complicated literary process, but it needs to be studied in its own right. Frye sees a sequence or dialectical progression in the Bible, consisting of seven main phases which form a chain of types and antitypes.

One feature of the literary approach has been a renewed interest in biblical narrative or story, which has led to the development of 'narrative theology'. Some see this as part of 'the collapse of history' in recent biblical studies. A popular slogan is that the Bible is not 'history' but 'story' and some scholars deny any referential function to biblical narrative. Many scholars engaged in the literary study of the Bible are either indifferent or even opposed to a religious understanding of the text. A literary approach need not, however, be based on secular presuppositions and a number of scholars, such as L. Ryken and T. Longman, have shown that it is quite compatible with more conservative presuppositions, including a high view of the historicity of the text. By looking at biblical stories and poems as literary wholes as well as locating them in their wider, literary, canonical context, biblical literary criticism has the potential to make an important contribution to biblical theology.

The latter part of the 20th century also saw a surprising interest in the *canon of Scripture, a subject that has not usually been regarded as of first importance in biblical studies. J. A. Sanders' form of 'canonical criticism' can be seen as a reaction against a historical-criticism that frequently treated only the (reconstructed) original form of a biblical text as 'authentic'. In his studies of the nature and function of canon Sanders stresses the importance of the whole process of transmitting, editing and shaping the material up to and including its final canonical form. In his view the canonical process was marked by both stability and adaptability.

Significantly different from this is the 'canonical approach' of B. S Childs first enunciated in his *Biblical Theology in Crisis* (1970) and worked out in canonical introductions to both OT and NT. Childs does not reject historical criticism but is acutely conscious of the gap between such criticism and the use of the Bible as authoritative Scripture by the Christian community. Thus he argues that biblical theology must be based primarily on the final form of the canonical text. His approach is like that advocated in the methodology of G. F. Hasel, who sees biblical theology not as merely historical in its approach but rather as 'theological-historical', and as based on the canonical form of the biblical texts.

Another recent trend is the sociological approach to Scripture. This can be seen as an extension of the historical-critical approach, and it shares some of that approach's limitations, as it tends to be based on hypothetical reconstructions of the social situations out of which the biblical texts emerged. Moreover, a sociological approach is no more free from presuppositions than any other. Sociologists transfer models from other societies, and this procedure may not be valid in relation to biblical societies of two or three millennia ago. Nevertheless a sociological approach can provide a different perspective and can complement other methodologies.

Related to this approach has been a new interest not just in the context of the original writer but also in that of the modern interpreter. One criticism of the so-called 'biblical theology movement' was its irrelevance to the emerging social, economic and political issues of the 1960s. Since then various types of 'liberation theology' (Latin American, Third World, black, feminist) have sought a biblical-theological basis. Some of these focus on the Exodus as a key event which demonstrates that God is on the side of the oppressed and downtrodden; others, on the OT prophets' calls for social justice. A striking example is the work of N. Gottwald (*The Tribes of Yahweh*, 1979), who draws on Marxist analysis to present the early history of Israel not in terms of the traditional 'conquest' but rather primarily as a peasant revolt within Canaanite society. Feminist biblical theologians stress the thoroughly patriarchal nature of biblical society which in contemporary hermeneutics needs to be radically reinterpreted if not totally rejected. Others, however, see a basically egalitarian approach within Scripture, in the teaching and example of Jesus and possibly in Paul (but not in the Pastorals), an approach that was smothered by re-emerging patriarchalism even within the NT period. All forms of liberation theology combine biblical interpretation with a call to radical action in terms of contemporary social, political and economic structures. Such 'contextual theologies' need not be seen as reading contemporary concerns back into Scripture; rather, they can serve the very useful purpose of bringing out neglected aspects of biblical theology. Nevertheless the obvious focus on a 'canon within the canon' raises serious concerns as to how adequately these approaches can serve as the basis for a truly 'all-biblical' theology.

The rebirth of biblical theology

In the midst of a wide variety of new approaches in biblical studies there are signs that rumours of the death of biblical theology may have been exaggerated. In recent years a number of attempts have been made to bridge the rigid division between OT and NT studies and to return to some form of 'biblical' theology.

One such attempt can be seen in the 'history of traditions' approach associated especially with the German scholars H. Gese and P. Stuhlmacher. This is based on the assumption that in the time of Jesus the OT canon was not yet closed, and that biblical theology is concerned with a continuous history of tradition. Divine revelation is not to be located only in the earliest forms of the tradition but in the entire process, which was long and complex as traditions were continually selected, edited and reinterpreted. This approach has been demonstrated in studies of such themes as 'wisdom', 'law' and 'righteousness'. Critics, however, point out that this type of tradition-history depends on a particular view of the canon (a subject that is currently very much under debate), that its use of non-canonical material is open to question, and that locating revelation in the process of tradition history fails to identify the norm of Christian faith.

Further evidence of a renewed interest in biblical theology in the 1980s and 1990s may be seen in the Fortress Press series *Overtures to Biblical Theology*, Abingdon's *Biblical Encounters* series and the *New Studies in Biblical Theology* series published by Inter-Varsity Press. Many of these studies do biblical theology by tracing biblical themes through both OT and NT, not ignoring diversity, but also seeking unity or at least continuity, in the biblical material.

The 1980s and 1990s also saw vigorous scholarly debate on topics such as 'Paul and the law' (J. D. G. Dunn, L. Gaston, H. Hübner, H. Räisänen, E. P. Sanders, P. Stuhlmacher), a theme that demands consideration of the place of the law in the OT as well as in other NT writings.

One unresolved tension in biblical theology is that between the academy and the believing community. The increasing use of the ecumenical lectionary in worship, for example, highlights the fact that for the church biblical theology is not an academic discipline but an integral part of its faith and life. F. Watson has argued cogently that a true biblical theology must bridge the gaps that presently exist not only between OT and NT specialists but also between biblical scholars and theologians. Such a biblical theology must emphasize 'both the ultimate coherence of the two Testaments and the theological dimension of the interpretative task' (*Text and Truth: Redefining Biblical Theology*, p. 8). Some see biblical theology as an activity to be practised in the exegesis of biblical passages or in studies of individual books, authors or themes.

Whether it is possible to go beyond this and produce an 'all-biblical theology' (*gesamtbiblische Theologie*) is a matter of debate. Some (*e.g.* H. Hübner) have argued that the present state of scholarship rules out such an enterprise, which in any case would be beyond the competence of any one individual. Despite this, however, the late 20th century saw a revival of interest in the possibility of writing a 'biblical theology' encompassing both OT and NT. Two early 20th-century examples come from opposite ends of the theological spectrum. M. Burrows' *An Outline of Biblical Theology* (1946) is written from a liberal Protestant viewpoint, but is more akin to a dictionary of biblical themes than a full-fledged 'theology'. The *Biblical Theology: Old and New Testaments* (1948) of G. Vos is written from a strongly conservative perspective, though it acknowledges a progressive revelation; it is worth reading, though unfortunately it is incomplete. Of major importance is S. Terrien's *The Elusive Presence: The Heart of Biblical Theology* (1978), which uses the theme of divine presence as a hermeneutical key in a study of each of the main units of the biblical canon, and which seeks to uncover what the author calls 'a certain homogeneity of theological depth' which binds the biblical books together. Other biblical theologies include Horst Seebas' *Der Gott der ganzen Bibel* (1982) which presents a sketch rather than a full biblical theology; H.-R. Weber's *Power: Focus for a Biblical Theology* (1989), another example of the one-theme approach, and the more conservative and popular volume by G. Goldsworthy, *According to Plan: The Unfolding Revelation of God in the Bible* (1991). The most significant 20th-century biblical theology is B. S. Childs' *Biblical Theology of the Old and New Testaments* (1992), which is the culmination of the author's 'canonical approach'. This volume first presents the 'discrete witness' of the OT and the NT, tracing the development of traditions in each of the main units of the canon; then it proceeds to theological reflection on the Christian Bible, discussing the biblical material under ten major topical headings, and concluding by relating these to contemporary theological discussion.

Despite the criticism levelled at these works from various quarters they demonstrate that it is possible once again to attempt the writing of a truly 'biblical theology', and they suggest both some of the pitfalls to avoid and some of the approaches that are worth pursuing.

See also: CHALLENGES TO BIBLICAL THEOLOGY; RELATIONSHIP OF OLD TESTAMENT AND NEW TESTAMENT.

Bibliography

G. Bray, *Biblical Interpretation: Past and Present* (Leicester and Downers Grove, 1996); B. S. Childs, *Biblical Theology in Crisis* (Philadelphia, 1970); W. Harrington, *The Path of Biblical Theology* (Dublin, 1973); G. F. Hasel, *New Testament Theology: Basic Issues in the Current Debate* (Grand Rapids, 1978); *idem*, *Old Testament Theology: Basic Issues in the Current Debate* (Grand Rapids, ⁴1991); R. Morgan, *The Nature of New Testament Theology* (London, 1973); J. Reumann (ed.), *The Promise and Practice of Biblical Theology* (Minneapolis, 1991); H. G. Reventlow, *Problems of Biblical Theology in the Twentieth Century* (Philadelphia, 1986); J. Sandys-Wunsch and L. Eldredge, 'J. P. Gabler and the distinction between biblical and dogmatic theology: Translation, commentary and discussion of his originality', *SJT* 33, 1980, pp. 133–158; J. D. Smart, *The Past, Present and Future of Biblical Theology* (Philadelphia, 1979); P. Stuhlmacher, *How To Do Biblical Theology* (Allison Park, 1995); F. Watson, *Text and Truth: Redefining Biblical Theology* (Grand Rapids and Edinburgh, 1997).

C. H. H. SCOBIE

Challenges to Biblical Theology

Introduction

The discipline of biblical theology has faced challenges of various kinds since the end of the 19th century. In 1897, William Wrede published an essay entitled *Über Aufgabe und Methode der sogenannten Neutestamentlichen Theologie* in which he argued that the discipline of NT theology should be replaced by study of 'the history of early Christian religion and theology' (ET; in *The Nature of New Testament Theology*, p. 116). Heikki Räisänen's programmatic study, *Beyond New Testament Theology* (1990), and his numerous subsequent articles have revived Wrede's proposal. Although these works focus primarily on NT theology, their effect is to undermine biblical theology as a whole.

Biblical theology is also challenged implicitly by those who do not want to move 'beyond' the discipline but rather to modify it to such an extent that its traditional name can hardly be justified. For example, there is a widespread view that the diversity of the Bible's theological ideas rules out any unified biblical theology (see *e.g.* P. Pokorný, 'The Problem of Biblical Theology', *HBT* 15, 1993, pp. 83–94, esp. 87).

Thus, there are two main challenges to biblical theology: first, the argument against confining study to the 'Bible' as defined in the canon; and secondly, the argument against the basic theological unity of the biblical authors and books.

There are also challenges which do not question the discipline of biblical theology as such, but which criticize some of the ways it has been practised. For example, in his article 'Revelation through history in the Old Testament and in modern theology', James Barr argues that the idea of revelation through history should not be overemphasized against other forms of revelation in the Bible, for example, the 'verbal self-declaration of Yahweh' (*Int* 17, 1963, pp. 193–205, quote from p. 197). He does not deny that salvation-history, *Heilsgeschichte*, is a central theme of the Bible, but stresses 'that there are other axes through the biblical material which are equally pervasive and important' (p. 201).

Similarly, Barr repeatedly criticizes the biblical theology movement that lay behind Kittel's *Theological Dictionary of the New Testament*, for grounding the unity and distinctiveness of the Bible in the alleged theological distinction between Hebrew and Greek thought and in the supposed rejection by the biblical writers of natural theology. However, even in his major work, *The Semantics of Biblical Language* (Oxford, 1961), Barr affirms that his purpose 'is not to criticize biblical theology or any other kind of theology as such, but to criticize certain methods in the handling of linguistic evidence in theological discussion' (p. 6). His main criticism is that Kittel's *Dictionary* places too much emphasis on single words at the expense of combinations of words or sentences. Barr has put forward his thesis as follows (p. 263): 'It is the sentence (and of course the still larger literary complex such as the complete speech or poem) which is the linguistic bearer of the usual theological statement, and not the word (the lexical unit) or the morphological and syntactical connection.'

Scholars engaging in biblical theology ought to learn from such criticism in order to improve their methods; rather than abandoning the enterprise altogether they should attempt to write better biblical theological works.

In the present article we survey and attempt to answer some of the challenges to biblical theology. Many of these are related to hypotheses which, by virtue of their having become a majority view, are often presented as assured results of biblical scholarship. Our focus will be on NT theology. We shall briefly state the major challenges relating to the development of the NT canon and to the unity of its basic theology, and marshal some arguments in favour of studying biblical theology at the level of historical, descriptive inquiry.

Religious experience instead of doctrine?

The history-of-religion approach presents a challenge to biblical theology in its emphasis on experience over doctrine. Wrede argued against the dominant approach to NT theology in his day, *i.e.* the attempt to isolate doctrinal concepts, *Lehrbegriffe* (in *The Nature of New Testament Theology*, p. 73).

Räisänen has taken up this argument, claiming that 'religious thought is only one, relatively small, part of religion' (*Beyond*, p.

105). Although he suggests that for pragmatic reasons a 'comprehensive history of early Christian religion' should begin with the study of religious thought, he qualifies his statement (p. 106): 'A history of early Christian thought as I see it ought to make abundantly clear the connections of the thoughts and ideas with the experiences of individuals and groups. The development of thought is to be analysed precisely in the light of the interaction between experiences and interpretations.'

In response, it should be said that the theology of the Bible and its doctrinal concepts are not identical. Theology should be defined more widely as affirmations and actions involved in relationships between God and humans.

Furthermore, there is no need to exclude from the field of 'theology' what Räisänen calls 'aspects' or 'branches' of religion: 'cult, rite, myth, communality' including 'historical, psychological and social realities' (*Beyond*, p. 105). Inasmuch as these were part of the early church's beliefs about God they belong to a biblical theology. In other words, such a theology can include a wide range of religious phenomena; it is not limited to doctrine.

Thus it seems that the study of experience does not pose a challenge to biblical theology if we accept a wider definition of that theology, one which includes experiences relating to religious beliefs. Biblical theology should describe the experiences of God recorded in the Bible as well as the doctrine contained therein.

No distinction between canonical and non-canonical early Christian literature?

The claim that there is no historical justification for distinguishing a 'canon' of Scripture from other early Christian writings is a serious challenge to biblical theology.

According to Wrede and Räisänen, one particularly problematic issue is the relationship between early Christianity and Christianity as reflected in the canonical NT. They argue that NT theology should not be confined to the canonical writings. We shall focus on the problem of distinguishing between early Christian literature in general and the NT canon in particular; for discussion of the OT canon, see *The canon of Scripture.

Is 'orthodoxy' a late phenomenon?

One major argument against the separation of canonical writings from non-canonical ones is drawn from the (supposed) history of the process whereby orthodoxy was distinguished from heresy. In what follows we retain the usual meaning of the terms 'heresy' and 'orthodoxy', as defined by the 2nd century church.

Walter Bauer, renowned for his Greek lexicon, wrote an important study in 1934 entitled *Rechtgläubigkeit und Ketzerei im ältesten Christentum*. Georg Strecker summarizes Bauer's thesis in the preface to the second edition of Bauer's work, as follows: 'In earliest Christianity, orthodoxy and heresy do not stand in relation to one another as primary to secondary, but in many regions heresy is the original manifestation of Christianity' (ET, p. xi). This thesis would render the distinction between heresy and orthodoxy irrelevant for the historian, and undermine the distinction between canonical and non-canonical writings.

Bauer argues that heresy in Edessa, Egypt and some parts of Asia Minor (especially central and eastern Asia Minor) was earlier and stronger than orthodoxy. However, he concedes that in some other parts of Asia Minor (*e.g.* Ephesus) and in Rome, orthodoxy was early and strong.

In his essays published in 1971 under the title *Trajectories through Early Christianity*, Helmut Koester revived and further developed the thesis of Bauer. He agrees with Bauer that 'Christian groups later labelled heretical actually predominated in the first two or three centuries, both geographically and theologically' ('*GNOMAI DIAPHOROI*: The origin and nature of diversification in the history of early Christianity', in *Trajectories*, pp. 114–157, quote from p. 114). Koester focuses 'on those developments which begin in the earliest period' (p. 119), that is, in 'the apostolic age', which 'is seldom considered in Walter Bauer's study'.

Koester's aim is to show how certain lines of development can be drawn in the history of early Christian traditions. These trajectories often start outside early Christianity and go beyond it. For example, in 'One Jesus and four primitive Gospels' (in *Trajectories*, pp. 158–204), Koester analyses the stage of gospel tradition prior to the writing of our four canonical Gospels. His detailed study of 'prophetic and apocalyptic sayings' (pp. 168–175), 'parables' (pp. 175–177), 'I-sayings' (pp. 177–179), 'wisdom sayings and proverbs' (pp. 179–184), *etc.* (in all of which he claims to find heretical developments), clarifies the various genres. But it does not prove that there can be no distinction made, among writings dependent on these sources, between canonical and non-canonical. It is possible that the oldest examples of these genres were thoroughly orthodox. Koester has not proved his thesis that the canonical Gospels were constructed on one pattern only, *i.e.* the kerygma of the death and resurrection of Jesus.

Thomas A. Robinson has presented a convincing refutation of Bauer's and Koester's thesis. In *The Bauer Thesis Examined: The Geography of Heresy in the Early Christian Church* (Queenston, 1988), he shows that the 'Bauer Thesis' proves to be indefensible with reference to western Asia Minor – an area from which there is plenty of evidence concerning orthodoxy and heresy. Robinson also argues that Bauer's thesis may be even more insecure with reference to areas from which we have little evidence. Thus the traditional view may be maintained, that heresy was later than orthodoxy in the early Christian church.

Different groups identified themselves by 'canons'

We may further argue for a legitimate distinction between the NT canon and other early Christian literature by pointing to different groups in early Christianity which identified themselves by their own group of sacred writings, *i.e.* by their 'canons'. There are three such groups apart from the 'orthodox'. These Christian groups – later labelled heretics – produced and treasured sacred writings which they regarded as Scripture.

First, Marcion produced a collection of writings (a Gospel and ten Pauline letters) which he and his followers held to be Scripture. Secondly, whilst it is uncertain as to whether the Montanists' canon presupposes the existence of the orthodox Christian canon, there is no doubt that they regarded their writings as 'Holy Scriptures'. Thirdly, Bardesanes wrote his own Psalms and had his own congregation with its own place of worship and order of service. Even Walter Bauer acknowledged that Bardesanes' congregation used its own 'Scripture'.

These three examples from the 2nd century point to the development by different Christian groups of their own sacred writings – their own 'canonical' Scripture – as an expression of their identity. It was through these 'canonical' writings that they could show how they differed from other groups. Since there were various groups in early Christianity that identified themselves by their 'canons', it is legitimate to study the theology of one particular group and its sacred writings. NT theology is justified in focusing its attention on one particular canon, that of the 'orthodox' group.

Is the canon a late decision of the church?

There is a widespread view that the canon was created by the decision of certain theologians and bishops of the earliest Christian centuries. It is also often claimed that their decision cannot be binding upon later generations. Such a claim challenges the focus of biblical theology on the canonical writings. For example, Wrede wrote that 'anyone who accepts without question the idea of the canon places himself under the authority of the bishops and theologians' of the first four Christian centuries (in *The Nature of New Testament Theology*, p. 71). Räisänen claims that it is 'arbitrary' to limit the scholar's work of interpretation to the NT canon (*Beyond*, p. 100).

In response to this challenge, arguments may be advanced for an early beginning to the process of 'canonization', and for a 'canonical awareness' on the part of the early Christians long before the 4th century, even if they did not use the term 'canon' to refer to a list of sacred writings until then.

Is the 'orthodox' canon an answer to Marcion's canon?

There is a widely accepted view that in the middle of the 2nd century the church found itself in a critical position because of the emergence of false teachers and sects. Thus it was necessary for the 'catholic' church to take action. Marcion produced his canon; the 'orthodox' section of the church created its own canon in response.

Against this view it is worth noting the case put forward by Theodor Zahn at the end of the 19th century. In his *Geschichte des Neutestamentlichen Kanons* (vol. 1.2, Leipzig, 1889), he argued as follows. Marcion held

that the message of the gospel was distorted (p. 650) and that this distortion had already happened in the time of Paul (pp. 593, 652). He opposed Christian tradition and the church's Scripture, but from this it is clear that he acknowledged the existence of a church canon (pp. 595, 626–671 *passim*). Recently, G. N. Stanton has argued that the very fact of four canonical gospels suggests they were not 'canonized' in response to Marcion; one gospel would have been a more effective answer ('The Fourfold Gospel', *NTS* 43, 1997, pp. 317–346, see esp. 336). Furthermore, we can argue for a 'canonical process' going on prior to Marcion's time (*i.e.* before the middle of the 2nd century), if we can show that the NT writers thought they were writing with an authority similar to that of the OT prophets.

The authority of apostolic writings

The apostles were 'sent' by Jesus, and their letters carried his authority (see *e.g.* P. Balla, *Challenges to New Testament Theology*, pp. 121–129). The early church believed that the gospels were written by apostles or followers of apostles. Paul, though not one of the Twelve, wrote with apostolic authority, as can be seen from the introductions to his letters. (For his awareness of the authority he shared with the Lord who sent him, see *e.g.* 1 Cor. 7:17, 25, 40; 2 Cor. 13:10; 1 Thess. 2:6–7.) For example, in the opening verses of Romans there are possible indications that Paul thought his writing was in some sense related to that of the OT prophets. In Romans 1:2, the phrase 'which he promised beforehand' (RSV) may well express Paul's belief that he was being used by God to declare the fulfilment of promises made long before. Again, the expression 'through his prophets in the holy scriptures' may indicate that Paul stands in the line of the prophets, inasmuch as there is a connection between a promise and its fulfilment. If a promise made by God was recorded in a sacred writing, then the witness to the fulfilment of the promise may also claim to be penning a sacred writing. If teaching about the Son of God made a writing sacred in the OT period, the same should be true in the new era (v. 3; *cf.* also 16:25–26; 1 Pet. 1:10–12).

This proposal is not unlikely historically; there are analogies. Slight but nevertheless significant pieces of evidence suggest there were Jews at the time of Jesus who believed that in the final days new sacred writings would be revealed and added to the 'canonical' OT. For example, the Qumran community most probably thought of one of their writings (the Temple Scroll) as a 'second Torah' (see Balla, *Challenges*, pp. 106–109). It could be argued that 4 Ezra also witnesses to a belief in the emergence of a 'second canon' in the end times. Ezra is inspired by God to dictate the Law (which had been burnt some time before). Twenty-four books (the then 'canonical' OT) are to be made public, and seventy others are to be kept secret for the use of the wise (4 Ezra 14:19–48; see Balla, *Challenges*, pp. 112–114; *cf.* also Deut. 29:29). Thus the apostles, who saw themselves as living in the end times, inaugurated by the coming of the Messiah, may have thought that they were writing sacred books that would become a 'second canon'.

The adoption of the codex in the process of canonization

A further argument in favour of an early beginning to the process of canonization can be based on the early adoption by Christians of the form of the codex, as opposed to the (then more favoured) roll. The emergence of the codex made it possible for certain writings to be bound or 'published' together. For example, the four Gospels could not be written on a single roll, but, as the manuscript evidence shows, they could be bound conveniently together in codices.

C. H. Roberts and T. C. Skeat have argued that 'it is impossible to believe that the Christian adoption of the codex can have taken place any later than *circ.* A.D. 100 (it may, of course have been earlier) … ' (*The Birth of the Codex*, London, 1987, p. 61). Unfortunately, we probably do not have any NT manuscripts from the 1st century, but on the basis of the use by Christians of the codex form in the 2nd century we may hold that 'Christians adopted the codex for their writings from the outset' (p. 45). The manuscript evidence shows that some codices contained groups of writings, for example, the four Gospels, the catholic (general) epistles, or the Pauline corpus. The adoption of the codex would have helped to promote the books which were held to be 'canonical' (to use the term anachronistically; see also J. K. Elliott, 'Manuscripts, the Codex and the Canon',

JSNT 63, 1996, pp. 105–123).

Thus, early Christians could have put short collections of writings into single codices even by the end of the 1st century. Such writings were published together because they were treasured as authoritative, perhaps even sacred, writings.

To sum up, the church did not 'create' the canon by some late 'decisions' of synods and bishops, but recognized the authority of the NT writings in a process that began in the 1st century. The focus of NT theology on the canonical writings can therefore be justified historically.

Biblical theology or biblical theologies?

Biblical theology is strongly challenged by a large number of scholars who argue that there is no theological unity in the Bible. In the 19th century, F. C. Baur claimed that there was radical disagreement in the early church between the parties of Peter and Paul, before the development of the NT canon. If this is true, NT theology represents the synthesis of a former antithesis.

More recently, Räisänen has argued that there is no single 'theology "of" the early Christian sources, for these sources contain divergent theological standpoints' (*Beyond*, p. 137). He implies that due to these divergences it is not possible to summarize the theology of the early Christians; hence the task should not even be attempted.

This challenge, when applied to the whole Bible, can be put as follows: biblical theology cannot be maintained if there is no (at least underlying) unity in the Bible's theology. The question of diversity and alleged contradictions in Scripture is addressed elsewhere (see *Unity and diversity of Scripture), so it suffices here to advance some positive arguments in favour of the basic unity of NT. (Concerning the theology of both Testaments, see *Relationship of Old Testament and New Testament.) It is appropriate to advance these arguments, because the task of writing biblical theology should not be based on blind faith in the theological unity of the text. In principle, a writer could discover that such unity does not exist and consequently give up the enterprise. It is sometimes argued that a true historian cannot write a biblical theology. Yet there is evidence to suggest that the task can be historically justified.

Credal formulae

The most widely held view among scholars is that the credal elements in the NT developed from simple to more complex forms. For example, H. Lietzmann classified the credal elements in this way (*Kleine Schriften III: Studien zur Liturgie- und Symbolgeschichte zur Wissenschaftsgeschichte*, Berlin, 1962, esp. pp. 230ff.).

1. Simple Jesus-creeds which state that Jesus is Lord or the Son of God; *e.g.* 1 Corinthians 12:3; Romans 10:9; 1 John 4:15; Acts 8:37 mg. (in some Gk. MSS only). These formulae were later developed into the *ichthys* formula. (*Ichthys* is the Greek word for 'fish'; in the early church it was an acrostic for 'Jesus Christ, Son of God, Saviour'.)

2. Christ-creeds of more complex form, *e.g.* Romans 1:3; 2 Timothy 2:8; 1 Corinthians 15:3–5; 1 Peter 3:18–22; Philippians 2:5–11 (*cf.* also Ignatius, *Letter to the Ephesians* 18:2; *Letter to the Trallians* 9; *Letter to the Smyrneans* 1:1–2).

3. Creeds referring to God and to Christ, *e.g.* 1 Corinthians 8:6; 1 Timothy 6:13; 2 Timothy 4:1.

4. The trinitarian creed (which became dominant), *e.g.* Matthew 28:19; 2 Corinthians 13:13.

The dates of the passages mentioned by Lietzmann under his various headings do not correspond to the projected development from simple to complex forms. For example, Romans is mentioned under both 'simple Jesus creeds' and more developed Christ-creeds. The trinitarian confession is thought to be late because it is complex, but 2 Corinthians is probably one of the earlier NT documents.

Some scholars argue that the end of the Gospel of Matthew was added by the early church. However, the saying as it stands is attributed to Jesus; many scholars believe that he spoke about the Spirit of God, and at least some that he believed God was his 'Father'. Thus a 'trinitarian' saying can be dated to the time of Jesus. (For a detailed argument for the view that 'trinitarian' theology is not a late development, see J. C. O'Neill, *Who Did Jesus Think He Was?*, esp. pp. 77ff. and 94ff.)

Moreover, it is possible that confessions of different types ('classes') existed in parallel, and do not necessarily represent various stages of a temporal development.

So credal elements may have formed part of the 'basic theology' of the early Christians, and been a unifying factor in their communities and among the NT writers. The existence of early creeds therefore points to the unity of NT theology.

Nomina sacra

Further evidence for the theological unity of early Christianity may be found in C. H. Roberts' study of *nomina sacra* (*Manuscript, Society and Belief in Early Christian Egypt*, London, 1979). Roberts has shown that 'a strictly limited number of words, at most fifteen', are abbreviated in Greek and Latin (biblical as well as non-biblical) religious writings (p. 26). Scholars call these words *nomina sacra*. Roberts classifies them in three groups (p. 27): four words (Jesus, Christ, Lord and God) 'the abbreviation of which in their sacral meaning may be said to be invariable'; three words (spirit, man and cross) 'of which the contracted form is found relatively early and relatively frequently'; and eight words (father, son, saviour, mother, heaven, Israel, David and Jerusalem) of which 'the contraction is irregular'.

Roberts argues that the abbreviations of these words have a Christian origin (p. 34). Behind the list 'lies a quite unmistakeable, if implicit, theology' (p. 41). He emphasizes that 'the system of *nomina sacra* presupposes a degree of control and organization' (p. 45). The Christian practice of abbreviating the *nomina sacra* may have originated in the Jewish Christian community of Jerusalem, 'probably before A.D. 70' (p. 46). Thus 'the *nomina sacra* may be plausibly viewed as the creation of the primitive Christian community, representing what might be regarded as the embryonic creed of the first Church' (p. 46).

If Roberts is right in seeing 'a summary outline of theology' (p. 47), or an implicit theology (p. 72) in the *nomina sacra*, then this is further evidence for the early origin of creeds and for the basic unity of early Christian theology. It is therefore a legitimate exercise to search for a single NT theology.

Literary and social sciences – or a historical enterprise?

In recent decades, biblical theology has faced some challenges from scholars who are dissatisfied with its exclusively historical character. Some argue for complementing, others for replacing, the historical approach with alternatives based on the literary and social sciences.

Robert Morgan has reflected on the problems involved in biblical theology, and especially NT theology, in numerous works, the most comprehensive of which is *Biblical Interpretation*. According to Morgan, 'acts of God cannot be spoken of, let alone established, by historical research' (p. 70). Since history is not capable of conveying theological judgments (*cf.* also p. 119), other approaches are needed (*cf.* also pp. 123, 197–198). According to Morgan's survey, recent developments in biblical interpretation suggest that the religious message of the text can be identified by interpreting the Bible within a literary framework (see *e.g.* pp. 143, 199). Sometimes the historical approach may even become 'subordinate' to the literary one (p. 287).

Morgan defines the literary approach as follows (p. 221): 'The literary frame of reference can be characterized as a shift in the focus of interest from past persons, events, traditions, literary forms, and conventions, to the now available texts and their impact upon present-day hearers and readers.'

However, there are good reasons for retaining a historical frame of reference for biblical theology. First, Morgan himself acknowledges that historical criticism has made 'positive contributions to constructive theological restatement' inasmuch as its 'negative theological role' forced theologians to 'restate the traditional faith' (p. 288). Secondly, historical study can control arbitrary interpretations. Consigning the historical approach to a secondary role and introducing non-historical approaches can undermine the accuracy of biblical interpretation. Morgan himself concedes that there may be occasions in theological work where 'the historical framework of research co-ordinates all the methods used' (p. 287). He also acknowledges that literary methods were used alongside historical ones in the past (*e.g.* by Wellhausen, p. 82).

It follows that the historical and the literary approaches do not exclude one another. It is best to combine them in the way suggested by Morgan (*cf.* p. 215).

In *Biblical Interpretation* Morgan identifies significant differences between the disciplines of history and sociology: 1. 'history attends to the individual and particular, sociology to what is general or typical' (p. 139); 2. history is diachronic, sociology is synchronic (pp. 139–140). For Morgan, these differences imply 'that the disciplines are complementary' (p. 140). Since in biblical theology we are more concerned with the 'unique' than with the 'typical', it follows 'that history rather than sociology should provide the framework for studying the biblical past'. A 'sociological theory', that is 'based on empirically grounded generalizations' such as might be discovered by 'observing many societies' may helpfully complement the insights of historical study. Morgan also argues that 'Since religion is a social phenomenon, the history of religion must be social history' (p. 140).

However, a distinction should be drawn between extending historical inquiry to include the societies of biblical times and using theories based on present-day sociological analysis. A historical framework for studying the Bible's theology may incorporate a social dimension without making use of modern sociological theories.

So it is possible to complement historical study with a sociological theory within the discipline of biblical theology, but this is only an option for the scholar. The validity of the historical approach to biblical theology is not dependent upon its being supplemented by sociology.

Conclusion

The foregoing argument suggests the term 'theology' can reasonably be retained as a description of the Bible's content. It may be used to refer to the biblical authors' (and characters') thoughts about God. Biblical theology is essentially historical, and may be justified as such, though the biblical theologian may also adopt frames of reference drawn from literary theory or the social sciences.

Judgments on the validity of the enterprise depend upon the presuppositions of scholars, the interpretation of key biblical passages and the exegetical reconstruction of historical events related in the Bible. For example, even if we find that much early Christianity shared a basic theology (perhaps expressed in short credal statements), we may still acknowledge diversity in the details with which early Christians filled out that theology.

It is likely that Christians with different theological views formed different canons from the 2nd century onwards. The orthodox group also formed a canon. The Christians of the 1st century may have written with a certain 'canonical awareness'. If as historians we find that the NT 'canon', in the form of a 'canonical process', is a historical fact of the first two Christian centuries (and not just the result of a decision made at a later date), and if we find that the NT claims authority for itself, perhaps even that of a 'canonical' text, then it is legitimate to look for the theology contained in the NT writings.

We do not have to move 'beyond' biblical theology. The discipline can be justified both in its focus on the canonical writings, and in its aim of describing the theology contained in the Bible.

Bibliography

P. Balla, *Challenges to New Testament Theology: An Attempt to Justify the Enterprise* (Tübingen, 1997; repr. Peabody, 1998); J. Barr, *The Scope and Authority of the Bible* (London, 1980); *idem*, 'Etymology and the Old Testament', in A. S. van der Woude (ed.), *Language and Meaning: Studies in Hebrew Language and Biblical Exegesis* (Leiden, 1974), pp. 1–28; W. Bauer, *Orthodoxy and Heresy in Earliest Christianity* (ET, Philadelphia and London, 1971, 1972); J. J. Collins, 'Is a critical biblical theology possible?' in W. H. Propp, B. Halpern, D. N. Freedman (eds.), *The Hebrew Bible and Its Interpreters* (Winona Lake, 1990), pp. 1–17; H. Koester and J. M. Robinson, *Trajectories through Early Christianity* (Philadelphia, 1971); L. M. McDonald, *The Formation of the Christian Biblical Canon* (Peabody, [2]1995); R. Morgan and J. Barton, *Biblical Interpretation* (Oxford, 1988); J. C. O'Neill, *Who Did Jesus Think He Was?* (Leiden, 1995); H. Räisänen, *Beyond New Testament Theology: A Story and a Programme* (London and Philadelphia, 1990); *idem*, 'Die frühchristliche Gedankenwelt: Eine religionswissenschaftliche Alternative zur "neutestamentlichen Theologie"', in Ch. Dohmen, Th. Söding (eds.), *Eine Bibel – zwei Testamente: Positionen biblischer Theologie* (Paderborn, 1995), pp. 253–265; *idem*, 'New Testament Theology?' in J. Neusner (ed.), *Approaches to Ancient Judaism*, vol. 9 (Atlanta, 1995), pp. 197–210; W. Wrede, 'The Task and Methods of "New Testament Theology"', in R. Morgan (ed.), *The Nature of New Testament Theology: The Contribution of William Wrede and Adolf Schlatter* (ET, London, 1973), pp. 68–116.

P. BALLA

The Canon of Scripture

Introduction: canonicity

Every book has a text, but not every book has a canon. Only a book like the Bible, which is also a collection of books, has a canon. The collection can be listed, and indeed needs to be listed for the avoidance of confusion and doubt, especially in a period like the biblical period, when the collection cannot yet be embodied in a single scroll or codex. 'Canon' is by origin a Greek word, denoting a straight rod or rule, and thus a criterion, and (together with its cognates 'canonical' and 'canonize') it began to be applied by Christian writers of the later 4th century AD to the correct collection and list of the Scriptures. This was a new usage; the common idea that this language had earlier been used by the Alexandrian grammarians for the select lists (*pinakeis*) of classical writers and artists which they drew up is a mistake. Such lists did exist, both among the Greeks and perhaps among the Babylonians, but calling them a 'canon' is a practice dating only from the 18th century, and was based upon the biblical canon, not the other way round.

It is interesting that this language first arose just at the time when it was at last becoming possible to put the Scriptures into a single volume. The great 4th-century codices, Codex Vaticanus and Codex Sinaiticus, are the earliest known examples. Among the Jews, the Pentateuch seems not to have been embodied in a single scroll before the Christian era, and at Qumran each biblical book (or regular and manageable combination of books) had its own scroll. The scrolls of the Greek OT, being made of papyrus not leather, seem to have been even less capacious. So lists were of great importance. The earliest Christian lists of the OT and NT, those of Melito and the Muratorian Fragment respectively, both date from the 2nd century AD, and the earliest Jewish list of the Hebrew Scriptures, found in a primitive tradition or *baraita* quoted in the Babylonian Talmud (*Baba Bathra* 14b), is probably older still. Before the term 'canon' was invented, a variety of names were already used by Jews and Christians for the collection of their sacred books, some, such as 'the Holy Scriptures', going back to the 1st century (Rom. 1:2; 2 Tim. 3:15; Philo; Josephus), and others, such as 'the Holy Books' and 'the Law and the Prophets', being even more ancient (1 Macc. 12:9; 2 Macc. 15:9). The terms 'Old Testament' and 'New Testament' began to be applied by Christian writers to collections of Scriptures in the 2nd and early 3rd centuries. What the language of 'canonicity' added was the idea of correctness; this correctness could now be embodied, for the first time, not just in lists but also in one-volume copies.

The biblical canon is not, of course, primarily a collection or list of literary masterpieces, like the Alexandrian lists, but one of authoritative sacred texts. Their authority derived not from their early date, nor from their role as records of revelation (important though these characteristics were), but from the fact that they were believed to be inspired by God and thus to share the nature of revelation themselves. This belief, expressed at various points in the OT, had become a settled conviction among Jews of the intertestamental period, and is everywhere taken for granted in the NT treatment of the OT. That NT writings share this scriptural and inspired character is first stated in 1 Timothy 5:18 and 2 Peter 3:16. Pagan religion also could speak of 'holy scriptures' and attribute them on occasion to a deity (see J. Leipoldt and S. Morenz, *Heilige Schriften* [Leipzig, 1953], pp. 21f., 28–30), but the Jewish and Christian claims were made credible by the different quality of biblical religion and biblical literature.

In a dictionary of biblical theology, the canon provides both boundaries and a basis. We are not engaged in producing a general survey of ancient Jewish and Christian religious ideas; if we were, all the surviving literature from the period would have an equal claim to our attention. Rather, we are engaged in interpreting the revelation of God, and for this the books which are believed to embody that revelation, and their text, are alone directly relevant. The accepted ways of arranging the canonical books are also significant, in so far as they highlight the historical progression of revelation and the literary forms in which it was given.

The history of the OT canon

The origin of the canon may be dated from the time that revelation first started being given in written form and being recognized for what it was. In both covenants, revelation was initially given through spoken words and outward signs, and in the new covenant through the person of the Lord Jesus Christ during his ministry on earth, but for the sake of permanence it soon started to be put into written form. The materials mainly used were books, *viz.* scrolls of papyrus or leather, and in NT times perhaps also small papyrus codices, but in OT times writing tablets might sometimes be used (Is. 30:8; Hab. 2:2), of which the tablets of the Ten Commandments, written by the finger of God and deposited in the ark of the covenant, are an illustrious example. Writing was used as a 'memorial' (Exod. 17:14) and as an abiding 'witness' (Deut. 31:26) which would last until 'the generation to come' (Ps. 102:18) and indeed 'for ever' (Is. 30:8). The finding of the law-book by Hilkiah in the temple showed vividly what happened when the written form of revelation was lost; the revelation itself was forgotten (2 Kgs. 22 – 23; 2 Chr. 34). In the NT one finds Luke writing a careful record of Jesus' life and work for the sake of his readers' 'certainty' (Luke 1:3–4.) and John correcting in writing a corrupt oral report (John 21:23).

On three great occasions in Israel's history, we see a smaller or greater part of the Pentateuch being recognized as having divine authority, and being accepted as a written rule of life for the nation: at the giving of the covenant at Sinai (Exod. 24:4, 7), at the reformation of Josiah (2 Kgs. 23:1–3; 2 Chr. 34:29–32) and at the re-establishment of the nation after the exile (Neh. 8:9, 14–18; 10: 28–39; 13:1–3). Deuteronomy contains provisions for the book to be regularly read, so that its laws may be known and obeyed (Deut. 17:18–20; 31:9–13).

There are many other references in the OT to the written law of Moses as a God-given rule (Josh. 1:7–8; 8:31; 23:6–8; 1 Kgs. 2:3; 2 Kgs. 14:6; 17:37; Hos. 8:12, etc.) and also to the written form of oracles uttered by the prophets (Is. 30:8; Jer. 25:13; 29:1; 30:2; 36:1–32, etc; Ezek. 43:11; Hab. 2:2; Dan. 7:1). In the later books of the OT, references start to be made to the earlier books with the expression 'as it is written', but without further explanation as to where 'it is written' (2 Chr. 30:5, 18; Ezra 3:4; Neh. 8:15; cf. Ps. 149:9), the meaning of the phrase being 'as it is written in the well-known and authoritative Scriptures'. This usage becomes common in the intertestamental literature, and also in the NT, especially as a way of introducing quotations. Every book of the Hebrew OT except perhaps the little Song of Songs is attested as authoritative in the intertestamental literature and the NT taken together, most of them several times over; there is no need to appeal to the rabbinical literature to demonstrate their authoritative status.

The fullest evidence is provided by the Jewish historian Josephus (late 1st century AD). He numbers the sacred books as twenty-two, a common variant on the standard Jewish number twenty-four (first attested about Josephus's time in 2 Esdras 14:44–48). The Jews reckoned Samuel, Kings, Chronicles, Ezra-Nehemiah and the twelve Minor Prophets together as one book each, giving a total of twenty-four books (instead of the familiar thirty-nine). But this figure was often reduced to twenty-two, to assimilate it to the number of letters in the Hebrew alphabet, by appending Ruth to Judges and Lamentations to Jeremiah. For the benefit of his Greek readers, Josephus provides a simple arrangement for the twenty-two books, putting all those with historical content into Moses and the Prophets (consisting of five and thirteen books respectively), and leaving just 'hymns to God

and precepts for human life' in the final section of four books (Against Apion 1:7f., or 1:37–43).

It has been widely believed that the Greek-speaking Jews of Alexandria had a larger canon, including the books (found in manuscripts of the Old Greek or Septuagint translation) which we call the Apocrypha. This theory arose from the assumption that the large 4th- and 5th-century Christian codices of the Greek Bible, in which the Apocrypha are found, went back to others, much older but equally capacious, produced by Jews. We now know that this assumption is mistaken. A contributory cause of the theory was the belief that the Apocrypha were mostly composed in Alexandria, and that their original language was Greek. These claims too are now widely doubted. Ecclesiasticus tells us that it was translated from Hebrew, and many believe that all the Apocrypha except Wisdom and 2 Maccabees were translated from a Semitic language and originated in Palestine. We can now explain the strange silence of Philo (early 1st century AD), the greatest of Alexandrian Jewish writers, in his voluminous works, where he quotes as divinely inspired many of the OT books but not one of the Apocrypha. The Jews of course read these books, and so did the early Christians, but the idea that they were Scripture is a purely Christian phenomenon, of slow and irregular development, and always opposed by the greatest scholars, such as Origen and Jerome. The NT never quotes the Apocrypha as Scripture, and the earliest Christian OT lists and biblical manuscripts contain few or none of them.

A better case could be made out for the canonicity of the so-called Pseudepigrapha (books under false names), such as 1 Enoch and Jubilees, which were cherished by the Essenes at Qumran; two of which are mentioned in the NT epistle of Jude. The Dead Sea Scrolls, however, never actually treat these books as Scripture, and the Essenes seem to have regarded them as an interpretative appendix to the standard canon, not as part of it. Jude's use of such books is best regarded as an argumentum ad hominem for readers influenced by them, i.e. an argument designed to take advantage of the readers' ideas (whether right or wrong) for a good purpose.

In the rabbinical literature there are discussions of the canonicity of five OT books – Ezekiel, Proverbs, Ecclesiastes, the Song of Songs and Esther. Some rabbis propose that these books should be withdrawn from use or should even be regarded as uninspired. The grounds they offer, such as contradictions, are also offered in the rabbinical literature against many other canonical books, including the books of Moses, and are refuted, but the books listed evidently presented specially intractable problems. It follows that the matter under discussion was that of removing books from the canon, not that of adding them to it, and the objections to these five books were eventually answered or dismissed. The theory that a synod at Jamnia about AD 90 added them to the Jewish canon is pure imagination. The academy at Jamnia did once discuss two of the books, Ecclesiastes and the Song of Songs, and confirmed their canonicity, but that is all.

The closing of the OT canon can hardly be dated later than the time of Judas Maccabaeus, in the second quarter of the 2nd century BC. Some books were probably recognized as Scripture more slowly than others, and the evidence of Ecclesiasticus (c. 180 BC) may indicate that the last to be recognized were Daniel and Esther. Ecclesiasticus seems to reflect a knowledge of Daniel, but the fact that its great catalogue of the 'famous men' of Scripture (Ecclus. 44 – 49) does not include either Daniel and his companions or Esther and Mordecai may indicate that there was not yet agreement to include Daniel and Esther among the Scriptures. By the time Ecclesiasticus was translated into Greek (c. 130 BC), the Scriptures had been organized in three sections and translated into Greek, as the prologue by the translator of the book shows, and the principles on which the threefold organization was made involved the arrangement of the books in order and a potential numbering of them (cf. 'The shape of the canon' below), so Daniel and Esther must by then have been included. These final steps may have been taken when Judas collected the scattered Scriptures after the Antiochene persecution (1 Macc. 1:56–57; 2 Macc. 2:13–15).

The history of the NT canon

Since the OT canon was closed more than two centuries before the NT canon was opened, it provided a model to which the NT canon could be conformed. By the 1st century, it was customary to think of all the authors of the OT books as prophets, but prophecy (in the full sense of the word) had ceased in the intertestamental period, as 1 Maccabees, Josephus and the rabbinical literature all bear witness. With the gospel, however, the long silence of prophecy was broken (Matt. 11:9; Acts 2:16–18; 11:27–28; 13:1; etc.), and written prophecy also was revived (Rev. 1:3; 10:11; 22:6–7, 9–10,18–19). With the NT prophets were linked the apostles (Luke 11:49; 1 Cor. 12:28–29; Eph. 4:11), as joint recipients of the mystery of the gospel and joint foundation stones of the Christian church (Eph. 2:20; 3:5), and the greatest Christian prophet of all was Jesus himself, the expected prophet like Moses (Mark 6:4; Luke 13:33; 24:19; Acts 3:22–23; 7:37).

At first the sayings of Jesus and the writings of the apostles were often quoted alongside the OT Scripture as having a similar authority but not as themselves constituting Scripture. The idea of scriptures in any language except Hebrew was alien to the Semitic mind, but the high reputation of the Septuagint must have made Greek Scriptures less unthinkable, and Paul's command that his epistles should be publicly read in the congregation (1 Thess. 5:27; cf. Col. 4:16) suggests that in his view they have scriptural status; the author of Revelation makes the same claim, more clearly, for his work (Rev. 1:3; 22:18–19.). In 2 Peter 3:16 Paul's epistles are actually called 'Scriptures', and a gospel is identified as 'the Scripture' in 1 Timothy 5:18. The use of 'Scripture(s)' to denote NT writings became increasingly common through the 2nd century and by the end of it was normal. By that date there was widespread agreement to accept as Scripture the four Gospels, the Acts of the Apostles, the thirteen epistles of Paul, 1 Peter and 1 John. The remaining seven books (the so-called 'Antilegomena', books spoken against) were still the subject of disagreement, and general agreement to include them was not reached until the end of the 4th century. A few extra books (notably the *Apocalypse of Peter* and the *Shepherd of Hermas*) were under consideration for a short time, but by the early 4th century it was agreed to exclude them. The three general criteria which the Fathers are known to have applied were origin in the apostolic circle, continuous use and orthodoxy.

There was already strong support for Hebrews and Revelation in the 2nd century, or even the late 1st, and a fair degree of support for Jude and 2 John. 3 John seems to have been little known, however, and James and 2 Peter, though rather better known, were seldom regarded as canonical. An international body like the Christian church would be bound to take time in reaching agreement on the canon, but the reason why it took longer with these seven books than with the others is that they all presented particular problems. In five cases there was doubt about apostolic authorship. Hebrews was anonymous and stylistically different from the acknowledged Pauline epistles. 2 Peter was stylistically different from 1 Peter, and Revelation from the other writings of John. The author of 2 and 3 John called himself 'the elder'. There was a second problem with Revelation: the Montanists claimed its support. (They also claimed the support of the Gospel of John, which caused some opponents of the Montanists to attack it, but it was so well established that the church simply brushed these criticisms aside.) Jude quoted the book of *Enoch*. The problem with James is not clearly recorded, but it probably related to the teaching given on justification in chapter two.

The church did not in the long run find these problems insuperable; nor need we. Hebrews is probably by an associate of Paul (*cf.* Heb. 13:23), though not by Paul himself. The stylistic differences between 1 and 2 Peter could be due to Peter's use of different scribes, and those between Revelation and the other Johannine literature due to John having no help with his Greek when in exile on Patmos. The use of 'the elder' does not exclude the possibility that the author of the Johannine letters was an apostle (*cf.* 1 Pet. 5:1). Revelation does not really give support to Montanism; Jude does not really recognize *1 Enoch* as Scripture; and James does not really agree with the Pharisees or disagree with Paul on justification.

Probably all these books were accepted as Scripture from an early period in some quarter of the church, even those whose acceptance is not recorded. Otherwise we would have to suppose that, at the end of the 4th century, some of them sprang suddenly from being canonical nowhere to being canonical everywhere, an implausible supposition.

The shape of the canon

The Hebrew OT is differently arranged from the Christian OT with which the English Bible has made us familiar. It is in three sections: the Law, the Prophets and the Hagiographa or Scriptures (probably meaning 'the *other* Scriptures'). The division is at first sight perplexing, especially with respect to the books assigned to each section, and until recently it was widely held to be a mere historical accident, due to the books having been recognized as Scripture (so it was supposed) at three different periods. However, the ancient order of the books, found in the Talmudic *baraita*, corrects this view. The arrangement is subtle, but fully intelligible. It is as follows (the five books of the Law, Genesis to Deuteronomy, being taken for granted): 'Our rabbis taught: The order of the Prophets is Joshua and Judges, Samuel and Kings, Jeremiah and Ezekiel, Isaiah and the Twelve ... the order of the Hagiographa is Ruth and the Book of Psalms and Job and Proverbs, Ecclesiastes and the Song of Songs and Lamentations, Daniel and the Scroll of Esther, Ezra and Chronicles' (*Baba Bathra* 14b).

An inspection of this list shows that each of the three sections contains narrative literature, covering three successive periods, and that each contains literature of another kind, differing from section to section. In the Law, the narrative runs from the creation to the death of Moses. The other kind of literature is law, but it is introduced into the context of the narrative, and the sequence is chronological throughout.

In the Prophets, the narrative books are distinct from the others; they are the first four, and they carry on the history, in chronological order, from where Deuteronomy leaves it, beginning from the death of Moses and ending with the end of the monarchy, at the start of the Babylonian Exile. The other four books in the Prophets are oracular literature, and they are arranged, not chronologically, but in descending order of size.

In the Hagiographa, there are four narrative books covering the period of the Exile and the return, and they are put after the others, probably so that the canon can begin with creation and end with the return, the beginning and end of biblical history. Chronicles, which recapitulates the whole of it, starting with Adam and ending with the return, is for that reason put last, after and not before Ezra-Nehemiah. Daniel, because of its first six chapters, is reckoned to be a narrative book. Ruth, which is really a narrative book relating to a quite different period, is treated in the Hagiographa as a preface to the Psalter, ending as it does with the genealogy of the psalmist David. The other six books are books of lyrics and wisdom, and once again they are arranged not chronologically but in descending order of size, a slight liberty being taken with the Song of Songs (which is really shorter than Lamentations, not longer), so as to keep the books relating to Solomon together.

This is by no means the only order in which the books of the Hebrew Bible have been arranged, but it is the oldest and most illuminating. In a modern printed Hebrew Bible, the three sections, with the books assigned to them, are maintained, but one will often find the oracular Prophets rearranged chronologically and the Hagiographa rearranged liturgically (with the five little books now read at Jewish festivals put together), though still ending with Chronicles.

Whether the Alexandrian Jews who translated the Septuagint made any alteration to the Hebrew arrangement we do not know, since no list that they produced has survived, though the way that Josephus simplifies the arrangement for the benefit of Greek readers, in his list mentioned earlier, is interesting. But when Christian lists and manuscripts of the OT begin to appear, we again find the subtle Hebrew arrangement simplified, and the books rearranged, according to literary character and chronology, as law, histories, poetical and wisdom books, prophecies (though not always in that order, and with the histories sometimes subdivided). The main difference is that, whereas Josephus put all the narrative books into the Prophets, Christians took all the narrative books out of the Prophets, and created a fourth section. This is the sort of arrangement that is found in Greek and Latin Bibles, and from there it was transferred to the English Bible. When books of the Apocrypha are included in Greek and Latin Bibles, they are usually assigned to the various standard categories in the same way. Following the Reformation, they were taken out and printed as a separate section between the Testaments in the English Bible. Among

modern English Bibles it is only those of Roman Catholic origin that still intermingle them with the canonical books.

The way Christians arranged the books of the NT was similar to the way they rearranged those of the OT. In ancient lists and manuscripts, as in modern printed Bibles, they are normally arranged as follows: the four Gospels; the Acts of the Apostles; two groups of epistles (either the Pauline epistles or the catholic epistles coming first); and the Revelation of John. The most basic books come first, another narrative book follows, and a prophetic book comes last, much as in the OT. The epistles take the place of the poetical and wisdom books, and it is here that the correspondence between the lists is most approximate.

Divergent forms of the canon

1. *The Samaritan canon.* The Samaritans have, from antiquity, recognized as canonical only the Pentateuch. This was at one time thought to indicate that when the Samaritans separated from the Jews in the time of Ezra and Nehemiah, the Jewish canon consisted simply of the Pentateuch. The Dead Sea Scrolls, however, have provided evidence that the Samaritans remained closely in touch with the Jews and conformed to most of their customs till the latter part of the 2nd century BC, when the Jews caused a permanent estrangement by destroying the Samaritan temple on Mount Gerizim. The Samaritans, it appears, reacted by rejecting the Prophets and Hagiographa, because of the recognition they give to the temple at Jerusalem.

2. *The Syrian canon.* When the standard Syriac translation of the Scriptures, the Peshitta, was made in the early 5th century, debate about the seven NT Antilegomena was still continuing in Syria, and only two of them, Hebrews and James, were included in the translation. The linguistic and political isolation of the Syrian churches was greatly accentuated by the Nestorian and Monophysite schisms of the 5th century, in which large parts of Syrian Christianity became separated for doctrinal reasons from the catholic communion of East and West. As a result, the status of the remaining five Antilegomena has continued to be doubtful in the Syrian churches.

The Ethiopian church, which was founded by missionaries from Syria, was further separated even from the other Monophysite churches for about 600 years, between the 7th and the 13th centuries, because of the Moslem domination of Egypt and Arabia. As a result its canon is quite eccentric, and today includes all the books generally recognized in East and West, with one possible exception, but also many of the Apocrypha, *1 Enoch*, *Jubilees* and certain late works, mainly of Ethiopian origin, which have been mistakenly identified with ancient books not available in Ethiopia.

3. *The Roman Catholic canon.* The Council of Trent, at its fourth session (1546), reacted to the Reformation by endorsing the list of the Scriptures first found in the 6th-century pseudo-Gelasian decree, and obliterating Jerome's distinction between the Hebrew Bible and the Apocrypha. Though later Roman Catholic writers sometimes speak of the Apocrypha as 'deutero-canonical', this is contrary to the official teaching of Trent, often reaffirmed since, most recently in the *Catechism of the Catholic Church* (120, 138). The church which really regards the Apocrypha as deutero-canonical (authoritative, but less so) is the Eastern Orthodox.

Bodies which have a defective canon obviously lack something of the full biblical message, but bodies which recognize additional books are probably in greater danger of going astray. Some books of the Apocrypha countenance a weaker view of original sin and of the need for salvation (Tobit 12:9; Wisdom 8:19–20; Ecclus. 1:14; 3:3, 30; 35:3); one recommends prayer for the forgiveness of those who have died in their sins (2 Macc. 12:39–45).

Text and versions

The language of the OT is Hebrew (and to a small extent Aramaic) and that of the NT is Greek. These were the languages in which the inspired authors wrote, and what they wrote is our starting point for study, faith and obedience. Thus the original text of what they wrote, in so far as it can now be recovered, is our starting point. But although it is our starting point, it is not therefore all that we need.

Well before the NT was written, the OT was translated into Greek, and the Septuagint translation has deeply affected the NT, both in its OT references and in its general religious phraseology. This fact shows the feasibility and

legitimacy of translating the Scriptures into other languages, and the importance of the Septuagint translation in particular.

Then again, the use that the NT makes of the OT shows that a transmitted text can have authority, and not just the original text. The NT writers quote the OT as it was in their day, and in translation, but even so attribute to it final authority. This indicates that the transmission of the text is firmly controlled by the providence of God, and that, though we should study all indications of what the original text may have been, we can have confidence that it has not been changed out of all recognition, so as to frustrate God's purpose of guiding his people through Scripture. These considerations would not apply to every aberration of an individual scribe, but they do apply to standard forms of the transmitted text, such as the Massoretic text of the Hebrew OT and the 'traditional' text of the Greek NT, and probably also to standard translations of them. At the same time, they do not give the transmitted text exclusive authority, or imply that it is identical with the original text.

As regards the original text itself, our search for it, though proper and important, is circumscribed in various ways. Even the oldest and most carefully written manuscripts are separated from it by a period of decades or centuries, and the study of them has convinced textual critics that they do not at every point correspond to the original. To get back further, conjecture is necessary, and though certain agreed procedures are employed by textual critics, they are such as can yield only possible or probable results and leave plenty of scope for disagreement. What is more, there is scope for disagreement as to what is being sought. Many of the biblical books show signs of having been edited or supplemented, sometimes by the original author, sometimes by another. Even when another hand has been at work, we seldom have the right to say that the changes it made were unnecessary. The edited text is often the only text for which we have manuscript evidence. What, then, are we looking for? The work as it originally left the hand of the primary author, or as it left the hand of the editor, whether the author or another? These doubts about the original text should make us humble enough to treat the transmitted text with a proper respect.

Since both the canon and the text are the forms in which it has pleased God to clothe his revelation, we accept them as his precious gifts, given to make us wise unto salvation, and use them with the confidence of believers.

Bibliography

R. T. Beckwith, *The Old Testament Canon of the New Testament Church* (London and Grand Rapids, 1985); *idem*, 'A modern theory of the Old Testament canon', *VT* 41, 1991, pp. 385–395; F. F. Bruce, *The Canon of Scripture* (Glasgow, 1988); S. Jellicoe, *The Septuagint and Modern Study* (Oxford, 1968); S. Z. Leiman, *The Canonization of Hebrew Scripture* (New Haven, ²1991); J. P. Lewis, 'What do we mean by Jabneh?', *JBR* 32, 1964, pp. 125–132; B. M. Metzger, *The Text of the New Testament* (Oxford, ²1968); *idem*, *The Early Versions of the New Testament* (Oxford, 1977); *idem*, *The Canon of the New Testament* (Oxford, 1987); J. D. Purvis, *The Samaritan Pentateuch and the Origin of the Samaritan Sect* (Cambridge, 1968); A. C. Sundberg Jr., *The Old Testament of the Early Church* (Cambridge, 1964); E. Tov, *Textual Criticism of the Hebrew Bible* (Minneapolis, 1992).

R. T. BECKWITH

Scripture

Introduction

Definitions

When Christians refer to the Bible as 'Scripture', they express their conviction that the Bible is the written word of God. The term 'holy Scripture(s)' was used by Jews to denote an established body of writings of divine origin, possessing authority for the people of God as well as for the individual (*cf. Epistle of Aristeas*, 155, 168; Philo, *Quis Rerum Divinarum Heres Sit* 106, 159; *Mishnah Yadayim* 3, 5). The early Christians shared this view: the (OT) Scriptures are 'utterances of God' (Rom. 3:2; *cf.* 1:2), even when the speaker is not God himself (*cf.* the quotation of Is. 28:11–12 in 1 Cor. 14:21). Jewish and the early Christian tradition agree that 'what Scripture says, God says'. Jewish and Christian interpretations of various statements in the Hebrew Scriptures differed, but the divine origin and the normative nature of Scripture were acknowledged by both groups. The first Christians extended the notion of the 'word of God' to the apostolic account and explanation of the person and ministry of Jesus Christ (*cf.* 1 Thess. 2:13), just as specific words of Jesus were regarded as authoritative (*cf.* 1 Cor. 7:10), and soon the term 'Scripture' was used for letters of the apostles (*cf.* 2 Pet. 3:16). The conviction that Scripture is the word of God was the undisputed tradition of the church until the 17th century.

Challenges

In the 17th century, philosophers and theologians began to challenge the truthfulness and authority of Scripture with reference to human reason (which was increasingly regarded as an independent source for truth about the world) and the nature of history (which was regarded as contingent, particularly in relation to the supposedly 'absolute' truths established by reason). René Descartes's method of establishing truth fundamentally changed the way 'progressive' theologians viewed Scripture, particularly its truthfulness and relevance. If on the one hand the insights of human reason are regarded as a priori correct and certain; if on the other hand the possibility of a contradiction between theology and philosophy is excluded; then Scripture must be open to criticism, unless such criticism is forbidden by clear dogmatic statements (K. Scholder). As such statements were soon regarded as inadmissible in an academic 'scientific' context, the appropriateness of the traditional concepts used to describe the nature of Scripture – word of God, revelation, inspiration, authority, canon – was challenged.

Today some critics abandon the traditional models for Scripture altogether, *e.g.* by attenuating the notion of an authoritative canon on the grounds that texts other than Scripture can mediate God's presence, and by suggesting a new view of how the Bible functions today (J. Barr). Others seek to redefine the traditional terms: revelation is seen as an 'occurrence' which happens within people and changes their self-understanding (R. Bultmann); the term 'word of God' is reserved for Jesus Christ (K. Barth); inspiration becomes the human experience of being inspired by someone to do something (W. J. Abraham), or a process whereby traditions are formulated, reshaped and transmitted within believing communities (P. J. Achtemeier), or an enhancement of one's understanding of God which is effected by the Bible (K. R. Trembath); biblical authority is limited to the saving purpose and effect of the Bible (D. K. McKim).

The problem with many of these approaches is that of establishing a clear and definite 'location' where humans may find truth, particularly truth about God. In the context of postmodern thinking, some scholars explicitly repudiate any appeal to normative 'readings' (of the Bible, or of any other text). More conservative scholars seek to preserve the notion that God speaks to humans; however, as some reject the traditional identification of Scripture as the word of God, and do not want to accord authority to an historical document, it is not clear which criteria might be used to establish where we may hear God's voice, unless one appeals to tradition, reason or experience. These alternatives all rely on the exercise of human reason in one form or another. As the history of humankind has made many people rather pessimistic concerning the competence of human reason to establish truth, the intrinsic subjectivity of these options does not give much ground for hope. As human reason is affected by the fall and thus by the malaise of sin, it cannot be the source of truth. If truth about God is not revealed to us, we have to remain agnostic. Without revelation we cannot know God. This is the reason why our understanding of Scripture as the word of God has to be derived from Scripture itself.

Consequences for biblical theology

The refusal to regard the Bible as Scripture, *i.e.* as the word of God, reflects the belief that the biblical documents, being historical in nature and diverse in outlook, do not constitute a coherent and established canon. As a result, biblical theology is thought to be impossible. The programmatic essay of W. Wrede (1859–1906) on 'The tasks and methods of NT theology' (in R. Morgan [ed.], *The Nature of New Testament Theology* [London, 1973], pp. 68–116) illustrates this view with reference to the NT. Wrede asserted that since 'logical thinking' cannot arrive at the conclusion that Scripture is a collection of inspired writings which constitute the revealed word of God, the traditional 'biblical theology of the NT' should be replaced by a 'history of early Christian religion and theology' which deliberately ignores the canon or any consideration of the question of revelation; the scholar who wants to deal with the NT in a scientific way must be guided by 'a pure, disinterested concern for knowledge, a concern that accepts every result that emerges', as the task of theology is not to serve the church but to pursue truth.

Today many critical scholars dismiss the possibility of biblical theology because they regard the Bible as a collection of diverse historical texts; they contain information and represent theological positions which are mutually contradictory, and revelation cannot be identified with historical documents anyway (*cf.* P. Pokorný, in *HBT* 15, pp. 83–94). Biblical scholars must work with a complex diversity of texts, sources, traditions and positions. Some believe that only confessionally bound 'scholars of the church' can attempt to formulate a biblical theology in the sense of a synthesis of 'early Christian thought' or an outline of the theologies of the whole Bible (H. Räisänen, *Beyond New Testament Theology*, p. 121).

The task

Biblical theology seeks to present a synthesis of the message of Scripture. It presupposes therefore a coherent and established canon of biblical books. It is precisely for this reason that the nature of the Bible as Scripture is of central importance. In order to understand what is entailed by the conviction that the Bible is Scripture, we need to understand the Bible as a collection of historical texts written over a long period of time, utilizing different literary forms and manifesting diverse perspectives, and as the word of God who spoke and continues to speak through its books. Biblical theology acknowledges the multidimensional nature of Scripture.

A brief note about theological method. With reference to the inductive procedures of the natural sciences during the 17th to 19th centuries, opponents of a high view of Scripture have often claimed that the only academically responsible approach to formulating a view of Scripture as God's word is on the basis of the historical, literary, theological and ethical features of the biblical books. Arguments from the nature of God are regarded as 'deductive', and thus related to dogmatic claims which may be appropriate in confessional statements of faith but which should be set aside in serious study of the Bible. Many scholars who work with these assumptions think it impossible to believe that Scripture is totally trustworthy in all respects, as the phenomena of Scripture allegedly reveal numerous errors and contradictions. Some who want to continue to accept the authority of Scripture for faith and practice believe that these conclusions as to the errancy of Scripture are unavoidable; but they have to admit that to adopt this position is to abandon the conviction of the Protestant Reformation that Scripture is the only valid norm which Christians acknowledge, to accept human reason as the only valid criterion in questions of interpretation, and to acknowledge that there is no absolute standard for truth and that Scripture might err in theological and ethical matters as well (cf. S. T. Davis). However, the history of biblical theology and biblical criticism shows that an emphasis on induction is no hindrance to a high view of Scripture. And more importantly, it is recognized in contemporary discussion of scientific theory that both induction and deduction have a place in the formulation of theories. Thus it is perfectly reasonable to begin one's enquiry with the nature of God and the state of humankind.

A relevant formulation of the nature of Scripture takes into account (1.) basic questions about the nature of God and the nature of humans, (2.) modern insights into the nature of language, (3.) the multidimensional nature of Scripture, as history, theology and literature, and, as an integrating model (4.) the nature of communication.

The nature of communication

We begin with the last point. The conviction that Scripture is the written word of God is based on the assumption that God has communicated and is communicating with human beings. In order to understand the nature of Scripture it is therefore helpful to focus first on the nature of communication and the various factors involved in the complex process of communication.

1. Interpersonal communication involves the use of language which utilizes symbols (words) to convey meaning. Meaning reflects the speaker's perception, experiences, intentions and construction of reality. Even though there is no consensus among theorists of language how the form of a word and its meaning are related, verbal communication is a commonplace experience and is usually carried out successfully.

2. The use of language in ordinary speech ('speech-acts') includes the following elements: locution, the act of speaking (using a particular language, choosing particular words, etc.); illocution, the use of speech to perform actions (e.g. informing someone of a situation, rebuking someone, etc.); proposition, the act of putting forward something for consideration (referring to some object or event and predicating meaning); and perlocution, the effect of an utterance on the actions or beliefs of the hearer (e.g. forgiving somebody). Illocutionary speech-acts include assertions, directives, commitments and expressions of emotion.

3. The source of the communication creates the message. The credibility of the speaker is linked to his or her competence, character and sociability. When the source is perceived to possess power, questions of control (the ability to apply sanctions), concern (the concern of the speaker for the listener), expertise (the superior knowledge of the speaker) and legitimation (the right of the speaker to exert control over the situation) become important.

4. The receiver is the person (or group of people) who is the target of communication. As the speaker seeks to get a reaction from an audience, she or he makes assumptions about

the listeners with regard to their age, social background, economic position, cultural situation and intelligence. Basic receiver skills include hearing, comprehension, retention and the willingness to give feedback.

5. The message involves reference to objects or events in the environment, translated into the symbolic code of language.

6. The medium or 'channel' of human communication may be spoken language, written texts, body movements or other non-verbal codes.

7. The transmission of the message can be disturbed or disrupted by unwanted stimuli ('noise') such as misunderstandings, psychological dispositions, previous experiences, selectivity or forgetfulness.

8. The response of the receiver to the message ('feedback') links the source to the receiver; it enables the speaker to adjust the message to fit the needs of the listener and the listener to adjust to the speaker.

God speaks

Our doctrine of Scripture as the word of God depends on our view of who God is and what he does. Here the temptation to focus on a single mode of God's nature must be resisted. God is both creator (implying his presence among his people and his fellowship with humans) and king (implying God's authority over history and human dependence), both transcendent Lord (implying God's omniscience and omnipotence and human finiteness) and ever active Father (implying God's love for his children and his acceptance of humans in virtue of his own nature), both perfect (implying God's total integrity and humanity's call to holiness) and merciful (implying God's forgiveness of wrongdoing and humanity's confidence of being accepted). A biblical doctrine of Scripture needs to take all these elements into account. A fundamental description of the nature of God as related to the nature of Scripture includes the following:

1. God is a person, *i.e.* he communicates, he speaks, he wills. When he reveals himself, he does so in an encounter with men and women, maintaining or establishing contact with his people. Encounter without verbal communication is limited and ambiguous. One of the most fundamental biblical assertions about God is that he speaks. Much of what he does, he does by speaking: warning and promising; commanding and prohibiting;

forgiving and comforting; informing and calling. When he reveals himself by uttering words addressed to human beings, he acts in accordance with his being (Jer. 23:29; Heb. 4:12). God continued to speak to humans after the fall (Gen. 3:9), when man and woman needed to be rescued from the consequences of their actions (Gen. 3:14–24). He promised to begin a new humanity with Abraham and his descendants (Gen. 17:3–16). He provided a new framework for fellowship with himself as the holy God when he spoke to Moses (Exod. 19:3–6). He spoke to the prophets; he spoke to the kings. He spoke through Jesus his Son (Matt. 11:27; 17:5; Heb. 1:2) who is his word in the flesh (John 1:14). And he spoke about a new earth yet to come (Rev. 21:5). God spoke directly to individuals: Abraham, Isaac, Jacob, Moses and Joshua, David and Solomon, Peter, Paul, John, and many others. And he spoke indirectly to the community of his people through intermediaries: such as the prophets and the apostles. God spoke through direct verbal communication and through dreams and visions. And he spoke through sacred documents such as the book of the covenant (Exod. 24:7) or the letters of the apostles.

2. God is transcendent spirit, *i.e.* he is not dependent upon anybody or anything; he is omnipresent in his creation; when he reveals himself, he cannot be limited as though he were only immanent (Exod. 20:4; 1 Cor. 2:14). When he speaks, his words reach their intended destination, and he can speak to any number of different people across time and space. Can the words of human authors convey divine truth? The answer is yes, if and when God chooses to use human words to communicate what he wants to say to people.

3. God is omniscient. As Creator and Lord, he knows the reality of creation and of human life; he knows the past, the present and the future; he knows what is real and what is possible; when he reveals himself, he does so in trustworthy and dependable ways (Ps. 119:89–90); he knows what humans need to know (Ps. 139:1–4). His words are true and reliable.

4. God is king. Nobody can resist his power; when he reveals himself, he is able to overcome all human obstacles to his disclosure (Is. 55:8–11). His words possess absolute authority.

5. God is lord. He rules history; when he reveals himself, he does so in space and time, in

the contingent circumstances of history and culture. His words are clothed in the thought patterns of distinct historical and cultural contexts.

6. God is holy. The distance between God and creation cannot be reduced from the human side. God abhors any rebellion against himself and any harm done to his creation. When he reveals himself, he is true to his pure nature and does so without sin (Ps. 12:6). His words are good and true. Because he wills his people to share in his holiness, his words offering forgiveness and salvation transform those who listen and respond.

7. God is faithful. He acts in accordance with his nature and his promises; when he reveals himself, he directs his interaction with humankind towards the restoration of the paradise which was lost (Deut. 7:9; 2 Cor. 1:20; Rev. 21:1–6). His words offer hope and effect salvation.

8. God is father. He is kind, loving and merciful; when he reveals himself, he seeks to save the lost, to make the wicked holy, to have fellowship with the human beings he created (Gen. 3:15, 21; 17:5–8; Exod. 19:3–6), so much so that he revealed himself in Jesus his eternal word who became a human being to establish his dominion over his creation (John 1:1, 14; 3:16; Phil. 2:6–11). When he reveals himself, his words are comprehensible, communicating with ordinary people in ordinary language and ordinary literary forms. The Reformers of the 16th century insisted that the Bible should be accessible to every Christian, not only to the professors at the universities. They translated Scripture into the vernacular, and wrote Bible commentaries and introductions. Since human beings, as finite creatures and guilty rebels, cannot recognize the truth about themselves or about God, God's words convey information on these matters, as God with his undeserved love seeks to bring humanity back to himself.

9. God is glorious, as creator and as redeemer, as Father of his people and as ruler of the nations. When he reveals himself, he is feared by his enemies and worshipped by his people.

10. God continues to speak. In the Bible he speaks (a) directly and subjectively, through Israel's recollection of his words (Deut. 6:6–9), and through the preaching of the gospel, which is the word of God (Acts 4:31; 1 Thess. 2:13; 1 Pet. 1:23), and (b) directly and objectively, through the Hebrew Scriptures, which continue to be the word of God (Matt. 5:17–18; 1 Cor. 10:11; 2 Tim. 3:16; 2 Pet. 1:20–21), through the apostolic letters (2 Pet. 3:16), and through the written Gospels and the other NT books. Today he speaks through the Christian Scriptures as a whole. God caused his word to be written down. He writes his commandments on tablets of stone. He commands Moses to write down his words (Exod. 34:27) and an account of his deeds (Exod. 17:14), so that coming generations would remember them, and so that God's people would know the basis and content of his covenant with them. A text can be both the word of God and the work of a human being, when God inspires it as such. God commands the individual Israelite to remember his words by reading written portions of it and by passing them on to the next generation. Many of the prophets wrote down the revelations they had received. The Jews of the Second Temple period in general, and Jesus and the early Christians in particular, regarded the documents of the Hebrew Bible as the written word of God. The church later included the NT in this category.

11. The credibility of God as he speaks to individuals and to communities is linked with his competence as creator, with his character as the holy and merciful Lord, and with his 'sociability' as the heavenly Father who speaks to ordinary human beings. Since God possesses power, humans have to acknowledge that God has the ability to apply sanctions if they do not listen to his word; that he is concerned for human beings despite the fact that humankind has chosen not to acknowledge him; that he alone may legitimately pronounce on fundamental topics such as reality, life and death, hope and destruction, promise and judgment.

Human beings listen

The targets of God's word are ordinary human beings. This is true when God speaks personally to people in concrete historical situations, and when he speaks through written documents which he has declared to be his word. When we consider God speaking to humans, the following points are fundamental.

1. Humankind was created by God. God called creation into existence through his sovereign word (cf. Gen. 1 – 2). This means that

humans are dependent upon God, created to live in fellowship with him, enjoying his presence, called to obey his glorious and caring will (Gen. 1:28; 2:16–19; Rev. 4:10–11).

2. Humankind was created in the 'image of God' (Gen. 1:27). This means that God's purpose for his creation involves his having continued contact with human beings; he speaks to them. Humans are created in God's image, which means that they too can speak, that they have a will, that they have a mind which can think, be creative and comprehend creation (*cf.* Gen. 2:19, and the OT wisdom literature), and that they can hear and understand God.

3. Humankind has lost God's presence. When humans disobeyed God's word concerning the knowledge of good and evil, they lost immediate fellowship with God and began to suffer pain, toil and mortality (Gen. 3). The barrier which has come between God the Creator and humanity the creature denies humans access to the truth about God and his creation (Rom. 1:18–23). But humans are still persons; they can still communicate; they continue to possess a will. But they cannot re-establish the perfection of paradise; they are unable to eliminate their own imperfections and those of creation. Without God taking the initiative in speaking to them, humans have no access to God, as neither experience (enthusiastic religion) nor reason (natural theology) are functioning 'interfaces' for communication between humans and God. Humans are dependent upon God, the merciful and holy Creator, revealing himself and his will. And this revelation has to be dependable.

Reference

The message of a speaker is focused on a particular event, object, person or process in the environment and verbalizes a proposition. It is the task of biblical theology to formulate the message of Scripture. Depending on one's view of God, and of humanity, different organizing principles may be used (*e.g.* salvation history, covenant, justification, reconciliation, creation, the people of God). The rich diversity of the message of Scripture needs to be heard.

Scripture as a medium of God's communication

The Bible declares that God has spoken in countless situations, and it claims to be a record of these divine communications. Scripture indicates various channels through which God spoke to people. Some heard God speak directly; some saw images through which God communicated (visions, dreams). God spoke through historical events (*e.g.* the Exodus) and personal experiences (*e.g.* those of Jonah). He spoke through people whom he had chosen to speak for him (prophets, apostles). God spoke through texts (*e.g.* the Book of the Covenant) written by people chosen for the task. And Christians are convinced that God speaks through Scripture. As a medium of divine communication Scripture can be described as a set of human-divine speech-acts, the diversity, literary contexts and historical settings of which need to be acknowledged.

Scripture as speech-acts

Scripture does not consist simply of timeless true propositions. It is not a collection of 'spiritual laws'. Besides assertions it contains questions and promises, riddles and parables, hymns and praise, commandments and warnings, laments and confessions, stories and letters.

1. The nature of Scripture has been described using the prophetic paradigm: Scripture communicates God's truths which people must believe and obey; Scripture reveals authoritative doctrine. This paradigm is appropriate with reference to propositions in assertive speech-acts. It explains some parts of Scripture (including important elements of the historical books; in the Hebrew Bible, Joshua, Judges, Samuel and Kings are regarded as prophetic books, indicating that it is God who declares what lessons are to be learnt from historical events). The authority of Scripture as God's word can be described in terms of intellectual belief; the proper response to assertive speech-acts is assent.

2. Scripture also contains directives which may be more or less forceful. Here the authority of Scripture requires categorical obedience (*e.g.* to the words of the Decalogue, to the laws in Lev.), or reflective observance (*e.g.* of the sayings of the wisdom literature, of the mandates of the Sermon on the Mount).

3. Scripture contains commissive speech-acts, in which God commits himself to a specific course of action in the future (*e.g.* promises). Here the proper response to the authority of Scripture is trust.

4. Scripture contains expressive speech-acts (psalms, hymns, songs, laments). Here the proper response to the authority of Scripture is to follow the invitation implicit in these texts to share and participate in their normative response to God's glory and revelation (*cf.* K. Vanhoozer, in D. A. Carson and J. D. Woodbridge, *Hermeneutics, Authority and Canon*, p. 94).

5. Some scholars limit the scope of biblical authority, restricting it to 'faith and practice' and claiming that it contains errors in historical and scientific matters. The roots of this position lie in the wedge driven between Scripture and science in the modern era. It is true that the main focus of much of Scripture is 'practice', the day-to-day living, of God's people, which results from their faith in God. But it is not possible to separate matters of faith from matters of history (*e.g.* the Exodus, or Jesus' death and resurrection). It is illegitimate to separate the authority of Christ from the authority of Scripture, or to oppose the one to the other. If Scripture is indeed the inspired word of God, *i.e.* authentic self-revelation, the questions of its authority and unity are settled. A 'high view' of Scripture is regarded as obscurantist by many; this charge is more an emotional reaction than the result of a responsible evaluation of the exegetical and theological consequences of the position. We must remind ourselves that appealing to and heeding authority is not irrational per se; it is an act of reason when it arises from an awareness of one's own limitations and from the acknowledgment that someone else has better understanding (H. G. Gadamer, *Truth and Method* [ET, London, 1975], p. 248).

Scripture as a collection of literary texts

When we speak of Scripture we speak of the OT and the NT, but we also speak of the Pentateuch, the prophetic writings, the psalms and the proverbs, the Gospels, the Acts and the letters. The character (or genre) of the biblical texts need to be taken into account when considering the nature of Scripture. J. Goldingay (*Models for Scripture*) points to four models:

1. The narrative books (Genesis to Esther, Gospels and Acts) characterize Scripture as witness: they pass on testimony to events in the history of Israel, of Jesus the Messiah and of his followers. Some have described the entire Bible as 'story': the story of God the creator and king working out human salvation. The biblical stories invite readers to believe that what God did for others, he might also do for them. The concept of witness implies reliability.

2. The commandments (in the Pentateuch, in the apostolic letters and elsewhere) characterize Scripture as authoritative canon: they stipulate normative behaviour for the people of God. The notion of authority which must be obeyed may be applied to other material; the Jews could refer to the entire Hebrew Bible as 'the Law'. Jesus cites a passage from Psalm 82:6 with 'is it not written in your Law', adding that as law 'Scripture cannot be broken' (John 10:34; for Paul *cf.* Rom. 3:19; Gal. 4:21–22).

3. The prophetic books characterize Scripture as inspired word: through the prophets God himself spoke (Heb. 1:1); as they experienced the activity of the Spirit of God they spoke the word of God (2 Pet. 1:21). The prophets repeatedly claim that they speak under divine prompting, that their words are framed by God, not by themselves (note the phrase 'thus says Yahweh'). The inspiration of God's Spirit guarantees that God's word will speak to the listener or reader in relevant ways. 2 Timothy 3:16 shows that the notion of inspiration was extended by the early Christians to all the biblical books (of the Hebrew Bible), notwithstanding their particular genre. In this they agreed with their Jewish contemporaries (*e.g.* Philo of Alexandria). The biblical texts carry the authority of God. Throughout salvation history God effected an identity between the words of the various biblical writers and his words through the process/event of inspiration. What the writers mean, God means.

4. The experiential books (the poetic books, various passages in the NT letters) characterize Scripture as experienced revelation: they offer insights into creation; they reflect on the experience of God's people in this world; they demonstrate the dynamic power of life in God's creation, however fallen and complex it might be.

These four 'models' represent very broad categories. If we take into account more complex analyses of the genres and forms used in Scripture, we may interpret the wisdom literature (Job, Prov., Eccles.) as revelation which explains creation, or the genre of biography (the Gospels) as people-focused revelation, or the genre of the letter as contextualized revelation. Furthermore, the category of 'inspired word' cannot be limited to the prophetic books (as understood in the Protestant tradition); the 'historical books' of the OT were regarded both in early Judaism and by Jesus and the apostles as having been written by prophets (the 'former prophets').

Implications of inspiration

The implications of the inspiration of Scripture may be listed as follows. 1. The inspiration of Scripture implies that God may be encountered in the words of Scripture. Since Scripture is the word of God, the ultimate goal of interpretation is primarily encounter with God rather than encounter with the human writers of the biblical texts. 2. The inspiration of Scripture forces us to recognize that theology is a discipline *sui generis* in which humans can participate only on the basis of adequate presuppositions. This implies that a specific *hermeneutica sacra* is necessary for the interpretation of Scripture. The inspiration of Scripture renders inappropriate any 'atheistic' methodology which acknowledges besides or 'above' Scripture other normative criteria for establishing truth (*e.g.* philosophical or general religious concepts of truth and reality, or scientific 'facts' which are more often than not just theories, or certain views of historical events or processes which are currently consensus views). Scripture must be interpreted by Scripture. 3. The inspiration of Scripture establishes its unity and legitimizes the attempt to harmonize discrepancies and tensions in the text. The unity of Scripture prohibits any criticism of the content of scriptural assertions ('*Sachkritik*'). The dissolution of the unity of OT and NT, of each individual Testament, and even of the individual books of Scripture, to which the biblical criticism of the last 200 years bears witness, has been partly a result of increased specialization, but more often a result of critical prejudices. 4. The inspiration of Scripture, which is in itself a historical event, demands historical exegesis of the text. Just as the evangelical doctrine of inspiration is not docetic, so evangelical exegesis is not docetic. 5. The inspiration of Scripture makes the faith of the interpreter significant. There is no 'neutral' interaction with the biblical text. 6. The inspiration of Scripture also liberates the interpreter from the tyranny of the historical method. True biblical interpretation is not concerned exclusively with historical questions, unlike much historical-critical scholarship. Dogmatic, dynamic, spiritual approaches to Scripture are acceptable, provided that they are tied to the wording of the text and do not introduce subjective ideas unrelated to its literal meaning. The inspiration of Scripture establishes a relationship between the academic, scholarly interpreter and the lay person who may also read and expound the Bible. 7. The inspiration of Scripture implies that Scripture may be applied to present circumstances. Scripture is the word of the unchangeable God; so it can and must be universally applicable. This universal applicability of Scripture makes preaching possible. 8. The inspiration of Scripture binds the interpreter, and thus the Christian community, to Scripture as God's word. Scripture is thus a protection against, and corrective for, any uncontrolled and subjective enthusiasm. At the same time it implies that the Bible can be a mere 'letter which kills' (2 Cor. 3:6), when it is handled not in the Spirit but in the flesh.

The process of inspiration

Various theories have been suggested to explain the process of inspiration. 'Plenary inspiration' focuses on the *extent* of the influence of God's Spirit over the content of Scripture: *all* Scripture is 'God-breathed' (2 Tim. 3:16). 'Verbal inspiration' affirms that the influence of God's Spirit over the content of Scripture cannot be limited to ideas or doctrines but extends to the smallest units of meaning (verbal inspiration is often, but wrongly, associated with a theory of mechanical dictation). It is a matter of debate among evangelicals whether the notion of the reliability and trustworthiness of Scripture carries with it the notion of 'factual inerrancy'. Questions about the definition, appropriateness and relevance of this term cannot be considered here.

The witness of the Spirit

How are we convinced that the Bible is indeed the written word of God that bears authoritative witness to his redemptive will, and that we should therefore view it as a unity? The answer of the Reformers, taking John 16:13 as the general principle for understanding divine revelation, is still valid: it is

God's Spirit who convinces us that the Bible is holy Scripture.

'Noise'

Communication can be disturbed or disrupted by unwanted stimuli ('noise'). As God speaks in and through Scripture, the following dispositions prevent his word from being heard as he wants it to be heard: misunderstanding (as when Sarah is promised a child); psychological dispositions such as fear (as with Israel in the wilderness); previous personal experiences (as with Pharaoh at the time of the Exodus); selectivity (as with some scribes and Pharisees in the Gospels); forgetfulness (as with the disciples of Jesus).

A more fundamental element of 'noise' is the specific historical and cultural circumstances in which God's word is conveyed. Many of these circumstances are not experienced today, at least not in the Western world (*e.g.* animal sacrifices, levirate marriage, the offering of meat to idols). Because God has revealed himself in history (note the introduction to the Decalogue, Exod. 20:1–2), and because the biblical books were written by recipients of or witnesses to such revelation, Scripture has to be interpreted historically, using the best available historical methods. Historical judgments deal with probabilities and certainty is not always possible; as a result hearing Scripture as the word of God can be difficult.

Another element of 'noise' is the need to interpret Scripture. An acceptance of the claims of Scripture concerning its own truthfulness does not guarantee true interpretations. Human interpreters can make, and have made, mistakes. Thus the meaning of Scripture has been disputed in many important and less important areas.

On a more general note, as Scripture is a collection of many books written over a period of more than a thousand years by authors who wrote for different audiences and had different objectives, it is not surprising that some statements or viewpoints seem to contradict others. Some critics regard such apparent contradictions as a reason why Scripture cannot be, in an unqualified sense, the word of God. (For possible responses to this view, see above, and also *Unity and diversity of Scripture.)

Effects

What Scripture does follows from what Scripture is, which is in turn tied to who God is. Because Scripture tells the story of God, the Creator of the world and King of his people, working out the salvation of humanity, and because God has inspired that story, written by different people at different times, so as to make it his word, Scripture draws its readers into the story and so transforms them. All Scripture, as it is God-breathed, is valuable for teaching, reproof, correction and training in righteousness, so that God's people may be complete, equipped for every good work (2 Tim. 3:16–17). The exhortation of J. A. Bengel which used to be printed on the first page of the *Novum Testamentum Graece*, is still valid: '*Te totum applica ad textum rem totam applica ad te*' ('Apply yourself totally to the text, apply the matter of the text totally to yourself').

The Jewish-Christian belief in God the Creator and Saviour, upheld in the medieval and Reformation churches until the 17th century, shaped their convictions about revelation and inspiration. The Deists' view of God and the resulting focus on the primacy of human reason gave rise to biblical criticism in the 18th century. The Romantic view of religion in the 19th century was more concerned with human religious experience than with divinely revealed truths. It is more than probable that the pluralistic and panentheistic parameters of contemporary (*e.g.* New Age) thinking will increasingly influence the way Christians will view and use Scripture; all sincere religious utterances and experiences will be treated as of equal worth, and the voice (or voices) of the Bible as just one (or some) of many. In this context it is as important as ever to maintain the traditional Christian view that Scripture is the word of God.

See also: BIBLICAL THEOLOGY; HISTORY OF BIBLICAL THEOLOGY; CHALLENGES TO BIBLICAL THEOLOGY; EXEGESIS AND HERMENEUTICS.

Bibliography

W. J. Abraham, *The Divine Inspiration of Holy Scripture* (Oxford, 1981); P. J. Achtemeier, *The Inspiration of Scripture* (Philadelphia, 1980); J. Barr, *Holy Scripture: Canon, Authority, Criticism* (Oxford and

Philadelphia, 1983); K. Barth, *Church Dogmatics* vol. 1 (ET, Edinburgh, 1956); R. J. Bauckham and B. Drewery (eds.), *Scripture, Tradition and Reason* (Edinburgh, 1988); D. G. Bloesch, *Holy Scripture* (Carlisle, 1994); R. Bultmann, 'The concept of revelation in the New Testament', in S. M. Ogden (ed.), *Existence and Faith* (London, 1964); D. A. Carson, 'Current issues in biblical theology', *BBR 5*, 1995, pp. 17–41; D. A. Carson, and J. D. Woodbridge (eds.), *Scripture and Truth* (Grand Rapids and Carlisle, 1996); idem, *Hermeneutics, Authority and Canon* (Grand Rapids and Carlisle, 1996); S. T. Davis, *The Debate About the Bible* (Philadelphia, 1977); J. D. G. Dunn, *The Living Word* (London and Philadelphia, 1988); J. Goldingay, *Models for Scripture* (Grand Rapids and Carlisle, 1994, 1995); C. F. H. Henry, *God, Revelation and Authority* (Waco, 1976–1983); I. H. Marshall, *Biblical Inspiration* (London, 1982); H. D. McDonald, *Theories of Revelation* (Grand Rapids, 1979); D. K. McKim, *What Christians Believe About the Bible* (Nashville, 1985); R. H. Nash, *The Word of God and the Mind of Man* (Grand Rapids, 1982); J. I. Packer in *NDT*, pp. 627–631; P. Pokorný, 'The Problem of Biblical Theology', *HBT 15*, 1993, pp. 83–94; H. Räisänen, *Beyond New Testament Theology* (London, 1990); P. E. Satterthwaite and D. F. Wright (eds.), *A Pathway into the Holy Scripture* (Grand Rapids, 1994); E. J. Schnabel, *Inspiration und Offenbarung* (Wuppertal, 1986); K. Scholder, *Ursprunge und Probleme der Bibelkritik im 17. Jahrhundert* (Munich, 1966); K. R. Trembath, *Evangelical Theories of Biblical Inspiration* (Oxford, 1987); K. Vanhoozer, 'God's mighty speech-acts: The doctrine of Scripture today', in Satterthwaite and Wright (eds.), *Pathway*, pp. 143–181; N. T. Wright, *The New Testament and the People of God* (London and Minneapolis, 1993).

E. J. SCHNABEL

Biblical History

Introduction

This article surveys the entire Bible from a 'biblical-theological' perspective; that is, from a perspective according to which the whole Bible is seen as describing the progressive unfolding of God's purposes of salvation for humanity. Clearly the Bible is a collection of books written at different times in different historical contexts. But a basic unity of theme may be detected in the Bible; the individual books contribute to one unfolding narrative, and later books clearly refer back to earlier ones. Advocates of this perspective, like those of the 'salvation-historical' view of the Bible, believe that later parts of the Bible take the form they do in part by building on traditions relating to earlier stages (J. Goldingay, *Approaches to Old Testament Interpretation*, pp. 66–96; L. G. Perdue, *The Collapse of History*, pp. 45–68). Further, in its tendency to use the outlines of the biblical account as its basic terms of reference in speaking about God, rather than, for example, relying on philosophical or abstract categories, their approach shares important features with that of 'narrative theology' (Perdue, *Collapse*, pp. 231–262).

From creation to new creation

In this section we give a 'broad-brush' presentation of the Bible's view of human history, and of God's unfolding purposes within that history. (If readers want more details on a particular biblical book, they should also read the article on that book.)

The Old Testament

Our treatment of the OT is structured around the narrative and prophetic books; the two corpora have a similar biblical-theological perspective (on the prophets, see D. E. Gowan, *Theology of the Prophetic Books*, esp. pp. 1–10). For the relationship of the Psalms and wisdom literature to this account, see below.

1. Key points in the OT account. The OT begins by describing God's creation of the world, all living creatures and, in particular, the first man and woman, who are blessed by God and charged with ruling the world in obedience to him (Gen. 1 – 2). Genesis 3 – 11 describe the disobedience of the man and the woman and its consequences, finishing in Genesis 11:1–9 with a picture of a world very like that of today, one in which men and women are alienated from God and each other and unable to remedy their circumstances. But the account of the spread of humanity does not focus simply on the spread of human wickedness; God's promise to the first woman (Gen. 3:15) suggests that her descendants will include 'offspring' ('seed': the term is ambiguous as to whether an individual or many descendants are in view) who will undo the destructive consequences of wickedness, and the genealogies of Genesis 3 – 11 pick up this promise by focusing on a particular line of descendants, from Adam through Seth, Noah and Shem, who are associated with hope, righteousness and blessing (Gen. 4:25–26; 5:29; 6:9; 9:26–27). A further genealogy takes this line down to Abram (Gen. 11:10–26).

In Genesis 12 Abram is called to leave his land and is given a promise of descendants who will become a great nation; they will not only enjoy God's blessing but also be the means of bringing blessing to 'all peoples on earth' (vv. 2–3). The terms of this promise imply a reversal of the negative developments described in Genesis 3 – 11: a man whose descendants will restore the blessing promised to the first man (*cf.* Gen. 1:28); a nation which will be used by God to address the plight of the scattered nations (cf. Gen. 11:1–9). Genesis 3 – 11 and 12 thus relate to each other as 'problem' and 'answer'. The rest of the Pentateuch traces the partial fulfilment of this promise (D. J. A. Clines, *The Theme of the Pentateuch* [Sheffield, 1978]). Abram's descendants become a multitude in Egypt (Exod. 1:6–7), are rescued from oppression in the Exodus, and, through Moses' mediation, enter into a covenant with God at Sinai, be-

coming a special nation, God's people Israel, who will acknowledge his kingship by obeying his laws, mirroring his holiness in their corporate life, and thereby acting as priests, revealing God's character to the nations and bringing blessing to them (Exod. 19:4–6; 20 – 23; Lev. 19:1–2; *cf.* Deut. 26:17–19). Israel's special relationship with God is reflected in their portrait in Exodus-Numbers; God is in their midst when they camp, and goes before them as they travel to the land he has promised them. By the time Moses addresses his last words to Israel in Deuteronomy, they are on the point of entering the land (Deut. 4:1–2; *cf.* Gen. 15:18–21). (On the Pentateuch see also W. J. Dumbrell, *The Search for Order*, pp. 15–55.)

The process of occupying the land begins under Joshua (Josh. 1 – 12). After problems in the land in subsequent generations (Judg., esp. 2:6 – 3:6), the conquest of the land is completed by David, Israel's second king, when he captures Jerusalem (2 Sam. 5:6–10). Since his reign sees the fulfilment of many of the promises given to Abraham, it is fitting that David should receive a promise concerning a line of rulers who would descend from him, the terms of which echo the earlier promises (2 Sam. 7:9–16, esp. v. 12; *cf.* Gen. 12:7; 15:4). During the reigns of David and Solomon Israel enjoys the 'rest' in the land anticipated by Moses (2 Sam. 7:1; 1 Kgs. 5:3–4; *cf.* Deut. 12:10); God's rule over Israel is made manifest by the bringing up of the ark to Jerusalem (2 Sam. 6) and the building of a temple there (1 Kgs. 6 – 8); and Israel starts to attract the admiring attention of the nations around her, again as Moses had hoped (2 Sam. 8:8–9; 1 Kgs. 5:1–2, 7; 10:1–9; *cf.* Deut. 4:5–8). From this point, the figure of the Davidic king (for whom another title is 'Messiah' or 'Anointed One'; *cf.* 1 Sam. 2:10) becomes important. Various texts in the Psalms, for example, develop the significance of the king's role, linking it to the theme of God ruling the nations justly from Zion (see below).

There follows a long period of decline: the division of the kingdom under Solomon's son Rehoboam, as a result of Solomon's unfaithfulness (1 Kgs. 11 – 12); the growing disobedience of both northern and southern kingdoms (1 Kgs. 16; 2 Kgs., esp. 16, 21; Hos. 4 – 5; Jer. 2 – 3); the outworking of the covenant curses (Deut. 28) against both kingdoms through enemy invasion (1 Kgs. 14:25–

26; 2 Kgs. 5:1–2; 10:32–33; 15:29; 24:1–2), siege and famine (2 Kgs. 6:24–25; 17:5; 25:1–3); and finally exile to Assyria and Babylonia respectively (2 Kgs. 17:6–23; 25:11). The Jerusalem temple is destroyed, God's glory having already departed from it because of the defilement of the people (2 Kgs. 25:9; Ezek. 8 – 10).

The prophetic books which record warnings of coming judgment also contain prophecies of restoration after judgment: of God pardoning his repentant people (Hos. 2; Jer. 31:18–20; *cf.* Deut. 30:1–10; 1 Kgs. 8:46–51); of the two kingdoms reunited in a purified land (Is. 11:11–16; Jer. 3:18; 30:1–11; Ezek. 37:15–23; 48:1–29) and enabled to obey God in a new way (Jer. 31:31–34; Ezek. 11:16–21; Zeph. 3:9–13); of Jerusalem and the temple rebuilt (Is. 54; Jer. 33:1–13; Ezek. 40 – 43) and God dwelling once again in the temple (Ezek. 43:1–4; 48:30–35); of a king from David's line who will rule the people justly (Hos. 3:5; Is. 11:1–9; Mic. 5:1–5; Jer. 23:1–6; Ezek. 37:24–28); of the nations coming to Zion to learn the ways of Israel's God (Is. 2:1–4; Jer. 3:17); and ultimately of a restored creation, as in Ezekiel's vision of a river flowing from the temple to revive the waters of the Dead Sea (47:1–12), or Isaiah's vision of a new heaven and new earth (65:17–25). Israel's restoration is sometimes described (metaphorically) in what appears to be resurrection language (Ezek. 37:1–14; *cf.* Hos. 6:1–3). It is important to stress that Israel's restoration is seen as part of a larger picture, the renewing of creation and the blessing of the nations, in fulfilment of God's purposes in calling Abraham.

One of the most extended restoration prophecies, Isaiah 40 – 55, introduces an individual described as '[the LORD's] Servant' (Is. 42:1; 49:5–6), who in some sense takes over the role of Israel (also denoted by the term 'servant' in these chapters: 41:8–10; 45:4), that of witnessing to God's power (43:10–13), when Israel in the misery of exile is too weak or stubborn to fulfil it (42:18–25; 48:1–11). This idea is especially clear in 49:3–6, where, speaking in the first person, the Servant declares that God said to him, 'You are my servant Israel' (v. 3), and that his appointed role is both to minister to Israel in exile (v. 5) and to be a 'light to the nations' (v. 6). In the most astonishing passage concerning the Servant, he is said, in language reminiscent of the Levitical sacrificial texts, to die for the sins of God's people (53:5–6, 8, 11–12). The identity of this figure is uncertain, and not only because he is unnamed. In some respects he resembles a king or prophet, and he also shares a number of features with Moses, particularly Moses as portrayed in Numbers (so G. P. Hugenberger in *The Lord's Anointed*, pp. 105–140). However, his role is essentially unprecedented. The time-frame of Isaiah 49 – 55 is also unclear; these chapters seem to look beyond the return from exile to a time when Zion's glory will be fully restored (ch. 54), and the Servant's ministry and death may be located in this distant future (R. E. Watts, 'Consolation or confrontation? Isaiah 40–55 and the delay of the new Exodus', *TynB* 41, 1990, pp. 31–59).

The books of Ezra and Nehemiah record what actually happened next: that Cyrus king of Persia, having defeated Babylon, permitted the exiles from the southern kingdom and their descendants to return to Judah (Ezra 1:1–4); that many of them did so, rebuilt the temple and celebrated the Passover in Judah again (Ezra 3; 6:13–22); that under Nehemiah the walls of Jerusalem were rebuilt in the face of opposition (Neh. 3 – 4, 6); that Jerusalem was re-inhabited (Neh. 11) and the walls dedicated with great joy (Neh. 12:27–43). These are significant achievements, yet a note of longing and disappointment is also sounded in these books. At the heart of the ceremonies described in Nehemiah 8 – 10 there is a long prayer of confession (ch. 9), which concludes with the Israelites lamenting their present situation; they remain slaves in the land God gave to their forefathers (v. 36), subject to foreign kings and 'in great distress' (v. 37). The books of Ezra and Nehemiah both conclude with chapters describing the sins into which some of the returned exiles fell: Sabbath violations (Neh. 13:15–22); failure to provide tithes (Neh. 13:10–13); and, most seriously, marriages with non-Israelite wives (Ezra 9 – 10; Neh. 13:23–28). It is clear that the events described in Ezra and Nehemiah fall well short of the hopes expressed by the 'restoration' prophecies.

Each of the post-exilic prophetic books concludes with passages which, in different ways, restate or develop the earlier prophecies of restoration (Hag. 2:20–23; Zech. 12 – 14, *cf.* ch. 8; Mal. 4), indicating that a complete fulfilment is still awaited.

The Psalms and wisdom literature. How may we relate the Psalms and wisdom literature, which together form a substantial portion of the OT, to the above account? We need to beware of flattening the distinctive perspectives of Psalms and wisdom in an effort to fit them into a biblical-theological framework (so Goldingay, *Approaches*, pp. 67–69). Nonetheless some possible connections may be suggested. (For much of what follows, see J. Goldingay, *Theological Diversity and the Authority of the Old Testament*, pp. 200–239).

Most obviously, many psalms refer to incidents from Israel's history or in other ways reflect a biblical-theological perspective (Pss. 66 – 69, 76 – 78, 105 – 107, 147, 149). Other psalms take up and develop themes found in the historical books and prophets: for example, psalms which stress the role of Zion (Pss. 46 – 48, 65, 132) or the king (Pss. 2, 18, 45, 69, 72, 110) in God's purposes. In many psalms there are no such external references: for example, some of the more obviously personal psalms. However, the final form of the Psalter perhaps reflects a desire to link the more individual themes of these psalms with the national issues raised in other psalms. It may be intentional, for example, that some of the psalms which express questionings, complaints or petitions in relation to the national sphere (Pss. 44, 74, 89, 90, 132) are juxtaposed with psalms similar in tone in which personal issues are more prominent (Pss. 42, 43, 73, 88, 130, 131). The figure of David, to whom about half the psalms are ascribed, is another clear link with the rest of the OT.

Similarly, while it is true that the wisdom literature hardly refers to events and people from Israel's history (but note the references to Solomon in Prov. 1:1; 10:1; *cf.* 1 Kgs. 3 – 5, esp. 4:32), wisdom has significant theological links with that history. One of the foundations of wisdom is the created order and its regularities (*e.g.* Prov. 8), the same created order which (the narrative and prophetic books declare) it is God's intention to restore. The very fact that wisdom sets out the ethical response God expects from all humans implies that it also describes the ethical response God expects from his people Israel, who are to display his wisdom to the nations around: hence the overlap which has been noted between the concerns of OT law and those of wisdom (M. Weinfeld, *Deuteronomy 1–11*, AB [New York, 1991], pp. 62–65). Finally, the questioning books like Job and Ecclesiastes handle issues (does God care? does God reward good and punish evil? is there a purpose to be discerned in life's ceaseless activity?) which also feature in the narrative books and prophets; though there the focus is more specifically the apparent frustration of God's purposes for Israel (in addition to Neh. 9:36–37, noted above, see Is. 63:7 – 64:12).

Important aspects of the OT account. (i) *Cross-textual allusions.* What was noted above about the Bible as a whole is also true of the OT alone; later books often allude to ideas in earlier books, and thus set what they say in a wider context. Zechariah 9:9–10 echoes Psalm 72 (esp. v. 17), which echoes 2 Samuel 7, which echoes Genesis 12 and 15; Jeremiah 4:23–26 alludes to the formless and dark state of the world before God set about the work of creation (Gen. 1:2) to suggest that Judah's history has run into the sands; Isaiah 26:16–18 picks up Genesis' idea of 'the line of promise' to similar effect. There are recurring themes: the promise to Abraham; covenant; the role of the king; the gift of the Promised Land (seen as a partial restoration of the blessings of the garden of Eden; *cf.* Deut. 8:7–9 and Gen. 2:9–14); Zion and the temple; the worship of God; sin and failure; the surrounding nations. Some later books clearly rework themes from earlier books; for example, Zechariah reworks themes from Ezekiel (I. Duguid, in *The Lord's Anointed*, pp. 265–280). Such reworkings, in which the 'ancestry' of ideas in later books is apparent, point to both consistency and development in God's purposes.

(ii) *What kind of restoration?* When the prophets speak of the return of all the tribes from exile, the repossession of the land, the nations flocking to a rebuilt and glorious Zion to learn from God, and so on, do they expect a literal fulfilment of their prophecies? In many cases there is no evidence that they do not; but in some texts it is possible that 'traditional' language (referring to entities familiar from Israel's past such as land, temple and tribes) is deliberately used in a hyperbolic way to suggest a non-literal fulfilment. Perhaps the clearest example is Ezekiel 47 – 48, which speaks of all twelve tribes dwelling in the land again, but in terms which appear, on closer examination, to be highly unrealistic: the new 'land of Israel' will be more extensive than even under David and Solomon (47:13–20); the new 'tribal territories' consist of twelve strips of land running from east to west, with a thirteenth reserved for the Levites and the temple, and no exact boundaries specified (48:1–29; contrast the detailed boundary descriptions of Josh. 13 – 21). Is this Ezekiel's way of saying that Israel has a future that will be as glorious as anything from Israel's past, but will also be qualitatively different from anything Israel has experienced so far? In the prophecies of the rebuilding of Zion in Isaiah 56 – 66 the promised restoration and glorification of Zion (see esp. chs. 60 – 62) seems to recede further and further into an unspecified future in which the 'new heavens' and 'new earth' dominate the final scene (65 – 66). Are these prophecies also meant to imply that Israel's future will be splendid, but unlike anything in her past? If so, then already in these passages there is some progress towards the NT's radical transformation of the OT hope.

(iii) *Disappointment.* Restoration, in any case, is far from complete when the OT comes to an end. D. J. A. Clines, in two essays on Genesis-Nehemiah ('What happens in Genesis' and 'The Old Testament histories: a reader's guide', pp. 49–66 and 85–105 of *What Does Eve Do to Help?* [Sheffield, 1990]), goes so far as to describe the books Genesis-Nehemiah as a 'narrative of unmitigated disaster' (p. 66), and an account of 'fair beginnings and foul endings' (p. 93). This may not do justice to the OT prophets' continuing hope for the future, but it is hard to dispute as a statement of Israel's fortunes up to this point. Even the more positive chapters of Israel's history hardly represent a full reversal of Genesis 3 – 11. Genesis' ending is relatively sunny, but the last verses of the book express an intense hope for the future fulfilment of God's promises (50:24–26). Leviticus represents Israel as a people whose holiness is constantly threatened by sin and defilement, so that even the tabernacle needs to be cleansed annually (Lev. 16); God dwells in the midst of the people, but the people must be 'insulated' from God's presence by the tabernacle and priestly mediation (Exod. 26 – 29; contrast the position in Gen. 2). More generally, what has happened to the hope of 'all peoples on earth' being blessed through Abraham's descendants? Not even in

the reigns of David and Solomon has this happened, still less under the later kings. What sort of an 'answer', in short, has Israel's history provided to the problem of human sin?

Between the Testaments

These questions become more serious in the intertestamental years (surveyed in J. H. Hayes and S. R. Mandell, *The Jewish People in Classical Antiquity* [Louisville, 1998]). This period sees the land of Israel passing from the hands of the Persians into those of Alexander, the Ptolemies, the Seleucids and finally the Romans. But apart from the successes of the Maccabean revolt (167–164 BC) and the period of Hasmonean rule that follows (ended by the coming of the Romans in 63 BC), little happens that even approximates to a fulfilment of the OT restoration prophecies. Jewish writings of the period attest to a sense that, though the Jews have returned to their ancestral lands, they are hardly better off than if they had not; in effect the exile continues (so N. T. Wright, *The New Testament and the People of God*, pp. 268–70, citing the [Qumran] *Damascus Document* 1:3–11; Tobit 14:5–7; 1 Baruch 3:6–8; 2 Macc. 1:27–29; along with Neh. 9:36–37).

The New Testament

The following account follows the narrative framework of the Gospels, Acts and Revelation (the last, of course, is not exactly straightforward narrative). Many of the NT letters, however, share the biblical-theological viewpoint of the Gospels, Acts and Revelation (*e.g.* Romans, Ephesians, Hebrews), though the immediate focus of their arguments may be somewhat narrower: for example, observance of the OT law (Galatians), apostasy (Hebrews), or ethics (1 Corinthians, 1 Peter). We shall, therefore, also refer to the letters.

Key points in the NT account. All four Gospels begin their accounts of Jesus with clear backward links to the OT: Matthew by tracing Jesus' genealogy back to Abraham, highlighting David and the Babylonian exile as significant stages in the genealogy (Matt. 1:1–17); Mark by relating John the Baptist's coming, which he sees as 'the beginning of the gospel about Jesus Christ', to two prophetic restoration texts (Mark 1:1–4; *cf.* Mal: 3:1; Is. 40:3); Luke by presenting the births of John the Baptist and of Jesus as a demonstration of God's faithfulness to Israel (Luke 1:46–55, 67–79; 2:29–32); John by echoing Genesis 1 (John 1:1–9). Jesus' call for repentance in the light of the coming of the kingdom of God (Matt. 4:17; Mark 1:15) seems similarly to pick up OT ideas of God's rule over the nations (*e.g.* Pss. 96 – 99) and God's forgiving Israel and restoring their fortunes (*e.g.* Is. 40:1–11; Jer. 31:34; Zeph. 3:14–20). Are the OT prophecies of Israel's restoration to be fulfilled in Jesus? Perhaps so, but not in any straightforward sense.

Jesus seems consistently to repudiate the idea that God's coming kingdom will include Israel's being restored to a position of pre-eminence among the nations. His teaching and actions can be seen as an attack on nationalistic views of the kingdom: his emphasis on non-violent ways of bringing in the kingdom (Matt. 5:5, 7, 9); his teaching of love for enemies (Matt. 5:43–48), which extends even to generous behaviour towards Roman soldiers (Matt. 5:41); his calling into question practices which are based on a strongly nationalistic view of holiness (Sabbath observance, Mark 2:23–27; ceremonial purity, Mark 7:1–23), and his association with those commonly held not to share in this holiness (Luke 5:27–32). He fiercely criticizes the Jewish religious leaders for leading their people astray (Matt. 23:1–32). He attacks the temple (Matt. 21:12–17), the centre of the nation's life, and perhaps even hints at the abolition of Mt Zion's special status as God's 'holy mountain' (Matt. 21:21–22; *cf.* Pss. 46 – 48). He prophesies the coming of judgment upon Jerusalem (Luke 21:5–24), which will leave the temple a ruin (vv. 5–6). It is hardly surprising that he is executed. (For extended discussion of many of these and the following points, see N. T. Wright, *Jesus and the Victory of God.*)

Yet Jesus' actions are consistent with his claim that the kingdom of God is at hand: his avoidance of fasting, implying that Israel's misfortunes are over (Mark 2:18–22; *cf.* Zech. 8:18–19); his dispensing of forgiveness, also related to Israel's restoration (Mark 2:1–12); his calling of twelve disciples, with its implication that Jesus is restoring Israel (all twelve tribes) around himself; the healings, at one point presented as signs that the exile is at last coming to an end (Matt. 11:2–6; *cf.* Is. 35, esp. vv. 5–6). Finally, he acknowledges that he is the promised Messiah, though only

privately to the Twelve, and with the immediate qualification that he is going to die (Mark 8:27–33). A later saying seems to imply that he understands his role as similar to that of the Servant in Isaiah (Mark 10:45; *cf.* Acts 8:26–35; 1 Pet. 2:24–25), and thus points to his coming death.

Jesus' resurrection is the unexpected vindication of his claims, the event by which he is publicly declared to be the Messiah (Acts 2:22–36; 4:8–11; *cf.* Rom. 1:3–4). Like the Servant in Isaiah, Jesus takes his people's sins on his own shoulders and emerges on the other side of death (*cf.* Is. 53:5–6, 11–12). He thus secures Israel's redemption (Luke 24:17–27; Acts 3:17–26), opens the way of salvation (Acts 4:12; 5:31) and begins the renewal of the entire creation (Acts 3:21; 2 Cor. 5:17). Appearing to his disciples after his resurrection, Jesus charges them to take the message of repentance and forgiveness in his name to all nations, beginning at Jerusalem (Matt. 28:18–20; Luke 24:47–48; Acts 1:8). When Jesus leaves them to go to the Father, his disciples are told that he will return (Acts 1:9–11); this hope is echoed in other parts of the NT (Acts 17:31; Rom. 13:11–14; 1 Thess. 4:13 – 5:10; Heb. 9:27–28). Thus the early church comes into being through the apostles' preaching, spreading out from Jerusalem around the Mediterranean world, until at the end of Acts Paul is preaching the message of Jesus in Rome (Acts 28:31).

In the account of the early church in Acts several OT ideas are developed and transformed. The command to 'make disciples of all nations ... teaching them to obey everything I have commanded you' (Matt. 28:18–19; *cf.* Rom. 1:5) takes up the idea of God ruling over the nations from Zion. The coming of God's Spirit at Pentecost, enabling people from many nations to hear the message of salvation (Acts 2:1–11), fulfils Joel's prophecy of the Day of the Lord (2:28–32); it is also a reversal of the Tower of Babel incident (Gen. 11:1–9) and a fulfilment of the promise to Abraham (Gen. 12:1–3), creating the possibility of people from many nations joining together to acknowledge, rather than to contest, God's kingship (*cf.* Rev. 7:9–10). The apostles' healings continue those of Jesus (Acts 3:1–10; 5:15–16; 14:8–10; 19:11–12): both are signs of a new, 'contagious' holiness which works outwards rather than, like the holiness described in Leviticus, being constantly under threat from sin. Clearly linked to this holiness is the welcoming of Gentiles into the church, and their endowment with the Holy Spirit (Acts 10:1 – 11:18; cf. Eph. 2:11–13); the link between Gentile inclusion and the transformation of OT ideas of holiness is made explicit in Peter's vision before he meets the Roman centurion Cornelius, in which unclean animals, representing Gentiles, are declared 'clean' by God (10:13–15, 28). Paul, writing to partly Gentile churches in Corinth and Ephesus, declares them collectively to be 'God's temple' (1 Cor. 3:16–17; Eph. 2:19–22; cf. John 2:19–22; 1 Pet. 2:4–8), a designation which, given the OT associations of the temple, has far-reaching implications: the Corinthian Christians are indwelt by God (cf. 1 Kgs. 8:10–11); they are the locus of God's rule over the nations (cf. Ps. 47:8); it is through them that the nations can approach God (cf. Is. 56:7).

By the end of Acts, Jesus' charge to baptize and make disciples of all nations is far from accomplished. The later letters speak of some in the churches turning aside to false teaching (1 Tim. 1:3–11; 2 Tim. 3:1–9; Jude 3–4; Rev. 2:14–16, 20–25), rather as the Israelites in the generations after Joshua turned to idolatry. It is clear as the NT draws to a close that the story of the church is not over, or even necessarily close to its end. But the last book of the NT presents a vision in which, at the close of human history, the enemies of God are finally defeated (Rev. 19 – 20), and God and 'the Lamb' (Jesus) reign in a 'new Jerusalem' which is part of a renewed heaven and earth (Rev. 21 – 22). The presence in the city of 'the river of the water of life' and 'the tree of life' (22:1–2) recalls the beginning of the biblical account (Gen. 2:8–14), just as their presence in a city, a human creation (cf. Gen. 4:17) recalls subsequent human history, now taken up into the new creation. The last note sounded in the NT is one of expectation and longing for the return of the Lord Jesus (Rev. 22:12–21).

Important aspects of the NT account. (i) *Continuity.* On the one hand, the NT writers regard Jesus' life, death and resurrection and the mission of the early church as the fulfilment of the OT promises. This view is reflected, for example, in the copious OT quotations and allusions in the NT, in the 'fulfilment' passages in Matthew (Matt. 2:15, 17–18, *etc.*), and in the 'typological' approach

of Hebrews, according to which the work of Christ is prefigured in the OT (see the discussion of typology in C. J. H. Wright, *Knowing Jesus through the Old Testament*, pp. 107–116). The church, continuing Jesus' work, is seen as taking over the task of OT Israel. This idea is implied in Paul's use of 'temple' imagery, noted above, and also in Peter's application to his readers of language used in Exodus to describe Israel's status (1 Pet. 2:9; cf. Exod. 19:4–6). Note also how in Revelation 21:10–14 the description of the new Jerusalem is reminiscent of Ezekiel's picture of the restored city of God (48:30–35) with twelve gates for the twelve tribes of Israel, but the twelve-fold foundation of the new Jerusalem is inscribed with the names of the 'twelve apostles of the Lamb' (Rev. 21:14). This verse seems clearly to imply that the prophetic hopes associated with the restoration of Israel are fulfilled through the apostolic (hence the church's) preaching of the message of Jesus.

(ii) *Discontinuity?* On the other hand, the NT writers seem to acknowledge that Jesus fulfilled the OT promises in an unexpected way, or at least not as the Jews of his day were expecting. This idea is expressed in John the Baptist's question to Jesus (Matt. 11:2–3); there are clear signs that Jesus is 'the one who was to come' (as Jesus implies in his response, vv. 4–6), but enough that is unexpected about Jesus to raise questions as well. Or again, resurrection was a familiar idea to the Jews of Jesus' day; in OT and later Jewish texts it is particularly associated with hopes of national restoration (Ezek. 37:1–14; Dan. 12:1–4; 2 Macc. 7; cf. N. T. Wright, *The New Testament*, pp. 320–334). But that one man should be resurrected apart from a general resurrection and the restoration of Israel was a startling development which entailed a radically revised understanding of God's faithfulness to his promises, particularly in respect to the nation of Israel. (Luke, Acts, Romans and Galatians all address this question in different ways.) For some, of course, Jesus was *too* unlike what was expected; many Jews of Jesus' day and later did not accept him as the promised saviour, a fact also acknowledged in the NT and addressed at length in Romans 9 – 11.

However, the startling and unexpected aspects of the NT message should not be over-emphasized. In a discussion of this issue C. J.

H. Wright (*Knowing Jesus*, pp. 70–77) uses the analogy of a boy whose father, in the period before motorized transportation, promises him a horse when he comes of age. By the time the boy grows up, the internal combustion engine has been invented, and the boy receives, not a horse, but a car. Has the father broken his promise? Most would say not; the car can do everything a horse could do and more, and expresses the father's love as clearly as the horse would have done. In a similar way, the restoration prophecies are not fulfilled literally, but the larger hope of which these prophecies were always no more than a part is realized: that of blessing for the nations and ultimately the renewal of the entire creation.

But is the biblical account history?

Is it historiography?

Implicit (and sometimes explicit) in many parts of the biblical account is the claim that the events narrated actually happened and that their having happened is significant. Thus, according to M. Sternberg, OT narratives everywhere claim the status of history (*The Poetics of Biblical Narrative* [Indiana, 1985], pp. 30–32). Similarly, Paul stakes his gospel on the historicity of the resurrection (1 Cor. 15:12–34).

Consideration of genre reinforces this conclusion. Thus, for example, K. L. Younger's study of Joshua 9 – 12 argues that the writer of Joshua constructs his account using language and concepts familiar to him from other ancient Near Eastern conquest accounts; if these accounts merit the title 'historiography', as they are usually held to do, then so does the account in Joshua (*Ancient Conquest Accounts* [Sheffield, 1990]). In a similar way, against earlier views that the Gospel writers' main concern was not the recording of traditions about Jesus, recent writers have stressed both that the Gospels fall into a recognized category of Hellenistic writing, the *bios*, or biography (R. A. Burridge, *What are the Gospels?* [Cambridge, 1992]), and that they were intended for wide circulation, precisely to the end that traditions about Jesus should become well known everywhere (R. J. Bauckham [ed.], *The Gospels for all Christians* [Grand Rapids, 1997]).

That does not mean that the Bible follows the conventions of modern historiography at all points. To mention only two issues: the writers of OT narrative show little interest in the question of how one evaluates historical evidence; and the frequent references in both Testaments to divine agency as an explanation of historical events would be felt by many today to disqualify the Bible from the category of historiography, though conservative Christians will naturally contest this point (see V. P. Long, *The Art of Biblical History*, pp. 120–135).

On any understanding, of course, the Bible's account is highly selective, as all history-writing must be. Although Genesis 1 – 11, the prophetic oracles against the nations (Amos 1 – 2; Is. 13 – 23; Jer. 46 – 51; Ezek. 25 – 32; Hab. 2), Daniel and Revelation together provide an outline interpretation of human history, countless events of world history recounted in other sources (*e.g.* most of Egyptian, Assyrian, Greek and Roman history) are not mentioned in the Bible. Furthermore, the Bible offers particular interpretations of the events it does narrate, interpretations which must always have been controversial, from the claim that Israel's god is the one true God, to the claim that the crucified Messiah Jesus was the focal point of his purposes. But from another viewpoint the biblical account is universal in scope, describing a divine purpose, the fulfilment of which will be the culmination of all human history (a Saviour who can meet all human aspirations, a judgment to which all will be subject, and so on).

Is it historical?

Recent decades have seen a growing scepticism towards the OT's presentation of Israel's history. The basis for this scepticism may be questionable, whether it be the older-style source criticism (as in Wellhausen's hugely influential documentary hypothesis of Pentateuchal origins) or the more recent tendency to treat much of the OT as Persian- or Hellenistic-period propaganda (*e.g.* N. P. Lemche, 'The Old Testament – A hellenistic book?', *SJOT* 7 [1993], pp. 163–193), but it is not always possible to mount a strong positive case for historicity. Often this case can be made only in the form of an argument concerning the general plausibility of the events narrated, as in J. K. Hoffmeier's work on Exodus (*Israel in Egypt: The Evidence for the Authenticity of the Exodus Tradition* [New

York, 1997]) or A. R. Millard's debate with J. M. Miller concerning the biblical account of Solomon's reign (in L. K. Handy [ed.], *The Age of Solomon* [Leiden, 1997], pp. 1–56).

In the case of the NT, contemporary external sources are more copious and more directly relevant to the biblical account. A. E. Harvey has used the phrase 'the constraints of history' to characterize one approach to the historical Jesus; given what is known of Palestine in the first centuries AD and BC, the historian can make some well-grounded claims about what Jesus must have done and said in order for the NT writers to attribute certain deeds and words to him (*Jesus and the Constraints of History* [London, 1982]; *cf.* N. T. Wright, *Jesus*, pp. 125–144). It is hard to think of similar constraints that apply in the case of the OT, or apply to the same degree; there are usually fewer extra-biblical data. Even in the case of the NT, historical argument of this sort will take the historian only part of the way to faith in Jesus.

We began this section by noting the frequent claim of both Testaments, explicit or implicit, to be giving an accurate account of events; we could go further and speak of the implicit biblical claim to be giving a divinely inspired account of events (see W. A. Grudem, 'Scripture's self-attestation and the problem of formulating a doctrine of Scripture', in D. A. Carson and J. D. Woodbridge [eds.], *Scripture and Truth* [Grand Rapids and Carlisle, ²1992], pp. 19–59). It must be acknowledged that both claims are often unsupported by any external data and often controverted in contemporary scholarship. But there is another range of 'extra-biblical testimony' which many find convincing: the intuitive sense that the biblical interpretation of human history, along with the insights that the Bible provides into the human condition and the workings of one's own heart, yields the best 'fit' with reality as one experiences it.

Conclusion

The biblical account gives us a narrative framework, a continuing story, in which we can, if we will, locate ourselves, and thereby find meaning in life (*cf.* C. E. Armerding, 'Faith and method in Old Testament study', in P. E. Satterthwaite and D. F. Wright [eds.], *A Pathway into the Holy Scripture* [Grand Rapids, 1994], pp. 31–49). Like the speakers in Nehemiah 9, we may feel dissatisfaction that the end of the narrative still seems far off, but in the light of Jesus' resurrection we have better grounds than they for confidence that the narrative will in due course end triumphantly.

Bibliography

W. J. Dumbrell, *The Search for Order: Biblical Eschatology in Focus* (Grand Rapids, 1994); J. Goldingay, *Approaches to Old Testament Interpretation* (Leicester, 1981); *idem*, *Theological Diversity and the Authority of the Old Testament* (Grand Rapids and Carlisle, 1987, 1995); D. E. Gowan, *Theology of the Prophetic Books: The Death and Resurrection of Israel* (Louisville, 1998); V. P. Long, *The Art of Biblical History* (Grand Rapids and Leicester, 1994); L. G. Perdue, *The Collapse of History: Reconstructing Old Testament Theology* (Minneapolis, 1994); P. E. Satterthwaite *et al.* (eds.), *The Lord's Anointed: Interpretation of Old Testament Messianic Texts* (Grand Rapids and Carlisle, 1995); C. J. H. Wright, *Knowing Jesus through the Old Testament* (London and Downers Grove, 1992); N. T. Wright, *The New Testament and the People of God* (London and Minneapolis, 1992); *idem, Jesus and the Victory of God* (London and Minneapolis, 1996).

P. E. SATTERTHWAITE

Exegesis and Hermeneutics

Introduction

How should one read the Bible so as to discover its theology? Because the task of biblical theology is to describe the theology of the Bible, it is vital for the biblical theologian to distinguish the theology of the text from the theology of this or that ecclesial reading, the message of the text from the tradition of its interpretation. Whether or not it is possible to recover the original meaning of a text on its own terms is the abiding question of hermeneutics. Questions about textual meaning and interpretation therefore lie at the centre of debates concerning the nature and method of biblical theology. To attempt biblical theology apart from reflection on hermeneutics and exegesis – the theory and practice of interpretation, respectively – is to risk a potentially idolatrous identification of one's own doctrine with that of the text.

Biblical theology and hermeneutics achieved the status of independent academic disciplines at roughly the same time, in the 18th century. Yet the connection between the two disciplines is much more than an accident of history. For biblical interpretation without biblical theology is (theologically speaking) empty; and biblical theology without biblical interpretation is (hermeneutically speaking) naive. It is thus no exaggeration to say that the fate of biblical theology at the turn of the new millennium is inseparably related to developments in hermeneutics, and to the fate of textual meaning in particular.

The viability of biblical theology as a discipline depends on the ability to interpret the biblical texts 'on their own terms'. It was this that set biblical theology apart from dogmatic theology insofar as the latter began from church confessions rather than the biblical canon. It remains to be seen, however, how the interpretation of the biblical theologian differs from that of the exegete and the systematic theologian. Hermeneutics both complicates and contributes to the project of biblical theology. The complication arises because of the historical distance that separates the text from readers today. How can interpreters know that they are recovering the original message rather than imposing their own ideas and agenda on the text? Yet hermeneutics also contributes to the project of biblical theology by showing more clearly how texts, thanks in large part to their literary forms, nevertheless communicate across distances in complex and often subtle ways.

The task of biblical hermeneutics, and hence of biblical theology, is to understand the biblical witness on its own terms. Despite the postmodern suspicion of all claims to correct interpretation, a number of recent developments in hermeneutics show how biblical theology might fulfil its role as a crucial mediating discipline between biblical studies and systematic theology.

Biblical theology and interpretation: meaning and method

If biblical theology is a form of biblical interpretation, how does it differ from other interpretative approaches? Specifically, does the interpretative method of the biblical theologian have more in common with that of the biblical scholar or that of the systematic theologian? Should the biblical theologian attend more to the original sense of particular passages, to the larger emerging patterns that cut across individual books, or to the Bible's overall message? On the one hand, the books of the Bible are historical documents; on the other hand, they are also the church's Scripture.

To be sure, the very name 'biblical theology' suggests the possibility (and actuality) of theologies that are *not* biblical, and of studies of the Bible that are less than theological. Where, then, does the biblical theologian stand with regard to the 'ugly ditch' that separates the work of the academic exegete from that of the confessing theologian? The challenge, and the hope, in thinking about hermeneutics and biblical theology together is to find a way of reading the Bible that will neither distort Scripture by reading it merely to confirm one's dogmatic theology, nor drain Scripture of theological significance by reading it in a historical-critical manner only. At its best, biblical theology bridges the yawning gap (an open wound, actually) between a theologically impoverished historical criticism of the Bible on the one hand, and an ecclesially motivated reading of the Christian Scripture on the other.

Why biblical theology is a hermeneutical discipline: meaning and interpretation

The task of biblical theology, as traditionally understood and as defined in this volume, is to present the theology of the Bible – the parts and the whole – in a manner that lets the texts, in all their peculiarity and particularity, set the agenda. In short, biblical theology is the attempt to provide a holistic yet historical account of the biblical testimony to the God of Israel and Jesus Christ. But what exactly is involved in this attempt? How does one set about presenting the theology of the Bible? Does it matter, for instance, whether one is a historian or a believer oneself? To paraphrase Bultmann's question to the exegete: is biblical theology without presuppositions possible?

J. P. Gabler

'Christian theology through the Middle Ages did not try to think the thoughts of the biblical writers *as distinct from their own*' (H. Boers, *What is NT Theology?* [Philadelphia, 1979], p. 16). By and large, medieval Christians did not take note of the cultural-historical distance separating the Bible from their lived faith. The Reformers' recognition that text and Christian tradition could come apart implied a distinction between the thought of the biblical authors and the thought of later theologians. In modern biblical studies, this conceptual distinction gave rise to a problem that has dominated the scholarly agenda, namely, how to overcome the cultural and historical distance that separates present-day readers from the original situation of the authors.

It is Gabler's 1787 lecture on the distinction between biblical and dogmatic theology, however, that is usually credited with the separation of the theological disciplines, and hence with the birth of biblical theology proper. Gabler sought to 'free' biblical study from the chains of church tradition and especially from the categories of dogmatic theology. He saw the goal of biblical theology as historical and descriptive, distinct from the didactic and normative goal of dogmatic theology. He thus called for an inductive approach that would yield a historically accu-

rate description of the religious thought-world of the biblical authors. At the same time, he wished to make biblical theology the foundation of dogmatics by uncovering the unchanging, divine concepts in the Bible. Hence he distinguished the objective description of its historical data ('true' biblical theology) from the attempt to sift out what was of permanent value for dogmatics ('pure' biblical theology).

Anthony Thiselton has recently called attention to an interesting parallel between biblical theology and hermeneutics at this point. Just as Gabler resists the captivity of exegesis to the categories of dogmatic theology, so H.-G. Gadamer resists the captivity of understanding to a single scientific method. Gadamer argues that human life invites understanding on its own terms, 'not in terms of some prior method predetermined in advance of engaging with the material' (A. Thiselton, in *The Modern Theologians*, p. 533). In other words, Gadamer gives properly *hermeneutical* rather than theological grounds for insisting on the primacy of the text.

Krister Stendahl

Some two hundred years after Gabler, Krister Stendahl reinforced the distinction between biblical and systematic theology with the hermeneutical distinction between 'what it meant' and 'what it means' (K. Stendahl, in *IDB* 1, pp. 418–432). It is the role of biblical theology, he argued, to describe 'what it meant' to the original author and to the original audience. The task of systematic theology is to say 'what it means' in a language and conceptuality intelligible to people living today. This division of interpretative labour represents a methodological schism in theology and hermeneutics alike. In theology, the net effect of this division of labour is to suggest that exegesis is somehow 'neutral' and 'objective' whereas dogmatics is 'biased' and 'subjective'.

Stendahl appears to have translated Kant's distinction between public fact and private values into the practice of biblical interpretation, with fateful results. The impact on hermeneutics is no less damaging. Once one distinguishes 'past facts' from 'present values', how may one then relate them? Stendahl's distinction between 'what it meant' and 'what it means' opens up a rift in biblical interpretation and hermeneutics alike, for it is not at all clear how one can move from description of the past to present or future application. It is one thing to say what the prophet Isaiah thought about God, quite another to say what present-day believers should think about God.

Truth and method in biblical theology: 'the descriptive task'

The idea of biblical theology as the task of giving historical descriptions of the biblical testimony gives rise to three important questions, all of which have become problematic. First, just what are we describing? What is the proper context within which to locate the meaning of the biblical text? Secondly, how do we get from historical descriptions of 'what it meant' – exegesis – to theological prescriptions of 'what it means'? And thirdly, is objective historical description really possible? Does not the interpreter always get in the way?

What are we describing?

It is not enough to define biblical theology in terms of ascertaining 'what it meant', for two reasons. In the first place, one must first specify the meaning of meaning, which is no small part of the task of hermeneutics. Just as importantly, one must also specify just what 'it' is. Is 'it' a word, a sentence, an event, a text, a group of texts, an entire Testament, or the whole canon? What exactly does biblical theology describe? The present article will first review various 20th-century options and then put forward an integrative model.

Can we move from historical descriptions of religion to norms for faith?

Can interpreters combine a descriptive-historical reading of the Bible with one that is prescriptive-theological? Solutions as to how to reconcile the descriptive and prescriptive have been in short supply. To a great extent, scholars in the academy have read the Bible in one way, while church members have read it in another. It has been far from apparent whether, and how, 'what it meant' to Moses, or Ezekiel, or even John and Paul should be considered authoritative for Christians today. While historians may be content with describing human religious experience, believers come to Scripture with the aim of knowing God. Indeed, the main tension in modern biblical studies results from a clash of two interpretative frameworks, the historian's and

the believer's. The ultimate goal of biblical theology, of course, is not to impose an alien framework onto Scripture but rather to let the Bible's own theological framework come to light.

Some biblical critics seek to locate authority in the historically-reconstructed religious experience that comes to expression in the text. This approach gives rise to two problems, however. First, it locates authority behind the text, that is, elsewhere than in the text. Secondly, it does not explain why the religious experiences and beliefs of an ancient people should be considered binding for contemporary people. True, the Bible is full of fascinating grist for the historian's or cultural anthropologist's mill, but how are believers looking for the word of God to separate the wheat from the chaff?

Modern biblical scholars have thus sought a hermeneutical alchemy that would somehow change the dross of historically conditioned religion to the gold of pure theology. R. Bultmann's 'demythologizing', for instance, was a hermeneutical process that restated and repackaged the kerygma in terms of existentialist philosophy, abstracting timeless truths of human existence from the 'primitive' stories that make up much of the NT. Such alchemy has more hermeneutical magic than science about it, however, and Bultmann's demythologizing sometimes appears as arbitrary as early Christian allegorizing (yet another attempt to extract a universally relevant 'what it means' from a historically conditioned particular 'what it meant').

Is biblical theology without presuppositions possible?

Since the Enlightenment, biblical exegesis has largely operated on the assumption that a neutral and objective description of 'what it meant' is both desirable and possible, at least in the academy. Upon closer inspection, this assumption is tied up with epistemological foundationalism and with the concomitant notion that the result of exegesis is objective knowledge. Any capable biblical scholar, in contemplating the historical evidence, should in principle reach the same conclusion. With the advent of modern hermeneutics, however, these unstated epistemological assumptions have now been challenged, if not wholly overturned. Today, hermeneutics deals with the general problem of human understanding, a problem that includes the historicity of the reader as well as the historicity of the text. Theories of textual interpretation now deal not only with questions of method (*e.g.* how to do exegesis) but also with questions about the interpreter. Hermeneutic philosophers such as Gadamer and P. Ricoeur, for instance, deny the objectivity and neutrality of historical description, preferring rather to speak of a 'fusion of two horizons' (text and reader). Two hundred years on, the fates of biblical theology and hermeneutics remain intertwined.

It was Bultmann himself who suggested that exegesis without presuppositions is impossible. Every reader of the Bible makes certain assumptions (presuppositions) about what is being said and about the right way of questioning the material so as to get understanding. For Bultmann, the true subject matter of the Bible concerns human existence, both sinful and faithful. He therefore read the text expecting to find existential truths. Indeed, his *Theology of the New Testament* is essentially an existential interpretation of the writings of John and Paul. For Bultmann, then, biblical theology is a matter of interpreting the Bible with categories drawn largely from outside the biblical text (*e.g.* existence, temporality, inauthenticity).

Karl Barth agrees with Bultmann that a purely 'historical' exegesis, unaffected by presuppositions, is a will o' the wisp. Yet he criticizes Bultmann, along with other historical critics, for not being critical enough, in that their historical reconstructions and existentialist applications ultimately fall short of engaging the real subject matter of the text. Understanding the book of Romans involves more than a disinterested knowledge of its language and composition; it involves a personal response to the object of the text's witness, the word of God. Barth here echoes the concern of Adolf Schlatter, for whom biblical interpretation is *historically* inadequate if it fails to recognize the personal address of God. *Contra* Gabler, one does not first do one's historical homework and only then begin to do theology. On the contrary, one's exegesis is already affected by one's dogmatic beliefs. The relationship between exegesis and theology is more a dialogical conversation than it is a linear or unidirectional process. Hermeneutics, in calling attention to the assumptions readers bring to the text, reminds us that theology is involved in the task of exegesis from the outset.

So-called postmodern thinkers (*i.e.* those who no longer trust reason's power to give us universal truths or a universal point of view) have intensified these doubts about the possibility of objective description, so much so that many deny the validity of historical criticism altogether. For postmoderns, the way one reads, and the meaning one finds, is thought more to reflect the *reader's* interests, aims and context than those of the author. Some feminist biblical scholars, for instance, use women's experience or the norm of equality for women as a criterion for evaluating the biblical text. They expose and decry the patriarchal ideology that lies behind many of the explicit laws and unspoken assumptions in Scripture. Do such exegetes hear the voice, and theology, of the text, or do they hear only their own voices, their own ideologies? Modernity's so-called hermeneutics of suspicion (*i.e.* the critical questioning of traditional interpretations) has now hardened into the postmodern suspicion of hermeneutics itself. Henceforth, all attempts to interpret – to say 'what it meant' – are seen as wilful impositions, on the text and on other readers. Postmodern exegesis has become a thoroughly pluralistic and political affair where no one is able to say why one interpretative community's reading should count more than another's.

What is at stake: the integrity of the theological disciplines

The postmodern challenge is simply stated: every attempt to describe 'what it meant' is in fact only an assertion of *what it means to me*, or worse, *what we will it to mean*. Stated in these terms, the real issue comes to light: the question of authority and the locus of the word of God. If all words are historically conditioned, and if all readings are ideologically conditioned, it is difficult, if not impossible, to believe in a word from God.

The postmodern suspicion of hermeneutics leads inexorably to the suspicion of biblical theology. The contemporary crisis in interpretation is simply the last stage of the story in which biblical studies and Christian theology have gone their separate ways. The rift that divides biblical studies from theology will be bridged only if we develop a theological hermeneutic – a theory of interpretation informed by Christian doctrine – and if we simultaneously recover the distinctive contribution of biblical theology to the project of biblical interpretation.

It is helpful to see the various theological disciplines in relation to their common interpretative task. 'Biblical theology' is the name of an interpretative approach to the Bible which assumes that the word of God is textually mediated through the diverse literary, and historically-conditioned, words of human beings. It is therefore an intrinsically hermeneutical endeavour, having to do with the interpretation of the variety of biblical witnesses that communicate the word of God. If theology is indeed largely a matter of biblical interpretation, what is the place of biblical theology among the theological disciplines? Just where do we situate biblical theology on the 'hermeneutical arch' from explanation to understanding? How can we move beyond the sterile dichotomy between historical exegesis and theological interpretation?

One way forward is to introduce the notion of different kinds and levels of textual description. There is an important *via media* between the critical fragmentation of the Bible into a hodgepodge of cultural and theological diversity on the one hand, and a simplistic systematization of the Bible into a single conceptual scheme on the other. It is important not to say that only some readers should read the Bible with a theological interest. To say this would be to make biblical theologians simply one more interpretative interest group. Biblical theology must be more than 'theologically motivated interpretation'. It would be to make a stronger claim to argue that any description that fell short of describing a text's theology remains incomplete. To state the claim more positively, biblical theology corresponds to the interests of the texts themselves (W. Jeanrond, *Text and Interpretation*).

New developments in hermeneutics (*e.g.* communicative action, genre criticism, narrative studies) have prepared the way for the 'second coming' of biblical theology in the 21st century by enabling us to attend to a level of textual meaning of which traditional historical-criticism was largely ignorant: the literary. Biblical theology, reinvigorated by a new appreciation of what it is to interpret texts, provides the missing link that permits the theological lion to lie down with the exegetical lamb. The promise of biblical theology lies in its ability to reconcile the systematic 'one' with the exegetical 'many'.

Levels of biblical theological description

Though biblical theologians have been adamant in distinguishing their own work from the more external interpretations of dogmatic and systematic theology, many believe that a description of biblical faith should also be normative for the faith community today. As we have seen, however, their difficulty lies in explaining how to proceed smoothly from a description of 'what it meant' to 'what it means' for the church today. Yet it is the text, considered at certain higher levels of description, which itself provides the decisive clue as to its continuing significance.

Describing biblical words: theology by dictionary

On its most basic level, exegesis consists in expounding linguistic meaning in its appropriate historical context. The aim of the exegete is, in the first instance, philological and historical: the recovery of what words meant in their original context.

If the aim of biblical theology is to derive theology from the Bible on the Bible's own terms, what better way to accomplish this task than to derive theology from the actual terms – that is, *words* – of the Bible? Surely on this level, one might think, the biblical theologian could attain to 'pure description'. The so-called Biblical Theology Movement, popular in North America in the 1940s and 1950s, was preoccupied with the notion that word studies and etymologies gave access to the distinctive mentality and theology of the biblical authors. The Hebrew language was evidence of the peculiarly Hebrew (biblical) way of thinking about God, it was claimed. Members of the Biblical Theology Movement argued, on the basis of word studies, that the biblical notions of time, history, and divine action were dynamic and concrete, in contrast to the static and abstract concepts of the Greeks. Members of the Biblical Theology Movement had a tendency to view theology *as* philology.

James Barr's *The Semantics of Biblical Language* (London and New York, 1961) is a formidable critique of the linguistic and hermeneutical presuppositions that lay behind several of the articles in the early volumes of G. Kittel's *TDNT*, a work that, like the Biblical Theology Movement, looked to words as the primary locus of the Bible's theology. First, Barr attacks the assumption that words have certain root meanings that remain constant, even across centuries of use. It is simply not the case that the 'basic' meaning of a word is present in each individual use of it. Many of the entries in *TDNT* were also guilty of what Barr called 'illegitimate totality transfer'. This refers to the error of reading all possible meanings of a particular term into a single occurrence of the word. While it is true that some words can have several meanings (*e.g.* in the phrase 'he's hot', the word 'hot' could refer to his temperature, anger, or tennis), it is wrong to think that the many possibilities are always contained in the one use.

Closely related to this first mistake is a second error: the etymological fallacy. The meaning of a word cannot be deduced from its etymology or origin. Instead, the meaning of a word must be determined in the concrete *context* of its use. Barr's work demonstrated that it is fallacious to move too quickly from word to concept (*e.g.* from biblical words to theological doctrines). The moral is clear; one cannot move from a study of words (*e.g.* 'salvation', 'to save') to biblical theology (*e.g.* soteriology).

Barr correctly observes that meaning is expressed at the level of a sentence (*i.e.* in the author's particular *use* of words) rather than at the level of the sign (*i.e.* in the individual words considered apart from the context of their use). The Biblical Theology Movement, we may conclude, ultimately foundered on a misleading picture of language and an inadequate theory of meaning. It is one thing to study the etymology of a word, another to study what an author meant when using it on a particular occasion. 'What it meant' has less to do with the origins or history of a word than with the circumstances of its actual use.

The lesson to be drawn from the short-lived Biblical Theology Movement is that, in Barr's words, 'It is the sentence (and of course the still larger literary complex ...) which is the linguistic bearer of the usual theological statement, and not the word (the lexical unit)' (*Semantics of Biblical Language*, p. 263). In short, the smallest unit of linguistic communication is not the isolated word but words as

used in the performance of 'speech acts' (see K. Vanhoozer, *Is There a Meaning in this Text?*, pp. 218–229).

Describing biblical events: revelation and historical interpretation

A second possibility is that biblical theology describes either revelatory events or religious experiences. Modern biblical critics, having discarded the assumption of supernatural inspiration, came to see the Bible as a collection of fallible human documents. The new theological presupposition (not always acknowledged) was that knowledge of God is mediated through the religious experience to which the Bible bears witness. As Hans Frei brilliantly demonstrated, the inevitable result was that theological significance was relocated *behind* the text (see H. Frei, *Eclipse of Biblical Narrative*).

According to a number of biblical critics, what we have in the Bible is an interpretation of salvation history from the perspective of the faith community. However, interpretations that substitute a description of events *behind* the text for a description of what the texts are actually saying generally teach only *religion*, not theology. Be that as it may, modern biblical critics are more interested in what may be found behind the text and in explaining the processes of the text's composition rather than in describing what lies in the text and its processes of communication. The result: critical interpretations that allegedly reconstruct 'what actually happened', but only at the cost of losing the perspectives of the biblical witnesses themselves.

Describing biblical books: literary genres and 'word views'

The Biblical Theology Movement failed in its attempt to derive theology from words. Similarly, modern biblical criticism has failed in its attempt to derive theology from extra-biblical events or experience. In each case, the error was as much hermeneutical as theological. To be precise, biblical scholars in the tradition of Stendahl failed to answer two vital questions: 1. what is the 'it' being described? 2. what is the meaning of 'meant'? Any adequate biblical theology must engage with hermeneutics at least long enough to answer the questions 'What is a text?' and 'How do we determine textual meaning?' For how one approaches an object of study depends in large part on the nature of the object to be known.

Modern biblical criticism, while professing to study the text scientifically, in fact approached the text with the anti-theological presuppositions of secular reason and hence with a bias against the unity of the text and an anti-narrative hermeneutic. Perhaps nothing is so typical of the historical-critical method than its tendency to fragment the text. By contrast, the most exciting developments in biblical theology are those that approach the texts with a sense of their literary integrity, a sense that stems from a postcritical hermeneutic which is open to being shaped by Christian perspectives (*cf.* Vanhoozer, *Is There a Meaning?*, Part Two).

1. *What is a text?* A text is an extended piece of discourse – something said by someone to someone else about something – fixed by writing. Literary texts are thus best viewed as communicative actions performed on a variety of levels for the reader's contemplation. To understand a text, one needs to do more than parse every verb. One needs to know what an author is doing. For texts have both matter (a message, a topic) and energy (the use to which an authors puts his message).

J. Barr and P. Ricoeur agree; the basic unit of meaning is not the individual sign or word but the sentence. For words are ambiguous until they are used in concrete instances of discourse. If biblical theology involves description, then it behooves the biblical theologian to use the right categories to describe the ways in which authors communicate their theologies. Biblical theologians need, first, categories for describing communicative action, and second, categories for describing different kinds of communicative action.

Properly to interpret biblical discourse requires one to develop an awareness of what authors are doing in their texts, of what the philosophers J. L. Austin and John Searle call 'speech acts' (J. Searle, *Speech Acts: An Essay in the Philosophy of Language* [New York and Cambridge, 1969]). In particular, one needs to attend not only to the words themselves but to what authors are *doing* with their words (the 'illocution'). One needs also to appreciate the way in which speech acts can be put together to form more sophisticated 'text acts' (*e.g.* stories, psalms, epistles). The discipline of biblical theology thus in-

volves not only linguistic and historical but also *literary* competence. In the words of N. T. Wright: 'If we are to be historians and theologians, we must also be literary critics' (*The New Testament and the People of God*, p. 25).

Biblical theology aims to give theological interpretations of the Bible on its own terms. It is precisely this aim that links the fate of biblical theology and that of hermeneutics. Far from being inimical to biblical theology, recent work in hermeneutics may provide the conditions for its contemporary renaissance. What is needed is a biblical theology that attends precisely to the level of the text as a complex communicative act, as a structured literary act with a certain kind of wholeness. The 'it' in Stendahl's 'what it meant', in other words, is the text, taken in all its literary integrity as a complex written communication.

2. *Literary genre and the forms of biblical discourse.* To focus on the higher, textual level of communicative action is to come to appreciate the importance of literary form. Only by attending to a text's literary form or genre does one learn what kind of thing, or communicative act, it is. Note that a number of exegetical approaches are necessary to accomplish the task of understanding the text as a whole. What interpreters ultimately seek to determine, however, is what an author is *doing* in a text: making a promise; giving a warning; stating how things are; expressing a personal preference; telling a story; or whatever. It follows that biblical theology should not treat biblical words out of their literary context, but rather describe how they are used in the context of the literary whole of which they are part. It also follows that our only access to the events to which the Bible bears witness is *in* and *through* the literary form, not apart from it. If the literary form of the Bible is essential to its theological and historical content, then biblical theology ignores the diverse literary genres of the Bible at its peril.

Hans Frei has argued that the significance of the Bible's literary forms was lost as modern biblical scholars, in their haste to find the truth (*e.g.* 'what actually happened', or a theological proposition) used the text as evidence for something *else*. The Bible gradually came to be read in the light of extrabiblical evidence, leading to what Frei terms the 'great reversal' in biblical hermeneutics, where the literary form of the text was eclipsed in favour of recovering its historical or doctrinal content. Such biblical interpretation, Frei argued, fails spectacularly to study the Bible on its own literary terms. By contrast, a hermeneutical approach that attends to the literary form of the biblical text reverses the 'great reversal' in biblical hermeneutics, and restores the possibility of theological interpretation. The traditional goal of biblical theology may be best achieved by attending to the diverse literary genres of the Bible – by describing the 'text acts' of Scripture. Every text is a kind of something, a particular kind of communicative act, and the genre of the text is often the best indication of the kind of point the author is making.

The concept of literary genre is much more than a device for classifying kinds of texts. Each literary genre represents a way of experiencing and representing some aspect of reality. Each genre is a communicative strategy that employs language to engage readers and render reality in different ways. Literary genres are language games, each with its own set of rules for making sense. For example, the rules for history differ from those for story, apocalyptic, proverb and myth. Indeed, genres are as much cognitive as communicative strategies, that 'map' reality in diverse ways. The Bible's theology is textually mediated, and together the rainbow of literary forms comprise the white light of truth. Biblical theology thus concerns not only words and concepts, not only narrated acts and witnessed events, but also the 'poetics' – the 'systematic working or study of literature as such' – of Scripture (Meir Sternberg, *Poetics of Biblical Narrative* [Bloomington, 1985]).

The urgent task of biblical theology is to undertake a biblical poetics in which the theology of the Bible would be described not primarily by means of etymology or history, but rather by interpreting the biblical message in terms of its communicative integrity as a particular kind of literature (*e.g.* apocalyptic, narrative, praise chorus, law, letter, *etc.*). In thus describing the Bible's 'word views', biblical theology serves as an indispensable tool for helping readers to indwell the words, and the worlds, of the Bible. Calvin was right to call Scripture the 'spectacles of faith', though we need to add that these spectacles are made up of a plurality of lenses.

Perhaps no single genre illustrates the significance of literary form better than narrative. Narrative is a unique cognitive instrument that is especially good at viewing a heterogeneous collection of people and events as evincing a certain wholeness. Indeed, with narrative we may have to say that the medium is the message; there is simply no way to identify the meaning (or referent) of the narrative apart from the narrative form. Readers can view the history of Israel, or of Jesus, as the story of divine providence, for example, only thanks to the narrative lenses of certain biblical books. Narratives communicate ways of seeing and thinking about God's involvement with the world that cannot be reduced to a set of concepts.

What precisely would a biblical theology that attends to the significance of literary form describe in dealing with the theology of, say, biblical narrative? The particular contribution of the narrative genre is that authors who employ it display worlds. A narrative displays a worldview, an interpreted world. In addition to relating a series of events, authors take up an attitude towards it. What the author communicates is a perspective on the world displayed in the text. The events displayed may be accompanied by any number of evaluative stances (*e.g.* praise, mockery, condemnation). The point is that narrative not only informs one about historical events, but also aids in the formation of one's attitude towards them. Narratives are powerful instruments for shaping the way we see, imagine and think about the world. Without the biblical narratives, for instance, we might not be able to see the world in its created and covenantal ordering. And just as we learn what it is to be a virtuous human by reading stories of heroes and villains, so we learn what it is to be a genuine follower of Jesus through the Gospel narratives.

The main point here is that the Bible is made up of a variety of texts that need to be described not only at the linguistic but also at the literary level. Each of the major genres to be found in Scripture – narrative, prophecy, apocalyptic, didactic, hymnic – contributes in its own way to the larger project of testifying to the God of Israel and of Jesus Christ. The recognition that the diversity of literary forms is essential to the content of the Bible need not prevent the biblical theologian from studying particular theological themes. Ricoeur, for example, has explored the ways in which the diverse literary forms of Scripture treat the topic of *time*, a well-known theme in biblical theology. The contrast between Greek and Hebrew concepts of time was a mainstay of the Biblical Theology Movement. What is most striking about Ricoeur's study, however, is that he is less interested in biblical words for time than in how the major biblical genres *depict* time (P. Ricoeur, *Figuring the Sacred* [ET, Minneapolis, 1995], pp. 167–180). Each genre configures or construes time in a distinctive way: as time immemorial; as historical time; as 'ripe' or 'eschatological' time. Attending to the level of genre allows us to pursue longitudinal themes across Scripture, then, with less danger of analyzing them out of (literary) context.

Describing the whole Bible: two Testaments, one testimony?

The remit of biblical theology – to understand the theology of the text on its own terms – leads us to attend to the nature of the biblical texts as literary wholes. There are other levels of wholeness, however, that are of great interest to the biblical theologian: the level of the Testament (*i.e.* OT theology, NT theology), and beyond that, still higher and all-encompassing, the level of the canon (*i.e.* biblical theology proper). On this level, the 'it' of 'what it meant' refers to the Christian Scriptures taken as a unified whole. With regard to interpreting the Bible as Scripture, perhaps the most important question with regard to literary context is: one lump or two? To be precise, what theological assumptions legitimate reading the two Testaments as *one* Scripture? Reading the Testaments together involves taking hermeneutical as well as theological positions. Most importantly, it means deciding that the God who raised Jesus from the dead is the same God who brought Israel out of Egypt. To read the Bible typologically or intertextually is to let Christian theology transform the presuppositions one brings to the text.

What new problems or possibilities does the concept of canon raise for the exegesis and hermeneutics of the Bible? What happens when one tries to describe the key themes or the message of the Bible considered as a unified whole? The problem is quickly stated: *diversity*. According to Walter Brueggemann, the canon represents a collection of such widely diverse ideas that all attempts to

perceive a coherent theological message results in interpretative violence and reductionism (*Theology of the Old Testament: Testimony, Dispute, Advocacy* [Minneapolis, 1997]). On the one hand, linguistic, historical, and cultural diversity hardens into what appears to be a theological discontinuity: old vs. new covenant. Christian hermeneutics is here stretched to the breaking point; is it really possible to read both Testaments *together*? On the other hand, the hermeneutic process bridging two Testaments was already the subject of explicit reflection by the authors of the NT. The appropriate hermeneutical question to ask is this: what is the significance for biblical theology of a theological exegesis of Scripture that takes seriously the canonical context?

1. Brevard Childs's canonical approach. For Childs, canonization refers to the process by which the traditions of Israel and the early church came to be shaped in a way that enabled them to function authoritatively for future generations, much like a *regula fidei* (rule of faith). What Childs sets out to describe, then, is the way in which texts have been shaped in order to function authoritatively in the life of the believing community.

In their final form, the Christian Scriptures include two Testaments, each of which is to be read in the light of the other. For Childs, it follows that the OT must not be described in abstraction from its connection to the NT. It is precisely this interdependence of OT and NT interpretation that constitutes the unique remit of biblical theology according to Childs. To interpret the OT as if it were an autonomous text is to *misinterpret* it; at the very least, it is to interpret it out of its proper (*i.e.* canonical) context. In speaking of a canonical context, Childs is referring both to the final form of each individual biblical book and to their position in relation to one another. Note that on Childs's view, 'what it meant' (*e.g.* the servant songs of Isaiah) shades into 'what it means' (*e.g.* Jesus Christ as servant of the Lord), precisely because the final form in its *canonical intention* serves as a rule of faith – as *Scripture* – for past, present, and future church members. This is the canonical version of the hermeneutical circle: read intertextually, the old in light of the new and new in light of the old. Childs has followed his own hermeneutical advice in his commentary on the Exodus (*The Book of Exodus*, OTL

[Philadelphia and London, 1974, 1979]), in which he deals with the 'NT context' of the story of Moses.

The most frequent criticism of Childs is that he exaggerates the importance of the final form. Some exegetes balk at carrying description to this level. Why, asks the biblical critic, should we describe OT words and texts in their canonical rather than their historical context? J. Barr and H. Räisänen, for instance, believe that it is arbitrary to limit the scholar's work to intra-canonical description; they prefer to march around the canonical walls, looking for extrabiblical information and parallels that might shed light on the text. Childs, for his part, is trying to mediate between the critical approach of the academy and the confessional approach of the church. He presents his canonical approach as a hermeneutic common to both saints and scholars. However, he does not provide an adequate argument to support his notion that the final form alone is theologically authoritative.

Childs has recently supplemented his literary argument about the canon's structure with a more properly theological argument about the canon's substance. Childs speaks of the 'hermeneutical role' of biblical theology, namely, to understand the 'two choirs' of voices within the Christian Bible 'in relation to the divine reality [Jesus Christ] to which they point in such diverse ways' (*Biblical Theology of the Old and New Testaments*, p. 85). Childs is not always clear, however, as to whether reading the Bible for its witness to Christ is a matter of the literary shape of the text or the interpretative interests of the community. Is 'canon' a fact about the text or about the interpreting community that looks to it for guidance? Stephen Fowl speaks for reader-oriented critics today when he suggests that we eliminate the concept 'meaning' and instead admit that we read the Bible with certain aims and interests (*Engaging Scripture* [Oxford, 1998], p. vii). The issue is whether the canonical reading is mandated by the text itself or arbitrarily chosen by an interpretative community.

Paul Noble believes that Childs's preference for the final form of the biblical text must ultimately be grounded in a doctrine of inspiration. What Childs calls 'canonical biblical theology of the Old and New Testaments' is more properly understood in terms of *divine* authorship. Childs's claim that the meaning of the text can only be arrived at in the context of the canon as a whole 'is formally equivalent to believing that the Bible is so inspired as to be ultimately the work of a single Author' (P. Noble, *The Canonical Approach*, p. 340). This idea is very significant for hermeneutics and biblical theology.

2. *Thick description: Scripture interprets Scripture.* If the 'it' in 'what it meant' refers to the whole Christian Bible, Old and New Testaments, then we cannot claim to have adequately described the text if we ignore the canonical level. To interpret isolated passages of the OT as evidence of the religious or cultural history of Israel is to give 'thin' descriptions only. Similarly, the use of NT texts to reconstruct the historical Jesus yields diluted descriptions only. Childs, along with his mentor Karl Barth, is absolutely right to insist on this point.

To read the Bible canonically is to read the Bible as a unified communicative act, that is, as the complex, multi-levelled speech act of a single divine author. It follows that biblical theology – not just OT or NT theology but the theology of the whole Bible – is the attempt to read Scripture as the word of God. To read the Bible canonically may be to read it according to its truest, fullest, *divine* intention. This is a most important point; the canonical approach is a matter not of how the church reads the Bible but of what the Bible *is*. To read the Bible as unified Scripture is not just one interpretative interest among others, but the interpretative strategy that best corresponds to the nature of the text itself, given its divine inspiration.

It is possible to describe texts, like actions, at various levels of complexity. One can speak of neural firings, of the movement of an index finger, of pulling the trigger, of assassinating a President – all might be descriptions of the same act, though they work on different explanatory levels. However, the first description is 'thin' when compared to the last. Thin descriptions are the result of using too narrow a context to interpret an intended action. A description fails to generate understanding if something essential is left out of the story. It is one thing to describe the biological mechanism of the tear duct, quite another to describe *why* someone is crying. Similarly, it is not enough to describe biblical words, events, or even books taken in isolation.

Thin descriptions of the text suffer from a poverty of meaning. While each level yields helpful descriptions, we cannot claim to have understood the true meaning of the action – what an author (human or divine) is doing – until we contemplate it in its final form, as a complete act. To remain on the level of words and concepts, or even of literary genres, does not yield a sufficiently 'thick' description of the message of Scripture. Only the final form of the text displays the divine communicative act in its completeness; hence the final form is the best evidence for determining what the authors, human and divine, are ultimately doing.

The canon, as a collection of divinely inspired texts, describes the unified communicative act of God as it takes up and coordinates the diverse human communicative acts performed at the comparatively lower levels of sentences and books. The canon is a great hall of witnesses in which different voices all testify to the Lord Jesus Christ. Over and above the laws and promises, the warnings and commands, the stories and the songs, is an all-embracing act, that of witnessing to what God was and is doing in Christ. When described at this higher level, the canon mediates the subject matter that unifies Scripture and emerges from, but cannot be reduced to, the smaller, less complex speech acts that comprise both Testaments (*e.g.* telling a story, prophesying, promising, *etc.*). Thanks to their overarching canonical context, the smaller communicative acts are caught up and reoriented to the larger purpose of 'making wise unto salvation'.

What biblical theology should describe is the multi-levelled, human/divine discourse of the Bible – the canonical texts as complex communicative acts (*cf.* C. Bartholomew, *Reading Ecclesiastes*, esp. ch. 7). When describing 'what it meant/means', it is perhaps best to think of a series of expanding interpretative frameworks. There is first the semantic range of what words could possibly have meant in their historical situation, then the historical context of what authors could have meant at a particular point in the history of redemption, then the literary context of what the words could have meant as part of a particular kind of literature, and finally what the words at a certain time in a certain kind of

text mean today when read as part of a unified canon that, taken as a whole, points to Jesus Christ.

In the final analysis, the best way to describe 'what it meant' is to interpret a given passage of Scripture in its linguistic-historical, literary, and canonical context. It is noteworthy that at the highest level, the Bible itself constitutes its own most adequate context. Hence the Reformation principle for biblical interpretation applies to biblical theology too; Scripture interprets Scripture.

Biblical theology and theological hermeneutics

One of the most prominent emphases of contemporary hermeneutics concerns the role of the reader in interpretation. Virtually no one in the field of hermeneutics today believes in the possibility of value-neutral interpretation. Biblical theology, however, despite its having achieved the status of an independent academic discipline about the same time as hermeneutics, has for most of its history made *pure description* of linguistic and historical data its goal. Can biblical theology survive in a hermeneutical age?

The inevitability of hermeneutics

To raise the question of hermeneutics is to raise the question of *who* it is that is undertaking the task of interpretation, and *why*. To be sure, communities of interpreters approach the Bible with diverse ideological interests. Is it possible, however, to approach the text with the interest of *understanding* it? This is the ultimate aim of biblical theology, and of interpretation in general: to receive the text on its own terms, not in terms of some method or scheme determined in advance. If one did have such an interest – of understanding the biblical text on its own terms – would it be primarily *historical* rather than *theological*? The suggestion of the present article is that having a theological interest, far from being arbitrary, is rather required if one is to do justice to the nature of the Bible itself, taken not only as a collection of human speech acts but also as a unified divine canonical act.

It is commonplace to be asked to choose between rival interpretative interests: 'I belong to Childs'; 'I belong to Eichrodt'; 'I belong to Ladd'. Or again: 'I belong to feminism'; 'I belong to liberalism'; 'I belong to evangelicalism'. Faced with such diversity, the postmodern reflex is to tolerate them all; to each exegete his or her own hermeneutics. In the face of such interpretative plurality, it is important to ensure that one's interpretative interest corresponds to the communicative intent of the text. Otherwise interpreters will describe not the theology of the text but only their own agendas and ideologies.

The biblical texts themselves have a theological interest, an interest in mediating the knowledge of God. To undertake theological exegesis is not a matter of arbitrarily deciding to read theologically rather than historically, but rather of specifying and respecting the appropriate context for 'thick' description. To do biblical theology is to take a multi-level, integrative approach to the text as a complex communicative act involving words, events, texts and Testaments.

Hermeneutics is inevitable, not because the biblical texts are unclear but because the aims and interests of the interpreter often are. One's readings, even the purported objective historical descriptions, are always governed by certain assumptions: about the kind of text one is reading, about the extent of its coherence or unity, about its relationship to other texts, about whether it is a human word only or also the word of God. If neither exegesis nor pure historical description without presuppositions is possible, then it is important to approach the biblical text with the right preliminary assumptions. It is important to develop a properly *theological* hermeneutic.

Biblical theology as theological interpretation

Christopher Seitz and Francis Watson, OT and NT theologians respectively, agree that the real issue behind the decision to read the Bible canonically is a theological one. For Seitz, it is a question concerning how confident modern liberal biblical critics are that the Scriptures of the OT and NT 'have the power to witness to divine reality' (C. Seitz, *Word without End*, p. 108). For Watson, it is a matter of the Christian conviction that the truth of Jesus Christ is textually mediated through both Testaments, 'according to the Scriptures'. No other justification is adequate for reading the OT and NT together than the theological conviction that these texts mediate the truth of the one God.

As we have seen, attempts to offer pure historical descriptions of the biblical texts in fact yield only thin descriptions with respect to theology. If one construes the 'it' of 'what it meant' too narrowly, one gets no further than non-theological exegesis. To limit biblical theology to historical description is to abandon the attempt to read the Bible as theologically normative for the church and to reject the notion of divine inspiration and divine authorship, and thus to refuse to read the Bible as the word of God. It is impossible to read the Hebrew Scriptures as OT without taking a stand on the relation between the two Testaments, a stand that ultimately follows from one's view of God and Jesus Christ: 'Where theological concerns are marginalized, the two Testaments fall apart almost automatically' (Watson, *Text and Truth*, p. 5). In short, neither exegesis nor biblical theology is possible apart from explicitly theological presuppositions, assumptions about the nature and identity of God. The academy has its assumptions too, but they are all too often either a-theological or based on radical revisions of Christian orthodoxy. Thanks to the postmodern critiques of objectivism, however, Christians need no longer fear the rhetoric of the academy which says that only its assumptions are rational ones.

As presented here, biblical theology is that approach which describes the 'word views' and literary shapes of the Bible, and especially that 'thick' description of the canon as a divine communicative act. Biblical theology is a description of the biblical texts on levels that display their theological significance. Accordingly, biblical theology is nothing less than a theological hermeneutic: an interpretative approach to the Bible informed by Christian doctrine. The biblical theologian reads for the theological message communicated by the texts taken individually and as a whole collection.

'Biblical theology is a theological, hermeneutical, and exegetical discipline, and its hermeneutical and exegetical dimensions are placed at the disposal of its overriding theological concern' (Watson, *Text and Truth*, p. vii). The theology of the texts is mediated through various kinds and levels of communicative action, all of which need to be acknowledged and described. Theological exegesis aims at recovering an intention that is historical, embodied in literary forms, and which ultimately aims (*i.e.* at the canonical level) at testifying to Jesus Christ.

Rather than take a stand with either the exegete or the systematician exclusively, then, the biblical theologian seeks instead to foster an interdisciplinary approach to biblical interpretation which aims at textually mediated theological truth. Biblical theology is nothing less than a theological hermeneutic, a *regula legei* (a rule of reading). As such, biblical theology is not merely a matter of repackaging the conceptual content of the Scriptures, but a way of having one's heart, mind, and imagination alike schooled in the ways of seeing and experiencing the world according to the many literary forms and the one canon, which together constitute the word of God written.

See also: BIBLICAL THEOLOGY; UNITY AND DIVERSITY OF SCRIPTURE; RELATIONSHIP OF OLD TESTAMENT AND NEW TESTAMENT.

Bibliography

J. Barr, 'Biblical Theology', *IDBSup*, pp. 104–111; C. Bartholomew, *Reading Ecclesiastes: OT Exegesis and Hermeneutical Theory* (Rome, 1998); B. Childs, *Biblical Theology of the Old and New Testaments* (London, 1992); H. Frei, *The Eclipse of Biblical Narrative: A Study in Eighteenth- and Nineteenth-Century Hermeneutics* (New Haven, 1974); W. Jeanrond, *Text and Interpretation as Categories of Theological Thinking* (New York, 1988); A. LaCocque and P. Ricoeur, *Thinking Biblically: Exegetical and Hermeneutical Studies* (Chicago, 1998); R. Lints, *The Fabric of Theology: A Prolegomenon to Evangelical Theology* (Grand Rapids, 1993); R. Lundin, C. Walhout and A. C. Thiselton, *The Promise of Hermeneutics* (Grand Rapids, 1999); R. Morgan with J. Barton, *Biblical Interpretation* (Oxford, 1988); P. Noble, *The Canonical Approach: A Critical Reconstruction of the Hermeneutics of Brevard S. Childs* (Leiden, 1995); C. Seitz, *Word without End: The OT as Abiding Theological Witness* (Grand Rapids, 1998); K. Stendahl, 'Biblical theology, contemporary', *IDB* 1, pp. 418–432; A. Thiselton, 'Biblical theology and hermeneutics', in D. Ford (ed.), *The Modern Theologians* (Oxford and Cambridge, MA, [2]1997), pp. 520–537; W. VanGemeren (ed.), *A Guide to OT Theology and Exegesis* (Grand Rapids, 1999); K. Vanhoozer, 'From canon to concept: the "same", the "other" and the relation between biblical and systematic theology', *SBET* 12, 1994, pp. 96–124; *idem, Is There a Meaning in this Text? The Bible, the Reader and the Morality of Literary Knowledge* (Grand Rapids and Leicester, 1998); F. Watson, *Text and Truth: Redefining Biblical Theology* (Edinburgh, 1997); N. T. Wright, *The NT and the People of God* (London, 1992).

K. J. VANHOOZER

The Unity and Diversity of Scripture

Introduction

Throughout most of the history of the church, the unity of *Scripture has been assumed and its diversity taken less seriously. Apparent contradictions or tensions between one part of Scripture and another have been harmonized. Typology has been seen as a key to understanding the NT use of the OT. Difficult passages have been allegorized, and the principle of the *regula fidei* ('the rule of faith') has led to clearer texts being used to interpret more opaque ones. Since the Enlightenment, however, much of this has changed. A salutary emphasis on biblical theology – hearing the message of each book and each author in its own terms – has developed, but in consequence the unity of the Bible has often been denied. The last 200 years of biblical interpretation have been dominated by claims that there are irreconcilable conflicts among the authors of Scripture, and by theories of the tradition history of both Testaments that conflict with the data presupposed by the canonical form of the Scriptures themselves.

A movement of the 1950s and 1960s, sometimes called simply the biblical theology movement, reacted against these trends and sought to identify 'centres' that unified either the OT or the NT or both. That quest, however, has been largely abandoned. Today unity in Scripture is perceived for the most part only by advocates of canonical criticism and by evangelicals who continue to believe that Scripture does not contradict itself as a theological corollary of their acceptance of its inspiration. D. N. Freedman (*The Unity of the Hebrew Bible*), J. Hultgren (*The Rise of Normative Christianity*) and J. Reumann (*Variety and Unity in New Testament Thought*) are among the most important recent exceptions from other theological traditions.

Of the many issues that could be profitably explored, we will focus on three: 1. the quest for a centre in each Testament and in the Bible as a whole; 2. a model for the unfolding unity of the biblical narrative; and 3. the question of how to respond to the diversity (especially the apparent contradictions of Scripture), including the issue of 'development'.

Centres in Scripture

The OT

Many different proposals have emerged for a unifying centre of the OT. Various scholars attempt to trace the predominance of a single theme, for example, covenant, promise, the mighty acts of God, communion, the life of God's people, dominion, justice or righteousness. Others identify pairs of themes, for example, law and promise, election and obligation, creation and covenant, the rule of God and communion with humankind or salvation and blessing. Some pairs of themes involve polarities, such as the presence versus the absence of God or the legitimation of structure versus the embracing of pain. It has been argued that holding together these antinomies is a key to finding unity within diversity. Still other writers point simply to Yahweh, or God, as the sole unifying element

within the older Testament.

Certain scholars find unity in a complex of multiple themes. Hasel concludes, 'A seemingly successful way to come to grips with the question of unity is to take the various major longitudinal themes and concepts and explicate where and how the variegated theologies are intrinsically related to each other' (*New Testament Theology*, pp. 218–219). One of the most ambitious and compelling proposals for finding a unifying structure comes from E. A. Martens (*God's Design: A Focus on Old Testament Theology* [N. Richland Hills, [3]1998]), who perceives a fourfold design of God in Exodus 5:22 – 6:8 which recurs in every major section of the OT: to bring deliverance; to summon a peculiar people; to offer himself for his people; to know and give them land.

The NT

Again, single themes have been suggested as a centre for the NT: kingdom, gospel, righteousness, justification, reconciliation, faith, new creation, salvation or salvation history, eschatology, Israel or the new Israel, the cross and/or the resurrection, the love of God, existential anthropology and covenant. Perhaps most common of all, Jesus (or Christology more generally) has been identified as a centre.

Again, various combinations of themes have also been proposed. C. H. Dodd (*The Apostolic Preaching and Its Developments*) turned to the speeches in Acts and the pre-Pauline creeds to find elements of an early kerygmatic summary of foundational doctrine. A. M. Hunter (*Introducing New Testament Theology* [London, 1957], p. 66) suggested that a reporter's digest of an early Christian sermon might have read like this: 'The prophecies are fulfilled, and the New Age has dawned. The Messiah, born of David's seed, has appeared. He is Jesus of Nazareth, God's Servant, who went about doing good and healing by God's power, was crucified according to God's purpose, was raised from the dead on the third day, is now exalted to God's right hand, and will come again in glory for judgment. Therefore let all repent and believe and be baptized for the forgiveness of sins and the gift of the Holy Spirit.'

D. Wenham ('Appendix', pp. 12–13) suggests a multiplex centre involving the *context* of God the creator's intervening through Jesus to complete his saving purposes for his people, the *centre* of Jesus as Spirit-filled Messiah and Son of God, the *community* of those who receive Jesus and his salvation by faith, having the Holy Spirit of sonship and being called to live as a restored community in loving fellowship with God and one another, and the *climax* of the mission of restoration completed at the Lord's return when he judges the world and finally overthrows evil to vindicate God's people and restore all creation. Finally, E. Lemcio (in *JSNT* 33, p. 6) finds a six-part kerygma which recurs in all major portions of the NT: '(1) God who (2) sent (Gospels) or raised (3) Jesus. (4) A response (receiving, repentance, faith) (5) towards God (6) brings benefits (variously described).'

The entire Bible

The most common examples of perceived unity in both Testaments combined can be described under the headings of promise–fulfilment, type–antitype, salvation history, a relationship with the living God, intertextuality and Christology. Some scholars point to narrower themes such as monotheism, God's covenant faithfulness, God's reign, righteousness, the covenants, election, grace and the response of obedience, the people of God, Exodus and new Exodus, creation and new creation or sin and salvation. Again, multiplex solutions have been proposed, for example, the existence of God, God as creator of a good world, the fall of humanity and the fact of election (Hanson and Harvey, in H. G. Reventlow, *Problems of Biblical Theology in the Twentieth Century*, p. 159). P. Stuhlmacher (*How to Do Biblical Theology* [Allison Park, 1995], p. 63) offers an excellent narrative summary of the story of both Testaments: 'The one God who created the world and chose Israel to be his own people has through the sending, the work, and the death and resurrection of his only Son, Jesus Christ, sufficiently provided once and for all the salvation of Jews and Gentiles. Jesus Christ is the hope of all creation. Whoever believes in him as Reconciler and Lord and obeys his instruction may be certain of their participation in the kingdom of God.'

Evaluation

Clearly the OT is necessary to an understanding of the background and meaning of both individual terms and broader concepts in the NT, not to mention the explicit quotations or allusions from the Old in the New. Conversely, for the Christian, the OT cannot be properly understood and applied without taking into account how NT revelation has or has not changed specific laws and principles from previous eras of salvation history. The broadest proposals for centres in each Testament, God and Jesus respectively, and a unifying theme for the entire Bible such as salvation history, best reflect the unity of the books. But one may ask how valuable this insight is, and whether such general themes significantly distinguish the canonical material from other Jewish and Christian literature of the time. Yet the narrower proposals all seem to exclude certain material within the canon or at least move certain books or portions of books to the periphery, if not to create an explicit canon within the canon, an approach methodologically inappropriate for those wishing to respect Scripture's own view of the inspiration and relevance of every section (*e.g.* 2 Tim. 3:16). Proposals combining several themes imply that the unity of Scripture may be likened to a picture album of a family over multiple generations – considerable diversity within a common gene pool (*cf.* R. L. Hubbard, Jr., 'Doing Old Testament theology today', in R. L. Hubbard, Jr., *et al.* (eds.), *Studies in Old Testament Theology* [Dallas and London, 1992], pp. 36–37). Clearly, there are 'family resemblances' (to use the language of Wittgenstein) among many of the proposed centres, despite there being no consensus on an exact theme or terminology.

Proposals like those of Lemcio or Stuhlmacher have the particular advantage of preserving *in nuce* the narrative form of the whole of Scripture. It is not often asked if it is necessary to reduce that which is couched in story form to a single theme or proposition. Perhaps it is more appropriate to consider how the story might be retold in its simplest form. Treating the Bible as narrative suggests a model for demonstrating in greater detail the unfolding unity and diversity within Scripture. One may summarize the plot line of the narrative literature, recognizing that other literary genres of Scripture are embedded in this larger 'historical' framework. Despite the diversity of Scripture, it is remarkable how if one follows the putative chronological sequence presented by the books themselves, each successive narrative consistently builds on antecedent Scripture in what seems to be a very conscious and straightforward fashion.

Stories typically lend themselves to the development of major themes through the eyes of their principal characters. Just as Jesus' parables consistently present a triadic model involving the interaction between a God-figure and contrasting subordinates, so one may posit a triangular structure for the whole narrative of Scripture, in which God in Christ relates to both his followers and his opponents. God's creative purposes, at first apparently thwarted, are followed by a plan of redemption and restoration which some people accept and others reject. The four major periods in this narrative are related to creation, the fall, redemption and the consummation of all God's purposes. Didactic material in the law, the prophets and the wisdom and epistolary literature describe how God's people should live within this broader historical framework.

The unifying plot of Scripture

The OT

The Bible begins with an account of creation and the primeval history of humanity (Gen. 1 – 11). In Genesis 12:1–3, God singles out the individual Abraham and promises him seed, land and a blessing for the nations. The rest of Genesis describes the obstacles to the immediate fulfilment of these promises and ends with Joseph and his brothers sojourning in Egypt. Exodus makes clear that God can deliver his people, but the golden calf (Exod. 32) and the wilderness wanderings (Num.) again delay God's blessing. Yet between Egypt and Canaan, God singles out the Israelites as his elect people and gives them the law in covenant form at Sinai, including promises and stipulations for their coming inheritance of the land (Exod. 20 – Lev. 27). Deuteronomy anticipates that inheritance by repeating and contextualizing the law, while Joshua describes the conquest, both books including covenant renewal ceremonies (Deut. 27 – 30; Josh. 5:2–12; 8:30–35).

But not all the nations are dispossessed. Hence Judges follows, with its 'Deuteronomistic' cycles of reward for blessing and punishment for disobedience. The book ends with God's people in near anarchy because

'Israel had no king' (Judg. 21:25). Samuel emerges as the first of the prophets and anoints the kings who will inaugurate the era of the monarchy. The books of Samuel and Kings narrate the rise and fall of that monarchy: the high point of Israel's enjoyment of its promised blessings; an extension of the covenant to include a Davidic dynasty (2 Sam. 7:14); and the downward spiral of disobedience during the period of the divided kingdom, with God's people finally taken away into exile.

Thus ends the first two of the four major sections of the OT according to the sequence of the Hebrew canon – the law (Gen. – Deut.) and the former prophets (Josh., Judg., 1 and 2 Sam., 1 and 2 Kgs.). Regardless of one's theory concerning the composition of these books, each successive narrative consciously builds on the previous one. The Pentateuch centres on God's promise of the land of Canaan to his people and culminates with their arrival on its borders. Yet Joshua, the first of the former prophets, follows so naturally from Deuteronomy that even critical scholars have spoken of a Hexateuch, uniting Joshua with the five books of the law. On the other hand, the theology of Deuteronomy so clearly pervades the former prophets that they have been linked by postulating a Deuteronomistic historian who wrote them all.

The third section of the Hebrew Scripture is the latter prophets (Is., Jer., Ezek. and 'the Twelve' [minor prophets]). These books supplement the 'primary history' of the first half of the OT. They can all be historically located within the chronological framework of the story of the divided kingdom, exile and restoration. References to prophets appear initially in the historical books (esp. important are Samuel, Nathan, Elijah and Elisha). These earlier, non-writing prophets resemble the later writing prophets in their powerful ministry of word and deed. Historical narrative (often parallel to antecedent Scripture – *cf.* esp. Jer. 52 and 2 Kgs. 25) is interspersed with prophetic oracles, suggesting that the latter prophets are consciously supplementing the stories that preceded them.

The prophetic rebukes of Israel are based on the Sinai covenant and especially criticize the Israelites' failure to respect the principles of social justice that permeate the Torah. Isaiah's suffering Servant passages develop the theme of sacrifice as necessary for forgiveness of sins, so central in the book of Leviticus. The latter prophets' concern for the nations prepares the way for the universal spread of the Gospel. Despite the distinctives of each prophetic book, one finds again and again an announcement of the Israelites' sin and of impending judgment, coupled with the promise of later restoration and comfort and that they will again obey God's word.

The 'writings', the fourth section of the Hebrew canon, is the most amorphous, yet it clearly belongs in the 'family'. The Psalms formed Israel's worship book. Their contents and even their superscriptions demonstrate that many emerged as responses to specific historical contexts. Especially noteworthy are detailed recountings of God's past deeds, as described in the earlier narrative literature (*e.g.* Pss. 44, 68, 78, 89, 105, 106, 136). Psalm 119, by far the longest of the Psalms, is entirely a meditation on Torah. The Proverbs offer more generalized wisdom for all walks of life, but centre on the fear of the Lord as the beginning of wisdom (Prov. 1:7). Like the Psalms, they share key themes, especially about creation, which presuppose the teaching of the Pentateuch. Job in part forms a counterpoint to the rest of the canon in affirming suffering as a mystery locked in God's inscrutable sovereignty, which cannot be explained merely as a punishment for sin, as it is so often in the Deuteronomistic history. Nevertheless, the canonical framework in which Job's narrative is embedded (chs. 1 – 2; 42:7–17) meshes with the rest of the OT, with Job's ultimate material reward even in this life for his faithfulness against all odds.

The five scrolls ('Megilloth') comprise Ruth, Song of Songs, Ecclesiastes, Lamentations and Esther. Ruth reflects God's care for Gentile women, yet is linked with the 'primary history' by Ruth's role as King David's ancestor. Song of Songs and Ecclesiastes are linked with King Solomon, whether or not he is the actual author of either work. As erotic love poetry, Song of Songs is unique in the canon, but it agrees with the rest in affirming the goodness of God's creation, even in its most material and earthy dimensions. Ecclesiastes, like Job, functions as 'protest literature', describing the insoluble mysteries of this transient life. But it too ultimately affirms enjoyment of God's good creation alongside fearing God and keeping the commandments (12:13). Lamen-

tations forms a fitting sequel to Jeremiah, bemoaning Israel in exile and Jerusalem in ruins. Esther too focuses on God's care for Jews in exile, through a Jewish queen in Persia, even though God never appears by name in the book.

The remaining writings are similarly disparate and yet are tied in with previous canonical literature. Daniel's ministry in Babylon recalls Joseph's role in Egypt and demonstrates the triumph of the kingdom of God over the kingdoms of this world, a formative theme for the NT as well. The Chronicler's work parallels that of the Deuteronomistic historian, but from a pro-Judah, pro-Davidic perspective. But it actually spans the whole period of history from creation to exile, after which comes the repatriation narrated in Ezra-Nehemiah. There are enough links between Chronicles and Ezra-Nehemiah to suggest to some common authorship. Interestingly, in the Hebrew Scriptures, Chronicles comes last, after Ezra-Nehemiah, as if to close the canon with its review of names and events from Adam onwards.

In numerous ways the OT remains self-consciously open-ended. The manifold promise of Genesis 12, elaborated in Exodus 5 – 6, supplemented by the law, transformed by the monarchy of Samuel/Kings, to be fulfilled in the coming Day of the Lord as predicted by the prophets, has not been fully consummated, certainly not in perpetuity. Thus Malachi (3 – 4) looks forward to a coming purification of the temple by the Lord himself, Jeremiah (31) to a new covenant with God's people, Ezekiel (36) to a new heart and spirit in Israel, Joel (2) to a new age in which the Holy Spirit is poured out upon all God's people indiscriminately and Isaiah (*e.g.* 2; 25; 65 – 66) to a glorious material world, an eschatological banquet and ultimately new heavens and a new earth. All this is clear, even apart from specific texts whose interpretation is disputed but which are taken in the NT as Messianic prophecies (*e.g.* Pss. 2; 16; 22; 45; Is. 7:14; 9:6; Mic. 5:2). And the end of the historical narrative finds Israel, while restored to her land, still subject to foreign nations and with a rebuilt temple whose grandeur pales in comparison with the temple of King Solomon (Hag. 2:3).

The NT

Neither the intertestamental period nor the

rabbinic era saw any greater fulfilment of these OT promises, though the century of liberation inaugurated by the Maccabees (167–63 BC) certainly raised Israel's hopes and rekindled Messianic fervour. Many of the details of OT prophecy are not literally fulfilled in NT events either, but there is reason to think that God intended the age of Jesus and the apostles to inaugurate their fulfilment. Some OT promises may have been forfeited through Israel's disobedience; others were meant to be interpreted spiritually; and the fulfilment of still others is postponed until Christ's return. No one could have deduced the NT from the Old or created all of its detail out of the Old. Yet the lines of correspondence are clear and impressive (H. H. Rowley, *The Unity of the Bible*, pp. 99–100).

Jesus came announcing the arrival of the kingdom of God. God would again rule over his people. By choosing twelve apostles, Christ was forming the nucleus of a new or true Israel. His teaching fulfilled the law, even while reinterpreting and transcending it (Matt. 5:17; Luke 24:44). His ethic centred on love, in clear continuity with the OT's double love-command for God and neighbour (Matt. 22:34–40; *cf.* Deut. 6:5; Lev. 19:18). His miracles demonstrated the presence of God's reign. His passion and death typologically fulfilled various passages in the Psalms and Prophets and more straightforwardly fitted the model of Isaiah's suffering servant (Is. 52:13 – 53:12). His resurrection is seen as the beginning of the general resurrection, already anticipated in Daniel 12:2. N. T. Wright (*Jesus and the Victory of God* [London and Minneapolis, 1996]) helpfully sums up Jesus' message as the announcment of the end of exile, despite the presence of Roman troops. The true enemy is Satan, not Rome, and the central element of liberation is the forgiveness of sins, not political independence. And all four Gospels agree that Jesus was the Christ, the Son of Man, the Son of God and the Lord.

The book of Acts is the only other historical narrative in the NT, carrying forward the story of the community Jesus established. It is an account of the transformation of a uniquely Jewish sect into a significant worldwide religion, in fulfilment of God's promise that Abraham's seed would be a blessing to all the nations of the earth.

The epistles comprise apostolic instruction for that ever-expanding community in diverse settings and circumstances. At first glance Paul seems to present a quite different message from that of Jesus, but they agree that Christianity is the fulfilment of Israel and that people are made right with God by faith in Christ, not by works of the law. Paul's infrequent references to the details of Jesus' life are balanced by his frequent allusions to his teaching. In writing to Christian individuals and churches, Paul presupposes knowledge of the Christian kerygma and builds on it. One may trace distinct theological trajectories across the spectrum of Judaism to Hellenism in Hebrews and the 'Catholic Epistles' (Jas.; 1 and 2 Pet.; 1, 2 and 3 John; Jude) but they are united to the kerygma by their core Christology (*e.g.* Heb. 1:1–4; 1 Pet. 2:21–25; 1 John 4:1–3). James is perhaps the most distinct of these letters, but it resembles the wisdom literature of Proverbs and frequently echoes Jesus' ethical instruction. And all the epistles fit into the broader historical narrative of Jesus and the churches that his followers created in the 1st century.

It is appropriate for both the NT and the Scriptures as a whole to end with the Apocalypse, prophesying the complete fulfilment of all the Bible's predictions, and full of allusions to Isaiah, Jeremiah, Ezekiel and Daniel. Revelation's final chapters expand upon Isaiah's new heavens and new earth (Rev. 21 – 22), and form an inclusio with Genesis 1 – 2, with frequent parallels between the original creation and the new creation.

All in all, the Old and New Testaments together provide a remarkably unified story-line considering the diverse authors, audiences and circumstances of their various books. 'In no other literature besides the Bible do some forty authors or editors, writing in a period of over a thousand years, in places and cultures as widely separated as Rome and Babylon, succeed in developing a body of literature that even at a first inspection gives an indication of being a unity' (D. P. Fuller, 'The Importance of the Unity of the Bible', p. 65).

The diversity of Scripture

In the midst of Scripture's unity, we must not lose sight of its diversity (*cf.* esp. J. Goldingay, 'Diversity and Unity in Old Testament Theology', and J. D. G. Dunn, *Unity and Diversity in the New Testament*). This takes several forms. The books of the Bible are written by different authors, in different times and places, to different audiences in distinct circumstances, using various literary genres. Each book thus displays unique purposes and themes. In some instances, different portions of Scripture are so closely parallel that we can postulate a literary relationship between them and assume that their differences are intentional: sometimes theologically motivated; sometimes merely for stylistic variation. Deuteronomy consciously updates various laws of Exodus and Leviticus for more settled life in the Promised Land. Chronicles retells significant portions of the Deuteronomistic history, adding, omitting and rewording to highlight its focus on the southern kingdom, its kings, the temple and the priestly service. Each of the four Gospels clearly has its own slant on the identity of Jesus and the nature of his ministry, while 2 Peter seems to have revised and supplemented Jude to combat a new group of false teachers in a new context.

It is important, therefore, to understand each biblical author or book in its own right. Identical words may be used differently by different writers in different contexts. Luke, for example, regularly uses 'apostle' to refer to one of the Twelve, whereas Paul uses it for a variety of individuals, including himself, who function as early Christian missionaries. He reflects the etymology of *apostolos*: 'someone sent on a mission'. The famous 'contradiction' between Paul and James is resolved once one understands that the authors use the key terms 'faith', 'works' and 'justify' in somewhat different ways.

Diversity may emerge within a given book of Scripture as well. Joshua 11:23 narrates how the Israelites 'took the entire land', whereas 13:1 observes that much of the land remained to be taken. These seemingly conflicting statements are better explained as complementary perspectives on one underlying reality. The Israelites had indeed dispossessed their neighbours of a substantial portion of Canaan (ch. 12), but their failure to follow up their victories kept them from conquering it all (13:3–6). J. G. McConville ('Using Scripture for theology') finds two kinds of unity and diversity within the OT, which might also be found in the NT. First, there are divergent but complementary data that may be combined into a larger, more complex whole. Here Scripture is prescriptive. Second, there are genuinely conflicting data

that reflect specific teaching for specific circumstances in biblical history. These obviously cannot all be equally normative in the same way at the same time, but sometimes function prescriptively in parallel contexts today, while at other times remaining merely descriptive.

The key to a proper appreciation of the diversity in biblical theology, therefore, is to interpret each book as a literary integrity in its own right, in the light of the unique circumstances and purposes that generated it, and of antecedent Scripture and other relevant historical background. On the other hand, the pervasive unity of Scripture means that if the resulting interpretations of two different passages or writers produce an irreconcilable contradiction, it is legitimate to ask if one has interpreted both correctly. That Jews and Christians have historically believed that no Scripture, properly interpreted, contradicts another, means that one should exhaust all reasonable options for harmonizing texts before announcing the discovery of an insoluble problem.

Illustrations of diversity

One of the most important kinds of diversity among the books of the Bible is their distinctive themes. Among the minor prophets, Amos highlights social justice; Joel, the coming day of the Lord; Haggai, the rebuilding of the temple; and Habakkuk, the problem of evil. In the Gospels, Matthew presents Jesus as the Son of David; Mark, the Christ incognito; Luke, the Saviour of all humanity; and John, the Logos, Lamb and God incarnate. In the Pentateuch, Genesis focuses particularly on God's promise to bless the nations through the seed of Abraham; Exodus on God's presence; Leviticus on sacrifice and holiness; Numbers on national failure; and Deuteronomy on the re-establishment of the covenant. Among Paul's epistles, Galatians emphasizes Christian freedom; Ephesians, the unity of the church; Philippians, rejoicing in all circumstances; and the Pastoral Epistles, church order.

There are also diverse genres, subgenres and literary forms. 1 Thessalonians is a letter of exhortation; 2 Corinthians, an epistle of apostolic self-commendation; Philippians, a family letter of friendship. Within a Gospel one finds parables, miracles, proverbs and pronouncement stories; in the Psalter, psalms of praise, lament, imprecation and prayer for deliverance. And all Scripture may be subdivided into prose and poetry.

Harmonization of diversity

Harmonizing apparently discrepant texts is a legitimate technique which most historians, ancient and modern, utilize. The fact that the church has at times proposed implausible harmonizations of Scripture does not invalidate the method. Interpreters of ancient texts must plead a cautious agnosticism if a majority of data falls together into a harmonious whole, but a minority seems at first glance not to do so. It is legitimate to leave certain questions open, particularly in the light of the vast amount of information about the ancient world which is simply unknown.

Many of the most plausible harmonizations of texts are not strictly additive; that is, they do not claim that two apparently discrepant statements are both part of a larger whole. Apparent contradictions may be due to a corrupt text, to a misunderstanding of unusual or literary forms or to a lack of historical or chronological precision among ancient writers. Apparent 'doublets' may reflect similar but distinct incidents. Rugged 'seams' may stem from divergent sources woven together somewhat loosely. Understanding the theological or redactional distinctives of a given writer may resolve other problems (For examples of all these types of harmonization, with reference to the OT, the NT and other ancient texts, see C. L. Blomberg, 'The legitimacy and limits of harmonization'.)

'Development' as a source of diversity

God's progressive revelation allows for development in Scripture in numerous ways. An excellent example is the OT's progressive understanding of an afterlife. Initially Sheol seems little more than the grave or a very shadowy existence beyond. But by Daniel 12, resurrection of both just and unjust is articulated, and the NT even more clearly delineates the nature and occupants of heaven and hell. Or again, God may act differently in different ages. In the OT, his Holy Spirit comes temporarily on special people for special acts of power. After Pentecost the Spirit permanently indwells all Christians (Rom. 8:9).

Less plausible theories of development include those that require the rearrangement of biblical chronology or the disregard of significant scriptural data: for example, the view that Israel evolved from a polytheistic to a monotheistic religion, or the idea that an older priestly emphasis on ritual was later supplanted by a prophetic stress on morality (*cf.* instead the mixture of holiness laws in Lev. 19 and contrast Ps. 51:16 with 19). Similarly, in the NT, theories of developing Christology must come to grips with Jesus' self-understanding and the high Christology of the early chapters of Acts and the pre-Pauline creeds. Theories of a developing institutionalization in ecclesiology must account for Matthew 18:15–20 on church discipline, 1 Corinthians 14 on the orderly use of *charismata* and the church officers of Philippians 1:1.

One must approach even more cautiously theories of theological development within one given writer over a very short period of time. It is not likely, for example, that Paul first thought he would live to see the parousia (1 Thess. 4:15, AD 50) but later changed his mind (Phil. 1:23, AD 62). In no passage of Paul's does he claim to know for certain that he will live until Christ's return (or that he will not). Where development clearly does appear in Scripture, it is better to speak of evolution than of revolution, of organic development than of mutation or distortion, or of the unity one finds in a robe with many fibres, not all of which extend the length of the twine, but each of which grows out of and is tied into a previous strand (I. H. Marshall, 'Climbing ropes, ellipses and symphonies: The relation between biblical and systematic theology', in P. E. Satterthwaite and D. F. Wright [eds.], *A Pathway into the Holy Scripture* [Grand Rapids, 1994], pp. 208–211).

Conclusion

In short, the unity and diversity of Scripture must be acknowledged and held in a delicate balance. More liberal scholarship tends to focus so much on diversity that the unity disappears. More conservative scholarship tends to focus so much on unity that the diversity disappears. Without a recognition of the unity of Scripture, the canon in its entirety cannot function as the authoritative foundation for Christian belief and practice as historically it has done. Without an appreciation of the diversity that comes from hearing each text, book and author on its own terms, one risks misinterpreting Scripture and not discerning what God intended to say to his people at any given point in their history. Theologically, the unity of Scripture marks out clear limits of thought and behaviour beyond which individuals or 'churches' may not legitimately be called Christian. On the other hand, the diversity of Scripture demonstrates how no one sect or ecclesiastical tradition has a monopoly of the truth. One can become heretical by being either too broad-minded or too narrow-minded!

See also: CHALLENGES TO BIBLICAL THEOLOGY; RELATIONSHIP OF THE OLD TESTAMENT AND NEW TESTAMENT.

Bibliography

P. Balla, *Challenges to New Testament Theology* (Tübingen, 1997); C. L. Blomberg, 'The legitimacy and limits of harmonization', in D. A. Carson and J. D. Woodbridge (eds.), *Hermeneutics, Authority, and Canon* (Grand Rapids and Carlisle, repr. 1995), pp. 135–174; R. B. Dillard, 'Harmonization: A help and a hindrance?' in H. Conn (ed.), *Inerrancy and Hermeneutic* (Grand Rapids, 1988), pp. 151–164; C. H. Dodd, *The Apostolic Preaching and Its Developments* (London, 1936); J. D. G. Dunn, *Unity and Diversity in the New Testament* (London and Philadelphia, 1977); R. T. France, 'Development in New Testament Christology', *Them*, 18.1, 1992, pp. 4–8; D. N. Freedman, *The Unity of the Hebrew Bible* (Ann Arbor, 1991); D. P. Fuller, 'The Importance of the Unity of the Bible', in R. L. Hubbard, Jr., *et al.* (eds.), *Studies in Old Testament Theology* (Dallas and London, 1992), pp. 63–75; J. Goldingay, 'Diversity and Unity in Old Testament Theology', *VT* 34, 1984, pp. 153–168; G. F. Hasel, *New Testament Theology: Basic Issues in the Current Debate* (Grand Rapids, 1978); *idem*, *Old Testament Theology: Basic Issues in the Current Debate* (Grand Rapids, ⁴1991); A. J. Hultgren, *The Rise of Normative Christianity* (Minneapolis, 1994); E. E. Lemcio, 'The unifying kerygma of the New Testament', *JSNT* 33, 1988, pp. 3–17; 38, 1990, pp. 3–11; J. G. McConville, 'Using Scripture for theology: Unity and diversity in Old Testament theology', *SBET* 5, 1987, pp. 35–57; J. Reumann, *Variety and Unity in New Testament Thought* (Oxford, 1991); H. G. Reventlow, *Problems of Biblical Theology in the Twentieth Century* (Philadelphia, 1986); D. Rhoads, *The Challenge of Diversity: The Witness of Paul and the Gospels* (Minneapolis, 1996); H. H. Rowley, *The Unity of the Bible* (London and Philadelphia, 1953); W. VanGemeren, *The Progress of Redemption* (Grand Rapids and Carlisle, 1988, 1995); D. Wenham, 'Appendix: Unity and diversity in the New Testament', in G. E. Ladd, *A Theology of the New Testament* (Grand Rapids and Cambridge, 1993, 1994), pp. 684–719.

C. L. BLOMBERG

New Testament Use of the Old Testament

Introduction

It is difficult to overemphasize the importance of the function and influence of the OT in the NT. There are quotations of or allusions to the OT in every NT writing except Philemon and 2 and 3 John. It is quoted with introductory formulas ('it is written') and without. Paraphrases and allusions appear; sometimes the allusions comprise no more than a word or two. In other places the NT reflects OT themes, structures and theology. The NT writers appeal to the OT for apologetic, moral, doctrinal and liturgical reasons. The evangelists seek in various ways to show how Jesus understood Scripture, fulfilled Scripture, and was clarified by Scripture. The OT is represented even more prominently in the writings of Paul and in Hebrews.

Of more importance than its use in the NT is the theology of the OT. The OT's view of God, of humanity, of covenant, of the election of Israel and of judgment forms the presupposition that underlies the theology of Jesus, his disciples, and the writings of the NT. Apart from the OT the NT would make little sense. Explicit quotations of the OT, as well as the numerous allusions, provide only a partial indication of the foundational function the OT plays in the theology of the NT. Careful consideration of the function of the OT clarifies at many significant points the foundational doctrines of the NT.

Functions of the OT

The OT is quoted with introductory formulas (*e.g.* 'in order that it be fulfilled'), and sometimes without; many paraphrases and allusions are made through the use of a few key words or phrases. With regard to exegetical style, scholars have pointed to possible parallels with *pesher* as practised at Qumran (esp. in Matthew, Paul and Hebrews) and parallels with rabbinic midrash (esp. in John and Paul). The OT seems to have three principal functions: 1. legal, 2. prophetic and 3. analogical. *Legal* interpretation has to do with determining what is required of the one who has faith in God (or in Jesus). *Prophetic* interpretation has to do with what has been fulfilled in Jesus' advent and what is expected to be fulfilled in the future. *Analogical* interpretation has to do with comparisons. Typology is a familiar form of analogical interpretation. Several examples of these principal functions are considered in the following sections.

Jesus and the Gospels

Jesus' use of the Scripture is at points similar to its use by the rabbis of his day. Therefore much of his teaching and use of the OT is familiar to his hearers. However, the eschatological orientation of Jesus' interpretation of Scripture parallels more closely scriptural interpretation at Qumran, while its pneumatic emphasis reflects Jesus' own experience of the Spirit in his life and ministry. Thus Jesus' understanding of the OT often struck familiar chords, which attracted hearers, and yet his understanding was at points distinctive and

unexpected, which challenged his hearers, including his closest followers.

Citations of the OT in the Gospels reflect the Hebrew (Matt. 11:10, 29; Mark 10:19; 12:30; Luke 22:37), the Greek (Matt. 18:16; 21:16; Mark 7:6–7; 10:8; Luke 4:18; 23:46; John 12:38), and the Aramaic (Matt. 4:10; Mark 4:12; 9:48) versions. Given the nature and origin of the material, the respective contexts of the evangelists, and the fact that they wrote their Gospels in Greek, such diversity is hardly surprising. But citations attributed to Jesus also reflect the same diversity. Since Jesus probably did not speak Greek, he probably did not quote the Greek version (LXX). But the Greek citations are not necessarily inauthentic, that is, deriving from the Greek-speaking Church after the time of Jesus. In many cases Jesus' citations of Scripture have been assimilated to the wording of the Greek, especially when the point that he makes is not lost in such assimilation.

Legal interpretation of Scripture

In most respects Jesus' view of the legal portions of Scripture was essentially that of his Palestinian contemporaries. When tempted by the devil (Matt. 4:1–11; Luke 4:1–13), Jesus responded with appropriate citations from Deuteronomy 8:3 ('Man shall not live by bread alone'), 6:16 ('You shall not tempt the Lord your God'), and 6:13 ('You shall worship the Lord your God', RSV). When asked what the greatest commandment was, Jesus cited Deuteronomy 6:4–5 ('Hear O Israel … love the Lord your God with your whole heart … '; *cf.* Mark 12:29–30) and Leviticus 19:18 ('You shall love your neighbour as yourself'; *cf.* Mark 12:31). Deuteronomy 6:4–5 was part of the Shema that an observant Jew was to recite twice daily (*cf. Mishnah Berakot* 1:1–4). The idea of loving one's neighbour as oneself and so fulfilling the whole law is found in Jewish sources: 'This [Lev. 19:18] is a great principle in the Torah' (*Sipra Leviticus* on Lev. 19:18; *cf. Genesis Rabbah* 24.7 [on Gen. 5:1]). There is probably an allusion to the two commandments in combination in the *Testaments of the Twelve Patriarchs*: 'Each of you speaks the truth clearly to his neighbour … Throughout all your life love the Lord and one another with a true heart' (*Testament of Dan* 5:2–3); 'Love the Lord and the neighbour' (*Testament of Issachar* 7:6); they are also linked by Philo: 'Among the great number of particular propositions and principles, two, as it were, stand as preeminent topics: one of duty toward God in piety and holiness, one of duty toward people in generosity and justice' (*On Special Laws* 2.15 §63). When the young man asked Jesus what he must do to inherit eternal life, Jesus responded, 'You know the commandments ...', and then cited approximately half the Decalogue (Mark 10:19; *cf.* Exod. 20:12–16 [Deut. 5:16–20]). In condemning legalism and hypocrisy (Mark 7:1–23), Jesus argued that the Pharisaic *korban* tradition (*cf. Mishnah Baba Qamma* 9:10; *Mishnah Nedarim* 1:1; 9:1) controverted God's commands: '"Honour your father and mother"; and "He who speaks evil of father or mother, let him surely die"' (Mark 7:10; *cf.* Exod. 20:12 [Deut. 5:16] + LXX Exod. 21:17). Herein we find an important difference between Jesus and the Pharisees. On another occasion Jesus cites Hosea 6:6, 'I desire mercy, not sacrifice' (Matt. 9:13; 12:7), to defend his habit of having fellowship with 'tax collectors and sinners' (Matt. 9:10). According to the rabbis, one was to avoid the company of sinners (*Tosefta Demai* 3:6–7; *Babylonian Talmud Berakot* 43b). But the citation of Hosea did not imply that Jesus was opposed to the cultus; he urges his followers to be reconciled before offering something upon the altar (Matt. 5:23–24). Moreover, implicit in Jesus' command not to take oaths is a profound respect for Jerusalem and the temple (Matt. 5:34–35; *cf.* Is. 66:1). Indeed, Jesus' action in the temple (Mark 11:15–17) was probably a call for greater respect for the cultus.

The Gospels, however, do recount several episodes where the activity of Jesus and his disciples was thought to break the law. Perhaps best known was the frequent charge that Jesus violated sabbath laws, even when he healed someone (*cf.* Mark 2:23–28; 3:1–6; Luke 13:10–17; 14:1–6; John 5:1–18; 9:1–34). To be sure, the rabbis taught that the 'saving of life overrides the sabbath' (*Mekilta* on Exod. 31:13), after all, 'the sabbath was given to [people], not [people] to the sabbath' (*Mekilta* on Exod. 31:14). This reasoning obviously parallels Jesus' claim that 'the sabbath was made for man, not man for the sabbath' (Mark 2:27). (It is possible, of course, that the tradition in *Mekilta* is dependent upon Jesus.) But in cases where a person's life was not in immediate danger, some rabbis felt that healing activity was unnecessary and so constituted a violation of the sabbath. Indeed, the Essenes were even more strict in their interpretation of Sabbath laws (*Damascus Document* 11:13–14: 'If a [beast] fall into a cistern or into a pit, let it not be lifted out on the sabbath'; *cf.* Matt. 12:11: 'What man of you, if he has one sheep and it falls into a pit on the sabbath, will not lay hold of it and lift it out?'). Obviously the difference between Jesus and his opponents lay in the interpretation and application of the sabbath laws; they did not dispute their validity.

Jesus applied Mosaic law to disputes among his disciples, enjoining that 'every word be confirmed by the evidence of two or three witnesses' (Matt. 18:16; *cf.* LXX Deut. 19:15). On the permanence of the marriage union, Jesus cited texts from Genesis: 'God made them male and female' (Mark 10:6; *cf.* LXX Gen. 1:27; 5:2); and 'For this reason a man shall leave his father and mother and be joined to his wife, and the two shall become one flesh' (Mark 10:7–8; *cf.* LXX Gen. 2:24). Jesus' legislation is clearly at variance with some of the more permissive interpretations of Deuteronomy 24:1: 'The School of Hillel says, "[Divorce is permitted] if she spoil the cooking"... Rabbi Aqiba says, "[Divorce is permitted] if he has found another more beautiful than she, as it is said..."' (*cf. Mishnah Gittin* 9:10). In this case the Essenes apparently adopted a position similar to that of Jesus (*cf. Temple Scroll* 57:17–18: 'And he must not select in addition to her another woman because she, and she alone, will remain with him all the days of her life'; *cf. Damascus Document* 4:20–21, where Gen. 1:27 is cited).

It is clear from his interpretation of the legal portions of Scripture that Jesus was committed to the essentials of the Jewish faith, even if some of his interpretations were apparently at variance with, at times even stricter than, those of his contemporaries. The chief difference between Jesus' interpretation of Scripture and that of many of his contemporaries is seen in his view of the relationship between the law and people. When it came to morals (*e.g.* divorce) Jesus' interpretation was stricter than that of most of his contemporaries. When it came to cultic laws (*e.g.* the sabbath and certain aspects of purity) Jesus' interpretation was comparatively lenient.

Prophetic interpretation of Scripture

Jesus cites Isaiah 61:1–2 as fulfilled in, and perhaps the occasion for, his public ministry: 'The Spirit of the Lord is upon me, because he has anointed me to preach good news to the poor' (Luke 4:18–19; *cf.* Luke 7:22 = Matt. 11:5). Jesus' interpretation of Micah 7:6 ('For I have come to set a man against his father, and a daughter against her mother...' [Matt. 10:35–36]) is similar to the messianic interpretation of this text in Jewish sources (*cf. Jubilees* 23:16, 19; *Mishnah Soṭa* 9:15; *Babylonian Talmud Soṭa* 49b; *Babylonian Talmud Sanhedrin* 97a). Apparently the rabbis also believed that division within families would take place in the time of the Messiah. The theme of division is reflected in the allusion to Psalm 6:8 ('Depart from me, you evildoers') in the sayings concerning false prophets (Matt. 7:23). The early Christian understanding of John the Baptist as the fulfilment of Malachi 3:1 apparently derives from Jesus ('See, I am sending my messenger ahead of you, who will prepare your way before you', Matt. 11:10, NRSV). Jesus explains the incomprehension and unbelief of his contemporaries in terms of Isaiah's strange commission from God: 'in order that they may indeed see but not perceive, and may indeed hear but not understand; lest they should turn again, and be forgiven' (Mark 4:12, alluding to *Targum of Isaiah* 6:9–10; *cf.* Matt. 13:14–15, which cites LXX Is. 6:9–10). But even Jesus' disciples are rebuked in similar terms: 'Having eyes do you not see, and having ears do you not hear?' (Mark 8:18; *cf.* Jer. 5:21; Ezek. 12:2; Is. 6:9–10). Jesus castigates Israel's religious leaders: 'This people honours me with their lips, but their heart is far from me; in vain do they worship me, teaching as doctrines the precepts of men' (Mark 7:6–7, citing LXX Is. 29:13).

Many of Jesus' prophetic statements looked forward to fulfilment in the future. In alluding to Isaiah's oracle against Babylon ('will you be exalted to heaven? You shall be brought down to Hades' [Is. 14:13, 15]) Jesus offered the cities that rejected him a grim warning of coming judgment (Matt. 11:23). Jerusalem herself received a warning no less foreboding in language borrowed from Jeremiah 22:5 ('Behold, your house is forsaken and desolate' [*cf.* Matt. 23:38]). The thought is completed in the reference to Psalm 118:26: 'Blessed is he who comes in the name of the Lord' (Matt. 23:39). The prophetic implication is that Jerusalem will be in a state of spiritual desolation until Jesus returns at the Parousia and is properly received. Jesus predicted Jerusalem's impending fate in terms of Daniel's 'abomination of desolation' (Mark 13:14; *cf.* Dan. 11:31; 12:11). The eschatological day will approach ' ... suddenly like a snare; for it will come upon all who dwell upon the face of the whole earth' (Luke 21:34–35; *cf.* Is. 24:17). When these things happen, 'they will begin to say to the mountains, "Fall on us"; and to the hills, "Cover us"' (Luke 23:30; *cf.* Hos. 10:8).

Jesus described his impending arrest and crucifixion in the words of Zechariah 13:7: '"I will strike the shepherd and the sheep will be scattered"' (Mark 14:27). He told his troubled disciples: 'And then they will see the Son of man coming in clouds with great power and glory' (Mark 13:26; *cf.* Dan. 7:13). Before the high priest, Jesus similarly predicted: 'you will see the Son of man seated at the right hand of Power, and coming with the clouds of heaven' (Mark 14:62; *cf.* Ps. 110:1 + Dan. 7:13). Jesus apparently understood himself in terms of Daniel's 'son of man', to whom the kingdom would be given (*cf.* Dan. 7:14; *1 Enoch* 69:29; *Psalms of Solomon* 17:44), and his disciples as the 'saints' to whom judgment would some day be given (*cf.* Dan. 7:22). This is probably what lies behind Jesus' saying, 'Truly, I say to you, in the new world, when the Son of man shall sit on his glorious throne, you who have followed me will also sit on twelve thrones, judging the twelve tribes of Israel' (Matt 19:28; *cf.* Luke 22:28–30: '... I assign to you, as my Father assigned to me, a kingdom, that you may ... sit on thrones judging ... '). It is likely that Psalm 122:3–5 ('Jerusalem ... to which the tribes go up ... There thrones for judgment were set, the thrones of the house of David') has also contributed to this eschatological saying; both passages, Daniel 7 and Psalm 122, are cited side by side in a rabbinic exegesis that anticipates the day when God and Israel's elders will sit in judgment upon the peoples of the world (*cf. Tanhuma, Qedoshim* 1.1). Elsewhere Rabbi Aqiba interpreted the plural 'thrones' of Daniel 7:9 as implying that the Messiah would take his seat next to God himself (*Babylonian Talmud Sanhedrin* 38b; *Babylonian Talmud Hagiga*

14a). Finally, Jesus warns his followers of the judgment of Gehenna: 'where their worm does not die, and the fire is not quenched' (Mark 9:48; *cf. Targum of Isaiah* 66:24). According to Jesus, when the Son of man comes, 'he will repay every person for what he has done' (Matt. 16:27; *cf.* LXX Ps. 61:13).

Analogical interpretation of Scripture

This category includes typology and other points of comparison. Jesus explicitly compared his ministry to those of Elijah and Elisha (Luke 4:25–27; *cf.* 1 Kgs. 17:1–16; 2 Kgs. 5:1–14). Later deeds resemble the exploits of these prophets of old (compare Luke 7:11–17 with 1 Kgs. 17–24 and 2 Kgs. 4:32–37; Luke 9:51–56 with 2 Kgs. 1:9–16; Luke 9:61–62 with 1 Kgs. 19:19–21). The kingdom is compared to the crop that grows of its own accord and then is harvested (Mark 4:29; *cf.* LXX Joel 3:13). Jesus enjoined his listeners to take his yoke upon them and 'find rest for [their] souls' (Matt. 11:29; *cf.* Jer. 6:16). He may have presented himself here as the personification of Wisdom (*cf.* Ecclus. 51:23–27; *cf.* Matt. 11:19, where Jesus apparently did identify himself with Wisdom). The rabbis spoke variously of taking upon oneself the yoke of the kingdom, the law, or repentance (*Babylonian Talmud Berakot* 10b; *Mishnah 'Abot* 3:5; *Babylonian Talmud 'Aboda Zara* 5a).

The comparison with Jonah is one of the most significant and one of the most debated: 'For as Jonah was three days and three nights in the belly of the whale, so will the Son of man be three days and three nights in the heart of the earth' (Matt. 12:40; *cf.* Jonah 1:17). In Matthew (12:38–39) the 'sign of Jonah' has something to do with Jesus' resurrection (*cf. 3 Macc.* 6:8). In Luke (11:31–32) it appears to be no more than Jesus' preaching. In a late rabbinic work Jonah's remarkable deliverance is described as a sign to the heathen (*Pirqe Rabbi Eliezer* §10). Not only is Jesus greater than Jonah, he is also greater than Solomon, who was visited by the 'queen of the South' (Matt 12:41–42; *cf.* 1 Kgs. 10:1–10).

When he took action in the temple, Jesus said: '"My house shall be called a house of prayer for all the nations." But you have made it a den of robbers' (Mark 11:17; *cf.* Is. 56:7 + Jer. 7:11). Isaiah 56 anticipates the day when all peoples will gather at Jerusalem to worship the Lord. By crowding the temple's court of the gentiles with sacrificial animals, the ruling priests made it difficult to pray and so showed callous disregard for gentile worshippers. Jeremiah 7 is a prophetic indictment of a violent and avaricious priesthood, one destined to come under divine judgment. In alluding to this passage Jesus implied that the ruling priests were corrupt and possibly violent. Other Jewish sources reflecting upon the pre-70 AD ruling priesthood paint a similar picture (*cf.* Josephus, *Antiquities of the Jews* 20.8.8 §181; 20.9.2 §206–207; *2 Baruch* 10:18; *Mishnah Keritot* 1.7; *Tosefta Yoma* 1.6–7; *Tosefta Menaḥot* 13.18–22; *Babylonian Talmud Pesaḥim* 57a). As a rejoinder to the chief priests' indignation over the children's shouts of acclamation (which recall the triumphal entry and the citation of Ps. 118:26, *cf.* Matt. 21:9), Jesus replied: 'Out of the mouth of infants and nursing babies you have prepared praise for yourself' (Matt. 21:16, NRSV; *cf.* LXX Ps. 8:3, one of the *Hallel* psalms that small children were taught; *Tosefta Soṭa* 6.2–3).

Jesus' parable of the wicked vineyard tenants begins with an important allusion to Isaiah's song of the vineyard: 'A man planted a vineyard, and set a hedge around it, and dug a pit for the wine press, and built a tower' (Mark 12:1; *cf.* Is. 5:1–2). Whereas Isaiah's original song indicted all of Judah (*cf.* Is. 5:3, 7), Jesus' parable limits the indictment to the Jewish religious leaders (*cf.* Mark 12:12). His application probably reflects exegetical traditions current in his time (*cf. Vineyard Text*; for later, but fuller explications, see *Targum of Isaiah* 5:1–7; *Tosefta Me'ila* 1.16; *Tosefta Sukka* 3.15, where the song's 'tower' is explicitly identified as the temple, and the 'wine vat' the altar). At the conclusion of the parable Jesus quotes Psalm 118:22–23: 'The very stone which the builders rejected has become the head of the corner; this was the Lord's doing, and it is marvellous in our eyes' (Mark 12:10–11). The rejected stone of Psalm 118 is to be understood as further explanation of the significance of the rejected son of the parable. The targum's paraphrase, 'the son which the builders rejected' (based upon a play on the words son [*ben*] and stone ['*eben*]), and the rabbis' custom of referring to themselves as the 'builders' (*cf. Babylonian Talmud Shabbat* 114a; *Babylonian Talmud Berakot* 64a [in a positive sense]; *Damascus Document* 4:19; 8:12, 18 [in a negative sense]; *cf*. 1 Cor. 3:10), probably facilitated Jesus' comparison. With the citation, 'The Lord said to my Lord, Sit at my right hand, until I put your enemies under your feet' (Mark 12:36, NRSV; *cf*. LXX Ps. 110:1), Jesus startled his hearers by suggesting that the son of David (*i.e*. the Messiah) is in fact greater than King David (not lesser as might be implied by his identification as the son of David). Jesus' interpretation of this verse provides important evidence that he understood his messiahship in terms very different from those of his contemporaries.

An apparently distinctive feature of Jesus' understanding of OT Scripture was that it was fulfilled: not soon to be fulfilled, as at Qumran, but actually fulfilled in his ministry. The casting out of demons was tangible evidence that the kingdom of God had come upon those in his presence (Luke 11:20). This proclamation of the kingdom ('The kingdom of God is at hand!') is drawn from passages in Isaiah (*e.g*. 40:9; 52:7; 61:1), through the interpretive lens of the Aramaic synagogue: 'The kingdom of your God is revealed!' (*Targum of Isaiah* 40:9; 52:7). Jesus' proclamation of the fulfilment of Scripture thus established the hermeneutical matrix, in the light of which the NT interprets and utilizes the OT.

Distinctive emphases in the four Gospels

Although the four Gospels cite and allude to many common Scriptures, their respective uses of the OT are distinctive and clearly serve their respective interests and purposes.

Mark. Mark apparently defines the 'good news' of Jesus Messiah in terms of the fulfilment of Isaiah's oracle of salvation and deliverance: 'See, I am sending my messenger ahead of you, who will prepare your way; the voice of one crying out in the wilderness: Prepare the way of the Lord, make his paths straight' (1:2–3, NRSV; *cf*. Mal. 3:1 + LXX Is. 40:3). In other words, the good news of the Christian message is the fulfilment of that for which Israel had for many years longed. Qumran (*Rule of the Community* 8:12–14; 9:19–20), as well as others (Baruch 5:7; *Testament of Moses* 10:1–5), also understood Isaiah 40:3 as a prophetic text that spoke of restoration. At his baptism the heavenly voice echoed the words of Psalm 2:7: 'You are my

Son, the Beloved; with you I am well pleased' (1:11, NRSV; *cf*. Gen. 22:2; Exod. 4:22–23; Is. 42:1). With this utterance Jesus' identity is made clear. Such recognition will not come forth from a human being until Jesus' death on the cross (*cf*. Mark 15:39). At the mountain of transfiguration, where Jesus conversed with Moses, the heavenly voice once again spoke, only this time addressing the disciples: 'This is my beloved Son; listen to him' (9:7; *cf*. Ps. 2:7; Gen. 22:2; Deut. 18:15). The injunction to listen is probably an allusion to Deuteronomy 18:15 ('The LORD your God will raise up for you a prophet like me [Moses] ... listen to him', NIV). These citations and allusions strongly suggest that Mark understood Jesus as the fulfilment of Jewish messianic expectation. As God's beloved Son and as the prophet who was to come (see 8:28), Jesus was the long-awaited Messiah of Israel.

Matthew. The extensive use of the OT in the Gospel of Matthew is well known. The Matthean evangelist was keenly interested in showing how Jesus fulfilled every aspect of the scriptures. All three components of the Bible, legal, prophetic, and wisdom/praise, have been fulfilled in Jesus. He not only has personally fulfilled the requirements of the law, but also is the law's master interpreter. He not only fulfilled messianic prophecies, but is also Israel's greatest prophet. Finally, he is the incarnation of Wisdom itself, an unparalleled master teacher. The evangelist's practice of finding new meaning in old tradition (whether OT or Christian tradition), which parallels that of Qumran, may very well be reflected in a verse found only in his Gospel: 'Every scribe who has been trained for [or by] the kingdom of heaven is like a householder who brings out of his treasure what is new and what is old' (13:52).

Luke/Acts. The OT functions in the writings of the Lukan evangelist in ways that are clearly distinct from its functions in the other three Gospels. He does not punctuate the tradition with proof texts as do Matthew and John; rather, he punctuates his narrative with speeches that are full of OT words and phrases (esp. the speeches in the birth narratives). Another distinctive feature is Luke's dependence upon the LXX. Indeed, the evangelist deliberately imitates the style of the Greek OT. But this imitation does not involve only style; it involves substance too. It is probable that the Lukan evangelist understood the story of Jesus (the Gospel) and the early church (the book of Acts) as the continuation of the biblical story. This is probably part of the meaning of the risen Jesus' statement to his disciples that 'everything written about me in the law of Moses and the prophets and the psalms must be fulfilled' (24:44–47; cf. 24:26–27).

John. At first glance John's use of the OT appears to be very much the same as Matthew's. Like Matthew, the fourth evangelist formally quotes the OT several times, many times with reference to the 'fulfilment' of something. But in other important ways the OT functions in John quite differently. Even in the case of the quotation formulas, John's purpose is very different. Unlike Matthew's, John's formulas appear to make up a pattern, a pattern that accentuates the theological development of the gospel narrative. In the first half of his Gospel, the evangelist introduces Scripture in a variety of ways, though usually using the word 'written' (1:23; 2:17; 6:31, 45; 7:38, 42; 8:17; 10:34; 12:14). In the second half he invariably introduces Scripture with 'in order that it be fulfilled' (12:38, 39–40; 13:18; 15:25; 19:24, 28, 36, 37). What is the meaning of this pattern? The answer may be deduced from the summary in 12:37 and the citation that follows in verse 38: 'Though he had done so many signs before them, yet they did not believe in him; it was that the word spoken by Isaiah might be fulfilled'. The 'signs' to which reference is made are those of the first half of the Gospel. The scriptural citations in the first half of the Gospel demonstrate that Jesus conducted his ministry in keeping with scriptural expectation ('as it is written'). For example, Jesus' zeal for the temple is related to Psalm 69:9; the feeding of the five thousand is related to Psalm 78:24; his appeal to the testimony of two witnesses is related to Deuteronomy 17:6 (or 19:15); his claim to be God's Son is related to Psalm 82:6; and his riding the donkey is related to Zechariah 9:9. In some of these instances the evangelist could have introduced the OT citation with reference to fulfilment (compare the citation of Zech. 9:9 in Matt. 21:4–5), but he did not. It is not until Jesus is rejected, despite his signs, that the Scriptures are said to be 'fulfilled'. It is in Jesus' rejection and crucifixion that the Scriptures find their ultimate fulfilment. Far from proving that Jesus did

not fulfil the Scriptures, and so could not be Israel's Messiah, Jewish unbelief and obduracy specifically fulfilled Isaiah 53:1 ('Lord, who believed ... ?') and Isaiah 6:10 ('He blinded their eyes ... '). In each action taken against Jesus, including the treachery of Judas, Scripture is fulfilled. It is apparent that the fourth evangelist wishes to show that it is in his passion, Jesus' 'hour of glorification' (17:1), that the Scriptures are truly fulfilled.

Paul

Paul cites the OT some one hundred times (slightly more, if the disputed letters are included). More than sixty of these quotations agree with the LXX, though many of these agree with both the LXX and the MT (some forty in all; *e.g.* Rom. 2:6; 3:4, 13, 18; 4:17, 18; *etc.*). Several quotations agree with the LXX, but not with the MT (some sixteen in all; *e.g.* Rom. 2:24; 3:14; 4:3, 7–8; 9:29; *etc.*). A small number agree with the MT and against the LXX (*e.g.* Rom. 1:17; 11:4, 35; 12:19; 1 Cor. 3:19; Gal. 3:11). A larger number of others disagree with both the LXX and the MT (*e.g.* Rom. 3:10–12, 15–17; 9:9, 17, 25, 27–28, 33; 10:6–8; *etc.*). Ten others are debatable (*e.g.* Rom. 3:20; 9:20; 11:1–2; 12:16–17; 1 Cor. 2:9; *etc.*). Paul's allusions to Scripture are as important for his theology as his formal citations, as will be seen in the following example.

One of the most intriguing instances of Paul's use of the OT is seen in the allusion to Deuteronomy 30:12–14 (and 9:4a) in Romans 10:6–8. Whereas Moses spoke of God's 'commandment' not being too far off (either up in heaven or beyond the sea), so that failure to obey it cannot be excused, Paul speaks of Christ. As unusual as Paul's exegesis appears, it is not entirely novel. The author of Baruch has alluded to this passage from Deuteronomy, and has applied it to Wisdom: 'Who has gone up into heaven, and taken her, and brought her down from the clouds? Who has gone over the sea, and found her ... ?' (Baruch 3:29–30). As already noted, comparisons between Christ and wisdom were sometimes made. But Baruch's parallel usage leaves some components of Paul's exegesis unclear. Scholars have called attention to the paraphrase of Deuteronomy 30:12–13 in the *Fragmentary Targum*, which reads (with italics showing departures from the Hebrew): 'The Law is not in heaven that one may say:

"*Would that we had one like the prophet Moses who would ascend to heaven and fetch it for us* and make us hear the commandments that we might do them." Neither is the Law beyond the Great Sea that one may say: "*Would that we had one like the prophet Jonah who would descend into the depths of the Great Sea and bring it up for us* and make us hear the commandments that we might do them.'" The point of the Hebrew is that the law has been given once and for all. There is no need for a prophet to ascend to heaven or to traverse the sea to obtain it. The Aramaic paraphrase illustrates this point with two biblical characters whose experiences roughly match the language of the passage. Moses, it was believed, had ascended to heaven when he received the law from God. For example, in *Targum Pseudo-Jonathan* Deuteronomy 34:5 we are told that Moses 'brought it [the law] from heaven'; and in *Pesiqta Rabbati* 4:2: 'Moses went up to heaven' (see also *Biblical Antiquities* 15:6; 2 Esdras 3:1–8). These traditions are based on Exodus 19:3, 20, where God summons Moses to meet him on the mountain. The reference to the sea, of course, provides the link to Jonah. In fact, the Targum's 'descend into the depths' draws the OT passage into closer alignment with Jonah's experience, for the prophet did not go across the sea; he went down into it (see the reference to 'abyss' in Jonah 2:3; *cf.* v. 6). In the NT, of course, both Moses and Jonah are compared to Christ, at points that are relevant to the traditions just reviewed. Like Moses, Jesus brings a new law from heaven (Mark 9:2–8; John 3:13–14; 1:17); like Jonah, Jesus descends into the abyss (Matt. 12:39–40; 16:4; Luke 11:29–30). Paul presupposes these Jewish and Christian traditions (*cf.* Eph. 4:8–10), and has combined them in his own way. His point in Romans 10:4–13 is that Christ has accomplished salvation. All that is now required is faith. No one needs to ascend to heaven to bring Christ down, for he has already descended. No one needs to descend into the abyss to raise him up, for he has already been resurrected. Redemption has been accomplished. All that remains is the confession of faith (Rom. 10:8–10, citing and interpreting Deut. 30:14). By faith in what God has accomplished through Christ, God's righteousness may be obtained.

Hebrews and the general epistles

The author of Hebrews explicitly cites the OT some thirty-six times, alludes to it another thirty-five times, and summarizes OT passages or stories another eighteen times. The author makes use of the LXX, but it is not clear exactly which version of it is used. Use of the OT in Hebrews is distinctly un-Pauline. Never is Scripture introduced with *gegraptai* ('it is written'). While several studies have looked to Philo or Qumran as the background against which Hebrews might be understood, the exegesis of its author is neither allegory nor *pesher*. He has developed his own style of typological exegesis, in which he compares Christ and the church against OT figures and institutions (figures such as Moses, angels and especially Melchizedek; institutions such as the priesthood and the sin offering). Unlike midrash, *pesher*, or even allegory, typology is primarily interested in biblical *events* and not in the biblical *text*.

Revelation

In the book of Revelation Scripture is never cited. No introductory formula appears (such as 'as it is written'), nor is Scripture (*graphē*) even mentioned. Yet Revelation is full of echoes and allusions to words and phrases drawn from the Bible. The seer envisages conflict with representative beasts (drawing upon Ezekiel and Daniel), a new Jerusalem, a new temple, and a new covenant (drawing on Ezekiel and Isaiah), and a return to the bliss of Paradise (drawing upon Genesis and the 'tree of life'). This expectation returns the end to the beginning, as earthly and heavenly history comes full circle and human and cosmic redemption is completed.

Continuity between the Testaments

One of the most important assumptions underlying the NT's use of the OT is that of fulfilment and continuity. NT usage of the OT cannot be reduced to mere proof-texting and apologetic. The purpose, structure and content of OT theology lie behind the major theological themes of the NT. Beliefs in and about the only God and Creator, who establishes a covenant with a chosen people and who promises redemption and salvation, are the beliefs presupposed in NT theology and its exegesis of specific OT passages.

The advent of Jesus not only fulfils prophetic and messianic expectations of the Scriptures of Israel; it also continues the story of Israel. Recognition of this important fact should warn Christians against neglect of the OT and failure to appreciate the inherently Jewish nature of Christianity. This means that Christian biblical theology must take fully into account the theology of the OT and never develop NT theology apart from it.

See also: RELATIONSHIP OF OLD TESTAMENT AND NEW TESTAMENT.

Bibliography

D. L. Bock, *Proclamation from Prophecy and Pattern: Lukan Old Testament Christology* (Sheffield, 1987); D. A. Carson and H. G. M. Williamson (eds.), *It is Written: Scripture Citing Scripture: Essays in Honour of Barnabas Lindars* (Cambridge, 1988); B. D. Chilton, *A Galilean Rabbi and His Bible* (Wilmington, 1984); D. Daube, *The New Testament and Rabbinic Judaism* (London, 1956); C. H. Dodd, *According to the Scriptures: The Substructure of New Testament Theology* (New York, 1952); E. E. Ellis, *Paul's Use of the Old Testament* (Grand Rapids, 1981); C. A. Evans, 'The function of the Old Testament in the New', in S. McKnight (ed.), *Introducing New Testament Interpretation* (Grand Rapids, 1989); J. Fekkes, *Isaiah and Prophetic Traditions in the Book of Revelation* (Sheffield, 1994); J. A. Fitzmyer, 'The use of explicit Old Testament quotations in Qumran literature and in the New Testament', *NTS* 7, 1960–61, pp. 297–333; R. T. France, *Jesus and the Old Testament* (London, 1971); E. D. Freed, *Old Testament Quotations in the Gospel of John* (Leiden, 1965); L. Goppelt, *Typos – The Typological Interpretation of the Old Testament in the New* (Grand Rapids, 1982); R. H. Gundry, *The Use of the Old Testament in St. Matthew's Gospel* (Leiden, 1967); A. T. Hanson, *Studies in Paul's Technique and Theology* (Grand Rapids, 1974); *idem*, *Living Utterances of God: The New Testament Exegesis of the Old* (London, 1983); R. B. Hays, *Echoes of Scripture in the Letters of Paul* (New Haven and London, 1989); G. Howard, 'Hebrews and the Old Testament quotations', *NovT* 10, 1968, pp. 208–216; B. Lindars, *New Testament Apologetic: The Doctrinal Significance of the Old Testament Quotations* (Philadelphia, 1961); R. N. Longenecker, *Biblical Exegesis in the Apostolic Period* (Grand Rapids and Carlisle, 1975, 1995); S. Moyise, *The Old Testament in the Book of Revelation* (Sheffield, 1995); B. Rosner, *Paul, Scripture and Ethics: A Study of 1 Corinthians 5–7* (Leiden and Grand Rapids, 1994, 1999); D. M. Smith, 'The use of the Old Testament in the New', in J. M. Efird (ed.), *The Use of the Old Testament in the New and Other Essays* (Durham, 1972); K. R. Snodgrass, 'The use of the Old Testament in the New', in D. A. Black and D. S. Dockery (eds.), *New Testament Criticism and Interpretation* (Grand Rapids, 1991); S. G. Sowers, *The Hermeneutics of Philo and Hebrews* (Richmond, 1965); K. Stendahl, *The School of St. Matthew and Its Use of the Old Testament* (Philadelphia, 1968).

C. A. EVANS

Relationship of Old Testament and New Testament

The nature of the problem

'Long ago God spoke to our ancestors in many and various ways by the prophets, but in these last days he has spoken to us by a Son' (Heb. 1:1–2, NRSV). Thus the biblical author poses the question of the relationship of the Testaments: how does the word of Christ relate to that of the prophets, and in broader terms, is the NT continuous or discontinuous with the OT? The history of biblical theology as a modern discipline, not to mention the history of its antecedents, shows that the question of the relationship between the two Testaments is of enduring importance and concern. H. G. Reventlow, in *Problems of Biblical Theology in the Twentieth Century*, p. 11, sees it as one of the key problems in 20th-century *biblical theology, and quotes N. H. Ridderbos as saying, 'The relationship between Old and New Testaments: that is just about the whole story; the whole of theology is involved in that.' The problem is manifested in a number of theoretical and practical ways: the use of the OT by Jesus and by the authors of the NT; the history of the Christian interpretation of the OT, and its effects on Christian doctrine; and the application of the OT to the Christian life, are but a few examples.

Biblical theology as a discipline presupposes that the Bible, notwithstanding its great diversity, has some kind of perceptible unity. However, the modern pursuit of a biblical theology has (almost inadvertently) created a problem. The overwhelming majority of biblical theologies written in the last century and a half have been theologies of either the OT or the NT. Some would argue that this is simply due to the necessary specialization demanded by the sheer volume of biblical literature. Whatever the reason, the result has been a tendency to treat the two Testaments as if they were independent of each other. This is more true in OT theologies than in NT, since the latter have to take into account the conviction common to all the NT authors that their message has its roots in the OT. All the books of the NT, with the possible exception of 2 John and 3 John, contain direct references and allusions to the OT, presupposing some continuity between the Testaments.

A number of OT theologians have attempted to address the problem in a theoretical way. For example, G. von Rad includes a lengthy section at the end of volume 2 of his *Old Testament Theology* (ET, Edinburgh, 1965, pp. 319–429), dealing with the OT and the NT. It gives a detailed exposition of a typological understanding of the unity of the Bible. Th. C. Vriezen, in his volume, *An Outline of Old Testament Theology* (ET, Oxford, 1958), devotes the first two chapters to his view of the OT as Christian Scripture, but it is not altogether obvious how this presupposition has affected his treatment of the OT itself. W. Eichrodt, in the opening chapter of his *Theology of the Old Testament* (ET, London, 1961, p. 27), states that OT religion must be seen as completed in Christ, but in the two volumes of this work there is little that displays an overt application of this principle. G. A. F. Knight wrote *A Christian Theology of the Old Testament* (London, 1957), and stated that his purpose was to 'seek to discover what the Old Testament has to say to the twentieth century in the light of the Christian revelation as a whole' (p. 10). Despite the title, one of the crucial issues concerning the continuity between the Testaments, that of Israel and the church, is relegated to a short appendix.

Some see the OT as providing authentic revelation and theology independently of the NT. For Christian writers this means that the OT reveals God as truly as does the New. But resistance to a Christological, and thus to a NT-based, interpretation of the OT can be seen in more extreme approaches to the diversity within it. Postmodernist trends not only follow modernism in denying transcendence, but refuse to allow any concept of a metanarrative, a comprehensive story and picture of reality in a word from God, which can unite the two Testaments into one meaningful canon of revelation. The notion that there is no transcendent authority or objective truth challenges the very basis upon which biblical theology has been built from biblical times.

So there is something of a continuum of approaches to the relationship of the Testaments which broadly follows a historical line of development. This continuum is also contemporary, in view of the ongoing existence of orthodox, historic Christianity which finds itself in substantial conflict with both modernism and postmodernism. First, attempts were made to understand the essential unity of the Bible by starting from the epicentre of the person and work of Jesus Christ. The early Christological interpretations of the OT were driven partly by the apologetic need to counter Judaism by asserting that the OT belonged to the church, and partly by the need to understand the OT presuppositions underlying apostolic doctrine. Early Christian apologetics also needed to counter Gnosticism by showing the unity of the Testaments, and at the same time to refute the Judaizers in the church by stressing the distinctions between the Testaments. Medieval Catholicism and Reformation Protestantism were both heirs of the Christological approach.

Secondly, with the Enlightenment and the advent of humanistic presuppositions in biblical and historical studies, the theological ties between OT and NT were loosened. The Bible was no longer regarded as a divinely inspired revelation of the mind of God, but as a purely human book which recorded certain ideas about God and his activity. Theological studies gave way to the study of the history of religion, and the religion of Israel was regarded as a matter for historical investigation almost without reference to the religion of Jesus and the early church. Thus, it was the philosophical influences of the Enlightenment, rather than practical issues, which led in the 19th and 20th centuries to the development of the parallel disciplines of OT theology and NT theology. Many OT theologies were produced from within the framework of certain Christian assumptions about the relationship of the Testaments, but with the clear aim of understanding what the OT was saying in its own right.

Thirdly, the postmodern age of religious pluralism encourages not so much the rejection of any connection between the Testaments, but rather a sense of either the freedom or the need to pursue the significance of the OT quite independently of its claimed or possible relationship to the NT. However, the task of writing OT theologies continues to be undertaken by those who also have some allegiance to the NT. It is remarkable that Jewish writers show little interest in writing theologies of the Hebrew Scriptures, which reinforces the conviction that the very nature of the Christian gospel as seen in the context of NT theology, however that is understood, provides the major impetus for pursuing an OT theology.

Unity and diversity in the history of interpretation

Simply put, the question is that of how two different Testaments can fit together to form one Bible with a unified message. It is generally recognized that the relationship of the two Testaments is one aspect of the unity and diversity, or continuity and discontinuity, within the canon of Scripture. This is one form of a philosophical and theological issue which underlies all attempts to understand reality: the relationship of the one to the many, of unity to plurality. This issue must be faced in every area of life, including the social and political sphere (how do the many individuals relate to the one state?), and human relationships and sexuality. In metaphysics and religion, the question is that of how the individual relates to the whole of reality. Some eastern religions aspire to have the individual lose all identity and eventually become absorbed into an undifferentiated divine unity. Christianity, on the other hand, has always maintained the distinction between God and the created order, even while also maintaining that human beings are made in the image of God.

While the natural tendency is to solve these problems by allowing either unity or diversity to dominate (an either–or solution), the Christian gospel suggests a distinctively Christian perspective embracing both unity and diversity (a both–and solution). The relationship of the Testaments is thus, from a Christian point of view, organically related to the Christological question of the relationship of the divine and human natures of Jesus. Long before the theologians of the early church had established formal ways of talking about the incarnation of Jesus as the God-human, the same basic issue was surfacing (in a different form) in their handling of Scripture. The relationship of the one and the many is integral to the theology of the OT.

The apostolic understanding of Jesus pointed to the mystery of the one person who was both fully God and fully human. It required a 'both–and', rather than an 'either–or' approach. Later the church formalized this perspective in the doctrine of the incarnation, and particularly in the formula of the Council of Chalcedon in AD 451. The doctrine of the Trinity is the epitome of 'both–and' formulation. God is conceived as both one and many (three). The early heresies about God tried to define his being in ways that compromised either the unity of the three Persons or their distinctiveness. Gnostic Christology opposed spirit and matter in a docetic view of Jesus as a divine spirit who had only the appearance of humanity. Similarly Marcion found his 'spiritual' ideas incompatible with the earthiness of the Bible's historical events, especially those in the OT, and removed the OT, and parts of the NT, from his canon of Scripture. Amongst more orthodox Christians the legacy of Hellenistic Gnosticism was seen in the recourse to allegory as a means of relating the OT to the NT. Whereas Marcion had removed the OT, the allegorists thought it contained a kind of judaistic overlay which hid from view the true spiritual meaning drawn from the NT and, later, from ecclesiastical dogma. While Marcion completely separated the Old from the New, the allegorists used a Hellenistic sleight of hand which effectively removed all differences and fused the two. Both solutions reflect an 'either–or' approach. The concern of these Alexandrine interpreters, such as Clement and Origen, for the literal or historical understanding of Scripture cannot be ignored, but their allegorical emphasis takes them away from the perspective of 'both–and'.

Running parallel with allegory, although developing later, was the historical approach of the interpreters of Antioch. Here there was a greater sense of the unity of the Testaments alongside that of the distinctions between them. Typology as a method of relating the Testaments was given great impetus, and it underlined both the unity and the diversity between them. Typology as a method of relating the Testaments has a variety of forms, but their essential feature is the recognition of parallel or repeated historical patterns. Rather than simply reading NT teaching or ecclesiastical dogma back into OT events, typology sees certain OT events as in some sense corresponding to later, significant gospel events.

Medieval interpretation maintained the struggle to understand the relationship without abandoning the historical meaning of the OT, but allegory prevailed as the major way of identifying the Christian meaning of the OT. This was a docetic approach in that it effectively disregarded the earthly and human nature of OT history and looked only for spiritual and eternal truths. It not only had ramifications for the relationship of the Testaments, but also de-historicized the gospel event. The medieval emphasis on the working of sacramental grace in the present life of the believer raised the question, which puzzled even the great Catholic theologian Thomas Aquinas, of how the OT believer could be saved in the absence of the church and its sacraments of grace. For Augustine the OT contained edifying material, which could be taken in its literal sense, and unedifying material which had to be allegorized. But by the later Middle Ages the distinction between edifying and unedifying was virtually coterminous with the distinction between the two Testaments.

Broadly speaking, one of the gains of the Reformation was the recovery of a more consistently Christological understanding of the relationship between the Testaments. This involved the understanding not only that the OT Scriptures truly testified to Jesus (John 5:39), but also that this unity existed in tension with the real diversity within and between the Testaments. It also meant that the unity-distinction formula of Chalcedon could be applied to the Word inscripturate in the same way as to the Word incarnate. This formula has multiple, in fact endless, applications. It addresses the nature of Scripture as both divine and human, and constantly reminds us that the Old–New relationship is only one aspect of the question of the one and the many: what does it mean for the Bible to be one yet to consist of two Testaments? It also addresses the questions of unity and diversity within and between the various corpora of the Bible, especially that of the progressive nature of revelation. But while the unity that exists between the Word incarnate and the word inscripturate is important for our understanding of the nature of the authority of the Bible, we must never overlook the very significant differences. The Bible is not divine in the way Jesus is. Biblical authority is derived from the authority of its divine author and from its content as God's word about Christ. The book is not inherently divine and bibliolatry has never been an acceptable option for Christians.

Luther's recovery of a more historical approach to the OT went hand in hand with his recovery of the historical and objective nature of the gospel. Justification by faith and the concept of an alien righteousness through faith made it possible for the believer in the 16th (or 20th) century to relate to the historic Christ who in turn related to God's acts in OT history. Christians could once again conceive of the word of God in the OT as a Christian word without resorting to allegory. Luther saw the question of the two Testaments as that of the relationship between law and grace. He went a long way towards removing the absolute divide between the Old and the New because he recognized that there was law and promise (*i.e.* gospel) in both Testaments. However, he continued to stress the predominance of law in the Old and of grace in the New. This rather negative understanding of the OT characterizes the Lutheran hermeneutic of law and grace, and helps to explain the negative assessment of the OT by the modern Lutheran theologian, Rudolf Bultmann.

John Calvin significantly places his discussion of the relationship of the Testaments in the wider context of the revelation of the Redeemer (*Institutes*, II). Book Two of the *Institutes* is entitled 'The Knowledge of God the Redeemer in Christ, First Disclosed to the Fathers Under the Law, and Then to Us in the Gospel'. In this section, Calvin first deals with the effects of the fall of the human race into sin and the need for divine grace. Chapter 7 is headed, 'The Law was Given not to Restrain the Folk of the Old Covenant under Itself, but to Foster Hope of Salvation in Christ until His Coming'. In this claim Calvin includes both the moral and the ceremonial law. The law was the means of revealing Christ to Israel even though it did so only as by a shadow. Calvin points to the essential unity of the Testaments while in no way ignoring the differences. Two chapters (*Institutes*, II, 10 and 11) are devoted to the similarity of the OT and the NT, and to the differences between them respectively. It is here that Calvin

expounds his influential view of the unity of the covenants, although he never arrives at the position of the 17th-century covenant theologians. There is however, something of this emphasis on unity in the thinking of the modern Reformed theologian, Karl Barth.

Unity and diversity in recent biblical theology

The relationship of the Testaments, then, is one aspect of the *unity and diversity of Scripture and overlaps with the *NT use of the Old. Against the background of the history of the Christian interpretation of the OT, which is essentially the question of the relationship of the Testaments, we can look at some of the more recent attempts to formulate this relationship. In our attempt to categorize the various approaches suggested by modern biblical theologians we recognize that their different emphases are just that: emphases and not mutually exclusive perspectives.

The dimensions of Scripture

The literary dimensions of the Bible include the language and genre of the various parts. Obvious distinctions exist between the OT corpus of Hebrew writings (including portions in Aramaic) and the NT writings which are all in Koine Greek. The existence of the Septuagint, a Greek Targum of the OT, does not eliminate the distinctions since this clearly has Hebrew sources. It does, however, reduce the differences by adapting the OT to the same linguistic milieu as the NT. Furthermore, while the NT introduces new literary genres not found in the Old, such as gospels and epistles, it also includes wisdom forms, historical narratives, prophecy and apocalyptic, which it shares with the Old.

The historical dimension, which is contained in the literary, shows both continuity and discontinuity between the Testaments. The undisputed continuity lies in the cultural and religious history of the ancient Near East, and in the fact that the central figure of the NT and his first adherents were members of the ancient race that is the focus of the OT. The fact that the movement which develops out of the life, death and resurrection of Jesus of Nazareth very quickly begins to include people of other races is seen in the NT to be continuous with the OT expectations concerning the nations of the world. Judaism, however, did not accept that the Jesus-movement was in fact continuous with the hope of Israel in the way it claimed. At best, Judaism allowed that Christianity was another sect started by messianic Jews.

The theological dimensions of the Bible are inseparable from the literary and historical dimensions. The NT writers constantly make connections between their message and that of the OT. They understand Christianity to be continuous with the OT, but the nature of the continuity can be defined only in relation to its discontinuity. Orthodox Christianity has always maintained that the God and Father of the Lord Jesus Christ is the Yahweh of the OT. The theological unity of the Testaments is asserted in the claim that the Bible as a whole contains the one word of the one God concerning his one way of salvation. Some kind of theological discontinuity between the Testaments is not thereby ruled out.

The canonical and theological status of Old and New Testaments

1. *The problem of the canon.* The subject of the *canon of Scripture is dealt with elsewhere. It will suffice here to mention the conclusions reached by Roger Beckwith in *The Old Testament Canon of the New Testament Church* (Grand Rapids, 1985), chapter 2, that Jesus and the primitive Christian church did not dissent from their Jewish contemporaries over which books constituted the authoritative canon of the Hebrew Scriptures. That being the case, and given the eventual acceptance of a body of literature as a NT canon, the question arises of how these two corpora were first perceived as comprising one canon of Christian Scripture. This is the historical question of the canon. The biblical-theological question concerns the internal theological evidence for the canonical status of the two Testaments.

2. *The OT has priority over the NT.* D. L. Baker (*Two Testaments, One Bible,* chapter 5) and Reventlow (*Problems of Biblical Theology,* pp. 54–64) have drawn attention to the view of some scholars that the OT is prior or superior to the NT. The scholars named are not Jewish theologians who reject altogether the authority of Jesus and the NT; rather, they are theologians who acknowledge the importance of the NT and claim adherence to the Christian faith. The best example of this position is provided in A. A. van Ruler, *The*

Christian Church and the Old Testament (ET, Grand Rapids, 1966). He adopts a salvation-history approach which sees the OT not only as the antecedent to the New but also as maintaining its own integrity, especially in setting forth the message of the kingdom of God. In a sense the gospel fulfils the promises of the OT, but at the same time it regresses from the fullness of the OT message. Thus the OT is apparently *the* canon of Scripture, and the NT is 'explanatory glossary' (p. 94). The distinction is not merely semantic, since van Ruler believes that important elements of the central theme of the kingdom of God are absent from the NT. In this, as Baker points out (p. 131), he oversimplifies in seeing the OT view of the kingdom as earthly and the message of the New as spiritual. Van Ruler's view that Jesus came as an emergency measure seems to ignore the NT's conviction that he was central to God's plan from the start. A similar position to van Ruler's is that of the Dutch theologian, K. H. Miskotte (*When the Gods Are Silent* [ET, London, 1967]).

3. *The NT has priority over the OT.* The most extreme example of this position is, of course, the rejection of the OT by such as Marcion. Marcionite tendencies in more recent times are seen in the *deutsche Christen* and the Nazis whose anti-Semitism was expressed in the rejection of the Jewish Scriptures (Baker, p. 49). There is also an incipient form of Marcionism which appears by default in the church and in individual Christian piety. Preachers and people alike find the OT problematic and its consequent neglect results in a 'canon within the canon' heavily weighted in favour of the NT. In theory, people maintain that the whole Bible is equally the word of God, but in practice, the difficulties of dealing consistently with the OT can lead to its eclipse if not to some intuitive, Christianizing approach.

There are, however, carefully considered and closely argued theological positions which place the OT on a lower level than the NT. An extreme developmental position was taken by Adolph von Harnack, who concluded that the early church was right to reject Marcionism, the Reformation was unable to avoid keeping the OT, but the modern retention of it 'results from paralysis of religion and the Church' (quoted in Baker, p. 49). The Lutheran dialectic of law and gospel failed to eradicate the medieval practice of imposing a hermeneutical divide between the Testaments. Rudolf Bultmann's existential approach led him to emphasize this hermeneutical gap to the point where he asserted that the significance of the OT was negative, not in the Marcionite or Nazi sense, but existentially. The OT is the presupposition of the NT. In his essay 'The Significance of the Old Testament for the Christian Faith', in B. W. Anderson, *The Old Testament and Christian Faith*, Bultmann rejects the old liberal notion of the development of religion as the basis for understanding the relationship of the Testaments. This view regards the OT as outmoded in the light of the purer NT religion. Bultmann preferred to ask how the OT presents human existence. He concluded that it reveals the demand of God (though this is not its only concern). It is necessary to understand that demand (*i.e.* to understand the Law) in order to grasp NT teaching on the grace given in the gospel. So Bultmann emphasizes the discontinuity of the Testaments: 'True, the Old Testament, in so far as it is Law, need not address us as direct Word of God and as a matter of fact does not do it. It speaks to a particular people who stand in a particular ethnic history which is not ours' (p. 17).

There is little doubt that Bultmann's position points to an important discontinuity between the Testaments. Carl Michalson (in Anderson, *The Old Testament and Christian Faith*, ch. 3) sees Bultmann's view as standing against Marcionism because it allows the OT to remain as it is. By contrast, traditional appropriations of the OT as Christian Scripture are a form of Marcionism because they exegetically absorb the Old into the New. But this argument ignores the question of how Jesus, the apostles, and the writers of the NT took over the OT.

4. *Both Testaments have equal status as Christian Scripture.* David Baker (*Two Testaments*, ch. 4) gives a number of examples of this position, but concentrates on that of Wilhelm Vischer, whose views have provoked rather strident criticisms. In his unfinished work, *The Witness of the Old Testament to Christ* I: *The Pentateuch* (ET, London, 1949), he assesses the complementarity of the Testaments thus: 'The Old Testament tells us *what* the Christ is; the New, *who* he is' (p. 7). Or again, 'In their preaching of Jesus the Messiah the apostles in no way desire to declare anything else than that which is written in the Old Testament' (p. 11). The continuity between the Testaments is emphasized in Vischer's essay 'Everywhere the Scripture is about Christ Alone' (Anderson, *The Old Testament and Christian Faith*, ch. 5): 'The New Testament asserts that God's deed in Jesus Christ is not merely one but rather THE decisive event for the history of Israel' (p. 97). In view of this, the question should probably not be that of the status of each Testament, for this is an elusive concept. Even if both Testaments are equally Christian Scripture, their relationship is still open to dispute. Vischer's approach gives priority in the interpretation of Scripture to the word about Christ in which the OT is fulfilled. Furthermore, the status of the OT as Christian Scripture is utterly dependent on its fulfilment in the NT.

Whether Vischer is guilty of extravagant use of typology or, as some would suggest, of allegorizing, is not the issue. He has pointed to the fact that Christians appropriate the OT as Christian Scripture and that the NT itself provides the grounds for doing so. To give both Testaments equal canonical and theological status is not at all to suggest that they function in exactly the same way. Vischer uses a basic model of promise and fulfilment which makes the person and work of Jesus Christ theologically central and pre-eminent. In this he adopts one of the thematic polarities which characterize attempts to assess the relationship of the Testaments.

Thematic polarities between the Testaments

A number of thematic approaches have been proposed which highlight the nature of the problem of defining the continuity and discontinuity between the Testaments. None can be seen as a total solution or as exclusive of all other proposals. Each involves a polarity which cannot be resolved by demolishing one or other pole. Once again the Christological and trinitarian analogies are helpful in warning against facile 'either–or' solutions. But merely to propose that the 'both–and' tension be maintained is not to solve the problem.

1. *Salvation-history and eschatological consummation.* The essence of salvation-history is the recognition that the books of the Bible, while not being uniformly historical in form, all relate to an overarching history in which God acts to bring salvation to his people. Beginning at the creation event the storyline

moves through the entry of sin to the history of Israel as the chosen people. This history leads eventually to Jesus Christ and finally to the consummation and the new creation. The OT, then, is the first part of this story. The tension in this polarity lies in the fact that biblical salvation-history comes to an end. History is goal- or end-oriented. It finds its true meaning in the nature of the end defined by the coming of Christ.

Oscar Cullmann, in *Salvation in History* (ET, London, 1965) sees salvation-history as focusing on Jesus, and includes in it the eschatological tension. It could certainly be argued that salvation-history, as a Christian approach to the appropriation of the OT, is found in the words of Peter (Acts 2:16–36), Stephen (Acts 7:2–56) and Paul (Acts 13:16–41). Each has a sense of the continuity between the salvific, historical events of the OT and Jesus of Nazareth, so that Jesus is claimed to be the crowning saving act of God. In 19th-century scholarship the name of J. C. K. von Hofmann is linked with the idea of salvation-history. It was seen as one implication of the Reformation's retrieval of the historical sense of the OT, but also as a rejection of the Enlightenment and the reduction of biblical theology to the history of religious ideas. It established one of the central tenets of much 20th-century biblical theology: the idea that God has acted in history, and consequently, that history is revelation.

Not all salvation-history approaches have such a strong sense of continuity. G. von Rad stresses discontinuity within the OT: there is a gap between what can be said to have happened and what Israel came to confess. The OT consists of a developed tradition of saving history and the record of Israel's response to that saving history. The processes of reinterpretation which took place in the OT continue in the NT's appropriation of the OT. This approach raises important questions about the historicity of salvation-history. In what sense has God acted in history if the events which are said to evidence this action cannot be taken as historical?

The polarity of salvation-history and eschatology is examined by Cullmann (*Salvation in History*, pp. 28–64). Implicit in the whole notion of God's acting in history is the goal towards which such history moves. History, to be saving history, must involve eschatology. But eschatology is the end of history as well as its goal. The continuity of the Testaments is usually conceived in terms of some kind of eschatological resolution in and through Jesus Christ. The question of how the kingdom of God comes is discussed elsewhere. We note here the connection between the resolution of the process of salvation-history and the nature of Christian existence between the two comings of Christ.

2. *Type and antitype.* The salvation-history approach is closely related to the revived interest in typology as a way of understanding the inner theological structures of the Bible. The connection was recognized by von Hofmann in his *Biblische Hermeneutik* (Noerdlingen, 1880; ET, *Interpreting the Bible* [Minneapolis, 1959], p. 135). The history recorded in the OT is the history of salvation as it proceeds towards its full realization. Hence the events recorded therein are to be interpreted teleologically, *i.e.* as aiming at their final goal, and thus as being of the same nature as the goal, though also shaped by their particular place in history. The typological principles applied by von Hofmann thus included the unity of salvation-history and the interpretation of individual events as part of the whole history (p. 145).

In broad terms, typology rests upon the recognition that the way God spoke and acted in the OT was a preparation for and anticipation of the definitive word and act of God in Christ. The nature of the anticipation can be variously understood. One view is that God acts in the NT in ways patterned by his actions in the OT. Thus his leading of people out of their captivity to sin and death shows some similarities to his leading of Israel out of captivity in Egypt. Another view is that the OT type predicts a fulfilling antitype to come. Typology is not the same as predictive prophecy, but nor is it simply the recognition of coincidences. In the purpose of God, he provides a preparatory shadow of the real saving events. The relationship between the type and the fulfilling antitype is such that grasping the shadow in the OT by faith, believing the promises of God, was the means by which the people of the OT grasped the salvation which is in Christ. Thus, von Rad is able to acknowledge on the basis of typology that 'One must therefore ... really speak of a witness of the Old Testament to Christ.' (See 'The Typological Interpretation of the Old Testament', in Westermann, *The Old Testa-*

ment and Christian Faith, p. 39.) The concepts of type and antitype express the organic relationship between the events of the OT and those of the NT: the former pattern and foreshadow their fulfilment in the latter. The heart of the antitype in the NT is the person and work of Jesus Christ, and especially the resurrection. Thus, both Peter and Paul can assert that Old Testament prophecy about Israel and its king is fulfilled in the resurrection of Jesus (Acts 2:29–36; 13:30–33).

3. *Promise and fulfilment.* Salvation-history and typology are connected also with the thematic polarity of promise-fulfilment. There are many variations on this theme, but essentially it goes beyond the fulfilment of promise or prophecy within OT history, and extends it to a definitive fulfilment in the NT. One implication of this is that the OT is incomplete with respect to the working out of God's purposes and thus cannot be fully understood apart from its fulfilment in the NT. The two Testaments are interdependent in that the New is needed to complete the Old, but also needs the Old to show what it is that is being fulfilled.

4. *Sensus literalis and sensus plenior.* A variation on the notion of typology, first propounded by Roman Catholic scholars, is the idea of a literal sense of the OT and a fuller sense (*sensus plenior*) which is mainly worked out in the NT. The *sensus plenior* of an OT text, or indeed of the whole OT, cannot be found by exegesis of the texts themselves. Exegesis aims at understanding what was intended by the author, the *sensus literalis*. But there is a deeper meaning in the mind of the divine author which emerges in further revelation, usually the NT. This approach embraces typology but also addresses the question of how a text may have more than one meaning. While typology focuses upon historical events which foreshadow later events, *sensus plenior* focuses on the use of words. Types are generally believed to find their antitypes in the NT. For some Roman Catholic scholars, the fuller sense can be found either in the NT or in ecclesiastical dogma. Most frequently, however, *sensus plenior* is a means of giving expression to the unity and distinction between the Testaments.

5. *Old covenant and new covenant.* Most covenant or federal theologians are heirs of the Calvinist Reformation. Their emphasis on the continuity of the Testaments contrasts with the Lutheran emphasis on discontinuity. The Westminster Confession provides a classic expression of their view. It speaks of one covenant which 'was differently administered in the time of the law, and in the time of the gospel: under the law it was administered by promises, prophecies, sacrifices, circumcision, the paschal lamb, and other types and ordinances delivered to the people of the Jews, all foresignifying Christ to come' (chapter VII, section V).

Some modern biblical theologians have seen the idea of the covenant as a unifying principle or centre of biblical theology. The first covenant is with Noah (although Westminster theology conceives of a covenant of works with Adam; *Westminster Confession of Faith*, chapter VII). The covenant is then given to Abraham, to Israel at Sinai, and then to the Davidic royal line. The prophets conceive of a new covenant which will rectify the failures of Israel to be faithful to the original covenant. The NT declares that the new covenant is established in Jesus, who is the representative head of a new Israel, and who by his resurrection demonstrates his acceptance by the Father.

6. *Law and gospel.* The emphasis on discontinuity fostered by the law–gospel polarity has been mentioned above. It could be said to extend back to Paul and his apparent ambivalence about the law, and to the different ways in which the word 'law' is used in the NT. An extreme form of discontinuity is found in earlier expressions of dispensationalism, in which the dispensation of law is completely separated from the dispensation of grace. The present age of the gospel is regarded as a parenthesis unseen by OT prophecy. This view presupposes an extremely literal view of prophetic fulfilment and finds continuity in what is yet to happen by way of fulfilment, rather than in what has already happened in Christ.

7. *Israel and the church.* Is the church the new Israel, and if so, in what sense? Some see continuity, in that the church virtually takes over all the roles of Israel as the saved people of God. Others, for example dispensationalists, see discontinuity, in that they expect the future fulfilment of the hopes of Israel to involve national restoration and salvation. A third view takes the OT ideas of the ingathering of the Gentiles to the restored Israel as being worked out in the gospel, which is to

the Jew first (Rom. 1:16); the church consists of restored or spiritual Israel (Christian Jews), plus converted Gentiles, who are privileged to share in Israel's blessings.

A way forward?

From a literary point of view, the relationship of the two Testaments involves the history of the Bible as canon. This in turn raises some internal historical questions relating to the biblical proclamation of the unity of the people of God and the work of God for their salvation. The NT's use of the OT is one important consideration. These literary and historical concerns point to the internal structures of biblical theology, which reveal something of the unity and diversity of the biblical message. Finally, the centrality of Jesus Christ to the NT's expression of its continuity with the OT points to the dogmatic formulations of the person and work of Christ. Christology demands that the whole question be addressed in the light of the revealed model of unity-distinction, and biblical theology provides the instrumental means for describing the nature of both the unity and the distinctions between the two Testaments. The heart of the issue lies in the fact that the historical Jesus who is at the centre of the NT's message is absent from the events of the OT. Yet he claims that the OT witnesses to him. Understanding the relationship of the two Testaments involves understanding that the God who has revealed himself finally in Jesus has also revealed himself in the OT in a way that foreshadows both the structure and content of the Christian gospel.

Bibliography

B. W. Anderson (ed.), *The Old Testament and Christian Faith* (New York, 1969); D. L. Baker, *Two Testaments, One Bible* (Leicester, [2]1991); J. C. K. von Hofmann, *Interpreting the Bible* (ET, Minneapolis, 1959); O. Cullmann, *Salvation in History* (ET, London, 1967); J. S. Preuss, *From Shadow to Promise: Old Testament Interpretation from Augustine to the Young Luther* (Cambridge, 1969); H. G. Reventlow, *Problems of Biblical Theology in the Twentieth Century* (ET, Philadelphia, 1986); C. Westermann (ed.), *Essays on Old Testament Hermeneutics* (ET, Richmond, 1964).

G. GOLDSWORTHY

Systematic Theology and Biblical Theology

To relate the nature and functions of systematic theology and biblical theology respectively proves distractingly difficult because various scholarly camps operate with highly divergent definitions of both disciplines, and therefore also entertain assumptions and adopt methods that cannot be reconciled with those of other scholarly camps. The permutations from these intertwined variables ensure the widest diversity of opinion; no analysis of the relations between systematic and biblical theology can sweep the field. Some of these difficulties must be explored before useful connections between the two disciplines can be drawn. Because more debate attaches to biblical theology than to systematic theology, and because biblical theology is the focus of this volume, that is where we must direct primary attention.

Biblical theology

Before attempting to sort out the conflicting definitions of biblical theology, we shall do well to consider the bearing of a number of topics on the discipline.

History of biblical theology

Because the history of biblical theology is surveyed elsewhere in this volume, here we may restrict ourselves to a mere listing of some of the turning points that have given rise to different apprehensions of biblical theology.

In one sense, wherever there has been disciplined theological reflection on the Bible, there has been a *de facto* biblical theology. The first occurrence of the expression itself, however, is in 1607, in the title of a book by W. J. Christmann, *Teutsche [sic] Biblische Theologie* (no longer extant). The work was apparently a short compilation of proof texts supporting Protestant systematic theology. This usage enjoyed long life; it was alive and well a century and a half later in the more rigorous four-volume work by G. T. Zachariae (1771–75). A century earlier, however, the German pietist P. J. Spener, in his famous *Pia Desideria* (1675), distinguished *theologia biblica* (his own use of Scripture, suffused with reverence and piety) with the *theologica scholastica* that prevailed in Protestant orthodoxy.

By the second half of the 18th century, the influence of the European Enlightenment and the rise of English Deism generated a small but influential group of theologians who sought to extract from the Bible timeless truths in accord with reason, truths that were largely still acceptable to the established orthodoxies but increasingly removed from the various confessional orthodoxies. The most influential of these figures was J. P. Gabler, whose inaugural lecture at the University of Altdorf (1787) captured this rising mood and proved seminal: 'An Oration on the Proper Distinction Between Biblical and Dogmatic Theology and the Specific Objectives of Each'. Contrary to what is commonly asserted about this address, Gabler only marginally called for what might today be called salvation-historical study of the biblical texts (*i.e.* the understanding and exposition of the texts along their chronological line of development). His fundamental appeal was to circumvent the endless debates among systematicians whose emphasis on diverse confessions and philosophical analysis kept them not only arguing but also several steps removed from the Bible. Gabler argued that close inductive work on the biblical texts themselves would bring about much greater unanimity among scholars, as all would be controlled by the same data. Systematic theology could then properly be built on this base.

The first part of the call was largely heeded (owing, no doubt, to many factors far removed from Gabler); the second part, the fresh reconstruction of systematic theology, was by and large ignored, or pursued by others with little interest in this new 'biblical theology'. With more and more emphasis on close study of individual texts, and with less and less emphasis on serious reflection on the relationship of these findings to historic Christian faith, the tendency was toward atomization. Thus G. L. Bauer produced not a biblical theology but an OT theology (1796) followed by a two-volume NT theology (1800–1802). What might be called 'whole Bible' biblical theologies continued to be written for the next century (with a handful in the 20th century), the most influential being that of J. C. K. von Hofmann (1886), whose work greatly influenced Adolf Schlatter. Nevertheless, the tendency was away from whole-Bible biblical theology, and towards OT theology and NT theology. By the 20th century, these works most commonly divided up their subject matter into smaller corpora (Pauline theology; Matthean theology; Q-theology; theology of the major prophets; *etc.*) or into organizing structures (the covenant for W. Eichrodt; a specialized understanding of salvation history for G. von Rad; a form of existentialism for R. Bultmann; *etc.*).

We will shortly mention some of the efforts to re-establish some form of whole-Bible unity. Within the so-called 'Biblical Theology Movement' in the middle of the 20th century, emphasis was often laid on 'the mighty acts of God' in history. Divorced from the rigour of adherence to exegesis of authoritative texts, however, it was soon perceived to be too ethereal, too insubstantial, to support the weight that was being placed on it.

Today, at the beginning of the 21st century, the situation is extraordinarily diverse. On the one hand, there is in Germany a renewed interest in *eine gesamtbiblische Theologie* ('a whole-biblical theology'), what James Barr calls 'a pan-biblical theology'. The journal *Jahrbuch für biblische Theologie* celebrated its fifteenth anniversary in 2000. Similar developments in Britain and America testify to mushrooming interest in biblical theology; *Horizons in Biblical Theology* has published now for more than twenty years. Not least significant is the 'whole Bible' biblical theology expressed most dramatically in the competing proposals of Brevard Childs and J. A. Sanders (see below). On the other hand, rising voices provide stern criticisms of these movements and provide detailed reasons for rejecting them or firmly domesticating them, while others continue to use the expression 'biblical theology' for approaches to the OT or NT that are radically atomistic or that are the product of highly creative, imaginative, allusive structures that self-consciously depend on a postmodern epistemology.

In short, the history of 'biblical theology' is extraordinarily diverse. Everyone does that which is right in his or her own eyes, and calls it biblical theology. In a situation so fluid it is necessary to state and justify what one means by 'biblical theology' before analysing its relation to systematic theology.

Exegesis

Barr has pointed out that in contemporary usage 'biblical theology' is largely contrastive: *i.e.* a substantial part of the definition, on any reading, is taken up with explaining how biblical theology is *not* exegesis, is *not* systematic theology, is *not* historical theology, and so forth. For Barr, that is a sign of its intrinsic weakness; biblical theology is not so much something in itself, he avers, as a distinction from a lot of other things with which it holds much in common. It might be argued, however, that the contrastive nature of biblical theology is not so much a weakness as a strength. True, biblical theology must be differentiated from other disciplines, but the fact that it can be is precisely what gives it its distinctiveness, while the fact that it must be is precisely what makes it such an excellent bridge discipline, building links among the associated disciplines and in certain respects holding them together.

Nowhere is the overlap more striking than between exegesis and biblical theology. Both are concerned to understand texts. It is impossible to have any sort of responsible biblical theology apart from careful, responsible exegesis. Moreover, responsible exegesis of entire texts (as opposed to a merely mechanical or atomistic approach) is the working material of biblical theology (on almost any definition of the latter). But exegesis tends to focus on analysis, and may therefore drift to details and specialized interests (source criticism, for instance) of little use to the biblical theologian; biblical theology tends towards synthesis: the theology of the book, the corpus, the canon, constructed out of the detailed exegesis of the book, the corpus, the

canon. Inevitably, the exegesis largely controls the biblical theology, though not every detail is taken up in the theology; on the other hand, the biblical theology, so far as it has been constructed, inevitably influences the exegesis, perhaps more so than is commonly recognized. Yet this circle is not vicious, provided the exegete and the biblical theologian share the common vision of trying to explicate the text.

Historical theology

Historical theology has been broadly understood to be the diachronic study of theology, *i.e.* the study of the changing face of theology across time. Insofar as biblical theology studies the changing face of the accumulating biblical documents across time, should it not be construed as nothing more than historical theology pushed back into the period before the 'closing' of the canon?

There is insight here, of course. The parallels between the two disciplines are striking. Yet before they are pushed too far, two observations are necessary.

First, those who want to demolish all distinctions between biblical theology and historical theology (save the obvious one of the range of material studied) are those who are most uncomfortable with notions of canon. To those for whom the distinctions presupposed by the canon are purely accidental and arbitrary, historical theology is merely a temporal extension of biblical theology; or, otherwise put, biblical theology is little more than an earlier version of historical theology, when all the assessments of earlier theological documents took place within documents which themselves came to be included (for whatever reasons) in the canon. But if the notion of canon is bound up with authority, or if a claim of revelation attaches to the documents judged canonical, then there is a fundamental distinction between biblical theology and historical theology, apart from the obvious distinctions in the time and place of the documents being studied. For under these assumptions historical theology, however much it builds upon or corrects or interacts with earlier theological reflections, draws the line at self-consciously correcting or abandoning the biblical documents. They are part of the given. By the same token, under these assumptions the internal developments within the canon will be seen in a different light, in comparison with, say, internal developments in the history of theology from the late medieval period to the early Reformation period, or from the early Reformation period to the Counter-Reformation. The former developments will be seen as part of the God-directed transformations that ultimately constituted the fundamental given; the latter developments will be seen as part of the ongoing task of coming to grips with the foundation documents, and being corrected by them.

Secondly, the point just made will prove persuasive only to those who, for whatever reasons, accept the authoritative uniqueness of the canonical books. But many scholars find that such a notion of the canon is precisely the problem. They are convinced that the NT documents themselves betray divergent and mutually contradictory theologies. To speak of a canonical wholeness or a canonical authority is to speak of a chimera. Very often such scholars have been influenced by one or both of two highly influential works. In *Rechtgläubigkeit und Ketzerei im ältesten Christentum* (1934), Walter Bauer argued that heresy preceded orthodoxy, that earliest Christianity was far more diverse than its later forms, and that to read unified theology into the earliest decades is sheer anachronism. Despite telling responses, Bauer's thesis still has many followers. Helmut Köster's 1957 dissertation, *Synoptische Überlieferung bei den apostolischen Vätern*, argued that, judging by the pattern of quotations among the Apostolic Fathers, the synoptic tradition enjoyed no fixed wording until well into the second century, thereby demonstrating that the tradition itself is late and historically unfounded. Building on an array of criticisms of these books, Peter Balla has shown that Köster's arguments are without foundation, and that Bauer's thesis, once the sources are carefully examined in location after location (Edessa, Egypt, Asia Minor, Rome), is simply invalid.

The functional parallels between biblical theology and historical theology need not be denied. Nevertheless they should not be developed beyond the evidence, and must not be permitted to stand against the abundant interlocking considerations (canon, revelation, authority) that demand distinctions.

Historical criticism

The interplay between biblical theology and the historical criticism of the last two centuries or so is extraordinarily convoluted. But here, five observations must suffice.

First, as intimated by the historical survey of the changing meanings of 'biblical theology' across the last four centuries, the major impulse has been toward fragmentation and atomization. In this century, the number of whole-Bible biblical theologies has been small and their content frail and hesitant, compared with the number of OT theologies and NT theologies. Moreover, most of the NT theologies do not offer us a theology of the NT, but a treatment of the distinctive theology that the scholar finds in each NT corpus, with the shape and contents of that corpus determined by the scholar's historical-critical conclusions. (Something similar could be said of OT theologies.) To take one recent example, Georg Strecker's NT theology, after examining various influences on Paul and other NT writers, devotes chapters to Paul, the Synoptics as a whole, Mark, Matthew, Luke-Acts, 2–3 John, 1 John, John, and so forth. The influence of more-or-less standard historical criticism is obvious. Moreover, parts of his book read less like a theology, biblical or classical, than a theological introduction to the NT: he devotes 106 pages to an overview of the historical John the Baptist, the historical Jesus, the early Palestinian church, the Hellenistic church, and Q-material. None of this leads towards whole-NT biblical theology, still less towards whole-Bible biblical theology.

The *second* observation shows that the issue lies deeper. The historical-critical method exemplified by Strecker presupposes that this approach is capable, in principle, of uncovering assured results grounded in unassailable premises. Rational arguments and appropriate historical-critical methods generate neutral results that can be tested by other workers in the field. The fact that historical criticism has generated a wide diversity of results merely leaves scope for further work, in the hope of achieving greater scholarly unanimity. But postmodern thought, whatever difficulties it has cast up (see below), has effectively exploded the myth of neutrality in studies in the humanities. Daniel Patte argues convincingly that historical-critical studies presuppose a worldview not itself a result of critical biblical exegesis but rather its foundation. Though not all their arguments and analogies are convincing, R. A. Harrisville and W. Sundberg trace the rise of 'rationalist biblical criticism' and fault it for thinking it can 'go beyond the reach of cultural presuppositions and philosophical commitments to establish the historical meaning of biblical texts once and for all' (*The Bible in Modern Culture*, p. 263). Thus another set of scholars, using the same historical-critical tools deployed by Strecker, may emerge with very different historical-critical reconstructions, and therefore with very different biblical-theological conclusions. For instance, if one historical-critical construction sees Paul as the author of seven NT letters, the shape of 'Pauline theology' may be rather different from the work of a scholar who thinks Paul wrote ten of the NT letters that bear his name, or all thirteen. A scholar who thinks the canonical evangelists, while betraying their own theology, nevertheless bear faithful witness to the teachings and deeds of Jesus, will not only interpret the Synoptics rather differently from his or her more sceptical colleagues, but will develop the chronology of dominant influence rather differently; Jesus himself will be seen to be the fountainhead of NT thought (P. Barnett, *Jesus and the Rise of Early Christianity*).

A *third* observation about the influence of historical criticism on biblical theology depends on a distinction between a 'narrow' view of history and a 'wider' view of history (this terminology is Balla's, but many writers develop the same distinction using different categories). A 'narrow' definition of history (so, for instance, H. Räisänen) excludes even the possibility of accepting as true any biblical affirmation of God acting in history. It operates, in fact, on naturalistic assumptions. In other words, it does not deny the possibility of the existence of God, but denies that history can find any evidence of him. History is a closed continuum. A 'wider' definition of history allows that God may well have operated in the domain of what 'really happened' in space and time, observable to human witnesses (*e.g.* the resurrection). Adherents to the former definition call for a 'purely historical' approach to the study of the NT documents; the latter definition is prepared to blend history and theology.

Of course, what it means to blend history and theology is itself rather elusive. It means more than to study what happened and what 1st-century participants *believed* to have happened (the latter being cast in theological terms); such study may still be narrowly 'historical'. The blending of history and theology in any useful sense presupposes two things: first, that the Christianity portrayed in the NT documents is inescapably historical, *i.e.* its entire structure depends on the veracity of its claims that certain events actually took place in history, and therefore these events are in principle open to historical investigation; and secondly, that the theological beliefs espoused and advanced by the NT writers belong to a matrix of thought that corresponds to reality, *i.e.* these writers are telling us true things about God, about Jesus, about his resurrection, about the significance of his cross, and so forth. Similar points could be made about OT theology.

Fourthly, just as historical-critical judgments, as we have seen, shape the outcome of one's attempts to do biblical theology, so also one's conclusions regarding biblical theology can shape one's historical-critical conclusions. If years of studying, say, NT Christology, or Paul's use of the OT, have shaped one's conclusions about who the historical Jesus is and how the church came to ascribe an array of titles to him, or how the NT documents are related to the Old, inevitably such judgments will influence one's historical-critical stances. That is not necessarily a bad thing; it is frequently an unacknowledged thing.

Fifthly, there is one place where the interests of historical criticism and the interests of biblical theology tend to part company. Historical criticism includes in its purview research into sources, extra-canonical influences, and the like; biblical theology in almost all of its forms focuses on the final form of the biblical texts, and may then ask how these texts cohere and complement one another theologically.

The history-of-religions movement

The history-of-religions movement that flourished at the end of the 19th century and the beginning of the 20th aspired to an ostensible neutrality that was frequently 'narrowly' historical, but which was also usually comparative, synchronically descriptive, and interested as well in diachronic development. By and large the movement was eclipsed by the influence of Barth and Bultmann. Bultmann in particular insisted that faith, and with it biblical theology, was necessarily divorced from all historical claims. Faith could never become contingent on the probabilities of historical probing.

Apart from some pockets of resistance, however, Bultmann's view, which held sway for almost half a century, has itself been eclipsed. Barr, depending in part on the work of Rainer Albertz, is entirely right to argue that any biblical theology worthy of the name (*i.e.* theology that purports to reflect the biblical texts at all) must be grounded in history. Christian theology, including biblical theology, is in this respect unlike Buddhism; its essential theological structures depend absolutely on claims about God's activity in history. Biblical theology will always be attracted to historical questions precisely because of the nature of the biblical documents. After making allowances for 1st-century conceptual structures, many passages in the NT (*e.g.* Luke 1:1–4; 1 Cor. 15:6) are close to what we mean by 'scientific history', tightly joining the textual witness to what happened. Contemporary scholars may believe that witness to be true, and advance their reasons, or they may believe that witness to be false, and justify their unbelief; in the latter case Christianity is no longer (for them) credible. But biblical theologians do not have the right to disallow historical reflections. Moreover, insofar as the history-of-religions movement focuses on diachronic development, it has obvious links with biblical theology. In short, history-of-religions study need not be 'narrowly' historical; biblical theology dare not be narrowly 'theological', understood in some exclusively non-historical or even anti-historical sense.

Literary genre and speech-act

Most systematic theologies that have tried to be biblically based have sought first and foremost to be faithful to biblical truth. At one level, this is highly commendable. But the search for theological truths to be integrated into a *system* may unwittingly ride roughshod over two related realities. First, Scripture is written in many different literary genres, and the way these genres carry their message is highly diverse; secondly, speech-act theory has taught us that texts (oral or written) actually do many different things apart from conveying truth, so that a focus on extracting truth or truths in order to build a system may

unwittingly blind the reader to a large part of what is actually there. (Moreover, the notion of 'truth' has itself become slippery, but I shall deal briefly with that point below.)

We may begin with the latter point. Speech (oral or written text) may provide truths, but it may rebuke the reader/listener, complain, offer a lament, serve as a private solioquy, ask a question, pronounce a curse, pronounce forgiveness, tell a story (true or made up; with or without extra-textual referents), and so forth. Of course, some of these speech-acts may, in addition to whatever else they are accomplishing (effectively or otherwise), presuppose certain truths, or convey certain truth, even though to do so is not their primary intent. Further, such utterances may betray, say, the 'truth' of a fractured personality exploring the apparent meaninglessness of the universe (*e.g.* Qoheleth), the substance of which can be put into a propositional truth. But that propositional truth has nothing of the power of the original text. Thus there is a sense in which all systematic theology, for all its strengths and legitimacy (on which more below), is necessarily in some measure a distortion of the biblical texts.

To a lesser degree, the same is doubtless true of biblical theology; it easily distorts the very texts it seeks to explicate. But it is intrinsically less distorting, because methodologically it stands closer to the text than systematic theology, aims to achieve genuine sensitivity with respect to the distinctiveness of each corpus, and seeks to connect the diverse corpora using their own categories. Ideally, therefore, biblical theology stands as a kind of bridge discipline between responsible exegesis and responsible systematic theology (even though each of these inevitably influences the other two).

Similarly, the sheer diversity of the Bible's literary forms demands a sensitivity to more than (though certainly not less than) propositional truth, and to the diverse ways that different genres convey meaning (*cf.* K. J. Vanhoozer, *Is There A Meaning in This Text?*). The point is not that all literary genres simply convey truth plus something else, as if it were a matter of quantity or percentage. Rather, some genres focus their priorities rather differently. Narrative, for instance, over against the more discursive forms of Scripture, focuses on plot, character development, themes and subthemes. It has a capacity to follow change in characters, to maintain certain competing or complementary themes in tension, to leave some questions open. Simply to reduce the significance of an extended narrative to a number of propositions, or to ignore the narrative almost entirely, is an interpretative failure. Similar things could be said about wisdom and other genres. Moreover, building on the work of M. Bakhtin (*The Dialogic Imagination* and *Speech Genres*), it is now widely recognized that genre is not a closed, abstract, linguistic phenomenon (like the grammatical notion of a genitive absolute), but an historically and culturally conditioned way of producing and interpreting texts in specific contexts. This bespeaks not only the need for literary sensitivity, but also the importance of historical criticism.

Once again, biblical theology is admirably suited to build a bridge between the texts of Scripture and the larger synthesis of systematic theology. Precisely because it overlaps with the relevant disciplines, ideally it enables them to hear one another a little better. Moreover, its commitment to unpacking the texts of Scripture along the historical axis of the Bible's plot-line makes it eager to reflect on what it means to be historically and culturally conditioned, in a way that the synchronic emphasis of systematic theology tends to ignore.

Strictly speaking, of course, both biblical theology and systematic theology carry a moral obligation to grasp the nettle of the Bible's literary genres. Working so closely and inductively from the texts, however, responsible biblical theology necessarily attempts to grasp the communicative genius or rationality of each genre, *i.e.* the rules of each 'language game' and the way in which each genre conveys meaning, and thus what the meaning of a passage is, all of this set within the twin frameworks of, on the one hand, the emphases of the particular corpus and, on the other, the plot-line of the entire canon. In contrast, systematic theology tends to focus on the relationships among these various rationalities in its pursuit of the large-scale synthesis.

This is not to suggest that legitimate influence runs only one way, from exegesis to biblical theology to systematic theology. For instance, insofar as systematic theology accurately summarizes some important things that the Bible as a whole actually does say, it may

serve as a helpful grid that disciplines the task of the interpretation of, say, narrative. Narrative stripped from its context and thrown open to an active imagination is patient of far more uncontrolled interpretations than narrative safely embedded in its literary, historical, and canonical context. The insistence of many postmodern interpreters that individual narratives (*e.g.* the fall, Gen. 3) must be interpreted independently of the rest of the book of Genesis, let alone the rest of the storyline in the entire canon, fuels the imagination and produces articles and books for publication, but cannot serve the interests of biblical theology or systematic theology, or even, in the long run, responsible exegesis. Competent systematic theology usefully curbs such excesses.

Unity

The definition of biblical theology is profoundly tied to the way in which its unity is perceived. Nothing controls one's perception of the entire discipline more than this point, and yet no point is more controverted. The recent studies of D. L. Baker and of Christoph Dohmen and Thomas Söding disclose the main lines of debate and the intricacy of many of the issues. The bearing of these debates on one's approach to biblical theology may be clarified if a few of the competing positions are identified.

1. Philip Davies may be taken as a rigorous example of those who think that biblical theology in any sense is impossible for those who are not confessionally committed. He argues that there are two quite different strategies for reading biblical texts, the confessional method and the non-confessional method. The task of the interpreter who adopts the former is to affirm the values and claims made by the text; the task of the interpreter who adopts the latter is to accept or reject claims made by the text at his or her own discretion. Clearly the former assumes or finds some sort of internal coherence; the latter does not. Davies insists that the two methods are mutually incompatible. They should never be intermingled. They generate opposed polarities: Scripture versus biblical literature; Bible study versus biblical studies; and theology versus non-theology.

As stimulating as is his work, the fundamental bifurcation is not convincing. Every human being engaged in study of any sort operates with some sort of framework, a confessional stance. In practice, there are countless scholars who do not think that everything in the Bible is to be affirmed, but are broadly 'confessional' with respect to its main emphases. Davies may consider this a hopeless methodological mess, but that, after all, is a reflection of his own 'non-confessional' confessional stance.

2. A second group, often highly influenced by postmodern epistemology, finds the unity of biblical theology in the discipline itself, not in the texts, in the results, or in communitarian interests. Dennis Olson, for instance, argues (along with most biblical theologians) that the primary starting point of biblical theology is the present form of the biblical text, but the discipline must then proceed, he asserts, by appreciating and explicating 'the wide diversity of biblical witnesses as a first step'. It then engages in some 'thematizing, summarizing, generalizing, and analogizing', inevitably succumbing to a degree of reductionism. The discipline is further enhanced by engagement, dialogue, and debate with co-readers of the texts from different backgrounds: Christian, Jewish, secular, ancient, modern, *etc*. Completely missing from Olson's treatment is any sense of moving towards wholeness (however provisional), or of unity of content. Thus the unity of biblical theology becomes the unity of the methods of the discipline, so much so that he can, rather amazingly, put Childs and Brueggemann in the same camp.

3. Canonical unity has been understood in four distinguishable ways.

First, whatever the legitimacy or otherwise of the canonical boundaries, some scholars develop their biblical theologies by observing those boundaries for no other reason than that they are traditional. This much could be said for the majority of OT and NT theologies produced in the past century. Their writers do not attempt a 'whole-Bible' biblical theology; indeed, most are profoundly suspicious of such attempts. For many, even their NT theologies (for instance) focus attention on what they perceive to be irreconcilable differences among the NT corpora, or even within each corpus. Thus for these scholars the unity of the enterprise of biblical theology is formal. It is bound up with the canon as the collection of documents on which they are focusing attention. Whether or not their theological analyses (only rarely is there much synthesis) conform to the shape of historic orthodoxy, or any other unity, is thus independent of their views on the canon.

Secondly, a more communitarian unity is displayed in the 'canon criticism' of J. A. Sanders and his disciples. Sanders is not content to restrict himself to the final form of the biblical texts. It is precisely their growth and development, and the changing communitarian experiences and interests that such changes reflect, that interest him, and shape his approach to biblical interpretation. All sides recognize, of course, that such study is intrinsically less secure and more speculative than that which focuses on the final documents. Continuing the study of such change beyond the canonical documents holds similar interest, but historical limitations on the canon provides some sort of a boundary, *at least for the individual scholar*. For after all, there are other scholarly communities that adopt a slightly different canon (Roman Catholic and Protestant disparities on this point are merely the most obvious).

Thirdly, the 'canon criticism' of Childs (though he does not use the expression of his own work) is currently far more influential than that of Sanders, and, inevitably, attracts the most systematic criticism (especially Barr). While Childs adopts more-or-less standard critical positions with respect to the biblical documents, they influence relatively little of his biblical theology because he allows only the final form to shape his theological synthesis. The Christian church has recognized a restricted canon (whose borders are a little blurred), and if we are Christians that must be the framework in which we do our theological reflection. Unlike Sanders, Childs is not much interested in trying to delineate the communitarian interests that produced the documents, and not at all interested in ostensible extra-canonical influences. To some extent he deals with how the documents relate to each other (*i.e.* how later ones use earlier ones and reshape what they have received), but he is most interested in using the canonical documents to show how, together, they ground and justify a more-or-less traditional, orthodox theology, as judged by post-biblical categories. Much of his work is stimulating and refreshing. Nevertheless, because he completely rejects any traditional view of Scriptural authority, his reason for using the canon as his boundary is not well defended, and has led to some critics charging him with 'canonical fundamentalism'. Because Childs is happy to admit a diversity of historical-critical perspectives, but can scarcely tolerate *theological* criticism, Barr prefers to charge him with 'theological inerrancy'. In any case, as useful and stimulating as many parts of his work are, many suspect it is not epistemologically consistent or secure (see especially P. R. Noble, *The Canonical Approach*). Childs emerges with a unity of result, but it is less than clear how he gets there as long as the unity of the foundation documents is affirmed by little more than the results, and is more or less adopted by assuming ecclesiatical tradition regarding the boundaries of the canon.

Fourthly, those with a high view of Scripture insist that what gives the canonical documents their unity is that, for all their enormous diversity, one Mind, one Actor, stands behind them; they constitute a truly revelatory base. Inevitably there are differences of opinion about how this revelation interacts with other material (*e.g.* natural revelation, providential leading, tradition). Whatever the outcome of such debates, however, the unity here envisaged is a unity of substance in the source documents themselves. The efforts of 'whole-Bible' biblical theology may sometimes be thwarted by the complexities of the task, and sometimes mocked by inadequate work, but they are not intrinsically doomed to frustration; there is an intrinsic unity that is to be pursued and explored. In the final analysis, those who cannot agree to some kind of intrinsic unity in the Scriptures will always find their attempts at 'whole-Bible' biblical theology, however admirable, to be the fruit of either accident or pragmatism.

4. A rather different kind of unity is a kind of *ad hoc* subscription to certain post-biblical confessional bases, which are then found to have adequate support in Scripture, such that this support then functions as the appropriate unity of Scripture and thus of biblical theology. This stance may overlap with two or three of the options already listed. Many biblical theologians operate with this view, but only rarely with the self-critical awareness of Robert Morgan. He seeks to show, for instance, that for all the diversity of the NT documents, visible not least in their Chris-

tological pluralism, 'there is also a Christian doctrinal unity, encapsulated in some words from Chalcedon' (in *Words Remembered, Texts Renewed*). To justify this stance is to write a NT theology. This 'relatively loose version of traditional Christianity' allows 'a legitimate theological pluralism without abandoning doctrinal boundaries as some forms of this religion do'. On this view, however, one cannot escape the conclusion that the adopted theological synthesis is finally warranted by the accidental historical adoption of certain themes in the Bible, while others may be safely discarded. The view provides comfort to those who want to be broadly orthodox without providing greater justification for their orthodoxy than the commitments of other Christians at another time. Under this perspective it is difficult to imagine how biblical theology has any authority to reform certain views. This vision of unity will inevitably prove unstable.

One may in fact analyse the importance of canon for biblical theology along a slightly different set of axes. Some biblical theologians tend to adopt what might be called a linear hermeneutic, a developmental hermeneutic. They may disagree on whether the results sanction or refute a 'whole-Bible' biblical theology, but they tend to operate in the temporal framework of the history-of-religions school, or of the history of tradition, or of salvation-history. Other biblical theologians adopt the canon as a starting point, and the divisions of the canon become the controlling hermeneutic: law, prophets, gospels, *etc.* Once again, this group of scholars disagree as to whether the results tend toward unity or disunity. Among those who acknowledge the revelatory nature of the scriptural documents, however, these two axes run parallel to each other and are mutually supportive.

Use of the OT in the New

The questions surrounding the unity of the canon can be explored a little further by examining one subset of this topic, *viz.* the use of the OT in the New. During the last four decades, a vast quantity of work has been done in this area. Here we may merely identify three aspects of this work that have a bearing on biblical theology, without probing any of them very deeply.

1. One of the most intriguing aspects of this subject is the warrant provided, if any, by

the NT writers, when they draw theological conclusions from the OT. While many scholars have shown that the NT writers' appropriation techniques find parallels in the Jewish writers of the second temple period when they use the Hebrew canon, such observations do not adequately account for the different conclusions reached by Christian Jews like Paul and by non-Christian Jews. Some scholars (*e.g.* D. J. Moo) have advanced the debate by distinguishing between appropriation techniques and hermeneutical axioms; the former may be shared by Christians who wrote the NT and by Jews, but disjunctions surface when the latter are studied closely. For instance, many conservative Jews saw in the law given at Sinai not only a body of instruction but a hermeneutical key to the rest of Scripture. In contrast, some NT writers insist that the proper place of the law-covenant can be grasped only when it is properly located in the stream of redemptive history (hence Paul's argument in Gal. 3, or the argument of Heb. 7). It follows that the kind of biblical theology that is profoundly grounded in tracing out the Bible's plot-line is intrinsically more likely to pick up this kind of inner-canonical hermeneutical distinctive than either systematic theology or those kinds of biblical theology that rarely ask diachronic questions.

2. More challenging, certainly more technical, are the countless quotations from, allusions to, and echoes of the OT found in the NT. Many, of course, are straightforward. But many raise fundamental questions. Psalm 2:7 is quoted three times in the NT, once to justify the claim that Jesus has been raised (Acts 13:32–33), once to prove that Jesus is superior to angels (Heb. 1:5), and once to demonstrate that Jesus did not take on himself the authority of high priest, but was appointed to the task by his Father (Heb. 5:5). At the surface level, Psalm 2:7 warrants none of these conclusions. Indeed, the disparity prompts many scholars to conclude that the NT writers frequently use the OT in an irresponsible proof-texting way that badly rips texts out of their contexts (*e.g.* B. Lindars). Others reverently appeal to the revelatory stance of the NT authors, who thus found more in the OT text than was actually there on the surface. The NT writers thus deployed an approach to textual citation that cannot be duplicated today by readers of the OT (*e.g.* R. Longenecker). Still others hold that close scrutiny of these challenging passages discloses some profound assumptions, themselves grounded elsewhere in exegesis, regarding interlocking typologies having to do with David, the temple, the priesthood, and other subjects. If these latter approaches are valid, they have an enormous bearing on how one should properly read the Bible. Moreover, they are the very stuff of biblical theology that seeks to track the Bible's storyline and explore the significance of the canon.

3. During the last two decades many have come to speak of 'intertextuality' in preference to 'the use of the Old Testament in the New'. In some usages, the two expressions are roughly synonymous. More commonly, however, intertextuality refers to a broader phenomenon, not only because it includes in its purview the use of earlier texts by later texts *within* each Testament, but also because it explores how the later texts, duly absorbed by the contemporary interpreter, cast a shadow back on the meaning the interpreter finds in the earlier text. Among some exponents of intertextuality, this generates blatant anachronisms. Such anachronisms are inoffensive, however, to those with the strong postmodern conviction that meaning rests primarily with the interpreter and not with either the author or the text. Among more cautious exponents of intertextuality, anachronism is carefully avoided, while the interpreter seeks to identify textually based markers that attest an earlier passage as truly an adumbration of something that will develop only later, an anticipation of something still obscure, the beginnings of a typology that develops across the sweep of redemptive history. Carefully exploited, intertextuality proves to be one of the lashings that hold biblical theology together.

Postmodernism

Notoriously difficult to define, postmodernism has many faces and many degrees. For our purposes, its focus is primarily the domain of epistemology, and it offers itself in part as a rejection of the epistemology of the Enlightenment, a rejection of approaches that are positivist, rationalistic, exclusive, certain.

Yet postmodernism has many degrees. In the first half of the last century, avant-garde thinkers argued, with great persuasiveness, that for finite human beings there can be no uninterpreted facts. In the second half of the 20th century, many extrapolated this argument to conclude that there are no facts, only interpretations. The former reminds us of our finitude and contingency, even our fallenness, and checks our hubris; the latter insists we are confined to a quagmire of relativity, and exults in the disappearance of any possibility of objective truth.

It is not uncommon for postmodernists to criticize both the earlier 'biblical theology movement' and its critics for being too 'modernist' in epistemology (*e.g.* D. Penchansky). Perhaps the most articulate of those who define postmodern biblical theology is Werner Jeanrond. His multi-faceted definition is too complex to be probed very deeply here. Suffice it to say that for him biblical theology is 'a multi-disciplinary theological exercise which aims at retrieving the theological dimensions of the biblical texts as part of the larger project of interpreting the communicative potential of these texts' (*BI* 6, p. 245). It is interested in discovering 'the theological diversity within the biblical texts', and is thus a continuing 'challenge to all systematic theologies insofar as it calls for an always new test of any preconceived or traditionally assumed concept of the God to whose self-revelation in history the texts of the Hebrew Bible and the New Testament witness in various ways' (p. 246). It 'encourages all non-dogmatic models and paradigms of discussing continuities and discontinuities in the complex development and religious challenge of biblical monotheism' (p. 246). By definition, although it begins its work by interpreting the documents of the biblical canon, it is not limited to those texts. Moreover, it encourages 'not only the critique of hidden or open ideologies in the act of interpretation, but also the critique of ideologies in the biblical texts themselves' (p. 246). The only thing that Jeanrond will apparently not permit biblical theology to critique is his own far-reaching postmodern epistemology.

Similarly, it has been argued (*e.g.* by T. L. Thompson) that the true God (if there is one) must remain unknown; gods are created by our interpretations. The historicism which was tied to the biblical theology movement in the mid 20th century was more modern than biblical; the reality is that all we have are texts which we interpret in many different ways. The Bible itself gives us no access to history, but only to a tradition.

Here we find a strange mix of the more radical wing of historical criticism combined with a postmodern definition of history that makes the discipline of history incapable in principle of saying anything true about extra-textual referents.

The degree to which these stances control the outcome varies considerably. Some members of the so-called Yale School write energetically and challengingly about being more 'biblical', but they find it difficult to confess to much extra-textual referentiality: *i.e.* there is a great deal of biblically informed God-talk, but it is less than clear that one is to think in terms of a God who is actually 'there', a God who is to be thought of in biblical terms. After all, it is what God has accomplished on the cross that saves us, not the biblical ideas about what God has accomplished on the cross. Similarly, Francis Watson's suggestion that the Gospels be regarded as 'narrated history' cries to be teased out a little further. At one level, of course, what he says is obvious. But to speak of the Gospels as imaginative presentations of Jesus which, for all their literary quality, may exert a powerful truth claim on us because they are *our* story, the story of our community, our only access to Jesus, is sooner or later to duck the toughest question of all: do these stories in some way *refer* to a real Jesus, an extra-textual Jesus, who is never reducible to the Jesus of the text but to whom the texts bear faithful and responsible witness? If not, in what sense is the substance of our proclamation anything more than the proclamation itself? This view really would be the most terrible bibliolatry. It would command adherence to the text, the story in the text, and not to the Jesus to whom the text bears witness. In a postmodern world, it is important to keep saying that we are not saved by ideas, not even biblical ideas, but by the Jesus whom God sent to the cross on our behalf.

In a rather different vein (but certainly this side of the postmodern divide), the recent OT theology by Brueggemann greatly stresses the virtue of imagination, eschews attempts at a broad 'fit', and organizes its material into core testimony, countertestimony, unsolicited testimony, and embodied testimony. The tension between the first two are nicely seen in his treatment of Exodus 34:6–7. This 'credo', according to Brueggemann, embraces a besetting tension, not between opposing theological traditions, but in 'the very life, character, and person of Yahweh': between, on the one hand, Yahweh's solidarity with his people and gracious fidelity, and, on the other, his sovereign, sometimes excessive, and destructive self-regard.

Part of the problem here is that most postmodern work either tacitly assumes or robustly defends the legitimacy of one particular antithesis, *viz.*: either a finite knower can know some things absolutely and exhaustively, or such knowers are necessarily lost in a sea of relativity (D. A. Carson, *The Gagging of God*). If we buy into the legitimacy of that antithesis, we are lost, for it can always be shown that human beings, finite knowers all, cannot ever know anything absolutely and exhaustively. The only alternative, then, is some form or other of relativism. In fact, however, this antithesis must be rejected, for there are other options. Human beings may know some things truly, if nothing exhaustively. They may approach greater and more accurate knowledge, even though they can never gain absolute knowledge (omniscience is not a communicable attribute of God!).

Postmodernism does its most honourable work when it exposes the most arrogant epistemological claims of the 'modern' period, and especially the hollow pretensions of 'independent' or 'autonomous' reason. It functions honourably when it reminds us that we operate in contexts (linguistic, cultural, religious, racial, individual), and that these inevitably shape us. Precisely because of the worldview-forming power of systematic theology (see below), no biblical theology can be pursued apart from the 'systematic' stances already adopted by *every* person (including those who incessantly disparage 'systematic theology'). But postmodernism succumbs to a new arrogance when, misled by the antithesis outlined in the previous paragraph, it tells us we are nothing more than our contexts, and proclaims the absoluteness of the relative. There are alternatives. Biblical theology apart from such alternatives is in our time likely to sink into creative but undisciplined flights of fancy loosely tied to the texts of Scripture, supporting them or opposing them, in line with personal preference and current cultural agendas.

Definition

The foregoing discussion was designed in part to set out the wide spectrum of opinion regarding the history, definition and roles of biblical theology. The discussion repeatedly hinted at the lines that must now be drawn.

'Biblical theology' is not usefully applied to all theological reflection on the Bible. It may still be used to refer generically to OT theology and NT theology, inductive disciplines that seek to articulate the theologies of the diverse books and corpora within their domains. But ideally, biblical theology, as its name implies, even as it works inductively from the diverse texts of the Bible, seeks to uncover and articulate the unity of *all* the biblical texts taken together, resorting primarily to the categories of those texts themselves. In this sense it is canonical biblical theology, 'whole-Bible' biblical theology; *i.e.* its content is a theology of the whole Bible, not a theology that merely has its roots in the Bible, or merely takes the Bible as the place to begin (Hasel). Such biblical theology is overtly theological, *i.e.* it makes synthetic assertions about the nature, will and plan of God in creation and redemption, including therefore also the nature, purpose and 'story' of humanity. But it is not narrowly theological. Rather, precisely because so many of the theological claims of Scripture are claims about revelation in history, biblical theology is committed to using rigorous and responsible historical methods. Equally, because the texts are literary pieces, diverse in genre and other features, biblical theology seeks to be sensitive to literary structures.

While acknowledging that it can never be autonomous, biblical theology focuses on the inductive study of the biblical texts in their final form, seeking progression towards greater and greater faithfulness. While some part of the biblical theological enterprise may focus on the theology of one corpus, or on one or two themes across the corpora of Scripture, the discipline as a whole must strive toward the elucidation of the biblical documents along the axis of redemptive history, the canon itself providing the boundaries of the primary source documents (however much we must be open to 'hear' how these documents have been understood and applied in later centuries). On the one hand, biblical theology will try to preserve the glorious diversity of the biblical documents; on the other, it will try to uncover all that holds them together, sacrificing neither historical particularity nor the unifying sweep of redemptive history. It will marshall the resources of rigorous exegesis, and it will try above all to uncover and understand how words and themes in earlier canonical texts are used in later canonical texts. Recognizing their finiteness, biblical theologians will want to pursue their calling not only in interaction with the work of twenty centuries of Christian witness, but in community with the living church. Moreover, insofar as the biblical theologian holds that the boundary of the canon is valid because the canonical documents are, finally, God-given and God-authorized, so far also must biblical theology become not only a descriptive enterprise (a description of the theology one finds in the Bible) but also a normative enterprise, a confessional enterprise.

Such considerations ensure that there will never be unanimity about the discipline; there are too many disputed variables. But that is no reason to retreat into endless discussions of definition and method. Rather it is a call to work out, among those who share this approach or something akin to it, a faithful, penetrating, self-correcting biblical theology.

Systematic theology

Many, but not all, of the subtopics explored in connection with biblical theology could be usefully canvassed again with respect to systematic theology, doubling the length of this essay. Here we can attempt only the briefest probing of some of the definitional issues.

As its name suggests, systematic theology attempts to organize, to systematize, theological reflection. When the primary authoritative source for that theological synthesis and reflection is the Bible, systematic theology attempts to organize what the Bible says according to some system. The traditional tenfold division of topics is certainly not the only possiblity. But even to choose topics, to hierarchialize them, is to impose a structure not transparently given in Scripture itself. In any case, such theological reflection inevitably emerges out of one epistemology or another, out of a particular cultural consciousness, and such matters will become correspondingly more influential in the system to the degree that the theologian is unaware of them or

holds, naively, that they have little or no influence.

Such systematic theology will seek to be faithful to Scripture. That means careful exegesis is essential, along with the panoply of the interpreter's tools. But because the ordering vision is not dictated by inductive study of the text within the categories of the text, corpus by corpus, the danger of simplistic proof texting becomes proportionately greater, and the difficulty of deciding which ordering principles will control the system correspondingly greater and more disputable. Moreover, most systematic theology includes some sort of canvassing of earlier work by seminal theologians (Irenaeus, Anselm, Augustine, Aquinas, Calvin, and so forth). That means that many of the categories, not to mention the priorities for discussion and reflection on how various theological strands cohere, have been laid down by the ecclesiastical tradition, and it is very hard work to be informed by them without being controlled by them. Further, systematic theology worthy of the name, more so than biblical theology, seeks to articulate what the Bible says in a way that is culturally telling, culturally prophetic. The alternative is to write a systematic theology that is of merely antiquarian interest, or that appeals to the most traditionalist voices in the culture. Such concerns for contemporaneity and relevance, entirely legitimate, may nevertheless cast more influence than is sometimes recognized on the shape of the systematic theology, such that the concern for relevance and prophetic voice may unwittingly distance it from a faithful portrayal of what the Bible says.

There are deeper issues. The Bible speaks in highly diverse literary genres that play upon our hearts and minds in a great variety of speech acts. To encapsulate this diversity and power within the form of a systematic theology is to demand too much of the discipline. But the systematic theologian can mitigate the most obvious dangers by wide reading in the literature of exegesis and by delving deeply into biblical theology as a mediating discipline. The systematician must recognize, further, the inherent limitations of systematic theology. For all its strengths, there are many things it cannot do. It can analyse a lament within the biblical corpus, but it cannot evoke a heart-felt lament in the way a lament itself can. It may expound the meanings of some parables, but it cannot explode the reader's worldview in the way the most striking of the narrative parables can.

Still more importantly, systematic theology, precisely by its efforts at systemic wholeness and by its engagement with the culture, openly attempts worldview formation, worldview transformation. (Something of the same can be accomplished by steady, thoughtful, repeated Bible reading, but in that case there is obviously no attempt in the text to address *this particular culture* as opposed to some other.) Thus unlike biblical theology, systematic theology is not so much a mediating discipline as a culminating discipline. Nevertheless, once a particular systematic theology has been deeply absorbed, precisely because it is worldview forming it is likely to exercise significant influence on the disciplines that nurture it: exegesis, biblical theology, historical theology. The hermeneutical circle is joined, but not vicious.

This discussion of systematic theology has so far assumed that the systematician is at least attempting to systematize what is found in the Bible. But it must be frankly admitted that the label 'systematic theology' has often been attached to approaches far removed from such commitments. Sometimes the Bible, ecclesiastical tradition, and an ostensibly autonomous reason have been understood to have equal authority in the discussion. Very commonly, the judgments of the more sceptical varieties of historical criticism have been adopted, not least the conviction that a systematic theology of the whole Bible is in principle impossible; there are too many intrinsic contradictions. In that case, the systematic theologian may self-consciously attempt a synthesis based on those parts of the Bible he or she is able to accept as valid. Systematic theology may also begin to overlap with historical theology, as competing positions are evaluated. Countless books that ostensibly belong to the domain of systematic theology are in fact an evaluation and critique of some theologian or of some theological position, based on criteria that are an interesting mix of tradition, Scripture, reason, philosophical structures and internal coherence.

So deep was the suspicion that what might be called 'whole Bible' systematic theology is in principle impossible that many theologians devoted most of their work to prolegomena, to hermeneutical and other methodological questions, to evaluation and critique of other work. During the past decade and a half, however, a fresh interest has arisen in what has come to be called 'constructive theology', *i.e.* not merely interaction with and critique of the work of others, but attempts at articulating doctrine that is meant to be normative. One thinks, for instance, not only of the work of a handful of scholars such as Colin Gunton, but also of the new Edinburgh series.

What is transparently clear about all such systematic theology, however, is that its organizing principles do not encourage the exploration of the Bible's plot-line, except incidentally. The categories of systematic theology are logical and hierarchical, not temporal.

Relationships between systematic theology and biblical theology

Most of the relationships between systematic theology and biblical theology have been teased out in the defining discussions of the previous pages. A summary will crystallize the conclusions.

As currently discussed in the literature, both 'systematic theology' and 'biblical theology' can refer to wildly diverse ideas of the nature of the respective disciplines. Ideally, however, the two expressions serve best when certain defining restrictions are adopted. Systematic theology and biblical theology enjoy a common base of authority, *viz.* canonical Scripture. This does not mean that other voices (*e.g.* historical theology) play no role. It means rather that the theologian cannot treat them as if they enjoyed the same revelatory status as Scripture. Both systematic theology and biblical theology are provisional and in principle correctible, as virtually all products of finite human enterprise must be. Although in terms of authority status there needs to be an outward-tracing line from Scripture through exegesis towards biblical theology to systematic theology (with historical theology providing some guidance along the way), in reality various 'back loops' are generated, each discipline influencing the others, and few disciplines influencing the others more than does systematic theology, precisely because it is so worldview forming.

The distinctions between systematic and biblical theology are perhaps more striking. Although both are text based, the ordering principles of the former are topical, logical, hierarchical, and as synchronic as possible; the ordering principles of the latter trace out the history of redemption, and are (ideally) profoundly inductive, comparative and as diachronic as possible. Systematic theology seeks to rearticulate what the Bible says in self-conscious engagement with (including confrontation with) the culture; biblical theology, though it cannot escape cultural influences, aims to be first and foremost inductive and descriptive, earning its normative power by the credibility of its results. Thus systematic theology tends to be a little further removed from the biblical text than does biblical theology, but a little closer to cultural engagement. Biblical theology tends to seek out the rationality and communicative genius of each literary genre; systematic theology tends to integrate the diverse rationalities in its pursuit of a large-scale, worldview-forming synthesis. In this sense, systematic theology tends to be a culminating discipline; biblical theology, though it is a worthy end in itself, tends to be a bridge discipline.

See also: BIBLICAL THEOLOGY; HISTORY OF BIBLICAL THEOLOGY; CHALLENGES TO BIBLICAL THEOLOGY; UNITY AND DIVERSITY OF SCRIPTURE; NEW TESTAMENT USE OF THE OLD TESTAMENT.

Bibliography

A. K. M. Adam, *Making Sense of New Testament Theology: Modern Problems and Prospects* (Macon, 1995); R. Albertz, *A History of Israelite Religion in the Old Testament Period*, 2 vols. (London, 1994); D. L. Baker, *Two Testaments, One Bible: A Study of the Relationships Between the Old and New Testaments* (Leicester, [2]1991); M. Bakhtin, *The Dialogic Imagination: Four Essays* (Austin, 1981); idem, *Speech Genres and Other Late Essays* (Austin, 1986); P. Balla, *Challenges to New Testament Theology: An Attempt to Justify the Enterprise*, WUNT (Tübingen, 1997); P. Barnett, *Jesus and the Rise of Early Christianity: A History of New Testament Times* (Downers Grove, 1999); J. Barr, *The Concept of Biblical Theology: An Old Testament Perspective* (London and Minneapolis, 1999); G. L. Bauer, *Theologie des Alten Testaments* (Leipzig, 1796); idem, *Biblische Theologie des Neuen Testaments*, 2 vols. (Leipzig, 1800–1802); W. Bauer, in R. A. Kraft and G. Krodel (eds.), *Orthodoxy and Heresy in Earliest Christianity* (Philadelphia, 1971); M. Bockmuehl, 'Humpty Dumpty and New Testament theology', *Theology* 101/803, Sept/Oct 1998, pp. 330–338; W. Brueggemann, *Theology of the Old Testament: Testimony, Dispute, Advocacy* (Minneapolis, 1997); R. Bultmann, *Theology of the New Testament*, 2 vols. (London, 1952–1955); M. Burrows, *Outline of Biblical Theology* (Philadelphia, 1946); D. A. Carson, *The Gagging of God: Christianity Confronts Pluralism* (Grand Rapids and Leicester, 1995); idem, 'New Testament theology', in *DLNTD*, pp. 796–814; D. A. Carson and H. G. M. Williamson (eds.), *It Is Written: Scripture Citing Scripture* (Cambridge, 1988); B. S. Childs, *Biblical Theology in Crisis* (Philadelphia, 1970); idem, *Biblical Theology of the Old and New Testaments* (London, 1992); P. R. Davies, *Whose Bible Is It Anyway?*, (Sheffield, 1995); C. Dohmen and T. Söding (eds.), *Eine Bibel – zwei Testamente: Positionen biblischer Theologie* (Paderborn, 1995); W. Eichrodt, *Theology of the Old Testament*, 2 vols. (London, 1961, 1967); W. A. Foley, *Anthropological Linguistics: An Introduction* (Oxford, 1997); R. J. Gibson (ed.), *Interpreting God's Plan* (Carlisle, 1998); J. B. Green and M. Turner (eds.), *Between Two Horizons: Spanning New Testament Studies and Systematic Theology* (Grand Rapids, 2000); C. E. Gunton (ed.), *The Cambridge Companion to Christian Doctrine* (Cambridge, 1997); W. Harrington, *The Path of Biblical Theology* (Dublin, 1973); R. A. Harrisville and W. Sundberg, *The Bible in Modern Culture: Theology and Historical-Critical Method from Spinoza to Käsemann* (Grand Rapids, 1995); G. F. Hasel, 'Proposals for a canonical biblical theology', *AUSS* 34, 1996, pp. 23–33; S. Hauerwas, *Sanctify Them in the Truth: Holiness Exemplified* (Nashville and Edinburgh, 1998); J. C. K. von Hofmann, *Biblische Theologie des Neuen Testaments* (Nördlingen, 1886); W. Jeanrond, 'The significance of revelation for biblical theology', *BI* 6, 1998, pp. 243–257; H. Köster, *Synoptische Überlieferung bei den apostolischen Vätern* (Berlin, 1957); B. Lindars, *New Testament Apologetic: The Doctrinal Significance of the Old Testament Quotations* (London, 1961); R. N. Longenecker, *Biblical Exegesis in the Apostolic Period* (Carlisle and Grand Rapids, 1995, [2]1999); U. Mauser, 'An anniversary for biblical theology', *TT* 53, 1996, pp. 74–80; D. J. Moo,

The Old Testament in the Gospel Passion Narratives (Sheffield, 1983); R. Morgan, 'On the unity of Scripture', in Jon Davies *et al.* (eds.), *Words Remembered, Texts Renewed* (Sheffield, 1995); J. D. Morrison, 'Trinity and church: An examination of theological methodology', *JETS* 40, 1997, pp. 445–454; S. T. Neill, *The Interpretation of the New Testament 1861–1986* (Oxford, ²1988); P. R. Noble, *The Canonical Approach: A Critical Reconstruction of the Hermeneutics of Brevard S. Childs* (Leiden, 1995); D. T. Olson, 'Biblical theology as provisional monologization: A dialogue with Childs, Brueggemann and Bakhtin', *BI* 6, 1998 pp. 162–180; D. Patte, *Ethics of Biblical Interpretation: A Reevaluation* (Louisville, 1995); D. Penchansky, *The Politics of Biblical Theology: A Postmodern Reading* (Macon, 1995); G. von Rad, *Old Testament Theology*, 2 vols. (Edinburgh, 1962–1965); H. Räisänen, *Beyond New Testament Theology: A Story and a Programme* (London, 1990); J. A. Sanders, *Torah and Canon* (Philadelphia, 1972); *idem, From Sacred Story to Sacred Text: Canon as Paradigm* (Philadelphia, 1987); A. Schlatter, *The History of the Christ: The Foundation of New Testament Theology* (ET, Grand Rapids, 1995); *idem, The Theology of the Apostles: The Development of New Testament Theology* (ET, Grand Rapids, 1997); G. Strecker, *Theologie des Neuen Testaments* (Berlin, 1995); P. Stuhlmacher, *Biblische Theologie des Neuen Testaments* (Göttingen, 1992); T. L. Thompson, *The Bible as History: How Writers Create a Past* (New York, 1999); K. J. Vanhoozer, *Is There a Meaning in This Text? The Bible, the Reader, and the Morality of Literary Knowledge* (Grand Rapids and Leicester, 1998); G. Vos, *Biblical Theology: Old and New Testaments* (Grand Rapids and Edinburgh, 1948, 1975); F. Watson, *Text and Truth: Redefining Biblical Theology* (Grand Rapids, 1997); G. E. Wright, *God Who Acts* (London, 1952).

D. A. CARSON

Preaching and Biblical Theology

The relationship of biblical theology and preaching

Biblical theology demands a preacher

The Bible commands its readers to communicate its message. So true biblical theology will reflect this imperative, and the true biblical theologian will want to communicate to others the truths of the Bible. A good pragmatic test of any theology is whether or not those who believe it want to pass on what they have learnt. Preaching, or any other means of explaining the message of the Bible, attempts to communicate it to others.

We can summarize a biblical theology of preaching in these words: *God has spoken, It is written,* and *Preach the word* (P. Adam, *Speaking God's Words*, pp. 15–56).

God has spoken. The self-revelation of God is always either expressed or explained through words. It is by the words which God has spoken that we know who he is, that he has made the universe, and the meaning of his works, his saving acts. It is by these words that we know of the identity and significance of his Son Jesus, of his plan of salvation, and of the gospel. It is by these words that we know how we should respond to God's grace with the obedience of faith, and look forward to the return of Christ and the consummation of God's kingdom. God has accommodated himself to us and condescended to speak in human language, with perfectly true words, so that we can respond to him in faith as we hear his voice. When God is present, he is present to speak. Whereas he once spoke on earth, he now warns us from heaven (Heb. 12:25).

The idea of God's revelation as 'speaking' or 'words' is so powerful that it is used as metaphor for God's self-revelation in his Son. So in Hebrews 1 we read that 'In the past God spoke ... at many times and in various ways by the prophets, but in these last days he has spoken to us by his Son'; Paul writes of Jesus that he 'preached peace'; and John describes Jesus as 'the Word' (Heb. 1:1–2; Eph. 2:17; John 1:1, NIV). God uses words to reveal the Word.

It is written. When God has spoken he has sometimes also caused the words to be recorded for future generations. Throughout the Bible we see him doing this. Moses not only speaks to the people of Israel the words that God has spoken, he also writes them down, so that later generations, who are constituted as the people of God by the same saving acts, can know that he is in a covenant relationship with them. Moses' sermons on the plains of Moab are written down, not only for the immediate hearers, but also for the subsequent generations of God's people. When these ancient writings are rediscovered, read, and obeyed, as in the times of Josiah and Ezra, there is revival. God's words were also written down for us 'on whom the fulfilment of the ages has come' (1 Cor. 10:11).

As we become part of the people of God we inherit these promises, covenants, and warnings. In NT times, some of the teaching of Jesus and his followers was written down for the benefit not only of the original readers but also of subsequent generations of God's people. All these words are preserved, or *inscripturated*, for God's people who live in the last days, which began with Jesus' first coming and will end with his return. As God's saving acts are complete, so also is the verbal revelation that explains them.

Preach the word. The call to preach the word is heard throughout the Bible in many different ways. Abraham as a prophet is to teach his household, and Moses the prophet is to speak, write and read the words of God for the people of God. The priests of the old covenant have the duty of teaching the law given through Moses, and prophets apply the law to their own generation. Wise men and women teach others the way of wisdom; the disciples of Christ preach the kingdom of God; apostles, pastors and teachers speak the truth in order to bring people to faith in Christ, and to present them mature in Christ. The great need in the post-apostolic church is for teachers, who can teach the truth and refute error. Ordinary believers have the responsibility of encouraging one another with God's words (1 Thess. 4:18); as they do so 'the word of Christ' dwells richly among them (Col. 3:16) and this mutual encouragement is God's remedy for the deceitfulness of sin (Heb. 3:13). It is therefore unsurprising that Paul instructs Timothy to preach the word (2 Tim. 4:2).

As Edmund Clowney points out, biblical theology reflects the authority, character and content of preaching: 'We bear in our hands the words which Moses carried on the tables of stone down the thundering mountain ... We bear the whole witness of the Father to the Son: those things that are written in the law of Moses, and the Prophets, and the Psalms concerning him. In our hands we hold the inspired *kerygma* and *didache* of the witnesses who testify of Christ' (*Preaching and Biblical Theology*, p. 61). Those who receive the biblical revelation also receive the command to become speakers of God's word.

Preaching and biblical theology need each other

Gerhard Ebeling has expressed this mutual need in these words: 'Theology without proclamation is empty, proclamation without theology is blind' (*Theology and Proclamation*, p. 20). He is saying that theology can never be a satisfactory end in itself, and that preaching that is not informed by reflection on the content of revelation is destructive.

So theologians should never be satisfied when their theology serves only the needs of the academy. Any theology, including biblical theology, must serve the Christian ministry of the word. Likewise preachers should not be satisfied when they have communicated only their own insights, the ideas of contemporary sociologists, political commentators, or psychologists, or even current theories of Christian or church life. Nor should they be content with the ritual repetition of a text of Scripture, reference to a token Bible verse, or preaching on a text to which they have not first applied Paul's instruction to Timothy: 'Reflect on what I am saying' (2 Tim. 2:7).

The dangers of the Western academic tradition are its assumptions that knowledge can be discovered only by those who share secular, naturalistic, or contemporary world views, and that knowledge is a satisfactory end in itself. These are damaging assumptions for any Christian academic to adopt, but particularly damaging for the theologian. Many preachers today, even many who know the Bible, do not use it in their preaching, or use it in a trivial way. We should not meet the challenge of postmodernism by abandoning the Bible, but by using it carefully, theologically and effectively. If we abandon theological reflection on the meaning of the text of the Bible, we will indeed be blind guides.

Preachers always practise good or bad biblical theology

Theologians can avoid the demands of biblical theology. They can ignore the Bible, or base their theology on their favourite verses. Bible commentators can avoid biblical theology by concentrating on the pre-history of the text, by assuming that the Bible has no intellectual coherence, by isolating one Testament from the other, or by commenting on other commentators rather than on the text itself.

The preacher has nowhere to hide: every sermon presupposes a good or bad biblical theology. The pitfalls are legion, and the wise preacher tries to avoid them. How can I preach on 'Do not commit adultery' without implying that salvation is achieved by moral perfection? How can I preach on the gift of the land to the people of God in the OT without raising the question of the ownership of that same land today? How can I preach on the OT in its own right and also use it to point to Christ? Is physical prosperity a NT blessing? We communicate biblical theology as much by our silence as by our words. We must work hard at communicating good biblical theology.

People learn how to use the Bible mostly from their teachers in church, so preachers have a better opportunity than anyone else to teach good biblical theology and to model a hermeneutically sound use of the Bible. Brevard Childs writes: 'Christian pastors continue to do their own Biblical Theology', and because this is the case 'some directions may come from the experience of pastors in the front line' (*Biblical Theology in Crisis*, pp. 95–96).

If the preacher is using a text, then that text must be placed not only in the *literary context* of chapter, book, Testament and Bible, but also in the *theological context* of that same Bible, *i.e.* in the context of both the developing revelation and the whole revelation. If the preacher is using a story from the Bible, then that story must be placed in the context of the great story of the Bible, the sending of God's Son for the salvation of the world. If the preacher is using a parable of Jesus, Jesus' explanation of the purpose of parables must be taken into account. Preachers need to teach good biblical theology, making good use of the Bible, and not misusing it.

Jesus, preacher of biblical theology

Jesus' debates with the Pharisees, Sadducees, and the leaders of his nation were mainly concerned with the interpretation of the Bible. Their interpretations were wrong, and as a result they did not believe in him.

Jesus not only told them that they were wrong, but on many occasions told them *why* they were wrong. He frequently prefaced his explanation of their error with the question 'Have you not read?' On one level this was simply a way of reminding them of the *content* of Scripture, and of pointing out to them that the truth would be found in that Scripture. On another level the question 'Have you not read?' challenged them to question their understanding of the *meaning* of Scripture. If they had read it carefully, and understood it as God intended, then they would believe in Jesus, and not oppose him. Even his own disciples were 'foolish', and 'slow of heart to believe all that the prophets have spoken'; Jesus had to open both their minds and the Scriptures for them to believe in him and understand the OT revelation (Luke 24:25–27).

Christian preachers should make sure that they teach the same biblical theology as Jesus taught. His interpretation of the OT, and his summary of his own teaching is found in Luke 24:44–47: 'This is what I told you when I was still with you: Everything must be fulfilled that is written about me in the Law of Moses, the Prophets, and the Psalms ... The Christ will suffer and rise from the dead on the third day, and repentance and forgiveness of sins will be preached in his name to all nations ...' Jesus attempted to teach true biblical theology; that is, to interpret the OT as pointing to him.

Luke described Paul's ministry in Rome in similar terms: 'From morning till evening he explained and declared to them the kingdom of God and tried to convince them about Jesus from the Law of Moses and the Prophets ... he preached the kingdom of God and taught about the Lord Jesus Christ' (Acts 28:23, 31). Paul provides another useful summary of his message in speaking to the Ephesian elders. His message was that they 'must turn to God in repentance and have faith in our Lord Jesus'. He then describes his ministry as 'the task of testifying to the gospel of God's grace', 'preaching the kingdom', and points out that he has told them 'the whole will of God', by which he means God's plan of salvation (Acts 20:21–27).

Preachers need biblical theology in order to preach the text in context

We all know the saying 'A text without a context is a pretext', which points to the danger of trying to interpret words out of their context. However the task of understanding a text in context is more complex than many realize. To place a text in context we must identify its *literary context* in the book, its *theological context* in the writings of the author, and the *historical context* of the book. Then to place a text in the context of the whole biblical revelation will involve understanding its *context in OT or NT theology*, its *context in God's progressive revelation* within each period of salvation-history, and its *context in biblical theology*. In sum, context must be theological as well as literary, and context must include the whole biblical revelation, as well as the book in which the text occurs.

In the words of Geerhardus Vos, biblical theology is: 'the exhibition of the organic progress of supernatural revelation in historic continuity and multiformity'; and 'the specific character of Biblical Theology lies in this, that it discusses both the form and contents of revelation from the point of view of the revealing activity of God himself' (in *Redemptive History and Biblical Revelation*, pp. 15, 6–7). When God chose to reveal his saving will in the Bible, he did not use a systematic theology, a dictionary of useful texts, or an anthology of current debates. He used progressive revelation in word and explained deed, at intervals during the history of his chosen people. The OT declares God's promise; the NT relates its fulfilment. Salvation in Christ was first revealed in shadow, and then in substance (Col. 2:16–17). In preaching Scripture we are not dealing with timeless truths but with coherent, progressive, historical and theological revelation.

The study of biblical theology will help the preacher to preach from the text in the context in which it was placed by God. There is great need for such preaching today, when so many think that the OT provides nothing more than background to the NT, that it is just a part of its social and cultural context. On the contrary, the OT is the essential basis of the complete biblical revelation, and we cannot understand the NT without it. There can be no local cultural substitute for the OT, and those who read the NT without the OT are sure to misread it.

Preachers need biblical theology for application

A widespread problem for theologians in the 20th century has been 'the pastness of the past', the great gulf between the world of the 1st century and our own world. The challenge has been to develop a hermeneutic or principle of interpretation that manages to bridge that great gulf. The assumption has been that we live in such a different age that we need to work very hard at listening to both the word (the Bible) and the world (our own very different world).

While it is true that from the perspective of sociology we live in very different worlds, from the perspective of biblical theology we live in the same age, the last times. There is not much difference between reading the Bible as a Gentile in the 21st century, and reading it as a Gentile in the 1st century. The task of *internal hermeneutics* (i.e. biblical theology) needs to be addressed first, and only then the task of *external hermeneutics* (the meaning of the text today). Without biblical theology, we will frequently misapply the text. As C. S. Lewis pointed out, when we are studying an ancient text it is that which we think we understand which we are most likely to misread.

We need biblical theology for appropriate application. This is not because the Bible is an ancient book, because although it was written long ago, it is also a contemporary book. It is contemporary because it is God's message for those who live in the last days. In the Bible God speaks today. The difficulty in application does not lie primarily in the pastness of the past, but in the progressive and diverse nature of the revelation itself. A NT Gentile would have had as much difficulty as a contemporary Christian in knowing what to do with the OT instructions about not boiling a kid in its mother's milk. Preachers in different centuries will have the same difficulty in piecing together what the Bible teaches about marriage and divorce. The church at Laodicea may have had as much difficulty as we do in understanding Paul's teaching in Romans. If understanding biblical theology helps the preacher to apply the text, then every reader of the Bible needs to learn some biblical theology in order to understand and apply the Bible. Preachers should not only use biblical theology, but also teach it to others.

Let the text speak!

Biblical theology and preaching have the same aim: to let the text speak. As von Rad instructed young preachers: 'every text wants to speak for itself' (G. von Rad, *Biblical Interpretation*, p. 18). We should not only try to find out what the text means; we should also ask: 'What is the passage trying to do?' (D. Buttrick, in *EA* 1, p. 91). In the words of Gerhard Ebeling: 'The sermon is the execution of the text ... it is the proclamation of what the text has proclaimed' (*Theology*, p. 109). This is why biblical theology is so useful for the preacher; because both have the same aim, 'to allow God to address man through the medium of the text' (R. W. Funk, *Language, Hermeneutics and The Word of God*, p. 11). The text provides both information and proclamation (S. T. Logan, in *The Preacher and Preaching*, p. 137), and as the Bible is read and preached, God speaks to us today. If biblical theology and preaching have the same aim, then the preacher should take advantage of the insights of biblical theology.

Using biblical theology in preaching

Text in theological context

Most preachers have been trained to read a text in its literary context, a verse in the context of a paragraph, a paragraph in the context of a chapter, a chapter in the context of a book, a book in the context of the thought of the author. However not every preacher has been trained to read a text in the context of theology, much less biblical theology. To do so is to ask the following questions: How does this text fit into the progressive revelation that God gives in the Bible? Is it related to any major biblical themes? Is its theme one in which there is significant development between the OT and NT? What relationship does it have to the gospel? How does the gospel form a context for it? How does it relate to the revelation of Jesus Christ, to the promise or the fulfilment? Is it used or interpreted elsewhere in the Bible? In which major theological category does it occur, *e.g.* promise, law, prophecy, wisdom, instruction, blessing, curse, people of God, gospel?

This is a more difficult exercise than studying the literary genre and context. But to attempt it will make it less likely that a stirring call to build the temple will be applied to the church building programme, that a call to discipleship will become a proclamation of justification by works, or that adulterers will be stoned. Only biblical theology can save us from misusing the Bible, as we read each text in the context of the progressive revelation of God's saving work in Christ.

Biblical theology and expository preaching

Although all preaching ought to include an exposition of the Bible, I am here referring to the practice of preaching through books of the Bible sequentially, verse by verse and chapter by chapter. Augustine and John Chrysostom followed this model of preaching in the early church, and Zwingli, Luther and Calvin rediscovered it at the Reformation. It is the obvious way to preach the Bible, as it reflects the way in which God caused Scripture to be written (in books, not isolated texts or paragraphs). It enables us to imitate God in respecting the humanity of the authors and their style and historical context. It also reflects the usual way of reading books, and models a good use of Scripture to the congregation.

However, as Peter Jensen has pointed out, preaching consecutively through the whole Bible is not necessarily to preach the whole Bible: 'The goal of "preaching the whole Bible" is attained when we so preach Christ that every part of the Bible contributes its unique riches to his gospel' (in *When God's Voice is Heard*, p. 64).

A decision to use both expository preaching and biblical theology will enrich and invigorate our ministry, for both imply commitment to Scripture as a whole. Expository preaching implies commitment to the literary extent of Scripture, and biblical theology to its theological depth. The preacher who is using both will be a true preacher of Jesus Christ.

Biblical theology and topical preaching

While the greater part of our preaching should be expository, topical preaching is also important. Every day Christian people face many issues on which they need biblical wisdom. The preacher can provide good models for analysing issues and thinking biblically about them. But to do this the preacher needs biblical theology, which can place each relevant text in its theological context in the light of the whole Bible, and which can be used to evaluate the way the issue has been set out and to point towards an answer.

Inexperienced preachers should not try to preach topical sermons, because they are the most difficult to prepare, and require an extensive biblical theology. Not every preacher has enough biblical theology to preach on 'love', or 'divorce' or 'prayer'. The pressure to preach on only one text that addresses the topic, or to take a text out of context, is unbearable; the sermon can become nothing more than a repetition of contemporary clichés. Experienced preachers should include topical series in their programme; they will benefit the preachers as well as the people.

Planning a sermon series

The preacher who tries to cram into one sermon everything that the people need to know about the historical and literary context of a text, its place in the thought of the author, its meaning, and its role in the unfolding revelation of the Bible, will undoubtedly over-feed the congregation. One great advantage of preaching a series on a book of the Bible is that we can distribute teaching on the historical context, the intentions of the author, and biblical theological themes throughout the series. So a sermon series on the first chapters of 2 Samuel could include historical background (in the sermon on chapter 1), the context of 1 and 2 Samuel (ch. 2), biblical theology relating to David (ch. 3), the biblical theology of kingship (ch. 4), the biblical theology of Jerusalem (ch. 5), and the historical background and biblical theology of the ark and temple (ch. 6). Biblical theology should

always be in the mind of the preacher; but the preacher should not put everything in his or her mind into the sermon.

Useful resources?

Brevard Childs asserts that many commentaries discuss everything about the text but its theology. He illustrates this point from a commentary on 1 Kings 13, on the story of the man of God from Judah, which deals with different kinds of trees in Palestine, varieties of lions, and furniture in Early Bronze Age family tombs, but never tackles the theology of the text. Many modern commentaries reflect 'tone deafness to theological issues', whereas some old commentaries include 'highly significant models for the doing of theological exegesis' (Childs, *Biblical Theology*, pp. 142, 144).

The preacher who wants to use biblical theology will need to be discriminating in the use of commentaries. A good assessment can be made by looking at what the commentary says on a significant theological passage. If there is no theology here, it is unlikely to be found elsewhere. If it is hard to find commentaries that discuss theology, it is even more difficult to find any that discuss biblical theology. Because of this, one author has even written on 'The superiority of pre-critical exegesis' (D. Steinmetz, in *EA* 1, pp. 74–82). For useful commentaries, see the bibliographies to the Part 2 articles. For a good introduction to biblical theology, see E. P. Clowney, *The Unfolding Mystery*, G. Goldsworthy, *According to Plan*, and J. A. Motyer, *Look to the Rock*.

Key themes of biblical theology

Another way of teaching biblical theology is to preach on themes that reveal the structure of that theology, and so explain most parts of the Bible. Here are some themes that may be useful: covenants, the kingdom of God, the gospel, the temple, promise and fulfilment, the people of God, the land and the inheritance, the promise of the Messiah, the promises to Abraham, atonement, resurrection, creation and new creation. We can also study these themes in seminal books of the Bible such as Genesis, Deuteronomy, Psalms, Isaiah, John, Romans, Galatians, Hebrews, 1 Peter and Revelation.

Content and mood

The aim of the preacher is to let the text speak not only in terms of its content, but also in terms of its mood or intended emotional impact. The insights of biblical theology do not alter the emotional direction of a text, nor do they diminish its passions; rather they serve to intensify it. The preacher should ask not just 'what does the text say?', but also 'what is the text trying to do?' (Buttrick, in *EA* 1, p. 91).

As Calvin points out, one of the aims of the preacher is to increase the emotion of the text: 'we add there withal a vehemency to the end that doctrine may touch their hearts to the quick, that they not only know what is good but be moved to follow it' (J. Calvin, *Sermons on Timothy and Titus*, p. 419). David Day comments that the text is 'content embodied in a form', and encourages preachers to express the form and emotion of the text as well as the content (in *Anvil* 14, p. 278; and see also Peter Adam, in *The Anglican Evangelical Crisis*).

The task of the preacher is to release the eloquence of the text. Whether the text is making an appeal, giving information, rebuking, encouraging, or demanding obedience, the preacher should release the emotion as well as the meaning of that text.

Dangers to be avoided

Preaching biblical theology rather than the text. The particularity of the text can be lost in the discussion of its great theological themes. We need to make use of the great themes, but then find out which particular aspect of the themes is found in the text. Our aim is not to muffle the particular message of the text, but to let it speak with its own purpose, emotion, and power.

Just as we should avoid preaching from the text without also communicating its biblical theology, so we should avoid bypassing the text in order to preach the biblical theology that lies behind it. Our task is to preach the text and to use its biblical theology to illuminate it, not to overshadow it.

Slow motion biblical theology. Sometimes a preacher preaches a complete sermon on every word of a text, including a complete biblical theology of each word drawn from all its occurrences in Scripture. To do this is to lose the movement and particularity of the text, so that it becomes a peg on which to hang a series of theological sermons. Each word is used as an exercise in biblical theology. William Gurnall's *The Christian in Complete Armour* exemplifies this approach (W. Gurnall [Glasgow, 1864; repr. London, 1964]).

Failing to apply the text. In 2 Timothy 3:16 Paul affirms the usefulness of Scripture for 'teaching, rebuking, correcting and training in righteousness' and in 4:2 he instructs Timothy to use Scripture to 'correct, rebuke, and encourage'. Because it is useful, Scripture should be applied to those who hear so as to achieve its God-given purpose in their lives. Biblical theology should not distract from this application, but should be a means to appropriate application.

In sum, preachers should not become so intoxicated with biblical theology that they fail to preach the particularity of each text.

The benefits of biblical theology

Coherence

When the preacher uses biblical theology, the congregation learns more about the coherence of the Bible. They learn to recognize and identify the shape of God's plan for the human race, revealed in two stages (the OT and the NT) and focused on Christ. In an age in which knowledge is more and more specialized and fragmented, they learn the meta-narrative that explains human existence and purpose in the context of God's saving will and the coming of Christ. Biblical theology helps them to learn the message of the Bible, and to understand the universe.

Paying attention to biblical theology is an effective means of turning people away from the ultimately destructive postmodern question 'What does this text mean to me?' to the more fruitful question 'What does this text mean?' Only when this primary question of the text's meaning has been answered can the other, secondary question of the application of the text to our lives be addressed to advantage.

Variety and humanity

Preachers who use biblical theology will be better able to use the great variety of biblical revelation, exploring every genre of writing, every stage of biblical revelation, and every style of revelation. Their preaching will be alert to each stage of salvation history, and will be sensitive to the human context of every part of the biblical revelation. Awareness of what Vos calls 'the organic structure of the truth' (in *Redemptive History*, p. 21) will enable the preacher to respect the humanity of every part of Scripture, and also to express the unity of the revelation as it comes from the mind of God. The message of the sermon will thus reflect both the humanity and the divine origin of the message, in all its rich variety. The message includes the medium, and God has spoken in many ways. The use of biblical theology makes for interesting preaching.

Effective apologetic

It is not possible to 'take captive every thought to make it obedient to Christ' (2 Cor. 10:5) without teaching a biblical world view, and we cannot do this without biblical theology. We cannot help people to address the pervasive worldviews of humanism, postmodernity, secularism, materialism and pantheism by providing them with a few helpful texts or pious ideas. They must begin to 'think God's thoughts after him', and they do this by learning the shape of God's self-revelation in history and in the Bible. This biblical theology is the best corrective for false worldviews, just as it is the best corrective for destructive heresy. By teaching and using biblical theology in all our Bible teaching we point people to the objective and historical reality of God's progressive and purposeful revelation. Through this revelation, God speaks a transcendent message to people in every age, and shapes their minds, hearts and lives so that they can know and serve him, and speak his truth to others.

Conclusion

Without biblical theology we cannot understand the Bible as God intended; with a sound grasp of biblical theology we can both read and preach the Bible so as both to convert people and to build up the body of Christ to maturity. When Jesus taught in the synagogue at Nazareth, he explained that the Scriptures were fulfilled in himself; the people wondered at the gracious words that came from his lips (Luke 4:16–22). We too can speak these gracious words if we follow the example of Jesus Christ in our teaching, and show how the Scriptures point to him and to God's mighty work of salvation in his death and resurrection.

We can use biblical theology to preach the whole Christ and the whole gospel from the whole Bible. We may then dare to say with the apostle Paul: 'I have not hesitated to proclaim to you the whole will of God' (Acts 20:27).

Bibliography

P. Adam, 'Preaching and pastoral ministry', in M. Tinker (ed.), *The Anglican Evangelical Crisis* (Fearn, 1995); *idem*, *Speaking God's Words* (Leicester and Downers Grove, 1996, 1998); D. Buttrick, 'Interpretation and preaching', *EA* 1, 1985, pp. 83–91; *idem*, *Homiletic* (London, 1987); J. Calvin, *Sermons on Timothy and Titus* (ET, Edinburgh, 1983); B. Childs, *Biblical Theology in Crisis* (Philadelphia, 1970); E. P. Clowney, *Preaching and Biblical Theology* (Grand Rapids and London, 1961, 1962); *idem*, 'Preaching Christ from all the Scriptures', in S. T. Logan (ed.), *The Preacher and Preaching* (Darlington and Phillipsburg, 1986); *idem*, *The Unfolding Mystery* (Leicester, 1990); D. Day, 'Preaching the epistles', *Anvil* 14:4, 1997, pp. 273–282; G. Ebeling, *Theology and Proclamation* (London, 1966); R. W. Funk, *Language, Hermeneutics and the Word of God* (New York, 1966); R. J. Gibson (ed.), *Interpreting God's Plan* (Carlisle, 1998); G. Goldsworthy, *According to Plan* (Leicester and Homebush West, 1991); *idem*, 'The pastoral application of biblical theology', in D. Peterson and J. Pryor (eds.), *In the Fullness of Time* (Homebush West, 1992); W. J. Harrington, *The Path of Biblical Theology* (Dublin, 1973); P. F. Jensen, 'Preaching the whole Bible', in C. Green and D. Jackman (eds.), *When God's Voice is Heard* (Leicester, 1995); H. Krabbendam, 'Hermeneutics and preaching', in S. T. Logan (ed.), *The Preacher and Preaching* (Darlington and Phillipsburg, 1986); S. T. Logan, 'The phenomenology of preaching', in S. T. Logan (ed.), *The Preacher and Preaching* (Darlington and Phillipsburg, 1986); J. A. Motyer, *Look to the Rock* (Leicester, 1996); G. R. Osborne, *The Hermeneutical Spiral* (Downers Grove, 1991), pp. 263-285; H. Ott, *Theology and Preaching*, (ET, London, 1965); G. von Rad, *Biblical Interpretation in Preaching* (ET, Nashville, 1977); D. Steinmetz, 'The superiority of pre-critical exegesis', *EA* 1, 1985, pp. 74–82; G.

Vos, *Biblical Theology* (Grand Rapids and Edinburgh, 1948, 1975); *idem*, 'The idea of biblical theology as a science and as a theological discipline', in R. B. Gaffin (ed.), *Redemptive History and Biblical Revelation* (Phillipsburg, 1980).

P. J. H. ADAM

PART TWO

GENESIS TO KINGS

The books of Genesis to Kings may rightly be viewed as forming the foundation upon which everything else in the Bible rests. Comprising almost one-third of the entire biblical corpus, they form a continuous narrative which describes events from the creation of the world to the 6th century BC. The events selected for inclusion within this narrative focus almost exclusively on the early history of the Hebrew people. While the contents of the books of Genesis to Kings are far from homogeneous, with different types and styles of material having been incorporated into the whole, the entire corpus displays a remarkable coherence.

Two main plots, which are themselves closely related, link together Genesis to Kings: 1. the promise of *land and 2. the promise of a royal deliverer. While the former is usually traced from the call of *Abraham in Genesis 12:1–3, it has antecedents in Genesis 1 – 11 where the themes of expulsion and *exile appear in various episodes. Although the early chapters of *Genesis are integral to the development of both plots, we shall focus initially upon how the books of Genesis to Kings trace the fortunes of the Hebrew nation from the time of the patriarch Abraham to the release of the Judaean king Jehoiachin from prison in Babylon in 561 BC.

The promise of nationhood

In Genesis Abraham is promised by Yahweh, the Lord, that his descendants will become a great nation in the land of Canaan (e.g. Gen. 12:2; 15:1–21). This promise is later renewed to Abraham's son, Isaac, and his son, *Jacob (whose name is changed to Israel). However, before it can be fulfilled, Jacob's family must migrate to Egypt, from where, after a period of oppression, they are miraculously delivered by *God, under the leadership of *Moses (Exod. 3 – 15). Following their *Exodus from captivity in Egypt, the Israelites are invited by the Lord to enter into a *covenant relationship with him (Exod. 19 – 24). At the heart of this agreement is the requirement that they should acknowledge, through love and *obedience, the sole lordship of Yahweh as their God.

The formal establishment of this covenant between Yahweh and the Israelites leads to the construction of a 'royal' tent or tabernacle, which becomes the locus of God's presence among his people (Exod. 25 – 31; 35 – 40). However, it has significant ramifications for the Israelites. New structures and customs have to be set in place in order for the people to live in safety close to Yahweh. These are described in considerable detail throughout the book of Leviticus. *Holiness is particularly important; the Israelites must sanctify themselves and maintain an appropriate state of holiness in order to remain in the presence of the Holy One.

While the books of *Exodus and *Leviticus focus on the transformation of *Israel into a 'holy nation', this stands in tension with the people's failure to live up to their covenant obligations. Whereas the record of Israel's time at Mt Sinai highlights the immense privilege which Yahweh bestowed upon the Israelites by choosing them to be his 'treasured possession' out of all the nations (Exod. 19:5), the story of the Israelites' journey from Egypt to the promised land contains a long catalogue of failures. Indeed, the book of *Numbers graphically reveals that of all the adult Israelites who experienced God's deliverance from slavery in Egypt and witnessed the spectacular theophany at Mt Sinai, only Joshua and Caleb survive to enter the promised land (cf. Num. 26:63–65). Even Moses, the faithful servant of the Lord, is condemned to die outside the land, having struggled to lead the people for forty years in the wilderness.

After the untimely death of those who entered into the covenant relationship at Mt Sinai, Moses invites the next generation of Israelites to make a similar commitment to Yahweh. The book of *Deuteronomy describes in detail the renewing of the covenant, this time 'in the desert east of the Jordan' (Deut. 1:1). Here the Israelites stand on the threshold of the land God promised centuries earlier to Abraham, Isaac and Jacob.

In Deuteronomy the obligations of the covenant are set out by Moses in several lengthy speeches which abound in exhortations challenging the people to be faithful to Yahweh. When he has finished speaking, Moses records this '*law' – the Hebrew term torâ is best translated 'instruction' or 'teaching' – in a book and gives it to the priests and elders of Israel (cf. Deut. 31:9, 24). Moses commands them to read the book to the people regularly so that future generations will 'learn to fear the LORD' (Deut. 31:13).

The concluding sections of Deuteronomy, however, clearly predict, in a variety of ways, further acts of disobedience; see for example the long list of curses (Deut. 28:15–68; *cf.* 27:15–26) and the contents of the 'Song of Moses' (Deut. 32:1–43).

Although the final chapter of Deuteronomy concludes with the burial of Moses, his birth and death framing the books of Exodus to Deuteronomy, further developments are expected; the Israelites have yet to occupy the land of Canaan, an event anticipated by much of the material in Genesis to Deuteronomy. In the light of this, it is apparent that the opening verses of *Joshua have been deliberately composed to continue the story. The divine commissioning of Joshua as Moses' successor echoes Deuteronomy 31:1–8 (*cf.* Josh. 1:1–5), and Joshua's success as a leader will depend upon his obedience to the 'Book of the Law' (Josh. 1:7–8)

While the book of Joshua describes how the Israelites succeed in taking possession of much of the land of Canaan, the next book, *Judges, provides a contrasting sequel. No longer does the occupation of the land proceed smoothly. On the contrary the Israelites find themselves losing ground to their enemies. Whereas their success under Joshua was due to their obeying the Lord, failure thereafter is the result of disobedience. Even the divinely appointed and spirit-empowered 'judges' are increasingly tainted by the *sin of the people as a whole.

The pattern of events described in Judges continues into the opening chapters of *Samuel, climaxing in the capture of the ark of the covenant by the Philistines. This would have symbolized the total defeat of Yahweh himself but for the fact that he permitted it to happen. When the ark of the covenant is brought as a trophy of victory into the temple of Dagon in Ashdod, Yahweh's power is demonstrated through the falling over of Dagon's stone image (1 Sam. 5:1–5).

Subsequent developments lead to a new phase in God's dealings with the Israelites, involving the creation of a monarchy. While most of 1 Samuel focuses on the establishing of Saul as the first king of Israel, he is overshadowed by the figure of *David, the one anointed by the prophet Samuel to replace Saul as king.

2 Samuel records how, after Saul's death in battle, David becomes king over all Israel and establishes *Jerusalem as his capital. To confirm his divine appointment as monarch, David transports the ark of the covenant to Jerusalem. Soon afterwards, when he expresses a desire to construct for Yahweh a *temple in Jerusalem, the Lord intervenes and delays the project. However, in response to David's desire to build a 'house' or temple for God, the Lord promises that David's 'house' or dynasty will be established for ever. The importance of David is underlined by the fact that all of 2 Samuel is devoted to describing his period as king.

Attention shifts in the opening chapters of 1 *Kings to *Solomon, who succeeds to his father David's throne. Through the divine gift of wisdom Solomon extends the boundaries of the *kingdom and brings peace, prosperity and justice to the Israelites. He then constructs a splendid temple to Yahweh in Jerusalem. As a result, the impression is conveyed that the promise of nationhood made centuries earlier by God to Abraham has come at last to fulfilment.

Yet the account of Solomon's life concludes on a dark note by highlighting how his many wives lead him into idolatry. Consequently, after his death, God divides the kingdom between Solomon's son Rehoboam and one of Solomon's officials, Jeroboam. While Rehoboam retains control of the region around Jerusalem, known as '*Judah', Jeroboam becomes king of the much larger portion of Solomon's kingdom designated 'Israel'.

The fortunes of these two kingdoms, and in particular the activities of their kings, are recorded in the rest of 1 and 2 Kings. Whereas the northern kingdom of Israel is ruled by a series of short dynasties, control of the southern kingdom remains in the hands of David's descendants. Although both kingdoms are portrayed as failing to remain loyal to Yahweh, the apostasy of Israel is much greater, resulting in its downfall at the hands of the Assyrians by 721 BC. While Judah survives on this occasion, a similar fate befalls it just over a century later when the Babylonians invade the country, destroy the temple, and carry away many of the population into exile. Once again, the blame is placed upon the failure of the monarchy and people to remain loyal to Yahweh.

Although the narrative in Genesis to Kings ends with the subjugation of Judah, there are indications that the story is not finished. The concluding chapters of Deuteronomy anticipate God's *judgment coming upon the Israelites, climaxing in their exile from the land. However, Deuteronomy 30:1–10 also describes a subsequent return to the land. This theme is echoed later by Solomon in his prayer at the dedication of the temple (1 Kgs. 8:46–51). It is noteworthy that the final episode in Kings focuses on the release of Jehoiachin from prison in Babylon and his kind treatment by the Babylonian king, Evil-Merodach. Does this offer a glimmer of *hope for the future?

The promise of a royal deliverer

We have observed that the books of Genesis to Kings are bound together by God's promise to Abraham that his descendants will become a great nation, occupying the land of Canaan. This, however, is only one part of what Yahweh promises Abraham, and possibly not the most important. Alongside the promise of nationhood is the promise that Abraham will be a source of *blessing to the *nations of the earth. Not only does this promise play a very significant role within the Abraham narrative and subsequent narratives; it also links this material with the opening chapters of Genesis.

The divine promise of blessing through Abraham, introduced in Genesis 12:1–3, is clearly set against the background of Genesis 1 – 11. These chapters open with the *creation of the earth and humanity. All living creatures are blessed by God (Gen. 1:22, 28) and everything is described as 'very good' (Gen. 1:31). However, Genesis 3 concludes with the expulsion of the human couple from the Garden of Eden, Yahweh having punished them for disobeying his instructions. Various curses are listed in Genesis 3:14–19, which have the effect of reversing, in part at least, the blessings previously announced by God. As the following chapters reveal, *humanity, alienated from God, struggles to survive in a world that is dominated by *evil. Eventually the growth of human wickedness is so great that God intervenes, destroying through a flood all human beings apart from Noah and his closest relatives. In spite of this, however, the sinful nature of humanity remains essentially unchanged (Gen. 8:21). People continue to challenge and reject God's authority over them.

While the events of Genesis 3 – 11 highlight the disastrous consequences of living under God's curse or disfavour, the call of Abraham offers hope. Yahweh promises to bless all those who bless Abraham (Gen. 12:3). Much later, in response to Abraham's obedience, this promise is confirmed by a divine oath which guarantees that God's blessing will come to 'all the families of the earth' through one of Abraham's descendants (Gen. 22:16–18).

This guarantee of future blessing is linked to a unique line of '*seed', which begins with Seth (cf. Gen. 4:25) and is traced downwards through two linear genealogies to Abraham (Gen. 5:1–32; 11:10–26). (Significantly, the Lord has already announced that this 'seed' will overcome the '*serpent' [Gen. 3:15]). From Abraham it proceeds through Isaac to Jacob/Israel and then *Joseph. In spite of his brothers' actions against him, Joseph is protected by God and, from being a prisoner in an Egyptian jail, is dramatically exalted to become prime minister of Egypt. In this capacity he is a source of blessing to many nations during a seven-year famine.

Although Genesis undoubtedly makes much of Joseph's place within the family line descended from Abraham, attention is drawn also to Judah, especially in Genesis 38. Of note here is Tamar's determination to continue the line of 'seed' (38:6–26) and the remarkable account of the birth of twin boys in which the younger breaks out ahead of the older (38:27–30). The reader is clearly meant to reflect upon the significance of this event in the light of other birth stories in Genesis. Later, Jacob's blessing of Judah highlights the importance of his descendants, suggesting that from them shall come a royal line (49:8–12).

While there are indications that Judah's descendants may include a future royal dynasty, the line of 'seed' is initially traced from Joseph to his younger son Ephraim (cf. Gen. 48:1–22). Jacob's blessing of Ephraim ahead of his older brother Manasseh is reminiscent of Jacob's own experience in relation to his older twin brother Esau. After the Israelites' Exodus from Egypt under Moses, Joshua from the tribe of Ephraim successfully leads the people into the promised land, establishing a central sanctuary at Shiloh in the territory allocated to the Ephraimites (Josh. 18:1).

Thereafter, however, the Ephraimites gradually lose control of the nation as the people forsake Yahweh for other gods. Through Samuel God moves to establish a monarchy in Israel, and this leads, after Saul's failure as king, to the creation of a Davidic dynasty from the tribe of Judah. Interestingly, the divine rejection of Ephraim coincides with the departure of the ark of the covenant from Shiloh and the death of the high priest Eli and his sons (*cf.* Ps. 78:56–72).

Whereas Joshua had established Shiloh as the location for Israel's central sanctuary, David selects Jerusalem and proceeds to transport the ark of the covenant there. Although he prepares for the building of a temple in Jerusalem, the actual task of construction is left to his son Solomon. These activities confirm God's choice of David and his descendants as the lineage through whom God's blessing will come to all the families of the earth. However, although much of Solomon's reign is portrayed positively (through wisdom he brings blessing to the Israelites and is admired by foreigners) his many wives eventually lead him into idolatry. As a result, God divides the kingdom between Solomon's son, Rehoboam and Jeroboam, an Ephraimite.

Although the appointment of Jeroboam as king may have been interpreted by some as heralding the restoration of the line of Joseph, the book of Kings continues to focus upon the fulfilment of God's promises to David. While different dynasties come and go in the northern kingdom of Israel, David's descendants remain upon the throne in Jerusalem. Nevertheless, the unrighteous activities of some of David's descendants place the nation of Judah in jeopardy, resulting in its punishment at the hands of the Babylonians.

With the destruction of the temple and the apparent demise of the Davidic dynasty, the book of Kings comes to its conclusion. In contrast to the promise of nationhood, God's promise to bless the nations of the earth through a royal descendant of Abraham has remained unfulfilled. However, Jehoiachin's release from prison in Babylon possibly suggests that the story is not finished.

The literary unity of Genesis to Kings

The preceding survey provides grounds for believing that the books of Genesis to Kings form a unified literary composition. To say this is not to claim that their style is uniform throughout; the individual books have their own distinctive features, and even within each diverse material may be found. To the reader this presents a challenge, for it is easy to lose sight of the big picture. Yet throughout Genesis to Kings a rich variety of components has been worked together to produce a remarkable literary collage.

These observations on the literary unity of Genesis to Kings have important implications for our understanding of this material, and this may be contrasted briefly with other approaches. Within Judaism, it has been traditional to view the books as forming two distinctive blocks: the Torah (Genesis to Deuteronomy) and the Former Prophets (Joshua to Kings). However, because greater authority was given to the first of these, a division was created between Deuteronomy and Joshua. With the development of critical approaches to the OT scholars began to question seriously the value of treating Genesis to Deuteronomy as a unity. Observing that Deuteronomy had no account of the Israelites taking possession of the promised land, they soon included the book of Joshua in discussions regarding the composition of the Pentateuch. This marked an important shift, from thinking of a Pentateuch to thinking of a Hexateuch. A further development was the introduction by Martin Noth of the concept of a Deuteronom(ist)ic Historian, who composed the books of Deuteronomy to Kings in the exilic period. Focusing on the unity of these books, Noth dismissed the concept of a Pentateuch, favouring instead that of a Tetrateuch. While Noth's proposals have been very influential, the process by which the books of Genesis to Kings were composed continues to be the subject of intense debate among scholars, and new theories regarding their composition continue to be offered. This should not distract us, however, from considering how all these books, viewed as a unified narrative, contribute to a Christian understanding of biblical theology.

Although absolute certainty is impossible, it seems likely that the books of Genesis to Kings were given their present shape shortly after 561 BC, the date of Jehoiachin's release from prison (2 Kgs. 25:27). While the process by which these books were composed remains obscure, they were probably written to give hope to those affected by the destruction of

Jerusalem and the temple, the demise of the Davidic dynasty, the deportation of many leading Judaean citizens to Babylon and the flight of others to Egypt.

The books of Genesis to Kings not only offer an explanation for these traumatic events by focusing on the nation's failure to be *faithful to Yahweh, but also preserve the hope that God will one day raise up a descendant of David through whom he will bless all the nations of the earth. Similar optimism is found in other writings, some of which originate prior to the exile (*e.g.* Is. 9:1–7; 11:1–5; Jer. 23:5–6; 30:8–9; Ezek. 17:22–24; 34:23–24; 37:24; Amos 9:11–12).

Thus, although the books of Genesis to Kings narrate the past history of the Hebrew people, they are firmly orientated towards the future. By tracing the line of 'seed' from Seth to Jehoiachin, the narrative highlights God's ongoing faithfulness to his promises in spite of many obstacles to their fulfilment. Moreover, a picture is gradually drawn of the one who is yet to come, for the reader is given to expect that he will resemble and excel the prominent figures in Genesis to Kings. Like Abraham, he will trust and obey God. Like Joseph, he will save 'many lives' (Gen. 50:20). Like Joshua, he will do everything written in the 'Book of the Law'. Like David, he will be divinely exalted from humble circumstances. Like Solomon, he will rule with great wisdom.

In the light of this expectation, it is easy to understand how *Jesus is portrayed in the NT as the one who fulfils the Law and the Prophets (*e.g.* Matt. 5:17; Luke 24:27, 44; John 1:45; Acts 26:22–23; 28:23). He is the promised 'seed' of Abraham and of David (e.g., Acts 3:25–26; Rom. 1:2; Gal. 3:16). Although Genesis to Kings contain other themes of significance for biblical theology, there is an urgent need to recognize afresh that these books point, above all else, to the coming of one through whom the nations of the earth will be blessed.

Conclusion

Thus far, our main purpose has been to show that the narrative in Genesis to Kings is bound together by two interrelated plots which centre around the divine promises of nationhood and a royal deliverer. However, by the end of Kings the latter promise is at best only partially fulfilled, thus creating the expectation that its fulfilment still lies in the future.

In line with this expectation, it is apparent that other elements in Genesis to Kings have a paradigmatic function, pointing forward to and/or anticipating events that have yet to take place. Probably the most important of these elements is the account of the deliverance of the Israelites from slavery in Egypt and their taking possession of the promised land. These events, viewed in the light of the expulsion of Adam and Eve from the garden of Eden, provide a preview of the greater deliverance which God has planned for the whole earth. Thus, although the Israelites enter into a special covenant relationship with the Lord at Mt Sinai and, consequently, are distinguished from all other nations by having God come and dwell in their midst, they enjoy at most only a partial restoration of the idyllic conditions which existed on earth prior to the rebellion of Adam and Eve. While the building of the tabernacle enables the Lord to live among the Israelites, direct access to him is still very restricted, and numerous provisions must be made in order for the people to atone for their ongoing sins. Moreover, as the books of Genesis to Kings bear witness, these arrangements by themselves provide no permanent solution to the fractured relationship between God and humanity. They do, however, provide an important guide to the means by which a lasting solution will be achieved.

In the light of the preceding observations, the importance of the books of Genesis to Kings for biblical theology is evident. As numerous articles elsewhere in this dictionary demonstrate more fully, these books not only introduce a rich variety of theological ideas, but also provide the foundation upon which everything else rests.

Bibliography

T. D. Alexander, *From Paradise to the Promised Land: an Introduction to the Main Themes of the Pentateuch* (Carlisle and Grand Rapids, 1995, 1998); *idem*, 'Royal expectations in Genesis to Kings: their importance for biblical theology', *TynB* 49, 1998, pp. 191–212; D. N. Freedman, 'The earliest Bible', in M. P. O'Connor and D. N. Freedman (eds.), *Background for the Bible* (Winona Lake, 1987); J. G. McConville, *Grace in the End: A Study in Deuteronomic Theology* (Carlisle and Grand Rapids, 1993); M. Noth, *The Deuteronomistic History* (ET, Sheffield, 1981); R. N. Whybray, *The Making of the Pentateuch: A Methodological Study* (Sheffield, 1987).

T. D. ALEXANDER

WISDOM BOOKS

Introduction

In the context of the historical-critical paradigm, wisdom theology has been much neglected until recently. The strong historical interests of Wellhausen and his followers made wisdom literature seem marginal, with little to offer to OT theology. The OT was supposed to be about God's acts in history, and since OT wisdom literature appears to say little or nothing about God's great saving acts, its secondary status was confirmed for many.

However, recent decades have witnessed renewed interest in wisdom. Scholars have become increasingly aware that OT wisdom is not secular and human-centred, but based on the doctrine of *creation and (like other ancient Near Eastern wisdom) deeply religious. Today it is recognized that wisdom has a major contribution to make to OT theology, although there is considerable disagreement about how the different strands of the OT are interrelated. The rise of literary criticism as a technique of biblical interpretation has made possible an examination of the OT wisdom books as literary entities, and this is proving a most fruitful source of theological insights. It is also acknowledged that wisdom schools may have played a key role in the final editing of the canon, and that OT wisdom is an indispensable part of the background to the Jesus tradition and thus of any satisfactory biblical theology.

The fear of the LORD

*Proverbs, *Job and *Ecclesiastes all assert that the *fear of the LORD is the beginning of wisdom (Prov. 1:7; 9:10; 16:6; 31:30; Job 28:28; Eccles. 5:7; 12:13). The wisdom books of the OT include some references to its historical literature, but not many. However, the assertion that the fear of Yahweh is the beginning of wisdom indicates that the writers assumed the validity of the historical and *prophetic traditions. Yahweh (see Exod. 3 and 6) is the name of *Israel's redeemer *God who rescues the nation from slavery in Egypt and brings them to himself (see Exod. 19).

Thus from a canonical perspective wisdom begins with a holy reverence for the One who has rescued Israel and brought her to himself. Wisdom in this sense is not separate from Yahweh's *redemptive acts but a response to them. The close canonical link between wisdom and *Solomon (1 Kgs. 3–4; Prov. 1:1; Eccles. 1:1) confirms the link between wisdom and Israel's history. (See also *Genesis to Kings.)

The fear of Yahweh as the beginning of wisdom should be understood in two ways. First, if wisdom is about knowing how to live a successful *life in God's world, then the fear of the LORD is the indispensable starting point. The route to true wisdom will not be found apart from the particularity of God's *salvation of Israel. The OT here firmly rejects human autonomy as the path to *truth and thus delineates a pre-theoretical epistemology. The OT wisdom writers often appeal to observation to support their views, and this might appear to contradict their taking Yahweh as their starting point. However, as M. Fox rightly points out (*Qoheleth and His Contradictions*) wisdom's epistemology is not empiricism. It is not neutral observation which is used to support wisdom, but observation through Yahwistic glasses.

Wisdom's stress on the fear of the LORD as *the* starting point for wisdom presupposes that alternative starting points are a real possibility. Indeed, the doctrine of the two ways is fundamental to the theology of the wisdom books: ultimately one follows either Yahweh's ways or those of folly (*cf.* Ps. 1). Thus the wisdom books assume the context of a fallen world in which folly is a constant temptation.

Secondly, the fear of the LORD is the beginning of wisdom in that it is the start of a journey rather than a final destination. God's acts of salvation, from this perspective, are the basis of a journey of exploration and discovery constrained only by the limits God has placed upon his creation. Wisdom based on the fear of Yahweh enables humans to use their resources to explore God's *world.

From such a perspective it is clear that wisdom holds redemption and creation closely together and knows nothing of the modern sacred/secular divide. For OT wisdom Yahweh the redeemer is the creator; those who start with him are led to a right understanding of how his world works.

Creation and OT wisdom

In Proverbs, underlying the metaphors of the two ways, the two houses and the two women, is an understanding of creation as ordered by God. Finding wisdom means discovering how to follow the order that God has built into his world. In Proverbs the foundation of wisdom in creation is discussed in two places in particular: 3:19–20 and 8:22–31. Job 28 includes a hymn about wisdom and creation, and Job 38 – 41 reflects at length on creation. The earth, according to Proverbs, was 'founded by wisdom' and Lady Wisdom was present throughout God's creation of the world and delighted in it. In Proverbs 8 (as elsewhere in Prov. 1 – 9), wisdom is personified as Lady Wisdom, but it is unclear how this figure is to be understood. Some see her as a personification of Yahweh's own wisdom by which he created the world. However, the poem distinguishes her from Yahweh, just as elsewhere in the OT the angel of the LORD, the word of the LORD and the name of the LORD are associated with but distinguished from Yahweh. The main points of the chapter are that Yahweh founded the world by this 'wisdom' and that true human wisdom is found by following it. Like the major cultures of the ancient Near East, the OT wisdom books affirm an overall order in creation.

Because the fabric of creation comes from God, wisdom is found and is to be sought in every area of human life. Wisdom is not restricted to family and cultic life. Proverbs stresses that wisdom's call is heard in the city centres: the city gates which were the place of government and justice, and the market squares, which were the economic centres (e.g. Prov. 8:1–3). God's people are called to be wise in all areas of life by locating and living according to his norms.

The woman of Proverbs 31 is placed at the end of the book as a paradigm of the wise person. Scholars have struggled to understand how this woman can be an example of a person who fears the LORD when the activities in which she engages are all 'secular'. The Reformers achieved a breakthrough in the interpretation of this passage by realizing that all life is sacred and that this wise woman's fear of the LORD manifests itself in her activities as housewife, international trader in high quality fabrics and estate agent. In these ca-

pacities she is hailed as a hero in language normally used of God. Job affirms this celebratory view of creation, as does Ecclesiastes with its language of eating and drinking and joy, which is best understood not as hedonistic but as shalomic.

Retribution and theodicy

Wisdom's belief in the order of creation and in its accessibility to the Israelites raises the issue of theodicy (see *Suffering). If wisdom is the key to a successful life, then how are experiences like Job's to be explained? There has been considerable discussion about the views of the different wisdom books with respect to retribution. It has often been argued that whereas Proverbs teaches that wisdom leads automatically to blessing and success – that it has what R. C. Van Leeuwen calls an 'act-consequence' structure (in HS 33, pp. 25–36) – Job and Ecclesiastes pose radical challenges to this naïve view.

Reading Proverbs as a literary whole has shown this interpretation to be too simplistic. Wisdom *does* teach that wise acts generally lead to success and *blessing. This is clear from Proverbs 1 – 9, the hermeneutical key to the whole book. However, this general truth is not worked out in every individual case, and in the later chapters the exceptions come more clearly into focus (cf. Prov. 15:16; 16:8). Job is the story of such an exception. Job is a thoroughly wise man whose wise acts lead not to blessing but to disaster of the worst sort. In its canonical form, however, the book asserts that this wise man is led ultimately into a deeper knowledge of God through his sufferings and into material blessing.

Ecclesiastes wrestles with the fact that an act–consequence pattern is not evident in every aspect of life. Law courts, for example, are sometimes unjust. If one's approach to life does not start with the fear of the LORD, one will fail to put these exceptions in the context of God's purposes and God's justice and will inevitably conclude that all is *vanity.

In neither Job nor Ecclesiastes are the authors' difficulties in understanding what precisely God is doing in the mysteries of life resolved by means of logic alone. In Job the resolution comes through Job's encountering God existentially as the great Creator. In Ecclesiastes the resolution comes as Qoheleth realizes that trying to discover the meaning of life by reason and experience alone leads one to see everything as enigmatic or absurd, and that this does not do justice to the goodness of life as God has made it. Ecclesiastes concludes by returning to the starting point of the fear of God.

Theologically the wisdom books have much to offer. They are connected with the other types of OT literature through the themes of creation and *covenant. Covenant, like wisdom, is rooted in creation. The history central to the covenantal literature is part of God's dynamic creation order; different parts of this order come into focus in different types of literature. God's laws reflect how God has made the world. Prophetic literature is based on covenant, and the psalms celebrate creation and God's other great acts, acknowledging that two ways of life are open to worshippers (cf. Ps. 1). The OT wisdom writers do not focus on God's acts and laws, but they are aware of them (cf. Prov. 2:21–22; 10:30; 22:28; Job 15:18–19; Eccles. 5:1–7).

Bibliography

J. Day, R. P. Gordon, and H. G. M. Williamson (eds.), *Wisdom in Ancient Israel: Essays in Honour of J. A. Emerton* (Cambridge, 1995); M. Fox, *Qoheleth and His Contradictions* (Sheffield, 1989); R. P. Knierim, *The Task of Old Testament Theology* (Grand Rapids, 1995); G. von Rad, *Wisdom in Israel* (London, 1972); R. C. Van Leeuwen, *Context and Meaning in Proverbs 25–27* (Atlanta, 1988); idem, 'The Book of Proverbs', in *NIB* V (Nashville, 1997); idem, 'Wealth and poverty: System and contradiction in Proverbs', *HS* 33, 1992, pp. 25–36; L. Wilson, 'The book of Job and the fear of God', *TynB* 46, 1995, pp. 59–79; A. Wolters, 'Nature and grace in the interpretation of Proverbs 31:10–31', *CTJ* 19, 1984, pp. 153–166; idem, 'Proverbs XXXI 10–31 as heroic hymn: A form-critical analysis', *VT* 38, 1988, pp. 448–457.

C. G. BARTHOLOMEW

PROPHETIC BOOKS

Introduction

The classical or 'writing' prophets form a distinct and important part of the OT. It consists of major and minor prophets. The former group consists of *Isaiah, *Jeremiah, *Lamentations, *Ezekiel and *Daniel, and the latter of the twelve books from *Hosea to *Malachi. This distinction between major and minor books is based on length and not on significance, and the sequence of the books is largely determined by length and chronology. The longer books (Isaiah, Jeremiah [with Lamentations], Ezekiel and Daniel) come first, and in the best attested sequence are arranged in chronological order from the earliest to the latest. Lamentations follows Jeremiah since Jeremiah was believed to be its author. The minor prophets follow, and are arranged in roughly chronological order, with Hosea being the earliest and Malachi the latest.

The rise of classical prophecy

The process which produced the prophetic books began in the middle of the 8th century BC and ended some 300 years later. It marked a watershed in the history of *prophecy. There had previously been significant stories about prophets (1 Sam. 3; 1 Sam. 7 – 15; 1 Kgs. 13; 1 Kgs. 17 – 2 Kgs. 13), and these stories contained a few oracles (1 Kgs. 13:2–3; 17:14), but prophetic speeches were not circulated in isolation from their narrative context. Although Samuel, *Elijah and *Elisha were prophets of gigantic stature, they did not produce written collections of their sayings. Scholars often make a sharp distinction between these great figures (and their disciples) and the later classical prophets, but it is a false one. Classical prophecy probably evolved naturally from the earlier form. Just as the writing of much of the Torah followed Moses' vision of *God at Sinai (Exod. 33 – 34), so classical prophecy began to flourish soon after Elijah's similar experience on the same mountain centuries later (1 Kgs. 19). These two revelatory figures would much later join *Jesus on a mountain, after which prophecy again flourished and the NT was produced (Matt. 17:1–8).

The emergence of the 'literary' prophets coincides with the destruction of the northern and southern kingdoms of *Israel and *Judah and the restoration of the latter. The prophetic books record both the largely unheeded prophetic announcement of divine *judgment, made to a sinful and self-confident people, and the prediction of *salvation beyond the judgment, made to a chastened and discouraged people.

Language and style

The prophetic books in the OT are distinguished from other canonical volumes on the basis of form and content. They constitute a distinct class of literature. They preserve the prophets' words, which were written down by the prophets themselves, their scribes or their disciples.

The main genre or literary form found in the literature is the prophetic oracle, which is often marked by an introductory formula such as 'Thus says Yahweh' (Amos 1:3, 6; Mic. 3:5). Such oracles clarified the prophet's role as a messenger of God. These pronouncements can be subdivided into two classes, oracles of woe (judgment) and oracles of weal (salvation). The former consist of an announcement of judgment and of reasons for it (e.g. Amos 1:3–5). In the latter there is a bare announcement of salvation (e.g. Is. 2:1–4). The prophets also used many different literary forms borrowed from diverse social contexts to communicate their message. The use of these forms, which include allegories (Is. 5:1–7), proverbs (Ezek. 18:2), lamentations (Amos 5:1–2) and prayers (Hab. 3), reveal the prophets' resourcefulness; they were able to use every known literary convention to communicate with their audiences. They spoke the divine *word, and were deeply committed to it.

The style of their writing attests to the passionate involvement of these messengers. It is often raw with emotion: in Jeremiah's painfully honest cries (8:18 – 9:1); in Ezekiel's shocking statements (20:21–26); in Isaiah's lyrical rhapsodies (40:12–31); in *Habakkuk's incredulous questioning (1:12–17); in Amos' sarcasm and irony (3:12). The prophets were often so personally involved with their message that their lives as well as their words conveyed it.

The prophets and/or their disciples committed their divinely inspired oracles to writing. Generally the sayings were preserved as anthologies in which different principles of arrangement were used: thematic (Jer. 23:9–40; Ezek. 12:21 – 13:23); chronological (Hag. 1:1; 2:1, 10, 20); formulaic expressions (Amos 3:1; 4:1; 5:1); questions and answers (Mal. 1:2, 6, 13, 2:10, 13; 17; 3:7, 13). Rarely are individual oracles given a specific historical context. This explains Luther's famous comment regarding the prophets that they 'have a queer way of talking, like people who, instead of proceeding in an orderly manner, ramble off from one thing to the next, so that you cannot make head or tail of them or see what they are getting at' (Works, XIX:350; cited in G. von Rad, Old Testament Theology, p. 33).

Very little is known about the production of a prophetic scroll. (The book or codex was not invented until the beginning of the Christian era.) Nonetheless, there is preserved in the book of Jeremiah an account of the production of a scroll of his oracles, which provides some insight into the process (Jer. 36). Jeremiah was told by the Lord to write out all the oracles he had ever spoken and to read them in the temple, thus providing a more ominous warning than any individual saying could convey; his words were intended to bring the people to *repentance. Jeremiah recited all the oracles from memory to his scribe, Baruch, and the latter recorded them on a scroll and read them in the temple. As a result, the document was destroyed (burned) by the king, and a warrant was issued for the prophet's arrest. Jeremiah and his scribe escaped and were commanded to make another scroll to which 'many other words were added' (36:32). Jeremiah's prophetic ministry continued for many years, and many other oracles were added to the scroll. The document was completed by editors during the *exile, years after the prophet's death (Jer. 52).

The publication of a large number of prophecies was a last attempt to lead the people to repentance. It was a powerful witness to the truth of the prophetic word. This concept of witness as a means of verifying the truth of prophetic words is illustrated in other passages in the prophets. Isaiah told his disciples to seal up a scroll for a later day in order that the next generation should be confronted with the truth of his prophetic revelation (Is 8:16–18; 30:8–11). Similarly the editorial inscription of the book of Amos pointed to the fulfilment of the prophetic prediction of an earthquake, which authenticated it (Amos 1:1–2).

One of the structural arrangements used in the prophetic scrolls is that of judgment and salvation, *death and resurrection. Salvation oracles are often juxtaposed to judgment oracles. For example, in the book of *Micah an oracle announcing the future exaltation of Zion immediately follows an oracle of doom spoken against the present Zion (3:11–12; 4:1–5); even the book of Amos, which largely consists of judgment oracles, concludes with two salvation oracles (9:11–13, 14–15). This arrangement indicates how the prophets' words functioned as canonical literature. The prophetic books contained a distinct message; their authors 'comforted Jacob and delivered them by assured hope' (Ecclus. 49:10).

Each prophet had a distinctive message, but some themes recur repeatedly in all the prophetic books.

1. *Sub specie aeternitatis.* The prophetic vision of life was radically different from the norm. Theologians use the Latin term *sub specie aeternitatis* to describe it. The prophets saw human life 'under the gaze of eternity', and this perspective led them to a fundamentally different evaluation of human life. What others saw as monumental, the prophets saw as miniscule, and vice versa. Jeremiah recognized the absolute poverty of wealth, power and intelligence and the inestimable value of *love, *righteousness and justice (9:23–24). Isaiah and Ezekiel announced a levelling of all that was 'tall' and proud in human life (Is. 2:9–22; Ezek. 17:24). The classic metaphor for pride was the lofty tree which would be cut down in Yahweh's coming judgment (Ezek. 17:24). Similar motifs are found in *Obadiah (3–4), Habakkuk (2:5–20), *Nahum (1:2–15) and *Zephaniah (1:12–18).

2. The transcendence of God. The transcendence of God, and the consequent vulnerability and dependence of human beings, is integral to the prophetic vision. In Isaiah 31:1–3 the prophet warns the Israelites not to make a treaty with the Egyptians, 'for they are human and not God; their horses are flesh and not spirit' (NRSV). These two sets of terms are opposites: 'human' and 'flesh' represent weakness and 'God' and 'Spirit' strength. This view of transcendence is found also in Ezekiel, in the account of his vision of resurrection (ch. 37); in Jeremiah, in the command to make an absurd commercial transaction by buying Israelite real estate when Jerusalem is surrounded by Babylonian armies (ch. 32); in Hosea, in the declaration of God's willingness to *forgive the Israelites despite their unfaithfulness (ch. 11); in Amos, in the prediction of a powerful earthquake (9:1–4); and in Nahum (ch. 1) and Habakkuk (ch. 3), in the records of their *theophanic visions.

3. Love, righteousness, justice. Isaiah describes Israel's reason for being as rooted in Yahweh's *covenant love. But the purpose of this love was that Israel should produce justice and righteousness (5:1–7) as Yahweh's beckoning light to the *nations. 'Righteousness' generally refers to Israel's living in a right relationship with Yahweh, keeping the terms of his covenant. Sometimes this relationship is disrupted and needs to be restored; when one does this, one 'does justice'. Frequently the prophets confront Israel with its failure to live in righteousness and do justice. They are often advocates for the powerless in society; it is the rights of these little people that are violated by the mad lust for power. Some books (*e.g.* Amos) consist mostly of such advocacy, but it forms part of most prophetic books. Widows, orphans and the *poor have only the lonely voice of prophetic protest to help them (Is. 1:17; Jer. 22:15–16; Zech. 7:8–10). The call to love, justice and righteousness is sometimes used to summarize the entire prophetic message (Jer. 9:23–24; Is. 5:7; Hos. 4:1–3; 6:1–3; Mic. 6:8; Amos 5:7, 11, 21–24).

4. Repentance. The prophetic message could also be summed up in one word: *šûb* ('repent'), a word which signified that the people whom the prophet was addressing needed to change the moral direction of their lives (2 Kgs. 17:13). The use of this word was the primary difference between a true and a false prophet (Jer. 23:22): the true prophet stressed repentance; the false one did not. By abandoning the Torah and love, justice and righteousness, the people had terminated their communion with Yahweh. Jeremiah said that the people had given their backs to God and not their faces (Jer. 2:27); they needed to turn.

5. The transformation of human nature. Even though the prophets were preachers of repentance and social reform, it is wrong to think of them as the ancient equivalents of a Martin Luther King, Jr. Their shared dream of a better society was not based on an optimistic reading of *human nature. Rather, they saw human beings as fundamentally flawed, with *sin engraved on the tablets of their hearts (Jer. 17:1). Just as Ethiopians and leopards could not change the colour of their skins, so human beings could not change their sinful nature (Jer. 13:23). Often the prophets declared that the people had become so corrupt that not even famous, righteous individuals would be able to intercede successfully

on their behalf (Jer. 15:1; Ezek. 14:14–21). The people were beyond hope and judgment could not ultimately be averted. This was a common theme of the later prophets, those who prophesied immediately before and during the exile. But even in earlier times it was predicted that God's divorce of the incorrigible Israel would be followed by a new 'honeymoon' in the desert, in which the new bride would be given righteousness as a dowry (Hos. 2:19). Jeremiah and Ezekiel shared the conviction that human effort could never suffice to save Israel; its heart was too corrupt. What was needed was a heart transplant, the gift of a new heart which had Yahweh's Torah written all over it (Jer. 31:33; Ezek. 36:26–27). Nothing less than a transformation of human nature was required.

6. Restoration of Israel. The restoration of Israel is a pervasive theme in the prophetic literature. Not only will God judge his people and chasten them; afterwards he will restore them to their land, from which they have been uprooted and exiled (Hos. 3:5; Amos 9:14; Jer. 3:18). 'Building' and 'planting' are two of the key terms used to describe this restoration (Jer. 1:10; Amos 9:15).

7. Universalism. Since Yahweh is the great Creator of all human beings, he is concerned not only for the future of his people Israel, but also for that of the nations. In each of the major prophetic books much space is devoted to judgment oracles against the nations (Is. 13 – 23; Jer. 46 – 51; Ezek. 26 – 32), and many of the minor prophets include this universalistic theme in their teaching (Joel 2 – 3; Amos 1 – 2; Obad.; Hab. 1 – 3; Nah. 1 – 3; Zeph. 3; Zech. 9 – 14). But the prophets predict salvation as well as judgment for the nations. Astonishingly, the Assyrians and Egyptians, as well as the Israelites, will one day be called Yahweh's 'people' (Is. 19:19–25). *Jonah's message of salvation for Nineveh tempers Nahum's message of doom.

8. A new age preceded by judgment. When read collectively, many of the prophets' judgment oracles against nations point not only to a temporal judgment but also to an *eschatological, universal judgment. Similarly the concept of the Day of Yahweh sometimes signifies a temporal manifestation of Yahweh's judgment, but within the broader context of prophetic literature it becomes almost a technical term for a final manifestation of judgment and salvation.

Many metaphors are used for judgment: cosmic disasters (Is. 13:10; Joel 2:30–31); natural disasters such as earthquakes (Joel 2:10), storms (Zeph. 1:15) and locust plagues (Joel 2:1–11); spiritual disasters such as a famine of Yahweh's word (Amos 8:11–12); personal disasters such as the loss of an only child (Zech. 12:10) or an encounter with a wild beast (Amos 5:19). The most common image is that of a final battle in which Yahweh destroys his enemies and establishes a new world order (Joel 3:1–17; Ezek. 38 – 39; Zech. 14:1–15). The prophetic vision of the new age includes the following features: the preeminence of the *temple, which as the symbol of God's presence becomes the source of all life (Ezek. 40 – 48; Joel 3:18); the leadership of a new *David, a just king who will exercise Yahweh's perfect rule (Hos. 3:5; Amos 9:11–12; Is. 11:1–10; Jer. 30:3–22; Ezek. 34:23–25); the renewal of nature, described in terms of new heavens and a new earth (Is. 65:17) or a return to Edenic conditions (Ezek. 36:35; 47:1–12); the forgiveness of sin and a transformed human nature marked by the desire to do Yahweh's will (Jer. 31:31–34; Ezek. 36:25–28).

9. Messiah. The victory in the final eschatological battle is achieved by a Messianic figure, who is the final fulfilment of the prediction in Genesis 3:15. The seed of the woman will struggle with the seed of the deceiving *serpent, and will finally overcome it. The new age will be inaugurated by the crushing of the serpent (Is. 27:1). A regal 'David' will conquer the forces of *evil in a final battle. A great warrior, he will slay the wicked with the breath of his mouth (Is. 11:4) and set up a universal *kingdom (Mic. 5:4; Is. 9:6–7). Yet he will also be weak and will suffer: he will be like a tender plant (Is. 53:1), like a shoot out of dry ground (Is. 53:2), a man who suffers intense pain (Is. 53:3), a man who is 'pierced' (Is. 53:5; Zech. 12:10), an exalted figure coming in the clouds of heaven but yet also like a mere human being (Dan. 7:13). The tension between the predictions of conquering king and suffering servant is not resolved in the prophetic books. The NT resolves it in Jesus Christ. He has smitten the serpent's head by being himself smitten. Whereas OT prophecy looked forward to one Day of the Lord, the NT divides this event into two phases: 1. a day of forgiveness and reconciliation during which Jesus atones for sins by his death, and

2. a coming day of judgment when the regal Christ will return to the earth. The inauguration of the first phase is the beginning of the end; hence the urgency of the NT's message.

The canonical place of the prophets

The position of the prophetic books in the overall arrangement of the Christian Bible emphasizes the prophetic hope for the future and consequently imparts to the entire OT a note of eager anticipation. To explain this point it is necessary to describe the differences between the first three-quarters of the Christian Bible (the OT) and the Jewish Bible, sometimes called the TaNaK. (TaNaK is an acronym based on the first letter of the Hebrew name for each section: T = *Torah* [Law], N = *Nevi'im* [Prophets], K = *Ketuvim* [Writings].) These two collections of sacred books are identical in content, but are organized differently. The arrangement of the TaNaK, which was most likely the Bible of Jesus, clearly predated that of the OT. It was probably as follows: *Torah* (5 books: Gen., Exod., Lev., Num., Deut.); *Nevi'im* (8 books: Josh., Judg., 1–2 Sam., 1–2 Kgs., Jer., Ezek., Is., the 'Twelve' [the minor prophets in one book]; *Ketuvim* (11 books: Ruth, Ps., Job, Prov., Eccles., Song, Lam., Dan., Est., Ezra-Neh., Chr.). This arrangement produces only twenty-four books, but more importantly it imposes a hermeneutical framework on the literature. This framework makes the Torah central and combines history and prophecy in a second section. It resembles a temple with the *Torah* occupying the Holy of Holies, the *Nevi'im* the sanctuary proper and the *Ketuvim* the outer court. The arrangement of the Jewish scriptures therefore points to the hermeneutical dominance of the Torah and imparts to them a fundamentally ethical orientation.

Textual evidence suggests that Christian scribes transmitting the Greek translation of the Hebrew Bible probably made changes in the arrangement of the books in order to show more clearly the conceptual link between the ancient scriptures and the NT documents. (They also may have adopted an already existing, different arrangement which suited their purposes.) Not only are there more books in the OT (39 instead of 24); the sequence is different. Like the TaNaK, the OT has three sections. Law and history point to the past (17 books: Gen., Exod., Lev., Num.,

Deut., Josh., Judg., Ruth, 1 Sam., 2 Sam., 1 Kgs., 2 Kgs., 1 Chr., 2 Chr., Ezra, Neh., Est.), poetry to the present (5 books: Job, Ps., Prov., Eccles., Song.), and prophecy to the future (17 books: Is., Jer., Lam., Ezek., Dan., Hos. – Mal. [12 books]). In this radically altered sequence, the writing prophets are a distinct section and are placed prominently at the end of the canon, while the law is placed with the historical books. The new arrangement may be likened not to a temple but to an arrow. The base of the projectile is the law and historical books, the shaft the poetic books, and the tip (pointing to the future) the prophetic books. The ethical orientation of the Hebrew Bible has been replaced by an eschatological one (J. Barton, *Oracles of God*, pp. 16–29). The placing of the apocalyptic book of Daniel as the fourth of the major prophets reinforces this orientation. Thus the announcement at the beginning of the NT that the time is fulfilled and that the kingdom of God is near (Matt. 3:1; Mark 1:15) indicates that the events described in the NT are the fulfilment of the OT *hope. The end of the OT (prophecy) and the beginning of the NT (fulfilment) complement each other perfectly.

Bibliography

J. Barton, *Oracles of God: Perceptions of Prophecy in Israel after the Exile* (London, 1985); T. Collins, *The Mantle of Elijah* (Sheffield, 1993); D. Gowan, *Theology of the Prophetic Books: The Death and Resurrection of Israel* (Louisville, 1998); A. J. Heschel, *The Prophets* (New York, 1962); K. Koch, 'Is Daniel also among the prophets?' *Int* 39. 1985, pp. 117–130; G. von Rad, *Old Testament Theology*, vol. 2 (ET, Edinburgh and New York, 1962); H. Ridderbos, *The Coming of the Kingdom* (Philadelphia, 1962); C. Westermann, *Basic Forms of Prophetic Speech* (ET, London and Philadelphia, 1967).

S. DEMPSTER

SYNOPTIC GOSPELS

Although it is of great importance to give full heed to the distinctiveness of each Synoptic Gospel, it is clear that they share not only a common framework but also a basic theological perspective. To a considerable extent, of course, this may be explained as the result of the literary interdependence of the documents. But they also represent a single *gospel, and each includes its core elements. Not without reason did the early church refer to the (one) Gospel *according* to *Matthew, *Mark and *Luke, rather than to three Gospels. The theological perspective common to these foundational documents may be summarized under a few main headings.

The dawning of the kingdom of God

The main theme of the Synoptic Gospels is found in *Jesus' announcement that the long-awaited promise concerning the *kingdom of God is coming to fulfilment in and through his own ministry and mission. This contrasts with the main theme of the Gospel of John, the announcement of the gift of life/eternal life. Like the epistles of the NT, John focuses on the fruit of the kingdom of God rather than upon the message of the dawning of the kingdom *per se*.

The prominence of the theme of the kingdom of God in Mark (where the phrase occurs 13 times) and Luke (32 times) is obvious. While Matthew uses the phrase 'kingdom of God' in four passages, he prefers the equivalent 'kingdom of heaven' (32 occurrences) as a circumlocution, reflecting Jewish sensitivity to the use of the name 'God'. Thus Matthew regularly substitutes 'heaven' for 'God' when he takes up the phrase from Mark. The equivalence of 'kingdom of God' and 'kingdom of heaven' can be seen from the use of the phrases consecutively in the parallel lines of Matthew 19:23–24.

In the Synoptic narratives, it is *John the Baptist who first announces the imminent arrival of the kingdom (Matt. 3:2). This message is taken up by Jesus at the very beginning of his ministry according to Mark 1:15: 'The time is fulfilled, and the kingdom of God is at hand' (RSV) (*cf.* Matt. 4:17; Luke 4:43). From that time onwards the whole ministry of Jesus – his words as well as his deeds – relates in one way or another, implicitly if not explicitly, to the announcement of the dawning of the kingdom. His deeds manifest the kingdom; his words define it. The result is that the present dawning of the kingdom (the gospel, or 'good news', of the kingdom, as Matthew calls it [4:23; 9:35; 24:14]) serves as a hermeneutical key for understanding the Synoptic Gospels. For example, it explains the character of Jesus' ethical teaching, which may be understood only as the ethics of the kingdom.

The kingdom of God is not to be understood as a realm so much as a state or condition that can be described as the experienced rule or reign of God. That reign has not only 'drawn near' (the literal meaning of *engizō*), but is said to be already present: 'If it is by the finger of God that I cast out demons, then the kingdom of God has come [the literal meaning of *phthanō*] upon you' (Luke 11:20; Matt. 12:28). This emphasis on the presence of the kingdom is a recurring element in the narratives (*e.g.* Matt. 11:2–6; 13:16–17; 22:1–10; Mark 2:19; Luke 4:16–21; 17:20–21; 19:9).

Fulfilment of the promises of Scripture

All three Synoptic writers are excited by the fact that the fulfilment of the OT scriptures has taken place. The stress on fulfilment is more prominent in Matthew and Luke than it is in Mark. Even Mark, however, stresses fulfilment at the beginning of the story (Mark 1:15) and at its climax: 'But let the scriptures be fulfilled' (Mark 14:49). Mark frequently quotes the OT (*e.g.* 1:2–3; 7:6–7; 12:10–11; 14:27).

Matthew's stress on the fulfilment of the scriptures, by means of his famous 'fulfilment formula' quotations (1:22–23; 2:15; 2:17–18; 2:23; 4:14–16.; 8:17; 12:17–21; 13:35; 21:4–5; 27:9–10; *cf.* 13:14–15; 26:56), is the most frequent and striking among those of the Synoptic writers. It is clear that for Matthew what God had promised in the scriptures of *Israel has come to pass in Jesus Christ. The same must be said for Luke. In addition to the remarkable story of Jesus' reading Isaiah 61:1–2 in the synagogue and then announcing 'Today this scripture has been fulfilled in your hearing' (Luke 4:21), Luke at the end of his narrative puts great stress on the fact that what has been described in his narrative is the fulfilment of the scriptures. In 24:27, at the end of the story concerning the Emmaus disciples, Luke states that 'beginning with Moses and all the prophets, he interpreted to them in all the scriptures the things concerning himself'. A few lines later Jesus says to the disciples, 'These are my words which I spoke to you, while I was still with you, that everything written about me in the law of Moses and the prophets and the psalms must be fulfilled' (24:44). The last words are probably a deliberate allusion to the three parts of the Old Testament canon: the Law; the Prophets; and the Writings.

Future eschatology

For all the emphasis in the Synoptic Gospels on the presence of the kingdom and the fulfilment of the promises of the OT, there is at the same time a recognition that not *all* the promises have been fulfilled, and that the end of the present age has not yet come. In other words, the kingdom has come, but in mystery, or veiled form, visible only to those who believe in the message of Jesus (*cf.* Matt. 13:11; Luke 17:21). The wicked have not yet been *judged; the righteous do not yet enjoy the wholeness of *salvation that is to be theirs. The fulfilment brought by Jesus accordingly involves an overlap of the ages; the new has begun, but the old has not yet passed away. God's purposes have been fulfilled, but not consummated. Thus the Jesus who announces the presence of the kingdom can also teach his disciples to pray, 'Thy kingdom come' (Matt. 6:10). Matthew addresses the problem of the present form of the kingdom, which involves a delay in judgment, in his collection of parables in chapter 13.

Each of the Synoptic Gospels, unlike John, has an *eschatological discourse that deals with the future. The exegesis of the discourses presents a challenge to interpreters. We may say at least that at the core of each version of the discourse is a strongly apocalyptic expectation focusing on the return of the Son of Man (Mark 13:24–27; Matt. 24:29–31; Luke 21:25–28), with strong motifs of judgment. The writers are confident of a final denouement, despite the fact that its date cannot be known, and are therefore convinced of the need for constant preparedness.

The centrality of the passion

One of the most remarkable features of the Synoptic Gospels is the primacy given to the passion narrative. Nearly half of each Gospel is devoted to the story of Jesus' death. The Gospels have appropriately been described as passion narratives with extended introductions. A major turning point at approximately the middle of each narrative is the confession of Peter concerning the identity of Jesus as the Messiah and the immediately following announcement of the death of Jesus (Mark 8:31; Matt. 16:21; Luke 9:22). This first prediction of the passion is followed by two more (Mark 9:30–32; 10:32–34; Matt. 17:22–23; 20:17–19; Luke 9:43–45; 18:31–34), so that each Gospel has a threefold announcement of its central event. Since the common expectation was that the Messiah would come as a triumphant king, a great shift in understanding was required by the idea of a Messiah who must suffer and die.

At the heart of the story of Jesus, then, is neither the teaching nor the *healings he performed, but the cross. Jesus came not mainly to teach or to heal but to die as a sacrifice (*cf.* Mark 10:45; Matt. 20:28). Far from being a tragic accident of history, the death of Jesus fulfils the will of God (*e.g.* Mark 14:49; Matt. 26:24; Luke 24:26, 46). On the mount of transfiguration the conversation is devoted to Jesus' 'departure, which he was to accomplish at Jerusalem' (Luke 9:31). The word translated 'departure' is the Greek word *exodos*, which literally means 'Exodus', and thus contains an allusion to the *redemptive work to be accomplished by the death of Jesus. At the last supper Jesus, referring to his imminent death, says, 'This is my blood of the covenant which is poured out for many [Matthew adds: 'for the forgiveness of sins']' (Mark 14:24; Matt. 26:28; *cf.* Luke 22:20). (See *Atonement.)

Christology

The Synoptic Gospels share a high Christology, *i.e.* estimate of the person of Jesus. For none of these writers is Jesus merely a wonderful teacher or healer, or even *prophet. He is for them a figure without parallel. Their Christology is conveyed not only through the titles that they assign to Jesus, but also indirectly through the whole of their narratives, where Jesus is consistently portrayed as possessing an unparalleled authority.

It is clear that for all three writers Jesus is the Messiah (Mark 8:29; Matt. 16:16; Luke 9:20). This Messiah is, as expected, the Son of David, but he is also paradoxically David's Lord, and thus more than a human Messiah (Mark 12:35–37; Matt. 22:41–45; Luke 20:41–44). He is uniquely the Son of God, enjoying a unique relationship with his Father (see especially Matt. 11:25–27; Luke 10:21–22; also Matt. 10:32–33; Luke 12:8–9). At times this title is almost an affirmation of deity (*e.g.* Matt. 14:33). He is furthermore the apocalyptic Son of Man of Daniel 7:13, a quasi-divine figure. Jesus is often addressed as *kyrios*, 'Lord', which has a range of meanings in the Synoptic Gospels, from a reverential

'Sir' to a divine figure who calls forth worship (*e.g.* Matt. 14:30, 33). Matthew can refer to Jesus as 'Emmanuel', that is, 'God with us' (Matt. 1:23), a title which his church surely understood to mean more than merely 'representative of God'. To the risen Lord, of course, divine power and authority are readily ascribed (Matt. 28:18).

In the Synoptic Gospels, Jesus is best described as the unique representative or agent of God, who stands so close to God that he assumes a quasi-divine status. Pre-existence is not yet consciously articulated, however; nor is there a doctrine of incarnation or outright reference to Jesus as God, such as are found in the Gospel of John. The Christology of the Synoptics, nevertheless, may be said to be on the same high trajectory, so that it verges on that of John. Given the relatively late date of these Gospels (compared, for example, to that of the Pauline letters), it is a tribute to the authors' exercise of historical control that the Christology of the Synoptics is so restrained.

Salvation for the Gentiles

Jesus comes into an exclusively Jewish context, proclaiming the gospel of the kingdom exclusively to Jews. He brings the fulfilment of the promises to Israel in the Jewish scriptures. Matthew delights in emphasizing this point to his Jewish readers (*cf.* 10:5–8; 15:24). But in all three Synoptics the mission to the Gentiles is on the horizon even in the ministry of Jesus, and the writers stress the universal significance of Jesus' mission.

Despite the express limitation of the proclamation of the gospel to the Jews in Matthew, the Gentiles are already in view in the magi of 2:1–12, the centurion of 8:5–13, and the Canaanite woman of 15:21–28. The limitation was only temporary, as the statements in 24:14 and 28:19 indicate. Mark and Luke were written with Gentile readers in mind, so it is not surprising that they too have the universal proclamation of the gospel in view (Mark 13:10; *cf.* 11:17; Luke 24:47). This comes to expression in Luke's second volume, most impressively in the missionary work of Paul. (See *Nations.)

The importance of faith

Often unnoticed is the importance of *faith in the Synoptic Gospels. The two words 'faith' and 'believe', which come from the same root in the Greek language, occur frequently. The first words of Jesus according to Mark call for faith: 'The time is fulfilled, and the kingdom of God is at hand; repent, and believe in the gospel' (Mark 1:15). Throughout the Synoptic narratives Jesus calls for faith, from those who would be healed and from those who would be his disciples (*e.g.* Mark 5:36; 9:23; Matt. 9:28; Luke 8:50). To those who are healed Jesus says that their faith has made them whole (*e.g.* Mark 5:34; 10:52; Luke 7:50; 17:19; *cf.* Matt. 9:29; 21:22). Jesus instructs his disciples to 'have faith in God' (Mark 11:22) and the disciples ask Jesus to increase their faith (Luke 17:5).

This emphasis on faith provides important continuity between the Gospels and the letters of Paul. Both call for a turning from one's own resources to trust in the grace of God. Though not altogether lacking in Matthew and Mark (since the kingdom is itself a gift of God's grace brought to the unworthy), this motif of salvation by faith comes to clearest articulation in the parable of the prodigal son in Luke 15:11–32, and in the remarkable statement of Jesus in Luke 18:14 that the tax collector rather than the Pharisee 'went down to his house justified'. The verb here is *dikaioō*, a word used frequently by Paul in his articulation of the gospel.

Bibliography

L. Goppelt, *Theology of the New Testament*, vol. 1 (Grand Rapids, 1981); G. E. Ladd, *A Theology of the New Testament*, rev. D. A. Hagner (Grand Rapids and Cambridge, 1993, 1994).

D. A. HAGNER

LUKE-ACTS

Introduction

These two canonical books constitute the largest collection of NT material written by any NT author. Traditionally ascribed to Luke, the volumes are probably from the hand of one of Paul's companions, though this has been disputed recently. (For the debate and a defence of Lukan authorship, see D. L. Bock, *Luke 1:1 – 9:51*, BECNT [Grand Rapids, 1994], pp. 4–7.) These volumes are the only NT works that explicitly link the life of *Jesus to the origins of the early *church.

What is Luke trying to do in these two

volumes? He is in a new religious movement that is part of a culture which values its rich, ancient heritage more than innovation. He is in a movement that claims to have its roots in Jewish *hope but which is receiving a hostile reaction from Jews and is becoming increasingly more Gentile. He is in a movement that claims to originate with the one true *God and yet has a leader who was crucified. How can he explain all this and reassure members like Theophilus (Luke 1:3–4) that they belong in this movement and that it is really from God? Luke-Acts attempts to explain how God has acted in the life of Jesus and the early church to do a work he promised long ago in the OT scriptures (Luke 24:44–49). Two key elements make up the bulk of Luke's case: the life of Jesus and the gift of the *Holy Spirit. Given who Jesus is and what he does from his *exalted place at God's right hand, Theophilus and other readers of Luke-Acts can know that the message of *forgiveness and inclusion the church preaches is a genuine message of *salvation sent from God.

Why a hyphen in Luke-Acts?

Though separated in the canon (because *Luke is a gospel and *Acts is not), Luke-Acts clearly should be seen as a united work. This unity is signalled in Acts 1:1, when the author refers to Luke as 'the first book'. Luke overlaps with the beginning of Acts; both tell the story of the ascension. The key theme of the Messiah as the bringer of messianic *blessing in the gift of the Spirit runs through both volumes (Luke 3:15–17; Acts 10 – 11). Finally, the use of geography in both volumes reveals their unity. The movement from *Jerusalem to Galilee, back to Jerusalem, and then from Samaria to the ends of the earth shows how the gospel has moved beyond the nation of *Israel to encompass all humanity (Acts 1:8; Luke 3:4–6; Is. 40:3–5; Ps. 72:8). This point is important for biblical theological reasons. The volumes were intended to be read as containing one story and a unified theological argument.

Key themes

God's activity in fulfilment

Dominating Luke-Acts from the beginning is an emphasis on how the events of Jesus' life and that of the church result from the divine initiative and realize the divine promise. In the very first verse, Luke speaks of 'events fulfilled among us'. Luke 1 – 2 presents the births of John the Baptist and Jesus in a style reminiscent of Jewish Scripture and using many citations and allusions to the history of Israel. Everything about these opening chapters, which form a prologue to the two volumes, tells the story in a way that declares that God is again at work in a powerful way. Whether through the invoking of prophetic hope or the acknowledgment of recurring patterns of divine activity, Luke proclaims and explains how God is powerfully at work again. Even the *suffering of Jesus and the early community are explained in these terms, so that Luke-Acts is preaching, apologetic and theodicy. How can God's people suffer as the church does? Is not that suffering really a sign of God's judgment and rejection of their claim? Luke asserts that suffering was part of God's design from the start. Whether in the announcement that the Son of Man must suffer in Jerusalem, or in the accounts of the persecution of leaders like Peter and the career of Paul, the narrative makes clear that suffering is a key part of God's plan (Luke 9:22, 44; 17:25; 18:32–33; 24:7, 46; Acts 4:25–31; 26:15–18).

In addition, the presentation of Jesus' identity is accompanied by references to the ancient Scriptures, whether in citation or allusion. Jesus is the Son (Ps. 2:7; Luke 3:21–22). He is the one at the right hand of God (Ps. 110:1; Luke 20:41–44; 22:69; Acts 2:30–36). He is the rejected stone that is none the less exalted (Ps. 118:22; Luke 20:17; Acts 4:11). He is to be the returning Son of Man (Dan. 7:13–14; Luke 21:27). In fact, he is Lord of all, so the gospel can go to all (Luke 20:41–44; Acts 2:30–39; 10:34–43).

That the activity of ministry is a fulfilment of Scripture also emerges in Jesus' answer to John's question in Luke 7:18–22. Here Jesus uses several *eschatological texts from Isaiah to show that his ministry is one of fulfilment and so marks him out as 'the one to come' (Is. 29:18; 35:5–6; 42:18; 26:19; 61:1). The activity and preaching of the early church, including the outreach to Gentiles and the rejection of much of Israel, are also explained in these terms (Acts 2; 3; 10 – 11, 13; 15; 26:12–23).

The Messiah as the bearer of forgiveness and the Spirit

Another key theme running through the two volumes is the offer by Christ to all people of forgiveness and the Spirit. References to forgiveness are linked to related images of the one who comes as the bringer of *peace and the one who leads people out of darkness (Luke 1:76–79; 24:46–47; Acts 13:26–41). The Messiah is the distributor of the Spirit (Luke 3:15–17; Acts 2:30–36; 10 – 11); the gift of the Spirit demonstrates that the inclusion of Gentiles in the messianic blessing results from the divine initiative. John the Baptist identifies the eschatological sign of Messiah's presence as his baptizing 'with Spirit and fire'. Peter's Pentecost address endorses this view: Israel can know that God has made Jesus both Lord and Christ because the promised Spirit has been poured out by Jesus from on high (Luke 24:49; Acts 2:32–34). The gift of the Spirit to Cornelius is the sign that Gentiles have been included in the fullness of messianic blessing (Acts 10:44–48; 11:15–18), a point supported by Luke's account of Paul's ministry. The Spirit is seen as the source of enablement and of direction for the church in its mission, the one through whom Jesus oversees its life (Luke 24:49; Acts 13:1–2).

The response of repentance, reaching out to those outside

Another key theme is that of response to the message, summarized in terms of *repentance or turning. The people of God are called to reach out to those who previously were thought to be excluded from the hope of salvation (Luke 3:8–14; 5:32; Acts 3:19; 5:31; 26:18). Jesus actively pursued outsiders: he taught lepers, tax collectors, immoral people, the blind, the poor, the humble and the lost in general (Luke 1:46–55; 4:16–21; 7:22–50; 15:1–32; 19:1–10). The church's commission is to preach the message of repentance and the forgiveness of sins (Luke 24:47). Eventually even non-Jews were included, as God worked actively to extend his blessing to the end of the earth (Acts 1:8; 10 – 11; 15:14–21; see *Nations).

As the Messiah suffers, so must the church

Yet another interesting theme is how the task and suffering of the Messiah become those of the church. Nothing reveals this more vividly than Paul and Barnabas' defining their ministry in terms of the Servant (Acts 13:47; Is. 49:6). Their activity, like that of the church, is an extension of the work of Jesus, the original

Servant. Thus the rejection of the church by the nation and by the world as it appears in Acts 4:24–30 should not be surprising. This is also a part of the church's call.

A people different from the world

Their reception of God's blessing requires those allied to Jesus to be different from the world. The church is to serve in the world without expecting blessing from others in return (Luke 6:20–49). Their behaviour is to go beyond what sinners do for one another. They are to concern themselves with ministry to people who cannot pay them back (Luke 14:12–14). A glance at the church's ministry in Acts, in which people go to places where they know the reaction will be hostile, shows that this message was taken seriously.

Conclusion

Luke-Acts teaches that God is at work in the new entity called the church. The church has old roots, as it results from God's activity in fulfilment of his ancient promises. Even the death and resurrection of Jesus show that he is now at God's right hand administering the promised blessings, such as the Spirit, which are made available to those who repent and seek his gracious forgiveness. Those who respond can share in the calling and enablement of the messianic Lord and become light to a world that otherwise would not know how to please God.

Bibliography

D. L. Bock, *Proclamation from Prophecy and Pattern: Lukan Old Testament Christology* (Sheffield, 1987); F. Bovon, *Luke the Theologian: Thirty-three Years of Research (1950–1983)* (Allison Park, 1987); P. F. Esler, *Community and Gospel in Luke-Acts* (Cambridge, 1987); I. H. Marshall, *Luke: Historian and Theologian* (Exeter, [3]1988); I. H. Marshall and D. Petersen (eds.), *Witness to the Gospel: The Theology of Acts* (Grand Rapids, 1998); R. F. O'Toole, *The Unity of Luke's Theology: An Analysis of Luke-Acts* (Wilmington, 1984); M. Strauss, *The Davidic Messiah in Luke-Acts: The Promise and Its Fulfillment in Luke's Christology* (Sheffield, 1995); R. C. Tannehill, *The Narrative Unity of Luke-Acts: A Literary Interpretation*, 2 vols. (Philadelphia, 1986, 1990); D. L. Tiede, *Prophecy and History in Luke-Acts* (Philadelphia, 1980); M. M. B. Turner, *Power* from on High: The Spirit in Israel's Restoration and Witness (Sheffield, 1996); J. B. Tyson (ed.), Luke-Acts and the Jewish People: Eight Critical Perspectives (Minneapolis, 1988); J. A. Weatherley, Jewish Responsibility for the Death of Jesus in Luke-Acts (Sheffield, 1994).

D. L. BOCK

THE JOHANNINE WRITINGS

Substantial and independent articles on the contribution made to biblical theology by the three (or five) elements of the Johannine corpus (viz. the Gospel of *John, the three *letters of John, and the *Revelation of John) appear elsewhere in this Dictionary. This article is focused on what may be gleaned from the corpus as a whole. The special contribution of this corpus can be usefully considered under two headings: the biblical-theological significance of the Johannine writings construed as a corpus; and a selection of themes that are found in two or more books of the corpus and that have some importance for biblical theology.

The biblical-theological significance of the Johannine corpus

The Johannine corpus provides us with something unique in the NT. Like the *Pauline corpus, it includes letters; like the *Luke-Acts corpus, it includes a Gospel. Unlike any other, however, it is made up of a Gospel, three letters (two short and in line with common epistolary form, and one apparently a tractate letter), and an apocalypse.

The significance of this diversity turns on several highly contested matters. If there is only diversity among the documents, then the label 'Johannine writings' is nothing more than a flag of convenience imposed by erroneous patristic tradition, and the significance of the documents must be evaluated separately, one by one. But if there is some measure of deep unity or commonality shared by the five documents, then the tension between this unity and their transparent diversity provides invaluable insight into several matters (as we shall see). The extent and nature of this unity, however, are precisely what is contested. There are three overlapping disputes.

1. Authorship. If all five of the Johannine documents were written by separate individuals with minimal connection, or by at least three authors (the three letters sharing one author), then the degree of unity is considerably weakened. More energy will then be spent isolating what is theologically distinctive in each document, than in trying to treat the documents as part of a corpus defined by authorship.

2. Johannine community. Many who deny that the same person wrote the Fourth Gospel, the three letters of John and the book of Revelation, nevertheless argue that all the authors emerged from one 'Johannine school' or 'community'. This is probably the majority view today. It provides a different sort of continuity. It does not so much encourage the integration of 'Johannine theology' grounded in the documents, as an exploration of the diversity from document to document, so that the scholar can attempt to isolate different strands of thought within the ostensible community, and perhaps even reconstruct something of the community's history.

3. History. Apart from the usual debates regarding the dating of each document, not a few scholars insist that the Fourth Gospel tells us little of what happened in the days of *Jesus. Rather, it deploys a theological narrative to deal with problems in the church or community or school that 'John' is addressing towards the end of the 1st century. It may convey some useful pieces of information about the historical Jesus (shards of historical flotsam accidentally cast up, as it were), but its focus is on the church of the ninth or tenth decade. If this view is correct, then the time span ostensibly covered by the Johannine corpus is seriously diminished. Conversely, if the Fourth Gospel, however stylized its presentation and however interested its author may be in addressing readers at the end of the 1st century, is nevertheless a faithful witness to what happened 'back then' in Jesus' time, then the Johannine corpus as a whole spans the first six or seven decades of the church's life.

It is impossible to argue each disputed point here. For the record, in line with the majority view among Christian students during the past two thousand years (though out of step with today's majority), I think it highly probable that John the apostle wrote the Fourth Gospel and the three letters that traditionally bear his name. That he is also the 'John' of Revelation (Rev. 1:4) is plausible but much less certain, though there is certainly some sort of personal connection between this book and the other documents of the Johannine corpus. Even if John hoped for very wide readership of his Gospel (*cf.* R. Bauckham, *The Gospels for All Christians*), he had certain kinds of readers in mind, and his approach was shaped by those readers. Similarly, the three letters presuppose particular pastoral situations in concrete churches; moreover, however disputed the precise historical context of Revelation may be, few doubt that John is dealing with particular churches (Rev. 2 – 3) towards the end of the 1st century, as those churches find themselves in various spiritual, doctrinal and moral conditions but on the verge of systematic Roman persecution.

What we have, then, is a single corpus which takes us from sketches of the very beginning of the ministry of Jesus and the inauguration of the new covenant, through doctrinal and moral conflicts in defined churches, to the last document of what became the New Testament canon, a document that depicts Christianity's growing conflict with the wider world, and in apocalyptic imagery anticipates its ultimate resolution. God himself reigns, and through the triumph of the Lamb introduces the new heaven and the new earth, the home of righteousness.

Thus the Johannine writings constitute a microcosm of early Christianity, and a microcosm of the final defining documents of biblical theology. This is not to say that the Johannine writings are so complete that the rest of the NT is scarcely needed. Indeed, in some ways the themes defined by the Johannine writings are rather restricted; John is given to focusing on a small number of themes in their interplay and complexity, rather than to casting a wide net. In that sense, the Johannine contribution to biblical theology tends to be deep rather than broad. Nevertheless, as the next section shows, themes treated in various ways in the Johannine writings are often connected with emphases in the rest of the canon. Not only are there thematic connections with other NT books, but there are many linkages with the OT that suggest how inner-canonical connections should be drawn.

A selection of themes found in two or more books of the Johannine writings

Among the themes in which the Johannine writings are especially rich is Christology.

Only John directly assigns the title 'the *Word' to Jesus (John 1:1; Rev. 19:13; possibly 1 John 1:1), though very similar theology is found elsewhere (*e.g.* Heb. 1:1–4). Many NT writers find ways of bearing witness to Jesus' uniqueness as a person: he is to be worshipped as *God; he is a perfect *human being, the historical man who is the product of miraculous incarnation (see *e.g.* Phil. 2:5–11). Yet perhaps the Johannine writings are the most insistent on this point. Jesus is directly described or addressed as God (John 1:1; 20:31); he shares the throne of God (Rev. *passim*). Yet he is the Word, God's self-expression, who becomes flesh (John 1:14); he is the *life that was manifested in such a way that people could hear him and see him and touch him (1 John 1:1–4). Moreover, this corpus that so strongly affirms his deity is also the corpus that most strenuously insists on his functional subordination to the Father (*e.g.* John 5:16–30; 8:29; 14:31; Rev. 5), as part of its rich treatment of the 'Son of God' title. Other NT documents insist on the uniqueness of Jesus and his exclusive ability to save lost men and women (Acts 4:12), but the Johannine writings are especially emphatic about this (*e.g.* John 14:6; 1 John *passim*; Rev. 5).

In all five of the Johannine writings there is a formal dualism that sets out fundamental issues with stark clarity. The polarities of this dualism (*light and darkness, *truth and lie, from above and from below, *faith/*obedience and unbelief/disobedience) are unambiguously present in the Fourth Gospel, become tied to crucial pastoral and ecclesiastical issues in the Johannine letters, and then take on apocalyptic overtones in Revelation. In the latter book, the contest between good and *evil includes new polarities: *Babylon and the new *Jerusalem; the whore and the bride of the *Lamb; the mark of the beast and the mark of the Lamb. In no case does the dualism of the Johannine writings jeopardize the sovereignty of the one God; Johannine dualism never becomes ontological dualism. But its stark antitheses convey one supreme benefit. Though they cannot deal very adequately with the shadings of good and evil and with the confusion of ambiguity, they absolutely forbid the fuzzy thinking and relativism that are characteristic of our age. In short, they identify and highlight the content of the fundamental issues.

Among those who study the NT it is a commonplace that there is a running, complementary tension between rejoicing in what God has already done through Christ (realized *eschatology) and anticipating what God will finally do through Christ (futurist eschatology). The subtleties and shadings of the various emphases found in the NT are reflected, in various ways, within the Johannine writings. With its emphasis on eternal life secured *now* by faith, the Fourth Gospel falls on the side of realized eschatology. Nevertheless, it looks forward to the time when the Son of God will raise the dead on the last day (5:21, 25; 6:39–40). While not denying that there is an ultimate antichrist, 1 John insists that many antichrists have already gone out into the world, a fact which proves that it is already the 'last hour' (2:18). On the other hand, even though the Revelation of John teaches the whole church to look to God's final triumph and to cry in anticipation, 'Come, Lord Jesus' (Rev. 22:20), that futurist eschatological stance is intended to teach believers to be faithful and persevering now.

Especially strong in the Gospel and first letter of John, though not absent elsewhere, is the emphasis on faith. More precisely, John's emphasis is on believing rather than faith; he avoids the noun, and uses the verb lavishly. Despite blunt antitheses (*e.g.* John 3:36; 1 John 5:1–5), John is not naïve; he is fully aware of the dangers of spurious faith, and does his best to warn against them, as he is also aware of the dangers of spurious *love (1 John 3:16–20). In such passages he reminds us of James. Nevertheless, John 5:24 ('I tell you the truth, whoever hears my word and believes him who sent me has eternal life and will not be condemned; he has crossed over from death to life', NIV) has strong connections with the Pauline formulation of justification by grace through faith.

John's teaching regarding the *Holy Spirit, while it frequently overlaps with emphases found elsewhere in the NT, embraces several noteworthy features. Some of these have more to do with the distinctiveness of the formulation than with the uniqueness of the thought. Only John refers to the Holy Spirit as the 'Paraclete' (John 14 – 16, 'Counsellor'), whose task it is to call to mind and unfold all that Jesus taught, along with its significance; to convict the world of sin and righteousness and judgment; to be with and in the disciples, substituting for Jesus after his departure. Implicitly, of course, this latter point suggests that Jesus is the first 'Paraclete', which is explicitly affirmed in 1 John 2:1–2. 1 John makes a further contribution by insisting that all believers have received an 'anointing' (2:24–27), almost certainly a reference to the Holy Spirit. Some have linked this 'anointing' with what Paul regards as the witness of the Spirit (Rom. 8:15–16), though arguably in the context of the Johannine letters the anointing of the Holy Spirit is not some quasi-independent 'witness' but is manifest precisely in the teaching and conduct which (John insists) invariably attend true believers. References to the Spirit in Revelation are sparser. Either they are rather casual (*e.g.* Rev. 1:10), or they abound in subtle symbolism. For instance, at least some of the 'seven spirits' references may in fact refer to the Holy Spirit (*e.g.* Rev. 1:4), though admittedly the point is disputed.

The Johannine writings are rich in the theme of persecution, *i.e.* in picturing the people of God as necessarily facing some opposition from a world that does not know God, not least because this is the way the Master went. Although the treatments of the theme in the Fourth Gospel have their own flavour (*e.g.* John 15:18–25), they have their Synoptic counterparts (*e.g.* Matt. 10). In 1 and 2 John, the dominant opposition springs from a group that had once belonged to the church but had abandoned it, apparently in favour of some proto-gnostic heresy. Such a stance aligns the seceders with 'the *world', about which nothing good can be said (1 John 2:15–17). Of course, John recognizes that the very vigilance he commends with respect to dangerous heresies and unchristian conduct may become an excuse in the hands of some to build little exclusivistic ecclesiastical empires, and this he roundly condemns and seeks to expose (3 John). But the Johannine writing that devotes most sustained thought to the status of the people of God as targets for the wrath of the dragon and of his associated beasts is Revelation. However the book is interpreted, it is recognized to be a sustained encouragement to believers to be faithful to the end, in the assurance that God is in control, not Rome or any other pagan or satanic empire.

The two largest books of the Johannine corpus make important contributions to the biblical-theological theme of *worship. When they cross over from the pages of the OT to the pages of the NT, worship terminology and emphases shift, on the whole, from a focus on the tabernacle/temple, the sacrificial system, priestly mediation, and prescribed feasts and fasts, to the uniqueness and finality of Jesus' *sacrifice, and with it a corresponding enlargement of horizons. Worship is no longer bound up with the ancient temple cultus and priestly system, still less with an activity restricted to Sunday mornings; rather, it embraces all of life, as Christians learn to offer themselves to God as a continuing living sacrifice, so that everything they do is done to the glory of God. The Fourth Gospel contributes substantially to this development. Jesus insists that the true worshippers whom the Father seeks, in this new 'hour', are no longer tied to Jerusalem and its temple (or to any other geographical site), but worship him 'in spirit and in truth'. This expression means much more than 'sincerely'. Not only is the locus no longer constrained by the requirements of the Mosaic covenant, but true worship will be bound up with the 'truth', the truth of the revelation that has come exclusively through Jesus, through him who is 'the truth' (14:6). The worship theme in Revelation is sometimes subtle and sometimes explicit. Certainly John is implicitly inviting his readers to participate in the worship songs of heaven (e.g. 1:7; 4:11; 5:9–10, 12, 13; 11:15, 17–18; 12:10–12; 15:3–4; 19:1–3, 5, 6–8), singing that becomes for them not only God-centred adoration but a confession of God's sovereignty and of eschatological confidence. It is not for nothing that from Revelation 5 these hymns are devoted 'to him who sits on the throne and to the Lamb'.

Although some have argued that the Fourth Gospel depicts the death of Jesus solely in revelatory terms and with little grasp of such central NT themes as substitution and expiation, this view is clearly mistaken, as many have recognized. The presentation of Jesus Christ as substitutionary sacrifice in the Fourth Gospel is necessarily set forth in symbol-laden categories, as befits the pre-resurrection setting, but it is no less compelling for that. For instance, in John 6 Jesus is the bread of life. In the first century, bread was one of two staple foods: one either ate bread, or one died. Moreover, in an agrarian society everyone knew that virtually everything that human beings eat is the husk of what has died, whether meat or fish or barley or corn. So when Jesus

says that he is the true bread from heaven who gives his life for the life of the world (6:51), he means that either he dies or we do, and unless he dies and we 'eat' him we will never have eternal life. Here, then, is substitution of the most rigorous kind. In John 10 Jesus is the good shepherd who gives his life for the sheep. In John 11, God providentially talks through Caiaphas so that the high priest speaks better than he knows; it is indeed better 'that one man die for the people' (11:50–51). However flexible the background of 'lamb of God' language (1:29), the Fourth Gospel as a whole surely indicates that Jesus is a sacrificial lamb. Small wonder, then, that in Revelation the vision of Revelation 4 – 5 figures so prominently. The only person who is capable of bringing about God's purposes for blessing and judgment (symbolized by the scroll in his right hand) is the lion who is also the lamb, who emerges from the very throne of God. The symbolism depicts him as simultaneously a warrior-lamb (the seven horns, indicating perfection of kingly authority) and a slaughtered sacrifice, brutally slain yet now alive. The whole of Revelation could be titled 'The Triumph of the Lamb'. 1 John shows that Christian assurance (5:13) is tied at least in part to transformed conduct and belief, but here too the fundamental *ground* of human acceptability before God is never human conduct, but 'Jesus Christ, the Righteous One', who is the propitiation for our sins (1 John 2:1–2).

Finally, something must be said of the use of the OT Scriptures in the Johannine corpus. John's Gospel cites the OT much less frequently than does Matthew. The Johannine letters never quote the OT, and refer to only one OT figure (viz. Cain, 1 John 3:12). The book of Revelation is almost as sparing of direct quotations. Yet to say only this is to say far too little. Although the word 'covenant' occurs only once in the entire Johannine corpus, it has been shown that its thought (especially that of the Gospel) is profoundly covenantal (J. Pryor, *John*). Moreover, whether or not John's Gospel quotes the OT on each point, it takes enormous pains to portray Jesus as the antitype of the temple, the manna, the great feasts of Israel, and more. 1 John makes telling use of Jeremiah 31 and related passages (for details, see *Johannine Letters). And Revelation, for all that it is reluctant to quote the OT extensively, is saturated with the OT. Scarcely a verse is free from OT allusions or echoes. Sometimes merely the OT language is picked up; sometimes John constructs his argument to show that what he sees in visionary form is the fulfilment of OT anticipation. In short, scrupulous study of the use of antecedent Scripture in the Johannine writings contributes to a grasp not only of Johannine theology, but also of the ways in which the biblical documents cohere and depend on one another, and thus of genuinely *biblical* (*i.e.* 'whole bible') theology.

Bibliography

C. K. Barrett, *The Gospel According to St. John* (London and Philadelphia, ²1978); R. Bauckham, *The Climax of Prophecy: Studies on the Book of Revelation* (Edinburgh, 1993); *idem* (ed.), *The Gospels for All Christians: Rethinking the Gospel Audiences* (Grand Rapids, 1998); G. K. Beale, *The Book of Revelation*, NIGTC (Grand Rapids and Carlisle, 1999); R. E. Brown, *The Community of the Beloved Disciple* (New York, 1979); D. A. Carson, 'John and the Johannine Epistles', in D. A. Carson and H. G. M. Williamson (eds.), *It Is Written: Scripture Citing Scripture* (Cambridge, 1988); D. A. Carson, L. Morris and D. J. Moo, *An Introduction to the New Testament* (Grand Rapids and Leicester, 1992); J. M. Lieu, *The Theology of the Johannine Epistles*, NTT (Cambridge, 1991); L. Morris, *Jesus Is the Christ: Studies in the Theology of John* (Grand Rapids, 1989); D. G. Peterson, *Engaging with God* (Leicester, 1992); J. Pryor, John: *Evangelist of the Covenant People* (London, 1992); D. M. Smith, *Johannine Christianity: Essays on its Setting, Sources, and Theology* (Columbia, 1984); D. G. Vanderlip, *Christianity According to John* (Philadelphia, 1975).

D. A. CARSON

PAUL

Introduction

The contribution of Paul of Tarsus to biblical theology is immense. Called by *God through the dramatic Damascus Road experience to be 'apostle to the Gentiles', Paul engaged in a missionary career celebrated in the latter part of the book of *Acts. Thirteen of the letters Paul wrote during that missionary career have become books of the Bible. He therefore contributes more to the NT than any other writer except Luke, who is himself something of a disciple of Paul. But more important than the quantity of the material is its significance. Used by the Lord to open up the Gentile world to the gospel, Paul hammered out his teachings in the midst of change and controversy. The first Christians make up a Jewish messianic sect. By the time the NT period comes to an end, Christianity is a worldwide, Gentile-dominated religion. Paul is in no small measure responsible for that transformation. Indeed, Paul has been called the 'second founder' of Christianity and even by some the true founder of Christianity. This, however, is a gross overestimate. For all his pioneering theological thinking, Paul himself insisted that he was dependent on a tradition of apostolic teaching that existed before his time (*e.g.* 1 Cor. 15:1–11). And his dependence on the teaching of *Jesus is greater than many have been willing to recognize (see particularly D. Wenham, *Paul: Follower of Jesus or Founder of Christianity?*). Nevertheless, Paul remains a gigantic figure, whose impact on the history of theology is probably greater than that of any other biblical author.

In this brief introductory survey we will begin with some comments on the theological significance of Paul personally, and then move on to an examination of the theology of his letters.

The theological significance of the person of Paul

Paul and eschatology

Paul's theological significance owes a great deal to the pivotal role God called him to play in the incorporation of Gentiles into the people of God. While Luke tells us that God initially called Paul to minister to both Jews and Gentiles (Acts 9:15), and Paul never abandoned his work among Jews (Acts 28:17–23), he soon focused his work on Gentiles (Gal. 2:1–10). He not only opened up several vital mission fields (southern Asia Minor, Macedonia, Achaia, the province of Asia), but he also developed, as need arose, theological categories that would explain and give guidance to the many Gentiles that he converted. Paul is justly remembered as *the* 'apostle to the Gentiles'. (See *Nations.)

But several scholars, most notably Johannes Munck, think Paul's view of his personal significance goes much farther. On their view, Paul saw himself as an *eschatological figure, whose ministry to the Gentiles would actually usher in the final kingdom of God. Paul, so these scholars argue, found in the prophets predictions that God's final restoration of Israel would cause Gentiles to flock to Jerusalem in worship of the true God (*e.g.* Is. 60:1–7). Paul, however, found matters to be working out differently: Jews were largely rejecting the gospel, while Gentiles were flocking into the church. So he revised the eschatological sequence: now, he believed, God was using him to bring Gentile converts as an 'offering' to Jerusalem so that Jews would be stimulated to repent, and thus the end would come. (Rom. 9 – 11 and 15:17–20 are cited in support of this view.)

We can agree that Paul is, indeed, an eschatological figure, remembering that 'eschatology' is rightly applied to the entire church age, the 'last days' when God is fulfilling his promises. But, despite repeated claims to the contrary, there is little good evidence that Paul thought the return of Christ and end of history would come as the immediate result of his own ministry. Moreover, the cautious optimism expressed in passages like Romans 11:14, where he expresses only the hope of saving 'some' of his people Israel, counters any idea that Paul thought he would bring about the mass conversion of Israel for which he hoped (Rom. 11:25–26).

Paul's conceptual background

A 'search for the historical Paul' would turn up almost as many divergent views as does the 'search for the historical Jesus'. Scholars have repeatedly tried to read between the lines of the limited information in the NT in the interests of constructing all kinds of more or less plausible pictures of the 'real Paul'. Particularly important for our purposes is the question of Paul's conceptual background. As he developed his theology, what categories of thinking influenced him? The categories of the Greco-Roman world, where he spent his first years in the cosmopolitan city of Tarsus? Or the categories of the OT and the Jewish world, taught to him by his parents (Acts 26:4–5; Phil. 3:5) and by Gamaliel in the rabbinic school in Jerusalem (Acts 22:3)? Early in this century, under the influence of the 'history of

religions' approach to the NT, scholars thought that Paul imported many Greek ideas into his theology. But reaction quickly set in, as it was demonstrated again and again that Paul's basic categories are derived from his Jewish background. Paul certainly claims a Jewish background for himself repeatedly in the NT. Moreover, as Paul's almost ninety explicit quotations and countless allusions indicate, the OT was a determinative source for his theology. This does not mean we should dismiss influence from the wider Greek world entirely. God caused Paul to be born and raised in such an environment so that he could draw from both the Jewish and the Greek worlds for his theology. Ultimately, under the inspiration of the Spirit, Paul sought to bring all his thinking – whatever its origin – into captivity to Christ (2 Cor. 10:5).

The theological significance of the letters of Paul

Methodological considerations

Paul's theology is not expressed in a systematic treatise but in thirteen letters, written over a period of at least fifteen years to at least seven different churches and two individuals. None of these letters is systematic, in the sense of a general and logical development of theological ideas – not even Romans. Each is written against a specific background and with a specific purpose. In a word, all the letters of Paul are 'contingent'. How one can deduce from this welter of occasional pastoral advice a 'coherent' theology is an issue of great importance for the church. (J. C. Beker analyses particularly clearly this problem of 'contingency and coherence' [*Paul the Apostle* (Edinburgh and Philadelphia, 1980), pp. 11–36]). We may cite one much-debated example: is Paul's prohibition of women teaching in 1 Timothy 2:12 'contingent' only (advice only for the first-century Ephesian church), or part of the 'coherent' core of his thinking (mandatory for the church in all times and places)?

The problem is more easily posed than solved, and scholars continue to struggle to arrive at a clear and agreed methodology. But several points are clear.

1. The contingent nature of every letter of Paul must be given due weight. We cannot, without looking carefully at the context, simply 'read off' systematic theological conclu-

sions from the text of the letters. Always we must ask questions, such as why Paul wrote what he did, and what specific circumstances gave rise to the teaching. For instance, a reading of Galatians by itself would yield a very negative picture of the Mosaic *law. But once we recognize that Paul in this letter is dealing with false teachers who are paying far too much attention to the law, we can understand why what he says about it is so uniformly negative. To use Galatians by itself to establish a Pauline – or Christian – theology of the law would be shortsighted.

2. On the other hand, one must not dismiss what Paul says because it is written in a polemical context or for a specific purpose. Some modern interpreters of Paul tend in this direction, accusing Paul of giving contradictory advice depending on the circumstances he is addressing. Such an approach means that no 'theology' of Paul could ever be written; all would be contingent and nothing coherent. A careful reading of Paul will show that so pessimistic an appraisal of the task is unnecessary. In the case already cited, while we should not use Galatians by itself to build a Pauline theology of law, we must take seriously what it says about the law and integrate it into a larger picture drawn from all the Pauline evidence.

3. Integration of what Paul says in his different letters will ultimately require conceptual categories capable of bringing together the variety of language and ideas that he expresses. Biblical theology generally seeks to use the actual categories supplied by the biblical authors themselves. But even in analysing a single author, like Paul, it will sometimes be necessary to use a broader term than any the author uses. For instance, Paul usually uses the word 'justify' to denote God's initial acceptance of the sinner. But he can also, on occasion, use it in typical Jewish fashion to refer to the final judgment (*e.g.* Rom. 2:13). Treating such passages together under the heading of 'justification' would result in a skewed and perhaps even contradictory understanding of Paul's teaching. (See *Righteousness, justice and justification.)

The centre of Paul's theology

One potentially very helpful step in the search for coherence in Paul's theology would be the identification of a 'centre' in his thought that could integrate all he teaches. Scholars have proposed many different 'centres' over the

years, some of the most popular being justification by *faith, eschatology, the *church as the body of Christ, reconciliation, participation in Christ, *salvation history, and Christ. Unfortunately, many of the proposals are reductionistic and have the ultimate effect of distorting Paul's thinking by forcing all he says into too restrictive a mould. But two of the suggestions have merit.

Salvation history is not a 'centre' for Paul's thought in the true sense of the word, for it denotes a framework of thinking rather than a dominating idea. But a correct interpretation of Paul's theology demands recognition of the conceptual approach called 'salvation history'. The term (German *Heilsgeschichte*) is used in a variety of ways in contemporary theology. Here we use it very simply to denote the historical and corporate dimension of Paul's theology. Paul starts from the assumption that God has accomplished *redemption as part of a historical process. The OT, and God's dealings with *Israel recorded in it, lead to Christ, the climax of history. The Christ event therefore divides history into two epochs, an old age and a new. Paul presents his theology from within this framework, explaining the significance of Christ frequently by contrast with the old age of *sin, *death and the Torah that came before him. The framework also makes Paul's thinking more corporate than modern Western interpreters often recognize. The inclusive significance of *Adam and Christ, for example (Rom. 5; 1 Cor. 15), is quite understandable from within a salvation-historical framework. (H. Ridderbos's book *Paul: An Outline of his Theology* is an outstanding example of the salvation-historical approach to Paul.)

If we are forced to identify a 'centre' of Paul's theology in the true sense of the word, then the only category broad enough to encompass the incredible range of Paul's teaching is 'God's act in Christ'. Here, Paul clearly teaches, is the very heart of the world's significance. All can be derived from it; all must be related to it. As many scholars have noted, Paul himself was confronted with precisely this point on the Damascus road, when the one whom he had scorned and rejected was revealed to him unmistakably as the Messiah of God and Lord of the universe. This Copernican revolution is the mainspring for Paul's own faith and for his theology as well. (See particularly on this point, S. Kim, *The Origin of Paul's Gospel*.)

Specific theological themes

Paul's rich theological contribution cannot even be surveyed in the space available here. We will single out some of his most distinctive contributions to biblical theology.

Salvation history

If salvation history is the determinative framework for Paul's theology, it is also a central topic in its own right. Paul, more than any other biblical author, helps us to understand the unity of God's plan as revealed in Scripture by integrating the various parts of the biblical revelation. Faced with Judaizers on the one hand who sought to impose the Mosaic law on Gentile Christians (*cf.* Galatians) and Gentile Christians on the other who downplayed their importance of the Israelite heritage (*cf.* Romans 9 – 11), Paul highlighted the ultimate significance of Christ and the new covenant without rejecting the old. As Paul explains in Galatians 3:15–29, salvation history is rooted in the promise of God to *Abraham, a promise fulfilled in Christ, the '*seed' to whom the promise was made. The Mosaic law, given centuries after the promise, could not modify this basic arrangement. Salvation has therefore always been, as it was for Abraham, based on faith. The law was only a temporary stage in salvation history, as God used it to preserve Israel until the promise should be fulfilled.

But salvation history also has a future. Messiah has come, but he is to come again. Christians live in the 'overlap of the ages', still in the flesh, subject to temptation and death, but also, by faith, participating in the new age of salvation. The *Holy Spirit provides critical support for the believer in this period of tension and also stimulates in the believer a deep assurance of the deliverance to come (Rom. 8:14–30).

Faith and works; Judaism

Generations of Pauline scholars, rooted in the reformation paradigm, viewed Paul as a champion of *freedom and faith versus the legalism of the Judaism of his day. Jews, so the stereotype ran, believed that people were saved by works; Paul countered with the gospel of salvation by *grace and faith. This scenario can no longer be accepted without careful argument and/or qualification. In a landmark study, E. P. Sanders argued that the Judaism of Paul's day was not legalistic, but taught that sinners were saved by God's *election expressed in the covenant (*Paul and Palestinian Judaism*). Most interpreters have accepted Sanders' basic view of Judaism, inaugurating what is being called 'the new perspective on Paul'. What then becomes of Paul's polemic against people who argued that justification was based on the law? Some scholars take the radical position that Paul was simply wrong. Others, such as J. D. G. Dunn, take the much saner route of seeking to re-interpret Paul in light of this new consensus about Judaism.

But we should be somewhat cautious about accepting Sanders' view in its entirety. He is undoubtedly right in claiming that many Christian interpreters have been guilty of misunderstanding and caricaturing ancient Judaism. But we find evidence both in Jewish writings of the time and in the NT that there were some Jews who had strayed into legalism. And even on Sanders' viewpoint, Jews still believed that obedience to the law was necessary for salvation. So caution about adopting the 'new perspective' is called for at this point. We think that the traditional reformation antithesis of 'works' versus 'faith' is solidly grounded in Paul and should still be seen as a cardinal contribution of the apostle to biblical theology.

Christ

Paul did not see Jesus in the flesh, but his many allusions to the teaching of Jesus reveal that he knows of and values Jesus' earthly existence. Paul's most often-used title for Jesus is 'Christ', which never completely loses its underlying meaning of the Messiah, the promised heir of David who fulfils God's promises to Israel. Nevertheless, Jesus' value for Paul is found particularly in his resurrected state as Lord (see Rom. 1:3–4). This title has far-reaching significance for Paul, for it comes from the OT, where it is applied to God. Paul therefore implies an extremely close relationship between Jesus and God. Note, for instance, the quotation of Joel 2:32 in Romans 10:13, where Paul applies a passage about God to Jesus. What this title implies, Romans 9:5 appears to state explicitly, for the probably correct punctuation of the verse has Paul calling Jesus 'God' (*cf.* NIV; NRSV; and see also Titus 2:13). As Lord, Jesus is ruler of the universe, with all things 'put under his feet' (1 Cor. 15:26–27, quoting Ps. 110:1; *cf.* also Col. 1:15–17). But the title 'Lord' is important more for its relational than its ontological significance. 'Jesus is Lord' (1 Cor. 12:3) is the basic Christian confession, in which believers acknowledge Jesus as the one to whom they owe *worship and *obedience.

The cross

Jesus' death on the cross is the most (though not the only) decisive point in the redemptive plan of God for *humanity. Paul uses many images to convey to his readers the significance of Jesus' death. Sacrificial imagery, drawn from the OT, is particularly prominent. God set forth Jesus as a '*sacrifice of atonement' (Rom. 3:25), and his shed *blood (symbolizing sacrificial death) brings forgiveness (Eph. 1:7; Col. 1:14), justification (Rom. 5:9) and reconciliation (Eph. 2:13). The language of 'redemption' suggests that Christ's death is viewed by Paul as the costly price by which God purchased freedom for human beings enslaved to sin (Rom. 3:24; *cf.* 1 Cor. 6:20). Paul can also present the cross as a victory over evil *spiritual powers (Col. 2:15).

The return of the Lord

While Christ rules even now as Lord, Paul anticipates eagerly the day when his lordship will be extended over all the world (*e.g.* Phil. 2:11). Paul's theology, while oriented decisively toward the cross and the resurrection, also looks forward to the return of Christ in glory, the parousia ('coming' or 'presence'). The parousia will bring final deliverance for all believers: 'we will all be changed' (1 Cor. 15:51). Those who have died will be resurrected in transformed bodies (1 Thess. 4:16; 1 Cor. 15:21–23; Rom. 8:13). And those who are still alive at the parousia will also be 'changed' as their 'earthly dwelling' is exchanged for a 'heavenly' one (2 Cor. 5:1–10; 1 Thess. 4:17).

The church as the body of Christ

Paul never views Christians in isolation but always as members of a community: the church (*ekklēsia*), those who have been 'called out' of the world to exist as God's eschatological people. While Paul frequently addresses the church as it exists in a given location, he ultimately sees the church as a single, universal entity that embraces all who believe. This idea is particularly prominent in Ephesians and Colossians (Eph. 1:22–23; 4:4; Col. 1:18). Also prominent in these books, as well as in 1 Corinthians 12 and Romans 12, is the idea of the church as 'the body of Christ'. The metaphor is rooted in Christ's own body given on our behalf and is used by Paul especially to convey the diversity in unity that should characterize the body. The body is one, Paul stresses, for Christ cannot be divided. But the body has many parts, and the Spirit has appointed *men and women to serve very different roles within the unity of the body. Paul's grand conception of the single body with diverse parts should inform the church in our own age, warning us against unnecessary divisions and encouraging us to celebrate and learn from the diversity within our communities.

Bibliography

F. F. Bruce, *Paul, Apostle of the Free Spirit* (Exeter and Grand Rapids, 1977); J. D. G. Dunn, *A Theology of Paul the Apostle* (Edinburgh and Grand Rapids, 1998); S. Kim, *The Origin of Paul's Gospel* (Grand Rapids, 1981); J. Munck, *Paul and the Salvation of Mankind* (London, 1955); H. Ridderbos, *Paul: An Outline of his Theology* (Grand Rapids, 1974); E. P. Sanders, *Paul and Palestinian Judaism* (London, 1977); D. Wenham, *Paul: Follower of Jesus or Founder of Christianity?* (Grand Rapids, 1995).

D. J. MOO

GENESIS

Introduction

Genesis centres on the faithfulness of God in carrying out his promises to the chosen fathers of the nation *Israel (Gen. 11:27 – 50:26; Acts 7:1–18). The triad of divine promises were: 1. a nation of numerous descendants (seed), 2. a country (land) and 3. the *blessing of the nations (12:1–3). These elements of the promised blessing are the building blocks of the theology of Genesis and form the threads which connect the destiny of Israel and the mission of the church. The promises repeatedly appear, and are the theological touchstone of Genesis, showing God's love for Israel (Deut. 7:7–8) by his original commitment to *Abraham (12:1–3,

7; 13:15–17; 15:7–21; 17:4–8, 15–16; 18:18; 22:16–18), Isaac (26:3–4) and *Jacob (28:13–14; 35:9–12; 46:3–4). By these promises God swore an oath to make of Abraham a great nation through his union with *Sarah (18:10; 22:16; 24:7; 26:3; 50:24; Exod. 6:8; Num. 14:16; Deut. 7:8; 9:5; 34:4; Luke 1:73; Acts 7:17; Heb. 6:13–18). The purpose of bestowing the promises upon the ancestors of Israel was ultimately to mediate the blessing to all *nations (12:2b–3; 18:18; 22:18; 26:4), thus realizing God's intention for all *humanity at *creation (1:28; 9:1, 7). Genesis shows how the promises were partially realized in the experiences of the patriarchal family. The nature of the promises assumed that a full realization could be known only by future generations (e.g. 15:7–15; 17:7–8; 35:11; 48:19). Thus, Genesis is oriented toward the future.

Generations

The theology of Genesis is reflected by the book's literary structure. The key feature of this is the recurring phrase 'these are the generations of' (NRSV, eleven times) which introduces new sections (2:4; 5:1; 6:9; 10:1; 11:10, 27; 25:12, 19; 36:1, 9; 37:2). The book profiles Israel's forefathers from Adam to Abraham, who were the chosen recipients and mediators of the promises (5:1–32; 11:10–26). The phrase also functions as the framework of the book, indicating a continuum between the act of creation and the subsequent events of human history, such that the revelation given to Israel at Sinai has both universal and future implications.

Genesis and Israel

As part of the Pentateuch, the theology of Genesis must be understood in the context of the theology of the five books. The primary concern of the Pentateuch is the revelation of God to Moses at Sinai (Exodus 19 – Numbers 10). Genesis functions as the introduction to the Sinai revelation by recounting how the ancestors of Israel received the promises of God intended also for their descendants (e.g. Exod. 3:13–17). Genesis 1 – 11 provides the cosmic setting for the role of the patriarchs and their offspring as Israel prepared to enter Canaan, the land of promise. People and events described in Genesis, such as Abraham's descent into Egypt (12:10–20), prefigured the experiences of Israel.

Genesis and the church

As the Mosaic community had viewed Genesis as prefiguring its experiences, the church found in the Pentateuch an anticipation of Jesus as the last *Adam and the second Moses (e.g. Deut. 18:15, 18–19; John 1:21, 25, 45; 5:46; 6:14; 7:40; Acts 3:22–26; 7:37; Rom. 5:12–21; 1 Cor. 15:45–49). Also, the community of Israel was understood to be a type of the church (e.g. 1 Cor. 10:1–13; 1 Pet. 2:9–10). The promise that in Abraham's seed all the nations of the earth would be blessed was judged to have been fulfilled by Christ and the church (Rom. 4:16–18; Gal. 3:6–9, 16).

Creation and blessing

The idea of blessing dominates the theology of Genesis; the word 'bless' in its verbal and noun forms occurs eighty-eight times, more than in any other biblical book. Divine blessing in Genesis typically consisted of procreation or material prosperity. Important blessings included the giving of life at creation and the prosperity of the patriarchal family through children and riches.

Life (blessing)

Genesis 1:1 – 2:3 includes three divine declarations of blessing (1:22, 28; 2:3). In the creation week God 'blessed' only the seventh day and 'sanctified' it, showing divine approval of his 'good' creation (2:3). Creation was achieved by divine fiat ('then God said') by which the earth became capable of sustaining life (days 1–3) and inhabited with innumerable life forms (days 4–6). The Creator on the fifth day brought forth life and 'blessed' the sea creatures and birds, directing them to reproduce (1:20–23). On the sixth day God created human life and 'blessed' the male and female so that they too would procreate (1:26–28). Human life, however, was specially honoured, for it represented the rule of God by virtue of the male and female's being made in the divine *image (1:26–27).

Procreation (seed)

Procreation indicated divine favour and imparted life-giving power. '*Seed' in its metaphorical sense, meaning 'offspring', occurs commonly in Genesis (e.g. 4:25). The first instance of the word, however, is in its literal sense, and occurs in the account of the land's producing vegetation (1:11–12; *cf.* 1:29). The significant point here, given the book's central theme of promise, is the establishment of a pattern found in life, where the parent reproduces itself abundantly ('kinds', *e.g.* 1:21) in accordance with the creation ordinance which guaranteed prosperity in perpetuity for all life forms ('Be fruitful and increase ... fill the earth', 1:22, 28).

Dominion (earth/land)

God's rule over creation was delegated to the luminaries which governed (*māšal*) the heavens (1:16–18) and the human couple, the divine image, who through procreation and ownership subdued (*kābaš*) and ruled (*rādâ*) the earth with its life forms (1:26–28; Ps. 115:16b). These terms for rule are used also of royal dominion (*e.g.* 2 Sam. 8:11; 1 Kgs. 4:21, 24; Ps. 72:8), inferring that the human creature had the honoured role of representing the Creator as his vice-regent over the earth (Ps. 8:5–8). Human dominion over the earth is described in the Eden narrative (chs. 2 – 3), for God created the man from dust and placed him in the garden, which he tended as caretaker (2:7, 15). The man's subjection of the animal world is indicated by his naming of the beasts (2:19). The creation of the woman as the man's helper anticipated the blessing of procreation which is shown by the use of the anachronism 'father and mother' prior to their union as 'one flesh' (2:24). It was by human procreation that dominion could be achieved.

Crime and curse

Although God placed the man and his wife in a bountiful garden, the LORD restricted them from one tree, 'the tree of the knowledge of good and evil' (2:16–17). The penalty for transgressing God's only law was death. In the garden the *serpent impugned the goodness of God and promised the woman that she and her husband could obtain divine wisdom through the forbidden fruit. In consequence of the woman's deception and the man's rebellion, they ate of the tree and unlawfully obtained wisdom (3:1–7, 22). By their *sin the human couple jeopardized the blessing and disrupted the good creation. Now, the relationship they had enjoyed with God was fractured; their own relationship as husband and wife became competitive; and their dominion over the earth was resisted.

Punishment (blessing)

The LORD declared three *judgments against the culprits (3:14–19). He spoke a curse against the serpent, condemning it to a life of humiliation. As for the woman and the man, God brought sorrow upon them in the exercise of their primary roles as childbearer and farmer. The woman faced pain in childbirth and difficulty in her relationship with her husband. The man encountered a field that was cursed and produced thorns and thistles which he had to control in order to reap an edible crop. Also, he was condemned to the ultimate punishment for his crime; he returned to the dust from which he was made.

Deliverer (seed)

Although the serpent was 'cursed' by God (3:14), the man and the woman were not. The LORD cursed the ground from which the man was formed (3:17), but there was no curse relating to the woman. This reflected the value the woman held as God's instrument for preserving the blessing for the human family. This blessing would be effected by the victory of the woman's 'seed' over the serpent (3:15). Therefore it was not made obsolete by the couple's sin; rather, God graciously preserved them, ensuring procreation and promising a deliverer. That the promise of a deliverer had implications for the future was indicated by the language of the judgment oracles against the serpent and the man which speak of 'all the days of your life' (3:14, 17). The future struggle between the seed of the serpent and the seed of the woman (3:15) was first manifested by wicked Cain's murder of righteous Abel (4:8). When the evil of the Cainites became pervasive in the earth (6:1–13), God purged it by the waters of a flood. And again God in his grace preserved the blessing, for the family of Seth and through the deliverer Noah (5:29–32; 6:8–9), who offered atoning sacrifice (8:20) and whose son Shem fathered the chosen line of Abraham (9:26–27; 11:10–26). However, a complete victory over sin awaited a future deliverer, for the human heart remained inclined towards sin (8:21) as was shown by Noah's son, Ham (9:22–25).

Exile and death (land)

Since the man and woman had transgressed the law of God, the LORD imposed upon them the penalty of *death, as he had forewarned by expelling them from the garden. Their exile barred them from access to 'the tree of life' which provided the means for the renewal of life (3:22–24). Although the LORD graciously delayed their death, the refrain 'and he died' in the genealogy of Adam shows that Adam and his descendants experienced the penalty (5:1–32). That the sin of Adam condemned all his offspring was shown not only by his death and that of his descendants, but also by the murder of Abel by his brother, Cain (4:8). As the sin of his parents in the garden had meant banishment to the east (3:24), Cain's deed resulted in a divine curse, a further breakdown in his relationship with the ground, and his further exile from the land and from the 'presence of the LORD' towards the east (4:11–16). Nonetheless, God's grace continued in the life of his human creatures as shown by the gift of Seth (4:25), their increased numbers (5:4), and the hope afforded by Enoch's translation (5:24).

Blessing for all nations

Following the judgment of the flood, the descendants of Noah gathered in the east in Babylonia and built a city with a tower reaching to the heavens to 'make a name' for themselves (11:4). Their actions challenged God's authority; so he confused their language. This resulted in their migration, in groups who formed various nations (10:1–32; 11:1–9). As God had shown mercy to sinful humanity in the past, so he now set in motion the creation of a nation by choosing Israel's fathers descended from the line of Shem (9:26; 11:10–26).

Call of Abraham (blessing)

The promised blessings bestowed on all humanity would be fulfilled exclusively through the family of Abraham. The LORD would be for ever known as the 'God of Abraham'. The word 'bless' occurs five times in the call of the patriarch (12:1–3); this was the gracious counterbalance to the five 'curses' against fallen creation and humanity (3:14, 17b; 4:11; 8:21; 9:25). Abraham, as the mediator of blessing to all 'peoples' (mišpaḥâ), was himself the progenitor of a 'great nation' (gôy), which inherited a promised land ('ereṣ). This divine agenda was a gracious response to the formation of the nations at Babel according to their 'peoples' (mišpaḥâ) and 'nations' (gôyim) which had scattered across the face of the 'earth' ('ereṣ) (10:5, 20, 31–32).

Promise of a nation (seed)

The promise of a 'great nation' (12:2) implied a large population, but Sarah was barren (11:30). The question of an heir for Abraham and Sarah is the major tension in the Abraham story. Although the prospects for the promise's fulfilment were dim, Abraham believed God and responded obediently (15:6; also 12:4; 22:16–17). A decade later Isaac was born to Sarah as the appointed heir of the blessing (21:12b). The creation ordinance called for humanity to increase in number (1:28; 9:1, 7), and in the patriarchal promises God said that Abraham's descendants would flourish as the 'dust of the earth' (13:16; 22:17; 28:14; 32:12) and the 'stars of the sky' (15:5; 22:17; 26:4). Genesis anticipated the founding of Israel as the future realization of this promise (Exod. 1:7; 3:15–17; 6:2–8; 32:13; Deut. 1:10; 10:22).

Canaan homeland (land)

For the LORD to make Abraham into a 'great nation', the Hebrew people required a homeland. Repeatedly the LORD assured Abraham and his successors of a promised land, the land of Canaan, which the LORD himself would 'give' them (12:7; 13:15, 17; 15:7, 18; 17:8; 24:7; 26:3; 28:13, 15; 35:12; 48:4; 50:24). 'Go from your country … to the land I will show you' is the first recorded command to Abraham (12:1; 15:7). Abraham obeyed the LORD by migrating to Canaan (12:4), but the patriarch had only a tentative foothold in the land. Famine forced his immediate departure to Egypt, but he returned enriched by Pharaoh (12:10–20). Israel's future claim to the land was prefigured by the journeys of Abraham, who traversed the land (12:4–9), entered into treaties with neighbours (21:22–34), and purchased the family burial site at Machpelah (ch. 23; 25:7–11; 50:13). The chief tension in the Jacob narrative is the patriarch's absence from Canaan. Fearing for his life because he had stolen Esau's blessing, he fled to Aram where he lived for twenty years (31:38). Later, he also left Canaan for Egypt with his sons (46:26–27). Yet the LORD brought Jacob back from Aram to the land of his father (28:15; 31:3; 35:12; 48:4); as a portent of better days when God would bring back the people of Israel from Egypt (46:4), Jacob's body was returned to Canaan for burial with his fathers in Machpelah's cave (49:29; 50:4–14).

Abraham, *David and Israel

Although the LORD delivered the nation from Egypt and returned them to the land as promised, the expectations of an autonomous state governed by a royal dynasty remained unfulfilled. The promised seed had been depicted in royal terms: Abraham and Sarah would be the ancestors of 'kings' (17:6, 16; also Ishmael, 25:16 and Esau, 36:15–43). Abraham's successful engagement against warring kings in his rescue of Lot (ch. 14) and his treaty with the Philistine king Abimelech (21:22–34; also Isaac, 26:1–33) showed the international status of Abraham as a powerful player in regional politics. Proleptically, Jacob spoke of Judah's household as bearing 'the sceptre' for ever over his brothers and achieving victory over their enemies (49:8–12). Mosaic legislation built on this expectation by establishing the regulations whereby Israel's king would govern (Deut. 17:14–20). The growing desire for such a ruler resulted in the premature offering of kingship to Gideon (Judg. 8:22–23) and the foolish submission of the Shechemites to the kingship of Gideon's son, Abimelech (Judg. 9:1–57). Despite Samuel's protestations, the people turned to a king to fight their battles (*e.g.* 1 Sam. 8:1–22; 10:17–19; 12:1–25), but Saul's reign collapsed and the LORD, again out of grace, chose a deliverer, David, through whom he would rule his people (1 Sam. 16:7–13).

Israel's patriarchs and kings (seed)

The idea of an elect family through whom exclusively God would work is integral to Genesis both structurally and theologically. As noted above, Jacob's blessing upon *Judah (49:8–12) pointed to a future royal house springing from the patriarchs. With the rise of the Davidic monarchy, this early expectation became central to Israel's theological reflection. David's credentials as a descendant of Judah, as shown by his royal genealogy (Ruth 4:18–22; 1 Chr. 2:5–15), satisfied the Genesis prophecy. The linear form of the ten-name genealogy for David is the same as that of the two chief genealogies in Genesis, tracing the line from Adam to Abraham (5:1–32; 11:10–26). In creating a ruling house, the Davidic covenant (2 Sam. 7) interpreted the promises made to David as the fulfilment of the Abrahamic blessing. Similar forms and language underline the close relationship between the two covenants. Their form was that of the royal land grant in which a king bestowed a royal possession upon a loyal subject. This grant was a one-time gift which was perpetually possessed by the recipient's family. The LORD blessed Abraham and his royal descendant David with a promised 'name', 'seed' and 'land'. The promise of a great 'name' occurs for only these two leaders in the OT (12:2; 2 Sam. 7:9). The LORD promised David a dynastic 'house' (2 Sam. 7:11, 16) of kings 'for ever' (2 Sam. 7:13, 15–16). 'House' and 'household' were common terms in the *covenant of circumcision made with Abraham (17:12, 13, 23, 27). Psalm 89's memorial to God's covenant with David emphasized his eternal line of royal 'seed' (Ps. 89:3–4, 29, 34–37). 'Seed' was also the language of patriarchal expectation (12:7; 13:15–16; 15:3, 5, 13, 18; 16:10; 17:7–12, 19; 21:12–13; 22:17–18; 24:7; 26:3–4, 24; 28:13–14; 32:12; 35:12; 48:4, 19). Another echo of the Abraham story in the Davidic covenant was the promise that only a child from the forefather's own body would receive the inherited blessing (15:4; 2 Sam. 7:12).

Promised Land and exile (land)

While the word 'land' occurs in Genesis' prediction that Israel will inherit Canaan (*e.g.* 12:1, 7; 13:14–17; 15:7, 18; 26:3; 28:13, 15; 48:21), the Davidic covenant uses the words 'place', 'kingdom' and 'throne' in its reformulation of the promise (2 Sam. 7:10, 12–13, 16; Ps. 89:29, 36, 44). Much of the Jacob and *Joseph stories concerns the life of the patriarchs outside Canaan, and in the remainder of the Pentateuch the Hebrews are in exile and in the wilderness. During the conquest and monarchy, the people lived in the land for the longest continuous period recorded in the OT. However, dispossession and dispersion remained a threat from Abraham to the time of the prophets, even during the reigns of David and Solomon. God foretold to Abraham his descendants' four-hundred-year exile in Egypt (15:12–16), and Moses' final message to Israel predicted their apostasy and exile (Deut. 28:49–52, 62–68; 31:15–21; *cf.* 1 Kgs. 8:33–34). In a manner reminiscent of Deuteronomy, the Davidic covenant provided for the chastening of any future king who transgressed the law of the

LORD (2 Sam. 7:14; Ps. 89:30–32). Foreign oppression and exile resulted from the wickedness of the kings and the nation's apostasy (Ps. 89:38–51; 2 Kgs. 17:5–23; 21:11–12).

A banner for the nations (blessing)

Despite their expulsion, Israel could take heart that the prophets also had foreseen their return to the land and the establishment of a worldwide kingdom by a future heir of David (e.g. Is. 2:2–4; 11:1, 10–12; Jer. 23:5; Zech. 6:12). Through this new David the psalmist's ideal of a realm maintaining global peace and blessing would be realized (Ps. 72:8–17). Genesis had given birth to this expectation of blessing for the nations which would come through Abraham's progeny (12:2b–3). The treatment of the patriarchs by their neighbours, for good (blessing) or ill (curse), determined whether or not those nations benefited from the promised blessings. Pharaoh suffered, as did the Philistine king Abimelech, because of their mistreatment of Abraham and Sarah (12:10–20; 20:1–18; cf. 31:24), but outsiders benefited by making friends with the patriarchs (21:22–32; 26:28–29; 30:29–30; 39:2–5; 47:20).

Jesus Christ and the nations

The apostolic interpretation of the ancient promises proclaimed that their fulfilment was in Jesus Christ and his church. The OT images of seed and blessing were foundational to the way the early church understood Jesus and his mission of salvation for the nations. Since the Davidic promise concerned primarily the individual 'seed', the relationship of Christ to the patriarch David was more important in the Gospels and Acts than the epistles. The apostle Paul's concern was the identity of the church as Abraham's many 'nations' and 'descendants'.

Royal descendant (seed)

The promise of 'seed' made to Abraham is said explicitly to refer to Christ (Gal. 3:16, 19) but also to those who believed (Rom. 4:16–18; 9:8) by virtue of their relationship to him by faith (Gal. 3:29). Jesus was of the 'seed of David' (Rom. 1:3; 2 Tim. 2:8) and hence of royal stock (Matt. 1:1; Luke 1:32). Jesus accepted the messianic title, the 'Son of David' (Matt. 12:23; 21:9; 22:42; Mark 12:35), who as the promised royal descendant would save his people (Luke 1:69–74; Acts

13:23, 33–39; 2 Tim. 2:8). Only in one place, however, do the names 'Abraham' and 'David' occur together with 'Jesus' (Matt. 1:1). The linkage of the patriarchal promises with the future kingdom of David occurs in the prophets (Jer. 33:22, 26; Ezek. 37:25), and in the NT both covenants appear together in the review of God's promises handed down through Israel's history (Acts 7:2–53; 13:16–41). Paul, in his defence of justification by faith, appealed to Abraham's faith and the forgiveness granted to David (Rom. 4:1–8). In the NT the language 'our father' (sing.), when not referring to God, is used only of the patriarchs Abraham (Luke 1:73; John 8:39, 53; Acts 7:2; Rom. 4:1, 12; Jas. 2:21), Isaac (Rom. 9:10) and Jacob (John 4:12), and once of King David (Mark 11:10). Similarly, 'patriarch' is used only of David (Acts 2:29) and Abraham (Heb. 7:4) and the twelve sons of Jacob (Acts 7:8–9). These patriarchs were viewed as the principal ancestors who received the promises, founded Israel and its royal house and prepared the way for the Messiah.

Salvation to the Gentiles (blessing)

The outpouring of the Spirit upon the Gentiles who came by faith to inherit the blessing could be explained by the Abrahamic promise which included all nations (12:2b–3; Gal. 3:8–9, 14; Rom. 4:9; 15:8). The church, made up of Jews and Gentiles, constituted the 'many nations' who were Abraham's promised offspring (Rom. 4:17–18). Nevertheless, the Jews had the first opportunity to experience the blessing through Jesus (Acts 3:25–26; Rom. 1:16).

Inheriting the earth (land)

The NT's expansion of the original promise of land to include the whole earth (Rom. 4:13; Matt. 5:5; cf. Ps. 37:9) was foreshadowed by messianic passages in the psalms and prophets (e.g. Ps. 72:8; Is. 55:3–5; Zech. 9:10). Inclusion of all nations was implied by the language of 'families' (12:3) and 'nations' (22:18). Jewish interpretations of the patriarchal promises before the Christian era reflected this same understanding (Ecclus. 44:18–21; Jubilees 19:21). Jesus Christ's future dominion will involve the renewal of the creation blessing lost in the garden (Rom. 8:19–23; Heb 2:5–9). The author to the Hebrews spoke of spiritual realities corresponding to the promise of the land: 'a better country, that is, a heavenly one' (Heb. 11:16; *cf.* v. 10).

Conclusion

The theology of Genesis is the prelude to God's election of Israel and her monarchy, whose purpose was to channel the divine blessing for all nations. Although Israel enjoyed prosperity during the golden years of David and Solomon, the blessings were secured only with the coming of Christ and the founding of the church. Since the promises were intended ultimately for all nations, they were appropriately interpreted in the universal setting of creation and early civilization in which they were first made. The promises to Abraham were God's gracious response to human sin which had jeopardized the blessing he intended to provide. Genesis then is the first act in the meta-story of God's purposeful creation and the salvation of fallen humanity through Abraham's seed, the son of David, our Lord Jesus Christ, the last Adam.

Bibliography

T. D. Alexander, 'Genealogies, seed and the compositional unity of Genesis', *TynB* 44, 1993, pp. 255–270; D. J. A. Clines, *The Theme of the Pentateuch* (Sheffield, 1978); T. W. Mann, '"All the families of the earth": The theological unity of Genesis', *Int* 45, 1991, pp. 35–53; K. A. Mathews, *Genesis 1 – 11:26* (Nashville, 1996); C. W. Mitchell, *The Meaning of BRK 'To Bless' in the Old Testament* (Atlanta, 1987); G. J. Wenham, *Genesis 1 – 15 and 16 – 50, WBC* (Waco, 1987).

K. A. MATHEWS

EXODUS (BOOK)

Introduction

Exodus is far more than simply the story of Israelite slaves led to *freedom. Indeed, to read Exodus as such is to miss not only the theology of the book itself, but also the transfiguration of that theology in the NT. Rather, Exodus is a story of the lengths to which *God is willing to go to create for himself a *people, 'a kingdom of priests and a holy nation' (Exod. 19:6), through whom his plan of universal *blessing, promised to Abraham in Genesis 12:1–3, will one day be realized.

Exodus, therefore, is not really a story in its own right, but the continuation of the story begun in *Genesis and a bridge to what follows. The theology of the book of Exodus is central to a right understanding of redemptive history, not only the unfolding of Israel's story in the OT, but also the climax of that story in the death and resurrection of Jesus Christ.

Main theological themes in Exodus

The broad theological concerns of Exodus can be discerned by looking at the basic structure of the book. Exodus may be divided into three parts: the departure from Egypt and the journey to Sinai (1:1 – 18:27); the arrival at Sinai and the giving of the *law (19:1 – 24:18); further instructions from Sinai and the building of the tabernacle (25:1 – 40:38).

This outline highlights the three central events that form the basic structure of the book: departure; law; tabernacle. When we add to these the explicit and repeated connection the author of Exodus makes between Exodus and Genesis (specifically, *creation and the patriarchs), a theme that underlies all three events, we have a basic outline of the theology of Exodus that governs the entire book.

Exodus: the continuation of a story

Exodus begins by inviting the reader to read the story in the light of what comes before, the stories of Genesis. The very first word of Exodus is the Hebrew letter *waw* which means 'and'. English translations routinely leave this word untranslated, perhaps for stylistic reasons (*e.g.* NIV: 'These are the names ...'). The presence of 'and' at the very beginning of the book, however, is striking. Moreover, Exodus 1:1 as a whole cements the connection to Genesis: 'These are the names of the sons of Israel who went to Egypt.' This verse is essentially a repetition of Genesis 46:8, which announces Israel's journey to Egypt. The same words are now used to announce Israel's departure from Egypt. The fact that Exodus 1:1, including 'and', repeats Genesis 46:8 indicates that the story of Israel's departure from Egypt must be understood as a continuation of the story told in Genesis. Israel's presence in Egypt is no product of chance. The Israelites in Egypt are to view their present *suffering and oppression in the light of God's larger, unchanging picture. God chose a people for himself and brought them down into Egypt. He will bring them out again.

The connection between Exodus and the patriarchs becomes explicit in Exodus 2:24–25: 'God heard their groaning and he remembered his covenant with Abraham, with Isaac and Jacob. So God looked on the Israelites and was concerned about them.' The reason why Israel was redeemed from Egypt is that God made a promise to the patriarchs. The Exodus is not due to any merit on Israel's part. The relationship, then, between the Exodus and the patriarchs is that the Exodus is the next stage of the plan God announced to the patriarchs. This connection to the patriarchs is also seen in *Moses' announcement to the Israelite slaves: 'The LORD, the God of your fathers – the God of Abraham, the God of Isaac and the God of Jacob – appeared to me ...' (3:16; see also 4:5). The Exodus is not an afterthought. The God of the Exodus is the God of the patriarchs.

Departure: the creation of a new people

Exodus is not only a continuation of a past story but also the beginning of a new one. In Exodus 1 a theme is introduced that will prove to be central throughout Scripture; Israel's redemption from Egypt is described in creation language. Redemption is an act of 're-creation' (see below).

We read in 1:7 that the Israelites were settled in Egypt and that as time passed they were 'fruitful and multiplied greatly and became exceedingly numerous' (NIV). The Hebrew is even more explicit than the NIV: 'Be fruitful and swarm; increase in number and become exceedingly strong.' These words are clearly reminiscent of language found in Genesis 1:28 and 9:1 (compare also Exod. 1:7 with Gen. 47:27). 'Swarm' is used also in Genesis 1:21 and 8:17. 'Swarming' is something that God's created beings do.

The story of Moses' birth (2:1–10) is also told in creation language. When his mother looked at the child after his birth, she saw that he was 'good' (tob; 2:2). This is a curious comment, and it has exercised commentators since before the time of Christ. The entire Hebrew phrase, however, is ki tob, which is an echo of the refrain in Genesis 1, where God pronounces what he has created 'good'. The birth of Moses is not merely about the birth of one man, but represents the beginning of the birth of the people. The saviour of the people is born, and it is through him that God's people will be given a new beginning. Their slavery will end and their saviour will bring them safely into their *rest, the Promised *Land.

Moreover, the boy is set in an 'ark' (tebâ) and set afloat on the Nile (2:3). The Hebrew word is found only here and in the flood story (Gen. 6:11 – 9:17). The theological connection between these two events is evident. Both *Noah and Moses are specifically selected to escape a tragic, watery fate. Both are set on an 'ark' treated with bitumen and are carried to safety on the very *water that brings destruction to others. Both Noah and Moses, in other words, are re-creation figures. They serve as the vehicles through whom God 'creates' a new people for his own purposes.

The role Pharaoh plays in Exodus becomes clearer in light of this creation theme. Pharaoh is opposed to the Israelites' increasing in number, which is to say that he is opposed to their fulfilment of the creation mandate to be fruitful and increase (compare Pharaoh's words in 1:9 with what is said in 1:6–7). This is Pharaoh's sin, not simply that of enslaving the people. In this respect, Pharaoh represents not only a force which is hostile to God's people and enslaves them (vv. 11–14), but also a force hostile to God himself, who wills that his people multiply. Pharaoh, in other words, is presented as an anti-God/anti-creation figure; he repeatedly places himself in direct opposition to God's purpose for his people, and this behaviour is anticipated in the opening chapter of Exodus. The battle in Exodus, therefore, is between the true God who calls his people to *worship him on Mt Sinai and the false god Pharaoh who wishes to keep Yahweh's people under his own power. His efforts prove futile, however. Oppression merely results in further increase and, as if to emphasize this point, 1:12 repeats the 'increase' language of 1:7. Pharaoh is no match for the creator-God. Verse 12 is an early hint as to the eventual outcome of their battle.

The use of creation language continues in the narratives of the plagues and the parting of the Red Sea. The plagues are not just a display of God flexing his muscles. They are the unleashing of God's creative forces against the enemies of God's people (and therefore the enemies of God himself). In the abstract one can imagine God using a variety of other means to bring Egypt to its knees, ways that have biblical precedent. He could have sent an angel dressed for battle. He could have used a foreign army as his pawn to plunder the land. But he chose rather to fight with weapons that no one but he had, that only he could command, and against which there was no defence. The series of attacks upon Egypt removes all doubt as to who the *victor in the battle will be.

God also chose this means of punishment as a just recompense for the crime perpetrated against Israel. Pharaoh poses as an anti-God force, and the decree to kill the male children (1:22) is nothing less than a challenge to God's creation mandate in Genesis 1. Hence, quite properly, the plagues are an undoing of creation, a series of creation reversals, at Egypt's expense: beasts harm rather than serve humanity; *light ceases and darkness takes over; waters become a source of *death rather than *life; the climax of Genesis 1 is the creation of humans on the last day of creation, whereas the climax of the plagues is the destruction of humans in the last plague. The plagues do not run rampant, however; they eventually cease (although the narrative does not always say so explicitly), and each cessation is another display of God's creative power. He once again restores order to chaos as he did in the beginning: the waters are restored; the troublesome insects and animals retreat; light once again comes out of darkness. Each plague is a reminder of the supreme power of Yahweh, the creator. The one who will save Israel is also the one who holds chaos at bay, but who, if he chooses, will step aside and allow chaos to plague his enemies.

The parting of the Red Sea is another act of re-creation. In Genesis 1:9, the seas come together and separate themselves from the dry land. In Exodus 14, the seas are split open to expose the land beneath. In both episodes, the result is that 'dry land' (*yabbašah*) appears. In Genesis 1, the formation of dry land brings forth the myriad of creatures who will live there. In Exodus, however, the act of 'creation' is reversed against the Egyptians; it brings them death and not life. Thus it is not just a creation reversal, but also direct retribution for Pharaoh's attempt to kill the Israelite firstborn in the waters of the Nile. Just as Pharaoh attempted to destroy the Israelites, by water, so God now destroys the Egyptians. But for the Israelites, the separation of the waters from the land gives life, as it did once before in Genesis. Yahweh has once again tamed the waters of chaos, this time for the purpose of creating a new people for himself, a nation that will have a renewed relationship with their maker. The precise nature of this relationship becomes clear in the subsequent chapters of Exodus, which deal with the law and the tabernacle.

Law: God's will for a new people

The giving of the law is one of the reasons for which Israel was brought to Mt Sinai (the other reason is the building of the tabernacle, which is discussed below). The two main bodies of law that are given in Exodus are the Ten Commandments (20:3–17) and the book of the *covenant (21:1 – 23:19). These laws are not given in the abstract. They are given by God to a people he has just redeemed, God's newly created people, a point made clear in the prologue to the Ten Commandments: 'I am the LORD your God, who brought you out of Egypt, out of the land of slavery' (Exod. 20:2). This prologue precedes the law not just narratively but also theologically. The law has significance only for those already redeemed. It shows God's redeemed people how to be 'holy' (see 19:6); in other words, it reveals something of the nature of God himself. We see in the law not simply what Israel must do (*e.g.* to make themselves good citizens), but also that the reason why Israel must obey the law is because it reflects God's nature. The law is God's cosmic order which will now be reflected in Israel's daily life.

The giving of the law, in other words, is itself an act of re-creation. And both sets of law concern Israel's proper conduct towards God and towards fellow Israelites (*i.e.* vertical and horizontal dimensions). All of life is subsumed under these new-creation stipulations. The Israelites are to behave as new-creation beings, conforming themselves to God's standards in both the religious and the social spheres (no doubt a distinction that ancient Israelites did not recognize). How the Israelites act towards each other (horizontal) is a concrete expression of their devotion to the God of the Exodus (vertical).

Tabernacle: a microcosm of creation

Instructions concerning the tabernacle span

thirteen of the last sixteen chapters of the book of Exodus. Chapters 25 – 31 record the instructions for building the tabernacle. Chapters 35 – 40 record the actual building of the tabernacle. In the middle of these instructions is the famous story of the golden calf, a story of rebellion and eventual *forgiveness. And this is not a story of just any rebellion; the Israelites' attempt to set up an alternative cultic system to the one laid down in chapters 25 – 40.

The building of the tabernacle is more than simply the building of a place of worship in the desert. The tabernacle is a microcosm of creation, a piece of *heaven on earth. Even though the list of building materials, lampstands and incense altars may seem repetitive and tedious to modern readers, it is precisely the sheer mass of this material that alerts us to the fact that we have arrived at a central concern of the Exodus story. The cosmic character of the tabernacle is indicated by the manner of its construction. The cherubim worked into the blue, purple and scarlet yarn of the curtains (26:31) were to be an ever-present reminder that the tabernacle was an earthly representation of a higher reality. Moreover, the tabernacle was to be made according to a strict and precise heavenly pattern (see 25:8–9, 40; 26:30; 27:8; 31:11; 39:32, 42–43). As thoughtful readers of the OT have remarked for centuries, the precise, perfect dimensions of the tabernacle (essentially two cubes, the outer court and the inner court, which included the Holy Place and the Most Holy Place) convey a sense of heavenly order amid earthly chaos.

Significant also is the sevenfold repetition of the phrase 'The LORD said to Moses' in chapters 25 – 31. The first six occurrences concern the building of the tabernacle and its furnishings: 25:1; 30:11, 17, 22, 34; 31:1. The final occurrence is in 31:12, which introduces the *Sabbath command. The purpose of this repetition is to aid the reader in making the connection between the building of the tabernacle and the seven days of creation, both of which involve six creative commands (cf. the repetition of 'And God said' in Genesis 1) culminating in a seventh-day Sabbath rest. In the midst of a fallen world, in exile from the Garden, the original 'heaven on earth', God undertakes another act of creation, a building project signifying a return to pre-fall splendour. The tabernacle, therefore, is laden with

redemptive significance, not just because of the *sacrifices and offerings made within its walls, but also because of what it is: a piece of *holy ground in a world that has lost its way. If this is a correct understanding of the tabernacle, one can see why the writer of Exodus devoted so much space to its description.

The twofold repetition of the Sabbath command is also significant. The commands to keep the Sabbath are found in 31:12–17 and 35:1–3, at the end of the instructions for building the tabernacle and at the beginning of the account of the actual building. The golden calf episode (chs. 32 – 34) is framed by these Sabbath passages. The fact that 35:1 follows naturally from 31:18 suggests that the intervening episode of rebellion (chs. 32 – 34) and the threat by God to dissolve the covenant relationship (see 32:9–14) are forgotten. The framing of the rebellion narrative by the Sabbath law indicates that although God's plan has almost been destroyed, it is now proceeding undiminished. God will be with his people, no matter what happens.

The tabernacle is holy space. The Sabbath is holy time. By building the tabernacle and setting apart one day in seven, God is truly recreating heaven on earth in space and time. Weekly Sabbath worship is on holy ground in holy time. There was no more holy place on the face of the earth than the tabernacle on the Sabbath. The tabernacle, and later the *temple, were thus very important to Israel's identity as God's people; the destruction of the temple by the Babylonians in 587 BC was utterly devastating. By entering the tabernacle, Israel entered God's heavenly house. By keeping the Sabbath, Israel entered God's heavenly rest. By obeying the law, Israel engaged in heavenly conduct. Israel is holy as God is holy.

Exodus theology in the OT

The theology introduced in Exodus finds repeated expression in various forms throughout the OT. For example, one can hardly overestimate the importance that the law and the tabernacle (later the temple) have in Israel's identity throughout her history. These two elements, proper conduct and proper worship, make up the substructure of Israel's relationship to the God who redeemed her from Egypt. They are never a burden in themselves. Only when they become a perfunctory exercise do they become lifeless. The Psalms of Ascents

(120 – 134), the psalms extolling Zion (e.g. Pss. 74 and 87), and the psalmist's love of the law expressed in Psalm 119 only hint at Israel's heart-felt devotion towards these institutions.

The departure from Egypt appears in a number of contexts, but primarily in those books that deal with Israel's captivity in *Babylon and eventual release. Jeremiah, the prophet whose words are directed towards the *exiled generation, uses the departure story in a number of places to make a theological point about Israel's relationship with Babylon. For example, Jeremiah prophesies that God will hand Israel over to the Babylonians (Jer. 21:5–7). In fact, God himself will fight against the Israelites 'with an outstretched hand and a mighty arm', a phrase well known from the Exodus narrative (3:20; see also Deut. 4:34; 5:15; 7:19; 26:8). Israel's captivity in Babylon is described as a reversal of the Exodus. The Israelites are captives once again to a foreign power.

Such captivity will not be permanent, however. God will once again bring about an Exodus for his people. Jeremiah 16:14–15 is explicit: '"However, the days are coming," declares the LORD, "when men will no longer say, 'As surely as the LORD lives, who brought the Israelites up out of Egypt,' but they will say, 'As surely as the LORD lives, who brought the Israelites up out of the land of the north and out of all the countries where he had banished them.' For I will restore them to the land I gave their forefathers"' (see also 23:7–8). A similar expression is found in Jeremiah 31:32, which is quoted in Hebrews 8:9. The 'new covenant' that God will initiate with the released captives will not be like the Sinai covenant. It will be more lasting, and not threatened by disobedience, since the law will be written on the people's hearts (Jer. 31:33). The new Exodus will be accompanied by a new and better covenant.

Brief mention should also be made here of the Exodus theme in Isaiah. Not only does Isaiah speak of the departure from Babylon as an Exodus event, but he also ties together redemption and creation as in Exodus. Israel's confidence that God will indeed deliver them from Babylon is founded on two previous acts of God: the Exodus (e.g. Is. 43:14–19); and the creation (e.g. Is. 42:5; 44:24; 45:11–12). In other words, it is because God is the creator as well as the 're-creator' (as in Exodus) that Israel can now receive with confidence Isaiah's words and know that their redemption is near.

Exodus theology and the NT

The theological contours of the book of Exodus are both continued and transformed in the person and work of Christ. The connection between the two is perhaps most explicitly, if briefly, made in Hebrews 3:1 – 4:11. The writer of Hebrews compares Moses to *Jesus. His conclusion, as he explains in the somewhat complex analogy of 3:1–6, is that Jesus, the better Moses, is here. Thus he continues the 'Jesus is better' theme introduced in chapter 1 with regard to angels and to which he returns throughout his letter (e.g. in his claims that Jesus is a better high *priest and a better tabernacle). This new and better Moses has come to bring his people, the church, the new Israel, out of a slavery far worse than that imposed by Egypt – a slavery to *sin and death. And by his death and resurrection he has defeated an anti-God figure much more heinous than a mere human pharaoh – Satan himself. And, having himself proceeded to a new, heavenly country, he will one day return to bring his people to a land far better than Israel's piece of land in the Middle East – heaven itself. In the meantime the church, having experienced its own Exodus from sin and death, is now in its desert march awaiting that final redemption (see Heb. 3:7 – 4:11).

Echoes of Exodus in the NT are by no means restricted to Hebrews. For example, Jesus is said to be the manna from heaven (John 6:25–40, esp. vv. 32–35). His death is called an *exodos* in Luke 9:31 ('departure' in NIV). The Last Supper is overtly linked to the Passover meal (Matt. 26:17–29; Mark 14:12–25; Luke 22:7–23), thus indicating that the events about to occur will inaugurate a new Exodus.

The two other main theological themes of Exodus, law and tabernacle, also appear in the NT. The relationship between the gospel and the OT law is a matter of continued debate. Still, it seems quite clear that Jesus, in some sense, fulfils the law rather than simply abrogating it (Matt. 5:17–20). The content of Jesus' teaching does not so much replace the OT law as make explicit its proper application, to the heart and not just to external behaviour. Further, despite Paul's negative comments on the law, it is equally clear that for the apostle the demands of the law are not simply to be brushed aside. Rather the Christian's new status in Christ makes law-keeping possible. The law is not dismissed, but can now be properly followed, for it is now written on the heart (Jer. 31:33; Heb. 8:10). The purpose for which the law was given has been fulfilled.

The tabernacle theme too is transformed in the NT. In at least two places Jesus is described as either the new temple or the tabernacle (although only the tabernacle is mentioned in Exodus, the two structures are clearly connected). Jesus' words in John 2:19 are well known: 'Destroy this temple, and I will raise it again in three days.' This statement was misunderstood by the Jews as a claim to be able to rebuild the literal temple, but John adds that the temple of which Jesus spoke was his body (v. 21). John 1:14 is also important here, although its impact is completely lost in English: 'The Word became flesh and made his dwelling among us.' The Greek verb translated 'made his dwelling' is *skēnoō*. This verb is related to the noun *skēnē*, which is the word used throughout the Septuagint for the tabernacle. John is saying that Jesus came and 'tabernacled' among his people. Clearly, his intention is that Jesus be seen as the new and improved tabernacle/temple. He does not reject the OT structures as places for mere ritual, now (fortunately) obsolete. Rather he recognizes the reality to which the OT structures pointed, a reality that has finally reached its climax in Christ. Jesus embodies more clearly what the OT structures did truly but only partially. Hence, John continues in John 1:14 'We have seen his glory'. The *glory that resided above the ark in the Most Holy Place, to which the high priest alone had access once a year, is now walking the streets of Jerusalem for all to see, a truly 'portable' tabernacle.

At Christ's return, another chapter will be written on this theme. We read in Revelation 21:22, in the account of the descent of the new Jerusalem, that there will be no temple in the new city. This is because 'the Lord God Almighty and the Lamb are its temple'. At the end of our age and at the dawn of the new, what the tabernacle and temple represented in the OT, the very presence of God, will be in the midst of God's people without mediation. God himself will dwell with his people. These words are no doubt written in imagery intended to provoke the imagination rather than to satisfy our intellectual curiosity. John does make clear, however, that at the consummation the tabernacle/temple, that shaped to a large extent Israelite identity, will no longer be needed, because something better will be here.

Between the first and second comings of Christ the position is different. Christ, the new temple, has ascended to the Father. His presence, however, has not left his people. He has sent his Spirit to abide with them. In fact, he himself abides in them. This is what Paul means in his description of the *church in 1 Corinthians 3:16–17: 'Don't you know that you [the Greek is plural] yourselves are God's temple and that God's Spirit lives in you? If anyone destroys God's temple, God will destroy him; for God's temple is sacred, and you are that temple.' The church has become God's holy dwelling, God's temple. Paul develops this thought in 6:19: 'Do you not know that your body is a temple of the Holy Spirit, who is in you, whom you have received from God? You are not your own'. Paul here seems to identify the temple with the individual Christian (sexual conduct is the topic, and the pronoun 'you' is singular). In the period between the first and second comings of Christ, the church both collectively and individually should be understood as realizing the intimacy between God and his people that was first experienced at the building of the tabernacle.

Further, Christ is himself holy and sacred ground in whom the glory of God resides. With the spread of the gospel, God's glory can now be seen in new temples everywhere, wherever men and women repent, come to know him, and gather to worship. God's sacred space is no longer restricted to a building in one part of the world. Nor is it embodied only in his Son, as it was for a brief time two thousand years ago.

Finally, just as Israel's redemption from Egypt was described in creation language, so is the redemption in Christ. For example, John's Gospel begins with the words 'In the beginning'. John's prologue is an explicit attempt to link the person and work of Christ and creation. The redemption soon to come in Christ is a new beginning. Similarly, Paul twice presents Jesus as a 'new Adam' (Rom. 5:12–19; 1 Cor. 15:20–28). Jesus is like

Adam in that both are representatives of a larger group. The continuity between the two, however, is not absolute, since they represent very different groups of people. Through Christ life is given to his people, whereas through Adam's disobedience came condemnation. Yet with the coming of Christ we are taken back to the very beginning of human history. The second Adam does what the first did not do; he is *obedient to God and thus brings life to his people.

The redemption of the individual believer is likewise described in creation language. The most notable example, perhaps, is in 2 Corinthians 5:17: 'Therefore, if anyone is in Christ, he is a new creation [kainē ktisis]; the old has gone, the new has come!' Being in Christ means being a 'new creation'. By virtue of the church's relationship to Christ the creator, the Christian's salvation is a new beginning. And the end will be as the beginning. The final chapter of the book of Revelation brings us back to the Garden of Eden, complete with the tree of life (22:2). At that time, the curse pronounced in the first Garden scene will no longer exist (v. 3). After a long and costly detour, that required the blood of God's Son to correct, creation is set back on track. The church's Exodus is complete. God's holy people have truly entered the Promised Land.

Bibliography

P. E. Enns, *Exodus* (Grand Rapids, 2000); T. E. Fretheim, *Exodus*, Interpretation (Louisville, 1991); D. E. Gowen, *Theology in Exodus: Biblical Theology in the Form of a Commentary* (Louisville, 1994); C. Houtman, *Exodus*, 3 vols., HCOT (ET, Kampen, 1993); J. G. Janzen, *Exodus* (Louisville, 1997); J. Plastaras, *The God of Exodus: The Theology of the Exodus Narratives* (Milwaukee, 1966); N. Sarna, *Exodus* (Philadelphia, 1991).

P. E. ENNS

LEVITICUS

The book

Leviticus is the third book of the Pentateuch, following *Exodus and preceding *Numbers. Its name derives from the Latin form of the Greek word *leuitikon*, which indicates that the book concerns *priests of Levite origin. In Jewish tradition the book is named after its first word, *wayyiqrā'* ('And he called').

Some elements of Exodus–Numbers (including Leviticus) point to the unity of the Pentateuch. Exodus concludes with three verses (40:36–38) that foreshadow the wandering of the Israelites in the desert. This wandering, however, is described not in Leviticus but in the following book of Numbers (ch. 9). But Leviticus is the sequel to Exodus in that it gives rules for the *sacrifices and offerings to be performed in the sanctuary, the construction of which is described in Exodus, and the instructions in Exodus 29 are carried out in Leviticus 8. Furthermore, the fiery manifestation of the Lord in the burning bush in Exodus 3 foreshadows the appearance of the *glory of the Lord not only in Exodus (Exod. 24:16–17) but also in Leviticus (9:24) when Aaron and his sons, assisted by *Moses, offer sacrifices to the Lord in a service on 'the eighth day' (9:1; see below).

Leviticus is based on the promise of the Lord's dwelling in the midst of the *Israelites (Exod. 29:45–46). It addresses the question of how *humans can live in proximity to the *holy *God. (See *temple.)

Structure and themes

Exodus 25 – 40 deals with the construction of the tabernacle; then in Leviticus 1 – 7 five types of offering are prescribed for it (see below for details). Chapters 1 – 7 can be subdivided into two subsections, 1:1 – 6:7 and 6:8 – 7:37. The first is concerned with how to approach the Lord with offerings, the second with safeguarding the holy things. Chapter 8 describes the installation of the priests, and chapter 9 recounts the first service, on 'the eighth day' (*i.e.* after the seven-day ordination of the priests). The ritual described in chapters 8 – 9 takes place in the outer court, while the subsequent story of Nadab and Abihu demonstrates the need for *atonement to be made in the tabernacle.

Chapter 10 recounts the death of Nadab and Abihu, two of Aaron's sons, at the same service. The sin of the priests cannot be dealt with at the altar of the burnt offering; atonement must be made for them in the tabernacle itself (ch. 16).

Chapters 11 – 15 deal with cleanness and uncleanness and with the regulations for the ritual of purification. Uncleanness, unless properly handled, disqualifies the Israelites, including the priests, from approaching the

Lord and thus defiles the tabernacle (15:31).

Chapter 16 concludes the series of regulations which began in Exodus 25. It describes the ultimate atonement ritual, thus establishing literary and theological links with chapters 4 (vv. 6, 17), 9, 10 and 15 (v. 31).

Chapters 17 and following are normally called the 'holiness code' by scholars because they include the refrain 'I am Yahweh your God', and because of their focus on holiness (qdš). However, it is not certain that these commandments constitute a 'code'.

Chapters 18 – 26 consist of religious and ethical commandments. These are addressed not just to the Israelites but also to the foreigners living with them, and they concern not just the camp and the sanctuary but also the *land.

Chapters 18 and 20 deal with illegal sexual unions; chapter 20 lists their consequences and punishments. Chapter 19 lays down fundamental principles in relationships between humans, the sum of which is to be found in verse 18, 'Love your neighbour as yourself.' This chapter also shows that holiness includes both justice and *love. (Compare 19:15, 17 with 19:18.)

Chapter 21 contains rules concerning priests. Although the priests were holy by virtue of their anointing, they were capable of desecrating that holiness. Chapter 22 is closely related to chapter 21; it deals with the cleanness and uncleanness of the priests themselves and of the holy food.

Chapters 23 and 25 deal with 'holy *time': the former with religious festivals (see *Sacred meals); the latter with sabbatical years and the Year of Jubilee. Chapter 24 is composed of laws concerning the lampstand and the twelve loaves of bread, and the case of a blasphemer. The connection between the laws and the narrative in this section is unclear; however, the divine *grace symbolized by the lampstand and the twelve loaves contrasts sharply with the blasphemy. The enormity of blaspheming the Lord highlights the magnitude of God's grace.

Chapter 26 sets God's *blessing and curse before the Israelites, the blessing for *obedience to his commandments and the curse for disobedience. The blessing is presented only briefly, the curse in greater detail and at greater length. The climax of the curse is the threat to destroy the land (vv. 31–33), which is expressed ironically in terms of *redeeming it (cf. ch. 25). Despite the numerous curses, the Lord promises that the people will not perish utterly, as he remembers his covenant with the patriarchs (26:40–45).

Chapter 27 is largely composed of basic principles concerning people and things dedicated to the Lord, such as offerings, houses, real estate, the firstborn, items devoted to destruction and tithes. It lists the items devoted to the Lord which can be returned to their ordinary use, and under which conditions, and those which cannot be returned to their ordinary use under any circumstances.

Thus from chapter 18 onwards Leviticus is concerned with how an Israelite, whether priest or lay person, becomes holy. Holiness is not something given, but an ideal towards which the people ought to aspire.

On the usual critical view, the holiness of the so-called 'holiness code' is different in kind from that of the sacrifices and sanctuary described in Leviticus 1 – 16. In fact, the difference is more a matter of emphasis. The major concerns of chapters 1 – 16, which deal with the holiness of the sacrifices and sanctuary, are defilement and purification. In chapters 18 – 27, which assume the background of chapters 1 – 16 and deal with holy living, the legislation centres on the relationship between the holy God and human beings.

The fact that the chapters dealing with the holiness of such things as altars come first in Leviticus indicates that priority is to be given to creating and maintaining the appropriate environment for God's holy presence.

Theology

Leviticus consists mostly of prescriptions and rules, but these reflect a distinct theology. This theology may be considered under the following headings: sacrifices and offerings; cleanness and uncleanness; holy living.

Sacrifices and offerings

The first five chapters of Leviticus prescribe the way in which the Israelites are to approach the Lord with their offerings. The meaning of each offering is not explained in detail, not because the legislation is concerned only with external acts, but because the participant's sincerity of heart (thanksgiving, *joy, penitence, etc.) when making an offering is presupposed.

The material of the offerings are the Israelites' ordinary foodstuffs. God does not need to be fed (*cf*. Ps. 50:8–13); rather an offering expresses the belief that the Israelites need to be fed (and so be given *life) by God.

As the first act of the sacrificial ritual, the Israelite lays a hand on the animal to be offered, thereby symbolizing that the animal is going to take his/her place. The animal's *blood represents that of the *worshipper. The blood rites performed by the priests enable the offerer to approach the Lord; without the shedding of blood a person cannot approach God. Except in the burnt offering, in which everything is burnt, part of the offering is burnt; the rest is eaten by the priest as his due. In the case of the *peace offering the choicest parts go to the priest and the rest is eaten by the offerer.

There is some overlap in the rites associated with the various offerings (*e.g.* blood, the burning of fat); the meaning of each offering is to be found in the elements most strongly emphasized. The primary functions of the five main offerings in Leviticus 1:1 – 6:7 are as follows.

The burnt offering (Lev. 1). The motives for making a burnt offering are various (atonement for sin, joy, thanksgiving, *etc*.), but it primarily symbolizes the total dedication of the offerer.

The grain/cereal offering (Lev. 2). The emphasis here is on the pleasing aroma which is the culminating element of the burnt offering. It stresses the renewal of one's dedication to the Lord.

The peace/communion/well-being offering (Lev. 3). The emphasis of this offering lies in the eating of the meat with the priest, though Leviticus 3 gives no account of this rite (see 7:15–16). The sacrifice emphasizes communion following reconciliation with the Lord, and/or the dedication of the offerer to the Lord.

The sin/purification offering (Lev. 4:1 – 5:13; 12:8, *etc*.). This sacrifice expiates inadvertent sins, so-called 'sins of negligence' and severe types of natural uncleanness. That these sins and uncleannesses defile the holy things (*e.g.* the altars) is presupposed in the ritual.

*The *guilt/reparation offering* (Lev. 5:14 – 6:7). This sacrifice expiates transgressions such as those against the holy things, those against the divine commandments, and those against God himself (*i.e.* the violation of an oath). Underlying the ritual is the idea of compensation for the damage done both to the neighbour and to God.

Leviticus 17:11 is the key passage on the blood ritual, giving the rationale for it. Two fundamental principles are set out in this passage. 1. God has provided animal blood, which contains life, so that atonement might be made for the sins and uncleanness of the Israelites. 2. The blood can serve as an element in atonement because it is the carrier and symbol of life. Although blood is said to contain life, the blood in sacrificial rites represents a life that has been taken away: that is, it represents *death or, to be more exact, a substitutionary death. This kind of death should not be confused with that symbolized by uncleanness (see below).

The priests' work at the altar is summed up by the Hebrew term *kipper*, normally translated 'atone, make atonement, expiate'; its possible etymologies include the Arabic *kafara* ('cover'), the Akkadian *kuppuru* ('cleanse', 'wipe out'), and the Hebrew noun *kôper* ('ransom'). Although the exact connotation of *kipper* eludes modern scholars, a careful examination suggests that while the term is primarily associated with the blood ritual, it is more comprehensive, including other ritual elements such as the burning of fat. The term appears most frequently in the rituals of the sin-offering (purification offering); the most complicated and solemn of these offerings is performed on the day of atonement (Lev. 16). On this occasion all the sins of the people are expiated and carried into the *wilderness by the Azazel goat.

Cleanness and uncleanness

The cause of the uncleanness discussed in Leviticus 11 – 15 has long been debated. Three basic explanations have been proposed for the uncleanness of the animals in Leviticus 11. The first is the hygienic explanation, that the forbidden animals are harmful to human health; however, harmful plants are not mentioned. The second is the cultic explanation: for instance, pigs are forbidden because they are offered to the Canaanite deity. However, most of Israel's sacrificial animals were sacrificed in Canaan. The third is the symbolic explanation, which is of three kinds: clean animals represent the *righteous and unclean animals the ungodly; unclean animals are associated with death; the uncleanness of an animal is related to its divinely ordained role within *creation and to its mode of locomotion. If an animal transgresses its proper habitat (land, sea, air), it is unclean. Animals with normal locomotion are clean, whereas animals with abnormal locomotion are unclean. This last theory, associated especially with Mary Douglas, is based on anthropological study. However, whilst it was well received at first, there is now some debate as to whether it can satisfactorily explain the evidence of Leviticus.

Uncleanness should certainly be understood in a ritual rather than a physical sense. Therefore it seems appropriate to see the motif of death (including the idea of abnormality) behind the various regulations on uncleanness, since uncleanness is clearly related to death. Carnivorous birds are unclean because they carry the dead bodies of their prey or carrion which they happen to have found. Such dead bodies bear the contagion of uncleanness, which attaches even to a clean animal after it dies.

In Israel natural uncleanness is restricted to discharges of the sexual organs and to skin disease. It seems that the rationale for these rules is closely related to creation and the fall, particularly the latter. For instance, the fact that giving birth defiles the mother (Lev. 12) can be explained best in terms of the curse of God regarding childbirth (Gen. 3:16; *cf.* 1:28). By observing the cleanness/uncleanness laws, the Israelites were reminded of the consequences of the fall, and thus of their sinful nature, as well as their calling to be a holy *people.

Holy living

God is holy and the Israelites are called to become holy (19:2). Some of the characteristics of holiness are revealed in Leviticus.

The opposite of 'holy' is 'common' (10:10). However, holiness is usually contrasted with uncleanness, the former being associated with life and the latter with death. Thus any contact between the holy and the unclean is fatal (Num. 1:51; 3:10; *cf.* Lev. 7:19–20). Not only holy things, such as sacrifices and offerings, but also priests, who are holy by consecration, are to be strictly separated from the unclean (21:10–11).

The idea of holiness also includes that of wholeness/perfection. Thus sacrifices and offerings, which are called 'holy', should be outwardly perfect, without blemish (*e.g.* 1:3,

10), and so should the priests (21:17–23).

On the other hand, sacrifices, altars and various utensils used in the rituals are also called 'holy'; these function mostly in making atonement, thus representing/substituting for the people of Israel.

While holiness is sometimes seen as threatening to the unclean and the sinful, it is also inherently gracious in that all holy things and people (*i.e.* priests) are made holy in order that the Lord may dwell among the people. This suggests that God, who is holy, is also gracious. The exhortations in chapter 19 imply that self-sacrificial love and justice are the essence of holy living (see 19:18).

To live a holy life it is essential to keep the Lord's commandments. In chapter 19 various commandments are given, some of which are negative and others positive. Both kinds must be kept; both bring people closer to the Lord. Leviticus provides both minimum standards and the ideal towards which every individual ought to aspire. To infringe a negative injunction not only brings a penalty; it also indicates that because one always falls short of the ideal, one has something of which to repent.

Holiness is to pervade all areas of Israelite life, both individual and national. It ought to be exhibited not only in the ethical realm, but also in such everyday matters as eating (ch. 11), wearing clothes, the breeding of animals (19:19) and reaping of fruit (19:23). At the centre of life stands the holy God, who redeemed the Israelites from servitude in Egypt.

The Levitical legislation assumes that the world is fallen but is formulated to promote the renewal of human nature and servanthood among the Israelites.

Christian use of Leviticus

Rituals and rules for the purification of uncleanness are foreign to the modern mind. However, it is assumed in the NT that *Jesus Christ fulfilled and superseded every type of sacrifice and offering in his death on the cross. Thus the rules and prescriptions of Leviticus may be read as foreshadowing the work of Christ. For instance, the Azazel goat in chapter 16 takes away the guilt of the Israelites into the wilderness, thus foreshadowing the suffering of Christ outside the gate (*cf.* Heb. 13:12). The Christian reader can also learn from the way in which general principles are tangibly expressed in detailed regulations (*e.g.* the enormity of human sin expressed in laws of cleanness and uncleanness).

As stated above, God's holiness is representative/substitutionary, making possible a relationship between the holy God and the sinful/unclean. This suggests that the holy people and holy things in the Levitical rituals represent the incarnate God before Christ's coming, and that his condescension and graciousness are revealed in the book's rules and prescriptions. The 'severe' OT God and the 'gracious' NT God are one and the same.

The cross of Jesus Christ also can be linked to the OT: his death allows even a lay person (not just a high priest) to enter the eschatological Holy of Holies. To read Leviticus, and to recognize the huge gap that separates the holy from the sinful/unclean, enables Christians better to appreciate the grace of Christ.

Bibliography

R. E. Averbeck in *NIDOTTE* 4, pp. 907–923; R. T. Beckwith and M. J. Selman (eds.), *Sacrifice in the Bible* (Carlisle, 1995); J. Hartley, *Leviticus*, WBC (Dallas, 1992); P. P. Jenson, *Graded holiness: A key to the priestly conception of the world* (Sheffield, 1992); N. Kiuchi, *The purification offering in the priestly literature: Its meaning and function* (Sheffield, 1987); G. J. Wenham, *The Book of Leviticus*, NICOT (Grand Rapids, 1979).

N. KIUCHI

NUMBERS

Numbers follows *Exodus and *Leviticus and relates the history of the people of *Israel for the next 40 years or so, by the end of which they are on the plains of Moab on the border of Canaan. *Deuteronomy, which follows Numbers, consists largely of an account of *Moses' sermon there. The message and theology of Numbers are most clearly seen when it is considered as part of the narrative from Genesis to Kings, which begins with the promises made to *Abraham in Genesis 12 – 22. (See *Genesis to Kings.)

The promises to Abraham and the theology of Numbers

*God's promises to Abraham were twofold: 1. 'through your offspring all nations on earth will be blessed' (Gen. 22:18, NIV; *cf.* 12:3); 2. 'I will make you into a great nation' (Gen. 12:2). This second promise is made up of two components: a. the promise of very numerous descendants (13:16; 15:5; 17:2, 6; 22:17); and b. the promise of the *land of Canaan (13:15, 17; 15:18; 17:8). The fulfilment, and delay in the fulfilment, of these promises are the organizing principle of the remainder of the Pentateuch and of Joshua. (In Judges, Samuel and Kings, though they are not the organizing principle, they are still prominent.) The need for *faith in the ability of God to fulfil his promises is emphasized (see especially the statement that 'Abraham believed God, and he credited it to him as righteousness' [15:6]), and then, later, the climactic testing of Abraham's faith in the promises when he was commanded to sacrifice Isaac (Gen. 22).

The remainder of Genesis and Exodus tell how the fulfilment of the promises of numerous descendants and the land of Canaan were often under threat. But by the end of Exodus the Israelites are numerous and the promise of the land is about to be fulfilled. A rapid advance into Canaan is expected; in chapters 1 – 10 of Numbers final preparations are completed and the people set out. But in the next section (chs. 11 – 21) the people fail to trust in God to give them the land, and all are sentenced to die in the desert. The fulfilment of the promise is deferred for forty years. But this is not the end of the story, which now moves from Israel's disobedience and unbelief to God's faithfulness to his promise. In chapters 22 – 24 God forces the pagan prophet Balaam to proclaim *victory for Israel, and then in chapters 26 – 36 he prepares the new generation to enter Canaan; they are numbered and told how to allot the land among the various tribes and clans. The book ends with Canaan in sight.

So the book of Numbers continues the story of the outworking of God's promises to Abraham, analysing both Israel's tendency to unbelief and, over against this, God's faithfulness to his promises.

Chapters 1 – 10

This first part of the book describes how the Israelites, following God's instructions given through Moses, prepared to leave Mount Sinai to occupy the land of Canaan. A census was held of those able to serve in the army. This was in preparation for war: the commanders needed to know the numerical strength of their army, and the Israelite men realized that war was coming and so prepared themselves mentally and physically (ch. 1). The layout of the camp was carefully organized: the tribes formed an outside circle and the *priests an inner one, with the tabernacle at the centre, and this arrangement is related to the people's marching order (ch. 2). Instructions were issued to the Levites about how the tabernacle was to be transported (ch. 4), and carts were donated for this purpose (ch. 7). New rules were given to prevent the camp from being defiled by ritual or moral sins; such defilement could jeopardize the occupation of the land (ch. 5). The people were led by a cloud above the tabernacle (ch. 9). Silver trumpets were made to announce the start of each journey (ch. 10). There is a small amount of other material in this section which does not appear to be directly related to the imminent journey and war or to the occupation of Canaan; for example, the detailed instructions for the appointment of the Levites (chs. 3 and 8). But the emphasis on preparations is so strong, and the people are being so *obedient, that the long-awaited fulfilment of God's promise to Abraham concerning the land of Canaan appears to be imminent. This impression is reinforced as the Israelites set out from Sinai in chapter 10:11, by three optimistic speeches from Moses: to Hobab he said: 'If you come with us, we will share with you whatever good things the Lord gives us' (10:32); and to God he prayed: 'Rise up, O Lord! May your enemies be scattered; may your foes flee before you' (10:35), and 'Return, O Lord, to the countless thousands of Israel' (10:36).

Chapters 11 – 21

After ten chapters of complete harmony between the Israelites and God, and of constructive activity, there follow eleven chapters of rebellion on the part of the people, *anger on the part of God, and major destruction. The suddenness of the transition from the last verse of chapter 10 to the first verse of chapter 11 vividly draws attention to the fickleness of the Israelites.

The rebellion took the form of refusal to trust God; seven cases are described. In four instances the people refused to accept the difficult conditions God was making them endure, especially with regard to food and water (at Taberah, 11:1–3; at Kibroth-Hattaavah, 11:4–34; at Meribah, 20:1–13; and between Hormah and Oboth, 21:4–9). In two cases they refused to accept the leaders he had provided (Moses, 12:1–16; or Moses and Aaron and the Aaronite priesthood, ch. 16). Then, in the incident which is presented as by far the most serious, when the spies returned from their exploration of Canaan, the people refused to trust God's promise to give them the land. God said that this represented a refusal to believe in him (14:11). The fulfilment of the Abrahamic promise was postponed; God's plan for the nation was disrupted; all adult Israelites were sentenced to die in the desert (chs. 13 – 14). These chapters reflect both the promises of God in Genesis and the accompanying call for faith in God's ability to fulfil his promises.

Most of the other material in this section of Numbers is linked to the rebellions. In 15:22–31 the laws about deliberate *sins (as distinct from unintentional ones) serve to indicate that the people's refusal to believe God was deliberate sin and that God was being entirely consistent when he imposed the death penalty for it. And the material in chapters 17 – 19, i.e. the budding of Aaron's staff and the rules for priests and Levites, is a reassertion of the authority of the Aaronic priesthood in the face of the rebellion against it by Korah, Dathan and Abiram (ch. 16).

Yet even in the midst of this overwhelmingly dark picture there are glimmers of light. The fulfilment of the promise was postponed for forty years, but the promise was not abrogated. Immediately after the catastrophic chapters 13 and 14, God says, 'After you enter the land I am giving you as a home ...' (15:2); and there follow instructions about offerings which assume that the people will have land on which they will be able to grow crops of grain and grapes. In the last chapter of this section there is the story of God's merciful provision of the bronze snake and of the people believing God's promise in relation to it, and also that of the first military victories, over Sihon and Og; the second of these is explicitly attributed to the power of God (ch. 21). The faithfulness of God, never completely hidden, is now being revealed more clearly.

Chapters 22 – 36

The account of Israel's journeys in chapters 20 and 21 implies that by this stage the old unbelieving generation had all died out. The

157

faithfulness of God, and his continuing intention to fulfil his promise concerning the land, now come to the fore. These themes are dramatically presented in the remarkable account of the activities of Balaam (chs. 22 – 24). Balak king of Moab, afraid of the advancing Israelites, hired Balaam to curse them. But Balaam found himself unable to do anything but *bless them. On four separate occasions he predicted good for Israel, even quoting God's promises to Abraham (23:10, *cf.* Gen. 13:16; 15:5; Num. 23:21, *cf.* Gen. 17:8; Num. 24:9, *cf.* Gen. 12:3; Num. 24:17, *cf.* Gen. 17:6). The inability of a pagan prophet to nullify the promises of God to Israel underlined the fact that those promises were sure; the Moabites, standing between Israel and Canaan, would not be able to stop their fulfilment. (There is delightful irony and humour in the account: the region's greatest authority on spiritual matters cannot see an angel standing in the middle of the road in front of him, but his donkey can!)

The following chapter (25), a story of sexual immorality and idolatry, is very disappointing, but the disappointment is probably outweighed by optimism: the narrative emphasizes the intense loyalty to God of Phineas, a grandson of Aaron, suggesting that with young leaders like this the new generation will do well.

The census of chapter 26 confirms that the disbelieving generation has died out; this reinforces the impression that the promise of the land will now be fulfilled. Almost all the following material concerns preparation for battle and for arrival in the land of Canaan. The urgent question of who would succeed Moses and lead Israel into the Promised Land was answered with the appointment of Joshua (ch. 27). It was decreed that women would be allowed to inherit land (ch. 27), provided that they married within their own tribe (ch. 36). A complete programme of *sacrifices to be offered every day of the year was provided, since the people would soon have a settled lifestyle and an abundant supply of animals, flour, wine and oil (chs. 28 – 29); these instructions must have been very exciting for people struggling for subsistence. Provision was made for releasing people from vows which had created unforeseen problems (ch. 30). Why such laws were required at this time is not immediately obvious, but G. J. Wenham (*Numbers* [1981], p. 207) suggests

that vows were often taken in time of war (*cf.* 21:2; Judg. 11:30–31; 21:1–7); Israel was facing a long war.

The attack on the Midianites is recorded in chapter 31 (25:16–18), while given its own justification in 25:16–18, is also linked to the theme of preparation for Canaan. The narrative concentrates less on the battle itself and more on the treatment of the enemy and the spoils. Moses' instructions, given in response to mistakes made by the Israelites, pointed forward to those given by God to Joshua during the conquest. Not a single Israelite life was lost in this major battle; it was a striking testimony to the faithfulness of God to his people. Reuben and Gad were given permission to settle on the east side of the Jordan, provided that they helped with the conquest of Canaan (ch. 32). Chapter 33 contains a list of forty places where the Israelites camped between leaving Egypt and arriving on the plains of Moab. This fits well with the theme of expectancy and confidence: the lengthy description of the long journey suggests that the people are now near their journey's end; and 'If God has helped Israel thus far, then he will surely enable them to reach their goal, the land of Canaan' (Wenham [1981], p. 217). The boundaries of the land to be possessed by the Israelites were clearly defined, as were the names of the leaders who would divide it among the various tribes (ch. 34). Special arrangements were made for the Levites: they were not to receive a single large tract of territory like the other tribes did, but instead forty-eight cities scattered throughout the territories of the other tribes. Six of these cities were designated 'cities of refuge', places of safety for anyone who accidentally killed another person (ch. 35).

The failure of Israel to believe seemed to threaten the fulfilment of God's promise of the land, but by the end of Numbers the picture is bright again. God has not revoked his promise; he is bringing his people into Canaan.

The artistry of the writer

The author of Numbers used his literary skill and craftsmanship to communicate his message more powerfully. The arrangement of the book is broadly chronological, but in chapters 1 – 10, although the author gives the dates of the various events, they are not recounted in chronological order. Instead the narrative progresses three times from the outer circle of the camp (the tribes) to the inner circle (priests and Levites) and twice to the tabernacle in the centre: first, in chapters 1 – 4 the tribes and then the Levites are numbered; secondly, in chapters 5 – 8 the camp and then the priesthood and tabernacle are consecrated; thirdly, in chapter 9 the Passover is observed throughout the camp and then the cloud appears over the tabernacle. In this way the layout of the camp, which symbolizes the presence of God at the centre of the nation, is given additional emphasis. (See P. J. Naylor, in *NBC*, pp. 160–161.)

In the middle section of the book no dates are given for the seven 'rebellions', but the accounts are ordered symmetrically (*i.e.* in a chiasm) as follows: A. 11:1–3, general difficulties; B. 11:4–34, monotonous food; C. 12, leadership; D. 13 – 14, enemies in the land; C[1]. 16 – 17, leadership; B[1]. 20:1–13, lack of water; A[1]. 21:4–9, general difficulties. (For this analysis *cf.* R. Schultz, *NIDOTTE* 1, p. 190.) This arrangement emphasizes the rebellion of chapters 13 – 14. (J. Milgrom, *Numbers*, JPSTC [Philadelphia, 1992], finds shorter chiasms in nearly every chapter of the book.)

The theology of Numbers in the context of the whole Bible

The theological pattern which emerges in Numbers, *i.e.* harmony between God and Israel, followed by unbelief and disobedience, followed by God's *judgment, followed by God once again working graciously with Israel to fulfil his promises to them, repeats itself over a much longer time frame in the subsequent history of Israel. Samuel and Kings, and Amos, Micah, Isaiah, Jeremiah and Zephaniah tell a story of harmony followed by disobedience and then judgment; Isaiah 40 – 66, Ezekiel 24–48 and Haggai, and Chronicles, Ezra and Nehemiah tell of how God did not abandon his people but once again began to pursue his purpose of blessing them. So the theological themes of Numbers are attested throughout the OT.

Both Matthew (4:1–11) and Luke (4:1–13) saw a parallel between *Jesus' forty days in the *wilderness and Israel's forty years in the desert. The temptations Jesus faced were almost identical, relating to food, protection and *idolatry. But Jesus did not give in to the temptations. His replies to the devil were quotations from Deuteronomy, which originally referred to the wilderness experience recorded in Numbers. Jesus was the new Israel who succeeded where the old Israel failed (Wenham [1981], p. 51). (See *Testing.)

The insistence throughout the NT that salvation is by faith alone sits very easily with Numbers' theology. Indeed, it might even be said that the faith which the gospel requires is faith in the promises of God, whether these are the promises of Jesus (*e.g.* Matt. 11:28) or promises of God in relation to Jesus (*e.g.* John 3:16; Acts 2:38–39; Rom. 8:1)

In a few places believers are warned against 'a sinful, unbelieving heart that turns away from the living God' (Heb. 3:12, a reference to Numbers) or against falling away through disobedience (Heb. 4:11). But more frequent are assurances that God will be faithful to those who have become his children and will complete his loving purpose for them (John 10:28–29; Phil. 1:6; 1 Thess. 5:24).

Bibliography

T. D. Alexander, *From Paradise to the Promised Land* (Carlisle, 1995); P. J. Budd, *Numbers* WBC (Waco, 1984); P. J. Naylor in *NBC*, pp. 158–197; G. J. Wenham, *Numbers*, TOTC (Leicester and Downers Grove, 1981); *idem*, *Numbers*, OTG (Sheffield, 1997).

I. HART

DEUTERONOMY

Introduction

The book of Deuteronomy, which consists mostly of *Moses' final 'sermon' stands at a crucial juncture not only in the history of the infant nation of *Israel, but also in the unfolding of *God's revelation. It both provides a fitting climax to the Pentateuch, bringing the theology of promise and *covenant to its fullest and most mature expression, and lays the theological foundations for much of what follows in both OT and NT. The most significant contribution of Deuteronomy to biblical theology lies in its view of God's *grace. Much of the book is devoted to explaining that even God's *people are intrinsically *sinful, and the inevitability of their moral failure. Despite all that God has done for his people, they will surely disobey. Moses, however, goes on to anticipate the later prophetic discussions of the 'new covenant'. The grace which God has shown to Israel in the past will one day be surpassed by his provision of a lasting solution to the problem of human sin. At the deepest level, the theology of Deuteronomy is a theology of grace, and thus anticipates the coming of Christ to deal with human sin.

Grace that demands a response

The role of the covenant in Deuteronomy

Considerable efforts have been made to identify the genre of the book by comparing it to other extant covenant documents (whether Egyptian, Hittite or Assyrian). Of much more importance than the templates possibly used in the composition of the book is the way in which Moses takes common covenantal ideas and applies them to the unique situation in which Israel finds itself forty years after leaving Egypt. Yahweh's inauguration of a 'covenant' with Abraham and his offspring had, from the very beginning (Gen. 12:1–3), carried with it the obligation to make a choice. This same basic covenantal choice lies at the heart of the theology of Deuteronomy, as the call of 30:19–20 makes clear: 'Now choose life, so that you and your children may live and that you may love the LORD your God, listen to his voice, and hold fast to him' (NIV). That the whole book is an exposition of this choice is made very clear in chapters 27 – 29, where the rituals to be enacted on entering the *land and Moses' own words on Israel's prospects both centre on the themes of '*blessing' and 'curse'. If Israel obeys, the people will enjoy the blessings of the covenant. If Israel disobeys, they will experience the curses of the covenant. God has acted in grace, but now Israel must choose which way to go.

The prophets return time and time again to this most basic consequence of Israel's relationship with God (see *e.g.* 1 Sam. 8; 12; 1 Kgs. 8; 18; 2 Kgs. 22 – 23; Neh. 9; Jer. 2 – 4 *et al.*; Ezek. 18; Dan. 9; Hos. 4; Amos 5). The teaching of the NT reflects a similar perspective. Much of *Jesus' ministry is predicated on a Deuteronomic understanding of covenant. The 'Sermon on the Plain' in Luke 6, with its blessings and woes, and many of the parables, reflect the fundamental dichotomy between choosing *life and choosing *death in a covenantal context (see *e.g.* Matt. 22:1–14; 25:14–30). John, both in his Gospel (light/darkness) and in Revelation (blessing/-curse, see 22:3, 7) works with similar categories, but it is Paul, particularly in Galatians 3:10–14, who draws most explicitly on these chapters. He understands Christ's redeeming work to consist in freeing people from the curse of the covenant, actualized by their inability to keep the *law (see also Rom. 3:20).

In Deuteronomy, then, covenant language serves to highlight the decisions which now face Israel as a result of Yahweh's gracious intervention in their national life. This raises one very obvious question: of what exactly does this 'decision' consist?

Israel's journey of obedience

In Deuteronomy, two kinds of response are demanded of Israel. The first is quite obvious: Israel must reverse the mistake made at Kadesh Barnea forty years earlier (see Num. 13 – 14). This time they must not simply send a reconnaissance mission, but take the decisive step of settling down in the land. This initial step of *obedience must then be followed by a more far-reaching response. Israel must live in obedience to Yahweh in the land.

To convey the nature of this life of obedience, in his preaching Moses introduces the theological idea of Israel's journey of obedience. The book opens with a pointed reassessment of Israel's recent journey out of Egypt. It may take only eleven days to travel from Horeb to Kadesh Barnea (1:2), but it had taken God's new people forty years. They were allowed to take their own decisions (1:9–18), but this led only to a cowardly and catastrophic resolution to remain where they were, made on the basis of far-fetched tales of mythical giants ('Anakites') living in Canaan. In fact, the journey of Israel to the land stopped before it had even properly started, and soon the people of God found themselves in retreat (2:1).

However, the rebellion of Israel is ultimately met not with rejection, but with grace. After consistently caring for them in the desert (2:7), God finally sets his people moving in the right direction once more (2:2). His desire to see them, like their 'cousins', Ammon, Edom and Moab, settled in the land given to them is unabated. God will not simply leave Israel to conquer Canaan unassisted. Just as by his grace he cleared the hostile kings Sihon and Og from their path (2:24 – 3:7), so he will ensure that their advance continues.

There is, however, no guarantee that the Israelites will reach their 'destination', whether that is simply occupation of the land or sustained obedience within it. God's insistence that Moses himself cannot enter the Promised Land (3:21–29) is a stark reminder of that fact. Even the new start offered to Israel under Joshua does not qualify the serious implications of Moses' *exclusion. The harsh reality of the choices occasioned by the covenant is plain for all to see. Israel's journey really does matter.

Chapter 4, which functions as an overture to the rest of the book, begins to spell out what this ongoing journey will involve. The key to a continuing, obedient response is 'listening' (4:1). In the same way that listening to God at Horeb and obeying was the precondition of progress through the *wilderness, obedience to the divine *word holds the key to Israel's 'progress' into Canaan. After that, living 'successfully' in Canaan (i.e. enjoying a right relationship with Yahweh and thus being the envy of all other nations, 4:5–8) depends on obedient listening to God. To keep 'moving', Israel must keep listening and obeying.

The Deuteronomic version of the Decalogue in chapter 5 builds on the identification of Moses' preaching in Moab with God's words at Horeb. In 5:2–3, Moses even goes so far as to say that God made the covenant at Horeb 'with us', not with 'our fathers'. This seems a rather strange statement, as 2:14 asserts that by this stage (Moses, Joshua and Caleb apart) there were no adult survivors of the *Exodus. However, it is Moses' way of urging his contemporaries at Moab to remember that God's self-revelation is not something only in the past. God is still speaking, and his people must continue to respond. In Moab, God through Moses is taking the essence of what was said at Horeb, and reapplying it to the radically different circumstances of settled life in Canaan (5:22– 31). The words of the 'Shema' at the beginning of chapter 6 underline the continuity between past and present. Israel's primary responsibility is still to 'listen' to God's gracious words, for only then will they keep moving on with God and be satisfied in the land (6:3), experiencing in full measure the

fulfilment of the covenant promises.

Chapters 7 – 11 are one long call to Israel to choose life over death and blessing over curse as they continue to move forward into the land, and to progress in obedience within it. *Election (ch. 7), the past action of God (ch. 8) and the past failures of Israel (chs. 9 – 10) are the basis for a series of plaintive appeals (e.g. 10:12–22) for wholehearted commitment to Yahweh.

It is in this context that the command to destroy the Canaanites must be understood. God has given the land into the hands of the Israelites. As a response to this divine initiative, the first decision they must make on entering the land is to destroy all vestiges of Canaanite civilization. Several reasons are given for this command. First, Israel must realize that they are acting primarily as agents of God's *judgment on a wicked people (9:4). In addition, God makes it clear that Israel could not resist the temptations with which life in a pluralistic environment would present them at this stage in their national development (e.g. 7:3–6). The account of Joshua – 2 Kings supports this assertion. Moreover, Moses frequently insists that this *war is unique. Once Israel is settled in the land, the rules of engagement change (see ch. 20). Deuteronomy is not a charter for military expansionism. It presents the war of judgment against the Canaanites, shocking though it may be, as one aspect of the ongoing choice between blessing and curse which Israel must make as they continue their journey.

At several points in the book (e.g. chs. 4, 29 – 31), the outcome of the journey upon which Israel has embarked is anticipated. The journey began in Egypt, and has taken Israel haltingly to the edge of Canaan. This onward movement will continue into and in the land. But Moses also predicts that this journey will one day take them back out of the land, even back to 'Egypt' (e.g. 28:58–68). From there, the journey will once more restart, bringing Israel back into the land, where this time a consistent walk with God will be a reality, rather than a vain hope (30:1–10).

The course of this 'ethical journey' is charted in the rest of the Bible. The account does not always make pleasant reading, as Israel eventually returns to 'Egypt' (the exile), before God intervenes decisively to make obedience a real possibility for his people in Christ. The journey of God's people, however, does not end with the coming of Christ. The writer of Hebrews, in particular, uses the metaphor of journeying to describe the Christian life. In chapters 3 and 4, the experience of Israel in the wilderness is used to urge Christians to press on, making every effort to enter the 'sabbath rest of God'. (Paul often uses similar language, drawn from the world of athletics [*e.g.* 2 Tim. 4:7] to emphasize that believers must persevere to the end.) The long list of 'people of faith' in Hebrews 11 makes the same essential point, that life with God is always a journey, in which people respond to his grace by making conscious choices to follow him into the future, and it will continue to be so until they find rest in the new heavens and the new earth.

The life of faith throughout the Bible involves an initial commitment (or act of *repentance), followed by a lifetime consisting of similar decisions to submit to the Sovereign Lord, constantly reorienting one's life to conform with the pattern he has laid down. Deuteronomy's concept of the journey of discipleship stands in a tradition extending from Abraham's departure from Haran to the apostolic injunction to persevere to the end.

The nature of obedient response

Deuteronomy contains many general descriptions of the response sought by Yahweh from his people (see *e.g.* 10:12–13), but it is in the collection of laws in chapters 12 – 26 that the specifics of obedience are defined. The laws present Israel with the opportunity to keep moving forward in obedience to God, even after they have settled in the land. At some points the theological dimension of this legal material is extremely clear, while at others it is well hidden in what appears to be a jumble of very specific case law (*e.g.* 25:11–12). Overall, however, these chapters provide clear evidence of how the Deuteronomic theology of covenant and journey shapes the ethics of God's people. The ethical demands of these chapters can be summarized under three broad headings.

Obedience and worship. The laws consistently declare that the primary responsibility of Israel in Canaan is to *worship Yahweh, and to worship him at the place and in the way that he chooses (see ch. 12). This worship is regulated by divine revelation; the place and the manner of worship are both determined by God's sovereign choice. Israel

must constantly listen to the divine word, allowing it to shape their worship, and must keep on the move, regularly going to the place chosen by God to enjoy his presence. Conversely, Israel must repudiate the ways of Canaan. As God's chosen people, their whole life must reflect the distinctiveness which God requires. This is the only way to live obediently in the land.

Obedience and the land. In Deuteronomy, worship is inseparably connected to land, for the land is pre-eminently the place where God is encountered. Yahweh brings Israel out of Egypt and gives them the land, first that they should enjoy its bounty, but ultimately that his people should enjoy his company (12:7; 16:1, 13–14). This is why the nation is called to the place of Yahweh's choice; there, at the heart of the land, they can enjoy the presence of the Lord. Enjoyment of the milk and honey of Canaan, won in the dark night of the Passover, is intimately linked to enjoyment of a relationship with Yahweh himself. It is vital, then, that nothing is done to defile this land; such defilement must inevitably affect the people's relationship with the owner of the land.

Obedience and human relationships. Not only defilement of the land interrupts Israel's relationship with God, but also the breakdown of relationships among the people. They are one people serving one God in one land, they must do everything in their power to maintain justice and right relationships, equality and equity, so that the relationship for which they have been set apart can be enjoyed in all its fullness.

These three simple distinctives are all direct theological consequences of the Exodus event. The nation has been *redeemed, and now belongs to God. As his unique people, they must submit to him in worship. He has redeemed them from Egypt to enjoy a relationship with him, and to do so in his land. They must not treat one another in a way which is incompatible with how he has treated them in redeeming them. Now that they have become an Exodus people, a people of journey, they are destined to keep moving forward with Yahweh, their redeemer God.

In the Exodus, Israel experiences God's grace. At Horeb, God explains that experience and begins to describe what it means to be his people. In Moab, Moses, God's spokesman, applies the theology of the Exodus and the laws of Horeb to the new life facing Israel in Canaan. Israel must respond to the ethical demands which these laws place upon them.

This reading of the laws is supported by the content of chapter 26 with which it is concluded. 26:1–11 describes a paradigmatic response not only to the grace of Yahweh, but also to the declaration of his laws. At the place God has chosen, Israel is to make their response to God. The basic affirmation to be made by the worshipper (v. 3) is that the land is the gift of Yahweh. The longer credal statement (vv. 5b–10a) is focused on the starting point and destination of Israel's journey. The transition from landless rabble to landed nation is, in one sense, complete; Israel now has a new land and a 'new' law. 'Law-code' is an inadequate title for Deuteronomy 12 – 26, which is not a list of legal statutes, but law pressed into the service of theological preaching, law set in the context of a response to grace. In this respect Deuteronomy is the prototype of all the Bible's subsequent ethical teaching.

The all-embracing obedient response to grace envisaged here is reflected in much of the NT. Paul in Romans 12:1–2 declares that an obedient response to God consists of worship, but this worship is expressed in the details of life (rather than in temple rituals). Whilst in Christ the land is no longer the locus of God's relationship with his people, the integrity and purity of their relationship with Christ, which is conceived in personal terms, must be guarded carefully (e.g. 1 Pet. 1:14–16; 2:9–11), not least for evangelistic reasons. The third dimension of the obedient response (human relationships) is the most prominent in the NT. In view of the mercy God has shown to his people, they are to love one another (e.g. John 15:12–17; 1 Cor. 12 – 13; 1 John 3:16–20). Thus the theological-ethical content of Deuteronomy makes an important contribution to the theology of the whole Bible.

Grace that provides a solution

At one level, Deuteronomy is a thorough-going call to covenantal obedience in the light of God's grace. In practice, however, Moses knows that Israel's future life will not be that simple, for God's people will inevitably fail.

The strange paradox of the book is that whilst calling for obedient choices to be made, Moses also seems convinced that Israel will fail to deliver the faithful response which Yahweh seeks. As Israel failed in the desert (see chs. 1 – 3), so they will fail in the land. The heavy irony of chapter 2, which makes an unfavourable comparison between Israel and the Moabites and Ammonites, shows how little can be expected from God's people. In chapters 4 – 11, where one might expect Moses' preaching to be more positive, he continues in the same style. Chapter 4 rests on the assumption that appeals to Israel's 'better nature' will never suffice to guarantee a life of perpetual bliss in the land (4:25–26). The uncertainty of Israel's future will be unhappily resolved: Israel will disobey; God's people will be expelled from God's land; the nation is already on the road to judgment. Moses believes that the standards he preaches are ultimately beyond the reach of Israel; therefore he regards them as only interim measures. As a true prophet, he preaches and waits for God's solution to the problem of Israel's disobedience.

This pessimism is expressed throughout chapters 5 – 11. The repeated calls to obey or remember (see e.g. 5:1, 31–33; 6:1–14; 7:12–15) reveal an underlying negative expectation. Israel may be God's chosen nation, but not because of their moral stature (7:6–9). In fact, God has chosen a 'stiff-necked' people who are prone to idolatry and disobedience (5:29; 7:25–26; 8:2–5; 9:22–24). Even at Horeb they made an idol in the shape of a calf (9:16). God has given them yet another chance (10:1–9), but it is doubtful whether the same people will be able to keep the same law. Israel may have had the Decalogue for forty years, but the revelation at Horeb has done nothing to solve their basic problem; will the new revelation in Moab solve it? Israel will not respond to the appeal to *circumcise their hearts (10:16) and reject the stubbornness of the past in the face of both the grace and the *holiness of Yahweh. God's people stand on the boundary of the land, confronted by a choice between blessing and curse (11:26–28). On the basis of chapters 1 – 11 there is little reason to suggest that their future will be bright.

After setting out the laws, Moses returns to this basic question, but his words in the closing chapters of the book are no more positive. The list of curses in chapters 27 – 28 is far longer than the list of blessings, and deepens the gloom created by chapters 1 – 11. However, in chapters 29 and 30 Moses turns to the solution that God will eventually provide to the problem of his people's disobedience.

In 29:1 Moses inaugurates a new covenant. He begins with a piercing analysis of Israel's moral, intellectual and spiritual incapacity (see especially 29:4). In so doing, he makes it clear that this new covenant cannot wholly solve Israel's problems, for laws cannot open minds, eyes or ears. 29:5–6 remind Israel that Yahweh has the power to provide a covenant which can deal with the deepest of Israel's problems, their own flawed nature. The chapter then returns to the people's past failures, and culminates in the most severe curse against covenant-breakers in the entire book (29:19–28). According to 29:29, even this Moab covenant (the 'revealed things') will not solve Israel's problems, but God's ultimate covenant (the 'secret things') will one day be revealed.

This new covenant is then anticipated in chapter 30, which speaks of the day when both curse and blessing have been experienced in the life of the nation. Then the 'secret things' will be revealed, and God will act to change his people. At the centre of 30:1–10 stands verse 6, which picks up the command given to Israel in 10:16, and states that, in the wake of their persistent refusal and inability to conform to Yahweh's laws, he will himself circumcise their hearts. Only then will repentance and obedience (30:2–3, 8–10; cf. 6:3–4) be a realistic possibility for God's people, and the full potential of life with God in the land be realized for Israel.

This is the beginning of 'new covenant' thought, developed by Jeremiah and Ezekiel, and an important part of biblical theology. One day Yahweh will solve the problem of the human heart. Then, obedience will be a real possibility (30:11–14). Until Yahweh's climactic (eschatological) action, the only satisfactory option open to Israel is to strive to obey the law which they have been given (30:15–20), making wise decisions in the light not only of their failures in the past, but also of the *hope for the future held out in chapter 30.

The 'postscript' of chapters 31 – 34 confirms this interpretation of the book, returning in both narrative and poetic sections to the problem of Israel's 'nature' and God's solution to it. After Moses' prediction of Israel's apostasy in 31:16–18, Yahweh himself confirms it. The context of the Song of Moses (32:1–43) is therefore one of strong negative expectation. In 32:19–21, God states that he knows the *yeṣer* (sinful nature) of Israel, and Moses points out that the law functions only to convict people of sin (31:26). Moses repeats this assertion in 31:28, before developing these themes in Yahweh's song (e.g. 32:5–6, 15, 16–18, 20–21, 23–27, 28–29), which finishes with the one reference to atonement in the entire book (32:43).

It is not surprising then that in his last words, Moses the lawgiver insists that the law is not the way of *salvation for Israel (32:46–47). The key to enjoying life in the land in the short term is indeed to follow the words of Yahweh recorded in Moses' book (31:24). But the ultimate function of the law is not to enable obedience, but to expose disobedience, paving the way for the divine intervention which will eventually enable real obedience, and a new intimacy with God himself.

Despite the evident significance and holiness of Moses, he dies outside the land as a result of his disobedience. The inference can be only that there is little hope of Israel as a whole surpassing him. His death outside the land is an eloquent illustration of the theology which he preached. J. Sailhamer has forcefully argued that the narrative strategy of the Pentateuch as a whole contrasts Abraham, who lived by faith before the law, and Moses, who failed to keep the law once it had been given. He argues that *the Pentateuch itself* presents the way of Abraham as better than the way of Moses (*Introduction to Old Testament Theology*, p. 270). My reading of Deuteronomy supports his case.

Ultimately, there is hope only in the intervention of God for Israel. The law cannot be kept, even by the greatest of humans. As Israel stands in Moab, faced with a lifetime of decision in the land, Moses' message is simply that lasting obedience can be maintained and lasting prosperity achieved only by trusting in the grace of Yahweh to provide the solution to Israel's problem for which Moses longed.

As the OT unfolds, it becomes apparent that this 'solution' would take a personal form. In Jesus Christ we see that it takes the form of God himself. Much of the theological framework needed to understand the significance of Jesus' coming, life and death was put in place by Moses in his writing, and perhaps above all in Deuteronomy. For it is here that the theology of blessing and curse which lies at the heart of Jesus' sin-bearing work is first articulated. It is here that the hopelessness of humanity trapped in sin, even when chosen by God, is exposed. It is here that the prospect of a divine intervention so radical that it changes people at the very core of their being first appears. This book is a thrilling exposition of grace, grace which we have now seen in all its glory in the Lord Jesus Christ, who demands a response which embraces all of life.

Bibliography

P. C. Craigie, *Deuteronomy*, NICOT (Grand Rapids, 1976); J. G. McConville, *Law and Theology in Deuteronomy* (Sheffield, 1984); J. G. McConville and J. G. Millar, *Time and Place in Deuteronomy* (Sheffield, 1994); J. G. Millar, *Now Choose Life: Theology and Ethics in Deuteronomy* (Leicester and Grand Rapids, 1998); D. T. Olson, *Deuteronomy and the Death of Moses* (Minneapolis, 1994); J. Sailhamer, *Introduction to Old Testament Theology: A Canonical Approach* (Grand Rapids, 1995); C. J. H. Wright, *Deuteronomy*, NIBC (Peabody and Carlisle, 1996).

J. G. MILLAR

JOSHUA

The book of Joshua forms a bridge between the Pentateuch and the books of Judges to Kings. In particular, Deuteronomy 1 – 5 and 27 – 34 include texts that are repeated and developed in Joshua. Themes that continue from the preceding books include Joshua as *Moses' successor, exhortations to faithfulness and courage (ch. 1) that resemble similar exhortations and commands in *Deuteronomy, the experience of the twelve tribes of *Israel in passing through the wilderness and going on to possess the Promised Land, their *obedience to the laws of the 'ban', the allocation of Canaan to them, and the renewal of the *covenant. With the burial of the bones of Joseph at Shechem (24:32), the story of Israel's journey from Canaan to Egypt and back again is completed.

The book of Joshua also anticipates important theological themes found in the succeeding books. Among the most important are the gift of the *land to Israel, and the permission given to non-Israelite outsiders, such as Rahab, to become members of the covenant community. The figure of Joshua also serves as a prominent embodiment of many of the promises of God and receives special attention here.

Holy war and the 'ban'

Israel's *victories in their conquest of the Promised Land readily spring to mind when Joshua is mentioned: in particular, the destruction of Jericho (ch. 6), the conquest of Ai (ch. 8) and the defeat of the southern (ch. 10) and northern (ch. 11) coalitions. God had promised the ancestors of Israel that the land of Canaan would be theirs (Gen. 13:14–17; 15:16–21; 17:8; 35:11–12; 50:24; Exod. 3:8; 6:8; 23:23–31). Despite the failure through unbelief of an earlier attempt (Num. 13 – 14), the occupation of the Promised Land remained a key part of God's covenant promise (Deut. 1:6–8).

Israel's conquest of the land is portrayed as a series of victories in which God directs the operation and Israel responds in obedience. In the case of Jericho, the *war was fought entirely by the Lord; it was he who destroyed the fort's defences, leaving Israel with no task but to enter and take possession of it. With Ai there was an initial failure through the disobedience of one of the warriors (ch. 7). However, once this was addressed, it was God's instructions to Joshua at the critical moment in the battle that enabled the tide to turn and Israel to defeat their opponents (8:18–19). The southern coalition was defeated and destroyed by miraculous interventions (10:10–14). Even in the battle with the northern coalition it was God who handed the enemy over to Joshua and Israel (11:6, 8). All these battles are to be seen as holy wars, not because of the form in which they are recorded, but because they represent the will and power of the Lord God of Israel.

Many question the justice (see *Righteousness, justice and justification) of the divinely approved and assisted slaughter of so many of Canaan's inhabitants. How can a loving and just God allow so many innocents to die? The answer lies in the nature of the holy war commanded by God in Deuteronomy 7 and 20. God is *holy and cannot tolerate *sin. His decision about the Canaanites, held back for many years (Gen. 15:16), was that he would destroy them unless they gave their allegiance to him (as *Rahab did in 2:9–11) and offered no opposition to his people in their conquest of the land (9:2–3; 11:1–5). The 'ban' commanded Israel to destroy every living person in the Promised Land who did not *worship the God of Israel. Animals and property were destroyed, or devoted to the tabernacle, but not in every victory that Israel enjoyed; the divine instructions varied. Holy war was not unique to Israel but was practised by every nation in the ancient Near East. The deity of the winning side was always supposed to have commanded the war, and received rewards for assistance in the victory. The 9th-century BC inscription of King Mesha of Moab records that he devoted conquered Israelite towns and citizens to the 'ban', and uses the term found in the Hebrew Bible.

Was Joshua cruel to put all of Canaan to the sword? Like other nations at the time, Israel adopted a military policy in which defeated enemies were slain in obedience to a putative divine command. In Israel this was called the 'ban'; it involved returning to God that which belonged to him but had rebelled against him in disobedience and disloyalty (Deut. 7:1–6, 20–26; 20:1–20), as had the Canaanites whose land was given to Israel. Rahab knew of the 'ban'; she used the term in her confession of Israel's God as the true God (2:10). The wholesale destruction of every living thing at Jericho (6:16–19) was followed by less drastic destructions at Ai and elsewhere (though at Hazor also the destruction is described as complete). Nevertheless, the impression is given that all people were put to *death and that this was commanded by Moses (11:12–14). The exception of Rahab was not an act of disobedience on the part of Joshua but an example of the way in which anyone who saw the acts of God and believed could *repent, confess the God of Israel and find *salvation and *life. No Canaanite who confessed the lordship of Israel's God was subsequently put to death, even when deceit was involved (as with the Gibeonites in ch. 9).

It is not clear how many non-combatants were put to the sword. From the archaeological evidence it appears that some of the Canaanite cities were primarily military fortresses rather than homes for the local population. Perhaps this is why the Jericho and Ai narratives mention men and women (both as warriors?) but make no explicit reference to children (Josh. 6:21; 8:22–24). Moreover, those who knew that Israel's army was approaching and that it was virtually undefeated may have taken the opportunity to escape. Nevertheless, the 'ban' did command everyone to be put to death, and whilst there are variations regarding booty, there are none which permit the sparing of people.

But little is said about the victims and the circumstances of their deaths. The text is concerned rather with Israel's obedience, with God's holiness, with the opposition of other peoples to him, and with divine and human *mercy for those who confessed faith in him.

The land as inheritance

The land of Canaan was Israel's inheritance, promised to their ancestors (see above) and given by God in the covenant. Gratitude and praise to God were expressed by bringing the firstfruits of the produce to God (Deut. 26). Obedience to the covenant would lead to a long and peaceful life in a fruitful and productive land (Deut. 28:1–14), while disobedience would bring famine, usurpation by others of the produce of the land, and ultimately expulsion from it (Deut. 28:30–68). The promised land of Canaan did not include the regions east of the Jordan that were allotted to Reuben, Gad and the half tribe of Manasseh (13:1 – 14:5). Although this territory was given to them as a special privilege, the tribes were still obliged to participate with the rest of Israel in the conquest of Canaan (1:12–18) and to worship God in the Promised Land, only at the place where he would command the building of an altar (ch. 22).

The land of Canaan was allocated by Joshua. First he gave the greater part of the occupied territory to *Judah (15:1–12, 20–63), Ephraim (16:1–10) and Manasseh (17:1–2, 7–11). Caleb was of the tribe of Judah and he was awarded a special place in the south (i.e., Hebron) for his faithfulness (14:6–15). The remainder of the land was divided by map-makers into seven parts, one for each of the seven tribes who were still to receive an inheritance of land (chs. 18 – 19). After all Israel had received the land promised to them, they gave back some of the towns for the protection of those accused of murder and for use by the Levites, who were dedicated to God's service and were not to possess any tribal land (chs. 20 – 21). Like the offering of the firstfruits already noted, the return of some of the towns and land for these purposes was an acknowledgment that all things belonged to God, and that although he had given his people use of some of them, it was appropriate to confess his ownership by returning a portion to him.

The covenant

According to 1:8, God commanded Joshua to preserve the Book of the *Law by meditating on it and obeying it. The key to his success, and that of Israel throughout the book, was their faithfulness (see *faith) to the covenant. Disobedience, even by one member of the community, could bring about disaster (as in ch. 7). Obedience included observance of the covenant symbol of *circumcision that God gave to Abraham in Genesis 17 (5:1–9). The covenant also required that the feasts (see *sacred meals) be kept; preeminent among them was the Passover, which Israel celebrated as it entered the new land (5:10–12). The renewal of the covenant, the book of the Law of Moses, is remembered in 8:30–35; the Israelites gathered on Mt Ebal and an altar was built there just as Moses commanded in Deuteronomy 27:1–26. The final chapter of the book records a renewal of the covenant in which Joshua led the people at the end of his life. Following a structure resembling a vassal treaty between an overlord and a subject nation, Joshua related the major elements of the treaty/covenant: the identification of the parties (24:2); the review of the past history of the overlord (God) and the vassal (Israel; 24:2–13); the stipulations, summarized in the command to worship and obey the one God of Israel and no other (24:14–15); the curses for disobedience (24:19–20); the witnesses (see *Testimony/witness) of the covenant agreement (24:22, 26–27); the writing of the covenant (24:25–26).

The covenant with God that the people made and renewed stood in contrast to that between the Gibeonites and Israel (9:1–27). The latter was based on deception. The Gibeonites persuaded the Israelites to make a treaty ('covenant' in Hebrew) with them, even though Israel was forbidden to have dealings with other nations near them. The Gibeonites succeeded because they were able to convince Israel that their nation was not close but far away. However, the root of their success lay in the failure of Israel to enquire of the Lord as to whether or not they should make the treaty (9:14). Having been deceived, the leaders of Israel were obliged to allow the Gibeonites to live among them. The people were discontented, and Joshua had to deliver the Gibeonites from the hands of an angry Israelite mob who threatened to kill them (9:26). But Israel honoured the covenant, and it became the catalyst for their war with the southern coalition (10:6–7). It is ironic that Israel's failure to make use of its own covenant with God led them to make another agreement with a group of people with whom they were supposed to have no relations.

Israel, the *people of God

Israel, already a people of God through their deliverance from Egypt (see *Exodus [event]), the Red Sea crossing, the giving of the law at Mt Sinai and the forty years of wilderness travelling, now became a people united in holiness before God.

The unity of the people is illustrated at the beginning and end of the book by a focus upon the group most likely to separate and create division: the tribes who received their inheritance east of the Jordan. These tribes had the least to gain by risking war in the land of Canaan west of the Jordan. Therefore, their oath to participate in the conquest (1:16–18) established the integrity of the whole nation. This continued even when there was a misunderstanding regarding the building of an altar (ch. 22). Disunity in Israel was also a problem when the sin of Achan caused the nation to lose the first battle of Ai. The identification and death of the transgressor and his family was the essential remedy for this sin (ch. 7) and allowed Israel again to be completely united before God and to achieve success in war (ch. 8). A dangerous disunity also appeared during the Gibeonite incident (ch. 9). The leaders were responsible for making a treaty of which the people, when they found out about it, disapproved (9:18, 26). At no other time in the period of conquest did the nation come so close to overthrowing its leadership. Yet even here the word of Joshua was followed and the people were ready to go to war on behalf of Gibeon a short while later (10:6–7).

External threats to Israel's holiness and unity are identified in the book. The general threat posed by the peoples of Canaan was so great that Israel had to exterminate them in order to avoid falling away from God and worshipping other deities. Both the record of wars fought and kings and cities conquered (chs. 1 – 11), and that of the land not yet conquered (13:1–6) underline this threat. The holiness of God's people might also appear to have been threatened by the inclusion of Rahab and her family among the Israelites (6:17, 22–25). However, it is made clear that Rahab was a believer in the God of Israel and acted on Israel's behalf (ch. 2). Therefore her inclusion was not a threat to the holiness of the nation but an example of how other peoples and nations of the world could find blessing through Israel's God. The Gibeonites also confessed the power of God (9:9–10) and became willing servants of the Israelites (9:26–27). Even though no other Canaanite cities followed their example (11:19), they illustrate how other nations might be saved without Israel's holiness being defiled.

The people of Israel practised their holiness through obedience to their leader, Joshua, and the word he received from God. In addition to waging wars of conquest, allocating the land, and observing covenants (see above), Israel engaged in ceremonies which involved the ark of the covenant, the symbol of the presence of the Lord God among his people. One of these took place at the crossing of the Jordan (chs. 3 – 4): a special line of march was created, and a circle of stones was raised to commemorate the event. Another occurred at the first victory in Canaan, the destruction of Jericho: a procession around the walls was made for seven days in accordance with detailed instructions (6:2–5). In fact, the whole series of events in chapters 3 – 6 may be understood as the march of the ark of the covenant across the Jordan and through its first obstacle in the land of Canaan. After that the ark may have settled at the cult centre of Gilgal where Joshua and the army proceeded from and returned to at time of battle (9:6; 10:6–7, 15, 43; 14:6). Like Mt Ebal and Shechem (8:30–35; 24:1, 32) and Shiloh (18:1, 10; 19:51; 21:1–2), it was also a place where later meetings of Israel were held and where Joshua spoke to the people (14:6).

Joshua, God's faithful servant

'Joshua' in the Greek OT (the Septuagint) is spelled exactly the same as 'Jesus' in the Greek NT. Joshua first appears as an assistant of Moses and a warrior (Exod. 17:8–13; 24:13; 32:17). As one of twelve spies he re-

turned an optimistic report on the land of Canaan (Num. 14). He is presented as an example of God-given *leadership; his appointment as Moses' successor was made by God, confirmed by Moses (Num. 27:18–23; 34:17; Deut. 1:38; 3:28; 31:6–7, 23; 34:9; Josh. 1:1–9) and acknowledged by the people. This acknowledgment was based on the successes he had in war, but primarily on the miraculous crossing of the Jordan (3:14), an event which recalled the Exodus from Egypt a generation earlier and the miraculous crossing of the sea ahead of Pharaoh's chariots (Exod. 14 – 15).

Joshua was the successor of Moses and the person divinely chosen to lead the nation of Israel across the Jordan, to take the land of Canaan and so to realize the covenant blessings that God had given to Israel. He was faithful to the LORD, and the Bible makes no explicit criticism of him. The figure of Joshua may be considered from four perspectives that are productive of theological insight: his rise to leadership; his role as military leader; his role as saviour and life-giver; and his service as covenant mediator.

The rise of Joshua to leadership

Joshua appears for the first time as an assistant in Israel's war with the Amalekites (Exod. 17:8–13). Under Moses' direction and with his intercession before God, Joshua led Israel to victory. When Moses received the law it was Joshua who accompanied him up Mt Sinai (Exod. 24:13) and who informed him of the noise of the Israelite's idolatrous worship (Exod. 32:17). Joshua and Caleb were the only two of the twelve spies who gave a positive evaluation of their investigation of Canaan (Num. 14). Whether as a leader or standing apart from the crowd, Joshua was the faithful servant of God and of his appointed leader, Moses. It was no doubt Moses' recognition of this that led him to choose Joshua as his assistant.

Numbers 13:16 describes how Moses renamed Joshua. His earlier name was Hoshea, meaning, 'He has delivered'. 'Joshua' means, 'the LORD has delivered'. Though both names refer to an act of salvation, 'Joshua' specifies the Saviour as the God of Israel. The name may have been Moses' own confession, but it also suggests the promise that Moses saw in Joshua, that of someone who would lead Israel in waging wars decreed by God. It is ironic that the only time that Joshua is described as 'saving' anyone is when he delivered the Gibeonites from the angry Israelites who wished to put them to death despite the covenant that Gibeon deceived Israel into making (9:26). Nevertheless, the renaming of Joshua (like that of Abram and Jacob) represented election by God to a special role in the deliverance and salvation of God's people.

In the Pentateuch Joshua appears most frequently in the descriptions of his appointment by Moses as the latter's successor (Num. 27:18–23; 34:17; Deut. 1:38; 3:28; 31:6, 7, 23; 34:9). In this role Joshua is largely passive as one who is given charges and promises. Similarly, in his initial appearance in the book of Joshua he is the passive recipient of the leadership of Israel as the nation prepares to cross the Jordan and take possession of the land (1:1–9). This charge given to him included both a reaffirmation of the promise to the patriarchs of the land (vv. 1–5) and most importantly, the promise of the acquisition of that land by means of God's presence with Joshua (vv. 6–9). It is this latter promise that was the basis for Joshua's courage and strength. God's presence enabled Joshua to attain the victories and to meditate upon the law of the Lord (v. 8). The divine presence promised to Joshua is explicitly compared with that granted to Moses, the servant of the Lord. Joshua was the successor of Moses and all that God had promised and given to Moses was renewed in God's presence with Joshua (vv. 3, 5).

The establishment of Joshua as leader of Israel was not completed until the crossing of the Jordan (3:14). However, all the elements of his leadership are already present in the first chapter of the book. Its basis lay in the divine commissioning of Joshua as successor to Moses. But this was worked out as Joshua instructed the leaders of the people, who conveyed his words to all Israel (1:10–11), and as he received an oath of loyalty from the part of Israel least likely to follow him, those tribes who had already received their lands in the region east of the Jordan River (1:12–18).

Military leader

As military leader, Joshua followed Moses' basic strategy for the conquest of the land. In so doing he showed that he was first the obedient servant of God and then the loyal warrior. First, he sent out spies or scouts be-

fore the wars against Jericho (ch. 2) and Ai (7:2). This was both an information gathering exercise and an opportunity to identify supporters of Israel and their God, such as Rahab and her family (ch. 2). Joshua's deliverance of Rahab (6:17, 22–25) was not a disobedient act of mercy (see on the 'ban' above), but rather the fulfilment of a covenant between Israel and Rahab that was made as a result of her confession of faithfulness and her acting upon it.

More important than the sending of scouts, however, was the way in which Joshua followed Moses as a recipient of divine instructions and his precise obedience to them. The first military expedition was the movement across the Jordan, through which the warriors, arrayed for battle, marched on dry land. This was a miracle brought about by obedience to the instructions given by God to Joshua (3:7–8; 4:1–3, 15–16). The same principle was illustrated in the victories over Jericho (6:2–5), Ai (8:1–3, 18), the southern coalition (10:8) and the northern coalition (11:6). All these were accompanied by encouraging promises, which Joshua received as a result of God's abiding presence with him. The account of the failure at Ai (ch. 7) and the making of the Gibeonite treaty (ch. 9) are notable for the absence of God's *word. Interestingly, Joshua does not play the same key role in these passages. In the Gibeonite story, he appears as part of the leadership group (9:14–15), and so is not solely responsible for the failure to consult the Lord.

There is, correspondingly, an emphasis in the account of Joshua's military leadership upon God's gracious acts and words. In fact, there was often little that Joshua needed to do other than reap the rewards of victory. This was especially true at Jericho, where the collapse of the walls seemed to signal the end of all resistance and the Israelites needed only to enter the city and 'take' it (6:20). At Ai Joshua followed the divine instruction to hold out his javelin, and at once the whole battle turned, with the burning of Ai and the destruction of the army (8:18–19). In the southern campaign, God threw the enemy into confusion, sent down huge hailstones from heaven and caused the sun to stand still (10:10–14).

The Israelites were thus able to overcome all opposition. In the northern campaign also, Joshua and the Israelite army met no opposition, but rather 'the LORD gave them into the hand of Israel' (1:8, NIV). God was able to perform miracle after miracle (see *Signs and wonders) as Joshua and Israel responded in faith and obedience.

One incident in Joshua's role as military leader is most mysterious: his confrontation with the commander of the army of the LORD on the eve of the Jericho campaign (5:13–15). Although this incident resembled Jacob's wrestling with the stranger at Peniel (Gen. 32:22–32), the closest parallel is with Moses' confrontation with God at Horeb (Exod. 3:1–5). Both accounts begin with an encounter between the leader and one who speaks. The leader is commanded to remove his shoes; there then follows a divine commissioning that prepares him for the struggle ahead. The figure in Joshua 5 was associated with God and the charge was intended to equip Joshua for what was to come.

Saviour and life-giver

Although Joshua is explicitly described as 'saving' only the Gibeonites (from the Israelites, 9:26), he also continually saved Israel from their enemies, including internal corruption like that of Achan (ch. 7). Further, he delivered Rahab and her family. Even in the opening chapters of the book, Joshua is seen delivering Israel. The nation was in danger of fragmentation and disintegration because of the two and a half tribes of Transjordan (1:12–18). Moreover, the Jordan was in its flood stage, and Israel needed to cross it (3:15). In both cases Joshua delivered the people by acting according to the instructions of God.

Joshua also gave *life to Israel in that through him the covenant promises that the land would be theirs were fulfilled. It seems that Joshua supervised the distribution of the whole Promised Land to all the remaining tribes (14:1, 13–15; 17:15, 17–18; 18:3–9) and allocated both the towns of refuge (20:1–3) and the towns set aside for the Levites (21:1–3). Israel received the land and they and all future generations were given the opportunity to live in it and to enjoy it.

This covenant promise generated the warnings that Joshua gave to the people at the end of his life (ch. 23); in doing so he again acted as a life-giver. He warned the people to obey God and love him. Serving other deities in Canaan would bring an end to their lives and those of their children.

Covenant mediator

Covenant as a relationship between God and the people of Israel is a theme that reaches its climax in Deuteronomy where the details of Israel's covenant are set out. In Joshua this covenant is recalled and reaffirmed throughout. Foremost among its requirements is the command to worship the LORD God alone and avoid all other deities (Deut. 5:8–9). This was the basis for the destruction by Israel of *nations who could lead them into idolatry. The words of the covenant are recalled in the first chapter as Joshua is commanded to preserve, obey and teach them (1:8–9). These were his last deeds in the presence of the people: he wrote down the covenant and then set up a large stone as a witness to Israel's confession (24:26–27). The conquest episodes in the first half of the book of Joshua are interspersed with expressions of Joshua's concern that the people should maintain their covenantal relationship with God. Thus after crossing the Jordan and in preparation for the assault on Jericho, the people of Israel were circumcised and celebrated the Passover in the Promised Land (5:1–12). Circumcision is the sign of God's covenant with Abraham's seed (Gen. 17), while the Passover is the great festival of Israel's birth, recalling how God brought the nation into being. In leading the people in these activities Joshua renewed their identity as the holy people of a holy God. The Passover festival took on new meaning; the celebration of Israel's Exodus from Egypt became also that of Israel's presence in the Promised Land.

After the victory at Ai and Israel's entrance into the hill country, Joshua and Israel came to Mt Ebal (8:30–35), where Joshua copied the covenantal law of Moses and read it to the people in fulfilment of Deuteronomy 27:1–8. This was the first instance of covenant renewal; there was another at the end of Joshua's life (ch. 24).

Between the covenant-making texts of Joshua 8 and 24 are chapters detailing the distribution of allotments to Israel. This was a covenantal promise and blessing. Many ancient Near Eastern treaties included the granting of lands and towns by a lord to faithful vassals. Thus the covenant integrates both the book of Joshua and the life of its principal figure. Faithful to God as assistant to Moses, warrior and leader of Israel, giver of life and land, and covenantal mediator between God and his people, Joshua exemplified life lived in the covenant.

Joshua stood between Moses, the leader of the people and their lawgiver, and the judges and kings. He was unique as Moses' successor, not only because he remained faithful to God like Moses but also because he alone (with the possible exception of Caleb) remembered and was present from the birth of the nation of Israel in the Exodus to the realization of its full covenantal blessings in the settlement of the Promised Land. Like Moses, Joshua received at the end of his life the special designation, 'servant of the LORD' (24:29). Unlike the priestly figures of Aaron and Eleazar, however, Joshua is not recorded as having descendants. His unique role as successor of Moses could not be repeated. Succeeding generations would have to depend on leaders who had not witnessed first-hand the mighty acts of God by which he created the nation. The covenant would henceforth require those who followed it to walk by faith. With the possible exception of Samuel, none of those whose lives are recounted achieved the same level of faithful obedience to God and his covenant as did Joshua. David was commended for the way he followed God; so were Hezekiah and Josiah; but most of the other kings of Judah and Israel were not. The expectation of a leader who would lead God's people to victory over all their enemies became focused in the hope of a messiah. This began to be realized in the first coming of Jesus, and will be perfectly fulfilled in the second.

Joshua and the NT

Joshua prefigures Jesus Christ in many ways. They had the same name. As a military leader Joshua organized the people and led them in wars against their enemies. Jesus' enemies were not simply the powers of this world but the spiritual struggles that led him to victories over demons (Matt. 9:33; 17:18; Mark 7:26–30; Luke 4:35; 9:32; 11:14) and would ultimately lead to the defeat of Satan (Rev. 19 – 21) (see *Spiritual powers). He also instructed his disciples and empowered them for this struggle (Matt. 10:1–8; 21:21; Mark 3:14–15; 6:13; 16:17).

Jesus follows Joshua as a Saviour and life-giver to his people (Luke 2:11; 4:40). He *heals and so delivers individuals, such as

Rahab, from physical death (John 12:1–17). However, his greater power is to provide spiritual salvation by experiencing for his people the death of the cross and the resurrection, the results of which are promised to all who will believe and follow him (Luke 24:46) (see *Atonement). As Joshua distributed the inheritance of land, so Jesus distributes the spiritual *blessings and power of the resurrection to give an everlasting inheritance to his people.

Joshua gave a covenant written on stone and plaster to the people of Israel. Jesus also gave a new covenant to his followers. This covenant was not written on stone but was his body broken and blood shed for his followers (Matt. 26:26; Mark 14:22; Luke 22:19–20; 1 Cor. 11:25). Like the covenant of Joshua it required the obedience of the people and their faithfulness for them to appreciate the fullness of its blessings. These blessings were no longer an inheritance of land but the fullness of a personal relationship with God.

Bibliography

T. C. Butler, *Joshua*, WBC (Waco, 1983); R. S. Hess, *Joshua*, TOTC (Leicester and Downers Grove, 1996); J. P. U. Lilley, 'Understanding the *ḥerem*', TynB 44, 1993, pp. 169–177; T. Longman and D. G. Reid, *God Is a Warrior* (Carlisle, 1995); M. H. Woudstra, *The Book of Joshua*, NICOT (GrandRapids, 1981); C. J. H. Wright, *God's People in God's Land* (Grand Rapids and Exeter, 1990); K. L. Younger Jr., *Ancient Conquest Accounts* (Sheffield, 1990).

R. S. HESS

JUDGES

Introduction

The book of Judges, an important part of Israel's historical epic literature, is easily divided into major sections, each consisting of one or more cycles (stories), to which have been added two editorial introductions and two conclusions (see Structure, below). The short stories, which are among the finest in any literary corpus, are easily remembered, but consistently contradict contemporary moral principles. The culture of the entire period covered by the book is often regarded as sub-Christian, or seen as the low point of Israel's moral life, a matter of merely academic interest to the person reading theologically.

But the stories are more significant than this, and in interpreting them, the biblical theologian must consider their literary context. Three common mistakes must be avoided. The first is that of viewing each of the major stories of the judges as nothing more than a morality tale, illustrating bad behaviour to be avoided. The second is that of viewing the entire period of the judges as one of unbroken failure. The third is that of seeing in the accounts of the period a rejection of the charismatic principle of *leadership. A close look at the book, and at its theological importance, should enable the reader to avoid these errors.

A first step, then, is to avoid moralizing the stories of the judges. Far from being an unbroken series of failures, the period of the judges highlights the importance of biblical charismatic activity and leadership. Charismatic leadership is leadership that derives its authority from the working of the Spirit of God (see *Holy Spirit) in gifting or anointing. The fact that each of the judges was raised up by charismatic means gives the book its special place in biblical theology. The failures of the judges, some of which are very serious, are an important part of the story, but are not what gives the book its place in biblical theology.

A second important step towards a theological understanding of Judges is to see in the book the progress of tribal *covenant failure, the evidence for which is found in each tribe's disobedience (see *Obedience) to the divine command to drive out the inhabitants of the land. Nowhere in the OT is the result of disobedience so starkly reflected. In concentrating on the major storyline, i.e. the individual cycles of the judges, readers often ignore the secondary theme, that of covenant requirements, primarily reflected in the accounts of the tribal occupation of the land (see ch. 1). The tribes' failure to conquer is a subtheme of each cycle, and of the prologue and epilogue.

A third step is to see the period of the Judges as a divinely ordained transition from centralized leadership in the desert under Moses and Joshua to the centralization of leadership in Jerusalem under David and Solomon. This transition, and the way in which it was viewed by those who lived through it, those who came after, and the writers of Scripture, illuminates the study of divine covenants, the raising up and preparation of leaders, and kingship. The statement that 'there was no king in Israel in those days; each man did what was right in his own eyes' (Judg. 17:6; 21:25; cf. 18:1; 19:1) summarizes the period, but also points to transition. (See *Kingdom of God.)

Judges in the canon

In the Hebrew canon Judges is the second of the former prophets; in the Christian OT, it is the second of the historical books. Earlier canonical questions have in recent decades been incorporated into the discussion of whether a Deuteronomic history was published during the exile. Those who believe that this putative document existed, claim that its basic themes were the failure of kingship in *Israel and the need for covenant renewal through exile. Judges is said to embody these themes, partly in its cyclical stories, but more clearly in its editorial framework (see below).

That a Deuteronomic history existed as a distinct document can never be proved, but there is little doubt that Judges formed part of a connected narrative, which recounted the various attempts, from the time of Moses until the exile, to establish divinely ordained leadership. The theme of royal failure is part of this story, but the latter is far more complex and paradoxical than the former. From a canonical perspective, however one finally evaluates judgeship and the judges, it is inconceivable that the so-called Deuteronomic historical epic could have omitted the period and its contribution to Israel's search for God's kind of covenant leader. Judges makes a significant contribution to Israel's national epic, explaining theologically the transition from conquest leadership under Joshua to royal leadership in David.

Despite the fact that many of the stories in Judges seem to mock traditional customs, there is no evidence that the keepers of Israel's tradition ever doubted the book's right to be included in what became the canonical Scriptures. In one of the earliest clear references to normative Israelite traditions, the Wisdom of Ben Sira 46:11–12 (2nd century BC) includes the judges in a list of heroes, placing them after Joshua and Caleb and before Samuel:

The judges also, with their respective names,
  those whose hearts did not fall into idolatry
and who did not turn away from the Lord –
  may their memory be blessed!
May their bones revive from where they lie,
  and may the name of those who have been
  honoured
live again in their sons! (RSV)

Within the NT, several judges are listed in Hebrews 11, being remembered for their deeds of valour rather than for their moral failure. It is beyond question that their stories, as we have them, were part of the canon from its formation.

Structure

The theological impact of a narrative is made by the story itself, its structure and the nuances of its telling. The medium shapes the message. Nowhere is this more evident than in the book of Judges. Beginning with two prologues (1:1 – 2:5 and 2:6 – 3:6), featuring respectively the key theological themes of the work (see below), Judges goes on to develop these themes in a series of short stories, or cycles, in which an individual hero raised up by Yahweh delivers the nation. A clear progression can be seen in the cycles, from the periods of *rest (Othniel through Gideon), to the periods of sporadic deliverance (Jephthah through Samson). In the middle (chapter 9) stands the story of the anti-judge, King Abimelech, and interspersed are vignettes of shadowy, but still epic, figures called (for narrative reasons) minor judges. The book ends with two epilogues (chs. 17 – 18 and 19 – 21), in which the dominant themes are illustrated in reverse sequence. Held together by an editorial framework, the book of Judges presents a clear and powerful literary and theological message.

Judges in criticism

Until the modern era, Judges was considered to be a unified series of short stories, brought together by unknown editors at some time in the early monarchy. Very little of the book need be dated any later.

Two chronological references at the end of chapter 18 indicate when the text may have reached its settled form, but the precise interpretation of the references is disputed. The chronology of the editorial process has implications for other critical issues, which in turn bear upon the question of the theological concerns behind the final edition of the book.

Judges 18:31, the clearer of the two references, appears to point to a *terminus ad quem* for the narrative some time after the destruction of the tabernacle shrine at Shiloh, which most scholars date at the end of the period of the judges, following the capture by the Philistines of the ark (then based in Shiloh; 1 Sam. 4). If so, the book's theology must be associated with the rise of kingship and the centralizing of worship *vis-à-vis* the Danite sanctuary. A more complex problem arises with verse 30, considered by many scholars to be a Deuteronomic gloss, in which the apostate Danite priesthood is said to have lasted 'until the captivity of the land'. Assuming that this reference is to the Assyrian conquest of the northern kingdom in 733 BC, it is easy to envisage the editorial work on the book of Judges continuing until the Babylonian exile, (cf. the chronological markers at the end of the so-called Deuteronomic history, 2 Kgs. 25:27–30, dated 561 BC). If so, the book's primary theological concern would be that of the exiles, *i.e.* the demise of kingship, not its inception.

The latter view is consistent with the dominant critical hypothesis, noted above, which posits a theologically motivated historical work, completed during the exile, in which the demise of kingship is attributed to the Judean monarchy's failure to keep the covenant statutes of Deuteronomy. Such a theory may help to explain features common to Judges and the rest of the corpus, but does insufficient justice to those features which are either unique to Judges (*e.g.* the absence of Deuteronomic language from most cycles), or more relevant to the inception of kingship than to its demise.

An alternative view is that both verses refer to the destruction of Shiloh in the 11th century. If so, Judges can be understood more simply as a theological reflection from an early period of Israel's history. In any case, the canonical question cannot be separated from the critical one.

Recent critical interest has moved away from sources to the literary value of the finished work and the way in which it has been read through the years. Literary devices, plots and themes, such as irony, have been explored, while reader-response critics, particularly feminist critics, have investigated the gender issues raised by (for example) the Jephthah cycle and the narrative of the Levite's concubine. Some of this work has proved fruitful in identifying both the literary and the theological concerns of the book.

Theological themes in Judges

Two major themes dominate Judges. The first is the development and varying fortunes of the nation's charismatic leadership, exercised by a succession of individual heroes. A second theme, related to the tribal life of Israel, is that of covenant *faithfulness. A third theme, derived from the other two, and developed only in the succeeding narrative (the books of Samuel), is the rise of kingship.

Charismatic leadership

Charismatic leadership, as generally understood by scholars since Max Weber, is leadership which gains its authority by virtue of divine gifting or spiritual 'filling'. Charismatic leaders are raised up by God, often with supernatural powers or gifts, and are recognized as leaders by their followers. They need not be appointed to their office, since the gifting proves itself in action, usually in the face of some crisis, and popular acclaim follows. In the editorial framework of Judges (*e.g.* in the second prologue), God is said to have 'raised up judges', to deliver his people (2:16, RSV). The various cycles, beginning with that of Othniel (3:9), outline the careers of these judges. Again and again a leader is 'raised up' and endued with the Spirit, faces a challenge and emerges victorious. The general is then transformed from a military hero into a judicial or administrative functionary.

The book of Judges, far from simply showing the weakness of the various leaders, celebrates the quality of charismatic leadership, from the affirmation in the second prologue of its divine origin (see especially 2:16–19) to the celebration, not only in narrative but also in poetry (*cf.* ch. 5), of the judges' heroic feats. Charismatic leadership becomes a fundamental building block for divinely ordained kingship. Yahweh's ideal king is raised up by Yahweh, filled with the Spirit, endued with power, and popularly acclaimed. He is, in short, the ideal charismatic leader. But despite its celebration of charismatic leadership, Judges also reminds the reader of its weaknesses. In the first epilogue (chs. 17 – 18) the only leaders left in Israel are Micah the idol-maker and his wandering Levite, a pathetic figure for sale to the

highest bidder. Something more than charismatic leadership is needed.

Covenant faithfulness and disobedience

A second theme of the story, is that of covenant. This theme is highlighted in Deuteronomy and much of Joshua, but recedes into the background in Judges, thus leading many scholars to overlook its role in both the larger story and the individual stories. The first of the two prologues (1:1 – 2:5) is in fact all about covenant faithfulness, or more properly, the absence of it. Beginning as it does with the death of Joshua, the initial prologue refers only obliquely to charismatic heroes (vv. 11–15), instead focusing on the tribes of Israel and their covenant duty. The narrative of Joshua concludes with the covenant renewal at Shechem, during which the people are challenged to take the land which Yahweh, in covenant faithfulness, has given them (Josh. 23 – 24). Now it is their responsibility, having been sent away to their own inheritance (Josh. 24:28) to prove the Lord's faithfulness.

At first sight, then, Judges appears to be concerned only with charismatic leaders, but the first prologue reveals that it also continues the covenant theme. Only Judah, and possibly Simeon, truly fulfil the covenant, most notably in the conquest of Jerusalem (Judg. 1:8). Judah even foreshadows the charismatic heroes, both male and female (Caleb, Achsah and Othniel), because Yahweh is with them (1:19). Others fare less well. First Benjamin, then the house of Joseph and the smaller tribes (Zebulun, Asher, Naphtali, Dan), all fail fully to dislodge the Canaanites. Other tribes are not even mentioned in the narrative. The conclusion of the first prologue (2:1–5) condemns the weeping people to continued Canaanite occupation of the land, as divine covenant curses are activated to thwart their progress.

The second prologue (2:6 – 3:6) also begins with the death of Joshua. Although it focuses on the raising up of the charismatic deliverers, it makes absolutely clear that behind the story of each hero is a nation that has violated the covenant and has not listened to Yahweh (Judg. 2:20). In the cycles of the individual heroes, this covenant disobedience is corrected only during those short periods when the power of a deliverer's charisma is so evident that the people follow Yahweh in spite of themselves. Even then, some tribes do not support the leader and others are lukewarm (5:15–17; 12:1–6; 15:11–13). Finally, in the second epilogue (chs. 19 – 21), the tribal coalition is said to be threatened with dissolution, from which no ordinary charismatic leader can rescue it. The danger demands some new institution, which will guarantee both charismatic leadership and covenant-keeping. That institution, as the editorial commentary makes clear (17:6; 18:1; 19:1; 21:25), is kingship.

Kingship

The theme of kingship is derived from the book's two major themes, but it is always present in the background. When kingship is offered to Gideon (8:22–23), it becomes clear that the hero shares the widespread conviction that to set up a human king, especially with the right of hereditary succession, would be to supplant Yahweh as Israel's head. It is ironic that Gideon begins immediately to act in ways appropriate to ancient Near Eastern kings, especially in the light of the subsequent events described in chapter 9.

Gideon's son, ironically the son of a concubine, has no qualms about claiming the kingship, though his realm is a mere Canaanite city-state within the larger pan-Israelite nation. Abimelech's pathetic attempt at kingship becomes a model for the kind of kingship rejected in the Judges–Samuel epic, and serves primarily to highlight the depths to which Israel could sink during this period when there was no charismatic leader.

It is often claimed that Judges clearly rejects kingship, presumably in favour of the non-hereditary, charismatic model of leadership exemplified by the judges. Yet four times in the dual epilogue of chapters 17 – 21 the statement that 'there was no king in Israel in those days' appears, and twice is followed by the assertion that 'every man did what was right in his own eyes'. Whether or not this is an implicit request for kingship is still debated by Judges scholars, but it is difficult not to see in these statements a longing for what was to come.

Summary

According to both Ben Sira and the letter to the Hebrews, the Spirit of God was active, and his power was manifest in the time of the judges. These charismatic men and women were raised up by Yahweh, and had they been supported by the tribes' complete faithfulness to the covenant, who can say what might have happened? But partly because of the weakness inherent in charismatic leadership itself, and partly because of the fatal disregard of the covenant amongst Yahweh's tribes, the covenant promise of security and prosperity in the land was never realized. The unique theological contribution of Judges is to show the potential of charismatic leadership, and to find it insufficient. Its deficiences are remedied in the institution of kingship, and especially in the further covenant promises given to the ultimate charismatic king, David. The new 'royal theology', in turn, provides the model for the final charismatic King, in whom all the promises to Abraham are fulfilled.

Judges and the NT

The NT develops and refines each of the theological themes of Judges in the context of the promise and fulfilment model by which the NT writers interpret the OT documents. Jesus and all the early apostolic leaders are portrayed as purely charismatic leaders, having no authority other than that accorded to one in whom the Spirit's presence is discerned. Themes of covenant faithfulness and disobedience also feature prominently in the NT, where the people of God are enjoined to keep themselves from idols (1 John 5:21). But the most striking development is seen in the prominence given to kingship; Jesus is presented not merely as the ideal judge, but also as the one anointed by the Spirit (Luke 4:16–22), the great antitype of all the expectations attached to charismatic, covenant kingship in the OT. The search for the elusive ideal judge has come to an end.

Bibliography

C. E Armerding, 'A charismatic theology of Judges', in H. Burckhardt and M. Bockmuehl (eds.), *Gott lieben, und seine Gebote halten; in memoriam Klaus Bockmuehl* (Giessen and Basel, 1991); W. J. Dumbrell, '"In those days there was no king in Israel; every man did what was right in his own eyes." The purpose of the book of Judges reconsidered', *JSOT* 25, 1983, pp. 23–33; J. C. Exum, 'The centre cannot hold: thematic and textual instabilities in Judges', *CBQ* 52, 1990, pp. 410–431; D. W. Gooding, 'The composition of the book of Judges', in B. A. Levine and A. Malamat (eds.), *Eretz Israel, Archaeological, Historical* and *Geographical Studies,* vol. 16 (Jerusalem, 1982); F. E. Greenspahn, 'The theology of the framework of Judges', *VT* 36, 1986, pp. 385–396; L. Gros and R. R. Kenneth, 'The book of Judges', in R. R. Kenneth, L. Gros, J. S. Ackerman and T. S. Warshaw (eds.), *Literary Interpretations of Biblical Narratives* (Nashville, 1974); D. M. Gunn, 'Joshua and Judges', in R. Alter and F. Kermode (eds.), *The Literary Guide to the Bible* (London, 1989); L. R. Klein, *The Triumph of Irony in the Book of Judges* (Sheffield, 1988); R. H. O'Connell, *The Rhetoric of the Book of Judges* (Leiden, 1996); P. E. Satterthwaite, '"No king in Israel": narrative criticism and Judges 17–21', *TynB* 44, 1993, pp. 75–88; P. Trible, *Texts of Terror: Literary-Feminist Readings of Biblical Narratives* (Philadelphia, 1984); B. G. Webb, *The Book of Judges: An Integrated Reading* (Sheffield, 1987); M. Wilcock, *The Message of Judges,* BST (Leicester, 1992); G. A. Yee (ed.), *Judges and Method: New Approaches in Biblical Studies* (Minneapolis, 1995).

C. E. ARMERDING

RUTH

The book of Ruth tells of a Judahite family's migration to escape famine. All the males die in Moab leaving Naomi with two widowed daughters-in-law. The story develops around the return of Naomi with Ruth to Bethlehem, and the events that lead to Ruth's marriage to Boaz, by which she becomes part of the genealogy of *David.

Principal themes

*Prayer and *blessing

Ruth has been considered theologically sparse since only 1:6 and 4:13 provide narrative statements of Yahweh's activity, but as B. Rebera notes, Ruth prefers to embed theological evaluation in dialogue (*The Book of Ruth,* esp. pp. 181–244). Thus, prayer, and its answers, constitute a significant part of the book's theology. Prayers or blessings include: (a) Naomi's plea for Yahweh's ḥeseḏ (kindness) in providing husbands and security for Orpah and Ruth (1:8–9); (b) Naomi's lament before the Bethlehemite women that Yahweh has embittered her by bringing her back empty, thus presenting a challenge to Yahweh

to redress her situation (1:20–21); (c) Boaz' blessing and prayer that Ruth will receive her reward from Yahweh, to whom she has come as a proselyte (2:11–12) – later she will challenge Boaz to fulfil this role (3:9, *cf.* Gen. 15:1–5; 30:16, 18; Ps. 127:3 where reward is linked with progeny); (d) Naomi blesses Boaz for his kindness (2:19–20); (e) Boaz blesses Ruth for seeking him out as redeemer (3:10–11); (f) the community (LXX 'elders') prays for the fruitfulness of the marriage comparing Ruth to Rachel and Leah (4:11–12); (g) the women acknowledge Yahweh's role in Naomi's restoration and praise Ruth for her part while praying for the fame of their posterity (4:14–15). All these prayers have their outworking in the marriage of Ruth and Boaz and the birth of Obed.

*Providence

God's providence is seen not only in answered prayer, but also in the ending of the famine (1:6), which leads to Naomi's return with Ruth. There are no overt narrative theological statements in chapters 2 and 3, but the beginning of chapter 2 introduces Boaz, and then says that Ruth happened upon the field of Boaz, so conveying another hint of divine overruling – the meeting was unintentional on the humans' part but overseen by a caring providence. This probably echoes Genesis 24:12–27 where Yahweh overruled the meeting of Abraham's servant and Rebekah. There is *concurrence* between divine and human activity; although God is the unseen actor, this is very much a human story, and it is 'people, living as they are to live under God's sovereignty, who proceed to work it out' (E. F. Campbell, *Ruth,* p. 29). This is seen in chapter 3 where Naomi counsels Ruth to take bold action concerning her relationship with Boaz. Ruth plays her part, but when she returns home in the morning, Naomi counsels her to wait and see how the matter develops. Boaz can be relied on to do his part but ultimately the result is in the hand of God. Chapter 4 also points to this concurrence. Boaz does his part by marrying Ruth but we are told it is Yahweh who gives conception (4:13).

Reversal motif

In the OT, Yahweh is the one who 'makes poor and makes rich', who 'lifts the needy from the ash heap' (1 Sam. 2:7–8, NRSV). In the book of Ruth there is a movement from emptiness to fulfilment. Elimelech migrates because of famine; he dies; his sons marry but also die. Naomi is widowed and childless, alone with two childless widows. The news of Yahweh's providence prompts her return. This introductory section (1:1–7) reflects the whole book in microcosm in its movement from deprivation to restoration. In the remainder of the story, Naomi's immediate needs are met through Ruth's industry and Boaz' generosity, while the levirate marriage of Boaz and Ruth and the birth of Obed restores the lineage.

Conversion / inclusion

Ruth's ethnicity is a significant element of the book. The sons of Elimelech marry 'Moabite women' (1:4), and when the action moves to Bethlehem, where Ruth is a foreigner (see *Nations), her race becomes an issue (so esp. Rebera, pp. 156–159; see 1:22; 2:2, 6, 10, 21; 4:5, 10). But the story moves by stages towards her inclusion among the people of God. When Naomi counsels Ruth to return to her own god/s and people, Ruth vows to follow Naomi in life and death, declaring, 'your people shall be my people and your God my God', a clear acknowledgment of her conversion to Yahwism. Thereafter, whenever mention is made of Ruth's Moabite origins, this is followed by a kin term linking her to her Judahite family – she is referred to as 'daughter-in-law of Naomi', and described by both Naomi and Boaz as 'my daughter'. Chapter 2 highlights how Boaz acts to include Ruth, approves her actions, and gives her protection (2:8–16). The issue is essentially settled in chapter 2; hence her ethnicity is not mentioned in chapter 3. Twice in the legal case Ruth is described as a Moabite, but in each case this is balanced by the fact of her *marriage to Mahlon, hence the marriage of Boaz and Ruth is leviratic and legally justified. When the women give their final blessing at the birth of a son, Ruth's ethnicity has dropped entirely from sight; now she is 'your daughter-in-law who loves you ... who is worth more to you than seven sons'(4:15).

Kindness (ḥesed)

This motif was early recognized. R. Ze'ira suggested that Ruth was written 'to teach how great is the reward of those who do deeds of kindness' (*Ruth Rabbah* II:14). Naomi ac-

knowledges Ruth and Orpah's ḥesed (1:8) and Boaz mentions it (3:10; cf. 2:11). Early studies of ḥesed described it as the loyalty expected in reciprocal relationships, and therefore as an obligation. But ḥesed in the OT contains a gracious element; in references to human relationships it 'mainly describes exceptional acts of one human to another, meeting an extreme need outside the normal run of perceived duty, and arising from personal affection or goodness' (F. I. Andersen, 'Yahweh, the Kind and Sensitive God', in P. T. O'Brien and D. G. Peterson (eds.), *God Who is Rich in Mercy* [Homebush West, 1986], p. 81). AV comes close to this sense with the translation 'loving-kindness'. God in his grace and mercy shows this kindness to humans; he does not owe salvation but gives it freely. The nature of the divine–human relationship means we cannot give ḥesed to God, but if we have experienced God's loving-kindness we can, like Ruth and Boaz, show it in our relationships with others (cf. Mic. 6:8; Matt. 25:34–40; 1 John 4:7–12).

Women

Whether or not the author was female (cf. Campbell, *Ruth*, pp. 22–23) the book of Ruth is unique amongst ancient literature in its celebration of female friendship (cf. D. Daube, *Ancient Jewish Law* [Leiden, 1981], pp. 35–37). Moreover, the book is focused largely upon the female characters. The story begins with Elimelech, his wife and sons, but the males soon die. Thereafter Ruth and Naomi are the main characters, with Boaz being given only a supporting role. This is highlighted by 3:9, where Ruth, not Boaz, proposes marriage. Boaz has the leading role in the legal case, but the women again come to the fore in 4:13–17. In the final patrilineal genealogical material (4:18–22) Ruth drops from view, but this should not be seen negatively. The outsider has been integrated and is now part of Israelite history.

Davidic / Messianic purpose

Two views of the book's purpose may be discounted: that it was written (a) as a celebration of ḥesed (kindness/loyalty); or (b) to encourage the performance of the levirate. It is the person doing kindness who is praised, not the ideal itself, and the levirate is portrayed as a recognized institution, not as something under evaluation. Views in which the marriage of an Israelite to a Moabite is identified as the central theme, and is linked in some way to the genealogy of David, are more credible. Thus the book may be seen as (c) a refutation of ethnic exclusiveness, showing the possibility of the inclusion of Gentiles among the people of God; or (d) an attack on Ezra's and Nehemiah's rigid rejection of mixed marriage; or (e) a justification of the marriage of Boaz to Ruth, a believing Gentile, and hence as a defence of the claim of the Davidic family to the throne. Recent scholarship favours (e) (*e.g.* Gerleman, Gow, Hubbard, Bush, Nielsen). The book may be described as *messianic history* in that it reveals God's control over the events that produced the Davidic dynasty.

Contemporary value

The book of Ruth may be expounded at a number of levels: (a) as a story of divine providence in the lives of ordinary people going about the ordinary tasks of life; (b) as an illustration of divine co-operation with people who pray and then make things happen; most of the prayers are fulfilled by the human participants; (c) as an example of people who do acts of loving kindness; (d) as a story about women; (e) as an example of the inclusion of the outsider, in particular of the inclusion of believing Gentiles amongst the people of God; (f) as part of a larger messianic story, partially fulfilled in the Davidic monarchy but extended to include blessing to the whole world through a future descendant of David (*cf.* Gen. 12:1–3; Matt. 1:1; Rom. 1:3).

Bibliography

D. Atkinson, *The Message of Ruth*, BST (Leicester and Downers Grove, 1983); F. W. Bush, *Ruth, Esther*, WBC (Dallas, 1996); E. F. Campbell, *Ruth*, AB (Garden City, 1975); H. Fisch, 'Ruth and the Structure of Covenant History', *VT* 32, 1982, pp. 425–437; M. D. Gow, *The Book of Ruth: Its structure, theme and purpose* (Leicester, 1992); R. M. Hals, *The Theology of the Book of Ruth* (Philadelphia, 1969); R. L. Hubbard, *The Book of Ruth*, NICOT (Grand Rapids, 1988); *idem*, *NIDOTTE* 4, pp. 1153–1157; K. J. A. Larkin, *Ruth and Esther*, OTG (Sheffield, 1996); E. H. Merrill, 'The Book of Ruth: Narration and Shared Themes', *BS* 142, 1985, pp. 130–141; K. Nielsen, *Ruth*, OTL (London, 1997); B. Porten, 'The scroll of Ruth: A rhetorical study', *Gratz* 7, 1978, pp. 23–49; W. S. Prinsloo, 'The theology of the book of Ruth', *VT* 30, 1980, pp. 330–341; B. Rebera, 'The Book of Ruth: Dialogue and Narrative' (PhD diss. Macquarie University, 1981); P. Trible, *God and the Rhetoric of Sexuality* (Philadelphia, 1978); E. van Wolde, *Ruth and Naomi* (ET, London, 1997); P. D. Wegner, in *EDBT*, pp. 694–696.

M. D. GOW

SAMUEL

Introduction

The main events covered in 1 and 2 Samuel (hereafter *Samuel*) are: the rise of the prophet Samuel and Israel's partial restoration in his lifetime (1 Sam. 1 – 7); the people's choice of Saul as their first *king (1 Sam. 8 – 12) and Saul's rejection by *God (1 Sam. 13 – 15); the rise of *David, chosen by God to replace Saul as king (1 Sam. 16 – 31); David's acceptance as king by all *Israel (2 Sam. 1:1 – 5:5); his conquest of *Jerusalem (2 Sam. 5:6–10); his victories over the Philistines (2 Sam. 5:17–25); his bringing of the ark of God up to Mt Zion (2 Sam. 6); God's promise to David concerning his descendants (2 Sam. 7); David's victories over the nations round about (2 Sam. 8 – 10); his sin with Bathsheba and its consequences of death and *violence within his own house and civil *war in Israel (2 Sam. 11 – 20).

From a biblical-theological point of view a key aspect of *Samuel* is how the earlier promises given to the patriarchs and to Israel are partially fulfilled in the reign of David. David's achievements, and particularly God's promise to him, which builds on the earlier promises, are seen as highly significant by later OT writers, and are taken up by the NT writers in their proclamation of the gospel of *Jesus Christ. David's reign is thus a turning-point in the outworking of God's purposes of salvation. The rise of the Israelite monarchy, however, held potential for both good and evil, and *Samuel* is concerned to do justice to both sides of the picture. *Samuel* can in fact be seen as a sustained theological reflection, in narrative form, on the implications of the coming of monarchy to Israel. In the body of this article we shall follow the successive stages of the narrative, tracing the theological significance of the developments described.

Leading themes of 1 and 2 Samuel

1 Samuel 1 – 7: Israel's disarray; God's sovereignty

The book of Judges has closed with Israel in disarray: though the Israelites live in the *land promised by God to the patriarchs (Gen. 15:17–21), their hold on it is threatened by the Philistines (Judg. 13 – 16), who are only the last of a series of foreign enemies sent as a *judgment on Israel's unfaithfulness (Judg. 2:10–19). In some respects the situation is unchanged at the beginning of 1 Samuel: the Philistines remain a threat (ch. 4), and the corrupt leadership of Eli's sons continues the moral anarchy of the earlier period. However, the narratives of Hannah and Samuel (chs. 1 – 3) mark a fresh start for Israel (W. Brueggemann, '1 Samuel 1: A sense of a beginning', *ZAW* 100, 1988, pp. 33–48). The reference to '[God's] king' and 'anointed' in Hannah's song of praise (2:10) suggests that this will be bound up with the coming of a king.

Hannah's song also depicts God as uncompromisingly sovereign, bringing down the mighty and exalting the humble (2:1–10). These verses are programmatic for all of *Samuel*. In chapter 4 God brings judgment on the Israelites at Aphek. This is followed by judgment on the Philistines, the notional 'captors' of God's ark (5:1 – 6:12). But the return of the ark to Israelite territory does not imply that God is now bound to bless Israel: rejoicing turns to dismay as men from Beth Shemesh are killed for impiously looking into the ark (6:13–20). The ark remains at Kiriath Jearim (7:1), on the Judah-Benjamin border, until the early years of David's reign; no attempt is made to restore the ark to a central sanctuary like Shiloh. It is as though the Israelites feel themselves estranged from God. The subsequent narrative describes the Israelites mourning, seeking God and putting away their false gods (7:2–4). Then at last they experience God's deliverance in battle (vv. 10–11). *Blessing comes only from *faithfulness and *obedience. This will be true also for Israel's kings.

1 Samuel 8 – 15: Saul's kingship

The coming of a king has been anticipated in previous OT texts: the promises to the patriarchs (Gen. 17:6, 16; 35:11); Balaam's oracles (Num. 24:7, 17–19); and Deuteronomy 17:14–20, which lays down the conditions on which Israel may appoint a king after entering Canaan.

The account of Saul's rise (chs. 8 – 12) begins with the people's request for 'a king to lead us, such as all the other nations have' (8:5, NIV). Both Samuel and God greet this request with disapproval (8:6, 8; *cf.* 10:17–19; 12:17). This is surprising, in the light of the earlier passages just cited. The people, indeed, are requesting no more than what Deuteronomy 17 permitted (*cf.* esp. Deut. 17:14), with the additional justification that Samuel's sons were not fit to lead Israel (8:3, 5). It is often supposed, on the basis of 1 Samuel 8 – 12, that kingship was a concession on God's part to Israel, something God never really desired. But that view seems hard to reconcile with the largely positive presentation of David's kingship in *Samuel* (see below). No more satisfactory, though once a standard view, is the suggestion that 1 Samuel 8 – 12 is a conflation (without harmonization) of pro- and anti-monarchical sources (see V. P. Long, *The Reign and Rejection of King Saul*, pp. 173–194).

It appears, rather, that what is criticized in 1 Samuel 8 – 12 is a request for a king made for the wrong reasons. The people's motives are laid bare in 1 Samuel 8:19–20, where they repeat their request in an expanded form: 'We want a king over us. Then we shall be like all the other nations, with a king to lead us and to go out before us and fight our battles'. Their main interest in the king is as military leader. This form of the request retains some of the wording of Deuteronomy 17, but with a very different overall sense: Israel's king was meant to be different from other kings, not a point of similarity with the other *nations; and military prowess was not among the attributes required of him. It is understandable, then, that Samuel later accuses the people of failing to trust God (10:18–19; 12:6–12). Perhaps the people find such trust too demanding and see the king as a way of finding security without having to meet God's requirements (*cf.* the treatment of 7:2–4 above). But this is not a good basis for choosing a king: as Samuel notes, leaders other than kings can win battles, with God's help (12:11); conversely, unless the king is obedient to God, he will offer Israel no security at all (12:14–15, 24–25). In a way true to Deuteronomy 17, then, 1 Samuel 8 – 12 clarifies the issues of kingship. These chapters are not anti-monarchic in an unqualified sense, but express strong opposition to a kind of kingship that, in effect, undermines God's kingship (*cf.* the account of Gideon and Abimelech in Judg. 8 – 9).

Saul does not fulfil all Samuel's negative prophecies (8:11–18); nonetheless he fails as king. The failure is not primarily military: chosen by God to 'deliver my people from the hand of the Philistines' (9:16), he does enjoy some success (14:47–48, 52). Crucially, however, having been charged with obeying and serving God (12:14, 24), he twice disobeys God's command to him through Samuel (13:1–15; 15:1–28; the earlier incident is, admittedly, a severe test of his obedience). On this basis he is rejected as king (15:26–29). The consistent view of *Samuel* is that the king must be subject to the prophetic word (*cf.* 2 Sam. 7:1–17; 12:1–14; 24:11–25).

1 Samuel 16 – 2 Samuel 4: Saul's decline; David's rise

In God's eyes, Saul's reign is now over (see 16:1). In Saul's place David is anointed as king, God's Spirit coming upon him and departing from Saul (16:13–14). Nearly twenty chapters separate the account of this incident from that of his acceptance as king by all the Israelite tribes (2 Sam. 5:1–3). The lengthy account of David's rise and Saul's decline has at least two functions. First, it makes clear that God was with David during his rise to power, granting him a striking victory over a Philistine champion (1 Sam. 17), protecting him in various ways (19:18–24; 23:1–6, 9–12, 24–29; 27; 29) and, in short, establishing him as king over Israel (2 Sam. 5:12). Second, the section shows us something of David's character: his first spoken words mark him out as one zealous for God (1 Sam. 17:26); he quickly wins the love of the people and also of Jonathan and Michal (18:1–21); he refuses to avenge himself against Saul when he has the opportunity (24:3–7; 26:7–11); after Saul's death, he distances himself from the deaths of Saul's adherents (2 Sam. 3:28–35; 4:8–12), and in the case of Abner's death, at least, the people are convinced of his innocence (2 Sam. 3:36–37).

In all this there is a clear contrast with Saul. Saul has an increasingly destructive influence within Israel (note esp. 1 Sam. 22:6–23), ne-glecting national interests in his desire to eliminate David (23:26–28), and ultimately leading Israel to defeat against the Philistines (ch. 31). He is a man under judgment, troubled by 'an evil spirit from God' (16:14; 18:10; 19:9; *cf.* Judg. 9:23), and Israel as a whole is caught up in his judgment (1 Sam. 28:16–19; *cf.* 12:25). Does the narrator mean to imply that Saul would have avoided this personal and national disaster if he had renounced the kingship after Samuel's denunciation? We may perhaps contrast David's behaviour when he later falls under a judgment like Saul's (see below). Certainly, this section shows us something of the difference between a king chosen by God (16:1) and one chosen by the people (12:13; Saul is also said to be appointed by God [9:16; 10:24], but it is clear that God gives the people the kind of king they want [8:22]).

2 Samuel 5 – 10: David's achievements

As noted above, many promises and hopes associated with earlier stages of Israel's history find their fulfilment during David's reign. Under David the Israelites finally end the Philistine threat and take possession of the land (chs. 5, 8; *cf.* also ch. 10). They thus finally enjoy the '*rest' in the land which Deuteronomy anticipated (7:1; *cf.* Deut. 12:10), and of which they only had a foretaste in Joshua's days (Josh. 14:15; 21:44). Earlier, the Song of Moses spoke of God's taking possession of a *mountain in the Promised Land as his 'sanctuary' and thereby establishing his rule (Exod. 15:17–18). This happens when the last Canaanite stronghold in the land is captured (2 Sam. 5:6–8) and the ark is brought up into it (6:1–19). It could be said that David thus makes God's kingship visible in Israel, though it is as true to say that God validates David's kingship by allowing him to bring the ark into 'David's city' (6:12; *cf.* C. L. Seow, *Myth, Drama and Politics*, pp. 79–144).

Deuteronomy 12 looked forward to the time of Israel's 'rest' as one in which the Israelites would worship God at 'the place that the LORD your God will choose as a dwelling for his name' (Deut. 12:11). This passage clearly lies behind 2 Samuel 7, in which David (implicitly) proposes to build a *temple for God (v. 2). Underlying this proposal is the understanding, common in the ancient Near East, that if a ruler is permitted to build a temple for a deity, that implies the deity's blessing upon his rule (*cf.* T. Ishida, *The Royal Dynasties in Ancient Israel*, pp. 85–88). God tells David that, instead, David's son will build a 'house [temple] for my name' (v. 13). David himself is promised a different sort of 'house', a royal dynasty which will be established over Israel (v. 12) and will 'endure for ever before me' (v. 16). Using terms familiar from ancient Near Eastern kingship language, God promises to be 'father' to David's son and, by implication, to his subsequent descendants (A. A. Anderson, *2 Samuel*, WBC [Waco, 1989], p. 122). God's refusal to allow David to build a temple seems to underline a theological principle (reinforced in the Hebrew by the word-play on 'house'): just as God has taken the initiative in choosing David and bringing him to power over Israel, so God's 'house-building' must come first, with any 'house-building' by David's line distinctly in second place. To put the point differently, David's line is always going to depend on God's *grace.

The presence of the ark, rich in associations with Israel's earlier history, in 'David's city' (6:12), clearly suggests that David's kingship, though a new development, does not represent a break with Israel's previous history. The clear echoes of the promises to Abraham in 2 Samuel 7 similarly suggest that David, in receiving a promise from God concerning his descendants, also inherits the promises given to Abraham ('name', v. 9, *cf.* Gen. 12:2; 'offspring ... from your own body', v. 12, *cf.* Gen. 15:4–5; 'nation', v. 23, *cf.* Gen. 12:2; 'bless', 'blessing', v. 29, *cf.* Gen. 12:2–3). Thus 2 Samuel 6 – 7 stresses the continuity of God's dealings with Israel before and after David's accession to kingship. This suggests that monarchy was indeed God's will for Israel.

This period of David's reign brings blessing for Israel (*cf.* 5:12: David's kingship is 'for the sake of [God's] people Israel'). It is as though by accepting God's chosen king over them the tribes have also entered anew into a life of obedience to God (5:1–3). Most importantly, God's presence is restored to the Israelites: the bringing up of the ark to Zion formally restores a relationship between God and the people that has been marred since the time of Eli. (It has been suggested that the narratives dealing with the ark [1 Sam. 4 – 6; 2 Sam. 6] originally formed a separate 'Ark Narrative', but everything that happens to the ark in

Samuel fits perfectly with other developments in the narrative, and there are no convincing grounds for seeing these chapters as coming from a separate source; see R. P. Gordon, *1 and 2 Samuel*, pp. 29–37.) God's granting of *victories to David is one indicator of the restored relationship (chs. 5, 8, 10; *cf.* Deut. 28:7). The distribution of gifts of food after the bringing up of the ark also seems significant (2 Sam. 6:19): the Israelites have now entered a period in which they will enjoy the material blessings of the land (*cf.* Deut. 28:3–6). Even the list of David's officials indicates another blessing of his reign: just administration (8:15–18; *cf.* 23:1–7; Deut. 16:18–20; 17:8–13). One has only to compare Israel's state in 2 Samuel 5 – 10 with those of earlier periods (see, *e.g.*, Judg. 17 – 21; 1 Sam. 2 – 4; 1 Sam. 31) to see the change David's kingship has brought. This section of *Samuel* clearly lies at the root of later biblical texts which see the line of David as a focus of *hope for the future, or which see in Zion a symbol of God's rule over the nations (see below).

2 Samuel 11 – 20: David's decline

The second part of David's reign is less happy. David's sin with Bathsheba and Uriah, a serious abuse of royal power, draws down a prophetic condemnation which recalls Saul's rejection (compare 1 Sam. 15:17, 26, 28 and 2 Sam. 12:7, 9–11). Having earlier been given a promise concerning the 'house' he will inaugurate (7:11, 16), David is now told that 'the sword will never depart from your house' (12:10). The result is a widening circle of death and violence which spreads from David's household throughout Israel: the death of David's son by Bathsheba (12:14–23); the rape of Tamar (13:1–22); the murder of Amnon (13:23–33); Absalom's revolt (15:1–12). Rape and civil war were singled out by the last chapters of Judges as two of the greatest evils of the pre-monarchic period (Judg. 19 and 20), and attributed to the *lack* of a king (Judg. 17:6; 21:25); they now reappear in David's kingdom and even in his own household. However, David and his followers leave Jerusalem, preventing the destruction of the city (2 Sam. 15:14). Unlike Saul, David refuses to cling to power or to try to compel God to support him (15:25–26). Nonetheless, many Israelites are lost in the battle between David's and Absalom's supporters (18:7), and Absalom himself is killed, to David's great grief (18:15, 33). David's return to Jerusalem is full of a sense of what has been lost (19:8 – 20:3). The account of the later stages of David's reign concludes on a note of tribal hostility and sordid pragmatism (ch. 20). It also hints at the division of the kingdoms which will occur in the reign of David's grandson Rehoboam (1 Kgs. 12; compare 2 Sam. 20:1 and 1 Kgs. 12:16).

2 Samuel 21 – 24: The summing-up

Both the positive and the negative sides of David are represented in 2 Samuel 21 – 24, which should be seen as the true conclusion of the account of David (Gordon, *1 and 2 Samuel*, pp. 95–97). On the one hand, the two poems at the centre of these chapters (David's thanksgiving, ch. 22; David's last words, 23:1–7) present David at his best: *righteous and blameless (22:21–27; 23:5); upheld by God (22:5–7, 17–20); victorious over the nations (22:38–51); ruling his people justly (23:3–4). In these poems he represents the ideal ruler of Israel; it is an ideal which he has often fulfilled (P. E. Satterthwaite, in *The Lord's Anointed*, pp. 43–47). On the other hand, the reference to Uriah at the very end of the list of David's warriors (23:39) is a reminder of one occasion when David acted with brutal injustice. Finally, the account of David's census (ch. 24) shows how royal pride brings a plague on Israel; the incident is almost a parable for the destructive potentialities of the royal establishment (though also for the forgiveness that the king may obtain by penitence).

Samuel, then, leaves the reader with the question: is the monarchy a real blessing for Israel? The answer seems to be: yes, if the king is someone like the obedient David; no, if he is like Saul or like David when he abuses his power. A good king can lead the people in being faithful to God, unite the Israelite tribes into a single nation and provide for their needs through royal administrative structures. If his descendants follow his example, these benefits will be secured for many generations. Such a king, then, can bring blessing of unprecedented scope and continuity to Israel (contrast the judges, Judg. 2:19). The last chapters of 2 Samuel, however, leave the reader asking how often the ideal depicted by David's thanksgiving and last words will be embodied in the lives of David's descendants.

Further links with other OT books

As already noted, ideas first introduced in *Samuel* are enormously influential later in the OT. Only a brief sketch of this huge topic is possible here (see also C. J. H. Wright, *Knowing Jesus Through the Old Testament*, pp. 88–97).

Narrative books

In 1 and 2 Kings, though the kingdom of David and *Solomon is divided and greatly weakened during the reign of Rehoboam (1 Kgs. 12), the promise to David remains a factor in the long survival of the kingdom of *Judah (1 Kgs. 11:36; 15:4; 2 Kgs. 8:19). Even after the destruction of Judah, David's line remains a focus of hope (2 Kgs. 25:27–30). It has been suggested that the promise, having been stated with no conditions attached in 2 Samuel 7, is made conditional in Kings (see 1 Kgs. 2:2–4; 8:25; 9:4–5). This may be a false opposition (*cf.* Wright, *Knowing Jesus*, pp. 77–80), but it is clear by the end of Kings that, if the promise has a future, this is more a matter of God's grace than of human faithfulness. For Kings also portrays at length the evils which have arisen under the kings of both Israel and Judah, including some which had not appeared before the monarchy, such as institutionalized idolatry (1 Kgs. 16:29–33; 2 Kgs. 8:25–27; 16; 21:1–9) and injustice (1 Kgs. 21; 2 Kgs. 21:16). As in *Samuel*, so in Kings, a king who does not obey God offers his people no security.

The books of Chronicles, like those of Kings, note the failings of the kings of Judah (*e.g.* 2 Chr. 16; 28; 33:1–12), but also emphasize God's continuing commitment to David's line (2 Chr. 13:4–5). The very length at which David and Solomon are treated (1 Chr. 11 – 2 Chr. 9) suggests that for the Chronicler the promise to David continues to be significant in the post-exilic period.

Psalms

Many ideas in the Psalms develop ideas introduced in *Samuel*, *e.g.* the depiction of God as ruling Israel and the nations from Zion (Pss. 46 – 48; 65; 93; 96 – 99), and the view of the Davidic king as God's 'son', exercising God's authority over the nations (Pss. 2; 72). If the nations have mainly appeared in *Samuel* as Israel's enemies, to be defeated (*cf.* 2 Sam. 22:44–49), in the Psalms a more positive note, of blessing for the nations, is introduced

(Pss. 47:7–9; 72:17; 96:10–13; cf. Gen. 12:1–3). In some lament psalms the Davidic king is depicted as *suffering because of his calling to lead God's people, but he is then delivered by God (e.g., Pss. 3; 9 – 10; 22). There is a similar movement from humiliation and persecution to vindication in *Samuel's* depiction of David (1 Sam. 18 – 2 Sam. 5; cf. 2 Sam. 15 – 20). Both *Samuel* and the lament Psalms thus lay some of the groundwork for the NT's depiction of Jesus as a suffering and vindicated Messiah. Psalms 2 and 72, in fact, along with Psalms 89 and 132, form a sequence which traces in outline the history of David's line: inauguration (Ps. 2, esp. vv. 6–9); *glory (Ps. 72); humiliation (Ps. 89); restored hope after the exile (Ps. 132). Zion's history can similarly be traced in the sequence: Psalm 2 (inauguration; see esp. v. 6); Psalm 65 (glory); Psalm 74 (humiliation); Psalms 120 – 134 (hope after the exile). The placing of these royal and Zion psalms perhaps gives the Psalter a subtly messianic shape.

Prophetic books

The pre-exilic prophets combine critique of contemporary kings of Judah with a hope for a future descendant of David who will restore the line to its former splendour (Is. 7 – 9; 11; Jer. 22:1 – 23:8; Mic. 5:1–5). Similarly, Isaiah and Ezekiel contrast the disgrace and defilement of Zion and the temple in the prophets' own days (Is. 1; 29; Ezek. 8; 10) with the glory that will one day return to them (Is. 2:1–4; 54; 60; Ezek. 40 – 48). Both sets of ideas remain influential in the post-exilic prophets (Hag. 2:1–9, 20–23; Zech. 9:9–10; 13:1–3; 14; Mal. 3:1).

Links with the NT

The NT also makes significant use of ideas introduced in *Samuel*. Most obviously, the NT titles for Jesus, 'Christ' ('anointed one'; cf. 1 Sam. 16:13) and 'Son of God', have roots in *Samuel*. Many NT passages draw out the implications of the idea that Jesus is God's King, chosen to rule his people, but earlier ideas of kingship are often strikingly transformed. Thus Jesus enters Jerusalem as the promised king of David's line (Mark 11:1–10), but he comes to announce judgment on Jerusalem (Luke 19:41–44) and the temple (Mark 11:12–17; 13:1–2). Jesus preaches the arrival of the kingdom of God (Mark 1:14–15) but it arrives in an unexpected way (Luke

17:20–21); and Jesus' own kingship is established by his death on the cross (Mark 15:18–19, 25–26) and resurrection from the dead (Rom. 1:3–4). Similarly, in Revelation, the figure announced as the triumphant 'Lion of the tribe of Judah' and 'Root of David' proves to be 'a lamb, looking as if it had been slain' (Rev. 5:5–6). Later in Revelation, however, the visions of a king riding out to do final battle against the forces of evil (19:11–21) and of a new Jerusalem in which a temple is no longer needed (Rev. 21), seem to recall King David and his royal city in a more straightforward way, though with a splendour and power which quite transcends the OT archetypes.

Bibliography

R. P. Gordon, *1 and 2 Samuel* (Sheffield, 1984); T. Ishida, *The Royal Dynasties in Ancient Israel: A Study on the Formation and Development of Royal-Dynastic Ideology* (Berlin, 1979); V. P. Long, *The Reign and Rejection of King Saul: A Case for Literary and Theological Coherence* (Atlanta, 1989); P. E. Satterthwaite, 'David in the Books of Samuel: A Messianic Hope?' in P. E. Satterthwaite, R. S. Hess and G. J. Wenham (eds.), *The Lord's Anointed: Interpretation of Old Testament Messianic Texts* (Grand Rapids and Carlisle, 1995); C. L. Seow, *Myth, Drama and the Politics of David's Dance* (Atlanta, 1989); C. J .H. Wright, *Knowing Jesus Through the Old Testament* (London and Downers Grove, 1992).

P. E. SATTERTHWAITE

KINGS

Introduction

1 – 2 Kings tells *Israel's story from a time close to the end of *David's reign, when his sons Adonijah and *Solomon were locked in a struggle over the succession to the throne, to the period during which *Jerusalem fell to the Babylonian army and *Judah followed the northern kingdom of Israel into exile. Its theology can be summarized under the following headings.

The God of Israel

The primary theological theme in Kings is Israel's *God as the true and only God. The

LORD is not to be confused with the various gods worshipped within Israel and outside, for these are simply human creations (1 Kgs. 12:25–30; 2 Kgs. 17:16; 19:14–19). They are part of the created order, like the people who worship them; and they are powerless, futile entities (1 Kgs. 16:13, where the Heb. behind NIV's 'worthless idols' literally means 'insubstantial things'; 18:22–40; 2 Kgs. 17:15; 18:33–35). The LORD, by contrast, is the incomparable Creator of heaven and earth (1 Kgs. 8:23; 2 Kgs. 19:15). He is utterly distinct from the world which he has created (1 Kgs. 8:9, 14–21, 27–30, where he is neither truly 'in' the ark nor 'in' the *temple; cf. 18:26–38, where the antics of the Baal priests apparently imply belief in an intrinsic connection between their actions and divine action, while Elijah's behaviour implies quite the reverse), yet powerfully active within it. It is he, and no-one else, who controls nature (1 Kgs. 17 – 19; 2 Kgs. 1:2–17; 4:8–37; 5:1–18; 6:1–7, 27). It is he, and neither god, nor *king, nor *prophet, who controls history (1 Kgs. 11:14, 23; 14:1–18; 22:1–38; 2 Kgs. 5:1–18; 10:32–33; 18:17 – 19:37). This latter point is perhaps illustrated most clearly in the way that prophets generally function within the book, describing the future before God brings it about (1 Kgs. 11:29–39; 13:1–32; 16:1–4; 20:13–34; 2 Kgs. 19:6–7, 20–34). Nothing can hinder the fulfilment of this prophetic word – although God himself, in his freedom, can override its fulfilment for purposes of his own (1 Kgs. 21:17–29; 2 Kgs. 3:15–27, where the ending to the story is somewhat unexpected). There is only one living God, then: the LORD (1 Kgs. 18:15; 2 Kgs. 5:15).

True worship

As the only God there is, the LORD demands exclusive *worship. He is not prepared to take his place alongside the gods, nor to be displaced by them. He will not be confused with any part of the created order. He alone will be worshipped, by Israelite and foreigner alike (1 Kgs. 8:41–43, 60; 2 Kgs. 5:15–18; 17:24–41). Much of Kings therefore describes what is illegitimate in terms of worship. Most interest is shown in the *content* of worship, which must not involve *idols or images, nor reflect any aspect of the fertility and other cults of 'the nations' (1 Kgs. 11:1–40; 12:25 – 13:34; 14:22–24; 16:29–33; 2 Kgs. 16:1–4; 17:7–23; 21:1–9). A subsidiary concern is the *place*: ideally worship should be offered at the Jerusalem temple, and not at the local 'high places' (1 Kgs. 3:2; 5:1 – 9:9; 15:14; 22:43; 2 Kgs. 18:4; 23:1–20). The book also describes the moral wrongs which inevitably accompany false worship. For as the worship of something *other than God* inevitably leads on to some kind of mistreatment of fellow-mortals in the *eyes of God* (cf. 1 Kgs. 21, where abandoning God in the way envisaged in Exod. 20 leads on to wholesale breach of the other commandments described there; 2 Kgs. 16:1–4, especially v. 3; 21:1–16, especially vv. 6 and 16), so true worship of God is always bound up with more general obedience to the law of God. By the same token, true *wisdom is defined in terms of true worship and wholehearted obedience. It cannot be divorced from either (cf. 1 Kgs. 1 – 11, where there is an extended play on the nature of true wisdom). Worship and ethics are two sides of the same coin, in Kings as elsewhere in the Bible.

A moral universe

As the giver of the law which defines true worship and right thinking and behaviour, the LORD also executes *judgment upon wrongdoers. The world of Kings is a moral world, in which wrongdoing is punished, whether the *sinner be king (Solomon in 1 Kgs. 11:9–13; Jeroboam in 14:1–18), or prophet (the unnamed Judaean in 1 Kgs. 13:7–25; the disobedient man in 20:35–43), or ordinary Israelite (Gehazi in 2 Kgs. 5:19–27; the Israelite officer in 7:17–20). It is not a vending-machine world, however, in which every coin of sin which is inserted results in individually-packaged retribution. Even though people are told that they must obey God if they are to be *blessed by him (e.g. Solomon in 1 Kgs. 2:1–4; Jeroboam in 11:38), there is no neat correlation between sin and judgment in Kings. This is largely because of the compassionate character of the Judge, who does not desire final judgment to fall upon his creatures (2 Kgs. 13:23; 14:27), and is ever ready to find a reason to delay or mitigate it (1 Kgs. 21:25–28; 2 Kgs. 22:15–20). God's *grace is to be found everywhere in the book of Kings (1 Kgs. 11:9–13; 15:1–5; 2 Kgs. 8:19), confounding expectations which the reader might form on the basis of a simplistic understanding of *law. Sin can, nevertheless, accumulate to such an extent that judgment falls, not only upon individuals, but upon whole cultures, sweeping the relatively innocent away with the guilty (2 Kgs. 17:1–23; 23:29 – 25:26).

The divine promise

A promise is usually at the heart of the LORD's gracious behaviour towards his people in the book of Kings. The two most important divine promises mentioned are those given to the patriarchs, on the one hand, and to David, on the other.

The patriarchal promise to Abraham, Isaac, and Jacob, of descendants and ever-lasting possession of the *land of Canaan, clearly influences God's treatment of his people at various points in the story (2 Kgs. 13:23, and implicitly in 1 Kgs. 4:20–21, 24; 18:36; it also underlies Solomon's prayer in 1 Kings 8:22–53, as the king looks forward to the possibility of forgiveness after judgment). The future aspect of the promise in this passage is in tension with the story's ending as we find it in 2 Kings 25, where disobedience has led to expulsion from the land and *exile in a foreign empire. It seems that the true fulfilment of the promise is thought still to lie in the future, even though the promise has played a part in Israel's past as well.

There is a similar tension in the promise given to David that he will have an eternal dynasty; it appears in the book in a paradoxical form. For much of the narrative it explains why the Davidic dynasty survives, when other dynasties do not, *in spite of* the disobedience of David's successors (1 Kgs. 11:36; 15:4; 2 Kgs. 8:19). It is viewed, in other words, as unconditional. Judah's fate is not to be the same as Israel's, and Jerusalem's fate is to be different from Samaria's, because God has promised David a 'lamp', a descendant who will always sit on his throne. Thus when Solomon sins the Davidic line does not lose the throne entirely, but retains 'one tribe' (1 Kgs. 11:36), and has the prospect of restoring its dominion at some time in the future (11:39). When Abijam (or Abijah) sins, likewise, his son still retains the Judean throne (15:4). The background here is evidently the promise to David as it is recorded in 2 Samuel 7: the sins of David's descendants are to be punished by the 'rod of men' rather than by the kind of divine rejection experienced by Saul (2 Sam. 7:14–16). This promise makes the ultimate difference between Davidic kings and those of other royal houses

throughout the book of Kings: it makes the Judean dynasty unshakeable even while the dynasties of the northern kingdom are like 'reeds swaying in the water' (1 Kgs. 14:15). The dynasty survives *in spite of* the disobedience of David's successors. In other places, however, the continuance of the dynasty is made *dependent upon* the obedience of David's successors (1 Kgs. 2:4; 8:25; 9:4–5). The promise is treated as conditional. It seems that this latter view prevails as the book progresses: accumulating sin puts the unconditional nature of the promise under too much stress, and in the end brings God's judgment down upon Judah just as severely as it came upon Israel (2 Kgs. 16:1–4; 21:1–15; 23:31 – 25:26). And yet Jehoiachin lives (2 Kgs. 25:27–30). What is the significance of this fact?

A messianic hope

Interpreters of Kings have differed over the extent to which the book looks optimistically to the future, and what the nature of its future *hope might be. The closing verses of 2 Kings might of themselves be taken simply as the final nail in the coffin so skilfully prepared for Israel throughout the preceding chapters of the book. On this view Solomon's glory has finally departed to *Babylon; the empire has been dissolved; the Babylonian king has destroyed Solomon's city, his palace and his temple; he controls Solomon's empire, and he possesses all his wealth. Now Solomon's last-surviving successor (so far as we know) sits, amply provided for, at the Babylonian king's table, the great symbol of imperial power (*cf.* the high profile of Solomon's table in 1 Kgs. 4:27). He sits; he eats; and then (it is implied) he dies. The exiles (it is also implied) ought to behave in the same way, accepting the advice of Gedaliah to the people in Judah: 'Settle down ... serve the king ... and it will go well with you' (2 Kgs. 25:24).

In the context of the book of Kings taken as a whole, however (the immediate context in which 2 Kings 25:27–30 must be read), it is difficult to believe that this is all these verses mean. They tell us that Jehoiachin lived on (in contrast to Jehoahaz, 2 Kgs. 23:34), when he could have been left in obscurity (like Zedekiah, 2 Kgs. 24:18 – 25:7). Moreover, the fate of Jehoiachin's family (exile, 24:15) is clearly contrasted with that of Zedekiah's (death, 25:7). It is Zedekiah, and not Jehoiachin, who ends up as (in effect) the 'eunuch in Babylon' whom Isaiah had foreseen (2 Kgs. 20:18), a mutilated man deprived of heirs who might later claim the throne. Jehoiachin, by contrast, has living descendants. The significance of this fact is more clearly seen when the whole movement of the narrative in 2 Kings up to this point is considered.

Throughout the initial stages of this second section of the book of Kings, the reader still awaits the judgment which Elijah has prophesied for Ahab's house (1 Kgs. 21:17–29), a judgment unexpectedly delayed, in the first instance, by Ahab's own remorse when confronted by its announcement. The delay is sufficient for the kingdom of Judah to be drawn into Israel's sins. After two relatively righteous kings (Asa, Jehoshaphat), Judah finds itself with two kings who share with Ahab's children both their names (Jehoram, Ahaziah) and their penchant for idolatry (2 Kgs. 8:16–29). The disease in Ahab's household has proved infectious, having been carried south by his daughter (2 Kgs. 8:18). Intermarriage has again wreaked havoc (cf. 1 Kgs. 11:1–8; 16:31–33). Yet God has promised David a 'lamp' (2 Kgs. 8:19). Thus reappears the motif mentioned above, which has already featured twice in 1 Kings (11:36; 15:4), the promise which makes the ultimate difference between Davidic kings and others.

It is certainly this promise that makes the difference in 2 Kings 9 – 11. At first sight it seems that the house of David, mixed up through marriage with the most wicked of royal houses, has been caught up in divine judgment (2 Kgs. 11:1): after Ahaziah's death Athaliah the queen-mother 'proceeded to destroy the whole royal house'. Yet she does not quite succeed. One royal prince remains to carry on the line (11:2); and against the odds, he survives six years of his grandmother's 'foreign' rule to emerge once again as king in a land purified of the worship of foreign gods (11:3–20).

It is the Ahab story in particular which provides the framework within which 2 Kings 21 – 23 must be read. In these chapters the characters of both Manasseh and Josiah are so drawn as to recall, in different ways, the character of Ahab. Manasseh imitates Ahab by building altars to Baal (2 Kgs. 21:3; cf. also the Asherah pole in 1 Kgs. 16:33) and by worshipping idols (2 Kgs. 21:11; cf. 1 Kgs. 21:26).

The judgment that will fall on Jerusalem because of Manasseh's sins will be analogous to what happened to the house of Ahab (2 Kgs. 21:13). That judgment completely destroyed the royal house (1 Kgs. 21:21–22; 2 Kgs. 9 – 10; cf. 1 Kgs. 14:10 and 21:21 for the only occurrences prior to 2 Kgs. 21:12 of 'I am going to bring … disaster'). It seems from this that the Davidic line is to end after all, divine promises notwithstanding. It seems that there will be no escape, on this occasion, like the narrow escape of 2 Kings 11:1–3. What is said about the righteous Josiah does nothing to dispel this impression. Huldah's words to him in 2 Kings 22:15–20 simply confirm what has already been said by the unnamed prophets of 2 Kings 21. Because Josiah has humbled himself before the LORD (v. 19), he will not personally see all the disaster that is to fall on Jerusalem. There is to be a delay, as in the case of Ahab, whose house was also spared for a while because he tore his clothes and 'humbled himself' (1 Kgs. 21:27–29). Manasseh's grandson, in other words, is now being treated, as his grandfather was, like Ahab. Josiah's reaction makes a difference, but only to him. The judgment which has been announced will still surely fall, as it fell on the house of his apostate predecessor.

These parallels drawn between the house of David and the house of Ahab in 2 Kings 21 – 23 thus clearly imply that the destruction of David's house will be total. The full significance of the mere mention of Jehoiachin and his family in the closing chapters of Kings now becomes apparent. His reappearance is strikingly reminiscent of the appearance of Joash: he survives, unexpectedly, in the midst of carnage, and he represents the potential for the continuation of the Davidic line at a later time, when foreign rule has been removed. All is not yet necessarily lost, after all; the destruction of the family of the 'last king of Judah' (Zedekiah) does not mean that there is no Davidic line left. As the prayer of Solomon in 1 Kings 8:22–53 looks beyond the disaster of exile, grounding its hope for the restoration of Israel to her land in God's gracious and unconditional election of Abraham, Isaac and Jacob (cf. also 1 Kgs. 18:36–37; 2 Kgs. 13:23; 14:27); as it refuses to accept that God's words about the rejection of people, city and temple (e.g. 2 Kgs. 21:14; 23:27) are his final words; so too 2 Kings 25:27–30 in its narrative context hints that the unconditional aspects of the Davidic promise may still, even after awful judgment has fallen, remain in force. They express the hope that God may indeed be found to be, in the end as in the beginning, a God of grace and not only of commandment; the hope that, God's wrath having been poured out upon good Josiah's sons, his (admittedly wicked) grandson might still produce a further 'lamp for Jerusalem', as his (equally wicked) forefathers did (1 Kgs. 11:36; 15:4; 2 Kgs. 8:19). These closing verses of the book thus hang on tenaciously, in difficult circumstances, to the words of 2 Samuel 7:15–16 ('my love will never be taken away from him ... your throne shall be established for ever'), looking forward to the ideal Davidic king of the future. The two least criticized Judean kings, Hezekiah and Josiah, and the early Solomon (later criticized, but nevertheless blessed by God to an unparalleled extent), indicate the shape of the ideal towards which the authors of Kings were looking, as recognized by both Jewish and Christian interpreters of later times.

A 'Deuteronomistic' theology?

The theology of Joshua–Kings, and that of Kings specifically, is often referred to as 'Deuteronomistic' (or 'Deuteronomic'). The telling of the story of Israel in these books has clearly been greatly influenced by the language and theology of the book of *Deuteronomy, but it may not be helpful to think of the theology of Joshua–Kings as 'Deuteronomistic'. Some of the books display a much greater theological subtlety and complexity than one would expect to find within the framework of a 'standard' Deuteronomistic theology. Their theological emphases also seem to be different (cf., e.g., Judges with Kings). The construction of a 'Deuteronomistic theology' involves the blurring of all such subtleties, complexities and differences in order to extract an 'essence' which is said to lie beneath them and which reflects a relatively uniform ideological perspective on the world. It also runs the risk of obscuring theological and narrative themes shared with other OT books (e.g. the many and important connections between *Exodus and Kings). (See also *Genesis to 2 Kings.)

The book of Kings in the Bible

A centrally important feature of biblical narrative is its patterning. The biblical story is told in such a way that events and characters in the later chapters recall events and characters in the earlier chapters, by way of comparison or contrast. This is apparent within the book of Kings itself. The kings of Judah are compared and contrasted with David; Jeroboam is portrayed in the colours, first of Moses, and then of Aaron; both Manasseh and Josiah, in their own ways, remind us of Ahab; and so on. It is also apparent, however, in the NT, whose authors tell the story of *Jesus in ways that constantly remind us of earlier OT stories, including the story in Kings, whether at the general thematic level (God; worship and ethics; sin and judgment; grace and promise) or at the level of individual characters and events. The story in Kings, in other words, functions typologically in respect of the later NT story, preparing its way and gaining full significance only when read in the light of it. The God who is alone truly God, alone worthy of worship and reigning over a moral universe, is found to be the God and Father of our Lord Jesus Christ, who is himself the righteous son of David (the Messiah) for whom Israel has been looking, and the one in whom all God's grace and promises are focused. The story also functions typologically in respect of the people addressed by the NT (i.e. the readers). It invites them to read their own lives into the lives of its characters (i.e. to attach their story to its larger narrative whole), and it gains its full significance for them only as they begin to understand themselves in its context. Biblical theology 'reads together' the NT and Kings, allowing each to shed light on the other by their explicit and implicit connections, and thus arrives at a fulness of perspective that each body of literature cannot supply by itself.

One example, concerning human response to God, must suffice. It has been plausibly argued that the stories of Simon and the Ethiopian in Acts 8:9–40 are patterned after the story of Naaman and Gehazi in 2 Kings 5. The similarities between the texts, ranging from broad themes to tiny details, are certainly striking. Naaman arrives in Israel with royal backing, money and a scroll, but initially fails to do the one thing needful, to establish appropriate communication with God's prophet. The Ethiopian arrives in a similar way, and like Naaman, in a chariot. In both texts the foreign official washes and is renewed. In both texts the question arises of whether the gift of God can be exchanged for money. Elisha refuses Naaman's attempt to pay him, but Gehazi is happy to cash in on the miracle. Simon thinks that he can buy spiritual power. Both are confronted over their attempt to commercialize the gift; both are described as being (or fated to be) in the grip of a powerful negative force. By making the connection between the two testaments in this specific way, it is perhaps easier to see how 2 Kings 5 speaks more generally to the theme of Christian conversion. In this chapter Israel's God is acknowledged as the only real God, the God of Gentile (see *Nations) as well as Jew, and one prepared not only to be gracious to those 'outside the camp' (in this case someone who is not only a foreigner, but a leper as well), but also to pronounce judgment on 'insiders'. As throughout the Elisha stories, the humble (the servants, 2 Kgs. 5:2–3, 13) are presented as having more insight than the exalted (kings, army commanders, 2 Kgs. 5:1, 6–7); it is they, rather than the exalted, who are the channels of divine *salvation. It is through listening to their words, and indeed through becoming like them in submitting to authority, in becoming 'as a little child' (5:14), that the exalted come to know this salvation. The internal transformation is accompanied by the external sign of healing, the *water functioning as the medium of the move from old to new life. All these themes reappear and are of crucial importance in the NT (cf., e.g., Matt. 18:1–5; 19:13–15; Mark 9:33–37; 10:13–16; Luke 9:46–48; 18:15–17; John 3:1–8; Rom. 6:1–5; 1 Cor. 6:11; Col. 2:11–15; Titus 3:4–7).

Bibliography

B. S. Childs, *Introduction to the Old Testament as Scripture* (London, 1979), pp. 281–301; T. R. Hobbs, *1, 2 Kings*, WBC (Dallas, 1989); I. W. Provan, *1 and 2 Kings*, NIBC (Peabody, 1995); idem, 'The Messiah in the book of Kings', in P. E. Satterthwaite et al. (eds.), *The Lord's Anointed: Interpretation of Old Testament Messianic Texts* (Carlisle, 1996), pp. 67–85; idem, *1 and 2 Kings*, OTG (Sheffield, 1997).

I. W. PROVAN

CHRONICLES

Theology and the unity of Chronicles

Any summary of the theology of the books of Chronicles has to begin by identifying where that theology is to be found. Underlying this question, however, are at least three different issues. The first is the unity of the work. It is sometimes argued (e.g. by A. C. Welch, M. Noth) that the original Chronicler was responsible for a shorter version and that passages such as the genealogies of 1 Chronicles 1 – 9 and the lists of 1 Chronicles 23 – 27 are later supplements. The second issue is the extent of the work; some suggest that the Chronicler's history includes *Ezra and Nehemiah. The adoption of either or both of these views has resulted in scholars treating the Chronicler's theology as rather exclusive, even anti-Samaritan in tone. The third issue is whether the Chronicler's 'contribution' is confined to his own distinctive material or includes the extensive biblical and other sources which are such a prominent feature of the work. The simplest approach to all these issues, however, is to begin from the premise that the theology of Chronicles is the theology of the present form of the work. This approach has two advantages. It recognizes the vital contribution of the person responsible for Chronicles' overall design and purpose, and is consistent with the work of recent commentators such as S. Japhet and W. Johnstone who have taken the unity of Chronicles as a basis for their theological interpretation of these important books.

Theology and the nature of Chronicles

A second issue of principle concerns the nature of the books of Chronicles. Christians and Jews have traditionally assumed that they are historical books containing information about *Israel's history, like other historical books of the OT. On this view, the Chronicler's theology has more to do with his divinely inspired perspective on events than with the historical content of his work. It has often resulted in a minimalist view of the Chronicler's theology, however, irrespective of whether individuals have taken a positive (J. M. Myers) or negative (J. Wellhausen) view of the work's historical value. In contrast, since the 1970s Chronicles has increasingly been interpreted as primarily a theological work. This view is based on the Chronicler's approach to history (he uses speeches, prophecies and prayers rather than reports of events), on his frequent reinterpretations of earlier Scripture, and on his use of patterning and typological methods. It is also part of a wider recognition that all biblical history is to some extent theological in nature, though the theological perspective is most explicit and thorough in Chronicles. While the description of the Chronicler as 'the first Old Testament theologian' (P. R. Ackroyd, *JSOT* 2, 1977, p. 24) hardly does justice to his predecessors, it is increasingly recognized that Chronicles 'is a highly integrated theological statement, a single dominant complex of ideas, which binds the whole work together' (W. Johnstone, *1 and 2 Chronicles*, vol. 1, p. 10).

A theology of history

The Chronicler's interpretation of history highlights three areas where *God's activity was of special significance. Firstly, Israel's history from beginning to end belongs in the context of *God's purposes for the whole world*. The work accordingly traces Israel's origins and those of the *nations back to Adam (1 Chr. 1:1–54) and ends with a pagan emperor fulfilling *prophecy by inviting the Jewish *exiles to return to their Promised *Land (2 Chr. 36:22–23). In the Chronicler's post-exilic context where many Israelites believed that foreign empires had obliterated God's purposes for them, this idea was a direct challenge to a narrow theology; God's work is seen as part of a symbiotic relationship linking Israel with the rest of the world.

Secondly, the Chronicler is especially concerned with the *monarchy*. This subject dominates the entire work, though the Chronicler concentrates on the United Monarchy under *David and on *Judah during the Divided Monarchy, emphasizing two contrasting influences. On the one hand, Saul's kingship is removed because of his unfaithfulness to God and refusal to listen to God's word, and Judah is finally sent into exile for the same reasons (1 Chr. 10:13–14; 2 Chr. 36:14–20). On the other, God turns Saul's *kingdom over to David and preserves his dynasty throughout the period because of his *covenant promises (1 Chr. 17).

Thirdly, the perspective on Israel's past from which the Chronicler writes is that of the *exile*. Though the exile hung like a spectre over the whole of Israel's history (1 Chr. 5:26; 2 Chr. 30:6–9), it also formed a bridge between the disasters of Israel's past and their hopes for the future. Beyond the exile lay an opportunity to repopulate the Promised Land, to rebuild the *temple, and to restore the *worship of God (1 Chr. 9:2–34; 2 Chr. 36:23). The key to understanding the exile is found in the prophetic word. Although the exile had happened because the prophets' warnings had been repeatedly rejected (2 Chr. 24:19; 36:15–16), prophecy was also the means by which God's purposes were put into effect and could be renewed (2 Chr. 36:21–23).

A theology of the word of God

For the Chronicler, written Scripture is more important than individual prophecies. Chronicles is in effect a commentary on much of the rest of the OT, and 'stands apart in its attempt to interpret the Old Testament from beginning to end' (M. J. Selman, *1 Chronicles*, p. 42). The Chronicler aims to show the relevance of Scripture for his own period, though his method is that of quotation and allusion to earlier themes and passages rather than that of application to contemporary circumstances. In this process, the Law, the Prophets and the Writings are all included.

The Law in Chronicles

The Pentateuch is of special importance, above all because the Chronicler regarded the *law of Moses as the foundation for the life of God's people. First, however, the Chronicler combines material from Genesis on the themes of creation and election. He shows how the line of Abraham and Jacob grew out of the nations created by God and continued through the twelve tribes to the post-exilic community (1 Chr. 1:1 – 9:34). Thus the Chronicler's readers could see a direct connection between God's work in their own day and God's original creation of the human race.

The rest of the Pentateuch provides the Chronicler with two major emphases. Firstly, the Torah is the living word of God. The Torah is not a subject of antiquarian interest but a means by which people can obey God's will and learn how to worship him (2 Chr. 17:9; 19:4–11; 35:26). It must, however, be taught so that people's hearts can be turned back to the Lord (2 Chr. 19:4); neglect of the law leads to ignorance of God (2 Chr. 15:3; *cf.* T. Willi). The idea that *obedience to the law brings blessing is particularly important in relation to the temple. If *Solomon and the people follow God's laws, they will be successful in building the temple and will prosper in the land (1 Chr. 22:11–13; 28:8–10). If Israel disobeys, the Torah can even provide for their restoration and *forgiveness. The great promise in 2 Chronicles 7:13–14 that God will forgive the *sin and heal the land of those who *repent is closely based on Leviticus 26:40–42, a passage that was of special significance for the Chronicler; he also quotes verses 43–45 in relation to restoration after the exile in 2 Chronicles 36:21.

Secondly, the Torah provides a pattern for the worship of God. The building of Solomon's temple is based on the analogy of Moses' tent. Parallels include the basic shape of the buildings (2 Chr. 3 – 4; *cf.* Exod. 36:1 – 39:32), God's provision of a blueprint for their design (1 Chr. 28:11–19; *cf.* Exod. 25:9, 40), the people's generosity in making offerings for the construction (1 Chr. 29:6–9; *cf.* Exod. 35:20–29), and the appearance of God's glory preventing the priests entering the building at the dedication ceremony (2 Chr. 5:13–14; *cf.* Exod. 40:34–35). The Chronicler's main interest, however, is in the worshipping activities that took place in the buildings. He takes care to emphasize that the pattern of daily, weekly, monthly and annual worship in the temple follows the 'requirement for offerings commanded by Moses' (2 Chr. 8:13, NIV; *cf.* 1 Chr. 6:49; 2 Chr. 23:18; 31:3). Even though the Levites' role as musicians and worship leaders in the temple involved a substantial change from their previous activities, it conformed to the basic requirements of the law (2 Chr. 8:12–15; 30:16–17).

The Prophets in Chronicles

The historical books, or Former Prophets, provide the basic structure of the Chronicler's work. The underlying narrative comes from 2 Samuel and 1 and 2 Kings and covers the period from David to the exile, though the Chronicler offers his own interpretation of it. For example, he emphasizes that all twelve tribes recognized David's kingship (1 Chr. 11 – 12), and his preparations for the temple as a place of atonement and worship (1 Chr. 21 – 29). Solomon's role as the chosen temple

builder is given even greater prominence than in Kings, and the temple becomes the focus of the people's relationship with God throughout Judah's turbulent history. The Former Prophets are placed within a framework taken from Ezra and Nehemiah, which were probably the most recent books of Scripture available to the Chronicler. Both the genealogies and the narrative sections of Chronicles end with material based on Ezra and Nehemiah. They bring the main story down to post-exilic times by explaining the exiles' authority for returning home (2 Chr. 36:22–23; *cf.* Ezra 1:2–4) and recounting the story of their repopulation of the land (1 Chr. 9:2–34; *cf.* Neh. 11:4–19).

The rest of the prophetic literature is also prominent in Chronicles. Sometimes the Chronicler envisages the prophetic literature as a single entity. For example, acceptance of the prophets' words will bring success ('Have faith in his prophets and you will be successful', 2 Chr. 20:20; *cf.* Is. 7:9), but rejection of them makes Israel liable to God's *judgment (2 Chr. 24:19; 36:16). These general statements are supplemented by messages from a variety of individual prophets and even non-prophets, and by more frequent references than are found in Kings to the use of prophetic documents among the writer's historical sources (*cf.* 2 Chr. 9:29 with 1 Kgs. 11:41; 2 Chr. 32:32 with 2 Kgs. 20:20).

Prophecy is one of the main means by which Israel's history is interpreted in Chronicles. The replacement of Saul's kingdom by David's is interpreted in the light of prophecy (1 Chr. 10:13–14; 11:3), and the theological foundations of the Davidic monarchy and the temple are established through messages from God (1 Chr. 17:1–15; 2 Chr. 7:11–22). The prophets are more than just interpreters of history or messengers of prosperity and judgment, however. They have a special role in calling Israel to repentance, precisely in order that God's people should avoid judgment (S. Japhet, *The Ideology of the Books of Chronicles*, pp. 176–191). The Chronicler uses the message of repentance in Ezekiel 18 to interpret the lives of certain kings. Joash, Amaziah and Uzziah all begin in faith but then fall into sin, thus exemplifying the circumstances described in Ezekiel. 18:24–32 (2 Chr. 24 – 26). The next three kings then mirror the description in Ezekiel 18:1–20 of a righteous man (= Jotham, 2 Chr. 27) with a violent son (= Ahaz, 2 Chr. 28) who in turn has a righteous son (= Hezekiah, 2 Chr. 29 – 32). Finally, Ezekiel's emphasis on the life-saving nature of repentance (Ezek. 18:30–32) is exemplified by a further trio of kings; Manasseh's and Josiah's changed attitudes are contrasted with Amon's stubbornness (2 Chr. 33 – 35).

The Psalms in Chronicles

The Psalms are important for the Chronicler in illustrating Israel's worship in the temple, though they are quoted less frequently than the Law and the Prophets. (With the exception of Ezra and Nehemiah, the rest of the Writings hardly appear.) The Psalms are used in two different ways. Firstly, psalms are quoted at key points in the narrative as the ark is installed in Jerusalem and when the temple is built (Pss. 96, 105 and 106 are quoted in 1 Chr. 16:8–36; there is an allusion to Ps. 145 in 1 Chr. 29:10–13; and Ps. 132 appears in 2 Chr. 6:41–42). Secondly, the refrain 'for his steadfast love endures for ever' occurs several times, apparently reflecting the writer's major theme of Israel's praise in the temple (1 Chr. 16:41; 2 Chr. 5:13; 7:3; 20:21).

Chronicles and the development of Scripture

What role, then, does the notion of Scripture play in Chronicles? It is the chief means by which the Chronicler expounds his understanding of history, but it also provides a highly important contribution to the developing theology of Scripture in the OT. Firstly, the Chronicler assumes that the Torah, the Prophets and the Psalms exercise authority in the life of God's people. Though this kind of canonical awareness is paralleled elsewhere in the OT, the range of authoritative literature quoted in Chronicles is much greater than that quoted in any other OT book. Secondly, the written nature of this material and the assumption that it was familiar to the readers suggests it was already functioning as Scripture. 'The Law of Moses' and 'the Prophets' appear to have been recognized and accepted as the word of the Lord by the community for which the Chronicler was writing.

Thirdly, the Chronicler assumes that this received Scripture has already been considerably integrated. The prophetic literature is simply 'the prophets' (2 Chr. 20:20) and Samuel's prophecies concerning Saul are 'the

word of the LORD' (1 Chr. 10:13). The Pentateuch is called 'everything written in the Law of the LORD, which he had given Israel' (1 Chr. 16:40), or just 'the Book of the Law of the LORD' (2 Chr. 17:9). These designations are still accurate even if they do not refer to the final versions of the Law and the Prophets. The Law and the Prophets also speak with one voice. In sharp contrast to the rest of the OT where the 'word of the LORD' is mostly identified with prophecy, six of the twelve non-synoptic uses of this phrase in Chronicles refer to the prophetic word and six to the Mosaic law (cf. 1 Chr. 10:13; 15:15; 2 Chr. 12:7; 35:6; cf. W. M. Schniedewind, The Word of God in Transition, pp. 133–138). Prophetic interpretation confirms the written law (2 Chr. 34:18–28), and prophets and law speak together on issues such as the priority of seeking God (1 Chr. 28:9; 2 Chr. 25:2 quoting Deut. 4:29; Jer. 29:13–14).

Fourthly, Chronicles supplies considerable evidence that this written Scripture was capable not only of application but also of further development. New circumstances could lead to fresh applications of existing laws: for example, those concerning the right way to transport the ark (1 Chr. 15:12–15, based on Num. 7:9; Deut. 10:8) or those dealing with the Passover celebration in the second month (2 Chr. 30:2–3 based on Num. 9:9–13). Also the Chronicler is unafraid to adapt the law himself, for example with respect to the role of the Levites at the Passover. Whereas the elders slaughtered the original passover animals (Exod. 12:21), at Hezekiah's Passover the Levites carried out this task for the ceremonially unclean, and at Josiah's Passover they did so for every worshipper (2 Chr. 30:17; 35:5–6). Even more significantly, David is portrayed as having authority to change Moses' commands, and being able to introduce new arrangements for the priests and the Levites (2 Chr. 8:12–15; 29:25–30). For this reason, he is sometimes described as a 'second Moses'.

For the Chronicler, then, the word of God is both authoritative and dynamic, written and oral. Schniedewind has argued that Chronicles represents a change from oral prophecy to scribal prophecy or 'inspired inspiration of texts' (The Word of God, p. 231). But although Chronicles strongly emphasizes the interpretation of existing

Scripture, it is not clear that this replaces traditional prophecy. The importance given to oral prophecy alongside the interpretation and fulfilment of written prophecy, and to new adaptations of existing Scripture, suggests that the Chronicler saw a vitality in Scripture that allowed it to develop in response to current issues and to promote active faith.

The central theme of Chronicles

The lack of any explicit statement about the theme or purpose of the work has led to a wide variety of proposals on this issue, though several authors have argued that no one theme is predominant (notably Japhet, *Ideology*; H. G. M. Williamson). Recent scholarship has increasingly focused on the central role played by the Davidic monarchy and the cultus of the Davidic temple (*e.g.* B. E. Kelly, W. Riley, M. J. Selman), but other proposals merit serious consideration. These include: that Chronicles is an extended parable about seeking God as a way of life (C. T. Begg); that it is a pointer to Israel's restoration after the disaster of exile and judgment (Ackroyd); and that 'the themes of guilt and *atonement, derived from Leviticus, provide the Chronicler with the interpretative key by means of which the whole sweep of Israel's history within world history is to be understood' (Johnstone, vol. 1, p. 130).

The theme of seeking God is mentioned over thirty times in Chronicles (*e.g.* 1 Chr. 28:9; 2 Chr. 1:5; 7:14). Since it occurs throughout the work, and its use is very different from that in the Deuteronomic history, it seems that the Chronicler wanted particularly to emphasize this idea. Seeking God involves looking to God in all circumstances, emphasizing the importance of the divine–human relationship, and acknowledging the need for human repentance and divine assistance. It involves practical activity as well as an inner attitude, and results in specific actions such as building and restoring the temple or renouncing idolatry. However, the idea that Chronicles is just a parable on this theme gives insufficient weight to the historiographical intent of the Chronicler, and since the theme is sometimes treated alongside other aspects of repentance and restoration (*e.g.* 2 Chr. 7:14) it is questionable whether it is quite as dominant as has been claimed.

There is perhaps more evidence that Chronicles is about the relationship between judgment and exile on the one hand and the restoration of the community around the temple on the other. The climax of the genealogies (1 Chr. 9:2–34), God's promise of national restoration through prayer (2 Chr. 7:13–14) and Cyrus' edict inviting the exiles to return all reflect this theme and occur at key points in the work. Similarly, the idea that Israel's guilt needed to be atoned for is certainly a major theme, but it is perhaps too narrowly conceived to encompass the breadth of the Chronicler's thought. The temple services were concerned with more than just the removal of sin, and the Chronicler's concept of restoration includes more than atonement.

The overall structure of Chronicles reveals that the work is dominated by the Davidic monarchy and Solomon's temple. The central section is devoted to the united monarchy of David and Solomon (1 Chr. 10 – 2 Chr. 9), which actually occupies more space than the whole of the Divided Monarchy (2 Chr. 10 – 36). Two passages dominate the central section, the promise of the Davidic covenant (1 Chr. 17) and Solomon's prayer and God's promises at the dedication of the temple (2 Chr. 6 – 7). These two passages contain the longest messages from God in the entire work. The account of the Divided Monarchy also focuses on David's dynasty, especially its relationship with temple activities and personnel.

Several different interpretations of this material have been proposed, though they can be reduced to two main approaches: the first limits the Chronicler's horizon to acceptance of the status quo; the other emphasizes the Chronicler's eschatological hope. Three main variations of the view that the Chronicler was preoccupied with his own time have been advocated. According to the first of these, the Chronicler saw his community as the culmination of God's theocratic rule on earth, in the form of a religious community centred on temple worship. The Davidic emphasis is understood as a claim to the legitimacy of the Davidic house, in opposition to the rival claims of the Samaritans (W. Rudolph, O. Plöger). According to the second variation, the temple and its cultus outlived and replaced the Davidic monarchy (Riley). The cultus was established to provide atonement for Israel's sins, and was necessary even for good kings like David or Jehoshaphat (1 Chr. 2:7; 21:8; 2 Chr. 19:2; Johnstone). The third variation is a royalist one: the Chronicler looked for the Davidic line to be restored, perhaps in association with the restoration of the Jerusalem community in the late 6th century BC (D. N. Freedman).

Each of these interpretations seeks to link the Chronicler with the political and religious circumstances of post-exilic Israel, but since the Chronicler makes no mention of his own context, they can be only provisional. According to a further important variation on this theme, the Chronicler is concerned to promote the theory of immediate retribution (R. Dillard, Japhet). According to Japhet, *I and II Chronicles*, 'Reward is mandatory, immediate and individual. Every generation is requited for its own deeds, both good and evil, with no postponement of recompense; there is no accumulated merit' (p. 44). Though the Chronicler does indeed put more emphasis than other OT writers on individual blessing or punishment as a consequence of one's behaviour, the Chronicler's position is considerably more nuanced than Japhet recognizes, as illustrated by the various reasons he gives for the exile, which go back at least as far as Ahaz (2 Chr. 28).

One of the key interpretive issues is how the Chronicler's presentation of David and Solomon should be understood. While the chief feature of both kings is clearly their association with the temple, it is also often argued that they are presented in an idealized way, with their faults obliterated and their achievements magnified. Since, however, the Chronicler omits many positive as well as negative features of these two kings, this assessment must be questioned, especially as the Chronicler summarizes and indeed occasionally magnifies their failures (1 Chr. 13:9–13; 21:1 – 22:1; 2 Chr. 10:1–14). The Chronicler's greatest interest is in fact in God's covenant promises to David and Solomon, which he sees as initially fulfilled in Solomon's succession and the dedication of the temple.

The Davidic covenant plays a particularly significant role in Chronicles, in sharp contrast to the very restrained references to the Exodus, the Sinai covenant, and the entry into the Promised Land. It is mentioned repeatedly (*e.g.* 2 Chr. 6:16–17; 13:4–8; 21:7), and is even associated with the kingdom of God (1 Chr. 28:5; 2 Chr. 9:8). Three distinctive features are highlighted. Firstly, God's promises

can be realized through obedience, as exemplified especially by Solomon's commitment to building the temple (1 Chr. 28:8–10; 2 Chr. 6:14–17). Secondly, the temple becomes the chief symbol of the Davidic covenant. Rather than the temple replacing the monarchy, regular temple worship draws attention to the very promises which brought both temple and monarchy into being. Thirdly, the Davidic promises are permanent. The association between the eternal line of David, the kingdom of God, the repeated promise of an eternal kingdom, and the strong hint in Cyrus' edict that the task of building God's house still continues, all support the view that the Davidic line contained a genuine hope for the future as well as reminding the people of a glorious past. The claim that this hope is messianic is usually based on the Chronicler's supposed idealization of David (G. von Rad, R. North), and is therefore open to question. A more realistic view is that Chronicles does envisage a real hope for the future, but that its precise details remain open. Its conditional element depends on the readers' response, which the Chronicler expresses in terms of humility and repentance. However, the scope of this hope is potentially very broad. It incorporates the whole people of Israel represented by all twelve tribes, and envisages their occupation of the Promised Land and their being in relationship with God, a relationship expressed through joyful worship centred on the temple. In fact, far from the Chronicler's hope being limited to a messianic-type figure, it involves the full restoration of the whole community of God's people.

The purpose of Chronicles

The Chronicler is not explicit about the purpose of his work, but several features indicate that his aim involved more than the reinterpretation of Israel's past. His distinctive vocabulary emphasizes the value of seeking God, the importance of humility and repentance, and the attention to be given to praise and prayer in the temple. The extensive speeches, whether by kings, prophets or priests, are strongly hortatory, and the design of the work has the same purpose. The Chronicler was writing to a post-exilic community whose relationship with God was still characterized by the experience of exile. Though some had returned to their homeland, Israel's cumulative unfaithfulness over the generations had left them in a position before God where there was (lit.) 'no healing' (2 Chr. 36:16).

Having underlined the enormity and seriousness of the problem, the Chronicler then sets out the principle of restoration, describes the means for atonement, illustrates from the life of the kings of Judah how the principle works, and concludes with an invitation to participate in the restoration. The principle of restoration is described in detail at one of the key points of the book, namely the account of God's response to Solomon's prayer, and is characterized by God's promise to forgive sin and (lit.) 'heal their land' (2 Chr. 7:14). The means of forgiveness is the temple, whose atoning function is symbolized by the temple's location at the place where David sinned (1 Chr. 21:26 – 22:1; cf. 2 Chr. 29:20–35). Illustrations of how God restores those who repent are found in the account of the Divided Monarchy. Whereas in Kings, Rehoboam, Abijah and Manasseh are all described as notorious sinners, in Chronicles they become repentant sinners. Chronicles ends with an invitation to the readers to return to the Promised Land and build the house of the Lord (2 Chr. 36:23), and in order to emphasize this invitation, the quotation from Cyrus' edict is broken off in mid-sentence ('let him go up'; cf. Ezra 1:2–4). For the Chronicler, to build the house of the Lord was to make the temple function properly as a place of worship rather than to make it structurally complete, just as Solomon's dedication was not finished until the full pattern of worship commanded by Moses and David was established (2 Chr. 7:1–10; 8:12–16). The Chronicler could be satisfied that his purpose was accomplished only when all Israel were worshipping in the temple and living in accordance with the word of the Law and the Prophets throughout the land.

Chronicles in the NT

Quotation from the books of Chronicles in the NT is rare, and many commentators do not recognize any reference to them at all. But the NT is not silent with respect to Chronicles. 1 Chronicles 17:13, which is parallel to 2 Samuel 7:14, is quoted in 2 Corinthians 6:18, Hebrews 1:5, and Revelation 21:7. Only the writer to the Hebrews preserves the sense of the original promise, that a son of David is also a son of God, and he applies it to *Jesus as the unique Son of God. The other two passages extend the meaning of the original promise by making it refer to the *people of God, who in 2 Corinthians 6:18 specifically include daughters as well as sons.

Moreover, some NT writers affirm the Chronicler's general point that the Davidic covenant remained valid long after the collapse of the Judean monarchy. They preferred to support their view by quotations from the Psalms (especially Pss. 2:7; 110:1, 4) and the Prophets rather than from Chronicles, but there is no doubt that these quotations are consistent with the Chronicler's underlying thought. However, the NT authors' view of the Davidic covenant affected not only their Christology, but also their ecclesiology; for them the various OT promises about the Davidic covenant were just as much concerned with the nature of the *church as with the person and work of Christ. The ecclesiological significance of the covenant is seen not just in the application of 1 Chronicles 17:13 to the church in 2 Corinthians 6:18 and Revelation 21:7 but also in the NT's development of the temple theme so important to the Chronicler. Paul acknowledges that the church is both God's living temple and God's family in 2 Corinthians 6:16–18 by quoting from important OT covenant passages. It is perhaps no accident therefore that the concluding section of the Bible (Rev. 21 – 22) contains a quotation from the Chronicler, the OT writer who was most concerned to provide an interpretation of the whole of human history. That history, which for the Chronicler began with Adam (1 Chr. 1:1), and which was bound up with David's line and with the temple, will ultimately involve the complete renewal of the whole people of God (Rev. 21:7) as the supreme Son of David is reunited with his covenant people.

Bibliography

P. R. Ackroyd, *The Chronicler in his Age* (Sheffield, 1991), pp. 273–289; C. T. Begg, '"Seeking Yahweh" and the purpose of Chronicles', *LS* 9, 1982, pp. 128–142; R. Braun, *1 Chronicles*, WBC (Waco, 1986); R. Dillard, *2 Chronicles*, WBC (Waco, 1987); D. N. Freedman, 'The Chronicler's purpose', *CBQ* 23, 1961, pp. 436–442; S. Japhet, *The Ideology of the Books of Chronicles and its Place in Biblical Thought* (Bern, ²1997); *idem*,

I and II Chronicles, OTL (London, 1993); W. Johnstone, *1 and 2 Chronicles*, 2 vols. (Sheffield, 1997); B. E. Kelly, *Retribution and Eschatology in Chronicles* (Sheffield, 1996); R. Mosis, *Untersuchungen zur Theologie des chronistischen Geschichtswerkes* (Freiburg, 1973); J. M. Myers, *1 Chronicles, 2 Chronicles*, AB (New York, 1965); R. North, 'The theology of the Chronicler', *JBL* 82, 1963, pp. 369–381; M. Noth, *The Chronicler's History* (ET, Sheffield, 1987); O. Plöger, *Theocracy and Eschatology* (ET, Oxford, 1968); G. von Rad, *Das Geschichtsbild des chronistischen Werkes* (Stuttgart, 1930); W. Rudolph, *Die Chronikbücher*, HAT (Tübingen, 1955); W. M. Schniedewind, *The Word of God in Transition* (Sheffield, 1995); M. J. Selman, *1 and 2 Chronicles*, TOTC (Leicester and Downers Grove, 1994); A. C. Welch, *The Work of the Chronicler* (Oxford, 1939); J. Wellhausen, *Prolegomena to the History of Israel* (ET, Edinburgh, 1885); T. Willi, 'Thora in den Chronikbüchern', *Jud* 36, 1980, pp. 102–105, 148–151; H. G. M. Williamson, *1 and 2 Chronicles*, NCB (London, 1982).

M. J. SELMAN

EZRA-NEHEMIAH

Form

The books of Ezra and Nehemiah appear in our Bibles as separate works, but they originally formed a single composition (hence 'Ezra-Nehemiah') and should be read as such. Until recently it was generally believed that Chronicles and Ezra-Nehemiah had also originally comprised a single composition (usually called 'the Chronicler's History Work') which was subsequently divided into the present corpora. This view is increasingly rejected in modern scholarship as significant differences in outlook and presentation between *Chronicles and Ezra-Nehemiah are recognized. Nevertheless, both works come from the same postexilic community and should be read in the light of each other.

Ezra-Nehemiah recounts episodes in the history of the Judean community from 538 BC, 'the first year of Cyrus, king of Persia' (Ezra 1:1), until Nehemiah's second term as governor of Judah (c. 430 BC, Neh. 13:6–7). The subjects of the narrative are as follows:

1. Ezra 1 – 6: the return of Jewish exiles from Babylonia to restore worship and rebuild the temple in *Jerusalem (a task finally completed in 516 BC, Ezra 6:14);

2. Ezra 7 – 10, Nehemiah 8 – 9: the return of Ezra the scribe from Babylon in 458 BC with a royal mandate to teach and enforce the law of Moses in Judah;

3. Nehemiah 1 – 7, 10 – 13: Nehemiah's governorship from 445 BC, and his building work and social reforms.

Ezra-Nehemiah is composed from a variety of historical sources (including personal memoirs of the reformers, official letters in Aramaic, and various citizen lists) which were edited into the present work probably around 400–300 BC. It is a work of historiography, albeit a highly selective one which concentrates on the significance of a few decisive events in the period 539–432 BC or thereabouts. For example, the narrative describes Ezra's mission immediately after its account of the dedication of the *temple, passing over an interval of almost sixty years with the terse comment 'After this' (Ezra 7:1, NRSV). Whereas the modern historian sees no causal connection between these events, the biblical writer understands them as clearly related within God's redemptive activity, and so proceeds at once to the next significant event in the life of the restored community.

The historical materials in the work have been purposefully arranged (in some cases, apparently more according to theme than to strict chronology) to convey a distinctive theological outlook. Thus the literary shape of the book in its final form is intrinsic to its message: from the perspective of faith it connects separate or temporally distant historical events and interweaves accounts of the work of various community leaders to indicate the essential unity of their work within God's purposes, from the days of Zerubbabel until Nehemiah's time (*cf.* Neh. 12:47).

Theological themes

The overall themes are God's restoration of the *Judean community to the Promised *Land and their reorganization as his faithful covenant people (see *People of God). These two broad themes provide us with basic perspectives for exploring the theology of the work and its connections with other parts of Scripture.

God's activity in history on behalf of his people

Each of the three sections of the work noted above represents a definitive stage on the way to the Judean restoration.

First, the *reinstatement of *worship* according to the Mosaic law and the rebuilding of the temple are accomplished through the governor Zerubbabel and the high priest Jeshua, with the encouragement of the prophets Haggai and Zechariah (Ezra 6:14, 18).

Second, Ezra's *teaching of the *Law* leads to the people's confession of sin (Ezra 10:2). Those who had taken non-Jewish wives agree to divorce them, and the people commit themselves anew to the Mosaic covenant (Neh. 10:30–39).

Finally, the *dedication of Jerusalem's wall* (Neh. 12:27–43) marks the culmination of Nehemiah's labours to provide security and self-respect for the embattled community by rebuilding the wall and further repopulating the city (Neh. 1 – 7; 11).

Thus, a movement of spiritual and social revival that begins in Jerusalem with the repair of the ruined altar of Solomon's temple (Ezra 3:2) extends, in time, to encompass the city, literally and figuratively. At each point the ideals of the leaders are adopted by the people, in a context of joyful worship and commitment (Ezra 3:4; 6:22; Neh. 8:12; 12:27).

The whole process is attributed to God, who fulfils his promise through Jeremiah (Ezra 1:1; *cf.* Jer. 29:10–14) and effects a (partial) reversal of the *exile. There are no outward miracles in the work; instead, changes occur at the psychological level of decision-making. God initiates events: he 'stirred up the spirit' of Cyrus to encourage a return of exiles to rebuild the temple (Ezra 1:1; *cf.* Is. 41:25; 45:13). Subsequently God 'put ... into the heart' of Cyrus's successors, Darius and Artaxerxes, to assist the community, in the face of powerful local enemies, to complete the temple, maintain its services and promote the Mosaic law (Ezra 7:27; *cf.* 6:22; 9:9). Finally, Nehemiah's mission is carried out under royal protection and patronage, granted through God's favour (Neh. 2:7–10). Thus, the Persian kings are presented as God's agents for the benefit of his people (H. G. M. Williamson, *Ezra-Nehemiah*).

God is equally at work among his covenant people, whom he inspires and graciously enables to fulfil his plans (Ezra 1:5; 5:5; 7:28; 8:18; Neh. 2:12, 18; 6:16; 7:5). They are co-opted into God's purposes through their faith and prayerfulness. Nehemiah's example is particularly instructive. He is outstanding as a man of both earnest prayer (*cf.* Neh. 1:4–10) and decisive action, and the book perceives no incompatibility between these two characteristics. Instead, human responsibility in the form of wise planning and practical action is readily combined with a keen sense of divine sovereignty guiding and protecting the community (*cf.* Neh. 2:7–9; 4:9, 14–15). Thus what God proposes, he also disposes, whether through Gentile kings or his faithful people.

Israel restored and reformed

Ezra-Nehemiah signals therefore the resumption of '*salvation', in the classical OT sense of living as God's people in the Promised Land with his worship and law at the centre of the community's life. However, there are some significant differences from the pre-exilic period in view of the post-exilic political conditions. The pre-exilic state and Davidic monarchy are now irrevocably gone, and the community is numerically much reduced. It must adjust to living as a minor portion of the ethnically diverse province of Trans-Euphrates, itself a part of the vast Persian empire. Under such conditions, many small peoples were assimilated and disappeared for ever, but Ezra-Nehemiah indicates how 'Israel' (in the form of the restored community) succeeded in preserving its existence and identity. This was achieved in three interrelated ways: by establishing continuity with the people's past; by drawing firm boundaries – spiritual, social and physical – around the community; and by the creative interpretation of Scripture to regulate the people's life.

1. Continuity with the pre-exilic period is expressed first in worship. The new temple is constructed in the style of Solomon's building (Ezra 6:4; *cf.* 1 Kgs. 6:36; 7:12); it is furnished with the pre-exilic vessels which Cyrus returned (Ezra 1:7–11; 6:5); and its forms of worship are those prescribed by the Mosaic law or by David (Ezra 3:3–6, 10; 6:18; Neh. 8:13–18; 10:29–30; 12:45). These details make deliberate contact with Israel's past so as to overcome the breach caused by the destruction and exile. The second temple is thus

depicted as the legitimate continuation of the first. It had the same sacramental significance as its predecessor, as the primary means through which God mediated grace and forgiveness to his people (cf. 1 Kgs. 8:29–45). Within the relatively small post-exilic community the temple played a central role, and the rhythm of worship focused on the building connected the people to their spiritual roots.

Participation in the popular festivals (see *Sacred meals) also reinforced the community's self-understanding as Israel. Nehemiah 8:17 records that, in response to Ezra's teaching, 'all the assembly (qāhāl) of those who had returned from the captivity made booths and lived in them' in a celebration of the Feast of Tabernacles. The verse indicates that the people were deliberately re-enacting the Israelites' wandering in the wilderness after the Exodus (cf. Lev. 23:43) and understood their own return from 'captivity' as a second Exodus. The editor of the work has also echoed this theme in his description of the initial return, which calls to mind the spoiling of the Egyptians (Ezra 1:4–6; cf. Exod. 12:35–36), and in his account of Ezra's 'going up' from Babylon (Ezra 7:9; cf. Exod. 12:2).

Finally, continuity with the past is reflected in the people themselves. Membership of the community depended principally on establishing one's physical descent from pre-exilic Israel (Ezra 2:2–63 = Neh. 7:6–65; 13:3). The positive significance of this condition was that it affirmed the identity of the community as the legitimate heirs of old Israel: they were the 'escaped ... *remnant' (Ezra 9:15) whom God had gathered once more to the land (Neh. 1:9).

2. Ezra-Nehemiah shows that the boundaries of the community were tightly drawn. The negative side of the preoccupation with genealogy and physical descent was a rigidly separatist attitude taken towards the neighbouring peoples in the land whenever they sought involvement with the Jewish community (Ezra 4:1–3; Neh. 2:20), or whenever intermarriage had been practised (Neh. 9:2; 13:1–3, 23–28). However, the community was not wholly exclusive, for Ezra 6:21 indicates that non-Jews who separated from their neighbours' ways and converted could participate in its life.

It was essential to protect the small and vulnerable community from religious syncretism and from absorption by its more numerous and economically powerful neighbours; thus, a policy of compelling the divorce of foreign wives and confining *marriage to within the Jewish community was adopted (Ezra 10:11–17; Neh. 10:30; 13:23–25). It is important to note, however, that the basis of this policy was not racial but religious: Deuteronomy's law of marriage for pre-exilic Israel, which banned liaisons with the pagan Canaanites (cf. Deut. 7:1–4 and Ezra 9:12), was now invoked and applied as a means of ordering the post-exilic community's life in relation to its non-Jewish neighbours (Ezra 9:1–2; Neh. 13:23; see below). The community leaders perceived that Israel's potential and actual status as 'the holy *seed' (Ezra 9:2; cf. Is. 6:13), that is, a people chosen and preserved by God for covenant loyalty, was gravely compromised by intermarriage, for such liaisons would lead to the adoption of pagan practices and an ignorance of Scripture in the following generation. Nehemiah was shocked to discover that the children of mixed marriages could not converse in Hebrew and thus could not understand the Scriptures (Neh. 13:24). 'A single generation's compromise could undo the work of centuries' (F. D. Kidner, Ezra and Nehemiah).

3. Scripture, in particular the Torah (law/instruction) of Moses, plays a profound role in Ezra-Nehemiah in determining the life of the community and shaping its identity. This is especially evident from the time of Ezra with his specific mission to teach the law (Ezra 7:25–26). As a result of Ezra's endeavours, culminating in the public reading of the Torah (Neh. 8), a veritable reformation was instituted, leading to a concerted effort to regulate the community according to the law in its membership, practice of marriage, worship and commerce (cf. Neh. 10:28–39; 13:1–3, 15–25). The resultant reform was not simply legalistic, for it involved profoundly religious motives of repentance and worship (Neh. 8 – 9). Significantly, Ezra did not enforce the law autocratically, but rather allowed its teaching to do its own work among the people, convincing and reforming them (cf. Ezra 9:1–2; Neh. 9:38 – 10:39).

Scripture thus came to assume a more normative role, and the Jewish community became more consciously defined as a 'people of the book', than was the case in pre-exilic times. We see in Ezra-Nehemiah, and pre-eminently in the figure of Ezra, the beginnings of scribalism, the first attempts to interpret and apply the pre-exilic Mosaic Torah in the circumstances of the present (cf. Ezra 7:10). This trend continues into NT times, where Jesus' disputes with the religious authorities frequently turn on the correct interpretation of scripture (cf. Mark 2:23–26; 10:2–9).

Conclusion

Ezra-Nehemiah is thus the record of the restoration and reformation of God's covenant community. From the perspective of biblical theology, it is significant that the book marks the end point, chronologically speaking, of the OT narrative. The people of God, who were constituted at Sinai, have passed through all the vicissitudes of the monarchy and the catastrophe of the exile, to be gathered once more, in chastened circumstances, around the temple and under the Mosaic Torah. They have been restored as God promised, but the achievement is only partial, and in no sense does the restored community represent the fulfilment of God's purposes for his people. The earlier Davidic-Messianic hope of the prophets, which promised a glorious and peaceful future for the people (cf. Is. 9:6–7; Jer. 33:15–22; Ezek. 37:24–28), is apparently dormant in a period preoccupied with the survival and consolidation of the covenant community. It is clear that many things are far from ideal in the community's present circumstances. Thus, Ezra 4:6–24 and other passages indicate that the people frequently faced opposition from their neighbours, while the prayer in Nehemiah 9:36–37 reflects the oppression they endured from their Persian overlords. Ezra 9 – 10 and Nehemiah 13 also indicate the propensity of the community to fall back into sin, despite the experience of exile and the work of reform.

Against these facts, the work sets out the ideal to which the people may aspire in the hope of a fuller salvation, by living as 'the assembly of God' with God's worship and word at the heart of their community life (Neh. 12:44 – 13:3). The NT makes no reference to Ezra-Nehemiah, nor to the work of the reformers, but the Judaism we encounter there some centuries later, with its characteristic concerns for purity and for the exegesis and application of Scripture, in large measure grew directly from their labours, and so provided the context for Jesus' own ministry of teaching and reconstituting the people of God. With his coming, the unfulfilled hope of the prophets began finally to be realized.

Bibliography

B. S. Childs, Introduction to the Old Testament as Scripture (London, 1979); F. D. Kidner, Ezra and Nehemiah, TOTC (Leicester and Downers Grove, 1979); J. G. McConville, Ezra, Nehemiah and Esther, DSB (Edinburgh, 1985); H. G. M. Williamson, Ezra, Nehemiah, WBC (Waco, 1985); idem, Ezra and Nehemiah, OTG (Sheffield, 1987).

B. E. KELLY

ESTHER

Introduction

The book of Esther is unique in the reactions it has attracted. Some have praised it as one of the most worthy books of Scripture; others, particularly some Christian commentators, have reacted violently against it, even questioning its canonicity.

The main reason for such doubts lies in the fact that the book nowhere refers to God, either by direct reference or by allusion. In addition, God's people are consistently referred to as 'the Jews'. In the past this caused consternation among some Christian scholars. So too did the Jews' treatment of their enemies at the end of the book.

Themes in Esther

A close examination of the book reveals that it possesses great spiritual and theological depth. This may be seen particularly in its main themes.

Divine *providence

The character of Haman in the book of Esther is representative of the pagan, anti-God society in which Esther and the Jews live. He is both self-absorbed (6:6) and self-indulgent (3:5–6). Of great significance for the message of the book is Haman's dependence upon chance. Having decided to pursue his plan of genocide against the Jews, he casts lots daily for almost a full year in order to determine a lucky day on which to put the plan into action (3:7, RSV). Haman, however, is shown to be subject to a power much higher than that of chance. A long series of *chance* events places him at the mercy of King Ahasuerus and Queen Esther. This results in his execution and the abysmal failure of his plan (7:10; 9:1–17).

Proverbs 16:33 states, 'The lot is cast into the lap, but the decision is wholly from the LORD.' There is no 'chance'. The book of Esther clearly demonstrates that Almighty God has human affairs firmly under his control. It does so by reference to the surprising number of *coincidences* which serve to thwart Haman's plans. Vashti's deposition (1:10–22), Ahasuerus' choice of Esther as his queen (2:17), Mordecai's discovery of the plot against the king (2:21–22), Ahasuerus' insomnia on a certain night (6:1), and so on, all serve to highlight the transcendence of God, without once mentioning his name. Human responsibility

In Esther 4:13–14, Mordecai enunciates the belief that God has a plan for Esther's life; and that she has been placed in her present position as part of that plan. Esther must make a choice: to act, or not to act, on behalf of God's people by approaching the king without having been summoned into his presence. Thus within the context of God's plan, Esther must choose what to do. She has the responsibility to carry out God's will. If she does not do so, she is culpable and will be punished (v. 14). It is her responsibility to find God's plan for her life and to act accordingly.

The reversal of fortunes

The reversal of fortunes is a significant theme in Esther, as it is elsewhere in Scripture. Esther, an insignificant Jewish girl, is elevated to the position of First Lady in the mighty Persian Empire (2:15–18). Mordecai, a regular at the king's gate, is promoted to be Ahasuerus' right-hand man (8:2). Meanwhile Haman, Ahasuerus' Grand Vizier, is suddenly abased, forfeiting his position, his wealth and his life (7:9 – 8:1).

The theme of God exalting the humble and bringing low those in high position may also be observed in the stories of Jacob (Gen. 25:23), Joseph (Gen. 41:39–44), Ephraim (Gen. 48:14–20), Gideon (Judg. 6:14–16), David (1 Sam. 16:6–13) and many others throughout both Old and New Testaments. It is found in Hannah's song of praise (1 Sam. 2:1–10), Psalm 113 and Mary's *Magnificat*

(Luke 1:46–55). The book of Esther is frequently compared with the *Joseph narrative of Genesis 37 – 45. Both Joseph and Esther are exalted to lofty positions in the royal household in order to bring salvation to God's people.

The importance of this theme in Scripture relates directly to the ultimate reversal of fortunes: salvation through Christ. Esther and Joseph are exalted to royal position in order to bring temporal salvation, but Jesus abases himself to bring eternal salvation: 'though he was rich, yet for your sake he became poor, so that by his poverty you might become rich' (2 Cor. 8:9). The exaltation of the humble also anticipates the exaltation of Christ after his conquest of sin and death at Calvary (*e.g.* Phil. 2:5–11). The elevation of Esther and Mordecai points forward to Christ and reveals the hand of a God who is infinitely more powerful than the whole Persian Empire, a God who is truly the King of kings.

Mordecai and Esther

The role of Mordecai

Many commentators emphasize the role of Mordecai. Yet although Mordecai is promoted (8:15), and has an important role in the Jewish community (9:20–23), the focus of the text is clearly the character of Queen Esther. Mordecai is her link with the world outside the walls of the royal harem, with the community of God's people, with her life before entering the king's palace. It is Esther, however, who is the central figure in the text.

The character of Esther

Esther is an epitome of purity and guilelessness. She goes into the presence of the Gentile king, saying '"… if I perish, I perish"' (4:16). She is prepared to lay down her life for the sake of God's people. Indeed her self-sacrificial attitude in many ways prefigures the sacrifice of Christ, whose death achieves the ultimate liberation for God's people because of his sinless purity. Esther is one of the OT pointers to Calvary and to the coming of the Messiah, through whom the redeemed will one day enter unhindered the presence of Almighty God.

Conclusion

The dialogue between Mordecai and Esther in 4:10–16 encapsulates the message of the book. It expresses a firm assurance that God's people will be delivered from the hand of Haman and their enemies because divine providence is at work on their behalf. The only question to be resolved is by what human agency God will bring salvation. The outworking of the story reveals that Esther, whom God has elevated, will be the one to fulfil his plan.

God is never mentioned in the book of Esther, but his imprint is everywhere. He is the unseen force behind every apparent coincidence which brings victory and deliverance to his people. Esther acts faithfully to fulfil God's plan, and God honours her faithfulness. The book is a practical demonstration of Romans 8:28: 'We know that in everything God works for good with those who love him, who are called according to his purpose.'

Bibliography

J. G. Baldwin, *Esther*, TOTC (Leicester and Downers Grove, 1984); S. B. Berg, *The Book of Esther: Motifs, Themes and Structure* (Missoula, 1979); J. Craghan, *Esther, Judith, Tobit, Jonah, Ruth* (Wilmington, 1982); K. J. A. Larkin, *Ruth and Esther*, OTG (Sheffield, 1996).

G. KEYS

JOB

The story

The book of Job consists of a prologue, a dialogue in three acts, a *wisdom poem, three monologues and a concluding epilogue. In the prologue the author lays the foundation for both the dialogue and the epilogue. He introduces Job, a man who seems to have had only success in life. He has a prominent social position and great wealth, but his joy lies in his fellowship with *God. He is a just and honourable man, who fears God and avoids *evil.

Then the action switches to heaven and a scene between God and Satan (see *Spiritual powers). God points Satan's attention to his humble and faithful servant Job, but Satan is unimpressed. Job is not pious for nothing, he suggests. Given all the earthly wealth that Job has received, it may be that his faith is self-interested. Satan claims that Job will rebel against God if he loses all his possessions or is struck with a terrible disease (1:11; 2:5). To prove that Job is trustworthy, God allows Satan to take away all the man's possessions

and children and to strike him with a severe disease. But Satan is not allowed to take Job's life, since that would make the test impossible. Job maintains that God is *righteous.

As Job suffers severely, three of his friends (Eliphaz, Bildad and Zophar) come 'to console and comfort him' (2:11, NRSV). But they do not even recognize him, so severe is his disease. Deeply distressed, they express their grief and sorrow in a traditional way. But in their attempt to comfort their friend, they are hampered by their ignorance of the scene which has taken place in heaven. Their words of comfort turn into accusations against Job; they conclude that because he has suffered all these catastrophes, he must have *sinned. Job, however, protests strongly against his friends' increasingly harsh accusations. After a while, the dialogue reaches an impasse; indeed, in the final sequence of exchanges Zophar does not speak.

Before Job presents his final plea to God, there is a song in praise of wisdom (ch. 28), which declares that true wisdom and insight can be found only in God; *humans apart from God live in ignorance.

In his final contribution to the discussion, Job summarizes his life, his past happiness (ch. 29), his present misfortune, and finally, his innocence. He does not give way to despair in the face of the misfortunes that have come upon him; nor does he accept his friends' explanation of his predicament.

Suddenly and unexpectedly a young man called Elihu speaks. He aspires to judge between Job and his friends, but he is far from being impartial. He speaks of the purpose of *suffering, but not of its cause; it is intended to purify and to save people. According to Elihu, God's purpose is to judge Job's pride (33:15–30; 36:5–16). But God does not appear in person to Elihu: 'The Almighty – we will never find him – is high in power and justice, great in righteousness, he does not answer!' (37:23, author's translation). But Elihu is wrong; God does answer Job from out of the whirlwind.

In the epilogue, Job is fully restored to his original blessedness (42:10). His old friends return; he has more children, as many as he had before, and he lives another 140 years. Job is still as dear to God as he was at the beginning of the story. Nothing has changed in their relationship because of what Job has said and done. His material restoration is a sign of his personal restoration to fellowship with God.

Structure

1:1 – 2:10	Prologue
2:11 – 42:6	Dialogue
3	Job curses the day of his birth
4 – 14	Act I
15 – 21	Act II
22 – 31	Act III
28	Song of Wisdom
32 – 37	Speeches of Elihu
38:1 – 42:6	Speeches of God
38:1 – 39:38	Speech I
40:1 – 42:6	Speech II
42:7–17	Epilogue

The theology of Job's friends

The God of Job's friends is a God of retribution. God's main function, according to Eliphaz, Bildad and Zophar, is to uphold the law of retribution in relation to all people. This principle was commonly taught in Israel (see *e.g.* Prov.; Ps. 18:20–28). God will be good to the one who does good, but he will also bring harm upon the one who does evil. Job's friends base their whole view of God and the world on this principle of retribution (4:8). They emphasize that it is not their own invention, but based upon the experiences of past generations, the wisdom of the elders (8:8–13; 15:17–20). They try to comfort Job with it: since no innocent person ever suffered, all he needs to do is to think hard about what he has done and find out what he has done wrong (4:6–7). But as the dialogue proceeds, their tone becomes harsh, and they accuse Job of sin (15:4; ch. 22).

There is of course some support for the principle of retribution in the OT, but Job's friends work backwards in their reasoning. The OT writers reason from cause to effect: observing a sin, they conclude that it will have an unfortunate result. Job's friends, however, reason from effect to cause; they observe his suffering and conclude that he must have sinned. This conclusion cannot be sustained in the light of the OT as a whole. Much of the suffering recounted in the OT is unconnected to the sufferer's own sin. The suffering of Naboth, who loses his life when Ahab robs him of his vineyard, is clearly not the result of his own sin (1 Kgs. 21). Job's friends see God and humans as being like a pair of marionettes, who automatically act and react to the pulling of their strings, and God himself as bound by the principle of retribution. Yet their view of God is not entirely wrong. There is a pattern or structure in the world; it is not chaotic. There is a God, who is the supreme *judge (5:8–16). He judges wisely (11:5–12), and so provides much-needed stability for humankind. Life can to some extent be foreseen; it is not true that anything can happen at any time, without consequences. But Job is not convinced by his friends' arguments.

The theology of Job

The theology of Job is not a considered standpoint. It is a cry in the dark, a deeply felt anxiety that his God may not listen to him.

Job affirms the principle of retribution (6:24; 13:23). His argument with his friends and his God is over whether or not he has sinned. Job believes in the moral order, but in his case God has repaid good with evil, and this throws his worldview into crisis. His friends conclude from his suffering that he is a sinner; Job knows that he is innocent. Since he is suffering, and has not sinned, God is making a mockery of his own righteousness: 'It is all one; therefore I say, he destroys both the blameless and the wicked. When disaster brings sudden death, he mocks at the calamity of the innocent. The earth is given into the hand of the wicked; he covers the eyes of its judges – if it is not he, who then is it?' (9:22–24).

Job does not accuse God of actually doing evil, but of standing by passively while it happens. This means that God contributes to suffering. God may not be among 'the wicked' (9:24), but by not actively hindering their evil-doing, his effect upon the sufferer is the same as if he were. Job is aware that this view takes him to the brink of blasphemy (13:13–14; 31). But he has nothing to lose by accusing God, and he is sure of his own innocence.

According to Job's friends, God upholds the moral order consistently. To Job, who is innocent and yet suffers, God is an almighty tyrant, who mocks at the suffering of his *creation (10:3). God is absent and cannot be found; his absence contributes to the chaos of the world (13:24; 23:8). The world is without meaning, since its purpose has been frustrated by its creator. In the story of creation (Gen. 1:3), God creates light by saying, 'Let there be light.' When Job curses the day of his birth, he says 'may it be dark' (3:4–5, author's translation). These are the words of a nihilist, who may not have lost his faith in the existence of God, but who has ceased to believe in the order and meaning created by God. His God has now become his opponent, responsible for his suffering (19:8, 10; 30:21–23). This is not a detached 'theology of suffering', but the view of one who *is* suffering and cannot understand why.

The message from the whirlwind

God has been the focus of every speech in the dialogue, but has been silent throughout. Finally he speaks to Job, and Job responds by withdrawing his accusations (40:3–5; 42:1–6). Job receives an answer which reduces him to silence; he no longer wishes to voice his anger and frustration. God takes Job back to the very moment of creation, and describes poetically how he created an ordered world. God's own theology of creation reveals to Job that there is indeed order in the world, ordained at creation. This beauty and perfection in creation is, however, fully appreciated only by its creator. Since Job was not present at creation, he has only limited insight into the order of the world, which makes it a safe place in which to live (38:4–7). Job's horizon is very restricted because of his short lifespan. God assures him that there is an order in the world that he cannot see; he can only trust God's word that it is there. Evil powers are at work in the world, and God acts against them, but Job, a mortal, cannot perceive God's activities (38:8–11). God has imposed order even over death (38:16–17).

In his second speech, God talks of how he tamed wild animals, the leviathan and the behemoth. These animals, symbolizing evil and chaos, were tamed by God in his struggle against evil. So how can Job speak of God being unrighteous, when he was not even present when God struggled against the forces of evil? God asks Job a poignant question, 'Will you even put me in the wrong? Will you condemn me that you may be justified?' (40:8).

Job has earlier accused God of making a mockery of his own righteousness by standing by when the righteous suffer. But God points out that Job simply does not know enough to make such a claim. His argument is not that Job has sinned but does not know how (as his friends claimed), but that he cannot know the reason for his suffering at all. Reasoning from effect to cause is invalid. God asks whether Job will really condemn him in order to maintain his own innocence (40:5–9). God does not deny the principle of retribution, but puts himself beyond it. The principle is part of the order of creation, and the knowledge of how it works belongs only to God, its maker (40:4). God cannot reveal to Job, with his limited perspective, what can be understood only from the standpoint of the creator. Job is not wrong to seek *truth and justice, but as a mortal he simply cannot understand. Recognizing this, Job abandons his case against God (42:3).

Summary

In the book of Job the suffering of the innocent is not treated as a philosophical problem. Job's friends consider it to be impossible; Job knows it is real; most modern readers regard it as a fact, hard to understand. Undoubtedly Job suffers, and not as a result of his sin. But the main theme of the book is not suffering; it is the relationship of righteous people and their God. Satan questions the existence of unselfish righteousness. Does Job really fear God without any thought of his own well-being (1:9)? If Job turns his back on God when he is deprived of earthly possessions, then he is not unselfishly righteous, and if he fears God for selfish reasons, his suffering is not without a cause (2:3). Satan and God make a bet over Job: Satan claims that no one is righteous except for selfish reasons; God denies this. If Job blasphemes or rejects God because of his suffering, Satan has won. If Job persists in asserting his innocence while still confessing his faith in God, then his earthly gains have not been the motive for his righteousness. Job suffers, then, in order that the cause of his righteous actions might be revealed.

Therefore, the purpose of the book of Job is not to resolve the problem of suffering, but to define the proper relationship between humans and God as based on divine *mercy and human *faith, which sometimes doubts but always trusts.

There are few theologically significant references in the book of Job to other parts of the OT. However, the author parodies the message of Psalms 8 and 107, inverting it into a message of despair (Job 7:17–18; Ps. 8:4–6). The most appropriate genre for accusation is that of the psalm of individual complaint; the book makes extensive use of this.

The figure of Satan in the prologue is one of various traditions of personified evil in the OT, the intertestamental literature and the NT. However, Satan in Job is not equal to God; nor is he a member of his court (he is asked his business there). Job's righteousness, however, must be demonstrated to Satan without divine intervention. This explains God's initial silence in spite of Job's pleas for a response from God. A similar alienation is reflected in Christ's outcry upon the cross, 'My God, my God, why have you forsaken me?' (Matt. 27:46). Through his suffering, Christ, the truly righteous one, overcomes Satan, bringing to fulfilment the judgment pronounced by God upon the serpent in Eden (Gen. 3:15; Rev. 12:9; 20:2).

But the closest parallel to the book's central theological theme is found in the suffering servant of Isaiah (Is. 42:1–9; 49:1–7; 50:4–9; 53:1–12). There does not seem to be a formal link, but in both Job and the Isaianic servant songs the righteous one who suffers is also the one who is closest to God. The early Christians used this theme to explain the suffering of Christ. His suffering did not alienate him from God, as though he had sinned; eventually it brought him closer to his Father. In James 5:11 the endurance of Job to the end is used as an example for the readers. The experience of Job, the suffering servant and Christ reveals that suffering ought not to separate humans from God. Indeed, it can be a means of drawing them close to God, who may be their only refuge in the hour of suffering.

See also: WISDOM BOOKS.

Bibliography

F. I. Andersen, *Job*, TOTC (London and Downers Grove, 1976); D. J. A. Clines, *Job 1–20*, WBC (Dallas, 1989); N. C. Habel, *The Book of Job: A Commentary*, OTL (London,

1985); J. E. Hartley, *The Book of Job*, NICOT (Grand Rapids, 1988); J. G. Janzen, *Job*, Interpretation (Westminster, 1985); R. B. Zuck (ed.), *Sitting with Job: Selected Studies on the Book of Job* (Grand Rapids, 1992).

Å. VIBERG

PSALMS

Theology in the context of devotion

The book of Psalms is a collection of literary items written over some centuries by a number of different authors and generally devotional in tone. It contains a number of earlier collections, and yet it has a coherent theological perspective, shaped by the final editor or editors who took all the material into the final compilation, the canonical book of Psalms. This means that although the immediate literary context for any one word, phrase, verse or stanza is the particular psalm in which it is to be found, each psalm needs also to be interpreted within the context of the whole book. In some ways, therefore, a theology of the psalms is like a biblical theology, for the Bible's separate literary units find their place within the canon as a whole. Incidentally, the psalm headings (which were part of Jesus' Bible) were in the book's text as it emerged from this final editorial process, so for our purposes they must be taken seriously.

The theological message of the whole book

In recent years much attention has been given to the structure of the book, which is of considerable theological importance. The psalms are divided into five books, probably on the Pentateuchal model, showing clear evidence of deliberate structuring. Each book has a praise conclusion, and the whole ends in a full praise psalm. Other obvious structural features are the Egyptian Hallel (Pss. 113 – 118) and the Songs of Ascents (Pss. 120 – 134). Book 1 and, to a lesser extent, Book 2 are dominated by psalms headed 'a psalm of *David', while Book 3 consists mostly of psalms associated with Levites like Asaph and the sons of Korah. Book 4 has several psalms of *God the universal *King (Pss. 93 – 100) and Book 5 climaxes with a great praise series.

Scholars have recently highlighted other structural features. For instance, kingly psalms close Books 1 to 3, perhaps as a reminder that kingship is an important theme. This is more obvious in Psalms 72 and 89 than in Psalm 41, but the latter mentions several characteristics appropriate for a godly king, like concern for the weak of the land. If, as some suggest, Psalm 2 functions with Psalm 1 as a general introduction, it emphasizes this royal theme, for here God the supreme King promises support for the Davidic king.

Most of Book 1 and much of Book 2 consist of psalms associated with David. Views as to how many are Davidic in authorship range from none at all, through a select number (*e.g.* Holladay argues for Pss. 2, 23, 18 and 110 [*The Psalms*, pp. 9, 10, 23, 24]), to all those headed 'a psalm of David'. The Hebrew preposition translated 'of' in the phrase 'a psalm of David' may indicate authorship but need not have so definite a meaning and may simply suggest some kind of association with him. Some scholars who deny his authorship of all or most of these psalms nevertheless see them as referring to David; the compilers apparently wished to employ him as a role model for the life of *faith, especially in the way he brought his trials to God.

Psalm 72, headed 'a psalm of Solomon', is followed by the words, 'the prayers of David, son of Jesse are ended'. The genealogical form of this reference may suggest that this psalm is both Davidic and *Solomonic, possibly one used by successive monarchs to pray for their successors in the anointed line, and a reminder that the promise to David was not simply individual but dynastic.

Book 3 includes many individual and communal laments expressing puzzlement at God's ways, and it may have reached its present form during the exile. All but one of its psalms are associated with Levitical names, and the Levites would have been deeply grieved by the *temple's destruction. As musicians and leaders of the temple's praise, they may well have used the exile to compose and compile psalms reflecting the nation's plight and its feelings about this. Book 3 ends with Psalm 89, which expresses confidence in the Davidic *covenant but great perplexity at the events that seem to be undermining it.

Psalm 90 opens Book 4 and, as 'a psalm of Moses', recalls the people's roots as a redeemed nation. The promises to David, although important, do not represent the beginning of God's dealings with Israel; he is God of all the ages and called them out of Egypt through Moses. Book 4 builds faith, stressing divine rather than human kingship and calling all nations to praise the true God. If it is post-exilic in compilation, the people, at their rebuilt temple, would have sung once more the songs of Zion and, although a small community, would have celebrated their God's universal lordship.

Book 5 is the longest. Its two pilgrim collections were used at the annual festivals and furnished the people with another reminder of their Mosaic roots, thus strengthening their sense of being God's *redeemed, the people of the *Exodus. Between these two collections stands Psalm 119, which is in a significant position as a great celebration of the Torah (see *Law) revealed at Sinai. After what appears to be a miscellaneous section, the whole book of Psalms ends with a great praise group.

This structure highlights a number of important theological ideas.

Kingship. God had established the Davidic line and no eclipse of it could be total. Psalms like 110 and 132 clearly promise a future king. Even those written about contemporary monarchs were based on the dynastic promise, and could be appropriately related to the messianic hope which would confirm that promise for ever. Hebrews 7 makes much of Psalm 110 as showing that *Jesus would be both king and priest, and in Acts 2:25–32 and 13:35–37 both Peter and Paul argue that Psalm 16 goes beyond David's experience and is fulfilled in Christ's resurrection.

Kingship brought affliction to David, and so psalms describing his affliction, when this was a result of his loyalty to God and his will, could be applied to Jesus Christ, who faced the ultimate in suffering to fulfil his Father's will and purposes. So the NT applies Psalms 69 and 22 to him (John 2:17; 15:25; Acts 1:20; Rom. 11:9–10; Heb. 2:12). The agonies of psalmists and others who feel themselves to be suffering unjustly were summed up, yet utterly transcended, in his agonized cry, 'My God, my God, why have you forsaken me?' (Matt. 27:46), in which he used the words of Psalm 22:1. Although formulated as a question, this is still an utterance of faith, for he cries '*My* God'.

Faith. Believers may be battered and perplexed, but they can still trust God, proving their faith by bringing their questions to him.

The theme of refuge is important from Psalm 2 onwards, and God is seen as the Protector who can be trusted. Faith should be realistic, taking the form of strong *hope in an *eschatological fulfilment of God's promises.

Obedience. The book moves from obedience to praise (see W. Brueggemann, 'Bounded by Obedience and Praise: the Psalms as Canon', *JSOT* 50, 1991, pp. 63–92). The psalmists became aware, like Abraham when called to sacrifice his son, that understanding may wait but obedience cannot. Believers who faced trial and, although puzzled, continued in faith and obedience, found their faith reshaped in the light of their experience. This reorientated faith is expressed in thanksgiving psalms, which become more frequent towards the book's close.

As now arranged, Psalms is a book of *prayers, arising out of the experience of God's people, and well fitted for use both by ancient Israel and the church of all ages, Israel's God is also God of the church, and, despite historical, geographical, and religio-cultural changes, the human heart with its wide range of emotions has not altered.

Psalms is also a book of praise, and one which shows that praise, like prayer, is responsive, for it is based on God's revelation of himself and his ways. It also shows that praise needs to be honest, embracing the negative experiences of life as well as the positive.

Finally, it is a book of instruction. At least Psalm 1 and perhaps Psalms 1 and 2 were written to introduce it. The basic meaning of 'Torah', translated 'law' in Psalm 1:2, is 'instruction'. For the original writer the term may have referred to the Mosaic Torah, but for the compilers, who would be aware of its wider sense, it probably functioned as a call to the reader to approach the book as Scripture, with a readiness to learn from God. The presence of psalms of the law and of *wisdom at various points in the book are reminders of this.

The God of the psalmists

Teaching about God is basic to all theology and in the psalms it is very rich. His name is 'Yahweh' ('the LORD', Pss. 68:4; 83:18, NIV), a name which expresses 'all the mystery and wonder of revelation, the object of all prayer, praise and reflection' (H.-J. Kraus, *Theology of the Psalms*, p. 20). It occurs well over six

hundred times, about twice as frequently as 'Elohim' ('God'), and much more often than any other designation. Being a personal name, it is particularly apt in a devotional collection. 'Yahweh' dominates Book 1, while 'Elohim' is more frequent in Book 2.

The martial 'LORD Almighty' (NIV), or 'Yahweh of hosts', occurs fairly often, particularly in Psalms of Zion such as Psalms 24, 46 and 84, for it was a military action which took the city for David. It is absent from the historical books prior to 1 Samuel, and it is in this name that David confronted Goliath (1 Sam. 17:45). 'God Most High', or simply 'the Most High', is often found in these psalms, reminding us that Melchizedek, king of Salem (identified with Zion in Ps. 76:2), was priest of God Most High (Gen. 14:18). It is appropriate that such phrases, which speak of power and supremacy, should occur frequently in a book of praise and prayer.

God is also the 'maker of heaven and earth' (Pss. 124:8; 134:3), and in both spheres he is to be praised (Ps. 148). Figurative terms suggesting power and protection, such as 'rock', 'fortress', 'shield' and 'deliverer' (Ps. 18:2), as well as more intimate expressions like 'shepherd' (Ps. 23:1) and 'redeemer' (Ps. 19:14), are also used.

God is 'the living God' (Pss. 18:46; 36:9; 84:2) and as such is contrasted with the dumb and inactive *idols of the nations (Pss. 96:5; 135:13–18), much as he is in Isaiah 40 – 48. The Canaanite mythological terms 'Leviathan' (used once of a sea-creature, perhaps the whale, in Ps. 104:26) and 'Rahab' are strikingly employed of Egypt as an enemy utterly vanquished by God (Pss. 74:14; 89:10), for 'what Baal had claimed in the realm of myth, God had done in the realm of history – and done for His people' (F. D. Kidner, *Psalms 73–150*, TOTC [London, 1975], on Psalm 74:13–15 *ad loc.*). His name alone is exalted (Pss. 83:18; 148:13).

God and his people

Yahweh is Israel's God, and most instances of 'the Holy One of Israel' outside Isaiah are found in this book (Pss. 71:22; 78:41; 89:18). In Genesis 32:28, 'Israel' is Jacob's new name; however, 'God of Jacob' in the psalms is no mere synonym for 'God of Israel', but emphasizes the people's weakness (Pss. 20:1; 46:7, 11). There is historical continuity in his self-revelation, for he is the God of the patriarchs

(Pss. 47:9; 105:9–11, 42), of Moses (Ps. 103:7) and, by implication, of Joshua (Ps. 78:54–55), as well as of David and Solomon and of Levites like Asaph and the sons of Korah. Constant reference is made to his activities, both nationally and in relation to individual psalmists, in which his nature was revealed.

References to the history of Israel and Judah are mostly about the nation's early days, with a strong emphasis on the Exodus, the wilderness wanderings and the entry to Canaan. God's promises to the patriarchs feature in Psalm 105, and there are both explicit (Pss. 89 and 132) and implicit (Ps. 2:6–9; 78:68–72) references to God's covenant with David and his dynasty. Allusions to events after David are rare, although it is evident that Psalm 137 comes from the time of the exile.

God has spoken to his people. They hear his voice in the thunderstorm (Ps. 29), in the heavens (Ps. 19:1–4), and clearly in Scripture (Pss. 33:4), which has the reliability so often lacking in the human *word (Ps. 12:5–6). The Torah (law) is of special importance (Pss. 19:7–11; 119) as instruction from God. Psalm 1:2 is probably given its primary literary position to indicate that, like the Mosaic Torah, the book of Psalms should be approached as divine instruction. Some psalms, such as Psalm 50, are like prophetic oracles.

God is his people's Redeemer. This role, established at the time of the Exodus from Egypt (Exod. 6:6; 15:13; Pss. 74:2; 77:15), is revealed in further acts of deliverance (Ps. 107:2). God is also his people's Judge: judgments occurred in the wilderness (Pss. 95:7–11; 106:13–33) and at other times when Israel sinned (Pss. 78:9–11, 56–64; 106:34–46). Psalm 95 is used in Hebrews 3 and 4 to warn the readers of judgment if they rebel as Israel did.

God and the individual: the two ways

The Psalms are very practical. Wisdom psalms (such as 37 and 49) and psalms of the Torah (like 19 and 119) remind the reader of the importance of obedience and walking in the light that comes from God the Teacher (Pss. 25:4–15; 32:8). Paul's words, 'In my inner being, I delight in God's law' (Rom 7:22), reflect the delight shown throughout Psalm 119. Psalm 1, a psalm of the Torah and of wisdom, shows obedience as the one way to fruitfulness. It implies that the enemies of God's ways are not only foreigners but also Israelites who choose the wicked way.

The characteristics of these two ways are revealed whenever the psalmist is confronted by his enemies. They are aggressive (Pss. 10:2; 17:10–12), liars (Pss. 12:1–4; 41:5, 6) and opposed to God's purposes (Pss. 2:1–3; 74:4–10, 18–23). He, on the other hand, has committed himself to God and to truth (Pss. 16; 17). Passages such as Psalms 17:3–5 and 18:20–28, in which the psalmist seems to be self-righteous, are best seen either as claims to be innocent of the particular charges levelled against him by his enemies, or as assertions of decisive commitment to God, rather than as claims to absolute sinlessness.

In Matthew 4:5–7, Satan quotes Psalm 91:11–12 in an unsuccessful attempt to persuade Jesus to do something spectacular but contrary to God's will for him. However, the psalm's contents reveal that it is concerned with those who trust and *love God, so Satan's application is clearly invalidated by the context of the quoted verses.

Prayer and trial

The psalms are honest: there is no easy triumphalism and no attempt to disguise the trials that beset believers. The psalmists believed Yahweh to be a God of order, whether in *creation (Ps. 104), redemption (Ps. 107), covenant (Ps. 132), or in his moral government (Ps. 1), but with respect to the last two their faith was sometimes severely tested. Psalm 89:49 asks where God's former great love and faithfulness are, for contemporary events have raised questions about his covenant commitment to David. Often the psalmists faced threats to an ordered life, whether from danger (many psalms in Books 1 and 2) or depression (Pss 42; 43). They ask why God does not quickly come to their aid (Ps. 13) or why the wicked prosper (Pss. 49; 73).

At times the psalmists are facing God's judgment for their sins (Pss. 38; 51). In Romans 3:10–18 Paul quotes a number of psalms that speak of human sinfulness before going on in Romans 4:6–8 to cite Psalm 32:1–2 as evidence that there was justification by faith in the OT period. There were times, however, when the psalmists could find no moral explanation for their *sufferings (Ps. 44:17–22). Psalm 22 is the most moving of these psalms. Here a sense of being forsaken by God is contrasted with God's blessing on past generations and even formerly on the sufferer himself (vv. 1–11).

Yet every lament is brought to God. Like Job or Jeremiah, the psalmists sometimes complained to God, because they recognized his sovereignty (see *Providence) over events. The phrase, 'My God', occurs twenty-three times in the psalms, eighteen times in laments, underlining the fact that lament, even complaint, was uttered within a conscious, personal relationship with God. Sometimes complaint moves into praise, as in Psalm 22. At times this is because the situation had been altered, rather as the psalmist describes in the thanksgiving Psalm 34, while at other times (as in Ps. 6) God gave a deepened certainty that he would ultimately put things right.

Psalm 1:6 affirms, 'the LORD watches over the way of the righteous, but the way of the ungodly shall perish.' This kind of statement may seem to promise what life itself does not deliver. The book as a whole, however, fully recognizes that it is often the wicked who prosper and the righteous who suffer; thus it provides appropriate exegesis of the statement in Psalm 10. This may therefore be understood eschatologically, as a statement about what will ultimately be seen to be true.

In some psalms (e.g. 73) the psalmist's faith is reorientated by the union of experience and eschatological hope. Occasionally the means of this reorientation are revealed. Psalm 18 is not a lament, but its use of language reminiscent of the Exodus and of Sinai (vv. 7–15) shows that personal faith was strengthened by remembering these events. In Psalm 77, a deep personal lament in which God's ways are questioned, the memory of these great deeds, possibly even reading about them in Scripture, renews the psalmist's faith, for verses 13–15 seem to echo the language of the song of Moses and Miriam in Exodus 15:11–13. In Psalm 73 the psalmist's faith is given its new perspective in the house of God. A Christian, tempted to give up Bible reading and attendance at *worship when beset by trials and doubts, may learn much from these psalms.

The prayers of imprecation, in which the psalmist calls on God to destroy his enemies, often trouble Christians deeply. Antagonism was often directed against an official, representative person, a king or Levite, who was doing the work of God; in such circumstances the need was for rectoral divine justice rather than for personal forgiveness from the psalmist. The OT often uses graphically concrete language, which can sound shocking. Yet the concluding verse of the most shocking of these psalms, Psalm 137, would sound appropriate if it read, 'May God use alien warriors to bring the wicked, arrogant, oppressive Babylonian dynasty to a full end!'; this is what it means.

Thanksgiving and worship

The psalms are full of praise, both corporate and individual, and were thus fit for use in Israel's worship. This praise is wholehearted (Ps. 103:1), often exuberant (Pss. 98; 148) and consistently responsive, because it was based on what God had done, whether for the whole world (Ps. 96), the nation (Ps. 48), the individual believer (Ps. 40) or some combination of these (Pss. 66; 147). The Egyptian Hallel (Pss. 113 – 118) and the Songs of Ascents (Pss. 120 – 134), by their use at the festivals that celebrated the nation's origin in the great, divine, saving events of the past, show how even material making only brief references to these events could be employed to extol the God who had liberated and blessed his people. Psalm 118, the climax of the Egyptian Hallel, is quoted and alluded to several times in the NT (e.g. in Matt. 21:42; Acts 4:11; Heb. 13:6) and, because it was read at the Passover, could well have been the last Scripture read or heard by Jesus before his death.

Some psalms declare God's acts, while others describe him. Even these descriptions, however, are often based on his acts, for they affirm that he is the kind of God who does such things. Description relates to what is present and permanent, and declaration to what is historical or biographical. So, for instance, Psalm 18 proclaims that God has intervened powerfully in the psalmist's life, but includes the descriptive verse, 'You save the humble but bring low those whose eyes are haughty' (Ps. 18:27). God's attributes are revealed in his acts, and both elicit praise. Some psalms, such as Psalm 113, are purely descriptive.

Many psalms of petition and lament move into thanksgiving, revealing the conviction of the writer that God either has answered or will answer his prayer (Pss. 13; 56). Some thanksgiving psalms contain no element of lament, but ponder gratefully some act of personal divine deliverance (Pss. 18; 34).

The people loved to visit Jerusalem's temple to celebrate God's great saving deeds (Ps. 122), and the psalms emphasize not ceremonial but moral fitness (Pss. 15; 24). Those prevented from attending for some reason long to be there (Pss. 42; 63; 84). Psalm 50, like many a prophetic passage, attacks sacrificial formalism, here with reference to the insulting idea that Israel's God needed to be fed just like some pagan deity.

The God of the future

The psalmists often give praise because God, the supreme Judge, will act eventually to put all things right (Pss. 50:6; 94:2; 98:7–9). They call him to judge Israel's enemies (Pss. 83:9–18; 129:5–8) and assert that the way of the (Israelite) wicked will perish (Ps. 1:4–6). God is King over all the earth (Pss. 93; 97; 99) and many psalms call all *nations to worship him, while in Psalm 87 alien peoples, even former oppressors of Israel, are welcomed into relationship with him, as in Isaiah 19:18–25. Romans 15:8–11 applies to Christian Gentiles psalms in which Gentiles are called to praise God.

The psalms also contain an individual eschatology. Sheol, the place of departed spirits, is mentioned explicitly about a dozen times (NIV margin). The view that the OT does not distinguish the place of the unrighteous dead from that of the righteous is under challenge, with P. Johnson arguing (in *The Lord's Anointed*, pp. 213–222) that Sheol is for the ungodly (Ps. 9:17) and that the righteous are apprehensive of it only when under extreme trial (Ps. 18:5) or preoccupied by their sins (Is. 38:17–18). At other times they eagerly anticipate seeing God's face (Pss. 17:15; 49:13–15; 73:24–26). (See *Death and resurrection.)

The theme of a future Messiah which, in the final arrangement of the book, is given an important place, has already been addressed. This theme accords well with the way in which the NT applies many psalms to Jesus as the Christ.

Bibliography

L. C. Allen, *Psalms*, WBT (Waco, 1987); W. Brueggemann, *The Message of the Psalms: A Theological Commentary* (Minneapolis, 1984); W. L. Holladay, *The Psalms through Three Thousand Years* (Minneapolis, 1993); P. Johnson, '"Left in Hell": Psalm 16, Sheol and the Holy One', in P. E. Satterthwaite, R. S. Hess and G. J. Wenham (eds.), *The Lord's Anointed: Interpretation of Old Testament Messianic Texts* (Carlisle, 1995), pp. 213–222; H.-J. Kraus, *Theology of the Psalms* (ET, Minneapolis, 1986); T. Longman III, *How to Read the Psalms* (Leicester, 1988); J. L. Mays, *The Lord Reigns: A Theological Handbook to the Psalms* (Westminster, 1994); J. C. McCann (ed.), *The Shape and Shaping of the Psalter* (Sheffield, 1993); D. C. Mitchell, *The Message of the Psalter: An Eschatalogical Programme in the Book of Psalms* (Sheffield, 1997).

G. W. GROGAN

PROVERBS

The problem of wisdom in biblical theology

The book of Proverbs belongs to the wisdom literature of the OT, along with *Job, *Ecclesiastes, certain *psalms and, in the view of some, the *Song of Songs. For many biblical theologians the wisdom literature has presented certain difficulties because its authors display little interest in the main biblical themes of covenant and salvation-history. In more recent scholarship it has been suggested that the wisdom literature belongs rather with the doctrine of *creation than with the doctrine of salvation. There are at least two inherent dangers in this approach. One is that of ignoring the links between creation and salvation, especially in the prophets where salvation is sometimes set out in terms of a new creation. The other is that of ignoring the links between wisdom and salvation-history that are to be found, not in the main wisdom corpora, but in the historical narratives.

The history of wisdom and the Solomonic traditions

The book of Proverbs goes under the title of 1:1, 'The proverbs of *Solomon the son of David the king of Israel'. This is an intentional link with the narratives in 1 Kings 3 – 10 concerning Solomon as the exemplary wise man. Here Solomon's wisdom is seen in relation to his prayer for understanding in order to govern well (1 Kgs. 3:9; 4:29). His wisdom compares favourably with that of famous non-Israelites, including the Queen of Sheba

(1 Kgs. 4:31, 34; 10:1–5). His literary activity as a wise man includes the writing of many songs and proverbs (1 Kgs. 4:32–33).

Similar kinds of wisdom writing existed among Israel's neighbours, notably Babylon and Egypt, long before Israel became a nation. Traditions of pre-Solomonic wisdom in the Bible include references to proverbial sayings in Genesis 10:9, 1 Samuel 10:12, 19:24 and 2 Samuel 5:8, and the reference by Stephen to Moses' education in all the wisdom of Egypt (Acts 7:22). Why, then, did it take so long for wisdom to flower in Israel? Why do the traditional origins of Israelite wisdom lie with Solomon, while the completion of the canonical book of Proverbs postdates Hezekiah (Prov. 25:1)?

The biblical-theological answer lies partly in the Solomonic narrative. The whole section 1 Kings 3 – 10 presents a composite picture of the relationship of wisdom to salvation-history. It stands together with the Davidic narrative as the account of an important development in the outworking of salvation-history in the experience of the people of Israel. The covenant promises to Abraham lead eventually to his descendants' being released from the Egyptian bondage in the Exodus. They are constituted as the people of God by the Sinai covenant. A new generation of Israelites enters the Promised Land under Joshua and, eventually, the rule of the judges and the prophet Samuel leads to the establishment of kingship. David, the king after God's heart, captures the Jebusite city of Jerusalem which becomes the holy city, Zion. David then installs the ark of the covenant in the city. God's covenant with David (2 Sam. 7) establishes David's dynasty in relation to the temple and the throne.

In the middle of the pericope of Solomon's wisdom is the account of the building and dedication of the temple. The priestly ministry at the temple is recognized by the Queen of Sheba as part of the wisdom of Solomon (1 Kgs. 10:5). Wisdom flowers under Solomon when the whole plan of salvation is revealed in Israel's history. It is not so much that a more settled existence allowed time for intellectual pursuits. Rather, rest within the land is seen as the goal of God's savings acts (1 Kgs. 4:25). With Solomon and the temple, God is in the midst of his people in Zion, and rules through his anointed king who is the son of David. In short, the revelation of God's wisdom in his plan of salvation is the only framework within which authentic human wisdom can flourish. Grace provides the epistemological basis for the interpretation of human experience. However, the historical kingdom and the saving events leading to it are only shadows of the reality which is to come. The process begun with Abraham and climaxing with Solomon's temple goes into reverse, paradoxically, with the subsequent apostasy of Solomon himself. But it is, nevertheless, the framework within which the knowledge of God is given to his people.

The theological framework of Proverbs

The theological problem of wisdom is most marked in Proverbs. Not only are there hardly any references to Israel's salvation-history in the book, but many of the individual sayings do not refer explicitly to God or to anything religious. However, most commentators believe that the introduction to the book (1:1–7) is an explanation of the intended purpose of the whole corpus. This statement concludes with a proverbial statement that 'the fear of Yahweh is the beginning of knowledge'. In Proverbs 9:10, 'the fear of Yahweh is the beginning of wisdom' (so also in Ps. 111:10 and Job 28:28).

These passages speak of the *fear of the Lord (Heb. *yhwh*). This is the reverential response of faith to the God of Israel who reveals himself in his word as it interprets his saving deeds. The use of the personal name, 'Yahweh', identifies himself as the God of salvation-history who makes and keeps covenant with his people (see Exod. 6:2–8). The whole book is placed within the Solomonic tradition (1:1), and thus within the salvation-history framework of 1 Kings 3 – 10.

The theological function of the wisdom forms in Proverbs

There are two main types of wisdom saying in Proverbs. The 'instruction' is the longer saying typical of chapters 2 – 9. This form, involving directives, motive clauses, and predicted outcomes of wise behaviour, supports explicit theological reflection, but at times avoids it. The 'proverbial saying', which is found in chapters 10 – 22 and 25 – 29, usually consists of two lines involving some form of parallelism in which the second line restates, develops, or is in contrast with the first. Many proverbial sayings explore the

opposites of wisdom and folly, or righteousness and wickedness, in the context of daily
life. Some make explicit comparisons; others
simply place things side by side. A third literary form is the 'numerical saying' (*e.g.* 30:15–
31) which involves listing things or situations
which have some common feature. The *n*,
n+1 formula (usually 3, 4) appears to invite
the reader to add other items which share the
same characteristics.

The theological presuppositions of the book of Proverbs

1. The *world is orderly. Wisdom does have
links with the theology of creation. God has
made the world and orders all things. This
ordering of relationships and functions in all
their complexity is presupposed in daily *life
and social structures. By linking aspects of
experience which may otherwise seem to be
unconnected, wisdom shows that life in fellowship with God ultimately makes sense.
The relationship of deeds to their outcome at
times appears to be a purely natural retribution, but in it God is at work (16:1–7, 9) and
he, the Creator, is sovereign (20:12; 21:1–2;
22:2). (See *Providence.)

2. Human beings have a rational capability
which reflects what is often called the cultural
mandate (Gen. 1:28). They have the responsibility, in the course of seeking to exercise
God-given dominion in the world, to understand the nature of the orderliness of the
universe. The essence of this empirical wisdom is, by reflecting on experience in the light
of God's self-revelation, to learn of what each
circumstance consists, so as to know the best
way to relate and respond to it. Since the fear
of the Lord is the beginning of wisdom, Proverbs sets out a view of wisdom that cannot be
equated with native intelligence. An understanding of life's experiences can be achieved
only if the Lord of life is acknowledged.

3. The confusion of order, which has been
introduced because of human sin, has not
been allowed to assume catastrophic propor-
tions. Chaos does not reign, and a (natural)
law of retribution exists. Thus, in normal
daily experience the predictable relationship
between deeds and their outcomes remains
the principal way in which to learn about life,
and to determine how to pursue the good life.
The bulk of the book of Proverbs consists of
self-contained sayings reflecting on human
experience within the framework of the

knowledge of God. Thus individual proverbial sentences deal with such matters as
being wise (or righteous) and not foolish (or
wicked) (10:1–32); the nature of kingship
(16:10, 12–15); *family and community relationships (19:13–14, 17–19; 21:21); sloth
(6:6–11; 19:15, 24; 20:4); the power of words
to inflame or to cool passions (15:1–2, 4, 7,
23, 28; 21:23; 25:11); right dealing in commerce and society (20:10, 23; 21:6; 22:16, 22–
23; 25:8–10); *humility (11:2; 25:6–7); contentment, self-control and sobriety (15:16–17;
19:1; 23:1–3, 17, 30–35; 25:28), and many
other themes.

4. There are limits to human wisdom. Empirical wisdom, which is that gained through
experience of life, is the focus of Proverbs. It
assumes that the orderliness of the universe,
though to some extent confused by sin, is
nevertheless perceptible if people take the
trouble to learn wisdom. But human empirical wisdom is limited by two factors. First,
the framework of the fear of the Lord indicates that the empirical data cannot be rightly
understood or interpreted without the wisdom of God given in his covenant of
redemptive revelation. While sinfulness limits
understanding, human beings were always
dependent upon God's giving them the interpretation of the universe and of their
relationship to it. Secondly, there is mystery in
the universe because God does not reveal all.
Sometimes the normal relationships between
deeds and their outcomes do not seem to exist; the proper response is to trust the
sovereign God.

5. The quest for empirical wisdom is not
an optional exercise for dilettantes. Proverbs,
and the wisdom literature in general, counter
the idea that being spiritual means handing all
decisions over to the leading of the Lord. The
opposite is true. Proverbs reveals that God
does not make all people's decisions for them,
but rather expects them to use his gift of reason to interpret the circumstances and events
of life within the framework of revelation that
he has given. Yet when they have exercised
their responsibility in decision-making, they
can look back and see that the sovereign God
has guided. Ultimately, to learn wisdom is to
choose life, while a life of folly is a deliberate
choice of destruction (10:2, 16–17, 29;
13:21).

Proverbs in biblical-theological perspective

Proverbs, then, must be understood in the context of creation, the fall and redemption. The creation narratives in Genesis 1 – 2 depict Adam and Eve's being addressed by God, whose word sets the boundaries of their existence (Gen. 1:28–30). Being created in the image of God and having dominion over the rest of the creation implies the use of rational faculties, as does the task of naming the animals (Gen. 2:19). The serpent tempts the couple to reject the authority of God's word and thus to dismiss his interpretation of reality. Human rationality and intelligence are misused when humans interpret the world of experience apart from the revelation of God. The result is a different and erroneous view which may work well at the mundane and pragmatic level of human wisdom but which is ultimately self-destructive.

Proverbs points to the redemptive revelation of God to which humans must respond with 'fear', *i.e.* awe, reverence and faith. Within this framework of revelation they are able to learn from experience about the good life. When Solomon the wise forsook the fear of the Lord, the ultimate result of his apostasy was the destruction of the nation, Jerusalem and the temple. During the period of decline the prophets predicted another son of David who would be filled with wisdom. The vocabulary associated with wisdom in Proverbs 1:1–7 and 8:12–15 is similar to that used in Isaiah 11:1–5. In Israel wisdom was limited; in the new Israel it is established fully by the one who is greater than Solomon. Luke sees Proverbs 3:4 as being fulfilled in the boy Jesus (Luke 2:52). As an adult, Jesus uses the wisdom forms of proverb and parable for much of his teaching. He is not only the truly wise man, but he is the wisdom of God itself. The framework for true human empirical wisdom is the revealed wisdom of God in the gospel (1 Cor. 1:18 – 2:7). The fear of the Lord now includes faith in and intellectual apprehension of the gospel.

See also: WISDOM BOOKS; WISDOM.

Bibliography

R. L. Alden, *Proverbs*, EvBC (Grand Rapids, 1983); G. Goldsworthy, *Gospel and Wisdom: Israel's Wisdom Literature in the Christian Life* (Exeter and Homebush West, 1987); idem, *The Tree of Life: Reading Proverbs Today* (Sydney, 1993); H.-J. Hermisson, *Studien zur israelitischen Spruchweisheit* (Neukirchen-Vluyn, 1968); D. A. Hubbard, *Proverbs*, CC (Dallas, 1989); G. von Rad, *Wisdom in Israel* (ET, London, 1972); U. Skladny, *Die ältesten Spruchsammlungen in Israel* (Göttingen, 1962); R. N. Whybray, *Proverbs*, NCB (London and Grand Rapids, 1994).

G. GOLDSWORTHY

ECCLESIASTES

Introduction

The theology of Ecclesiastes is more difficult to synthesize than that of any other OT wisdom book, since the interpretation of the book as a whole and of many of its individual verses is highly disputed. Qoheleth (Heb. = one who assembles others in order to address them), as its speaker or author is usually designated, has been described contrarily both as a 'preacher of joy' (so R. N. Whybray, similarly M. A. Klopfenstein) and as a rationalist, agnostic, sceptic, pessimist and fatalist (so R. B. Y. Scott, *Proverbs, Ecclesiastes* [Garden City, 1965], p. 192), who questions the benefits of *wisdom and the meaningfulness of *life. Divergent, seemingly contradictory, voices discerned within the book should be attributed to the author's intellectual and spiritual wrestling with the jarring realities of everyday life rather than to the work of a pious editor. S. Holm-Nielsen has shown that early Christian interpretation of the book was unduly influenced by the early translations, for its key words and phrases have more negative connotations in Greek and Latin than they have in Hebrew. Regardless of how one decides questions of authorship (*Solomon or a pseudonymous author who views life through Solomonic eyes) and date of composition, Ecclesiastes can be understood as a life-affirming book which challenges its readers to joyful celebration and vigorous effort, despite the brevity, uncertainty, *mysteries and injustices of life.

Purpose and structure

Ecclesiastes 12:9–14 offers the reader a hermeneutical guide to the book, summarizing the author's approach and procedure (vv. 9–10), the effect of wisdom sayings (vv. 11–12), and his basic message (vv. 13–14). Qoheleth's words are ordered and reliable; they are authoritative ('given by one Shepherd', NIV) even though based upon his own wisdom and experience; and they encourage reverence towards and *obedience to *God in the light of coming *judgment. The author frames his discourse with his basic thesis: everything is utterly 'temporary' (Heb. *hebel*, 1:2; 12:8, a keyword occurring 38 times in Eccles.; see D. C. Fredericks, who argues that the word's basic meaning is 'transient' rather than 'vain' [see *vanity] or 'senseless'). He sets out to analyse and assess the activities of life 'under the sun' ('sun' occurs 33 times in Eccles.) in order to discover what has lasting value ('profit', Heb. *yitrôn*, 15 times in Eccles.) in such a world (1:3–11, especially v. 3). He considers human achievements and wisdom (1:12 – 2:26), time and eternity (3:1–22), social interactions (4:1–16), and wealth (5:10 – 6:9, following a brief warning against wrong attitudes towards God and government in 5:1–9; see *Poor, poverty). As a result of his investigation, he comes to understand: that 'bad' days can bring about good (6:10 – 7:14); that '*righteousness' and wisdom can offer only limited protection in this world (7:15–29); that one must submit to the government despite its injustice (8:1–17); that, in the light of *death, one must fully use one's opportunities (9:1–12); and that one should embrace wisdom and avoid folly (9:13 – 10:20). This leads to his final charge to be bold (11:1–6), *joyful (11:7–10) and reverent (12:1–7) while there is still time.

Major themes

On the basis of repeated words and questions within the book, a number of interrelated themes can be identified.

Creation and fall

Several leading OT theologians have emphasized that wisdom theology is best characterized as '*creation theology'. God is explicitly called 'Creator' in 12:1 but his creative work is emphasized throughout the book; he has formed *humans out of the dust of the ground, and has imparted 'spirit' (or breath, Heb. *rûah*) to them (12:7; 3:20–21), which returns to him at death. Everything has been made 'beautiful in its time' (3:11). Humans,

too, were created 'upright' (Heb. *yašar*) but now seek out 'many schemes' (7:29); now there is no righteous person on earth 'who does [only] what is right and never sins' (7:20). In the fallen world, work has become 'toil' or 'trouble' (*'amal*, 33 times in Eccles., *cf.* especially 1:13) and produces only temporary (Heb. *hebel*) results.

God as the giver of good gifts and as sovereign judge

Though some commentators have described the God of Ecclesiastes as distant, unknowable or even despotic, there is no compelling basis for distinguishing the 'god of the sages' from the covenant God of Israel, though the covenant name for God (Yahweh or LORD), never occurs in the book (so S. de Jong, in *VT* 47, pp. 154–167). The activity most frequently ascribed to God in Ecclesiastes is 'giving' (Heb. *natan*, used 13 times of God); he is the giver of everything, both toil (1:13; 2:26; 3:10) and enjoyment in life (2:24, 26; 3:13; 5:18), wisdom and knowledge (2:26; *cf.* 12:11), wealth (5:19; 6:2), honour (6:2) and the very days of one's life (5:18; 8:15; 9:9). God is sovereign (6:10; 9:1) and his work is incomprehensible (3:11; 7:14; 8:17; 11:5). Nothing can be added to his work (3:14), and what he has 'made crooked', none can straighten (7:13; *cf.* 1:15). Both the pleasant and the unpleasant days come from him (7:14). Sooner or later, every person will encounter him as judge (3:15, 17; 5:6; 8:5–6; 7:16–17; 11:9; 12:14). Ecclesiastes 5:2b provides a succinct and powerful summary of this theme: 'God is in heaven and you are on earth, so let your words be few.' Qoheleth, though not questioning the existence of divine justice, is troubled by its timing (3:10–11; *cf.* 8:6–8). Observed exceptions to the principle of justice (*e.g.* 7:15) do not weaken his conviction that justice will ultimately be done (8:11–12; 11:9; 12:13–14; *cf.* R. Lux). Indeed, it is Qoheleth's conviction that God is good and just, though his ways are inscrutable, that enables him to find meaning and joy in this often brutal and disappointing world (2:24–26; 5:18–20).

Human responsibilities

Though God's work is unfathomable, he has placed 'eternity' (*'ôlam*) within the human heart (3:11) and he and his will are knowable. The appropriate human response is twofold.

First, people are to *fear God, not recoiling in terror (as some have suggested) but revering him. His sovereign work and authority command respect (3:14; 5:7), and fear of God elicits his favour (8:12–13). Secondly, people are to obey his commandments (12:13) and avoid evil (7:18, 26).

The reverent person is cautious in approaching and addressing God, not making empty promises (5:1–2, 4), and is obedient to the ruler (8:2). Ecclesiastes refers to the person who is properly related to God as 'righteous' (3:17; 7:15–16, 20; 8:14; 9:1–2), and (employing a more easily misinterpreted expression) as 'one who pleases him' (literally: 'one who is good before him', 2:26; 7:26; 8:12–13; 9:2), as distinct from the 'sinner'.

The call to reverence is balanced, however, by Qoheleth's dominant call to joy (2:24–25; 3:12–13; 5:19–20; 8:15; 9:7–8; 11:8–10), which recurs like a refrain; initially it is cast in the form of an assertion, but later in that of a command. Ecclesiastes 9:7–9 emphasizes that finding enjoyment in one's food, drink and partner is not simply a sedative against the disappointments of life, but rather expresses an attitude that has divine approval (cf. also 5:20). One is to enjoy one's work (3:22; 5:18–19), be diligent in it (9:10; 11:1–6) and do good (3:12). Without these twin characteristics (reverence for God and joy in everyday experiences), life is reduced to futility (i.e. chasing the wind: 1:14, 17; 2:11, 17, 26; 4:4, 6, 16; 5:16; 6:9); joy is empty (2:1–2; 7:3) and there is no *rest (2:23; 4:6; 5:12; 8:16), satisfaction (4:8; 5:10; 6:3, 7, 9) or meaning in life (2:17–23; 4:8); instead, there is envy (4:4), hatred (2:17–18) and despair (2:20; 5:17; 9:3).

There are, however, significant obstacles to a joyful life, above all, the ephemeral nature of all human endeavours (as expressed by Heb. hebel). Death is the unavoidable equalizer and terminator of human existence (2:16; 3:2; 5:15–16; 6:3, 6; 7:2, 15; 9:5–6, 10), against which none can prevail (8:8; 9:12). Since animals and humans, righteous and wicked, share one fate (2:14, 16; 3:19–20; 6:6; 9:2–3), and it even appears at times that death is preferable to life (4:2–3; 6:3–5; 7:1), Ecclesiastes affirms that ultimately righteousness will be rewarded (3:17, 21; 8:12–13; 12:14). Furthermore, the wickedness of others so imperils the life of the righteous (3:16; 4:1; 5:8; 7:7; 8:11; 9:2) that, at least temporarily,

the wicked seem to have the upper hand; all that people can do is enjoy those gifts of creation that are available (8:14–15). Uncertainty regarding the future (3:22; 6:12; 7:14; 8:7; 9:1, 12; 10:14), success (11:1–6) and the work of God (3:11; 7:24; 8:17) can lead to debilitating confusion and doubt, even despair, and one can expect repeatedly to be confronted by that which is impossible or unattainable, no matter how wise or righteous one may be (1:15 [cf. 7:13]; 3:14; 7:24; 8:8).

Living 'gainfully'

Qoheleth affirms repeatedly that despite these difficulties, gain (Heb. yitrôn, advantage, cf. 1:3; 3:9) can be had by following his counsel. Apart from joy, there are a number of acquisitions which can assist one in dealing with the challenges and uncertainties of life. Wisdom is portrayed in Ecclesiastes as a divine gift (2:26), though also as something acquired gradually (1:16), and as beneficial (2:13; 7:11–12) if esteemed and employed at the right moment (4:13–14; 9:13–16; 10:10–11). Wisdom is both the means (1:13; 2:3, 9; 7:23) and the object (2:12; 7:25) of Qoheleth's investigation. It can enhance and preserve life in a variety of ways (2:19, 21; 8:1, 5; 12:9, 11), despite its limitations (it causes mental anguish, 1:18; it is soon forgotten, 2:16; it is easily undermined, 7:7; 10:1; it can become pretentious, 7:16; it does not enable one to comprehend everything, 8:16–17; it does not guarantee success, 9:11). Wisdom manifests itself both in actions and in speech (9:17; 10:12); its supreme value is seen most clearly when it is contrasted with folly (2:14; 4:13; 7:4–6; 10:2–3).

Ecclesiastes also acknowledges the (lesser) value of wealth (5:19–20; 7:12; 10:19) with contentment (4:6, 8), strength (9:16, 18; 10:10) and government (5:9; 10:17), despite its frequent abuse of power (4:13; 8:9; 10:4). Like Proverbs, Ecclesiastes emphasizes the value of discerning the proper action to take at a particular moment (3:1, 11; 8:5–6; 10:10–11, 17) while recognizing that divine timing and 'chance' lie outside one's control (3:17; 9:11–12). Even 'bad' days can be good for deepening one's wisdom and understanding, for both pleasant and unpleasant days are under God's control (7:1–14). In the midst of the difficulties and confusion of life, Qoheleth counsels individuals to accept their lot (Heb. heleq), not out of resignation but as an affirmation that a life lived in wisdom before God 'under the sun' can be meaningful and enjoyable (2:10; 3:22; 5:18–19; 9:9), especially so in the light of the brevity of life (9:3–6, 10). Though interpreters dispute whether Qoheleth's repeated references to 'afterwards' (Heb. *'aḥ⁺rê*, 2:12, 18; 6:12; 7:14; 9:3; 10:14; 12:7) are eschatological or merely chronological, the book affirms the existence of an eternal dimension (3:11) and a future (final?) judgment (3:17; 8:12–13; 11:9; 12:14), possibly hinting at an ultimate reunion with God (3:21; 12:7).

Canonical relationships

Although Ecclesiastes has been regarded as a unique book within the canon, and even as heretical, its major themes develop and are developed by the teaching of other biblical books. Since it is an OT wisdom book, Ecclesiastes' closest conceptual links are to *Proverbs. Its emphasis upon the limitations of wisdom for explaining and helping one avoid *suffering and injustice parallels one of Job's central themes. Though it clearly enjoins obedience to the Torah (12:13–14), even explicitly quoting Deuteronomy 23:21–23 in 5:4–6, its primary theological roots are to be found in the Genesis creation account. D. M. Clemens claims that the book is 'best understood as an arresting but thoroughly orthodox exposition of Genesis 1 – 3', (*Themelios* 19, p. 5; *cf.* also H. W. Hertzberg, *Der Prediger* [Gütersloh, 1963], p. 230). Genesis 3 thus forms the textual backdrop for Qoheleth's assessment of work as toil (*'āmal*) and life as ephemeral (*hebel*, possibly a word-play on 'Abel', the name of the first person to die). Ecclesiastes 3:11 may allude to the divine assessment of creation in Gen. 1:31, while 3:20b takes its description of the 'return to dust' from Genesis 3:19 (*cf.* Eccles. 12:7 and 5:15; compare also Gen. 2:7 with Eccles. 3:19). Qoheleth's familiar encouragement to 'eat, drink and enjoy your work' is not hedonistic, but refers to the fulfilment of the covenant promises of national blessing, as described in 1 Kings 4:20 (referring to the Solomonic era): 'The people of Judah and Israel were as numerous as the sand on the seashore; they ate, they drank and they were happy.' Thus Ecclesiastes enjoins the joyful response to God's good gifts which is required at Israel's annual and special festivals (Deut. 16:11, 14; 26:11; Neh. 8:10–12). Sev-

eral psalms concur with Ecclesiastes that acknowledgment of the brevity of life (Pss. 39:4–6; 144:3–4; both psalms use *hebel*) should lead not to gloomy pessimism but to trusting reliance upon the giver of life (Pss. 39:6–7; 144:1–2). (For further links to OT themes, *cf.* R. L. Schultz, *TynB* 48.)

Ecclesiastes is never quoted explicitly in the NT, though Romans 8:20 echoes Ecclesiastes' *hebel* theme in claiming that all creation is subject to 'frustration' (NIV; Gk: *mataiotēs*, the usual LXX translation of *hebel*). Though it may discuss personal eschatology and theodicy (see above), Ecclesiastes lacks the 'new creation' theme, which is introduced elsewhere in the OT (Is. 65:17–25; *cf.* Pss. 51:10) and which permeates the NT. While Qoheleth clings to the conviction that justice will ultimately be done (8:12–13), the NT associates the establishment of justice not simply with the future reign of God and his agent (as in the OT prophets) but specifically with the return of Jesus Christ. Verses in the NT which condemn an 'eat, drink, and be merry' attitude (Matt. 24:38; Luke 12:19; 1 Cor. 15:32) are not directed against Ecclesiastes' call to enjoy life; Qoheleth also demands reverence before God. He affirms, as does Paul, not only that God is the supplier of good gifts but also that they are to be enjoyed with contentment (1 Tim. 6:6–8, 17). Ecclesiastes' discourses on wealth (5:10 – 6:9) and government (Eccles. 8) are fully consonant with Paul's later development of these themes in 1 Timothy 6 and Romans 13, respectively. Qoheleth's charge to enjoy one's God-given material possessions and opportunities, while accepting one's lot, which may involve suffering and injustice, but not to seek ultimate meaning in the goods and achievements of this present world, is as pertinent today as when it was first issued.

Bibliography

D. M. Clemens, 'The law of sin and death: Ecclesiastes and Genesis 1 – 3', *Them* 19, 1994, pp. 5–8; S. de Jong, 'God in the book of Qohelet: A reappraisal of Qohelet's place in Old Testament theology', *VT* 47, 1997, pp. 154–167; M. A. Eaton, *Ecclesiastes*, TOTC (Leicester and Downers Grove, 1983); M. V. Fox, *Qohelet and his Contradictions* (Sheffield, 1989); D. C. Fredericks, *Coping with Transience: Ecclesiastes on Brevity in Life* (Sheffield, 1993); S. Holm-Nielsen, 'On the interpretation of Qoheleth in early Christianity', *VT* 24, 1974, pp. 168–177; M. A. Klopfenstein, 'Kohelet und die Freude am Dasein', *ThZ* 47, 1991, pp. 97–107; R. Lux, '"Denn es ist kein Mensch so gerecht auf Erden, daß er nur Gutes tue ..." Recht und Gerechtigkeit aus der Sicht des Predigers Salomo', *ZThK* 94, 1997, pp. 263–287; R. E. Murphy, 'Qoheleth and theology?' *BTB* 21, 1991, pp. 30–33; R. L. Schultz, 'Unity or diversity in Wisdom theology? A canonical and covenantal perspective', *TynB* 48, 1997, pp. 271–306; R. N. Whybray, 'Qoheleth, preacher of joy', *JSOT* 23, 1982, pp. 87–98; G. H. Wilson, '"The words of the wise": The intent and significance of Qohelet 12:9–14', *JBL* 103, 1984, pp. 175–192.

R. L. SCHULTZ

THE SONG OF SONGS

The Song of Songs is a joyous, poetic celebration of *love, romance, beauty and sexual intimacy. As poetry, it seductively draws the reader into its world of longing and desire. Its metaphors and images are often somewhat extravagant and strange to western ears, and need to be handled with taste and delicacy. The Song has virtually no plot or story-line; its poetic genre allows it to be cyclical, repetitive and somewhat rambling. The Song bombards our hearts and minds, stimulates our imaginations and desires, and often leaves us gasping for breath, longing wistfully for the fulfilment of our private dreams. After such an assault upon our senses of sight, sound, scent, taste and touch, we need, having wallowed in the Song's luxuriousness, to reflect more calmly on its implications. Its teaching is oblique and indirect, and fleshes out, in metaphorical language, that which is more formally stated, explicitly or implicitly, elsewhere in Scripture. It is a living visual aid adorning the doctrine of the goodness of *creation.

Before we explore this further, it is necessary to mention another hermeneutical approach, which sees the Song as exhibiting types or allegories of the spiritual realm. The behaviour of the two lovers is used to illustrate the relationship between either Yahweh and *Israel, or *God and his *church, or *Jesus Christ and the individual believer. In the last case, the Song becomes a manual for advanced spirituality or the higher life. Some of the themes that are often interpreted allegorically are: seeking and finding; the desire for intimacy; the happiness of uninterrupted communion; the raptures and ecstasies of consummation; hindrances to fellowship; the threats of external and internal assaults; maintaining intimacy; holding fast; slowness in responding; restoration after rupture; the power of praise; the sins that spoil. Whilst the NT never quotes or alludes to the Song, it is nevertheless true that the OT uses the love and loyalty of the lover–beloved relationship as an illustration of the relationship between God and his *people. The parable of Hosea's marriage to Gomer acts as a prophetic symbol of how Yahweh deals in love and discipline with his fickle and *adulterous people Israel. The parable of the foundling child in Ezekiel 16, describing how Yahweh entered into a marriage covenant with her, is used to portray the long salvation history of Israel. Jeremiah 31:32 speaks of Israel's breaking the covenant with Yahweh 'though I was a husband to them' (NIV). A well-known passage in the NT, Ephesians 5:22–27, speaks of the church as the bride of Christ; and the book of Revelation (Rev. 19:7–9) looks forward to the consummation of all things under the metaphor of the marriage supper of the Lamb, in which the church is again the bride of Christ. Thus there is some biblical justification for a moderate typological approach. But the danger of this hermeneutic is that of thinking that the relationship between the believer and God is highly emotional or even erotic. It is far safer to look for spiritual stimulus, encouragement and rebuke concerning the spiritual life in the straightforward and explicit admonitions of the NT. The typological approach also almost inevitably leads to excessive allegorization, which has a long history in the church, beginning from the early fathers. It has included the interpretation of 'a spring enclosed, a sealed fountain' (4:12) as the virgin Mary; of 'the little foxes that ruin the vineyards' (2:15) as the little sins that spoil the church; of 'your navel' (7:2) as the baptismal font or the cup of communion, *etc.

But why has it been thought necessary to reinterpret the explicit references in the Song to lovemaking, caressing, kissing, beauty, breasts and passion? The western church has been influenced by a Greek philosophical worldview in which the spiritual realm is on a higher moral plane, eternal and substantial, while the created order is on a lower level, impermanent, subject to corruption and under judgment. In popular religion the body's functions have been regarded as second-rate, and the body itself as the prison-house of the soul, from which the soul needs to be liberated to soar unshackled into the immediate presence of God. But this dichotomy is not biblical. It has led some in the Christian church to exalt the doctrine of salvation at the expense of the doctrine of creation.

The Song is often classified under the OT genre of wisdom literature (see *Wisdom books). The characteristics of this (even though they are not always very explicit) are as follows: a strong doctrine of the sovereign *providence of the unseen God; a strong doctrine of creation; and an emphasis on *human initiative in and responsibility for achieving *šalôm*, the good life (see *Peace). There is no explicit mention of God in the Song (perhaps one or two rather obscure allusions), but it is never 'secular'. Its worldview is entirely Hebraic: human life is an integrated whole, lived under the rule of a creator God, who superintends the whole order of creation, upon which he has pronounced the verdict, 'It was very good' (Gen. 1:31). The ancient Hebrews had a wholehearted attitude to life, embracing with enthusiasm all that the created order had to offer, and uninhibited by false ideological presuppositions.

We will briefly explore a number of distinctive themes that occur throughout the Song, and their treatment in the wider biblical corpus: physical attraction; *joys and tensions; erotic arousal; betrothal and *marriage; sexual consummation.

That the lovers are physically attracted to each other hardly needs saying. The articulation of this deep, mutual appreciation cements their relationship. They find delight in praising each other's physical attributes. Nowhere else in the Bible is metaphor used so extravagantly. But these similes need to be handled sensitively; our modern translations often lead us astray. For example, in 7:1, 'Your graceful legs are like jewels, the work of a craftsman's hands', the point is not that the woman's rounded thighs glitter and sparkle, but that they are exquisitely smooth, well-rounded and proportioned as if shaped by a skilful craftsman. Elsewhere in the Bible, description of physical beauty is severely restrained, leaving much to the imagination. David is 'ruddy, with

a fine appearance and handsome features' (1 Sam. 16:12). Rachel is beautiful (Gen. 29:17). Abigail has a beautiful countenance (1 Sam. 25:3). Some verses in the Bible seem at first sight to deny the value of beauty; *e.g.* 'charm is deceptive, and beauty is fleeting, but a woman who fears the LORD is to be praised' (Prov. 31:30). The point here is that beauty is ephemeral; to be a God-fearing woman is far more important than being preoccupied by external appearances. Similarly Peter's admonition (1 Pet. 3:3–4) warns against an obsession with fashion at the expense of cultivating 'the unfading beauty of a gentle and quiet spirit'.

Courtship consists of both the relaxed joys of mutual companionship and adjustment to the minor tensions and frustrations of a growing relationship. For example, the girl delights 'to sit in his shade' and to eat of his fruit (2:3). On the other hand, she is terrified of losing him and fears his loss: 'I looked for him but did not find him' (3:1). But there is also room for playful teasing: 'I have taken off my robe, must I put it on again?' (5:3); and for playing hide and seek: 'Catch for us the foxes …' (2:15). The initiatives of the girl in seeking romantic encounter and stimulating desire are far more numerous in the Song than those of the boy. This subtle disproportion may be a deliberate attempt by the author gently to challenge the pronounced patriarchalism of OT Hebrew society. (See *Man and woman.)

The Song is full of metaphorical allusions to erotic arousal and lovemaking. In 1:2 the word translated 'love' (NIV) refers more specifically to physical arousal. It is used in Proverbs 7:18 for the advances of the wayward wife, and also in the allegory of the foundling child in Ezekiel 16:8: 'I saw you were old enough for love.' Kissing is with the mouth, erotic, and not the formal peck of social convention. The girl delights that her lover's 'left arm is under my head, and his right arm embraces me' (2:6; 8:3). The only other biblical reference to romantic fondling is in Genesis 26:8, where Abimelech sees Isaac caressing his wife Rebekah. A state of undress is presupposed by the descriptions of the girl's breasts (7:3), her waist (7:2), her graceful legs (7:1) and her navel (7:2). There are also a number of possible euphemisms associated with the references to the navel, the bolt, the polished ivory.

The canonicity of the Song, as well as the

sexual mores of ancient Hebrew culture, demand that the couple's relationship be understood as a marriage. There is no hint of any illicit sexual activity. However, the almost complete absence of a credible, continuous story-line makes it very difficult to discern just what is happening at any stage of the relationship. Solomon's wedding carriage is mentioned (3:7–11), but who, if anybody, is in it, and what bearing this has on the couple's romance is a matter of much debate. In the scenes of greatest intimacy (4:9–12), the girl is called (literally) 'my sister-bride', which puts the couple in the marriage bed. But it is also obvious that the girl in her courtship chafes under the constraints of the social conventions of the ancient world. She longs to be able publicly to demonstrate her affection for her betrothed (8:1), but she will have to learn to live temporarily with frustration and not 'to arouse or awaken love until it so desires' (2:7).

The intimacies and delights of love are experienced within the bond of a secure relationship: 'For love is strong as death, its jealousy unyielding as the grave' (8:6). There must be no intruders; so in biblical terms, adultery is a most serious offence, the breaking of a bonded relationship. Love is a quality that can be neither bought nor sold (8:7); it is not a commodity for trade (8:12). 'Many waters cannot quench love; rivers cannot wash it away' (8:7). This constancy is the very opposite of the lust of Amnon when he raped Tamar. It is poignantly written of him, after the deed was done, that 'the hatred with which he hated her was greater than the love with which he had loved her' (2 Sam. 13:15, RSV).

The Song reaches its sexual climax in 4:16 – 5:1. Using the metaphor of eating fruit from a luscious garden, full sexual union is described. This delicate euphemism is used to refer to what is described in Genesis 2:24 as becoming 'one flesh'. Other biblical metaphors for intercourse include 'to know' (Gen. 4:1, 17, 25), 'to enter' (Ruth 4:13) and 'to lie with' (Gen. 19:32; 29:23, 30; 38:26; *etc.*).

Finally, there are a number of literary and thematic parallels between the Song and the garden of Eden story in Genesis 2. Both contain imagery of luscious vegetation and of beautiful and mouth-wateringly sweet fruit. Both refer to a garden watered by springs or wells. There is joyful complementarity and union between the man and his wife. There is

nakedness and no sense of shame. The Song seems to look back on and recapture these scenes of primal innocence, and reaffirms the doctrine of the goodness of God's creation. However, there is a snake in the garden in Genesis, and the idyllic dream is shattered. A curse is pronounced, and the resulting disruption is mirrored in some of the tensions and frustrations of the Song as the lovers pursue their relationship east of Eden. And so we are led inevitably from the doctrine of creation and the fall to the necessity of the doctrine of redemption and re-creation.

Bibliography

G. L. Carr, *The Song of Solomon*, TOTC (Leicester and Downers Grove, 1984); M. V. Fox, *The Song of Songs and the Ancient Egyptian Love Songs* (Madison, 1985); T. D. Gledhill, *The Message of the Song of Songs*, BST (Leicester and Downers Grove, 1994); M. D. Goulder, *The Song of Fourteen Songs* (Sheffield, 1986); F. Landy, *Paradoxes of Paradise: Identity and Difference in the Song of Songs* (Sheffield, 1983); R. E. Murphy, *The Song of Songs*, Hermeneia (London and Minneapolis, 1990); M. H. Pope, *The Song of Songs*, AB (Garden City, 1977).

T. D. GLEDHILL

ISAIAH

Introduction

Although it is surely a coincidence that the number of chapters in the book of Isaiah corresponds exactly to the number of books in the Christian Bible, there is no other book in either Testament which comprehends the whole of biblical theology so completely as does Isaiah. Here the terrifying *holiness of *God is depicted as clearly as it is anywhere in the OT, but also the unchanging *grace of God is depicted as clearly as it is anywhere in the NT. Thus in many ways the book of Isaiah offers a summary of biblical theology.

Theology of the book as a whole

Recent studies of the book of Isaiah have rediscovered its thematic unity. Earlier work, dominated by hypotheses of multiple authorship, tended not to see the complex interplay of themes which is a special characteristic of this book. Themes such as *judgment and *hope, blindness and deafness, rebellion and trust, and even highways and trees, not to mention obvious ones like 'the Holy One of Israel', have been utilized throughout the book to tie the various units together. Clearly, the parts of the book have been structured in the light of the whole.

Chapters 1 – 6

In the present form of the book, chapters 1 – 5 function as an introduction. As such, they contrast the rebellion and corruption of *Judah and *Israel in Isaiah's own day (1:1–31; 2:6 – 4:1; 5:1–30) and the future holiness and *blessedness which the nation will enjoy (2:1–5; 4:2–6). One of the chief marks of the rebellion is the tendency to glorify *humanity at the expense of God. But such folly can result only in the humiliation of humanity, for it is only God's *glory that fills the earth. Nevertheless, God will not be content to leave his people in their humiliation. But this raises a question: how can the promised holiness and blessedness replace rebellion and corruption? Chapters 1 – 5 do not provide an answer.

The answer is found in chapter 6, which explains why the *prophet's call is narrated only after the five preceding chapters. Just as the man of unclean lips had to abandon all hope before being cleansed by fire, so too must the nation. In many ways the rest of the book describes the outworking of the components of Isaiah's experience on a national scale. Just as Isaiah needed to see both God and himself correctly (6:1–5), so did the nation (chs. 7 – 39). Just as Isaiah needed to receive the fiery, but ultimately gracious cleansing of God (6:6–7), so did the nation (chs. 40 – 55). And just as Isaiah needed to receive God's commission (6:8–13), so did the nation (chs. 56 – 66).

Chapters 7 – 39

The vision of God and of Israel in chapters 7 – 39 revolves around the question of trust (see below). The people of Judah are called to trust God and to be delivered from the nations. In so doing they will demonstrate God's unique glory to the nations. But instead, they tend to be impressed by human glory and to trust the *nations instead of God. As a result, they will be captured and destroyed by the very nations they trust. Nevertheless, God is so trustworthy that even after the people of Judah have brought upon themselves the re-

sults of their own failure to trust, God will still offer himself to them.

These ideas are represented in an A-B-A structure. Chapters 7 – 12 (A) recount Ahaz's refusal to trust God and the immediately tragic and yet ultimately hopeful results of that choice. Chapters 13 – 35 (B) show in detail why it is folly to trust the nations rather than God. The nations are all under God's judgment, both in the short term (13 – 23) and in the long term (24 – 27). Only woe lies ahead for those who rush to ally themselves with the nations and refuse to wait for God, who is the true King of the universe (28 – 33). The stark contrast between the alternatives is summed up in chapters 34 (trusting the nations) and 35 (trusting God). In chapters 36 – 39 (A¹) Ahaz's son Hezekiah is given the same test. Will he succeed where his father failed? Has he learned the lessons contained in the intervening chapters? The answer is both yes and no, for although he trusts God to deliver him from the Assyrians and experiences a mighty confirmation of God's trustworthiness, he also succumbs to the temptation to parade his wealth and power before the visiting Babylonians. These chapters conclude the section and prepare for the following one, which will address issues raised by the Babylonian captivity.

Chapters 40 – 55

Chapters 40 – 55 are addressed to a people in despair. They are asking whether history has not made a mockery of God's promises to those who trust him. Has not God been defeated by the Babylonian gods, or if not by them, by his people's *sins? Isaiah's response to these questions is twofold. First, God demonstrates that he alone is God (see below, Uniqueness of God). He does this by showing that the gods of the nations are not really independent of the world, that they did not create it and cannot say what will become of it. He is the sole creator and he is able to do new things as he wishes. Secondly, God declares that he will use Israel as the evidence for all this. He is no more defeated by Israel's sin than he is by the Babylonian gods. Far from being cast off, the Israelites are his chosen servants who will declare his glory to the world.

But sinful Israel cannot automatically become servant Israel. Just as Isaiah's lips were made clean, so the nation must be cleansed.

Mere return from *exile will not automatically produce different behaviour. In chapter 42 Isaiah begins to address this issue with a brief reference to another servant. In language very much like that used to describe the coming king in chapters 9, 11, 16 and 31 – 32, it is said that this servant will 'bring justice to the nations' (42:1, 3–4) and will be 'a covenant to the people' (42:6) 'to open the eyes of the blind [Israel]'(v. 7). This is surely not a description of the nation healing itself. In chapters 49 – 55 Isaiah says that God will find a way of reconciling himself to his people and of restoring them to fellowship. Here the unidentified servant is described in much greater detail, and it is clear that he is not Israel personified. Instead of being rebellious and corrupt, this servant is obedient and pure-hearted. Instead of being self-protective, this servant is self-surrendering for the sake of others. The climactic description of this servant is found in the enigmatic 52:13 – 53:12. Here he is said to *suffer and die for the sin and rebellion of people whom the prophet calls 'us'. This section is immediately followed in chapters 54 – 55 by lyrical invitations to Israel to come and receive restoration and cleansing. Clearly it is the substitutionary suffering of the servant in 52:13 – 53:12 which makes this invitation possible.

Chapters 56 – 66

There is a striking change of emphasis in chapter 56. In chapters 40 – 55 the people are invited to *experience* the *righteousness of God (his deliverance) which is made available to them freely. Now, in language very reminiscent of chapters 1 – 39, they are challenged to *do* righteousness. They are told in no uncertain terms that obedient foreigners and eunuchs are more pleasing to God than pure-bred Judeans who pride themselves on their worship practices. These Judeans are quoted as saying that they are unable to do justice no matter how hard they try, and God responds that he himself will come in the person of a divine *warrior who will do in them what they cannot do in themselves. As a result Israel will become a light to the nations, through whom the Spirit-anointed Messiah can declare his good news to the whole world.

Two ideas are highlighted. On the one hand, merely being among the chosen people does not make one a servant of God;

*obedience is required. But on the other, no one should think that obedience is merely a result of human effort. It is divine enabling that makes obedience possible.

Key themes

Judgment and hope

This is the most dominant theme in Isaiah; it is presented in every chapter and gives the book its structure. Even the prophet's breathtaking vision of God, from which his teaching on judgment and hope is derived, is not so prominent.

One of the book's distinctive features is the intertwining of the themes of judgment and hope. The Israelites and Judeans thought, as many modern people do, that judgment and hope are mutually exclusive. But Isaiah shows that they are complementary. It might be said that chapters 1 – 39 focus on judgment and chapters 40 – 66 on hope, but when these two sections are examined closely, it becomes clear that this is only partially true; the theme of hope appears in 1 – 39 and that of judgment in 40 – 66. The interdependence of the two themes is apparent in chapter 1 and in the rest of the introductory unit. Judgment is certain; God announces that he will rid himself of his adversaries and take vengeance on his enemies, who are identified as his people (1:24–25). But what is the purpose of these acts of judgment? It is not destruction, but purging; once again Jerusalem will be called the city of righteousness, the faithful city (1:26). Hope for Judah is not to be found in the avoidance of judgment, but in judgment. If the people could somehow escape the fire, then in their present condition, they would have no hope of ever becoming what they were designed to be (*cf.* 6:9–10). As noted above, this seems to be the significance of the alternation between the announcements of judgment and the declarations of hope in chapters 1 – 5. Judgment cannot be avoided, but the people should not despair. It is through a 'spirit of judgment and a spirit of burning' (4:4, NRSV) that Zion can experience the presence of God in its midst, which was the goal of the Exodus.

The same point is made in chapter 6; the devastating experience of uncleanness before God is not intended to result in dissolution, but in cleansing and calling. In chapters 7 – 12 it is through the failure of the house of

David and the consequent destruction of the land at the hands of the Mesopotamians (7:13–25) that Immanuel will be revealed and the new age will be inaugurated by the budding of the stump of Jesse (11:1). Even the judgment of the nations (13 – 23) is intended to result in the permanent removal of the veil of death from all nations (25:7–8). And if the foolish advisers of the Judean monarchy turn the nation into nothing more than a tattered flag waving on a hilltop (30:17), this is in order that all God's blessings, especially the blessing of the true king, might come to his people (30:18–26; 32:1–8).

If chapters 1 – 39 are not only about judgment, neither are chapters 40 – 66 only about hope. In particular, in chapters 56 – 66 the prophet uses strong words to pronounce judgment on anyone who persists in thinking that the gracious *salvation of God described in chapters 40 – 55 simply follows from Israel's *election such that righteousness is not necessary as a response to that salvation (57:8–13; 58:1 – 59:15a; 63:10 – 65:15; 66:3–4, 14–17).

But the theme of judgment is found even in chapters 40 – 55, which speak so lyrically about God's deliverance. Unbelief is repeatedly denounced, and judgment pronounced on those who refuse to believe that judgment is meant to issue in hope and who have succumbed to despair (42:18–25; 43:25–28; 45:9–19; 46:8–13; 48:1–19; 50:1–3, 10–11; 51:12–16).

The uniqueness of God

Perhaps more than any other book in the canon, Isaiah insists on the uniqueness of God. This theme is especially prominent in chapters 40 – 48, in the prophet's insistence that the Babylonian gods can do nothing to prevent the restoration of Judah and Jerusalem, but it is not restricted to that section. In chapter 2 Yahweh is said to be God of all nations, not just of Judah; it is by his Torah that all nations will be judged (vv. 1–4). Later in that chapter it is said that all humanity and the *idols made in the image of humans will be humiliated before the unique glory of the Lord (vv. 6–22). In 5:26–30 all the nations are portrayed as subservient to his call. But God's uniqueness was most clearly expressed to the prophet in his call experience. The triple 'Holy, holy, holy' is an assertion that God is supremely, uniquely holy. Only of him is this an accurate description. He alone is truly

other than this world, truly transcendent. The gods are not holy at all. They are made of wood and stone, and covered with precious metal by a human craftsman (cf. 2:8–9, 20; 17:7–8; 31:7; 40:18–20; 44:6–20). How can such things be called holy? The most common appellation of God in this book (26 times out of a total of 31 in the OT) is 'The Holy One of Israel (or Jacob)'. The God of Israel is the uniquely holy one.

These ideas are developed further in 13 – 23, where all nations are depicted as suffering the judgment of God. They are not merely his tools, subject to his purposes; they are also accountable to him, and will be judged by his standards. It is this God alone who will bring history to its appointed end, in which the nations will experience either healing or final destruction (chs. 24 – 25; cf. also 34).

The implications of these assertions are made explicit in chapters 40 – 48, which directly address the challenge to Israel's faith occasioned by the exile. It appears that God has been defeated by the Babylonian gods. But God calls them into court and challenges them to prove that they are gods (cf. 43:8–13). He demands specific evidence; they are to explain 'the former things' and the latter things. According to the philosophy of paganism, the gods are part of the ceaseless cycles of the cosmos, and for them there is no past or future; they explain neither the purpose nor the destiny of the cosmos. Their identity with the cosmos is evidenced in the practice of idolatry, in which a 'god' is nothing more than an expensively decorated block of wood. But God 'sits above the circle of the earth' (40:22) in absolute transcendence. He is the sole creator, the one who brought the cosmos into existence for a good purpose. Not only can he explain the purpose and meaning of existence; he also knows the future before it occurs and can do what has never been done before. Only a divine being who is separate from the cosmos can do all this. He alone can say, 'I am'.

Trust

Trust is the main subject of chapters 7 – 39, but the theme is found in other parts of the book as well. Unless the people of Israel will entrust their future to God and let him demonstrate through them that he is the unique creator and saviour, their mission to the world can never be fulfilled.

The initial challenge to trust God is given to Ahaz (7:1–7), but the king has already decided to put his hope in Assyria, as 2 Kings 16:7–9 indicates. Isaiah declares that by doing this Ahaz has delivered his nation up to destruction at Assyria's hand. Nevertheless, God will demonstrate his genuine trustworthiness by bringing Assyria under judgment, rescuing his people from captivity and appointing a true son of David to rule Judah and Jerusalem. The appropriate response of the people is to 'trust, and not be afraid' (12:2). As mentioned above, chapters 13 – 35 provide lessons in trust, demonstrating the folly of trusting the nations of the world, which are all under judgment and will be helpless against superior forces. God alone can be trusted in all circumstances (26:3–6). When humans have made a desert of the world through trying to meet their needs by themselves (ch. 34), God will still be trustworthy and will bring those who 'wait' for him out of the desert into a garden (ch. 35).

After Hezekiah's deliverance from his military enemy (chs. 36 – 37) and his deliverance from the enemy of illness (ch. 38), it is very surprising to see him succumbing to the enemy of pride in chapter 39. Whereas Ahaz's refusal to trust (ch. 7) issued in hope (ch. 12), here Hezekiah's trust issues in judgment. Chapters 36 – 39 seem to be saying both that trust is a way of life, and that hope does not lie in the perfectibility of any human. Thus the reader is prepared for the next section of the book; the trustworthiness of God has been amply demonstrated, and it has been made quite clear that Hezekiah is not Immanuel. (See *Faith, faithfulness.)

Creation

Probably no OT book apart from Genesis discusses *creation so fully as Isaiah does. In chapters 40 – 48 the prophet argues that since Yahweh alone is the creator of the universe, he alone directs history, and he alone is the saviour. God made the world without assistance or counsel (40:12–14; 44:24). He is the creator of the whole earth (40:28), and in it Israel is a special creation (43:7). Everything that exists is ultimately the work of God; no one else can take credit for the origination of anything (44:6–8). In the pagan 'creation' stories all things originate in chaos and humanity is an afterthought. In contrast, Isaiah insists that God created the world in order

that humans should inhabit it (45:18–19). Because pagan gods have been made by human ingenuity, they must be carried by their *worshippers (46:1–2). But God, the Maker, carries his worshippers (46:3–9). Because God is the creator, he can do new things, things never heard of before (48:6–7).

Salvation

Like many of the other themes in the book, that of salvation is developed in some detail. The concept is directly related to Israel's problem. The problem is rebellion, self-exaltation, injustice, alienation, and resultant devastation; the solution must deal with all of these. Furthermore, the problem has both physical and spiritual dimensions; a full solution must embrace both. Salvation must produce people who submit to God, trusting him to supply all their needs. It must result in reconciliation between God and humans, and between humans. It must include deliverance from physical and spiritual bondage. It must involve *forgiveness and cleansing. It must produce people who are committed to the justice prescribed in their *covenant with God. It must issue in a glad desire to declare the glory, the uniqueness and the salvation of God to all the world.

The basis for this salvation is found in the trustworthiness of God. Even when his people have rejected him and trusted in the empty glory of the nations, he will not reject them. Instead he reaches out to *comfort them in the tragedies which have justly befallen them, and declares to them that their sin is forgiven and that they are restored to his favour. The means of this forgiveness and restoration are twofold. On the one hand, the fires of judgment themselves are cleansing if they are received as such and not allowed to destroy faith in the one who sent them. But fire cannot atone for sin; Leviticus makes clear that only a life can atone for sin. Thus the ideal Servant gives his life for the transgression of the people. In him God renews the covenant with them; he is the means of their healing. Isaiah does not explain how all this is possible, but the first Christians came to believe that God himself was in the servant.

Messiah-servant

From the beginning of the book it is clear that corrupt leadership is one of the main causes of Israel's failure to be the obedient people they were called to be (1:10, 23). This point is made more explicit in chapter 7 where Ahaz and the house of David are accused of lacking faith (7:2, 13). It is repeated several times in the succeeding chapters (see *e.g.* 22:15–19), but is especially prominent in chapters 28 – 33. Priests and prophets are drunk, both literally and figuratively (28:7–13; 29:9–10), and the princes are the worst of sinners, scoffers who mock the truth and cynically plan to save themselves when trouble comes (28:14–19; 29:15–16). The problem is not only with Israelite leadership, but with any human ruler who exalts himself against God, as chapter 14 so graphically shows.

It is against this backdrop that Isaiah depicts another kind of leader, one who will rule with the righteousness and justice which the ancient Near Eastern kings often pretended to bring (1:26; 9:7; 11:4–5; 16:5; 32:1–8). He will be of the tribe of Jesse (11:1) and the house of *David (9:7; 16:5), and yet somehow he will be all that his predecessors in that line had failed to be. He will do what they had only promised to do: his *kingdom will be free from war, danger, evil and oppression (9:4–5, 7; 11:1–9 [*cf.* 65:17–25, where God is said to create the kingdom]; 32:1–8). His kingdom will have no end (9:7), because he will be the evidence of God's presence with his people, even being called 'Wonderful Counsellor, Mighty God, Everlasting Father, Prince of Peace' (9:6). The reader or hearer of these words may well ask who such a person could be.

Perhaps it is to be Hezekiah, Ahaz's son, who learned the lesson which his father never learned, that God is trustworthy. Could he not be the son born to the 'virgin', the one upon whose shoulder government would rest? Chapters 38 – 39 make clear that he is not. Hezekiah is mortal (38). He is given an additional fifteen years, but he will die, and his rule will die with him. Furthermore, Hezekiah is tragically fallible (39). He parades his wealth and power, and trusts in his own achievements.

Is the Messiah to be found in chapters 40 – 66? Many scholars would say not. The language of kingship found in the early chapters is largely absent. On the other hand, in 61:1 an anointed one is introduced. He is anointed by Yahweh to announce the salvation of God to the world, and will make it possible for the people to be called 'trees of righteousness'

(61:3). This reference to righteousness recalls the promise of the king in 11:1–5 and elsewhere in chapters 1 – 39, which in turn recalls the description of the servant in 42:1 and 49:6, where he is said to bring justice to the nations and God's deliverance to the end of the earth.

But if this is the same person as the one promised in the earlier chapters, why is the royal imagery absent? Chapters 1 – 39 emphasize the *humility of the messianic figure. God's answer to the arrogance of Assyria and the stubbornness of the Judean court is a baby. Throughout chapters 7 – 12 children are presented as the signs of God's promised kingdom. Chapter 11 says that the coming King will rule not by the trappings of power, but in the power of righteousness. Chapter 32 emphasizes this point; his power will not compel, but rather attract. One of his functions will be to give sight to the blind and hearing to the deaf (32:3–4) as in 61:2–3.

Thus the messianic figures in the two parts of the book are not contradictory, but complementary. The king will be the servant and the servant will be the king. This paradox underlines one of the key points in the book: only God is high and lifted up. To exalt humanity against him leads to utter humiliation. But one of the principal marks of God's 'high' holiness is his delight in dwelling with the lowly and the contrite (57:15). God's power is at its greatest not in his destruction of the wicked but in his taking all the wickedness of the earth into himself and giving back love. Only one who has utterly abandoned himself in service to God and his people can take the crown upon his head.

Isaiah in the NT

Like Psalms and Deuteronomy, Isaiah is a favourite among NT authors. There may be as many as 115 quotations from or allusions to it in the NT. While some of the supposed allusions may be questionable, there are fifty-eight direct quotes, in which forty-one different verses or passages are represented. The most frequently quoted passage is 6:9–10 (Matt. 13:14–15; Mark 4:12; Luke 8:10; John 12:40; Acts 28:26–27). Clearly the apostles saw a parallel between Isaiah's experience and theirs: the preaching of the good news seemed to turn people away. 8:14 is used in Romans 9:33 and 1 Peter 2:8 to explain why so many Jews stumbled over Christ. In his discussion of the fate of the Jews in Romans 9 – 11 Paul quotes from Isaiah no fewer than eleven times (Rom. 9:29 = Is. 1:9; 9:27–28 = 10:22–23; 11:26–27 = 27:9; 11:8 = 29:10; 11:34 = 40:13; 10:15 = 52:7; 11:26–27 = 59:20–21; 10:20 = 65:1; 10:21 = 65:2). These references point both to Israel's propensity to sin and to God's determination to deliver them.

All four Gospels utilize 40:3–5 to show that Christ's coming was foreseen by Isaiah. They do so by identifying John the Baptist as the voice crying in the wilderness (Matt. 3:3; Mark 1:3; Luke 3:4–6; John 1:23). Matthew's well-known quotation of Isaiah 7:14 in relation to the virgin birth (Matt. 1:23) also identifies Jesus as the fulfilment of OT promises. Matthew shows that Jesus' Galilean ministry fulfilled Isaiah's prediction in 9:1–2 (cf. Matt. 4:15–16). Jesus himself cited Isaiah 61:1–3 to identify himself as the promised Messiah (Luke 4:18–19).

There are ten quotations from or allusions to chapter 53 in the NT; the servant's substitutionary suffering and death is a prominent theme (see esp. Matt. 8:17; Luke 22:37; Acts 8:32–33; Heb. 9:28; 1 Pet. 2:22, 24–25). This chapter may have had a formative effect upon the early church's understanding of the meaning of the cross.

Moreover, the book of Isaiah influenced the church's understanding of its mission to the Gentiles. The mysterious plan of God (29:14 = 1 Cor. 1:19; 40:13 = 1 Cor. 2:16; 66:4 = 1 Cor. 2:9), in which God's people would declare salvation to the entire world (11:10 = Rom. 15:12; 49:6 = Acts 13:47; 52:5 = Rom. 2:24; 52:15 = Rom. 15:21), is another Isaianic motif which helped early Christians to make sense of their experience.

Bibliography

J. N. Oswalt, 'Key themes in the book of Isaiah: their relevance for Christian theology', in T. Dwyer (ed.), *The Newell Lectureships* vol. 3 (Anderson, 1996); B. Webb, *The Message of Isaiah*, BST (Leicester and Downers Grove, 1996); H. M. Wolf, *Interpreting Isaiah: The Suffering and the Glory of the Messiah* (Grand Rapids, 1985).

J. N. OSWALT

JEREMIAH

Introduction

The book of Jeremiah contains more biographical and autobiographical information about the life of an ancient Hebrew *prophet than any other OT *prophetic book. This is because it contains Jeremiah's personal written record, as well as the work of Baruch, Jeremiah's scribe and disciple. It is not clear in all instances which parts come directly from the pen of Jeremiah and Baruch, and which parts are the product of later Jewish communities. Historical minimalists attribute little to the historical Jeremiah and his friend, and some (*i.e.* Carroll) suggest that no such prophet ever lived. On the other hand, historical maximalists attribute a large proportion of the book of Jeremiah to a prophet of that name and his associate, Baruch. Unravelling the complex layers of tradition in a book like Jeremiah is no easy process. It seems quite likely that in the generations after the prophet's death his materials were collected and edited into their final form.

Historical context

The setting of the book of Jeremiah is the late 7th and early 6th centuries BC. Jeremiah was a young man from the village of Anathoth, near the vicinity of *Jerusalem. His call to be a prophet to the nations (1:5) as a young man (1:6) has been dated to either 627 or 609 BC. Both were years of upheaval in the ancient Near East. In 627 BC, Ashurbanipal, the king of Assyria, died, which further weakened what was left of the former Assyrian empire, and made room for a new political threat from the north (1:14) – *Babylon. In 609 BC, the Israelites suffered a tragedy when Josiah, their king from the line of David, was killed by Egyptian forces. Either scenario could have necessitated the commissioning of a prophet. The traditional date of Jeremiah's call to be a prophet is 627 BC. If this is correct, his ministry covered a substantial period of ancient Near Eastern political history. The traditional date is assumed in what follows.

Some knowledge of the historical context of Jeremiah's ministry is necessary for an understanding of his book. He lived in a volatile time for Jerusalem, *Judah and the surrounding nations. The book bears witness to the most devastating events in OT Hebrew history.

These include the Babylonian invasion which culminated in the capture of Jerusalem, the destruction of Solomon's *temple and the forced exile of many Judeans into Babylon. The year was 587 BC, a date embedded in the memory of succeeding Jewish generations, and a cause of introspection in later OT books.

The times of the prophet Jeremiah may be broken down into five periods. Assuming that the call of Jeremiah took place in 627 BC, the first period began on this date and ended in 622 BC. Jeremiah was therefore called to action because of the political crisis resulting from the growth in Babylonian power after the death of Ashurbanipal. This first period ended on a good note five years later when King Josiah implemented domestic reforms following the discovery of a lost book, presumed to be a portion of the Mosaic law (2 Kgs. 22 – 23).

The second period might be called 'the silent years'. Jeremiah quietly observed the reform movement of Josiah without conducting an obvious public ministry. In the meantime, Nineveh, the capital city of Assyria, was besieged and conquered in 612 BC. This further cleared the way for Babylonian domination and imperialism. Assyria and Egypt had kept the power of Babylon at bay to some extent, but after the defeat of Nineveh their resistance crumbled. By 609 BC Jeremiah could keep silent no longer. Tragically, King Josiah resisted the Egyptians as they marched through his land on the way to do battle with Babylon, and this resulted in his death. The national emergency called for a prophet, just as the unstable days of Ahab had called for Elijah (1 Kgs. 17:1).

The third period of Jeremiah's ministry was from 609 to 597 BC. This proved to be the most trying time for the prophet, whose task it was to convince Josiah's successor that submission to the rule of Babylon was the will of *God. It was this theological conviction that provoked such serious resistance to Jeremiah's ministry, not only by kings, but also by the populace. Josiah's immediate successor was his son, Jehoahaz, who was deported to Egypt only three months after taking the throne. His brother Jehoiakim followed him, and became Jeremiah's greatest enemy (22:13–23; ch. 36). During this third period, the final consolidation of Babylonian power was completed in 605 BC when their general Nebuchadnezzar, who later became

king of Babylon, defeated the Assyrian-Egyptian coalition at the Battle of Carchemish. As a result, Jeremiah was commanded by God to write his message on a scroll (36:1–3).

The fourth period of Jeremiah's ministry lasted ten years. It began in 597 BC after the death of Jehoiakim and ended in 587 BC with the Babylonian conquest of Jerusalem during the reign of Zedekiah, Josiah's third son.

The final period of Jeremiah's ministry began after the fall of Jerusalem and extended into the 570s BC. During this time Gedaliah, a righteous Jew, was appointed acting governor of Judah by the occupying Babylonians. But Gedaliah was soon murdered by a fellow Israelite, a crime which incurred further Babylonian wrath. Finally Jeremiah was forced into Egypt against his will by his own people. The prophet continued his ministry, but faded into oblivion, largely disregarded by the people whom he tried to persuade to obey the will of God.

Theology

The historical background to the book of Jeremiah is crucial in that Jeremiah preaches non-resistance to the expanding Babylonian empire. His message contradicts previous Israelite experience, such as that of king Hezekiah, who through piety and a miracle thwarted a foreign invasion of Jerusalem (Is. 36 – 37; 2 Kgs. 18 – 19). But this is not to happen in Jeremiah's day. In his famous temple sermon (chs. 7, 26), the prophet warns that Jerusalem is not invincible, thus opposing conventional 'Zion theology' that trusts in God's promise to David to protect David's throne in Jerusalem (2 Sam. 7:8-16). Jeremiah's thought-world is not dominated by Zion theology, even though many of those to whom he preached in Judah accept it. The two most important factors influencing Jeremiah's thinking are the *Exodus from Egypt (Exod. 11 – 14) and the *covenant given to Moses at Sinai (Exod. 20 – 40). In this respect Jeremiah is a typical Hebrew prophet who calls the people back to obedience to the Sinai covenant (11:1–13). In fact, Jeremiah appears to be most powerfully influenced by the earlier ministry of Hosea to the north. He may have had close contact with Hosea's disciples, and possibly even a thorough knowledge of the writings Hosea left behind.

Jeremiah's message has two aspects, first identified in 1:10:

> See, I have appointed you
> > this day over the nations
> > and over the kingdoms,
> > *To pluck up and to break*
> > *down,*
> > *To destroy and overthrow*
> > [first aspect],
> > *To build and to plant*
> > [second aspect]
> > (NASB; author's italics).

Jeremiah's ministry is to the international world of his day, where God is subjugating all the nations, including his own, to the rule of Babylon for a time. Because he lives and preaches at this crossroads of Israelite history, Jeremiah becomes one of the most resisted and rejected of the Hebrew prophets. He is often referred to as the 'weeping prophet' (9:1; 13:17; 14:17). His distress is not limited to his relationship with his people, but extends also to his perplexing relationship with God. He speaks quite candidly with God on a number of occasions about the difficulty of his task (especially in chs. 12 – 20, which contain what are known as Jeremiah's five 'Confessions'). At one point he accuses God of taking advantage of his youthfulness in calling him to be a prophet (20:7). He even finds it within himself to curse the day of his birth in the manner of Job (20:14–18; *cf.* Job 3:1).

The troublesome nature of Jeremiah's call and ministry are a reflection of the heart of God, who is burdened with the sin, idolatry and eventual punishment of his people. The prophet must identify with God in order fully to comprehend his ministry. In the story of the ruined waistcloth (13:1–11), the clinging of the waistcloth to Jeremiah as *Israel and Judah clung to God (13:11) does more than symbolize punishment. It represents the oneness, the closeness, the attachment that exists between God and his covenant people. Jeremiah's act of buying and putting on the waistcloth (13:1–2) is central to the meaning of the passage; for God himself has purchased Israel and attached himself to her, as recorded in the Pentateuch. In this scenario, the prophet must learn to feel for himself God's intimate attachment to Israel. Jeremiah must learn of God's grief in having to spoil what is very precious to him. Through this role-playing drama,

Jeremiah comes to understand that God is the redeemer of Israel who in the earliest stage of their relationship enjoyed intimacy with his people.

Jeremiah is called further to identify with God in his being obliged to forgo marriage and children so as to symbolize the barrenness of a land under judgment (16:1–4). God signifies the complete end of his relationship with Israel by his representative prophet's not having a wife or bearing children. Natural life as the Israelites know it is becoming extinct. Jeremiah himself is called to extinction. By his life he symbolizes the death of his people. Hosea's marriage to a prostitute is shocking (Hos. 1:2), but not unheard of. Jeremiah's bachelorhood, however, is so unusual among the Jews that the OT has no word for bachelor, and it undoubtedly reinforces questions about him. God is attempting to shock the people through the prophet's identification with God. In the suffering of the prophet is reflected the suffering of God over his people.

In Chapter 18 Jeremiah is commanded to go down to the house of a potter to learn a theological lesson. In this symbolic action Jeremiah identifies with the purpose and mind of God; it proclaims that Judah can become like a marred pot that is in need of breaking down and reworking in a manner pleasing to the potter, God. However, the key theological point in the story of Jeremiah at the potter's house is that God's promises of blessing and warnings of judgment are not irrevocable. Everything depends upon how people respond: human repentance can avert a threatened disaster, while human wrongdoing can lead to the forfeit of a promised blessing. God responds to the response of humans. Like human relationships, a relationship with God is mutual, and is therefore dependent upon interaction and response. Jeremiah works hard to evoke this response, but in the end only those already sent into Babylonian exile are spared (ch. 24).

Conflict

Distinguishing an authentic prophet from a counterfeit is an important task in the time of Jeremiah (14:13–16; 23:9–40; 28:1–17). For Jeremiah, the true prophet is one who attempts to turn the people away from evil by emphasizing God's moral and covenantal demands (23:14, 22). To identify true prophets, one must examine their moral life and message. Further, the tone of the message should be analysed. The true prophet patiently *stands* in the council of the Lord (23:18); the false prophet hurriedly *runs* without having been sent (23:21). Personal discernment and intuition must be employed when judging prophecy. This problematic issue of who does and who does not speak for God is central to the book of Jeremiah, and casts a shadow over both Old and New Testaments (1 Cor. 14:29). There is no simple solution (28:11), and it is an issue relevant to every generation. Much of the conflict which surrounds the OT prophets concerns the use of the term 'prophet'; Sometimes it refers to those who speak falsely (e.g. in 1 Kgs. 13; 22:1–40). Whether a prophet is true or false must be determined by the biblical context and by criteria such as those mentioned above.

Theological terminology

The first two verses of Jeremiah 4 string together for the first time some important concepts which appear together a number of times thereafter (9:24; 22:3, 13, 15; 23:5; 33:15). The verses capture the essence of chapters 2 and 3, which discuss Israel's idolatry and need for *repentance. The call to 'return' is issued in chapter 4; it is to be accomplished in '*truth', 'justice' and '*righteousness'.

'Turning', a term used (in various forms) nearly a hundred times in Jeremiah, is the literal meaning of the Hebrew word for repentance. It involves turning from one's own way back to the familiar paths (6:16) of God's moral and covenantal norms. The prophet calls the community to a wholesome life in which the needs and rights of all under God are recognized and met.

Often the turning is to 'truth', 'justice' or 'righteousness'. These terms are used together many times and reinforce each other, which almost suggests that they should be regarded as synonyms. They denote a firm reliability, a moral soundness, a covenant-keeping loyalty, an unswerving straightness, all of which uphold community relations and responsibility.

In 17:1–11 Jeremiah identifies the seat of society's problems as the human heart. It is described as a rock-hard object, permanently engraved with sin (17:1). According to Hebrew thought the heart is the central faculty within the human person. More than once Jeremiah asserts that at all levels of society evil arises from the deceit of the human heart (6:13;

8:10b). Self-seeking and falsehood are at the foundation of human thought and action. Therefore, Jeremiah calls for a breaking up of fallow ground (4:3) and a removal of the foreskins of the heart (4:4). God alone can see into the depths of the human heart and understand it (17:9–10). Therefore, it is he who must initiate change (3:15; 31:31; 32:40).

The knowledge of the Lord is also important in Jeremiah's thinking (8:7; 24:7; 31:31–34). Only Ezekiel and the Psalms use the term 'know' in the OT more than Jeremiah's seventy-seven times. He speaks of it most poignantly in his address to King Jehoiakim (22:13–17; esp. v. 16). Concern for the afflicted and needy, and the practice of justice and righteousness, are equated with the knowledge of God.

Hope

The theology of Jeremiah, which highlights plucking up and breaking down (1:10), also includes a promise to build and plant (1:10). Ultimately, God will give back to his covenant people the life and well-being that they once enjoyed. Every aspect of Jewish life will be restored after a seventy-year exile (25:11; 29:10). A collection of promises for the new Jewish community is found in chapters 30 – 33, known to scholars as 'The Book of Consolation'. It describes Israel's *hope for the future.

Imagery of God wounding and healing is employed in 30:12–17, and occurs not only in other poetic sections of Jeremiah (8:22; 10:19; 14:17), but also in the language of the prophet Hosea (Hos. 5:13; 6:1; 7:1; 11:3). As the compassionate physician of his people, God will cause new flesh to grow (30:17); a similar picture is found in Ezekiel (Ezek. 37:6). God's remedy for the sick heart (17:9) will be to put his law directly on the heart of the new community (31:31–34). This passage, known as the 'New Covenant', has an important place in early Christian writings (Luke 22:20; Heb. 8:8–12; 10:16–17). The term 'New Testament' was coined by the early church father Origen.

In 'The Book of Consolation' God invites his people to realize his good intentions for them, at a time when the Babylonian army was beseiging Jerusalem (33:3). God's good intentions are based on a predetermined love for Israel which existed before the covenant itself (31:3). Jeremiah's purchase of land in chapter 32 illustrates in a practical way the exiles' hope of restoration.

The final section of the book (chs. 46 – 51) is composed of oracles against foreign nations. First, the prophet celebrates Babylon as God's instrument of judgment (chs. 46 – 49); then, he dismisses Babylon utterly (chs. 50 – 51). Thus the book reaches a climax in the total reversal of 1:14 (*cf.* also 6:22–23 and 50:41–42) and the future hope of Israel.

Jeremiah and the NT

Although Jeremiah is not quoted as often in the NT as Isaiah, the longest quote from the OT in the NT is from the book. The writer to the Hebrews quotes the 'New Covenant' passage of Jeremiah 31:31–34 to support his claim that the first covenant is obsolete (Heb. 8:8–13).

In Jeremiah's preaching of a new era, involving a new work of God in which he gives the nations into the hand of Babylon, is revealed the possibility of God's doing something remarkable, even seemingly inconceivable. The coming of Christ and the NT is just such a new, remarkable work of God. The Jerusalem of Jeremiah's day could not grasp a work of God outside the limits of 'Zion theology'; neither could the Jerusalem of Jesus' day submit to the work of God in Christ.

Jeremiah calls for repentance and true knowledge of God. The NT uses similar terminology in pointing to Jesus Christ (John 6:29). The falsehood to which Jeremiah so often refers continues to be a threat for the NT writers, who call people to faith in Jesus Christ (1 Tim. 4:1; Jas. 3:1; 2 Pet. 2:1; 1 John 4:1).

Bibliography

W. Brueggemann, *A Commentary on Jeremiah: Exile and Homecoming* (Grand Rapids, 1988); R. P. Carroll, *From Chaos to Covenant* (London and New York, 1981); *idem, Jeremiah* (London, 1986); B. S. Childs, *Introduction to the Old Testament as Scripture* (London and Philadelphia, 1979); *idem, Old Testament Theology in a Canonical Context* (Philadelphia, 1985); J. Goldingay, *God's Prophet, God's Servant* (Carlisle, 1996); W. L. Holladay, *Jeremiah,* 2 vols, Hermeneia (Minneapolis, 1986, 1989); G. J. Janzen, *Studies in the Text of Jeremiah* (Cambridge, 1973); D. R. Jones, *Jeremiah,* NCB (Grand Rapids, 1992); J. G. McCon-

ville, *Judgment and Promise* (Leicester, 1993); J. A. Thompson, *The Book of Jeremiah,* NICOT (Grand Rapids, 1980).

J. R. SOZA

LAMENTATIONS

Introduction

The book of Lamentations is an emotional response to the aftermath and tragedy of the destruction of *Jerusalem in 587 BC. It bewails the day, warned of by the prophets, in which Yahweh became 'like an enemy', destroying Israel 'without pity' (2:2, 5, NIV). This destruction was accomplished by King Nebuchadnezzar's Babylonian army. The historical narratives of 2 Kings 25 and Jeremiah 52 give the facts; the five poems of Lamentations capture the emotions.

The Septuagint and Jewish tradition both ascribe the writing of Lamentations to the prophet Jeremiah. But since the text itself records nothing of its authorship, it seems best to assign the composition to an unknown eyewitness of the fall of Jerusalem.

The title of the book is derived from the first word of chapters 1, 2, and 4, which, in English, is translated into the lament 'how'. It evokes the wailing customary in a Hebrew funeral dirge. Chapters 3 and 5 are, respectively, an individual lament and a community lament.

The first four poems are alphabetical acrostics (*cf.* Pss. 25; 34; 37; 119; Prov. 31:10–31). Chapters 1 and 2 contain twenty-two verses of three lines each, and the first word of each verse begins with a different Hebrew letter. In chapter 4 each verse has two lines. Chapter 3 is the most tightly constructed, for its sixty-six verses are divided into twenty-two groups of three verses each, and each of the three begins with the appropriate letter. Even chapter 5, which is not in alphabetical form, seems to have been affected by the acrostic pattern; it also has twenty-two verses of one line each.

The artistic acrostic structure may serve a threefold purpose. First, it could have mnemonic value (*i.e.* to serve as a memory device). Second, it might be intended to convey a full expression of grief over Jerusalem's destruction ('from A to Z'). Included in this expression is a total confession of *sin which brings about a complete cleansing of the conscience. Third, the acrostic places constraints on the lament, thus adding a gentle dignity to what could have become an unfettered display of grief.

The theology of Lamentations

Lamentations is by no means theologically barren. In the opening verse of the book Jerusalem is personified. The city, once a proud and dignified woman, is now brutally raped and abandoned by treacherous friends. This image is intensified in the use of words and phrases like 'widow' and 'queen' (1:1), and 'daughter of Zion' (1:6), a term of endearment that could be translated as 'cherished Jerusalem' or 'fair Zion'. Christian liturgy and hymnody has sometimes heard in the agony of the personified city an anticipation of the agony of the personified God, that is, the crucifixion of Jesus.

The lengthy lament is a funeral dirge for an irrecoverable past. The Davidic monarchy had survived for four centuries in Judah even during the upheavals of the split with the northern kingdom and the Assyrian conquests. This stability had led to a belief that no enemy attack could ever humble Jerusalem. After all, the one true God lived there, and he would never let an enemy ransack his home. But those days were gone. The laments express a longing for 'the good old days'. The people of Judah must have been very surprised that the hand of God had brushed aside King Josiah's reforms so lightly. But Jeremiah had warned that the earlier abominations of King Manasseh (Jer. 15:4) outweighed the righteousness of Josiah. Sin and disobedience (see *Obedience) are punished severely (Rom. 6:23). It is a widespread human characteristic to desire the recovery of the irrecoverable.

Even where God is chided for his severity (ch. 2), the *guilt which permeates the book is evident (1:5, 8–9, 18, 22; 2:14; 3:40–42; 4:13, 22; 5:7). The sense of tragedy is heightened by the recognition that the *judgment was avoidable. The many descriptions in Lamentations of the wrath of God (1:12; 2:1–9, 20-22; 3:1–18; 4:6, 11) make the book a key source for any study of this aspect of God's nature. The second poem describes the vehemence of God's *anger against Jerusalem; the third is a complaint about the author's personal *suffering, which reflects the suffering of the nation, and the fourth shows that punishment for sins has been completed (4:22). Lamentations clearly illustrates the retributive aspect of human suffering and the notion of divine abandonment. God is seriously opposed to disobedience and will withdraw his presence and blessing from those who disobey him. Human sorrow is therefore a major aspect of the theology of Lamentations. It can come to an individual (ch. 3), or to a whole nation. Chapter 5 may date from somewhat later in the exile, when the sharp pains of defeat had dulled into the chronic ache of captivity.

Judah's plight is desperate but not hopeless. Her reason for *hope is cogently stated: the *faithfulness of a covenant-keeping God (3:19–39). Human guilt, accompanied by sorrow, suffering and an irrecoverable past, can be superseded by judgment, *repentance and a God who brings hope out of a seemingly hopeless situation.

Themes from Lamentations in the NT

The events in Jerusalem of 587 BC highlight the larger biblical issue of humanity's ruin as a result of sin and disobedience to God (Rom. 5:18a). As Israel's future can be found only beyond death and destruction, so also humankind's hope can be found only in the finished work of Jesus, and what he accomplished in his death. His final words from the cross, as recorded in the gospel of John, are, 'It is finished!' (John 19:30).

With the death of Jesus there is hope for all (John 12:24). As the structure of Lamentations suggests that the time of mourning and hopelessness will be limited, so also the NT gospel of Jesus predicts a time when the tragedy of rebellion will be removed to make way for a new era of hope (Rev. 21:4).

Conclusion

Lamentations weaves together the three great strands of Israel's literature and faith: the prophets' insights into the judgment and *grace of the covenant Lord; the priests' liturgical expressions of contrition and hope; and the wise teachers' wrestlings with the mysteries and difficulties of human suffering. It captures in brief form these major strands of Israel's distinctive theological tradition.

Bibliography

N. K. Gottwald, *Studies in the Book of Lamentations* (London, 1954); D. R. Hillers, *Lamentations*, AB (Garden City, 1972); W.

C. Kaiser Jr., *A Biblical Approach to Personal Suffering* (Chicago, 1982); I. Provan, *Lamentations*, NCB (Grand Rapids and Carlisle, 1991, 1996); C. Westermann, *Lamentations: Issues and Interpretation* (Edinburgh and Minneapolis, 1994).

J. R. SOZA

EZEKIEL

Introduction

The book of Ezekiel is a prophecy which was delivered during the *exile in Babylon. The dated oracles in the book range from 593 to 571 BC. Written from the perspective of exile, it predicts and explains the final fall and destruction of *Jerusalem by the Babylonians in 587 BC, and the future for God's people after that world-shattering event. The book itself is made up of four main parts: 1. The call and commissioning of the prophet (Ezek. 1 – 3); 2. Oracles of judgment against Judah and Jerusalem (Ezek. 4 – 24); 3. Oracles of judgment against the nations (Ezek. 25 – 32); 4. Oracles of restoration for Judah and Israel (Ezek. 33 – 48).

Central themes in Ezekiel

Because of the fundamental twofold structure of the book as a declaration of *judgment and restoration, it is not surprising to find that the major themes in Ezekiel generally have a similar twofold aspect.

Uncreation – re-creation

There are many points of contact between Ezekiel's opening vision of the *glory of God and the opening chapters of Genesis. Ezekiel sees a mighty windstorm (*rûaḥ sᵉ'ârâ*, 1:4) approaching from the north, the traditional source of Judah's enemies. This windstorm recalls the activity of God both in *creation, where the spirit (*rûaḥ*) of God was hovering over the waters (Gen. 1:2), and in the re-creation of the earth after the flood, when God sent a wind (*rûaḥ*) to dry up the floodwaters (Gen. 8:1). At the centre of this windstorm, Ezekiel sees living creatures (*ḥayyôt*; *cf.* Gen. 1:24, 28), which in a later vision are explicitly identified as cherubim (10:1), those who enforce divine judgment in Genesis 3:24. Over the heads of the cherubim is an awesome 'expanse' (*râqîaʿ*, 1:25, NIV), like that of Genesis 1:6. The

aura of God's radiance is compared to a rainbow in the clouds on a rainy day (v. 28), a description which evokes Genesis 9:13–16, the only other passage in the OT which speaks of God's setting his bow in the clouds. Together, these references set the tone of the entire book of Ezekiel as an account of uncreation – re-creation.

The re-creation aspect is most evident in the 'new *Adam' theme which emerges in two places. Ezekiel himself is characteristically addressed in the book as *ben-'ādām* a phrase normally translated 'son of man', but which literally means 'son of Adam'. Just as the first Adam received the breath of life from God (Gen. 2:7), so Ezekiel as 'son of Adam' receives an infusion of divine spirit (*rûaḥ*) (see *Holy Spirit) which raises him from the prone position to which the vision of God's fearsome glory reduced him (Ezek. 2:1–2). Like the first Adam, he faces a test of *obedience which revolves around the idea of eating, though in his case he is to eat whatever the Lord commands him to eat (2:8), rather than to abstain from eating what the Lord prohibits. In another reversal of the original sin, what Ezekiel is given to eat is anything but 'good for food and pleasing to the eye, and also desirable for gaining wisdom' (Gen. 3:6): it is a scroll covered on both sides with words of lament and mourning and woe (Ezek. 2:10). Yet though its appearance is unattractive, to the obedient eater it tastes as sweet as honey (3:3), and through eating it the 'new Adam' becomes equipped to bring *life to many (3:16–21). As the 'new Adam', Ezekiel is the founder member and firstfruits of the renewed community (see *People of God), whose re-creation is the theme of Ezekiel 37:1–11. This re-creation of the community from the valley of dry bones involves first the forming of the raw material into bodies and then their being filled with breath, resulting in life, as at the creation of the first Adam.

Covenant curse – covenant establishment

The idea of Israel's relationship with the Lord as a *covenant is prominent throughout the OT. Like typical ancient Near Eastern suzerainty treaties of this period, the covenant made between God and his people at Mt Sinai comes with *blessings and curses attached. If the people obey the stipulations of the covenant, then they will experience the blessings of the covenant relationship, blessings which include fertility, abundant rainfall, peace and security, and the life-giving presence of the Lord in their midst (Lev. 26:3–13). On the other hand, if they break the terms of the treaty, they can expect to experience the curses of the covenant, namely: plagues of wild animals, drought, famine, pestilence, the sword and exile among the nations (Lev. 26:14–39).

The prophets often acted as messengers from the Lord convicting the people of breaches in the covenant, and Ezekiel is no exception. His indictments of the people's sin are frequently drawn directly from the language of the Pentateuchal laws, especially Leviticus 18 – 20 (cf. Ezek. 18:5–17), and his message of judgment depicts the threats of the curses of Leviticus 26 being actualized (cf. Ezek. 5:10–17). Not only the Sinai covenant has been breached; the Davidic covenant also has been broken by the unfaithfulness of David's descendants. As a result, the central blessing of both covenants, God's dwelling in the midst of his people, will be removed. God will abandon his earthly *temple on Mt Zion, leaving Jerusalem defenceless against the Babylonian invaders (9 – 11).

But this abandonment is neither full nor final. God's covenant purpose cannot be broken, even by repeated human unfaithfulness, for the honour of the Lord's holy name depends on its fulfilment (36:20–32). So he has preserved for himself a *remnant of his people. The remnant are not those who remain in the *land after Jerusalem's destruction; though these may think of themselves as Abraham's heirs, they are not his true children (33:24–29). But the glory of the Lord which departed from Jerusalem was seen by Ezekiel in the land of exile (1:1), in keeping with God's promise to be 'a little sanctuary' (AV) (or 'a sanctuary … for a little while', NRSV) to those in exile (11:16). They are the true heirs of the promise, who will return to possess the land and the blessings of the covenant, not because they deserve it but through sheer sovereign grace (36:24–32).

In that day, there will still be tribulations, depicted in the imagery of the cosmic struggle with Gog from the land of Magog (38 – 39). These, however, will no longer be the result of covenant curses as their previous tribulations were (39:23). Now the Lord will act to rescue his people from all their difficulties, pouring out his wrath not on Israel but on their enemies (38:18–19). This cosmic victory

over the forces of chaos is the precursor to a cosmic reordering of the universe, through the reestablishment of the temple and the return of God's glory to inhabit it (40 – 46), which in turn leads to a renovation of the entire Promised Land, watered by the new River of Life (47 – 48). The heart of this visionary renovation is, however, just what has already been promised in Ezekiel 37:26–28: the fulfilment of the covenant promise of God's dwelling peacefully in the midst of his people.

Sin and judgment

Those who are condemned most prominently in Ezekiel 1 – 39 on account of their *sin are pushed to the margins of the renewed society envisaged in Ezekiel 40 – 48. No one escapes criticism entirely in the opening chapters of the book: the kings and princes, priests, prophets and lay leadership are all faulted for their sins, but not all equally. Similarly, all those who are permitted access to the renewed Promised Land are privileged, but not all equally. Ezekiel envisages a hierarchically graded society, in which status is determined by access to the central holy spaces. No one, not even the prophet himself, is permitted access to the Most Holy Place at the centre of the temple. The most privileged class of people are the Zadokite priests, who alone have access to the Inner Court. Next in rank and access are the Levites and the prince. At the outskirts are the laity, whose access to the temple and its services is extremely limited. Even such limited access is itself a precious privilege, however. The 'outsiders' such as the false prophets, will not enter the land at all (13:9). The Lord will return upon the head of all the people their ways (9:10).

Themes from Ezekiel in the New Testament

Uncreation – re-creation

The note of impending judgment found in the opening vision of Ezekiel recurs in its NT analogue, the vision of John on the island of Patmos (Rev. 1:1–20). The allusions to Ezekiel 1 in *Revelation 1 include the images of blazing fire and glowing bronze, a human figure surrounded by radiance, and the noise of rushing waters. Other images from Ezekiel 1 appear in the vision of the heavenly throne room in Revelation 4: a throne on a surface like crystal, four living creatures covered with eyes, and partaking of the likeness of a lion, an eagle, an ox and a human being. Yet along with the similarities there are also striking differences. The 'expanse' becomes a 'sea of glass'. The four living creatures now each take on the likeness of one kind of animal, instead of their having the faces of all four, and now they have six wings instead of four. The eyes have moved from the wheels, which have disappeared, on to the living creatures themselves. The message remains one of judgment to come on the unrepentant, as well as hope for those who persevere, but now it is no longer directed to Israel and Judah but to the seven churches of Asia Minor.

God's re-creative work has also widened in scope with the coming of the new 'son of man', *Jesus Christ. He is the second Adam, who by his obedience undoes the effects of the first Adam's fall (1 Cor. 15:44–49; Rom. 5:19). He is the one on whom the Spirit rested in fullness of power and through whom the Spirit is poured out upon the *church, to create the new community of his people. He acts as the precursor and firstfruits of the new community, experiencing first the *death that is rightly ours, and then the *victory which will ultimately be ours also. If we have died with Christ, we shall certainly live with him (Rom. 6:8). Because Christ has been raised physically and gloriously, we also shall be raised physically and gloriously: the first fruits provide the assurance of the full *harvest, and even now we are indwelt by the Spirit who is at work in us, changing us into what we ought to be (Rom. 8:11). The Christian hope is not merely a hope of resurrection in general but is focused concretely on Christ in us, the hope of glory (Col. 1:27). This life-giving Spirit (1 Cor. 15:45) is now poured out not only on renewed Israel but on the Gentiles as well. They too, though once 'far away', now have access with Israel to the Father by the same Spirit (Eph. 2:18).

Covenant curse – covenant establishment

By nature, all humankind stands in breach of a covenant relationship with God. This is true not simply of Jews, who have broken the Sinaitic covenant (Rom. 2:17–27), but even of Gentiles and pre-Mosaic humanity who, because of their genetic relationship to Adam, stand under condemnation for Adam's sin (Rom. 5:14). Thus in the vivid pictorial imagery of Revelation, the wrath of the Lamb

upon the earth is expressed in the form of four horsemen, symbolizing the covenant curses of conquest, the sword, famine and death (Rev. 6:1–8). However, all of the OT covenants find their consummation in Christ. He is the one who fulfils the conditions of the covenant for us, enabling us as his people to experience every blessing in him (Eph. 1:3). He is the one who took upon himself the curse which we deserved as covenant breakers, so that we might be redeemed (see *Redemption) by his blood (Eph. 1:7). The blessing of life in God's presence is for all those whose names are written in the Lamb's book of life (Rev. 21:27).

The fulfilment of the covenant promise of the dwelling of God in the midst of his people is also found in the person of Christ. He is the glory made manifest, the dwelling of God among humanity (John 1:14). Jesus spoke of his body as the temple in John 2:19, when he said 'Destroy this temple and I will raise it again in three days.' There on the cross, God's abandonment of his chosen temple found its fullest expression, as Jesus was forsaken by his Father, not for his sin but for the sins of his people.

This world continues to be a place of tribulation for God's people (Acts 14:23). This is depicted in a variety of ways in the book of Revelation, including the assault of Gog and Magog, a final battle loosely based on Ezekiel 38 – 39. Revelation's description of the final state of believers, the new Jerusalem, is also clearly influenced by the vision of the heavenly temple in Ezekiel 40 – 48. Like Ezekiel, John is carried away to a great and high mountain to see this city (Rev. 21:10) and is accompanied by an angel with a measuring rod (21:15). The city is square, with a great high wall around it and prominent gates, like Ezekiel's temple, while a river of life flows from its centre (22:1). There the Lord will dwell in the midst of his people, in fulfilment of the central promise of the covenant. Yet the differences from Ezekiel's vision are equally striking. The city of Revelation has no temple (21:22); in addition, there are twelve gates around the perimeter, not the three gates of Ezekiel's temple, and they stand perpetually wide open to the nations (21:12, 25).

Sin and judgment

In Ezekiel, those who have been most faithful (the Zadokites) are rewarded with the greatest access to God, while those who have been less faithful (Levites, princes, people) are progressively at a greater distance from the throne. This graduation of *reward should be neither over-stressed nor under-stressed; there is real differentiation on the basis of merit, but the renewed people all receive the fundamental blessing of being restored to God's land, with God's dwelling in their midst.

Both of these aspects of Ezekiel's teaching are present in the NT. In the vision of the new Jerusalem in Revelation 21, the fundamental equality of all the saints is stressed. All are made perfect and stand in the very presence of God himself, in the heavenly Most Holy Place itself, which is the entire city. This is true because of the perfect *righteousness given to all who are in Christ, which forms the basis for their full inheritance. In him, through *faith, every Christian receives the righteousness of God (Rom. 3:22). Similarly, in the parable of the workers in the vineyard, those who have worked hardest and longest receive the same reward as those who are hired at the eleventh hour (Matt. 20:1–16).

Yet there are also texts which seem to affirm a gradation in reward. In 1 Corinthians 3, Paul draws a contrast between two builders. Both are Christians, building on the only foundation, Jesus Christ (1 Cor. 3:11), but one builds with gold and precious stones, while the other builds with wood and straw (3:12). The works of both will be exposed on the day of judgment, and their quality will be tested with fire (3:13). If what has been built survives, the builder will receive a reward. If it is burned up, the builder will suffer loss (3:15). In both cases the builder is saved; only the rewards are different.

Intriguingly, the two versions of the parable of the talents present complementary pictures. In Matthew, the focus is on the sameness of the reward which the faithful stewards receive: the one who has been faithful with two talents hears his master say exactly the same words as the one who was faithful with five: 'Well done, good and faithful servant! You have been faithful with a few things; I will put you in charge of many things. Come and share your master's happiness!' (Matt. 25:21). Both have been equally responsible with different amounts and so receive the same reward. In Luke's account, on the other hand, the servant whose faithful stewardship of the money resulted in a ten-fold increase is rewarded with charge of ten cities, while the one whose stewardship resulted in a fivefold increase is awarded charge over five cities (Luke 19:17, 19). They start with the same amount, but their fruitfulness is different, and so they receive a graded reward.

Conclusion

The main images and themes found in the book of Ezekiel are frequently picked up in the NT, even though Ezekiel is not explicitly cited as often as some other OT books (e.g. Isaiah). Yet these images are rarely borrowed entirely intact or treated as 'literal' prophecies. What the NT typically does is to show how Ezekiel's themes look when viewed through the lens of fulfilment in Christ. This is perhaps most evident when the new Jerusalem of Revelation 21 – 22 is compared with Ezekiel's heavenly temple. The points of contact are numerous and detailed, but key emphases have shifted, because with the coming of Christ the final temple has changed shape and taken on flesh.

Bibliography

D. I. Block, *The Gods of the Nations* (Grand Rapids and Leicester, [2]2000); I. M. Duguid, *Ezekiel and the Leaders of Israel* (Leiden, 1994); J. D. Levenson, *Theology of the Program of Restoration of Ezekiel 40 – 48* (Missoula, 1976); K. R. Stevenson, *The Vision of Transformation: The Territorial Rhetoric of Ezekiel 40 – 48* (Atlanta, 1996).

I. M. DUGUID

DANIEL

The opening verses of the book of Daniel (1:1–2) present the reader with what several scholars see as the main theme of the book: the sovereignty of God (e.g. D. N. Fewell, *Circle of Sovereignty*; R. S. Wallace, *The Lord is King*). Here we read of two human kings, Jehoiakim of Judah and Nebuchadnezzar of *Babylon. Nebuchadnezzar has besieged and captured Jerusalem and looted its temple. The natural conclusion to draw would be that behind Nebuchadnezzar's triumph lay the power of his god. That is why he puts the vessels taken from the Jerusalem temple in his god's treasury. However, Daniel 1:2 asserts that his triumph came about because the Lord (the God of Israel) gave Jehoiakim into Nebuchadnezzar's power. So we are introduced to the themes of human sovereignty and divine sovereignty, and to the relationship between them.

The sovereignty of *God

The references to God in Daniel are significant (P. R. Davies, *Daniel*, pp. 82–83). It is only in Daniel's prayer in chapter 9 that we find the personal name Yahweh. Its alternative, 'the Lord', is also limited to this chapter and 1:2. Elsewhere the general term 'god' is used. This expresses the fact that 'the God of Daniel' (6:26) is not just the God of the Jews (Yahweh) but is *the* God, who is God of all nations. In a pagan context this is expressed in terms of Daniel's God being the supreme God of the pantheon, and so he is called 'the Most High (God)' (4:17; 5:18), and 'God of gods' (2:47). For the faithful Jews these titles express the belief that their God is the unique and absolute divine sovereign. By use of these titles the pagan rulers are brought to confess that the God of the Jews is at least the one who exercises ultimate sovereignty among the gods.

Because the God of the Jews is God of gods he is also 'Lord of kings' (2:47). This truth is driven home time and again in Daniel, but perhaps is expressed most explicitly in chapter 4. Here we are told that because of his hubris in thinking that his royal power and glory are all his own achievement, Nebuchadnezzar is struck with some form of madness and driven away from human society to live with the animals for 'seven times' until he learns that 'the Most High has sovereignty over the kingdom of mortals, and gives it to whom he will' (4:25, NRSV). The importance of this lesson is reinforced by the fact that in the next chapter Daniel reminds Belshazzar of it and reproaches him for not taking heed of it (5:18–22).

As 'the Lord of kings' God is the God of history. In this regard three characteristics of God are emphasized in Daniel: 'God *knows* all, he *controls* all, and he *rescues*' (Davies, *Daniel*, p. 86). In chapter 2 we see the close connection between God's knowledge of history and his control of it. Through Daniel God reveals to Nebuchadnezzar the future course of history. Only the God who controls the future can know it and reveal it. God's control of history is expressed in the vision in

chapter 7, where God is seen on the throne of the universe deciding the fate of the superpowers of history and giving dominion to whom he will. But the God of Daniel is not a remote sovereign. He acts within history, especially to deliver those faithful to him when they are oppressed. In Daniel there are two stories of miraculous deliverance, each of which ends in a royal confession of this divine characteristic. After the deliverance of Shadrach, Meshach and Abednego from the furnace, Nebuchadnezzar is moved to confess concerning their God that, 'there is no other god who is able to deliver in this way' (3:29). When he finds Daniel safe after a night in the lions' den, Darius says of Daniel's God, 'He delivers and rescues, he works signs and wonders in heaven and on earth' (6:27). The ultimate act of rescue will come at the end of time when, as an angel says to Daniel, 'But at that time your people shall be delivered, everyone who is found written in the book' (12:1). The dead will be raised so that the righteous can receive their reward and the oppressors their punishment.

Belief in Yahweh's control of history is a characteristic of the OT, but elsewhere it is usually expressed in terms of his control of specific historical events (*e.g.* Is. 10:5–19; 45:1–13; Hab. 1:5–11). However, 'It is expressed here with a universality that is unusual. Daniel's testimony extends to God's control of history as a whole' (J. E. Goldingay, *Daniel*, WBT, p. 24) (see *Providence).

God's control of history is not always evident. Often it is the beasts of the human superpowers which seem to be in control. Daniel asserts that the time will come when all human sovereignty will be replaced by the rule of God (see *Kingdom of God). So, in the dream of chapter 2, the climax of history is the coming of a stone 'cut out, not by human hands' (v. 34) which demolishes the statue representing human empires and becomes a great mountain filling the whole earth. The vision of chapter 7 ends with the destruction of the little horn and the giving of an everlasting kingdom to 'the people of the holy ones of the Most High'.

Human sovereignty

The witness of Daniel is that, until the end comes, divine sovereignty normally operates through human rulers. God 'deposes kings and sets up kings' (2:21) and gives the kingdom of mortals to whom he will (4:17), but the human rulers do have considerable power. Although God sometimes has to exercise his sovereignty *over* human rulers because of their hubris (*e.g.* chs. 5, 7), he wants to exercise it *through* human rulers. This is the implicit message of Daniel 4. As Goldingay says, 'Actually the chapter assumes that if God's kingship is acknowledged, human sovereignty can then find its place. At the end of the story, even the majesty and glory of human kingship are affirmed' (*Daniel*, WBT, pp. 27–28).

The book of Daniel draws a number of explicit and implicit contrasts between human kingdoms and God's kingdom. In chapter 2 the statue speaks of the transience and fragility of human kingdoms compared with the kingdom God will set up, which 'shall never be destroyed, nor shall this kingdom be left to another people ... it shall stand for ever' (2:44). In chapter 3 Nebuchadnezzar asks, 'who is the god that will deliver you out of my hands?' (3:15), assuming that the answer is, 'there is none', only to find that the real answer is 'the God of Shadrach, Meshach and Abednego' (3:28). In chapter 6 Darius discovers that once he has signed a decree which consigns Daniel to the lions' den he is powerless to deliver him from it, whereas Daniel's God does have that power.

The greatest contrast is found in chapter 7. To a degree chapter 4 prepares the way for the message of this chapter. In chapter 4 we see that when a human ruler fails to acknowledge the sovereignty of God and gives way to hubris he becomes subhuman. He becomes like a beast of the field. So, in chapter 7 the human superpowers, all of which to some extent do give way to hubris, are depicted as beasts. In contrast to this, the kingdom of God which replaces the rule of the beasts is depicted by 'one like a human being' (7:13). The giving of 'dominion, glory and kingship' to this figure echoes Genesis 1:26–28 and Psalm 8:5–8 (see the discussion of the 'Adamic' background to Dan. 7:13–14 in A. LaCocque, *Daniel in His Time*, pp. 143–161). It implies the culmination of God's purpose for human beings in creating them in his image and likeness to exercise dominion over the earth as his representatives. It is when we recognize, and live under, the sovereign rule of God that we become truly human and fulfil our destiny.

The theology of history

The explicitly more universal view of God's control over history which is found in Daniel is a characteristic of other more clearly apocalyptic books. A distinction is often made between the deterministic view of history held by the apocalyptists and a more open view held by the Hebrew prophets (see *Prophetic books; also D. S. Russell, *The Method and Message of Jewish Apocalyptic* [London, 1971], pp. 230–234). Even when the prophets declared what seemed to be a settled decision of God (*e.g.* Jonah declaring the destruction of Nineveh) the possibility of the hearers' responses changing things seems always to have been implied.

How far the view of history in Daniel is deterministic is debatable. Clearly the framework of history seems fixed in the dream of chapter 2 and the vision of chapter 7. The long survey of history in chapter 11 deals with specific events in the reigns of specific rulers, and the statement 'for what is determined shall be done' (11:36) seems quite deterministic. However, the equally deterministic language of 4:17 is followed by Daniel's plea to Nebuchadnezzar in 4:27 which implies that this is a warning of something which need not happen if the king responds rightly. Also, the long prayer of repentance in chapter 9 assumes that human response to God can affect the course of history. Goldingay seems to strike the right balance when he says, 'Daniel assumes that human beings make real decisions which do shape history, yet that human decision-making does not necessarily have the last word in history. Daniel affirms the sovereignty of God in history, sometimes working via the process of human decision-making, sometimes working despite it' (*Daniel*, WBT, p. 24).

In some exilic and post-exilic books of the OT (Ezekiel, Zechariah) angels (see *Spiritual powers) play a significant role in the mediation of revelation. This is so in Daniel, but here angels also apparently play an active role in the historical process. While this could be taken to imply a distancing of God from human history, it is more likely that it is simply a more nuanced way of speaking of God's involvement in history than that used by the Hebrew prophets. Isaiah 43:1–3 promises that God will be present with his people when they pass through the fire. The presence of an angelic being ('a son of the gods', 3:25 mg.) with the three young men in the furnace is not a diluting of that promise, but a fulfilment of it. The angel mediates God's presence in those particular circumstances. Talk of angels in Daniel seems to be a more formalized way of portraying God as really involved in the world, while safeguarding God's transcendence over history, than the references to 'the angel of the Lord' or the 'Spirit of the Lord' that are found in earlier OT literature.

The rather allusive references in Daniel (10:13–14; 10:20 – 11:1; 12:1) to heavenly powers which correspond in some way to earthly powers can be seen as developing the assumption found earlier in the OT that the outcome of battles on earth reflects the involvement of heaven. Usually this is a matter of heavenly forces aiding Israel against otherwise overwhelming odds (*e.g.* Josh. 5:13–15; Judg. 5:19–20; 2 Sam. 5:22–25; 2 Chr. 20:22–23). What is being expressed here, and comes out even more clearly in Daniel, is that there is more to history, indeed to reality, than we can see. History is not merely the outworking of human decisions and actions, though these play an important part in it. Nations, and other entities which embody power, are more than purely human and earthly. There is a suprahuman, spiritual realm that 'meshes' in some way with the human, earthly realm. Because of this, conflicts on earth have their counterpart in heavenly conflicts. However, it is important to note that Daniel does not fall into a simple dualism. The Most High God is not matched by some equally powerful opponent. The opposition comes only at the level of the 'princes' of the nations. God remains the supreme sovereign in heaven and on earth.

Although the Hebrew prophets sometimes use what appears to be 'end of the world' language, it seems to refer to events *within* history rather than those at the *end* of history (*e.g.* Is. 13:10; 34:4). This is true even of the reference to a 'new heaven and a new earth' in Isaiah 65:17; 66:22. However, Daniel 12:1–3 does seem to envisage the end of history, with its reference to resurrection, judgment and the transformation of 'those who are wise' (see *Eschatology).

Living under God's sovereignty

There is a general consensus that the original purpose of the stories in Daniel 1 – 6 was to commend a particular lifestyle. (W. L. Humphreys, 'A life-style for diaspora: A study of the tales of Esther and Daniel', *JBL* 92, 1973, pp. 211–223). This is the lifestyle of those who are seeking to live under the sovereignty of God. Such a lifestyle is based on *faithfulness to God in the face of competing claims for loyalty. In chapter 1 Daniel and his companions are under pressure to become 'good Babylonians'. They decide, for the sake of their own integrity as much as for any public display, that they need to draw a line and remain faithful to their God. Faithfulness to God becomes a matter of defying human sovereignty in chapters 3 and 6. Such faithfulness calls for trust in God when faced with threats intended to undermine loyalty to him. In the stories in Daniel God proves to be worthy of such trust by being faithful to Daniel and his companions. One way of expressing trust is through *prayer, and so it is not surprising that prayer is one of the characteristics of Daniel throughout the book. When faced with problems he seeks the answer through prayer (2:17–18; 9:3). It is his habit to pray daily (6:10).

Living under the sovereignty of God means accepting responsibility for the consequences of rebelling against that sovereignty. Daniel does this in the prayer of confession in chapter 9. He recognizes the justice of God's dealing with Israel (v. 7) and that the disaster of the *exile was the result of their continual *sinful rebellion (vv. 9–10). His plea for forgiveness and restoration is based purely on God's mercy (vv. 9, 18).

Although Daniel 3 and 6 tell of the prompt deliverance from peril of faithful Jews, no Jew could have read those stories in a simplistic way. They knew, as 3:17–18 indicates, that although their God *could* deliver them promptly and miraculously from any situation, it was not the case that he always (or even usually) did so. The laments among the Psalms testify to this. In 7:21, 23; 8:24; 11:32–35 it is made clear that there are times when the faithful people of God are called upon to endure *suffering, sometimes even martyrdom. It is in response to the seeming injustice of this, and the apparent impugning of either God's faithfulness to his people or his sovereignty, that the promise of resurrection (see *Death and resurrection) and *judgment comes (12:1–4). Death is no barrier to either God's faithfulness or his sovereignty.

Daniel and the NT

Probably the most important influence of Daniel on the NT lies in the role of Daniel 7:13 in the development of the 'Son of Man' tradition. This is a complex topic which cannot be discussed in any detail here (for a good survey see the essay by A. Y. Collins on 'The Influence of Daniel on the New Testament' in J. J. Collins, *Daniel*, pp. 90–112). Despite arguments to the contrary, many would agree with C. F. D. Moule that 'there is a strong case ... for the view that the phrase belonged originally among *Jesus' own words as a reference to the vindicated human figure of Dan. 7' (*The Origin of Christology*, [Cambridge, 1977], p. 17). If so, it throws important light on his understanding of himself and his mission. The 'Son of Man' sayings in the Synoptic Gospels fall into three groups, each with an emphasis that is rooted in Daniel 7. There are those in which Jesus is speaking about his earthly ministry, which tend to speak of his authority (*e.g.* Mark 2:10, 28). In a second, larger group of sayings, Jesus speaks of his rejection, suffering, death and resurrection (*e.g.* Mark 8:31; Luke 9:44). The third, and largest, group speaks of Jesus' eschatological glory, including his acting as judge on God's behalf (*e.g.* Matt. 13:41–43; Mark 14:62).

Another phrase from Daniel that has left its mark in the NT is 'the abomination that desolates' (9:27; 12:11; *cf.* Matt. 24:15 and Mark 13:14). This is more than simply the borrowing of a phrase. It points to an understanding of history according to the pattern found in Daniel.

The book of *Revelation contains many allusions to Daniel. There are allusions to Daniel in Revelation 1:7a, 13; 14:14. The vision of the beasts in Revelation 13 clearly draws on the imagery of Daniel 7:2–8. Whereas in Daniel four beasts rise out of the sea, in Revelation 13:1–10 a single beast rises out of the sea, but combines characteristics of each of the four beasts of Daniel. Clearly this empire represents an epitome of all that is worst in rebellious human powers. Yet for John, as for Daniel, despite all appearances on earth, God remains the sovereign on the throne. In both the vision of the heavenly throne room (Rev. 5:11) and the vision of final judgment (Rev. 20:12) there are allusions to Daniel's vision of the heavenly throne room with God acting as judge of the human empires (Dan. 7:10).

Bibliography

J. J. Collins, *Daniel* (Minneapolis, 1993); J. J. Collins, 'The Danielic Son of Man', in *idem* (ed.), *The Sceptre and the Star* (New York, 1995), pp. 173–194; P. R. Davies, *Daniel* (Sheffield, 1985); D. N. Fewell, *Circle of Sovereignty: Plotting Politics in the Book of Daniel* (Nashville, [2]1991); J. E. Goldingay, *Daniel* (Dallas, 1989); *idem*, *Daniel*, WBT (Dallas and London, 1989); A. LaCocque, *Daniel in His Time* (Columbia, 1988); R. S. Wallace, *The Message of Daniel*, BST (Leicester, 1979).

E. C. LUCAS

HOSEA

Hosea's life and God's message

Hosea was a *prophet with a message for his own people. He was from the northern kingdom of *Israel and prophesied there. The second verse of the book may be a reference to his call. It speaks of the 'beginning' of *God's word to Hosea, which is a command to take to himself a woman of harlotry. This unconventional formulation points to the nature of Hosea's ministry. He was called not only to proclaim a message; his personal life was to dramatize God's relationship with his faithless *people.

As with most OT prophets, not much is known about Hosea. It was their message, not their life story, that was considered important and so was preserved. The information in the first three chapters about Hosea's *marriage(s) and his children is supplied only because it signifies God's broken relationship with his people. Hosea's personal circumstances must have strongly influenced both the man and his message, as well as other people. (See *Prophetic books.)

Hosea's God

Hosea usually calls God 'YHWH', a name which signifies the unique relationship between God and his people Israel. The allusion in 1:9 to the initial revelation of the divine name to Moses (Exod. 3:14 is formulated as an abrogation of the *covenant between God and his people: 'You are not my people and I am not your I AM.'

No other book in the OT includes such a detailed description of God's inner feelings as Hosea does. The prophet uses a variety of striking metaphors to depict God and his people. God is portrayed primarily as the deceived and forsaken husband with Israel as his faithless but still beloved wife. In a moving allegory, Hosea describes Yahweh as a loving parent who bemoans the fate of a persistently rebellious child who brings punishment upon itself (11:1–9).

Hosea's style, message and metaphors influenced later prophets, especially *Jeremiah and *Ezekiel. This influence is evident especially in their use of marriage and *love metaphors to express the relationship between God and his people, and also in their idealizing of the period of *wilderness wanderings (Jer. 2:2–8; 3:6–13; Ezek. 16; 20; 23).

Prophet of doom

In contrast to the popular prophets, many of the canonical prophets proclaimed imminent disaster for a faithless people. The message Hosea had to deliver to his contemporaries was dominated by oracles of *judgment and included little *hope. However, in the first three chapters each group of judgment oracles is followed by the promise of a future era of obedience and re-established relationship with God (1:10 – 2:1; 2:14–23; 3:5). This redactional arrangement is evident also in the other two sections of the book (11:10–11; 14:5–9).

Hosea's message must be understood in its historical context. The period of his ministry is described in biblical documents (2 Kgs. 14 – 17; 2 Chr. 25 – 28) and in Assyrian annals and royal inscriptions. Hosea became a prophet in Jeroboam II's reign, *i.e.* some time before 745 BC, and his active ministry probably ended shortly before the destruction of Samaria in 721 BC; nothing in the book suggests that the nation has already fallen.

Hosea became a prophet at a time when both Israel and *Judah were politically stable and economically prosperous. Assyria was the local superpower, but was content at this stage to limit its direct rule to territories east of the Euphrates. However, the religious life of the nation was unsatisfactory: Baalism threatened the *worship of Yahweh. This is the background of the first four chapters. Hosea denounces Israel, describing the nation as a faithless wife engaged in harlotry.

The political situation soon changed dramatically, as reflected in Hosea's message from 5:8 onwards. In Assyria a powerful ruler, Tiglath-Pileser III, ascended the throne and in a short time had greatly expanded Assyrian rule in the Middle East. In Israel political instability weakened the nation. Foreign policy in the following decades was a choice between accommodation to Assyrian rule or resistance with support from Egypt. Hosea condemns this kind of political manoeuvering (7:8–12). The need is for *repentance and a return to the LORD, the God of Israel.

In the 730s anti-Assyrian elements took over Israel and (with Syria) tried to force Judah into an alliance against Assyria. This led to the humiliating subjugation of Israel, and Hoshea, the last king, had to pledge obedience to Assyria. In these chaotic circumstances Hosea played an active prophetic role. In 5:8–14 the prophet steps forward like a watchman to announce imminent disaster for both Israel and Judah. No political strategy can avert it, for it is God's punishment of his rebellious people.

Chapter 13 portrays Israel without a king and close to annihilation, probably in the late 720s after further rebellions against Assyria (2 Kgs. 17:4). These led to the final destruction of the northern kingdom. Hoshea was imprisoned; Samaria fell and a large proportion of the people was deported. These tragic events were evidence that Hosea was a true prophet. His messages were collected as a warning to Judah and to future generations; they made it clear that the ultimate reason for the fall of the northern kingdom was neither political circumstances nor Yahweh's inability to save, but the faithlessness of the people.

It must have been a painful task for Hosea to prophesy doom to his own people. One short passage reflects his personal experience of scorn and hostility (9:7–8). The saying 'The prophet is a fool, the man of spirit is mad' is clearly a quotation from his opponents. Like so many prophets and godly people, Hosea never gained the response he sought from his nation.

The first commandment

The dominant message of Hosea's oracles is the necessity of strict adherence to the first commandment. The prophet's marriage underlines the impossibility of compromise.

Hosea reinstitutes and radicalizes the 'Yahweh alone' movement led by the prophet Elijah in the preceding century.

Like *Amos, his contemporary, Hosea speaks against social injustice and violence, especially in relation to specific places, but he relates these evils more explicitly to the lack of '*faithfulness, devotion and knowledge of God' (4:1–3). These are relational-theological terms for *truthfulness, *obedience and responsibility. Two of them recur several times in the book: ḥesed, translated 'devotion' (2:19; 6:4, 6; 10:12; 12:6), and 'to know/knowledge of God' (2:8, 20; 4:1; 5:4–6; 6:3, 6; 8:2; 11:3; 13:4).

Hosea strongly emphasizes the responsibility of the nation's leaders, both religious and political. Priests, prophets, kings and others are repeatedly accused of leading the people astray (4:4–9; 5:1, 10–11; 10:5–8; 13:9–11).

A crucial issue underlying Hosea's message is the relationship between Yahwistic religion and Baalism. The prophet condemns a syncretistic religion incorporating Yahwism and Baalism. The people even call Yahweh 'my Baal' (2:16). Evidently Elijah's 'Yahweh alone' movement has not produced lasting results.

Our knowledge of Canaanite religion is limited. The biblical texts are strongly polemical and yield little information. Even the Ugaritic texts are of only limited help in reconstructing the Baal cult. The common depiction of Canaanite religion, largely derived from Hosea, is of a fertility cult to which sacred prostitution and licentious sexual behaviour were integral. This view has been increasingly contested, mainly because of the lack of clear evidence for it (see e.g. R. Albertz, *A History of Israelite Religion in the OT Period*, I, pp. 171–177).

An important metaphor in Hosea's oracles is that of 'harlotry' (the root znh occurs fourteen times). It signifies that Israel, by turning to other gods, has broken its historical bond with the Lord who led them out of Egypt and made them his people. Explicit sexual imagery is frequently used, especially in the early chapters. But does this language refer to sexual behaviour in the context of a fertility cult, or is it merely metaphorical? In Hosea 4:11–19 people gather at high places for worship. The detailed description of sexual activities indicates that the sexual language had a double function: it served as a metaphor for defection from Yahweh but it also referred to sexual behaviour that was part of the Canaanite cult.

H. W. Wolff has argued that it was traditional in Hosea's time for young women to engage in a Canaanite bridal rite involving cultic prostitution. The theory is largely dependent on comparisons with ancient Mesopotamia and late sources such as Herodotus. According to this view, Hosea's wife Gomer was called a woman of 'harlotries' because she had taken part in such practices. J. L. Mays claims that Gomer was a cult-prostitute while G. I. Davies argues that she was a common prostitute. If the term is purely metaphorical it signifies simply that Hosea's wife and children took part in the syncretistic religion of the day (so D. Stuart).

The woman in chapter 3 may be the 'Gomer' of chapter 1. Hosea's renewed relationship with her would then symbolize the reunion between the Lord and his people. But the text does not make this identification explicit, and the terminology in chapter 3 differs from that in chapter 1. Hosea is told again to love a woman (unspecified) who has a lover and is an *adulteress (3:1). Israel is 'without king' (3:4), which indicates that this command was given late in Hosea's ministry, near to the time of the nation's demise. Gomer may have left Hosea at some point, in which case the description in chapter 3 could be appropriate for her at this time. Whether the women are the same or not, the focus of the oracles is on the irrationality of a love that extends to the unworthy. Hosea's actions symbolize the love of a holy God for his people, which continues in spite of their unfaithfulness. Their breach of the first commandment might have led to the covenant's being annulled; only because of Yahweh's love is it maintained.

Covenant

Scholars debate whether the Mosaic covenant and law had been established by the eighth century. The references to God's 'covenant' and 'law' in 8:1 indicate an awareness at this time of a treaty between God and Israel (cf. Amos 2:4). The breach of this formal agreement was the basis for the prophets' bold accusations against Israel. It also explains why Hosea's use of the marriage metaphor is so appropriate: Israel has broken a formal relationship with its God

Hosea in the NT

Hosea's radical message about allegiance to the one God is echoed in the preaching of later prophets and in the NT, where *Jesus extends our understanding of the God who loves his people but also asks for their 'faithfulness, devotion and knowledge of God'. And Paul widens the meaning of *idolatry (Eph. 5:5; Col. 3:5) to include the whole lifestyle of the world without God.

Hosea's depiction of a loving and almighty God in deep anguish because of humankind's rebellion and the tragic consequences this brings upon them is embodied by Jesus when he weeps over a Jerusalem heading for destruction (Luke 19:41–44; Matt. 23:37; Luke 13:34–35). Here, as in Hosea, 'the suffering God' appears, and his involvement in the world eventually leads him to the cross.

The words 'out of Egypt I called my son' in Hosea 11:1 refer to the *Exodus and the early days of the nation. In one of Matthew's 'fulfilment quotations' (2:15) this passage is applied to the return, after Herod's death, of Jesus and his parents to Israel from their sojourn in Egypt. The meaning of the text has been extended to apply to another, analogous event. The common element is that of God as a father caring for his son. In Hosea the *redemption of the nation is described in terms of God's *adoption and care of a little child. In the NT God literally brings a little child out of Egypt, and it is through this child that all humankind will be redeemed from slavery.

Hosea prophesied about an era when those who were 'not God's people' would be called 'sons of the living God' (1:10; 2:23). Paul sees the fulfilment of this prophecy among the followers of Jesus, who constitute the new people of God that knows no ethnic or national barriers (Rom. 9:25–26). (See *Nations.)

Bibliography

R. Albertz, *A History of Israelite Religion in the Old Testament Period*, 2 vols. (London, 1994); G. I. Davies, *Hosea*, NCB (Grand Rapids, 1992); J. L. Mays, *Hosea*, OTL (London, 1969); J. M. Miller and J. H. Hayes, *A History of Ancient Israel* (Philadelphia, 1986); D. Stuart, *Hosea–Jonah*, WBC (Waco, 1987); H. W. Wolff, *Hosea*, Hermeneia (Philadelphia, 1974).

N. E. L. BOSTROM

JOEL

Introduction

The book of Joel is written in the context of a cataclysmic plague of locusts which have ravaged the Judean countryside (1:2–4). The message of the book deals with the immediate circumstances but also looks beyond them to the eschatological 'Day of the Lord' when God will judge the nations.

Contents

The countryside has been devastated by the worst infestation of locusts in living memory; indeed the worst in the nation's history (1:2). Apparently, the problem has been exacerbated by drought and fire (1:19–20). As a result of the devastation, drunkards are told to weep because there is no wine (1:5), priests to mourn because there are no sacrifices (1:9), and farmers to despair because the harvest is ruined (1:11). The message to the priests is expanded: they are commanded to wear sackcloth, to declare a fast and to lead the nation in prayer at the temple (1:13–14).

Although the circumstances of the nation are dire, the prophet warns that there is worse to come; the Day of the Lord is near (1:15). Contrary to popular belief, the Day of the Lord will be a day of terrible destruction (*cf.* Amos 5:18). The locust invasion is used as a metaphor for God's universal day of *judgment when he will lead his 'large and mighty army' against the nations (2:1–11). The Day of the Lord is a 'day of darkness and gloom' (2:2, NIV) when nations are in anguish (2:6), the earth shakes, the sky trembles and the sun, the moon and the stars stop shining (2:10). This great and dreadful day of God's judgment is inevitable unless the people *repent (2:12–17). This repentance must involve a genuine change of heart and not merely an external show of rending garments (2:13).

However, the message of Joel is not one of unrelenting doom; the book also contains a message of hope for God's people. God promises national security (2:20), productive crops (2:19, 24), abundant rainfall (2:23), and a close relationship with himself (2:26). Even the animals will benefit because of the renewed harmony between God and his people (2:22). This harmonious relationship will culminate in spiritual renewal, so that 'sons and daughters will prophesy', 'old men will dream dreams' and 'young men will see visions' (2:28). The Day of the Lord will be a day of darkness and blood – 'a great and dreadful day' – but it will also be a day of salvation for those who call on the name of the Lord (2:30–32). In particular, *Jerusalem will be the place of God's deliverance (2:32).

The Day of the Lord will involve the judgment of the surrounding *nations who have mistreated Israel (3:1–16). They have scattered Israel among the nations, divided its land, cast lots for its people, and sold its children (3:1–3). The Lord will judge those nations in the valley of Jehoshaphat (which means 'the Lord will judge'). Further indictments are brought against Tyre and Sidon and all the regions of Philistia who, without provocation, raided Israel's wealth and sold its inhabitants to the Greeks (3:4–6). These nations will suffer the same fate as they inflicted on Israel (3:7–8).

Very graphic and powerful images describe these nations as they gather to await God's decision about them: 'Multitudes, multitudes, in the valley of decision' (3:14). The accompanying signs (the sun and moon becoming dark while the stars no longer shine) and the metaphors used ('the Lord will roar from Zion'), indicate that the judgment will be carried out by God himself (3:16).

The book concludes with a description of Israel as a restored Eden. In contrast, Edom will be a desert and Egypt desolate (3:17–21).

Theological message

The Lord is sovereign and powerful

The book of Joel emphasizes the greatness of God in terms of his powerful activities in the created order. The declaration, 'Surely he has done great things' is repeated to highlight its importance (2:20–21). Far from being remote and passive, the Lord controls the rain, sending it or withholding it (2:23–24). He uses locusts as a general would deploy soldiers (2:25), and he decides the destiny of the nations (3:1–16). Sin and rebellion are no match for the Lord and cannot thwart his sovereign purposes. He performs 'wonders', not only on earth but also in the heavens where the sun becomes dark and the moon blood (2:31). However, it is in God's dealings with his people that his greatness is particularly evident. He performs wonders for them, drives

away their enemies and lives among them as their refuge (2:26–27).

Divine wrath and compassion

Joel is a sobering book that warns about the seriousness of *sin. The nations have incurred the Lord's wrath, and natural disasters (such as the swarms of locusts) are harbingers of worse to come. Joel urges the Israelites to lament, to mourn and to cry to the Lord. Although he is a God of wrath, he is also 'a gracious and compassionate' God who 'relents from sending calamity' (2:13). Joel regards genuine repentance as the most appropriate response in times of trouble. He does not emphasize sacrifices because to some people the cult had become no more than a formality (cf. Is. 1:11–14; Amos 4:4–5). Like Jeremiah (Jer. 17:1, 9, 10), Joel argues that external religious activity, such as tearing garments, is not enough; true repentance must come from the heart. If the people repent the Lord will bless them with good harvests and they, in turn, will be able to bring their offerings to him in thanksgiving (2:14).

The relationship between people and their environment

The Genesis account of the Garden of Eden describes a state of harmony between God and the human beings whom he had created (Gen. 2:1–25). One corollary of this harmony was a close relationship between human beings and their environment (see *Creation). There was no animosity between animals and humans (Gen. 2:19) and the land was fertile and well watered (Gen. 2:8–14). These idyllic conditions were ruined when the human beings rebelled against their Creator (Gen. 3:1–19). In the new atmosphere of alienation, God pronounced curses, including a curse on the ground which made it less fertile (Gen. 3:14–19).

It follows that the Creator *blesses those who are living in harmony with him but curses his rebellious subjects. When Israel prepared to enter Canaan they were informed about the two possibilities: 'See, I am setting before you today a blessing and a curse – the blessing if you obey the command of the LORD your God that I am giving you today; the curse if you disobey' (Deut. 11:26–28). Joel argues that Israel is suffering because of her disobedience and that this is reflected in environmental catastrophe: the *land has been 'invaded' (1:6), ruined and dried up (1:10); fire and drought have caused suffering for both human beings and animals (1:19–20). The people are not living in harmony with God and this is affecting their environment. If Israel repents God will restore his blessing and be 'jealous' (zealous) for his land (2:18).

Joel envisages a repentant and obedient Israel, living in harmony with God and enjoying the fullness of his blessing in a fertile land (2:14; 3:17–18). The main element in this blessing is a close relationship with God, in which the people enjoy his protection and abundant provision. Jerusalem will be claimed by the Lord as his personal property and will be known as 'my holy hill', with the result that 'never again will foreigners invade her' (3:17). The land will be very fertile and well watered (3:18).

The Lord is the judge of the nations and will vindicate his chosen people

Israel's disobedience has led to the withdrawal of divine protection and, consequently, to foreign invasion. However, although God has withdrawn his protection from Israel, he has never abandoned them, and he is aware of all the atrocities that the nations have committed. The restoration of Israel will be accompanied by the chastening of the nations who have humiliated her. God, the universal judge, will gather the nations to the valley of Jehoshaphat, and with great signs and wonders the nations will be repaid in kind for their war crimes against Israel (3:1–16). Throughout this passage indicting the nations, the use of first person possessive pronouns, with God as the subject, emphasizes that the treacherous actions taken against Israel have been against the Lord himself: 'my inheritance' (3:2), 'my people' (3:2–3), 'my land' (3:2), 'my silver and my gold' (3:5), 'my finest treasures' (3:5). Thus even though Israel's judgment was deserved, God identifies with his people in their suffering. The nations are invited to beat their ploughshares into swords and their pruning hooks into spears. This symbolizes a life or death struggle, and is in sharp contrast to the picture of international peace and harmony envisaged by Isaiah and Micah (Is. 2:4; Mic. 4:3).

The Spirit of the Lord

The Spirit (see *Holy Spirit) of the Lord comes upon certain people in the OT, usually to enable them to carry out a specific task (Exod. 31:1–5). The Spirit is linked in particular with prophecy. Moses longs for a day when this gift will be available to all the Israelites (Num. 11:29). Joel sees this pouring out of God's Spirit as a prelude to the 'great and dreadful Day of the Lord' (2:31). Peter refers to this passage to explain the pouring out of God's Spirit at Pentecost (Acts 2:14–21). He declares that the Messianic age has arrived and that God is giving his Spirit to all who call on him in the name of Jesus Christ (Acts 2:22–36). Paul also quotes Joel, pointing out that his prophecy applies not only to Jews but also to Gentiles: 'For there is no difference between Jew and Gentile – the same Lord is Lord of all and richly blesses all who call on him, for, "everyone who calls on the name of the Lord will be saved"' (Rom. 10:12–13).

The use of Joel in the NT

Besides the direct references mentioned above, there are various allusions to Joel in the NT. In particular, the prophet's graphic description of the 'Day of the Lord' is echoed in the eschatological language of the early church. The following examples show the similarity in imagery and content: trumpets are used to herald significant eschatological events (2:1, cf. 1 Cor. 15:52; 1 Thess. 4:16; Rev. 8:6 – 11:19); the nations will be judged by the Lord (3:1–14, cf. Matt. 25:31–46); there will be unusual signs in the heavens (2:30–31; 3:15, cf. Luke 21:25; Rev. 8:12); the earth and the heaven will be shaken (3:16, cf. Heb. 12:26). God's judgment is compared to harvesting a crop (3:13, cf. Mark 4:29); a locust army is compared to horses (2:4–5, cf. Rev. 9:7–9). For further examples see D. A. Hubbard, *Joel and Amos*, p. 38.

Bibliography

L. C. Allen, *The Books of Joel, Obadiah, Jonah and Micah*, NICOT (Grand Rapids, 1976); D. A. Hubbard, *Joel and Amos*, TOTC (Leicester and Downers Grove, 1989); D. Stuart, *Hosea–Jonah*, WBC (Dallas, 1987).

J. MᶜKEOWN

AMOS

Amos's message

The book of Amos begins with a startling lion's roar that withers the fertile fields and forests (1:2). With this image the prophet set the tone for his message. The LORD was coming in *judgment, bringing destruction in his wake. The 'day of the LORD' (see *Eschatology) anticipated by the northern kingdom of Israel was imminent (see 5:18). The fire of judgment would sweep over the surrounding nations, including Judah to the south (1:3 – 2:5). But much to Israel's shock, Amos suddenly turned on his northern audience. The 'day of the LORD' would not be sunny, but dark (see 5:18–20). Israel was the primary target of divine judgment because Israel had offended the LORD more than had all the other nations (2:6–16).

In the central section of the prophecy (chs. 3 – 6), Amos develops the related themes of Israel's *sin and divine judgment. Israel's special relationship to the LORD did not insulate it from judgment, but rather made the nation more responsible to follow the LORD's demands. When Israel failed to live up to the LORD's standard, it became more culpable in his sight than others who had not received as much revelatory light (3:1–2). But the LORD is not emotionally volatile and unpredictable. Before striking in anger, he communicates his intentions through his prophets (3:3–8). The LORD would judge Israel for its socio-economic injustice, materialism and religious hypocrisy (3:9 – 4:5). The LORD had tried unsuccessfully to get Israel's attention; now he was ready to confront them personally (4:6–13). The LORD places a higher priority on *obedience than sacrifice. If Israel would not repent of its sinful ways, revamp its economic and legal systems and repudiate its hypocritical religious ritualism, the LORD would bring death and destruction upon the nation (5:1 – 6:14).

In the final section of the prophecy (chs. 7 – 9) Amos highlights the coming judgment. Israel's blatant rebellion against the LORD, so vividly illustrated by Amaziah the priest (7:10–17), had exhausted the LORD's patience and made judgment necessary (7:1–9; 8:1–3). Though divine judgment would be severe, bitter and inescapable, it would also be appropriate and discriminating (8:4 – 9:10).

Judgment would sweep away the sinful majority, but the nation would not be annihilated. When the smoke of judgment cleared, the LORD would restore his people to their land, revive the Davidic dynasty and bless the nation with unprecedented prosperity (9:11–15).

Amos's portrayal of the LORD

Amos depicts the LORD (see *God) as the sovereign ruler of the world who exercises absolute authority over the nations of the earth and his people Israel. The divine king is concerned that all people recognize his authority and obey the covenantal laws he has established to govern human relationships. When these laws are violated, the king will make war against those who have rebelled against his authority.

Divine names and titles

The divine names and titles used by Amos reflect his emphasis on the LORD's royal position and sovereign authority. Amos employs 'Yahweh' ('the LORD'), the covenantal name of Israel's God, eighty-one times. On twenty-one of these occasions the name is preceded by 'Adonai' ('Sovereign' or 'Master'). This compound name ('the sovereign LORD') emphasizes the LORD's royal authority. Three times the title 'Adonai' is used by itself to refer to Israel's God (7:7–8; 9:1).

Amos highlights the LORD's role as warrior (see *Warfare) by his choice of names and titles. Eight times he identifies the LORD ('Yahweh') or 'the sovereign LORD' ('Adonai Yahweh') as the 'God of Hosts' (or 'Armies') (3:13; 4:13; 5:14, 15, 16, 27; 6:8, 14). In 9:5 the compound name 'The sovereign LORD ("Adonai Yahweh") of Hosts' appears.

The LORD as warrior-king

The dominant role in which the prophet casts the LORD is that of warrior-king. As the 'God of Hosts', the LORD leads his armies against the rebellious nations. He descends in the storm clouds and 'treads', as it were, on the peaks of the mountains (4:13). As the LORD roars like a lion (1:2; 3:8) and the darkness of judgment settles over the land (5:20; 8:9), the whole cosmos shakes with fear (8:8; 9:5). The LORD uses fire (1:3 – 2:5; 7:4), famine (4:6), drought (4:7–8), pestilence (4:9; 7:1–2), disease (4:10) and the sword (4:10; 7:9; 9:4) as his instruments of destruction.

The LORD as creator

Amos also depicts the LORD as the creator (see *Creation) of the world. The LORD formed the mountains (4:13), made the constellations (5:8) and constructed the heavens (9:6). The entire cosmos lies within his sovereign juridisdiction (9:2–4). He controls the forces of nature, including the wind (4:13) and rain (5:8; 9:6), and determines whether the land will experience agricultural prosperity or suffer famine and drought (1:2; 4:6–10; 7:1–2; 9:13–14).

Amos's description of the LORD as creator and ruler of the physical world must not be viewed in isolation. These portrayals come at strategic points in the prophecy and have a powerful rhetorical function. In 4:12 the LORD, having pointed out that Israel had refused to respond positively to a series of divine judgments (4:6–11), exhorts the nation, 'Prepare to meet your God, O Israel' (NIV). Amos then pictures this God as the creator of the mountains and the wind who comes in the storm in his role of warrior. Here the reminder of God's creative acts emphasizes that he possesses both the authority and the power to judge Israel.

The same is true in 5:8, which is embedded within a speech (5:1–17) that displays a mirror or chiastic structure. The sights and sounds of death and mourning dominate the introduction (vv. 1–3) and conclusion (vv. 16–17) to the speech as they picture the effects of the coming judgment. Exhortations to 'seek' the LORD and his ethical standards appear before (vv. 4–6) and after (vv. 14–15) a central section (vv. 7–13), which focuses on Israel's sin. Within this section the prophet abruptly inserts a description of the LORD as the creator and ruler of the natural world. Because of its syntactical awkwardness, some regard this hymnic insertion as a later addition to the prophecy. However, its very abruptness grabs one's attention and contributes to its rhetorical power. All of a sudden one is confronted with the sovereign creator who clearly possesses the authority and power to carry out his threats and destroy his enemies (see v. 9).

Another hymnic portrayal of the LORD as creator and ruler of the physical world appears in 9:6, following a vision depicting his severe and inescapable judgment (vv. 1–4). The mighty warrior who comes in judgment (v. 5) has both the authority and power to punish sinners, for he is the creator and ruler of the world. Once more the portrayal of the LORD as creator validates the announcement of judgment and effectively complements the image of the LORD as warrior.

The LORD and the nations

According to Amos, the LORD controls the history and destiny of the *nations (9:7). He determines when disaster will overtake a city (3:6) and can summon a nation to be his instrument of judgment (6:14).

The nations are responsible for keeping the LORD's demands. When they violate his standard, he decrees that they should be punished. Amos's six oracles against the nations (1:3 – 2:3) illustrate this well. Each of the oracles begins with the formulaic statement, 'Because [name of nation] has committed three rebellious acts – make that four! – I will not revoke my decree of judgment' (author's translation). The oracles assume the nations are accountable to the LORD. The Hebrew noun pešaʿ, 'rebellious act', has a covenantal flavour and may suggest the nations have violated a formal agreement or treaty. (Note the use of the related verb in 1 Kgs. 12:19; 2 Kgs. 1:1; 3:5, 7; 8:22. See also S. Paul, Amos, pp. 45–46.) But on what formal basis does the LORD exercise authority over the nations and hold them guilty? The divine mandate to Noah, from whom all nations descend (Gen. 10), is perhaps in view. (See J. Niehaus, in The Minor Prophets, p. 340.) In this mandate the LORD commands Noah and, by extension, his offspring to populate the earth (Gen. 9:7). Consistent with the mandate, all people must respect the divine image resident in each human being. But the nations violated this mandate. The atrocities mentioned in the oracles – excessive cruelty, slave trade, kidnapping, wholesale slaughter of women and children, and the desecration of an ancestral tomb – were, at least in principle, violations of the Noahic mandate.

Like Amos, Isaiah views the nations as being in a permanent covenant relationship with the LORD. The nations have broken this 'everlasting covenant' and defiled the earth (Is. 24:5) by shedding the blood of their fellow human beings (Is. 26:20–21). Because this covenant has been violated, the LORD will bring judgment, in the form of a covenant curse, upon the perpetrators (see Is. 24:1–13).

Isaiah, like Amos, assumes that the nations of the earth have violated a formal agreement with God. To what 'everlasting covenant' does he refer? A possible referent is the Noahic mandate, which has attached to it a promise that is called an 'everlasting covenant' (Gen. 9:16). By ironically transferring the phrase 'everlasting covenant' from the promise to the mandate, Isaiah stresses the enduring importance of the mandate and the severe consequences of its being violated. (See R. B. Chisholm, Jr., 'The "Everlasting Covenant" and the "City of Chaos": Intentional Ambiguity and Irony in Isaiah 24', *CTR* 6, 1993, pp. 237–253.)

Though the nations had rebelled against the LORD's authority and would suffer judgment, the LORD intends to incorporate them into his theocratic kingdom. According to Amos 9:11–12, the revived Davidic dynasty would conquer the surrounding nations, including Edom. This would be appropriate, for the LORD is their sovereign ruler. The statement used to describe the nations in verse 12 ('the nations that bear my name', literally, 'the nations over whom my name is called') indicates that the LORD owns the nations. The Hebrew expression is idiomatic; when a name is 'called over' an object, it means the object belongs to the owner of the name (see 2 Sam. 12:28; Is. 4:1).

In Acts 15:16–17 James cites a variant textual form of this passage as a proof text in support of his argument that God always intended to reach out to the Gentiles. The Hebrew text of Amos 9:12a reads, 'so that they may possess the remnant of Edom and all the nations that bear my name.' The Old Greek translation of the passage misreads 'possess' (Heb. *yāraš*) as 'seek' (Heb. *dāraš*), misinterprets 'Edom' as 'mankind' (Heb. *'aḏām*) and makes 'the remnant of men and all the nations' the subject of the verb, rather than its object. The resulting reading, 'that the remnant of men and all the nations, over whom my name is called, may seek', is strangely elliptical (the verb 'seek' requires an object but has none) and textually corrupt. Later Greek witnesses supplied an object (either 'me' or 'the Lord'). James's citation follows the second of these secondary readings, taking the passage as a positive prophecy of the Gentiles' seeking God. In its original context the passage may perhaps have envisaged a day of vengeance on Edom

and others (*cf.* Amos 1:11–15) and a new era of Davidic rule.

The LORD and Israel

The LORD's relationship to *Israel is the focus of Amos's prophecy. The LORD chose Israel to be his special covenant people (3:2). He delivered them from Egypt, led them through the wilderness and enabled them to defeat the Amorites who lived in the land of Canaan (2:9–10).

But Israel had rejected the LORD's authority and broken his covenant. The nation's royal, bureaucratic leadership was guilty of socio-economic injustice and characterized by greed and materialism (2:6–8; 3:9–10, 15; 4:1; 5:7, 10–12; 6:4–6, 12; 8:4–6). They were proud of their wealth and displayed an air of self-sufficient pride (6:1–3, 8, 13). They had no respect for the LORD's prophets (2:11–12; 7:10–17), but nevertheless hypocritically maintained a semblance of religion, though it was characterized by hollow ritualism and tainted by syncretism and idolatry (4:4–5; 5:21–26; 8:14).

In accordance with the Mosaic law, the LORD had begun to implement the threatened judgments (or 'covenant curses'). As the LORD had warned, the nation suffered famine, drought, pestilence, disease and military defeat because of its sins (compare 4:6–11 with Lev. 26:16–20 and Deut. 28:16–27, 35, 38–42, 49–51). But the people did not repent; so the LORD's patience had run out (7:1–9; 8:1–3). He would bring widespread destruction on the land, culminating in the exile of its leaders and people (compare 2:13–16; 3:11–15; 4:2–3; 5:1–3, 5, 16–17, 27; 6:7, 9–11, 14; 7:9, 17; 8:7–14; 9:1–6 with Lev. 26:30–31, 33–39 and Deut. 28:26, 36–37, 42, 52, 63–68). The nation would be reduced to a humiliated, miserable remnant (3:12; 6:9–10) as the LORD's inescapable judgment swept through (3:14; 5:19; 9:1–4).

But Israel's story would not end in judgment. As always divine judgment would be discriminating and purifying (9:8–10). It would remove the 'sinners' among the covenant community, but a faithful *remnant would be preserved. In fulfilment of his unconditional oath to David (2 Sam. 7:16; Ps. 89:27–29), the LORD would one day restore the Davidic dynasty to its rightful place and revive the glory of the Davidic era (9:11–12). As Moses had foreseen (Deut. 30:1–10), the

LORD would bring the exiles back to the land and give them abundant agricultural prosperity (9:13–14). True to his promise to Abraham, the LORD would give them permanent possession of the land (9:15). Amos's eschatological vision is partially fulfilled in Jesus Christ's present heavenly reign (Acts 2:32–36). Its complete fulfilment awaits the second coming, when Christ establishes the new covenant with Israel (Rom. 11:26–27), annihilates all opposition (Rev. 19:11–21) and inaugurates his earthly rule over the nations (Rev. 20:1–6).

Bibliography

T. J. Finley, *Joel, Amos, Obadiah*, WEC (Chicago, 1990); G. F. Hasel, *Understanding the Book of Amos* (Grand Rapids, 1991); J. H. Hayes, *Amos* (Nashville, 1988); P. J. King, *Amos, Hosea, Micah – An Archaeological Commentary* (Philadelphia, 1988); J. A. Motyer, *The Message of Amos*, BST (Leicester and Downers Grove, 1974); J. Niehaus, 'Amos', in T. McComiskey (ed.), *The Minor Prophets* (Grand Rapids, 1992), pp. 315–494; S. M. Paul, *Amos*, Hermeneia (Minneapolis, 1991); G. V. Smith, *Amos* (Grand Rapids, 1989); D. Stuart, *Hosea–Jonah*, WBC (Waco, 1987); H. W. Wolff, *Joel and Amos*, Hermeneia (ET, Philadelphia, 1977).

R. B. CHISHOLM, JR.

OBADIAH

The book in its setting

Although it is the shortest OT book (twenty-one verses), Obadiah still raises questions, including those of its authorship and date. The author is one of two *prophetic writers identified only by name, Malachi being the other. There are many Obadiahs in Scripture, but the name could describe rather than identify this messenger of *Israel's *covenant *God; it can be translated 'servant of Yahweh', which elsewhere is a prophetic title (1 Kgs. 14:18; 2 Kgs. 17:23). This role, and the author's association with Yahweh, are both relevant to the book's theological message.

The prophecy condemns Edom, Israel's eastern neighbour in Transjordan. Descended from Esau (Gen. 36), Edom antagonizes Israel (also called '*Jacob', vv. 10, 17–18) throughout its history, reflecting the conflicts between their founders, Jacob and Esau (Gen. 25:19–34; 27; 32). Edom has been involved in an attack on Jerusalem (Obad. 10 – 14); if this is a reference to the city's destruction by Babylon in 587 BC, it probably places the prophecy in the mid-sixth century BC (see D. W. Baker, *Obadiah*, pp. 21–23). Edom is castigated as a representative of all the *nations mistreating Israel, which are the subject of the book's latter section.

Israel's God

Yahweh, Israel's covenant God, formed them into a people (Exod. 20:2). His presence and person are evident in the prophecy from beginning to end. Yahweh is repeatedly identified as the origin of the message delivered by his servant (vv. 1, 4, 8, 15, 18), which implies that it has divine rather than human authority. This authority is emphasized by the application of hierarchic, judicial and royal imagery to Yahweh. He is 'sovereign' (NIV), Obadiah's master (v. 1; see above). The equity of the just *judge will be shown to the Edomites, who will receive on their own heads what they heaped on Israel (v. 15). Ultimately Yahweh may dispose of all lands and peoples as he wishes, since he is also the universal *king (v. 21).

Yahweh's absolute power and authority are not, of course, introduced here for the first time in Scripture; the Bible begins and ends with his *creative (Gen. 1 – 2; Rev. 21 – 22:2) and judgmental (Gen. 3; Rev. 20; 22:3–19) acts. All nations are under his control; Israel and Edom provide examples of the weal or woe which can come to any nation, depending on its acceptance or rejection of Yahweh's authority (*e.g.* Gen. 12:3; Is. 2:2–4; Amos 9:7; Gal. 3:8).

Yahweh's power is not solely transcendent and other-worldly, but also immanent, irrupting into human history. It can harm the daily life and eternal destiny of godless nations like Edom who stand against the universal King. On the other hand, oppressed Israel will have their promised boundaries restored by their Sovereign (vv. 17–21); they will possess the inheritance promised by Yahweh to the patriarchs (*e.g.* Gen. 12:1–3; 15:1–6; 17:8; *cf.* 2 Sam. 7:10–13). Here the covenant promises are unconditional. Elsewhere Yahweh makes demands of those who enter a covenant relationship with him (Exod. 20 – 23), but he does not do so in Obadiah.

The prophet anticipates that the covenant-establishing God will effect his promised restoration, without regard to whether or not the other covenant signatory has kept any of its obligations. Israel is restored and their foes judged not because of Israel's actions, but due to the *grace of their covenant God. Israel was *exiled as a punishment for their sins (2 Chr. 36:13–21; Ezek. 12:1–16; cf. Deut. 30:1), but was restored through God's grace following their repentance (2 Chr. 36:22–23; cf. Deut. 30:2–3).

Israel and her enemies

Obadiah shows that punishment of one's enemies can be a *blessing. Israel, as the wronged party (vv. 10–14), will receive blessing indirectly, being avenged when her tormenter, the haughty Edom, is brought low. Edom, resting in the false security and apparent impregnability of their high, impenetrable crags across the Dead Sea to the east of Judah (v. 3), will be humiliated (much like proud Capernaum [Matt. 11:23; cf. 23:12]). Looking down with scorn at its lowland foes, Edom does not realize that the true enemy of the ungodly does not come from below, or in a manner that can be countered by human arms or stratagems. Rather, the threat to the godless is from above (v. 4). When the transcendent God becomes immanent, he surpasses the real or imagined grandeur of his foes (v. 8). Edom's unassailable stronghold is all too vulnerable to the creator of the mountains (Ps. 104:8).

Pride in position or power is a danger to which many succumb in Scripture. A self-sufficient attitude is found among God's own people (2 Chr. 32:26; Is. 28; Jer. 13:8–11; Mark 9:34; 10:37), as well as among those who oppose him (Is. 10:12, Assyria; 14:12–23, Babylonia; 16:6 and Jer. 48:29, Moab; Ezek. 27, Tyre; 32:12, Egypt). The humble know from whence their help comes (Prov. 3:34; Jas. 4:6).

Edom's collusion in violence is condemned in vv. 10–14. This starts with their enjoyment of the calamity falling on others, and develops into gloating, looting and physical oppression. This response to the misfortune of others is wrong in itself, but is particularly unacceptable when there is a bond of kinship with the oppressed. This should lead to solidarity and support rather than rapaciousness.

God's blessing is not only negative, however. Israel's restoration and elevation is a positive good, a beneficent gift from their gracious King, and a contrast to the fate of their despotic neighbours.

Bibliography

D. W. Baker, et al., Obadiah, Jonah and Micah (Leicester and Downers Grove, 1988); R. J. Coggins, 'Judgment between brothers: A commentary on the book of Obadiah', in R. J. Coggins and S. P. Re'emi, Israel Among the Nations (Edinburgh and Grand Rapids, 1985).

D. W. BAKER

JONAH, BOOK OF

Introduction

Jonah, a Judean prophet, ministered during the reign of Jeroboam II in the eighth century BC (2 Kgs. 14:25). The book of Jonah describes how God commissioned the prophet to preach a message of doom to the wicked inhabitants of Nineveh (1:1–2). Rejecting this commission, Jonah boarded a ship going in the opposite direction (1:3). A violent storm pummelled the ship until the sailors were forced to throw Jonah overboard (1:12–16). After being brought to land by a large fish, Jonah complied with God's renewed command and warned the people of Nineveh about their impending doom (1:17 – 3:4). The Ninevites responded with repentance, and consequently God graciously averted the threatened destruction of their city (3:5–10). Jonah complained bitterly and God used a fast-growing plant, a hot east wind and a hungry worm to chastise and instruct him (4:1–11).

Genre

Although Jonah is one of the twelve 'Minor Prophets', the text is unlike any other *prophetic book. It is the only one of the twelve written in narrative form. There is no prophetic pronouncement for Israel and the only record of Jonah's preaching to Nineveh is the brief proclamation, 'Forty more days and Nineveh will be overturned' (3:4, NIV). The differences between Jonah and the other prophetic writings have led to extensive discussions about the 'genre' of the book.

Several options have been explored. Some

scholars view it as a historical record of a particular incident in the prophet's life; it deals with a historical figure and refers to historical places. However, this interpretation has been challenged on the basis that some of the events recorded in the book are (supposedly) highly improbable; these include the incarceration of Jonah in the great fish, the repentance of the Ninevites en masse and the remarkable growth of the plant. Furthermore, it is argued that the book includes historical inaccuracies, such as the reference to the size of Nineveh and the use of the title 'King of Nineveh'. For these and other reasons many regard the book of Jonah as fiction and describe it as a midrash, a myth, an allegory, a didactic story, *etc.*

A study of the genre of Jonah lies outside the scope of this article but most commentaries include a detailed discussion. For example, a defence of the historical approach is found in D. W. Baker, T. D. Alexander and B. K. Waltke, *Obadiah, Jonah and Micah*, pp. 69–77.

Message and implications

The sovereignty of God

The first main theological statement in the book is forced from the lips of Jonah by the intense questioning of the sailors. In a creed-like statement Jonah confesses, 'I worship (Heb. 'fear') the LORD, the God of heaven who made the sea and the land' (1:9). In this confession, Jonah condemns himself: knowing this about God, he still chose to disobey. The statement describes the nature of God as revealed to Israel. The Exodus from Egypt had demonstrated that the Lord was the God of the sea and the land: the plagues, the deliverance at the Red Sea and the provision in the barren wilderness all manifested his remarkable control of nature.

God's sovereignty over the sea and the land is demonstrated in several ways in the book of Jonah. He 'sends' the storm (1:4); the verb means to cast or throw and it is used again when the sailors throw Jonah overboard. He calms the storm (1:15). He prepares a great fish to swallow Jonah, and later speaks to it causing it to vomit up its hapless passenger (2:10). The phenomenal growth of the plant shows that fertility is the gift of God (4:6). Even a worm furthers his plans (4:7).

God's power over nature is unrivalled:

other gods are useless during the storm, and in the psalm of Jonah (ch. 2) idols are described as 'worthless'. Jonah's declaration that God is the maker of heaven and earth reflects Israel's faith in the Lord as the supreme authority. As the psalmist declares, 'The sea is his, for he made it, and his hands formed the dry land' (Ps. 95:5).

Divine retribution and divine compassion

On the one hand, the Bible portrays God as, 'compassionate and gracious, slow to anger and abounding in love' (Ps. 103:8). On the other hand, it portrays him as a holy and jealous God who will not forgive rebellion and sin (*e.g.* Josh. 24:19). The book of Jonah shows that these concepts of divine retribution (see *Judgment) and divine compassion (see *Mercy) are not mutually exclusive. The theme of judgment and retribution dominates the first half of the book. God is the universal judge who will not tolerate the wickedness of the heathen city of Nineveh. Neither will he tolerate the disobedience of his servant Jonah, whose rejection of his divinely appointed task endangers not only his own life, but also the lives of innocent sailors. The turning point of the book is Jonah's repentance and his declaration that 'salvation is of the Lord' (2:9); here the tone changes from one of judgment to one of compassion. Jonah, rescued from drowning, receives a second opportunity to obey the Lord and through his ministry the people of Nineveh hear God's warning of impending doom. Their acceptance of this message and subsequent repentance leads to forgiveness. The book of Jonah ends on a note of compassion with God's declaring, 'should I not be concerned about that great city?' (4:11).

Thus, although the book of Jonah endorses a view of God as a righteous judge who will punish the wicked, it balances this with the message that God responds to those who cry to him for mercy (4:2; *cf.* Joel 2:13). His love extends not just to Israel but to people of every nation. All the human beings who feature in the book cry for mercy and God answers them: the sea grows calm for the sailors; Jonah is delivered from drowning and the people of Nineveh are pardoned. God is not like those earthly monarchs who, having made a decree, cannot change their decisions (*cf.* Dan. 6:15); he responds to humble repentance and earnest prayer.

Jonah's relationship with the Lord

The sailors and the Ninevites are very uncertain about the character of God. They have no assurance of God's mercy, only a vague hope. Thus the captain exhorts Jonah to call on his God because 'Maybe he will take notice of us' (1:6). The King of Nineveh proclaims a fast and says, 'Who knows? God may yet relent' (3:9). In contrast, Jonah is blessed with the knowledge of God.

Jonah's knowledge of God comes from God himself by direct speech. The sailors, on the other hand, must deduce what they can about God from the storm and eventually from Jonah. The people of Nineveh likewise learn about God's plans through Jonah. Only Jonah knows that God is the maker of heaven and earth and that he is 'a gracious and compassionate God, slow to anger and abounding in love, a God who relents from sending calamity' (4:2). Jonah has a close relationship with God: he is the only one who is said to 'pray'. The Ninevites and the sailors call to God in emergencies but he is a stranger to them. Jonah knows God personally and has no doubt that he will be gracious and forgiving to those who repent, even to a heathen nation (4:2). In spite of all his privileges, Jonah's response is contrasted unfavourably with that of the sailors and the Ninevites. All the other characters in the story, including the animals, obey God without hesitation.

There is, therefore, tremendous irony in the story: although Jonah has the privilege of being in direct communication with God, he refuses to learn from God's word and has to be taught by natural events. The storm and the fish teach him that he cannot escape God's commission and that his attempt to run away from God is pointless and ineffective (cf. Ps. 139). The divine provision of the gourd, followed by its untimely destruction, reveal that Jonah's behaviour is irrational. He cares for a single plant and objects to its demise but demands the destruction of thousands of human beings and animals.

The irony in Jonah's story reflects that of Israel's history. The nation had the privilege of direct communication from God of a kind that no other nation had experienced. Israel had failed to obey and had to learn its lesson the hard way through the bitter experiences of history. These included the destruction of the northern kingdom of Israel and the later exile of Judah to Babylon. If Israel had obeyed God's direct communication these events would not have been necessary, just as Jonah's incarceration in the fish and the destruction of the gourd would not have been necessary had he responded obediently to God's commands.

Israel – a source of blessing for others?

We are not told the reason for Jonah's antagonism towards the people of Nineveh. Perhaps he perceived (accurately) that within several decades the Assyrians would destroy Israel. For whatever reason, Jonah wanted Ninevah to be overthrown. He knew, however, that God was gracious and that he intended to use him to give the Ninevites an opportunity to repent. God was going to use Jonah to be a source of *blessing to his enemies, and the prophet could not countenance this, especially when it would result in the demise of Israel.

The message of the book for Israel and for the church today is that those who have been blessed by the Lord have the potential and, indeed, the responsibility to be a blessing to others, even their enemies (Matt. 5:43–47). There is no nation or people beyond the range of the Lord's compassion and concern (John 1:10–13).

NT use

There are three NT passages which refer to Jonah: Matthew 12:38–41, paralleled in Luke 11:29–32, and Matthew 16:1–4. In these passages Jesus states that his contemporaries shall receive, in response to their request for a 'sign', only one, 'the sign of Jonah'. Although Jesus' comments have been interpreted in various ways, he clearly views his own ministry as paralleling that of Jonah. Since Jesus condemns the unbelief of his contemporaries, he is possibly reflecting on the consequences of Jonah's ministry to Ninevah which resulted in the destruction of the northern kingdom of Israel at the hands of the Assyrians. Here, as elsewhere in the Gospels, Jesus may be indicating that the positive reception given to his ministry by Gentiles will be accompanied by disaster for the Jewish nation. For those who reject Jesus, this will be the only 'sign' given to them. (See *Jonah (person) for a fuller discussion of the 'sign of Jonah'.)

Bibliography

L. C. Allen, *The Books of Joel, Obadiah, Jonah and Micah*, NICOT (Grand Rapids, 1976); D. W. Baker, T. D. Alexander and B. K. Waltke, *Obadiah, Jonah and Micah*, TOTC (Leicester and Downers Grove, 1988); J. Limburg, *Jonah* (London, 1993); R. B. Salters, *Jonah and Lamentations*, OTG (Sheffield, 1994); J. M. Sasson, *Jonah* (New York, 1980); D. Stuart, *Hosea–Jonah*, WBC (Dallas, 1987).

J. McKEOWN

MICAH

The superscription to this book places the start of Micah's ministry during Jotham's reign, which was from 750 to 732 BC, and the end during Hezekiah's, which was from 716 to 687 BC. Micah, who came from the southern kingdom, and preached mostly in *Jerusalem, was certain that the Spirit of God had come upon him, was helping him to see clearly the *sinfulness of *Judah, and was giving him the courage to speak out against it (3:8).

Social sins

It appears that Micah had seen many rich people obtain permanent ownership of *poor people's *land. This was against the rules. The assignment of land to each tribe, clan and family was enshrined in the regulations associated with the Sinai *covenant. Land was not to be bought or sold permanently; nor was its ownership to pass permanently in any other way to any other tribe or person (*e.g.* Lev. 25:23; Num. 36; 1 Kgs. 21:3). But by some means, rich people in Micah's day were forcing poor people off their land; possibly when the poor got into debt the rich forced them to sell their land in order to pay the debt. Apparently the jubilee provision for such land to return to its original owner was ignored. This abuse is described precisely in 2:1–2, 9 and more generally in 3:1–3. When the poor person tried to prevent it by going to a judge, the judge accepted a bribe from the rich person (3:9–11; 7:2–3).

Micah also condemned cheating in business: the use of a light weight when weighing out a commodity, or a heavy weight when weighing gold, or a small measure when selling something by volume. This is another case of the rich (the merchant) exploiting the poor (the customer; 6:10–12). Both injustices were connected with greed, for money and property.

Micah was undoubtedly angry at this ill-treatment of the poor. He was also aware, from his knowledge of the Sinai covenant, that such ill-treatment was against the laws of *God, and that God had promised to punish the breaking of his laws. But the main reason why the prophet preached as he did, denouncing the evils and promising the imminent *judgment of God, was that in his personal communion with God, God confirmed that these practices constituted covenant-breaking and that he would soon punish them (1:1–2; 3:8).

Sins involving the perversion of worship practices

Micah spoke against the *worship of Canaanite idols, in both the northern kingdom (1:7) and the southern (5:13–14; also possibly 1:5b, if the MT reading, which labels Jerusalem a 'high place', *i.e.* a pagan shrine, is the correct one), and against witchcraft (5:12).

He also denounced peace *prophets (3:5–7, 11). These prophets had succumbed to the fascination with money mentioned above, and were prepared to give favourable oracles in order to ingratiate themselves with the rich and powerful; they pointed to God's promise to *David to protect Jerusalem (2 Sam. 7:16), and chose not to say anything about the conditions attached to it. Again Micah's own observations and his awareness of the laws and threats in the Sinai covenant were no doubt important reasons for his preaching, but his primary motivation was the direct revelation he received from God.

Judgment

Micah announced that God would punish these sins. In chilling oracles he predicted that Samaria would become 'a heap of rubble' (1:6, NIV), and that Jerusalem would be 'ploughed like a field' (3:12). This latter prophecy, when originally spoken, was understood by its listeners to be conditional; Jeremiah 26:18–19 says that Hezekiah repented on hearing Micah's oracle and that God relented and did not bring disaster upon him. However, this does not mean that Micah's words had done their work and ceased to be relevant; the threat remained, warning subsequent generations that if Judah broke the covenant Jerusalem would be ploughed like a field. Eventually this judgment came to pass. (This passage in Jeremiah provides remarkable evidence of how a Hebrew prophet's sayings were preserved and transmitted so effectively that a century later people could quote them in conversation.)

In other messages Micah added further detail to his description of the judgment which would come if there was no *repentance; it would involve *exile in *Babylon (4:10). In Micah's day Babylon did not seem to pose any threat to Judah, but at the time of a visit to Jerusalem by Merodach-Baladan, king of Babylon, in 705 BC (Is. 39:1–8), God revealed also to Micah's contemporary, Isaiah, the prospect of the nation going into exile in Babylon.

Most of Micah's descriptions of the judgment to come were not as specific as these. He often represented it as corresponding precisely to the sin, in the spirit of the ancient talion rule of an eye for an eye, a tooth for a tooth. Against those who 'plan iniquity' God would 'plan disaster' (2:1, 3). Those who robbed others of their land would themselves be robbed of theirs (2:4–5). Those who ignored the cries of the poor would in their turn be ignored when they cried out to the Lord (3:1–4). (See also 1:7b.)

Hope

If the canonical anthology of Micah's oracles is representative of his preaching, he must have spent almost as much time preaching *hope as preaching doom. Having preached the judgment of God, he went on to insist that that judgment would not be the end of Judah's story. Destruction would not be total; a '*remnant' would remain (2:12; 4:7; 5:7–8; 7:18). Micah's use of this word conveyed both bad news (only a remnant would survive) and good news (at least some would survive). (This promise of a remnant is found also in Isaiah, e.g. in Is. 7:3.)

Micah also promised that God would rescue and *redeem Judah from Babylon (4:10); the people will return to Jerusalem (4:6–8). In the last days many *nations would look to Jerusalem for 'the word of the LORD', and as a result there would be *peace; nations would beat their swords into ploughshares (4:1–5;

cf. Is. 2:1–5).

Moreover, a new ruler will be born in Bethlehem; he will reign 'in the majesty of the name of the LORD'; his people will dwell securely and 'his greatness will reach to the ends of the earth' (5:1–5). There are a number of similarities between what is said here about the coming ruler and the messianic expectations of other OT writers: for his ruling not in his own strength but in the strength of Yahweh, cf. 1 Samuel 2:10; for his providing security for his people, cf. 2 Samuel 7:10; for the worldwide extent of his reign, cf. Psalm 2:8; for the peace he will bring, cf. Isaiah 9:6; 11:6–9; the cryptic phrase 'whose origins are from of old' and the reference to Bethlehem may be intended to indicate that the coming ruler is descended from David without connecting him with David's decadent line, cf. Is. 11:1. Micah's prophecy is unique in identifying Bethlehem as the birthplace of the coming ruler.

Many of Micah's expressions of hope find their fulfilment in the new covenant. With regard to 4:1–5, the letter to the Hebrews speaks of believers in *Jesus now having come 'to the heavenly Jerusalem, the city of the living God', because they have access to the presence of God (12:22). The promise 'he will teach us his ways' (4:2) was fulfilled when Jesus explained what God had done and what he required of his people (Matt. 28:18–20; Mark 1:22).

With regard to 5:1–5, John 7:42 shows that the Bethlehem prophecy was understood messianically in the 1st century AD, and Matthew used it to confirm that Jesus was the Messiah (2:6). The NT claims that Micah's promise that the coming one would 'shepherd his flock' was fulfilled in Jesus (Matt. 2:6; John 10:1–18; 1 Pet. 2:25; 5:4; Rev. 7:17). Paul too draws upon these verses: in Ephesians 2:14 he applies Micah's promise 'and he will be their peace' to Jesus. For Micah this peace consisted of the re-unification of *Israel and Judah (5:3) and peace with their external enemies. Paul proclaims a greater re-unification, of Jews and Gentiles, and peace with God.

Paul also believed that in his own time, as in the time of Micah, God's plan of *salvation included a significant role for a remnant within Israel (Rom. 9:27; 11:5).

The interplay between doom and hope in Micah

Micah is not the only prophetic book to include both oracles of doom and oracles of hope; so do Isaiah, Jeremiah and Ezekiel. But in Micah the rapid alternation between the two is striking, especially the movement from judgment to salvation at 2:12 and 7:7. Most commentators think that Micah's material has been arranged in three sections, chapters 1 – 2, 3 – 5, and 6 – 7, each section beginning with the command 'Hear' (1:2) or 'Listen' (3:1; 6:1). If this is correct, then each section consists of oracles of doom followed by oracles of salvation: 1:2 – 2:11 followed by 2:12–13; 3:1–12 followed by 4:1–5:15; 6:1 – 7:7 followed by 7:8–20. Is this arrangement significant?

By placing the salvation oracles after the doom oracles the compiler (who may have been Micah himself, 3:1) has given them greater weight; salvation, not doom, is Micah's and God's final word. This holds true even if the book is divided up in some other way, because its last verses are about salvation. The same pattern is seen in all three major prophets and in Hosea, Amos, Zephaniah, Haggai and Zechariah. B. S. Childs has found it also in many psalms and in the two historical works, Deuteronomy–Kings and Chronicles–Ezra–Nehemiah (Childs, *Old Testament Theology in a Canonical Context*, pp. 238–239). It reveals that God's *mercy is stronger than his wrath; his sending of his Son would confirm this. It may also reveal the ultimate triumph of mercy and *grace, an important theme of OT *eschatology. Micah's emphasis on hope is based on the covenant made long before between God and Israel, to which he alludes many times: 6:1–8 is a covenant lawsuit; nine times God calls Israel 'my people'; and the last verse of the book indicates that the prophet's hopes for the future are founded upon God's promises to 'our fathers'.

Moreover, the arrangement of doom and salvation oracles is intended to prevent readers from thinking of one theme without the other. God's judgment and his redemption are closely linked; they are both part of his single purpose. Each is best understood in connection with the other. Though the people of Judah are sinners, justly under punishment, Yahweh is incomparable (note the pun on Micah's name in 7:18; who is like Yahweh?) as the one whose *forgiveness is more powerful than their sins; he delights in mercy and will not persist in *anger. Yet his mercy can be properly understood only if his wrath is also properly understood. Similarly his wrath should not be considered in isolation from his mercy.

In the death of Christ both the wrath and mercy of God are revealed; the reader of the NT is confronted by both simultaneously and must grasp both.

Bibliography
L. C. Allen, *The Books of Joel, Obadiah, Jonah, and Micah*, NICOT (Grand Rapids, 1976); B. S. Childs, *Old Testament Theology in a Canonical Context* (London, 1985); J. L. Mays, *Micah*, OTL (Philadelphia, 1976); R. L. Smith, *Micah–Malachi*, WBC (Waco, 1984); B. K. Waltke, in D. Baker, D. Alexander and B. K. Waltke , *Obadiah, Jonah and Micah*, TOTC (Leicester and Downers Grove, 1988).

I. HART

NAHUM

The book

The prophet Nahum is unknown apart from the opening verse, the only occurrence in Scripture of the name (which means 'comfort') being here. The location of his home town, Elkosh, is uncertain; none of the suggestions of sites in Galilee (*cf.* Capernaum, 'Nahum's city'), *Judah or Assyria is convincing. His period is more definite, as he looks back to the destruction of Thebes (Heb. No Amon, 3:8–10) in Egypt, which was sacked in 663 BC, and anticipates the fall of Nineveh, the capital of the once mighty Assyrian Empire, which captured the northern kingdom of Israel in 722 BC. The city fell to the Babylonians in 612 BC, and since from the prophet's wording (*e.g.* 2:1) the event seems to be imminent, a date for these prophecies of the last third of the 7th century BC is most likely.

Nineveh is the main subject of the book (1:1). The Assyrians, enemies of *God and his people *Israel, merit destruction. Nahum probably did not address Assyria directly, as had *Jonah, his near canonical neighbour (Jonah 3). In fact, Assyria was not the recipient of the message at all, but simply its subject. Numerous OT prophecies are delivered to Israel and Judah concerning the enemy nations who beset them (*e.g.* Is. 10:5–34; 13 – 21; Jer. 46 – 51; Ezek. 21:18–32; 25 – 32; Joel 3; Amos 1:3 – 2:3; Obad.; Jonah). They are messages of hope for the oppressed (Nah. 1:15), since they proclaim *judgment upon the oppressor.

The message

The initial portrayal of Yahweh in this prophecy is problematic. In one verse (1:2) he is presented as jealous, vengeful and *angry, in addition to being a fierce destroyer who has enemies. His global power renders nature and *nations powerless. Everything convulses before his wrath (1:3–6). One would be reluctant to approach or worship such a God. However, these verses serve an important foundational function for the rest of the book, presenting an aspect of God's being which is too easily forgotten: his justice and *righteousness in not countenancing sin. Whoever opposes his will, whether a pagan or one of his own people, is in danger of encountering this aspect of God's nature (*cf.* Amos 1:3 – 2:16; Acts 5:1–11).

Fortunately, wrathful judgment is not the only aspect of God's nature encountered either in this book or in the lives of those who seek him. Judgment is tempered by *grace, and is at times delayed, though not cancelled (1:3). Ultimately, justice and righteousness will result in peace (1:15; Is. 52:7; Acts 10:36; Rom. 10:15); this can be most clearly seen in the cross of Christ, where God is proved to be just and the justifier of those who believe in Jesus (Rom. 3:26). However, unregenerate Assyria recognizes neither Yahweh ('the LORD') as anything more than the God of Israel, nor that what they are doing is wrong (*cf.* 2:12); they deal with all their conquests in the same way (3:19). This precludes *repentance, which must include acknowledgment of wrongdoing.

Nahum pronounces unmitigated judgment upon Nineveh not because of personal animosity towards Assyria, though that would be understandable in the light of his historical context. Rather the judgment follows from the character of Yahweh described in the opening verses (1:1–6). Even though Yahweh had originally appointed Assyria as the instrument of punishing his own rebellious people (Is. 7:17; 10:5–6), they will be held corporately responsible for atrocities which go beyond what God intended (Is. 10:7–19). Being under the orders of another does not preclude responsibility for actions which are transparently wrong. The curses called down on Israel's enemies (*e.g.* in Ps. 137:7–9) do not reflect a low view of them as people, but a high view of the importance of right and wrong.

This message was theologically necessary for Judah to hear, since they were living in fear of a seemingly irresistible enemy who had already destroyed their northern neighbour. There was no human reason for Judah to be anything but pessimistic about their own future in the light of the overwhelming forces arrayed against them. In fact, Judah had some reason to fear for their own existence, but this was not due to the nature of their enemy, which, though humanly omnipotent, would meet more than its match when confronted with the truly Omnipotent (1:3–6; Is. 40 – 55; Obad. 4). Rather it was due to their choosing to ignore God and their promises to him, though this is not Nahum's focus (*cf.* Amos 2:4–5; Zeph.). From this prophecy Judah is able to appreciate the sovereignty of their God.

This sovereignty is not restricted only to those who faced Nineveh, but is evident universally. Each generation facing seemingly insurmountable obstacles, whether human or circumstantial, needs to be reminded of the one who is in control. This is proved historically by the fall of Nineveh in 612 BC, and of the Assyrian Empire as a whole in 605 BC, as it is existentially whenever God's children turn to him, from Nazi Germany to South Africa, from Iraq and Iran to Northern Ireland. He makes possible what is humanly impossible. God controls not only humans, but also natural forces, since sea and river are under his control (1:4; Ps. 104:6–7; Is. 50:2; Luke 8:24–25), wind and storm show his power (1:3), and the whole earth is unstable while he is unchangeable (1:5; Joel 2:10). However, God's sovereignty is not only good news. In what must be terrifying words to hear, Yahweh can also say (2:13) 'I am your enemy' (NLV), 'I am against you' (NIV). While Yahweh's patronage shields from all harm those who honour him (Gen. 12:2–3a; Rom. 8:31), those who oppose him (Gen. 12:3a; 2 Pet. 3:3–10) experience unmitigated woe.

Bibliography

E. Achtemeier, *Nahum–Malachi*, Interpretation (Atlanta, 1986); C. E. Armerding, 'Nahum, Habakkuk', *EBC* (Grand Rapids, 1985); D. W. Baker, *Nahum, Habakkuk, and Zephaniah*, TOTC (Leicester and Downers Grove, 1988); W. A. Maier, *The Book of Nahum: A Commentary* (Saint Louis, 1959).

D. W. BAKER

HABAKKUK

The setting

Nothing is known of the person of Habakkuk. An apocryphal text (Bel and the Dragon) describes him as a Levite who assists Daniel in his distress, but this has no historical value, apart from reflecting the respect in which the prophet was held by later writers. However, his character as a sincere believer in Yahweh and his covenant, as well as his courage, shine brightly through his prophecy.

The events mentioned indicate that the book was written towards the end of the seventh century BC, when the political power of the Babylonians (also called Chaldeans, 1:6) was increasing. It probably predates the capture of the Assyrian capital, Nineveh, in 612 BC, and must predate the complete downfall of the Assyrian empire in 605 BC.

The book consists of two sections. First there is a double complaint by the prophet (1:2–4; 1:12 – 2:1) countered by God's double response (1:5–11; 2:2–20). This is followed by a prayer in the form of a psalm (ch. 3). Though some suggest that these two sections were originally separate, thematic links between them point to the unity of the book.

The message

Habakkuk is unique among the prophets (see *Prophetic books). The primary role of a prophet was to take *God's people to task for neglecting the covenant with Yahweh initiated at Sinai. Habakkuk reversed this role, however, by taking Yahweh himself to task for what the prophet perceived as laxity in keeping the terms of the covenant. He asked the opposite question to that of *Job, another questioner of God. Both experienced a tension between their concept of how God should act, and the way in which he actually behaves (*cf.* Job 7:11, 20–21). Job asked why a righteous person should suffer. Habakkuk, on the other hand, wondered why the *evil were able to continue unpunished in their wickedness and perversion (1:2–4). The irony in his questioning is that the wicked in this case were not the pagan nations surrounding Israel, but rather Israel herself. The recipients of the good law (*tôrāh*, 1:4) had rendered it, their very constitution, powerless and ineffective. Habakkuk is calling judgment down upon the head of his own people.

Yahweh's response, that he was preparing a nation to punish his rebellious children (1:5–11), caused another moral dilemma for Habakkuk. Yahweh's instrument for punishing wicked Judah was the even more wicked Babylon. Habakkuk could not see how a *holy God could use such a vile tool (1:13a), people who mercilessly piled atrocity upon atrocity, apparently for their own perverse enjoyment (1:15, 17). Did not Yahweh realize that these were pagan people (1:16)? Habakkuk was convinced that the answer to his original question raised more problems than it solved.

Yahweh's use, for his own ends, of those who do not believe in him is not without parallel. He used such people both as a means of punishing Israel (*e.g.* Assyria, Is. 8; Babylonia, Jer. 4:5–31; 6:1–30; Egypt, Hos. 9:5–7) and as a means of saving them (Cyrus, Is. 44:28 – 45:4). He also held liable those who arrogantly used excessive violence in their treatment of Israel, even if it was he who had ordained the punishment (Assyria, Is. 10:5–19; Babylonia, 14:4–23). He assured Habakkuk that he would judge Babylon (2:2–20). The prophet could rest assured that (contrary to his initial perception) Yahweh was still holy (2:20), and did not condone evil.

The best known expression of Habakkuk's assurance is cited in the NT. He contrasts the wicked, who will get their just deserts (by implication, death: *cf.* Prov. 14:12; 16:25), with the *righteous, who will live through *faithfulness (2:4, cited in Gal. 3:11; Rom. 1:17; and Heb. 10:38). This faithfulness, as indicated by the immediate context (Hab. 2:3), is patient waiting, trusting in God to fulfil his will. The Septuagint, in one version, attributed the justifying faithfulness to God himself ('my faith[fulness]') , while in another version it is God's 'righteous one' who will live. The latter interpretation seems to be that of the writer to the Hebrews, who encouraged readers by the promise of a 'Coming One', that is, the Messiah (Heb. 10:37).

Romans 1:17 also is ambiguous with regard to 'the one who is righteous', but it is clear that the righteousness is given by God as a gift, and is not an inherited characteristic. Galatians 3:11 is even clearer in its contrast between self-righteousness, sought by human effort through following the law, and true righteousness, which derives from faith in God.

Habakkuk realized the audacity of his questioning this mighty God, the one who came to Israel at Sinai (3:3–4), who sent powerful plagues against Egypt (3:5), who parted the Red Sea and Jordan before the people (3:8, 15), and who crushed their enemies with his mighty power (3:12–15). When Habakkuk finally understood that it was in front of this God of power and majesty that he stubbornly stood awaiting an answer to his questions (2:1), he was filled with dread and terror (3:16).

God does not respond to the confrontation by destroying the doubter, any more than he did in the case of Job (see also John 20:24–29). The Creator's position is not threatened by honest questioning from the creature. Instead, unlike Job, the prophet receives an answer to his questions. Both of them are forced to acknowledge the creating and saving power of God, the giver of life and vitality (Hab. 3:17–19; Job 1:21). This is an encouragement to all people comforted by the apparent absence of moral or theological absolutes. This absence is illusory; the instruction of God has not lost its power and efficacy, nor has God changed his character.

Bibliography

D. W. Baker, *Nahum, Habakkuk, Zephaniah*, TOTC (Leicester and Downers Grove, 1988); F. F. Bruce, 'Habakkuk', in T. E. McComiskey (ed.), *An Exegetical and Expository Commentary on the Minor Prophets* (Grand Rapids, 1993); D. J. Clark and H. A. Hatton, *The Translator's Handbook on the Books of Nahum, Habakkuk, and Zephaniah* (New York, 1989).

D. W. BAKER

ZEPHANIAH

The book in its setting

Zephaniah's prophecy, dated in the reign of Josiah (640–609 BC), *Judah's sixteenth king (2 Kgs. 21:26 – 23:30; 2 Chr. 33:25 – 35:27), was contemporary with those of *Nahum, *Habakkuk and *Jeremiah. The major nation of the period, and *Israel's overlord, was Assyria (2:13–15). It had exiled the northern kingdom of Israel in 722 BC, but was itself defeated by Babylonia at the end of the 7th century. Since its destruction is still only anticipated, the prophecy must date from before 612 BC, when the capital city fell. Other nations who had oppressed Judah are also warned of coming punishment: the Philistines (2:4–7), Moab and Ammon (2:8–11), and Cush or Ethiopia (possibly a reference to Egypt, since in the 25th Egyptian dynasty [716–663 BC] Ethiopia controlled Egypt [2:12]).

Zephaniah's genealogy is the longest in the *prophetic books, stretching back to Hezekiah (1:1) (716–686 BC), Josiah's great-grandfather. He restored Yahwistic worship, which had fallen into disfavour (2 Kgs. 18:4–6). But his reforms were effective only during his lifetime, since his son, Manasseh (2 Kgs. 21:1–18), and grandson, Amon (2 Kgs. 21:19–26), reinstated forbidden practices. Josiah himself was the next great reformer, re-establishing true Yahwistic worship by approximately 621 BC. It could be argued that Zephaniah's prophecies, especially those of 1:4–9, precede this reformation, since he condemns pagan practices. This does not necessarily follow, however, since the ideal of fidelity to the *covenant demanded by the prophets was never completely realized in the life of the people. Again and again new prophets were raised up to proclaim the same message.

The message

The overarching theme of Zephaniah's message is the Day of the Lord (see *Eschatology), a concept introduced by his predecessors (Amos 5:18–20; 8:9–14; Is. 2; 13; 24; Joel 2) and developed by his successors (Jer. 46 – 51; Ezek. 7). In no other book, however, is the idea such a major part of the message as it is in Zephaniah.

The Day of the Lord has two aspects. It is

both a day of weal and a day of woe, a day of *blessing for those who serve Yahweh (3:9–20), and a day of *judgment upon those who do not (1:8 – 3:8). Israel misunderstood the Day; they thought that as they were *God's 'chosen people', it must be a day of blessing and light for them. However, because they had broken the covenant, it would rather be a time of darkness and judgment (Amos 5:18–20). Birth into the family of Israel is no guarantee of future blessing, since Judah, as well as the pagan nations around it, is subject to judgment (Zeph. 1:2–6, 8–18; 2:4 – 3:8). Judah will find that there is no such thing as a second generation child of God; each person and generation must make a commitment to him and his covenant.

Israel's chauvinism is subverted also with respect to blessing from God. This blessing is not reserved for Israel alone; all peoples and nations who *repent of their paganism can become God's children and benefit from that relationship (3:9–10; Is. 2:1–5; Amos 9:7; Mic. 4:1–5). Since Judah's neglect of the first covenant commandment against having other gods than Yahweh (1:4–5; cf. Exod. 20:3; Deut. 5:7) makes them *de facto* pagan, they also need to repent (3:11–13), rather than arrogantly presuming on God's blessing (*cf.* 2:3). The nation (1:4–6, 12) and their leaders, those charged with keeping them close to God (3:3–4), break the covenant. It is especially troubling that this *sinful state elicits no response; foolishly, the people do not care (1:12), thinking that God also does not care and will not react.

The Day of the Lord has two time frames. It is near at hand and coming suddenly (1:7, 14, 18), but will also be realized in a more distant, unspecified, eschatological future (3:8–9, 11, 13–17). In this respect it is similar to the kingdom of God (or of heaven) which was inaugurated with Jesus' first advent (*cf.* Matt. 11:2), but is also still anticipated (H. Ridderbos, in *NBD*, pp. 656–659).

God's control over all *creation, to bless or to punish, is reflected in the deliberate description of those destined for destruction (1:2–3) in the words of the creation account (Gen. 1:20, 24–25, 26–28). In fact, their punishment could be seen as an 'uncreation', since the order of destruction in Zephaniah exactly reverses that of creation in Genesis. Since only he is creator and lord, Yahweh is jealous of his position as Israel's sole object of *worship (1:4–6). In his battle for theocracy,

the rule of God, he brooks no rivals.

God's bounty also is unrivalled, since his *grace is available to all. Any penitent, Israelite or foreigner, can enter into the blessings of God's covenant with Noah, which included all creation (Gen. 9:9–11), just as he or she can enter the new covenant inaugurated by the cross of Christ (1 Cor. 11:25; Heb. 9:15). People are called to respond, to 'seek the Lord' (2:3; *cf.* 1:6). The statement that 'perhaps' there will be shelter from God's judgment (2:3; *cf.* Exod. 32:30; Amos 5:15) is theologically significant. God's justice and *righteousness demand that wrongdoing be punished, but he is also characterized by *forgiveness and *love. The 'perhaps' is a warning to the wrongdoer that God cannot be manipulated, and that grace should not be taken for granted, lest it be cheapened and trivialized. The word protects God's sovereignty, his choice to forgive or not in any and every case. Repentant sinners should always be surprised at God's forgiveness.

Bibliography

D. W. Baker, *Nahum, Habakkuk and Zephaniah* (Leicester and Downers Grove, 1988); P. C. Craigie, *Twelve Prophets* (Edinburgh and Philadelphia, 1985); J. A. Motyer, 'Zephaniah', in T. E. McComiskey (ed.), *An Exegetical and Expository Commentary on the Minor Prophets* (Grand Rapids, 1998); H. Ridderbos, 'Kingdom of God, kingdom of heaven', *NBD*, pp. 656–659.

D. W. BAKER

HAGGAI

Historical background

The Babylonian army destroyed Jerusalem in 586 BC and exiled many of its inhabitants. Jerusalem lay in ruins until the fall of Babylon in 539. The Persian king, Cyrus, permitted exiled peoples to return to their homelands, and a small group of Jews made the 900-mile journey to Jerusalem in 538. Intending to rebuild the *temple, they laid the foundation-stone in 537, but strong opposition forced them to abandon the project. One discouragement followed another and by 520, hampered by economic hardship, political uncertainty, and spiritual depression, they had made little progress. In these apparently hopeless circumstances the prophet Haggai addressed the community in the name of 'the Lord Almighty'.

The prophet and his message

Apart from two brief references in Ezra 5:1 and 6:14, Haggai is not mentioned elsewhere in the OT. The book named after him comprises four prophetic messages, each of which is assigned a specific date.

Haggai's first message (1:1–11)

Addressing Zerubbabel, the governor, and Joshua, the high priest, Haggai declared that the adverse conditions facing the small community – inflation (1:6), poor harvests (1:9), and drought (1:11) – were the direct result of their failure to rebuild the temple. God had not only refused to help them, but was working against them because they had given priority to beautifying their own houses while the temple lay in ruins (1:9–11). In the light of this, the leaders and the people were urged twice to 'give careful thought to your ways' (1:5, 7, NIV).

The response (1:12–15)

Following Haggai's message, the Lord powerfully motivated ('stirred up') both leaders and people (1:14). The people recognized that the Lord was speaking through the prophet and they obeyed with reverent fear (1:12). Work on the temple began just twenty-three days after the first message (1:15). Haggai encouraged the workers by assuring them of God's presence (1:13).

Haggai's second message (2:1–9)

Less than a month after building had commenced, some of the elderly people who had seen Solomon's temple made unfavourable comparisons (2:3). The prophet reassured the people and their leaders that the Lord was with them (2:4), that they were his covenant people whom he had brought out of Egypt (2:5) and that his Spirit was among them (2:5). God was at work in the world, declared Haggai, and he would shake the nations until their silver and gold poured into Jerusalem, so that the glory of the second temple would be greater than that of the first (2:6–9).

Haggai's third message (2:10–19)

This enigmatic message dealt with the priestly issues of holiness and defilement. In a dialogue with the priests, Haggai emphasized that holiness was not transferable from one object to another or from an object to a person, whereas defilement was contagious (2:11–13). Lack of enthusiasm for the temple and its worship had defiled them and thus everything they did had been defiled (2:14–18). Building the temple would not automatically make them holy, but it did give them an opportunity to make a new start. Three times Haggai urged them to 'give careful thought' to their terrible predicament, on the grounds that a dramatic change was taking place (2:15, 18), made possible by the renewal of the covenant blessing: 'from this day on I will bless you' (2:19).

Haggai's fourth message (2:20–23)

Haggai's final message was delivered on the same day as his third message. It was addressed to Zerubbabel, governor of Judah. Earlier the Judean king, Jehoiachin, had been likened to a discarded signet ring: God had rejected him as the leader of his people (Jer. 22:24). Now the declaration that Zerubbabel was like God's signet ring heralded the renewal of God's promise to bring blessing through the Davidic line (2:23, cf. 2 Sam. 7:8–16).

Important themes and concepts from Israel's rich theological heritage

Lord Almighty (Lord of Hosts)

The term 'Almighty' (literally, 'hosts') refers to the greatness of *God and to his supreme power and authority. The 'hosts' in this context are probably armies of heavenly beings under God's command who protect the people and the temple from their enemies (cf. 2 Kgs. 6:15–17).

Although not found in the Pentateuch or the book of Judges, the title occurs frequently in the rest of the OT – almost 300 times, including fourteen occurrences in Haggai. Some passages link it with Jerusalem and with King David; when David decided to bring the ark to Jerusalem it was referred to as 'the ark of God, which is called by the Name, the name of the Lord Almighty' (2 Sam. 6:2). Furthermore, the covenant with David was prefaced with the declaration, 'This is what the Lord Almighty says' (2 Sam. 7:8); Haggai employed the same phrase several times (1:2, 5, 7; 2:6, 11). By his use of this terminology, so clearly linked with the past, Haggai indicated that the great God of Israel's history, the God of the covenant, was the same God who spoke to the post-exilic community.

Divine *blessing

Divine blessing was pronounced at creation in the context of perfect harmony between God and his subjects (Gen. 1:22, 28; 2:3). When this harmony was disrupted by the rebellion of human beings, God pronounced curses (Gen. 3:14–19). Thus blessing is associated with harmonious relations between God and his subjects but cursing is God's reaction to rebellious subjects. Haggai argued that the rebuilding of the temple was the beginning of renewed harmony with God and would result in a new era of blessing (2:19). The NT announces that harmony with God is possible only through the sacrifice of Christ. Through his suffering on Calvary, Christ became a curse on behalf of sinful human beings, to reconcile them to God and to make them heirs of the blessing promised to Abraham (Gal. 3:10–14).

*Remnant

Earlier prophets who taught that Israel would be punished by God also affirmed that a remnant would survive (Is. 7:3; 46:3; Amos 5:14–15). Haggai applied the term 'remnant' to those living in Jerusalem, to assure them that they were heirs to the rich heritage of the covenant people (1:12, 14).

Temple

The temple represented God's presence in harmony with his people (Ps. 132:13–14; 1 Kgs. 6:13). It was closely associated with the Davidic monarchy: David wanted to build God a house (temple) but God built David a house (dynasty) (2 Sam. 7:11, 16). It symbolized not just peace with God but also peace within the land (1 Kgs. 5:3–4). In contrast, the destruction of the temple was associated with Israel's alienation from God, the apparent end of the reign of David's line and the loss of the Promised Land to the nations (2 Kgs. 25:8–21). In this context the enthusiasm of Haggai for the rebuilding may be understood. The new temple represented the renewal of divine favour towards Israel: God's protective presence would once again be manifest in a harmonious relationship among his people (1:13; 2:4); the promises to David,

represented by God's acceptance of Zerubbabel the Davidic prince, would be fulfilled (2:23; *cf.* Matt. 1:12); and God's purposes for the nations would be revealed (2:6–9).

Christ's ministry was closely associated with the temple. He taught and healed within its precincts and prophesied its destruction. More importantly, the person and work of Christ brought into sharper focus the profound theological truths that the temple represented. For example, the temple represented God's presence in harmony with his people, but Christ made reconciliation between humankind and God a reality through his sacrificial death at Calvary (Matt. 12:6). Furthermore, the close association between temple and David was presupposed in Christ's continuation of David's line as universal King (Rev. 5:5). Finally, Christ rendered the Jerusalem temple obsolete by dwelling through his Spirit within the body of each believer (1 Cor 6:19).

Bibliography

J. E. Baldwin, *Haggai, Zechariah, Malachi*, TOTC (Leicester and Downers Grove, 1972); D. L. Petersen, *Haggai and Zechariah*, OTL (London, 1984); P. L. Redditt, *Haggai, Zechariah, Malachi*, NCB (London, 1995); R. L. Smith, *Micah–Malachi*, WBC (Dallas, 1984).

J. McKeown

ZECHARIAH

Introduction

The book of Zechariah contains a series of visions and oracles received after the return from *exile in Babylon. The dates given in the book range from 520 BC (1:1) to 518 BC (7:1). The basic structure of the book is as follows:

Part I: Zechariah 1 – 8

1. Introduction and prophetic call narrative (1:1–6)
2. A cycle of eight night visions, and accompanying oracles (1:7–6:8)
   a. the four horsemen (1:7–17)
   b. the four horns and smiths (1:18–21)
   c. the man with a measuring

line (2:1–13)
d. cleansing of Joshua the
High Priest (3:1–10)
e. the lampstand and two
olive trees (4:1–14)
f. the flying scroll (5:1–4)
g. the woman in the ephah
(5:5–11)
h. the four chariots (6:1–8)

3. The crown for the High
Priest (6:9–15)

4. Oracles in response to a
question about fasting
(7:1–8:23)

Part II: Zechariah 9 – 14

1. First oracle (9 – 11)
a. judgment upon the nations
(9:1–8)
b. peace for God's people
(9:9–17)
c. return from the nations
and restoration (10:1–12)
d. the foolish shepherd
(11:1–17)

2. Second oracle (12 – 14)
a. first assault upon Jerusalem leading to judgment
upon the nations (12:1–9)
b. transformation of God's
people (12:10–13:9)
c. second assault upon Jerusalem leading to judgment
upon the nations (14:1–9)
d. transformation of the entire world (14:10–21)

Themes in Zechariah

The fundamental context of Zechariah is the return from the exile, which represents a state of partial restoration for God's people. The exile was the result of the sinful disobedience of the forefathers (1:2–6). But now through repentance and return a new beginning had been made possible (1:6b), and the returnees were part of God's plan of cosmic transformation. Yet the realities of everyday life in the ravaged land to which they returned seemed depressingly mundane and difficult. The exiles found themselves, like the ephah of 5:9, caught up between two worlds, between the

promises of heaven and the realities of earth. They were living in the 'now' but longing for the 'not yet'. Indeed, at risk of oversimplification, we may say that the first half of the book (chs. 1 – 8) focuses on the 'now', especially on signs in the present 'day of small things' (4:10, NIV) which point forward to the reality of the 'not yet'. On the other hand, the latter half of the book (9 – 14) points the attention of the people onward to the 'not yet' and encourages them with the vision of the final *victory of God.

God's presence

In the aftermath of the exile, when God abandoned his people and his *temple because of the people's sin (Ezek. 8 – 11), the issue of God's presence was pressing. Ezekiel himself had prophesied that the Lord would return to dwell among his people (Ezek. 37:27) and that the glory would return to a renewed temple (43:1–5). But was that promise part of the 'now' or of the 'not yet'? Zechariah's visions proclaimed that the 'now' was the time for rebuilding.

The initial visions of Zechariah declare that the Lord's scouts have traversed the earth and found everything 'at *rest', which is the prerequisite for temple building (1:10–11; cf. Deut. 12:10; 2 Sam. 7:1). The Lord has promised to return to Jerusalem and have his house rebuilt (1:16). The *glory will once more be within *Jerusalem (2:5), which will again be God's dwelling place and the city of God's choosing (2:11–12). The two central visions of the cycle also concern the temple and its functionaries. In the first, Joshua the high priest is cleansed from his defilement by an act of the divine council, thus enabling him to fulfil his duties and supervise the temple ministry (3:1–7). In the second, the menorah, which was one of the central symbols of God's presence in the temple, is fully functioning once more, now fed with an inexhaustible supply of oil from two olive trees (4:1–14). The consequence of this restoration of the cult will be a cleansing of the land from its iniquity (5:1–11) and the final defeat of all God's enemies (6:1–8). The end result will be God's Spirit (see *Holy Spirit) at rest (6:8), which contrasts starkly with the motion of the preceding visions.

The 'now' aspect of this section is evident. The angelic watchers have found the world to be at rest (1:11) at a particular point in his-

258

tory, the second year of Darius. The vision of the cleansing of the *priesthood so that it can undertake its proper ministry concerns a particular historical individual, Joshua (3:1). The prophet names another individual, Zerubbabel, as the one who has laid the foundation of the temple and will himself complete it (4:9). This is not a message for the distant future but an encouragement to set to work at that historical moment, no matter what the apparent obstacles (4:7).

Yet there is also a 'not yet' aspect to all of this. The vision concerning Joshua is also a sign of things to come (3:8). Specifically, 'my servant, the Branch' will come, who will bring about the cleansing of the *land in a single day and will usher in the final *blessing (3:9–10). Ultimately it is he who will build the temple of the Lord (6:12–13). The cleansing of the land and the Lord's final victory (5:1 – 6:8) are assured realities but they are not present realities. Indeed, both are central themes in the second part of Zechariah, where they are depicted as events which will happen in the future. 'On that day' the land will be cleansed (13:1–9) and the Lord's final victory established (14:1–21).

The Messiah

The vital event which will initiate the blessings of the 'not yet' is the coming of the Messiah (see *Jesus Christ). This epoch-transforming figure appears under a number of designations. He is 'my servant, the Branch' (3:8) or simply 'the Branch' (6:12); he is Jerusalem's king (9:9), 'my shepherd' (13:7), 'the one they have pierced' (12:10). These images are familiar from earlier prophecies of a future king. For example, 'the Branch' (ṣemaḥ) refers to the future righteous scion of the line of *David in Jeremiah 23:5 and 33:15 (cf. similar imagery in Is. 11:1 and Ezek. 17:22). The promise of a new good shepherd to replace the former bad shepherds is found in Jeremiah 23:4 and Ezekiel 34:23, while the theme of mourning over the pierced one recalls Isaiah 53, which describes the affliction of 'my servant' (Is. 52:13) who grew up like a tender shoot (Is. 53:2).

The coming of the messianic figure clearly belongs to the 'not yet' in both the earlier prophets and Zechariah, yet the unique contribution of Zechariah is the connecting of this future event to the 'now'. The present reality of Joshua and his associates is a portent of the

coming of the Branch (3:8), while in chapter 6 Joshua is symbolically crowned as a sign of the future rule of the Branch (6:9–15).

The final victory of God

The importance of these present tokens, which assure the people that final victory is certain, is emphasized by the pervasive tone of struggle in Zechariah's writings. The reality of conflict is everywhere present in the 'now', both on the angelic level, where the adversary (śāṭān) stands ready to accuse Joshua (3:1), and on the human level where the foes include the 'four horns' (1:18) and the 'mighty *mountain' which faces Zerubbabel (4:7). Nor will the future be free from struggle. Enemies remain, both outside (12:2–3) and within (11:4–16). Indeed, the events which usher in the 'not yet' will take the form of a cataclysmic assault by the nations on Jerusalem (12:2–6; 14:2–5; cf. Ezek. 38 – 39).

But the struggle, though real and intense, is not God's final word. The enemies are merely the foils which serve to demonstrate clearly God's commitment to his people (see *People of God) and his city. The adversary stands rebuked by the Lord himself (3:2); the mountain becomes level ground (4:7); and those who assault God's people touch the apple of his eye (2:8). God himself will be a wall of fire around Jerusalem in the present (2:5), and will intervene to give them victory over the nations that come against them (9:8; 12:2–4; 14:3–5). Because the Lord is on Israel's side, final victory is secure.

This final victory will bring about a transformation in the inhabitants of God's land. Joshua's transformation from a state of defilement to one of purity is symbolic of a similar work which God is doing all around him. The people will be purified (5:1–4) (see *Holiness); their iniquity will be taken away (5:5–11); a spirit of *grace and supplication will be poured out upon them (12:10); a fountain of cleansing will be opened for them (13:1); and false prophets will be banished (13:2–6). Then, finally, the people will enter their rest, in which they will be seated under vine and fig tree, enjoying length of days and bountiful *harvests, and an endless supply of living *water (3:10; 8:3–13; 10:6–12; 14:8–9, 20–21). This transformation will have implications not just for the Promised Land but also for the entire world. The *nations appear in Zechariah not just as God's enemies but as a future part of

God's people, joining wholeheartedly in *worship (2:11; 8:20–23; 14:16–19).

Themes from Zechariah in the NT

The presence of God and the Messiah

The conviction of the NT writers is that the 'not yet' of the prophets has now arrived. With the coming of Christ, the 'last days' have broken into history (Acts 2:16–17). This means that God's presence among humans is now experienced in a new way, in Jesus the Messiah. Thus, the separate themes of Zechariah coalesce into a single theme in the NT. Jesus is himself the new temple (John 2:19–21), the glory of God in the midst of his people (John 1:14). He is the 'Root of David' (Rev. 5:5). He is the one whose coming brings 'rest' to his people (Matt. 11:28; Heb. 4:1–11). He is the one who reclothes his people in clean garments of fine linen (Rev. 19:8).

But he does so at great personal cost. In order to clothe his church with priestly garments, our great high priest must himself be stripped naked and hung on a cross, where he bears the *sins of his people on their behalf. Indeed, the majority of the direct citations of Zechariah in the NT appear in the passion narratives. Matthew and John both quote Zechariah 9:9–10 in their accounts of Jesus' triumphal entry into Jerusalem on a donkey (Matt. 21:4–5; John 12:14–15). Jerusalem's king (see *Kingdom of God) has finally come. Matthew further cites Zechariah 13:7 as a prediction of Jesus' abandonment by the disciples (Matt. 26: 31; cf. Matt. 9:36; the theme of Jesus the Good Shepherd in John 10:11); John also points to Zechariah 12:10 as a prophecy of the soldier's piercing of Jesus' side (John 19:37; cf. Rev. 1:7). Matthew relates the fulfilment of Zechariah 11:12–13 in Judas' betrayal of Jesus for thirty pieces of silver and its subsequent use to buy a potter's field (Matt. 27:9). The NT thus depicts Jesus as being the Messiah of whom Zechariah spoke.

The final victory of God

Even though the end of the ages has broken into history in Christ, history continues. There is in the NT also a 'now' and a 'not yet'. In the 'now', trials and tribulation continue (Acts 14:22). Only in the 'not yet' will the final victory of God be seen, when all things are put under the feet of Christ (1 Cor. 15:24–25). Then at last we shall be in the place where there is no more *suffering, no more sorrow, only the unhindered presence of God in the midst of his people (Rev. 21:3–4). In the meantime, the onslaught of Satan and his forces (see *Spiritual powers) against God's people continues with ever greater ferocity (Rev. 20:7–8). But the final victory of God is already assured because of the coming of Christ. God will not stand by and watch his people devastated; instead, he will intervene and fight for them, destroying the forces of the evil one and bringing about a recreation on a global scale as the nations flock to the heavenly Jerusalem. The vision of Zechariah that the whole Promised Land will be holy to the Lord (14:20–21) finds its fulfilment in the heavenly Jerusalem, depicted as a gigantic Most Holy Place, with cubic shape and ubiquitous pure gold (Rev. 21:16, 18).

Bibliography

I. M. Duguid, 'Messianic Themes in Zechariah 9–14', in P. E. Satterthwaite, R. S. Hess and G. J. Wenham (eds.), The Lord's Anointed: Interpretation of Old Testament Messianic Texts (Grand Rapids and Carlisle, 1995) pp. 265–280; E. M. Meyers and C. L. Meyers, Haggai, Zechariah 1–8, AB (Garden City, 1987); idem, Zechariah 9–14, Malachi, AB (Garden City, 1994); D. L. Petersen, Haggai, Zechariah 1–8, OTL (Philadelphia, 1984); idem, Zechariah 9–14, Malachi, OTL (Louisville, 1995).

I. M. DUGUID

MALACHI

Malachi was probably the last of the named OT prophets, chronologically as well as canonically. He ministered long after the exile, since service in the *temple, completed in 516 BC, had already become perfunctory (1:6–14). This period shows a striking pattern of spiritual fervour punctuating years of decline and apathy. Restoration and revival were led by Sheshbazzar in 539 (Ezra 1 – 3), Zerubbabel, *Haggai and *Zechariah in 520 (Ezra 5 – 6), *Ezra in 458 (Ezra 7 – 10), Nehemiah in 445 (Neh. 1 – 12), Nehemiah again after 433 (Neh. 13:6–31) and, sometime in this period, Malachi himself. Devotion to Yahweh was threatened less by apostasy and idolatry, largely dealt with by the cataclysm of exile, and more by lax *worship and loose morals.

The parallel with some Christian history, not least today, means that we can learn much from *God's post-exilic messengers.

'Malachi' means, appropriately, 'my messenger'. It could be a cover for anonymity (cf. 3:1), but this would make Malachi unique among the *prophetic books; more probably it is a name. The prophet's character comes across in the confrontational question and answer style (or 'prophetic disputation') used throughout the book. Perhaps he was a lawyer! This style distinguishes him from other post-exilic leaders and other prophets, and reminds us of the diversity of personalities God uses. While Malachi has his distinctive style and makes his own contribution to the prophetic corpus, his main themes can also be seen as a summary of the prophetic message, indeed of the whole OT, and are ever relevant.

1. *Covenant love (1:2–5)*. The categoric assertion of the Lord's *love contrasts markedly with the opening condemnation of most other prophetic books. This love is the very basis of the nation and faith of *Israel, and was emphasized in the *covenant at Sinai (cf. Exod. 19:5 and particularly Deut. 4:37; 7:7–8; 10:15). While the term 'covenant' is not used here (but cf. 2:10, also 2:4, 14), its core element of personal relationship is clear in the mention of the two brothers, Jacob and Esau. Love for Jacob, reaffirmed in Israel's restoration after exile, is highlighted by 'hate' for Esau – the term covers the range of emotions from implacable enmity to second preference (e.g. Gen. 29:31 RSV, Leah is 'hated'). The oracle given to Rebekah before the twins' birth mentioned only reversal of roles, but as the centuries progressed Edom became Israel's unrelenting enemy and even participated in its downfall (cf. Obad. 10 – 14). Thus God's wrath (1:3–4) was revealed in Edom's irreversible destruction, fulfilled by the Babylonians and/or Nabateans. This passage is cited by Paul in defence of God's sovereignty (Rom. 9:13), though as with Pharaoh, also quoted, human responsibility is inextricably intertwined.

2. *Devotional integrity (1:6 – 2:9; 3:6–12)*. The temple which had been rededicated with such enthusiasm (Ezra 6:16–18) now witnessed only slovenly *sacrifice from bored *priests and stingy, cheating worshippers. Better to suspend the whole sacrificial system! Unless things improved, the priests would be cursed and discarded along with the animal offal and dung (2:3). By contrast, renewed financial *faithfulness would bring uncontainable blessing (3:10). As an encouragement, Malachi presents two cameos. First, there is a glorious vision (1:11, already hinted at in 1:5) of all the *nations of the world presenting true sacrifice to the Lord (cf. Ps. 113:3; Is. 19:18–25; Zeph. 2:11). As in the divine promises from *Abraham's time onwards, God's purposes centre on Israel but extend far beyond. Secondly, the prophet describes a model priest like Levi, a reverent, upright and effective teacher (2:5–7). Both prophetic vistas are clearly fulfilled in the NT, the latter in both Christ and his apostles (cf. 2 Cor. 5:11, 20).

3. *Faithful relationships (2:10–16)*. Partnership in covenant involves faithfulness to partners, within both the covenant community and *marriage (2:10, 14). But many men were abandoning their older Jewish wives in favour of foreigners. (2:11 seems at first sight to be a discussion of religious apostasy, but the textual and historical contexts point more to the theme of mixed marriages.) Penitence without faithfulness is futile. Verse 12 may invoke the example of Abraham (NIV footnote), an implicit backdrop to much of Malachi, or may provide a divine rationale for faithful marriage within the covenant *people (NIV text). Either way, God hates divorce, which violently disrupts this plan as well as provoking untold misery. Some think this categorical statement must place Malachi before Ezra and Nehemiah, who both presided over divorce from foreign wives (Ezra 10; Neh. 13). But the statement occurs in the context of men's divorcing their Jewish wives. And the recurrence of the problem between Ezra and Nehemiah shows that Malachi could have addressed the same issue again later still. The principle of permanent marriage is reaffirmed by *Jesus (Matt. 19:4–9) and that of partners' sharing the faith by Paul (2 Cor. 6:14, though the verse has a wider application). Malachi's repeated injunction to 'guard yourself' is as apposite as ever.

4. **Fearful *hope (2:17 – 3:5; 3:13 – 4:6)*. Tying these threads together, and in response to the prevailing sense of futility, Malachi portrays the sudden, startling appearance of the Lord in *judgment, preceded by his messenger. Some see the three descriptions in 3:1 as referring to the same person, but the Hebrew structure and the mention in 4:5 of

*Elijah as precursor argue against this. On the one hand, fiery judgment will bring purification of the temple personnel, vindication for God's treasured possession and *healing from the 'sun of righteousness'. On the other, it will consume the ungodly, who are guilty of religious, moral and social *sin. The NT identifies 'Elijah' as *John the Baptist (Luke 1:17; 7:27), and reiterates that judgment involves purification and punishment (e.g. 1 Cor. 3 and 1 Pet. 4, both of which echo Malachi). And it also gloriously reveals the Lord, coming to his temple – both building and people.

And so Malachi (and our OT) ends with an exhortation to *obedience, a reminder of the future, and a warning against unfaithfulness.

Bibliography

J. G. Baldwin, *Haggai, Zechariah, Malachi*, TOTC (London, 1972); R. L. Smith, *Micah–Malachi*, WBC (Waco, 1984); P. L. Redditt, *Haggai, Zechariah, Malachi*, NCB (London, 1995); P. A. Verhoef, *The Books of Haggai and Malachi*, NICOT (Grand Rapids, 1987).

P. S. JOHNSTON

MATTHEW

The Gospel of Matthew has been widely understood from the beginning as reflecting a form of Jewish Christianity. It is the Jewish-Christian character of Matthew that largely accounts for both its unique richness and its problematic character. Although Matthew has universal relevance, it clearly articulates the story of *Jesus especially with Jewish readers in mind, and this is clearly an indispensable key to a correct understanding of the Gospel and its theology.

The life-setting of the Gospel

Although the point is much debated, Matthew reflects a time when Jewish Christians had broken with the synagogue. Such a conclusion does not necessitate a date as late as the 80s, contrary to the consensus among scholars. There was great tension between Christians and Jews from a very early stage, and it is not difficult to imagine the situation presupposed by Matthew if a relatively early date is accepted, e.g. one in the late 60s.

Matthew and his Jewish readers found themselves in a difficult position. On the one hand they had to defend their *faith to the non-Christian Jewish community, which criticized them for departing from the faith of *Israel. On the other hand they knew that they had become part of a new entity that united them with Gentile Christians. The challenge they faced was to show the continuity of their faith with the OT scriptures, i.e. to affirm the old, while at the same time acknowledging the unprecedented character of what had now occurred in Christ – to affirm the new. For this reason, many have seen the words of Jesus in 13:52 as describing what Matthew himself is doing: 'Therefore every scribe who has been trained for the kingdom of heaven is like the master of a household who brings out of his treasure what is new and what is old' (NRSV). For Matthew, a proper understanding of the *gospel entails the affirmation of both new and old, and thus there is a tension between continuity and discontinuity throughout the Gospel. If we are to understand the evangelist we must think of him first of all as a Jew who believes that his Jewish faith has not been abolished, but rather fulfilled in Christ.

Theological tensions in Matthew

On several key theological topics Matthew reveals tensions that reflect the delicate balance between old and new. The new does not cancel out the old; the old may be taken up into the new, to be sure, but it is always preserved in some form.

Particularism and universalism

Unquestionably among the most difficult material in Matthew is that which affirms a particularism that stands in sharp contrast to what we understand as NT Christianity. According to Matthew, when Jesus sends out the twelve on their missionary journey, he instructs them that they are to 'go nowhere among the Gentiles, and enter no town of the Samaritans, but go rather to the lost sheep of the house of Israel' (10:5–6). Similarly, when the Canaanite woman pleads with Jesus for the healing of her daughter, he refuses and responds with the words 'I was sent only to the lost sheep of the house of Israel' (15:24).

At the same time, Matthew is clearly aware of and affirms the Gentile *mission, which is explicitly referred to in 24:14 and is the heart of the commission given to the apostles by the risen Jesus in 28:19. Indeed, the Gentile mission is anticipated at various points in Matthew's narrative: the Magi in 2:1–12; the centurion in 8:5–13, and especially the statement of Jesus in 8:10–11, 'Truly I tell you, in no one in Israel have I found such faith. I tell you, many will come from east and west and will eat with Abraham and Isaac and Jacob in the kingdom of heaven'; the statement of 12:21, 'And in his name the Gentiles will hope' (drawn from the LXX of Is. 42:4); the definition of 'the field' as 'the world' in 13:38; the parables of the tenants (21:33–43) and the marriage feast (22:1–10).

What then is the point of the particularist statements, found in the Gospels only in Matthew? They are of course historically accurate descriptions of Jesus' restriction of his work and that of his disciples to the Jews. But why does Matthew bother to include these statements which conflict so strongly with the ultimate goal of Jesus' mission? The answer is that Matthew is eager to underline the fulfilment brought by Jesus as in the first instance the manifestation of *God's *covenantal faithfulness to Israel.* Far from being disloyal to the faith of the patriarchs and the hope of Israel, Jesus comes precisely to fulfil it and to fulfil it for the Jews exclusively. Only subsequently would the Gentiles be part of the fulfilment (*cf.* Paul's perspective in Rom. 1:16). (See *Nations.)

Israel and the church

If Jesus came in the first instance to Israel, neither during his mission nor afterwards did Israel as a whole receive his message. The result is that together with its very Jewish character, the Gospel includes a bitter polemic against the Jews who rejected Jesus and his message.

Early in the Gospel *John the Baptist indicates that descent from Abraham can guarantee nothing, but that God can raise up sons for Abraham from stones (3:9). These words suggest that a new entity is on the horizon, one that will transcend Israel. This comes further into focus in the strong words of 8:11–12: 'I tell you, many will come from east and west and will eat with Abraham and Isaac and Jacob in the kingdom of heaven, while the heirs of the kingdom will be thrown into the outer darkness, where there will be weeping and gnashing of teeth.' The heirs of the *kingdom, the Jews, will not inherit the kingdom, except in and through Jesus Christ.

The new entity in which God's purposes will ultimately find their fulfilment is the community established by Jesus in 16:18, his '*church' (the Greek word *ekklēsia* is used only here and in 18:17 in the four Gospels). That the church is meant to represent a new Israel (a phrase not used by the evangelist) is already clear from the fact that Jesus chose twelve disciples (10:1–4), who reflect the twelve tribes of Israel.

Towards the climax of the Gospel, three successive parables elaborate the movement away from Israel as the locus of God's *salvific purposes to the new entity being created by Jesus. In the first of these (21:28–32), the son who said he would work in the vineyard but did not do so symbolizes the disobedience and unbelief of the Jewish leaders. Tax collectors and prostitutes, on the other hand, receive the message of the kingdom.

The second parable, the parable of the tenants (21:33–43), is the most graphic of the three. The workers in the vineyard, the Jews, not only fail to bring forth fruit, but eventually kill the son of the vineyard owner. When Jesus asks the Jewish authorities what the owner of the vineyard will do to the tenants, they answer, 'He will put those wretches to a miserable death, and lease the vineyard to other tenants who will give him the produce at the harvest time' (21:41). This conclusion is reinforced by Jesus with the words 'Therefore I tell you, the kingdom of God will be taken away from you and given to a people that produces the fruits of the kingdom' (21:43). Here in dramatic sharpness is the theme of the transference of the kingdom from Israel to the church. The kingdom is the salvation that Christ brings, and it is now the possession not of Israel but of a new entity that has taken Israel's place.

In the third parable (22:1–10), those invited to the wedding banquet (a metaphor for eschatological fulfilment) decline the invitation, upon which the king concludes: 'The wedding is ready, but those invited were not worthy. Go therefore into the main streets, and invite everyone you find to the wedding banquet' (22:8–9). Because they did not receive Jesus and his message, the Jews (those who initially were the privileged recipients of the covenant promises) lose their place at the banqueting table. A new group that responds positively to the invitation takes their place.

Although Matthew does not use the language of a new Israel, it is fairly clear that he has something like this in mind. For Matthew the new entity, the community founded by

Jesus, is the fulfilment of the scriptures and hence stands in continuity with Israel as the heir to the promises. The church is therefore the demonstration of God's faithfulness to Israel.

The transference of the kingdom from Israel to the church is often thought to involve 'displacement theology', *i.e.* the displacement of Israel by the church. This is not, however, language that Matthew would find acceptable. The church does not take the place of Israel; rather Israel finds its true identity in the church. This may sound like a subtle point, but it is an important one. In this connection it is useful to remember that the earliest church was entirely Jewish. These first Jewish Christians, including Matthew, would have argued vociferously that their Christian faith was consistent with, and the fulfilment of, the faith of Israel. As Matthew notes in 1:21, Jesus came to 'save his people from their sins'.

It is obvious that the tension between Jewish Christians, such as those represented by Matthew, and Jews who did not accept Christ or his teaching, was very great as the first century progressed. This is reflected in the tone of Matthew's narrative at several points. The evangelist refers to '*their* synagogues' (4:23; 9:35; 10:17; 12:9; 13:54), '*their* scribes' (7:29), and simply 'the Jews' (28:15), thus setting himself and his readers clearly apart from their non-Christian Jewish brothers and sisters. The hostility is reflected in such passages as 3:7 and 6:1–18, the vitriolic chapter 23, and the notorious statement of 27:25, where the people say: 'His blood be on us and on our children.'

It should immediately be pointed out that this hostility reflects an intramural debate (*i.e.* one between Jews and Jews), and that to an extent it reflects the polemical conventions of the day. It is in principle little different from the blistering polemic against the Jews that can frequently be found in the prophets, except that here the stakes are higher. It must be made absolutely clear, however, that these passages provide no warrant whatsoever for anti-Semitism. They reflect historical circumstances of the first century and are conditioned by the identity of the participants. Anti-Semitism can have no place in the church if the church is to follow the teaching of her Lord. Real and deep differences between Christians and Jews need not, and must not, lead to hatred and hostility. Indeed, the church must vigorously combat anti-Semitism wherever and whenever it rears its ugly head.

Law and grace

The strength of Matthew's commitment to the *law of Moses is unique among the Gospels, indeed, in the entire NT. Matthew alone records Jesus' words, 'Do not think that I have come to abolish the law or the prophets; I have not come to abolish but to fulfil … not one letter, not one stroke of a letter, will pass from the law until all is accomplished. Therefore, whoever breaks one of the least of these commandments, and teaches others to do the same, will be called least in the kingdom of heaven' (5:17–19). To the young man who wants to know what he must do to gain eternal life, Jesus responds: 'If you wish to enter into life, keep the commandments' (19:17). Consonant with this is Matthew's emphasis on reward for good deeds (*cf.* 6:1–6; 10:41–42; 16:27; 25:31–46).

This emphasis on the law is unsurprising in a Gospel written for Jewish Christians. It was important for Matthew to stress that Jesus remained fundamentally loyal to the law. Matthew understandably portrays Jesus in a much less radical light than does his main source, *Mark. He will, for example, have nothing of the Markan editorial insertion 'thus he declared all foods clean' (Mark 7:19), in his version of Jesus' answer to the question about defilement. Instead, he turns readers' attention away from the issue of kosher food to that of eating with unwashed hands (15:10–20). Matthew's loyalty to the law is so strong that he can even note that Jesus approved of the Pharisees insofar as they correctly interpreted the law (23:2–3).

Yet with all of this, even Matthew can hardly avoid the dramatically authoritative stance that Jesus takes in his interpretation of the Mosaic law. It is not the law of Moses *per se* that must be kept, but rather the law *as now interpreted by the Messiah*. Jesus does not bring a new law; he has come to reveal the intended meaning of the law, to provide its definitive interpretation (*cf.* the antitheses of 5:21–48). This is how he fulfils the law (*cf.* 5:17). The *eschatological turning point has been reached, with the dawning of the kingdom of God now announced by the Messiah. It was the authority with which Jesus taught that so impressed those who heard him (*cf.* 7:28–29); in and through his teaching the intent of the law comes to expression. The law is not abolished, but brought to expression the uniquely authoritative teaching of Jesus. The result is that the one who obeys the teaching of Jesus, which penetrates to the very essence of the law, has in effect faithfully obeyed the Torah in its entirety. For this reason, at the end of the Gospel Jesus commissions his disciples to teach not what the Torah commands, as one might expect, but 'everything that *I* have commanded you' (28:19–20). Those who follow Jesus' teaching will truly embody the *righteousness of the Torah.

Because of its strong emphasis on *demand,* Matthew has often been misunderstood as setting forth a salvation by works theology. Indeed, there are a number of strong statements which, if isolated from the larger context, can be taken that way. Counterbalancing the stress on demand, however, is the significance of *gift* in Matthew. Full weight should be given to the framework of the entire Gospel, which rests upon the overwhelming announcement of *grace in the arrival of the promised kingdom and God's promised Messiah. The kingdom of heaven (= the kingdom of God; see the synonymous use in 19:23–24) is the gift of God's grace, brought to the unworthy and the needy, who have only to receive it. Indeed, isolated from the context of the entire Gospel and from the beatitudes with which it begins, the Sermon on the Mount (chs. 5 – 7) presents a required standard of righteousness so high that it may well terrify the reader. Yet at the beginning of the Sermon the beatitudes offer the kingdom freely, by grace, to those who will merely receive it with empty hands.

This point is underlined throughout the ministry of Jesus as recorded in the Gospel narrative. Jesus offers the kingdom to the unworthy, for example, to 'tax collectors and sinners' (9:10–13; 11:19), who respond positively to his message of grace. He says that he came 'to call not the righteous but sinners' (9:13; *cf.* 21:31). 'Both good and bad' are invited to the wedding feast, according to the parable in 22:1–10. Grace can be clearly seen also in the parable of the workers in the vineyard, where those who come at the last hour are paid the same as those who worked the whole day (20:1–16). And the parable of the unforgiving servant concerns one who had

been forgiven an unimaginably huge debt (18:23–35). Forgiveness of *sins is at the heart of grace, and Matthew defines the gospel in terms of forgiveness: 'For he will save his people from their sins' (1:21). This is indeed the work of the Son of Man according to Matthew, for he came 'not to be served but to serve, and to give his life a ransom for many' (20:28). At the last supper he says, 'this is my blood of the covenant, which is poured out for many for the forgiveness of sins' (26:28). At the centre of the Sermon on the Mount stands the Lord's Prayer with its petition for the forgiveness of sins (6:12). More than once in the narrative the forgiveness of sins is highlighted: 9:2, 6; 12:31. (See *Reconciliation.)

In short, grace is the very basis of Matthew's narrative. As in Paul, so in Matthew, the imperative is grounded in the indicative of God's grace. The demand in fact presupposes the gift, and is impossible to fulfil without it. For Matthew the law is to be fulfilled in following the teaching of Jesus. But the call to discipleship is based on the gift, the grace of God, that is the heart of the gospel. Thus Matthew finds room for *both* law *and* grace.

Other important theological motifs in Matthew

There are a number of other theological motifs which, though shared by other Gospel writers, have a distinctive character in Matthew. In these we will again see Matthew, the Jewish-Christian interpreter of Jesus, writing to Jewish Christians with their interests and concerns particularly in mind.

Fulfilment: the distinctive formula quotations

Fulfilment is a matter of keen interest to Matthew and his Jewish readers. The main announcement of the Gospel concerns what is called 'the gospel of the kingdom' (4:23; 9:35; 24:14; *cf.* 26:13). This is the good news that the promised rule or reign of God has begun to be realized in history. It is a given for Matthew that Jesus, the Messiah, comes in fulfilment of the promises of Scripture. Matthew contains more than sixty explicit quotations from the OT, not to mention a great many allusions. This is more than twice as many as in any of the other Gospels.

Most striking are the ten quotations introduced with a slightly varying formula employing the passive of the verb *plēroun*, 'so that the word was *fulfilled*' (1:22–23; 2:15; 2:17–18; 2:23; 4:14–16; 8:17; 12:17–21; 13:35; 21:4–5; 27:9–10). An eleventh quotation uses the synonymous *anaplēroun* (13:14–15). The *plēroun* formula occurs again in 26:56, but without a quotation, referring instead to the events of the passion narrative. Other quotations stress fulfilment without using the formula (*e.g.* 3:3).

Many of Matthew's quotations involve a Christological exegesis of the OT, starting from the *a priori* conviction that Jesus is the fulfilment of the promises. This makes possible an approach known as *sensus plenior*, that is, the discovery of a 'fuller meaning' in texts beyond that intended by the authors.

Christology

All the main Christological titles occur more frequently in Matthew than in the other two Synoptic Gospels (except for *kyrios*, which is found most often in *Luke), and Matthew may be said to have a very high Christology (*i.e.* estimate of the person or identity of Jesus) second only among the Gospels to that of *John.

The identity of Jesus as the Christ (= the Messiah) and Son of David (another messianic title; see 22:42), is very important to Matthew and his readers. He is identified as such in the opening words of the Gospel (1:1). The title 'Son of David' occurs throughout the narrative (*e.g.* 12:23; 15:22; 20:30; 21:9), as does 'Christ'. Jesus' healing ministry is summarized in 11:2 as 'the deeds of the Christ'. Most striking is Peter's confession in 16:16 that Jesus is the Christ. The answer of Jesus to the high priest's question as to whether he is the Christ (26:64) is taken by most scholars to be a qualified affirmative (*i.e.* he is the Messiah, but not the kind that the high priest was expecting).

The titles 'Son of Man' and 'Son of God' are both important in Matthew. They do not refer to the humanity and deity of Jesus respectively. The first has an exceptionally wide range of meaning, referring commonly, for example, to the suffering and death that Jesus must undergo. But in many instances the apocalyptic Son of Man is in view (in dependence upon Dan. 7:13), and in references to the parousia and eschatological judgment, 'Son of Man' overlaps with 'Son of God'. 'Son of God' is arguably the most im-

portant title for Jesus in Matthew. It occurs at key points in the narrative (*e.g.* 14:33; 16:16, in connection with 'Messiah'; 27:54). The title of 'the Son' is equivalent to it (3:17; 11:27; 17:5). Along the same lines, but more nearly explicit affirmations of the deity of Jesus, are the reference to him as 'Emmanuel' = 'God with us' (1:23), the *ego eimi* statement, 'it is I' (literally 'I am'; 14:27, alluding to Exod. 3:14), and the passages that refer to Jesus' future presence among his disciples (18:20; 28:20).

The title *kyrios* (Lord) is parallel to 'Son of God', since it too often points to the deity of Christ (see especially 22:41–45). Although in places it is probably to be translated 'sir', it functions occasionally as a confessional title, and is found only on the lips of the disciples.

Righteousness and discipleship

Matthew alone among the Synoptic Gospels uses the word 'righteousness' (*dikaiosynē*), except for the hymnic use of the word in Luke 1:75. In most of its seven occurrences the word refers to the ethical conduct to which disciples of Jesus are called (5:10; 5:20; 6:1; and 6:33). It is clear that the idea of ethical righteousness is extremely important in Matthew. In some instances, however, the word may carry another meaning. Thus if 5:6 is read in context, *dikaiosynē* can be translated 'justice'. And in 3:15 and 21:32 righteousness in the sense of God's saving activity, rather than ethical behaviour *per se*, may be in view.

The word for 'righteous' or 'just' (*dikaios*) occurs more often in Matthew (17 times) than in the other three Gospels combined. It refers to conduct in accordance with the law, as interpreted by Jesus, and to the doing of the Father's will (*e.g.* 7:21; 12:50; 21:31).

The word for 'disciple' (*mathētēs*) occurs far more often in Matthew (73 times) than in the other Synoptic Gospels, and the verb 'to make disciples/be discipled' (*mathēteuō*) is found only in Matthew among the four Gospels (13:52; 27:57; 28:19). This underlines the importance of discipleship for Matthew.

The church

Matthew alone among the four Gospels uses the word 'church' (*ekklēsia*). In the famous 16:18, Jesus says to Peter, who has just confessed him as the Messiah, 'you are Peter, and on this rock I will build my church'. Since Jesus would have been speaking to Peter in

Aramaic, he would not have used the Greek word *ekklēsia*, but an Aramaic word for 'community'. Jesus promises to build his new community upon the first disciple of the Twelve; indeed, the Twelve as representative of the twelve tribes of Israel are the nucleus of that new community. He adds that 'the powers of death shall not prevail against it'. The church will survive and Jesus will be present with it until the end of the age (28:20).

The word 'church' occurs again, twice, in 18:17, where a matter of community discipline is in view. A person who does not listen to the church is to be ostracized from the community. In this passage the authority given to Peter in 16:19 is also given to the other members of the community, as the plural form of the verbs in 18:18 attests. In their exercise of this authority, under the leadership of Christ, the community is promised that Jesus will be present with them: 'where two or three are gathered in my name, I am there in the midst of them' (18:19–20).

In other respects too Matthew can be described as an 'ecclesiastical' Gospel. Not only because of the section on church discipline in chapter 18, but also (more importantly) because of the five lengthy discourses (5 – 7; 10; 13; 18; 24 – 25), Matthew has been regarded as a kind of handbook for the church and for teachers in the church. The needs of the church seem to be constantly in the evangelist's mind, and he has very skilfully shaped the Gospel for its instruction and edification.

Eschatology

It is obvious that eschatology is of great importance to Matthew and his Jewish-Christian readers. These readers would have needed to be assured that the apocalyptic expectations of their scriptures were going to be fulfilled. The importance of eschatology is immediately apparent when the amount of space given by Matthew to the so-called apocalyptic discourse (chs. 24 – 25) is compared to Mark 13. But there is much more on eschatology unique to this Gospel (*e.g.* 13:24–30, 36–43; 20:1–16; 22:1–14). The technical word for the second coming of Christ, *parousia* (lit. 'presence'), is found in the four Gospels only in Matthew (24:3, 27, 37, 39).

In all this material the theme of the coming eschatological judgment plays a special role. Matthew's eschatological teaching is not intended primarily to satisfy ·curiosity concerning the future, *i.e.* to provide information for its own sake, but rather to motivate the church to appropriate conduct. Thus eschatology is closely related to discipleship; believers must be prepared for the coming of the end.

Indeed, eschatology is related to all the main themes of Matthew's theology, and unifies them all. Everything depends for Matthew upon the announcement of the dawning of the kingdom of God, itself a fundamentally eschatological concept, and the coming of the promised Messiah, the Son of God. Herein lies the possibility of moving beyond Jewish particularism to the new community that includes Gentiles. In the dawning of eschatology come grace and salvation, the forgiveness of sins, and a new, authoritative reading of the law by the one messianic Teacher. This beginning of eschatology takes up into itself what Israel's scriptures foretold while at the same time transposing it into a new and higher key.

Bibliography

R. T. France, *Matthew: Evangelist and Teacher* (London, 1989); D. A. Hagner, 'Law, righteousness, and discipleship in Matthew', *WW*, 1998, pp. 364–371; *idem*, 'The Sitz-im-Leben of the Gospel of Matthew', in D. R. Bauer and M. A. Powell (eds.), *Treasures New and Old: Contributions to Matthean Studies* (Atlanta, 1996); *idem*, 'Matthew's eschatology', in T. E. Schmidt and M. Silva (eds.), *To Tell the Mystery: Essays on New Testament Eschatology in Honor of Robert H. Gundry* (Sheffield, 1994); *idem*, 'Apocalyptic motifs in the Gospel of Matthew: continuity and discontinuity', *HBT*, 1985, pp. 53–82; J. D. Kingsbury, *Matthew: Structure, Christology, Kingdom* (Minneapolis, ²1989); U. Luz, *The Theology of the Gospel of Matthew* (Cambridge, 1995); G. N. Stanton, *A Gospel for a New People: Studies in Matthew* (Edinburgh, 1992).

D. A. HAGNER

MARK

Introduction

The Gospel of Mark has received a great deal of attention since a majority of scholars concluded that in all probability it was the first of the NT Gospels to have been written and circulated. This brief Gospel, which early patristic tradition ascribes to John Mark, companion and secretary to the apostle Peter (*Fragments of Papias* 3; Eusebius, *Historia Ecclesiastica* 3.39.15), offers a fast-paced, dramatic narrative of the ministry, teaching, death and mysterious resurrection of *Jesus. At the same time, however, the Gospel of Mark develops a sophisticated apologetic designed to show that Jesus is Israel's Messiah and a true divine hero, for whom Romans should have high regard.

The genre of Mark

Mark is the only Gospel to call itself a 'gospel' (see 1:1, 'The beginning of the gospel', or 'good news'). This word has its origins in Isaiah (see 40:9; 41:27; 52:7; 61:1), but carried other important connotations in the Greco-Roman world (see commentary on 1:1–8 below). The genre of Mark is for the most part biography, similar to the biographies of Elijah and Elisha in the OT (1 Kgs. 17 – 2 Kgs. 9), or to the popular biography found in the Pseudepigrapha (such as *Lives of the Prophets* or *Joseph and Aseneth*). The distinctive features of Mark's biography are the exclusive focus on Jesus and the emphasis on the proclamation of his message. The 'good news' has been realized with the appearance of Jesus. Now the story must be told and the message must be proclaimed (see R. A. Guelich, *Mark*, pp. xix-xxii).

Mark may be a somewhat novel form of biography (and its novelty has sometimes been exaggerated by scholars), but one must not expect of it what we moderns usually expect of biography. Mark tells us nothing about Jesus' birth and upbringing (some details of which are supplied by Matthew and Luke). The evangelist says absolutely nothing about Jesus himself; not one word describes Jesus' appearance or personality. Mark tells us nothing of Jesus' habits, likes, dislikes or interests, apart from his teaching and one or two details. The evangelist is principally concerned with Jesus' public ministry, the impact he had on others, and his fate in *Jerusalem. But the account is not in a strictly chronological, developmental order. The order is thematic. The events and teachings are sometimes clustered around common themes. When and where these things hap-

pened or were spoken often cannot be determined. The Markan presentation is largely guided by literary and theological interests. Jesus is presented as a remarkable, even stunning figure.

Occasion and purpose of Mark

Careful study of Mark 13 and a few related passages suggests that the Gospel of Mark was published in the early stages of the Jewish war with Rome (AD 66–70; see M. Hengel, *Studies in the Gospel of Mark*, pp. 14–28). Mark 13 begins with Jesus' prediction of the complete destruction of the Herodian *temple (v. 2). The disciples ask when this will happen (v. 4) and the long discourse that follows describes various signs that will precede the coming of the 'son of man' (v. 26). Among these signs will be the appearance of various false messiahs and false prophets (vv. 5–6, 21–22) and wars and rumours of war (vv. 7–8). But the major sign that will warn Jesus' followers that the end is near will be the setting up of the 'abomination that desolates' the temple (v. 14).

The events of the 40s – 60s correspond in many ways to these signs. But if Mark wrote after 70, as many scholars assume, then the prediction of the abomination could not be fulfilled. Sensing this problem, some interpreters argue that the abomination was the occupation of the temple precincts by the rebels, or Titus's entry into the sanctuary as it burned. But these proposals are unconvincing. Jesus tells his disciples to flee from Jerusalem when they see the abomination set up. But as it happened, it was too late to flee the city when the rebels occupied the temple precincts, and certainly too late to flee when the Roman army stormed the temple mount and General Titus himself entered the sanctuary. Moreover, verse 18 urges believers to pray that the crisis not happen in winter. But the taking of Jerusalem and the horrors that resulted in fact occurred in the summer. On any fair reading of Mark 13, the actual events of AD 70 do not seem to lie behind these warnings.

It is more probable that Mark 13 reflects the very beginning of the war, possibly even a time shortly before the war began. It was a time of rumours of war, perhaps the early stages of the revolt itself; a time when various would-be prophets and deliverers proffered signs of salvation; a time when Christians believed that the abomination of which Jesus spoke would be set up in the temple, thus making worship there impossible; a time to flee the city, for judgment and the appearance of the son of man was quite near (vv. 14–27).

If the Gospel of Mark was indeed written in the middle 60s, then it was written at a time of severe Christian persecution at the hands of the megalomaniac Nero (ruled AD 54–68). This emperor, increasingly hated and despised by his own people, promoted his deification (which at his death was denied by the Senate). More than any emperor before him, he encouraged the use of the honorific titles 'god', 'son of god', 'lord', 'saviour' and 'benefactor'. Writing in the last two or three years of Nero's life, when the Jewish rebellion was in its early stages, when persecution of Christians was severe, and when many 'prophets' and 'deliverers' were making themselves known, the Markan evangelist puts forward Jesus as the true son of *God, in whom the good news for the world truly has its beginning.

Mark's opening verse makes the Gospel's purpose clear: 'The beginning of the good news of Jesus Christ, the son of God' (Mark 1:1, RSV). The evangelist has very carefully chosen his language, for it deliberately echoes the language of the imperial ruler cult, as seen in the Priene inscription in honour of Caesar Augustus: 'the birthday of the god Augustus was the beginning for the world of the good news'. The evangelist Mark has challenged the imperial myth, claiming that the good news for the world began with Jesus Christ, the true son of God (see Mark 15:39, where the Roman centurion admits upon seeing the impressive death of Jesus: 'Truly this man was the son of God').

Theology and themes of Mark

Mark's theology consists primarily of Christology and represents an attempt to bridge the gulf between the Jewish and Roman worlds. The evangelist achieves this by drawing upon OT language, imagery and structures, and by presenting them in ways that will capture Roman interest. His purpose is to demonstrate that Jesus is indeed Israel's Messiah and that his death on the Roman cross did not nullify either his identity or his mission.

The OT in Mark

Unlike Matthew and John, Mark rarely quotes the OT outside what is probably the tradition that he received. Other than the conflated quotation of LXX Exodus 23:20/Malachi 3:1/LXX Isaiah 40:3 at the opening of his account (1:2–3), and a few allusions in the passion narrative (15:24, 29, 36), OT quotations are limited to statements of Jesus (4:12; 7:6–7, 10; 8:18; etc.). Even the citation in 1:2–3 and the allusions in the passion story are probably traditional elements. But this is not to say that the OT is unimportant to the evangelist. Isaiah 40:3 plays an important role in defining the 'gospel' (cf. Is. 40:9) for both Jewish and Roman readers. Moreover, in many places OT passages and themes underlie the Markan narrative. It has been suggested, for example, that the miracle stories of Mark 4:35 – 8:26 reflect God's mighty acts of deliverance eulogized in Psalm 107.

A specific example of the allusive presence of the OT is found in the transfiguration story (9:2–8), which at several points parallels Sinai tradition. 1. The phrase 'after six days' (v. 2) alludes to Exodus 24:16, where after six days God speaks. If such an allusion is not intended, the chronological reference at this point in the Markan narrative is without meaning. 2. Just as *Moses is accompanied by three companions (Exod. 24:9), so Jesus is accompanied by Peter, James, and John (v. 2). 3. In both accounts, the epiphany takes place on a mountain (v. 2; Exod. 24:12). 4. Moses appears in both accounts (v. 4; Exod. 24:1–18). It is interesting to note that on one occasion Joshua (LXX 'Jesus') accompanied Moses up the mountain (Exod. 24:13). 5. Jesus' personal transfiguration (v. 3) probably parallels the transfiguration of Moses' face (Exod. 34:29–30). Matthew and Luke have apparently seen this parallel, for they draw a closer correspondence by noting the alteration of Jesus' 'face' (Matt. 17:2; Luke 9:29). 6. In both accounts the divine presence is attended by a cloud (v. 7; Exod. 24:15–16). Some believed that the cloud which had appeared to Moses would reappear in the last days (see 2 Macc. 2:8). 7. In both accounts the heavenly voice speaks (v. 7; Exod. 24:16). 8. Fear is common to the stories (v. 6; Exod. 34:30; cf. Tg. Ps.-J. Exod. 24:17). 9. Mark's 'Hear him' (v. 7), unparalleled in Exodus 24, probably echoes

Deuteronomy 18:15. Again it is likely that Luke has noticed the parallel, for he makes the word order correspond to that of the LXX (Luke 9:35). These parallels, especially that of the injunction to hear, may suggest that the voice that spoke with authority from Sinai now speaks through Jesus the Son.

For Jewish readers and hearers, these biblical images and themes would be arresting. Some no doubt found them compelling. Mark defines the 'good news' of Jesus Messiah in terms of the fulfilment of Isaiah's oracle of *salvation and deliverance: 'See, I am sending my messenger ahead of you, who will prepare your way; the voice of one crying out in the wilderness: Prepare the way of the Lord, make his paths straight' (1:2–3, NRSV; cf. Mal. 3:1 and LXX Is. 40:3). In other words, the good news of the Christian message is the fulfilment of that for which Israel had for many years longed. Qumran (*Rule of the Community* 8:12–14; 9:19–20), as well as others (Baruch 5:7; *Testament of Moses* 10:1–5), also understood Isaiah 40:3 as a prophetic text that spoke of restoration. At Jesus' baptism the heavenly voice echoed the words of Psalm 2:7: 'Thou art my beloved Son; with thee I am well pleased' (1:11; cf. Gen. 22:2; Exod. 4:22–23; Is. 42:1). With this utterance Jesus' identity is made clear. Such recognition does not come forth from a human being until Jesus' death on the cross (cf. Mark 15:39). At the mount of transfiguration, where Jesus conversed with Moses, the heavenly voice once again spoke, only this time addressing the disciples: 'This is my beloved Son; listen to him.' These citations and allusions strongly suggest that Mark understood Jesus as the fulfilment of Jewish messianic expectation. As God's beloved Son and as the prophet who was to come (see 8:28), Jesus was the long-awaited Messiah of Israel.

Themes in Mark

The principal message of Mark is the divine sonship of Jesus, a divine sonship that inhabitants of the Roman Empire will find impressive. This point will be treated separately below. Other important themes in Mark's Gospel include the *kingdom of God and conflict with Satan, faith and salvation, the Jewish *law, and the Twelve and discipleship.

The kingdom of God and conflict with

Satan. The essence of Jesus' message, according to Mark 1:15, is 'The time is fulfilled, and the kingdom of God is at hand; repent, and believe in the gospel.' In Mark it is clear that the kingdom of God is directly opposed to Satan and his minions. Indeed, the two kingdoms are at war with one another. According to Mark 3:27, Jesus implies that he is the one stronger than the strong man (*i.e.* Satan himself): 'No one can enter a strong man's house and plunder his goods, unless he first binds the strong man; then indeed he may plunder his house.' John the Baptist earlier had predicted, 'After me comes he who is mightier than I, the thong of whose sandals I am not worthy to stoop down and untie. I have baptized you with water; but he will baptize you with the Holy Spirit' (1:8). Answering this expectation, Jesus shows that he is indeed the stronger one, powerful in the Spirit, for the evil spirits cower before him (1:24, 34; 3:11; 5:6–10; 9:20, 25). So impressive is his power that the crowds exclaim, 'With authority he commands even the unclean spirits, and they obey him' (1:27).

As the stronger one who plunders Satan's 'house', or kingdom, Jesus begins the liberation of Israel. He casts out demons, *heals, purifies and reclaims the lost. These activities are manifestations of the kingdom of God, that is, the powerful presence of God. The 'beginning of the good news' (1:1), as inhabitants of the Roman Empire would have understood it, would have to entail restoration and renewal. Jesus' remarkable ministry, in which he overpowers Satan and his allies and brings about healing and restoration, dramatically validates his message. (See *Spiritual powers.)

Faith and salvation. A distinctive feature in the Markan presentation of Jesus is his call for *faith and his linking of healing, or salvation, to faith. At the outset of his ministry Jesus commanded Israel to 'believe in the gospel' (1:15). The need for faith becomes axiomatic. When Jesus sees the faith of the paralysed man and his friends who lower him through the roof, he declares: 'My son, your sins are forgiven' (2:5). Jesus assures the woman who has touched his coat: 'Daughter, your faith has made you well; go in peace, and be healed of your disease' (5:34). Moments later Jesus assures the ruler of the synagogue, who has just learned that his daughter has died: 'Do not fear, only believe'

(5:36). When Jesus asserts, 'All things are possible to him who believes', the panicked father cries out: 'I believe; help my unbelief!' (9:23–24). The same point is made in reference to the rich young man, who was unable to give away his wealth and follow Jesus (10:17–22). The astonished disciples ask, 'Then who can be saved?' Jesus replies, 'With men it is impossible, but not with God; all things are possible with God' (10:26–27). In Jericho Jesus says to blind Bartimaeus: 'Go your way; your faith has made you well' (10:52). After the discovery of the withered fig tree, Jesus enjoins his disciples, 'Have faith in God' (11:22), and then goes on to teach that one who asks without doubting, but in faith, will receive whatever he asks in prayer (11:23–24). Faith in God will be needed all the more because of the difficult and dangerous days that lie ahead. Jesus warns his disciples that they 'will be hated by all' for his 'name's sake. But he who endures to the end will be saved' (13:13). The time of persecution will be so severe, 'if the Lord had not shortened the days, no human being would be saved' (13:20).

The ruling priests, however, reject Jesus' ministry and have no faith in his message or in John's before him (cf. 11:31). Indeed, when Jesus hangs dying on the cross, the ruling priests mock him by saying, 'save yourself, and come down from the cross!' (15:30); and again, with the scribes: 'He saved others; he cannot save himself. Let the Christ, the King of Israel, come down now from the cross, that we may see and believe' (15:31–32). The ruling priests and scribes thus exhibit the precise opposite of what the Markan evangelist demands.

The Jewish law. The Markan Jesus speaks comparatively little about the Jewish law, but what is said is quite significant. As 'son of man' Jesus claims to have authority 'on earth to forgive sins' (2:10), an authority delegated by God to the priests (cf. 2:7). Again, as son of man Jesus is 'lord even of the sabbath' (2:27–28). Jesus directly challenges Pharisaical interpretation of the law when he heals on the *sabbath (3:1–6). The implication is that it is always lawful 'to do good and to save life', even on the sabbath. In 7:1–13 Jesus' teaching regarding purity is a declaration (the Markan evangelist says parenthetically) that 'all foods' are clean (7:20; cf. vv. 14–23). In the same context, Jesus condemns the practice of *korban* ('gift [to God]') whereby one denies material assistance to one's aging parents. Jesus views this oral tradition as a direct contravening of the command of God to honour one's parents (7:9–13; cf. Exod. 20:12; Lev. 20:9).

Jesus criticizes the Pharisees' interpretation of Deuteronomy 24:1–4; their oral traditions too easily permit divorce. Jesus infers from Genesis 1:27 and 2:24 that it is God's will that marriage be permanent (Mark 10:2–12). Because God is God of the living (cf. Deut. 5:26; 1 Sam. 17:26; Hos. 1:10), Jesus infers the truth of the resurrection from God's declaration from the burning bush (Mark 12:18–27; cf. Exod. 3:6). When asked which is the greatest commandment, Jesus responds with his famous 'double commandment', to love God with all that one is and has, and to love one's neighbour as dearly as one loves oneself (Mark 12:28–34; cf. Deut. 6:4–5; Lev. 19:18). Impressed, the scribe is forced to admit that obeying the double commandment is more important 'than all whole burnt offerings and sacrifices' (Mark 12:33). In the Markan context, this is a stunning concession on the part of the scribe. He concedes that Jesus' teaching outweighs the very assumptions operative on the temple mount. Accordingly, Jesus assures the scribe that he is 'not far from the kingdom of God' (v. 34).

Jesus further attacks tradition and practice in the temple precincts, when he warns his disciples of the scribes, 'who like to go about in long robes, and have salutations in the market places and the best seats in the synagogues' (12:38–39). These are the ones who 'devour widows' houses' and offer up long, counterfeit prayers. For this they will receive the greater condemnation (12:40). Indeed, the widow who throws her last penny into the treasury should be viewed (12:41–44), in the Markan context, as one of those widows whose house (or estate) has been consumed by the avarice of the scribes, not assisted, as the laws of Moses command.

The Twelve and discipleship. Jesus calls Simon and Andrew, and then James and John the sons of Zebedee, and 'immediately' they follow him (1:16–20). The abruptness of the call and the promptness of compliance casts Jesus in an impressive, commanding light; he summons people and they obey. Out of his disciples, Jesus appoints 'twelve', a symbolic number surely meant to imply the restoration of Israel. Jesus empowers the Twelve 'to preach and have authority to cast out demons' (3:13–15). Later, Jesus summons the Twelve, sends them out two by two and gives them 'authority over the unclean spirits' (6:7; *cf.* v. 13).

The Markan disciples, however, have much to learn. The storm on the Sea of Galilee frightens them, so much so that Jesus asks: 'Why are you afraid? Have you no faith?' (4:40). The disciples have no understanding of the meaning of the loaves (in reference to the feeding of the five thousand and the feeding of the four thousand), and therefore are scolded by Jesus (6:47–52; 8:14–21). The Markan disciples, despite private explanation (4:11–20; 7:17–23), are slow to understand the full significance of the person and mission of Jesus. Nowhere is this portrayed more dramatically than in Peter's confession in Caesarea Philippi. Most people view Jesus as one sort of prophet or another, but Peter declares that Jesus is 'the Christ' (8:28–29). But when Jesus asserts that he must 'suffer many things, and be rejected', Peter takes him aside and rebukes him (8:31–32). Peter is then rebuked in turn, for he is 'not on the side of God, but of men' (v. 33). From this point the disciples are uncomprehending or frightened when Jesus speaks of his impending passion (9:9–10, 31–32; 10:32–34). Failing to grasp the necessity of *suffering and *humility, the disciples discuss among themselves who is the greatest (9:33–37); later James and John wonder if Jesus might assign them seats on his right and left, the positions of greatest honour in the coming kingdom (10:35–40). This ill-timed request only causes rancour among the disciples, requiring Jesus once again to teach them about humility and service (10:41–45).

The evangelist's purpose in portraying the disciples in this way is not to denigrate them, or to correct an unhealthy triumphalist Christianity that identifies with them. The purpose is to highlight the contrast between the masterful, commanding Jesus on the one hand, and the much weaker and less comprehending disciples on the other. The evangelist wishes to present Jesus to the Roman world as a compelling figure, as the true saviour.

Jesus, the Son of God for the Roman Empire

As already mentioned, the evangelist alludes in his opening words to the imperial religion and its worship of the emperor. There is a further allusion to the imperial gospel in the exclamation of the Roman centurion, 'Truly this man was the son of God' (Mark 15:39). But its Christian import has by this point in the Markan narrative been amply attested.

Jesus' divine identity and mission is confirmed by the heavenly voice, which twice speaks, identifying Jesus as God's 'son' (1:11; 9:7). The demonic world also recognizes the divinity of Jesus and is terrified (1:21–28, 34; 3:11; 5:6–7). The 'wind and sea obey him' (4:41); Jesus walks on water (6:47–52), and multiplies loaves and fishes (6:35–44).

With ease Jesus heals every manner of illness and infirmity. Because of their divinity, it was believed that the Roman emperors could in some instances effect healing. According to Suetonius: 'A man of the people, who was blind, and another who was lame, together came to [Vespasian] as he sat on the tribunal, begging for help for their disorders which Serapis had promised in a dream; for the god declared that Vespasian would restore the eyes, if he would spit upon them, and give strength to the leg, if he would deign to touch with his heel. Though he had hardly any faith that this could possibly succeed, and therefore shrank even from making the attempt, he was at last prevailed upon by his friends and tried both things in public before a large crowd; and with success' (*Divus Vespasianus* 7.2–3). In Mark's Gospel healings are especially prominent (a significant proportion of the Gospel is devoted to miracle stories: 1:21–28, 29–31, 32–34, 40–45; 2:1–12; 3:1–6, 7–12; 4:35–41; 5:1–20, 21–43; 6:35–44, 47–52, 53–56; 7:24–30, 31–37; 8:1–10, 22–26; 9:14–29; 10:46–52). Jesus' use of spittle to heal the blind (Mark 8:22–26; *cf.* John 9:1–12) and the deaf-mute (Mark 7:31–37) parallels Vespasian's use of spittle to heal the blind man.

After his death the successful and respected emperor was deified, that is, enrolled among the gods. Among the most respected emperors was Julius Caesar, whose military prowess was greatly admired, and his nephew Caesar Augustus, whose remarkable, lengthy and successful reign laid the foundation on which the Roman Empire – and the emperor cult – would rest for generations to come. According to Suetonius: '[Julius Caesar] died in the fifty-sixth year of his age, and was numbered among the gods, not only by formal decree, but also in the conviction of the common people. For at the first of the games which his heir Augustus gave in honour of his apotheosis, a comet shone for seven successive days, rising about the eleventh hour, and was believed to be the soul of Caesar, who had been taken to heaven; and this is why a star is set upon the crown of his head in his statue' (*Divus Julius* 88.1). A similar legend grew up around Augustus. After describing the death and cremation of the emperor, Suetonius relates: 'There was an ex-praetor who took oath that he had seen the form of the Emperor, after he had been reduced to ashes, on its way to heaven' (*Divus Augustus* 100.4).

In Mark's Gospel Jesus repeatedly foretells his death and resurrection (8:31; 9:31; 10:33–34), while he confesses to Caiaphas that he will be seen seated at God's right hand, coming with the clouds of heaven (14:62). The centurion's confession that Jesus was 'truly' the son of God (15:39) is the equivalent of Roman deification of their deceased emperors, but the discovery of the empty tomb and the (angelic?) announcement that he has risen (16:4–7) provide divine confirmation of the truth of Jesus' predictions.

The good news of Isaiah 40:3, fulfilled in Jesus of Nazareth, has now become the good news for the entire world. As the true son of God, Jesus offers the world genuine good news, which no Roman emperor could ever hope to offer or make a reality. It is in this context that the Markan evangelist boldly sets forth his apologetic. Despite rejection at the hands of his own people (and the most important people, according to contemporary measures of importance) and a shameful death at the hands of the most powerful people, Jesus was indeed the son of God, humanity's true Saviour and Lord. Mark's purpose is to narrate the story of Jesus in such a way that such a confession will appear compelling and plausible to Jews and Romans.

Bibliography

E. Best, *Disciples and Discipleship: Studies in the Gospel According to Mark* (Edinburgh, 1986); E. K. Broadhead, *Prophet, Son, Messiah: Narrative Form and Function in Mark 14 – 16* (Sheffield, 1994); R. A Guelich, *Mark 1 – 8:26*, WBC (Dallas, 1989); R. H. Gundry, *Mark: A Commentary on His Apology for the Cross* (Grand Rapids, 1993); M. Hengel, *Studies in the Gospel of Mark* (Philadelphia, 1985); M. D. Hooker, *The Gospel According to Saint Mark*, BNTC (London, 1991); H. C. Kee, *Community of the New Age: Studies in Mark's Gospel* (Philadelphia, 1977); J. D. Kingsbury, *The Christology of Mark's Gospel* (Philadelphia, 1983); W. L. Lane, *The Gospel of Mark*, NICNT (Grand Rapids, 1974); J. Marcus, *The Way of the Lord: Christological Exegesis of the Old Testament in the Gospel of Mark* (Louisville and Edinburgh, 1992, 1993); R. P. Martin, *Mark: Evangelist and Theologian* (Grand Rapids, 1972); R. P. Meye, 'Psalm 107 as "horizon" for interpreting the miracle stories of Mark 4:35 – 8:26', in R. A. Guelich (ed.), *Unity and Diversity in New Testament Theology* (Grand Rapids, 1978); F. Neirynck, *The Gospel of Mark: A Cumulative Bibliography 1950–1990* (Leuven, 1992); R. Pesch, *Das Markusevangelium*, 2 vols., HTKNT (Freiburg, 1990–91); V. Taylor, *The Gospel According to St. Mark* (London and New York, 1966); T. J. Weeden, *Mark – Traditions in Conflict* (Philadelphia, 1971); W. Wrede, *The Messianic Secret* (Cambridge and London, 1971).

C. A. EVANS

LUKE

Luke's theological and pastoral concerns are evident in his emphases. In particular, he is concerned to show the continuity in God's plan, even though there are some apparent surprises in what has taken place. These surprises include a Messiah who is crucified and, in his second volume of Acts, the inclusion of Gentiles in God's *people without any attempt being made to relate them to the law. This emphasis also appears in the Christology of the Gospel, in an emphasis on the authority of Jesus, as seen in his work and declarations. In addition, his resurrection-exaltation is God's vindication of his claims and sets the stage for the declaration in Acts of Jesus as the exalted Messiah-Lord, who will be the judge of the living and the dead.

Another surprise is Jesus' conscious pursuit of the fringe of society, including the immoral, the poor and those who suffer. While urging them to turn to God, he also makes it clear that God is ready to accept and empower them, as the Spirit emerges at the Gospel's end as an important gift. The surprises in Jesus' teaching provoke opposition from the Jewish leadership and require perseverance in faith in the face of such opposition. To walk in the ways of the Lord is not easy, given the opposition one faces. None the less, Luke wishes to reassure Theophilus concerning his place among the Lord's people and to make clear that the difficulty of the walk is worthwhile.

The God of design and concern: the plan

Luke's reassuring of Theophilus involves detailed discussion of *God's plan. Luke treats this theme more than the other Synoptic evangelists. His concept of a plan involves both a connection to scriptural hope and divine design and elements of structure and progress within the Gospel's story.

A number of uniquely Lucan passages include this theme (1:14–17, 31–35, 46–55, 68–79; 2:9–14, 30–32, 34–35; 4:16–30; 13:31–35; 24:44–49), while one text overlaps with the other Gospels (the enquiry of *John the Baptist, 7:18–35). Luke utilizes the *suffering Son of Man texts, a few of which are unique to him (9:22, 44; 17:25 [L]; 18:31–33 [L]; 22:22 [L]; 24:7 [L]). Acts also highlights the plan (Acts 2:23; 4:27–28; 13:32–39; 24:14–15; 26:22–23). Its major elements are the career of *Jesus, the hope of the spiritually humble and needy, the offer of God's *blessings, the new era's coming, the suffering of Jesus and the division of *Israel.

Supporting the theme of God's plan is that of promise and fulfilment, especially as it relates to the Scriptures. Three areas are key: Christology, Israelite rejection/Gentile inclusion, and *eschatological justice. The latter two themes are more prominent in Acts. Nonetheless, the theme of Gentiles and non-Jews responding to the gospel, while Israel stumbles, is present in numerous gospel texts (2:34; 3:7–9; 4:25–27; 7:1–10; 10:25–37; 11:49–51; 13:6–9, 23–30, 31–35; 14:16–24; 17:12–19; 19:41–44). (See *Nations, *Righteousness, justice and justification.)

Various themes delineate the plan. The 'today' passages show the immediate availability of the promise (2:11; 4:21; 5:26; 13:32–33; 19:5, 9; 19:42; 23:42–43). John the Baptist is the bridge between promise and inauguration (1 – 2; esp. 1:76–79; 3:4–6; 7:24–35; 16:16), the forerunner predicted by Malachi and the greatest prophet of the old era (7:27). However, the new era is so great that the *kingdom's lowest member is higher than the greatest prophet of the old (v. 28). Here is the basic Lucan structure: the era of promise-expectation followed by the era of inauguration. The message of the gospel and Jesus' teaching about the end clarify the timing and structure of the new era. The plan still has future elements (17:20–37; 21:5–36; 2:38), but the basic turning point has come. So the plan's second portion is subdivided, even though all of that era represents fulfilment. The subdivisions are inauguration (Acts 2:14–40) and consummation (Acts 3:1–26), the already and the not yet.

Jesus' *mission statements outline his task. Jesus preached good news to those in need (4:18–19), healed the sick (5:30–32) and was to be heard, whether his message was communicated through him or through his representatives (10:16). He came to seek and save the lost (19:10). The geographical details trace the growth of the Jesus movement, *e.g.* the progress of the gospel from Galilee to *Jerusalem and the necessity of Paul's going to Rome in Acts (Acts 1:8; 19:21; 23:11). Many passages declare that 'it is necessary' (*dei*) that something occur. In fact, 40 of the 101 NT uses of *dei* occur in Luke-Acts. Jesus *must* be in his Father's house (2:49), preach the kingdom (4:43) and heal the woman tormented by Satan (13:16). Certain events *must* precede the end (17:25; 21:9). Jesus *must* be numbered among the transgressors (23:33). The Christ *must* suffer and be raised, and repentance for the forgiveness of *sins *must* be preached. The Son of Man's suffering is a divinely set forth necessity (24:7); the Christ *must* suffer and come into glory (24:26). At the climactic conclusion of the gospel (24:44), it is also noted that all of this took place because Scripture *must* be fulfilled. The fact that so many of these references appear in the last chapter of Luke underlines the importance of this theme.

Christology and salvation

Jesus and deliverance stand at the heart of the plan. Central here are the themes of Jesus as Messiah-Lord, his teaching and work, and the blessings of the plan that come through him. In addition, Luke issues a call to respond to the opportunity Jesus' invitation creates.

Christology: Messiah-Servant-Prophet to Lord

Some say that Luke's Christology is more a

patchwork than a unified whole; it is a collection of various traditions, the most variegated Christology in the NT. However, there is a unity to the whole. Jesus is introduced as a regal figure (Luke 1 – 2). The announcement to Mary and Zechariah's words make a *Davidic connection explicit (1:31–33, 69). The anointing of Jesus at his baptism recalls two OT passages, Psalm 2 and Isaiah 42, fusing regal and *prophetic images. The images of servant and prophet are combined in Simeon's words (2:30–35), but the idea of a leader-prophet is a dominant Christological theme in Luke. Jesus' sermon at Nazareth (4:16–30) also conjoins regal and prophetic motifs. Though Elijah and Elisha are patterns for Jesus' work (4:25–27), the anointing described in the language of Isaiah 61:1 refers to Jesus' baptism with its regal-prophetic motifs. The people recognize that Jesus is a prophet (7:16; 9:7–9, 19), but Peter confesses him as the Christ (9:20). Jesus further explains that he is a suffering Son of Man. In a tradition unique to his Gospel, Luke relates Jesus' title as 'Son' to Jesus' messianic role (4:41). The regal-prophetic mix reappears with the heavenly voice at the Transfiguration (9:35; Ps. 2:7; Is. 42:1; Deut. 18:15). Jesus is presented as a leader-prophet, one like Moses. The themes of rule and direction are fundamental.

Jesus' messianic role is foundational for Luke. He spells out the nature of Jesus' messiahship, placing it alongside other Christological categories. The prophetic motif is important in the woes against the scribes (11:46–52), the mourning for Jerusalem (13:31–35) and the conversation on the Emmaus road (24:19, 21). Yet even in Luke 13:31–35, the appeal to Psalm 118 includes a regal allusion (19:38), since 'the one who comes' is for Luke fundamentally an eschatological and messianic deliverer (3:15–18; 7:22–23; 19:38). On the Emmaus road the disciples associate their perception of Jesus as a prophet with the hope of national redemption (24:21). For Luke the deliverer-regal imagery merges with the prophetic.

Luke emphasizes Jesus' elevated status. The authority of the Son of Man is introduced as early as 5:24, and this authority and his status as Lord become the focus of dispute in 20:41–44, 21:27 and 22:69 (Acts 2:30–36; 10:36). The significance of Psalm 110 and its reference to Jesus is of crucial importance. In three

steps, the issue is raised (20:41–44), Jesus responds (22:69) and the message of Jesus' authority as Lord is proclaimed (Acts 2:30–36). The Synoptics share the first two texts, but Luke's sequence, ending with the detailed exposition of Acts 2, shows the importance of the dispute. Luke 22:69 makes it clear that 'from now on' Jesus – the Messiah-Servant-Prophet – will exercise his lordship at the right hand of God. This is not to deny that Luke uses other titles. Jesus is Saviour, or one who delivers (2:11; 1:70–75; 2:30–32), as well as Son of David (1:27, 32, 69; 2:4, 11; 18:38–39) or King (19:38). He is the Son, who relates to God as Father, just as the divine testimony declares (1:35; 2:49; 3:21–22; 3:38; 4:3, 9, 41; 9:35; 10:21–22). Yet he is also Son of Adam, who grows in grace (3:38; 2:40, 52). He is compared to Jonah and Solomon (11:29–32). As Son of man he not only suffers and is *exalted, but also ministers (5:24; 6:5, 22; 7:34; 9:58; 11:29–32; 12:8; 19:10). Another frequently used title is 'Teacher' (7:40; 8:49; 9:38; 10:25; 11:45; 12:13; 18:18; 19:39; 20:21, 28, 39; 21:7; 22:11). Luke's portrait of Jesus is variegated, but also organized. Jesus bears authority as well as promise.

The kingdom in Jesus' teaching and work

The Messiah brings the kingdom of God (4:18, 43; 7:22; 8:1; 9:6; 10:11). The kingdom is present now, but it comes in the future. It includes earthly hope, and yet has spiritual dimensions. The kingdom as present reality is associated with Jesus' authority, shown in his command over evil forces. Jesus can speak of the kingdom as 'near' (10:9). He sees Satan fall as the seventy(-two) disciples exercise authority over demons (10:18–19). He says that if he casts out demons by the finger of God, then the kingdom has come (11:20 – 23). He can say that the kingdom is 'among you' (17:21). A king, in one parable, departs 'to receive a kingdom' (19:2). In his hearing before the council of Jewish elders, Jesus says that from now on he will be at God's side (22:69). Finally, the appeal to Psalm 110 depicts a regal authority, ruling from the side of God.

But the kingdom is also future. Luke 17:22–37 describes the *judgment preceding its consummation. Luke 21:5–38 describes the 'time of redemption'. Here the imagery of the Day of the Lord abounds; evil is to be decisively judged. In Luke 21:25–27 allusions appear suggesting the cosmic disturbance associated with the Day of the Lord (Is. 13:10; Ezek. 32:7; Joel 2:30–31; Pss. 46:2–3; 65:7; Is. 24:19, LXX; Hag. 2:6, 21; Dan. 7:13). Jesus will return to fulfil the rest of the promise, showing himself visibly on earth to all humanity while giving eternal benefits to believers.

The kingdom is earthly. Jesus will rule as a Son of David on the earth and yet will bring about total deliverance in the ministry that will follow that of John the Baptist (Luke 1:32–33, 46–55, 69–75). All this activity, both present and future, is Jesus' promised messianic work. The eschatological discourses and the statements of Acts 1:11 and 3:18–21 show that the future hope has not been absorbed in the theme of present inauguration, but remains alive, connected to its OT roots. God brings all his promises to fruition. Spiritual deliverance also comes from him. Zechariah's song (1:78–79) speaks of Jesus as the rising sun who leads those in darkness into peace. The promise of the *Holy Spirit (3:15–17; 24:49; Acts 1:8) and the hope of forgiveness of sins (24:47; see *Reconciliation) are elements of this deliverance. Jesus' authority over demons shows that he is able to fulfil these promises.

The subjects of the kingdom, who benefit from its presence, are the disciples of Jesus (18:26–30). Anyone who wishes to enter is a potential beneficiary (13:23–30; 14:16–24). But there are also unwilling subjects, those who are accountable to Jesus now and who one day will face his rule (19:27; 21:24–27; Acts 3:20–26; 10:42; 17:30–31).

The coming of the Spirit is promised (3:15–17). He empowers and testifies to Jesus (3:21–22; 4:16–20). Later the Spirit will fall on all believers as the last days come (24:49; Acts 2:1–41). The Spirit is power (or enablement) from on high (24:49; Acts 2:30–36; 10:44–47; 11:15–16; 15:8). His presence is evidence that Jesus is raised and that Jesus directs his new community from the right hand of God. Though the Messiah has died and seems to be absent, he is present in the gift and presence of the Spirit. The Spirit becomes the enabler of the kingdom, sent by the Messiah-Lord as the evidence that he has come and is active (3:15–17; Acts 2:14–39).

At the centre of God's provision of *salvation is the resurrection/ascension of Jesus.

Among the Gospel writers, only Luke describes the ascension; it links Luke 24 and Acts 1. A risen Saviour is one who can both rule and consummate his promise. He is one who can forgive and signify forgiveness by bestowing blessings (Luke 24:47; Acts 2:21; 4:12; 10:43). He is one who can receive and give the Spirit, who empowers God's people to testify to him (Acts 2). In short, the ascension shows that Jesus is both Lord and Christ (Acts 2:36).

Salvation in Jesus' teaching and work

Jesus brings both promise and salvation. Salvation involves sharing in *hope, experiencing the kingdom, tasting forgiveness and partaking in the Spirit's enabling power. As we have seen, Jesus' teaching focuses on the offer of the kingdom. This offer is pictured as the release and *healing of Jubilee (4:16–21; Lev. 25:10; Is. 61:1–2), but it also includes a call to ethical honour reflecting the experience of blessing (6:20–49). The parables show the same dual concern. A few parables deal with God's plan (13:6–9, 23–30; 14:16–24; 20:9–18), and in some of these a meal or feast scene is included. The feast displays the joy of salvation and the table fellowship of the future.

Thus the offer of salvation includes a call to an ethical way of life. The life of relationship with God, engagement in mission and ethical honour involves *love, humility, service and righteousness – the subject of most of the other parables (10:25–37; 11:5–8; 14:1–12; 12:35–49; 15:1–32; 16:1–8, 19–31; 18:1–8; 19:11–27). Jesus did not come just to rescue people for heaven, but also to have them know God's transforming presence. This is why commitment is so prominent in Jesus' teaching (9:21–26, 57–62; 14:25–34; 18:18–30).

In his survey of Jesus' work and teaching, as well as in his treatment of salvation, Luke says little about the cross. Why is this, especially since Paul makes so much of it? It is because Luke gives Jesus' ascension and exaltation more prominence. Luke emphasizes the 'who' of salvation: it comes from the exalted Lord who functions as the promised Messiah. Paul explains how Jesus accomplished salvation from sin. Though the cross is less prominent for Luke than for Paul, it has more than an ethical or historical function; it occupies an important theological position in

Luke's teaching. Jesus is the righteous sufferer (Luke 22 – 23). His death inaugurates the new covenant (Luke 22:20), and the church is 'purchased' with his blood (Acts 20:28). Covenant inauguration and a saving transaction take place in Jesus' death. Two other images reinforce this view. The substitution of Jesus for Barabbas illustrates the fact that Jesus took the place of the sinner (23:18–25). Jesus' offer of paradise to the thief as they die together (23:43) shows that Jesus, despite his death, can offer life. (See *Atonement.)

Not only the resurrection, but also the miracles, in their demonstration of the arrival of the new era, authenticate Jesus' authoritative role in the divine plan that brings salvation (7:22; Acts 2:22–24). In fact, the scope of Jesus' healings show the breadth of his authority. He heals the sick, exorcising evil spirits and curing a variety of specific conditions: a flow of blood; a withered hand; blindness; deafness; paralysis; epilepsy; leprosy; dropsy; and fever. He resuscitates the dead and exercises power over nature. The fact that Acts records the disciples' continuing to perform some of these works (Acts 3:6, 16) shows that Jesus' authority, and its authentication, continue after his ascension.

Luke's portrayal of Jesus is focused on his authority and the promise he brings. Jesus' saving work inaugurates the kingdom, delivers the sinner, secures forgiveness of sin, provides the Spirit, and calls for a committed and faithful life lived in the context of hope in the future consummation. Theophilus should be reassured that Jesus can and does fulfil these promises. But who makes up the new community? How does Christology relate to the task of this new community?

The new community

The new community formed around Jesus (see *Church) is not really an organized entity. There are the Twelve and the Seventy (-two), but beyond these basic groups there is no formal structure in Luke. Rather, those who will become the new community of Acts are called 'disciples'. This group is mostly Jewish, but a few hints reveal that Jesus' programme can extend to Samaritans and non-Jews (3:4–6; 4:22–30; 7:1–10; 13:23–30; 14:16–24; 17:12–19; 20:15–16; 24:47). This multiracial theme becomes prominent in Acts, but in the Gospel the key fact is that Jesus' message touches the fringe of society.

Luke focuses on outcasts as members of this blessed community: the *poor, sinners and tax collectors. In addition, women receive special treatment. The poor are materially and spiritually impoverished (1:50–53 and 6:20–23, where the condition of the poor and humble is related to that of God's prophets). The poor or rejected are mentioned in several texts (1:46–55; 4:18; 6:20–23; 7:22; 10:21–22; 14:13, 21–24; 16:19–31; 21:1–4). Sinners are the special targets of the gospel (5:27–32; 7:28, 30, 34, 36–50; 15:1–2; 19:7). Tax collectors, regarded by most Jews as traitors, are potential beneficiaries as well (5:27–32; 7:34; 18:9–14; 19:1–10).

Finally, Luke features women (7:36–50; 8:1–3; 8:43–48; 10:38–42; 13:10–17; 24:1–12). Often widows are mentioned, since they are the most vulnerable of women (2:36–37; 4:25–26; 7:12; 18:3, 5; 20:47; 21:23). Most of these women in the Gospel are sensitive to Jesus' message. Though on the fringes of 1st-century society, women are at the centre of Luke's story. Often they are paired with men (2:25–28; 4:25–27; 8:40–56; 11:31–32; 13:18–21; 15:4–10; 17:34–35; Acts 21:9–10). (See *Man and woman.)

In short, the make-up of the new community knows no boundaries. The good news is available to all, but society's weak and vulnerable are often most able to respond. Jesus shows them a special concern, just as the world seems to ignore or rebuke them. Luke uses three terms to describe the response to the message that brings one into the community: '*repent', 'turn' and '*faith'. The term translated 'repent' is rooted in the OT word 'to turn around' (24:44–47). Repentance involves a reorientation of perspective, a fresh point of view. For Luke the fruit of repentance expresses itself concretely. In material unique to Luke, the Baptist replies to those who enquire 'What should we do then?' by teaching that repentance expresses itself in everyday life, especially in how men and women treat each other (3:7–14).

Four pictures of repentance are specially memorable. Luke 5:31–32 portrays Jesus as a physician healing the sick. Luke 15:17–21 describes the repentance of the prodigal and indicates that a repentant heart makes no claims, recognizing that only God and his mercy can provide relief. At the end of his Gospel, Luke summarizes the essence of the good news: 'Repentance and forgiveness of sins will be preached in his name' (24:47). The parable of the tax collector who in the temple cries out 'God, have mercy on me, a sinner' (18:9–14) demonstrates the penitent's response to God, though the term 'repentance' is not used (also 19:1–10). The word 'turn', while rarely used in the Gospel (1:17; 17:4; 22:32), becomes prominent in Acts, where it denotes the fundamental change of direction that accompanies repentance (Acts 3:19; 9:35; 11:21; 14:15; 15:19; 26:18–20; 28:27). Faith for Luke expresses itself concretely, whether the faith of the paralytic's friends (5:20), the faith of the centurion (7:9) or the faith of the sinful woman who anoints Jesus (7:47–50). The Samaritan leper and the blind man also have faith that Jesus can restore them to wholeness (17:19; 18:42). Faith believes and so acts. In short, faith is the recognition and conviction that God had something to offer through Jesus: forgiveness and the promised blessings. Such people 'call on the name of the Lord' (Acts 2:21; Rom. 10:13).

Various terms denote the blessings given to community members: forgiveness or release (1:77; 3:3; 4:18; 24:47); life (10:25; 12:15, 22–25; 18:29–30); *peace (1:79; 2:14; 10:5–6; Acts 10:36); the kingdom; and the Spirit.

The opponents of salvation

Luke identifies spiritual and human opponents of the new community. At the transcendent level the spiritual forces of evil are resistant, though powerless to frustrate the plan (4:1–13, 33–37; 8:26–39; 9:1; 10:1–12, 18; 11:14–26; 22:3). God's struggle involves not only reclaiming humanity's devotion, but also reversing the effects of the presence of evil forces (see *Spiritual powers). On a human level the opponents are primarily the Jewish leadership of scribes and Pharisees. After Jesus claims authority to forgive sin and challenges the sabbath tradition (5:24; 6:1–11), their opposition becomes a regular feature of the narrative. Its roots go back to their rejection of John the Baptist (7:29–30; 20:1–8). Three times Jesus warns the Pharisees (7:36–50; 11:37–52; 14:1–24). Often the leaders are the object of Jesus' condemnation (11:37–52; 12:1; 14:14; 15:1–2; 16:14–15; 19:45–47; 20:45–47). While the few exceptions, such as Jairus (8:41) and Joseph of Arimathea (23:50–53), catch the attention, the Jewish leadership as a whole opposes

Jesus and plots his demise (6:11; 11:53–54; 20:19; 22:1–6, 21; 23:3–5).

The crowd's reaction to Jesus is mixed. They are interested, but their response is superficial and fickle. A transition occurs in Luke 9 – 13. Jesus issues many warnings in Luke 12:49 – 14:24. He rebukes 'this generation' in 11:29–32, condemns various cities of Israel in 10:13–15 and tells a few parables about the failings of the nation (13:6–9; 20:9–19). The crowd's eventual response typifies the response of most people in Israel. Their rejection of Jesus brings warnings of judgment, yet he weeps for those he warns (19:41–44). In the end the crowd share the responsibility for Jesus' death by asking for Barabbas (23:18–25). So Jesus delivers a prophetic message of judgment to the daughters of Jerusalem and their children (23:27–31).

The response of most of Israel is a tragic one. The nation was offered blessing, but has missed its day of visitation and now awaits judgment (19:44). Now it is the 'time of the Gentiles' (21:24). Israel has not lost its place in God's plan, for the faithfulness of God's promise cannot be denied, but it is 'desolate' until it acknowledges the Messiah (13:34–35; Acts 3:13–21). Luke has been wrongly accused of anti-Semitism; rather, he claims that the new community was persecuted by those rejecting the message of hope. Jesus and the disciples offered the *gospel to the nation and suffered for it. The disciples did not create the division or bring violence to Israel. The new community was not anti-Jewish; it was pro-promise. Its enemies were to be loved and prayed for, as Jesus made clear (6:27–36; 23:34; Acts 7:60).

One source of tension was the issue of the *law. Luke's precise understanding of this issue has been a subject of ongoing debate in Lucan scholarship. It has been properly argued that Luke understands the law to be part of the old era, and portrays the church in Acts as slowly coming to recognize that truth. The law was not regarded as binding, though the missionary praxis of the early church allowed its observance where issues central to the new faith were not at stake. So Gentiles did not need to be circumcised (Acts 15), but Jews could continue to be. The law and its associated traditions, especially the sabbath regulations (6:1–11), are a major source of conflict in Luke's Gospel. Jesus' challenge to the sabbath regulations comes after his proclamation that new wine must come in new wineskins and that those who like the old will not try the new (5:33–39). This remark is part of a dispute centred on Jesus' neglect of Jewish traditions related to cleansing. Jesus challenged the law, or at least its 1st-century Jewish interpretation. Luke regards this challenge as the occasion for Jewish opposition.

In the face of opposition disciples were called to a strong commitment to Jesus. Opposition would come. Indications of division come early in the Gospel (2:34–35) and continue throughout (8:14–15; 9:21–23, 61–62; 12:8–9, 22–34; 22:35–38). The disciples are pictured shrinking back from a bold response, as in the account of Peter's denial. The exhortation to steadfast discipleship reveals one facet of the Gospel's origin. For Theophilus and others the pressure of conflict was the occasion for reassurance.

Response: Luke's call

Luke is clear about how his readers should respond to Jesus and the difficulties arising from opposition to him. The community is called to a fundamental reorientation towards God expressed in faith, repentance and commitment. This attitude of trust both initiates and sustains their walk with God (5:31–32; 15:17–21; *cf.* 12:22–32). The path is difficult and requires self-examination, total commitment, daily dedication and cross-bearing (9:23, 57–62; 14:25–35). The community is called to mission. While Acts details the early missionary activity of the community, the call to preach repentance and forgiveness to all nations, beginning at Jerusalem, is spelled out in the Gospel (24:47). The parables of Luke 15:1–32 reflect Luke's focus on the lost, as do the clear statements of Luke 5:31–32 and 19:10. Jesus' disciples are to follow him in reaching out to others.

Love for God and for one's neighbour, including one's enemy, is part of the call. Luke 11:1–13 describes devotion to God expressed in dependent *prayer. Devotion to Jesus is shown in Mary's choice to sit at his feet, absorbing his teaching and enjoying his presence (10:38–42). In this she is an example of love for God and his way. In addition, the care of one's neighbour is enjoined in Luke 10:25–37. Jesus in his ministry demonstrates what he calls his disciples to be: neighbours to

all, without distinction of race or class. The cross, as the expression of his willingness to die for others, shows him acting in love towards those who are his enemies.

Jesus encourages prayer (11:1–13; 18:1–8, 9–14; 22:40). Prayer does not demand; it requests, humbly relying on God's mercy and will. It trusts in God's care and provision of basic needs. And it looks with expectation to the eschatological consummation of God's kingdom.

Under the pressure of opposition, the community is to remain steadfast and faithful (8:13–15; 9:23; 18:8; 21:19). Disciples are to fear God, not mortals (12:1–12), recognizing that the Lord will return and that they are responsible to him (12:35–48; 19:11–27; 18:8). Like the seed on good soil, they hear the word, cling to it, persevere and bear fruit (8:15). Jesus' promises are for both the present and the future. Those which remain unrealized will eventually be fulfilled (17:22–37; 21:5–38). The coming judgment on Jerusalem is the guarantee and picture of the final judgment. The return of Jesus will be horrific for unbelieving humanity, who will be severely judged. Luke emphasizes that the coming of the Son of Man places a responsibility on his disciples to be faithful and on all humanity to respond to the gospel. While the time of Jesus' return is unknown, it will come suddenly and the disciples must be prepared (12:35–40).

The Lucan view of wealth warns against attachment to possessions (8:14; 12:13–21; 16:1–15, 19–31; 18:18–25), but some examples are given of the positive uses of money (8:1–3; 19:1–10; 21:1–4). Scholars have debated whether Luke decries wealth *per se*. Zacchaeus, who generously gives half of his possessions to the poor and repays those he has wronged, does not divest himself of every asset. His example suggests that the issue is what people do with their possessions and how they view possessions – do they hoard them or use them generously? The disciples are said to have 'left all' for Jesus (18:28–30), family as well as resources. Yet later in the Gospel, under the pressure of Jesus' arrest, they are afraid and deny him. The issue with resources, as with the other demands of discipleship, is not the perfection of the response, but rather its fundamental orientation. Disciples are called to recognize that all life belongs to God and comes from his hand. The rich man rejects Jesus' request to sell all, while the disciples and Zacchaeus begin to relinquish their possessions. Luke warns that hindrances to discipleship include not only confidence in resources, but the fear of others' opinion (12:1–12) and the cares of life (8:14).

Conclusion

Luke's Gospel is pastoral, theological and historical. God's plan affects how individuals see themselves and the community to which they belong. The message of Jesus is one of hope and transformation. Anyone, Jew or Gentile, can belong to the new community. At the centre is Jesus, the promised Messiah-Lord, who sits at God's right hand exercising authority from above. He will return one day and all are accountable to him. His life, ministry and resurrection/ascension prove that he is worthy of trust. Just as he has inaugurated the fulfilment of God's promises, so he will bring it to completion. In the meantime, being a disciple is not easy, but it does bring many rich blessings which transcend anything else this life can offer.

Bibliography

D. L. Bock, *Luke 1:1 – 24:53*, 2 vols., BECNT (Grand Rapids, 1994, 1996); C. A. Evans, *Luke*, NIBC (Peabody and Carlisle, 1990, 1995); C. F. Evans, *Saint Luke*, TPINTC (Philadelphia and London, 1990); J. Fitzmyer, *The Gospel According to Luke*, AB 2 vols. (Garden City, 1981, 1985); J. B. Green, *The Gospel of Luke*, NICNT (Grand Rapids, 1997); I. H. Marshall, *Commentary on Luke*, NIGTC (Grand Rapids and Carlisle, 1978); J. Nolland, *Luke*, WBC, 3 vols. (Dallas, 1989); H. Schürmann, *Das Lukasevangelium*, HTKNT (Freiburg, 1969).

D. L. BOCK

JOHN

John's Gospel, together with the letter to the Romans, can justifiably be called 'the Mount Everest of NT theology'. From its peaks it is possible to survey much of the territory of biblical revelation, including the OT, the *Synoptics, and other portions of the NT. The following essay surveys: 1. the Fourth Gospel's historical setting; 2. its literary features; 3. its theological emphases; 4. its

place in the canon; and 5. its contemporary relevance.

Historical setting

The Gospel's internal evidence suggests that the author is an apostle (1:14; *cf.* 2:11; 19:35); one of the Twelve ('the disciple whom Jesus loved': 13:23, NIV; *cf.* 19:26–27; 20:2–9; 21, esp. vv. 24–25); John, the son of Zebedee ('the disciple Jesus loved' is associated with Peter in 13:23–24; 18:15–16; 20:2–9; 21; *cf.* Luke 22:8; Acts 1:13; 3 – 4; 8:14–25; Gal. 2:9). External evidence supports this identification (Irenaeus, *Adversus Haereses* 3. 1. 2). The Gospel was probably written in Ephesus and aimed (like the other Gospels) at a universal readership (see *e.g.* R. Bauckham, 'For whom were the Gospels written?' in *The Gospels for All Christians*). John's original audience appears to have been made up primarily of diaspora Jews and proselytes.

The purpose statement in 20:30–31 indicates that John wrote with an (indirect) evangelistic purpose, probably expecting to reach his unbelieving audience via Christian readers (Bauckham, *Gospels*, p. 10). The most probable occasion for writing is the destruction of the Jerusalem *temple in 70 AD, a traumatic event that left Judaism in a national and religious void and caused Jews to look for ways to continue their ritual and worship. Seizing the opportunity for Jewish evangelism, John presents *Jesus as the temple's replacement (2:18–22) and the fulfilment of the symbolism inherent in Jewish feasts (esp. chs. 5 – 12). If this hypothesis is correct, the Gospel could have been written any time after AD 70. If Thomas' confession of Jesus as 'my Lord and my God' is intended to evoke associations with emperor worship under Domitian (AD 81–96), a date after 81 AD would appear most likely.

Literary features

John demonstrates that the Christ, the Son of *God, is Jesus (20:30–31; *cf.* D. A. Carson, in *JBL* 106, pp. 639–651) by weaving together several narrative strands. The prologue places the entire Gospel into the framework of the eternal, pre-existent *Word who became flesh (see *Incarnation) in Jesus (1:1–18). The first half of John's narrative sets forth evidence for Jesus' messiahship by way of seven selected *signs (1:19 – 12:50; *cf.* 20:30–31; A. J.

Köstenberger, in *BBR* 5, pp. 87–103). John also includes Jesus' seven 'I am' sayings (6:25–59; 8:12 = 9:5; 10:7 = 9, 11; 11:25; 14:6; 15:1) and calls numerous witnesses (see *Testimony/witness) in support of Jesus' claims (including *Moses and the Scriptures; the Baptist; the Father; Jesus and his own works; the Spirit (see *Holy Spirit) and the disciples; and the fourth evangelist himself). Representative questions concerning Jesus' messiahship serve to lead the Gospel's readers to the author's own conclusion (*i.e.* that Jesus is the Christ; *e.g.* 1:41; 4:25; 7:27, 31, 52; 10:24; 11:27; 12:34).

The second half of John's Gospel shows how the Christ ensures the continuation of his *mission by preparing his new messianic community (see *Church) for its mission. The section opens with Jesus' farewell discourse (13 – 17): the new messianic community is cleansed (by the footwashing and Judas's departure; ch. 13), prepared (by instructions regarding the coming Paraclete and his ministry to the disciples; 14 – 16), and prayed for (ch. 17); the disciples are made partners in the proclamation of *salvation in Christ (15:15–16) and taken into the *life of the Godhead which is characterized by perfect *love and unity (17:20–26). The Johannine passion narrative (18 – 19) presents Jesus' *death both as an *atonement for *sin (*cf.* 1:29, 36; 6:48–58; 10:15, 17–18), though without the Synoptic emphasis on shame and humiliation, and as a stage in Jesus' return to the Father (*e.g.* 13:1; 16:28). The resurrection appearances and the disciples' commissioning by their risen Lord constitute the focal point of the penultimate chapter (20), where Jesus is cast as the paradigmatic sent one (*cf.* 9:7), who has now become the sender of his new messianic community (20:21–23). The purpose statement of 20:30–31 reiterates the major motifs of the Gospel: the 'signs'; believing (see *Faith); (eternal) life; and the identity of Jesus as Christ and Son of God. The epilogue portrays the relationship between Peter and 'the disciple whom Jesus loved' in terms of differing yet equally legitimate roles of service within the believing community.

Theological emphases

The Christ and his mission

In keeping with its Gospel genre, John's narrative focuses on Jesus and his messianic

mission. At the very outset, John's account is based on OT theology. The Gospel's opening phrase, 'In the beginning', recalls the beginning of Genesis, which recounts the *creation of the world (1:1; *cf.* 1:3). According to John, the Word's coming into this world and becoming flesh in Jesus constitutes an event of comparable magnitude (1:1, 14). Jesus is presented as the Word sent from heaven to accomplish a mission and, once the mission has been accomplished, to return to the place from which he came (*cf.* Is. 55:11). John's use of the term *logos* ('Word') with reference to Jesus also serves to contextualize the Christian message in the evangelist's culture.

Another OT concept taken up in John's prologue is that of *light and darkness (1:4–5, 8–9; *cf.* 3:19–21; Gen. 1:3–4). There is a superficial parallel here with the Qumran literature. But there this contrast is set within the framework of an eschatological dualism, while in John Jesus is presented as the Word, active in creation, who has now brought final *revelation from God. This revelation, in turn, is compared and contrasted with the revelation received by and mediated through Moses (1:17–18; *cf.* Exod. 33 – 34). Jesus brought 'grace instead of grace' (1:16, author's translation): while the *law given through Moses also constituted a *gracious gift from God, *truth – final, eschatological truth – came only through Jesus (1:17). And no one, not even Moses, truly saw God (1:18; *cf.* Exod. 33:20, 23; 34:6–7); but now Jesus, already with God at the beginning (1:1), and always, even during his earthly ministry, at the Father's side, has 'exegeted' (explained) him (1:18, author's translation).

The Jewish milieu of John's Gospel and the firm grounding of its theology in OT antecedents are also borne out by the various component parts of the Fourth Gospel's Christological teaching. John's favourite designation for Jesus is that of the Son sent by the Father (3:17, 35–36; 5:19–26; 6:40; 8:35–36; 14:13; 17:1). This metaphor is taken from Jewish life and the halakhic concept of the *šāliaḥ*, according to which the sent one is like the sender himself, a faithful representative of his interests (*cf.* 13:16, 20). The image of the descending bread from heaven develops OT teaching on God's provision of manna in the wilderness (*cf.* Jesus as the antitype of the serpent in the wilderness, 3:14); the figure of the descending and ascending Son of Man (*cf.*

the 'lifted up' sayings in 3:14; 8:28; 12:34) probably derives from apocalyptic passages featuring 'one like a son of man' (Dan. 7:13). Jesus is also shown to fulfil the symbolism of the Jewish feast of Tabernacles (chs. 7 – 9) and the Passover (ch. 19) (see *Sacred meals), as well as that of Jewish institutions such as the Jerusalem temple (2:14–22; see 'Historical Setting' above, and further below).

Central to John's presentation of Jesus' work (esp. in chs. 1 – 12; see 'Literary features' above) is the concept of signs (Köstenberger, in *BBR* 5, pp. 87–103). The trajectory of antecedent OT theology reaches back as far as the 'signs and wonders' performed by Moses at the exodus; Jesus' signs point to a new exodus (*cf.* Luke 9:31). In John, however, the miraculous character of Jesus' works is blended with, and even superseded by, their prophetic symbolism (*cf.* Is. 20:3). As with those of Moses and later prophets, the signs' function is primarily to authenticate the one who performs them as God's true representative. People are severely criticized for demanding spectacular evidence of Jesus' authority (4:48); yet signs are offered as an aid to faith (10:38). And while blessing is pronounced on those who 'have not seen and yet have believed' (20:29), Jesus' signs are clearly designed to elicit faith among his audience, and when they fail to do so, the people are held responsible.

Another crucial motif in John's theology is Jesus' fulfilment of the symbolism inherent in Jewish feasts and institutions. By pronouncing himself to be the 'light of the world' (8:12; 9:5) and the source of 'living water' (4:10–14; 7:38), Jesus claims to fulfil the torch-lighting and *water-pouring ceremonies which formed part of the feast of Tabernacles. By dying during Passover week, Jesus is revealed as the prototype of the Jewish Passover (19:14). By pointing to his own crucified and resurrected body as the true embodiment and replacement of the Jerusalem temple (2:14–22), Jesus indicated that Judaism was merely preparatory, anticipating the coming of God's Messiah. True worship must be rendered, not in any particular physical location, but in spirit and truth (4:23–24).

One final striking feature deserving comment is John's inclusion of seven 'I am' sayings of Jesus. According to John, Jesus is: 1. the bread from heaven (6:25–59); 2. the light of the world (8:12 = 9:5); 3. the door for the sheep and 4. the good shepherd (10:7, 9, 11); 5. the resurrection and the life (11:25); 6. the way, the truth, and the life (14:6); and 7. the vine (15:1). This terminology recalls God's self-identification to Moses at the outset of the exodus: '"I AM WHO I AM ... I AM has sent me to you"' (Exod. 3:14). It is also reminiscent of Isaiah's consistent portrayal of the sovereign Lord God (*e.g.* Is. 43:10–13, 25; 45:18; 48:12; 51:12; 52:6). In places 'I am sayings' and signs are linked (6:35; 11:25). Like the background to the Johannine 'signs', the background to Jesus' self-designation as the 'I am' is therefore to be found in a trajectory ranging from Moses and the exodus to the OT prophets, particularly Isaiah (*cf.* also 12:38–41).

The new messianic community and its mission

Like his portrait of Jesus, John's presentation of the new messianic community follows a salvation-historical pattern (J. W. Pryor, *John: Evangelist of the Covenant People*). In keeping with OT typology, believers are described as a 'flock' (ch. 10) and as 'branches' of the vine (ch. 15). Yet John does not teach that the church replaces *Israel. Rather, he identifies Jesus as Israel's replacement: he is God's 'vine' taking the place of God's OT 'vineyard', Israel (Is. 5). John acknowledges that 'salvation comes from the Jews' (4:22). Yet he portrays Israel as part of the unbelieving world which rejects Jesus. Jesus' 'own' (*i.e.* 'the Jews') did not receive him (1:11). In their place, the Twelve, who are now 'his own', become the recipients of his love (13:1; *cf.* ch. 17). The Jewish leaders, on the other hand, are said not even to belong to Jesus' flock (10:26).

Another instance of John's drawing on OT antecedents is Jesus' parting preparation of his followers in terms reminiscent of Moses' deuteronomic farewell discourse ('love', 'obey', 'keep ... commandments', *etc.*; 13 – 17; *cf.* 1:17). However, at this salvation-historical juncture it is not Israel but believers in Jesus who represent the core group through which he will pursue his redemptive purposes. The community is formally constituted in the commissioning narrative, where Jesus' breathing upon his gathered disciples marks a 'new creation', recalling the creation of the first human being, Adam (20:22; Gen. 2:7). Jesus' dependent and obedient relationship to his sender, the Father, is made the paradigm for the disciples' relationship with their sender, Jesus (Köstenberger, *Missions of Jesus and the Disciples*, pp. 190–198).

In John's treatment of individual disciples, particular attention is given to two of Jesus' followers: Peter and 'the disciple whom Jesus loved'. These two characters are regularly featured together (see 'Historical Setting' above; K. Quast, *Peter and the Beloved Disciple*, 1989): in the upper room (13:23–24); in the courtyard of the high priest (18:15–16); at the empty tomb (20:2–9); and at the Sea of Tiberias subsequent to Jesus' resurrection (ch. 21). While Peter is considered to be the leader of the Twelve (*cf.* 6:67–69), he is presented as second to 'the disciple whom Jesus loved' in terms of access to revelation (13:23, RSV) and faith (20:8). In the end, the ministry of 'the disciple Jesus loved' is shown to be equally legitimate to that of Peter. The ministries of both Peter and John are portrayed by the fourth evangelist in terms which recall Jesus' ministry: in Peter's case, the analogy is found in the death by which he would glorify God (21:19; *cf.* 12:33); in the case of 'the disciple whom Jesus loved', the parallel consists in his position 'at the breast of Jesus', which qualified him supremely to 'narrate' the story of his Lord (13:23, author's translations; *cf.* 1:18). Thus the role of (eye)witness to Jesus' ministry may take forms as different as martyrdom and writing a Gospel, but witness must be borne, according to each person's calling (15:26–27).

Place in the canon

Relationship with the Synoptic Gospels

The relationship between John's Gospel and the Synoptics has been described in terms of mutual independence or varying degrees of literary interdependence. Historically, it seems difficult to believe that John had not at least heard of the existence of the Synoptics and read at least some portions of them. But whether or not John knew these Gospels, he clearly did not make extensive use of them in composing his own narrative. Apart from the feeding of the five thousand, the anointing and the passion narrative, John has little in common with the Synoptic Gospels (but note the 'interlocking traditions' enumerated in D. A. Carson, D. J. Moo, and L. Morris, *Introduction to the New Testament* [Leicester and Grand Rapids, 1993] pp. 161–162).

Moreover, unlike the Synoptics, John has no birth narrative, no Sermon on the Mount or Lord's Prayer (but neither has Mark), no accounts of Jesus' transfiguration or the Lord's Supper, no narrative parables, and no eschatological discourse. Clearly, John has written his own book. This, however, does not make his a sectarian work apart from the mainstream of apostolic Christianity (D. Wenham, in *TynB* 48, pp. 149–178). Rather, John frequently transposes elements of the Gospel tradition into a different key. The synoptic teaching on the kingdom of God corresponds to the Johannine theme of 'eternal life'; narrative parables are replaced by extended discourses on the symbolism of Jesus' signs. Moreover, all four Gospels present Jesus as the Messiah fulfilling OT predictions and typology. Thus the differences between the Synoptics and John must not be exaggerated.

Relationship with the other Johannine writings

John's first epistle (see *Epistles of John) is designed to defuse an early gnostic threat to the message of John's gospel by showing that Jesus has come in the flesh. John's Gospel portrays Jesus along similar lines, albeit without specific references to proto-Gnosticism. The striking similarities between John's Gospel and his first epistle include the following: the contrast between light and darkness (John 1:4–9; 3:19–21; 12:35–36; 1 John 1:5–7; 2:8–11) and the negative view of 'the *world' (*cf.* esp. 1 John 2:15–17), which must be 'overcome' (John 16:33; 1 John 5:4–5); the use of the term *paraklētos* (for the Spirit, in John 14:16, 26; 15:26; 16:7; for Jesus, in 1 John 2:1); the emphasis on truth (John 1:14, 17; 3:21; 4:23–24; 5:33; *etc.*; 1 John 1:6, 8; 2:4, 21; *etc.*); 'eternal life' (John 3:15–16, 36; 4:14, 36; *etc.*; 1 John 1:2; 2:25; 3:15; 5:11, 13, 20) and references to believers' having already passed from death into life (John 5:24 = 1 John 3:14); the description of Jesus as the Christ, the Son of God (John 20:30–31; 1 John 2:22; 4:15; 5:1, 5); God's sending of his Son into the world in order that those who believe in him may have life (John 3:16–17; 1 John 4:9); and the frequent use of substantival participles ('the one who'), of 'just as' comparisons, and of important terms such as 'know', 'keep the commandments', 'abide', 'love', and the designations 'born of God' and 'children of God'.

The book of *Revelation is addressed to seven churches in Asia Minor (Rev. 2 – 3), and is intended to strengthen believers in the face of suffering at the end of the first century. Common features of John's Gospel and the Apocalypse include: the Christological titles 'Lamb' (John 1:29, 36; twenty-eight times in Rev.) and Logos (John 1:1, 14; Rev. 19:13); the eschatological images of shepherding (John 10:1–16; 21:15–17; Rev. 2:27; 7:17; 12:5; 19:15) and living water (John 4:14; 6:35; 7:37–38; Rev. 7:17; 21:6; 22:1, 17); statements regarding God's dwelling with humans (John 1:14; Rev. 7:15; 21:3) and the absence of the temple (John 2:19, 21; 4:20–26; Rev. 21:22); the importance assigned to the number seven (in John, signs and 'I am' sayings; in Rev., seals, trumpets and bowls); the identification of Satan as the chief protagonist of Jesus (John 6:70; 8:44; 13:2, 27; Rev. 2:9–10, 13, 24; 3:9; 12:9, 12; 20:2, 7, 10); the contrast between believers and the world in John and between those with God's seal and those with the mark of the beast in Revelation; the quotation of Zechariah 12:10 in John 19:36–37 and Revelation 1:7; the terminology of 'witness' and '*glory'; and both the necessity of perseverance and the sovereignty and predestinating counsel of God (theodicy).

Relationship with the Pauline writings

John's Gospel and *Paul's epistles reflect different but not contradictory perspectives. Both emphasize love (John 13:13–14; 1 Cor. 13), consider the world to be in darkness and its wisdom futile, and use the phrase 'in Christ' or 'in him'. They also depict Israel's destiny using similar imagery, whether branches of a vine (John in ch. 15) or of an olive tree (Paul in Rom. 11). Both subordinate the Law to faith in Jesus (John 1:17; Rom. and Gal.), and both depict God as 'the Father', with John stressing the Father's role in believers' conception ('born of God'; see *Regeneration) and Paul emphasizing his role in adoption. For both writers the gospel is centred on Jesus Christ crucified, buried, and risen (John 18 – 20; 1 Cor. 15:1–4), and they both teach divine sovereignty and predestination in the context of theodicy (John 12:37–40; Rom. 9 – 11).

But John and Paul differ in many respects.

Unlike Paul, John nowhere elaborates the relationship between sin and the law; thus John lacks an equivalent to the Pauline antithesis between works and faith. The Pauline term 'flesh' in contrast to the Spirit is without parallel in John (John 3:6 is no real exception). Likewise, John has no explicit doctrine of justification (though see A. H. Trotter, in *Right with God*, pp. 126–145); neither does he feature fully fledged versions of the Pauline corollaries to justification, such as reconciliation, calling, election (though see R. W. Yarbrough in *The Grace of God, the Bondage of the Will*, vol. 1, pp. 47–62), adoption into sonship, and sanctification.

Relationship with other NT writings

John shares with *Hebrews a high Christology, particularly in the prologues. Both books stress that Jesus is the locus of God's final revelation (John 1:18; Heb. 1:2), and both set God's redemptive work through Christ in parallel to his work of creation (John 1:1; Heb. 1:3). Both also stress that Jesus is the last in a long series of divine emissaries and bearers of revelation (John 4:34; Heb. 1:2). Both emphasize faith (John throughout; Heb. 11) and portray Jesus as *exalted subsequent to his *suffering. But John's eschatology is mostly realized while Hebrews accentuates hope; Johannine 'in Christ' language is absent from Hebrews; and Hebrews portrays the Christian life more in terms of struggle, owing to the readers' weariness and reluctance to suffer.

John and Peter are associated in ministry in the early portions of the book of Acts. It is therefore not surprising that they have similar perspectives on a number of issues. Both emphasize that the fall of Judaism is part of God's plan (John 12:37; 1 Pet. 2:8). Both present Jesus simultaneously as Lamb and as shepherd (John 1:29, 36; 10:11; 21:15–17; 1 Pet. 1:19; 2:25; 5:4). Both portray believers as those who are 'in Christ' (1 John 2:5–6; 1 Pet. 5:14) and who believe in Jesus although they do not now see him (John 20:29; 1 Pet. 1:8). Both emphasize mutual love (John 13:34; 15:9, 12, 17; 17:26; 1 Pet. 1:22; 2:17; 4:8), regard Jesus' death as the norm for Christian conduct (John 15:13; 1 Pet. 2:21–25; 3:17–18), challenge the church to suffer joyfully for Christ (John 15:18–25; 1 Pet. 2:13 – 4:2), and acknowledge the Spirit as the witness to Jesus (John 15:26; 1 Pet. 1:11–12) and the life-giver (John 6:63; 1 Pet. 3:18). Finally, neither discusses the law or the constitution of the church. (See *1 Peter.)

Relevance

John's Gospel accentuates Jesus' divinity more strongly than do the other Gospels (*cf.* esp. 1:1, 18; 20:28–29), thereby expanding the horizons of Jewish monotheism. As in John's day, his emphasis on Jesus' exclusive claims and unique person and work (*cf.* esp. 1:18; 14:6) confronts alternative claims to (religious) truth. John's Christology, particularly regarding Jesus' deity and his human and divine natures, has profoundly influenced the way Christians think about their Lord, particularly though the early church councils and creeds.

By contextualizing the good news about Jesus, John shows Christianity to be a world religion, transcending its Jewish roots. Faith in Jesus as Messiah and Son of God is presented as the entrance into a personal relationship with God the Father in Christ and into the messianic community, which is no longer defined by ethnic boundaries. The most well-known verse of the Gospel, John 3:16, tells of God's love for the (sinful) world which led him to send his Son, so that whoever believes in him should not perish but have eternal life.

According to the commissioning passage in 20:21–23, the church has entered into Christ's mission and is charged to proclaim the message of forgiveness in Jesus' name to a dark and hostile world. But as Christ has overcome the world, believers in the exalted Christ, after having borne testimony to the world regarding Jesus' messiahship, are certain to join their Lord in his eternal glory (17:24).

Bibliography

J. Ashton, *Understanding the Fourth Gospel* (Oxford, 1990); C. K. Barrett, *The Gospel According to St. John* (London and Philadelphia, 1978); R. Bauckham (ed.), *The Gospels for All Christians* (Edinburgh and Grand Rapids, 1997); R. E. Brown, *The Gospel According to John*, 2 vols., AB (New York, 1966, 1970; London, 1971); *idem*, *The Community of the Beloved Disciple* (New York, 1979); R. Bultmann, *The Gospel of John* (ET, Oxford and Philadelphia, 1971); D. A. Carson, *The Gospel According to John*, PNTC (Leicester and Grand Rapids, 1991); *idem*, 'The purpose of the Fourth Gospel: Jn 20:31 reconsidered', *JBL* 106, 1987, pp. 639–651; R. A. Culpepper, *The Anatomy of the Fourth Gospel* (Philadelphia, 1983); M. Hengel, *The Johannine Question* (ET, London and Philadelphia, 1989); *idem*, *Die johanneische Frage* (Tübingen, 1993); J. L. Martyn, *History and Theology in the Fourth Gospel* (Nashville, 1979); A. J. Köstenberger, *The Missions of Jesus and the Disciples according to the Fourth Gospel* (Grand Rapids, 1998); *idem*, 'The seventh Johannine sign: A study in John's christology', *BBR* 5, 1995, pp. 87–103; J. W. Pryor, *John: Evangelist of the Covenant People* (Downers Grove, 1992); H. Ridderbos, *The Gospel of John* (Grand Rapids, 1997); A. Schlatter, *The Theology of the Apostles* (ET, Grand Rapids, 1999); R. Schnackenburg, *The Gospel According to St. John*, 3 vols. (ET, New York, 1990); D. M. Smith, *Johannine Christianity* (Columbia and Edinburgh, 1984, 1987); A. H. Trotter, 'Justification in the Gospel of John', in D. A. Carson (ed.), *Right with God: Justification in the Bible and the World* (Carlisle and Grand Rapids, 1992), pp. 126–145; D. Wenham, 'The enigma of the Fourth Gospel: another look', *TynB* 48, 1997, pp. 149–178; R. W. Yarbrough, 'Divine Election in the Gospel of John', in T. R. Schreiner and B. A. Ware (eds.), *The Grace of God, the Bondage of the Will*, vol. 1 (Grand Rapids, 1995), pp. 47–62.

A. J. KÖSTENBERGER

ACTS

This article aims to investigate the contribution that Acts makes to the canon of Scripture and to the unfolding message of the Bible. Although it is not possible to delve extensively into Lucan theology here (for which, *cf.* I. H. Marshall and D. Peterson, *Witness to the Gospel*), certain key themes that are central to Luke's purpose will be highlighted. (See also *Luke–Acts, *Luke.)

Literary genre and relationship with Luke's Gospel

Although the common authorship of Luke and Acts is generally acknowledged, the relationship between these two books continues to be debated. For example, M. C.

Parsons and R. I. Pervo insist that the two works belong to distinct literary genres. At the discourse level, it is inappropriate to speak of a narrative unity: 'the two works are independent narratives with distinct narration, that is, they each tell the story *differently*' (*Rethinking the Unity of Luke and Acts* [Philadelphia, 1993], p. 62). They rightly argue that Acts is a sequel to the Gospel, rather than a simple continuation. But they play down the theological links between Luke's two volumes. It is important to recognize that these works are different in type and to explore the consequences of that conclusion. At the same time, it is necessary to explain the links between the volumes at the level of story and theology.

On the evidence of the prologues, literary and thematic links between the Gospel and Acts, and the ending of the Gospel, I. H. Marshall ('Acts and the "Former Treatise"', in B. W. Winter and A. D. Clarke (eds.), *The Book of Acts in its Ancient Literary Setting*, pp. 163–182) proposes that Luke–Acts is a two-part work (whatever the timescale involved in the production of the whole). The Gospel cannot be adequately understood by comparing it only with its synoptic companions; it must also be compared with Acts. The Gospel points forward in certain respects to the outworking of the story in Acts and the latter points back in various ways to what preceded it.

As for the length, scope, focus and formal features of Acts itself, D. W. Palmer ('Acts and the ancient historical monograph', in Winter and Clarke, *The Book of Acts*, pp. 1–29) has argued that it fits best into the category of 'historical monograph'. In modern study, this term is applied to ancient writings which deal with a limited issue or period. Acts tells some parts of the story in great detail and others only in broad outline. There are many gaps in the story: Peter and the other apostles soon disappear from the scene and the focus turns to *Paul and his mission. Acts is a highly selective history and the presentation is carefully controlled by the author's summary statements and transitional notes.

The prologue in Luke 1:1–4 is best read with reference to Luke–Acts as a whole. The first few words of Acts recall this prologue and indicate the author's intention to begin a second volume. Such an arrangement, with a common preface and then brief introductions to subsequent volumes, was not uncommon in the ancient world. In Christian circles, however, Luke was doing something novel, writing a second book as a sequel to his Gospel. With the words 'fulfilled among us' (v. 1, NRSV), he connects his readers with the first generation of *Jesus' followers, particularly with 'those who from the beginning were eyewitnesses and ministers of the word' (v. 2). Luke intends to give his patron Theophilus and those he represents some 'assurance' or 'certainty' concerning the things of which they have been 'informed' (v. 4, Gk. *katechēthēs*). Although it is possible that this expression may refer to the correction of inaccurate reports about Christianity received by an outsider or of defective instruction received as a new convert, it is much more likely that Luke writes to give his readers certainty about Christian instruction properly given. He seeks to 'add some new dimension to what (his predecessors) have taught, which will help to reassure his readers of the significance of what they have believed' (R. Maddox, *The Purpose of Luke–Acts*, p. 13).

A key element in this preface is the motif of fulfilment, which will be discussed below. Here it is sufficient to note that Luke proclaims the accomplishment of God's purposes in the person and work of Christ *and* in the events he records in Acts. Luke's distinctive concern, by comparison with the other evangelists, is to consider the outcome of the Jesus-story in the life and witness (see *Testimony/witness) of the early *church. By referring to fulfilment, Luke suggests that these things can be understood only in the larger biblical framework he intends to provide.

There is one further point of comparison between the Gospel and Acts which is worth highlighting. 'The Gospel focuses on the vertical (up and down the social scale) universalization of the gospel, while Acts focuses on its horizontal universalization (to all peoples through the Empire)' (B. Witherington, *The Acts of the Apostles*, p. 69). In this way Acts shows that Jesus is the universal saviour. Those who believe in him are brought into the new community of the *people of God, consisting of both Jews and Gentiles. There is a continuity of the Jesus-movement with *Israel and her Scriptures but also a discontinuity caused by the universalistic agenda of Jesus and his apostles.

Luke–Acts and the OT

Luke's interest in the theme of fulfilment and his emphasis on the divine control or guidance of sacred history would have been familiar to readers who knew the Jewish Scriptures. Indeed, he seems to have modelled his work to some extent on the historical books of the OT. There, 'past history is regarded as expressing the purpose of God, and future history is the object of prophecy by men with an insight into the intentions of God' (I. H. Marshall, *Luke*, pp. 104–105). But in Mediterranean antiquity more generally the belief was widespread that divine necessity controls human history. *Providence was a central theme in Hellenistic literature, as was the concept of history's fulfilling oracles, whether written or oral. Although the primary audience for which Luke wrote was the Christian community, his apologetic method offered Christians a 'missionary tool', to assist them in evangelism. Even the prominence of the Hebrew Scriptures and the insistently Jewish practices of Jesus and the earliest Christians in Luke–Acts 'reinforce the notion (essential in the Hellenistic context) that Christianity was "no mere novelty", but was able to claim a long antiquity in Israel' (J. T. Squires, *The Plan of God in Luke–Acts* [Cambridge, 1993], p. 191). Luke's attempt to outline the continuity between Christians and Israel and between the events of Jesus' career and OT prophecies was an important aspect of his response to criticisms of Christianity that may have been made, whether by Jews or by pagans.

The theme of fulfilment

The terminology of fulfilment is used extensively throughout Luke–Acts, beginning with the prologue and birth narratives, where Luke introduces some of the main themes of his Gospel. Here there is a transition from the story of Israel to the story of Jesus, with godly characters proclaiming the realization of Israel's hopes with the birth of John the Baptist and Jesus the Messiah. Angelic revelations (1:11–20, 26–38; 2:9–14) are combined with prophetic declarations by those 'filled with the *Holy Spirit' (1:41–45 [1:46–55]; 1:67–79; 2:25–35 [2:36–38]) to explain the significance of the great events to follow.

These chapters parallel in some respects the Spirit-inspired interpretation of Jesus and his ministry found in the speeches of Acts.

Both volumes are concerned to show that Jesus' rejection and *suffering was no accident of history but part of the plan of God, as revealed in specific passages such as Isaiah 53 (*cf.* Luke 22:37; Acts 8:26–35), and in the OT more generally (*cf.* Acts 2:23; 3:18; 17:3; 26:22–23). In Luke 24, Jesus speaks about himself as the suffering Messiah of whom *Moses and all the prophets had written (vv. 25–27) and proclaims that *everything* written about him 'in the law of Moses, the prophets and the psalms must be fulfilled' (v. 44). There are many strands of Scripture that have to be linked together for a full understanding of Jesus and his ministry. Nevertheless, it is clear from what follows that the need for the Christ to suffer and be raised from the dead is at the heart of what Jesus was teaching his disciples (vv. 45–46). Far from disqualifying him as the Messiah of Israel and saviour of all, his *death and resurrection make it possible for *repentance and forgiveness of sins to be 'proclaimed in his name to all nations, beginning from Jerusalem' (vv. 46–47). With this last clause, the *mission that is committed to the disciples is also related to the fulfilment of Scripture. The unfolding of events in Luke's second volume is thus meant to be viewed against the background of OT expectations and Jesus' own predictions.

The opening verses of Acts recapitulate the emphases of Luke 24 and outline what is to follow. Resurrection appearances are the context in which Jesus teaches the apostles and commissions them, reassuring them that they will soon be 'baptized with the Holy Spirit' (Acts 1:1–5). The central theme of Jesus' teaching continues to be 'the *kingdom of God', but with a new emphasis. From the parallel account in Luke 24 it is clear that Jesus was teaching his disciples how to interpret his death and resurrection in the light of Scripture, demonstrating how these events are at the heart of God's plan for Israel and the nations. In so doing he was outlining for them how to understand the Scriptures christologically and in terms of 'the kingdom of God', a short-hand way of referring to Israel's hope for a decisive manifestation of God's rule in human history. This theme is at the heart of the apostolic preaching in Acts (*e.g.* 8:12; 19:8; 28:23, 31), where 'preaching the kingdom' (20:25) is actually equated at one point with declaring 'the whole purpose' or plan of God (20:27, Gk. *pasan tēn boulēn tou theou*). In the light of Easter and Jesus' own instruction of his apostles, preaching the kingdom is now a matter of preaching Jesus and his resurrection within the framework of biblical prophecy (*cf.* Acts 2:14–36; 13:16–41; 20:20–21; 28:31).

Acts 1:6–8 suggests that God's sovereignty, which was decisively manifested through the death and resurrection of Jesus, would be further demonstrated through the preaching of the *gospel and the bringing of men and women from all nations under God's rule by the power of his Spirit. The phrase 'to the ends of the earth', which is critical in Jesus' commissioning of the apostles in 1:8, appears to be an allusion to Isaiah 49:6 (*cf.* Luke 2:29–32). This text is actually quoted by Paul in Acts 13:47 as a justification for his pattern of preaching to the Jews first and then turning to the Gentiles. Thus it is implied in Acts that there are aspects of the ministry of the Servant of the Lord that must be carried out by the disciples of Jesus. His 'fulfilment' of the Servant's role in his death and resurrection does not exhaust the meaning and application of the Servant Songs in the messianic era. Acts 1:8 is a prediction of the way the divine plan will be fulfilled through the witness of the apostles. The rest of the book shows how that happened, first in Jerusalem (Acts 2 – 7), then in all Judea and Samaria (Acts 8 – 11), and in principle 'to the ends of the earth' (Acts 13 – 28). In other words, the selection of events in Acts illustrates the beginning of the fulfilment of Jesus' promise in 1:8.

The speeches in Acts

The speeches in Acts proclaim that there is an unfolding plan of God in the OT, which culminates in Christ and his work. Thus they offer a broad perspective on biblical theology or 'the whole purpose of God' (Acts 20:27). Indeed, Scripture provides a theological perspective for understanding all the activities and events that Luke records.

Peter's Pentecost discourse is foundational to Acts because it interprets the gift of the Holy Spirit in the light of Joel 2:28–32a, the teaching of Jesus and the fact of his heavenly *exaltation. Despite his rejection and crucifixion, Jesus has been raised from death and enthroned by God at his right hand (2:22–36). This fulfils what *David foresaw about the resurrection of the Messiah and his heavenly exaltation (*cf.* Pss. 16:8–11; 110:1; 132:11–12). The linking of Jesus' resurrection and ascension with the pouring out of the promised Holy Spirit indicates that Joel's prophecy has been fulfilled and that Jesus is 'the Lord' on whom Israel is to call for *salvation, 'before the coming of the Lord's great and glorious day' (compare Acts 2:20–21 with 2:36–40).

The gift of the Spirit at Pentecost marks the beginning of a process of restoration in Israel that fulfils a range of *eschatological prophecies (*e.g.* Joel 2:28–29; Ezek. 36:26–27; 37:1–14; Jer. 31:31–34). The Spirit enables repentance and *faith in Christ through the preaching of the gospel (Acts 2:37–41), creates a unique fellowship of *prayer, praise (see *Worship) and generosity based on devotion to the apostolic teaching (Acts 2:42–47) and empowers the disciples of Christ for ministry (*cf.* M. M. B. Turner, 'The "Spirit of Prophecy" as the power of Israel's restoration and witness', in Marshall and Peterson, *Witness*, pp. 327–348). Acts shows how this *blessing of Israel progressively overflows to the nations, with 'extensions' of the Pentecostal event marking the breakthroughs with the Samaritans (8:14–17) and the Gentiles (10:44–46).

Peter's sermon in the temple precincts (3:12–26) presents an even broader framework for understanding the work of Christ, based on the declaration to *Abraham of God's saving purpose (3:25–26, citing Gen. 12:3; 22:18; *cf.* Luke 1:55). This takes the reader back behind the eschatological and messianic prophecies to the foundational *covenant promises of Scripture. Israel is being blessed and the nations also will be blessed because 'the God of Abraham, the God of Isaac, and the God of Jacob, the God of our ancestors has glorified his servant Jesus' (3:13). Jesus is the messianic servant of the Lord who accomplishes God's saving purposes for Israel and the nations by dying and being raised to glory. 'All the prophets' may be hyperbolic (3:18; *cf.* 3:24; 10:43) but, following the lead of Jesus himself, the earliest Christians took passages from a variety of OT books as typological or prophetic of the sufferings of the Messiah (*cf.* the use of Psalm 2:1–2 in Acts 4:24–28). The testimony of the prophets from Moses onward was that God's ultimate plan for Israel and the nations would be fulfilled in the raising up of a particular individual, here identified as a prophet like Moses (3:22–23, citing Deut. 18:15–16), but also as 'the Holy and Righteous One' and 'the Author of life' (3:14–15).

The healing of the crippled man in Acts 3:1–10 is taken by Peter to be a pointer to the saving power of Jesus, understood in its widest sense (3:16; cf. 4:10–12). The apostle then tells his audience how they can share in the messianic salvation by repentance towards God and faith in Christ (3:17–21). The immediate promise is for *sins to be 'wiped out' and for 'times of refreshing' to come from the presence of the Lord (3:19–20). This appears to parallel the offer in 2:38 for sins to be forgiven and for the gift of the Holy Spirit to be received. But the consummate experience of salvation will come when Christ returns, 'who must remain in heaven until the time of universal restoration that God announced long ago through his holy prophets' (3:21). The healing of the crippled man anticipates the renewal of the whole created order which is the ultimate hope of the prophetic Scriptures (e.g. Is. 35:1–10; 65:17–25; Ezek. 47:1–12). Peter's sermon thus sets the work of Christ within a framework bounded by the covenant with Abraham and promises of a new or renewed *creation.

In Stephen's speech the picture is filled out, especially in connection with the role of Moses and the bearing his story has on the rejection of Jesus and his representatives in the messianic era (7:1–53). Sacred history is used to make sense of present-day events and Scripture is used in a polemical way, against Jewish opponents of the gospel, as well as in a positive way, to expound the significance of Jesus and his saving work. Stephen's speech also examines the place of the temple in God's plan. It asserts that the promise to Abraham finds its fulfilment, not in the law given to Moses nor in the temple, but in the exalted Lord Jesus Christ, to whom everything in the OT points.

Paul's sermon in the synagogue at Pisidian Antioch offers another survey of salvation history (13:16–41). More attention is paid here to David and to God's promise to maintain the Davidic kingship, bringing to Israel from David's posterity 'a Saviour, Jesus, as he promised' (vv. 22–23, 32–37; cf. Lk. 1:32–33; Acts 2:25–36). Because of the resurrection of Jesus, Paul can bring the good news to Jews everywhere that 'what God promised to our ancestors, he has fulfilled for us, their children, by raising Jesus' (vv. 32–33). Here there is a familiar emphasis on the fulfilment of prophecy in the rejection of Jesus by his people and the details of his suffering. However, a broader interest in the way biblical theology reaches its climax in Jesus is revealed in the pattern of the sermon as a whole and particularly in the reference to the fulfilment of 'what God promised to our ancestors' in the resurrection of the Messiah. This important example of Paul's 'diaspora' preaching ends with a quotation from Habakkuk 1:5, warning the synagogue audience not to be counted amongst the scoffers, who reject the deeds of God with unbelief and so perish (13:40–41).

Gospel growth and the structure of Acts

The sermons to Jewish audiences explain the gospel in the light of Scripture and show how this 'word' is the climax of a whole pattern of revelation stretching back to Abraham's time. Structurally, all the discourses in Acts show how the gospel was adapted for different situations, as the mission of Christ proceeded 'to the ends of the earth'. Even Paul's address to the pagans in Athens (17:22–31) concludes with a proclamation of the resurrection of Jesus and an explanation of what this means in terms of biblical eschatology.

Fundamentally, however, the placing of such discourses at key points in the narrative is a reflection of Luke's special interest in the way 'the *word' is preached, received and 'grows' in Jerusalem (2:41; 4:4, 31; 6:7) and in all Judea (8:4) and Samaria (8:14, 25; 9:31), and 'to the ends of the earth' (10:44; 11:1, 19; 12:24; 13:5, 7, 44, 48–49; 14:3, 24–28; 15:35–36; 16:6, 32; 17:11, 13; 18:5, 11; 19:10, 20; 28:31). Luke's concern is to emphasize the triumph of 'the word of the Lord' in face of many difficulties and much opposition. In particular, he focuses on the way the message of salvation sent to Israel reaches the Gentiles (see *Nations), thus fulfilling the plan of God revealed in the OT. Three important editorial summaries (6:7; 12:24; 19:20) climax sections of the narrative, recording the resolution of some conflict or the cessation of opposition and persecution.

The gospel is shown to prosper in spite of, and even because of, suffering. Allied to these summaries are important statements about the church's or churches' growing (9:31; 16:5). The following broad outline of Acts is thus suggested:

(1:1 – 6:7) Development of the church in Jerusalem under the leadership of the Twelve. The transitional summary in 6:7 indicates that 'growth' of the word followed the satisfactory resolution of conflict in the church with the appointment of the Seven (*cf.* 6:1–6).

(6:8 – 9:31) Unplanned expansion in Judea, Samaria and Gentile areas, with a widening of the church's ministry to include the Seven and others scattered because of the persecution in Jerusalem. The church throughout this region enjoys peace, encouragement and strengthening when Saul is converted and the persecution for which he is responsible ceases (9:31).

(9:32 – 12:24) Further movement of the gospel into Gentile territory is accompanied by a hardening of the opposition in Jerusalem. The transitional summary in 12:24 indicates that growth of the word followed the release of Peter from prison and the death of Herod, the persecutor of the church (*cf.* 12:1–23).

(12:25 – 16:5) Planned and organized geographical expansion into Asia Minor, under the leadership of Paul and Barnabas, initiated from Antioch in Syria. This section concludes with the observation that the south Galatian churches were strengthened in the faith and 'grew daily in numbers' because Paul revisted them with Silas and Timothy, delivering the decisions reached by the council in Jerusalem.

(16:6 – 19:20) Gospel expansion into Europe, with churches planted in significant locations, before Paul returns to Antioch. The climax of the section is the account of Paul's influential ministry in Ephesus. The transitional summary in 19:20 indicates that growth of the word was specifically related to the overcoming of demonic opposition in Ephesus (*cf.* 19:11–19).

(19:21 – 28:31) The word of the Lord continues to grow and prevail, even though Paul is persecuted and arrested. The focus is on Paul's testimony to the gospel when he is on trial, climaxing with the statement about the free course of the word when he is under arrest in Rome (28:30–31). At the same time,

various travel companions are mentioned, suggesting that the progress of the word will continue through such as these.

Acts and the rest of the NT

In the NT canon, the function of Acts is to reveal the outcome of the story of Jesus contained in the fourfold Gospel and to introduce the rest of the apostolic writings, especially the letters of Paul. As well as providing an historical context for some of those writings, it yields 'clues to the deeper logic of the Pauline letters, beginning with Romans' (R. Wall, 'Israel and the Gentile mission in Acts and Paul: A canonical approach', in Marshall and Peterson, *Witness*, p. 440). Acts does this by focusing on the role of the apostles as witnesses and by giving particular attention to the significance of Paul and his ministry.

The witness of the apostles to Jesus

The Twelve whom Jesus appointed from amongst a wider group of disciples (*cf.* Luke 6:13–16) were 'sent out' (Luke 9:2) to preach the kingdom of God and to heal. Since others shared in this task and were not called apostles (Luke 10:1–20), there must have been something more distinctive about the role of the Twelve. The number twelve suggests that Jesus intended them to be patriarchs or leaders of a restored and renewed Israel (*cf.* Luke 22:14–30, especially v. 30). Presenting himself alive to them for forty days after his resurrection 'by many convincing proofs', and 'speaking about the kingdom of God' (Acts 1:3), he qualified them to be eyewitnesses and authorized interpreters of that event for unbelievers and for the earliest Christian communities (1:6–8).

The word 'witness' is applied almost exclusively to the apostles in Acts, though related terms are used in connection with the ministry of others. The apostles occupy a unique place in history as witnesses of Christ because of the time they spent with him, especially after his resurrection, and because of their direct commissioning by him. The narrative concerning the appointment of Matthias makes it clear that in Luke's view such qualifications are critical for apostleship (1:21–26). The apostles could not be Messiah's witnesses unless they represented in their number the ideal of a reunited and renewed people of God, Israel in its fullness, not a remnant (*cf.* Jer. 31:1–34; Ezek. 37:15–28; Rev. 21:12, 14). Once the Spirit had been bestowed and the Twelve had been definitively constituted at the heart of this renewed Israel, there was no need to replace them when one of them died (*cf.* 12:1–2).

Christians today cannot be witnesses in the same foundational sense that the apostles were. Yet Luke shows how those who were converted through the testimony of the apostles came to share in the task of testifying to Jesus and the fulfilment of God's saving plan in him (*e.g.* 8:4; 11:19–21). The authoritative witness of the apostles is available for readers of Acts, particularly in the summaries of the apostolic preaching, and in the other NT writings, to inspire and guide them in their witness to Christ.

Acts and the ministry of Paul

Luke does not normally identify Paul as an apostle, although in Acts 14:4, 14 the title is applied to both Paul and Barnabas. Here Luke shows an awareness of a wider usage of the term in early Christian circles. Moreover, his threefold presentation of Paul's encounter with the risen Christ shows that Paul fulfilled the basic requirement of apostleship, by being a witness of the resurrection with a special commission of his own in God's eschatological plan (9:1–19; 22:1–21; 26:2–18). The impression is given that he was an 'extraordinary' apostle, as in Paul's own accounts (1 Cor. 9:1–2; 15:5–9; Gal. 1:12–17).

Paul is chosen to be a 'witness to all' of what he has seen and heard of the risen Christ (22:14–15; 26:16; *cf.* 22:18; 23:11). The legal and religious dimensions of his witness are stressed in the trial scenes in Acts 22 – 26. Yet even Paul defers to the witness of the Twelve in his preaching (13:31). At one level, concentration on Paul and his troubles with the Jews in the last half of Acts is an inspiring example to Christians under pressure in their own discipleship and mission. It is less likely that these chapters were designed to establish Paul's authority in churches where it was in doubt or dispute. More profoundly, Paul embodies the continuity of the gospel from the period of the Twelve to that of Luke's readers. Luke wished to highlight Paul's distinctive calling and role in the outworking of the divine plan. Paul plays a critical part in establishing the gospel in the Gentile world, while continuing to persuade Jews that the hope of Israel is fulfilled in Jesus (*e.g.* Acts 28:17–31).

Bibliography

J. B. Green and M. C. McKeever (eds.), *Luke–Acts and New Testament Historiography* (Grand Rapids, 1994); R. Maddox, *The Purpose of Luke–Acts* (Edinburgh, 1982); I. H. Marshall, *Luke: Historian and Theologian* (Exeter, 1970); I. H. Marshall and D. Peterson (eds.), *Witness to the Gospel: The Theology of Acts* (Grand Rapids and Cambridge, 1998); R. C. Tannehill, *The Narrative Unity of Luke–Acts: A Literary Interpretation, vol. 2: The Acts of the Apostles* (Minneapolis, 1990); B. W. Winter and A. D. Clarke (eds.), *The Book of Acts in its Ancient Literary Setting* (Grand Rapids and Cambridge, 1993); B. Witherington, *The Acts of the Apostles: A Socio-Rhetorical Commentary* (Grand Rapids and Carlisle, 1998).

D. G. PETERSON

ROMANS

Introduction

*Paul's letter to the Romans, claimed 17th-century Puritan Thomas Draxe, is 'the quintessence and perfection of saving doctrine'. This high estimation of the theological significance of Romans is echoed throughout the history of Christianity. Augustine's mature theology derived its key categories from Romans, along with other Pauline letters. Romans, judged Luther, presented the 'purest gospel' of the Scriptures. Calvin built his *Institutes* on the logical progression of Romans. Karl Barth developed his theological programme through interaction with Romans. And millions of Christians have found in Romans a particularly compelling presentation of the way of *salvation, the nature of sanctification (see *Holiness), and the requirements of Christian *obedience.

But all this interest in theology can obscure an important fact that must be kept in mind if Romans is to be properly understood. Romans is a letter. Paul writes to a specific audience in a certain historical context with a definite and limited purpose. The occasional nature of Romans explains why the selection of theological topics is so limited. Far from being, as

Melanchthon called it, a 'compendium of Christian doctrine', Romans concentrates on certain issues to the exclusion of others. A correct understanding of the theology of the letter must therefore derive from a recognition of the overall purpose of the letter. That purpose is, however, debated, and the general shape of the theology of Romans is, for that reason, given quite distinctive shapes by different modern interpreters.

Occasion, purpose and theme

Paul writes Romans on his third missionary journey from Cenchrea, near Corinth, probably in about AD 57. He has undoubtedly heard about circumstances in the church at Rome from friends and missionary companions such as Priscilla and Aquila (see 16:3–5). But Paul did not found, nor has he ever visited, the Roman Christian community, so he treads warily in the letter, seeking by diplomatic language to get his points across without causing needless offence (see 1:11–12; 15:14–15). The reason Paul writes so densely theological a letter to a church he has never visited remains controversial. At least four theories deserve attention.

1. Paul uses the occasion of the letter to sum up his own theology. Romans, as G. Bornkamm put it, is 'Paul's last will and testament' (the title of his essay, found in K. P. Donfried, *The Romans Debate*).

2. Paul uses the occasion of the letter to rehearse the speech he is planning to give in Judea when he brings the money he has been collecting from the Gentile churches to the poor Jewish believers (see 15:25–33).

3. Paul's plans to evangelize in Spain require him to establish a new logistical base in the western Mediterranean. He writes Romans to explain and defend his theology in order to create a basis for financial support from the Roman church (15:24).

4. Paul has heard of a split in the Roman community between Jewish and Gentile believers. He develops a theology in the letter that will serve as a basis for his plea that the two groups 'accept each other', which is the real point of the letter (14:1 – 15:13).

Each of these proposals has merit, although we think that a combination of the latter two provides the best explanation for the letter. But what is important in these proposals for understanding the theology of Romans is their common feature: the issue of Jewish–Gentile relationships, along with its theological backdrop, the issue of continuity and discontinuity in *God's plan of *redemption. Paul had fought over this issue throughout his ministry (notably in Galatia). His collection for the saints in Judea was intended to bring Jew and Gentile together. His theology created controversy because of his concern to include Gentiles. And the Roman community was apparently split between Jewish and Gentile Christian factions. And so the great theological 'occasion' of Romans is this quite basic matter of the relationship between the testaments, an issue of vital importance in the early church and of great significance in the construction of a truly biblical theology. (See *Israel, *Nations.)

Granted this basic occasion, interpreters have debated over the years the real centre of Paul's theology in Romans. In a general way, the history of this debate could be traced in terms of a movement from an emphasis on the earlier parts of the letter to one on the latter parts of the letter. The Reformers, and Luther especially, highlighted the doctrine of justification by *faith in Romans 1 – 4. In this approach, still very popular among some scholars and many lay people, Romans is basically a letter about individual salvation. In reaction to what they perceived to be an overemphasis on the legal category of justification, interpreters such as W. Wrede and A. Schweitzer at the beginning of the 20th century insisted that the real heart of Romans was to be found in chapters 5 – 8. Here Paul uses the category of 'participation' in Christ to present Christian experience in more personal terms. Some contemporary scholars, such as E. P. Sanders, thinks that this is a better starting point for a fair evaluation of Paul's theology. The Holocaust and the creation of modern Israel focused renewed attention on Romans 9 – 11. These chapters, which had sometimes been relegated to the status of an appendix on predestination (see *Election), were now viewed by some scholars as the centre of the letter. Romans was therefore not so much about individual salvation as about the history of God's dealings with different people groups. And, finally, the renewed focus on Romans as a letter has brought with it the realization that Paul has some very practical goals in view, goals which are spelled out in the 'practical' section of chapters 12 – 16, and especially in 14:1 – 15:13. Here, many scholars believe, is the real climax of Romans: a plea that Jewish and Gentile Christians accept each other and so glorify God by living as the one people of God that he has brought into being through Christ.

How are we to evaluate these proposals? Three brief responses will suffice for our purposes here. First, Paul's practical concern to bring unity to the Roman Christian community is obvious. But he expresses concerns about other matters as well in 12:1 – 13:14, and these should not be minimized. Moreover, this focus does not obviate interest in determining the *theological* centre of the argument. On this matter, then, secondly, an unwarranted reductionism is to be avoided. Romans is a long and complex letter, no one part of the letter, nor any one of its themes, should too easily be elevated above all others. Indeed, we think that only a concept as broad as 'the *gospel' can legitimately be regarded as the theme of the letter. Thirdly, we must say something concerning the most basic, and theologically significant, point of debate about the theological centre of Romans. Simply put, this debate is between those who think that Romans is basically about the salvation of the individual human being and those who think that it is basically about the incorporation of one people (Gentiles) into another (the Jews) to form a new *people of God. It is no doubt true that some interpreters have underestimated the importance of the 'people' question in Romans. They have been so concerned with deriving systematic theological categories directly from Romans that they have neglected Paul's historical situation, in which the issue of the nature and basis of Gentile inclusion in the previously Jewish-centred people of God was the major theological question. But these interpreters, in turn, can easily miss the fact that Paul seeks to deal with this question by stripping it to its essentials: the plight of and divine provision for every individual human being. Paul's gospel, the theme of the letter, is 'the power of God for [the] salvation' (1:16, NIV) and, as such, has a basically individualistic orientation. But that gospel, Paul is at pains to emphasize in Romans, is 'first for the Jew, then for the Gentile' (1:16). Confronted with a church divided between Jew and Gentile, and against the backdrop of a *mis-sionary enterprise that was quickly turning the church into a Gentile-dominated group, Paul in Romans has to focus especially on the salvation-historical and corporate implications of his gospel. This is why, in addition to the sinfulness, justification and salvation of the individual that Paul delineates in Romans 1 – 8, he also deals at length with the question of Israel and God's plan for history in Romans 9 – 11. And this is why he also makes constant reference to the Jew–Gentile controversy and to its theological counterpart, the relationship of the OT to the NT. Indeed, Romans derives much of its power and enduring relevance from its focus on these critical theological issues of the continuity and discontinuity in the plan of God.

Individual themes

Salvation history

Before considering any single theological theme, however, we need to consider the theological framework within which Paul expresses many of these themes: salvation history. The salvation-historical approach emphasizes that God has accomplished redemption as part of a historical process. *Jesus Christ is the centre of history, the point from which both past and future must be understood. With Christ as the climax of history, history can be divided into two 'eras', or 'epochs', each with its own founder – *Adam and Christ, respectively – and each with its own ruling powers: *sin, the *law, flesh and *death on the one hand; *righteousness, *grace, the *Holy Spirit and *life on the other. All people start in the old era by virtue of their participation in the act by which it was founded, the sin of Adam (*cf.* Rom. 5:12, 18–19). But one can be transferred into the new era by being joined to Christ, the founder of that era, thereby participating in the acts through which that era came into being, Christ's death, burial, and resurrection (*cf.* 6:1–6). This *corporate* element in Paul's thinking is vital to an understanding of his argument at a number of points in Romans.

The division of history into two ages was popular in Jewish apocalyptic, and Paul probably drew his conception from that background. But his understanding of God's work in Christ introduces a key qualification into the scheme. Although Jewish apocalyptic conceived of the transition from old age to new as taking place in the field of actual history, Paul's conception is necessarily more nuanced. For, contrary to Jewish expectation, the Messiah has accomplished the work of redemption, the Spirit has been poured out, yet evil has not been eradicated, the general resurrection is still future and the final state of God's kingdom has not been established. In other words, the new era has begun, has been inaugurated, but it has not yet replaced the old era. Both ages exist simultaneously, and this means that 'history', in the sense of temporal sequence, is not ultimately determinative in Paul's salvation-historical scheme. Thus, the 'change of aeons', while occurring historically at the cross (*cf.* 3:21), becomes real for the individual only at the point of faith. (See *Time.)

The human predicament

In the structure of Romans, 'plight' comes before 'solution'. That is, Paul delineates at some length the sinful condition of all *human beings (1:18 – 3:20) before going on to show what God has done to deal with this dire problem (3:21–26). Given the purpose of this letter, Paul is especially concerned to show that Jews and Gentiles are equally helpless victims of sin's power and the condemnation it brings. Gentiles have turned from the *revelation God has given them in nature and are accountable (1:18–32); Jews, likewise, have disobeyed God's revelation in the Torah and are equally guilty (2:1 – 3:8). And so, Paul concludes, all people are 'under sin', slaves of a harsh and cruel master. For Paul, the basic problem that human beings face is not simply that they commit sins; it is that they are held as captives by sin, conceived of as a power. The 'solution' to this 'plight' then follows as a matter of course. People do not need a teacher, to tell them what sin is and is not; they require a liberator to free them from their slavery.

Another distinctive element in the presentation of sin in Romans is Paul's corporate focus, typical of his salvation-historical perspective. All people are held captive by sin because they share a common experience in the original sin of Adam. As a corporate figure, Adam's sin is seen by Paul to be at the same time the sin of all human beings. The death and condemnation that came as a result of that sin therefore apply to all people (5:12–21).

The 'righteousness of God' and justification

Despite its long pedigree in Protestant, and especially Lutheran, theology, 'justification by faith' is not the overarching theme of Romans. There is simply too much in Romans that cannot, without distortion, be subsumed under the heading of justification. But while it is not the theme of Romans, justification by faith is nevertheless of critical importance in the letter. As most contemporary interpreters, both Protestant and Roman Catholic, now recognize, justification is a metaphor for salvation drawn from the legal world. A judge 'justifies' a defendant by declaring that person to be innocent of the charges brought against him or her. So in Romans Paul presents God's justification of the sinner as the opposite of the condemnation under which the sinner suffers because of sin (2:12–13; 3:9–20; 5:16–19; compare 5:1 with 8:1). Six aspects of justification in Romans deserve mention.

1. God justifies people through faith and not through 'works of the law' (a literal translation of the Greek in 3:20 and 3:28). 'Works of the law' refer to obedience to the OT law, the Torah. Interpreters of Paul have traditionally thought that, while highlighting works done in obedience to the Mosaic law because of the context, Paul intended by the phrase also to exclude all works. The Reformers therefore used these texts as key evidence for their contention that justification was 'by faith' and not 'by works'. Many contemporary scholars, however, think that the phrase must be restricted to the Jewish context and that Paul's point is that justification cannot come through the OT law or its *covenant (see especially J. D. G. Dunn, in *BJRL* 65, pp. 107–111). The contrast, then, is not between two different human responses (faith versus works) but between two different divine provisions (law versus Christ). While the traditional view can sometimes be faulted for missing the Jewish elements in Paul's presentation of justification, we think it is still the best interpretation of his language.

2. Closely related to the first point is Paul's insistence that justification is available for all human beings, Jew and Gentile, on the same basis of faith (1:16; and esp. 3:27–30). Were access to God based on Torah, Gentiles

would be virtually excluded, for they have not been given Torah. Faith, however, is a response to God's gracious work in Christ that is open to all people.

3. God justifies people by a completely free act of his will: in a word, by 'grace' (3:24). Indeed, it is because God relates to the world by grace, freely and without any compulsion of any kind, that justification must be by faith rather than by works (4:3–6). That God relates to the world he has created as a totally free agent is a theological postulate in Paul, and comes to expression at critical points in Romans (3:24; 4:4–6; 5:1, 15–16; 9:14–18; 11:5–7).

4. Justification by faith is rooted in the OT. In the initial statement of the theme of the letter, Paul quotes Habakkuk 2:4 to confirm his insistence that a person can be justified by faith 'from first to last': 'It is the person who is righteous by faith who will live' (1:17, author's translation). But especially important is *Abraham, whose experience Paul describes in some detail in Romans 4. Critical to Paul's argument is Genesis 15:6, which asserts that Abraham's faith was 'counted' as righteousness before he was circumcised (4:9–12) and without any basis in his obedience to the law (4:13–16). As he does throughout Romans, Paul seeks to demonstrate that his gospel is firmly rooted in the OT.

5. Justification is the product, or extension, of 'the righteousness of God'. It is important to stress that 'justify' (*dikaioō*) and 'righteousness' (*dikaiosynē*) are closely related in Greek. 'The righteousness/justice of God' is a key theological phrase in Romans, occurring eight times (1:17; 3:5, 21, 22, 25, 26; 10:3 [twice]) and only once elsewhere in the letters of Paul (2 Cor. 5:21). The phrase has been a focus of theological debate. Most Protestant interpreters think that in 1:17, 3:21–22 and 10:3 it refers to a status of righteousness given to the human being by God (note the NIV rendering 'righteousness *from* God'). But the phrase 'righteousness of God' has its roots in OT *eschatological expectation, where it is virtually synonymous with 'salvation of God' (see esp. Is. 46:13; 51:4–6). Since Paul claims that the righteousness revealed in Christ is testified to by 'the Law and the Prophets' (3:21), it is more likely that 'righteousness of God', at least in 1:17, 3:21–22, and 10:3, refers to an activity of God: his acting to put people in right relationship to himself. What

the prophets anticipated has taken place in Christ: God has intervened in human history to establish his salvation.

6. Justification by faith in based in the *sacrifice of Christ on the cross. In the supremely important 3:21–26, Paul explains that people can be justified freely (v. 24) because God has presented Christ as 'a sacrifice of atonement'. This phrase translates a Greek word, *hilastērion*, that has been another centre of controversy. 'Propitiation', which suggests the idea of God's wrath being appeased, has been the traditional rendering. But many contemporary scholars, partly because they have difficulty with the notion of God's acting to appease his own wrath, argue for the translation 'expiation', which refers more broadly to the wiping away of sins. In fact, however, Paul's language is again rooted in the OT. *Hilastērion* occurs in the Greek OT (the Septuagint) as a description of the '*mercy seat', the place in the tabernacle where the blood of sacrifice was sprinkled on the Day of *Atonement (Lev. 16). In a bold metaphor, Paul claims, in effect, that Christ is now the final, eschatological 'mercy seat', the place where God draws near to human beings for their redemption.

While not the centre of Romans, justification by faith is nevertheless a critical component of Paul's presentation of the gospel in Romans. The doctrine expresses, in the sphere of anthropology, a crucial element in Paul's understanding of God's work in Christ: its entirely gracious character. Not only, then, does justification by faith guard against the Jewish attempt to make works of the law basic for salvation in Paul's day; it expresses the resolute resistance of Paul, and the NT authors, to the constant human tendency to make what people do decisive for salvation.

The law

The word *nomos* ('law') occurs more times in Romans (74) than in all the other letters of Paul combined (47); Paul devotes an entire chapter to it (ch. 7), and it recurs in relation to almost every topic he treats (*cf. e.g.* 2:12–16; 4:13–15; 5:13–14, 20; 6:14–15; 8:2–4; 9:31 – 10:5; 13:8–10). The 'law' that Paul discusses in Romans is the OT law, the body of commandments that God gave to Moses at Sinai. To be sure, Israel's experience with the law of Moses is in many ways paradigmatic for the experience of all people with 'law' of various kinds (see esp. 2:14–15). But Paul's focus is on the Jewish law, the Torah. He deals with this topic as a central issue in the larger debate in the early church about continuity between the OT and Judaism on the one hand and Christianity on the other. That Gentiles were to enter the new covenant people of God was relatively uncontroversial. But the basis on which they were to enter was greatly debated. Since they were now considered to be part of the people of God, should they not be expected to obey the rules that God had set forth for his people in the law of *Moses? What was the status of Torah now that the Messiah had appeared? Different factions in the early church took dramatically different viewpoints on this issue. Paul was immersed in the controversy from the beginning of his apostolic ministry, and the issue has now appeared in the Roman church. This is evident particularly in Romans 14:1 – 15:13, where the 'weak' are mainly Jewish Christians who insist on continued observance of much of the Torah, while the 'strong' are mainly Gentile Christians who see no need to keep Torah any longer. And because both sides are represented in the community, Paul's teaching on the law in Romans is more even-handed than it is in Galatians, where he must emphasize one side of the matter because of the polemical context. He makes several points.

1. The law, though good and holy (7:12) does not deal with the problem of human sin. Human beings are weak and sinful, unable to obey the law that God has given them. The history of Israel (7:7–25) reveals this problem particularly clearly.

2. Not only does the law not deal with the problem of sin; it exacerbates it. The law, by confronting human beings with a detailed list of God's requirements, increases their accountability. It has therefore had the effect of revealing even more clearly the degree to which people fall short of God's demands (3:20; 4:15; 5:20; 7:7–12).

3. Because of the close connection between the law and sin, Christians must be released from its authority (6:14–15; 7:1–6). Many interpreters think these texts refer to deliverance from the condemnation pronounced by the law. But Paul seems to go further, suggesting that the law of Moses is no longer a binding authority on people who live in the age of fulfilment.

4. However, their not being under the Torah does not mean that Christians are free to do whatever they want. Grace itself constrains people to follow God (6:15–16), and obedience to the *love command satisfies all the demands of the law (13:8–10).

Israel

Paul's generally negative perspective on the law could be taken to imply that he is equally negative about the role of Israel in God's plan of redemption. But in response to Gentiles who seemed to be asserting such a negative view (see 11:17–24, 25), Paul in Romans 9 – 11 asserts a positive one. Paul writes these chapters to vindicate God's word to Israel in the light of the widespread rejection of the gospel among his Jewish contemporaries (9:1–6). He first makes clear that the exclusion of many Jews from the people of God because of their refusal to embrace Christ does not contradict God's promise to Israel, for he has always determined to save only some (the '*remnant') from among physical Israel (9:6b–29). Nor does the inclusion of Gentiles violate God's word, for he had always intended to do this also. But does this inclusion of Gentiles now mean that the old idea of Israel is obsolete? Many interpreters argue so, insisting that Paul replaces physical Israel with spiritual 'Israel', the church. Thus what Paul predicts in 11:25–26 is the ultimate salvation of all, Jew and Gentile, who constitute the 'new Israel'. But this interpretation ignores the way in which Paul continues carefully to distinguish Gentiles from Jews (and Israel) in this part of his argument. Probably, then, 11:25–26 predicts a turning to Christ of many Jews ('all Israel' in a corporate sense) at the time of Christ's return in glory. God is faithful to his promise to Israel, saving many Jews during this period of history as they are integrated into the church (11:1–10) and intending to bring even greater numbers to faith in Christ at the end of history (11:11–32).

The Christian life

Justification brings people into the family of God, and God will eventually *glorify those whom he has justified, saving them from wrath and delivering them from sin and suffering (5:1–11; 8:18–30). But what about the period between these events? Paul deals with this question in Romans 5 – 8. He wants first to assure believers that their justification secures their final salvation: they need not fear the verdict of the last day (see esp. 5:9–10; 8:29–30). But he also wants to assure them of God's provision for them during their earthly pilgrimage. In Christ, they have been removed from the lordship and mastery of sin. Sin no longer compels the believer to act in ways contrary to God's will. A new obedience, prompted by the believer's submission to Christ as Lord, is now possible and, indeed, required (ch. 6). Nor does the law, used by sin to stimulate disobedience to God, have any hold on the believer (ch. 7). Positively, God sends the Holy Spirit to assure believers of their new status (8:14–17), to stimulate *hope (8:18–25) and to empower for works of service (8:5–13).

Theology and ethics

No analysis of the theology of Romans would be complete without recognition of the very practical outcome of the theology that Paul unfolds in the letter. Paul summons believers, 'in view of God's mercy' (set out in chs. 1 – 11), to offer their bodies as sacrifices to God (12:1). Comprehension of the benefits God has secured for us in Christ should stimulate a life of sacrificial obedience, some aspects of which Paul spells out in 12:3 – 15:13.

Bibliography

K. P. Donfried (ed.), *The Romans Debate* (Edinburgh and Peabody, 1991); J. D. G. Dunn, 'The new perspective on Paul', *BJRL* 65, 1983, pp. 95–122; *idem, Romans*, WBC (Waco, 1988); D. J. Moo, *The Epistle to the Romans*, NICNT (Grand Rapids, 1996); H. Ridderbos, *Paul: An Outline of his Theology* (Grand Rapids, 1974); S. Westerholm, *Preface to the Study of Paul* (Grand Rapids, 1997).

D. J. MOO

1 CORINTHIANS

Recent research

A flood of recent research, mainly in the 1990s, has substantially changed perceptions of this epistle and its theological importance. Research on the social world of Corinth in the era of *Paul has revealed striking resonances with secular cultures of our own day: an obsessive concern about reputation and status in the eyes of others; self-promotion to win applause and to gain influence; ambition to succeed, often by manipulating networks of influence. Rhetoric was more concerned with audience-approval ratings than with truth; people valued autonomy and 'rights'. Such a social background places Paul's message of divine *grace and the cross of *Jesus Christ into the sharpest possible focus. Contrary to cultural expectations at Corinth, the cross offered not status-enhancement but an affront, a reversal of the whole value-system of non-Christian Corinth.

It is not the case, as older modern commentators often suggest, that Christian behaviour at Corinth simply 'relapsed' into pagan habits, or was influenced unduly by new teaching. Rather, Christians' appropriation of the cross had insufficiently pervaded their attitudes. Hence, in his excellent commentary, W. Schrage (*Der erste Brief an die Korinther*) observes that Paul proclaims the cross not simply to the world but also as 'ground and criterion of church and apostle' (vol. 1, p. 165). The cross addressed Corinth in ways which resonate with its message for today's *churches. No longer should 1 Corinthians be overshadowed by a supposedly more 'theological' Romans.

The theology of the cross and the social world of Corinth

Roman Corinth and the power of patrons

Research in the 1990s has shown more clearly than ever before that after 44 BC (when the city was refounded and resettled by Julius Caesar) we should regard Corinth as primarily a Roman city, even if its location was in Greece. Caesar settled his Roman veterans and their households there, and these set the tone until after Paul's lifetime. However, since the city was situated on a narrow isthmus with its harbour of Lechaeum serving the West, and its port of Cenchreae the East, Corinth stood at a north–south/east–west crossroads for shipping and for commercial business. A mixture of entrepreneurs, traders, freedmen and slaves soon swelled the population to expand a Roman nucleus of settlers into a city where people hoped to make their fortune, win power and gain honour. Plutarch (c. AD 50–120) observes that in such a culture the Roman system of patronage provided an all too easy route to fame and fortune. To enjoy the mutual benefits of the client–patron relation permitted the less influential to climb 'just as ivy climbs by twining itself around a strong tree' (*Moralia*, 805 E–F). On one side, patrons provided their clients with influence and contacts. On the other side 'the recipient of a *beneficium* was expected to publicize the generosity of his patron' (A. D. Clarke, *Secular and Christian Leadership in Corinth*, p. 32; *cf*. pp. 8–39). Extensive research on this aspect and its impact on our epistle has been carried out by Clarke, J. K. Chow (*Patronage and Power*) and others. Against this background Paul declares, 'Let no-one glory in human persons' (1 Cor. 3:21; author's translation).

Obsession with status and self-promotion

Archaeological evidence reveals inscriptions which publicized the generosity of benefactors as a means of promoting their reputation. Yet the research of B. Witherington (*Conflict and Community in Corinth*) and others demonstrates that self-promotion ran through every level of society: 'Self-promotion had become an art form ... People ... lived within an honour–shame orientation. Corinth was a magnet for the socially ambitious ... status-hungry people' (Witherington, *Conflict and Community*, pp. 8, 20, 24). Paul exposes the huge gap between such 'worldly wisdom' and the proclamation of the cross. The Corinthians, judging from their behaviour, apparently perceived even their Christian status as a tool for self-affirmation and self-promotion: 'You have been made rich ... You reign as kings – if only you did!' (4:8); whereas the apostles are working-class 'manual labourers ... the world's scum ... the scrapings from everyone's shoes' (4:12–13). The cross addresses not moralism (*cf*. Galatians and Romans) but the self-absorption which characterizes much of secular and even 'church' attitudes today.

New perspectives on the cross

By contrast, Paul insists that if the *gospel is used manipulatively for self-esteem, 'the cross of Christ becomes nullified' (1:17). To those whose horizons are those of 'the wisdom of the world' the cross is 'folly' (1:18). *God destroys worldly *wisdom. If some find the cross 'an affront ... folly ... to those who are

called [it is] God's power, God's wisdom' (1:24). The cross passes *judgment on those who perceive themselves as 'something' but lifts up 'the nothings' (1:28). '*Glory' is not for patrons, social climbers, or those who claim special 'knowledge' (8:1) or special 'gifts', for with regard to 'gifts' (Gk. *charismata*) 'what do you have that you did not receive?' (4:7). Hence, 'let the person who glories, glory in the Lord' (1:31). 'Status' is found in Christ, not in one's own aspirations (1:30). Grace through the cross is no less prominent here than in Romans, but it is addressed to a social situation which offers special resonances with society today (*cf*. 1:6; 1:30–31; 3:2–3; 4:7–8; 6:11; 15:10).

Alexander Brown and Raymond Pickett place this cross-centred theology in sharp focus. Brown urges that the proclamation of the cross constitutes a transforming and formative speech-act (*The Cross and Human Transformation*, pp. 13–30). The theology of the cross expounded in chapters 1 – 2 is 'inseparable from the ... combined love and service outlined in chs. 3 – 14 and from the ... transfigured body in ch. 15' (p. 12; *cf*. pp. 107–152). Pickett shows how 'Christian identity' in this epistle is seen 'in terms of ... response to "the word of the cross"' as against 'the wisdom of the world'. An identity crisis arises from many at Corinth's 'belonging to two discrepant universes of meaning' (*The Cross in Corinth*, pp. 59–62).

Research on rhetoric: some implications for preaching, ministry and the church

A rhetoric of audience-applause

Quintilian disapproved of the kind of audience-pleasing rhetoric which departed from earlier Roman traditions: 'Every effusion is greeted with a storm of ready-made applause ... The result is vanity and empty self-sufficiency' (*Institutio Oratoria* 2:2:9–12). S. Pogoloff has shown how at Corinth rhetoric was intertwined with status and the 'game' of audience-approval. As with chat-show hosts today, people became 'fans' of particular orators. Many at Corinth would have liked Paul to turn 'professional' and win prestige and admiration with his cleverness (just as some today want ministers to ape chat-show hosts). They wanted Paul to be like 'the sophists, those "visiting professional preachers" who relied upon ... admirers, all expert talkers ... The Corinthians are competing for status ...' (Pogoloff, *Logos and Sophia*, pp. 191, 203). However, Paul consciously 'did not come with high-sounding rhetoric or a display of cleverness (Gk. *ou kath' hyperochēn logou ē sophias*) in proclaiming to you the mystery of the gospel ... I came to you in weakness with much fear and trembling ... not with enticing, clever, words ... that your faith should rest not on human cleverness but on God's power' (1 Cor. 2:1, 3–5). Far from playing to the gallery, the apostles fight like those who have become a shameful, bloodied, spectacle (*apedeixen*) in the arena (4:9). They are 'on exhibit' as 'fools', not 'clever people' ... the world's scum, the scrapings ...' (4:9–13). By contrast, the Corinthians make their assessments from the gallery, glutted with self-ascriptions of status and power (4:8).

Rhetoric and leading 'personages'

Clarke shows how disastrous this role for rhetoric could become for issues of church *leadership and the unity of the church. Corinthian Christians 'selected' their favourite church leaders and gathered around them, or used their name. Apollos, for example, perhaps spoke more 'boldly' (Acts 18:26, 28); his Alexandrian connections may have made him popular with a specific group, although Paul did not regard the ministry of Apollos as differing from his own in any significant way (1 Cor. 3:6–7). At all events, Paul received a report from Chloe's people that 'splits' (Gk. *schismata*) had emerged under such slogans as ' "I, for me, am of Paul's people"; "I, for my part, am for Apollos"; "I am a Peter person"; "As for me, I belong to Christ" ' (1:12). Clarke describes this as 'personality-centred politics' (*Secular and Christian Leadership*, p. 93). The church had absorbed secular leadership styles.

Pleas for unity within the church

These 'splits' were not doctrinal divisions. Paul does not distinguish between right and wrong groups, and rebukes the 'Paul' group no less than others. Perhaps each of several house groups (the largest house could accommodate about 30–40) evolved its own 'ethos', claiming some 'name' as its model or 'patron'. We cannot be certain. Margaret Mitchell, however, has shown that Paul uses 'stock phrases[s] in Greek literature for

political order and peace' (1:10) and concludes (with Clarke) that the major issue turns on inflated 'boasting' in human personages (*Paul and the Rhetoric of Reconciliation*, p. 95). While he rejects an applause-orientated rhetoric, Paul does employ a deliberative rhetoric of truth to argue for future policy and action, to elucidate the 'beneficial' consequences of diversity-in-unity for all. Here he understands 'beneficial' as what tends to be the good of 'the other person' (*cf.* 8:7–13; 10:23 – 11:1; 13:1 – 14:40).

The role of ministers and the agency of apostles

On one side Paul guards against too high a view of those who serve as apostles or ministers. He asks, 'What (Gk. neuter *ti*) is Apollos? What is Paul?' and answers, 'Servants, through whom you came to faith' (3:5). It is God, not ministers, who gives life and growth to the church (3:6). On the other side Paul equally rejects too low a view of ministers. They provide conditions ('planting and watering') through which God chooses to give growth (3:6–9a). Theirs is a shared ministry: although each has a distinctive task, under God they are fellow-workers (*theou ... synergoi*, v. 9a) and are 'one' (v. 8a). They 'build up' the Christian community together, and the day of judgment will disclose whether their work has been solid, or 'fire-proof' (3:12–15).

Apostleship, too, points away from the apostle's own person to that to which the apostle bears witness, namely the crucified and raised Lord Christ. E. A. Castelli (*Imitating Paul* [Louisville, 1991]) has argued that Paul's call to imitate him as a model (1 Cor. 4:16; 11:1) functions as a bid for power (pp. 89–117). However, a different view, from Chrysostom and Calvin to J. A. Crafton (*The Agency of the Apostle* [Sheffield, 1991]), urges that apostleship points away from the agent to that to which he bears witness. 'While an agent calls attention to himself, an agency gives itself wholly to the task ... and therefore points all attention away from itself' (Crafton, pp. 62, 63). The context of 11:1 confirms this. It is precisely concern for the other, not for the self, on which the *mimēsis* of Paul and especially of Christ consists. 9:1–23 is not a 'defence of apostleship', but an integral part of the argument of 8:1 – 11:1 which calls believers to forgo their 'rights' for the sake of 'the other'. Apostles need to be witnesses of the resurrection (15:3–11) because apostolicity points away from the self to witness to Christ as crucified and raised. (See *Mission.)

The church as one body with many members

The metaphor of the body and its diversity of members is explicated in 12:12–30. (Perhaps Christ's identification with his people in Acts 9:4–5 gave an impetus to this theme.) On one side Paul reassures those whose status as part of the body is called into question. Mistaken comparisons with the more 'gifted' should not lead them to conclude, 'because I am not a hand, I do not belong to the body' (12:15). The body does not simply consist of 'gifted' members, let alone of a single stereotypified member defined in the interests of some 'gifted' exclusivist group. Conversely he rebukes the 'strong' or self-styled 'wise', 'gifted', or socially influential: 'The eye cannot say to hand, "I have no need of you"' (12:21). Single-cell organisms are a very primitive life-form. Paul's use of 'body' imagery receives elucidation in recent research from D. B. Martin (*The Corinthian Body*) among others. Both unity and diversity remain essential.

The *Holy Spirit, ethics and *love for the other person

The transcendence of the Holy Spirit: *revelation and transformation

Paul's first reference to the Spirit of God in this epistle occurs in the context of a need for divine disclosure: 'God revealed these things to us through the Spirit. For the Spirit searches out everything, even the depths of God's own self' (Gk. *ta bathē tou theou*, 2:10). Paul takes pains to explain that this is no mere immanental spirit which animates the world in a Stoic sense, but 'the Spirit who issues from God' (Gk. *to pneuma to ek tou theou*, 2:12) The gift of the Spirit entails ceasing to live 'on an entirely human level' (2:14). Indeed the Corinthian self-congratulatory claim to be 'people of the Spirit' (3:1) is invalidated by their involvement in 'jealousy and strife' and 'behaving like any merely human person' (Gk. *sarkikoi*, 3:3). The Christian community is corporately the holy shrine of God among whom 'the Spirit of God dwells' (3:16). Similarly the Spirit indwells the individual 'body' (Gk. *sōma*) *i.e.* our public, everyday life (6:19).

*Holiness of life, love, and the limits of freedom

The section 5:1 – 11:1 concerns the public face of the transformed life, both individual and corporate, in the world. Some suggest that the case of incest had to do with patronage or property-rights which were of benefit to the community. The ethical 'lists' of 5:9–11 may well allude to the 'two ways' of Christian catechetical instruction. The issue of taking a fellow-believer to law most probably presupposes a social situation in which local civil magistrates could readily be influenced by networks of patronage, or the socially 'strong'. Hence the ethical issue in 6:1–11 turns not on going to law as such, but more probably on manipulation on the part of the socially 'strong' to exploit more vulnerable fellow-believers.

6:12 contains a quotation from Corinth: 'I have the right to do anything – I am no longer under the law as a new creation.' Paul does not deny the '*freedom' of the gospel outright, but he seriously qualifies and redefines what such freedom entails. It is precisely not 'autonomy', freedom to choose what I want to do. Paul first explains that indulgent freedom begins to exercise 'rights over me' (note the cognate Gk. *exesti*, 'it is lawful', v. 12a; *exousia*, 'authority' or 'right'; *exousiazō*, v. 12b). One clear limit-situation is that of a sexual relation with a prostitute. This is incompatible with the very union with Christ which allegedly provided the supposed ground for 'freedom' (6:16–17). There is no 'autonomy' for the purchased slave of Christ (6:20). Christ has the care of the believer's conduct in the public domain (Gk. *sōma*): the believer is no longer his or her own master. Freedom is always to be qualified in the light of what promotes the gospel (9:19–23) and what serves the well-being of the other (8:2–13; 10:23 – 11:1; 13:1–13).

Vocation, the progress of the gospel, and respect for 'the other' in grey areas

The issues in 7:1–40 are too complex for detailed treatment here. Some relate chapter 7 to Stoic-Cynic views of what is 'beneficial' in a given context. A. C. Wire (*The Corinthian Women Prophets*) argues from a feminist perspective that Paul seeks to restrict the power and freedom of women by placing them in the private domain of the home. This does not cohere well, however, with Paul's acceptance of women's role in proclamation or 'prophecy' (11:5). Indeed Witherington discerns here 'Paul's attempt to reform the patriarchal approach to *marriage and singleness' (*Conflict and Community*, p. 177; cf. pp. 170–181). Rosner underlines the major point that in line with OT traditions Paul gives priority both to 'contentment in one's life-situation' and to a positive view of the physical order as part of 'the goodness of creation' (*Paul, Scripture and Ethics*, pp. 147, 153). (See *Man and woman.)

In 8:1 – 11:1 the welfare of 'the other', especially the more vulnerable believer, becomes paramount. We do not have space to allude to the vast literature on 'food offered to idols'. However, archaeological evidence about the use of dining rooms in the precincts of pagan temples and historical records about temple sources of supply for the meat market serve to bring the three chapters to life as a difficult 'grey area'. Here 'the strong' felt that they could act with freedom in the secure knowledge that there existed only the one God (8:6) and everything was subject to him (8:4–6); 'the weak' remained troubled in their sensitivities. Paul distinguishes between different levels of situation (8:7–13 and 10:23–32, as against 10:1–22) and defends the vulnerable, subject to certain contextual factors. Two important studies come from K.-K. Yeo, *Rhetorical Interaction in 1 Cor. 8 and 10*, and P. D. Gardner, *The Gifts of God and the Authentication of a Christian*, while on background, see J. Murphy-O'Connor (*St Paul's Corinth*). The translation and meaning of Gk. *syneidēsis* remains controversial. Does it mean 'conscience' or (more probably) 'self-awareness'? 'Those "weak in their conscience" were people who ... felt insecure ... Their weakness was not in moral decision-making [but] weakness in self-awareness' (Gardner, *The Gifts of God*, pp. 44–48). The 'strong' regarded 'knowledge' (Gk. *gnōsis*), as the key; Paul saw it as *love* (8:1); 'the weak' must not be damaged.

Gifts of the Holy Spirit and issues of worship and the sacraments

Gifts of the Holy Spirit

The opening of 12:1 – 14:40 on the agency of the Holy Spirit in prompting the confession 'Jesus is Lord' (12:3) is fundamental. The gifts (Gk. *charismata*, gifts freely given without condition or desert) of the Spirit serve diverse means for a single end: to make visible the lordship of Jesus Christ as crucified and raised, and to build up the whole community. Since all gifts come from the same Spirit, these should not manifest self-contradiction (in time or place), or serve mere self-affirmation. 'Different apportionings of gifts "serve" the same Spirit ... the same Lord ... the same God' (12:4–6). Paul clearly places these gifts in a 'Trinitarian' frame: they are not even to bring 'the Spirit' into prominence, but to serve God in Christ through the Spirit. The criterion of authenticity is the 'common advantage' (Gk. *to sympheron*), not of an elite group but of all believers (12:7). Hence gifts which relate to speech (*prophetic speech, tongue-speaking) must constitute intelligible communicative events or else should be reserved for a context outside public *worship (14:13–17). An unintelligible utterance in a tongue is addressed not to fellow-believers but to God (14:1; cf. Rom. 8:26, 'sighs too deep for words'). There is no evidence in 12:1 – 14:40 that Paul regarded speaking in tongues as a kind of coded message to the congregation. Presumably its 'building' or 'common advantage' when tongues were put into plain speech (14:13) consisted in their facilitating a depth of corporate praise or prayer prompted by a heart welling up with deep yearnings, passion or visionary insight.

In a public context utterance must be articulated, *i.e.* involve mental reflection (14:14–21). Strange sounds put other believers in the position of feeling like outsiders rather than 'at home', as if tongues gave a sign of their status as unbelievers, like Israel exiled under judgment (14:22). By contrast prophetic speech may include straightforward proclamation or preaching, as T. W. Gillespie (*The First Theologians*), following D. Hill (*New Testament Prophecy* [London, 1979]) and U. B. Müller (*Prophetie und Predigt im Neuem Testamentum*

[Gutersloh, 1975]), convincingly argues. It can convict and convert the outsider (14:24–25), just as it can build up the believing community by comfort or exhortation, or encouragement (14:3–4). There is no evidence that all prophecy had to be 'spontaneous'. In OT traditions Jeremiah reflected on the almond tree before speaking as prophet. The charisma of celibacy (7:7) and the charismata of teaching administration (Gk. *antilēmpseis*) or church strategy (*kybernēseis*, 12:28) do not appear to fall from heaven independently of reflective processes. Although he accepts a conventional view of 'tongues', C. Forbes (*Prophecy and Inspired Speech*) rightly warns us against making assumptions about the nature of 'inspiration' (*e.g.* in prophecy) from alleged parallels in Hellenistic religions.

Public worship and the wearing of hoods by women

In the compass of this article we cannot address the breathtakingly huge array of research articles on 11:2–16. Aline Rouselle's research on the Roman world, however, is helpful. In Roman society (see above) 'one sees only the face' of women, Horace observes, who are 'respectable'; that is, 'A veil or hood constituted a warning: it signified that the wearer was a respectable woman' who was not to be approached (propositioned) by men (A. Rouselle, 'Body politics in ancient Rome', in G. Duby and M. Perot [eds.], *A History of Women in the West*, vol. 1 [Cambridge, MA, 1992], pp. 296–337; quotation from pp. 314–315). A related discussion about the meaning of 'head' (Gk. *kephalē*, 11:3) cannot be solved merely by translating it as 'source' (see J. Murphy-O'Connor, *St Paul's Corinth*). J. M. Gundry-Volf rightly perceives a triple 'map' of creation, convention and eschatology in which headship and mutuality stand in tension ('Gender and creation in 1 Cor. 11:2–16', in J. Adna *et al.* [eds.] *Evangelium, Schriftsauslegung, Kirche: Festschrift für P. Stuhlmacher* [Göttingen, 1997], pp. 151–171). G. W. Dawes shows that Gk. *kephalē* means 'head' in the physiological sense, even if with diverse metaphorical applications which include 'head', 'source' and above all differentiation from an 'other' (*The Body in Question: Metaphor and Meaning in the Interpretation of Eph. 5:21–33* [Leiden, 1998], pp. 122–149).

Baptism and the Lord's Supper

Paul clearly does not over-value the role of *baptism (1:14–16) and approves of the baptism of a 'household' (Gk. *oikon*, v. 16). As in Romans 6:3–11, it signifies solidarity with, and allegiance to, the one in whose name someone is baptized. Arguably in 10:2 it signifies sharing in the privileges of the 'visible' church. Allusions to the Lord's Supper (see *Sacred meals) occur in a context of exclusive covenant loyalty to Christ (10:14–22) which heightens the dreadful seriousness of apostasy, disloyalty or double allegiance: inappropriate reception is not only counter-productive; it leads to harmful and destructive effects (11:27–32). The seriousness of these verses is too often ignored today. Yet in the Lord's Supper every believer has the opportunity to 'proclaim the Lord's death' as a witness and proclaimer through personal participation in the corporate act of public identification with the body and blood of Christ with the five physical senses (11:26; *cf.* 11:17–34).

*Eschatology and the resurrection

On the way to salvation

The Corinthian concern for self-promotion showed itself in a premature triumphalism of those who had 'arrived' and already received their thrones (4:8), and been given all 'knowledge' (8:1–2) and every 'freedom' (6:12; 10:23). Paul reminds them that they are still 'on their way to full *salvation' (Gk. *sōzomenois*, present tense, 1:18), still 'merely human' (3:4), and unable to pronounce definitive judgments about the quality of Paul's work or their own (4:4–5; *cf.* 3:13–15; 13:8b–13). Paul insists they should 'judge nothing before the time' when 'the secrets of hearts will be disclosed' (4:5). Only love will never become obsolete (13:13).

The resurrection: its credibility

Paul leaves this subject virtually to the end because through chapters 1 – 14 he places the church under the cross. Paul draws on a public tradition of witness (15:3) to establish the reality of the resurrection of Christ as 'of first importance' (Gk. *en prōtois*, v. 3; *cf.* 15:1–11). His resurrection is 'according to the Scriptures' (15:3–4) in the sense that it epitomizes and fulfils a fundamental biblical pattern and promise. In 15:12–34 Paul shows the untenable consequences of denying the resurrection: apostolic witness would be bias, and faith would be groundless or 'empty'; believers who have already died would be 'lost' (15:15–19). Their solidarity would be with sinful Adam, rather than with the raised Christ who in fact is their Lord and their new 'Adam' (vv. 21–22).

The resurrection: its conceivability

How can resurrection be conceived (vv. 35–49)? The answer rests not on any human capacity to imagine what the resurrection mode of existence might be like, but on whether the God who has already proved his resourcefulness in the wonders of creation is capable of raising the new creation in Christ to the fullness of life that resurrection entails. The 'hinge' of the argument comes in verse 34: 'Some remain ignorant of God.' Paul uses the analogy of seeds (vv. 36–38) to demonstrate how we can conceive of a continuity of recognizable identity co-existent with radical transformation. God has proved his capacity to create creatures appropriate to a variety of different environments (fish in the sea, birds in the sky, stars in space, vv. 39–41). The fallenness, sin and physical limits of human beings can be transformed, and yet the humans remain 'themselves', unfettered by shame, weakness, decay, or imperfect response to the Holy Spirit (Gk. *sōma … pneumatikon*, v. 44). As 'somatic' (Gk. *sōma*, body) persons, these glorious beings will be able to communicate, act, interrelate, experience, no less than they could in the physical realm (*cf.* further A. C. Thiselton, in *The Bible, the Reformation and the Church*, pp. 258–289).

Paul envisages no 'thinning down' of existence to that of a mere 'soul', but resurrection life in the fullest possible mode of existence: 'more' but not 'less' than 'body' (Gk. *sōma*). The model or paradigm is that of Christ's own resurrection body (15:45–49), which primarily denotes bearing the restored 'image' (v. 49) of his holiness and love (*cf.* 13:9–13). The metaphor of the trumpet signals the waking of a sleeping army to action (v. 52). Paul reiterates that it is victory over sin through the cross that constitutes the ground of this rich promise of splendour to come (15:56–57). This provides the ground for present realism and present action (v. 58).

Paul's use of the OT in 1 Corinthians

Citations and versions

It has often been argued that Paul resorts to citing OT texts only as an *ad hoc* argument when his opponents are Christians who still view the gospel as a sect within Judaism. Appeal is sometimes made to Paul's language about freedom from the Jewish law in such a way as to imply that he no longer thought of the OT as divine revelation authoritative for practical conduct. In 1 Corinthians, however, Paul cites OT texts explicitly at least a dozen times. Rosner rightly insists that 'Paul's Scriptural inheritance may thus be regarded as having priority over other sources, such as pagan law, Stoicism ... and Graeco-Roman mystery religions' (*Paul, Scripture and Ethics*, p. 17). In his detailed study of Paul's citations of the OT, C. D. Stanley discusses twelve in 1 Corinthians. Of these, three precisely follow the LXX wording (1:31 cites Jer. 9:24; 6:16 cites Gen. 2:24; 10:7 cites Exod. 32:6). Four citations reproduce LXX texts but also make a minor change, often only to a particular word, usually to bring out an emphasis or clarification relevant to Paul's argument. In 1:19 Paul cites Isaiah 29:14 with one change of word (*athetēsō*) 'to drive this point home' (Stanley, *Paul and the Language of Scripture*, p. 186); in 3:20 Paul specifies 'human beings' (in Ps. 94:11) as 'the wise' for the same reason; 9:9 cites Deuteronomy 25:4 with a different word for 'muzzle'; 15:27 offers a minimal adaptation of Psalm 8:6.

Other examples are more complex. Probably the most difficult is the quotation of Isaiah 28:11–12 in 1 Corinthians 14:21, where Paul does seem to reshape a text which corresponds precisely neither with the Hebrew Massoretic Text nor with the LXX. 1 Corinthians 15:45 is also a looser citation of the LXX, while 3:19 retains echoes of the Hebrew MT of Job 5:13 or more probably of a different Greek version (see Stanley, *The Language of Scripture*, pp. 189–194, 197–209). Stanley concludes that various Greek text-types may have been used, although Paul's 'primary text' is what we know as the LXX. He makes minor changes from time to time for the purposes of clarification or emphasis, including the exclusion of irrelevant directions of application. It is possible that Paul may have collected his own anthology of OT texts for use in the life of the churches, but this cannot be proved.

The purpose of OT citations

The OT does not serve for Paul merely as a source of *ad hominem* argument addressed to more 'Jewish' readers. The OT remained the Scripture of the Christian church. A sustained case for the use of the OT as a foundation for Christian ethics and lifestyle in 1 Corinthians is made by Rosner. An initial survey shows that even some of those scholars who are specialists in the OT or Jewish background pay insufficient attention to this point, while other specialists acknowledge it (*e.g.* C. K. Barrett, *A Commentary on the First Epistle to the Corinthians*; B. S. Rosner, *Paul, Scripture and Ethics*, pp. 3–25). Rosner pays particular attention to the role of OT thought behind the ethical issues of incest, *exclusion, sexual immorality and marriage in 1 Corinthians 5 – 7. Thus 5:1–13 draws on the holiness motif of Deuteronomy 23:1–9, and in turn on its re-actualization and further explication in Ezra, in which issues of covenant and corporate identity arise (*Paul, Scripture and Ethics*, pp. 61–93). No less, 'the Scriptures were an indispensable and formative source for 1 Corinthians 6:1–11' (p. 121).

Typology in 1 Corinthians 10:7–13?

In 10:6 Paul uses the Gk. word *typos* as a term to denote a corresponding sense borne by an OT passage or events (*cf. typikōs* in 10:11). In L. Goppelt's view this decisively disposes of the notion that Paul appeals to the OT only as a piece of contextual apologetics or polemics against 'Judaizers'. Paul cites the 'craving' of the majority of Israelites, redeemed from Egypt, which caused them to fall and to incur God's displeasure (*cf.* Exod. 32:1–6; Num. 14:22–30; 25:1–9; as well as further allusions in Exod., Deut. and Ps.). All shared in God's destruction through mis-directed desire. These events occurred as *typoi*, 'examples' (NRSV, NIV, NJB, KJV/AV) or 'warnings' (REB). In 10:11 Paul explicitly states that the accounts of self-indulgence and destruction in the wilderness were 'written also for our sake' (the title used by J. W. Aageson for a book on these issues). Paul adds that this becomes all the more critical because it is the Christian community 'on whom the ends of the ages have come' (v. 11). Paul's use of the OT identifies and reflects both continuity between Israel and the church as God's covenant people, and contrast between them, since the church confesses Christ as Lord and belongs to the 'last' days, or at least to the period 'between the times' of Christ and the end. Some scholars emphasize the eschatological frame of OT 'application' to Christians, but we must be cautious about appeals to a 'pesher' exegesis on analogy with Qumran. In spite of its rejection by some, we are on safer ground with Goppelt's distinction (*Typos*) between so-called *allegorical* interpretation as a more speculative correspondence only between *ideas*, and *typology* as a firmly historical correspondence between *events*. This seems to be the case in 1 Corinthians 10.

The theology of 1 Corinthians in relation to the Pauline corpus and the NT

The priority of grace

We have demonstrated that to regard Romans as centred on justification by grace, and 1 Corinthians on ethics or conduct in daily life, is wide of the mark. In 1 Corinthians the critique of the cross stands in judgment upon all human pretensions to generate 'wisdom' or 'status'. Indeed, it speaks more subtly than any other NT writing of the seduction of using 'religion', even the Christian religion, as an instrument for mere self-affirmation. Even the 'gifts' bestowed by the Holy Spirit can be misconstrued as conferring 'power' or 'status'. Hence in this epistle Paul presses a Christocentric and Christomorphic criterion of 'spirituality'. The spiritual gifts of 1 Corinthians 12 – 14 remain *gifts*: 'What do you have that you did not receive? And if you received it, why do you boast as though you did not?' (4:7). This clearly coheres with major themes in Romans and Galatians. In Romans the figure of Abraham provides a classic paradigm (Rom. 4:4–16), which is applied to Christian believers (Rom 5:15–21). In Ephesians this becomes a central summarizing theme (*e.g.* Eph. 2:6–8; 3:7–8). However, the theme also runs throughout the NT (*e.g.* John 1:14–17; Heb. 4:16; 1 Pet. 1:5–12).

The work of Christ and Christ-union

In 1 Corinthians 1:18 Paul defines the very nature of the gospel as 'the proclamation of the cross' (1:19–31). The death of Jesus

Christ constitutes a Passover sacrifice, which together with his resurrection brings new life (5:7). Paul speaks of this as a 'purchase price' which redeems believers from bondage into the new lordship of Christ (6:20) with whom they are now 'one' (6:15, 19; 10:16–17). That 'Christ died for our sins according to the Scriptures, that he was buried, and that he was raised ... ' (1 Cor. 15:3–4) is part of the pre-Pauline tradition transmitted to Paul (Gk. *paredōka ... paralabon ...* 15:3) and common to the churches. Similarly the theme of being 'in Christ' (15:22) as an objective state of salvation (*cf.* also 6:15, 19; 10:16–17 cited above) finds parallels in most of the Pauline writings (*cf.* Rom. 3:24; 8:1, 39; 2 Cor. 5:17; Gal. 4:19; 5:5; Phil. 3:9). The epistle to the Hebrews uses different imagery of 'drawing near' through the mediating priesthood and sacrifice of Christ, but the vine imagery of John 15 expounds the theme of union with Christ in one single life-entity.

God and Christ

1 Corinthians firmly defines Christian existence in terms of a practical commitment to Christ as Lord (1 Cor. 12:3). The redemption imagery of being purchased from bondage to evil forces into being Christ's own person (1 Cor. 6:19–20; 7:23) underlines this. Again, this entirely coheres with the notion elsewhere in Paul that the believer is not only committed to serve Christ with practical obedience but also that the believer enjoys a related freedom because Christ has taken responsibility for his or her welfare (*cf.* Rom. 14:7–12). On the other hand, 1 Corinthians reflects a clearer notion of an 'ordered' relation between God, Christ and the Holy Spirit than perhaps any other epistle or NT writing: 'You belong to Christ, and Christ to God' (3:23); 'God the Father from whom are all things ... One Lord Jesus Christ through whom are all things ...' (8:6); 'Christ's "head" is God' (11:3); and especially 'Then comes the end when Christ delivers up the kingdom to God the Father ... He is destined to reign until God has put all enemies under his feet ... Then the Son will also be made subject to God who made all things subject to him, and thus God will be all in all' (15:24–28). Two reasons may be suggested for this emphasis in 1 Corinthians. First, it is possible that the Corinthians focused too readily on a more self-affirming 'Lord' of their assembly than the awesome

transcendent God of universal judgment and grace. Corinth demonstrates the danger of a 'local' theology. Second, again and again concern for 'the other' and refusal to stand on one's own 'rights' assertively runs through every ethical and pastoral concern, and Christ and the cross stand as a definitive critique of this. In his stance towards the weak on one side, and towards God on the other, Christ voluntarily gives place to the other for the sake of God's larger purposes for all. Hence the climax of redemption is 'that God may be all in all'. This in no way diminishes the status of Christ, but rather defines it in Christological (as against worldly) terms (*e.g. power* is redefined in terms of the cross. Further, as against today's political egalitarianism and post-modern fragmentation, Paul insists in this epistle on 'orderedness' and a concern for the universal. Even so, this is not the only NT writing to convey this angle of vision. Philippians 2:6–11, the pre-Pauline 'hymn', insists that it is God whose power and authority lie behind the acclamation 'Jesus Christ is LORD' (2:9, 11). In the fourth Gospel a similar dialectic stresses both the 'oneness' of Christ and the Father (John 14:6, 20; 17:21–22; *cf.* also John 20:28; Heb. 1:8), and also the correlation of the 'order', 'God, Christ, believers'. Hence 'As the Father sent me, so I send you' (John 20:21; *cf.* 17:22). In John the Father 'glorifies' the Son, but this action is also reciprocal (17:1–5, in part-parallel with 1 Cor. 15:24–28).

The Holy Spirit, the church, eschatology

All three themes achieve considerable prominence in 1 Corinthians. The transcendence of the Holy Spirit is emphasized in 1 Corinthians 2:10–12, and whereas the church fathers appealed to 1 Corinthians 2 to underline the deity of the Holy Spirit, the Reformers appealed to this chapter to emphasize revelation by the Holy Spirit. The unity and diversity of the gracious operations of the Spirit in the corporate believing community receive their fullest treatment in 1 Corinthians 12 – 14. Here Paul insists that self-affirming status is not conferred by the most spectacular kinds of gift, but that the Holy Spirit makes a sovereign choice about how gifts will be 'apportioned' for the good of the entire community. If any criterion of authenticity is needed, it emerges from the Christlike character of the 'gift': does it promote Christ's Lordship (12:3) and 'build' the whole community (12:12 – 14:25)? The crown of the epistle is the resurrection chapter (ch. 15), which is the most detailed exposition of the subject in the NT. The three major 'last things' – the parousia, the last judgment, and especially the resurrection – all find place here. Again, this coheres with the expositions of these themes elsewhere in Paul and the NT. With the possible exception of John and Hebrews, God (or the Spirit of God) is the active agent who brings about Christ's resurrection (*cf.* Rom. 8:11; Phil. 2:9; Eph. 1:20; and the passives of 1 Cor. 15:15, and of vv. 12–17). The emphasis of the unity of the gifts of the Spirit in 1 Corinthians 12 – 14 finds a parallel in Ephesians 2:11–22, while the 'appointment' of gifts is further reflected in Romans 12:3–8. The theme of 'building' for the eschatological goal finds expression also in 1 Thessalonians 5:12–22 and Colossians 3:12–17.

Other theological themes

We do not have space to explore other themes. It should be noted, however, that bodily obedience in the public domain is fundamental to Paul's theology of humanness and Christian lifestyle in this epistle (see above). (For further parallels with other Pauline epistles, see sections 71–145 in F. O. Francis and J. P. Sampley, *Pauline Parallels* [Philadelphia, 1979], pp. 104–183).

See also: DEATH AND RESURRECTION.

Bibliography

J. W. Aageson, *Written Also for our Sake* (Louisville, 1993); C. K. Barrett, *A Commentary on the First Epistle to the Corinthians*, BNTC (London, ²1971); A. R. Brown, *The Cross and Human Transformation* (Minneapolis, 1995); J. K. Chow, *Patronage and Power* (Sheffield, 1992); A. D. Clarke, *Secular and Christian Leadership in Corinth* (Leiden, 1993); R. F. Collins, *First Corinthians*, Sacra Pagina (Collegeville, 1999); H. Conzelmann, *1 Corinthians*, Hermeneia (ET, Philadelphia, 1975); G. D. Fee, *The First Epistle to the Corinthians*, NICNT (Grand Rapids, 1987); C. Forbes, *Prophecy and Inspired Speech* (Tübingen, 1995); P. D. Gardner, *The Gifts of God and the Authentication of a Christian: An Exegetical Study of 1 Cor. 8:1 – 11:1* (Lanham, 1994); T. W. Gillespie, *The First Theologians: A Study in Early Christian Prophecy* (Grand Rapids, 1994); L. Goppelt, *Typos* (Grand Rapids, 1982); R. B. Hays, *Echoes of Scripture in the Letters of Paul* (New Haven, 1989); *idem*, *First Corinthians*, Interpretation (Louisville, 1997); D. G. Horrell, *The Social Ethos of the Corinthian Correspondence* (Edinburgh, 1996); R. A. Horsley, *1 Corinthians* (Nashville, 1998); D. B. Martin, *The Corinthian Body* (New Haven, 1995); M. M. Mitchell, *Paul and the Rhetoric of Reconciliation* (Tübingen, 1991; Louisville, 1992); J. Murphy-O'Connor, *St Paul's Corinth: Texts and Archaeology* (Wilmington, 1983); R. Pickett, *The Cross in Corinth* (Sheffield, 1997); S. M. Pogoloff, *Logos and Sophia: The Rhetorical Situation of 1 Corinthians* (Atlanta, 1992); B. S. Rosner, *Paul, Scripture and Ethics: A Study of 1 Cor. 5 – 7* (Leiden, 1994); W. Schrage, *Der erste Brief an die Korinther*, 3 vols. (Neukirchen-Vluyn and Zurich, 1991, 1995, 1999); C. D. Stanley, *Paul and the Language of Scripture* (Cambridge, 1992); G. Theissen, *The Social Setting of Pauline Christianity: Essays on Corinth* (ET, Philadelphia and Edinburgh, 1982, 1990); A. C. Thiselton, *1 Corinthians: A Commentary on the Greek Text*, NIGTC (Grand Rapids and Carlisle, forthcoming); *idem*, 'Luther and Barth on 1 Cor. 15: Seven Theses', in W. P. Stephens (ed.), *The Bible, the Reformation and the Church: In Honour of J. Atkinson* (Sheffield, 1995); A. C. Wire, *The Corinthian Women Prophets* (Minneapolis, 1990); B. Witherington, *Conflict and Community in Corinth* (Carlisle and Grand Rapids, 1995); K.-K. Yeo, *Rhetorical Interaction in 1 Cor. 8 and 10* (Leiden, 1995).

A. C. THISELTON

2 CORINTHIANS

2 Corinthians falls into three sections: chapters 1 – 7 contain *Paul's explanation of his recent conduct and of the apostolic ministry in general; in chapters 8 – 9 Paul exhorts the Corinthians to complete their contribution to the collection for destitute believers in Jerusalem (*cf.* Rom. 15:25–26); chapters 10 – 13 are Paul's defence and vindication of his apostolic authority (see *Mission). Some scholars argue that the

canonical 2 Corinthians is a composite letter, comprising two or more separate letters, but a strong case can be made for its integrity and its being despatched as a simple composition, even if the actual writing of the document occurred over a period of time during which the situation at Corinth changed.

Chapters 1 – 7

The major theme of these chapters is 'comfort in the midst of affliction' (cf. 1:4).

Suffering

In this epistle there are two lengthy lists of Paul's apostolic *sufferings (viz. 6:4–10 and 11:23–29) but his theology of Christian suffering is most apparent in 1:3–11. He had recently experienced some unspecified affliction in the province of Asia that caused him to be so utterly and unbearably crushed that he was forced to renounce all hope of survival (1:8). But *God had graciously intervened to deliver him and would do so again provided the Corinthians cooperated in *prayer (1:10–11). Several principles emerge from Paul's discussion.

1. Suffering endured patiently deepens our appreciation of God's character, in particular his limitless compassion and never-failing *comfort (1:3–4; cf. Ps. 145:9; Is. 51:3, 12).

2. Suffering drives us to trust God alone. Paul's desperate plight had undermined his self-reliance and compelled him to depend totally on the God who raises the dead and who can therefore rescue the dying from the grip of *death (1:9).

3. Suffering leads to identification with *Jesus Christ. Paul could identify his sufferings as 'the sufferings of Christ' (1:5) probably because they befell him as 'a person in Christ' (12:2) who was engaged in the service of Christ (4:11). They were *Christ's* sufferings because they contributed to the fulfilment of the suffering destined for the Body of Christ (Acts 14:22; Col. 1:24), or because Christ continued to identify himself with his afflicted *church (Acts 9:4–5).

4. The experience of God's comfort (his help, consolation and encouragement) in our suffering qualifies, equips and obliges us to comfort others undergoing any type of suffering (1:4, 6). The apostle's thought seems to imply four stages: Paul's own sufferings (which are Christ's sufferings; 1:4); his experience of God's comfort mediated

through Christ (1:5); the Corinthians' sufferings; their experience of God's comfort mediated through Paul (1:6–7).

5. Suffering is not for ever. In comparison with the weighty and eternal *glory that is produced by suffering patiently endured, suffering is both light and momentary (4:17; cf. Rom. 8:17–18). Glory follows suffering (cf. Luke 24:26; 1 Pet. 1:11; 5:9–10).

Death and resurrection

Paul's disconcerting encounter with death (1:8–11), his incessant suffering (11:23–29; cf. 1 Cor. 15:31, 'Not a day but I am at death's door,' Moffatt), and his progressive physical debilitation (4:16) prompted him to reflect as never before on the nature of death for the Christian. Negatively, death means the destruction of the earthly tent-dwelling (5:1), the loss of both physical corporeality (we are no longer 'in the flesh') and earthly corporateness (we are no longer 'in Adam', although we remain 'in Christ', 1 Cor. 15:18; 1 Thess. 4:16). Positively, death brings departure from mortal embodiment to the presence of the Lord (5:8; cf. Phil. 1:23). A departure implies a destination as well as an evacuation, a 'to' as well as a 'from'. At death, believers are not left homeless but experience a change in their place of residence. Earthly embodiment means spatial distance or exile from the immediate presence of the Lord (5:6), since the Christian pilgrimage is in the realm of faith, not the realm of sight (5:7). But the same moment of death that marks the dismantling of the transitory tent of the physical body also marks the entrance into permanent residence 'with the Lord' (5:8) and therefore the enjoyment of active and mutual fellowship with him.

Although the terms 'raise' and 'resurrection' are not found in 5:1–10 (but see 4:14) it is clear, as Paul describes the sources of divine comfort that are afforded the believer who faces the possibility of death, that these include not only the assurance that death brings enriched communion with Christ (5:7–8) but also the certainty of the future possession of a 'spiritual body' (5:1; cf. 1 Cor. 15:44) and the knowledge that the indwelling Spirit (see *Holy Spirit) is God's pledge of a resurrection transformation (5:4–5). This splendid hope (5:1–8), along with accountability to Christ (5:10), prompt the believer to seek the Master's constant approval (5:9).

Other important themes

1. *Church discipline (2:5–11)*. Apparently Paul or one of his representatives at Corinth had been verbally insulted by someone in the Corinthian church. The precise nature of the offence is not known, but it clearly involved Paul since he offers his personal forgiveness (2:10). At first the congregation had not rallied to Paul's defence but, stung by his 'severe letter' which called for the punishment of the wrongdoer, the majority of them inflicted some unspecified penalty on the man. Now Paul calls for them to terminate the penalty and reaffirm their love for the man (2:8). For offences serious enough to warrant corporate church *discipline (such as overt immorality not repented of [1 Cor. 5:1–11], false teaching actively propagated [Rom. 16:17], or divisiveness [Tit. 3:10]), there would seem to be five stages in the process, stages that are not only necessary but should also occur in a fixed order: 1. The wrongdoing (2:5), which implies an offending party (7:12) and sometimes an offended party (7:12). 2. The punishment (2:6), which is inflicted by 'the majority'. 3. The pain or sorrow (2:5, 7), which is suffered by the wrongdoer, and in a different sense, is felt by the whole congregation (2:5). 4. Repentance (implied in 2:6), which is the outcome of 'godly sorrow' (*cf.* 7:9–10). 5. Forgiveness (2:7, 10) and restoration (2:8), which are granted by the congregation as well as by the offended party.

2. *The two covenants (3:7–18)*. The expression 'the old covenant' (3:14) may be a phrase coined by Paul; it follows naturally from Jeremiah's 'new covenant' (Jer. 31:31) and from the eucharistic tradition of the cup as 'the new covenant' ratified by Christ's blood (1 Cor. 11:25). The paragraph 3:7–11 is basically a comparison of the two *covenants that establishes the surpassing glory of the new covenant. Both covenants are glorious (3:7–8), but the new is far more glorious than the old (3:9–11). The old was engraved on stone tablets (3:3, 7); the new is written on hearts-of-flesh tablets (3:3). One was a death-dealing written code; the other involves a life-giving Spirit (3:6). The era of the old covenant was a dispensation of death (3:7) and condemnation (3:9), a fading order (3:7, 11), whereas the era of the new covenant is a dispensation of the Spirit (3:8)

and of righteousness (3:9), a permanent order (3:11).

The second paragraph, 3:12–18, is an allusive homily based on Exodus 34:29–35, the account of *Moses' regular encounters with Yahweh in the 'tent of meeting' before his speaking with the Israelites. In 3:18 Paul draws his conclusion regarding the superiority of the new covenant. Under this new economy, 1. not one man alone, but all believers see and then reflect the glory of the Lord; 2. unlike the Jews, who still read the law with veiled hearts, Christians, with unveiled faces, see the glory of Yahweh, which is Christ, in the mirror of the gospel; 3. glory is displayed inwardly in the character, not outwardly on the face; 4. so far from waxing and waning, the glory progressively increases until the believer acquires through resurrection a 'glorious body' comparable to Christ's (Phil. 3:21).

3. *Evangelism (5:11–21)*. From one perspective evangelism is 'try(ing) to persuade people' (5:11, NIV) of the truth of the *gospel. Paul's motivation for his evangelistic effort was, in part, 'the fear of the Lord' (5:11), that is, the sobering awareness of people's ultimate accountability to the Lord Christ (5:10). But other impulses for proclaiming the foolishness of the cross (*cf.* 1 Cor. 1:18) were the honour of God (5:13) and the love of Christ (5:14). Conversion involves gaining a new view of Christ – he is no messianic pretender, nor simply an exemplary moralist, but God's promised Messiah – and consequently a new view of other people (5:16), who are seen 'according to the Spirit' or in the light of the cross. The converted person also has a new relation to Christ, being 'in Christ' (5:17a), that is, in personal union with the risen Christ and incorporated within the body of Christ, the church. There has been a new act of divine creation (*cf.* 4:6) and a new set of relationships has been permanently established (5:17–18a). As for the content of the evangel, reconciliation to God has been achieved by the work of Christ (5:18b–19a) so that *forgiveness of sins is granted (5:19b) and a right standing with God is acquired (5:21) by those who are reconciled to God (5:20b). The function of evangelists is threefold. They are trustees of a message (5:19c), ambassadors for Christ, and advocates for God (5:20).

4. *Holiness of life (6:14 – 7:1)*. Structur-

ally, this is a minor digression within Paul's major digression describing the apostolic ministry (2:14 – 7:4). He calls for the Corinthians to avoid getting into 'double harness' with unbelievers (6:14a; *cf*. Deut. 22:10; Lev. 19:19), that is, to sever all close attachments with non-Christians (such as membership of local pagan cults) that would compromise their professed loyalty to Christ or jeopardize the consistency of their Christian witness. This is not an injunction against all association with unbelievers (see 1 Cor. 5:9–10; 7:12–16; 10:27). However, Christianity and heathenism (especially idolatry) are incompatible, as Paul shows by five rhetorical questions (6:14b–16a). Such discerning separation from the world (6:17) leads to fellowship with God and his people (*cf*. Jas. 4:4). If Christians corporately are the temple of the living God (6:16; *cf*. 1 Cor. 3:16), individually they are the sons and daughters of a Father who is the Lord Almighty (6:18). The privilege of being a dwelling place of God (6:16) and the benefits of compliance with the divine will (6:17–18) Paul calls 'promises'; they motivate believers to avoid every source of possible defilement and so bring their *holiness to completion by this proof of their reverence for God (7:1). Living for the honour of Christ (5:15) involves not only separation from outward evil (6:17) and from inward defilement (7:1) but also fellowship with the living God and with his family (6:16, 18).

Chapters 8 – 9

From AD 52–57 a large proportion of Paul's time and energies was devoted to arranging a collection among his Gentile churches for 'the poor among the saints in Jerusalem' (Rom. 15:26). He regarded this collection as an act of fraternal love (Gal. 6:10) that expressed the interdependence of the members of the Body of Christ (1 Cor. 12:25–26), that symbolized the unity of Jew and Gentile in Christ (Eph. 2:11–22), and that dramatized for Gentile believers in material terms their spiritual indebtedness to the mother church in Jerusalem (Rom. 15:19, 27).

As Paul encourages the Corinthians to finalize their contribution to the collection, he appeals to a variety of motives which should prompt them to generous giving (8:1–15). There is the example of other believers (8:1–5, 8), their own promising start and desire for

spiritual excellence (8:6–7), and the supreme example of Christ himself who showed eagerness and generosity in giving as a demonstration of his love (8:8–9). Christ 'became poor' by the act of incarnation that followed his preincarnate renunciation of his 'wealth', the glory of heavenly existence (*cf*. Phil. 2:6–8). Paul then shows that Christian stewardship does not aim at the exchange of financial burdens so that the rich become poor and the poor rich, but rather at equal sharing of burdens that will lead to an equal supply of the necessities of life (8:13). Moreover, voluntary mutual sacrifice maintains that equality of supply (8:14), an equality which was enforced when God miraculously provided manna to the Israelites in the wilderness (8:15, citing Exod. 16:18).

Having spoken of the need for generosity (8:1–15), Paul proceeds to illustrate the twofold result of generosity (9:6–15). First, 'cheerful givers' who sow generously will also reap generously in God's provision of both spiritual grace and material prosperity ('all grace') that will permit them constantly to dispense spiritual and material benefits to others (9:6–11a). Second, because generous giving is evidence of God's grace (9:14; *cf*. 8:1–4), it prompts 'many expressions of thanks to God' (9:11b–13).

These two chapters highlight several characteristics of genuine Christian stewardship. It is voluntary, not enforced (8:3; 9:5, 7); generous, not parsimonious (8:2; 9:6, 13); enthusiastic, not grudging (8:4, 11–12; 9:7); deliberate, not haphazard (9:7); and sensible, not reckless (8:11–15).

Chapters 10 – 13

If the tone of chapters 1 – 7 is apologetic, and that of 8 – 9 hortatory, in 10 – 13 the tone is polemical, as Paul vigorously defends his authority as an apostle against the counterclaims of certain intruders from Palestine, who were 'false apostles, deceitful workmen, masquerading as apostles of Christ' (11:13). Here the chief theme is 'strength in the midst of weakness'. Divine power (10:3–5) finds its full scope and potency only in acknowledged human weakness (12:9; *cf*. 13:4).

Although Paul's letters to Timothy and Titus are commonly called 'the Pastorals', 2 Corinthians may justly be described as the pastoral epistle *par excellence*. Paul's theology of pastoral service may be discerned especially in these last four chapters, as he exhibits the characteristics of a spiritual father (1 Cor. 4:14–15) who has been entrusted by God with the care of his children.

1. *Adaptability*. As Paul seeks to persuade his 'children' to open their hearts wide to him (6:13) and to close their hearts against his adversaries, he uses a delicate blend of meekness (10:1; 13:10) and boldness (10:2, 11; 11:13). Because the immature Corinthians were dazzled by the pompous boasting of the Judaizers about their credentials, Paul was forced to indulge in boasting as they did (10:8; 11:1, 16–18, 21–27; 12:1, 11), although he chose to boast in matters that showed his weakness (11:30), namely his humiliating nocturnal escape from Damascus (11:31–33) and his debilitating 'thorn in the flesh' (12:7). He uses biting irony (11:4, 19–21; 12:11, 13) that stops short of sarcasm. He shows sensitivity to the needs of the situation, in refusing to forgo his financial independence from his converts (11:7–12).

2. *Jealousy*. Paul was jealous for the Corinthians' undivided loyalty to Christ during the period between their betrothal to Christ (*i.e.* their conversion) and their presentation to him, their heavenly bridegroom (*i.e.* their glorification) (11:2–3). Paul pictures himself as the father of the bride, whose aim was to preserve her virginity, her 'sincere and pure devotion to Christ' (11:3), until her marriage. Whereas human jealousy is sinful, to share divine jealousy (11:2) is virtuous.

3. *Devotion*. Indicative of Paul's paternal devotion to his children was 'the daily pressure' of his anxious concern for all his churches (11:28), as he sympathized with their weakness in faith, conduct and conscience (11:29; *cf.* 1 Cor. 8:7–13; 9:22; 12:26). In this 'anxious concern' (*merimna*) Paul was not violating Jesus' teaching about anxiety (Matt. 6:25–34, where the verbal form of *merimna* occurs six times), since he was, in fact, seeking first the kingdom of God and grappling with present not future problems, and was free of anxiety about relatively trivial matters such as food and clothing (see 11:27).

4. *Affection*. Like parents who work hard and save up for their children (12:14), Paul was willing 'to spend and be spent' for the benefit of his spiritual children (12:15). Neither property nor energies would be spared in his endeavour to win their devotion

to Christ. When he asks, 'Am I to be loved the less because I love you the more [that is, so intensely]?' (12:15), he is seeking from his readers an appropriate response of filial love to his own paternal affection (*cf.* 6:11–13; 11:11).

5. *Fear*. As he contemplated his forthcoming third visit (12:14), Paul was fearful that it might lead to mutual embarrassment (12:20), that sin might continue to be rampant in the church (12:20), and that he might again be humiliated and grieved because of certain unrepentant Corinthians (12:21). These fears induced Paul to issue a warning of impending discipline (13:1–4) and a plea for self-examination (13:5–10). In each case he reverts to the theme of 'strength in weakness'. As a result of being 'in Christ', Paul shared the weakness of his Lord who was 'crucified in weakness' (13:4), the 'weakness' of non-retaliation and of obedience to God. But as a consequence of his fellowship 'with' Christ, Paul shared in the power of the risen Christ (13:4), which would be shown, if necessary, in his 'not sparing' any erring Corinthians (13:2–3). But if the Corinthians were 'strong' in Christ, giving evidence of robust and mature Christian character, Paul would be able to come to them in the 'weakness' of a 'gentle spirit' (1 Cor. 4:21, and then he would rejoice (13:9).

The letter ends with the famous trinitarian benediction (13:13) that is noteworthy for its unusual 'economic' order of Son–Father–Spirit that reflects Christian experience. It is through the grace exhibited by Christ (8:9) in his selfless devotion to others in life and death that God demonstrates his love (Rom. 5:8) and the Spirit creates fellowship among believers (Eph. 4:3).

Bibliography

P. Barnett, *The Second Epistle to the Corinthians*, NICNT (Grand Rapids, 1997); V. P. Furnish, *II Corinthians*, AB (Garden City, 1984); A. E. Harvey, *Renewal Through Suffering* (Edinburgh, 1996); J. Murphy-O'Connor, *The Theology of the Second Letter to the Corinthians*, NTT (Cambridge, 1991); K. F. Nickle, *The Collection* (London, 1966); T. B. Savage, *Power Through Weakness* (Cambridge, 1996); M. E. Thrall, *The Second Epistle to the Corinthians*, vol. 1, ICC (Edinburgh, 1994); W. J. Webb, *Returning Home* (Sheffield, 1993); F. M. Young and D.

F. Ford, *Meaning and Truth in 2 Corinthians* (Grand Rapids, 1987).

M. J. HARRIS

GALATIANS

The theology of this letter is seen both in its explicit message and in the foundational presuppositions and implicit premises upon which the argument is built. The letter addresses a situation in which *Paul's Gentile converts are being told by a new group of teachers that in order to be integrated fully into God's *covenant people they need to enter into the Mosaic covenant by *circumcision (2:3; 5:2–6, 11–12; 6:12–13, 15).

Foundational issues

Some of the key theological foundations for Paul's argument are found in the first paragraph of the letter (1:1–5). Due to our sins we were all captives to this present evil age, but *Jesus (who is the Christ and clearly a divine figure) sacrificed himself for our sins in order to free us from it. *God raised him from the dead, and now we experience *grace and *peace from God, who is our Father, and from Jesus Christ, who is our Lord. All this was accomplished according to God's will, for which he deserves unending praise. God also sent Paul, through Jesus Christ, as a messenger and interpreter of these events. The references to Christ (Messiah), God the Father, the resurrection from the dead and 'this evil age' establish the apocalyptic, messianic-Jewish (Christian) theological framework in which Paul's argument will be developed.

Eschatology and apocalyptic

Galatians reflects a salvation-historical perspective in which the coming of Christ is seen to be the climactic fulfilment towards which the whole history of *Israel has been leading. Key elements of this perspective include God's promise to *Abraham (3:7–8, 16–17, 29; 4:22–23), the giving of the *law (3:17, 19; 4:24–25), the execution of the curse of the law in Israel's exile (3:10, 13; 4:24–25), and the prophetic promise regarding the future *salvation and restoration of God's people (the '*gospel'; 1:6–9).

The letter also reflects an 'apocalyptic' perspective inasmuch as it focuses on the revelation of the dramatic and climactic in-breaking of the *eschatological age of salvation which heralds the end of pre-resurrection history. Typically apocalyptic elements in Paul's thought include the spatial or cosmic dualism which separates heaven from earth (4:25–26) and God from humanity (1:1), the piercing of the barrier by a divine intermediary (1:12), the resurrection of the dead (1:1), the pouring out of the *Holy Spirit (4:6) and the new *creation (6:15). But the most important of these elements is the eschatological dualism in which the present evil age is contrasted with the age to come (1:4). In the light of this eschatological dualism Paul draws a sharp distinction between the *times before and after the coming of Christ. The former time when God did not yet justify the Gentiles (see *Nations) by faith is contrasted with the present time when he does (3:8–9). The time before the coming of the promised *seed is contrasted with the present time when the promise is fulfilled (3:19, 22). The time before *faith came stands in contrast with the time when faith has come (3:23, 25). Formerly we were slaves of the elements of the world but now we are redeemed children (4:3–5). Similarly, Paul's life is divided into the time before God revealed Christ in him and the time after he did so (1:13–15; 2:20), and the Galatians' lives are divided into the time when they did not know God and the present time when they do know God and are known by him (4:8–9).

The radical nature of the transformation accomplished by the coming of Christ is such that Paul can say that both the former world and his former existence came to an end with the crucifixion of Christ (6:14; 2:20; 5:24), and that now 'neither circumcision counts for anything, nor uncircumcision, but a new creation' (6:15, RSV), which is seen in faith expressing itself through *love (5:6). The radical contrast between the two ages is such that many distinctions between people that seemed fundamental before the coming of Christ, including the difference in status between Jews and pagans, are now inconsequential (3:28; 4:3–9).

Paul begins by drawing a sharp distinction between two possible sources of his apostleship: the divine and the human. Many other such distinctions are found in the letter. Some of them are explicitly worked out, others are implicit:

311

Receiving the Spirit by works of law	Receiving the Spirit by faith
Curse	Blessing
Receiving teaching from humans	Receiving teaching from God
Not walking according to the gospel	Walking according to the gospel
Being justified by works of law	Being justified by faith
Slaves	Children
Children of the slave woman	Children of the free woman
The present Jerusalem	The Jerusalem above
Flesh	Spirit
Under law	Led by the Spirit
Vanity	Love

Jesus Christ and God the Father

The eschatological and apocalyptic orientation of the letter also reflects the Christological focus of its theology. The coming of Christ, and his *death and resurrection, mark the turning point between the ages. These events have transformed the world and brought the promises of Abraham, of the Spirit, *redemption, grace and *freedom to both Jews and Gentiles.

It is God the Father who sent his Son to redeem us (4:4–5), who raised him from the dead (1:1) and whose will has been fulfilled through all that has been done for our redemption (1:4). He offers us that which has been made available through his Son Jesus Christ.

Paul as a figure of theological significance

In the process of establishing the divine origin and authority of his ministry and message (1:11 – 2:21), Paul reveals that he considers himself to be a figure of considerable theological importance. God had set him apart before his birth and having now called him by his grace (1:15) he has sent him, through a special revelation of his Son (1:11, 16), to preach Christ to the Gentiles (1:16).

Paul's calling is modelled on that of OT prophets. He is one of two key figures in God's missionary strategy: he was given a special grace (2:9), being entrusted with the ministry to the Gentiles just as Peter was entrusted with the ministry to the Jews (2:7). His description of his own life (1:13–24) reflects the same apocalyptic structure that he sees in the history of creation: two distinct periods, radically different from each other, with the revelation of Jesus Christ serving as the dividing point between them.

The church of God and the Israel of God

Paul seems to understand the *church as the eschatological Israel in whom God's prophetic promises are being fulfilled. His reference to 'the church of God' (1:13) strongly suggests that the church is the eschatological equivalent of the OT assembly of the Lord or assembly of God (Deut. 23:1–3, 8; 1 Chr. 28:8; Mic. 2:5; Neh. 13:1; see esp. the LXX). In Qumran the equivalent Hebrew expression was used to refer to the eschatological company of God.

The Galatian churches have been 'redeemed' and 'called' by the God of Israel (3:13; 1:6), terms which evoke the exodus of Israel from Egypt (Hos. 11:1–2). They have received the gospel (1:6–9), the good news which Israel had been waiting to hear (Is. 40:9–11; 52:7–10). The Christ (Messiah) is *their* Lord and they have received grace and peace from him and from God their Father (1:3). They are the children and heirs of Abraham (3:7, 29) and the children and heirs of God (3:26; 4:5–7). They have received the Spirit (4:6) whom God promised to pour out on his people Israel (Is. 44:3; Ezek. 36:26–27). Although the point has been debated, given the theological background above it seems most likely that the reference to the 'Israel of God' in 6:16 is a reference to the church as the eschatologically restored people of God, which now clearly includes both Jews and Gentiles.

Faith and its benefits

There is a serious debate in Pauline studies over the meaning of the expression *pistis Christou*, traditionally translated 'faith in Christ'. A growing number of scholars have been arguing that it should be translated 'the faith of Christ' or 'Christ's faithfulness' and understood as a reference to Christ's death on the cross, the act of obedience which is the ground of the justification (see *Righteousness, justice and justification) available to those who believe in him. One of the key texts in the debate is Galatians 2:16 where the expression appears twice in the same verse (see also 3:22). Supporters of the traditional view believe that the clause 'we have believed in Christ Jesus' makes clear that the other expressions refer to believers' faith in Christ (see *e.g.* J. D. G. Dunn, *The Theology of Paul's Letter to the Galatians*, pp. 57–58). Supporters of the alternative position believe that such an interpretation makes part of the verse overly redundant and that it is actually making two different affirmations: that we are justified by Christ's faithfulness (his obedient death on the cross), and that we believe in him in order to enter into the justification that his faithfulness has made available to us (see *e.g.* the studies by R. B. Hays and B. W. Longenecker listed in the bibliography). In either case it is clear that our salvation was made possible by Christ's death for us (3:2; 6:14), a self-*sacrifice of love (1:4; 2:20) in which he became a curse on our behalf to redeem us from the curse of the law (3:13) (see *Blessing/curse).

Paul's argumentation in 2:15 – 4:31 reveals that for him, being justified, receiving the Spirit and becoming children of Abraham and of God are all interrelated benefits given to those who have faith in Christ. They affirm (and confirm) that one is truly a member of God's special *people. Thus Paul begins by speaking of being justified by faith (2:16–21); then to prove that justification is by faith he points out that it was by faith that the Galatians received the Spirit (3:1–5). Paul identifies God's promise to bless the nations in Abraham (3:8) with the Gentiles' experience of both justification (3:8–9) and the Spirit (3:1–6, 14) on the basis of the faith they have in common with him. The faith they share with Abraham proves that they are indeed his children (3:7, 9).

Paul then clarifies that God's promise to bless all nations through Abraham's 'offspring' referred to a single individual, Christ (3:16). Those who have faith in Christ are Abraham's seed by means of their union or identification with Christ, who is the single son of Abraham in whom the promises are fulfilled (3:29). Not only are they Abraham's seed, but also God's children and heirs by

means of that same identification with Christ (3:26–29; 4:5–7; see also *Adoption). It is this identification with Christ in his death and resurrection that brings the believer into the blessings of new life in the new creation (2:20; 5:24–25; 6:14–15).

The law

The difference between Paul's view of the law and that of the other teachers in Galatia is based on the greater discontinuity implied in Paul's more apocalyptic perspective. He does not expect the Mosaic covenant (and its laws) to survive the transition to the new age. Although the law was given by God to serve his purposes (3:19–24), it pertained to the former age to which Christ and his community have died (2:19; 3:25). They now live in a new world where the old law is fulfilled even while it is no longer in force (5:13–23; 6:2).

Unlike the law, the promise given to Abraham was not limited to the former age and always referred to and awaited an eschatological fulfilment (3:8). The law does not annul that promise (3:17), and the coming of Christ brings about its long-awaited realization (3:14, 29).

The meaning of Paul's references to the 'works of the law' (2:16; 3:2, 5, 10) is now clearer in the light of the Qumran document *Miqṣat Ma'aśê ha-Torah*, where the phrase is used to refer to what Rabbinic Judaism later called *halakah*: the precise interpretation of the Mosaic law, which was to be kept by those living under the Mosaic covenant and which distinguished Israel from other peoples. Thus 'those who rely on the works of the law' are people who see their acceptance of the Mosaic covenant and law as the basis for their membership in God's people. Paul says such people are under a curse (3:10). The meaning of this verse has been debated, but in the light of the reference to 'the curse of the law' in verse 13 it seems most likely that Paul believes Israel still to be suffering the curses associated with their disobedience to the law, which resulted in their exile (Deut. 27:26; Dan. 9:11). This would explain the reference in 4:25 to *Jerusalem's being in slavery (see Ezra 9:9; Neh. 9:36).

Thus the Mosaic covenant and law is not a means of justification because this was never its purpose. In fact, those who enter into it enter into the curse that has fallen on Israel because of disobedience. It belongs to the former, pre-Christ, pre-resurrection age which has been superseded by the new age of the Spirit. The letter to the Galatians suggests that in Paul's view the gospel has displaced the law in some significant ways. Paul represents the situation of the Galatians as one of impending *apostasy (1:6–9). His attitude to the uniqueness of the gospel is reminiscent of what the OT says about God himself: there is only one; anything else that claims the name is false; and whoever preaches anything other than the only true one is to be anathematized (see Ciampa, *The Presence and Function of Scripture in Galatians*, pp. 169–170, 238–239). Apostasy from Paul's gospel is to be dealt with in the same way as apostasy from God and his law. The displacement of the law by the gospel is reflected also in the way Paul speaks of the behaviour of Peter and the other Jewish Christians: 'they were not acting in line with the truth of the gospel' (2:14, NIV). This indicates that the gospel is the standard for the 'walk' of the Christian community. That is, Paul establishes the gospel and its interpretation as the standard of judgment for the Christian community, in place of the interpretation of the Mosaic law and its commandments.

The life of freedom through the Spirit

In the last two chapters of the letter Paul focuses on the issues of freedom and its proper manifestation by means of the Spirit. He has already referred to 'the freedom we have in Christ Jesus' in 2:4. In Galatians 4:21–31 he establishes that Christians, as children of the heavenly Jerusalem, enjoy a freedom not shared by those who are under the Mosaic law. He then summarizes much of the theology of the letter with the phrase 'for freedom Christ has set us free' (5:1). Christians must guard their freedom from those who would have them become enslaved again by taking on the Mosaic law (2:4; 5:1–2). But that freedom is not to be abused by indulging the flesh; rather, it should be used in serving each other in love (5:13). This is achieved by means of the Spirit. 'Flesh' and 'Spirit' are not anthropological, but eschatological terms. The 'flesh' represents the weakness of human nature living on the resources of this age (4:23). It promotes moral and spiritual corruption and divisiveness (5:19–21). The 'Spirit', on the other hand, represents the presence and the power of the age to

come (4:29) with its supernatural ability to promote the moral and spiritual health of the community (5:22–23). It is by walking in the Spirit, and not by keeping the law, that one will overcome the problem of the flesh (5:16–17) and manifest the love and character that is the true fulfilment of the law of Christ (5:14, 22–23; 6:2).

The theology of Galatians as a biblical theology

Paul presents a scripturally based message to his Galatian readers. This is evident in his basing many of his arguments on Scripture passages cited in the text (Gen. 15:6 in Gal. 3:6; Gen. 12:3 in Gal. 3:8; Deut. 27:26 in Gal. 3:10; Hab. 2:4 in Gal. 3:11; Lev. 18:5 in Gal. 3:12; Deut. 21:23 in Gal. 3:13; Gen. 12:7 in Gal. 3:16; Is. 54:1 in Gal. 4:27; Gen. 21:10 in Gal. 4:30; Lev. 19:18 in Gal. 5:14). Even where he is not quoting Scripture his arguments are informed by his understanding of the Scriptures (see Ciampa, *Presence and Function*). The theology of the letter reflects a messianic and apocalyptic reading of the Scriptures in the light of the coming of Christ, which is governed by the conviction that the church represents the fulfilment of God's promise to restore his people and that, in agreement with the promise to Abraham, Gentiles also participate in the blessings of that restored people. The transition from 'this age' to 'the age to come' has already been accomplished by the death and resurrection of Christ; the church participates in that transition and in the blessings of redemption, justification, adoption and the Spirit through identification and union with Christ by faith.

Bibliography

J. M. Bassler (ed.), *Pauline Theology*, vol. 1 (Minneapolis, 1991); J. M. G. Barclay, *Obeying the Truth* (Edinburgh, 1988); R. E. Ciampa, *The Presence and Function of Scripture in Galatians 1 and 2* (Tübingen, 1998); J. D. G. Dunn, *The Theology of Paul's Letter to the Galatians*, NTT (Cambridge, 1993); R. B. Hays, *The Faith of Jesus Christ* (Chico, 1983); B. W. Longenecker, 'Defining the faithful character of the covenant community' in J. D. G. Dunn (ed.), *Paul and the Mosaic Law* (Tübingen, 1996); J. M. Scott, '"For as many as are of works of the law are under a curse" (Galatians 3.10)' in C.

A. Evans and J. A. Sanders (eds.), *Paul and the Scriptures of Israel* (Sheffield, 1993).

R. E. CIAMPA

EPHESIANS

Introduction

The letter to the Ephesians was probably a circular letter to a number of churches in Western Asia Minor. Its theology needs to be interpreted against this background. The letter has a unique, almost synoptic, relationship with *Colossians, which was probably written earlier. Quite possibly Ephesians *is* Colossians re-written (perhaps within days or weeks of its completion) for a similar, yet slightly different audience: similar, in the sense that both letters were intended for Christian recipients in danger of syncretism; different, in the sense that Ephesians appears to be addressed to a more Jewish-minded (or even Judaizing?) audience. It is Ephesians' extensive use of OT material which sets it apart from Colossians. It is true that Colossians refers to some typically Jewish identity markers (Sabbath, festivals, circumcision and food laws), but these were so well known that any community tending towards syncretism could have appropriated them. Ephesians, however, makes assumptions which point to a greater interest in Jewish matters on the part of its recipients.

If so, Ephesians provides an insight into the re-contextualizing of the theology contained in Colossians. Paul's determination to do this by employing OT traditions encourages the commentator to relate the theology of Ephesians to the text of the OT or to the history of the OT motifs appropriated in the letter. Apart from Colossians, the letter's closest parallels in the NT are Romans and 1 Peter. There is evidence of traditional material in the eulogy (1:3–14), the intercessory prayers (1:15–23), the doxology (3:20–21), the so-called 'hymnic' remnants in 2:14–16 and 5:14, the catechesis in 4:22 – 5:20, the lists of vices and virtues (4:31–32; 5:3–4, 9), the household codes (5:21 – 6:9) and the confessional material in 1:20–23; 4:4–6 and 5:2, 25. This encourages the attempt to relate Ephesians to similar NT texts.

Celebrating divine grace

*God's *grace pervades the Bible. (For grace as a major covenantal theme *cf.* G. Wenham, *Law, Morality and the Bible*, pp. 3–23.) The importance of this theme in Ephesians is demonstrated by the extensive praise section in Ephesians 1:3–14. The fact that much of this opening eulogy – which appears to be fashioned on the pattern of a Jewish *b°rakâ* – employs power and *revelation language is indicative of Paul's attempt to praise God's grace in terminology appropriate to the religio-cultural context of his intended readership. (For a detailed discussion of this context *cf.* C. Arnold, *Ephesians: Power and Magic*, pp. 13–40.) Paul returns to this theme in Ephesians 3:2–13, even though he has to interrupt the flow of his previous argument (3:1; for a digression for similar reasons *cf.* 1:19). The major manifestation of divine grace is Christ's *exaltation (1:20–23), following his humiliation which involved 'descent to the lower parts of the earth' (4:9, author's translation). This humiliation–exaltation pattern is encountered also in Philippians 2:5–11 and John 3:13. Believers participate in this transfer of status by grace alone, a theme which recalls Romans 3:23–28. The transfer is symbolized by *baptism (4:5; 5:14b, 26).

God's salvific interest in his creation

Like Romans 8:18–22, Ephesians 1:10 expresses the hope that *creation will be redeemed (*cf.* Col. 1:20). Ephesians abounds with 'new creation' terminology (*cf.* also below, 'Christian existence as growth'). This terminology is bound up with the existence of the *church in which, as a result of Christ's 'creative' *death (Eph. 2:15; *cf.* 2:10), the separation between *Israel and the Gentiles (see *Nations) is destroyed (*cf.* Rom. 9:25–33; 11:25–26; Gal. 3:28; 4:25–27; 6:15–16; for the reversal theme in Jesus' teaching *cf.* esp. Luke 12:13 – 20:19). God's *salvific interest in creation also means that any 'powers' that claim to exercise authority over creation are faced with the existence of the church (3:10), a clear sign that their days are numbered (*cf.* 1:21 – 2:5). Christ has been exalted to God's sphere (2:6). Paul concedes that the 'so-called powers' (this is probably a legitimate rendering of the implied polemic of 1:21) still need to be resisted (6:10–17), making the point with the help of OT traditions. He implies that the expansion of God's control over his creation involves the equipping of the church to withstand *evil with the weaponry of the divine warrior (cf. Is. 11:4–5; 52:10; 59:17). (See *Spiritual powers, *Warfare.)

Christ as the centre and goal of history

In line with Pauline Adam Christology, Ephesians presents *Jesus Christ as the centre (2:13–19) and the goal (1:10) of history. He forms the hinge between the age of the Torah and the Christocentric reconstitution of humanity achieved on the cross. In those verses which affirm the present realization of *eschatology (1:20–23; 2:6, 13–19; 3:3–11; 4:8–10; 5:32; 6:19), the centre and the goal of history appear to converge. Naturally this emphasis on present realization is found especially in the praise sections, although Ephesians 5:5, 16 may also refer to the present. References to the future benefits of God's grace are comparatively few (1:14; 2:7; 4:30), though not as few as in Galatians (Gal. 5:5). However, being seated with Christ in heaven becomes a synonym for experiencing the 'overflowing riches of his grace' (2:7) until 'the day of redemption' (1:14; 4:30; cf. 6:13, a possible reference to persecution), a grace experienced in all areas of life (4:6, 10). The manifestation of God's grace is presented within a 'now but not yet' framework. The decisive 'summing up' has already occurred, but further, future benefits are expected as a result (1:10).

The Spirit as the exclusive seal of salvation

Until the day of salvation believers are sealed with the *Holy Spirit (4:30). The sealing itself occurs when the good news is accepted in faith (1:13). Its significance can be understood against the background of the recipients: various forms of mysticism in which seals were needed in order to traverse the various levels of heaven. The loss of the appropriate seal would result in one's having to abandon the spiritual quest for the divine presence, or worse, in mental disturbances which result from interrupting the state of trance required for the mystical ascension. Paul anticipates no such problems with the seal of 'the Spirit of promise' (cf. Is. 44:3; Joel 2:28–29). It is unlikely that believers will lose it; impossible if they remain 'in Christ'. In

view of the victorious exaltation of Christ over all the powers (1:21–22; 4:8–10), the seal of the Spirit suffices as the exclusive 'guarantee of our inheritance' (1:14) or change of status (2:5–8).

Heaven as an expression of divine kingship

The celebration of divine grace is occasionally phrased in 'heavenly' language. 'Heaven' stands for spiritual blessings (1:3); it is the sphere of Christ's presence following his resurrection (1:20) and exaltation (2:6; 4:10), which together constitute the realized aspect of Christ's summing up of all things (1:10). This is not contradicted by the rhetorically motivated use of the phrase 'the heavenlies' for spiritual realm of both good (3:14–15) and evil (3:10; 6:12). God's grace manifests itself in his all-encompassing kingship. The polemical nature of this claim cannot have escaped the attention of the letter's intended readers. The goddess Artemis was regarded by many as the queen of heaven, but according to Paul it is Christ who exercises divine kingship throughout the cosmos.

Grace, election and salvation

Ephesians 1:3–8 contains *election and predestination language. This must be understood on the author's own terms; its point is missed when it is interpreted individualistically. God elected to provide both salvation and ethical transformation in Christ alone (1:4, 11; cf. 1 Pet. 1:2, 20). Paul is not saying that some individuals were predestined for eternal punishment and others for salvation. Predestination here means God's gracious determination to provide *forgiveness through Christ's blood (1:5–7, 11; cf. Rom. 8:29–30). Paul's praise language derives from his Christocentricity and from his desire to prepare the ground for the ethical directives in the second half of the letter. It must not be pressed into the service of individualistic soteriologies. The 'helmet of salvation' (6:17) is linked with the cross (2:13–16) and expresses a movement from past to present. Ephesians 2:11–22 applies this theme to the church and to Israel, 2:1–3 and 4:17–24 to the individual.

God's people in this world

A major ecclesiological question is whether the term *ekklēsia* (1:22; 3:10, 21; 5:23–32) denotes the so-called 'universal church', or whether Paul's corporate use of 'church' simply reflects the fact that this letter is a circular intended to be read by a number of local churches.

Local church or universal church?

Appeal is commonly made to Ephesians to support the idea of the church as a universal worldwide organism. This would be an advance from the position elsewhere in the Pauline corpus, where *ekklēsia* is used of local church(es), including small household gatherings (Col. 4:15–16). However, it is quite possible that *ekklēsia* in Ephesians denotes the heavenly (or kingly) dimension of local churches, in line with the references to the exaltation of both Christ and believers (2:6; *cf.* Col. 3:1–4; *pace* A. Lincoln, *The Theology of the Later Pauline Epistles*, pp. 92–93). Local churches are earthly manifestations of a heavenly reality, the exaltation of Christ and of believers (Eph. 3:21), in the midst of religio-cultural adversity. Elsewhere Paul appeals to Christ's relationship to the church as a model for *marriage (5:23–32). The passage celebrates the locus of God's power in the world, which is the (local?) church. Perhaps it should not be tamed by being read as referring to the abstract notion of a universal church.

Walking in Christ

Ephesians accounts for more than a quarter of the exhortations in the Pauline corpus to conduct oneself (*peripatein*) not like the enemies of the gospel do, but in a way worthy of Christ (2:2, 10; 4:1, 17; 5:2, 8, 15; *cf.* Col. 1:10; 2:6; 3:7; 4:5 and 1 Thess. 4:12). These exhortations are paralleled in Romans 6:4; 8:4; 13:13; 14:15; 1 Corinthians 3:3; 6:17; 2 Corinthians 4:2; 5:7; 10:2–3; 12:18; Galatians 5:16; Philippians 3:17–18; 1 Thessalonians 2:12; 4:1, 12 and 2 Thessalonians 3:6, 11. Believers are to walk in accordance with the good works prepared by God (Eph. 2:10), worthy of the calling of God (1:4; 4:1; 5:2, 8, 15), not as the Gentiles do (2:2; 4:17).

Distinctive ethics

More specifically Paul highlights the foundation of the believer's *hope (1:12, 18; 2:12; 4:4; 5:25–27) in Christ and the need to give expression to the unity of Christ's body (4:1–6) as crucial elements of distinctively Christian ethics. Another such element is following the example of Christ (5:1–2), thus reflecting divine grace and *love (1:5; 3:17–19; 4:15–16; 5:1–2, 25–33; 6:24) to each other and the world. This teaching recalls Paul's appropriation of Jesus' teaching on relating to others (*cf.* Luke 6:27–38) in Romans 2:1–4; 12:9–21; 1 Corinthians 4:12 and 13:5. To follow Christ's example requires spiritual strengthening (3:16; 5:18; *cf.* 1:13 and 4:30; 5:18 polemically contrasts the state of fullness in the Spirit with getting drunk with alcohol, a strategy used in the Dionysus cult to internalize the deity). The ethical outworking of this theology is expressed in the language of early Christian parenesis (*cf.* Introduction), and in the language of the OT. Thus Paul draws on Genesis 2:24 to illustrate how Christian marriage embodies more fully the ideal of mutual love which is already part of God's created order (5:31–32). In Ephesians 6:2–3 he appeals to Exodus 20:12 (part of the Decalogue) in support of respect for parents. The supposedly hymnic character of Ephesians 5:14b betrays an indebtedness to Isaiah 26:19 and 60:1–2, another parallel between Christocentric ethics and the values of the old covenant (a discussion of this with reference to Ephesians 4:25–30 is found in T. Moritz, *A Profound Mystery*, pp. 87–96). The *people of the fulfilled *covenant have no less a responsibility to behave ethically than the Jewish people before Christ. This is not contradicted by the fact that, in line with Galatians 2:19; 3:24–25 and Romans 6:14; 7:4–6; 10:4, the old *law is said to have been superseded by the cross (2:15; *cf.* the polemical implications of 4:8–10 discussed in Moritz, *A Profound Mystery*, pp. 74–76) and apostolic teaching: the apostles and prophets replace the law and the prophets (2:20; 3:5 and 4:11); the new *temple replaces the old (2:21–22). It is true that Paul continues to appeal to the OT, as in 6:1–3, but he uses it not as a binding covenant document, but rather to demonstrate the continuity between God's covenantal expectations for his people then (in the Torah) and now (in Christ). God's ethical expectations may not have changed fundamentally, but believers' means and motivation for meeting them are derived from Christ, not the Torah. This point was important for Paul (Rom. 7 and 8) and the early church (Acts 15:19–29) in their defence against Jewish and Jewish-Christian challenges on more than one occasion. It explains to some extent the apparent tension between the claim that the Torah has been superseded and the use of the Torah in early Christian ethical exhortation. The Torah expresses certain ethical expectations; being in Christ must be even more ethically demanding.

Spiritual opposition

The intended recipients would have been familiar with the 'powers' language that Paul employs (1:21; 2:2; 3:10; 4:8; 6:12). Having affirmed God's kingship through Christ in the opening eulogy (1:3–14) and thanksgiving (1:15–23) and in the praise section in 3:14–21, Paul describes the connection between these 'powers' and the spiritual and ethical struggles that face believers until the day of redemption (4:30; for the 'evil day' cf. 6:13). The thrust of the main passage on this subject (6:10–17) is clearly defensive: believers are to withstand (vv. 11, 13, 14). An attack has already been effected in Christ's exaltation over the powers (4:8), in which believers share (2:6). The imagery of Ephesians 6:14–17 may be that of a Roman soldier. More likely, however, it is drawn from the arena, where believers sometimes had to defend themselves against superior enemies, even to the point of death. This context is suggested by the term 'struggle' or 'wrestling match' used in verse 12. The defensive tone of the passage would sit awkwardly alongside the metaphor of the attacking Roman army. If, however, imagery comes from the arena, the commonly perceived need to speak of a 'paradox of peace' (the tension inherent in the call to use weapons to secure peace) largely disappears. Peace here is not that which one secures by means of weapons; it is the spiritual attitude which makes it possible to stand in the face of evil and be victorious.

Christian existence as growth

'In Christ' is not a static concept. Ephesians is full of growth language. In the face of a hostile environment, it is not enough to exist as a believer. Growth is necessary, especially in the areas of spirituality (1:16–19; 3:14–19) and church life (2:20–22; 4:11–16).

Past and present: God's people

The theological basis for corporate growth is the removal of the distinction between Jew and Gentile, in Christ and the church, through the cross (2:15–16). The apostle's own mission to the Gentiles is a reflection of this (3:2–8). Because of the cultural background of the readers, the nature of the church is expressed in '*mystery' language (1:9; 3:3, 4, 9; 5:32; 6:19; cf. C. Caragounis, The Ephesian Mystērion, pp. 124–127), but also in language drawn from Isaiah 52:7 and 57:19. Paul appeals to scriptural passages which reveal God's intention to provide for non-Jews. The realization of this intention is symbolized also by the imagery of a new temple (2:21–22), which stands for the church. This is an implicit reminder that the new temple replaces not just the old, but also that of Artemis. The new temple, or church, is then described as the locus of unity and growth (4:1–16). The 'mystery' language in chapters 1 and 3 specifically recalls Daniel 2 and 7; in both books the revelation of the mystery is a truly eschatological event involving the subjecting of everything under the Son of Man/Christ and the endowment of God's reconstituted people with wisdom. Whereas Daniel does not disclose the content of the mystery (cf. Eph. 3:5), Ephesians reveals it as the redefinition of God's people around the person of Christ, a relationship reflected in the mystery of marriage (Eph. 5:31–32; cf. Gen. 2:24). Both relationships grow only on the basis of love (1:4; 4:15–16 and 5:25–29).

Past and present: a new person

This theme of eschatological restoration, expressed in the contrast between past and present, operates also on the level of the individual. The old person is to be put off in favour of the new person that is created in God's likeness (2:1–3; 4:22–24; 5:14). The contexts indicate that the envisaged transformation is ethical. The closest parallel is with Paul's Adam Christology (Rom. 12:5; 1 Cor. 12:12–13; 15:22–49; Gal. 3:27–28 and Col. 3:10–11), which involves the incorporation of believers into Christ. In Ephesians 1:21–22 Adam typology is implied in the use of Psalms 8:6 and 110:1 (cf. 1 Cor. 15:20–28). The principle 'having been justified we will be saved' is found also in Romans 5:9 (cf. Eph. 2:3–9; 5:14b).

The church as the context for growth

Paul regards the church as Christ's fullness (1:23), but this does not prevent him from calling for growth, through love, towards Christ's fullness (4:13, 16). This dialectic is found also in Ephesians 2:20–22: believers are built on the foundation of the apostles and the prophets, with Christ being the cornerstone; but the building still needs to grow into a more complete spiritual temple (cf. 4:11–16). God provides the gifts needed to build up the church. These gifts are probably functions rather than offices (cf. vv. 8–10). This functional diversity is meant to operate in a context of theological unity (4:1–6). (See *Spiritual gifts.)

Mutual responsibility

Colossians encourages mutual edification in teaching, exhortation and worship (Col. 3:16–17). This is followed by a brief household code (Col. 3:18 – 4:1). Ephesians extends the code (Eph. 5:21 – 6:9) by incorporating OT material (5:31–32 and 6:2–3), thus framing the exhortation with scriptural reminders that mutual responsibility has been a covenant sign through the ages. It has now become a symbol of believers' new status in Christ.

Bibliography

C. Arnold, *Ephesians: Power and Magic* (Cambridge, 1989); C. Caragounis, *The Ephesian Mystērion* (Lund, 1977); A. Lincoln, *The Theology of the Later Pauline Epistles,* NTT (Cambridge, 1993); T. Moritz, *A Profound Mystery* (Leiden, 1996); G. Wenham, *Law, Morality and the Bible* (Leicester, 1978).

T. MORITZ

PHILIPPIANS

Philippi was the first major town in ancient Macedonia to be visited by *Paul and Silas when they crossed over into Europe from Asia (Acts 16:11–40), but Paul's letter to the church dates from a later time when he was in prison, most probably in Rome (cf. Acts 28:16–31). The story in Acts of the foundation of the church unfortunately sheds little or no light on the circumstances of the composition of the letter. The letter is essentially expressive of the friendship, or better fellowship, between Paul (with Timothy) and the congregation in Philippi, who were regarded with affection by him as

sharers in the common task of Christian mission (Phil. 1:5); the congregation had helped him by its prayers (1:19) and its giving (4:10–19). Paul shares news about his own situation as a prisoner with the aim of encouraging his readers (1:12–26), and writes about his contact with the congregation through Timothy and Epaphroditus (2:19–30). He also makes a strong pastoral appeal to the congregation to avoid dissension and to cultivate unity so that they will not be weak and unable to resist the powerful temptation, caused by active opposition, to give up their faith (1:27 – 2:18; cf. 4:2–9). The church was in danger also from a group of people (rival travelling preachers) who appear to have been encouraging Jewish ritual and legal practices as the path to spiritual perfection or maturity (3:1 – 4:1). Paul's response in his letter to this situation is deeply theological and represents a typical use of his profound theology for pastoral purposes.

The centrality of Jesus in Paul's experience and theology

As in all Paul's letters, *Jesus Christ plays a crucial role in the argument. In contrast with 1 and 2 Thessalonians, but in harmony with his other letters, Paul names Jesus Christ at the beginning of the letter, here to define his own role as Christ's servant and the Christian status of his readers (1:1), who are 'saints in Christ Jesus'. If the first part of this phrase uses OT language to identify the readers as the people of God, set apart to belong to him as his own distinctive people and to demonstrate this status by various specific characteristics, the latter part of the phrase shows that they owe their status to their relationship to Jesus Christ. Similarly, when Paul prays in his opening salutation for the divine blessings of grace and peace to be part of their experience, the Lord Jesus Christ is named alongside *God the Father as the source of these gifts (1:2; cf. 4:19).

The phrase 'in Christ' (and variants such as 'in him') recurs frequently in the letter. Sometimes it is the natural complement to a verb (as in the phrases 'to rejoice, be confident in Christ', *i.e.* on the basis of Jesus and who he is; 2:19, 24; 3:1). At other times it expresses the way in which Christian conduct ought to be determined by the fact that Christ is the Lord of his people and requires a certain kind of behaviour from them (2:29; 4:2). It is also used to identify the person through whom God acts for the good of his people, calling them to salvation (3:14), protecting them (4:7) and generously meeting their needs (4:19). In several of these instances the phraseology indicates that the readers have a close relationship with Jesus through their faith in him (*cf*. 3:9b), and this relationship is emphasized even more clearly when they are said simply to be in Christ (as in 1:1, 14; 3:9a; 4:21). Here the language suggests the idea of union with Christ (perhaps similar to Paul's view of believers as parts of the body which belongs to Christ and of which he is the head, or again to John's concept of believers being in Christ and Christ being in them).

This idea of close relationship to Christ emerges again when Paul writes about his desire to know Christ and the power of his resurrection, and to participate in his *sufferings (3:10). Plainly he is referring not simply to knowledge about somebody but to a personal experience in which he shares the actual experiences of Jesus. He lays great emphasis on the powerful effects of this union with Christ, in which the resurrection life of Christ is shared with him, both in the present and after physical death. At the same time the experience involves Paul in sharing in the sufferings of Christ. This reference is presumably to the pains and hardships associated with the Christian existence of all believers (1:29–30) and those of Paul's missionary work (*cf*. 2 Cor. 11:23–33), but we should surely see also a parallel to the way in which Paul writes elsewhere of being united with Christ in his *death and resurrection as the experience of all believers (Rom. 6:1–14; Col. 2:20 – 3:4). There is, accordingly, an intense sense of personal relationship with Christ in this letter. For Paul Christian existence is not to be understood simply in terms of belief in a set of doctrines or as a way of life, although these are integral parts of it; it is also a spiritual experience of a relationship with God through Christ. One of the major contributions of Philippians to biblical theology is the stress laid on this relationship.

In the light of this view of Christian experience we can now understand what Paul has to say about his attitude to death in the first chapter. It is evident that he had been in some situation in which the possibility of his own death (whether through illness or through physical violence) was very real. In that situation he was brought up sharply against the question of what mattered most to him. He emphasizes that for him life is Christ, *i.e.* the opportunity to know Christ and experience his love (1:21). But if so, it follows that physical death is a better state than physical life, since it brings a believer into even closer union with Christ. This conviction placed Paul in a dilemma, since he was aware that he was called to be a missionary during his life on earth and to share the life of Christ with other people. Therefore, he accepted that he must be prepared to continue in the body for as long as God required instead of longing to go to be with Christ before the time God had set for him to do so (1:19–26).

Jesus, the divine servant

All this raises in the most pressing manner the question of what kind of person Jesus could be that Paul could talk about him in this astonishing way. How can this person be the channel through whom God operates, a person with whom one can have this kind of spiritual relationship? The answer is provided by another passage of the letter. When Paul comes to deal with the problem of rivalry leading to disunity in the congregation, he uses various arguments (2:1–4), and then draws his readers' attention to the attitude of Christ Jesus. Jesus is described as a person who existed in the form of God and did not regard his equality with God as something to be held on to or exploited (2:5–8). This language appears to set Jesus on the same level of authority as God the Father (as God is called in 2:11). It is true that some scholars have suggested that nothing more may be meant here than that Jesus in his earthly existence shared the same status as that with which Adam was created, but chose not to take advantage of it. However, the use of the verb 'being' and the clear contrast between the original state of Jesus and the way in which he then took the nature of a servant and adopted a human likeness and appearance indicate fairly decisively that here Paul is describing what has come to be known as the 'pre-existent' state of Jesus, *i.e.* the way in which he existed before God the Father sent him into the world to be born of a woman (Gal. 4:4) and live a human life. The language used is not surprising, given that Paul had earlier spoken of Jesus as the one

Lord alongside the one God the Father who shared with him in the task of creation (1 Cor. 8:6), and that he would repeat the description in all essentials in another letter (Col. 1:15–17). Paul's thinking may well have been influenced by the way in which Wisdom was personified in Jewish wisdom literature as God's helper at creation and his messenger sent into the world (Prov. 8:22–31). It is often suggested that this passage was composed by somebody other than Paul and then incorporated into the letter to express Paul's own sentiments, but the arguments against it being Paul's own composition are not compelling. For Paul, then, Jesus was a divine being, and, although strictly speaking the name 'Jesus' was given to him at his birth, Paul was able to use it for the same person in his existence with God before his birth.

Paul's purpose in this description is not simply to discuss the status of Jesus before his human birth for its own sake. The whole aim of the passage is to contrast the position of supreme authority enjoyed by him with the way in which he became a human being and, even more to the point, a human being who plumbed the depths of self-negation and obedience to God by being prepared to die. Paul does not explain here why Jesus had to die, or rather why God required him to die (since his obedience was to God; to say that he was 'obedient to death' as if death were the master is to misinterpret the text).

Elsewhere Jesus' death is identified as a means of salvation (*e.g.* Rom. 3:25; 5:6–10), but here Paul's point is the willingness of Jesus to do nothing out of the selfish ambition and vain conceit which were spoiling the life of the congregation in Philippi (Phil. 2:3). It is then made clear that such saying 'No' to self is what God approves. Because Jesus was prepared to die, God subsequently not only *exalted him to the highest place in the universe, to where he was previously, but also made him the object of universal worship by all people. They will recognize him as the Lord, and the language used, which is obviously based on Isaiah 45:22–24, indicates clearly that the term 'Lord' here is the title of God the Father himself which he has bestowed on Jesus. (The term is, of course, used elsewhere in the NT simply as a respectful title for a human being, but there are passages, such as this one, where it carries the connotation of divine authority.) The

immediate point of the passage is that the humble will be exalted, in other words, that God himself approves of the self-denying, self-negating spirit and will reward it. Yet this should not be understood to mean that self-seeking people ought to be willing to forgo selfishness for a season in order to be finally and permanently exalted by God; such behaviour is only a parody of self-negation. Moreover, the context makes plain that there is no virtue in self-denial, in the sense of asceticism, for its own sake; what Jesus did was for the benefit of other people, and is an example to Paul's readers of looking 'to the interests of others' (2:4).

It is as a result of this V-shaped career (from God 'down' to earth and back 'up' again) that Jesus now has what has been called a 'post-existence' in which, without losing his humanity, he is an omnipotent (3:20), spiritual person, able to enter into relationships with those who believe in him. Consequently, he is able to act as the mediator of God's blessings to his people. To say that 'The Lord is near' (4:5) is to acknowledge his availability to help his people in their needs. Such relationships will be fully realized when he returns in a glorious bodily form from heaven to earth to be the Saviour of his people from their imperfect life in this corruptible world and to share his new existence with them (3:20–22).

As the risen and exalted Lord, Jesus is the dispenser of the *Holy Spirit (*cf.* Acts 2:33), and the blessings bestowed by God on his people may be attributed both to him and to the Spirit. So when Paul refers to the way in which he is being sustained and delivered from danger by God in his present sufferings, he does so in terms of the help given by the Spirit of Jesus Christ, indicating how closely the Spirit is associated with Jesus (Phil. 1:19). The 'one spirit' in which believers should stand firm (1:27) is the Holy Spirit who strengthens Christians (the phrase is not merely metaphorical). In Philippians 2:1 the phrase 'fellowship with the Spirit' unambiguously refers to the way in which Christians together share in the blessings bestowed by the Spirit and are thus united with one another; it is striking that Paul uses very similar language to refer to participation in Jesus Christ (1 Cor. 1:9). Worshipful Christian service of God also takes place through the agency of the Spirit (Phil. 3:3).

Although our discussion has been shaped by Paul's understanding of Jesus Christ, it has given us some idea of his understanding of God and also of his theological understanding of the Christian life. Yet while Jesus Christ is quite literally the beginning and end of the letter and of the theology which it contains (1:1; 4:21–23), nevertheless the letter reaches its climax in a statement of the extraordinary generosity of the God who acts in Jesus and in a doxology to him (4:19, 20; *cf.* 2:11).

Bibliography

K. P. Donfried and I. H. Marshall, *The Theology of the Shorter Pauline Letters*, NTT (Cambridge and New York, 1993); G. D. Fee, *Paul's Letter to the Philippians*, NICNT (Grand Rapids, 1995); P. T. O'Brien, *The Epistle to the Philippians: A Commentary on the Greek Text*, NIGTC (Grand Rapids and Carlisle, 1991); G. F. Hawthorne, *Philippians*, WBT (Waco, 1987); I. H. Marshall, *The Epistle to the Philippians*, EPC (London, 1991); R. P. Martin, *Carmen Christi: Philippians 2:5–11 in Recent Interpretation and in the Setting of Early Christian Worship* (Grand Rapids, ²1983)

I. H. MARSHALL

COLOSSIANS

There are two main theological focal points in Colossians. One is the person and work of *Jesus Christ; the other is the believer's new life in Christ. They are linked by the proclamation of the *gospel.

Much of the Christological teaching in the letter is a response to the 'Colossian heresy' (*cf.* 2:4), which may have been a Phrygian variety of nonconformist, Gnosticizing Judaism. The advocates of this unorthodox teaching claimed that it had a Christian basis (see 2:4), but it denied Christ his proper place (2:8, 16–17, 19), exhibited Judaistic and ritualistic tendencies (2:16–17), was philosophic or theosophic in approach (2:8, 18), advocated the worship of angels (2:18), and emphasized asceticism (2:18, 20–23).

The person of Christ

The famous 'hymn' of 1:15–20 establishes the supremacy of Christ, both in *creation (vv. 15–17) and in *redemption (vv. 18–20). A similar link between nature and *grace,

cosmology and soteriology, is found in John 1:1–18 and Hebrews 1:1–4 and is common in the OT (*e.g.* Is. 43:1; 44:24–28).

First, Christ is *supreme in creation*: as 'the *image of the invisible God' (v. 15a, NIV), the exact and visible expression of *God; as 'the firstborn over all creation' (v. 15b), a title which denotes his pre-eminence in rank and priority in time; as the creator of the entire universe, including the angelic occupants of heavenly thrones and all supernatural potentates (v. 16a, b); as the goal of the whole universe (v. 16c; *cf.* Eph. 1:10); as the person who is 'before' everything in time and status (v. 17a); and as the sustainer of the universe (v. 17b), maintaining its permanent order, stability and productivity. In OT thought, Wisdom existed at God's side before creation and acted as his master craftsman in his creative work (Prov. 8:22–31). Paul may have had this passage in mind in his description of Christ's role in creation, but there are crucial differences between Colossians 1 and Proverbs 8. In Paul's view, Christ is more than the embodiment or personification of Wisdom, for unlike Wisdom he is the uncreated image of God and sustains what he once created (vv. 15–17), and he is the focus of all creation (v. 16c; *cf.* Eph. 1:10) and himself embodies all the divine attributes.

Second, he is *supreme in redemption*: as 'the head of the body, the church' (v. 18a), its authoritative ruler and director; as 'the beginning' (v. 18b), the originating cause of the *church and the constant source of its life; as 'the firstborn from among the dead' (v. 18c), the pioneer of a resurrection to immortality (*cf.* Acts 26:23; Rom. 6:9); as the possessor of all God's fullness (v. 19); and as the agent of God's reconciliation (v. 20).

This emphasis on Christ's unchallenged superiority is also found elsewhere. Christ is ruler over every cosmic power and authority (2:10). He is the source of the nourishment, unity and growth of his body, the church (2:19), where he is everything, all that matters (3:11). As the Son whom God dearly loves, he possesses and rules over a *kingdom of light (1:12–13). Being 'seated at the right hand of God' (3:1) he occupies a position of unparalleled dignity, honour and power (*cf.* Ps. 110:1). He is the source of corporate peace in his church (3:15) and will dispense to believers their inheritance as a *reward for their service (3:24). Also it is in Christ and

Christ alone that the full treasury of God's *wisdom and knowledge is stored (2:2).

Colossians 1:19 and 2:9 together form an unambiguous statement of Christ's deity. It was by God the Father's choice and at his pleasure that all the divine attributes and powers resided in the person of Jesus; in him God in all his fullness (*pan to plērōma*) was pleased to dwell (1:19). Paul has the post-*incarnational state of Christ in mind when he says that in him the whole fullness of deity (*pan to plērōma tēs theotētos*) dwells in bodily form (2:9). Two distinct affirmations are being made: 1. the total plenitude of the Godhead dwells in Christ eternally ('dwells' is a timeless present); 2. this fullness now permanently resides in the incarnate Christ in bodily form. Here, then, both the eternal deity and the permanent humanity of Christ are implied.

The work of Christ

In both Testaments God is portrayed as a God who saves (Ps. 68:20; *cf.* 1 Tim. 2:3–4). But the NT is distinctive in its claim that '"[s]alvation belongs to our God ... and to the Lamb"' (Rev. 7:10). The source of *salvation is God the Father and the agent in its procurement is Christ (*cf.* 1 Cor. 8:6). In Colossians this salvation is portrayed in two ways. It is through union with Christ that believers enjoy the possession of *redemption* (1:14), that is, release from the bondage of *sin, or as 1:13 expresses it, rescue from the dominion of darkness. Thus Paul can define redemption as simply 'the *forgiveness of sins' (1:14; *cf.* 2:13; Eph. 1:7), an equation that is totally in line with OT teaching (*e.g.* Pss. 32 and 51). *Reconciliation* is God's act of restoring *humankind and nature to their proper relationship to himself, through the *death of Christ. God is the reconciler (1:19–20, 22) and the goal of his action is the harmony of all creation with himself (1:20; *cf.* Rom. 5:10). This harmony was achieved through Christ (1:20a) and through him alone (1:20c, where there is an emphatic repetition of 'through him'), that is, 'through his blood, shed on the cross'. Reconciliation embraced the entire universe (*ta panta*, 1:20a), including inanimate nature, the world of human beings, and *spiritual powers that were at variance with God (1:20b, 'whether things on earth or things in heaven'; *cf.* 1:16). But 1:21–23, and especially 1:23a ('if you continue in your

faith'), make it clear that although the universe in its totality has now regained its divinely appointed direction (that was frustrated by the effects of human sin, Rom. 8:20–22) in an objectively real reconciliation, the benefits of this reconciliation are not experienced by individual humans automatically, apart from their faith. By nature they were alienated from God and at enmity with him (1:21; *cf.* 2:13), but now reconciled, they will be presented blameless before God (1:22), assuming that they persist in faith and refuse to shift from the hope generated by the gospel (1:23). This insistence on the necessity of faith for the receipt of divine blessing reflects an OT emphasis (see *e.g.* Pss. 22:4; 28:7; 37:40).

Two further aspects of the work of Christ on the cross are mentioned in 2:14–15. God has completely cancelled the statement of indebtedness – the sinner's IOU to God – and its particulars (broken regulations), that was a threat to sinners, and has set it aside by nailing it to Christ's cross (2:14). In doing this God was acting in accordance with his nature declared centuries earlier: '"I, even I, am he who blots out your transgressions, for my own sake, and remembers your sins no more"' (Is. 43:25; *cf.* 44:22; Ps. 51:1, 9). In addition, after disarming 'the powers and authorities' whose demonic aim is to enslave the human race (2:20–22; *cf.* Gal. 4:3, 9), he boldly exposed them to public display by leading them in Christ's triumphal procession as his captive enemies (2:15).

The gospel

The OT is certainly not devoid of 'good news', but the OT gospel that declares Yahweh's universal victory and reign (Is. 40:9; 41:27; 52:7), inaugurating a new era of salvation, was given principally to God's people (Pss. 40:9–10; 68:11). '[I]n the LORD our God is the salvation of Israel' (Jer. 3:23). Only with the coming of the Messiah could all those in need (Is. 61:1; *cf.* Luke 4:16–21), or all those who called on the name of the Lord (Joel 2:32; *cf.* Acts 2:16-21), expect to receive the good news of salvation. The good news or gospel brought by Jesus, the Messiah, involved among other things the inclusion of Gentiles in the people of God (1:27; *cf.* Eph. 3:2–6; Is. 42:1–4).

In 1:5 the good news is identified as 'the word of truth', the message that has the stamp of *truth on it. Part of its content is the 'hope' (here, by metonymy, almost 'inheritance') that is stored up for believers in heaven (1:5a). This gospel has intrinsic potency (*cf*. Rom. 1:16) for it is continuing to produce all over the world the same kind of harvest and increase it has been yielding in the Colossians ever since they heard it (1:6).

The gospel generates a hope that must never be abandoned, and it has already been proclaimed 'to every creature under heaven' (that is, to every type of person in every place; 1:23). Paul himself is an agent in its proclamation, which involves 'warning and teaching everyone with all wisdom, our aim being to present every believer mature in Christ' (1:28, author's translation).

In several passages the gospel is implicitly identified. It is 'the *word' (4:3, NRSV), or 'the word of God' (1:25) in the sense of 'the message about or from God', or 'the word of Christ' (3:16) in the sense of 'the message spoken by or concerning Christ'. It is the sacred secret of God's plan of salvation ('the *mystery') that was hidden for ages and generations past but now has been disclosed to God's people (1:26; *cf*. Eph. 3:3–6); this 'mystery' is Christ himself (2:2; 4:3) or his indwelling of Gentiles (and all believers; 1:27). Also 'truth' (1:5) and 'grace' (1:6) are virtual synonyms for the gospel. Negatively, the gospel of Christ is not based on human tradition (2:8) and does not consist of human rules and regulations (2:20–22; *cf*. Is. 29:13).

The believer's new life in Christ

In the OT the call to humans to be holy was based on God's own holiness and his gracious intervention to save his people. '"I am the LORD who brought you up out of Egypt to be your God; therefore be holy, because I am holy"' (Lev. 11:45; *cf*. 11:44; 19:2; 20:7, 26). In a similar way, at the heart of Pauline ethics (and of NT ethics in general) is the relationship between theological proclamation and moral exhortation, between affirmation and appeal, between the indicative and the imperative: 'you are ... therefore be!' 'You have died [*apethanete*]' (3:3, NRSV) '... Put to death, therefore (*nekrōsate oun*) ...' (3:5). The doctrinal indicative of 'the forgiveness of sins' (1:14) is the basis and stimulus for the ethical imperative, 'forgive ... one another' (3:13). That is, 'you are forgiven; therefore be forgiving'. God's action

prompts and demands a human response. 'Since, then, you have been raised with Christ [to be seated with him in the heavenly realms, Eph. 2:6], set your hearts on things above, where Christ is, seated at the right hand of God' (3:1). This paradoxical dialectic is common in Paul (*e.g.* Rom. 6:2, 12; Gal. 5:25; Phil. 2:12–13).

The indicative

God the Father has granted believers an entitlement to inheritance in the kingdom of light (1:12), has rescued them from the power and domain of darkness, and has transferred them safely into the kingdom of his dearly loved Son (1:13). In Christ, the embodiment of God's fullness (2:9), believers have come to completeness (2:10), the satisfaction of every spiritual need. In him they have experienced a spiritual *circumcision (2:11). Physical circumcision is an external act performed by human hands on a mere portion of the flesh eight days after birth, while in contrast heart-circumcision is an inward, spiritual act carried out by divine agency on the whole fleshly nature at the time of regeneration (*cf*. Rom. 2:28–29). Certainly the OT writers are aware of the danger of being circumcised in body but uncircumcised in heart (Jer. 9:25–26), and stress the need for a circumcision of the heart (Deut. 10:16; 30:6; Jer. 4:4; Ezek. 44:7), but Paul describes this divesture of the old self as distinctly Christ's (or Christian) circumcision, spiritual surgery performed on Christ's followers.

Paul's love of the motif of identification with Christ is shown in his use of the preposition 'with' (*syn*), often found in compound verbs such as 'be crucified with' (Gal. 2:20) or 'suffer with' (Rom. 8:17), where Christ is the object. In Colossians believers are said to have died with Christ (2:20; *cf*. 3:3), to have been buried with Christ (2:12), and to have been raised with Christ (2:12; 3:1), a sequence which represents an advance on Romans 6:1–11 where the concept of spiritual resurrection with Christ is merely implied. Once they have been spiritually raised with Christ, believers' new life lies hidden with Christ in the safe keeping of God (3:3) until the time when they are identified with Christ in resurrection glory (3:4). There is nothing in the OT that begins to match this description of believers' spiritual resurrection with the Messiah at the time of their conversion and baptism (2:12; 3:1), leading to their sharing first in his resurrection life (3:4a) and then in his messianic glory (3:4b).

Christian renewal is the theme of 3:9–11. At *regeneration Christians stripped off their old nature or self (or the old humanity) like a garment needing to be discarded (3:9; cf. 3:5, 8) and put on their new nature or self (or the new humanity) which is being constantly renewed in conformity with the image (i.e. Christ) of its creator (i.e. God) (3:10). This process of sanctification will issue in a full knowledge (epignōsis) of God (3:10). In this new humanity, the church, distinctions based on nationality or custom or social status count for nothing, for here Christ amounts to everything and indwells all believers without distinction (3:11). The emphasis on the comprehensiveness of the new spiritual order created in Christ and the abolition of distinction between people represents a significant advance on the OT and 1st-century Judaism, in which national identity signified by circumcision, the sabbath and food laws counted for everything.

The imperative

When Paul divulges to the Colossians the content of his intercession for them (1:9–12a), he is describing the features of the normal or ideal Christian life and indirectly exhorting them to conform to various patterns of behaviour. In essence his intercession is a request that God should give them every form of spiritual wisdom and discernment and thus fill them with a knowledge of his will (1:9). The outcome will be a life that is worthy of the Lord, pleasing to him (1:10a), and marked by four characteristics (each expressed by a present participle that denotes contemporaneous action): fruitfulness in good deeds; growth in knowledge of God (1:10b); empowerment for endurance and patience of every kind (1:11); and gratitude to God (1:12a; cf. 2:7; 3:16–17). Other ideal character or behavioural traits are living in union with Christ (2:6), firm rootage in him and continuous building on him (2:7), along with the various Christian virtues listed in 3:12–17. In this latter list, *love-in-action (articular agapē) is seen as binding together and perfecting all the other virtues (3:14).

There is a focus on interpersonal relationships within the household in 3:18 – 4:1.

Paul issues a series of commands to three pairs of people (wives and husbands, children and fathers, slaves and masters), addressed in descending order of intimacy. In each case the emphasis rests on obligations to be met rather than rights to be asserted, and invariably the motivation is Christological, for 'the Lord' is always the point of reference. Christian conduct is motivated and determined by Christ the Lord. Wives are to submit to the leadership of their husbands (3:18), while husbands are to love their wives constantly, avoiding harshness and bitter feelings (3:19). These apostolic injunctions do not imply the inferiority or superiority of either party, for the whole relationship is between equals and is based on love. (See *Man and woman.) Children are directed to obey their parents in every respect (3:20), and fathers (or parents) are to avoid exasperating their children (presumably by over-correcting them or scorning their efforts), lest they become disheartened and sullen (3:21). Slaves' obedient service to their earthly masters is to be given with heartfelt sincerity and enthusiastically, out of reverence for the Lord and as a service to him (3:22–23). It is from their heavenly Master that they will receive the glorious inheritance of believers as their due and full recompense (3:24). Wrongdoers will be duly requited for the wrong they have done, and this Master will show no favouritism in dispensing rewards and punishments (3:25). Finally, masters are to give their slaves just and even-handed treatment, aware that they too are accountable to a Master in heaven (4:1). This whole section demonstrates that the pursuit of the realm above (3:1) and preoccupation with its affairs (3:2) do not prompt an ascetic otherworldliness, but rather lead to an enthusiastic commitment to the routine duties of this world out of 'reverence for the Lord' (3:22).

Relationships with those outside the church come into focus in 4:2–6. The elements of effective *prayer are persistence, vigilance and thanksgiving (4:2), and petition for opportunities to proclaim Christ (4:3) and for appropriate boldness in proclaiming him (4:4). The elements of powerful witness are tact and resourcefulness in using opportunities (4:5), and conversation that is invariably winsome, penetrating and tailored to the needs of each individual (4:6).

When Paul mentions the Christian qualities

of certain believers, he is indirectly holding them up as models to emulate. He identifies Epaphras in 1:7 as 'our dear fellow servant' and 'a faithful minister of Christ', a true exponent of the gospel and an effective representative of Paul. Then in 4:12–13 he is depicted as a constant warrior in prayer and a tireless pastor of the Lycus Valley Christians, evidence of his being 'a servant of Christ Jesus'.

Bibliography

R. E. DeMaris, *The Colossian Controversy: Wisdom in Dispute at Colossae* (Sheffield, 1994); J. D. G. Dunn, *The Epistles to the Colossians and to Philemon*, NIGTC (Carlisle and Grand Rapids, 1996); J. G. Gibbs, *Creation and Redemption: A Study in Pauline Theology* (Leiden, 1971); M. J. Harris, *Colossians and Philemon*, EGGNT (Grand Rapids, 1991); E. G. Hinson, 'The Christian household in Colossians 3:18 – 4:1', *RevExp* 70, 1973, pp. 495–506; C. F. D. Moule, 'The new life in Colossians 3:1–17', *RevExp* 70, 1973, pp. 481–493; P. T. O'Brien, *Colossians, Philemon*, WBC (Waco, 1982); T. J. Sappington, *Revelation and Redemption at Colossae* (Sheffield, 1991); A. J. M. Wedderburn and A. T. Lincoln, *The Theology of the Later Pauline Letters*, NTT (Cambridge, 1993); N. T. Wright, 'Poetry and Theology in Colossians 1:15–20', *NTS* 36, 1990, pp. 444–468.

M. J. HARRIS

THESSALONIANS

Although there is a strong case for the view that Galatians is the earliest of Paul's letters, most scholars think that this position should be assigned to 1 Thessalonians. It is generally understood to have been written from Corinth during *Paul's extended stay there (Acts 18), although some would date it much earlier (*c.* AD 41) on the basis of a radical reinterpretation of the evidence (E. J. Richard, *First and Second Thessalonians*). Certainly the theology of 1 Thessalonians gives an impression of simplicity and lack of development compared with that of the major letters (including Galatians), but this may be due in part to the lack of a polemical situation and the consequent need to develop in depth a theology of the law, the cross and justification

by faith. The letter is in fact a mixture of consolation, instruction and encouragement for a young church which has experienced some opposition in the community, felt the pressures of a typical Greco-Roman religious environment with its temptations to immorality, and suffered a loss of confidence in the future owing to the death of some of its members.

2 Thessalonians has traditionally been interpreted as a follow-up letter to 1 Thessalonians, written to help the readers cope with an increase in opposition to the church, but also with a fresh problem in the church caused by some people thinking that the countdown to the end of the world was already far advanced, with consequent effects on their lifestyle. The purpose of the letter is again to comfort and encourage the church but centrally to insist that the end of the world cannot happen before the Satanic opposition to God has reached a climax. There is a contrast between the stress on the imminence of the coming of Christ in 1 Thessalonians and the damping down of expectation in 2 Thessalonians, and there is a curious combination of the repetition of material from the former letter with some subtle differences in theological expression. These points have led many scholars to argue either that 2 Thessalonians is a pseudonymous letter from the end of the first century (R. F. Collins, *Studies on the First Letter to the Thessalonians*; Richard, *Thessalonians*), written at a time of strong apocalyptic expectation (*cf.* Rev.), or that it is the work of a collaborator using Paul's authority shortly after 1 Thessalonians (K. P. Donfried [and I. H. Marshall], *The Theology of the Shorter Pauline Letters*). Although it is questionable whether the evidence is strong enough to warrant a theory of non-Pauline authorship, the two letters will be considered separately in what follows.

The theology of 1 Thessalonians

1 Thessalonians does not contain any explicit citations of the OT, but its thought stands squarely in the early Christian tradition of a theology which is thoroughly Judaic and reflects the OT way of thinking.

The Judeo-Christian understanding of God

The Christian faith embraced by the recipients is summed up as a turning away from pagan gods, represented concretely in the idols worshipped in pagan temples and shrines, to serve the living *God, *i.e.* the God revealed in the OT and worshipped in Judaism, and to wait for the coming of this God's Son from heaven (1 Thess. 1:9–10). This God is the author of the 'good news' (1 Thess. 2:8) preached by his co-workers (1 Thess. 3:2) and messengers, the apostles of Christ (1 Thess. 2:4, 6). He it was who helped them to preach his message in a hostile environment (1 Thess. 2:1–2). Consequently, when the good news is made known, it is not simply a human communication but simultaneously God speaks his word through it (1 Thess. 2:13). Moreover, it is through the power of God that those who believe the gospel are enabled to stand fast despite all the difficulty and opposition (see *Suffering) which they face. Paul therefore records his prayers to God for his readers that he will make it possible for Paul and his colleagues to visit them (1 Thess. 3:11), and that the readers themselves will be strengthened in their faith and grow in Christian character (1 Thess. 3:12–13). God has a purpose for the readers, which is that they will be 'sanctified' or made *holy (1 Thess. 4:3; 5:23): this phraseology refers to the development of a character which honours God by freedom from immorality, especially as regards self-control in sexual desire (1 Thess. 4:4–6), and which grows in the love which God has called his people to show to one another (1 Thess. 4:9–10). They are now God's people, like Israel in the OT period (1 Thess. 2:14; 5:26), and in contrast to the Gentiles who do not know God (*cf.* Jer. 10:25).

Moreover, God holds the future in his hands (see *Eschatology). 1 Thessalonians stresses the resurrection of the dead and the coming of Christ as integral parts of the Christian faith and thus reminds its readers of the future dimension of *salvation which can easily be forgotten in a materialist environment. This thought is developed especially with regard to the fate of those in the congregation who had died. It appears that the survivors were uncertain about them, since they had not grasped the significance of the fact that God had raised Jesus from the dead and realized that at the coming of Christ God would raise up the dead in Christ and bring them with him (1 Thess. 4:13-18; *cf.* Is.

26:19; Dan. 7:13; 12:2; Zech. 9:14). The fact is that God has appointed believers to receive salvation instead of wrath at the judgment which will come upon all people and bring destruction for those who live in the darkness of evil deeds and foolishly imagine that they are safe from *judgment (1 Thess. 5:3, 5, 9).

We thus have a genuine '*theo*-logy' in this letter in which the readers are the *people of God, called and protected by him, and under obligation to live lives befitting their God. It is not difficult to see how all that has been said about this relationship is a continuation of the way in which the relationship of God and his people is described in the OT.

Jesus Christ and the church

However, we must now observe how all this is expressed in a Christian way through the constant references to *Jesus Christ as the co-functionary with God. The readers constitute a 'congregation' (*ekklēsia* – a term that is similar to 'synagogue' in referring to a company of God's people) which is 'in God the Father and the Lord Jesus Christ' (1 Thess. 1:1, NIV). Three points are striking here.

First, there is the qualification of God as 'Father', a term which is rarely used of him in the OT but which becomes the preferred way of speaking of him in the NT as a result of the speech-habit of Jesus (*cf.* 1 Thess. 1:3; 3:11, 13); it expresses the loving relationship which he has to his people.

Second, the *church is said to be 'in God', an unusual prepositional phrase which is evidently an extension of the phrase 'in Christ/the Lord' which characterizes Paul's writings and expresses the new relationship that Christians have to Jesus: their existence is determined by him and they are entirely committed to him, to such an extent that they may be said to be incorporated in him (*cf.* 1 Thess. 2:14; 3:8; 4:1, 16; 5:12, 18).

Third, Paul places God the Father and the Lord Jesus Christ side by side without any suggestion of novelty or tension; by the time that he writes this letter the fact that God and Jesus are ranked alongside each other 'on the divine side of reality' has become for him a self-evident truth, and one which he does not need to demonstrate to his readers (*cf.* 1 Thess. 3:11). Jesus is the source of spiritual blessings (1 Thess. 5:28) and God's gifts are granted in association with him (1 Thess. 3:12).

It is characteristic of this letter to refer to

Jesus as 'the Lord'. A number of factors have contributed to the use of this phrase, including Jesus' own usage and the way in which other people referred to him. But Paul's use reflects that of the Septuagint, in which the term is the Greek equivalent for the Hebrew *'donay*, 'Lord', used by the Jews as a substitute for God's name, *Yahweh*. Thus Paul can refer to 'the day of the Lord' (1 Thess. 5:2) for the day when the Lord will come (1 Thess. 4:15-17); in both cases OT language about the future day of God's judgment when God will 'come' is being echoed (*e.g.* Joel 3:14; Is. 40:10), with the implication that this function of God has been transferred to Jesus.

Similarly, 'the word of the Lord' (1 Thess. 1:8, NRSV) echoes OT phraseology (*e.g.* Jer. 1:4). The precise relationship between God and Jesus Christ which justifies the use of such language is expressed by saying that Jesus is God's Son (1 Thess. 1:10). If in the OT it is God himself who is the Saviour of his people, in the NT this function is also transferred to Jesus who 'rescues us from the coming wrath' (1 Thess. 1:10) and through whom God destines us for salvation (1 Thess. 5:9). This destiny is closely tied to the fact that he died for us (1 Thess. 5:10) and that he rose again (1 Thess. 4:14). Although at first sight it might seem that God is the author of wrath and Jesus of salvation, this is a false conclusion. It is true that the juxtaposition indicates that it is because of the death of Jesus for us that we are saved from the wrath, but 5:9 indicates clearly enough that, as elsewhere in Paul, it is God who initiates the process of salvation. If in the OT God himself is the author of the covenant obligations to holiness which are laid upon his people, so here the Lord Jesus becomes the agent of God's will (1 Thess. 5:18) and the judge of sinners (1 Thess. 4:6).

The reception of salvation is dependent upon acceptance of the message (1 Thess. 1:6), an acceptance expressed in faith (1 Thess. 2:10, 13), and salvation is equally accessible to both Jews and Gentiles (1 Thess. 2:16). Although, therefore, in a context where there was no need to face up to Judaizers who insisted that Gentile converts must be circumcised and keep the law of Moses, the language of justification by grace through faith and not by the works of the law is absent, the implicit theology of this letter is clearly in line with that of the later letters.

The role of the Holy Spirit

Alongside Jesus Christ as God's agent we also find a prominent role assigned to the *Holy Spirit. The Spirit is active in the powerful proclamation and joyful reception of the gospel to make the preachers persuasive and the hearers receptive (1 Thess. 1:5-6). In 4:8 it is implied that the Spirit is also active in the sanctification of believers, so that it is God, who gives the Spirit (*cf.* Ezek. 36:27; 37:14), who is being resisted when believers persist in sin. Within the congregational meetings the Spirit is powerfully active in moving believers to prophesy and probably also in prayer and praise (1 Thess. 5:17-18).

The theology of 1 Thessalonians can thus be clearly recognized as trinitarian in the sense that God the Father, the Lord Jesus Christ and the Holy Spirit are all involved in the process of salvation. From this springs the paradox which is inherent in Pauline theology. On the one hand, the conferring of salvation and the sanctifying of believers are ascribed to the agency of God the Father and his co-functionaries; Paul prays to God to act in the lives of the readers (1 Thess. 3:12-13; 5:23-24) and seeks their prayers for him (1 Thess. 5:25), and he gives thanks to God for their safekeeping and growth (1 Thess. 1:2; 3:9). On the other hand, Paul also acts in a human way to help them in their difficulties (1 Thess. 3:1-5), and he can urge them to live in a way that pleases God (1 Thess. 4:1-10; 5:6, 11, 12-22). There is evidently no tension for Paul between these two ways of speaking.

The theology of 2 Thessalonians

In 2 Thessalonians the theological framework is very much the same as in 1 Thessalonians. God the Father is again the ultimate agent in salvation and judgment. In this letter his function as judge is particularly stressed in view of the injustices which are being suffered by his people. There is a strong element of retribution expressed in a reversal of positions. Those who inflict trouble on believers will themselves suffer in that they will be excluded from the presence of the Lord when he comes (2 Thess. 1:9-10; for the OT background *cf.* Is. 66:4, 15; Zech. 14:5); but God's people will share in the glory of their Lord (*cf.* Pss. 68:35; 89:17).

Underlying the letter is a belief in powerful spiritual opposition to God (see *Spiritual powers) and the gospel. Associated with the type of thinking known as apocalyptic, a form of prophecy based on access to God's plans through visions and heavenly journeys, was the belief in an evil spiritual organization opposed to God and his good heavenly agents. It was headed up by 'the evil one' (2 Thess. 3:3), otherwise Satan (2 Thess. 2:9), who was able to inspire human agents to evil. Apocalyptic prophecies stressed the increase in evil activity preceding the final showdown with God (*cf.* Mark 13; Rev.).

This strand of thinking is drawn upon to deal with a major problem in the congregation. In 1 Thessalonians Paul expressed a lively hope in the imminent coming of the Lord as something which could take place in the foreseeable future within the lifetime of himself and his readers (1 Thess. 4:17), although he does not delimit the time in any way. He warned the readers to be alert and ready so that the day would not take them by surprise (1 Thess. 5:4-6). With such encouragement from Paul it is not surprising that some readers came to believe that the coming of the Lord was about to take place and longed for the relief from their opponents that it would bring; it is also likely that the tendencies to idleness on the part of some in the congregation were due to, or were accentuated by, their acceptance of this doomsday scenario (2 Thess. 3:6-15). To counter this imminent expectation Paul had to claim that he had been misinterpreted in some way. In fact he had told them that a prior stage before the End would be the advent of a powerful movement of opposition to God led by a specific figure who would set himself up as equal to God; but for the time being he could not appear openly because there was a force at work to restrain him. Attempts to identify more closely what Paul meant are beset with almost insuperable difficulties, but the restraining force may well be God himself providing opportunity for the gospel to be heard everywhere. What the passage expresses, therefore, is the ultimate control of God over the course of history. This control extends not only to the restraining of evil and to its final defeat but also to the people whom God has chosen to be saved and whom he will preserve until their final salvation (2 Thess. 2:13-14). Knowing that they are, as it were, 'on the winning side', they can take courage as they face the difficulties of living as believers in a hostile world.

God's control of the universe and his protecting power for his people is accordingly a major theme of this letter. As in 1 Thessalonians, Jesus Christ is closely associated with the Father as the source of blessings (2 Thess. 1:2, 12; 2:16; 3:5). In 2 Thessalonians 1:12 it is possible that the NIV margin is correct to render 'our God and Lord, Jesus Christ', but this rendering is less likely than the text. Those who oppose believers are people who do not know God and do not obey the gospel of our Lord Jesus (2 Thess. 1:8). Both God and the Lord Jesus are agents of the judgment on the wicked (2 Thess. 1:6, 7-8.) and both are involved in the salvation and preservation of believers (2 Thess. 2:13). The Lord Jesus Christ is the authority behind the practical, ethical instruction to believers (2 Thess. 3:6, 12). And the concept of the Christian's life being 'in Christ/the Lord' is clearly expressed (2 Thess. 1:1, 12; 3:12; *cf.* 3:4). The one reference to the Holy Spirit (2 Thess. 2:13) echoes the teaching of 1 Thessalonians about his role in the sanctification of believers.

2 Thessalonians is among the most difficult books of the NT for the modern reader with its apparently bizarre future scenario in chapter 2. However, apocalyptic language is an attempt to express the inexpressible using vivid imagery that is not meant to be understood literally. Those who have lived through the Holocaust and other examples of mass genocide in the 20th century should not need much persuasion that there are 'principalities and powers' hostile to God at work in the world, sometimes on a terrifying scale; they need the reminder of this letter that an integral part of Christian faith is the certain hope of the final victory of God's justice and goodness.

Bibliography

R. F. Collins, *Studies on the First Letter to the Thessalonians* (Leuven, 1984); R. F. Collins (ed.), *The Thessalonian Correspondence* (Leuven, 1990); K. P. Donfried and I. H. Marshall, *The Theology of the Shorter Pauline Letters*, NTT (Cambridge and New York, 1993); H. Hübner, *Biblische Theologie des Neuen Testaments*, Band 2 (Göttingen, 1993), pp. 41–56, 376f.; R. Jewett, *The Thessalonian Correspondence: Pauline Rhetoric and Millenarian Piety* (Philadelphia,

1986); I. H. Marshall, *1 and 2 Thessalonians*, NCB (London and Grand Rapids, 1983); L. Morris, *1, 2 Thessalonians*, WBT (Dallas and London, 1989); E. J. Richard, *First and Second Thessalonians* (Collegeville, 1995); C. A. Wanamaker, *Commentary on 1 and 2 Thessalonians*, NIGTC (Grand Rapids and Exeter, 1990).

I. H. MARSHALL

THE PASTORAL EPISTLES

The question of authorship

In Pastoral Epistles scholarship, assumptions about authorship influence the way in which the theology of these letters is understood. Until early in the 19th century, the *Pauline authorship of the Pastoral Epistles was not seriously questioned. Thus, whether the letters are best placed in the period following Paul's (possible) release from his first imprisonment (*cf.* 1 Clement 5:7; so Guthrie, Kelly, Fee, Knight), or in gaps in the chronology of Acts and the earlier Pauline correspondence (Robinson), or are regarded (most wisely) as additions to the incomplete picture which can be assembled from Acts and the earlier Paul (Johnson), the traditional view is that they were written by Paul (either through an amanuensis or in collaboration with a co-worker) and contain Pauline theology. At the start of the 21st century, however, proponents of this view are very much in the minority.

The controlling assumptions of the majority view, greatly refined from but still indebted to the critical pioneers F. C. Baur and M. Dibelius, are as follows: 1. the Pastoral Epistles are pseudepigraphical, written in the name of Paul by a later 'paulinist' (Donelson); 2. they form a unique literary corpus within the NT, which reflects a fully developed theological and ecclesiastical situation in contrast to that of the genuine Paul; 3. they belong to an early 2nd-century setting, in which the expectation of Christ's return no longer clearly influenced the life of the *church, and in which the main issues included those of how the church could coexist peacefully with secular society, how it should respond to heresy, and how 'Paul' might be made to speak to these new circumstances. In contrast to earlier critical views which regarded the Pastoral Epistles as a collection of traditions and (possibly) some Pauline fragments (Harrison, Hanson, Miller), the majority view sees in the letters a coherent message to a real church somewhere in time (Young, Bassler, Marshall). But the theology of the Pastoral Epistles has to be understood in terms of Pauline tradition (*Paulustradition*), not Pauline theology.

Neither view is without problems, but which is the least problematic? The majority view rests precariously on a web of unproved assumptions that are rarely acknowledged: 1. To view the Pastoral Epistles as a late fiction that somehow acquired canonical (apostolic) status requires one to imagine a tremendously complicated process of writing and reception; after all, the early Fathers consistently rejected late-emerging documents as unauthentic, and there is no evidence (apart from the Pastoral Epistles) for the sort of Pauline community or school supposed to be behind the letters. 2. The majority interpretation emphasizes differences from the early Paul as if a uniform Pauline 'style' were identifiable in the earlier letters. In fact, differences might well be expected: a. there is much uncertainty about the writing process that produced Paul's letters; b. in terms of style, although the Pastoral Epistles differ from the earlier letters, the latter themselves exhibit a good deal of stylistic variety; and c. the Pastoral Epistles are written, uniquely, to individual co-workers. The case made by the majority is not so compelling as to remove the Pastoral Epistles from the orbit of the historical Paul. Neither the letters' different 'look' (see below) nor their references to journeys not mentioned in the earlier letters (*cf.* 2 Cor. 11:23–29; *cf.* L. T. Johnson, *Letters to Paul's Delegates*, pp. 8–11) necessarily rule out a substantial link with Paul. 2 Timothy is most easily placed at the end of Paul's life, for he is in Rome (1:17) and anticipates a sentence of death (4:6–8). 1 Timothy and Titus are more difficult to place. In each letter, Paul indicates that he is moving freely (1 Tim. 3:14–15; Titus 3:12), possibly after a first, or prior to an only, Roman imprisonment.

Choice of literary style and the shape of theological expression in the Pastoral Epistles

It is now widely acknowledged that the Pastoral Epistles belong to the category known as letters of moral exhortation (parenetic letters), although 2 Timothy is sometimes regarded as 'testamentary' in style. The extant 'testaments' are clearly fictional portrayals of the last message of a dying religious leader to a faithful follower (*Testament of Abraham*; *Testaments of the Twelve Patriarchs*; etc.), but in 2 Timothy the recipient is not so conspicuously removed from the 'hero'. However, the exploration of literary forms has revealed other possible options. In Paul's time there were various types of letter styles on which he might have drawn, depending on his readership and purpose. The mixture of public and private materials in 1 Timothy and Titus resembles that of the 'mandate letter', typically used to convey the orders of a ruler to a newly commissioned delegate in the hearing of those within his administrative purview. By means of such a letter, Paul would authenticate and empower his delegate (Timothy, Titus) and publicly obligate him to embody the ethical instructions contained therein. 2 Timothy, which lacks some of the distinguishing marks of the testamentary genre, is better classified as a letter of private parenesis, which aimed to encourage the pursuit of acceptable conduct in common situations of life and the avoidance of unacceptable conduct. If the Pastoral Epistles are taken as what they purport to be, letters written by Paul to individual co-workers to establish their position within the churches and to exhort them privately, their different appearance from that of the earlier Paulines is not so surprising. The Hellenistic cast of the ethical language is more puzzling, but the fact that Timothy and Titus almost certainly had had access to a Greek education (Acts 16:1; Gal. 2:3) goes some way towards explaining this turn in the Pauline articulation of Christian ethics (Johnson, *Paul's Delegates*). What might appear to be 'remedial' teaching or unnecessary reminders are features of the exhortatory style employed.

The material in the Pastoral Epistles probably came from a variety of sources. Duty codes (1 Tim. 3:1–13; Titus 1:5–9), modified household codes (1 Tim. 2:8–15; 5:1–2; 6:1–2; Titus 2:1 – 3:8) and teaching addressing particular groups (1 Tim. 5:3–16; 5:17–25; 6:17–19) are employed. Theological material (1 Tim. 1:15–16; 2:3–6; 3:16; 2 Tim. 1:9–10; 2:8–13; Titus 2:11–14; 3:5–7) and didactic formulae (1 Tim. 1:15; 3:1; 4:9; 2 Tim. 2:11;

Titus 3:8) appear in various forms. Allusions are made to the Jesus tradition (1 Tim. 5:18; 6:19), to the OT and Jewish traditions (1 Tim. 6:7–8; 2 Tim. 2:19; 3:8), to secular wisdom (Titus 1:12; 1 Tim. 6:10), and perhaps to Paul's earlier letters (1 Tim. 5:17; 2 Tim. 2:11, 20). The language Paul employs to express his ethical message is distinctively Hellenistic.

The emergence of heresy as the setting for the theology of the Pastoral Epistles

One shared feature of the letters is instruction for confronting false teachers and restoring the stability of the churches. There are similarities between these opposition groups and those Jewish-Christian groups that troubled Paul elsewhere in Asia Minor, but at the time of writing the opponents are within the churches: thus they come within the scope of the delegates' authority (1 Tim. 1:3; 6:2; 2 Tim. 2:14; 4:2; Titus 1:13; 3:10); they are said to have deviated from the *faith (1 Tim. 1:6; 6:21; 2 Tim. 2:18); specific false teachers are identified (1 Tim. 1:20; 2 Tim. 2:17–18); the *apostasy was anticipated in prophecy (1 Tim. 4:1; 2 Tim. 3:1; *cf.* Acts 20:28–31). Some of the apostates may have been church *leaders (1 Tim. 3:1–13; 5:17–25).

The Jewish element of the opposition is most dominant: the opponents made peculiar use of the OT ('myths and endless genealogies', 1 Tim. 1:4; 'myths', 1 Tim. 4:7; 2 Tim. 4:4; 'Jewish myths', Titus 1:14; 'genealogies', Titus 3:9; see J. E. Quinn, *The Letter to Titus*, pp. 100–101, 245–248); they claimed to be 'teachers of the law' (1 Tim. 1:7), and were absorbed with matters of ritual purity (1 Tim. 4:3; Titus 1:15–16).

The false teaching included both theological doctrine and ethical practice. Little of the false doctrine can be retrieved. In Ephesus, a distorted view of the resurrection of believers was taught (2 Tim. 2:18), perhaps a central element in the heretics' ('falsely called') 'knowledge' (1 Tim. 6:20). This belief is paralleled in 1 Corinthians 15:12–58, where it is linked to the view that spiritual 'fullness' is available in the present (1 Cor. 4:8; *cf.* Phil. 3:12). Paul was more interested in the effects of the false teaching on the stability of the churches, which took the form of unacceptable behaviour among women (1 Tim. 2:9–15; 5:15; 2 Tim. 3:6; Titus 2:3–5; *cf.* 1 Cor. 11:2–16; 14:33–35; see *Man and woman) and unrest among slaves (1 Tim. 6:1–2; Titus 2:9–10). Doctrines with direct ethical implications included the prohibition of *marriage (1 Tim. 4:3; *cf.* 5:11; 1 Cor. 7:1–7; Irenaeus, *Adversus Haereses* 1. 24. 2; Philo, *Apologia* 380), and the observance of ritual purity regulations in relation to foods and things clean and unclean (1 Tim. 4:3; Titus 1:14–15; *cf.* Rom. 14:1–5; 1 Cor. 8:1–13; Col. 2:16). On both the theological and the ethical level, the indication is that the heretics failed to distinguish between the 'already' and the 'not yet' dimensions of *salvation. This confusion was not something new to Paul. The false resurrection belief and the doctrines of ritual purity and sexual asceticism form a pattern that corresponds to one that Paul had encountered earlier. Thus the historical Pauline ministry remains the best context within which to understand the developments reflected in the Pastoral Epistles.

Although theological refutation appears in several places (*e.g.* 1 Tim. 1:8; 4:3–5, 7–8; 6:5–10) in response to the opposition, the blanket characterization of the false teachers by means of vice lists, stereotypes and harsh adjectives is far more frequent (1 Tim. 1:6, 9–10; 4:1–2, 7; 6:4–5; 2 Tim. 2:23; 3:2–5, 13; Titus 3:9). This sort of polemic created a vivid picture in the minds of the faithful that would keep them from associating with the false teachers and their doctrines.

The theological message of the Pastoral Epistles

Salvation in Jesus Christ

At the centre of the theology of the Pastoral Epistles is the theme of salvation. Paul develops this theme in each letter in poetic clusters of his own teaching or traditional material that he has reshaped (1 Tim. 1:15; 2:4–6; 2 Tim. 1:9–10; 2:8–13; Titus 2:11–14; 3:4–7). Each text declares that salvation is a present reality because *Jesus Christ entered history and accomplished his *redemptive work. Within this theme of redemptive action, several aspects of traditional Christology intersect in the 'epiphany' concept (Gk. *epiphaneia*; 1 Tim. 6:14; 2 Tim. 1:10; 4:1, 8; Titus 2:11, 13; 3:4). This idea, which is different from earlier Pauline emphases, portrays Christ's earthly ministry and future parousia as divine 'appearances' to bring aid

(Lau, Towner). The deity of Christ is implied; it is affirmed unequivocally in Titus 2:13. Epiphany Christology also presumes the pre-existence of Christ, which may be implied in 1 Timothy 1:15 (*cf.* Phil. 2:5–11; Col. 1:15; *cf.* John 9:39; 11:27; 16:28; 18:37). Christ's first epiphany is equated with his *incarnation and human existence, which are confirmed by other texts (1 Tim. 2:5; 3:16; 6:13; 2 Tim. 2:8; *cf.* Rom. 1:3; Gal. 4:4). The close association of *God and Christ made in the epiphany concept (Lau) is reinforced by Paul's designation in conspicuous juxtaposition of each of them as Saviour (Titus 1:3–4; 2:10, 13; 3:4, 6; see also 2 Tim. 1:10 [of Christ]; *cf.* Eph. 5:23; Phil. 3:20; and 1 Tim. 1:1; 2:3; 4:10 [of God]). The connection between the sacrificial self-offering of Christ's *death 'for us' and redemption from sin is depicted in Pauline terms (1 Tim. 2:6; Titus 2:14; *cf.* Gal. 1:4; 2:20). The strong abnegation of any role for human effort in the salvation process (Titus 3:5; 2 Tim. 1:9) also corresponds to the earlier Pauline writings, where the issue is explored both in terms of 'works of the law' (*e.g.* Rom. 3:27–28) and, as in the Pastoral Epistles, in a more general sense (*cf.* Rom. 9:11–12; Eph. 2:4, 8). In contrast to the false teachers, whose optimistic view of the present age and over-realized view of salvation diverged from the Pauline *gospel (*e.g.* 2 Tim. 2:18), the Pastoral Epistles follow the Pauline pattern, holding in tension the evil and transitory nature of the present age in which salvation has begun to unfold (2 Tim. 3:1; 1 Tim. 4:1; *cf.* Rom. 12:2; 1 Cor. 10:11; Gal. 1:4) and the necessity of the return of Christ for the completion of that salvation (Titus 2:13; 1 Tim. 6:13–15; 2 Tim. 4:1; *cf.* 1 Thess. 2:19; 2 Thess. 2:8; Phil. 3:20).

The Pauline gospel and mission

The importance of the gospel message and the *missionary enterprise are underlined in these letters. Two factors shape the way in which the apostolic teaching is described. Terms such as 'sound teaching' (1 Tim. 1:10; 2 Tim. 4:3; Titus 1:9) and 'word of truth' (2 Tim. 2:15, 18) reflect the conflict with opponents and the need to set the Pauline gospel in stark contrast to the false teachings being spread in the churches. The term 'deposit' (*paratheke*) implies that the gospel is a commodity entrusted by God to Paul and by Paul to Timothy (and others). In 2 Timothy (1:12,

14) this idea is part of the broader theme of the handing over of the Pauline mission and gospel to Timothy. The use of the term is intended to protect the message from the dangers posed by heresy (1 Tim. 6:20). The *parathēkē* language reflects a development in the notion of '*tradition' from the letters of the earlier Paul. Earlier discussions of 'tradition' focused on 'accepting' and 'maintaining' the apostolic gospel (1 Cor. 11:2; 15:1; Gal. 1:14; Col. 2:6; 2 Thess. 2:15; 3:6). But in the Pastoral Epistles, with the imminence of the apostle's departure and the threat posed by heresy in view, the accent shifts to the idea of the secure transmission of 'the deposit' to the next generation. The concept is absent from Titus.

In various ways, the Pastoral Epistles articulate a theology of mission. First, 1 Timothy and Titus respond to a threat to the Pauline gospel and mission: 1 Timothy 2:1–7 (2:1 – 3:16) grounds the universal mission in the fact that Christ died for 'all' (2:5–6), and Paul's Gentile mission provides the framework for the letter to Titus (1:1–3). The theme of witness that underlies much of the ethical teaching reveals one important way in which the Christian communities are to participate in the mission to the Gentiles (1 Tim. 3:7; 5:14; 6:1; Titus 2:5, 9; 3:2, 8). But this point is made even more graphically by means of a subtle but unmistakable allusion to the OT in 1 Timothy 2:8. Following the theological argument for universal mission made in 2:1–6, and the strong reminder of Paul's calling to the Gentiles in 2:7, men are commanded 'to pray in every place'. The phrase 'in every place' (*en panti topō*) occurs in the NT only in Paul (1 Cor. 1:2; 2 Cor. 2:14; 1 Thess. 1:8), in each case in relation to the proclamation of the gospel of Jesus Christ, and in ways that pick up the theme introduced in Malachi 1:11 of the universal Gentile worship of God in the future ('For from the rising of the sun to its setting my name is great among the nations, and *in every place* incense is offered to my name, and a pure offering; for my name is great among the nations, says the LORD of hosts', NRSV). These echoes place the Ephesian church in the salvation-historical position of 'fulfillers' of the OT promise that the *nations will worship God. Paul's own mission to the Gentiles (1 Tim. 2:7; 2 Tim. 1:11) has become the church's mission as well.

Instructions to Timothy develop his role in terms of the Pauline mission, and 2 Timothy is written specifically to prepare the younger co-worker to carry on the apostle's mission (2 Tim. 1:6–14; 2:1–7; 3:10–17; 4:1–5, 6–18). In fact, the command to Timothy not to be ashamed (2 Tim. 1:8) is extraordinarily 'missiological' and *eschatological. On the one hand, in this command and with the language of 'shame', Paul consciously connects Timothy and his ministry with himself and his stand for the gospel (2 Tim. 1:12), and in doing so the echoes of Romans 1:16 are impossible to miss. In that verse the 'I am not ashamed' announcement echoes OT themes associated with God's promise to vindicate his people (Is. 50:7–8; 28:16), which Paul sees being fulfilled in the revelation of God's righteousness in the gospel he preaches (see Hays). Thus Timothy also is involved in the fulfilment of the eschatological promise which Paul understood to be occurring in his mission to the Gentiles.

The Holy Spirit

It is often held that the *Holy Spirit, so dominant in the early Paul, is lacking in the picture of the spiritual life that emerges from the Pastoral Epistles, but the five references to the Spirit reflect a Pauline understanding (1 Tim. 3:16; 4:1; 2 Tim. 1:7, 14; Titus 3:5). Titus 3:5 reflects on the role of the Holy Spirit in salvation, as the agent whose 'washing' brings about '*regeneration' and 'renewal'. 2 Timothy 1:6 depicts the Spirit as the source of power for ministry. 2 Timothy 1:14 speaks of the Spirit's indwelling of believers. In 1 Timothy 4:1 the Spirit is seen as the Spirit of *prophecy in accordance with tradition. Finally, 1 Timothy 3:16 characterizes the resurrection existence of Christ with the term 'in Spirit' (*cf.* Rom. 1:4). Thus the Spirit is not absent from the Pastoral Epistles, even if they articulate a theology of the Christian life using other terms.

The Christian life

In a way similar to that of Paul's teaching in Philippians 4:8–9, though more extensively, the Pastoral Epistles use Hellenistic vocabulary to construct a model of the Christian life. Three concepts sum up this life: 'faith', 'godliness' and 'good works', of which the most striking is godliness (or piety; Gk. *eusebeia*). This term conceptualizes Christian existence as a balance between faith in God/Christ and the appropriate response of *love and service towards others. The term 'piety' had already been adapted for use in Hellenistic Judaism to describe a life lived in response to God's *covenant loving-kindness, so there is no reason to think that it is at odds with Pauline theology. At the same time, the Pastoral Epistles employ various other terms that were well known in secular ethics to describe the outward life (prudence, moderation, discretion and self-control [Gk. *sōphrosynē*]; seriousness or respectability [Gk. *semnos*]), along with 'love', 'patience', 'endurance' and '*hope', whilst explaining that all these characteristics of faithful living are grounded in Christ's appearance and the salvation it introduced (Titus 2:11–14). Whether through magnifying the cognitive and 'spiritual' dimensions of the faith or through rigid adherence to regulations governing ritual purity, the opponents had driven a wedge between faith and practical living. It may be asked why Paul chose such a distinctively Greek way of articulating this aspect of his message, but the difference between the Pastoral Epistles and Philippians 4:8–9 is one only of degree; the thought is continuous.

Church and leadership

The degree to which the Pastoral Epistles focus on church structure and the degree to which this differs from the community life reflected in earlier Pauline correspondence have been overemphasized by some writers. 2 Timothy does not discuss the subject. Two sections in 1 Timothy (3:1–13; 5:17–25) and one in Titus (1:5–9) address the issue of church leadership. The nomenclature of leadership includes overseer/bishop (Gk. *episkopos*), deacon/deaconess (Gk. *diakonos*) and elder (Gk. *presbyteros* in 1 Tim. 5; *cf.* 4:14), but both the language (Phil. 1:1; Rom. 16:1) and the phenomenon of authoritative church leadership (*e.g.* Rom. 12:8; 1 Cor. 6:2–6; 12:28; 1 Thess. 5:12; Phil. 4:3) are found in earlier letters, and little about the actual structure of the church in Ephesus is evident from 1 Timothy. The stress is on the character that such leaders should have; gifts recede into the background (1 Tim. 3:2, 4; Titus 1:9). In the case of Ephesus, the importance of character is seen against the background of the apostasy of some leaders from an already existing church, while in

Crete the church is newly planted and in need of leaders (*cf.* Acts 14:23).

Theological description of the church is most evident in 1 Timothy where household imagery provides the dominant components. The church is God's household (3:15; Gk. *oikos theou*). This phrase ties together related concepts in key places to describe God's rule in life in terms of household order (1:4; Gk. *oikonomia theou*) and the overseers' leadership in terms of household management (3:4–5). Subsequent discussion of relationships pertinent to both household and church show how the fundamental social institution has come to serve as a model for understanding the obligations of believers within the community of faith. The concept is not pervasive in Titus (1:7), although basic household relationships and duties overlap with those of believers in the Christian community (2:2 – 3:2). In 2 Timothy the household metaphor (2:20) relates to the church less directly.

2 Timothy was written to prepare Timothy for joining the apostle in Rome. It prepared him for *suffering (1:8; 2:3; 4:5) and included instructions designed to ensure that gifted leaders were selected to continue his work in Asia Minor (2:2–6). In 2:2, ministering gifts are stressed alongside character ('faithfulness'). The leadership profile in the Pastoral Epistles includes three related elements: qualifications for leadership; personal commitment to the mission; personal *holiness. Timothy himself is to follow the example of Paul by perseverance in godliness, suffering and trust in God (1 Tim. 4:6–16; 6:12–14; 2 Tim. 1:6–14; 3:10–17; 4:1–5).

The authority and use of Scripture

2 Timothy 3:16 makes a very strong statement about the authority of Scripture and its use. The declaration of Scripture's divine inspiration is probably directed against the tendency of the false teachers to put forward strange teachings, which Paul calls 'myths' (4:4), and implies that Timothy should be diligent in his use of the OT writings. The point of the statement in 3:16, which underlines the divine nature of Scripture, is to demonstrate the superior effectiveness of the OT for teaching and correction in the church. The implications of this passage for an understanding of Scripture in general cannot be denied, but Paul's aim at this juncture was not to propound a doctrine of Scripture.

Nevertheless, Paul's view of the OT's supreme usefulness in teaching is amply demonstrated in various ways throughout his earlier letters, and also in the Pastoral Epistles. Although there are no sustained quotations, such as are found in Romans, short direct citations occur at 1 Timothy 5:18–19 and 2 Timothy 2:19, and OT allusions and echoes, sometimes produced by words and phrases rather than whole texts, are more numerous, even if they are more difficult to spot and are therefore more open to question (*e.g.* 1 Tim. 2:8, alluding to Mal. 1:11 [see above]; 6:1 alluding to Is. 52:5 [*cf.* Rom. 2:24]; 6:7 alluding to Job 1:21 and Eccles. 5:15; 6:16 alluding to Exod. 33:20; 2 Tim. 2:7 alluding to Prov. 2:6; 4:16–18 contains several allusions to Ps. 22; Titus 2:14 echoes Ps. 130:8, Ezek. 37:23, Exod. 19:5, Deut. 7:6, 14:2). Some allusions may be incidental, arising simply from the use of scriptural language. But use of language found in OT texts is often intended to evoke the readers' recollection of those OT texts. The allusion to Malachi 1:11 in 1 Timothy 2:8 illustrates this intentional echoing of OT themes in order to interpret the present situation in the light of prophetic promise. The various echoes in Titus 2:14 invite the readers to understand the death of Christ as the outworking of God's faithfulness to his covenant promises.

It is somewhat less clear how the apostles understood the teaching of Jesus, or, for that matter, their own correspondence, in relation to the authority of the OT. 1 Corinthians 7:10 and 11:23–26 indicate that Paul regarded the Lord's teaching as authoritative; yet where the accepted tradition did not touch on the local situation, he spoke equally authoritatively as an apostle (7:12), and believed the source of his teaching to be the Lord (2 Cor. 13:3; *cf.* 1 Cor. 7:40). In 1 Timothy 5:18, which discusses the support of ministers, there is an intertextual web woven of an explicit OT quotation in 5:18a ('You shall not muzzle the threshing oxen', Deut. 25:4) and a saying of Jesus in 5:18b in which he alluded to related teaching about the proper wages of the Levites in Numbers 18:31 ('a workman is worthy of his wages'; Luke 10:7; *cf.* Matt. 10:10). Interestingly, Paul employed this same combination earlier, in 1 Corinthians 9:9–14, citing first the Deuteronomy text (v. 9), then alluding to the passage in Numbers (v. 13), and finally referring to the saying of Jesus (v. 14) in confirmation of his point. Thus the apostle brings together the relevant, authoritative OT text and the Lord's authoritative expansion, and reinforces them with his own apostolic authority. He does the same in 1 Timothy 5:18, though in a more compressed form. The assumption of some that the formula preceding the quotation of Deuteronomy 25:4 ('For the Scripture says') identifies the Jesus material as Scripture is unlikely; moreover, the authority of that material is not dependent upon it. Although the Jesus tradition was no doubt already being written down and collected, and regarded as authoritative, the canonical Gospels had not yet emerged. But this is not to say that the teaching of Jesus would be accorded a sub-scriptural authority (the Messiah was the supreme interpreter of the Scriptures), merely that what is not written cannot, in the strictest sense, be regarded as Scripture. In this repetition of an earlier pattern, Paul adds to the authority of the OT and the Jesus tradition that of his own earlier apostolic use. Timothy, the immediate recipient of this letter, would surely have understood the force of Paul's argument (*cf.* 1 Cor. 16:10). Since Paul wrote 1 Corinthians from Ephesus, it is reasonable to assume that the Ephesian believers would also hear the echoes of earlier, authoritative, apostolic teaching.

Common themes but three separate messages

Within the Pauline corpus as a whole, the Pastoral Epistles clearly reflect some new interests. But there is little in them that cannot be explained by the new situations, the new choice of literary forms, and the transition the author himself perceives to be under way as the universal Gentile mission is passed from Paul to Timothy and the next generation.

In spite of the overlap of themes and language, it is clear that each letter is unique. 1 Timothy clearly addresses a problem of heresy, which has troubled an established church in various ways. The solution is to reassert the sound apostolic gospel, resist unruly behaviour (2:8–15; 5:9–15; 6:1–2), maintain strong leadership in the church (3:1–13; 5:17–25), pay attention to *prayer and other aspects of orderly *worship (2:1; 4:13) and model the life of godliness that others must live.

Titus's role is very similar, but the needs of his church are not entirely the same. In the face of false teaching, he is to set in place a strong leadership (1:5–9), but the main concerns of the letter seem to be the stability (2:1–10) and public image (3:1–2) of the church, each of which requires respectable behaviour. The theological basis given for the ethical instruction (2:11–14; 3:5–7) makes it clear that the behaviour enjoined was to be understood as the appropriate outworking of the *grace of God in human relationships through various forms of godliness (Gk. *eusebeia*; 2:12).

2 Timothy shares themes and language with 1 Timothy and Titus, and the heresy in Ephesus is a continuing concern (2:14–18; 3:1–9). However, this letter is far more personal and more concerned with Timothy's welfare and calling. It begins by reminding Timothy of his relationship with Paul and his similar calling. He is to follow Paul's example (1:11–13; 2:8–10; 3:10–17; 4:6–7) as he prepares to join him. Both in coming to Rome to be with Paul and in continuing the apostle's ministry, Timothy will encounter suffering (1:8; 2:3; 3:12; 4:5). He must get to Rome before the end and (presumably) carry the mission on to completion from there. 2 Timothy concludes the Pauline story in the NT.

Bibliography

J. M. Bassler, *1 Timothy, 2 Timothy, Titus*, ANTC (Nashville, 1996); M. Dibelius and H. Conzelmann, *The Pastoral Epistles*, Hermeneia (ET, London and Philadelphia, 1972); E. E. Ellis in *DPL*, pp. 658–666; L. R. Donelson, *Pseudepigraphy and Ethical Argument in the Pastoral Epistles* (Tübingen, 1986); G. D. Fee, *1 and 2 Timothy, Titus*, NIBC (Carlisle and Peabody, 1988); D. Guthrie, *The Pastoral Epistles*, TNTC (London and Grand Rapids, ²1990, 1991); A. T. Hanson, *The Pastoral Epistles*, NCB (Grand Rapids, 1982); P. N. Harrison, *The Problem of the Pastoral Epistles* (Oxford, 1921); R. B. Hays, *Echoes of Scripture in the Letters of Paul* (New Haven, 1989); L. T. Johnson, *Letters to Paul's Delegates* (Valley Forge, 1996); J. N. D. Kelly, *A Commentary on the Pastoral Epistles*, BNTC (London and New York, 1963); G. W. Knight, *The Pastoral Epistles*, NIGTC (Carlisle and Grand Rapids, 1992); A. Y. Lau, *Manifest in Flesh* (Tübingen, 1996); I. H. Marshall, *The Pastoral Epistles* (Edinburgh, 1999); J. D. Miller, *The Pastoral Letters as Composite Fragments* (Cambridge, 1997); M. Prior, *Paul the Letter-Writer* (Sheffield, 1989); J. E. Quinn, *The Letter to Titus*, AB (New York, 1990); J. A. T. Robinson, *Redating the New Testament* (Philadelphia, 1970); P. H. Towner, *The Goal of our Instruction* (Sheffield, 1989); *idem*, *1–2 Timothy and Titus*, IVPNTC (Leicester and Downers Grove, 1994); D. C. Verner, *The Household of God* (Chico, 1983); F. Young, *The Theology of the Pastoral Epistles*, NTT (Cambridge, 1994).

P. H. TOWNER

PHILEMON

We may surmise that this letter, the shortest and most occasional of *Paul's extant letters, was included in the New Testament canon because of its distinctive contribution to several areas of Christian thought.

1. Although not a disquisition on slavery, the letter reflects the apostle's attitude towards slavery. Paul does not demand that Philemon release Onesimus, nor even assume that Philemon will set him free (see v. 15). The apostle accepts slavery as an existing social and legal condition (see v. 12), but when he emphasizes Onesimus's true identity as a dearly loved Christian brother (v. 16) he sets the master–slave relationship on a new footing, thereby undermining the discriminatory hierarchy of social relations that is at the heart of slavery and putting the institution itself in jeopardy among Christians. Acceptance of the status quo did not amount to endorsement of it.

2. This letter contains a potent illustration of the breaking down of social and cultural barriers in Christ (*cf.* Gal. 3:28). Here is Paul, a highly educated Roman citizen, championing the cause of a destitute runaway slave whose life was potentially forfeit because of his flight and his theft (*cf.* v. 18). *Love must be shown to the slave as much as to the free person.

3. It shows a pastor skilfully shepherding his sheep. Paul forgoes his apostolic right to give commands (vv. 8–9) and chooses to ask

for Philemon's voluntary consent to his wishes (v. 14). He identifies himself with Onesimus, his spiritual son (v. 10), to the extent of calling him 'my very heart' (v. 12) and guaranteeing to repay his debts (vv. 18–19). He expresses confidence in Philemon's compliance (v. 21) with his basic request that Onesimus be given a ready welcome on his return to Colossae (v. 17), but beyond this Paul leaves Philemon free to follow the dictates of his Christian conscience in deciding how his love (vv. 5, 7) should be expressed. And it is in the context of the whole local church that Philemon must make his decision (vv. 1–2).

4. In Paul's requests on behalf of Onesimus, the essence of the gospel is reflected. When we come to God in repentance and faith, he welcomes us as if we were Christ (*cf.* v. 17) and gives us a new status (*cf.* v. 16). What we owe God, Christ debited to his own account (*cf.* v. 18). He assumed personal responsibility for the full payment of our debt to God (*cf.* v. 19a). Thus the letter illustrates the nature of substitution.

5. It demonstrates the power of the gospel to transform life. The one who had previously been 'useless' (*achrēstos*) had become, as a result of conversion (v. 10), '(really) useful' (*euchrēstos*), now living up to his name. (Onesimus means 'useful' in Gk.)

Bibliography

J. D. G. Dunn, *The Epistles to the Colossians and to Philemon*, NIGTC (Carlisle and Grand Rapids, 1996); M. A. Getty, 'The theology of Philemon', in *SBLSP*, 1987, pp. 503–508.

M. J. HARRIS

HEBREWS

Introduction

The letter to the Hebrews was traditionally attributed to Paul, and since the Reformation has sometimes been ascribed to Apollos. But it is now most widely believed that in this writing we hear an unnamed voice, distinct from those of Paul and the other NT writers, making its own contribution to the normative expression of the Christian faith.

The letter is carefully constructed, with skilful and smooth transitions. It is written in some of the best literary *koinē* Greek in the NT. Its central theological theme, that of the high-priestly self-sacrifice of *Jesus, is introduced in passing (1:3; 2:17; 3:1), and later developed in detail.

The date of Hebrews is disputed. Many continental European scholars place it after the fall of Jerusalem in AD 70, primarily because of its advanced Christology. Most Anglo-Saxon scholars, however, and some others, place it a few years before that date, arguing that if Jerusalem had already fallen, the writer would have strengthened his statement that the old covenant 'will soon disappear' (8:13, NIV).

The place of writing is unknown. So also is the destination, though the phrase 'those from Italy' (13:24) may perhaps most naturally be understood of Italian expatriates sending greetings to friends at home, principally in Rome. If this is so, references to the 'wandering people of God' (3:7 – 4:13), and to Abraham as 'a stranger in a foreign country' (11:9), may have had a special resonance for the writer.

The situation to which the letter is addressed can be inferred only from the writing itself. The original readers were part of a community suffering persecution (13:3), though not yet martyrdom (12:4). The writer makes extensive use of the OT (see below), suggesting that many of his readers were almost certainly of Jewish origin. The indefinite expression 'the fathers' (1:1; the reading '*our* fathers' is very weakly attested) suggests, however, that the community included some Gentile members. The avoidance of expressions related specifically to either Gentiles or Jews, and the generally non-polemical tone of the letter, indicate that the writer was sensitive to feeling in a mixed community, and possibly that there was a danger (of which he was aware) of reopening some past controversy.

The writer by implication disclaims the authority of an apostle or eye-witness (2:3), and does not write as a leader. He refers to 'your leaders' (13:7,17) in the third person, which suggests that the letter may be addressed, not to an entire local church, but to a group within it. If so, this reflects the personal concern for the readers' salvation which fills the writing.

We refer to Hebrews as a letter; but although it ends like a letter, it does not begin like one. Some have suggested that it is a sermon to which epistolary features have been added. Conversely, an epistolary opening or covering note may have been deleted when the writing was forwarded to a community other than its original addressees. In either case, it is clear that the writing was seen from very early times to have theological significance for others besides those to whom it was first sent.

We also refer to the author as 'he'. Occasionally, female authors have been suggested, but the use of a masculine singular form in 11:32 makes it very likely that the author was male.

The purpose of the letter

Hebrews consists of alternating sections of teaching and exhortation. Different views have been taken about which type of writing expresses more directly the author's purpose, and which is a means to that end. It is more likely that his purpose is primarily pastoral, but that he finds himself impelled, in order to meet his readers' spiritual needs, to develop profound and distinctive teaching, especially about the person and work of Christ.

As already stated, the readers are threatened by persecution; but the author appears to see as the main threat to their faith a certain slowness to learn (5:11) or laziness (6:12; the same Greek word is used in both places). This has been held to imply that they are second- or third-generation Christians; but that is not necessarily so.

The author's purpose is thus twofold. On the one hand, negatively, it is to prevent his readers from falling back into their pre-Christian state, which for some may have been traditional Jewish belief. On the other hand, positively, it is to encourage them, with the help of the advanced teaching he offers, to go on to maturity (6:1); essentially, to a fuller understanding of the person and work of Christ. There is for the writer no halting-place on the Christian way; one must either go forward, or risk falling short (4:1) of participation in what God has promised, and which is now available through Christ.

Hebrews' relation to other writings

Non-biblical writings

Points of contact have from time to time been noted between Hebrews on the one hand, and

gnostic writings, Philo and Qumran on the other.

Fully developed Gnosticism is known only from post-NT times, but it may be that the writer's avoidance of the word *gnōsis* and related terms is a form of defence against pre- or proto-gnostic currents liable to mislead or confuse his readers.

Similarities between Hebrews and the voluminous writings of Philo (*c.* 20 BC – *c.* AD 50) have been found since the 17th century, and it is probable that the thought of both writers developed in a similar Hellenistic, Jewish diaspora environment. Yet the points of contact fall short of convincing evidence that the writer of Hebrews had personally read works by Philo. Hebrews' almost complete avoidance of allegory is in striking contrast to Philo's practice.

Points of contact between Hebrews and the Qumran writings, most notably Melchizedek. (*cf.* Heb. 7:1–19), probably indicate currents of theological speculation circulating both at Qumran and in the milieu in which Hebrews was written; but whereas the Qumran community appears to have been closed and reformist, Hebrews addresses primarily a Judaism revolutionized and transformed by the coming of Christ.

Biblical writings

The OT is easily the most important literary source of Hebrews. Hebrews contains thirty-five direct quotations, together with numerous allusions and historical references. Quotations are drawn most commonly from the *Psalms and the Pentateuch, especially *Genesis and the final chapters of *Deuteronomy. The writer shows no preference for earlier historical accounts over the products of later reflection on them (*e.g.* in Ps. 95), but he never uses allegory in order to bypass history or spiritualize it away. There is cumulative evidence that even where the writer quotes selectively, he is aware of the context of his quotations; for example, he systematically excludes polemical references in such contexts.

The author's implied theology of the OT may be summarized as follows. Christ, by whom God has now spoken his final word (1:1–2), was active in creation (1:2) and throughout Israel's history. Any part of the OT may therefore in principle be understood as speaking about Christ, or as spoken to or by him. Since Christ was already active in OT times, even an OT text without a future reference, such as Psalm 40:6–8 (= Heb. 10:5–7), may be applied to Christ. There is no conflict between the authority of (OT) Scripture and the authority of Christ: Scripture, sensitively explored, provides Christians with language which they can appropriately use of Christ, and because of the coming of Christ, believers are enabled to read and interpret the OT in fresh ways.

God

In the Authorized or King James Version, 'God' is the first word in Hebrews; its opening sentence begins 'God, who at sundry times and in divers manners spake in time past unto the fathers by the prophets.' 'God' does not come first in the Greek but KJV is not wrong in implying that the writer, like any good teacher, begins where his readers are, in this case by presupposing belief in the one true *God of the OT.

The writer's main purpose is thus not to develop any fresh doctrine about God the Father; yet what he says about God includes distinctive emphases. God created the universe (1:2; 2:10) by his word (11:3; cf. 'God said', Gen. 1:3, etc.) and established it (3:4). He spoke through the prophets, and has now spoken by his Son (1:1–2). He speaks in Scripture (1:3, 6, 8, etc.). He called OT priests to their office (5:4), as he called Jesus to his high priesthood (5:5–6). He confirmed by miraculous signs the message of salvation brought by Christian evangelists (2:3–4; cf. 13:7). He raises up the Christian community (2:13), disciplines believers as sons (12:7), and makes it possible for them to offer true worship (12:28; 13:15–16), which is the purpose of human life (9:14). To fall away from him leads to death (3:12; cf. 12:15). He is the source of peace, and the one who raised Jesus from the dead (13:20). Hebrews repeatedly refers to God as the living God (3:12; 9:14; 10:31; 12:22) and as the judge of all (12:23; cf. 4:12; 10:31; 13:4). God speaks and acts through his Son (1:2; cf. 4:14; 7:2; 10:29). His grace is active in his Son's death (2:9) and resurrection (13:20).

Christ

This is the central theme of Hebrews, and it is in this area that the writer makes his most distinctive and fully developed theological statements. The opening chapters are largely devoted to demonstrating from Scripture the supremacy of the Son over angels (ch. 1), Moses (3:1–6), Joshua (4:8), and more generally the OT priesthood. The purpose of this teaching is made clear by exhortations and warnings, for example in 2:1–4; 3:1, 12; 4:1–2, 11–13. (See also below: 'The "rigorism" of Hebrews'.)

The writer is not concerned to make precise statements, in the style of later creeds, about the relationship between the divine and human natures of Christ. He does, however, combine a general interest in what happened 'in the days of [Christ's] flesh' (5:7; cf. 2:17–18; 5:2) with a strong emphasis on his present status at the right hand of God. The human name Jesus is used sparingly but with emphasis, especially in the early chapters of the letter. The reinterpretation of Psalm 45:6–7 in Hebrews 1:8–9, including the words 'Your throne, O God', is one of the NT texts which comes closest to affirming the divinity of the Son, though in a context of worship rather than dogmatic statement.

The author's thinking about Christ revolves principally around two titles. The first is the traditional 'Son', probably already in common use within the community to which Hebrews is addressed. The other is 'high *priest', not explicitly used elsewhere in the NT (though the high-priestly work of Christ is implicit, for example, in John 17). The author's use of this title is probably the result of his meditation on Psalm 110, moving from v. 1, 'The LORD says to my Lord: "Sit at my right hand ..."' (the OT text most often quoted in the NT), to v. 4: 'The LORD has sworn and will not change his mind: "You are a priest for ever, like Melchizedek"', and supported by the only other OT reference to *Melchizedek, in Genesis 14:17–20 (cf. Heb. 7:1–20). Different aspects of the key text Psalm 110:4 are highlighted at different stages of the letter (5:6, 10; 6:20; 7:3, 17, 21). Except in quotation and direct exposition, the writer of Hebrews adapts the text to refer to Jesus as 'high' priest, to reflect his supreme dignity. There is however no suggestion of a hierarchy including subordinate Christian priests, of any successor to Jesus in the office of high priest, or of a succession of non-levitical priests linking Melchizedek and Jesus.

The author does not separate Christ's

person from his work. Both the key titles of Son and high priest are functional; specifically, they relate to his death (see *Atonement) and *exaltation to the right hand of God (which in Hebrews virtually subsumes his *resurrection, referred to in traditional language at 13:20) (see 1:3; 7:26; and especially 5:5–6). The single act (the words *hapax* and *ephapax*, 'once [for all]', are prominent in Hebrews: 6:4; 9:7, 12, 26–28; 10:2, 10) by which Christ 'became the source of eternal *salvation for all who obey him' (5:9) is closely linked with both his sonship (v. 8) and his high priesthood (v. 10), and both ultimately depend on the activity of God. Yet the effect of that one act is to initiate a continuing ministry of intercession (*Prayer) in the heavenly tabernacle (9:24). Christ's exaltation is related to his *faithfulness in the office of high priest (3:2), and especially to his final act of *obedience to the will of God (10:5–10); but the writer also speaks of Christ's own conquest of death (2:14–15) and of the 'power of [his] indestructible *life' (7:16).

It is therefore possible for the writer, without detracting from the uniqueness of Christ's sonship, to speak of him as 'bringing many sons [and, by implication, daughters], to *glory' (2:10). This metaphor of relationship is used alongside that which describes believers, in the language of Isaiah 8:18, as 'the children God has given me' (Heb. 2:13). The writer never uses the terms 'son' and 'child' in the singular in speaking of believers.

Apart from the key titles of Son and high priest, the most remarkable feature of Hebrews' Christological language is his use of the name 'Jesus'. This is most often used alone (2:9; 3:1; 4:14; 6:20; 7:22; 10:19; 12:2, 24; 13:12; 'Jesus Christ' in 10:10; 13:8, 21), and usually in an emphatic position at the end of a clause. In many places the name is avoided (though modern translations sometimes insert it, for example NIV, in 3:3). This economical use of the name enhances its effectiveness when it is used, and illustrates the author's reverence for the human figure of Jesus.

In his opening sentence, the writer speaks of the Son as 'the radiance of God's glory and the exact representation of his being' (1:3); the language recalls that used of divine *wisdom in Wisdom of Solomon 7:22 – 8:1. Elsewhere, the writer, uniquely in the NT,

describes Jesus as 'the apostle and high priest of our confession' (3:1, author's translation), a phrase which may be best understood as 'the high priest whom we acknowledge as the one sent by God'. Jesus is also called 'the author [*archēgos*] of ... salvation' (2:10; *cf.* 12:2), and as our forerunner (6:20; NIV 'Jesus, who went before us'). These terms refer to Christ's passage through death to exaltation on behalf of humanity.

Hebrews' other Christological language is mostly traditional. The writer sometimes (2:3; 7:14; *cf.* 1:10 = Ps. 102:25) refers to Jesus as Lord, but this title is more often used of God. It is remarkable that the writer can assume, rather than having to argue for, the pre-existence of Jesus; the Son was active in *creation (1:2, 10 = Ps. 102:25) and rules justly over the world (1:8 = Ps. 45:6).

Salvation

The flexibility of Hebrews' thought and language has already been noted in his description of believers as Christ's brothers and sisters and as his children. This flexibility is shown on a larger scale, especially in the central teaching section of the letter (8:1 – 10:18), in which Christ's death is described as a *sacrifice in which he also acts as high priest, thus offering himself as a willing sacrifice to God. In this way Hebrews represents Christ's death as gathering into itself all the significance of the levitical cultus, especially the ritual of the Day of Atonement. Christ's death indeed surpasses that cultus, because it is a willing human sacrifice rather than an involuntary animal offering (9:12–14), because it purifies the conscience rather than merely dealing with external impurities (9:9–10), and because it does not need to be constantly repeated, but is valid once for all (9:24–28).

Christ's death is thus 'for everyone' (2:9); more specifically, for 'purification for sins' (1:3). His sacrifice is cosmic in scope, extending even to the purification of 'heavenly things themselves' (9:23). Jesus is the pioneer of salvation for his 'many sons and daughters' (2:10), and the source or cause of their salvation (5:9).

What remains in doubt is whether the readers will benefit from the 'things that accompany salvation' (6:9). Salvation thus has an unrealized aspect; the writer uses the future tense, saying that the blood of Christ 'will ... cleanse our consciences' (9:14). Conversely, though, the writer can speak of the sanctification (see *Holiness) of believers in the past tense (10:10; *cf*. 10:14, 29). Faith is essential in appropriating the benefits of Christ's sacrifice (10:22 and ch. 11).

The writer uses a rich variety of language in speaking of salvation. Sometimes he speaks simply of *forgiveness (10:18), sometimes of purification (10:22), sometimes in cultic terms of 'drawing near' to God (7:19, 25; 10:22), sometimes of being 'made perfect' (10:14; 11:40) or sanctified (10:14), sometimes of sharing in Christ (3:14) or in God's holiness (12:10, 14).

In accordance with the purpose of the letter, the writer frequently uses the language of movement and pilgrimage. This is particularly prominent in 3:7 – 4:13, a meditation on Psalm 95:7–11 which highlights the theme of entry into God's *'rest' or resting-place. Similar language is found in chapter 11, where the OT examples of faith are interpreted as pointing towards the future (vv. 1, 13–16, 39–40). An exodus theme underlies the references to inheriting what God has promised; that is, taking permanent possession of a gift from God (6:12; *cf*. 9:15; 10:36; 11:39).

The writer does full justice to the past event of Christ's sacrifice of himself, the present experience of believers, and the *hope of future fulfilment: 'Jesus Christ is the same yesterday and today and for ever' (13:8). Believers are already identified as God's 'house' or household (3:6), yet the object of their hope is not yet fully in their possession (6:18–20). Moreover, the fulfilment of their hopes has implications for the OT heroes of faith (11:40; see also below: 'The church').

The *Holy Spirit

Hebrews accepts, but does not develop, traditional Christian teaching about the Spirit; the writer assumes that his readers also accept it. The 'gifts of the Holy Spirit' (2:4) are part of the 'great salvation' which the readers neglect at their eternal peril. The Spirit is the author of the Scriptures (3:7; 10:15; *cf*. 9:8). Believers are those 'who have shared in the Holy Spirit' (6:4). He is 'the Spirit of *grace' (10:29). 'The eternal Spirit' (9:14) may be either the Holy Spirit or the spirit of Christ himself.

The *church

Hebrews is addressed to a Christian community with a structure and recognized leaders (13:7, 17, 24), though we are told little of its organization. References to 'baptisms' (6:2; 9:10; *cf*. 10:22) probably but not certainly refer to Christian *baptism, as also may those to 'enlightenment' (6:4; 10:32). Some have argued that the addressees did not celebrate the Lord's Supper; but an argument from silence, especially the silence of a single letter, is weak.

The writer almost certainly knew members of the community to which he wrote, though he does not mention any of them by name. His repeated use of expressions such as 'any [one] of you', 'none of you' (3:12–13; 4:1, 11; 12:5–6) is not a mere rhetorical device but an expression of pastoral concern.

Yet the writer's concern stretches out beyond individuals to include the entire *people of God. Although the old or first covenant is 'obsolete and ageing' (8:13), there is continuity, within God's purpose, between his people under the old and new dispensations. His constant intention for his people is that they should enter his resting-place (4:9; *cf*. 4:4). The purpose of Christ's self-sacrifice was to deal with the sins of God's people (2:17; *cf*. 1:3; 13:12), not just those of isolated individuals. God's promise through Jeremiah, 'they will be my people' (8:10 = Jer. 31:33), is realized in Christ. The sacrifice of Christ entails a different kind of priesthood (7:13–15), and thus a change in the law (7:12); but God's purpose for the salvation of his people remains unchanged.

The 'rigorism' of Hebrews

A special problem is posed by three passages in Hebrews (2:1–4; 6:4–6; 10:26–31) which appear to state that those who, after becoming Christians, then lose their faith, and have no further hope of salvation. These passages may have constituted one reason for the slow acceptance of Hebrews by some parts of the early church. (The conditions on which lapsed but penitent Christians could be readmitted to the Lord's Supper were more than once a subject of controversy, as the question of the final perseverance of believers has been in modern times.)

When the 'rigorist' passages are placed in the context of the entire letter, the following statements may be made: 1. The writer places no limits on the scope and effectiveness of Christ's sacrifice (1:2–3; 2:8–9). 2. The benefits of that sacrifice are appropriated only by faith (5:9). 3. The readers appear to be in real danger of losing their faith, though the writer never affirms that any of them have done or will do so. 4. There is no intermediate position between faith in Christ and apostasy; to lose hold on Christ (3:14) is 'to fall away from the living God' (3:12). 5. The writer includes himself in discussing the danger of losing faith in Christ (note 'we' forms in 2:1, 3; 10:26). 6. Warnings are always followed by words of encouragement (6:9–12; 10:32–39). 7. The writer does not state simply that *apostates cannot be saved, but rather that they cannot 'be brought back to repentance' (6:6), that is, repeat the act by which they would return to faith and so be saved. 8. Apostasy is described both passively, as 'ignor[ing] such a great salvation' (2:3), and also actively, as a deliberate sin (10:26) against the sacrifice of Christ and 'the Spirit of grace' (10:29).

The seriousness of these passages, and the real danger of apostasy, should not be understated; yet they are set in the context of a 'word of exhortation' (13.22) or 'encouragement', and are pastoral rather than dogmatic in intent.

The world to come

Hebrews is not an apocalyptic writing; its purpose is not to present a comprehensive picture of things to come. Yet the future dimension of salvation is prominent. God has appointed his Son heir of all things (1:2); that is, he will in the end place everything in Christ's possession. Similar language is used of believers, who 'will inherit salvation' (1:14). From one point of view 'the world to come' (2:5) is the theme of the letter. Hope itself, especially the object of Christian hope, is a recurring theme (3:6; 6:11, 18; 7:29; 10:23; cf. 11:1); hope is the human counterpart to God's promises (4:3). The promise of entering God's resting-place remains open (4:1). The readers are repeatedly exhorted to hold fast to their faith (6:12; 10:23, 32, 36), particularly since 'the Day', the final day of *judgment, is approaching (10:25; cf. 12:29, quoting Deut. 4:24). There will be a final shaking of both heaven and earth (12:26; cf. Hag. 2:6), 'so that what cannot be shaken may remain' (12:27). (See *Eschatology.)

Bibliography

H. W. Attridge, *The Epistle to the Hebrews*, Hermeneia (Philadelphia and London, 1989); F. F. Bruce, *Commentary on the Epistle to the Hebrews*, NICNT (Grand Rapids and London, ²1990); P. Ellingworth, *The Epistle to the Hebrews*, Epworth (London, 1991); idem, *The Epistle to the Hebrews*, NIGTC (Grand Rapids and Carlisle, 1993); O. Hofius, *Katapausis: Die Vorstellung vom endzeitlichen Ruheort im Hebräerbrief* (Tübingen, 1970); W. L. Lane, *Hebrews 1–8, 9–13*, WBC (Waco, 1991); J. Swetnam, *Jesus and Isaac: A Study of the Epistle to the Hebrews in the Light of the Aqedah* (Rome, 1981); A. Vanhoye, *Situation du Christ: Hébreux 1–2* (Paris, 1969); idem, *La Structure littéraire de l'épître aux Hébreux* (Bruges and Paris, ²1976); H.-F. Weiss, *Der Brief an die Hebräer*, KEK (Göttingen, 1991); R. Williamson, *Philo and the Epistle to the Hebrews* (Leiden, 1970).

P. ELLINGWORTH

JAMES

The epistle of James is a literary letter, written perhaps about AD 61–62 to conserve the teaching of the Lord's brother James after his martyrdom. Although it is an edited work, consisting of the sayings and homilies of James, it presents a unified outlook which reflects the historical setting of the Jewish-Christian church in Judea in the decades preceding the Jewish War of AD 66–70.

The perspective of James is shaped by 1. contemporary Jewish interpretations of the OT, in particular Jewish expansions of OT narratives, and 2. the teaching of Jesus. No other NT book contains as many allusions to the teaching of Jesus, though there is only one identifiable quotation (5:12, and even this is not attributed). Therefore one must read the theology of James in the light of the theology of the Jesus tradition, especially that found in the sayings tradition ('Q'). James does not show any awareness of written Gospels.

In short, James is a pastoral application of the teaching of Jesus and other Christian and Jewish material to the contemporary problems of the church.

Testing

James begins with the issue of *testing (1:2–4), which he addresses twice more in the book

(1:12–15; 4:13 – 5:11). The experience of the church is that the righteous suffer as a direct result of their Christian faith and of economic oppression by unbelievers. This experience of *suffering for the faith recalls that of the Jewish martyrs of the Maccabean period (167–164 BC) and is anticipated in the teaching of Jesus (*e.g.* Mark 13:9–13). In James, as in other NT literature, 'suffering/testing' refers to those negative experiences that one endures as a result of one's Christian faith. These may include 1. the disadvantages one experiences in the world as a result of following the Christian ethic, 2. the effort one puts into spreading the Christian gospel (*e.g.* 2 Cor. 11:23–29), and 3. the emotional, economic or physical pain inflicted by those opposed to the Christian gospel. They do not include internal pain, *i.e.* sickness, about which James provides a separate discussion (5:14–18).

In James, the Maccabean literature, and Jesus, as well as in Paul and 1 Peter, the theme is treated in the same way. First, the reality of suffering as a result of faithfulness to God is recognized; the painfulness of the experience is not denied. Secondly, the suffering is set in an eschatological context. In James, 'the Judge is at the door' (5:9; author's translation) and 'the coming of the Lord is near' (5:8); the letter includes references to inheriting the coming kingdom (2:5). A proper eschatological perspective enables one to realize that God/Jesus (whether 'the Judge' and 'the Lord' is God or Jesus is debated) is going to come and set things right. Injustice will not prevail; instead the justice of God will have the final word. Furthermore, this setting of everything to rights is 'near' or 'at the door'; there is to be no specified or indefinite delay. In the light of these facts Christians are to endure injustice (1:3–4; 5:7–11), not out of resignation, but on the grounds that their *righteousness will result in a reward. The example of Job is cited (5:11); but the reference is not to the biblical Job, who does not appear to be very patient (the term 'patient endurance' does not appear in the canonical book), but to the traditions behind the *Testament of Job* (*i.e.* the stories about Job current in James' Jewish world); this whole book is based on the theme of patient endurance, and the term occurs many times.

The result of such patient endurance is that one 'counts it all joy' when one experiences 'various tests' (1:2). This statement is patently a pastoral adaptation of Jesus' command to rejoice when one is persecuted (*e.g.* Matt. 5:11–12). Neither statement commends masochism or the seeking of persecution in order to increase one's reward. The idea is rather that individuals who are so sure of the coming kingdom of God and its righteousness that they can virtually 'taste' it in the present have an inward joy in that knowledge in the midst of pain and tears. This is eschatological, anticipated joy.

The failure to endure and to develop the associated virtues (*e.g.* 'maturity' or 'perfection', 1:4) leads one instead to choose one's desires (often translated 'lusts', though they are only negative insofar as they lead one away from obedience to God) (1:13–15; 4:1–6). In a classic presentation of Jewish *yēṣer* theology James presents desire as in conflict with both the human person and God. For the Jews *yēṣer* was the sum of the impulses or drives in the human being. They were evil in that they knew no boundary. Thus hunger might lead one not only to provide food for oneself, but also to steal the food of a neighbour. Since these drives knew no boundaries, their tendency was to draw the person away from following God. In James failure begins in blaming God for adverse circumstances (1:13); the person is then drawn down the path of desire to sin and ultimately death. The antidote for such desire is patient endurance and the wisdom of God.

James denies that God ever sends tests (1:13). (Sometimes the Gk. word is translated 'temptations', but this narrows the focus of the discussion and obscures the author's use of the same word to mean 'tests' elsewhere in the chapter.) Thus he denies a literal interpretation of Genesis 22:1 (in both its Hebrew and Greek versions). He can do this because, like the author of 1 Chronicles 21:1 who reinterprets 2 Samuel 24:1, and like many Jews of his own day, he interprets the Abraham story in the light of Job, understanding Satan as the agent of testing who is excluded from the Genesis narrative by the strict monotheism of its author. That James understands Satan as standing behind desire is clear from 4:7, where in a discussion of desire (4:1, 3), his call to submit to God has as its counterpart resisting, not desire, but the devil. Thus in James' view only good comes from God (1:16–18, the counterpart of 1:13–15), while evil comes from desires within us, stirred up by the devil. We must take responsibility for our actions and cannot simply say, 'The devil made me do it', but neither can we say, 'God is to blame for putting me to the test' (*cf.* the Lord's Prayer, 'Do not lead us to the test').

The ideal result of testing is that the eschatological joy which leads to patient endurance in the light of the coming of the Lord becomes the basis not only for resistance to overt persecution, but also for dealing with the challenges of speech and wealth. For James, as for the NT in general, eschatology is the basis for ethics.

Speech

The most difficult of James' theological themes to summarize is that which we have labelled 'speech'. It could equally well be labelled '*wisdom', for speech-ethics and wisdom are closely connected in both James and Proverbs (which draws on traditions of speech-ethics circulating in the ancient Near East). But the aspect of wisdom with which James is most concerned is that of speech-ethics and the resulting community solidarity.

Wisdom

For James wisdom is what one needs if one lacks something when being tested (1:5). Furthermore, the 'wisdom from above' produces good fruit (3:13, 17; *cf.* Paul's fruit of the Spirit, Gal. 5:22–23). For James, therefore, wisdom functions very much as the Spirit does for Paul, and as in the wisdom pneumatology that is found, for example, in Wisdom 7:7, 22 – 8:1. It is the gift of God that leads the Christian into a righteous life, which includes the ability to stand in the test (*cf.* Mark 13:11 and parallels).

The results of wisdom listed in 3:17 reflect James' view of God. God gives generously, not complaining about our need to return to him again and again (1:5). God gives only good, for his character is unchanging; he gave us new birth, not accidentally, but purposefully (1:17–18). God gives more grace when we fail, rather than condemning us (4:6). Thus while there are indications in the letter of God's role in future judgment (*e.g.* the cries of the defrauded workers enter into the ears of the Lord of hosts, 5:4; the coming one is described as 'the Judge', 5:9), the God of

James is good to his people, gives freely, gives only good, and heals (5:15). It is this God who gives the divine wisdom.

Anger

What James calls 'not the wisdom from above' (3:15) is associated with community destruction. It is not surprising, then, that it is also associated with negative speech. The importance of this topic for James is seen clearly in 3:1–12, a long denunciation of the destructive power of the tongue (*i.e.* speech). That it begins with a warning to teachers may indicate that the biggest problem in the communities to which James was writing was teachers being critical of one another; the negative 'wisdom' is characterized by 'selfish ambition' or 'party spirit' as well as by 'disorder'.

Chapter 3 is not the only place where the destructive power of speech is mentioned. In 1:19–20 Christians are counselled to listen rather than to express *anger. (James, like other NT writers, concerns himself with the expression of anger, not angry feelings.) This section concludes with the observation that true religion includes controlling one's speech (1:26). The following chapter has two examples of negative speech, the partiality of 2:3 and the useless words of 2:16, although speech is not its main theme. Chapter 4 returns to the topic, referring to verbal struggles as 'wars and fighting' (4:1–2). The readers are explicitly commanded not to 'speak evil of' or 'judge' one another (4:11–12) and not to 'grumble' against one another (5:9). All this recalls Jesus' condemnation of angry outbursts and critical speech in Matthew 5:21–26.

The theological reason given for rejecting destructive speech is twofold. First and foremost, speech that judges or criticizes a fellow-Christian usurps the place of God. The Jews believed that God was the judge of the world. In the NT only John modifies the idea, and then only by the identification of Jesus as God's designated judge (John 5:22, 27). Thus the human being who criticizes or judges his or her fellow-believer is usurping God's throne. Given that the real Judge is 'at the door', this is not a good idea. Secondly, negative speech insults the image of God and by extension God himself (3:9). It is such speech rather than pious words in the Christian assembly, which reveals the true state of one's heart (3:10–12).

Two further examples of negative speech should be mentioned. The first is the confident speech of 4:13–17; these people assume that they can carry out their plans but fail to consult God about them. The second is the oaths of 5:12, with reference to which James echoes the teaching of Jesus in Matthew 5:33–37. In Matthew the stated reason for avoiding oaths is that anything more than a clear 'yes' or 'no' comes from the evil one, apparently because taking oaths at least tempts one to usurp prerogatives of God. In James the reason is that an oath can bring one under condemnation (presumably divine) for having violated it. All speech should be truthful, and there should be no levels of truthfulness (*i.e.* absolutely truthful speech if under oath and not so truthful speech if not).

Prayer

The proper use of speech is *prayer. This topic is discussed in three places in the book. First, in 1:5–7 the readers are urged to ask God for the wisdom they need. Such prayer should be 'in faith' without 'doubt'. The OT and Jewish literature clearly indicate that double-minded or double-hearted people are those who do not really trust God. They are trying both to trust in the world and their own resources, and to pray to God. Such duplicity is not prayer 'in faith'; it is trust in the world with God as an insurance policy. And it will receive nothing.

This principle is stated another way in 4:1–5. The people addressed here are praying that God will fulfil their selfish desires. They want to get on in the world; they want God to help. God will not answer such prayer. The people are rightly called to repent; they are 'double-minded' (4:8).

Proper prayer is described in 5:13–18, in three scenarios. The first is of a person who is being persecuted ('suffering'), and who is to pray, presumably for 'wisdom' (1:5) or endurance (5:7–11). The second is of a person who is happy, and who is to sing songs, presumably songs of praise to God.

The third scenario is of a person who is sick. James gives two sets of instructions, one involving prayer by elders, the other applying to the whole church. In the first the elders (the leaders of James' church) are to be called, probably because the person is too ill to attend the church meeting. They are to use

acted prayer (anointing with oil) and spoken prayer (the 'prayer of faith'), and God will respond with healing. While the form of prayer is based on the practice of Jesus' disciples (Mark 6:13), the focus of James' teaching is the response of God to prayer. The prayer is 'the prayer of faith', one made out of confident trust in God, not from mixed motives (which reveal that the person does not really trust God but looks on prayer as a last resort 'just in case'; *cf.* 1:7–8). God will respond to such a prayer in character, that is, with his good gifts of healing and forgiveness. The example of Elijah is cited to direct the readers' focus away from their human weakness and towards God.

James is well aware that *some* sickness is connected to sin (note the conditional clause, 'if'). Indeed, the confession of sins within the community ('to one another') is a prophylactic against illness. Yet he clearly implies that not all sickness is caused by sin, and that sin is no barrier to healing, for God as gladly forgives sin as he heals.

The elders have no special prerogatives, for when a person can attend the communal gathering all are exhorted to pray for healing; they are also to listen to the confessions of others. The reference to Elijah ('a human being just like us') encourages all Christians to expect their prayers to be effective.

Wealth

James' final theological contribution is to the Christian view of wealth. Here again he is building on the teaching of Jesus in the Sermon on the Mount (Matt. 6; Luke 6, 12). However in James the teaching is applied to a community experiencing economic persecution.

Sharing

The principal purpose of wealth, for James as for Jesus, is that it be shared with those in need. True religion is that which shares with the *poor (1:27). The works discussed in 2:14–26 involve sharing (2:15–16). Abraham and Rahab are cited because they are regarded by the Jews as models of charity (the binding of Isaac is viewed as the culmination of Abraham's works, and the sparing of Isaac as a response to Abraham's charity). The merchants in the community should not focus on their own plans for making money, but should do what they know to be good (4:17),

i.e. share with others. The rich are denounced because they take from the poor instead of sharing with them (5:1–6).

As James echoes Jesus' teaching about the use of wealth, so he shares Jesus' attitude towards wealth. The rich should rejoice in being humbled (1:9), for they will pass away like grass (1:10–11). They persecute the poor Christians (2:6–7), and are condemned for their deeds in 5:1–6 (of course, the people denounced in 5:1–6 did not think of their own deeds as evil, but as normal, legal business practices). No Christian is called 'rich' in the letter, and when Christians act like the rich (2:6) or try to increase their wealth (4:13–16) they are criticized. Wealth for James is dangerous at best and those who hold onto it instead of sharing it are not viewed positively.

James has a different view of the poor. The poor Christian is 'exalted' (1:9) and is an heir of the kingdom (2:5; *cf.* Luke 6:20). The poor are persecuted by the rich, but they should be patient, for the coming Lord will take up their cause (5:6–8). Thus for James 'poor' is an honourable name for people within the community, while 'rich' is reserved for those outside. The community itself is condemned when it favours the wealthy over the poor, for it is then taking the part of the rich, who persecute the church (2:1–6; note that the wealthy believer is obviously well-off, but never called 'rich').

The epistle of James, then, reveals a theology of the poor in line with the teaching of Jesus and significant strands of Jewish tradition before him, including that found in the Dead Sea Scrolls (which refer to their own community as 'the poor').

Faith

James discusses *faith in the context of his teaching on wealth. He uses the term in at least three ways. Sometimes, as in Paul and John, it refers to commitment to or confident trust in Jesus or God (*e.g.* 1:7–8). Elsewhere, as often in the pastoral epistles, it refers to Christian belief (2:1). But in 2:14–26 James defines faith as intellectual belief in the Jewish creed, the *Shema* ('God is one'). Such faith, devoid of works of charity, saves no one.

This passage has often been thought to reflect a conflict between James and Paul. While it is very likely that James is responding to an antinomian distortion of Paul's teach-

ing, he is not being critical of Paul himself. Not only is his definition of faith different from that of Paul; he also uses 'works' to refer to charity rather than to the ethnic markers of Judaism: circumcision and the observance of feast days and purity rules. Thus James is not debating with Paul, but with those who think that believing the right things about God and Christ is enough to save them. Saving faith, James says, includes obedience to Christ, the doing of works. Demons believe the truth; the true Christian obeys the truth.

Bibliography

W. R. Baker, *Personal Speech-Ethics in the Epistle of James* (Tübingen, 1995); A. Chester and R. P. Martin, *The Theology of the Letters of James, Peter, and Jude*, NTT (Cambridge, 1994); P. H. Davids, *A Commentary on the Epistle of James*, NIGTC (Grand Rapids and Carlisle, 1982, 1995); L. T. Johnson, *The Letter of James: A New Translation with Introduction and Commentary* (Garden City, 1995); R. P. Martin, *James*, WBC (Waco, 1988); T. C. Penner, *The Epistle of James and Eschatology* (Sheffield, 1996).

P. H. DAVIDS

1 PETER

Introduction

1 Peter is not a systematic treatment of Christian theology; nor does it present a complete picture of Petrine theology. The epistle is a practical document, in which the author expounds those theological themes most relevant to the circumstances of the readers. The first readers/hearers of the book were recently converted Christians (1:3, 18–19, 22–23; 2:2) who lived throughout the Roman provinces of Asia Minor (1:1). They were mostly Gentiles, who had recently abandoned an idol cult with its attendant debauchery (4:3; 1:14). Their rejection of the civic religion practised by their families and their radical change of lifestyle brought them into acute conflict with their contemporaries, an experience described as a 'painful trial' (4:12, NIV). While government officials may have been involved in the persecution at some point (2:13–17 may reflect official disapproval of the Christian sect), the hostilities

mainly took the form of social pressure against the Christian community, expressed publicly in both verbal and physical abuse. Christians were reviled (3:9), slandered (3:16), maligned (4:4) and denounced as criminals (2:12, 14; 4:15). Particularly where close social ties existed, such as those between masters and believing slaves (2:18–20) or husbands and Christian wives (3:1–7), there was the danger of physical hostility (4:1).

The reaction of the new Christians was grief (1:6; 2:19), fear (3:6, 14), bewilderment (4:12) and anxiety (5:7). The dishonour they suffered in their communities made them ashamed of their new faith (4:16), and they were tempted to retaliate in order to regain their honour (3:9; cf. 2:23). Some contemplated returning to their former lifestyle and abandoning their faith in Christ (4:2–3; 1:14); this was the goal of their adversary, the devil (5:8–9).

The setting in *salvation-history

1 Peter is addressed to Christians who, under pressure from the surrounding society, are tempted to relapse morally or to apostatize. The author shows them the true grace of *God and calls them to stand in it (5:12; cf. 1 Thess. 3:8; Eph. 6:11, 13–14). This 'grace' reflects the nature of God (5:10), and is expressed in his saving activity predicted by the prophets (1:10; see *Prophetic books) and to be realized fully at the future *revelation of Christ (1:13). The principal demonstration of this grace is the '*sufferings of Christ and the *glories that would follow' (1:11). Thus Peter emphasizes the transcendent saving activity of God which embraces past, present and future. He lifts his readers beyond their immediate temporal and social concerns and helps them to understand their place within the eternal purposes of God.

This plan, centred in *Jesus Christ, was generated before creation (1:20) and includes God's sovereign choice of his *elect (1:2) according to his determinative 'foreknowledge' (cf. 1:20). Issuing from this plan came the promises given by the 'Spirit of Christ' through the OT prophets (1:10–12), who predicted both the 'sufferings' and the 'glories' of Christ, the benefits of whose work are received by Christians in the present through the preaching of the gospel (1:12). The cross, resurrection, ascension and future revealing of Christ are the fundamental saving events in God's plan (see *Death and resurrection, *Exaltation). While the incarnation is mentioned briefly (1:20), there are several references to the 'sufferings of Christ and the glories that would follow' as the fulfilment of God's salvation (1:2, 3, 11, 18–21; 2:21–25; 3:18–22; 4:1, 13; 5:1; and implied in 2:4–8; 3:15; 4:11; 5:10). The 'sufferings of Christ' include his death on the cross for sins (2:24) as well as the sufferings he endured beforehand (2:21–23). The 'glories' are his resurrection (1:21), ascension and authority over all powers (3:18–20, 22), and his reappearance (1:13). The importance of these events is underlined by the author's eyewitness testimony to Christ's sufferings (5:1) and by the prophetic and angelic interest in the fulfilment of the prophetic hope (1:11–12). Christians have become participants in this saving plan: salvation is 'to/for' them (1:10, 12, 20, 25; 2:7, 9) and is 'now' realized in the time of fulfilment (1:12; 2:10; 3:21). The 'last times' are upon them (1:20; 4:7).

1 Peter also links the present and the future. Future salvation is one with present salvation (1:5, 9, 10–12; 3:21). Similarly, the *judgment of God also is realized in the past, present and future (3:20; 4:5, 17–18). The resurrection of Christ and his glorification are one with the glory of his future revealing (1:21; 4:13), and the grace of God in which Christians now stand (5:5b, 12) will be brought to them in full when Christ is revealed (1:13). The community's present praise and joy will continue beyond the end (1:3; 2:5; 4:11 and 1:6, 8; 4:13). The eschatology in 1 Peter is both realized and future (cf. 1:20 and 1:5) with the future being proleptically manifested in the present.

God

The sovereignty and transcendence of God dominate the theology of the epistle, and are important for its readers, who have emerged from paganism and are undergoing persecution. God is the faithful creator (4:19), the author of salvation-history (1:2, 20), the eternal one (implied in 1:25; 4:11; 5:10), the Almighty (4:11; 5:6, 11), and the God of glory (4:11, 14; 5:10), who keeps for believers their final inheritance (1:4), and who is judge of both the living and the dead (4:5; 1:17; 5:5b).

Yet despite this emphasis on God's transcendence, the author is also keenly aware of his presence with his people. He is the source of their life (1:3, 23) and guards them for their final salvation (1:5). His eyes are constantly upon them and his ears are open to their petitions (3:12; Ps. 34:12–16); he is invoked as their Father (1:17; *cf.* Matt. 6:9), who has chosen them (1:2) and given them new birth according to his great mercy (1:3). He supplies his grace for believers to serve one another (4:10–11). His Spirit rests on those who suffer (4:14), and he gives grace to the humble and the oppressed (5:5, 10). Christians are conscious of his presence (2:19), and Christ, like a shepherd, leads them to God (3:18). In their adversity, believers can be assured of God's care for them (5:7). Yet Peter reminds his readers that the one whom they call Father is also their impartial judge (1:17; 4:17), whom they should honour with reverential fear (1:17; 2:17; 3:2). He is the holy one (1:15–16; Lev. 19:2).

Christ

Christ is the pre-existent one (1:20), who is 'revealed in these last times' and whose Spirit spoke through the prophets (1:11). In describing the activity of Christ, the author focuses on his sufferings and glories (1:11), which include his redemptive suffering (2:24; 3:18), his resurrection from the dead (1:3, 21; 3:18) and the proclamation (at his ascension) of his victory and authority over all demonic forces (3:19–20, 22; *cf.* 5:8–9; see W. J. Dalton, *Christ's Proclamation to the Spirits*). At present Christ is not 'absent'; he is 'veiled' from sight until the time of his revealing (1:13; Peter does not speak of his 'coming', *parousia*). The time of this 'unveiling' is not far distant (1:7, 13; 4:7, 13; 5:4); Christ will bring both salvation and reward for the believers (1:4–7; 5:4) and judgment for their oppressors (4:5). Though Christ is not seen, faith and love can penetrate the 'veil' which hides him (1:8). Believers have tasted his kindness (2:3, possibly a reference to the eucharist) and have come to him (2:4); Christ in turn brings them to God (3:18). It is through Christ that the worship of the community is acceptable to God (2:5).

1 Peter includes an extremely high Christology. Jesus is both Christ and Lord (1:3), and in 3:15 Peter applies the reference to YHWH (LXX *kyrios*) in Isaiah 8:13 to Christ: 'But in your hearts set apart Christ as Lord.' In 2:6 he interprets the 'stone' in Isaiah 28:16 messianically; people's relationship to it

determines their eternal destiny (so also Paul in Rom. 9:33). In verses 7–8 he links this prophecy with Isaiah 8:14 and Psalm 118:22. But the transcendent and authoritative Christ also tenderly shepherds his sheep (2:25; 5:4) and has become their guardian (2:25).

The author's descriptions of Christ's character are full of OT imagery. He is called 'the righteous (one)' (3:18; Is. 53:11); as the suffering servant of Isaiah 53 (Is. 53:9, 7, 4 and 12, and 6a are echoed in 1 Pet. 2:22–25) he 'committed no sin' (2:22). He inaugurates the new covenant through the sprinkling of his blood (1:2; *cf.* Exod. 24:3–8), and just as the paschal lamb was a ransom paid for the deliverance of Israel from Egypt (1:18–19; Exod. 12:5–7), so his sacrifice redeems believers. He became a sin offering who bears the sins of the people (2:24; Heb. 9:28; Lev. 16:15–16).

The Spirit

Peter seldom refers to the Holy Spirit; yet he ascribes to the Spirit a significant place in salvation history. In 1:11 the Spirit, called here the 'Spirit of Christ' (which implies that Christ is pre-existent), is said to have inspired the OT prophets to foretell the sufferings and glories of Christ (*cf.* 2 Sam. 23:2; Acts 1:16; 28:25; 2 Pet. 1:21). These key events of salvation-history were then proclaimed to Peter's readers in the gospel 'by the Holy Spirit sent from heaven' (1:12; *cf.* Acts 1:8; 1 Cor. 2:4; 1 Thess. 1:5; Heb. 2:3–4). The Spirit's work also includes conversion or 'the sanctifying work' (1:2, perhaps an allusion to his activity in baptism; *cf.* 3:21). The persecuted believers are assured that the Spirit rests upon them (4:14) and indwells the community (2:5; *cf.* 1 Cor. 3:16).

The Christian community

Peter does not use the word '*church' (*ekklēsia*), but he identifies the Christian community with the OT *people of God. He sees the Christian community as the true *Israel of God and heir to the promises of God. Believers have entered into the new covenant (1:2; *cf.* Exod: 24:1–8) and await their inheritance (1:4; *cf.* Deut. 15:4; Dan. 12:13). They are the elect (1:1; *cf.* Deut. 4:37; Ps. 105:6) and 'strangers' of the Dispersion (1:1; Gen. 23:4; Lev. 25:23), and are properly called by titles previously ascribed to the people of God: 'chosen people, royal household, priesthood, holy nation, people of God's possession' (2:9, author's translation; Exod. 19:6; Is. 43:20–21). Christian women are called 'daughters of Sarah' (3:5–6) and typology connects baptized believers with Noah and others who were saved through the flood (3:20–21). Believers were formerly 'not a people' but now they are 'the people of God' (2:10; Hos. 2:23). They have been chosen by God (1:2) and their new existence as the people of God has given them the social stigma of being non-citizens and resident aliens (2:11; 1:1, 17). Although Elliott (*A Home for the Homeless*) argues that the readers were non-citizens before their conversion, Peter links their alien status with their election (1:1; 2:10–11). They are part of the 'dispersion' (1:1) scattered in this world and separated from their true inheritance, which is kept in heaven for them (1:4). Though rejected by their contemporaries, the Christians have a new social identity which is in continuity with that of the OT people of God and based on their new faith in God.

Peter reminds his readers that although they have no visible temple, they are 'being built into a spiritual house' (temple), and that they constitute a 'holy priesthood' who offer up 'spiritual sacrifices' (2:5 and 9). Christians are also witnesses in the communities in which they live, even in the face of severe opposition. They are called to 'declare the praises of him who called you out of darkness into his wonderful light' (2:9). They are not to disengage from society, but are to witness both in word and conduct (2:12; 3:16) in order both to silence their accusers (2:15) and to make them ashamed (3:16). Peter tells the believers that their conduct should in no way justify the ill treatment they receive (4:14–16; 2:18–20); rather it should be such that those who oppose them may be won to the faith (3:1–2; implied in 2:12). The despised Christians are even called to become benefactors in the communities in which they live (2:13–15; see Winter, *Seek the Welfare of the City*).

The sufferings believers endure are set within the larger framework of salvation-history. Peter presents Christ as the paradigm of those who suffer unjustly and do not then act unjustly themselves (2:21–23), though some aspects of Christ's suffering are inimitable (2:24–25). Believers are called to suffer (2:20b–21) according to the will of God (3:17; 4:19; 1:6), and in so doing they

'participate in the sufferings of Christ' (4:13). But just as his sufferings gave way to glory (1:11) so in their sufferings 'the Spirit of glory and of God' rests on them, and they are called to God's 'eternal glory in Christ' (5:10, 4). While they experience extreme dishonour in their towns and villages, they receive supreme honour from their God.

The community is exhorted to imitate the holiness of God (1:15–16; Lev. 11:44–45) and this call becomes the controlling imperative of the epistle. They should be 'holy in all [their] way of life' (1:15, author's translation); this is defined as 'doing good' (2:12, 15, 20; 3:6, 11, 13, 17), and is God's will for them (2:15; 4:2). The indicative of God's character contains within itself the imperative of their conduct. Similarly the indicative of Christ's innocence and non-retaliatory response to suffering (2:22–24) becomes an imperative for the community (2:21). Peter's call to those who contemplated a return to their pagan lifestyle is to 'act as God acts'. But he also exhorts them to live according to their new nature 'as obedient children' (1:14) and as those who have been 'purified' (1:22). Their lifestyle should reflect their existence as 'aliens and strangers' (2:11). Peter urges them, 'Act in accordance with your new identity!'

Bibliography

P. J. Achtemeier, *1 Peter*, Hermeneia (Minneapolis, 1996); D. L. Balch, *Let the Wives be Submissive* (Chico, 1981); F. W. Beare, *The First Epistle of Peter* (Oxford, [3]1970); E. Best, *1 Peter*, NCB (London and Grand Rapids, 1982); A. Chester and R. P. Martin, *The Theology of the Letters of James, Peter, and Jude*, NTT (Cambridge, 1994); W. J. Dalton, *Christ's Proclamation to the Spirits* (Rome, [2]1989); J. H. Elliott, *A Home for the Homeless* (Philadelphia, 1981); L. Goppelt, *A Commentary on 1 Peter*, MeyerK (ET, Grand Rapids, 1993); J. N. D. Kelly, *A Commentary on the Epistles of Peter and Jude*, BNTC (London and New York, 1969); E. G. Selwyn, *The First Epistle of St Peter* (London, [2]1955); C. H. Talbert (ed.), *Perspectives on 1 Peter* (Macon, 1986); B. W. Winter, *Seek the Welfare of the City* (Carlisle and Grand Rapids, 1994).

G. L. GREEN

2 PETER

2 Peter is presented as a farewell letter from the apostle, in which he seeks to combat the teaching of unethical behaviour and the denial of the return of *Jesus Christ and final *judgment. It makes extensive use of *Jude (virtually the whole content of Jude appears in the same order and often in the same words in 2 Peter 2) and focuses on the much debated topic of *eschatology.

Ethics

According to 2 Peter, human culture is corrupted by desire (cf. Jas. 1:14; see *James). Christian faith makes it possible to escape from these desires and to share in the divine nature. This unique expression is not explained in 2 Peter, although similar ideas are found in the Johannine literature (e.g. 1 John 3:9). It does not imply the divinization of the individual, but a sharing of the divine nature by the believer (perhaps equivalent to Paul's indwelling of God's Spirit or John's 'birth from above'). This participation in the divine nature is not something earned through human rites or effort, but is a gift of God that leads in turn to ethical living.

The teachers condemned in chapter 2 have, through their sexual indulgence, denied Christ (2:1; the denial is ethical rather than theological, as in 1 John), and have been trapped by desire once again (2:19–22). Secondary accusations made against them include greed and the slandering of fallen angels (cf. the same charges in Jude). The readers are exhorted instead to grow in virtue; this growth confirms their 'calling and election' and thus their eternal reward or entry into 'the eternal kingdom of our Lord and Saviour Jesus Christ' (1:3–11; 3:11, 14, NIV).

Eschatology

Apocalyptic eschatology is central to 2 Peter, since the false teachers reject the return of Christ and final judgment, instead teaching a steady-state universe (3:4). The argument is in six parts. First, in chapter 1 the expectation of Jesus' glorious return is based upon the apostolic *testimony to a proleptic glorification of Jesus in the transfiguration (1:16–18), which confirms previous prophetic announcements. Secondly, the final judgment with fire has already been prefigured by the judgment with water of Noah's time (3:5–7). Thirdly, the parousia (Christ's return) has not been delayed, for God works to his own timetable. He is patient, seeking the repentance and salvation of all people (3:8–10, 15). Fourthly, the Christian life is lived in the light of the transitory nature of the world as we know it and the permanence of the new heavens and new earth. Thus the promise of Isaiah 65:17–25, reflected in Revelation 21 – 22, is also found here. Fifthly, since Christians do not know God's timetable, 'the day of the Lord' will come as 'a thief', that is, unexpectedly; this echoes the teaching of Jesus (Matt. 24:36–44; cf. 25:1–13). Sixthly, Christian living seems to have an effect upon God's timetable, in that Christians not only wait for but also hasten the coming of the 'day of God' (3:12). This idea may be similar to the later rabbinic view that the purity of Israel would determine whether God brought the Messiah on schedule or delayed his coming. While the meaning of 2 Peter on this point is uncertain, the letter clearly teaches that the Lord will come, that the present world is impermanent, that it will be transformed and that there will be a final judgment. Thus the false teachers will receive their punishment, while the faithful believers will receive their reward.

Scripture

The basis for this eschatology is twofold. First, the *prophetic teaching of the OT warns of God's judgment. This teaching is not mere human insight, but divinely inspired (1:19–21). We do not know which scriptures the author regards as prophetic. Interestingly, he tones down or eliminates Jude's references to non-canonical writings, and like Jude his explicit references to the canonical books are all to the Pentateuch, with only allusions to the OT prophets. As a good Jew he takes the Pentateuch as his focal point and Moses as his chief prophet, using the rest of the OT to support their teaching.

Secondly, the apostolic witness to Jesus includes warnings of judgment; of all NT figures it is Jesus who spoke most extensively on the subject. This witness comprises narratives about Jesus (e.g. the story of the transfiguration, cited above) and the teachings of Jesus (3:2).

2 Peter is the first work to refer explicitly to part of the NT, namely the letters of Paul.

These were probably being used by the teachers to justify their immorality as 'freedom in Christ'; thus Peter notes that these letters, as well as the OT prophets, have been misinterpreted by the teachers he is condemning. Since 1:20 and 3:15 are the only place where 2 Peter uses the Greek term *graphē* (writing, Scripture) he obviously thinks it permissible to group Paul's writings with those of the OT prophets, just as in 3:2 he groups the OT prophetic writings with the (largely oral) teaching of the apostles. This represents the first stage in the development of a written NT canon. We do not know what is meant by 'all his letters' (3:16), that is, whether the author is aware of a collection of Paul's letters or knows only that Paul has written several; so we cannot tell which letter or letters are being misinterpreted by the teachers.

Bibliography

R. J. Bauckham, *Jude, 2 Peter*, WBC (Waco, 1983); A. Chester and R. P. Martin, *The Theology of the Letters of James, Peter, and Jude*, NTT (Cambridge, 1994); J. H. Neyrey, *2 Peter, Jude*, AB (New York and London, 1993); A. Vögtle, *Der Judasbrief, der Zweite Petrusbrief* (Solothurn/Neukirchen-Vluyn, 1994).

P. H. DAVIDS

THE JOHANNINE LETTERS

Introductory matters

As brief and as apparently simple as they are, the three Johannine letters have stirred enormous controversy, both academic and popular. The Greek is deceptively simple; two of the three letters boast fewer than three hundred words; some of the principal themes of 1 John are elucidated in the Fourth Gospel. Nevertheless disputes abound, focused not least on the following areas.

1. *The setting of the letters.* The majority view, probably correctly, argues for a setting towards the end of the 1st century, as the church (probably in Asia Minor) is beginning to face the pressure of incipient Gnosticism. That stance has a bearing on how we understand some of the biblical-theological issues, especially in 1 and 2 John.

2. *The concrete setting of 3 John* is particularly difficult to construct, with its sharply polemical language by the 'elder' regarding Diotrephes and those he controls. All reconstructions, of course, involve some 'mirror reading', the attempt to infer what the other side is saying when one can listen in to only one side of a debate or a conversation. In this instance, the most radical proposal is that Diotrephes represents the 'orthodox' church leader who is attempting to hold the line against an invasive and power-hungry 'elder'. Thus the 'wrong' side made it into the canon. That sort of reconstruction necessarily makes a number of judgments about the *Johannine writings generally that are far from persuasive. In any case, the issue is not merely technical; one's perception of the contribution of 3 John to biblical theology depends rather heavily (as we shall see) on one's conclusions regarding such debates.

3. Somewhat less important, from the perspective of grasping these letters' biblical theology, is *their chronological relation to *John's Gospel.* Were they written before the Gospel, or after? Or some before, and some after? Judgments on these matters affect some of the 'fine tuning' of the exegesis (and therefore of the biblical theology), but do not significantly modify the most central points.

4. *The assumption that they are written by the same hand, and by the same hand that wrote the Fourth Gospel,* enables the interpreter the more easily to appeal to parallels among these documents for mutual clarification; but these two assumptions are constantly challenged.

The biblical theological contribution of 2 John and 3 John

Of the three Johannine letters, 1 John and 2 John are the closest in terms of theme, while 2 John and 3 John are the closest in terms of form and brevity. Unlike the first two Johannine epistles, 3 John makes no specific mention of heretical beliefs or practice. The elder assumes that Diotrephes ought to receive his messengers, but that he does not do so because he 'loves to be first' (v. 9, NIV) and is engaged in a power play that has manipulated his local *church into a stance that excludes the elder and his emissaries.

This much is undisputed. But these raw elements have a bearing on three important issues. *First,* the most reasonable answer to the question of why the elder thinks he should have a fundamental hearing in the church where Diotrephes is in charge is that this particular elder is the apostle John. Like Peter, John thinks of himself as a fellow elder (1 Pet. 5:1). Just as Paul faced opponents in a variety of churches he oversaw, and insisted on obedience (*e.g.* 1 Cor. 14:37–38), so also here; John knows that Diotrephes' love of preeminence is not only intrinsically evil in the church of the crucified Redeemer, but if it leads to excluding the authority of the apostolic witness the dangers are extreme. *Secondly*, this brief epistle offers a vignette of church governance just before a major shift took place. Since the work of Lightfoot, it has been widely recognized that during the NT period there were only two offices in the local church: the deacon, and the elder-pastor–overseer (= bishop). In other words, extension of the bishop's work to include oversight of other elder-pastors did not take place until the second century, after the writing of the NT documents was complete. The apostles and their emissaries maintained a supervisory role, but their status could not, in the nature of the case, be institutionalized. But as John faces dangers towards the end of the 1st century, dangers from powermongers within (3 John) and from schismatic heretics without (though they had originally split off from the church; 1 John and 2 John), his solution is not to introduce a new level of supervisory administration, but to call the church back to what was 'from the beginning' (a recurrent phrase) and was tightly bound up with apostolic witness. In later centuries, the church often tried to identify itself through its succession of bishops; John insists that the church identify itself by its maintenance of what was 'from the beginning' and taught by the founding apostles. *Thirdly*, the elder's denunciation of Diotrephes discloses what should be clear from any careful reading of the NT documents; qualifications for Christian *leadership include not only doctrinal firmness but also a certain gentleness, a transparent humility, even when strong action must be taken (*cf.* 2 Cor. 10 – 13; 1 Tim. 3:1–7; Titus 1:5–9). This is not an optional extra for specially endowed leaders. Rather, it is mandated for all leaders of the followers of the Crucified. The desire to be first is a disqualification for Christian leadership.

If 3 John finds the elder threatening a church that has become too narrow because of the manipulative control of a Diotrephes, 2 John finds him warning a church (under the guise of 'the chosen lady and her children', v. 1) to be careful of itinerant preachers who are full of what we would today call 'spirituality' but who have left behind what the Christians had learned 'from the beginning' (v. 6). The love of novelty combined with admiration for piety easily breeds an irresponsible tolerance for theological rubbish. One remembers the wisdom of the old preacher: 'You say I am not with it? / My friend, I do not doubt it. / But when I see what I'm not with / I'd rather be without it.'

The biblical theological contribution of 1 John

Readers who pay close attention to the text of 1 John cannot fail to notice the close similarity between its language and the language of John's Gospel. Yet the differences are at times almost as striking. 1 John 1:1 seems at first glance, like the Johannine prologue (John 1:1, 14), to assign the title 'Word' to the incarnate Son who was heard and seen and touched. Yet 1 John 1:2 promptly takes a slightly different direction: it is the 'life' that appeared and was seen, rather than the Word. Again, both documents insist that the purpose of writing was to encourage people to believe; yet the Gospel casts this in terms of fundamental mandate (John 20:30–31), while the first epistle tells us it was written to grant *assurance to those who believe (1 John 5:13).

Even a quick and superficial reading of 1 John discloses that John circles around three themes. He insists that genuine believers hold certain *truths about *Jesus, in particular that he is the Christ, the Son of God, while those who deny this point are liars and deceivers (2:22–23; 4:2). Moreover, genuine believers are *obedient to Christ's commands (2:3–6; 3:7–10); the heretics whom John condemns and who were once members of the church (2:19) are conspicuous for their disobedience. And finally, genuine believers are characterized by transparent and practical *love for one another (2:9–11; 3:11–18), while the defectors display a haughty condescension.

Since the time of Robert Law (*The Tests of Life*), these three themes have often been referred to as John's three 'tests': the truth test, the moral test, and the social test; or, otherwise put, the test of doctrine, the test of obedience, and the test of love. Yet one must recognize that in John's hands these 'tests' are not so much presented as standards by which the church may exclude certain people (for in this case the defectors have already withdrawn and do not need to be excluded), even though they could conceivably exercise that role. Rather, John writes 'these things', *i.e.* about these tests, so as to reassure the genuine believers (5:13). It appears that these believers, perhaps under the pressure from those who had left them for a more 'advanced' spirituality, were in danger of doubting their status.

Four additional characteristics of these so-called 'tests' may illuminate John's contribution to biblical theology. *First*, although it is common to speak of three discrete tests, in the last two chapters of his first epistle John intertwines them. If Jesus commands us and we must obey, one of his commands (indeed, his primary command) is to love. Moreover, if one loves God, then of course one will obey him (5:2). Thus the test of obedience and the test of love are tightly tied together. Moreover, it is the person who believes the truth (that Jesus truly is the Christ) who is born of God, and whoever is born of God will surely love others who are born of God (5:1). Further, the person who overcomes the world and therefore obeys God's commands is none other than the one who believes 'that Jesus is the Son of God' (5:5). Thus the truth test is interlocked with both the love test and the obedience test. In fact, John multiplies such links, so that one should perhaps not speak of three tests so much as of three facets of one comprehensive vision. One cannot pass one or two out of three of these tests; in John's view, they stand or fall together. Christian authenticity can never rightly be negligent of love while virulently defending the truth, or vice versa. John sees the holism of the Christian vision. Moreover, he is in line with other NT passages that threaten the severest penalties for those who teach major doctrinal deviation (*e.g.* Gal. 1:8–9), who conduct themselves in massive disobedience to God (1 Cor. 6:9–11), or who prove persistently loveless and divisive (Titus 3:10); the so-called three tests of 1 John carry many faces in the NT documents. Intertwined, they make it clear to the Christian believer that the presence of these elements of Christian belief

and conduct makes its own contribution to Christian assurance (1 John 5:13), and, further, that the only alternative to the total bundle is sheer idolatry (5:21).

Secondly, although contemporary scholars commonly speak of three tests in 1 John, a handful add a fourth. For several passages speak either of an 'anointing' (presumably of the *Holy Spirit) that has been given us, or of the Holy Spirit directly (2:20, 27; 3:24), in contexts designed to engender assurance: 'But you have an anointing from the Holy One, and all of you know the truth' (2:20); 'And this is how we know that he lives in us: We know it by the Spirit he gave us' (3:24). Some link such passages to the 'witness of the Spirit' theme of which Paul speaks (Rom. 8:15–16). But the question that must be asked is this: does 1 John present this 'anointing' or this work of the Spirit as something discernibly different or at least distinguishable from the three tests that lie on the surface of the text? In other words, does the anointing constitute a fourth and separate evidence for the work of God? Or does the context of each passage suggest that the manifestation of the Spirit's anointing is precisely in the observable three tests to which reference has already been made? Contextually, the latter appears to be the more defensible position. In any case, to add or subtract one more test is not of ultimate importance in a book which so diligently intertwines its tests in order to emphasize that Christian doctrine, life and love stand or fall together.

Thirdly, although the three tests are used by John to engender assurance (5:13), and although all of them are in the domain of observable conduct, it would be quite mistaken to infer that John ultimately *grounds* Christian assurance on personal conduct. It is not as if John is saying, 'Your beliefs, your obedience, and your love are so rich that you are entitled to Christian assurance.' After all, he recognizes that the Christian's confidence before God, when we sin, finally turns on Jesus Christ and what he accomplished on the cross (2:2), and this in turn is grounded in God's matchless love in sending his Son (4:7–12). On this point, John is in entire agreement with Paul. But John insists that there is another element in Christian assurance, viz. the evidence of a transformed life. Such evidence provides not the ultimate ground of confidence (that is reserved for Christ and his cross), but a subsidiary appeal to the confirmation of a life transformed by the gospel, since it is unthinkable that a life that has truly known the power of the gospel should not have been changed by it.

Fourthly, John's style of writing, not least the implacability and absolutism of his tests, serve as a necessary complement to other canonical writings. Not for John the anguished searching of Ecclesiastes or Job; not for him the intricate theological argumentation of Romans. Nevertheless, his voice is not less important than theirs. True, absolute criteria without the voices of anguish or of even-handed evaluation could easily become harsh, legalistic, even demeaning; on the other hand, anguished voices and even-handed evaluation ('on the one hand', 'on the other hand') easily dissolve into moral relativism without the absolutes of a John to stiffen their spine. Christianity is not infinitely plastic. It embraces truth, the denial of which merely proves one is not a Christian; it defines conduct, the systematic flouting of which demonstrates one is outside the camp. Precisely because our age thinks that ambiguity and relativism are signs of intellectual and even moral maturity, John's immovable tests are the more necessary as we seek to construct inductively-shaped biblical theology.

Other themes come to unique expression in 1 John, even though they are tied to broader NT structures. 'Remaining in' is a favourite locution: the truth remains in believers, believers in Christ, and so forth. In common with much of the NT, John lives with the tension between inaugurated and futurist *eschatology, but he applies it not only to the Christian's hope (3:1–3) but also to the antichrist; the antichrist expected at the end (whose coming John does not deny) has already appeared in many antichrists (2:18). Many biblical writings describe the love of God, but only this epistle sums the matter up with the declaration 'God is love' (4:8), which can never be reduced to mere sentimentalism because the ensuing discussion presupposes that the most spectacular display of God's love is in the cross. Numerous phrases and expressions connect this letter with the Fourth Gospel and its larger theological framework (*e.g.* 'No one has ever seen God', 4:12, *cf.* John 1:18; 'the Saviour of the world', 4:14, *cf.* John 4:42).

Finally, although 1 John never cites the OT in an unambiguous and extensive citation, and although the only OT person named in the epistle is Cain (3:12), there are several deeper links that are sometimes overlooked. Some of these are *covenantal in nature (see J. Pryor, *John*). One of the most important is bound up with John's strong and repeated insistence that his readers, because of the anointing from the Holy One, already know the truth, and do not need anyone to teach them (2:20, 27). Sceptical critics (*e.g.* R. E. Brown) detect in such passages little more than Johannine hypocrisy: after all, what is John doing but teaching them himself? But that question misses the point. John is almost certainly thinking of passages such as Jeremiah 31:31–34. They promise that under the new covenant the people of God will no longer need teachers to tell them, 'Know the Lord', for they will all know him, from the least to the greatest. Within the framework of the old covenant there were appointed prophets, priests and kings whose first task was to mediate God to the covenant community at large. Under the new covenant, however, all would have genuine knowledge of God. Jeremiah does not so much anticipate the abolition of teachers as the abolition of mediating teachers, teachers with privileged access to God. Under the new covenant, there is no need for mediating teachers, for all know God, any more than for priests, for all are priests. Such teachers as the new covenant prescribes are seen as members of the body rather than as priestly mediators. John's readers, intimidated by those who claimed some sort of super-spiritual access denied to others, needed to be reminded of this fundamental feature of the new covenant: no one may legitimately claim a privileged status with God, on the basis of some role or office or experience. It is a biblical-theological emphasis not uncommon in the NT (however variously it is shaped), and it is needed no less today than in John's day.

Bibliography

R. E. Brown, *The Epistles of John*, AB (New York, 1982); D. A. Carson, *The Epistles of John*, NIGTC (Grand Rapids and Carlisle, forthcoming); R. Law, *The Tests of Life: A Study of the First Epistle of St. John* (Grand Rapids [3]1979); J. M. Lieu, *The Second and Third Epistles of John: History and Background* (Edinburgh, 1986); *idem*,

The Theology of the Johannine Epistles, NTT (Cambridge, 1991); J. B. Lightfoot, *Saint Paul's Epistle to the Philippians* (Grand Rapids [12]1953); I. H. Marshall, *The Epistles of John*, NICNT (Grand Rapids, 1978); J. Pryor, *John: Evangelist of the Covenant People* (London, 1992); R. Schnackenburg, *The Johannine Epistles* (New York and Tunbridge Wells, 1992); J. R. W. Stott, *The Letters of John: An Introduction and Commentary*, TNTC (Leicester and Grand Rapids, [2]1988).

D. A. CARSON

JUDE

Written by Jude, the brother of James (who was a leader of the Jerusalem church in the mid-1st century), this letter points to some of the difficulties facing the church in that period, *i.e.* teachers who have entered the local Christian community from outside and who practise an immoral lifestyle. The style of the letter is that of prophetic denunciation, making Jude sound like one of the OT prophets.

Ethics

Jude's major concern is ethics. The false teachers are accused of denying Christ (v. 4), who is described as 'our only Master and Lord' (NRSV). But the specific charges Jude brings indicate ethical rather than doctrinal departure from Jesus: to call Jesus 'Lord' and reject his ethical teaching is just as much a denial of him as to deny he is 'Lord'. Two types of ethical departure are described: 1. sexually immoral living and 2. personal greed. Both were temptations for the early church. The concept of liberty in Christ and the treating of all female believers as sisters could lead to self-justified sexual encounters. The model of paying teachers in the Hellenistic world often led to similar demands within the church (rabbis did not receive reimbursement during the 1st century).

Scripture

In condemning the false teachers Jude draws heavily on the OT as interpreted by his Jewish contemporaries. Specifically, he cites examples of judgment from the pre-patriarchal period (*e.g.* Noah) through to the end of the wilderness wanderings (*e.g.* Balaam). All except two of these examples are from the Pentateuch, but no teaching of Moses himself is cited. There are only allusions to the prophets. Jude also cites *1 Enoch* 1:9 (vv. 14–15), alludes to *1 Enoch* (*e.g.* v. 6), and refers to a story from the *Testament of Moses* (v. 9). Jude expects these narratives to be accepted as evidence that God judges evil, and thus as warnings not to engage in the practices of the false teachers.

Theology and angelology

Concerning angelology (see *Spiritual powers), we learn that the 'sons of God' of Genesis 6:1-4 were angels, whose liaisons with human women were evil and who will be judged in the final *judgment. Angelic hosts are associated with the coming of 'the Lord' (v. 14). One archangel, Michael, is named (*cf.* Dan. 10:13, 21), and is seen defending the reputation of Moses against the devil.

While this world is the scene of conflict, both between the true faith and that of the false teachers and between Michael and the devil, God is above the conflict. God exists as God, the Holy Spirit, and 'our Lord Jesus Christ'. Since every unambiguous instance of the word 'Lord' (vv. 4, 21, 25) refers to Jesus, it is probable that 'the Lord rebuke you' (v. 9, *cf.* Zech. 3:2) and 'the coming Lord' (v. 14) also refer to him, in contrast to their OT background. The false teachers feel they can curse and defeat dark powers on their own, but Michael, the glorious archangel, appeals to the Lord to execute justice. It is precisely this Lord who will come in judgment at the end of the age.

While Jude speaks of judgment, he also knows of *grace. While the primary exhortation is for the believers to remain firm in the faith, they are also to 'have mercy on' or 'save' others, even if it means 'snatching them out of the fire [of hell]'. Thus even if some are teetering on the brink of the fire, they can still be saved, although those who persist in their error will certainly face the ultimate judgment of God.

Bibliography

R. J. Bauckham, *Jude, 2 Peter*, WBC (Waco, 1983); A. Chester and R. P. Martin, *The Theology of the Letters of James, Peter, and Jude*, NTT (Cambridge, 1994); J. H. Neyrey, *2 Peter, Jude*, AB (New York and London, 1993); A. Vögtle, *Der Judasbrief, der Zweite Petrusbrief*, EKK (Solothurn/Neu-kirchen-Vluyn, 1994).

P. H. DAVIDS

REVELATION (BOOK)

Introduction

Revelation, which comes at the very end of the biblical canon, combines three distinctive literary types to form a most remarkable book. As its opening sentences reveal it is, at the same time, an 'apocalypse' or '*revelation', a '*prophecy' and a 'letter'. The first of these terms has now become a technical term for a body of literature, mainly Jewish, which developed in the two centuries before the birth of *Jesus Christ, although the style is probably best exemplified in the much earlier book of *Daniel. These apocalyptic writings were viewed as revealing heavenly secrets, normally inaccessible to human beings, sometimes focusing on *God's *judgment of the wicked and his deliverance of the righteous. As a prophecy Revelation claims to be a message from God which invites a response of trust and *obedience from John's contemporaries. Finally, the book is presented in the form of a letter, sent from John to those churches 'in the province of Asia' for whom he had a special concern. The distinctive nature of the book of Revelation must always be borne in mind when reading it, especially as John develops a number of significant theological themes by utilizing OT scripture, Jewish interpretative traditions on the OT and early Christian tradition.

Suffering and victory

As in John's Gospel, so in John's Revelation, the death and defeat of Christ is, in reality, his *victory over Satan (see *e.g.* 5:5–6). The *Lamb's followers are to recapitulate the model of his ironic victory in their own lives; by means of *enduring* through *tribulation* they reign in the invisible *kingdom* of the Messiah (see 1:6, 9). They exercise kingship in the midst of their *suffering just as Christ did from the cross; Christians are called to be conquerors by emulating in their own lives the archetypal messianic triumph of Jesus. Though the Christian's outer body is vulnerable to persecution and suffering, God has promised to protect the regenerated inner spirit of true

saints (see 11:1–7). And at the end of the sojourn of Christ's body (the *church) on earth, its presence, like his, will be completely removed, and then it will be resurrected (see 11:7–12 and *cf.* 20:11 – 22:5).

Conversely, the church's opponents defeat themselves spiritually when they persecute God's *people in the same manner as Satan (see *Spiritual powers) was defeated at the cross, though it appeared that he had won a physical victory over Christ (*cf.* Col. 2:14–15). Acts of oppression against the saints, when not *repented of, lay an increasing foundation for the oppressors' final judgment, and even become expressions of a judgment of *hardening by God upon permanently recalcitrant people.

The main goal of the argument of John's Revelation is to exhort God's people to remain *faithful to the calling of following the Lamb's paradoxical example and not to compromise, in order that they may inherit final *salvation. The major theological theme of the book is that God receives *glory, as a result of accomplishing full salvation and final judgment (see 1:6; 4:11; 5:11–13; 19:1, 5, 7; *cf.* 11:17). Even the notion of Christ and the church reigning ironically in the midst of their suffering and the idea of unbelieving persecutors experiencing spiritual defeat in the midst of their physical victories demonstrate the *wisdom of God, and point accordingly to his glory (see 5:12 for the link between the slain Lamb, wisdom and divine glory, which is not found in the hymns of praise at the end of ch. 4).

Revelation 4 – 5 form the introduction to the remainder of the book's visions up to 22:5; this introduction overshadows everything in 6:1 – 22:5. Therefore a clear understanding of the main point of Revelation 4 – 5 is essential; God and Christ are *glorified* because Christ's resurrection demonstrates that they are sovereign over *creation to judge and to redeem. The focus of this primary point in chapters 4 – 5 is upon the glory of God and the Lamb. The clear deduction from these two chapters is that the Lamb is in the same divine position as God, a point reiterated throughout the remainder of the book, and intimated earlier (*cf.* e.g. 1:13–14).

The theological significance of the image of the throne

The vision of Revelation 4 – 5 portrays a

*heavenly world in which God and the Lamb's throne are the centre and everything else is configured in a series of outer circles around the throne apparently in the following order: 1. a rainbow aura; 2. the 'living creatures' who guard the throne; 3. the twenty-four elders sitting on twenty-four thrones in a second outer circle; 4. all other creatures in the universe. Seventeen of the thirty-four references in the book to God's 'throne' occur in chapters 4 – 5, a fact which underlines the centrality of God's sovereignty (see *Providence) for which he is given glory climactically in 4:9–11 and 5:12–13.

All the following visions flow out of this introductory vision and are to be seen as the historical consequences of divine sovereignty. For example, the visions of the seals and trumpets, the unnumbered visions (chs. 12 – 14) and the visions of the bowls (together with the appended visions of chs. 17 – 19) show the results in past, present and future history of divine sovereignty in its *redemption and judgment.

Therefore God and Christ are in ultimate control of all the woes of both believers and unbelievers. Their absolute sovereignty over such unpleasant events poses a theological problem: how can the *righteousness, goodness and *holiness of Christ and God be maintained if they are so directly linked, as the ultimate cause, to all the judgments, and to their associated demonic agents who actually carry out many of the destructive judgments under ultimate divine supervision?

Some commentators do not think that there is a theological problem, since they do not view Christ and God as the ultimate cause of the judgments. Some scholars use theological presuppositions about God's holiness and love in order to deny the direct link, and consequently assert that Christ only 'permits' or 'tolerates' such characters as the four horsemen to execute their woes (e.g. G. B. Caird, Revelation, pp. 81–83). However, not only does Revelation see the divine throne as ultimately behind the trials of believers and woes of unbelievers, but the major OT passages formative for the visions of the seals, trumpets and bowls, without exception, portray God as the ultimate cause of the ordeals (so Zech. 6:1–8; Ezek. 14:21; Lev. 26:18–28 and their use in 6:2–8).

The answer to the theological difficulty lies in the ultimate purpose of the woes being that of refining the faith of believers and punishing unbelievers. For example, the four horsemen's woes of 6:1–8 are an effect of Christ's death and resurrection (chs. 4 – 5). He transformed the suffering of the cross into a triumph, gained sovereignty over the powers of evil who crucified him (cf. Rev. 1:18; Col. 2:15), and subsequently uses them to achieve his purposes of refining his people and punishing those recalcitrant in their wickedness.

As at the end of chapters 4 and 5, so also towards the end of the visionary segment in Revelation 19:7–8, the author affirms that saints are to glorify God. This glorification occurs at the conclusion of history because of the consummation of the marriage of the Lamb with his bride, who will be perfectly adorned for the occasion; focus on the adorned bride is intended to lead the saints to glorify God. This notion of divine glory is central also to Revelation 21:1 – 22:5, since the new *Jerusalem (God's people) can be defined only in relation to its luminescent reflection of God's glory. Indeed, the central feature of the city is God and the Lamb who shine as a lamp upon the city (cf. 21:22–23; 22:5), so that the more complete definition of the new Jerusalem includes God's people in full fellowship with God and Christ, the former reflecting the glory of the latter.

The new creation as the goal of redemption and history

The portrayal of the new *covenant, new *temple, new *Israel and new Jerusalem affirms the future fulfilment of the main prophetic themes of the OT and NT, which all find their ultimate climax in the new creation. The new creation itself is the most overarching of these themes, of which the other four are but facets (see W. J. Dumbrell, The End of the Beginning). John's repeated allusions to the OT historical form of these five concepts expresses a typological interpretation of history which views OT institutions and other realities as prophetic foreshadowings of escalated and equivalent NT realities: e.g. Genesis 1 creation, the *Exodus as fulfilment of the divine covenant and as new creation, the tabernacle, Solomonic temple, old Jerusalem, etc. These typological and prophetic themes suggest a belief in God as the sovereign designer of all history, which is planned to result in his glory. All five of the central biblical ideas of new covenant, new temple, new Israel, new Jerusalem and new creation are metaphorical ideas which refer to the same reality, God's intimate, glorious presence with his people.

These same five themes together culminate in 21:1 – 22:5 and form the climax and major goal of the entire book up to Revelation 22:5. In particular, the central notion of God's glorious presence is introduced in Revelation 4 – 5 and developed throughout the book, and finally culminates in the last visions of Revelation 21:1 – 22:5. These concluding visions of Revelation, however, do not express the main point of the whole book. 21:1 – 22:5 is placed at the conclusion of John's work to underline John's ultimate purpose in writing: to encourage and admonish Christians to remain faithful. This is why the book concludes with a non-visionary, auditory epilogue of repeated promises, exhortations and affirmations of Christ's imminent coming, and warnings to the saints in 22:6–21. The vision of the future, perfected people of God in unending fellowship with his glorious presence is intended to encourage and motivate them to persevere through temptations (see *Testing) to compromise. The prospect of final victory should provide impetus to win partial victory now by not compromising.

The main reason that the bride is contrasted with the prostitute in 17:1 – 22:5 is to encourage and admonish the faltering churches, troubled by compromise with the whore, to stop compromising and reflect in greater measure the features of their coming, consummated excellence in anticipation of it. This point is suggested by the antithetical correspondence between the imperfections of the churches in chapters 2 – 3 and the perfections found in 21:1 – 22:5.

Furthermore, an exegetical analysis of 21:1 – 22:5 reveals that a number of the OT prophecies which are viewed as reaching fulfilment at the conclusion of history are viewed elsewhere in the NT as having already begun to be fulfilled in Christ and the church: e.g. new creation, new temple, apostles as a foundation of the temple, new Jerusalem, the promise of God's tabernacling presence in 21:3, and the kingship of the saints. Even elsewhere in Revelation it is apparent that these prophecies have already begun to be fulfilled in the latter part of the 1st century: e.g. new creation (3:14), new temple

(cf. lampstands of 1:12–13, 20, exalted saints in the heavenly temple in 6:9–11), and kingship (1:5b–6, 9, 13; 2:27; 3:21; 5:10). New creation, as the broad redemptive-historical theme, subsumes the promissory ideas of new temple, new covenant, new Israel and new Jerusalem.

The new temple

The paradisal city-temple of Revelation 21:1 – 22:5 encompasses the entirety of the newly created earth: 1. Isaiah 54:2–3, together with several Jewish references, supports the notion of a new Jerusalem or end-time temple greater than the former Jerusalem and temple. 2. John says in Revelation 21:1 that he saw 'a new heaven and new earth', and then in 21:2 and 21:9 – 22:5 he, in fact, sees only a paradisal city-temple. It is possible that he first saw the whole heavens and earth in 21:1 and then subsequently the city-temple which is part of that new cosmos. It is, however, more likely that the 'new heaven and new earth' of 21:1 is defined by and equated with the paradisal city-temple of 21:2 and 21:9 – 22:5. The allusion to Isaiah 65:17 in Revelation 21:1 supports this view.

The rationale for the world-encompassing nature of the paradisal temple lies in the ancient notion that the OT temple was a microcosmic model of the entire heaven and earth. Josephus and Philo discuss various ways in which the tabernacle or temple or parts of it symbolically reflect the cosmos (Philo, De Vita Mosis 2:71–145; Josephus, Antiquities of the Jews 3:123, 179–187; in Jewish Wars 4:324 priests are referred to as leading the 'cosmic worship' [tēs kosmikēs thrēskeias]. While it is true that Philo and Josephus had different interpretations of the symbolism, it is probable that they both testify to a general cosmological understanding of the temple held in mainstream contemporary Jewish thought (see also M. G. Kline, Images of the Spirit, pp. 41–47, and V. S. Poythress, The Shadow of Christ in the Law of Moses, pp. 13–35, who make many of the same and similar observations about the temple and the priestly garments as do Philo and Josephus). Ancient Near Eastern literature also relects the notion that temples of the gods were microcosmic models of heavenly temples or of the universe.

This cosmic understanding of the temple

implicitly suggested that its purpose was to point to a future time when it would encompass the whole world (much like an architect's model of a newly planned building is but a small replica of what is to be built on a much larger scale). Since the OT temple was the localized dwelling of God's presence on earth, the temple's correspondence with the cosmos pointed to the *eschatological goal of God's presence tabernacling throughout the earth, an eschatological goal which Revelation 21:1 – 22:5 appears to describe (*cf.* 21:3).

Revelation 22:1–5 suggests that the author is aware of an earlier cultic interpretation of Eden. The Garden of Eden was the archetypal temple in which the first human worshipped God. Israel's temple was the place where the *priest experienced God's unique presence, and Eden was the place where Adam walked and talked with God. Genesis 2:15 says that God placed Adam in the Garden 'to cultivate (work) it and keep it'. The two Hebrew words for 'cultivate and keep' are usually translated 'serve and guard' elsewhere in the OT, often in association with priestly service in the tabernacle/temple. The writer of Genesis 2 possibly suggests that Adam was the archetypal priest who served in and guarded God's first temple. When Adam failed to guard the temple by sinning and letting in an unclean serpent to defile the sanctuary, Adam lost his priestly role and the two cherubim took over the responsibility of 'guarding' the Garden temple: God 'stationed the cherubim ... *to guard* the way to the tree of life' (so Gen. 3:24). Probably their role was recalled in Israel's later temple in the two cherubim stationed on either side of the ark of the covenant in the Holy of Holies. The 'tree of life' itself was probably the model for the lampstand placed directly outside the Holy of Holies. That the Garden of Eden was the first temple is also suggested by the fact that Israel's later temple had wooden carvings which gave it a garden-like atmosphere (1 Kgs. 6:18, 29, 32, 35; 7:18–20). The entrance to Eden was from the east (Gen. 3:24), which was also the direction from which one entered the tabernacle and later temples of Israel.

According to Genesis 1:28, not only was Adam to 'guard' this sanctuary, but he was also to subdue the earth. It seems that he was to extend the geographical boundaries of the Garden until Eden extended through-out and covered the whole earth. What Adam failed to do, Revelation pictures Christ as finally having done. The Edenic imagery beginning in Revelation 22:1 shows that the building of the temple which began in Genesis 2 will be completed in Christ and his people and will encompass the whole new creation.

The new covenant

The affirmation in Revelation 21:3–4 that God's dwelling is now with human beings and that 'they will be his people, and God himself will be with them and be their God' (NIV) indicates that the new creation, towards which history is moving, will bring to fulfilment the new covenant promised in the book of Jeremiah and inaugurated by Jesus Christ. In essence, like the Sinai covenant which foreshadows it, the new covenant binds together in a special relationship God and his people. However, while the Sinai covenant made it possible for God to come and dwell uniquely in the midst of the Israelites, access into the very presence of God was limited to the high priest and then only briefly on one occasion during the year, the Day of *Atonement. These limits will not exist in the new creation, for through the new covenant all those 'whose names are written in the Lamb's book of life' will see God's face and take delight in being in his presence.

The new Israel

The new creation unveiled in Revelation 21 – 22 is presented in images which clearly indicate that its inhabitants are to be viewed as a new Israel. This picture is created by an interesting 'fusion of tribal and apostolic imagery' (Dumbrell, *The End*, p. 119). Thus on the gates of the holy *city are 'the names of the twelve tribes of Israel' (12:12), and 'the wall of the city had twelve foundations, and on them were the names of the twelve apostles of the Lamb' (21:14).

The continuity between tribal 'Israel' and apostolic 'Israel' builds on God's desire to create for himself a special people. In Exodus 19:6 God offers to those whom he has just delivered from slavery in Egypt the prospect of becoming 'a kingdom of priests and a holy nation'. While this conditional promise is never fully realized by OT Israel, the same opportunity is extended to those who believe in Christ. Thus the apostle Peter, writing to

God's elect in Asia Minor, states, 'But you are a chosen people, a royal priesthood, a holy nation, a people belonging to God, that you may declare the praises of him who called you out of darkness into his wonderful light' (1 Pet. 2:9). While God's people will include individuals 'from every tribe and language and people and nation', this inclusion is based on the understanding that they are the spiritual seed of Abraham (*e.g.* Gal. 3:29). For this reason they may legitimately be considered to be the new Israel. Furthermore, the idea of a new Israel is reinforced by the designation 'new Jerusalem' given to the city at the heart of the new creation (Rev. 21:2).

The new Jerusalem

John's vision of 'a new heaven and a new earth' centres on the descent from heaven of the 'Holy City, the new Jerusalem'. The new city, radiant with God's glory and constructed from the most precious of minerals, dominates the landscape. Indeed, such is the light emanating from it that there is no need for sun or moon. To this new Jerusalem the nations will bring their glory and honour in *worship of the Lord God Almighty and the Lamb.

The image of the city at the heart of the new earth clearly draws upon OT passages which highlight the special significance of Jerusalem/Zion in the purposes of God. A close relationship exists between the divine appointment of David as king over Israel, the choice of Jerusalem as the capital of the new kingdom, and the construction of a temple in the city. This relationship between king, city and temple continues to be important even after the destruction of the temple and the removal of the Davidic monarchy at the time of the Babylonian exile. The *hope remained that there would yet be a restoration involving all three. In the light of this the Gospels give special attention to the relationship between Jesus, Jerusalem and the temple. However, just as Jesus is much more than a son of David, so too the NT writers develop a new understanding of Jerusalem/Zion and the temple. While the earthly Jerusalem is doomed to destruction, believers are encouraged to come 'to Mount Zion, to the heavenly Jerusalem, the city of the living God' (Heb. 12:22).

The place of Christians in the present age of the world

In the light of the above discussion and of an exegetical analysis of the entire book, the main idea of Revelation can be roughly formulated as follows: the sovereignty of God and Christ in redeeming and judging brings them glory, which is intended to motivate saints to worship God and reflect his glorious attributes through obedience to his word. It is not coincidental that the passages in which the most significant expressions of worship are recorded occur just at the points where God's glory is highlighted (*cf.* Rev. 4 – 5; 7:9–12; 11:15–19; 15:2–8; 19:1–8; where words for 'worship' are also found). *Idolatry in Revelation is not merely worshipping other false gods, but 'the failure to worship the one who is Lord of all' (M. M. Thompson, in *EA* 8, p. 51). People may claim that they are religiously neutral and worship no god, but in John's mind this is still idolatry.

The book portrays an end-time new creation which has irrupted into the present old *world through the death and resurrection of Christ, as well as through the sending of the Spirit at Pentecost. John's vision communicates values that run counter to the values of the old world and which provide 'a structure of meaning that grounds' the lives of Christians in the new world (so L. L. Thompson, in *Sacred Places and Profane Spaces*, p. 120). The symbols which describe the new world spell out the eternal significance and consequences of Christ's life, death and resurrection, and of the present choices and behaviour of the readers. Part of John's purpose is to motivate the readers not to compromise with the world but to align their thoughts and behaviour with the God-centered standards of the new creation. They are to see their own situation in this world in the eternal perspective of the new world which is now their true home.

So the churches are to read and re-read the book in their assemblies in order that they may continually be reminded of God's real, new world which stands in opposition to the old, fallen system in which they presently live. Such a continual reminder will cause them to realize that their home is not in this old world but in the new world portrayed parabolically in the heavenly visions of Revelation. Continual reading of the book will encourage genuine saints to realize that what they believe is not strange, but truly normal from God's perspective. They will be prevented from being discouraged by worldliness, including that which has crept into the churches, which always makes godly standards appear odd and sinful values seem normal (for this concept see D. Wells, *God in the Wasteland*, pp. 35–59, and *passim*, as well as Wells, *No Place for Truth*). John refers to true unbelievers in the book as 'earth-dwellers' because their ultimate home is on this transient earth. They cannot trust in anything except what their eyes see and their physical senses perceive; they are permanently earthbound, trusting only in earthly security, and will perish with this old order at the end of time when the corrupted cosmos is finally judged and passes away.

On the other hand, Christians are like pilgrims passing through this world. As such they are to commit themselves to the revelation of God in the new order, so as progressively to reflect his image and increasingly to live according to the values of the new world, not being conformed to the fallen system, its idolatrous images and associated values (similarly *cf.* Rom. 12:2).

In this connection it may be profitable to ask why Christ addresses the churches in the letters of chapters 2 and 3 through their angelic representatives, especially since it does not seem logical to blame and reproach angels for the sins of the churches. One answer to this question is that essential to the idea of corporate representation is the accountability of the representative for the group and the accountability of the group for the actions of the representative. So there is a sense in which the angels are responsible for the churches; yet the churches also benefit from the position of the angels.

Thus the existence of the churches in heaven is represented and embodied in their representative angels. In fact, one of the reasons for the presence of so many angels throughout the visions of Revelation, and especially for God addressing the churches through their representative angels, is to remind true Christians that a dimension of their existence is already in the heavenly realm, that their real home is not with the unbelieving 'earth-dwellers', and that they have heavenly help and protection in their struggle not to be conformed to the pagan environment. And the purpose of the weekly gatherings of the church on earth (as in 1:3, 9–10), in addition to the purposes noted above, is to be reminded of its heavenly identity by the modelling of its worship on that of the angels' and heavenly church's worship of the exalted Lamb. This is why scenes of heavenly liturgy are woven throughout Revelation, especially as part of concluding sections which serve as interpretations of preceding visionary narratives. It is from these passages that the churches are to learn how to worship in their gathered meetings and to be given a zeal for worship of the true God. The intended consequence is that believers in the churches should develop an attitude of worshipful reverence for God, not only in their assemblies, but in their bowing to divine sovereignty in every aspect of their lives and in every area of its outworking.

The theological meaning of the use of symbols

John's method of symbolizing the heavenly world and other invisible forces, such as demonic powers, is theologically significant. The literary form of symbolic parable appears whenever ordinary warnings are no longer heeded, and no warning will ever be heeded by people who are spiritually callous and intent on continuing in disobedience (*cf.* G. K. Beale, in *A Vision for the Church: Studies in Early Christian Ecclesiology*, pp. 167–180). The parabolic aspect of OT prophets' messages is closely linked to the hardening commission of Isaiah 6:9–10 and, therefore, may be considered one of the means by which people are to be blinded. Yet the parables are also intended to have a jolting effect on the remnant who have become complacent among the compromising majority; in addition, a remnant of pseudo-believers are woken up and genuinely converted. Parables function in the same manner in Ezekiel and in Jesus' ministry. Therefore the appearance of parables in redemptive history signals judgment on the majority of the covenant community.

John's repeated use of the hearing formula is thus not novel but in line with the prior prophetic pattern. John's use of the phrase 'the one having ears, let him hear' is linked to Isaiah 6:9–10, as well as to Ezekiel 3:27 (*cf.* Ezek. 12:2), and is a development of the

Gospels' use of the phrase (*e.g.* Matt. 13:9–17, 43), which itself builds upon Isaiah 6:9–10. As also in the case of the OT prophets and Jesus, the expression about hearing indicates that parabolic communication has the dual purpose of opening the eyes of the true remnant but blinding counterfeit members of the covenant community.

There is a consensus that this repeated formula 'the one who has an ear, let him hear' in Revelation 2 – 3 is an allusion to the Synoptic formula. Therefore, as in Isaiah 6, Ezekiel and the Synoptics, the formula refers to the fact that Christ's message in Revelation will reveal truth to some but conceal it from others. John addresses the formula to the church, which is the continuation of the true Israel and the genuine covenant community. But, the church, like Israel, has become spiritually dull and has begun to compromise by associating with idolatry. The parabolic method of revelation is instituted in Revelation because many among the churches have become intractable in their compromising stance. The symbols in Revelation have both a hardening effect on the unbelieving and a shock effect upon genuine saints caught up in the church's compromising complacency. For example, the symbols reveal the terrible, satanic essence of the idolatrous institutions with which God's true people are beginning to associate, in order that they may realize the horrific nature of these institutions and immediately break off their association with them.

The hearing formulas at the end of each of the letters anticipate the visionary parables of chapters 4 – 21. A very similar formula in 13:9, 'if anyone has ears, let him hear', is a further hint that John intends the symbolic visions of Revelation 4 – 21 to have the dual revelatory function mentioned above.

This means that the symbolic visions of chapters 4 – 21 are parabolic portrayals of the more abstractly expressed material in chapters 2 – 3. Therefore the letters broadly interpret the symbolic visions and *vice versa*. The twofold spiritual function of the symbols is further indicated by the parallel between the series of trumpets and bowls and the Exodus plague *signs, which functioned originally to harden the Egyptians but to give insight and redemption to Israel. Yet it needs to be recalled that a remnant among the Egyptians responded positively to the plagues

and left Egypt with Israel; it should also be remembered that the majority of Israelites who left Egypt were characterized by unbelief and hard hearts (see Psalm 95). Consequently, as probably in the case of the OT prophets and Jesus, the symbols used by John not only harden the reprobate, but also both jolt genuine believers out of their spiritual anaesthesia and shock a remnant among the unbelieving mass so that they truly believe. John applies the Exodus model to the church and the world. Consequently, the large amount of symbolic material in Revelation is due primarily to John's theological intention, of identifying his relationship to the situation of the Asia Minor churches with the relationship of the OT prophets and Jesus to the plight of Israel.

Conclusion

Many consider Revelation (esp. chs. 4 – 22) to be primarily a map of future events which have yet to happen. While there are significant sections which look to the future, there are also many which refer to the past and the present. This is to say, in view of the preceding discussion, that the book of Revelation is not merely a futurology but also a redemptive-historical and theological psychology for the church's thinking throughout the age before Christ's final coming.

See also: THE JOHANNINE WRITINGS.

Bibliography

R. Bauckham, *The Theology of the Book of Revelation*, NTT (Cambridge, 1993); G. K. Beale, Review of W. J. Dumbrell, *The End of the Beginning: Revelation 21–22 and the OT*, in *Themelios* 15, 1990, pp. 69–70; *idem*, *The Book of Revelation* (Grand Rapids, Cambridge and Carlisle, 1998); *idem*, 'The hearing formula and the visions of John in Revelation', in M. Bockmuehl and M. B. Thompson (eds.), *A Vision for the Church: Studies in Early Christian Ecclesiology in Honour of J. P. M. Sweet* (Edinburgh, 1997); G. B. Caird, *A Commentary on the Revelation of St. John the Divine* (London and New York, 1966); U. Cassuto, *A Commentary on the Book of Genesis* (ET, Jerusalem, 1989); W. J. Dumbrell, *The End of the Beginning: Revelation 21–22 and the Old Testament* (Homebush West, 1985); C. H. T. Fletcher-Louis, 'The destruction of the temple and relativization of the old covenant: Mark 13:31 and Matthew 5:18', in K. E. Brower and M. W. Elliott (eds.), 'The Reader Must Understand': Eschatology in Bible and Theology (Leicester, 1997); R. H. Gundry, 'Angelomorphic Christology in the book of Revelation', in SBLSP 33, 1994, pp. 662–678; W. Hendricksen, More Than Conquerors: An Interpretation of the Book of Revelation (Grand Rapids, 1962); M. G. Kline, Images of the Spirit (Grand Rapids, 1980); idem, Kingdom Prologue (South Hamilton, 1989); J. D. Levenson, Creation and the Persistence of Evil: The Jewish Drama of Divine Omnipotence (San Francisco, 1988); J. J. Niehaus, No Other Gods (Grand Rapids, forthcoming); V. S. Poythress, The Shadow of Christ in the Law of Moses (Brentwood, 1991); L. L. Thompson, 'Mapping an apocalyptic world', in J. Scott and P. Simpson-Housely (eds.), Sacred Places and Profane Spaces (New York and London, 1991); M. M. Thompson, 'Worship in the book of Revelation', EA 8, 1992, pp. 45–54; D. Wells, No Place for Truth (Grand Rapids and Leicester, 1993, 1995); idem, God in the Wasteland (Grand Rapids and Leicester, 1994); G. J. Wenham, 'Sanctuary symbolism in the Garden of Eden story', in PWCJS, Division A, 1986, pp. 19–25; idem, Genesis 1–15, WBC (Waco, 1987).

G. K. BEALE

PART THREE

AARON, see PRIESTS

ABRAHAM (ABRAM)

Introduction

The figure of Abraham, or Abram as he is initially known, dominates the book of Genesis and casts a shadow which extends across the whole Bible. Pre-eminent as a man of *faith, and as such a model for others, he receives from *God various promises which permeate both the OT and the NT. These promises involve the establishment of Abraham's descendants as a 'great nation' in the land of Canaan, and the blessing of all the nations of the earth through a future *king descended from Abraham.

Abraham in Genesis

Of the human characters in Genesis, Abraham is by far the most important. This is reflected both in the length of the narrative devoted to him, and in the key theological concepts associated with him. Since the material concerning Abraham, beginning with the tôlᵉḏôṯ heading in 11:27 ('This is the account of'; NIV) and concluding with the report of his death in 25:7–11, forms an integral part of the book of Genesis, our reading of the Abraham narrative will take into account this broader context (see *Genesis).

Abraham and the line of 'seed'

The book of Genesis traces, through the use of tôlᵉḏôṯ headings and linear genealogies, a unique family line. This lineage is traced from *Adam to Ephraim, later, beyond Genesis, being associated with Joshua. In the time of Samuel, however, it is divinely rejected (cf. Ps. 78) in favour of an alternative line traced through *Judah (cf. Gen. 38:1–30; 49:8–12) to the royal house of *David (cf. Ruth 4:18–22). The members of this lineage enjoy a special relationship with God and play a central role in the outworking of God's *redemptive plan for *humanity. In Genesis Abraham is a key figure in the lineage.

At the outset of the Abraham narrative, we learn that his wife is unable to have children (11:30). *Sarah's barrenness prevents the continuation of the family line, and considerable attention is paid to the resolution of this problem. When the LORD assures Abraham that he will have a son of his own (15:1–5), Sarah persuades him to have a child by her maidservant *Hagar (16:1–4). As a result Ishmael is born, and Abraham, by naming him, acknowledges him as his own son (16:15). Afterwards, however, God reveals on two occasions that Sarah herself will have a son (17:15–21; 18:9–15). When Isaac is eventually born (21:1–7), he is established as Abraham's main heir through the divinely approved expulsion of Hagar and Ishmael (21:8–21). Remarkably, Sarah gives birth to Isaac well beyond the natural age for a woman to have children – she is ninety years old. Here, as elsewhere in Genesis, the continuation of the line of 'seed' is attributed to God's intervention (25:21; 30:22–24; cf. 4:1; 29:33; 30:6).

Central to the Hebrew concept of 'seed' is the idea that the progeny resembles its progenitor. Since Abraham is the most prominent member of the line of 'seed' in Genesis it is anticipated that his descendants will resemble him. For this reason it is no coincidence that Isaac's stay in Gerar (26:1–33) parallels closely that of his father (20:1–18; 21:22–34). More significant, however, is the fact that Abraham is sometimes portrayed as having royal attributes. This is reflected in the account of his victory over the eastern kings (14:1–24), the desire of Abimelech king of Gerar to enter into a *covenant with him (21:22–34), and his designation 'prince of god' by the inhabitants of Hebron (23:6). These factors suggest that the line of 'seed' traced in Genesis anticipates the establishment of a royal dynasty (cf. 17:6, 16; 35:11; 36:31; 37:8–11; 41:39–43; 49:8–12).

Abraham and the promise of nationhood

Closely linked to the continuation of Abraham's family line is the divine promise that he will become a 'great nation' (12:2). Implicit in this promise of nationhood is the idea that Abraham will have numerous descendants who will possess a particular land; the Hebrew term gôy, 'nation', denotes people inhabiting a specific geographical location and forming a political unit. Significantly, the promise of nationhood follows on from the LORD's initial command to Abraham to leave his own country, people and family, and 'go to the land I will show you' (12:1). When Abraham subsequently arrives in Canaan, the LORD states, 'To your offspring [seed] I will give this land' (12:7). Later, after the separation of Lot from Abraham, the LORD repeats this promise, emphasizing the extent of the land to be possessed by Abraham's descendants (13:14–17). The topic of nationhood reappears in chapter 15 where a new element is introduced; Abraham's descendants will possess the land of Canaan only after a period of four hundred years, during which they will be slaves in another country (15:13–14). This announcement of a delay in the acquisition of the land possibly explains why the promise of land, which is very prominent in chapters 12 – 15, is mentioned less frequently in the rest of the Abraham narrative (*cf.* 17:8; 22:17). Although later episodes record Abraham's acquisition of a well at Beersheba (21:22–34) and a tomb at Hebron (23:1–20), we must look far beyond these to see God fulfilling his promise to Abraham that he will become a great nation.

Within the Abraham narrative the promise of nationhood comes to an important climax in chapter 15. Here God, by means of a special ritual, makes a covenant with Abraham to give his descendants the land 'from the river of Egypt to the great river, the Euphrates' (15:18). Through this covenant the LORD guarantees unconditionally all that was previously promised to Abraham regarding land and descendants. Nowhere, however, is it suggested that the fulfilment of this covenant is dependent upon the actions of either Abraham or his descendants. Rather God commits himself unreservedly to fulfil his promise that Abraham's descendants will become a 'great nation' in the land of Canaan. The account of this covenant's being honoured by God is recorded in the books of Exodus to 2 Samuel (*cf.* 2 Sam. 8:1–14). (See *Israel.)

Abraham and the blessing of the nations

Taking Genesis as a whole the divine speech in 12:1–3 is exceptionally important. It not only marks a new phase in God's relationship with human beings, but also sets the agenda for the entire Abraham story and subsequent events. In calling Abraham to leave his own people and country, God promises that he will be a source of divine blessing, or possibly cursing, to others. The LORD says to Abraham, 'Be a blessing, so that I may bless those who bless you, and curse the one who disdains you, and so that all the families of

the ground may be blessed through you' (12:2b–3, author's translation).

God's desire to bless Abraham, and through him to bless others, stands in sharp contrast to the events described in Genesis 3 – 11. Whereas these earlier chapters are dominated by the effects of divine punishment inflicted as a result of human disobedience, the Abraham narrative emphasizes the theme of divine blessing. This is underlined in 12:1–3 by the fivefold repetition of the Hebrew verb *bārak*, 'to bless'.

The climax of God's call to Abraham comes in the statement 'so that all the families of the ground may be blessed through you'. The promise that Abraham will become a 'great nation', which comes in the first part of the divine speech in 12:1–3, is subservient to God's principal desire to bless all the families of the ground. The prime motive behind the call of Abraham is God's intention to bless humanity and reverse the disastrous consequences of Adam and Eve's rebellion in the Garden of Eden.

Although the idea that all the families of the ground will be blessed through Abraham is introduced in 12:3, it is not until chapter 17 that it is developed further by means of the covenant of *circumcision. From God's perspective this covenant focuses on Abraham as 'the father of many nations'. God states, 'As for me, this is my covenant with you: You will be the father of many nations. No longer will you be called Abram; your name will be Abraham, for I have made you a father of many nations. I will make you very fruitful; I will make nations of you, and kings will come from you' (17:4–6).

Later God says regarding Sarah: 'I will bless her so that she will be the mother of nations; kings of peoples will come from her' (17:16). The mention of nations coming from Abraham and Sarah presents a problem if taken to mean those nations directly descended from both of them; strictly speaking, only the Israelites and Edomites fall into this category. However, the idea of Abraham's being the father of many nations is not restricted here to physical descendants; in Genesis the term 'father' does not always denote a biological relationship (in 45:8 Joseph is described as 'father to Pharaoh'; *cf.* Judg. 17:10; 2 Kgs. 2:12). Furthermore, in chapter 17 God instructs Abraham to circumcise not merely his own family members but every male 'including those born in your household or bought with your money from a foreigner – those who are not your offspring (seed)' (17:12). This suggests that circumcision enables those who are not biologically related to Abraham to become his 'children', and hence to benefit from the divine blessing mediated by Abraham. Later, in the account of the rape of Dinah, it is noteworthy that the men of Shechem circumcise themselves in order to establish a kinship relationship with *Jacob's family (34:14–23). These factors suggest that the covenant of circumcision is primarily concerned with the mediation of God's blessing to all the nations of the earth.

Whereas the promissory covenant of chapter 15 is unconditional, the establishment of the covenant of circumcision is dependent upon Abraham's continuing *obedience to God. This is highlighted in the introduction to chapter 17. After identifying himself as 'ēl šadday ('God Almighty'), the LORD says to Abraham, 'Walk before me and be blameless so that I may confirm my covenant between me and you and increase you greatly' (17:1–2, author's translation). The covenant of circumcision will be confirmed only if Abraham walks before God and is blameless. For the ratification of the covenant we must look to the divine oath which concludes the account of the *testing of Abraham in chapter 22.

God's speech in 22:16–18 is not only the climax to the account of the testing of Abraham but also closes the main section of the Abraham narrative by echoing his initial call in 12:1–3. The solemnity and importance of this speech in chapter 22 is underlined by the fact that only here in Genesis does the LORD swear by himself. Much of what was promised conditionally in 12:1–3 is now guaranteed unconditionally by divine oath. While the first mention of 'seed' in 22:17 denotes 'descendants' in the plural, the remaining references to 'seed' are ambiguous; they could refer either to many descendants or to a single descendant. On syntactical grounds (see T. D. Alexander, 'Further observations on the term "seed" in Genesis', *TynB* 48, 1997, pp. 363–367), God's comment in 22:18, 'Your seed will take possession of the cities of his enemies and through your seed all nations on earth will be blessed', is best understood as referring to a single descendant (*cf.* Ps. 72:17).

The idea that the nations will be blessed

through a single descendant of Abraham is associated in Genesis with those who receive the blessing given to the firstborn. Thus, although Esau and Jacob are both the biological 'seed' of Isaac, it is Jacob alone who experiences God's blessing in an extraordinary way and imparts it to others (*cf.* Gen. 29:32–33; 30:6, 17–18, 20, 22–24, 27–30; 32:3–21; 35:9). Similarly, of Jacob's twelve sons *Joseph, treated by his father as the firstborn (*cf.* 1 Chr. 5:1–2), is the one through whom others are divinely blessed (*cf.* Gen. 39:2–6, 20–23; 41:56–57; 47:13–26). While this line is continued initially through the tribe of Ephraim (Gen. 48:1–20; 49:22–26), it is later transferred to the tribe of Judah (*cf.* Ps. 78:67–72), and comes to fulfilment in *Jesus Christ (*e.g.* Acts 3:24–26; Gal. 3:8–18).

Abraham's faith, obedience and righteousness

The Abraham narrative provides an interesting picture of the interplay between divine word and human faith and obedience. Initially, the LORD makes a series of promises, the fulfilment of which is conditional upon Abraham's obedience (12:1–3). By commanding him to leave his homeland and be a blessing, God requires Abraham to respond positively in order that the promises concerning nationhood and the blessing of others may be fulfilled. As Abraham in faith obeys and journeys to Canaan, God declares that he shall have both land and descendants (12:7; 13:14–17). Later, when Abraham seeks reassurance from God, these statements are divinely guaranteed by a promissory covenant (15:1–21). The narrative, however, goes on to highlight Abraham's continuing faith in and obedience to God, as revealed in the establishment of the eternal covenant of circumcision (17:1–27), a covenant which focuses on the blessing that will come through Abraham and his 'seed' to all nations. Significantly, this covenant is ratified only after Abraham is tested by being required to sacrifice his only son Isaac (22:1–19). From beginning to end, faith expressed in obedience is the hallmark of Abraham's relationship with the LORD.

In all this Genesis 15:6 stands out as particularly significant: 'Abram believed the LORD, and he credited it to him as righteousness.' The rarity in Genesis of such comments by the narrator makes them especially important. Here Abraham is viewed as *righteous in God's sight because he believes unreservedly that the LORD will fulfil his promise regarding a son and numerous descendants. Abraham is reckoned righteous on account of his faith in God's promise, rather than because of any deeds performed by him.

Abraham's faith is all the more remarkable when the following factors are taken into account. First, the divine promises concerning nationhood and the blessing of all the families of the earth will never be fulfilled in Abraham's lifetime; at the very most Abraham will experience only the firstfruits of their fulfilment. Secondly, circumstances exist or develop which militate against the fulfilment of these promises. Sarah's barrenness, linked to her advancing years, is a major obstacle, and, even when all seems assured with the birth of Isaac, God himself places the future fulfilment of the promises in jeopardy by demanding that Abraham sacrifice Isaac. Yet in spite of these difficulties Abraham displays exemplary faith in God.

While the writer of Genesis highlights Abraham's virtues, lapses of faith are also noted. This is especially evident when Abraham pretends that Sarah is his sister (12:10–20; 20:1–18). Although Abraham's lack of trust in God is revealed on these occasions, and possibly also in connection with the birth of Ishmael (16:1–16), it is outweighed by the faith in God which he demonstrates elsewhere.

Abraham in the rest of the OT

Outside Genesis there are forty-three references to Abraham in the OT, and two to Abram (1 Chr. 1:27; Neh. 9:7). Abraham is frequently mentioned, usually with Isaac and Jacob, in connection with the covenant which God made regarding the land of Canaan (Exod. 6:8; 32:13; 33:1; Lev. 26:42; Num. 32:11; Deut. 1:8; 6:10; 9:5; 29:13; 30:20; 34:4; 2 Kgs. 13:23; 2 Chr. 20:7; Ezek. 33:24). The fulfilment of the divine promise of land is viewed as resulting from Abraham's special relationship with God; twice he is called God's friend (2 Chr. 20:7; Is. 41:8). Since the Israelites come to possess the land of Canaan because they are Abraham's descendants, descent from Abraham is viewed as especially important. This conviction is even more evident in the NT.

Abraham in the NT

Many references to Abraham in the NT focus either directly or indirectly on his status as father of the Jewish people (Matt. 3:9; Luke 1:55, 73; 3:8; 16:24, 30; John 8:39, 53, 56; Acts 7:2; Rom. 4:12, 16; Jas. 2:21; cf. Exod. 3:6; Josh. 24:3; Is. 51:2). According to various passages, some Jews considered their descent from Abraham as a guarantee of God's blessing. In the Gospels such thinking is challenged by John the Baptist (Matt. 3:9; Luke 3:8) and Jesus (Luke 16:19–31; John 8:31–59). Jesus stresses that Abraham's children will resemble him (John 8:39), and *Paul develops the same point at length in *Romans 4 and *Galatians 3 by observing that the true children of Abraham are those who 'share the faith of Abraham' (Rom. 4:16; Gal. 3:7). However, within the NT, especially in Romans, Galatians, *Hebrews and *James, the most noteworthy aspect of Abraham's life is his faith.

Abraham in Romans and Galatians

There can be little doubt that Paul's understanding of the gospel was heavily influenced by his reading of the Abraham narrative in Genesis. This is particularly apparent in his letters to the churches in Galatia and Rome. In these he focuses on Abraham in order to challenge the view of his opponents that Gentile believers must be circumcised and obey the *law of Moses in order to know God's *salvation.

In his letter to the Galatians Paul responds at length to those who were emphasizing the necessity of observing the law for salvation. Quoting Genesis 15:6, 'Abram believed the LORD, and he credited it to him as righteousness,' he observes briefly that Abraham's righteousness was achieved not by keeping the law but by believing God. Furthermore, he says, 'those who believe are children of Abraham' (Gal. 3:7).

Paul, however, does not conclude his argument at this point. He underlines three further aspects of the Abraham narrative in order to drive home his case that Gentiles who believe in Jesus Christ now receive God's blessing. First, he sees in the justification of the Gentiles the fulfilment of the divine promise to Abraham that all nations would be blessed through him (Gal. 3:9). By highlighting the emphasis which Genesis places on all nations being blessed through Abraham, Paul challenges the view of his opponents that God's salvation was only for those who were circumcised and kept the law of Moses.

Secondly, Paul argues that the divine promises made to Abraham find their ultimate fulfilment in Jesus Christ. To arrive at this conclusion he notes that the promises were given to Abraham and his 'seed'. For Paul this 'seed' is Jesus Christ (Gal. 3:16). At first sight Paul's identification of this 'seed' with Jesus Christ seems contrived. However, the Hebrew word *zera*', 'seed', is a keyword in Genesis, and while it sometimes denotes a group of people, it may also refer to a single individual (*e.g.* Gen. 4:25; 21:13). This latter possibility is significant, especially given that the book of Genesis highlights a particular line of 'seed' which formed the early ancestry of the Davidic dynasty. Since Genesis anticipates a future royal 'seed' through whom God will fulfil his promise to Abraham to bless all nations, Paul's interpretation of the term *zera*' as referring to Jesus Christ is in keeping with the common NT understanding of Jesus as the Davidic Messiah. A similar view is proclaimed by Peter in Acts 3:25–26.

Finally, Paul argues in Galatians that the divine promise/covenant made with Abraham takes precedence over the law given several centuries later at Mt Sinai (Gal. 3:15–25). Whereas his opponents were claiming that believers must keep the law in order to be righteous, Paul responds by noting that the law, given later to fulfil a temporary role until Christ came, could never make anyone righteous; it merely indicated the righteousness required by God, and was not the means of achieving such righteousness. Thus it underlined the necessity of becoming righteous through faith.

A similar, but not identical, argument is advanced in Romans 4. Here, as in Galatians, Paul is concerned to argue that the righteousness by which an individual is justified comes from God through faith in Jesus Christ (Rom. 3:21–22). Once again the argument centres on Genesis 15:6. For Paul, the sequence of events in the Abraham story is all important. Since Abraham was credited as righteous prior to being circumcised, it must follow that circumcision is not necessary in order for an individual to be reckoned righteous by God. Furthermore, Paul stresses that Abraham is the father of those who have faith, whether they are his natural descendants or not (Rom. 4:9–12; *cf.* Rom. 9:6–8). Thus he concludes that Jews and Gentiles can be justified only by faith.

Abraham in Hebrews

Abraham's faith is highlighted also in Hebrews 11, the detailed list of those 'ancients' who were commended for having faith. Approximately one-third of the chapter is devoted to Abraham (Heb. 11:8–19), making him by far the most important person listed; Moses, who is next in importance, receives about half the space given to Abraham (Heb. 11:23–28). Fittingly, the author of Hebrews highlights Abraham's faith as an example of 'being sure of what we hope for and certain of what we do not see' (Heb. 11:1).

In keeping with the overall theological emphasis in Hebrews, Abraham is portrayed as living 'like a stranger in a foreign country' (Heb. 11:9), 'looking forward to the city with foundations, whose architect and builder is God' (11:10; *cf.* 12:22). This city is located in 'a better country – a heavenly one' (11:16). These descriptions resemble the picture in the final two chapters of Revelation. With the creation of a new heaven and a new earth, John sees 'the Holy City, the new Jerusalem, coming down out of heaven from God, prepared as a bride beautifully dressed for her husband' (Rev. 21:2).

While the book of Genesis does not reveal explicitly what expectations Abraham may have had concerning the future, a deliberate contrast is made between him and those who sought to build a city, Babel, with a tower that reached to the heavens (Gen. 11:1–9). In spite of God's promises concerning the land of Canaan, Abraham did not attempt to found a city there. Indeed, towards the end of his life, he described himself to the people of Hebron as 'an alien and a stranger among you' (*cf.* Gen. 23:4).

Abraham in James

Abraham's faith is discussed also in James 2:20–24. Here, however, the context differs from that found in Romans and Galatians. Whereas Paul seeks to demonstrate the priority of faith over circumcision and keeping the law, James is concerned to clarify the nature of saving faith: 'What good is it, my brothers, if a man claims to have faith but has no deeds? Can such faith save him' (Jas.

2:14)? At the heart of James's discussion is the desire to show that true faith in God will exhibit itself in righteous actions. Thus, he focuses on Abraham and in particular the offering of Isaac on the altar (Jas. 2:21–23). In doing so James reveals how faith in and obedience to God cannot be separated. While James accepts that Abraham was justified by faith, as stated in Genesis 15:6, he views his later actions as visible expressions of this inner faith. Undoubtedly he focuses on Genesis 22 because of the way in which Abraham is rewarded for his willingness to sacrifice Isaac. For James there can be no separation of faith and deeds. Thus, he views Abraham's actions in Genesis 22 as the fulfilment or culmination of what was described in Genesis 15:6.

Although James writes that 'a person is justified by what he does and not by faith alone' (Jas. 2:24), it is clear from the context that he does not contradict what Paul says in Romans and Galatians. They are addressing different situations and therefore highlight different aspects of Abraham's faith. On the one hand, Paul concentrates on Genesis 15:6 because he is responding either directly or indirectly to those who wish to emphasize the necessity of circumcision and/or keeping the law for salvation. On the other hand, James is concerned to show that Abraham's faith, by which he was justified, produced righteous actions. Thus, he writes, 'faith without deeds is dead' (Jas. 2:26). Undoubtedly Paul and James would have agreed wholeheartedly with what the other had to say, given the different problems that confronted them.

Conclusion

Of the many and varied figures to appear in the Bible Abraham is clearly one of the most significant. Our survey reveals four main ideas that dominate the way in which he is portrayed. 1. Abraham's trust in and obedience to God is exemplary; his inner faith demonstrated itself in ongoing obedience to God. 2. Abraham was reckoned righteous by God on account of his faith prior to being circumcised. 3. All who exhibit similar faith are Abraham's children and share in the blessing associated with the divine promises made to Abraham. 4. The divine promises to Abraham anticipate the coming of a royal descendant who will impart God's blessing to all the nations of the earth. Although the Genesis nar-

rative does not identify this future king, the NT writers, building on the rest of the OT, share the belief that he is Jesus Christ, the son of David. While the story of Abraham's life appears first in Genesis, it is obvious that this account influenced significantly the thinking of the early *church regarding the nature of Jesus Christ's mission to the world and its understanding of personal salvation.

See also: BLESSING / CURSE; LAND; NATIONS; SEED.

Bibliography

T. D. Alexander, *Abraham in the Negev: A Source-critical Investigation of Genesis 20:1–22:9* (Carlisle, 1997); *idem*, 'Abraham reassessed theologically: the Abraham narrative and the New Testament understanding of justification by faith', in R. S. Hess, P. E. Satterthwaite and G. J. Wenham (eds.), *He Swore an Oath: Biblical Themes from Genesis 12 – 50* (Grand Rapids and Carlisle, [2]1994), pp. 7–28; G. W. Hansen, *Abraham in Galatians: Epistolary and Rhetorical Contexts* (Sheffield, 1989); J. Muilenburg, 'Abraham and the nations: blessing and world history', *Int* 19, 1965, pp. 387–398; L. A. Turner, *Announcements of Plot in Genesis* (Sheffield, 1990).

T. D. ALEXANDER

ACTS, see Part 2

ADAM AND EVE

Introduction

Adam and Eve are the progenitors of the *human race in Jewish, Christian and Islamic tradition (in the Qur'an, see 2:28–36; 4:1; 7:18–26; 20:114–121). The Judeo-Christian tradition is rooted in the Bible's opening chapters, which Luther called 'doubtless the foundation of the whole Scripture'.

Biblical references to Adam and Eve

References are spread unevenly through the canonical books, and in some cases there is no scholarly consensus as to the meaning of the text. In order properly to understand the NT references intertestamental developments must be considered.

In the OT

The noun Adam, '*adam*, occurs 562 times in the OT, but in most instances it refers to generic 'humankind' and not to the first man and father of the race. Although the references in *Genesis 1:26 and 27 are interpreted as proper names in the Targums of Jonathan and Onqelos respectively, in these verses the word is used generically. The LXX begins to use 'Adam' as a proper name in Genesis 2:16, and Jerome's Vulgate in 2:20 following the Masoretic vowel-points; most scholars, however, do not translate '*adam* as such until 4:25 or even 5:1. R. S. Hess has shown that '*adam* functions as the *title* of the first human, 'The Man', in Genesis 2 and 3 ('Splitting the Adam: The usage of '*adam* in Genesis i–v', in J. A. Emerton (ed.), *Studies in the Pentateuch* [Leiden, 1990], pp. 1–15, 12).

Opinions vary as to the meaning of the word in other passages. The older rendering of Hosea 6:7, 'Like Adam, they have broken the covenant' (NIV) is also the more natural one. Psalm 82:7a reads literally: 'Surely you will die like '*adam*'; for judges inflated with pride because they bear the divine *image a reference to Adam would be appropriate (H. N. Wallace, *The Eden Narrative* [Atlanta, 1985], p. 185: 'the reference to '*adam* would certainly recall to the hearers of this psalm the fate of Adam in Gen. 2–3'). Similarly, but with an explicit reference to Eden, Ezekiel's oracle of and dirge over the king of Tyre compare him to the first prince of *creation, using the phrase 'You '*adam*' (28:9; 'You will be but a man'). Job 15:7–8 may be translated 'Were you born the first man ('*adam*) ... did you grab for yourself wisdom?', a reference to a usurping of knowledge which recalls the sin of Adam in Genesis (*cf.* 31:33). Ecclesiastes 7:29 uses the article with '*adam*, in a phrase possibly equivalent to the Genesis 2 – 3 'title' ('Few, if any, other OT texts provide so succinct and precise an account of the fall,' D. M. Clemens, 'The law of sin and death: Ecclesiastes and Genesis 1–3', *Them* 19.3, 1994, p. 7). Some suggest that there is an allusion to Adam in Deuteronomy 32:8, which refers to a primeval event: 'When the Most High ... divided all mankind', literally 'the sons of '*adam*' (a primeval event reminds one of Adam). It is a moot point whether the common phrase 'the sons of '*adam*' usually includes a reference to Adam.

Adam gives his wife her generic name of *woman* (Gen. 2:23) and, later, her proper name of *Eve* (Gen. 3:20). In Genesis 4 she gives birth to sons (vv. 1–2, 25), and then recedes into the background. Clemens argues that 'the archetypal woman envisaged in [Ecclesiastes] 7:26 is Eve, whose hands picked the fruit' (in *Themelios*, p. 7).

Between the Testaments

Jews of the Second Temple period were interested in the stories of Genesis, and the figure of Adam became very important. If the Wisdom of Solomon (2:23–24) focuses on the devil's part in Adam's fall (see *Spiritual powers), Ecclesiasticus, which acknowledges Adam's pre-eminence over other people (49:16), focuses on the woman: 'Woman is the origin of sin, and it is through her that we all die' (25:24 NEB; *cf.* 40:1–2). The *marriage-prayer of Tobit 8:6 reads: 'Thou madest Adam, and Eve his wife to be his helper and support; and those two were the parents of the human race' (NEB).

Pseudepigrapha, like later rabbinical literature, credit Adam with great ability and glory, and some texts describe in catastrophic terms the disaster his disobedience brought. Occasionally, as in the *Life of Adam and Eve*, Eve is made the main culprit (21:6), a view born of asceticism and misogyny. Two writings identify Adam and Eve as the fountain-head of corruption and *death: 2 Baruch refers to their inheritance of death (23:4; 48:42–43; 54:15), and 4 Ezra teaches something like 'original *sin' (4:30; 7:118–119).

In the NT

Explicit references to Adam are spread unevenly across the NT corpora, but throughout the NT the significance of Adam is reassessed in the light of *Jesus Christ.

The Synoptic Gospels offer only hints of an Adam–Christ typology, most clearly in Luke's juxtaposition of Jesus' genealogy and temptation (Luke 3:23 – 4:13). The Johannine references to the fall focus on the 'ancient serpent' (Rev. 12:9; *cf.* John 8:44; Rev. 20:2). In Paul's theology, on the other hand, Adam has a major role. In 1 Corinthians he draws the parallel between the first, earthly human, Adam, in whom all die and the final, heavenly human, Jesus, in whom all will be made alive (15:21–23, 44–49). In Romans 5:12–21 he uses the condemnation brought by the trespass of the one human Adam to demonstrate that salvation, justification and life are brought (how much more!) by the righteous deed of the one human, Jesus Christ. Paul refers obliquely to Adam in Romans 8:20; the phrase 'not by their own choice' is equivalent to 'by Adam's fault'. Scholars have detected the Adam-Christ typology in many passages in Paul's writings (see C. M. Pate, *The Glory of Adam*). Eve is mentioned twice, in the context of warnings against seductive doctrines (2 Cor. 11:3; 1 Tim. 2:12–14), and Paul refers to Adam and Eve as the model for *men and women (1 Cor. 11:3–12; *cf.* Eph. 5:31–32).

The names 'Adam' and 'Eve'

'aḏām 'is attested as a Northwest Semitic personal name ... with exact parallels in Amorite and the texts from Ebla' (S. C. Layton, 'Remarks on the Canaanite origin of Eve', *CBQ* 59, 1997, p. 22, *cf.* p. 30). Despite other proposals, the traditional etymology (Josephus, *Antiquities of the Jews*, I, 1, 2) is still the most convincing: Adam is 'the *red* one', and the name may be connected to *dām*, *blood. The main association, and wordplay, is with *ᵃdāmâ* (red?), earth or soil (Gen. 2:7; 3:17, 19); humankind is defined by the relationship of the 'earthling' to the earth (*cf.* 1:28).

The name *hawwâ*, Eve, is unique. Layton (pp. 22–32) offers a convincing analysis: no link with the Aramaic *hwh*, 'serpent', is warranted; the name is derived from the root 'to make alive' (as implied in Gen. 3:20) and should be translated '*life-giver.'

'Woman', *'iššâ*, is not derived from 'man', *'îš*, but it sounds like the feminine form of *'îš*. Did the wordplay on the feminine indicate movement (*cf.* English *wards*: woman is man*wards*)? For S. A. Meier, *'aḏām* comes from *ᵃdāmâ* and *'iššâ* from *'îš*; the man goes *to* the earth in death (3:19) and the woman goes *to* the man to bring forth life ('Linguistic clues on the date and Canaanite origin of Genesis 2:23–24', *CBQ* 53, 1991, pp. 20–21).

Adam and Eve and history

The traditional reading of Genesis took Adam and Eve to be real individuals who once lived in time and space. This is the view of many evangelicals and the official position (often called 'monogenism') of the Catholic magisterium (*Humani generis*, 1950), though some believe the account contains figurative elements. Almost everyone else assigns Genesis 2 – 3 to the category of myth and draws from it only a general truth about the human predicament. The main reasons are modern philosophical attitudes towards history, the influence of evolutionary perspectives and the discovery of affinities between Genesis and myths of origin. Many have abandoned belief in Scripture as revelation and cannot credit the writer with reliable information on events so remote.

Those who presuppose, by faith, that Scripture is the word of God have framed some cogent counter-arguments. The use of common words and symbols, and the writer's intention to counter one view of origins with another, account for the similarities between Genesis and myths. But the genre, function and intention of the Genesis narrative are quite different from those of other creation accounts, and its place in the structure of the book implies that it stands in continuity with the subsequent history. Paul's argument in Romans 5 requires an individual, historical Adam.

Among those who believe in evolution, opinions on Genesis vary; some find room for monogenism and the first transgression. To do this is hard but not impossible; the most attractive hypothesis is that of J. J. Davis ('Genesis, inerrancy and the antiquity of man', in R. R. Nicole and J. R. Michaels [eds.], *Inerrancy and Common Sense* [Grand Rapids, 1980], pp. 137–159), who sees Adam as the first *homo sapiens sapiens*. Whatever the solution, the historicity of Adam is vital: the biblical view of *evil and of salvation (which is also a historical event) hangs upon it.

Other issues

Death and immortality

It was once thought that Adam and Eve were created immortal, but that they were capable of losing their immortality. This they did, as a penalty for their sin; had they eaten the fruit of the tree of life they would have become irreversibly immortal. But the opposite view is now common: they were created mortal (like animals), and the penalty for their sin was a new kind of death, in anguish and pain; the tree of life would have given them immortality, but this was not intrinsic to their nature. It seems better not to draw conclusions about human nature from the first couple's fellowship with God, nor to reason from their spiritual to their bodily immortality. Genesis 2:17 and 3:19 and Romans 5:12 (*cf.* 6:23) do not favour the view that Adam was mortal by nature, but neither do they say that he was immortal. Since access to the tree of life was free (Gen. 2:16), Adam must have eaten of it daily; this signifies the constant renewal of life, body and soul, through fellowship with the LORD. But this renewal was incompatible with sinfulness (as indicated by the flaming sword), and so was lost at the fall.

The relationship of the sexes

Genesis 1:27 highlights the difference of the sexes, while Genesis 2:18–23 stresses their common nature.

Controversy surrounds the subordination of the woman to the man: was it only a consequence of the fall? ('Rule', *mashal*, in Gen. 3:16 may refer to benevolent government, as in Gen. 45:26, *or* to harsh, oppressive dominion, as in Gen. 4:7; *cf.* 37:8, Is. 3:12.) G. Bray ('The significance of God's image in Man', *TynB* 42, 1991, p. 221) ties 'submission' to the fall but affirms a 'hierarchical principle' *before* the fall. While Genesis 1 mentions only the authority of man and woman together over the earth, and says nothing about their relationship, the main argument in favour of an original subordination seems to be the naming of the woman by Adam (2:23). Phyllis Trible, in *God and the Rhetoric of Sexuality* (Philadelphia, 1978), while granting that name-giving implies authority, denies that Adam gave his wife her name. G. W. Ramsey ('Is name-giving an act of domination in Genesis 2:23 and elsewhere?', *CBQ* 50, 1988, pp. 24–35), argues the opposite: Adam did name his wife, but this does not imply subordination. Yet in all biblical instances of name-giving, the authority-bearer names the subordinate (except Genesis 16:13, where a human being gives God a name). The word 'Helper', often applied to God, involves no inferiority; in Genesis 2:18, however, it is used to define the woman's essential role and status. In 2:24 the man is said to take the initiative. Paul's arguments in 1 Corinthians 11:3–12 and 1 Timothy 2:13–15 must also be taken into account. A cautious conclusion is that *mashal*, 'rule', would have been too strong a word to describe the relationship before the fall, but that there was some difference in authority, which sin embittered as it did child-bearing and cultivation of the ground.

The couple's sexual activity in the Garden is also a matter of debate. Rabbinical tradition, following earlier teaching (*Jubilees* 3:2–6), emphatically affirmed that Adam and Eve consummated their union, whereas the ascetically inclined church mostly denied it. Pregnancy occurs only after the fall (Gen. 4:1) though it has been argued from the word order in this verse that the translation should be 'Adam *had known his wife*', in the Garden). The 'one flesh' of 2:24 implies consummation straight after the marriage. There is no hint in the OT that Adam and Eve were less than fully mature, even with respect to their morals. The 'knowledge of good and evil', as study of the phrase has shown, does not refer to moral awareness, without which the idea of *obedience becomes meaningless.

Probation and representation

Reformed theologians since Calvin (Commentary, *Institutes* II, i, 14) have interpreted Genesis 2:16–17 as a *test of obedience*, to which Adam was put as head and representative of humankind: the tree of good and evil was forbidden to him for a time and (supposedly), had he passed the test, God would have raised him to a higher form of life. Some scholars (G. C. Berkouwer, *Man: The Image of God* [Grand Rapids, 1962], p. 345; H. A. G. Blocher) find no hint of probation in the text. The idea may stem from embarrassment at the apparent disproportion between Adam's action (eating a fruit) and God's response, a disproportion which disappears if the tree is understood as a literary symbol. It may also arise from the desire to explain the appearance of sin; the fall seems less scandalous as one of the possible outcomes of a test.

The concept of headship, rather than the less adequate 'corporate personality', reveals the communal nature of humankind and Adam's role within it. This is a key element in the biblical doctrine of original sin.

Bibliography

J. N. Aletti, 'Romains 5, 12–21: Logique, sens et fonction', *Bib* 78, 1997, pp. 3–32; G. Anderson, 'Celibacy or consummation in the

Garden? Reflections on early Jewish and Christian interpretations of the Garden of Eden', *HTR* 82, 1989, pp. 121–148; H. A. G. Blocher, *In the Beginning: The Opening Chapters of Genesis* (ET, Leicester and Downers Grove, 1984); *idem*, *Original Sin: Illuminating the Riddle* (Leicester and Grand Rapids, 1997); C. M. Pate, *The Glory of Adam and the Afflictions of the Righteous: Pauline Suffering in Context* (Lewiston, 1988); W. H. Shea, 'Adam in ancient Mesopotamian traditions', *AUSS* 15, 1977, pp. 27–41; D. P. Wright, 'Holiness, sex, and death in the Garden of Eden', *Bib* 77, 1996, pp. 305–329.

H. A. G. BLOCHER

ADOPTION

Adoption is the legal establishment of a kinship relationship between two people that is recognized as being equivalent to one based on physical descent. There are few references to the practice of adoption in the Scriptures, but the concept was employed to explain the nature of *God's relationship to his *people and to their *king.

Divine adoption in the OT

God and his adopted son, Israel

*Israel's status as God's son is based on the *covenant relationship established at the time of the *Exodus and due to be renewed at the future restoration (see *Eschatology). That relationship is frequently affirmed through the covenant formula 'you shall be my people, and I will be your God' (*cf.* Exod. 6:7; 29:45; Lev. 26:12; Deut. 29:13; 2 Sam. 7:24; 1 Chr. 17:22; Jer. 7:23; 11:4; 30:22; Ezek. 36:28; Hos. 1:9).

In several texts God adopts Israel as his son at the time of the Exodus (Exod. 4:22; Deut. 32:10; Hos. 11:1). God's parental relationship with Israel explains the way he treated them in the desert (Deut. 8:2–5) and serves as a basis for Israel's *obedience (Deut. 14:1–2). The memory of the way he raised Israel, with the tender love of a father (Deut. 32:10–14; Hos. 11:1, 3–4), makes the nation's idolatrous infidelity even more painful and incomprehensible (Deut. 32:15–18; Is. 1:2; Hos. 11:2). That infidelity provokes the anger of their father (Deut. 32:16, 19–20) and threatens the integrity of their status as God's children (Deut. 32:5).

Still, Israel counts on their father's tender heart to show *mercy and grant *forgiveness (Is. 64:6–12), and in the end his *love will not let him give up on his wandering children (Hos. 11:8–9). His compassion leads him to call them home again (Is. 43:6; Jer. 3:12–14; Hos. 11:10–11) and to promise them *blessings and a better future (Jer. 3:15–19; 31:9) in which they will also finally respond to him as loving and faithful children (Jer. 3:19).

God and his adopted son, the king of Israel

In 2 Samuel 7:14 God promises *David, 'I will be a father to him, and he shall be a son to me' (NRSV), speaking of David's offspring. The promise is repeated verbatim in 1 Chronicles 17:13 and then is clearly applied to *Solomon in 1 Chronicles 28:6. Referring to that promise, Psalm 2:7 says, 'I will tell of the decree of the LORD: He said to me, "You are my son; today I have begotten you."' Although they have been much debated, it seems that 2 Samuel 7:14 and Psalm 2:7 are best understood as based on adoption formulae; thus God's relationship to the king was understood in terms of adoption (see esp. J. M. Scott, *Adoption as Sons of God*, pp. 96–104; M. Weinfeld in *IDBSup*, pp. 190–191). 2 Samuel 7:12 establishes that the father–son relationship between God and the king will be established with David's offspring after his death, and in the second part of 7:14 it is implied that God will take over the father's role in raising the son. This adoption probably serves as the legal basis for the gift of the eternal dynasty (7:13–16); this is confirmed by the reference to an inheritance following the adoption formula in Psalm 2:7–8: 'I will tell of the decree of the LORD: He said to me, "You are my son; today I have begotten you. Ask of me, and I will make the nations your heritage, and the ends of the earth your possession."'

Already in 2 Samuel 7 the adoption formula v. 14 is contextualized by the covenant formula (v. 24, 'And you established your people Israel for yourself to be your people forever; and you, O LORD, became their God'), such that God's covenant with David and the adoption of the Davidic king is 'a case of special election within the covenant relationship between Yahweh and his people

Israel' (Scott, *Adoption*, p. 209).

In time God's relationship with his people came to be portrayed by combining the covenant formula with the adoption formula. In Hosea 1:9–10 a reversal of a previous rejection of the covenant formula (Israel will be 'my people') is conjoined with the recognition of Israel as God's children.

Divine adoption in the intertestamental literature

In early Jewish traditions the adoption formula found in 2 Samuel 7:14 was applied to the Messiah (*Florilegium* 1:11), to God's people as a whole in the time of restoration (*Jubilees* 1:24), and to both (*Testament of Judah* 24:3; see Scott, *Adoption*, pp. 104–117). This development may have been encouraged by the proximity of the adoption formula to the covenant formula in 2 Samuel 7 (Scott, *Adoption*, pp. 104–105), and by the fact that the Davidic king represented his people and came to be identified, in some sense, with his people (compare Dan. 7:13–14 with its interpretation in Dan. 7:27).

In early Jewish literature (and in the NT, as we shall see) the expectation of the re-establishment of God's covenant adoption of his people became closely tied to the prophetic promises of the outpouring of God's Spirit (see *Holy Spirit) on his Messiah and on his people in the time of restoration (Is. 42:1; 44:3; Ezek. 36:27; 37:14; 39:29; Joel 2:28–29; Zech. 12:10; *cf. Jubilees* 1:24–25; *Testament of Judah* 24:3).

Divine adoption in the NT

In Acts 13:33 and in Hebrews 1:3–5 and 5:5 the resurrection/*exaltation of Jesus is understood to be his enthronement as God's king and son, in agreement with a messianic interpretation of 2 Samuel 7:14 and of Psalm 2:7. That Paul has a similar understanding of these events is indicated by his allusion to the former passage when he says that Jesus, who was 'descended from David according to the flesh' was designated 'Son of God' (Rom. 1:3–4). The second affirmation appears to be a circumlocution for the adoption formula of 2 Samuel 7:14.

Paul is the only author in the NT to use the word 'adoption' (*hyiothesia*, sometimes translated 'sonship') in his writings (Rom. 8:15, 23; 9:4; Gal. 4:5; Eph. 1:5). Although there has been great debate regarding the contextual background and meaning of the word in Paul, the evidence suggests that it refers to the process or state of being adopted, and that an OT and Jewish background probably lies behind Paul's usage (see especially the studies of Scott).

In Romans 9:4 Paul recognizes adoption to be one of Israel's special privileges; evidently he is thinking of the adoption which the nation received at the Exodus, as discussed above. In the other four places where the word is used it refers to the status of believers as God's adopted children in and through *Jesus Christ. One of the motives for praising God in Ephesians 1:3–14 is that 'He destined us for adoption as his children *through Jesus Christ*' (1:5). For Paul it is clear that the adoption of Christians is derived from that of Jesus who is God's Son in a unique sense. In Galatians Paul says that 'God sent his Son' so that believers 'might receive adoption as children' (4:4–5). It is through the work of Jesus Christ, *the* seed of *Abraham and *the* son of God, and by their union or identification with him, that they are adopted as God's children (Gal. 3:16, 26–27; 4:4–5; Rom. 6:5).

Paul associates adoption as God's children with the reception of the Spirit (Gal. 4:4–6; Rom. 8:15) whom he even calls the 'Spirit of adoption' (Rom. 8:15). In both Romans and Galatians it is by the Spirit that believers participate in the adoption of the Son of God and join in his cry of 'Abba! Father!' (Rom. 8:15; Gal. 4:5–6; *cf.* Mark 14:36).

In the OT God promises that at the time of restoration he will transform the hearts of his people by his Spirit so that they will fulfil his law rather than rebel against it (Deut. 30:6; Jer. 31:33; Ezek. 36:26; see *Freedom). In the passages surrounding Galatians 4:4–6 and Romans 8:15, Paul takes up this theme. Galatians 4:6 explicitly says that because believers are his children 'God has sent the Spirit of his Son into our hearts'. Galatians 5:16–25 affirms that it is through this Spirit that the flesh can be overcome and God's will accomplished. The argument of Romans 8:1–14 is similar to that of Galatians 5:16–18, explicitly affirming that God sent his Son 'in order that the just requirement of the law might be fulfilled in us, who walk … according to the Spirit' (8:4; see also Rom. 5:5; 6:17). Thus when Paul speaks of the 'Spirit of adoption' in 8:15 he may have fused together promises linking the Spirit with divine adoption and with the spiritual and moral transformation of the restored people of God.

The references to adoption in Galatians 4:5 and in Romans 8:15 both occur in contexts that explicitly establish a strong connection between adoption and the status of heirs: heirs of God, fellow heirs of Christ and of the promises given to Abraham (Rom. 8:17; Gal. 3:18, 29; 4:1, 7). For Paul it is through divine adoption as God's children, made possible by the *redemptive work of God's unique Son, that believers are able to participate in the rich inheritance promised to the seed of Abraham and of David.

In Romans 8:23 Paul refers to another aspect of divine adoption in which the Spirit plays a different role. Here he says that believers have the 'first fruits of the Spirit', but are still awaiting their adoption, which is now identified as 'the redemption of our bodies' (8:23). This is a reference to the future revelation of the *glory of the children of God (Rom. 8:18–21). When Jesus comes, those who are already God's children through the Spirit of adoption will 'participate in Jesus' resurrection to messianic Son of God in power (Rom. 1:4)' through the Spirit, as they in turn are resurrected (Scott, Adoption, p. 266). At that time they will enter into a fuller and more glorious participation with Christ and conformity to his *image 'in order that he might be the firstborn within a large family' (Rom. 8:29).

While other passages in Paul's writings that speak of believers as God's children should be understood in the light of what he says about adoption, equally the significance of divine adoption for Paul should be understood in terms of what he says about the children of God, since it is by adoption that one enters into that status.

In 2 Corinthians 6:16–18 Paul cites a number of OT texts that he understands as promises given to Christian believers (7:1). Bound together in this list of 'promises' are the covenant formula in v. 16 (from Lev. 26:12) and the adoption formula in v. 18 (2 Sam. 7:14 modified by Is. 43:6; cf. also Rev. 21:3, 7). He cites Hosea 2:23 and 1:10 (with its combination of elements from the covenant and adoption formulae) in Romans 9:25–26 to explain the inclusion of the Gentiles in God's eschatological people.

For Paul it is God's unique Son, Jesus Christ, who has made believers' adoption as God's children possible. That adoption takes place through their Spirit-mediated identification with Christ, and entails participation in God's restored people and (as heirs of God and of Christ) in the blessings and benefits of the promised time of eschatological *salvation.

Bibliography

H. Haag in TDOT 2, pp. 147–159; V. P. Hamilton in NIDOTTE 4, pp. 362–364; F. W. Knobloch in ABD 1, pp. 76–79; F. Lyall, 'Roman law in the writings of Paul – Adoption', JBL 88, 1969, pp. 458–466; H. Ringgren in TDOT 1, pp. 1–19; J. M. Scott, Adoption as Sons of God (Tübingen, 1992); idem, in DPL, pp. 15–18; M. Weinfeld in IDBSup, pp. 188–192.

R. E. CIAMPA

ADULTERY

Adultery in the literal sense

In both OT and NT, adultery is regarded as a serious *sin. Adultery presupposes the existence of *marriage. When *God formed Adam and Eve, our first parents, he initiated the marriage relationship, a relationship in which 'a man will leave his father and mother and be united to his wife, and they will become one flesh' (Gen. 2:24, NIV).

In Matthew 19:5–6 Jesus quotes this verse from Genesis, and states that it is the Creator who has made the pronouncement. Then Jesus adds, 'So they are no longer two, but one flesh. Therefore what God has joined together, let no one separate' (NRSV). The 'one flesh' relationship of marriage involves a joining together of the *man and the woman at all levels, social, economic, emotional, and physical. Adultery is the violation of this one-flesh relationship, the intrusion of an outsider into the total, unique and exclusive commitment which husband and wife are to have to each other.

Thus in its literal sense, 'adultery' refers to the act in which a spouse engages in sexual behaviour with a third party. In common with all sexual behaviour outside marriage, adultery is inconsistent with God's intention that sexual expression be restricted to the marriage relationship. Adultery is also an expression of disloyalty to the marriage partner, to whom alone one is to be united through sexual encounter: 'she is your partner, the wife of your marriage covenant ... do not break faith with the wife of your youth' (Mal. 2:14–15, NIV).

The first explicit mention of adultery is the prohibition in Exodus 20:14, one of the Ten Commandments. This prohibition is repeated in numerous places in both OT and NT.

In most places where the word 'adultery' is used, it refers to a physical act. However, *Jesus also applied the term (Matt. 5:27–28) to the thought and intent of the heart. The act of adultery most frequently results from allowing an illicit attraction to move from thought into action, and Jesus identifies the lustful look as the beginning of the sin. That first step, the lustful mental dalliance, is in itself disloyalty to one's spouse. The sin of adultery begins in the mind and heart (Matt. 15:19; Mark 7:21); adultery usually takes place because, to use Jeremiah's vivid picture (5:8), people are like 'well-fed, lusty stallions, each neighing for another man's wife', or another woman's husband. Job (31:1–12) recognized the temptation which results from letting one's eyes and imagination linger upon the sexual attractiveness of another person (*cf.* Prov. 6:23–29). And 2 Peter 2:14, possibly in an allusion to the words of Jesus, speaks of those who have 'eyes full of adultery'.

Adultery, cultic prostitution, and idolatry

'Adultery' is also used in the Bible in a spiritual sense, with reference to the disloyalty of the covenanted *people of God who turned from Yahweh to *worship and serve other gods. The origin of this spiritual adultery is in the cultic prostitution and associated *idolatry which confronted *Israel in Canaan.

In ancient fertility rites, devotees would engage in sexual intercourse with the shrine prostitute and by this means, through imitative or 'sympathetic' magic, would seek to ensure that the land and its creatures brought forth in abundance. The shrine prostitutes were highly respected because of their (supposed) role in bringing prosperity to the land. This practice of cultic prostitution is attested from Babylon to Cyprus, and from Greece to Canaan, where it was a particularly prominent feature of Baal worship.

The book of Exodus records how Yahweh repeatedly warned Moses of the danger which would be posed to the Israelites by the people already living in the land to which he was leading them (Exod. 23:23–24, 33; 34:12–16; Lev. 18:3; 20:23; Deut. 7:1–5; 12:29–31; 29:16–18). The Lord predicted that the people would prostitute themselves to other gods and so incur his wrath (Deut. 31:16–21).

Yet even in the wilderness in the days of Moses, the people were making sacrifices to idols, to whom they 'prostituted' themselves (Lev. 17:7; Deut. 32:15–18). They were enticed by the Moabite women into sexual immorality and sacrificing to Baal and worshipping him (Num. 25:1–3; Deut. 4:3; Ps. 106:28; Hos. 9:10). To sacrifice to Moloch (Lev. 20:5), or to turn to mediums and spiritists (Lev. 20:6), is to prostitute oneself by following them.

In the Law of Moses Israelites are forbidden to become shrine prostitutes (Deut. 23:17).

After the conquest of Canaan under Joshua, significant Canaanite communities remained in the land (Judg. 1:27–36; 1 Chr. 5:25), and ever thereafter were a snare and temptation to the Israelites. All too easily Israel was persuaded that the god of the land, Baal, and not Yahweh, was the source of nature's gifts. The people came to believe that to have sexual intercourse with sacred prostitutes was to share in the divine. In consequence, Baal worship, with its attendant sexual practices, was a problem against which prophets and godly Israelites had constantly to contend (*e.g.* 2 Chr. 25:14–16; *cf.* Elijah's confrontation with Ahab and the prophets of Baal on Mt Carmel, 1 Kgs. 18:16–46; and Jehu's destruction of Baal worship in Israel at the same time, 2 Kgs. 10:18–28).

Judges 2:7–17 notes that 'the people served the LORD throughout the lifetime of Joshua and of the elders who outlived him ... After that whole generation had been gathered to their fathers, another generation grew up who knew neither the LORD nor what he had done for Israel. Then the Israelites did evil in the eyes of the LORD and served the Baals .... they would not listen to their judges but prostituted themselves to other gods and worshipped them.' Even Gideon, through whom Yahweh delivered Israel from the Midianites, fashioned a gold ephod and 'All Israel prostituted themselves by worshipping it there, and it became a snare to Gideon and his family' (8:27); and furthermore, 'No sooner had Gideon died than the Israelites again prostituted themselves to the Baals' (8:33).

The Israelites were prohibited from marrying the people of the land, and were warned of the consequences of doing so: 'when you choose some of their daughters as wives for your sons, and those daughters prostitute themselves to their gods, they will lead your sons to do the same' (Exod. 34:15–16; also Deut. 7:4). This principle was never more clearly exemplified than in the life of Solomon, who began his reign by asking for God's wisdom but who disobeyed his command and married many foreign wives, with the result that 'As Solomon grew old, his wives turned his hearts after other gods' (1 Kgs. 11:1–11). After the return from exile, Nehemiah took a very strong line against intermarriage, citing the tragedy of Solomon's foreign wives (Neh. 13:23–27).

Hosea describes (4:14) how the Israelite men 'consort with harlots and sacrifice with shrine prostitutes'. Israel is portrayed as going after other gods like an adulterous wife goes after her lovers; the people attribute the fertility of the land to these other gods (2:5), and do not acknowledge that all its blessings have come from Yahweh (2:8). But, says Yahweh, though the people engage in fertility rites with the cultic prostitutes, their prosperity will not increase (4:10–12). Rather, God's judgment will cause Israel's abundance to wither away (2:9–13); Yahweh will withhold the increase of the land to show that he, not Baal, is its source.

Spiritual adultery

Participation in cultic prostitution led Israel into idolatry. As the Canaanite religious rites involved sexual intercourse with shrine prostitutes, so the prophets spoke of Israel's *apostasy from Yahweh as 'spiritual adultery' (Is. 57:3–9). The actual adultery of many Israelites with the cultic prostitutes generated the language of spiritual adultery, which denotes the turning away of Israel from Yahweh to foreign gods.

Jeremiah portrays the relationship of the people of Israel to God at the Exodus as that of a bride who loved her husband and followed him through the desert (Jer. 2:2; 31:32; cf. Is. 54:5; 61:10; 62:5; Hos. 2:15). But then she turned away to other gods,

'worthless idols' (Jer. 2:5, 8, 11); this behaviour is compared to that of a prostitute (2:17–33; cf. 2:20). Jeremiah develops further the theme of Israel as an adulterous wife (3:1–21), though he declares that Yahweh will receive her back if she turns from her idols (3:22 – 4:4). But Israel is guilty of forgetting God and of trusting instead in false gods, and is condemned because of its 'adulteries and lustful neighings' and 'shameless prostitution' (Jer. 13:25–27; 9:2).

Ezekiel also depicts Israel as the bride of Yahweh who became an adulterous and promiscuous wife (chs. 16 and 23). In the punishment of exile they will remember how God has 'been grieved by their adulterous hearts, which have turned away from me, and their eyes, which have lusted after their idols' (Ezek. 6:9). They will be restored, if they will 'put away from me their prostitution and the lifeless idols of their kings' (43:7–9).

Hosea, prophesying before the Assyrian attack upon the northern kingdom of Israel, is the earliest and the most impassioned of the prophets who speak of the spiritual adultery of Israel. At Yahweh's command, Hosea marries an adulterous woman, and thus his own life becomes a vivid representation of the relationship of God and unfaithful Israel. Hosea then reviews Israel's history from this perspective.

Hosea's prophecy is not a calm intellectual discussion of Israel's sin. Rather, Hosea portrays God as devastated by Israel's betrayal, and in turmoil within himself, just as a loving husband is when his wife commits adultery. As Hosea disowns adulterous Gomer, so Yahweh disowns his people (1:6, 8–9; 2:2). Just like a human husband betrayed by his wife, Yahweh feels pain because of the unfaithfuness of his people. It tears at his very heart; they must be punished for their betrayal, but how can he give them up? Yahweh debates within himself, and says (11:8–9), 'My heart is changed within me; all my compassion is aroused. I will not carry out my fierce anger, nor will I turn and devastate Ephraim. For I am God and not man – the Holy One among you. I will not come in wrath.' He makes this decision because of his *love for Israel (1:7, 10–11; 2:23). He will again court and woo them, and betroth them to himself (2:14–20). So Yahweh instructs Hosea (3:1), 'Go, show your love to your wife again, though she is loved by another and is an adulteress. Love her as the LORD loves the Israelites, though they turn to other gods and love the sacred raisin cakes.' But the people of Israel must turn from their spiritual adultery, return to Yahweh, and seek his forgiveness (14:1–4).

The imagery is used to describe the relationship between the Lord and his people in the NT too. Christ is pictured as the bridegroom, and the people of God as his bride (Matt. 9:15; 25:1–10; Mark 2:19–20; Luke 5:34–35; John 3:29; 2 Cor. 11:2; Rev. 19:7; 21:2, 9; 22:17), and a parallel is drawn between the relationship of husband and wife and that of Christ and his *church (Eph. 5:22–33).

Although Israel is no longer guilty of idolatry, the NT writers regard them as still guilty of unfaithfulness to God, spiritual adultery. Addressing the scribes, Pharisees and Sadducees (Matt. 12:39; 16:4), and then the crowds (Mark 8:38), Jesus condemns them and the nation in general as an 'adulterous generation'. Some commentators take this phrase in a literal sense; there is some evidence to suggest that such a condemnation was well merited. But the primary sense of Jesus's words is spiritual; the leaders and people were spiritually unfaithful to God, and this was most clearly seen in their rejection of Jesus.

James certainly has spiritual adultery in mind when he writes (4:4, NKJV), 'Adulterers and adulteresses! Do you not know that friendship with the world is enmity with God?' (cf. Rev. 2:20–22; 14:8; 17:1–5; 18:3, 9; 19:2).

The theme of spiritual adultery is very significant theologically. It focuses attention upon the close relationship between God and his people, and in particular the great love he has for them; and it is a reminder of the seriousness of spurning that love and turning away from him, whether to cultic prostitution and the worship of idols, or to love of this *world and indulgence in its pleasures.

See also: FAITH, FAITHFULNESS.

Bibliography

R. C. Ortlund Jr, *Whoredom: God's Unfaithful Wife in Biblical Theology* (Leicester and Grand Rapids, 1996).

B. W. POWERS

AGE, see TIME
AMOS, see Part 2
ANGELS, see SPIRITUAL POWERS

ANGER

The nature of anger

Anger is a state of disturbing and energizing passion in which strong negative emotion is triggered by a perception of wrong done to oneself or others or both. The capacity for anger, like that for *joy and grief, is ours as moral and relational beings made in God's *image, for Scripture frequently depicts joy, grief, and anger in *God as well as in his *human creatures. Anger asserts itself in attitudes of indignation and acts of aggression, both expressing a sense of outrage and a wish that appropriate punitive hurt overtake the wrongdoer. Anger threatens human self-control, prudence, and good judgment: ordinary speech describes angry people as having lost their 'temper' (equable balance) and 'head' (wisdom) and as being 'mad'. Yet Scripture speaks of anger as motivating admirable action too (see 2 Cor. 7:11; Is. 59:16; 63:3–6).

Analysing anger in any particular instance requires that we review our apprehension of the offending events, the arousal of our hostile reaction, our approval of our negative feelings, and our assault, such as it was, on the object of our anger (perhaps God, as with Jonah [Jonah 4]; perhaps oneself, as with Judas [Matt. 27:3–5]). This assault may stop at cherishing ill-will, or break out in verbal or physical violence; or, if the object of our anger is also an object of our *love, it may issue in tragic, frustrated distress at the good that has been lost and the harm that has been done; and if we are already committed to serve God and others, anger may teach us to be more careful in future. So anger may be *righteous or unrighteous, justified or unwarranted, virtuous or vicious, constructive or destructive in its effects, depending on what one is angry at, and on one's own prior character and commitments. The biblical writers view anger, human and divine, within this frame of understanding throughout.

The vocabulary of anger

Anger is multiform, and both OT Hebrew and NT Greek have a variety of words for its various expressions. The commonest Hebrew noun is *'ap̄*, which means first the nose or nostril (Num. 11:20; Is. 2:22) and then the quivering, snorting and flaring of the nostrils that indicate anger (Gen. 27:45; Job 4:9). 'Slow to anger' in Proverbs 14:29; 15:18; 16:32 (NRSV) is literally 'long of nose'. The imagery of heat and of burning is also drawn on, as is the vocabulary of fury, hostility and the quest for revenge. In the LXX and, echoing it, the NT, *thymos* and *orgē* are used as synonyms, often paired, to render all the Hebrew anger-words in application to both God and humans, and these are the commonest NT words for the idea. In secular usage *orgē* is more suggestive of thoughtful deliberation and *thymos* of thoughtless outburst, but in biblical Greek these distinctions of nuance do not apply.

Anger and sin

The loss of control and wisdom that anger brings lets loose what is worst in fallen human nature, namely love's opposite, the revengeful *hatred of thwarted and wounded pride. Thus in Genesis Cain kills Abel (4:3–8), Lamech threatens wholesale slaughter (4:23–24), Esau plans Jacob's death (27:41–45), Simeon and Levi massacre the Hivites (34:7, 25–29; 49:5–7), and Joseph's brothers hate and sell him (37:4, 8, 11, 18–28). Small wonder, then, that James says Christians should be 'slow to become angry, for man's anger does not bring about the righteous life that God desires' (1:19–20, NIV), and that Proverbs constantly represents the indulging of anger as the trouble-making style of the cruel fool (12:16; 14:17, 29; 15:18; 19:19; 27:3–4; 29:22; 30:33; *cf.* Eccles. 7:8–9). NT surveys of *sins regularly include angry attitudes and behaviour patterns (rage, envy, jealousy, hatred, fury, malice, murder) as habits to abjure and to replace by goodwill, self-control, patience, and peaceable purposes (Mark 7:22; Rom. 1:29–31; Gal. 5:20, *cf.* 22–23; Eph. 4:31, *cf.* 26–27; Col. 3:8; 1 Tim. 1:9; Jas. 3:14–18). Proneness to anger is specified as unfitting a man for eldership (Titus 1:7).

The anger of Jesus

Indications of anger on *Jesus' part appear in Mark 1:43 (at the prospect of unwelcome publicity), 3:1–5 (at the Pharisees' ill-will and indifference to suffering), 10:14 (at the disciples' arrogance towards children), 11:15–17 (at the desecration of the temple; *cf.* John 2:13–17), 12:24–27 (at the Sadducees' complacent errors about resurrection); Matthew 16:23 (at Peter's rejecting of his prediction of the cross), 23:13–36 (at the Pharisees' sham religiosity); and John 11:33–38 (at the repellent legacy of sin, namely death). In light of the NT insistence that Jesus, the Son of God incarnate, was totally sinless (John 8:46; 2 Cor. 5:21; Heb. 4:15; 7:26; 1 Pet. 2:22), these passages must be held to show that anger at what dishonours God, so far from being sinful, may be just the reverse – a truth already modelled in the Psalms and prophets (Ps. 139:21–22; Jer. 15:17).

The anger (wrath) of God

Though God is 'slow to anger' (Exod. 34:6) in relation to what his human creatures deserve, his anger at sin ('wrath' in most EVV) is frequently highlighted in both Testaments. Conceived in a way that excludes the fitfulness, arbitrariness, waywardness and foolishness that disfigure human anger, God's wrath is viewed as a judicial expression of *holiness repudiating unholiness, as it must. God's wrath is retribution re-establishing righteousness where unrighteousness was before, so vindicating God's goodness. Divine wrath touches both individuals and groups – family units (Num. 16:25–34; Josh. 7:24–26), urban units (Gen. 19:1–29; Luke 21:20–24) and national units (2 Kgs. 17:1–23; 24:20). Israel's lapses into apostasy brought drought, bad harvests and captivity, as Leviticus 26:14–45 and Deuteronomy 28:15–68 had warned; Revelation anticipates wrath in world history until it ends (Rev. 2:5; 11:18; 15:1; 19:15, *etc.*); Romans 1:18–32 diagnoses divine wrath in the spiritual and moral degenerating of society. Also, Jesus and the NT writers proclaim a coming 'day of wrath, when God's righteous *judgment will be revealed', when everyone will receive a destiny matching his or her personal life-choices (Rom. 2:5–16; 2 Cor. 5:10). So 'leave room for God's wrath, for it is written: "It is mine to avenge; I will repay," says the Lord' (Rom. 12:19 [NIV], citing Deut. 32:35).

God's anger pacified

A significant NT word group expresses the thought of propitiating (satisfying, and so quenching and pacifying) the anger of God against sinful human beings. The words are: the noun *hilasmos* (propitiation, that which propitiates: 1 John 2:2; 4:10); the verb *hilaskomai* (with dative, be propitious to: Luke 18:13; with accusative, make propitiation for: Heb. 2:17); the adjective *hilastērios* (having a propitiatory effect: Rom. 3:25); and the noun *hilastērion* (technical term in LXX for the propitiatory covering, the 'mercy-seat', in the tabernacle; Heb. 9:5). As the context in each case shows, it is the sacrificial death ('blood') of Jesus Christ, God's incarnate Son, that quenches divine anger against sinners, just because Christ's death was a vicarious enduring of the penalty that was our due. The once popular view that expiation of sins is all that this word group signifies rested on the supposition that there is no wrath of God needing to be dealt with, rather than on linguistic or contextual considerations, and is now largely abandoned. The NT idea of propitiation is that of pacifying God's judicial anger by removing sin from his sight, which is what the *atoning blood of Christ has done. Sinners with faith in Christ are no longer in the hands of an angry God (to echo Jonathan Edwards' famous phrase), but enjoy the forgiveness and favour of the God who quenched his own wrath by sending his Son to be the propitiation for our sins (1 John 4:10).

Bibliography

J. Fichtner *et al.* in *TDNT 5*, pp. 382–447; H. C. Hahn in *NIDNTT 1*, pp. 105–113; L. Morris, *The Apostolic Preaching of the Cross* (London, ³1965); *idem*, *The Cross in the New Testament* (Exeter, 1967); R. V. G. Tasker, *The Biblical Doctrine of the Wrath of God* (London, 1951).

J. I. PACKER

ANOINTED, see JESUS CHRIST
ANTICHRIST, see ESCHATOLOGY

APOSTASY

Introduction

The category 'apostasy' functions in theological discourse for the open and final repudiation of one's allegiance to *God in Christ. Consideration of the theme is warranted by the language and logic of the biblical writers and also by church life and pastoral concern.

John Owen, writing from the atemporal perspective of Puritan thought, defines the essence of apostasy as 'a total renunciation of all the constituent principles and doctrines of Christianity'. This entails a 'voluntary, resolved relinquishment of ... the *gospel, the *faith, rule and *obedience thereof'. A distinction is generally drawn between apostasy and backsliding, a less radical decay of one's Christian integrity, for the latter does not involve 'resolved relinquishment'. This distinction is useful in some contexts, but the Bible does not always separate the two neatly. For example, the same Hebrew noun (*m'šûbâ*) in Jeremiah 2:19; 5:6 and 14:7 is translated 'backsliding[s]' in the NIV and 'apostasies' in the NRSV. At what point in real life does backsliding degenerate into apostasy? Biblical theology may not offer an easy answer, but it can provide a framework of conceptual and historical models to which one can look for analogies to one's own historical situation.

The biblical language evoked by the category 'apostasy' is various and suggestive. The verbs 'forsake' (Deut. 31:16, NRSV), 'turn aside [from following God]' (1 Kgs. 9:6), 'wander' (Jer. 14:10), 'rebel [against God]' (Ezek. 2:3), 'cast [God behind one's back]' (Ezek. 23:35), 'commit treachery' (Dan. 9:7), 'commit whoredom' (Hos. 1:2), 'fall away' (Matt. 24:10), 'neglect' (Heb. 2:3), 'turn away' (Heb. 3:12), 'shrink back' (Heb. 10:39) and 'go out' (1 John 2:19) occur in contexts concerned with spiritual decline so egregious as to merit consideration as apostasy.

Biblical imagery adds to this richness of expression. Jerusalem's silver becomes dross and her wine is mixed with water (Is. 1:22). *Israel degenerates from a choice vine to a wild vine (Jer. 2:21). She is an unfaithful wife to her husband Yahweh (Hos. 1 – 3). The nation is like a defective bow that can no longer shoot straight (Hos. 7:16). Apostates in the Christian *church are like well-watered ground that produces not a good crop but thorns and thistles, the end of which is to be burned (Heb. 6:7–8).

Apostasy in the OT

Beginning with the fall of *Adam in Genesis 3, the apostate impulse in the human heart becomes the salient feature of the race. But apostasy finds its most pungent expression among the *covenant *people, by reason of the covenant itself, especially when apostates reach a sort of 'critical mass' in the corporate soul of the community so that the whole nation departs from its allegiance to God. This ominous development among the chosen nation is apostasy in the fullest sense. After a long-standing pattern of spiritual defection was established in the course of Israel's history, the nation was eventually abandoned to itself and allowed to be swallowed up in foreign *exile.

Early indications of Israel's intractable apostasy include their *worship of the golden calf (Exod. 32), their yoking themselves to the Baal of Peor (Num. 25) and the period of the judges (cf. Judg. 2:11–19). That these events were not isolated anomalies but true indications of the nation's apostate soul is implied by Psalm 106. The poet reviews Israel's record of resistance to God and identifies it as national uncleanness and prostitution (v. 39), which so angers God that 'he gave them into the hand of the nations' (v. 41).

During the period of the monarchy, apostasy in Israel developed with ultimately devastating effect. It was manifested in flirtation with the fertility religion of the Baals, and entanglement in political alliances with foreign powers. By the first Israel rejected the *loving provision of God; by the second they rejected his protective security. The prophet Hosea, addressing the northern kingdom in its latter decades, exposes the moral offensiveness of both in the language of spiritual harlotry. He unveils a shocking vision of Yahweh as a husband rejected by his adulterous wife (Hos. 1 – 3, et passim). Jeremiah, addressing the southern kingdom, laments that nation's lust for idols and alliances (Jer. 2), borrowing from Hosea's marital imagery. In 3:6–12 Jeremiah boldly identifies Israel as Apostasy incarnate (mᵉšûḇâ yiśra'el) and *Judah, the even more guilty offender, as Treachery (bogedâ yᵉhûdâ). Ezekiel 16 embellishes the prophetic vision still further. The nation was like a pitiful, abandoned infant girl, rescued by Yahweh and raised up to be an exquisite young woman, favoured by him with rich privilege and, indeed, married to her kind benefactor. But she used his gifts to finance liaisons with other lovers. In Ezekiel 23 the prophet re-tells the stories of both northern and southern kingdoms in terms of two sisters who corrupted themselves from their youth, but with the greater guilt falling upon Judah.

Interestingly, the prophetic language for apostasy suggests that it is, as it were, the photographic negative of *repentance. For example, in Jeremiah 3:12 the prophet calls apostate (mᵉšûḇâ) Israel to return (šûḇâ). In 3:14 and 22 he calls the apostates (šôḇâbîm) to return (šûḇû). In 8:5 the prophet agonizes over why the people apostatize (šôḇᵉḇâ) with perpetual apostasy (mᵉšûḇâ), refusing to return (lašûḇ). Both repentance and apostasy are acts of turning (šûḇ), but one is turning towards God and the other is turning away from him. Apostasy is a kind of perverse anti-conversion.

With some conspicuous exceptions, the overall history of the OT people of God is one of their refusing the *grace of God and turning away from him. This can be seen in passages like Ezekiel 20:1–39, Nehemiah 9:6–37 and Daniel 9:4–19, which review Israel's history with a sweep of the prophetic eye and discover there a damning pattern of defection which must be regarded as apostasy. But remarkably, condemnation is not the end for the apostate people of God. Yahweh may 'divorce' his adulterous wife (Hos. 1:9; 2:2), but he will win her heart again (Hos. 2:14–15). He will betroth her to himself again in re-created moral virginity (Hos. 2:19–20). He will heal Israel's apostasy and love them without any pre-condition (Jer. 3:22; Hos. 14:4). God shuts them up to disobedience, that he might show them *mercy, and the nation's mouth be stopped (Ezek. 16:59–63; cf. Rom. 11:1–32).

Apostasy in the NT

Although the Christian church is receiving the promised outpouring of the *Holy Spirit (Acts 2:14–21) and has inherited better arrangements for its life and worship than Israel enjoyed (Heb., passim), apostasy is very much within the scope of NT concern. Indeed, *Jesus predicted that the present, age-long delay before the end would be characterized by tribulation, such that many will 'fall away' (Matt. 24:10; cf. D. A. Carson, 'Matthew', in EBC, pp. 495, 498–499). The disciples themselves confirmed Jesus' prophetic word when they deserted him in Gethsemane (Matt. 26:56), although they were later restored. Within this historical framework of tribulation, which increases the temptation to fall away, the danger of apostasy remains until the end. (See *Eschatology.)

Any consideration of apostasy in NT teaching must begin with the conviction that Jesus Christ occupies the ultimate position in the *redemptive purposes of God (Heb. 1:1–4). As the consummation of OT *revelation, Jesus is the final and greatest God-revealer. With all lines of redemptive history converging on him, calculated repudiation of the all-sufficiency of Jesus must be regarded with the utmost seriousness.

The letter to the Hebrews solemnly insists upon the irreversibility of apostasy after exposure to the power of the Christian gospel (Heb. 6:4–6; cf. 12:16–17). Wilful persistence in sin after having received the knowledge of the *truth, such that one shrinks back from fixing one's faith upon the Son of God, exposes one to 'a fury of fire' (Heb. 10:26–31). A perfect faith is not required. The people of God are 'ignorant and wayward' (Heb. 5:2). But Jesus is able to help his people when they are *tested (Heb. 2:18). He can sympathize with their weakness, having been tested himself, and is therefore approachable (Heb. 4:15–16). To refuse his resources of mercy and grace in time of need could lead to an apostate condition, in which one holds the Son of God up to contempt (Heb. 6:6) – hardly consistent with 'things that belong to salvation' (Heb. 6:9). Such a view may not preclude a church's or denomination's recovery, but it offers no encouragement for individuals who apostatize. The author's position may be summed up, according to Paul Ellingworth, as follows: 'Nowhere does the writer of Hebrews leave his readers any room for the hope that, if they abandon faith in Christ, they may find, so to speak, a fallback position in their former (in particular, Jewish) beliefs and practices. Christ has made the old covenant old (8:13), so that there is now nowhere else to go. To abandon Christ, or to accord him anything but the highest place in the universe, is not to adopt an alternative religious option, but simply "to fall away from the living God" (3:12).' ('Hebrews and the anticipation of completion', *Themelios* 14, 1988, p. 10.)

The apostle Paul is amazed to see the Galatians 'deserting' the one who called them in the grace of Christ for another gospel (Gal. 1:6), and he condemns anyone who 'perverts' the true gospel (1:7–9). He also warns against hypocritical teachers who advocate asceticism (1 Tim. 4:1–5), glorifying physical depriv-

ation and denying the goodness of God. The apostle anticipates a time when church people will have 'itching ears' and so will turn away from the truth to myths (2 Tim. 4:3–4). He cautions the Ephesian elders against 'savage wolves' and those who will distort the truth to mislead the church (Acts 20:29–30; cf. 2 Pet. 2:1–2; Jude 3–4). These passages accurately illustrate the troubling spiritual atmosphere in which believers must demonstrate the genuineness of their faith and avoid apostasy.

Personal illustrations of apostasy may include Judas Iscariot (Luke 22:22), Hymenaeus and Alexander (1 Tim. 1:19–20) and Demas (2 Tim. 4:10). The immoral man in 1 Corinthians 5:1–5 is not an apostate; his continuing identification with the church is aggravating the scandal.

Paul's prophecy of 'the lawless one' (2 Thess. 2:1–12) who will draw the world away into rebellion against God may not describe apostasy in the strict sense. This agent of evil intrudes himself into the temple of God (2:4), but the interpretation of this 'temple' is an arguable point. He holds sway over 'all who have not believed the truth' (2:12), as distinct from the church (2:13–17).

Apostasy and perseverance

Jesus insisted that some who experience real spiritual power and name him 'Lord' will be rejected as 'evil-doers' (Matt. 7:21–23; cf. Heb. 6:4–6). He discerned in some an unconvincing faith (John 2:23–25). He posited various responses to the gospel, some of which are initially promising but prove hollow in the end (Luke 8:11–15). It is the believer's perseverance to the end that validates a claim to Christian faith and authenticates spiritual experience (Col. 1:21–23; Heb. 3:14; 6:11–12; 2 John 9). The apostle John accounts for those who walk away from their former identification with Christ in this way: 'They went out from us, but they did not belong to us; for if they had belonged to us, they would have remained with us. But by going out they made it plain that none of them belongs to us' (1 John 2:19).

Larger theological systems, Calvinist or Arminian, may unintentionally blunt the edge of the biblical witness either by diminishing one's sense of the need to persevere or by subverting one's confidence in God's commitment to and provision for the struggling saint.

Scripture affirms both God's active work in his people and their own responsibility to pursue *salvation (Phil. 2:12–13). Ultimately, the believer lays hold of God himself as 'him who is able to keep you from falling' (Jude 24). But the hypocrisy of apostates is eventually exposed, however impressive their profession of faith may be for a time.

See also: ADULTERY; FAITH.

Bibliography

D. A. Carson, 'Reflections on Christian assurance', *WTJ* 54, 1992, pp. 31–46; J. M. Gundry Volf, *Paul and Perseverance: Staying in and Falling Away* (Tübingen, 1990); I. H. Marshall, *Kept by the Power of God: A Study of Perseverance and Falling Away* (Minneapolis and Carlisle, 1975, 1995); *idem*, 'The problem of apostasy in New Testament theology', in *Jesus the Saviour: Studies in New Testament Theology* (London, 1990); R. C. Ortlund, Jr., *Whoredom: God's Unfaithful Wife in Biblical Theology* (Leicester and Grand Rapids, 1996); R. Wakely, in *NIDOTTE* 2, pp. 1121–1123; J. Owen, *The Nature and Causes of Apostasy from the Gospel*, in *The Works of John Owen*, vol. 7 (Edinburgh, repr. 1979).

R. C. ORTLUND, JR.

APOSTLE, see MISSION
APPEARANCE, DIVINE, see THEOPHANY

ASSURANCE

Assurance: terminology in the OT

Although since the Reformation the term *adsecurus* and its cognates have given much scope to the church for teaching about doubt and *faith and the need for a spiritual inner sense of the *Holy Spirit, and also for something like a practical syllogism, it is less easy to see much conceptualizing of the issue in the Bible. Of course in the OT we do find the idea of a reinforcement of faith which comes from *God. In its least technical sense we can see assurance in Genesis 15:1–6, where God reassures Abra(ha)m by a dream, or in Exodus 4, where he strengthens the wavering Moses by signs and words. Joshua seems to have received special treatment in

the form of divine intervention in battle and encouragement (Josh. 1:6–9; 5:13–15; 7:10–15; 8:1–20), as did Gideon in Judges 6:22–24 and 36–40. Given that 'standing' in Isaiah 7:9b ('if you will not believe you will not be made to stand'; author's translation) is the opposite of stumbling, in Isaiah 8:14 the sense seems to be that of mature faith doing without present signs, but hearing the prophetic word, trusting in God's character, and thus receiving an assurance which is both dignity and 'uprightness', an ability not to cower before God or anyone else. Hezekiah in 2 Kings 20:1–7 is an object lesson here. Assured faith is more than assent but is an attitude, incorporating belief and the positive emotion of steadfastness (as against despondency), lived out in a sense of 'quiet trust'. Related to this is Isaiah 28:16: 'he who believes will not be in haste' (RSV). This corresponds to what immediately precedes: 'I am laying … a precious cornerstone of a sure foundation'. Whether this 'cornerstone' is best understood as the Messiah or the responding faith is uncertain. Furthermore, Habakkuk 2:4b affirms: 'the righteous shall live in assurance'; this expression implies taking one's position in some already secure structure and not moving from it.

Assurance and inner witness: NT

Romans 8:16 speaks of the Holy Spirit giving 'immediate and direct' *witness; one should not rely on reflection or syllogism to prove to oneself that one is a Christian. The effect of the Holy Spirit's witness is the believer's ability to call God 'father' (Rom. 8:15). In 1 Corinthians 2:5 the foundation for faith is the power of God, and not only at the time of conversion. As in John 16, the work of the Holy Spirit is seen positively by Paul as reassurance and strengthening, bringing *joy where the initial stage of faith involved sorrow and some uncertainty. However, 2 Corinthians 13:5 sounds a rare call to self-examination, indicating that for Paul, faith was a matter for the depths as well as for the surface of a person's being. The assurance or certainty of faith is thus not like the certainty of knowledge, *e.g.* that of a scientific interpretation which may be challenged for a time by conflicting evidence. For assurance of faith it is moral disposition that counts, the 'love of a pure heart and good conscience and sincere faith' (1 Tim. 1:5). In 2 Timothy 4:17 Paul speaks of the gospel's being confirmed by the Lord's sustaining and rescuing him; here assurance is born of an objective, outwardly visible confirmation by God.

In Colossians 2:2 we find the phrase *plērophorias tēs syneseōs* ('all the riches of assured understanding', NRSV). In Colossians 4:12 Epaphras is said to wrestle in prayer so that the Colossians 'may stand mature and fully assured [*peplērophorēmenoi*] in everything that God wills'. Paul has already used the passive participle 'was being assured' when describing Abraham's saving faith (Rom. 4:21). The slightly odd expression in Romans 14:5 'let each be encouraged [*plērophoreisthō*] *in* his own mind' refers to the need of the individual to have a faith which is personal, not buttressed by comparisons with the apparent spirituality of others.

Steadied faith: Hebrews

For the writer to the Hebrews too there is a sense in which faith has to have the fullness of 'assurance' (6:11; 10:22) if it is to be a faith which perseveres and saves. But Hebrews takes us a step further by introducing the term *hypostasis* in relation to faith and *hope. In the LXX this word translates various Hebrew terms. In 2 Corinthians 9:3 and 11:17 *hypostasis* refers to a certainty in the mind (in these verses, that Paul is boasting of his foolishness). However, in Hebrews 11:1 and 3:14 *hypostasis* in its *function* is the antithesis of *apostenai*; it is what keeps one standing firm when one is tempted is to give up on God and his hope. *Hypostasis* is used in Hellenistic philosophy (to refer to the actualization of the invisible hopes to which people must hold) and in legal discourse (to refer to the warranty of future possession). Thus in Hebrews it can be used to refer to a guarantee of obtaining the future hope/*kingdom, in parallel with *bebaiōsis* (3:14). It includes the idea of the fragrance of that which will one day become empirically present, in contrast to that which merely seems to exist. Furthermore, in secular usage *hypostasis* may be that which remains after something has been strained through a sieve. In the context of Hebrews' theology, it is that which lasts, enables one to stand (*cf.* Is. 7:9) and connects the believer's faith now to the far-off hope of *heaven.

Against the view that *hypostasis* must mean 'confidence' rather than 'reality' or 'the effect or act of grace', the evidence suggests that in the Middle Platonism of the time of Hebrews (unlike that of later neoplatonists, Augustine included) hopes which were merely subjectively rooted were regarded as illusory; there had to be something more. Faith lends full certainty to our hope. But this faith is a *working* faith (*fides qua*) not 'the faith'; it was '*by* faith' that the heroes of Hebrews 11 were enabled to persevere. Faith does not move us towards assurance; rather (post-Pentecost) assurance is the start of faith, but it is also that which makes faith continue and endure, because it is a knowledge of God's good purposes. We are not assured of God's existence or providence but of Christ's ability to change humans. 'I believe; help my unbelief' (Mark 9:24) is faith because it recognizes that one's own unbelief does not make it impossible for him to act.

Confidence and conviction

The term *parrēsia* (confidence) which appears in Ephesians 3:12 is associated with 'faith' and is paralleled in that text by the idea of a right of access (*prosagōgē*). The LXX uses it once in Leviticus 26:12, but otherwise only in those books which were translated relatively late; it belongs to the world of Hellenistic trade and of religious and nationalistic confidence (*cf.* the many occurrences in 1–2 Macc.). The term is paralleled also (at Rom. 5:1) with *eirēnē*; assurance is linked with a sense of *peace, of being 'on the right side of God' through faith. Paul speaks in Romans 8:38 of his being persuaded (*pepeismai*), echoing Abraham's conviction, not just that *salvation was promised, but that it was promised *for him*. In Romans 4:21, it is said that 'Abraham did not waver in unbelief before the promise of God but was strengthened in faith, giving glory to God and convinced [*plērophoretheis*] that what God had promised he was able to do and would bring it about'. Likewise in 1 John 4:17 it is *love, the active outworking of faith, that will lead to believers having *parrēsia* on the day of judgment.

Assurance also relates to conscience, as is clear from Hebrews. The question that the testimony of a good conscience addresses is not, 'Do I have a gracious God?' but rather, 'Is my faith in the grace of God sincere or hypocritical?' The ability to be confident (*cf.* 2 Cor. 13:5) after self-examination is also reflected in the Lukan notion of the Holy

Spirit as the source of restoration after sin or even apostasy and thus perhaps of a stronger, tested, more assured faith. Likewise in Luke 12:10 ('the one who blasphemes against the Holy Spirit will not be forgiven') the implication is that assurance is *re*assurance and requires continual 'topping-up'.

The 'medieval' view that God's will is ultimately unknowable implies that assurance is none too desirable, since one's uncertainty should keep driving one to the sacrament. Assurance is the subjective side of the objective hope of heaven. Yet since the object of that assurance is not yet present, assurance needs constant renewal from God's promise. The NT instructs believers to play their part, to 'hurry to make firm your election and calling' (2 Pet. 1:10). It is as one lives as an elect person that one is and shall be assured of one's *election. Assurance is the result of faith reflecting on its object so as to become more like certainty; faith becomes more certain than reason by trying itself out against reason. Yet this knowledge is personal and involves the will, since assurance, as faith strengthened through doubt, is like the 'second naivety' of those who have learned again to trust completely and unselfconsciously in love, like little children.

Conclusion

For a *biblical* theology, the focus of assurance is not a decree, nor a 'personal relationship with God', but God's love, on which such a relationship may be built. A doctrine of assurance is contained *in nuce* in Matthew 28:5: 'do not be afraid ...' OT parallels include those of Elijah after Mt Carmel (1 Kgs. 19) and many Psalms in which God reassures his servant when all other noises have subsided. A quest for certainty may only reinforce doubt; receiving assurance as a gift allows God's faithfulness to be demonstrated in action.

Bibliography

O. Betz, 'Firmness in faith: Hebrews 11:1 and Isaiah 28:16', in B. P. Thompson (ed.), *Scripture, Meaning and Method* (Hull, 1997); D. A. Carson, 'Reflections on Christian Assurance', *WTJ* 34 (1992), pp. 31–46; I. H. Marshall, *Kept By the Power of God* (London, 1969); A. Schlatter, *Die Grunde der christlichen Gewissheit* (Giessen, 1998).

M. W. ELLIOTT

ATONEMENT

Introduction

'Atonement' may be defined as God's work on sinners' behalf to reconcile them to himself. It is the divine activity that confronts and resolves the problem of human *sin so that people may enjoy full fellowship with God both now and in the age to come. While in one sense the meaning of atonement is as broad and diverse as all of God's saving work throughout time and eternity, in another it is as particular and restricted as the crucifixion of *Jesus. For in the final analysis Scripture presents his sacrificial death as the central component of God's reconciling *mercy. This explains why Revelation 22:3, for example, shows not only God but also the *Lamb – slain to atone for sin – occupying the throne of heaven in the age to come.

Why is atonement needed? The Bible portrays a personal and loving yet *righteous God who created a 'very good' world (Gen. 1:31, NIV). But human faithlessness plunged creation into a state of estrangement from him (Gen. 3). Human unrighteousness thus brought the punishment of divine curse (see *Blessing/curse) (Gen. 3:14–19). Yet in God's great mercy, even his curse does not leave the world languishing in darkness. Latent in the curse is a ray of future redemptive light, the so-called Protoevangelion (Gen. 3:15; *cf.* Rom. 16:20, Heb. 2:14). The banishment of Adam and Eve from Eden underscores God's ultimately benevolent purpose (Gen. 3:22–23). He does not abandon his fallen creation; rather he moves to redeem and restore it. 'Atonement' is the saving act of God which according to Scripture makes possible, and in a sense constitutes, his redeeming and restoring work. It is the means by which his righteousness is re-established in a cosmic order marred temporarily by rebellion against its Creator and King.

In the NIV, the word 'atonement' occurs in the NT only three times (Rom. 3:25; Heb. 2:17; 9:5). 'Atoning' occurs only twice (1 John 2:2; 4:10). But the thing denoted by the word is often present when the word itself is not. Hebrew words of the *kpr* word group (*cf.* words translating *exhiloskomai* and cognates in the LXX) are widespread in the OT, the NIV translating a form of 'atone' some 112 times (Torah 96×, Prophets 10×,

Writings 6×). In the NT, atonement ideas are present with a wide range of words and their cognates, among them ransom, redemption, *covenant, sacrifice, reconciliation and *victory. These are dealt with in various connections below.

The need for atonement

Just as the Christian Scriptures assume the existence of God, they assume the sinful nature of humans since the fall. The programmatic NT statement 'all have sinned' (Rom. 3:23) is amply attested in the OT as well (e.g. 1 Kgs. 8:46; 2 Chr. 6:36; Job 14:4; Ps. 14:1–3; Prov. 20:9; Eccles. 7:20). In intertestamental Judaism we find a number of sectarian strategies to address the widely acknowledged problem of personal and corporate guilt. The angel announces Jesus as the one who will 'save his people from their sin' (Matt. 1:21).

John the Baptist declared in effect that the whole Jewish population was cut off from its covenant God; only those who would repent and renew their hope in the coming kingdom could expect God's mercy on the day of judgment. From the Bible's point of view, if there was no hope for Abraham's descendants unless they cried out for divine assistance, the larger pagan world was far worse off. And this is exactly what Paul affirms: before their conversion the (non-Jewish) Ephesians were 'excluded from citizenship in Israel and foreigners to the covenants of the promise, without hope and without God in the world' (Eph. 2:12). Jesus assumed the fallenness of those he encountered: 'If you, then, though you are evil … ' (Matt. 7:11). The apostles' zeal to take the gospel to the ends of the earth made sense only if they shared Jesus' conviction of his universal lordship. He commanded them to take the good news to all humanity, since everyone needed to hear and accept it in order to be saved (cf. Rom. 10:14–15).

Alongside the conviction of humanity's condemnation is the certainty of divine *judgment. God's wrath is not petty or capricious, but neither is it to be regarded as a barbaric legacy of unsophisticated antiquity. A profoundly disturbing subplot of the whole OT is impending (and sometimes unfolding) divine judgment, whether direct or indirect. This is seen in the Genesis flood, the ruin of Sodom and Gomorrah, the plagues and defeat that befell the Egyptians, the destruction of Can-aanite settlements, David's military conquests, and the divine punishment of God's own people at the hand of the Assyrians and later the Babylonians. And the NT counsels no lessening of vigilant readiness in the light of an imminent, great, and terrible Day of the Lord (e.g. Matt. 24:44; 1 Thess. 1:10; 2 Thess. 1:7–9; Rev. 22:7, 12). God's verdict on human rebellion against himself is symbolized by the blackness that covered the whole land in the hour of Jesus' crucifixion (Luke 23:44).

Humanity's abject and seemingly incurable spiritual separation from God, and God's inexorable movement to 'bring every deed into judgment, including every hidden thing, whether it is good or evil' (Eccles. 12:14), are twin truths seen in the unfolding biblical history of redemption. They are also the foundations for an understanding of the biblical doctrine of atonement. They pose the problem to which God responded with both OT and NT atoning sacrifice.

The means of atonement: Old Testament

Many OT passages speak of atonement in terms of the sacrifice and offering up of the blood of a suitable victim. The people's inadvertent sin, which deserved death, could be atoned for through the death of a prescribed animal duly chosen and offered in their place. (The system did not make explicit provision for brazen or 'high-handed' sin.) From the Torah's point of view, 'without the shedding of *blood there is no forgiveness' (Heb. 9:22). At the onset of the Mosaic era, 'Moses said to Aaron, "Come to the altar and sacrifice your sin offering and your burnt offering and make atonement for yourself and the people; sacrifice the offering that is for the people and make atonement for them, as the LORD has commanded."' (Lev. 9:7). Aaron's disobedience to this mandate was on pain of death (Lev. 8:35). The destruction of Nadab and Abihu illustrated this (Lev. 10:1–2). Sacrifice to atone for sins was at the heart of the religious system which God instituted for his people and as a witness to the surrounding world.

The prophets understood that atonement did not amount to a bribe offered to God in exchange for forgiveness. God says disparagingly of Israel, 'They offer sacrifices given to me … but the LORD is not pleased with them' (Hos. 8:13). Micah's sarcasm is palpable:

'With what shall I come before the LORD and bow down before the exalted God? Shall I come before him with burnt offerings, with calves a year old? Will the LORD be pleased with thousands of rams, with ten thousand rivers of oil? Shall I offer my firstborn for my transgression, the fruit of my body for the sin of my soul?' (Mic. 6:6–7). Sacrifice as nothing more than a ritual act did not excuse transgression. Rather it was to be the expression of a contrite heart, and appealed to God for the mercy that he and he only could provide: 'The sacrifices of God are a broken spirit; a broken and contrite heart, O God, you will not despise' (Ps. 51:17). This was confirmed to Isaiah when the seraph announced the forgiveness of his sin, not because of Isaiah's religious act but by the atonement which God's angel provided: 'With [the live coal] he touched my mouth and said, "See, this has touched your lips; your guilt is taken away and your sin atoned for."' (Is. 6:7). Throughout the OT, God provides the sacrifice and ensures the atoning efficacy of the ritual he prescribes: 'I have given [the blood of the sacrifice] to you to make atonement for yourselves on the altar' (Lev. 17:11).

Expiation or propitiation?

It has been argued (*e.g.* by C. H. Dodd) that atonement should be understood as expiation for sin. 'Expiation' in this sense means 'cancellation' or 'dismissal'. God simply waives the threatened penalty for transgressions. R. Averbeck argues that there is good ground for understanding the piel Hebrew verb form of *kpr*, often translated as 'atone' or 'atonement', as denoting 'to wipe away, wipe clean, purge' (see *e.g.* Lev. 16:20, 33; Deut. 32:43; Dan. 9:24; Is. 47:11). He suggests that 'the underlying rationale of OT *kpr* was wipe away, not ransom' (*NIDOTTE* 2, p. 708). Averbeck's lengthy discussion makes little mention of either divine wrath or human sinfulness, though these are prominent in the background of OT atonement passages.

Others point out that atonement seems rather to involve 'propitiation', the turning away of wrath by an offering. It does not merely expiate in the sense of dismissing sin; it propitiates in the sense of averting God's punishment. Linguistic work by L. Morris and others appears to have refuted the expiation theory as Dodd and his supporters have presented it. Recent Romans commentators like Moo, Mounce and Stott have upheld Morris' arguments, as have I. H. Marshall and others. Current Septuagint lexicography points in the same direction (J. Lust, E. Eynikel, K. Hauspie, *A Greek-English Lexicon of the Septuagint*, pp. 160–161).

The key to this discussion is the fact that since at least the Enlightenment the notion of a wrathful God has been widely rejected by many theologians. Dodd (*The Epistle of Paul to the Romans* [London, 1932], p. 23) echoes the sentiments of F. Schleiermacher and A. Harnack (both of whom rejected not only a wrathful God but the whole OT as authoritative for Christians) in arguing that in Jesus' teaching, 'anger as an attitude of God to men disappears, and His love and mercy become all embracing'. Even in Paul, Dodd continues, the wrath of God describes not 'the attitude of God to man, but … an inevitable process of cause and effect in a moral universe'. At a time when humanity has come to be seen as basically good, the concept of divine wrath seems obscene. The nobly intentioned affirmation of God's goodness and therefore of the absence of wrath from his being are of a piece with post-Christian theories of the innate innocence of humanity and the minimal significance of sin in human nature.

The danger of overemphasizing God's wrath does exist. But it hardly justifies the impossible programme of trying to expunge the attribute from the NT record. God's coming wrath is a persistent theme of Jesus' parables. In non-parabolic discourse Jesus spoke repeatedly of 'the fire of hell' (Matt. 5:22) and 'eternal fire' (Matt. 18:8). He urged his followers, 'Fear him who, after the killing of the body, has power to throw you into hell' (Luke 12:5). The double-edged nature of Jesus' ministry is well summarized in John 3:36: 'Whoever believes in the Son has eternal life, but whoever rejects the Son will not see life, for God's wrath remains on him.' Those who reject God's righteousness become targets of his wrath (Rom. 1:18, 24, 26, 28; Eph. 5:6; Col. 3:6; Heb. 10:26–31; Rev. 19:11–21). God's wrath is not a minor or isolated biblical theme.

Atonement takes on its importance, urgency, and poignancy precisely because God's righteous judgment is coming upon humans and their unrighteous ways. Jesus' death not only expiates sin (wipes away its penalty); it also propitiates (turns away the wrath of)

God's promised punishment of sin and sinners whose transgressions are not atoned for. In the current climate of scepticism about a wrathful God, the biblical view has recently received strong support from philosopher H. Cassirer, who persuasively calls Christians away from modern sentimentalism and back to the God of whom the prophets, apostles and Jesus spoke (*Grace and Law* [Grand Rapids, 1988], pp. 99–107). Propitiation is not a peripheral but a vitally important implication of their references to atonement and its absolute necessity.

Shed blood: life or death?

Debate also surrounds the exact meaning of Hebrew animal sacrifice with respect to atonement. (Some sacrifices were festive or devotional rather than penitential in nature; in such cases the notion of atonement was secondary or absent.) A time-honoured view is that certain atoning sacrifices (*e.g.* the high priestly ritual of the Day of Atonement; *cf.* Lev. 16) carried substitutionary imagery; the sacrificial victim endures the (divine) punishment due to the sinner, enabling the sinner to go free. In recent times this view has been rejected as reading NT theology back into OT religion. Instead, it is proposed that the pouring out of blood symbolized the release of *life. The life given up by the animal is somehow freed to provide life for the people who offer sacrifice.

Given that God commanded sacrifice as a means of avoiding the punishment of death (*e.g.* Num. 18:32), and that wrongful sacrifice occasionally caused death by God's direct act (*e.g.* Num. 16:35), it seems hard to avoid the conclusion that when intelligent worshippers in OT times presented animals for atoning ritual slaughter they understood their sacrifices to involve an element of substitution. 'The ritual retains the note of an objective guilt which can only be removed through sacrifice or substitution' (Childs, *Biblical Theology of the Old and New Testaments*, p. 507). And while the sacrifice did result in life for the worshipper, this was not because poured out blood opened a fount of poured out life. If it did, we should expect a ritual in which the victim gave up only a cup, or perhaps a litre, of blood, not its very life. Rather it was because the shedding of blood leading to loss of life satisfied Yahweh's just demand that violation of his holy will results in death:

'The soul who sins ... will die' (Ezek. 18:4; *cf.* Gen. 2:17). Shedding the blood (extinguishing the 'life'; *cf.* Lev. 17:11, 14; Deut. 12:23) of the animal was required in exchange for sparing the life of the worshipper. The *death (not only symbolized but actually experienced in the fatal shedding of blood) of a sacrificial victim was necessary for the benefit of the guilty. Such OT convictions are only intensified under the new covenant (Heb. 10:28–31). The release-of-life view is grounded in the modern West's exalted view of humanity and disapproval of a God who demands death for sin, but it lacks convincing support in biblical texts.

The means of atonement: New Testament

Jesus' death is consistently presented as an atoning sacrifice for sins. He fulfils (provides the basis for and completes) what OT sacrifices could grant only by way of anticipation. While Jesus' teachings and miracles are of obvious importance, the Gospels do not present them as the primary means of the salvation he offers. Jesus is 'Saviour' not in the sense of spiritual visionary or miraculous power broker but as sacrificial victim, the just for the unjust (1 Pet. 3:18), his life poured out a ransom for many (Mark 10:45).

There is no single definitive NT explanation of the atonement. Jesus is presented as having paid the penalty for sin (Rom. 3:25–26; 6:23; Gal. 3:13). He died in place of sinners so that they might become God's righteousness (2 Cor. 5:21). He redeemed sinners through his blood (Eph. 1:7). He paid the price for sinners to go free (1 Cor. 6:20; Gal. 5:1). He won the victory over death and sin, sharing with believers the victory (1 Cor. 15:55–57) that he paraded in spectacular fashion by his cross (Col. 2:15). He put an end to the hostility between warring human factions, most notably Jews and Gentiles (Eph. 2:14–18), with implications for all other ethnic divisions. His example of patient suffering according to God's will and the demands of his kingdom is a precedent for his people to follow (1 Pet. 2:21–23). Peter's statement captures well the means and importance of Jesus' ministry of atonement: 'He himself bore our sins in his body on the tree, so that we might die to sins and live for righteousness; by his wounds you have been healed' (1 Pet. 2:24).

In the light of such passages the historic

status of the cross as the symbol of the Christian faith is fitting. The cross is where Jesus died, and Jesus' sinless death is why sinners can have life. In NT parlance 'atonement' and 'cross' are very nearly synonymous.

The varied NT atonement language has given rise in church history to numerous theories of the atonement. Here 'theory' refers to *how* God accomplished atonement through the cross. Some have stressed the effect that the atonement has on those who believe in it. This has been called the moral influence view and is commonly attributed to Abelard (1070–1142). It has been popular in modern theological liberalism. It contains an element of truth, but taken alone it is inadequate to capture the depth and richness of NT statements. Others, from patristic times onwards, have stressed the victory over sin, death, and the devil (see *Spiritual powers) that the atonement accomplished. Christ is conqueror. This theory, too, preserves an important truth, but like the moral influence view it is too limited in scope. In medieval times Anselm (1033–1109) proposed the so-called satisfaction theory: sin is such an affront to God that only one who is both God and man can remedy the problem. Like the other theories Anselm's has commendable aspects. But its focus is too restricted, in part because Anselm worked within the categories of philosophical reasoning with too little input from biblical theology. The same can be said of other theories proposed since.

The NT seems to give greatest direct support to the 'penal substitution' and 'sacrifice' theories. It is obvious throughout Scripture that God atones for sin via sacrifice. The problem with the theory lies in explaining *how* sacrifice saves. No universally accepted answer has been advanced, despite the impressive range of biblical texts using sacrificial terminology. Among these are passages referring to Jesus as the mediator of a new covenant, a covenant sealed with his blood (*e.g.* Matt. 26:28 par.). This implies (self-) sacrifice. So do numerous other, often overlooked, references to Jesus' 'blood' denoting his (sacrificial) death for sin (*e.g.* Acts 20:28; Rom. 5:9; 1 Cor. 10:16; Eph. 1:7; 2:13; Col. 1:20; 1 Pet. 1:2, 19; 1 John 1:7; Rev. 1:5; 5:9; 12:11). The prominence of sacrificial language or imagery elsewhere in the NT, whether in the Gospels (Jesus' passion predictions and the passion narrative itself), in Paul (*e.g.* Rom. 3:24–26; 1 Cor. 5:7; Eph. 5:2), or throughout Hebrews (*passim*), argues strongly for the centrality of sacrifice to NT atonement teaching. One reason for scepticism towards sacrifice theories is perhaps the view, held by many biblical scholars, that Jesus was no more than human. If this is so, and Jesus was at best perhaps a martyr, why should his death, even granting that he intended it somehow to be for others, be any more significant than the deaths of other people for their fellow humans? On the other hand, if Jesus truly was God incarnate, sent by the Father to achieve a goal determined in eternity (*cf.* Rev. 13:8: 'slain from the creation of the world'), there is no reason why his death could not bear the atoning significance that biblical language invests in it.

The penal substitution view is likewise strongly supported by numerous biblical authors (*cf. e.g.* allusions to Isaiah 53 in various NT passages) and was advanced aggressively by the Reformers. It asserts that atonement primarily involves Jesus' taking the sinner's place ('substitution') in bearing the penalty (hence 'penal') for his or her sin. That penalty was no less than God's wrath and the sinner's death. Various objections have been lodged against this theory, especially in modern times by theologians who disapprove of a God who is not only loving but wrathful and who not only pours out blessing but exacts penalties for transgressions. Yet this view, carefully and positively formulated, is indispensable to an accurate interpretation of the dominical and apostolic witness.

The scandal of the atonement

There are continual challenges to the biblical theology of atonement sketched above. Recently M. Winter (*The Atonement*, pp. 1, 116, 124) has argued that the crucifixion was, in fact, unnecessary. All humans must do to be reconciled to God is ask sincerely. Moral conversion is enough. For his part, Jesus 'atoned' for sin by asking God for this favour. 'Basically nothing more or less is required for the atonement' than Jesus' intercession (Winter, *Atonement*, p. 90). R. Funk (*Honest to Jesus* [San Francisco, 1996], p. 312) forthrightly demands the abandonment of the doctrine of atonement through the shedding of blood; it is time to 'give Jesus a demotion' (*ibid.*, p. 306). Other accounts of the meaning of atonement resort to martyrdom as chief explanatory category, or seek to replace 'atonement' with 'incarnation' or 'resurrection' as the essential core of Jesus' saving work, or understand 'atonement' in terms of primarily revelatory rather than propitiatory work. In this latter view salvation comes as human ignorance is dispelled, not as human sin is dealt with via the sacrificial death of God's own Son. The similarity to ancient Gnosticism is remarkable.

It is no surprise that the biblical writers' view of atonement causes consternation in the so-called postmodern climate. It has always called forth reactions ranging from polite rejection to rage. Atonement – the cross – has long been scandalous. Yet in different cultures around the world many continue to embrace the biblical witness, as Christians always have. The doctrine of the atonement retains its dramatic force and explanatory power as a summary of what Jesus came to earth to do (Heb. 10:9–10).

See also: FORGIVENESS AND RECONCILIATION; REDEMPTION; SACRIFICE; SALVATION.

Bibliography

R. E. Averbeck, '*kpr* [4105/4106]', in *NIDOTTE* 2, pp. 689–710; B. S. Childs, *Biblical Theology of the Old and New Testaments* (Minneapolis and London, 1992, 1996); F. Godet, A. Harnack, A. Sabatier *et al.*, *The Atonement in Modern Religious Thought: A Theological Symposium* (New York, 1902); J. E. Goldingay (ed.), *Atonement Today* (London, 1995); M. Hengel, *The Atonement* (ET, London, 1981); H.-G. Link, C. Brown, H. Vorlander, 'Reconciliation, Restoration, Propitiation, Atonement', in *NIDNTT* 3, pp. 145–177; J. Lust, E. Eynikel, K. Hauspie, *A Greek-English Lexicon of the Septuagint*, Part I (Stuttgart, 1992); I. H. Marshall, 'The Development of the Concept of Redemption in the New Testament', in I. H. Marshall (ed.), *Jesus the Saviour* (Downers Grove, 1990); H. D. McDonald, *The Atonement of the Death of Christ* (Grand Rapids, 1985); L. Morris, *The Apostolic Preaching of the Cross* (London, ³1965); C. M. Tuckett, 'Atonement in the NT', *ABD* 1, pp. 518–522; M. Winter, *The Atonement* (London and Collegeville, 1994, 1995).

R. W. YARBROUGH

BABEL, see LANGUAGES

BABYLON

The city of Babylon and the surrounding region in south-eastern Mesopotamia played a significant role in biblical history and thought. Though the site existed in the 3rd millennium BC, it was not until the famous Old Babylonian king, Hammurapi, elevated the role of the city in the 18th century BC that it came to play a dominant role in ancient Near Eastern history. Over a millennium later, Babylon was the capital of the short-lived Neo-Babylonian empire under Nabopolassar and his son Nebuchadnezzar, and it once again became the centre of political power in the region (625–539 BC). Its political and cultural significance continued into the Persian and Hellenistic periods.

The origin and meaning of the name itself are lost in antiquity. It may have had Sumerian origins, but the oldest Akkadian form of the name means 'gate of God' (*Bâb-ilim*) and was a development from popular etymology. Its plural form was the basis for the Greek *Babylōn*, and ultimately for the modern name (B. T. Arnold, in *Peoples of the Old Testament World*, pp. 43–44). The Bible makes mention of the city, the region or its inhabitants nearly 400 times and in a variety of ways. The most common term used in the OT is *Bābel*, which is translated 'Babylon', or 'Babylonia'. The ethnically precise designation *kaśdîm*, 'Chaldea/n/s', occurs ninety times, and the eight occurrences of the appellation *šin'ār*, 'Shinar' appear to denote southern Mesopotamia generally. Because of its international and cultural significance in the early biblical period, and its role in destroying *Jerusalem and deporting large numbers of its citizens, Babylon acquired theological significance for the OT writers alongside its obvious historical importance.

The first mention of Babylon, and the only one in the Pentateuch, is cloaked in the Hebrew term 'Babel' (Gen. 10:10; 11:9). The tower of Babel episode (Gen. 11:1–9) serves as the literary climax of the primeval history, which traces the vitiating consequences of *sin in humankind (Gen. 3 – 11). The tower is to be understood as a Mesopotamian ziggurat, or stepped pyramid; these were developed in the early stages of Mesopotamian urbanization. Even before the city played an important historical role, Babylon came to symbolize the worst kind of *idolatry, involving the dishonouring of the deity in pagan polytheism (J. H. Walton, in *BBR* 5, pp. 155–175). The narrative concludes in an ironic wordplay. Though Akkadian speakers understood the name of the city as 'gate of God', the Israelites knew better. God turned humankind's gate of heaven into confusion: 'Therefore it was called Babel, because there the LORD confused (Hebrew *balal*) the language of all the earth' (11:9, NRSV).

The historical books contain many references to events in which Babylon plays a central role. But it is in the prophetic literature of the OT that Babylon comes consistently to symbolize *evil power, though at times God used her to accomplish a wider purpose. In Jeremiah, Babylonia is cryptically denoted by the divine warning that disaster will break forth 'out of the north' (1:14 and 6:1, 22–23). But ultimately the prophet is comforted by the knowledge that Babylon will one day encounter its own enemy from the north, when Medo-Persian forces come upon it to destroy it (50:41–42).

The downfall of the king of Babylon is celebrated in Isaiah 14:4–23 in terms that came to symbolize the destruction of any hostile enemy of God. In the second literary unit of Isaiah (chs. 40 – 55), Babylon is a symbol of the evil oppressor. In Isaiah 47, Babylon is described as a beautiful woman reduced to slavery: 'Come down and sit in the dust, virgin daughter Babylon! Sit on the ground without a throne, daughter Chaldea!' (v. 1). The longed-for return from exile in Babylonia is described as a miraculous event comparable to the crossing of the Red Sea (Is. 51:9–11). The role of Babylon in Daniel 1 – 5 is that of a ferocious human empire capable of many atrocities, yet vulnerable and ultimately doomed because of God's opposition. Belshazzar's writing on the wall illustrates the outcome of obstinate royal opposition to God's will (Dan. 5). In OT poetic passages, Babylon comes to represent the place of *exile and alienation: 'By the rivers of Babylon – there we sat down and there we wept' (Ps. 137:1).

The history of the OT period led Israelite authors to characterize Babylonia as the place of religious hubris and degrading idolatry, tantamount to a refusal to worship or acknowledge the rightful place of the deity. In the NT Babylon continues to symbolize avaricious power, the evil influences of sin and idolatry, and all anti-God predilections. The derogatory reference to 'Babylon' in 1 Peter 5:13 is probably an allusion to the pretensions of Rome (D. F. Watson, in *ABD* 1, pp. 565–566).

The final biblical references to Babylon are in Revelation (specifically 16:17 – 18:24). Babylon is portrayed as the great prostitute seated on many waters, representing the various nationalities that Babylon subjugated (17:1, 15). She is 'Babylon the great, mother of whores and of earth's abominations' (17:5). Because of her great pride and luxurious living at the expense of those she tormented, Babylon's downfall is swift and total: 'For in one hour your judgment has come' (18:10; *cf.* vv. 17 and 19).

First-century readers of Revelation would have undoubtedly understood 'Babylon' as a cipher for Rome, which could not have been openly criticized (Watson, *ABD*). Just as ancient Babylon had been the wicked and ruthless enemy of God's people in OT times, so now the Roman Empire was the enemy of Christians. The passage thus symbolizes the rapacious and violent nature of the imperial power sought by many earthly kingdoms. Nations have continued to satiate their relentless appetite for secular power, but the practices of *Realpolitik* will not succeed for ever. Just as the early Christians celebrated the downfall of Rome, so every generation of believers waits expectantly for the end of oppressive world empires.

Bibliography

B. T. Arnold, 'Babylonians', in A. J. Hoerth, G. L. Mattingly and E. M. Yamauchi (eds.), *Peoples of the Old Testament World* (Grand Rapids and Cambridge, 1994, 1996); H. W. F. Saggs, *The Greatness That Was Babylon* (New York, 1962); J. H. Walton, 'The Mesopotamian background of the tower of Babel account and its implications', *BBR* 5, 1995, pp. 155–75; D. F. Watson, 'Babylon in the NT', in *ABD* 1, pp. 565–566; D. J. Wiseman, 'Babylon', in *NIDOTTE* 4, pp. 430–433; D. J. Wiseman, *Nebuchadrezzar and Babylon* (Oxford, 1985).

B. T. ARNOLD

BAPTISM

Introduction

Baptism is the act by which a person is declared to be a member of the body of Christ, 'in the name of *Jesus Christ' (Acts 2:38) or 'in the name of the Father, and of the Son, and of the *Holy Spirit' (Matt. 28:19). Baptism is an outward act which signifies inward *grace received by the believer. There is some debate about the earliest mode of baptism; it may have been pouring, or sprinkling, or immersion in water. Possible historical antecedents of Christian baptism are the Jewish rite of *circumcision, proselyte baptism, baptism in the Qumran community and the baptism of *John. The theology of baptism may be presented in terms of the uses to which the NT authors put it; most often they consider its present implications for Christians. Baptism is relevant to Christian living and Christian ethics. Believers are reminded of their baptism to strengthen their *faith, to call them to unity and to exhort them to live lives worthy of the *gospel, that is, to 'walk in newness of life' (Rom. 6:4).

Baptism and salvation

In Matthew 3:7, Mark 1:4 and Luke 3:3; 7:29 (*cf.* Acts 19:3) baptism is mentioned with reference to the ministry of John, who baptized with water in the Jordan. His baptism was a preparation for the eschatological kingdom ('Repent, for the kingdom of heaven is at hand', Matt. 3:1, RSV), and hence a pointer to the advent of the messianic era. John emphasized the need for *repentance. He warned the Jews not to boast in being the children of Abraham; the kingdom is not to be inherited on the basis of race. His baptism was 'for the forgiveness of sins' (Mark 1:4; Luke 3:3); it anticipated its eschatological fulfilment in Christ, who alone has the prerogative to baptize with the Holy Spirit (Matt. 3:11; Mark 1:8; Luke 3:16; John 1:33). In Mark 10:39 'baptism' is used figuratively by Jesus, but again in the context of the events of *salvation history, in a prediction of his vicarious *suffering and (perhaps) the suffering of his disciples.

Several references to baptisms administered in the early Christian community are found in the book of Acts. In each case baptism was a vital part of people's response to *God's gracious offer of salvation. Those baptized include: the believers on the day of Pentecost (Acts 2:41); the Samaritan believers (Acts 8:12–13); Saul (Acts 9:18); Cornelius and his household (Acts 10:48); the Philippian jailer and his household (Acts 16:33); and Crispus with his household (Acts 18:8). In all these instances baptism was administered only after the people had heard the gospel and confessed the lordship of Christ. Baptism was the seal of their faith.

Galatians 3:27, the only explicit reference to baptism in Galatians, occurs in a passage crucial to Paul's argument. His purpose is to establish a Christological foundation for the inclusion of Gentiles (including the Galatians) within the *covenant community. For Paul, the relationship of believers to Christ by faith is the premise from which their participation in the blessing promised to Abraham may be inferred. But since his Jewish Christian opponents do not approve of this teaching, which gives to Gentile Christians a status equal to their own, he has to appeal to an experience shared by all Christians, namely baptism. Baptism is the proof of believers' incorporation into the *death and resurrection of Christ, which is the basis on which they participate in Abraham's blessing.

Half the references to baptism in 1 Corinthians are found in 1:13–17. Party spirit among the Corinthians had, it seems, generated a mistaken view of baptism, in which more importance was attached to the identity of the baptiser than to baptism itself as a seal of believers' conversion experience. Paul had baptized some of his readers; therefore, they believed, he should be given a position of honour, perhaps equal to that of Christ himself. In response, Paul places baptism in its proper perspective; he strongly denies any view which would focus attention on himself at the expense of Christ, who is the embodiment of Paul's good news.

Paul's concern in 1 Corinthians 10:2 is to warn the Corinthians not to regard baptism (and the Lord's Supper) as conferring upon them immunity from divine judgment. Just as the Israelites, who enjoyed various privileges, fell in the wilderness because they lived wantonly, so the Corinthians will suffer the same disaster if they presume upon God on the basis of their vaunted 'spiritual' life. Whilst this passage has sometimes been thought to express a relationship between the sacraments of baptism and the Lord's Supper, it should be noted that here Paul uses 'baptism' metaphorically, and makes no explicit reference to either practice.

In 1 Corinthians 15:29, in the context teaching on the resurrection, Paul refers to the practice of being baptized for the dead. The Corinthians conceived of baptism as a sacrament which united them to Christ and thus gave them protection from all spiritual powers, unlimited authority and a confident hope of final resurrection. This erroneous view may have led some of them to be baptized on behalf of their dead, unbelieving relatives. Paul does not approve the practice; he merely points out that it is evidence for the bodily resurrection (which his readers regard as impossible).

Baptism and the body of Christ

The Corinthian *church was exercising one spiritual gift to the exclusion of all others, and regarded as 'spiritual' only those who did so. In 1 Corinthians 12 Paul argues that the true basis of his readers' spirituality is the Spirit in whom they all share, and that all gifts should be given equal recognition. To make these points he appeals in 12:13 to baptism. The Corinthians have all confessed the lordship of Christ at conversion, and therefore have new *life in him by the Spirit. On the basis of their confession they have all been baptized into Christ. Their baptism is thus a proof and reminder of what the Spirit has done in them; it demonstrates that they are all 'spiritual'. All their gifts come from the Spirit, and none should be exalted at the expense of others so as to cause discrimination and division among believers. Far from expecting baptism to be an issue of contention in the body, Paul appeals to it as a basis for church unity.

Similarly, in Ephesians 4:5 baptism is used to remind believers of the essential unity of the body of Christ. It is the seal of an inward work of divine grace, a work made apparent in believers' complete break with their past, sinful life, their confession of the lordship of Christ, and their receipt of new life in him. Through their faith in the one Lord, they have been incorporated into Christ's death and resurrection. By their one confession, conversion and incorporation into Christ, depicted in baptism, they belong to one God. They are children of the same Father, who has called

them into a relationship with himself and one another, and they are to walk in accordance with that calling. Thus baptism reveals the foundation on which the unity of the church, and hence the church itself, is built.

Baptism and the new life

The context of Romans 6:4 suggests that Paul's teaching on *sin and grace in Romans 5:12–21 has been misconstrued: 'Are we to continue in sin that grace may abound?' (Rom. 6:1). For Paul, baptism indicates that the Christian life has begun; so it is logical for him to appeal to his readers' baptism to correct the misunderstanding. Baptism demonstrates that believers in their temporal existence should consider themselves dead to sin and alive to God under the reign of grace. It thereby determines the proper content of the Christian life in the present age.

Likewise, in Colossians 2:12 Paul appeals to his readers' baptism to show them the basis of their new life in Christ and to urge them to reject any philosophy which calls into question the fullness of that life. False teachers are denying the sufficiency of Christ; Paul insists against them that fullness of life is found only in Christ, the object of the believers' faith, and not in the activities of spiritual powers. The Colossians are reminded by their baptism of the complete break they have made with their old pagan life (lived under the control of those powers) and of the need to go on in their walk with Christ, living in him just as they have received him.

In Hebrews 6:2 the author exhorts his readers to progress in their Christian faith by moving beyond its foundational principles, including baptism. They have appropriated the message of salvation by faith and the attendant new life in Christ; their baptism proves that they have done so. Now consistent spiritual growth is expected of them; they are to reject spiritual mediocrity and go on to maturity.

In 1 Peter 3:21 the author uses baptism to encourage his readers to stand firm in their confession in the face of unpleasant experiences. Sometimes believers are persecuted because of their obedience to God's will (cf. 1 Pet. 4:12–19), and they may be tempted to avoid such suffering by returning to their former, sinful way of life. But their baptism marks the end of that old life and the beginning of a new one. Therefore they are to repudiate sin. Having confessed Christ by faith at conversion and been raised to new life, their call is to acknowledge his lordship by following in his steps, accepting the suffering which results from doing good (1 Pet. 2:21).

Conclusion

Baptism is a symbolic event representing the death and resurrection of Jesus Christ. In it the church confesses that the baptized person has died to sin and has received a new spiritual life by the grace of God. Through it believers of all races are welcomed into the one body of Christ, where they are expected jealously to guard their new spiritual state.

Bibliography

J. Baillie, *Baptism and Conversion* (London 1964); C. K. Barrett, *Church, Ministry and Sacrament in the New Testament* (Carlisle, 1993); K. Barth, *Church Dogmatics*, vol. 4.4, ed. by G. W. Bromiley and T. F. Torrance (ET, Edinburgh, 1969); G. R. Beasley-Murray, *Baptism in the New Testament* (Grand Rapids and Carlisle, repr. 1990, 1997); E. J. Christiansen, *The Covenant in Judaism and Paul: A Study of Ritual Boundaries as Identity Markers* (Leiden, 1995); O. Cullman, *Baptism in the New Testament* (London, 1950); J. D. G. Dunn, *Baptism in the Holy Spirit* (Philadelphia, 1970); M. O. Fape, *Paul's Concept of Baptism and its Present Implications for Believers: Walking in Newness of Life* (Lampeter, 1999); W. F. Flemington, *The New Testament Doctrine of Baptism* (London, 1948); A. Gilmore, *Christian Baptism* (London, 1959); G. W. H. Lampe, *The Seal of the Spirit* (London, 1967); H. G. Marsh, *The Origin and Significance of the New Testament Baptism* (Manchester, 1941); R. Schnackenburg, *Baptism in the Thought of St Paul* (ET, Oxford, 1964); A. J. M. Wedderburn, *Baptism and Resurrection* (Tübingen, 1987).

M. O. FAPE

BARRENNESS, see CHILDLESSNESS
BIBLICAL HISTORY, see Part 1
BIBLICAL THEOLOGY, see Part 1

BLESSING/CURSE

Blessing and cursing are both key concepts in Scripture. Biblical writers and characters wish or *pray that good, beneficial and desirable things, or bad, disadvantageous and undesirable things, will happen to others. In some instances the blessing or curse is understood to be in itself a powerful and effective mechanism for ensuring that such good or bad things will happen to others. The words of blessing and cursing are thought to have inherent, autonomous power, so that once spoken they cannot be recalled, and unless some greater power is invoked to combat them the good or bad that they have called for is bound to happen. Both of these senses are found in other ancient Near Eastern literature as well as in the Bible. However, there are significant differences between the ideas of the surrounding societies and the way in which the terms were understood by the biblical writers. These differences are largely related to the *Israelite conviction that whereas people can wish that good or bad things might happen to others, *God as sovereign is the only one who can make such things happen and his hand cannot be forced. Also, although curses and blessings are contrasted, particularly in Deuteronomy, in Scripture as a whole they are neither presented nor understood simply as two sides of the same coin.

Mesopotamian views

In the ancient Near East in general, life was dominated by the need to cope with the terrifying threat of curses and omens. Such curses were invoked by individuals who were at enmity with the one cursed or who acted in self-defence, seeking to pre-empt any curse being placed on themselves. The actions called for by the curses were thought to be performed by the gods, but the gods had no real choice. Once the words had been uttered, using the correct form and accompanied by the correct ritual, then the actions *had* to be performed. The accompanying rituals were often symbolic actions believed to reinforce the power of the curse in a way more reminiscent of magic than of religious faith as understood within Israel. Thus in the minds of the people a curse was 'power-laden', and their *fear was understandable. In theory blessings too were inherently powerful, but they did not dominate society in the same way, and there was not the same conviction that a blessing once invoked would automatically be realized.

One indication of the extent to which life was ruled by curses is the massive amount of liturgical material comprising rituals for the revoking of curses. The people could live normally only because there was a possibility of such revocation. For example, the Shurpu series of penitential prayers (*cf.* W. Beyerlin [ed.], *Near Eastern Texts Relating to the Old Testament* [London, 1978], p. 131) are incantations designed to undo or reverse the effects of a curse.

Legal codes were often validated by a system of curses. Legal documents governing treaties or *covenants included blessings and (more significantly) curses which would be realized if the requirements listed in the documents were kept or broken. The blessings were the benefits which the suzerain or lord would provide for his subjects if they accepted his lordship and kept his rules. However, if having entered into this covenant relationship (whether that entry was voluntary or not) they betrayed the suzerain or failed to keep his requirements, then their fate was clearly predetermined by the curse sections of the treaty document.

Deuteronomy

The curses and blessings found in Deuteronomy, which relate to the breaking and keeping of the covenant between God and Israel, are thus part of a known system of covenant validation. In Deuteronomy 27 – 28, which follows a detailed description of the covenant obligations that Israel are required, as God's covenant people, to keep, the consequences of keeping or failing to keep those obligations are clearly set out in the form of specific blessings and curses. The lists of curses are substantially longer than the lists of blessings; yet the curses serve primarily as a backdrop to the blessings. Deuteronomy as a whole is a kind of national constitution explaining what it means for Israel, both as a nation and as individuals, to live as the *people of God. The primary focus of this life as God's people is relationship; they belong to God, and are chosen and blessed by him. They are to exhibit a *holy lifestyle, keeping the *law, not for the law's own sake but because God is holy and the law exhibits something of his character, a character which

they are called to reflect. In other words, the law is an indication of how their life in relationship with God can and should be worked out. To live in relationship with God, expressed in this holy lifestyle, is to be blessed. This blessing is not portrayed as a reward for keeping the law; it rests on God's promise and is an automatic consequence of being in relationship with him.

There is no doubt that this blessing is expressed in material terms. The people are led to expect that material benefits, of fertility, prosperity, *peace and *victory, will be theirs as a result of remaining in relationship with God. However, the ultimate blessing is not the material benefits but the relationship itself. To be part of God's covenant people, to belong to God in this way, is to be blessed. In a similar way, to be out of relationship with God is to be cursed. The curses also are presented in materialistic terms. If the people reject God they will suffer famine, ill-health, defeat and general ignominy. However, it is unlikely that this principle was meant to be applied in a literalistic or mechanistic way, as though the breaking of one law automatically realized a curse. Rather it was designed to convince the Israelites that God must be taken seriously, that rejecting God or his will for them would have terrible, devastating consequences, and that being 'outside Yahweh' was a state to be avoided at all costs. In this context the curse is not so much a punishment as an illustrative description of what it means to be out of relationship with God and to lack God's blessing. Deuteronomy 27:26, 'Cursed be anyone who does not uphold the words of this law by observing them' (NRSV), can be seen as summarizing the more detailed curses, supporting the view that there is a unified curse and that all who break the law and thus take themselves out of relationship with God face that curse.

If this understanding is correct, then the focus of any interpretation of the blessings and curses in the covenant documents should not be on the individual elements of the blessing or curse narratives. Attention should rather be directed to the single and significant blessing of being in relationship with God and the single curse of being outside God's sphere, no longer in relationship with him. Deuteronomy includes a single joyful affirmation of covenant *life and a single solemn warning against any kind of rejection of God's covenantal reign. This, along with the understanding of God's total sovereignty which allows him to show *mercy when and where he wills, explains why individual blessings and cursings were not automatically realized when on a literalistic interpretation they should have been. Not every *righteous person lived a long and happy life; not every wicked person suffered devastation and loss. This was a major problem to the Israelites at times, with which psalmists and prophets alike struggled, but it was not usually seen in terms of the failure of covenantal curses to be effective.

Legalism and an understanding of the curse as direct retribution were sometimes apparent in the thinking and practice of ordinary Israelites. This, however, does not seem to be what Deuteronomy intended, and the book certainly does not seem to be interpreted in this way elsewhere in Scripture. It is true that everyone who breaks the covenant stands under the threat of the curse. That is a self-evident corollary of two facts: that to break the covenant is to be outside the covenant; and to be outside the covenant is what it means to be cursed. However, God's sovereign mercy also must be taken into account. At the heart of the book is relationship with the living God, not the mechanistic application of *rewards and punishments. Deuteronomy presents in contemporary terms what relationship with Yahweh means.

Elsewhere in the OT

The concept of God as the one who blesses is presented at the start of the OT; God gives a blessing and a purpose to human beings at the beginning of time (Gen. 1:28). However, the disobedience of *Adam and Eve results in various divine curses being pronounced. These contrast sharply with the picture of divine blessing presented in Genesis 1 – 2. The events in Eden lead to a dramatic transformation of *creation. Afterwards, *human beings are conscious of God's displeasure with them. Unfortunately, the unrighteous activities of the first generations of people lead to the curse of the flood (cf. Gen. 8:21). While the divine covenant with Noah offers hope for the future, humanity continues to have at best only a limited experience of God's blessing. The tower of Babel incident is a further reminder of their alienation from God. Against this background God's promise

to bless *Abraham, and through him the nations of the earth, takes on special significance.

Israel's understanding of themselves as a people who are blessed stems from the blessing and promises given to Abraham in Genesis 12:2–3 and developed and expanded in Genesis 15 and 17. Their very existence as a nation was a confirmation that God had kept his word to Abraham, that he would make him 'into a great nation'. Their hope for ongoing blessing was also based on these promises. God was going to continue to work through them, bringing blessing to 'all peoples on earth'. It is blessing, not cursing, that dominated Israel's thinking. Israel, as the people of God, are inheritors of the blessing given originally to Abraham, confirmed in the *Mosaic covenant to Abraham's descendants and reaffirmed at the time of *David. Their confidence is not unfounded; they are blessed. Prophets and psalmists alike expounded the meaning of that blessing and revelled in it (e.g. Pss. 1:1; 32:1–2; 34:8; 65:4; 84:12; 106:3; 112:1–2; 128:4; Is. 19:25; 30:18; 56:2; 65:23; Jer. 17:7; Ezek. 34:26; Mal. 3:12). The NT presents the coming of Jesus as the ultimate fulfilment of the promises to Abraham, and the way in which both Israel and all the nations receive the greatest blessing possible (see below).

Problems arose only when Israel assumed that the blessing was automatic and forgot that they were totally dependent on their continuing relationship with God. Jeremiah's fierce denunciation of those who took it for granted that the possession of the *temple guaranteed national security (Jer. 7:4) shows that such assumptions were mistaken.

The differences between the understanding of curses and blessings in Israel and that found elsewhere in the ancient Near East are more apparent in the OT outside its formal covenant documentation. In ancient Mesopotamia life was dominated by the fear of curses, but not in Israel. Nowhere in the Bible is a curse-removing ritual put into effect or even mentioned. In fact there is very little discussion of the concept of cursing outside the stylized treaty chapters. Blessing, not cursing, was significant for Israel. Although the OT abounds with instances of God's blessing being bestowed – on individuals, on families, on the nation – only rarely does God specifically curse any human being or artefact. God is the one who blesses. The Israelites were convinced of their position as those blessed by God.

Language of *judgment and punishment is used in the context of the people's *sin, particularly by the prophets, but language of cursing is not. It is true that many of the curses outlined in Deuteronomy are identical to judgments proclaimed by the prophets. However, these judgments are never presented as simply unavoidable fulfilments of previously issued curses. They are rather a description of what will happen if the people depart from the way that God has outlined for them. The books of Joshua to Kings use curse narratives and the prophets use judgment oracles to make essentially the same point: to desert the covenant by breaking its requirements is to move out of relationship with God, and that leads to disaster.

In both cases there is an element of conditionality, in that God in his mercy can choose to lessen or delay the impact of judgment or even, inexplicably, to bring blessing when judgment is deserved. Similarly, promised blessings depend on a continuing relationship. One cannot be out of relationship with God and receive the blessing of being in relationship with God, nor in relationship with God and miss out on that blessing. God himself, not the blessing or the curse as such, is sovereign. When action is taken against children who curse their parents or citizens who curse leaders, it relates to the dishonour involved in the curses rather than any fear of their consequences. (Exod. 21:17; 22:28; 2 Sam. 16:9; Eccles. 10:20, *etc.*) In cases where sin leads to disease and *death, or where such disasters are predicted – for example in the cases of Nabal (1 Sam. 25), Jehoram (2 Chr. 21), David and Bathsheba's first baby (2 Sam. 12) or Hezekiah (2 Kgs. 20) – they are said to be sent from God rather than the automatic result of a curse. God continues to be in control. Prayer may, as in Hezekiah's case, or may not, as in David's case, result in circumstances being changed, but because God is sovereign it is always worth praying. God may choose to bless. It is perhaps because of this that David's response to the cursing of Shimei (2 Sam. 16:5–14) is so matter-of-fact. In effect he says that if Shimei has rightly understood God's intentions and he is to be punished, then this is unavoidable; if Shimei has not, then his cursing will make

no difference. Proverbs 26:2 emphasizes the point: 'Like a fluttering sparrow or a darting swallow, an undeserved curse does not come to rest' (NIV).

In the OT, and frequently in some psalms, writers say bad things about other people or pray that God will do bad things to other people. However, these statements and requests are cursing prayers rather than curses. As with any other prayer, God's answer is his own prerogative. In no sense are the imprecatory psalms seen as setting in motion an unchangeable course of events. God has the power to act as he sees fit whatever the desires of the psalmist.

In their reflections on the new covenant the prophets recognized that without specific divine intervention God's blessing would inevitably be lost. It was not possible for people to remain in relationship with God without his help. Jeremiah says that *obedience to the law (and in the light of passages like Mic. 6:8 this must be taken as referring more to a just and righteous lifestyle than to mere adherence to a legal code) will be built into his renewed people by God. So the requirement of a godly lifestyle remains an essential part of relationship with God, but because that lifestyle is built into God's people, there is no question of a curse. If God guarantees and enables the relationship, people of God will not forfeit the blessing by failing to keep the covenant. In the passages which refer to the new covenant there is no reference to curses.

The NT position

As in the OT, the language of blessing is far more common than the language of cursing, and that blessing is seen in relational terms. References are varied, but there is a marked emphasis on relationship. Those who belong to God, who are part of the *kingdom of God, who keep the words of God, whose sins are *forgiven, who are invited to the wedding feast – these are the ones who are blessed (Matt. 5:3–11; 25:34; Luke 6:20–22; 11:28; Rom. 4:7–8; Eph. 1:3; Jas. 5:11; Rev. 19:9; 20:6; 22:14). These blessings are closely linked to the work of Jesus. It is Jesus who, through his life, death and resurrection, enables Jew and Gentile alike to inherit the blessings promised through Abraham.

The word 'curse' is used to refer to bad language and unpleasant statements about people. Luke 6:28, 'Bless those who curse you', and 1 Corinthians 4:12, 'When we are cursed, we bless', seem to use the term in this way, though the theological concept may underlie what is said. There is no indication that curses had effects that needed to be nullified by some kind of ritual, or that blessing was the means of escape from otherwise unavoidable effects. Jesus and Paul are both making the point that the language of blessing is more appropriate for the Christian than the language of cursing and that bad attitudes should be met by good ones.

Some NT passages speak of the curse of the law, or of certain people as being in a cursed state. In 1 Corinthians 5:5 Paul uses curse language when he instructs his readers to 'Hand this man over to Satan'. Similarly in 1 Timothy 1:20 he says of Hymenaeus and Alexander that 'I have handed them over to Satan'. This appears to refer to some kind of expulsion from the community, but the intention is clearly not to harm the individuals concerned but to encourage renewal and restoration. Perhaps Paul is arguing that anyone who behaves in a certain way cannot be in relationship with God. It is important to acknowledge that such a person is not part of the community of those who are blessed by being in relationship with God, but is under a curse. To pretend that blessing exists when it does not will not help the community and may deny the individual concerned an opportunity to *repent and to become a real member. In 1 Corinthians 11:27–29 Paul speaks of those who eat and drink 'in an unworthy manner' as eating and drinking judgment against themselves. All those who have not appropriated the blessings which come through Christ and are therefore not in relationship with God stand under judgment. They are under the curse, and participation in the communion meal will not change that. It seems unlikely that Paul is referring to a separate curse which falls upon those who take part in the eucharist when they should not. Rather he is acknowledging people's existing state, and insisting that the communion service is not a magic rite which will remove them from that state. Again, 'If anyone does not love the Lord' (1 Cor. 16:22) or if anyone should preach 'a gospel other than what you accepted' (Gal. 1:8) then the church must 'let that person be cursed'. Anyone who does not love Christ or who

preaches a different *gospel is not part of the community of Christ. The form of words may indicate that Paul is not simply stating a fact but calling on his readers to recognize those who are under the curse and not pretend that such people can still be part of the community.

Galatians teaches that the only way to come into relationship with God, the only way to come into the sphere of the blessing and the promise, is through *faith in Christ Jesus. In Galatians 3:10–13 Paul quotes Deuteronomy 27:26 and takes it for granted that all the curse narratives can be summed up in these words. No-one can keep the law and therefore all are cursed. The only way for this curse to be removed is through Christ's *redemptive *sacrifice, which enables Jew and Gentile alike to come out of the sphere of the curse and into relationship with God, thus receiving the blessing. The quote from Deuteronomy 21:23 about the curse which rests on those who are hanged on a tree adds force and poignancy to his argument.

NT teaching echoes the OT view of blessing and cursing as relational. The ultimate and only important blessing is that of belonging to God, being part of his people, a member of his family. The only real curse is being out relationship with God, outside of the community of blessing. In temporal contexts both blessings and curses can be described in material terms, but their material dimension is secondary. Although bad things can and do happen to those who belong to the kingdom, those who are part of God's people cannot be under the curse; rather they are blessed.

See also: JESUS CHRIST; NATIONS.

Bibliography

T. G. Crawford, *Blessing and Curse in Syro-Palestinian Inscriptions of the Iron Age* (New York, 1992); J. G. Gager (ed.), *Curse Tablets and Binding Spells from the Ancient World* (Oxford, 1992); C. W. Mitchell, *Meaning of* brk *'to bless' in the Old Testament* (Atlanta, 1987); C. Westermann, *Blessing: In the Bible and in the Life of the Church* (Philadelphia, 1978).

M. J. EVANS

BLOOD

Blood in the OT

Blood: a question of life and death

Blood is essential for bodily *life: as long as it flows in a body, the body is alive, but blood outside the body indicates loss of life. Because God is life and to be acknowledged as sovereign over life and *death, blood outside the body is a serious matter. Most of the blood mentioned in the OT is outside the body, and the word is therefore frequently associated with (violent) death.

God requires a reckoning for any human blood shed by either animals or human beings (Gen. 9:5–6; *cf.* Gen. 4:10). Spilled blood pollutes the land (Num. 35:33; Ps. 106:38), where it remains 'uncovered' until it is avenged (Gen. 37:26; Ezek. 24:7; Job 16:18). It is said to be on the hands of the one who has taken life (Is. 1:15; 59:3); that person's life is demanded in return (*e.g.* 2 Sam. 4:11; see Num. 35:30–34 for a combination of the two ideas). Murderers are to be put to death by a member of the victim's family, who is the 'avenger of blood' (Num. 35:19, 21; Deut. 19:6, 12; *cf.* Deut. 32:43; 2 Kgs. 9:7; Ps. 9:12 for God as the ultimate avenger). If the murderer cannot be found, an animal has to die instead (Deut. 21:1–9). Blood shed in war is not regarded as murder (see 1 Kgs. 2:5), but it still disqualifies David from building the temple (1 Chr. 22:8). If people are responsible for their own death, their blood shall be upon their heads (Josh. 2:19; 2 Sam. 1:16; *cf.* Matt. 27:24–25; Acts 18:6).

After the flood, God permits humans to eat meat, but they are to respect the distinction between life and death and, therefore, are allowed to consume neither animals with the blood still in them nor the blood itself (Gen. 9:3–4; *cf.* Lev. 3:17 where the same rule applies to fat as the substance of an animal's life; Lev. 17; Deut. 12:16; 1 Sam. 14:32–35). According to Leviticus 17:4, the person who slaughters animals inappropriately 'shall be held guilty of bloodshed; he has shed blood, and he shall be cut off from the people' (NRSV). The best context in which to eat meat was therefore a sacrifice, when the blood could be offered to God (Lev. 17; Deut. 12).

The association of loss of blood with loss of life may underlie the regulations which specify that menstruation, post-natal discharge and other discharges of blood disqualify a woman, for a specified period, from participating in the worship of the community (Lev. 12; 15; *cf.* 18:19). Yet blood not only defiles; it can also be used to *remove* defilement.

The use of blood in ritual acts

Blood has a very important role in OT rituals, not because of any inherent quality, but because the Lord has ordained that it be used for cleansing (Lev. 14) and as a means of *atonement (Lev. 17:11). Just as shed blood marks the transition from life to death, so blood is used ritually to effect a transition from the realm of death to the realm of life.

In rituals of atonement, the blood recalls the fact that an animal has given is life and proclaims that therefore no further bloodshed is required (*cf.* Exod. 12:13, 23). The precise ways in which the blood is used, especially on the Day of Atonement (Lev. 16), are beyond the scope of this article, but in general terms the blood serves as a substitute, being able to ransom the life of the one who brought the animal (see *Redemption).

In rituals of cleansing, blood is the means of removing impurities that compromise the holiness of the sanctuary and altar. It has been called a 'ritual detergent' by Milgrom, who argues that blood absorbs sin and becomes unclean itself. However, Kiuchi argues persuasively that it is rather the priest who bears the guilt associated with uncleanness. The blood draws attention to the transition from the realm of death (uncleanness) to the realm of life (*holiness), which takes place not in the sprinkling of the blood as such, but in the ritual act as a whole. Similarly, blood is used to indicate that a cleansed 'leper' is free to return to the realm of the holy (Lev. 14).

Blood is used also in rituals of consecration for *priests (Exod. 29; Lev. 8) and for the altar (Ezek. 43:20). Together with the purification offering, it is used for cleansing, but probably also symbolizes the close connection between the priesthood and altar and the sacrifices.

Blood and covenant

The last act in the sealing of a *covenant was usually a sacrifice that provided the opportunity for a common meal. Exodus 24 describes a covenant ceremony in which the covenant between the Lord and his people is confirmed on the twofold basis of the blood of the covenant and the book of the covenant. The book of the covenant speaks of the requirement to live and act in loyalty to the covenant partner. The blood of the covenant is often seen as an oath rite, but is more likely a reminder of the need and provision of forgiveness (see *Righteousness, justice and justification), since the altar does not represent God, but the sacrificial act. Zechariah 9:11 and Hebrews 12:18–29 refer to this passage. In Zechariah, the reference to 'the blood of the covenant' shows that God still offers forgiveness in spite of the enactment of the covenant curses. Hebrews compares and contrasts the old and new covenants (see below).

Blood in the NT

Blood in non-sacrificial contexts

As in the OT, 'blood' is frequently used to refer to violent death (*e.g.* Matt. 23:30–35; 27:4–8, 24–25; Heb. 12:4; Rev. 6:10; 17:6; 18:24; 19:2) and blood imagery is used in the context of *judgment (Acts 2:19–20; Rev. 6:12; 8:7, 9; 11:6; 14:20; 16:3–6 with which *cf.* Exod. 7). Those who are responsible for a death are said to have the blood of the victim on their head (*cf.* Acts 5:28; 18:6) or to be responsible for their blood (*cf.* Acts 20:26).

The phrase 'flesh and blood' (Matt. 16:17; 1 Cor. 15:50; Gal. 1:16; Eph. 6:12; *cf.* John 1:13), as distinct from the simple 'flesh' used in the OT, was used in the intertestamental period (*cf.* Ecclus. 14:18; 17:31) to denote *human beings in their frailty. According to Hebrews 2:14 Jesus took on 'flesh and blood' in order to confront death.

In Acts 15 the Jerusalem Council instructs the early church to abstain from blood (*cf.* Acts 21:25). While it is possible to interpret the Hebrew text of Genesis 9:4 as prohibiting only the consumption of blood from living animals (so S. D. Sperling in *ABD* 1, pp. 761–763), the council accepts what is apparently the current Jewish interpretation (*cf.* Acts 15:21), seeing the same prohibition in Genesis 9:4 as in Leviticus and therefore making no distinction between what is forbidden to Jews and what is forbidden universally.

The blood of Jesus Christ

Justification, atonement and redemption 'by the blood of Christ' (*e.g.* Rom. 3:25; 5:9; Eph. 1:7; 2:13) means justification, atonement and redemption by the death of *Jesus Christ, as shown by references to the cross and to death in the same contexts. In the NT no magical power is attributed to the blood itself and there is no trace of blood mysticism. Salvation is not linked to the blood itself, but to the bloodshed, *i.e.* to the death of Christ. Some have interpreted the significance of Christ's death as the release of his life, on the basis that blood stands for life. But Christ's blood is not used in any way after his death, and as we have seen, 'blood' is generally used to denote *lost* life (*cf.* A. M. Stibbs, *The Meaning of the Word 'Blood' in Scripture*, and L. Morris, *The Apostolic Preaching of the Cross*). The NT writers speak of the 'blood' as well as the 'death' of Jesus Christ because they interpret Christ's death as a sacrifice. The phrase 'the blood of Christ' combine the ideas of purification and forgiveness associated with different sacrifices in the OT. Just as in the OT, 'blood' speaks of a ransom paid (*e.g.* Rev. 5:9) and of cleansing (*e.g.* 1 John 1:7). The references in 1 John 5:6–8 to the water and the blood that testify are probably references to the baptism and the death of Christ respectively.

The blood of the covenant and the eucharist

In the Pentateuch we find the expression 'blood of grapes' (Gen. 49:11; Deut. 32:14) and a reference to the use of red wine in sacrifices to represent blood (Deut. 32:38). The imagery of a wine press and of intoxicating wine is frequently used in the OT to refer to bloodshed (Deut. 32:42; Is. 49:26; 63:2–3; Ezek. 39:19; Joel 3:13). It is therefore not entirely surprising that Jesus uses a cup of wine to denote the 'blood of the covenant' (Matt. 26:28; Mark 14:24; Luke 22:20; *cf.* 1 Cor. 10:16; 11:25, 27), as well as using bread to represent his body. Whoever eats and drinks the eucharistic bread and wine disregarding the proclamation of salvation through the death of Christ 'will be answerable for the body and blood of the Lord' (1 Cor. 11:27), *i.e.* will be held liable for the death of Christ.

It is disputed whether there is an allusion to the eucharist in John 6:53–56. The imagery of eating probably speaks first of the life-giving acceptance of Christ through faith, but towards the end of the chapter most Christian readers will find it hard to avoid thinking of the eucharist as the context in which this faith is proclaimed and union with Christ is celebrated. The eucharistic overtones are not meant to imply that participation in the Lord's supper is necessary for salvation; rather, they denote the life-giving effect of appropriating by faith the human death of the one 'from above'. 'It is the Spirit that gives life' (John 6:63a). (See *Sacred meals.)

An important feature of this new covenant is the inclusion of those 'who once were far off' (Eph. 2:13). The separation of Gentiles and Jews which was marked in the flesh by circumcision (Eph. 2:11) is now abolished through the blood and the flesh of Christ Jesus (Eph. 2:13–15), *i.e.* through Christ's death on the cross (*cf.* Col. 1:20–22).

In Hebrews 9 – 10, the writer contrasts the priesthood of Christ with that of the old covenant. The blood of the animal sacrifice brought by the Levitical high priest opened the way from the unclean to the holy area of the physical sanctuary. But Christ brings his own blood, which purifies the conscience and opens the way into the heavenly sanctuary. Christ's death inaugurates a covenant of eternal redemption (*cf.* Heb. 13:20) and makes it possible for all sins to be forgiven. No further sacrifices are required, because Christ's sacrifice, being the culmination of a life of voluntary obedience, brought about a definitive and permanent purgation that animal sacrifices were unable to effect. This is why Christ's sacrifical blood 'speaks a better word than the blood of Abel' (Heb. 12:24) which was unable to effect reconciliation.

See also: SACRIFICE.

Bibliography

N. Kiuchi, *The Purification Offering in the Priestly Literature: Its Meaning and Function* (Sheffield, 1987); B. A. Levine, *In the Presence of the Lord* (Leiden, 1974); J. Milgrom, *Leviticus 1–16*, AB (New York, 1991); L. Morris, *The Apostolic Preaching of the Cross* (London and Grand Rapids, ³1965); A. M. Stibbs, *The Meaning of the Word 'Blood' in Scripture* (London, ³1962); G. J. Wenham, *The Book of Leviticus*, NICOT (Grand Rapids, 1979).

T. RENZ

BODY, see HUMANITY
CALL, see ELECTION
CANON OF SCRIPTURE, see Part 1
CHALLENGES TO BIBLICAL THEOLOGY, see Part 1

CHILDLESSNESS

Introduction

Although childlessness in contemporary societies may be either voluntary or involuntary, the biblical concept of childlessness focuses upon involuntary childlessness or barrenness. It can be understood only against the background of the importance placed upon children in the Bible: 'Behold, children are a gift of the LORD; the fruit of the womb is a reward. Like arrows in the hand of a warrior, so are the children of one's youth. How blessed is the man whose quiver is full of them' (Ps. 127:3–5, NASB; *cf.* Ps. 128:1–4). In the ancient Near East, children were needed to care for aging parents, attend to the *family's work and inherit the family name and estate. In addition, children were a sign of God's *blessing. Having no children brought shame (Gen. 16:5; Gen. 30:1; 1 Sam. 1:6–7; Luke 1:25), while having children brought *joy and vindication (Gen. 21:6; 30:23; 1 Sam. 2:1, 7–8; Luke 1:25). In ancient Israel, childbearing was important for several reasons. First, the Israelites believed that procreation was commanded in Genesis 1:28; secondly, the blessing of procreation was linked to God's promises to Abraham (Gen. 15:5; 17:1–6; 26:3–5; 28:14); and finally, it was thought that through childbearing the redemptive purposes of God, including the birth of the Messiah, would be manifested.

Childlessness is closely linked in the Bible to God's purposes for humankind in salvation history, and to *marriage and procreation. Several important questions arise. Is there biblical warrant for considering procreation to be a requirement, either in general or in particular marriages? Is childlessness understood as a punishment for sin? Does it mean that something essential to marriage is lacking? What is the significance of childlessness in the light of Christ?

Marriage and procreation in Genesis 1 – 2

The command to be 'fruitful and multiply'

(Gen. 1:28) is thought by some to lay a duty of procreation upon each person or each marriage. However, this interpretation is cast into doubt by the words which follow: 'and fill the earth, and subdue it; and rule [over it]'. In addition, 'be fruitful and multiply' is also said to the birds and the sea creatures (Gen. 1:22). Thus, while Genesis 1:28 affirms that procreation is a blessing given by God, it is not declared to be the primary purpose of marriage. Genesis 2:18–25 declares marriage to be a relationship of 'one flesh', and no mention is made here of procreation. The explicit purpose of marriage, according to verse 18, is to provide companionship. Indeed, too much emphasis upon procreation in marriage can actually divert attention from the spouse and make procreation a project rather than the result of shared love. Genesis 1:28 is best understood as a blessing and a promise given to humankind, rather than as a command and a duty.

Procreation and barrenness in the fallen world

Though procreation is neither a duty, nor the primary purpose of marriage, children are nevertheless a gift from God. It is therefore proper to seek to understand the significance of barrenness as a human experience in the fallen world. There are two main elements in the biblical view of barrenness. First, barrenness is associated in a general sense with human *sin, and is a cause for despair. Secondly, in some cases barrenness is taken up in God's purposes of reconciliation, which gives hope to those who are barren.

Barrenness in relation to human sin

Genesis 3 lists the results of human sin, emphasizing both spiritual and physical consequences; these are in sharp contrast to the blessings listed in Genesis 1. Although barrenness is not mentioned explicitly, the process of procreation is cursed by additional pain in childbirth (v. 16), and it is also affected by the more wide-ranging curses. Indeed, just as the ground is cursed, becoming more difficult to harvest (vv. 17–19), so all creation is thrust into a state of futility, awaiting redemption (Rom. 8:20–22). It is in this context that barrenness is to be understood as a consequence of humankind's sin and rebellion against God, in contrast to the blessing of procreation in Genesis 1. In

God's relationship with Israel, the blessing of fruitfulness and the curse of barrenness are related to Israel's obedience and disobedience. Fruitfulness, and the absence of barrenness, are promised to Israel in exchange for obedience (Exod. 23:26; Lev. 26:3, 9; Deut. 7:14; 28:11), while barrenness or childlessness is threatened as a punishment for disobedience (Gen. 20:17–18; Lev. 20:20–21; Job 18:19; Is. 14:22; Jer. 15:7; 22:30; Ezek. 5:17; Hos. 9:11–17). Yet these texts do not make a direct connection between barrenness and individual sin. Blessings and punishments are primarily related to the nation's obedience, not that of individuals; blessings and suffering fall upon the just and the unjust alike (Pss. 13:2; 38:19; 73:12; 82:2; Matt. 5:45; Luke 13:1–5). Indeed, Luke makes clear that barrenness is not directly attributable to sin by asserting that Elizabeth and Zechariah 'were both righteous in the sight of God, walking blamelessly in all the commandments and requirements of the Lord. But they had no child, because Elizabeth was barren' (1:6–7).

Stories of barren women

Undoubtedly barrenness is a cause of great despair. Yet in the Bible's depiction of barren women (which extends through its narrative from Genesis to Luke), the emphasis falls upon God's grace and his purposes for the people of Israel in the face of seemingly insurmountable difficulties. The experiences of *Sarah (Gen. 11 – 21), Rebekah (Gen. 25), Rachel (Gen. 29 – 30), the wife of Manoah (Judg. 13), Hannah (1 Sam. 1 – 2), the Shunnamite woman (2 Kgs. 4) and Elizabeth (Luke 1) are recorded. Taken together, the stories indicate in various ways that barrenness is not depicted as a punishment for individual sins. First, barrenness is stated simply as a fact; it is not said to be the result of sin (Gen. 11:30; 25:21; 29:31; Judg. 13:2; 1 Sam. 1:2; 2 Kgs. 4:14; Luke 1:7). While it may be a problem in human experience, it is presented as an opportunity for the outworking of the divine purpose. Secondly, barrenness is attributed to divine causation (Gen. 16:2; 30:2; 1 Sam. 1:5). The reason for barrenness is not stated, perhaps because it is not the most important issue. Each story unfolds according to the divine purpose. Thirdly, just as God closes the womb, so he also opens it (Gen. 21:1, 6; 25:21; 30:22; 29:31; *cf.* Judg. 13:3; 1 Sam. 1:17; 2:1–10; 2 Kgs. 4:16; Luke

1:13). Fourthly, the children who are eventually born to barren women, with one exception, are important figures in Israelite history, and are used in the purposes of God (Isaac, Jacob, Joseph, Samson, Samuel and John the Baptist, the exception being the son born to the Shunnamite woman). This shows that God gives children to certain barren women not for their purposes, but according to his purpose, and that he has compassion on the downcast. Finally, these accounts relate barrenness to *faith in God and God's faithfulness.

Childlessness in the light of Christ

The biblical view of barrenness, then, is not that it is a punishment for individual sin, but rather that it is a consequence of human sin in general, and that it is a difficult human experience through which God can act. But it is important also to ask how barrenness should be understood in the light of Christ, and whether it is good or even necessary for childless couples to take all morally acceptable steps in order to have children.

Hope beyond children

Isaiah does not see physical barrenness as the worst of calamities, nor does one need to overcome it in order to participate in the purpose of God and experience true joy. '"Shout for joy, O barren one, you who have borne no child. Break forth into joyful shouting and cry aloud, you who have not travailed. For the sons of the desolate one *will* be more numerous than the sons of the married woman," says the LORD' (Is. 54:1; *cf.* Is. 56:4–5). Fruitfulness does not necessarily signify God's favour; nor does it merit any spiritual reward. Conversely, it is not the childless as such, but rather those who lack faith in God, who will experience divine disfavour. God desires faithfulness and obedience, not simply adherence to sacrificial rituals or outward signs of devotion (1 Sam. 15:22; Prov. 15:8; Hos. 6:6). The barren woman in Isaiah 54 sings not because she has been given children, but because God has given her supernatural offspring (J. Motyer, *The Prophecy of Isaiah* [Leicester, 1993], p. 445). This spiritual reward is part of an eschatological *hope associated with the coming Messiah, and anticipates the relief of suffering and a joy greater than that brought by any number of children (*cf.* Is. 65:17–25).

The 'problem' with barrenness, then, is not the condition itself, but the significance attributed to it.

The fruit of faith in Christ

Jesus Christ offers both present and eschatological hope for the childless. Paul's assertions that 'the time has been shortened' (1 Cor. 7:29) and that 'the form of this world is passing away' (7:31) are presented as reasons for remaining single; they demonstrate the relative insignificance of the human institutions of marriage and family in comparison to 'undistracted devotion to the Lord' (7:35). Marriage and family are not thereby rendered unimportant; they continue to reveal God's goodness. Yet the NT writers show surprisingly little interest in the biological family. Where the family is addressed, it is with reference to its conduct (Eph. 5:21 – 6:4; Col. 3:18–21). The importance of the biological family is qualified by that of the spiritual family, which consists of those who follow Jesus (Matt. 12:46–50; Eph. 3:14–15). The priority is not physical generation but spiritual regeneration; 'spiritual kindred' are emphasized (Augustine, 'On the good of marriage', p. 403). Thus a change in values is required of those who follow Christ, but they have a hope for the future of greater value than anything temporal, including children.

Theological and ethical implications of childlessness

Those who suffer childlessness are encouraged to focus 'on the things above, not on the things that are on earth' (Col. 3:2), and to place their hope in God and find comfort in his mercy (2 Cor. 1:3–8). These exhortations are not purely religious platitudes (the suffering of those who are childless is not denied); rather, they spell out the significance of the gospel message. Despite childlessness, marriage can still be made outward-looking by serving God (1 Cor. 7:35), practising hospitality (Rom. 12:13; Heb. 13:2), and *adoption (which reflects God's action towards us: Rom. 8:15; 9:4; Gal. 4:5; Eph. 1:5). These considerations do not rule out the use of reproductive technology *per se* (though some forms of it may be morally unacceptable), but they should guide the way it is used; having children should not become a person's greatest goal. The Bible indicates that childlessness is not a condition which *must* be overcome. God has acted on behalf of his people in such a way that those who are childless may experience true joy, despite their suffering, and may receive a spiritual reward which merely having children cannot provide.

Bibliography

R. S. Anderson, 'God bless the children – and the childless', *CT* 31, p. 28; Augustine, 'On the good of marriage' (*De bono conjugali*), in P. Schaff (ed.), *A Select Library of the Nicene and Post-Nicene Fathers of the Christian Church* (Edinburgh and Grand Rapids, 1980, 1988); K. Barth, *Church Dogmatics*, (ET, Edinburgh, 1936–1981); J. R. Baskin, 'Rabbinic reflections on the barren wife', *HTR* 82, 1989, pp. 101–114; M. Callaway, *Sing O Barren One: A Study in Comparative Midrash* (Atlanta, 1986); D. Daube, *The Duty of Procreation* (Edinburgh, 1977); J. Van Seters, 'The problem of childlessness in Near Eastern law and the Patriarchs of Israel', *JBL* 87, 1968, pp. 401–408.

K. T. MAGNUSON

CHRIST, CHRISTOLOGY, see JESUS CHRIST
CHRONICLES, see Part 2

CHURCH

Introduction

Although the church is often thought to be a human institution, a social arrangement to facilitate the interests and mission of like-minded people, as indeed it is, the Bible presents it as primarily a consequence of the character and purposes of the trinitarian God. Its origins lie in God's desire to have a people of his own (Deut. 7:6). It is a community of those who acknowledge Jesus Christ as Lord (1 Cor. 12:3). It is a fellowship where the Holy Spirit lives (1 Cor. 3:16), directing and energizing its community life. (See Clowney, 'Biblical Theology', p. 15.)

The church in the OT

The church traces its roots back to the OT people of God. The new covenant community, although in some ways radically differ-ent from the community of the old covenant (Jer. 31:31–34), nonetheless has much in common with it.

The people of God

God chose Abram (Gen. 12:1–3) to receive his special blessing and to be a blessing to 'all peoples on earth'. The basis of the relationship was God's sovereign and gracious choice of Abram, expressed in a binding *covenant (Gen. 17:1–14). God was to be his God, providing protection and a fruitful future. In turn, Abram was to keep the stipulations of the covenant and walk blamelessly before God.

The covenant embraced subsequent generations of Israel, and God's gracious initiative remained the basic element in their constitution as a people. 'The Lord did not set his affection on you and choose you because you were more numerous than other peoples, for you were the fewest of all peoples. But it was because the Lord loved you ... ' (Deut. 7:7–8, NIV). Their obligation was to love and obey him, avoiding any disloyalty. Deuteronomy spells out the details of the covenant which was periodically renewed in a united gathering (Deut. 29; Neh. 8).

The church has entered a new covenant with God (2 Cor. 3:4–18), also initiated by divine grace (Eph. 1:3–14; 2:1–10). This covenant is sealed by the blood of Jesus (1 Cor. 11:25) and instituted by his sacrifice as a great high priest (Heb. 8 – 10).

A holy *priesthood

Worship was to be at the heart of Israel's life. Moses demanded the release of the Israelites from Egypt so that they might worship their God in the desert (Exod. 7:16). After the Exodus they gathered at Mount Sinai where God called them his 'treasured possession' and pronounced them 'a kingdom of priests and a holy nation' (Exod. 19:5–6; see also Is. 61:6), subject to their continuing obedience. As priests, they were to worship God, to live holy lives (Lev. 19:1–2; 20:7–8), and to be intermediaries between God and the world. With the creation of the Tabernacle, or divine tent, the role of priest devolved on a few specially chosen from the house of Aaron and tribe of Levi, although a collective priestly responsibility remained with all the people.

The calling to be 'a royal priesthood' (1 Pet. 2:9) has passed to the church of Christ where the concept of 'the priesthood of all believers' has assumed a richer significance. All believers may now enter the presence of God without the need for any human mediator; the purifying effect of the blood of Christ qualifies them to do so (Heb. 9:14; 10:19–22; 1 Tim. 2:5).

A gathered assembly

The usual Greek word for church is *ekklēsia*, a non-technical word which means 'gathering' or 'assembly'. It is used in LXX to translate the Hebrew word *qāhāl*. It is used of ordinary crowds (*e.g.* in Gen. 49:6; Num. 22:4), but also designates the assembling of Israel before God to hear the reading of the law, confess their sins, express repentance and renew the covenant (Deut 4:10, 33; Josh. 8:33–35; Judg. 20:1–2; 1 Chron. 28:8; 2 Chron. 20:5; 23:3; 29:20–31; Neh. 8). Leviticus 23 provides details of the annual round of assemblies given to Israel to celebrate the deliverance, provision and guidance of their God. In later Judaism the emergence of the synagogue indicates the continuing importance of the community gathering.

Ekklēsia does not refer to abstract entities like a society but to actual gatherings of people. As a result, some have seen the church almost exclusively as the meeting of a local congregation and deny that it has any real existence beyond this. However, whilst valuable in its insistence that the church is a real human gathering, this view is too restricted to do justice to the use of the word in the NT.

A *remnant

Whilst God's intention had been that Israel should be a theocracy, a holy nation set apart for and governed only by himself, the persistent sin of the people and their leaders eventually caused the division of the kingdom, the punishment of the Exile and the refining of the people of God. Consequently, some prophets posited a theology of a remnant who were faithful to God (Is. 10:20–22; 37:31–32; Mic. 2:12; 5:7–8; Zeph. 3:12–13; Zech. 8:11–12) and in whom Israel's future lay.

Paul adopted this vision when he asserted that 'not all who are descended from Israel are Israel' (Rom. 9:6) and claimed that the church is the true Israel of God and comprises the real descendants of Abraham, the man of faith (Gal. 6:16). There are many other allu-sions to the church as the true successor of Israel (W. S. Campbell, in *DLNTD*, p. 212) (Matt. 3:9–10; 19:28; John 15:1–8; Eph. 2:11–22; Jas. 1:1; 1 Pet. 1:1).

The crucial significance of *Jesus Christ

The plan of God was not completely fulfilled under the old covenant but came to full realization in Jesus Christ (Eph. 1:3–10; 2:11–22). He it is who brings the church into being. It is his church (Matt. 16:18). The church of the new covenant is entered by faith in him (Gal. 3:1–14; Eph. 2:1–10) and, consequently, is international in membership and allows no ethnic, gender or social divisions (Gal. 3:28; Eph. 2:11–22; Col. 3:11). The church is his body on earth, and he is the head (Rom. 12:5; 1 Cor. 12:12–31; Col. 1:18). The church takes its alignment from him as a building takes its alignment from the cornerstone (Eph. 2:20–21). It derives its unity and growth from him (Eph. 2:19–22; 4:15–16). The life of the church is maintained by its vital union with him (Rom. 6:1–4; Eph. 2:21–22; 4:15–16, and by contrast, Col. 2:19) and exists only insofar as it is 'in him'. The person and work of Christ, then, are at the heart of the NT view of the *ekklēsia*. They enable us to understand both the continuities and the discontinuities between the old and new covenant people of God. It is a fuller analysis of the NT teaching to which we now turn.

The church in the Gospels

The church in the Synoptic Gospels

At first sight the Synoptic Gospels appear to be focused on the *kingdom of God rather than the church, giving rise to Alfred Loisy's famous comment, 'Jesus foretold the kingdom and it was the church that came.' But this is a misjudgment, based on the belief that the writers expected the kingdom to be fully realized immediately after Jesus' death and resurrection. This view prevented many from seeing that the Gospels did teach about the church even though the word was rarely used. The kingdom of God is the sphere in which he reigns; it presupposes a community of people who have submitted to his rule and who act as both its agent and its sign. The kingdom is not abstract but is embodied in the lives of people on earth. Its outworking necessarily takes place not only in the lives of individuals but also in the life of a group. So

Jesus calls twelve disciples to be with him (Mark 3:13–19) and evidently has many other followers who assume a common identity (Luke 8:1–3; 10:1–24). He frequently uses communal language. His disciples are a *family (Mark 10:29–31; Luke 8:19–21); a fraternity (Matt. 23:8); a little flock (Luke 12:32); and a city (Matt. 5:14). They are a synagogue which, unlike contemporary Jewish synagogues, does not require ten males for legitimacy; Jesus will be present with two or three (Matt. 18:19–20). These images all once referred to Israel; Jesus is presented as reconstituting Israel. The Twelve are to be the new patriarchs who will judge the twelve tribes of Israel (Matt. 19:28). In the meantime their apostolic role is to spread the gospel and teach the believers (Matt 13:52; 16:16–19; 23:34; 28:19–20), without seeking status for themselves (Matt. 23:9–12).

Matthew twice refers to 'the church' (16:18; 18:15), but these are the only instances of the word *ekklēsia* in the Gospels. Evidently some form of ongoing and organized congregation of believers is in mind. In 16:18 Jesus commits the privilege of interpreting his teaching authoritatively to his disciples and assures them that the church will never be defeated by any natural or supernatural, earthly or cosmic, opposition. In 18:15 the theme is the life of the local congregation. It is to be a community in which broken relationships are restored, and only after several attempts at reconciliation have failed is it to become a community which enforces *discipline and draws clear boundaries.

John's Gospel

While John's Gospel stresses the individual relationship between a believer and the Lord, it equally stresses the communal aspects of faith. The disciples are portrayed as a flock led by a shepherd (10:1–18); guests in the Father's house (14:1–3); branches of a vine (15:5) and chosen and intimate friends (15:15–16). John explores the quality of relationships required of disciples. They are to be characterized by love and servanthood (13:1–17, 34; 15:9–17), as well as by obedience to Christ's commands (14:15–24). They are the community of the Paraclete, the *Holy Spirit (14:15–31; 16:5–16), and as such are not only taught and sanctified by him but brought into painful conflict with the unbelieving world.

John depicts the disciples in sharp contrast to the world. He especially emphasizes the hostility which will be shown by the Jews (9:1–41; 15:18 – 16:4), probably reflecting the circumstances of his original readers as they suffered ostracism and persecution from Jewish synagogues. So, although there is no systematic teaching about ecclesiology in John's Gospel, there is much which is relevant to a biblical theology of the church.

The writings of Paul

Introduction

There can be no doubting the centrality of the church in the writings of Paul. According to Ephesians 5:25–27, '... Christ loved the church and gave himself up for her to make her holy ...' It is through the church, of which Christ is the head (Eph. 1:22; 5:23; Col. 1:18), that God's wisdom is 'made known to the rulers and authorities in the heavenly realms' (Eph. 3:10). Paul's own ministry concentrated on the planting of Christian communities among the Gentiles and then, by visit, letter and intermediary, on instructing them more perfectly in their faith. Even when relationships were strained, as with the Corinthian church, Paul never reduced his commitment to the churches he had founded and to others, like Colossae and Rome, which he had never visited. His teaching must be pieced together from the 'shifting panorama' (Minear) of vivid images, deep theological insights and urgent pastoral advice which he offers.

Developments in Paul's writings

Paul's writings reflect developments in both his thinking and the position of the church. Consequently, Paul's letters are not monochrome. Margaret MacDonald has differentiated between his earlier writings which relate to the period of community-building, mature writings which relate to the period of community-stabilizing (Colossians and Ephesians) and later writings which relate to community-protecting (the Pastoral Letters).

The meaning of ekklēsia

Of the 114 references to *ekklēsia* in the NT, sixty-two are to be found in Paul. In his earlier writings he uses *ekklēsia* mostly with reference to the gathering of the local congregation (Rom. 16:5; 1 Cor. 1:2; 1 Thess. 1:1; 2 Thess. 2:1; Philem. 2), which usually meets in someone's home. When he wants to describe more than one local congregation he uses the plural (1 Cor. 16:1, 19; Gal. 1:2; 1 Thess. 2:14). There is little reason to believe that Paul thought of the church as some abstract or other-worldly entity. When he uses the term 'the church' generically, as he does in 1 Corinthians 10:32; 15:9; Galatians 1:13, he is referring to all the Christians on earth, to the entire Christian community which finds expression in many varied local congregations. But the one is never disconnected from the other after the manner of Platonic substance and form.

In Colossians and Ephesians his concept of church is more developed and applies to something wider than the local congregation. The distinctive element in these letters (Eph. 1:22; 2:6; 3:10; 5:23–27, 29, 32; Col. 1:18; 3:1–2) is the connection between the church on earth and the heavenly realm, which should determine the nature of the church in the present age.

Whether Paul's writings provide any justification for the existence of denominations is a matter of debate. Traditionally it has been argued that in Paul the church was local and universal and that there was little room for anything in between. More recently it has been recognized that various NT churches formed special associations (Rom. 16:4, 16; Gal. 1:22; 1 Thess. 2:14). These affiliations probably arose from Paul's calling as a missionary to the Gentiles (Gal. 2:8). The need for any such group to submit to the wider church, and not to work in arrogant isolation, is underlined by Acts 15.

Imagery for the church

The church is the *temple of the living God and so should be neither destroyed nor defiled (1 Cor. 3:16–17; 2 Cor. 6:16–18; Eph. 2:21). It is a new *humanity, taking its origin from the second Adam rather than the first (Rom. 5:12–17; Eph. 2:15). It is a body where each member is significant and which must keep closely in touch with its head (Rom. 12:4–5; 1 Cor. 12:12–31; Col. 1:18). As a body it can grow and mature (Col 2:19; Eph 4:16). It is the household of God (1 Tim. 3:15) where certain rules of conduct apply. Further images speak of the church as God's field (1 Cor. 3:9), the bride of Christ (2 Cor. 11:2), an army of the Spirit (Gal. 5:25 – 6:5), the pillar and foundation of truth (1 Tim. 3:15).

Life and organization

The life and worship of the early church is portrayed in Acts and, in Paul, especially in 1 Corinthians 11 – 14 and Colossians 3:16. Paul is concerned more with the quality of relationships within the church than with its programme. It must be characterized by mutual love and upbuilding as well as by holy living and practical concern for the poor (2 Cor. 8–9; Eph. 4:17 – 6:9; Phil. 2:1–18; Col. 3:5 – 4:1; 1 Thess. 4:1–12). No blueprint is given for the *leadership structure of the Pauline churches, which seems to have been flexible (within certain spiritual guidelines), involving both apostles, prophets, teachers and evangelists, and elders or overseers and deacons (1 Cor. 12:28; Eph. 4:11–13; Phil. 1:1; 1 Tim. 3:1–16; Titus 1:5–9). Whilst some development in organization is evident between the early years of the Gentile *mission and its later more settled period, earlier charismatic ministries (see *Spiritual gifts, *Languages) should not be seen in opposition to later structured offices. Both charisma and structure are apparent and essential throughout.

Later NT writings

Hebrews views the church through the lens of the OT cult and offers a distinctive understanding of it as the *worshipping community of the New Covenant brought into being through the sufficient sacrifice of Jesus as the great High Priest. Stressing the importance of meeting together (10:25), it contrasts the worship of the new community with that of the old and relates it to heavenly worship (12:18–29). Leaders are mentioned in passing at 13:7 and 17.

James speaks of the church as the scattered twelve tribes (1:1) and wants it to be an egalitarian community (2:1–13) which values the *poor as much as the rich, and a *healing community which experiences the restorative power of prayer (5:13–16).

1 Peter does not use the word 'church', but the writer sees the Christian community as composed of '*elect strangers' (1:1) who are constituted as the new Israel (2:9–10) through the liberating work of the suffering Christ. Instructions are given to elders and to other sections of the church community (5:1–9).

John's letters stress the need to distinguish the genuine from the false church. In 3 John there is a repeated emphasis on faithfully walking in *truth (1, 3, 4, 8, 12). 1 John spells out the essentials of the truth about Jesus.

Revelation is addressed to the seven churches of Asia (1:1 – 3:22); the writer designates the church a kingdom and a priesthood (1:6; 5:10). The role of *prophet is especially significant (10:7; 16:6; 18:24; 22:6, 9) as the church is undergoing severe persecution. The writer presents the true destiny of the church, unseen in this world, as a reason for hope and perseverance (19:9–10; 21:1 – 22:21). He envisages the church composed of people from every people and nation (5:9), and the creation fully restored to its creator (21:1 – 22:21)

Conclusion

Recent discussions of the church have reflected two major concerns. First, theologians have explored the trinitarian nature of *God as the origin and basis of the church, thus providing a theological justification for both its unity and its diversity. Secondly, postmodern culture has led to impatience with the church as an institution and has encouraged many to be 'post-denominational' in their desire to experience the church as true community. Both these concerns have contributed to a rediscovery of important elements of biblical ecclesiology.

See also: ISRAEL; PEOPLE OF GOD.

Bibliography

R. Banks, Paul's Idea of Community: The Early House Churches in their Historical Setting (Grand Rapids and Exeter, 1980); W. S. Campbell, 'Church as Israel, People of God', in DLNTD, pp. 204–219; W. Chow, 'The Church in the Old Testament', in B. J. Nicholls (ed.), The Church: God's Agent for Change (Exeter, 1987); E. P. Clowney, The Church (Leicester and Downers Grove, 1995); idem, 'The biblical theology of the Church', in D. A. Carson (ed.), The Church in the Bible and the World: An International Study (Exeter and Grand Rapids, 1987); A. Dulles, Models of the Church (Dublin, 1976); J. D. G. Dunn, Unity and Diversity in the New Testament (Philadelphia and London, 1977); K. Giles, What on Earth is the Church? A Biblical and Theological Enquiry (London, 1995); C. E. Gunton and D. W. Hardy, On Being the Church: Essays on the Christian Community (Edinburgh, 1989); H. Küng, The Church (London, 1968); P. Kusmic, 'The Church and the Kingdom of God', in B. J. Nicholls (ed.), The Church: God's Agent for Change (Exeter, 1987); M. Y. MacDonald, The Pauline Churches: A Socio-Historical Study of Institutionalisation in the Pauline and Deutero-Pauline Writings (Cambridge, 1988); P. Minear, 'Idea of church', in IDB 1, pp. 607–617; A. Snyder, The Community of the King (Downers Grove, 1977); M. Volf, After Our Likeness: The Church as the Image of the Trinity (Grand Rapids, 1998).

D. J. TIDBALL

CIRCUMCISION

The Jews were not the only people who practised circumcision in ancient times. It is not clear how widespread the practice was, but male circumcision was usually seen as one of the practices that clearly distinguished Jews from those around them. Infant circumcision became the rule for all male Jews; see Genesis 17:12; 21:4 and Leviticus 12:3.

The precise origins of circumcision are debated by scholars. Circumcision initially became theologically significant through its role in Judaism as a mandatory sign of covenant membership. It is first described in Genesis 17:1–14, where *God commands its practice as the sign and seal of his covenant with *Abraham. The command is given in the context of God's ongoing relationship with Abraham following the establishment of a covenant in Genesis 15. In Genesis 17, God promises Abraham that he will become 'the father of many nations' (vv. 4–6). Abraham will be a means, a channel, of God's *blessing to many people. Verses 11–13 indicate that circumcision was a physical expression of *faith which distinguished those who belonged to the Lord from those who did not. Further, God's instruction that Abraham should circumcise every male connected with him, including any 'slave born in your house and the one bought with your money from any foreigner who is not of your offspring' (v. 12, NRSV), suggests that circumcision was not meant to be understood as a sign of racial purity. Rather it was a necessary 'mark', a physical indicator, of God's people (as in Gen. 34 where, before the men of Shechem could marry into Jacob's family, they had to be circumcised – see v. 16). However, the essence of this covenant is probably to be seen not so much in its sign as in the promise that through Abraham God will bless many nations.

The relationship between covenant and circumcision is expressed in the structure of Genesis 17 (esp. vv. 9–14). Circumcision involved both the confirmation and the taking possession of the covenant. Thus it also functioned as 'God's indispensible branding of his people' (L. C. Allen, in NIDOTTE 4, p. 474), without which a male would be 'cut off' from the people of God (v. 14).

The importance of circumcision is further seen in Exodus 4:24–26. *Moses had to be circumcised before undertaking a mission on God's behalf. The passage is not easy to interpret, but the divine attack of verse 24 seems to have been prompted by Moses' being uncircumcised; Zipporah then circumcises their son as a vicarious act (for discussion of this passage, see R. G. Hall, in ABD, pp. 1026–1027). That circumcision is absolutely necessary in order for a man to be part of the worshipping community is further underlined by Exodus 12:44, 48, in which circumcision is a condition for participation in the Passover. In Joshua 5:2–8 the necessity of circumcision is again underlined, as God commands that the generation of Jews born on the journey through the wilderness, who had not been circumcised, should now undertake the rite. Verses 6–7, and 11–12 may also indicate that the people should re-dedicate themselves to the Lord before occupying the land promised in the covenant.

But while these passages focus on the literal, physical meaning of 'circumcision', the word is also used in a metaphorical sense. It is clear even from these passages that circumcision is never merely a physical act. It is not sufficient merely to be physically circumcised. The Israelites are instructed in Deuteronomy 10:16 to circumcise their hearts as a spiritual response to God's choice of them as his *people. This response involves *fearing, serving and holding fast to him (v. 20); it is the opposite of stubbornness. Heart commitment is a necessity, not an option. Similarly, Deuteronomy 30:6 indicates that on their return to the land after exile, there will be a new start. God will circumcise the people's hearts so that they will *love him 'with all

their heart' (cf. 29:4, and Lev. 26:41, which refers to the humbling of Israel's 'uncircumcised heart', seen in their rejection of God's *laws, v. 43).

Further, Jeremiah encourages the people to ensure that they are acting in a spiritual way as a corollary to the physical act of circumcision. They must put into practice the meaning of the rite in order to show appropriate commitment to the Lord. The limitations of the mere physical act are underlined in Jeremiah 9:25–26, where the prophet plays down the value of circumcision as merely an end in itself; to rely on it could lead to false confidence and therefore Israel should become circumcised in heart. A Jew with an uncircumcised heart is no different from a Gentile whose nation practises circumcision (cf. Ezek. 44:9, where entry to the rebuilt temple is forbidden to those who are not circumcised in heart and flesh).

So while circumcision gave the Jews a sense of national identity (particularly when they faced 'uncircumcised' nations; see e.g. Judg. 14:3; 15:18; 1 Sam. 14:6; 17:26, 36), the physical act of circumcision always had to be accompanied by spiritual qualities of *obedience and consecration, to the Lord and to the moral teaching of the covenant, of which *holiness was foundational (Lev. 11:44).

In NT times circumcision was still a fundamental indication of covenant membership. Thus John the Baptist, *Jesus and Saul of Tarsus were all circumcised (Luke 1:59; 2:21; Phil. 3:5) on the eighth day. While circumcision is rarely mentioned in the Gospels (and the references are only to the physical rite), John 7:22–24 may show Jesus casting doubt on its importance. He suggests that his healings make people completely whole, and contrasts himself with Moses, implying that the blessing he brings is far greater than that of circumcision.

The fact that the words denoting circumcision in the NT occur mainly in Acts and the Pauline epistles (e.g. the noun 'circumcision' occurs 36 times, 32 times in Paul; see further H. C. Hahn, in NIDNTT) indicates that it is in the early *church that there was debate on the subject. Stephen reinforces the OT idea that the mere physical act is of no value when he accuses the Jewish people of the same weaknesses that Jeremiah had criticized – uncircumcision of heart and ears and thus opposition to the work of God (Acts 7:51).

In the primitive church problems began to arise when the gospel was preached to Gentiles and they began to respond. Was circumcision necessary for these people? How did what God was doing in Christ relate to what he had done in the past through Abraham's covenant of circumcision? Some believed that what God was doing in Christ was part of what he had done in Abraham. Hence circumcision was necessary for all; it was a necessary condition of *salvation as well as its guarantee (see Acts 15:1, 5).

But others rejected this view of salvation, especially when uncircumcised Gentiles were filled with the *Holy Spirit (Acts 10:44–48). Clearly God had given to the Gentiles the '*repentance that leads to life' (Acts 11:18). At this point there was no discussion over whether converted Gentiles should be circumcised. Perhaps it was perceived that this event was a fulfilment of Joel's proclamation that God would pour his Spirit out on all flesh (Joel 2:28; cf. Acts 2:17), and thus that circumcision in the spiritual sense had been realized by this act of God's *grace, making the physical rite unnecessary.

However, the view of some believers who belonged to the sect of the Pharisees (Acts 15:5) that circumcision was necessary for salvation, became a source of considerable tension and debate in the early church, as this chapter of Acts and Paul's letters indicate. The tension was between some 'believers from among the circumcised' (Jewish Christians; see Acts 10:45; 11:2) and those called 'the uncircumcision' (Gentile Christians; see Acts 11:3). Peter opposed these Jewish Christians and affirmed that salvation was 'through the grace of the Lord Jesus' (Acts 15:11), thus denying that the Gentile converts needed to be circumcised. Paul and Barnabas consulted with the Jerusalem assembly (the apostles and elders) and it was agreed that Gentiles should not have to be circumcised (Acts 15:13–21).

But the controversy followed Paul throughout his ministry. He was concerned with more than merely the cultic act. For Paul, the presence of the Spirit in the lives of Gentile Christians, without their being circumcised or keeping any other parts of the law, indicated that keeping the law was unnecessary for membership of God's people (Gal. 3:1–5). The Galatians had received the Spirit apart from circumcision, so clearly the latter was not required for justification (Cf. Gal. 2:16).

Paul supports his argument against the need for circumcision by reference to Abraham. Genesis 15:6, he says, shows that Abraham was justified by faith, not by his performance of the law (Gal. 3:6–9; Rom. 4:1–8). Circumcision could not have been a necessary part of Abraham's becoming a member of God's people, because he was already regarded as *righteous in God's eyes before he was circumcised (Rom. 4:9–12). Thus circumcision is irrelevant, and Abraham is equally 'father' of both Jewish and Gentile Christians. Abraham's circumcision was a 'seal' of his righteousness, gained by faith before he was circumcised. So for Paul those who think they can become righteous before God by receiving circumcision (Gal. 5:2–6) which is a work of the law, are deceived (cf. Rom. 2:25). No one can perform perfectly the works required by the Law (Gal. 5:3), and faith in Christ alone is all that is needed for justification (cf. Gal. 3:10–14).

So circumcision could never have the place in the church that it had had in Judaism. As far as Paul was concerned, 'We are the circumcision, who worship in the Spirit of God and boast in Christ Jesus and have no confidence in the flesh' (Phil. 3:3). Paul does attach some value to circumcision in Romans 3:1–2, but this is because the promises attached to it are fulfilled through faith, quite apart from circumcision. God will 'justify the circumcised on the ground of faith and the uncircumcised through that same faith' (Rom. 3:30). It may be that Paul's agreeing to circumcise Timothy (perhaps to facilitate his mission, Acts 16:3) indicates that he did not forbid Jews from practising the law (Acts 21:21–26; cf. 1 Cor. 9:19–23). As a cultural practice, Paul did not object to circumcision. But to say that it was required for salvation was another matter altogether.

Thus for Paul, circumcision is not an issue with respect to acceptance in God's sight. The major issue is how a person responds to God's claims. The events of the cross, resurrection and new creation in the Spirit nullify any advantage resulting from circumcision (Gal. 5:6; 6:15). Faith working through love, and obedience to God, are everything (cf. 1 Cor. 7:19). The only circumcision which matters is circumcision of the heart through the Spirit (Rom. 2:29).

Jesus Christ has made one the circumcised

and the uncircumcised (*cf.* Eph. 2:14–16). *Baptism may be seen as the visible confirmation of justification by faith and is therefore called 'the circumcision of Christ made without hands' (Col. 2:11). Thus Paul did not need to circumcise Titus (Gal. 2:3), no longer preached circumcision (5:11), and treated any demand that Gentile Christians be circumcised as anachronistic; likewise as Jewish Christians did not need to reverse their circumcision (*cf.* Gal. 6:12; 1 Cor. 7:18). In Christ the distinction between circumcision and uncircumcision is eliminated (Col. 3:11).

Thus in Scripture the physical act of circumcision was never an end in itself, and its spiritual importance was frequently emphasized. The necessity of faith as a prerequisite to the physical rite in the OT led the early church to conclude that circumcision was no longer required of God's people, and that the work of Christ united Jewish and Gentile Christians without distinction.

See also: COVENANT; ISRAEL; NATIONS.

Bibliography

L. C. Allen, 'Circumcision', in *NIDOTTE* 4, pp. 474–476; P. Borgen, in M. D. Hooker and S. G. Wilson (eds.), *Paul and Paulinism: Essays in Honour of C. K. Barrett* (London, 1982), pp. 85–102; M. E. Glasswell, 'New Wine in Old Wine Skins: VIII. Circumcision', *ExpT* 85 (1974), pp. 328–332; H. C. Hahn, 'Circumcision', in *NIDNTT* 1, pp. 307–312; R. G. Hall, 'Circumcision', in *ABD*, pp. 1025–1031.

P. D. WOODBRIDGE

CITY, CITIZENSHIP

Introduction

From the period of rapid urbanization near the beginning of the Early Bronze Age (3300–2000 BC), city life was common in the ancient Near East. Most cities were small by modern standards, and except for Babylon and Nineveh, they may be more appropriately called 'towns' rather than 'cities' (J. D. Price, in *NIDOTTE* 3, p. 398). As city life was an important element of ancient society, we should not be surprised that the Bible discusses it and even uses it as a metaphor for important revealed truths.

The historical experiences of the OT Israelites are marked by two tensions, both having significant implications for the theological concept of citizenship. First, in the early period there is a tension between nomadic or semi-nomadic and urban life. Secondly, the OT prophets contrast Babylon and Jerusalem, which symbolize two ways of life.

Semi-nomadism and urban life in the OT

In the early period there is a tension between nomadic and urban life, the first traces of which can be seen in the primeval history. Cain built the city of Enoch, named after his son (Gen. 4:17); Cain's settled agricultural life is contrasted with the nomadic, pastoral life of Abel. After the Flood, some of the descendants of Noah built great cities from which the Mesopotamian empires developed (Gen. 10:10–12).

The tension between urban and nomadic is also evident in Israel's ancestral traditions. *Abraham was called to forsake one of the greatest cities of Mesopotamia and begin a life of nomadism, in which he depended exclusively on God's provision and protection (Gen. 12:1–3). He journeyed from Ur of the Chaldeans in southern Babylonia to Haran, the traditional ancestral city. From Haran, God directed him to Canaan, where he settled down, pitching his tent between Bethel and Ai (Gen. 12:8). He continued to live in tents for the rest of his life, exchanging an urban-based life for a semi-nomadic life with no permanent home (A. R. Millard, in *ABD* 1, p. 36). At the time of Sarah's death, Abraham described himself to the neighbouring Hittites as 'a stranger (*gēr*) and an alien (*tošab*) residing among you' (Gen. 23:4, NRSV). He purchased the cave of Machpelah from the Hittites as a burial place for Sarah; this was the only piece of land he acquired. Elsewhere the term 'stranger, sojourner' is used to describe the experience of the Israelites' ancestors in Canaan (Gen. 17:8; 28:4; 47:9; Exod. 6:4). Abraham and his family continued to live in tents as semi-nomadic, resident aliens on the fringes of urban Canaanite society (Gen. 13:3, 12, 18; and *passim* in Gen. 12 – 35, and see Heb. 11:9).

We can assume that the descendants of Abraham were more sedentary during their sojourn in Egypt, since they built the fortified Egyptian cities of Pithom and Rameses (Exod. 1:11). But after the Exodus, the Israelites once again lived as nomads, awaiting the day when they would inherit the Canaanite cities (Exod. 33:8 and Lev. 23:42–43). Part of the attraction of the Promised Land was the agricultural life it could afford, and the cities and towns in which the Israelites could dwell (Deut. 11:10–12; 19:1 and Josh. 24:13). But this new urbanized life could easily entice the Israelites into the sins of Canaan. So after giving them towns, homes and plantations built and planted by someone else, God warned the Israelites that they were still aliens: 'The land shall not be sold in perpetuity, for the land is mine; with me you are but aliens and tenants' (Lev. 25:23; and see 1 Chr. 29:15; Pss. 39:12; 119:19). Furthermore, the prophets declare that the cities of Israel can become as perverse and corrupt as they were under the Canaanites (Amos 3:9–11; 5:4–7; Is. 1:21–23). In fact, Jerusalem can become like Sodom and Gomorrah (Is. 1:8–10; Jer. 23:14).

Jerusalem and Babylon in the OT

This prophetic warning about the potential for evil, even within Jerusalem itself, brings us to the second tension resulting from the historical experiences of the OT Israelites. The OT's prophetic *eschatology contrasts Jerusalem and Babylon.

Jerusalem is specially significant for the prophets as the religious centre of the restored holy land (Ezek. 45:1–6). Yahweh has placed his name on Mount Zion, and it shall receive the gifts and adoration of many peoples (Is. 18:7; Zech. 8:22–23). In this way Jerusalem represents the *people of God, who will enjoy the *salvation of God after a period of punishment for their sins. The word of God issues forth from Jerusalem (Is. 2:3); peoples gather to honour him (Jer. 3:17); and the messianic king will appear victoriously (Zech. 9:9–10). It is not always clear within what time-frame these oracles of salvation are to be fulfilled; some promises refer to the distant future. In the age to come, Yahweh's rule will be firmly established in Jerusalem (Is. 24:23; 65:18–19). Jerusalem will finally become a holy city and will never again be conquered by foreign nations (Joel 3:17). In these prophetic passages, Jerusalem has become more than a political centre. It now serves as a symbol of the final and ultimate consummation of Yahweh's plan of salvation (T. L. Brensinger, in *NIDOTTE* 4, pp. 774).

Conversely, Babylon serves for the OT prophets as a symbol of wickedness. For Isaiah, Babylon is the proud and wicked city that will be left uninhabited and in ruins (Is. 13:20). Its name will be cut off for all time (Is. 14:22–23). Jeremiah also predicts severe punishment for Babylon and its deities (Jer. 50 – 51). Habakkuk comforts himself with the knowledge that Babylon will one day receive due retribution for all its crimes against Judah (Hab. 2:4–20). In this way, the OT prophets see Babylon and Jerusalem as confronting each other and representing the two 'cities' between which humankind is divided.

Babylon served the prophets especially well because of its brutal treatment of Judah and other nations in the late seventh and early sixth centuries BC. Furthermore, there is reason to believe that Babylonian nationalism was of a particularly rancorous kind not found in other nations of the ancient Near East (Sheriffs, in *TynB*, p. 38). This is borne out by the boastful claim of Nebuchadnezzar: 'Is this not magnificent Babylon, which I have built as a royal capital by my mighty power and for my glorious majesty?' (Dan. 4:30). Modern archaeologists have shown that Nebuchadnezzar's pride was not without justification, even if his personal role was overstated. During his reign, Babylon was transformed into the greatest city of the ancient world, leaving ruins spread over two thousand acres (B. T. Arnold, in *Peoples of the Old Testament World*, p. 63).

The citizenship of Abraham in the NT

Echoes of Abraham's sojourn in Canaan may be heard in Paul's statement that Christians are citizens of 'the Jerusalem above' (Gal. 4:21–31). Peter's description of believers is reminiscent of the terms used for Abraham in Genesis. They are 'temporary residents' ('refugees', *parepidēmois*) whose time on earth is a brief stay among strangers ('time of temporary residence', *paroikia*, 1 Pet. 1:1, 17).

The author of the letter to the Hebrews makes more explicit references to Abraham's experiences. In Hebrews 11:8–16, the lesson drawn from Abraham's faith is that while he, Isaac and Jacob were living in tents in Canaan, they were actually seeking the 'city that has foundations, whose architect and builder is God' (11:10). This reference to the semi-nomadism of the ancestral sojourn states clearly that Abraham's faith was rewarded beyond his comprehension. The city he inherited was the 'the heavenly Jerusalem', the city of the living God (Heb. 12:22–23), which is the capital of an unshakeable kingdom (Heb. 12:28). He expected to inherit the cities of Canaan, which were difficult to defend and vulnerable to many aggressors, but was rewarded with a far greater city. Likewise, Christians 'have no lasting city, but we are looking for the city that is to come' (Heb. 13:14).

The two cities in the NT

The eschatological picture of the two cities, Jerusalem and Babylon, had significant implications in the NT and subsequent Christian theology. The clash between the city of God and the city of Satan will come to a head in the eschaton.

The clearest expression of this eschatological conflict is found in the book of Revelation, where both the fall of the new Babylon and the arrival of the new Jerusalem are described. The horrors of the new Babylon are detailed in Revelation 17 – 18 (specifically 16:17 – 18:24). First-century readers would have undoubtedly understood 'Babylon' as a code name for Rome. As ancient Babylon had been the wicked and ruthless enemy of God's people in OT times, so here she symbolizes the evil and violent thirst for power so typical of earthly kingdoms. But Babylon's downfall will be swift and total (18:10, and see vv. 17 and 19).

Most of the book of Revelation is an account of persecution and death (chs. 6 – 20). But in chapters 21 – 22, the book moves from time into eternity as it foretells the glorious outcome of God's redemptive plan. The first paragraph (21:1–8) describes the new heaven and new earth in general terms, relying largely on images from the prophecy of Isaiah (65:17; 66:22). The old creation has passed away, making room for this new creation, 'the holy city, the new Jerusalem, coming down out of heaven from God' (Rev. 21:2). The second literary unit describes the new Jerusalem in more detail (21:9–21). The holy city of Jerusalem will be the new home for God's people. It is described as perfectly symmetrical, and radiant like pure jewels. Finally, the book gives a glimpse of life in the eternal city (21:22 – 22:5). Some things necessary and taken for granted in the former

city will be absent from the new Jerusalem. It has no temple, for the temple represented the presence of God in the midst of Jerusalem. Instead, God himself will be the temple in the new city (21:22). It has no sun or moon, for it will have the glory of God (21:23); no night, because the Lord God will be light for its inhabitants (21:25; 22:5). Life in the new city will surpass the experiences of the first couple in the Garden of Eden, for this city has 'the river of the water of life', and 'the tree of life' (22:1–2).

The contrast between the two cities encourages believers of every generation to have the faith of Abraham, who was a resident alien in Canaan, but whose citizenship was in heaven (Phil. 3:20). While living in tents here below, we must live a life worthy of our calling, aware that our time here is brief and that we are on a journey to that eternal city.

See also: BABYLON; JERUSALEM.

Bibliography

B. T. Arnold, 'Babylonians', in A. J. Hoerth, G. L. Mattingly and E. M. Yamauchi (eds.), *Peoples of the Old Testament World* (Grand Rapids and Cambridge, 1994, 1996), pp. 43–75; T. L. Brensinger, 'Jerusalem', in *NIDOTTE* 4, pp. 772–776; A. R. Millard, 'Abraham', in *ABD* 1, pp. 35–41; J. D. Price, ''îr' in *NIDOTTE* 3, pp. 396–399; D. C. T. Sheriffs, ' "A Tale of Two Cities" – Nationalism in Zion and Babylon', *TynB* 39, 1988, pp. 19–57.

B. T. ARNOLD

CLEAN, see HOLINESS

CLOTHES

Clothes serve a number of important functions in Scripture: to denote community identity; to signal social status; to enact legal, binding agreements; and to illustrate God's *redemptive activity towards his people.

Prescribed blue tassels sewn on the edges of Israelite garments define community identity and serve as tangible reminders prompting obedience to the *covenant commands of the Lord (Num. 15:38–40). Communal alienation and restoration are symbolized by actions performed on garments. Lepers quarantined outside the camp wear torn clothes (Lev. 13:45), but once healed and declared clean, they bathe their bodies and wash their clothes in order to be restored to the community (Lev. 14:8–9; cf. Luke 8:35).

Clothes signify the social status of individuals within the community, serving as an external expression of the established social order. *Kings (1 Kgs. 22:10; Jer. 13:18; Mark 15:17–18), queens (Est. 5:1), princes (Ezek. 21:26; 26:16), and princesses (2 Sam. 13:18) are distinguished by their royal attire and accoutrements. *Prophets often wear garments of hair (2 Kgs. 1:8; Zech. 13:4; Matt. 3:4). Priests minister in tunics of linen (Exod. 28:40–42), and the high priest is robed in splendid apparel made of gold embroidery and precious stones (Exod. 28:6–39). The bride (Jer. 2:32) and bridegroom (Is. 61:10), and perhaps those in attendance (Matt. 22:11) don ceremonial dress and ornamentation. *Men and women are differentiated by their respective garments (Deut. 22:5). Widows (Gen. 38:19; Deut. 24:17), mourners (2 Sam. 14:2), and others on the margins of the community are identified by their dress, as are prostitutes (Gen. 38:15) and prisoners (2 Kgs. 25:29).

Agreements considered legally binding are enacted through symbolic actions performed on clothes. *Marriage involves the spreading of a cloak over the woman to be wed, bringing her under the covering, protection and provision of her husband (Ruth 3:9; Ezek. 16:8). Conversely, the dissolution of the marriage covenant is effected by stripping off the wife's garments (Ezek. 16:37; Hos. 2:3, 9). Garments represent inheritance (Gen. 37:3; Luke 15:22), and are often given in pledge to represent the property belonging to an individual (Deut. 24:12–13, 17). Furthermore, acts of redemption or transfer of property are legalized by the acceptance or rejection of a sandal (Ruth 4:7). Installation to royal, prophetic and priestly offices is accomplished by the act of investiture (Gen. 41:42; Lev. 8:13, 30; Num. 20:26; 1 Kgs. 19:19; Dan. 5:29), whereas abdication or removal from office is signified by divestiture (1 Sam. 18:3–4; Is. 22:21).

Woven throughout Scripture, the exchange and provision of garments portray God's redemptive initiative. In the first act of *mercy extended to fallen humanity, the Lord covers Adam and Eve with clothes, replacing the inadequate fig-leaf covering their own hands have made with garments of skin (Gen. 3:21). From this time, proper garments are required when coming into the presence of the holy God (Exod. 19:10, 14; Ezek. 44:17; Matt. 22:11–12; Rev. 3:18; 7:9, 14). Israel's high priest is clothed with sacred garments of glory and splendour (Exod. 28:2), which, through their rich symbolism, foreshadow a re-created *humanity (Ps. 132:16; Rev. 21:10–20). These vestments secure entrance into the innermost chamber of the sanctuary and bring the nation representatively into the presence of God. Upon the breastpiece the high priest bears the names of the tribes of Israel inscribed on precious stones (Exod. 28:29) and upon his turban he bears their *guilt (Exod. 28:38). Prophets describe Jerusalem's redemption and restoration using images of clothing. In a heavenly scene, angelic attendants strip the high priest Joshua of his filthy raiment indicative of the *sin of the nation (Zech. 3:1–9), and exchange his defiled garments for pure ones: 'See, I have taken away your sin and I will put rich garments on you' (Zech. 3:4, NIV). Jerusalem's garments have become soiled by her own self-righteousness (Is. 64:6) and only the Lord can provide clean ones for her to wear. After the judgment of exile, her sin will be removed from her and she will be clothed with garments of splendour (Is. 52:1), adorned with returning exiles as bridal ornaments (Is. 49:18). She will be garbed in bridal attire, and so be restored to her status of God's bride (Is. 62:1–12). The Messiah will effect this. He will bestow a crown of beauty upon her head, which was once covered with ashes of mourning, and clothe her with 'a garment of praise instead of despair' (Is. 61:3; cf. Luke 4:18–19). Zion will exult: '… he has clothed me with garments of salvation and arrayed me in a robe of righteousness' (Is. 61:10).

Redemption symbolized by the exchange of garments culminates in the person and work of *Jesus Christ. Believers are charged to disrobe themselves of the old self in order to put on as a garment (endysasthai), the new self created in *righteousness (Eph. 4:22–24). This new self is not merely an external covering of Christian virtues (Col. 3:12), but a putting on of Christ himself (Gal. 3:27). Believers are exhorted, 'clothe yourselves with the Lord Jesus Christ' (Rom. 13:14). Having dressed themselves with Jesus Christ, they are transformed into his likeness, conformed to his ethical image, and become partakers of his nature (Col. 3:10). Those clothed with Christ will have entrance into the presence of God and fellowship with the worshipping community (Rev. 3:5). The crowning act of redemption will come when the bride of Christ is graciously granted fine, white linen to wear; that is, when she is clothed in the eschatological dress which 'stands for the righteous acts of the saints' (Rev. 19:8). At the end of the age, the community of the redeemed will be clothed with an imperishable, immortal, heavenly dwelling (1 Cor. 15:53; 2 Cor. 5:3). They will no longer be identified by perishable tassels, but by the imperishable righteousness of the Lamb.

See also: PRIESTS.

Bibliography

J. Gamberoni, *TDOT* 7, pp. 457–468; M. G. Kline, 'Investiture with the image of God', *WTJ* 40 (1977), pp. 39–62; H. Weigelt, *NIDNTT* 1, pp. 314–316.

C. E. PALMER

COLOSSIANS, see Part 2

COMFORT

Comfort in the ancient world

Comfort or consolation is the encouragement or sympathy given to someone who is grieving or sad. In both the Jewish and the pagan world it was considered the duty of a relative or neighbour to give comfort by visiting, or by writing a letter if the distance was too far to travel.

The many letters of comfort which have survived suggest that the normal message was 'do not lament long'. It was argued that 'lamenting is useless', and that people should 'set an example' by mourning for a short period. The reading of philosophy and poetry was encouraged, and philosophers attended the sorrowful like physicians attended the sick. Sometimes diversions such as wine, song or even riddles were encouraged. Assurances of immortality or of the peacefulness of eternal nothingness were given, depending on the

beliefs of the comforter.

Hardly ever was invocation or reference made to the gods. Comfort was not regarded as a divine function, and no pagan deity was associated with it. Indeed, the biblical concept of a God who comforts was otherwise virtually unknown in the ancient world.

Comfort in the OT

The concept of comfort is expressed most often by the Hebrew root *nḥm*. This is used in the *niphal* form for sorrow and regret, and in the *piel* form for comfort or consolation. Sorrow is comforted by visiting (Gen. 37:35; Job 2:11; 42:11) and by bringing food and wine (Jer. 16:5, 7; Gen. 14:18). Consolation is given mostly to those who are bereaved (Gen. 24:67; 37:35; 38:12; 2 Sam. 10:2; 12:24; 1 Chr. 19:2; Is. 61:2; Jer. 16:7; 31:15).

The book of Job shows how friends are expected to comfort. Eliphaz, Bildad and Zophar come to sit with the sorrowful Job, and share his sorrow. They give encouragement through talking, especially about philosophical aspects of life and death, punishment and reward. They surround Job with support as troops surround their king (Job. 29:25), though on this occasion they give poor comfort (Job 16:2).

The Psalms and prophets emphasize that comfort comes from God. God comforts individuals (Pss. 22:5; 86:17; 94:19) and the people of God (Is. 40:1–31; 52:9; 54:11–15). He comforts like a shepherd (Ps. 23:4; Is. 40:11) and like a mother (Is. 66:13). His consolation is mediated through Scripture (Ps. 119:52, 76, 82; *cf.* 2 Macc. 15:9), and especially through his Servant (Is. 61:2). The Septuagint of Isaiah 57:18 calls the comfort of God, 'true comfort'.

Development of comfort/consolation in Judaism

The consolations of Isaiah, which open with Isaiah 40:1 'Comfort, O comfort my people' (NRSV), became very important in Judaism. The Messiah (see *Jesus Christ) was called 'the consolation of Israel' (a designation based on Is. 61:2), and the end time (see *Eschatology) was called the 'the time of consolation'. 'Consolation' was also used to refer to preaching, and to the subject of the second synagogue reading (from the Prophets), the *haftorah*. Before the lectionary of the *haftorah* was finalized, the reader could choose any passage from the Prophets which had links with the Torah reading, or any passage about the consolation of Israel.

Comfort in the NT

The idea of comfort or consolation is almost always expressed using *parakalein* and its cognates. The normal meanings of *parakalein* outside the Septuagint and Christian writings are 'to summon' someone and 'to beseech/exhort' a person or a god. The word occasionally means 'to comfort' in pagan literature, but this meaning is much more common in Jewish and Christian writings. These were both influenced by the Septuagint which as a rule used *parakalein* to translate *nhm*.

The use of *parakalein* in the Gospels and Acts is influenced by the Jewish use of 'consolation' to refer to the Messiah and the eschatological hope. The rich have their comfort now (Luke 6:24), but the righteous wait for eternal consolation (Matt.5:4; Luke 16:25), 'the consolation of Israel' (Luke 2:25). In Acts the word is used to refer to the second synagogue reading and to preaching based on these passages of consolation (Acts 13:15, 31; 15:31).

In the epistles, as in the Septuagint, comfort comes from other people and especially from God. Hebrews and Paul find comfort in the word of God (Heb. 6:18; 12:5, referring to Prov. 3:11; Rom. 15:4). Paul also associates comfort with the visit of Tychicus (Col. 4:8; *cf.* Eph. 6:22), the love of Philemon (Philem. 7) and the return of Timothy from Thessalonica (1 Thess. 3:7); Timothy himself is comforted when at Corinth (2 Cor. 7:4, 7, 13). Paul points out that when we receive comfort, we can give it to others, especially when that comfort comes from God (2 Cor. 1:3–7). Although the epistles speak mostly about receiving comfort from each other and from God in this life, Paul also looks forward to the eternal consolation (2 Thess. 2:16).

The Holy Spirit as paraclete

The traditional translation of *parakletos* as 'comforter' is probably mistaken. It was popularized by many early translations (especially Wycliff and King James, and perhaps Luther), but later translations have favoured the more accurate 'advocate' or a more neutral 'paraclete'.

The normal meaning of *parakletos* in Greek literature is 'advocate', usually in the sense of one who speaks in court on someone else's behalf. Rabbinic literature refers to Michael or other angels as advocates for Israel in the heavenly courts. Good deeds and repentance are a person's advocates before God.

Parakletos clearly means 'advocate' in 1 John 2:1, where Jesus stands before the Father interceding for the sinner. This idea is consistent with other NT teaching about Christ as intercessor (Rom. 8:34; Heb. 7:25; Matt.10:32–35).

The *Holy Spirit is called *parakletos* in the farewell discourses of John 14 – 16. Here too a courtroom theme of judgment and conviction is present (John 16:7–11). This makes the translation 'advocate' very apt, but to use it is not to detract from the role of the Holy Spirit as one who comforts the disciples when Jesus leaves them (cf. Acts 9:31).

Bibliography

O. Schmitz, 'Parakaleo, paraklesis', in *TDNT 5*, pp. 773–799; J. Behm, 'Parakletos', in *TDNT 5*, pp. 800–814; M. Butterworth, 'NHM', in *NIDOTTE 3*, pp. 81-83; J. Mann and I. Sonne, *The Bible as Read and Preached in the Old Synagogue* (Cincinnati, 1940–66).

D. INSTONE BREWER

COMMAND, see LAW
COMPASSION, see MERCY
CONDEMNATION, see JUDGMENT
CONFESSION, see TESTIMONY/WITNESS
CONFIDENCE, see ASSURANCE
CONSECRATION, see HOLINESS
CONSOLATION, see COMFORT
CORINTHIANS, see Part 2

COVENANT

Theological significance

The 'covenant' concept is one of the most important motifs in biblical theology. As well as being reflected in the traditional title of the two parts of the Christian Bible, the Old and New *Testaments* (*i.e.* covenants), the covenant idea looms large at important junctures throughout the Bible. The concept underpins *God's relationship with Noah, the patriarchs, *Israel, the Aaronic *priesthood, and the Davidic dynasty. It is also used with respect to God's relationship with the reconstituted 'Israel' of the future. Therefore, while 'biblical' and 'covenant theology' are not synonymous, the covenant concept is undoubtedly one of the Bible's core theological themes.

Terminology and meaning

The Hebrew term for covenant, *berît*, is of uncertain derivation. It is commonly connected with *berîtu*, an Akkadian noun meaning 'bond' or 'fetter'. Others associate it with the Akkadian preposition *birit*, meaning 'between'. Still other suggested sources are the Hebrew roots meaning 'to eat' and 'to select', which associate covenant with the ideas of eating together (*cf.* Gen. 26:30; 31:54) and election respectively. Here, as elsewhere in biblical theology, contextual usage of a word is more important in determining its meaning than etymology. Actual usage of the term (occurring some 285 times in the OT) suggests that it conveys the idea of a solemn commitment, guaranteeing promises or obligations undertaken by one or both covenanting parties. While the term applies predominantly to divine–human commitments, it is also used of various agreements between humans (*cf.* Gen. 21:22–24; 1 Sam. 18:3; 1 Kgs. 5:1–12; 2 Kgs. 11:17), including marriage (Ezek. 16:8; Mal. 2:14; Prov. 2:17), and even in a figurative sense for solemn commitments made with oneself (Job 5:23; 31:1; 41:1–4; Is. 28:15–18).

While *berît* is the primary term for covenant in the OT, other terminology is also used (*e.g.* *ḥesed* = steadfast *love, lovingkindness). Moreover, the absence of the term *berît* does not, of itself, exclude the concept of covenant (*e.g.* while 2 Sam. 7 is not explicitly described as the making of a covenant, it is so understood elsewhere, *cf.* 2 Sam. 23:5; Pss. 89:3, 28, 34; 132:12).

The term used in the NT is *diathēkē*, the word used to translate *berît* in the LXX. Although the term occurs only some thirty-three times, almost half of which occur in OT quotations, many other NT passages reflect covenantal ideas (*e.g.* Rom. 9 – 11). While the use of this word rather than *synthēkē* the Greek term for 'treaty', may suggest that a 'covenant' is not simply a mutual agreement, the fact that *diathēkē* is deployed in the LXX even for covenants between equals suggests

that too much can be read into the use of this term. On two occasions in the NT *diathēkē* is apparently used in its strict Greek sense of a 'will' or 'testament' (Gal. 3:15; Heb. 9:16–17, NRSV), a connotation somewhat different from that of the Hebrew concept of a *berît* yet perhaps intended to facilitate Hellenistic understanding.

Number and relationship

There is no consensus over the precise number of divine covenants in Scripture. While many note only those divine–human relationships to which covenantal terminology is expressly applied, others, chiefly those within the Reformed school, identify several additional covenants, including an overarching 'covenant of grace'.

Hypothetical/'implicit' divine covenants in Scripture

Although 'Reformed' or 'covenant' theology has correctly underlined the centrality of the covenant concept in biblical theology, it has tended to go beyond the exegetical evidence. The primary example of this tendency is the introduction into the discussion of non-biblical terminology and ideas (*e.g.* covenants of redemption, creation, works and grace). Such hypothetical covenants are without solid exegetical support, and primarily serve to bolster the unnecessary premise that all God's actions must be understood within a covenantal framework. While this is indeed how God's saving purpose has been given historical expression in a number of significant ways, to see all God's salvific activities in terms of covenant is unwarranted.

The idea of a 'covenant of redemption' through which the Father and the Son agreed to save elect sinners does not sit easily with trinitarian theology, and applies a historical concept to a theological construct which is clearly ahistorical.

The covenant with creation postulated by Dumbrell and others does have at least some exegetical foundation. Dumbrell's argument is essentially twofold: 1. the way that the Noahic covenant is introduced in Genesis 6:18 implies that a previously established covenant is being renewed; 2. the Noahic covenant clearly alludes to important themes in Genesis 1 – 3. While initially impressive, however, Dumbrell's arguments do not stand up to close scrutiny. Neither the causative verb (*hēqîm* = establish) nor the possessive pronoun ('*my* covenant') demands that an existing covenant is being mentioned in Genesis 6:18. The allusions in the Noahic covenant to the material in Genesis 1 – 3 do not necessarily mean that the latter must be understood covenantly. Others (*e.g.* Niehaus) find support for such a hypothetical creation covenant in Jeremiah's references to a 'covenant with day and night' (Jer. 33:20, 25), but these allusions are perhaps better understood in relation to the Noahic covenant, a covenant which expressly encompasses God's creative ordinances. Niehaus also defends a covenantal framework in Genesis 1 – 2 on the basis of form-critical arguments, but his case is rather too circular to be convincing. Thus, despite the efforts of these scholars, the burden of proof still rests with those who maintain the existence of such a 'covenant with creation'.

Exegetical support for the posited 'covenant of works' or 'Adamic covenant' is sought in Hosea 6:7. This text, however, is open to a wide range of interpretations, the most likely of which reads 'Adam' as the name of a geographical location and the event as an otherwise unrecorded breach of the Mosaic covenant by Israel. Given the exegetical difficulties with the key phrase, Hosea 6:7 is a rather tenuous basis on which to construct the otherwise unattested concept of a 'covenant of works with Adam'. Interestingly, even some Reformed theologians seem to concede this; for example, Van Groningen prefers Dumbrell's idea of a 'covenant with creation'.

The concept of a 'covenant of grace' clearly lies at the very heart of 'covenant theology'. In fact, this concept so pervades Reformed thinking that it is sometimes inadvertently read into Ephesians 2:12, a text which speaks not of one overarching biblical covenant (as supposed by many Reformed theologians), but rather of the 'covenants (pl.) of promise'. Admittedly, the concept of a single, overarching 'covenant of grace' serves to keep the continuity and relationship between the various divine-human covenants in focus. However, it does so at the expense of introducing non-biblical and misleading terminology into the discussion. While all the divine-human covenants ultimately serve the same overarching divine purpose, that *purpose* is better described as simply and unambiguously as possible.

Historical/explicit divine covenants in Scripture

Depending on how one views the Noahic, Abrahamic and Mosaic covenants, there are between five and ten divine covenants (the higher figure involves counting with Beckwith, covenant 'renewals' such as Exodus 34 and Deuteronomy 29 – 30 as separate covenants). While the following discussion assumes a total of nine (and does not include some covenant renewals by Israel such as those described in Josh. 23 – 24; 1 Sam. 12; 2 Chr. 29 – 31; 2 Kgs. 22 – 23), the covenants will be delineated under the following convenient headings: Noahic, Abrahamic, Mosaic, priestly, Davidic and new.

The Noahic covenant. The first explicit mention of a 'covenant' is found in Genesis 6:18. Although some distinguish between this covenant and the post-diluvian covenant established between God and Noah (Gen. 8 – 9), it seems more likely that 6:18 anticipates the latter covenant made on behalf of all living creatures. As well as lacking even the most basic covenantal aspects (*e.g.* a promissory oath of some kind), God's initial speech to Noah (Gen. 6) reads more like a series of preliminary instructions. The mention of 'covenant' at this point is simply explanatory, highlighting God's purpose in the selection of Noah and his family.

Thus understood, the establishment of the post-diluvian covenant with Noah (Gen. 8:20 – 9:17) serves to reaffirm God's original creational intent which had been 'disrupted' by the flood. The promissory and obligatory emphases of the Noahic covenant may be explained in the same way. God solemnly promises that humanity's creational mandate (*cf.* 9:1–7; 1:26–30) will never again be interrupted by a suspension of the natural order (8:21–22; 9:11–15). Significantly, this covenant is described as 'everlasting', a term which, in the context, appears to signify at least 'as long as the earth endures' (8:22).

The occasion for the establishment of the Noahic covenant was the offering of *sacrifices. Given that this is so, and that such a ritual was apparently anticipated (*cf.* 7:2–3), it would seem that the offering of a sacrifice was a crucial element in the making of this covenant. The Noahic covenant is by no means unique in this respect.

The introduction of additional divine

commands (9:4–6) is initially puzzling. However, in the context of a tremendous loss of life, this emphasis on the value of life generally, and of human life especially, is of considerable significance. Rather than suggesting that 'life is cheap', the deluge signifies precisely the opposite: the seriousness of the problem that had precipitated the flood. In any case, this emphasis on the preservation of life reflects the primary rationale for the establishment of the covenant: the preservation, without further divine interruption, of life on earth. It is at least implicit from this that God's redemptive goal will ultimately encompass not just one people or nation, but rather the whole earth. The universal emphasis of Genesis 1 – 11 is not lost entirely in the subsequent chapters of Genesis (or beyond), despite their narrowing focus.

The 'sign' of the Noahic covenant was God's 'bow in the clouds' (9:12–17). While this visible symbol in the sky would undoubtedly reassure humankind, its express intent was to remind God himself to keep his covenantal promise(s), although the reminder may be just an anthropomorphic way of expressing the reassurance. The fact that there was a covenant sign (see below), along with the strategic placing of divine instructions between the sacrificial ritual and the formal establishment of the covenant, strongly suggests that the Noahic covenant was not simply promissory, but involved bilateral obligations.

The Abrahamic covenants. Most scholars understand God's covenant with Abraham as a single covenant instituted in a number of stages (between two and four). These 'stages' have been viewed diachronically by critical scholarship in terms of different sources or traditions which allegedly lie behind the final form of the Abraham narrative. Thus, for example, Genesis 12:1–3 = 'J'; Genesis 15:17–21 = 'E'; Genesis 17 = 'P'. These chapters, therefore, contain variant accounts from different periods of what is essentially the same event. However, this approach is fundamentally flawed; as well as being built on the increasingly unstable foundation of the Documentary Hypothesis, it involves numerous presuppositions that do not stand up under close examination. More importantly, however, it actually evades the important issue of how these passages relate to each other in the final form of the text.

Synchronically, for those who believe in a single Abrahamic covenant, the staged revelation of it has been understood by most scholars in terms of Abraham's spiritual pilgrimage. The covenant is initially established in either Genesis 12 or 15, and then amplified in subsequent chapters. On this view, Genesis 17 is not an alternative account of the establishment of the Abrahamic covenant, but is either a renewal of the previously established covenant, or simply the next phase in the establishment of the covenant, supplementing its promissory aspects with important obligatory dimensions that had not been disclosed previously. However, none of these suggestions explains adequately the significantly different emphases of Genesis 15 and 17.

The only way to account for these is by a radically different synchronic explanation; the two chapters (Gen. 15 and 17) focus on two separate covenants, each of which takes up different aspects of the promissory agenda outlined in Genesis 12:1–3. The two main promissory aspects in this programmatic text are 'nationhood' (*i.e.* descendants and land) and international blessing, and these are also the primary emphases in Genesis 15 and 17 respectively. Thus two distinct covenants were established between God and Abraham. The first (Gen. 15) solemnly guaranteed God's promise to make Abraham into a 'great nation'. The second solemn guarantee (anticipated in Gen. 17, but not actually given until Gen. 22) related to God's promise to bless the *nations through Abraham and his '*seed'. These two Abrahamic covenants, while different, are nevertheless related by the theme of Abraham's 'seed'. The second covenant, guaranteeing international *blessing through one of Abraham's royal descendants, clearly assumes the fulfilment of the promise of nationhood.

As with the Noahic covenant, the occasion for the establishment of both Abrahamic covenants was sacrificial ritual (*cf.* 15:9; 22:10–14). The ritual in Genesis 15 has generally been interpreted as a self-maledictory curse akin to Jeremiah 34:18, although salient objections have been raised against such an interpretation (*cf.* G. J. Wenham, in *JSOT*, pp. 134–137). Whatever the precise symbolism, however, the important point to note is that God alone (represented by the theophanic imagery of fire and smoke) passed between the dissected animals, indicating the unilateral nature of the covenant. God alone took on obligations; Abraham remained a passive spectator of the ritual. Interestingly no covenant 'sign' is expressly mentioned (admittedly the stars and the ritual were visual aids for Abraham), although this fact is probably explained by the complete absence of human obligations and by the temporal nature of the covenant.

In contrast to Genesis 15, the subsequent covenant passage incorporates two human obligations, one ethical and the other ritual. Irreproachable behaviour (17:1) is a prerequisite for the establishment of this covenant (in the Hebrew text of Gen. 17 references to the covenant are consistently in the future tense), and the rite of physical male circumcision is necessary in order 'keep' the covenant and enjoy its benefits (17:9–14). Circumcision also functions as the 'sign of the covenant' (17:11), a feature quite in keeping with a covenant which is not just promissory in nature.

The bilateral nature of this second covenant between God and Abraham is further emphasized in its establishment (Gen. 22:16–18). Here God reiterates his promises to bless Abraham, but the covenant promises are firmly placed within the framework of Abraham's *obedience (vv. 16, 18b). Moreover, when this occasion is mentioned later (in God's speech to Isaac, Gen. 26:2–5), Abraham's obedience is presented as the crucial factor which prompted God's solemn oath (v. 5). Together this evidence suggests that whereas the 'covenant between the pieces' was a unilateral obligation on the part of God, the covenant announced in Genesis 17 involved bilateral obligations.

As well as this significant difference in the nature of the two Abrahamic covenants, there is also a clear distinction in their promissory elements. As noted above, the promises solemnly guaranteed in Genesis 15 are those relating to posterity and territory, themes which Alexander helpfully labels 'nationhood'. There is no mention in Genesis 15 of any international dimension, or indeed of royal descendants or a perpetual divine–human relationship. The promises relate solely to the establishment of a 'great nation' (12:2) in a carefully defined geographical region (15:18–21). Moreover, the chronology for the fulfilment of this covenant is stated quite explicitly (15:13–16). Nothing is revealed (at least in Gen. 15) of events subsequent to the establishment of nationhood.

In Genesis 17 the promissory element is markedly different. Even though the promises of Genesis 15 are not altogether absent (cf. vv. 2b, 8), the stress in chapter 17 is on 'nations', 'kings' and a perpetual divine–human relationship with Abraham's 'seed' (vv. 4–8, 16–21). The emphasis on these new promises is brought out even more clearly by the fact that Ishmael is in some sense excluded from this 'everlasting covenant', even though he is promised the blessings of numerous posterity, status and nationhood (v. 20), and receives the covenant sign of circumcision (v. 26). From the contrast between the future prospects of Isaac and Ishmael, it appears that the covenant of Genesis 17 (involving nations, kings and a divine–human relationship) will be perpetuated exclusively through Isaac's line (an inference apparently confirmed in Gen. 21:12), although its benefits will be enjoyed by all who, like Abraham's household, submit to its fundamental requirements. The preservation of Abraham's 'seed' through Isaac was therefore crucial if the promises of Genesis 17 were to be fulfilled. Without Isaac there would be no posterity, no 'great nation', no kings, and consequently no blessing for the nations.

This claim accentuates the rigour of the divine test in Genesis 22; God was commanding Abraham to destroy the foundational element of the divine promise. Ironically, it was through Abraham's willingness to surrender this that the ultimate fulfilment of the divine promise was guaranteed; all the nations of the earth would be blessed through Abraham's 'seed' (here a single individual and, in view of Gen. 17:6, 16, probably a royal descendant; cf. Ps. 72:17). Through his obedience to God's command, Abraham supremely demonstrated his irreproachable behaviour, and so fulfilled the stated prerequisite for the establishment of the covenant. Clearly the narrator means us to understand Abraham's behaviour as typifying and anticipating the kind of behaviour later demanded of his descendants (Gen. 26:5). Contrary to what is sometimes thought, the concept of an ethical code was not introduced by the Mosaic covenant, but was already implicit in the Abrahamic covenant. The 'great and mighty nation' descended from Abraham was, from the beginning, 'to keep the way of the LORD by doing righteousness and justice, so that the LORD may bring about for Abraham what he has promised him' (Gen. 18:18–19, NRSV; cf. Gen. 26:5).

The Mosaic covenant(s). As with the earlier divine covenants, the inauguration of the Mosaic or Sinaitic covenant involved sacrifice (Exod. 24:3–8). It also conformed to the now established pattern for covenants involving bilateral obligations; it had a 'sign', *sabbatical rests (Exod. 31:13–17; cf. Is. 56:4; Ezek. 20:12, 20). The fact that the stipulated covenant sign is identified as such only after the instructions concerning the tabernacle and the priesthood are given (Exod. 25:1 – 31:11) may suggest that the latter elements were also intrinsically related to the Mosaic covenant (cf. 24:12; 31:18). The primary concern of the Mosaic covenant was the maintaining of the unique divine–human relationship between Yahweh and Israel, and thus some means of sustaining communion between a holy God and a sinful people was required.

The Mosaic covenant was established after the first stage of the 'covenant between the pieces' had been realized: the deliverance of Abraham's descendants from oppression in a foreign land. Indeed, God's intervention was clearly motivated by the promises made in Genesis 15, to which there are several clear allusions (cf. Exod. 2:23–24; 3:7–8, 16–22; 6:4–6; 13:5, 11). Significantly, nowhere in the Mosaic covenant is the actual inheritance of the Promised *Land placed in any doubt. The focus is not on what Abraham's descendants must do in order to inherit the land (this had been guaranteed unconditionally in Genesis 15), but rather on how they must conduct themselves within the land as the special kind of nation that God intended them to be (Exod. 19:5–6).

It is clear from the conditional framework (*i.e.* 'If you obey … then …', NIV) of this text that the covenant involved bilateral obligations. For his part, God would make Israel unique among the nations; they would be his 'special treasure', a 'priestly kingdom' and a 'holy nation'. To be such, however, Israel must 'keep God's covenant' by fulfilling her obligations (*i.e.* the divine commands of the Decalogue [Exod. 20:1–17] and the ordinances of the 'Book of the Covenant' [Exod. 21 – 23]). These, and indeed the rest of the Sinaitic obligations (*i.e.* as disclosed in Leviticus), had a revelatory purpose. Just as

ancient *law-codes generally made a statement about the king who had promulgated them, so the covenant obligations revealed at Sinai disclosed something of the nature and character of Yahweh. Being in special relationship with Yahweh involved more than privilege; it also entailed responsibility. Only by maintaining the ethical distinctiveness enshrined in God's instructions to Abraham (Gen. 17:2, 9–10) could Israel, the patriarch's promised descendants, enjoy the divine–human relationship anticipated in that chapter (Gen. 17:7–8). For Yahweh to be their God, Israel had to be like him (cf. Lev. 19:2). Like their ancestor, Israel must 'walk before God and be blameless' (Gen. 17:1). Thus the primary concern of the Mosaic covenant was the way in which the divine–human relationship between Yahweh and the 'great nation' descended from Abraham should be maintained.

It was vital that Israel remained distinct from other nations, especially those they were about to dispossess. While the point is not made explicitly until later (Lev. 18:24–29; although cf. Exod. 23:20–33), Israel's distinctiveness was also a prerequisite for retaining possession of the territorial inheritance. Expulsion from the Promised Land would in turn jeopardize the fulfilment of God's ultimate objective, the blessing of all nations through Abraham's royal 'seed'. Therefore, just as the Noahic covenant had guaranteed the preservation of life, in particular human life, on earth, so the Mosaic covenant guaranteed the preservation of Israel, Abraham's national posterity, in the land until the arrival of Abraham's ultimate seed and covenant heir (cf. Gal. 3:19).

However, this guarantee was not unconditional, a fact illustrated by the crisis that arose from the golden calf episode (Exod. 32 – 33). Significantly, while appeal to the unconditional promise of nationhood prompts God not to annihilate Abraham's descendants (32:7–14), the seriousness of this breach of the covenant is highlighted not only by the punishment meted out immediately (32:28), but also by the ominous threat of divine *judgment in the future (32:33–34). Moreover, it was only on the condition of loyal obedience to his commands that Yahweh agreed to maintain his special relationship with Israel (34:27–28). While the latter chapter is generally viewed as a covenant renewal, it is perhaps better understood as the making of a new and separate covenant which served the same purpose as the first, but with more emphasis on the covenant fidelity (human and divine) that was essential if the relationship between Yahweh and Israel was to be maintained.

The covenant in Deuteronomy is likewise a distinct development in God's relationship with Israel (*cf.* Deut. 29:1); the new generation had to commit themselves to the Mosaic covenant before taking possession of the Promised Land. Although in one sense this was a renewal or remaking of the Sinaitic covenant with a new generation, there are some significant differences in emphasis, which may suggest that this covenant qualifies the conditional nature of Israel's unique relationship with Yahweh, especially in relation to their future tenure of the Promised Land. Yahweh had earlier guaranteed the staged removal of the Canaanites (Exod. 23:30; 34:11). He had also indicated that Israel would likewise be expelled, if she failed to meet her covenant obligations (Lev. 18:24–30). However, now it is disclosed that even exile to the most remote parts of the earth (Deut. 30:4) will not thwart God's ultimate purpose; rather, the promises made to Abraham will find further fulfilment (30:5), and the divine–human relationship will be sustained by an inner change (30:6). Thus the covenant in Deuteronomy is not simply a remaking of the Sinaitic covenant with a new generation. It is a reaffirmation of obligations laid out in the 'covenant of circumcision' (Gen. 17; *cf.* Deut. 30:6–10) for all future generations (29:14–15), and an anticipation of the 'new covenant' which will guarantee that a divine–human relationship between Yahweh and Abraham's 'seed' will be maintained for ever (*cf.* Jer. 31:31–34) by facilitating the fulfilment of the important ethical obligations.

The priestly covenant. Although the ordination of Aaron and his sons as priests (Exod. 28 – 29) is not related in expressly covenantal terminology, the immediate context is certainly covenantal. Moreover, a number of other passages apply covenantal language to the Levitical priesthood (Jer. 33:21–22; Neh. 13:29; Mal. 2:1–9). In Numbers 18 the priestly 'gratuities' are described as 'a covenant of salt forever' (v. 19), which suggests that the arrangement was intended to be permanent. In 25:10–13 Phinehas, Aaron's grandson, is awarded a 'covenant of peace' for his loyalty to Yahweh. This is further defined as a 'covenant of perpetual priesthood'. It appears that the latter was a reaffirmation of the covenant initiated with Aaron, the ancestor of the Zadokite priesthood (1 Chr. 6:3–15) and perhaps the Maccabean priesthood (1 Macc. 2:54).

All this suggests that the priestly covenant was closely related to the Mosaic covenant, serving the same general purpose: the priests facilitated the maintenance of the divine–human relationship between Yahweh and Abraham's descendants. Significantly, it was when they failed to do this that they were accused by Malachi of having 'corrupted the covenant of Levi' (Mal. 2:8). Thus the priestly and Mosaic covenants, while remaining distinct, run in parallel with one another, and are closely related in purpose: the perpetuity of the relationship between God and Israel.

The Davidic covenant. This also appears to be closely coupled with an earlier covenant; viz. the Abrahamic. The chapter (2 Sam. 7) in which the establishment of the Davidic covenant is described (while the term *berît* is not found here, the use of the term *ḥeseḏ* is significant) is full of allusions to the divine assurances given to Abraham. For example, both Abraham and David are promised 'a great name' (Gen. 12:2; 2 Sam. 7:9); victory over enemies (Gen. 22:17; 2 Sam. 7:11 *cf.* Ps. 89:23); a special divine–human relationship (Gen. 17:7–8; 2 Sam. 7:14 *cf.* Ps. 89:26), and a special line of 'seed' through which their name will be perpetuated (Gen. 21:12; 2 Sam. 7:12–16). In addition, the descendants of both are obligated to keep God's laws (Gen. 18:19; 2 Sam. 7:14; *cf.* Pss. 89:30–32; 132:12), and a unique descendant of both will mediate international blessing (Gen. 22:18; Ps. 72:17).

Given these clear connections between the Abrahamic and Davidic covenants, there can be no doubt that they are inextricably related. In the Davidic covenant the promises made to Abraham become more focused. The Davidic dynasty inherits the promises of the patriarchal covenant; the special divine–human relationship and attendant blessings now belong primarily to the Davidic royal lineage. Thus the Davidic covenant serves to identify at a later stage in Genesis–Kings the promised line of 'seed' that will mediate blessing to all the nations of the earth.

Thus with the Davidic covenant there is a subtle change of focus, namely from the promises enshrined within the 'covenant between the pieces' (Gen. 15) to those of the 'covenant of circumcision' (Gen. 17). In the Davidic–Solomonic empire the former covenant finds its most extensive fulfilment (2 Sam. 7:1, 23–24; *cf.* 1 Kgs. 4:20–21). With the promise of a 'great nation' now realized, attention shifts from Abraham's national descendants to his royal descendants, the 'kings' to whom attention was drawn in Genesis 17:6, 16. The importance of this royal line, which had already been traced explicitly through Jacob (Gen. 35:11) and Judah (Gen. 49:10), and implicitly through Perez (Gen. 38; *cf.* Ruth 4:18–22), lay in the fact that its most illustrious descendant would be the individual, conquering 'seed' of Genesis 22:18. Thus the Davidic covenant identifies the royal dynasty from which the anticipated victorious 'seed' of Abraham would come.

Nevertheless, notwithstanding the foreshadowing of the 'blessing of the nations' in the Davidic–Solomonic empire, this promise still awaited its ultimate fulfilment. The history of the Israelite monarchy illustrates why this was so. Though a few kings made reforms, none of the Davidic dynasty, not even David himself, fully complied with the crucial criterion for divine–human relationship: irreproachable behaviour. None had, like Abraham, 'obeyed God's voice and kept his charge, his commandments, his statutes, and his laws' (Gen. 26:5). Thus while the divine promise to bless the nations in Abraham's seed would be fulfilled in a scion of David, ultimately that fulfilment depended on a Davidic king who would be a son of Abraham in the fullest possible way, and not merely biologically (*cf.* Ps. 72).

The new covenant. Although the concept of a 'new covenant' is especially associated with Jeremiah 31:31–34 (the only passage in the OT that specifically mentions a 'new covenant'), several other texts allude to an everlasting covenant that will be established between God and his people in the future (see esp. Jer. 30 – 33; Ezek. 34, 36 – 37; Is. 40 – 66; *cf.* Is. 42:6, where covenant language is applied to the enigmatic 'servant of Yahweh', a figure whose mission closely parallels that of the 'seed' of Abraham and David). For this reason, and because of the future, visionary character of this covenant as described in the OT, drawing together the various threads of the OT witness is rather more difficult in this case than with the earlier covenants. Even so, the following points can be made.

1. The 'new covenant' will be both national and international. The covenant described by Jeremiah and Ezekiel is primarily nationalistic (*cf.* Jer. 31:36–40; 33:6–16; Ezek. 36:24–38; 37:11–28). Against the historical backdrop of the Babylonian exile, such an emphasis is unsurprising; the catastrophe of 587 BC raised significant questions concerning the fulfilment of God's earlier promises to the nation and its king. Therefore the repatriation of a reunified Israel in a renovated land with a Davidic king was inevitably a dominant motif in the prophetic hope associated with the new covenant.

However, the scope of this new covenant clearly transcends national and territorial borders. While Jeremiah and Ezekiel both allude to the international significance of the new covenant (Jer. 33:9; Ezek. 36:36; 37:28), its universal scope is depicted most clearly in Isaiah. National blessing is still envisaged (*cf.* Is. 44:28; 45:13), but this covenant will extend to the ends of the earth, ultimately encompassing all nations (Is. 42:6; 49:6; 55:3–5; 56:4–8; 66:18–24). Thus the new covenant projects the ultimate fulfilment of the divine promises onto an ideal Israel (*i.e.* a community of faith) located in a rejuvenated universe (Is. 65:17; 66:22).

This ideal Israel is not, however, a novel concept foreign to the original promises. Rather, from the beginning of the nation's history it had been made clear that ethnic descent from Abraham was neither sufficient (Gen. 17:14) nor essential (Gen. 17:12–13) for inclusion among the *people of God. Moreover, ethnic Israel is clearly depicted in the Bible as a foreshadowing of the new covenant people, the 'Israel of God' (Gal. 6:10). Thus while the restoration of the Jews in the Promised Land marked the beginning of the fulfilment of the new covenant promises, it was *only* the beginning. The best was yet to come, when the 'rest' foreshadowed in Joshua would find its ultimate consummation in the new heavens and the new earth.

2. The 'new covenant' will involve both continuity and discontinuity. Several features

underline the new covenant's continuity with previous divine covenants: its emphasis on the divine Torah (Jer. 31:33; Ezek. 36:27; Is. 42:1–4; 51:4–8); its focus on Abraham's 'seed' (Jer. 31:36; Ezek. 36:37; Is. 63:16), particularly his royal 'seed' (Jer. 33:15–26; Ezek. 37:24–25; Is. 55:3); its use of the covenant formula 'I will be their God, and they shall be my people' (Jer. 31:33; Ezek. 37:23, 27; *cf.* Is. 54:5–10). Thus although some sort of break with the past is clearly understood, 'the newness of the new covenant must not stand in absolute contradiction to the previous covenants. A factor of continuity must be recognised' (O. P. Robertson, *The Christ of Covenants*, p. 281).

Yet the newness of the new covenant must not be underestimated; it incorporates novel elements in radical discontinuity with the past (*cf.* Jer. 31:32): the complete removal of *sin (Jer. 31:34; Ezek. 36:29, 33); inner transformation, of the heart (Jer. 31:33; Ezek. 36:26); an intimate relationship with God (Jer. 31:34a; Ezek. 36:27). Significantly, all these aspects of the new covenant emphasize the most important of its novel elements: its indestructibility. Unlike previous covenants, the new covenant cannot be broken unilaterally. This suggests, therefore, that:

3. The 'new covenant' will be both climactic and eternal. In some sense previous divine covenants culminate in the new covenant, for this future covenant encapsulates the key promises made throughout the OT era (*e.g.* a physical inheritance; a divine–human relationship; an everlasting dynasty; blessing on a national and international scale), while at the same time transcending them. Thus the new covenant is the climactic fulfilment of the covenants that God established with the patriarchs, the nation of Israel, and the dynasty of David. The promises of these earlier covenants find their ultimate fulfilment in the new covenant, and in it such promises become 'eternal' in the truest sense.

According to the NT's witness, the new covenant was ratified by the sacrificial death of *Jesus. While the textual evidence may cast some doubt over the originality of the word 'new' in Matthew and Mark's accounts of the institution of the Lord's Supper, the presence of the adjective in 1 Corinthians 11:25 (perhaps our earliest account of the Last Supper) and Luke 22:20 suggests that it was at least implicit in what Jesus said. In any

case, Jesus was clearly referring to something other than the covenant with which his Jewish disciples were familiar. The allusions to both the *forgiveness anticipated by Jeremiah (Matt. 26:28; Jer. 31:34) and the blood associated with the establishment of the original Mosaic covenant (Luke 22:20; Exod. 24:6–7), further underline the fact that Jesus understood his death as the inauguration of the new covenant.

In keeping with this premise, the Gospels (esp. Matthew) present Jesus as the climax of the OT's covenantal promises. Through Jesus the promises made to Abraham find their ultimate fulfilment (Matt. 1:1, 17; 3:9; 8:11–12; *cf.* Luke 1:55, 72–73; John 8:31–59). He is the one anticipated in the Pentateuch, and in whom the obligations of the Mosaic covenant have been both fulfilled and transcended (Matt. 3:15; 5:17–48; 9:16–17; 11:28–30). He is the royal son of David (Matt. 1:1; 3:17 [*cf.* Ps 2:7]; 4:15–16 [*cf.* Is. 9:1–2]; 15:22; 16:16; 21:5; 22:41–45; *cf.* Luke 1:69–70), who will shepherd the people of God (Matt. 2:6; 9:36; 15:29–39 [*cf.* Ezek. 34:11–16]; *cf.* John 10:1–16). He is portrayed as the remnant, the 'true Israel' through whom *salvation will come to the nations (Matt. 2:15; 4:1–11; 5:13–16; 8:11; 12:18–21; 13:47; 21:42–44; 24:14; 25:31–34; 28:19; *cf.* Luke 2:14, 32), and in whom 'new covenant' blessings such as cleansing and forgiveness are experienced (Matt. 1:21; 8:1–4, 17; 9:1–8; 11:2–5).

However, as well as this positive emphasis in the Gospels on the fulfilment of covenant blessings, there is also a more negative theme: the fulfilment of covenant curses (judgment) on unbelieving Israel (Matt. 8:12; 13:12–14; 21:43; 23:37–39; *cf.* Luke 16:19–31). In order to inherit the covenant promises, more is required than mere biological descent (Matt. 3:9).

Therefore, although the 'new covenant' is mentioned explicitly only at the institution of the Lord's Supper, the Gospels are pregnant with associated ideas. Indeed, from his opening genealogy to his concluding paragraph, Matthew declares that the OT's covenant promises find their fulfilment through Jesus. While the other evangelists may not place quite so much emphasis upon fulfilment, they nevertheless bear eloquent testimony to the fact that Jesus is the anticipated Messiah, the one through whom salvation comes not only to Israel, but to all who come to him in *faith.

While the term 'covenant' appears only twice in Acts (3:25; 7:8), the book clearly presents Jesus as the fulfilment of the OT's messianic hope and the *church as the true Israel, the genuine heirs of the covenant promises in the OT (cf. 2:30, 39; 3:25; 7:52; 13:16–39; 15:14–17; 26:6, 23). Significantly, this true covenant people includes not only believing Jews, but also believing Gentiles (see esp. 10:1 – 11:18; 15:1–29), thus reflecting the international dimension of OT hope.

In the Pauline corpus the term 'covenant(s)' is used nine times (Rom. 9:4; 11:27; 1 Cor. 11:25; 2 Cor. 3:6, 14; Gal. 3:15, 17; 4:24; Eph. 2:12). Some have found support in Romans 9 – 11 for a 'two-covenant' theology (*i.e.* rather than replacing God's covenant with physical Israel, God's covenant in Christ with the church merely parallels it), interpreting the key verses (11:25–27) as predicting a future, large-scale salvation of ethnic Jews. However, given the overall purpose of Romans, to encourage unity in the church by demonstrating how God has been faithful to his covenant promises to Abraham (see N. T. Wright, *The Climax of the Covenant*, p. 234), the emphasis in Romans 9 – 11 is surely on the fact that God's covenantal promises *vis-à-vis* Israel will indeed be fulfilled, but only in the genuine heirs of the covenant(s), Abraham's spiritual descendants (whether Jew or Gentile; *cf.* Eph. 2:11–22). Thus Paul highlights the fact that, although 'Jewish Israel' had enjoyed some tremendous spiritual privileges (Rom. 9:4–5), God had never promised that *all* Abraham's physical descendants would inherit the covenant promises (Rom. 9:6–13). Rather, through Jesus God has done exactly what he had promised Abraham (Gen. 12:3) and later reiterated in the prophets; viz. extended blessing to all the nations of the earth. Thus Romans 9 – 11 graphically reinforces the point that Paul made earlier in this epistle (*cf.* Rom. 4:16–19), that the *gospel was the means by which the covenant promise made to Abraham would be realized; references to Abraham's 'fatherhood of many nations' and multitudinous descendants related to the extension (beyond Israel) of the people of God. But Paul is at pains to stress in Romans 9 – 11 that this fact does not negate nor abrogate the fulfilment of the covenant promises in relation

to ethnic Israelites. Biological descendants of Abraham are in no way disadvantaged under the new covenant, as some of Paul's protagonists were apparently suggesting (*cf.* Rom. 11:13–22). Rather, they (like the Gentiles) could respond positively to the Gospel message, and so 'all Israel' (*i.e.* all Abraham's seed, whether Jew or Gentile) 'will be saved' (Rom. 11:26). Hence the covenant promises had been inherited not by Israel in an exclusively ethnic or biological sense, but by true Israel, composed of those united to Abraham primarily through faith in Jesus Christ.

Significantly, the inheritance of true Israel appears to include even the territorial promise, albeit in a cosmic sense (Rom. 4:13; *cf.* Matt. 5:5). Thus understood, the promise of land, while including the territory of Canaan, ultimately encompasses much more; viz. the 'new heaven and the new earth' anticipated by the prophets (Rom. 8:17–25; *cf.* 2 Pet. 3:13).

The Corinthian passages in which the 'covenant' is explicitly mentioned are important because of their use of the associated adjectives 'new' and 'old', calling to mind the contrast between the old and new covenants anticipated by Jeremiah. Whatever the precise contrast in Paul's mind in 2 Corinthians 3 (see W. S. Campbell, in *DPL*, pp. 180–181), the 'new covenant' is identified as the gospel of Jesus Christ (2 Cor. 4:3–6).

Paul's use of covenant terminology in Galatians serves primarily to establish the significance of the Abrahamic over against the Mosaic covenant. Once again, however, the crucial point to note is that Abraham's genuine 'heirs' are not simply those who can claim biological descent from the patriarch, but rather 'those who believe' (Gal. 3:7). This chapter is particularly important in view of its discussion of how the covenant promises are inherited by Abraham's 'seed'. Significantly, Paul interprets this aspect of the divine promise in terms of Jesus Christ and those who, through faith, are united to him (Gal. 3:16–17, 29). While Paul's exegesis in verses 16–17 has often been dismissed as fanciful or midrashic, careful examination of the Abrahamic covenant of circumcision (see above) certainly lends exegetical credibility to Paul's logic at this point. As the individual, royal descendant promised to Abraham, Jesus Christ is in a unique position to mediate blessing to all who, through belonging to him, become 'heirs according to the promise' (Gal. 3:29, NRSV).

The most developed 'new covenant theology' in the NT is found, however, in Hebrews. Indeed, this is a subject to which the writer returns repeatedly (*cf.* Heb. 7:22; 8:6 – 10:31; 12:18–24; 13:20), twice quoting the Jeremiah passage directly (8:8–12; 10:16–17). The writer contrasts the old and new covenants by emphasizing the superiority of the promises, sacrifice, mediator, blessing and inheritance involved in the latter. While the necessity of the new covenant demonstrates that the old was in some sense deficient, the fault was not in the covenant itself but in those who failed to keep it. Not surprisingly, therefore, it is this intrinsic inadequacy that is rectified by the Spirit in the new covenant, a fact which the writer is keen to underline (8:10–12; 10:16–17). Thus the contrast in Hebrews between the covenants is similar to that of Paul; it is not between something evil and something good, but between something good and something better.

While the new covenant has certainly been inaugurated in the NT era, the ultimate eschatological reality awaits the 'new heavens and new earth, where righteousness is at home' (2 Pet. 3:13, NRSV).

See also: ABRAHAM; CIRCUMCISION; DAVID; LAW; MOSES; NOAH.

Bibliography

T. D. Alexander, 'Abraham reassessed theologically', in R. S. Hess, G. J. Wenham, P. E. Satterthwaite (eds.), *He Swore an Oath: Biblical Themes from Genesis 12–50* (Carlisle and Grand Rapids, [2]1994); *idem*, 'Further observations on the term "seed" in Genesis', *TynB* 48, 1997, pp. 363–367; R. T. Beckwith, 'The unity and diversity of God's covenants', *TynB* 38, 1987, pp. 93–118; W. S. Campbell, 'Covenant and new covenant', in *DPL*, pp. 179–183; W. J. Dumbrell, *Covenant and Creation: An Old Testament Covenantal Theology* (Exeter, 1984); D. E. Holwerda, *Jesus and Israel: One Covenant or Two?* (Leicester, 1995); S. Lehne, *The New Covenant in Hebrews* (Sheffield, 1990); A. McCaig, 'Covenant, The New', in *ISBE* 1, pp. 795–797; T. E. McComiskey, *The Covenants of Promise: A Theology of the Old Testament Covenants* (Nottingham, 1984); J. J. Niehaus,

God at Sinai: Covenant and Theophany in the Bible and Ancient Near East (Carlisle and Grand Rapids, 1995); C. C. Newman, 'Covenant, New Covenant', in *DLNTD*, pp. 245–250; R. Rendtorff, *The Covenant Formula: An Exegetical and Theological Investigation* (ET, Edinburgh, 1998); O. P. Robertson, *The Christ of the Covenants* (Phillipsburg, 1980); J. A. Thompson, 'Covenant (OT)', in *ISBE* 1, pp. 790–793; G. Van Groningen in *EDBT*, pp. 124–132; J. Walton, *God's Covenant, God's Purpose* (Grand Rapids, 1994); G. J. Wenham, 'The symbolism of the animal rite in Genesis 15: A response to G. F. Hasel', *JSOT* 22, 1982, pp. 134–137; P. R. Williamson, *Abraham, Israel and the Nations: The Patriarchal Promise and its Covenantal Development in Genesis* (Sheffield, 2000); N. T. Wright, *The Climax of the Covenant: Christ and the Law in Pauline Theology* (Edinburgh, 1991); J. Zens, 'Is there a covenant of Grace?', *BRR* 6.3, 1977, pp. 43–53.

P. R. WILLIAMSON

CREATION

Creation in the OT

Inevitably the early chapters of *Genesis dominate the biblical doctrine of creation simply by virtue of their location in the text. However, the doctrine is certainly not found only in these chapters. Belief in creation is implicit in many parts of the OT. It informs the concern for the environment demonstrated in parts of the Pentateuch. It underlies the creation imagery used in the *Psalms and, indeed, becomes a major theme in several psalms (notably Pss. 8, 19, 104, 139, 148). It is assumed in important prophetic passages (see *Prophetic books). And it appears at several points in the *wisdom books (*e.g.* Job 38 – 41).

Creation by *word

At eight points in Genesis 1 God speaks creatively: 'And God said, "Let ... "' (vv. 3, 6, 9, 11, 14, 20, 24, 26). By using speech as a metaphor the biblical authors are indicating that the divine activity of creation is voluntary, effortless and rational. In marked contrast, the creation myths of neighbouring cultures characterize creation as a process of inevitable struggle and conflict.

God commands and it is so. The very effortlessness of the fulfilment indicates God's sovereignty. God is presented as a king issuing broad injunctions rather than as an architect issuing detailed instructions (the favoured image of God as creator in recent centuries). Thus the Genesis account of creation possesses a degree of openness that is missing from the more deterministic readings common in Christian theology.

Creation from nothing?

It has to be admitted that the OT is less than explicit in its support for the Christian doctrine of *creatio ex nihilo*. The Hebrew text of Genesis 1:1–2 is much less clear than is suggested by most English translations. These verses could be interpreted as speaking of uncreated raw material from which God moulded the heavens and the earth.

Against this view, it is worth noting that the translators of the LXX avoided the use of *dēmiourgos* when referring to God as creator. Further, the majority of contemporary OT scholars interpret verse 1 as a principal sentence prefixed to the chapter as a whole (C. Westermann, *Genesis 1–11*, pp. 94–97). Thus the first verse of the Bible makes an assertion quite unprecedented in ancient Near Eastern literature: it ascribes the entire work of creation exclusively to the one God. While this does not amount to an explicit statement that God created all things from nothing, it does lend support for the later development of such a doctrine as a means of defending divine sovereignty against Hellenistic insistence on the eternity of matter.

Creation, time and history

Another striking feature of the Genesis account of creation is the priority given to the category of *time. Light and darkness are the first of all God's creations because from their alternation flows the temporal succession which is the fundamental context of created reality. That time is, indeed, fundamental to creation is demonstrated by the fact that the activity of creation is placed within a clear temporal sequence.

The pervasive temporality of the biblical doctrine of creation clearly distinguishes it from the cosmological myths of the ancient Near East. In contrast to the essentially atemporal (hence mythological) creation accounts of other cultures, the Hebrew account speaks of God's creating the world over a period of seven days, which is clearly related to subsequent history.

This does not mean that the text need be taken literally. Since Augustine, commentators have recognized that the pattern of days in Genesis 1 is a literary device. The number seven occurs repeatedly in the passage, *e.g.* seven days, seven fulfilment formulae, seven approval formulae. Its significance is symbolic: it indicates the completeness, the perfection, of God's creative activity. Nor are the days defined as twenty-four-hour periods.

The effect of this temporal framework is to bind creation and temporality together. God creates time but also creates over a period of time. Creation becomes a process moving towards a goal in time. Thus creation is transferred from the mythological realm of transcendent realities; it is integrated into history (or, more precisely, pre-history), and the way is opened for creation to be seen as continuing in history. This supports the idea of continuing creation that was already an important part of Israelite worship and wisdom.

Creation, order and goodness

Again in contrast to the elaborate cosmogonies of the ancient Near East, the OT paints a stark picture of creation as a process of ordering by separation. Creation is thus presented as a differentiated totality (H. Blocher, *In The Beginning*, p. 71): its very diversity is part of the process that God declares to be good. Seven times in the course of Genesis 1 God declares this process of differentiation in response to the divine command to be good (vv. 4, 10, 12, 18, 21, 25 and 31). This does not mean that creation is good in itself; rather, it is a divine judgment about creation. The creature is good by virtue of its standing in appropriate relationship to its creator. Thus the divine perspective which enables God to make this judgment is not that of detached contemplation but that of active engagement. Bonhoeffer rightly relates this divine act of seeing to the preservation of creation: 'It does not sink back again into the moment of becoming, God sees that it is good and his eye resting upon the work preserves the work in being ... The world is preserved not for its own sake but for the sake of the sight of God' (D. Bonhoeffer, *Creation and*

Fall: A Theological Interpretation of Genesis 1–3 [ET, London, 1959], p. 23).

Belief in this divinely ordained order in creation pervades the OT. While rarely explicit, it was one of the assumptions on which faith in the social order of the Hebrew monarchy was founded. Thus creation imagery is invoked to guarantee the social order in Psalms 74, 77 and 89. The prophetic use of creation imagery is even more striking in many parts of Isaiah 40 – 55; the prophetic promise to the exiles is built upon reminders of God's creative activity. If God can bring the cosmic order into being God can certainly restore order to Judah. The correspondence between cosmic order and social order is also implicit in the OT concept of *šalôm*.

In contrast to the largely anthropocentric Christian tradition, the biblical story of creation unequivocally declares non-human creatures to be good without reference to *humankind. They have their own place in God's good creation and were not created merely for our benefit.

The pivotal role of humankind in the created order

Traditional readings of the primeval history stress the special status it appears to confer on humankind. The creation of humankind is seen as the climax of Genesis 1, and this impression is reinforced by the prior creation of Adam in Genesis 2. God appears to give us a special blessing; we are portrayed as made in the *image of God (in contrast to other creatures); and we are given dominion over the other creatures. But while the primeval history clearly distinguishes humankind from the rest of creation, and elevates us above it, several elements stress the intimacy of the relationship between humans and the non-human creation.

First, humankind is created on the same day as the land animals, suggesting a certain kinship. Secondly, it is simply wrong to regard the creation of humankind as the climax of Genesis 1; that privilege is accorded not to humankind but to the establishment of God's *sabbath communion with creation as a whole. Third, the appearance of humankind's creation in the same passage as the creation of the non-human contrasts with the ancient Near Eastern tendency to separate accounts of cosmic and human origins. Finally, it is not clear that the divine *blessing of verse

28a by itself distinguishes humans from the non-human. God has already pronounced a similar blessing upon sea creatures and birds (v. 22), and it is arguable that the blessing of verse 28a is actually inclusive of the land animals created in verses 24 and 25.

This impression of interdependence is further reinforced by the more detailed account of the creation of humankind in Genesis 2. Adam is placed in the garden in order to maintain it. Elsewhere this role is used to distinguish humankind from the rest of creation. For example, Psalm 104 contrasts God's direct provision for non-human creatures with our God-given responsibility to provide for our own needs. However, this distinction is placed in the larger context of a common dependence on God's *providential care.

The command to have dominion is closely related to the divine blessing, 'Be fruitful and increase in number; fill the earth and subdue it. Rule over the fish of the sea and the birds of the air and over every living creature that moves on the ground' (Gen. 1:28, NIV). Many environmentalists see this command as a mandate to trample nature underfoot. However, it does not give humankind carte blanche to exploit the environment. The human race is permitted to subdue the earth, but this is a warrant for agriculture and nothing more. We are given the fruit of the earth to be our food. In Genesis 1, dominion does not even extend to the killing of animals for food (or clothing). The command has the effect of qualifying the divine blessing, transforming it (at least as far as humankind is concerned) into a divine vocation. And that vocation to dominion over nature must be interpreted in terms of the concept of kingship (see *Kingdom of God) familiar to the ancient Israelites, which includes responsibility for one's subjects.

Judgment and the reversal of creation

Adam's disobedience in Genesis 3 and its ecological consequences highlight the ambivalence in nature experienced by the Hebrews (and which people experience to this day). It is to be received gladly as a gift of God, but it is also a place of thorns and thistles, of stinging insects and predatory animals. Above all, it threatens us with personal extinction through disease and natural disaster. Remarkably, this ambivalence is explained not in terms of the recalcitrance of matter but in terms of human disobedience. The disobedience of Adam consisted in his rejection of the divine boundaries placed upon his dominion of the earth. It was thus a rebellion against the good order of creation established by God in Genesis 1.

The result, expressed in terms of divine judgment, is the disruption of the relationships established by God (specifically between God and humankind, between man and woman, and between humankind and other creatures). Adam no longer has a harmonious relationship with God, Eve, or nature: he has lost his dominion over the earth. Furthermore, there is no way in which he can regain that dominion for himself: he is barred from Eden by the cherubim.

The environmental implications of human disobedience are further highlighted by the flood narrative. It portrays a world in which the vocation of humankind to be stewards of creation has been supplanted by their quest for autonomy. This quest is characterized by the spread of human violence. The unique status of humankind means that this violence contaminates the whole of creation.

Since humans have disrupted the good order of creation in their quest for self-deification, the judgment is appropriately a temporary suspension of that order. The temporary withdrawal of the active divine care implicit in Genesis 1 leads to a virtual return to the initial 'waste and void'. Indeed the flood narrative parallels the creation story of Genesis 1, presenting God's judgment as the mirror image of his creative activity.

At the same time, the faithful Noah is called to exercise human dominion over creation precisely in the preservation of representative animals from the judgment that is about to overwhelm the world. However, there is no suggestion that God has abdicated responsibility for the earth to humankind. Although Noah cooperates willingly with the divine plan, the initiative remains firmly with God.

Similar imagery is used elsewhere in the OT to portray divine judgment. It is particularly prominent in the writings of the pre-exilic prophets. God is presented as revoking or suspending the harmonious order of creation as an act of judgment upon a faithless Israel. This usage reflects the wisdom tradition of a correspondence between the moral and the natural: disharmony in the former is presented as having serious consequences for the latter. A stark example of this principle is found in Isaiah 24:1–13. The prophet envisages the judgment of the Lord in terms of an ecological catastrophe. Similarly Hosea presents desolation as a direct consequence of human sinfulness: 'Because of this the land mourns, and all who live in it waste away; the beasts of the field and the birds of the air and the fish of the sea are dying' (Hos. 4:3). The same theme appears in Zephaniah and frequently in Jeremiah.

The continuation and renewal of creation

The flood narrative concludes with the establishment of an everlasting covenant between God and the inhabitants of the ark: Noah and his descendants and every living creature. Covenants which include the non-human are a recurring theme in the OT, particularly amongst the prophets (*e.g.* Hos. 2:18; Jer. 33:20–25; Ezek. 34:25). It is symptomatic of the pervasive anthropocentrism of our culture that so many commentators simply overlook this fact.

What is the content of this covenant? Generally speaking, covenants are ceremonies that give binding expression to relationships that already exist between the covenant partners. Here the relationships which receive formal expression are those which endured through the flood, including Noah's care for the animals. The wording of the covenant recalls the divine blessing of Genesis 1. But, in addition to the blessing, God now gives an unconditional promise to maintain for all time the basic conditions of order which are a precondition for response to the blessing.

Finally, it should be noted that the issues raised in the primeval history are not settled there. Human violence and the ambivalence of nature continue into the patriarchal history, and thence to the present. The primeval history leaves us with the promise given in the covenant with Noah. This covenant has *redemptive implications which concern not only humankind but also the rest of God's creation. It is an everlasting covenant with the human and the non-human. Thus the final consummation of all things concerns the non-human as well as the human.

Echoes of the covenant with nature instituted at the end of the flood narrative are heard elsewhere in the OT. For example, this covenant is the positive corollary to the prophets' use of the theme of creation reversal. It reminds the reader that judgment does not result in final destruction. On the contrary, a faithful remnant will be preserved. And, says Yahweh to that remnant, 'I will make for you a covenant on that day with the beasts of the field, the birds of the air, and the creeping things of the ground' (Hos. 2:18, RSV). For Jeremiah the certainty of such promises is based upon God's prior covenant with the forces of nature (Jer. 33:25). Once again we see how the Israelites interrelated the social, moral and ecological orders. The relationships between God and humankind, within humankind, and between humankind and the non-human creation cannot be separated. A failure in any one of these areas implies a breakdown elsewhere.

Perhaps the best known creation passages in the entire prophetic tradition are those of Isaiah 40 – 55. Here creation imagery is used to express God's promise of redemption to the captives in Babylon. The less certain is guaranteed by the more certain. The very use of such imagery implies an existing faith in a God who created and sustains the natural world. Without such a faith, Isaiah's promises of redemption would be incomprehensible.

But the OT speaks of a redemption for the non-human creation as well as for the faithful remnant. The writers of the OT simply cannot envisage an immaterial eschaton. Thus creation figures clearly in their *eschatological vision. The remnant share the eschatological Sabbath with the non-human, and that sharing is prefigured in the respect for the non-human demanded by the sabbatical laws (Exod. 20:8–11; 23:10–12; Lev. 25:8–55; *cf. Jubilees* 2:19–24).

Creation in the NT

By and large, the NT reaffirms the view of creation presented by the OT. Thus at several points we are reminded that creation took place by the will and word of God (*e.g.* Rom. 4:17; Heb. 1:3; 11:3; Rev. 4:11). However, many NT perspectives on creation are implicit rather than explicit. Thus, for example, *Jesus illustrates his admonition not to worry with reference to the birds of the air and the flowers of the field (Matt. 6:25–34). This is not an assertion of God's care for creation but it is built upon the assumption that God cares even for the lowliest sparrow (Luke 12:6).

Christ and creation

Like the OT, the NT views creation as thoroughly theocentric. But this very theocentricity entails a transformation of the OT doctrine. That Jesus Christ is the centre of history implies that he is also the centre of creation. The biblical texts do not recognize the modern distinction between history and nature. His significance for creation is implicit in the creative power demonstrated in many of his miracles. His healing the sick, raising the dead and stilling of storms all show him restoring order and harmony to human bodies or natural systems that have become disordered.

Christ's significance for creation becomes explicit in the prologue to John's Gospel. It is none other than the Word by which God created that has become incarnate as Jesus Christ (John 1:14). He is the agent of creation and the source of life (John 1:4), and is thus not only involved in the original creative act but also intimately associated with God's continuing providential care for creation.

Perhaps the most explicit statement of this christological transformation of creation is the hymn cited in Colossians 1. It begins by claiming that Jesus Christ 'is the image of the invisible God, the firstborn of all creation' (v. 15). Both titles provide perspectives on the relationship between creation and redemption.

As the image of God, Jesus Christ is the point of contact between the creator and his creation. He is the one who reveals God to creation and, as such, is naturally associated with the creator rather than the creation. Any suggestion that he is in some respect inferior to the creator (*e.g.* merely the visible image of God) is ruled out by the synonymous parallelism with 'firstborn'. This term, which implies pre-existence, is characteristically Jewish and ascribes to Jesus Christ the role reserved in pre-Christian Judaism for divine wisdom (*e.g.* Wisdom of Solomon 9:4, 9; Prov. 8:22; Ecclus; 1:4; 24:9).

Since Jesus Christ is the image of God, the restoration of the image of God in humankind becomes part of the Christian vocation: we are called to be conformed to Christ, the paradigmatic image of God. At the same time the close connection made in the OT between the divine image and humankind's dominion over the material creation means that the

433

latter must undergo a similar transformation. The only dominion open to the Christian is that exercised by Christ, a dominion expressed in humble service. Thus the NT radicalizes the servanthood already implicit in the OT notion of dominion.

In expounding 'firstborn', the subsequent verses present Christ as the agent of God's creative activity: all things were created through him. Furthermore, they present Christ as the frame of reference for creation: all things were created in him, *i.e.*, with reference to or in relation to him. In other words, Christ is the context of creation.

Christ is not only the origin of the cosmos; he is also its goal. All things were created for him, *i.e.*, to be subject to and to glorify him. The cosmos is envisaged as being in movement towards its eschatological end, namely, Jesus Christ.

In expanding on the creative agency of Christ, verse 17 adds that 'in him all things hold together'. The use of the perfect tense here makes it clear that the reference is to a continuing activity. All things continue and cohere in Christ. He is the sole basis of unity and purpose in the cosmos. Again the hymn has substituted Jesus Christ for divine wisdom: he becomes the personal basis of unity which allowed the Hebrews to discern a real correspondence between the moral and natural orders. He is the foundation upon which God has established the earth. Indeed for Christian theology the very notion of 'cosmos' must be Christocentric (*i.e.* it must be defined with reference to Christ as its basis). By thus making Christ the basis of the order of nature this passage appropriates to Christ the creative activity of ordering the cosmos which we noted in both the primeval history and Psalm 104. In other words his role in creation is by no means limited to *creatio ex nihilo* but includes the continuing maintenance of the cosmic order. Thus Christ is also presented as the divine agent of the preservation of the cosmos.

The christocentric nature of the NT view of creation has important implications for any contemporary theology of creation. It provides a theological rationale for once again treating creation as a central and distinctively Christian doctrine. Thus it leaves no place for an autonomous natural theology within the framework of Christian dogmatics.

Creation and renewal

As the centre of history, Christ holds out the promise of a new future. Thus, since he is also the centre of creation, it is natural for NT writers to express this as a promise of a new creation. Because they associate this new creation closely with the life of the believer, both individually and in community, it is tempting to interpret the NT promise in purely anthropocentric terms. However, the cosmic scope of Christ's renewing activity is underlined by a well-known passage from Paul's letter to the Romans: Romans 8:18–25.

Paul's use of 'creation' in this passage has been interpreted in many different ways. However, the involuntary nature of the bondage to which he refers (v. 20) suggests that any interpretation which includes the angelic and/or human dimensions of creation must be ruled out. We must conclude that *ktisis* denotes the subhuman created order.

Paul uses the strange image of nature's suffering. Even more remarkably, nature itself is looking forward eagerly to an eschaton which will bring an end to its bondage.

What does Paul mean when he speaks of the subjection of nature to 'futility'? *Mataiotēs* stands in contrast to *telos* and means emptiness, futility, meaninglessness, lack of purpose. It is the Septuagint's translation of *hebel* or 'vanity' (*e.g.* Eccles. 1:2). Here, it appears to be synonymous with 'bondage to decay' (v. 21). In referring to 'groaning and travailing', the passage clearly points us to Genesis 3 for an explanation of the term. Thus it seems likely that creation's inability to achieve its *telos*, to fulfil the purpose of its existence, is a direct result of the disorder envisaged in Genesis 3:17.

If this is the case, the one who subjected it in hope must be God. However, the responsibility for the 'futility' lies with humankind: our place in the created order is such that our disobedience brings with it ecological consequences. Paul does not teach that nature is in itself fallen; rather its *telos* is inextricably bound up with the destiny of humankind. Our disobedience prevents the natural order from achieving its goal: creation 'is cheated of its true fulfilment so long as man, the chief actor in the drama of God's praise, fails to contribute his rational part' (C. E. B. Cranfield, 'Some observations on Romans 8.19–21' in R. Banks (ed.), *Reconciliation* and Hope: The Leon Morris Festschrift [Exeter, 1974], p. 227).

In spite of this statement of the cosmic repercussions of evil, Paul emphasizes that this divine subjection does not exclude hope. On the contrary, the subhuman creation was subjected 'in hope'. The present suffering of creation is a 'groaning and travailing': it represents the birth pangs which will ultimately give way to joy and fulfilment. Paul sees Christ's redemptive activity as effecting not just the reconciliation of humanity with God but also, through that reconciliation, the consummation of the entire created order. The non-human part of creation is not merely a backdrop to the human drama of salvation history but is itself able to share in the 'glorious liberty' which Paul envisages for the covenant community. What we have here is a Christological and pneumatological (and, hence trinitarian) transformation of the OT concept of the *dominium terrae*.

This hope for the whole of creation is graphically portrayed by the apocalyptic vision of the book of Revelation. John promises not a spiritual eschaton, but a new heaven and a new earth. This typically Jewish idiom clearly refers to the transformation and renewal of creation as a whole. Even when John changes his imagery to that of a city, the non-human creation is still represented. The heavenly Jerusalem is no work of humankind standing over against an alien wilderness. Rather John's portrayal of the city with a garden at its centre (a renewed Eden once again open to humankind) reveals it as a divine city in which the human and the natural are reconciled.

See also: GOD.

Bibliography

B. Anderson (ed.), *Creation in the Old Testament* (London, 1984); H. Blocher, *In The Beginning: The Opening Chapters of Genesis* (Leicester, 1984); W. Brueggemann, *Genesis: A Bible Commentary for Teaching and Preaching*, Interpretation (Atlanta, 1982); D. Fergusson, *The Cosmos and the Creator: An Introduction to the Theology of Creation* (London, 1998); C. E. Gunton (ed.), *The Doctrine of Creation: Essays in Dogmatics, History and Philosophy* (Edinburgh, 1997); C. Westermann, *Creation* (ET, London, 1974); *idem*, *Genesis 1–11: A Commentary* (ET, London, 1984).

L. H. OSBORN

CURSE, see BLESSING/CURSE
DANIEL, see Part 2
DARKNESS, see LIGHT

DAVID

Introduction

*Israel's greatest king, David, is esteemed in Scripture as a great ruler, warrior, poet and musician, and most of all, as a man after God's own heart. Subsequent kings in Israel are compared, either favourably or unfavourably, with David. Most significantly, David is the prototype of the ideal coming king – the Messiah. God's promise to David of a perpetual line (2 Sam. 7) becomes in the royal psalms and the prophets the expectation of an ideal king from David's line. The NT sees in *Jesus Christ, the son of David, the fulfilment of these hopes. (See *Kingdom of God.)

The David narratives in Samuel

The rise of David

The drama and detail of the David story in 1 and 2 *Samuel make it a literary masterpiece, one of the finest extended narratives of the ancient world. The twin themes which permeate the account of David's rise are God's favour and David's sincere and passionate heart for God. When Samuel is directed to Jesse's home to anoint the new king of Israel, it is the youngest and least significant of eight brothers who is chosen. Samuel is informed that while 'man looks at the outward appearance, the LORD looks at the heart' (1 Sam. 16:7, NIV). God's gracious choice is confirmed by the sincerity of David's heart.

David's rise is counterbalanced by the decline of Saul, whose self-centred jealousy is in contrast to David's trust and patient waiting on the Lord. From his anointing onwards, David's star rises while Saul's falls. David's defeat of Goliath and his subsequent victories bring public acclaim, provoking jealousy and rage in Saul, who repeatedly attempts to kill David (1 Sam. 17 – 19). In contrast the fugitive David, though the rightful king, repeatedly refuses to harm the Lord's anointed (2 Sam. 24:26). David's patient waiting on the Lord receives its reward following Saul's suicide after being wounded in battle (1 Sam. 31). Even here David demonstrates his respect for the office of king, first, by executing an Amalekite for his presumption in killing the Lord's anointed (2 Sam. 1:1–16), and secondly, by composing a stirring lament in honour of the heroism of Saul and Jonathan (2 Sam. 1:17–27).

Following the death of Saul, David is anointed king over Judah and reigns in Hebron for seven and a half years. *War ensues between *Judah and Israel, pitting David's forces against those of Saul's son Ishbosheth. After David's forces prevail and Ishbosheth is assassinated by conspirators, the elders of Israel anoint David as king (2 Sam. 2 – 5). For thirty-three years David reigns over a united kingdom, giving him a reign of forty years in all. David's rise to power is summed up in 2 Samuel 5:10; he was successful because 'the LORD God of hosts was with him'.

The zenith of David's power and the Davidic covenant

The account of David's reign begins with four theologically significant events. 1. David's conquest of the Jebusite stronghold of *Jerusalem establishes a strong and neutral site for a capital over all Israel (2 Sam. 5:6–9). Jerusalem also provides a single central sanctuary for Israel's corporate worship. 2. David brings the ark to Jerusalem, and thereby establishes the city as the locus of the nation's religious as well as political life (2 Sam. 6). 3. David's *victories over his enemies, especially the Philistines, consolidate his power and provide the 'rest' which forms the context for the Davidic *covenant (2 Sam. 6, 8). 4. The Davidic covenant itself (2 Sam. 7) establishes David's seed and dynasty in perpetuity.

The oracle of Nathan in which the Davidic covenant is set provides the primary foundation upon which the messianic idea arose in Israel. The account in 2 Samuel 7 finds its poetic counterpart in Psalm 89. The context is David's consolidation of power, the 'rest from all his enemies around him' (2 Sam. 7:1), and his desire to build a temple for the Lord. In a play on words, Nathan informs David he will not build a 'house' (i.e. a *temple) for the Lord; rather the Lord will build a 'house' (i.e. a dynasty) for David. David is promised the perpetuity of his seed, God's eternal lovingkindness (ḥesed) (despite the failures of David's son[s] and the discipline administered by the Lord), a unique father-son relationship between the Lord and David's seed, and an eternal throne for David. Also in 2 Samuel 7 there is the promise that Solomon will build the temple (v. 13). This promise will be taken up by subsequent generations when the temple lies in ruins (as in Zechariah and the rabbinic writings), or when the current temple leadership is viewed as corrupt (as at Qumran, where the community becomes the 'temple'). Finally, God promises *peace and security for Israel in the land. This, in turn, implies a united kingdom and freedom from foreign domination. The promise of a place of *rest and security for Israel following the Exodus (Deut. 3:20; 12:9–10; Josh. 1:15) is here expanded and applied to the Davidic dynasty. The Davidic promise thus becomes an extension and individualization of the Lord's covenant relationship with the nation Israel.

David's sin and subsequent decline

The highlight of David's life (the Davidic covenant) is followed by his greatest fall. David's sin with Bathsheba and the murder of her husband Uriah become a crucial turning point in the David story in 2 Samuel, inaugurating a period of devastating decline. The *sin is attributed to both complacency and the abuse of power. It is David's failure to go to war which results in his temptation, and his disregard for the law which results in adultery and murder. The king in Israel was not meant to be above the law, but to act as God's faithful vice-regent, providing for the people a model of righteous adherence to the Torah. Disaster upon disaster follows in David's life as a result: the death of Bathsheba's child; the rape of Tamar by Amnon; the subsequent murder of Amnon by Absalom; Absalom's conspiracy and seizure of the throne; David's humiliating retreat from Jerusalem, and war with Absalom resulting in the young man's death (2 Sam. 11 – 18). Throughout much of this David remains on the sidelines, powerless to stop the cycle of violence which his action has provoked.

Though tragic and devastating, David's sin and restoration also serve to highlight God's grace and the eternal loving-kindness promised to him. When David repents, he is forgiven and restored, and God's promise is not revoked. David's song of praise (2 Sam. 22) and the 'last words of David' (2 Sam. 23) serve as fitting summaries of the author's assessment of David's life. Throughout both passages the Lord is given credit for the successes and victories in David's life. It is the Lord who 'gives his king great victories; he shows unfailing kindness to his anointed, to David and his descendants for ever' (2 Sam. 22:51).

The Davidic dynasty in Kings

The book of *Kings demonstrates how each successive king after David dealt with his covenant responsibilities before the Lord. The overriding prophetic theme is that faithfulness to God and his covenant brings success, while unfaithfulness brings failure and judgment. The standard of *righteousness is always David, and subsequent kings are judged according to whether each serves God 'as David his father had done' (1 Kgs. 11:6; 14:8; 15:3, 11; 2 Kgs. 14:3; 16:2; 18:3; 22:2).

The pattern is established by Solomon, who starts with the enormous potential provided by David's legacy: a united and consolidated kingdom, a central place of worship for the construction of the new temple, great *wisdom from the Lord, and great material prosperity. Yet Solomon's heart is not fully devoted to the Lord 'as the heart of David his father had been', and in his old age his foreign wives turn his heart away (1 Kgs. 11:4–5). God's mercy in postponing the division of the kingdom until Solomon's death and in sparing a single tribe (Judah) for Solomon's son is only 'for the sake of David my servant' (1 Kgs. 11:12–13).

'For the sake of David' is essentially the same as 'for the sake of my promise'. It is God's good name which is at stake. Even when the Davidic king falls into sin, God remains faithful to his promise (2 Sam. 7:15). When the kings of Aram (Syria) and Israel attempt to depose Ahaz of Judah and place the son of Tabeel on the throne, God intervenes, prophesying the destruction of Israel and Syria (Is. 7:1–25). It is surely not wicked King Ahaz whom God is protecting, but rather the heritage of the 'house of David' (Is. 7:2, 13), that is, the dynasty promised to David.

Ideal (Davidic) kingship and the royal psalms

The royal *psalms express and elaborate the significance of David's reign and of the Davidic covenant. There has been much discussion of the supposed distinction between 'messianic' and 'royal' psalms, the former supposedly prophetic, pointing to the coming 'Messiah', the latter supposedly historical and related to court occasions (births, marriages, accessions, etc.) of the Davidic dynasty. Such a dichotomy, however, is unnecessary. In one sense all royal psalms are 'messianic' since they express the hope that the present king will fulfil the Davidic promise and restore the glories of the Davidic era.

The royal psalms affirm and elaborate the major components of the Davidic promise. God's faithfulness to his 'covenant' (Pss. 89:4, 29; 132:12) guarantees the perpetuity of David's line (Pss. 18:50; 45:6, 16–17; 132:10–12, 17). The Davidic king's divine sonship is affirmed (Ps. 2:7), together with his enthronement on Mount Zion (Pss. 2:4–6; 110:2), his reign in justice and righteousness (Pss. 45:7; 72:1–4, 7), his victory over enemies through the Lord's power (Pss. 2:1–9; 18:31–42; 20:1–9; 21:1–13; 45:5; 72:9–11; 110:1–2, 5–6) and material prosperity in the land (Ps. 72:16). New features introduced include worldwide dominion (Pss. 2:8; 72:8–11), a privileged position at the Lord's right hand (Ps. 110:1), and a perpetual *priesthood 'according to the order of Melchizedek' (Ps. 110:4, NRSV). Though not of Levitical lineage, the Davidic king oversees the temple cult and serves as a priest in his own right.

Davidic messianism in the prophets

Pre-exilic prophecy

Some scholars assert that there are no true messianic prophecies before the Babylonian exile. Only after the Davidic dynasty had collapsed could the prophets predict that God would raise up a Davidic king to restore and renew the nation. Yet the Nathan oracle and the royal psalms suggest that hopes for Davidic restoration may be traced to the period of the monarchy, and even to expectations surrounding Solomon himself. It is in the 8th-century prophets, however, that these hopes reached their most sublime expression. Isaiah prophesies the coming of a new David, a 'shoot from the root of Jesse'. Like David (1 Sam. 16:13) this king will be permanently endowed with the Spirit of the Lord, and so will have extraordinary wisdom and insight (Is. 11:2–3). With a word – the breath of his lips and the rod of his mouth – he will destroy the wicked (Is. 11:4). He will protect the poor and oppressed, establishing an eternal era of peace, justice and righteousness, and reigning on David's throne for ever (Is. 9:1–7; 11:1–16). He is given extraordinary royal titles: Wonderful Counsellor, Mighty God, Everlasting Father, Prince of Peace (Is. 9:6).

Micah's prophecies are similar to Isaiah's. He predicts a Davidic ruler who will shepherd his people, adding that the king will come from Bethlehem, the birthplace of David (Mic. 5:2–4; cf. 1 Sam. 17:12). Since the current Davidic kings were associated with Jerusalem, Micah, like Isaiah, may here be foretelling the rejection of the present Davidic line in favour of a new 'David'.

Prophecies of exile and restoration: Jeremiah and Ezekiel

With the collapse of the Davidic dynasty and the Babylonian exile, the expectation that the dynasty would be restored became a common (if not universal) feature within the more general hope for Israel's renewal. While preaching the judgment and destruction of Jerusalem, Jeremiah asserts the Lord's faithfulness to his covenant promises, including his promises made to David. Though the Davidic covenant is surpassed by the promise of a new covenant (Jer. 31:31–34), this is an expansion rather than an abrogation of earlier covenants, and God remains faithful to his promises to David and his seed for ever. As in Isaiah, an individual Messiah rather than a perpetual dynasty appears to be in view (but see Jer. 33:17). He is the righteous 'shoot' of David who will reign as king wisely and will establish justice and righteousness in the land (Jer. 23:5–6; cf. 33:14–26).

Ezekiel declares that following the exile the Lord will regather and restore his people (Ezek. 34 – 37). They will be sprinkled clean and given a new heart and a new spirit. They will live in peace and prosperity as a united nation (Ezek. 36:24–38). The Lord will dwell with them as their God, and they will be his people. He will set over them one king and

one shepherd, 'my servant David', who will feed them and be their prince for ever (Ezek. 34:22–24; 37:24–28). Ezekiel here brings together elements of the Davidic and Sinai covenants. The 'I their God, they my people' formula of the Sinai traditions becomes 'I, the LORD, will be their God, and my servant David will be prince among them' (Ezek. 34:24).

It is evident from these texts that the details of the Davidic hope vary from prophet to prophet. In some texts an ideal king who reigns for ever in righteousness is envisaged (Is. 9:7); in others, a perpetual line or dynasty appears to be in view (Jer. 33:17–22; Ezek. 45:8–9; 46:16–18). In some texts the Messiah is portrayed as a new 'David' (or even a David *redivivus*?), a shoot from Jesse (Is. 11:1; *cf.* Ezek. 34:23–24; 37:24–25; Jer. 30:9–10; Hos. 3:5); in others he is a Davidic descendant, a shoot from David (Jer. 23:5–6; Zech. 6:12). In some texts he seems to be merely human. Elsewhere extraordinary royal titles (Is. 9:6) suggest pre-existence and divine status. Despite these variations, the predominant hope remains essentially the same: a restoration of the glories of the Davidic era, when the king after God's heart served not as a despot but as the Lord's vice-regent, establishing *his* justice and righteousness.

Post-exilic prophecy

The return of the exiles under the decree of Cyrus and the subsequent appointment of Zerubbabel, Davidic heir and grandson of Jehoiachin, as governor of Judah, raised hopes among some that God was about to fulfil his covenant promises to David. Both Haggai and Zechariah recall the promise that David's son will build a house for the Lord, to embolden Zerubbabel and Joshua the high priest to return to the task of temple building. Zechariah's prophecies have strong messianic overtones. In the account of the investiture and crowning of Joshua the high priest, the prophet speaks of one called 'Shoot' or 'Branch' who will rebuild the temple (Zech. 6:12–13; *cf.* Jer. 23:5–6). Some scholars consider this figure to be Joshua himself; others, Zerubbabel and Joshua together; still others, a future messianic figure who will combine the offices of king and priest (see Ps. 110:4). In any case, the interaction between the royal and priestly messianic offices found here will play a prominent role in Second

Temple Judaism (where two messiahs, royal and priestly, sometimes appear) and in the Christology of the early church (where Jesus Christ assumes both offices). Though Zerubbabel completes the second temple (Zech. 4:9), he and Joshua serve as types for the longed-for deliverer who will unite the royal and priestly offices and will build the true temple of God.

David and his dynasty in Chronicles

The Davidic legacy, positively assessed in Samuel and Kings, is idealized even further in Chronicles. In the context of disillusionment and the national identity crisis following the Babylonian exile, the Chronicler writes to affirm the central components of Israel's national existence. He emphasizes God's choice of David, Jerusalem, the Levitical priesthood and the centrality of the temple for Israel's life and worship. While acknowledging the disastrous consequences which resulted when the Davidic kings failed in their duty towards God, he insists that God remains faithful to his promises to establish David's seed for ever.

In line with this emphasis, Chronicles presents an idealized portrait of David, emphasizing his religious affections and his preparations for the building of the temple. The account of his sin with Bathsheba is omitted and the story of his decline greatly reduced. David the great king and man after God's heart becomes the solid foundation upon which the Davidic dynasty is built, guaranteeing its perpetuity and the perpetuity of Israel's national existence. In line with this Davidic emphasis, Chronicles follows only the Davidic line in Judah in the south, omitting the accounts from Kings of the non-Davidic kings of the north. Only in Judah is a legitimate, God-ordained king on the throne.

The psalms of David and Israel's corporate worship

While David's idealized kingship left the most enduring mark on Israel's religious life, his musical talents and ordering of *worship also had a profound impact. David's name appears in the superscripts of almost half the psalms. Fourteen refer to incidents in David's life.

According to Chronicles, David also had a leading role in Israel's corporate worship. He made musical instruments used in temple worship (2 Chr. 7:6) and developed the order of worship (2 Chr. 8:14). David's prescriptions for worship are followed in the revivals of both Hezekiah and Josiah (2 Chr. 29:25–30; 35:4, 15). When the exiles return to build Jerusalem and the temple they follow the order of worship prescribed by 'David, the man of God' (Neh. 12:24, 36, 45–46; Ezra 3:10).

David and Davidic messianism in Second Temple Judaism

David in Second Temple Judaism

The idealization of David found in the former prophets and in Chronicles continues in Second Temple Judaism. Especially prominent are David's roles as warrior, psalmist and faithful servant of God. In his 'praise of our ancestors' section, Jesus ben Sirach (c. 180 BC) extols David for his great valour and complete reliance on God. As a young shepherd David 'played with lions as though they were young goats and with bears as though they were lambs' (Ecclus. 47:3, NRSV). By slaying Goliath he took away the people's disgrace (Ecclus. 47:4, NRSV). Yet 'in all that he did he gave thanks to the Holy One ... proclaiming his glory; he sang praise with all his heart and he loved his Maker' (Ecclus. 47:8, NRSV). As in Chronicles David is extolled for his musical talents in arranging the music for the Temple and for Israel's festivals (Ecclus. 47:9–10, NRSV). David's sin with Bathsheba is mentioned only in the context of God's forgiveness: 'The Lord took away his sins, and exalted his horn for ever ...' (Ecclus. 47:11, NRSV).

God's victory over Goliath through 'your servant David' is repeatedly recalled to embolden God's people to faith and perseverance (1 Macc. 4:30, NRSV; *War Scroll* 11:1–2; *Psalms Scroll* 28; Ps. 151, LXX). Also recalled are David's musical talents. In the Psalms scroll from Qumran, it is said that David wrote 4,050 psalms through the prophecy that the Lord gave him (*Psalms Scroll* 27).

Josephus provides a long and detailed account of David's life which closely follows the biblical narrative (Josephus, *Antiquities* 6 §156 – 7 §394). Though he does not ignore the sin with Bathsheba, he presents it as an isolated incident in an otherwise exemplary life (7 §391). David had all the qualities of an ideal ruler: a man of excellent character and bravery, wise and prudent in his national affairs, and kind and righteous in his dealings with others (7 §390, 391).

The *Damascus Rule* also views the Bathsheba incident as an isolated event. The 'deeds of David rose up [to God], except for the murder of Uriah, and God granted forgiveness' (*Damascus Rule* 5:2–3). While David is also said to have broken the law against a king's multiplying wives (Deut. 17:17), this is excused because 'David had not read the sealed book of the Law which was in the ark' (*Damascus Rule* 5:2).

Davidic messianism during the Second Temple period

Though David was honoured as a model of faith in Second Temple writings, expectations for a Messiah from his line ebbed and flowed with the changing political and social climate in Israel, and varied according to the diverse agendas of the sects (or 'Judaisms', Neusner *et al.* (eds.), *Judaisms and Their Messiahs*) within Judaism. The resurgence of Davidic hopes at the time of Zerubbabel and the rebuilding of the temple inevitably diminished when Zerubbabel passed from the scene. During the Persian period the authority of the high priest increased as he took over administrative functions previously performed by the Davidic king. During the Maccabean period the Hasmonean priest-kings assumed both royal and priestly offices.

This is not to say that the covenant with David was forgotten, or that expectations for a Davidic king disappeared completely, but increasingly such hopes were set aside or postponed to an indefinite future.

This apparent decline in Davidic expectations appears to have been reversed in the late Second Temple period. Growing disenchantment with the corruption of the Hasmoneans and the subsequent subjugation of Israel by Rome renewed hopes for a great king from David's line who would judge unrighteous rulers and expel foreigners from the land. This is most strongly expressed in the *Psalms of Solomon,* a 1st-century BC document probably composed in Pharisaic circles. In these psalms a group of Jewish pietists cry out against certain 'sinners' (the Hasmonean priest-kings) who have arrogantly usurped the Davidic throne and have defiled the temple of God (*Psalms of Solomon* 1:6–8; 2:3–5; 8:8–

13; 17:5–9, 19–22). In response God has sent a foreign conqueror (*Psalms of Solomon* 17:8) – probably a reference to the Roman general Pompey (63 BC) – to defeat the city and lay waste the land (*Psalms of Solomon* 2:3–8; 7:2; 8:14–22; 17:8–20). The psalmist beseeches the Lord to raise up the 'son of David' to rule over Israel (*Psalms of Solomon* 17:21ff.). The characteristics and functions of the Davidic king listed here are drawn from the OT Davidic promise tradition, and especially from Isaiah 11. He destroys the wicked, purges Jerusalem, restores the nation's boundaries, gathers a holy people and faithfully and righteously shepherds them. He judges and rules in wisdom, understanding, strength and righteousness. At the same time the king is wholly subordinate to the Lord, 'his king', judging, leading and ruling according to God's word and spirit (*Psalms of Solomon* 17 – 18).

Similar expectations for a powerful and conquering messianic king appear in the Qumran scrolls, though here a second messiah, a priestly one, appears beside the Davidic one, at times taking precedence over him (see *Rule of the Community* ix 11; *Messianic Rule* ii 11–21; *cf. Testament of Judah* 21:1–3). Particularly in the cave 4 documents, the Davidic king plays a more prominent and executive role, acting as God's agent to defeat Israel's enemies. He is a warrior king after the model of Isaiah 11:1–5, who slays the ungodly with the breath of his lips, and whose mighty sceptre ravages the earth and rules the nations (*Florilegium* i 10–13; *Pesher on Isaiah* fr. D 1–8; *Patriarchal Blessing* 1–5; *cf. Rule of the Blessings* v 24–26). Yet unlike the Hasmoneans, he never acts as a despot, but is wholly submissive to the will of God. His loins are girded with righteousness; he upholds the Law and learns at the feet of the priests: 'As they teach him, so shall he judge' (*Pesher on Isaiah*).

It should be noted that Judaism at the dawn of Christianity included a great diversity of eschatological expectations. In some texts, no messianic figure appears; God himself acts as Saviour. In others, an agent of deliverance appears, but is not a Davidic figure. In still others, imagery is drawn from the Davidic tradition but without reference to David's seed. In general, however, there appears to have been a widespread (if not universal) expectation that God's promise to

David still stood, and that he would soon raise up the 'son of David' to deliver Israel and re-establish righteousness and justice in the land.

David and Davidic messianism in the NT

As in the literature of Judaism, David appears in the NT as a mighty king, inspired psalmist, man after God's heart, and ancestor of the Messiah. For the NT writers Jesus is the messianic king and saviour from David's line, the fulfilment of Israel's hopes. Yet the prominence given to his Davidic descent varies from writer to writer. In some it is assumed but not emphasized. In others it becomes a crucial feature in the author's presentation of Jesus.

Paul and pre-Pauline formulas

Paul assumes rather than defends Jesus' Davidic descent and messianic office. The description 'seed of David' (KJV) appears in Romans 1:3–5 in what is probably a pre-Pauline hymn. The original meaning of the hymn has been debated, with some claiming that it represents an early two-stage Christology. Jesus, born as a son of David, became at his resurrection the son of God. It is more likely that the hymn was originally a two-stage proof of Jesus' messiahship based on the Nathan oracle (2 Sam. 7:12, 14). Jesus' messiahship is confirmed *both* by his legitimate Davidic ancestry ('seed of David') *and* by his vindication as God's Son. Paul quotes the traditional hymn as an expression of the faith he holds in common with the church at Rome. For Paul the emphasis changes, however, with his introductory phrase, 'concerning his Son' (NRSV), and the qualification 'according to the flesh'. Though the title 'seed of David' confirms Jesus' messianic status, it more importantly characterizes the humble incarnation of the pre-existent Son (Gal. 4:4; Rom. 8:3; Phil. 2:7). This relative lack of interest in Davidic messianism is characteristic of the Pauline tradition. Apart from the similar confessional formula in 2 Timothy 2:8, it is mentioned only incidentally, in Romans 15:12, where Isaiah 11:10 is cited to defend the Gentile mission.

The Gospel of Mark

In Mark, as in Paul, Jesus' Davidic lineage is assumed rather than defended. In the account of the healing of blind Bartimaeus, the acclamation 'son of David' (Mark 10:47–48) prepares the reader for the pilgrim cry at Jesus' entrance into Jerusalem (Mark 11:10). The general reference to 'the coming kingdom of our father David' now carries for the reader specifically messianic significance and points to Jesus. Some commentators have interpreted Mark 12:35–37 as a denial of Jesus' Davidic descent; Jesus cannot be the son of David since he is David's Lord. This is unlikely in the light of Mark 10:47 and 11:10. Jesus' question indicates that the title 'son of David', though an accurate description of the Messiah, is insufficient to describe his exalted status. Jesus is not a warrior king restoring the glories of the Davidic era through conquest. He is rather David's Lord, who will bring in a new era of salvation history through suffering as the righteous servant.

David is also mentioned, though without messianic implications, in Mark 2:25–27 (pars.) where his action in eating the bread of the presence (1 Sam. 21:1–6) serves as proof that the needs of a human being may supersede certain commandments. Hence, 'the Sabbath was made for man, not man for the Sabbath' (Mark 2:27).

The Gospel of Matthew

In the first Gospel the Davidic ancestry of the Messiah emerges as a crucial element in Matthew's prophecy-fulfilment motif. In Matthew's carefully structured genealogy, Abraham and David – the covenant receivers – stand together as central figures in salvation history (Matt. 1:1, 17). While in Mark only Bartimaeus addresses Jesus as 'son of David', in Matthew this becomes a common acclamation of those seeking help from Jesus (Matt. 9:27; 15:22; 20:30). When the people see Jesus' miracles they wonder 'Could this be the son of David?' (Matt. 12:23) and at Jesus' entrance into Jerusalem the crowds now shout 'Hosanna to the son of David!' (Matt. 21:9, 15). As in later rabbinic thought the title 'son of David' is equivalent to that of 'Messiah', but provides a more explicit link to the Davidic roots of OT messianic expectation.

Luke-Acts

Luke's emphasis on the continuity of salvation history, like Matthew's on prophetic fulfilment, means that David and Davidic messianism occupy a prominent place in his two-volume work. In Stephen's speech in Acts 7 David is said to have found favour (*charis*) with God and to have sought to build a house for him (Acts 7:46). In Pisidian Antioch Paul provides a summary of Israel's history, which reaches its climax with David, the man after God's heart who consistently did his will (Acts 13:22). 'From this man's seed God brought to Israel the Saviour, Jesus, as he promised' (Acts 13:23, author's translation). Jesus will fulfil the Davidic promise, reigning on David's throne over the house of Jacob for ever (Luke 1:32–33). He is the Lord's anointed, born in Bethlehem the 'town of David' of Joseph, a descendant of David (Luke 1:27; 2:4, 11, 26). Luke's birth narrative applies the Davidic promise to the infant Jesus; the speeches in Acts explain its fulfilment (Acts 2:29–36; 13:22–23, 32–37; 15:16–18). Only Luke among the NT writers explicitly links the fulfilment of the Davidic promise with Jesus' *exaltation-enthronement at God's right hand (Acts 2:33–36).

Also significant for Luke is David's role as prophet of the Christ. While David's prophetic gift is elsewhere implied with reference to his composition of psalms (Heb. 4:7; Rom. 4:6; 11:9), in Acts it is explicitly stated. In Psalm 2 the Lord spoke '*by* the Holy Spirit *through* the mouth of ... David' (Acts 4:25). David's prophetic testimony is crucial in the apologetic argument of Peter's Pentecost speech. Since David was a prophet (and since he neither rose from the dead nor ascended to heaven), Psalms 16 and 110 may be interpreted as predictions of the resurrection and ascension of the Christ (Acts 2:29–31). This emphasis on David as prophet reflects Luke's belief in the continuity of salvation history. The whole of the OT revelation – 'all that the prophets have spoken ... in all the Scriptures' – points forward to the coming of the Christ (Luke 24:25–27).

The Gospel of John

John's emphasis on the divine Son, 'the one who comes from above', is reflected in his lack of interest in Jesus' earthly origins. His Davidic descent is mentioned only in John 7:41–44, where Jesus' messiahship is questioned by the Jews because of his (supposed) Galilean origin and non-Davidic lineage. While some suggest that John is ignorant of Jesus' Davidic ancestry, the passage more probably reflects the Fourth Gospel's characteristic irony. Two traditional messianic expectations are expressed by the Jews: first, the Messiah's hiddenness (John 7:27; *cf.* 2 Esdras 7:28; 13:25–26; 2 Baruch 29:3), and second, his Davidic and Bethlehemite origin (John 7:42). For some, Jesus cannot be the Messiah since they know where he is from; for others, he cannot be the Messiah because he is apparently from Nazareth, not Bethlehem. But both are wrong. The first group does not know where he is from, since he is from heaven. The second does not know his earthly origins, since he was indeed born in Bethlehem and from the line of David. John ironically affirms that traditional expectations cannot adequately express the person of the Son.

Hebrews

The writer of the epistle to the Hebrews also accepts but goes beyond traditional messianic categories. Though he is aware of Jesus' Judahite ancestry (Heb. 7:14), and hence of his Davidic lineage, he mentions it only to demonstrate that Jesus' Melchizedekian priesthood is distinct from and superior to that of the Levitical line. Citations from the Nathan oracle (2 Sam. 7:14; Heb. 1:5) and the royal psalms (Pss. 2:7; 45:6–7; 110:1–2; Heb. 1:5, 8–9, 13; 5:5) show that as the Son Jesus is superior to angels, and the author's repeated references to Psalm 110:4 confirm that Jesus' Melchizedekian priesthood is superior to that of Aaron (Heb. 5:6; 6:20; 7:17, 21).

Revelation

David is mentioned three times in Revelation; two of the references are explicitly messianic. The author's penchant for OT allusion and imagery provides a remarkable synthesis between Jewish messianic expectations and Christian reflection on their fulfilment in Jesus Christ. In Revelation 5:5–6 Jesus is both the 'Lion of the tribe of Judah, the root of David' and the Lamb who was slain. The allusion to the 'lion' refers to Jacob's blessings in Genesis 49, where Judah is a 'lion's cub' from whom the sceptre of rulership will not pass 'until Shiloh comes' (vv. 9–10, NIV fn.). This first biblical prediction of the Davidic dynasty became an important messianic text in Second Temple Judaism (*Patriarchal Blessing* 1–5). The reference to the 'Root of

David' draws on the 'shoot' and 'root' imagery of Isaiah 11:1, 10. The Lamb, slain but standing in readiness, represents both sacrifice and victory. Jesus is the Messiah from David's line who suffers and then conquers as the sacrificial lamb of God.

In Revelation 22:16 Jesus is again identified as 'the Root and the Offspring of David', but also as 'the bright morning star'. The star imagery comes from the fourth oracle of Balaam (Num. 24:17), which was also interpreted messianically in Second Temple writings (*Testament of Levi* 18:3; *Testament of Judah* 24:1–6; *Rule of the Blessings* v 27–29).

In short, Revelation brings together traditional Davidic messianic images to confirm that the Lamb, slain but now victorious, is indeed the consummation of God's plan. The eternal destiny of all of creation comes to fulfilment in Jesus, who is not only the Davidic Messiah but also the Alpha and Omega, the Lord of all.

See also: SOLOMON.

Bibliography

W. Brueggeman, *David's Truth in Israel's Imagination and Memory* (Philadelphia, 1985); K. Berger, 'Die königlichen Messiastraditionen des Neuen Testament', *NTS* 20, 1974, pp. 1–44; C. Burger, *Jesus als Davidssohn: Eine traditionsgeschichtliche Untersuchung* (Göttingen, 1970); K. R. Crim, *The Royal Psalms* (Richmond, 1962); D. M. Gunn, *The Story of King David* (Sheffield, 1978); E. O'Doherty, 'The organic development of messianic revelation', *CBQ* 19, 1957, pp. 16–24; D. N. Freedman, 'The Chronicler's purpose', *CBQ* 23, 1961, pp. 436–442; D. M. Howard Jr., 'The case for kingship in the OT narrative books and the Psalms', *TJ* 9, 1988, pp. 19–35; E. Lohse, 'Der König aus Davids Geschlecht: Bemerkungen zur messianischen Erwartung der Synagoge', in O. Betz *et al.* (eds.) *Abraham Unser Vater: Juden und Christen im Gespräch über die Bibel* (Leiden, 1963); J. L. McKenzie, 'The dynastic oracle: II Samuel 7', *TS* 8, 1947, pp. 187–218; *idem*, 'Royal Messianism', *CBQ* 19, 1957, pp. 25–52; T. N. D. Mettinger, *King and Messiah: The Civil and Sacred Legitimation of the Israelite Kings* (Lund, 1976); S. Mowinckel, *He That Cometh* (ET, Oxford, 1956); J. Neusner *et al.* (eds.), *Judaisms and Their Messiahs at the Turn of the Christian Era* (Cambridge, 1987); L. Rost, *The Succession to the Throne of David* (ET, Sheffield, 1982); M. L. Strauss, *The Davidic Messiah in Luke-Acts* (Sheffield, 1995).

M. L. STRAUSS

DEATH AND RESURRECTION

The resurrection of *Jesus Christ is central to the documents of the NT, to apostolic preaching and to Christian faith (1 Cor. 15). However, this is part of the radical newness of the *gospel. Paul affirms that 'our Saviour Jesus Christ ... destroyed death and brought life and immortality to light through the gospel' (2 Tim. 1:10, NIV). So until Christ's resurrection the afterlife was an unknown quantity, truly 'in the shadows'. This is the key to a biblical theology of death and resurrection, at once affirming the light shed by the gospel and the relative ignorance of pre-Christian times (*cf.* also Mark 9:10).

Death

Punishment

The creation accounts are ambiguous concerning death. On the one hand, the sentence of death for disobedience (Gen. 2:17) suggests its original absence. On the other, the need to eat from the tree of life to live for ever (Gen. 3:22) implies mortality. The latter view is apparently confirmed when the death sentence is fulfilled not immediately but by banishment from the tree of life. The subsequent limitation of a normal lifespan to 120 years (Gen. 6:3) may be a further punishment. Elsewhere in the OT death is occasionally connected to *sin, as (implicitly) in Psalm 90:7–10. The NT develops this theme extensively (*e.g.* Rom. 5:12; 6:23; 1 Cor. 15:21). It is to death as divine punishment that the death and resurrection of Christ makes such a potent response. (See *Judgment.)

An enemy

A related approach to death is found in a few prophetic texts. Hosea 13:14 toys with the prospect of Yahweh's ransoming Israel from the power of death, but apparently draws back from this and instead invites a personified Death to unleash his plagues. In *God's resurrection of Christ from the dead as the firstfruit of his people, Death's plagues are neutralized and Paul can legitimately quote the same words with a quite different, now triumphant, emphasis (1 Cor. 15:55). According to the 'Little Apocalypse' of Isaiah, Yahweh 'will swallow up death for ever', removing the covering from the nations (either shroud or veil of mourning, Is. 25:7–8), and in the next chapter his dead are said to come to life again (Is. 26:19, see below). The NT cites this swallowing of death in relation to Christ's *victory over it (1 Cor. 15:54; Rev. 21:4). For the Christian, death is not a terror but a transition.

Natural end

However, the above themes are rare in the OT. Overwhelmingly death is treated simply as the end of life. Sometimes this is peaceful and contented, as with Abraham and Jacob (Gen. 25:8; 49:33). Sometimes it is violent and troubled, whether attributed to divine intervention ('the LORD smote Nabal', 1 Sam. 25:38) or not. Often death is simply recorded without further comment, as with Samuel (1 Sam. 25:1). The NT echoes the theme of peaceful death in using the term 'fall asleep' for the death of believers. However, the NT does not portray death simply as the natural end of life, perhaps partly because it lacks narrative extending over many generations, but mainly because of the new and distinctively Christian understanding of death.

Present experience

Some psalmists in great distress speak graphically of being already in the clutches of Sheol, the underworld (e.g. Ps. 18:4–5; 88:3–8). This metaphor is so powerful and evocative that some scholars think the Israelites viewed death as a power which invaded life, such that any illness, enforced absence or other misfortune was an actual experience of Sheol. However, this misreads the typically Hebraic hyperbole. Even in the bleakest of all psalms the poet can still pray to God, an activity impossible in Sheol (Ps. 88:1–2; cf. 6:5). The NT can also speak of death invading life (Eph. 2:1), as well as of present eternal life (John 3:36).

The dead

OT underworld

The only afterlife articulated in the OT is Sheol. This term, with its synonyms 'pit' and 'destruction', indicates a realm of sleepy, shadowy existence in the depths of the earth. In one description, formerly mighty kings now in Sheol need to be roused to greet a newcomer, the mighty king of Babylon, who has become weak like them (Is. 14:9–11). In another, various conquering armies lie in groups in a great cavern (Ezek. 32:17–32). This is similar to the underworld in much other ancient Near Eastern literature. However, the OT shows a striking disinterest in the fate of the dead. There are only about one hundred occurrences of 'Sheol' and its synonyms in the OT, and even fewer passages, since the different terms often occur in parallel. In the psalms, laments frequently describe misfortune and thanksgivings often rejoice in deliverance without recourse to underworld terminology. For Israel, Yahweh was the God of the living; faith was for this life, and what followed it was unimportant.

Underworld terms occur almost exclusively in 'first-person texts': psalms, proverbs, prophetic writings, and direct speech in narrative. (The only exception is Num. 16:33, where the narrator echoes the direct speech of v. 30.) In all the many accounts of the deaths of patriarchs, judges, kings and others, the underworld is ignored. Clearly it is a concept of personal involvement, not of detached description.

For most scholars, the Israelites thought everyone was destined for Sheol, since no other fate is described. Nevertheless, in the OT Sheol is predominantly noted as the fate of the wicked rather than that of the righteous, and this is explicit in Psalm 49:14–15. On four occasions godly men *fear they will go there (Gen. 37:35; Is. 38:10; Ps. 88:4; Job 14:13), but probably because they interpret their extreme misfortune as divine punishment. Jacob envisages going to Sheol when separated from his favourite sons, but when he eventually dies, after the family is happily reunited, Sheol is never mentioned (Gen. 47 – 50). Only two texts seem to indicate that everyone goes to Sheol, and these are set in negative contexts, those of divine punishment (Ps. 89:48) and human futility (Eccles. 9:10). Whatever Israelites in general thought, the OT writers clearly viewed the underworld negatively.

When the dead Samuel is consulted by Saul he 'comes up' from the earth (1 Sam. 28:8, 11, 13). It is usually assumed that Samuel comes up from Sheol, though no underworld term is used. But this may not be right if the Israelites instinctively reserved underworld terminology for the wicked while accepting the grave as the destiny of all. The finality of death is confirmed in Peter's Pentecost sermon, where he describes David as dead and buried, and asserts that he did not ascend to heaven (Acts 2:29, 34).

OT phrases for death

'To be gathered to one's people', which occurs alongside notices of death and burial, implies joining one's ancestors in the afterlife. But it occurs only ten times, and only of the nation's ancestors and leaders (Abraham, Ishmael, Isaac, Jacob, Moses, Aaron). Elsewhere there are a few similar, probably derivative phrases (Judg. 2:10; 2 Kgs. 22:20; Ps. 49:19). 'To sleep with one's fathers' is also used restrictively, of kings of Israel and Judah who died peacefully, regardless of their assessment as good or evil or their place of burial. (The one exception of Ahab may be due to scribal error.) Whatever the phrase's origin, this usage suggests that it came to indicate a type of death rather than afterlife reunification.

OT alternatives?

Alongside this general picture, there are occasional glimpses of a more positive afterlife. God 'took' *Enoch (Gen. 5:24), and *Elijah ascended to heaven in a fiery chariot and whirlwind (2 Kgs. 2:11). But these fates are unique, and never become paradigms for the aspirations and prayers of others. However a few OT passages seem to envisage some form of continued communion with God beyond death, however ill-defined and unlocated (Ps. 16:10; 49:15; 73:24). This aspect of Psalm 16 is cited by Peter, though as prophetic of Christ rather than as personal to the psalmist (Acts 2:27). Job's defiant wish in 19:25–27 is often cited in this connection, but the severe textual difficulties in this passage make any theological conclusion tenuous. The idea of continued communion with God beyond death is affirmed by Paul in his longing to 'be with Christ, which is better by far' (Phil. 1:23).

Later Jewish thought

Intertestamental literature displays a spectrum of views on the dead. The more traditionally Jewish Ecclesiasticus (17:28–30) echoes the OT's perspective on mortality and Sheol, while the more Hellenistic Wisdom of Solomon affirms that 'the souls of the righteous are in the hands of God' (3:1–6) until 'the time of their visitation', *i.e.* the resurrection (3:7–8). Various words are used to refer to someone in the resultant intermediate state, notably 'angel' (*cf.* Acts 12:15) and 'spirit'. These terms are used synonymously in Acts 23:8, where Sadducees believe in 'neither resurrection nor angel nor spirit', but Pharisees acknowledge 'both'. (This last term always means 'both of two' in the NT, so 'angel' and 'spirit' must be identical here.)

A growing belief in resurrection led to views of the dead existing in different compartments. In an early section of the composite *1 Enoch*, the seer is shown the dead divided into four (or possibly three) separate groups in Hades awaiting judgment (ch. 22). The fate of the wicked is uncertain: in this section it is said that they will be punished with torment for ever (22:11), as an eternal spectacle for the righteous (27:3), but elsewhere the seer asserts that 'those who walk in the path of iniquity will be destroyed for ever' (91:19).

The NT

With its focus on the resurrection of Jesus to life, and of everyone else to eternal life or punishment, the NT gives less attention to the pre-resurrection state of the dead. Jesus' story of the rich man and the beggar (Luke 16:19–31) reflects one strand of current Jewish belief, with the dead already experiencing torment or bliss. The nameless rich man is clearly in Hades while Lazarus is probably in heaven. (He is carried to Abraham's side by angels, and the rich man looks up to see him far away.)

In his early letters, Paul seems to expect an imminent parousia, and focuses on the resurrection body (1 Thess. 4; 1 Cor. 15, see below). Later, after his own brush with death (2 Cor. 1:8), he contrasts the present earthly tent with the clothing of 'our heavenly dwelling'. Being thus clothed is far preferable to being naked or unclothed (2 Cor. 5:1–4). Given the contrast between present and future, 'nakedness' might refer to this life, but it is usually interpreted as an undesirable disembodied intermediate state. Elsewhere Paul seems to ignore the state of believers between death and resurrection; 'falling asleep' (nine times in 1 Cor. and 1 Thess. 4) refers primarily to their death (see M. J. Harris in *Them*. pp. 47–52), though it may be suggestive of their subsequent state. In his late letters, Paul speaks of being immediately in Christ's presence (Phil. 1:23), or being brought safely to the heavenly kingdom (2 Tim. 4:18), without further detail.

There are a few references in later NT books to the ungodly dead's awaiting judgment (2 Pet. 3:7, Jude 6–7). After his death Christ 'preached to the spirits in prison' (1 Pet. 3:19), proclaiming their judgment rather than offering them *salvation (see R. T. France, in *New Testament Interpretation*, pp. 264–281).

Resurrection

The OT

A few prophetic passages use the imagery of resurrection for national restoration after the cataclysm of *exile (Hos. 6 and passim; Ezek. 37; possibly Is. 26:19). More startlingly, two texts suggest individual resurrection; Isaiah 26:19 where Yahweh's people awake to joy, and Daniel 12:2 where some awake to everlasting life and some to everlasting contempt. However, these texts are marginal to the OT, at least theologically and perhaps also chronologically. If the texts are indeed authentic to the 8th-century prophet and the exilic sage respectively, then their startlingly revolutionary concept remained unappropriated and undeveloped. It was simply ignored by subsequent prophets, psalmists and sages. If instead these texts reflect later post-exilic periods of developing apocalyptic, then further theological reflection was restricted to subsequent, non-canonical writings.

In the past, scholars often suggested that post-exilic Israel absorbed Persian notions of resurrection and post-mortem judgment. More recently, some scholars have proposed an earlier influence from Canaanite notions of Baal as a dying-and-rising god, as attested in the Ugaritic texts. For example, J. Day traces this influence progressively, with the concept 'demythologized' to refer to the nation in Hosea and Isaiah and 'remythologized' to refer to individuals in Daniel. In contrast, others argue for an inner-biblical development: reflection on God's creative power prompted belief in his recreative, resurrecting power. For instance, B. C. Ollenburger notes this strong motif in the 2nd-century martyr account of 2 Maccabees 7, and traces it back to the OT. These approaches are not mutually exclusive. It was the threat and then the reality of exile which led to the prophetic development of the motif, perhaps one already known from Canaanite religion(s). But the development was a distinctly Israelite one – not of a dying and rising deity, but initially of a moribund and revived nation, and then of dead and resurrected individuals.

Later Jewish thought

In the mid 2nd century BC, a developing belief in the physical resurrection of God's faithful, with restored and rejuvenated bodies, bolstered martyrs (2 Macc. 7:9, 11, *etc.*; 14:46) and led to prayers and sin offerings for the dead (12:43–45). In 2 Maccabees, resurrection is envisaged only for the righteous; for the tyrant Antiochus 'there will be no resurrection to life' (7:14). By the late 2nd century BC, *The Testaments of the Twelve Patriarchs* affirms a total resurrection: first the patriarchs will rise to God's right hand in gladness, then 'all men will rise, some to glory and some to disgrace' (*Testament of Benjamin* 10:6–8).

By NT times, belief in resurrection was common among Pharisees and many other Jews (Acts 23:8). Resurrection was envisaged as God's restoration of Israel in the present transformed and recreated world, not in an ethereal heavenly realm. However, some Jewish groups were less sure. The Qumran scrolls contain only one fleeting reference to resurrection (*Messianic Apocalypse* ii. 12, where 'revive the dead' is inserted between allusions to Ezek. 37:16 and Is. 61:1). And the Sadducees denied the resurrection (Acts 23:8), ostensibly because it is not mentioned in the Torah, which alone was authoritative for them, but probably also because such belief encouraged insurrection and martyrdom which threatened their establishment position.

The Gospels and Acts

Jesus categorically opposed the Sadducees with their trick question regarding a hypothetical widow's six levirate marriages, and described a resurrection state where marriage and procreation were superfluous and death unknown. Jesus then countered with a fresh interpretation of Exodus 3:6. Israel's God was the God of the living, so his relationship with the patriarchs was not broken by death and the dead must therefore rise (Luke 20:27–38 and par.). Elsewhere Jesus could speak of 'the resurrection of the righteous' (Luke 14:14), but his teaching on final judgment clearly implies universal resurrection (Matt. 25:31–46).

Despite their incomprehension, Jesus repeatedly told his disciples of his forthcoming death and resurrection (Mark 8:31, *etc.*). John typically focuses on the implication of these events: Jesus himself is resurrection and life, and this implies resurrection and eternal life after death for all believers (John 11:25–26). From Pentecost onwards, the focal point of apostolic preaching was the resurrection of Jesus, which vindicates him as Lord and Messiah and necessitates human repentance and transformed faith (Acts 2:24–36, *etc.*).

Paul

For Paul, the resurrection of Christ is the foundation of Christian life in the present and of hope for the future, as he explains at length in *1 Corinthians 15. He first establishes the historical fact of Jesus' resurrection by noting his subsequent appearance to hundreds of disciples and ultimately to Paul himself (vv. 1–10). He then notes the universality of early Christian resurrection belief and the absurdity of non-belief for Christian faith (vv. 11–19). If Jesus did not rise, he was just another failed Jewish messiah. But if he did, then God's new kingdom has dawned. Next Paul reworks typical Jewish motifs into a distinctly Christian perspective. Death came through *Adam, resurrection through Christ, who now reigns in heaven having defeated his enemies (a distinguishing feature of the Messiah, though the enemies were normally identified as political; vv. 20–28). This should profoundly affect the way believers live (vv. 29–35). Paul then describes both the continuity and the difference between the present and future bodies using several analogies (vv. 35–49), and summarizes this discussion with two adjectives which are difficult to translate concisely and have often been misunderstood (v. 42). The contrast is not between physical/material and disembodied/immaterial, but between different bodies, the present one *psychikon*, *i.e.* animated by soul, the future one *pneumatikon*, *i.e.* animated by spirit. The perishable flesh-and-blood body is transformed into an imperishable immortal body, and so death itself is swallowed up (vv. 50–55). Christ's resurrection is thus the prototype of Christian experience.

Other epistles and Revelation

1 Peter echoes Pauline themes in grounding its opening doxology on Christ's resurrection and in contrasting the perishable and the imperishable (1 Pet. 1:3, 23). Hebrews similarly lists resurrection as a basic tenet of faith, and even ascribes the belief to Abraham (Heb. 6:1–2; 11:19). Revelation, for all its apocalyptic imagery and eschatological focus, only speaks cryptically of a 'first resurrection' of martyrs to a millennial reign with Christ (Rev. 20:5–6). Different terminology is used for the final judgment: the sea, death and Hades 'give up' their dead to stand before God's throne (20:12–13). Here death and the realm of the dead are not just defeated but forced to surrender all their captives, and finally destroyed. The wheel has come full circle.

See also: HEAVEN AND HELL; LIFE.

Bibliography

T. D. Alexander, 'The Old Testament view of life after death', *Them.* 11.2, 1986, pp. 41–46; L. R. Bailey, *Biblical Perspectives on Death* (Philadelphia, 1979); J. Day, 'Resurrection imagery from Baal to the Book of Daniel', in J. A. Emerton (ed.), *Congress Volume Cambridge* (Leiden, 1997); R. T. France, 'Exegesis in Practice: two examples', in I. H. Marshall (ed.), *New Testament Interpretation* (Exeter, 1977); M. J. Harris, *Raised Immortal* (Basingstoke, 1983); *idem*, 'The New Testament view of life after death', *Them.* 11.2, 1986, pp. 47–52; P. S. Johnston, '"Left in Hell"? Psalm 16, Sheol and the Holy One', in P. E. Satterthwaite *et al.* (eds.), *The Lord's Anointed* (Carlisle, 1995); L. J. Kreitzer, 'Intermediate State', 'Resurrection', in *DPL*, pp. 438, 441, 805–812; R. N. Longenecker (ed.), *Life in the Face of Death* (Grand Rapids, 1998); G. W. E. Nickelsburg, *Resurrection, Immortality, and Eternal Life in Intertestamental Judaism* (Cambridge, 1972); *idem*, in *ABD* 5, pp. 684–691; B. C. Ollenburger, 'The Old Testament and resurrection', *EA* 9, 1993, pp. 29–24; G. R Osborne in *DJG*, pp. 673–688.

P. S. JOHNSTON

DECREE, see LAW
DELIVERANCE, see SALVATION
DEMONS, see SPIRITUAL POWERS
DEUTERONOMY, see Part 2
DEVIL, see SPIRITUAL POWERS

DISCIPLINE

'Discipline' in Scripture covers a wide range of meaning, for it can connote training (Eph. 6:4), education (Deut. 8:5), reproof (Prov. 9:7), correction (Zeph. 3:2, 7), warning (Is. 8:11), chastening (Prov. 3:11, AV), and punishment (Hos. 10:10). As a concept discipline is in the OT intimately connected with *God's *covenant with Israel and with his covenant *law. Since discipline is located within the context of covenant it is to be understood theocentrically, for all discipline comes ultimately from God, and its goals and means are determined by him.

Discipline has both a corporate and an individual dimension; it can be the discipline of a community (*Israel in the OT, the *church in the NT) or of an individual believer. In the OT discipline is understood mostly in corporate terms (e.g. Deut. 8:5), though the individual dimension is not lacking (e.g. Prov. 3:11–12). While in the NT the corporate aspect is certainly present (e.g. 1 Cor. 11:27–32), the individual dimension assumes greater prominence, especially in the letter to the Hebrews where it is connected with the *suffering that discipleship entails and the *holiness that God wills for believers (Heb. 12:3–11).

Vocabulary

In the OT the most frequently used words for discipline are the verb yāsar and the related noun mûsār. Less frequently used of discipline is the verb yākaḥ ('to contend'), which in the hiphil form means 'give reproof, reprove' (see Gen. 21:25, where it is translated 'complained' by NIV, NRSV, and Prov. 3:12, where it is used in parallel with 'the Lord's discipline' [mûsār]: 'for the LORD reproves the one he loves' [NRSV]).

In the NT paideuō and paideia are the words most commonly used of discipline. On occasion elenchō ('to convict, reprove', Eph. 5:11) and elegmos ('rebuking', 2 Tim. 3:16, NIV) are used in contexts relating to discipline.

Discipline in the OT

In the OT discipline is particularly associated with God's disciplinary action with regard to his covenant *people, although he is also said to discipline the *nations (Ps. 94:10).

In the law

In the book of Deuteronomy discipline is an important sub-theme, as a number of key passages indicate. In 4:35–36 it is made clear that God's voice from heaven was not only revelatory ('so that you might know that the LORD is God; besides him there is no other') but also disciplinary ('to discipline you'). The discipline that God exercises is ethical. Its purpose is that the covenant people might know Yahweh (cf. Jer. 24:7). The discipline of Yahweh is taught through his 'decrees and commands' (Deut. 4:39) which Israel is to 'keep ... so that it may go well with you and your children after you'. The 'good life' that God wills for his people will be possible only as they live by the given tôrāh (v. 40, 'instruction') that is bound up with the covenant God has made with them.

Behind God's covenant with his people, indeed the very ground of it, is his electing *love (Deut. 4:37). It is this gracious, unmerited love (7:7–11) which provides the motive for the responsive love and *obedience (v. 9) which should characterize the life of Israel (v. 11).

In Deuteronomy 8:5 the nature of God's covenant discipline is made clear. It is not so much the discipline of a suzerain towards a vassal, as the discipline of a father towards his child. It is therefore prompted by a tender love and a deep concern for the child's development as a person. Though fatherly discipline may involve 'admonition, correction, and severity' (P. C. Craigie, The Book of Deuteronomy, p. 186), it is always educative and loving in a way that military discipline never could be. However, the covenant curses of chapters 27 and 28 warn us against sentimentalizing God's love so as to preclude the exercising of severe discipline, of which the destruction of Jerusalem and the Babylonian exile constitute the paradigm.

In context Deuteronomy 8:5 indicates that the *wilderness period was 'the time of adolescence in Israel's history, when the people learned to understand by experience the way in which God wanted them to walk' (Craigie,

Deuteronomy). It was a time of humbling, testing and teaching (vv. 3–4), all of which are expressions of God's fatherly discipline. Thus *redemptive history is seen to be the sphere in which God operates to discipline his people.

In 11:2 'the discipline of the LORD' is even more clearly related to the wilderness period. The events of the *Exodus are seen as an important part of Israel's education. God displayed 'his majesty, his mighty hand, his outstretched arm' in the overthrow of Pharaoh and his army (vv. 3–4), *and* his severe *judgment in 'what he did to Dathan and Abiram' (v. 6; *cf.* Num. 16:1–3, 23–35). Yahweh's discipline is pedagogical, teaching Israel both by his *gracious acts and by acts of judgment.

Though in Deuteronomy the main focus is on divine discipline, there are places in which *yasar* is used of human discipline (see 21:18; 22:18).

In the wisdom literature

Discipline is a prominent theme in the book of *Proverbs. As in Deuteronomy 8:5 it is set within the father/child relationship, which serves as the main vehicle for the imparting of ethical instruction, though Proverbs 1:8 brings in the mother/child relationship as well. The use of this familial metaphor points to the same metaphor as employed to describe God's relationship to Israel (Deut. 8:5).

In 3:11–12 the father appeals to his child not to despise 'the LORD's discipline'. As in Deuteronomy this proceeds from his love, which determines all his disciplinary action, however severe it may sometimes have to be. As will be seen, this passage is quoted by the author of Hebrews and applied to believers who were growing weary and losing heart because of the opposition they were experiencing (Heb. 12:3–6).

In contrast to the child who accepts discipline, some refuse to do so. Such people are variously described as fools (*i.e.* morally reprobate people lacking the fear of Yahweh; *e.g.* 1:7), scoffers (9:7), and wicked (5:22–23). They have no disposition to accept discipline and, knowing nothing of the *fear of the Lord, they cannot be taught *wisdom (14:6). In sum, 'he who ignores discipline (*mûsār*) despises himself [lit. his life], but whoever heeds correction gains understanding' (15:32).

Closely connected with discipline in Proverbs is 'rebuke' (*tôkahat*), a term used

thirteen times. In 5:12 it is used in apposition to *mûsār*. In the majority of instances it is employed negatively, to denote the rejection of reproof, but it can be '*life-giving' (15:31) and impart wisdom (29:15).

Discipline in Proverbs is aimed at the shaping of godly character, character that reflects something of the wisdom and *righteousness of God.

The book of Job has comparatively little to say on the subject of discipline, but what it does say is significant. It prefers the verb *yākah* to *yāsar*. In 6:25–26 Job protests to his friends: 'But your reproof, what does it reprove? Do you think that you can reprove words?' (NRSV). However, God reminds him that his own words to God have been unwise, to say the least. '"Will the one who *contends* (*yissôr*) with the Almighty correct him?"' (40:2). Yahweh may correct humans, but they must not presume to correct him, hence Job's confession (42:3).

In the prophets

In Hosea God threatens drastic discipline against his unrepentant people. He will bring them down like netted birds and discipline them (7:12, NRSV), for they are incorrigibly wayward (10:10).

Jeremiah charges Judah with repeatedly refusing Yahweh's correction. As the judgment of *exile looms over the nation, all hope that there will be a positive response to correction has vanished. The uniform lament is that the people have refused correction (5:3; 7:28; 17:23; 32:33). There is no possibility that judgment can be avoided through genuine *repentance. The axe is about to fall.

In the Psalms

Here the emphasis falls on the disciplining of the individual believer, although it is recognized that Yahweh also disciplines the nations (94:10). Prayer is made that discipline should be unnecessary (6:1; 38:1); yet God's discipline is seen as a *blessing (94:12), even though it may be severe (118:18).

Discipline in the NT

The NT follows the OT in giving prominence to corporate discipline, but this is now *church* discipline, not the discipline of the people of Israel (Matt. 18:15–17; 1 Cor. 5:1–5). Individual self-discipline certainly receives greater emphasis, for it is demanded of all disciples of

Jesus, who are called to deny themselves, take up the cross and follow him (Matt. 16:24).

Self-discipline

Various images are used to express the idea of self-discipline. The Christian is an athlete in strict training (2 Tim. 2:5) and a soldier who endures hardship (v. 3). The body is to be kept under strict control (1 Cor. 9:27), for there are fleshly (*sarkikos*) desires which war against the soul (1 Pet. 2:11). From these the believer must abstain and flee (2 Tim. 2:22). Day by day Christians are to put off their pre-conversion way of life and put on the new self (Eph. 4:22–24).

Self-discipline is the Spirit-enabled discipline of those who know that their bodies are temples of the Holy Spirit (1 Cor. 6:19). It covers attitudes (Phil. 2:5) and speech (Eph. 4:25, 29) as well as desires.

The discipline of suffering

The letter to the *Hebrews sees suffering as God's discipline for his children (12:5–11) Even God's Son was not exempt from such suffering, for he learned obedience through what he suffered (5:8). 'As the incarnate Son ... it was absolutely necessary for him to learn obedience, since his obedience was essential for the offsetting of our disobedience' (P. E. Hughes, *A Commentary on the Epistle to the Hebrews*, p. 187).

Those who are united to Christ by faith must expect to experience the discipline (*paideia*) of suffering. When they do, they are not to lose heart (12:3), but to take heart (v. 5), for 'the Lord disciplines those whom he loves' (v. 6). The discipline of suffering flows from the love of God, is proof that we are his children (vv. 8–10), and is 'for our good, that we may share in his holiness'. To view suffering for the sake of Christ as evidence of God's fatherly work of perfecting us is a needed corrective to the all too common idea that our happiness, *as defined by us*, is his chief concern. God would have us holy rather than happy.

Disciplinary suffering may be painful but it has a blessed outcome: 'it produces a harvest of righteousness and *peace for those who have been trained by it' (v. 11).

Church discipline

The community of faith exercises discipline over its members. They are members one of another, fellow members of the body of Christ (Eph. 4:25). This body is to be marked by unity (Eph. 4:3), 'orthodoxy' ('one faith', v. 5) and purity. When believers refuse to be reconciled they deny the unity of the church and thus become subject to discipline by the assembly (Matt. 18:17). When the truth of the gospel is denied church discipline is to be exercised (2 John 7–11; *cf.* 1 Tim. 1:20). When there is open and scandalous *sin it cannot be tolerated; severe action must be taken (1 Cor. 5:1–5) but always with a view to bringing about repentance.

Excommunication is the end of the disciplinary process, not its beginning, and is to be imposed only reluctantly. Galatians 6:1–5 suggests that the first step in the disciplining of an erring brother or sister is personal, private and gentle.

In Revelation God threatens to discipline an entire church very severely (Rev. 3:16), yet even when he is about to do so he calls for repentance (v. 19), reminding its members that 'those whom I love I rebuke and discipline'.

Bibliography

D. L. Christensen, *Deuteronomy 1 – 11*, WBC (Dallas, 1991); P. C. Craigie, *The Book of Deuteronomy*, NICOT (Grand Rapids, 1978); P. E. Hughes, *A Commentary on the Epistle to the Hebrews* (Grand Rapids, 1977); K. J. Muller, *The Concept of Discipline in the Book of Proverbs* (ThM thesis, Dallas Theological Seminary, 1973); C. J. H. Wright, *Deuteronomy*, NIBC (Peabody and Carlisle, 1996).

D. P. KINGDON

ECCLESIASTES, see Part 2
EDEN, GARDEN OF, see TEMPLE

ELECTION

Election in the OT

The election of *Abraham must be integrated with the storyline of the scriptures. *God's promise that victory would come through the *seed of Eve (Gen 3:15) reveals God's intention to bring about *salvation. The seed of the serpent appears to triumph in the subsequent chapters of Genesis, for Cain slays Abel, only Noah and his family survive the flood, and human civilization descends into the idolatry of trying to make a name for itself (Gen. 11:4). God intervenes to save, however, by calling and choosing Abraham.

Some statements in the scriptures could be interpreted to say that God chose the fathers by virtue of their merits (Deut. 7:8; Rom. 11:28). Such a view is a bad misreading of the biblical evidence. Joshua says that Abraham and his family were idolators (Josh. 24:2), and Abraham's new life is attributed to the work of God, 'I took your father Abraham from beyond the River' (Josh. 24:3, NRSV). The narrative in Genesis (chs. 12 – 25) confirms the words of Joshua, for Abraham – though sometimes faltering – learns to trust God by believing that God is working on his behalf. The call of Abraham, of course, is not merely individual. God promises Abraham *land, seed, and universal *blessing (Gen. 12:1–3), and these promises are confirmed to Isaac and *Jacob (Gen. 26:3–4; 28:13–15; 35:11–12). By choosing Abraham God is choosing a people whom he would save and through whom he would bring salvation to all peoples (Gen. 12:3).

Since God elected a people in choosing the patriarchs, we often read that Yahweh has chosen *Israel to be his own (e.g. Ps. 33:12; 135:4). Isaiah, in particular, speaks of Israel as God's elect (eklektos in LXX, cf. Is. 42:1; 43:20; 45:4; 65:9, 22; cf. 1 Chr. 16:13; Pss. 105:6, 43; 106:23) whom God has chosen (eklegomai in LXX; cf. Isa 41:8–9; 43:10; 44:1–2; 49:7). The election of Israel as God's special people (perousios in LXX; cf. Exod. 19:5; Deut. 7:6; 14:2; 26:18) is attributed to Yahweh's *love (Deut. 4:37; 7:7–8; 10:15). God's love for Israel preceded his choosing them. Indeed, his love is the reason he chose Israel to be his own. God did not choose Israel because Israel loved him; he chose Israel because it was his good pleasure to do so. Israel was the servant by whom Yahweh would fulfil his promise to bless all *nations. The OT also often speaks of God's electing people to an office or a ministry. Yahweh chose Aaron (Num. 16:5, 7; Ps. 105:26), the Levitical *priests (Deut. 18:5; 1 Chr. 15:2), *David as king (1 Sam. 16:8–12; 1 Kgs. 11:34; Pss. 78:70; 89:4, 19), Solomon to build the temple (1 Chr. 28:10), Jeremiah (Jer. 1:5) and Isaiah (Is. 6:1–13) as *prophets, etc.

Even though Israel was God's elect nation, not everyone in Israel genuinely belonged to the *people of God. Both the northern (722 BC) and the southern (586 BC) kingdoms were exiled because of their sin. The prophets often emphasize that only a *remnant of the nation is truly God's people (cf. Is. 10:20–22; 46:3; Jer. 31:7; Mic. 2:12; Zeph. 3:13). The Elijah narrative (1 Kgs. 17:1 – 2 Kgs. 2:14) reveals that only a small remnant of Israel remained faithful to Yahweh during the days of Elijah's prophetic ministry. Only those with circumcised hearts truly belonged to Yahweh (Deut. 30:6; Jer. 4:4). Physical *circumcision alone was no guarantee of Yahweh's blessing.

Election in the NT

Israel fulfilled their role as God's elected servant and son poorly in the OT period. They regularly disobeyed Yahweh, and both the northern and southern kingdom were sent into exile for their sins. Yahweh extends his mercy to his people and brings them back from Babylon. But at the beginning of the NT period, the promises of salvation given to Israel had not yet been fulfilled. The gospels emphasize, however, that *Jesus of Nazareth is the man whom God has chosen as his Messiah. He is the true son of Abraham and the true son of David (Matt. 1:1), the fulfilment of the promises made to Abraham and David. Israel in the OT is the son of God's favour (Exod. 4:22) and God's servant (e.g. Is. 41:8–9; 42:1, 19; 43:10; 44:1–2, 21; 45:4). The gospels teach that Jesus is God's servant and son (Mark 1:9–11 par.; cf. Matt. 12:18–21). Jesus is the true Israel, succeeding where Israel failed. Jesus is the son liberated from Egypt (Matt. 2:15). He is the one who resists the temptations of Satan in the wilderness (Matt. 4:1–11 par.). When Jesus chooses the Twelve, therefore, he reconstitutes Israel (Mark 3:13–19 par.). Those who belong to his community are part of the true Israel. Membership of the people of God does not belong to those who are part of the twelve tribes of Israel but to those who believe in Jesus the Messiah and are part of the community of the twelve chosen apostles. Jesus is the elected cornerstone of God's new building (1 Pet. 2:4, 6).

This idea that the *church is God's new people is confirmed by Paul. He speaks of the church as elect (Rom. 8:33; Col. 3:12; 2 Tim. 2:10; Titus 1:1), called (e.g. Rom. 1:6–7; 8:28, 30; 9:7, 12, 24–26; 1 Cor. 1:2, 9, 24;

Gal. 1:6; 5:8; 1 Thess. 5:24; 2 Thess. 2:14; 1 Tim. 6:12; 2 Tim. 1:9), chosen (1 Cor. 1:27–28; Eph. 1:4) and beloved (Rom. 1:7; 9:25; Col. 3:12; 1 Thess. 1:4; 2 Thess. 2:13). Designations which belonged to Israel are now applied to the church of Christ. Those who belong to Christ are saints (*e.g.* Rom. 1:7; 1 Cor. 1:2; 2 Cor. 1:1; Eph. 1:1), beloved, children of Abraham (Gal. 3:7, 29; Rom. 4:11–12, 16–17), the true circumcision (Rom. 2:28–29; Phil. 3:3; Col. 2:11–12), and the Israel of God (Gal. 6:16). Peter speaks in a similar way, claiming that believers in Christ are God's elect race, royal priesthood, holy nation, and special possession (1 Pet. 2:9–10). In Revelation the one hundred and forty-four thousand from the 'twelve tribes' probably designates the worldwide people of God from every cultural-linguistic group (Rev. 7:1–8; *cf.* Rev. 14:1–5). The promise of universal blessing which was first made to Abraham is fulfilled in the church of Jesus Christ, which is comprised of the elect from every nation.

A theology of election

The nature of election is the subject of a longstanding debate. Some have understood the scriptures to teach that God has chosen a people, *i.e.* the church of Christ, for salvation, but has not chosen individuals. Similarly, it has been suggested that God has chosen Christ to be the means by which people are saved (Eph. 1:4), but has not determined which individuals will actually be incorporated into Christ.

Such a view rightly acknowledges that God is calling out a people for himself, and correctly emphasizes that the elect are chosen in Christ. None the less, the attempt to separate corporate from individual election is unsuccessful. John focuses on the individual in his teaching that any and all who are drawn by the Father will come to the Son (John 6:37; *cf.* John 17:2, 6, 9). Conversely, individuals cannot come to or believe in (*cf.* John 6:35) Jesus unless God grants them the ability to do so (John 6:44, 65). Such texts cannot be adequately explained if corporate election is separated from the election of individuals. Moreover, God's electing work begets *faith in his people. John 10:26 says, '[Y]ou do not believe because you do not belong to my sheep.' It is tempting to reverse the syntax, to make the verse say that one is

not Jesus' sheep because one does not believe. The text, however, says just the opposite, conveying the idea that being chosen as one of the sheep is the means by which God's people come to believe. Luke articulates the same theology when he says that all those in Pisidian Antioch who were ordained to eternal life believed (Acts 13:48; *cf.* Matt. 11:25–27). The syntax of the verse clearly indicates that God's ordaining work precedes, enables, and secures human belief. In Ephesians 2:8–9, Paul says that the salvation event 'is the gift of God'; this event includes the whole saving process of *grace, faith and salvation. Scholars, of course, continue to dispute this reading, but Romans 8:30 seems to confirm that faith is a gift. Here Paul contemplates God's saving work from beginning to end, affirming that those whom God has foreknown he will also glorify. The list of God's saving works includes the statement, 'those whom he called he also justified'. It is immediately evident that the word 'called' (*kaleō*) cannot possibly be translated as 'invited to believe in Christ'. Otherwise, the verse would say that all those who are summoned to believe in Christ are justified (see *Righteousness, justice and justification). Paul does not believe this, for he often insists that justification is only by faith (*e.g.* Rom. 5:1), and not all people believe in Christ. In Paul the word 'called' refers to God's effective call, which produces or begets faith in those to whom it is addressed. All who are called are justified, since the calling is performative, bringing people into a saving relationship with God. If this is so, then the calling must produce faith and be limited in scope. All those who are called are justified because God's effective call begets faith in them, and by virtue of their faith they are justified. James also identifies faith as God's gift, teaching that God has chosen the *poor to be rich in faith (Jas. 2:5).

That God's call is effective is confirmed by 1 Corinthians 1. The *gospel is preached indiscriminately to both Jews and Greeks (1 Cor. 1:23), but only those called among Jews and Greeks embrace it as the wisdom and power of God (1 Cor. 1:9, 24). Paul then describes the 'calling' of the Corinthians (1 Cor. 1:26–31). Three times in 1 Corinthians 1:27–28 he explains 'calling' in terms of God's choosing (*eklegomai*) the Corinthians, indicating that the call is a powerful work of grace which inducts believers into the kingdom and confers faith in Jesus Christ.

In 1 Corinthians 1:30 Paul refers to believers' induction into Christ. Some understand Ephesians 1:4 to say that God chose Christ, and that those believers who choose to be part of Christ are thereby 'elect'. Such a reading ignores the syntax of Ephesians 1:4, for the text does not actually say that God chose Christ, but that he chose 'us' to be 'in Christ'. The reading also seems to ignore 1 Corinthians 1:30, which clearly teaches that believers are in Christ because of God's work (*ex autou*, 'of him'). No room is left for the idea that believers themselves are ultimately responsible for their faith. Paul, of course, does not teach election to provoke intellectual debates. In both Ephesians 1:3–14 and 1 Corinthians 1:26–31 he emphasizes that God elects his people in order to bring glory, praise, and honour to his name. God's election is 'to the praise of his glory' (Eph. 1:6, 12, 14). He chose some and not others so that no one would boast in human beings (1 Cor. 1:29) and so that we would boast only in the Lord (1 Cor. 1:31).

Probably the most controversial text on election is Romans 9 – 11 (especially Romans 9). In these chapters, Paul emphasizes God's saving plan in history, affirming that God is faithful to his word (Rom. 9:6). A strong view of divine sovereignty is found throughout chapter 9. Some have said that the text refers only to corporate and not to individual salvation, but this distinction is not made elsewhere in the NT (see above). In addition, the separation of individual and corporate election is illogical, for all groups are comprised of individuals. Others suggest that chapter 9 relates to the historical destiny of Israel, Ishmael, Esau, Jacob and Pharaoh, and thus they conclude that Paul's discussion is not about salvation at all. Such arguments are unconvincing. Paul is indeed concerned about the historical destiny of Israel, but that destiny is inextricably intertwined with salvation. Paul's deep grief and willingness to suffer for Israel is precisely because the nation is unsaved (Rom. 9:3; 10:1) in contrast to the Gentiles (Rom. 8:28–39). It is this which precipitates Paul's discussion in the first place, and he does not leave the issue of salvation behind in Romans 9:6–23. Indeed, in Romans 9 he uses soteriological terms: 'Abraham's children' (Rom. 9:7); 'children of God' (9:8);

'children of the promise' (9:8); 'election' (9:11); the contrast between 'works' and 'call' (9:12); 'loved' and 'hated' (9:13); 'mercy' (9:15–16, 18); 'special use' and 'ordinary use' (9:21); and 'objects of wrath' and 'objects of mercy' (9:22–23). Thus historical destiny must not be divorced from salvation. In fact, chapters 9 – 11 have a single theme: God's promise relating to Israel's salvation, and the conclusion of the argument is that 'all Israel will be saved' (Rom. 11:26).

Romans 9, therefore (*cf.* Rom. 11:1–10), emphasizes God's sovereignty in salvation. He will surely accomplish what he has ordained. Since he chooses people by virtue of his own good pleasure and from his *mercy, not on the basis of foreseen works or foreseen faith, his promises will certainly be fulfilled. Those who are dead in trespasses and sins have no ability or inclination to believe (Eph. 2:1–10), and thus the only means by which new life may be obtained is a powerful resurrection work of God.

The biblical teaching on election makes clear that salvation is God's work, that his purpose will be accomplished, and that his promise to bless all nations will be fulfilled. Of course, such teaching raises questions about human responsibility and divine justice. The scriptures do not provide a complete answer to such questions. They do, however, teach a form of compatibilism in which human responsibility is assumed, even though God has predestined everything which will occur. This tension between divine sovereignty and human responsibility is articulated in Acts 2:23 and 4:27–28. The death of Jesus was predestined before the foundation of the world, and yet the people who did the evil deed were held responsible for their motives and actions. Nowhere do the scriptures teach that if events are predestined, then those who do what is evil are free from responsibility. Rather, they present God as sovereign over all things, even the toss of the dice (Prov. 16:33), and the choices of human beings as real and significant; people are held responsible for their actions.

Bibliography

D. A. Carson, *Divine Sovereignty and Human Responsibility: Biblical Themes in Tension* (Atlanta, 1981); P. K. Jewett, *Election and Predestination* (Grand Rapids, 1985); W. W. Klein, *The New Chosen*

People: A Corporate View of Election (Grand Rapids, 1990); C. H. Pinnock, The Grace of God, the Will of Man: A Case for Arminianism (Grand Rapids, 1989); idem (ed.), Grace Unlimited (Minneapolis, 1975); J. Piper, The Justification of God: An Exegetical and Theological Study of Romans 9:1–23 (Grand Rapids, [2]1993); T. R. Schreiner and B. A. Ware (eds.), The Grace of God, the Bondage of the Will, 2 vols. (Grand Rapids, 1995); R. K. M. Wright, No Place for Sovereignty: What's Wrong with Free Will Theism (Downers Grove, 1996).

T. R. SCHREINER

ELIJAH

Introduction

In the Gospels, *Jesus is portrayed not only as Son of God and Messiah, but also as a sage with a *prophetic ministry. Many parallels are drawn between his ministry and those of Elijah and *Elisha. Jesus describes his predecessor John the Baptist as the second Elijah (Matt. 11:13–14; cf. Mark 9:11–13), and his own concern for widows and Gentiles (see *Nations) reflects that of Elijah and Elisha, whom he cites as models for his ministry (Luke 4:24–27). At the transfiguration of Jesus, Elijah appears next to *Moses, possibly representing the prophets alongside the representative of the law, or reflecting the expectation of Elijah's coming at the end of the age. Both Moses and Elijah were prophetic figures who suffered rejection and persecution, but were vindicated by God, and in this they prefigure Jesus's own fate. In 1–2 Kings, Elijah is portrayed as a single-minded and solitary figure, but there are indications that Elijah's own view of his role did not correspond exactly to God's view (cf. Rom. 11:2–4), and Jesus on at least one occasion refused to emulate Elijah (Luke 9:54–55; cf. 2 Kings 1:10, 12). What then are the characteristics of Elijah and his ministry?

The beginning and high point of Elijah's prophetic ministry

Elijah appears quite suddenly in 1 Kings 17, predicting a drought to Ahab. Remarkably, the initiative does not seem to have come from God, but from Elijah himself. Neither a prophetic call nor a divine oracle is recorded.

Instead, James concludes, 'Elijah was a human being like us, and he prayed fervently that it might not rain, and for three years and six months it did not rain on the earth' (Jas. 5:17, NRSV). However, Elijah's prayer is not arbitrary. The *covenant between the Lord and Israel challenged the people to expect the blessing of rain from the Lord and threatened the withholding of rain in the event of apostasy (e.g. Deut. 11:16–17). Elijah asks that this threat be carried out in response to the royally sanctioned worship of Baal, the Canaanite storm and fertility god (cf. 1 Kgs. 16:31–33).

Elijah is first recognized as a man of God by a widow in the heartland of Baal worship, but only after having brought back her son to life. Both the widow and Elijah refuse to acknowledge death as an independent force that could challenge Yahweh, but make Yahweh directly responsible for the death. This is in contrast to Canaanite religion in which Mot ('Death') is seen as a god to whom Baal succumbs from time to time. Like Jesus, Elijah demonstrates that God can use death (cf. John 11:4), and that his word is effective beyond the boundaries of Israel (cf. Mark 7:24–30; Matt. 15:21–28).

When Yahweh asks Elijah to present himself to Ahab and to announce the return of the rain (1 Kgs. 18:1), Elijah uses the opportunity to challenge Israel to repent of their Baal worship. He does this by means of a public confrontation on Mt Carmel with the Baal prophets. Pointedly, he erects a twelve-stone altar (for the twelve tribes of Israel) and prays to the covenant God, 'O LORD, God of Abraham, Isaac, and Israel' (1 Kgs. 18:36–37; cf. Jas. 5:18), reminding the people of their true identity as the covenant people of Yahweh (cf. Exod. 24:1–11). Elijah's prayer is answered and he is vindicated against the Baal prophets who are slaughtered (the Hebrew word in 1 Kgs. 18:40 is used elsewhere to refer to the slaughter of sacrificial animals) as a punishment for their apostasy (cf. Deut. 13:12–15). However, Elijah flees when he realizes that even after the events on Mt Carmel, Ahab is still in submission to his wife Jezebel rather than to Yahweh. For the first time since he announced the drought, Elijah acts not in response to a word from God, but on his own initiative.

The turning point of Elijah's prophetic ministry

Some of Elijah's actions parallel those of Moses (*e.g.* the encounter of Moses with Pharaoh's magicians). Like Moses, Elijah flees from enemies into the wilderness, but this time in a 'reversal' of salvation history. He journeys for forty days and forty nights (far longer than necessary) from Beersheba, at the border of the Promised Land, to Horeb, *i.e.* Mt Sinai, symbolizing Israel's forty years' journey in the wilderness. Yet when he arrives at a cave (Moses was in the cleft of a rock when he saw the glory of Yahweh passing by in Exod. 33:18–23), Yahweh asks him what he is doing there (1 Kgs. 19:9). Elijah claims to be the only faithful person left in Israel, and it seems that God will have to make the same offer to Elijah as he once did to Moses, namely to make a great nation of him (Exod. 32:10).

Elijah experiences the tangible signs of a *theophany: a strong wind; an earthquake; and fire (for the latter two at Sinai, see Exod. 19:18). These are also frequently associated with Baal. But this time Yahweh does not reveal himself by these means. Instead it is 'a sound of sheer silence' (1 Kgs. 19:12), either a barely audible sound or what we might call 'a pregnant silence', which entices Elijah out of the cave to meet Yahweh. Elijah does not experience another Sinai theophany for two reasons: firstly, because contrary to what he thinks, God has preserved a *remnant (*cf.* Rom. 11:2–4), and secondly, because the LORD is not merely a god of natural forces, but reveals himself also in history and through his word. The Sinai theophany served to legitimize Moses as a unique spokesman of Yahweh (*cf.* Deut. 34:10–12); later prophets were to be judged by their faithfulness to Mosaic teaching and by the fulfilment of their word (*cf.* Deut. 18:15–22), not by the signs that legitimized Moses.

Elijah is ordered to return and to anoint three successors: one for the King of Aram; one for the King of Israel and one for Elijah himself. This new order will bring the victory over Baal-worship. Baal will be defeated not through more spectacular demonstrations of divine power in the natural realm, but through a historical process. Elijah has to be content with being the one who began the fight against Baalism rather than one who

sees its completion. Elijah, however, apparently did not anoint any of the three people he was told to anoint (Elisha commissions both Hazael and Jehu, see 2 Kgs. 8:7–15; 9:1–13; differently Ecclus. 48:8). When Elisha becomes his servant (rather than his successor), one wonders whether Elijah has merely postponed the anointing or is not prepared to give way to a successor. In 1 Kings 20 Yahweh continues to reveal himself as the true God of Israel in a victory over the Aramean king Ben-Hadad ('Son of Hadad', the storm god) and announces Ahab's doom, yet he does both *without* Elijah. There are, however, another three occasions on which Elijah acts as God's spokesman.

The close of Elijah's prophetic ministry

The story of Naboth in 1 Kings 21 reveals the profound difference between Israelite covenant law (*cf.* Lev. 25:23; Deut. 27:17) and the principles of Canaanite kingship. By appropriating Naboth's land as crown property, Ahab acts more like a Canaanite than an Israelite king, and even instigates the judicial murder of Naboth, who refuses to violate the covenant. This time Elijah is asked to confront Ahab, which he promptly does with a message that seems even harsher than the word of Yahweh itself (*cf.* 1 Kgs. 21:19 with 20–24; see 1 Kgs. 22:37–39 and 2 Kgs. 9:30–37 for the fulfilment of these prophecies).

The last two recorded confrontations are with Ahaziah, the son of Ahab, and with Jehoram, Ahab's son-in-law, who introduces Ahab's apostasy into the southern kingdom. Ahaziah is condemned to death for inquiring of Baal-zebub ('Lord of Flies', probably a distortion of the original name intended to ridicule the Syrian deity) rather than of Yahweh. Elijah challenges the king's messengers to recognize him as a 'man of God' (rather than merely addressing him as such) by twice destroying fifty men with fire (2 Kgs. 1). Jehoram, in the southern kingdom, is condemned by letter (2 Chron. 21:12–15).

At the end of his prophetic career, Elijah moves in stages to Bethel, to Jericho and to the Jordan, each time trying to leave Elisha behind (2 Kgs. 2:2, 4, 6). Finally, he crosses the Jordan into the same region where Moses died, having re-enacted one of the most symbolic moments in Israel's history, the dividing of the Jordan (*cf.* Exod. 14:15–31). Even now, Elisha's persistence is tested; he has to ask for the 'double share' of Elijah's spirit that will confirm him as the legitimate successor (*cf.* Deut. 21:17). In the past Elijah has been confident that he knows the will of God, but he is strangely reticent about whether God will grant Elisha his request. Is this another sign of Elijah's reluctance to accept God's plan? In any case, Elisha witnesses Elijah's departure up to heaven in a whirlwind and proves by his subsequent actions that he is the true successor. To Elijah's mysterious translation to heaven corresponds an eschatological return: 'See, I will be sending you the prophet Elijah before the great and terrible day of Yahweh comes' (Mal. 4:5, author's translation). On that day, the people will repent, and Elijah will not need to pray for the enactment of the covenant curses. Rather, 'he will turn the hearts of fathers to their sons and the heart of sons to their fathers, so that I will not come and strike the land with a curse' (Mal. 4:6, author's translation).

The lasting significance of Elijah's prophetic ministry

In early Jewish tradition, Elijah is remembered especially for his zeal. His mysterious rapture (according to 1 Macc. 2:58 the reward for his great zeal for the law) signifies to many that he has a role to play in God's ultimate victory, and apocalyptic writings are attributed to him (see O. S. Wintermute, 'Elijah, Apocalypse of', *ABD* 2, pp. 466–469). This tradition may explain John the Baptist's refusal to be (directly) identified with Elijah (John 1:21, 25). He is 'Elijah' only in a figurative sense. An alternative explanation is that John had similar difficulties accepting his God-given role.

Elijah's name, which means 'Yahweh is (my) God', was his programme. His single-mindedness can inspire us to similar loyalty in the face of apostasy. We should, however, remember that Elijah was never as isolated or indispensable as he thought he was, and his zeal for God did not always bring him closer to God (the same was true for the apostle Paul who may have meditated on the Elijah narratives after his conversion; see N. T. Wright, 'Paul, Arabia, and Elijah [Galatians 1:17]', *JBL* 111, 1996, pp. 683–692). Like Moses, Elijah died outside the land before the work was completed. Their appearance at the transfiguration is perhaps meant to suggest that Jesus's death completes the work they began, although a witness similar to that of Moses and Elijah is still required in the struggles of the church (see Rev. 11, esp. vv. 5–6).

See also: JOHN THE BAPTIST.

Bibliography

J. R. Battenfield, 'YHWH's Refutation of the Baal myth through the actions of Elijah and Elisha', in A. Gileadi (ed.), *Israel's Apostasy and Restoration: Essays in Honor of Roland K. Harrison* (Grand Rapids, 1988); D. L. Bock, 'Elijah and Elisha', in *DJG*, pp. 203–206; A. J. Hauser and R. Gregory, *From Carmel to Horeb: Elijah in Crisis* (Sheffield, 1990); P. J. Kissling, *Reliable Characters in the Primary History: Profiles of Moses, Joshua, Elijah and Elisha* (Sheffield, 1996); I. W. Provan, *1 and 2 Kings*, NIBC (Peabody and Carlisle, 1995); J. T. Walsh, 'Elijah', *ABD* 2, pp. 463–466.

T. RENZ

ELISHA

The story of Elisha, along with that of his predecessor *Elijah, occupies the central section of 1–2 *Kings (1 Kgs. 17 – 2 Kgs. 13), in which is described a time of special *prophetic intervention in the life of Israel directed against widespread apostasy to the god Baal and his consort Asherah. The authors of Kings characterize Elijah's leadership role in this period as like that of Moses, and his successor Elisha's (unsurprisingly) as like that of *Joshua (*cf. e.g.* 2 Kgs. 2:1–18, where Elisha inherits Elijah's leadership in a scene partially reminiscent of Moses at the Sea of Reeds [Exod. 14:15–31] and of Joshua's crossing of the Jordan and entering the land of Israel near Jericho [Josh. 3]). Like Elijah, Elisha brought life in the midst of death (1 Kgs. 17:17–24; 2 Kgs. 4) and mediated *salvation even to foreigners (1 Kgs. 17:8–16; 2 Kgs. 5). Having asked of Elijah a *double* portion of his spirit, he went on to perform many more miracles than his predecessor did, especially for the benefit of the humble, who were generally more in touch with and open to what God was doing through his prophet than were the great. As a true prophet of God, however, he brought not only blessing, but also cursing (his first two prophetic actions were a blessing and a cursing; 2 Kgs. 2:19–25); not only salvation, but also *judgment (as his name implies: Elisha ['God saves'] son of Shaphat ['judgment']). Though he could function as a mediator of salvation to King Jehoram (2 Kgs. 5:7–8; 6:8 – 7:20), ultimately he was a mediator of judgment to the royal house (2 Kgs. 9:1–10). Thus the process which Elijah had initiated was, in God's own time, brought to completion, as the house of Ahab was destroyed and the war against Baal-worship was won. That for which Elijah had prepared the way was, in Elisha's time, made a reality.

Elisha is mentioned only once in the NT (Luke 4:27), where he functions typologically in relation to *Jesus. Jesus' mission embraces the Gentiles, as the mission of Elisha did: what Jesus does is analogous to what Elisha did when healing Naaman (2 Kgs. 5). Various implicit connections are made elsewhere in the Gospels. Jesus heals lepers, just like Elisha (2 Kgs. 5; Matt. 8:1–4; 10:8; 11:5; Mark 1:40–45; Luke 5:12–14; 7:22; 17:11–19; cf. also John 9:1–12 for a different kind of healing story reminiscent of the Naaman narrative). He transforms water (2 Kgs. 2:19–22; John 2:1–11) and suspends the laws of gravity in relation to it (2 Kgs. 6:1–7; Matt. 14:22–33; Mark 6:45–51; John 6:16–21). He raises the dead (2 Kgs. 4:18–37; Mark 5:21–24, 35–43; Luke 7:11–17; John 11:17–44) and multiplies food (2 Kgs. 4:1–7, 42–44; Matt. 14:13–21; 15:29–39; Mark 6:30–44; 8:1–10; Luke 9:10–17; John 6:1–14). He does all this mainly for the benefit of the humble, who are generally more receptive to God's salvation than are the great. He mediates salvation; but he also brings judgment. He utters prophetic curses (2 Kgs. 2:23–25 and Matt. 21:18–22; Mark 11:12–14, 20–21, noting also Matt. 25:41). He comes so that those who see will become blind, even as those who are blind receive their sight (2 Kgs. 6:8–23; John 9:35–41; 12:37–41). He inaugurates God's kingdom, in which everyone will experience divine justice (Matt. 13:36–43, etc.). Jesus is thus presented in the Gospels not only as the true son of David, but also as the supreme prophet, the one who truly mediates God's rule on earth.

Given that the names 'Joshua', 'Elisha', and 'Jesus' have the same basic meaning ('God saves'), that John the Baptist is so clearly identified in the Gospels with Elisha's predecessor Elijah (cf. e.g. Matt. 3:4; 11:1–19; 17:11–13; Mark 1:6; Luke 1:11–17), and the many links between Jesus and Elisha, it is intriguing that a more explicit connection between them is not made in the NT. The transition from the era of Elijah, when it was established (again reflecting the prophet's name) that 'the LORD is God' (1 Kgs. 18:39), to the era of salvation under Elisha, is suggestive of the transition from John the Baptist's era to that of Jesus. Yet both Joshua and Elisha were the successors of more famous men, and the early church was anxious to avoid the suggestion that Jesus was John's successor in any sense which detracted from his pre-eminence (cf. e.g. John 1:1–42 for evidence that this was a live issue in some quarters). It is not surprising, in such circumstances, that the typological significance of Elisha in relation to Jesus is downplayed in the NT.

There are few explicit references to Elisha in the NT as someone from whom Christian believers can learn. Hebrews 11:34–35 (and possibly v. 36, if the boys from Bethel in 2 Kgs. 2 are in mind) refers to him, and the early church certainly exercised faith of the kind described in Hebrews 11 in mediating both salvation and judgment in the manner of Elisha and Jesus (cf. Acts 5:1–11; 9:36–43). An interesting case of implicit typology appears in Luke 9:57–62 (cf. Matt. 8:18–22), with its allusion to 1 Kings 19:19–21. The point appears at first to be that disciples of Jesus must have a greater commitment to service in God's kingdom than Elisha had to his work. Yet the mention of the plough reminds us of Elisha's decisiveness in leaving his home (he burned the ploughing equipment, his previous means of sustenance), which in a sense demonstrates greater commitment than that of Jesus' first disciples (they 'left' only their nets, Mark 1:16–20, and were later to return to them, John 21:1–14). This is a good example of the way in which taking the OT seriously in its own terms can lead us to ask deeper questions about a particular NT passage, prompting us to relate it to others (e.g. Matt. 21:28–32; Luke 14:25–35). The biblical theologian must hear the distinctive voices of the biblical witnesses before moving to any synthesis of them and any application of the biblical message to the present.

Bibliography

R. D. Moore, *God Saves: Lessons from the Elisha Stories* (Sheffield, 1990); I. W. Provan, *1 and 2 Kings*, NIBC (Peabody and Carlisle, 1995); P. E. Satterthwaite, 'The Elisha narratives and the coherence of 2 Kings 2–8', *TynB* 49, 1998, pp. 1–28.

I. PROVAN

ENOCH

The theological significance of Enoch lies in: the meaning of his name; his walking with God and being taken by God, understood in their ancient Near Eastern context and in the light of the importance attached to them in Scripture and elsewhere; the similarities and differences between the genealogies in Genesis 4 and 5, with respect to the achievements of those listed and Enoch's position as seventh from Adam.

Enoch, the seventh in the line from Adam, is known as the one who walked with God (lit. 'the *'elōhîm*') and was taken by God such that he was no longer present on earth (Gen. 5:18–24). There are ancient Near Eastern parallels with Enoch and other persons named in the pre-flood genealogies of Genesis 4 and 5. These figures are described as sages whose wisdom is important for the development of civilization. In one account, a certain Utuabzu is even said to have been taken up to heaven by the gods. The name of Enoch comes from a Hebrew root meaning, 'to introduce, initiate'; he is introduced to the truths of God as he walks with him. Enoch is 365 years old when God takes him; he lives one year for every day in a solar year. Whether this is significant or not is a matter of dispute; it may mean that God took Enoch to be with himself in the fullness of time. In any case, Enoch is remembered for his wisdom and piety.

In the intertestamental period several books credited to Enoch appeared, which described in great detail various events from nesis 1 to 6, and which told of a tour by Enoch of heaven and hell. In the epistle of *Jude verses 14–15 this literature is quoted: Enoch prophesies the coming of God with his holy ones to render judgment and punishment. In Hebrews 11:5–6 Enoch is remembered as one of the heroes of faith who pleased God and was privileged to escape from death. He did this through his faith which enabled him to believe in the existence of God and in the reward which God gives to those who seek him. Both NT texts identify Enoch as a believer and God-fearer, in contrast to others of the pre-flood generation who did not believe in God so as to fear his judgment. This may be a reference to the sons of God and Nephilim of Genesis 6:1–7 whose conduct angered God so much that he brought about the flood.

In Genesis 4:17–24 another Enoch is born, the son of Cain. Cain builds a city (Gen. 4:17) and names it after Enoch (though some commentators suggest that it was named after Irad). The name 'Enoch' in Genesis 4 may thus be related to the Sumerian 'UNUG', the name of the city of Uruk. The Sumerians are one of the oldest civilizations on earth, and Uruk was thought to be one of their oldest cities. However, this Enoch, like others in the line of Cain, is not a warrior of faith but a hero of culture who benefits humanity with new discoveries. In contrast, the line of Seth (from which comes the Enoch who walked with God) is known for its godliness and spirituality rather than for its material discoveries. Thus Lamech prophesies concerning his son, Noah, that he will bring comfort after the curse the Lord has placed on the ground. Methuselah, the son of Enoch, lives 969 years, the longest life span of any mortal in the Bible; Enoch's son, like Enoch himself, is blessed by God.

The genealogical lines of Cain and Seth stand side by side for a purpose. The Sethite Enoch is the seventh in the line from Adam; the seventh in the Cainite line from Adam in Genesis 4:18–24 is Lamech. The names of Enoch and Lamech appear in both lines but theologically they represent completely different people. The Cainite Lamech is a murderer who brags that his violence surpasses that of his ancestor Cain, who slew his brother Abel. Lamech's song describes the brutality which issues in vengeance and death. In contrast, the Sethite Enoch gives life to his long-lived son Methuselah, and his piety and faithfulness lead him to the highest level of communion with God. Cain's line ends with Lamech's immediate family, while Seth's line through Enoch leads to Noah and the preservation of the human race (see *Seed).

Bibliography

R. Borger, 'Die Beschwörungsserie *Bit Meseri* und die Himmelfahrt Henochs', *JNES* 33, 1974, pp. 183–196; R. S. Hess, 'Enoch', in *ABD* 2, p. 508; idem, *Studies in the Personal Names of Genesis 1–11* (Kevelaer and Neukirchen-Vluyn, 1993); J. M. Sasson, 'A genealogical "convention" in biblical chronography?', *ZAW* 90, 1978, pp. 171–185; G. Wenham, *Genesis 1-15*, WBC (Waco, 1987).

R. S. HESS

EPHESIANS, see Part 2

ESCHATOLOGY

Definition

The word 'eschatology' is derived from the Greek *eschatos* = 'last'; hence, 'the doctrine of last things'. But this definition is too narrow. Biblical eschatology cannot be confined to those parts of Scripture addressing the post-mortem fate of individuals, nor understood simply in terms of the end of our time-space continuum.

The term has several connotations, but the idea of *telos* is common to them all. Biblical eschatology may be defined as 'the direction and goal of God's active covenant faithfulness in and for his created order' (K. E. Brower, 'Temple' in *The Reader Must Understand*, p. 119). This broader definition better fits the evidence. It is Trinitarian in shape, Christocentric in focus, *creation-affirming and future-orientated, describing the way *God's good purposes in history correspond to God's ultimate reality.

Eschatology is not an inevitable process, however. God is moving history forward: he gives it direction and purpose. This goal might be described as 'new creation' (see G. K. Beale, 'Conception' in *The Reader Must Understand*, pp. 11–52). Eschatology thus describes the outworking of God's sovereign rule against the backdrop of the fundamental questions of human existence – 'What is God doing about our predicament and what does the future hold?' Underlying these questions are two premises: that God's purposes are good and that he will bring them to fruition.

In fact, his purposes on earth are already being realized, and their manifestations reflect his character.

The covenant-making God

God is involved with his creation. The entire biblical narrative, from creation to consummation in Christ, shows the ways in which God's purposes intersect with history. There are, however, a number of nodal points.

Strictly speaking, eschatology does not feature in the creation narratives, but consummation cannot be understood apart from creation. The creation stories describe God's activity in bringing light and peace out of darkness and chaos. Life, reaching its zenith in the creation of *humankind, comes from God. The man was lovingly fashioned from the dust of the earth and given the 'breath of life' (Gen. 2:7). He was a being created in continuity with the rest of God's created order.

But humankind was also different. God is a being-in-communion, and humans were made in the image of God, created as male and female (Gen. 1:27). Humans were created to live in community and to exercise stewardship over God's creation, mirroring the care of God himself (Gen. 1:29–30; 2:15; *cf.* Ps. 8:3–8; Heb. 2:6–9). In this harmonious relationship, creation was pronounced 'very good' (Gen. 1:31). In contrast, isolation was 'not good' (Gen. 2:18). Most important was the loving fellowship between the Creator God and humans, the climax of his creation, in Eden. Clearly, creation reflects God's good purposes.

Disruption soon followed. Tempted by the serpent who, in this narrative, symbolizes the cosmic opposition to God which is later focused in the Satan or devil, humans refused to accept their creatureliness, putting themselves on the slippery slope to destruction. The consequences were catastrophic. All relationships were distorted (Gen. 3:14–19). Suspicion and estrangement entered into relations between the man and the woman; fratricide soon followed. Existence itself became fraught with pain and sorrow. Humans are pictured as wresting sustenance from a recalcitrant creation. Most importantly, the relationship between God and humankind was seriously attenuated. Whereas at the beginning, the human couple walked and talked with God, now they hid from God because they were afraid (Gen. 3:8–10). Humans were expelled from the Garden, away from the tree of life, and death became their enemy. *Evil was unleashed in creation.

Despite the *judgment that followed, God's good purposes had not been exhausted. Even at the point of disaster, God provided for and protected his creatures (Gen. 3:21, 24). Indeed, the narrator already hints at God's ultimate triumph over evil (Gen. 3:15). But this was not immediate. Although there were signs of God's grace at work, evil flourished. Humanity fumbled in the darkness to reach God. As people slipped ever further into the mire of rebellion, chaos returned, and creation was overwhelmed by the flood (Gen. 6).

Judgment was not God's final word, however. Noah and those with him became the building blocks of a new society. God established a *covenant with Noah in which he promised never again to return creation to a watery chaos (Gen. 8:21; 9:11–17). But human nature remained corrupt after the flood. Consequently 'God created a corporate Adam, Israel, who was to be obedient to God in the promised land' (Beale, in *Reader*, p. 26).

The beginning of God's eschatological purposes centred in Abraham. He was called to leave his ancestral homeland and go to a new land. God promised Abraham that he would give him a land, and would make him a great nation and a blessing to the whole world (Gen. 12:1–3). God covenanted himself to Abraham (Gen. 15); Abraham was called to walk blamelessly before God (Gen. 17:1). Abraham became the progenitor of the *people of God through whom God would rescue creation.

When Abraham's children found themselves enslaved in Egypt, Yahweh rescued them. Through this deliverance, *Israel came to understand itself as the chosen people by the gracious provision of God. Their election was purposeful. They were to be a kingdom of priests and a holy nation (Exod. 19:3–6), on God's mission and modelling his holiness amongst the nations. God himself would dwell in their midst, but community purity and holiness were prerequisites of this. God's gracious gift of Torah provided the means whereby he might safely dwell with them and they might fulfil his mission (see G. J. Thomas, 'Holy God' in *Reader,* pp. 53–69).

The reign of David was Israel's golden era.

To him was promised a dynasty (2 Sam. 7:14–16). But kingship itself was a mixed blessing. On the one hand, the choice of a king was a rejection of theocracy (1 Sam. 8:7–9). On the other, David's kingship led to an idealized hope for a new scion who would reign in righteousness.

The subsequent story of Israel was riddled with failure. Separation from the nations became an end in itself, and the idea of election for service gave way to a sense of superiority. Though Israel suffered, the people were confident that God would vindicate them on 'the Day of the Lord'. After all, they were his elect and Zion was inviolate because it was God's dwelling (Jer. 7:4, 8–11). But Amos warned them that the 'Day of the Lord' was a day of judgment on their disobedience, a day of darkness and not light (Amos 5:18–20; see also Joel 1:15; 2:1–2; Zeph. 1:14–15). They could not live disobedient lives with impunity (Amos 5:21–24; Mic. 6:6–8).

Time and again the people were warned that doom was pending unless they repented. But they refused, and punishment inevitably followed (Jer. 7:12–15). First, Israel disappeared into oblivion, and although Judah enjoyed a brief revival, by the mid 6th century Jerusalem was razed, the temple destroyed and the people exiled. The future looked bleak indeed.

Biblical eschatology reached a new stage in these desperate conditions. In the midst of exile, *hope was reborn (see esp. Is. 40 – 66). God would act to restore the throne of David. The people would return in triumph (Is. 41); Jerusalem and the temple would be rebuilt and God would dwell again in their midst (Is. 60). God would do all this, either rescuing his people himself (Ezek. 34:12–16) or through his anointed one who would again sit on David's throne, administering justice to the nations and bringing peace (Is. 9:6–7; 11:1–10).

Central to Israel's hopes was the promise of a new covenant. This covenant would be written on the hearts of the people (Jer. 31:33). They would be given a new heart and God would put his Spirit within them (Ezek. 36:26–28; 37:13–14). Indeed, in the last days, the Spirit would be poured out on all flesh (Joel 2:28–29). The nations would come flocking to Zion, the city of God (Is. 61:5–6). God would create a new heaven and a new earth (Is. 65:17–18; 66:22) and all would come to worship him (Is. 66:23; see Mic. 4:2–4). God would make all things new, an event described in terms of the idyllic beginning in Eden.

In reality, the return and restoration were rather less glorious. Apart from a brief period after the Maccabaean revolt, Judah was not even moderately powerful. But this did nothing to dampen hopes. A 'transcendental eschatology, which expects a direct and universal act of God, beyond the possibilities of ordinary history' (R. Bauckham, in *NBD*, p. 333) became one response to these disappointing circumstances in which 'the present state of affairs had not yet (to put it mildly) seen the full realization of the purposes of the covenant god for his people' (N. T. Wright, *The New Testament and the People of God*, p. 149). The unshakeable conviction that God would act for his people prevailed.

Jesus and the eschatological Spirit

Into this context of hope and uncertainty came *Jesus of Nazareth. Clearly the NT writers saw his coming as the fulfilment of OT eschatological hopes. 'His incarnation is *the* eschatological nodal point' (Brower, in *Reader*, p. 142). Biblical eschatology begins and ends with Christ because all God's purposes are focused in him. The 'last days' have arrived in Christ's coming (Heb. 1:1–4; Rev 22:13).

Matthew's birth narrative is instructive: Jesus is born of the virgin and is called Emmanuel; his birth is in Bethlehem; the nations, represented by the Magi, come to worship him; the infanticide by Herod raises weeping in Ramah; Jesus and his parents escape to Egypt from where Jesus returns to Nazareth. Matthew links each point to the OT by citation or allusion. He also demonstrates Jesus' lineage from Abraham through David. For Matthew, the OT promises of the son of Abraham and son of David through whom God will effect his rescue are fulfilled in Jesus.

Luke links the titles 'Son of David' and 'Holy One' in his birth narrative, while Mary's song and the song of the angels speak of *salvation and peace on earth. Jesus' conception itself is a new creation through the *Holy Spirit, with echoes of Genesis (Luke 1:35; *cf.* Gen. 1:2). Luke traces Jesus' lineage to Adam (Luke 3:23–38). For John, Jesus

actually is the Word, who was God (John 1:1–3) become flesh (John 1:14) and living in the midst of the people.

The Baptist precedes Jesus and fulfils the role of Elijah (Matt. 11:14). He proclaims a coming one who will purify Israel and exercise judgment (see Mal. 3:1–3). This 'restoration eschatology' (see E. P. Sanders, *Jesus and Judaism*), uses language taken from OT passages expressing the hope of restoration and applies it to Jesus (Mark 1:2–3). In John's Gospel, the Baptist proclaims another aspect of Jesus' role, that of taking away the *sins of the world (John 1:29), while the voice from heaven echoes the royal psalms and the Servant Songs (Mark 1:11). Jesus' obedience is immediately tested, and the Gospels hint that the issues at stake go well beyond Israel's national aspirations.

Jesus begins his ministry by proclaiming the arrival of the *kingdom of God (Mark 1:14–15). Jesus invites all Israel to join the restoration movement, but only a few respond. He calls twelve disciples, a highly evocative number and explicitly linked to Israel by Luke (Luke 22:30). They are to be with him and on his mission (Mark 3:14), representing the new beginning of the people of God, in continuity with the past but now the instrument of God's purpose in the age of fulfilment.

In Luke, Jesus explicitly identifies his ministry with that of the Isaianic Servant (Luke 4:18–19; *cf.* Is. 61:1–2). The Matthean Sermon on the Mount contains the words of Jesus Messiah set in the context of his deeds (Matt. 4:23 – 9:35). They call for 'a new way of being Israel' (see Wright, *Jesus and the Victory of God, passim*). Jesus' answer to the Baptist's question from prison (Luke 7:18–23) is a further indication that God is now accomplishing his good purposes through his anointed one (Is. 35:5–6). Jesus' exorcisms not only confirm his identity (Mark 1:24) but also show the cosmic dimension of his struggle against evil, symbolically personified in the opposition of the devil (Matt. 4:1–11). The accounts of the nature miracles echo OT teaching on the authority of God; those of the feedings, the record of God's care for his people inside and outside Israel (Mark 6:30–44; 8:1–9). In John, Jesus is the Good Shepherd, who knows and is known by his sheep and lays down his life for them (John 10:11–15).

The Gospels are clear that Jesus' *redemptive death was the expected outcome of his ministry. As the perfectly obedient Son, in Gethsemane Jesus accepts the will of his Father. At Passover, during the final meal with the Twelve, Jesus symbolically constitutes the new covenant community in his blood (Mark 14:24). They are the beginning of the new people of God. Matthew makes the restoration motif explicit with his added words 'for the forgiveness of sins' (Matt. 26:28). (See *Atonement.)

Jesus was opposed primarily by the religious establishment. On the historical level, Jesus' vision of God's restoration of Israel was either misunderstood by, or incompatible with, those of the temple establishment. This was to have dire historical consequences, clearly seen in Jesus' apocalyptic teaching when it is read in the context of Second Temple Judaism (Mark 13). Unless Israel repented, it would ultimately be destroyed, and 'not one stone upon another' would remain of the temple. According to the Evangelists, Jesus' crucifixion set in motion a chain of events leading inexorably to AD 70. But the fall of Jerusalem could scarcely be seen as the conclusion of God's good purposes.

At another level, judgment is executed at the cross. Darkness at noon symbolized the darkness of 'the Day of the Lord' over the entire world, and the cry of dereliction demonstrated Jesus' full identification with human estrangement from God (Mark 15:33–34). The conflict with the temple establishment 'brought God's judgment on the very heart of the temple system through the death of the messiah, the Son of God. This judgment also carried with it the conviction that God's purposes for the temple would be realized through Jesus and His new covenant community' (Brower, in *Reader*, p. 143). The temple veil was rent; from that moment on the dwelling place of God amongst his people was Jesus and the new community. Matthew again makes this explicit by adding 27:51–53 'to signal to his readers that Christ's death was the beginning of the end of the old creation and the inauguration of a new creation' (Beale, in *Reader*, p. 19).

Had the cross been God's final action, there would be no future hope; the resurrection is the key to God's purposes. In Second Temple Judaism, belief in resurrection was linked, not merely to personal survival beyond death, but rather to the good purposes of God in restoring his creatures to their proper destiny. (See Wright, *New Testament*, pp. 267–268.) 'So the unexpected resurrection of the one man Jesus ahead of all others determined the church's conviction that the End had already begun' (Bauckham, in *NBD*, p. 334). In the resurrection the whole story from creation onwards has reached its climax. Jesus came announcing, effecting and embodying the kingdom of God. The last days are here and the day of deliverance is at hand. Jesus is actually 'God with us' in his saving power. 'He is the embodiment of God's eschatological purposes, promised by the prophets and realized in the new covenant community with the promised in-the-heart Torah' (Brower, in *Reader*, p. 143).

Among the NT writers Paul gives the most sustained expression to the supreme significance of Christ's resurrection (1 Cor. 15). The resurrection confirms that Jesus is God's final solution to the plight of humanity. Through Christ death has suffered its first and decisive reversal, and in Christ the eschatological future of humanity has already been realized. Christ is the paradigmatic new creation and those who are in Christ are also new creatures (2 Cor. 5:17). The coming of Christ marks the decisive turn of the ages; the age to come has already dawned and is being experienced in the midst of this present age. In Christ all God's promises find their fulfilment.

Paul is also very clear that the resurrection of Christ is but the first fruits (1 Cor. 15:20). Humanity awaits the resurrection, 'the redemption of our bodies' (Rom. 8:23). Likewise, creation itself awaits the final re-creation which will be the culmination of God's good purposes (Rom. 8:19–21). In the meantime, a proper understanding of God's love for his created order, experienced through his love poured out in the hearts of his people, inevitably leads to their sharing his love for the created order and to the renewal of the stewardship given to them in creation.

The Christian hope: the presence of the kingdom

The NT writers believe that the kingdom is a present reality. Before Jesus ascended to his Father, he promised to send the Spirit. The same Spirit who had been with Jesus would now be poured out on all flesh, again in fulfilment of OT promises and as a public confirmation that the 'last days' had arrived (Acts 2:16–17). The outpouring of the Spirit upon the gathered community both prepares and empowers them for mission. In the power of the Spirit, Jesus' followers bear witness to him, continuing his mission, engaging in conflict with the powers of this present age (Eph. 6:12–13) and hastening the day when God's good purposes will finally be accomplished (2 Pet. 3:11–13). They advance God's purposes in the world through the abiding presence of Christ in their midst (Matt. 28:16–20). Through the presence of the Spirit indwelling believers, the power of the age to come impinges upon the present. Those who are 'born from above' are new creatures in Christ. They live as part of the new people of God, called to be a kingdom of priests and a holy nation (1 Pet. 1:15; 2:9), on God's mission as agents of his reconciliation (2 Cor. 5:18–21) and, through the power of the Spirit, modelling his holiness in their individual and corporate life (2 Cor. 6:14 – 7:1). The love of God poured out in their hearts through the Spirit (Rom. 5:5) creates in them the very unity present within the Holy Trinity (John 17). They are set free from the domination of sin (Rom. 6:5–14) and the sting of death has been drawn (Heb. 2:15; 1 Cor. 15:55). Life is lived in the power of the resurrection and the people of God experience freedom in Christ.

However, the people of God still live in mortal flesh; they are subject to weakness, decay and death, and open to temptation. They are still on a pilgrimage (Heb. 13:14). Even the manifestation of the Spirit's presence in their midst is but a foretaste of God's ultimate good purposes (1 Cor. 13:8–13; Eph. 1:13–14). They see clear evidence that the new creation is not yet fully formed. God's people still live in an environment which is under the hostile dominion of evil. They suffer for their witness to the truth, even to the point of martyrdom (Rev. 6:9–11; cf. Heb. 12:4).

Cosmic opposition to the kingdom is still manifest in a variety of personal and societal forms. 'Antichrist' is only 'one of many designations used for one or several human representatives of the devil or Satan who actively oppose the Messiah. For that reason the term "eschatological antagonist" is preferable ...' (D. E. Aune, *Revelation 6 – 16*, p.

752). Indeed, the NT writers believe that this opposition will become more virulent as the culmination of God's good purposes draws ever nearer. Evil will be personified in grotesque caricatures of the good, such that many 'antichrists' will arise before opposition is concentrated in one final otiose fling of 'Antichrist'. (See *Spiritual powers.)

The Christian hope: the consummation of the kingdom

The dynamic tension between the 'already' and the 'not yet' is integral to biblical eschatology: the kingdom is present and coming. The resurrection of the body, the defeat of death, the end of all opposition to God's reign, and the redemption of the whole created order in a new heaven and a new earth all await the consummation of God's good purposes.

The variety of images in the NT used to depict this consummation should warn against overly literal readings. Timetables or catalogues of 'end-time events' are unhelpful. Significantly, Jesus did not claim to know 'about the day or the hour' (Mark 13:32) and did not give a date for 'restoring the kingdom to Israel' (Acts 1:7), all of which was in the Father's hands. But neither did he limit his vision to Israel. Views which restrict Jesus' teaching to the historical events of AD 70 are too narrow. The evangelists pay such careful attention to the destruction of the temple because it is 'confirmation that God's good purposes are now centred in Jesus and the new people of God. These purposes are being accomplished and vindication of his people will also be accomplished: the End will be found in the climax of God's good purposes in Christ' (Brower, in *Reader*, p. 142).

The evangelists agree that Jesus expected the gospel to be proclaimed in all God's creation (Matt. 28:18–20; Mark 13:10; Luke 24:47 with Acts 1:8; John 20:21, 29). This proclamation would elicit increasing opposition, centred in human resistance but not confined to it. The cosmic dimension of the struggle is portrayed in a vast array of imagery in Matthew 24 and parallels, 1 and 2 Thessalonians and particularly in the book of Revelation. There are references to war and violence, famine and persecution, suffering, tribulation and apostasy, portents in the heavens and catastrophes on earth.

Some students of Scripture have linked

these and other biblical images to particular events in *church or world history. But these prosaic interpretations of Jesus' teaching, Paul's rather restrained remarks and the book of Revelation should be resisted because they fail to take seriously the nature of apocalyptic imagery and the Second Temple context of Jesus' teaching. Rather, the message of this imagery is twofold. First, Christians of all ages, as agents of God's good news who live as his holy people, should expect opposition. But secondly, despite all evidence which might suggest that evil has triumphed (see especially Revelation), vindication is certain. In the face of such opposition, and maintaining their hope, the people of God are to remain alert (Mark 13:37; 1 Thess. 5:6).

There are some key elements in the future hope. First, Christ remains at the centre (Eph. 1:20–22). Whether in Paul's 'summing up all things in Christ', or in the evangelists' coming of 'the Son of Man with the holy angels and in the glory of the Father' (Mark 8:38), or in John's 'Alpha and Omega' (Rev. 22:13), Christ is the agent and embodiment of God's purposes. 'If Jesus was the centre of God's decisive eschatological act whereby He established His kingdom in the midst of history, then Jesus will also be the centre of God's final act' (G. B. Caird and L. D. Hurst, *New Testament Theology*, p. 256, n. 31). Jesus Messiah, who came first in weakness, poverty and humiliation, will come again in great power and glory, exercising universal authority and dominion, all to the glory of God (1 Thess. 4:16; Rom. 8:38–39; Phil. 2:10–11). This hope gave rise to the prayer of early Christians: 'Come, Lord Jesus' (Rev. 22:20).

Second, the end includes a final judgment. 'Justification is the foundation [of salvation], but what we build upon it is exposed to judgment' (Bauckham, in *NBD*, p. 338). All human activity is scrutinized to determine its alignment with God's purposes. This judgment was inaugurated in the coming of Christ and is already happening. The last judgment will confirm the verdict already reached. Those who are in Christ are freed from all condemnation (John 5:24; Rom. 8:1–3, 33–39). Those who are finally impenitent, who put themselves outside the ultimate purposes of God, have no part in God's future. Their fate is described in a variety of ways, but it is clear that their self-chosen destiny is not God's intended purpose for them. They suffer

the fate of those cosmic forces implacably opposed to God, 'the devil and his angels' (Matt. 25:41), being separated from the source of light and life (Rev. 20:15).

Third, biblical eschatology ends in the *victory of God in Christ (1 Cor. 15:28). The new heaven and new earth in which the holy God dwells in the midst of a holy people (Rev. 21 – 22) is the glorious hope of those who are in Christ. With this hope in view, the people of God face the present with confidence in God. They can 'perceive God's purpose in the present situation and the role that Christians are called to play in that purpose with a view to the coming of the kingdom' (Bauckham, *The Theology of the Book of Revelation*, p. 158). Those who suffer now, hope for the future described in Revelation 20:1–6 and often called 'the millennium'. 'John expects the martyrs to be vindicated, but the millennium depicts the meaning rather than the manner of their vindication' (Bauckham, *Theology*, p. 108).

Even if countless details of biblical eschatology are open to different interpretations, its central principle is clear enough: that God's good purposes for his created order are fulfilled in Christ, the perfect representative of redeemed humanity. 'As it is, we do not yet see everything in subjection to him, but we do see Jesus' (Heb. 2:8–9). Herein lies the Christian hope.

See also: DEATH AND RESURRECTION; HEAVEN AND HELL.

Bibliography

D. E. Aune, *Revelation 6 – 16*, WBC (Nashville, 1998); J. C. Beker, *The Triumph of God: The Essence of Paul's Thought* (ET, Edinburgh and Minneapolis, 1989, 1990); R. Bauckham, 'Eschatology' in *NBD*, pp. 333–338; idem, *The Theology of the Book of Revelation*, NTT (Cambridge, 1993); K. E. Brower and M. Elliott (eds.), *The Reader Must Understand: Eschatology in Bible and Theology* (Leicester and Downers Grove, 1998); G. B. Caird and L. D. Hurst, *New Testament Theology* (Oxford, 1994); E. P. Sanders, *Jesus and Judaism* (London, 1985); N. T. Wright, *The New Testament and the People of God* (London, 1992); idem, *Jesus and the Victory of God* (London, 1996).

K. E. BROWER

ESTHER, see Part 2
ETERNAL LIFE, see HEAVEN
ETERNAL PUNISHMENT, see HELL
EVE, see ADAM AND EVE

EVIL

Introduction

Every language contains words for 'evil' – that which ought not to be. A distinction is sometimes made between physical/metaphysical evil (misfortune, woe) and moral evil (offence, wrong), and the Bible includes terms for both kinds. The Hebrew *ra'* occurs about 640 times, and 40 per cent of these cases refer to some calamity. There are many other words both for mishaps (*e.g. šô'â*, trouble, storm) and for moral fault or *sin. In NT Greek, the word *kakos* has a wide application: it is used to denote Lazarus' *poverty and sores (Luke 16:25), the harm caused by a venomous snake-bite (Acts 28:5), and the moral evil of which Jesus and Paul are innocent (Mark 15:14; Acts 23:9) and which issues from the human heart (Mark 7:21); the word and its cognates occur 121 times. The other common NT words for evil are *ponēros* and *ponēria* (derived from *ponos*, toil or pain, Col. 4:13; Rev. 16:10–11), which occur 85 times; these refer to physical evil, to the bad condition of the eye (Matt. 6:23) and to pain resulting from plague (Rev. 16:2), but more often to that which is wicked and worthless, the store from which men and women, being evil, draw the evil things they do and say (in Matt. 12:35 *ponēros* is used three times; *cf.* v. 34). In classical Greek, *ponēros* may have been the stronger term, suggesting hardened malignity (R. C. Trench, *Synonyms of the New Testament* [London, ⁸1876], pp. 304–305), but in the NT, while it is used more frequently than *kakos* to refer to moral evil, the latter is an equally strong word (*cf.* Mark 7:21 and the parallel Matt. 15:19).

Lexical studies are illuminating; however, the Bible's treatment of the theme is distinctive.

Biblical contrasts

The biblical view of evil is finely balanced between pessimism and optimism. Several intriguing contrasts may be noted.

Essential good and real evil

The Bible powerfully affirms the goodness of all that exists. The refrain in the prologue (Gen. 1), 'and *God saw that it was good', is heard seven times, with a concluding superlative (v. 31). Scripture contains countless songs of praise and (from the wisdom writers) commendations of cosmic orderliness, summed up in Paul's statement that 'Everything God created is good' (1 Tim. 4:4, NIV; *cf.* Titus 1:15a). Since in biblical monotheism only God and his *creatures exist, this means that everything is good.

At the same time, the Bible stands out among sacred texts for its preoccupation (some might say 'obsession') with evil. From Genesis 3 (the Fall) to Revelation 22 it repeatedly denounces human unrighteousness (see Rev. 22:11, 15, 18; *cf.* Mic. 3:8). Prophetic and apocalyptic discourse overflows with descriptions and predictions of calamities, bloodshed and destruction. People of God shudder at the pervasive nature of evil: 'The whole world is under the control of the evil one' (1 John 5:19); this age is 'the present evil age' (Gal. 1:4). The Lord's declaration 'that every inclination of the thoughts of [man's] heart was only evil (*raq ra'*) all the time' (Gen. 6:5) proves to be true in every generation (Ps. 14:1–3; Rom. 3:9–18; Matt. 12:34, 39). And at the centre of the biblical narrative is the horrendous instrument of torture invented by Rome for its slaves, the cross.

God both hates and causes evil

This second contrast is almost a formal contradiction. Evil, in biblical theology, is totally alien to God: his 'eyes are too pure to look on evil' (Hab. 1:13); he is perfectly upright (Deut. 32:4); he 'is light; in him there is no darkness at all' (1 John 1:5); 'God cannot be tempted by evil, nor does he tempt anyone' (Jas. 1:13). On the other hand, this God claims to 'form the light and create darkness', to 'bring prosperity and create disaster (*ra'*)' (Is. 45:7). Amos 3:3–8 denounces the shortsightedness of those who do not perceive the origin of devastating blows: 'When disaster (*ra'â*) comes to a city, has not the LORD caused it?' (v. 6). Isaiah ironically reminds diplomats that the Lord 'too is wise and can bring disaster (*ra'*)' (Is. 31:2). The King James Version translates Genesis 22:1 as

'God did tempt Abraham'. 2 Samuel 24:1 plainly states that the LORD 'incited David against [Israel], saying, "Go and take a census"', *i.e.* to commit a grievous sin, though 1 Chronicles 21:1 attributes that temptation to Satan. Ezekiel 14:9 says, 'If the prophet is enticed to utter a [false] prophecy, I the LORD have enticed that prophet.' Other passages make similar points.

Does Scripture contain conflicting theologies? The evidence rules out this facile solution. The very texts that portray God as the author of evil also declare his indignation against evil: 2 Samuel 24 depicts the plague that God sent as punishment for David's sin (and thus agrees with 1 Chr. 21); the second part of Ezekiel 14:9 emphasizes that God holds the enticed prophet liable to capital punishment. Biblical writers employ paradox to signify mystery.

The nature of evil

It is important to define evil. Two biblical insights are relevant here: 1. evil has no independent existence but is a perversion of what is good; 2. sin is the greatest of evils, the root of all evil.

Evil as perversion

If only God and his creatures exist, and they are good, it follows that evil has no independent existence. This view, taught by Origen and by Augustine after he broke from Manichaeism (in which evil is an eternal substance), is firmly grounded in Scripture. Several Hebrew terms relating to evil connote nothingness or vacuousness, *e.g.* the four words in Zechariah 10:2 translated 'deceit', 'lie', 'false' and 'vain' in NIV. The first of these, *āwen* (fraud, *vanity) was linked to *'ayin* ('there is not'), by Gesenius' etymology, and is paired with it in the parallel of Isaiah 41:24 and 29 (J. A. Motyer, *The Prophecy of Isaiah* [Leicester, 1993] p. 318). The gods of heathenism are *'elîlîm*, worthless nothings (Ps. 96:5), not *'ēlîm* nor *'elōhîm*. In Greek, the prefix *a-* is negative (*adikia, anomia, etc.*), as are the common symbols of evil: darkness; disease; destruction.

To view evil as the loss or absence of good yields no ground to minimizing theories. Evil is no optical illusion, no mere local imperfection that promotes universal harmony. Evil is real, drawing its reality from created things; it is the *perversion* and *corruption* of the good. This makes it more heinous than it would be if it had independent existence. B. Hebblethwaite expounds the meaning well: 'The monstrous and, in a sense, positive fact of a malicious and perverted human will is still not, in itself, a substance. It is the perversion of something inherently and in God's intention good, namely a human being' (in *Christ, Ethics and Tragedy*, p. 135). Biblical evidence supports this theory (by key words, metaphors and statements, *e.g.* in Eccles. 7:29; Deut. 32:5, 'a warped and crooked generation', echoed in Phil. 2:15).

This analysis of evil corresponds to the biblical account of its appearance in history. The Genesis narrative separates the origin of evil from the act of creation: evil entered the world later, as a 'foreign body' and parasite; it was not present in the beginning. Evil entered history in the abuse of created *freedom (cf. Matt. 19:8; Rom. 5:12).

Sin as radical evil

If evil is perversion, its original locus is the perversion of freedom: the primary evil is sin. Genesis 3 traces life's ills to *humankind's disobedience: shame and *fear (vv. 7, 10); pain in childbearing and the distortion of male–female relationships (v. 16, see *Adam and Eve, *Man and woman); the painful relationship between humans and the ground; and finally *death (vv. 17–19). Paul agrees that death entered the world through sin (Rom. 5:12; see C. E. B. Cranfield's essay 'Death understood as the consequence of sin', in his *The Epistle to the Romans* [Edinburgh, 1979], 2, pp. 844–845), and declares that everything has been made subject to frustration (*mataiotēs*, Rom. 8:20).

Scripture does not encourage speculation regarding the changes that followed the fall. Only human death is mentioned as a direct consequence. The curse on the ground resulted from human exploitation. Nowhere is there any hint of prodigious mutations among the animals, *e.g.* that only then were they given fangs and claws; on the contrary, God's creation order included the lions' seeking their food from God (Ps. 104:21; *cf.* Job 38:39–41; 39:27–30) and the terrifying features of the beasts of prey (Job 41). Original human powers, as long as they remained attuned to the Lord's will, were presumably sufficient to protect people from earthquakes or viruses.

Evil and divine government

Assertions that God is the cause of evil fall into two categories.

Evil as punishment

Some of the most frightening biblical calamities are attributed to God's judgment. Judgment itself is not evil, but a necessary expression of goodness. 'Penal evil' is evil only in a restricted sense, in comparison with the well-being and fulfilment of creatures as defined in creation. Since sin entered the world, justice demands punishment, which restores God's holy order and glorifies his holy name (Lev. 10:3; Ezek. 38:16); its infliction is good in itself and for the person involved. Even reprobates will acknowledge this at the last (H. A. G. Blocher, 'Everlasting punishment and the problem of evil', in N. M. de S. Cameron (ed.), *Universalism and the Doctrine of Hell* [Carlisle and Grand Rapids, 1992], pp. 281–312).

Evil as divine permission

One form of punishment is the giving over of a sinner to more vile sins (Rom. 1:21, 24, 26), *e.g.* in cases of '*hardening' (1 Sam. 2:25). However, this model does not fit all the biblical statements which make God the cause of moral evil. The intention of these statements is to magnify divine sovereignty (see *Providence) and rule out creaturely independence. Evil does not proceed from God but does depend on his decrees. Theologians speak of God's (sovereign) *permission*: when humans do what is evil, God is *not* at work in them to will and to act according to what is good (*cf.* Phil. 2:13). Thus, for example, God 'left' Hezekiah to test him (2 Chr. 32:31).

To label God's relationship to evil as 'permission' is to highlight the asymmetry of good and evil; it is not to resolve the mystery. The book of Job and Romans 9:19–24 offer no hope of a complete solution to the 'problem of evil'.

The ultimate agents of evil

Scripture reveals that evil appeared in heaven before it entered the world (2 Cor. 11:3; John 8:44; Rev. 12:9; 20:3). One called the Devil, Satan or the Evil One apostatized and tempted Adam and Eve. However, his role does not explain the fall, for Adam and Eve had no reason to yield, and his own fall from integrity is shrouded in mystery (though Jude 6 proves that the idea is biblical). With the spirits that followed him, the powers of darkness, Satan has set up an empire of evil; evil has dimensions beyond those of the individual human will. (See *Spiritual powers.)

The power of Satan will express itself supremely in 'the coming (*parousia*) of the lawless one' (2 Thess. 2:9), who may be identified with the final Antichrist (1 John 2:18) and the first beast of Revelation (Rev. 13). His forerunners, present-day antichrists, appear as teachers of pseudo-Christianity (1 John 2:18–23). 'Antichristianity', the Devil's lie in Christian disguise, is the most pernicious evil conceivable.

Conclusion

The gospel declares that the powers of evil have been defeated by the blood of Christ's cross (Rev. 12:11; Col. 2:15). For God's people the burden of *guilt is lifted and the bondage of sin broken. On Calvary faith beholds both God's hatred of sin (radical evil) and his sovereignty over it, which issues in victory. Evil, having entered history, is overcome in history by perfect goodness.

Bibliography

H. A. G. Blocher, *Evil and the Cross: Christian Thought and the Problem of Evil* (ET, Leicester, 1994); B. Hebblethwaite, 'MacKinnon and the problem of evil', in K. Surin (ed.), *Christ, Ethics and Tragedy: Essays in Honour of Donald MacKinnon* (Cambridge, 1989); A. Gesché, *Dieu pour penser*, I: *Le Mal* (Paris, 1993); J. Wenham, *The Enigma of Evil: Can We Believe in the Goodness of God?* (Leicester, ²1985).

H. A. G. BLOCHER

EXALTATION

Exaltation is one of the most significant and pervasive themes the Bible employs to portray the majesty and greatness of *God and of *Jesus Christ.

The OT

In the OT God is frequently presented as exalted above all beings. He is lifted up and supreme in his power and authority, over

467

Israel and all the nations of the earth (1 Chr. 29:11; Pss. 46:10; 113:4). He is the Most High, the great *king over all the earth and exalted far above all gods (Pss. 47:2; 83:18; 97:9). He alone rules over humankind and grants dominion to whomever he wishes (Dan. 4:17, 25, 32; 5:21). Thus Israel's response must be to exalt him in *worship and praise and give him honour above all others (Exod. 15:2; 2 Sam. 22:47; Neh. 9:5–6; Ps. 57:5; Is. 25:1). In fact, all nations and all creation are called to praise the Lord for his *glory and majesty (Ps. 148:13). All of life is put in its proper perspective only when God is exalted in this way.

Over against God, who deserves exaltation, is proud humanity that lifts itself up in self-sufficiency and disobedience (Gen. 3:5; Deut. 8:14; Ps. 75:4–7). God desires humble faith and raises to leadership those who honour him (Josh. 3:7; 2 Sam. 5:12; Ps. 89:27). While arrogant people may wield authority for a time, the day will come when they will be humbled and the Lord alone will be exalted (Is. 2:11, 17). This is especially true of Gentile nations and their rulers who exalt themselves over God and his people (Exod. 9:14–17; Num. 24:7; Is. 14:12–15; Ezek. 28:1–10; Dan. 8:25; 11:36–37). So all humanity faces a paradox, that the proud will be humbled while the lowly will be exalted (1 Sam. 2:7–8; Ps. 138:6; Is. 57:15).

The NT

Much of this OT background is assumed in the NT. God is the Most High and he alone should be worshipped and exalted. The Synoptic statement, 'whoever exalts himself will be humbled, and whoever humbles himself will be exalted' (Matt. 23:12, RSV; Luke 14:11; 18:14) is exactly consonant with OT ideas. This principle is the basis for one of the NT's descriptions of Jesus' course of life: he was humbled in his *incarnation, *suffering and death, but God highly exalted him in his resurrection, ascension and enthronement. This paradoxical path then becomes the way of discipleship for all his followers: suffering and then glory; obedient service and then greatness (Mark 8:34–38; 10:42–45; Phil. 2:1–11).

In the NT the theme of God's exaltation of Jesus after his suffering and death is one of the most important and pervasive ways of reflecting on who Jesus is and what he has accomplished. It is taken up by virtually every NT author and is found in both early and late writings. But the theme is expressed by five different motifs, which in some passages overlap with one another.

Resurrection

Paul points to Jesus' death and resurrection as the foremost themes of his *gospel preaching (1 Cor. 15:3–4). He readily acknowledges that in this he mirrors what others have preached before him (v. 3a), and the early sermons in Acts reflect a similar focus on the cross and resurrection of Jesus (e.g. Acts 2:22–24, 32–36). Likewise in introducing his letter to the Romans Paul immediately defines his calling from God as one focused on 'the gospel concerning his Son, who was descended from David according to the flesh and designated Son of God in power according to the Spirit of holiness by his resurrection from the dead, Jesus Christ our Lord' (Rom. 1:3–4). The resurrection of Jesus confirmed his divine sonship and constituted not just a restoration to physical life, but his transformation to a position of such heavenly power and glory that he becomes a 'life-giving spirit' who offers the hope of resurrection to all who are in him (1 Cor. 15:20–22; 45–49; cf. Rom. 6:3–11; Phil. 3:20–21). The resurrection, as the constant counterpart to the cross in Paul's thinking, demonstrates God's acceptance of Jesus' death as the means of justification and propitiation (Rom. 3:24–26; 4:24–25). Jesus' exaltation to highest glory and universal lordship came only by the path of humble obedience 'unto death, even death on a cross' (Phil. 2:8–11).

Luke also commonly ties Jesus' suffering and glory or suffering and resurrection together (Luke 24:26, 46; Acts 3:18; 17:3; 26:23). That this theme is drawn from the Suffering Servant passages in Isaiah (cf. 52:13; 53:11–12) can be seen in Acts 3:13–18, where Messiah's suffering as something 'God foretold by the mouth of all the prophets' is connected with God's glorification of 'his servant Jesus'.

For Paul this truth is certainly rooted in the experience which changed everything for him: his conversion on the Damascus Road (Acts 9:1–22; 22:6–16; 26:12–23; 1 Cor. 9:1; 15:8). His encounter with the risen Lord completely transformed Paul's understanding of who Jesus was and what he had accomplished: he was not a criminal justly put to death for blasphemy, but the exalted Lord. Jesus' death was actually the expression of God's power and wisdom, the crucifixion of 'the Lord of glory', as a means of redemption foreordained by God but never understood by merely human wisdom (1 Cor. 1:18–25; 2:6–8). Thus for Paul, Jesus' resurrection ultimately demonstrates not just that God had exalted an obedient human who served to the point of death. It shows that Jesus is the preexistent one, who reflects the invisible God because God's fulness dwells in him, and he 'existed in the form of God' before he humbled himself to become human (Phil. 2:6–11; Col. 1:15–20).

Ascension

Explicit accounts of the ascension of Jesus are given only by Luke, but more general references are made to it elsewhere, and it is presupposed in other texts, especially those that speak of Jesus' enthronement at God's right hand (see 'Session/Enthronement' below). Luke records Jesus' departure from earth to *heaven as a visible phenomenon occurring forty days after the resurrection (Luke 24:50–51; Acts 1:2–3, 9–11). In both passages this is linked with the promise that his followers would receive 'power from on high' in the form of the *Holy Spirit, and in Acts it brings with it the expectation that 'he will come in the same way as you saw him go into heaven' (1:11).

Paul only rarely mentions the ascension (Rom. 10:6; 1 Tim. 3:16), but in one text he too connects it with the bestowal of the gifts of the Spirit from on high (Eph. 4:7–11). John speaks of Jesus' 'ascending' to heaven (3:13; 6:62; 20:17), but also of his 'going', or 'going away' to the Father (14:2, 12, 28; 16:7, 28; 7:33; 8:14, 21; 13:33, 36; 14:4; 16:5, 10, 17). This also is linked to the sending of the Spirit (14:16–18; 16:7). In addition, John portrays Jesus' ascension in several places as a return journey 'to where I was previously', or 'to the Father who sent me', or as presupposing his prior descent from heaven to earth in the incarnation (3:31; 6:38, 62; 8:23; 13:3; 16:28).

Glorification

The Gospel of John contributes a unique nuance to the portrayal of Jesus' exaltation in the NT. While John, as others, uses the term 'exalt' or 'lift up' (Gk hypsoō) to describe Jesus' lofty status, he uses it with a typical Johannine double sense. In one sense to be 'lifted up' is to be crucified, raised up on the cross to die; but in another sense it is to be exalted to heavenly honour. In Jesus' fulfilling of his mission from God the two are inexorably tied together: 'As Moses lifted up the serpent in the wilderness, so the Son of man must be lifted up' (3:14); 'When I am lifted up from the earth, I will draw all men to myself' (12:32; cf. also 8:28; 12:34). The same can be said for Jesus' glorification in John's Gospel: the cross is his ultimate glorification, the event in which God magnifies and honours him (7:39; 12:16, 23, 28; 13:31–32; 17:1–10). In his death and its effects Jesus' true glory is seen, 'glory as of the only Son from the Father, full of grace and truth' (1:14–15), the glory that he shared with the Father before the world began (17:5). (See *Atonement.)

Session/Enthronement

Jesus' enthronement at the right hand of God is the extraordinary theme the early Christians found in Psalm 110:1, the OT verse most often quoted or alluded to in the NT (some 33 times): 'The LORD said to my Lord, Sit at my right hand, till I put your enemies under your feet.' The application of this psalm to Jesus was highly influential in the development of NT Christology and is a primary expression of his exalted status, sometimes assuming and eclipsing the motifs of resurrection and ascension (e.g. in Hebrews resurrection is hardly ever mentioned, since it is assumed in the references to Jesus' heavenly session).

This use of Psalm 110 began with Jesus' own teaching on two occasions as recorded by all three Synoptics (Matt. 22:44/Mark 12:36/Luke 20:42–43; Matt. 26:64/Mark 14:62/Luke 22:69). It is a significant theme in the early sermons in Acts (2:33–35; 5:31; 7:55–56). Paul also utilizes the psalm (Rom. 8:34; 1 Cor. 15:25; Eph. 1:20; 2:6; Col. 3:1), often combining it with Psalm 8:6 to speak of Jesus having 'all things subjected under his feet' (1 Cor. 15:27; Eph. 1:22; Phil. 3:21). Jesus' session at God's side is also described in 1 Peter 3:22 and Revelation 3:21.

A number of these texts emphasize the benefits that derive from Jesus' exalted status at God's side: his authority over principalities and powers and ultimately over all things (1 Cor. 15:25; Eph. 1:20; 1 Pet. 3:22); his intercession on behalf of Christians (Rom. 8:34); the giving of the Spirit and forgiveness of sins (Acts 2:33–35; 5:31). They also connect these blessings with the fulfilment of OT promises, first the promise that a son of David would reign in his line for ever (Acts 2:30, quoting from 2 Sam. 7:8–17; Ps. 89:3–4, 19–37) and also the promise of a new covenant providing full forgiveness and internalizing of the law through the Spirit (Jer. 31:31–34, alluded to in Acts 2:33–35; 5:31). In the inaugurated *eschatology of these passages Jesus is seen as already enthroned on high and providing salvific benefits to his people, but as not yet exacting the complete submission of his enemies. The consummation of his rule over all creation is expected in the future.

The most extensive use of Psalm 110 in the NT, however, is found in Hebrews, where verse 1 is evoked five times (1:3, 13; 8:1; 10:12–13; 12:2) and verse 4 nine or ten times (5:6, 10; 6:20; 7:3, 8 [?], 11, 15–17, 21, 24–25, 28). This psalm is so central to the argument of Hebrews that virtually the whole sermon (*cf.* 13:22) is a theological exposition of these two verses. The writer has come to see Jesus as God's Son and High *Priest, exalted now to the position of greatest honour in God's presence. This view of Jesus' sitting in God's very presence after offering himself for sins is the basis for the author's whole argument about the eternal efficacy of Jesus' sacrifice and the need for Christians to hold firmly to their faith in him. The insight that this exalted position is rooted in a priesthood different from the Levitical one, and eternal, is the basis for all that is said about the change from old to new in God's saving work. The recognition that Jesus' path to this heavenly status required costly obedience learned 'through the things that he suffered' (5:8) is the foundation for all the exhortations to faithful endurance, for which Jesus is the model (12:1–3).

For this last point the writer relies also on Psalm 8:4–6 (Heb. 2:6–8), to show that Jesus' status of glory and honour is the result of his suffering and death for the sake of humankind, in whose fleshly likeness he had shared. This was God's design to perfect him as the merciful and faithful high priest: faithful to God and sympathetic to all those who are weak and tempted (2:10, 17–18; 4:14–16).

Another striking OT theme, the stone testimonia found in Psalm 118:22, Isaiah 8:14–15, 28:16 and Daniel 2:34–35, is used also to expound Jesus' central importance as the one exalted after suffering and death. These passages are interpreted individually (Matt. 21:42–44; Mark 12:10; Luke 2:34; Acts 4:11) or in combination (Luke 20:17–18; Rom. 9:32–33; 1 Pet. 2:4–8) to show that Jesus was the 'stone' rejected by those who should know about such things, the one who has now become the 'head of the corner'. God has made him the precious cornerstone, the tested foundation stone, and those who rely on him will never be put to shame. On the other hand, he will be a stumbling stone for those who ignore him, causing the fall of many and the crushing of all on whom it falls.

Return

The hope of Jesus' return to earth in glorious triumph is another NT motif expressing the theme of his exaltation. The expectation of return entails a previous absence, and several verses make clear that Jesus will come down or come back from heaven (John 14:2–3; Acts 1:11; Phil. 3:20; Col. 3:1–4; 1 Thess. 1:10; 4:16).

Jesus' exalted status also reveals his authority to *judge and produces an anticipation that his reigning power, which has already been inaugurated, will one day be consummated and acclaimed in all creation. The coming of the Son of Man in power and glory is anticipated in several passages in the Synoptics (Matt. 24:30; Mark 13:26; Luke 21:27). It is linked explicitly with his session at God's right hand in Matthew 26:64 and with his prerogative to judge in Matthew 16:27 and Mark 8:38.

It is appropriate then that the book of Revelation, which most graphically portrays the return of the exalted Christ, should provide the final scenes of the canonical scriptures. All of Revelation reveals Jesus as exalted to heavenly glory, rightly sharing with God the status of Alpha and Omega, the beginning and end: from John's vision of the resplendent Son of Man in chapter 1; to the surprising view of the heavenly throne room in chapters 4 – 5, in which the one worthy of all worship and authority together with God is the Lamb who was slain to provide redemption; to the unveiling of judgments on sinful humanity that constitute the wrath of God and of the Lamb; all the way through to the pictures of the return and reign of Jesus as King of kings and Lord of lords and the eternal blessedness of all the redeemed centering on the presence of the Lord God and of the Lamb. The exaltation of God and of Jesus Christ is the proper and joyful focus of all of existence.

Bibliography

D. L. Bock, *Blasphemy and Exaltation in Judaism and the Final Examination of Jesus* (Tübingen, 1998); B. K. Donne, *Christ Ascended: A Study in the Significance of the Ascension of Jesus Christ in the New Testament* (Exeter, 1983); M. Gourgues, *A la droite de Dieu: Résurrection de Jésus et actualisaton du Psaume 110:1 dans le Nouveau Testament* (Paris, 1978); D. M. Hay, *Glory at the Right Hand: Psalm 110 in Early Christianity* (Nashville, 1973); W. R. G. Loader, 'Christ at the right hand: Ps. CX.1 in the New Testament', *NTS* 24, 1978, pp. 199–217; J. F. Maile, 'The Ascension in Luke-Acts', *TynB* 37, 1986, pp. 29–59; C. C. Newman, *Paul's Glory-Christology: Tradition and Rhetoric* (Leiden, 1992); M. C. Parsons, *The Departure of Jesus in Luke-Acts: The Ascension Narratives in Context* (Sheffield, 1987); M. C. Parsons, 'Son and High Priest: A study in the Christology of Hebrews', *EvQ* 60, 1988, pp. 195–216; M. Saucy, 'Exaltation Christology in Hebrews: What kind of reign?', *TJ* 14, 1993, pp. 41–62; P. Toon, *The Ascension of Our Lord* (Nashville, 1984); A. W. Zwiep, *The Ascension of the Messiah in Lukan Christology* (Leiden, 1997).

B. M. FANNING

EXCLUSION

The word 'exclusion' could be used to translate a host of biblical terms. In 1 Corinthians 5 alone the command to exclude the incestuous man is given in five different ways, using the verbs 'to remove', 'to drive out', (not) 'to eat with', 'to deliver' (to Satan) and 'to purge away'. Ironically, for this very reason, the concept of exclusion from the community of God's people is relatively neglected in lexicons and theological dictionaries, especially those which do theology one word at a time. Yet as a concept exclusion covers a wide range of biblical material, including both laws, which treat the subject in theory, and narrative, which works it out in practice. The laws in *Deuteronomy, the case of Achan, and the examples of *Ezra and of Paul (in 1 *Cor. 5) will provide the key texts for discussion.

The subject may be treated from a number of angles, for example, who is excluded (and for which *sins and heresies)? How does the exclusion take place (*i.e.* what procedure is to be followed)? Who authorizes it (a leader, the congregation or God)? And what does it involve (the withdrawal of certain social contacts or permanent excommunication)? This article concentrates on the theologically central question of the rationale of exclusion. Why are sinners to be expelled? What are the reasons for exclusion? The material is covered under the headings of *community*, *holiness*, *covenant*, *restoration* and *salvation*. These five motifs or images are drawn directly from the Bible and serve as a framework for our reading of the relevant texts.

The solidarity of the community

The foundational texts for a biblical theology of exclusion are found in Leviticus (see next section) and Deuteronomy. Those guilty of idol worship, contempt for the Lord, sexual offences and a variety of social crimes are condemned in Deuteronomy with the formula, 'you must purge the *evil from among you' (NIV, *cf.* 13:5; 17:7; 19:19; 21:21; 24:7; *cf.* Judg. 20:13; 1 Cor. 5:13b), which denotes the most extreme form of exclusion, *i.e.* execution. However, in the history of its transmission and interpretation, a curse (see *Blessing/curse) of exclusion is substituted for the death penalty in this formula (regularly in Targum Onkelos, Targum Pseudo-Jonathan and Sifre and usually in the LXX). Similarly, in 1 Corinthians 5:13b we find that 'the evil man' rather than 'the evil' is to be put away.

The notion of corporate responsibility is associated with the formula in Deuteronomy 19:13 and 21:9, which concern murder. The reason for the expulsion/execution of the offender is 'so that it may go well with you', *i.e.*, the nation (19:13, *cf.* 21:8). The community, it seems, is held responsible for the sin of the offender while he or she remains within it. The lesson is reinforced in Deuteronomy 23:14b where Israel is warned to deal with sin in the camp, lest the Lord 'see among you anything indecent and turn away from you' (*cf.* 29:19–21). The same solidarity is evident in a number of incidents throughout the OT, involving Sabbath breaking (Exod. 16:27–28), the sin of Korah, Dathan and Abiram (Num. 16:24–27), Achan's sin (Josh. 7:1–26; 22:20), and the Reubenites, Gadites and Manassites' supposed sin in setting up an altar east of the Jordan (Josh. 22:16–18). Like the pagan sailors who felt compelled to eject Jonah in order to obtain a safe passage for their ship, the *people of God removed certain offenders as an exercise in corporate responsibility, in order to avoid impending *judgment and to preserve the harmonious relationship between the community and God.

The prayers of Ezra (ch. 9), Nehemiah (chs. 1, 9) and Daniel (ch. 9) also express the idea of association with the *guilt of others. In each case the leaders mourn (LXX *pentheō*) over the unfaithfulness of the exiles (*cf.* Ezra 10:6; Neh. 1:4; Dan. 10:2), just as Paul enjoined the Corinthians (1 Cor. 5:2) to 'mourn' (*pentheō*) over the sin of the incestuous man. When used in connection with sin, *pentheō* signifies mourning in the sense of confessing the sin of others as if it were one's own. It is not that the community is guilty of the sin itself, but it is held responsible for purging the evil from its midst.

Such judgments are to take place in the presence of the whole community and of the Lord (*cf.* Deut. 19:16–20). The 'entire assembly' is to stone the Sabbath-breaker (Num. 15:35) and the blasphemer (Lev. 24:14, 16), and to judge the murderer (Num. 35:24), just as the decision to exclude the sinner in 1 Corinthians 5:4 is to be made when the *church is 'gathered together'. Indeed, Paul addresses the church as a body throughout the chapter (*cf.* the nine occurrences of the second person plural pronoun) and directs them to act as a group. Exceptions to this principle appear in 2 Corinthians 13:1–3, 1 Timothy 1:19–20 and 3 John 9–10, where apostles act individually.

In the Bible exclusion from the community is normally effected by the community and for the community's sake. Upon what basis does the solidarity of the community rest? The following section suggests that holiness guarantees its essential unity.

The maintenance of holiness

Whereas in OT teaching on exclusion social crimes are associated with the notions of 'purging' or 'utterly removing' the evil and the curses of Deuteronomy 27 and 28, the term 'to cut off' has to do with ritual offences (*cf.* Gen. 17:14; Exod. 12:15, 19; 30:33, 38; 31:14; Lev. 7:20, 25–27; 17:4, 9, 14; 19:8; 22:3; 23:29; Num. 4:18; 9:13; 19:13, 20; 1 Sam. 2:33) and is related to the cult and holiness. In Leviticus, 'unclean' individuals are removed from the camp, which is meant to be a holy place. A process of cleansing is necesssary to restore unclean people at the end of their period of exclusion, a practice which highlights the incompatibility of the holy and the unclean. However, it was the laws of admission to the *temple which did most to establish the link between exclusion from the community and the maintenance of holiness.

The origin of these restrictions is in the exclusion of individuals from the 'assembly of the Lord' on the basis of physique and descent in Deuteronomy 23:1–8. Ezra 9:1–2 and Nehemiah 13:1–3, 23–27 allude to this passage as the basis for the exclusion of foreign wives. The lamentation over the destruction of Jerusalem in Lamentations 1:10 also recalls it. However, as revelation progresses, moral conditions for admission become more important. Biblical evidence for this evolution includes the 'entrance-torot' (Pss. 15; 24:3–5; Is. 33:14–17), the exclusion of rebels from the eschatological congregation (Ezek. 20:38–40), and the indictment of Israel for admitting the 'uncircumcised in heart' to the sanctuary (Ezek. 44:6–9). Josephus and Philo interpret Deuteronomy as excluding not only aliens but also gravely-offending Jewish sinners.

Concerning 1 Corinthians 5, it is no coincidence that the idea of the community as God's holy temple is introduced only twenty-three verses earlier in 3:16–17. In calling for the incestuous man to be removed Paul in effect cleanses the temple, calling for his destruction (5:5), for 'if any one destroys God's temple, God will destroy him; for God's temple is sacred' (3:17).

In biblical thought, holiness and unholiness do not mix, and the danger of contamination is taken seriously, not only in the laws in Leviticus but also in the ban, a curse of exclusion on people and objects resulting from their contact with foreign gods (cf. Deut. 7:26; 13:12–18); whoever takes possession of a devoted thing must also be devoted. Likewise for Paul the sinner must be removed because holiness and unholiness cannot co-exist: 'a little leaven leavens the whole lump' (1 Cor. 5:6, RSV). After cleansing the temple it was customary, at least in OT times, to celebrate the Passover (see 2 Chr. 29:5, 35; 30; 35:1–19; 2 Kgs. 23:1–23; Ezra 6; cf. Matt. 21:12–13; Mark 11:15–18; Luke 19:45–47; John 2:13–22). Paul seems to endorse this practice. In 1 Corinthians 5:7–8 he calls on the Corinthians to keep the festival (spiritually) once they have got rid of the old yeast (a metaphorical reference to the exclusion). The death of Christ is the basis for Paul's demand that the community maintain its sanctified status: 'For Christ, our Passover lamb, has been sacrificed.' As Titus 2:14 observes, 'Christ gave himself ... to purify for himself a people that are his very own.'

The community's solidarity and the maintenance of its holiness make the practice of exclusion a necessity. But this practice is also just with respect to the offender, because he or she has breached God's covenant.

Breach of covenant

In both the Deuteronomic expulsion formulae and the curses listed in chapters 27 and 28 (cf. Lev. 26), which censure virtually the same offences, *discipline is exercised because of failure to keep the covenant obligations. Deuteronomy 17:2–7, for example, demands that evil be purged because the offender has 'done evil in the eyes of the Lord your God in violation of his covenant' (17:2). Likewise, in the case of Achan, *Joshua 7:15 declares that, 'he [Achan] has violated the covenant of the Lord' (cf. Josh. 23:16). Ezra conceives of his reform in terms of a return to covenant obligations (Ezra 10:3; cf. Neh. 9:32–34). Building on such teaching the *Damascus Document* at Qumran also gives breaches of the covenant as grounds for expulsion from the community.

These examples underscore the notion of personal responsibility. Certain rules, when broken, automatically exclude the offender. The sins in 1 Corinthians 5:11 are remarkably similar to those connected in Deuteronomy to the formula Paul quotes in 5:13b. People are excluded primarily for the sake of others, but

they have no one but themselves to blame. As Titus 3:10–11 says of a divisive person who is to be avoided, he or she is 'self-condemned'. The gracious gift of membership in the community carries with it certain demands. In neither testament is open rebellion against God tolerated among his people.

Another reason given for exclusion is to deter a further breach of covenant in the community. Deuteronomy 19:19b–20a states: 'You must purge the evil from among you. The rest of the people will hear of this and be afraid and never again will such an evil thing be done among you.' (See *Deut. 13:12–18; 17:2–7, 12–13; 21:18–21.) In the NT too this reason for exclusion is cited in 1 Timothy 5:20 ('Those who sin are to be rebuked publicly, so that the others may take warning'); in the case of Ananias and Sapphira (Acts 5:1–11), when following their deaths 'great fear seized the whole church' (presumably at the prospect of further divine judgment); and in the yeast proverb in 1 Corinthians 5:6 and Galatians 5:9, which has a modern equivalent in the saying, 'one bad apple spoils the whole barrel'.

Exclusion reminds us how seriously the Bible takes the setting of both a good and a bad example. Even in material which stresses the offender's personal responsibility his or her effect on others is never far from view.

The hope of restoration

The OT supplies the key texts dealing with exclusion on the basis of community solidarity, maintenance of holiness and breach of covenant, though these ideas are confirmed in the NT. However, the notion of exclusion for the purpose of bringing about the *repentance and restoration of the sinner, although not absent from the OT (cf. David's sin with Bathsheba) and anticipated in some strands of Judaism, becomes prominent only in Christian teaching.

The remedial function of exclusion is implied in Galatians 6:1 ('If someone is caught in a sin, you who are spiritual should restore him gently'; cf. Jas. 5:19–20) and explicit in 2 Thessalonians 3:14–15 ('If anyone does not obey our instruction. . . Do not associate with him. . . Yet do not regard him as an enemy, but warn him as a brother'). That such continuing concern for the one under discipline was meant to lead to reinstatement is clear in 2 Corinthians 2:5–9, where Paul tells his readers that since the one who has been punished has shown genuine repentance he should be lovingly restored to the fellowship.

In Matthew 18:15–18 the main concern is for the restitution of the sinner, at least up until the point of exclusion, rather than for the purity of the church. The point of the cautious steps leading up to the excommunication (private, then semi-private, than open rebuke before the church) is obviously to 'gain the brother' (18:15b). We need not interpret this in opposition to a passage like 1 Corinthians 5, however, since we are introduced to the Corinthian story at a late stage, probably after such appeals for repentance have already taken place. There is an implicit promise in the 1 Corinthians 5 exclusion; if he repents, he will be restored. Whereas in the Pentateuch a single act of transgression brings exclusion, in 1 Corinthians 5 the character and lifestyle of the sinner, not an isolated offence, provoke the penalty (5:10–11).

One text in the NT which appears to be inconsistent with the idea of the remedial purpose of exclusion is 1 Corinthians 5:5 where Paul says that the man is to be, literally, 'handed over to Satan for the destruction of the flesh'. This sounds as if exclusion is a final and irrevocable punishment. It is commonly held that Paul here enjoins the pronouncing of a curse on the immoral man that will lead to physical suffering and ultimately to death (cf. NEB, 'this man is to be consigned to Satan for the destruction of the body'). However, this is not the best interpretation of the verse. To hand the man over to Satan is to turn him back out into Satan's sphere, outside the edifying and caring environment of the church where God is at work. In other words, verse 5 states metaphorically what Paul says literally in verses 2 and 13: the man is to be excluded from the community of faith. A similar metaphorical elaboration is found in verse 7: 'get rid of the old yeast'. 'The destruction of the flesh' refers not to the man's death but to his turning from evil desires, the destruction of 'the sinful nature'. When Paul contrasts flesh and spirit, as here in verse 5, he is contrasting evil and good tendencies (cf. Rom. 8:5–17 and Gal. 5:16–24). 'Flesh' refers to the person oriented away from God and 'spirit' to the person oriented towards God. It is the man

viewed as one at enmity with God who is to be 'destroyed'. That the man in 1 Corinthians 5 is not expected to die, at least immediately, is clear from verse 11 where the Corinthians are told not to 'associate with' him and from 1 Timothy 1:19–20, where Hymenaeus and Alexander are 'handed over to Satan to be taught not to blaspheme' (that is, to change their behaviour). The incestuous man is handed over to Satan to be taught not to commit sexual immorality, in the hope of his restoration to the Christian community. Of course the work and intent of Satan is evil and may even involve the infliction of suffering, but it serves God's ultimate purpose, the salvation of the sinner.

The prospect of salvation

Exclusion is not always undertaken, however, with a remedial intent. Sometimes individuals are excluded or exclude themselves, usually on the basis of false belief rather than conduct, because they do not belong to the company of the saved. 2 John 10–11 gives one example: 'If any one comes to you and does not bring this doctrine, do not receive him into the house or give him any greeting; for he who greets him shares his wicked work' (RSV, cf. 1 John 2:19). The expulsion of Adam and Eve from Eden and, hence, from proximity to God is perhaps the first example of this punitive exclusion. Such texts raise the issue of how exclusion is related to an individual's salvation, on which there is surprisingly little NT material.

On the one hand, damnation can be perceived as the ultimate 'exclusion', as a final and retributive exclusion from God's presence (cf. 2 Thess. 1:9): in 1 Corinthians 6:9–10, Ephesians 5:5 and Colossians 3:5–6 those who have no future with God are said to be guilty of roughly the same sins as those who should be excluded from the community according to 1 Corinthians 5:11. On the other hand, there is no hint that the act of excluding people damns them. On the contrary, in 1 Corinthians 5:12–13 such judgment is explicitly said to be God's exclusive prerogative.

Exclusion from the community and salvation are linked in 1 Corinthians 5:5b, but the former does not lead to the loss of the latter. On the contrary, the express purpose of this expulsion is the offender's salvation. Paul's ultimate aim in excluding the man is his own good. How is this purpose to be understood? Paul assumes (see 6:9–11) that those who persist in flagrant sin have no future with God; in this sense 6:9–11 clarifies 5:5b. Yet he is confident that God's faithfulness will confirm believers 'until the end ... blameless on the day of our Lord Jesus' (1 Cor. 1:8). However, future salvation is not a forgone conclusion for one 'who calls himself a brother but is sexually immoral' (v. 11). The passage does not teach that ethical failure results in the loss of salvation, but that assurance of salvation depends in part on ethical progress; cf. 6:11: 'that is what some of you *were*'. Paul does not answer the question of whether the man is currently 'saved'. His point is that so-called brothers who engage in blatant sexual misconduct will be finally saved 'on the day of the Lord' only if 'the sinful nature is destroyed'. According to 5:5b exclusion is undertaken not only to benefit the community and the individual in the present, but also to secure the salvation of the sinner in the future.

Conclusion

Few topics do more to emphasize the corporate dimension of the Christian faith, the seriousness and consequences of sin and the holiness of God, than exclusion. In the Bible serious offenders are excluded from the community because of its solidarity, in order to maintain its holiness, because of a breach of covenant, in the hope of their restoration and to secure their future salvation.

Exclusion teaches us something about both God and the people of God. It reveals how the holiness of God works itself out in relation to his purposes. It reminds us that God's grace in election cannot be taken for granted and that certain standards of conduct cannot be continually transgressed with impunity. The gift of being included in God's people demands appropriate behaviour. In the present evil age, in anticipation of the age to come, God uses various means to call out and purify a people for himself, one of which, ironic as it seems, is exclusion. He deals with this people, not only as individuals, but also and primarily as groups. Exclusion is a powerful reminder that such groups, or churches, are responsible to one another as well as to God. Their behaviour, whether doing good or committing sin, affects the community's well being; exclusion underlines the profound interrelation and interdependence of believers in the body of Christ.

Bibliography

G. Forkman, *The Limits of the Religious Community* (Lund, 1972); J. M. Gundry Volf, *Paul and Perseverance* (Tübingen, 1990); W. Horbury, 'Extirpation and Excommunication', *VT* n.s. 35, 1985, pp. 13–38; I. H. Marshall, *Kept by the Power of God: A Study of Perseverance and Falling Away* (London, 1969; repr. Carlisle, 1996); C. Roetzel, *Judgement in the Community: A Study of the Relationship Between Eschatology and Ecclesiology in Paul* (Leiden, 1972); B. S. Rosner, *Paul, Scripture and Ethics: A Study of 1 Corinthians 5–7* (Leiden, 1994); idem, ' "Drive out the wicked person": A biblical theology of exclusion', *EvQ* 71.1, 1999, pp. 25–36.

B. S. ROSNER

EXCOMMUNICATION, see EXCLUSION
EXEGESIS AND HERMENEUTICS, see Part 1

EXILE

Introduction

Although the exile of Israel as a nation did not occur until relatively late in the OT period, the theological concept of exile is present virtually from the beginning of biblical revelation. Exile, in theological terms, is the experience of pain and *suffering that results from the knowledge that there is a home where one belongs, yet for the present one is unable to return there. This existential sense of deep loss may be compounded by a sense of *guilt or remorse stemming from the knowledge that the cause of exile is *sin.

The exile foreshadowed

The expulsion of Adam and Eve from the garden of Eden is the archetype of all subsequent exile (Gen. 3:24). Paradise has been lost because of their sin, and now they must live as strangers in a land from which they have become alienated (Gen. 3:17–19). Throughout the rest of the Bible, the state of God's *people is one of profound exile, of living in a world to which they do not belong and looking for a world that is yet to come. Abraham was already aware that, even though he was dwelling in the land *God had promised to give to him, he lived there as a stranger and alien (Gen. 23:4; *cf.* Heb. 11:8–10). Jacob's deception of his father Isaac and his stealing of his brother's birthright compelled him to flee the Promised Land and live in exile with his uncle Laban for many years. In the time of Joseph, famine brought Abraham's descendants down into Egypt, where they would subsequently experience the bitterness of servitude in a land that was not their own. On the other hand, that bitterness and the correlative sense of exile was not quite universal among the Hebrews. From his privileged position growing up in Pharaoh's household, Moses became aware of his status as an alien only after he left behind the luxuries of Egypt. His new sense of being an exile was expressed in the name he gave to his first son, 'Gershom'; he recognized that he had now become an alien in a foreign land (Exod. 2:22).

Even before God's people entered the land he had promised them under the leadership of Joshua, the prospect of their exile from that land as a punishment for disobedience was in view. The land, which had been given to Israel as a gift, would be removed from their care if they were disobedient. If the people failed to keep the terms of the *covenant, they would be scattered among the *nations (Lev. 26:33; Deut. 28:64; 30:3–4). The possibility of exile is taken into account in Solomon's prayer at the dedication of the *temple; exile is the seventh, climactic example of circumstances in which prayers may be made towards the temple, seeking *forgiveness and restoration from the Lord (1 Kgs. 8:46–50).

However, for Israel exile is not simply the loss of the land. More importantly, it is the loss of the Lord's presence with them. For that reason, even though the land had not been lost, the loss of the ark to the Philistines in 1 Samuel 4 can be described as the glory of the Lord 'going into exile' (*gālâ*; 1 Sam. 4:22). This prefigured the visionary departure of the *glory of the Lord from the *Jerusalem temple in Ezekiel 10, which itself preceded the historical exile in 586 BC. After the Lord had abandoned the land, it was only a matter of time before the people would go into exile.

The exile as historical and theological reality

This threatened *judgment of God came upon his people in two stages. First, the northern kingdom of Israel was carried into captivity by the Assyrians in 722 BC. Then the southern kingdom of *Judah followed them into exile at the hands of Nebuchadnezzar and the *Babylonians in 586 BC. In the providence of God, the time delay meant that exile had significantly different consequences for Israel and Judah. The Assyrians had a policy of resettling captured lands with replacement people groups, so producing a mixed population. The Babylonians, on the other hand, moved the skilled members of captive peoples from the edges of the empire to the centre. Thus the people of Judah had the prospect of returning to a relatively empty homeland; the people of the former northern kingdom did not.

The exile was not simply a historical event, however; it had profound theological significance. In the same way that Jewish thought in the later 20th century had to deal with the impact of Auschwitz, even on those who were not yet born in 1945, so also the exile had an enormous impact on all subsequent OT writings. After the exile, life could not simply return to the way it was before. How could there be joy when all that was sacred and precious had been defiled and destroyed by the invaders?

The first result of the exile was, naturally, an outpouring of grief. The exiles sat down by the rivers of Babylon and wept (Ps. 137:1). They wept both because of the consequences of exile, *i.e.* Jerusalem in ruins and her infants slaughtered (Ps. 137:7–8), and because they recognized the fundamental cause of exile: their own sin and the sin of their forefathers (Lam. 3:42, 49). Because of the close connection between the Lord and the Promised Land, they may have felt that to be isolated from their land was also to be abandoned by their God. For that reason, the prophet Ezekiel was given a vision of God's glory by the river Kebar, in Babylon itself (Ezek. 1:1). The good news that the prophet brought to the exiles was that God himself would be a sanctuary for them where they were, in Babylonia (Ezek. 11:16). In abandoning the land, God had not turned his back on all his people.

Yet, paradoxically, the recognition that God had sent his people into exile because of their sin caused the exiles not only to mourn but also to *hope and to dream. The one who had bruised them could also bind up their wounds; the one who had rejected his people could restore them to himself (Lam. 5:21). Indeed, the ancient covenant documents that threatened Israel with exile for disobedience also spoke of a restoration for the exiles (Lev. 26:44; Deut. 30:3). Because of God's covenant faithfulness to his people, the exile could not be the end of Israel's story. The Lord's enduring ḥeseḏ, his covenant *love, was the basis of their hope for the future (Lam. 3:21–22). The Lord had associated the honour of his name with the fortunes of his people, and for the sake of that name he would once again restore them (Ezek. 36:23–24).

In the meantime, the exiles were able, indeed obliged, to reinvent Israel. The captives dreamed not simply of a return but of a renewal, a rebirth of Israel in greater conformity to God's original design. Much of the exilic writing focuses, therefore, on critiquing the past and drawing up plans for a better future, a future in which Israel's sins will no longer come back to haunt them. With everything reduced to rubble, a radically new future could be conceived in which *obedience to the Lord would no longer be a dream but a reality. Indeed, the Lord promised that he would bring about such a change in the hearts of his people that there would be, in effect, nothing less than a new covenant (Jer. 31:31–34; Ezek. 36:16–28). This 're-visioning' of the future also served the present needs of the people, by providing an alternative construction of reality from the dominant model in the culture around them. Although they saw a world firmly in the grip of Babylonian imperialism, by faith they beheld a different ruler on the throne and believed that their narrative would have a better conclusion.

Exile in the NT

Although the return from exile that occurred in the time of Cyrus is viewed in several passages of Scripture as a fulfilment of the promises of restoration and the end of the exile, it fell short of the great expectations raised by the visions of Jeremiah and Ezekiel. Israel's land was still governed by foreigners, not by a descendant of the line of David; many (the diaspora) were still scattered through other lands;, and those who returned persisted in all kinds of sin, obdurately resisting God's word. Because of the people's hardness of heart, the exile was in some respects still a reality. A further action on God's part would be necessary to deal with Israel's sin, to inaugurate a genuinely new covenant, as promised in Jeremiah 31:31–34, and to bring about the full *salvation of God's people.

In the light of that sense of continuing exile and the expectation of a new work of God to redeem his people, the NT's interest in the concepts of exile and restoration is explicable. The exile's importance as a historical event is immediately clear in the structure of Jesus' genealogy in Matthew 1, where the three major reference points of *redemptive history are Abraham, David and the exile (Matt. 1:17). Moreover, as a child Jesus himself experienced exile, going down to Egypt to flee the wrath of Herod (Matt. 2:13). There Jesus grew up as a sojourner, far away from God's people and land.

In this, as in other respects, Jesus was partaking of the same experience as that of his fellow human beings (Heb. 2:14) and especially that of his fellow Israelites. For God's new-covenant people, the Israel of God, are, like their forefather Abraham, strangers and exiles in this world (1 Pet. 1:1; 2:11; Heb. 11:13). They are the true diaspora, those who are scattered among the nations (Jas. 1:1; 1 Pet. 1:1). This term denotes not only their physical location but also, more profoundly, their theological location (cf. the LXX of Deut. 30:4; Ps. 147:2). Christians are the true exiles, living in a world to which they do not belong and with which they are not to fall in love (1 John 2:15), while they long for a world which they do not yet see but to which they look forward in hope (Heb. 11:1). They live in a world that is seduced by the political and economic attractiveness of 'Babylon' (Rev. 17 – 18), but they dwell there as the children of the Jerusalem that is above (Gal. 4:26). That is why God's people can never feel fully at home in this world.

However, the decisive act in the ending of exile and the restoration of God's people has now taken place in Christ. While life in exile is still painful, its sting has been drawn by the cross. At the cross, *Jesus experienced the sting of exile – punishment for sin – in its fullness for his people. The one who had never sinned was made sin for them (2 Cor. 5:21), and the one who for all eternity had dwelt in the bosom of the Father was thereby exiled from his presence. In the midst of that experience of exile, he cried out 'My God, my God, why have you forsaken me?' (Matt. 27:46). But his exile has redemptive power. By it, his people are once and for all reconciled to God.

For that reason, even though NT believers are physically absent from the Lord, yet spiritually he is always with them (Matt. 28:20). He walks among the lampstands and knows intimately what is happening in the seven churches of Asia Minor (Rev. 1:13; 2:1 – 3:22). Indeed, the visions of Revelation are given to one who is himself in exile for the sake of Jesus, his servant John (Rev. 1:9).

Moreover, Paul was optimistic that the redemptive work accomplished in Christ would in the fullness of time be applied not simply to the Gentiles but also to the Jews. Because of their disobedience and *hardness, the Jews were still experiencing exile (Rom. 10:21). But ultimately exile could never be the end of the story for God's chosen people. The ancient promises of God could not be nullified. Through their continuing exile, salvation had come to the Gentiles (Rom. 11:11), but God's overarching purpose was to move his own people to jealousy. This jealousy would in turn lead to a still greater restoration and the incorporation of Jews and Gentiles into a single olive tree, the one Israel of God (Rom. 11:12–31). Then indeed all the prophecies of the OT would be completely fulfilled.

Like the exiles of the OT, NT believers dream of home, a new Jerusalem where the sin and suffering of their present existence will be no more and the time for weeping will finally be past. There they will no longer be exiles but rather will be at home with the Lord (2 Cor. 5:8). There Jew and Gentile will be united in a single, sin-free people, to the glory of God the Father. This new heavenly home is depicted in all its glory in Revelation 21 – 22, as an encouragement both to dream passionately of the future, and to live obediently and with perseverance in the present.

See also: ISRAEL; LAND.

Bibliography

P. R. Ackroyd, *Exile and Restoration: A Study of Hebrew Thought of the Sixth Century BC* (Philadelphia 1968); W. Brueggemann, *Cadences of Home: Preaching among Exiles* (Louisville, 1997); T. C. Eskenazi, 'Exile and dreams of return', *CurrTM* 18, 1990, pp. 192–200; R. W. Klein, *Israel in Exile: A Theological Interpretation* (Philadelphia, 1979); J. M. Scott, 'Restoration of Israel', in *DPL*, pp. 796–805.

I. M. DUGUID

EXODUS

Introduction

There are over 120 explicit OT references to the Exodus in law, narrative, prophecy and psalm, and it is difficult to exaggerate its importance. Foundational to *Israel's self-perception (Deut. 6:20–25) – they are here first designated a *people (Exod. 1:9) – it is recalled in liturgy (*e.g.* Pss. 78, 105; Exod. 12:26–27), prayer (*e.g.* 2 Sam. 7:23; Jer. 32:16–21; Dan 9:4–19), and sermon (*e.g.* Josh. 24; Judg. 2:11–13; 1 Sam. 12:6–8; 1 Kgs. 8). As the preeminent saving event in their history (Deut. 4:32–40), the Exodus profoundly shaped Israel's social structures, calendars, remembrance of the ancient past, and *hopes of future restoration. Because of their conviction that *Jesus fulfilled Israel's destiny, the NT authors couch their works in Exodus language, albeit on a cosmic scale and with reference to all peoples.

Beginnings

The Exodus cannot be understood apart from Genesis. It fulfils the patriarchal promises of progeny and *land (Gen. 12:7; 13:14–17; 15:18) and begins a new *creation, albeit in microcosm, whereby *God establishes a new *humanity, provides them with a new Edenic land, and dwells among them. The first overt reference to the Exodus occurs in the *covenant ratification of Genesis 15:7–21. Abram is warned that his descendents will be enslaved for three generations, but in the fourth, when Amorite wickedness is complete, they will go free with great wealth (Exod. 3:22; 12:35–36). The confirming *theophany of a smoking brazier and a flaming torch passing through the split animals adumbrates the pillar of fire and cloud (Exod. 13:21) and (possibly) Yahweh's causing Israel to pass through the split sea (Ps. 136:13–14). (Joseph, aware of this promise, later requires that the people take his bones with them when they leave Egypt, Gen. 50:25.) But as the reference to the Amorites' *sin indicates, possession of the land is tied to behaviour: if Israel fails to be *obedient, she too will be expelled.

The Exodus

The Exodus comprises three fundamental elements: Israel's deliverance from Egypt; the journey through the *wilderness; and the arrival in the Promised Land (Josh. 24:5–13; Exod. 3:7–21). It is bracketed by the beginning and end of *Moses' life, by the miraculous crossings of the Reed Sea and the Jordan (Exod. 14 – 15; Josh. 1:2; 3 – 4; Pss. 114:1–5; 66:6), and by the defeat of Pharaoh and the Canaanites (Josh. 24:16–18).

The patriarchal promise of offspring

The account of the Exodus begins with the introduction of a central motif, that of Yahweh's covenant *faithfulness: the patriarchal/creation promise of offspring is fulfilled (Exod. 1:1–20; Gen. 1:28; 15:5; 46:8–20). Pharaoh, however, with serpent-like cunning (Exod. 1:10a), embarks on a policy resulting in hard service, pain in childbearing, and *death, all of which are associated with life outside the garden of Eden (Gen. 3:16–19). Emulating the murderous line of Cain, Lamech, and the sons of the gods (Gen. 4:8, 23–24; 6:5), he pretends to deity, presiding over an anti-Eden (Exod. 1:13; Gen. 2:15; 13:10). But Yahweh hears Israel's cry and remembers his covenant (Exod. 2:23–25; 3:7–10, 16; Gen. 50:24). In an act of new creation, he provides Moses (Exod. 2:1; lit. 'she saw that he was good'; Gen. 1:4, 10, etc.), who like Noah is preserved through waters by an ark (Gen. 6:14–19).

The revelation of the divine name

Yahweh appears to the exiled Moses (Exod. 3:1 – 4:17), announcing that he will redeem Israel with an outstretched hand and great wonders (3:20; 6:6). As God of the patriarchs, he reveals his name, I AM WHO I AM, which denotes his dynamic and personal presence. He is incomparable, and comprehensible only in terms of his self-generating and self-sustaining being (3:14; 6:3). The sign promised to Moses, that Israel will worship Yahweh on Mt Sinai (3:12), emphasizes that their identity is grounded not in their independence and liberty but, as God's son, in Yahweh's presence with them and their *worship of and loyalty to him. After initial reluctance, Moses returns to Egypt to demand the release of Yahweh's firstborn (4:22–23).

The hardening of Pharaoh's heart: creating Pharaoh in his own image

Integral to the Exodus is the *hardening of Pharaoh's heart (Exod. 4:21; 7:3; by Pharaoh, 8:15, 32; and by Yahweh, 9:12; 10:1; etc.). His inability to control even his own thoughts mocks his idolatrous pretension to deity (Pss. 115:5–8; 135:15–18; Is. 44:17–18) and reflects the principle of lex talionis: as Pharaoh hardens his heart to Israel's hard labour (Exod. 1:14; Deut. 15:7; 26:6) so Yahweh's hard hand (Exod. 3:19) hardens him so that, ironically, he finally drives Israel out with his own hard hand (6:1). Pharaoh's hardness, in the face of many signs and wonders, becomes the occasion for acts of *judgment intended to show all Egypt that Israel's God is Yahweh (7:3–5).

Signs and wonders: (un)creating Egypt in Pharaoh's image

Through ten plagues Yahweh displays his mighty hand and outstretched arm (Exod. 6:6; 13:3–16; Deut. 9:29), humbling Egypt, Pharaoh, and her gods (Exod. 12:12; Num. 33:4). So the Nile, deified as the god Hapi and the source of Egypt's life, having been filled with the blood of Israel's sons, now turns to blood and brings death to Egypt. The sun, deified as Re (Amon-Re), is humilated by the plague of darkness. Pharaoh's words of death are turned back on him by the judgments of Yahweh the creator. Just as murderous Cain was cursed from the ground, so Pharaoh's anti-Eden is (un)created in his own distorted moral image, disintegrating into pre-creation chaos. Only when he submits to Yahweh's word does the good order of creation return. Nevertheless, his continued idolatrous arrogance culminates in the final plague, the death of Egypt's firstborn (Exod. 12:29), and for Israel in the institution of Passover (12:1 – 13:16).

The Passover and the firstborn

The narrative implies that the term 'Passover' derives from Yahweh's angel passing over his people (Exod. 12:13–27). The final plague is the only one in which Israel has to be distinguished from the Egyptians; this suggests that Israel is inherently no different from Egypt and that the people are just as likely to be killed by the destroyer as are the Egyptians (Josh. 24:14; Ezek 20:7–8). Key to the ritual are the slaughter of a *lamb or kid, the smearing of its *blood on the doorposts, and the eating of its meat. The special instructions regarding the animal indicate that Passover is an *atoning *sacrifice, the smearing of the blood with hyssop suggests purification (Exod. 12:22; Lev. 14:4–6; Ps. 51:7), and the parallels with the stipulations for the Aaronic priests, and the requirement of *circumcision imply an act of consecration (Exod. 29:20–34; Lev. 8:23–32): Passover sanctifies all Israel to God (Exod. 19:6). That the participants eat in readiness for departure stresses the centrality of Passover to Israel's deliverance (12:11). It is in remembrance of this that Passover is to be celebrated annually (12:14–20; 13:3–10; Deut. 16:1–8). The emphasis on the firstborn is noteworthy (Exod. 13:2–15; 22:29b–30; 34:19; Num. 3:12–13, 40–45; 18:15). First, the plague against them is in response to Pharaoh's attempt to destroy Yahweh's firstborn, Israel (Exod. 4:22). Secondly, it demonstrates that Yahweh alone is the great King who creates and sustains life. According to the requirements of tribute, not only do Israel's firstborn, both human and animal, belong to him, but Israel is the firstfruits of Yahweh's harvest (Jer. 2:3; cf. the minḥâ or tribute offering in Gen. 4:3–5). Thirdly, the connection with entry into the Edenic-land reminds Israel that their inheritance is dependent on their loyalty to Yahweh (Exod. 13:5, 11–16). Yahweh, in disinheriting the 'Cainite' Pharaoh, and later the Amorites, in favour of his firstborn, Israel, declares that only as his faithful son will Israel inherit his world. (See *Sacred meals.)

Crossing the sea: a new creation

Israel, driven out, plunders (disinherits) Egypt as they go (Exod. 11:2; 12:35). Again Pharaoh changes his mind, but now the Lord himself appears in a pillar of fire and cloud (13:21–22; cf. Gen. 15:17). The paradigmatic miracle of the Exodus is the parting of the Reed Sea, beyond which lies chaos. The language of darkness and *light, *waters divided by the wind, and the appearance of dry land, mark this as moment of new creation (Exod. 14:20b–21; Gen. 1:2–4, 9–10; 8:3–4; cf. the metaphor of hovering in Gen. 1:2 and Deut. 32:10–11). The song of Moses fuses the motifs of creation and conquest as Yahweh's defeat of the primeval sea is linked with his shepherding his people to *victory in Canaan and to his Edenic holy *mountain (Exod. 15:1–21; Pss. 74:13–14; 78:53–54). Just as the Cainite dynasty was judged by God through water (Gen. 6 – 7), so too is Pharaoh. Having drowned a potential Israelite army in the Nile (Exod. 1:22), he now witnesses the watery demise of his own forces while Israel, like the child Moses, passes to safety. Parallels with the flood, along with Israel's plundering of the Egyptians, the loss of the firstborn, and the dispossession of the Amorites, suggest that this is a trial by water (cf. Is. 43:2) in which Israel's inheritance rights, as Yahweh's firstborn, are vindicated.

Journey to the mountain of God

The journey through the wilderness is characterized by Yahweh's faithful provision (e.g. Exod. 15:22–25; 16 – 17), notably of manna (16:4) and water from the rock (17:1–7), and by Israel's *grumbling (e.g. 15:24; 16:2; 17:2–3). The climactic moment is the ratification of Yahweh's covenant with Israel, his '*kingdom of priests and holy nation' (19:5–6). After rigorous preparations by Israel, Yahweh descends with the blast of a horn, fire, thunder, and storm clouds (19:10–19; 24:17; Deut. 4:11; cf. Exod. 3:2; Gen. 15:17). His holy presence distinguishes Israel from other *nations, and reverses the separation caused by the expulsion from Eden. In accepting the ten words (Exod. 20:1–17) and the covenant (20:22 – 23:33), God's son Israel renounces the autonomy sought by Adam and Eve at the tree of knowledge (Gen. 3). In keeping the commandments and the covenant, Israel will be recreated in the image of God their father (Gen. 1:26), and so will inherit the land through the guidance of Yahweh's mysterious angel, who bears his name (Exod. 23:20–22). The covenant of blood, which represents God as the author of life and provides atonement for Israel, is ratified (24:8) by the elders of Israel sharing a covenant meal on the mountain in God's presence (24:9–11).

The tabernacle

The material sign of Yahweh's dwelling among his people is the tabernacle. He too lives in a tent with a stove (altar), water, lamp, bread, and a footstool. The camp is arranged in a rectangular battle formation, like the military camp of Rameses II. As it moves towards the Promised Land, the tabernacle at its centre indicates that Yahweh is Israel's warrior-king. The tabernacle resembles the sanctuary of Eden, with its ark of the presence and guardian cherubim (Exod. 25:18–22; 26:31; Gen. 3:24; Ezek. 28:13–14), bread symbolizing bountiful provision (Lev. 24:5–9; Gen. 2:9a), stylized candelabra symbolizing the tree of life and the law that gives knowledge (Exod. 25:31–36; Deut. 10:1–5; 4:6; Gen. 2:9b), *priests who are to guard and keep the sanctuary (Num. 3:7–8; 8:22; 18:5–6; cf. Gen. 2:15), and precious materials (Gen. 2:12). Comparable to Yahweh's Edenic mountain (Ezek. 28:14, 16), it is a moveable Mt Sinai with graduated levels of *holiness and a central place in which is the cloud of Yahweh's presence (Exod. 40:34–38). The creation account is recalled in the Spirit's anointing of Bezalel (Exod. 31:1–11; Gen. 1:2), the six divine speeches concluding with a statement about the *sabbath (Exod. 25:1 – 31:11, 12–17; Gen. 2:1–3), the tabernacle's being finished in all its array (Exod. 39:32; Gen. 2:1), Moses' seeing that all had been done in accordance with God's command (Exod. 39:43; Gen. 1:31), and the dedication of the tabernacle on New Year's Day (Exod. 40:2, 17). That the sabbath is then explained in terms of creation (20:11; 31:12–17) and *rest from hard labour in Egypt (Deut. 5:13–15) reinforces the presentation of the Exodus as a new creation.

The golden calf, Israel's fall and an atoning servant

Nevertheless, like Adam, Israel falls by engaging in *idolatry. In implicit opposition to the tabernacle, the golden calf is an attempt to make Yahweh's presence concrete (Exod. 32:1–6; Deut. 9:7–17). Moses' destruction of the tablets symbolizes the consequences of Israel's faithlessness (Exod. 32:19), while the water ordeal (32:20), resembling that for *adultery (Num. 5:11–31), divulges the true character of Israel's *apostasy (Exod. 34:16; Jer. 3:1–5; Ezek. 16; Hos. 2). For the first time a plague is visited on Israel (Exod. 32:35). Moses, Yahweh's servant (Exod. 4:10; 14:31; Num. 12:7–8; Deut. 34:5), seeks to make atonement (Exod. 32:30), and Yahweh reveals his *glory as the compassionate one, abounding in *love and covenant faithfulness (34:6–7). New tablets are written, the tabernacle is completed using Egypt's riches (35:4–9, 22–29; 3:21–22; 11:2; 12:35–36), and the cloud of Yahweh's glory descends (40:34–38).

Faithful Yahweh and grumbling Israel

The subsequent journey is again characterized by Yahweh's provision and Israel's grumbling (e.g. Num. 11:1–4; 14:36–37; 20:3–5; 21:4–5), culminating in unbelieving Israel's refusal to enter the land (Num. 13:26–33; Deut. 1:26–28). The nation is sentenced to wander for forty years (Num. 14:29–34) before a purified *remnant and the new generation enters the land under the guidance of Joshua; Moses is forbidden to enter because of his high-handed autonomy in striking the rock a second time (Num. 20:11–13; Deut. 3:21–28). But as Deuteronomy explains, Israel's possession of the Edenic sanctuary (8:7–9; 11:10–12; Exod. 15:17) and enjoyment of the creation *blessings (Deut. 28:1–14) is contingent on their faithfulness (26:16–19; Lev. 26:1–13). Faithlessness will incur the plagues wrought upon Egypt and Israel will be expelled, as were the nations (Deut. 28:15 – 29:28; 32; Lev. 26:14–39), and will even return to Egypt (Deut. 28:68). Nevertheless, on account of the covenant with their fathers, there will be hope for a *repentant remnant (30:1–10; Lev. 26:36–45).

A new era

The Exodus demonstrates that Yahweh is the creator who controls nature and whom none can resist. He has not abandoned his creation, but directs history in keeping with his promises to Abraham (Gen. 15:13–14). A God of justice and great *mercy, he is known by Israel supremely as the one who redeemed them from Egypt (Exod. 6:6; 15:3; 20:2). As the moment of her creation, Israel's New Year is relocated to the Exodus (Exod. 12:2); the sabbath days and years celebrate it (Deut. 5:14–15; Exod. 23:10–12; the yearly feasts recall it (Exod. 23:14; Lev. 23:42–43; Deut.

16:9–12), and the food laws are based upon it (Lev. 11; especially v. 45). The impact of the Exodus on Israel's social relationships is seen in the following requirements: care for the stranger (Exod. 22:21; Lev. 19:33–34; Deut. 10:17–19); a rest day (Deut. 5:13–15); justice and concern for the weak (Deut. 24:17–22); Hebrew slaves should not be ruled with cruelty (Lev. 25:43); they are to be freed at the Jubilee (Lev. 25:42); they must not go empty-handed (Deut. 15:13–15); even the Egyptian is not to be abhorred (Deut. 23:7).

Exodus in the former prophets

The earlier fusing of the Exodus and conquest themes (Exod. 15:13–18) continues as Joshua is presented as a new Moses (Josh. 3:5–17; 4:14; 5:14–15; Exod. 3:5; 23:20–23). In the context of Passover and the cessation of manna (Josh. 5:10–12), he presides over the Jordan crossing (3:9–17; 4:18–24; Ps. 114:3) and his actions at Ai reflect those of Moses against Amalek (Josh. 8:18–19, 26; Exod. 17:8–11). The Exodus events cause Jericho and the Gibeonites to cower (Josh. 2:10–11; 9:9), undergird Joshua's call at Shechem to covenant faithfulness (Josh. 24:5–13), and shape the account of the ark's sojourn in Philistia (1 Sam. 4:8; 5:2–4, 6–12). Solomon's building of the temple is the only OT event dated from the Exodus (1 Kgs. 6:1): 480 years, forty years for each tribe's wandering in the desert. The Shekinah's presence at the dedication of the *temple (1 Kgs. 8:10; 2 Chr. 5:13b; Exod. 40:34–35) marks the culmination of the Exodus (8:21; 2 Chr. 6:11; cf. Exod. 15:17; Deut. 12:9–11). Yahweh had enabled David to purge the land (1 Kgs. 5:3–5), and now Yahweh's presence dwells among his people who, as his new humanity called to be a blessing to the nations (e.g. the Queen of Sheba, 1 Kgs. 10:1–13; 2 Chr. 9:1–12), are settled and at peace in a new Eden. But Yahweh warns that covenant-breaking will result in *exile (1 Kgs. 9:9; 2 Chr. 7:22), while the nation's hope of return is founded on the *election the Exodus signifies (1 Kgs. 8:51, 53). The rot begun under Solomon (1 Kgs. 11) continues under Rehoboam. His oppression recalls Pharaoh's (12:8–11; Exod. 1:14; 5:1–21): he threatens to increase the burden on the builders of his store cities (1 Kgs. 9:15–19; Exod. 1:11). Yahweh's intervention recalls the Exodus motif of hardening (1 Kgs. 12:15). Forced by

Solomon's murderous plot to flee to Egypt (1 Kgs. 11:28, 40; Exod. 2:15), Jeroboam, like Moses, returns on the king's death to deliver his people (1 Kgs. 12:2–4; Exod. 4:19; cf. Hadad, 1 Kgs. 11:14–22), but directly his Exodus occurs he becomes an Aaron, fashioning golden calves 'who brought [Israel] up out of Egypt' (1 Kgs. 12:28–33; Exod. 32:4). In the end, the northern kingdom's exile is directly related to their abandoning the Exodus covenant (2 Kgs. 17:7–23) and, like Adam and Eve, they are expelled from Yahweh's Edenic land. In the case of Judah, Manasseh exceeds the wickedness of the Amorites (2 Kgs. 21:11–16) and, despite the exemplary Hezekiah and Josiah (both of whom are noted for their Passover celebrations; 2 Chr. 30; 35; 2 Kgs. 23:21–23), the same fate is inevitable.

The latter prophets

Here the Exodus theme is most influential, serving both as a foil to Israel's faithlessness and as a paradigm for future hope. In protest against Israel's faithless response to Yahweh's Exodus redemption, Hosea's marriage to an adulterous wife recalls Israel's Exodus apostasy (Hos. 2; 11; Exod. 32:20; Num. 5:11–31). Yahweh reverses his earlier declaration: Israel becomes 'Lo-Ruhamah' (i.e. 'not loved') and 'Lo-Ammi' (i.e. 'not my people'; Hos. 1:6–9; Exod. 5:1; 6:5), and is returned to Egypt (Hos. 8:3; 9:1–3), but not for ever. Those said not to be God's people will again be called his children (1:10 – 2:1). In a new Exodus Yahweh will gather Israel from the nations (11:1, 10–11), and woo her in the desert (2:14), and the site of her first infidelity in Canaan (that of Achan at Achor, Josh. 7:1; 1 Chr. 2:7) will become a doorway of hope (Hos. 2:15).

Amos says that although at the Exodus Yahweh chose Israel as his special possession (3:1–2), they have become like the Amorites. Having refused to respond to a visitation of Egypt's plagues (4:10; Joel 1:1 – 2:11), they will be driven from the land (Amos 2:6–16; 5:27; Deut. 28). But the Exodus not only provides the basis for judgment; it also offers hope for a remnant (Amos 9:7–8, 14–15; Deut. 30:1–10).

Micah likewise recalls Yahweh's Exodus redemption to rebuke Israel's faithlessness (6:4), and announces a new Exodus of the lame and the exiles (4:6–7; 5:3b). Compassionate Yahweh (7:18–20; cf. Exod. 34:6–7) will again show his wonders and humble the nations just as he did the Egyptians (Mic. 7:15–16); their wealth too will be devoted to him (4:13b; 1 Sam. 6:4; Exod. 11:2).

Isaiah describes Yahweh as recovering a second time the exiled remnant from the four corners of the earth (11:11–16), as he smites the sea and his people cross dry-shod (11:15–16; Exod. 14:21; 15:3–5). The Exodus paradigm of salvation is now extended to Egypt (Is. 19:19–25): when they cry out because of their oppressors, Yahweh will send them a deliverer; they will build an altar as a sign so that they might know him and sacrifice to him, and they will be his people (cf. Exod. 3:7–9). Indeed, all nations will come to Zion, the new Sinai, enshrouded in the fire and cloud of God's presence, to be taught by the Lord (Is. 2:2–4; 4:2–6; 19:23–25).

For Jeremiah the Exodus evokes the faithfulness of Israel's youth, and Yahweh's jealous protection (2:2–3). But the people have forgotten their deliverer (2:6), and have forsaken the living water for other rivers (2:13; Exod. 17:1–7). Because of Israel's breach of the Sinai covenant (Jer. 7:22–26; 11:3–7; 32:20–23), their land will (like Egypt) revert to chaos (4:23–26), and they will go into exile as Yahweh's mighty arm is turned against them (21:2–6). But God, like a shepherd leading his firstborn son, will redeem his scattered people (31:7–11) and establish a new covenant with them, writing his law not on stone tablets but on their hearts (31:31–34). This new Exodus will supplant the old as the paradigmatic moment of *salvation (16:14–15; 23:7–8).

Habakkuk, perplexed over Yahweh's mysterious dealings with Israel, consoles himself with a song recalling the Exodus and conquest (Hab. 3:2–15). For Ezekiel the Exodus is a tragedy of rebellion: he traces Israel's idolatry back even to Egypt, and claims that only Yahweh's constant mercy averted annihilating judgment (Ezek. 20:7–26; 23:3; cf. Josh. 24:14). Drawing on God's word to Moses (Exod. 6:6–8), he announces that Yahweh will gather Israel from the nations, where he has scattered them with a mighty hand, but this will be a gathering in the desert and, as in Israel's wilderness chastisement, he will purge them thoroughly (Ezek. 20:33–38; 11:19–20). In this new

Exodus, envisaged as a resurrection (37:1–14) and recovery of Eden (36:33–36), Yahweh returns to the restored temple mountain (44:4; 48:35; cf. 10:18), on which Passover is celebrated (45:21–24) and from which a river flows (47:1–12; Gen. 2:10; cf. Zech. 14:8).

The most extensive new Exodus/new creational material occurs in Isaiah's prophecy of the return from *Babylon (51:9–11; cf. 27:1; 44:24–28). As in Jeremiah, this new deliverance, journey, and arrival become the paradigm of redemption (43:9; 42:9). The prophet begins with a summons to prepare the way for Yahweh (40:3–11). Israel's warrior shepherd (40:10–11; 51:9–10; Exod. 15:13; Pss. 77:20; 78:52–53) and redeemer (Is. 41:14; 44:22–23; etc.; Exod. 6:6), will deliver his plundered people from the strong man of Babylon (Is. 49:24–25; 42:24). But this time they will not go out in haste (52:11–12; Exod. 12:11). Just as he once divided the sea (Is. 43:16–17) so the compassionate Yahweh (49:10–13; Deut. 30:3), his people's front and rear guard (Is. 52:11–12; Exod. 13:21–22), provides them with food and water (Is. 43:19–21; 48:20–21; 35:7), and leads blind and deaf Israel (42:16–22) through waters and fire (43:2, 16–19) along a way that they do not know (42:16; Deut. 1:33; cf. Is. 35:8; 57:14; 62:10). Just as Moses once sang a victory song (Exod. 15), so hymns accompany this new deliverance (Is. 42:10–12; 44:23), and it is all to Yahweh's glory among the nations (40:5; cf. 52:10; Exod. 9:16). The healed blind, deaf, and lame (Is. 35:5–6) arrive in a restored *Jerusalem (35; 54; 60 – 62; cf. Exod. 3:12; 15:17) and a renewed Eden (Is. 41:17–20; 51:3), to which the nations bring their wealth (45:14; 60:5; 66:12). The agent of the Lord's arm (53:1; 51:9; Exod. 6:6) is his Spirit-anointed servant (Is. 42:1–9; 49:1–13; 50:4–11; 52:13 – 53:12; 61:1–3) who not only Moses-like atones for Israel's rebellion (Is. 52:13 – 53:12; Exod. 32:30) but also makes a covenant both with Israel and with the nations (Is. 42:6; 49:12; 52:15; cf. Exod. 24:8). Yahweh will pour out his Spirit upon his people (Is. 44:3; Num. 11:24–25), and they will become a kingdom of priests (Is. 61:6; 56:6–8; 66:21; Exod. 19:5–6). As Yahweh again marries the fomerly barren Jerusalem (Is. 62:5), she will look in wonder at the multitude of her children (54:1–3; 51:2; cf. Gen. 15:5; Deut. 10:22).

However, in spite of Yahweh's constant declaration of his presence (lit. 'I AM'; Is. 44:6; 45:18; *etc.*; Exod. 3:12–14), fearful Israel (*cf.* Is. 40:9; 41:10–14; *etc.*) rejects the good news (45:9–10; 48; Deut. 1:26–35). Concluding with a lament recalling the time of the Exodus (Is. 63:7 – 64:3), the prophet remembers that even then Israel rebelled by grieving Yahweh's holy spirit (63:10), but asks that Yahweh might again rend the heavens and do 'awesome' things (64:1–3).

Haggai too exhorts the returnees not to fear, declaring that I AM, the warrior, is with them and, recalling Sinai, that his presence will shake the nations and their wealth fill his house (Hag. 2:4–9). But in Malachi's day Israel's faithlessness (Mal. 3:7) delays Yahweh's coming (2:9b). Nevertheless, Yahweh has not abandoned his covenant (*cf.* 4:4) and promises to send his angel (Elijah, 4:5, see above) to prepare his way (3:1; Exod. 23:20; Is. 40:3), lest when he come the people's wickedness causes him to curse the land (Mal. 4:1–6; 3:2–3).

Psalms

Numerous psalms recall Yahweh's redemptive love in the Exodus. Hymns of praise celebrate it (66:6–12; 68; 103:7; 105; 114; 135:8–9) and laments appeal to it (74; 77; 80; *cf.* 44). The splitting of the Reed Sea is the most common motif (66:6; 74:13–14; 77:16–20; 78:13, 53; 106:9–11, 22; 114:3, 5; 136:13–15), with the Exodus being seen as a new creation (136:5–9; *cf.* 135). Having brought his vine out of Egypt (80:4–16), Yahweh as Israel's warrior-shepherd (77:15, 20) moves his presence from Sinai to Mt Zion (68:15–18). While Psalm 105 is the most complete recital of events, the most extensive treatment focuses on the mystery of Israel's constant unfaithfulness (see 106; 95:7–11), and concludes with a celebration of David's shepherding kingship as God's solution (78:70–72). The Exodus engenders praise, repentance (81:5–7, 10–16), and faithfulness by reminding Israel both of Yahweh's powerful deeds of mercy on her behalf and of her frequently faithless response.

The Gospels and Acts

Mark's Gospel opens with allusions to Exodus traditions (1:1–3). Its good news (Is. 52:7; 61:1–2; *cf.* 40:9) is that Jesus fulfils Isaiah's prophecy of a new Exodus (Is. 40:3).

But Israel must obey Yahweh's Elijah, John the Baptist, who comes to prepare his way (Mal. 3:1; 4:5; Exod. 23:20); otherwise the land will be cursed (Mal. 4:6). At Jesus' *baptism the rent heavens and descent of the Spirit provide an answer to Isaiah's last lament (Is. 64:1), while the heavenly voice and Jesus' passing through the water into the desert (which recapitulates Israel's experience) designate him as Yahweh's true servant Israel ('my beloved son', Exod. 4:22) and thus exiled Israel's messianic servant deliverer (Ps. 2:7; Is. 42:1).

In this new Exodus, Jesus, Israel's bridegroom (Mark 2:19; Is. 54:5–8; 62:5), delivers his people (Mark 1:14–8:21), leads his 'blind' followers along the way (8:22 – 10:52), and arrives in Jerusalem (11:1 – 16:8). His exorcisms fulfil Yahweh's promise to bind the strong man (3:27; Is. 49:24–25) (here the demons, not Babylon, are the oppressors), and after defeating the sea, he drowns the enemy host (Mark 4:35–41; 5:9–13; Is. 43:16–17; Exod. 14–15). Isaiah's new Exodus expectations are fulfilled in the miraculous feedings (Mark 6:34–44; 8:1–10; Is. 49:9b–10; 48:21), the healings of the blind, deaf, dumb, and lame (Is. 35:5–6; 61:1–2 LXX; 32:3–4), the *forgiveness of sins (Mark 2:5; Is. 43:25; 33:24), and the reversal of the defilement and death of daughter Israel (5:25–41; Is. 64:6–7; 65:19–20). The calling of the Twelve on a mountain signifies the reconstitution of Israel (Mark 3:13–19). Consequently, for Israel to reject Jesus is to blaspheme the Spirit (3:29), and thus to repeat the sin of the first Exodus (Is. 63:10). As in Isaiah, this new Exodus is effected by a suffering servant (Mark 10:45; *cf.* 8:31; 9:31; 10:33–34; Is. 53:6–12). And like blind Israel (Is. 42:18–20), the disciples, having recognized that Jesus is the Messiah (Mark 8:27–38), have their eyes touched a second time (*cf.* Mark 8:22–26), as he leads them along a way they do not know (8:31–38; Is. 42:16; 53:1). On the way, Jesus' transfiguration after six days recalls Moses' experience on Sinai (Mark 9:1–7; Exod. 24:12–16; 34:29–35; *cf.* Mal. 4:4), and he too descends to encounter faithlessness (Mark 9:19; Exod. 32).

Jesus' arrival in Jerusalem, accompanied both by the healed and cleansed blind man (Bartimaeus means 'son of uncleanness') and by the praising crowd (Mark 10:46 – 11:10), fulfils the prophecy of Yahweh's return to

Zion (Is. 35:3–10). However, the authorities reject Jesus and God's plan for the temple to be a house of prayer for all nations (Mark 11:17; Is. 56:6–8; 66:19–20). As a result the temple is cursed (Mark 11:12–14, 20–21), the care of Yahweh's vine is given to others (12:1–12; Is. 5:1– 7; 3:11; Ps. 80), and the nation is subjected to a reverse conquest (Mark 13). But Jesus' bloody death in great darkness (*cf.* Gen. 15:11–12) inaugurates a new covenant (Mark 14:24; Exod. 24:8), and the future now lies in Galilee of the Gentiles (Matt 4:15; *cf.* Is. 9:1).

Matthew and Luke frequently follow Mark's narrative pattern (see parallel passages) but with additional emphases. Like Moses, Jesus is threatened by a ruler, and he flees (ironically to Egypt), returning on the news of his enemy's death (Matt. 2:13–20; Exod. 2:11–15; 4:19). Jesus' departure fulfils Jeremiah's promise of a new Exodus (Matt. 2:18; Jer. 31:15 and context), and his return that of Hosea (Matt. 2:15; Hos. 11:1). After his baptism, Jesus' responses to temptation recall Israel's wilderness wanderings, but the true Israel, the true Son of Yahweh, does not fail (Matt. 4:1–10; Deut. 8:3; 6:16, 13; *cf.* 8:2–9). (See *Testing.)

In Matthew, Jesus' healings are explicitly related to his servant role (8:17; Is. 53:4) and to Isaiah's new Exodus (Matt. 11:5; Is. 35:5–6; 61:1–2 LXX; 32:3–4). His gentleness as the Servant brings new creational sabbath rest to Israel and the nations (Matt. 12:18–21; Is. 42:1–4; *cf.* Matt. 2:1–12; 8:5–13; 10:18; 28:18–20). But again, Israel's hard-heartedness leads to judgment (13:15; Is. 6:9–10).

For Luke, Jesus' birth (1:51, 70–75 [Exod. 4:31; 7:16; Ps. 106:4, 10], 76, 79 [Is. 40:3–4; 59:8] and 2:30–32 [Is. 40:5 LXX; 52:10; 42:6; 49:6]) and inaugural proclamation initiate Yahweh's new Exodus salvation (4:18–19; Is. 61:1–2; 58:6; *cf.* Luke 3:4–6; Is. 40:3–5). In his account of the Beelzebul controversy, Luke's use of the phrase 'finger of God' indicates that Jesus' exorcisms constitute a new Exodus (11:20; Exod. 8:19), while the sending of the seventy(-two) recalls the anointing of elders to assist Moses (Luke 10:1; Num. 11:16–17, 24–25). At his transfiguration, Jesus is presented as undertaking a new Exodus (Luke 9:31; *cf.* 24:27), and his subsequent way (9:51 – 19:48), which includes many calls to faithfulness reminiscent of those in Deuteronomy, leads finally to his

death in Jerusalem. Forty days later he ascends (Acts 1:3).

The Pentecost theophany in Acts recalls Sinai (2:2–3; Exod. 19:16–19). Jesus is the prophet like Moses who is rejected just as was Moses (Acts 3:22; 7:20–41; Deut. 18:17–19; Exod. 2:14). As in Isaiah, the new Exodus is effected by a Servant (Acts 8:32–33; Is. 53:7–8, 12; Luke 23:37), who through his own *suffering servants brings light to the nations (Acts 1:8; 9:15; 13:47; Is. 49:6; Luke 2:32; 24:47). Sadly it is Israel, likened to the crooked Exodus generation (Acts 2:40; Deut. 32:5), whose heart is hardened (Acts 28:25–31; *cf.* 13:16–46; Ps. 78).

Following the ancient pattern, John links Exodus with creation. The eternal word tabernacles among us in glory, 'full of grace and truth' (John 1:14; Exod. 25:8 LXX; 33:19–22; 34:5–7), as the Baptist prepares his way (1:23; Is. 40:3). The law came through Moses, but Jesus, the prophet about whom Moses wrote (John 6:14; 7:16–17, 40; Deut. 18:15–19), brings grace and truth, thereby fulfilling Israel's Exodus feasts. At the Passover he is revealed as the new temple (John 2:19; 4:20–24; Exod. 3:12), the one whose lifting up makes available to all people the fulfilment of Israel's wilderness *healing (John 3:14; Num. 21:4–9), Israel's true bridegroom (John 3:29; Hos. 2:14ff; Is. 54:6ff), the I AM (John 8:58; Exod. 3:14; Is. 44:6; 45:18) who feeds Israel and controls the sea (John 6:5–59), and the Passover lamb whose death seals Israel's new Exodus redemption (19:36; *cf.* 1:29; Exod. 12:46). On the sabbath, he inaugurates Israel's eschatological sabbath restoration (John 5:16–18). At Tabernacles (Lev. 23:33–43) he is revealed as the light (John 8:12; Exod. 13:21) and water (John 7:37–39; *cf.* 4:13–14; Exod. 17:1–6) of *life (the promised new creational river flows not from the temple but from those who trust him; *cf.* Ezek. 47) and as Israel's true shepherd (John 10:1–18; Ps. 80:1). Nevertheless, in spite of Jesus' numerous signs, Israel, like hard-hearted Pharaoh, rejects this new Exodus revelation of Yahweh's 'arm' through his servant (John 4:48; 12:37–40; Exod. 7:3–4; *cf.* Is. 53:1; 6:10).

Paul

Although Paul's writings include few explicit references to the Exodus, his language of new creational redemption from slavery into adopted sonship reflects its influence (Rom. 3:24; Gal. 4:3–8; Col. 1:13–14; Exod. 6:6; Deut. 7:8). Christ, our Passover lamb (1 Cor. 5:7b; Exod. 12:21), established the new covenant (1 Cor. 11:25; Exod. 24:8) by giving himself as an atonement (Rom. 3:25; Lev. 16:14–21) for sins (Rom. 4:25; 2 Cor. 5:21; Gal. 1:4; Is. 53:10–12). Just as Israel was baptized in the cloud and sea and ate the manna and drank from the rock, so too Christians are baptized into Jesus, passing from death into new creational life (2 Cor. 5:17; Rom. 6:3–4) and sharing spiritual food and drink (1 Cor. 10:1–4). But believers are warned against the leaven of wickedness (1 Cor. 5:6–8; Exod. 12:18–20); they should recall God's judgment on Israel's infidelities, and not presume upon his grace (1 Cor. 10:5–13; Exod. 32:6; Num. 25:1–9). Sinai's law was incapable of dealing with sin (Rom. 7; 2 Cor. 3:6–9), but the new covenant of unfading glory (2 Cor. 3:7–11; Exod. 34:29–35) is written by the Spirit on the 'tablets' of the heart (2 Cor. 3:3–6; Jer. 31:31–34; Ezek. 11:19–20; Exod. 31:18).

Fulfilling barren Jerusalem's new Exodus hope (Gal. 4:24–27; Is. 54:1), the gospel of peace (Rom. 5:1; Gal. 1:3–5; Eph. 6:15; Is. 52:7; 61:1) brings together those near and far, both Jew and Gentile, to be God's new humanity (Eph. 2:13–17; Gal. 3:26–29; 6:15; Is. 57:19; 52:7; cf. Rom. 4:16–17), his elect people (Eph. 1:4; Col. 3:12; Deut. 4:37; 10:15). In this Exodus, however, Yahweh's presence resides not in a building but in his new temple, i.e. his people (1 Cor. 3:10–17; 2 Cor. 6:16; Exod. 25:8; Jer. 32:38; Is. 52:11), his new congregation (ekklēsia, Deut. 4:10; 31:30). And as in the Exodus the victory spoils adorned Yahweh's dwelling and enriched his people, so too the church benefits from Christ's victory (Eph. 1:18; 4:8; Ps. 68). As the new Israel (Gal. 6:16; 2 Cor. 6:18; Phil. 3:3; Is. 43:6–7; Jer. 31:9), who walk in the new Exodus way of the Spirit (Rom. 8:4; Gal. 5:16; Eph. 5:8), believers are exhorted to awake (Eph. 5:14; Is. 52:1; 60:1) and to join Yahweh the warrior in effecting the new creational Exodus (Eph. 6:13–18; Is. 59:17; 52:7). Ministers of the new covenant, however, must also enter the fellowship of the sufferings of its servant mediator (Phil. 2:6–11; 3:10; Col. 1:24). Surprisingly, the Gentiles' salvation fulfils the new Exodus promise to Hosea's 'not my people' (Rom. 9:25–26; Hos 1:10b, 2:23) while only a remnant of Israel joins the nations (Rom. 9:27–29; Exod. 12:38): as in the first Exodus Yahweh has compassion on whom he will (Rom 9:15; Exod. 33:19). Like Pharaoh, Israel's hard-heartedness is used to glorify Yahweh (Rom. 9:17; Exod. 9:16).

Other

More directly than any other NT book, Hebrews argues for the superiority of the new epoch. In this new Exodus (3:7–19), Jesus, attested by signs and wonders and gifts of the Spirit (cf. Is. 63:11; Num. 11:25), is greater than both the angels who gave the first covenant (Heb. 2:1–4) and Moses who mediated it (3:2–6; cf. 8:5–6). We should therefore heed the warning example of the generation who through unbelief failed to enter the promised rest (3:12–19; cf. Jude 5). Further, since Joshua did not provide new creational rest (Heb. 4:8), it still remains for us (4:1–11; Ps. 95:7–11). Bearing the sins of many (Heb. 9:28; Is. 53:11–12), Jesus, our new Moses and new Joshua, has gone ahead to provide perfect access to the Father (Heb. 12:2; 8:1; 10:19–20; 4:16) through his blood of the new covenant (13:20; 12:24; Exod. 24:8). We, however, are exiles, still on the journey (Heb. 11:13–14; 13:14); it requires faithful endurance (11:39 – 12:3), and wilful disobedience will be punished (6:4–12; 10:26–31; Num. 15:30; 16:35; Deut. 17:12, 20). Our coming not to Sinai but Mt Zion the heavenly Jerusalem means joy and not terror for us (Heb. 12:18–24; Deut. 9:19; Exod. 19:16–19). But if those who disobeyed the voice that shook the earth were punished, how much more those who disregard the heavenly voice that will shake both the heavens and the earth (12:25–29; Deut. 4:24)? Nevertheless, we are comforted by the great shepherd of the sheep who came through death as Moses came through the Reed Sea (Heb. 13:20–21; Is. 63:11).

In 1 Peter, the Gentiles, who were once not God's people (2:10; Hos. 1:8–10), are now a chosen people, a royal priesthood (2:5, 9; Exod. 19:4–6; Deut. 14:2; Is. 43:20–21), called into the light (1 Pet. 2:9b; Is. 49:6) to be holy (2:15–16; Lev. 11:44–45). Sanctified by the sprinkling of blood (1 Pet. 1:2; Exod. 24:8; Is. 52:15) Christians are urged to prepare for action (1:13; Exod. 12:11). Their exilic affliction (1 Pet. 1:1) and fiery ordeal

(4:12; Deut. 4:20; Is. 43:2) is likened to that of Isaiah's Servant (1 Pet. 2:22–24; Is. 53:7–9), whose new Exodus suffering as a Passover lamb (1:19; Exod. 12:5) redeemed them (1:18; 2:25; Is. 53:4–12).

For Revelation the church is a kingdom of priests (1:6; 5:10; Exod. 19:6), beset by false teachers who follow the path of Balaam (Rev. 2:14; Num. 31:16). Those who remain faithful in the new Exodus are promised hidden manna (Rev. 2:17) and a conqueror's name (3:5; Exod. 32:32). With a trumpet blast and amidst thunder and lightning, the prophet enters God's presence (4:1–6; Exod. 19:16; 24:10). Here he sees creation's heir: Jesus, the slain Passover lamb (5:6–10; Exod. 12:6–7; Is. 53:11), who has ransomed his priest-kings from every nation (Exod. 19:6; Is. 35:10; 51:11; 56:6–8). The two series of seven plagues associated with the trumpets and bowls resemble those of the Exodus (Rev. 8:6 – 9:21; 15:1 – 16:21; cf. the seven plagues in Ps. 105:27–36), and the city in which the two witnesses die is named 'Egypt' (Rev. 11:8). The woman Israel escapes into the desert on eagles' wings (12:14; Exod. 19:4) and is rescued from the serpent's river (Rev. 12:15–16; cf. Exod. 14:23–31; Num. 16:32). But in the new Exodus true Israel proves a faithful witness (Rev. 12:17; 17:6; 19:10; Is. 43:10–12; 44:8). Although the beast is celebrated in a parody of Moses' song (Rev. 13:4; Exod. 15:11), the ultimate victory belongs to reconstituted Israel (12 times 12,000) who, standing beside the sea, sing the song of Moses and the Lamb (Rev. 15:1–4) as the tabernacle is revealed (15:5–8). Judgment scenes recall Yahweh's descent on Sinai (8:5; 11:19; 16:18–21). Rome's downfall (17 – 18) and the Lord's 'Alpha and Omega' declarations (1:8, 17; 21:6; 22:13) recall Babylon's demise (Is. 47) and Yahweh's victorious affirmation (Is. 41:4; 44:6) in the context of Isaiah's new Exodus. The designation of God as 'the one who is ...' recalls Yahweh's self-revelation to Moses (Rev. 1:4, 8; etc.; Exod. 3:14). The holy army of saints (14:4a; Deut. 23:9–14) is called to be faithful during its new Exodus (Rev. 20:1–6; Ps. 90:4; 2 Pet. 3:8), and even to share in the Lamb's sufferings (Rev. 7:4–14; 14:4b; 20:4). The glorious new Jerusalem appears as described by Isaiah (Rev. 21:9–11; Is 54:1–3; 60:3–20; Ezek. 48:30–35) descends upon the great and high Edenic mountain (Ezek. 28:14; 40:2; Is.

65:25). Isaiah's new Exodus/new creational cry 'I am making everything new!' (Rev. 21:5; Is. 65:17) concludes the story.

See also: REDEMPTION; SIGNS AND WONDERS.

Bibliography

R. Beckwith and M. J. Selman, *Sacrifice in the Bible* (Exeter, 1995); F. F. Bruce, *New Testament Development of Old Testament Themes* (Exeter, 1969); D. Daube, *The Exodus Pattern in the Bible* (London, 1963); M. Fishbane, *Text and Texture* (New York, 1979); M. Kline, *Kingdom Prologue* (South Hamilton, 1993); R. E. Nixon, *The Exodus in the New Testament* (London, 1963); N. M. Sarna, *Exploring Exodus* (New York, 1986); W. Swartley, *Israel's Scripture Traditions and the Synoptic Gospels* (Peabody, 1994); R. E. Watts, *Isaiah's New Exodus and Mark* (Tübingen, 1997); Y. Zakovitch, *The Concept of the Exodus in the Bible* (Jerusalem, 1991).

R. E. WATTS

EXODUS, BOOK OF, see Part 2
EZEKIEL, see Part 2
EZRA-NEHEMIAH, see Part 2

FAITH, FAITHFULNESS

Introduction

In the waning years of the 6th century BC *God made the following promise to the post-exilic community: 'I will bring them to live in Jerusalem. They shall be my people and I will be their God, in faithfulness and in righteousness' (Zech. 8:8, NRSV). For all its tenderness, the promise, as it stands, contains ambiguity and tension. It is ambiguous because the final phrase, 'in faithfulness and in righteousness', can modify 'God', 'people' or both in relationship. If either of the latter two options is chosen, there is tension, because Zechariah does not reveal how a faithful *Israel is a possibility. The final phrase, 'in righteousness', simply exacerbates the problem, for how can a *righteous God be faithful to such a promise when it was made to a faithless and unrighteous *people?

The ambiguity and tension inherent in Zechariah's formulation underlie the use of the concept of faith/faithfulness in the Christian canon. And within that canon they are resolved only in the person of *Jesus Christ.

Vocabulary

English-speaking readers may well wonder why faith and faithfulness are being discussed in the same article. After all, 'faithfulness' generally denotes a settled disposition or character, a virtue, that expresses itself in a full range of activities such as *obedience, promise-keeping and patient endurance, while 'faith' denotes a frame of mind, a mental, or even wholehearted, assent that has no necessary relationship to a virtue or a character trait. At least since the Reformation, crucial doctrines have rested on the conceptual distinction underlying the two terms. But whereas English equips us with different terms for each concept, neither Hebrew nor the biblically dependent Greek of the NT affords us a similar luxury. It is not that the conceptual distinction is entirely missing from the biblical tradition; close attention to context can, in fact, uncover the different concepts. Rather, it is that the difference between the concepts is minimized by a more relational framework. While the English terms are typically used to describe a person's or group's character and mental orientation, the biblical terms are typically applied to people in relationship.

The biblical concept of faith/faithfulness stands at the heart of the relationship between the God of the Bible and his people, a relationship which, in its essential bi-polarity, is intensely personal, dynamic, and multiform. A characteristic terminology is employed whenever the relationship is in view. In the OT, for example, there is the Hebrew 'aman group ('ĕmûnâ and 'ĕmet). These are often used interchangeably, and mean 'steadfastness', 'truthfulness', 'faithfulness' and sometimes 'faith'. Other Hebrew verbs are frequently used in parallel with the verb, such as bāṭaḥ ('to trust', 'to believe in'), ḥāsâ ('to take refuge in', 'to trust'), or qāwâ ('to wait for', 'to hope in'). Forming a penumbra around this terminology are other terms belonging to other, closely associated semantic domains: ḥeseḏ ('steadfast love', 'covenant faithfulness'), and ṣedeq ('righteousness', 'salvation', 'faithfulness'), for example.

The NT vocabulary is largely determined by the Septuagint (LXX), the Greek translation(s) of the Hebrew Bible. Noteworthy among the words used to translate the Hebrew terms such as those listed above are alētheia ('*truth', 'faithfulness'), and elpizein ('to *hope in') and its cognates, dikaiosynē ('righteousness', 'faithfulness'; see Is. 38:3–19, LXX) and its cognates. But most common are those with the pist- root: pistis ('faith'), pistos ('faithful'), pisteuein ('to believe', 'to trust in') and certain tenses of the cognate peithein ('to trust in', 'to be persuaded', 'to obey').

But a biblical-theological concept cannot be approached merely by delineating the relevant terminology and its meaning. This is especially true in this case, where 'faith' and 'faithfulness' define the sine qua non of the God/people relationship. Indeed, the biblical writers exploit a number of images and metaphors to elucidate this trust-shaped relationship: marriage; father and son; king and people; parties to a covenant; to name only the most prominent. As a result, and precisely because God's relationship with his people is an intensely personal and all-consuming one, a biblical-theological exposition of faith/faithfulness can be attempted only by tracing connections with other ideas derived from the people of God's experience of God at discrete times and places. A history of faith/faithfulness is required.

Abraham and Yahweh: an ambiguous paradigm

Although the writer of *Hebrews (with good reason) begins his homily on faith with the examples of Abel, Enoch and Noah (Heb. 11:4–7), the explicit terminology of faith/faithfulness does not appear in the biblical narrative until the story of *Abraham and his family. In this foundational cycle of stories both the certainty and the anxiety, the clarity and the ambiguity of the faith-shaped relationship between God and his people stand out.

First, it is clear that the relationship existed because of God's initiative and persisted because of God's faithfulness. God called Abraham out of Chaldea and on successive occasions assured him of his intention to bless him, his seed, and through him all nations (Gen. 12:1–4, 7–8; 13:14–18; 15:1–6). Abraham's responses to these promises, and supremely his response to God's command to sacrifice Isaac (Gen. 22:1–18), can be explained only on the assumption that at crucial junctures in his life he took God to be utterly faithful. It is Abraham's trusted slave, however, who first speaks explicitly of God's faithfulness. When, after a long journey to find a wife for Isaac, he chanced on Rebekah at the well, he expressed the fundamental conviction of Abraham's household: 'Blessed be the LORD, the God of my master Abraham, who has not forsaken his steadfast love (*ḥesed*; LXX *dikaiosynē*) and his faithfulness (*ʾmet*; LXX *alētheia*) toward my master' (Gen. 24:27). Isaac continued (at least at crucial points in his life) to live out the conviction that the God of his father was faithful (Gen. 26:1–6, 24–25; 27:28–29). *Jacob too, unlike his brother, Esau, apparently shared the family conviction: his steadfast pursuit (at Rebekah's instruction) of the birthright, and the deceiving of his father, bear paradoxical testimony to that. Years later, humbled by his experiences and facing the crisis of reunion with Esau, Jacob appealed to God's faithfulness once more, admitting that he was 'not worthy of the least of all the steadfast love [*ḥesed* / *dikaiosynē*] and all the faithfulness' (*ʾmet* / *alētheia*) that God had shown to him (Gen. 32:10). The faithfulness of God to his covenant promises is here stated in no uncertain terms.

However, the other side of the relationship is more ambiguous and complex. Genesis 15:6 makes an apparently clear statement: 'And [Abraham] believed (*ʾāman* / *pisteuō*) the LORD; and the LORD reckoned it to him as righteousness.' The simplicity here is stark. Abraham took God at his *word, responding in the only fitting manner to the word of Yahweh. Yahweh conferred upon Abraham the status of being rightly related to him, not on the basis of a righteous deed, but solely on the basis of Abraham's trust in the divine promise. In its starkness, this verse is unique among OT statements concerning faith.

However, it is not clear how this exchange between Abraham and Yahweh is related to the preceding and subsequent sections of the narrative. In particular, it is not clear that Genesis 15:6, in context, really does establish a distinction between a singular, decisive act of believing, which alone secures the divine verdict of righteousness and the promises, and a more settled disposition of faithfulness. Had not Abraham taken God at his word before, for example, in leaving Haran (Gen. 12:1–4; *cf.* Hebrews 11:8–9)? Was Abraham's response of obeying a divine command any

different in kind from his response of believing a divine promise? Moreover, the subsequent narrative does not attach unique significance to the response described in Genesis 15:6. Indeed, in confirming the promises to Isaac after Abraham's death, Yahweh recalled Abraham not as a 'believer' but as one who 'obeyed my voice and kept my charge, my commandments, my statutes, and my laws' (26:3–5). In fact, it was this obedience that was cited as the basis for extending the promises to Isaac. Similarly, in the covenant between God and Abraham described in Genesis 17:1–14, 'walking blamelessly' and circumcision were enjoined upon Abraham and his descendants (17:1, 9–14). This fits well with the final statement of God's promises to Abraham in Genesis 22; the stipulations of the promise were framed by two causal clauses: 'because you have done this, and have not withheld your son' (22:16) and 'because you have obeyed my voice' (22:18; *cf.* also 18:17–19).

The story of Abraham, then, at least in its first telling, is not unambiguously the story of human faith – excluding works – responding to God's faithfulness, but rather the story of God's faithfulness calling forth Abraham's faithfulness, a full-bodied response of trust and obedience.

This is how later Jewish readers understood the story. In his prayer of confession Ezra prefaced the list of Israel's sins with the following: 'You are the LORD, the God who chose Abram and brought him out of Ur of the Chaldeans and gave him the name Abraham; and you found his heart faithful [*pistos*] before you, and made with him a covenant' (Neh. 9:7–8). In the post-biblical period Abraham was remembered as one who 'kept the law of the Most High, and entered into a covenant with him; he certified the covenant in his flesh, and when he was tested he proved faithful' (*pistos*, Ecclus. 44:20; compare *Jubilees* 13:25–27; 15:1–2; 16:20–31; *Prayer of Manasseh* 8:1). Genesis 15:6 was usually understood to mean that Abraham was 'found faithful [*pistos*] when tested, and it was reckoned to him as righteousness' (1 Macc. 2:52).

This is very close to the understanding of the verse expressed in James 2:21–23: 'Was not our ancestor Abraham justified by works when he offered his son Isaac on the altar? You see that faith was active along with his works, and faith was brought to completion by the works.' (*Cf.* Heb. 11:17.) In the light of these interpretations, *Paul's use of the Abraham story in Romans 4 and Galatians 3 must be seen as unusual.

It is, however, this emphasis on Abraham's faithfulness which introduces into the biblical account of faith/faithfulness the tension noted at the beginning of this article. Abraham is not presented in the Genesis account as invariably faithful. His stay in Egypt (12:10; contrast 26:1–3), his repeated dissimulation over Sarah's status as his wife (12:11–20; 20:2–18), and his attempts to father an heir through another woman in his household (16:2–4, 15; *cf.* 25:1–6) all reveal him to be a man swayed by doubt and capable of unfaithfulness. Perhaps this is why the prophets rarely glorify Abraham and indeed Isaiah speaks of 'the LORD, who redeemed Abraham' (29:22), and Micah at the end of his prophecy expresses only the hope that God will show *his* 'faithfulness [*ʾemet / alētheia*] to Jacob and unswerving loyalty [*ḥesed / eleos*] to Abraham' (Mic. 7:18–20).

Thus even at this foundational, paradigmatic level the tension between two possible views of the relationship between God and the people of God emerges. The two views are encapsulated by the two English words that form the title of this article. On the one hand, the relationship could be construed asymmetrically as involving faithfulness on God's part and mere faith ('faith alone') on the part of his people. This schema is, no doubt, more comforting and, at first glance, more consistent with the NT witness, but it is at best only hinted at here. It is certainly not developed in any sustained and programmatic way. Much more prominent in Abraham's story is a view of the divine–human relationship as one of mutual faithfulness. This view is more dominant in the OT as a whole, but it tends to throw the entire relationship into doubt.

Faithful Yahweh and faithful Israel: the idealized relationship

Yahweh as faithful God

The subsequent story of God and his people is based on the clearest affirmation of the Abrahamic paradigm: God is faithful. This was the climactic statement of the Exodus, delivered to Moses on Sinai in the wake of the

people's apostasy: 'The LORD descended in the cloud and stood with him there ... The LORD passed before him, and proclaimed, "The LORD, the LORD, a God merciful and gracious, slow to anger, and abounding in steadfast love [*ḥesed / polyeleos*] and faithfulness [*ʾemet / alēthinos*], keeping steadfast love [*ḥesed*; LXX 'keeping righteousness and doing mercy'] for the thousandth generation, forgiving iniquity and transgression and sin"' (Exod. 34:5–7a). Yahweh had indeed remembered his promises to Abraham and been faithful to his word (see Gen. 15:13–14) even in the face of his people's iniquity and transgression.

This language is found throughout the Hebrew scriptures. Deuteronomy 32:4 describes Yahweh as 'a faithful God [*ʾel ʾemûnâ*], without deceit, just and upright'. Psalm 86:15 echoes the language of Exodus 34 verbatim, while other psalms celebrate God's faithfulness in similar terms (see Pss. 25:6–10; 92:1–2). In the prophets Isaiah 25:1–9 is typical: God is praised for his 'faithful [*ʾōmen*] and sure [*ʾemûnâ*] plans', which include subduing the nations, sheltering the needy, providing a banquet for the nations on Mount Zion, and swallowing up death for ever. 'It will be said on that day,' exclaimed Isaiah, 'Lo, this is our God; we have trusted in [or 'hoped in', *qāwâ*] him, so that he might save us. This is the LORD in whom we have trusted [*qāwâ*]; let us be glad and rejoice in his salvation.'

With the rise of the *Davidic dynasty all this was transposed into a new key; henceforth God's faithfulness to Abraham and his offspring was bound up with his faithfulness to the line of David. God 'will appoint a place for ... Israel and will plant them' (2 Sam. 7:10), but only through the ministrations of David's offspring to whom God guaranteed, with 'a sure [*ʾemet / alētheia*] oath', a perpetual throne (Ps. 132:11; 2 Sam. 7:15–16; 1 Chr. 17:11–14; Is. 55:3).

Israel as faithful people

Apprehension of the faithfulness of God called forth response from his people. Those who lived 'in the shelter of the Most High', could indeed say to and of Yahweh, 'my refuge and my fortress; my God, in whom I trust [*bāṭaḥ / elpizō*]' (Ps. 91:1–2). This was not a contrived or detached confession, for Yahweh's faithfulness had proved to be 'a shield and a buckler', and his people could expect deliverance from the 'terror of the night' and the arrows of the enemy (91:3–5); they could expect to trample on 'the lion and the adder' (91:13). God would preserve all their bones (Ps. 34:20; see also the language of trust in Ps. 37). This confession was at the heart of the royal ideology (Ps. 31:1–17; 34:1–8; 40:11) and was also the testimony of Israel's wisdom literature: 'Trust [*baṭaḥ / peithō*] in the LORD with all your heart ... and he will make straight your paths' (Prov. 3:5–6). This heartfelt faith was pictured in a multitude of ways, using a number of synonyms and images: *joy and gladness in Yahweh's presence (Is. 25:1–9), continuous praise (Pss. 57:9–10; 71:22), peaceful sleep (Ps. 4:5–8), lack of fear (Ps. 56:3–4; Is. 43:1–10). In short, truly to understand God's faithful character was to have faith in him: 'those who know your name [the name proclaimed on Sinai] put their trust [*baṭaḥ / elpizō*] in you' (Ps. 9:10).

Unfaithful Israel and 'unfaithful' Yahweh: a troubled relationship

Israel's faithlessness

Nevertheless, there were solemn reminders that the relationship between Yahweh and his people was not merely one of divine faithfulness and human affirmations of faith, but also one of mutual faithfulness. The God proclaimed on Mount Sinai as 'abounding in steadfast love and faithfulness ... forgiving iniquities' would also 'by no means clear the guilty' (Exod. 34:6–7). As the psalmist affirmed, 'All the paths of the LORD are steadfast love [*ḥesed / eleos*] and faithfulness [*met / alētheia*]', but only 'for those who keep his covenant and his decrees' (Ps. 25:10). Even the unconditional language of the Davidic covenant was qualified. On his deathbed David related God's promise in these terms: 'If your heirs take heed to their way, to walk before me in faithfulness [*met / alētheia*] with all their heart and with all their soul, there shall not fail you a successor on the throne of Israel' (1 Kgs. 2:1–4; see also 9:4–9; 1 Chr. 28:7). The requirement of an inward, wholehearted faithfulness was, contrary to Solomon's eulogy (see 1 Kgs. 3:6; cf. 2 Chr. 15:17 – 16:12; Is. 38:3), one that even David failed to achieve constantly, for the confession of Psalm 51 acknowledges a lack of 'faithfulness [*met / alētheia*] in the inward parts' (v. 6).

The language of mutual faithfulness necessarily has a conditional tone, and neither Israel nor her king could meet the condition (Neh. 9:33–34). On the eve of the exile Jeremiah proclaimed: 'This is the nation that did not obey the voice of the LORD ... Faithfulness [*mûnâ / pistis*] has perished; it is cut off from their lips' (Jer. 7:28, author's translation; cf. Hos. 4:1–9). This conclusion was not drawn late in the story; in Deuteronomy Moses predicted that Yahweh would 'hide his face from them ... for they are a perverse generation, children in whom there is no faithfulness [*ēmûn / pistis*]' (Deut. 32:15-20; see also 32:3-5).

Yahweh's 'faithlessness'

The faithlessness of Israel and the hiddenness of Yahweh occasioned a great crisis of faith: could the faithlessness of Israel defeat the faithfulness of God? Of course, the faithfulness of God could be said to have triumphed in his judgment upon Israel (Neh. 9:32; cf. Ps. 119:75). But in the light of God's unconditional promises of blessing, that was hardly a satisfying answer to this vexing question.

Even the unthinkable was entertained: perhaps Yahweh could not be trusted after all. This sentiment was expressed clearly in several psalms. Psalm 89:1–37 comprises one of the most sustained and intense panegyrics on the faithfulness of Yahweh; the language of faithfulness abounds. But verse 38 reveals that Yahweh has been set up for the charge of unfaithfulness: 'You have renounced the covenant with your servant ... which by faithfulness you swore to your servant David' (vv. 39–51). The parting blessing (v. 52) simply adds insult to injury. (See also Ps. 44.)

Even Jeremiah contemplated the unthinkable. In Lamentations he turned Israel's language of faith in God upside down: God was the one who had brought him into the terror of darkness (Lam. 3:2, 6), broken his bones (3:4), and made his paths crooked (3:9). God was the lion tearing him to pieces (3:10–11), the archer shooting the arrows (3:12). And yet Jeremiah was able to hold on to this confession: 'The steadfast love [*ḥesed*] of the LORD never ceases, his mercies never come to an end; they are new every morning; great is your faithfulness [*mûnâ / pistis*]' (Lam. 3:22–23; cf. Jer. 12:1–4).

Continued hope

Jeremiah's affirmation of God's faithfulness in the face of the apparent breakdown of the covenant represents the authentic prophetic response of the OT. This is what God called Habakkuk to understand: God's promissary vision concerning his ultimate victory would surely come to pass in God's time; meanwhile the righteous person should not faint, but rather 'live in the light of its faithfulness' [*mûnâ / pistis] (Hab. 2:4, author's translation). Yet ambiguity and tension are obvious even in Habakkuk's statement. Who is 'the righteous person'? Is the prophet referring to one who is justified by faith? Or does he really agree with Ezekiel, his contemporary who said (using very similar language): he who 'follows my statutes, and is careful to observe my ordinances, acting faithfully [*met] – such a one is righteous; he shall surely live' (Ezek. 18:9)?

Ezekiel's language of mutual faithfulness is found throughout the prophets. Even Isaiah formulated his glorious vision of Israel's redemption in terms presupposing Israel's faithfulness. 'On that day this song will be sung in the land of Judah: We have a strong city ... Open the gates, so that the righteous nation [gôy ṣadîq] that keeps faith [*mun] may enter in' (Is. 26:1–2). The throne of the future Davidic king would 'be established in steadfast love [ḥesed]', and he would rule 'in faithfulness [*met / alētheia]' and 'do what is right [ṣedeq / dikaiosynē]' (Is. 16:5.) How Israel or her king could ever merit such descriptions remained a mystery. God himself would have to intervene (Ps. 40:10–11; Hos. 2:19–23) and change the hearts of his people (Deut. 30; Jer. 31:31; Ezek. 36:24–28), thereby making them faithful.

The faithfulness of God in Christ

At the coming of Jesus Israel was still unfaithful. Echoing the words of Deuteronomy 32:15–20, Jesus called his contemporaries, including his disciples, a 'faithless and perverse generation' (Luke 9:40–41; Mark 9:19; Matt. 17:17). But with Jesus' life, death and resurrection, and the giving of the Spirit to the Gentiles, it became clear that God was doing a new work. The pressing question was, however: was this new work in any way continuous with what the God of Abraham, Moses and Isaiah had done and promised, or

was it so novel as to 'nullify the faithfulness [pistis] of God' (Rom. 3:3-4)? The letter to the Romans was written to affirm the former. Paul was 'not ashamed of the gospel', for in it the righteousness of God, his saving faithfulness promised through the law and prophets, was actually realized and clarified (Rom. 1:16, read in the light of Ps. 98:3; Is. 51:4–5; Is. 50:7–8; Is. 28:16 LXX; Rom. 3:21–22). It is a righteousness that proceeds from God's faithfulness and engenders faithfulness (Rom. 1:17, read in the light of 1:5; 16:26). As Paul summed up his argument: 'For I tell you that Christ has become a servant of the circumcised on behalf of the faithfulness [alētheia] of God in order that he might confirm the promises given to the fathers, and in order that the Gentiles might glorify God for his mercy' (Rom. 15:8–9; author's translation). John made much the same point when he insisted that the 'steadfast love [charis] and faithfulness [alētheia]' embodied by Jesus Christ were the only adequate explication of the Father (John 1:14–18, read in the light of the allusion to Exod. 34 in v. 17). In Christ, as it were, Yahweh was no longer holding his peace but was finally crying out in answer to his critics, 'I have not forsaken them; I am faithful!' (see Is. 42:14–16).

But the wonder of the gospel is deeper still. In Christ Jesus the faithfulness of God was not vindicated by a last-minute revision of the relationship between God and his people. Mutual faithfulness (not mere faith) remained the *sine qua non* of the relationship, but only because Yahweh the faithful God, contrary to every expectation and at great cost, entered the story of his people and, in the person of his Son, established faithfulness there as well (Gal. 4:4–5; Phil. 2:5–8). In Christ God played out faithful roles, as it were, on both sides of the relationship. Foundational to NT theology is not only the conviction that Jesus was 'God with us', but also that Messiah Jesus was 'Israel summed up'. On the cross the story of unfaithful Israel came to an end under the curse of the law (Gal. 3:13), so that the story of faithful Israel might continue as the story of the faithful Messiah. It was the summation (and continuation) of Israel in the Messiah that accounted for the fact that Gentiles could, by virtue of union with the Messiah, enter into the story and blessings of faithful Israel (Gal. 3:17–29). In Christ, then, the ambiguity and the tension first found in the story of Abraham were emphatically, if surprisingly, resolved: 'steadfast love and faithfulness [*ḥesed* and *ʾemet* / *eleos* and *alētheia*] met; righteousness and peace kissed each other' (Ps. 85:10, author's translation).

Christ's faithfulness and human faith

The NT, unlike the OT, is full of the language of faith as 'believing' rather than that of faithfulness. According to the Gospels, this language originated in Jesus' own ministry and teaching. Jesus would sometimes say to those who called out to him: 'your faith has made you well' (lit. 'has saved you'; Matt. 9:22, 29; Mark 10:52; Luke 8:48; 18:42). On most of these occasions, the faithfulness of the supplicant was not an issue. This emphasis was maintained, according to the Acts of the Apostles, in the early preaching of the church (Acts 9:42; 10:43; 16:31; 20:21). And Paul, above all, sought to establish a church composed of Jews and Gentiles on the basis of a gospel of simple trust and reliance on God's faithful and gracious work in Christ (Rom. 4:5; 10:10; Gal. 2:16; Eph. 2:8–9). 'Faith' as the only saving, or justifying, response to the good news about Christ, is the general and undeniable testimony of the NT.

But a doctrine of 'faith alone' must be explicated and lived out in the light of the larger story of faithfulness, a story that reaches its climax in Jesus, the faithful Messiah. Indeed, the idea of 'faith alone', and even Paul's use of the OT in the service of that idea, makes sense only if the faith is an outworking of that climax. This is why there is in the NT a very intimate and complicated relationship between faith (*pistis*) and Jesus Christ. However one understands the Pauline phrase 'faith of Christ' (and equivalent phrases: Rom. 3:22; 26; Gal. 2:16, 20; Phil. 3:9; Eph. 3:12), it is clear that the NT presents Jesus as more than the object of faith. He is also the very embodiment or personification of faith and faithfulness (Gal. 3:23–25; 1 Tim. 1:14; 2 Tim. 1:13; Rev. 1:5; 14:12; 19:11). As such, Christ constitutes the necessary and sufficient condition of Christian faith (Acts 3:16; Heb. 12:2; 2 Pet. 1:1). It is only because Christ has 'done it all' that the sinner's faith is possible and can be a saving response to God.

Moreover, a clear-sighted focus on the story of faithfulness reminds us that God's salvation calls us beyond an absorption with our own faith or even with our own individual redemption. Faith involves 'looking to Jesus, the pioneer and perfecter of faith' (Heb. 12:2). Likewise salvation in the present, before the consummation of all things, involves union or relationship with the Messiah and, through him, inclusion in the people of God. Within the framework of that relationship, with all its personal and corporate dimensions, the Spirit of the Messiah nurtures the initial response of faith to the gospel message into a continuing life of joyful praise and obedience to God (Rom. 1:5; 16:26), and loving service to the neighbour (Gal. 5:6, 13–14; 6:1–2). When Christian faith matures in this manner the story of faith is finally complete, having proceeded from God's faithfulness to the faithfulness of the people of God.

See also: ADULTERY; MARRIAGE.

Bibliography

T. D. Alexander, 'Abraham re-assessed theologically: The Abraham narrative and the New Testament understanding of justification by faith', R. S. Hess, P. E. Satterthwaite and G. J. Wenham (eds.), in *He Swore an Oath: Biblical Themes from Genesis 12 – 50* (Grand Rapids and Carlisle ²1994); R. A. Harrisville, *The Figure of Abraham in the Epistles of St Paul: In the Footsteps of Abraham* (San Francisco, 1992); R. B. Hays, *Echoes of Scripture in the Letters of Paul* (New Haven, 1989); idem, *The Faith of Jesus Christ: An Investigation of the Narrative Substructure of Galatians 3:1 – 4:11* (Chico, 1983); J. J. M. Roberts, *Nahum, Habakkuk and Zephaniah: A Commentary*, OTL (Louisville, 1991); J. A. Sanders, 'Habakkuk in Qumran, Paul and the Old Testament', in, C. A. Evans and J. A. Sanders (eds.), *Paul and the Scriptures of Israel* (Sheffield, 1993); M. Silva, *Explorations in Exegetical Method: Galatians as a Test Case* (Grand Rapids, 1996); N. T. Wright, *The Climax of the Covenant: Christ and the Law in Pauline Theology* (Edinburgh, 1991).

S. S. TAYLOR

FALLING AWAY, see APOSTASY
FALSE PROPHETS, see PROPHECY, PROPHETS

FAMILY

Introduction

The family is central to the Bible's message: the Hebrew Bible tells the story of one set of families, while the extended household of the Greco-Roman world provides the backdrop to the NT. Moreover, family imagery is used to articulate the meaning of belief in *God.

The OT

Contemporary western understandings of 'family' derive from the Enlightenment, and no single Hebrew term directly corresponds to this. Three terms denote social groups of various sorts: *ševet* (conventionally translated as 'tribe') denotes ethnic origins; *bêt 'ab* and *mišpaḥâ* can both be translated as 'family', though generally they have wider connotations than the English term. *Bêt 'ab* can mean 1. a nuclear family consisting of parents and their children, living together in the same home (*e.g.* Gen. 50:7–8); 2. a wider grouping, consisting of one or two generations of close relatives (*e.g.* Gen. 7:1; 14:14); 3. relatives more generally (*e.g.* Gen. 24:38; 1 Kgs. 12:19; Is. 5:7). *Mišpaḥâ* usually refers to a wide group of relatives, and for that reason is sometimes translated as 'clan', often with a territorial as well as a relational significance (*e.g.* Num. 27:8–11; Judg. 18:11).

OT families

The family was clearly very important in the OT, though the text includes few, if any, distinctive insights into its nature: for the most part the OT takes for granted the cultural norms of its day. At the centre of all kinship groups was a leading male, and members of the 'household' were under his authority, along with animals and property (Exod. 20:17). The family was held together by the traditional concerns common to all cultures prior to the emergence of the nuclear industrial family; providing employment, together with education and socialization for children, and a religious identity for all (Exod. 10:2; 12:26; 13:8; Deut. 4:9; 6:7; 32:7; Prov. 1:8; 6:20). Duty and responsibility, rather than romance and friendship, were the undergirding principles. The head of the family normally expected his first-born son to succeed him, and took it for granted that he would arrange all marriages and could

usually divorce his wife (Deut. 24:1; *cf.* 22:19, 29). In the patriarchal period the head of the household had a theoretical power of life and death over family members, though he might choose not to exercise it and even to defer to them (*e.g.* *Abraham gives way to Lot in Gen. 13).

At its best, this social structure provided security and support for family members (Deut. 25:5–10), and women could be valued, at least as providers for their husbands (Prov. 31). The reality, however, rarely matched the ideal. The fall so disrupted the marriage relationship (Gen. 3:16) that men and women were sometimes unable to realize God's intention for it (Gen. 2:24), becoming unfaithful to one another. One story after another shows the integrity of the family being threatened by brutality and violence. Isaac's family disintegrated, as *Jacob cheated his brother Esau (Gen. 27:1–45), and his sons in turn sold their brother *Joseph into slavery (Gen. 37:1–36). The same pattern of family dysfunction later brought ruination to the royal houses of both *Israel and Judah, with the cycle broken only when Joash was removed from his home and raised by a foster parent (2 Kgs. 8 – 12). Nor are these isolated episodes: there are many examples of such dysfunctional family relationships throughout the OT.

Family styles

Most of the OT stories concern leading families, whose lives were part of the power politics of the day, and who were under considerable economic pressure to produce large numbers of children; the oldest male could be the heir, while the rest would enhance national prestige by marrying into the ruling families of neighbouring nations. Rulers therefore needed many wives. Solomon famously had 700 wives and 300 concubines (1 Kgs. 11:3), though even Ahab had 70 sons, so must have had more wives than Jezebel (2 Kgs. 10:1–11).

Stories about more ordinary families present a different picture, supported by archaeological evidence which suggests the average house was occupied by no more than six or seven people in all. The story of Ruth implies that monogamy was the norm, though other stories suggest that it was known for men to take a second wife if their first was infertile. With the centralization of the state in David's time, the rights of ordinary households were restricted, and the public authority took over the control and regulation of family behaviour. At first, this change limited the autocratic powers of family heads, but as the state itself was undermined through constant invasion, the tension between small-scale rural families and the ruling élites of the urban centres increased to the point where poorer families found themselves dispossessed, even selling their own members into slavery to pay their debts (Is. 5:8–10; Amos 2:6–8; 4:1–3). After the exile, ethnicity dominated the renewed quest for national identity, and references to the family in this period imply largely bureaucratic models that could deal with the Persian empire on the one hand and the Palestinian population on the other (Neh. 7:5–38). There is clearly 'no biblical blueprint, no once-and-for-all model, of the family' (R. Clapp, *Families at the Crossroads*, p. 15).

The NT

Jesus

*Jesus challenged many of the accepted norms of family life within later Jewish culture, not least by insisting that the demands of discipleship could take precedence over the requirements of traditional families (Matt. 10:34–39; 12:46–50; Mark 3:31–35; Luke 12:49–53). He called for an end to divorce practices which gave women no rights, arguing instead that the OT norm was monogamy, understood as an equal relationship between a man and woman (Mark 10:2–12; *cf.* John 4:7–29; 7:53 – 8:11). Furthermore, he affirmed that women could be spiritual leaders as well as domestic workers (Luke 8:2–3; 10:40–42), and recognized the intrinsic value of children, using them as examples of true discipleship and thereby challenging both Jewish and Hellenistic culture, in which childhood was regarded as an immature and inadequate form of existence (Mark 9:33–37; 10:13–16 par.). It is clear, though, that his intention was not to make the family redundant, but to challenge conventional assumptions about family loyalties (Mark 7:9–13; 10:1–12; Luke 18:18–30; John 19:26–27).

Household codes

The Greco-Roman social structure was similar to that of ancient Israel. The household (*oikos*) was the basic social unit, consisting of property as well as people, though generally with less emphasis on biological relationship than in the Hebrew family. The Roman family could include slaves and their children, and was often extended by the adoption of (usually) adult males, while divorce and remarriage were easier for both men and women. Nevertheless, the family was a microcosm of the state, and the *paterfamilias* had absolute power, though this was generally exercised benevolently in return for absolute loyalty from family members.

A key element in Jesus' approach was his argument that God's original intention for humankind was a monogamous relationship of equals, as depicted in the OT *creation stories (Gen. 1:27, where women and men are both 'made in God's image'). This clearly implies that he regarded exploitation of one by the other as part of the fallen world, and not integral to the order of creation (*cf.* Gen. 3:16, where as a consequence of the fall Eve is told that 'your husband shall rule over you'). Paul seems to edge towards a similar view in 1 Corinthians 7, where he appears to treat women and men as equal partners, though in a context in which marriage and family life have already been depicted as having drawbacks compared to singleness. In other NT passages, especially the so-called household codes (Col. 3:18 – 4:1; Eph. 5:22 – 6:9; 1 Pet. 2:18 – 3:7; 1 Tim. 2:8–15; 6:1–2; Titus 2:1–10), the conventional, hierarchical family structures of the ancient world are mostly accepted. There has been considerable debate about the significance of the codes. They are sometimes seen as evidence that the early Christians simply did no original thinking on family life and just accepted the cultural norms they knew. Yet they are remarkable for the fact that they address women, slaves and children alongside men, masters and fathers, which suggests that the former were accepted as equal members of the household.

Historically, these codes of behaviour were intended to avoid the criticism that Christianity undermined family loyalties and, therefore, threatened the stability of society. But the NT writers also seem to have wished to affirm that social convention was not the only factor that determined relationships in the Christian family. Since the typical

Christian household would be both an economic unit and a *church, there may well be some tension here between appropriate relationships in the household as church (Gal. 6:10; Eph. 2:19) and the household as part of the socio-political structures of the wider community (Acts 16:15; 18:8).

Theological concerns

For modern readers, the OT and household codes raise some thorny questions. While Genesis 1 emphasizes marriage as a monogamous and loving relationship, many subsequent narratives highlight episodes of family dysfunction, often taking it for granted as an unavoidable part of life. The wider culture of biblical times was patriarchal in the literal sense, and outside the teaching of Jesus this arrangement is seldom challenged specifically in Scripture. No doubt the uncritical acceptance of cultural norms found in the NT household codes can be explained either as an example of the eschatological tension between this fallen world and the ideals of God's kingdom, or in terms of what it was possible and worthwhile for a minority group like the church to question in the social context within which it had to operate. The issues raised here are similar to questions that surface over the NT's treatment of slavery, for example, in which the cultural norm was not challenged, though underlying trends within NT teaching implicitly undermined its rationale.

But that leaves other questions for today's Christians. For example, a descending social hierarchy of God–men–women–children may imply a spiritual hierarchy in which women and children are denied direct access to God, which on the face of it is a form of idolatry, and a sign of fallenness, not of salvation.

Similarly challenging questions arise with regard to the way family images are applied to relationships between humans and God, especially in the OT. There the nation is God's household (Exod. 4:22; Hos. 1:2–11), and Jerusalem and Samaria are God's daughters (Is. 1:8; Jer. 6:2), while God can be regarded as both father (Is. 63:16; 64:8) and mother of the people (Hos. 11:1–9; Is. 49:14–17), as well as their husband (Hos. 1 – 3, Jer. 2:2–13; Ezek. 16:1–43). In the historical circumstances of the day, this imagery gave the prophets a useful way of explaining the meaning of Israel's national fortunes, seeing their many defeats as punishment for their neglect of family duties and responsibilities. But in the broader sweep of Christian theology and contemporary family life, some aspects of it can be problematic. For example, God is sometimes portrayed as an angry father punishing his children, and even (occasionally) as a husband beating his wife. Some men, believing that they are in the place of God in a way that women cannot be, and ignoring the biblical command to love their wives, have used these passages as a justification for violence. A responsible biblical theology will recognize the potential pastoral implications of such images, and will interpret them in the light of the whole Bible.

See also: MAN AND WOMAN; MARRIAGE; SEED.

Bibliography

D. L. Balch, *Let Wives be Submissive: The Domestic Code in 1 Peter* (Chico, 1981); S. C Barton, *Discipleship and Family Ties in Mark and Matthew* (Cambridge, 1994); idem, 'Living as families in the light of the New Testament', *Int*, 1998, pp. 130–144; idem, (ed.), *The Family in Theological Perspective* (Edinburgh, 1996); L. S. Cahill and D. Mieth, *The Family* (London, 1995); R. Clapp, *Families at the Crossroads* (Downers Grove and Leicester, 1993, 1994); L. W. Countryman, *Dirt, Greed and Sex* (Philadelphia and London, 1988, 1989); J. E. Crouch, *The Origin and Intention of the Colossian Haustafel* (Göttingen, 1972); J. A. Dearman, 'The Family in the Old Testament', *Int*, 1998, pp. 117-129; H. Moxnes (ed.), *Constructing Early Christian Families* (London, 1997); C. Osiek and D. L. Balch, *Families in the New Testament World: Household and House Churches* (Louisville, 1997); L. G. Perdue, J. Blenkinsopp, J. J. Collins and C. Meyers, *Families in Ancient Israel* (Louisville, 1997); D. C. Verner, *The Household of God* (Chico, 1983); C. J. H. Wright, *God's People in God's Land: Family, Land and Property in the Old Testament* (Carlisle and Grand Rapids, 1990).

J. W. DRANE

FATHERHOOD OF GOD, see GOD
FAVOUR, see GRACE

FEAR

Introduction

Fear is a pervasive concept in both Testaments, and in every major literary corpus within them. Fear can be directed to various objects, but the most important kind of fear in the Bible is that of *God and/or *Jesus Christ. As the writer of Proverbs states, the fear of God is the beginning of wisdom (Prov. 1:7; *cf.* 8:13; 9:10; Ps. 111:10; Eccles. 7:16–18). Humans and institutions may be objects of fear; the biblical writers also speak of an unfocused fear resulting from human circumstances. But whilst fear is a pervasive force within this world, the *peace of God or Christ, which stems from due fear or reverence of God, is its most potent adversary, banishing fear. Not all fear is that of terror in the face of overwhelming and threatening circumstances, however. The fear of God may well include a recognition of the futility of human opposition to the divine, especially for those who are God's enemies, but for those who follow God, fear grows from the respect and honour of which God is worthy as God.

Fear of God and of Christ

In the OT, written before the coming of Christ, all fear of the divine is fear of God. The NT also speaks of this fear. So just as early in Genesis Abram can be told by God not to fear, because God is his protector (Gen. 15:1), the writer of Revelation can admonish the reader to fear God, and give him *glory (Rev. 14:7). One of the distinguishing features of God's people is their fear of God. To fear God is to revere him and give him due respect and honour (Gen. 20:11). In Deuteronomy, fear of God is linked to *love of God, and *obedience to his commandments.

Numerous biblical passages describe or express fear of God, or call upon others to fear him. In the OT, the Psalms and prophets in particular are full of such language. The Psalms begin from the premise that fear of God and service and *worship of God go hand in hand (Pss. 2:11; 5:7; 19:9), so that people who fear and serve him are worthy of honour (15:4). In consequence, the psalmist calls on everyone else to fear God (33:8). The prophets similarly call upon the people of

Israel to fear God (Is. 11:2; Jer. 5:24).

In the Gospels fearing God is not mentioned as often, but clearly it was advocated by Jesus. For example, in Matthew's Gospel he tells his followers that they should fear not the one who can destroy the body but rather God, who can destroy the body and soul (Matt. 10:28; Luke 12:5). For Paul, both Jews and Gentiles stand condemned before God, as sinners who do not fear God (Rom. 3:18, quoting Ps. 36:1), and the foundation of his ministry is fear of the Lord (2 Cor. 5:11). In the later Pauline letters, fear of the Lord clearly becomes fear of Christ (Col. 3:22), and is the basis of Christian behaviour (Eph. 5:21). In a direct link with the fear of God in the OT, in the book of Acts those Gentiles who are attracted to Jewish belief but are unwilling to become complete proselytes are called God-fearers, reflecting their own reverence for God but also the reverence which characterizes true belief.

Fear of humans

Fear of other humans ranges from appropriate fear and respect given to a highly-regarded person such as a parent (Lev. 19:3), to fear of one's enemies (Deut. 3:22). This fear is mentioned in many places in the OT, but is less apparent in the NT, though still present (*e.g.* John 20:19). The broad semantic range of such language makes it difficult to generalize about its theological purpose, but there is certainly a shift of emphasis from the OT to the NT. Whereas in the OT people fear God, who stands outside the human sphere, in the NT they also fear Jesus, who is present in the world. In several places Jesus either speaks directly to relieve fear (Matt. 10:28), or is spoken of as the one who overcomes fear (Acts 27:24).

Fear of human institutions

Two of the passages which mention appropriate kinds of fear are controversial: Romans 13:7, which speaks of giving due fear or respect; and 1 Peter 2:17, which commands the reader to fear God and honour the king. The problem is that the language of offering due respect seems to be applied equally to God and to rulers. But the difficulty can be resolved if fear is understood as the appropriate level of respect. Romans 13 is a set of instructions for Roman Christians concerning their obedience to the state. The authorities are owed obedience only if they are just. Due respect or fear is thus owed only to authorities which attempt to act justly. In 1 Peter 2, God is supreme over earthly powers, including kings.

Fear of circumstances

The language of fear is used most frequently in the Bible to refer to fear resulting from circumstances. Often the circumstances are adverse: people face an unexpected turn of events, such as Mary's becoming pregnant (Matt. 1:20; Luke 1:30), or live in the shadow of *death (Heb. 2:15). This fear is the normal human reaction to the unknown or incomprehensible. However, the context of such language is noteworthy. Often the frightened person is told not to fear. In other words, although the fear is not denied, the person is told not to dwell upon it. Moreover, fear is often set in the context of God's overriding plan, purpose and power. Thus the angel brings good news of great *joy to many (Luke 2:10), because in God's eyes all his followers are valued (Matt. 10:31; Luke 12:32).

Conclusion

The language of fear in the Bible is part of a larger picture of God's controlling and guiding purposes. God demands obedience, but he frees his followers from fear of circumstances, their enemies and everything else, so long as they fear (*i.e.* respect and honour) him. When traditional values, such as respect and honour, are under attack, it is perhaps wise to reflect on the importance of fearing God. This fear puts other values into their appropriate perspective.

Bibliography

S. E. Porter in *DPL*, pp. 291–93; *idem* in *DLNTD*, pp. 370–373; W. Zimmerli, *Old Testament Theology in Outline* (ET, Edinburgh, 1978).

S. E. PORTER

FEASTS, see SACRED MEALS
FLOOD, see CREATION

FORGIVENESS AND RECONCILIATION

The meaning of forgiveness

In Scripture, 'forgiveness' occurs whenever humans who have violated *God's will cry out for and receive his *mercy. It is different from mercy itself, which is God's staying his hand of deserved *judgment. He has mercy to some extent on all people (*cf.* Matt. 5:45), but not all people are forgiven in a full and saving sense. Forgiveness begins with the acknowledgment of one's *guilt (1 John 1:9) in God's eyes. It is completed when the offender is restored to full fellowship with God, experiencing his healing *love, and with other people, to the extent this is possible (Matt. 5:23–24; Rom. 12:18).

The terminology of forgiveness

The frequent occurrence of 'forgiveness' and its cognates in Scripture points to its importance (NIV, 150 occurrences; RSV, 153). To this can be added occurrences of the closely related word 'pardon' and related forms (NIV, 7; RSV, 24).

In the OT, the major Hebrew words for 'forgiveness', and their basic meaning, are as follows: *slḥ* (to forgive, pardon, send away), *nś'* (to bear, take away), *kpr* (to cover), *mḥh* (to wipe away), and *ksh* (to cover). The Septuagint translators found it necessary to expand this vocabulary considerably, and use nearly twenty words and expressions: *aphiēmi* (to forgive, *e.g.* Gen. 50:17a), *dechomai* (to receive, pardon, *e.g.* Gen. 50:17b), *prosdechomai* (to accept, pardon, *e.g.* Exod. 10:17) *aphaireō* (to take away, *e.g.* Exod. 34:7), *hileōs einai* (to be favourably inclined, propitious, *e.g.* Num. 14:20), *exhiloskomai* (to propitiate, make atonement, *e.g.* Num. 15:28), *euilateuō* (to be merciful, *e.g.* Deut. 29:20), *aniēmi* (to forgive, *e.g.* Josh. 24:19), *airō* (to forgive, *e.g.* 1 Sam. 15:25), *hilaskomai* (to pardon, be merciful, *e.g.* 2 Kgs. 5:18), *katharizō* (to cleanse, *e.g.* Ps. 19:12), *euilatos ginesthai* (to be merciful, *e.g.* Ps. 99:8), *hilasmos* (expiation, atonement, *e.g.* Ps. 130:4), *athōoō* (to let go unpunished, hold guiltless, *e.g.* Jer. 18:23), *hilateuō* (to be gracious, Dan. 9:19), *lambanō* (to remove, *e.g.* Hos. 14:2), *hyperbainō* (to overlook intentionally, *e.g.* Mic. 7:18), and *apoluō* (to acquit, remove; used with this connnotation in OT apocrypha only, *e.g.* 3 Maccabees 7:7). Three of these terms are Septuagint neologisms (words occurring only in the LXX and works based on it): *euilateuō*; *athōoō*; *hilateuō*. The vocabulary of forgiveness is complex and rich in both the Hebrew and the Greek OT.

The NT uses a much more limited selection of words. Most common is *aphiēmi* (used with the theological connotation of 'forgiving' some forty times), which is the chief verb for 'forgive' found in the Gospels (but see Luke 6:37) and the only one found in James (5:15) and 1 John (1:9; 2:12). Less frequent but characteristic of Paul is *charizomai* (to grant *grace to, forgive, *e.g.* Eph. 4:32); Paul may have been the first to use the word in this sense (see Shogren in *ABD* 2, p. 835). Luke uses the unusual *apoluō* (to pardon) in 6:37. The lone noun for forgiveness in the NT is *aphesis* (*e.g.* Mark 3:29; Heb. 10:18), often used in the phrase 'forgiveness of sins' (*e.g.* Matt. 26:28; Luke 1:77; Acts 2:38; 5:31; Col. 1:14).

The language of forgiveness in the OT history of redemption

The reality of forgiveness is often present in Scripture when explicit words for it are absent. It could be that God extended forgiveness to Adam and Eve when he covered them after the Fall (Gen. 3:21). He forgave Noah and his kin in order to spare them from the flood (Gen. 6:17–18). *Covenant promises to Noah and his descendants (Gen. 9:8–11), made in the wake of *sacrifices (Gen. 8:20), imply forgiveness; so also the promises to Abraham (Gen. 15:1–18). Having faith credited as *righteousness (Gen. 15:6) bespeaks full pardon for *sin, a point made and enlarged on by Paul (Rom. 4:1–16). While forgiveness was implicitly present prior to and during the patriarchal period, the first explicit mention of forgiveness in the OT is in the story of Joseph. His brothers relate the news (true or not) that their father Jacob's dying wish was for Joseph to forgive them (Gen. 50:17). Joseph not only forswears revenge but expresses love and benevolence towards them (Gen. 50:19–21). These are hallmarks of true forgiveness.

Forgiveness is prominent in the life and legislation of Moses. Pharaoh asks Moses to forgive him and to pray that God might halt the plague of locusts (Exod. 10:17); human-

ity's awareness of the need for divine forgiveness is universal and not limited to God's chosen *people. Moses warns the people that rebellion against God's angel will not be forgiven, since the angel bears God's own Name (Exod. 23:21); people are not to presume on God's forgiveness. Forgiveness is frequently mentioned in the cultic sections of the Pentateuch, where animal sacrifice is said to atone for sin, resulting in forgiveness for the *worshipper (*e.g.* Lev. 4:20, 26, 31, 35; *cf.* P. House, *Old Testament Theology*, pp. 128–133). Through the OT sacrificial system forgiveness was freely promised and granted, provided that the worshipper approached the altar with a contrite heart expressed in the shedding of the *blood of a suitable victim (N. Kiuchi, in *TynB* 50, pp. 23–31). In Moses' writings God is portrayed as 'maintaining love to thousands, and forgiving wickedness, rebellion and sin' (Exod. 34:7, NIV; *cf.* Num. 14:18). At the same time, those who turn away from God, who say 'I will be safe, even though I persist in going my own way' (Deut. 29:19), must expect not forgiveness but rejection: 'The LORD will never be willing to forgive him; his wrath and zeal will burn against that man' (Deut. 29:20; *cf.* *Jesus' reference to unforgivable sin [Mark 3:28–29; Matt. 12:31–32; Luke 12:10]). Forgiveness can be sought in *prayer and granted by God, however, even when God's people as a whole are ripe for judgment (Num. 14:19–20).

God's willingness to forgive and the need for his people to seek forgiveness are prominent themes throughout the OT's historical books. Nehemiah echoes Moses' words regarding God's gracious, compassionate, and forgiving nature (Neh. 9:17). Solomon mentions God's forgiveness numerous times in his prayer at the dedication of the temple (1 Kgs. 8:30, 34, 36, 39, 50; *cf.* 2 Chr. 6:21, 25, 27, 30, 39). God responds with a promise to forgive his people when they humble themselves, pray, seek him and turn from their *evil ways (2 Chr. 7:14).

The prophets dramatize two truths about forgiveness. One is that God is indeed a forgiving God, pardoning his people's sins in the long run even if judgment is necessary in the present (Dan. 9:9; Is. 33:24; Jer. 33:8; 50:20; Mic. 7:18). The other is that while God's patience and forbearance are vast, they have limits. There comes a time when forgiveness is no longer possible (Jer. 5:7; Hos. 1:6; *cf.* Josh. 24:19; 2 Kgs. 24:4).

The Psalms are perhaps the capstone of the OT's eloquent testimony to the God who forgives. The psalmist has found the only source of forgiveness and cries out to the Lord in order to receive it (Pss. 19:12; 25:11; 32:5; 65:3; 78:38). David's famous beatitude becomes a foundational truth for Paul a millennium later: 'Blessed is he whose transgressions are forgiven, whose sins are covered' (Ps. 32:1; *cf.* Rom. 4:7). God's forgiveness is not inconsistent with his punishment; both together constitute his loving guidance and care for his covenant people (Ps. 99:8; *cf.* 130:4), whether as individuals (like the various psalmists) or as a corporate body.

An important bridge between OT and NT is the God who forgives; the famous 'new covenant' passage in Jeremiah looks ahead to a time when the Lord will forgive his people's wickedness and remember their sins no more (Jer. 31:34). That time was graphically and explicitly foreshadowed in the OT, but came only with Jesus.

Intertestamental testimony to the need and possibility of divine forgiveness

Jesus did not enter a world ignorant of the need and possibility of forgiveness. Even pagan writers were aware of the problem of human sin (Horace, *Odes* 3.6), though they offer little help in solving it. Stoic appeals to reason's greatness were counsels of despair given the impersonal and mechanistic Stoic cosmology, and in any case resignation, not forgiveness, was the Stoic means of dealing with intransigent people or difficult circumstances. Most Jewish writers concurred with Philo (*On the Unchangeableness of God* 16.75) that 'there has never been a single man who, by his own unassisted power, has run the whole course of his life, from the beginning to the end, without stumbling'. The sense of need for forgiveness was present (though as understood in a Christian sense, not prominent, *contra* Charlesworth in *ABD* 2, pp. 833–835) in the Jewish world out of which the early church emerged.

A Qumran document speaks of perfect compliance with the law of Moses, the intentional violation of which leads to expulsion from the community for ever (*Rule of the Community* 8.20–9.2). Yet the same document expresses the hope that God will pardon

sins through 'the greatness of his goodness' (11.11–15). Another pre-NT Jewish writing extols God's 'forgiveness for those who turn to him', promises forgiveness 'in the hour of [God's] visitation', and praises God's mercy and 'his forgiveness for those who turn to him!' (Ecclus. 18:19–21; 17:29; *cf.* 2:11). But in those documents God is said to judge according to works, not by the grace that Abraham's faith affirmed (Ecclus. 16:11–14), which implies that forgiveness is in part a matter of human merit (*cf.* Ecclus. 28:2). Low-born people may be forgiven, but not rulers (Wisdom of Solomon 6:6).

One of the clearest Jewish expressions of the need for forgiveness is the Prayer of Manasseh 7: 'Thou, O Lord, according to thy great goodness hast promised repentance and forgiveness to those who have sinned against thee ...' The prayer is fictional rather than historical, but it shows that a hope for divine absolution of guilt before God existed at the time of Christ's appearing. The same hope surfaces in Luke 1 – 2 as numerous figures await 'the redemption of Jerusalem' (Luke 2:38) that the Christ child's arrival signified.

Forgiveness in the NT history of redemption

The messianic expectation presupposed particularly by Matthew and Luke is of a Christ who will win forgiveness for sinners; 'he will save his people from their sins', says the angel of the Lord (Matt. 1:21). Zechariah prophesies that Jesus will give God's 'people the knowledge of salvation through the forgiveness of their sins' (Luke 1:77). The message of the cross that would achieve forgiveness was latent in the pronouncements that attended the nativity. N. T. Wright's claim, that 'to a first-century Jew' forgiveness of sins 'is not in the first instance the remission of individual sins, but the putting away of the whole nation's sins' (*The New Testament and the People of God*, p. 273), is hardly compelling; the body politic that looked sincerely for corporate deliverance was the sum total of individuals maintaining dogged hope in their (personal) covenant God, *e.g.* Zechariah, Elizabeth, Joseph, Mary, Simeon, and Anna (Luke 1 – 2).

Forgiveness (of individuals and thereby, if at all, of the nation) was prominent in Jesus' earthly ministry. John the Baptist laid a foundation by 'preaching a baptism of repentance for the forgiveness of sins' (Mark 1:4). Forgiveness is mentioned in the Lord's Prayer (Matt. 6:12 par.), and is the subject of both instruction and parable (Matt. 18:15–35). But Jesus not only taught forgiveness; he also granted it (Matt. 9:2), to the displeasure of sceptical listeners, who pointed out that only God can forgive sin (Matt. 9:3; *cf.* Mark 2:7). He prayed for forgiveness for his persecutors as he hung on the cross (Luke 23:34). The blood he shed there would be, he declared, 'my blood of the covenant ... poured out for many for the forgiveness of sins' (Matt. 26:28). After his resurrection he granted special authority to the apostles to remit sins (John 20:23); perhaps this was exercised particularly in gospel preaching and early church discipline. The story of Jesus' life, from infancy to ascension, is dominated by the account of his mission to provide forgiveness.

That forgiveness was proclaimed repeatedly during the several decades spanned by the book of Acts, which reports that the core of the apostolic preaching was 'forgiveness of sins' (2:38; 5:31; 10:43; 13:38; 26:18; *cf.* 8:22; see also C. Stenschke, in *Witness to the Gospel*, pp. 132–135). 'Forgiveness' as a theological term is relatively rare in Paul, whose preferred term *dikaiosynē* (righteousness, 58 times in the Pauline corpus) includes the less comprehensive concept of 'forgiveness'. But forgiveness is assumed as a *conditio sine qua non* of Christian fellowship (2 Cor. 2:7), a condition which Paul himself sought to satisfy (2 Cor. 2:10). In two of his prison letters Paul defines *redemption in terms of 'the forgiveness of sins' (Eph. 1:7; Col. 1:14), and in the same epistles he deduces the necessity of forgiveness among Christians from the fact that 'in Christ God forgave' them (Eph. 4:32). Therefore Christians are to forgive as the Lord forgave them (Col. 3:13). In Romans 3:25 God is said to have presented Christ as an atoning sacrifice 'to demonstrate his justice, because in his forbearance [*paresis*] he had left the sins committed beforehand unpunished'. *Paresis* is however a stay of judgement, not full forgiveness. Paul tells the Lycaonians that in past times God 'let all nations go their own way' (Acts 14:16; *cf.* Acts 17:30), thus testifying to a God who forgives, but not extending the status of 'forgiven' to his listeners unless they accept his message.

Hebrews expresses the doctrine of forgiveness inasmuch as it centres on Christ's *priestly ministry. The word itself, however, appears only in a quotation from Jeremiah 31:34 (Heb. 8:12), in a statement of the OT law's requirement for blood to be shed in order for sin to be forgiven (Heb. 9:22), and in a summary statement explaining the results of Christ's death; God forgives the sinful acts and guilt of those who put their trust in the *gospel message, so that continuing sacrifice for sin is no longer required (Heb. 10:18). John's first epistle states that forgiveness follows confession and is not granted to those who deny their personal sinfulness (1 John 1:9–10). But though confession is important, sins are forgiven not because of a human act but because of 'the name' of the one who has won forgiveness (1 John 2:12).

The means and goal of forgiveness

'But if there is anything in the whole of religion that we should most certainly know, we ought most closely to grasp by what reason, with what law, under what condition, with what ease or difficulty, forgiveness of sins may be obtained!' (Calvin, *Institutes* III. iv. 2).

The objective means of forgiveness is Christ's atoning death on the cross: 'He forgave us all our sins, having cancelled the written code, with its regulations, that was against us and that stood opposed to us; he took it away, nailing it to the cross' (Col. 2:13–14). The OT belief that God provides both the atoning sacrifice (Lev. 17:11: '"I have given [the sacrifice] to you to make atonement for yourselves on the altar"') and the resulting forgiveness is a fundamental assumption of the NT writers. They appeal to it every time they describe the death of Christ as the payment for sin which sinners themselves could never have made. As for the OT saints, Hebrews declares that OT sacrifices for sin, while sufficient to mediate God's grace to them (note the high status accorded to OT believers in Heb. 11), looked ahead to a final and climactic priestly gesture, one in which the high priest both presided over and was himself the ultimate sacrifice for sins (Heb. 10:11–12). The whole Bible proclaims a single objective means of forgiveness.

The subjective means of forgiveness have been disputed by different schools of interpretation through the centuries. According to

501

the NT, the first means is *faith, *i.e.* informed personal trust. A person hears of or otherwise discerns what Paul calls 'God's invisible qualities – his eternal power and divine nature' (Rom. 1:20), and is led to accept the message of Christ's death for sin, not merely as a general truth, but as a fact of personal significance. The person comes to understand something of God's *holiness and his or her own abject unworthiness. This personal, compliant apprehension of God in his holiness may thereupon lead immediately to *repentance, the only sane response when sinful flesh glimpses transcendent holiness (*cf. e.g.* Job 42:5–6; Is. 6:5; Luke 5:8; Rev. 1:17). Following the person's acknowledgment of his or her guilt – not a merely academic admission but a plea for transformation supported by deeds (*cf. e.g.* Zacchaeus' example, Luke 19:8) – forgiveness is granted (Luke 19:9; *cf.* 1 John 1:9). The process of forgiveness may therefore be summarized as faith–repentance–forgiveness.

The goal of forgiveness is far broader than the individual sinner's rescue from eschatological woe, though that is a benefit not to be minimized. Forgiveness fully appropriated should result in the renewal of the will (Rom. 6:17–18). The forgiven person is more motivated and able to live a holy life, which comprises a comprehensive and growing trust in and love for God, love for others, and heartfelt compliance with God's commands (see *e.g.* 1 John *passim*). Love is the goal of all Christian instruction (Matt. 22:37–40; 1 Tim.1:5), and love as modelled by Christ (*cf.* 1 John 2:6) follows from forgiveness, as sinners estranged from God and other humans are cleansed from guilt and their broken fellowship is restored. Other goals of forgiveness, corollaries of divine love, include humble regard for others (Matt. 7:1–5; Titus 3:1–5), engagement in Christian *mission to the world (Matt. 28:18–20; Jude 21–23), and the eternal praise of God. Such praise is mentioned in numerous passages in which his mercy or covenant love (the basis of forgiveness) is extolled (*e.g.* Ps. 136; Rom. 11:32–33; 15:9; 1 Pet. 1:3).

The double fruit of forgiveness: reconciliation with God and with others

'Reconciliation' in Scripture pertains most directly to the atonement proper, but it also has direct links with the idea of forgiveness. It may be defined as the restoration of fellowship between estranged parties.

The word is rare in (if not absent from) many modern translations of the OT (*e.g.* NIV; but see NRSV 1 Sam. 29:4). The concept is however present throughout the OT as God speaks and acts to fulfil the promise of Genesis 3:15, to abolish the enmity (alienation, estrangement) that sin introduced into human existence, both between God and humanity and in human relationships.

OT apocryphal writings foreshadow the NT use, with theological connotations of the 'reconcile' word family. But in 2 Maccabees 1:5 (*cf.* 2 Macc. 5:20) God is said to be reconciled to sinners; in canonical Scripture sinners are reconciled to God. 3 Maccabees 5:13 calls God 'easily reconciled' (*eukatallaktos*); this implies not only that it is God who is reconciled, but that the process of reconciliation is unproblematic; the NT stresses the great cost involved in the reconciling sacrifice of God's own Son.

The word 'reconcile' and its cognates occur some sixteen times in the NT, mostly in Paul's writings, where they are found in three clusters. In the first, Paul stresses that believers were reconciled to God through Christ's death while they were still 'God's enemies'; this is a ground for rejoicing (Rom. 5:10–11). In the second, Paul calls the whole gospel ministry of apostolate and church 'the ministry of reconciliation' (2 Cor. 5:18); it is grounded in the fact that 'God was reconciling the world to himself in Christ, not counting men's sins against them' (2 Cor. 5:19). It is therefore incumbent on Paul's readers to 'be reconciled to God' (2 Cor. 5:20). A third cluster of Pauline references is found in the prison epistles. In one passage Paul stresses the outcome of God's saving work in Christ, *i.e.* sanctification, through which believers are presented to God 'holy and without blemish and without reproach' (Col. 1:22, author's translation). In another he focuses on the universal scope of the blessedness ('peace') effected by Christ's cross (Col. 1:20). In yet another he underlines the social dimension of Christ's death; by it Jew and Gentile, paradigmatic for all humankind and the fractured creation, are made into 'one new man ... through the cross, by which he put to death their hostility' (Eph. 2:15–16).

The words that Paul uses (the noun *katallagē* and verb *katallassō* in Romans and

2 Corinthians, the verb *apokatallassō* in Colossians and Ephesians) all connote the estrangement between God and humans being brought to an end through Christ. The alternative is a needlessly barren (and contentious) life in this age and divine judgment in the age to come.

Jesus points to the need to be to be reconciled (*diallassomai*) 'to your brother' as a precondition of true worship (Matt. 5:23–24). He implies that his listeners should be reconciled (*apallassō*) to God in the light of the signs of the times (Luke 12:58; *cf.* vv. 54–59).

The correlation of forgiveness and reconciliation

While there is always much good in God's world for which to be thankful, the 20th century ended on the same note of social disintegration, strife, warfare and religious persecution that characterized the whole century. Reconciliation, realized in concrete acts of human forgiveness, whether between individuals or between groups, seems to be increasingly rare. *De facto* tribalism and ethnic feuding are rampant and highly destructive, in places too numerous to list. Atrocities that forgiveness might have averted have been seen in virtually every part of the world. A recent study concludes that 'churches have rarely exercised their ministry of reconciliation' (G. Baum and H. Wells (eds.), *The Reconciliation of Peoples*, p. 185). It also asserts (p. 189) that 'the process of reconciliation demands ... conversion, a change of mind and heart'.

Only where Christ's death for sin is taken with apostolic seriousness can the rains of divine restoration wash human hate away and moisten seeds of love. The prospects for real and lasting forgiveness in the many trouble spots of the postmodern world depend on the grace God grants as the gospel of his reconciling Son is proclaimed, believed and applied.

See also: ATONEMENT.

Bibliography

G. Baum and H. Wells (eds.), *The Reconciliation of Peoples: Challenge to the Churches* (Geneva and Maryknoll, 1997); P. B. N. Eugene, 'Christ as reconciler in Pauline theology and in contemporary Rwanda', *AJET* 15.1, 1996, pp. 19–28; P. House, *Old Testament Theology* (Downers Grove, 1998); J. Kselman, J. Charlesworth and G. Shogren, 'Forgiveness', in *ABD* 2, pp. 831–838; N. Kiuchi, 'Spirituality in offering a peace offering', *TynB* 50, 1999, pp. 23–31; R. Martin, *Reconciliation: A Study of Paul's Theology* (Atlanta, 1981); A. Schlatter, *Das christliche Dogma* (Stuttgart, ²1923); C. Stenschke, 'The need for salvation', in I. H. Marshall and D. Peterson (eds.), *Witness to the Gospel: The Theology of Acts* (Grand Rapids and Cambridge, 1998); V. Taylor, *Forgiveness and Reconciliation* (London, ²1948); N. T. Wright, *The New Testament and the People of God* (Minneapolis and London, 1992).

R. W. YARBROUGH

FREEDOM

Freedom is the state of being free from (or unfettered by) undesirable controls, or restrictions and especially from the state of bondage or slavery. *God sets his *people free to live in *covenant relationship with him. In Scripture freedom is always a qualified concept: God's people are set free in order that they might serve him, Christ, *righteousness, *etc.* The *Exodus is the supreme paradigm of freedom in the Scriptures.

Old Testament

The primary context of freedom in the OT is the contrast with the (individual or communal) state of slavery. While 'freedom' language is not common, the concept is found in the language of slavery and *redemption from slavery.

Pentateuch and historical books

*Israel's slavery in Egypt and their redemption is central to biblical thought on freedom. In Genesis 15:13–14 God warns Abraham that his descendants will be enslaved for four hundred years, but then promises, 'I will bring judgment on the nation which they serve, and afterward they shall come out with great possessions' (RSV). Henceforth the Exodus is seen as the fulfilment of God's promise to Abraham.

The importance of Israel's redemption from slavery is indicated by the fact that the first fifteen chapters of Exodus are dedicated to narrating the event. Thereafter God is identified primarily as the one who set Israel free from slavery in Egypt. That deliverance is the basis for the Mosaic covenant and the principal motivating force for obeying the covenant stipulations. The laws dealing with the treatment of slaves, sojourners and the *poor are based upon Israel's liberating experience in the Exodus (Deut. 5:15; 15:15; 24:18, 22). An Israelite could not have his freedom denied indefinitely, since Hebrew slaves were to be released after six years of service (Exod. 21:2; Deut. 15:12; Jer. 34:8–17) and treated very generously, for 'you were a slave in the land of Egypt, and the LORD your God redeemed you' (Deut. 15:13–15). Once every fifty years Israel was to celebrate the Year of Jubilee, blowing the trumpet and proclaiming 'liberty throughout the land' (Lev. 25:8–55). At that time Hebrews who had sold themselves into debt slavery were to have their freedom restored, and land that had been sold was to be restored to its original owner.

The Mosaic covenant established that living securely and enjoying freedom and other *blessings were dependent upon fulfilling the conditions of the covenant (Lev. 26; Deut. 28). The historical books of the OT reflect the same Deuteronomic theology, according to which faithfulness or unfaithfulness towards the Mosaic covenant results in the blessings of freedom and prosperity or the curses of captivity and exile (e.g. 1 Sam. 30:1–5; 1 Kgs. 8:46–50; 2 Kgs. 15:29; 24:14–16, 19–20; 2 Chr. 6:36–38; 28:1–17; 29:6–9; Ezra 9:6–9; Neh. 9:26–37).

Prophets

Prophetic oracles of *judgment and *salvation were based upon the application of the curses and blessings of the covenant as they related to the future *exile and restoration of God's people.

Several passages in Isaiah portray the future release from Babylonian captivity as a new Exodus (e.g. 43:16–21; 51:9–11). Isaiah 61:1 proclaims 'liberty to the captives, and the opening of the prison to those who are bound'.

Jeremiah 31:31–34 and Ezekiel 11:17–20 and 36:24–27 develop the theme of Deuteronomy 30:1–6 according to which God will do a special work in the heart of his people at the time of post-exilic restoration. These passages imply that there has been a problem with the heart of God's people which has resulted in rebellion and unfaithfulness. Jeremiah 31:31–34 says that God will write his *law upon their hearts, while Ezekiel says that God will give them a new heart (11:19; 36:26) and put his Spirit within them (11:19; 36:26–27). This theme of God's transformation of the heart of his people through the gift of his Spirit in the time of restoration may be reflected in a number of NT passages that speak of freedom from the power of *sin.

New Testament

Gospels

The authors of the Synoptic Gospels presuppose that *Jerusalem is awaiting its ultimate liberation and restoration (Matt. 1:21; 3:2–3; Mark 1:1–4; Luke 1:68–77; 2:25, 38), to be realized with the coming of a promised messianic *king. Although many Jews hoped for a political liberation from Rome, the Gospel authors indicate that *Jesus' teaching offered a spiritual and moral freedom that was not contingent upon an alteration of the political situation.

Luke tells us that Jesus inaugurated his Galilean ministry by proclaiming the fulfilment of Isaiah's promise of good news to the poor, freedom for the captives, release from darkness for the prisoners, and the arrival of the year of the Lord's favour (Luke 4:16–21; cf. Is. 61:1–2). While freedom was not a common theme in Jesus' teaching, liberation is an appropriate description of what people experienced when they encountered the kingdom of God through his ministry, perhaps especially through his ministry of exorcism and *healing.

John 8:31–38 records Jesus' promise that those who continued in his teaching would know the *truth and be set free by that truth. His Jewish listeners object that they had never been in bondage. Jesus makes clear that he is referring to their slavery to sin, and that only the Son can provide freedom from that bondage. Here the subjection of the Jews (and of all those outside Christ) is strongly affirmed, but the bondage that calls forth the sending of the Son is defined as moral slavery to sin rather than political subjection to Rome.

Paul

It is Paul who most fully develops the idea of freedom in Christ, and in particular the idea of freedom from the dominion of the law and the power of sin. In Galatians 5:1 Paul can summarize the 'indicative' of salvation (and the argument of much of Galatians 3 – 4) with the phrase 'for freedom Christ has set us free'.

Paul's concept of freedom reflects a scriptural and Jewish understanding of salvation as deliverance out of a state of slavery and into a state of freedom. Its principal background is the scriptural traditions which depicted the Exodus as the fundamental paradigm for liberty, and the prophetic tradition that portrayed post-exilic redemption and restoration as a second Exodus (Isaiah 40 – 55). For Paul, all those who do not know Jesus Christ are living in slavery since true freedom is found only in the coming of Christ and the *Holy Spirit.

Paul ties Christians' freedom from slavery to sin directly to their identification with Christ's *death and resurrection (Rom. 6:5–8). Through union or identification with Christ those 'who were once slaves of sin' are now able to be '*obedient from the heart' (Rom. 6:17). They have been 'set free from sin' (Rom. 6:18, 22) and have become 'slaves of righteousness' (Rom. 6:18) and 'slaves of God' (Rom. 6:22). Romans 7:5 – 8:11 contrasts the slavery to sin and captivity to the flesh which the law could not overcome with 'the law of the Spirit of life in Christ Jesus' which sets one 'free from the law of sin and death' (8:2). It is through the 'new life of the Spirit' (7:6) that one has the potential to fulfil 'the just requirement of the law' (8:4). This sounds like a paraphrase of the OT contrast between the inability of God's people to fulfil his law before he transforms their hearts in the time of restoration and their capacity to fulfil his law after that transformation (Deut. 30:1–6; Jer. 31:31–34; Ezek. 11:17–20; 36:24–27).

In 2 Corinthians 3 Paul discusses the Corinthians' manifestation of that which the Spirit has written on their hearts (3:2–3, alluding to Jer. 31:33 and Ezek. 36:26–27). In this context Paul declares that 'where the Spirit of the Lord is, there is freedom' evidently referring to the freedom to see Christ in the Scriptures and be transformed by that vision (3:14–18).

Paul affirms that those who are in Christ have been freed from the dominion and curse of the law by having died to the law and entered into the resurrection age through their identification with Christ (Rom. 6:14; 7:4–6; 10:4; Gal. 2:19; 3:23–24; 5:18). It was Christ who became a curse for us and opened the way to the new age of the Spirit through his death and resurrection (Gal. 1:4; 3:13–14). Galatians 4:21–31 is a powerful re-reading of Genesis 21 which establishes that those who are bound to the Mosaic covenant and law and to the earthly Jerusalem are children of slavery while those who are (Christian) children of promise and of the heavenly Jerusalem are not slaves but free (Gal. 4:21–31).

For Paul freedom in Christ is a present reality, but it is not automatically manifested in the lives of believers. They are still capable of yielding themselves to sin and of letting it reign over them (Rom. 6:12–13, 16; 8:12–13; Gal. 5:13). Freedom may also be lost or surrendered by those who are not vigilant or willing to defend their freedom from those who would have them become enslaved again (Gal. 2:4; 5:1–2). Paul exhorts his readers to live out the life of righteousness and the freedom from sin that Christ has made possible. Here we encounter the tension between the 'indicative' which affirms that which Christ has accomplished for his people and the 'imperative' in which they are exhorted to realize their potential in the fallen world.

Although Paul affirms the freedom that is already present in this age he awaits that complete freedom from the power and presence of sin which will only be experienced at the time of the resurrection of believers (Rom. 6:5; 8:11, 18–23). At that time the rest of *creation will also be 'set free from its bondage to decay and obtain the glorious liberty of the children of God' (8:21).

For Paul (as in the OT) the freedom of God's people is not absolute; rather they are freed from bondage in order that they might serve God (Rom. 6:22), righteousness (Rom. 6:18), and others. In 1 Corinthians 9 Paul affirms both his freedom (9:1) and his willingness to be 'a slave to all' (9:19). In 1 Corinthians 10:25–33 he teaches that one's freedom with respect to food ought to be employed in such a way as to glorify God and avoid offending others (10:31–33). In 1 Corinthians 7:22 he uses the Christian's paradoxical status as one who has been freed by the Lord and yet is a slave of Christ in order to relativize the importance of one's social status as slave or free.

General epistles and Revelation

In 1 Peter 2:16 the readers are exhorted to live as free people but to avoid using their freedom 'as a pretext for evil'; rather they are to 'live as servants of God', recognizing that their freedom in Christ is limited by the spiritual and moral purpose for which it was given (as in Gal. 5:13 and Rom. 6:22).

2 Peter 2:19 deals with false teachers who 'promise [their disciples] freedom' but who are themselves slaves of corruption, 'for whatever overcomes a man, to that he is enslaved'. It was 'through the knowledge of our Lord and Saviour Jesus Christ' that these people had 'escaped the defilements of the world', but now they have fallen away (2:20).

James declares the blessedness of the one who perseveres in doing 'the perfect law, the law of liberty' (1:25), and exhorts his readers to act as people who will be judged according to that law of liberty (2:12). Here he seems to have applied a Jewish understanding of the law as a means of liberty to the Scriptures as interpreted by Jesus and understood in the light of his ministry.

Conclusion

As God set Israel free from slavery through the Exodus, so those who are in Christ are freed from their bondage to *spiritual powers, sin, death and the law. They enter into this freedom through their knowledge of and identification with Christ. Guided and transformed by their reading of Scripture, they are not to abuse their freedom through sinful or destructive behaviour but are to serve God and others in all righteousness as they await the complete liberty that all creation will enjoy at the second coming of Christ.

Bibliography

F. F. Bruce in *ISBE* 3, pp. 118–122; J. K. Chamblin in *DPL*, pp. 313–316; J. D. G. Dunn, *Christian Liberty* (Carlisle and Grand Rapids, 1993); R. L. Hubbard, Jr. in *NIDOTTE* 1, pp. 789–794 and 3, pp. 578–582; F. S. Jones in *ABD* 2, pp. 855–859; K. Niederwimmer in *EDNT* 1, pp. 432–434; J. P. J. Olivier in *NIDOTTE* 1, pp. 986–989, and 2, pp. 238–239; H. Ringgren in *TDOT* 2, pp. 350–355; H. Schlier in *TDNT* 2, pp. 487–502.

R. E. CIAMPA

FRUIT, see HARVEST
FRUIT OF THE SPIRIT, see HOLY SPIRIT
GALATIANS, see Part 2
GENEALOGIES, see SEED
GENESIS, see Part 2
GENESIS TO KINGS, see Part 2
GENTILES, see NATIONS

GENTLENESS

Gentleness is a somewhat ambiguous concept in Hebrew and Greek as well as in English. The ambiguity arises from the fact that the term can denote both strength and vulnerability. Thus gentleness may be understood as a positive or a negative characteristic: on the one hand, as forbearance and kindness towards the helpless, or purposeful and self-chosen powerlessness; on the other, as oversensitivity and timidity in the face of everyday life. Deuteronomy 28:56 uses the term negatively in its ironic description of the gentle woman, too sensitive to put her foot to the ground. More usually, however, in the OT and in the NT, gentleness is portrayed as a positive quality. It is a characteristic of peaceable and controlled kindness, the opposite of arrogance or domination. It is contrasted with harshness (2 Sam. 18:5), wildness (Job 41:3), drunkenness, violence and self-serving greed (1 Tim. 3:3).

Because of this conceptual ambiguity, translation of the related Hebrew and Greek terms is difficult. In Greek *epieikeia, epieikēs, ēpios, praupatheia, praus, prautēs* and *chrēstotēs* all include the idea of gentleness, but also connote graciousness, clemency, kindness, humility, consideration, courtesy and meekness. In Galatians 5:22–23 both the KJV and the NIV include gentleness among the fruit of the Spirit (see *Holy Spirit), but the KJV uses the term to translate *chrēstotēs* which in the NIV and the NRSV is rendered 'kindness'. The NIV and the NRSV, on the other hand, use 'gentleness' to translate *prautēs* which the KJV translates as 'meekness'. In Hebrew there is a similar range of related word groups: *'nh, 'nw* conveying the notion of forbearance and humility, and *ḥsd* conveying that of loving-kindness. Therefore the idea of gentleness is present in the biblical texts far more often than the actual word appears in the English versions.

Gentleness is an aspect of the character of *God, and is particularly apparent in the way he speaks to his people. Job 15:11 speaks of God's gentleness demonstrated in his providing consolation (cf. also Is. 40:1–2) and 1 Kings 19:11–13 describes God's speaking to Elijah in the gentle whisper. Zechariah 9:9 prophesies the future king's coming not with military pomp and splendour but in gentle humility. *Jesus' fulfilment of this prophecy goes far beyond his symbolic entry into Jerusalem, 'gentle and riding on a donkey' (Matt. 21:5, NIV). When he calls his followers to take his yoke on their shoulders (Matt. 11:29), he describes himself as a gentle, humble servant who provides comfort and rest for them. Paul appeals to his readers 'by the meekness and gentleness of Christ' (2 Cor. 10:1), and in Philippians 2:6–11 he presents the gentle character and behaviour of the one who is now enthroned as Lord as an example for his readers (although the word 'gentle' or its cognates are not used here).

Paul understood the importance of behaving towards church members with the same kind of gentleness as that shown by Jesus (1 Thess. 2:7; 1 Cor. 4:21) (even though in practice he sometimes struggled to express it). Gentleness is described in Galatians as part of the fruit of the Spirit borne by the Christian (Gal. 5:22–23), and thus by implication as evidence of the indwelling of the Spirit of Christ. In Colossians gentleness is presented alongside other spiritual fruit as necessary 'clothing' for all God's chosen people (Col. 3:12). To be gentle, therefore, should be the ambition of all Christians (Eph. 4:2; 2 Tim. 2:24), and should characterize the whole community of believers (Phil. 4:5; Titus 3:2), women (1 Pet. 3:4) and men, leaders and led. It is a particularly important quality for *leaders: Jesus taught that leadership among his disciples was to be quite different from that in the world (Mark 10:42–45), more a matter of *suffering and service than of power and authority. Timothy is exhorted to strive for gentleness (1 Tim. 6:11), and it is an essential qualification for the office of bishop or overseer (1 Tim. 3:3). Leaders have to communicate, and gentleness makes communication more effective. Indeed, 'a gentle answer turns away wrath, but a harsh word stirs up anger' (Prov. 15:1) and 'through patience a ruler can be persuaded, and a gentle tongue can break a bone' (Prov. 25:15; cf. also James 3:17–18). All answers are to be given 'with gentleness and respect' (1 Pet. 3:15).

Gentleness includes the flexibility which allows a distinction to be drawn between the spirit and the letter of the law and *mercy to be shown as a result. David displays this mercy in enjoining his commanders to be gentle with Absalom. Gentleness requires *humility or 'stooping down' (2 Sam. 22:36; Ps. 18:35) and a willingness to submit like that of a *lamb going to slaughter (Is. 53:7; Jer. 11:19). It also demands a generous-hearted attitude towards others (Col. 3:12; 2 Cor. 6:6; Eph. 2:7; Titus 3:3), and the kind of compassionate forbearance and loving-kindness exhibited by the Lord himself.

The challenge that gentleness presents to the Christian is, therefore, a difficult one. To be truly gentle the believer must imitate Christ.

Bibliography
J. K. Chamblin in *EDBT*, p. 286; P. H. Davids in *DBTE*, p. 301.

M. J. EVANS

GIFT, see GRACE

GLORY

The OT

'Glory', 'honour' and related verbs and adjectives translate several OT words, primarily a group stemming from the Semitic root *kbd* (which means 'weight' or 'heaviness'). This word group, particularly the noun (*kābôd*), has the concrete sense of 'abundance', 'wealth' (Gen. 31:1, NIV: 'Jacob ... has gained all this wealth ...'; Is. 61:6: '... in their riches you will boast') and 'splendour', whether of people (e.g. Joseph in Egypt, Gen. 45:13; David as king, 1 Chr. 29:28) or things (e.g. chariots, Is. 22:18; the trees of Eden, Ezek. 31:18; the temple, Hag. 2:3, 9), and the more abstract sense of 'dignity' (Ps. 112:9; Prov. 29:23; Jer. 48:18) and 'respect' or 'reverence' (for Hezekiah as king, 2 Chr. 32:33; for Yahweh, Is. 42:12; for a father, Mal. 1:6).

Glory is pre-eminently a divine quality; ultimately only *God has glory. In view of his sovereignty as the creator of heaven and earth (Is. 42:5; *cf*. 40:12–28), which is exercised for Israel's deliverance through his anointed servant (Is. 42:1–5) and excludes all idol worship, the Lord declares, 'I will not give my glory to another' (Is. 42:8). However, he grants glory; it exists derivatively among his creatures. In the words of David's prayer, 'Yours, O LORD, is … the glory and the majesty and the splendour, for everything in heaven and earth is yours', and 'Wealth and honour come from you' (1 Chr. 29:11–12).

Not surprisingly, then, the phrase 'the glory of the LORD' (*k^e bôd yhwh*) occurs frequently in the OT; it is virtually a technical term (*e.g.* Exod. 16:7; 1 Kgs. 8:11; Ps. 63:2). God's glory is his visible and active presence. His glory fills the entire *creation (Ps. 19:1; Is. 6:3) and is seen by the *nations (Ps. 97:6). But, more specifically, his glory is his presence in the midst of his *covenant people *Israel (Exod. 16:7). Used in this sense, the word is clearly associated with God's name (Exod. 33:18–19; Ps. 115:1). Related to his grandeur and power as Creator and Redeemer, it is often associated with the phenomenon of *light or fire, sometimes of such overwhelming brilliance and unendurable intensity that it is shrouded in a cloud (Exod. 16:10; 24:17; *cf*. 33:22–23; 34:29–35).

The association of glory with God's self-*revelation is seen in the exchange between the Lord and Moses, which involves a word play on *paneh*, in Exodus 33:7 – 34:35. The Lord customarily speaks to Moses, as Israel's leader, 'face to face [*paneh*], as a man speaks with his friend' (33:11; *cf*. Num. 12:8). This happens within the tabernacle as the pillar of cloud, which envelops the Lord's glorious presence (*cf*. Exod. 13:21–22 with 16:10), remains at the entrance (33:9–10).

Responding to Moses' request for assurance, the Lord promises, 'My Presence [*paneh*] will go with you, …' (33:13–14). Moses, in turn, replies, 'If your Presence does not go with us …' and then asks, 'Now show me your glory' (33:15, 18). To this the Lord says, 'I will cause all my goodness to pass in front of you [*paneh*], and I will proclaim my name, the LORD, in your presence [*paneh*] … But … you cannot see my face [*paneh*], for no

one may see me and live' (33:19–20). Accordingly, the Lord makes provision, apparently with a view to what will soon happen on Mount Sinai, to protect Moses 'when my glory passes by'. He promises to cover Moses with his 'hand' as he passes by, so that Moses will see his 'back'; 'but my face [*paneh*] must not be seen' (33:21–23).

Afterwards Moses' face (*paneh*) has a radiance which, though tolerable for others, is also intimidating, so that when he has finished speaking the Lord's commands to Israel, he veils his face (Exod. 34:29–33). Subsequently, whenever he enters the Lord's presence (*paneh*), he removes the veil and his face remains unveiled until he has come out and spoken the Lord's word to the people (34:34–35; *cf*. the commentary on this passage in 2 Cor. 3:13–18).

The interchangeableness or close association in this passage of God's glory and his presence/face, his goodness, his name and his radiance, both veiled and unveiled, and the fact that Moses both does and yet may not see the Lord's face, indicates that God's glory is his manifest presence which, without further mediation, will destroy his creatures, but which admits of mediated expressions involving the most intimate fellowship with him. In the NT *Jesus Christ is the ultimate and permanent expression of divine glory (*e.g.* John 1:14; 2 Cor. 3:13–14).

God's glorious presence, whether for salvation or destruction, is prominent in the decisive moments and central institutions of Israel's history: Moses and the Exodus, monarchy and temple, exile and return. In the prophets, divine glory becomes messianic and eschatological. In the latter part of Isaiah, for example, the prophet foretells the coming and activity of the Lord's anointed servant (42:1–4; 49:1–12; 52:13 – 53:12; the NT explicitly applies such passages to Jesus, as the Christ, *e.g.* Matt. 12:18–21; Luke 2:32; 2 Cor. 6:2; Acts 3:13). Accordingly, the preparatory 'voice of one calling in the desert' (40:3, NIV mg., applied in the NT to John the Baptist, Matt. 3:3 par.) will announce a time when 'the glory of the Lord will be revealed' to the whole of humanity (Is. 40:5). This future revelation of messianically mediated glory will mean not only the full, eschatological restoration of Israel (Is. 58:8; 60:1–2, 19; 62:2–3), but will be universal (66:18), including the *salvation of the nations ('From the west …

and from the rising of the sun, they will revere his glory,' 59:19). To that end the Lord will send some from among Israel's restored remnant 'to the nations ... that have not heard of my fame or seen my glory. They will proclaim my glory among the nations' (66:19). This prophetic expectation of the final, saving revelation of the divine glory through the messianic servant is expressed most comprehensively in the hope that 'the earth will be filled with the knowledge of the glory of the LORD, as the waters cover the sea' (Hab. 2:14).

The NT

The translation of *kābôd* as *doxa* in the Septuagint caused a substantial semantic change in the latter (in secular Greek it meant 'opinion', 'reputation', 'praise'). That change is seen in the NT use of 'glory' vocabulary, especially in John and Paul; well over half of its occurrences are in the latter's writings.

The Gospels and Acts

In the Gospels glory is pre-eminently messianic. In the Synoptics, at the birth of Jesus 'the glory of the Lord' appears as dazzling light (Luke 2:9), evoking praise from the heavenly host, 'Glory to God in the highest' (2:14). Accordingly, the infant Jesus is himself 'a light for revelation to the Gentiles and for glory to your people Israel' (Luke 2:32; *cf.* Is. 49:6; 46:13). When Jesus is tempted by the devil to prostitute his messianic calling ('If you are the Son of God ...', Luke 4:3, 9 par.), he is offered 'all the kingdoms of the world' with 'their authority and splendour' (4:5–6 par.).

In the accounts of Jesus' earthly ministry his future messianic glory is emphasized. Previewed in the transfiguration (Luke 9:31–32), this glory is attained in his resurrection (Luke 24:26), and will be displayed in the future 'when he comes in his glory and in the glory of the Father and of the holy angels' (Luke 9:26 par.), 'in a cloud with power and great glory' (Luke 21:27 par.). His disciples' share in messianically mediated glory is entirely future, to be received when Christ is revealed (Matt. 19:28; Mark 10:37). None the less, in Acts, at critical points in the narrative, the divine glory of the ascended Christ is seen by Stephen (7:55) and Paul (22:11; *cf.* 1 Cor. 15:8), and is experienced by the latter in a powerful and transforming way.

In John's Gospel the glory of Jesus is prominent from the outset. As the *Word, who 'in the beginning ... was God' and 'was with God' (1:1–2) and has 'become flesh', his is 'the glory of the Only Begotten' (1:14, NIV mg.). In him the revelation of the divine glory has found its ultimate expression. Foreseen by Isaiah (John 12:41), it is marked pre-eminently by 'grace and truth', in contrast to the revelation granted to Moses (1:17; *cf.* 7:18). Accordingly, his miracles manifest 'his glory' (2:11) as 'the glory of God' (11:4, 40).

Akin to the Synoptic idea of future messianic glory is John's distinctive view of the glorification of Jesus as his being 'lifted up' in his *death (John 3:14; 12:32, 34), resurrection and ascension. With this culmination of his earthly ministry in view, he prays to the Father, 'Glorify your Son, that your Son may glorify you' (17:1). To that end, his further prayer is 'glorify me in your presence with the glory I had with you before the world began' (17:5, *cf.* v. 24b). By this impending glorification, the now incarnate Word-Son will be invested with the glory he has shared eternally with the Father. This will happen so that he, in turn, may share his glory with believers, 'that they may be one as we are one' (17:22; *cf.* v. 24a).

Integral to this process are the *Holy Spirit and his activity. His presence in believers is contingent on Jesus' own glorification (John 7:39); when Jesus ascends to the Father, he will send the Spirit as 'Counsellor' (14:12–26; 15:26; 16:7). This subsequent activity of the Spirit is Christologically focused; specifically, he ministers Christ's glory: 'He will bring glory to me by taking from what is mine and making it known to you' (16:14).

Paul

Glory terminology provides a window on virtually the whole of Paul's theology; nowhere are its OT roots more apparent. His gospel is 'the gospel of the glory of Christ' (2 Cor. 4:4) and may be viewed as a message of restored and consummated glory.

Through their sinful rebellion, human beings have forfeited the privilege (given to those who bear God's image; 1 Cor. 11:7) of reflecting God's glory (Rom. 3:23). But they have not frustrated God's eternal plan of salvation in Christ, 'to the praise of the glory of his grace' (Eph. 1:4–6, 12, KJV; *cf.* Rom. 8:29–30). Christ is the climactic revelation of

God's glory. His glory, mediated through the Spirit, is the glory of the new covenant (2 Cor. 3:3 – 4:6). It is surpassing and permanent; in a word, eschatological. In comparison, the glory of the old covenant, though real, is transitory and virtually non-existent (2 Cor. 3:10–11). The light of Christ's glory recalls the light of the original creation; his is the splendour of a new and final creation (2 Cor. 4:6, quoting Gen. 1:3; cf. 5:17).

The status of Christ as 'the Lord of glory' was veiled in his crucifixion (1 Cor. 2:8), but has been openly revealed in his resurrection. Rewarded with life for his obedience to death (Phil. 2:6–9), he has been 'vindicated by the Spirit ... taken up in glory' (1 Tim. 3:16). The resurrection gives him an unprecedented relationship with the Holy Spirit; 'raised in glory' (1 Cor. 15:43), as the 'last Adam' he has become 'life-giving Spirit' (1 Cor. 15:45; cf. 2 Cor. 3:17). The Spirit ministers Christ's resurrection life and glory to his *people (cf. Rom. 8:9–11).

Christ's glorification, then, is not only for himself but others. 'Raised from the dead through the glory of the Father', he is the source of 'a new life' (Rom. 6:4), so that the church too might be 'radiant' (endoxos, Eph. 5:27). This glorification takes place as the image of God's glory, universally defaced and perverted in Adam, is restored and consummated first in Christ and then in believers. Already, they 'are being transformed into the same image from glory to glory', as they 'reflect [or 'behold'] the Lord's glory' (2 Cor. 3:18), in 'the light of the gospel of the glory of Christ, who is the image of God' (2 Cor. 4:4).

This present glory of the *church, paralleling the experience of its Lord prior to his resurrection, is veiled by *suffering and adversity. Fundamental to the Christian life is that 'we share in his sufferings in order that we may share in his glory' (Rom. 8:17b; cf. 2 Cor. 1:5; 4:10–11; Phil. 3:10). Paul's prayer is that believers might be powerfully strengthened 'according to [God's] glorious might so that you may have great endurance and patience' (Col. 1:11). The 'light and momentary troubles' involved in renewal of glory in the present are producing 'an eternal glory that far outweighs them all' (2 Cor. 4:17; cf. Rom. 8:18).

Christ, indwelling the church, is 'the hope of glory' (Col. 1:27). When Christ returns, believers 'will appear with him in glory' (Col. 3:4; cf. Rom. 2:7, 10). Then, Christ, 'the firstfruits' of the resurrection harvest (1 Cor. 15:20, 23), will transform the present, 'lowly' bodies of believers to be 'like his glorious body' (Phil. 3:20–21; cf. 'raised in glory', 1 Cor. 15:43). This final, open revelation of 'the glorious freedom the children of God' (Rom. 8:21) will be cosmic in scope, and will release creation from futility and corruption (Rom. 8:19–21).

At Christ's return unbelievers will be punished with 'everlasting destruction', consisting of separation from him and 'the majesty [doxa] of his power' (2 Thess. 1:9). On that 'day' he will also 'be glorified in his holy people' (2 Thess. 1:10). To that end Paul prays for the church, that from the present time until then, 'the name of our Lord Jesus Christ may be glorified in you, and you in him ...' (2 Thess. 1:12).

Other NT writings

In Hebrews, the eternal glory which is ascribed to God in the closing doxology (13:21) is at the outset predicated of the Son as 'the radiance of God's glory and the exact representation of his being' (1:3). Subsequently, however, the writer emphasizes the glorification experienced by the incarnate Son (e.g. 2:14, 17) as high *priest (5:5), a distinctive theme in Hebrews. In being permanently seated at the right hand of God in the heavenly sanctuary (7:26 – 8:2), he is 'now crowned with glory and honour because he suffered death' (2:9, applying to him Ps. 8:4–6, quoted in 2:6–8). As the ascended Son (3:6) he has been 'found worthy of greater glory than Moses' (3:3); in comparison to him 'the cherubim of the Glory' above the ark in the tabernacle (9:5) were but a shadow and type (8:5; 10:1). His high priestly 'perfecting' (as the Son), through his sufferings, death and ascension, was not simply for himself, for his own glory, but for the salvation of others, understood as 'bringing many sons to glory' (2:10).

In James, the reason why believers should not show favouritism is that they believe in Christ as 'the Lord of glory' (2:1). His glory as Lord leaves no place in the life of the church for discriminatory attitudes and actions, particularly preferential treatment of the rich at the expense of the poor (2:2–4).

In 1 and 2 Peter and Jude, glory, as

elsewhere in the NT, is ascribed to Christ and mediated through him. His sufferings and consequent 'glories' (the plural probably denotes the fullness of glory), and their saving significance, are the unifying preoccupation of the prophets (1 Pet. 1:10–11). Witnessed in advance by Peter and the others present at the transfiguration (2 Pet. 1:17), this resurrection glory (1 Pet. 1:21; *cf.* 1:3), sustains believers in their present sufferings, the fiery testing of their faith that will result in 'praise, glory and honour' at Christ's return (1 Pet. 1:7), when they will 'share in the glory to be revealed' (1 Pet. 5:1; *cf.* 5:4, 10; Jude 24). Even now, by faith, they are 'filled with an inexpressible and glorious joy' (1 Pet. 1:8). They have been 'called by [God's] own glory and goodness' to a life of godliness (2 Pet. 1:3) that will cause a watching world to 'glorify God on the day he visits us' (1 Pet. 2:12).

Suffering is associated with glory in 1 Peter 4:12–19 (*cf.* Rom. 8:17). In those sufferings which do not result from their own sins (v. 15), believers are to rejoice because they 'participate in the sufferings of Christ'. This solidarity in suffering will result in even greater joy in the future 'when his glory is revealed' (v. 13). In their present suffering God's Spirit is with them, as 'the Spirit of glory' (v. 14). Because of this involvement of Christ and the Spirit in their suffering as Christians, they ought to 'praise [lit. 'glorify'] God that you bear that name' (v. 16).

There is no glory vocabulary in the letters of John.

In Revelation, the glory of God and of the exalted Christ is prominent in numerous doxologies (*e.g.* 1:6; 4:11; 5:12–13; 7:12; 19:1). Accordingly, the exercise of God's power and wrath in apocalyptic judgment, reminiscent of the display of his glory in the OT (15:8; 18:1), evokes the response of 'giving glory' to God (11:13; 14:7) or, alternatively, of refusing to do so (16:9). The eschatological *Jerusalem and the *temple within it will be illumined only by 'the glory of God' (21:11, 22). Then, as it reflects that glory (21:24) and so fulfils the prophetic vision (*e.g.* Is. 60:3, 5, 19–20), 'the glory and the honour of the nations will be brought into it' (Rev. 21:26).

See also: THEOPHANY.

Bibliography

S. Aalen in *NIDNTT* 2, pp. 44–52; C. J. Collins in *NIDOTTE* 2, pp. 577–587; G. Kittel and G. von Rad in *TDNT* 2, pp. 233–255; J. Schneider in *TDNT* 8, pp. 174–180; C. Spicq in *TLNT*, pp. 362–379, N. Turner, 'Glory and glorification', in *Christian Words* (Edinburgh, 1980), pp. 185–189; C. Westermann in *TLOT* 2, pp. 590–602.

R. B. GAFFIN, JR.

GOD

The ultimate author and principal subject of the Bible. In the broadest sense, the whole of Scripture is a *revelation of God, though it is customary to distinguish between what God does outside himself and who God is in himself. As most of the Bible concentrates on the former, it is often said that a truly biblical theology ought to approach God from the standpoint of his acts, but this is not always or necessarily appropriate. The Bible often speaks of who God is as well as of what he does, so that to think in such ontological terms cannot be regarded as 'unbiblical'. Furthermore, the scope and significance of what God does depends on who he is, and cannot be properly understood otherwise.

The knowledge of God

According to the Bible, every living creature has an innate knowledge of God, because God is the *creator of all things (Ps. 14:1; Rom. 1:21). In the case of angels (see *Spiritual powers) and of *human beings this knowledge extends to a conscious recognition of God's lordship over them, even though this lordship has been rejected by some angels and by all human beings. The disobedient angels, who are called demons or devils, are aware of God's purposes and may even be in contact with him at some level in spite of their fallen state (Job 1; Jas. 2:19). Human beings are not as aware of God as the fallen angels are, but they are still without excuse for their disobedience. Both their reason and their conscience point to the existence of God and remind them of their separation from him. This separation has led human beings to create substitutes for the true God, which the Bible calls *idols. It is not altogether clear whether these idols are evil spirits or merely creatures of the human imagination (Jer. 10:3–5; 1 Cor. 10:19–20), but whatever they may be, they have no power when set against the true God.

It is possible for human beings to acquire some knowledge of God by looking at the works of his creation (Ps. 19:1), but this is not enough for them to come into that relationship with him which is enjoyed by his *covenant people and which is necessary for salvation from sin. In order to enjoy that relationship, people must hear God's '*word' and accept it by faith (Rom. 10:14–17). The 'word of God' is an expression which is used in different senses, but in its most basic terms it is God's communication to his people. This communication comes in words and can be expressed in any human language, even though it cannot be understood or accepted without the persuading power of the *Holy Spirit. In the OT, God spoke to Israel in many different ways, but in the NT these have ceased and given way to the fullness of God's revelation, who is *Jesus Christ, his Son (Heb. 1:1). Christ is not only the vehicle of the message; he is also its content, and therefore the term 'word of God' can be applied directly to him. The Bible is the written expression of this 'word' and has the force of divine utterance (2 Tim. 3:16; 2 Pet. 1:21), as can be seen for example in the story of the temptations of Jesus, where he quotes Scripture as God's reply to Satan (Matt. 4:4).

Ancient Israel was distinguished from its neighbours by the fact that it worshipped only one God, whom it identified as the creator of the universe and therefore as the supreme and ultimate reality. Whether the ancient Israelites believed that their God was the only divine being in existence, or whether they attributed some kind of being to the gods of other nations has been a matter of controversy. The former view is strict 'monotheism', and was certainly the position of the Jews in NT times. The other view is known as 'henotheism', which may have prevailed in the pre-exilic period. From a theological point of view, however, there is little or no difference between the two options. Whatever the Israelites may have thought about the gods of the nations around them, they always regarded their own God as supremely powerful and thus 'real' in a way that the others were not. We may therefore conclude that Israel practised a *de facto* monotheism

from earliest times, even if this was not fully clarified until the time of the exile or later.

God was known to Israel by his presence among them as a people. This presence was signified by the use of the term 'name', which expresses God's power as well as his identity. God placed his 'name' in the ark of the covenant, which was a large wooden chest in which were kept the ten commandments and other precious signs of the covenant which God had made with Moses in the desert. In the early days the ark had no permanent home, but travelled from place to place and was protected by a tent, called the 'tabernacle'. In the time of King David (c. 1000 BC) the ark was moved to Jerusalem, with the intention that a permanent home should be built for it. That home was the temple constructed by David's son Solomon, which from then on became the chief symbol of God's presence among his people. It was destroyed in 586 BC when Jerusalem fell to the Babylonians, but it was reconstructed seventy years later and remained in existence until its final destruction in AD 70. It is not known whether the ark survived the catastrophe of 586 BC or not, but the idea that God was present in the temple was very much alive in NT times.

This is made clear by Jesus, who identified himself with the temple (John 2:19), a statement which was equivalent to affirming that he was God in human flesh. Later on, the Apostle Paul took up the same theme when he reminded Christians that their bodies are the temple of the Holy Spirit, because God dwells in them (1 Cor. 6:19–20). These statements about the temple are theologically important because they reveal the difference between the way in which God was known in the OT and the way in which he is known by Christians now. Before the coming of Christ, God dwelt among his people, but not in them. The Jews knew that God was in their midst, but they could not enter the so-called 'holy of holies', the room in the temple where the ark was kept. Only the high priest could do that, when he presented the sin offering of *atonement for the sins of the people once a year. But when Christ died on the cross, reconciling God with his people by *sacrificing himself as an atonement for sin, the veil which separated the holy of holies from them was torn in two and the people were given direct access to God's presence.

One way of expressing this is to say that whereas the ancient Israelites knew God on the 'outside', Christians know him on the 'inside', having entered into his inner life. The NT supports this picture by saying that Christians are seated in heavenly places in Christ Jesus (Eph. 2:6) and have access to God through him (Eph. 2:18). It is this access which makes the Christian experience of God fundamentally different from the Jewish one; it forms one of the main themes of the NT proclamation.

The names of God

In the Bible, God is defined both generically and specifically. Generically, he is called '*ēl* or *'lōhîm* (which is the plural form of '*ēl*) in Hebrew and *theos* in Greek. The Hebrew word is related to the Arabic '*allah* and is common to the Semitic language family. In the OT, the plural form occurs about ten times as often as the singular, but this should not be understood as implying that the Israelites believed that there was some kind of plurality inside God. Most likely, the plural form is used to emphasize his majesty, and it should be noted that it has not been carried over into Greek or any other language. The Greek word *theos* is related to the Latin *deus* and to similar forms in other Indo-European languages. They all seem to be derived from an overarching *time concept, more or less synonymous with words like 'age' or 'eon' and probably related to the word 'day'. In Old English, the equivalent of *theos* became restricted to the pagan god of war ('Tiw') and now survives only in the word 'Tuesday', though the word 'god' turns up in Russian with the meaning 'year', which reinforces the theory that such Indo-European words were originally time concepts. God of course is timeless in himself (although this has been disputed by some), which shows that the Bible employs analogical language even at the most fundamental level of revelation.

As words, both '*ēl* and *theos* can be used to refer to any supernatural power, of which there may be many, as well as to the supreme or absolute supernatural being. Because of this, translators of the Bible have felt free to use similar words in other languages which have a corresponding breadth of meaning (*e.g.* 'God' in English). This is in contrast to Islamic translators of the Qur'an, for example, who retain the word '*Allah* as an untranslatable proper name, even though there is no semantic justification for this. The Bible's willingness to use generic words of deity to refer to the unique God of Israel confirms its assertion that some knowledge of him is innate in every rational creature and that pagan deities are but pale and corrupt reflections of this knowledge.

In the Bible God also reveals himself by the name *YHWH*, which is usually vocalized as 'Yahweh', but which at some point ceased to be used by the ancient Israelites. Instead, they substituted another word, usually *'dōnāy* ('my Lord') which they read in place of the sacred name. By combining the vowels of *'dōnāy* with the consonants *YHWH*, the hybrid Y*hōwāh* was created, which has come into English via its Latinized form as 'Jehovah'. The claim made by Jehovah's Witnesses that this is the true name of God is thus based on a misunderstanding of ancient Hebrew practice. The substitution of *'dōnāy* was so widely accepted that the Greek translators of the OT put the Greek equivalent (*kyrios*), or sometimes *theos*, wherever *YHWH* appeared in the Hebrew text, and this practice is reflected in the NT also, where the Hebrew *YHWH* is translated in the same way. Modern translations generally respect this tradition, though many of them put LORD or GOD in capital letters when they represent the Hebrew *YHWH*.

The ultimate origin of the name *YHWH* has been disputed by modern scholars but the biblical account of its meaning is clear enough. The name was given by God to Moses at the burning bush, and was linked to the Hebrew verb *hāyāh* ('to be'). God defines himself as 'I am' and the word *YHWH* therefore means 'he who is'. This point is of particular importance in the teaching of Jesus, who also referred to himself as 'I am' in a way which is clearly intended to identify him with God.

YHWH is the special covenant name of God, given only to Israel and associated in a special way with the promises made to that nation, but it would be a mistake to suppose that the Israelites saw any real distinction between *YHWH* and '*ēl* / *'lōhîm*. This is apparent from Hebrew personal names, which use the two words interchangeably (*e.g.* Elnathan = Jonathan). Since personal names are usually among the most conservative elements of any language, this must reflect a very early identification of the two which persists throughout the Bible. As a matter of interest, *YHWH* occurs almost three times as often as *'el / *lōhîm* in the OT.

God is also referred to by a number of epithets, which generally reflect his attributes or are associated with particular events in the history of Israel. Of particular significance is the name *'el šadday* (Gen. 17:1), which is given in Greek as *pantocratōr* (Rev. 1:8) and is usually translated in English as 'God Almighty'. This name emphasizes God's supreme power and total sovereignty over the creation. Another name which is frequently used in the OT is 'God of Hosts', referring to the angelic armies at his command. Sometimes the word 'hosts' is left untranslated as 'Sabaoth', a reminder that this is a personal name as much as a description of who God is. The Pentateuch is especially rich in such names for God. For example, he is called *'el 'elyôn* ('God most high') in Genesis 14:18–22, *'el 'ôlām* ('the eternal God') in Genesis 21:33, *yahweh yir'eh* ('Yahweh will see/provide') in Genesis 22:14 and *yahweh nissî* ('Yahweh my banner') in Exodus 17:15–16. Such forms occur less frequently later in the OT, but they are not entirely absent, *e.g. yahweh ṣidqēnû* ('Yahweh our righteousness') in Jeremiah 23:6 and 33:16. On the other hand, they do not appear in the NT, except in direct allusion to the OT (*e.g.* Rev. 1:8).

There are a number of other ways in which God's power and majesty are described in the Bible. Many of these analogies are anthropomorphic, but a number refer to elements of the material universe. Among the anthropomorphisms, we may note that God is referred to as a bridegroom (Is. 61:10), a father (Deut. 32:6), a *king (Is. 33:22), a shepherd (Ps. 23:1) and as a physician (Exod. 15:26). In addition to this, parts of the body and human actions are frequently attributed to him. He is said to have a face (Exod. 33:20; Rev. 22:4), eyes (Ps. 11:4; Heb. 4:13), ears (Ps. 55:1), a nose (Deut. 33:10), a mouth (Deut. 8:3), hands (Num. 11:23) and a heart (Gen. 6:6). He is described as knowing (Gen. 18:21), seeing (Gen. 1:10), hearing (Exod. 2:24), smelling (Gen. 8:21), tasting (Ps. 11:5), sitting (Ps. 9:7) and walking (Lev. 26:12).

Among the sub-human and material analogies used of him, we may mention that he is compared to animals like the lion (Is. 31:4), the eagle (Deut. 32:11), the *lamb (Is. 53:7) and even the hen (Matt. 23:37). He is called a fire (Heb. 12:29), and related images like the sun (Ps. 84:11), the *light (Ps. 27:1) and the torch (Rev. 21:23) are also used of him. In addition he can be called a rock (Deut. 32:4), a tower (Prov. 18:10), a shield (Ps. 84:11) and a shadow (Ps. 91:1).

Some modern scholars have detected remnants of paganism in these analogies, but it must be said that any such suggestion is firmly contradicted by the Bible itself, which frequently insists that God cannot be reduced to any creaturely shape. Nor have these analogies ever been a problem to believers, whether Jews or Christians, who have instinctively known that they must be understood in a metaphorical way. They are intended to highlight certain aspects of God's character and activity, and remind us that he is present with his people in the most intimate and seemingly ordinary aspects of everyday life. He teaches us and protects us in a way which, although it can be illustrated by earthly examples, ultimately goes beyond all human understanding.

The personhood of God

There is no doubt that the God of the Bible is what we would call 'personal', although this word never appears in the text of Scripture and the concept seems to have been unknown in biblical times. But if we define a person as a rational agent capable of establishing interactive relationships with other rational agents, then God is certainly portrayed as a person in the OT. Furthermore, although he sometimes speaks in the plural, and there are grounds for thinking that some of his attributes, like his 'word', are occasionally personified, he is a single person with no superiors, equals or rivals. His only personal relationships are with his creatures, both angels and human beings.

In his personhood, God is clearly 'masculine', although the Bible is careful to point out that both men and women have been created in his *image (Gen. 1:27). In himself, God is beyond the limitations of human gender or sexuality, but that does not mean that his masculinity is purely conventional. Female deities were common in the ancient world, and there is no *a priori* reason why the God of the Bible should not have revealed himself in a female form. Had gender been completely irrelevant, there might have been a mixture of usage in Scripture, or even a third form created specially for him. As it is, his masculinity is consistently maintained, even if he is sometimes credited with apparently 'female' characteristics, such as the ability to give birth (Ps. 2:7; Heb. 1:5).

When we look at the NT, the issue of God's personhood takes on an entirely new dimension. The unique oneness of God is unquestioned, but the appearance of the Son and of the Holy Spirit raises questions as to how this must be understood. The Son is described as being eternally present with God (John 1:1–14), as being equal to him (Phil. 2:6), as taking part in the creation of the universe (John 1:3; Col. 1:16) and as becoming human in Jesus Christ (John 1:14). This Jesus claims the power to forgive sins, which is a divine prerogative (Mark 2:5–11). He calls himself 'I am' (John 8:58), which is the special covenant name of God. He is tempted to do things which only God is capable of doing (Matt. 4:3–10), and he performs miracles which testify to the possession of divine power, even if they do not prove that he must be God. Finally, and from the theological standpoint most importantly, he becomes the sinless sacrifice for sin (Heb. 4:15; 9:26) and then rises from the dead, before ascending into heaven to claim his kingdom.

Each of these things, taken individually, can be (and has been) questioned, but taken together they provide a powerful argument in favour of Christ's divinity, unless we are prepared to conclude that the Gospels are completely fictitious. No prophet, priest or king in the OT does anything like the kind of thing claimed or done by Jesus, and even his worst enemies recognize that he has some kind of supernatural power (Mark 2:5; Luke 11:15–19).

The evidence for the divinity of the Holy Spirit is less obvious, but it is there nevertheless. The Spirit is called Lord, in a way which recalls the use of the term *YHWH* (2 Cor. 3:17). He is portrayed as a *life-giver (Rom. 8:2), and spiritual life can be given only by God. He is described as proceeding from the Father (John 15:26), he is worshipped and glorified along with the Father and the Son (Matt. 28:19) and he is credited with having inspired the people who wrote the Scriptures (2 Pet. 1:21), which are elsewhere described as having been inspired by God (2 Tim. 3:16).

Putting these things together, it is clear that both the Son and the Holy Spirit have a strong claim to divinity which is difficult to satisfy without some restructuring of the OT picture of *YHWH*. Superficially it seems most natural to equate *YHWH* with the Father of Jesus Christ, but there are various reasons why this identification is not as obvious or as satisfactory as it might appear at first sight. First of all, although the fatherhood of *YHWH* is not totally foreign to the OT (Hos. 11:1; Ps. 2:7), it was not customary for Israel to address God as Father. When Jesus did so, it was regarded as a peculiarity, and led to accusations that he was making himself equal to God (John 5:18). Second, Jesus claimed to be identical with the Father (John 10:30; 14:9), although they are clearly distinct persons. If the Father is *YHWH*, the Son must therefore be *YHWH* as well, or else there would be two gods.

The NT resolves this problem by contrasting the different perceptions of the divine being, which we have labelled the 'outside' and the 'inside' perspectives. From the 'outside' God appears to be one, totally unique in his absolute and mysterious supremacy. This is how the ancient Israelites perceived him. But Christians, having entered into his inner life, see him differently – as three co-equal persons sharing the one divine being. These three persons interpenetrate each other in such a way that, although they can be distinguished from each other, they cannot be separated. This is brought out most clearly in the opening chapters of the book of Revelation. Who is speaking in Revelation 1:8, the Father or the Son? Who is seated on the throne? At first it appears to be the Father, but in Revelation 1:17–18 it becomes clear that the writer is talking about the Son. Similarly, although it is the Son who addresses the letters to the seven churches, each of them concludes with the assertion that this is what the Spirit is saying to them (Rev. 2 – 3). In John's Gospel, we are told by Jesus that when the Holy Spirit comes to dwell in our hearts, the Father and the Son will accompany him, so that all three will dwell together with us (John 14:23). The three persons are nowhere confused, but neither are they separated from one another, and it is this dual reality which forms the basis for the subsequent development of the orthodox doctrine of the Trinity.

Whether or to what extent that doctrine is found in the NT is a matter of dispute, but there is plenty of evidence that it is. Quite apart from the formulas in Matthew 28:19 and 2 Corinthians 13:14, both of which are explicitly trinitarian, there are a number of indirect references to the three persons which are difficult to explain in any other way. A classic example is Galatians 4:6, which was one of the earliest passages of the NT to have been written. It says: 'Because you are sons, God has sent the Spirit of his Son into our hearts, crying "*Abba*, Father".' The complementarity of the persons could hardly be clearer than this, and the doctrine of the Trinity may rightly be understood as an extended interpretation of this and other similar NT texts, like Ephesians 2:18 and 1 Peter 1:2.

The attributes of God

From the persons of the Godhead we pass naturally to his attributes, many of which are described in the various titles which God is given. Theologians traditionally distinguish between the 'communicable' attributes of God, by which they mean divine characteristics which can be shared with human beings, and the 'incommunicable' attributes, which belong to him alone. Ultimately, of course, there is no such distinction, because all God's attributes are essentially incommunicable. Whatever likeness there may be between him and us is purely relative and must be interpreted within the perspective of the fundamental differences which separate his being from ours. In theological terms, what God is by nature we can only become by *grace, which is God's free gift bestowed on us according to his will and pleasure.

Most of the so-called 'incommunicable' attributes of God are not really characteristics of his being; references to them are intended as denials of any similarity between God and his creatures. On the whole, they are implied in the Bible rather than stated explicitly, although this does not make them unimportant or irrelevant to a biblical theology. As an example, we may choose God's invisibility. This word is never used in Scripture, but it is quite clear from any number of passages that it expresses an important truth about God. However, it is inadequate to do justice to the biblical witness because all it means is that God cannot be seen, and it is therefore a purely negative term. We might equally well say that atoms are invisible, as are leprechauns, but this does not make God like either of them. The Bible does not say that God is invisible because he is too small to be seen, or because he is fictitious – quite the opposite. There is no general characteristic of 'invisibility' which can be regarded as an attribute of God.

Nevertheless, God's invisibility is fundamental to the biblical witness and very important theologically, because it argues against any form of idolatry. To picture God, physically or mentally, is to limit him, and this is a denial of his essential character. The same is true of his infinity, his incomprehensibility and so on. These truths about God are not stated in those terms in the Bible, but their substance is conveyed in other ways, *e.g.* by frequent warnings not to put limits on God, or to imagine that he can be understood in purely human terms.

A very important attribute of God is his eternity, with its implied immutability. This is frequently referred to in the Bible, where it appears as a guarantee of his reliability in maintaining the laws of his creation and the promises of his covenant (Ps. 102:27). In recent years this characteristic has been objected to on the grounds that to call God eternally unchanging denies something fundamental about the relationship which the covenant has established between him and us. To put it simply, how can God answer prayer if he is immutable? Presumably his response to our needs implies a willingness to adapt to our situation, which in turn might involve changing his mind, but if God can do these things, how can it be said that he does not change? Furthermore, those who object to the traditional theological teaching claim that the Bible reveals a God who changes, and that assertions to the contrary are based on an unrepresentative selection of biblical statements taken out of their context.

Superficially there appears to be some truth in these arguments, since the Bible does portray God as '*repenting' of his intentions (usually to destroy people) because of prayer made to him (Exod. 32:14; Jonah 3:10). But closer examination of the evidence reveals that the situation is more complex than these objections to the traditional understanding allow. For example, when Moses pleads with God to spare Israel, he does so on the understanding that God has established a covenant with the nation and that he has made promises to them which he will not revoke or ignore. In other words, Moses is not asking God to do what Moses wants, but to accomplish what God himself has proclaimed is his purpose (Exod. 32:11–13). The threat to annihilate Israel because of its sins is a reminder that God cannot tolerate the presence of sin, which must be eradicated if the covenant promises are to be realized. Both the fulfilment of the promises and the need to remove sin remain constant factors throughout. Furthermore, it is also true that it was always God's intention to achieve the second of these aims by using a substitute – the sacrifice of a lamb in the OT and the sacrifice of his *incarnate Son in the NT.

On balance therefore, it must be said that when the Bible speaks of God's 'repentance', it does so in the context of his personal relationship with human beings. In that context, human repentance leads to a different experience of God but does not involve any change in the divine being. God's response to human good and evil remains the same, and if we perceive a change in the way he works it is because we have changed, not God. The language of divine 'repentance' can only be used in the framework of our personal relationship with him, and is an example of the way in which God accommodates himself to the limitations of human understanding. It does not compromise God's fundamental immutability, a concept which remains necessary to describe the permanent, unchanging nature of the other attributes of his eternal being.

Another divine attribute which has been questioned on the basis of biblical evidence is God's 'impassibility', or inability to suffer. It is claimed that in the Bible God is portrayed as sharing in the sorrows of his people, and ultimately, as *suffering and dying on the cross for their salvation. Once again, however, we are faced with a confusion of categories which creates a misunderstanding of what Scripture actually teaches about God. God is impassible because there is no created power which can overpower him. Suffering involves subjection to an oppressive force, and God could not experience this without losing sovereignty over his creation. But this is not to say, as many of those who object to the notion of divine impassibility do, that

God is incapable of understanding his people's suffering. The Bible clearly states that he is, and what is more, that he has done something about it (Ps. 106: 41–46). The proper analogy here is not that of a fellow-sufferer, but rather that of a doctor and his patient. A good doctor is not called upon to acquire the illnesses of those who come to see him, but rather to understand what they are and provide the cure. In this context, God's impassibility is a guarantee that he will never become incapacitated or unable to function in this way – unlike a human doctor, there is no chance of his being 'off sick' himself.

How this relates to the suffering and death of Jesus is a question which preoccupied the greatest minds of the early church and which was not resolved until the council of Chalcedon in 451. The understanding adopted then was that Christ, the divine Son of God, took on a human nature in order to be able to suffer and die for the sins of the world. Scriptural support for this was found mainly in Philippians 2:5–11 and in Hebrews 4:15. Although the precise Chalcedonian formulation was rejected at the time by many Eastern Christians, mainly because they were used to a different terminology, it has come to be regarded as the classical, orthodox interpretation of Scripture in both the Protestant and the Roman Catholic traditions. It protects the impassibility of God's nature but allows for the suffering and death of a divine person in a second (human) nature, thereby making it possible to hold the doctrines of the incarnation and the atonement together.

Of the divine attributes which have traditionally been regarded as 'communicable', the most fundamental is that of God's *holiness. This word means 'separation' and is used to remind us that God is both totally different from anything which he has created and morally perfect. He is not bound by the limitations which he has imposed on his creation, and can do whatever he chooses. In practical terms, holiness in the Bible is used to describe God's absolute goodness, in contrast to the sinful state into which the human race has fallen (Lev. 22:31–33; Eph. 1:4). When he chose Israel to be his people on earth, God intended them to become morally perfect as well, though in practical terms this perfection was not (and could not be) exactly the same as his own holiness. According to the law of Moses, the holiness of the people was to be achieved by a rigorous self-discipline which involved severe discrimination in every area of life, but especially in the use of the senses. The Israelites were told that they could not eat or touch certain things, either because the things were holy (*i.e.* set apart) to God, like the ark of the covenant, or because they would defile the people in God's sight (Lev. 11:44–45; 21:6–7).

The tendency to describe holiness in external terms is perhaps understandable in the light of the Israelite experience of God on the 'outside', but it should not be forgotten that even in the OT, the external signs of holiness were meant to reflect an inner, spiritual reality. It was the perceived absence of this among those who were most zealous in promoting the ideals of holiness among the Jews which brought Jesus and later on, his Christian followers, into conflict with them. Jesus and his followers preached that the only way to attain to the biblical ideal of holiness was by repentance and spiritual *regeneration, both of which were works of the Holy Spirit and not of human beings, however well-intentioned they might be (John 3:1–8). Spiritual rebirth in Christ was a new experience of God which separated Christians from any form of Judaism, and this consequently made it essential for them to develop a new understanding of holiness as well. Rather than seeing the call to be holy in terms of external acts and obligations, Christians were to understand the call to be holy in terms of internal commitment and attitude, reflecting their own knowledge of God on the 'inside' (Matt. 15:11–20; Mark 7:15–23). The NT writers did not see this as a contradiction of what the OT taught, but rather as a revelation of the latter's true meaning. Even the law of Moses was essentially spiritual in character (Rom. 7:12), which is to say that it spoke of knowing God on the 'inside', but the Israelites were unable to appreciate this and perverted its true meaning because of their own spiritual blindness.

Because God is an invisible and supernatural being, his holiness is also invisible and supernatural. It can be known only as a gift of the Holy Spirit working in the heart, not by the external application of the Mosaic law or any other ritual observance. What this means to believers is a freedom from the power of sin which enables us to have fellowship with a God who cannot tolerate sin in his presence (Hab. 1:13). But important though this freedom is, it cannot be equated with God's own holiness, which is much more than sinlessness, including as it does a glory which encompasses heaven and earth (Is. 6:3). In essence therefore, God's holiness is and remains fundamentally different from anything which human beings can acquire or achieve.

Another 'communicable' attribute is God's justice, or *righteousness. In English, the former term tends to be used in an external, legal sense, whereas the latter is regarded as an inner quality, but the Bible makes no semantic distinction between them. All human beings have a sense of right and wrong, and therefore a notion of justice as well, but the Bible is ambiguous about how this relates to God. On the one hand, there is no doubt that God is just and that he demands justice from those who serve him, but his standards of justice are not necessarily the same as ours. The real problem is not that God defines right and wrong in a different way (although that may sometimes be true) but that his treatment of wrongdoing is often at variance with what most human beings think is just. For example, he may tolerate evil, even to the point where his own people suffer from it. In theological terms, this is known as the problem of 'theodicy', and it is a major theme of the Scriptures, with whole books like Job and Jonah being dedicated to it. Why the wicked should prosper and the righteous suffer is a mystery which is not fully explained in the Bible, although it is quite clear that God's sovereignty is not diminished as a result (Ps. 73; Hab. 3). It is also clear that, in the end, the righteous will be vindicated and the wicked will be punished, and there is at least a hint that suffering is permitted by God in order to demonstrate that those who are truly righteous will worship him in (and in spite of) any adverse personal circumstances.

Another way in which God's justice is called into question is his willingness to pardon and even reward those who repent, regardless of the evil which they have committed. God does not have a hierarchy of sins, but regards every form of disobedience as equally wrong, and therefore also as equally forgivable. The Bible makes it clear that, although this conflicts with human notions of justice, it does not compromise

God's essential righteousness, because he is free to pardon or to punish whomever he wills (Matt. 20:1–16). In strictly objective logic, all *salvation is unjust, because no human being has done, or can do, anything to deserve it. The message of the Bible is that God's justice is tempered by *mercy, without which no-one would be saved (Ps. 143:2; Rom. 9:14–18).

Similar to mercy is God's grace, a concept which also expresses his free favour towards us (Eph. 2:7–8). Very often the two terms are interchangeable, though grace is a wider term which is also applied to God's gifts to the church (Rom. 1:5). The key point however is that both mercy and grace are unmerited, and are distributed at God's pleasure.

God's mercy forms an essential part of his covenant relationship with his people, but although it tempers his justice, it must not be understood so as to conflict with it. Even if sin can be forgiven, it must still be paid for, and this is the reason why sacrifice plays such an important part in the Bible. Christians are pardoned by God not because he has decided to ignore their sins, but because in Christ he has taken the penalty for sin on himself (2 Cor. 5:21). It is that act which makes God's mercy towards us possible and which gives it its meaning. Because of the principle of sacrifice, God's justice is not compromised but affirmed and strengthened.

Both the justice and mercy of God operate within the framework of his *love, and nowadays most people regard the latter as his most fundamental characteristic. This is probably right, but it has to be said that the modern emphasis on love has produced its own distortions. At one extreme, it is sometimes claimed that God's love will not allow any of his creatures to perish, although that is not how the Bible understands the concept. It is also sometimes thought that God's love is synonymous with tolerance, which is also false. There is admittedly such a thing as divine forbearance, but this is intended to give people time to repent and is not to be regarded as acceptance of sinful behaviour (Rom. 3:25). The love of God must be understood in the context of his demands for obedience (John 15:14). Love is not a quality in itself, but the working out of a relationship which is fully realized only inside God himself, in the love which the Father has for the Son and which the Son returns to the Father. That love is manifested in the Son's obedience to the Father's will, above all in his willing acceptance of death. Those human beings who are saved in Christ are the beneficiaries of this divine love, which makes sense only in that context. Salvation by God's grace is not a licence to sin, but rebirth into a new life in which sin has no place (Rom. 6:1–2).

The counsel of God

Fundamental to the biblical revelation is the assertion that God has a mind which has prepared a plan for the created order. Traditionally, this has been known as his 'counsel', and it embraces both what he has done in the past and what he intends to do in the future (Eph. 1:4–10). The Bible does not say why God created the world in the first place, nor does it speculate on whether or not things could have been made differently. To the extent that questions like these are considered at all, they are regarded as presumptuous and therefore not to be asked of God by mere human beings (Job 38:2–5; Rom. 9:20–21). The Bible concentrates on what God has actually done, and explains that there is a purpose in everything he has made, whether that is immediately apparent to us or not.

God created the universe in order to manifest his *glory, but there was no inner necessity which compelled him to do so. He made it out of nothing, not (as many pagans believed) by subtracting parts from, or by adding elements to, his own being. God is supremely *wise and rational, and his creation reflects these qualities, albeit within the limits imposed by creaturely finitude (Ps. 19:1–6). The human mind, for example, can comprehend something of God's plan, but many parts of it are hidden from our eyes, either because they have not been revealed to us, or because we are unable to understand the revelation which has been given (Rom. 11:33–34). This revelation includes what we think of as 'predictive prophecy', which is a major theme of the Bible. In the OT the Jews were promised a Messiah who would save them, but the details were sufficiently unclear that when he finally came he was not generally recognized. Similarly, we are given a broad outline of God's plan for the future *judgment and *redemption of his creation, but we cannot say precisely when or how it will be worked out.

God retains his sovereignty over everything he has made, and is therefore in complete control of events. Nothing can happen without his consent, even if he is not the primary cause of every event. This is true even of evil, which exists by God's permission and cannot exceed the bounds which he has appointed for it (Job 1; 1 Cor. 10:13). The fall of Adam and Eve must therefore also be regarded as part of God's purpose, and yet they were entirely responsible for their own actions, for which God cannot be blamed in any way.

To account for this apparent paradox, a distinction is sometimes drawn between God's 'foreknowledge' and 'predestination'. According to this way of thinking, God knew in advance what would happen but did not actually plan it. Thus the existence of evil in the world is not something which took God by surprise, but neither did he actively will it. Ultimately this explanation is unsatisfactory, however, because either God is in control of events or he is not. The Bible, of course, says that he is (Matt. 6:28–34), and nowhere suggests that he merely intervenes in the world's affairs from time to time in order to rescue a situation which has got out of hand. This control is called '*providence' by theologians, and is typified by the sign of the rainbow, which was given to Noah after the flood. At that point, God promised that he would never again destroy the earth because of the evil in it, but would allow good and evil to co-exist until the final judgment and the consummation of all things (Gen. 8:21).

Within the bounds thus established by his providence, God chose Abraham and his descendants for salvation. In line with the difference between the OT and the NT, Abraham's descendants are reckoned by blood relationship in the former and by spiritual affinity in the latter. It is not altogether clear to what extent the second of these replaces the first, but whatever the ultimate fate of the historical Israel may be, it is quite plain from the NT that no-one can be saved apart from Christ (John 14:6). The only question is whether he will eventually be revealed to the whole of historical Israel, or whether the word 'Israel' must now be restricted to those who believe the promises of God in the way that Abraham did, whether they are physically descended from him or not.

Those whom God has chosen he has also predestined to inherit eternal life and to share with him in the government of his kingdom (2 Tim. 2:11–12). Faith is the key to entering into this experience, but there is no human explanation as to why this faith is given to some and not to others. The story of the twins Esau and Jacob is archetypal in this respect. Although they came out of the same womb at the same time, Jacob was chosen and Esau was not, even though he was both the younger and the weaker of the pair (Rom. 9:10–16). The Bible tells us that God's people are few in number and without many of the characteristics which would define a human elite (1 Cor. 1:26–27; Deut. 7:7), but we know no more than this. Neither human poverty nor the kind of inverted snobbery expressed by such phrases as 'a bias to the poor' is any guide to the divine plan of *election – whatever criteria God may have used in his selection, they are unknown to us.

God's plan includes the salvation of his chosen ones (the 'elect') but there is no indication in the Bible that this will include the entire human race. On the contrary, the logic of election as revealed in Scripture points in the exact opposite direction – only a remnant will be saved. For the time being, God is allowing the wheat and the tares – the good and the bad – to grow together, but the harvest will eventually come, and at that point the tares will be rejected (Matt. 13:40). The indications are that when this happens, the number of the faithful on earth will be few (Luke 18:8).

To conclude, we learn from the outline of his plan in Scripture, that God is both a loving father to his people and a just judge of those who have disobeyed his law. These two descriptions are not contradictory, because those who have been saved have been shown mercy on the basis of the sacrifice of Christ, not because they have deserved it in any way. It is the totally unmerited character of salvation which shows us both the greatness and the *freedom of God, thereby bearing the fullest and ultimate witness to his true nature.

Bibliography

A. W. Argyle, *God in the New Testament* (London, 1965); D. Bloesch, *God the Almighty* (Leicester, 1994); G. L. Bray, *The Doctrine of God* (Leicester, 1993); D. A. Carson, *Divine Sovereignty and Human*

Responsibility (London, 1981); L. W. Hurtado, *One God, One Lord. Early Christian Devotion and Ancient Jewish Monotheism* (London, 1988); G. A. F. Knight, *A Biblical Approach to the Doctrine of the Trinity* (London, 1953); G. H. Parke-Taylor, *Yahweh: The Divine Names in the Bible* (Waterloo, 1975); A. W. Wainwright, *The Trinity in the New Testament* (London, 1962).

G. L. BRAY

GOODNESS, see LOVE

GOSPEL

OT antecedents

Verbal

The word 'gospel' translates the Greek *euangelion* which, together with its verbal cognate *euangelizomai* (= to evangelize), occurs more than 120 times in the NT. It has also some synonyms, such as *witness* (see *Testimony/witness*) (*martyria* and its verbal cognate), which is the preferred term in John's Gospel. The verbal antecedents of these words are partly revealed by the Septuagint's usage of *euangelion* and cognates to translate the Hebrew noun *bᵉśôrâ* and its verbal cognate *mᵉbasser*. The root *bsr* is used in a number of OT texts to indicate news of a significant nature (*e.g.* 1 Sam. 4:17; 1 Kgs. 1:42; Jer. 20:15). In Isaiah and certain Psalms it has the more specific meaning of good news concerning *salvation (Pss. 40:10; 68:11; 96:2; Is. 40:9; 41:27; 52:7; 61:1). Here the proclamation is specifically religious: a messenger of God declares the coming of God's *kingdom.

Theological

In Mark 1:14–15 Jesus is said to proclaim the gospel in terms of the fulfilment of the times and the coming of the kingdom of God. This 'fulfilment' is presumably a reference to the expectations of Israel recorded in the OT. Paul also defines his gospel in Romans 1:1–4 and 1 Corinthians 15:1–4 as the message of the OT. Both he and Peter are recorded as preaching their first sermons about the fulfilment by Jesus of all the OT expectations (Acts 2:16–36; 13:16–41). The gospel was promised 'beforehand through his prophets' (Rom. 1:2, NRSV). The gospel was declared beforehand to Abraham: 'All the Gentiles shall be blessed in you' (Gal. 3:8).

What, then, is the specific content that the OT gives to the gospel? It is, as the preaching of Jesus indicates (Mark 1:15), the gospel of the coming of the kingdom of God. The link with the OT places the gospel squarely into the realm of history: it emerges as an event, and as the proclamation of that event. Paul's references to Abraham in Galatians 3 and Romans 4 also show that the gospel of the kingdom comes through the acts of God in the history of his people. There are two significant perspectives in the OT: re-*creation of a fallen world, and *redemption of the *people of God from judgment and death. The promises to Abraham involve his descendants, their possession of the promised land, and their relationship with God as his people (Gen. 12:1–3; 15:5–6, 13–16). And, as indicated in Genesis 12:3 and Galatians 3:8, the promises to Abraham's descendants also have saving ramifications for all the peoples of the world.

The promises to Abraham take on a redemptive significance when his descendants, the nation of Israel, are enslaved in Egypt. The redemptive event of the Exodus is based on the *covenant promises made to Abraham (Exod. 2:23–25; 6:6–8). The goal of this event is the kingdom of God in the promised land. The problem of human rebellion is seen in the inability of Israel to remain faithful to its saviour-God. The historic kingdom of Israel, which reaches the high-point of its glory in the reigns of David and Solomon, nevertheless fails and disintegrates. Then the prophets recapitulate the promises of God and his past saving acts as the basis for a future and glorious coming of the kingdom of God. Thus, the prophets proclaim the gospel beforehand (Rom. 1:2).

The OT gospel is the proclamation of the coming kingly rule of God, which will have a defined form and a defined means. However, this gospel of the salvation of a remnant of Israel and of a great multitude of Gentiles is inseparable from a stern message of judgment. The coming of the kingdom and the salvation of God's people are consistently portrayed in the OT, as in the NT, as involving both the saving act of God and his judgment on all who oppose his kingdom and reject his gracious offer of salvation.

The gospel is thus given two major 'beforehand' expressions in the OT: the historic and the prophetic. The historic expression is the instrumental means by which OT believers are saved and made inheritors of the kingdom. In it the promises to Abraham are fulfilled, in the emergence of the nation of Israel and the redemption from Egypt leading eventually to the kingdom of David and Solomon. It is clear from Paul's use of Abraham as the paradigmatic example of justification (see *Righteousness, justice and justification; *Atonement) by faith (Gal. 3:6–14; Rom. 4:1–5, 13, 23–25) that salvation was available in the OT to those who grasped by faith the promises of God.

But the OT revelation of the gospel is incomplete, for it merely anticipates the true salvation and kingdom, and the means of that kingdom's coming is not yet fully revealed. The problem of human sin has yet to be properly resolved. Until it is, the people of God are sustained by prophetic promises of the coming day of the Lord when salvation will come fully and gloriously. When Jesus said, 'Abraham rejoiced that he would see my day; he saw it and was glad' (John 8:56), he indicated that, in God's eyes, for an OT believer to grasp the shadow by faith was to grasp the reality of Christ. The promises and acts of God for Israel's salvation link the OT believer to the effective basis of salvation, Jesus' death and resurrection.

The gospel as God fulfilling his promises

Although the four Gospels post-date most of the epistles, they must be studied as our main source of information about the life and teaching of *Jesus. Just as in the OT the abstraction of the kingdom of God is given concrete expression in God's dealings in history with the nation of Israel, so also in the NT the gospel of the kingdom has its concrete expression in the person and work of Jesus of Nazareth. The four Gospels relate the process by which the fulfilling event emerges through the life, death, resurrection and ascension (see *Exaltation) of Jesus. In doing so they share the OT's anticipation of the completed event and the full message of salvation in Christ. Mark possibly points to this incompleteness when he begins his account with the words, 'The beginning of the gospel of Jesus Christ,

the Son of God' (Mark 1:1). Jesus' preaching of the gospel at the beginning of his ministry is thus, like the prophetic message in the OT, an anticipation of the full message. The difference is that the locus and means of the fulfilment of the OT promises is now being revealed specifically as Jesus himself.

Although the person and work of Jesus cannot be separated, we can distinguish them theologically. He is declared to be Son of God which, against the OT background, is not so much a claim to deity as one to true humanity and to be the authentic people of God. But there are also claims to deity which mark Jesus out as unique, and which show that some aspects not yet clear in the OT promises are clarified in the revelation in Jesus. Thus, according to John's prologue, Jesus is the Word of God, who is true God himself, come in human flesh. The gospel involves the mystery of the *incarnation of the Word, who is, in himself, the final revelation of God. He is full of grace (the unmerited saving power of God) and truth (wisdom and knowledge of God), says John (John 1:14).

The deeds of Jesus reveal who he is and what he has come to achieve. His teachings must be seen in the light of his overall strategy of establishing the kingdom and saving his people. Thus the miracles are signs of his saving power to release people from sin, sickness, subjection to the evil power of demons and death. These anticipate the ultimate deed of Jesus by which they are saved, his death and resurrection. When John the Baptist seems to have second thoughts about Jesus, he asks him if he really is the Messiah. The answer is given in terms of Jesus' healing miracles and of the poor being evangelized (Matt. 11:2–6). Luke records the beginning of Jesus' ministry in Galilee when he reads from Isaiah 61 in the synagogue and claims to be fulfilling it: 'The Spirit of the Lord is upon me, because he has anointed me to evangelize the poor' (Luke 4:16–21).

All four gospels concentrate on the last days of Jesus and the events leading to his condemnation and execution. He interprets this impending suffering and death as service of others and as the needed ransom for many (Mark 8:31; 9:31; 10:45; Luke 22:15). The resurrection and ascension of Jesus complete the gospel event. Indeed the resurrection encapsulates the gospel, for it implies both the death of Jesus and his perfectly obedient life.

In the light of these events, the risen Christ is able to explain to his disciples the meaning of the OT promises (Luke 24:25–27, 44). He points to a new kind of presence of the Spirit of God, and to the consequent witnessing of his disciples to him in all the world (Luke 24:45–49; Acts 1:6–8), as the fruit of this finished event.

The gospel as the proclamation of the primitive church

The Acts of the Apostles enables us to understand something of what Jesus told his disciples in his post-resurrection meetings (Luke 24). The series of apostolic addresses beginning with Peter's Pentecost sermon mark the beginning of the world-wide *mission of evangelization. As C. H. Dodd has pointed out, a consistent pattern emerges in the apostolic preaching (see *The Apostolic Preaching and its Developments*, pp. 7–34.) This includes: 1. the fulfilment of the OT promises; 2. the ministry of Jesus culminating in his death; 3. his resurrection and exaltation; 4. the gift of the Spirit; and 5. the call to repentance and faith. Not everything in an evangelistic sermon will be, strictly speaking, the gospel. There may be reference to the need for the gospel (alienation from God), to the appropriate response to the gospel (repentance and faith), and to the fruits of the gospel in the believer's life (*Holy Spirit, *regeneration, sanctification [see *Holiness] and good works). The gospel is the proclamation of what God has done in Christ, and needs always to be distinguished from the fruit of the gospel, which is God's work in those who believe. Obedience to the gospel is first and foremost faith (Rom. 1:5). But the faith which is the instrument of justification will never exist alone without the fruit of the Spirit. Hence James' linking of justification and good works (Jas. 2:26), and the reference to the gospel as if it were something people do (Acts 14:15).

Other important statements of the essence of the gospel in the apostolic testimony are Romans 1:1–4, 1 Corinthians 15:3–5, and 2 Timothy 2:8. In many places reference is made to the gospel without its being defined. The writers assume that its content is known or, as in many of the epistles, they expound the essence of the gospel as the grounds of acceptance with God and the basis for holy living. The gospel is essentially what has been done, and its proclamation is in the indicative. The fruit of the gospel is achieved by the Spirit, working in and through people, including their minds and wills. There is, therefore, a right place for the imperatives which flow from the gospel. The call to repentance and faith is a biblical imperative, but the gospel itself can only be addressed to people as an indicative, for it is done for them and is past, finished and perfect.

Because gospel proclamation is broader than the gospel itself, another word group in the New Testament is relevant: *keryssein* and *kerygma,* signifying 'to herald, to cry out,' etc. In the Septuagint version of Isaiah 61:1 *keryxai* is used in parallel with *euangelisasthai* and, here at least, the two are synonymous. This eschatological proclamation is the means by which release and liberty are achieved. This proclamation is an essential part of the ministry of Jesus (Mark 1:38; Luke 4:18–19, which quotes Is. 61:1–2; and Luke 4:43–44, which links *euangelizomai* with *keryssein*). It is also the frequently reported activity of those who have been touched by Jesus as he demonstrates his saving and *healing power (Mark 1:45; 5:19–20). The relationship of this activity to the gospel is clearly seen in Luke 24:46–48, where Jesus links his death and resurrection with proclamation (*kerychthenai*) and witness (*martyres*). The apostolic *kerygma* is the proclamation of the gospel of the crucified Christ to the end that faith may rest on the power of God (1 Cor. 2:2–5). The *kerygma* is also related to the resurrection (1 Cor. 15:14) and is synonymous with the evangel (1 Cor. 15:1–4).

Because the gospel concerns the work of the historical Jesus Christ as the one who fulfils the OT promises, it is at the heart of biblical theology. When the plain meaning of the OT was lost to parts of the early church, often through the adoption of a dehistoricizing, allegorical interpretation of the Bible, the gospel ceased to be regarded as primarily what God has done in the historical Christ. The emphasis shifted to what God does inwardly in the human soul through piety and the sacramental ministrations of the church. The Protestant reformers of the sixteenth century recovered the historical meaning of the OT and, with it, the historical gospel. A biblical theology which had its roots in the apostolic gospel was thus re-established.

The gospel as literary genre: the four Gospels

*Mark begins his Gospel ambiguously, by saying that the beginning of the gospel of Jesus Christ is as it is written in the prophets. He quotes from Malachi 3 and Isaiah 40 and links these with the preaching of John the Baptist as the forerunner to Jesus. None of the four Gospels actually uses the word *euangelion* as a title; yet it has been attached to them as such by the Christian church. *Luke refers to other written accounts of the events 'that have been fulfilled among us' (Luke 1:1), and indicates his own intention to write an orderly account for Theophilus, 'so that you may know the truth concerning the things about which you have been instructed' (Luke 1:4). This suggests that the motivation for writing such an account included the need for an historical record which would function in instruction and perhaps evangelism. *John indicates his evangelistic motivation, 'that you may come to believe that Jesus is the Messiah, the Son of God, and that through believing you may have life in his name' (John 20:31).

The four canonical Gospels (see *The Synoptic Gospels, *The Johannine writings), while having significant differences, share a common focus which, presumably, accounts for the later attaching of the name 'Gospel'. They are all concerned with the historical event of Jesus of Nazareth. Two begin with events surrounding his birth (*Matthew and Luke), one with the adult ministry of Jesus (Mark), and the fourth (John) focuses on the incarnation of the Word of God. All are concerned to tell of the ministry of Jesus, of what he said and did. All agree on the primary significance of the last week of Jesus' life leading to his death and resurrection. All agree that this gospel event is the fulfilment of the promises of God, and that the salvation-history of the OT is brought to its climax in the death and resurrection of Jesus. It is entirely consistent with the apostolic testimony to the gospel that these written documents should come to be called Gospels. They share features with biography, aretalogy and, according to some, midrash, but constitute a unique genre which is characterized by its relationship to the historic Jesus; what he was as the God-man, what he taught, and what he achieved for the salvation of his people.

The word *gospel*, then, is used in several

ways. First, the NT uses it to describe the heart of the OT promises of salvation. Secondly, it is used of the saving event of Jesus of Nazareth as the grounds of salvation for all who believe. Thirdly, it designates the proclamation of that saving event as the means by which people are confronted with the truth about Christ. Finally, it is the name applied by the early church to the distinct literary genre, found in the New Testament, by which the story of Jesus is told and preserved for posterity.

Bibliography
J. C. Chapman, *Know and Tell the Gospel* (Sydney, 1981); C. H. Dodd, *The Apostolic Preaching and its Developments* (London, 1965); M. Green, *Evangelism in the Early Church* (London, 1970); P. Stuhlmacher (ed.), *The Gospel and the Gospels* (ET, Grand Rapids, 1991).

G. GOLDSWORTHY

GRACE

Terminology

The words most relevant to an understanding of the biblical concept of grace include the Hebrew roots *ḥnn* ('to be gracious' or 'to show favour') and *ḥsd* ('lovingkindness' or 'goodness') (others are *rḥm, 'hb, śn* and *'mn*) and the Greek term *charis* ('grace'). *ḥnn*, which appears some 200 times in the OT, connotes favour, usually by a superior to an inferior, including but not limited to care for the *poor, deliverance of those in distress, and other acts of compassion. Such beneficence is given freely, and thus can be requested, received and even withdrawn, but never claimed, coerced or possessed. The term often appears in the idiom, 'to find favour in someone's eyes', so that the prayer that Yahweh might 'make his face shine upon you' is tantamount to a request for him to extend his graciousness (Num. 6:25; for the opposite, see Pss. 27:7–9; 30:6–10). *ḥsd*, which appears some 245 times in the OT, refers to compassionate acts performed either spontaneously or in response to an appeal by one in dire straits. Acts of *ḥesed* are not grounded in perceived obligation or contract, nor can they be coerced; rather they arise out of affection and goodness. Acts of *ḥesed* pertain to *covenantal relations (*cf.* the translation, 'covenant love'), but *God enters into covenant with human beings freely; the establishment of the covenant is itself an act of *ḥeseḏ* on God's part (F. I. Andersen, in *God Who is Rich in Mercy*, pp. 41–88). At the same time, *ḥeseḏ* includes notions of loyalty and constancy not always associated with *ḥnn*. In Hellenistic Greek, *charis* connotes favour and friendship, as well as beneficence; gifts of benefactors are acts of *charis* in the latter sense. In the LXX, *charis* typically translates *ḥēn*, while *eleos* ('mercy') generally translates *ḥeseḏ*.

The vocabulary of 'grace' thus connotes spontaneous kindness and acts of generosity grounded in dispositions of compassion toward those in need. 'Grace' as a characteristic of God grounds divine-human relations in God's generous initiative and sustaining *faithfulness culminating in the powerful, restorative activity of God on behalf of humanity.

Of course, the concept of 'grace' can be present, and often is, even when these and related words are absent.

Witness of the OT

One starting-point for consideration of the graciousness of God to humanity in the OT is the self-revelation of God in Exodus 34:6–7:

> The LORD, the LORD, a God merciful and gracious,
> slow to anger, and abounding in steadfast love and faithfulness,
> keeping steadfast love for the thousandth generation,
> forgiving iniquity and transgression and sin,
> yet by no means clearing the guilty …
> (NRSV)

The importance of this pronouncement is underscored by its status as Yahweh's self-revelation and by its reappearance in Numbers 14:17–19; Deuteronomy 5:9–10; 7:9–13; Psalms 77:8–9; 86:5, 15; 103:8–12, 17–18; 111:4; 116:5; 145:8–9; Joel 2:12–14; Jonah 3:10 – 4:2; Nehemiah 9:17–19, 31–32; 2 Chronicles 30:9. Numerous affirmations flow from this confession, all of which reflect the fundamentally relational character of the concept of grace. God's graciousness is foundational to his character; hence, it outlasts his wrath and spills over in abundance in activity that saves and sustains life. Moreover, that Yahweh attributes 'steadfast love and faithfulness' to himself in the immediate aftermath of the episode of the golden calf (Exod. 32) points to the persistent, everlasting quality of the *love he lavishes on his people.

Although divine favour may be sought by individuals (see especially the Psalms, *e.g.* 123:3; also Is. 30:19; Mal. 1:9), God is sovereign in his giving of grace: 'I will be gracious to whom I will be gracious, and will show mercy on whom I will show mercy' (Exod. 33:19). God's graciousness is thus neither rooted in nor dependent on people's prior acts or foreseen responses; nor is it subject to human calculation. God's gracious activity results from his own dispositions, and he can be graciously disposed even towards the unrighteous (see Jonah 4:2, 11).

The OT allows for no dichotomy between '*law' and 'grace', just as the Bible as a whole does not resolve the tension between human responsibility and divine sovereignty; the two coexist at times in delicate balance, but more often than not the law is a gift, itself an expression of divine grace. Before the commandments are enumerated in Exodus 20, Yahweh reminds Israel, 'You have seen what I did to the Egyptians, and how I bore you on eagles' wings and brought you to myself' (Exod. 19:4), and identifies himself as 'the LORD your God who brought you out of the land of Egypt, out of the house of slavery' (Exod. 20:1). The character of God is thus manifested in his compassionate response to the cries of Israel (see Deut. 26:5–10), in his *redemptive initiative in rescuing Israel from slavery, in their transformation by him into a people, in his choosing them from among the nations (see *Election), and by his gift of Torah by which their relationship with him would be sustained. Set against comparable practices in the ancient Near East, the laws enumerated in the Pentateuch are characterized by their humaneness. Rather than levying interest rates of thirty, forty, even fifty percent, for example, the people of Israel are to charge the poor no interest at all. Just as God had cared for Israel and rescued them from slavery, so they are to care for the alien, the orphan, and the widow among them. *Obedience to the covenant is rooted in the priority and prevenience of God's grace. In subsequent years, Israel sees their liberation from Egypt as a portrait of divine sovereignty and mercy, as they yearn again not only for assurances but also for demonstrations of Yahweh's continuing favour.

Witness of the NT

Pauline usage

Some two-thirds of all NT references to *charis* occur in the *Pauline correspondence (*i.e.* 100 of 154 occurrences). Here there is the fundamental affirmation that the whole of *salvation rests on God's initiative, that the single source of salvation is God, and that God's salvific purpose comes to expression in the one event of grace, the redemptive act of *Jesus Christ. Perhaps the Pauline emphasis comes to sharpest expression in Ephesians 2:8–9: 'For by grace you have been saved through faith, and this is not your own doing; it is the gift of God ...' The grace of God is overwhelming in its abundance (*cf.* Rom. 5:15, 17; 6:1; 2 Cor. 4:15; 8:9; 9:8, 14), an important point for those living in the context of economic scarcity who might be tempted to think of grace as limited, and for those living in a society based on patronal ethics who might believe that they must (or might) somehow repay God for his beneficence. 'Gratitude' (another translation of *charis,* see, *e.g.* 2 Cor. 2:14; 8:16; Rom. 6:17; 1 Cor. 10:30; 15:57) is appropriate as a response to the graciousness of God, but never repays it.

For Paul, grace as the salvific act of God in Christ is also ethically powerful. The life of *holiness is itself a manifestation of the powerful work of grace in the life of God's people (see Rom. 6:14). But although grace calls forth and enables a human response of faith, salvation and holiness should never be mistaken for human achievement: 'The love of Christ compels us!' (2 Cor. 5:14; *cf.* Titus 2:11–14). Paul grounds ethical conduct in the grace God has already given (2 Cor. 8:1–7), and in the grace shown by the Lord (2 Cor. 8:9).

Those who have received and are being transformed by the grace of God should be willing also to acknowledge that same grace at work in the lives of others. One's experience of divine grace ought to transform the standards by which one evaluates others (see 2 Cor. 5:16). Generosity ought to characterize relationships within the Christian community, not only because God may be at work even in the midst of frailty and suffering, but also because the grace of God reveals itself in a variety of gifts. God's power is evident sometimes in surprising ways (see *e.g.* 2 Cor. 4:1–12; 12:7b–10), and all believers as recipients of the grace of God, make essential, albeit different contributions to the life of the community (see Rom. 12:1–8; 1 Cor. 12 – 14).

The rest of the NT

Although it is possible to read the so-called 'catholic letters' of the NT as a counter-balance to the Pauline interpretation of the gospel, no substantive distinction in the meaning of grace can be drawn by comparing the two collections. For James, God is the giver of every perfect gift, whose generosity is extended above all to those who are poor according to worldly standards (Jas. 1:5, 17–18; 2:5; 'the humble', 4:6; *cf.* 1 Pet. 5:5; Prov. 3:34). The graciousness of God calls for robust faith, which proves its vitality in action on behalf of the poor. The epistles of John emphasize both the priority and primacy of God's love and its implications for morality: 'God is love', he writes (1 John 4:16), summarizing the essence of the OT view of the gracious God

In the Gospel of John, the word *charis* is rare, but the fourth evangelist everywhere highlights the significance of God's love for an unperceptive, intractable, and undeserving world (*e.g.* John 3:16–21). The Son of God dwells in the love of the Father, and mediates that love to the world (see John 3:36; 5:20; 14:31; 15:9–10); he calls on his followers to love one another (15:17). From a different perspective, Revelation portrays the invincible love of God, sovereignly at work, spanning the period from creation to new creation, bringing his gracious purpose to consummation. (See *Providence.)

If in Paul 'grace' can refer to 'the redemptive act of Christ', in Luke-Acts 'grace' can be used as a parallel for 'the *gospel' or 'salvation'. Thus, Jesus' sermon at Nazareth is summarized as 'words of grace' (Luke 4:22; *cf.* Acts 14:3; 20:32; also 1 Pet. 5:12); and believers can be said to have received 'grace' or to be 'full of grace', and be challenged to continue in 'grace' (*e.g.* Acts 6:8; 11:23; 13:43; *cf.* 20:24, 32). The missionaries in Acts proclaim the grace of God, and it is through this grace that people are able to respond with faith (see Acts 14:3, 26; 15:40; 18:27;

20:24, 32). More important than these uses of the term *charis*, however, is the way in which Luke consistently grounds salvation in the ancient purpose of God, which comes to fruition at God's own initiative, with the result that God must be viewed as the great benefactor who pours out his blessings on 'all people' (see Luke 3:6; Acts 2:17, 21). Even the opportunity to repent is God's own gift (Acts 5:31; 11:18). The three parables concerning seeking and finding what was lost in Luke 15 illustrate divine grace: it is embodied in the person who is willing to leave the ninety-nine to restore the one lost, and in the (costly) celebration when it is recovered. The ministry of Jesus is nothing less than the giving of God's salvific *blessings to all who will receive them, and especially to those whose lot in life locates them on the margins of society (*e.g.* Luke 4:18–19; 6:20–26).

Indeed, throughout the Synoptic Gospels one finds evidence of the extravagant grace of God at work in and available through the ministry of Jesus. The seed of the word of God is sown without discrimination, even if responses to the word vary (Mark 4:1–20). In Matthew 8 – 9 Jesus is depicted as one who makes available the presence and power of God's dominion to those dwelling on the periphery of Jewish society in Galilee: a leper, the slave of a Gentile army officer, an old woman, the demon-possessed, a paralytic, a collector of tolls, a young girl, and the blind.

Conclusion

From a biblical-theological perspective, 'grace' is fundamentally a word about God: his uncoerced initiative and pervasive, extravagant demonstrations of care and favour for all. On the one hand, his favour is poured out indiscriminately ('to the ungrateful and the wicked', Luke 6:35); on the other, those in dire straits, the poor and marginalized, can be assured that his compassion reaches especially to them. God's grace is given freely, but it also enables and invites human response, so that people are called to behave towards God with worship, gratitude and obedience; and towards one another in ways that reflect and broadcast the graciousness of God.

See also: MERCY.

Bibliography

F. I. Andersen, 'Yahweh, the kind and sensitive God', in P. T. O'Brien and D. G. Peterson (eds.), *God Who Is Rich in Mercy: Essays Presented to Dr. D. B. Knox* (Homebush West, 1986); G. B. Caird, *New Testament Theology* (Oxford, 1994); G. R. Clark, *The Word* Hesed *in the Hebrew Bible* (Sheffield, 1993); R. M. Hals, *Grace and Faith in the Old Testament* (Minneapolis, 1980); C. Spicq, '*charis*' in *TLNT*, vol. 3, pp. 500–506.

J. B. GREEN

GRIEF, see SUFFERING

GRUMBLING

Grumbling is a word that well describes the behaviour pattern of the *Exodus generation. Three stories in Exodus 15:22 – 17:7 set the tone for much of *Israel's subsequent behaviour. The Israelites leave Egypt under the most miraculous of circumstances; then, within one month of their departure, they forget the lessons they learned from the Exodus experience.

The first instance of grumbling (Heb. usually *lûn*, occasionally *rāgan*) concerns the provision of *water at Marah (Exod. 15:22–27). As the harsh realities of a desert march set in, the people begin to fear that they may die of thirst. Then, when they finally come to water, they find it is 'bitter' (Heb. *mārâ*). And so the grumbling against *Moses begins: 'What are we to drink?' But *God, rather than rebuking the people, responds in a manner reminiscent of the plagues and the Exodus; he performs another water miracle. The wood thrown into the water is clearly reminiscent of the wood of the staff that Moses used to perform the two great water miracles of the departure narrative: the first plague and the parting of the sea. By sweetening the bitter waters, God is showing his continued *faithfulness to his people despite their grumbling and despite apparent evidence to the contrary.

One month after the departure from Egypt, the Israelites arrive in the desert of Sin and renew their grumbling against Moses and Aaron. The Israelites bring an absurd charge against their leaders, well in keeping with their absurd behaviour in this passage as a whole: 'you have brought us out into this desert to starve this entire assembly to death' (16:3, NIV). But more surprising than this example of spiritual decline is the response that God makes. Rather than punishing his people, God again provides for them, this time with bread (manna) and quail.

The people are to gather only as much bread as they need for each day, but not everyone obeys this simple instruction (16:20). The Israelites continue grumbling, and receive a stunning rebuke from Moses: 'How long will you refuse to keep my commands and my instructions?' (v. 28; author's italics). The only other time Moses utters this phrase, it is addressed to Pharaoh: 'How long will you refuse to humble yourself before me?' (10:3; author's italics). God's patience seems to be reaching its limit. Israel's stubbornness is so similar to Pharaoh's that it warrants a similar rebuke. In their grumbling the Israelites are in danger of becoming more like the Egyptians than the *holy people God has called them to be.

The third grumbling episode is the famous provision of water from the rock at Rephidim (17:1–7). The people again complain that they have no water. Moses is exasperated: 'What am I to do with these people? (NIV, but perhaps better translated 'What have I done to these people?', or as 'What have I done to deserve this?'). In response to his question, Moses is instructed to walk ahead to Horeb with some of the elders and to strike the rock with the staff with which he struck the Nile (vv. 5–6). The coming of water from the rock is another Exodus-like event; a staff touches water and the people are saved. The power that brought the Israelites out of Egypt is the same power that is sustaining them in the desert and that will eventually bring them safely into the land God promised to Abraham.

The grumbling of Exodus 15:22 – 17:7 is, astonishingly, repeated in Numbers 11:1–35. Once again, the Israelites complain of lack of food. Specifically, they are tired of manna and want meat to eat. The grumbling reaches a climax in Numbers 14, 16, and 17 (see also Deut. 1:27 and Ps. 106:25). According to chapter 14, the Israelites are only about two years into the wilderness journey. The grumbling of God's people reaches such a level that

God reacts in a way that would have been unthinkable in the Exodus narrative. All those twenty years old or older will not be permitted to enter the promised land. They will be made to wander in the desert until the last rebel is dead (Num. 14:26–35). This is certainly a low point in Israel's once victorious march to Canaan. By human standards, the entire plan seems to be hanging by a frayed thread. Israel's grumbling is beginning to take its toll.

Echoes of the grumbling theme are heard in the NT. In John 6:25–59, *Jesus claims to be the 'bread of life'. This statement follows his miraculous feeding of the five thousand (6:1–15). Jesus, like Moses before him, provides bread and meat (fish) for the people. But his purpose is not simply to fill their stomachs, but to teach them that a greater 'bread' is among them. Having witnessed the miracle earlier in the day, the crowd begin to discuss with him what God requires of them. Jesus tells them that they are 'to believe in the one he has sent' (v. 29). But the people require a *sign which will prove to them that Jesus is worthy of such attention. After all, as they argue in verse 31, Moses gave his people a sign, bread from heaven. What is Jesus' proof? Jesus responds: 'I tell you the truth, it is not Moses who has given you the bread from heaven, but it is my Father who gives you the true bread from heaven. For the bread of God is he who comes down from heaven and gives life to the world' (vv. 32–33). The benefits to those who 'eat' this bread from heaven are greater than the benefits to those who ate the manna; those who eat the bread of God will never hunger or thirst again, and they will be raised up at the last day (vv. 35, 40).

The crowd, however, responds in a manner reminiscent of the Exodus generation; they grumble (gonguzō, vv. 41, 43, 61). Even some of the disciples grumble, to the point of no longer following Jesus (vv. 61–66). Ironically, whereas the Israelites grumbled because they did not have bread, this crowd grumbles because they do have it. Jesus, the true bread, has come and the people respond by grumbling. Even though this bread far exceeds anyone's expectations – it does not merely fill the stomach and give life for a day, but brings eternal life – they will have none of it. But it is the only means by which they have any hope of life. In the same way that the manna was the only food available to keep the Israelites alive each day, Christ, the bread from heaven, is now the only way to life eternal.

Christ's life of faithfulness to the Father stands in stark contrast to Israel's grumbling. Christ, the perfect Israelite, never falters by grumbling against God. His groanings in Gethsemane are not faithless grumblings but honest, heart-felt expressions of spiritual torment and loneliness. Christ never wavers. Indeed, unlike Israel, Christ is perfectly *obedient to the Father, 'obedient to death – even death on a cross' (Phil. 2:8).

The obedience of Christ is what secures the salvation of his people. It is also the foundation of his people's conduct before God. Hence Paul applies the grumbling theme to the church at Corinth (1 Cor. 10:5–11). Recounting Israel's rebellions in the desert, he warns his readers, 'do not grumble [gonguzō], as some of them did – and were killed by the destroying angel. These things happened to them as examples and were written down as warnings for us, on whom the fulfilment of the ages has come' (vv. 10–11) The lesson to be learned from Israel's rebellions in the desert is that the church is not to follow their example. In view of the coming of Christ, such grumbling should be unthinkable.

Finally, Christ's obedience provides a model not only for the church's behaviour towards God but also for the behaviour of Christians towards one another. James admonishes his readers not to 'grumble [stenazō] against each other' (Jas. 5:9). Likewise, Peter tells his readers to 'offer hospitality to one another without grumbling [gonguzō]' (1 Pet. 4:9). Neither grumbling against God nor grumbling against God's people is acceptable for those who have been raised in Christ's image. The pattern of behaviour exhibited by the Exodus generation must be transcended by those who have partaken of the new Exodus in Christ.

See also: TESTING; WILDERNESS.

P. E. ENNS

GUILT

In biblical language and thought guilt and sin are closely related. While sin usually denotes an action of personal failure (in deed, word or thought), guilt is a legal term that denotes the state resulting from this action. Guilt is an objective fact and arises when God's standards (see *Law) have not been met, when the creator's claim on his creation is neglected or refused whether wilfully or unintentionally. According to Scripture, guilt is a universal human state and experience (Rom. 3:23).

Guilt in the OT

Guilt is essentially a forensic term (Ps. 109:7; Prov. 18:5; 30:10; Is. 5:23; 50:9; Ezek. 23:45) which is widely applied to the spiritual sphere. 'Doing any one of the things that by the Lord's commandments ought not to be done' (Lev.4:13, 22, 27, NRSV) incurs guilt: trespasses related to the cult (Exod. 28:43; Lev. 17:3–4); to moral (Num. 5:6; Jer. 30:14–15; 33:8; Ezek. 22:4) and ritual failure (cf. the connection of uncleanness and guilt e.g. in Lev. 5:2–3.; Num. 6:11). People 'transgress and become guilty' (Hab. 1:11). God knows of guilt (Gen. 44:16) and holds guilty people accountable (Exod. 23:7; 34:7; Num. 14:18; Jer. 2:3 [cf. the question of Jer. 12:1]; Hos. 13:16; Joel 3:21; Jonah 1:14; Nah. 1:3). The guilty are condemned in *judgment when God brings their conduct on their own head (1 Kgs. 8:32; 2 Chr. 6:23; cf. Is. 3:11; 24:6); guilt can lead to death (Exod. 28:43; Num. 18:22; Jer. 25:31; Ezek. 18:24; Hos. 13:1). The lifestyle of God's enemies is described as 'walking in guilty ways' (Ps. 68:21; Prov. 21:8; in Hos. 5:5 Ephraim 'stumbles' in his guilt). It is also possible to bring guilt upon others (Gen. 20:9; 26:10; Lev. 4:3; Hos. 4:15; cf. Josh. 7). Guilt can be incurred before other people (2 Sam. 19:19; 2 Kgs. 7:9), requiring restitution (Lev. 6:5) on the human level and *sacrifice to God 'because when we sin against others and incur "indebtedness" to them, we violate the order that God prescribes for his world and his people, and have thus incurred a debt toward him also' (S. Motyer, in EDBT, p. 319).

Guilt cannot be removed by the offenders themselves; guilt requires a guilt offering (Lev. 5:5–19, 15–19; 6:6; 22:16; Num. 5:8). The connection between them is emphasized by the use of the same word ('āšām) to denote both 'guilt' and the guilt/reparation offering (cf. Jer. 51:5 and Lev. 5:14–19). The word 'āšām occurs thirty-nine times in the OT, and twenty-five times in Lev., mainly chs. 5 – 7 and 14; see also Ezra 10:19 and NIDOTTE 1, pp. 553–566. In neither of its meanings does it occur in the context of the day of atonement in Lev. 16. God provides the means of *grace whereby guilty people may be restored and live in his *holy presence. God removes guilt (Jer. 33:8 'I will cleanse them from all the guilt of their sin'; Zech. 3:4, 9); he will make the life of the servant of Isaiah 53:10 a guilt offering for others (*cf.* Mark 10:45 for Jesus as the 'ransom' for indebtedness; also John 1:29). Such sacrifices are to be accompanied by recognition of guilt and confession of sin (Lev. 5:5; 6:4–5; Ezra 9). Fools mock the guilt offering (Prov. 14:9). David confesses his guilt (Ps. 51:3–5) and prays for its removal (2 Sam. 24:10; 1 Chr. 21:8; *cf.* Pss. 25:11; 32:5).

Guilt in the NT

While various Greek words are translated as 'guilt' or 'guilty' (*cf. NIDNTT* 2, pp. 137–145) occurrences are comparatively scarce. There are three technical terms for legal guilt (for *enochos* see *e.g.* Matt. 5:21–22; 26:66; for *opheilo* see Matt. 18:24, 28, 30; Luke 7:41; Rom. 4:4; for all occurrences of *aitia* or *aitios*, see *BAGD*); the first two also denote guilt before or indebtedness to God and people. According to Mark 3:29 the blasphemer of the Spirit is guilty (*enochos*) of an eternal sin which cannot be removed by forgiveness. Unworthy participants in the Lord's supper become guilty (*enochos*) of the Lord's body and blood (1 Cor. 11:27). Failing in one point in keeping the law renders one guilty (*enochos*, 'accountable' in NRSV) of it all (Jas. 2:10). Thus universal human guilt before God derives from failure to follow his will. The Lord's prayer asks for the forgiveness of debts (*opheilēma*, indebtedness to God through sins, Matt. 6:12; Luke 11:4a has 'sins'). Those killed under tragic circumstances were not worse 'debtors' (*opheiletai*, sinners) than others. Irrespective of quantifiable guilt, all need repentance to escape judgment (Luke 13:4–5; Rom. 6:23).

Guilt is not a key concept in NT teaching on sin and salvation. While the nature and seriousness of guilt as portrayed in the OT continues undiminished, they are expressed differently. As the NT's focus is on God's *salvation in Christ for all guilty people, it is less interested in guilt itself than in its removal through *faith in Jesus. The NT demands that deliverance from guilt through God's *forgiveness be reflected in uncon-

ditional readiness to forgive those who have offended us or are indebted to us (without restitution); we cannot rightly ask for ourselves what we deny to others (Luke 11:4; Matt. 6:12; 18:21–35).

The objectivity of guilt

The Bible contains moving descriptions of emotions of guilt following failure (*e.g.* Ps. 32:1–5; Peter in Luke 22:61–62; Judas in Matt. 27:3–5). Such a response indicates the recognition of guilt (*cf.* the different responses of Judas and Peter!) and should prepare the way for its acknowledgement and confession (Lev. 5:5; Hos. 5:15). However, in view of the overall biblical evidence it needs to be stressed, against the limited secular understanding, that guilt is always an objective fact *irrespective* of corresponding emotional response. Though guilt frequently spawns corresponding feelings, its presence is not dependent on them. Feelings of guilt are often not in proportion to the transgression (being too intensive or 'meagre') and are influenced by personal experience (including upbringing), character and culture. While the experience of forgiveness should include emotional relief, alleviation of *feelings* of guilt – apart from *forgiveness* – does not dispose of guilt itself.

See also: EVIL; SIN.

Bibliography

R. E. Averbeck in *NIDOTTE* 1, pp. 557–566; G. W. Bromiley, 'Sin. VI-IX', *ISBE* 4, pp. 520–522; B. Bron, 'Schuld', *EKL* 4, pp. 114–118; C. Brown *et al.* in *NIDNTT* 2, pp. 137–145; E. Carpenter and M. A. Grisanti in *NIDOTTE* 1, pp. 553–557; R. C. Cover, 'Sin, Sinners. OT', *ABD* 6, pp. 31–40; R. Glei *et al.*, 'Schuld', *HWP* 8, pp. 1442–1465; H. Hanse in *TDNT* 2, p. 828; F. Hauck in *TDNT* 5, pp. 559–566; *Louw-Nida* nos. 88, pp. 310–317; B. Kedar-Klopfstein in *TDOT* 3, pp. 234–250; D. Kellermann in *TDOT* 1, pp. 429–437; L. L. Morris in *NDT*, p. 285; *idem*, 'Sin, Guilt', *DPL*, pp. 877–881; S. Motyer in *EDBT*, p. 319; J. C. Moyer, 'Guilt, Guilty', *ISBE* 2, pp. 580f.; G. Quell *et al.* in *TDNT* 1, pp. 279f.; K. H. Rengstorf in *TDNT* 1, pp. 317–335; H. Schwarz, *Im Fangnetz des Bösen: Sünde – Übel – Schuld* (Göttingen, 1993), pp. 56–65; V. Taylor, *Forgiveness and Reconciliation: A Study in*

New Testament Theology (London, ²1946); P. Tournier, *Guilt and Grace* (ET, New York, 1962); Th.C. Vriezen *et al.*, 'Sühne und Schuld. II.–IV.', *RGG* 6, pp. 478–489.

C. W. Stenschke

HABAKKUK, see Part 2

HAGAR

Introduction

Hagar, the Egyptian slave of Sarai (*Sarah), bore to Abram (*Abraham) his first son, Ishmael, from whom were descended twelve Bedouin tribes (Gen. 25:12–16; 1 Chr. 1:29–31). The name 'Hagar' occurs twelve times in *Genesis (16:1, 3, 4, 8, 15 twice, 16; 21:9, 14, 17 twice; 25:12) and twice in *Galatians (4:24–25). The Genesis narratives (chs. 16; 21) present an ambiguous picture of Hagar and Ishmael; they are portrayed negatively as rivals to Sarah and Isaac, but also the Lord blesses them by virtue of their relationship to Abraham. In the intertextual context of the Pentateuch, Hagar and Sarah typify *Israel's servitude and expulsion from Egypt, but ironically in reverse (15:13; 16:6, 12; 25:18). Paul uses Hagar typology of slavery and expulsion to combat the Judaizers in Galatia (Gal. 4:21–31).

The Egyptian who sees

Hagar is repeatedly identified as 'the Egyptian slave girl' (NRSV, 16:1, 3; 21:9; 25:12) of her 'mistress' Sarai (16:4, 8). Although Hagar and her son ridicule Sarah and Isaac (16:4; 21:9), Genesis depicts Hagar favourably by reference to God's double appearance through his 'angel' (16:7–12; 21:17–19). The Lord both 'sees' and 'hears' the plight of the outcasts, as the names 'El Roi' (the God who sees) (16:13) and 'Ishmael' (God has heard) (16:11; 21:17) indicate. In this respect Hagar is more honoured than Sarah, who did not receive the same *theophanic attention (18:15). Also, Ishmael is the first person to undergo covenant *circumcision (17:23), and he is promised descendants (16:10; 21:13, 18). The position of Hagar and Ishmael in the household of Abraham is ambiguous until, at the direction of the Lord, they are expelled (21:12). Hagar's Egyptian identity is also

ambiguous, since 'Egypt' in Genesis indicates both a threat to the patriarchal seed (12:10–20) and a refuge for the preservation of Jacob's house (chs. 47 – 50); the patriarchal couple emerge from Egypt enriched with possessions, perhaps including Hagar herself (who is the daughter of Pharaoh in *Genesis Rabbah* 45.1.5).

The place of Hagar is paralleled in the future of Israel, which involves hostility (Gen. 16:6; Exod. 1:11, 12), expulsion (Gen. 21:10; Exod. 12:39) and flight (Gen. 16:6; Exod. 14:5) (*cf.* Joseph and the Ishmaelites, Gen. 37:28). The historical irony was that the roles of Hagar and Sarah were reversed when the mistress's children became enslaved to the people of Hagar's nation. Abraham's descendants were 'oppressed' (Gen. 15:13) by Egypt, the same term used of Sarah's mistreatment of Hagar (16:6). Ishmael's taunt against Isaac functions as a prototype for the later Egyptian threat to the children of the Hebrews (21:9; Exod. 1:16). Also, Hagar and *Moses have parallel experiences, including oppression (Exod. 2:11–15a), flight into the desert where they meet *God (Exod. 2:15b; 3:2), return, eventual expulsion and miraculous deliverance (Exod. 10:11; 11:1; 15:22–27) (T. B. Dozeman, in *JBL* 117, pp. 29–32).

The 'foreigner' motif is enhanced when Hagar acquires a wife for her son from Egypt (Gen. 21:21). The ambiguity of Ishmael as the offspring of a foreigner typifies Israel's treatment of foreigners who undergo circumcision prior to participation in the Passover (Exod. 12:43–49). The 'in-between' position of foreigners, and in particular of Egyptians, is revealed by the condition of their acceptance into the sacred assembly (Deut. 23:7–8) (R. Syrén, *The Forsaken First-born*, pp. 39–40). Although Hagar and Ishmael are included in the household of Abraham, it is God who relieves the narrative tension by specifying that the inheritance will be through Isaac alone (21:12).

The ancestress of wilderness slaves

Although Hagar is identified as Abraham's 'wife' (16:3), she is treated in the passage as inferior to Sarah. The contrasts between the two women are pronounced; Hagar is a young slave woman and fertile, whereas Sarah is old and barren. The pregnancy of Hagar is not unusual (16:4), but the birth of Isaac in Sarah's old age is remarkable. Hagar has a socially peripheral place in the household of Abraham and is twice in the *wilderness, indicating her status as an outcast. Even her sexual relationship with Abraham seems to be limited to one occasion (16:4; *cf. Genesis Rabbah* 45.4.1). The Bedouin lifestyle of Ishmael's tribal descendants in the region of Syria-Arabia (25:12–18) contrasts with the urbanized life of Canaan. Sarah is located in the 'tent' of Abraham (18:6, 9–10), and it is in Sarah's 'tent' that Isaac resides (24:67).

Paul presents a typology of Hagar and Sarah in his argument against the Judaizers in Galatia (4:21–31). The two women represent two *covenants: Hagar the slave the Mosaic covenant, and Sarah the *free woman the new covenant. The birth of Ishmael and the promise concerning him were 'according to the flesh', *i.e.* after the normal pregnancy of Hagar. Isaac, however, was born 'through the promise', which was made before Sarah's exceptional pregnancy. One Jewish tradition depicts Hagar as a converted proselyte who chose to observe the *law (Philo, *De Abrahamo* 247–253; *Genesis Rabbah* 61.4.1), but Paul focuses on her inferior position; her children are born into slavery (P. Borgen, in *New Testament and Hellenistic Judaism*). Paul then ties the motif of her slavery to the geographical locations of Mt Sinai and *Jerusalem. Hagar represents Mt Sinai where the law was given and the present Jerusalem under Roman oppression. The typology of Hagar and Moses associates her with Sinai, and Sinai was located in the region known in Paul's day as Arabia. Some believed that the Arabians were descended from Hagar (Baruch 3:23). Those of the covenant of the flesh are descendants of Hagar; their home is outside the land of promise, which shows that they are outcasts from the household of Abraham. The identity of Sarah as the superior 'Jerusalem above' (Gal. 4:26) is derived first from her status as a free woman and secondly from Abraham's testing at Mt Moriah (Gen. 22:1–2), the site of the temple in Jerusalem (2 Chr. 3:1). The agitators in Galatia are indeed circumcised descendants of Abraham, as was Ishmael, but like Hagar and Ishmael they are outside the household of faith (Gal. 4:31).

Bibliography

P. Borgen, 'Some Hebrew and pagan features in Philo's and Paul's interpretation of Hagar and Ishmael', in P. Borgen and S. Giversen (eds.), *New Testament and Hellenistic Judaism* (Peabody, 1997); T. B. Dozeman, 'The wilderness and salvation history in the Hagar story', *JBL* 117, 1998, pp. 23–43; R. Syrén, *The Forsaken First-born: A Study of a Recurrent Motif in the Patriarchal Narrative* (Sheffield, 1993).

K. A. MATHEWS

HAGGAI, see Part 2

HARDENING

Introduction

In biblical theology, words from the 'hard' root denote a state of spiritual obduracy. To be 'hard' is to be insensitive to *God, his *word, and his work. The 'hardened' person is unable to respond to God and thus cannot enter into a saving relationship with God.

Three Hebrew words (from the roots *ḥzq*, *qsh*, and *kbd*) and two Greek words (from the roots *sklēr-* and *pōr-*) are significant for the theological idea of 'hardening'.

The critical passages

Spiritual 'hardening' is referred to in about thirty OT and twenty NT texts. Some of the references occur in isolation. 'He [Zedekiah] also rebelled against King Nebuchadnezzar, who had made him take an oath in God's name. He became stiff-necked and hardened his heart and would not turn to the LORD, the God of Israel' (2 Chr. 36:13, NIV). But the theologically most important occurrences occur in, or in relationship to, three OT passages: the story of Pharaoh's hardening in Exodus 4 – 14; the prophecy of spiritual obduracy in Isaiah 6:9–10; and the reflection on *Israel's rebellion in the wilderness in Psalm 95:7–11. Each deserves separate consideration.

Psalm 95:7b–11 is a warning, attributed to Yahweh, to the people of the psalmist's own day. He wants them to avoid the spiritual rebellion of an earlier generation who 'hardened' their hearts when they were presented with the opportunity of going in to possess the Promised Land.

The author to the Hebrews uses this text as the basis for his similar warning to Jewish

Christians whose sufferings were bringing them to the point of *apostasy (Heb. 3:7 – 4:11). The hardening of the 'heart', standing in Scripture for the very essence of a person, denotes a deep-seated insensitivity to the word of God. In this tradition, clearly, the individual is responsible for his or her own hardening.

Individual responsibility is less clear in the other two passages, and this creates the cardinal theological issue in the biblical presentation of hardening. When God appoints the prophet Isaiah, he announces that his task will be a negative one: 'Go and tell this people: "Be ever hearing, but never understanding; be ever seeing, but never perceiving." Make the hearts of this people calloused; make their ears dull and close their eyes. Otherwise they might see with their eyes, hear with their ears, understand with their hearts, and turn and be healed' (Is. 6:9–10). This text becomes programmatic in early Christianity. Jesus uses it to explain his parabolic teaching (see esp. Matt. 13:13–15; also Mark 4:11–12 and Luke 8:10), John cites it to explain why so many people who had seen Jesus' 'signs' nevertheless turned from him (12:40), and Paul finds the disbelief of Jews in Rome to be a fulfilment of this prophecy (Acts 28:25–27). In each of these passages, though with varying degrees of emphasis, the 'hardening' comes about as a result of divine initiative. People are hardened because God has determined, through his word and his messengers, to harden them.

How are we to explain the confluence of divine purpose and human responsibility that we find in these first two sets of hardening texts? The third set, many think, supplies the answer.

In Exodus 4 – 14, God's intention to bring his people out of slavery in Egypt is repeatedly thwarted by Pharaoh who, despite increasingly spectacular miracles, refuses to let the people go. The text explains that Pharaoh acted as he did because his heart was 'hardened'. Six times the text uses a passive form, leaving it unclear whether God or Pharaoh was responsible for the hardened condition of the Egyptian ruler's heart: see, *e.g.*, Exodus 7:13: 'Yet Pharaoh's heart became hard and he would not listen to them, just as the LORD had said' (see also Exod. 7:14, 22; 8:19; 9:7, 35). But three times Pharaoh is said to harden his own heart, as in

Exodus 8:15: 'But when Pharaoh saw that there was relief, he hardened his heart and would not listen to Moses and Aaron, just as the LORD had said' (see also Exod. 8:32; 9:34). But, as the phrase 'just as the LORD said' hints in each of these verses, there is another, dominant note in this passage. Ten times God himself is said to harden Pharaoh's heart. Indeed, God warns Moses that he plans to do just that: 'When you return to Egypt, see that you perform before Pharaoh all the wonders I have given you the power to do. But I will harden his heart so that he will not let this people go' (Exod. 4:21; see also 7:3; 9:12; 10:1, 20, 27; 11:10; 14:4, 8, 17). Some scholars insist that God's role here is responsive, confirming Pharaoh's decision to harden his own heart; others insist that God's role is creative, causing Pharaoh to harden his heart. The debate is heated because these passages in Exodus form the backdrop for the most famous hardening text, Romans 9:18.

In Romans 9:6–13, Paul vindicates God's promises to Israel by arguing that God had always selected from within physical Israel a smaller number of people to inherit his blessing. In response to an objection that God's so choosing some and passing over others would be unfair, Paul defends God's right to do just that. After mentioning God's purpose with Pharaoh, Paul concludes, 'Therefore God has mercy on whom he wants to have mercy, and he hardens whom he wants to harden' (9:18; see also Rom. 11:7). Paul appears to be suggesting that God is responsible both for choosing those who will be saved and also those who will be damned. The text has thus been used as a key exegetical basis for the doctrine of 'double' predestination (see *Election). But does the text clearly support such an idea? Those who resist this conclusion sometimes appeal to the Exodus texts to suggest that behind God's hardening lies a prior human decision to refuse to respond to God. But this is an unlikely reading of Exodus, and an even more unlikely reading of Romans. More telling is the objection that Paul appears to present 'hardening' in Romans 11 (see vv. 11–24) as a condition that can be reversed. The spiritual obduracy denoted by 'hardening', in other words, while ultimately caused by God, is not clearly presented as a permanent condition. On this view of the matter, the condition of being 'hardened' is one that can change through the work of God's grace. As Paul puts it in Romans 11, those among the Jews who have been 'hardened' (v. 7) have not stumbled 'so as to fall beyond recovery' (v. 11). By their faith, they can be restored again to the olive tree, the people of God (v. 23). And this faith, as the argument of Romans has made plain, is faith in Christ and the good news that he has brought (see *e.g.* 3:22, 26; 10:8-13).

See also: REPENTANCE.

Bibliography

G. K. Beale, 'An exegetical and theological consideration of the hardening of Pharaoh's heart in Exodus 4 – 14 and Romans 9', *TJ* 5, 1984, 129-154; J. L. Kuyper, 'The hardening of heart according to biblical perspective', *SJT* 27, 1974, pp. 459–474; H. Räisänen, *The Idea of Divine Hardening: A Comparative Study of the Notion of Divine Hardening, Leading Astray and Inciting to Evil in the Bible and Qur'an* (Helsinki, 1972).

D. J. MOO

HARLOTRY, see ADULTERY

HARVEST

Harvest, the reaping of the ripened agricultural produce of the land, is a rich biblical motif with a wide range of theological and symbolic connotations. But it is never merely agricultural, for the ancient Israelites embraced a holistic worldview, in which the Creator God, the covenant people and the *land formed one interrelated framework. This is reflected in the overarching concept of the covenant, in both creation and redemption, and underlies the biblical theme of the harvest.

After the flood, Yahweh solemnly promised: 'As long as the earth endures, seedtime and harvest, cold and heat, summer and winter, day and night will never cease' (Gen. 8:22, NIV). In other words, as long as the temporal world exists, the cycle of the seasons will continue. This promise serves as a guarantee of Yahweh's covenant with David (Jer. 33:20–21). Yahweh made his covenant with the elect nation, and the book of Deuteronomy describes the covenantal blessings

for his obedient people: 'The fruit of your womb will be blessed, and the crops of your land' (Deut. 28:4); '[t]he LORD will send a blessing on your barns and on everything you put your hand to' (Deut. 28:8). But this was no unconditional promise. Only if his covenant people cleaved to Yahweh in faithful love would he guarantee prosperity. If they did not, he would implement the covenant curses such as Deuteronomy 28:38, 'You will sow much seed in the field but you will harvest little, because locusts will devour it'. The warnings of the prophets were all based on the principle expressed in Micah 6:15, 'You will plant but not harvest; you will press olives but not use the oil on yourselves'. Hosea in the 8th century BC verbalizes Yahweh's complaint against Israel's apostasy in favour of the Canaanite fertility gods: 'She has not acknowledged that I was the one who gave her the grain, the new wine and the oil' (Hos. 2:8).

Harvest was a time of celebration, joy and thanksgiving. Two of the three great annual pilgrimage festivals, Weeks and Tabernacles (see *Sacred meals), were closely associated with the agricultural harvest, and were celebrations of Yahweh's covenant bounty. 'For the LORD your God will bless you … in all the work of your hands, and your joy will be complete' (Deut. 16:15). This munificence was to be shared equitably by all the people, both rich and poor. The aliens, widows and sojourners were all entitled to share in God's generosity, as the laws of gleaning made clear (Lev. 19:9–10).

Virtually every aspect of harvesting and the growth of fruit is pressed into service by the biblical writers to illustrate various truths about the spiritual life, both individual and corporate. The selection of seed inevitably influences the expected outcome. Choicest vines should produce luscious grapes (see Is. 5:2). Jesus asked 'Do people pick grapes from thornbushes or figs from thistles?' (Matt. 7:16). So also if we sow to the flesh, we shall reap a harvest of corruption, if we sow to the Spirit, we shall reap a harvest of eternal life. It is a simple law: in the process of sanctification we reap what we sow (see Gal. 6:7). Similarly, the magnitude of our sowing inevitably influences the outcome. 'Whoever sows sparingly will reap sparingly' (2 Cor. 9:6) in both Christian activity and personal spiritual progress. The type of soil in which the seed is sown will also influence the size of the harvest. The owner of the vineyard clears it of stones as a preparation to planting (Is. 5:2). In the parable of the sower (Mark 4:1–20), seed which falls on rocky ground which allows for no deep roots is unproductive.

The preparation of the ground is an act of backbreaking labour, of sweat and pain. This is part of the curse on *creation: 'By the sweat of your brow you will eat your food' (Gen. 3:19). But there is hope beyond the tears, as the Psalmist writes: 'Those who sow in tears will reap with songs of joy. He who goes out weeping carrying seed to sow, will return with songs of joy, carrying sheaves with him' (Ps. 126:5–6). However, laziness will produce no fruit: 'Whoever watches the wind will not plant; whoever looks at the clouds will not reap' (Eccles. 11:4). Even the process of growth needs to be supervised. The ailing fig tree needs to be fertilized with manure (Luke 13:8); the vine needs to be pruned in order that it may bear more fruit (John 15:2).

The time lapse between sowing and reaping is part of the natural order of things, and demands patience on the part of the farmer. 'So we shall reap if we do not lose heart' (Gal. 6:9). There is a season for fruit bearing (Ps. 1:3) that cannot be made to happen by human beings. Rain and sunshine are required to produce growth and ripening and it is 'only God who makes things grow' (1 Cor. 3:6–8). To the farmer, this is a mystery; while he sleeps night and day, the soil produces corn, 'all by itself', though he does not know how (Mark 4:28). Since the process of growth is slow, the sower, the waterer and the reaper may not be the same. Paul says 'I planted, Apollos watered' (1 Cor. 3:6). It is often true in Christian ministry that 'one sows and another reaps' (John 4:37). Those involved in the cultivation should be rewarded: 'The hardworking farmer should be the first to receive a share of the crops' (2 Tim. 2:6). Paul establishes this as a principle for the payment of the Christian worker: 'If we have sown spiritual seed among you, is it too much if we reap a material harvest from you?' (1 Cor. 9:11).

The close of the age is portrayed as the eschatological harvest. 'Swing the sickle, for the harvest is ripe' (Joel 3:13). Both judgement and redemption are involved. This is seen in both Revelation 14:14–20, where the image of reaping the harvest is used in the context of God's wrath and deliverance, and the parable of the weeds of the field (Matt. 13:24–30, 36–43), which speaks of a great separation at the end of the world.

T. D. GLEDHILL

HATRED

Hatred is described by G. M. Hagan as 'a tangible measurement of *evil in the world' (in *EDBT*, p. 326). This is a fair assessment of the biblical witness, for every *human has the potential to hate (Eccles. 3:8); indeed hatred is one of the acts of the *sinful nature (Gal. 5:20; *cf.* Titus 3:3). All relationships can be scarred by it. Parents can hate their children (Prov. 13:24) and a husband his wife (Gen. 29:31). There are three distinct categories of hatred to be discussed in considering the biblical view of hatred and hate: cosmic, human and divine.

Cosmic. While much can be said about human and divine hatred, no discussion of hatred is quite complete without some reference to its cosmic dimensions. These are perhaps most explicit in the Johannine writings, in which hate clearly belongs to the realm of darkness and has no place in the kingdom of light (1 John 2:9–11). This point is picked up in the ethical teaching of James, in which he warns that 'friendship with the world is hatred towards God' (4:4, NIV). It is also affirmed by Paul in Romans, in which evildoers are described as 'God-haters' (1:30). Genesis perhaps hints at this cosmic dimension to hatred (and to sin in general; Gen. 3:15).

Human. The hating of one human being by another is the one explicit prohibition within the OT with regard to hatred (Lev. 19:17; Deut. 19:11–13). These texts do not preclude hatred only of a physical brother, but also of all those included in the *covenant people of Israel.

The biblical witness is candid about the various reasons for hatred: jealousy (Gen. 37:11), rejection (Judg. 11:7), and even the seemingly legitimate desire to avenge evil can all spiral out of control if hatred is left unchecked. It would seem that there is no such thing as the legitimate hatred of one human by another.

The Bible is clear: hatred is wrong. But

why is it a particularly odious sin? The answer lies in the fact that hatred of fellow humans mars the image of *God in them, thus denying them their rightful status in God's creation. Indeed, to hate another is to deny God's very involvement with humanity.

G. F. Hasel's contention that 'a lack of *love is equal to hate' (in *ISBE* 2, p. 630; Prov. 13:24) does not take into account the covenant-breaking nature of hate. The *righteous hate what God hates because these 'hated things' 'threaten the very foundation of all human order' (Hasel, p. 630). This point is made particularly clear in the Psalms (69:22–25; 59:5; *cf.* Rom. 11:9–10). For example, both the prophets and Christ hate idolatry and religiosity, which result from the breaking of the covenant between God and humanity (Is. 1:11–14; Matt. 23:5–6; Luke 11:39–42).

*Jesus teaches that the world will hate those who follow him because of its dislike of him (John 15:18–20). This hatred perhaps stems from the fact that people's responses to Jesus divide families, races, and nations (Matt. 10:34–36). The disciple is asked to put Jesus not only before these things, but also before him or herself. Jesus is explicit: the love that Christians are to have for their Lord is to make even their love for themselves look like hatred (Mark 8:34–35 and par.).

Divine. The idea of God's hating someone or something is more perplexing. It appears to contradict the maxim: 'God is love' (1 John 4:8b). Yet God's hatred of those who have broken his covenant is demonstrated throughout the OT (Exod. 32:31–33; Deut. 12:31; Is. 1:11–14; 61:8; Jer. 44:4–5; Hos. 9:15; Amos 5:21). Moreover, divine hatred is not absent from the NT (*contra* F. W. Young, in *IDB*, p. 536). In Revelation Jesus is depicted as hating the works of the Nicolaitans (Rev. 2:6). The writer to the Hebrews picks up on Psalm 45:7 in his discussion of Christology, suggesting that Christ hates lawlessness (Heb. 1:9); this statement may reflect the covenant theme. Indeed Paul, quoting from Malachi, confirms that God loved Jacob, while hating Esau (Rom. 9:13). While such texts must be considered in their specific context (in this case Paul's discussion concerning the election of Israel), they must not be rendered invisible by exegetical gymnastics.

To attempt to distinguish (as Young and Hasel do) between hating the sin and hating the one who sins is to make divine hatred far too clinical. It is to deny his justice and *holiness, 'two essential qualities of God' (Hagan, p. 326), and to ignore the hostility with which the covenant-making God views those who break his covenant. Sinful hatred is an expression of that which God is not. The witness of both the Testaments roundly condemns the evil and pain that hatred can cause. Christians are called to hate what is evil (Rom. 12:9), even while loving those who hate them because of Christ.

Bibliography

L. L. Belleville, 'Enemy, Enmity, Hatred', in *DPL*, pp. 235–238; G. M. Hagan in *EDBT*, p. 326; G. F. Hasel in *ISBE* 2, pp. 629–633; F. W. Young in *IDB* 2, p. 536.

K. S. ELLIS

HEALING

Scripture as a whole affirms the image of Yahweh as healer, and the NT adds to this the portrait of *Jesus as *God's agent of healing. Healing at the hand of others – whether Elijah or Peter or some other – is consistently attributed to God, or to 'the name' of the exalted Lord Jesus, or to the *Holy Spirit. The biblical texts invariably reject recourse to magic as a means of recovery, and generally view physicians with disdain. This is in part a commentary on the state of health care in ancient times, but more a recognition that Yahweh is the source of *life and, therefore, the source of renewed health.

Health and sickness

People in the modern world of the West often misconstrue the nature of healing in Scripture by reading into the Bible alien notions of health and disease. Two interrelated points of orientation are therefore vital. First, *humanity was created in the *image of God (Gen. 1:26–27), and this includes relationships of harmony within the human community as well as with God and the entire cosmos. 'Healing' from a biblical perspective cannot therefore be focused on the physical body alone but must comprise restoration to health in the fullest sense. Secondly, different cultures think of sickness and healing in different ways (see R. A. Hahn, *Sickness and Healing*), with the result that for most people to read the biblical accounts of healing is to engage in an exercise in cross-cultural communication. Modern western people tend to think of disease as an abnormality located within the body, in or beneath the skin; thus healing requires physical or biomedical intervention. People in the biblical accounts tend to think of sickness in more holistic ways. The source of sickness for them lies not only in the bodies of the sick, but also and sometimes especially in their social environments and in the larger universe. Thus healing may require an alleviation of the pressure of one's social relationships, bodily intervention, and/or redress of cosmic imbalances.

This cross-cultural perspective on sickness and healing is important for understanding many of the biblical accounts of healing and when working with broader categories of healing. For example, in the Bible 'leprosy' is rarely if ever true leprosy, or 'Hansen's Disease', but may refer to any of a number of skin conditions. According to Leviticus 13 – 14, leprosy is a sign of God's curse on a person; hence someone who is diagnosed as a leper by a *priest is thrust to the periphery of human existence, being forced to dwell outside the human community. Their 'leprosy' is not life-threatening; nor are they likely to pass their skin disease on to others; rather it is their ritual impurity that is contagious. 'Leprosy' is thus a good example of how religious, social and physical maladies coalesce in a single set of symptoms. Jesus' intervention in such cases is classified as 'cleansing' rather than healing, since religious impurity is the primary problem, and intervention is followed by such instructions from Jesus as those found in Luke 5:12–14: 'Go, show yourself to the priest, and make an offering for your cleansing as Moses commanded' (author's translation). In such an instance, the priest functions not as a healer but as a kind of health-care consultant, validating the cure and mediating the former leper's return to the community of God's people.

Accounts of exorcism similarly correlate spiritual, social, mental and physical factors, both in the presentation of the disorder and in its resolution. The Gerasene demoniac (Luke 8:26–39) lives not in a house but among the tombs (apart from the human community, as though he were dead, ritually unclean), is naked and uncontrollable (thus lacking human identity), and his speech includes both 'I'- and 'we'-statements (so fully is he demonized). Following the exorcism, he sits at the feet of Jesus (submission), clothed and in his right mind (restored to human identity), and Jesus sends him back to his home to declare what God had done for him (restored to his community, with a vocation).

In more straightforward accounts, too, such as the healing of the woman with a haemorrhage (Mark 5:25–34 par.), forms of social and spiritual restoration are clearly linked with physical recovery. This is also true in the larger biblical worldview in which healing and sickness are indicators of Yahweh's favour and displeasure. Although one cannot assume that health is necessarily the direct result of God's favour, or that sickness is necessarily the direct result of divine punishment, it is nevertheless true that for ancient Israel there is a causal link from *sin to sickness. (For examples, see Deut. 28; 1 Kgs. 13:1–25; Prov. 3:28–35; 11:19; 13:13–22; 1 Cor. 11:29–30. This position is eloquently represented by Job's interlocutors in Job 8:1–22; 11:6; 22:1–30, in a book where such logic is undermined!) In John 9, the disciples assume the causal relationship of sin to physical disorder, but Jesus makes no general pronouncement on the subject; elsewhere, his actions presuppose that healing one man's paralysis and forgiving his sin are equivalent (Mark 2:1–12 par.). A holistic approach to healing is thus demanded by the biblical evidence, which refuses the easy segregation of physical from spiritual, or communal from physical disorder.

That the biblical material disallows any easy categorization of sickness or healing can be illustrated further from Matthew 8 – 9. Miraculous events are recounted one after the other, as Matthew depicts Jesus as one who makes available the presence and power of God's dominion to those dwelling on the periphery of Jewish society in Galilee: a leper; the slave of a Gentile army officer; an old woman; the demon-possessed; a paralytic; a toll-collector; a young girl; and the blind. At the same time that Matthew recounts the restoration to physical health of those who are diseased, he also chronicles the restoration of people to status within their families and communities, the re-ordering of life based on faith in God, and the driving back of demonic forces (see *Spiritual powers). The cleansing of a leper allows him new access to God and to the community of God's people (Matt. 8:1–4); the healing of a paralytic is tantamount to forgiving his sins (Matt. 9:2–8); the extension of God's grace to tax collectors and sinners is the work of a physician (Matt. 9:9–13); and, as throughout the biblical tradition, recovery of sight is a metaphor for the insight of faith (Matt. 9:27–31).

Yahweh the healer

Throughout the OT, Yahweh's role as healer is paramount: 'I, Yahweh, am your healer' (Exod. 15:26; see 2 Kgs. 5:7). The context of this self-affirmation is important, for it follows the narration of the incredible lengths to which Yahweh has gone to liberate *Israel from Egypt. 'I am your healer', Yahweh declares, but Israel must hearken to his voice and heed his commands. Again in the Torah, as proof of his unique status, Yahweh declares, 'I kill and I make alive. I wound and I heal' (Deut. 32:39). God's role as healer is even more prominent in the prophetic writings, where appeals are made to God to come and heal both individuals and the nation. Hezekiah appeals to God to restore his health (Is. 38:16), and Ezekiel portrays Yahweh as healer of the weak, the sick, and the lost (34:16). The Servant of Yahweh, Isaiah writes, will effect the healing of the people of God (53:5). The Writings, too, portray God as healer. In the Psalms a recurring motif is God's restoring the faithful, sometimes by means of *forgiveness, liberation or renewal (Pss. 30:2; 41:4; 103:3; 107:19–20). Yahweh binds up and heals the wounded (Job 5:17–18).

In the NT, the role of God as healer is confirmed, though with important amendments. Healing is a sign of the inbreaking *kingdom of God, reminding the reader that behind the healing ministry of Jesus and others stands Yahweh the healer. It is nonetheless true, especially in the Gospels and Acts, that restoration is typically mediated, first through Jesus and then through his disciples and witnesses. In Acts Peter says that God worked deeds of power, wonders and signs through Jesus so as to accredit him as God's authorized agent of *salvation (2:22); in the same way, the Lord authorized the word of his grace by 'granting signs and wonders to be done' through Paul and Barnabas (14:3). Others may participate in God's healing activity, then, but this does not detract from the more fundamental affirmation that Yahweh is the one doing the healing. Indeed, the phrase so popular in Acts, '*signs and wonders', is woven into the fabric of the OT; there, as in Acts, it signals the actualizing of God's *redemptive purpose on behalf of his *people and testifies to his commanding influence in history (e.g. Exod. 7:3; Deut. 4:34; 7:19; 26:8; 29:3; 34:11; Jer. 32:20–21; Dan. 4:2–3; 6:27; Acts 2:19, 22, 43; 4:30; 5:12; 6:8; 7:36; 8:6, 13; 14:3; 15:12; cf. H. C. Kee, *Medicine, Miracle and Magic in New Testament Times*, p. 11).

Jesus, agent of God's power to heal

The portrait of Jesus as healer is central to the Synoptic Gospels. They contain multiple versions of the same episodes, but include six independent accounts of exorcism and seventeen of healing (including three of resuscitation). Compared with that of such Jewish holy men as Honi the Circle-Drawer and Hanina ben Dosa, Jesus' activity as a healer is distinctive in two ways: 1. the degree to which healing was central to or typical of his ministry, and 2. his unmediated exercise of the saving power of God. He did not ask God to intervene on behalf of the sick, but pronounced healing directly, in speech-acts that assumed his possession of divine authority to do so. He also often emphasized faith in his ministry of healing: so much so, in fact, that one of the characteristic assertions of Jesus was, 'Your faith has made you well.'

Jesus often healed merely by pronouncement, but the Gospel writers also mention his laying on of hands or touching the sick in the context of his healing. This was a boundary-crossing gesture of compassion which reflects the extension of God's own 'hand' which acted in *creation and deliverance in the OT, and so signifies the power of God at work in and through Jesus. That this practice is continued by Jesus' emissaries in Acts identifies them also as instruments of divine power.

According to the Synoptic Gospels, some who recognized Jesus' status as a healer did not see in his work divine credentials. Instead, they attributed his ministry of exorcism to association with Satan. In dialogue with these people, Jesus interprets his exorcisms as a sign of the work of the Spirit in his mission, and as a demonstration of God's kingdom at work among them (Matt. 12:24–33; Mark 3:22–30; Luke 11:14–26). Here, as elsewhere, the healing ministry of Jesus is portrayed as a sign of the inbreaking kingdom of God, as the divine *blessings of salvation come near in the ministry of Jesus. His healing ministry marked the coming of the new aeon, the long-awaited era of salvation (see Luke 4:18–19 [citing Is. 58:6; 61:1–2]; Matt. 8:14–17 [citing Is. 53:4]).

Prophets and other healing agents

Priests, as we have noted, were not healers but served rather as health-care consultants, verifying when a healing had taken place. *Prophets, on the other hand, were sometimes portrayed as agents of healing. *Elijah was instrumental in restoring a widow's son to life (1 Kgs. 17:8–24), and *Elisha told Naaman, commander of the Syrian army, how to be cured of leprosy (2 Kgs. 5:1–14). Interestingly, in Luke 4 Jesus mentions both of these episodes in articulating the nature of his own *mission. In the NT, during the course of Jesus' ministry, his disciples participate in his ministries of healing and exorcism (Mark 6:7–13 par.), and in Acts the ministries of the apostles, as well as those of Stephen, Paul, and Barnabas, are characterized by signs and wonders, including healing. Such healing is performed explicitly in the name of Jesus (e.g. Acts 3:1–10; 9:34; 16:16–18); he has been vindicated as Lord through his exaltation to the right hand of God, and the benefits of salvation are now available through him (see Acts 2:33–36). Both Peter and Paul repudiate any notion that they have power to heal apart from Jesus (Acts 3:12–16; 14:14–15). For Luke, the healing activity of people like Stephen and Peter functions not only to convey the blessings of salvation now available through the risen Lord, but also to prove that they are the Lord's authorized emissaries.

In 1 Corinthians 12, Paul lists gifts of healings and working of miracles as manifestations of the work of the Spirit in the life of the *church. The use of the plural, 'gifts of healings', suggests that each occasion of healing is a manifestation of this gift; no individual permanently possesses the power to heal. In 2 Corinthians, Paul speaks of his having performed 'the signs of an apostle' (12:12; cf.

Rom. 15:18–19; 1 Thess. 1:5), which presumably included healing, but otherwise he is reticent in speaking of such matters autobiographically. His own weakness is an occasion for identifying with the suffering of Jesus and for communicating the power of the gospel (e.g. Gal. 4:13; 2 Cor. 12:7).

James directs those who are sick to call for the elders of the church to pray over them, anointing them with oil in the name of the Lord (5:14–16); almost certainly, 'the Lord' in this directive is 'the Lord Jesus' (see Jas. 1:1; 2:1). James does not assume that illness is necessarily caused by sin, but does allow that sin may be a factor. In any case, sin must be confessed and it will be forgiven; the healing James envisages is complete.

Physicians in the ancient world

Only rarely do physicians appear in the OT. They are typically seen as negative alternatives to Yahweh (e.g. 2 Chr. 16:12; Jer. 8:22 – 9:6) or as people who offer worthless advice (Job 13:4). This is consistent with the biblical portrait of Yahweh as the only God. It is also consistent with the mysteries of the human body and its processes, which led ancient peoples to find hope in magic and/or miracle in cases of disorder. OT faith explicitly excluded magic (or sorcery, the manipulation of the spirits) as a remedy used in preference to divine intervention and care (e.g. Lev. 19:26–28; Deut. 18:10–14; Ezek. 13:17–18).

In the world of the NT, physicians occupy a place sufficiently central to enable Jesus to allude to their activity metaphorically: 'Those who are well have no need for a physician ...' (Mark 2:17 par.). Only the wealthy could afford the care of a trained physician, however, with the result that people in the villages were vulnerable to abuse by charlatans who took what little money they had but provided little by way of a cure. Mark 5:26 is illustrative: 'She had endured much under many physicians, and had spent all that she had; and she was no better, but rather grew worse' (NRSV). This is not to say, however, that wealth could always buy medically competent treatment. Hippocratic treatises on diseases might speak with hostility about 'root-cutters, drug-sellers, and purveyors of amulets, incantations, and charms' (J. C. Vallance, in Oxford Classical Dictionary, p. 945), but even the best physicians understood little of the body's elements and processes. Of course, the Greco-Roman world also supported healing cults and shrines. The goddess Isis, for example, was credited with healing and life-restoring drugs, and her shrines were found throughout the eastern Mediterranean and, indeed, the larger Roman world. Healing was also believed to be available by means of a whole range of magical paraphernalia. Luke records the burning of magical books at Ephesus by former magicians who had become believers (Acts 19:18–19), thus disclosing what must have been the characteristic Christian response to such practices.

Conclusion

From the perspective of biblical theology, the scriptural evidence underlines the identity and role of Yahweh as original giver and restorer of human life. This is true for individuals (whose recovery, however, must be set within the network of their relationships with others and with God), but also for the people of God, who depend upon him for renewal. Within this worldview, Jesus functions first as the authorized agent of Yahweh's healing beneficence, the presence of which in Jesus' ministry signals the presence of God's end-time rule. As exalted Lord, however, Jesus is co-regent with God and dispenses the divine blessings of salvation, including both restored health (for which *prayers are to be offered on behalf of the sick) and the Holy Spirit who enables gifts of healing.

This dual affirmation of Yahweh as healer and Jesus as agent of divine healing leaves little room for human agency, apart from that of those who administer the healing presence of God and those who seek healing for others through prayer. Sorcerers and even physicians are regarded as ineffective in the alleviation of suffering and the restoration of health. This attitude is mitigated only slightly by Paul's reference in Colossians 4:14 to 'Luke, the beloved physician', a favourable reference that portrays Luke as a respected person of some significant medical training and education.

At the start of the 21st century, it is easy to ignore the theological significance of healing as set out in Scripture, and to imagine that our biomedical knowledge is on the verge of rendering obsolete Yahweh's self-disclosure to his people, 'I am your healer'. To do so would be to adopt a myopic perspective indeed, not least by reducing human life and health to

biological processes internal to the body. Such a perspective neglects the fact, underlined repeatedly in Scripture, that healing and health must be conceived in ways that reflect the interconnectedness of the human being with larger human communities and, indeed, with the whole human family, as well as with God and with the whole of creation. Scripture speaks prophetically in the modern world, challenging our limited views of sickness and recovery and calling us to patterns of health in which we are fully alive.

See also: SUFFERING.

Bibliography

H. Avalos, *Health Care and the Rise of Christianity* (Peabody, 1999); R. A. Hahn, *Sickness and Healing: An Anthropological Perspective* (New Haven and London, 1995); H. C. Kee, *Medicine, Miracle and Magic in New Testament Times* (Cambridge, 1986); H. Remus, *Jesus as Healer* (Cambridge, 1997); G. H. Twelftree, *Jesus the Exorcist: A Contribution to the Study of the Historical Jesus* (Tübingen and Peabody, 1993); idem, *Jesus the Miracle Worker: A Historical and Theological Study* (Downers Grove, 1999); J. T. Vallance, 'Medicine', in S. Hornblower and A. Spawforth (eds.), *Oxford Classical Dictionary* (Oxford, ³1996), pp. 945–949.

J. B. GREEN

HEAVEN

The term 'heaven' is used differently in the Bible and in Christian theology. In the Bible it has two main referents: the sky above the earth, and the place where *God dwells. But in theology 'heaven' usually refers to the eternal destiny of Christians, especially when juxtaposed with '*hell'.

The terms translated 'heaven(s)' are *samayim* (Heb.), *s^emayin* (Aramaic) and *ouranos* (Gk.). The former two are always plural, the last sometimes. This Greek plural is peculiar to Jewish and Christian usage and probably derived from the plural Semitic terms, though perhaps also from intertestamental Jewish writings which subdivided the heavens into three, five, seven, or even ten layers (see J. Lunde, in *DJG*, p. 307). The term 'paradise' comes directly from the Greek *paradeisos*, which in turn comes from a

Persian word for 'garden'. It is the Greek term used for the garden of Eden. In inter-testamental literature paradise is often located in heaven (or its third layer, *cf.* Paul's experience in 2 Cor. 12:2).

Physical sky

'In the beginning God made the heavens and the earth' (Gen. 1:1). Frequently 'heaven' refers to the sky, often envisaged as a vast dome or firmament with various lights, windows for rain, and supporting pillars. Heaven and its elements are simply part of God's *creation, neither to be worshipped nor seen as influential over human destiny. While heaven's permanence was proverbial (Deut. 11:21; Ps. 89:29), some prophecy envisaged its vanishing like smoke and God's creating new heavens and earth (Is. 65:17; 66:22).

The NT similarly refers to heaven as the physical sky created by God, realm of birds and clouds, indicator of imminent weather, and theatre of future cataclysm. However, given the NT's heightened eschatological emphasis, there is also greater awareness of heaven's future dissolution (Matt. 5:18; Mark 13:31), destruction (2 Pet. 3:7, 13) and replacement (Rev. 21:1), or alternatively of its liberation (Rom. 8:21, implicitly).

Divine abode

In the OT 'heaven' often refers to the dwelling place of God and his attendant beings. From there God looks down on *humanity, hears their cry and sends *blessing or judgment. In post-exilic literature he is called 'the God of heaven' (Ezra 1:2; Neh. 1:4), or by metonymy simply 'Heaven' (Dan. 4:26).

In the NT also, heaven is the abode of God and his angels. The Son descended from heaven, ascended to it, and will return from it. The *Holy Spirit also descended from heaven at *Jesus' baptism, and at Pentecost (*cf.* 1 Pet. 1:12). As in the OT, 'heaven' often means God himself, hence Matthew's 'kingdom of heaven' and the prodigal son's sin 'against heaven'.

Christian destiny?

The OT has no clear concept of future unimpaired communion with God and perfect harmony with others, though it occasionally glimpses some undefined form of positive afterlife. By contrast, the NT has many refer-ences to such a future life for the followers of Jesus Christ. This life is portrayed variously and evocatively as a celebration banquet (Matt. 8:11; 22:2; 25:10; *cf.* Rev. 19:9), an inheritance (Matt. 25:34), a secure city (Heb. 11:10; 12:22–24), and above all as eternal life.

This future life is traditionally called 'heaven', for several reasons. God dwells in heaven, so those who live with him after death will be in heaven. Jesus spoke of reward or treasure in heaven (Matt. 5:12; 6:20; Mark 10:21), and the apostles echo this in speaking of Christians' unspoiled inheritance there (1 Pet. 1:4; Heb. 10:34 implicitly). The disciples should rejoice that their names are written in heaven (Luke 10:20); later this truth is a source of comfort and encouragement (Heb. 12:23; Rev. 21:27). Paul similarly asserts believers' heavenly citizenship (Phil. 3:20). Jesus went to his Father's house to prepare a place for his disciples, and would take them there (John 14:2–3). On the cross, Jesus assured his dying companion that he would join him immediately in paradise (Luke 23:43). Paul juxtaposes being on earth and being with Christ (2 Cor. 5:6; Phil. 1:23). John's breathtaking vision of God and the lamb enthroned in heaven and worshipped by all (Rev. 4 – 5) is a paradigm of future heavenly *worship.

At the same time, this future life is never called 'heaven' in Scripture, nor is death ever described as 'going to heaven'. Many writers progress immediately from the biblical data to the Christian concept without noting this (*e.g.* Lunde, *DJG*, p. 308). The traditional the-ology is not necessarily incorrect; theological concepts can legitimately be extrapolated from the textual evidence, as with the doc-trine of the Trinity. But the different uses of the term in the Bible and theology should be noted.

New heaven and earth

The OT presents several vistas of a renewed physical, animal and human *world, where all will live together in harmony and bliss (Is. 11:6–9; 65:17–25), and where even death itself may be 'swallowed up' (Is. 25:8; though *cf.* 65:20). This picture of a renewed world is developed in inter-testamental literature and found also in the NT (Matt. 19:28; Rom. 8:21), sometimes in the Isaianic phraseology of 'a new heaven and a new earth' (2 Pet.

3:13; Rev. 21:1). Further, John's final vision presents the new Jerusalem descending *from* heaven so that God may dwell with his people. These texts imply a future life for the people of God not in heaven but on a transformed earth.

Given this perspective and the lack of biblical reference to a heavenly future, some writers argue strongly that the traditional view of heaven is mistaken, and that believers should instead anticipate eternity in a new creation. In particular, N. T. Wright argues: heaven is not a future state but a present reality; *salvation 'kept in heaven' (1 Pet. 1:4) is hidden from present sight, not reserved for future experience; heavenly citizenship (Phil. 3:20) indicates one's ultimate allegiance, not one's future home, like Roman citizenship in Philippi; immediate transfer to Christ's presence is to the intermediate state; and the goal of salvation is the renewal of the cosmos (Rom. 8).

This view implies that Christians should respect the present creation, even though at present it is deeply marred by sin and in the future it will be radically renewed. In any case, whether eternity is envisaged in heaven or on a renewed earth, its essential feature will be the unlimited experience and untarnished worship of God.

The intermediate state

The two OT texts which mention personal resurrection envisage it for those long dead, *i.e.* as a distant prospect (Is. 26:19; Dan. 12:2). This concept became widespread in Judaism, as Martha's reaction at her brother's tomb illustrates (John 11:24). At the same time, some Jewish literature explored the concepts of an intermediate state between death and resurrection, with the inhabitants of Sheol/Hades in different compartments or already in paradise or torment (*cf.* Luke 16:23).

The NT likewise seems to envisage an intermediate state: Christ promised immediate paradise to the crucified criminal; Paul sensed that death was but the door to Christ's presence; Hebrews evokes an unseen cloud of witnesses (Heb. 12:1); and John glimpsed the souls of martyrs longing for vindication (Rev. 6:9–10). This state is one of *rest and peace with God, and is presumably disembodied since it precedes resurrection as a spirit-animated body (1 Cor. 15:44). But no further details of it are given.

Some Christian writers and religious groups (notably Adventists and Jehovah's Witnesses) deny the existence of an intermediate state, and argue instead that there is no moment of consciousness between death and resurrection, due either to 'soul-sleep' or to the dead moving out of human time. Thus the dying thief and Paul will immediately experience resurrection, Hebrews evokes a hall of memory rather than a spectator's gallery, and John's vision is imaginative rather than realistic. This view raises philosophical problems (*cf.* J. W. Cooper) and has often been called heresy. However, it is no different from 'orthodoxy' with respect to the final state of eternal bliss.

See also: DEATH AND RESURRECTION; ESCHATOLOGY; LIFE.

Bibliography

J. W. Cooper, *Body, Soul and Life Everlasting* (Grand Rapids, 1989); L. J. Kreitzer, 'Intermediate State', in *DPL*, pp. 805–812; A. T. Lincoln, *Paradise Now and Not Yet* (Cambridge, 1981); J. Lunde, 'Heaven and Hell', in *DJG*, pp. 307–312; N. T. Wright, *New Heavens, New Earth* (Cambridge, 1999).

P. S. JOHNSTON

HEBREWS, see Part 2

HELL

Hell is a difficult topic. Many Christians would agree with C. S. Lewis: 'There is no doctrine which I would more willingly remove from Christianity' (*The Problem of Pain* [Glasgow 1951], p. 94). And yet, logically and biblically, a gospel of salvation for some means condemnation for others; eternal life for believers implies death for unbelievers; God's presence for the righteous involves his absence from the unrighteous.

Biblical references to hell

In the OT, Sheol, the abode of the dead, is never pictured as a place of punishment, even if it is a fate the righteous wish for their enemies but not for themselves. Later Jewish literature speculated on the fate of the unrighteous, sometimes in different ways within the same book. For instance, the composite *1 Enoch* variously describes the wicked as punished with torment for ever (22:11), as an eternal spectacle for the righteous (27:3), yet *also* destroyed for ever (91:19).

Most NT references to hell are in the Synoptic Gospels, and all those in Mark and Luke are paralleled in Matthew except for the parable in Luke 16:19–31. Two words are translated 'hell'. The first, 'Gehenna' (12 times), comes from the 'valley of Hinnom' (Heb. *ge'hinnom*) near Jerusalem, a notorious site of Israelite idolatry and child sacrifice (2 Kgs. 16:3; 21:6; 23:10; *cf.* Jer. 7:32), where corpses and ashes were thrown (Jer. 31:40), and where Isaiah's concluding vision of rotting and smouldering corpses was probably set (Is. 66:24). This association of fire, *judgment and death led to the NT concept of Gehenna as a place of punishment. The term is almost unique to Jesus, and is used in connection with: insults (Matt. 5:22); causes of sin (5:29–30); 'the Destroyer' (10:28); the Pharisees and their converts (23:15, 33); and the misuse of the tongue (Jas. 3:6). No verse specifies the duration of the punishment. In Mark 9:43–48 the term 'life' for the obedient may imply its opposite, 'death', for the disobedient; conversely the quotation from Isaiah 66 may imply continued existence in hell. In Matthew 10:28 destruction of body and soul may imply cessation of existence.

The other word, 'Hades' (11 times), was the common Greek term for the world of the dead, and was used for 'Sheol' in the Septuagint and other Jewish writings; for example, *1 Enoch* 22 envisages all the dead in Hades in separate compartments. Hades is mentioned with reference to: unbelieving Capernaum (Matt. 11:23); the church's invincibility (Matt. 16:18); the rich man and Lazarus (Luke 16:23); Jesus' resurrection (Acts 2:27, 31, quoting Ps. 16:10); Christian resurrection (1 Cor. 15:55, quoting Hos. 13:14); and supernatural symbolism (Rev. 1:18; 6:8; 20:13–14; here Hades is always paired with 'death'). Matthew 11:23 and Luke 16:23 associate Hades with punishment, and the latter associates it with torment, treating the term as similar in meaning to 'Gehenna' (despite their different origins and usage elsewhere). The duration of the punishment is not specified in these texts, though Revelation 20:14 may portray the end of Hades itself.

Fire is the only feature of hell commonly mentioned in the NT. There are references to it in the Synoptic Gospels, some catholic epistles (Heb. 10:27; 2 Pet. 3:7; Jude 7) and Revelation. Other features are mentioned only occasionally, mostly in Matthew: darkness, weeping and gnashing of teeth.

Other biblical references to the fate of unbelievers

Large parts of the NT present the fate of unbelievers with no direct reference to hell. John's Gospel and letters often contrast eternal life with death and perishing, though they also contain two references to judgment (John 5:29; 1 John 4:17). Acts proclaims salvation with only occasional reference to judgment (Acts 10:42; 24:25). Paul repeatedly refers to the wrath of God, judgment, condemnation, perishing, destruction and death, but hardly ever to what follows judgment (only in 2 Thess. 1:9). And James refers only to destruction and death.

Hell as eternal conscious punishment

The most widely held view throughout Christian history, expounded notably by Tertullian, Augustine, Anselm and Jonathan Edwards, and by many others in the past and present, *e.g.* G. Bray, K. S. Harmon (in N. M. de S. Cameron [ed.]), D. Pawson and R. A. Peterson, is that hell is eternal conscious punishment. Many portray the punishment and torment as physical; others see it as mental or spiritual. The main arguments are: 1. In the NT, fire (Matt. 25:41; Jude 7), punishment (Matt. 25:46), destruction (2 Thess. 1:9), and judgment (Heb. 6:2) are all described as 'eternal', and all associated with hell. In Jesus' parable, eternal punishment parallels eternal life (Matt. 25:46), and 'eternal' must have the same meaning in both phrases. This argument is often seen as conclusive. 2. *Sin against an infinitely glorious God, though committed by finite humans, is infinitely *evil and so deserves infinite punishment. 3. Those in hell continue to sin in refusing to worship God, so they deserve continuous punishment.

Hell as limited conscious punishment

On this view, the unrighteous are resurrected for judgment, confined to hell, and there punished and annihilated. They experience conscious punishment in hell, but for a limited period. This view is often called 'annihilationism' (though annihilation occurs not at death but after resurrection and judgment), 'conditional immortality' (though the word 'immortality' is more commonly used to refer to the eternal life of the righteous), or simply 'conditionalism'.

Until recently, only a small minority of writers have held this view. It was first explicitly defended by Arnobius of Sicca (c. AD 310), though some scholars have detected it earlier, at least in outline. It emerged seriously in English-language theology in the late 19th century and in evangelical theology in the late 20th century, and has recently been defended in detail by E. W. Fudge, J. W. Wenham (in Cameron [ed.]), E. E. Ellis and D. Powys. The main arguments are: 1. The NT frequently speaks of death, perishing and destruction, which imply the end of existence. It also often mentions fire, the main purpose of which is to destroy rather than to cause pain. Thus the effect of hell is eternal, but the process of punishment is not. There is no biblical reference to eternal conscious punishment; in Revelation 14:11 'eternal' refers only to the smoke of the torment of God's enemies, not to the torment itself, and in 20:10 it is the symbols of hostility to God who are tormented for ever. 2. God's justice cannot demand infinite punishment for finite sin. 3. Several NT texts stress the final universal reign of God the Father and/or the Son (1 Cor. 15:28; Eph. 1:10; Phil. 2:10–11; Col. 1:20), and this is hard to reconcile with the continued existence of evil in hell.

These two views appear contradictory; yet both have some biblical support. However, proponents of both use words and images from the present space-time world to portray a destiny which lies beyond it. Yet we now know that space and time are relative, even in the present universe, that time is experienced differently at different velocities, and that visibility is affected by gravity. D. C. Spanner suggests intriguingly that one recently discovered feature of the universe may be illustrative of hell. A spaceship travelling into a black hole would be sucked in and annihilated. Yet an observer would continue to see the ship appear to hover above the horizon of visibility, gradually fading but without definite end. Similarly, hell might be experienced as annihilation but observed as continuing punishment, gradually fading from view.

Conclusion

Finally, it must be stressed that evangelical proponents of both views see hell as real and horrific. On both views the unrighteous realize the enormity of their sin and are aware of their everlasting separation from God. In biblical theology, hell is ultimately the absence of God.

See also: DEATH AND RESURRECTION; ESCHATOLOGY.

Bibliography

ACUTE, *Death, Judgment and Hell* (Carlisle, 2000); G. Bray, 'Hell: eternal punishment or total annihilation?', *Evangel* 10.2, 1992, pp. 19–24; N. M. de S. Cameron (ed.), *Universalism and the Doctrine of Hell* (Carlisle, 1992); E. E. Ellis, 'The New Testament teaching on hell', in K. E. Brower and M. W. Elliott (eds.), *The Reader Must Understand* (Leicester and Downers Grove, 1997); E. W. Fudge, *The Fire That Consumes* (Carlisle, [2]1994); T. Gray, 'Destroyed for ever: an examination of the debates ...', *Them* 21.2, 1996, pp. 14–18; D. Pawson, *The Road to Hell* (London, 1992); R. A. Peterson, 'Does the Bible teach annihilationism?', *BibSac* 156, 1999, pp. 13–27; D. Powys, 'Hell': A Hard Look at a Hard Question (Carlisle, 1997); D. C. Spanner, 'Is hell for ever?', *Churchman* 110.2, 1996, pp. 107–120.

P. S. JOHNSTON

HIGH PRIEST, see PRIESTS
HISTORY OF BIBLICAL THEOLOGY, see Part 1

HOLINESS

Introduction

Throughout Scripture, holiness is pre-eminently a characteristic of *God himself. The terminology is used to signify that God is wholly other, distinct and separate from everything that he has made, and different from the gods of human imagination. As the Holy One, he acts in *judgment against human *sin and its consequences. Remarkably, however, he also chooses to dwell amongst those whom he has redeemed. They are 'sanctified' or made holy by God's manifesting himself to them, drawing them into a special relationship with himself and making provision for their sinfulness. The holy people of God are then called to live in a way that demonstrates the reality of their relationship with God and with one another. A pattern of sanctification is established for *Israel under the Mosaic covenant that foreshadows the definitive work of *Jesus Christ and the operation of the *Holy Spirit for believers under the new *covenant. Indeed, the notion of a holy God among a holy *people in a holy place is 'the enduring eschatological hope of the Scriptures' (G. J. Thomas, in 'The Reader Must Understand', p. 55).

The holiness of God

God is frequently identified in the OT as 'the Holy One' (e.g. Job 6:10; Is. 40:25; 43:15; Hos. 11:9; Hab. 1:12; 3:3; Ezek. 39:7) or 'the Holy One of Israel' (e.g. 2 Kgs. 19:22; Is. 1:4; 43:3; Jer. 50:29; 51:5). Isaiah describes him more completely as 'the high and lofty one who inhabits eternity, whose name is Holy' (Is. 57:15, NRSV), who nevertheless dwells with 'those who are contrite and humble in spirit'. God's name, God's 'arm', God's word and God's spirit are all holy because they belong to him (e.g. Amos 2:7; Is. 52:10; Ps. 105:42; Is. 63:10).

The root meaning of the Hebrew noun 'holiness' (qōdeš) and the adjective 'holy' (qādôš) is hard to determine etymologically. One common suggestion is 'set apart', since the opposite is 'profane' or 'common' (Heb. ḥōl, cf. Lev. 10:10). Fundamentally, however, the terminology is used to connote 'the essential nature that belongs to the sphere of God's being or activity and that is distinct from the common or profane' (J. A. Naude, in NIDOTTE 3, p. 879). God's holiness is particularly associated with his majesty, sovereignty and awesome power (e.g. Exod. 15:11–12; 19:10–25; Is. 6:1–4; cf. Rev. 4:8–11; see *Providence). As the one who is supreme over all, he is transcendent, exalted and different from everything he has made. He cannot be compared with the gods of the nations or be judged by human standards. God alone is holy in himself.

An important dimension to God's separateness and distinctness is his moral purity and perfection. He is presented in the OT as

ethically unique, 'too pure to behold evil' and unable to tolerate wrong (Hab. 1:12–13; cf. Is. 1:4–20; 35:8). He must act with holy justice when his people rebel against him; yet his *love will not allow him to wipe them out. Speaking through Hosea, he explains their restoration in these terms: 'for I am God and no mortal, the Holy One in your midst, and I will not come in wrath' (Hos. 11:9). This means that his love is also 'holy'. God loves with an incomparable and distinctive love.

In the *Exodus from Egypt, the Lord was recognized as being 'majestic in holiness, awesome in splendour, doing wonders' (Exod. 15:11). The Holy One had been encountered in his saving acts and in the *revelation of his *glory associated with those wonderful deeds. At Mt Sinai, the revelation of his holiness made him seem threatening and unapproachable (Exod. 19:10–25; cf. Josh. 24:19; 1 Sam. 6:20). But the giving of the *law was an expression of his mercy and grace and a sign of his intention to dwell among his people (cf. Exod. 29:42–46; Hos. 11:9; Is. 57:15). After the encounter at Sinai, the tabernacle and later the temple were to be the physical means of recognizing and responding to his kingly presence in their midst.

The holiness of Israel

For Israel, holiness was to be found in a relationship with the Holy One. The Lord effectively 'sanctified' Israel, by rescuing them from Egypt, bringing them to himself at Mt Sinai, and giving them his law (Exod. 19:1–6; 20:1–6; cf. 31:13). A common factor in the terms describing Israel's vocation in Exodus 19:5–6 is the note of separation from the nations, so as to be uniquely at God's disposal. As 'a holy nation', they were to demonstrate what it means to live under the direct rule of God, with God's sanctifying presence in their midst. As 'a priestly kingdom', they were to serve the Lord exclusively and thus be a people through whom his character and will might be displayed to the world. In this way, God's original promise to bring blessing to all the nations would be fulfilled (cf. Gen. 12:1–3).

When Israel came to Sinai, Moses was told to consecrate them ritually, to prepare them for a unique encounter with God (Exod. 19:14). The Hebrew verb to 'sanctify', 'consecrate' or 'be holy' (qdš; Gk. *hagiazein*) refers to 'the state of that which belongs to the sphere of the sacred' or 'the transition into/move towards a particular grade of holiness' (Naude, *NIDOTTE* 3, p. 877). The Israelites were already a holy nation because God had drawn them to himself, but at Sinai they were to discover the awesome implications of being in such a relationship with him. Even the *priests were required to 'consecrate themselves', lest he 'break out against them' (Exod. 19:22). The point of these instructions was to teach Israel about God's overpowering holiness. Even 'a holy people' could approach him and relate to him only on the terms that he laid down. A system of mediation was necessary to prevent the Israelites from being destroyed by God's holiness (vv. 22, 24).

After Sinai, the ritual provisions of the covenant were meant to sustain Israel as a holy nation. Elaborate instructions were given for consecrating Aaron and his sons as priests (Exod. 28:3, 41; 29:1, 21, 27; *cf.* Lev. 8). Here the emphasis was on separation, purification and initiation into a distinctive role before God, as representatives of the people. Levites were also set apart 'to do service' for Israel and assist the priests (Num. 8:14–19). Both groups were consecrated to God from within Israel, so that Israel could remain a consecrated people and continue to draw near to God in his holiness.

The tabernacle, and later the temple, represented God's holy presence in the midst of his people and his rule over them. The covenant relationship established by God contained at its heart the assurance that he would be their God and they would be his people (*e.g.* Gen. 17:7–8; Exod. 6:7). Consequently, he would be uniquely with them, to fulfil his purposes and bring blessing to them (*e.g.* Gen. 28:13–15; Exod. 3:7–8). God's sanctifying presence would continue to mark them as a holy people and demand holiness of life in response.

Since the Holy One had brought the Israelites into a special relationship with himself by redeeming them and dwelling amongst them, the fundamental demand of the levitical code was 'You shall be holy, for I am holy' (Lev. 11:44–45; 19:2; 20:7, 26). By keeping his ritual, moral and social laws, the people of Israel would not profane his holy name before the nations. Rather, they would demonstrate God's virtues and the benefit of being 'a people holy to the LORD ... chosen out of all the peoples on earth to be his people, his treasured possesion' (Deut. 14:2). Pollution and sin were to be avoided in every area of life, and there was to be a complete break with every form of *idolatry and false religion. Separation from the nations and consecration to God were two different facets of Israel's exclusive relationship with the Lord. When transgression occurred, rites of purification were available for the restoration of 'cleanness' and holiness.

There are different ideals of holiness in the OT. 'For the prophets it was a cleanness of social justice, for the priests a cleanness of proper ritual and maintenance of separation, for the sages it was a cleanness of inner integrity and individual moral acts' (J. G. Gammie, *Holiness in Israel*, p. 196). Nevertheless, in various parts of the canon these ideals are blended into a unified demand for purity before God. This is expressed in different ways, according to the context. But the common element is an awareness of God's initiative in making himself known as the Holy One, taking possession of Israel as his own, and requiring his people to live in the light of his self-revelation in their midst.

The fulfilment of God's sanctifying purpose

In the face of Israel's failure to live out the implications of her calling, the prophets reveal God's intention to act in judgment. So, for example, Isaiah has a vision of the holiness of God and confesses that there is no hope for him or for rebellious Israel in the presence of such a God (Is. 6:1–5). With a burning coal from the altar of incense, however, a seraph expresses God's extraordinary mercy: 'now that this has touched your lips, your guilt has departed and your sin is blotted out' (vv. 6–7). The paradox of holiness is that God acts to judge everything that is unholy and yet provides a way of cleansing and sanctification for sinners. Even beyond terrible devastation and destruction, God's purpose for his people would continue. The cleansing and preservation of the prophet himself anticipated the *salvation of a remnant, identified here as 'the holy seed' (v. 13). God's 'offspring' would be holy because of his actions on their behalf.

This last point emerges most powerfully in

Ezekiel's prophecy about the return of the exiled Israelites from Babylon to *Jerusalem. God promises to sanctify himself or manifest his holiness among them in the sight of the nations, by rescuing them and restoring them (Ezek. 20:41; 28:22, 25). God had to sanctify his great name in this way because it had been profaned among the nations by his people and he wished the nations to know that he is the Lord (36:23). Ezekiel goes on to indicate that this revelation of God's holiness will involve the restoration of his covenant with Israel, the re-establishment of Davidic *kingship and the setting up of his sanctuary or dwelling place among them for evermore (37:24–28). The promise of cleansing and spiritual renewal that is given in Ezekiel 36:25–27 is paralleled in Jeremiah's prediction of a new or renewed covenant (Jer. 31:31–34).

Sanctification in Christ

Just as Israel was made holy by God's saving activity in the time of Moses, and again in the restoration after the Babylonian *exile, so sanctification in the NT is an integral part of the redemptive work of Jesus Christ. It is regularly portrayed as a once-for-all, definitive act and is primarily to do with the holy status or position of those who are 'in Christ'. This sanctifying work of God becomes the basis for an appeal to lead holy lives and to anticipate the ultimate experience of sanctification in the new creation.

Sanctification according to John's Gospel

Jesus uses the language of sanctification in connection with his role as the Son sent by the Father to be the saviour of his people (John. 10:36; 17:19; Gk. hagiazein). When he claims to sanctify or set himself apart 'for their sakes' (Gk. hyper autōn), the language recalls *atonement passages elsewhere in the NT (e.g. Mark 14:24; Luke 22:19; John 6:51; 1 Cor. 11:24). Jesus dedicates himself to become a *sacrifice for sins. As 'the Lamb of God who takes away the sin of the world' (John 1:29, 36) and as 'the good shepherd', who 'lays down his life for the sheep' (10:11, 17–18), the Messiah must die to deliver Israel from God's judgment and to make it possible for believers to be drawn together to God from every *nation (11:49–53; 12:20–33). Disciples are separated from the *world and from 'the *evil one' (17:15–16), by being

consecrated in 'the *truth' that Christ proclaims and lives out (17:17). By this means they are liberated to bring blessing to the world as the agents of Christ (17:18), thus fulfilling the Abrahamic promise. Jesus' prayer for his followers is that they might be kept from being overwhelmed by the world and its values, so that they might be devoted or 'sanctified' to the Father and his values (vv. 17–19). Witness and mission are the goal of sanctification in John 17.

Sanctification according to Hebrews

Hebrews 10:5–10 indicates that, when Christ came into the world, he took upon himself the task of fulfilling the plan of God described in Psalm 40:6–8. In the body that was 'prepared' for him, the Son of God lived a life of perfect obedience to the Father, culminating in his death as an unblemished sacrifice for sins (cf. 4:15; 7:26–27; 9:14). He came to set aside the ancient sacrificial system by expressing the *obedience which was always the intention behind the rituals. His complete self-consecration to God brought about his death, making possible a consecration of God's people in a new way. Hebrews proclaims that by the will of the Father, revealed in Scripture and carried out by the Son, 'we have been sanctified through the offering of the body of Jesus Christ once for all' (10:10). The Greek periphrastic perfect here (hēgiasmenoi esmen) points to a state or condition made possible by the self-offering of Christ in death. No further sacrifices or rituals are required to keep people in that sanctified condition. The preceding context suggests that this involves a once-for-all cleansing from sin that the law of Moses could not provide (10:1–4). As in OT teaching, purification and sanctification are closely related (cf. 9:13–14): purification is the basis of sanctification. By his sovereign action in Christ, God sets apart and binds to himself those who have been purified from the defilement of sin. This objective, consecrating work of God has profound implications for the attitude and behaviour of those who believe (cf. comment on 9:14 below).

Hebrews 10:10–18 suggests that the verb 'to sanctify' is employed primarily in a covenantal sense. Christ's sacrifice binds men and women to God in a new relationship of heart-obedience, fulfilling the promise of Jeremiah 31:31–34. The covenantal dimension is highlighted again in verse 29, where it is said that the readers were sanctified by 'the blood of the covenant'. The writer recalls the language of Exodus 24:1–8; the relationship between God and Israel was confirmed as Moses poured 'the blood of the covenant' on the altar and on the representatives of the people gathered with him on Mt. Sinai. Hebrews 9:18–21 actually speaks about the first covenant's being 'inaugurated' by Moses on this occasion. By implication, the new covenant was inaugurated by the shedding of Jesus' blood (cf. 13:12).

The sanctifying work of Christ in Hebrews has inward as well as outward aspects. His saving work brings about a cleansing of the conscience 'from dead works to serve the living God' (9:14; cf. 10:22). When the message about his completed and eternally effective work is applied to the heart or conscience of believers, it brings about an inner conviction of forgiveness, acceptance and hope. A life of dedicated service or worship results. Consecration as a human response is made possible by God's initiative through his Son, cleansing people and consecrating them to himself for eternity.

Sanctification according to Paul

Paul addresses the Corinthians as 'those who are sanctified in Christ Jesus' (1 Cor. 1:2). They were a holy and distinct people in that corrupt and godless city because of God's initiative, drawing them into an exclusive relationship with himself. Here the perfect passive participle 'sanctified' (Gk. *hēgiasmenois*) should be understood as another way of speaking about conversion and incorporation into Christ. It can hardly refer to holiness of character or conduct, since Paul spends much time in this letter challenging the Corinthians' values and behaviour, calling them to holiness in an ethical sense. He does this on the basis that they are already sanctified in a relational sense, but need to express that sanctification in lifestyle.

The apostle also reminds the Corinthians that they were 'called to be saints' (Gk. *klētois hagiois*). The designation 'holy ones' or 'saints' is a shorthand way of referring to those who have been sanctified in Christ. The term has its origin in OT descriptions of Israel as 'a holy nation' or 'holy people'. It was later used more narrowly to describe the elect in Israel who would share in the blessings of the messianic kingdom (*e.g.* Dan. 7:18–27; *Psalms of Solomon* 17; Qumran). 'Saints' becomes Paul's regular way of describing Christians in general (*e.g.* Rom. 1:7; 8:27; 2 Cor. 1:1; Eph. 1:1; Phil 1:1; Col. 1:2), though he sometimes uses the term to refer more specifically to the believers in Judea (*e.g.* Rom. 15:25–26, 31; 1 Cor. 16:1; 2 Cor. 8:4; 9:1, 12). It was peculiarly applicable to the primitive Jewish church, whom God had preserved and sanctified to be the channel of his light and life for the whole world. As the first Jewish believers received the *gospel and proclaimed it to the nations, Gentiles were brought to share in the inheritance of 'the saints' (*cf.* Col. 1:12; Eph. 2:17–22).

The theme of sanctification emerges again in 1 Corinthians 1:30, where Paul writes that Jesus became for us 'wisdom from God, and *righteousness and sanctification and redemption'. Here the noun 'sanctification' (Gk. *hagiasmos*) is used as one of three metaphors to explain how God has made Jesus the *wisdom that leads to eternal salvation. This text is not describing a sequence by which God justifies, sanctifies, then redeems. Rather, it draws on three different but related strands of OT thought to describe the same reality, namely believers' status or standing with God through Jesus Christ.

1 Corinthians 6:11 similarly affirms, 'you were washed, you were sanctified, you were justified in the name of the Lord Jesus Christ and in the Spirit of our God'. Again, three metaphors are used to explain the benefits of Christ's saving work. Paul's overall meaning is this: 'Your own conversion, effected by God through the work of Christ and the Spirit, is what has removed you from being amongst the wicked, who will not inherit the kingdom …Therefore, live out this new life in Christ and stop being like the wicked' (G. D. Fee, *The First Epistle to the Corinthians* [Grand Rapids, 1987], p. 245). A profound change of attitude and behaviour on the part of the Corinthians is acknowledged in the context (6:9–11). But the language of sanctification here refers quite specifically to the separation from a godless lifestyle that has come about by their being attached to the Father through the redemptive work of the Son. Christ is the source of everything they obtain, which is communicated to them by the Spirit, who is God's sanctifying presence

amongst the people of the new covenant.

The Holy Spirit not only brings the benefits of Christ's saving death to bear on the lives of believers at conversion but also effectively empowers them for holy living. Other NT passages which suggest that the sanctifying work of Christ is applied through the ministry of the *word/gospel and the operation of the Holy Spirit include 2 Thessalonians 2:13–14, Ephesians 5:25–27, Romans 15:16, Acts 20:32 and 1 Peter 1:2.

Pursuing holiness

Divine discipline

Hebrews 12:3–11 speaks of God's fatherly care for his children. He *disciplines us 'for our good, in order that we may share his holiness' (v. 10b; Gk. *tēs hagiotētos autou*). This rare term for holiness here denotes the sanctity of God's character and life. To share God's holiness is to enjoy life in his presence (*cf.* 12:9) and to be transformed into his likeness (*cf.* 1 John 3:2). It is to be brought 'to glory' through Christ in the age to come (Heb. 2:10), and even now, by *faith, to experience some of the blessings of that age in anticipation (*cf.* 6:4–5; 12:22–24). So Hebrews 12:9–10 suggests that as believers learn to submit to God's will in *suffering, something of his holiness is reflected in their lives. They learn to acknowledge him as the Holy One, who is supreme over all, perfectly loving, wise and righteous. At the same time, he moulds and shapes them into the kind of people he wants them to be. Trials of various kinds are necessary for the formation of godly character (*cf.* Rom. 5:3–5; Jas. 1:2–4; 1 Pet. 1:6–9). But they are also necessary to keep Christians firm and faithful to the end, when by God's grace they will fully share his holiness. God 'exercises' or 'trains' his people in the present (Heb. 12:11), to produce in them the signs of a transformed and sanctified life.

Holiness as a goal of Christian living

The exhortation in Hebrews 12:14, to 'pursue peace with everyone, and the holiness without which no one will see the Lord', picks up the note of 'peace' from verse 11 and the challenge of verses 12–13 to move *together* in the direction set by God. This prepares for the warning in verses 15–17 to care for any member of the church who may be in danger

of committing apostasy. Although a different Greek word is used in verse 14 (*ton hagiasmon*), the note of 'holiness' from verse 10 is also picked up. The wonderful prospect of seeing God, which is equivalent to living in his presence, is highlighted. This motif is elaborated in verses 18–24, as the basis for a final challenge not to forfeit the grace of God and the blessings of the coming kingdom (vv. 25–29). Christians are to seek holiness as a practical expression of their sanctification in Christ, at the same time remembering the promise that God is disciplining his children so that they might 'share his holiness'. Hebrews 13 illustrates some of the dimensions of a holy or consecrated lifestyle.

Abounding in holiness

Paul's prayer in 1 Thessalonians 3:12–13 indicates that abounding in love is the means by which believers' hearts are, literally, 'established blameless in holiness before our God and Father, at the coming of our Lord Jesus with all his saints' (v. 13). God must fortify them with love at the very centre of their being if they are to stand before him on the day of judgment 'blameless in holiness'. The word for holiness here (*hagiōsynē*) is used on only two other occasions in the NT (Rom. 1:4; 2 Cor. 7:1), though the related noun *hagiotēs* in Hebrews 12:10 is doubtless a synonym. Both terms refer to *a quality of life and character* arising from a relationship with the Holy One. The goal of those who are consecrated to God through the saving work of Christ and the ministry of the Holy Spirit can be nothing less than blamelessness in word and action (*cf.* Phil. 2:15). God himself is pure and blameless and he desires his children to reflect his character. Since the Spirit brings believers together into a dedicated and distinctive relationship with the Father, love for one another in the *family of God will be a vital expression of true holiness. Moreover, love for those outside the Christian community will be a powerful revelation of the character of God to an unbelieving world.

Love and holiness are two related aspects of the Christian life. Holiness will be pre-eminently expressed in love and love will be the essential means by which holiness is maintained. In effect, holiness abounds when love abounds. But there is no suggestion that a second 'crisis of faith' can immediately perfect people's love or bring them to a new level of spirituality where practical holiness becomes more attainable.

Holiness, love and sexuality

1 Thessalonians 4:1–8 emphasizes that holiness must be exhibited in the sexual realm. 'Chastity is not the whole of sanctification, but it is an important element in it, and one which had to be specially stressed in the Greco-Roman world of that day' (F. F. Bruce, *1 and 2 Thessalonians*, WBC [Waco, 1982], p. 82). In our world too, it is radical to claim that holiness must be expressed by abstaining from 'fornication' (v. 3). Paul explains what he means by this in verses 4–7, where it appears that any form of sexual relationship outside marriage is covered by the Greek term *porneia*. If our bodies belong to the Lord, we are no longer free to use them selfishly or in accordance with the accepted values of the time (*cf.* 1 Cor. 6:12–20).

Some have argued that the apostle introduces a new subject in verse 6, warning against the exploitation of a 'brother' in the field of commerce. It is certainly critical to see God's call for holiness as extending to every sphere of life, where covetousness tempts everyone to defraud or manipulate others. There are no compelling reasons, however, to conclude that Paul moves away from sexual matters in this verse. Indeed, the mention of 'impurity' in verse 7 confirms that the subject of the preceding verse is sexual rather than commercial behaviour. Paul warns against the *social consequences* of sexual indulgence in verse 6. Christians must beware of trespassing against others by behaving covetously. By crossing forbidden sexual boundaries, they enrich themselves at someone else's expense. The Lord Jesus himself is 'an avenger in all these things' and will inflict the appropriate judgment on those who disregard his will (v. 6b; *cf.* 2 Thess. 1:6–10). The flow of the argument in verses 6–7 suggests that the coming judgment and God's initial calling of believers 'in holiness' are to be the ground and motivation for holy living. God did not call them 'for impurity' but, by setting them apart for himself, he indicated his desire for them to live differently, as those who belong to him. The strength to do this is experienced by those who know that they are loved and possessed by God's Spirit (v. 8; *cf.* Gal. 5:16–24).

Entire sanctification

Paul's wish-prayer in 1 Thessalonians 5:23, like the one in 3:11–13, is oriented towards the return of Christ (see *Eschatology) and has as its object the condition of believers at that decisive time. God is addressed as the source of harmony and wholeness and asked to sanctify his readers 'entirely' (Gk. *holoteleis*). The apostle desires that 'spirit and soul and body' may be ready to stand in the presence of God ('kept sound and blameless at the coming of our Lord Jesus Christ'), and he assures his readers that 'the one who calls you is faithful, and he will do this' (v. 24). 'Entire sanctification' is not a crisis moment in the process of Christian maturation, as some have proposed. The Greek aorist (*hagiasai*) is used in a summary way here, as Paul asks for the complete expression in his readers' lives of what it means to be the holy people of God. Sanctification is not a second work of grace, though it clearly has a present and a future aspect. Paul speaks about the consummation of God's sanctifying work in a way that anticipates his later teaching about glorification (*cf.* Rom. 8:17, 29–30; 2 Cor. 3:18).

See also: TEMPLE.

Bibliography

G. C. Berkouwer, *Faith and Sanctification* (Grand Rapids, 1952); M. E. Dieter, A. A. Hoekema, S. M. Horton, J. Robertson McQuilkin and S. F. Walvoord, *Five Views on Sanctification* (Grand Rapids, 1987); J. G. Gammie, *Holiness in Israel* (Minneapolis, 1989); J. A. Naude in *NIDOTTE* 3, pp. 877–887; J. I. Packer, *Keep in Step with the Spirit* (Old Tappan and Leicester, 1984); D. G. Peterson, *Possessed by God: A New Testament Theology of Sanctification and Holiness* (Leicester and Grand Rapids, 1996); G. J. Thomas, 'A holy God among a holy people in a holy place: the enduring eschatological hope', in K. E. Brower and M. W. Elliott (ed.), *'The Reader Must Understand': Eschatology in Bible and Theology* (Leicester and Downers Grove, 1997), pp. 53–69.

D. G. PETERSON

HOLY SPIRIT

In the OT

Introduction

The OT uses the term 'Holy Spirit' (*rûaḥ qādoš*) only three times (Ps. 51:11; Is. 63:10–11; in contrast there are some 90 instances in the NT). More usually, divine Spirit is denoted by such expressions as 'Spirit of God/the LORD', 'my/his Spirit', *etc.*

The word *rûaḥ* itself perhaps originally denoted air in movement, but by the time of the earliest OT writings it carries a variety of senses, including: a. wind; b. breath (including the 'breath of life' [Gen. 6:17; *cf.* Job 12:10; Is. 42:5, *etc.*]); c. human vitality (as in, *e.g.*, 1 Sam. 30:12), mood/emotion, inclination, or character; as in, *e.g.*, a 'grief of spirit' (Gen. 26:35), 'spirit of adultery' (Hos. 4:12); d. mind, inner being (Is. 40:13; Ezek. 11:5; 20:32, *etc.*). Common connotations include 'energy' and 'invisibility'; hence the metaphoric extension of *rûaḥ* to denote, e. *God's* activity, or the extension of his vitality, in *creation and among humankind (like the 'arm/hand of the Lord').

Broadly speaking, God's *rûaḥ* is represented: 1. as God's power in the creation of the cosmos (Gen. 1:2; Ps. 33:6, *etc.*); 2. as God's sustaining power immanent in *all* *life (Gen. 6:17; 7:15; Job 33:4; Ps. 104:29–30, *etc.*); 3. as the invisible activity of God in power through and amongst his *covenant people, whether in dramatic irruptions or more sustained endowments; and 4. as his presence in many types of *revelation, charismatic *wisdom and invasive speech.

Of these, 1. and 2. are only ambiguously related to 'Holy Spirit', for in these cases *rûaḥ* may denote (variously) 'wind' (Gen. 1:2), the breath used in issuing the creative command (Ps. 33:6), the 'breath of life' (Gen. 6:17), or some combination of these; however, the LXX and most Jewish intertestamental literature tend to interpret such references as being to 'the Spirit' (*cf. Judith* 16:14; Wisdom of Solomon 1:7; *Apocalypse of Moses* 43:4; *2 Esdras* 6:38–41; *2 Baruch* 21:4, 23:5; Philo, *etc.*). In contrast, unambiguous examples of God's Spirit as 3., 4., and combinations of the two, are numerous. Typically they refer to God's *covenantal* activities *in and on behalf of *Israel* (only very exceptionally is the Spirit

conceived as active outside Israel, and even then for her benefit: *cf.* Num. 24:2 and possibly Is. 45:1).

The Spirit in Israel's experience

The Spirit may come as God's apparently impersonal power to seize and transport a *prophet (1 Kgs. 18:12; 2 Kgs. 2:16; Ezek. 2:2; 3:12, 14; 8:3; 11:1, *etc.*), or to provide blatantly supernatural force for overcoming dangers/enemies (*e.g.* to Samson in Judg. 14:6, 19; 15:14–15), or more generally to enable strong rule / military might in Israel at times of crisis (Judg. 3:10; 6:34; 11:29, *etc.*).

Working in a more personal way, the Spirit of the Lord is an endowment for *Moses (Num. 11:17, 29) and Joshua (Num. 27:18), through which they liberate Israel and lead the people at God's direction (*cf.* Num. 11:25–29). The same endowment for the seventy elders (Num. 11:25–29) also gives them wisdom (with Moses) to resolve Israel's disputes (*cf.* Neh. 9:20). God's Spirit similarly gives special wisdom to the craftsmen who make the tabernacle and its furnishings (Exod. 28:3; 31:3; 35:31). Later, the Spirit is perceived to effect God's righteous rule through her kings, such as Saul in 1 Samuel 10:1–11 and notably through *David from 1 Samuel 16:13 onwards (*cf.* Zech. 4:6).

In the majority of OT incidents involving the Spirit, the Spirit acts as the channel of communication between God and a human person. In this role, the Spirit was understood in Judaism to be the 'Spirit of prophecy'. That is, the Spirit was considered to make God's will and wisdom known to his people, especially through the phenomenon of oracular speech called 'prophecy', in which a message of the Lord was granted by the Spirit in a dream, vision or word. This view of the Spirit can be traced from early prophecy (as in Num. 11:25–29; 24:2; 1 Sam. 10:10; 19:20) into classical prophecy and beyond (*cf.* Mic. 3:8; Hos. 9:7; Is. 48:16; 61:1–3; Ezek. 11:5–25; Zech. 7:12, *etc.*).

The Spirit in Israel's hope

In contrast to the past, when Spirit-endowment appeared to be restricted to *leaders and prophets, a future is awaited in which *all* Israel will share in the Spirit of prophecy (Joel 2:28; *cf.* Num. 11:29). At the heart of the hoped-for new covenant lies universal and immediate knowledge of God;

each will 'know the Lord' for himself or herself (Jer. 31:34). Israel thus awaits a epoch of 'new *Exodus' *salvation characterized by the lavish outpouring of God's Spirit (as in Is. 32:15; 44:3; Ezek. 39:29) and by the revelation of his *glory and power (Hab 2:14). As the self-manifesting, transforming presence of God amongst his people, the Spirit is expected to accomplish deep existential renewal that recreates the very heart of humankind in obedience (Jer. 31:31–40; Ezek. 36:24–29; cf. Ps. 51:10–14; Is. 44:3–5). In some expressions of this *hope, it is to be fulfilled in part through a righteous prophetic liberator (Deut. 18:15; Is. 42:61) and king endowed with the Spirit of wisdom and power (Is. 11:1–9).

The Spirit in the Synoptic Gospels and Acts

In the Gospels

With the exception of two references to speaking by the Spirit (David in Mark 12:36; par. Matt. 22:43; the disciples in Mark 13:11; par. Matt. 10:20; Luke 12:12), all the references to the Spirit in Mark (total = 6) and Matthew (total = 12) relate to *Jesus and his work. With approximately twenty references to the Spirit in his Gospel (and a further sixty in Acts), Luke is the Synoptic writer with the greatest interest in the Spirit, and his teaching is Christocentric. Other pious figures experience the Spirit of prophecy in revelation and inspired speech (in Luke 1 – 3), but only as those who await the messianic salvation and recognize or testify to its inauguration in Jesus (so Zechariah, 1:67; Simeon, 2:25–27; John the Baptist, 1:15, 17 [80?]).

The portrait of Jesus and the Spirit in the Gospels functions primarily to confirm to readers that Jesus is indeed the Messiah anticipated by the OT (see above) and inter-testamental Jewish writings. The latter tended to draw especially on Isaiah 11:1–4 in their anticipation of a ruler endowed with the Spirit of prophecy, and so with revelation, wisdom, redoubtable *righteousness and power to cleanse Israel (see esp. 1 Enoch 49:2–3, 62:1–2; Psalms of Solomon 17:37; 18:7; Rule of the Blessings 5:24–25, [4Q] Testament of Naphtali, etc.). The same picture probably informs the Baptist's promise that the coming one will baptize (= cleanse/purify) with Holy Spirit and fire (Matt. 3:11; par. Luke 3:16); the following verse sets this baptism in the context of the cleansing restoration of Israel.

Another vital aspect of the Synoptic portrait, however, draws on the great Isaianic 'new Exodus' themes. It is these that explain the main features of the prelude to Jesus' ministry. 1. *John the Baptist chooses the wilderness as his location and Isaiah 40:3 (a key new-Exodus chapter) as his prime explanatory text (Mark 1:2–3; par. Matt. 3:2–3; Luke 3:4; John 1:23). 2. The Spirit descends upon Jesus at his baptism and is interpreted by a heavenly voice in terms of the anointing of the Servant of Isaiah 42:1–2 (Mark 1:11; par. Matt. 3:17; Luke 3:22). 3. Jesus is led by the Spirit in the wilderness (cf. esp. Luke 4:1) in a replay of the temptations that faced Israel in the exodus-wilderness traditions of Deuteronomy 6 – 8. 4. Having overcome, he returns in the power of the Spirit (Luke 4:14), and in the programmatic sermon of Luke 4:16–30, he announces himself as the Spirited-anointed liberator, proclaiming the 'good news' of Isaiah 61:1–2. In the Isaianic context the essence of this good news is the *forgiveness of Israel's sins, the end of her historical chastisement, and the joyful proclamation to Zion that, with the return of Yahweh to them, their God reigns, and the nations will see the salvation he works in and from Jerusalem (cf. e.g. Is. 52:7–10; 40:1–11; 44:1–8; 49:6, etc.). It is mainly these ideas that inform the preaching of the forgiveness of sins, and the announcement of the *kingdom of God, by the Baptist and especially by Jesus. Luke has already expressed the same set of hopes in the prophecies of Zechariah (Luke 1:68–79), Mary (1:46–55) and Simeon (2:29–32), and in his designation of the Spirit in the conception of Jesus as 'the power of the most High' (Luke 1:35, evoking Is. 32:15–20 with its promise that Israel would be restored when God's Spirit was 'poured out on us from on high'; and see below on Acts 1:8).

Outside their introductions, the Synoptic Gospels have surprisingly little to say about the Spirit. Both Mark and Q (the non-Markan source shared by Matt. and Luke) include a tradition which warns that 'blasphemy against the Spirit' is unforgivable (Mark 3:28–29; Matt. 12:31–37; Luke 12:10). The immediate Markan and Matthean contexts suggest that this blasphemy consists in an absolute resistance to the idea that it is God at work through Jesus, which leads, in this instance, to his opponents attributing his exorcisms to demonic powers instead. It is implicit in Mark that Jesus works rather by the power of the Spirit. Such a view is made explicit in Q ('If I by the Spirit of God cast out demons, the kingdom of God has come upon you'; Matt. 12:28), and Matthew too clearly attributes Jesus' *healing miracles to the Spirit (cf. Matt. 12:15–18). Such a view is sometimes denied to Luke, on the grounds that he understands the Spirit as 'the Spirit of prophecy', and so cannot attribute to the Spirit either 'works of power' or 'ethical effects' (so, esp., E. Schweizer and R. P. Menzies). But this argument reflects a misunderstanding of what Jews meant by the Spirit of prophecy, especially in relation to messianic figures like the Branch of Isaiah 11:1–4, and it misrepresents Luke (see M. Turner, *Power From On High*). At the very beginning of his Gospel, the Spirit is portrayed as the creative power of God that miraculously brings about the conception of the 'holy' Son of God (1:35; cf. also Matt. 1:18, 20). The 'power of the Spirit', in which Jesus returns from the wilderness (4:14), enables both his proclamation and his mighty acts. The same double perspective is maintained in Luke 4:16–21, and in the account of its dramatized fulfilment in Luke 7:21–22 (cf. also Acts 10:38). Luke understands Jesus' exorcisms and healings as examples of God's new-Exodus, liberating reign which Jesus is anointed by the Spirit not merely to proclaim, but also to enact.

The Synoptic evangelists show little interest in what the Spirit meant for Jesus' interior life before God; they are concerned only with what the Spirit accomplished through him. Thus even Luke, who includes a reference to Jesus 'rejoicing' in the Spirit (10:21), and perhaps depicts the Spirit providing Jesus with the charismatic wisdom that enables him to defeat Satan in the wilderness (cf. 4:1), nevertheless does not explain how the Spirit relates to Jesus' experience of sonship. Did the Spirit leave Mary and Jesus after the event mentioned in 1:35? Or is the wisdom /understanding of the messianic son in 2:47, 49–51, 52 to be understood as an ongoing 'fullness' and 'growth' in the Spirit, like John the Baptist's (cf. 1:15, 80)? How does this experience of the Spirit, if such it is, relate to Jesus' baptismal experience of the Spirit (3:21–22)? And how much of this is paradigmatic for the experience of disciples after Easter? Matthew and Mark are almost silent about the disciples' experience of the Spirit; they mention only the Baptist's promise, and an assurance of the Spirit's guidance in times of trial (Mark 13:11; Matt. 10:20; Luke 12:12). Luke's Gospel offers further hints (24:49, and, perhaps 11:13), but not until Acts is the experience described in any detail. The Synoptic evangelists are more concerned to demonstrate that Jesus fits Judaism's identikit picture of the Messiah of the Spirit than they are to explore such interesting theological questions.

In Acts

Nothing could be clearer than that the gift of the Spirit in Acts is what we have called the 'Spirit of prophecy'. Not only does Peter interpret the Pentecost gift in terms of Joel 2:28–32 (Acts 2:17–18, redactionally emphasizing prophecy in 18b), but also nearly all subsequent references to the Spirit in Acts are related to the prototypical gifts of the Spirit of prophecy, namely charismatic revelation (whether in visions, dreams, words, or a mixture of these), charismatic wisdom (sometimes evoking *joy), immediately inspired speech of different kinds, and acts of power (8:39; 10:38). These statements, and the key transitional references to the Spirit as 'power from on high' in Luke 24:49 and Acts 1:8, have led some (e.g. Schweizer, Stronstad, Menzies, Penney) to conclude that for Luke the Spirit is *essentially* an empowering for *mission, and nothing else. It is a *donum superadditum* (second blessing) given to the community *subsequent* to their experience of salvation.

Closer inspection of the text, however, suggests that Luke has a broader soteriological and ecclesiological view of the Spirit of prophecy promised to all (2:38–39).

1. The Baptist's promise, invoked in the form 'you will be baptized with Holy Spirit' in Acts 1:5 and 11:16, refers not primarily to empowerment for mission, but to the restoration/cleansing of the messianic people of God (cf. the parallel between 11:16 and 15:8–9). This interpretation is confirmed by the clear allusion to Isaiah 32:15 in Acts 1:8.

2. For Luke, 'salvation' is not merely 'justification', but also participation with the Israel-of-fulfilment in the presence of the

kingdom of God and of its transformative power, which *results* from the 'forgiveness of sins'. During Jesus' ministry, this was partially experienced, but only through the Spirit bestowed on the Messiah. His removal through death, resurrection and ascension might thus be expected to bring to a close any experience of the kingdom of God before the parousia (so Conzelmann). However, the Gospel of Luke (and the opening paragraph of Acts) anticipates, instead, a *fuller* experience of God's reign/salvation, consequent on Jesus' enthronement. In this respect, the *exaltation of Jesus described in Acts 2:33–36 fulfils the hopes expressed in Luke 1:32–33 and elsewhere. But it is precisely through the gift of the Spirit that this salvation is poured out; only through the Spirit can the people of Jesus continue to experience his ongoing messianic/transformative reign (and hence the Holy Spirit is now called 'the Spirit of Jesus'; *cf*. Acts 16:7).

3. If Jesus' death fulfils the Passover and looks forward to the new covenant (Luke 22:14–20), Pentecost is portrayed as the fulfilment of Sinai (Acts 2), including a corresponding ascent on high of Israel's leader to receive a foundational gift for the people of God.

4. Given the above, the new, radical and paradisal community life depicted as the immediate consequence of Pentecost (2:42–47 and *cf*. 4:32–35) should almost certainly be interpreted as a result of the *church's reception of the Spirit (*pace* Schweizer *et al*.). This is confirmed in Acts 5, where the sin of Ananias and Sapphira against the community is described as 'putting the Spirit to the test' (5:9), *i.e*. rejecting what the Spirit is leading the community to do.

5. For Luke (as J. D. G. Dunn showed in *Baptism*), conversion-initiation normally involves *repentance and belief (see *Faith, faithfulness), crystallized in submission to *baptism, and reception of the Spirit. Acts 2:38–39 is thus paradigmatic (though the order of the elements may vary according to circumstances; thus, *e.g*., it is the Gentile Cornelius' evident reception of the Spirit that justifies his baptism and that of his household). This close connection with conversion-initiation suggests that the gift of the Spirit is fundamental to Christian life, not merely empowering for mission (indeed, with the exception of Paul, converts are not depicted as being immediately involved in mission). The apparent exceptions, if anything, prove the rule. a. The Samaritans (the first converts outside Judaism) in Acts 8 do not receive the Spirit until some days after their repentance and baptism, when the apostles come from Jerusalem. But if Luke and his readers considered such a delay as 'normal', he would not have needed the cumbersome 'explanation' in 8:16. b. Saul certainly comes to belief on the Damascus Road before he receives the Spirit at the hands of Ananias (9:17), but from a Lukan perspective he is not a member of the Messiah's *ekklēsia* until he responds to the vision with formal repentance and baptism, also at the hands of Ananias (*cf*. 22:16), and the assumption is that he is filled with the Spirit in the latter context. c. In 19:1–7 Paul encounters a group of 'disciples' awaiting the Messiah and he initially assumes them to be Christians (like Apollos in 18:24–28). Unlike Apollos, however, they have not even heard of the Spirit; so Paul asks questions about their baptism (19:2–3; the question assumes that *Christian* baptism and Spirit-reception *normally* belong together). It transpires that their baptism was John's, and Paul has to inform them that the coming one about whom John preached is Jesus. So it would appear that they were not yet Christians, which is why Paul re-baptizes them (contrast Apollos). And it is in that context that they receive the Spirit through the laying on of hands (19:5–6). In short, all these passages suggest that Spirit-reception was *normally* part of conversion-initiation, not a 'subsequent' experience.

6. It is clear that many of the activities attributed to the Spirit are orientated towards believers (individuals and congregations) and their life before God, not merely towards mission (*cf*. Acts 5:1–11; 6:3–6; 9:31; 11:28; 13:52; 15:28; 19:2; 20:22–23, 28; 21:4, 11).

It is unclear whether Luke thought Spirit-reception was *regularly* attended by tongues (see *Languages), or prophetic speech (*cf*. 2:4; 10:46; 19:6), or some other manifestation (8:18?), or whether he thought this should only be expected when some kind of attestation was 'required' by the situation (*e.g*. would the Jerusalem church readily accept that Samaritans and Gentiles had received the Spirit if there were not clear parallels with the initial outpouring?).

We may now address the question of how

a. Jesus' experience of the Spirit, and b. that of his disciples, might provide a pattern for Christian Spirit-reception after Pentecost. With respect to a., the above analysis suggests that the Pentecost gift corresponds loosely not merely to Jesus' Jordan experience of empowering, but also (in its soteriological dimension) to Luke 1:35. But there are clearly unique salvation-historical elements in Jesus' experience of the Spirit (and in the way it is bifurcated), and it is the church corporate, rather than every individual, that is anointed to continue the task implied by Luke 4:18–21. With respect to b., the disciples' experience of first coming to know 'salvation' through Jesus (during his ministry), and only subsequently receiving the Spirit (at Pentecost), cannot be paradigmatic. After the ascension the first part of their experience cannot be repeated, because it is no longer possible to know Jesus or to experience salvation through him *except by receiving the Spirit*.

The Spirit in John's Gospel

For John, too, the Spirit is very much a Christocentric version of the Spirit of prophecy, but he has a much more developed view of the soteriological and missiological dimensions of the gift.

The Spirit in John 1 – 12

Because humankind is alienated from God, people exist in a state of 'death' and 'darkness'. In contrast, *to know* the Father and the Son is by definition 'eternal life'/salvation (17:3). Jesus' essential mission is thus to *reveal* the Father (1:18), and so to bring light into darkness (1:4–9; 3:19–21; 8:12; 9:5), and life where there was death (5:24). Precisely *as* the manifestation of the Father (14:9–11), the Son not merely gives but *is* the 'bread of life' (6:35–51), the 'light of the world', the 'way, the truth, and the life' (14:6), *etc.*

But *how* is the Son the revelation of the Father? While this revelation is grounded in the eternal, intimate unity of the Father and the Son, it comes to expression in Jesus' works and in his teaching (14:8–11), and above all in his self-giving at the cross (3:14–16; 8:28–29; 10:14–17, *etc.*).

The Spirit is directly related to all these. Jesus hears and speaks the word of God because the Father gives him the Spirit without measure (3:34–36). Hence Jesus

claims he could have given the Samaritan woman 'living water' (= Spirit-imbued revelatory wisdom/teaching) had she asked for it, for although the definitive giving of living *water/Spirit lies beyond Jesus' 'glorification' (7:38–39), his teaching is already at least a foretaste of cleansing 'Spirit and life' (6:63; 13:10) to those who receive it. For them 'the hour' when they will worship God in Spirit and truth is not merely 'coming' but in some sense 'now (already) is' (4:23). But the primarily future orientation of 4:23 points forward to the cross as the definitive saving revelation of the divine wisdom, and this is the main theme of 3:14–16 and 6:35, 51, 53–58. Thus the cross is portrayed as the 'lifting up'/ascension/glorification of Jesus which will draw all people to him (3:14–15; 8:28–29 and 12:32). Of course, John is aware that this crucifixion/ascension is deeply paradoxical (6:61–62). Seen from the purely human perspective it is nothing but an ugly execution. Only by the *Spirit's revelation* to the individual can it be understood as the saving divine self-disclosure (so 6:63, concluding 6:35–63). But the transformation effected by that moment of revelation is so great that John can portray it as 'birth from above' (3:3). It is seeing Jesus 'lifted up' *with the eyes of faith* (3:14–15; *i.e.* by faith enabled by the Spirit) which brings about 'birth of water-and-Spirit' (3:5; an allusion to Ezek. 36:25–27). So the definitive giving of the Spirit is beyond the cross (7:38–39). Thus, in part one of John's Gospel (chs. 1 – 12), the Spirit is depicted primarily as the soteriological Spirit of prophecy/wisdom which enables the decisive revelation through Jesus. But the Spirit is not yet given to the disciples; they only partially experience the Spirit through Jesus' inspired teaching (6:63; *cf.* 13:10b).

The promise of the Spirit-Advocate

In the farewell discourses (John 13 – 17), the disciples are promised that they themselves will receive the Spirit. In three passages (14:16–26; 15:26–27; 16:7–15) John speaks of a coming gift of the Holy Spirit (14:26), or 'Spirit of truth' (14:17; 15:26; 16:13), to act as 'another Paraclete' (*paraklētos* = advocate; 14:16, 26; 15:26; 16:7) in Jesus' place.

The problem posed by the coming 'departure' of Jesus is that of how salvation, understood as knowing the Father and the Son (17:3), can continue, when Jesus, the

Revealer, is withdrawn into heaven. It is in this context that Jesus promises the Spirit to mediate the presence of the Father and the glorified Son (14:16–26). Thus, having assured the disciples of the gift of the Spirit in 14:16–17, in verses 18 and 19 Jesus promises that he will not leave them as orphans, but will come to them in such a way that 'the world' will not see him; he will manifest himself to any disciple who loves him (14:21). When Judas asks for an explanation (14:22), Jesus asserts that if a disciple loves him, he *and* the Father will come and make their home with that disciple. This promise cannot refer to Jesus' 'second coming' (for then the world *shall* see him), nor to resurrection appearances (which cannot be described as the coming of the Father and the Son *to dwell* with the disciple). As it is sandwiched by the promises of the Spirit-Paraclete (14:14–17; 14:25–26), and as (in Judaism) the Spirit of prophecy was regarded as the presence of God in revelation, *it must be the promised Spirit that will mediate the presence and self-revelation of Father and Son.* So the Paraclete/Advocate is the Holy Spirit in a special role, namely as the personal presence of Jesus in the Christian while Jesus is with the Father (see R. E. Brown, in *NTS* 13).

Overlapping with this role is the Paraclete's mission as teacher and revealer (14:26; 16:12–14). The disciples cannot really comprehend (16:12) what Jesus has said and done until he is glorified (16:25); consequently the Spirit-Paraclete will be given to *remind* them of Jesus' teaching (14:26), and to *interpret* it to them. His task is to lead them into the truth which Jesus has already incarnated (16:13), and into 'the things [yet] to come' (especially the cross and resurrection-glorification; 16:13–14).

In performing these tasks in and through the community of disciples, the Spirit-Paraclete makes them witnesses. The disciples are now 'sent' as Jesus was (20:21; *cf.* 17:17–18), and the Spirit is given to them to take over the earthly Jesus' advocacy of his case (15:26–27; 16:7b–11), that the life of the Father is savingly revealed in the Son.

A closing scene (20:22; matching 1:32–33) depicts Jesus insufflating the disciples with the Spirit and recalls Genesis 2:7 and Ezekiel 37:9 (each passage uses the rare verb 'to insufflate'). This event is probably not the giving of the Paraclete (*contra* G. M. Burge), which

is to happen only *after* Jesus' ascension/glorification, but the climax of the life-giving pneumatic wisdom/understanding they have already tasted in Jesus' ministry. But John envisages no two-stage reception of the Spirit in the period of the church. The experience of 20:22 cannot be repeated after the ascension, as Jesus can then come to the disciple only in the saving, sanctifying and empowering gift of the Paraclete.

Paul

For Paul, as for Luke-Acts and John, the Spirit is a Christocentric, soteriological and ecclesiological version of the Spirit of prophecy. Salvation is not merely 'justification', but deliverance from the whole 'realm' of Satan, the flesh and sin, and transfer to the realm/reign of God's beloved Son (Col. 1:13), with all that this entails, including reconciliation and reunification with God in Christ, sonship, membership in and fellowship with the new people of God, the restored Israel anticipated in (*inter alia*) Ezekiel 36 – 37, and ultimately resurrection into new creation (see *Death and resurrection). It can be argued that Paul sees the Spirit as the key to all of these blessings (there are 115 references to the Spirit in his small corpus of writings). Thus:

1. The Spirit initially reveals the Christ-event (*e.g.* through preaching) as God's saving wisdom (1 Cor. 2; Gal. 3:1–5; 2 Cor. 3:14–16), eliciting repentance, belief and reception of the Spirit in a single complex event (*cf.* esp. Gal. 3:1–5). Charismatic revelation/wisdom is thus at the foundation of the Christian life, and continues to play an important role (*cf.* 2 Cor. 3:18; Eph. 1:17–20; 3:16–20, *etc.*; and see below).

2. For Paul, this initial and ongoing experience of Christ by the Spirit is essentially transformatory, and he interprets it in the light of Ezekiel 36:24–27 as washing, sanctifying and justifying in the Spirit (1 Cor. 6:11; *cf.* Titus 3:5). Accordingly, in 1 Thessalonians 4:8 he reminds his readers (using the unusual wording of Ezek.) that ongoing sin frustrates the very purpose of the gift, which was for Israel's *eschatological cleansing/restoration.

3. In response to Judaizing pressures, Paul sharply radicalizes this pneumatology developed from Ezekiel 36 – 37:

a. in the great Torah/Spirit antithesis of 2 Corinthians 3, Galatians 3 – 6, and its refinement in Romans 7 – 8. For Israel, the law has led only to bondage to sin and death; the Spirit alone brings 'life' (as the one in whom the life-giver, God himself, indwells his people, and as the one who enables pleasing service to God) and freedom. Not to have the Spirit is to be on the wrong side of this antithesis, and to be in need of salvation, while to receive the eschatological gift of the Spirit is *ipso facto* to enter salvation.

b. in the great flesh/Spirit antithesis in Galatians 3 – 5 and Romans 7 – 8. Here again, belonging to 'the flesh' is the great disaster from which humankind needs salvation, while the Spirit is the means of 'putting to death' the flesh/deeds of the body (Rom. 8:13) and the source of ethical 'fruit' (Gal. 5 – 6). A related antithesis is that of uncircumcision/*circumcision of the heart in Romans 2:25–29; Philippians 3:3.

c. in the old creation/new creation antithesis of 2 Corinthians. 5:17 and Galatians 6:15. The language of new creation is bound up with that of Adam and Christ, and the injunctions to 'put off' the old self and 'put on the new' are paralleled and explained by the injunctions to 'put on Christ' (*cf.* Gal. 3:27; Rom. 13:14; Col. 3:9–10; Eph. 4:24, *etc.*), an action which Paul considers to be possible only 'by the Spirit'.

4. At the heart of Paul's view of salvation, however, is not so much new 'performance' as new *relationship*: *i.e.* restoration *to God*. Israel looked forward to 'salvation' as the lavish pouring out of the Spirit upon them (Is. 32:15; 44:3; Ezek. 36 – 37; Joel 2), because this was to be the *return of God* to Israel in transforming *grace. Accordingly:

a. Paul describes both the church and the individual as the eschatological temple which God now indwells by his Spirit (1 Cor. 3:16; 6:19; Eph. 2:22, *etc.*), and the believer is said to have access *to God* through the Spirit (Eph. 2:18; *cf.* Rom. 8:26–27).

b. However, these ideas are Christocentric. Paul's writings are dominated by a rich 'in Christ' mysticism, and his understanding of 'salvation' is summarized in such passages as Galatians 2:19–20: 'I have been crucified with Christ, and it is no longer I who live, but it is Christ who lives in me. And the life I now live in the flesh, I live by faith in the Son of God who loved me and gave himself for me' (NRSV, *cf.* 1 Cor. 12:13; 2 Cor. 5:17; Phil. 1:21; 3:10, *etc.*). Christ, as much as the Father, is the indwelling, self-revealing presence of God, but only through the Spirit of God, now experienced as the Spirit *of Christ* (Rom. 8:9–11; Phil. 1:19; *cf.* Gal. 4:6). If salvation is above all 'union with Christ', that union is effected and maintained only through the Spirit. The corollary is stated in Romans 8:9b: 'anyone who does not have the Spirit of Christ, that person does not belong to him'. Fundamentally, then, the Spirit is 'the Spirit of *adoption/sonship' (Gal. 4:6; Rom. 8:15).

5. For Paul, 'salvation' has a corporate dimension. The erstwhile alienated person experiences fellowship/communion in the 'body' of Christ. In Ephesians this amounts to a restructuring of the very notion of personhood. But even in the earlier letters it is clear that to be the Spirit-people is to live in a different sort of society, one marked by *love, unity and mutual service in the pattern of the cross (so Gal. 5 – 6; 1 Cor. 12 – 14; Rom. 12 – 14; Phil. 2:1–11, *etc.*). The new life is summed up in the expression 'fellowship of the Spirit', which denotes a sharing with each other in a unity enabled by the Spirit and/or joint participation in the Spirit (Phil. 2:1; 2 Cor. 13:14).

6. For Paul believers have now only the *firstfruits* of the Spirit (Rom. 8:23); the final element of salvation is resurrection transformation as a *sōma pneumatikon* like Christ (1 Cor. 15:45–49; *cf.* Phil. 3:21), and this too is by the Spirit. Paul appears to see resurrection to new creation life as the final great saving act of the Spirit. The Spirit in the believer now is the guarantee or first instalment of that future resurrection, because the Spirit himself will bring it about (2 Cor. 1:22; 5:5; Rom. 8:11, 12–25; Eph. 1:13–14; 1 Tim. 3:16).

7. Everywhere in Paul the Spirit is clearly the charismatic Spirit of prophecy, who builds the church, inspires its worship, and empowers its mission through a variety of spiritual gifts (notably Gal. 3:3–5; 1 Thess. 5:19–20; 1 Cor. 12 – 14; Rom. 12, Eph. 4:7–16, *etc.*). But these charismata are not a distinct set of workings of the Spirit, dependent on some 'second blessing'; they are an integral part of the new covenant relationship, sonship and service, which are charismatic throughout.

In the rest of the NT

Luke-Acts, John and Paul provide the most profound theologies of the Spirit in the NT.

The remaining writings add little to their witness. Not surprisingly, 1 John echoes the fourth Gospel; the Spirit is teacher/interpreter (2:20), who enables fellowship with the Father and the Son (1:6) and *assurance of their indwelling presence (3:24; 4:13), and who bears witness to the incarnate Son (4:1–6; 5:6–8). For Hebrews, the Spirit is the power working signs that confirm the gospel (2:4) and the one who once spoke, and now speaks anew, through Scripture (3:7; 9:8; 10:15; cf. 2 Tim. 3:16 and 2 Pet. 1:21). Through the same Spirit, Jesus made his self-offering (Heb. 9:14), and his disciples thereby participate in the eschatological new-covenant Spirit (6:4), who is 'the Spirit of grace', but who nevertheless must not be outraged by backsliding into Judaism (10:29).

In Revelation, the Spirit is again a Christocentric version of the Spirit of prophecy. In 19:10 this is explicit, but it is implicit elsewhere. 1. references to the apostle being 'in the Spirit' (1:10; cf. 4:2) lead into a Christocentric vision; 2. the repeated 'Let him who has ears hear what the Spirit says to the churches' (2:7, 11, 17, 29; 3:6, 13, 22) relates to oracular words of the risen Lord directed to the seven churches (oracles which amply demonstrate the active involvement of the risen Lord in the churches' affairs); 3. in 22:17, the Spirit, through the prophetic people (the bride), bids Christ 'come'; 4. the references to 'the seven spirits before the throne of [God]' (1:4; 4:5; cf. 3:1 and 5:6), which some interpreters have taken to be the angels of presence, more probably symbolize the omnipresent Holy Spirit (cf. Zech. 4:1–14; (see R. Bauckham, The Climax of Prophecy, ch. 5).

The Spirit as divine 'person'

In the OT, the Spirit is 'personal' only in the sense that rûaḥ is the self-manifesting activity of God himself, the extension of his personal vitality. The phrase 'Spirit of the Lord' is thus a synecdoche for God himself in action (cf. 'hand', 'finger', 'arm' of the Lord). But the NT modifies this understanding in a trinitarian direction. The Son may petition the Father to send the Spirit (John 14:16, 26), but he also commissions the Spirit (John 15:26; 16:7; cf. Luke 24:49; Acts 2:33) as the 'Spirit of Jesus/Christ'. There is thus a sense in which (using spatial metaphors to represent relationships) the Son steps between the Father and the divine Spirit, and becomes 'Lord of the Spirit' (i.e. to echo Johannine language, the Spirit now glorifies the Father and the Son together, and mediates their presence and activity in the disciple). That one step, however, reveals the one God as three persons. It is not then surprising that the whole 'grammar' or 'deep structure' of NT assertions about Father, Son and Spirit is implicitly trinitarian; this is not confined merely to such explicitly triadic passages as Matthew 28:19; John 14 – 16; 2 Corinthians 13:14, etc.

See also: SPIRITUAL GIFTS.

Bibliography
R. Bauckham, The Climax of Prophecy: Studies on the Book of Revelation (Edinburgh, 1993); R. E. Brown, 'The Paraclete in the fourth Gospel', NTS 13, 1966–67, pp. 113–132; G. M. Burge, The Anointed Community: The Holy Spirit in the Johannine Community (Grand Rapids, 1987); H. Conzelmann, The Theology of St. Luke (London, 1960); J. D. G. Dunn, Baptism in the Holy Spirit: A Re-examination of the New Testament Teaching on the Gift of the Spirit in Relation to Pentecostalism Today (London, 1970); idem, Jesus and the Spirit (London, 1975); G. D. Fee, God's Empowering Presence: The Holy Spirit in the Letters of Paul (Peabody, 1994); E. Franck, Revelation Taught: The Paraclete in the Gospel of John (Lund, 1985); W. Hildebrandt, An Old Testament Theology of the Spirit of God (Peabody, 1995); R. P. Menzies, Empowered for Witness: The Spirit in Luke-Acts (Sheffield, 1994); G. T. Montague, The Holy Spirit: Growth of a Biblical Tradition (New York, 1976); J. M. Penney, The Missionary Emphasis of Lukan Pneumatology (Sheffield, 1997); J. Schaberg, The Father, the Son and the Holy Spirit: The Triadic Phrase in Matthew 28:19b (Chico, 1982); E. Schweizer, 'Pneuma, ktl.', in TDNT 6, pp. 389–455; R. Stronstad, The Charismatic Theology of Saint Luke (Peabody, 1984); M. Turner, The Holy Spirit and Spiritual Gifts Then and Now (Carlisle, 1999); idem, Power From On High: The Spirit in Israel's Restoration and Witness in Luke-Acts (Sheffield, 1996).

M. TURNER

HONOUR, see GLORY

HOPE

Introduction

While the topic of hope appears in many different contexts within the biblical texts, with both positive and negative connotations, the Bible as a whole provides true hope to disorientated *humanity by revealing how *God, out of *love, will renew all *creation following the disruption caused by the rebellion of Adam and Eve in the Garden of Eden. While the early chapters of Genesis look back to the first creation to explain the present state of the cosmos, the final chapters of Revelation look forward to the re-creation of a new *heaven and a new earth. Throughout the Bible hope is closely associated with God himself and the outworking of his purposes in history.

Hope in the OT

Although hope is clearly associated with various Hebrew roots, the concept is present in many OT texts even when these roots are absent. For this reason, it is important to look beyond the distribution of specific vocabulary when assessing the importance of hope in the OT.

Fundamentally, Yahweh himself is the theological ground of human hope in the OT (e.g. Pss. 25:3; 31:24; 71:5; 131:3; Lam. 3:21–26), just as Christ is in the NT (esp. 1 Tim. 1:1). More accurately, hope is 'in Yahweh' (e.g. Ps. 37:9). As Preuss observes, 'Yahweh may well be "the foundation of hope"' (H. D. Preuss, *Old Testament Theology* II, p. 152). This explains the frequent use of the metaphor of 'rock' in relation to him.

When hope is mentioned in the Psalms a strong element of dependent relationship appears. Emphasis is thus put on a state or place of security, coupled with confidence in a person, a confidence which inspires patience and makes it possible. In difficult circumstances, hope provides a bubble-like safe place in which to exist for the time being. Moreover, while the OT has relatively little to say about life after *death, there are indications that those who enjoy a positive relationship with Yahweh in this life will continue to enjoy this experience beyond death. For this reason, confidence in Yahweh provides hope for every OT believer regardless of personal circumstances.

While specific references to hope are found most frequently in Psalms and in the wisdom books, the prophetic corpus is also full of hope, although possibly as a tonic in the midst of doom-laden prophecies. Isaiah 40 – 66 has passages of sheer hopefulness which presuppose a change in the whole political structure of the world; Ezekiel's temple-centred vision points to a paradise and so interprets the present experience of a desolate *Jerusalem as a foretaste of something wonderful. Joel and Jeremiah 31 – 33 speak of a new age of the Spirit.

From a biblical theology standpoint the OT is the text of promise which points ahead to a greater reality. There is, however, as much in the OT about the structure of history as about promise and fulfilment, with past promises already being fulfilled (e.g. in the Exodus and the monarchical expansion) and serving as evidence that the future too will see the fulfilment of divine promises.

Since true hope is intimately associated with God and his saving purposes, the divine promise regarding the blessing of all the nations of the earth through the '*seed' of Abraham takes on special significance. Given first in Genesis, this promise is associated with a future king who shall be descended from the tribe of Judah. As the books of Samuel and Kings reveal, hope of universal blessing is later tied to the house of David, and this continues to be the case even when the actions of David's descendants bring upon themselves divine judgment. Thus in spite of the removal of the Davidic dynasty from the throne in Jerusalem, and the associated destruction of the *temple, the exilic prophets, like those of the immediately preceding generations, hold out hope of a future restoration through a descendant of David. This hope undergirds later messianic expectations and comes to fulfilment with the coming of *Jesus Christ.

The NT: hope as interim gift and provision

In the NT, *hypomeneō* ('persevere/endure') has a slightly different meaning from that of the word used in the LXX (*elpizō*, 'wait expectantly'). *Hypomenē* seems more often to denote the effort involved in the human response to God, while *elpis*, 'hope', is reserved for the gift of God. Hopelessness seems to define the unbelieving world in that its hopes are empty (1 Thess. 4:13). Christian hope, however, is more solid than '*assurance'; the firstfruit of the Holy Spirit gives believers hope (not assurance). They shall be saved by hope: the reality and the subjective trust together (Rom. 8:23–25). In the *locus classicus* of Pauline teaching on hope, Romans 5:1–5, the apostle assures his readers that hope does not put 'us' to shame, *i.e.* cause us to be exposed at any time as shams, because the Spirit gives God's love into 'our' hearts.

One could argue that Paul, who refers to the 'God of hope' (Rom. 15:13), looks more to the future and God's plan for it ('*eschatology') than do his mainstream Jewish contemporaries, who are polarized between the extremes of apocalypticism (cataclysm now!) and anti-apocalypticism. *Faith needs to be allowed to direct hope, *i.e.* it is in God and to him that believers must trust and look (*cf.* 1 Pet. 1:21). This reflects the fact that the overcoming of evil is (logically) prior to the overcoming of death. Hope of the resurrection is the existential outworking of faith, the psychology-controlling gift accessed by faith which in turn issues in works of love. Hope can be 'against hope' (Rom. 4:18), as in the case of Sarah whose hope contradicts the best of human expectations. Hope as an ultimate reality, giving a shape and meaning to the present, is a distinguishing feature of Christians; unbelievers 'have no hope' (1 Thess. 4:13; Eph. 2:12). Paul (Phil. 1:23) looked forward to being 'with Christ'; Christ's presence was Paul's hope. This leaves room for other 'proximate' hopes, but it also imposes order on them. They are subordinate to the ultimate hope: fellowship with Christ himself.

'In Hebrews (with special reference to 11:1), "hope" never describes a subjective attitude but always denotes the objective content of hope, consisting of present and future salvation' (W. Lane, *Hebrews*, WBC, 2 vols. (Dallas, 1991), pp. 325–326). While love differs from faith and hope in being directed towards other humans and because it survives beyond the *eschaton* (1 Cor. 13:13), hope is different from love and faith because it is the ground for faith and the occasion for love

from the *Holy Spirit; hope is not empty belief, as it would be without love (Rom. 5:5). In 1 Thessalonians 1:3 the three are again tied together: '... your work of faith, your trial of love and the endurance of hope of our Lord Jesus Christ before our God and father' (author's translation; *i.e.* it is something of Christ's in which the readers participate). In 1 Thessalonians 5:8 the hope of *salvation is described as a helmet (something intellectual, forming one's 'worldview'), while faith is a breastplate (something affective and moral). These last two passages suggest that hope is the eschatological reality as it registers conceptually in a believer's mind.

Hope is like a safety net, the presence of which encourages us to take risks, not presumptuously, but only in humility and prayer. Thus 1 John 3:2 says: 'what we will be has not yet been made known, adding that 'we shall be like him'.

The focus of biblical hope

Being future-oriented is double-edged; it creates a God-given striving which is often corrupted into anxiety. It needs to build on a salvation experienced in the past and present to have the right viewpoint on the unknown designs of God for the future. Through the incarnation hope has come to be a part of life, or at least its potential is at hand to be actualized. Therefore we should not forget the 'already attained' quality of Christian hope; the Lord is near (Phil. 4:5; *cf.* Luke 19:13; Matt. 10:32–33; *etc.*). It is the future which gives sense to our lives, but it is freeing and therefore an open future. God has built into humanity a longing. 'Just as hearing and speaking are man's specific characteristics, so the expectation of the future is the distinctive mark of human life in time, (H. W. Wolff, *Anthropology of the Old Testament*, p. 153). Therefore God is not *Deus spes* ('the god Hope', an idol which according to Aristotle and his medieval Arab commentators promises humans their own divinity) but *Deus spei* ('the God of hope'). What makes the content of biblical hope distinctive is that God meets us (more than) halfway. Quite aside from questions of the certainty of individuals' salvation, certainty of hope (*i.e.* that an afterlife will follow and God's justice will be done) is guaranteed. Such hope inculcates a forward-looking attitude; one is caught up in a story bigger than oneself.

Bibliography

G. B. Caird, *New Testament Theology* (Oxford, 1994); W. Brueggemann, *Hopeful Imagination: Prophetic Voices in Exile* (Minneapolis, 1986); D. Hubbard, 'Hope in the Old Testament', *TynB* 34, 1983, pp. 33–59; G. Nebe, *'Hoffnung' bei Paulus: Elpis und ihre Synonyme im Zusammenhang der Eschatologie* (Göttingen, 1983); H. D. Preuss, *Old Testament Theology*, 2 vols. (ET, Edinburgh and Louisville, 1995, 1996); H.-W. Wolff, *Anthropology of the Old Testament* (ET, London, 1974); W. Zimmerli, *Man and His Hope in the Old Testament* (ET, London, 1971).

M. W. ELLIOTT

HOSEA, see Part 2

HOSPITALITY

Hospitality is at the heart of the gospel and practice of the early church; its themes and language pervade the NT. Implicit in the stories of Jesus and in NT descriptions of human relationships with God and other people, hospitality is also explicitly required and commended in practice. Although there is no word for hospitality in the Hebrew vocabulary, the practice is evident in the welcome, food, shelter and protection-asylum that guests received in OT times. Commands in the Torah and exhortations in the prophets to care for strangers attest to the importance of hospitality in the OT. Narratives demonstrate that hospitality was closely connected to the recognition of Yahweh's lordship and to covenant loyalty. Stories provide evidence of God's presence and provision in the context of hospitality.

OT stories

The story of *Abraham and the three guests in Genesis 18 is the most significant OT text on hospitality. The writer of Hebrews attaches special importance to this story in 13:2: 'Do not neglect to show hospitality to strangers, for thereby some have entertained angels unawares' (RSV).

Abraham graciously welcomed three unexpected visitors and, with *Sarah and their servant, hurriedly prepared a lavish meal for them. While the reader is told that the Lord appeared to Abraham in this meeting, it seems that Abraham only gradually recognized this encounter as being with the divine. In this context of welcome, Abraham and Sarah received the promise of a son.

Abraham welcomed his guests as any Near Eastern host would. Hospitality was highly regarded, often associated with promise and blessing, and necessitated by social and geographical conditions. In Genesis 19, two of the visitors ('angels'), arrived in Sodom and were given hospitality by Lot. Later, the men of Sodom surrounded Lot's house and demanded that he give up his visitors for sexual exploitation. Lot pleaded with the crowd to do 'nothing to these men, for they have come under the shelter of my roof' (Gen. 19:8).

In ancient times hospitality included protection. When one household provided hospitality, the entire community was bound to protect the guest. However, Lot's plea was unheeded by the men of Sodom, who dismissed him as an alien without authority. The guests/angels rescued Lot from the crisis. Hospitality, when offered against the will of the larger group, could be dangerous: an act of defiance; a challenge to the unity and expectations of the community. In a supportive environment, it was taken for granted as an act of mutual aid. Hospitality to male guests sometimes intensified the vulnerability of women (Gen. 19; Judg 19).

In several OT stories, women had important roles as hosts. *Rahab offered protection and lodging to Israelite spies (Josh. 2), demonstrating her loyalty to Israel's God. Abigail, despite her ill-mannered husband, provided hospitality for David and his men (1 Sam. 25). The widow of Zarephath provided hospitality for *Elijah when facing starvation herself, and God, through Elijah, provided her household with food until the drought passed (1 Kgs. 17:8–16). *Elisha received the hospitality of a Shunammite woman who provided him with a furnished guest room to use whenever he passed by (2 Kgs. 4:8–10).

In most of the OT stories, guests brought their hosts into close contact with God, but this often resulted in other forms of blessing as well: a longed-for child; marriage; protection; or provision. Acts of hospitality or inhospitality revealed the underlying good or evil of a person or community (Gen. 19; Judg. 19; 1 Sam. 25).

Israel as alien and Israel's treatment of aliens

The experience of being an alien or sojourner (*gēr*), vulnerable to others and dependent on God as host, was fundamental to Israel's identity. When receiving God's promises, Abraham was told that his descendants would be 'sojourners in a land that is not theirs' (Gen. 15:13). Israel lived as sojourners/aliens (*gērim*) in Egypt (Exod. 22:21; 23:9). In the wilderness, God miraculously supplied the Israelites with manna (Exod. 16:4, 15, 32), a daily confirmation of their dependence on God as host. When Israel finally inherited the land, God reminded them that the land belonged to him and 'you are strangers and sojourners with me' (Lev. 25:23; also 1 Chr. 29:14–15).

Israel's sojourner status was a reminder of their dependence on God and a basis for gratitude and obedience. This status also supplied the experiential foundation from which the Israelites could recognize and respond to the needs of aliens and powerless people in their midst (Exod. 23:9; Deut. 10:19). In the ancient Near East only Israel had explicit legislation protecting, and providing for, the resident alien. The command to love the alien parallels the command to love the neighbour (Lev. 19:18, 33–34). Laws on gleaning, the triennial tithe and Sabbath-keeping made reference to the sojourner (Lev. 19:9–10; Deut. 24:19–22; 14:28–29; 26:12–13; Exod. 20:10; Deut. 5:14). Judges were instructed to deal impartially between aliens and Israelites (Deut. 1:16; 24:17). Cities of refuge were open to alien and native born alike (Num. 35:15; Josh. 20:9). Sojourners were often classed with widows, orphans and the *poor as those deserving the community's provision and just treatment (Exod. 22:21–24; Deut. 24:17–18). Economic provision and protection did not depend on individual hospitality alone, but became the responsibility of the community.

The covenantal structure of their faith framed Israel's response to the alien. Just as God 'executes justice for the fatherless and the widow, and loves the sojourner', so Israel was to act with a justice that could not be corrupted by bribery and with a love that welcomed and provided (Deut. 10:18–22). However, foreign practices and people that might subvert commitment to God were rigorously excluded. Those strangers who, by maintaining ties to their foreign religion and community, might threaten Israel's social organization and loyalty to Yahweh were sometimes tolerated, but were more often seen as enemies and rejected (Exod. 17:8–16; 34:10–16; Deut. 7:1–6; 18:9–14; Josh. 23:12–13; 24:14–24).

NT hospitality

The idea of God as guest or stranger in the world is an important element in the NT theology of the *incarnation, and the practice of Christian hospitality is inextricably linked to it. Jesus experienced the vulnerability and rejection of the stranger (Luke 2:7; 4:16–30; 9:58; John 1:10–11). He and his disciples were dependent on the hospitality and support of others (Luke 8:1–3; 9:1–6; 10:3–12, 38–42).

Jesus had the dual identity of stranger-guest and host. As host, he proclaimed welcome to all who would come to him and enter the kingdom. As both guest and host, he challenged the prevailing but often unrecognized socio-religious patterns of *exclusion (Luke 5:27–32; 7:36–50; 19:1–10). Jesus' ministry of welcoming the lost was often expressed in his eating with people who ordinarily would have been excluded from fellowship. His willingness to be their guest provoked strong criticism.

Jesus' teaching on hospitality is distinctive in its emphasis on welcoming those who appear to have nothing to give in return. In Luke 14:12–14, Jesus challenged the conventional understanding of hospitality which assumed reciprocity and focused on family and friends. Rather than inviting those who could repay hospitality, he said, hosts should invite the poor and needy, who are unable to do so. Recompense is God's responsibility and hosts will be blessed and repaid at the 'resurrection of the just'. Just as God is gracious in welcoming people to the feast in the kingdom, so earthly hosts should welcome to their tables those who cannot repay the kindness.

The presence of the kingdom was prefigured and revealed most clearly in the context of shared meals. In his encounter with two disciples on the road to Emmaus, Jesus came to them as a stranger and accepted their offer of hospitality. In the context of the meal and of fellowship, he became their host and they recognized him as their risen Lord (Luke 24:13–35).

The most important passage for the Christian tradition of hospitality to strangers is Matthew 25:31–46. With Genesis 18, Hebrews 13:2, and Luke 14:12–14, it has shaped traditional Christian practice in this area. The passage identifies Jesus with the 'least of these' and links hospitality towards human beings with love for Jesus. Those who welcomed strangers and met the needs of people in distress had welcomed and ministered to Christ himself. Despite the ambiguity of the passage with regard to who is being judged and who is included in the 'least of these', it is clear that entry into the kingdom is tied to the practice of hospitality in this life.

Hospitality in the early church

The earliest Christian fellowship and church growth depended on household-based hospitality among believers. The first missionaries travelled widely and found a welcome in various homes (Acts 16:15, 32–34; 18:1–11), which also provided meeting places for the local community of believers. Hospitality was a virtue, and a practice appropriate for the church as the household of God, and particularly important for church *leaders (1 Tim. 3:2; 5:10).

In the earliest communities, the practice of hospitality had three dimensions. First, it was an expression of respect and recognition, a physical symbol of the destruction of those status boundaries irrelevant in the community of the new covenant. The early church struggled with determining appropriate boundaries and with transcending the socio-religious and socio-economic distinctions among its members. This struggle was often expressed in the language of welcome and hospitality. Shared meals were significant because they represented common life and equality; the practice also brought to the surface tensions and inequality (Acts 10 – 11; 1 Cor. 11:17–34; Gal. 2:11–14; Jas. 2:1–13).

Secondly, hospitality provided the structure for meeting the physical needs of strangers, travelling Christians, and the local poor. Many of the NT's direct instructions regarding hospitality were related to meeting the needs of travelling missionaries and other Christians. Caring for the needs of the poor, widows and orphans in the local community

often took the form of hospitality. The Greek word for hospitality, *philoxenia,* is used in Romans 12:13, Hebrews 13:2, 1 Peter 4:9, 1 Timothy 3:2 and Titus 1:8. It combines the general Greek word for *love or affection, *phileō,* which denotes love among people connected by kinship or faith, and the word for stranger, *xenos.* Hospitality is a concrete and personal expression of Christian love, intended to include strangers in a circle of care. Hospitality, though important, could also become burdensome; practices were developed to limit abuses (letters of reference; Acts 18:27; Rom. 16:1–2).

Thirdly, hospitality was expressed in the hosting of local assemblies of believers (Rom. 16:3–5, 23; Col. 4:15). In hospitable households, the gospel was preached and propagated, Christian identity was forged and reinforced, and social bonds were established and sustained. Christians denied welcome to two categories of people who claimed to be believers: those who persisted in immoral lifestyles (1 Cor. 5:9–11) and those who spread false teaching (2 John 9–11). Early struggles over authority and doctrine found expression in the extension or denial of welcome (3 John).

In Romans 15:7, Paul urged believers to 'welcome one another' as Christ had welcomed them. The experience of divine hospitality and the practice of the early church were dynamically related. In the Lord's Supper, the costliness of that divine welcome is regularly remembered.

Bibliography

J. Koenig, *New Testament Hospitality* (Philadelphia, 1985); A. J. Malherbe, *Social Aspects of Early Christianity* (Philadelphia, ²1983); C. D. Pohl, *Making Room: Recovering Hospitality as a Christian Tradition* (Grand Rapids, 1999); D. W. Riddle, 'Early Christian Hospitality', *JBL* 57, 1938, pp. 141–154; G. Stählin, '*xenos*', *TDNT* 5, pp. 1–36; C. van Houten, *The Alien in Israelite Law* (Sheffield, 1991).

C. D. POHL

HOUSE OF JESSE, see DAVID

HUMANITY

Christian writing on humanity has changed significantly in the last generation. Traditional terminology is no longer suitable; 'the doctrine of man' has become unsuitably gender specific, while the term 'anthropology' (formerly used alongside 'soteriology', 'ecclesiology', etc.) risks confusion with another discipline whose insights often inform biblical study. More importantly, the focus has shifted from the person to the community, with less emphasis on the physionomy and psychology of individuals and more on the interrelatedness of humanity. However, given the richness of human life and of biblical witness, these perspectives should be seen as complementary rather than as competing.

Creation of humanity

Humanity is the focus of the two *creation accounts, though in different ways. In Genesis 1 the creation of humanity is the longest section and the apex of the account. The important verb bārā', 'create' occurs three times (v. 27; cf. vv. 1, 21), and is the only instance when God blesses his creation. Human dominion over all other creatures is noted, and the creation of humanity precedes God's assessment of creation as 'very good'. In Genesis 2 it is the dominant element. The account includes the creation of *man from the dust, his physical setting and moral restriction, and the creation of woman from man. Genesis 1 implies parity between the sexes, with humanity created male and female. Genesis 2 implies complementarity, with woman created as man's helper at the climax of the account, and is unique among ancient Near Eastern creation accounts in its focus on woman. Here and elsewhere in Scripture, humans are clearly like other living things in being created by *God and hence subject to him, but also unlike them in being made in God's image and owing him obedience.

The Hebrew text hints at individual and collective aspects of humanity in ways difficult to translate. Throughout the OT 'ādām is a common noun for '(hu)man', usually preceded by the definite article ('the'), while in Genesis 'ādām also means '*Adam'. Thus the 'ādām in Genesis 1:27 refers to humankind, who are further differentiated as male and female, while 'ādām in Genesis 5:1, 3–5

refers to Adam. However, in Genesis 2 – 4 'ādām is used both with and without the article to refer to both humanity and Adam; the demarcation between them is unclear. P. Trible has argued influentially that before the account of the creation of woman (Gen. 2:21–23) 'ādām indicates a sexually undifferentiated earth creature. However, the narrative (Gen. 2:22) assumes the continuity of 'ādām before and after the creation of woman.

The image of God is clearly foundational to the biblical concept of humanness. It is a fundamental feature of humanity in Genesis 1, and is not obliterated by the fall (Gen. 5:1; 9:6; 1 Cor. 11:7; Jas. 3:9). Various suggestions have been made concerning the locus of the image: 1. reason, or some other human attribute like conscience; 2. relationship, with the other sex, other humans and God; and 3. role, as God's representative in creation. Further discussion is omitted here only because of separate treatment elsewhere (see *Image of God).

In the NT, the ultimate image of God is revealed as the eternal Son (Col. 1:15; cf. Heb. 1:3). In contrast with the one disobedient man (Adam) through whom sin entered the world, *Jesus Christ is the one obedient man through whom God's grace overflows to many (Rom. 5:12–17; cf. 1 Cor. 15:22, 45). The resultant change in status for Christians is so radical that it is described as death and resurrection (Rom 6:1–11), and leads in turn to their conformity to the image of God's Son. Thus both the model and the goal of humanity are seen in Christ.

Humans as individuals

Nepeš, the most common Hebrew term for the whole person, essentially means 'living being' (Gen. 9:5; Lev. 4:2). It sometimes indicates inner desires, from physical appetite to a longing to serve God (Prov. 23:2; Deut. 6:5). The traditional translation 'soul' is misleading, since this has connotations of a (later) dualism. Rûaḥ has the basic sense of 'breath', 'wind', 'spirit'. Human rûaḥ is linked to divine rûaḥ (see *Holy Spirit), sometimes explicitly (Ps. 104:29) but usually implicitly. Frequently rûaḥ denotes non-physical attributes such as ability and thought (Exod. 28:3; Is. 29:24). Thought and will are also often located in the heart (Gen. 6:5). Emotions also may be linked to the heart, but are often located lower in the body, in the liver, kidneys or bowels.

The OT clearly presents the human person as a psychosomatic unity, and does not distinguish between material body and immaterial 'soul'. This is due partly to the authors' holistic approach to *life, and partly to their dominant interest in the present life and the relationship of the living with God. Nonetheless, the OT also indicates in several ways that humans continue to exist in some ill-defined form after physical death. Necromancy is repeatedly condemned rather than dismissed as nonsensical (Deut. 18:11); the dead Samuel can be 'brought up' to advise the living Saul (1 Sam. 28); 'shades' (r'pā'îm) of dead kings in Sheol (the underworld) are roused to greet the newly descended king of Babylon (Is. 14:9–11); some shades will return to life (Is. 26:19), as will the multitude who sleep in the earth (Dan. 12:2). By NT times, developments within Judaism and the influence of Hellenism had led to much more speculation about the state of the dead. (See *Death and Resurrection.)

The NT reflects these developments. On the one hand, the teaching and healing ministry of Jesus and his apostles emphasizes the importance of the whole person (Matt. 6:30–32, etc.). On the other, there is a vital interest in the non-physical aspect of the person, in both the present and the future. True worship must be 'in spirit' (John 4:24), and Jesus' disciples should not fear 'those who kill the body but cannot kill the soul' (Matt. 10:28). The words psychē, 'soul' and pneuma, 'spirit' are sometimes used synonymously (cf. 'the spirits of just men made perfect', Heb. 12:23; the souls of martyrs under the altar, Rev. 6:9–11). However, the words may sometimes point to different aspects of non-physical human nature, psychē in relation to the world and pneuma in relation to God. This distinction may be reflected in Paul's phrase 'body, soul and spirit' (1 Thess. 5:23), and is seen more clearly in the contrasted adjectives psychikon, 'natural' and pneumatikon, 'spiritual' (1 Cor. 2:14–15; 15:44).

Traditional Christianity has usually viewed the human person as dichotomous, with both physical and non-physical aspects. (Early Eastern tradition maintained a trichotomous view, distinguishing further between soul and spirit.) However, dichotomy has been increasingly attacked, from the philosophy of Hobbes and Spinoza in the 17th century to scientific and biblical study in the later 20th century, and has now been largely abandoned. In science, the linking of mental and emotional activity to electro-chemical impulses in the brain has been taken to imply that the non-physical cannot persist without the physical. And in biblical study many scholars, following O. Cullmann, have contrasted the Hebraic, holistic view of the person with the Platonic dualism which has dominated much traditional Christian thinking. But the two views need not be diametrically opposed. J. W. Cooper argues cogently for 'holistic dualism', in which a person is understood as a psychosomatic unity in life, while an immaterial element continues after death.

Humans in relationship

The relational aspect of humanity, less developed though not ignored in older studies, has been increasingly emphasised in recent biblical study. It has several important aspects.

Sexual

The creation accounts note the differentiation and complementarity of male and female, the incompleteness of one without the other, and the norm of sexual intimacy. Plural human creation ('male and female') results from plural divine speech ('let us make', Gen. 1:27), and later revelation allows this gender complementarity and interrelatedness to be seen as a reflection of the trinitarian God, even if the writer of Genesis was hardly aware of this. Sexuality is intrinsic to humanity and vital for its continuation on earth. Its very preciousness leaves it vulnerable to abuse. But it is limited to this life, as Jesus indicates in his rebuttal of the Sadducees' disbelief in the resurrection (Mark 12:25). In heaven procreation will be unnecessary and inappropriate, while *love will be perfected in all relationships.

The 'pre-fall' accounts distinguish the human genders but do not attribute to them different roles; still less do they indicate a hierarchical relationship. In Genesis 1 male and female are created together and assigned their role together (vv. 27–28). In chapter 2 the man is created and placed in the garden to till and keep it (v. 15). Then his solitude is noted, and woman is created as 'a helper opposite him' (*'ēzer kᵉnegdô*, v. 18). But neither the order of creation here nor the rationale for the creation of the woman indicates a difference of status. As in chapter 1, the final element of the account can be seen as its climax. And the term 'helper' is often used of God himself, so hardly supports the traditional view of subordination, as Trible (*God and the Rhetoric of Sexuality*, p. 90) and others have argued. Separate roles are mentioned and hierarchy is stipulated for the first time in the divine judgment on disobedience (Gen. 3:16–19).

Pre-Israelite and Israelite society was clearly hierarchical, and the OT predominantly reflects a male perspective. The ministry of Jesus represented a profound challenge to this, notably in his affirmation of female enquirers (John 4) and followers (Luke 8:1–3) and his non-condemnation of the adulteress (John 8:1–11). His own celibacy and his encouragement of celibacy for the sake of the kingdom (Matt. 19:12) questioned the traditional view of *marriage as necessary for human completeness. This was particularly liberating for women, who feature prominently in the Gospel accounts. The gender roles reflected in the epistles have been the subject of intense scrutiny. Most commentators believe that the NT writers sought reformation of *family structures rather than revolution, though the extent of that reformation and its paradigmatic nature are debated. Further, as B. Witherington comments: 'Paul's constant use of family language to refer to his fellow believers indicates that he, like Jesus, saw the family of faith as the central and controlling social reality' ('Women [NT]', in *ABD* 6, p. 959).

Communal

The symbiotic relationship between individual and community in the creation accounts has already been noted. Throughout the OT the dominant theme is that of Israel as God's community, living together in fellowship with him. The importance of the community is demonstrated forcefully in the punishment of being 'cut off from one's people', used particularly for cultic sin (Lev. 7:20, *etc.*). While not as immediate as the death penalty, its effect could be equally profound. In laments psalmists often grieve over their solitude and the rupture of human relationships; in thanksgivings they inevitably invite the congregation to share their joy. Faith in Yahweh was essentially a community faith.

The NT similarly stresses human solidarity. The fatal effect on humanity of Adam's *sin is countered by the revivifying effect of Christ's resurrection (1 Cor. 15). And the new people of God are no less a community than the old. Mutual love is its distinctive feature (John 15:17), and the motivation and goal of its members (Rom. 8:35; Heb. 13:1), while exclusion is the community's ultimate sanction (1 Cor. 5:2).

Spiritual

W. Brueggemann rightly observes that the OT 'has no interest in articulating an autonomous or universal notion of humanness' (*Old Testament Theology*, p. 450). Rather, he notes that humanness is conceived only in relation to Yahweh, and its fundamental characteristics are seen only in this relationship: obedience, discernment and trust; complaint, petition and thanksgiving; praise and hope. (These three groups echo Brueggemann's focus on orientation, disorientation and new orientation in the psalms.) Certainly historical, legal, liturgical and prophetic texts take the spiritual dimension of humanity as axiomatic. The wisdom material seems to give a more detached and autonomous portrayal of humanity, due to proverbial wisdom's atomistic nature and its appeal to human reason. But even here the fear of the Lord is fundamental, and issues of relationship with God lie at the heart of Job and Ecclesiastes.

The NT likewise understands humanity in terms of its relationship with God, and focuses specifically on the rupture, restoration, present experience and ultimate perfection of this relationship. Humans individually and collectively are weak, mortal and sinful, as Paul explains at length (Rom. 1:18 – 3:20). But their condition has been changed dramatically in Christ (Rom. 3:21–26), the only human to be perfect in his unbroken relationship with God the Father (Heb. 5:8–9). Believers together form the new humanity, citizens of earth and of heaven, and living in expectation of the new heavens and the new earth.

Bibliography

F. W. Bridger in *NDCEPT*, pp. 21–27; W. Brueggemann, *Old Testament Theology* (Minneapolis, 1997); G. Carey, *I Believe in*

Man (London, 1977); J. W. Cooper, *Body, Soul and Life Everlasting* (Grand Rapids, 1989); O. Cullmann, *Immortality of the Soul or Resurrection of the Dead?* (ET, London, 1958); R. H. Gundry, *Sōma in Biblical Theology* (Cambridge, 1976); P. E. Hughes, *The True Image* (Grand Rapids and Leicester, 1989); P. K. Jewett, *Who We Are: Our Dignity as Human* (Grand Rapids, 1996); H. D. McDonald, *The Christian View of Man* (Basingstoke and Westchester, 1981); C. Sherlock, *The Doctrine of Humanity* (Leicester and Downers Grove, 1996); W. F. Taylor, 'Humanity, NT View of', *ABD* 3, pp. 321–325; P. Trible, *God and the Rhetoric of Sexuality* (Philadelphia, 1978); H. W. Wolff, *Anthropology of the Old Testament* (ET, London, 1974).

P. S. JOHNSTON

HUMILITY, PRIDE

Introduction

The various Hebrew words (translated 'afflicted', 'needy', 'poor', *etc.*) associated with humility (Heb. *'anaw, 'anî*) are derived from an anthropocentric view of *humanity in which humility is weakness caused by oppression or mismanagement. However in Scripture a theocentric worldview controls the connotations of the term, which refers primarily to submission to *God. Such submission is the appropriate attitude before the divine majesty and is a necessary condition for accepting his *grace. Even God himself is willing to stoop low to save the humble. In the NT, humility is taught by both example (in the incarnation, the foot-washing and the passion) and word to *Jesus' disciples. Grace is given only to the humble.

Pride (*ge, ga'on, gbh*) with its associated words (translated 'loftiness', 'height', 'majesty', 'exaltation', *etc.*), is not always a negative quality in the OT. God is *exalted high above all he has made. *Blessings given by his gracious hand, when acknowledged as such, are properly viewed with pride. It is when theocentricity becomes anthropocentricity and the divine majesty is usurped that pride becomes *sinful. Pride is therefore a direct opposite of humility. In the NT Paul can take pride in his work for God since that work is all of grace. In contrast, self-centred pride is a symptom of depravity. In heaven, God is fully, finally and perfectly exalted and all sinful human pride is banished for ever.

Humility in the OT

In the patriarchal period, while humility is not explicit in people's approach to God, it is implied in the physical posture of bowing low in *worship (Gen. 24:26; *cf.* Exod. 4:31, *etc.*). Though Abraham speaks with God as friend with friend, when pleading for Sodom he acknowledges that he is 'nothing but dust and ashes' (Gen. 18:27, NIV). Aged Jacob, in whom the afflictions of his long life have evidently worked humility, abases himself before Pharaoh, albeit as a spiritual colossus blessing a potentate (Gen. 47:7–10). Moses, once accused of elevating himself above his fellow Hebrews (Exod. 2:14), learns humility during the years of his exile (Exod. 3:11, *etc.*) The principle is therefore established that God uses modest human instruments to accomplish his salvific purposes, lest his people should boast in themselves and rob him of his *glory (Judg. 7:2). The insignificant Gideon (Judg. 6:15) and David (1 Sam. 16:11; *cf.* 18:23) are chosen, and the latter points forward to another modest leader (Is. 11:1; 53:2).

The Hebrew verb *'anâ*, which implies physical self-abasement is used in levitical regulations prescribing fasting (Lev. 16:29, 31; *cf.* Num. 29:7). A hand laid on the sacrifice's head in the sin and guilt offerings (Lev. 4 – 6) indicates a humbling of the sinner before a *holy God. The afflictions of *Israel in the wilderness were intended to humble them and so teach them to depend on God (Deut. 8:2–5). They must guard against pride when the exigencies of their wanderings give way to the prosperity of Canaan (Deut. 8:13–17). Thus what has already been implied in the stories of their forebears becomes a divine requirement of the elect nation which can never have cause for human pride (Deut. 7:6–7).

In the Psalms, a pious humility is described for which Moses, the meekest man in all the earth (Num. 12:3), is paradigmatic. The afflicted (Heb. *'anî*) are those brought low by injustice or exploitation; they constitute an economically destitute class (Lev. 19:10; 23:22) whose sole defender is God (Deut. 10:17–18). A distinction begins to appear between these people and the spiritually afflicted (*'anaw*, *'niyyîm*; mostly *prays*, *tapeinos* in LXX), in whom life's trials have done their proper work and wrought humility (Pss. 69:32–33; 119:67, 71, 75, 92, *etc.*), and who have learned to depend on God, who comforts them (Ps. 22:24; *cf.* Prov. 22:4). The psalmist daringly portrays God as humbling himself by stooping down to save the humble (Pss. 18:27, 35c; 113:5–8). In Psalm 22 the company of Israel who *fear (v. 23) and seek the Lord (v. 26) are the *suffering humble (v. 24) whose deliverance will be proclaimed universally (v. 27) to a people yet unborn (v. 31). Psalm 22 refers prophetically to David's greater Son who will provide the supreme example of inward humility in suffering.

In Isaiah, Zion is the refuge for the humble (14:32) who are comforted by divine compassion (49:13). The Servant who takes their afflictions upon himself (53:7) also proclaims good news to the meek (61:1). All God's *people are now called *'niyyîm*. In Zephaniah, a humble, *righteous remnant (2:3), marked out by their ethical integrity (3:12–13), are sharply distinguished from a shameful nation (2:1) of haughty oppressors (3:1, 11) who will be excluded from the city of God. In post-exilic Zechariah (9:9–10), the victorious king is humble, riding on a foal rather than a war horse. Thus the scene is set for him who was *gentle and lowly (*prays kai tapeinos*) in heart (Matt. 11:29).

Pride in the OT

In Moses' song and blessing (Deut. 32 – 33), pride is presented positively, with reference to the exalted majesty of God, and negatively, with reference to rebellion against him. God is the Most High (32:8) who rides on the clouds (33:26; *cf.* Exod. 15:1, 11), subduing his enemies, who cower before him, and trampling down their lofty places (33:29). He caused Israel also to ride on the heights (32:13). But Israel arrogantly 'kicked', abandoning the God who made them (32:15). Pride had caused Egypt to treat Israel harshly (Exod. 18:11), and Israel must beware lest the same stubborn pride beguile them into disobeying the Torah (Lev. 26:19). Even a high priest could be ensnared by spiritual arrogance and scorn the divinely ordained cultus (1 Sam. 2:29).

In the Psalms, 'pride' sometimes has positive connotations. God had subdued (humbled) nations and thereby given Israel an inheritance, 'the pride of Jacob' (47:3–4); its city was beautiful in its loftiness (48:2). But the term has negative associations too. In pride the wicked oppress the *poor and weak (humble) (9:12; 10:2), as they throw off all humility and scorn the righteous (17:10; 31:18; 123:3–4), whose only defence is in God (36:11).

In the prophets, pride is variously traced to military might (Ezek. 30:6), material wealth (but the Lord will humble the rich [Is. 23:8–9]) and the desire to be like God (Ezek. 28:2, 6, 17; Ezek. 28:1–19 has traditionally been interpreted as referring to an attempt by Satan to usurp the divine glory and has thus led some commentators to regard pride as the sin of sins). In sharp distinction to the meekness of the poor and needy, pride is marked by empty boasting (Jer. 48:29–30; Zeph. 2:10) and heedlessness to the plight of the afflicted (Ezek. 16:49). Even the sanctuary becomes the object of pride and false confidence; therefore God hands it over to desecration (Ezek. 7:20–24; 24:21).

The wisdom literature frequently contrasts the proud with the humble (Prov. 16:19; 29:23). Pride is also contrasted with fear of the Lord (Prov. 8:13) which in some places is linked with humility (Prov. 22:4; *cf.* Ps. 22:23–26). Those who, like Nebuchadnezzar, vaunt themselves will either have their arrogance subdued by God (Dan. 4:28–37) or be destroyed as Belshazzar was (Dan. 5:22–23, 30; *cf.* Prov. 16:18, *etc.*), for God opposes the proud but gives grace to the humble (Prov. 3:34; *cf.* Jas. 4:6).

Humility in the NT

Mary's song of praise acknowledges that God has looked with favour on her humble state (Luke 1:48; *cf.* 1 Sam. 2:7–8), and in choosing her to be the mother of the Christ, has scattered the proud and lifted up the humble (Luke 1:51–53). Humility is to know one's true position before God (Matt. 5:3–5) as a dependent child (Matt. 18:1–4). The messianic mission is therefore directed towards humbling the proud and exalting the humble.

In the OT, humbling of oneself is before God (except in Prov. 25:6). However, Jesus' explicit teaching adds a horizontal dimension to the concept; he was among his disciples as one who served (Luke 22:27, *etc.*). Anyone who would be the first (godly ambition is not forbidden in the church; *cf.* 1 Tim. 3:1) must be the last, the servant of all (Mark 9:35, *etc.*). God will humble those who exalt themselves but those who humble themselves will be exalted. The Hebrew root of 'pride' is 'lofty, high', yet humility as the opposite of self-exalting pride is prescribed by Jesus. It is not to be displayed outwardly, but is a hidden condition of the heart (Matt. 6:16–18). Indeed, he who calls the burdened to learn from him is meek and lowly in heart.

The Pauline teaching on the person and work of Christ presents his self-emptying and humiliation in death on a cross as the pathway to exaltation and 'the name above every name' (Phil. 2:6–11). Paul, slave of Christ, humbles himself by preaching the gospel without cost (2 Cor. 10:1; 11:7), but by his self-humbling the Corinthians are elevated (*cf.* 1 Cor. 4:10; 2 Cor. 4:12). He is but an earthen vessel (2 Cor. 4:7). Moreover, he has learned humility through material want, but thereby has been strengthened through Christ's power (Phil. 4:12–13).

Christian fellowship can be maintained only by humility of spirit. The disciples must follow their Lord's example and wash each others' feet (John 13:14–15). When believers humbly count others better than themselves they have the mind of Christ (Phil. 2:3–5). Both leaders and led must show humility towards each other (1 Pet. 5:5–6; *cf.* 3:8, *etc.*). God gives grace to and exalts the humble (Jas. 4:6).

Pride in the NT

As in the OT, 'pride' has both positive and negative connotations in the NT. Paul quotes from Jeremiah 9:24, 'Let him who boasts boast in the Lord' (2 Cor. 10:17). When God is given the glory, boasting in his blessings is appropriate. Thus Paul can take godly pride in the authority given to him to build up the *church (2 Cor. 10:8), in the progress of his converts (2 Cor. 7:14; 9:3–4), and supremely in the cross (Gal. 6:14). At the parousia, his glory will be those he has won for Christ (1 Thess. 2:19–20). This boasting in the Lord is connected to the apostle's personal abasement; sharing in the humiliation of Christ's suffering has been the means of new life (Eph. 3:13; 2 Cor. 4:10–12, 17).

On the other hand, when God is not given his due place in society, the inevitable outcome is an evil form of pride. This pride (vain conceit) is incompatible with the humility of Christ (Phil. 2:3–8) and is classified with shameful acts of depravity (Rom. 1:30; *cf.* Mark 7:22). It leads to foolish presumption and bragging about the unknown future (Jas. 4:13–16), and has a demonic source – the boasting tongue is set on fire by hell (Jas. 3:6). Believers are by no means immune from the dangers of pride. A young convert too hastily given office in the church may become conceited and so suffer the same judgment as was meted out to the devil (1 Tim. 3:6).

Paul exposed the futility of Jewish boasting in the law; those who rely on the law dishonour God by breaking it (Rom. 2:17, 23). Moreover, proud people rely on themselves, seeking their own glory before God. Abraham had nothing to boast about before God, for he was justified by faith (Rom. 4:1–12). For Paul, the shed blood of Christ excludes all human boasting (Rom. 3:27).

In Revelation, the final victory of God and his Christ is encapsulated in the subjugation of fallen, earthly pride and the universal ascription of highest praise and honour to him who is exalted on his throne. Those who refused to repent and give God the glory are judged (16:9), together with the woman dressed in purple and scarlet who boasted in her carnal glory – 'Fallen, fallen is Babylon the Great!' (17:4–6; 18:2–8). In the divine presence, the living creatures prostrate themselves before God (5:13–14; *cf.* 11:13; 14:7). Because God is all and in all, the nations rightly bring into the heavenly city their glory and honour and the kings their splendour (21:24, 26). The book concludes with the prayer that the day when the divine majesty is acknowledged by all creation will come quickly (22:20).

Bibliography

R. Bultmann, '*kauchēma*', *TDNT* 3, pp. 645–654; I. Cornelius, '*gā'ôn*', *NIDOTTE* 1, p. 789; W. J. Dumbrell, '*ānāw*', *NIDOTTE* 3, pp. 454–464; W. Grundmann, '*tapeinos*', *TDNT* 8, pp. 1–26; F. Hauck, '*prays*', *TDNT* 6, pp. 645–651; G. V. Smith and V. P. Hamilton, '*gbh*', *NIDOTTE* 1, pp. 797–799; *idem*, '*gē*' *NIDOTTE* 1, pp. 786–789.

D. C. SEARLE

IDOLATRY

The concept of idolatry in the Bible is

powerful and complex, diverse and problematic. Even though, as M. Halbertal and A. Margalit note, 'the central theological principle in the Bible is [the refutation of] idolatry' (*Idolatry*, p. 10), ironically the 'category that is supposed to be the firmest and strictest of all ... [exhibits] an astonishing fluidity' (p. 250). A theological treatment of the subject must consider the close association of idolatry with sexual immorality and greed and attempt to answer fundamental questions, such as 'What is idolatry?' and 'What constitutes a god?'

Opposition to idolatry

In the Bible there is no more serious charge than that of idolatry. Idolatry called for the strictest punishment, elicited the most disdainful polemic, prompted the most extreme measures of avoidance, and was regarded as the chief identifying characteristic of those who were the very antithesis of the *people of God, namely, the Gentiles (see *Nations). Fundamental to *Israel's life and faith were the first commandment and its exposition in the Shema (Deut. 6:4–5), which from early in the nation's history were thought to touch every aspect of its life. The early *church likewise treated idol *worship with the utmost seriousness.

Idolatry is the ultimate expression of unfaithfulness to *God and for that reason is the occasion for severe divine punishment (*cf.* Lev. 26:27–33; Num. 33:51–56; Deut. 29:16–28). The portrayal of the kings in 1 and 2 Kings is especially revealing. Kings are assessed as either good or bad purely on religious grounds, that is, on whether they destroyed or introduced idols. Omri, one of the greatest kings of Israel, is a case in point. In spite of his political achievements and the 'power that he showed' (1 Kgs. 16:27, NRSV), he is mentioned only briefly, because of 'the sins that he caused Israel to commit, provoking the LORD, the God of Israel, to anger by their idols' (1 Kgs. 16:26). The theme of *judgment on idolatry is widespread also in the NT (Acts 7:41–43; 17:29–31; Rom. 1:18–23; 1 Cor. 5:10–13; 6:9; 10:5–8, 14–22; Gal. 5:19–21; Eph. 5:5–6; Col 3:5–6; 1 Pet. 4:3–5; Rev. 2:20–23; 14:9–11; 16:1–2; 19:20; 21:8; 22:15).

The theological ground for the judgment of idolatry is the jealousy of God. The belief that idolatry arouses God's jealousy is a pervasive OT theme with a long history. It is introduced in the second commandment (Exod. 20:5; Deut. 5:8–10) and in Exodus 34:14 ('for you shall worship no other god, because the LORD, whose name is Jealous, is a jealous God'), and it explains the divine name, 'Jealous'. In fact, all the Pentateuchal references to God's jealousy have to do with idol-worship. An idol worshipped in Jerusalem in Ezekiel 8:3 is called 'the image of jealousy, which provokes to jealousy' (*cf.* Ezek. 16:38, 42; 23:25).

The conviction that God's jealousy inevitably leads him to stern action is also deeply rooted in the OT. God's jealousy, based upon his *love for those he has redeemed at great cost, motivates him to judge his people; *cf.* Nahum 1:2, 'A jealous and avenging God is the LORD.' The OT is full of texts in which God's jealousy leads him to destroy the faithless among his people (*cf.* Deut. 6:14–15; Josh. 24:19–20; Ps. 78:58–64; Zeph. 1:18). The warning of 1 Corinthians 10:22 echoes this teaching.

A common strategy in the OT for opposing idolatry was ridiculing polemic, in which the idols are portrayed as powerless and deceptive. The main examples are Psalms 115:4–8; 135:15–18; the words of Elijah (1 Kgs. 18:27); the prayer of Hezekiah (Is. 37:17–20; 2 Kgs. 19:16–19); and especially the teaching of certain prophets (Hab. 2:18–19; Jer. 14:22; 10:3–5; Is. 44:9–20; Hos. 8:4–6). Such material stresses the perishable nature of the idols, their human origin (in the mind and skills of the maker) and their lifelessness; the writers insist that idol worship leads only to the disappointment and embarrassment of those who trust in them. Habakkuk 2:18–19 contains all these elements.

The most commonly-used Greek term for idol, *eidōlon*, which occurs almost 100 times in the LXX, lends itself to such polemic and is in effect a term of derision. The established association of the word with insubstantiality and falsehood provided its pejorative element. Paul uses it pejoratively in Romans 1:18–32 and in 1 Corinthians 12:2 ('idols that could not speak'). To worship idols is both an error and a foolish vanity (*cf.* 1 Thess. 1:9–10; Acts 14:15; and esp. 1 John 5:21 where idols are contrasted with the living and true God). By contrast, the usual Greek term for cultic image, *agalma*, had positive associations of joy and beauty. Disgust and contempt for idolatry is also conveyed by several derogatory terms used to denote idols. Idols are 'unclean things', a common designation in Ezekiel, 'weak/worthless things', 'that which is insubstantial', and a '*vanity' or 'emptiness'. The Israelites were not simply to avoid idolatry; the language of prohibition could hardly be more emotive and urgent. They are to 'utterly detest and abhor' the heathen gods (Deut. 7:25–26).

The call to resist pagan pressure for Jews to compromise their religion by contact with idolatry is nowhere more clear than in Daniel, where the king's rich and presumably idolatrous food is shunned (ch. 1), Daniel's three companions refuse to worship the king's golden image (ch. 3) and Daniel refuses to *pray to the king (ch. 6). According to this book, earthly, pagan kingdoms will ultimately give way to the everlasting kingdom of the one true God (cf. 2:44; 4:3, 34; 6:26; 7:1–27).

It is not just that idolatry was one vice among many of which the heathen were guilty; rather, idolatry is a defining feature of the heathen, whose way of life is characterized inevitably by this *sin. 1 Thessalonians 4:3–5, read in conjunction with 1:9, is an early Pauline witness to this conviction. The characterization of the heathen by the three sins of sexual immorality, idolatry and greed comes through consistently in the Pauline vice catalogues. Furthermore, these three sins are the only vices in the Pauline letters that are considered to be such a threat that they must be 'shunned' or 'fled' (1 Cor. 6:18; 10:14 and 1 Tim. 6:10–11 respectively). In Romans 2:22 Paul takes it for granted that Jews abhor and detest idols. Opposition to idolatry was in effect a drawing of group boundaries for the people of God, set within the wider framework of their identity and self-definition. In making clear what they stood for, they emphasized what they stood against.

The worship of idols

Israel's neighbours used images in worship, but in Israel their use was prohibited (Exod. 20:4–5, 23; 34:17; Lev. 19:4; 26:1; Deut. 4:15–19, 25–26; 5:8; Jer. 10:3–5; 11:10–13). In Deuteronomy 4:12–18 it is said that God chooses to make himself known through words rather than through a visible form, and in Isaiah 40:18, 25 the prophet reasons that because the Lord is incomparable, all representative forms are inadequate. None the less, on numerous occasions the nation failed to keep the second commandment (cf. e.g. the golden calf in Exod. 32 – 33; Micah's image in Judg. 17 – 18; and Jeroboam's bulls in 1 Kgs. 12:28–33).

The term 'idolatry' can be defined as either the worship of images or the worship of foreign gods. Both definitions are valid. The second commandment extends and applies the first. At least in Israelite understanding, a pagan deity was present in its image (cf. Exod. 20:23, 'gods of silver' and 'gods of gold'; Lev. 19:4 RSV, 'molten gods'; Josh. 24:14, 'put away the gods'). Disagreement over the division of the Ten Commandments also obscures the close relation between the first and second commandments. Whereas the conventional Jewish division takes the opening verse as the first commandment and the prohibition of the worship of other gods and of images as the second, Augustine and the Roman Catholic and Lutheran traditions consider all this material to be the first commandment. In most cases the OT authors do not distinguish between the worship of other gods, the worship of images and the worship of the Lord using images. While a formal distinction between having gods and having images is possible, and may be useful, especially in discussion of images, for our purposes 'idolatry' is taken in the broadest sense to include both.

Just as keeping the first commandment was expected to lead one to obey all the commandments, so idolatry was thought to lead to other sins (Rom. 1:18–32; cf. Wisdom of Solomon 14:27: 'The worship of idols ... is the beginning and cause and end of every evil'), including and in particular sexual immorality. In one sense the link between sexual immorality and idolatry could not be more concrete. Pagan temples were often the venue for illicit sexual activities. Religious prostitution was commonly practised in the cults of the ancient Near Eastern fertility religions, and was a problem for Israel from the moment they entered the promised land (Num. 25:1–3; cf. Judg. 2:17), becoming especially prevalent in Judah and Israel during the divided monarchy (from Rehoboam, 1 Kgs. 14:22–24, to Josiah, 2 Kgs. 23:7). According to Exodus 34:11–16 the extermination of the inhabitants of the land was commanded so that the Israelites would avoid the practice. In Deuteronomy 23:17 cult prostitution is forbidden in Israel (*cf.* Amos 2:7).

Prostitution at cultic festivals is well attested in places like Corinth and is even mentioned in the OT. In the ancient Near East orgies commonly took place at heathen festivals. Hosea 4:13–14 probably refers to this kind of activity; mountaintop sacrifices, suggestive of pagan altars, and prostitutes are juxtaposed. Further possible references in the OT to this practice include Numbers 25:1–15, where Phineas' slaying of Zimri for sexual immorality occurred in the context of pagan sacrifice, and Isaiah 57:3–10, Jeremiah 2:20; 3:6 (*cf.* 2 Macc. 6:4–5). In Judges 21:19–23 even a feast to the Lord at Shiloh was the occasion for the Benjamites to take wives by force. The description of the cult of the golden calf can be considered as an archetype of such events (Exod. 32). During the celebrations 'the people sat down to eat and drink, and rose up to revel' (Exod. 32:6). The verb 'to revel' in Hebrew is clearly a euphemism for sexual activities. According to both pagan and Christian writers feasting and sexual immorality inevitably went together.

There seems little doubt that the discussion of idol food in 1 Corinthians 8 – 10 also addressed the problem of sexual immorality. Paul's response to the problem of the prostitute in 1 Corinthians 6:12–20 should probably be read in this light. Apparently some Corinthians were eating in pagan temples and using the prostitutes on offer on such occasions, and were defending both kinds of behaviour with the slogan, 'all things are lawful for me' (6:12). As already noted, the phrase 'rise up to revel' in 10:7 (an allusion to Exod. 32:6) is probably a reference to prostitution on a festive occasion in a pagan temple. Revelation 2:14 may be evidence of such activity in Asia Minor: the church in Pergamum is guilty of eating food sacrificed to idols and of sexual immorality. All this suggests a close association between sexual immorality and idolatry.

The concept of idolatry

Idolatry is defined by a number of 20th-century theologians in terms of making that which is contingent absolute. For Reinhold Niebuhr, for example, idolatry occurs when we 'make some contingent and relative vitality into the unconditioned principle of meaning' (*The Nature and Destiny of Man*, p.

178). In fact Niebuhr defines not just idolatry but sin itself in such terms: 'sin is the vain imagination by which man hides the conditioned, contingent and dependent character of his existence and seeks to give it the appearance of unconditioned reality' (pp. 137–138). Sin consists of placing such a high value on something that in effect it replaces God. Both the strength and weakness of this view of idolatry lie in its being so general. It can be readily applied to almost anything. Labelling all sin idolatry, attractive as this may sound, does not do justice to the variety and depth of the Bible's treatment of sin. Law-breaking, lawlessness, impurity and the absence of love are just a few of the many other ways in which Scripture defines sin. Romans 1 does not in fact take idolatry to be the pattern of all subsequent sins, but rather portrays indulgence in further sin, being given up to various vices, as the appropriate punishment for giving up God in idolatry. In attempting to understand idolatry, theologians like Niebuhr take a top-down approach, focusing on God as the absolute one. Another way of proceeding is from the bottom up, looking at what idolaters do with their idols, of what the charge of idolatry consists and to what the sin of idolatry is compared.

Two models of idolatry

The Bible uses a number of anthropomorphic metaphors to elucidate the way in which God relates to humankind. God is king, father, bridegroom, woman in labour, judge, and so on. The relevant metaphor for the dominant and most familiar conception of idolatry in the OT is that of marital relations (see *Marriage). The depiction of idolatry as sinful sexual relations is introduced in the Pentateuch (Exod. 34:15–16) and is used extensively in the prophets, especially Hosea, Jeremiah and Ezekiel. Common to all uses of the image is the idea that Israel is married to God but is unfaithful to her husband. The betrayed husband experiences both a fierce desire for revenge and a strong urge to win back his beloved wife. If Hosea describes idolatry as prostitution, Ezekiel is even more daring; for him it is outright nymphomania. However, the marital model is not the only understanding of idolatry found in the OT.

Another model of idolatry appears in the prophets, namely, the political model, in which God is seen as *king, and his people as his subjects. When God is understood as a husband, he demands exclusive love and devotion; as king, he demands trust and confidence in his ability to provide for and protect those under his care, and loyal service and *obedience. In both the marital and political models the choice of metaphor was reinforced or perhaps even occasioned by a potent association. Temple prostitution and the deification of human leaders made the marital and the political models of idolatry respectively all the more appropriate.

When the Israelites requested a king in 1 Samuel 8, Samuel was displeased and prayed to the Lord. The Lord's comforting reply in 8:7–9 compares their rejection of God's kingship to idolatry. Likewise the prophets Isaiah, Jeremiah and Ezekiel denounce Israel's treaties with Assyria and Egypt in terms that add up to nothing less than a charge of idolatry, even though the literal worship of other gods is nowhere in view. In Isaiah 31:1–3 the prophet chides the nation for its treaty with Egypt against the threat of Assyria. The reliance upon Egypt is regarded as a form of deification. Since God is Israel's ruler, the nation is supposed to seek protection only from him. To seek it elsewhere is in effect to look to another 'god' ('The Egyptians are human, and not God'). Isaiah 30:7 describes Egyptian help against the Assyrians as 'worthless'; the same Hebrew word is employed in Isaiah 57:13 and Jeremiah 2:5 to condemn the idolatry of the fathers. Jeremiah 2:17–19 describes the treaties with the Egyptians and with the Assyrians as a forsaking of God in favour of someone else. The nation is guilty of idolatry because they sought protection from and relied upon something other than God. In Ezekiel the political and marital models merge, with the treaties being described in the familiar language of marital unfaithfulness: 'You played the whore with the Egyptians, your lustful neighbours, multiplying your whoring, to provoke me to anger' (16:26); 'You played the whore with the Assyrians' (16:28). In this case the request to foreign powers for protection is compared to *adultery and the relation between God the king and the nation to that of a husband and wife.

With a throne room, from which God rules the world, and twenty-four elders who sit on thrones and wear crowns, ruling the heavenly world on God's behalf, the book of Revelation is not short of political imagery. Revelation portrays God's rule over against that of the Roman empire which, like most political powers in the ancient world, represented its power in religious terms, claiming for itself the ultimate, divine sovereignty over the world. Its state religion, which featured the worship both of the deified emperors and of the traditional gods of Rome, expressed political loyalty in terms of religious worship (cf. R. Bauckham, *The Theology of Revelation*). Revelation presents an alternative, theocentric vision of the world, referring frequently to worship in its graphic portrayal of the conflict of sovereignties. Glimpses of worship in heaven punctuate the reports of God's victory over false worship on earth. Christians are called to resist the deification of military and political power, represented by the beast, and of economic prosperity, represented by Babylon (see Rev. 18:2–17), by worshipping the true God and living under his rule.

Texts including the terms usually translated 'to serve' and 'to worship' supply unambiguous evidence that idolaters (and believers) were thought to serve and obey their deities. Even in ceremonial contexts these words signify more than just isolated acts of cultic worship. When it is said that the people 'worship' Baal (Judg. 10:6, 10, *etc.*) or other gods (Judg. 10:13, *etc.*) or the Lord (Judg. 10:16, *etc.*) the term implies not only the exclusive nature of the relationship but the total commitment and, in effect, obedience of the worshipper. That to 'serve' a deity involved doing its bidding is made clear in passages like Matthew 6:24/Luke 16:13, where the 'service' is that rendered to a master, and in the Pauline phrase 'bow/bend the knee(s)' (Rom. 11:4; 14:11; Eph. 3:14; Phil. 2:10), which is a synonym for worship.

Although it is difficult to reduce biblical teaching on idolatry to a simple formula, one element common to both models, the marital and the political, is worth noting. In both cases the notion of *exclusivity* is central: in one the exclusive claims of a husband to his wife's love and affection; in the other the exclusive claims of a sovereign to protect and provide for his subjects and receive their trust and obedience in return. Thus idolatry is an attack on God's exclusive rights to our love, trust and obedience.

Greed as idolatry

With this definition in mind, what then qualifies as idolatry? Although a number of possibilities, including pride, come to mind, the NT unambiguously judges only one thing to be idolatry, outside of the literal worship of idols, namely greed. The charge that greed is idolatry appears in four places. It is stated in Colossians 3:5 ('greed ... is idolatry') and Ephesians 5:5 ('one who is greedy [that is, an idolater]') and implied in the mammon saying in Matthew 6:24 and Luke 16:13. Whether worship of the belly in Romans 16:18 and Philippians 3:19 refers to Jewish preoccupation with food laws or circumcision, fleshly egocentricism, or gluttony and by extension greed, is difficult to say. Although the passage falls short of explicitly branding greed as idolatry, the two sins are treated as comparable in character and gravity in Job 31:24–28. Philo of Alexandria's repeated warnings against the idolatry of the love of money suggests that the provenance of the idea is Jewish. According to Philo the first commandment 'condemns strongly the money-lovers who procure gold and silver coins from every side and treasure their hoard like a divine image in a sanctuary, believing it to be a source of blessing and happiness of every kind' (*On The Special Laws* 1:21–22).

In what sense is greed idolatry? Matthew 6:24, understood in context, gives clear support to the idea that the worship of mammon instead of God involves love and devotion (using these very words), and service and obedience (using the notion of rival masters). It also implies a negative judgment on trusting in wealth since the verses which verse 24 introduces, 6:25–34, point to the birds and lilies in order to inspire trust in God's providential care.

Another indication that the greedy are idolaters because they love, trust and serve money rather than God is seen in the condemnation of the greedy in the Bible for their inordinate love, misplaced trust and forbidden service. A virtual synonym for 'greed', *pleonexia*, found in a broad range of material, is 'love of money', *philargyria* (*e.g.* Luke 16:14; 1 Tim. 3:3; 6:10; 2 Tim. 3:2), which is sometimes expressed in the form of an admonition (*e.g.* Heb. 13:5: 'Keep your lives free from the love of money'). Furthermore, in the OT the rich are not 'to set their heart',

the spiritual organ of love and devotion, on their riches (Ps. 62:10; *cf.* 2 Pet. 2:14). That such love should be reserved for God is spelt out in *Testament of Benjamin* 6:1–3: 'the good man ... does not accumulate wealth out of love for pleasure ... the Lord is his lot.'

Numerous texts not only observe that the rich trust in their riches, but warn against such reliance as being incompatible with and an unacceptable alternative to trust in God. Jeremiah accuses Israel of trusting in her 'strongholds and ... treasures' (48:7; *cf.* 22:21; 49:4; Ezek. 28:4–5; Hos. 12:7–8). Psalm 52:7 states that the one who 'would not take refuge in God ... trusted in abundant riches' (*cf.* 49:5–15). In Proverbs 'the wealth of the rich is their fortress' (10:15) and 'their strong city' (18:11); but 'Those who trust in their riches will wither' (11:28). On the other hand, God is the only trust of the *poor and those of humble means (Pss. 34:6; 40:17; *cf.* 68:10; 86:1; Is. 66:2). Proverbs 18:10–11 suggestively juxtaposes trust in God and trust in money. In Proverbs 28:25 a 'greedy person' is contrasted with 'whoever trusts in the LORD'.

Such teaching is also found in the NT, where the parable of the rich fool in Luke 12 warns against all active striving for the increase of material possessions as a means of security and 1 Timothy 6:17 counsels the rich not to trust in their riches but in God. In the NT the notion of trusting God, not money, is also apparent in the instructions to the disciples in the mission charges (*e.g.* Mark 6:8–9), in the story of the widow's offering (Mark 12:41–44 par.), in the calling of Peter and Matthew to leave all and follow Jesus (Mark 1:16–20; Luke 5:27–28), in the example of Zacchaeus (Luke 19:1–10), in the call to store up treasures in heaven, not on earth (Matt. 6:19–21), and supremely in Matthew 6:25–34, the Lukan version of which is introduced by the parable of the rich fool (12:13–34). Hebrews 13:5–6 encourages its readers, with the promise of the Lord's help, not to love money, implying that *faith in God is the alternative to finding security in money.

Evidence of the greedy serving their wealth is less direct. It is implied in the Bible's frequent condemnation of the greedy for ignoring social justice and oppressing the poor. Furthermore, the notion of sin as a ruling power can be seen in John 8:30–36 and

Romans 6. Jewish moral teaching in *Testament of Judah* 8:6 indicates that the love of money is 'contrary to God's commands' and 'enslaves' a person.

Greed is idolatry because the greedy contravene God's exclusive rights to human love, trust and obedience.

Conclusions

The fundamental question of theology, 'What do we mean by "God"?', can be answered from a variety of angles by exploring God's various relations to the world and to ourselves. Ironically, the study of idolatry also gives us some insight into the nature of the true God. What constitutes a god? Martin Luther's answer, as he reflected on the first commandment in his larger catechism, was 'whatever your heart clings to and relies upon, that is your God; trust and faith of the heart alone make both God and idol'. We wish to confirm his view, but also to emphasize love and service: a god is that which one loves, trusts and serves above all else. This definition suggests both the possibility and the urgency of making clear the relevance of idolatry to the modern world.

In one sense idolatry is the diagnosis of the human condition to which the gospel is the cure. The root problem with humans is not a horizontal 'social' problem (like sexual immorality or greed), but rebellion against and replacement of the true and living God with gods that fail (which lead to these destructive sins). If the story of the human race is a sorry tale of different forms of idolatry, the height of human folly, the good news is that God reconciles his image-bearers back to himself in Christ. It is no coincidence that the prophets envisage a time when idols will finally be eradicated and replaced by true worship.

See also: SPIRITUAL POWERS.

Bibliography

R. Bauckham, *The Theology of Revelation*, NTT (Cambridge, 1993); E. M. Curtis in *ABD* 3 pp. 376–381; M. Halbertal and A. Margalit, *Idolatry* (Cambridge, 1992); R. Niebuhr, *The Nature and Destiny of Man*, vol. 1 (London, 1941); V. Ramachandra, *Gods that Fail: Modern Idolatry and Christian Mission* (Carlisle, 1996); B. S. Rosner, *Greed, the Second Idolatry: The Origin and Meaning of a Pauline Metaphor* (Tübingen, forthcoming); *idem*, 'Temple prostitution in 1 Corinthians 6:12–20', *NovT* 40, 1998, pp. 336–351.

B. S. ROSNER

IMAGE OF GOD

The term 'image' can translate both the Hebrew *ṣelem*/Greek *eikōn*, and the Hebrew *d^emut*/Greek *homoiōsis*, though the latter is more usually rendered as 'likeness'. For many centuries it was generally assumed that the 'image' of God comprises the human characteristics of personhood which remain after the fall of *Adam, whereas the 'likeness' comprises those removed or destroyed at the fall. This distinction reflected intertestamental Jewish speculation, which held (in direct contradiction of Genesis) that *God's image gave the human soul the ability to distinguish between good and evil. As time went on, the rabbis argued, this ability diminished, and so the image was corrupted.

In the 16th century, Hebrew scholars concluded that the two words were synonymous, but the influence of the ancient tradition generated the (unfortunate) belief that the image/likeness was lost, or severely corrupted, by the fall. In recent years it has generally been agreed that the Bible nowhere speaks of a loss of the image/likeness, and that there are passages which imply that it is still intact. Human beings are created in God's image; therefore they should not be killed (Gen. 9:6) or cursed (Jas. 3:9). Neither of these texts would have any meaning if the image/likeness had been lost at the fall, and so the traditional view cannot be sustained.

The appearance of the words in Genesis 1:26–27 is of the greatest importance for biblical anthropology. There it is said that both male and female are created in the image and likeness of God, a statement which reinforces the equality of the sexes. However, this must be balanced against 1 Corinthians 11:7 where Paul explains that a man must not cover his head because he is the image of God, whereas a woman (see *Man and woman) ought to cover hers, because she is the image of the man. This does not contradict the Genesis statement, because it is through the man that the woman shares in God's image, given that she was created out of him.

It is possible that the biblical picture reflects the ancient Near Eastern idea of images as statues representing the king and therefore partaking of his authority in some way. If that is true, the designation of Adam as the image of God might mean that he was intended to be God's viceroy on earth.

In the Genesis passage, God says 'Let *us* make man in *our* image' (NIV; author's italics). Augustine believed that the plural referred to the Trinity, and developed a number of theories about the supposed threefold nature of the human soul. It has also been suggested that the plural refers to the angels, and that they are therefore also created in God's image, a view which was supported by Thomas Aquinas, though the Bible nowhere confirms it. Paul says that we shall judge the angels (1 Cor. 6:3), so although we are lower in the order of creation than they are (Ps. 8:5–6), there is no indication that we are dependent on them in any way.

In the NT, the word 'image' occurs twenty-three times, but 'likeness' appears only once, in James 3:9 (see above). The ten occurrences of 'image' in Revelation and the one in Hebrews are irrelevant to our subject. In the Synoptic Gospels, 'image' is used in the parallel passages about paying taxes to Caesar (Matt. 22:20; Mark 12:16; Luke 20:24). Possibly Jesus meant to imply that, just as the coins belonged to Caesar because his image was on them, so human beings belong to God because his image is in us. This is true, but as it is not explicitly stated in the text, we must be careful not to build too much on it.

This leaves nine occurrences of the word in the Pauline corpus, only one of which (1 Cor. 11:7, already mentioned) is undoubtedly connected with the Genesis doctrine. Romans 1:23 may well contain a pun based on it: Paul claims that after the fall we exchanged the glory of the immortal God for the likeness (*homoiōma*) of the image of mortal man; but as this 'likeness' is immediately coupled with those of birds, animals and reptiles, the reference is probably to idols and not the image of God in us.

The other occurrences are of two kinds. Some refer to Christ (see *Jesus Christ), as the 'image of God' (2 Cor. 4:4) or 'the image of the invisible God' (Col. 1:15); the rest refer to us, who are being remade in his image. The latter reminds us of the *creation account, but the term 'image' is used somewhat differently by Paul. In 1 Corinthians 15:49, for instance, he says that whereas we have previously borne the image of the earthly, we shall be recreated in the resurrection, so that we shall then bear the image of the heavenly. Here 'image' clearly refers to our humanity, which we have inherited from Adam, and which will be transformed by Christ, and not to our link with God, which is the meaning of the word in Genesis 1:26. It has sometimes been argued that the 'image of God' in Christ reflects his status as the second Adam, but the real point of the passages which refer to it is to explain Christ's relationship to God the Father, not his relationship to the human race. In his case, being the image of the invisible God means that he is fully divine, which Adam was not.

It must be concluded that the 'image (likeness) of God' refers to a permanent aspect of our created nature, which was not affected by the fall. It is the special characteristic of the human race, which distinguishes us from other creatures and makes our salvation a matter of supreme concern to God. At the same time, the word 'image' is often used in the NT so as to allude to the creation account in Genesis, without specifically referring to it.

See also: HUMANITY.

Bibliography

G. C. Berkouwer, *Man, the Image of God* (Grand Rapids, 1952); G. L. Bray, 'The significance of God's image in man', *TynB* 42.2, 1991, pp. 195–225; D. J. A. Clines, 'The image of God in man', *TynB* 19, 1968, pp. 53–103; A. A. Hoekema, *Created in God's Image* (Grand Rapids and Carlisle, 1986).

G. L. BRAY

IMMANUEL, see Jesus Christ
IMMORTALITY, see LIFE

INCARNATION

The English term 'incarnation' is derived from a Latin word developed from *in* + *caro* [flesh], which means 'being in flesh', and is used in

Christian theology with reference to the way in which the Son of God assumed a *human form in *Jesus. Through this act *God was revealed in a personal way to humankind, and thus in a way which is more adequate for a personal God than *revelation through the display of his *glory as Creator in the created world (Ps. 19:1) or even through personal communication in the words of prophets, law-givers and the wise. At the same time it enabled God to be united with humanity and so to bear their sins, die and make *atonement for them in one act of *sacrifice and reconciliation (2 Cor. 5:19–21). What humanity itself could not do was thus done in a human being by the Son of God, and simultaneously God demonstrated his saving love by himself bearing the consequences of sin (Rom. 5:8). Furthermore, through this union of the divine with the human Jesus became the author and head of a new humanity in which those who believe in him are united with him, share in his divine sonship, become co-heirs with him of glory, and participate in the divine nature (Rom. 8:17, 29–30; 2 Pet. 1:4). It follows that the doctrine of the incarnation is the essential foundation for the Christian doctrine of *salvation and renewal.

Jesus as the Word in the Gospel and epistles of John

Although the noun 'incarnation' is not found in the Bible, the concept represented by it is a familiar one in the NT. It receives classical expression in *John 1:14 where the author of the Gospel states that 'the Word *became flesh* [Latin: *verbum caro factum est*] and dwelt among us'. Here '*Word' is the designation for an entity which existed in the beginning and which paradoxically both 'was with God' and 'was God' (John 1:1–2.). The Word was the source of *light and *life for all who received him and could be said to be 'in the world'. But then the writer claims that the Word became flesh, 'flesh' here being the physical, living substance of which human beings are made.

The statement is not to be taken with wooden literalness to signify that the divine Word was *turned into* flesh, or rather into a creature made of flesh, in the way that a human being might be turned into a pillar of salt (Gen. 19:26). The meaning is clearly that the Word took on a human identity. Nor does it mean that the Word *merely assumed* a physical human body and nothing more, so that, for example, it did not have a human soul; 'flesh' is intended to refer to all that pertains to human life. Nor again does it mean that the Word was united with *an existing human being* so that the latter lost its identity and became simply the carrier of the divine being, perhaps by the unity of a human body with a divine soul.

John himself does not attempt to explain these matters. He emphasizes that those who saw the incarnate Word saw his glory, and that he was full of *grace and *truth which he conveyed to people. No reader would have understood the grace and truth as visible entities; they would have thought rather of the kind of character displayed by the Word and the quality of what he said and did. Equally, his glory is not some kind of visible radiance or accompanying splendour (like that of a king wearing royal apparel). John means rather that Jesus' character displayed those qualities for which people give praise to God and in which they see the character of God; the glory of the Word was seen supremely in his being lifted up on the cross to die, in humiliation and *humility, rather than in any kind of human *exaltation (John 12:23). The purpose of the incarnation is accordingly to make the invisible God 'visible' by showing what he is like and how he behaves.

The prologue to the Gospel thus explains who the Word was and how he became incarnate. The opening statement of 1 John begins with a statement somewhat similar to that of the Gospel, about the Word of life or simply 'the life' itself, which 'appeared' in the world so that it could be heard, seen and touched by human beings (1 John 1:1–4). But then the writer goes on to talk rather about Jesus and to uphold the claim that 'Jesus Christ has come in the flesh' (1 John 4:2, NIV) or that 'Jesus is the Son of God' (1 John 4:15; 5:5). When 2 John 7 comments on deceivers 'who do not acknowledge Jesus as coming in the flesh', the same meaning is probably intended. It is also possible that people were denying that Jesus would come again in the future in the flesh. Here the thought is of the original coming of the Son of God into the world and of his identity with Jesus. The human Jesus is the Son of God. A 'Jesus Christ who has come in the flesh' is a

Jesus who is really human as compared with a Jesus who merely appeared to be human. (See *Epistles of John.)

The paradoxical nature of the concept is now emerging. The texts so far discussed emphasize that a divine being, the Word or the Son, became really human, and that the person named 'Jesus', *i.e.* the 'Jesus of Nazareth' whose life, death and resurrection uniquely identify him, was this divine being. The writers are also claiming that his humanity was real in the sense that whatever can be affirmed of human beings in general was true of him: he had typical, normal human physical characteristics and experiences. He was thus not a divine being 'disguised' as a human being, like a human being temporarily wearing a monkey-suit. There was a real union of the divine being with a human person.

This picture presented by the author of the Gospel and reinforced by 1 John is in harmony with the portrayal of Jesus in the body of the Gospel. Jesus refers to himself as the Son of God, he speaks of God as his Father and he professes to have a hotline to God so that he knows what God wants him to say and do; he speaks of a very close relationship between himself and the Father. These are all things that the followers of Jesus also could say about themselves, but Jesus goes further. He talks about himself as existing before Abraham (John 8:58) and sharing glory with his Father before the world began (John 17:24). He speaks of being sent by the Father and coming from the Father in a way that goes beyond that in which a Christian missionary might say that he or she had been 'sent by God' to a particular area of the world. All this and other evidence might suggest that John thought of Jesus as a human disguise for a divine being that retained its self-consciousness and was 'pretending' to be human. Such a conclusion, however, would clash with other texts in which Jesus appears to have genuinely human experiences, such as hunger, thirst, and sorrow (John 4:6–7; 11:35).

Antecedents to the concept

What lay behind this theological understanding of Jesus? The ancient world acknowledged the possibility of gods, goddesses and other supernatural beings assuming a human (or sometimes animal) bodily form; Greek and Roman mythology testifies abundantly to this. There is little, if any, reflection on what exactly was supposed to happen. Usually the divine beings retain their self-consciousness and simply assume human form in order to communicate visibly and audibly with human beings; their temporary manifestation in human form is an extension of their heavenly life, just as an actor assumes a mask and then discards it again. The gods thus simply *appear* to be human.

It would, then, be possible against this background to think of the divine Word as temporarily assuming a visible and tangible form for the purpose of communicating with human beings. But the NT writers clearly mean something different. Whereas the gods temporarily take on a human form, the Word is united permanently with a human body to be a specific person, Jesus of Nazareth, and it is inconceivable that what God has joined together should ever be sundered.

Some of the great men of the ancient world were regarded as being the offspring of the gods and mortal women, so that they possessed a nature which was part human and part divine. But in these cases there is no suggestion of an existing divine being becoming human; rather an entirely new person comes into existence.

There is nothing fully comparable to the NT idea in the OT. Visible and/or audible manifestations of God are rare, though it was possible for God to visit the Garden of Eden and for Adam and Eve to hear the sound of his voice (Gen. 3:8), and in Exodus 33:18 – 34:9 Moses is permitted to see the back of God but not his front as his glory passes by. Sometimes God sends his angel, who may appear in human form (Gen. 18:2) like a Greek god; the narrative is ambiguous over the relationship between God and his angel. There are also *theophanies, in which God is powerfully present (as in a storm) and may speak, but does not appear in visible form.

One important concept is that of the *wisdom of God, which is personified as a female figure in Proverbs 8 – 9 and the later wisdom literature; she is at God's side during the creation of the world and she comes and sojourns among his people, apparently in the form of the law (Ecclus. 24; *cf. 1 Enoch* 42). But this is merely a literary personification, and there is certainly no thought of Wisdom taking a human form. Nevertheless, the language used of the coming of God's Son into the world in the NT appears to owe something to the way in which Wisdom is described.

The development of the concept in the Pauline corpus

The idea of incarnation emerges in the earlier letters of Paul. God sent his Son, born of a woman, into the world, and then he sent his Spirit to be in the hearts of believers (Gal. 4:4–6). The parallelism between the two sendings and the use of the concept of sonship indicate that the thought here is of something more than the authorization of a human prophet to speak in the name of God. The same idea is probably present when Paul speaks of the way in which the Lord Jesus, though he was rich, became *poor, so that we through his poverty might become rich (2 Cor. 8:9). Although the fact that Jesus was a materially poor person colours the language, the saying clearly does not refer to any act of Jesus surrendering wealth (of whatever kind) in the course of his earthly life; the established interpretation of the text, as a reference to an exchange of the glory of his pre-existent state with the Father in order to share the poverty of sinners so that they might share his 'wealth', is demanded. This ties in with the references elsewhere to believers becoming joint-heirs with Christ of the glory of God, which is what is signified by the metaphor of 'wealth' (Rom. 8:17).

The concept of Jesus Christ as the Son of God dominates the Christology of Romans in that it is emphatically expressed in the summary of the gospel in the opening salutation (Rom 1:3–4). The gospel is about the Son of God (cf. Rom. 1:9) who was humanly a descendant of David but was also appointed the Son of God with power by the resurrection from the dead. These descriptions are not in tension with each other, for example as successive stages in the career of Jesus Christ, so that he becomes the Son of God only at the resurrection; the resurrection is God's powerful seal on his existing sonship. Rather, God sends his Son in the likeness of sinful humanity (Rom. 8:3). When Paul speaks of Jesus as God's Son in this way, the language expresses the closeness of the relationship between them and the scale of the sacrifice made by the Father in sending his own Son to be a sacrifice for sin (Rom. 8:3).

The concept of incarnation thus incorporates that of pre-existence, i.e. that an existing being became a human being, rather than that a human being was conferred with the title or character of the Son of God in the way that human beings who believe in Christ are given the new status and character of children of God by an act of adoption. That this is Paul's understanding there can be no real doubt despite some recent attempts to argue otherwise.

Similarly, when Paul speaks of the one God the Father who created all things and places alongside him the 'one Lord, Jesus Christ, through whom all things came and through whom we live' (1 Cor. 8:6), the parallelism between the two figures and the roles of each in relation to the creation of all things indicate that Paul is thinking of a pre-existent figure whom he names 'Jesus Christ', even though strictly speaking these names apply first to the earthly human being.

Again, Philippians 2:6–11 is an account of a being who existed in the form of God but did not hold on to equality with God and took on the form of a slave by taking the likeness of a human being. The use of the terms 'form' and likeness' does not imply that the being merely *resembled* God or a human being but is rather an attempt to contrast the way in which the being was originally like *God* in nature and appearance and then was like *a human being* in nature and appearance. The contrast does not imply that the figure ceased to be divine when he became human; the idea of a divine being's ceasing to be divine and becoming something else simply did not exist. The point is that the being surrendered those privileges that belong to deity and assumed the role of a slave, even to the extent of being *obedient to God to the ultimate point of dying.

The same Christology reappears in Colossians where Jesus Christ is said to be the Son of God (Col. 1:13), the *image of God, through whom creation took place. In this letter Paul emphasizes that the fullness of God is in Christ (Col. 1:19); in Christ all the fullness of divine being dwells in a bodily form (Col. 2:9). This remarkable statement is evidently intended to exalt Jesus Christ above all the supernatural beings which might be thought to have some influence over humanity and to emphasize that whatever belongs to the essence of God is present in Christ. The term 'bodily' is surprising, since Paul is presumably thinking primarily about the exalted Christ (note the present tense!), but it reflects his belief that the resurrection is a bodily resurrection (1 Cor. 15:44; Paul also refers to Christ's physical body in Rom. 7:4; Phil. 3:21; Col. 1:22), and therefore the point is that the exalted Christ is still a bodily being in whom all that there is of God is to be found. There is thus an identity between God (the Father) and God (the Son) despite the fact that they are separate beings.

In 1 Timothy 3:16 there is a carefully formed statement introduced by a relative pronoun and consisting of six short clauses about 'the mystery of our religion'. At first sight the *mystery is the purpose of God, hidden in past ages, but now revealed in the *gospel message (Eph. 3:4–6). Here, however, although the word 'mystery' is neuter in Greek, the linking relative pronoun is masculine (Gk *hos*, translated as 'he' rather than 'who' in most English versions); it is generally assumed that the pronoun is the introduction to the remnant of a pre-formed statement which might have run something like 'Jesus Christ, who appeared in a body …', but it is more likely that the pronoun is intended to identify 'the mystery of our religion' with the person who 'appeared in a body' (NIV; lit. 'in flesh'). As elsewhere in the Pastoral Epistles, the saving event, the gospel which enshrines it, and the person in whom it is centred, tend to be dynamically identified; thus in Titus 2:11 (*cf.* 3:5) it is 'the grace of God' which has appeared, but in Titus 1:3 it is 'his word' and in 2 Timothy 1:10 God's grace is revealed 'through the appearing of our Saviour, Christ Jesus', whereas in 1 Timothy 1:15 'Christ Jesus came into the world'. Against this background it is likely that 1 Timothy 3:16 is an incarnational statement that ties in naturally with the earlier teaching of Paul.

In some texts a contrast is drawn between the 'now' of the present time in which Christ is revealed and the 'then' of the primeval time when God made his plan of salvation or 'grace was given us in Christ' (even before we came into existence, 2 Tim. 1:9). Outside the Pauline corpus, in 1 Peter 1:20 there is the same contrast between the time before creation when Christ was chosen and 'these last days' in which he has been revealed. Of itself the phraseology does not demand that this revelation is the appearance of an existing being, but in the light of the parallels it is probable that this idea lies behind Peter's expression.

The humanity of the Son in Hebrews

In the letter to the Hebrews the author indicates how God has spoken in a superior way to his earlier messages through the prophets by describing the Son in exalted terms at the very beginning of the letter. He is the 'firstborn' of God, a term that implies his exalted status; it does not imply that there were any subsequent sons and daughters other than those human beings whom God adopts into his family (Heb. 2:10). The status of sonship is strongly emphasized in order to assert the superiority of Jesus both to the angels (Heb. 1:5–14) and to Moses (Heb. 3:5–6). It is significant that some of the details of the description of the Son prior to his making purification for sins are taken from the language used of Wisdom (Wisdom of Solomon 7:24f.) and are also used by Philo when speaking of the Word (*Logos*). The author then says that 'God brings his firstborn into the world' (Heb. 1:6), and the words of Psalm 8:4–6 are applied to him (Heb. 2:6–8), so that his humble status as a human being who suffered death – making him temporarily lower than the angels – may be explained. He had to become a human being in order to experience death on behalf of everybody. Since human beings are composed of flesh and blood, he too had to share in them if he was to defeat the devil who has the power of death over people. The writer emphasizes that he became 'in every way' like his brothers and sisters. Despite being a son, he learned obedience to God from his human experience of *suffering and temptation (see *Testing). Inasmuch as he was an individual human being, he experienced representatively what it was to be human; thus, although he was not married nor did he father children, he was nevertheless fully human. He experienced what all human beings experience in being tempted, but with the important difference that he did not yield to it (Heb. 4:15); this crucial exception, however, does not make him any less human since he fulfilled God's original intention for humanity.

Jesus in the Synoptic Gospels

In the first three Gospels the presentation of

Jesus is somewhat different. For Mark Jesus is certainly the Son of God (Mark 1:1), but his actual story is more like that of a human agent of God akin to a prophet. Yet Jesus is still the recipient of a divine declaration that he is the Son of God (Mark 1:11), and the subject of the mysterious and glorious transformation seen by his disciples at the so-called transfiguration (Mark 9:2–7). Matthew and Luke both tell the story of the birth of Jesus; the child is conceived in Mary without the intervention of her husband but by the agency of the *Holy Spirit (Matt. 1:20; Luke 1:35), so that the child who is born bears the OT titles of Son of God (Luke 1:35) and 'Immanuel', *i.e.* 'God is with us' (Matt. 1:23; Is. 7:14). Matthew and Luke both understand Jesus to be the Son of God, although they appear to think of a creative act brought about by the Holy Spirit rather than the Word or Son of God being implanted in Mary.

In attempting to understand the apparently different perspective in the Synoptic Gospels it is significant that Paul, who believed that Jesus was the pre-existent Son of God who had been sent by God into the world, also affirmed that Jesus was born of a woman, and saw no tension between the two facts. The recording of the birth of Jesus in the Gospels is thus not in itself a ground for affirming that the Evangelists did not believe in his pre-existence. There has been discussion as to whether the Son of Man, with whom Jesus is identified by the Evangelists, was a figure who existed before he appeared in the world, but the debate is unresolved. It is more fruitful to consider what the term 'Son of God' would have implied for the Evangelists. It is most unlikely that they thought that God had a Son by the human mother Mary; such ideas belong to pagan mythology. Further, since the Gospels are later than the epistles of Paul, it is likely that they were conversant with the concept of incarnation which we have traced through every other major part of the NT. It is therefore most probable that by naming Jesus as the Son of God they were affirming that in him the Son of God had become incarnate. Their reticence is due to the fact that essentially they were telling the story of Jesus in terms of what he said and did, and their record did not include his self-disclosure as Son of God except to his disciples on rare occasions. Admittedly there is some tension at this point with the much more open sayings attributed to Jesus in the Gospel of John, for which there may be various explanations. Nevertheless, there is a genuine unity between the main New Testament witnesses in affirming that the human being Jesus is at one and the same time the Son of God who has come into the world in order to deliver sinful human beings from their sin and its consequences and to share the life of God with them.

Bibliography

D. B. Capes, 'Preexistence', in *DLNTD*, pp. 955–961; M. De Jonge, *Christology in Context: The Earliest Christian Response to Jesus* (Philadelphia, 1988); J. D. G. Dunn, *Christology in the Making* (London, [2]1989); *idem, The Theology of Paul the Apostle* (Edinburgh and Grand Rapids, 1997); *idem, The Christ and the Spirit* 1: *Christology* (Edinburgh, 1998), esp. pp. 30–47, pp. 405–423; R. H. Fuller, 'The Conception/Birth of Jesus as a Christological Moment', *JSNT* 1, 1978, pp. 37–52; J. Hick (ed.), *The Myth of God Incarnate* (London, 1977); S. Kim, *The Origin of Paul's Gospel* (Tübingen, 1981); I. H. Marshall, 'Incarnational Christology in the New Testament', in H. H. Rowdon (ed.), *Christ the Lord* (Leicester and Downers Grove, 1982), pp. 1–16; *idem*, 'God Incarnate: Myth or What?', in *Jesus the Saviour* (London, 1990), pp. 181–196.

I. H. MARSHALL

INHERITANCE, see LAND
ISAIAH, see Part 2

ISRAEL (NATION)

The themes relating to 'Israel', the chosen *people of God, take us to the heart of biblical theology. For, as many now maintain, the fundamental structure of biblical theology is a *story*, and Israel is one of the principal characters in that drama. The story of Israel's relationship with Yahweh ('the LORD' in some translations) reveals the basic principles on which the church's relationship with him also rests.

The 'prototypical' story in Genesis 32:22–32

Traditionally, biblical theology has started

with the main *covenant-making passages in its search for an understanding of 'Israel': the covenant made with *Abraham in Genesis 15:1–21 and 17:1–8; the covenant commitment to rescue Israel from Egypt in Exodus 6:2–8; and the covenant with the house of *David in 2 Samuel 7:4–17. These passages are certainly vital, and are all picked up in the NT in connection with *Jesus, who reshapes the identity of Israel (as we shall see). However, it can be argued that the story in Genesis 32:22–32 is prototypical; that is, it reveals the underlying dynamic of Israel's relationship with Yahweh so as to set a pattern for the nation's whole history.

This is the profound and mysterious story of *Jacob's battle with a 'man', whom he eventually identifies as *God himself, during the night before he crosses the river Jabbok to meet his brother Esau. The prototypical nature of this story is indicated in several ways: 1. it describes the origin of the name 'Israel'; 2. it declares that all future generations of Israelites will identify themselves with it, through an eating custom (32:32); 3. it is twinned with the story of Jacob's reunion with Esau (33:1–17), which is similarly 'typical', expressing Israel's future tense relationship with Edom; 4. it takes place at the crossing of a river, and is thus connected with all the other water events which mark significant encounters with God in the Bible (the crossing of the Red Sea, the coming of water from the rock, the crossing of the Jordan at the entry into the promised *land, and of course the baptism of Jesus); 5. it is treated as typical of Israel's relationship with Yahweh by Hosea (Hos. 12:2–5). So what does this story say about Israel, from a 'biblical-theological' perspective?

'Israel' as 'Jacob'

The last thing that Jacob expects, at this point in his life, is to find that God is his enemy. He is deeply afraid of his brother, Esau, because of his theft of Isaac's *blessing years before (Gen. 27), and is doing his best to show Esau his deep repentance, by sending lavish gifts ahead of him (32:13–21). We know that this repentance is genuine (albeit prompted by fear), because of his prayer in 32:9–12, where he confesses his unworthiness and prays for deliverance from Esau. He puts his trust in God's promise of blessing (32:12; cf. Gen. 28:12–15). But this story reveals that he has a

far more threatening enemy than Esau – God himself.

Why does God suddenly fight him, and try to wrestle him into submission? The encounter with Esau is the climax of God's fourteen-year strategy to turn Jacob the schemer into someone after whom God himself can be named (32:9; cf. Exod. 3:15). God has been 'wrestling' with him throughout the story (Gen. 27 – 32), ever since he obtained the 'blessing' by trickery. Now, at last, he is seeking it in the right way, as a gift from God (32:12), with desperate determination (32:26). But he cannot have it so long as he remains 'Jacob', who wangles blessings by subterfuge. And he cannot have it so long as he regards God as there simply to serve *his* agenda, deliverance from Esau. He needs to realize that he is there to serve God, not vice versa.

The whole history of Israel can be conceived in this way. The burden of Amos' message, many years later, was that the God whom the Israelites thought would guarantee their future actually despised them, hated their religion, and would destroy them rather than deliver them (see esp. Amos 5:1–7, 18–27). It turned out that the God they called 'theirs' actually had a complaint first and foremost against *them,* and not against their enemies (*e.g.* Amos 2:4–5; Hos. 4:1; 12:2; Is. 1:1–9; Mic. 6:1–2; Jer. 2:9–13; Ezek. 20:33–36). Amos vividly described how Yahweh sought to 'wrestle' Israel back into faithfulness: 'I gave you cleanness of teeth in all your cities, and lack of bread in all your places, yet you did not return to me, says the LORD!' (Amos 4:6, NRSV). In the end, it was *their* God, not the gods of the nations, who brought deadly enemies against them and tore them out of the land he had given them.

For 'Israel' is always inclined to be 'Jacob', the deceiver and idolater who, instead of submitting to God, tries to obtain power over him. Even after confessing his true nature by admitting his name (32:27), Jacob (now Israel) tries to discover God's name (32:29). The essence of *idolatry is the desire for control and for power, often thought of as embodied in the name of the deity. Thus far, God has simply been known by the relationships he has entered: he is 'the God of Abraham and the Fear of Isaac' (Gen. 31:42). His name is not known, and will not be revealed until Exodus 3:13–15. So Jacob cannot use it to make himself secure against Esau's threats. The Israelites' persistent temptation will be to idolatry, to use their God for their own ends, even when this does not involve exploiting the divine name. So they take the ark into battle as a talisman (1 Sam. 4:3–4), build royal prestige out of the cult (Amos 7:10–17; 2 Kgs. 16:10–16), flaunt their God-given strength in the world (2 Sam. 24; Is. 39), use the *prophets to legitimize their expansionist ambitions (1 Kgs. 22) or bolster their national security (Jer. 7:1–15); above all, as Paul saw it, they seek to establish their own righteousness (Rom. 10:3), by putting themselves forward as 'a guide to the blind, ... a corrector of the foolish, a teacher of children ...' (Rom. 2:19–20).

Ultimately, the idolatrous desire to control God, to turn him into an insurance policy against enemies, natural disasters and an uncertain future, will destroy Israel. At the time of Jesus, the widespread view was that *Jerusalem was secure, because the Lord would finally defend city, land and people against any threat, whatever the quality of Israel's life and *obedience. So, once again, as Jesus foresaw (Mark 13), Israel's God became Israel's enemy, and the great city was destroyed. The 'Jacob' in Israel finally won, just as Jacob prevailed in his battle against the 'man', and forced his opponent to display his power by dislocating Jacob's hip (Gen. 32:25).

But is this the end of Israel's story?

'Jacob' as 'Israel'

The story, of course, does not allow us to say that 'Jacob' has the last word. That word is the 'blessing' spoken by his divine antagonist (32:29). In a wonderful twist, just as Jacob seems to be winning, pinning his opponent to the ground (32:26a), his desire for victory evaporates and is replaced by a desire for blessing. He recognizes that this enemy has something he wants, something that he can receive only as a gift. So the struggle against God is wonderfully transformed into a struggle for blessing from God.

It was C. S. Lewis who gave the classic modern formulation of the insight that all desire, even introverted, corrupt desire, is fundamentally desire for God, directed away from its true object. Jacob was consumed with a desire for blessing, for which he was willing to sacrifice his father's respect, lose his

place in the family, and incur his brother's murderous hatred (Gen. 27:41). Amazingly, he still received God's promise of blessing (28:13–15). Jacob's sojourn in Paddan Aram (Gen. 29 – 31) is the story of how God keeps his promise, although at first his wives recognize it much more clearly than Jacob. He thinks he has earned his wives and children (30:26). At last, however, the staggering reproductive patterns among his sheep convince Jacob that God is blessing him (31:4–13), though he still tries to secure his wealth through deception (31:20). It is not until the midnight battle that Jacob finally abandons his own resources, and clings with desperation to his God.

This is the moment at which 'Israel' is born, the moment of grace and disclosure, for which God himself has 'wrestled'. At this moment, 'God wrestles' (the meaning of 'Israel') becomes the new name that defines Jacob's new outlook.

This is the paradox at the heart of Israel's life. God is both their enemy, fighting against them, and their Saviour, striving to bless (cf. Is. 63:9–10). The moment of movement from enemy to friend is the moment at which Israel recognizes Yahweh, and reaches out towards him in *worship and *love. The covenant relationship is established wholly by God's initiative, and is pictured as an act of creation equivalent to the creation of the world. This is the great burden of Isaiah 40 – 55: the God who is distinguished from the idols because he made the world has determined as Creator to make Israel his own. Israel's rebellion will not be the last word, and the mysterious work of the 'Servant' (Is. 53) is vital to the success of God's plan.

Jeremiah uses the name of 'Jacob' in his presentation of this idea. Yahweh is the true God (Jer. 10:10), who as Creator stands in contrast to the idols who did not make the heavens and the earth (10:11–13). The idols are a worthless fraud (10:13–14), but 'he who is Jacob's possession is not like these, for he is the Maker of everything, including Israel, the tribe of his inheritance. "Yahweh of hosts" is his name!' (10:16, author's translation). God refuses to reveal his name to Jacob, when Jacob's motivation is to gain power and control; but it is his intention to reveal his name to Israel, and ultimately to be known as 'Jacob's possession' (his 'portion', or 'lot'). He made Israel, and yet deigns to be possessed by Israel, a possession indicated by the revelation of his name. He is 'the God of Israel'.

This relationship, at the heart of the covenant with Israel, was symbolized that night beside the Jabbok when God seemed to be overpowered by Jacob, but then turned Jacob's hostility into the yearning to which blessing is the response. That yearning, the knowledge of God which is also a longing to know him, is Israel's great vocation in the OT, as seen in the Psalms. The Psalms come to us from the worship of the *temple, the place where Israel meets with God, just as Jacob came face to face with Yahweh that night, and they express Israel's yearning for God, that longing for blessing made sharper by the experience of blessing already received. In line with Jacob's direct encounter with God, the Jerusalem temple sits at the heart of Israel's life, as the place specially chosen by God for his 'name' to dwell (Deut. 12:5; 1 Kgs. 8:27–30).

But this vocation was also Israel's great peril, for they could deny knowledge of God, and fail to live in accordance with their relationship to him. This theme is prominent in Hosea: 'There is no truth, no love, no knowledge of God in the land, but cursing, deception, murder, stealing, and adultery ... my people are destroyed for lack of knowledge!' (Hos. 4:1–2, 6, author's translation). Like an adulterous wife, Israel has turned her back on the husband who loves her. But God will woo her and win her again (Hos. 2:14–23; 11:8–11), horrible though her rejection of him has been.

One of the particular horrors which Hosea bemoans is self-deception: 'They cry out to me, these Israelites, "My God, we know you!" But Israel has rejected what is good. An enemy will pursue them!' (Hos. 8:2–3, author's translation). The cult can give a false assurance of knowledge which is not really there: 'I desire mercy, not sacrifice; and the knowledge of God, rather than burnt offerings' (Hos. 6:6, author's translation). 'The knowledge of God' is not detailed obedience to the rules of ritual, but an intimate awareness of God, touching each member of the nation individually, and leading to personal prayer and a lifestyle of trust and obedience. This is 'the friendship of the LORD' which, says the Psalmist, is 'for those who fear him' (Ps. 25:14).

John picks up this theme in the NT, and uses it ironically. The Jews' claim to know God, and therefore accuse Jesus of the sin that marks out the false prophet, preaching a god 'whom you have not known' (Deut. 13:2, 13). Ironically, Jesus accepts the charge: indeed, they do not know the God he proclaims to them (John 7:28; 8:55).

Can Israel ever truly respond to Yahweh? The prophets expect such a response, but only *after* a terrible experience of *judgment for *sin and rebellion (Deut. 30:1–14; Joel 2:12–18; Is. 63:10–19; Jer. 31:31–34; Ezek. 36:22–32; *etc.*). Hosea pictures Israel saying, 'Come, let us return to the LORD, for it is he who has torn us, and he will heal us ... let us know, let us press on to know the LORD!' (Hos. 6:1, 3). But none of the prophets believed that they saw this response in their own day, not even those who ministered after the return from exile.

In this respect, Malachi is the saddest, as well as the latest, book in the OT. Malachi accuses the post-exilic community of the same sins which caused the exile 150 years previously: half-hearted worship conceived as mere performance of the cult (1:6–14); corruption among the priests (2:1–9); social and sexual unfaithfulness (2:10–17). The people have not changed (3:7). But Malachi insists also that Yahweh is unchanging: 'I, Yahweh, do not change: therefore you, children of Jacob, are not finished!' (3:6, author's translation). Yahweh is still wrestling with Jacob, determined to make the new name stick. And Malachi looks forward to the coming of 'the messenger of the covenant', who will refine and purify Israel's worship and bring judgment on the corrupt (3:1–5).

So the OT ends on a note of paradox: Israel is still Jacob, but Jacob is still Israel. The covenant stands, but the covenant promises both *salvation and judgment, both a blessing and a curse (Deut. 28). How will Yahweh's commitment to save Israel be realized, in the face of the nation's constant failure to respond to him?

Jesus as Israel

This is biblical theology's first answer to this question. Jesus appears, not just as the Saviour of Israel in fulfilment of prophetic expectation, but also as an embodiment of Israel as they should be. Matthew makes this point dramatically in his opening chapters, first by applying the Exodus verse Hosea 11:1 to Jesus (Matt. 2:15), and then by telling the story in a way that makes Jesus re-enact Israel's history: the *Exodus from Egypt (2:19–20), the crossing of the Red Sea (3:13–17), the temptations (see *Testing) in the desert (4:1–11), even the arrival at Mt Sinai to receive the *law (5:1–2). Perhaps most pointedly, it is Jesus on whom the Spirit descends (Matt. 3:16), although the prophetic expectation was of an outpouring of the Spirit upon Israel (Is. 44:2–3; Ezek. 36:25–27). Where Israel had failed the temptations in the desert, Jesus now remains faithful to God.

Here, at last, is a Son with whom God is truly pleased (Matt. 3:17). 'I have not come to abolish [the law and the prophets], but to fulfil [them]', he claims (Matt. 5:17): part of the meaning of this must be that, in Jesus, we see at last Israel's true response of obedience, worship and love.

John develops the same thought, but from a different angle: he presents Jesus as the temple, the focus of Israel's life, the place where sin is dealt with and prayer is truly offered and heard (John 2:19–22; 8:34–36; 16:23–24). Paul's approach to the same idea is to see Jesus as the seed of Abraham, the one who truly and supremely inherits the covenant promises given to Abraham (Gal. 3:16, 19). Israel fell under the curse of the covenant (Gal. 3:10, quoting Deut. 27:26); but the promise of blessing is not made void, because Jesus stepped into the position of those born 'under the law' to 'redeem' them (Gal. 4:4–5), and so the promises are realized in him (3:8–9, 22).

But if Israel's role and position are supremely fulfilled in the Lord Jesus, what then is the position of his followers? Again, the various NT authors give different perspectives, but these produce a coherent picture. Matthew focuses on Jesus' role as King and Judge of Israel, and therefore associates his followers with that rule (Matt. 19:28–30). Though rejected at present, his followers escape from the judgment coming upon Israel (7:24–27; 21:40–44; 24:27–31), and enter into eternal life (25:31–46). Matthew hints clearly that God's kingdom will be peopled by Gentiles (see *Nations) as well as Jews (8:10–12; 28:18–20).

Similarly John boldly applies to Jesus and his followers some of the great images of Israel. 'Vine' and 'flock' were frequently-used pictures of Israel in contemporary literature. In line with his presentation of Jesus as the temple and as the true meaning of the Jewish festivals, John clearly believed that, as 'the good shepherd' who gathers and cares for the flock (10:11–16), and as 'the true vine' in whom alone fruit can be produced for God (15:1–5), Jesus now gathers the 'true' Israel around himself.

Luke emphasizes Jesus' role as the Saviour promised by the prophets. In line with prophetic expectation, he presents Jesus as the Saviour not just of Israel but of the Gentile nations as well. This perspective dominates Luke's whole presentation of Jesus, in both his volumes (compare Luke 2:30–32 with Acts 28:17–28). He is well aware of the theological difficulties of his position and shows the early church wrestling with the question, 'If Jesus is the promised Saviour of Israel, then how are the Gentiles saved? Do they need to become members of Israel, or not?' (Acts 15:1–21). Luke's answer is in line with Paul's: the Spirit does not require Gentiles to become Jews in order to be saved (e.g. Acts 10:44–48). But it was Paul who strove to work out the covenant theology underlying this principle.

The church as Israel (and as Jacob)

Paul does not shrink from the implication to be drawn from the equal outpouring of the Spirit on Jews and Gentiles alike: God has abolished the distinction between them, and offers salvation to all on the same basis – faith in Jesus Christ (Rom. 3:27–30; 10:11–13; Eph. 2:11–22). As a missionary, therefore, though he felt impelled to offer the gospel first to Jews (Rom. 1:16; cf. Acts 13:46), he felt equally under obligation to all (Rom. 1:14–15). But does this mean that God has repudiated the *election of Israel in favour of an equal, universal commitment?

Paul cannot bring himself to say this. It would amount to saying that 'the word of God has failed' (Rom. 9:6). Instead, he consistently applies to the church – that is, the mixed Jewish and Gentile congregations to whom he writes – the great covenant ideas and terms which had previously belonged to Israel. They are the elect (1 Thess. 1:4–5), the people called to *holiness (1 Cor. 1:2), the justified who are objects of God's saving *righteousness (1 Cor. 6:11; Rom. 3:22–24), the *redeemed (Rom. 3:24; Eph. 1:7), who inherit the *kingdom of God (1 Cor. 6:10, Col. 1:12). They are the children of God (Rom. 8:14; *cf.* Exod. 4:22), on whom the *glory of God rests (Rom. 5:2; 8:30), who offer pleasing worship (Rom. 12:1–2; Eph. 5:1–2), and who can rightly appeal to the covenant *faithfulness of God, now revealed in Christ (Rom. 8:31–39). In all likelihood, when Paul calls God's *peace and *mercy upon 'the Israel of God' in Galatians 6:16, he is referring to the church.

When he theologizes about this enjoyment of Israel's blessings by the church, Paul points to the universal fatherhood of Abraham (Gal. 3; Rom. 4). He argues that an exclusive enjoyment of covenant blessings by Israel does *not* fulfil the promise to Abraham that he would be a source of blessing to the whole earth. Because Jesus is the seed of Abraham (Gal. 3:16), those who belong to him, whether Jews or Gentiles, are also 'the seed of Abraham, and heirs according to promise' (Gal. 3:29, author's translation). Paul's olive-tree analogy puts it differently: unbelieving Israel (Israel who is still Jacob) are like fruitless branches cut off from the stock, and believing Gentiles are like wild shoots grafted in to feed from the richness of the tree (Rom. 11:17–18).

By focusing upon Jesus as the fulfilment of the covenant relationship, the NT is able to resolve the tension of the OT between 'the kindness and the severity of God', as Paul puts it in Romans 11:22. Israel experienced both: God's kindness in that they became 'Israel' at all, and his severity in so far as they remained unredeemed 'Jacob'. And now, because it is Jesus, rather than the church, who fulfils the covenant relationship, the church faces the same moral demand as Israel did, to 'put to death what is earthly in you, sexual immorality, impurity, passion, evil desire, and covetousness which is idolatry' (Col. 3:5, author's translation). Paul knows that Israel's besetting sin of idolatry is an option for the church too, disguised, as always, as inordinate desire which is not longing and love for God. Christians live with the tension between Israel and Jacob within themselves until the final redemption comes (Rom. 8:23, *etc.*).

Israel as Israel?

The question whether Israel as an ethnic entity – that is, as the Jews – has a continuing covenant relationship with God is one over which Christians disagree. Some argue that the logic of the NT requires a termination of the covenant with Israel, because the 'blessings' are transferred to the church (see above). Others argue that this is the view against which Paul argues in Romans 9 – 11, where he insists that God's word to Israel has not failed (9:6), that 'the gifts and the calling of God are irrevocable' (11:29), and that one day 'all Israel will be saved' (11:26). Still others argue that, if the OT promises are irrevocable, then we must freely allow the independent validity of Judaism as a separate way of living in unity with God, and therefore not seek or expect Jewish conversions, whether individual or large-scale.

For many 'replacement' has become a loaded word, indeed a test of 'orthodoxy': does the church 'replace' Israel in the purposes of God? But this question crudely over-simplifies the issues. As far as the NT is concerned, the only candidate for 'replacing' Israel is Jesus himself. But he replaces *Jacob*, rather than Israel, by finally effacing the twistedness and idolatry which had ruined Israel's side of the covenant relationship. And he replaces, or rather displaces, all (whether Jews or Gentiles) who reject him and refuse to enter the 'friendship of the Lord' through him (*cf.* John 15:14–15). But when people enter that friendship through faith in him, and through the gift of the Spirit (*cf.* Rom. 5:5), then Israel's destiny and hope has been realized, not set aside. On this basis, Israel's Scriptures become the Scriptures of the church, and the unity of the biblical covenant is secured.

See also: CHURCH; NATIONS.

Bibliography

W. Brueggemann, *Theology of the Old Testament: Testimony, Dispute, Advocacy* (Minneapolis, 1997); E. M. Curtis, 'Structure, style and context as a key to interpreting Jacob's encounter at Peniel', *JETS* 30, 1987, pp. 129–137; F. C. Holmgren, 'Holding your own against God! Gen 32:22–32 (In the context of Gen 31–33)', *Int* 44, 1990, pp. 5–17; D. E. Holwerda, *Jesus and Israel: One Covenant or Two?* (Leicester, 1995); S. Motyer, *Israel in the Plan of God* (Leicester, 1989); D. Sheriffs, *The Friendship of the Lord*

(Carlisle, 1996); G. J. Wenham, *Genesis 16–50*, WBC (Dallas, 1994).

S. MOTYER

ISRAEL (PERSON), see JACOB/ISRAEL (PERSON)

JACOB/ISRAEL (PERSON)

Introduction

The primary biblical data on Jacob is found in Genesis 25:19 – 35:29. What follows in the rest of Genesis focuses on Jacob's family, especially *Joseph; in this account Jacob appears only occasionally. The Jacob story is bracketed by genealogies of the non-chosen: the sons of Ishmael (Gen. 25:12–18) and the descendants of Esau (the Edomites) (Gen. 36:1–43). This serves to put the *election of Jacob/Israel into proper perspective. The chosen are selected in order that the non-chosen, *e.g.* Ishmaelites and Edomites, also may know God's *blessing (Gen. 12:3b; 18:18b; 22:18; 28:14b).

Jacob in Genesis 25:19 – 35:29

Another bracket, so to speak, in the life of Jacob is formed by the first and last occasions on which the Lord speaks to him (Gen. 28:13–15; 46:2–4) and by the similarities between the two experiences. Both theophanies are nocturnal, and include an unconditional promise from God (like those given to *Abraham; compare Gen. 12:1–3 with Gen. 22:15–18). These promises include numerous progeny, mediation of blessing to others, God's presence and protection, and restoration to the *land of promise. God's first set of promises to Jacob is remarkable because it follows extremely unethical behaviour on Jacob's part: 1. his opportunistic securing of his brother's birthright by the exploitation of Esau's hunger and consequent vulnerability; and 2. his disguising himself as Esau and deceiving his aged, partially-sighted father into giving him the blessing that Isaac thought he was extending to Esau (27:1–29).

When the Lord first speaks to Jacob (when Jacob is by himself for the first time in the story), he says nothing about these reprehensible actions. The Lord's silence may be compared to that of Jacob's father Isaac when first he speaks to Jacob as Jacob (28:1–4). Isaac gives his son advice on seeking a wife (28:1b–2), and invokes God's blessing on his future life (28:3–4).

Such silences are not meant to imply approval of lying, cheating or deceiving and exploiting others. Certainly the elect are not free to act autonomously without regard for consequences. Rather, silences are the Scripture's way of teaching that the Lord's selection of Jacob over Esau is not based on merit but on *grace, not on performance but on promise. If God's choices are based on human character, Jacob is no more an ideal candidate than Esau; both are repugnant.

Jacob's life has its origin both in the prayers of his childless father Isaac (25:21) and in the sovereign choice of the electing Lord God (25:23). The Lord's revelation about Jacob's pre-eminence over Esau comes not unbidden, but in response to Rebekah's prayer (25:22b).

Jacob's name (Heb. *ya*ᶜ*qōb*) is connected by the narrator with the Hebrew word for 'heel,' *ᶜeqēb* (25:26), and later by Esau with the Hebrew verb for 'supplant,' ᶜ*qōb* (27:36). Jacob enters the world by fighting his way out of the womb. The name is not necessarily sinister or demonic, but it anticipates the plethora of conflict scenes to come, in the midst of which Jacob will find himself. Jacob alone of all OT characters is asked by God 'What is your name?' to which he gives a one-word answer 'Jacob' (32:27, NRSV).

Jacob's first conflict is with Esau (25:19–34; 27:1 – 28:9), and his second with Laban (29:1–30). Laban's deceit of Jacob may make the latter more sensitive to how Esau felt when Jacob victimized him. Conflict continues with Jacob's wives, especially Rachel. Throughout the account of the birth of Jacob's sons and Dinah (29:31 – 30:24), the mothers (not Jacob) name the children and speak of the powerful ways of God. Jacob's only reference to God in these birth scenes is not a salutary one: 'Can I take the place of God?' (30:2, author's translation) he sneers at Rachel.

Jacob's last conflict is with a 'man' whom the narrative will later identify as the Lord himself (32:22–31). It is a conflict in which God, not Jacob, takes the intiative. The text witnesses to the tenacity of Jacob (Gen. 32:25, 26b, 28). Jacob's new name 'Israel' refers not to what Jacob will become, but to what he has already done ('...because you have struggled with God, and with humans have you succeeded' [32:28, author's translation]).

But there are some things Jacob cannot do. He cannot give himself a new name, but God can (v. 28). He cannot bless himself, but God can bless him (v. 29b). God is also the source of Jacob's limp (vv. 31–32), which testifies to God's graciousness. Jacob has seen God, and should have died; instead, he is limping, but still living.

Jacob in the rest of Genesis

Jacob appears in much of the Joseph story. He is portrayed as a doting father (37:3), a father concerned for his family in time of drought (42:1), a distraught father (43:6), a stunned father (45:26), a relieved father (46:30), and a prophetic father (49:1–28). Since Jacob's life began with a prophecy, it is fitting that his last words are prophecies (about his sons and the tribes of Israel that will come from them).

Although Jacob is renamed 'Israel' in 32:28 and 35:9, the new name appears in the Jacob story only in 35:21–22. However, in the Joseph narrative both 'Jacob' and 'Israel' are used, sometimes in adjacent verses (46:1, 2) or the same verse (46:5). In contrast Abraham, after receiving his new name (17:5), is never again called 'Abram'. In this respect Jacob is like Simon of the NT whose name, says Jesus, will be 'Cephas/Peter' (John 1:42), but who is later addressed by Jesus as 'Simon, Simon ...' (Luke 22:31). The use of both the old name and the new testifies to the presence of the old Jacob alongside the new Israel, to one individual who is *simul iustus et peccator* ('at the same time justified and a sinner'). But why is 'Abram' not used for Abraham who, even after he receives his new name (ch. 17), is not above moral turpitude (ch. 20)? Possibly 'Jacob' also represents the suffering, human, feeling side of the patriarch, while 'Israel' underscores his office and role as progenitor of the chosen nation (hence 'the sons of Israel' [42:5; 45:21; 46:5, 8] rather than 'the sons of Jacob' [49:2; 50:12]).

Jacob in the rest of the OT

Jacob is associated with Abraham and Isaac as those with whom God made a covenant. This happens most often in Deuteronomy (1:8; 6:10; 9:5; 29:13; 30:20). In this book,

one of whose major themes is that God honours *obedience with blessing, the gift of the land has absolutely nothing to do with the obedience of the people. On the contrary, God is giving them the land only because he promised it by oath to Abraham, Isaac and Jacob.

In Deuteronomy 26:5 (as part of the first-fruits ceremony, Deut. 26:1–11) Israel confesses that 'my father was a Syrian about to perish' (NKJV); 'a wandering Aramean' (NIV); 'a fugitive Aramean' (JPSV). The expression 'my father' could refer to Jacob or, less probably, to Jacob's family, when Jacob went down to Egypt. But is Jacob perishing (NKJV), wandering (NIV), or a fugitive? A case can be made for each, and they all draw attention to the times of rootlessness and uncertainty in the life of Jacob. Those who now possess securely a rich, fertile land recall, by this recitation, the homeless, landless beginnings of Israel.

For Hosea (Hos. 12:2–6) Jacob is one who has passed his unsavoury characteristics to his descendants. But if Hosea's audience will turn from their Jacob-like duplicity and self-sufficiency, God will deliver them as he did Jacob (v. 6). Jacob is also the one God loves (Mal. 1:2).

Jacob in the NT

Jacob has a place in two great families, the family of Messiah (Matt. 1:2), and the family of the faithful (Heb. 11:21). Using Isaac/Ishmael and Jacob/Esau as illustrations (Rom. 9:10–13), Paul argues srongly that both Jewish election (Rom. 9:6–23) and Gentile election (Rom. 9:24–26) depend on God's *mercy. (cf. 9:15 (twice), 16, 18, 23; 11:30, 31 (twice), 32.)

Bibliography

W. Brueggemann, *Genesis*, Interpretation (Atlanta, 1982); M. Fishbane, *Text and Texture: Close Readings of Selected Biblical Texts* (New York, 1979); T. E. Fretheim, 'The book of Genesis', in *NIB* 1, pp. 592–674; J. Gammie, 'Theological interpretation by way of literary and tradition analysis: Genesis 25--36,' in M. Bus (ed.), *Encounter with the Text* (Philadelphia, 1979); V. P. Hamilton, *Genesis 18–50*, NICOT (Grand Rapids, 1995); R. Hendel, *The Epic of the Patriarch: The Jacob Cycle and the Narrative Traditions of Canaan and Israel* (Atlanta, 1987); G. A.

Rendsburg, *The Redaction of Genesis* (Winona Lake, 1986).

V. P. HAMILTON

JAMES, see Part 2
JEREMIAH, see Part 2

JERUSALEM

The OT

Jerusalem plays a key role within biblical history. It is never expressly mentioned in the Pentateuch (though the references to 'Salem' and 'Moriah' in Gen. 14:18 and 22:2 were later connected with the city: see Ps. 76:2; 2 Chr. 3:1). Early Egyptian Amarna texts, (from the second millennium BC) however, refer to 'Urushalim'. As the Canaanite *city of Jebus (Josh. 18:28; Judg. 19:10) it was taken by Joshua (Josh. 15:63 and Judg. 1:21), but it came to the fore only when *David made it his capital (2 Sam. 5). From then on the city's significance began to increase.

Situated on the borders of the two tribes of Benjamin and Judah, and without any prior Israelite associations, Jerusalem was an ideal choice for a capital designed from the outset to signify the unity of the tribes of *Israel; it was the 'cornerstone of the religious and cultic unification of Israel' (S. Talmon, in *Jerusalem*, p. 195). Yet with the breaking away of the northern kingdom after Solomon's death it soon became the capital of just the southern kingdom. The city designed to bring unity now pointed instead to Israel's division (see *e.g.* 1 Kgs. 12:27–28).

Despite its lack of pedigree, the city became a centre for Yahwism, not only because of Solomon's building of the *temple but also because his father David had brought to Jerusalem the ark of the covenant (2 Sam. 6; 15:29; *cf.* Pss. 50; 132; 68:8, 17). Thus Jerusalem became the place where the Sinai covenant (Exod. 19 – 34) was remembered and cultivated. This link between Sinai and Zion (the term used for Jerusalem especially in Isaiah and the Psalms) encouraged the belief in the election of Zion; as the dynasty of David was chosen by *God (2 Sam. 7:4–17), so too was Jerusalem (see Pss. 2; 110). Moreover Zion was understood to be the place where Yahweh had put his 'name' (1

Kgs. 11:36; 14:21; 2 Kgs. 21:4; *cf.* Deut. 12:5, 11). The city of David was thus the city of Yahweh, and its temple the place where he dwelt (Ps. 135:21). Such ideas needed to be stated with caution (see 2 Sam. 7:5–7; 1 Kgs. 8:27). Yet they passed into the heart of Israel's worshipping life, as seen later in the Psalms (especially the 'Psalms of Ascent' such as 122; 125; 128): Jerusalem is the 'city of our God, the city of the great King' (Ps. 48, NRSV). Similarly Isaiah speaks frequently of Zion as Yahweh's holy hill, the place where he lives (4:5; 8:18; 10:12; 12:5–6; 14:32; 24:23; 30:19; 31:9).

A distinctive 'Zion-theology' developed involving various related elements: Jerusalem as the abode of Yahweh, the great *king; Zion (not Sinai) as his chosen mountain located at the centre of the world; the coming to Jerusalem of other *nations to acknowledge the sovereignty of Yahweh (J. M. Roberts, in *JBL* 92, p. 329). The dramatic survival of the city when besieged by Sennacherib in 701 BC (2 Kgs. 19:35–37; fulfilling the prophecy of Is. 31:4–5) may have strengthened these convictions, leading to the further conclusion that, because of the divine presence and kingship, the city was inviolable.

This view was denounced by prophets such as Micah (3:12) and Jeremiah (7:1–15; 26:1–6). The Lord might indeed be 'in Zion' (Jer. 8:19), but that was no guarantee that the city would be spared divine *judgment. God's covenant with his people was never without conditions (*cf.* Deut. 4 – 5). Far from fighting a 'holy war' in defence of his city, Yahweh was now its enemy (Jer. 21:4–7). Messages of disaster and judgment for Jerusalem are therefore a major element in the prophetic writings. Beneath the superficial issues of local politics, the prophets discerned divine judgment upon the city, and they denounced it for its disregard of Yahweh (Is. 22:11), its idolatry (Jer. 7:17–18; Ezek. 8:3), the corruption of its leaders (Jer. 13:13; Mic. 3:10), the oppression of the poor (Mic. 6:9–16), and its failure to observe the Sabbath (Jer. 17:19–23). Isaiah had likened the city to 'Sodom' (1:9), but Ezekiel went further, portraying Yahweh's contending with a city which was now to be called 'Oholibah', an Egyptian prostitute (23:1–49).

The catastrophic destruction of the city by the Babylonians in 587 BC (described in 2 Kgs. 25 and Jer. 52, and mourned in

Lamentations) vindicated this critique. After the accession of Cyrus (539 BC) many *exiles returned to the city; the temple was rebuilt by Zerubbabel (Ezra 6) and the walls by Nehemiah (Neh. 1 – 6).

These key events within Israel's history inevitably occasion much reflection within the OT as to the nature of God's purposes towards Jerusalem, Israel and the world. First, there is a continued re-evaluation of the supposed 'inviolability' of Zion. For example, Psalm 89:1–37 speaks extravagantly of Jerusalem's security, but then describes its destruction in anguished terms (vv. 38–51). Significantly this concludes Book 3 of the Psalter, a book in which Psalms 74 and 79 also reflect on Jerusalem's destruction and which paves the way for Book 4, which bases its view of God's faithfulness and kingship not on Zion's restoration but on creation (see Pss. 90; 91; 93; 96 – 99). And Psalm 87, while emphasizing Zion (vv. 1–3), clearly sees God's purposes as more universal in scope: Yahweh declares that those who were 'born in Zion' will include even Israel's enemies (v. 4).

Secondly, although the prophets in the midst of their warnings had predicted *salvation and deliverance for Jerusalem in the short term (e.g. Is. 30:19; 44:26–28; Jer. 30 – 33; Ezek. 14:22; Zech. 1:16), increasingly God's purposes for the city in the long term were increasingly depicted as embracing something far bigger. The return of the exiles under Cyrus was indeed a fulfilment (especially of Jeremiah's prophecy in 25:12; 29:10; cf. 2 Chr. 36:22; Ezra 1:1), but in some ways it was disappointing (Neh. 9:32–36), thereby fuelling the hope that God might yet do something better (cf. Hag. 2:9). Isaiah and Micah had foreseen the day when '*word of the Lord' would 'go out from Jerusalem' (Is. 2:3; Mic. 4:2) and the nations would gather there to honour him (cf. Jer. 3:17). Jeremiah had spoken of the city's being called 'The Lord our Righteousness' (33:16). This larger, more apocalyptic vision was now augmented in grandiose and colourful terms. God's new work for Jerusalem would usher in a new age (Is. 65:18–19; Joel 3:17–18); the city would serve as a source of living *water (Zech. 14:8). The book of Ezekiel concludes with an extended depiction of the rebuilt temple in highly stylized terms with water flowing down to revitalize the Dead Sea and the city's

being renamed 'The LORD is there' (48:35) – a dramatic picture of the Lord's presence amongst his people.

The OT closes with these issues unresolved. In one sense the exile was over; Jerusalem could be told that her 'penalty was paid' (Is. 40:2), but in another sense it was clear that much of the prophetic hope remained to be fulfilled. Ezekiel had spoken of the departure of the Shekinah glory of the Lord from the temple (chs. 8 – 11) at the time of the exile, but it was unclear whether his vision of its return (43:1–5) had since been fulfilled; and Isaiah had spoken of the Lord's redeeming Jerusalem and returning to Zion as King (Is. 52:7–10), but in what sense, if any, had this occurred? Jerusalem was thus supposedly the place of God's presence and his kingship, but it appeared instead that Israel's God was absent and not yet truly King, Jerusalem not redeemed, Israel not restored and the exile not truly over.

Such concerns are widespread in the intertestamental period, especially after the end of independent Hasmonean rule (167–63 BC). Not surprisingly, then, Luke sets his Gospel against the background of godly Jews who longed for the '*redemption of Jerusalem' and the 'consolation of Israel' (Luke 2:38, 25; cf. 1:71). Some of those prophecies for Jerusalem were connected with expectations of a Messiah. Jerusalem would one day welcome her long-awaited king (Zech. 9:9), a new branch from David's line (Jer. 33:15–16); at that time the city's people would be cleansed and her temple visited (Mal. 3:1–4), and God's Spirit would be poured out (Joel 2:28–32). When would these prophecies be fulfilled?

The NT

The NT writers, convinced that *Jesus was truly Israel's Messiah, understand these Jerusalem-connected prophecies to have been fulfilled in him. Jerusalem plays a central role within the story of the NT, and this is no accident. If Jerusalem at the dawn of the NT period was associated with the presence of the divine Name, the throne of the true King, the place of true *sacrifice, the centre of Israel's life and the focus of its eschatological hope, then it was inevitable that the mission of Israel's Messiah would be integrally connected with this unique city. The more important question becomes: in what way are these biblical motifs concerning Jerusalem affected by the coming of Israel's Messiah? Do they continue unchanged, or is their significance reforged as a result of God's revelation in Jesus?

The key role of Jerusalem within previous salvation-history is clearly affirmed within the NT. Jesus describes it as the 'city of the great King' (Matt. 5:35) and affirms the idea that God in some sense dwells in its sanctuary (Matt. 23:21; cf. Luke 2:49?). Matthew twice describes it as the 'holy city' (Matt. 4:5; 27:53). For all the evangelists it is the ultimate goal of Jesus' ministry. This is seen most notably in Luke with its extended 'travel narrative'; Jesus 'set his face to go to Jerusalem' as early as 9:51.

Yet this very focus on Jerusalem reveals a deeper truth and a great irony. Jesus must go to the city, not to receive popular acclaim as Messiah, but to be rejected by its rulers and ultimately to die (Mark 8:31 etc.). Again it is Luke who makes this point most clearly. Jerusalem is the city which 'kills the prophets'; 'it is impossible for a prophet to be killed away from Jerusalem' (Luke 13:33–34). The infant Jesus had been welcomed by those who longed for the 'redemption of Jerusalem' (2:38), but now as he arrives in the city the adult Jesus weeps over it and pronounces a fearful judgment (19:41–44). This is repeated in the apocalyptic discourse (21:20–24 par.). He had longed to 'gather [the city's] children together' (13:34), but now the city will be surrounded instead by the Roman armies (19:43). Why? 'Because you did not recognize the time of your visitation from God' (19:44).

This becomes the key window through which to perceive Jerusalem from the standpoint of Jesus: the city which missed its moment of destiny; the city prepared by God to welcome his presence but which now rejects him who embodies that presence; in sum the 'city of God' which does not recognize its visitation by the Son of God.

This dramatic encounter between Jesus and Jerusalem, which inevitably must cast Jerusalem in a whole new light, can be seen in all the Gospels. They all record Jesus' cleansing of the temple – a dramatic, prophetic act, almost certainly pointing to the forthcoming destruction of the temple (Mark 11:15–17 par.). In Matthew Jerusalem is the 'city of the great King' but it becomes clear that Jesus is that King (25:31, 34), the one whom the city

does not welcome, the owner's 'son' who is thrown 'out of the vineyard' (21:39). Jesus is the embodiment of God's presence ('Emmanuel' in 1:23; cf. 18:20; 28:20) who pronounces that the temple, previously associated with that Shekinah presence (23:21), will now be 'left desolate' (23:38); and, with that, Jesus removes his own presence from the temple (24:1). He is the one 'greater than the temple' (12:6). His provocative and enigmatic statement ('destroy this temple, and I will raise it in three days', as in John 2:19) is used against him both at his trial and on the cross (Matt. 26:61; 27:40), but what happened on the third day? Was the risen Jesus the true temple? If so, what then would happen to the physical temple?

John affirms that Jesus is indeed the true embodiment of the temple (1:14; 2:21; cf. 1:51; 4:21–24) and the fulfilment of its festival symbolism (8:12; 10:36; etc.). Meanwhile Jerusalem is the city at the centre of his 'own country' (4:44), but when he 'came to what was his own', 'his own people did not accept him' (1:11). So Jerusalem proves to be the place which epitomizes the 'world' in its hostile response to God's truth and light. The crucifixion of the Messiah outside the walls inevitably casts a shadow over the city in the minds of the evangelists. How could this have come to pass? Could Jerusalem ever be the same again?

This new understanding of Jerusalem, drawn from a reflection on the life and ministry of Jesus, is then developed throughout the NT. The writer of Hebrews not only sees Jerusalem's temple sacrifices as now fulfilled in Christ (chs. 7 – 10 etc.); he also senses the contrast in the passion narrative between Jerusalem and Golgotha: 'let us then go to him outside the camp … for here we have no lasting city, but we are looking for the city that is to come' (13:13–14). He weans his readers away from the earthly Jerusalem and focuses their attention on the 'heavenly Jerusalem' (12:22; cf. 11:10, 16).

Acts tells a story in which (in deliberate contrast to that of Luke's Gospel) Jerusalem is gradually left behind, and it includes an extended critique of the temple and its hierarchy (Stephen's speech: Acts 7:2–53). Admittedly Paul returned to the city on several occasions (Acts 11:30; 15:2–4; 18:22?; 21:17), but despite his generous gift for the Jerusalem church (1 Cor. 16; 2 Cor. 8 – 9), he considered the 'present Jerusalem' to be 'in slavery with her children' (Gal. 4:25), influenced no doubt by the activities of the Judaizers who looked to the city for support (Gal. 2:1). It was indeed the place of the Messiah's great act of obedience and deliverance (Rom. 9:33; 11:26), from which the gospel message had gone out to the world (Rom. 15:19), but his converts were to focus now on the 'Jerusalem above; she is free and she is our mother' (Gal. 4:26). The book of Revelation completes the picture with its focus on the 'New Jerusalem' (3:12; 21:2). As for the physical city where the 'Lord was crucified', this is seen as comparable to 'Sodom and Egypt' (11:8). Even the description of the fall of *Babylon (ch. 18) appears to reflect the recent fall of Jerusalem, as predicted by Jesus in the apocalyptic discourse (Mark 13, reworked in Rev. 6).

The coming of Jesus, his death and resurrection in Jerusalem, result in a new theology of Jerusalem, with the city's losing its distinctive theological status as the 'holy city' or 'city of God'. In part this is because of divine judgment (see *e.g.* Luke 13:33–35; 19:41–44; 21:20–24; 23:28–31), but it is also because in the economy of salvation the city need no longer serve the same function within God's purposes. Christ is now in his own person the locus of God's presence on earth, and his death the fulfilment of the temple sacrifices; the temple's 'dividing wall' between Jew and Gentile is now broken down in Christ (Eph. 2:14), and by the Spirit God can be present with his people throughout the world: true worshippers need not 'worship the Father ... in Jerusalem', but 'worship in spirit and truth' (John 4:21, 24). This is a foretaste of the heavenly *worship in the New Jerusalem, where there is no temple (Rev. 21:22). Just as the temple, according to Hebrews, was a shadow of the heavenly reality, so too the city of Jerusalem points forward to that which lies ahead.

The *election of Zion thus speaks powerfully of God's involvement with his people and his desire to reveal himself in concrete ways. Moreover, the fact that the ultimate goal of salvation-history is depicted not as a garden but as a city (albeit in ways reminiscent of Eden: see Rev. 22:1–3) may indicate that God appropriates for his own ends the human instinct to build cities, even though since Babel (Gen. 11:1–9) this had

been a mark of human fallenness, a sign of humanity's proud 'counter-creation' (see J. Ellul, *The Meaning of the City*). Nevertheless the new perspective in the NT is also a powerful warning. That which God has given may be taken away when the divine gift is abused. And Jerusalem's fall serves as an advanced paradigm of God's ultimate judgment upon the world. The predominant note, however, is one of fulfilment in Christ. Jerusalem points to the greatness of Jesus. The one who visited the city on a donkey was indeed Zion's true King, the one in whom the city's chequered history was to find resolution, the one who held its destiny in his hand. Truly this was its 'hour of visitation'. It could never be the same again.

Bibliography

J. Ellul, *The Meaning of the City* (Grand Rapids, 1970); B. Ollenburger, *Zion, City of the Great King: A Theological Symbol of the Jerusalem Cult* (Sheffield, 1987); J. J. M. Roberts, 'The Davidic origin of the Zion tradition', *JBL* 92, 1973, pp. 329–344; S. Talmon, 'The biblical concept of Jerusalem', in J. M. Oesterreicher and A. Sinai (eds.), *Jerusalem* (New York, 1974); P. W. L. Walker, *Jesus and the Holy City: New Testament Perspectives on Jerusalem* (Grand Rapids, 1996); *idem* (ed.), *Jerusalem Past and Present in the Purposes of God* (Grand Rapids, and Carlisle, ²1994); I. Wilson, *Out of the Midst of the Fire: Divine Presence in Deuteronomy* (Atlanta, 1996); J. C. de Young, Jerusalem in the New Testament (Amsterdam, 1960).

P. W. L. WALKER

JESUS CHRIST

The OT as a book about Jesus

A study of Jesus Christ in a volume dedicated to biblical theology must necessarily devote some attention to the place of Jesus Christ in the OT.

On the one hand, it is obvious that the framework of early Christian thought is provided by the *revelation of *God in the history and experience of the Jews as it is recorded in the OT and interpreted in inter-testamental Judaism. Moreover, the actual content of Christian theology is largely based on a fresh understanding of texts and concepts from the OT on the assumption that it is a book which prepares for and prophesies the coming of the Messiah and the new *people of God. A 'biblical theology of the NT' will accordingly be sensitive to these roots of early Christian theology and will demonstrate their existence and significance.

On the other hand the OT must itself be understood as a part of Christian Scripture which testifies to Jesus Christ. Judaism also claims this canon of sacred books as its own Scripture, but rejects the idea that it points forward to Jesus (as distinct from an unidentified Messiah) or is in any sense a book about him. The OT *became* a Christian book once early Christians read it both in the light shed on it by Jesus and also for the light that they believed that it could shed upon him, but in what sense, if any, *was* it *already* a Christian book before it was interpreted in this way? In what sense, if any, is the OT a 'book about Jesus'?

The OT story

In the OT the main storyline which runs through the entire collection of books is the creation of God's people, the Jews, and their continuing relationship with God. In some parts of the OT the concept of the *covenant is of fundamental importance, defining the relationship between God and his chosen people; the narrative shows how the people were given the obligations of the covenant (Exod.) and how they sometimes failed to keep them and in consequence suffered divine chastisement and judgment, while at other times they acknowledged their sin and experienced God's favour and forgiveness (as in Judg.). But the narrative of God's people is taken right back to the *creation of the universe and put in the broader context of the creation of humankind and its sinfulness almost from the beginning. In this context is found the divine promise that the offspring of Eve will crush the head of the serpent (Gen. 3:15), although no hint is offered as to how this will happen, whether as one decisive event or in a continuing warfare. Thus the hope of future *victory over the serpent emerges.

In the narrative of the Exodus from Egypt and the establishment of the covenant there are various significant points. The first is that God promises through *Moses that he will raise up a future *prophet who will lead the people after Moses is no longer there to guide them (Deut. 18:15–20); the immediate thought is doubtless of a succession of leaders inspired by God. The second point is that an elaborate system, consisting of place of worship (the tabernacle, superseded by a fixed temple), *priesthood and the offering of *sacrifices for various purposes including the making of *atonement for sin, is established, through which the people maintained their relationship with God and repaired it when it was broken by sin.

The story of the people from this point onwards, after they have entered the land which God promised to them, is one of apostasy, *judgment, repentance and the restoration of God's favour in a repeated cycle. Alongside the prophets and priests a third type of leader emerges: the people are given a *king to rule over them, who is presented as God's appointee. After Saul the monarchy is put on a firm footing by *David, to whom God promises that he will be followed by a son (or descendant) who will be the object of God's special concern and that his house and kingdom will be established for ever (2 Sam. 7:8–16). Eventually the sins of the people and God's judgment upon them reach a climax with the taking of the people into exile by the Babylonians and the consequent end of the monarchy. From about this time onwards there develops the hope, expressed in prophecy, that at some time God will restore his favour to the people by renewing his covenant with them (Jer. 31:31–34), by raising up a new, righteous King in the line of David (Is. 9:2–7; 11; Ezek. 34), and by re-establishing the people in their own land. This hope is often called 'messianic' (from Heb. *māšîah* = 'anointed'), because it involved the anointing of a future ruler over the people. It is mainly in some of the prophets, whose writings (see *Prophetic books) and the underlying oral material cover a lengthy period and can often not be dated with precision, that these promises for the future are developed, and they continued to develop even after a small number of the people had returned to Jerusalem and set up a tiny state which was a pale shadow of its predecessor (at least in their nostalgic estimation). Particularly significant is the material in Isaiah 40 – 55, in which the people of Israel are presented as God's servant with a *mission to declare his greatness in the world; there are places where this vision appears to focus on a particular individual who is the Lord's servant (Is. 42:1–7; 49:1–7; 50:4–9; 52:13 – 53:12), but the poetic language makes it very difficult to discern exactly what the prophet was envisaging. The collection of hymnic material known as the *Psalms contains several references to an anointed person (Pss. 2:2; 18:50; 84:9; 132:10, 17; *et al.*). Although at the time of composition these texts probably referred to the reigning monarch, there is good reason to believe that by the time the psalms were collected they were being reinterpreted as referring to a future ruler, the Messiah. Elsewhere in the OT the term 'Messiah' is never applied to the future ruler, with the possible exception of the enigmatic Daniel 9:25–27.

Understanding the story in relation to Jesus

What are we to make of the OT in the light of this rapid survey? For most of the story the Jews had a relationship with God based on the Mosaic covenant, maintained by the sacrificial system, and focused in the relationship of the king to God. Within this community individuals could have their own relationship with God. Religion was thus focused very much on the present and based on the past, although there was also an element of future hope. From the exile onwards this hope assumes an ever more important place in the writings of the prophets. The belief in the future coming of God on 'the day of the Lord' for the judgment of sinners and the *salvation of his faithful people was an integral part of this hope.

It follows that the OT can hardly be called 'a book about Jesus' as if he were the principal subject. Where there is a future hope, it is centred on God himself and in some places on a messianic figure who is not identified. Jesus is not explicitly present. But two positive points can be made.

The first is that the OT bears witness to an ongoing revelation by God and a relationship with *humankind (more especially with the Jews) which from a Christian point of view reaches its culmination in the coming of Jesus and the establishment of the *church. Thus there is continuity in the history of God's dealings, so that the early Christians could view the OT story as the story of their ancestors and thus claim it as their own (*e.g.* Rom. 15:4; 1 Cor. 10:6).

The second point is that the fulfilment of Israel's various hopes for the future, centred especially on the Messiah and the renewal of God's people, are understood to be fulfilled in the experience of the followers of Jesus. Thus the OT is seen by the NT writers as the book which looks forward to what was now in process of fulfilment (*e.g.* Luke 24:46–47). This fulfilment was understood in more than one way.

First, there were passages in which it was believed that a prophet had been given insight by God into what would happen in the future (whether conditionally or absolutely; *cf.* Acts 2:30–31).

Second, it may be that some passages were regarded as having been fulfilled at one level in the history of the Jews but then as having a deeper fulfilment in Christian experience (Matt. 2:15; Acts 3:22–26).

Third, in some passages the description of an ideal person was seen as fulfilled most perfectly in Jesus (Mark 15:34).

And, fourth, there was the phenomenon known as typology. The word 'type' in its biblical usage signifies a correspondence between a past event chronicled in Scripture and a later event in which God acted in a similar but more profound way. For example, the prophet Jeremiah sees a correspondence between the Mosaic covenant and the new and better covenant which God was to make with his people in the future, and Christian writers drew a parallel between the *redemption of Israel from Egypt and the redemption from sin wrought by Christ (*cf.* Luke 9:31).

We may note here the way in which in the letter to the Hebrews the relationship between the high priest and Christ is developed at length. Whereas the concept of Jesus' death as a sacrifice for sin is found elsewhere in the NT, it is here that Jesus is identified explicitly as having a role which typologically fulfils that of the high priest (Heb. 7:1 – 8:6), who was responsible for the principal sacrifices offered in the temple, particularly those made on the Day of Atonement. Jesus is understood to have made a sacrifice of himself, which he then offered as a once-for-all offering to God in heaven (which is symbolically understood as being the 'true' temple; Heb. 9:23–28).

The book that prepares for the coming of Jesus

These two points, however, indicate that from a Christian point of view the OT is seen as a chronicle of the ongoing 'history of salvation' which culminates in the coming of Christ and therefore forms 'Part 1' of the whole Christian story. At the same time, since it is a book which records complex prophecies and fore-shadowings of Christ and the church, it is believed that God inspired its writers to record material which would find its fulfilment in Christ although the writers themselves, still less the original hearers and readers, could hardly have been aware of its significance. This point finds classic expression in 1 Peter 1:10–12, where Peter asserts that the prophets tried to find out the significance of what the Spirit of Christ in them was moving them to write, but were told that what they were writing was for the benefit of future generations. But if God was so working in them, it follows that the OT is in a sense a Christian book, some parts of which are about Jesus and the church, but that it could not be appreciated as such until the time of fulfilment. A biblical theology of the OT must recognize its dual role, as a book which would be understood on one level (or series of levels) by its original, pre-Christian readers, and on another level by those who had the 'key' to a new reading of it.

Accordingly, we see that within the OT there is a select group of passages, mainly in the prophets and the Psalms, which can be interpreted with hindsight as references to Christ on the basis of prophetic or typological fulfilment. Certainly there are places where the Christian reader may want to argue that a passage is unintelligible or yields no satisfactory meaning unless it is seen in the light of its fulfilment; one might argue this in the case of Isaiah 53 and point to the general inability of commentators to provide a convincing interpretation of the passage if they exclude the Christian one. Such passages might be taken as evidence for, or pointers to, the need to understand the OT as Christian Scripture, but it may be wiser to say that this view of the OT is in the end a tenet of faith.

It follows that the OT is perhaps not best described as 'a book about Jesus', but it is rightly seen as a Christian book by Christians. Without it the writers of the NT would not have had the resources which they needed for expressing their understanding of Jesus.

Jesus Christ in the NT

In contrast to the OT, the NT is a book in which Jesus Christ is the explicit subject virtually everywhere and his influence is implicit throughout. Although God is mentioned more frequently and remains the ultimate actor, to whom even Jesus is subject (1 Cor. 15:28; *cf.* Phil. 2:9–11), it is Jesus who is everywhere visible, so that the NT is a collection of books about Jesus.

As it stands, the NT is a combination of the Gospels and the letters (Rev. has the outward form of a letter, although its genre is complex) with *Acts forming a bridge between the two.

The first three Gospels

1. *The centrality of Jesus in the Gospels.* The NT begins with four books whose central theme is unambiguously Jesus Christ. It has been observed that he is the subject or the speaker in almost every individual unit in the Gospels; they are books about Jesus rather than God or even the message of Jesus. It is theologically significant that the Christian faith required a new literary genre, the Gospel, to express its distinctive character. The content of Christian faith is the founder of the religion rather than his message, even if the message and the founder belong inextricably together. The slogan that 'the Proclaimer became the Proclaimed' is essentially true.

Each of the Gospels tells the story of the significant part of Jesus's life, which begins with the arrival of his forerunner, *John the Baptist, and terminates with his death and resurrection. The greatest amount of space is given to the final period, spent in Jerusalem, thus justifying the famous description of Gospels as 'passion narratives with extended introductions' (M. Kähler, *The So-called Historical Jesus and the Historic, Biblical Christ* [Philadelphia, 1964], p. 80). The rest of the NT reflects this emphasis. In the letters virtually no attention is given to the events of Jesus's life, though there are some strong echoes of his teaching; the writers' interest is in his status as God's agent and in his death and resurrection, his present position as Lord, and his future role at the end of the world (see *Eschatology). The *gospel preached by Paul is summarized thus: 'that Christ died for our sins according to the Scriptures, that he was buried, that he was raised on the third day according to the Scriptures, and that he appeared to Peter, and then to the Twelve' (1 Cor 15:3–5, NIV). This centrality of Jesus' death and resurrection to the gospel is reflected in the shape of the Gospels, but the evangelists set these events in the context of what precedes them.

2. *Telling the story of Jesus.* The story of Jesus can be read as that of a wandering teacher and prophet who made people ask the question 'Who is this?' The development of partial understanding on the part of those who became his followers, and of the opposition that led to his arrest and trial by those who for various reasons saw him as a public danger who had to be stopped, can both be traced. So the story in the Gospels enables the reader to trace the way in which Jesus' actions and sayings revealed who he was.

At the same time, however, the reader already knows who Jesus is. The *Synoptic Gospels make this clear at the outset, so that as the story begins the reader (Christian or otherwise) is given the 'secret' of Jesus' identity as the evangelists understood it. In *Matthew and *Luke this is achieved by the stories of Jesus' birth and the events leading up to it. In Matthew he is named at the outset as 'Jesus Christ', a descendant of Abraham through David and his adoptive father Joseph. He is born through the action of God's Spirit on *Mary, who is a virgin in that she conceives him without intercourse with a male human being. Consequently, he is God's Son, and the prophecy of a child who bears the name Emmanuel, 'God with us', is fulfilled in him (Matt. 1:23; Is. 7:14). Luke's account gives a different version of events; it is told from Mary's point of view, whereas Matthew focuses on Joseph. Nevertheless, theologically it makes the same impression. *Mark begins with Jesus' adult life, but in his opening verse he declares that his concern is with 'the gospel about Jesus Christ, the Son of God' (Mark 1:1; note that some manuscripts do not have the last four words); for Mark, then, Jesus is the Messiah. The story of Jesus' encounter with John the Baptist, during which the Holy Spirit descended upon him in some visible and symbolic manner, and a heavenly voice confirmed his identity as the Son of God, called to be his servant (*cf.* Ps.

2:7; Is. 42:1), is also part of Mark's introduction. All three Gospels thus are concerned with the identity of Jesus, and the reader is privileged, as the actors in the story are not, to know the solution of the mystery and can measure the progress of the actors towards an understanding of it.

On the whole, the evangelists give a plausible account based on their premiss that Jesus was who they claimed him to be. They tell the story of Jesus as he travelled around the Jewish villages in Galilee and eventually made his way to Jerusalem (which he had previously visited briefly on the occasion of Jewish pilgrim festivals). During this period Jesus spoke about the arrival of the kingdom of God (Mark 1:14–15), which is to be understood as the future realm of justice and peace announced by the prophets (rather than simply the eternal heavenly rule of God over the whole world). His announcement was startling, in that he understood the kingdom to be already present and working powerfully in the world towards its consummation, whereas the prophets saw it as future (Matt. 10:7 par.; 12:28 par.; Luke 17:21). Further, the kingdom in Jesus' teaching was obviously different from the future realm of popular Jewish expectation, which involved the destruction of Israel's enemies and the unrighteous within the nation; this kingdom was a combination of the spiritual, political and national, and it was sometimes understood as something to be brought about by armed warfare. For Jesus, however, the kingdom had the nature of a spiritual force working upon individuals and communities, through which people would be set free from their unrighteous ways and summoned to a new way of life characterized by unqualified *love, even for their enemies, and was a matter of a changed heart rather than simply an outward conformity to new rules (Matt. 5 – 7; Luke 6:20–49). This ethic was not significantly different from that of the OT prophets, but it did carry with it criticism of the way in which observance of the regulations in the Torah had become a matter of outward obedience to a highly elaborate code of minute instructions that could get in the way of genuine fulfilment of the law of love (Matt. 23:23–24). Thus, although Jesus was not what we would understand as a social and political reformer, his message was very much concerned with social and political righteousness. Finally, the message of the kingdom was tied closely to Jesus himself; he summoned people who accepted his message to follow him as his disciples (Mark 1:16–20; Luke 9:57–62). His speech implied a claim to divine authority as God's spokesman (*cf.* his use of introductory 'Amen', Mark 3:28 and frequently), and he can be regarded as not so much a commentator on the kingdom as the agent through whom it was coming to pass. In short, his message, supported as it was by various mighty works (see *Signs and wonders) (Mark 1:27; 4:41), raised the question 'Who is he?'

3. *Who is Jesus?* This question was answered in various ways. One group of people was gradually convinced by Jesus; their response is summed up in the words of Peter, 'You are the Christ' (Mark 8:29 par.), although they did not fully understand at first how Jesus was filling this term with new meaning. So in the second half of the Gospel story we see Jesus trying to show them that he would have to be put to death; he was to be a *suffering Messiah in accordance with the divine purpose already attested in the Scriptures (Mark 8:31 par.; 9:31 par.; 10:33–34 par.). Other people simply did not understand what was going on and made no response. But there were still others who from an early stage took issue with Jesus for a variety of reasons: some no doubt because they felt condemned by his accusations of hypocrisy (Luke 11:45); some because Jesus' teaching about the Jewish law appeared to be an attack on it (Mark 2:23 – 3:6); some because they saw that he was implicitly claiming to be the Messiah and refused to believe him (Luke 23:2); some because they regarded him as a dangerous impostor who misled the people (John 11:47–48). On the human level, this was why Jesus had to face opposition and ultimately execution.

The manner of Jesus' teaching was such as to force people to think out for themselves what exactly was happening and who he was. His speech conveyed a sense of authority conferred by God, and it was natural that people should see him as a teacher like their other religious leaders and, more aptly, as a prophet. His own words confirmed this understanding of his role. He prayed to God as his Father, using the intimate Aramaic form *Abba* (Mark 14:36; *cf.* Matt. 11:25–27 par.). But Jesus did not refer to himself openly before the people as the Messiah or as God's Son, although he was less reticent in the presence of his close followers. Instead he used the phrase 'Son of Man'. There are two main points of view regarding the evangelists' understanding of this enigmatic phrase. First, there is the theory, built upon the fact that in the Aramaic spoken by Jesus 'Son of Man' could be simply a circumlocutory way of referring to oneself, that in some if not all cases even in the Greek Gospels it was nothing more than this. However, secondly, most scholars recognize that in at least some passages the term carries strong echoes of the tradition starting from Daniel 7 in which the Son of Man is a powerful figure who will come and exercise sovereign authority granted by God (Mark 13:26; 14:62; Luke 12:8–10). This set of associations would then also have been present where the term was used by Jesus in other contexts and indicated that he was a person already possessing authority (to *forgive sins and to legislate over the Sabbath [Mark 2:10, 28]), but whose authority was rejected by the Jewish leaders (Mark 9:12). It may well be that these associations were not immediately apparent on every occasion and that therefore the term baffled some of Jesus' hearers (John 12:34) and also the readers of the Gospels.

Part of the difficulty was that Jesus believed he must suffer in order to fulfil God's purpose for his life. He based this conviction on 'the Scriptures'. He saw himself as the 'rejected stone' of Psalm 118:22–23 (Mark 12:10 par.); he took upon himself the language used in the Psalms to refer to the righteous man who trusts in God but is afflicted even to the point of feeling that God has forsaken him (Ps. 22:1; Mark 15:34 par.); and he also saw himself as fulfilling the role of the Servant of Yahweh who was rejected and counted with evildoers (Is. 53:12; Luke 22:37). He saw a redemptive purpose being fulfilled in his suffering, interpreting his death as the payment of a ransom on behalf of humanity (Mark 10:45) and as a counterpart to the sacrifice which inaugurated the old covenant (Mark 14:24).

Following the story of Jesus' death, the Gospels conclude with an account of how the tomb where his body had been placed was found to be empty (Mark 16:1–8 par.), and of how various of his followers had encounters with him, from which they inferred that God had brought him back to life. In this way, the identification of Jesus as Messiah was believed to have been vindicated by God (Luke 24:19–27), and the final picture in the Gospels is of a lordly figure commanding his followers to engage in a worldwide mission (Matt. 28:16–20; Luke 24:44–49).

The Gospel of John

The Gospel of *John offers a somewhat different approach to its subject from that of the Synoptics. The content is different with respect both to the incidents related (before the last week in Jerusalem John and the Synoptics have in common only the feeding of the five thousand and Jesus's walking on the lake, John 6), and to the content and style of the teaching; the result is a different picture of Jesus. The first three Gospels provide something like a photograph, while John provides an artist's portrait, in which Jesus is seen more explicitly in the light of who Christians knew him to be after the resurrection. The Gospel is based upon a solid foundation of traditions which did not find their way into the other Gospels (together with some which did), but which are of essentially the same character as those underlying the Synoptics. John's aim is to draw out the inner meaning of the story of Jesus.

Like the other Gospel writers, John lets his readers into the secret at the outset. He begins with a stately piece of elevated prose (John 1:1–18), speaking of the *Word who was with God before creation and is the source of *light for the world. This Word became *incarnate; John does not state explicitly that he became incarnate in Jesus, but leaves the reader to draw this conclusion (John 1:17). In this Gospel Jesus is portrayed much more frequently as the Son of God and as speaking of himself openly as such (e.g. John 5:16–23; cf. 10:33). He gives a much stronger impression of having supernatural knowledge acquired from God and he is open about the close relationship between himself and God as his Father. He remains the teacher (John 13:13) and the prophet (John 6:14), and people recognize him as the Messiah (John 1:49; 4:29). He speaks of himself using the term 'Son of Man', but this figure is one who has come down from heaven (John 3:13). He uses powerful imagery in a series of 'I am' sayings, in which he is the bread of life, the way, the truth and the life, the good shepherd, and so on. As (nearly) always in the NT, the imagery is rooted in the language of the OT. He also speaks at some length regarding the coming of the *Holy Spirit, the Counsellor, who will come after he has departed (John 14:16–17, 26; 15:26; 16:7–15), whereas in the other Gospels there are only a few, isolated references to the Spirit.

The picture of Jesus in John is thus that of the Word made flesh in whom the glory of the Father can be seen. He is much more evidently a divine figure (John 1:1, 18), although he is also fully human (e.g. John 4:6). He can be the object of adoration and worship (John 20:28; cf. how prayer is addressed to the *exalted Jesus in Acts 7:59).

The Acts of the Apostles

The Gospels all conclude with a group of Jesus' disciples' being taken by surprise by his resurrection. This event is presented as the vindication of Jesus by God, the demonstration that he is in truth the Messiah. In both Matthew and Luke it is the occasion for Jesus to exercise his authority by commanding his followers to make disciples and to be his witnesses (see *Testimony/witness) throughout the world. What happened next is described in the continuation to Luke's Gospel, the narrative in the Acts of the Apostles. Acts refers to the Gospel's relating 'all that Jesus began to do and teach' (Acts 1:1); the second book relates all that Jesus continued to do and teach through his followers who acted 'in his name' (Acts 3:6, 16; 16:18). This language is used with reference to God himself in the OT (e.g. 2 Sam. 6:18), and thus has implications for the status of Jesus. Perhaps Jesus's most important action, according to Acts, occurs on the day of Pentecost when the powerful descent of the Holy Spirit on the disciples is explicitly ascribed by Peter to Jesus (Acts 2:33). Again this has implications for the writer's understanding of Jesus, since the pouring out of the Spirit is an action ascribed to God in the OT (Joel 2:28). Jesus is the Lord of the Spirit, and the Spirit can be referred to as 'the Spirit of Jesus' (Acts 16:7). It is accordingly through the Spirit that Jesus is active in the early Christians and their mission.

The understanding of Jesus found in Acts links together his earthly life and what happened afterwards. This is seen most clearly in Peter's speech to Cornelius, which contains the fullest summary in Acts of the life of Jesus and then relates how God raised him from the dead and appointed him to be the judge of all people (another role ascribed to God in the OT which is now fulfilled by Jesus; Acts 10:34–43).

The resurrection is understood as being not only the reversal by the power of God of the death sentence on Jesus but also the conferring of the highest rank upon Jesus (Acts 3:13–15; 5:31). The command of God in Psalm 110:1, 'Sit at my right hand', was addressed to Jesus and fulfilled at his resurrection (Acts 2:34–35). The followers of Jesus who could testify that he was alive on the basis of their post-resurrection meetings with him recognized that he was no longer on the earth (he was not simply a resuscitated body, like Jairus's daughter or Lazarus), but that he must have gone to be with God. They took over Jesus' own use of this Psalm (Mark 12:35–37) and interpreted it to mean that he was now enthroned alongside God; their belief that he was the Messiah and the Son of Man, God's chief agent, would have strengthened this belief. So more than one speech addressed to the Jews in Jerusalem claims that they had crucified Jesus in accordance with God's plan, but that God himself had then undone their action by resurrecting and exalting Jesus (Acts 2:23–33; 3:15).

This is the basic understanding of Jesus in Acts. The idea of Jesus' existence in some form before his earthly life (expressed in John in terms of the Word's becoming incarnate in the human Jesus), is not mentioned. This might be thought to support the view that Jesus' exaltation raised him to a level which he had not previously enjoyed, but the inference is invalid. It is true that Jesus is thought to be *humiliated in his earthly life and vindicated and exalted thereafter; at the same time the resurrection is understood as confirmation that Jesus was already the Messiah and Lord in his earthly life rather than as evidence that he has just been installed in this position.

The term 'Son of Man' appears in Acts 7:56, where Stephen designates Jesus in this way, thereby showing how the prophecies in the Gospel have been fulfilled (Luke 22:69 par.). Jesus is also shown to be the suffering Servant of Yahweh from Isaiah 53:7–8, when Philip explains the meaning of this passage to the Ethiopian traveller (Acts 8:30–35). A common practice in early Christian evangelism among Jews is to show from the Scriptures that the Messiah must suffer, and then to argue that Jesus fulfils this prophecy and is the Messiah (Acts 17:2–3). Jesus is also identified by Paul as the Son of God (Acts 9:20), on the basis of Psalm 2:7 (Acts 13:32–33).

Finally, the term 'Lord' is frequently used for Jesus, sometimes in compound phrases ('the Lord Jesus'; Acts 1:21; 4:33; 7:59; 8:16; *et al.*) and sometimes by itself ('the Lord'; Acts 2:36; 9:27; 11:16; *et al.*). However, Luke uses this term also to refer to God (Acts 2:39; 4:26; *et al.*), and sometimes it is unclear whether the reference is to God or to Jesus. This usage of 'Lord' puts Jesus on a level with God and hints at his divinity. In Luke's Gospel the narrator refers to Jesus as 'the Lord' but no character in the story ever does so (Luke 7:13, 19; 10:1; *et al.*). (When people address Jesus as 'Lord' in the Gospels, this is often no more than a customary polite form of address, although the amount of respect intended by it varies from occasion to occasion.)

The NT letters

If Acts describes in narrative form how the early Christians understood Jesus, the letters tell the same story in a more didactic manner.

In the writings of *Paul there are few, if any, passages the theme of which is 'Jesus', even though he is present almost everywhere. It is almost as if Paul did not need to instruct his readers about the Christian understanding of Jesus. When he writes about him, he takes it for granted that what he is communicating is already known and that nobody will disagree with it. Further, essentially the same understanding of Jesus is present throughout his letters, indicating that by the time he came to write the earliest of them (within about twenty years of the death of Jesus) he and his congregations had come to a mature and firm set of convictions on the matter. However, there is some progress and development in his thinking.

1. *Jesus Christ and his people.* Paul's understanding of Jesus is that he lived as an ordinary human being, born of a human mother, a member of the Jewish people (Gal. 4:4), having brothers (1 Cor. 9:5), giving teaching which his followers regarded as

authoritative (1 Cor. 7:10; 9:14), suffering death and subsequently being raised from the dead and exalted by God (1 Thess. 4:14). His exaltation led to his 'reign', which will continue until the time when all opposition to him has been overcome and he hands over his kingdom to his Father (1 Cor. 15:24–25).

Jesus is thus primarily a living Lord who exercises a spiritual influence from heaven (Col. 4:1). Consequently when his followers 'believe in' him, they are not simply expressing a belief about him, or placing their trust in what he has done in the past, but rather committing themselves to a living person (Gal. 2:16; Eph. 1:13; Phil. 1:29). They thus enter into a spiritual relationship with him, analogous to a *marriage relationship. Marriage is not only a physical and social union but also a spiritual relationship of love and trust between two people, as a result of which it is possible to talk of 'the Macdonalds' or 'the Patersons' as a new entity formed by the marriage. In the case of Christ, believers in him form a new entity called his 'body': the bond between Christ and every believer creates a mutual relationship between the members of the body (Rom 12:4–8; 1 Cor 12:12–27). Christ is accordingly a cosmic figure.

Another way of expressing this, characteristic of Paul but rare elsewhere, is the use of the preposition 'in' in such phrases as 'in Christ' and 'in the Lord', to express the way in which the lives of believers are determined by the crucified and risen Lord; in some places the phrase is used adjectivally, implying that believers are somehow closely bonded to Christ or incorporated in him, yet without any loss of their individuality and identity (Rom. 8:1; 1 Cor. 1:30; *et al.*). In John also believers are said to be in Christ and he in them (John 14:20); they are also in the Father (John 17:21; 1 John 2:24). Here the language of mutual indwelling reveals the close relationship between Christ and believers, similar to that between the Father and his Son (John 17:21).

Yet another characteristic Pauline expression is that of believers' having died and been buried with Christ and now living a new *life just as Christ was raised from the dead (Rom. 6:1–11; Gal. 2:20); they will also share in his resurrection in the future, and in a sense they have already been raised with him (Eph. 2:6; Col. 2:12; 3:1). This language demonstrates the cosmic role of Christ and his function as the representative of the human race, in whose death and new life believers participate.

2. *Jesus and Adam.* It is not surprising in the light of all this that Paul draws a comparison between *Adam and Christ. In 1 Corinthians 15:45–49 there is a simple contrast between the 'first man' and the 'second man'; believers who have borne the likeness of the former will also bear the likeness of the latter. Paul envisages some kind of unity between Adam and the human race in their sin and consequent death, and then a unity between Christ and believers in their justification (see *Righteousness, justice and justification) and eternal life (Rom. 5:12–21; 1 Cor. 15:22).

The Adam/Christ parallel is important not only because it illustrates yet again how Paul's thought is rooted in Scripture, but also because it shows how important it is for him that Jesus was a real human being, representative potentially of the human race and actually of believers. This raises the question of whether Paul compares and contrasts Jesus with Adam in other texts.

The crucial passage is Philippians 2:5–11 where, it has been argued, Christ is presented as being made, like Adam, in the *image of God and then, unlike Adam, resisting the temptation to misuse his position and being content to live a life of *obedience to God as a human being, even to the point of being willing to die.

Although some echoes of the story of Adam are present, it is likely that this passage depicts a pre-existent figure (like the Word in John 1) who is prepared to give up a heavenly position of equality with God in order to take on human form. The book of Proverbs contains a literary personification of *Wisdom as God's helper in the work of creation (Prov. 8:22–31), and this concept was developed in inter-testamental literature where Wisdom comes into the world to give instruction to God's people, taking concrete form in the law of God (Ecclus. 24). Although Wisdom is presented as a female figure (Prov. 7:4) and the language used is that of literary personification, there are many parallels with the descriptions of the Word in John 1 and the coming of Christ into the world in Paul (*1 Enoch* 42:2; Wisdom of Solomon 7:27). Paul, like John, believes that God sent his Son into the world as a visitor from outside (Gal. 4:4).

The alternative interpretation of this language, that the pre-existent wisdom of God somehow found expression in Jesus, is unnecessarily cautious and does not adequately reflect Paul's view of the incarnation. 2 Corinthians 8:9 refers to a pre-existent being's giving up the *glory of heaven so that by his earthly life human beings might share in that glory. In short, Christ became what we are in order that we might become what he is (Irenaeus), through a glorious exchange in which Christ, without ceasing to be what he was by nature, the Son of God, became like sinful humanity, *i.e.* became a man without being a sinner, in order that he might bear human sin and die on behalf of sinners (Rom. 8:3; 2 Cor. 5:21). Paul maintains that Christ is a real human being and yet fully divine (Col. 2:9); in a rhetorical flourish he asserts that Christ is superior over all the created universe, which was created through him and is upheld by him, and similarly he is head over the church and the whole universe to God (Col. 1:15–20).

3. *Jesus and God*. Paul uses a variety of designations when referring to Jesus. He uses the simple name occasionally, but much prefers compounds, 'Jesus Christ', 'Christ Jesus' and variations on 'the Lord Jesus Christ'. These combinations probably reflect early Christian confessions in which believers ascribed an exalted status to Jesus. Just as in Acts Paul is said to have argued that Jesus was the Christ, so it is likely that believers declared 'Jesus is the Christ' or 'the Christ is Jesus' as a public expression of their faith. Certainly they said 'Jesus is Lord' (Rom. 10:9; 1 Cor 12:3) or 'Jesus Christ is Lord' (*cf*. Phil. 2:11). The wording of Philippians 3:8 ('Christ Jesus my Lord') indicates that this was a confession of one's personal acceptance of Christ rather than simply a statement of his cosmic lordship. Throughout Paul's writings Christ's lordship is a dominant theme. It finds clear expression in 1 Corinthians 8:5–6 where Paul says that Christians have one God (the Father) and one Lord (Jesus Christ), both of whom participated in the creation of the universe and to both of whom believers are related. This is a remarkable statement in that Paul deliberately places the Father and Jesus alongside one another. The title 'Lord' here distinguishes Jesus from the Father, but elsewhere it recalls its OT use as a substitute for the name of God, indicating that Paul ascribes to Jesus a rank equal to that of the Father. Paul uses almost stereotyped language in his greetings to his readers, in which the Father and the Lord are coupled as the source of *grace and *peace (*e.g.* 1 Cor. 1:3). The natural way in which Paul so expresses himself shows how much it is taken for granted that Jesus is the source of divine *blessings alongside his Father. However, the term 'God' is rarely used for Jesus (Rom. 9:5; Titus 2:13); not only might it have caused confusion between the Father and Jesus, but also the early Christians' Jewish monotheism would have deterred them from stating their new and complex understanding of God (which was later to find expression in the doctrine of the Trinity) in such a way.

Implicit in all this is that Jesus bears the image of God and is his Son. There is a distinction between the image of God borne by Adam, which is also borne by all human beings, and the image of God borne by Christ (2 Cor. 4:4; Col. 1:15) to which believers are conformed (2 Cor. 3:18; Col. 3:10). The background to the idea of God's image in Christ (*e.g.* in Heb. 1:3) is probably to be found in the description of Wisdom as the image of God's goodness (Wisdom of Solomon 7:26). Jesus is thus an exact copy of God's being; if the invisible God could be seen, he would look like Jesus. Jesus is thus God's son, made in his image, just as Adam was the father of a son 'in his likeness, according to his image' (Gen. 5:3, NRSV). Paul does not use the term 'Son' of Jesus very often (Rom. 1:3–4; 1 Cor. 1:9; Gal. 2:20; *et al.*), but in doing so he expresses the closeness of Jesus to God and above all the greatness of the sacrifice made by the Father in giving up his own Son (like Abraham with Isaac; *cf.* Gen. 22:2, 12, 16) to death for us all (Rom 8:32).

Bibliography

R. J. Bauckham, *God Crucified: Monotheism and Christology in the New Testament* (Carlisle, 1998); M. Casey, *From Jewish Prophet to Gentile God* (Cambridge, 1991); O. Cullmann, *The Christology of the New Testament* (London, ²1963); M. De Jonge, *Christology in Context: The Earliest Christian Response to Jesus* (Philadelphia, 1988); J. D. G. Dunn, *Christology in the Making* (London, ²1989); *idem, The Theology of Paul the Apostle* (Edinburgh and Grand

Rapids, 1997); M. J. Harris, *Jesus as God: The New Testament Use of* Theos *in Reference to Jesus* (Grand Rapids, 1992); M. Hengel, *The Son of God* (London, 1976); L. W. Hurtado, *One God, One Lord: Early Christian Devotion and Ancient Jewish Monotheism* (Edinburgh and Philadelphia, 1988); I. H. Marshall, 'Jesus Christ, titles of', *NBD*, pp. 575–583; *idem, The Origins of New Testament Christology* (Leicester, ²1990); C. F. D. Moule, *The Origin of Christology* (Cambridge, 1977); M. A. Powell and D. R. Bauer, *Who Do You Say That I Am? Essays on Christology* (Louisville, 1999); B. Witherington III, *The Christology of Jesus* (Minneapolis and Carlisle, 1990); *idem, The Many Faces of the Christ: The Christologies of the New Testament and Beyond* (New York, 1998).

I. H. MARSHALL

JOB, see Part 2
JOEL, see Part 2

JOHN THE BAPTIST

Introduction

Born in the hill country of Judea to godly parents of priestly origin (Luke 1:5–6), John seems to have been attracted to the restoration movements so characteristic of *Israel during the late Second Temple period, especially those which gravitated towards the *wilderness as a place of either refuge or expectation. Like Hannah, Elizabeth (John's mother) was barren, but waited upon God to bring her honour (Luke 1:24–25) by giving her a child (1:7). An angel revealed to Zechariah (John's father) that Elizabeth would indeed become pregnant and give birth to a child, who was to be named John (1:13), and who would be filled with God's Spirit and announce the restoration of Israel (1:14–17). Elizabeth was a relative of *Jesus' mother, Mary (1:36, 39–45).

The evidence from the Dead Sea Scrolls has led many to think that John had some connection to the Qumran community. The following parallels are often drawn: 1. they lived in the same deserted area; 2. they shared an intense interest in Isaiah 40:3 (*cf.* Mark 1:2; *Rule of the Community, Manual of Discipline* 8:14); 3. they both focused on ritual purity; 4. they were both anti-materialistic (*cf.* Luke 3:11 and *Rule of the Community* 3:2; 5:2); 5. they may have had a similar diet (*cf.* Mark 1:6 and *Damascus Document* 12:13–14); 6. they both believed God's wrath was about to fall on Israel; and 7. they both had priestly connections (C. H. Kraeling, *John the Baptist*, pp. 1–32). However, recent scholarship has argued that the link is not as direct as was once supposed. For instance, the Qumran exegesis of Isaiah 40:3 is different from that of John, since he did not expect his followers to join him in the wilderness (see J. E. Taylor, *The Immerser*, pp. 25–29). Furthermore, John's practice of *baptism, a once and for all act of immersion in conjunction with a decisive repentance of *sins, differs markedly from the Qumran purification practices (calling into question parallel 3. above), which consisted of frequent self-administered baptisms. So although John and the Qumran community had a similar view of Israel (the nation and its leaders were corrupt and in need of restoration), of *eschatology (God will soon come to judge the nation and restore the true Israel), and of ethics (Israel must repent and practise *righteousness), these shared perceptions do not prove that John was a former Qumran member. John and Qumran understood God's will for the nation of Israel in the same terms, and as a result they were both drawn into the wilderness around the Jordan.

John was imprisoned by Herod Antipas for fearlessly declaring Herod's marriage to be illicit (*cf.* Josephus, *Antiquities* 18.118–119 and Mark 6:17–29), and was imprisoned at Machaerus (across the Jordan). During a sensual party, Herod's daughter-in-law pleased him so much that he promised her whatever she wanted. Much to her mother's delight, she asked for John's head on a platter. John's death made an immediate impression on Jesus (*cf.* Matt. 14:13). John had followers for some time after his death (Acts 19:1–7).

A prophet

Not all *prophets are the same, as Robert Webb has shown (*John the Baptizer and Prophet*, pp. 219–348), and John is probably best classed as a 'leadership popular prophet'. He led a large peasant movement, faced opposition from and death at the hands of the

Roman authorities, focused his efforts on the deliverance of Israel, and gathered his followers for a symbolic event which recalled significant themes from Israel's history and prophetic expectation. Many Jews may have believed that prophecy had ceased (or that it was extremely rare and open to question [cf. 1 Macc. 9:27]); when John announced the coming *judgment of God he may have changed people's minds and led many to think that the last days had arrived.

John's ministry was directed both to the nation, as a call to restoration through baptism and conversion, and against its corrupt leadership (Luke 3:7–14 par.; Matt 3:7–10). As a prophet, he would have expected to experience opposition from religious leaders, and in Matthew 3:7–10 he denounces both Pharisees and Sadducees. (In Luke 3:7–14 his audience is less specific.)

John's message was focused on the *kingdom (Matt. 3:2), or (if Matthew is projecting Jesus' language onto John) on Israel's final deliverance, so clearly expressed in the idea of the kingdom. His conviction that the final days were about to arrive drove John to demand from his listeners a heart-felt and effective repentance of sin, regardless of their station in life. Specifically, John exhorted his audience not to rely on Israelite privilege as against moral reformation, to share their clothing and food, to collect only what was due, and to practise social justice (Luke 3:10–14). Baptism, then, expressed one's acceptance of John's vision for Israel, of Israel's need for repentance, of the individual's participation in Israel's covenant guilt, and of a fundamental dissatisfaction with what the temple could offer to Israel.

John's threat was that the judgment of God would come on all those who did not repent, turn from their sinful ways, and so receive his baptism of repentance (Matt. 3:11–12 par.; Luke 3:15–18). John expected God to act soon and decisively in judgment of the nation through a messianic figure. This person would baptize with the Holy Spirit (effecting God's gracious salvation) and fire (effecting God's holy judgment upon the unrepentant). He would not winnow, but clean the threshing floor after the winnowing; he would gather the wheat into the barn and throw what remained on the threshing floor into the fire to be destroyed (R. Webb, *John the Baptizer*, pp. 261–306). From these descrip-

tions it appears that John's vision of the future was not as bright as Jesus': John seems to have thought that the kingdom and judgment were about to arrive and that Israel needed to repent at once, or be judged; Jesus envisaged a period during which the kingdom was inaugurated prior to God's judgment.

As a prophet, John bore a striking resemblance to Elijah. Many Jews believed that Elijah must come before the Messiah (cf. Mark 9:11–13), a conviction probably based upon Malachi 3:23–24 (cf. *Babylonian Talmud 'Erubin* 43a-b and *Vision* from Qumran Cave 4). Jesus associates John with Elijah. When asked by his disciples, after his transfiguration, why the leaders think Elijah must come first, he claimed that Elijah has already come: he was seen in John the Baptist (Mark 9:11–13; cf. also Matt. 11:14). John's role as Elijah is thus associated with rejection, a theme reflected also in his humble attire (Mark 1:6).

A baptizer

John's baptism had two distinctive features: first, it was in the Jordan, and secondly, it was a once and for all baptism. While John may have baptized in the Jordan simply because it was close to the desert, it is far more likely that he did so to evoke the ancient Jewish tradition of entry into the land as the new *people of God (R. Webb, *John the Baptizer*, pp. 360–366). Having been baptized in the Jordan, the people came out of the *water, re-entered the land and sought once again to take it for God as the now pure Israel. That the Jordan was chosen may also have been due to its being 'living' or running water; running water was used in the OT only for purification from serious conditions (Lev. 15:13).

Baptism signified purification from sin, a removal of sin's contamination. But there is still no solid evidence to suggest that proselyte baptism, at least as an unrepeatable initiation rite, had developed by the time of John (S. McKnight, *A Light Among the Gentiles* [Minneapolis, 1991], pp. 82–85). In fact, as J. E. Taylor has shown, it is far more likely that Jews would have understood John's baptism as a purification of the body following repentance of sins (*The Immerser*, pp. 49–100). That is, John preached a baptism in which repentance was publicly demonstrated and which purified the body from impurity. That John saw his baptism as effecting repentance and forgiveness may mean that he regarded the temple's means of forgiveness (through sacrifices) as ineffective for the true Israel.

John's actual role in the baptisms is unclear, though Christian tradition has quite easily assimilated John's practices to its own: thus some Christian art depicts John pouring water on his subjects while others have him immersing them. It is well known that in later Judaism the one being baptized immersed himself/herself and was naked to ensure that every part of the body was purified. We cannot be sure how John baptized: he may have immersed people himself, or helped them immerse themselves, or simply supervised the rites. It is highly unlikely, however, that the people were naked, given that they were of both sexes and the acts were public. The focus given to John, however, probably suggests that the repentant Israelites saw John as mediating forgiveness through this baptism of repentance.

Consistent with the theme of repentance expressed in baptism, John was known as the one who called sinners into the 'way of righteousness' (Matt. 21:28–32). John announced that Israel must turn from its sin and do the will of God, and that this way of *obedience was open to all. In fact, John's proclamation was heeded more by tax collectors and prostitutes than by the religious leaders, and so it is the former who entered the kingdom. This reveals an important connection between John and Jesus: they both called sinful people to repent and form the new people of God.

Relationship to Jesus

John was a relative of Jesus (*cf.* Luke 1:36) and so probably knew Jesus prior to their (overlapping) ministries. Jesus publicly identified himself with John's call and so received John's baptism of repentance (Matt. 3:13–17). That Jesus was baptized for the remission of sins did not mean that he was sinful. Rather, it reflected his belief that the nation was in a disastrously sinful state and that baptism for the remission of sins was needed. In accepting John's baptism, Jesus became a disciple of John in the sense of joining his movement for the restoration of Israel (B. F. Meyer, *The Aims of Jesus* [London, 1979], pp. 115–128).

Either as a result of John's arrest or for some other reason (perhaps a disagreement), Jesus eventually separated from John and formed his own movement, based on the idea of the kingdom of God (*cf.* John 3:22–36). This separation indicates that John and Jesus played different roles in the inauguration of the kingdom (Matt. 11:2–19). When asked if he was the expected one (Matt. 11:3), Jesus told John's disciples that he was inaugurating the eschaton by fulfilling the expectations of Isaiah (*cf.* Matt. 11:5–6 with Is. 29:18–19; 35:5–6; 61:1). But John, who prepared Israel for the new era, was superior to any other member of the old covenant (Matt. 11:11). In fact, from the time of John until the time of Jesus' statements about him, the kingdom had been under assault and violent people were seeking to prevent its arrival (11:12). Both John's ascetic lifestyle and Jesus' celebratory ministry were unacceptable to their contemporaries (11:16–19). Their ministries were successive stages in the coming of God's eschatological kingdom in Israel.

The Fourth Gospel depicts John as a witness to Jesus, who is the very Word of God. John confessed that he himself was not the Messiah, Elijah, or the prophet (John 1:19–21); instead, he was a witness (see *Testimony/witness) to the one who comes from the desert declaring the fulfilment of Isaiah 40:3. This coming one is in fact the Lamb of God, the one who can redeem people from their sins. This was recognized by John at the baptism of Jesus; it convinced him that Jesus was the Son of God (1:29–34).

See also: ELIJAH.

Bibliography

C. H. Kraeling, *John the Baptist* (New York and London, 1951); J. E. Taylor, *The Immerser: John the Baptist within Second Temple Judaism* (Grand Rapids and London, 1997); R. L. Webb, *John the Baptizer and Prophet: A Socio-Historical Study* (Sheffield, 1991).

S. McKnight

JOHN, LETTERS OF, see Part 2
JOHN, see Part 2

JONAH (PERSON)

For discussion of the figure of Jonah in the OT, see *Jonah (book of) in part 2.

The sign of Jonah

Throughout the NT a rich variety of OT themes and ideas are presented as having their fulfilment in *Jesus Christ. One of the more unusual of these is the 'sign of Jonah'.

The Synoptic Gospels describe several occasions on which opponents of Jesus came looking for a '*sign' (sēmeion) in order that they might determine the true nature of his ministry. While Mark observes briefly that Jesus refused to provide any sign (Mark 8:11–12), the parallel account in Matthew 16:1–4 records that Jesus added the following: 'A wicked and adulterous generation looks for a miraculous sign, but none will be given it except the sign of Jonah' (NIV). A further episode in Matthew 12:38–42 (cf. the parallel account in Luke 11:29–32) also includes the statement that no miraculous sign will be given 'except the sign of the prophet Jonah' (v. 39). Jesus expands upon this and concludes by affirming that 'one greater than Jonah is here' (v. 41). (A similar comparison with *Solomon is made in v. 42.)

In seeking a 'sign' from Jesus his opponents were not looking merely for a miracle; it may be inferred from Matthew 12:22–24 that the Pharisees did not dispute the fact that Jesus had already healed a 'demon-possessed man who was blind and dumb'. Rather, they were looking for something much more significant which would confirm that Jesus acted with divine approval. Jesus clearly viewed the demand for such a sign as not only unnecessary but wicked; it arose from an attitude of unbelief and hostility towards God. Only a 'wicked and adulterous generation' would seek such a sign (Matt. 12:39; 16:4; cf. Luke 11:29).

What Jesus meant by the 'sign of Jonah' is difficult to determine, and the problem is compounded by the different emphases found in Matthew 12:38–42 and Luke 11:29–32. While Matthew draws attention to the 'three days and three nights' which Jonah spent in the belly of the fish (12:40), and thereby creates a link with the death and resurrection of Jesus, Luke omits this idea completely. By focusing on the material common to both Matthew and Luke the concepts of preaching,

*repentance and *judgment appear most prominently. Scholarly discussion of the 'sign of Jonah' has focused on these various possibilities.

The preaching of repentance

It has been suggested, in the light of his unwillingness to accommodate the Pharisees, that the only sign which Jesus will give them is the call to repent. Undoubtedly repentance lay at the heart of his preaching (e.g. Matt. 4:17), but it is difficult to imagine that he would have classified the preaching of repentance as a 'sign'. Furthermore, why should such preaching be associated with Jonah in particular? The call to repentance was by no means unique to Jonah; it was an important feature of John the Baptist's ministry (Matt. 3:1–12; Mark 1:4–5; Luke 3:2–14). The 'sign of Jonah' is, therefore, likely to be something more than a summons to repent.

Deliverance from death after three days

Matthew 12:40 suggests that there is a parallel between Jonah's experience in the fish and Jesus' resurrection from death. It has to be asked, however: in what way was Jonah's experience a 'sign'? According to J. Jeremias (in TDNT), Jonah's deliverance confirmed to the people of Nineveh his divine calling and so persuaded them to repent. In the light of this the resurrection of Jesus will authenticate his ministry. However, Jonah acknowledges that he initially fled to Tarshish because he anticipated that the Ninevites would repent (Jonah 4:2). This suggests that he saw no need for a sign in order to convince the Ninevites of his divine authorization. Also, the absence of any reference in Luke to Jonah's time in the fish suggests that the 'sign of Jonah' must involve more that the resurrection of Jesus.

Other parallels between Jonah and Jesus

While Jesus and Jonah both preached repentance and reappeared alive after three days, several other parallels may be noted. First, by going to preach to the Gentile inhabitants of Nineveh Jonah became the agent of God's mercy to the very *nation that within several decades destroyed the northern kingdom of *Israel in 722 BC. Is it possible that in his reference to the 'sign of Jonah' Jesus anticipated that his own ministry would lead to the outpouring of God's *mercy and judgment upon Gentiles and Jews respectively? Such an interpretation is certainly in keeping with Jesus' negative description of 'this generation' and his comments about Gentiles' standing up at the judgment and their condemnation of unbelieving Jews (Matt. 12:41–42; Luke 11:31–32).

Second, is it possible that Jesus saw in the story of Jonah an example of a prophet sacrificing his own life in order to save others? According to *Mekhilta Exodus* 12:1: 'R. Jonathan (c. 140 AD) said: The only purpose of Jonah was to bring judgment on himself in the sea, for it is written: "And he said to them, Take me and cast me into the sea" [Jon. 1:12]. Similarly, you find that many patriarchs and prophets sacrificed themselves for Israel.' If such a view of Jonah existed in the 1st century, Jesus might have been alluding to the fact that he was willing to die for the nation of Israel. Interestingly, the early Christian biblical scholar Jerome linked Jonah's willingness to die at sea with the fact that he 'knew, by inspiration of the Holy Spirit, that the repentance of the Gentiles would be the ruin of the Jews'.

In the light of Matthew's overall presentation of Jesus as the Messiah who inaugurates the *kingdom of God/heaven through his death and resurrection, it is likely that Matthew saw in the 'sign of Jonah' a picture of God's mercy being extended to the Gentiles and divine judgment coming upon the present unbelieving generation of Jews. By adopting this perspective we may come closest to what Jesus meant when he referred to the 'sign of Jonah'.

Bibliography

D. W. Baker, T. D. Alexander and B. K. Waltke, *Obadiah, Jonah and Micah*, TOTC (Leicester and Downers Grove, 1988); R. A. Edwards, *The Sign of Jonah in the Theology of the Evangelists and Q* (London, 1971); J. Jeremias, "*Iōnas*' in *TDNT* 3, pp. 406–410; J. Woodhouse, 'Jesus and Jonah', *RTR* 43, 1984, pp. 33–41.

T. D. ALEXANDER

JONAH, BOOK OF, see Part 2

JOSEPH

Introduction

The account of Joseph's life, apart from his birth (30:22–24) and first seventeen years (37:2), is set in Egypt. This geographical setting performs three functions. First, it provides a parallel to the first section of Genesis (1 – 11), and marks off the beginning and end of Genesis (1 – 11; 37 – 50) which take place outside of Canaan, from the middle section (12 – 36) which is set in Canaan. Secondly, it draws attention to the fact that the God of Israel is active beyond the borders of Israel. Indeed, the Lord's song can (and must) be sung 'in a foreign land' (Ps. 137:4, NIV). Thirdly, the Egyptians of Joseph's time provide a contrast with those of *Moses' time. There is no brutality or oppression of the Hebrews in Genesis 37 – 50. Rather, Joseph (an outsider), becomes the second most powerful man in the land (41:41). Joseph's Egyptian steward brings a word of reassurance to the brothers (43:23). Pharaoh welcomes Joseph's family to Egypt (47:5–6). An Egyptian party accompanies Joseph to Canaan to bury Jacob (50:7–9). Such favorable references to the Egyptians should restrain those within the community of faith from demonizing or developing xenophobic attitudes towards those outside.

Connections with Genesis 12 – 36

Joseph's life is different in three ways from those of Abraham, Isaac and Jacob. First, Joseph experiences no theophanies. God speaks only once in the Joseph story, to Jacob (46:2–4). This raises the question of whether or not God is as real and active when there are no overwhelming dreams or powerful theophanies, but only silence.

Secondly, unlike his ancestors, Joseph is guilty of no egregious sin. In fact, he is the one person in Genesis who flees from sin (ch. 39). In Genesis 12 – 36 the greatest threat to the promises of God is the bearers of the promises. By contrast, in Joseph's time the threat to the promises is not Joseph's reprehensible behaviour, but a devastating famine that has spread from Canaan to Egypt. Will such a famine so decimate God's people that they will never become a great nation?

Thirdly, more than his forefathers Joseph fulfills the divine promise that God's chosen people will be the means of blessing to the non-chosen. The only non-covenant person in Genesis expressly said to be blessed because of the presence and gifts of an individual from the faith community is Potiphar (39:5). Furthermore, when Joseph, upon identifying himself to his brothers, mentions that God sent him to Egypt 'to save lives' (45:5), we know that these include Hebrew lives and Egyptian lives.

Connections with Exodus

The ominous threat to the well-being of God's people in Joseph's day is a famine. The threat to the well-being of God's people in Moses' early days is a Pharaoh who is intent on either eliminating the Hebrews or brutalizing them. In both cases the survival of the chosen family is in jeopardy. During the first crisis the instrument of God's *salvation is Joseph; during the second, it is Moses.

Joseph and the Messianic line

In Genesis 12 God begins to forge a chain of redemption whose last link will be Jesus (Matt. 1:1–17). Genesis 12 onwards provides the first five links in this chain – Abraham, Isaac, Jacob, Judah, Perez. Conspicuously absent is Joseph; the covenant line goes through Judah, his brother. For this reason Joseph's name does not appear in Matthew 1:1–17. And yet Joseph receives as much attention in Genesis (most of 37 – 50) as does his father Jacob (25 – 36) and his great-grandfather Abraham (12 – 25:11). This may be Scripture's way of teaching us that God has a vital place in the work of his kingdom not only for his Judahs, but also for his Josephs, for the 'main cogs' and the 'support staff'.

But Joseph is not a marginal figure in the account of Jacob's blessing on his sons (49:22–26). Jacob speaks of Joseph as a growing, spreading vine (49:22), more than able to withstand opposition (49:23–24b), because of divine aid (49:24c–26). Interestingly, Jacob speaks of God only when speaking of Joseph (using no fewer than five images for God), and he uses the word 'blessing' (six times in 49:25–26) only for Joseph, making Jacob's blessing on Joseph richer than that on any of his other children (except possibly Judah). Note also that Jacob's blessing on Joseph resembles Moses' blessing on the Joseph tribes (of Ephraim and Manasseh) (see Deut. 33:13–17), a closer

parallel than any other between Genesis 49 and Deuteronomy 33.

Joseph and providence

In Genesis 45:6–8 and 50:19–20 Joseph affirms bluntly his belief in the providential plan of God for his life. On one hand the text states that the brothers 'sold' Joseph to a caravan heading to Egypt (37:28; 45:4–5), an action which they themselves recognized as a sin (42:22; 50:17) and a wrong (50:15, 17). On the other hand, Joseph can say 'God sent me' (45:7), and 'God planned it for good' (50:20). Joseph does not deny human agency in favour of divine, or vice-versa; he is neither determinist nor deist. Rather he regards the action of God within the destructive, sinful behaviour of the brothers as decisive. It is surely this liberating perspective that saves Joseph from capitulating to temptations such as anger, resentment or bitterness.

Joseph and the NT

In Acts 7:9–16 Stephen recounts Joseph's life. His primary point is that God's presence with Joseph was a saving presence in the midst of much painful abuse. And by extension God's presence with any of his *suffering people (Jesus, Stephen, ourselves) is a saving presence. Joseph, Jesus and Stephen chose the path of reconciliation rather than that of retribution.

Hebrews 11:22 comments briefly on Joseph's *faith. On his deathbed he made mention of the Exodus from Egypt, and requested that his remains be a part of that Exodus. Hence, Joseph's faith is in a future for the people of God beyond their present circumstances. Egypt is a temporary dwelling, not a home.

See also: JUDAH; NATIONS; SEED; BLESSING/ CURSE.

Bibliography

G. W. Coats, *From Canaan to Egypt: Structural and Theological Context for the Joseph Story* (Washington, D.C., 1975); T. E. Fretheim, 'The book of Genesis', in *NIB* 1, pp. 592–674; V. P. Hamilton, *Genesis 18 – 50*, NICOT (Grand Rapids, 1995); W. L. Humphreys, *Joseph and his Family: A Literary Study* (Columbia, 1988); R. E. Longacre, *Joseph: A Study of Divine Providence: A Text Theoretical and Textlinguistic Analysis of*

Genesis 37 and 39–48 (Winona Lake, 1989); D. B. Redford, *A study of the biblical story of Joseph* (Leiden, 1970); J. Vergote, *Joseph én Égypte* (Louvain, 1959); C. Westermann, *Joseph: Eleven Bible Studies on Genesis* (ET, Edinburgh and Minneapolis, 1996).

V. P. HAMILTON

JOSHUA, see Part 2

JOY

Vocabulary

There is a wealth of Hebrew words for joy, and this points to the exuberant character of Israel's personal and religious life (*cf.* Zeph. 3:14, 17, in which eight different words are used for joy or rejoicing). The basic and most common Hebrew root is *śmh* (noun *śimḥā*, verb *śāmēaḥ*), which describes not only the state of joyful well-being, but also its expression, rejoicing. The root word *gîl* (noun and verb) is used less often, and includes the notion of exultation (Is. 35:2); while the Hebrew *hêdad* refers to sounds of joy, such as cheering or shouting (Jer. 48:33; *cf.* Ezek. 7:7).

The Greek vocabulary in the NT is more limited: the usual nouns are *chara* (verbs *chairō*, or *synchairō*), and *agalliasis*, meaning intense joy. The latter is often used in the LXX, and corresponds to *śimḥā*. The verb *euphrainō* (noun *euphrosynē*) is used rarely in the NT, and mostly by Luke. It is associated with festive joy, and good cheer.

In the OT

Joy is characteristic of the life of *faith; it marks out both the community, and the individual believer. Joy is a quality, and not simply an emotion, of which God is both the object (Ps. 16:11; Phil. 4:4), and the giver (Rom. 15:13).

Personal

The OT recognized the personal joys involved in human existence. Birthdays should be joyfully celebrated (*cf.* by contrast Job 3:1–7); people, young and old, are to rejoice in their years (Eccles. 11:8–9); a wise son will make his parents happy (Prov. 23:24–25); and young married couples can express their *love

for each other with joy (Prov. 5:18–19). The writer of Proverbs adds that 'an apt answer is a joy to anyone' (15:23, NRSV). The *Psalms express spontaneous, personal joy in a way that is distinctive in the OT (*cf.* Ps. 16:8–9). We can rejoice in God individually, they assert, because of his forgiveness (Ps. 51:12), his favour (Ps. 4:7–8) and his fellowship (Ps. 63:4–5).

National

More obvious, in the OT, is an emphasis on national and cultic rejoicing. Israelites share with everyone else a sense of communal joy at times of feasting (Ezra 6:22), dedication (2 Chr. 7:10), coronation (1 Sam. 11:15) and military victory (Judg. 16:23). But Israel's distinctive rejoicing is expressed in the cultic and corporate *worship of Israel's God which is centred in the temple (*cf.* Ps. 42:4; 84:1–2). This theme also is especially dominant in the Psalter. The people of God rejoice in the Lord their God, not only because he is the King of all the earth (Ps. 98:4–6), but also because he lives among his chosen in Zion (Ps. 132:8–16). As a result, God makes available to his people, for their joy and praise and thanksgiving, wholeness (Hab. 3:18), victory (1 Chr. 29:10–13) and prosperity (Ps. 118: 24–25; *cf.* Zech. 8:3–8).

Joy and gladness are inspired not only by God's *activity* in the nation of Israel, but also by his very *being*. The faithful rejoice in Yahweh's justice (Pss. 1 – 4), his steadfast love (Ps. 90:14; Jer. 31:2–4), his faithfulness (Ps. 33:1–4), his goodness (Exod. 18:9), his power (Ps. 47:1–7; *cf.* Dan. 2:20-23), his word and commands (Pss. 119:74, 111–112) and his all-embracing healing (Is. 12:2–6; Ps. 27:1–6).

Messianic

When God blesses his people, they rejoice; and with their joy are closely associated both praise and thanksgiving. By contrast, joy *departs* from Israel when God's judgment, as announced by the prophets, prevails (Ezek. 7:2–12; Joel 1:15–16); the nations around Israel have the same experience (Jer. 48:33; *cf.* Is. 16:9–10).

But, as well as being expressed in individual and corporate attitudes of thankful rejoicing for God's salvific goodness in the past and present, Israel's joy anticipates the future. The prophetic literature of the OT is strongly marked by an eschatological hope, which looks beyond current suffering, notably in the exile, to the joy of new blessing and fulness of life in the messianic age (Is. 26:19; Jer. 31:12–13; Joel 2:21–24; Zech 9:9; 10:6–7). At this time the whole of creation joins with God's people in rejoicing. The heavens, the earth, the mountains and the islands, are called upon to participate in the jubilation of the new age, or are said actually to do so (Pss. 19:4–5; 89:5–18; Is. 35:1–10; 42:5–16; 49:11–13). Moreover, God himself rejoices, and takes joy in his people (Is. 65:19; Jer. 33:9).

The possibility of future, messianic joy, achieved where necessary through present *suffering, gives special depth to the Hebraic attitude of thankful rejoicing in the OT. It also anticipates the NT understanding of joy.

Later Judaism

Allusions to joy appear in the literature of Qumran, echoing those in the OT. For example, the believer may have joy in God himself (*War Scroll* 4:14), in his powerful hand (*War Scroll* 13:12–13) and in his gifts of redemption (*Thanksgiving Hymns* 11:23, 30). Joy also derives from knowledge of the truth; that is, from knowing God as righteous and merciful (*Thanksgiving Hymns* 11:30). Salvation is for the Qumran community a present joy (*War Scroll* 1:9); yet it is also experienced for all time. Thus, 'eternal joy' is a constant theme in the Dead Sea Scrolls (*e.g. Rule of the Community* 4:7); so too is joy through suffering (*Thanksgiving Hymns* 9:24–25).

In most Rabbinic Judaism joy still has religious importance (*cf. Testament of Levi* 18:5). Joy in God himself, and therefore in his Law, becomes prominent (*Genesis Rabbah* 98:9; *cf.* Pss. 19, 119). The Jewish festivals, especially Passover and Tabernacles, are occasions of joy (*Bez* 15b); the Sabbath is also to be celebrated joyously, and should include at least three meals (*šabbat* 117b), while sabbatical mourning is not encouraged (*šabbat* 12b). Finally, perfect joy and rejoicing will characterize the future world (*Midraš Pss.* 75:2).

In the NT

The NT writers are clear that Israel's messianic expectations are joyfully fulfilled in Jesus, the Christ. In him can be found a spiritual joy which is personal (both individual and corporate), attained through suffering, and not from this world.

Personal

In the NT, as in the OT, religious joy is personal. However, expressions of joy from the early Christian period have an additional dimension, introduced by the coming of Jesus Messiah, who brings in the eschatological age of salvation.

Joy is evident in the Gospels even before the advent of Jesus. The angel promises Zechariah that at the birth of his son (John the Baptist, the forerunner of Christ), there will be joy and gladness and rejoicing (Luke 1:14); and the child in Elizabeth's womb expresses that joyfulness actively (Luke 1:44). Mary rejoices in her Saviour because she has been allowed to participate in his salvific purposes (Luke 1:47).

Joy surrounds the actual birth of Jesus; and Mary's rejoicing is shared by the shepherds, on behalf of all the people (Luke 2:10; *cf.* 2:14), and by the wise men, who are said to be 'overwhelmed with joy' (Matt. 2:10). John the Baptist declares that the coming of Jesus causes his joy to be fulfilled (John 3:29).

The ministry of Jesus, according to the evangelists, is marked by joyfulness. There are references in the parables to corporate festivity, and to the enjoyment of eating and drinking (Luke 12:19; 16:19). Jesus himself shares in this enjoyment, eating even with outcasts (Mark 2:15-17); but he makes it clear that the joy which comes from God is more important. This idea is especially prominent in *Luke's Gospel. For example, the seventy return with joy from their mission because the demonic powers are submissive to them in the Lord's name; but Jesus tells them rather to rejoice because of their redeemed status (Luke 10:17, 20). In Luke 15:23 the father of the prodigal son initiates celebrations to mark his return; and the elder son apparently longs for such a joyous feast on his own behalf (15:29). The crowds rejoice at the wonderful deeds of Jesus (13:17). Zacchaeus is happy to welcome Jesus to his house, when this action is suggested to him (19:5-6). The people are full of praise as Jesus approaches Jerusalem for the last time (18:43), and as he enters the city in triumph they rejoice at all the deeds of power which they have witnessed. In all this Jesus, as the agent of salvation, both encourages his followers to be joyful, and rejoices himself in spirit, because the kingdom of God is being inaugurated (Matt. 5:12; Luke 10:21).

Ecclesial

The personal experience of joy in Christ (both individual and corporate) to which the evangelists testify is given a more significant theological expression elsewhere in the NT, where it is related to the life of the church, the community of faith. Here again the NT echoes the OT, although now the firstfruits of the new Israel, of which Jesus Christ is the head, are God's covenant people.

In Acts, joy marks the life of the early church, through which the rule of God is disclosed. The basis of the church's rejoicing is in the death and resurrection of Jesus (Acts 2:26, quoting Ps. 16:9–10, where Peter declares that David's joy is grounded in the Christ event; cf. 2:22–24). Joy accompanies the eucharistic meal (Acts 2:46), miracles performed in Christ's name (8:8), the gift of the Spirit to disciples (13:52), and the conversion of Gentiles (15:3) and of the Philippian jailer and his family (16:34). The reference to joy resulting from the divine gifts in creation (14:17) has an Hebraic ring.

In John's Gospel the use of the term 'fullness of (or perfect) joy' (chara peplēromenē) is distinctive (and see below). The eschatological hour of salvation has arrived (John 3:29), and Jesus is already experiencing perfect joy because he is doing the will and work of the Father in complete communion with him (4:34; 14:20). This fulfilled happiness will be given to his followers in the church, after the resurrection and through the Spirit-Paraclete (15:11; 16:24), provided that they abide in him (15:4–11).

Paul sees joy as a dynamic gift of the *Holy Spirit (Gal. 5:22, 25), stemming from God's love and ours; so that love and joy (and peace) are closely associated in the list of the Spirit's fruit (Gal. 5:22–23). Growth in the faith by members of the body of Christ, especially those Paul himself has brought to Christ, gives him reason to rejoice (Rom. 16:19; 2 Cor. 7:15–16; cf. 2 John 4); indeed, such believers are described as 'our joy' (1 Thess. 2:20). But joy is not static; Paul summons the church to a daily practice of rejoicing in the knowledge of Christ and his salvation (Phil. 3:1; 4:4; cf. 1 Pet. 1:6, 8).

Paul acknowledges (with other NT writers) that suffering can produce joy. This possibility is anticipated in the OT, but Christian rejoicing in adversity is distinctive in being effected through the suffering and vindication of Jesus himself, and indeed it reflects them (Col. 1:24; 2 Cor. 6:10; Heb. 12:2). There is joy in suffering because it leads to a heavenly reward (Matt. 5:12); it produces character (Rom. 5:3–4) and endurance (Jas. 1:2–3); and, above all, it is for the sake of Christ Jesus and his body (Acts 5:41; Phil. 2:17–18). The paradox of Christian faith is that sorrow may be transformed into gladness by the Spirit (2 Cor. 7:4).

Eschatological

Although joy through Christ is expressed in the church on earth, sometimes during adversity, ultimately the rejoicing of believers does not belong to this world. In the Johannine farewell discourse, Jesus assures his disciples that their sorrow at his departure will turn to joy (John 16:16, 20), as do the pangs of childbirth (16:21). Such enduring joy (16:22) is characteristic of the kingdom of God, which is similarly 'not from this world' (18:36). In Pauline terms, the kingdom of God is about 'righteousness and peace and joy in the Holy Spirit' (Rom. 14:17).

Christian joy also anticipates the end of the age. The church already experiences, through the Spirit, the joy of the messianic kingdom heralded by the prophets of Judaism. But that joy is still to be consummated. In the future there will be rejoicing because evil, and opposition to God, will have been finally overcome (Rev. 12:7–12); God's salvific purposes will have been accomplished through judgment (Rev. 19:1–8); and the church will be presented blameless in the presence of God's glory, with rejoicing (Jude 24–25).

Bibliography

E. Bayreuther and G. Finkenrath in NIDNTT 2, pp. 352–361; H. van Broekhoven in ISBE 2, pp. 1140–1142; E. G. Gulin, Die Freude im Neuen Testament, 2 vols. (Helsinki, 1932, 1936); W. G. Morrice, Joy in the New Testament (Exeter, 1984).

S. S. SMALLEY

JUBILEE, see SABBATH

JUDAH

The name

The name 'Judah' first appears in the OT text in Genesis 29:35. Leah, who had given birth to three sons and was still unloved by *Jacob, turned from seeking her husband's praise to praising the Lord, and named her fourth son 'Judah'. How the term $y^e h \hat{u} \underline{d} \hat{a}$ is related to the verb ascribed to her ($yad\hat{a}h$, 'I will praise') is unclear. Throughout the OT, derivatives from ydh express praise and thanksgiving. A prophetic nuance is present in Leah's naming of her son; Judah became the ancestor of Jesus Christ, to whom praise and thanksgiving is given.

Incidents in Judah's life

Various incidents in Judah's life are recorded in Genesis. He advised his brothers not to kill *Joseph since he was their 'own flesh and blood' (Gen. 37:27), and interceded on behalf of his brother Benjamin before Joseph, offering to become a slave himself (Gen. 44:18–34). After Joseph was sold into Egypt, Judah left his brothers and married a Canaanite woman named Shua. This in itself should not be considered wrong for there were evidently few women available for Jacob's sons to marry. Shua gave birth to Er, who died because of his wickedness; Onan, Er's brother, refused to marry Er's widow Tamar, and also died. A third son Shelah, was not given to Tamar (Gen. 38:1–11). When Shua died, Tamar presented herself as a prostitute and became pregnant by her father-in-law Judah. She gave birth to Zerah and Perez, who became an ancestor of David (Gen. 38:12–30).

Jacob's prophecy concerning Judah

Jacob prophesied on his deathbed that Judah would be praised ($y\hat{o}\underline{d}\hat{u}\underline{k}\hat{a}$) by his brothers. From him would come one whose right it was to rule (Gen. 49:8–12). Jacob had expected Joseph to be the one to succeed him as the clan head. Joseph had been the morally upright son (Gen. 39:1–9) and had a regal position (Gen. 49:26); his father bestowed the double birthright on him (Gen. 48). The Lord's election of Judah, who had moral lapses, surprised Jacob: 'Judah, you are the one!' (Gen. 49:8, author's translation). Jacob's prophecy of Judah as the dominant son became reality. The tribe of Judah numbered 74,600 men (Num. 1:26) and was given the leading role in the arrangement around the tabernacle and in the marching order of the twelve tribes in the desert (Num. 2:3; 10:14).

Caleb of the tribe of Judah, who was sent by Moses to spy out Canaan, demonstrated leadership when he brought a positive report and urged the people to take possession of the promised land (Num. 13:30; 14:6–9). By the Lord's direction the tribal descendants of Judah were given a leadership role again after Joshua died, in the removal of the Canaanites left in the land inherited by the tribes. The Lord gave the Judahites victory, except in the plains where the enemy had iron chariots (Judg. 1:3–4, 19). The tribe inherited a large section of the land in southern Canaan, between the Salt Sea on the east and the Mediterranean Sea on the west and surrounding the inheritance of Simeon (Josh. 15:1–12; 19:1).

The nation of Judah

Judah became a small nation when the northern tribes, led by Jeroboam I, revolted and established their own monarchy (1 Kgs. 12:16–17). Benjamin joined Judah (1 Kgs. 12:21–23), and *Jerusalem, the city where the Lord chose to put his name (1 Kgs. 11:36), remained the capital city. Thus the *temple, the symbol of God's dwelling among his people, was in Judah's territory. The nation of Judah was invaded and defeated by King Nebuchadnezzar of Babylon in 986 BC, when most of its citizens were either killed by war or famine or exiled to Babylon. The nation disappeared for all time; the dynasty of David was overthrown, and no human descendant sat on an earthly throne again.

But a remnant of Judah survived the exile (Neh. 1:2). Ezra refers to the family heads of Judah and Benjamin who went back (with others) to Jerusalem to build the temple (Ezra 1:5) and eventually to rebuild Jerusalem's walls (Neh. 1 – 4). Two princes of the house of David are mentioned, Zerubbabel (Hag. 1:1) and Sheshbazzar (Ezra 1:8) though neither regained royal prerogatives or a crown.

The term 'Jew', believed to be derived from $y^e h \hat{u} \underline{d} \hat{i} m$ (2 Kgs. 16:6), was used to refer to the people of Judah (Jer. 32:12; 34:9; 52:28). Thus Jesus and the first Christians were known as Jews.

The messianic role of Judah in the course of the history of revelation and redemption can be traced. God promised Adam and Eve in the Garden of Eden that the seed of the woman would crush the head of the serpent/Satan (Gen. 3:15). The concept of seed is a major theme in the Bible. God promised Abraham that seed would issue from him and bring blessings to many (Gen. 12:1–3). The seedline included Judah, from whom the royal seed was to come (Gen. 49:8–12). David, born and raised in Bethlehem, a town in the land of Judah, was elected by God and anointed by Samuel (1 Sam. 16:12–13) to be the royal representative of the seedline. God promised David, the king, that from his house would come the Son who was to reign (2 Sam. 7:12-16), and that his *kingdom was to be eternal. The prophets repeat and expand on the theme that King David, from the tribe of Judah, was to be the ancestor of the Christ (Mic. 5:2; Is. 9:6–7). The Gospel writers state that Jesus was a descendant of David, that he was of the tribe of Judah and was born in the land of Judea (Judah) (Matt. 1:2; 2:1; Luke 2:4, 11; 3:23, 31, 33).

See also: DAVID; SEED; JESUS CHRIST.

Bibliography

H. E. Ellison in *NBD*, pp. 617–621.

G. VAN GRONINGEN

JUDE, see Part 2

JUDGMENT

Judgment is a comparatively simple topic, but it bears upon every aspect of biblical theology: *God (Deut. 32:4; Ps. 94:2; Mal. 2:17), the individual (Is. 1:17; Mic. 6:8), the ordering of society (Amos 5:15), the way history operates (Is. 26:8–11; Jer. 1:16) and the moral realities of the last day (Ps. 96:13; Rev. 20:12). The OT emphasizes judgment within history, while the NT emphasizes *eschatological judgment, filling out the concept of the Day of the Lord (Amos 5:18) with the larger perspectives of the Day of Christ (2 Thess. 1:5–10; 2 Pet. 3:7–13).

Vocabulary

The OT has a rich vocabulary of judgment.

As well as *šāpaṭ* (see below) there are the verbs *dîn* and *rîb*, the former dealing with lawsuits from the point of view of the judge (Gen. 30:6; Ps. 50:4), the latter with lawsuits from the point of view of the litigants (Ps. 43:1). They express the specificity of the charges brought, as does *pāqaḏ*, which conveys the idea of enumeration and therefore of attention to detail, inspection, visitation (Exod. 20:5; Num. 16:29; Is. 24:21–22). *Yāqaḥ* is arbitration between parties for the settling of disputes (Gen. 31:37; Is. 1:18). In contrast, the NT on the whole confines itself to the *krinō* family of words (*anakrinō*, 1 Cor. 2:15; *diakrinō*, 1 Cor. 11:31). Homer used *krinō* to mean 'to sift, separate out'. Later it came to be used of value judgments: to judge, decide; to reach a *krima* or verdict (Matt. 7:2; John 9:39); and to exercise the function of a *kritēs*, or 'judge' (Matt. 5:25; Acts 10:42).

Judges, judgment and jurisprudence

'Judgment' as an earthly exercise, a necessary function in society, belongs to the Lord. His people are to 'do my judgments' (Lev. 18:4, author's translation) and their justices are to recognize that 'the judgment is God's' (Deut. 1:17). The individual member of the Lord's people must act in any given situation as the Lord himself would act if so placed, and the magistrate must decide causes as the Lord would do were he sitting. Earth is to be a reflection of heaven and, in its jurisprudence, is to provide a window into heaven and into God.

'Judges' (šōpᵉṭîm) and 'judging' (šāpaṭ)

For a proper understanding of the meaning of *šāpaṭ* – whether it means 'to rule', or 'to follow custom' and 'case law', or 'to discriminate' – the important question is why the 'judges' in the book of *Judges were so named (šōpᵉṭîm, Judg. 2:16–18). What was it about people raised up to be 'saviours' (2:16; 3:9, 31) that caused them to be called 'judges'? The record itself reveals the answer. Certainly the judges were famous for stirring deeds of '*salvation' (Judg. 2:16), but Deborah was also active as 'judge' before (Judg. 4:4–5) she summoned Barak to battle; Samson was 'judge' throughout his impulsive career (16:31), and Jephthah for six years after effecting deliverance (12:7). Thus they had an on-going function of arbitration, which involved hearing cases, deciding issues and apportioning penalties, as judges were instructed to do (*cf.* Deut. 1:16; 16:18–20; 17:8–11; 1 Sam. 7:15–17). The judges, however, also preserved good order in society: they gave the land '*rest' (Judg. 3:11, 30; 5:31; 8:28); the verb (*šāpaṭ*) indicates freedom from war (Jos. 11:23) or from oppression or threat (Is. 14:7), undisturbed conditions (Job 3:13), or the absence of unsettlement or restlessness (Ruth 3:18) or interference (Judg. 18:7). And thirdly, the judges had a religious function, in that while there was a judge the people were *faithful; they lapsed into unfaithfulness only after the judge's hegemony (3:12; 6:1; 8:33).

Judgment (*mišpaṭ*), therefore, is to be defined as 'setting things to rights'. In Isaiah 1:17 it is the due ordering of society; in Isaiah 5:7 *mišpaṭ* and its partner '*righteousness' (*ṣᵉdāqâ*) are the opposite of *mišpāḥ* (whatever precisely that means) and *ṣeʿāqâ*, a howl of pain (*cf.* Amos 5:7), that is to say, social disruption and disorder. In OT 'judgment' there is no particular emphasis on 'passing adverse sentence' or 'condemnation'. Psalms 96:11–13 and 98:8–9 are typical in calling all creation to rejoice before the coming Judge, which is strange if judgment means condemnation. But if (as is the case) judgment is 'setting everything to rights', it is no wonder that all creation exults in the prospect (Rom. 8:18–21).

This view of the work of the judge well reflects the ambience of the *šāpaṭ*/*mišpaṭ* word-group: *mišpaṭ* is correct, discerning decision meeting the requirements of the situation (Is. 28:26; 30:18); *šāpaṭ* is the work of the *king, ordering society, crushing oppressors (Ps. 72:1–4). Religiously, *mišpaṭ* is part of the vocabulary of revelation: on earth it is authoritative, royal decision (2 Sam. 18:5), and in heaven it is what the Lord has settled and revealed to his people for their compliance (Deut. 4:1; 5:1; 67:1; 12:1; Is. 42:1, 3–4).

Basic principle

OT *law is extensive and complex – the Decalogue (Exod. 20:2–17; Deut. 5:6–21), *covenant law (esp. Lev. 17 – 26) – but considered as a judicial system it rests on one basic principle, that of absolute equity. At one level equity overrode both national (Lev. 24:22; Num. 9:14) and social discrimination

(Exod. 23:3; Lev. 19:15; Deut. 1:17; 16:19; 27:19), but at a deeper level it demanded an absolute equivalence between crime and punishment.

The *lex talionis* which enshrines this principle of equity is stated three times (Exod. 21:23–24; Lev. 24:20; Deut. 19:21). It was given as a directive for the court, not (as in the misunderstanding Jesus counters in Matt. 5:38) as a permission for private revenge. There is no evidence that the OT writers considered the *lex* to specify how punishment should be *inflicted*; it was a dramatic statement of how punishment should be *assessed* so that it neither exceeded the offence (by the imposition of a savage reprisal designed as a deterrent) nor fell below the offence (by a false leniency which would bring law itself into disrepute). The *lex talionis* was not primitive savagery but a non-negotiable principle, safeguarding jurisprudence and forging the path to a purged society (*cf.* Deut. 19:20).

Judgment and revelation

The enactments of Leviticus 19 are as varied as life itself. There is, however, a single binding thread: fourteen times a command is reinforced with the words 'I am the LORD your God'/'I am the LORD'. This sounds like an authority claim, and it would be false to the OT to deny divine 'authoritarianism' in ethics and jurisprudence (Deut. 4:1; 17:8–13). The Lord's status gave him the right to command the world (Ps. 50:1–4), and the work of *redemption gave him a special claim on Israel's compliance (Exod. 20:2–3). Yet this is not the point of Leviticus 19:3, 10, 12, *etc.* 'The LORD' is 'Yahweh', which means (Exod. 3:14) 'I am who/what I am'. To enforce a law by affirming 'I am Yahweh' is the same as to say 'I give you this command because I am what I am', that is, 'because it reflects and expresses my nature'.

The law, therefore, whether in the Decalogue, in the social, national and *holiness codes or in the muddle of Leviticus 19, is a *revelation of the Lawgiver. What exists as a principle within the divine nature is expressed as a precept in order that 'you shall be holy as I the LORD your God am holy' (Lev. 19:2). The law is intended to fulfil *humankind's essential nature as the image of God.

'God is the Judge' (Ps. 75:7)

When Isaiah says that 'the LORD is a God of

judgment' (Is. 30:18) his primary reference is to the discerning *wisdom of God who knows exactly when and how to act, but his words, understood more broadly, summarize the discussion so far. OT law is a reflection of the divine nature. God can be seen in all its principles, provisions and enactments. Since 'judgment' is 'setting everything to rights' he is seen as a God of order and perfection; this is part of what the Bible calls 'the beauty of (his) holiness' (cf. 1 Chr. 16:29; 2 Chr. 20:21; Pss. 29:2; 96:9; 110:3; etc.). In all its aspects judgment is an out-shining of the divine holiness (Ps. 50:1–6). Thus Isaiah 5:16 links the key words together. 'The LORD of hosts is exalted in judgment and God the Holy One displays his holiness in righteousness.' When 'judgment' (mišpāṭ) and 'righteousness' (ṣeḏāqâ) are paired like this (cf. Gen. 18:19; 2 Sam. 8:15; Pss. 33:5; 89:14; 99:4; Is. 1:21, 27; 5:7; etc.) 'righteousness' refers to principles and 'judgment' to practice. So, for example, in Isaiah 32:1 'righteousness' belongs to the king and 'judgment' to the princes; the throne embodies righteous principle and the executive arm practises just government. So it is also with the heavenly throne and its occupant (Is. 5:16): he is, in himself, holiness; in his rule he embodies righteous principles and displays his holiness in acts of 'judgment' whereby he puts everything to rights.

Since, however, judgment is an application of holiness it involves punishment as well as *reward, condemnation as well as approbation.

Judgment in history

The motif of the law court is a familiar one (e.g. Pss. 50:6; 75:7; Is. 3:13–15; 41:1–7; 43:8–13). It is based on the belief that 'the judgments of God are abroad in the earth' (Is. 26:9) and that the law-court is a reflection of history. The same ideas animate the imprecatory psalms: in dire straits the psalmists lifted up holy voices to God the Judge, neither entertaining animosity nor intending retaliatory action, but resting their case, so far as human action was concerned, on prayer, and, so far as divine rule was concerned, on their confidence that he who promulgated the lex talionis would himself best know how to enforce it (cf. Rom. 12:19), and that he who required earthly judges to bring an unjust accusation back onto the head of the accuser

(Deut. 19:16–19) would best know how to apportion a just requital.

Psalm 1 rests on the assumption that this divine judgment is the governing principle of the *world (cf. Ps. 103:6). The psalm, of course, is a creed, not a description, an affirmation of how biblical faith sees a world which belongs to the holy God and in which he rules as Judge. In such a world it must be well with the righteous (v. 3), and the way of the wicked must perish (v. 6). The same affirmation is made in those passages where Job voices the opinions of his friends (24:18–24; 26:5–14; 27:7–28). It is unnecessary to attribute these sentiments to the friends, for Job would not have disagreed with the basic 'faith' they espoused. They were right in their theology, but wrong in their theodicy. Job, like his friends, held that the only way to live in the world of the holy God is to believe with Abraham that 'the Judge of all the earth does right' (Gen. 18:25).

Ezekiel saw such divine judgment as impinging upon the life of the individual (18:1–32; cf. his teaching about the 'stumbling-block', 3:20; 7:19; 14:3; cf. Jer. 6:21); Isaiah (8:14) would concur though he is rightly more renowned for his understanding of judgment in history. The locus classicus is Isaiah 10:5–15 with its three fundamental 'positions': 1. even earth's superpowers are tools – stick, saw and axe (vv. 5, 15) – in the hand of God; 2. the Lord of history sovereignly directs its 'forces' to accomplish his moral purposes (v. 6); and 3. the powers he uses are moral agents in their own right, and since they are motivated not by obedience to the Lord of the earth but by their own imperialism they in turn must be judged.

Judgment and salvation

When Psalm 71:15 sets righteousness and salvation in parallel it speaks for the whole Bible. Thus Jerusalem must be redeemed with judgment and righteousness (Is. 1:27), and Jerusalem's bloodguilt purged with a Spirit of judgment (expressing divine justice) and a Spirit of burning (expressing divine holiness) (Is. 4:4); Paul's 'just and the justifier' (Rom. 3:26) derives from Isaiah's 'just God and Saviour' (45:21; cf. 1 Jn. 1:9); when God comes to save he 'arises in judgment' (Ps. 76:9); the Lord's garments of salvation are garments of vengeance (just requital) and include a breastplate of righteousness (Is.

59:16; *cf.* salvation and righteousness in 61:10; 63:1; *cf.* 63:4–5). In Hebrews 12:23 'the spirits of just men made perfect' live without fear in the presence of 'the Judge of all' because justice is satisfied and citizenship provided by the 'blood of sprinkling'.

Judgment and eschatology

In the OT period every new king was awaited as possibly the messianic king, every new prophet as possibly the prophet like Moses, and every new historical trial as possibly the 'day of the Lord' (*cf.* Is. 13:6, 9; Jer. 46:10; Ezek. 30:2–3; Joel 1:15; 2:1, 11, 31; 3:14; Amos 5:18; Obad. 15; Zeph. 1:14–16; Zech. 14:1). In the NT this becomes the last day, the Day of Christ, the great day of God the Almighty (*cf.* John 6:39; Rom. 2:5; 1 Cor. 1:8; 5:5; Eph. 4:30; 2 Thess. 1:10; 1 Pet. 2:12; 2 Pet. 3:12; Rev. 6:17; 16:14). Both Testaments refer to the finality, just requital and joyful salvation of that day and to the establishing of a new heaven and a new earth.

The Lord *Jesus spoke plainly about the dreadful aspects of the last day (Matt. 10:28; *cf.* 5:29; 23:33; Luke 12:5), and placed himself at the centre of the eschatological events. His coming signals the ingathering (Mark 13:26–27) and 'out-gathering' (Matt. 13:41–42). All will stand before him, to receive either eternal life (Matt. 25:34, 46) or eternal fire (Matt. 25:41, 46). The supposed problem of the judgment of those who have never heard the gospel is unreal, because these people will not be judged by the gospel but (as in Amos 1:3 – 2:3) by their works, their failure to be human. For this reason Jesus says that all judgment is committed to him 'because he is the Son of man' (John 5:27), the truly human one; judgment is consequent upon falling below his standard. Believers will appear before the judgment seat of Christ (Matt. 25:14–30; Luke 19:12–27; 1 Cor. 3:12–15; 2 Cor. 5:10; *cf.* Rom. 14:10; 1 Pet. 1:7; Rev. 20:12). The same Paul who says that at this judgment seat salvation is not in doubt (1 Cor. 3:15) himself anticipated it with terror (2 Cor. 5:10–11). Here is a true Christian ambivalence. On the one hand, the Lamb's book of life, the guarantee of elect status (Rev. 20:12, 15; *cf.* 3:5; 13:8; 17:8; Exod. 32:32; Is. 4:3; Dan. 12:1; Luke 10:20; Phil. 4:3), provides assurance of eternal security; on the other hand, the Fatherhood of God (1 Pet. 1:17) and the costliness of re-demption (1 Pet. 1:18–19) induces dread lest he not be delighted (Eph. 5:10; Col. 1:10) in respect of the gifts he gave (Matt. 25:14–30), stewardship of the gospel (Luke 19:11–27) or the gold of good works (1 Cor. 3:12–14).

Bibliography

K. E. Brower and M. W. Elliott, *The Reader Must Understand* (Leicester and Downers Grove, 1997); J. L. Crenshaw (ed.), *Theodicy in the Old Testament* (London, 1983); R. B. Girdlestone, *Synonyms of the Old Testament* (Grand Rapids, 1963); V. Herntrich in *TDNT* 3, pp. 921–924; W. Kaiser, *Towards Old Testament Ethics* (Grand Rapids and Carlisle, 1991); F. D. Kidner, *Hard Sayings*, (Leicester, 1972); L. Morris, *The Biblical Doctrine of Judgment* (Leicester, 1960); J. A. Motyer, *Law and Liberty in Biblical Ethics* (London, 1976); A. W. Phillips, *Ancient Israel's Criminal Law* (Oxford, 1970); W. Schneider, H. Beck and T. McComiskey in *NIDNTT* 2, pp. 361–367; K. W. Whitelam, *The Just King* (Sheffield, 1979); C. J. H. Wright, *Living as the People of God* (Leicester, 1983).

J. A. MOTYER

JUDGES, see Part 2
JUSTICE, see RIGHTEOUSNESS, JUSTICE AND JUSTIFICATION
JUSTIFICATION, see RIGHTEOUSNESS, JUSTICE AND JUSTIFICATION
KINDNESS, see LOVE
KING, KINGSHIP, see KINGDOM OF GOD

KINGDOM OF GOD

Jesus and the kingdom

The kingdom of God is a term which occurs mainly in the Gospels of Mark and Luke; it is synonymous with Matthew's 'the kingdom of heaven'. There are about one hundred references to the kingdom of God/heaven in the *Synoptics. There are two references in John (3:3, 5), where Jesus also speaks of 'my kingdom' (John 18:36). The kingdom of God is mentioned six times in Acts and eight times in Paul's letters. Three passages indicate that the kingdom of Christ is the same as the kingdom of God (Eph. 5:5; Rev. 11:15; 12:10).

The kingdom of God in the Gospels

Our starting point must be the concept of the kingdom in the Gospels. Jesus began his ministry with the announcement, 'The time is fulfilled, and the kingdom of God is at hand' (Mark 1:14–15, RSV). The use of 'fulfilled' (Gk. *peplērōtai*) suggests that this kingdom answers to well-known expectations based on past promises. The Gospels expound what it means for this kingdom to be 'at hand'. It would thus be a mistake simply to isolate the kingdom sayings of Jesus without reference to the broad strategy of all four Gospels which, notwithstanding the distinctives of each, can be simply stated: Jesus is declared to be the bringer of the kingdom through his life (which includes his miracles and his teachings), his death and his resurrection.

Matthew begins by identifying Jesus as the son of David (Matt. 1:1), thus immediately placing kingship on his agenda. In his birth narrative he stresses the Davidic link in Jesus' family tree (1:20), and the perception that Jesus is born to be king (2:1–2) as a fulfilment of prophecy (2:6). Jesus' message is the 'good news of the kingdom' (4:23). He speaks frequently of those who will partake in the kingdom (5:3, 10, 19; 6:33; 7:21). To enter it requires child-like trust (18:3–4; 19:14), while the self-righteous and self-sufficient will find great difficulty in entering (7:21; 19:23–24; 21:43; 23:13). His miracles are *signs that the kingdom has come near (9:35; 12:28). Matthew records a series of parables of the kingdom (*e.g.* 13:24, 31, 33, 44–47; 18:23; 20:1; 22:2; 25:1) which use the wisdom form of comparison, usually likening the kingdom to some event in daily life in which wise perceptions lead to spiritual enrichment or some other desirable outcome. Yet the parables also reinforce the hidden, spiritual and distinctive characteristics of the kingdom which make it accessible only to those who are initiated into its truth (13:11). The natural heirs of the kingdom, the Jews, and especially the religiously self-righteous, are often shown to be on the outside (5:20; 8:12; 21:31, 43; 23:13).

Mark moves from the announcement of his theme (Jesus' proclamation of the kingdom) to an outline of the coming of the kingdom in the ministry of Jesus. Like Matthew, Mark sees the kingdom in the miracles. Jesus exercises his dominion in nature, over people, over sickness and over the powers of darkness. The healing miracles are specifically linked with the forgiveness of sins (2:1–12). Mark also shares the perspective of the secret of the kingdom being hidden from the outsider through parables (4:11, 33–34). The kingdom grows in secret and unexpected ways (4:26–32); yet Jesus also demonstrates his rule in the miracles, which show him to be the saviour-king (4:35–41).

Luke's distinctives are partly in his unique introduction and structure. Whereas Matthew begins on a kingly note, Luke looks at the priestly pedigree of Jesus as he concentrates on the ministry of the temple as the context of Jesus' birth. The priestly and royal roles are related: in the annunciation to Mary, Jesus is designated son of *God, son of David, and ruler over the house of Jacob (Luke 1:30–33). Circumstances decree that Jesus is born in the city of David, his royal ancestor. Both Matthew and Luke record the baptism of Jesus and the accompanying word from heaven that almost certainly picks up the teaching of Psalm 2:7 that the son of God is the ruler of the kings of the earth (Luke 3:22). In Acts, which builds on Luke's Gospel, the kingdom is presented as the central message of the risen Christ and then of the apostles (Acts 1:3; 8:12; 14:22; 19:8; 20:25; 28:23, 31).

John's distinctive teaching links perception of and entrance into the kingdom to the miracle of birth from above (John 3:3, 5). Jesus is also quoted as pointing to the kingdom which comes without the usual displays of worldly power (18:36).

Definition of the kingdom

As we assemble the various data on the kingdom of God, certain difficulties arise in defining its nature.

1. *The manner of its coming.* The Gospels highlight two main points of tension between Jesus and his contemporaries. The first is the widening gap between Jesus and the religious teachers of his day, and especially the Pharisees. The second is the difficulty he has in persuading his own followers to forsake certain stereotypes and misconceptions of the kingdom of God. The rebuke given by the risen Christ to the two disciples on the road to Emmaus (Luke 24:25–27) suggests that the information they needed was available in the OT but that even his devoted followers had to

a degree misunderstood the kingdom: the Messiah had to become a suffering servant before being glorified as king. As Luke continues the narrative in Acts 1 it appears that the disciples are ready to acknowledge their mistake since they are now confronted by the fact of the resurrection. But their perceptions of the kingdom do not seem to have changed much: they ask, 'Lord, is this the time when you will restore the kingdom to Israel?' (Acts 1:6, NRSV). The answer points them to the manner of the kingdom's coming; it is through the Spirit-empowered witness to Christ in all the world (Acts 1:7–8).

2. *Reign or realm?* The variety of Jesus' references to the kingdom of God recorded in the Gospels contributed to the tension between Jesus and his hearers. Certain expectations about the kingdom of God had developed among religious Jews as a result of their traditions and their historical experiences. Jesus' teaching focuses on dimensions of the kingdom that were not altogether anticipated and which thus clashed with popular views. If some Jews had come to expect a political solution to their affairs as the essence of the kingdom of God, the words of Jesus, which point to the presence of the kingdom without a political solution having been effected, would have caused tension. The disciples' question in Acts 1:6 may well reflect an expectation of imminent political *salvation, which is then corrected. The dying thief who asks Jesus to remember him, 'when you come into your kingdom' (Luke 23:42), seems also to express the expectation that, despite present evidence to the contrary, Jesus will one day be king. Jesus' answer focuses on the present, 'Today ...', indicating that the crucifixion is the means by which he enters the kingdom.

Because the teaching of Jesus about the kingdom virtually ignores the expectations of a renewed Jewish political realm in which God's anointed is king, some commentators have proposed that Jesus taught a purely dynamic, spiritual kingdom. This is seen in ethical terms: the will of God is to be done 'on earth as it is in heaven'. Almost all the kingdom sayings in the Gospels can be interpreted in this way. Even the many statements qualifying entry into the kingdom do not require us to adopt a spatial interpretation. The kingdom has not only come near; it is currently among Christ's people (Luke 17:21), who have already been transferred into the kingdom (Col. 1:13).

There are, however, some references which are not so easily internalized and spiritualized. Many will come from east and west to eat with the patriarchs in the kingdom (Matt. 8:11), while others will be thrown out into darkness (Matt. 8:12). There will be a time when evildoers will be collected and excluded from the kingdom (Matt. 13:41). The Son of Man will be seen coming in his kingdom (Matt. 16:28). Jesus speaks of a day when he will eat and drink with his people in the kingdom (Matt. 26:29; Luke 22:16, 18, 30). This idea of a realm is reinforced by the emphases of the book of Revelation. God's people are made a kingdom of priests who will reign on earth (Rev. 5:10). The kingdom of the world becomes the kingdom of God (11:15). The final vision is of the new heaven and earth with a new *Jerusalem let down from heaven to earth (21:1–4). The kingdom of God is finally seen to be located in the new earth, inhabited only by people whose names are written in the Lamb's book of life (21:27).

3. *Present or future?* Closely connected with the question of the nature of the kingdom is that of the timing of its coming. It has long been recognized that the kingdom sayings imply both a present and a future perspective. A number of variations on the two major themes of present and future kingdom have been suggested. Some have tried to deal with this apparent contradiction by proposing that Jesus taught that the kingdom is fully present. This 'realized eschatology' was suggested by C. H. Dodd, who took Mark 1:15 to mean that the kingdom of God has come. It is not unlike the 'liberal' view of von Harnack, who accepted the idea of the ethical development of religion, especially in the Hebrew prophets, which led finally to the ethical religion of Jesus.

Some theologians, for example A. A. Hoekema (*The Bible and the Future*, pp. 1–75), have suggested that 'inaugurated eschatology' is a better term in that it allows for both a present and a future dimension to eschatological fulfilment. This position is to be favoured as most consistent with the NT evidence, and will be considered below in more detail.

In contrast to realized eschatology is the view (sometimes termed 'consistent eschatology') that Jesus believed the kingdom to be wholly future. Albert Schweitzer, following Johannes Weiss, stressed the influence of apocalyptic on the futurist eschatological views of Jesus. Jesus' ethical teachings constitute an interim ethic until the imminent kingdom arrives. He dies a disappointed man, because the expected kingdom does not come.

OT antecedents

The evidence of the NT overwhelmingly supports the view that Jesus and the apostles understood the kingdom of God as the fulfilment of the hopes and promises recorded in the sacred Scriptures of the OT. The fact that the term 'the kingdom of God' does not occur in the OT is not significant. The idea of the rule of God over *creation, over all creatures, over the kingdoms of the *world and, in a unique and special way, over his chosen and redeemed *people, is the very heart of the message of the Hebrew scriptures.

God the creator Lord

The Bible begins with references to God, who freely creates by his word all that now exists. He creates the universe out of nothing, and this creation is 'very good' (Gen. 1:31). God is not driven by any necessity to create, and all that he does is based solely on his sovereign will. Because God is the creator of all, he is the sole ruler to whom allegiance is owed by all his creatures (Gen. 14:19, 22; Exod. 20:11; Deut. 32:6; 2 Kgs. 19:15; Job 38:1 – 42:6; Is. 37:16; 40:12–28; 42:5; 43:15; 45:5–18). A number of Psalms celebrate the kingship of Yahweh on the basis of his being the creator (Pss. 93:1; 96:4–10; 104:1–35; 136:1–9).

Rule and dominion

The creation narratives in Genesis 1 – 2 establish a number of important concepts which relate to God's kingship. At the heart of these accounts is the primacy of the *human race among all creatures. Created in the *image of God and given dominion over the rest of creation, the human pair have a unique role in the purpose of God (Gen. 1:26–28). The dominion of the human race is subject to the sovereign will of the creator who sets bounds on human freedom (Gen. 2:17). The privileged position of humanity is later celebrated in Psalm 8. The relationships expressed in these creation narratives are neither abstract nor purely ethical. Human beings are created as physical beings and are placed in a physical environment. The garden of Eden is the focal point of the creation, for it is in this place that the human pair relate both to God and to the rest of creation. These conditions are a prototype of the kingdom of God, and certainly involve both reign and realm.

Rebellion

The biblical teaching on the *sinfulness of humanity is a reminder of the rightful rule of God over the whole creation, which is rejected by the human race in the garden of Eden and elsewhere. Sin is essentially rebellion against the claims of absolute lordship and rule which the Creator makes on his creatures. The early chapters of Genesis relate events which indicate that the whole human race is in rebellion against God and comes under the *judgment of death. Judgment also involves the confusion of all the relationships in creation. The relationship of husband and wife is confused, and the dominion of humankind over the rest of creation is challenged (Gen. 3:16–19). Paul reflects on this dislocation of relationships in Romans 1:19–32 and 8:20–23.

Sovereignty and redemption

Scripture consistently makes a distinction between the sovereignty of God over the whole creation and over all history, and the coming of his kingdom in the context of a rebellious creation. The Bible teaches that God is not only rightfully Lord over all but also that, despite human rebellion, he has not lost control and works all things according to his sovereign will. This sovereignty is not merely one of a general *providence in the world, an overall control of history, but has two principal outworkings: judgment and *redemption. These are complementary truths. On the one hand, the kingdom of God will exclude all *evil and rebellion. On the other hand, it will include all that is redeemed according to the gracious will of God. Eventually, when all evil is put down, the renewing process of redemption will result in the fullness of the kingdom of God. The OT story points towards this consummation; the gospel effects it.

The pattern of the kingdom in Israel

This kingdom is revealed in the OT in terms of a number of factors which make up the redemptive process. Following the loss of the Edenic kingdom, redemption is linked to the election out of the mass of humanity, of a people, the descendants of Abraham, to be the chosen people of God. They are promised a land to dwell in and that they will themselves be the means of *blessing flowing out to all nations of the world. The fulfilment of these *covenant promises leads to Abraham's descendants (through Isaac and Jacob) becoming captives in Egypt. Under Moses the *Israelites are led to freedom through a miracle which becomes a paradigm of redemption. At Sinai this people is constituted as a theocratic nation of God's people. Though rebellion leads to a disastrous delay, the nation is eventually given possession of the promised *land of Canaan. Here the structures of government develop towards a kingship under the dynasty of David ruling from Jerusalem. Solomon builds the *temple in Jerusalem which becomes the focal point of the promised land as the place where reconciliation and fellowship with God are established. The rule of the Davidic kings is representative of the rule of God over his kingdom.

The kingdom in prophecy

Again human sin becomes a problem, especially among the kings of Israel. Solomon builds the temple but soon falls into apostasy. The kingdom divides, and both realms begin the decline that will lead to their respective destructions. During this decline a new form of prophecy emerges as the so-called 'writing prophets' point to the coming destruction and renewal which the faithful God will effect. The overall pattern of renewal is seen as a recapitulation of the past history of redemption: a new Exodus; a new covenant; a new entry into the land; a new Jerusalem with its new temple; and a new Davidic king to rule in a perfect, glorious, and eternal kingdom. Some of the prophets designate a 'day of the Lord' as the time when judgment and salvation will bring the fullness of the kingdom of God.

Apocalyptic

A feature of the book of Daniel is its use of apocalyptic imagery to describe the coming kingdom of God. Its theme is the eventual demise of all the godless kingdoms of the world as the kingdom of God is established. In Daniel 7 this human challenge to God is represented by the imagery of four beasts, and the kingdom of God is brought in by the mediation of a heavenly Son of Man, a human figure who restores dominion to the people of God. One significant difference from prophecy is that the focus is not so much on the renewal of the land and the institutions of Israel; rather, apocalyptic emphasizes the coming universal rule of God.

The coming of the kingdom in the NT

Against the background of the OT expectations of the coming rule of God, the NT declares that Jesus of Nazareth is the bringer of the kingdom. While the proclamation of Jesus concerning the kingdom is not novel and is based firmly on OT antecedents, there are nevertheless some surprises. The prophets consistently present the 'day of the Lord' in terms of one coming. The gospel presents the Lord's coming in at least three distinct but related ways.

The kingdom has come in Jesus

The meek servanthood of Jesus which leads eventually to his suffering and death, despite being liberally punctuated with demonstrations of power, prevented many from perceiving the nature of the kingdom's coming. While Jewish expectations focused on political solutions to the problem of foreign domination, Jesus was the kingdom in person. By claiming to be the temple of God (John 2:19–21) he expressed the truth of his being both God and human perfectly related in one person. He was at once both creator and creature, king and obedient subject, Word of God and listening servant. Thus Jesus of Nazareth not only brings the kingdom; he is the kingdom in himself.

The kingdom is coming to the people of God

Before his death, Jesus tells his followers that he will shortly leave them but that he will come to them as another counsellor, the *Holy Spirit (John 14:18–26). Pentecost marks the transition from the time when Jesus was present in the flesh to the period of his presence in the world by his Spirit. The Spirit controls the preaching of the *gospel of the kingdom by the people of God and gathers the subjects of the kingdom to Jesus by faith. The reign/realm contrast is most obvious in this period because the subjects of the kingdom are not confined to any particular place. Even though they gather in fellowship as a *church, the true, visible locus of the kingdom is at best ambiguous. But while the present, earthly expressions of the kingdom are imperfect, the gathering is described as having been raised with Christ to sit with him in heavenly places (Eph. 2:5–6), and as having come to Mt Zion (Heb. 12:22–24). Thus the resurrection and ascension of Jesus, and the sending of the Holy Spirit, inaugurates an overlap of the ages. While believers belong through faith to the kingdom of God and the new age, they go on living in the old age, and will do so until Christ returns.

The covenant promise to Abraham (Gen. 12:3) concerning the blessing of the *nations was confirmed by prophetic oracles such as Isaiah 2:1–4 and Zechariah 8:20–23. The coming of God's kingdom is accompanied by the great ingathering of the nations to Jerusalem and to the temple. The apostolic mission of the present age fulfils this prophecy as the new temple, Jesus, gathers the new living stones into himself through the Spirit-empowered preaching of the gospel.

The kingdom will be consummated at Christ's return

The third way in which the kingdom comes in the NT is the future or eschatological consummation. Thus the one coming of the Lord in the OT is shown to involve the coming of the end (the kingdom of God), in three ways: representatively for God's people in Jesus of Nazareth; in them through the gospel and the Spirit; and finally with them at the consummation of the kingdom with the return of Jesus in glory to judge the living and the dead. In this way we see the 'either-or' polarity between reign and realm, present and future, resolved in terms of 'both-and'.

The kingdom as a central theme

The kingdom comes through the ministry of Jesus and the preaching of the gospel in all the world. It is both the reign and the realm of God for, although in the present age the locus of the kingdom in the world is diffuse, it is defined by the presence of Jesus

at the right hand of the Father. It is both present and future until its consummation at Jesus' return. It is also at least one possible theme by which biblical theology can be integrated. It is the focus of both creation and redemption: God's plan of redemption is to bring in a new creation. The entire biblical story, despite its great diversity of forms and foci, is consistent in its emphasis on the reign of God over his people in the environment he creates for them. The kingdom depicted in Eden is lost to humankind at the beginning of the biblical account. The history of redemption begins immediately the kingdom is lost, and tells of the way the kingdom of God will finally be established as a new people of God in fellowship with him in a new Eden, a new Jerusalem, a new heaven and a new earth.

See also: DAVID; ESCHATOLOGY; JESUS CHRIST; SOLOMON.

Bibliography

G. R. Beasley-Murray, *Jesus and the Kingdom of God* (Grand Rapids and Carlisle, 1986, 1988); C. H. Dodd, *The Parables of the Kingdom* (London, 1935); J. Fuellenbach, *The Kingdom of God* (New York, 1995); G. Goldsworthy, *Gospel and Kingdom* (Exeter, 1981); A. von Harnack, *What is Christianity?* (ET, New York, 1901); A. A. Hoekema, *The Bible and the Future* (Grand Rapids and Exeter, 1978 and 1979); G. E. Ladd, *Jesus and the Kingdom* (London, 1966); A. Schweitzer, *The Mystery of the Kingdom of God* (ET, London, 1913).

G. GOLDSWORTHY

KINGS, BOOKS OF, see Part 2
KNOWLEDGE, see WISDOM

LAMB

The word 'lamb' is used in the Bible in both a literal and a symbolic sense. In the OT the main Hebrew term is *kebeś*, which occurs approximately eighty-seven times in Exodus, Leviticus and Numbers, and a number of times in Ezekiel (*e.g.* Ezek. 46:4,11). It is often used, with the qualification 'of the first year', in connection with sacrifice, in which the lamb was the main victim. Lambs were offered by the Israelites in *worship each morning and evening in the burnt offering (Exod. 29:38–42; Num. 28:3–8; doubled on the Sabbath, vv. 9–10), on the first day of each month (Num. 28:11), on all seven days of Passover (Num. 28:16–24), at the Feast of Weeks (Num. 28:26–27), on the Day of Atonement (Num. 29:7–8) and at the Feast of Tabernacles (Num. 29:13–38). The main purpose of these burnt offerings and sacrifices (*cf.* also Lev. 9:3 and Num. 15:5) was to make *atonement for and cleanse either an individual or the people as a whole.

The lamb was often seen by Israelites as a symbol of innocence and *gentleness, as opposed to cunning and viciousness. While normally the wolf and the lamb have little in common, in the Messianic age they will lie together (*cf.* Is. 11:6; 65:25). The defencelessness of lambs is mentioned in Jeremiah 51:40, and Jeremiah refers to himself as a gentle lamb (Jer. 11:19).

The ascription of meekness, gentleness and innocence to the lamb is probably derived from the sacrificial system. All three characteristics are predicated of it in Isaiah 53 (a passage which illuminates the NT meaning of the term). In verse 7, the patiently suffering Servant of the Lord is compared to a lamb which is led to slaughter. Here, for the first time in the OT, a person is said to fulfil the task of a sacrificial lamb, and this lamb is not identified with the Passover lamb. Did the writer consider the *sufferer to be the Messiah? The lamb is not just an innocent sufferer; it suffers on behalf of others (*cf.* vv. 4–6). These verses recall the account of the sacrifice of Isaac (Gen. 22) and that of the sparing of the firstborn of Israel as a result of the blood smeared on the doorposts and lintels (Exod. 12:7, 13, 23). NT writers take up the theme of this verse in considering the message of *Jesus Christ (*cf.* Acts 8:35).

Three words are used in the NT for 'lamb'. *Amnos* is used in four places with reference to Jesus: John 1:29, 36; Acts 8:32 and 1 Peter 1:19. *Arnion* is used in John 21:15 and Revelation 13:11, and in its 27 other occurrences (all in Rev. 5 – 22), to refer to Christ. *Arēn* is found only in Luke 10:3.

*John the Baptist declares that Jesus is the Lamb of God who takes away the sin of the world (John 1:29, 36). What would this statement have meant to the Baptist? And can it have meant more than this to the writer of the

Gospel, as a result of later reflection (*cf.* John 2:22; 11:49–52)?

Among the various interpretations are the following (see especially the commentaries on John by D. A. Carson and L. Morris):

1. The word used for 'lamb' here (*amnos*) is used approximately 75 times in the LXX, often referring to the lamb which was sacrificed daily as a gift offering 'to make atonement' (Lev. 1:4). So the daily offering in the *temple was behind John's words (although it is not clear that the offering was ever called 'God's lamb').

2. Another suggestion is that the reference is to the lamb of the Passover offering. This is supported by the apparent identification of Christ's sacrifice with the Passover in John 19:33, 36 and at the Last Supper. (See also John 18:28; 19:14, 31; it was at the Passover when Jesus was put to death.) Paul identifies Jesus with the Passover offering in 1 Corinthians 5:7. Some scholars say that the Passover was not an atonement sacrifice, but some Jews may have viewed it as such, and in any case the Exodus which it commemorated was often understood in terms of deliverance from the power of *sin in early Christian thought, and a *redemptive action (see also 1 Pet. 1:19). Some object that the animal to be killed at the Passover was not necessarily a lamb; it could be a goat.

3. A further possibility is to see in this verse a Christian application of Isaiah 53 to Jesus. The parallel with verse 7 ('like a lamb that is led to the slaughter', LXX *amnos*, as in John) and verse 11 ('he shall bear their iniquities'), are particularly striking (*cf.* verses 4 and 12). John's 'takes away' corresponds with the meaning of the Hebrew term translated 'bear' in NRSV. Also Jesus is tacitly identified with the Servant in John 12:38.

It is difficult to be certain which of these interpretations is correct. Perhaps the writer deliberately used an expression that cannot be restricted to any one meaning. It is probably a general allusion to sacrifice. The figure of the lamb may be intended to recall several of the OT themes. 'All that the ancient sacrifices foreshadowed were perfectly fulfilled in the sacrifice of Christ' (Morris, *The Gospel According to John*, p. 148). (See Carson for a plausible suggestion: a historical statement by John the Baptist is given a fuller sense by the writer as a 'post-resurrection Christian'.)

The phrase 'takes away sin' may be interpreted in either of two ways. The Evangelist may be thinking of the setting aside of sin by the expiatory death of Christ, so that the reference is to the taking away of the sin of the world by the atoning power of Jesus' blood (*cf.* 1 John 1:7 and 1 Pet. 2:24 – 'by his wounds you have been healed'). Alternatively, the phrase may allude to the removal of sin by a substitute, a representative, who bears instead of others the penalty attached to it (*cf.* Is. 53:12, thus the reference is to the Servant of the Lord). (See J. Jeremias, in *TDNT* 1, p. 186.) These explanations complement one another; both meanings may be intended.

Isaiah 53:7 is quoted in Acts 8:32 and afterwards interpreted by Philip as referring to Jesus. How 1st-century readers would have understood this text, and what precise significance the quotation would have had for them, is open to question. It may be that the emphasis here is on the Servant's patience and waiting on God while he suffers persecution, rather than specifically on Christ's death on behalf of others. However, Luke may assume that his readers are familiar with the rest of Isaiah 53; if it was widely used in the early church (as seems likely), then this quotation may have reminded them of the whole passage.

In 1 Peter 1:19 Peter introduces the simile of the lamb in order to make clear the effect of Christ's sacrificial death: 'You were ransomed ... not with perishable things ... but with the precious blood of Christ, like that of a lamb without blemish or defect' (NRSV). Thus Christ's blood is compared to that of a sacrificial animal, unblemished as required in the *law. It may be that Peter has in mind the spotless lamb sacrificed in the Passover ceremony (*cf.* Exod. 12:5), but perhaps he is referring to the unblemished lamb required for most regular OT sacrifices (*e.g.* Num. 6:14; 28:3, 9), and thus to the perfection of the sacrifice (*i.e.* to the sinlessness of Christ).

In Revelation the blood of a slaughtered Lamb has ransomed people for God (5:6, 9, 12; 7:14; 13:8). This Lamb may be an antitype of the Passover lamb (with possible allusions to Is. 53:7) whose blood delivers those who belong to God from the coming plagues (*cf.* Rev. 7:14). But not only is Christ the Lamb whose blood redeems people from all races for God; he also has great power. The Lamb's seven horns and seven eyes are symbols of strength and power; the images are borrowed from other apocalyptic texts, such as *1 Enoch* 90:9, 12, 37, in which the Messiah is portrayed as a powerful king and warrior.

Thus the term 'lamb' evokes the idea of a mighty conqueror (*cf.* Rev. 14:10, the Lamb as a judge; 17:14, the Lamb victorious in war). Jesus Christ is both Lamb and Lion: the great Lion of Revelation 5:5 turns out to be also a slain Lamb, with the characteristics of both. The wrath from which all wish to hide is that of the Lamb (Rev. 6:16). The blood of the Lamb has cleansing power: the martyrs' robes have been made clean solely by the blood of the Lamb (Rev. 7:9, 14, 17). Thus the Lamb in Revelation is both Redeemer and Ruler, the Judge who died for his people, the Lamb-God, who is both slain and triumphant, Lord of lords and King of kings (Rev. 17:14; 19:16).

The OT image of the lamb is taken up and developed in the NT as it is applied to the Messiah and all that he came to do. The work of the sacrificial Lamb is accomplished by his patient suffering (Acts 8:32), the perfection of his death (1 Pet. 1:19) and the expiatory effect of his blood (John 1:29) which deals with sin. Just as the blood of the Passover lambs was vital in the redemption of Israel from Egypt, so Christ has accomplished redemption from sin by his blood (1 Pet. 1:18). But his work (unlike that of the passover lamb) is not limited to Israel; rather his death deals with the sin of the world (John 1:29).

See also: BLOOD; SACRIFICE.

Bibliography

C. K. Barrett, 'The Lamb of God', *NTS* 1, 1955–56, pp. 210ff.; D. A. Carson, *The Gospel According to John*, PNTC (Leicester and Grand Rapids, 1991); N. Hillyer, 'The Lamb in the Apocalypse', *EvQ* 39, 1967, pp. 228–236; J. Jeremias, '*amnos, arēn, arnion*', in *TDNT* 1, pp. 338–341; L. Morris, *The Gospel According to John*, NICNT (Grand Rapids, 1971); R. Tuente, 'Lamb, Sheep', in *NIDNTT* 2, pp. 410–414.

P. D. WOODBRIDGE

LAMENTATIONS, see Part 2

LAND

Introduction

The major problem facing any biblical-theological discussion of 'land' is that the theme seems, at first glance, to be limited almost entirely to the OT. A cursory glance at a concordance reveals that the NT writers have little interest in 'land' as a theological category. Just as surprising is the fact that at no point do *Jesus or any of the NT writers explain why this is so. (In marked contrast, there is a lengthy NT discussion of how Jesus has removed the need for sacrifice.)

Chris Wright has suggested that this basic discontinuity is actually anticipated within the OT (e.g. Is. 56:3–7; Ezek. 47:22), where it is envisaged that outsiders (viz. Gentiles) will share in the inheritance of Israel by right (*God's People in God's Land*, pp. 110–111). This way of thinking clearly demands the replacement of the 'land of promise' by another *covenant *blessing. Paul, in Ephesians 2:11 – 3:6, argues that occupation of a particular piece of real estate has been superseded by membership of *God's new community. In God's new covenantal economy loving fellowship (*koinōnia*) has replaced land tenure. Israel was to stand out in a hostile world through covenant *faithfulness in the land of promise (Deut. 4:5–8). Now God's people are to stand out in a hostile world through loving one another in the church (John 13:34–35). The context for *obedience is no longer limited to one ethnic group in one place; it is now the new covenant community scattered throughout the earth. Having noted this basic discontinuity, this article will discuss the theology of land in the OT, and then attempt to show how this theology, though often only implicit in the text, forms an important part of the theological framework of the NT.

Land in the OT: land and promise

Land is an important theological category in the Bible. From Genesis 12, Yahweh's commitment to give land to *Abraham and his descendants is often expressed (see e.g. 12:1–3; 13:14–16; 15:18–21; 17:8; 26:3, 4, 24; 28:3–4, 13–15; 35:9–12). Genesis focuses on the promise of 'seed' (descendants), but as the Pentateuch unfolds, its focus shifts increasingly to the land which Yahweh has sworn to give to Abraham and his progeny.

God's right to give the land to his people derives from his ownership of the whole earth (e.g. Exod. 19:5; Ps. 24:1). In fact, in Hebrew the same word denotes both 'land' and 'the world' ('ereṣ). It is not surprising, then, that the Bible insists that the land ultimately belongs to God (see Lev. 25:23; Deut. 32:43; Josh. 22:19; Is. 14:2, 25; Jer. 2:7; Ezek. 36:5; 38:16; Joel 1:6; 3:2). The gift of land to Yahweh's people is an expression of his covenantal commitment to them.

This commitment is the dominant feature of land theology in the OT. Israel is repeatedly told that they have been given the land because God in his *grace is committed to their good. Nowhere is this claim made more clearly than in Deuteronomy (see e.g. 1:20–21, 25, 35; 3:18, 20; 4:1, 40; 6:1, 10, 18; 7:1, 8, 12; 8:1, 18; 9:5; 10:11; 11:9, 21; 12:1; 19:8; 26:3, 15; 27:3; 30:20; 31:7, 21, 23; 34:4). It is important to understand, however, the nature of the good to which the land points. The often repeated description of the land as 'flowing with milk and honey' reveals that the land which the Israelites are about to enter is a new paradise (see 6:3; 11:9–12; 26:9, 15; 27:3; 31:20; cf. Exod. 3:8, 17; 13:5; 33:3; Lev. 20:24; Num. 13:27; 14:8; 16:13–14; for parallels in Ugaritic, see *ANET*, p. 140; P. D. Miller, *Int* 23, p. 457). This is a theological rather than an agricultural point; Israel's land is so good because it is the long-awaited gift of God in fulfilment of his promise. The promise of land guarantees the restoration of intimacy with God in terms which recall the description of Eden. The theology of land in the early part of the OT anticipates the final chapters of the Bible, where the apostle John describes the new heaven and earth in language taken from Genesis 1 – 3.

The fact that the land belongs to God, and is given to Israel in trust, obviously entails ethical obligations. This is made very clear by the ritual described at the conclusion of the laws regulating life in the land in Deuteronomy 12 – 25. In 26:1–11, the divine ownership of the land and the response demanded of Israel (i.e. to live in the land as faithful stewards) are explicitly connected.

Land in the OT: land and obedience

The land, then, is the good gift of God, given as an inheritance to Israel as an expression of their filial relationship to Yahweh. It is pre-eminently a locus for relationship with God. However, the land can be forfeited. Although it is a gift of God's grace, given unconditionally to his people as part of the fulfilment of the patriarchal promises, the fulfilment of those promises demands a response from Israel. Enjoyment of life with Yahweh in the land requires obedience. This is the conditional element in what God says about the land.

Some have tried to drive a wedge between the conditional and unconditional elements in the land/promise tradition (most famously Gerhard von Rad in *The Problem of the Hexateuch and other Essays*). Any such attempt, however, rests on two arbitrary and extremely questionable assumptions: 1. that an emphasis on promise and gift necessarily excludes the idea that the land ultimately belongs to Yahweh, who demands obedience; 2. that the presence of unconditionality necessarily excludes all conditionality. It is far better, with Wright, to say that conditionality and unconditionality co-exist in any relationship, particularly that of sonship: 'What kind of relationship can it have been to produce this duality in which the indicative of God's grace is explicitly unconditioned yet requires Israel's obedience and response? The answer, it seems, is to be found in the relationship of Israel's "sonship of Yahweh" which is expressed in many parts of the Old Testament. As a living, personal relationship, Israel's "sonship of Yahweh" involved this organic tension or duality by its inherent nature' (*God's People*, p. 15, also D. J. McCarthy, *CBQ* 27, pp. 145–146). The 'indicatives' and 'imperatives' concerning the land dovetail in a graphic exposition of the covenantal decision which Israel faces at all times.

P. Diepold (*Israel's Land*, p. 91) lists several distinct ways in which the land is related to the ethical injunctions laid upon Israel. The land is the context of Israel's obedience, and obedience is the condition both of entering the land and of continued occupation of it. These points can easily be illustrated from the book of Deuteronomy, which is the fullest exposition of the theology of the land.

The land as the context for obedience

The land is the place where Israel has the opportunity to obey God's commands. This is made abundantly clear at almost every significant point in Deuteronomy: *e.g* 'These are the decrees and laws you must be careful to follow in the land that the LORD, the God of your fathers, has given you to possess – as long as you live in the land' (12:1 NIV, see also 6:1; 26:1; 27:1–3). The land, given by God, is the place in which Israel must make their ethical choices and live in obedience. This is in keeping with the role of the land in the covenantal relationship between God and Israel (see above).

Obedience as the condition for entry into and occupation of the land

From Genesis 12 it is perfectly clear that Israel can enter the land promised to them only if they take Yahweh at his word. The chaos ensuing from the bad decisions taken at Kadesh Barnea (Numbers 13 and 14) is evidence of that fact. This same perspective is carried through into Deuteronomy. From the outset, it is clear that only if Israel obeys will they be able to enjoy the fulfilment of the promise to the patriarchs. Only by reversing the failures of the past and faithfully negotiating the challenges of the future will the infant nation enjoy this divine *reward (e.g. 'Hear now, O Israel, the decrees and laws I am about to teach you. Follow them so that you may live and may go in and take possession of the land that the LORD, the God of your fathers, is giving you' [4:1], also 8:1; 11:8, *etc.*). But the relationship between the fulfilment of promise and obedience extends beyond the successful subjugation of Canaan; this is only a first step towards fulfilment of the promise. Entry into the land and long-term successful occupation are repeatedly linked (see *e.g.* 6:1–3; 8:1–3; 11:8–9; 12:1); obedience is the condition of both. Enjoyment of life with Yahweh in the land (in fulfilment of the covenant promise) is open-ended and dynamic. To realize it, Israel must continue to obey. This idea of a promised land, which is first to be occupied and then enjoyed by an obedient people, is a powerful incentive to make the right decisions. Deuteronomy treats the concept of the land as a powerful rhetorical device to press home the urgency and importance of the decision facing the nation on the plains of Moab. The land is not simply the reward for obedience; it is part of the motivation to obey.

God has given Israel a land; now Israel must give God their wholehearted obedience.

It is not easy to see how the 'givenness' of the land and the necessity of Israel 'taking' it fit together. However, the challenge of holding divine grace and human response in tension is at the heart of all biblical theology. Miller articulates the link between God's action and Israel's in a helpful way, highlighting Israel's responsibilities in occupying the land: 'The two notions of Yahweh's giving and Israel's taking are brought together in the expression "the land which Yahweh gives you to possess" (Deut. 3:18; 5:31; 12:1; 15:4; 19:2, 14; 25:19; *cf*. 1:39; 4:1; 17:14; 26:1). In a similar way 7:1f. juxtaposes *Yahweh's bringing* Israel into the land and *Israel's coming* into the land, *Yahweh's giving over* of the enemy of Israel and *Israel's smiting* of the enemy. The ideas of divine gift and human participation are not incompatible but rather a part of the whole' (Miller, *Int* 23, pp. 455–456).

There are strong parallels with NT soteriology here. God has done all the work. He has assured Israel that the land is theirs. He will fight for them. Yet they must obey. They must take possession of what has been given to them, remembering always that their doing so is entirely the work of God on their behalf.

Occupation of the land as measure of obedience

Deuteronomy also lays down a principle which dominates discussion of the land throughout the rest of the OT. The one reliable way of gauging Israel's faithfulness and obedience in future will be their continuing occupation of the land; the primary consequence of faithlessness and disobedience will be loss of land. This is made clear in Deuteronomy 4 and 30, where the exile is predicted, and in chapters 27 – 28, where it is made clear that disobedience will actualize the curses of the covenant, which involve expulsion from the land and much else besides (see also Lev. 26:32–39). Moses puts the issue of land at the forefront of national consciousness; land represents, in many ways, the spiritual state of the nation.

This point is confirmed in Joshua, which is concerned with the 'success' of the conquest. The dubious infiltration of Jericho (ch. 2), is followed by the setback at Ai. The nation is then deceived by the Gibeonites (ch. 9), and despite the assertion in 11:23 that the entire land had been taken and 'the land had rest from war', it transpires that this is not the whole story (see 13:1). In fact, no tribe has taken its complete 'inheritance'; the implication is that no tribe has been entirely obedient. This does not bode well for the future of Israel.

It took many generations for this incipient disobedience to reach its fullness. Yahweh was very patient with his people, but eventually the inevitable came to pass (see *e.g.* Jer. 25:1–11); the land was lost. The initial shock at the fracture of the Israel–land–Yahweh 'triangle' (Wright) gave way to a realization that it was the unavoidable consequence of centuries of disobedience. It was only when the land was lost that the idea of a new covenant, transcending geographical boundaries, was developed in detail (see *e.g.* Jer. 30 – 31; 32:36–44; Ezek. 36 – 37), though there are earlier hints of it in Leviticus 26:40–45 and Deuteronomy 30:1–10.

Land in the OT: land and relationship

Throughout the history of Israel, it is clear that the relationship between God and his people is intricately linked to the land which he has given to them. 'Israel's involvement is always with the land and with Yahweh, never only with Yahweh as though to live only in intense obedience, never only with land as though simply to possess and manage' (W. Brueggemann, *The Land*, p. 52). This intimate link is most obvious in the deliberate use of the language of 'inheritance' in connection with Yahweh's gift of the land to Israel.

Land was not, strictly speaking, 'owned' in Israel. The family patrimony was not to be transferred at will, but was to be passed on to succeeding generations (see *e.g.* the story of Naboth's vineyard in 1 Kgs. 21). Each family's inheritance (*naḥ⁽a⁾lâ*) had been entrusted to them by God and was to be guarded at all costs (see *e.g.* Lev. 25:23–28; Num. 36:6–8; Josh. 19:51; 2 Sam. 14:4–16; Mic. 2:1–2). However, the word *naḥ⁽a⁾lâ* is not used to refer only to one family's inheritance; the whole land is often described as the 'inheritance' of the entire *people of God (as in Deut. 26:1 above). In giving his people his land as *naḥ⁽a⁾lâ*, God reveals that he considers Israel to be his 'son'.

This language of inheritance is pervasive in the OT (see *e.g.* Num. 26:53; 36:2; Deut. 4:21, 38; 15:4; 19:10; 24:4; 25:19; 26:1; Josh.

11:23; 1 Kgs. 8:36; 1 Chr. 16:18; 2 Chr. 6:27; Pss. 105:11; 135:12; 136:21; Is. 58:14; Jer. 3:19; Ezek. 45:1; 47:14; 48:29). It invests the occupation of the land with greater significance: occupation involves the enjoyment of a filial relationship with God; it is not merely the possession of a piece of real estate.

This claim is supported by the OT's complementary insistence that the land is also Yahweh's inheritance, which makes sense only if the language of inheritance connotes the idea of Israel's 'sonship'. In Exodus 15:15–17 (see also 1 Sam. 26:19; 2 Sam. 20:19; Jer. 2:7; 50:11; Pss. 68:9; 79:1), Moses explains that Yahweh can give the land of Canaan to the people of Israel because it ultimately belongs not to the current inhabitants, but to him. The land, then, represents Yahweh's solidarity with the nation to which he has bound himself in covenant.

This intimacy is mirrored in the assertion elsewhere that it is not only the land which is Yahweh's inheritance, but the nation of Israel itself (*e.g.* Deut. 4:20; 32:8–9; 1 Sam. 10:1; 2 Sam. 20:19; 1 Kgs. 8:51; Pss. 28:9; 33:12; 78:71; Jer. 10:16; 51:19). The gift of the land was never intended to be an end in itself, but a means of developing the relationship between God and his people.

In Deuteronomy the primacy of the relationship between God and Israel over any place is exhibited in Moses' teaching on the way in which Israel should *worship (see esp. ch. 12). This legislation (often referred to as the 'altar law') has often been misread as an attempt to promote the claims of one sanctuary (whether Jerusalem, Gilgal, Bethel or Shiloh) over against all others. However, when the chapter is read in the wider theological context of Deuteronomy (and that of the biblical theology of land), it becomes clear that the *law is given to dissuade Israel from becoming too attached to *any* place (like the Canaanites did). God's people are not to become preoccupied with places, but with Yahweh, the one to whom all places belong.

When the people come to the 'place which Yahweh shall choose', the characteristic of their gatherings is to be shared *joy in the presence of God (12:7, 12, 18, also 16:11, 14; see J. G. Millar, *Now Choose Life*, p. 153) which is a feature of all genuine theism. According to Deuteronomy, although God is transcendent and sovereign, he is also immanent and personal. As Moses declares in 4:39: 'Acknowledge and take to heart this day that the LORD is God in heaven above and on the earth below. There is no other.' This sovereign God gives his land to his people, and comes to meet with his people in that land.

Once the OT theology of God's land is understood, the enormous sense of national dislocation produced by the loss of the land at the time of the exile becomes comprehensible. The exile for Israel involved much more than their being reduced to the status of refugees; it undermined their entire theological tradition. The possibility that they might be 'disinherited' had played no part in their national consciousness. Therefore, when Judah was overrun by the Babylonians, it sparked an urgent reconsideration of the nature of God's relationship with his people.

Israel had always been convinced that the Father–Son relationship established by God with his people was inviolable (see *e.g.* Deut. 9:26, 29; 1 Kgs. 8:52–53). Until now, the land was seen as an essential part of this arrangement, and so it too was thought to be inviolable. Then came the exile, and the consequent questioning (see *e.g.* Jer. 12:7–9 with its threefold use of *naḥ*lâ, and the use of the divorce metaphor in Jer. 3:6–25). Israel seems to have concluded that their sonship remained intact, even though the outward sign of their familial relationship with God had been taken away. Israel had lost the land, but they still believed that they were the people of Yahweh, who would find blessing through obedience. However, the removal of the land from the heart of their relationship with God was a preparation for the broadening of his purposes in the world to embrace the Gentiles in a way that Israel had never envisaged. Ezekiel 47:22–23 predicts that the *nations will share in the inheritance from God that was previously reserved for Israel (see also Zech. 2:11). This is anticipated also by Isaiah in 60:3ff., and Paul develops the idea at some length in Galatians 3 and 4. He discusses the new Gentile mission in terms of inheritance and sonship. It was possible only because possession of the land had previously been removed from the heart of Israel's relationship with God.

Conclusion: the NT and the land

The theology of land in the Old Testament

enshrines relationship with Yahweh at the very heart of the national experience. Israel yielded to the temptation to become preoccupied with the gift (the land) rather than the giver (Yahweh), but the dislocation that followed led to God's initiation of the new covenant in Christ.

It is true that the NT devotes little space to the theology of land, but the formative influence in biblical theology of the relational ideas associated with land must not be underestimated. For example, in expounding the nature of the *kingdom in the beatitudes, Jesus draws explicitly on a promise of land from Psalm 37 (Matt. 5:5). A similar idea, this time couched in terms of inheritance, appears in Matthew 25:34. Gary Burge has argued that the imagery in John 15, and Jesus' injunctions to 'abide in me', point to the fulfilment of the land motif in the OT in the person of Jesus himself (G. M. Burge, 'Territorial Religion, Johannine Christology, and the Vineyard in John 15', in J. B. Green and M. Turner (eds.), *Jesus of Nazareth, Lord and Christ* [Carlisle and Grand Rapids, 1994], pp. 384–396).

It is not only Jesus who uses such ideas. Paul's understanding of the church as a community of both Jews and Gentiles is based on his reading of the OT teaching on land (see above). He too draws on the inheritance theme, in Colossians 1:13–14, in explaining the nature of salvation in Christ, as does Peter in 1 Peter 1:3–5. The theology of land, then, provides a basis for the NT doctrine of *adoption; it was as God's sons that the people of Israel received their inheritance. The link is most explicit in Romans 8:14–25, which also links the theology of land with the theology of *creation. Both the creation mandate to 'fill the earth and subdue it' (Gen. 1:28), and the theology of land in the OT find their ultimate fulfilment in the new creation brought together under Christ.

The writer to the Hebrews takes a slightly different approach, comparing the Christian life to the experience of Israel during their initial occupation of the land, when the experience of '*rest' depended on an obedient response to the grace of God (Heb. 4:1–11). In the closing chapters of the Bible this 'rest' is portrayed in terms which recall the description of the Garden of Eden; the people of God again take up residence in God's presence, a residence described in terms of both a new city and a new heaven and earth. At the centre of this new cosmic order is the Lord Jesus Christ. The theology of land provides the conceptual background for the description of life with Christ in this new environment, in which all restrictions on believers' intimacy with him are taken away and they see him face to face. This inheritance is anticipated by the theology of land. The inheritance in Christ is no doubt different from the land received and lost by Israel, but it is greater, not less, than that land.

See also: EXILE; ISRAEL.

Bibliography

W. Brueggemann, *The Land* (Philadelphia, 1978); W. D. Davies, *The Gospel and the Land* (Berkeley, 1974); P. Diepold, *Israel's Land* (Stuttgart, 1972); N. C. Habel, *The Land Is Mine* (Minneapolis, 1995); E. A. Martens, *Plot and Purpose in the Old Testament* (Leicester, 1981); D. J. McCarthy, 'Notes on the love of God in Deuteronomy and the father–son relationship between Yahweh and Israel', *CBQ* 27, 1965, pp. 145–146; J. G. McConville, *Law and Theology in Deuteronomy* (Sheffield, 1984); J. G. Millar, *Now Choose Life: Theology and Ethics in Deuteronomy* (Leicester, 1998); P. D. Miller Jr., 'The gift of God: The Deuteronomic theology of the land', *Int* 23, 1969, pp. 454–465; G. von Rad, *The Problem of the Hexateuch and Other Essays* (ET, London, 1966), pp. 79–93; H. E. von Waldow, 'Israel and her land: some theological considerations', in H. N. Bream, R. D. Heim and C. A. Moore (eds.), *A Light Unto My Path: Old Testament Studies in Honour of J. M. Myers* (Philadelphia, 1974); C. J. H. Wright, *Living as the People of God* (Leicester, 1983); idem, God's *People In God's Land* (Exeter, 1990); idem, 'erets', in *NIDOTTE* 1, pp. 518–524; idem, 'nah°lā', in *NIDOTTE* 3, pp. 77–81.

J. G. MILLAR

LANGUAGES

The biblical writers do not reflect on theoretical linguistics. They take the phenomenon of language itself, and the plurality of language forms, largely for granted. At two points, however, the nature of 'languages' is brought into sharper theological focus: 1. in the account of the *confusion* of languages in Genesis 11, and 2. in NT accounts of the charisma of 'speaking in [other/new] languages/tongues' in Acts and 1 Corinthians.

The confusion of languages in Genesis 11:1–9

The setting of this account is the story of the deepening alienation that follows the fall (Gen. 3). In Eden, Adam and Eve strive to be 'like God' (3:5, NIV) in wisdom, but to achieve this goal independently of him, and in a manner which is against his expressed will. Thus the harmony of communion with him is shattered, and they are banished from the garden of his presence (3:23–24; cf. 3:8). The independence they sought now becomes their fate, in the ugly form of alienation from God, from each other (cf. the accusation of 3:12) and from creation (3:14–19). This alienation is intensified by Cain's murder of Abel (Gen. 4) and the widespread corruption and violence God judges by the flood (Gen. 6 – 8). Even the bright new start with Noah's family (Gen. 8:20 – 9:19) soon falters (9:20–27), and humanity reaches its nadir in 11:1–9. In an exquisitely crafted story (often parodying *Babylonian narratives) the descendents of Noah, one people with one tongue (11:1, 6), combine to gain access to heaven (and a proud name for themselves) by building a high temple-tower. Unimpressed by this puny edifice, God comes down to inspect it (11:5). Perceiving that their arrogant endeavour is made possible only by their common language, he acts. In mockery of their words 'Come, let's make bricks (*nilbenah*)...' (11:3), God says 'Come, let us mix up (*nabelah*) their language, so that they will not understand one another's speech' (11:7, author's translation). The project is thereby brought to an abrupt halt, and the city ('Babel' = 'mixed, confused'; 11:9) left deserted as the peoples are scattered over the face of the earth. This divine 'gift' of different tongues is clearly portrayed as a *judgment, the deepening of the alienation which began at the fall. The corresponding hope of Zephaniah 3:9 is that the Lord will one day restore pure (unified?) speech to all nations, that they may call on his name and serve him with one accord.

The gift of tongues/languages in the NT

In the book of Acts

Whatever the phenomenon of Pentecost may have been (some take it as merely a 'hearing' miracle), Luke portrays it as including Spirit-inspired praise of God's great deeds (Acts 2:11), uniquely given here by Galilean believers in what was (for them) the *un*learned languages/dialects of the migrant Jewish pilgrims (2:4, 6–8). He interprets these 'tongues' (elsewhere only 10:46 and 19:6) as belonging to a broader class of *prophetic speech (cf. 2:16–18, 33; also 19:6), but nowhere else does he suggest that they are languages understood by the hearers, or serve evangelistic ends. He mentions the phenomenon only with reference to the moment of receiving the Spirit, but there is no clear evidence that he thinks tongues attend this event *normatively*; rather, with Judaism, he appears to believe that 'initial evidence' is given mostly when some form of public 'legitimation' of Spirit-reception might be anticipated, *e.g.* to confirm the granting of the Spirit not merely to pious believing Jews but to 'outsider' Samaritans (8.17–18), to Gentiles (10.46) and to the twelve Ephesian 'disciples' (19:6). As to whether most (or any) of these recipients *continued* to experience tongues, and what role it played in their lives, service and witness, Luke is silent.

Noting some parallels between Acts 2 and Genesis 11, J. G. Davies (*JTS* 3, pp. 228–231) argued that the gift of tongues at Pentecost deliberately echoed the Babel incident, and so supplied its hoped-for *eschatological reversal. But the verbal parallels are very slender, and the phenomenon described in Acts is not the gift of a single universal language (a spiritual Esperanto). A plurality of languages, with their potential for alienating misunderstanding (cf. 2:13), is maintained. Indeed, if Luke shares Paul's view, even the tongues-speakers themselves do not understand the words they speak (see below).

Altogether, surprisingly little may be learned from Acts about the nature and purposes of tongues.

In Paul

The issue of tongues is raised by the Corinthians, and Paul addresses the question in 1 Corinthians 12 – 14 (nowhere else).

Careful exegetical reconstruction suggests that the Corinthians considered tongues to be the most spiritual of gifts, because they were the declaration of (heavenly) '*mysteries' (cf. 14:2), in 'the languages ... of angels' (cf. 13:1; see *Spiritual powers), untrammelled by the human mind (cf. 14:14), and exhibiting divine *mania* (cf. 14:23). Accordingly, a number were vaunting their elite status by dominating the assembly with (uninterpreted) glossolalia. Paul's response robustly asserts the spiritual value of tongues (14:18; cf. 14:5, 15), especially as a form of private *prayer (14:2, 4, 14–15), but also – *providing the tongue is interpreted* – for the congregation (14:5, 13). At significant points Paul concurs with the Corinthian understanding of tongues; he appears to affirm that they are Spirit-enabled angelic and human languages (13:1; cf. 'different kinds of tongues' 12:10), used to celebrate divine mysteries, sing God's praise, or (perhaps) intercede (14:15a; cf. Rom. 8:26). His sharpest differences with his readers centre on his assessment, 1. that 'tongues' are *less* significant than other comprehensible charismata, and 2. that *uninterpreted* (public) tongues are uncomfortably close to the 'strange tongues' (*i.e.* foreign language) of Isaiah 28:11–12 (cf. 1 Cor. 14:20–23). In that passage, the prophet declares that God will speak through the incomprehensible language of an invader, but only because his people are acting like 'unbelievers' by refusing to listen to him speaking in their own language.

Origins and conceptual setting

As C. B. Forbes has shown (*Prophecy and Inspired Speech*), the widespread attempt to 'explain' tongues as a minor variant on ecstatic speech in hellenistic religions (cf. most recently G. Theissen, *Psychological Aspects of Pauline Theology*) has proved to be misguided. There is also no pre-Christian parallel in Judaism to the NT gift of unlearned language (*Testimony of Job* 48 – 50 provides the closest parallel in Jewish literature, but these chapters are *Christian* additions), incomprehensible to the speaker. The Christian phenomenon of 'tongues' is thus a 'new' phenomenon in the contemporary literary world (cf. 'new tongues' in the spurious ending to Mark [16:17]). Some apocalyptic writers do, however, expect that the final revelation of God will evoke Spirit-

inspired praise (cf. *1 Enoch* 61:11–12; 71:11), and *Apocalypse of Zephaniah* 8 anticipates that such praise will involve the use of angelic languages (but learned, and understood by the speaker). This may suggest that Paul understood the gift of tongues as an anticipation of the cosmic praise that would greet the Parousia. But tongues remain paradoxical in Paul, illustrating the 'now' and 'not-yet' of *salvation. Through the Spirit, men and women receive a foretaste of the heavenly *worship that marks the reunification of all things; yet this reveals their present weakness and distance from God, for it comes as *incomprehensible* language, understood only (if at all) through 'interpretation'.

Bibliography

J. G. Davies, 'Pentecost and Glossolalia', *JTS* 3, 1952, pp. 228–231; G. D. Fee, 'Toward a Pauline theology of glossolalia', in W. Ma and R. P. Menzies (eds.), *Pentecostalism in Context: Essays in Honor of William W. Menzies* (Sheffield, 1997); C. Forbes, *Prophecy and Inspired Speech in Early Christianity and Its Hellenistic Environment* (Tübingen and Peabody, 1995, 1997); G. Theissen, *Psychological Aspects of Pauline Theology* (Edinburgh, 1987); M. Turner, *The Holy Spirit and Spiritual Gifts: Then and Now* (Peabody and Carlisle, 1998, 1999); idem, 'Tongues: an experience for all in the Pauline churches?', *AJPS* 1, 1998, pp. 231–253.

M. TURNER

LAST SUPPER, see SACRED MEALS

LAW

Introduction

In fulfilment of his promises to *Abraham, Isaac and *Jacob, God brought forth the Israelites out of Egypt (see *Exodus [event]). At Sinai God made a covenant with them, setting out obligations which have often been understood as 'laws' although no single term adequately defines them. These laws were among Israel's most precious possessions. *Obedience to them distinguished the people from other nations. They covered all aspects of life, regulating relationships and dealing with both personal and economic matters. They laid down guidelines for the way Israel should relate to other nations. Above all, the laws regulated the cult and its *sacrifices through which the Israelites related to God, and by which their *sins could be *forgiven.

The Israelites' obedience to these laws was irregular. Sometimes they observed them carefully and experienced God's *blessing in their national life. At other times they disregarded God's laws and brought sanctions upon themselves; they were overrun by other nations, and eventually suffered *exile. The *prophets of Israel called upon the people to return to God through obedience to his laws, but the people rarely listened to them. Eventually, the prophets spoke of a time when God himself would write his laws, not on tablets of stone as before, but upon the tablets of his people's hearts. Then they would walk in his statutes and obey his commandments.

When *Jesus Christ came, he said that his purpose was not to destroy the law and the prophets, but to fulfil them. Not one jot or tittle would pass from the law until all was fulfilled. With Jesus' death and resurrection, his exaltation and the sending of the *Holy Spirit upon the church, that time of fulfilment came. That which the law foreshadowed was now fulfilled. The law had come through *Moses, grace and truth now came through Jesus Christ.

No one in the early church understood the implications of what Jesus Christ had achieved better than the apostle Paul. He recognized that Jesus' coming marked the changing of the times. In the past the marks of membership of the *people of God were being born a Jew (or becoming a proselyte), *circumcision (if a male) and obedience to the Mosaic law. But now the marks of membership were *faith in Jesus Christ and participation in his Spirit. Circumcision and law observance were no longer required. However, the *love of God and love of neighbour, which summed up what the law required, were to be produced in those who walked in the Spirit. This did not mean that all the demands of the law were to be obeyed, or that people were to relate to God through the law. Rather they were to relate to God through faith in Jesus Christ and in his Spirit. The Mosaic law was not their law, any more than the Mosaic covenant was their covenant.

However, the OT in its entirety, including the law, was their Scripture, and that meant that it was useful for 'teaching, rebuking, correcting and training in righteousness' (2 Tim. 3:16 NIV), as long as it was read paradigmatically and not applied literally.

As one reads through the major corpora of the Bible this development in the law's role becomes evident.

The Pentateuch

The patriarchal period

The patriarchs, living well before the giving of the law at the time of Moses, appear to have observed the local customs in place at the time. For example, Rachel's possession of the Teraphim possibly reflects provisions in the Nuzi tablets (whereby the possession of household idols ensured leadership of the family and a claim on the family inheritance, Gen. 31), as also does the barren Sarah's giving of her slave girl to Abraham (so that he might have children by her, Gen. 16). However, when Genesis was written, Abraham's faith response to God was described, not only in terms of keeping the way of the Lord by doing what is right (Gen. 18:19), but also in terms of his obedience to God's commandments: in Genesis 26:5 God is said to have fulfilled his promises because Abraham 'obeyed me and kept my requirements, my commands, my decrees and my laws'. It was in fulfilment of God's promises to Abraham, Isaac and Jacob, that he brought the Israelites out of Egypt (Gen. 50:24) and led them to Sinai, where he entered into a covenant with them and gave them his laws.

The Sinai covenant

At Sinai God made a formal covenant with the Israelites and provided them with laws and instructions by which they were to order their lives in covenant relationship with him (Exod. 19:3–9). The laws and instructions given by God to Israel at Sinai represented one of their greatest possessions. No other nation had 'such righteous decrees and laws' as those Moses set before them at Sinai (Deut. 4:5–8). These laws were to govern the Israelites' relationship to God, with one another, and with the peoples living around them. The laws regulated the cult by which they approached God and by which forgiveness for their sins could be obtained.

Obedience to the laws, by which the Israelites' covenant relationship with God was sustained, ensured that the blessing of God would continue to be experienced, while wilful disobedience to the laws was tantamount to an abrogation of the covenant.

Several different Hebrew words are used to refer to the laws given to Israel. The most common is *tôrāh*, which means 'instruction, direction, or guidance'. The term is later used to denote not only the prescriptive parts of the Pentateuch, but its narrative sections as well, all of which provide guidance for the reader. However, within the book of *Deuteronomy the word *tôrāh* refers to the law book itself, consisting of the stipulations, decrees and laws Moses gave to Israel (*cf.* Deut. 4:44–45).

Covenant obligations

The covenant obligations of Israel are set out in several passages in the Pentateuch: 1. the Decalogue (Exod. 20:1–17; Deut. 5:6–21), both forms of which begin with a prologue in which God, who gives the law, is described as the one who brought them out of Egypt; 2. the Book of the Covenant (Exod. 20:23 – 23:19), comprised mostly of an assortment of commandments, case laws and responsibilities, but including some moral imperatives (Exod. 22:21 – 23:9); and 3. the Deuteronomic Code (Deut. 12 – 26), possibly the 'law' found in the temple in Josiah's time (2 Kgs. 22:8 – 23:3), which comprises cultic laws, regulations regarding the appointment of judges, kings, priests, and other miscellaneous laws. (The contents of *Leviticus, which includes cultic matters, qualifications for *priests, regulations regarding festivals [see *Sacred meals], *sabbatical years and jubilee etc., do not appear to have been included in the covenant making ceremony of *Exodus 34 or the covenant renewal ceremony of Deuteronomy 29 – 30.)

Two significant passages from Deuteronomy

Deuteronomy 6 is particularly significant for an understanding of the status and function of God's laws and instructions within Israel. God, who led the Israelites out of Egyptian bondage, gave them his laws, and obedience to the laws would ensure their prosperity in the land of Canaan (Deut. 6:3, 12). Central to these obligations was the command to love God with all one's heart, soul and strength (Deut. 6:4–5). Deuteronomy 30 looks into the future. It foreshadows the Israelites' failure to observe God's laws which would result in their dispersion among the nations. But afterwards God would bring them back to their promised land. He would circumcise their hearts and they would again obey his commandments and prosper (Deut. 30:1–6).

The Decalogue

The Decalogue is particularly significant because it forms the moral and spiritual basis of Israel's covenant relationship with God. It opens with a brief description of the relationship between God and his people, followed by the 'ten words' setting out what was expected of them in their relationship with him. The first four 'words' deal with the Israelites' relationship with God; the last six with their relationships with one another. The commands are apodictic in nature, *i.e.* they are absolute commands, which are mostly, but not entirely, negative in nature. The Decalogue differs from other sets of 'legal' material in the Pentateuch in a number of ways. First, the words of the Decalogue are spoken directly by God to Israel, whereas all the other laws are given through Moses as mediator. Secondly, only the Decalogue is inscribed in stone by the finger of God. Thirdly, unlike many of the other laws the Decalogue does not include prescribed punishments for disobedience. Whilst the Decalogue can be distinguished in these ways from the other 'legal' material in the Pentateuch, it is nevertheless connected to it in so far as it provides the moral and spiritual background for the more detailed covenant obligations laid upon Israel elsewhere.

The former prophets

The former prophets (Josh. – 2 Kgs.) illustrate the outworking of the promises and sanctions of the law found in the Pentateuch. These books show how obedience to the laws of God is rewarded with God's blessing and how disobedience attracts his *judgment. When the Israelites were obedient they enjoyed security and prosperity in the land. When they were disobedient the rains were withheld, they were overrun by their enemies, and finally suffered exile.

The books of 1 and 2 Kings include the stories of *Elijah and *Elisha, 9th-century prophets, who called Israel to abandon their alliance with Baal and to give their allegiance wholly to God. Elijah rebuked King Ahab for his failure to act in accordance with God's laws by ignoring the legislation about inalienable land rights (1 Kgs. 21:1–29).

The second book of Kings includes a description of the reforms carried out by Josiah. The king led his people back into the ways of righteousness, and gave instructions that the house of the Lord should be repaired. While carrying out this task those responsible found 'the book of the law' in the temple. It was taken to the king and read in his presence (2 Kgs. 22:8–10). This book of the law is usually identified with the Deuteronomic Code (or part of it). When Josiah heard the book of the law read, and realized how far Israel had departed from its requirements, he was deeply disturbed. He led the people in an act of covenant renewal (2 Kgs. 22:11 – 23:3). He himself tried harder than any king before or after him to obey all that was written in the book of the law (2 Kgs. 23:25). He destroyed pagan shrines, offered sacrifices to God, and kept the Passover which had long been neglected (2 Kgs. 23:4–23). This national *repentance produced a stay of judgment (2 Kgs. 22:14–20).

One passage, 2 Kings 17:13, reflects the relationship between the prophets and God's laws: 'The LORD warned Israel and Judah through all his prophets and seers: "Turn from your evil ways. Observe my commands and decrees, in accordance with the entire Law that I commanded your fathers to obey and that I delivered to you through my servants the prophets."' Here the mission of the prophets is defined in terms of calling Israel back to obedience to God's laws.

The latter prophets

Many of the writing prophets (see *Prophetic books) called Israel back to their covenant obligations to God. Amos and Hosea prophesied in the northern kingdom. Amos rebuked the people for their failure to practice justice and Hosea called upon them to abandon *idolatry. Micah and Isaiah did the same in the southern kingdom. Micah castigated the people for their injustices, and called upon them 'to act justly and love mercy and to walk humbly with your God' (Mic. 6:8). He promised a time when the Lord himself would teach them his law and bring

in a period of *peace and prosperity (Mic. 4:1–5). Isaiah 1 – 39 speaks against the corruption, injustice and violence in society, and warns of the Babylonian invasion. Both Micah and Isaiah contain visions of the last days: a time when many peoples would go up to the mountain of the Lord to learn his ways, and when the law would go out from Zion (Is. 2:2–3; Mic. 4:1–2).

Jeremiah prophesied the downfall of the southern kingdom because of its idolatry and injustice, and spoke of a time when God would make a new covenant with his people and write his law upon their hearts (Jer. 31:31–34). Ezekiel was a prophet of the exile. He said that the reason for the banishment of the people from Judah to Babylon was their failure to keep the covenant, in particular their failure to observe its ethical requirements, and the desertion of their God in favour of pagan *worship. Ezekiel, like Jeremiah, looked forward to a time when God would bring his people back from exile, cleanse them from their sins, remove their idols, and put a new heart within them. Ezekiel went further than Jeremiah in saying that God would put his Spirit within his people and cause them to obey his laws and teachings (Ezek. 36:24–28). Isaiah 40 – 55 also looks forward to the restoration of Israel following her exile in Babylon. After the sanctions of the law had been applied to Israel for her sins, God would turn to them again and restore their fortunes. In Isaiah 56 – 66 a bright future is promised to those who are faithful to God in practising justice, observing the law and worshipping God with sincerity.

Malachi was a prophet of the restoration. He called upon Israel and her priests to act faithfully. They must cease worshipping other gods, offer acceptable sacrifices to the Lord, pay the tithes, and be faithful to their marriage partners. When Israel was faithful to their covenant with God by obeying his laws, God would open the windows of heaven and pour out his blessing upon them. In Malachi 4:4 the prophet calls upon the people to 'remember the law of my servant Moses, the decrees and laws I gave him at Horeb for all Israel'.

The writings

The book of Daniel, reflecting the life of the exiles during the Babylonian and Persian periods, does not say much about the law, but in relating the faithfulness of Daniel and his friends, it indicates that this consisted in their refusal to defile themselves with unclean food. In this way the steadfastness and wisdom of Daniel and his friends is related to their obedience to God's laws.

The books of Ezra and Nehemiah reflect the period following the return of the Jews from the Babylonian exile, and describe the rebuilding of the *temple and the city walls of Jerusalem. Ezra himself was an expert in the law. He is described as one who 'had devoted himself to the study and observance of the Law of the LORD, and to teaching its decrees and laws in Israel' (Ezra 7:10).

Ezra came to Jerusalem to ensure that the laws of God were obeyed. Those who had married foreign women put them away in accordance with the law, so that God's blessing might rest once more upon Israel. It was Ezra who read the Book of the Law (probably the Pentateuch or part of it) to the people, while others went among them explaining the meaning of what was read (Neh. 8:1–8). This led to national repentance, an agreement not to allow their daughters to marry foreign men, to refrain from trading on the Sabbath, to let their fields lie fallow on the seventh year, and to provide for the needs of the priests and the temple worship (Neh. 8:9 – 9:3; 9:38 – 10:34).

The book of Psalms contains what in recent times have been identified as 'torah songs' (Pss. 1, 15, 24, 119). Psalm 1, which extols the virtues of the person 'whose delight is in the law of the LORD', is set at the beginning of the whole Psalter, perhaps to indicate that Israel's worship is to be predicated upon the law. Psalms 15 and 24 say that those who can approach God are those who are obedient to him. Psalm 119, the longest of all the psalms, is acrostic in form, and each successive letter of the Hebrew alphabet is used to begin eight verses, all of which extol the virtues of the law and the advantages of ordering one's life by it.

The book of Proverbs has few explicit references to the law, but the way of wisdom which it extols is often couched in terms reminiscent of Deuteronomy. Two explicit references indicate how wisdom is related to the law. The first (Prov. 6:23) depicts the commandments as a lamp that guides; the second (Prov. 29:18) calls those who keep the law

'blessed'. The book of Ecclesiastes explores the limits of wisdom and concludes that the whole duty of human beings is to 'fear God and keep his commandments' (Eccles. 12:13).

The books of 1 and 2 Chronicles tell the story of Israel from the time of the death of King Saul down to the Babylonian exile, and conclude with a record of Cyrus' edict allowing the Jews to return to Jerusalem. Like 1 and 2 Kings, these books attribute the disasters which befell the Israelites to their disobedience to God's laws (though the primary focus of 1 and 2 Chronicles is upon the dynasty of David and the temple worship). The discovery of 'the book of the law' in the temple during Josiah's reign, and the subsequent actions taken by Josiah, are recounted at some length. Josiah realized that Israel's disobedience to God's laws had laid them open to God's judgment. This was postponed when Josiah led his people in a covenant renewal ceremony in which the people promised to do what the laws of God required (2 Chr. 34:8 – 35:19).

Jesus and the Gospels

The four Gospels in their various ways provide us with a picture of Jesus' attitude to the Mosaic law. Jesus was generally obedient to the law (there is no evidence that he violated it). He did not go out of his way to transgress the *traditions of the elders, except where their teaching was at variance with a proper understanding of the laws of God. When he healed lepers he told them to go and show themselves to the priests and offer the sacrifices which the law prescribed (Matt. 8:4; Mark 1:44; Luke 5:14). Also it was his custom to attend synagogue services each Sabbath day (Luke 4:16), not a requirement of the law, but a Jewish tradition. However, where traditions came into conflict with his understanding of the law he was forthright in his condemnation. For example, he accused those who said that the money they would otherwise use to support their parents was a gift devoted to God, of breaking the commandments of God in order to preserve their traditions (Mark 7:8–13).

Areas of conflict

In two areas in particular Jesus came into conflict with the Jews because of his attitude to the law. The first was in relation to Sabbath observance. Conflict arose largely because of the healings which Jesus performed on the Sabbath. He did not accept that his actions were in contravention of the Sabbath law, asserting rather that his opponents had not understood the intention of the law: it was made for humankind, not humankind for the Sabbath (Mark 2:27). The second was his statement about what defiles people. He said that it was not what goes into people (what is eaten) that defiles them, but what comes out of them (evil desires) (Mark 7:14–23). Whether Jesus intended by these words to suspend the food laws is not clear. But this was how they were understood later by the evangelist who added, 'In saying this, Jesus declared all foods "clean"' (Mark 7:19).

Another area in which it might appear that Jesus negated the law is that of divorce. When asked by his opponents what he thought of Moses' provision for a man to divorce his wife so long as he gave her a bill of divorce, Jesus said that this provision was given to them by Moses only because of their hardness of heart, and that it was not God's intention from the beginning (Matt. 19:3–9). However, this is not the negating of a law so much as the recognition that it was a concession to human sinfulness, something that ought not to be necessary among those who know the power of the *kingdom.

The six antitheses

Particularly important for an understanding of Jesus' attitude to the law are the six antitheses of Matthew 5:21–48. Here Jesus contrasts his teaching with what was said to the ancestors. At first sight it seems that Jesus was doing away with the law in favour of his own teaching. However, closer examination reveals that in four cases he was extending the application of the law, sometimes including within its purview attitudes as well as actions. But in the cases of divorce and swearing oaths Jesus taught something different from the law's teaching. In the first case he says that the Mosaic legislation was only an accommodation to human sinfulness, and that divorce was not God's original intention (Matt. 5:31–32). In the second case he says that the Mosaic provision for oaths ought not to be necessary; a person's 'yes' should be sufficient (Matt. 5:33–37). In both these cases the Mosaic law is being superseded by the higher ethics of the kingdom.

'I came to fulfil the law'

Before the six antitheses a very important statement is made by Jesus concerning his relationship to the law: 'Do not think that I have come to abolish the Law or the Prophets; I have not come to abolish them but to fulfil them. I tell you the truth, until heaven and earth disappear, not the smallest letter, not the least stroke of a pen, will by any means disappear from the Law until everything is accomplished' (Matt. 5:17–18). The key issue here is what Jesus meant by fulfilling the law (and the prophets). Several different interpretations have been proposed: 1. Jesus fulfilled the law by explaining fully its original intent; 2. Jesus fulfilled the law by extending its application; 3. Jesus fulfilled the law by bringing to fruition what it foreshadowed; 4. Jesus fulfilled the law by personally carrying out its demands. In the light of the fact that Jesus said he came to fulfil both the law and the prophets, and of the way 'fulfilment' is used in the gospel of Matthew as a whole, i.e. of bringing into being what was spoken of beforehand, it seems best to understand Jesus' statement about coming to fulfil the law to mean his bringing into being of that which the law foreshadowed. In Luke 16:16 Jesus is quoted as saying: 'The Law and the Prophets were proclaimed until John. Since that time, the good news of the kingdom of God is being preached, and everyone is forcing his way into it.' This suggests that Jesus believed that the law remained in force until the coming of the kingdom of God, but that when the kingdom arrived the law's role as a regulatory norm would cease, being superseded by the coming of the kingdom.

Jesus' independence from the law

It is striking that Jesus makes very little appeal to the law in his own ethical teaching. His references to it are for the most part found in controversies with his opponents. His own positive teaching was not an exposition of the law but was given on his own authority. This suggests that Jesus' teaching took precedence over the law. He expounded its true meaning to those who had misconstrued it, but otherwise he ignored it, concentrating rather on explaining to people the implications of the coming kingdom of God. The important question is not that of

Jesus' relationship to the law, but that of the law's relationship to Jesus. The law foreshadowed what Jesus came to do, and in doing it he fulfilled the law and the prophets (Luke 24:27, 44).

The Acts of the Apostles

Even though Jesus taught that the time of the law was coming to an end, it took the church a long time to recognize the fact.

A law-observant church

The Acts of the Apostles depicts the Jerusalem church as law-observant. It consisted of thousands of Jews who were zealous for the law (Acts 21:20). Many of them continued as members of the Pharisaic party (Acts 15:5), and others continued to function as priests (Acts 6:7). They practised circumcision (Acts 11:2–3), and some believed it was necessary for salvation (Acts 15:1). They attended Jewish festivals (Acts 20:16), participated in temple ceremonies (Acts 2:46; 3:1) and sacrifices (Acts 21:23–26), and continued to observe the food taboos (Acts 10:9–16).

Admission of Gentiles

It is not surprising that such a church experienced difficulties when Gentiles (see *Nations) gave their allegiance to Jesus Christ. Some Jewish Christians insisted that the new Gentile converts submit to circumcision and take upon themselves the yoke of the law (Acts 15:1, 5). This led to dissension, and the Council of Jerusalem was convened to resolve the issue. Following reports from Peter, Paul and Barnabas, the council eventually decided in favour of *freedom for Gentile believers, *i.e.* that circumcision and law observance would not be required of them (Acts 15:2–21). For the sake of fellowship between Jewish and Gentile Christians the Gentiles were asked to avoid certain things that would offend Jews (Acts 15:19–21). Thus the gospel was able to advance among the Gentiles. Most Jewish believers appear to have seen this as a concession for Gentile believers only. Few of them recognized that this freedom applied also to Jewish believers; they believed that Jewish Christians were still required to keep the law.

The Pauline corpus

It was the apostle Paul who was left to work out in theological terms the relationship of believers, both Jew and Gentile, to the Mosaic law.

*Galatians

In the churches of Galatia Jewish Christians tried to convince Paul's Gentile converts that they must submit to circumcision and observe certain aspects of the Mosaic law if they were to be true members of the people of God, true descendants of Abraham. Paul strenuously resisted this imposition, arguing that the mark of the people of God was no longer circumcision and law observance, but faith in Jesus Christ and participation in his Spirit. And all this was in fulfilment of the promise God made to Abraham long before the law was given (Gal. 3:1–22). Now that faith had come, Paul argued, even Jewish believers were no longer under the discipline of the law. They were like people who were once children under the supervision of guardians, but who had now reached their maturity and were no longer under guardians. Jewish believers were once under the discipline of the law, but now that faith in Christ had come they were under that discipline no longer. Instead they were free from the law to walk in the Spirit (Gal. 3:23 – 4:7). If Jewish believers were no longer obliged to live under the law, then certainly there was no need for Gentile believers to do so.

*Romans

The relationship of believers to the law of Moses was spelled out in greater detail in Romans, where the apostle expounded and defended the gospel he preached. Paul demonstrated that works of the law could not bring justification (see *Righteousness, justice and justification), but only a consciousness of sin (Rom. 3:19–20). He argued that people were justified by faith without works of the law (Rom. 3:21–24). He also claimed that believers no longer lived under the law; they had died to the law so that they might live to God (Rom. 7:1–6). Contrary to what people might expect, this freedom from the law did not lead to moral anarchy, rather it was the doorway to a life of *holiness (Rom. 6:1–11, 15–19). Believers needed to be free from the law so that they might bear fruit for God (Rom. 7:4–6). The law itself was not sinful, but holy, spiritual and good. However, sin seized the opportunity it provided and brought human beings into deeper bondage

(Rom. 7:7–25). It became part of the problem not part of the solution. The answer was a life of faith in Jesus Christ and walking in his Spirit (Rom. 8:2–4).

Believers and the OT

Freedom from the law did not mean that believers had nothing to learn from the law. In fact the whole OT, including the Mosaic law, was 'God-breathed' and 'useful for teaching, rebuking, correcting and training in righteousness' (2 Tim. 3:16). While believers were not obliged to carry out all the demands of the Mosaic law, they could nevertheless draw from the OT, read paradigmatically, lessons for Christian living.

The rest of the NT

Of the remaining letters of the NT it is the letter to the *Hebrews which is most germane to our topic.

Hebrews

Hebrews was written to believers who were in danger of giving up their Christian faith because of the pressure of persecution. Part of the writer's strategy in seeking to keep his readers from succumbing to this temptation was to explain to them the advantages that were theirs as believers, and in particular the excellencies of the new covenant under which they now lived. It was a covenant under which their sins were remembered no more and the law of God was written in their hearts (Heb. 8:6–13). The writer sought to show them that the provisions of the new covenant were the substance of which the law was but a shadow (Heb. 10:1). The earlier commandments in regard to sacrifice were abrogated, because the law made nothing perfect (Heb. 7:18–19). In its own way the letter to the Hebrews makes clear that the earlier regime operative under the Mosaic law had come to an end, and had been replaced with the provisions of the new covenant: sins were remembered no more and the law of God was written on people's hearts.

Conclusion

In the patriarchal period people's relationship with God was not governed by law, though Abraham's faith response to God was later described in terms of keeping God's commandments and decrees. Following the Exodus from Egypt, God made a formal covenant with Israel at Sinai and gave them laws by which their relationship with him was to be sustained. Obedience to these laws was to be the distinguishing mark of the people of God. With the coming of Jesus Christ a new phase in God's relationship with his people was introduced. Jesus' own teaching was not an exposition of the law; nor did he abrogate the law. He virtually ignored it except when dealing with the questions of his opponents, or when explaining to his disciples how the law and the prophets actually foreshadowed what he was to do, or when showing how his own teaching extended the application of the law; he concentrated on explaining the meaning of the kingdom of God. After the coming of Christ, obedience to the Mosaic law was no longer the distinguishing mark of the people of God. They were now distinguished by their faith in Jesus Christ and participation in his Spirit. The law continued to have an educative role for them, but it was no longer the regulatory norm under which they lived. Christians were not bound to the actual demands of the law but had much to learn from the principles and values underlying them.

See also: COVENANT; ISRAEL.

Bibliography

T. D. Alexander, *From Paradise to the Promised Land: An Introduction to the Main Themes of the Pentateuch* (Carlisle, 1995); R. Banks, *Jesus and the Law in the Synoptic Tradition* (Cambridge, 1975); W. Brueggemann, *The Message of the Psalms* (Minneapolis, 1984); R. E. Clements, *Old Testament Theology: A Fresh Approach* (London, 1978); T. E. Fretheim, *The Pentateuch* (Nashville, 1996); R. K. Harrison, 'Law in the OT', in ISBE 3, pp. 76–85; C. G. Kruse, *Paul, the Law and Justification* (Leicester and Peabody, 1996, 1997); D. Patrick, *Old Testament Law* (Atlanta, 1985); E. P. Sanders, *Paul, the Law, and the Jewish People* (London, 1983); S. Westerholm, *Israel's Law and the Church's Faith: Paul and his Recent Interpreters* (Grand Rapids, 1988).

C. G. KRUSE

LEADERSHIP

Leadership in the Bible is framed within the

overarching context of divine sovereignty. In this context Christ's supremacy is not simply over his *church (Matt. 16:18–19; Eph. 1:22–23; 4:15; 5:23; Col. 1:18; 2:19). Rather, all human government is necessarily derivative of and circumscribed by his sovereign leadership (Eph. 1:20–21; Phil. 2:9–10; Col. 2:10).

In the light of *God's overall headship, not only are the leaders of the *people of God chosen by him (Deut. 17:14–15), but also secular authorities are instituted by him (Dan. 2:37–38; 4:31–32; Rom. 13:1). Furthermore, to promote or demote those in positions of leadership is the prerogative of God alone (Pss. 2; 75:6–7). God neither abdicates his position of supremacy nor completely delegates that authority to human leaders, but desires that the world be governed through human beings in accordance with his will (Gen. 1:28). All leaders are, therefore, ultimately accountable to God (Luke 12:48; Heb. 13:17). On many occasions in the OT, when human leaders resist God's directing, he variously uses his prophets (Hag. 2:20–23), the leaders of foreign nations (2 Chr. 36:15–17; Is. 45:1), and even natural disasters (Exod. 7:4) to instruct them, to *judge them or to impose his sovereign will on them.

Similarly, those who are subject must submit to the human powers whom God has appointed over them (Titus 3:1; 1 Pet. 2:13–14). Consequently, resistance to such authorities is interpreted as resistance to God (Rom. 13:2, 4–5). As a further consequence of God's overall sovereignty, when *obedience to human authorities conflicts with obedience to God, it is God who must be obeyed (Acts 4:19).

In the course of the biblical account numerous examples of human leadership are portrayed – good and bad; religious and political; godly and pagan. From these varied examples, the reader can discern both *principles* and *structures* of biblical leadership.

Principles of leadership

Many of the principles which characterize biblical leadership are timeless. They surface frequently and remain foundational in widely differing contexts in both OT and NT.

In biblical times and during the course of later church history, godly principles of leadership and, by implication, God's overarching leadership, are habitually rejected by his people, and attempts made to adopt 'worldly' models of leadership, sometimes with catastrophic results (Exod. 17:1–7; 1 Sam. 8:7–8; 1 Cor. 2:8). For a number of reasons these attempts repeatedly prove to be flawed. First, those patterns of leadership endorsed in the Bible are different from those widely practised by the surrounding nations (1 Sam. 8:5; Mark 10:42–44; 1 Cor. 1:20). Significantly, much of Jesus' ministry is characterized by conflict with both the religious and the political leaders of his day (*e.g.* Matt. 23; Mark 15:1–15). Secondly, the qualifications for godly leadership are frequently highlighted in the biblical text precisely because they are somewhat unexpected (1 Sam. 16:7). God's selection of Moses, who lacked eloquence (Exod. 3:9 – 4:16), of Gideon, who was hiding out of fear and cowardice (Judg. 6:11–12), of David, who was the youngest of Jesse's sons (1 Sam. 16:11), and of Simon Peter, who lacked education (Luke 5:1–11), exemplifies his choice of individuals who appear to lack the typically accepted credentials for such a role.

There is a recognition in Scripture that godly leadership is a gift which derives from God and, therefore, is not something about which the leader can boast (1 Cor 1:26–31; 3:21; 4:6–7). In OT times, *kings and *priests were anointed before God to perform their task of leadership (Exod. 28:41; 1 Sam. 15:1; 1 Kgs. 1:34). In the NT, leadership is portrayed as a gifting (Rom. 12:8; 1 Cor. 12:28) and, therefore, should not be grounds for boasting (1 Cor. 4:7). On occasions the gift of leadership within the church is recognized by the 'laying on of hands' (Acts 6:5–6; 13:2–3; 1 Tim. 4:14; 5:22).

A consequent characteristic of the godly leader is, therefore, the desire continually to seek and respond to the revealed will of the God who is recognized as sovereign over human affairs (1 Sam. 13:14; Acts 13:22). A number of leaders of the *Israelite nation, including Abraham, Jacob, Moses, Samuel, Gideon, and David, are instructed directly by God (*e.g.* Exod. 19:7), and Solomon is heralded as a leader who is gifted by God with *wisdom by which to rule (1 Kgs. 10:23–24; 2 Chr. 1:11–12). In addition, God employs the canonical *prophets as channels through whom to challenge human leaders (Is. 7:3–9; Dan. 9:6), and Nehemiah's *fear of the Lord influences the way he governs the people of Judah (Neh. 5:15). In the Acts of the Apostles the decisions of the church leaders are guided by God (Acts 13:2–3; 14:23; 16:7–10), and in the epistles this desire to seek the will of God is demonstrated in the leaders' dependence on *prayer and their search for godly, as distinct from human, wisdom (1 Cor. 2:1–7; Jas. 1:5; 3:13, 17). A similar dependence on God's leading is seen in the life of *Jesus (Mark 1:35); indeed John's Gospel particularly highlights the closeness of the relationship between Jesus and his heavenly Father (John 5:17–20; 8:28; 10:18, 38; 12:49–50; 14:10–11).

Spiritual leaders in both the OT and NT were often noted not only for their seeking of God's will, but also for their ability to teach or communicate it. In their message the prophets applied the OT law, and the priests also were called to teach (Lev. 10:11; 2 Chr. 15:3; Ezra 7:10). Jesus is clearly presented as a teacher (Mark 1:22; John 13:13), and it is noteworthy that teaching is a skill highlighted in a list of qualifications commended in the pastoral letters specifically for Timothy, but also more generally for church overseers (1 Tim. 3:2; 2 Tim. 2:24).

The godly leader is also one whose lifestyle provides an example appropriate for others to emulate. Jesus attracts followers, both individuals and large crowds (Matt. 4:18–25; 8:18–23; 9:9; 16:24), and sets an example for his disciples to follow (John 13:15). A number of OT heroes of faith are listed as examples in the NT (Rom. 4:12; Heb. 11:4–40; Jas. 5:10). The NT writers also repeatedly encourage those in their congregations both to imitate good contemporary models of Christian living and set an example themselves, but ultimately they are to lead others to imitate Christ himself (Acts 20:19–35; 1 Cor. 4:16; 11:1; Eph. 5:1; Phil. 3:17; 4:9; 1 Thess. 1:6; 2:14; 2 Thess. 3:7, 9; Heb. 6:12; 13:7; 1 Pet. 2:21; 3 John 1:11). Thus, in correspondence with Timothy, Paul draws attention to his own life and example (2 Tim. 3:10–17) and urges the young church leader likewise to set an example for other believers (1 Tim. 4:12). Consistently with this principle of the leader being an example, in the pastoral letters the qualifications for positions of church leadership are repeatedly framed in terms of moral character (1 Tim. 3:1–13; Titus 1:5–9).

Godly leadership is also characterized in the Bible by humble service (Luke 22:26–27; Acts 20:19) in contrast to self-exaltation (Exod 10:3; Deut. 17:20; 1 Pet. 5:3) and a seeking after personal glory (1 Cor. 4:8–13). This is not only *humility in relation to God (2 Chr. 33:23), but significantly it is also humility before those who are being led (Matt. 21:5; 2 Cor. 12:21). The supreme model of such humility in leadership is found in Jesus (Mark 10:42–45; 2 Cor. 10:1). His leadership was not only costly and self-giving (John 10:15; Eph. 5:25), but also involved a rejection of personal glory (Phil. 2:6–8).

Humility in leadership, however, is not to be confused with weakness. Isaiah can at once portray God as a mighty ruler and a caring shepherd (Is. 40:10–11). Jesus reconciles humility with authority (Matt. 7:29; 9:8), the call to obedience (John 14:15), submission (Mark 1:34; 1 Pet. 5:5), and *anger (John 2:14–17). Paul, as he responds to a critical congregation, directs the Corinthians to the example of Jesus who could reconcile power and weakness (2 Cor. 13:2–4). In following Jesus' example, Paul is himself able to exercise an authority of which the goal is edification (2 Cor. 10:8; 13:10). Thus the godly leader has learnt how human weakness can be tempered by God's strength (1 Cor. 1:27; 9:22; 2 Cor. 12:10). At the heart of resolving this apparent dichotomy between strength and weakness is the way in which authority is exercised (2 Cor. 1:24) and consequently rewarded by obedience and respect (1 Thess. 5:12).

Structures of leadership

In contrast to these abiding principles of biblical leadership, many of the structures of leadership or government which are presented in Scripture differ according to the particular context in question (whether household, tribe, nation, temple or church). Some of the categories change over time as political horizons develop (e.g. prophet, judge, king); some of the categories are transformed in the new covenant (e.g. priest, king); and other categories remain constant (e.g. the familial relationships of husband-wife and parent-child).

From earliest times, leadership of the Israelite nation was patriarchal. A tribal system dominated, with authority vested in the elders of the community (Exod. 3:16; Num. 11:16–17). Elders continued to be influential in local civic leadership throughout OT times (Ezra 10:8, 14). They were supplemented at a national level by a series of judges, appointed by God to deliver the people during times of national crisis (Judg. 2:16). The Israelites, however, sought to be led instead by a monarch (Judg. 9; 1 Sam. 8:5). The concession was reluctantly made, but with the proviso that the king, together with his subjects, should seek to follow God as the ultimate Lord (1 Sam. 12:13–15). The subsequent biblical history of Israel is a catalogue of kings, and later governors, the success of whose reigns is measured by the degree to which they followed the commands of God.

The religious leadership of the nation included a chief priest and a hereditary priesthood comprising the sons of Aaron (Lev. 8), with the tribe of Levi to assist (Num. 1:50). Priests continued to serve in the tabernacle and the later Jerusalem temple into the first century AD. The role of the priest was to mediate between God and his people (Exod. 28:29–30), to offer sacrifices to make *atonement for them (Lev. 16), and to communicate God's laws (Lev. 10:11; Deut. 33:8–10; Jer. 18:18; Mal. 2:1–9). Spiritual guidance was given to the kings often by means of the prophets, as God's spokespersons (1 Kgs. 22:14).

In NT times, we see Jesus gathering to himself a small band of apostles. Filled with the Spirit, they are charged with proclaiming the kingdom as the church grows after the resurrection of Jesus (Acts 1:8). In both Acts and the epistles, numerous titles are used to refer to the tasks of church leaders – apostle, prophet, pastor, teacher, evangelist, deacon, bishop/overseer, elder, servant, steward and guardian. These titles are used to denote function; the focus is on task rather than office or status. NT writers refer to different combinations of offices in different communities, and it seems that certain titles may have been used interchangeably. This is consistent with the view that the ecclesiastical structures of leadership as they emerge in the NT at different times and in different contexts are not intended to be prescriptive.

The context of leadership significantly affects the way in which that leadership is rightly exercised. Whilst being described as a labourer (1 Cor. 15:10; 16:15–16), the godly leader is nonetheless to equip (Eph. 4:11–13),

care for (1 Thess. 2:7, 1 Tim. 3:5), guide (1 Cor. 4:15) and mobilize God's people that they in turn may serve. It should be noted that, whereas commanding or ruling is fundamental to the task of the monarch (1 Kgs. 3:9), the military leader (Matt. 8:9), and the secular leader (Rom. 13:1–7), it has a comparatively small place in the role of the church leader. Consequently, whilst believers are to obey and be subject to their church leaders (1 Cor. 16:16; Heb. 13:17), the NT says little about church leaders demanding or exacting obedience from believers.

From a salvation-historical perspective, there are two structures of OT leadership which are clearly fulfilled in Christ and are not, therefore, characteristic of Christian leadership in the church. These are the roles of the representative priest (Heb. 2:17; 3:1; 4:14; 5:5–6; 6:20; 9:11) and king (Matt. 21:5; 27:37; 1 Tim. 1:17; 6:15; Rev. 17:14). Under the new covenant there is no human mediator between the believer and God (1 Tim. 2:5), and the Christian leader does not, therefore, fulfil such a priestly role for fellow believers in the community. Direct access to God is through Christ as the great high priest (Heb. 4:14–16; 10:11–22). The sins of individuals are atoned for by the 'once for all' sacrifice of Christ himself as priest (Heb. 7:23–28). It should be noted, however, that continuing through OT and NT is the principle of a priesthood of all believers. This is not exclusive, like the levitical priesthood, and in the NT it becomes a royal priesthood (Exod. 19:6; 1 Pet. 2:9; Rev. 1:6). Also under the new covenant, the Davidic line of kingship is fulfilled in Christ himself, whose kingdom shall never end (Is. 9:6–7; 2 Pet. 1:11; Rev. 11:15).

Two metaphors frequently used of leaders in both Testaments and embodied in Christ do have a prescriptive value for all Christian ministry. The first is the metaphor of a servant or slave (Luke 22:26). Samuel is instructed to use the term of himself (1 Sam. 3:9–10). Jesus is depicted as a servant in some of the messianic songs of Isaiah (Is. 42; 49; 50; 53), and he came to earth in order to serve (Mark 10:45). Jesus' servanthood is dramatically seen in his act of washing the feet of his disciples (John 13:1–15), and is eloquently expressed in Paul's hymn of Christ (Phil. 2:6–11). One of Paul's favoured self-descriptions is that of the slave (Rom. 1:1).

The primary direction of this relationship, in both Testaments, is towards God, but the relationship is expressed also in terms of the leader serving those who are led.

The second metaphor is that of a shepherd. A number of shepherds were chosen to be significant leaders of God's people, namely Joseph (Gen. 37:2; 47:1–4), Moses (Exod. 3:1) and David (1 Sam. 16:11; 17:15; Ps. 78:70–72). God himself is repeatedly described as a shepherd over his people (Gen. 49:24; Pss. 23:1; 28:9; 80:1; Is. 40:10–11; Ezek. 34; Mic. 2:12; Matt. 25:32–33), and Jesus is the chief shepherd of the sheep (John 10:1–18; Heb. 13:20; 1 Pet. 2:25; 5:4; Rev. 7:17; *cf.* also Matt. 15:24). Bad shepherds are rebuked for their lack of care for their flock (Zech. 11:4–17), and both Jeremiah and Ezekiel are used by God to chastise those who have been bad shepherds over his people. God himself will gather the flock back into the fold and will appoint new shepherds who will care for it (Jer. 23:1–4; Ezek. 34:23–24). He calls leaders to be shepherds (2 Sam. 5:2; 7:7), and the role of the godly leader is to watch over, care for, feed, and protect the sheep (Jer. 3:15; John 21:15–17; Acts 20:28; 1 Pet. 5:1–3).

The place of women (see *Man and woman) in leadership is a contentious issue. In the predominantly patriarchal cultures of OT and NT times, women lead only occasionally (Judg. 4:4; Rom. 16:1). Many scholars consider that the relatively small number of women in positions of leadership reflects an abiding biblical principle which derives from the creation ordinance (1 Cor. 11:3–10; 1 Tim. 2:11–14) and is also expressed in the patriarchal priesthood and the maleness of the incarnate Christ. Other scholars class leadership by women as one of the transient structures of biblical leadership, and believe that in different cultural contexts women may rightly be seen more frequently in positions of leadership.

Bibliography

D. W. Bennett, *Metaphors of Ministry: Biblical Images for Leaders and Followers* (Carlisle, 1993); A. D. Clarke, *Serve the Community of the Church: Christians as Leaders and Ministers* (Grand Rapids, 2000); *idem, Called to Serve: A Pauline Theology of Church Leadership* (Leicester and Downers Grove, forthcoming); L. O. Richards and C. Hoeldtke, *A Theology of Church Leadership* (Grand Rapids, 1982); D. A. Steele, *Images of Leadership and Authority for the Church* (Lanham, 1986).

A. D. CLARKE

LEGALISM, see LAW
LEVIATHAN, see SPIRITUAL POWERS
LEVITICUS, see Part 2

LIFE

In the Mediterranean world during the time when the Bible was composed, where people were not insulated from death as they are in modern Western culture, fear and curiosity gave rise to numerous stories explaining life and the afterlife. The Bible offers its own story of life. The degree to which the Bible interacts with or argues against other stories is not easily demonstrable, so this article seeks to synthesize the biblical stories without examining their polemical nature (on various Near Eastern, Jewish and Greek views in antiquity see K. Corrigan, in *Classical Mediterranean Spirituality*, pp. 360–383; R. N. Longenecker, *Life in the Face of Death*, pp. 21–95; G. Riley, *Resurrection Reconsidered*, pp. 7–68; E. P. Sanders, *Judaism: Practice and Belief*, pp. 279–303). Numerous Hebrew, Aramaic, and Greek synonyms in the Bible connote life (*e.g.* words for flesh, body, breath, soul, *blood; see A. R. Johnson, *Vitality*, and the standard theological dictionaries), as do several metaphors (*e.g.* bread, *water, tree). The purpose of this article is not to define these synonyms and metaphors, but to describe the biblical story of life as one part of a theology of the whole Bible. The headings below point to the broad and remarkable coherence of the biblical plotline concerning life, but they do not deny that different and often apparently contradictory views are to be found in the canon. Deviations from the main plot offer correctives to an oversimplified presentation of this important theological story. The article traces the theme through the various corpora of biblical literature, but does not assume a chronologically linear development of the story; intertextual connections are clearly shown.

God creates life

Without defining life, the Bible everywhere assumes that all life comes from *God. He alone is the living God (1 Sam. 17:26; Is. 40:18–26; Acts 14:15) who has life in himself, as opposed to idols that have no life (Is. 41:21–24; Jer. 10:1–16; 1 Tim 6:16). He alone is the uncreated Life who speaks life into existence (Gen. 1:1, 24; Rev. 4:8–11). God gives life and takes it away (Gen. 6:3, 7; Deut. 32:39; 1 Sam. 2:6; 25:38; Ps. 104:27–30; Hos. 1:10); hence, life is sacred (Exod. 20:13). God opens the womb and shuts it (Gen. 29:31; 30:2, 17, 22; Judg. 13:3; 1 Sam. 1:19; Luke 1:13). Genesis 1 – 2 describes the beginning of life on earth, and the rest of the Bible assumes and in places alludes to these stories of *creation and procreation (e.g. Job 10:8–12; 34:14–15; Eccles. 12:7; 1 Pet. 1:23–24).

God defines life by his *word. Moses, pointing to the Torah, says, 'This is not an idle word for you, it is your life' (Deut. 32:47, author's translation; cf. Is. 55:11; Rom. 7:10). Human life is frail and finite, but God's word stands for ever (Is. 40:6–8). This is why humans must not seek life apart from God (Jer. 2:13; 17:13). Humans cannot live on bread alone; their life is dependent on what proceeds from the mouth of God (Deut 8:3); 'in him we live and move and exist' (Acts 17:28).

*Human life is the same as animal life (characterized by nepeš or psyche, often translated 'soul', but probably best rendered as 'life' or 'self'; Gen. 1:20, 24; Rev. 16:3). Humans have the breath or spirit of life dwelling in them (Gen. 2:7), as do animals (Gen. 7:22). It is this breath of life which separates animals from plants, for when it is gone the animal is dead (2 Sam. 1:9; 1 Kings 17:21–22). Blood is the sign of life in both animals and humans (Gen. 4:10; 9:4–6), and the pouring out of blood signals loss of life (Lev. 17:11, 14).

Human life is also differentiated from animal life (Gen. 7:21), especially in terms of its function. Humans are to rule over and care for other forms of life, i.e. fish, domesticated animals, wild animals, creeping things, and birds (Gen. 1:28; 6:19–20; 8:17, 19; 9:2; Ps. 8:6–8). But Genesis 2:7, where God breathes into humans the breath of life (a sign of great intimacy; the same is not said of animals, cf.

Gen. 2:19), and Genesis 3:20, where Eve (a form of the Hebrew word for 'life') is given her name because she is the mother of all life (certainly human life), may indicate an onto-logical distinction as well.

Life is often pictured in terms of its length and quality. The best life is one that is long, prosperous, and lived before God in *peace (šalôm) in the *land of promise (Gen. 47:9; Deut. 30:20; Pss. 23:6; 91:16). Hence the *exile is pictured as death (Is. 5:13–14). The best life is that lived in the community of the *people of God. Hence premature death and being cut off from God's people are nearly the same (Exod. 12:15; Lev. 7:20; Ezek. 14:8). Life is preserved through progeny (as seen in the laws of levirate marriage; Deut. 25:5–10; Ruth 4:5), but not only through progeny.

The best life is received by following God's word (Josh. 1:8; 1 Kings 3:14; Pss. 1:3; 119:144; Is. 1:19–20), which is sometimes symbolized as a tree. In the Garden of Eden the tree of life symbolizes the source of the life that comes from God (Gen. 2:9). Its fruit is not magical; no long quest is required to find it; it is simply available (H. Blocher, In the Beginning, pp. 122–125). In a passage reminiscent of the Garden, God sets before *Israel life and death and admonishes them to choose life (Deut. 30:19; cf. Jer. 21:8). So life is not inherent in humanity and it is not something earned; it is received through 'eating' the fruit of God's tree, which the first man and woman probably did. Humans are not naturally immortal; all life comes from God. Later in the Bible a tree and a fountain symbolize *wisdom or God's word as the source of life (Prov. 3:18; 11:30; 13:14; 15:4; Ps. 36:9); 'eating' the fruit or 'drinking' the water gives life.

The best life is a prominent theme in Proverbs. Wisdom defines and leads to the ethical character that is true life (Prov. 1:33; 2:1–22; 8:35; 10:17; passim). Significantly, most proverbs are community oriented. The wise life consists in more than possessions; it involves a good and pious reputation (Prov. 8:18–21). Wisdom preserves the best life, life as designed by God. But wisdom does not work mechanistically, leading to life by an automatic process. Job and Ecclesiastes show that the universe is not a machine. *Suffering raises questions about the fairness of life (Job 7:11–21; 10:18–22), and can even cause one to wish for a shortened life (Job 3:20–22). At times death seems better than life (Eccles. 4:1–3). Life is a mere vapour (Eccles. 2:17) and a prisoner of time (Eccles. 3:1–11). A meaningful life, based on wisdom, is one lived in *obedience to the personal Creator God, not by mechanical processes (Job 28:28; Eccles. 12:13–14).

Life flows towards death because of sin

In the Bible life and death are often portrayed as the opposite ends of a continuum or as enemies continually struggling against one another. A living person moves towards one end or another, or gains or loses quality of life. Sickness or *poverty are pictured as a movement towards death or as death winning the struggle with life (Pss. 18:5; 33:19; Prov. 9:18). *Healing is *salvation or restoration to life. Premature death is a victory of the enemies of God. But death at the end of a long and righteous life can also be considered as merely the end of that life; it is to be asleep with those who have died before (see below). The Bible is notably reticent in recording funeral lamentations for leaders, although it does lament the death of the nation (Lamentations). Thus individual death is not an enemy to be feared or even necessarily avoided, but one that must inevitably be faced (Pss. 89:48; 90:10) and can even be mocked (Eccles. 12:1–8).

Life is threatened in the Garden when God tells Adam that, should he eat from the tree of the knowledge of good and evil, he will certainly die (Gen. 2:9, 17). When Adam and Eve sin by eating the fruit of the forbidden tree they are banished from the source of life (Gen. 3:22–24). Death is rampant in Genesis 4 – 11. Cain kills Abel; Lamech kills a man. In spite of their longevity, the life of Adam and his descendants (except Enoch) ends in death (Genesis 5). Humankind is wicked, and all except *Noah and his immediate family are wiped out in the flood (Genesis 6 – 9). The righteous Noah is appointed to keep living creatures in the ark during the flood, and afterwards to release them again onto the dry ground (Gen. 6:19–20; 8:17–19). After the flood God changes the order of life for everything that lives. For Noah and his descendants, the flesh of animals is now available for food, but the blood must be thoroughly drained from the animal before it is eaten (9:1–5). This is because life is in the blood. When an animal loses its blood it dies, because its blood gives it life. But blood when it is poured out, because it contains life, can also make atonement (pay a ransom) for another life. This is not merely because of the cost of life; one life is actually substituted for another. So, out of respect for life and because life is given in exchange for life, humans are not to eat flesh with its blood still in it (Lev. 17:10–14; Deut. 12:23). It is because of its connection with life that blood is sprinkled on the altar to consecrate it. (Exod. 29:12; Lev. 1:5; Ezek. 43:18). This connection is further developed in the NT (cf. Heb. 9:22; John 6:54; Luke 22:19–20).

In the new order after the flood, God gives the human community the responsibility of avenging human life poured out by murder (Gen. 9:6–7). In spite of this new order and the cleansing of the earth, even Noah dies (9:29). The genealogy of Shem (11:10–32) is different from that of Adam in that before the story of Terah, Abraham's father (11:28, 32) it does not mention the death of any person. The implication is that even in this genealogy that contains the promise of life, death reigns. All the patriarchs of Israel die, but their being buried in the land (Gen. 23:1–20; 25:10; 49:29; 50:25; Josh. 24:32; cf. 1 Sam. 26:20) implies hope. In the biblical story, burial outside the land separates one from life in the community. Even Moses dies, although the Lord buries him (Deut. 34:5–6). A future life may be intimated in the saying that at death someone is gathered to his people or sleeps with his fathers (Gen. 35:29; 49:29–33; Judg. 2:10; 1 Kings 1:21; 2:10). Again the communal aspects of life and death are evident. Jesus argues from Exodus 3:6 that the God of the patriarchs is the God of the living (Mark 12:18–27 par.).

Life is a gift from God

In the midst of the reign of death stand the promises of life (Ps. 22; Is. 53:7–12). Although humans were banished from the source of life (Gen. 3:24), God has not abandoned them to death (Ps. 16:10). In keeping with his covenant love he promises the gift of life (Is. 44:21). This life is a good life with God's people in the land of promise (Deut. 30:1–20) and in fellowship with the Creator (Job 42:5; John 17:3). In the same way, although Israel sinned and God cut them off from life in the land, he promised to bring them back (Is. 40:1–5), to give them life

(Ezek. 37:1–14). He alone will give life to the parched and barren land (Is. 35:1–10; 41:17–20). As water gives life to the desert, so God's Spirit (see *Holy Spirit) gives life to his people (Is. 44:3–4; John 7:37–39). This life comes through mediators like Noah (Gen. 6:19–23) and *Joseph (Gen. 45:5) who preserve life in the face of death. It also comes through *sacrifice; one life is given for another, an exchange symbolized in the laying on of a hand (Lev. 1:4, *passim*). But ultimately life comes as a gift through the Messiah, the possessor of the Spirit, the pioneer of life, who restores God's people to life (Is. 9:1–7; 11:9–11; 61:1–9; John 6:68; Acts 3:15; Rom. 6:23; 2 Tim. 1:10). He holds the keys of death and Hades (Rev. 1:18) because he was dead but now lives (Rev. 1:5, 17–18). This restoration to life is salvation (Is. 12:1–3). It is communal as well as individual (Ezek. 37:1–14; Dan. 12:2). Ultimately it is a return to the Garden where life began (Is. 65:17–25; Rev. 21:22 – 22:5). The tree of life is found in the new Jerusalem and supplies healing for the nations (Rev. 22:2). (See *Eschatology.)

Thus redeemed human life is pictured as having present and future (eternal) aspects (as distinct from material and non-material aspects). In the present, life is subject to pain, sorrow, *sin, disease and decay, which cause believers to groan as they wait for the future life (Rom. 8:18–23). In the future, life will include none of these ills. There will be no more death or pain or tears (Is. 25:6–9; 1 Cor. 15:54; Rev 21:4). The promised life is one of *worship lived beyond death (Pss. 16:11; 22:29; 49:15; 73:23–28; Is. 26:19; Rev. 20:4, 6, 15; *cf.* W. Eichrodt, *Theology of the Old Testament*, 'The common factor linking all these witnesses to the conquest of death in the life of the individual is that their certainty is built on the gift of fellowship with God here and now', p. 525), and it will last for ever, *i.e.* it is immortal (Luke 20:36).

The message of the NT is that the future aspects of life have begun to appear even while the present aspects still exist. Although the resurrection life is still future (John 5:28–29), whoever believes in the one who sent the Saviour has eternal life in the present because life is in him (John 1:4; 5:24–26; 11:25–26; 2 Cor. 5:17; *cf.* D. H. Johnson, in *DJG*). Life is more than a promise; it has become a reality because *Jesus has been resurrected (John 14:19). For those who trust in Christ,

the life now lived 'in the flesh' (in the old age) is not the old life under the *law, but the new life in Christ; it is Christ's life (Gal. 2:19–20). Although dead in trespasses and sins, they have been raised and seated with Christ (Eph. 2:5–6). God is now in the process of making all things new (Rev. 21:5). The fountain of the water of life is now open (Rev. 21:6). Jesus came to give abundant life in the present (John 10:10). He has restored God's people to the place of *blessing, which is not a geographical location, but a relationship with God and with each other, like that in the Garden before human disobedience caused humankind to be cut off from God, the source of life. Whether this life will be lived in a new (Is. 65:17; 2 Pet. 3:10–13; Rev. 21:1) or renewed (Matt. 19:28; Acts 3:21; Rom. 8:18–25) earth is unclear. Perhaps the two notions are complementary (M. Harris, *Raised Immortal: Resurrection and Immortality in the New Testament*, p. 170).

The NT teaching about life is concerned primarily with eternal life. The phrase 'eternal life' does not denote a never-ending life so much as the 'life of the age to come' (D. Hill, *Greek Words and Hebrew Meanings*, pp. 163–201). Since the first coming of Christ this life has been present, but it is also still to come (Col. 3:3–4). The testimony of the NT is that the future has invaded the present in the coming of the Messiah (Luke 17:21). All people in the old age are dead in their sins (Eph. 2:1–3; 1 John 3:14); thus eternal life is a gift of God's *grace (John 3:16; Eph. 2:8–9). It has three basic characteristics.

First, eternal life is given and sustained by the Spirit of life (Rom. 8:2). It is life in Christ and Christ's life in the believer (John 15:5; Gal. 2:20; Eph. 1:13–14). As God created life in the Garden of Eden, so he is the source of restored or reborn life (John 4:14; Titus 3:5). The Spirit is the down payment or firstfruits guaranteeing the future inheritance (Rom. 8:23; 2 Cor. 5:5). God gives life to the believer in the present and will continue to sustain life in the age to come (Rom. 8:10–14; 2 Cor. 3:6).

Secondly, eternal life lasts for ever; it is immortal life free from decay. In one sense believers receive immortality at their resurrection (1 Cor. 15:52; *cf.* Harris, *Raised Immortal*, pp. 196–197). But in another sense, eternal (and thus immortal) life begins as people eat the bread of life (believe in

Jesus; John 6:48–51) and so participate in the divine nature (2 Pet. 1:4). (Although unbelievers may suffer eternal conscious punishment, this is not called 'immortality'.) Death is only a temporary foe, confined to this life. Through his own death Jesus destroyed the devil (see *Spiritual powers) who held the power of death (Heb. 2:14). His life-giving work lasts for ever because he is a priest in keeping with the power of an indestructible life (Heb. 7:16, 21–25). That is, his resurrection guarantees the hope of eternal life (1 Pet. 1:3). In the end death shall be swallowed up by life for those who have followed the Spirit (1 Cor. 15:54; Gal. 6:8). The mode of the immortal life is different from that of the present life (1 John 3:2). It is lived in a body, but a different kind of body (1 Cor. 15:35–49; 2 Cor. 5:1–4; Phil. 3:20–21).

Thirdly, eternal life is lived in community with the people of God both now and in the future. Eternal life is not lived in isolation. Just as believers have come to belong to the *church of the firstborn (Heb. 12:22–24), so all believers will be raised and share with Christ in the new heavens and the new earth (1 Thess. 4:13–18; Rev. 20:6; 21:3). There are no passages in Revelation dealing with the future life in which believers are described as being alone (Rev. 6:9–11; 7:9–17; 14:1–3; 15:2). In the Garden of Eden it was not good for Adam to be alone, so God made a companion for him (Gen. 2:18–25). The ideal life is lived in a community.

See also: DEATH AND RESURRECTION; HEAVEN AND HELL.

Bibliography

H. Blocher, *In the Beginning* (Leicester and Downers Grove, 1984); K. Corrigan, 'Body and soul in ancient religious experience', in A. H. Armstrong (ed.), *Classical Mediterranean Spirituality: Egyptian, Greek, Roman* (New York and London, 1989); W. Eichrodt, *Theology of the Old Testament*, vol. 2 (ET, Philadelphia and London, 1967); M. J. Harris, *Raised Immortal: Resurrection and Immortality in the New Testament* (Grand Rapids, 1983); D. Hill, *Greek Words and Hebrew Meanings: Studies in the Semantics of Soteriological Terms* (Cambridge, 1967); W. Janzen, *Old Testament Ethics: A Paradigmatic Approach* (Louisville, 1994); A. R. Johnson, *The Vitality of the Individual in the Thought of Ancient Israel* (Cardiff, 1964); D. H. Johnson, in *DJG*, pp. 469–471; R. N. Longenecker (ed.), *Life in the Face of Death: The Resurrection Message of the New Testament* (Grand Rapids, 1998); G. Riley, *Resurrection Reconsidered: Thomas and John in Controversy* (Minneapolis, 1995); E. P. Sanders, *Judaism: Practice and Belief: 63 BCE – 66 CE* (Philadelphia and London, 1992).

D. H. JOHNSON

LIGHT

Light is a universal phenomenon of the physical world. It generally signals the presence of illuminating sources such as lamps, torches, the sun and radiating light bulbs powered by steam, water or atomic energy.

The Bible, however, provides some fascinating insights into the origin and nature of light. Unlike in scientific analyses, in the phenomenological description of *creation in Genesis 1 light is called forth by *God (Gen. 1:3–4) prior to the establishment of the luminaries (1:14–18). Thus, for the inspired writers, light is tied inseparably to the powerful presence and activity of God as the ultimate source of the first creation. Moreover, at a time when the sun, moon and stars were worshipped as deities, the Bible rejects such worship and represents light and the luminaries as part of creation.

The themes of light and its opposite, darkness, have been used in many cultures and by people groups throughout history to describe the two basic contrary philosophical and theological principles of reality. For instance, in Mesopotamian Zoroastrianism and its Gnostic successor Manicheanism, there were two gods: Ahurimazda, the good god of light, and Ahriman, the *evil god of darkness. These two were locked in a constantly repetitive wrestling match, paralleling the seemingly endless cycle of night and day. The devotees of these religions hoped that when death came the god of light would take them to his resplendent realm.

While the Bible does not teach a metaphysical dualism of two eternal deities, the writers certainly employ the themes of light and darkness. The Psalms and the wisdom literature of the OT contain many references to these themes. In reflecting on his *life in God, the psalmist rejoices that God is his light and his *salvation (Ps. 27:1), that the encompassing darkness of night is not to be feared because light and darkness were both under God's control (139:11–12), and that God is his fountain of life in whose light we see light (36:9). Therefore he begs God to support his cause by sending out divine light and *truth to lead him (43:3).

In contrast the author of Job struggles to find meaning in the midst of *suffering, when light and darkness seem to be confused and when the light of hope appears to be gone (Job 3:3–9; 30:26). While his companions use the imagery of light to propose easy answers to Job's pain (e.g. in 22:28), Job himself wrestles honestly with the question of how God can bring light out of darkness (12:22–25; 28:11). Elihu, on behalf of God, reminds him that the awesome God is able to restore him even from Sheol in order that he may see the light of life (33:29–30). Finally, God reminds Job that the answers to his questions are hidden in the very mystery of creation, when God called forth the world out of the depths of darkness into the light of day (38:4–12).

These themes of light and darkness are further developed by the NT writers to distinguish people and activities aligned with God from those opposed to God and aligned with Satan and the demonic (see *Spiritual powers).

John describes God's gracious act of creation as light shining into darkness, and darkness as unable to resist or counter such divine activity (John 1:5; cf. the first creative act of God in calling forth light to banish confusion, Gen. 1:3). Evil people are described as loving darkness rather than light (John 3:19). Indeed, those who lie and hate are said to walk in darkness and are like blind people (1 John 1:6; 2:9–11; cf. John 12:40; Is. 6:9–10). But since God is equated with unapproachable light (1 Tim. 6:16) in whom there is no darkness (1 John 1:5), those who have confessed their *sins and been made clean by the blood of Jesus are said to walk in the light (1 John 1:7, 9; John 8:12).

The coming of *Jesus is viewed by Matthew (4:16) and Luke (2:32) as the fulfilment of God's covenant with Israel through which not only Israel would be enlightened but also the Gentiles (cf. Is. 42:7). The opposition to and rejection of the messianic Jesus is interpreted by the NT writers using the imagery of darkness (cf. Eph. 6:12; Jude 13), whilst John describes the betrayal by Judas and his capitulation to Satan with the vivid statement that 'it was night!' (13:30).

Since Jesus is the light of the world (John 8:12; 9:5), his disciples have the light of life (8:12) in them (11:10). Not only are they to believe in the light (John 12:35) but all who come after them are to be sons or children of the light (Eph. 5:8; 1 Thess. 5:5; cf. John 12:36). Moreover, not only Jesus is called the light of the world, but also those who follow him (Matt. 5:14). They are to let their light shine among others (Matt. 5:16; Phil. 2:15) and by *loving are to live in the light (1 John 2:10). Paul admonishes Christians to throw off the works of darkness and put on the armour of light (Rom. 13:12). Peter states that in the struggle against evil believers are God's special people who have been called 'out of darkness into his wonderful light' (1 Pet. 2:9).

In the universal battle of good against evil, or of God against Satan, Paul warns, the enemy of God can disguise himself as an 'angel of light' (2 Cor. 11:14). Such a disguise is aimed both at blinding unbelievers so that they cannot recognize the light of the gospel (2 Cor. 4:4; 1 John 2:11) and at confusing the people of the world so that the light in them is great darkness (Matt. 6:23; Luke 11:35). Accordingly, Paul makes it clear that the substituting of innumerable idols for the immortal God and the consequent turning to all types of sinful and confused activity results from the darkening of the human heart or will (Rom 1:21). He reminds the Corinthians that there should be no fellowship between light and darkness (2 Cor. 6:14).

The result of people's following sinful ways and walking in darkness rather than light (John 3:19–21) is that the judgment of God will be visited upon them (Rom 1:18–20). Such condemnation is described in terms of being cast into outer darkness where there is great weeping (Matt. 8:12; 22:13; 25:30). It also means being part of the kingdom of the beast that will be condemned to darkness (Rev. 16:10) and ultimately to death in the lake of fire (21:14–15), a vivid contrast to the light of the fiery pillar which led the people in the wilderness and represented the saving presence of God (Exod. 13:21–22).

In contrast, the hope of heaven is described in terms of light. There is no need for luminaries such as sun and moon, because God is there and 'God is light' (Rev. 21:23). The heavenly Jerusalem is like a brilliant jewel radiating the light of the *glory of God (Rev. 21:11). The ultimate hope of the Christian is of life in the light of God.

Bibliography

E. Achtemeier, 'Jesus Christ, the light of the world: the biblical understanding of light and darkness', *Int* 17, 1963, pp. 439–449; G. Borchert in *DPL*, pp. 555–557; H. Conzelman in *TDNT* 9, pp. 310–358; S. Hunt in *DLNTD*, pp. 657–659; L. Morris in *ISBE* 3, pp. 134–136.

G. L. BORCHERT

LORD'S SUPPER, see SACRED MEALS

LOVE

'God is love', John writes (1 John 4:8), a statement the Bible makes about no other being. The truth of the statement is one of the glories of the Bible's picture of *God. It rules out impersonal pantheism; it denies the cogency of the deist vision, in which God is no more than powerful and distant. The God of the Bible is a person, and love, like *holiness, is so much bound up with who he is as a person that John can make this stupendous claim. Many have pointed out, rightly, that the statement cannot be reversed: 'Love is God' would depersonalize God as effectively as deism, for it would elevate 'love', an impersonal affection or impersonal willed sacrifice, to divine status. The reality is far more stunning: God is not only sovereign; he is a person, in whom love is so much constitutive of his being that he can no more abandon love than he can turn away from holiness.

For complex reasons, many in the Western world, both Christians and unbelievers, have drifted towards understandings of the love of God that are demonstrably sub-biblical, sometimes patently anti-biblical. To isolate three of these, and sketch something of a biblical response to each, will set us on a path towards a renewed understanding of some of the varied ways in which the Bible speaks of the love of God.

Some common misperceptions of the love of God

Word-based reductionism

Doubtless the most famous form of this error received its classic exposition by A. Nygren. He analysed love with reference to three Greek words: *erōs*, denoting acquisitive affection, often connected with sexual love; *philia* (and the cognate verb *phileō*, 'to love'), having to do with reciprocal friendship, including all the emotional life that sustains such friendship; and *agape* (and its cognate verb *agapaō*, 'to love'), denoting a self-sacrificing commitment to another's good. In some expositions, *agape* has no necessary emotional component. Precisely because it is primarily an act of will, such love can be demanded of people; when we are commanded to love, we are obliged to seek their good, even if we frankly dislike them.

This analysis is deeply flawed. R. Joly has shown that the relatively late flowering of *agapaō/agape* (and hence its spurt to dominance in the LXX and the NT) has to do with developments within the language itself. More importantly, even within these books the distribution of this word group vitiates Nygren's thesis. When Amnon incestuously rapes his half-sister Tamar (2 Sam. 13, LXX), twice we are told that he 'loved' her, once with *agapaō* and once with *phileō*. It is hard to see how this love differs from *erōs*, acquisitive and sexual love (though the word *erōs* is never found in the Bible). Twice John tells us that the Father 'loves' the Son, once using *agapaō* (John 3:35), once using *phileō* (John 5:20), and it is difficult to detect any difference in meaning. When Paul tells Timothy that Demas has forsaken him because he 'loved' this present, evil world (2 Tim. 4:10), the verb is *agapaō*; this love is scarcely a willed commitment to the good of the other. Most striking, perhaps, is the so-called love chapter, 1 Corinthians 13. There Paul tells his readers that if he were to give away all he possesses to the poor, and even submit his body to the torture of the flames (both willed acts for the good of others), it would be possible to do so without love (*agape*). This surely demonstrates that the love he has in mind is more sweeping than mere altruism, than mere commitment to the good of the other, however self-denying. Such considerations are easily multiplied.

In other words, although there are, as we shall see, unique and wonderful elements to the love of God, they cannot be univocally tied to one particular word-group.

The view that God becomes more loving as one moves from the OT to the NT

This second claim is no more valid than the first. Its superficial defensibility rests on the large number of OT chapters that pronounce *judgment, both on the covenant people and on their neighbours, primarily using the categories of war, famine and pestilence. By contrast, it is argued, Jesus tells us to turn the other cheek and to love our enemies. Moreover, some Christian theology has interpreted OT law primarily or exclusively in terms of strict accounting and unbending justice ('an eye for an eye'), and the new covenant in terms of grace and forgiveness.

This sort of contrast is achieved only by a highly selective reading of the evidence. It may be that we are impressed by the OT's pictures of temporal judgment because by and large we are a generation that focuses on the concerns of this world. But the NT is far more colourful in its descriptions of final judgment than is the OT, and many of the most colourful metaphors of hell are found on the lips of Jesus. To reflect on, say, Revelation 14 is to reject for ever the notion that God is somehow sterner under the old covenant than under the new, or that the God of the NT is a kinder, *gentler God. Moreover, even the inauguration of the old covenant is bound up with the revelatory declaration that Yahweh is 'the compassionate and gracious God, slow to anger, abounding in love and faithfulness, maintaining love to thousands, and forgiving wickedness, rebellion and sin' (Exod. 34:6–7, NIV). Indeed, the two words rendered 'love and *faithfulness' (ḥeseḏ and *meṯ) recur repeatedly in the pages of the OT; it appears that John renders them '*grace and *truth' (John 1:14–18, certainly within their semantic range).

But this does not mean that there is no development at all along the axis of redemptive history. Far from moving from an *angry God to a loving God, however, the framework is more sweeping. Just as the love of God becomes clearer as one moves from the history, literature and types of the OT to the revelation of the NT that culminates in Jesus and his cross and in the kingdom he brings, so the wrath of God becomes clearer as one moves from the history, literature and types of the OT to the revelation of the NT that culminates in Jesus and his cross and in the final sanctions that await all who reject the gospel.

The thesis that God hates sin but loves sinners

There is a small element of truth in this thesis. God always *hates sin; he is invariably and implacably opposed to it. And it is true that God loves sinners: God 'demonstrates his own love for us in this: While we were still sinners, Christ died for us' (Rom. 5:8; cf. John 3:16). Nevertheless the thesis, with its simplistic antithesis between the personal sinner and sin in the abstract, is mistaken. The same apostle who declares that God's wrath is revealed from heaven against 'all the godlessness and wickedness of men' (Rom. 1:18) also speaks of God's wrath against individuals (2:5); indeed we are all 'by nature children of wrath' (NRSV). The first fifty Psalms repeatedly describe the kinds of people on whom God's wrath rests, not just the kinds of sin. Indeed, the language can move from God's wrath to God's hate and abhorrence: 'The arrogant cannot stand in your presence; you hate all who do wrong. You destroy those who tell lies; bloodthirsty and deceitful men the Lord abhors' (Ps. 5:5–6, NIV).

None of this means that God's wrath is arbitrary or whimsical. In Scripture, God's wrath, however affective, is the willed and *righteous response of his holiness to sin. God's holiness, like God's love, is intrinsic to the very being of God; his wrath is not. To put the point another way: God has always been holy, as he has always been love; he has not always been wrathful. But where his holiness confronts the rebellion of his creatures, he must be wrathful (and the entire sweep of the Bible's storyline insists he is), or his holiness is anaemic. Yet for all that he is no less the God of love.

Some ways in which the Bible speaks of the love of God

The expressions 'love' and 'to love' have a wide range of uses when human beings are the subject: he loves his work; they fall in love; she loves her husband; they make love; he loves woodwork and milkshakes. Similarly, precisely because God is a person who enters into a variety of relationships, the Bible speaks of God's love in several distinguishable ways. To name but five:

Intra-Trinitarian Love

Twice John's Gospel speaks of the love of the Father for the Son (3:35; 5:20); elsewhere it speaks of the love of the Son for the Father (14:30–31). Clearly this is not the love of redemption. The Father's love for the Son is manifest in his determination to 'show' him everything he does, and to ensure that all honour the Son even as they honour the Father (5:16–30); the love of the Son for the Father is displayed in the perfection of his obedience (14:30–31; *cf.* 8:29). Thus in John's Gospel there is a profound sense in which the intra-Trinitarian love of God is not only temporally and logically prior to his love for his creatures, but is constitutive of the nature of God. Moreover, the cross-work of Jesus is first of all motivated by this intra-Trinitarian love of God, for the cross comes about, in John's theology, precisely because the Father determines that all will honour the Son, and because the Son obeys so perfectly that he accomplishes his Father's commission and goes to the cross. Ultimately this intra-Trinitarian love becomes the critical model of Christian unity under the lordship of Jesus (15:9–16; 17).

God's providential love

When he made everything, God declared that it was 'very good' (Gen. 1:31). It was, after all, the product of his own hand, of his very character, not least of his love. Even now, with his image-bearers in full-fledged rebellion against him, he rules with *providential care; he 'causes his sun to rise on the evil and the good, and sends rain on the righteous and the unrighteous' (Matt. 5:45). Thus he provides a model for Jesus' followers' love for their enemies (Matt. 5:44); God's providential rule is assumed to be a reflection of his love.

God's yearning, salvific love

God is the one who cries, 'Why will you die, O house of Israel? For I take no pleasure in the death of anyone' (Ezek. 18:31–32). God loved 'the world' (John 3:16), an expression which in John most commonly refers to the entire moral order of men and women in rebellion against their Creator. His most astounding display of love, the sacrifice of his Son, was in its potential sufficient 'for the sins of the whole world' (1 John 2:2).

God's elective love

'I have loved Jacob, but Esau I have hated' (Mal. 1:2–3), God declares. Referring to these words, the apostle Paul points out that they were uttered before either of the brothers was born, precisely so that 'God's purpose in election might stand' (Rom. 9:11–13). The Lord did not choose Israel because they were choice; rather, he set his affection on them because he loved them (Deut. 7:7–10). In other words, he loved them because he loved them: one cannot probe further back than that. Paul well understands the intervening, sovereign grace that reached into his own life (*e.g.* Gal. 1:15–16). The result is that he can scarcely make mention of Jesus and the cross without a personal confession of delight; *e.g.* he mentions the Son of God, and adds, 'who loved me and gave himself for me' (Gal. 2:20).

God's conditional, covenantal love

'Keep yourselves in God's love', Jude exhorts his readers (v. 21), clearly implying that it is possible for Christians *not* to keep themselves in the love of God. According to John, on the night that he was betrayed Jesus exhorted his followers to remain in his love, adding, 'If you obey my commands, you will remain in my love, just as I have obeyed my Father's commands and remain in his love' (John 15:10). Such texts do not tell us how people become Christians; rather, assuming that followers of Jesus are in view, they tell us that Christians remain in the love of God and of Jesus by obedience, in precisely the same way that children remain in their parents' love by obedience. Of course, in another field of discourse one might legitimately speak of the same parents' love as unconditional. Nevertheless, the child who explicitly disobeys his or her parents may well experience unpleasant sanctions, as opposed to remaining in the parents' love; that is one of several ways of speaking of familial love. The same emphasis is often found among the old covenant people of God. For instance, in the Decalogue the Lord declares he is a God who shows 'love to a thousand generations of those who love me and keep my commandments' (Exod. 20:6).

Three important implications

Numerous theological and personal inferences might legitimately be drawn from the evidence so far adduced. Here three points will suffice, all of cardinal importance.

The *first* is that if any one of the five ways just articulated in which the Bible speaks of the love of God is absolutized, not only are the others vitiated but theological nonsense is the inevitable result. Emphasize the last of the five, out of its rightful context, and the result is a return to the most egregious merit theology. Men and women will become painfully introspective, wondering if they have been good enough today to win God's love. Emphasize the fourth out of its rightful place, and the result will be hyper-Calvinism, a rather mechanistic view in which God has only love for the elect and only wrath for the reprobate, making the free offer of the gospel for the latter a presumptuous offence before God. Emphasize the third without recourse to the others, and the result is a rather pathetic Deity who has done all he can do, and now pleads for our repentance and loyalty, though there is very little he can do to elicit them. And so we might go on.

Secondly, not only must we take account of all the ways in which the Bible speaks of the love of God, but we must do so with an eye to proportion and function. In other words, these various ways of speaking about the love of God must have a voice in our theology in a fashion analogous to their roles in Scripture. This means we must do more than list them; we must see how they operate in Scripture, with what themes they are linked, what ethical inferences are drawn, and so forth.

Thirdly (and most important), it is essential to see how these various ways of talking about the love of God fit into the Bible's storyline and are related to the person and work of *Jesus Christ. If the mission of the Son is the result of the intra-Trinitarian love of God, so also it is the fruit of the Father's love for this lost world; the measure of that love is the Son himself (John 3:16). In love, the Father makes a gift of an entire people to his Son; in love, the Son perfectly performs his Father's will and preserves all who are given to him (John 6:37–40). The entire plan

of redemption finds as its wellspring the love of God, poured out on sinners who are God's enemies and far from being intrinsically lovely. This is one of the distinctives of God's love: while with only rare exceptions human love in this fallen world is poured out only on that which the lover finds lovely, God's love springs from within himself, and, at least in the second, third and fourth ways of speaking of his love, it is not dependent on the loveliness of the person or thing that is loved.

Christian love

Christian love can be understood, and best practised, only when it is seen to be a reflection of God's love in its varied dimensions. Moreover, like the love of God, the love believers are to display is not so much invented under the new covenant as sharpened or brought into clearer focus. Jesus' response to the person who asked him what the greatest commandment is (Mark 12:28–31), *i.e.* to love God with all your heart and soul and mind and strength, and your neighbour as yourself, was not entirely innovative; it brought together two crucial OT passages (viz. Deut. 6:4–5; Lev. 19:18).

Failure to love God lies at the heart of idolatry, and God's response is jealous wrath (*cf.* Exod. 20:4–5; Jas. 4:4–5). But if Christians love, whether God or fellow Christians, it is in response to God's love (Col. 3:12–15; 1 Pet. 1:8; 1 John 4:11). Although Christian love is invariably the obligation of Christians, it is the fruit of the Spirit (Gal. 5:13). It is characterized by *humility and gentleness (Eph. 4:1–2); in emulation of the Master, it eschews retaliation (1 Pet. 3:8–9). Inevitably self-restraint becomes a watchword (Rom. 14:13–15) as the Christian learns to love with heart and attitude no less than with action (1 Cor. 13).

The many connections between Christian love and the various ways in which the Bible depicts the love of God demand far more reflection than is possible here. But one telling example may be offered. Some have argued that the love on which 1 John insists within the community is inferior to the love that Jesus enjoins for enemies (Matt. 5:43–47). This judgment depends on what *we* find more difficult: in this case, loving enemies as opposed to loving (ostensible) friends. But the proposal is sterile. Love for one's enemies is analogous to the third and fourth ways in which the Bible speaks of God's love (listed above). By the work of the Spirit (Rom. 5:5), itself the fruit of the cross, we learn to emulate God in this respect: we love the unlovely, the love springing up from within, for we ourselves have been so loved. But love for others in the household of faith in some ways mirrors the intra-Trinitarian love of God (John 17). In both cases, God's love is the motive and standard of ours. In such a framework, to label some expressions of love 'inferior' and others 'superior' is presumptuous indeed, for behind all these various ways of speaking of the love of God is one God whose nature is love.

Bibliography

K. Barth, *Church Dogmatics*, IV/2 (ET, Edinburgh, 1957); E. Brunner, *The Divine Imperative* (ET, London, 1937); D. A. Carson, *The Difficult Doctrine of the Love of God* (Wheaton and Leicester, 2000); W. Gunther and H.-G. Link, in *NIDNTT* 2, pp. 538–551; R. Joly, *Le vocabulaire chrétien de l'amour est-il orginal?* (Bruxelles, 1968); C. S. Lewis, *The Four Loves* (Glasgow, 1960); J. Moffatt, *Love in the New Testament* (London, 1929); L. Morris, *Testaments of Love* (Grand Rapids, 1981); A. Nygren, *Agape and Eros* (ET, London, 1932–39); O. M. T. O'Donovan, *Resurrection and Moral Order* (Leicester, 1986).

D. A. CARSON

LUKE, see Part 2
MALACHI, see Part 2

MAN AND WOMAN

Introduction

A biblical theology of man and woman must explain how they relate to one another under *God, with respect both to their differences and to their similarities, in the course of biblical revelation. What does the Scripture teach regarding man vis-à-vis woman and woman vis-à-vis man, in the order of God? And how does the Scripture address the human distortions of that normative order and its divine *redemption? The following essay can survey only the most important of the passages which address the subject.

The author is aware of the vigorous discussion surrounding this subject but has no interest in mere controversy. Some readers of this article may not agree with everything proposed here, but it is hoped that all readers will find the evidences handled modestly and responsibly.

Man and woman at the creation

Genesis 1:27 initiates the biblical theology of man and woman:

> So God created man in his own image,
> in the image of God he created him;
> male and female he created them.
> (RSV, in poetic structure)

The divine intention declared in verse 26 is here fulfilled, but by shifting to poetic form in verse 27 the author conveys a sense of wonder at this climactic act in the sequence of *creation. The third line of the verse draws attention to itself by introducing a new thought, viz. the sexuality ('male and female') and plurality ('them') of the newly created 'adam. And the inner logic of the whole, bound together with the same verb ('created'), demands that both male and female alike be dignified as bearers of the divine image.

The use of 'male and female' rather than 'man and woman' highlights the sexuality of the race. It is 'male and female' who are blessed with fertility ('And God blessed them', v. 28) and commanded to reproduce in abundant measure ('Be fruitful and multiply'). Man and woman are more than sexual ('in the image of God', v. 27), but sexual nonetheless. And it is in their identity as 'male and female', together comprising 'man' in the image of God, that man and woman first appear in the biblical narrative; God endorses this identity as 'very good' (v. 31). There is no reductionism or prudery in the biblical account.

The dignity of the man and woman's shared station in the created order appears not only in the *imago Dei* but also in their authorization to rule together over the lower creation ('and God said to *them*', v. 28) and feed on its vegetation at will (v. 29). Psalm 8 rejoices in this vision of *human existence, interpreting it explicitly in terms of 'glory and honour' (v. 5). Man and woman *per se* are not mentioned by the psalmist, but the Genesis account awards the psalmist's 'glory and honour' equally to them without rank or distinction.

While Genesis 1 emphasizes the divine image in man and woman, defining them vertically in relation to God, Genesis 2 explains more fully their earthly relationship to one another. The only man-woman relationship in view here is marriage, and it is presented in the biblical narrative with a respectful tenderness unknown elsewhere in ancient Near Eastern accounts of human origins.

After the divine pronouncements in Genesis 1 that creation is 'good', the reader is struck in Genesis 2:18 by the reference to a flaw in the garden God has planted: 'Then the LORD God said, "It is not good that the man should be alone; I will make him a helper fit for him."' This 'helper' is not found in the lower creation (2:20) but only in the woman.

God defines the newly created woman with the phrase 'helper fit for him' ('ēzer kᵉnegdô), suggesting a twofold understanding of woman vis-à-vis man. On the one hand, 'helper' positions her in the garden as his supporter (cf. Ps. 20:2). On the other hand, 'fit for him' affirms her unique compatibility with the man. She alone answers his need, for she alone is his true counterpart in the creation.

The man, for his part, acknowledges in his own words this 'helper fit for him' by naming her. His outburst of joy requires the narrative to shift into a poetic mode:

> Then the man said,
> 'This at last is bone of my bones
> and flesh of my flesh;
> she shall be called Woman,
> because she was taken out of Man.'
> (Gen. 2:23)

The one with authority to name (2:19), in his climactic act, captures the essence of this newest creature. The name he chooses for her, 'iššâ ('woman') echoing 'îš ('man'), reveals how closely he identifies with her, for she is his very substance ('bone of my bones and flesh of my flesh'). The perfection and bliss of their union are signalled by Genesis 2:25: 'And the man and his wife were both naked, and were not ashamed.'

Man and woman at the fall

By disobeying God's command, man and woman squander their happiness and drag the creation down with them into futility. But their disobedience also entails a disordering of their own relationship. God sets forth two reasons for his cursing of the ground in Genesis 3:17:

> 'And to Adam he said,
> "Because [1] you have listened to the voice
> of your wife,
> and [2] have eaten of the tree of which
> I commanded you, 'You shall not eat
> of it',
> cursed is the ground because of you ..."'

This pronouncement is consistent with the temptation narrative earlier in chapter 3, where the couple's disobedience in relation to God and their confusion in relation to one another are woven together in one event. The *serpent engages the woman in a dialogue premised on the untrustworthiness of the Creator (Gen. 3:1–5). She tries to deflect his question rather than repudiating it directly, which concedes too much to the question. As the deception proceeds, her vision of God and her perception of the forbidden tree are shrewdly manipulated. Moreover, in approaching the woman the serpent addresses both the woman and the man ('you' in vv. 1, 4 and 5 is plural), leading her to speak on behalf of both her husband and herself ('*We* may eat', v. 2). But where is the man as this dialogue unfolds? The answer is unclear, but it would appear that he stands by and does nothing ('And she also gave some to her husband, *who was with her*, and he ate', v. 6, NRSV). The man and woman *sin against God by disobeying his command of 2:17, but in doing so they also disrupt the order of their own relationship. The man 'listen[s] to the voice of [his] wife' by following her lead (cf. v. 6), and the woman fails to be his 'helper' by taking the lead (cf. 1 Tim. 2:12–14). As a consequence, the harmony of man and woman in marriage disintegrates into tension (Gen. 3:16; see *Marriage).

Relieving the gloom, the man names his wife 'Eve' (3:20), 'because she [is] the mother of all living'. God's promise that the woman's offspring will crush the serpent (3:15) opens up to the eye of faith a future bright with triumphant human life. The man thus honours the woman he had scorned shortly before (3:12), bearing witness to the healing power of hope.

The sorrows of the man-woman relationship throughout the rest of Scripture are traceable to the fall of the first man and woman in Genesis 3. The Genesis narrative recounts subsequent abuses: the violence, egotism and polygamy of Lamech (4:19, 23–24); the cowardice of Abram (12:10–20; 20:1–18) and Isaac (26:6–11); the rivalry and heartache of Sarai in relation to Abram and Hagar (16:1–6); the deceiving of Isaac by Rebekah and Jacob (27:5–29); Shechem's rape of Dinah (34:1–31); and Judah's disgraceful relations with his daughter-in-law Tamar (38:13–18).

Man and woman under the law

Pentateuchal law enforces the protocols of manhood and womanhood as created by God, as to both their outer parameters (Lev. 18:22–23; 20:13, 15–16; Deut. 22:5) and their inner dynamics (Lev. 18, passim; 20:10–21). The question asked by the modern mind, however, is whether the law treats the sexes 'equally'. Some laws clearly do (Exod. 20:12; 21:28–32; Lev. 13:29, 38; 20:9, 15–16; Num. 5:6; 6:2; Deut. 5:16; 17:2–5; 27:16; 29:18; 31:12), but OT law in general does not lay out equal terms for both sexes with the scrupulosity expected of modern law (e.g. Lev. 12:1–5).

The atmosphere of OT law appears to be that of a benign patriarchy. Vows made by a woman while in her father's household, or by a wife, can be invalidated by the father or by the husband (Num. 30:1–16), while the vows of a single woman cannot be withdrawn (v. 9). And yet this social order also recognizes women's concerns (Num. 27:1–11) and protects women (Exod. 22:15, 17; Deut. 21:10–14). Indeed, a newly married man is exempted from military duty 'to stay at home and bring happiness to the wife he has married' (Deut. 24:5, NIV). The law looks askance at polygamy (Deut. 17:17) and guards the rights of the firstborn of the disliked wife (Deut. 21:15–17).

Because the Mosaic law, considered as old covenant, regulates the people of God only during their years of immaturity (Gal. 4:1–11), its social arrangements, although just, are not intended in every respect to be permanently binding. The historical perspective assumed in the law is one that looks back regretfully to the fall, around realistically at the present, and forward in anticipation of greater gifts from God. When applying the law to the NT church, therefore, one must take into account the law's context in the history of redemption. As will be affirmed below, woman is elevated under the new covenant, under which all God's children are granted adult status (Gal. 3:23–29).

The rest of the OT teaching on the significance of man and woman may be interpreted with reference to three hermeneutical touchstones: the ideal in Genesis 1 – 2; the fall in Genesis 3; and the Mosaic guardianship of God's under-age children in the law. The domestic happiness commended by the sages (Prov. 5:15–23), the excellent wife of Proverbs 31:10–31 and the marital bliss of the Song of Solomon indicate that the pre-fall ideal is not completely out of reach. The irony of a bold Deborah prodding a timid Barak into action (Judg. 4:4–9, 14) shows that God's purpose can move forward even under less-than-ideal conditions. And the OT's lack of finality points forward to a greater day when the prophetic Spirit of the Lord will fall upon all alike (Joel 2:28–29; cf. Num. 11:29), irrespective of sex or rank.

Man and woman in the NT

After Genesis 2, the most explicit biblical exposition of man and woman is found in the writings of Paul. On the one hand, he affirms that 'there is neither male nor female, for you all are one in Christ Jesus' (Gal. 3:28). The gospel dignifies all God's people as 'Abraham's offspring, heirs according to promise' (v. 29), without rank or distinction. To receive the redemption that is in Christ, mere faith is required. Therefore the human barriers of race and class, and even the divinely-created order of male and female, are transcended in Christ, producing a new oneness with respect to spiritual privilege. Paul cannot mean, however, that sexual distinctions are absolutely obliterated, for then he would have no logical warrant for condemning homosexuality in Romans 1:26–27. To quote F. F. Bruce, 'It is not their distinctiveness, but their inequality of religious role, that is abolished "in Christ Jesus"' (The Epistle to the Galatians, NIGTC [Grand Rapids, 1982], p. 189).

Consistent with Galatians 3:28 is the outpouring of the Spirit upon all believers alike. The results of this include a united prophetic voice (Acts 2:17–18), the divine empowering of each believer to serve the whole church (1 Cor. 12:7–11), a common baptism by the Spirit (1 Cor. 12:13) and the sharing of the burdens of church work (Rom. 16:1–23; Phil. 4:2–3). The NT breathes a spirit of inclusiveness created by the full revelation of the gospel of grace.

On the other hand, Paul nuances the unmistakable equality of man and woman in Christ by preserving male and female sexual identity within the oneness of all in Christ. In 1 Corinthians 11:3–15 (a difficult passage to interpret) the apostle's concern seems to be the blurring of sexual distinctions as members pray and prophesy in the assembly of the Corinthian church. Women are participating with their heads unveiled (v. 13), displaying an improper manliness (vv. 14–15). While affirming the delicate interdependence of man and woman under God (vv. 11–12), Paul also upholds the distinctiveness of the two sexes by reasoning from the relational dynamics within the Godhead (v. 3) and from human origins (vv. 7b–9; *cf.* Gen. 2:18–25). For a woman, therefore, to venture into male behaviour violates the transcendent ordering of relationships. She is to retain her feminine dignity, and the man his original headship, so that there is no falsifying of manhood and womanhood in the church.

The meaning of *kephalē* in verse 3 has attracted debate. The NRSV reads, 'Christ is the head of every man, and the husband is the head of his wife, and God is the head of Christ.' Playing in verses 4, 5, 7 and 10 on the literal usage of this word, Paul argues that something about God in relation to Christ, Christ in relation to every man, and a husband in relation to his wife, may be truly predicated with the assistance of the word *kephalē*. Some argue that the word means 'source' rather than 'leader' or 'authority', appealing to the logic of verse 8. The function of verses 8 and 9, however, is parenthetical (*cf.* RSV), validating the idea that woman is man's 'glory' (v. 7). Verse 8 does not function in Paul's argument as a gloss on verse 3. The view that *kephalē* means 'source' has also been encountered by sophisticated philological objections.

In 1 Corinthians 14:26–40 Paul sketches broad parameters for the meetings of the Corinthian church, giving special attention to tongues and prophecies. He instructs the women of the church to 'be silent', in keeping with their subordinate position (v. 34), and instead to talk to their husbands at home regarding prophecies spoken in the church meeting (v. 35). Neither the women's silence nor their subordination can be intended by the apostle to be absolute, however, for he himself acknowledges in 11:5 that women may pray and prophesy (properly adorned) in the church meeting. The difficulty may be resolved on the supposition that Paul's instructions in verses 34–35 have to do with the evaluating of the prophecies ('Let two or three prophets speak, *and let the others weigh what is said*', v. 29). Verses 30–33a expand upon the first part of verse 29 (the speaking of the prophecies), while verses 33b–36 explain what is required by the second half of verse 29 (the weighing of the prophecies). Given Paul's understanding of man and woman from 'the law' (v. 34, alluding to Gen. 2:18–25), the subordinate position of the woman is inconsistent with her 'weighing' a man's prophecies.

Paul authorizes Timothy to instruct the Ephesian church on 'how one ought to behave in the household of God' (1 Tim. 3:15). Included in his instructions are guidelines for men and women in church (ch. 2). Men are to pray without anger or argument (v. 8), and women are to adorn themselves with good works rather than with extravagant dress (vv. 9–10). Moreover, a woman is to 'learn in silence with full submission' (v. 11). Then Paul explains more fully what this silence with full submission entails: 'I permit no woman to teach or to have authority over a man' (v. 12).

While women served in many roles in the early church, the apostle sets two ministries apart for qualified men only, viz., teaching and exercising authority. The teaching ministry described in 1 Timothy 4:11–16 suggests that the teaching mentioned in 2:12 is the church's formal doctrinal exposition by those in the pastoral office (*cf.* 1 Tim. 3:2; 5:17). The exercise of authority is presumably the 'ruling' of the elder (5:17), which is comparable to the management of a household (3:5).

Some interpreters understand Paul's instructions to be intended for their original Ephesian context only, for the correction of abuses specific to that church. The weakness of this view is that Paul grounds his teaching not in the local situation, as he sometimes does (Titus 1:10–13), but in two primal human events: the creation of the man first, and then the woman (1 Tim. 2:13; *cf.* Gen. 2); and the deceiving of the woman, not the man (1 Tim. 2:14; *cf.* Gen. 3:1–7). His first rationale, analogous to his reasoning in 1 Corinthians 11:8–9, draws upon the divine intention that the woman would be a suitable helper for the man (Gen. 2:18), which implies that she has a supportive role. The significance of Paul's second rationale is more difficult to perceive. It is improbable that he is making a statement about the vulnerability of women to deception, since the Scripture nowhere teaches this and because his concern in this passage is woman's relation to man in the church, not woman's 'nature' in some abstract sense. Instead, Paul simply notes the fact that, at the fall, the serpent engaged Eve, not *Adam, in the deception (*cf.* Gen. 3:13). The tempter led her away from learning from her husband 'in silence with full submission' into the equivalent of teaching and exercising authority over him (*cf.* Gen. 3:6), so disrupting their divinely ordained roles; Paul wants the Ephesian church to reflect upon the negative consequences of this confusion.

1 Timothy 2:15 directs the Ephesian women to a sphere of activity where they can experience the salvation they desire in abundant measure: 'Yet she will be saved through childbearing, provided they continue in faith and love and holiness, with modesty' (NRSV). While the proper translation of this verse is not as obscure as our various English versions might imply, its interpretation is difficult. Paul may be using a strong soteriological term ('saved') to counter arguments that women can experience the fullness of what God has for them only if they discard their womanly roles (*cf.* 1 Tim. 5:14; Titus 2:3–5). He would not imply that only mothers can be 'saved'. But Paul does regard motherhood as a distinguished form of human experience, rich with saving potential, if the children born continue in faith, love, holiness and modesty. Indeed, sons marked by these qualities would provide church leadership in the next generation and thereby extend the woman's influence to the highest levels of church governance.

To sum up: the apostle affirms the oneness of the entire people of God, and he also demonstrates a sensitive alertness to the implications of sexual identity. His views on both the unity of the church and the distinctiveness of the sexes are rooted in biblical precedent and argued strongly against opposition.

Finally, the NT envisages an eternal state in which manhood and womanhood, while not erased, will be transcended in a final, heavenly order (Mark 12:25). The people of God will be 'like angels in heaven', in that the centre of their existence will be undivided communion with God. Then the beautiful and delicate interplay of man and woman with one another will give way to the ultimate reality of Christ and his church for ever at one (Rev. 21:2, 9–10).

See also: IMAGE OF GOD.

Bibliography

J. A. Fitzmyer, '*Kephalē* in I Corinthians 11:3', *Int* 47, 1993, pp. 52–59; S. J. Grenz, *Women in the Church: A Biblical Theology of Women in Ministry* (Downers Grove, 1995); A. J. Köstenberger, T. R. Schreiner and H. S. Baldwin (eds.), *Women in the Church: A Fresh Analysis of 1 Timothy 2:9–15* (Grand Rapids, 1995); R. C. Kroeger and C. C. Kroeger, *I Suffer Not a Woman: Rethinking 1 Timothy 2:11–15 in Light of Ancient Evidence* (Grand Rapids, 1992); J. Piper and W. Grudem (eds.), *Recovering Biblical Manhood and Womanhood: A Response to Evangelical Feminism* (Wheaton and Cambridge, 1991, 1992).

R. C. ORTLUND, JR.

MARK, see Part 2

MARRIAGE

Introduction

Discussion of marriage should go beyond the controversial questions of male and female roles, important as these are. Scripture elevates the subject to a more sublime level. Marriage is not merely a human institution, completely malleable in the hands of human custom. It is a divine *creation, intended to project onto the screen of the human imagination the beauty of a Saviour who gives himself sacrificially for his bride and of his bride who yields herself gratefully back to him.

Genesis 2: definition

The biblical concept of marriage is grounded in Genesis 2:23–24. After naming the animals and finding no suitable helper for himself, Adam encounters his newly created wife, given to him by God. He greets her with joy and relief, uttering the first recorded human words in poetic verse:

> Then the man said, 'This at last is bone of
>   my bones
>   and flesh of my flesh;
> this one shall be called Woman,
>   for out of Man this one was taken.'
>   (Gen. 2:23, NRSV)

Adam rejoices over her, because he identifies with her. He is no longer 'alone' (Gen. 2:18). But then the author arrests the progress of the narrative and addresses the readers directly in a one-verse explanatory comment: 'Therefore a man leaves his father and his mother and clings to his wife, and they become one flesh' (Gen. 2:24). Extrapolating ('therefore') from God's creation of the first woman as the first man's bone and flesh, taken from his very body, the author reasons that human marriage is a 'one flesh' union. Those two words are central to the biblical definition of marriage.

Genesis 2:24 makes two points in connection with the 'one-flesh-ness' of true marriage. First, in marrying, a man is to leave his father and his mother. Although the father and mother give a man his very life out of themselves, and although a man's early emotional attachment is to his parents, a married man's primary loyalty is to be directed elsewhere. Secondly, a married man is to cling to his wife. This is the positive complement of leaving his parents. The language suggests a profound union of husband with wife, so that his primary identification in all of life is with her. The outcome is that the *man and woman become 'one flesh'.

The 'one flesh' meaning of marriage calls a man and woman together into a fully shared life. Two things stand out here. First, this is a 'one flesh' union. Overriding even blood relationships ('his father and his mother') to create a new kinship, marriage is the most profound bond that exists between two human beings; within it nothing can be withheld. Secondly, this is a 'one *flesh*' union. Profound as it is, marriage is still less than ulti-

mate, for mortal 'flesh' (v. 24 has post-fall people in view) falls short of the divine (*cf*. Ps. 78:39).

Genesis 2, therefore, teaches that God created marriage when he made the first woman out of the flesh of the first man, so that the bond of marriage reunites man and woman as 'one flesh'. All other relational claims are subordinate to those of marriage. 'One flesh' entails a life-long, exclusive clinging of one man to one woman in one life fully shared. Marriage puts a barrier around a husband and his wife and destroys all barriers between them; they belong fully to one another, and to one another only.

Genesis 3ff.: distortion and restoration

After the fall of the man and woman into *sin against God, the Creator imposes parameters on the woman's existence:

> To the woman he said,
>   'I will greatly increase your pangs in
>   childbearing,
>   in pain you shall bring forth children;
> and your desire shall be for your
>   husband,
>   but he shall rule over you.' (Gen. 3:16,
>   author's translation)

The woman is condemned by an offended God to endure suffering in childbirth and in marriage. In the latter, her own desire and her husband's ruling will distort the beauty of their union. Her controlling impulse is matched by his lordly ego (*cf*. the logic of the analogous language in Gen. 4:7). In different ways and to different degrees, every marriage thereafter shows the effects of God's decree.

The distortion appears in various forms in the biblical narrative. For example, Genesis 4 records that 'Lamech took two wives' (4:19). He reappears in verses 23–24, boasting before them of his vengeful and murderous power. Male domination and violence are seen here in all their ugliness, and no comment is needed from the author. This brief scene, in its striking contrast with the tender monogamy of Eden, casts a shadow upon all subsequent polygamy as having arisen not from God's original design but when the race was tumbling from one level of ignominy to the next. As the biblical narrative continues, the story of marriage reflects that of human sinfulness; the institution can be only as beautiful as human moral character allows.

So Abram's cowardice puts his wife in jeopardy (Gen. 12:10–20), and Rebekah manipulates and deceives her husband (Gen. 27:5–17). The breakdown of marriages leads to the regulation of divorce and remarriage in the Mosaic law (Deut. 24:1–4). But this is only a concession to the hardness of the human heart; the original norm of 'one flesh' is not changed by human failure (Matt. 19:3–9). God openly declares that he hates divorce as a violation of the marital covenant (Mal. 2:13–16). It is God himself who binds the two into one (Matt. 19:6).

The post-fall picture is not entirely bleak, however, for the Bible tells the story of God's restoring grace. The entire *Song of Songs is devoted to celebrating married *love, assuring the covenant community that God's will is marital happiness. If, as seems likely, the final line of 5:1 ('Eat, friends, and drink, and be drunk with love'), is addressed to the two lovers, then whoever the speaker(s) may be, the larger (biblical) context invites the reader to hear the voice of God approving marital pleasure (cf. 1 Tim. 4:1–5). A note of warning is also heard, for marriage entails risk. Song of Songs 8:6 utters the heart-cry of the bride that her husband would make her ever near and dear to himself; love cannot be betrayed without pain. The partner who feels keenly her vulnerability yearns for the full realization of the one-flesh union. 'He loves me, he loves me not' cannot satisfy her heart. The Song of Songs supports the NT command that marriage be held in honour by all and the warning that the marriage bed must be kept undefiled (Heb. 13:4). Moreover, a wholesome view of marriage as wisdom's alternative to sexual folly is urged upon the young in Proverbs 5:15–23. Proverbs 31:10–31 exalts the virtuous wife as the living embodiment of Lady Wisdom.

Ephesians 5: the mystery

Ephesians 5:22–33 is the theological and hermeneutical intersection through which all biblical questions about marriage must eventually pass. In this passage Paul identifies the institution of marriage as a '*mystery' revealing Jesus Christ and the *church. Throughout his instructions to wives (vv. 22–24) and to husbands (vv. 25–30), he draws parallels between the Christian marriage of a man and a wife and the ultimate marriage of Christ and his church. It follows that the betrothal of the church to Christ (2 Cor. 11:1–3), and the union of the believer with Christ (1 Cor. 6:16–17), are not mere metaphors. They are the reality to which a Christian marriage points when it demonstrates the beauty described in Ephesians 5. In 1 Corinthians 7:27–38 Paul affirms that marriage is good, but also that the greatest human allegiance is to Christ himself.

Paul's statement that a man should love his wife as he loves his own body (Eph. 5:28) might be misunderstood as allowing base self-interest. He excludes this interpretation by pointing to Christ's love for his body, the church (vv. 29b–30), love which took him to the cross (v. 25). But Paul's declaration in verse 30 that 'we are members of [Christ's] body' gives him the opportunity to show a typological connection with Genesis 2:24 ('one *flesh*') in verse 31. His logic is striking. 'We are members of [Christ's] body. "*For this reason* a man will leave his father and mother and be joined to his wife, and the two will become one flesh"' (vv. 30–31). Christ's union with the church as his body is the reason why a man should become one flesh with his wife. It is the heavenly marriage that warrants and dignifies an earthly marriage. In Paul's reasoning, therefore, human marriage is not the reality for which Christ and the church provide a sermonic illustration, but the reverse. Human marriage is the earthly type, pointing towards the spiritual reality. This being so, the privilege of a Christian married couple is to declare the 'great mystery' (v. 32) by incarnating in their own marriage sacrificial divine love wedded to joyful human reverence (v. 33).

Revelation: ultimacy

After Babylon, the 'great whore who corrupted the earth with her fornication' (Rev. 19:2), has been judged by God, the victorious saints rejoice that 'the marriage of the Lamb has come, and his bride has made herself ready' (Rev. 19:7). It is granted to her to be clothed with 'fine linen, bright and pure', which is the righteous deeds of the saints (Rev. 19:8). The Husband of the bride presents the church to himself in splendour, without a spot or wrinkle or anything of the kind (cf. Eph. 5:26–27). The antitypical reality finally appears as the new *Jerusalem comes down out of heaven from God, prepared as a bride adorned for her husband

(Rev. 21:2). There will be no human marriages in heaven (Mark 12:25), for heaven will be *the* marriage. It is difficult to discuss this without using more lofty prose, as Jonathan Edwards illustrates (*Works* [Edinburgh, 1979 reprint], vol. 2, p. 22):

> Then the church shall be brought to the full enjoyment of her bridegroom, having all tears wiped away from her eyes; and there shall be no more distance or absence. She shall then be brought to the entertainments of an eternal wedding-feast, and to dwell for ever with her bridegroom; yea, to dwell eternally in his embraces. Then Christ will give her his loves; and she shall drink her fill, yea, she shall swim in the ocean of his love.

To sum up: the overall pattern of biblical teaching on marriage discloses typological symmetry from Genesis to Revelation, as the 'one-flesh-ness' of human marriage, sacred but provisional, points forward and upward to the eternal spiritual union of Christ with his bride, the church. The symbolism inherent in earthly marriage lends the relationship greater dignity; its significance goes beyond the human and temporal to the divine and eternal.

See also: ADULTERY; FAITH.

Bibliography

S. T. Foh, 'What is the woman's desire?', *WTJ* 37, 1975, pp. 376–383; R. C. Ortlund, Jr., *Whoredom: God's Unfaithful Wife in Biblical Theology* (Leicester and Grand Rapids, 1996); J. P. Sampley, *'And the Two shall become One Flesh': A Study of Traditions in Ephesians 5:21–23* (Cambridge, 1971).

R. C. ORTLUND, JR.

MARY

Introduction

Mary, the mother of *Jesus, has a unique place in salvation history and a vital role in the *incarnation. Given her later significance in the church, it is essential to distinguish between NT and subsequent depictions of Mary. This article will focus on the former. The term 'virgin birth' sometimes includes the extra-biblical idea that Mary was a life-long virgin; to avoid confusion, the term 'virginal conception' will be used. The virginal conception means Jesus was conceived in Mary by a creative act of the *Holy Spirit without the participation of a human father. The NT carefully describes the virginal conception in non-sexual language (Matt. 1:18, 20; Luke 1:35; R. E. Brown, *Birth of the Messiah*, pp. 124–125, 290–291). The role of the Holy Spirit in Mary's conception of Jesus must also be viewed against OT passages which associate Israelite kingship with the empowering action of the Spirit of the Lord (e. g. 1 Sam. 10:6–7; 16:13).

Paul

Paul does not refer to the virginal conception or to Mary by name. Since his letters address specific situations and make little mention of the life of Jesus before the cross, his silence is readily explicable. He asserts Jesus' Davidic descent (Rom. 1:3) and humanity ('born of a woman', Gal. 4:4, NIV).

The Synoptic Gospels

Mark begins his account from a time when Jesus is already an adult, and he too does not mention the virginal conception. The family of Jesus seriously misunderstand his ministry (Mark 3:20–21; 6:3–6; *cf.* John 7:5), but true discipleship as defined in Mark 3:31–35 is ascribed elsewhere to Mary (Acts 1:14), which suggests that she may not have fully agreed with others in the family against Jesus. Certainly she is never called an unbeliever. Mark 6:3, 'Mary's son', may testify to a life-long stigma attached to her, that Jesus was illegitimate (see also John 8:41).

Where Luke and Matthew agree in the details of their infancy narratives (Luke 1 – 2; Matt. 1 – 2) they have drawn independently from early material which contains the following elements: God reveals that a child will be born to a virgin, Mary, who is betrothed to Joseph, a descendant of David; he will be the Saviour, conceived through the Holy Spirit; he is to be named Jesus; he is born in Bethlehem in the reign of Herod the Great, and grows up in Nazareth. Mary is the most likely source of this material.

Mary is 'pledged' (*mnēsteuein*, Matt. 1:18; Luke 2:5), which means that she and Joseph have publicly exchanged consent, the first step in Jewish *marriage. Often the bride was under fifteen. The marriage was legally complete from the consent, so Mary is Joseph's wife (*gynē*, Matt. 1:20, 24). Sexual relations did not commence until the wife was received into the husband's home, about a year later (Brown, *Birth*, pp. 123–124). The Davidic descent of Jesus is established through Joseph, his legal father (Matt. 1:16; Luke 3:23). Mary's ancestry is never given, though she is related to Elizabeth, who is outside the line of David (Luke 1:5, 36).

In the account of the annunciation (Luke 1:26–38), the greeting 'highly favoured' (*kecharitōmenē*, Luke 1:28) identifies Mary as a recipient, not a source, of grace. Even most Catholic scholars now agree that 'full of grace', from the Vulgate, is a mistranslation (R. Laurentin, *A Short Treatise on the Virgin Mary*, p. 20). Because God has chosen her, she is 'blessed' (Luke 1:48). Her assent (Luke 1:38) is a powerful testimony of faith in God's will, despite her anxiety and uncertainty. Mary's song (Luke 1:46–55) draws deeply from the OT to portray her trust in the God who delivers his people. It is a song about what God has done for Mary.

Luke presents her as the first disciple, responding in trust and obedience to God's word (1:38). Elizabeth praises both her role and her faith in God (Luke 1:42–45). Her journey of faith is not without struggle and pain (Luke 2:19, 35). Her son even as a boy sets his mission above family claims, which is surely difficult for Mary (Luke 2:41–52). Texts traditionally taken as critical of her (Luke 8:19–21; 11:27–28) should be read in line with Luke's high view of her faith (1:38, 45), a faith which secures for her a place among the disciples (Acts 1:14).

John

Mary appears twice in John's Gospel. At Cana Jesus gently reprimands her unrealistic expectations which run against the priorities of his mission (John 2:1–11). His form of address, 'dear woman' (*gynai*, John 2:4), cannot be taken harshly as he uses it again in affection during his crucifixion (John 19:26). His word from the cross not only demonstrates his care for her, but also acknowledges her place in the believing community. The virginal conception may be implied in the irony of John 6:41–42.

Conclusion

The NT shows no interest in Mary's virginity after the birth of Jesus. Various passages speak of the brothers of Jesus, never implying they are not Mary's natural children (Matt. 12:46–47; 13:55–56; Mark 3:31; 6:3; Luke 8:19–20; John 2:12; 7:5; Acts 1:14; Gal. 1:19). Speculation that Mary remained a virgin is first attested sometime after 150 (*cf. Protevangelium of James*).

While the NT is mainly interested in Mary as the mother of Jesus, she stands in her own right as a major figure in the early church. Her maternity is often cited by Irenaeus, Tertullian and others to prove the humanity of the Saviour against docetism. She is also significant as an object of divine power and grace in being chosen by God. In affirming both of these as important theological roles for Mary, we must not overlook her own humble, obedient faith, which stands as a model for all believers.

Bibliography

R. E. Brown, *The Birth of the Messiah* (New York, ²1993); R. E. Brown *et al.* (eds.), *Mary in the New Testament: A Collaborative Assessment by Protestant and Roman Catholic Scholars* (London and Philadelphia, 1978); C. E. B. Cranfield, 'Some reflections on the subject of the Virgin Birth', *SJT* 41, 1988, pp. 177–189; D. Crump, 'The Virgin Birth in New Testament theology', in D. F. Wright (ed.), *Chosen By God: Mary in Evangelical Perspective* (London, 1989); H. Graef, *Mary: A History of Doctrine and Devotion* (London, ²1985); R. Laurentin, *A Short Treatise on the Virgin Mary* (ET, Washington, NJ, 1991); R. Longenecker, 'Whose Child is This?', *CT* 34, 1990, pp. 25–28.

E. B. MANGES

MATTHEW, see Part 2

MELCHIZEDEK

Although Melchizedek is mentioned only twice in the OT (Gen. 14:17–20; Ps. 110:4), this shadowy figure became the subject of much speculation in Jewish circles (*cf.* W. L. Lane, *Hebrews 1 – 8*, pp. 160–163). Given this background, the writer of *Hebrews appears to be quite restrained and independent in his use of the texts. Melchizedek is an historical figure whose priesthood serves as a precedent for that of *Jesus Christ. From a biblical-theological point of view it is important to note how Hebrews approaches the Genesis narrative typologically, guided by the perspective of the prophetic psalm text.

Melchizedek and Abram

Melchizedek is the first priest mentioned in Scripture. His origins are obscure, but as 'priest of God Most High' (Gen. 14:18, Heb. 'El 'elyôn) he serves the one whom *Abram acknowledges as 'the LORD, God Most High, maker of heaven and earth' (cf. 14:22). In traditional Near-Eastern fashion, Melchizedek combines priesthood with *kingship (Gen. 14:18; 'Salem' is probably to be identified with *Jerusalem, cf. Ps. 76:2, the Genesis Apocryphon [22:13] and Josephus [Antiquities of the Jews 1.10.2]). His *blessing (14:19–20) is a recognition of Abram's special relationship with God. It recalls the promise in Genesis 12:1–3 that the patriarch will be a blessing and that all the families of the earth will find blessing in him. Melchizedek is 'blessed' by Abram in the tithe that he pays him.

Melchizedek and the Messiah

Although Israelite kings sometimes exercised priestly functions, the distinction between the offices was much more definite in Israel than in neighbouring cultures. Psalm 110 therefore appears to be prophetic of a new situation in proclaiming that a *Davidic king will be 'a priest for ever according to the order of Melchizedek' (v. 4). The implied background for this promise is the capture of Jerusalem, by which the house of David succeeded to the kingship and somehow also to the priesthood of Melchizedek. In the first oracle (v. 1) the Lord speaks as the true king of Israel, inviting his human representative to act as his co-regent. As the Qumran texts and the Gospels show (cf. Mark 12:35–37 par.), this verse was interpreted messianically in Jesus' time. The promise of an eternal priesthood in verse 4 matches the assurance in 2 Samuel 7:16 that God will establish David's house and his kingdom for ever. Melchizedek appears in one Qumran text (Melchizedek) as an angelic figure who executes final judgment upon the

powers of evil, but his priestly function is not mentioned. The writer of Hebrews appears to be the first to link the two oracles in Psalm 110, considering what it means for the Messiah who sits at God's right hand to be 'a priest for ever according to the order of Melchizedek'.

Melchizedek and Jesus

Jesus' use of Psalm 110:1 stimulated much theological reflection on the part of early Christian preachers and writers (cf. D. M. Hay, Glory at the Right Hand, pp. 34–129). But Hebrews is the only NT book to cite Psalm 110:4 and expound its significance (cf. Heb. 5:6, 10; 6:20; 7:3, 8, 11, 15–17, 21, 24–25, 28; 8:1–2; 10:12–14).

Psalm 110:1 is first mentioned in Hebrews 1:3, and then cited in Hebrews 1:13, to show that the Messiah's heavenly enthronement (see *Exaltation) and eternal rule is the focus of discussion. Hebrews is particularly concerned to establish Christ's superiority with regard to the angelic world (1:4–14) and so to highlight the significance of the *salvation he has declared and made possible (2:1–4). Psalm 110:4 is first used in a passage which outlines certain qualifications for high-priesthood under the old *covenant as a basis for explaining how Jesus can be the high priest of the new covenant (Heb. 5:1–10). Just as Aaron did not presume to take the honour of high-priesthood upon himself but was called by God, so Christ 'did not glorify himself in becoming a high priest', but was appointed by the one who addressed him as 'Son' in Psalm 2:7 and as 'a priest for ever according to the order of Melchizedek' in Psalm 110:4 (NRSV). The messianic reference of both of these psalms is assumed. In Hebrews 1:5, Psalm 2:7 is one of the texts used in conjunction with Psalm 110:1 to affirm the heavenly rule of the Messiah. Jesus' priesthood is thus aligned with his ascension and enthronement (cf. also Heb. 6:19–20; 7:16, 26), as well as with his *suffering and death (see *Atonement; 5:7–10; cf. 2:17–18; 7:27). But just how Psalm 110:4 illuminates the nature of his priesthood is not fully disclosed until Hebrews 7.

Hebrews 7:1–10 reflects on the significance of Melchizedek and his encounter with Abraham in Genesis 14:17–20. True to the original text, the main emphasis in Hebrews is on the blessing of Abraham by Melchizedek and the paying of tithes to Melchizedek by the patriarch (7:1-2a, 4-10). The writer's aim is to establish the superiority of Melchizedek's priesthood over that of Levi, to prepare for the argument that Christ's priesthood brings the perfection unattainable through the levitical priesthood (7:11-28). Melchizedek's name is interpreted to mean 'king of *righteousness', and his title as king of Salem is taken to mean that he is 'king of *peace' (7:2b), thus anticipating the Messiah's reign of righteousness and peace (cf. 1:8-9 and Psalm 110).

It is also noted that, unlike other significant figures in Genesis, Melchizedek is introduced without genealogy and without reference to his birth or death (7:3). Since the legitimacy of a man's priesthood in the ancient world depended on such factors, the silence of Scripture at this point is remarkable. The implication is that Melchizedek did not obtain his priesthood because of hereditary rights. In God's providence, Melchizedek was (lit.) 'made to resemble [Gk aphōmoiōmenos] the Son of God, in that he remains a priest for ever'. Here the influence of Psalm 110:4 on the interpretation of the Genesis text is clear. This statement prepares for the argument in 7:15-16 that Christ's priesthood is 'not through a legal requirement concerning physical descent, but through the power of an indestructible life'. By means of his ascension and heavenly enthronement, Christ entered into the eternal priesthood of which Psalm 110:4 speaks (cf. Heb. 8:1-2; 9:11-12). This new order of priesthood was typified by Melchizedek as he is presented in Genesis. The writer does not mean that Melchizedek was an angelic figure or that he was a pre-incarnate manifestation of the Son of God.

As Psalm 110:4 is applied to Christ in Hebrews 7:11-28 it becomes clear that he holds his priesthood permanently because 'he continues for ever' and that this is confirmed by the divine oath in the psalm. His heavenly priesthood introduces 'a better hope through which we approach God' since 'he always lives to make intercession' for those who draw near to God through him.

See also: PRIESTS.

Bibliography

H. W. Attridge, *The Epistle to the Hebrews* (Philadelphia, 1989); D. M. Hay, *Glory at the Right Hand: Psalm 110 in Early Christianity* (Nashville, 1973); W. L. Lane, *Hebrews 1 - 8*, WBC (Dallas, 1991); M. J. Paul, in *NIDOTTE* 4, pp. 934-936.

D. G. PETERSON

MERCY/COMPASSION

Mercy is a quality fundamental to *God's interaction with *humankind. In the English Bible, the noun signifies concrete expressions of compassion and *love. Verbal phrases such as 'to be merciful', 'to have mercy on' or 'to show mercy towards' underline further the active and volitional character of mercy. The adjective 'merciful' denotes a quality of God and a requirement of his *people. The primary Hebrew term for mercy is *hesed*, which refers to the love, compassion and kindness upon which God's *covenant with Israel was founded. The *eleos* word group is the most frequently used to denote mercy in the Greek OT (LXX) and NT, but the semantic domain includes *oiktirmos/oikteiro* (compassion, pity, to show mercy) and *splanchna/splanchnizomai* (affection, sympathy, to show mercy, to feel sympathy for).

Mercy and compassion in OT thought

Mercy and compassion as divine characteristics

Mercy is a quality intrinsic to the divine disposition. It is so essential that in some situations the adjective 'merciful' alone could be used to refer to God (Ps. 116:5; cf. Tobit 6:17). The experience of God's people was that his mercy revealed in historical acts of *redemption was, unlike human mercy, inexhaustible (Lam. 3:22; 2 Sam. 24:14). Because of its expression in history, it becomes one of the qualities that God's people observe and describe (Exod. 34:6; Deut. 4:31; 2 Chr. 30:9; Ps. 86:15; Dan. 9:9; Jonah 4:2). Yet, while divine mercy is long-suffering and abundant, it is not blind; for generations God responded to *Israel's disobedience to the covenant with mercy (Jer. 3:12; Neh. 9:17, 19, 31), but mercy unheeded led ultimately to *judgment (Lam. 2:2, 21; Zech. 1:12). Then the people hoped for a renewed experience of God's mercy in their restoration (Is. 55:7; 60:10; Jer. 31:20; 2 Sam. 24:14; Ps. 57:1; Hab. 3:2; cf. Tobit 6:17).

People also have the capacity for showing mercy, especially towards those with whom a special relationship already exists (1 Kgs. 20:31; Is. 49:15; Jer. 31:20; Matt. 18:33; *cf.* 1 Macc 2:57). But a lack of mercy is more natural to the human condition (Prov. 5:9; 12:10; Is. 13:18; 47:6; Jer. 6:23; 50:42; *cf.* Wisdom of Solomon 12:5).

Mercy as the motive of God's covenant

Hesed expresses a complex of ideas which includes love, mercy and compassion. It is God's mercy that compels him to enter into the covenant with Israel (Exod. 34:6; Deut. 4:31; 13:17; Hos. 2:19). God's actions in freeing the people from slavery and creating the covenant reveal his mercy in historical events. Within the *hesed*-complex, mercy includes loyalty based on compassionate love, a loyalty that protects the covenant, though Israel despises it (Is. 63:7; Jer. 16:5; 42:12; Hos. 2:19; Joel 2:13; Zech. 7:9; Pss. 25:6; 40:11; 69:16). The mercy God has decided to give is unmerited (Exod. 33:19; Gen. 19:16; Jer. 42:12): thus in the covenant context God's mercy is closely linked to forgiveness (Exod. 34:9; Num. 14:19; Jer. 3:12; Dan. 9:9), a more basic disposition of compassion (Deut. 13:17) which generates the steadfast love by which God sustains the covenant and repeatedly passes over the people's *sins (Pss. 25:6; 40:11; 51:1; 69:16; 103:4; 119:77; Jer. 3:12; 16:5). Membership of the covenant community, with enjoyment of its attendant promises and *blessings, originates in the mercy/compassion of God.

Mercy and compassion in the NT

The imprint of mercy/compassion on the pattern of God's relationship with people in the OT also shapes the NT understanding of God in relation to his people. Mercy forms the foundation of the communion God desires with humankind. Not surprisingly, the NT interprets God's mercy largely in the light of the Christ event, the supreme expression of love, mercy and grace.

God's covenant mercy in NT perspective

Following the OT pattern, the NT affirms that mercy is a divine characteristic (2 Cor. 1:3; Jas. 5:11) expressed in abundance towards God's people (Eph. 2:4). This mercy invites humble people to cry out to a compassionate God who will intervene in time of need (2 Tim. 1:16, 18; Luke 18:13; *cf.* Matt. 15:22; 17:15). In the Magnificat, Mary celebrates the mercy of God, the *hesed*-love displayed tirelessly in his loyalty to Israel (Luke 1:50, 54; *cf.* 1:58, 72, 78). According to Paul, the same mercy shown in the OT to rebellious people has now been displayed in *Jesus Christ in the age of the Spirit both to the Jews and to the Gentiles (Rom. 9:15–16, 23; 11:31–32; *cf.* 15:9). The extension of mercy to the Gentiles (see *Nations) is also taken up in 1 Peter 2:10: 'Once you were not a people; but now you are God's people; once you had not received mercy, but now you have received mercy' (NRSV). Applied here with special emphasis to Gentile believers to remind them of their undeserved blessings, the fact is equally true of Gentiles and Jews: people come into relationship with God only because he shows mercy to them.

Christ as the fullest articulation of God's mercy

The mercy experienced by Israel through the great acts of God found articulate and personal expression in the ministry of Christ. He disclosed God's mercy at the level of human relationships. This is seen clearly in his acts of *healing. After expelling the legion of demons, Jesus tells the healed man to return home and recount his experience of divine mercy (Mark 5:19). Healing is given because God is merciful, and Jesus is the conduit through which mercy is poured out (Matt. 17:15; Mark 10:47–48 par.; Luke 17:13). The cry for mercy transcends religious and cultural barriers (Matt. 15:22), and Jesus' compassionate response foreshadows the abolition of those barriers in the universal display of God's mercy to the whole world. Jesus' ministry illustrates how mercy and compassion, in the form of practical help, produce tangible results in bringing people to wholeness.

Mercy as the basis of salvation

Jesus' demonstration of mercy in individual acts illustrates the redemption from sin and *death that God extends to the world through the *sacrificial death and resurrection of the Messiah. The OT story of God's covenant-making with Israel is recapitulated in the NT account of his gracious provision of *salvation through the work of Christ. These redemptive acts of God – the *Exodus from

Egypt and Jesus' crucifixion/resurrection – are interrelated. The one act grounds and shapes the other, initiating a process of redemption that reaches its climax in the NT. Mercy is fundamental to both acts: God's compassionate love for his creation moves him to do for it what it cannot do for itself. Now in Christ the new Exodus – salvation from sin – forms the basis for the relationship God desires with humankind. Thus by his mercy God forgives and liberates those who have no right to such blessings.

The NT story underlines that salvation rests upon God's mercy executed through the Christ-event. Paul's discussion with the Roman Christians about the Gentiles' place in God's redemptive plan spells this out plainly (Rom. 9:15–18); salvation originates only in God's mercy, and the extension of this gift to the Gentiles is another illustration of mercy: 'For he [God] says to Moses, "I will have mercy on whom I have mercy, and I will have compassion on whom I have compassion"' (9:15, NIV; quoting Exod. 33:19). Mercy is at the core of salvation: the 'saved' are called 'vessels of mercy' (9:23), while those who resist are the 'vessels of wrath' (9:22).

Peter implies that the new life in Christ is continuous with the OT story of the covenant with Israel: 'By his great mercy [Exod. 34:6; Num. 14:18; Ps. 86:5, 15], he has given us a new birth through the resurrection of Jesus Christ from the dead' (1 Pet. 1:3, NRSV). Titus 3:5 declares: 'he saved us not because of any works of righteousness that we had done, but according to his mercy'. Similarly, Ephesians 2:4–5 links the salvation of the Gentiles with God's abundant mercy.

Mercy as a human response and responsibility

God's mercy in Christ had a profound effect upon the *church. An apostle's testimony of his conversion from a life of rebellion and his calling to ministry centres on God's mercy (1 Tim. 1:13, 16). The privilege of serving God is a product of divine mercy (2 Cor. 4:1). Moreover, Paul perceived in mundane events the evidence of God's merciful intervention (Phil. 2:27). The belief in God's compassionate presence among those he loves and in his timely help caused prayers for mercy to become common among believers (2 Tim. 1:16, 18) and the term to be used in Christian greetings (1 Tim. 1:2; 2 Tim. 1:2; 2 John 3;

Jude 2; cf. Gal. 6:16). Examples like these illustrate the early Christians' awareness of being recipients of God's mercy through Jesus Christ, and of their living in daily anticipation of new 'mercies' from God. These new outpourings of mercy are the seal of his love for and claim on his people (cf. 2 Cor. 1:3; Rom. 12:1; all the greetings; cf. Lam. 3:22–23).

In response to past and present (and in anticipation of future) experiences of God's mercy (Jude 21), his people are to be channels of divine mercy in the church and in the world. Both Judaism and early Christianity were aware of the responsibility to show mercy through the practice of almsgiving (Gk eleēmosynē, a derivative of eleos). Although charitable giving might be driven by wrong motives (Matt. 6:2–4), as a proper response to God's mercy it is a mark of genuine spirituality (see Tobit 4:7; 12:8, 9; Ecclus. 3:30; 7:10; 17:22; 29:8, 12; 35:2; 40:17, 24). This is clear from Luke 11:41, where almsgiving is valued much more highly than matters of ritual purity. Equally, mercy expressed in charitable giving is a mark of true discipleship in Luke 12:33. This expression of mercy is highly respected in the early church (Acts 9:36; 10:2), and is considered a normal responsibility of Christians (cf. Acts 24:17). Such acts of compassion made Christians living emblems of God's mercy in Christ and pointed forward to the fulfilment of the promise of salvation (cf. Acts 3:3, 6).

Within Jesus' teaching about the *kingdom of God, mercy is a primary characteristic of life with God, a demonstration of kingdom power: the beatitude in Matthew 5:7 associates mercy (as a mark of righteousness) with the appearance of God's kingdom (R. A. Guelich, The Sermon on the Mount, p. 89). God's mercy has so transformed his people that they may be merciful, and the new potential must be realized in their lives. Their mercy provides a window through which the living God may be glimpsed (Luke 6:36; cf. the opposite picture Matt. 18:33; Jas. 2:13). To this end, the parable of the Good Samaritan elevates the importance of showing mercy, and implies that it is an essential response of God's people to his covenant (Luke 10:25–37; Deut. 6:4–5; Lev. 19:17–18), and to be valued much more than mere cultic acts (Hos. 6:6; Matt. 9:13). Compassion and merciful action towards those in need identify a person as belonging to God, while the absence of mercy indicates unbelief and rejection of God (Rom. 1:28, 31). Christ's compassion sent him among all kinds of people to help them (Mark 8:2 par.), and believers are to respond to the mercy shown to them in the same way.

See also: GRACE.

Bibliography

R. Bultmann in *TDNT* 2, pp. 477–487; *idem*, *TDNT* 5, pp. 159–161; J. D. M. Derrett, *Law in the New Testament* (London, 1970); H.-H. Esser in *NIDNTT* 2, pp. 593–601; N. Glueck, *Hesed in the Bible* (Cincinnati, 1967); R. A. Guelich, *The Sermon on the Mount: A Foundation for Understanding* (Waco, 1982); E. Käsemann, *New Testament Questions of Today* (ET, London, 1969); N. H. Snaith, *The Distinctive Ideas of the Old Testament* (London, 1944); F. Staudinger in *EDNT* 1, pp. 428–431; N. Walter in *EDNT* 3, pp. 265–266.

P. H. TOWNER

MESSIAH, see JESUS CHRIST
MICAH, see Part 2
MINISTRY, MINISTER, see SPIRITUAL GIFTS
MIRACLES, see SIGNS AND WONDERS

MISSION

Introduction

The subject of mission is often absent from treatments of systematic theology, and is frequently neglected even in theme studies of biblical books. But mission is an exceedingly important motif pervading virtually the entire course of biblical revelation, and must not be left to missiologists who are concerned primarily with the modern-day application of biblical teaching on the topic. A biblical–theological survey of mission in the OT, the intertestamental period, and the various corpora of the NT is needed to appreciate the diversity as well as the underlying unity of scriptural teaching on mission.

Mission in the OT

There was, no 'mission' in the Garden, and there will be no 'mission' in the new heavens and the new earth (though the results of 'mission' will be evident). Still, from the proto-evangelion (God's promise to the woman of a 'seed' who would bruise the serpent's head, Gen. 3:15) to the end of this age, mission is necessitated by humanity's fall into sin and need for a Saviour and is made possible by the saving initiative of God in Christ.

Genesis

Once fallen, humans are under the wrath of God. Their relationships with God and with one another are severely affected, and their exercise of dominion over creation through work and procreation is characterized by frustration and pain. The escalating spread of sin is depicted in the narratives following that of the Fall: Cain and Abel (4:1–16), the sons of God and the daughters of humans (6:1–4), the flood (6:5 – 9:19), and the tower of Babel (11:1–9). In judgment, God scatters humankind over the earth and confuses its languages. This shows how dramatically humanity falls short of God's creation design.

Yet God remains faithful to his creation, entering into covenants with Noah (9:9–13) and *Abra(ha)m (12:1–3; *cf.* 15:1–18; ch. 17). The latter is summoned to leave his native country on the basis of God's promise of a land, seed, and *blessing. Ultimately, this blessing extends not merely to Abraham's physical descendants but to all who are 'children of Abraham' through faith (Gal. 3:6–9, 26–29; Rom. 4:16–17). The Abrahamic covenant provides the framework for God's dealings with humanity in the rest of biblical history, which culminates in the new covenant instituted by Abraham's 'seed', Jesus Christ (Gal. 3:16).

The Exodus and Israel's role among the nations

Once the Israelites have been delivered from bondage in Egypt, they are to be God's treasured possession out of all nations, 'a priestly kingdom and a holy nation' (Exod. 19:5–6, author's translation). Israel is to mediate God's presence and blessings to the surrounding nations, as a people set apart to serve a holy God. This does not mean that OT *Israel is enjoined to engage in intentional cross-cultural mission. Rather, as the recipient of the divine blessings, the nation is to exalt God in its life and worship, attracting individuals from among the nations historically by incorporation and eschatologically by ingathering. In this way Rahab and her family and Ruth the Moabitess become part of Israel. Also, Mosaic legislation makes special provision for the *gēr*, the alien residing in Israel (*cf.* Exod. 12:48; 22:21). Still, intermarriage with foreigners is frequently limited, particularly in the post-exilic period (Neh. 13:23–27; Ezra 9 – 10). Overall, only a few individuals are incorporated in OT times, with a large-scale ingathering of Gentiles not expected until the end times (*cf.* esp. Is. 56:8).

The Davidic kingship and the eschatological pilgrimage of the nations

In 2 Samuel 7:13, *David is assured that his kingdom will be established forever. The establishment of the Davidic kingship is crucial for an understanding of Yahweh's rule over the nations and the fulfilment of his covenant promises to Abraham. Although the fulfilment of this promise was put in danger by Israel's disobedience, it is fulfilled in Jesus of Nazareth, the Son of David, and will be fulfilled completely at the time of Christ's second coming (Rom. 11:25–29; *cf.* Acts 1:6; Rev. 20:1–6).

During the reign of David's son Solomon, various promises to Abraham and David are fulfilled: the promised land is fully conquered; Israel becomes a great nation; and the Jerusalem temple is built (*cf.* Deut. 12:5–11). Jerusalem becomes a world centre, epitomized by the Queen of Sheba's visit to the city. This visit serves as a paradigm for the *eschatological pilgrimage of the nations to Zion in later prophecy (Is. 2:2–4; 60 – 62; *cf.* Mic. 4:1–5; Pss. 36:7–8; 50:2). Zion, in turn, is depicted in some OT apocalyptic passages as the centre of the new creation (Is. 35:1–10; 65:17–18).

In the last days, the nations flock to Jerusalem to learn about Yahweh and his ways (Is. 2:2–3; *cf.* Zech. 8:20–23; Mic. 4:1–2). As they come, they bring the scattered children of Israel with them (Is. 60:2–9). In an amazing reversal, the nations submit to Israel (Is. 60:14), bring their wealth into the city (Is. 60:11–22), and join in the worship of Yahweh, whose people they have now become. Thus the prophet's admonition, 'Turn to me and be saved, all the ends of the earth' (Is. 45:22) is fulfilled. Significantly, this

ingathering of Gentiles is depicted as an eschatological event, brought about by God, not by Israel. Moreover, the mode of this ingathering is attraction (the nations come to Israel), not active outreach (Israel's going to the nations). In addition to the anticipation of the universal scope of eschatological salvation, several prophetic books envisage the restoration of a Jewish remnant, including the inauguration of a new covenant (*cf.* esp. Jer. 31:31–34).

Jonah

The book of Jonah is regarded by some as a 'missionary tract' calling Israel to go to the nations, and is thus believed to be a precursor to the missionary mandate of the NT. Indeed, the book shows that God's saving concerns extend to people outside Israel (Jonah 4:11). But Jonah the prophet is not presented as a missionary whose preaching is intended to serve as a paradigm for Israel's outreach to the nations.

The Isaianic Servant of the Lord

The Servant of Yahweh, featured in the four 'Servant songs' of Isaiah (42:1–4; 49:1–6; 50:4–9; 52:13 – 53:12; *cf.* 61:1–3), is one of the most important OT figures whose ministry pertains to both Israel and the nations. While the Servant's work is in the first instance related to the redemption of Jerusalem and Israel's return to the holy city, eventually it will affect the entire world. The sequence of the Servant's ministry, directed initially to Israel but resulting in blessing for the nations, follows a pattern similar to that of the Abrahamic promises and constitutes a development of these.

The 'nations' in the Psalms

The 'nations' represent the great mass of humanity in rebellion against God and subject to divine judgment (Ps. 10:16). Yet they are still within the Creator's plan of grace, since he intends to bring blessing to the nations of the world. Fundamental to this inclusion of the nations is Israel's role as the people of God in whose privileges the nations will be invited to join. In the enthronement psalms (Pss. 47, 93, 96 – 97, 99), Zion is the permanent centre of the worship of Yahweh in Israel. Like the tabernacle and Mt Sinai before it, Zion is holy owing to Yahweh's presence, and if his people are 'holy' because of Yahweh's presence in Zion, then Israel is separated from the nations (*cf.* Ps. 78). Their salvation must therefore involve their coming out of the world to Zion in order to worship the Lord; this will happen in the end times (Pss. 72:8–11; 102:12–22).

Mission in the intertestamental period

The traditional view has been that intertestamental Judaism engaged in mission (*cf.* esp. D. Georgi, *The Opponents of Paul in Second Corinthians*; more recently L. H. Feldman, *Jew and Gentile in the Ancient World*). If so, the early church's mission would have operated within the parameters already established by Judaism. However, if mission is defined as a conscious, deliberate, organized, and extensive effort to convert others to one's religion by way of evangelization or proselytization, it is doubtful whether it was characteristic of intertestamental Judaism. For while the Jewish religion was doubtless successful in attracting converts or proselytes, the initiative in such instances usually lay with Gentiles who desired to join Judaism rather than in intentional Jewish missionary efforts (S. McKnight, *A Light Among the Gentiles*; M. Goodman, *Mission and Conversion*). Indeed, not all religious expansion is intentional (P. Bowers, in *NovT* 22, pp. 317–323).

The NT passage traditionally cited in support of the notion that intertestamental Judaism was a missionary religion is Matthew 23:15. There Jesus excoriates the Pharisees for 'travel[ling] about on sea and land to make one proselyte' and for then making that convert 'twice as much a son of hell' as themselves. But 'travelling about on sea and land' may denote extensive effort rather than geographical movement, and the term 'proselyte' does not necessarily pertain to non-Jews but may merely refer to a Jew converting to Pharisaism. And what Jesus condemns is in any case Pharisaic zeal in proselytization rather than Jewish mission as such.

Intertestamental Judaism should therefore not be regarded as a missionary religion. The operative paradigm was one of attraction rather than intentional outreach. While Jews did allow sympathizers and proselytes to participate in their religious practices to a certain extent, they were primarily preoccupied with national or sectarian concerns. The inclusion of Gentiles in the orbit of God's sal-vation was not expected until the end times, as a special work of God, which prevented intertestamental Jews from active outreach to Gentiles. Moreover, the absence of the prophetic voice in intertestamental Judaism left the Jews without an authorizing mandate equivalent to the 'Great Commission' in the NT. The missions of Jesus and the early *church thus did not merely build upon Jewish precedent but replaced the old paradigm of mission with a new mode of outreach.

Mission in the NT

Mission in the Synoptic Gospels and Acts

1. *Mark.* For Mark, following Jesus involves the renunciation of natural ties (3:31–35) and the taking up of one's 'cross' (8:34). While *Jesus' ministry is directed primarily to the Jews (*cf.* esp. 7:27a), he does have occasional contact with Gentiles, such as the Gerasene demoniac (5:1–20) and the Syro-Phoenician woman (7:24–30). Reference is also made to the future proclamation of the *gospel to the Gentiles (13:10; 14:9), and the fulfilment of Isaiah's vision of the temple as a house of prayer for all the nations (Mark 11:17 quoting Is. 56:7). The Gospel's climactic christological confession is uttered not by a Jew but a Roman Gentile (15:39). Nevertheless, Mark does not show Jesus embarking on a 'Gentile mission'. He rather presents him as following the pattern of OT (and intertestamental) Israel, whose presence was to attract the surrounding nations to its God without Israel's making a concious effort to reach them.

2. *Matthew.* Matthew's Gospel opens with the portrayal of Jesus' fulfilling Israel's destiny as the representative, paradigmatic Son of God, with the result that God's blessings to the nations, promised to Abraham, are to be fulfilled through Jesus in the mission of his followers. It concludes with the 'Great Commission' which calls Jesus' followers to make disciples of the nations (28:18–20). This stands in contrast with Jesus' earlier instruction to his disciples to limit their mission to Israel, according to his own practice (10:5–6; 15:24). Even at this time, however, Jesus is shown already to anticipate the bearing of witness (see *Testimony/witness), not merely in Jewish synagogues, but also to Gentiles (10:18).

Nevertheless Matthew, like the other evangelists, portrays Jesus' mission as proceeding along salvation-historical lines: first to the Jews; then to the Gentiles. Occasionally in Matthew Jesus ministers to Gentiles, but never at his own initiative (*cf. e.g.* 8:5–13; 15:21–27). Towards the end of his Gospel, Matthew refers to the preaching of the 'gospel of the kingdom' as a witness to all the nations (24:14; *cf.* Mark 13:10; *cf.* also Matt. 26:13).

3. *Luke–Acts.* Luke's Gospel tells the story of Jesus and his salvation; the book of Acts traces the movement of that salvation to the Gentiles. The first volume begins with a summary of God's promises to Israel which are about to be fulfilled in Jesus. This sets the stage for the second volume, which presents the regathering of 'Israel' and her mission as a *light to the nations. The infancy narratives of Luke 1 – 2 indicate that Israel's hopes for a Saviour of David's line are about to be realized (1:30–35; *cf.* 2 Sam. 7:12–13). Through the birth of Jesus, God will restore Israel and fulfil his promises to Abraham and his descendants. However, the Abrahamic promises are fulfilled not in national Israel but in those who fear God (1:50–55). Moreover, the Lord's Messiah fits the pattern of Yahweh's Servant (2:32; 4:18–19; *cf.* Is. 42:6; 49:6–9; 61:1–2). Luke's genealogy reaches beyond Abraham to Adam (3:23–28; contrast Matt. 1:1–17), pointing to Jesus' identification with all people, not just Israel. Jesus' healing of the centurion's servant, his first encounter with a Gentile in Luke's Gospel, foreshadows the expansion of his ministry to the Gentiles (7:1–10). Jesus' choosing and commissioning of first twelve, then seventy (-two) messengers show that the role of an apostle, includes a ministry of preaching and healing (6:12–15; 9:1–2; 10:1–24). Two Lukan parables, found in the extended 'travel narrative' (9:51 – 19:28), envisage Gentile participation in the messianic banquet (13:28–30; 14:23–24). After Jerusalem's rejection of her Messiah, the risen Christ commissions his disciples to proclaim the forgiveness of sins in his name (24:44–49).

The book of Acts presents what Jesus continued to do and teach (*cf.* 1:1) by his Spirit through the early church led by the apostles. The account follows geographical lines, tracing the progress of gospel proclamation from Jerusalem – the centre from which the word of the Lord goes forth – to Judea and Samaria, and 'even to the remotest part of the earth' (1:8). In a major paradigm shift from a centripetal movement to a centrifugal one, the Twelve are to function as 'witnesses' to Israel (in place of the restoration of the kingdom to Israel, 1:6), and subsequently Paul acts as 'witness' to the Gentiles. Events with major significance for the mission of the early church recorded in the book of Acts include the outpouring of the Spirit (see *Holy Spirit) at Pentecost (ch. 2), Stephen's martyrdom (ch. 7), the conversion of Paul (ch. 9), and the Jerusalem council (ch. 15). Nothing can hinder the irresistible progress of the gospel, and the church, by the Spirit, overcomes all obstacles. Paul and the apostolic church are now the 'light for the Gentiles' (13:47), and while proclamation still begins with the Jews (3:26; 13:46; 18:5; 28:25–28), no distinction is now made between Jews and Gentiles concerning salvation and reception into the church: faith in Jesus as Lord is all that is required (*e.g.* 16:31). The end of the book of Acts finds Paul 'preaching the kingdom of God and teaching concerning the Lord Jesus Christ with all openness, unhindered' in the capital of the Empire, Rome (28:31).

Mission in the Pauline writings

From the time of his conversion and calling on the road to Damascus, the gospel, the good news of salvation in the Lord Jesus Christ, became the determinative focus of Paul's whole life (Acts 9). His encounter with the risen Christ led to a 'paradigm shift' in Paul's thinking: if Jesus was the crucified and exalted Messiah, the divine curse on him was 'for us', 'in order that in Christ Jesus the blessing of Abraham might come to the Gentiles' (Gal. 3:13–14), and the Law was dethroned as the primary way of approaching God (Rom. 3:21 – 7:25). Paul knew himself to be entrusted with God's '*mystery', the eschatological revelation that now Jews and Gentiles alike would be gathered together into one body, the church (Rom. 16:25–26; Eph. 2:1 – 3:13; Col. 1:25–27). While Paul's ministry was primarily to the Gentiles, he ardently prayed for the salvation of his own people, the Jews, and believed that there remained a future for ethnic Israel in God's redemptive purposes (Rom. 9 – 11). It was Paul's ambition to go where the gospel had not yet been preached (Rom. 15:20–21). His strategy focused on preaching to and evangelizing Jews as well as Gentile proselytes and God-fearers in local synagogues. Paul's aim was to establish Christian congregations in strategic (urban) centres from where the gospel could spread further to the surrounding regions. In the Pastoral Epistles, Paul emphasizes that God is the Saviour of all (1 Tim. 2:3–4; 4:10; Tit. 2:10–11; 3:4) and provides the post-apostolic church with a pattern of organization and criteria which its leadership must satisfy (P. H. Towner, *The Goal of Our Instruction*, [Sheffield, 1989]).

Mission in John

John's teaching on mission focuses on Jesus who, as the sent Son, accomplishes his redemptive mission in complete dependence on and obedience to the Father 'who sent' him (*e.g.* 4:34). While the first part of John's Gospel shows Jesus' rejection by his own people Israel (1:11), the second part focuses on Jesus' preparation of his new covenant community to continue his mission following his crucifixion and resurrection (chs. 13 – 17). Anticipating his exaltation to the Father, Jesus promises to send 'another helper' (14:16) and to answer prayer in his name (14:13–14). He calls on his followers to glorify him by 'going' and bearing fruit (15:16), as they witness with the Spirit (15:26–27). Love and unity are to characterize their lives (13:34–35; 15:12, 17; 17:20–26). In the Johannine commissioning narrative, the crucified and risen Lord, Sent One now turned sender, breathes his Spirit on the disciples and charges them to proclaim forgiveness of sins in his name (20:21–23). The wording of Jesus' commission, 'As the Father sent me, so send I you' (20:21), makes his own relationship with the Father the basic paradigm for the disciples' relationship with Jesus in the pursuit of their mission (A. J. Köstenberger, *The Missions of Jesus and the Disciples according to the Fourth Gospel*).

Mission in the General Epistles and Revelation

1. *General Epistles.* In their struggle with heretical teaching, Jude, 2 Peter, and 1–3 John display an essential prerequisite for mission: zeal for the 'faith once for all entrusted to the saints' (Jude 3). John's second and third epistle deal with the issue of extending or refusing *hospitality to false teachers. But it is Hebrews and 1 Peter that contribute most to a biblical theology of mission. Addressing a congregation in danger of reverting back to Judaism, the author of Hebrews contends that God's final revelation occurred in his Son, Jesus (Heb. 1:1–3), and that his readers neglect 'such great salvation' at their grave peril (2:3; the 'warning passages'). Christians are portrayed as running a race following their forerunner, Jesus, into heaven (6:20; 12:1–3, 12–13), and as pilgrims and exiles in search of a homeland, a better country, and a 'city prepared by God' (11:13–16; *cf.* 12:22). As followers of the one who endured great hostility from sinners (12:3), believers are not to be afraid to suffer and identify openly with their crucified Lord (13:13; cf. 10:25–26).

Similarly, Peter describes believers as sojourners and 'resident aliens' in this world (1 Pet. 1:1, 17; 2:11; *cf.* Heb. 11:9,13). He exhorts his readers to view their suffering from an eschatological perspective (e.g. 1:4–6). The believing community is shown to fulfil the calling of OT Israel which was to 'proclaim the excellencies' of God as a mediatorial body (2:5–9; *cf.* Is. 43:21). Believers' mission is to take the form of verbal witness (2:9; 3:15), undergirded by a holy, spiritually separated life (1:13 – 2:10), a God-glorifying response to suffering (esp. 2:13–25; 3:8–18b), and proper submission to earthly authorities (2:13,18; 3:1; 5:1,5).

2. *Revelation.* Revelation depicts the result of mission: people from every tribe and nation gathered in heaven to worship God and the Lamb (1:7; 4:10–11; 5:9; 7:4–17; 14:1–5). This marks the fulfillment of God's covenants with Abraham (all nations are blessed in his seed, Christ) and David (the exalted Lord is the eternal ruler of his people). The book challenges believers to renewed spiritual zeal and commitment (chs. 2 – 3), and exhorts them to persevere in their suffering (14:12). The seer's apocalyptic visions depict an eternal state free from pain, suffering, and death (21:4); creation has come full circle, with the Edenic state not merely restored but superseded. God's vindication of the righteous (martyrs) and his judgment of the wicked are for the purpose of theodicy (G. R. Osborne, 'Theodicy in the Apocalypse', in *TJ* 14, 1993, pp. 63–77). John's four visions 'in the Spirit' (1:9 – 3:22; 4:1 –

16:21; 17:1 – 21:8; 21:9 – 22:21) are cast in terms of the pervasive evil influence of the Roman Empire ('the whore Babylon', chs. 17 – 18), a precursor of the anti-Christ. The concluding chapters depicting the 'New Jerusalem' and the new heavens and new earth portray the restoration of God's created order and the fulfilment of the divine purposes for his chosen people.

Conclusion

God takes the initiative in mission, for the effecting of salvation through Christ. The Abrahamic promises, the Davidic kingship, and the Isaianic Servant of Yahweh are major motifs that culminate in Jesus' coming and mission. While OT Israel was to serve as a mediatorial body displaying God's glory to the surrounding nations, and while even Jesus limited his earthly ministry to Israel, the time between Pentecost and Jesus' return marks the age of the church's active outreach. Believers are charged to preach the gospel of the kingdom to all the nations, to make them Christ's disciples, and to be his witnesses to the ends of the earth. In the pursuit of this mission, the church is promised the presence of Jesus and the aid of the Holy Spirit.

See also: NATIONS; SALVATION; FORGIVENESS AND RECONCILIATION.

Bibliography

D. Bosch, Transforming Mission: Paradigm Shifts in Theology of Mission (Maryknoll, 1991); W. P. Bowers, 'Religious propaganda in the first century', NovT 22, 1980, pp. 317–323; idem, in DPL, pp. 608–619; L. H. Feldman, Jew and Gentile in the Ancient World: Attitudes and Interactions from Alexander to Justinian (Princeton, 1993); D. Georgi, The Opponents of Paul in Second Corinthians (Edinburgh, 1986); M. Goodman, Mission and Conversion: Proselytizing in the Religious History of the Roman Empire (Oxford, 1994); F. Hahn, Mission in the New Testament (London, 1965); K. Kertelge (ed.), Mission im Neuen Testament (Freiburg-Basel-Wien, 1982); A. J. Köstenberger, The Missions of Jesus and the Disciples According to the Fourth Gospel (Grand Rapids, 1998); A. J. Köstenberger and P. T. O'Brien, Salvation to the Ends of the Earth: A Biblical Theology of Mission (Leicester and Downers Grove, 2001); W. J. Larkin and J. F. Williams (eds.), Mission in the New Testament: An Evangelical Approach (Maryknoll, 1998); S. McKnight, A Light Among the Gentiles: Jewish Missionary Activity in the Second Temple Period (Minneapolis, 1991); P. T. O'Brien, Consumed By Passion: Paul and the Dynamics of the Gospel (Homebush West, 1993); idem, Gospel and Mission in the Writings of Paul: An Exegetical and Theological Analysis (Carlisle and Grand Rapids, 1995); D. Senior and C. Stuhlmueller, The Biblical Foundations for Mission (Maryknoll, 1983).

A. J. KÖSTENBERGER

MOSES

Introduction

Moses is one of the primary characters in the Pentateuch, and a significant figure in later forms of Judaism, although curiously he is absent from much of the post-pentateuchal OT. The NT writers make use of Moses typology in framing their message; in particular, Matthew's version of the messianic gospel possibly uses the relationship between Moses and the *law as a commentary on *Jesus' reinterpretation and fulfilment of the Sinaitic law.

Moses in the book of Exodus

Most OT references to Moses are found in the Pentateuch. Of the 706 references in the Hebrew Bible, 593 appear in *Exodus (261), *Leviticus (eighty), *Numbers (216), and *Deuteronomy (thirty-six). Moses is a foundational character in the greatest event affecting *Israelite national formation and religious consciousness, the *Exodus from Egypt. He is also remembered posthumously in Deuteronomy as the greatest *prophet of Israel (Deut. 34:10–12). Because Moses appears most prominently in the book of Exodus, it will receive the most extensive treatment here.

The book of Exodus includes a partial biography of Moses. The accounts of various elements of Moses' bios – his birth, heritage (both Hebrew and Egyptian), vocation and career as representative of and intermediary between Yahweh and the Israelite community – take forward an already dynamic narrative. Certain aspects of his character are highlighted incidentally, such as his attitudes towards injustice and conflicts and his personal insecurities. Moses is remembered most often for the part he plays as lawgiver in the inception and integration of biblical law at Sinai.

Moses as narrative hero

The birth story in Exodus 2:1–10 provides information about the role of Moses in the plot of the Exodus story (ch. 1 – 14) and in the narrative of the entire Pentateuch. Literary form is a vital contributor to textual meaning, alongside conceptual content; the birth narrative belongs to a seemingly standard birth-of-a-hero sub-genre in which a virtually helpless infant who has been abandoned to the natural elements is miraculously rescued, granted a position of ascendancy, and eventually attains heroic status. Scholars have identified more than thirty occurrences of this literary form in the ancient Near Eastern and Graeco-Roman worlds. The closest parallel to Moses' story is the Legend of Sargon of Akkad, a Mesopotamian king in the middle of the third millennium BC.

These and other details in the early chapters of Exodus reinforce Moses' heroic status in the narrative plot, as the visible protagonist who represents Yahweh, the actual protagonist, against the antagonistic efforts of a deified Egyptian monarch to keep the Israelites in servitude and not recognize the universality of Yahweh's royal domain. The account of Moses' call in chapters 3 – 4, which also utilizes a stock literary form (the prophetic call narrative, seen elsewhere in Is. 6, Jer. 1, etc.), confirms his significant position as representative; it includes the call of Moses to represent Yahweh to the people, and formally introduces Yahweh into the plot. It is mainly through the eyes and experience of Moses as narrative hero that the reader hears the story, and the narrative of the Pentateuch, which forms the heart of the Hebrew Bible, ends with his death (Deut. 34:1–8).

Moses as patriarchal figure

The story of Moses contains allusive links with Genesis material. For example, the story of his birth includes a clear parallel with the creation narrative in its description of the child as 'good' (Heb. tôb, used in Exod. 2:2; cf. Gen. 1:4, 10, 12, 18, 21, 25, and especially

1:31), and also one with *Noah in its use of the Hebrew word tēbâ for the 'ark' or 'papyrus basket' (which appears only twice in the Hebrew Bible, in Exod. 2:3, 5, apart from the twenty-five instances in the Noah story in Genesis 6 – 9). Moses eventually preserves the lives of the Israelites through deliverance, just as Noah preserves his people. Furthermore, the etiology of Moses' son Gershom in the so-called betrothal type-scene in Exodus 2:22 ('I am/was/have become an alien/sojourner in a foreign land') serves to characterize not Gershom but Moses. Regardless of whether the 'land' refers to Egypt or to Midian, Moses is called an 'alien' or 'sojourner' (Heb. gēr). This term has been used for every one of the patriarchs in Genesis as they attempt to realize Yahweh's promise in their midst (for *Abraham in Gen. 17:8; 23:4; 28:4; 35:27, for *Isaac in 35:27; 37:1, and for *Jacob in 36:7; 37:1). The use of such loaded language in this patriarchal type-scene emphasizes Moses' continuity with his ancestors whose stories are told in Genesis.

Moses as leader

Although the Pentateuch venerates Moses with heroic status as a prophetically called patriarchal figure who propagates the law of Yahweh, its portrayal of his *leadership focuses on his weaknesses as well as on his strengths. Moses' recalcitrance and sense of inadequacy for his task (3:11; 4:13), described in terms of his being 'slow of speech' (4:10; to which God replies with creation language in 4:11–12) and having 'uncircumcised lips' (6:12, 30; contrasting with the description of Aaron as a fluent speaker in 4:14–16) has resulted in the tradition of Moses' speech impediment.

Many scholars have observed that Moses' self-assurance increases rapidly in the Exodus narrative, particularly in the plagues cycle, and that he becomes a confident leader. Aaron is initially appointed to act as Moses' mouthpiece (Exod. 4:14–16), in response to Moses' request that someone else be sent on the mission to emancipate the Israelites from Pharoah's despotic grasp (Exod. 4:13). From this request comes the shared leadership of Moses and Aaron who, shortly after assembling the Israelite elders and convincing them of the validity of their mission (Exod. 4:29–30; note that Aaron is described as performing the signs in 4:30 even though Moses was originally to have performed all three of them [4:2–5, 6–7, 8–9]), approach Pharaoh as negotiators with an initial request to leave the land (5:1–3). They are mentioned together in various of the Exodus episodes.

Moses as lawgiver

Moses is probably most often associated with the receiving of divine words of law and instruction from Yahweh on Mount Sinai, and with their dissemination among the Israelite community. This topic occupies a large block of the pentateuchal corpus, from Exodus 19 to Numbers 10:10, although Moses' juridical role is attested earlier (*e.g.* in Exod. 18:13–26, where his Midianite father-in-law suggests that he delegates the administration of justice in the Israelite community). Some scholars even argue that behind his murdering of the Egyptian in Exodus 2:12 lies an innate concern for justice. Because of the close connection between Moses and Sinai, early Jewish and Christian tradition ascribed to him the authorship of the Pentateuch, although this is disputed by many in current pentateuchal scholarship. It is clear from passages like Exodus 19 that in his receipt of the Sinai legislation Moses occupies a place of special privilege before Yahweh, a position not shared by the Israelite people or even the *priests (19:19–20; *cf.* vv. 23–24; 24:2, 15–18).

One of the most critically significant episodes in the Pentateuch, if not in the entire Hebrew Bible, which has direct implications for Moses' role both as leader and as lawgiver, is the dispute regarding the golden calf in Exodus 32 – 34. Impatient with Moses' long stay on Mount Sinai with Yahweh, the people persuade Aaron to create a golden image in the form of a calf (32:1–6), possibly, at least in part, with the gold that was plundered from the Egyptians immediately before the Exodus (Exod. 3:21–22; 11:2; 12:35–36; cf. Ps. 105:37). Aaron accedes to their request, and so threatens the continued presence of Yahweh with his chosen people (32:7–10). After Moses has interceded and deliberated with Yahweh, and received a new set of tablets to replace those that he had smashed in his anger (32:15–19), it is decided that the *covenant will be maintained instead of abrogated, and that Yahweh's presence, characterized by such qualities as mercy, compassion, steadfast love, faithfulness and

forgiveness (33:19; 34:6–7), will remain with his chosen people.

Moses in the rest of the Pentateuch

Moses in Leviticus

Moses appears in Leviticus largely as the mouthpiece of Yahweh, promulgating the ceremonial and other laws / instructions contained in the book. Often Moses relays instructions from Yahweh either to the Israelites directly (Lev. 1:1–2; 4:1–2; 7:22–23, 28–29; 12:1–2; 18:1–2; 19:1–2; 20:1–2; 23:1–2, 9–10, 23–24, 26, 33–34; 24:1–2, 23; 25:1–2; 27:1–2; summarized in 27:34) or to Aaron and his sons as priestly leaders of the community (Lev. 6:8–9, 24–25; 9:1–6; 17:1–2; 21:1; 22:1–2, 17–18). On a few occasions Yahweh gives instruction for the Israelites to both Moses and Aaron (Lev. 11:1–2; 13:1; 14:33; 15:1).

In chapters 8 – 9, Moses appears in the narrative of the appointment of the Aaronic priesthood (which occurs in a context comprised mostly of cultic regulations). Chapter 10 narrates the ensuing conflict, and demonstrates that the sacerdotal task must be discharged with strict attention to detail before Yahweh, the *holy *God of Israel. Already in the book of Exodus the line of Aaron has been identified as the levitical line from which the Israelite priesthood will be drawn (Exod. 28:1; 29:1, passim, 44; 30:30; 31:10), and Exodus 29 contains instructions for a ceremony, conducted by Moses, for the consecration of the priests to their special role in the community (cf. Lev. 8). The Levites are again identified as a special priestly tribe distinct from the other sons of Israel in Numbers 3 and 8 (cf. 1 Chr. 6:48–53).

Moses also issues specific decrees for the conduct of the priests, for example in chapter 16, which prescribes the annual Day of Atonement ceremonies; the purpose of these is to consecrate the tabernacle and its contents, along with the assembled priests and people (16:29–34). In chapter 21 Moses is commanded to relay a set of requirements for maintaining the sanctity of the priesthood (several of these are repeated in Ezek. 44:15–31).

Moses in Numbers

Moses is instrumental in initiating the censuses of Numbers (chs. 1, 26) from which the book is named, the symbolic arrangement of the tribes, and other legislation. From the departure from Mount Sinai in Numbers 10:1–12, through the desert wanderings, to the people's eventual destination in the plains of Moab in the transjordan area, several issues arise relating to Moses' leadership role within the Israelite community.

Various threats are posed to Moses' authority: the complaints and rebellion of the community (chs. 11, 14, 20, 21, and 25); the rebellion of Korah, Moses' cousin (ch. 16; cf. Exod. 6:18, 21); and the opposition of Aaron and Miriam (ch. 12). (Curiously, Moses is not mentioned at all in the Balak/Balaam episode in chs. 22 – 24.) These narratives seek to establish the divinely-ordained leadership role that Moses has received amongst his people, and reinforce the account of his prophetic calling to the task. He is not to exercise that role in a despotic way (cf. Num. 12:3), but in obedience to God's call (Num. 16:28).

Various other significant events are related in Numbers: the death of Aaron in 20:22–29 and 33:38–39; the death of Miriam in 20:1; and the prohibition against Moses' entering the promised land (Num. 20:12; cf. Deut. 32:51). It is rather ironic that the person from whom Yahweh wanted to make a nation (Exod. 32:10; cf. Num. 14:12), who reminded Yahweh of his promise of descendants made to the patriarchs (Exod. 32:11–14), and who even requested that Yahweh 'blot him out of the book' if he would not forgive the people (Exod. 32:32), is prohibited from entering Canaan. Instead, only the children of the wilderness generation (Num. 14:21–23, 26–35) would enjoy the fulfilment of the promise of *land. Joshua son of Nun, who had been Moses' aide for some time (Exod. 24:13; 32:17; 33:11; Num. 11:28), was to lead the people into the land (27:12–23).

Later in Numbers, Moses relates Yahweh's words regarding the initial allotments of land (ch. 32; to the transjordanian tribes of Reuben and Gad), lists the stages of the journey from Egypt to the plains of Moab (ch. 33), and delineates the ideal boundaries of Canaan.

Moses in Deuteronomy

The book of Deuteronomy is in the form of a sermon by Moses; it emphasizes, through rhetorical speech, the need for the Israelite community to take the words of Yahweh to heart 'this day'. It focuses on the present-day application of the divine instruction relayed by Moses. From a literary point of view, Deuteronomy concludes the Pentateuch, but theologically it sets the tone for the following books; its covenantal emphasis extends as far as 2 Kings.

Like Leviticus and Numbers, Deuteronomy reiterates much of the pentateuchal legislation (including the decalogue in 5:1–21), as its name, which refers to the second giving of the law, indicates. Chapters 12 – 26 comprise the Deuteronomic legal code, which forms the stipulations section of its covenantal structure. Characteristic themes like the one place of *worship (ch. 12) and the worship of Yahweh alone (ch.13) reinforce the idea that Yahweh's past salvific acts have implications for the daily life of the community. In Leviticus and Numbers Moses speaks Yahweh's words about the institution of the priesthood as one who is not himself a priest. But his words in Deuteronomy about the institution of prophecy (18:14–22) reflect his own role as the prophet par excellence (34:10–12). Part of the purpose of these words is to offer a means of distinguishing between authentic and inauthentic prophecy (13:1–5; 18:21–22).

Deuteronomy concludes with information already made known in Numbers, for example that Joshua will succeed Moses (Deut. 31:1–8; 34:9). But new information is given as well, particularly relating to the reading of the Torah in the assembly every seven years (31:9–13). After a hymnic recitation of a closing song (the words of which are to be a witness against the Israelites in the face of future apostasy; cf. 31:19–22), a command to the Levites to keep the book of the Torah (law) with the ark of the covenant, and an extended blessing of the Israelite tribes (33:1–29), Deuteronomy ends with an account of Moses' death (32:48–52; 34:1–8); this superlative prophet (34:10–12) sees the land only from a distance (32:49, 52; 34:1–4).

Moses in the rest of the OT

Of the 706 references to Moses in the OT, 113 occur outside the Pentateuch: seventy-two in the Prophets and forty-one in the Writings. It is somewhat surprising that a figure of his stature is mentioned so rarely in these two sections of the canon.

Most of the extra-pentateuchal references relate to his supposed authorship of the

Torah. The Torah is clearly associated with Moses in phrases such as 'the book of Moses' (2 Chr. 35:12; Ezra 6:18; Neh. 13:1), 'the law of Moses' (Josh. 8:31–32; Ezra 3:2; 7:6; Neh. 9:14; 10:29; 1 Kgs. 2:3; 2 Kgs. 23:25; 2 Chr. 23:18; 30:16; Dan. 9:11, 13; Mal. 4:4), 'the book of the law of Moses' (Josh. 23:6; Neh. 8:1; 2 Kgs. 14:6) and 'the law, in the book of Moses' (2 Chr. 25:4). More general references to his literary work are found in descriptions of the commandments, ordinances, *etc.* given through Moses (Josh. 4:10; 8:35; Neh. 8:14; 2 Chr. 8:13; 33:8), and in other allusions to his role as revelatory agent (Ps. 103:7). Specific taxes are ascribed to him (2 Chr. 24:6, 9), as is the placing of the tablets in the ark at Horeb (1 Kgs. 8:9; 2 Chr. 5:10).

References are made to the transfer of Moses' leadership role to Joshua (Josh. 1:1, 17; 3:7; 4:14; 11:15, 23), to his death (Josh. 1:1), to his lineage (1 Chr. 6:3; 23:13), to his descendants (Judg. 1:16; 4:11; 1 Chr. 23:14–17; 26:24), and to his role as 'servant of Yahweh' (Josh. 1:1–2, 7; 8:31, 33; 11:12; Neh. 1:7–8; 2 Kgs. 21:8; 2 Chr. 1:3); also to his military successes (Josh. 12:6; 13:12, 21), to his involvement in the allotment of the land (Josh. 1:13–15; 14:2; 17:4; 18:7; 22:9; Judg. 1:20), and to the promise of land which was made to him (Josh. 1:3; 9:24; 13:8, 24, 29, 32; 14:3; 22:7).

Moses and Aaron are described as priests who, like the prophet Samuel, communicated with Yahweh and faithfully kept his statutes and decrees (Ps. 99:6–7). But even if Moses and Samuel attempted to intercede for the people before Yahweh, says Jeremiah, their prayer would have no effect, because the people have broken the terms of the covenant (Jer. 15:1).

Moses in the NT

Moses is mentioned by name forty-three times in the NT: thirty-two times in the Gospels (in Matthew five times; in Mark five; in Luke four; in John seven) and Acts (eleven times); and eleven times in the epistles: in Romans (seven times), in 2 Corinthians (twice), and in Hebrews (twice). The Moses typology of the NT is an important part of its portrayal of Jesus as Messiah.

Moses in the Gospels and Acts

Moses is named with reference to aspects of the Torah's teaching: on purification (Matt.

8:4; Mark 1:44; Luke 2:22; 5:14); on divorce (Matt. 19:7–8; Mark 10:3–5); on marriage (Matt. 22:24; Mark 12:19; Luke 20:28); on respect for parents (Mark 7:10); on resurrection (Mark 12:26; Luke 20:37); on circumcision (John 7:22–23; Acts 15:1, 5); and on adultery (John 8:5). Moses' name also appears as an euphemism for the Torah itself (Luke 16:29, 31; John 1:17; 7:19; Acts 6:11, 14; 13:39; 15:21).

The Torah, which is assumed to contain the writings of Moses, is viewed as a source for messianic teaching about Jesus (Luke 24:27, 44; John 1:45; 5:45–46; 6:32; Acts 3:22; 7:37; 26:22; 28:23). In fact, both Matthew and John draw parallels between Moses and Jesus which typologically reinforce their claims about Jesus' messianic status. Matthew possibly presents Jesus, after his Exodus from the land of Egypt (Matt. 2:13–23) and subsequent *wilderness experience (4:1–11), as a second lawgiver who recontextualizes the stipulations of the Sinai covenant for his hearers from a mountain (5:1) as a prophet like Moses (chs. 5 – 7). Many interpreters, but not all, find a fivefold structure in Matthew's Gospel, and interpret it as an imitation of the Pentateuch's five-part scheme legitimated by its association with Moses. John alludes to the bronze snake from Numbers 21:9 which by Hezekiah's reign had become an idolatrous icon (2 Kgs. 18:4). In a similar context of unbelief, eternal life is offered to any of John's readers who look to the exalted Son of Man with faith (John 3:14).

At the transfiguration Moses, accompanied by *Elijah, appears before Jesus (Matt. 17:3–4; Mark 9:4; Luke 9:30, 33), and in Acts 7:20–44 Stephen rehearses the life of Moses in his speech before the Sanhedrin, with some details not found in the Pentateuch: that Moses was educated in all the wisdom of the Egyptians (7:22); and that he was forty years old when he visited his fellow Israelites (7:23).

Moses in the epistles

Moses is mentioned several times in the NT epistles, usually as the author of pentateuchal texts (Exod. 33:19 in Rom. 9:15; Lev. 18:5 in Rom. 10:5; Deut. 32:21 in Rom. 10:19; Deut. 25:4 in 1 Cor. 9:9), or as a euphemism for the Torah (2 Cor. 3:15; Heb. 10:28). Hebrews 7:14 declares that in connection with the tribe of Judah Moses says nothing about priests. In

Romans 5:14 death is said to reign from the time of Adam to the time of Moses. Moses is also a model of *faithfulness in difficult times (Heb. 3:2–5; 11:23–28). In Revelation 15:3 seven angels hold harps and sing the song of Moses from Deuteronomy 32 in worship of God.

Several events of Moses' time are mentioned, such as the Exodus from Egypt (Heb. 3:16), the Sinai revelation (Heb. 12:21), the covenant ceremony from Exodus 24 (Heb. 9:19), the veiled glory of Moses' face from Exodus 34 (2 Cor. 3:7), and the building of the tabernacle (Heb. 8:5). 1 Corinthians 10:2 is an allegorical description of the Exodus and subsequent wilderness journey with reference to Christian spirituality.

Moses is also mentioned in the reference in 2 Timothy 3:8 to his dispute with Jannes and Jambres, the magicians of Exodus 7:11, and in the reference in Jude 1:9 to the archangel Michael disputing with the devil about the body of Moses; this incident is not mentioned elsewhere in the canon.

Conclusion

Clearly Moses is an important biblical character, whose historical and literary significance is evident in both testaments and must be thoroughly understood in order to appreciate the theological significance of his role. Although many of the legal particularities of the Mosaic covenant were peculiar to their time and culture, the heart of Mosaic teaching remains relevant for Christians today, as summarized by Jesus in his call to love both God and the neighbour wholeheartedly (Matt. 22:37–40; Mark 12:29–31).

Bibliography

G. W. Coats, *Moses: Heroic Man, Man of God* (Sheffield, 1988); D. M. Gunn, 'The hardening of Pharaoh's heart: plot, character and theology in Exodus 1–14', in D. J. A. Clines, D. M. Gunn and A. J. Hauser (eds.), *Art and Meaning: Rhetoric in Biblical Literature* (Sheffield, 1982); P. E. Hughes, 'Moses' birth story: A biblical matrix for prophetic messianism', in C. A. Evans and P. W. Flint (eds.), *Studies in the Dead Sea Scrolls and Related Literature* (Grand Rapids, 1997).

P. E. HUGHES

MOUNTAINS

Biblical literature frequently uses the image of mountains and hills for rhetorical effect. Mountains are associated with the ideas of: endurance ('everlasting hills', Gen. 49:26, NRSV); stability (though it is regularly stressed that in the face of *God's powerful activity even the mountains may be removed, Pss. 18:7; 46:2–3; 97:5; Hab. 3:10); security (Gen. 19:17; Josh. 2:16; Ps. 11:1); desolation (2 Chr. 18:16; Jer. 13:16); and fruitfulness (Pss. 104:10, 13; 147:8; Amos 9:13). Individual mountains have particular characteristics: thus Carmel is a symbol of beauty and fertility (Song 7:5; Is. 35:2), and Hermon enjoys heavy dew, symbolizing the lavish *blessing that Yahweh is willing to bestow on his people (Ps. 133:3).

Some mountains are seen as having particular religious significance. Christ's transfiguration is said to have been witnessed on the '*holy mountain' (2 Pet. 1:18), while the same term is used nineteen times of *Jerusalem (particularly in connection with the restoration from the Babylonian exile, Is. 56:7; 65:25; Ezek. 20:40; Dan. 9:16, 20; 11:45; Zeph. 3:11; Zech. 8:3). Mt Gerizim (later the site for Samaritan worship, John 4:20) and Mt Ebal are important as the places where the *covenant is renewed after Joshua's entry into Canaan (Josh. 8:30–35), and *Elijah repairs an altar of Yahweh on Mt Carmel (1 Kgs. 18:30).

Two mountains, Sinai/Horeb and Zion, are singled out as being of particular importance for Israel's relationship with God. Israel looks back to Sinai/Horeb as the place where the foundational covenant between Yahweh and the nation was mediated by Moses and where the associated *laws were delivered (Exod. 19 – Num. 10). *Moses encountered God in a *theophany on this mountain and received his call to go back to Egypt, and Elijah's experience there revealed his role to be that of a new Moses ('Horeb, the mountain of God', Exod. 3:1; *cf.* 1 Kgs. 19:8). Yet, in the rest of the OT Mt Sinai/Horeb is only rarely mentioned.

Mt Zion comes to prominence after David captures the city from the Jebusites (2 Sam. 5) and transfers the ark to the site (2 Sam. 6). Solomon subsequently builds the *temple there (1 Kgs. 6). The close association of the mountain idea with Zion and its temple is reflected in such expressions as *har bêt YHWH*, 'the mountain of the house of Yahweh' (Mic. 4:1; Is. 2:2; 2 Chr. 33:15, author's translation) and *har habbêt*, 'the mountain of the house' (Mic. 3:12; Jer. 26:18).

Given Israel's location in the world of the ancient Near East, any understanding of the religious significance of mountains needs to take into account the role mountain ideology played in the religions of the surrounding peoples. The concept of a 'cosmic mountain' is well known from Mesopotamia, Syria and other parts of the region. R. J. Clifford (*The Cosmic Mountain*) examines the relationship between OT and Canaanite ideas about the 'cosmic mountain'.

While this concept is somewhat fluid, it denotes a place where the gods are to be encountered in a special way. Psalm 48 contains a description of Zion which emphasizes its impressive situation (vv. 1–3) and refers to it as being 'in the far North', lit. 'remote Zaphon' (v. 2) (*cf.* Is. 14:13). Zaphon is a mountain in Syria where the Canaanite god Baal had his temple and from where he made proclamations. Psalm 48:1–3 is probably best understood as a deliberate polemic against such claims for Zaphon, asserting rather that Zion is the dwelling place of the only God who is worthy of consideration in human affairs.

A series of *eschatological motifs is associated with Mt Zion. Scattered Israel will be gathered once more to the holy mountain (Ezek. 40 – 48; Jer. 31:1–25; Is. 35; 40 – 66); the nations will make pilgrimage to it to be taught the Torah, and it will be established as the centre of God's rule over the nations (Is. 2:2–4/Mic. 4:1–4; Is. 25:6–10; Zech. 8:20–23). During the Second Temple period these motifs were expanded and played an important part in forming expectations about the final appearance of God's *kingdom.

Against this background, mountains appear at important junctures in *Jesus' ministry. Matthew's Gospel has a sequence of six mountains: Temptation (4:8–10); Teaching (5:1–8;1); Feeding (15:29–31); Transfiguration (17:1–9); Olivet Discourse (24–25); and Power and Commissioning (28:16–20). T. L. Donaldson (*Jesus on the Mountain*) argues that while Sinai and Mosaic allusions appear in these accounts, the eschatological motifs associated with Zion, the mountain of

God's enthronement (see *Exaltation), are dominant, and that Jesus is portrayed as the one who brings about the consummation of God's kingdom.

In the allegory in Galatians 4:22–27 Paul contrasts Mt Sinai and Jerusalem, the former representing a past era of law and slavery, and the latter the new era of liberation (*cf.* Heb. 12:18–24).

Bibliography

R. J. Clifford, *The Cosmic Mountain in Canaan and the Old Testament* (Cambridge, 1972); T. L. Donaldson, *Jesus on the Mountain* (Sheffield, 1985).

W. OSBORNE

MYSTERY

Introduction

Scripture frequently speaks of hidden things and mysteries. From its depiction of *God as sovereign and omniscient, it is clear that nothing is hidden or mysterious to him, whether it be the workings of the universe (Job 38:1 – 39:30) or human hearts (1 Sam. 16:7; Ps. 139:1–4, 11–12; 1 Cor. 4:5; Heb. 4:13). There are, however, places in the Bible where something is disclosed to particular individuals or groups, but is hidden or mysterious to others. The following is an exploration of this concept of mystery.

The OT

The idea of mystery is most clearly seen in Daniel 2, the one place in the OT where the term 'mystery' (*rāz* in Aramaic, *mystērion* in Gk) is used. Explicit emphasis is placed upon it; Nebuchadnezzar's dream and its interpretation are both described as elements of a mystery that is to be revealed (Dan. 2:18–19, 27). Once Daniel has recounted the dream and given its interpretation, emphasis is once again placed on the idea of mystery; Nebuchadnezzar praises Daniel's God as a revealer of mysteries (Dan. 2:47) (G. K. Beale, *The Use of Daniel in Jewish Apocalyptic Literature and in the Revelation of St. John*, p. 13).

The content of mystery and its interpretative element are disclosed in Daniel 2. The content of mystery is the *revelation of God's present and future activity within history. This is seen in the establishment of Nebuchadnezzar's kingdom, and in many subsequent kingdoms which are then crushed by a 'stone' which establishes a divine kingdom (Dan. 2:36–45). The interpretative element of the mystery is seen in Daniel's function as an intermediary, explaining God's present and future activity within history to those who can understand it only as a mystery.

A similar understanding of mysterious and hidden things can be seen within other sections of the OT. Like Daniel, *Joseph interprets dreams (Gen. 40 – 41) and himself receives dreams (Gen. 37:5–11), that communicate the present and future plan of God. These dreams sometimes come in a mysterious form to people who initially do not understand them, i.e. to Pharaoh and his officials. Joseph, as the interpreter of these mysterious dreams, is used as an intermediary to discern and reveal God's future plan for the *blessing of his people (Gen. 45:4–11).

The *prophets' work also relates to mysterious and hidden things. In many places in their writings, the people of Israel are seen to be stumbling about in darkness and confusion (e.g. Is. 3:12; 49:9; 59:10; Jer. 23:12; Ezek. 32:8; Mic. 3:6). In response to this condition, the prophets often function as intermediaries making sense of Israel's mysterious condition and revealing the present and future purposes and plans of God (e.g. Is. 9:2; 29:18; 45:3; 60:1–2; Ezek. 34:12; Amos 3:7; Mic. 7:8–9).

The NT

A similar idea of mystery is found in the NT. Jesus speaks mysterious things in parables to his disciples and the crowds. He discloses the hidden aspects of the *kingdom of God, which baffle many, but which are interpreted by Jesus to his disciples so that they may understand God's present and future plans (Mark 4:10–12; cf. Matt. 13:11–17; Luke 8:9–10).

*Paul also speaks of mysteries with reference to the present and future purposes of God. He uses the term in two ways. First, he uses it to refer to all the saving purposes of God, which are summed up in the *gospel of Christ (1 Cor. 4:1; Eph. 1:9; 3:1–9; 6:19; Col. 1:25–27; 2:2; 4:3). Secondly, he uses it to denote particular details of God's plan, especially those relating to the future (Rom. 11:25–36; 1 Cor. 15:51–57). The hidden dimensions of these mysteries are initially known to a few but are dispensed to others by intermediaries like Paul (1 Cor. 2:6–10; cf. 2 Cor. 4:3–18) (M. N. A. Bockmuehl, *Revelation and Mystery*, pp. 225–227).

Other NT texts refer to God's mysterious and hidden plan in history. According to 1 Peter 1:10–12, that which was hidden to saints long ago has been revealed to Christians in the last days. The book of Revelation also refers to mysteries concerning the unfolding of God's present and future plan. The concept of mystery is found in relation to the *church, *Babylon the great, and the consummation of the kingdom of God (Rev. 1:20; 10:7; 17:5, 7; cf. 11:15). These mysteries are revealed through the intermediary figure of John.

Conclusion

From the many texts in which there is explicit use of the term 'mystery' or in which the theme of mystery is employed, some general conclusions can be drawn. What people initially perceive as mysterious or hidden is often explained to God's *people as divine revelation. This disclosure is usually performed by an intermediary figure. The content of the mystery is God's present and future purposes. In the NT a revealed mystery involves *Jesus Christ and his place within God's plan of *salvation.

This teaching about mystery indicates that God hides his plan of salvation from those who do not know him. While it remains hidden to others, God does, however, make his plan of salvation known to his people.

Bibliography

G. K. Beale, *The Use of Daniel in Jewish Apocalyptic Literature and in the Revelation of St. John* (Lanham, 1984); M. N. A. Bockmuehl, *Revelation and Mystery in Ancient Judaism and Pauline Christianity* (Tübingen, 1990); G. Bornkamm in *TDNT* 4, pp. 802–828.

H. H. D. WILLIAMS, III

NAHUM, see Part 2

NATIONS

Terminology

The most common designation for 'nation' in the OT is *gôy* (pl. *gôyîm*). The expression often occurs in conjunction with *'am* (pl. *'ammîm*), 'people'; *gôy* has political and *'am* kinship connotations. The LXX and the NT mostly use *laos* for the old or new *people of God, while other (pagan) peoples are generally called *ethnē* (pl.). *Gôy/gôyîm* is normally translated *ethnos/ethnē*. Where mention is made of more than one (non-Israelite) people, the plural *ammîm* is also translated *ethnē*. There is also a contrast between *Israel as the chosen people (*'am* or *laos*) and the Gentiles (*gôyîm* or *ethnē*). *Ethnē* occurs only rarely in Exodus, Leviticus, Numbers, Joshua and Chronicles, but much more frequently in Genesis, Deuteronomy, Psalms and the prophets.

Israel and the nations in the context of ancient perceptions of nationhood

The nation of Israel

Ancient perceptions of nationhood were largely a function of the following factors (D. I. Block, in *NIDOTTE,* pp. 967–970): ethnicity and language; territory; religion; kingship; and history. Israel's history can be understood in this context. The ancient Hebrews exhibited a strong sense of *ethnic cohesion*. This cohesion was reinforced by Israel's call to be distinct from the surrounding nations (*e.g.* Lev. 20:24, 26). *God's promise of *territory* to *Abraham followed from that of his descendants becoming a great nation (Gen. 12:1–3). In the Promised Land, the Israelites would experience fullness of life, prosperity and security.

Through the *covenant* at Sinai, God assumed the role of patron deity, pledging continued concern for Israel's welfare and safety. The people, in turn, were to abide by his moral code and worship no other gods, even though the neighbouring nations would entice Israel into *idolatry. Not only was Yahweh the only god the Israelites were to worship (Deut. 6:4), there was in fact no other god (Exod. 20:1–6; Deut. 4:35, 39): Yahweh alone was the true, living and eternal God (Jer. 10:10). Yet although Israel was his chosen people, non-Israelites also were wel-

come to worship Yahweh; for the scope of his rule is universal (Is. 54:5; Jer. 32:27).

Another element in ancient perceptions of nationhood was the *royal office*. The lack of a king in Israel's early history made the people feel inferior to the surrounding nations (Deut. 17:14; 1 Sam. 8:5, 19–20). Once Israel had become a monarchy, kings were to provide leadership in warfare, the administration of justice and the worship of Yahweh, embodying the nation's collective aspirations and exemplifying godly conduct. Their failure to live up to these high ideals in later years led to the disintegration of the Davidic kingdom and renewed bondage to foreign powers.

Every nation also looks back at defining moments in its *history*. In the case of Israel, such events include God's call of Abraham, the Exodus from Egypt and the making of the covenant at Sinai, the conquest of the Promised Land under Joshua, God's choice of David as Israel's king, the division of the kingdom in 931 BC, and the Assyrian and Babylonian exiles in 722 and 586 BC. The latter traumatic events brought into sharp focus the question of God's faithfulness to his covenant with Israel. In this context, prophets foretold the restoration of a believing remnant and the establishment of a new covenant (esp. Jer. 31:31–34).

Israel and the nations

Yet while God's electing purposes focused on Israel, the OT vision transcends this people to include the other nations as well. Thus, contrary to Israel's perceptions of Abraham as *their* ancestor exclusively, the table of nations in Genesis 10 places his call within the context of world history. Abraham will be a 'father of many nations' (Gen. 17:4–6), and God intends him to be a *blessing to 'all nations on earth', not merely Israel (Gen. 12:3; 18:18; 22:18; 26:4; 28:14). Likewise Israel was to fulfil a mediatorial role between God and the nations (Exod. 19:4–6). And while Yahweh sustains a special relationship with Israel, his rule extends to the entire universe. This rule even involves using pagan nations and their rulers as his instruments to chastise rebellious Israel, such as the Assyrian Shalmaneser (2 Kgs. 17:1–23) or Nebuchadnezzar king of *Babylon (Jer. 25:9; 27:6; 43:10).

In fact, God's treatment of Israel serves as a public display of his own character (Deut.

29:24): the laws demonstrate his wisdom (Deut. 4:6); the Exodus and other mighty acts his power (Lev. 26:45; Deut. 7:19; Jos. 4:24; Ps. 77:14); Israel's election his gracious, faithful love (Deut. 7:7–9; 10:15); his discipline of Israel his impartiality and holiness (Deut. 8:20; Jer. 46:12; Ezek. 38:23); and the universal offer of salvation his righteousness (Ps. 98:2; Is. 62:2). The ultimate purpose of Israel's existence is to reveal the greatness of God's name (2 Sam. 7:23; 1 Kgs. 8:43, 60; 1 Chr. 22:5; 2 Chr. 6:33; Is. 12:4).

Israel is repeatedly warned not to be like the nations in their idolatry (Deut. 12:30; 18:9; 2 Kgs. 17:15), and numerous prophetic oracles are directed against the nations, proclaiming divine *judgment of the utmost severity (Is. 13 – 23; Jer. 46 – 51; Ezek. 25 – 32). Yet despite all the nations' detestable practices, God is concerned also for their *salvation (e.g. Ps. 67:2; 98:2; Is. 52:10, 15: 'sprinkle many nations'). This is already implicit in the protevangelion of Genesis 3:15 (which predates the call of Abraham) and is made explicit in the blessing associated with Abraham (12:3) and his *seed (22:18).

Certain messianic texts are distinctly universal, such as the prediction that the '*obedience of the nations' will belong to the ruler from Judah (Gen. 49:10). Moreover, many prophetic texts envisage universal recognition of Yahweh (e.g. Is. 2:2–4; 66:18– 20; Joel 2:28–32): 'Then they will know that I am the LORD' (esp. in Ezek.). A key role is assigned to the Servant of the LORD who will be a light for the Gentiles and bring justice and salvation to the nations (Is. 42:1, 6; 49:6; 51:4–5; 52:10; 61:1–2). Prophets also envisage the pilgrimage of the nations to Mt Zion, 'the mountain of the LORD' (Is. 2:2–4; 25:6–8; 66:20; Jer. 3:17; Mic. 4:1–3; Zech. 8:3, 20–23; 14:16–19).

Jews and Gentiles in the NT

Jesus and the Gospels

The NT depiction of Jews and Gentiles is largely built on two major OT themes: the Abrahamic promise (Gen. 12:1–3) and the Isaianic Servant of the LORD (42:1–4; 49:1–6; 50:4–9; 52:13 – 53:12; cf. 61:1–3). Pervading the NT is the conviction that in *Jesus, the promised seed of Abraham, all the nations have been blessed (e.g. Acts 3:25; Rom. 4:17–

18; 15:8–12; Gal. 3:6–9, 13–14). The evangelists affirm at the very outset that Abrahamic descent is not confined to physical Israel (Matt. 3:9 par.). They also agree that Jesus operates consciously as the Servant of the LORD who, in keeping with OT prediction, came as a light to the Gentiles (Matt. 12:18–21; Luke 2:32; 4:18–19; cf. Acts 13:47; 26:17–18, 23). Though born in Bethlehem, Jesus begins his ministry, not in Jerusalem, but in 'Galilee of the Gentiles' (Matt. 4:15–16; cf. Is. 9:1–2).

To be sure, Jesus focuses his earthly mission on Israel (Matt. 10:5–6; 15:24), ministering to Gentiles only at their initiative (e.g. Matt. 8:5–13 par.; 15:21–28 par.; see A. J. Köstenberger and P. T. O'Brien, Salvation to the Ends of the Earth). While clearly anticipating the preaching of the *gospel to 'all nations' (Matt. 24:14; Mark 13:10; Luke 24:47; Matt. 28:19), Jesus does not envisage such universal proclamation until after the Jews have 'handed him over to the Gentiles' (e.g. Matt. 20:19). Israel's rejection of their Messiah will result in Jesus' crucifixion and exaltation but will bring judgment upon Israel, typified by the destruction of Jerusalem and the Jewish temple in AD 70. Jesus is aware that he must bring 'other sheep' (that is, Gentiles) as well (John 10:16), even though this will happen only through the efforts of his followers. They are commissioned by the risen Lord to 'go and make disciples of all nations' (including, but not limited to, Israel; Matt. 28:18–20), and are charged to emulate the dependent, obedient relationship he himself has during his earthly mission with the Father who sent him (John 20:21).

Paul and the early church

The apostle Paul was consumed by Jesus' vision of gospel proclamation to all the nations (e.g. 1 Tim. 3:16; 2 Tim. 4:17), being convinced that it was the purpose of Jesus' death that 'the blessing given to Abraham might come to the Gentiles' (Gal. 3:14). As apostle to the Gentiles (Acts 9:15; 22:21; Rom. 1:5, 13; 11:13; 15:16, 18; Gal. 1:16; 2:2, 7–8; Eph. 3:1, 8; 1 Tim. 2:7), although a Jew himself, he spearheaded the early *church's outreach to non-Jews (Acts 13 – 28). Perhaps his most significant theological contribution (of enormous practical significance) was his insistence that the Gentiles were to be accepted into the community of believers apart from Jewish legal observance (food laws, Sabbath observance, circumcision), solely on the basis of *faith in Christ (Acts 15; Rom. 9:30; Gal. 3:26–29; cf. Gal. 2). All barriers between Jews and Gentiles had been broken down (Eph. 2:11–22). This conviction was grounded in Paul's apprehension of the 'mystery', which until that time had been hidden in the wisdom of God, that 'through the gospel the Gentiles are heirs together with Israel, members together of one body, and sharers together in the promise in Christ Jesus' (Eph. 3:6, NIV; cf. Rom. 16:25–26; Col. 1:27). On a practical level, Paul assigned great symbolic significance to an offering taken up among Gentile congregations for the Jerusalem church (Acts 24:17; Rom. 15:25–28; 1 Cor. 16:1–4; 2 Cor. 8 – 9).

Yet Israel's salvation-historical distinctiveness is not obliterated. In Paul's (and the early church's) missionary practice, the progression was still 'first for the Jew, then for the Gentile' (Acts 3:26; 13:46; 18:6; 28:25–28; Rom. 1:16; 2:9–10). In his epistle to the Romans, the apostle wrestled with the implications of large-scale Jewish rejection of Jesus and the major Gentile influx into the church (Rom. 9 – 11). He concluded that 'salvation has come to the Gentiles to make Israel envious' (Rom. 11:11); 'Israel has experienced a hardening in part until the full number of the Gentiles has come in' (11:25); the fullness of the Gentiles will bring riches also to Israel (11:12); 'and so all Israel will be saved' (11:26: a reference to the second coming?).

The end of the NT era

The most striking and extensive application of OT terminology for Israel to the NT people of God (including both Jews and Gentiles) is found in Peter's first epistle, especially in chapter 2. This indicates that a paradigm shift has taken place and that it is now the church that is 'the Israel of God' (Gal. 6:16). The interval between Jesus' first and second coming is the 'time of the Gentiles' (Luke 21:24), marked by universal gospel preaching which issues in the worship of God among every people, tribe, language and nation (Rev. 5:9; 14:6; 15:4). After the evil world empire, seductress of the nations, and the devil (see *Spiritual powers), 'deceiver of the nations', have been judged

(Rev. 14:8; 16:19), Jesus the Son will rule all the nations (Rev. 12:5; 19:15), and believers with him (Rev. 2:26–27; cf. Ps. 2:9). In heaven, all distinctions of gender, ethnicity or social class will be swallowed up in believers' adoring relationship with God in Jesus Christ and their joint praise of the glory of their Lord and Saviour.

See also: ISRAEL; MISSION.

Bibliography

H. Bietenhard, 'People, Nation, Gentiles, Crowd, City', in NIDNTT 2, pp. 788–805; D. I. Block, 'Nations/Nationality', in NIDOTTE 4, pp. 966–972; idem in ISBE 3, pp. 492–496; D. L. Christensen, in ABD 4, pp. 1037–1049; E. J. Hamlin in IDB 3, pp. 515–523; D. R. de Lacey, 'Gentiles', in DPL, pp. 335–339; A. J. Köstenberger and P. T. O'Brien, Salvation to the Ends of the Earth: A Biblical Theology of Mission (Leicester and Grand Rapids, 2001); M. Liverani, 'Nationality and political identity', in ABD 4, pp. 1031–1037; S. McKnight, 'Gentiles', in DJG, pp. 259–265; idem, 'Gentiles, Gentile Mission', in DLNTD, pp. 388–394.

A. J. KÖSTENBERGER

NEW BIRTH, see REGENERATION
NEW COVENANT, see COVENANT
NEW HEAVENS AND NEW EARTH, see CREATION
NEW JERUSALEM, see JERUSALEM
NEW TESTAMENT USE OF THE OLD TESTAMENT, see Part 1

NOAH

The story of Noah in Genesis 5 – 9 is in four parts: the prophecy of Lamech at Noah's birth; the flood story; the covenant; and the drunkenness of Noah. The Hebrew root of the name 'Noah' means 'to comfort'. Although the term used in Lamech's prophecy is different, Noah's name reflects the purpose of his life (Gen. 5:29), to bring comfort to humanity after the cursing of the ground and the difficulties of obtaining a living from the land (Gen. 3:17–19). After the flood, Noah is described as 'a man of the soil' (Gen. 9:20, NIV), the earth having been cleansed of the defilement caused by human sin. However, the fulfilment of the promise was never completely realized, and remained open to a future scion of Noah who would bring 'comfort'.

The emphasis on the righteousness of Noah (Gen. 6:8–9) is set in contrast to the wickedness of the generation of Noah. This contrast is demonstrated throughout the flood story as Noah receives God's instructions and meticulously obeys them. The literary technique of repeating God's words in describing the actions of Noah underlines the statement (Gen. 6:22) that he is perfectly obedient. Although there has been much discussion regarding the literary form of the flood story, it is most probably centred on Genesis 8:1, 'But God remembered Noah...' It is God who remembers; all the action in the story occurs as a result of the divine initiative. Whereas God's wrath brings the judgment of the flood, his grace provides salvation for Noah. The act of remembrance is more than merely a recollection; here and throughout the biblical text, God's remembrance is the first step in his doing good to those remembered, delivering and encouraging them. Here God delivers Noah from the ark and returns him and his family to the earth. God's acceptance of the offering leads on to the divine promise that the seasons will remain and that never again will the world be destroyed by flood, despite the sinfulness of humanity.

The *covenant that God establishes with Noah and all humanity in Genesis 9:1–17 is an affirmation of God's creation of humankind in his image (Gen. 1:26–28; 9:1, 6). Thus murder is forbidden because it destroys the divine image and capital punishment for murder is commanded (Gen. 9:6). Further, the symbol of all animal life, its blood, must not be consumed. However, Noah receives permission to eat meat. God declares explicitly that animals as well as people are the recipients of the covenant (Gen. 9:10). This, and the command to be fruitful and multiply, link the covenant with the creation account of Genesis 1 and identify it as a renewal of God's creation. The appearance of the rainbow is a sign that the covenant and its promises are to last for ever.

The account of Genesis 9:18–27, set in Noah's later years, portrays him as less righteous than before. Whilst it anticipates the expansion of his descendants throughout the world (described in the Table of Nations in Gen. 10), it also tells of how he becomes drunk from the wine of his newly planted vineyard. The exact nature of Ham's sin in uncovering his father's nakedness is not clear, but the association of alcoholism and sexual sin seems to be established at the very beginning of the post-flood world. Noah's curse of Canaan looks forward to the promised rule of Israel over the land of Canaan and the command to exterminate the Canaanites. Thus Noah blesses Shem, the ancestor of Israel, as the master of Canaan. The promise that Japheth would dwell within the tents of Shem has no clear fulfilment in a specific biblical event but is echoed by the prophets, who see Jerusalem at the centre of the world and all nations coming to the city for instruction in the ways of God (Is. 2:1–4; Mic. 4:1–5).

Descended from Adam through Seth, Noah belongs to the special line which later includes the Hebrew patriarchs, *Abraham, Isaac and *Jacob. This family line is characterized by individuals who play an important role in the outworking of God's purposes to bring about the restoration of creation following the punishment of *Adam and Eve in the garden of Eden. This family line leads through the tribe of Judah to the house of *David and to *Jesus Christ.

Noah is remembered in the Bible as a figure of surpassing righteousness among the people of Israel (Ezek. 14:14, 20). His faith, and his obedience on the basis of that faith, enable him to escape the flood (Heb. 11:7). In the NT this deliverance is used as a picture of baptism, and of salvation through the resurrection of Jesus Christ (1 Pet. 3:20–21).

Bibliography

R. S. Hess, *Studies in the Personal Names of Genesis 1–11* (Kevelaer and Neukirchen-Vluyn, 1993); E. Van Wolde, *Words Become Worlds: Semantic Studies of Genesis 1–11* (Leiden, 1994); G. Wenham, *Genesis 1–15*, WBC (Waco, 1987).

R. S. HESS

NUMBERS, see Part 2
OBADIAH, see Part 2

OBEDIENCE

Meaning

The Hebrew expression that EVV regularly render 'obey' is *šāma' bᵉqôl*, literally 'hear the voice' of someone. Three thoughts are present: attending to the sound, understanding the utterance, and acting on it. Where any of these are lacking, listeners are said not to have 'heard'. Translators find themselves torn between 'hear' and 'obey' as the better rendering for this locution in particular cases. The corresponding Greek verb in the LXX and NT is *hypakouō*, a compound of *akouō*, the basic word for 'hear'. Etymologically, the *hyp-* prefix suggests the meaning 'hear *under*', that is, listen from a subordinate position in which compliance with what is said is expected and intended. Other 'obey' words in the NT are *eisakouō*, which etymologically suggests 'hear into', that is, listen with involvement; *peithomai*, which means 'respond to persuasion'; and *peitharcheō*, which carries the thought of bowing to a superior. The idea of obedience that this vocabulary builds up is of attentive and hearty compliance with the directives of someone with acknowledged authority, and that is what all these terms actually express in use.

Those to whom obedience is due must not only have a right to command but also be able to make known their requirements. The human duty to obey our Maker assumes both his dominion (lordship) and his revelation (words). The OT usually describes obeying God as hearing his voice (words of revelation), though Deuteronomy 11:27 speaks of obeying his commands (words of lordship), just as the Rechabites are said to have obeyed their ancestor's command (Jer. 35:8, 10, 14, 16, 18). In the NT, people obey not only authority figures (*God the Father, God the Son, parents, *church leaders, slaveowners) but also the doctrine, *truth, *gospel and *word that come from God (Rom. 6:17; 10:16; 1 Pet. 1:22; 3:1). Biblical religion in its historical unfolding is at every stage a matter of bonding with God by receiving and responding to his instruction, taking his word about the facts, trusting his promises and fulfilling his directives, and thereby experiencing with him both fellowship (sharing of life) and partnership (co-operation in tasks).

Scripture presents this pattern as most fully realized in being a disciple of *Jesus Christ, but in formal and structural terms it is there from Eden throughout. Obedience to God is always commended as pure religion (so with Abraham, Gen. 22:18; 26:5; *cf.* Heb. 11:8); disobedience is always condemned as radical impiety (so with Saul, 1 Sam. 15:13–26).

The obedience of Jesus Christ

Obedience is the hallmark of all God's servants, but the supreme instance is the incarnate obedience of the Father's flawless Son, Jesus Christ our Lord. Jesus' obedience on earth meant, positively, a purpose and practice of always pleasing his Father by doing his will, obeying his commands, faithfully relaying all he was told to say, and always seeking his *glory and honour, that is, that his name would be hallowed and praised (see John 5:30, 36; 6:38–40; 7:16–18; 8:27–29; 10:18; 12:49–50; 14:31; *cf.* Heb. 10:5–10). Negatively, it meant acting only on his Father's initiative as prompted, never cutting loose on his own (John 4:34; 5:19; *cf.* Mark 14:32–39; Luke 4:1–13; 12:50; 22:22; 23:37). The rock-like integrity of Jesus in refusing point-blank to fit into Jewish stereotypes and expectations, and insisting instead on following with complete consistency his own path of utterance and action, strikes readers of the Gospels, as it struck Jesus' own contemporaries, as awe-inspiring: it was clearly the outworking of his entire submission to the Father's will, immediately known every moment in each situation. The here-and-now gift of *righteousness (pardon of *sin, personal acceptance and permanent 'rightness' with God; Rom. 5:19) comes to us through Jesus' faultless obedience, learned – that is, perfected by practice – in the school of suffering (Heb. 5:7–9, *cf.* 12:2–3; Rom. 8:32; Phil. 2:8). The quality of Christ's obedience sets the standard by which Christians must measure theirs.

In Romans 5:12–19 and 1 Corinthians 15:21–22 and 45–49 Paul correlates and contrasts Jesus, 'the last *Adam', with 'the first man Adam' (1 Cor. 15:45) as the two representative people through whom God has dealt with humankind. Genesis 2 – 3 tells how our forefather's disobedience lost life with God for all his descendants; Paul proclaims how through Christ's obedience the gift of righteousness, guaranteeing glory, comes to all who are linked with him by faith, so that 'In him the tribes of Adam boast/More blessings than their father lost' (Isaac Watts). The moment of receiving this gift, on our receipt of Jesus Christ as Saviour and Lord, is also the moment of our justification by faith, when God the judge ceases to reckon our sins to us for retribution and instead reckons to us Christ's obedience (which includes the cross) as the basis for his present acceptance of us into eternal enjoyment of his forgiveness and favour (Rom. 3:21–26; 4:3–8; 5:1–11; Phil. 3:7–9).

Obedience and religion

Throughout the Bible story it is obedience to God's revealed will that pleases him, and that brings his *blessings of health, wealth, liberty, security and tranquillity, which in the OT are all embraced by the umbrella word šalôm. Noah obeyed God in building the ark (Gen. 6:22), Abraham in leaving Haran and offering Isaac (Gen. 12:1–4; 22:15–18), Moses in returning to Egypt to challenge Pharaoh and lead the people out (Exod. 3:10 – 4:20), and so on down the long line of faithful leaders in OT times. At Sinai, announcing his *covenant commitment to Israel, God charged the people to be obedient to all his requirements, and gave them the Decalogue and much else in writing to regulate their obedience (Exod. 19:5; 24:3–7, etc.). Samuel teaches Saul, who had not obeyed God's message through the prophet, that 'to obey is better than sacrifice' (1 Sam. 15:22) and that by disobedience he has lost his kingdom. So in NT times the rule of blessing is: 'We must obey God rather than men!' (Acts 5:29). '*Fear (reverence) God and keep his commandments' (Eccles. 12:13) is a biblical summary of biblical religion from first to last. Without obedience there is no pleasing of God, and failure to please God forfeits blessing. Much changes as the biblical story unfolds, but God's expectation of obedience to his revealed requirements at each particular time remains constant.

Old covenant obedience

The covenant relation whereby God binds himself and his people together in fidelity and fellowship for ever has been implemented historically in two main stages, which the writer to the Hebrews calls 'old' and 'new' (Heb. 8 – 10). The old covenant was the typical, temporary, educative, parabolic arrangement of *priests, sanctuary and *sacrifices that Moses instituted; it maintained fellowship with God despite the transgressions which typical sacrifices could not actually expiate. The new covenant is the better arrangement now superseding it through the all-sufficient priesthood and sacrifice of the God-man, Jesus Christ. Meticulous observance of the moral, political and ritual laws God gave was always required, not to gain acceptance (that was given already), but to show sincerity in seeking to please God (Pss. 26; 101; 119:1–16, 30–32; etc.). The Jewish self-justification by works that Paul had to fight (Rom., Gal., Phil. 3) was by OT standards an aberration.

New covenant obedience

*Faith in the gospel, and in Jesus Christ, is obedience, for God commands it (John 6:29; 1 Jn. 3:23); and unbelief is disobedience (Rom. 10:16; 2 Thess. 1:8; 1 Pet. 2:8; 3:1; 4:17). A life of obeying the Father and the Son is faith's proper fruit (Rom. 6:16–23; Jas. 2:14–26), by virtue of the sanctifying work of the *Holy Spirit (Rom. 7:4–6; 1 Pet. 1:2). Christian obedience means imitating God in *holiness (1 Pet. 1:14–16) and Christ in *humility and *love (John 13:13–17, 34–35; Phil. 2:5–13; Eph. 4:32 – 5:2). Gratitude for grace received (Rom. 12:1), plus knowledge of being called to holiness as a child of God (Eph. 4:20–24), plus finding in one's own regenerate heart a desire to please and glorify God (Rom. 7:22; Phil. 1:20), are the Christian's prime motives for obedience. Obeying divinely established authority in the family (Eph. 5:22–24; 6:1–3), the church (Phil. 2:12; Heb. 13:17) and the state (Matt. 22:21; Rom. 13:1–7; Titus 3:1; 1 Pet. 2:13–17) is part of the Christian's obedience to God. When claims clash, however, Christians must be ready to disobey human authority in order not to disobey God (Acts 5:29).

Bibliography

W. Mundle in NIDNTT 2, pp. 172–180; F. W. Young in IDB 3, pp. 580–581.

J. I. PACKER

ORDINANCE, see LAW
PAGAN GODS, see IDOLATRY
PARACLETE, see HOLY SPIRIT

PASSOVER, see EXODUS (EVENT)
PASTORAL EPISTLES, see Part 2

PEACE

Introduction

The concept of peace in the Bible is different in many ways from modern ideas of peace. Peace as the absence of strife, *war or bloodshed, so often sought by *humanity at any cost, is far removed from the focus of the biblical teaching. The biblical concept of peace is one in which *God's authority and power over his created order are seen to dominate his relations with his world, including both the material and the human spheres. In the OT, peace results from a person subjecting himself or herself appropriately to God (this subjection is often signified by *sacrifice) or to God's emissary, the promised Davidic *king. In the NT, which extends and modifies the OT imagery, the language of treaties between warring parties is used to speak of the way in which God relates to humans; he demands that strife be overcome through the death of Christ.

Peace in the OT

In any age in which strife is a reality, a wish for another to be in a state of peace and safety is much more than empty words. The OT is full of the language of peace, by which one person wishes peace upon another, or someone wishes to be and to live in peace, free from trouble from enemies and from other dangers. OT teaching on peace contains two distinct emphases, which reflect the different contexts in which the books were written, the historical development of the *people of *Israel, and the shape of the canon.

The first emphasis is found in the Pentateuch, which focuses on the sacrificial law as a means of making peace with God. Peaceful relations between humans, important as they might be, are not nearly so important as peace with God. In Exodus and Numbers there are several references to peace offerings (Exod. 20:24; 24:5; 29:28; 32:6; Num. 6; 7; 15; 29), and in Leviticus these are institutionalized (Lev. 3; 4; 6; 7; 9; 10; 17; 19; 22; 23). The occasion of these offerings is never given. Nevertheless, their general character gives insight into what is required in order to establish peace with God. The essential elements of the peace offering are the sacrifice of animals and the pouring out of their *blood. These actions strike the modern Western reader as almost grotesque, but they serve several useful purposes, including that of drawing attention to the costliness of peace. Peace is not simply an empty wish; it is the result of a process that, in this instance, exacts the high cost of *life. Peace is not confined to present circumstances but is part of a larger perspective on life and the *world, pointing towards the demands of a holy and righteous God on his followers, who are prone to strife with him and among themselves.

Although some of the sacrificial imagery relating to peace is found outside the Pentateuch (e.g. in Ezek. 45 – 46), in the prophet Isaiah the second OT emphasis emerges. It appears in the earliest strand of the Isaiah tradition (Is. 9:4–7 and 11:1–9), and reflects the historical troubles of the time. Despite God's provision of sacrifice as a means of making peace, the people had no peace, either in the land or with God. Isaiah predicts the coming of a *redeemer who will embody peace and bring it to the people; this will be the climax of Israel's history and the solution to their present difficulties. Various divine attributes are ascribed to this figure in the list of titles in Isaiah 9:6, the last of which is 'Prince of Peace'. But although he resembles God, he is also depicted in human terms; he will grow in power, sit upon the throne of David and establish an eternal kingdom (Is. 9:7). This imagery of the future Davidic king is developed more graphically in Isaiah 11, where the character of his rule is described; the chapter concludes with what many would see as a description of God's eternal or millennial kingdom (vv. 8–9). Although Christians have traditionally taken this language to refer to the coming of *Jesus Christ, it also has a corporate dimension; a faithful *remnant of Israel is tied to the 'shoot' from the stump of Jesse (see Is. 11:10–16).

Peace in the NT

In the NT, the concept of peace is extended, but still reflects the two emphases of the OT. Jesus is seen in the NT, especially by Paul, as the one who brings peace. His life and teaching, death and resurrection, are interpreted by his followers in terms of the peace they bring.

In the Gospels, Jesus reflects the OT concept of peace by prioritizing relations with God over those with other humans, including family. He says that he did not come to bring peace, but a sword (Matt. 10:34; *cf.* Luke 12:51). Jesus bestows peace on those who are troubled with afflictions, *healing them and telling them to go their way in peace (*e.g.* Luke 4:35; 7:50; 8:48), and he commands peace upon the physical elements (*e.g.* Mark 4:39). By so doing, he illustrates his relationship to the world and to humanity as God's agent. Jesus (not animal sacrifice) directly mediates the peace of God to those who are troubled; hence his appropriate use of the word 'Peace' to greet his disciples after the resurrection (Luke 24:36).

The Pauline letters present a fuller and more complex concept of peace; in several passages there is a sustained theological treatment of the subject. In the salutations of his letters, Paul wishes '*grace and peace' to his readers (Rom. 1:7; 1 Cor. 1:3; 2 Cor. 1:2; Gal. 1:3; Eph. 1:2; Phil. 1:2; Col. 1:2; 1 Thess. 1:1; 2 Thess. 1:2; Philem. 3; Titus 1:4; *cf.* 1 Tim. 1:2 and 2 Tim. 1:2, which include the word '*mercy'). 'Grace' is the unmerited kindness of God bestowed upon humans, and 'peace' the cessation of hostilities between warring parties, including God and humanity; these are two cardinal Christian concepts. Similar language is sometimes found at the close of Paul's letters. Paul's word for 'grace' is a cognate of the word of greeting used in many ancient Greek letters, but Paul has given theological content to this greeting and expanded it by the addition of 'peace'.

Elsewhere Paul defines his peace and reconciliation language. In four major Pauline passages (2 Cor. 5:18–21; Rom. 5:8–11; Col. 1:20–22; Eph. 2:14–17), the author draws upon the Greek language of exchange and treaty to describe the human relationship with God. Although Paul generally uses the language of peace or reconciliation quite consistently with its use in other Greek-language contexts, to speak of the process by which a ruptured relationship is restored, he also makes some noteworthy innovations. For example, the offended party (God) initiates the process of reconciliation with his enemy. It is not humans who approach God to make peace, but God who reaches out to humanity.

Paul also draws upon his Jewish background, making clear in all his reconciliation passages that it is by means of the sacrificial death of Jesus Christ that peaceful relations between God and humanity can be effected. (See *Atonement.)

The Johannine letters and Revelation, and the Petrine letters, reflect a similar orientation. In their salutations grace and occasionally mercy are linked to peace to make an appropriate greeting for fellow-Christians (1 Pet. 1:2; 2 Pet. 1:2; 2 John 3; 3 John 14; Rev. 1:4), which embodies the idea of peace as the cessation of hostilities between antagonists.

The essential message of the NT regarding peace, found in the Gospels on the lips of Jesus (and embodied in his actions towards others), in the letters of Paul and in the other NT writings, is twofold. First, God desires peace with humanity, to the point of acting to bring it about; secondly, the work of Christ upon the cross, in particular his death, has effected peaceful relations between God and humanity, and made possible peaceful relations between those who believe in him.

Conclusion

The difference in emphasis between the OT and NT concepts of peace should not be overlooked, but neither should it be overemphasized. The dominant theme in both Testaments is that of peaceful relations with God. In the OT, these peaceful relations are dependent on the sacrificial system, and later on the promised Davidic king. In the NT, peaceful relations between antagonistic parties are effected through the sacrificial death of Jesus Christ. According to the NT, what the OT sacrifices could not do (note the lack of specificity regarding when they were to be performed), and what the OT writers expected from the Davidic king, is realized through the death of Jesus Christ.

Bibliography

S. E. Porter, 'Peace, Reconciliation', in *DPL*, pp. 695-699; G. von Rad, *Old Testament Theology*, 2 vols (ET, London, 1975).

S. E. PORTER

PENTECOST, see LANGUAGES

PEOPLE OF GOD

Introduction

The message of the Bible, in essence, is that *God is at work to bring into being a people under his rule in his place. The idea of the people of God, therefore, stands at the heart of biblical theology. This is where the Bible starts and ends. In the Garden of Eden (clearly God's place) God creates the first couple, the protological people of God, and invites them to live under his rule. All too quickly they refuse to accept God's terms, and so are excluded from his presence. By the closing chapters of Revelation, however, the wheel has turned full circle. The story has returned to a 'garden' (comprising a new heaven and a new earth), which bears a striking resemblance to Eden. The primary characteristic of this new place is that here God's servants live in intimacy with him for ever, as his people, under his rule (Rev. 22:3–4). This is the overall trajectory of biblical theology. This article traces that trajectory through the canon, as the concept of the 'people of God' is developed.

The beginnings of the people of God

After the chaos arising from the tower of Babel incident in Genesis 11, God begins to create a people for himself, announcing his plans to the chosen progenitor of this nation/people, *Abraham. God promises to make Abraham into a great nation-state (gôy gādôl). This promise dominates the way in which the concept of the people of God is presented in Genesis (see e.g. 15:14; 17:20; 18:18; 21:18; 46:3). However, when the fulfilment of this promise is not being cited explicitly, Abraham's family group is referred to using the word 'am. In context, 'am often emphasizes kinship, but there is no strict distinction between these terms (they appear as synonyms in e.g. Gen. 17:6; Deut. 4:27; 1 Chr. 16:24; Ps. 47:8–9; Is. 1:4; Zech. 12:3).

The promise to create a nation from the *family of Abraham is fulfilled during their stay in Egypt, as the tribes of *Jacob become a distinct people. It is here that God begins to refer to Israel as his people (see Exod. 6:7, and also 3:7, 10; 5:1; 7:16; 9:1, 13; 18:1; 32:11; also Lev. 26:12). Yahweh assures Israel that if they are faithful to him, 'out of all nations you will be my treasured possession. Although the whole earth is mine, you will be for me a kingdom of priests and a holy nation' (gôy qādôš, Exod. 19:5–6, NIV) It is surprising that these words are repeated nowhere else in the OT (although 'am qādôš occurs in Deut. 7:6; 14:2, 21; 26:19; 28:9; Dan. 8:24), for they provide a seminal definition of the community of God. God's people are both to be distinct from the society in which they live, thus reflecting Yahweh's perfection (a *holy nation), and also to mediate God's blessing to the *nations (as a *kingdom of *priests). The phrase 'kingdom of priests' is difficult to interpret in its context, but the apostle Peter makes clear that it refers to the way in which God has always been committed to reaching the *world through his people (1 Pet. 2:9–10). A similar idea is present in Deuteronomy 4:5–8, where God's people function as an evangelistic model for the nations.

If there is a single, foundational moment for the people of God, then it comes on Mt Sinai. Moses, in Deuteronomy (9:10; 10:4; 18:16) refers back to this as 'the day of the assembly' (qāhāl, LXX ekklēsia). When God had brought his people out of Egypt, he brought them to the place of revelation, and in the making of the *covenant they were formally constituted as his people. From this point on, the people of God were to remember that God had freely chosen them and was going to establish them as an important player on the world stage, as a nation state, albeit one unlike any other (a gôy qādôš, 'a holy nation'). In addition, God's people were never to forget their essential kinship (i.e. that they were an 'am), but above all they were to understand that they were a people whose lives were centred on the divine *word, as on the original day of the assembly.

There are clear similarities between the people of God before and after Christ. God chooses his people, brings them into relationship both to himself and to one another, establishes a community centred on the word of God and uses this community to reach the world. However, there are also considerable differences between the people of God in the OT and in the NT. This becomes increasingly apparent as the narrative of the OT unfolds.

Israel as the people of God

The basic ideas of the assembly, kin-group descended from Abraham and nation-state can be traced throughout the history of Israel. However, the OT view of the people of God is more subtle than one which simply equates them with ethnic Israel. The historical books chart a steady downward trend in the fortunes of the people of God. Despite their being the covenantal people of Yahweh (see Jdg. 5:11,13; 1 Sam. 2:24; 2 Sam. 1:12, 6:21; 2 Kgs. 9:6), their behaviour falls consistently short of what is demanded of them. The book of Joshua charts their failure fully to take the land and eradicate Canaanite culture (see chs. 13 – 19 in particular). Judges records a downward spiral of disobedience, despite regular intervention from God. The shocking brutality described in Judges 19, and the internecine bloodletting which follows, reveal how far short of the divine ideal Israel falls.

The situation is made worse, if anything, by the demand of the people for a king in 1 Samuel 8. It is quite clear that this is an implicit rejection of the kingship of Yahweh (1 Sam. 8:19; 12:12), and it is presented as a most significant moment in the life of the nation. With a few brief interludes, the period of the monarchy brings ever-worsening disobedience and idolatry. The people of God are fractured after the 'golden age' of David and Solomon, and never recover. The northern kingdom is obliterated in 722 BC, whilst Judah in the south limps along as a minor player in the political ferment of the Fertile Crescent until 587 BC, when it is overrun by Babylon.

During this period a new dimension to the theology of the people of God was developed. Amos, Isaiah and Micah highlighted the widespread problem of hypocrisy in Israel, and drew a distinction between the kin-group or political state and the real people of God – those who lived for God in faithfulness to his covenant (see e.g. Hos. 1:1–11).

Isaiah, Amos and Micah all used the idea of the '*remnant'. Remnant theology was quite complex, bringing together the themes of judgment and salvation. At its heart, however, lay the conviction that even when Israel or Judah were at their worst, there was always a small group of faithful believers who held on to true religion (see e.g. Is. 11:11, 16; 28:5; 37:31–32; Mic. 4:7; 7:18; Amos 5:15;

9:12). The nation/people as a whole might have failed spectacularly, but there were still some who could provide a bridge to forgiveness and restoration. It was these people, the true people of God as it were, in whom God would work his eschatological resolution.

The language of remnant is picked up after the exile to denote those who have come back from the Babylonian captivity (see e.g. Hag. 1:12, 14; 2:2; Zech. 8:6, 11–15). However, hope for Israel was no longer seen to rest with a faithful remnant, but in the decisive intervention of God himself, acting to inaugurate a new covenant. Central to this new covenant (anticipated in Lev. 26 and Deut. 30, and developed in e.g. Jer. 30 – 31 and Ezek. 36 – 37) is the reiteration of Exodus 6:7: Israel would be God's people once more, as he would be their God (see Jer. 30:22; Ezek. 36:28).

The people of God, the kingdom of God and the church

*Jesus did not often speak explicitly about the people of God. As has often been pointed out, the dominant theme of his ministry (particularly as recorded in Matthew's Gospel) was rather the 'kingdom of God'. It is important to understand how 'the kingdom' is related to the doctrine of the people of God in the NT. G. E. Ladd has pointed out that the kingdom is not the new covenant community (for the kingdom is primarily the rule of God, and secondarily the sphere where that rule is experienced), but that it creates a community of God's people. As people 'enter the kingdom', a new covenant community is created on earth. This community (usually called the 'church' in the NT) then works to publicize the kingdom and extend its influence. It is in this anticipatory (or even preparatory) way that Jesus speaks about the people of God.

In the recorded ministry of Jesus, we have only two examples of him speaking specifically of the 'church' (Matt. 16:18; 18:17), the most usual NT designation of God's people. In both cases he uses classical OT language. Ekklēsia (used consistently in the LXX to translate qāhāl) was a non-sacral word denoting the gathering of God's people. It is the word that that was chosen by Jesus and the apostles to capture the nature of the new covenant community. The ekklēsia of

God was about to become the *ekklēsia* of Jesus Christ.

Jesus' (and the Gospel writers') understanding of his ministry rested firmly on conclusions drawn from the OT. He worked with a paradigm of fulfilment, rather than one of replacement. He came to the lost sheep of Israel (Matt. 10:6; 15:24; see also Luke 1:16, 68, 80; 2:25, 32, 34; 24:21; John 1:31), and to realize Israel's true destiny (see *e.g.* Matt. 19:28, Luke 22:30). Hence Jesus' inauguration of the new covenant (*e.g.* Matt. 26:28; Luke 22:20) means that his church can legitimately be described as the 'Israel of God' (Gal. 6:16) and the 'people of God' (Heb. 4:9; 1 Pet. 2:10, drawing on Hos. 1). It is on this simple foundation that the NT builds the rest of what it has to say about the nature of the people of God.

One of the most striking metaphors used of the people of God by Paul is that of the 'body (*sōma*) of Christ'. Although he uses the picture in two slightly different ways (*cf.* Rom. 12:5; 1 Cor. 10:16; 12:27, where Christ is the whole body and believers are in him, with Eph. 1:22; 5:23; Col. 2:17–19, where Christ is the body's *kephalē*, which could mean either 'head' or, perhaps more likely, 'source of life'), the point he is making with it is fairly clear. The life of the people of God is intimately bound up with the life of Christ (see Col. 3:3).

In the prophetic tradition, it was fairly common to describe the people of God as God's wife (see *e.g.* Is. 54:5–8; 62:5; Jer. 2:2 and R. C. Ortlund, *Whoredom*). Jesus' characterization of himself as 'the bridegroom' in Mark 2:18–20 develops this metaphor, which is also used by Paul and John as they reflect on the nature of the people of God. Paul, in a discussion of marital relationships, refers to the church as the bride of Christ, an image which is developed at the end of Revelation (21:2, 9; 22:17) as God's plan of salvation comes to a breathtaking climax.

A slightly more domestic image is that of the 'family of God'. Once more, this flows straight from an OT assertion, here that Israel is Yahweh's son (*e.g.* Hos. 11:1). Jesus himself insists that the incipient new community must see themselves as the family of God (*e.g.* Matt. 12:49–50), an insight which is developed in several ways in the rest of the NT. Paul exhorts Timothy to act as if

members of the local church were actually members of the same family (1 Tim. 5:1–2), and elsewhere explicitly asserts the fatherhood of God in relation to his people (2 Cor. 6:18; Eph. 3:14). John, throughout his first epistle, uses family language as he calls on believers to love one another (*e.g.* 1 John 3:1, 14–18).

However, the new community of people in Christ is not to be regarded simply as the family of God, but also as the house of God (usually *oikou tou theou*). The two ideas are not entirely separate, as is shown by Hebrews 3:2–6, where Christ is declared to be 'faithful as a son over God's house'. As in the OT, there is a close correlation between 'house' and '*temple', and in several NT passages the Christian community is compared to a building in which God lives (see *e.g.* Eph. 2:19–22; 1 Cor. 3:16; 1 Tim. 3:15; 1 Pet. 2:4–5; 4:17).

Other OT images used in the NT description of the people of God include the 'flock of God' (*e.g. cf.* Pss. 80:1; 95:7; 100:3; Ezek. 34:15 with John 10:1–30; 21:17; Acts 20:28; 1 Pet. 5:4; Heb. 13:20) and the 'vineyard of God' (*e.g. cf.* Ps. 80:8–19; Is. 5:1–7, with Mark 12:1–12 and John 15:1–8).

A degree of continuity between Israel and the NT people of God is undeniable, at least as far as Jesus and the apostles are concerned. There is still some question, however, over the precise relationship between the ethnic 'people of God' in the OT (*i.e.* Israel), and the international community of the church in the NT. This is a question which Paul addresses, particularly in the letter to the Romans.

Drawing on the 'remnant' theology of the OT, Paul insists in Romans 2:28–29 that membership of the people of God is not an outward or physical matter. On the contrary, 'a man is a Jew if he is one inwardly; and circumcision is circumcision of the heart, by the Spirit, not by the written code' (2:29). He follows through the logic of his argument in chapter 4, arguing that 'Abraham is the father of all who believe but have not been circumcised, in order that righteousness might be credited to them' (4:11). He returns to this theme in 9:6–8, confirming beyond all doubt that 'it is not the natural children who are God's children, but it is the children of the promise who are regarded as Abraham's offspring'. In other words, those who belong to the people of God (those who belong to Israel in the truest sense) are those who have believed in Christ and thus been included in the *ekklēsia* of the Lord Jesus Christ (see also Gal. 3:29; Phil. 3:3).

Ephesians 2 (especially vv. 14–16) makes perfectly clear that there is only one people of God, and that the new covenant community embraces all that has gone before, including both Jews and Gentiles on exactly the same basis. This is also reflected, as we have seen, in the way in which many of the OT pictures of the people of God are picked up and developed in the NT. Nowhere is this clearer than in Hebrews 8:7–13, where the writer clearly regards the church as the evidence that the promises of Jeremiah 31 (originally given to Judah) have been fulfilled.

Conclusion

In one sense, to write about the people of God is to attempt to encapsulate the whole of biblical theology. The entire Bible speaks of God's plan to create his people, in his place, under his rule. He commits himself to working with one people, and follows this commitment through to the end, though he extends the scope of his people infinitely through the work of Christ. The Bible ends not simply with Eden restored, but with the glorious realized vision of God with his covenant people in thrilling communion and a perfect, recreated environment.

See also: CHURCH; ISRAEL.

Bibliography

D. I. Block, 'Nations/Nationality', in *NIDOTTE* 4 pp. 966–972; R. E. Clements, 'gôy', in *TDOT* 2, pp. 426–433; W. A. Grudem, *Systematic Theology* (Leicester, 1994); G. E. Ladd, *A Theology of the New Testament* (Cambridge, 1975); E. A. Martens, *Plot and Purpose in the Old Testament* (Leicester, ²1981); J. G. Millar, *Now Choose life: Theology and Ethics in Deuteronomy* (Leicester and Grand Rapids, 1998); R. H. O'Connell ''am', in *NIDOTTE* 3, pp. 429–439; R. C. Ortlund Jr, *Whoredom: God's Unfaithful Wife in Biblical Theology* (Leicester and Grand Rapids, 1996); H. Strathmann, 'laos', in *TDNT* 4, pp. 50–57; C. J. H. Wright, *Living as the People of God* (Leicester, 1983).

J. G. MILLAR

PERSECUTION, see SUFFERING
PERSEVERANCE, see APOSTASY
PETER, LETTERS OF, see Part 2
PHILEMON, see Part 2
PHILIPPIANS, see PART 2
PLAGUES, see SIGNS AND WONDERS

POOR/POVERTY

Terminology

OT Hebrew has many terms for 'poor': *'anî* (76 times, 29 in Pss.), *'ebyôn* (61 times, 23 in Pss.), *dal* (48 times), *rwš* (21 times, 14 in Prov.), *miskēn* (4 times, only in Ecclus., but common in the Talmud and Midrash). The word *'anî* has a broad meaning, including 'weak', 'miserable', 'helpless' and 'suffering'. It can refer to the socially and materially poor who are dependent on support from other people (Exod. 22:21–27; Lev. 19:10; Is. 3:14–15; Hab. 3:14). But in the psalms of lament, where a common self-designation is 'I am poor and needy', the 'need' is never material poverty, *e.g.* lack of food or clothing or other necessities for life; it is persecution by enemies, illness and bodily weakness, or *guilt. The supplicants present themselves as helpless beggars before *God. In some contexts the *'anî* is contrasted with the 'proud'; '*humility' is presented as a positive moral quality (Prov. 3:34; Ps. 18:27; Zech. 9:9; Zeph. 2:3).

In the NT the most common word for 'poor' is *ptōchos*, which in classical Greek means 'poor like a beggar' as distinguished from *penēs* (not in NT), 'hard-working poor' or 'so poor that one cannot live on one's possessions'. In the LXX the two words can be used in synonymous parallelism. *Ptōchos* is the most frequent translation of *'anî*. The use of *ptōchos* in the NT is coloured in some contexts by the broader meaning of the Hebrew *'anî*.

There are many words which do not primarily refer to poverty, but to a social or medical status implying poverty or social misery. The *widow* and the *orphan* are liable to exploitation and are in need of help from others (Job 29:12–16; Jas. 1:27). They and the *stranger* are given special protection by the law (Exod. 22:21–25; Deut. 24:17–22). The *blind,* the *lame* and the *crippled* are further examples of socially weak people (Lev. 19:14; Jer. 31:8; Luke 14:21).

Thus in many texts the terminology of

'poverty' does not refer to the materially or socially poor, but has a broader meaning. On the other hand, many texts refer to social distress and poverty (*i.e.* people lacking sufficient food, clothing and housing) without using the terminology of 'poverty' (*e.g.* Job 30:3–8; Matt. 25:35–36).

It is important to make a clear distinction between the meaning of 'poverty' terminology and the social position of the poor, and attitudes to them. The idea of 'poverty piety' and groups of 'pious poor' in post-exilic Judaism results from the confusion of these two issues. The Psalms were used as a prayer book for all *Israel, including kings and high priests. There is no reason to connect these texts and their piety with specific social groups.

Poverty in the OT

Poverty as a social reality is never idealized in the OT. Poverty is need, distress and suffering, and contrary to the will of God. 'There will be no poor among you, for the LORD will bless you in the land which the LORD your God gives you for an inheritance to possess' (Deut. 15:4, RSV). Poverty is a curse; stability and prosperity are *blessings from God. But the experience of God's blessing should result in generosity and in care for the poor (Deut. 15:7–11).

Many commandments in the law are explicitly intended to help the poor. In Deuteronomy the sabbath commandment is socially motivated: the right to rest on the sabbath is also for servants and strangers (Deut. 5:12–15). During the harvest the corner of the field and the gleanings should be left for the poor (Lev. 19:9–10; Deut. 24:17–22). The law prohibits a creditor from taking interest or a garment from the indebted poor (Exod. 22:25–27; Deut. 24:12–13). In Deuteronomy 14:28–29 and 26:12 there are prescriptions for a special tithe for the poor, for the benefit of the Levite, the sojourner, the fatherless and the widows. In the sabbatical year the land was left fallow so that the poor could eat from it (Lev. 25:1–7; Deut. 15:1–11).

An example of social injustice is recounted in 1 Kings 21, where the prophet Elijah accuses the king of having killed Naboth and taken his vineyard. The problem of the rich man exploiting the poor is expressed in the parable of Nathan in 2 Samuel 12:1–4.

The prophetic books frequently accuse the rich of oppressing the poor (Amos 8:4–6; Is. 10:1–4; 32:6–7; Mic. 3:1–4; Jer. 5:26–29; Ezek. 18:12–13). True piety includes care for the poor and real fasting includes sharing bread with the hungry (Is. 58:5–10).

The wisdom literature contains both proclamations of God's blessing for those who care for the helpless (Prov. 14:21, 31; 19:17; 22:9; 28:8; 31:20; Eccles. 11:1) and warnings against closing ear and hand to the need of the poor (Prov. 21:13; 28:27). God is their protector, and those who mock or oppress the poor insult their creator (Prov. 14:31; 17:5). These expressions of God's identification with the poor cannot, however, be interpreted as a 'preferential option for the poor' in general. Normally God gives the *righteous person a prosperous life (Prov. 15:6). When the righteous are struck with poverty or illness or the wicked prosper, this presents a problem to the pious mind (Job; Ps. 73). The ideal picture of a righteous Israelite is of someone who helps the poor and gives freely, not of one who is dependent on others (Job 29:12–17; 31:13–32). The wisdom literature reflects the views of the leading circles of society. This makes its positive view of the poor all the more striking. The poor are never seen as immoral or as a threat to order and stability, but as fellow human beings created by God (Prov. 22:2; Job 31:15).

In the Psalms words for 'poor' are used as self-designations by the praying person (Pss. 25:16; 40:17; 69:29; 86:1; 109:22) or in promises of God's care (Pss. 18:27; 68:10; 140:12). This liturgical terminology is based on the metaphor of God as the righteous king of Israel, who cares for his people and for those who suffer (Ps. 146). Needy and helpless, the people appeal to the *mercy of God and honour him as the one who alone is rich and powerful.

Poverty terminology is used in this broader sense to refer to the people of Israel as beneficiaries of God's acts of *salvation (*e.g.* Is. 29:19; Zeph. 3:12). In Isaiah 61:1–3 God's salvation is described as a reversal of the *exile and its horrors. When the mercy of God is said to be directed towards the 'poor' (*ʿănāwîm*; LXX *ptōchoi*), the 'brokenhearted', 'captives', 'prisoners' (LXX 'blind') and 'those who mourn', these terms do not refer to different groups in Israel, but to the people as a whole. Later this promise was probably read as a word of eschatological *comfort to all Jews, both in Israel and in the dispersion, irrespective of their social status or physical *health.

This use of terms for 'poor' as a self-designation of a supplicant or as a religious description of Israel is found also in later literature of the second temple period (*Psalms of Solomon*; *Thanksgiving Hymns*; *War Scroll*). At Qumran terms for 'poor' were used to refer to the sect itself (*Pesher on Habakkuk* XII: 1–10; *Pesher on Psalm 37* II:2) and as a designation for Israel and the *remnant of Israel (*Messianic Apocalypse* frg 2 II:4–12).

Poverty in the NT

The Gospels

In the Synoptic Gospels the word *ptōchos* is used to refer to two groups: those who receive charity, and those who hear the *gospel and inherit the *kingdom of God.

The poor as recipients of charity. The rich man who asked *Jesus how to inherit eternal life was told to sell all he had and give it to the poor (Mark 10:21 par.). In this text the dominant concern is the rich man and his salvation; the need of the poor is not emphasized. The poor are also mentioned as recipients of alms in the anointing story (Mark 14:3–7 par.). Jesus and his disciples were normally able to give to the poor (John 12:5; 13:29). The duty to care for the poor and give alms is stressed especially in *Luke's Gospel (11:41; 12:33). In Matthew 6:1–4 Jesus warns against the public exhibition of almsgiving in order to gain honour and status.

The parable of the rich man and Lazarus urges the rich to listen to Moses and the prophets and open their heart to the suffering and destitute before it is too late (Luke 16:19–31). Charity and care for the poor follow from the double commandment of *love in which the law is summarized. Wealth is not to be an idol (Matt. 6:19–24); disciples are to love God with all their heart. Loving one's neighbour as oneself includes being generous to the needy.

The poor as recipients of the kingdom of God. In some very important sayings the 'poor' are those addressed by the gospel or the recipients of the kingdom. The expression 'good news is preached to the poor' in Jesus'

answer to the Baptist (Matt. 11:5; *cf.* Luke 7:22) is borrowed from Isaiah 61:1, which is the text for Jesus' inaugural sermon in Nazareth (Luke 4:18). In Nazareth it is applied to the congregation in the synagogue; in the answer to the Baptist it concludes a list of Jesus' healing miracles which includes terms used in Isaiah to refer to the salvation of Israel. The 'poor' are the people of Israel. In Isaiah 61:1 and in later texts alluding to it the meaning cannot be narrowed to people in social and economic need; the term denotes the whole people of Israel, in need of God's acts of mercy.

The Beatitudes are a poetic introduction to the Sermon on the Mount, which describes the people to whom the kingdom of God belongs. The first beatitude ascribes the kingdom to the 'poor'. But the blessings have a different form in Matthew 5:3–12 and Luke 6:20–26. Matthew has nine beatitudes, Luke only four; but Luke also has four woes which correspond exactly to his four blessings. Even though Luke's four blessings correspond to four of Matthew's, their meaning is not the same. Both the different wording and the different contexts of the extra blessings in Matthew and the woes in Luke show that the parallel blessings have different though related meanings.

Matthew 5:3 includes the expression 'poor in spirit', followed by a blessing on 'those who mourn'. To the fourth blessing, on 'those who hunger' is added 'and thirst for righteousness'. This makes clear that the blessings do not refer to material poverty or bodily hunger. The second blessing, on 'those who mourn', points to Isaiah 61:1–3 as the subtext for the two first beatitudes, and the addition 'in spirit' makes clear that the word 'poor' is used in a broad or transferred sense. Taken with 'those who mourn', the expression 'poor in spirit' should not, however, be read as a reference to humility as a virtue, but as a description of human distress. It refers to the 'poor' people of God as needy and helpless before God.

In Luke 6:20 the blessing of the 'poor' is followed by a blessing on 'those who hunger now'. In the following woes the poor and hungry are contrasted with those who are rich and well-fed in this world. The text no doubt refers to socio-economic poverty and physical hunger; those who *now* are poor, hungry, weeping and persecuted will be raised to glory and enjoy the abundance of the kingdom of God. It is, however, important to note that the beatitudes are in the second person plural. Jesus addresses them to *the disciples*. Their message is not that everybody who is poor is blessed, but that the disciples, in spite of their suffering now, are blessed because they are the recipients of the kingdom of God. Matthew's general blessing of the metaphorically 'poor' ('poor in spirit') is here applied to the disciples as a word of comfort in their sufferings or literal 'poverty'.

A general blessing of the poor and oppressed is not found in the canonical Gospel texts, but many scholars have tried to reconstruct such a text as a possible common source of the beatitudes in Matthew and Luke (see *e.g.* J. Dupont, *Les Béatitudes*). But the broader context of Jesus' proclamation of the kingdom does not point to the existence of a hypothetical text in which he offers a social message of comfort to all suffering and destitute people. He promised the kingdom to those who are like little children (Mark 10:14 par.), and he praised God for the revelation which is hidden from the wise and learned, but given to 'babes' (Matt. 11:25). The kingdom is thus assigned to the small and helpless, as against those who trust in their knowledge or obedience. The same point is made in the saying which justifies Jesus' table fellowship with tax collectors and *sinners: 'I came not to call the righteous, but sinners' (Mark 2:17). Of course Jesus does not in these sayings idealize the sin of the sinners or the ignorance of the 'babes'. Sayings like these underline that the kingdom is a gift given freely to those who are not able to repay it. When the recipients of the kingdom are called the 'poor', tax collectors are included, and they were not 'poor' in the modern sense of the word. The blessing of the 'poor' in the message of Jesus refers to the fundamental position of human beings before God, not to economic conditions or social position. It cannot be read as an expression of 'God's preferential option for the poor' in general, but is an application of the promise of Isaiah 61:1 to Israel and to the new community of the kingdom, which transcends borders set by class distinctions, nation, law, obedience or sex. Luke's blessings and woes may be seen as another application of the beatitudes intended to comfort the *church in times of poverty and persecution and as a warning to wealthy

people not to invest their lives only in this world.

The attitude of Jesus to poverty. In the Gospels Jesus' attitude to poverty is complex. He and his disciples were supported by some women (Luke 8:3) and by those who received them in their homes (Luke 10:38–42), but they were not beggars. Jesus was sometimes invited to eat with tax collectors and sinners (Matt. 9:10; Luke 15:1–2; 19:1–10) and his acceptance gave him a bad reputation when it was compared to the ascetic life of John the Baptist (Matt. 11:19; Luke 7:34). He healed a poor blind beggar, but also the daughter of a synagogue official and the servant of a Roman officer in Capernaum. He helped the poor, but also people of wealth and rank, and he did not idealize poverty.

On the other hand, he sent his disciples out in poverty. They were not allowed to carry money or extra clothes or shoes, but were totally dependent on those who listened to them and received their message (Matt 10:9–10 par.). But in Luke 22:35–38 Jesus refers to this sending and points to a new time, 'now', when they may take purse, bag and sword on their journeys. In the early church the ascetic demands of the first mission in Galilee were no longer valid. The first believers in Jerusalem 'had everything in common' and there was no needy person among them (Acts 2:44–45; 4:34–35), but the stories of Barnabas, Ananias and Sapphira (4:36 – 5:12) imply that not everybody sold their property.

Paul

Care for the poor was a concern laid upon Paul and Barnabas by their agreement with James, Peter and John (Gal. 2:10). The poor among the Christian Jews in Jerusalem were in need of support and the Gentile Christians had an obligation to them in return for the spiritual blessings received from Jerusalem (Rom. 15:26–27). The collection is mentioned in all Paul's principal letters; he strongly recommends the Corinthian church to participate (1 Cor. 16:1–4; 2 Cor. 8 – 9). The reason for the collection is evidently the social need among Christians in Jerusalem, possibly caused by hostility and persecution from the broader Jewish community. The collection also had a political function as a symbol of love and solidarity from the Pauline churches.

The majority of those in Paul's churches were poor people of humble origins (1 Cor.

1:26–28), but Paul stresses the abundance they had received in the gospel: 'as poor, yet making many rich, as having nothing, and yet possessing all things' (2 Cor. 6:10). When encouraging participation in the collection Paul also plays on the broader meaning of the words 'rich' and 'poor'. In 2 Corinthians 8:9 the 'rich' Christ has become 'poor' – a reference to the incarnation (*cf.* Phil 2:6) – so that believers can be rich and share with one another. Christ provides a new standard of values (Phil. 3:8), and the treasure of the gospel creates generosity in sharing with the needy (1 Tim. 6:17–19).

James

The letter of *James seems to reflect similar traditions to those of *Luke 6:20–26: the poor are chosen by God to inherit the kingdom and the rich are their oppressors. The stern warnings not to discriminate against the poor are derived from the command to love one's neighbour as oneself (Jas. 2:1–13). They are followed by a prophetic word of judgment against the rich, whose treasures will disappear and whose injustice against their labourers will confront them on the day of the Lord (Jas. 5:1–6).

Revelation

Who are the really poor and the really rich? That is the question raised in the letters to the churches in Smyrna and Laodicea. The Lord knows the afflictions and the poverty of his church in Smyrna, and yet he comforts them by a paradoxical proclamation: 'You are rich!' (Rev. 2:9). He also knows the self-deception of the Laodiceans; they believe they are rich and have no needs, but in fact they are 'wretched, pitiful, poor, blind and naked!' (Rev. 3:17–18). In both these texts the metaphorical use of words for 'rich' and 'poor' points to the reversal of all earthly values by the risen Christ, and in both texts the word 'rich' has positive connotations and the word 'poor' negative ones.

Bibliography

J. Dupont, *Les Béatitudes,* 3 vols. (Paris, 1969, 1969, 1972); M. Hengel, *Property and Riches in the Early Church; Aspects of a Social History of Early Christianity* (ET, London, 1974); H. Kvalbein, 'Jesus and the poor: two texts and a tentative conclusion', *Them* 12, 1987, pp. 80–87; S. J. Roth, *The Blind, the Lame, and the Poor: Character Types in Luke-Acts* (Sheffield, 1977); D. P. Seccombe, *Possessions and the Poor in Luke-Acts* (Linz, 1982); G. Theissen, *The First Followers of Jesus: A Sociological Analysis of the Earliest Christianity* (ET, London, 1978); *idem, The Social Setting of Pauline Christianity: Essays on Corinth* (ET, Edinburgh and Philadelphia, 1982).

H. KVALBEIN

POVERTY, see POOR/POVERTY
PRAISE, see WORSHIP

PRAYER

Prayer in the Bible addresses the personal *God who reveals himself to human beings, created in his image. When sin disrupted their communion with him, God took the initiative. He promised to reverse their rebellion against him, and to restore them to life with him. A son of the woman would crush the head of the serpent, bearing the wound that would bring deliverance (Gen. 3:15).

After Cain murdered Abel, *worship began in the line of Seth: 'At that time men began to call on the name of the LORD' (Gen. 4:26, NIV). That God is known by name implies that he may be personally addressed by his people. The narrative passages of the OT record many such prayers. These resemble common forms of inter-personal communication. God is addressed personally, as 'You'. Some petitions are brief: 'O God, please heal her!' (Num. 12:13). Longer prayers may include reasons for the petitions. One may be bold in speaking, and have confidence in being heard (Gen. 18:30). Confession of sin sometimes accompanies petitions (2 Sam. 24:10). Abraham's servant blesses God for answered prayer (Gen. 24:27).

The prayers of Israel in the poetic writings include more formal communal prayers that are not so closely related to specific circumstances. The psalmists praise God for his creation, and are confident of his power to accomplish his saving purposes (2 Kgs. 6:17; see Ps. 33:10–21). Biblical prayer is not patterned on incantational magic. Whether formal or informal, it addresses God as a person.

God's deeds of deliverance and salvation both invite and answer prayer. Because the initiative is with God, the effectiveness of prayer is not accomplished by a formula, nor by the eloquence of the one praying. Abraham laughed at God's promise that he would have a son, but Isaac, 'Laughter', was born (Gen. 18:14; *cf.* Luke 1:37). God made Abraham his friend, to whom he would confide his purposes (Gen. 18:17–19; Is. 41:8). God's relationship with the patriarchs enabled them to make intercession for others. Thinking of his nephew Lot, Abraham persuaded God to spare Sodom if ten righteous people could be found (Gen. 18:22–33). Job, after enduring the attacks of his friends, prayed for them at God's direction (Job 42:8).

Two aspects of prayer are highlighted in the story of Jacob. The first is the presence of God. Jacob's dream at Bethel reveals God's presence. God does not stand above the stairway, but over Jacob (Gen. 28:13 mg.; see 35:15), and promises to maintain his presence. Later, when Jacob returns to the land with vast wealth, he again prays (Gen. 32:9–12). He thanks God, confesses his unworthiness, and appeals to God's promise, asking the Lord to save him from Esau's anger. The presence of the Lord is again revealed to Jacob when the theophanic angel wrestles with him through the night. The Lord is the victor; his touch makes Jacob lame. Yet Jacob prevails, for he will not let go without receiving a blessing. In the morning, he sees the face of God in the angel.

The second aspect of prayer to which reference is made is the name of the Lord. Jacob is given his new name 'Israel', but when he asks the angel's name, the answer is not given. The name of the angel is the ineffable name of the Lord himself. The ordeal that will accomplish salvation awaits the coming of another 'Israel'. Agony in prevailing prayer has meaning because of our fellowship with *Jesus Christ (Col. 2:1–3; 4:12).

The names of God revealed in the patriarchal narrative decisively reveal the nature of the one to whom prayer is addressed. God is the creator; nothing is hidden from his sight (Gen. 14:22; 16:13). He is almighty, and intervenes in nature and history to accomplish his gracious purposes (Gen. 17:1). He is eternal (Gen. 21:33), but identifies himself as the God of Israel (33:20).

He provides a substitute for Isaac which points to his ultimate purpose (Gen. 22:13–14).

God's *covenant with Abraham undergirds prayer. God promised to bless him and to bless the families of the earth through him. Abraham responded in *faith (Gen. 15:6; Rom. 4). Later, God sealed his covenant with Abraham by taking an oath (Gen. 22:16–18; Heb. 6:13–18). When the Lord made his covenant with the people of Israel, he did so as the faithful God of Abraham, Isaac and Jacob.

God's deliverance of Israel in the Exodus was a response more to groans of affliction than to pleas of faith. Yet God came down to rescue and claim them. The fire in the bush revealed his presence and was a pledge of his deliverance. The presence of God is again linked to the name of God. The name I AM enabled Moses to identify the one who spoke as the God of his ancestors (Exod. 3:14).

The Exodus was not just liberation of the people from bondage; God brought them out to bring them to himself at Mt Sinai. The Lord's claim on liberated Israel provided a new covenantal setting for prayer. The prayers of *Moses were of central importance in God's dealings with Israel.

The terror that Israel experienced when God thundered from Mt Sinai turned into restlessness. Moses was long absent, receiving the plans for the tabernacle from God. The people induced Aaron to make a bull of gold, and were engaged in an idolatrous orgy when Moses came down from the mountain. Only the Levites, Moses' own tribe, responded to his call to put down the rebellion.

What prayer could Moses now make? He appealed to God's covenant promise to Abraham, Isaac and Jacob (Exod. 32:13), to the honour of God's name among the heathen (Exod. 32:12), and above all, to God's *ḥesed*, his covenantal love (Exod. 34:6). God said that he could not go in the midst of the people, because they were 'stiff-necked'. If he were to dwell among them, he would destroy them. God then proposed to go before them in the presence of his angel and to give them the land. He would meet with Moses outside the camp, but he would not pitch his tent in the midst of the tents of Israel. This meant that the tabernacle would not be built, for it was designed as God's dwelling in the midst of his people.

Moses was distressed. If God did not go in their midst, there was no point in going to Canaan. The land would have no temple; God would not be among them. Moses made two requests: he asked to know the name of the one God was sending with him (that is, the angel of the Lord), and to see the Lord's glory. God granted those requests, and proclaimed his name to Moses as the God who is 'abounding in love and faithfulness' (Exod. 34:6). John's Gospel renders the phrase 'full of grace and truth', and applies it to Christ (John 1:14). God would dwell in the midst of his people; the tabernacle would be built; his tent would be pitched in the centre of Israel's camp.

The prayer of Moses at the conclusion of this passage marks an *inclusio*. God had said that he could not go in the midst of the people because they were stiff-necked (Exod. 33:5). Now Moses prays, 'Go in the midst of us because we are a stiff-necked people.' (Translators have obscured this repetition.) But Moses adds, 'and forgive our wickedness and our sin, and take us as your inheritance' (not 'give us our inheritance'; Exod. 34:9).

The spiritual reality that Moses sought was made visible in a tent, later replaced by Solomon's *temple. The temple and the cultus served by the Aaronic priesthood represented an institutionalizing of covenant worship which contrasted with the intimacy of patriarchal prayer. Yet something was gained by the temple symbolism. God had appeared to the patriarchs only occasionally; in the temple God had a residence. Solomon dedicated the temple as the place to which the prayers of all the nations could be directed (1 Kgs. 8:41–43; Is. 56:7; Mark 11:17). The psalmist yearned for the courts of the Lord (Ps. 84:2, 10).

With the coming of Christ the worship of the OT reached its fulfilment, and the tension between personal and institutional worship was resolved. For the NT writers, it is no longer necessary to worship only at the Jerusalem temple (as opposed, for example, to the Samaritan temple on Mount Gerizim). Spiritual worship is not templeless worship, but worship at the true temple, the incarnate Son. The water he gives is his Spirit (see *Holy Spirit); he himself is the truth (John 4:23–26).

Peter quotes Exodus 19:6 in claiming that the people of the new covenant are a royal *priesthood (1 Pet. 2:9). In Christ, our ascended priest, we draw near to God and enjoy intimacy with him. Anna and Simeon, praying in the temple, echo the prayers of the OT saints for the coming of the Lord, and witness their fulfilment. The blend of personal devotion and corporate worship found in the *Psalms also appears in the prayer poems of Mary and Zechariah. Following the practice of the synagogue, the NT church joined in corporate prayer to the Lord.

God's covenant lordship shapes our prayer to him. The Lord God is jealous for his name, and will not tolerate prayers to other gods. Pluralism calls people to the worship of many gods; yet it is the exclusive demand of the true God which makes prayer real. He alone can enable us to speak freely with him. The Psalms comprise a treasure of united corporate prayer, and their use, with that of other forms of prayer, enables a group or congregation to pray in unison or in song. Paul writes that the richly indwelling word of Christ is the source of spiritual wisdom expressed in song, by which the congregation praises God and is built up (Col. 3:16; Eph. 5:19–20).

The God who seeks worshippers desires devotion; in prayer his people seek the accomplishment of his purposes. Jesus taught his disciples to pray, 'Thy kingdom come, thy will be done, in earth as it is in heaven' (Matt. 6:10, KJV).

Among modern biblical scholars, strong dissent has been expressed to the concept of submission to God's will. Christian orthodoxy has been described as a slavish fear of the Almighty that accepts all the blame for what goes wrong and dares not voice a protest. Appeal is made to laments in the OT: in Job, Jeremiah and the Psalms (Job 10:3, 9; 13:24; Jer. 20:7–18; Ps. 88), we find God not only questioned, but accused. His justice and faithfulness are challenged. It is suggested that to describe such language as hyperbole is to ignore the agony of the sufferers and the unanswerable questions which they raise. Some suggest that so long as blasphemy is directed to God, and not to others about God, it is an acceptable expression of piety. Sometimes God himself is thought to be under a cloud of suffering that has no ultimate answer. The influence of the 'death of God' theology and the claims that humanity has 'come of age' shape this challenge to orthodoxy. On the assumption that both OT and NT offer numerous contradictory theologies, it is said that we would do best to move away from Pauline dogmatism and adopt a theology shaped by the wisdom literature (see *Wisdom books), with its more cosmopolitan, humanistic outlook. (See W. Brueggemann, *In Man We Trust: The Neglected Side of Biblical Faith* [Atlanta, 1972].)

Such an approach fails to take account of the OT laments and the theology of the wisdom literature. Ecclesiastes shows that even the blessedness of Israel under Solomon cannot be God's ultimate goal. Suffering and death remain, and seem to contradict the covenant. God answers Job's charges by means of his presence, not by explaining himself. The teaching of Deuteronomy is that God's blessings are succeeded by his judgments. In exile, Israel laments. But following the blessings and the curse will come the triumph of God's good purpose. In the last days of restoration and renewal the hearts of God's people will be circumcised (Deut. 30:6). God himself will come (Is. 40:10–11; Ezek. 34:15), and so will the Servant of the Lord (Is. 49:6; Ezek. 34:23), for God will make a new covenant (Jer. 31:31–34).

Prayer in that day will receive God's answer 'Here I am!' (Is. 58:9). Before his people call, God will answer (Is. 65:24). The Servant of the Lord will be lifted up and exalted. Yet when he appears, he is disfigured beyond recognition (Is. 52:13–14). He is the suffering Servant who will justify many, and bear their iniquities.

The cry of Jesus Christ on the cross, 'Why have you forsaken me?' was the climax of all doubts and laments. Our laments are never as righteous as we think. We cannot justly ask 'Why?' for we deserve to be abandoned. Only Christ was faithful and had the right to ask that question. We cannot grasp the agony of his abandonment to the wrath we deserve; yet because he was abandoned, those who trust him will never be abandoned. Paul cites the lament of Psalm 44 to assure us that we are more than conquerors through God's love in Christ (Rom. 8:36). Our afflictions are transformed because we share in Christ's sufferings.

In prayer God's people submit to his saving grace. Psalmists and prophets confess their sin. David seeks not only forgiveness but restoration (Pss. 32; 51; 38:1–4). In the presence of the Holy One, the seraphs thunder, 'Holy, holy', but the prophet cries, 'Woe to me!' (Is. 6:3, 5). In the time of the judges repeated sin was repeatedly confessed; kings sometimes implemented reform, but not until the exile was the persistent apostasy of Israel fully acknowledged, in the prayers of Daniel (Dan. 9:3–19), Nehemiah (Neh. 1:5–11), and the Levites (Neh. 9:5–37).

In the historical books and the Psalms the people's major petition is for deliverance from their enemies, both personal and public. King Hezekiah spread before the Lord the letter of the Rabshekah, who is laying siege to Jerusalem (2 Kgs. 19:19). Israel celebrates God's past acts of deliverance while calling on him for rescue in the present. Psalms that call down judgment on the enemies of the people of God include the chilling language of retributive justice (Pss. 7:15–16; 109:6–16; 137:7–9). In contrast, victims often protest their righteousness (not sinlessness, but innocence). God did not sanction the wars of Israel so that his people might conquer the world, but only for the execution of his judgments. In the ancient Near East the sword symbolized divine justice and wrath against evil. As always in God's dealings with his covenant people, his giving went beyond their asking.

In the thanksgiving and praise of the Psalms, however, we reach the heart of prayer. Asaph's primary petition is not for deliverance from enemies, nor for provision of daily needs, but for the knowledge of God: 'Whom have I in heaven but you? And earth has nothing I desire besides you' (Ps. 73:25).

The Lord himself comes to consummate OT revelation. The full deity and the true humanity of Jesus Christ fulfils God's promises of his own coming and that of the Servant of the Lord. The primary prayer of God's people under the old covenant is answered: God comes in person. The great prayers for deliverance, for the restoration that brings us to God and God to us, are also answered. When two great praying prophets, Moses and Elijah, appeared with Jesus on a mountain top, they spoke of the 'Exodus' he must accomplish at Jerusalem (Luke 9:31). Jesus came to do what they could not. The 'lifting up' of Jesus in his resurrection and ascension began with his lifting up on the cross (John 12:32–33). Jesus is Lord because he conquered sin and death for us. He transforms prayer, because in him the communion with God which we seek in prayer becomes a reality. The psalmists sought the Lord in the temple; Simeon found him there.

The Lord answers prayer by coming in the person of Jesus. He is the righteous Servant of the Lord, the true Israel (Rom. 15:8–9; Is. 49:3). Jesus sang with Israel the songs of the people of God. He also cried in agony with David the king; yet he did so not merely as a righteous sufferer, but also as a substitute for sinners. He transformed the role of God's servant, even as he fulfilled it. He prayed, and was heard, as the incarnate Son who alone knows the Father (Matt. 11:27; John 11:41–42).

Jesus prayed constantly throughout his earthly ministry, particularly at its high points (Luke 3:21; 6:12; 9:18, 28; 11:1; 22:32, 41–45). He prayed for his disciples, and for those who crucified him. On the lips of Jesus, familiar forms of prayer gained new meaning. In his prayers of thanksgiving he rejoiced in the Father's electing love (Matt. 11:25; Luke 10:21). In Gethsemane he asked that, if possible, the cup of suffering might be taken away, but went on to pray, 'Yet not my will, but yours, be done' (Luke 22:42). He expressed his devotion to and intimacy with his Father in the name 'Abba'.

Jesus taught his disciples to pray in the (very brief) 'Lord's Prayer'. We pray to our Father to hallow his name in his Son, and to bring in his rule in the kingdom of his Son. Our Father will provide today our bread for tomorrow. We pray for forgiveness, forgiving others as we ourselves have been forgiven. Jesus overcame the devil when he was tempted for us, and he teaches us to pray for deliverance from the Evil One, as he prayed for Peter.

The mediators of the old covenant could not provide redemption. Moses saw a generation perish in the desert. Job cried out for a mediator to plead his case with God (Job 9:32–35). Isaiah's figure of the suffering Servant is presented as a more powerful mediator. He is identified with Israel, but also will be the Saviour of Israel and a light to the nations (Is. 49:5–6). As the suffering Servant, he will bear the sin of his people, and will intercede for transgressors (Is. 53:12).

Christ is the ultimate mediator, as prophet (Heb. 1:1–2), priest (Heb. 7:3, 25), and king (Heb. 2:8; 12:28). As prophet, he speaks the words given to him by the Father (John 15:15; 17:8). As priest, he mediates our worship and offers his atoning *sacrifice, ever living to make intercession for us (Heb. 7:24–25), and ever giving us confidence to approach his throne in prayer (Heb. 6:19–20). He is mocked as king of the Jews by Pilate, but his *kingdom is triumphant, for he is the truth (John 18:37). One with us in our humanity, he learned obedience through tears and suffering (Heb. 5:7–8). In corporate prayer, we approach Jesus and join the heavenly assembly (Heb. 12:22–29). The confidence which enables us to enter the most holy place by the blood of Jesus (Heb. 10:19–22) also moves us to keep meeting together to encourage one another (Heb. 10:23–25).

The Christ who gives us access to the Father in prayer also comes to us in his Spirit sent from heaven. He has not left us orphaned (John 14:18). The Spirit comes to possess us as Christ's inheritance, and also to be the deposit of our final inheritance, the foretaste of Christ's presence. Thus the Spirit seals our relationship with the Lord (Eph. 1:13–14; 2 Cor. 1:22; Rom. 8:23). To pray in the Spirit is to experience both aspects of his presence (Eph. 6:18). Boldness in prayer is a gift of the Spirit (Acts 4:29; Heb. 4:16), but the Spirit also prays for us (Rom. 8:18–27). As we wait for the Lord we groan with all creation. We have the Spirit to assure us of our adoption, but there is glory still to come. In our weakness, we do not know how to pray according to God's will for us. In our need, the indwelling Holy Spirit is our helper. He prays according to the will of God, for he knows that will. He prays *with* us as well as *for* us. He makes our groaning his groaning. God the Father, who searches our hearts, knows the mind of the Spirit which is expressed in his groaning within us.

By the presence of the Holy Spirit we become temples, both individually and corporately (1 Cor. 3:17; 6:19). Prayer requires consecration, the presentation of our bodies as living sacrifices (Rom. 12:1–2; 2 Cor. 6:16 – 7:1). Fellowship in prayer is fellowship in the Spirit. To be filled with the Spirit is to know the dimensions of the Spirit's presence and work, and to know the *love of Christ (Eph. 3:14–16). The fruit of the Spirit supports the prayers of the church: love for God leads us to seek him in prayer; love for others sustains persevering prayer on their behalf (1 Pet. 4:7–8). The strength to prevail in prayer comes from the faith which the Spirit gives (Jas. 5:13–18). Prayer in the power of the Spirit brings blessing. Paul prayed fervently for others, and asked others to pray for him (Eph. 6:18–20; Col. 4:3; 1 Thess. 5:25). The Spirit moves us to seek wisdom as we pray.

The Spirit who joins us to Christ our mediator also effects a living union with Christ, who is our life. We partake of Christ in the Spirit, but we are not absorbed into Christ. At the deepest level, his Spirit bears witness with our spirit that we are children of God (Rom. 8:16). Yet only by the Spirit can we experience the love of God for us (Rom. 5:5). The prayer of Moses is echoed in the prayers of Paul, who seeks for the saints the knowledge of the Lord (Eph. 1:17–23; Col. 1:9–11; Phil. 1:9). In prayer we rightly seek the joy which the presence of the Spirit brings, the knowledge of the Father and the Son. Yet the highest goal of prayer is not to claim the Lord as our inheritance, but to be claimed by him as his own.

Prayer leads us to the triune God. It is addressed not simply to a personal, but to a tri-personal God. In prayer, as in theology, we may misunderstand the mystery of the Trinity. But prayer draws us into communion with the living God, and makes it easier, not harder, to confess the Trinity. Calvin appreciated the words of Gregory of Nazianzen: 'I cannot think of the *one*, but I am immediately surrounded with the splendour of the *three*; nor can I clearly discover the *three*, but I am suddenly carried back to the *one*.' As the Spirit of adoption, the Spirit assures us of God's Fatherhood and our adoption. Since our sonship is in Christ, and the Spirit is also the Spirit of the Son, our understanding of prayer itself makes us aware of the triune mystery.

In prayer we address the Father, from whom his whole family in heaven and earth is named (Eph. 3:14–15). Even as we address him as Father, we are aware that we do so only through his Son, and in the Spirit who reveals him to us. Prayer to the Father does not exclude the Son or the Spirit, but confesses the purpose of the Father in sending them. In union with the Son we are made children, among whom there is no longer male or female, for 'you are all one in Christ Jesus' (Gal. 3:28). The prayer of adoption involves both dependence and assurance. We

come in urgent need, seeking the Father's will, kingdom and presence. We come to share the love of the Father who gave his Son for us.

Bibliography

S. E. Balentine, *Prayer in the Hebrew Bible: The drama of the divine–human dialogue* (Minneapolis, 1993); D. A. Carson (ed.), *Teach Us To Pray: Prayer in the Bible and the World* (Exeter and Grand Rapids, 1990); M. de Goedt, 'The intercession of the Spirit in Christian prayer', in C. Duquoc and C. Geffre (eds.), *The Prayer Life* (New York, 1972), pp. 26–38; M. Greenberg, *Biblical Prose Prayer As a Window to the Popular Religion of Ancient Israel* (Berkeley, 1983); E. Lohmeyer, '*Our Father*': An Introduction to the Lord's Prayer* (ET, New York, 1965); T. Longman III, *How to Read the Psalms* (Downers Grove and Leicester, 1988); P. D. Miller, Jr, *Interpreting the Psalms* (Philadelphia, 1986); W. R. Spear, *The Theology of Prayer* (Grand Rapids, 1979); C. Westermann, *Elements of Old Testament Theology* (ET, Atlanta, 1982).

E. P. CLOWNEY

PREACHING AND BIBLICAL THE-OLOGY, see Part 1
PREDESTINATION, see ELECTION

PRIESTS

Introduction

This article will concentrate on the theological implications of the priesthood, and on the functions of priests and other cultic officials. Answers to questions concerning the historical development of the priesthood in Israel tend to vary, according to scholars' dating of the various OT, especially Pentateuchal, materials. On many of these questions, no final answer or consensus has yet been reached.

Non-Israelite priests

Persons having functions similar to those of OT priests are known to have existed among Israel's neighbours. The OT names Potiphera, a priest in the Egyptian town of On or Heliopolis (Gen. 41:45, 50; 46:20); Jethro (or Reuel), a 'priest of Midian' (Exod. 2:16; 3:1; 18:1, NIV), who became Moses' father-in-law;

Mattan, (chief) 'priest of Baal' (2 Kgs. 11:18); and the mysterious Melchizedek, king of Salem (probably Jerusalem) and 'priest of the most high God', whose dealings with Abram are described in Genesis 14:18–20; *cf.* Psalm 110:4; the writer to the Hebrews (7:1–10; *cf.* below) emphasizes Melchizedek's independence from the later levitical priesthood. Other, unnamed foreign priests are mentioned as existing in Egypt (Gen. 47:22), Samaria (2 Kgs. 10:19), Philistia (1 Sam. 5:5; 6:2) and Moab (Jer. 49:3). All these, like Israelite priests, have the title *kōhēn*, the etymology of which is uncertain. A different word, *kᵉmarîm*, is also used occasionally (2 Kgs. 23:5; Hos. 10:5; Zeph. 1:4) of pagan priests. In the NT, the only reference to a non-Israelite priest is in Acts 14:13, where a priest of Zeus at Lystra attempts to offer sacrifice to Paul and Barnabas. These non-Israelite priests are introduced into the biblical narrative without explanation, and thus without distinguishing their functions from those of Israelite priests; the existence of priests outside Israel is presupposed and not questioned.

The rest of this article is concerned with priesthood in Israel and in the NT church.

The appointment of priests

The OT speaks of God's calling or choosing a prophet (*e.g.* Amos 7:14–15) or a king (1 Sam. 16:1), but not a priest. Micah of Ephraim is said to have 'installed' a Levite as his priest (Judg. 17:12), literally, 'filled [his] hand' (compare Exod. 29:1; 32:29; 1 Kgs. 13:33). The origin of this expression is uncertain, but it refers to appointment rather than to a religious rite of consecration. In Numbers 8:10, the Israelites lay their hands on the Levites 'as a wave offering from the Israelites', but this does not appear to have been a general practice, or to have had the significance of ordination. The high priest (Exod. 29:7; Lev. 8:12) and other priests (Exod. 40:12–15) were anointed, as were kings, to indicate their status in the community.

Despite there being no specific rite of ordination, priests and Levites were deemed to be 'consecrated' (Lev. 21:6; 1 Sam. 7:1), that is, made sacred or holy, by God for the work they did in the tabernacle, a place sanctified (see *Holiness) by God's special presence. This set them apart from the rest of the community (Num. 8:14; Deut. 10:8, of the Levites; 1 Chr. 23:13, of Aaron 'and his descendants for ever'); gave them special privileges, such as access to the sanctuary; and made them subject to special regulations related to their cultic duties (the wearing of 'linen undergarments', Exod. 28:43; washing, Exod. 30:17–21; 40:31–32; Num. 8:7; wearing the ephod, Lev. 8:7; abstinence from 'fermented drink' when on duty, Num. 10:8–11; attendance at funerals only of a close relative, Num. 21:1–6). The Aaronic priesthood, and especially the institution of the high-priest, are seen in the letter to the *Hebrews (see below) as a type of Christ's high priestly work.

Functions of priests

*Sacrifice

It is sometimes assumed that the essential function of priests was to offer animal and other sacrifices. Following the return from exile, this appears to have been the case (see below); but otherwise it is an over-simplification, in three respects.

First, in early times sacrifice could on occasions be offered by men who were not priests (Exod. 24:5; *cf.* 20:25–26). Sacrifices were offered by Gideon (Judg. 6:25–26); by Manoah, the father of Samson (Judg. 13:16–23), and by Elijah (1 Kgs. 18:30–33). None of these is called a priest. Sacrifice was also offered by kings such as Saul (1 Sam. 13:9–10), David (2 Sam. 6:13, 17–18; 24:25), repeatedly by Solomon (1 Kgs. 3:4, 15; 8:5, 62–64; 9:25), and by Ahaz (2 Kgs. 16:12–15). This last passage makes it clear that an inaugural sacrifice was made personally by Ahaz; he did not merely cause sacrifice to be offered by a priest. The implied rule appears to be that, at least until the early period of the monarchy, it was proper for the head of a family to offer sacrifice, and therefore *a fortiori* proper for the king as head of the nation. Later, however, King Uzziah is punished with leprosy for having entered the temple to burn incense at the altar, an act reserved to the priests (2 Chr. 26:18; *cf.* Num. 16:40; 1 Chr. 23:13). While others could offer sacrifices, they were not permitted to undertake the duties associated with the tabernacle.

Second (see below, 'Divination' and 'Instruction'), priests are sometimes represented as functioning in ways not related to sacrifice, notably in discerning and/or announcing God's will in particular circumstances.

Third, the actual slaughtering of a sacrificial animal was never the exclusive duty of priests. The animal had by law to be killed by the man offering it (Lev. 1:5, addressed to 'the Israelites'; 1:2, literally 'the sons of Israel'; similarly 3:2, 8, 13; also 4:22, 24, 'the leaders'; and 4:29, 33, 'members of the community'). The priest's role was to present the animal's blood, the holiest part of the victim (Lev. 17:11, 14) to God on the altar. In the case of a bird, however, the slaughtering itself had to be done on the altar, and therefore by a priest (Lev. 1:14–15; 5:8–10); similarly the priest was responsible for burning part of a meal offering on the altar (Lev. 5:11–13). The focus of the priest's sacrificial activity was thus the altar, not the killing of an animal as such.

Divination

Every time in the OT that the Urim and Thummim are mentioned (Exod. 28:30; Lev. 8:8; Num. 27:21; Deut. 33:8; 1 Sam. 14:41 LXX; Ezra 2:63; Neh. 7:65; cf. 1 Sam. 28:6), it is in connection with the activity of a priest. It is not known with certainty what the Urim and Thummim were, except that they were used in a formalized procedure for 'seek[ing] God's will' (Exod. 18:15). Exodus 28:30 and Leviticus 8:8 refer to their being carried or worn by a priest in his special garments, which included 'a breastpiece for making decisions' (Exod. 28:15–30; GNB 'a breast-piece for the High Priest to use in determining God's will') and an ephod (Exod. 28:6–14). Their close connection with priests suggests that the Urim and Thummim were not considered to have any intrinsic power, and were not used as mere instruments of chance (as for example in casting lots or throwing dice). Their value lay in their use by a priest deemed to be closely related to the God whose will was being sought. The Urim and Thummim disappeared at the time of the exile (Neh. 7:65), and were never recovered.

Instruction (tôrâh)

The announcement of God's will by a priest was not limited to the use of the Urim and Thummim. It was closely linked with the duty of instruction (tôrâh, Deut. 33:10, NIV 'law'), not only on cultic matters such as the distinction between the holy and the common

(Lev. 10:10; Ezek. 22:26; 44:23; cf. Hag. 2:10–14), but also on matters of right behaviour (Jer. 2:8; 18:18; Hos. 4:6). Priests thus exercised a mediatorial function, standing between God and human beings. Priests were called on to interpret the law, and to announce legal decisions. After the exile, however, these functions were exercised increasingly by scribes, the area of priestly activity becoming largely limited to the cultus. By NT times, teaching was physically separated from sacrificial worship and located in the synagogues.

Priests, Levites and *worship in Israel

An essential feature of priestly activity was the priest's relation to a shrine or place of worship. The story of Micah (Judg. 17:1–13) illustrates the assumption that a shrine required a priest, just as a ruler required servants at his residence. The priest may thus have been thought of as playing the role of an attendant or guardian (1 Sam. 7:1) at a place where God was believed to be particularly present. The priest became in this way an intermediary between God and those visiting the shrine; he announced God's will to the people, and presented their offerings to God.

There were no priestesses or female Levites in Israel, and it is unlikely (despite Exod. 38:8) that any women were included in the temple personnel. In this respect, Israel's cultic practice contrasts sharply with that of Assyria and other neighbouring countries.

The priests and Levites were organized in a hierarchical structure (cf. 1 Chr. 23 – 26). Many texts mentioning Aaron (e.g. Lev. 16:3–25; cf. v. 32) are to be understood as referring, not only personally to the brother of Moses, but also functionally to later high priests; some texts referring simply to 'the priest' (e.g. 1 Kgs. 4:2; 2 Kgs. 11:9; 12:9; 16:10–11; 22:10, 12, 14; cf. v. 8) are to be similarly understood.

Under the high priest (2 Kgs. 23:4; 25:18 = Jer. 52:24) were one or more 'priest(s) next in rank', literally, 'priests of the second [rank]', and three 'doorkeepers' (literally, 'keepers of the threshold', with financial responsibilities, 2 Kgs. 22:4, identified as priests in 2 Kgs. 12:9; cf. 'gatekeepers', Ezra 7:24).

The centralization of the cultus in *Jerusalem under Josiah entailed the abolition of all other sanctuaries, such as those at Gilgal (Josh. 4:19–20), Mizpah (Judg. 20:1, 3;

21:1, 5, 8), Ophrah (Judg. 6:24), Bethel (Gen. 28:18–19, 22; Judg. 20:18) and Dan (Judg. 18:30–31).

The fall of Jerusalem to the Babylonian armies in 587 or 586 BC, and the consequent destruction of the temple, were naturally disastrous for the priests and other temple personnel. The chief priest and his senior colleagues were deported and later executed (2 Kgs. 25:18–21; Jer. 52:24–27; cf. Jer. 39:6); some Levites or subordinate priests remained, and some sacrifices were offered in what was left of the temple (Jer. 41:4–5).

Among the first groups returning from exile in 538 BC, there were 4,289 priests, divided into four families, but only seventy-four Levites (Ezra 2:36–40; Neh. 7:39–43). There were probably two reasons for this disparity: first, that more priests than Levites had been taken into captivity; and second, that Levites had less incentive than priests to return to Jerusalem, where they would be mere 'temple servants' (Ezra 8:17).

The hierarchical structure of the priesthood corresponds to a differentiation between degrees of holiness attributed to various parts of the temple complex, and to particular days, the most holy place or 'holy of holies' being reserved to the use of the high priest on the Day of *Atonement (Lev. 16:32, cf. Heb. 9:6–7).

Priests and politics

From the foundation of the first temple in Jerusalem, the links between kings and priests were close. The kings were not priests, but on occasion performed sacral functions (see above). High priests were appointed (1 Kgs. 2:35) and could be dismissed (1 Kgs. 2:27) by the king; senior priests are included in a list of royal officials (1 Kgs. 4:2, 4–5), and took orders from the king, even on such matters as the design, installation, and use of a new altar in the temple (2 Kgs. 16:10–18).

There were, however, at times disputes between kings and priests. The priest Jehoiada led a successful rebellion against Queen Athaliah (2 Kgs. 11). Joash was assassinated in revenge for having had Jehoiada's son Zechariah stoned to death (2 Chr. 24:17–27). The high priest Jonathan was prominent in the Maccabean resistance to Greek rule (1 Macc. 10:69–74). The hope of 'harmony between the two', king and priest (Zech. 6:13; cf. Jer. 33:17–22), in the messianic age

remained alive, but was not always realized in the present.

Despite the close involvement of kings in the life of the Jerusalem temple, priests were materially supported not by the king, but directly or indirectly by the worshippers. Priests were entitled to at least a part of each animal sacrifice (except for the whole burnt offering or holocaust), once its fat had been offered to God by being burnt on the altar (Lev. 7:28–36; Deut. 18:1–5); also to the firstfruits of grain, new wine and oil, and the first wool from the sheep-shearing (Deut. 18:4). They also received a share of the money collected from worshippers; Joash made this right conditional on the priests' repairing (in fact paying workers to repair) damage to the temple (2 Kgs. 12:5–16; cf. 22:3–7).

During the Persian, Greek, and Roman occupations of Israel, the high priest became the focus of Jewish national consciousness, often exercising greater influence among the people than governors appointed by the imperial powers. Probably as a reaction to this, Herod the Great ended the life tenure of the high priest, and made his own appointments to that office whenever he chose; this power was later transferred to the Roman procurator.

Priests in the Gospels

It is against this background of the secularization of the high priesthood that the withdrawal of the Qumran community from Jerusalem, and the Qumran texts referring to 'the Wicked Priest' (for example, Pesher on Habakkuk XII), may be understood, and also negative references in the Gospels to chief priests and priests among the opponents of Jesus (Mark 8:31; 10:33; 15:11, 31 and parallels). Such negative evaluations recall condemnation of unworthy priests by OT prophets (e.g. Jer. 2:8; Ezek. 22:26; Mic. 3:11).

Even during the earthly lifetime of Jesus, only one high priest functioned at any one time; but members of a class of leading priests, some of whom, like Annas and Caiaphas, were linked by ties of kinship, are sometimes referred to collectively as 'the chief priests' (the plural of archiereus, translated 'high priest'). Within the generally negative assessment of priests in the Gospels, there stands the pregnant statement in John (11:49–

52; *cf.* 18:14), suggesting that because of his office, even a personally evil high priest such as Caiaphas could, 'not of himself', utter prophetic truth.

*Jesus as high priest

In the Gospels, leading priests are among those active in securing Jesus' condemnation to death, though after Pentecost 'a large number of priests' (Acts 6:7) are among those who become Christians. By a striking reversal, the writer to the Hebrews, alone among NT writers, claims the title of high priest for Jesus (Heb. 2:17; 4:14 – 5:10; 8:1–6), citing Genesis 14:18–20 and Psalm 110:4 in support of this claim. These texts in fact speak of a priest, but are interpreted by the writer of Hebrews as referring to the supreme priesthood realized in Jesus.

This argument is an integral part of the writer's interpretation of the death of Jesus as a sacrifice. Jesus is for the writer both a new and better kind of high priest, and also the sacrifice which he himself offers to God (Heb. 9:11–14, 23–28). The writer sees in the mysterious figure of Melchizedek (Heb. 7:1–17) a foreshadowing of a priesthood higher than that of Aaron, and fulfilled in Jesus. His death supersedes the OT cultus, as reality supersedes a mere foreshadowing (10:1–4); it effects in the conscience of the believer the forgiveness and purification that the OT cultus could effect only in an external manner (10:5–18). In particular, Jesus carries out on a cosmic scale the functions repeatedly and ineffectually performed by the high priest of the earthly sanctuary on the Day of Atonement.

Christian priesthood

Apart from Jesus, no individual member of a Christian community is described as a priest in the NT. Only in post-biblical times did some of the terms used to denote Christian leaders come to signify an office like that of the OT priesthood; these included the Greek *presbyteros*, properly 'elder', but also translated 'priest'. However, the Christian community (see *Church) as a whole is described as 'a royal priesthood' (1 Pet. 2:9, *cf.* v. 5), that is, a holy people devoted to the service of God and his kingdom. This language recalls that of Exodus 19:6; other OT texts, such as Genesis 12:1–3; Isaiah 2:2–4; and Psalm 96, represent *Israel as playing a mediatorial, and thus in a wider sense

priestly, role. (Philo, *On the Life of Moses*, II, XLI [224–225] similarly says that at the Passover, 'the whole nation is consecrated and officiates in offering sacrifice', being 'honoured by this participation in the priesthood'; this insight was not developed in OT times.) Exodus 19:6 has also probably influenced Revelation 1:6, '[Christ] has made us to be a kingdom and priests to serve his God and Father', and 5:10 and 20:6, which also refer to the royal and priestly dignity of the Christian community.

Conclusion

The OT writers had no inhibitions about normally using the same word, *kōhēn*, to describe both Israelite and foreign priests, leaving the context to make the reference clear. Similarly, NT writers use priestly language of Christ and of the Christian community. There is therefore no reason for such terms to be avoided today, on condition that they are used in their biblical senses, and that misleading associations are excluded. The traditional French Protestant translation of *kōhēn* and *hiereus* as 'sacrificateur' is thus unnecessary and indeed misleading, since sacrifice was only one of the functions of priests in OT times.

The OT sacrificial cultus ceased with the fall of Jerusalem in AD 70, or possibly some years later. Consequently, the Levitical priesthood, by that time identified with sacrifice, had as a body no continuing function, though individual priests could become scribes or teachers of the law. Thereafter, however, Jewish religious leaders would be rabbis, not priests.

Animal or other material sacrifices have no place in the life of the Christian community. But Christians continue to 'offer to God a sacrifice of praise', 'to do good and to share with others', and are described as 'sacrifices' with which 'God is pleased' (Heb. 13:15–16). Moreover, Christians, as the new people of God, fulfil the priesthood first entrusted to Israel, by proclaiming the one reconciling sacrifice of Christ, and by bringing to God their intercessions (see *Prayer) for the world.

See also: MELCHIZEDEK; TEMPLE.

Bibliography

A. Cody, *A History of Old Testament Priesthood* (Rome, 1969); *idem, Ezekiel, with* an Excursus on Old Testament Priesthood (Wilmington, 1984); R. Martin-Achard, 'Israël, peuple sacerdotal', in R. Martin-Achard (ed.), Permanence de l'Ancien Testament: Recherches d'exégèse et de théologie (Geneva, 1984); H. Valentin, Aaron: Eine Studie zur vor-priester-schriftlichen Aaron-Überlieferung (Freiburg, Switzerland and Göttingen, 1978); A. Vanhoye, Old Testament Priests and the New Priest, according to the New Testament (ET, Petersham, 1986); R. de Vaux, Ancient Israel: Its Life and Institutions (ET, London, 1961); D. P. Wright, 'The Spectrum of Priestly Impurity', in G. A. Anderson and S. M. Olyan (eds.), Priesthood and Cult in Ancient Israel (Sheffield, 1991).

P. ELLINGWORTH

PROPHECY, PROPHETS

Introduction

Prophecy is the most common means *God used to communicate with people throughout biblical history. The story of prophecy, from Genesis to Revelation, is the story of God speaking to people through human messengers, and thus it is the story of God's varying relationships with his people and with others. Speaking through the prophets, God guided kings and people by telling them how to act in specific situations, warned people when they disobeyed him, predicted events that he would bring about, interpreted events when they came about, and demonstrated that he alone was both ruler of history and a God who relates personally to his people.

The basic biblical principles regarding prophets and prophecy are found in the Pentateuch, especially in connection with *Moses, but a regular office of prophet, and bands of secondary prophets, are not fully established until the period covered by the later historical books and the prophetic writings. In the Gospels, *Jesus is seen as a great prophet, but much more than a prophet. The book of Acts and the epistles describe a gift of prophecy given to Christians which has lesser authority but much wider distribution than canonical prophecy, and prophecy is seen as the most valuable of the *Holy Spirit's many gifts to the church (see *Spiritual gifts). The Bible closes with a sobering yet magnificent picture of the future in the prophecy of Revelation.

Prophecy and prophets in the Pentateuch

While NT authors identify both Abel (Gen. 4:1–8; Luke 11:50–51) and *Enoch (Gen. 5:18–24; Jude 14) as prophets, the first explicit mention of a 'prophet' (Heb. nābî') in the OT occurs when God tells Abimelech that *Abraham 'is a prophet, and he will pray for you and you shall live' (Gen. 20:7, RSV). This suggests that a 'prophet' has a special relationship with God whereby his prayers will be answered, an idea that is revisited later in the OT (see below).

A messenger empowered by the Spirit of God

The nature of a prophet as a messenger of God is described by a human analogy in Exodus 7: 'And the Lord said to Moses, "See, I make you as God to Pharaoh; and Aaron your brother shall be your prophet. You shall speak all that I command you; and Aaron your brother shall tell Pharaoh to let the people of Israel go out of his land"' (Exod. 7:1–2). Moses is like God in that he gives a message to Aaron. Aaron is like a 'prophet' because he speaks the message that he has received. This fundamental idea of the prophet as a messenger of God pervades descriptions of prophets in both Old and New Testaments.

True prophecies are empowered only by the Spirit of God; only when the Lord places on the seventy elders some of the Spirit's empowering which has been on Moses are the seventy elders able to prophesy (Num. 11:25).

The prophet's message is not his own

What was implicit in the analogy of Moses and Aaron speaking to Pharaoh (Exod. 7:1) is made explicit in Deuteronomy: the prophet has no message of his own but can only report the message God has given him. God promises that whenever he raises up a prophet like Moses, 'I will put my words in his mouth, and he shall speak to them all that I command him' (Deut. 18:18). Even greedy and rebellious Balaam must submit to God; he says, 'Have I now any power at all to speak anything? The word that God puts in my mouth, that must I speak' (Num. 22:38).

The uniqueness of Moses

Moses has a more direct relationship to God

701

than that of any other prophet in the entire OT. He is also entrusted with greater responsibility: 'if there is a prophet among you, I the LORD make myself known to him in a vision, I speak with him in a dream. Not so with my servant Moses; he is entrusted with all my house. With him I speak mouth to mouth, clearly, and not in dark speech; and he beholds the form of the LORD' (Num. 12:6–8; *cf.* Deut. 34:10).

While there are other prophets in the Pentateuch, such as Abraham, Miriam (Exod. 15:20), Balaam (Num. 22:38) and the seventy elders who prophesied (Num. 11:25), no prophet is equal to Moses. However, Moses promises that another prophet like him will arise: 'The LORD your God will raise up for you a prophet like me from among you, from your brethren – him you shall heed' (Deut. 18:15). Although this promise was partially fulfilled in many subsequent OT prophets who spoke the words of the Lord, it was ultimately a messianic prediction fulfilled in Christ (John 6:14; 7:40; Acts 3:22; 7:37).

The expectation that one day all God's people would prophesy

The initial group of secondary prophets (the 70 elders who prophesied with Moses, Num. 11:25) provides a pattern for subsequent bands of prophets (see below) and also encourages an expectation that one day the gift of prophecy would be widely distributed among God's people: Moses says, 'Would that all the LORD's people were prophets, that the LORD would put his spirit upon them!' (Num. 11:29). Here Moses longs not just for a widespread prophetic gift but even more for the widespread personal relationship to God of which that gift would be a sign, for he knows by experience that prophets walk close to God. This expectation is restated in Joel's prophecy (Joel 2:28–29), and finds initial fulfilment in the NT *church on the day of Pentecost (Acts 2:16–18).

The problem of false prophets

Since a true prophet can speak only God's message, not his or her own, it follows that a false prophet is one who has no message from God but presumes to speak in God's name anyway (Deut. 18:20). If such false prophecy is joined with encouragement to serve other gods (Deut. 13:1–5; 18:20), the prophet 'shall

be put to death' (Deut. 13:5). However, contrary to much popular misunderstanding, there was no death penalty simply for speaking a false prophecy; Deuteronomy 18:20 requires capital punishment only for one who speaks a message God has not given *and* 'speaks in the name of other gods' (so the Hebrew text and the LXX, contrary to modern versions that translate the Hebrew *waw* as 'or').

False prophets are recognized both by their advocacy of other gods and by the failure of their predictions to come true (Deut. 13:2–3, 5; 18:22). Such false prophets may even work 'a sign or wonder', but their false doctrine reveals their true nature. By allowing false prophets to exist in Israel, the Lord is 'testing' his people, to know whether they love the Lord their God with all their heart and with all their soul (Deut. 13:3).

Prophecy and prophets in the post-Pentateuchal historical books and the writing prophets

Established, primary prophets

Just as in the Pentateuch Moses was established as the primary prophet of God, so in subsequent OT history there are prophets such as Samuel (1 Sam. 3:20), Gad (1 Sam. 22:5), Nathan (2 Sam. 7:2), *Elijah (1 Kgs. 18:22), *Elisha (2 Kgs. 2:15), Isaiah (2 Kgs. 20:1), Jeremiah (2 Chr. 36:12) and other writing prophets, who are established and recognized as prophets of the Lord. The pattern for such a recognized and prominent role was seen in Samuel when he was 'established as a prophet of the LORD' (1 Sam. 3:20), and the LORD 'let none of his words fall to the ground' (v. 19). It is frequently noted that such primary prophets were attested by miracles (1 Kgs. 18:24, 39; 2 Kgs. 5:3; see *Signs and wonders), true predictions (1 Sam. 9–10; 1 Kgs. 14:18; 16:12), and loyalty to the one true God.

Bands of secondary prophets

In addition to 'established' prophets who had recognized positions of *leadership, there were several bands of secondary prophets, such as those who met Saul after Samuel anointed him as king (1 Sam. 10:5), as well as the 100 prophets who were hidden by Obadiah (1 Kgs. 18:4), and the bands of prophets or 'sons of the prophets' in Bethel (2

Kgs. 2:3), Jericho (2 Kgs. 2:5, 7), and Gilgal (2 Kgs. 4:38).

These bands of prophets are viewed not as false prophets but as servants of the one true God, and were affiliated with true prophets such as Elijah (2 Kgs. 2:3, 5, 7). Therefore they must have received some kinds of message or revelation from God; this was the essential requirement for being called a 'prophet'. (For example, they had special knowledge from God that he would take Elijah on a certain day; 2 Kgs. 2:3, 5.) However, none of their prophetic utterances is preserved in the canonical Scriptures, which may suggest that their prophesying was not ordinarily counted equal in value or equal in authority to the messages of the primary, established prophets such as Samuel and Elijah. The distribution of prophecy to these bands of prophets foreshadows the outpouring of prophecy on 'sons and daughters ... menservants and maidservants' (Acts 2:17–18) in the new covenant.

The involuntary 'prophesying' and physical incapacity of Saul and his messengers (1 Sam. 19:20–24) is a unique incident in Scripture, and should not be generalized into a claim that there were 'ecstatic' bands of prophets throughout the land. (1 Sam. 10:5–13 indicates that prophecies were accompanied by music, but not that they were involuntary or ecstatic.)

Women as prophets

Several women are named as prophets in the OT: Miriam in the Pentateuch (Exod. 15:20); and in subsequent books Deborah (Judg. 4), Huldah (2 Kgs. 22:14–20; 2 Chr. 34:22–28), and the wife of Isaiah (Is. 8:3). (There is also a female false prophet, Noadiah, in Neh. 6:14.) These women prophets also foreshadowed the new covenant, when God would pour out his Spirit on all people, and 'sons and daughters' and 'menservants and maidservants' would all prophesy (see Joel 2:28–29; Acts 2:17–18).

Apart from Miriam's ministry in song and the song of Deborah and Barak, women prophets in the OT ministered privately to individuals rather than publicly to large groups; thus Deborah rendered private judgments (Heb. mišpāṭ, Judg. 4:5; see also 2 Kgs. 22:14; 2 Chr. 34:22). The activity of women as prophets was distinct from the activity of the OT *priests, who were male, and who

had the responsibility of teaching God's laws to the people (Mal. 2:7; cf. Deut. 24:8; 2 Kgs. 12:2; 17:27–28; 2 Chr. 15:3; Neh. 8:9; Hos. 4:6; Mic. 3:11), and was distinct also from the activity of kings, who ruled the people. Thus the OT also foreshadows both the NT's encouragement of women to prophesy in churches (Acts 21:9; 1 Cor. 11:5) and its prohibition of their teaching or governing the whole church (1 Tim. 2:11–15; 3:2; 1 Cor. 14:33–35). (See *Man and woman.)

Other names for prophets

Other names applied to prophets include 'man of God' (1 Sam. 2:27; 9:6; 1 Kgs. 13:1–10; 17:24; etc.) and 'seer' (this English term translates two different Hebrew words which seem to be nearly synonymous: rō'eh in 1 Sam. 9:9, 11; 1 Chr. 9:22; 29:29, etc., and ḥōzeh in 2 Sam. 24:11; 2 Kgs. 17:13; 1 Chr. 21:9, etc.). Another common title is that of God's 'servants' (1 Kgs. 14:18; 18:36; Jer. 25:4), and God himself calls them 'my servants the prophets' (2 Kgs. 9:7; 17:13; Amos 3:7), a title which suggests that God frequently sends them to perform various tasks.

How did prophets receive a message from God?

The OT records various means of receiving a message from God, including visions (1 Sam. 3:1, 15; 2 Sam. 7:17; Is. 1:1; 6:1–3; Ezek. 11:24; Dan. 8:1–2, etc.; cf. Num. 12:6). Dreams are also mentioned in the foundational passage, Numbers 12:6 ('If there is a prophet among you, I the LORD make myself known to him in a vision, I speak with him in a dream'), and Joel 2:28 promises dreams in connection with the future outpouring of a prophetic gift.

The most common means of communication from God to a prophet was a direct verbal message. Several times it is said simply that God put his words in the mouth of the prophet (Is. 51:16; Jer. 1:9; etc.; cf. Deut. 18:18). In places the message is called a 'burden' (Heb. māśā', commonly translated 'oracle'; Is. 13:1; 15:1; 17:1; 19:1; 21:1, 11, 13; Jer. 23:33–40; Nah. 1:1; Zech. 9:1; 12:1; Mal. 1:1), suggesting that a heavy sense of responsibility and perhaps reluctance was felt by the prophet who received it. In over a hundred cases the reader is told, without further explanation, that 'the word of the Lord came to the prophet ____' (1 Sam. 15:10; 2 Sam. 7:4; 24:11; Is. 38:4; Ezek. 1:3; Jonah 1:1, *etc.*). In several passages this is said to happen at a very specific time: 'And before Isaiah had gone out of the middle court, the word of the LORD came to him' (2 Kgs. 20:4; *cf.* 1 Kgs. 18:1; Jer. 42:7; Ezek. 3:16; Zech. 1:7). Sometimes the *word of the Lord comes in the form of a spoken question which the prophet immediately answers (1 Kgs. 19:9; Jer. 1:11, 13). Finally, in many long sections in the writing prophets, the content of the prophet's message is just presented, with no indication as to how the prophet received it.

The Holy Spirit (often called the Spirit of God, or the Spirit of the Lord) is seen as the personal agent who comes upon a prophet and makes God's message known to him (1 Sam. 10:6, 10; and note the general statements in Neh. 9:30; Zech. 7:12; *cf.* Num. 11:24–29).

The prophet is in a regular and unusually vital personal relationship with God and therefore in frequent personal communication with God. It is prophets who stand in the 'council' of the Lord (Jer. 23:18, 22), and the Lord makes known to them what he is going to do before he does it: 'Surely the Lord GOD does nothing, without revealing his secret to his servants the prophets' (Amos 3:7). Such statements connote an amazing picture of personal friendship with God, which is realized in the experience of Abraham (2 Chr. 20:7; Is. 41:8; *cf.* Jas. 2:23) and Moses (Exod. 33:11; Deut. 34:10). Because prophets are in such close communication with God, they will often just 'know' something that they could not have known using their natural faculties alone, but that had to be revealed by God (1 Kgs. 14:4–6; 2 Kgs. 5:25–26; 6:12; 8:12–13; note Elisha's surprise in 2 Kgs. 4:27 that there was something the Lord had not told him). In the light of such a close personal relationship between God and the prophets, it is noteworthy that the NT epistle of James presents Elijah's prayer life as a pattern for Christians to imitate (Jas. 5:16–18).

How did the prophets deliver their messages?

Most often prophetic messages were simply spoken aloud, with an affirmation that they were indeed words of the Lord. The prophetic messenger formula, 'Thus says the Lord' occurs hundreds of times throughout the OT.

From time to time, dramatic physical symbolism accompanied a spoken prophetic message. Ahijah tore a new garment into twelve pieces and gave ten to Jeroboam to symbolize the division of the kingdom (1 Kgs. 11:30–31); Elisha had King Joash shoot an arrow symbolizing victory over the Syrians (2 Kgs. 13:15–18); Jeremiah smashed a potter's vessel to symbolize irreparable *judgment coming on Jerusalem (Jer. 19:10–13); Ezekiel dug through the city wall and carried baggage out, symbolizing forthcoming *exile (Ezek. 12:3–6). Such symbolic acts did not merely make the message unforgettable; they were one form in which the message came.

The authority of the prophetic message

Throughout the OT the prophets' words are the very words of God. When a true prophet predicts events, those events surely come to pass, 'according to the word of the LORD which he spoke by the prophet ...' (1 Kgs. 14:18; 16:12, 34; 17:16; 22:38; 2 Kgs. 1:17; 7:16; 14:25; 24:2). It is easy to understand why this should be so: if an omniscient, omnipotent God predicts something, then it will surely happen.

The prophets' words are words of God; therefore the people have an obligation to believe and obey them. To believe God is to believe his prophets (2 Chr. 20:20; 29:25; Hag. 1:12), for the words of the prophets are the very words of God (2 Chr. 36:15–16). Therefore, to disbelieve or disobey a true prophet is to disbelieve or disobey God, and he will hold the hearer responsible (1 Sam. 8:7; 1 Kgs. 20:36; 2 Chr. 25:16; Is. 30:12–14; *cf.* Deut. 18:19).

Because many of these authoritative prophetic words were recorded in the OT Scriptures, they present a strong *prima facie* argument regarding the authority of Scripture. God's people throughout all ages are under obligation to treat all the words of the prophets as the very words of God, words which he requires his people to believe and (when understood and applied rightly with respect to the new covenant) also to obey.

The content of the prophetic message: God's words to guide, warn, predict, and interpret

All the kinds of messages needed in a relationship between God and his people are included in the words of the prophets. The prophets delivered to the people words sent by God for a wide variety of circumstances.

The message from God could include specific guidance about a particular course of action (1 Sam. 22:5). The prophet might declare God's choice of a king or another prophet, and confirm his declaration by the physical symbolism of anointing with oil, which established the person in the office (1 Sam. 15:1; 16:13; 1 Kgs. 19:15–16; 2 Kgs. 9:3–10). In some cases, individuals even went to a prophet seeking guidance from God (1 Sam. 9:6; 1 Kgs. 22:7; 2 Kgs. 3:11).

Moral guidance for a sinful people often turned to rebuke for sin and warning of punishment to come unless the people *repented (2 Chr. 24:19; Neh. 9:30; and frequently). In the context of such warnings, the prophets declared God's *law to the people (2 Kgs. 17:13; Dan. 9:10; Zech. 7:12); this is consistent with the dual role of Moses in earlier days as both primary lawgiver and primary OT prophet. The rebuking and warning activity of the prophets over many generations is summarized in 2 Kings 17:13: 'Yet the LORD warned Israel and Judah by every prophet and every seer, saying, "Turn from your evil ways and keep my commandments and my statutes, in accordance with all the law which I commanded your fathers, and which I sent to you by my servants the prophets."' But the prophets not only warned of punishment; they also offered promises of *blessing that would follow if the people *obeyed the Lord (Jer. 22:4; Zech. 6:15).

However, not all promises of blessings were conditional upon the people's obedience. Extensive parts of the prophetic books predict that the Lord will act, first to bring back his people from exile (Is. 35:10; 51:11; Jer. 30:10), and then one day to establish a new *covenant in which he will write his law on the people's hearts (Jer. 31:31–34; Ezek. 36:22–38). Many of the prophets' predictions look forward to a coming Messiah, and a complete list of such predictions would include all those explicitly mentioned in the NT (see Matt. 2:23; 4:14, *etc.*) and many not mentioned (see Luke 24:27). The prophets' ultimate vision is of a renewed earth with the Lord himself reigning as king (Is. 65:17; 66:22).

Finally, prophets interpret the events of history as they occur, telling the people God's perspective on what is happening. They do so frequently in the prophetic books, and also in their function as the official historians of the kings of *Israel (1 Chr. 29:29; 2 Chr. 9:29; 12:15; 13:22; 32:32). Their activity as such is not a mere recording of facts, separate from the prophets' ability frequently to understand God's purpose in and evaluation of historical events. No doubt the prophets who recorded the acts of the kings of Israel were qualified to do so precisely because God showed them his interpretation of those acts. In the extant historical narratives the prophets often give God's interpretation of events, and such divine interpretations of events will also have characterized the accounts of the 'rest of the acts of King ____' which are said to have been recorded in the books of various prophets (2 Chr. 9:29; 13:22; 20:34; 26:22; 32:32).

In these prophetic tasks of guiding, warning, predicting, and interpreting, God was demonstrating his sovereign rule over history and also his ongoing love and holiness in his personal relationship with his people.

Other tasks of prophets: musicians and intercessors

Because prophets receive revelations from God, it is not surprising that they participate in the musical aspects of the temple service, probably delivering messages from God in song, or singing songs which God had given to the people for use in *worshipping him (1 Chr. 25:1–3; *cf.* Deut. 31:19–22; 1 Sam. 10:5). Whenever such songs declared what God had done in the life of the people, and offered him praise for it, the prophets were again performing their task of giving God's interpretation of current or past history.

Prophets are sometimes seen in a somewhat distinct role as highly effective intercessors, *praying for specific situations (1 Sam. 12:23; 1 Kgs. 13:6; 2 Kgs. 20:11; 2 Chr. 32:20; Jer. 27:18; 37:3; 42:4; Hab. 3:1; *cf.* Gen. 20:17; Exod. 32:11–14). Because prophets have a close relationship with God, it is not surprising that he hears their prayers and that they are closely involved in this aspect of the relationship between God and his people.

False prophets

It seems that there were always false prophets alongside the true; in fact, as we have seen, God allowed false prophets to arise in order that he might test the people's hearts (Deut 13:3). However, God also gave guidelines to help his people know the true from the false. False prophets prophesy for personal gain (Mic. 3:5, 11) and tell the people only what they want to hear (1 Kgs. 22:5–13; Jer. 5:31). Their predictions do not come true (1 Kgs. 22:12, 28, 34–35; *cf.* Deut. 18:22); their 'miraculous signs' are inferior or nonexistent (1 Kgs. 18:25–29; but see also Deut. 13:1–2). Above all, they encourage the people to serve other gods (Jer. 23:13).

God repeatedly warned the people that he had not sent these false prophets, and that therefore they had no message from him. In fact, a false prophet is defined as someone who has not received a message from God, but simply prophesies out of his own mind (Neh. 6:12; Jer. 14:14–15; 23:16–40; 28:15; 29:9; Ezek. 13:2–3; 22:28; *cf.* Deut. 18:20).

The NT counterparts to the false prophets are 'false teachers' who speak 'false words' and bring 'destructive heresies' into the church (2 Pet. 2:1–3).

Frequent opposition to the prophets

Sometimes the people of Israel received and followed true prophets, but often the people were rebellious and did not want to hear God's words of rebuke and warning. Therefore true prophets often found themselves opposed and even persecuted by the people, especially by their leaders: 'but they kept mocking the messengers of God, despising his words, and scoffing at his prophets, till the wrath of the LORD rose against his people' (2 Chr. 36:16; *cf.* 2 Chr. 16:10; 25:16; Is. 30:10; Jer. 11:21; 18:18; 20:2, 7–10; 26:8–11; 32:2–3; 36:20–26; 37:15 – 38:28; Amos 2:12; 7:12–13). Some prophets were even killed (2 Chr. 24:20–21; Jer. 26:20–23). In the NT, Stephen says, 'Which of the prophets did not your fathers persecute?' (Acts 7:52). In enduring such persecution patiently while being faithful messengers for God, these prophets also foreshadowed Christ, and provided a pattern for Christians to imitate (Luke 13:33; 1 Thess. 2:15; Jas. 5:10).

Prophecy as a sign of God's favour

The existence of prophecy among the people of Israel was a great blessing, for it indicated that God cared about them enough, even in

their sins, to speak personally to them. While God was giving prophecies, he still had a relationship with them. On the other hand, the cessation of prophecy was a sign that God had withdrawn his favour from people who had strayed far from him (1 Sam. 3:1; 28:6; Lam. 2:9; Is. 29:10; Hos. 9:7; Mic. 3:7). The extensive outpouring of the gift of prophecy at the inception of the new covenant was thus an indication of God's abundant favour towards the new covenant church (Acts 2:16–18), and a functioning gift of prophecy is a sign of God's blessing on a church (1 Cor. 14:22).

Prophecy and prophets in the OT wisdom literature

Very little is said about prophets in the wisdom literature of the OT. There are only four explicit references to prophecy (Ps. 51 superscription; 74:9; 105:15; Prov. 29:18), plus a reference to Moses as the 'man of God' in the superscription of Psalm 90. The important role of prophecy in rebuking sin and encouraging obedience is emphasized in Proverbs 29:18: 'Where there is no prophecy [or 'prophetic vision,' *ḥazôn*], the people cast off restraint, but blessed is he who keeps the law.' Psalm 74:9 was apparently written at a late period when there was no more prophecy, a fact that is seen as evidence of the loss of God's favour and presence: 'We do not see our signs; there is no longer any prophet, and there is none among us who knows how long.'

Prophecy and prophets in the Gospels

Many of the themes introduced in the OT continue into the NT, but they are developed further. In many places the gospels show how the predictive prophecies of the OT pointed to Christ and now find their fulfilment in him (Matt. 2:23; 4:14; 26:56; John 12:38; 17:12; 19:36, *etc.*). Jesus is seen as the long awaited 'prophet like Moses' (John 6:14; 7:40; Acts 3:22–24; *cf.* 7:37), but he is not often explicitly called 'a prophet', and even when he is, it is usually by those who have little understanding of his person or mission (Matt. 21:11, 46; Mark 6:15; Luke 7:16; 24:19; John 4:19; 7:40; 9:17).

This is because Jesus is far greater than the OT prophets. While those prophets were messengers sent from God to the people, Jesus is not a mere messenger; he is God himself, come in the flesh. Therefore, while Jesus is indeed the 'prophet like Moses', he is more than that; he is the one to whom the OT prophecies all pointed: 'And beginning with Moses and all the prophets, he interpreted to them in all the scriptures the things concerning himself' (Luke 24:27; *cf.* Acts 3:18; 10:43; 26:22; Rom. 1:2; 1 Pet. 1:10). Moreover, while the OT prophets were messengers who declared, 'Thus says the Lord', Jesus is himself the author of his message, who has the authority to declare, 'But I say to you' (Matt. 5:28, 32, 34, 44). Hebrews 1:1–2 explicitly contrasts the many kinds of revelation that came through the OT prophets and the far superior, single revelation that has come in the last days through God's own Son: 'In many and various ways God spoke of old to our fathers by the prophets; but in these last days he has spoken to us by a Son.'

However, true prophets in the OT tradition do appear in the gospels, including Zechariah (Luke 1:67), Anna (Luke 2:36) and, pre-eminently, *John the Baptist (Luke 1:76; 3:2; *cf.* Matt. 11:14; 17:12). They appear at the time of Christ's coming, because they are God's messengers to proclaim what God has done in sending his Son into the world.

Regarding false prophets, Jesus warns that they are still to be expected; but they will be recognized by their fruit and by their false doctrine (Matt. 7:15; 24:11, 24; Mark 13:22).

The gift of prophecy in Acts and the epistles

Beginning with the pouring out of the Holy Spirit in new covenant fullness at Pentecost, the gift of prophecy was widely distributed in the NT church: 'but this is what was spoken by the prophet Joel: "And in the last days it shall be, God declares, that I will pour out my Spirit upon all flesh, and your sons and your daughters shall prophesy, and your young men shall see visions, and your old men shall dream dreams; yea, and on my menservants and my maidservants in those days I will pour out my Spirit; and they shall prophesy"' (Acts 2:16–18). The Pentecost outpouring was not an isolated event, but one that signified the beginning of much more widespread and frequent personal communication between God and his people, and thus it also signified that a more deeply intimate relationship between God and all his people would be one

of the rich blessings of the new covenant.

Although several definitions have been given of the gift of prophecy, the NT indicates that it should be defined not as 'predicting the future', nor as 'proclaiming a word from the Lord', nor as 'powerful preaching', but rather as 'telling something that God has spontaneously brought to mind'. The following material gives support for and explanation of this definition.

The NT apostles are the counterparts to OT prophets

Many OT prophets were able to speak and write words which had absolute divine authority (see above), and which were recorded in canonical Scripture. In NT times also there were people who spoke and wrote God's very words and had them recorded in Scripture; however, Jesus does not call them 'prophets' but uses a new term, 'apostles'. The apostles are the NT counterpart to the primary, established prophets in the OT (see Gal. 1:8–9, 11–12; 1 Cor. 2:13; 2 Cor. 13:3; 1 Thess. 2:13; 4:8,15; 2 Pet. 3:2). It is apostles, not prophets, who have authority to write the words of NT Scripture.

When the apostles want to establish their unique authority they never appeal to the title 'prophet' but rather call themselves apostles (Rom. 1:1; 1 Cor. 1:1; 9:1–2; 2 Cor. 1:1; 11:12–13; 12:11–12; Gal. 1:1; Eph. 1:1; 1 Peter 1:1; 2 Peter 1:1; 3:2, *etc.*). (See also *Mission.)

The meaning of 'prophet' in NT times

Why did Jesus choose the new term *apostle* to designate those who had the authority to write Scripture? One reason is that the gift of prophecy was going to be widely distributed to God's people at Pentecost, and it was appropriate to use another term to refer to the small group who would have authority to write NT Scripture. Another reason is that in NT times the Greek word *prophētēs* ('prophet') generally did not mean 'one who speaks God's very words' but rather 'one who speaks on the basis of some external influence' (often a spiritual influence of some kind), or even just 'spokesperson'. Titus 1:12 uses the word in this sense; Paul quotes the pagan Greek poet Epimenides: 'One of themselves, a prophet of their own, said, "Cretans are always liars, evil beasts, lazy gluttons."'

The apostles as 'prophets'

Of course, the words 'prophet'and 'prophecy' were sometimes used of the apostles when they were giving a 'prophecy', emphasizing that a special revelation from the Holy Spirit was the basis of what they said (Rev. 1:3; 22:7; Eph. 2:20; 3:5). But this was not the terminology ordinarily used for the apostles, nor did the terms 'prophet' and 'prophecy' in themselves imply that their speech or writing had divine authority, any more than Paul's calling himself a 'teacher' (2 Tim. 1:11) implied that all 'teachers' in NT times had authority equal to Paul's. With respect to the apostles functioning as 'prophets', Ephesians 2:20 and 3:5 speak of the 'foundational' role of a unique group of apostles (and perhaps also a limited group of prophets) who received the special revelation concerning the inclusion of Gentiles in the church (3:5). However, these verses have no direct relevance to the gift of prophecy as it functioned not in the 'foundation', but in the rest of the church, *i.e.* in thousands of ordinary Christians in hundreds of local churches in NT times. In other NT passages, the words 'prophet' and 'prophecy' are used more commonly with reference to ordinary Christians who spoke not with absolute divine authority, but simply to report something that God had brought to their minds (see discussion below).

The gift of prophecy to ordinary Christians

There are indications in the NT that 'prophecy' among ordinary Christians did not carry the same authority/power as Scripture.

1. *Acts 21:4*. In Acts 21:4, we read of the disciples at Tyre: 'Through the Spirit they told Paul not to go on to Jerusalem.' This seems to be a reference to prophecy directed towards Paul, but Paul disobeyed it. He surely would not have done this if the prophecy had been God's very words and had had authority equal to that of Scripture.

2. *Acts 21:10–11*. Agabus prophesied that the Jews at Jerusalem would bind Paul and 'deliver him into the hands of the Gentiles', a prediction that was nearly correct but not quite; the Romans, not the Jews, bound Paul (v. 33; also 22:29), and the Jews, rather than delivering him voluntarily, tried to kill him and he had to be rescued by force (v. 32). The verb used by Agabus in 21:11, *paradidōmi*, denotes the voluntary, conscious, deliberate giving over or handing over of something to someone else, but the Jews did not voluntarily hand Paul over to the Romans. The prediction was broadly true, but it included inaccuracies of detail that would have called into question the authenticity of any OT prophet.

3. *1 Thessalonians 5:19–21*. Paul tells the Thessalonians, 'do not despise prophesying, but test everything; hold fast what is good' (1 Thess. 5:20–21). If the Thessalonians had thought that prophecy equalled God's word in authority, Paul would never have had to tell them not to despise it; they 'received' and 'accepted' God's word 'with joy inspired by the Holy Spirit' (1 Thess. 1:6; 2:13; *cf.* 4:15). But when Paul tells them to 'test everything', this must include at least the prophecies he mentioned in the previous phrase. When he encourages them to 'hold fast *what is good*' he implies that prophecies contain some things that are good and some things that are not good. This could never have been said of the words of an OT prophet, or of the authoritative teachings of a NT apostle.

4. *1 Corinthians 14:29–38*. More extensive evidence on NT prophecy is found in 1 Corinthians 14. When Paul says, 'Let two or three prophets speak, and *let the others weigh what is said*' (1 Cor. 14:29), he suggests that they should listen carefully and sift the good from the bad, accepting some and rejecting the rest (this is the implication of the Greek word *diakrinō,* here translated 'weigh what is said'). An OT prophet like Isaiah would hardly have said, 'Listen to what I say and weigh what is said; sort the good from the bad, what you should accept from what you should not'. If the prophecy had absolute divine authority, it would be sin to do this. But here Paul commands that it be done, thus implying that NT prophecy did not have the authority of God's very words.

Paul implies also that no one at Corinth, a church in which there was much prophecy, was able to speak God's very words. He says in 1 Corinthians 14:36, 'What! Did the word of God come forth from you, or are you the only ones it has reached?' (author's translation).

All these passages indicate that the common idea that prophets spoke 'words of the Lord' when the apostles were not present in the early churches is simply incorrect. They also imply that prophecies today should not be prefaced with 'Thus says the Lord'; to do this is to claim an authority that new covenant prophets do not have.

Spontaneous 'revelation' differentiates prophecy from other gifts

If prophecy does not contain God's very words, then what is it? In what sense is it from God?

Paul indicates that God can bring something spontaneously to mind so that the person prophesying reports it in his or her own words. Paul calls this a 'revelation': 'If a revelation is made to another sitting by, let the first be silent. For you can all prophesy one by one, so that all may learn and all be encouraged' (1 Cor. 14:30–31). Theologians have used the word 'revelation' to refer to the words of Scripture, but here Paul uses it in a broader sense, to denote communication from God which does not result in written Scripture or words equal in authority to written Scripture (see also Phil. 3:15; Rom. 1:18; Eph. 1:17; Matt. 11:27).

Thus if a stranger comes in and all prophesy, 'the secrets of his heart are disclosed; and so, falling on his face, he will worship God and declare that God is really among you' (1 Cor. 14:25). In this way, prophecy serves as a 'sign' for believers (1 Cor. 14:22); it is a clear demonstration that God is definitely at work in their midst, a 'sign' of God's hand of blessing on the congregation. And since it will be effective for the conversion of unbelievers as well, Paul encourages the church to use this gift when 'unbelievers or outsiders enter' (1 Cor. 14:23).

Why did Paul value prophecy so highly (1 Cor. 14:1–5, 39–40)? Apparently because it was effective in 'building up the church' (1 Cor. 14:12), spontaneously revealing God's insight into someone's heart or into a specific situation, and thereby bringing 'upbuilding and encouragement and consolation' (1 Cor. 14:3). Even though it had to be tested and was never to be received as the authoritative 'words of the Lord' like the Bible (see above), through prophecies God was still manifesting his gracious presence in the day to day life of the church by guiding, warning, predicting, and giving his perspective on people's hearts and the events in which they were involved. In this way prophecy was a vivid expression

of the genuine personal relationship between God and his people.

However, Paul did not think that everything called 'prophecy' in the ancient world was like Christian prophecy. The Corinthians had previously been led astray to 'dumb idols' (1 Cor. 12:2), and Paul was well aware of demonic spiritual power at work in pagan temples; 'what pagans sacrifice they offer to demons and not to God' (1 Cor. 10:20). A failure to recognize this distinction leads to a fundamental error in the massive work of David Aune, *Prophecy in Early Christianity and the Ancient Mediterranean World* (Grand Rapids, 1983). He considers true Christian prophecy (which is empowered by the Holy Spirit) together with pagan prophecy (which is not) as one general religious phenomenon. Aune fails to consider the possibility that we can distinguish true from false prophecy on the basis of the prophet's willingness to acknowledge Jesus Christ as Lord (1 Cor. 12:3). No NT writer would have adopted Aune's perspective; nor should evangelical scholars today.

The difference between prophecy and teaching

Prophecy and teaching are always mentioned as distinct gifts (Rom 12:6–7; 1 Cor. 12:28–29; 14:6; Eph. 4:11), but what is the difference? Unlike the gift of prophecy, 'teaching' in the NT is never said to be based on a spontaneous revelation from God. Rather, 'teaching' is an explanation or application of Scripture (Acts 15:35; 18:11, 24–28; Rom. 2:21; 15:4; Col. 3:16; Heb. 5:12) or a repetition and explanation of apostolic instructions (Rom. 16:17; 2 Tim. 2:2; 3:10, *etc.*). (It is what people today would call 'Bible teaching' or 'preaching'.) The distinction between teaching and prophecy is thus quite clear. If a message is the result of conscious reflection on the text of Scripture, including interpretation of the text and application to life, then it is (in NT terms) a teaching. But if a message is the report of something God brings suddenly to mind, then it is a prophecy.

So prophecy has less authority than 'teaching', and prophecies in the churches are always to be tested by the authoritative teaching of Scripture. Timothy was not told to *prophesy* Paul's instructions in the church; he was to *teach* them (1 Tim. 4:11; 6:2). The

Thessalonians were told to hold firm not to the traditions which were 'prophesied' to them but to the traditions which they were 'taught' by Paul (2 Thess. 2:15). Some elders laboured in preaching and teaching (1 Tim. 5:17), and an elder was to be 'an apt teacher' (1 Tim. 3:2; *cf.* Tit. 1:9), but no elder is said to have the task of prophesying, nor is it ever said that an elder had to be 'an apt prophet'. James warned that those who teach, not those who prophesy, will be judged with greater strictness (Jas. 3:1). Contrary to the views of those who claim that 'charismatic leaders' governed the earliest churches, the evidence of the NT shows that it was teachers (in the role of elders), not prophets, who gave them leadership and direction.

The cessationist position

According to an alternative position within evangelical scholarship, the 'cessationist' position, the gift of prophecy in NT churches always had the same authority as Scripture, contained no errors, but only the very words of God, and therefore ceased to exist in the church around the end of the 1st century, when the canon of the NT was complete. For a defence of cessationism, see the books by R. B. Gaffin and O. P. Robertson listed in the bibliography, and the contributions by Gaffin and R. Saucy to W. Grudem, (ed.), *Are Miraculous Gifts for Today? Four Views.*

Prophecy and prophets in Revelation

Revelation 11 predicts the appearance on earth, for 1260 days, of two remarkable prophets. They will have great power and no one will be able to prevent them from carrying out their task: 'And if any one would harm them, fire pours out from their mouth and consumes their foes; if any one would harm them, thus he is doomed to be killed. They have power to shut the sky ... and to smite the earth with every plague, as often as they desire' (Rev. 11:5–6). Yet the writer also predicts the coming of a powerful 'false prophet' who will work deceptive miracles and ultimately be cast into the lake of fire with the beast and the devil himself (Rev. 16:13; 19:20; 20:10).

The book of Revelation as a whole is, as its name implies, a great 'revelation' from God, and the book itself is the last great prophecy in the Bible. From chapter 4 onwards it points towards the future, describing in sobering yet magnificent language both the judgments and the blessings which God has ordained. It closes with a reminder that its prophetic words, like the words God gave to the prophet Moses at the beginning of the Bible, and like the words of the prophets and apostles written in the rest of the Bible, are the very words of God, and no one may add to them or take from them (Rev. 22:18–19).

See also: REVELATION.

Bibliography

D. A. Carson, *Showing the Spirit: A Theological Exposition of 1 Corinthians 12–14* (Grand Rapids and Carlisle, 1987, 1995); J. Deere, *Surprised by the Voice of God* (Grand Rapids and Eastbourne, 1996); C. Forbes, *Prophecy and Inspired Speech in Early Christianity and its Hellenistic Environment* (Tübingen and Peabody, 1995); R. B. Gaffin, *Perspectives on Pentecost: Studies in New Testament Teaching on the Gifts of the Holy Spirit* (Phillipsburg, 1979); W. Grudem, *The Gift of Prophecy in 1 Corinthians* (Lanham, 1982); idem, *The Gift of Prophecy in the New Testament and Today* (Eastbourne and Westchester, 1988); idem (ed.), *Are Miraculous Gifts for Today? Four Views* (Grand Rapids and Leicester, 1996); D. Hill, *New Testament Prophecy* (Atlanta, 1979); W. Kaiser in *EDBT*, pp. 639–647. H. Krämer *et al.* in *TDNT* 6, pp. 781–861; J. A. Motyer and J. P. Baker in *IBD* 3, pp. 1276–1287; C. H. Peisker and C. Brown in *NIDNTT* 3, pp. 74–92; O. P. Robertson, *The Final Word* (Edinburgh and Carlisle, 1993); M. Turner, *The Holy Spirit and Spiritual Gifts: Then and Now* (Carlisle, 1996); W. A. VanGemeren, *Interpreting the Prophetic Word* (Grand Rapids, 1990); P. A. Verhoef in *NIDOTTE* 4, pp. 1067–1078; E. J. Young, *My Servants the Prophets* (Grand Rapids, 1955).

W. A. GRUDEM

PROPITIATION, see ATONEMENT
PROVERBS, see Part 2

PROVIDENCE

The term 'providence' as it is commonly used in theology normally identifies a cluster of biblical themes, rather than translating a particular word. A precise linguistic basis can certainly be found. For example, W. Eichrodt refers to Job 10:12, which tells of the 'divine superintendence or care by which creatures are preserved' (*Theology of the Old Testament*, vol. 2, p. 168); K. Barth derives a concept of providence from the story of the sacrifice of Isaac in Genesis 22:8, 14 (*Church Dogmatics*, vol. 3.3, p. 3). Generally, however, the notion of providence encapsulates the conviction that *God sustains the world that he has *created and directs it to its appointed destiny. Belief in God's providence evokes not only *humility and wonder, but also gratitude and trust, for believers know God as Father and believe that 'in all things God works for the good of those who love him, who have been called according to his purpose' (Rom. 8:28, NIV).

The natural order

The providential sustenance of God is mentioned in many places, with the books of Job and Psalms providing a rich quarry of texts in the OT and Matthew 6:25–30 being a notable passage in the NT. The idea goes beyond that of a general power which preserves cosmic life and order; the power is exercised specifically (Matt. 10:29). The development of the natural sciences over the centuries has increased human understanding of the causes operative within nature, but this leaves the biblical idea of providence unaffected. The Bible is concerned not with the mechanics of divine sustaining and the causal ordering of nature but with the knowledge, power, will and manifest activity of God. God's being and action is the basic reality which undergirds cosmos and history, and the biblical witness is interested in this fundamental fact rather than in its precise form and inner nature.

The notion of miracles (see *Signs and wonders) is connected with that of providence, and this too has occasioned difficulty. The miracles narrated in Scripture are set in the context not only of the conviction that God rules over nature, but also of the overarching story of Israel and the church, Jesus and the world. Miracles are variously defined as events which go against 1. the laws of nature, or 2. its laws as they are presently known, or 3. observed regularities (on the supposition that there are no strict laws). But

biblical reports are descriptive rather than conceptual. Divine miraculous power is an expression of the power of the one God who exercises providential sway. What are often called 'miracles' (regardless of the terms used in the various biblical accounts) can apparently be related in different ways to the providential order. Sometimes they involve its breach or suspension, as in the feeding of the five thousand or Jesus' walking on the water. But sometimes reference is made to 'coincidence miracles' which are extraordinary combinations of events, for each of which there is a straightforward natural explanation, but which are combined by God-given foresight and furnish an occasion for divine *revelation. The accounts of the catches of fish in Luke 5:4–7 and John 21:6–11 should surely be understood in these terms. However, the fact that the relation of different elements (natural, extraordinary and supernatural) may sometimes be unclear (as, *e.g.*, with the wind of Exod. 14:21 in the narrative of the crossing of the Red Sea) underlines the point that Scripture is relatively uninterested in secondary causes. Miracles are one form of providential ordering, integrating divine mastery over nature with divine purposes for the peoples. Theology's quarrel with sceptical philosophy and naturalistic science has to do ultimately with the nature and power of God.

The connection between the providential order and human history, the fact that 'the sustaining of the world ... is also related to His purposes for the future' (G. C. Berkouwer, *The Providence of God*, p. 83), has been noted in the history of theology by reference to the 'governmental' aspect of divine providence. This governmental aspect, which highlights the power of God, was one of the three most important lessons about God learned by Israel during the nation's history. The other two were the character of God and the nature of his purposes. These are both central to biblical teaching about providence.

The character of God

God's character is memorably set forth in Exodus 34:6–7: 'The LORD, the LORD, the compassionate and gracious God, slow to anger, abounding in love and faithfulness, maintaining love to thousands, and forgiving wickedness, rebellion and sin. Yet he does not leave the guilty unpunished ...' The subsequent narrative bears out this self-description in the story of Israel's disobedience, culminating in the exile of the southern kingdom of Judah, and it is reaffirmed by the prophets (e.g. Jonah 4:2). It by no means precludes the ascription to God of *judgment *holiness, implied in the reference to punishment, and about which OT and NT alike are emphatic. But it does assure believers of the gracious source and heart of the providential order, and Jesus specifically connected his teaching on divine fatherhood with the injunction to *rest in God's providential care (Matt. 6:25–34). God's purposes in history are revealed partially and progressively in the OT and come to focus, especially in the prophetic writings, on the deliverance of Israel, not just for its own sake, but also for the sake of the world and supremely for the glory of God himself. The story describes the unfolding of the promise given to Abraham that the nations should be *blessed through him (Gen. 12:2–3). In the NT, the promise is focused on Jesus Christ, through whom God's purposes for Israel, church and cosmos are executed, to the praise of God's glory. This is the unfolding of a design traceable back to creation itself (Col. 1:16; Eph. 1:10). Though the tragedy of perdition remains as a consequence of sin, the climax of *grace in the new heavens and new earth publicly vindicates the character of a God often concealed below the surface of the providential order. (See also *Righteousness, justice and justification.)

Personal purposes

The general question of the relationship of the divine character to the nature of divine purposes for individuals set within the providential order is posed, directly or indirectly, with special sharpness in the Israelite wisdom tradition. We shall look briefly at the way in which the question is handled in *Job and *Ecclesiastes. (See also *Wisdom books.)

Some theological and structural elements of the book of Job are unclear, notably the function of the Elihu cycle of speeches in chapters 32 – 37, but its overall structure has two intriguing features. The first is that the background and theological rationale of Job's *suffering are decisively set out in the opening two chapters of the book, with the account of God's granting Satan permission to test Job. But when God himself intervenes, late in the book, to respond to Job, that background and rationale are not disclosed to him. The reader's key for understanding the providential order, as far as it can be understood at all, is concealed from the participants in the drama. Secondly, the positive content of God's response seems initially puzzling for it does not seem to go beyond some of what Job's friends, or Job himself, have already said, and it falls short of the kind or fullness of explanation the reader may have expected. There is no reference to divine purpose; rather, there is reference to divine reality. The order in which Job is placed, and the suffering that occurs within it, are incomprehensible to him. But Job's moving confession after God has spoken (42:5–6) invites the reader to suppose that the purpose of meditation on the providential order is to instil in people a sense of God, not to provide reasons for every event. To find personal meaning is not primarily to discover patterns; instead, God wants to teach us humility before him. The book of Job is full of references to the providential order of the world (chs. 28 – 41). God's character is trustworthy though not yet luminous, his purposes largely hidden. The only NT reference to Job is in the book of James, where he is commended for his perseverance (Jas. 5:11). This text should not, of course, be taken to suggest that the restoration of worldly goods is always part of the providential order, and in the book of Job itself Job's acknowledgment of God precedes and takes place in ignorance of the restoration of his worldly prosperity.

Ecclesiastes was thought by the reformer Melanchthon to be basically a book about providence, and has also been adjudged to portray a God 'souverain à l'extrême' (Gorssen, quoted in R. E. Murphy, Ecclesiastes, WBC [Dallas, 1992], p. lxviii). Be this as it may, if God's speech is enigmatic in the book of Job, it is absent in the book of Ecclesiastes. The bulk of the book is a commentary on the words which enclose its body, and which appear frequently in the text: 'Meaningless! Meaningless! Everything is meaningless.' The author does not start where Job, or at least his friends, appear to start, with the assumption that in principle the order of life should be comprehensible, its meaning and purpose, causes and effects susceptible to rational and systematic explanation. Ecclesiastes, written on the basis of a lifetime's search for and exploration of wisdom, from the beginning entertains no such illusions. The meaninglessness of life is conclusive; the search for meaning and purpose, by scrutinizing immanent processes, yields nothing but futility (see *Vanity). So the contentment that is advocated – satisfaction in the intrinsic and immediate reward of labour, in food, drink, possessions and companions – seems to be based on the denial of cosmic meaning. It is tempting to conclude that this constitutes a denial of any providential order. But that judgment is contradicted at the end of the book. The author apparently is not so much aiming to promote a coherent and acceptable perspective on life as gathering a number of aphoristic and other remarks within a literary framework (Eccles. 12:9–12). In the injunction to '*fear God and keep his commandments for this is the whole duty of man. For God will bring every deed into judgment, including every hidden thing, whether it is good or evil' (12:13–14), the author indicates that in religious perspective, it is the moral that gives meaning to life. Meaning and purpose are not immanent in life's processes. They are given transcendently in relation to God, who is the creator and judge of every individual.

The problem of divine government

The question of God's government over history raises a number of vexing questions. Is the world genuinely open to more than one possibility, or is its future precisely determined? Is providence to be regarded as a determining power? It is within this context that the question of the relationship of God's activity to human agency and the problem of providence and *evil arise most sharply in the biblical account. Demanding exegetical, hermeneutical and philosophical issues arise in connection with these questions. We must confine ourselves to a broad description of the biblical parameters within which theology should operate.

The OT narrative, from the account of Abraham's calling to the return from exile, certainly on the face of it encourages the belief that history is genuinely open, according to whether people *obey or disobey God. For example, when Moses (Deut. 30:15–18) and Joshua (Josh. 24:14–24) set alternatives before the people, they appear to be free to follow alternative courses of action; history is presented as a theatre of genuinely alternative possibilities. In the very passage where Jeremiah likens God to the potter moulding the clay of Israel, he affirms that the execution of divine judgment or blessing is contingent on the disobedience or obedience of the people (Jer. 18:1–12). Divine declarations of what is to be often contain a tacit or an explicit condition, as in the account of the perpetuation of the Davidic kingdom through Solomon (e.g. 1 Chr. 28:6–7). Further, God seems to change his mind in response to petition (e.g. 2 Kgs. 20) and to acknowledge alternative futures (1 Sam. 23:9–13).

However, this must all be integrated into a wider picture.

First, human actions do not take place independently of God even when those actions are wicked. This fact emerges early in the Bible, both in the story of Joseph in Genesis 37 – 45 and in the accounts of the hardening of Pharoah's heart (Exod. 7 – 11). While the ways in which God is active may vary according to the evil or good in the human heart, biblical language signifies at the very least an active concurrence of divine and human action, not complete human autonomy. Yet while evildoers are responsible for their deeds, believers depend on God for their obedient actions (Phil. 2:13).

Second, God knows in advance what humans will do. As soon and as certainly as the fact of choice is established at a crucial juncture in Israel's history, so is the divine knowledge of what that choice will be (Deut. 31:16–18). The reduction or limitation of this principle cannot be justified on purely biblical grounds. (Philosophical arguments are beyond our scope here.) The prophetic literature, such as that of Isaiah, not only appears to suppose that divine foreknowledge is involved in the very logic of prophecy, but also exults in a God whose power is expressed in such foreknowledge (e.g. Is. 40ff.). In contrast to this, it is sometimes argued that statements in which God expresses ignorance, disappointment, regret or hope more or less strongly imply that some human actions are not foreknown by God and are even judged by him to be unlikely. The issue here is hermeneutical. Not only is it appropriate to read the biblical narrative in light of the progressive self-disclosure of God, but where such self-disclosure takes place, as in the high points of prophecy and apocalyptic in Isaiah and Daniel, the comprehensive scope of God's knowledge becomes increasingly clear. The account of Jesus' mission in the NT, in its eschatological context, militates against a view of God as one who takes risks with an unknown and unknowable future (*contra* J. Sanders, *The God Who Risks*).

Thirdly, the future is sometimes described as not just known to God but decreed by him. Certainly the Bible does not describe this decree in a monochrome way, as something which is always immutably antecedent to and independent of what humans decide to do. Nevertheless, the active responsibility for bringing history to its destiny lies with God and God's active decisions about what will or will not be. This raises the question of pre-destination, which is best approached in connection with the wider question of the providential government of world history.

The history of theology is littered with attempts to harmonize these and other biblical data, and even the very broad description of God's government set out above will be judged by some to be misleading and tendentious. But a comprehensive resolution is not necessary. Biblical theology is thoroughly practical; it emphasizes the application of its various truths to life more than their systematic relation to each other. The Christian's practice of adoration, trust, obedience, *repentance, *faith and perseverance does not depend on an understanding of how different theological ideas are to be woven together. Further, despite the perplexities involved, the dominant impression imparted by Scripture is that of a rich, if systematically elusive, coherence, not of a dismaying problem. God understands everything that is happening and directs history to its destiny with literally matchless power. The appearance of his actions varies according to their purpose and the relationships involved; he decides to act before he sees or when he sees or whatever he sees or according to what he sees, and in this respect is portrayed as the living and personal God that he is. But he is not caught out in ignorance or error, or prevented by human action from carrying out what he has determined, or manipulated by human entreaty into doing the unwise, the unjust or the unholy, and in this respect he is portrayed as the good and powerful God that he is.

Many passages illuminate divine providence. For example, the insight of Proverbs that 'In his heart a man plans his course, but the LORD determines his steps' (16:9) suggests that at the level of intention humans bear some responsibility, but whether or not intention comes to fruition is the decision of the Lord. It offers a way of discerning how evil acts are encompassed by an active providence and yet humans are accountable for them. Evil is radically mysterious, in the biblical account, right from its anomalous appearance in Eden. Where God's commands are flouted, the evil belongs to humans or to Satan. Scripture does not so much explain evil as assure readers that evil is intrusive in God's world and will finally be defeated. If, however, it is a matter of divine decision whether or not an evil deed is done, but the evil disposition is the responsibility of humans, then the divine decision is to enable the evil intention formed in the heart to be actively expressed. The freedom to will and the freedom to act are not the same thing (and freedom itself is not a transparent or undifferentiated notion). A person is rendered morally responsible not by a deed alone, but by its relation to the preceding nexus of will and intent. God is ultimately responsible in that evil occurs in a world over which he has power, although his disposal of it is in salient respects mysterious.

While faith seeks understanding, it does not live by understanding the providential ways of God. The confidence of the believer is born of the conviction that God is utterly trustworthy in character and promise, and this generates deep humility. Christians' relationship to providence becomes clearer when we consider *prayer. According to the Lord's Prayer (Matt. 6:9–13) God knows what we need before we ask him; he is our Father; we depend on him for our bread; we ask forgiveness when we fail; we petition him for the will and strength to do what he wants us to do and avoid what he wants us to avoid. In turn, the humility of the believer can issue in further confidence on the basis of the relationship of providence to world history as described in the last book of the Bible, Revelation. It is decided by God that the rebellion of kings and of beasts against his rule shall terminate; that the nations will be beneficiaries of healing justice and *mercy; that the decisive proof of his providence shall be the reappearance of Jesus Christ and the transformation of the world order. That God has determined all this does not eliminate the problems and tragedies from the story; it may even intensify them. But it means that providence ultimately finds its appropriate response in praise (see *Worship).

Bibliography

K. Barth, *Church Dogmatics*, vol. 3.3 (Edinburgh, 1960); G. C. Berkouwer, *The Providence of God* (Grand Rapids and Leicester, 1952); E. Brunner, *The Christian Doctrine of Creation and Redemption* (London, 1952); W. Eichrodt, *Theology of the Old Testament*, vol. 2 (London, 1967); P. Helm, *The Providence of God* (Leicester and Downers Grove, 1993); J. Sanders, *The God Who Risks: A Theology of Providence* (Downers Grove, 1998); E. Stauffer, *New Testament Theology* (London, 1955).

S. N. WILLIAMS

PSALMS, see PART 2
PUNISHMENT, see JUDGMENT
PURPOSE, see ELECTION

RAHAB

Rahab (1)

Within ancient Near Eastern mythologies, the picture of great sea monsters symbolizing pre-creation chaos is well known (*e.g.* Tiamat in the Babylonian stories). Similar but not identical imagery is found in the OT, where the 'chaos-monster' is known as Rahab (Job 9:13; 26:12; Pss. 87:4; 89:10; Is. 30:7; 51:9) or Leviathan (see *Spiritual powers) (Job 3:8; 41:1; Ps. 74:14; 104:26; Is. 27:1). The monster Rahab (the Heb. word is different from that used in the book of Joshua as a personal name), along with everything else in *creation, is presented not as a power equal to God and therefore a possible threat to his supremacy, but as totally under his control. In all the references to Rahab, the image is related more closely to God's powerful

conquest of Egypt at the time of the *Exodus than to the bringing of order out of chaos in creation. In an extension of the image, Pharaoh is described as a monster (Ezek. 29:3) and 'Rahab' is used as an alternative name for Egypt (Is. 30:7; Ps. 87:4). Egypt might appear to the much smaller and usually much weaker Israel to be an invincible monster. But the OT writers are convinced that before their God this monster will be crushed (Ps. 89:10), cut to pieces (Job 26:12; Is. 51:9) and left cowering (Job 9:13).

Rahab (2)

The account of the assessment of Canaan by two spies sent from *Joshua prior to the Israelite invasion (Josh. 2) is dominated by the story of their visit to a local brothel. In fact the only part of their trip about which we learn is their encounter with Rahab. Rahab's house may have been an inn, but Rahab herself was a prostitute. It may be that the Israelite spies deliberately sought out such a house as a place where they would be accepted without question and perhaps retain their anonymity. However, if that was their hope it proved to be unrealistic. The presence of strangers in Jericho, at a time when a very large contingent of foreign nomads was camped somewhat ominously nearby, aroused the interest of the local department of state (Josh. 2:2–3) and the two men were forced to hide and to flee.

Surprisingly, this prostitute from an enemy state risked her own life to protect the spies from discovery and to aid their escape. For whatever reason, she had been persuaded by rumours concerning the power of Israel's God, and the imminent destruction of Jericho (Josh. 2:9–11). Her conviction was stronger than her fear of reprisal from the local authorities; so she seized her opportunity and acted to protect herself and her family from what she saw as certain death. It may be that her motivation was primarily self-interest. She hid the spies beneath the flax on the roof as a mark of good faith, but she made sure that the men swore an oath to protect her before she let them depart. However, her actions are attributed to *faith (Heb. 11:31), and even interpreted as *righteousness (Jas. 2:25). Remarkably, it is Rahab who is placed alongside *Abraham as a key example of the significance of righteous actions in the life of the believer. Perhaps the underlying message, that even such an unlikely, unacceptable, underdog as this foreign brothel-keeper could, in God's providence, be used by him to fulfil his purposes, had been an encouragement to Israel in her own weakness and inadequacy. James may have wanted to reinforce that point; or perhaps he wanted to make sure his readers understood that believing actions were not the prerogative of those with an impeccable reputation or heritage.

Rahab, then, provides an illustration of God's interest and concern for those outside the covenant community (see *Nations), as do the widow of Zarephath and Naaman in later stories (1 Kgs. 17; 2 Kgs. 5; cf. Luke 4:25–27). Non-Israelites could be placed under God's protection. Furthermore, the development of Rahab's story in Joshua 6:23–25 (in which the oath to protect her was kept by the Israelites), shows that foreigners, even despised and scorned prostitutes, could not only receive blessing from God but could also be fully accepted and absorbed into the community. That community was not to be narrow or exclusive. Rahab's own acceptance was not immediate. Her kindred was initially restricted to 'a place outside the camp' (Josh. 6:23, NIV). However, her continuing life among the Israelites is noted (Josh. 6:25) and she eventually became an ancestor to both David and Jesus (Matt. 1:5).

There is no known reference in Jewish literature to the marriage between Salmon, son of Aaron's brother-in-law Nahshon (Exod. 6:23; 1 Chr. 2:11), and Rahab, but they would have been contemporaries. Matthew, in presenting Rahab as the mother of Boaz, was probably drawing on a tradition which is now lost. Of course Boaz was more than a generation removed from Rahab and Salmon (Ruth 4:20), but the foreshortening of genealogies in this way is a common practice in ancient writings. 1 Chronicles 2:51, 54 refers to a Salma, who was also associated with Bethlehem (Boaz's home town); this is a possible indication of an ongoing family link.

Bibliography

R. Bauckham, 'Tamar's ancestry and Rahab's marriage: Two problems in the Matthean genealogy', NovT 37, 1995, pp. 313–319; P. A. Bird, 'The harlot as heroine: narrative art and social presupposition in three Old Testament texts', Semeia 46, 1989, pp. 119–139; T. C. Butler, Joshua, WBC (Waco, 1983); J. Gray, Joshua, NCB (Grand Rapids, 1986); G. Mitchell, Together in the Land (Sheffield, 1993).

M. J. EVANS

RANSOM, see REDEMPTION
RECONCILIATION, see FORGIVENESS AND RECONCILIATION
RE-CREATIONS, see CREATION

REDEMPTION

Introduction

Popular parlance equates redemption with *God's plan of *salvation through *Jesus Christ. But the biblical term denotes only one important aspect of salvation. Redemption involves the release of people, animals, or property from bondage through outside help. Their social, physical, or spiritual weakness makes redemption necessary. Only someone strong or rich can effect it, so God plays a leading role in redemption. The language of redemption involves the Hebrew roots pādâ ('to redeem, ransom') and gā'al ('to redeem, serve as redeemer') and the Greek lytroō ('to redeem, ransom') and agorazō ('to buy'), often with the prepositions 'from' or 'in place of'.

OT law: the roots of redemption

Exodus 21 describes the two earliest kinds of redemption. Verse 8 requires an *Israelite man to permit the redemption (pdh) of his slave-wife, presumably by a repayment. Redemption ends her humiliation and restores her to her *family. It mediates divine *grace by protecting the weak from abuse by the powerful and by restoring a family's lost unity. Verse 30 permits the redemption of one condemned to *death because his ox killed someone through his irresponsibility, provided the victim's family consents. Here redemption extends *mercy toward the irresponsible.

Yahweh owns all firstborn (both human and animal) but permits the release of some (Exod. 13:2, 13; 34:19–20; Num. 3:12; Deut. 15:19–20). A sheep will redeem a donkey's life, while the sheep (and other unredeemable firstborn) is used as a *sacrifice or as meat for *priests (Num. 18:17–18). Owners may redeem or sell firstborn unclean animals, the proceeds going to the sanctuary treasury (Lev. 27:26–27; cf. vv. 13–20, 31). In place of firstborn sons, Yahweh accepted the tribe of Levi (Num. 3:49, 51; cf. Num. 8:15–18). In the redemption of firstborn, Yahweh waives his rights and cedes ownership to Israel. Theologically, this policy bespeaks divine generosity in two respects: through it God shares his property with Israel, and the firstborn in turn benefits Israel's family life; also, God's gift of the Levites and the five-shekel redemption price to the priests benefits them financially.

Redemption by a kinsman-redeemer (Heb. *gō'ēl*) is the most common kind of redemption in the OT. The redeemer was a close male relative (*e.g.* a brother, father, uncle, cousin) obliged under Israelite family law to assist relatives in distress. He would buy back their mortgaged property (Lev. 25:25–34; cf. Jer. 32:7–8) or buy them out of slavery (Lev. 25:48–52). These purchases restored the highly valued unity of family and property. Theologically, the divine mandate of redemption (vv. 23–24) implements on Israelite soil the redemption won by Yahweh in Egypt (vv. 42, 55), lest Israel produce its own cruel Pharaohs and impoverished slaves. To deny redemption is to infringe on Yahweh's rights (*i.e.* to enslave people belonging to him) and, in effect, to annul the gains of the Exodus. Here divine grace safeguards Israel's *freedom and social equality, and promotes Israel's ideal of family unity.

As 'avenger of blood' (Heb. *gō'ēl haddām*) the kinsman-redeemer would redeem the life of a relative by killing its killer (Num. 35:19; cf. 2 Sam. 14:11). He thus imposed the proper penalty of justice and rid the land of the defilement caused by the killing (Num. 35:33–34). To die without an heir was to weaken the whole clan, so the *gō'ēl* would also *marry a deceased's widow to produce an heir (Ruth 2:20; 3:9, 13; 4:1–14). Finally, several texts about Yahweh suggest that the redeemer also advocated the cause of a needy relative involved in a lawsuit (Prov. 23:11; Job 19:25) or illegally incarcerated (Jer. 50:34; cf. Ps. 72:14). The *gō'ēl* protected the family against weakness and restored its debilitating losses.

The divine Redeemer: the Exodus paradigm

God also redeems humans himself, classically in his liberation of Israel from Egyptian slavery. The Exodus introduces three theologically significant themes. First, this redemption frees slaves from brutal, oppressive captivity under Pharaoh (Exod. 6:6; Deut. 7:8; 13:5; Mic. 6:4). Until Yahweh intervenes, Pharaoh holds Israel against its will by force, cruelly controls its population, and demands impossible productivity in sweatshop conditions (Exod. 1:8–22). Secondly, this redemption happens, not through repayment of money owed or outright mercy, but because Yahweh overcomes Pharaoh's tight grip (Deut. 9:26; Neh. 1:10; Ps. 77:17). Finally, Yahweh redeems Israel because of his prior *covenant relationship as 'God of your ancestors' (Exod. 3:6, 15–16; 4:5) and because of his covenant promise to give them *land (6:4, 8; cf. Deut. 7:8; 9:26).

Exodus 6:6 and 15:13 use the root of family law (*g'l*) to describe this redemptive act. As elsewhere, the word may simply mean 'to rescue (from danger)'. But some scholars believe that it portrays Yahweh as a kinsman-redeemer, releasing his 'kinfolk' from slavery and restoring the 'family's' wholeness. The Exodus defined salvation for Israel as rescue from the cruel, resistant grip of an oppressive power. David later revels in the unprecedented and stunning nature of the Exodus (2 Sam. 7:23; cf. 1 Chr. 17:21), and the Exodus paradigm significantly shapes the NT's theology of salvation. Further, it created Israel's central ethical ideal, supporting Yahweh's demand that Israel supply departing Hebrew slaves generously (Deut. 15:13–15), leave food for the *poor to glean (24:19–22), and not abuse widows, orphans and aliens (24:17–18). On the other hand, it reassures Israel that Yahweh will remove the *guilt of an unexplained death (Deut. 21:8) and deliver them from their (and Yahweh's) foes (Ps. 74:2). Finally, the Exodus is the explanation given to children for the removal of leaven during Passover and the special treatment of firstborn animals and sons (Exod. 13:5–8, 11–15).

In light of the Exodus, *gō'ēl* ('Redeemer') becomes a popular title for Yahweh (Pss. 19:14; 78:35; Is. 49:26; 63:16). The title 'your redeemer' (often in the messenger formula) dominates Isaiah 40 – 66 (41:14; 48:17; cf. 44:6; 47:4; 49:7; 63:16). More theologically significant are the prophet's allusions to the first Exodus, including the root g'l ('to redeem'), to portray Israel's imminent release from *Babylon as a new Exodus (43:14–17, NRSV [but cf. NIV]; 51:10–11; 52:3–6, 9; 60:16–17; 62:12; cf. 63:9). Occasionally, the oracles juxtapose the language of redemption and *creation, creatively combining cosmic sovereignty and familial intimacy (Is. 44:21–23, 24–28). As Redeemer, it is Yahweh's duty to redeem his sons and daughters; as Creator he uses whole countries (Egypt, Ethiopia, Seba) as coins to pay for their release (Is. 43:1–7). As Redeemer, Yahweh will marry widowed Zion and bless her with many children; as Creator he has the power to do so (Is. 54:1–8).

The identity of the 'redeemer' in Job 19:25 is difficult to determine. Job clearly expects the gō'ēl ('vindicator') to vindicate him legally before his friends (cf. 16:19), but this is probably not an actual relative, since family and friends have abandoned him (19:13–19), and the vindication seems to occur on the earth after Job's death (v. 26). Many identify God as Job's advocate, but this makes God both the defendant and the plaintiff's lawyer. Others posit a resurrection in which Job serves as his own vindicator, but this is doubtful. Finally, D. J. A. Clines argues from Job 16:18–21 (Job 1 – 20, WBC [Waco, 1989], p. 459) that Job's 'champion' (i.e. gō'ēl) is his own cry of self-defence.

Redemption as rescue from danger

Redemption occasionally means simply 'rescue (from danger)' apart from any legal or social context. Friends may be rescuers (1 Sam. 14:45; Job 6:23), but Yahweh is the primary one. He rescues people from death (Ps. 103:4; Job 5:20; 33:28) or deadly dangers, both national (Ps. 25:22) and personal (Pss. 26:11; 31:5; 119:134; etc.; cf. 1 Macc. 4:11). Some prayers pair 'redeem' (g'l) with 'plead my cause' (rîb), metaphorically seeking Yahweh's advocacy as kinsman-redeemer (Ps. 119:154; cf. Prov. 23:11; Is. 51:10; Jer. 50:34; cf. Is. 35:9–10). The 'rescued' credit God for their deliverance (Lam. 3:58; Pss. 71:23; 107:2), and David twice swears oaths by Yahweh as rescuer (2 Sam. 4:9; 1 Kgs. 1:29). As at the Exodus, Yahweh's superior firepower overwhelms all

sources of danger. But the OT warns that no one, however rich, can buy a way out of death; the price is simply out of reach (Ps. 49:8). However, God will redeem the faithful from death by 'taking' them (v. 15). Since the accounts of Enoch's (Gen. 5:24) and Elijah's (2 Kgs. 2:10) departures both include the word 'take', Psalm 49 may allude to some form of afterlife (cf. 73:24–26).

Eschatological redemption

Yahweh's refusal to redeem signals the arrival of divine judgment against the northern kingdom. Unlike David, Ephraim will not be delivered from national death (Hos. 7:13; 13:14). On the other hand, the return from *exile is divine redemption, as Yahweh overpowers Israel's captors (Jer. 31:11; 50:33–34). Even the nations' conquest of Jerusalem is a prelude to redemption; later they will be plundered by Zion (Mic. 4:10). Isaiah 1:27 seems to imply that justice and *righteousness are Zion's purchase price, but clearly the return gladdens the 'redeemed' (Is. 35:9–10 = 51:11) and includes Ephraim (Zech. 10:7–8). In the end, restored Zion's new name will be 'the Redeemed of the LORD' (Is. 62:12).

Redemption from sin

In several texts the language of redemption refers to the forgiveness of *sin. Isaiah 44:22–23 seems to equate the blotting out of Israel's sin with divine redemption. On the other hand, in Isaiah 59:20 redemption apparently follows human repentance. Theologically, Psalm 130:7–8 contains the most far-reaching insight. Only Yahweh's power, not powerless Israel itself, offers hope for redemption (i.e. *forgiveness of sin). This insight into sin as an overpowering force anticipates the NT teaching on redemption as release from slavery to sin.

Redemption in the NT: introduction

The OT's two linguistic streams (g'l and pdh) flow into the NT's two linguistic word groups, agorazō ('to buy') and lytroō ('to redeem'). Familiar OT redemptive motifs, especially the Exodus from Egypt and the redemption of slaves, are used as metaphors for aspects of the work of Christ. Occasionally, themes from Hellenistic Judaism and Greco-Roman culture complement them. The epistles (especially Paul) and Revelation have more references to redemption than other NT texts.

Redemption in NT narratives

Except for Mark 10:45, Luke-Acts is the only narrative tradition to mention the theme. In the Lukan birth narratives, redemption denotes the realization of OT messianic hopes of political liberation and economic prosperity (Luke 1:68; 2:38). Ancient messianic hopes are echoed also in the words of the grieving disciples en route to Emmaus after Jesus' crucifixion (24:21). Controversy surrounds Mark 10:45 (par. Matt. 20:28), probably the earliest NT reference to redemption. Jesus models true kingdom greatness as a servant who gives 'his life a ransom (*lytron*) for many'. The question is whether this saying derives from Jesus himself or from early church teaching. In favour of the latter, scholars appeal to the prominence of redemption in Paul, the statement's allegedly more Hellenistic (rather than Semitic) language, and its close verbal similarity to 1 Timothy 2:6. The uniqueness of the Markan statement is certainly striking, but its language is Semitic, not Hellenistic, especially when compared to that of 1 Timothy 2:6 (see R. H. Gundry, *Mark*, pp. 587–591). Also, only Mark 10:45b uses the simple *lytron* ('ransom') while all other writers use the compound forms *antilytron* ('ransom', 1 Tim. 2:6) and *apolytrōsis* ('release, deliverance', Luke 21:28). This makes development of the latter forms from Mark 10:45 more likely than the reverse. So there is good reason to trace the roots of the NT's redemption theme to Mark 10:45b (I. H. Marshall, in *Reconciliation and Hope*, pp. 168–169).

The context of the Markan statement is Jesus' prediction of his betrayal and death (Mark 8:31–32; 9:31) and his question about what to exchange for *life (8:37), the latter an echo of Psalm 49:7–9. Death is inescapable, but Jesus will 'give his life as a ransom' (*i.e.* a 'price' paid to God) so that 'many' (*i.e.* an unspecified multitude; *cf.* Mark 14:24; Matt. 26:28) may escape death. The preposition *anti* ('in place of') means that Jesus' death is a substitute for all human deaths. But death results from human sin, so Jesus' ransom somehow removes the effects of sin, making forgiveness a possibility. There are no actual allusions here to the suffering servant (Is. 53), so Mark probably does not regard the ransom-death of Jesus in sacrificial terms as a sin offering. But Mark 14:24 ('my blood of the covenant ... poured out for many') suggests that Jesus understood his death as a covenant sacrifice. By linking his death to betrayal Jesus also seems to understand it as that of a martyr, which in some contemporary Jewish thought was seen as a ransom for the sins of others (see 4 Macc. 6:29; 17:21).

Redemption in Paul

Redemption is especially prominent in Paul's thinking. Drawing on OT themes, he affirms that 'Christ has redeemed us from the curse of the law' (Gal. 3:13). The curse is the death sentence for failure to keep the *law (v. 10; Deut. 27:26) which Christ absorbed in his public execution (Deut. 21:23). His death 'bought' release from death for believers at the 'cost' of his own life. Paul appears to interweave two familiar OT themes, the redemption of the firstborn (*i.e.* the substitution of one for many), and the redemption of one condemned to death (Deut. 21:8; but *cf.* Exod. 30:11–16). But in Galatians 4:5 redemption is clearly release from slavery to the law and the power of sin (*cf.* v. 3; 3:10; 4:8). The result is both freedom from repressive tyranny and *adoption as God's own children (4:5–7; 5:1).

Jesus' death produces a new spiritual paradox: slaves 'bought with a price' are not free but are slaves to a new owner (1 Cor. 6:20; 7:22). Thus redemption obligates Christians to glorify Christ in their daily living. The conduct of false teachers denies the rights of the kind slave-master who bought them and whom they should serve faithfully (2 Pet. 2:1). Paul also equates redemption with the believer's present possession of the forgiveness of sins (Eph. 1:7; Col. 1:14).

Redemption in the Pastorals and Hebrews

The Pastoral Epistles draw on Jesus' ransom statement (Mark 10:45) to support practical admonitions. 1 Timothy 2:6 seems to argue that as Christ died 'for all', he will answer prayers for pagan kings (vv. 1–2). According to Titus 2:14, the ransom freed believers from their sin and its penalty (*cf.* Ps. 130:8) and purified them as God's own, specially treasured *people (*cf.* LXX of Exod. 19:5; Deut. 7:6; 14:2; 26:18). The Day of

Atonement (Lev. 16), not martyrdom, shapes Hebrews' picture of Christ as the high priest obtaining redemption in the heavenly temple (Heb. 9:12–15). Here redemption amounts to full and final atonement for sin, as Christ's (not animal) *blood is substituted for the lives of sinful humans (v. 14; cf. 4:15). His superior sacrifice was acceptable to God and won 'eternal' redemption for sinners (vv. 12, 25–26). 1 Peter 1:18–19 stresses the value of Christ's blood, value based on his eternal existence (see vv. 20–21), and perhaps on his perfection as God. His blood easily pays the full 'price' for redemption from slavery to futile religions. Hebrews 11:35 mentions OT martyrs who refused to deny their *faith to buy 'release' from cruel, earthly captivity in order to win a better resurrection for themselves.

Redemption in the Apocalypse

Two victory songs in Revelation draw on OT motifs to comment on Christ's blood. The *Lamb is worthy of praise because its shed blood ransomed believers from all nations (5:8–9). The language appears to compare Christ to the Paschal lamb whose blood delivered the Israelite firstborn (Exod. 12; Mark 14:12–25, par.; cf. John 1:29) and to the lamb (i.e. the Suffering Servant) whose atoning death purchases believers from eternal death (Is. 53:7, 11). The second song focuses on the 144,000 redeemed as the 'first fruits' of humankind (Rev. 14:3–4; Jas. 1:18). The OT background (Lev. 23:9–14) suggests that these redeemed saints anticipate the larger, triumphant harvest of believers to follow (Rev. 14:14–16; R. Bauckham, The Climax of Prophecy, pp. 291–292).

NT *eschatological redemption

Like the OT, the NT foresees future aspects of redemption. Luke's apocalyptic discourse (Luke 21:28) anticipates a redemption of believers after Christ's second coming (i.e. deliverance from history's final distress; cf. 1 Enoch 51:2). In Paul, the future redemptive event is the consummation of God's past work (Eph. 1:13–14). In the seal of the *Holy Spirit, the sign of God's ownership (v. 13), believers already have a 'down payment' in advance of the 'day of redemption' (4:30), when God will claim his property and believers receive their full 'inheritance' (1:14; cf. v. 11). Remarkably, that day will see the release of their physical bodies from decay and suffering (Rom. 8:23; cf. v. 21 NIV); the same redemption will liberate the entire creation. The redemption/adoption of Christians will become complete, including body and soul, and it will be very personal and tangible. But until that day, Paul urges believers to 'redeem the time', i.e. to make the most of today's opportunities by wise conduct towards unbelievers (Eph. 5:16; Col. 4:5).

Conclusion

Theologically, redemption flows from the OT into the NT. As Redeemer, God lovingly demonstrates it in the Exodus, requires it in the law, and consummates it in Christ. Its sub-themes are rescue from harm, freedom from tyranny, the forgiveness of sin, and unbelievable *joy. Paradoxically, it frees slaves of sin to make them slaves of God. But in the end, the slaves become God's adopted children for all eternity. This is, indeed, a wonderful story.

See also: ATONEMENT.

Bibliography

R. Bauckham, The Climax of Prophecy (Edinburgh, 1993); A. Deissmann, Light from the Ancient East (ET, New York, 1927); R. H. Gundry, Mark (Grand Rapids, 1993); D. Hill, Greek Words and Hebrew Meanings: Studies in the Semantics of Soteriological Terms (Cambridge, 1967); R. Hubbard, Jr, 'g'l', in NIDOTTE 1, pp. 789–794; S. Lyonnet and L. Sabourin, Sin, Redemption, and Sacrifice (Rome, 1970); I. H. Marshall, 'The development of the concept of redemption in the New Testament', in R. Banks (ed.), Reconciliation and Hope (Grand Rapids, 1974), pp. 153–169; H. Ringgren, 'g'l', in TDOT 2, pp. 350–355; J. Schneider and C. Brown in NIDNTT 3, pp. 177–205; G. Shogren, 'Redemption (NT)', in ABD 5, pp. 654–657; J. Unterman, 'Redemption (OT), in ABD 5, pp. 650–654.

R. L. HUBBARD, JR.

REGENERATION

NT references

A biblical-theological approach to regeneration begins with an examination of the NT word and its related concepts; there is no word for regeneration in the OT. There are only two occurrences of the Greek word (*palingenesia*) of which 'regeneration' is the literal translation. These are found in Titus 3:5, which refers to the operation of the Holy Spirit on the believers as they begin the Christian life, and Matthew 19:28, where Jesus refers to the *eschatological renewal associated with the consummation of the *kingdom of God.

These two references point us in two directions: to the present personal renewal of believers, and to the future renewal of all things. The use of the same word does not necessarily indicate a common theological idea, and consequently we must seek for some conceptual unity. In this case, the theological concepts involved are the renewal of the fallen *creation and the coming of the kingdom of God. From these we can move towards a comprehensive picture of regeneration in the Bible. Revelation 21:5 refers to God 'making all things new' (NRSV); this involves the coming of the kingdom so that the people of God are gathered around the throne of God in the new *Jerusalem which comes from heaven.

Regeneration, new birth and new creation

Starting from the personal operation of the Holy Spirit in believers, the theme of personal renewal must include the biblical notions of new birth and new creation. Conceptual unity exists in that personal new birth is linked to entering the kingdom of God, which is described in OT terms of a renewed world with its centre in the new Jerusalem. Regeneration is frequently taken to refer exclusively to the personal and inward operation of the Spirit, but this notion, while valid as far as it goes, does not sufficiently explain the concept. It is, in fact, a mistake to start any theological investigation with the inward effects of *salvation since these are the fruit of a prior, objective work of God.

Both Matthew 19:28 and Revelation 21:5 point us to the renewal of the whole creation centring on the focal points of OT revelation and the fulfilment of these in Christ. The biblical theological background to regeneration in the NT is thus the creation of all things and the *redemption of all things revealed and foreshadowed in the OT. Thus,

an overview of regeneration would include the following: 1. The creation of the world and everything in it is called 'generation' in Genesis 2:4. 2. Although the term is not used, the effect of human sin in the fall is degeneration. This is not a total negation of creation because God, in his grace, is preserving the creation so that it might be redeemed. This is the force of Paul's statement in Romans 8:20–21. 3. The whole process of redemption, which includes the physical universe, unfolds in the rest of Bible and leads to the consummation described in Matthew 19:28 and Revelation 21:5. The entire biblical story may thus be summarized as involving generation, degeneration, and regeneration.

If it is legitimate to use the idea of regeneration in this way, the question remains as to how Titus 3:5 and the idea of personal and inner rebirth relates to Matthew 19:28 and the total or universal regeneration. Not only is the subjective–objective distinction involved here, but also the present–future and the instant–process tensions.

Biblical-theological context

Regeneration in the Old Testament

Biblical theology provides us with an answer to our question by giving us a total picture of revelation. The creation, or generation, involves a physical universe in which human beings are given titular rule. The sovereign work of God is to create freely by his word and through the agency of his Spirit. The rebellion of the first human pair harms not only themselves as the perpetrators of the crime, but also the whole creation as it is subjected to futility by the judgment of God (Rom. 8:20–23).

Without delay, God sets in motion his plan of redemption which will restore a people to himself and, in so doing, will see the whole creation caught up in this plan of renewal. The covenant promises to the descendants of Abraham include not only a restored relationship with God, but a land in which they will relate to God, a land which is portrayed as an Eden-like garden of plenty, of peace, and of restored relationships.

When the preliminary historical experience of these promises fails with the decline of the kingdom of Israel, the schism, and the eventual destruction of all the outward signs of God's blessing, the prophets have a message of renewal. They proclaim the faithfulness of God to his promises, so that what was experienced in the redemptive history from Abraham to Solomon one day will be completed in a perfect and glorious form as the eternal kingdom of God is established. At the heart of this message is the assurance of a new Israel and Jerusalem. But further, the whole universe will be regenerated. Thus Isaiah points to a day when the nations will stream to a new temple (Is. 2:1–4), when a new Davidic king will usher in an age of righteousness and harmony in nature (Is. 11:1–9), when the ravages of the fall in the natural universe and in the well-being of people will be abolished (Is. 35:1–10). This will be the kingdom of the everlasting God which goes beyond a regenerated people and a regenerated Israel. There will be a regeneration of the whole creation; a new heaven and a new earth (Is. 65:17–20).

The prophets also speak of an inner regeneration of the people of God so that there will be reconciliation and harmony with God's word. Jeremiah 31:31–34 tells of the law being written on their hearts, while in Ezekiel 36:25–27 a new heart and cleansing of the Spirit is promised to them.

Thus, the OT provides the background for both the personal regeneration of Titus 3:5 and the general regeneration in Matthew 19:28. It also enables us to understand the dialogue of Jesus with Nicodemus. The biblical concept is not confined to the usage of the one word *palingenesia*. But nor may we assume that regeneration is synonymous with the individual being born from above (*anōthen*), as Jesus describes it in John 3:3, 7, and with being born again (*anagennaō*) in 1 Peter 1:3, 23. The wonder of a radical personal transformation by the Spirit of God is enhanced when we see it as part of the whole process of renewal.

Objective regeneration in Christ

The Nicodemus narrative is instructive not least for Jesus' declaration that birth from above is necessary if one is to see and enter the kingdom of God. But also we see that Nicodemus is rebuked for failing to understand this even though he is a teacher in Israel. This implies that a knowledge of the OT Scriptures should have given him all the information he needed for understanding the initial statement about birth from above. Also, in John 3:5 'birth by water and Spirit' is almost certainly a reference to Ezekiel 36:25–27. Further, when Nicodemus presses the point about how such a thing can happen, Jesus answers by reference to the Son of Man's being lifted up as the object of saving faith. The real focus, reiterated in John 3:16, is the giving of God's son. There is an objectivity in this which points to the definitive locus of the regeneration: it is *Jesus.

A variety of OT themes are taken up in this teaching. The focal centre of the world in the OT becomes Zion and the *temple as the place where God meets his people and reconciliation is effected. In Ezekiel's vision of restoration the new temple is the centre of the earth, and from it comes life and a new Eden (Ezek. 47:1–12). The NT understands that Jesus is that temple (John 2:19–22); he is the regeneration.

This perspective fits with another significant passage, namely 2 Corinthians 5:17. The Greek text does not specify who is the new creation, Christ or the person who is in Christ. The answer must lie in the Pauline perspective of our union with Christ: being crucified with Christ (Gal. 2:19–20), being buried with him (Rom. 6:4–5), being raised with him and being made to sit with him in heavenly places (Eph. 2:5–6). This is not to deny the reality of the subjective regeneration in John 3 and Titus 3, but only to acknowledge that the locus of regeneration is not in us, but in Christ. By virtue of our faith-union with Christ, what belongs to his actual experience is putatively ours. This follows from the imputation of Christ's righteousness to all believers. We note also the complementary perspectives in 1 Peter 1. In verse 3 rebirth is said to come by means of the resurrection of Christ, whereas in verse 23 it is linked to the preached gospel. In that the resurrection of Christ is God's 'Amen' to the person and work of Jesus, his justification as the true covenant partner of God (Rom. 1:4), the beginning of this regeneration may be considered as the beginning of our regeneration. The incarnation, the conception and birth of Jesus, is the basis for our rebirth.

Universal regeneration

The climax of a biblical theology of regeneration comes in Revelation 21 and 22. Here a great number of the contributing themes are gathered up in one last dazzling description of the kingdom's consummation. Here the original generation, or creation, of the heavens and the earth in Genesis 1 – 2, which degenerated because of human sin, is fulfilled by the new heaven and the new earth (Rev. 21:1). At the centre of the new earth is the new Jerusalem which comes from heaven (v. 2). There is no temple built with hands because the new temple is there (v. 22). Ezekiel's vision of a new Eden is realized (Rev. 22:1–5). Regeneration is summed up in the glorious proclamation from the heavenly throne, 'See, I am making all things new' (Rev. 21:5).

Summary

Returning to our starting point we must conclude that personal regeneration in Titus 3:5 is part of the total picture which is implied by Matthew 19:28. The structure of NT theology suggests that there are at least three basic ways in which we must speak about this reality. They are not synonymous but they are linked in exactly the same way that justification, sanctification and glorification are linked: 1. *Objective regeneration*: this is the work of God in the person of Christ effected on our behalf. The new creation is where Christ is and it is imputed to all who believe in him. 2. *Subjective regeneration*: this is the sovereign work of the Holy Spirit in the believer as the Christian life begins and continues to its consummation. 3. *Comprehensive regeneration*: this is the renewal of all things, the corollary of the renewal of believers (Rom. 8:19–23). It is the fullness of the kingdom of God.

See also: HOLY SPIRIT.

Bibliography

H. Burkhardt, *The Biblical Doctrine of Regeneration* (Exeter, 1978); G. Goldsworthy, *According to Plan: The Unfolding Revelation of God in the Bible* (Leicester and Homebush West, 1991); P. Toon, *Born Again: A Biblical and Theological Study of Regeneration* (Grand Rapids, 1987).

G. GOLDSWORTHY

REJOICING, see JOY
RELATIONSHIP OF THE OLD AND NEW TESTAMENTS, see Part 1

REMNANT

OT terminology

In biblical history, the idea of a remnant goes back to Genesis, where only *Noah 'was left' (Gen. 7:23). The theme of a righteous *seed left over after the violent destruction of the many people was a common one in the ancient Near East. The threat to humanity's existence is answered by the assurance of the divine *salvation of the remnant. Thus L. V. Meyer defines remnant as 'what is left of a community after it undergoes a catastrophe' (*ABD* 6, p. 669). The same idea appears in the *Joseph story, where Joseph becomes saviour for the many (Gen. 45:7: 'God sent me before you to preserve for you a remnant on earth ...', NRSV). While the concept of remnant features occasionally in the Pentateuch, it is developed more fully in the prophetic writings.

The prophetic use

The context of the remnant idea is often that of *war; it can refer to return from battle and thus to survival in war (see 1 Kgs. 22:28; Jer. 23:3; Is. 10:22; *cf.* M. E. W. Thompson, *Situation and Theology*, pp. 23–28). In Amos 7:2 the prophet cries (after his vision of locusts devouring the grass): 'O Lord GOD, forgive, I beg you! How can Jacob stand? He is so small!' Since defeat at the hands of their enemies is frequently a means of divine punishment for *Israel, the nation's progressive diminution effectively means that the ethnic community becomes the 'ethical community', not only in Amos but also in the OT as a whole.

The tension between divine salvation and *judgment for Israel is resolved in the sense that belonging to the 'remnant' means survival. Amos holds out this small hope after warning that *God will be like a shepherd who tears away a remnant – two legs or a piece of an ear out of the predator's mouth (3:12). But the term may point, not forward to the residue, but, backwards to the ruin in which it was created and to the nation of which it was only a part.

Isaiah 7:3 mentions the remnant of a defeated army; yet it is not the defeat of *Judah but of her *enemies* to which the name *Shear-yashub* (lit. 'a remnant will return') refers here. In contrast Isaiah 10:20 refers to those (of the northern kingdom of Israel) who will return to Zion, as 'the remnant of Jacob' (Is. 10:21); only a remnant will return to Yahweh in *faith. But this oracle does not necessarily exclude the possibility of an externally visible return of *exiles as the expression or reward of a inward spiritual 'return' to God in faith or *repentance. In Isaiah 10 the prophet describes judgment on Israel as a warning to Judah so that they may do better. The *Shear-yashub* oracle declares that only a few from the northern kingdom will survive to return in penitence. Micah 5:6–7 too notes that the exilic remnant will affect the *nations by being among them 'like dew' and 'like a lion', in other words for *blessing and judgment. In the darkness are whispers of hope.

The movement towards a more positive concept of 'remnant' continues with Jeremiah. He makes the remnant concept into a theological doctrine, employing the term *ytr* which here means simply 'residue' (the primary meaning of *ytr* is 'surplus') and not yet 'saved remnant', *i.e.* those who remain in Jerusalem after the two deportations as distinct from the exiles in Babylon. Yet *ytr* does not connote an antecedent loss; where it is used, that which is left over (the 'excess') is often too substantial to be called a 'mere residue' and is sufficiently important to merit attention and possess dignity. The idea of continuity is to the fore. Yet Jeremiah, especially in chapter 44, can also focus on doom, by (ironically?) using the term 'remnant' (*š⁽ᵉ⁾ērît*) to refer to those who go astray.

In exilic times the 'nothingness' of the remnant becomes something out of which God can create, as with Noah and his remnant. The 'remnant' is a bridge concept mediating between those of doom and salvation both semantically and in the narrative flow of Genesis. In the later prophets, judgment must precede restoration. For Ezekiel, the idea is that of the survival of a purified Israel; thus Ezekiel 20:38 uses 'remnant' to refer to Israel as a whole. 'Remnant' is a way of preserving the dialectic of judgment and possible salvation. In Isaianic theology the remnant has equally positive and negative significance, depending on the context. All that is required of the people is faith in Yahweh to intervene. This faith cannot be separated from moral *holiness with an accompanying sense of the divine presence;

possibly the people are to be a prophetic community. 'The comparison with the trees [Is. 6:13; *cf.* Job 14:7–9] was originally concerned with the destruction of the branches and trunks, and not with what happened to the stumps. The later writer saw that the mention of the stumps left open the possibility of survival and hope for the future' (J. A. Emerton, in *Interpreting the Hebrew Bible*, p. 115). There must be deportation as a sure sign of punishment before restoration can begin.

But in Isaiah 40 – 66 in particular the idea of a remnant of Israel as a holy group, the (post)-exilic 'prophetic community', is developed. The existence of post-exilic survivors means that the pessimistic idea of decimation and gloom is left well behind, as the community looks to a brighter future. Even in the latest works of the OT there is no sectarian focus, but rather a concern for 'Israel' as a whole. The remnant is no longer understood as a very small and precious group, but as a composite and imperfect nation comprising returnees from Babylon and other places, and those who stayed in Judea. Only in Zephaniah 3:12–13 is there an idea of the remnant as a purified and united community after the exile ('the remnant of Israel shall not do evil.'). Whereas 'remnant' is used in Jeremiah to denote those who stayed in Jerusalem, 'the remnant of the people' (author's translation) is used in Haggai (1:12, 14; 2:2) and Zechariah (8:6, 11–12) to refer to those returning from exile.

The expectation of the Messiah possibly became associated with the community, the place of the presence of salvation (*cf.* Mic. 5:7–8 and Is. 66:19). The 'remnant' does not take the place of the Messiah but rather is to be understood as preparing for and bringing in the messianic age (*cf.* Mic. 5:2). However, Ezra 9:8, 13–15 sounds the warning that even the remnant will not be spared should they *sin again. There will be no remnant of the remnant. It was the failure of Israel to live up to the ideal of the purified community and the consequently disappointed expectations about it that led to the ideal being projected onto the future Messiah, with the remnant as witnesses to him and to God's *mercy.

The NT: the Gospels

In gathering the remnant of Israel destined for salvation, John the Baptist called all Israel, not all Israelites. Yet the remnant community was open to all Israelites in 'the recognition that a summons addressed to all may well be answered only by some' (B. F. Meyer, in *JBL* 84, p. 128). Those whom John gathered formed a provisional grouping which did not trust in its own repentance, because it was too busy being sorrowful for its sins. Unlike *Sanhedrin* 10.1 (all Israel has a share in the Kingdom to come', or the Pharisaic polar opposite (membership of the saved no more than 6,000, according to Josephus in *Antiquities of the Jews* 17.42), the NT provides a middle way. The term 'remnant' is not used in the Gospels, but as Jesus' ministry encounters more rejection, the theology of the 'little flock' (Luke 12:32) is developed. Yet Matthew 22:14, 'Many(= all) are called; few (= not all) are chosen', conveys more strongly the idea of 'remnant as *elect' than its parallel in *4 Ezra* 8:3: ('Many have been created but few will be saved'). To be 'called' is to take up the initial invitation; to be 'chosen' is to persevere to the end'. Jesus did not intend to restore the remnant of Israel during his earthly ministry, because the end-times had not fully arrived (*cf.* the parable of the tares, Matt. 13:24–30). Jesus was not exclusive; people excluded themselves.

The NT: Paul

According to H. Räisänen, it is only by introducing the idea of the remnant that Paul can change direction in Romans 9:27 and introduce the positive tone of Romans 10 (in *The Social World*, p. 186). This verse recalls Isaiah 10:21, but surely in both cases, *pace* Räisänen, the tone is negative. Paul in Romans 9:29 goes on to suggest that the remnant is a seed which will take time to grow. The basis for this claim is Isaiah 1:9 ('if the LORD had not left over for us a few survivors'), but the LXX and Paul use *sperma*, which in NT usage has clear Christological reference. In Romans 11:1–5 God's new people are discontinuous only with Israel as conceived by Paul's contemporaries; with the historical Israel there is continuity – Paul and Jewish Christians are the remnant. This remnant carries the name and nature of Israel (11:1–10). The root and branches are perhaps to be identified, not with Israel, but rather with Christ as the one who gives *life from the dead (Rom. 11:15–18). Jesus is the Messiah from Israel who links the *church

and Israel. The mark of remnant membership is not law-keeping (*cf. 4 Ezra*) but the Isaianic 'faith' (*cf.* Is. 7:9). 'The Israel of God' (Gal. 6:16) is not ethnic Israel but all Israel who believes, and is thus open to the Gentiles, though based on the Jewish believers of OT and NT.

One OT passage not mentioned above is 1 Kings 19:14–18 in which Elijah complains that he alone is left (LXX *hypoleleimmai*), and the Lord corrects his prophet's reckoning; there are in fact 7,000 left. In Romans 11:5 'a remnant saved by *grace' refers to believing Jews like Paul himself; their number may be enlarged through Jewish 'jealousy' of Gentile believers. The Pauline concept of the remnant is 'not about the vindication of ethnic Israel as she stands but about *forgiveness of sins the other side of the cataclysmic judgement on the temple' (N. T. Wright, *The Climax of the Covenant*, p. 251), as distinct from that of the intertestamental literature which portrays Israel as 'God's true humanity'.

Revelation

In Revelation, especially in 11:13, the theme of 'remnant' is applied to the whole of *humanity. In this passage, Revelation reverses the usual arithmetic; only a tenth (seven thousand) suffer the judgment, while the remnant (*hoi loipoi*) who are spared are the nine-tenths. Not the faithful minority, but the faithless majority are spared, so that they may come to repentance and faith. Thanks to the witness of the witnesses, the judgment is actually salvific. In Revelation 19:21 'the rest' are those put to death; which perhaps implies that the majority are saved. In any case the message is inclusivist, unlike that of contemporary sectarianism (*cf. War Scroll* 14:8–9: 'The remnant of thy people Israel').

Bibliography

R. J. Bauckham, *The Climax of Prophecy* (Edinburgh, 1993); R. E. Clements, '"A remnant chosen by grace" (Rom 11:5): The Old Testament background and origin of the remnant concept in Pauline studies', in *FS F. F. Bruce* (Exeter, 1980); *idem*, *š'r* in *TWAT* 6, pp. 933–950 (ET forthcoming); J. A. Emerton, 'The translation and interpretation of Is vi. 13' in J. A. Emerton and S. C. Reif (eds.), *Interpreting the Hebrew Bible: Essays in Honour of E. I. J. Rosenthal* (Cambridge, 1982); G. F. Hasel, *The Remnant: the History* and *Theology of the Remnant Idea from Genesis to Isaiah*, (Berrien Springs, 1972); T. Kronholm, '*ytr*', in *TDOT* 6, pp. 483–491; B. F. Meyer, 'Jesus and the remnant of Israel', *JBL* 84, 1965, pp. 123–130; *idem*, *The Aims of Jesus* (London, 1979); *idem*, 'Many (=All) are called, but Few (=Not All) are chosen', *NTS* 36, 1990, pp. 89–97; L. V. Meyer, 'Remnant', in *ABD* 6, pp. 69–71; H. Raïsanen, 'God, Paul and Israel: Romans 9–11 in Recent Research', in J. Neusner *et al.*, *The Social World of Formative Christianity and Judaism* (Philadelphia, 1988); M. E. W. Thompson, *Situation and Theology: Old Testament Interpretations of the Syro-Ephremite War* (Sheffield, 1984); *idem*, 'Remnant', in *IDBSup*, pp. 735–736; N. T. Wright, *The Climax of the Covenant: Christ and the Law in Pauline Theology* (Edinburgh, 1991).

M. W. ELLIOTT

REPENTANCE

The biblical notion of repentance refers to the radical turning away from anything which hinders one's wholehearted devotion to God, and the corresponding turning to God in *love and *obedience.

Repentance in the OT

With only a few exceptions (*e.g.* Jonah 3:10; Is. 19:22), repentance is associated in the OT with God's chosen people. Thus one should understand the concept, usually expressed metaphorically by the Hebrew verb 'to turn' (*šûb*), to be grounded in the gracious *covenant that God had previously established with Israel (Dan. 9:3–14; 2 Chr. 7:14a, 17–18; Neh. 1:5–7). Since the people who entered into this covenant were to reflect God's nature (Lev. 19:2; 20:22–26; Deut. 10:12–13), their turning away in unbelief and unfaithfulness implies a personal rejection of him (Deut. 4:23; 11:16; 1 Sam. 15:11; 1 Kgs. 9:6; 2 Chr. 7:19, 22; Ps. 51:4; Jer. 11:10; 34:13–16). In response to the people's *sin, God is presented as similarly turning away from them, bringing about the realization of the covenant curses (*e.g.* Deut. 4:15–28; 30:15–20; Dan. 9:11–14). But these curses are ultimately intended to move his people to repentance once again (Deut. 4:29–30; 1 Kgs. 8:33, 48). Thus, God initiates repentance

both through the call to remember the *blessings of the covenant and through the outworking of his covenantal justice (see *Righteousness, justice and justification) (Is. 44:22; 55:1–3; Neh. 9:26–31; Jer. 5:3; 29:10–14; 44:4–6).

Repentance therefore involves the turning away from those actions and attitudes that are offensive to God and his nature (1 Sam. 7:3; Jer. 4:1; Ezek. 14:6). It naturally includes the confession of sin, appropriately accompanied by mourning and regret (Joel 2:12–13; Jer. 3:13). Given the covenantal context, this is often expressed as 'turning back' to God, (which explains the frequent translation of *šûb* as 'return': Deut. 30:2; 2 Chr. 30:6–9; Is. 31:6; Jer. 3:22; 31:18–19; Lam. 3:40; Hos. 6:1; 14:1–2, NIV). While the condition of the heart is hardly ever explicitly discussed in the legislation governing *sacrifices for sin, the implicit assumption is that the offerers have humbled their hearts before God. This is confirmed elsewhere in the OT, where a sacrifice without a contrite heart is considered to be offensive to God and even sin (Amos 4:4–6; Hos. 6:6; Pss. 40:6–8; 51:16–17; 1 Sam. 15:22; Prov. 15:8; 21:3). Conversely, true repentance generates acceptable sacrifice (Ps. 51:18–19).

The behaviour resulting from true repentance is covenant love, purity and obedience that comes from the heart (see *e.g.* Deut. 30:6, 8, 10). The merciful divine benefits given in response to repentance include the *forgiveness (see *Mercy/compassion) of sin and the restoration of the covenant relationship (Deut. 4:30–31; 2 Chr. 7:13–16; Ps. 51:7–12; Is. 55:7; Jer. 15:19–21; 32:37–41; Ezek. 18:21–23; Hos. 14:5–8; Mal. 3:7, 10–12).

Repentance in the NT

*John the Baptist and Jesus repeat the OT covenantal call for repentance. In the NT the scope of this call becomes universal as the church goes out in mission to all nations (Matt. 28:18–20; Acts 1:8; 17:30; 2 Pet. 3:9). All have turned away from God (Rom. 3:9–18), so there is a universal need for the corresponding turning away from sin (Rom. 2:5–10; 2 Cor. 12:21) and to God (1 Thess. 1:9; Acts 14:15; 15:19; 1 Pet. 2:25). This notion is communicated principally through cognate words (*metanoeō / metanoia*) which express the complete reorientation of the person, although a verb which means 'turning' (epistrephō) is also used. As in the OT, God is understood to be the initiator of repentance both through the threat of *judgment and the gift of his *grace (cf. 2 Tim. 2:24–25).

Both John the Baptist and Jesus proclaim the need for repentance in light of the impending judgment associated with the kingdom's arrival (Luke 3:7, 9, 17; 13:1–5; Matt. 11:20–24; 12:39–42) – only those who have turned from their sinful ways will be forgiven (Luke 3:3; 7:47–50; 19:9; Mark 1:4; 9:45; cf. Acts 3:19; 5:30–31; 2 Tim. 2:24–25). Similar calls for repentance from sin can be found throughout the NT, often associated with the threat of judgment (Acts 3:19–26; 8:20–24; 14:15; 17:30–31; Rev. 2:5, 16; 3:3; 9:20–21; 16:9–11; cf. also Heb. 6:4–6).

But Jesus frequently presents the gracious goodness of God as the reason for repentance. Since with him the kingdom had already arrived in an inaugurated form (Matt. 12:28; 13:24–30, 33; Mark 4:26–32), salvific power was being mediated through his ministry, liberating people from Satan's stronghold (Matt. 12:29). Thus, Jesus' demand for repentance stresses God's covenantal grace, for he is its fulfilment and embodiment. Accordingly, Jesus' association with such despised groups as the tax collectors and harlots (Luke 7:37–50; 19:1–10; Mark 2:13–17) shows that he has come to seek out the lost (Luke 19:10; 15:4–32; Mark 2:17). Appropriately, then, *joy and celebration are often associated with repentance in Jesus' proclamation, evincing the grace which is its context (Matt. 13:44; 22:1–10; Luke 5:27–29; 19:6, 8; cf. also Rom. 2:4; Acts 9:35; 11:18, 21). Mourning and regret are also found, however (Luke 7:37–50; 15:17–20; 18:13–14; cf. 2 Cor. 7:9–10).

See also: HARDENING.

Bibliography

U. Becker et al. in NIDNTT 1, pp. 353–362; J. Behm and E. Würthwein in TDNT 4, pp. 975–1008; L. Goppelt, Theology of the New Testament, vol. 1, (Grand Rapids, 1981) pp. 77–138.

J. M. LUNDE

REQUIREMENT, see LAW

REST

In the OT the thematic treatment of the idea of rest consists of two main strands: the *sabbath rest (from routine labour) and the promise of rest (from wandering/journeying or enemy threat) in the land of Canaan. These two strands are combined in two NT passages that discuss the idea of rest thematically, namely Matthew 11:28–30 and Hebrews 3 – 4. The idea of rest appears in various other OT and NT passages.

Work

The language of Genesis 2:4–7 implies that *humanity's role will include the cultivation of the ground, especially irrigation. Further, Genesis 2:15 has Adam placed in the garden 'to work it and take care of it' (NIV), evidently as part of the dominion mandate in Genesis 1:26–28. Although it is possible to interpret the Hebrew of Genesis 2:15 as referring not to work as such but rather to 'work'-service, i.e. worship (e.g. J. Sailhamer, Genesis Unbound [Sisters, 1996], pp. 75–77), most interpreters understand the verse as a directive to cultivate the garden and keep (guard; cf. the use of the same verb in Gen. 3:24) it. Work is intrinsic to created human existence, reflecting the divine pattern of work and rest. A fundamentally positive view of work, including manual labour, is thus presupposed. (In the NT see Acts 20:34; 1 Thess. 4:11; 2 Thess. 3:6–13.) If, as seems likely, the garden is 'an archetypal sanctuary, prefiguring the later tabernacle and temples' (G. J. Wenham, Genesis 1–15, p. 61, cf. p. 67), then just as with the priests' service in the temple, Adam's 'work' in the garden would not have been something separate from his worship, and his 'guarding' function may have involved controlling access to and preserving the purity of the garden. But the idea found in the ancient Near Eastern myths about creation, that humanity was created to relieve the gods of undesirable labour, is nowhere present in Genesis. When *God completes his work, which is not portrayed as in any way wearisome or otherwise undesirable, he rests (Gen. 2:1–3). Humanity's labour does not function to meet any need in the deity.

The curse of Genesis 3:17–19 introduces a new phase of human work. The original couple's task (Gen. 2:15), evidently continuous with the earlier mandate (Gen. 1:28), takes on a new urgency (as they seek to survive in the face of certain death to come), which is coupled with the unprecedented experience of pain, difficulty, fruitlessness and recalcitrance. Humanity's sin has brought God's curse upon the ground (*cf.* also Gen. 5:29; 8:21–22 uses a different Hebrew word), which means that its fertility will be withheld from humanity, and the original couple are now expelled from the garden sanctuary into the outer regions, while the function of 'guarding' the garden is seemingly transferred from humanity to the cherubim and flaming sword (Gen. 3:24). Manual work itself is not made an evil, nor are the positive aspects of work (*e.g.* the enjoyment it can give) denied. Rather, a realistic view is taken of the experiences of painful toil and futility that have been characteristic of human existence ever since. Even at its best, work is bitter-sweet; this serves as a constant reminder of Genesis 2 – 3. Cain's sin brings a curse on him in Genesis 4:10–16 (in Adam's case the curse is on the 'ground'; the passage exhibits syntactical differences from, and similarities to, Gen. 3:17–24), with the result that his agricultural work is completely frustrated. Then the naming of Noah in connection with the curse on the ground (Gen. 5:29) evidently anticipates the deliverance that comes through him culminating in the divine speech of Genesis 8:20 – 9:17 (note the oath and *blessing referring to agriculture in Gen. 8:20–22) and probably the line of descent extending through Shem to Abraham.

The Edenic arrangement is paradigmatic for *redemption. When *Israel enters Canaan, the land is described in terms reminiscent of Eden, not least in its depiction as a banquet and lodging place, for which the people did not need to work, but which they are free to enjoy (Deut. 6:10–12), although of course the Israelites will work this fruitful land to their profit, and this too is a gift (Deut. 8:6–18). When Isaiah looks ahead to a reversal of the curse (though there is no reversal for the serpent), he describes it in terms of fruitful work rather than workless-ness (Is. 65:17–25). Ezekiel's vision of the new temple and the river proceeding from it includes fishermen at work and fruit trees producing fruit apparently without cultivation (Ezek. 47:7–12). Likewise, NT pictures

of salvation are of a place and a banquet prepared for the disciples (*e.g.* John 14:1–4; Rev. 19 – 22; *cf.* Rev. 22:2, recalling Ezek. 47 and Gen. 2 – 3). In these and other passages connected with divine *salvation the imagery is mixed, but at least in the OT passages human work in some form is regarded as consistent with the desired state of salvation.

After Genesis 3 human work takes novel forms (Gen. 4:2, 17, 19–22; 11:13), not all of which are legitimate (*e.g.* *warfare and associated *violence [Gen. 4:8, 23–24; 6:5, 11]) although the development of new forms of work is itself legitimate. Then in the account of the construction of the tabernacle, a tradition on which Paul may be drawing in 1 Corinthians 3:10, the divine bestowal of special skills is noted in connection with already existing forms of specialized labour (Exod. 31:1–11; 35:30 – 36:7). From passages such as the latter some might infer a generalized notion of individual 'callings' or 'vocations' (*e.g.* medical or domestic 'callings'), but this is hard to substantiate (W. J. Dumbrell, in *Crux* 24, p. 22).

A related theme is the interplay between divine provision and human responsibility. It is not discussed explicitly in Genesis 1 – 2 but is implied throughout the biblical narrative (*cf.* 2 Thess. 3:10; Matt. 6:11, 19–34). The continuing involvement of God in human work is reflected especially in his *covenantal relations: he blesses work (Deut. 2:7; 8:18; 14:29; 15:10; 2 Cor. 9:6–11; Job 1:10; *et passim*), or frustrates it (*e.g.* Deut. 28:15–48; Hag. 2:17) according to his purposes. An unbalanced focus on divine provision can lead to passivity; this tendency is corrected by Israel's sages, who emphatically favour indus-triousness and denounce laziness (*e.g.* Prov. 6:6–11; 10:4–5; 12:24; 13:4; 24:30–34; Matt. 25:26), though the relationship between diligence and success is not a simple one (Prov. 10:22; 16:1, 9), and there is more to life than a bounteous harvest resulting from one's labour (Prov. 15:16; 16:8).

Qoheleth (the Hebrew name used in Eccles. 1:12) would seem to agree with this view-point (Eccles. 4:5; 5:12; 11:6), but laments the meaninglessness of toil (*e.g.* 2:4–11). In the end, the ability to enjoy one's toil (or possibly the wealth acquired through toil) during life is what matters (Eccles. 2:24–25; 3:12–13, 22; 5:18–20; 8:15; 9:9–10). Interpreters have viewed this book in different ways, but according to T. Longman Qoheleth's outlook is expressive of the bitter experience of being denied this ability to enjoy his toil by God (*The Book of Ecclesiastes*, pp. 122f.), and Qoheleth's speculative, doubting wisdom is not endorsed by the author of the book, whose words frame Qoheleth's (Eccles. 1:1–11; 12:8–14). Qoheleth's 'hopelessness is the result of the curse of the fall without recourse to God's redemption' (Longman, *Ecclesiastes*, p. 39; he notes that Qoheleth's language seems to reflect that of Gen. 3). Another possible reading would be that Qoheleth's outlook *is* endorsed in the book; its real focus is on the value of a God-centred life over against the meaninglessness that results if life is centred elsewhere (*cf.* J. Walton, in A. E. Hill and J. Walton (eds.), *A Survey of the Old Testament* [Grand Rapids, 1991], p. 296).

There are references to mundane human work in the NT: to the occupations of Jesus and his disciples; in Jesus' parables; in the Baptist's preaching; and in Paul's practice and teaching. Mundane work is to be used in the service of the word (Acts 18:3; 1 Cor. 4:12; 7:29–31; 9:15–18; 2 Cor. 11:7–12; 12:14–15; 1 Thess. 4:11–12; 2 Thess. 3:6–13; 1 Tim. 5:3–16; *cf.* Eph. 4:28). The work of God and the work of redeemed humanity thus converge and move toward a common goal (John 5:17; Matt. 6:19–34). Such labour will not be in vain (1 Cor. 15:58).

Rest

Literal and figurative uses of the idea of rest are so widespread and varied in the biblical literature that it behoves us to restrict our discussion to two thematic strands in the OT before tracing their development by the NT writers.

The OT

1. *Sabbath.* The OT sabbath is a day free of work, a day on which even the slave can rest, just as God himself had been refreshed on the seventh day of creation (Gen. 2:2–3; Exod. 20:8–11; 23:12; 31:17; Deut. 5:12–15).

From early times work stopped on the seventh day to allow time for cultic activities, for rest and restoration, and in all of this, for undistracted reflection on creation, the Creator and humanity's place in the world. For this reason the sabbath was extended to slaves and beasts of burden (Exod. 20:10;

23:12; Deut. 5:14). As a result, 'on this day "the servant would walk side by side with his master," the rich would not become richer, and the poor would not become poorer' (N.-E Andreasen, *The Old Testament Sabbath*, p. 293). Yahweh's gift of 'rest in the land' (see below) would thus be realized for the whole community on each seventh day. The land's rest during its sabbaths (*cf.* Lev. 25; 16:31; 23:32; *cf.* Is. 61) functioned similarly: to remind the Israelites that the land was Yahweh's, that he was sovereign over it and them and that they lived in dependence on him. Even the weekly sabbath, inasmuch as it compelled the Israelites to stop working the ground, served as a reminder that the land was Yahweh's. In other words, the sabbaths were a way of teaching Israel that one 'does not live by bread alone but on every word that comes from the mouth of the LORD' (Deut. 8:3).

God's sabbath rest in Genesis 2:2–3 has the narrative function of concluding the creation account and is elsewhere cited as the basis of Israel's sabbath (Exod. 31:12–17; 20:8–11), possibly reflecting the idea that in the land God restores that which was lost in the garden. In Genesis 2, 'the creator, having completed his work, is at rest ... The whole creation is thus also at rest on the seventh day, a day characterized by completion, sanctity, and blessing' (Andreasen, *Sabbath*, p. 225). There is no clear indication that humanity shares directly in God's primordial sabbath, though the fact that he blesses and sanctifies 'the seventh day' suggests that the very work of creation, of which humanity is a part, reaches its climax then. Further, the notion of an '*eschatological Sabbath,' *i.e.* the rabbinic and Christian idea that the anticipated era of salvation would be a day that is 'wholly sabbath and rest for eternity' (*Mishnah Tamid* 7:4; *cf. Epistle of Barnabas* 15), is not formulated in so many words in the OT, but it seems to be rooted in the several ways in which the OT's eschatological hopes are expressed using sabbatical imagery (J. Laansma, *'I Will Give You Rest'*, pp. 65–67).

2. *The Rest Tradition.* A very important OT theme is Yahweh's gift of 'rest' to his people, from journeying or warfare, in the *land of promise, Israel's 'resting place'. This theme constitutes a powerful affirmation of Yahweh's continuing *faithfulness – as well

as being associated with Israel's faithfulness – and is a summary of his good gifts to his *people. In no way is the image one of blissful inactivity; rather it is one of unhampered constructive activity.

Deuteronomy speaks of the centralization of worship (12:9–10): when Yahweh gives his people rest from their enemies they will be obliged to take their offerings to the 'place' he chooses. This theme recedes somewhat, though not entirely, in Joshua (Josh. 23:1; *cf.* 21:44), before becoming central in 2 Samuel 7:1, 11, 1 Kings 5:3–5, and finally 1 Kings 8:56 in the context of *Solomon's dedication of the *temple (*cf.* Deut. 25:17–19; 28:65; Exod. 33:14). Elsewhere (*e.g.* 2 Chr. 6:41; Ps. 132:8, 14; *cf.* Num. 10:33–36) the link with the temple is strengthened by its designation as Yahweh's 'resting place'. Because this joining of themes is associated with *David and Solomon a strong connection is formed with the Davidic dynasty; this too is anticipated in Deuteronomy 12. With Solomon's dedication of the temple in 1 Kings 8 the unfolding of this theme reaches its climax.

The link between the Davidic dynasty and the rest motif is strengthened in Chronicles, where rest is associated even more closely with Solomon, a 'man of rest', than with David (*cf.* 1 Chr. 22:9, 18; 23:25; 28:2; *cf.* 6:31; 2 Chr. 6:41). In Chronicles this theme is taken up in connection with kings subsequent to Solomon, but they are all of the Davidic dynasty (2 Chr. 14:1, 5–6; 15:15; 20:30; *cf.* 32:22, where there is a textual problem). In the context of the Chronicler's theology of immediate retribution, the rest tradition is associated very strongly with covenant fidelity and 'seeking Yahweh.' Moreover, as was noted above, the idea of 'Yahweh's resting place' – the temple – becomes prominent, especially in the quote from Psalm 132 in the account of the temple's dedication (2 Chr. 6:41; *cf.* also 1 Chr. 6:31; 28:2).

Psalm 95:11, which is important to the author of Hebrews, belongs to this tradition. 'Rest' here is a tangible good (rather than a personal entering into God); so also in the closely related Psalm 81 (esp. Ps. 81:13–16). The psalm's oath therefore sums up the covenantal blessings promised to God's people – blessings of secure life in the land – which were bound up with God's presence among them. In its use of the perpetually present directive – '*today* if you hear his voice' – long after the occupation of the land, the text seems to contain an element of promise.

In the prophetic books of Isaiah (esp. 11:10; 14:3, 7; 28:12; 32:18; 63:14; 66:1), Jeremiah (esp. 6:16; 31:2; 50:34), Lamentations (1:3; 5:5) and Micah (2:10) many of the above ideas continue to appear, but new elements are present too. The loss of rest is a powerful symbol of God's *judgment; rest is an element of the prophets' eschatological *hope; it points towards šālôm ('peace'; *cf.* e.g. Is. 11:1–10; 32:17–18); and it is more closely connected with social justice, being the responsibility of the Israelites towards one another.

Although there is no direct or explicit link between the rest tradition and the theme of the OT sabbath rest, there are strong indications that the two themes are related in the OT. It is possible, then, that the association between Genesis 2 and Psalm 95 found in Hebrews 3 – 4 dates from the OT period, though this cannot be demonstrated.

The NT

1. *Matthew 11:28–30.* Matthew associates Jesus' promise of rest (*anapausis*) in Matthew 11:28–30 most directly with his Son of David Christology, under the influence of the OT rest tradition (for close OT parallels to the phrasing of Matt. 11:28–30 see Exod. 33:14; Jer. 6:16 [Heb.]; Ezek. 34:15 [LXX]; 2 Sam. 7:11 [LXX]; Deut. 5:33 [LXX]; Jer. 31:25 [Heb.]). The narrative of 1 Samuel 21:1 – 22:23 contains more than one parallel to Matthew 11 – 12 (1 Sam. 21:1–6 and Matt. 12:3–4; 1 Sam 22:2 and Matthew 11:28–30). The temple saying of Matthew 12:6 may be explained in terms of the OT complex of rest, Davidic dynasty and temple. Moreover, Matthew's placing of the rest saying just after an allusion to Isaiah 61 (Matt. 11:4–6; Is. 61 is phrased in terms of the sabbatical year of jubilee) and immediately before two sabbath controversies (Matt. 12:1–14) suggests that the idea of the sabbath rest was in his mind as well. Thus he blends the two primary OT traditions relating to rest (*cf.* Heb. 3 – 4), and connects them to the present and ultimately future work of the Messiah.

In the OT the promise of rest had a fairly extended range of application, depending on the circumstances in view; so also in Matthew the promise is shaped by the earthly ministry of the humble *king, the Son of David. As the ultimate Son of David, *Jesus announces the awaited rest, thereby claiming to bring to fulfilment Yahweh's OT promise. Soteriologically, this amounts to a claim that the total salvation God promised his people is being realized through Jesus as Messiah. Christologically, in promising rest Jesus stands in the place reserved for Yahweh in the OT. Oppressive forces once again threaten to overcome the powerless among God's people; Jesus in response uses an OT expression for Yahweh's salvation, but makes the promise in his own name. Ecclesiologically, Matthew views the Jesus movement as a 'new people' in some sense over against Judaism (cf. Matt. 21:43; G. Stanton, *A Gospel for a New People: Studies in Matthew* [Edinburgh, 1992]), and in view of its OT background, Matthew 11:28–30 could be read as announcing the formation of a new community. The OT promise of salvation takes on a new universality (it is no longer restricted to Israel), and particularity (it is conditional on coming to the Son).

2. *Hebrews 3 – 4*. In the context of a passionate warning against apostasy and an exhortation to listen obediently to God's definitive proclamation, the author of *Hebrews uses Psalm 95:11 in his Christ-centered discussion of God's OT promise. Behind the warning in Hebrews 3 – 4 stands the narrative of Numbers 14, which records the rebellion of the Israelites at Kadesh, but the author finds in Psalm 95:11 a reference to a heavenly and future salvation, a resting place (*katapausis*; the idea of place is found throughout this passage). Behind the offer made to the generation of Numbers 14, and in the implied offer of this psalm, he sees *one* promise, of entrance into God's own resting place at the time of Jesus' parousia. Joshua did not lead the second generation into *this* resting place; entry was denied until the completion of the ages. Only at that time would the heir of all things mediate the new covenant so that the faithful of all ages might together receive the promised eternal inheritance. Thus when the faithful community enters God's resting place at the parousia of Christ, it will finally be able to participate in the great sabbath *celebration* (this, rather than sabbath *rest*, is the meaning of *sabbatismos* in Heb. 4:9) around God's

throne (*cf*. Heb. 12:22–24); it will rest from the labours of a faithful life in this world (*e.g.* Heb. 6:10). In view of the irreversible destruction of the entire community because of the rebellion of a few at Kadesh, the author warns his community to respond differently: they must guard not only themselves as individuals but also one another, and in this way make every effort to enter together into God's resting place. The advent of the Son has brought the history of redemption to its climax. Unless the new covenant community recognizes that it stands at 'the end of the ages' (Heb. 9:26; *cf*. 1:1–2), and realizes the peril of refusing to obey the Son, the goal of that history will be denied to it.

3. *Other NT passages*. The rest motif became a feature of Jewish apocalyptic literature. It is therefore not surprising that it should appear in Revelation 14:13, (*cf. 4 Ezra* 7:88–94). This passage is concerned with the intermediate state as a foretaste of the final rest. The saints' works bring them a *reward. Their obedient service is ended; they enjoy rest and the fruit of their labours while the wicked have unrest and torment (Rev. 14:11–13; 2:2, 19, 23; 3:1–2, 8, 15; 22:12; *cf*. Heb. 3:6, 14; 4:10; 6:10; 10:36). 2 Thessalonians 1:7 draws on a similar apocalyptic tradition, and Acts 3:19–20 associates future 'seasons of refreshment' (*anapsyxis*) with the sending of the Christ and the 'restoration' of all things (*cf*. Acts 1:6–8; 3:21). The promise of rest is universalistic, but a nationalistic element is retained, *e.g.* in the word 'first' in Acts 3:26. The association of rest with the sending of the Messiah (Acts 3:20) recalls the OT connection between the Davidic dynasty and rest. The reference to the heavenly session of Christ and the exhortation to listen carefully to the prophet like Moses recall Hebrews.

Even closer to Hebrews is the speech of Stephen in Acts 7 (esp. Acts 7:49–50). A comparison of Acts 7:44–50 and Hebrews with reference to Isaiah 66 and other OT passages (Exod. 25:40; Ps. 132:4–5) strongly suggests some kind of connection. However, the exegesis and theology of Stephen's speech undergo several changes before their re-emergence in Hebrews.

The idea of an eschatological sabbath rest is found in John 5:17, where Jesus speaks of God's continuing sabbath activity, an idea familiar to the Jews (Philo, *De Cherubim* 86–90; *Legum Allegoriae* I:5f., 18; *cf*. also

Exodus Rabbah 30:9; *Genesis Rabbah* 11:10; *Babylonian Talmud Ta'anit* 2a), to justify *his* activity of making people whole on the Sabbath. The points of contact with Matthew 12:1–14 are obvious: Jesus, the Lord of the sabbath, rightly observes the sabbath by making people whole (*cf.* likewise Luke 13:10–17). It may be, then, that the phrase 'until now' (John 5:17; NIV 'to this very day') points to the day of resurrection, when the divine work of salvation will be completed and the sabbath will truly begin (O. Cullmann, *Early Christian Worship* [ET, Philadelphia, 1953], pp. 88–92). In this same vein, Luke 4:18–19 has been interpreted as a presentation of Jesus' ministry in terms of the OT year of jubilee, though some question whether Luke understood Isaiah 61 in this way.

There are various other allusions to mundane rest or refreshment in the NT (*e.g.* Mark 6:31; 1 Cor. 16:18; Philem. 7; 20; 2 Tim. 1:16), and some passages may picture salvific rest without naming it as such (*e.g.* Luke 16:22–23). While many Jewish Christians doubtless continued to observe the sabbath during the apostolic age, this was probably not normative, and the observance of the Lord's day was a quite separate practice. During the apostolic period the Lord's day was neither a Christian sabbath nor a day of rest.

Bibliography

N.-E. Andreasen, *The Old Testament Sabbath: A Tradition-Historical Investigation* (Missoula, 1972); D. A. Carson (ed.), *From Sabbath to Lord's Day* (Grand Rapids, 1982); W. J. Dumbrell, 'Creation, Covenant, and Work', *Crux* 24, 1988, pp. 14–24; O. Hofius, *Katapausis: Die Vorstellung vom endzeit-lichen Ruheort im Hebräerbrief* (Tübingen, 1970); E. Käsemann, *The Wandering People of God* (ET, Minneapolis, 1984); J. Laansma, *'I Will Give You Rest'* (Tübingen, 1997); T. Longman III, *The Book of Ecclesiastes*, NICOT (Grand Rapids and Cambridge, 1998); G. von Rad, *The Problem of the Hexateuch and Other Essays* (ET, London, 1966); G. Robinson, 'The origin and develop-ment of the Old Testament sabbath. A comprehensive exegetical approach' (Diss., Hamburg, 1975); R. B. Sloan, *The Favorable Year of the Lord: A Study of Jubilary Theology in the Gospel of Luke* (Austin, 1977); M. J. Suggs, *Wisdom, Christology, and Law in Matthew's Gospel* (Cambridge, MA, 1970); G. J. Wenham, *Genesis 1–15*, WBC (Waco, 1987).

J. C. LAANSMA

RESTORATION, see CREATION
RESURRECTION, see DEATH AND RESURRECTION

REVELATION

Revelation is the disclosure by *God of truths at which people could not arrive without divine initiative and enabling. The ubiquity and centrality of revelation are considerably more impressive than statistical study alone implies (though the NIV has nearly a hundred occurrences of the word or its cognates), and analysis of revelation in the Bible must extend beyond the use of the word. The Bible does not so much discuss or reflect on revelation as assume, embody, and convey it. The phenom-enon and concept as presented in Scripture can be discussed under the following head-ings: 1. types of revelation; 2. the means of revelation; 3. the stages of revelation; 4. the authority of revelation; and 5. the goals of revelation.

Types of revelation

In one sense God's disclosure of himself is as universal as *creation itself: 'The heavens declare the glory of God; the skies proclaim the work of his hands' (Ps. 19:1, NIV). Merely by observation of the natural *world, Job should have known better than to call God's ways into question (Job 38, 40). The things God has created, as people live in symbiotic dependence on them, reveal God's being and even aspects of his nature: 'Since the creation of the world God's invisible qualities – his eternal power and divine nature – have been clearly seen, being understood from what has been made, so that men are without excuse' (Rom. 1:20). *Jesus reasoned from the natural order to *truth about God: 'See how the lilies of the field grow ... If that is how God clothes the grass of the field, which is here today and tomorrow is thrown into the fire, will he not much more clothe you, O you of little faith?' (Matt. 6:28, 30). Theologians give the name 'natural revelation' to knowledge of God that in theory all people everywhere are capable of inferring from the phenomena of nature and human experience.

Yet the same biblical writers who posit a natural or universal revelation of God point also to a special or particular revelation. The psalmist who lauds creation's light speaks in still more glowing terms of God's law: 'The law of the LORD is perfect, reviving the soul' (Ps. 19:7). Nature alone, or unaided human apprehension of it, may point to God, but they do not mediate what the soul requires for *salvation: saving knowledge of God. Job's culpable ignorance was removed only when hearsay was superseded by direct, divinely disclosed, and personally appropriated knowledge (Job 42:5). Paul implies that while natural knowledge of God, the kind of knowledge common to world religions generally, is sufficient to prompt humans to affirm God's being and to seek him and to sense their guilt before him, that knowledge is insufficient to bring about reconciliation with him (Rom. 1 – 3). Jesus speaks in prayer of God's revealing heavenly truths to his followers, who presumably would have otherwise remained ignorant of them (Matt. 11:25, 27). He explicitly attributes Peter's recognition of his Messiahship to God's revelatory activity and not to Peter's reasoning alone (Matt. 16:17).

It is special revelation, divine disclosure of verities leading to saving knowledge of God (or, if such knowledge is spurned, to particularly harsh judgment by God [Ps. 7:12–16; Luke 10:13–14; 12:47; Heb. 4:2–3]), that is the main focus of the Bible. This revelation is made known by various means.

The means of revelation

The writer to the Hebrews declares, 'In the past God spoke to our forefathers through the prophets at many times and in various ways' (1:1). God's saving self-disclosure has taken various forms. These may be divided into two types: *word and deed. A subset of the latter is denoted by the word '*theophany'. A theophany occurs when God's presence is made visible and recognizable as a divine self-disclosure. It is not an appearance of God the Father in his essential being, whom no one can see this side of heaven (John 1:18; 1 Tim. 6:16), but it is a manifestation so fully revelatory of God that it bears his own authority and name. The Bible records appearances of

the theophanic Angel of the Lord to Hagar (Gen. 16:7), to Abraham (Gen. 18; 22:11–12), to Jacob (Gen. 32:29–30), to Moses (Exod. 3:2–6), to Joshua (Josh. 5:14–15), to Gideon (Judg. 6:11–14) and to David (1 Chr. 21:16, 18, 27) among others. This figure exercises divine functions such as predicting the future (Gen. 16:10–12), forgiving sin (Exod. 23:21) and receiving worship (Exod. 3:5; Judg. 13:9–20), yet is clearly distinguished from God. In the history of interpretation some have understood these appearances as not merely God-disclosures but specifically Christ-disclosures, or Christ-ophanies, pre-incarnate manifestations of the Son of God. Other instances of theophanic revelation include God's presence in Eden (Gen. 3:8), his presence with his people during the *Exodus (Exod. 13:21–22; 14:19, 24, etc.) and at Sinai (Exod. 24:15–18; 34:5), and his Shekinah glory in the tabernacle (Exod. 40:34–35) and later in the Jerusalem *temple at the time of Solomon (1 Kgs. 8:11; 2 Chr. 5:13–14).

A second means of divine revelation in deed is miracle. It is revelation not primarily as 'wonder', evoking awe, but as a *sign calling people to acknowledge and draw near to God. Both OT and NT record miracles, though neither lapses into a sensationalist preoccupation with them; God and his saving purposes remain the principal concern. The NT mentions nearly forty miracles performed by Christ alone, such as healings, exorcisms, acts of power over atmospheric disturbances, and resuscitations of the dead, and records Jesus' own resurrection. The Gospels may omit more miracles than they relate in detail (John 20:30; 21:25). On relatively rare occasions miracles are also part of early church life as recorded in Acts and the epistles.

Revelation occurs in the Bible also through dreams. Here God's deed, in granting the dream, and his word, in speaking through it, are combined. God guided Joseph and Mary through dreams before and during Jesus' infancy (Matt. 1:20; 2:12–13, 19, 22), and perhaps also touched the heart of Pontius Pilate's wife (Matt. 27:19). There are numerous OT instances of revelatory dreams: God appears to Abimelech (Gen. 20:3); Jacob (Gen. 28:12); Laban (Gen. 31:24); Joseph (Gen. 37:5, 9); Pharaoh (Gen. 41:1, cf. 41:32); Gideon (Judg. 7:13–15); Solomon (1

733

Kgs. 3:5); and Daniel (Dan. 7:1). The OT writers also speak of false dreaming, which is claimed by recipients to be revelatory but which is in fact deceptive and destructive of God's purposes (*e.g.* Is. 56:10; Jer. 23:25, 28).

Scripture also speaks of visions which, like dreams (*cf.* Num. 12:6), combine God's deed and word. Some visions are mere delusion (Is. 28:7; Jer. 14:14; 23:16; Ezek. 13:6; Zech. 10:2), but others are the means of major insight into God's workings and expectations for his people (*e.g.* Ezek. 1:1; 40:2). OT *prophets also received 'oracles' (or 'burdens', *maśśā'*) from God, usually warnings of disaster calling for immediate repentance (*e.g.* Is. 13:1; 14:28; 15:1; Nah. 1:1; Hab. 1:1; Zech. 9:1; Mal. 1:1). In the NT, visions are granted to Zechariah (Luke 1:22), Ananias (Acts 9:10), Paul (Acts 9:12; 16:9; 18:9), Cornelius (Acts 10:3), Peter (Acts 10:9–17) and John (Rev. 9:17).

Basil Mitchell has noted that 'behaviour unaccompanied by speech remains inherently ambiguous' (*The Making and Remaking of Revelation*, p. 182). God's revelatory acts in Scripture are important, but they need to be accompanied by revelatory words. While the exact processes by which God's words to Adam, Noah, Abraham, and many other OT figures were discerned, recorded and transmitted are not always clear, the overall claim of the OT writings to be mediating faithfully the very words and spoken will of God is undeniable. Even when David in the Psalms speaks *about* or *to* God (rather than using the formulaic 'thus says the Lord'), or when Solomon and others in Proverbs set forth wisdom rather than apodictic *law or prophecy in the most direct sense, the revelatory status of their writings may be affirmed by virtue of God's approval of the writers and of the substance of their utterances. The fact that the Son of God treats Scripture as revelation is not insignificant (J. Wenham, *Christ and the Bible*). When Paul refers to 'the oracles of God' (Rom. 3:2), and when Jesus and Peter refer to David's writings as coming through the *Holy Spirit by the mouth of David (Matt. 22:43; Acts 1:25, 30), they express the well-grounded conviction of God's people across many centuries that by God's direct act 'men spoke from God as they were carried along by the Holy Spirit' (2 Pet. 1:21), and that the Bible is the result.

Both Peter's statement above and Paul's reference to Scripture's God-breathed character (2 Tim. 3:16) refer most directly to the OT. But what are today called NT writings were viewed as divinely given, on a par with the OT oracles, at least as early as the AD 60s (2 Pet. 3:16). H. Ridderbos (*Redemptive History and the New Testament Scriptures*) has argued that the creation and recognition of NT writings by Jesus' disciples was one aim of his ministry and teaching. It is clear that from the time of 1 Clement (*c.* AD 95) and Papias (*c.* AD 95–110) at least some of the Gospels, 1 Corinthians, Hebrews, 1 Peter, and 1 John were in circulation, and that they were ranked alongside the OT writings well before the end of the 1st century. The appropriateness of this is supported by Paul's own high assessment of the God-given nature of his message (1 Thess. 2:13), the four Gospels' implicit and explicit claims to be recounting faithfully the truth of God's bodily and verbal self-disclosure in Jesus Christ, and the tone and content of the NT writings generally, all of which reflect an authorial consciousness of apostolic authority, even when their authors may not be apostles in the most thoroughgoing sense (Mark, Luke, the author of Hebrews, James, Jude).

The means of God's revelation are more complex and vast than we can comprehend (much less reconstruct in detail). They encompass a history and involve people of which we know only some parts. Yet evidence points to the Scriptures of Old and New Testament as very nearly congruent with 'revelation' in the sense of the revealed divine actions and words of God.

The stages of revelation

While it would be possible to attempt to draw fine distinctions between various eras in God's self-disclosure, from a NT point of view the decisive periods are simply BC and AD: 'In the past God spoke to our forefathers through the prophets at many times and in various ways ... but in these last days he has spoken to us by his Son' (Heb. 1:1–2). Despite the objections of modern writers like James Barr to the idea of 'revelation in history' (in *IDB*, pp. 746–749), it remains a defensible and necessary category for articulating the truths espoused by the biblical writers.

The foundational importance and abiding significance of OT revelation must not be minimized. Hundreds of NT quotations and thousands of allusions demonstrate the nature of what C. H. Dodd termed the OT substructure of NT belief. God's progressive self-disclosure in the time of Adam, Abraham, Moses, David, Isaiah, Daniel, and Ezra (to mention just a few prominent figures) came to comprise an enscripturated treasure, a monument to God's steadfastness in the past and a slowly accumulating record of his nearness to his people in the present. Even the writer to the Hebrews, who stresses Christ's supremacy over OT institutions, relies on (and assumes the truthfulness of) the accounts of God's OT dealings with the children of Abraham to make his case. Yet the OT ends with the promise of future deliverance: 'the sun of righteousness will rise with healing in its wings' (Mal. 4:2). Far from being a tacked-on appendix to OT revelation, Malachi's prophecy is related to other predictions of messianic deliverance which stretch back to the earliest times (see *e.g.* Gen. 3:15; 12:1–3; 49:10; Deut. 18:15; 2 Sam. 7; Pss. 2, 22, 110; Isa. 7:14; 9:1–7; 11; 53; Dan. 7:2–14; *etc.*).

God's personal self-disclosure to his people, largely though temporarily suspended after the completion of Malachi's ministry (see B. D. Sommers, in *JBL* 115, pp. 31–47), and renewed with the rebirth of prophecy in John the Baptist (Luke 3:2), reaches a climax in Jesus' own pronouncements, teachings, and presence. His use of 'amen' ('truly') (104 times in the Gospels, 50 of these in John where the 'amen' is always doubled) indicates that what follows is a transcendent word with unique authority. John's Gospel presents Jesus as speaking not his own words but the words of the one who sent him (12:49). Not only his words but his very being are divine in ultimate origin (John 16:30). All this implies a season of renewed divine revelation appropriate to the generation chosen to witness the onset of the fullness of the times (Gal. 4:4).

Revelation is an integrating component of the whole NT era. At the announcement of Jesus' birth in Luke's nativity narrative (1:26, 32, 35), John the Baptist says that he came 'that [Jesus] might be revealed to Israel' (John 1:31). Jesus is aware of the role of revelation in his followers' apprehension of his messianic and divine identity, sometimes actually using the word (Matt. 11:25, 27; 16:17) and at other times speaking of revelation parabolically, as in the parable of the sower: 'The secret of the kingdom of God has been given to you' (Mark 4:11). Jesus summarizes his ministry with the observation that he 'revealed' the Father to those whom the Father gave him (John 17:6). Apart from revelation the power of the *gospel history and its canonical recounting is inexplicable.

In Paul revelation is fundamental to the disclosure of the gospel, in which 'a *righteousness from God is revealed' (Rom. 1:17). His wrath (see *Anger) also is revealed (Rom. 1:18; 2 Thess. 1:7), and lends urgency to Paul's mission. Paul's whole gospel ministry, far from being based on his persuasiveness or power or on an historical accident, owes its effectiveness to revelation (Rom. 16:25–26; 1 Cor. 2:10). The '*mystery' (formerly hidden but now fully disclosed truth) that Paul proclaims 'was made known to [him] by revelation', and not to Paul only but 'to God's holy apostles and prophets' in general (Eph. 3:3, 5). Among these is Peter, who speaks of revelation primarily as future (1 Pet. 1:7, 13; 4:13). Yet revelation was involved in the disclosure of Christ to the prophets (1 Pet. 1:12), which is the foundation of both Jesus' ministry and the apostolic ministry. And revelation is for Peter an ongoing present fact: Jesus Christ 'was chosen before the creation of the world, but was revealed in these last times for your sake' (1 Pet. 1:20). This past-and-yet-future understanding of revelation undergirds the book of Revelation, given to John to make known the things to come, yet predicated on the conviction that Christ's future visible cosmic enthronement (see *Exaltation) will take place precisely because the 'righteous acts' of 'the Lord God Almighty ... have been revealed' (Rev. 1:1; 15:2–4).

Most evangelical theologians agree that revelation in the fullest sense of the term is now complete. Because of the finished nature of Christ's saving work and the uniqueness of the apostles and their associates, the possibility of further revelatory disclosure resulting in additions to Scripture is excluded. Yet the NT does not portray a dominical and apostolic age flooded with revelatory light, to be followed by a church age given over to darkness or dim memories of past glories. There remains a future element in Christ's revelation to be apprehended at his return 'on the day the Son of Man is revealed' (Luke 17:30; *cf.* Rom. 2:5). The darkness of the present world, which Scripture frankly acknowledges (Eph. 6:12), is offset by the first rays of the dawning future age (Rom. 13:11–12). Furthermore, the announcement of *redemption by God's *incarnate revelation in NT times is echoed in the preached word, *baptism, and the Lord's table (see *Sacred meals) 'until he comes' again (1 Cor. 11:26). While with the flowering and fading of earliest Christianity's witness the foundational voice of revelatory truth passed into history, the society it generated, like the truth it comprises, were not and cannot be silenced. Like revelation itself, the authority of revelation abides.

The authority of revelation

From the standpoint of biblical theology, revelation is not merely an interesting fact or even a major theological category. Far less is it an object of academic or political discussion, for example, between conservatives who see it as valid and unchanging and more liberal thinkers who recommend its ongoing revision in keeping with developing social or scientific standards of truth and relevance. It is rather a truth closely intertwined with several biblical convictions, all related to the authority of revelation, which give it its central place in the biblical writers' thinking. Without knowledge of these convictions the nature and importance of revelation as espoused in Scripture can be easily overlooked.

Revelation is authoritative because it is rooted in the very nature of God. Speaking of revelation Basil Mitchell has noted, 'Oxford colleagues may find it natural to think of a divine–human dialogue as a sort of never-ending tutorial in which a God of liberal sensibilities releases the truth in instalments with anxious care for the autonomy of the recipients, but this has little in common with the God of Abraham, Isaac, and Jacob' (in *Making and Remaking*, p. 185). The God of the biblical tradition is sovereign (see *Providence), in firm command of heaven and earth (Is. 40:12–26; 66:1). He is *holy (Lev. 11:45; Ps. 99:3, 5, 9; John 17:11; Rev. 4:8), and distinct from and unlike humans (Num. 23:19; Job 9:32; 10:4–5; 33:12; Ps. 50:21; Hos. 11:9), though he has deigned to commune with them, and they bear his image. He is partially distinct in character, as he is perfect in all his ways (Deut. 32:4; Ps. 18:30)

and just in all his dealings (Ps. 99:4; 111:7), unlike humans, all of whom have broken God's law (Rom. 3:23) and must face the consequences (Heb. 10:27). And he is *faithful (Deut. 7:9; Ps. 33:4; 1 Cor. 10:13). What he promises to do, he does (Ps. 146:6; 1 Cor. 1:9; 1 Thess. 5:24; 2 Thess. 3:3; Heb. 10:23). He has promised to forgive and *bless those who call upon him truly (Is. 55:7; Rom. 10:11–13), and to repay without *mercy those who ultimately reject him (Luke 12:5; Heb. 10:28–29).

God's sovereignty, his holiness, and his faithfulness comprise an urgent *apologia* for the revelation by which a saving personal relationship with him is established. Because it is the revelation of *this* God, it is very important as the means of entrance into God's eternal *kingdom for the peoples of humankind to whom it is addressed.

Revelation is authoritative because it is true. Of course it is perennially questioned and even cast aside; this is not new (Gen. 3:1; Ps. 2:2; Jer. 36:23; Matt. 28:17b; Jude 4). It is true because God, who cannot lie (Heb. 6:18), is its ultimate author. Further, its writers and chief figures repeatedly assert that their enscripturated claims are true and may be tested. Moses sets forth a truth criterion for OT prophets and prophecy (Deut. 13:1–3; 18:20–22; Num. 16:28–30; *cf.* 2 Chr. 18:27; Jer. 28:9). This criterion applies also to the NT writers to the extent that they are analogous to prophets in OT times. The implicit claim to be telling the truth is sometimes made explicit (Rom. 9:1; Gal. 1:20; 1 Tim. 2:7). Jesus appealed to the truthfulness of what he revealed (John 5:31–36). John swore to eyewitness experience of the Christ whose doctrine he propounded (1 John 1:1–3; *cf.* appeal to eyewitnesses in Luke 1:1–4). John pronounces a curse on any who might tamper with 'the words of the prophecy of this book', whether to add or to subtract (Rev. 22:18–19). NT writers are deeply impressed by the correlation of OT prophecy and NT fulfilment (*e.g.* Matt. 1:23; 3:3; 4:14–16; 27:9–10; Rom. 1:2; 11:8–10). Only God can foretell the future (Is. 44:8, 26; 45:21; *cf.* Ezek. 37:14), and in the fulfilment of OT Scripture by NT phenomena both Testaments bear witness to God's predictive truthfulness, much as Jesus assured his disciples of the truth of his utterances by exhibiting his foreknowledge of certain events, both in the immediate (Matt. 26:31; John 13:19; 16:4) and more distant future (see *e.g.* Jesus' passion predictions and *eschatological discourses).

Revelation is authoritative because of its agents. Attention has already been drawn to the place of God the Father and God the Son in the revelatory process and the dire implications of ignoring their counsel. The Holy Spirit, too, is active in revelation. He prepared Simeon to recognize the Christ-child (Luke 2:26). He was promised to the apostles to aid them in their recollection, interpretation, and dissemination of Jesus' teaching (John 14:26; 16:13). He divulged to Paul, and by extension to the wider church, abiding gospel truths (1 Cor. 2:9–13). He testifies to Christ (John 15:26) and reveals the saving meaning of Christ's *death to those who seek God (Acts 5:32). Apart from *regeneration by the Holy Spirit, revelation cannot be savingly apprehended (John 3:3–6); 'revelation, as true assertions about states of affairs, divine and human, is a gift of knowledge given to humans by the Holy Spirit' (G. Fackre, *The Doctrine of Revelation*, p. 221). The Holy Spirit's intimate involvement in revelation underlines the authority of that revelation. What the Spirit says or confirms must be heeded if God's favour is to be gained and his displeasure to be avoided. The book of Revelation's sombre, sevenfold 'hear what the Spirit says' (Rev. 2:7, 11, 17, 29; 3:6, 13, 22) emphasizes the authoritative nature of what he makes known.

The goals of revelation

John the Baptist, a personal recipient and authorized bearer of revelation, shrank back in humility from the *glory and wonder of what he proclaimed (John 3:30). Abraham was overcome by terror and darkness at God's revelatory presence (Gen. 15:12). Moses trembled (Deut. 9:19). Job was smitten with remorse (Job 42:6). Isaiah was terrified (Is. 6:5). Daniel was repeatedly mortified (Dan. 8:27; 10:8–9). The disciples fell to the ground in dismay (Matt. 17:6). Paul was struck blind (Acts 9:8). A major effect of revelation, and doubtless one of its primary goals, is to lead people to lower their innately high view of themselves and to give God due regard instead. No treatment of revelation should fail to point out the doxological imperative that biblical revelation conveys, at least as apprehended by its original recipients.

But bowing before God's fierce splendour is not necessarily a gesture of joyful worship, as even God's enemies will one day bend the knee (Is. 45:22–25; Phil. 2:10). In Scripture revelation's primary function is rather one of invitation to the delights of ever greater communion with the Lord (Is. 55; Rev. 22:17). The goal of the revelation of the truth of God is the expression of *love for God. The informational, cognitive value of revelation (often denied since Kant; *cf. e.g.* Bultmann's reflections on revelation, *What Is Theology?*, pp. 131ff.) should not be minimized, for there can be no saving faith apart from knowledge sufficient to generate and sustain faith. Revelation is knowledge of God. Yet revelation extends beyond what mortal minds will ever fully grasp. Its goal is not only to mediate truth but also to effect relationship with God. Revelation is the means, because it is the informing ground, of sinners' reconciliation to God.

Salvation is not by revelation *per se*; it is rather by God's promise enacted in Christ's justifying death and resurrection. God's work in Christ saves, not revelation (*contra* Gnosticism). But revelation is essential to the mediation of God's redemptive work (Rom. 10:17). Since biblical theology's mandate is to analyse and synthesize what the biblical writers affirm, its assessment of revelation will continue to play a cardinal role in its hermeneutical orientation, theological convictions, and historical observations.

Bibliography

P. Avis (ed.), *Divine Revelation* (Grand Rapids and Cambridge, 1997); P. Balla, *Challenges to New Testament Theology* (Peabody, 1998); J. Barr, 'Revelation in History', in *IDB* (Nashville, 1976), pp. 746–749; M. Bockmuehl, *Revelation and Mystery in Ancient Judaism and Pauline Christianity* (Tübingen, 1990); R. Bultmann, *What Is Theology?* (ET, Minneapolis, 1997); G. Fackre, *The Doctrine of Revelation* (Edinburgh and Grand Rapids, 1997); J. Goldingay, *Models for Scripture* (Grand Rapids and Carlisle, 1994); G. Maier, *Biblical Hermeneutics* (ET, Wheaton, 1994); B. Mitchell, 'Revelation Revisited', in S. Coakley and D. A. Pailin (eds.), *The Making and Remaking of Revelation* (Oxford, 1993); H. Ridderbos, *Redemptive History and the New*

Testament Scriptures (ET, Phillipsburg, 1988); B. D. Sommer, 'Did prophecy cease? Evaluating a reevaluation', *JBL* 115.1, 1996, pp. 31–47; B. B. Warfield, in *ISBE* 4, pp. 2573–2582; J. Wenham, *Christ and the Bible* (Guildford and Grand Rapids, [3]1994).

R. W. YARBROUGH

REVELATION, BOOK OF, see Part 2

REWARD

Rewards are gracious gifts given by God to those who render faithful service in his power.

Definition

There are a dozen words for reward(s) in the OT, but the root *śkr* is the one most frequently used. Often it refers to wages. After hiring Jacob for the price of mandrakes, Leah bore Issachar and declared, 'God has given me my wages' (Gen. 30:16, 18; author's translation). Pharoah's daughter paid Moses' mother wages for nursing him (Exod. 2:9). Zechariah asked for wages for shepherding God's rebellious people (Zech. 11:12). Less frequently *śᵉkār* is used to denote rewards. In cases involving God the word signifies his gracious gifts. God promises Abraham a great reward, that is, land and numerous descendants (Gen. 15:1). The Lord rewards the Levites with food for their service in the tabernacle (Num. 18:31). He rewards parents with children (Ps. 127:3). He promises rewards for those involved with religious reforms in Asa's day (2 Chr. 15:7).

In the NT eight Greek words are sometimes translated by 'reward(s)', producing forty-three occurrences in the NIV; twenty-nine of these come from *misthos*. Of the forty-three occurrences, sixteen have no theological significance, referring to the payment of wages to labourers in a vineyard (Matt. 20:1, 7, 8) or to hired servants (Mark 1:20; Luke 10:7; 15:17, 19; 1 Tim. 5:18; Jas. 5:4). Those instances with theological significance are discussed below. Though the terms for 'reward' can have unfavourable implications of *judgmental recompense (cf. Acts 1:18; Rom. 1:27; 2 Pet. 2:15), the majority of times they have the favourable sense of a reward for faithfulness (see *Faith)

(*cf.* Matt. 5:12; 1 Cor. 3:14). Revelation 22:12 is the only instance in which the reward most likely has both favourable and unfavourable aspects: 'Behold I am coming quickly, and my reward is with me to render to every one according to his work.' This article will deal only with the favourable sense.

In the OT most references to rewards appear to be bound within time. Although this is true of some rewards in the NT, there is an emphasis on future rewards which will last for eternity. Regardless of this distinction, rewards from God are always looked upon as gracious gifts (see *Grace). They are not earned, which would put God under obligation; rather, they are graciously given by him.

Time and place for bestowal of rewards

As stated, some rewards are given within earthly life. Jesus taught his disciples that those who parade their piety before people to receive immediate reward in the form of human praise will receive no reward from the Father who is in heaven (Matt. 6:1–2, 5, 16). His point was that true lasting rewards are those bestowed in heaven. However, he sometimes says that those who have forfeited their houses and land and left their families for his sake will be rewarded many times in this age as well as the age to come (Mark 10:28–30 = Luke 18:28–30; *cf.* Matt. 19:27–29).

Most rewards, however, are given on the future day of reckoning. In 2 Corinthians 5:10 Paul teaches that each believer 'must appear before the judgment seat of Christ in order that each may receive recompense for the things he has done in the body, whether it be good or bad'. In other words, what is done in this temporal life will be rewarded in eternity. Some argue that this is a declaration for all humanity, but the context speaks only of believers. Rewards are for believers, and are bestowed in eternity at the judgment seat of Christ, at a location which is not specified, but which seems to be in heaven.

Standards for rewards

According to 2 Corinthians 5:10, at the judgment seat of Christ believers will receive recompense for things done in the body, whether good or bad. The term 'bad' (*phaulos*) is not used to denote something intrinsically *evil, but rather something worthless, of no account, producing no gain. Inversely, 'good' (*agathos*) refers to things that are worthwhile. This is in keeping with Paul's discussion of rewards in 1 Corinthians 3:10–15. He states that he, as the skilled master builder, has laid the foundation of Jesus Christ, and every believer needs to take care how he or she builds on that foundation. In the future, presumably at the judgment seat of Christ, each believer's work will be revealed when it is tested by fire. If the work is good (gold, silver or precious stones), then it will survive and the person will receive a reward. If it is worthless (wood, hay or straw), it will be burned and the person will forfeit his or her reward. Paul makes it clear that the loss of reward is not a loss of *salvation; rather, the person will be saved, 'but as through fire'.

A 'good work' is an outward display which demonstrates an inward *obedience. Believers are instructed to *love God and their neighbours (Matt. 22:37–39 = Mark 12:30–31; Luke 10:27) and to love fellow believers (John 13:34–35; Eph. 4:1–2; 1 Pet. 2:17). This inward attitude is expressed by obeying God, specifically his commands to build up the body of Christ (Eph. 4:11–16; Col. 3:16–17) and to love one's neighbour (whether friend or enemy) as oneself (Matt. 5:43–44; Luke 6:27; 10:29–37). Each believer will be rewarded on the basis of how faithful he or she is in performing these tasks. As God's *kingdom is eternal, so also rewards are given for eternity. Efforts to build God's church and his kingdom will vary in the degree of personal sacrifice involved. Reward is promised to those who offer hospitality to servants of God (Matt. 10:41–42; Mark 9:41). Jesus also promised great reward to those who suffer persecution for his sake (Matt. 5:12). Even Moses, suffering for Christ by giving up the treasures of Egypt, looked forward to a reward (Heb. 11:26). On the other hand, a worthless work for which one forfeits any reward is one done in the energy of the flesh and/or with wrong motivation. Those who practised piety in order to impress others have already received their reward and will not receive a reward from the Father who is in heaven (Matt. 6:1–2, 5, 16).

Although salvation is based on grace (unmerited favour), it might appear that rewards imply merit. But on the contrary, rewards from God are not payment for services but a gracious gift from a generous God. They are independent of human achievement. This is illustrated in the parable of the labourers, where those who had worked one hour received the same pay as those who worked the entire day (Matt. 20:1–16). When the latter complained, the owner asked, 'Do you begrudge my generosity?' Thus, the bestowal of rewards is by God's grace on the basis of the believer's willingness to walk in the good works God has prepared beforehand (Eph. 2:10). Believers are promised power to enable them to do what is asked of them. Accordingly, Paul states that he will not speak of any accomplishments except those that Christ has done through him (Rom. 15:18). Any good work done through Christ in the power of the Spirit is an act of grace; any reward given by God at the judgment seat of Christ is also an act of grace. On the other hand, any work that is performed in the power of the flesh, even though good, will be considered worthless and will lead to loss of reward. Rewards, like salvation, are God's gracious gifts.

Variation in reward

There is NT evidence for degrees of reward (though some scholars dispute this). In the Beatitudes, Jesus states that those who are persecuted will receive a 'great' reward (Matt. 5:12; Luke 6:23). If believers love their enemies, do good and lend goods or money expecting nothing in return they will receive a 'great' reward (Luke 6:35). In the parable of the pounds (Luke 19:11–17; *cf.* Matt. 25:14–30), the nobleman gives a pound to each of his ten servants. When he returns, one servant has gained ten pounds by trading and is given authority over ten cities. Another servant has gained five pounds and is given authority over five cities. A third servant hides his pound and it is taken from him and given to the first servant. Thus the third servant receives no reward. This parable strongly suggests differences in rewards.

Will difference in rewards distinguish people in heaven for eternity? Biblical references to heaven suggest that entering will be far more important than any variation of rewards. Though these may exist, those in heaven will be glorified, and their values will be completely different from earthly values. There will not be envy or jealousy, but rather praise. It will not be, 'Why did you get more rewards than I?', but more likely 'It is wonderful how you allowed the power of the Lord to work in you,' or, 'It is amazing what persecution you endured for the Lord.' Finally, everyone in heaven will realize that rewards, like salvation, are of God's grace, and will give him praise accordingly.

Motivation for rewards

Believers' motivation in this life should not be the obtaining of rewards as an end in itself. Our motivation should be to please God wholeheartedly in gratitude for what he has done for us through Christ. Rewards will be given for the outward display which demonstrates an inward obedience. A soldier's primary motivation should be to serve his country, though he may receive medals as a reward for his service. In the same way, true servants of God should not be centred on themselves but on the Lord whom they love and serve. When Jesus speaks of 'the righteous' serving him by providing food, drink and clothing, he points out that they cannot remember when they did these things (Matt. 25:34–40). Paul enjoins believers to do all to the *glory of God and not for men and women (1 Cor. 10:31; Col. 3:23–24). In the end, rewards are a significant consideration in the life of believers, but not the ultimate goal, which is to glorify God and serve him wholeheartedly.

Bibliography

C. L. Blomberg, 'Degrees of Reward in the Kingdom of Heaven?', JETS 35, 1992, pp. 159–172; P. C. Böttger, B. Siede and O. Becker, 'Recompense, Reward, Gain, Wages', in NIDNTT 3, pp. 134–145; W. L. Gerig in EDBT, pp. 685–687; L. D. Hurst, 'Ethics of Jesus', in DJG, pp. 210–222; H. Preisker and E. Würthwein, 'misthos, k.t.l.', in TDNT IV, pp. 695–728; B. Reicke, 'The New Testament conception of reward', in O. Cullmann and P. Bonnard (eds.), Aux Sources de la Tradition Chrétienne: Mélanges offerts à M. Maurice Goguel à l'occasion de son soixante-dixième anniversaire (Neuchâtel, 1950), pp. 195–206; J. E. Rosscup, 'A New Look 1 Corinthians 3:12 – "Gold, Silver, Precious Stones"', MSJ 1, 1990, pp. 33–51; G. de Ru, 'The Conception of Reward in the Teaching of Jesus', NovT 8, 1966, pp. 202–222.

H. W. HOEHNER

RICHES, see POOR/POVERTY

RIGHTEOUSNESS, JUSTICE, AND JUSTIFICATION

Introduction

In English usage, the term 'righteousness' is associated with the idea of individual moral rectitude. 'Justice', on the other hand, generally signifies a right social order, that is, the proper distribution of goods and honour, including retribution for *evil. Thus the latter is often forensic, while the former is associated with personal ethics. Although such concepts are not foreign to the biblical authors, their concerns lie along other lines. The lexical distinction to which we are accustomed in English is absent from the Scriptures. The biblical terms often translated as 'righteousness' or 'justice' belong to a single word-group, that associated with the ṣdq root in Hebrew, or that based on the dik- root in Greek. Furthermore, the Hebrew usage, which influences that of the NT writers, tends to be relational and concrete; one is 'righteous' with respect to another human being or to *God, in a particular kind of conduct, or in a particular 'contention' which has arisen (e.g. Deut. 6:25; Ps. 106:31; Is. 5:7; Ezek 3:20; Luke 1:6; Rom. 2:13; 1 Pet. 3:10–12). The ṣdq root does not signify a proper inward disposition, even though it may presuppose it (usually other terms, especially the adjective yšr, express this idea). On the other hand, while ṣdq terms often carry forensic overtones (i.e. 'justice' and 'justification'), they generally signify the outcome of a 'contention' or 'lawsuit,' rather than the act of *judging or its content (e.g. Judg. 5:11; Ps. 40:10–11; Is. 51:6–8; cf. mišpaṭ). Furthermore, the verbal forms denote the dispensing of justice in a positive sense: 'to give someone justice' is to vindicate them, to grant them *salvation from injustice (e.g. Exod. 23:7; Deut. 25:1). Although in non-biblical Greek 'to do someone justice' had the sense of 'to punish someone', the NT authors adopt the Hebrew usage, which likewise appears in the Septuagint (e.g. Matt. 12:37; Gal. 2:16; Jas. 2:25; cf. dikē [punishment] Acts 28:4; 2 Thess. 1:9; Jude 7).

Biblical interpreters have long been concerned to describe the distinctiveness of biblical thought concerning righteousness over against the ancient Greek and Roman concepts, especially the idea of distributive justice. A comparison of these traditions is a task too large for this context. One fundamental difference lies in the centrality of the individual in Greek thought, where the question of conflict between individual duty and the demands of *law has a prominence unparalleled in Scripture. Likewise, 'righteousness' is discussed among the Greeks as an inward virtue, in a way not found in the Bible. For the biblical writers, God is the source of all righteousness, both in his saving intervention in *human affairs and in the requirements which he places upon the *world. While human beings acknowledge God's 'righteousness' and 'justice' as it is revealed, they cannot judge it according to their standards when it is hidden. To do so would be to reverse the roles of Creator and created (see, e.g. Job 32:1 – 42:17; Is. 45:8–25; Rom. 9:14–24).

'Righteousness/justice' as a creational concept

Since at least the end of the 19th century, interpreters have defined the biblical concept of 'righteousness' as 'covenant faithfulness'. God is thought to be 'righteous' in that he keeps his promises to save. Human beings, especially the people of Israel, are said to be 'righteous' in that they remain *faithful to the *covenant which God made with them. In this way, it is thought, one may account for the relational character of the biblical usage of righteousness language and its association with salvation. The definition seems, moreover, to be a useful tool for drawing together various strands of the biblical witness (e.g. N. T. Wright, *What Saint Paul Really Said*, esp. pp. 95–111). However, it fails to account adequately for biblical language and thought. In the first place, it conflicts with the biblical understanding of a 'covenant'. 'Covenant' is associated regularly with more strictly legal terms; one 'keeps', 'remembers', 'establishes', 'breaks', transgresses', 'forsakes', 'despises', 'forgets' or 'profanes' a covenant, but one does not, in biblical idiom, act righteously or unrighteously with respect to it. Furthermore, 'covenants' establish and maintain '*familial' relations. The obligations of those 'in' a covenant are *love and faithfulness, not merely a general rectitude (e.g. Hos. 6:6). A

transgressor of a covenant may thus be pictured as a rebellious child or an unfaithful wife (e.g. Is. 1:2; Hos. 1:2). In other words, a 'covenant,' despite its obvious forensic dimension, has to do with a narrower set of relations than that of *creation and 'righteousness'. The rare collocation of the terms 'righteousness' and 'covenant', despite their individual frequency, is one indication of this distinction in meaning. One might speak of 'faithfulness' as 'covenant righteousness', but one cannot properly speak of righteousness as 'covenant faithfulness'. On the infrequent occasions when 'righteousness' appears in association with 'covenant', it does not signify 'covenant faithfulness' (see Is. 42:6; 61:8–11; Hos. 2:16–20; Pss. 50:16; 111:1–10; Dan. 9:4–7; Neh. 9:32–33).

In biblical thought, 'righteousness' is simultaneously moral and creational, having to do with God's re-establishing 'right order' in the fallen world which he has made, an order which includes a right relationship between the world and its Creator (e.g. Is. 45:8, 23; Pss. 85:4–13; 98:1–9). The creational basis of the biblical understanding of 'righteousness' and 'justice' brings with it the notion of universal norms, such as the requirement that various implements of commerce (balances, weights, measures) be 'righteous' (e.g. Lev. 19:35–36; Ezek. 45:9–12). Likewise, the contrast between 'the righteous' and 'the wicked' has a universal application (e.g. Gen. 18:23; Exod. 23:7; Ezek. 33:12; Ps. 11:4–5). Noah and Job are named as righteous, even though they are not Israelites (Gen. 7:1; Ezek. 14:14, 20; cf. Heb. 11:4–7). Rulers establish 'righteousness' by means of the wisdom which has ordered creation (Prov. 8:15–16, 22–31). The biblical hope for justice embraces the salvation of the entire earth, a hope which comes to include an expectation of a coming Messiah (Pss. 72:1–19; 103:6; Is. 9:6; Jer. 9:23–24; Matt. 6:33; Acts 17:31). The close link between 'righteousness' and 'creation' is especially prominent in the various passages in which the establishment of righteousness is envisaged as the renewal of the created order and its elements (e.g. Is. 45:8; Pss. 89:1–14; 98:1–9; on this topic see H. H. Schmid, *Gerechtigkeit als Weltordnung*). The occasional instances in which 'righteousness' appears in a cultic context also very likely reflect a creational background, since cultic ritual represents the created order (*e.g.* Pss. 11:5–7; 118:19–20; Deut. 33:19).

'Righteousness/justice' as a forensic concept

The biblical concept of righteousness/justice is closely joined to that of the 'ruling and judging' by which 'right order' is re-established in creation. In the ancient world, the legislative and executive aspects of ruling were bound together with, and indeed often derived from, the judicial role of the king or leader. This connection may be seen from the biblical descriptions of the 'judges' who act on God's behalf in Israel (*e.g.* Judg. 2:16–18; 4:4–10). Kings in Israel, like the judges before them, were to mediate God's rule in the world, 'to effect just judgment and righteous-ness' (*aśâh mišpaṭ ûṣᵉḏaqâ*; 2 Sam. 8:15; Jer. 22:3; Ps. 72:1–4; *cf.* Is. 9:6). The basic vehicle for the administration of justice was the 'contention' or 'lawsuit' (K. W. Whitelam, *The Just King*). We need not enter into a discussion concerning the distinction between these two forms of dispute (see, with some qualifications, P. Bovati, *Re-establishing Justice*). It suffices to note that both have to do with the establishment of rights, and both are envisaged as two-party affairs; in rendering judgment, the king or another authority was to intervene in favour of the one in the right (*e.g.* Lev. 19:15; Deut. 16:20; Jer. 22:3). This essentially two-party judicial form is also found in the NT, despite the introduction of Greco-Roman procedures (see, *e.g.* Luke 18:1–8; Rom. 8:33–34; Acts 18:12–17).

A considerable portion of the biblical 'righteousness' language appears in the context of such 'contentions' and is therefore related to particular verdicts. When, for example, in the book of Genesis Judah says of Tamar, 'She is righteous, rather than I', he has in view his contention with her, not a general assessment of her character. Her way of becoming pregnant, deceptive though it was, conformed to the norm for preserving the familial line of her deceased husband; she was pregnant by Judah himself (Gen. 38:1–26; *cf.* Deut. 25:5–10). Judah's behaviour is called 'unjust' in that he had intercourse with Tamar incognito, supposing her to be a prostitute, and yet was prepared to execute judgment on his daughter-in-law for 'playing the whore' (Gen. 38:15, 24). Many

interpreters wrongly exclude the idea of a norm from the biblical understanding of righteousness, by speaking of it as 'relational' and *not* 'normative'. It is more accurate to say that the biblical concepts often involve the idea of justice in application, *i.e.* a norm or standard expressed in a particular relation-ship (*e.g.* Deut. 6:20–25; Ps. 7:6–11; 1 Sam. 26:23; *cf.* H. Cremer, *Rechtfertigungslehre*). In other contexts, where 'righteousness' is joined to such ideas as 'truth' and 'uprightness', it is clear that the idea of a standard or norm is included in the concept (*e.g.* 1 Kgs. 3:6; Is. 45:19; 48:1; Ps. 119:142).

We may further observe that the feminine noun *ṣᵉḏaqâ* (as opposed to its abstract masculine counterpart, *ṣeḏeq*) is generally concrete, signifying either a vindicating action on behalf of the one who has been judged in the right, or the deeds which warrant the claim to justification (on the former see, *e.g.* Is. 5:23, 2 Sam. 19:28; on the latter, Gen. 30:33; Deut. 9:4–5). Consequently, the psalmist appeals to God to 'answer in his righteousness' by defending him against his adversary, even as he asks God not to enter into contention with him, since 'no one living shall be justified before you' (Ps. 143:2). The profound tension between the hope for God's vindicating help over against an adversary and God's implicit contention with the psalmist is allowed to stand; it finds its resolution only in the NT. We find a further example of remarkable boldness in Psalm 51, where the psalmist asks for deliverance from *guilt and from the punishment which God justly visits upon him (Ps. 51:1–19). This deliverance will involve a new creation (Ps. 51:10). The tension between God's contention with the psalmist and his contention for the psalmist reaches its peak here; the writer expects the resolution to come from God himself.

It is of fundamental significance that the biblical writers regularly attribute the re-establishment of righteousness to God alone (*e.g.* Is. 45:24; 54:14–17; Jer. 23:6). The psalmists appeal to God to effect justice on their behalf or to grant 'his righteousness' to the king as his intermediary (Pss. 72:1–3; 24:5; 37:6). They await, expect and finally celebrate 'the righteousness of God', that is, his saving judgment in their cause (*e.g.* Pss. 31:2; 40:9–10; 71:15; 89:14–18; 143:11). They know that 'human wrath does not effect the righteousness of God' (Jas. 1:19–20, author's translation). The concreteness of the biblical language noted above, is evident here: where the feminine noun *ṣ'dāqâ* ('righteousness') is used the phrase 'God's righteousness' generally signifies his saving vindication of the oppressed (see also, *e.g.* Ps. 5:8; 71:2; Is. 51:6–8). Moreover, in accordance with its basis in a theology of creation, the biblical hope for 'righteousness' embraces the rectifying of the whole created order: 'Shower, O heavens, from above, and let the skies rain down righteousness; let the earth open, that salvation may spring up, and let it cause righteousness to sprout up also; I the LORD have created it' (Is. 45:8; NRSV). This is the theme which *Paul takes up when he announces that the righteousness of God has been revealed in the *gospel (Ps. 98:2; Rom. 1:17). It is also reflected in the Johannine promise that God is 'faithful and righteous to forgive our sins, and cleanse us from all unrighteousness' (1 John 1:8–9). The *holy love of God comes to perfection in rectifying *sinners.

Since the biblical usage of 'righteousness' is so strongly oriented towards the hope of God's saving justice, it is understandable that the presence of the concept of retributive justice in the Scriptures has been contested. Nevertheless, whenever a contention is resolved, one party suffers retribution for the evil which it has done, even as the other is vindicated. And in fact, a punitive 'righteousness of God' does appear in Scripture, mostly in the form of 'doxologies of judgment' in which those with whom God has been in contention admit his justice and their defeat: 'Yahweh is righteous, I and my people are the guilty ones' (Exod. 9:27; see also Lam. 1:18; 2 Chr. 12:1–6; Neh. 9:33; Dan. 9:7). Such confessions are also concrete admissions of guilt in the face of the punishment which God has meted out for particular failures. In other contexts, too, where a retributive righteousness is predicated of God, his ruling and judging activity is in view (Pss. 7:10–11; 11:5–7; Is. 1:27; 5:15–16; 10:22; 28:17; Dan. 9:16). The biblical writers treat the topic of 'righteousness' in the context of God's action, and not as an abstract idea.

'Justification' in biblical thought

In the light of the preceding considerations, the widespread claim that the biblical authors make no distinction between 'being declared righteous' and 'being made righteous' is to be rejected (*e.g.* E. Käsemann, *New Testament Questions of Today*, pp. 168–182). The rendering of biblical references to God's righteousness as 'salvation' is likewise unsatisfactory. In the various passages in question, the biblical writers speak of 'applied justice', the vindicating acts of God which in each instance presuppose that a verdict has been given. Such intervention represents not merely 'salvation', but God's 'saving justice' (*e.g.* Ps. 98:1–18; *cf.* Rom. 1:17).

According to the witness of the NT, this 'saving justice' of God has been decisively manifested in the resurrection of Jesus Christ from the dead. It is in this sense that Paul speaks of the 'righteousness of God' in the opening section of Romans, and at various other points in his letters (Rom. 1:17; 10:4; 2 Cor. 5:21). The new creation, in which righteousness dwells, has come into being in Christ (2 Cor. 5:17–21; 2 Pet. 3:13). Those who belong to Christ have died with him to sin and *death, and now live to God and to righteousness (Rom. 6:17–18). His resurrection, like his death, took place 'for us' (Rom. 4:25; 3:24). In Christ, the *kingdom of God, which consists in righteousness, eschatological *peace, and *joy, has entered the present, fallen and unjust world (Rom. 14:17; Gal. 1:3–4). The 'higher righteousness' of the kingdom of God which Jesus taught his disciples to seek is present in Jesus himself: formerly in his earthly presence, and now as it is distributed to people of faith through his resurrection (Matt. 5:10–11, 20; 6:33; 1 Cor. 1:30; 6:11; 2 Cor. 3:9; 5:21; Rom. 10:3; 1 Pet. 2:24). Participation in Christ and his righteousness thrusts one into the present 'contention' between God and the world (Rom. 8:18–39). In the fallen world, this new righteousness is under constant attack, not only from without, but also from within the believer, in whom 'the flesh' (the fallen person) persists even though it has been conquered (Rom. 8:12–14; Gal. 5:16–17). Only at the resurrection from the dead does Christ's vindication for us fully become his vindication in us (1 Cor. 15:50–58).

This understanding of justification appears especially in Paul's letters, but also is present also in other NT writings. It presupposes a 'contention' between God and the fallen world, as to whether or not the true God is in fact God, a theme which runs through the OT, but comes to special prominence in the latter chapters of Isaiah (see, *e.g.* Is. 41:1–29; *cf*. John 12:31; 16:8; Acts 17:31; Rev. 19:11). This 'lawsuit', which will be resolved at the final judgment, has also come proleptically to its conclusion in the resurrection of the crucified Christ. As the Righteous One sent by God, he was oppressed and afflicted, robbed of justice by unrighteous humanity (Acts 3:14; 22:14; 1 Pet. 3:18). Yet, although his death was the work of fallen humanity, it was simultaneously the work of God, who sent him as a 'propitiatory sacrifice' for sin (Rom. 3:25; 1 John 2:2). In *obedience to the will of God he willingly accepted the cross, and 'gave himself up for our sins' (Mark 10:45; Gal. 1:4; 2:20). In him God passed judgment upon fallen humanity, effecting the condemnation of 'sin in the flesh' in his death (Rom. 8:3). In raising Christ, God 'gave him justice', vindicating him over against the world (Acts 3:14–15; 1 Pet. 2:23; 3:18; 1 Tim. 3:16). With the resurrection, the exchange between fallen humanity and his Son is complete: 'he made him who knew no sin to be sin, that we might become the righteousness of God in him' (2 Cor. 5:21). The justifying action of God in Christ is twofold; in him God is justified in his contention with the sinner, and yet the sinner is justified. God is thus both 'just(ified) and justifier of the one who believes in Jesus' (Rom. 3:26).

God's dealings with the world in Christ were anticipated by the experience of *Israel, which more than once in its history was 'reduced to nothing' in order that God might bring it salvation (*e.g.* Hab. 2:4; Is. 6:9–13; 7:9; see H. G. Reventlow, *Rechtfertigung im Horizont des Alten Testaments* [Munich, 1971]). Paul sees this pattern being worked out in Israel's present rejection of the gospel, which will be followed by the salvation of *eschatological Israel (Rom. 9:1 – 11:36). God's dealings with Israel correspond to his work in Christ.

The justification of the fallen human being therefore takes place only in conjunction with condemnation (Rom. 4:25; 8:3). The 'ministry of righteousness, life and the Spirit' proceeds from the 'ministry of condemnation and death' (2 Cor. 3:4–11). In this way, the work of the gospel fulfils the work of the law (2 Cor. 3:12–18). According to Paul, the law

serves the divine purpose by pronouncing sentence upon fallen humanity (Rom. 7:13; 8:3–4). One can achieve only an outward conformity to its demands (Phil. 3:6; Rom. 7:7–13). To seek one's righteousness in the law is to ignore the work of God in Christ, who is the 'goal of the law' (Rom. 10:4). Here Paul's gospel corresponds to the message of Jesus, who 'did not come to call the righteous, but sinners' (Mark 2:17). To ignore this Jesus is to deny the true state of one's own heart and life, to hide behind a semblance of piety (Matt. 23:28; Luke 18:9–14).

Within the biblical witness, the righteousness 'reckoned' to faith appears as an extraordinary gift of God. It is contrary to expectations: first, it sets aside the standard of conduct which is usually regarded as 'righteousness' (Gen. 15:6; *cf*. 6:9; Ps. 106:31; Deut. 6:25); secondly, it grants the *blessing associated with justification in the form of a promise, which always stands in stark contrast to outward appearances (Rom. 4:18–25; Hab. 2:4). In both respects 'righteousness' and its resultant vindication spring from the *word of God itself, which out of nothing brings *life and blessing into existence (Rom. 4:17; Heb. 11:7). Those to whom the promises of God are given are called to the obedience of believing (Heb. 11:8; Rom. 1:5). In that they trust God and his word to them against all appearances, they acknowledge God as truly God (Rom. 4:20; *cf*. 1:23; 3:23; Is. 45:22–25). The 'righteousness' reckoned to faith is therefore (paradoxically) utterly gratuitous, yet the recompense for obedience to the first and highest commandment.

The declarations of Paul and *James on justification may be reconciled along these lines. James characterizes the divine declaration of *Abraham's righteousness as a prophetic utterance of Scripture, which was later fulfilled (Jas. 2:23; Gen. 15:6). It had its counterpart in Abraham's faith, which superintended his works and found its perfection in them (Jas. 2:22; see T. Laato in *TrinJ* 18). Abraham's vindication at his testing, when 'he offered up Isaac, his son' was the echo of the divine word already spoken. Likewise, the harlot *Rahab's treatment of the 'messengers' sent to her implicitly echoes the divine promise of the land to Israel (Jas. 2:25). Paul's announcement of justification by faith apart from the works of the law is a denial of the security of the fallen human being before

God on the basis of works (Rom. 3:27–31). He does not thereby exclude a final judgment according to works, which will reveal the secrets of the heart, and the 'work' (singular) of each person (Rom. 2:7, 16; 2 Cor. 5:10). Faith, which makes the crucified and risen Christ present within the sinner, is active in love (Gal. 2:20; 5:6). Christ's vindication for us has its counterpart in Christ's vindication within us at the final judgment (2 Cor. 13:5; Rom. 8:10–11). For Paul, final justification is therefore a mere echo of the justifying work of God in Christ, which is received by faith. Neither he nor James speaks of an increase of justification. Nor do they speak of a justification by faith and works. Rather, they both recognize that justifying faith in Christ necessarily has its own works.

See also: JESUS CHRIST.

Bibliography

P. Bovati, Re-establishing Justice: Legal Terms, Concepts and Procedures in the Hebrew Bible (ET, Sheffield, 1994); D. A. Carson (ed.), Right with God: Justification in the Bible and the World (Grand Rapids and Carlisle, 1992); H. Cremer, Die paulinische Rechtfertigungslehre im Zusammenhange iherer geschichtlichen Voraussetzungen (Gütersloh, 1900); R. B. Hays, 'Justification', in ABD 3, pp. 1129–1133; E. Käsemann, New Testament Questions of Today (ET, Philadelphia and London, 1969), pp. 168–182; T. Laato, 'Justification according to James: a comparison with Paul', TJ 18, 1997, pp. 43–84; J. Reumann, Righteousness in the New Testament: 'Justification' in the United States Lutheran-Roman Catholic Dialogue (Philadelphia, 1982); H. G. Reventlow, Rechtfertigung im Horizont des Alten Testaments (Münich, 1971); H. H. Schmid, Gerechtigkeit als Weltordnung: Hintergrund und Geschichte des alttestamentlichen Gerechtigkeitsbegriffes (Tübingen, 1968); idem, 'Rechtfertigung als Schöpfungsgeschehen', in J. Friedrich, W. Pöhlmann and P. Stuhlmacher (eds.), Rechtfertigung: Festschrift für Ernst Käsemann (Tübingen and Göttingen, 1976); M. A. Seifrid, Justification by Faith: The Origin and Development of a Central Pauline Theme (Leiden, 1992); idem, 'Righteousness language in the Hebrew Scriptures and early Judaism: linguistic considerations critical to the interpretation of Paul', in D. A. Carson (ed.), Paul and Variegated Judaism, vol. 1 (Grand Rapids and Tübingen, forthcoming); idem, Christ Our Righteousness: Paul's Theology of Justification (Grand Rapids and Leicester, 2000); P. Stuhlmacher, Gerechtigkeit Gottes bei Paulus (Göttingen, [2]1966); idem, Reconciliation, Law, and Righteousness: Essays in Biblical Theology (Philadelphia, 1986); idem, Biblische Theologie des Neuen Testaments: Grundlegung; Von Jesus zu Paulus (Göttingen, 1992); K. W. Whitelam, The Just King: Monarchial Judicial Authority in Ancient Israel (Sheffield, 1979); N. T. Wright, What Saint Paul Really Said (Oxford and Grand Rapids, 1997).

M. A. SEIFRID

ROMANS, see Part 2
RUTH, see Part 2

SABBATH

The theme of the Sabbath is often contentious. Yet throughout Scripture Sabbath legislation and theology are reapplied to new circumstances, so providing a clear trajectory of interpretation.

Sabbath in the Pentateuch

Genesis 2:1–3

'Thus the heavens and the earth were completed, and all their array, so that on the seventh day God had completed his work which he had done. He ceased on the seventh day from all his work which he had done, and God blessed the seventh day, and he sanctified it, because on it he ceased from all his work which God had created by making it' (author's translation).

There is no mention of the Sabbath here, nor of *rest. Instead we read of the 'seventh day' of *creation, and of *God 'ceasing' from his work. We should be careful not to read back into this passage more than it actually says.

The passage begins by describing all the work of creation as 'complete', and associates this completion with the Seventh Day (the capitals differentiate this Day from any other seventh day). God's 'work' is always carefully defined: the retrospective phrase 'which he had done' refers to the previous six days' work only, as does the verb 'created' (*br*'), which is picked up from 1:1 and reused to close the account. Was God doing another type of work on the Seventh Day, such as the work of sustaining his creation? We are not told (but *cf.* John 5:17).

'*Blessing' is associated in Genesis 1 with fruitfulness and dominion, both of which are expressions of what it means to be created in the *image of God (1:26, 28). We may conclude from its use in v. 3 that, just as God blessed what he created, he also blessed the fact of his creation: its completeness and its ongoing existence.

When God 'sanctified' the Seventh Day because on it he ceased creating, he was not celebrating or commemorating days one to six, but declaring his new state of not creating to be blessed and *holy. This is suggested by the close link between 'God had completed' and 'he ceased'. The end of God's creative work brought about a new type of *time, blessed and set aside, presumably in order that what was created could now *be*. The Seventh Day was to be a day for fruitfulness, for dominion, for relationship.

The created order is not commanded to sanctify the Seventh Day; the reason given involves God alone. The creation simply moves into the Seventh Day by default.

Exodus 16:21–30

The word 'Sabbath' first appears in Exodus 16:23: 'Tomorrow is a Sabbath feast, a holy Sabbath to Yahweh.' This was arguably the first Sabbath; the lenience shown in verses 27–29 suggests that the Sabbath-breaking was a first offence (*cf.* Num. 15:32–36). No explanation is given for the command. The statement in v. 30 that 'the people stopped working [*šabat*] on the seventh day' is the closest parallel to Genesis 2:1–3.

The fourth commandment

The biblical tradition of interpretation of Genesis 2:1–3 begins with the fourth commandment in Exodus 20:8–11, and is continued by Deuteronomy 5:12–15.

Exodus 20:8–11. The phrase 'the Sabbath day' appears only at the start and close of the commandment; the Sabbath day which Yahweh sanctified (v. 11b) is none other than the regularly recurring day which the Israelites were to sanctify (v. 8). The import

of verse 11 thus becomes clear. First, Exodus 20:11 does not simply cite Genesis 2:2–3, but explains it. Where Genesis 2:2–3 says that God 'ceased (*šabat*) from all his [creation] work', Exodus 20:11 uses the word 'rested' (*nwḥ*). Secondly, verse 11b is a quotation of Genesis 2:3a, but with the significant alteration of 'seventh' to 'Sabbath'. This alteration binds the two days closely together, but we should beware of the simple equation of the Seventh Day with the first Sabbath day. The Sabbath mentioned in verse 11b is, as we have seen, the *Israelites' weekly Sabbath, the subject of the commandment. The altered quotation compares the Israelite Sabbath to the Seventh Day, not in order to equate those two days in every respect, but rather to show that God's action of blessing and sanctifying applies equally to both. Verse 11b is a shorthand way of saying, 'which is why Yahweh blessed not only the seventh day, but also the Sabbath'.

Four conclusions follow. First, this commandment is not a mandate for Sabbath observance by all *humanity, for the lesson of creation is applied narrowly to the Israelite Sabbath. Secondly, the basic reason given for Sabbath observance is the imitation of God. God's example of work which finds its completion in rest should be the model for Israel. Thirdly, because there is no concept in Genesis 2:1–3 of a *cycle* of work punctuated by rest, its lesson is not that rest is good as a regular relief from work or as a means of making work more efficient, but that there is more to life than work; rest is the goal and the fulfilment of work. Fourthly, it will become clear that 'rest' is not inactivity. It involves living (and working) in fruitful harmony with God, as Adam did in the garden (*cf.* Amos 9:13–15). Thus the use of this word in verse 11 suggests that God did not 'cease' from all his activity either.

Deuteronomy 5:12–15. In Deuteronomy Moses interprets the law, expounding it to the new generation of God's people. The first addition to the Exodus text (v. 12b) refers back to the original giving of the fourth commandment. The additions in verse 14 stress that the cattle must not work, and explain why. Deuteronomy 5:12–15 *explains* Exodus 20:8–11, just as the latter explains Genesis 2.

The first imperative of Exodus 20:8, 'remember!', is changed to 'observe!' This is a *leitmotif* in Deuteronomy 5 – 6, and its regular partner, 'to observe' (a different word in Hebrew), occurs in verse 15b. The implication of the opening and closing lines is that this is not so much a fresh command to remember the Sabbath day, as an injunction to obey the Sabbath commandment of Exodus 20. It follows that verse 15b means, 'that is why Yahweh gave you the Sabbath commandment'. In other words, verse 15 provides the reason for the *law given in Exodus. The word 'remember' introduces the new material in both texts.

What, then, is the reason for the law? An analogy is drawn between Israel's six days of 'slaving' ('labour' in v. 13 translates *'bd*) and the time spent as 'slaves' in Egypt ('a slave' in v. 15 translates *'bd*); thus the seventh, work-free day symbolizes Israel's *redemption. Deuteronomy 5:15 is therefore answering two questions. With respect to verses 13–14, it explains why Israel was to keep the Sabbath: it was a memorial of their redemption out of a toilsome existence into a blessed existence as God's *covenant *people (*cf.* Deut. 5:1–6). And with respect to Exodus 20:11, it explains why the Seventh Day is the basis of the Sabbath day: there is a fundamental similarity between what God did on the Seventh Day (he rested) and what he did in the *Exodus (he brought Israel out of Egypt).

Three conclusions follow. First, whatever God's goal was in creating humankind was also his goal in redeeming Israel. Israel was to live as the image of God, bearing fruit and ruling over a good creation. Secondly, Deuteronomy 5:15 makes explicit the implicit restricting of the scope of Genesis 2:1–3 by Exodus 20:11. That is, the primeval blessing of the Seventh Day, which had all humanity in mind, is fulfilled in the redemption of a single people, so that the only mandate attached to it is that given to the redeemed. Thirdly, the blessing of the Seventh Day in Genesis 2 is fulfilled when Israel occupies the Promised *Land (*i.e.* enters into rest).

A covenant sign

In Exodus 31:12–17, the Sabbath is called a 'sign [...] that you may know that I am Yahweh who sanctifies you' (v. 13). The Sabbath is holy to Israel (v. 14) and to Yahweh (v. 15), a perpetual covenant (v. 16) and a sign for ever (v. 17). The covenant made with Abraham contained a threefold

promise of land, offspring and blessing (Gen. 12:1–3; 15:1–21), and although the land is the explicit goal of the fourth commandment, all three promises are implicit in it; the latter two are found in Genesis 2:1–3. The aptness of the Sabbath as a summary of the whole covenant relationship is reinforced by the rare reference to the sanctification of Israel in Exodus 31:13, which points back to God's sanctifying both of the Seventh Day and of Israel (Exod. 19:10–15). This verse prepares for the idea that Sabbath observance is as much about *righteousness as it is about rest.

The sabbatical year

Leviticus 25:1–7 legislates for a year in which the land itself was to observe a Sabbath to Yahweh. Crops were not harvested, but left in place for the benefit of the landless poor (*cf.* Exod. 23:10–11). The sabbatical year reinforced the fact that Israel had been set apart by God for rest (Lev. 25:12), and that this goal involved the way they lived as well as the place where they lived. Moreover, even the land itself was only a foretaste of what God had promised.

The covenant curses in Leviticus 26 speak of the exile as an opportunity for the land to enjoy the Sabbaths denied it by the people while they lived there (vv. 34–35, 43). The breaking of not just the Sabbath laws but the entire law is in view, suggesting that the land is denied Sabbath rest when the people are unfaithful to God.

Sabbath in the prophets

The former prophets provide only incidental material about the Sabbath and its observance, mentioning in passing various activities which were performed on the Sabbath (*e.g.* Judg. 14:12–18; 2 Kgs. 4:23; 11:5–9). In contrast, Sabbath theology is developed significantly.

Rest

The idea of Sabbath 'rest', whether God's (Exod. 20:11) or Israel's (Deut. 5:14), is tightly bound to the land. 'To give/have rest' usually refers to Israel's possession of the land arising from victory over her enemies (Deut. 3:20; Josh. 1:15; 1 Kgs. 5:4); the noun 'rest' can refer to the land itself (Deut. 12:9; *cf.* Ps. 95:11). It is a paradoxical idea, because rest is both achieved and not yet achieved. In part, this means simply that new enemies will arise, but it also reflects the theological idea that *peace is tied to covenant *faithfulness and the loss of rest is God's judgment (*cf*. Neh. 9:28).

Sabbath in the latter prophets

Unsurprisingly, looming exile precipitated a sabbatical crisis. For Isaiah, true Sabbath observance expresses solidarity with God's justice, *salvation and righteousness (56:1–2). The Sabbath is not a day for pursuing one's own immediate ends, but for taking delight in Yahweh. Only thus can one inherit the blessings of God's promise to Jacob (58:13–14). The book opens and closes with contrasting references to 'Sabbath' and 'New Moon', two festivals whose abuse brought down God's judgment (1:13), but which will be truly celebrated by all humankind in the new heavens and the new earth (66:23).

In Ezekiel 20:10–26, the profaning of Yahweh's Sabbaths is the direct cause of Israel's downfall, and the content of this profanation is idolatry (v. 16). Israel were called by Yahweh to make the sanctification of his Sabbath the sign of their renewed faithfulness (v. 20). In Ezekiel 46:1–12 the proper observance of the Sabbath is a central feature of the worship offered up by the Prince. The Sabbath thus stands for the nation's entire relationship with God, one which awaits restoration in the future.

It is not surprising that faithful Sabbath observance was such a big issue in Nehemiah's time (Neh. 13:15–22), given the recurrence of exactly the behaviour which had precipitated exile in the first place, including profanation of the Sabbath. But by the time of *Jesus, the primarily salvation-historical and *eschatological focus of the prophets had been blurred by a *halakhic* debate which attempted to eliminate every hint of Sabbath violation. The emphasis of the latter prophets, that the heart of Sabbath-breaking was idolatry, was lost.

Sabbath in the OT: conclusions

The OT presents a consistent theology of the Sabbath, but one which moves with the flow of salvation history. The original goal of a perfect (complete) creation in which humankind would rule fruitfully under God was never abandoned. The promise to Abraham pointed in the same direction: the fruitfulness in offspring and the blessing of a covenant relationship with God were to find a locus of expression in the Promised Land. The sacred time of the Seventh Day becomes the sacred place of the land; each in its own way is an expression of God's rest. The fourth commandment exhorted Israel to imitate God's creative and redemptive aim by living for a goal which transcended daily toil through fellowship with their covenant Lord.

Subsequent development was driven by the historical failure of Israel's possession of the land to achieve this goal. This failure was attributed on a political level to continued military struggle (the former prophets), and on a deeper level to idolatry (the latter prophets). Israel's real troubles were not military, but religious; her true debts were not economic, but spiritual. Rest was still in the future. A Sabbath day which would bring blessing was yet to dawn. Isaiah 66 hints at a universal Sabbath celebration, which takes us back to the original goal of Genesis 1 – 2.

Sabbath in the NT

The Gospels

When accused by the Pharisees of breaking the Sabbath law, Jesus did not point out that he was only breaking the oral tradition. Instead, he made the astounding claim that, just as King David and the priests were 'above the law' in certain respects, so he was not subject to the Sabbath law, but Lord over it (Luke 6:1–11; *cf*. Mark 2:23–28). Not only does this imply that Jesus has an authority at least as great as that of the Mosaic law, it suggests that Jesus is the one who will finally bring the blessings of the Sabbath to Israel.

The pericope in Matthew 12:1–8 reinforces the point by virtue of its position, following Jesus' call to the weary to find rest in him rather than in the Mosaic law (11:28–30). In the light of this, Jesus' taking authority over the Sabbath both wrests it from the legal framework in which it previously stood and realizes the rest which God's people were always intended to enjoy.

In all three Synoptics, the subsequent miracle is an example of what Jesus' lordship of the Sabbath will mean in practice: people delivered from the shadow of death and restored into the unblemished image of God.

John's Gospel pursues the Christological implications of Jesus' Sabbath activity. In the climactic statement, 'my Father is working until now, and I am working' (5:17), Jesus claims that the exemption from Sabbath law which applies to God applies to him also; it is the Father's work which the Son does. The discourse which follows reveals that God will realize his goal for humanity in the person and work of his Son. It is the Son who will give life to the dead, judge all people, and bring honour to himself and to the Father. He will realize the Sabbath by bringing an end to human rebellion and the reign of death. He participates with the Father in a second great work of creation, begun after the fall, from which there will be no resting until it is completed.

Paul, the Sabbath and the law

The Sabbath does not feature prominently in Paul's writings, except negatively. For the Galatians to observe it as if they were still subject to OT law would be to descend into gospel-denying slavery (Gal. 4:9–11); for the Colossians to observe it as part of a syncretistic system would be equally fatal (Col. 2:16). For the law belonged to an earlier era, and since the coming of Christ it is no longer binding (Col. 2:17). Even Sabbath observance 'for the Lord' was tolerated only for the sake of those whose faith was weak (Rom. 14:1–12). In short, those in Christ are beyond the jurisdiction of the OT law, which has been fulfilled in Jesus.

The Sabbath in Hebrews

Hebrews 3:7 – 4:11 continues the trajectory of interpretation begun in Exodus 20. Ever since the Seventh Day, there has always existed something called 'God's rest' (4:3–4). This rest is entered by responding to the good news of salvation (4:2), and was the true goal of God's redemption of Israel from Egypt. However, it was not attained by their entry into Canaan, since in David's time it still lay in the future (4:6–9). For Christians, therefore, God's rest is still a future hope, although unbelief will blight this hope as surely for them as it did for Israel (4:2, 11).

However, in two respects the trajectory is discontinuous. First, Psalm 95 referred to the Promised Land and the temple as the place of God's rest. But in Hebrews these copies have given way to the heavenly realities within which Christ now dwells (e.g. 9:11–12, 23–28). Secondly, and crucially, after centuries in which people failed to enter God's rest, one man now *has* entered his rest and ceased from his works as God did from his (4:10). And it is because Christ has already gone before that the writer can speak of Christians' *present* possession of this rest (4:3: 'we who have believed *enter* that rest'). They therefore 'observe the Sabbath' (*sabbatismos*, 4:9) by entering into God's rest (by faith, v. 3) and resting from their works (v. 10). This is a reference to those 'dead works' from which they turned to serve the living God (6:1; 9:14), although ultimately the Sabbath rest will involve the undoing of the curse on work.

Conclusions

In its original setting, the fourth commandment anticipated rest by prescribing rest, so that one kept the Sabbath by resting. However, the command soon escaped these confines, in part through its role as a sign of the whole law, and in part through the failure of Israel to find rest in the land. The stress in the prophets on faithfulness as the heart of Sabbath observance was taken up in the NT, but there it was viewed in the light of what Jesus had done. As God's perfect human, Jesus lived the Sabbath day for God, releasing his fellow humans from bondage, bringing them into blessing, and at the last entering himself into God's rest. Ultimately, as Lord of the Sabbath, Jesus made it possible for others to follow him into that rest. This means that the Christian's task is no longer to keep the Sabbath (Jesus has done that already) but to believe in him.

In its final setting, then, the fourth commandment is no longer a commandment for God's people, but its intent remains. The 'law of Christ' anticipates rest by prescribing belief, but now rest has been realized.

Postscript: the Sabbath and Sunday

We have said nothing about the Christian Sunday since we are convinced that there is no theological connection between Sabbath and Sunday, despite occasional attempts to prove the contrary (e.g. R. T. Beckwith and W. Stott, *This Is the Day*). There are hints in the NT that the first day of the week was set aside for evening worship, including the Lord's Supper (Acts 20:7; 1 Cor. 16:2); Revelation 1:10 refers to 'the Lord's Day'. There is, however, absolutely no indication either that the 'first day' replaced the 'Sabbath day' in practice (the first Jewish

Christians continued to attend the synagogue on the Sabbath), or that there was a transfer of Sabbath theology to Sunday worship. The Sabbath was a day of rest rather than a day of worship, and Sunday became a day of worship but was not initially a day of rest. Regularity, for which the seven-day week provided a ready-made framework, distinguishes (Sunday) worship (e.g. Heb. 10:25); completion, which was (and is) a final goal, distinguishes the Seventh Day. The Sabbath day, then, was a sign of this eschatological rest, whereas Sunday is not presented in the NT as a sign of anything, despite its connection to the resurrection. It is simply a well-chosen day upon which to gather to encourage one another in daily, unceasing striving to enter the Sabbath rest (Heb. 4:11). The only gathering which can truly be described as sabbatical is the gathering of the bond-servants who will reign with the Lamb for ever in the new creation (Rev. 22:3–6).

Bibliography

R. T. Beckwith and W. Stott, *This is the Day: The Biblical Doctrine of the Christian Sunday* (London, 1978); D. A. Carson (ed.), *From Sabbath to Lord's Day: A Biblical, Historical, and Theological Investigation* (Grand Rapids, 1982); G. N. Davies, 'The Christian Sabbath', *RTR* 42, 1983, pp. 33–41; G. F. Hasel in *ABD* 5, pp. 849–856; M. Tsevat, 'The basic meaning of the biblical Sabbath', *ZAW* 84, 1972, pp. 447–459; C. J. H. Wright, 'Jubilee, Year of', in *ABD* 3, pp. 1025–1030; *idem*, 'Sabbatical Year', in *ABD* 5, pp. 857–861.

A. G. SHEAD

SACRED MEALS

Introduction

Among humans friendship is often expressed in having a meal together. When the patriarch Isaac entered into a friendship-treaty with Abimelech, king of Gerar, the occasion was marked by a feast at which they ate and drank together (Gen. 26:30). Feasts appear to have developed among the ancient *Israelites as a means of celebrating their special relationship with Yahweh. At the time of the *Exodus from Egypt *Moses initially asked Pharaoh to let the Israelites hold a feast to the Lord in the desert (Exod.. 5:1; 10:9). When the Israelites eventually succeeded in departing from Egypt following the Passover, the Lord instructed them to commemorate the occasion by holding an annual festival.

Shortly afterwards, when the Israelites entered into a covenant relationship with Yahweh at Mount Sinai, the sealing of the *covenant was marked by a special meal at which Moses, Aaron and seventy elders 'beheld God, and ate and drank' (Exod. 24:11). While there is no suggestion that God ate and drank with them, the meal clearly performed a bonding function. From this point onwards, and especially with the building of the tabernacle, fellowship with Yahweh was to be an important aspect of the religious experience of the Israelites. Such communion was often closely associated with sacred meals. Furthermore, there are indications that the eating of *sacrificial meat was viewed as sanctifying those who participated in the meals.

Of the various sacrifices which individuals could offer to Yahweh, the peace or fellowship-offering is the most like a meal (Lev. 3:1–17; 7:11–21). Individuals might offer this kind of sacrifice when they made vows, had their prayers or vows answered, or just wished to enjoy a meal of meat with friends (Lev. 17:5). In all other sacrifices the *worshipper received nothing back, but in the fellowship-offering most of the flesh was shared out by the worshipper with his or her family and friends, thus making the sacrificial meal a joyful barbecue. Since the peace-offering was eaten by the priest and the family of the sacrificer, rejoicing before the Lord their God (Deut. 27:7) in the tabernacle/*temple complex, it represents the closest approximation in the OT to the idea of *God and human beings sharing a meal together. However, sacrifices and feasts alone did not guarantee fellowship with God, as the prophets said (cf. Is. 1:13–14).

An important feature of cultic worship was the three major yearly festivals of Israel: Passover or Unleavened Bread; the Feast of Weeks or Pentecost; and the Feast of Tabernacles. On these occasions all males had to appear before Yahweh with a gift. They were times of great joy, expressing gratitude to Yahweh for remembering his promises to the founding fathers. The most important emphasis during these three feasts was on looking back and remembering what Yahweh had done (Exod. 23:15; Lev. 23:43; Deut. 16:10–12). Furthermore, the cycle of Palestinian *harvests (indicative of Yahweh's blessing) was linked with Yahweh's *salvation events (*cf.* Exod. 23:14–17 with Lev. 23:4–44) for all time.

Passover and Unleavened Bread

One of the most important occasions for sacred meals was Passover and the feast of Unleavened Bread, which together formed a seven-day festival. The first part of the feast derived its name from the act of Yahweh 'passing over' the houses of the people of Israel when the first-born in every Egyptian household was slaughtered (Exod. 12:29). Exodus 12:1–27 records directions for the observance of the first Passover which were unique to it. In future commemorations of Passover the original model was slightly modified; for example, the blood of the lamb/goat was no longer smeared on the door-posts of the house. In the second and subsequent Passovers Yahweh required all the men of Israel to come together at the place of his choice (Deut. 16:2). The males probably appeared as representatives of their families, and women were not necessarily excluded. Whereas in the first observance of the Passover special attention was given to the *blood of the *lamb as protection from Yahweh's wrath, in all later Passover celebrations the lamb's bloodless carcass provided the centrepiece of a communal meal before Yahweh.

Immediately following the Passover came the feast of Unleavened Bread. The rationale for this feast was that on the first day of the Exodus Yahweh brought Israel's armies out of Egypt (Exod. 12:17), and they left in haste eating the 'bread of affliction'. The annual re-enactment of the events of the night on which they escaped from Egypt was instituted in order that throughout their lives they might remember their departure from Egypt (Deut. 16:6). It was a sacred meal with a distinct theological purpose. The backward historical glance would result in thankfulness to God, like the remembrance of the Lord's death in the communion service.

The Passover in the NT

Of all Israel's festivals, Passover (including the days of Unleavened Bread) was the most important theologically. It was this feast that

*Jesus chose to transform into a new institution to mark his coming substitutionary death for the nation. Just as the Passover blood functioned as a shield against Yahweh's wrath, so in the new age ('the last days') Jesus' blood would serve the same purpose. But instead of handing the meat of the Passover lamb to his disciples with the words: 'this is my body' (thus making a logical connection), he took the lowly unleavened bread, an adjunct to the meal, and gave it a significance it had never had before. He acted astutely in presenting himself under the form of unleavened bread, given the objections of his Jewish opponents to the idea that he was God's spiritual manna from heaven; also his many future disciples from all nations would find the bread acceptable food. His actions indicated that the death of the Passover lamb was about to become redundant; 'Christ our Passover is sacrificed for us' (1 Cor. 5:7). The Passover, in this sense, could never be repeated.

In portraying himself as 'the Lamb of God' who was selected from the foundation of the world to die on behalf of his people in all ages, Jesus sought to focus their attention away from the physical death of the Passover lamb to the need to find spiritual nourishment in him, and he succeeded in doing so by overlaying the Passover with his own Supper. He saw himself as the bread that came down from heaven. Eating the Passover lamb was no longer sufficient for maintaining fellowship with God. It was superseded by eating the body and blood of Christ, symbolized in the bread and wine of the Lord's Supper. To be excommunicated from the church was to be denied access to the supreme sacred meal that Jesus shared with his people.

Because the Passover Festival lasted seven days Paul, acutely aware that he was living in the 'last days' and that the Lord could return any day, followed the chronological logic of 1 Corinthians 5:8 by urging his hearers to 'celebrate the festival' of Unleavened Bread. He believed that the church was living in the period immediately following the Passover day. These were days of unleavened bread – newly harvested grain which had never been in contact with yeast – and this fact suggested to him an analogy with the new teaching brought by Christ from heaven (which was not mixed with the old Mosaic leaven, *cf.* Gal. 5:7–9). Using this analogy, Paul stressed the need to keep the new life in Christ (unleavened bread) completely distinct from the pre-Passover life, which he likened to leavened bread (*i.e.* bread with yeast in it). For Paul, in this context, yeast stands for the old life characterized by wickedness.

Feast of Firstfruits or Pentecost

The second major feast came fifty days after 15th Nisan. It marked the end of the cereal grain harvest when the people came with their tithes and gifts to the central sanctuary. The feast gave expression to their gratitude to and dependence on God (Lev. 23:9–14). Like the first and last days of the feast of Unleavened Bread, the day of Pentecost was a *Sabbath. The whole family, sons and daughters, male and female servants, were encouraged to come to this feast. The Israelites were told to observe it in order to remember that they were slaves in Egypt (Deut. 16:12). This sacred meal also included a backward glance at Yahweh's goodness, and this remembrance was intended to draw the people back into an attitude of deep gratitude to God for his kindness.

Pentecost in the NT

Pentecost was the day on which the Spirit was poured out on the church. It has been suggested that Pentecost was chosen for this momentous event because in the passage from Joel (2:28–31) which Peter said was fulfilled on that day, the prophet spoke in the context of a failed harvest. Joel 1:7–12 says that every kind of crop, including grapes, olives, wheat, barley, figs, pomegranates and apples, had been ravaged by a terrible plague of locusts. But typically, Yahweh pleads with his people to come to their senses and return to him; then he will replace the lost harvests with an abundant *pouring out* of his rains. And then, as if that were not a sufficient inducement, Yahweh promises to *pour out* his Spirit on all flesh, presumably to prevent their wandering away from him again.

Passover and Pentecost are inseparably joined by a fixed space between them; what was promised by Christ on Passover night (John 14:16–20; 16:7–14) was fulfilled at Pentecost with the outpouring of the *Holy Spirit.

The Feast of Trumpets

The seventh month (Tishri, Sept/Oct) contained several important sacred feasts. The first of these was held on the first day of the month. Since the first day of every month was a New Moon, and so a Sabbath day, marked by the blowing of trumpets, it would appear that 1st Tishri was special in some other way. The month marked the 'going out' of the agricultural year (Exod. 23:16), and consequently the first day was New Year's day (as it is for Jews today). This may explain why it is selected for special treatment. It also marked the start of the regnal years of the kings of Israel and Judah. The Jubilee and Sabbatical years began in Tishri (Lev. 25:9). The Gezer Calendar (ca. 925 BC) also begins its list of months with the olive harvest in autumn. The Feast of Trumpets probably marked the end of the agricultural and festival year.

Trumpets are associated with the *theophany on Sinai (Exod. 19:16, 19). Priests sounded trumpets prior to the destruction of Jericho (Josh. 6:16), and soldiers did so after battle (2 Sam. 2:28). Consequently the prophets often referred to trumpets as heralding warnings of *judgment and destruction to come (Jer. 4:5; 6:1; Ezek. 33:3). Trumpet blasts also signalled the beginning of a new era, such as the reign of a new king (1 Kgs. 1:34). The Feast of Trumpets was a signal to Israel that they were entering a very sacred month. The agricultural year was at an end. It was a time to take stock, not only of their farm produce, but also of the *sins that had accumulated over the previous year.

The Feasts of Trumpets in the NT

A loud, penetrating blast on a trumpet would both waken those asleep and interrupt the lives of those going about their ordinary business. It was a deliberately intrusive sacred sound demanding attention. The Feast of Weeks marked the end of one year and the beginning of another; Jesus announced that the present age would be separated from the awesome day of judgment by an impressive trumpet blast (Matt. 24:31). The NT possibly associates trumpets with the end of one age and the opening of another, or with a time of reckoning with God. Revelation describes apocalyptic judgments in terms of a series of trumpet blasts (Rev. 8 – 9). Paul writes that trumpets will introduce the day of resurrection (1 Cor. 15:52; 1 Thess. 4:16), which will mark the end of the age and the introduction of a new heaven and a new earth in which righteousness will dwell.

The Feast of Tabernacles

This feast took place on 15th Tishri, five days after the nation re-committed itself to Yahweh on the Day of *Atonement, and was forgiven and purified from past sins, pollution and shame. The feast restored their fellowship with God. Their thoughts were turned to the privations they endured when they left Egypt by the command to live for seven days in flimsy structures built out of palm fronds and branches from leafy trees. The feast was one of the most expensive and lavish of the year, celebrated in gratitude for the people's *freedom from slavery. In the temple the offering for the first day was thirteen bulls, two rams and fourteen sheep. Each day thereafter the number of bulls was reduced by one. The total offering was 71 bulls, 15 rams, 105 lambs and 8 goats. By eating God's food in a state of purity the people enjoyed real fellowship with their God.

The Feast of Tabernacles in the NT

On the last day of the Feast of Tabernacles, a *priest would draw *water from the pool of Siloam and carry it in a solemn procession to the altar where, it is suggested, he poured it out. This ritual apparently lies behind Jesus' statement that if anyone would come after him, that person would experience streams of living water flowing from within (John 7:37–39), a reference to the promised Holy Spirit (John 14:16–17; 16:7).

The fact that three important religious occasions occurred within the space of three weeks in the seventh month, one of which had to be attended by all the male members of the community, gave this season a special place in the life of the nation. The Feasts of Trumpets announced the end of one year and the beginning of another. Every kind of harvest had been gathered in; the animals had multiplied and the farmers had time to take stock of their blessings. Next came the Day of Atonement and the opportunity to make a new beginning spiritually. Lastly came the Feast of Tabernacles and the opportunity to take stock of the nation's progress since leaving the privations of Egypt so long ago. During these three weeks Israel reassessed its life; this is probably how the first Christians interpreted the period.

With the abolition of the entire OT sacrificial system through the death of Jesus, a different kind of sacrifice is now required of God's people. Paul says: 'I serve like a priest in preaching the Good News from God, in order that the Gentiles may be an offering acceptable to God, dedicated to him by the Holy Spirit' (GNB, Rom. 15:16). All sacrifices are now spiritual; they are acts of faith done in the name of Christ. The only acceptable sacrifices are the living bodies of Christians presented to God in spiritual worship (Rom. 12:1). Christ's death is a real sacrifice (despite appearances), bringing all sacrifice to an end. There is no continuous sacrifice offered in the eucharist. Calvin spelled out the relationship between the sacrificial victims offered under the *law and Christ's sacrifice: 'They pre-figured a true sacrifice such as was finally accomplished in reality by Christ alone; and by him alone, because no other could have done it' (*Institutes* 4, 18, 13).

The marriage supper of the Lamb

The fellowship with God conveyed by the old sacrificial system has been superseded by the fellowship experienced in the Lord's Supper. This meal both brings believers into closer fellowship with God in this world, and anticipates a greater sacred meal, the marriage supper of the Lamb. This feast, at the end of the age, will be an occasion of great rejoicing when 'many will come from the east and west, and will take their places at the feast with Abraham, Isaac and Jacob in the kingdom of heaven' (Matt. 8:11; *cf.* Matt. 22:1–14; Luke 14:15–24). Indeed, such will be the intimacy of the fellowship enjoyed between Christ and all believers that the feast is described as a marriage banquet (Matt. 22:1–14; Rev. 19:9; *cf.* Eph. 5:25–27).

Bibliography:

R. E. Averbeck, 'Offerings and Sacrifices', in *EDBT*, pp. 574–581; T. Holland, *The Contours of Pauline Theology* (Fearn, forthcoming); A. Kanof, 'Passover', in *EJ* 13, pp. 163–173; L. Morris, 'The Passover in rabbinic literature', *ABR* 4, 1954–55, pp. 57–76; G. J. Wenham, *The Book of Leviticus*, NICOT (London, 1979).

L. McFall

SACRIFICE

Introduction

Sacrifice is a form of *worship. It is of very ancient origin and very widespread use, and is found from one end of the Bible to the other.

The general biblical language of sacrifice is, in Hebrew, *qorbān* (that which is brought near, gift), *zebaḥ* (that which is slain, sacrifice), *minḥâh* (gift, also used more specifically for the cereal offering), *'iššeh* (offering made by fire, sacrifice), together with the more specific terms indicated below and a variety of (often cognate) verbs; and in the Greek of the NT, following the LXX, *prosphora* (offering), *dōron* (gift), *thysia* (sacrifice, also cereal offering), and the verbs *prospherō* and *anapherō* (offer), together with the more specific terms *holokautōma* (whole burnt offering), *thymiama* (incense), *spendō* (pour out as a drink offering), and others mentioned below. The Hebrew verb *kipper* (atone), which expresses one of the primary purposes of sacrifice, is usually rendered in the LXX by *exilaskomai* (make propitiation); the NT uses the related verb and nouns *hilaskomai* (make propitiation), *hilasmos*, *hilastērion* (propitiation), or paraphrases from the language of reconciliation, *redemption and ransoming.

The origin of sacrifice

It used to be much discussed, and the question remains relevant, as to whether or not sacrifice was originally instituted by *God. It first appears at the beginning of biblical history in the offerings (*minḥâh*, gift) of Cain and Abel, in Genesis 4, but no direct institution of the practice is recorded. If it was not of divine institution, it was presumably modelled on gifts between humans, and there is an early example of their being compared in the account of Jacob's gift to Esau, of which Jacob speaks in religious terms (Gen. 32:20; 33:10).

However, this connection would not explain the remarkable fact that gifts to God, unlike gifts to humans, characteristically involve the death of animals, and that when God starts making direct regulations about sacrifice this characteristic is further emphasized. Attention has often been directed to the fact that, after our first parents sinned, God clothed them with the skins of animals (Gen.

3:21), thus underlining the link between *sin and *death (*cf*. Gen. 2:17; 3:3, 19, 22). Perhaps the right answer to the question of the origin of sacrifice is that, by clothing them in this remarkable manner, God instituted sacrifice indirectly rather than directly. If so, Abel, a man of faith (Heb. 11:4), saw here an indication that, when approaching God with a gift, sinners should acknowledge their *guilt in the same way, by the death of an animal.

This is not to say that the reason why God accepted Abel's sacrifice and rejected Cain's was that one brought an animal sacrifice and the other a vegetable one (Gen. 4:3–5). Vegetable offerings are afterwards included in the Sinaitic legislation, though they have a subsidiary place. The real reason was that Cain, unlike his brother, was an unrepentant sinner (Gen. 4:7; *cf*. 1 John 3:12). We see here the beginning of another great principle of sacrifice, much emphasized by the prophets, psalmists and wisdom writers, that the inward disposition of worshippers must be right if their 'outward' gift is to be accepted. Nevertheless, insofar as Abel's manner of sacrifice was an indication of his inward disposition, it was not unrelated to the acceptance of his gift.

If sacrifice had been of human origin, its widespread presence among the races of humankind could be explained as having a variety of sources, though doubtless with some degree of imitation between one race and another. If, however, it is of divine origin, and goes back to the beginning of human history, it is one of those primeval ordinances which humankind carried with it in its dispersion across the world, modifying and in some respects distorting it in the process. Imitation of one race by another remains possible, and in view of the evidence from comparative religion, is likely. A comparison between Israel and their neighbours reveals interesting similarities, as well as differences, in sacrificial practice and language, and this should not surprise us, for divine revelation is always given in a particular human context.

The development of OT sacrifice

Once introduced, sacrifice continues throughout the patriarchal age, and altars are recorded as having been built, or sacrifice as having been offered, by Noah, Abraham, Isaac and Jacob. The gift offered is a basis for *prayer, for calling on the name of the Lord

(Gen. 12:8; 13:4; 26:25). The link with prayer continues throughout the OT, and when the *temple is dedicated, Solomon requests that it may be the place at which prayer is answered (1 Kgs. 8); Isaiah describes it as a house of prayer for all peoples (56:7).

Only clean animals are offered in sacrifice (Gen. 8:20), and *Moses later specifies which clean animals are to be offered. Those offering sacrifice must first cleanse themselves and change their clothes (Gen. 35:1–4). According to later restrictions, sacrifices are to be unblemished (Exod. 12:5; Lev. 22:17–25; Mal. 1:6–14), and if eaten, they are to be eaten only by those who are ceremonially clean (Lev. 7:19–21; 22:2–7; Num. 9:6–14) and only within a specified time (Exod. 12:10; Lev. 7:15–18).

Another principle is that those offering sacrifice must first divest themselves of anything relating to *idolatry (Gen. 35:1–4), for the Lord whom they worship is a jealous God (Exod. 20:4–5), requiring the heart of his worshippers to be fully devoted to him (1 Kgs. 11:4; 15:3, 14). Hence his command to the Israelites to blot out everything connected with Canaanite worship from the Promised Land (Exod. 34:12–17; Deut. 7:5–6; 12:2–3), and the struggle of the prophets against Israel's inveterate tendency to syncretism (1 Kgs. 18; Jer. 7; Ezek. 8; Hos. 1 – 5).

Sacrifice begins in Genesis as worship by individuals, on behalf of themselves or their families, and the role of the individual still continues to have a central place in it even after a sanctuary has been established for the whole nation and communal sacrifices instituted. Even the sanctuary regulations refer mostly to individuals ('when any man brings an offering', 'if any one sins', *etc.* [Lev. 1:2; 2:1; 4:2. 22, 27; 5:1, 15, 17; 6:1; RSV]). Sacrificial provision is made for the accidental uncleanness of individuals (Lev. 12 – 15; Num. 19), for a wife suspected of unfaithfulness (Num. 5) and for an individual undertaking a Nazirite vow (Num. 6). The offering of tithes and firstfruits is the responsibility of individuals (Deut. 14:22–29; 26:1–15). The motives that individuals may have in offering a sacrifice include freewill, the fulfilment of a vow and thanksgiving (Lev. 7:12–13, 15–16; 22:18, 21; Num. 15:3, 8).

The earliest communal function of sacrifice is to establish *covenants between the Lord and his creatures. The covenant with Noah, which extends to humankind and animals (Gen. 8:20 – 9:17), the covenant with Abraham, which extends to his seed (Gen. 15), and the covenant of Sinai, between the Lord and Israel (Exod. 24), are all effected by sacrifice. In Genesis 15, the sacrifices are divided and the Lord passes symbolically between the pieces. In Exodus 24, the blood of the sacrifices is sprinkled both on the altar and on the people (vv. 6–8), and the representatives of the people are then admitted to a *sacred meal (v. 11). The principle expressed by these sacrifices is that a covenant involves death, to atone for human trespasses (Heb. 9:15–20). They all take place before the establishment of the tabernacle and *priesthood, though the third of them only just before.

At the establishment and anointing of the tabernacle and priesthood, sacrifice is used for a second communal purpose, to consecrate them, and in this consecration atonement is once again prominent (Exod. 29 – 30; 40; Lev. 8 – 9; Heb. 9:21–22). The tabernacle, or dwelling, of the Lord enables God to 'dwell among the people of Israel' (Exod. 29:45–46) in the pillar of fire and cloud. It is also called the 'tent of meeting', because the Lord meets with Israel there (Exod. 29:42–43; 30:36). But because the Lord dwells among them in the midst of their sins and uncleannesses (Lev. 16:16), they cannot approach him directly, but only through permitted intermediaries, the priests, whose role is to bear the guilt of drawing near to God in his sanctuary (Exod. 28:38; Lev. 10:17; Num. 18:1). For the same reason, atonement needs to be made for the sanctuary and the priesthood, not just when they are first consecrated, but also regularly, on the Day of Atonement (Exod. 30:10; Lev. 16:6, 11, 16–20, 24, 33; Heb. 9:23). Once the altar is consecrated, it in turn sanctifies the gifts offered in sacrifice upon it (Exod. 29:37; 30:29; Matt. 23:19). (See *Holiness.)

After the sanctuary and priesthood are established, sacrifice is turned to a third communal purpose, the statutory offerings of every day, every *Sabbath, every New Moon and every annual feast or fast (Exod. 29:38–42; Lev. 23; Num. 28 – 29). These offerings are primarily the responsibility of the priesthood, but the law says that all male Israelites are to appear before the Lord on the three pilgrim feasts of Passover, Pentecost and

Tabernacles, and are not to come 'empty'/'empty-handed', *i.e.* without a gift (Exod. 23:14–17; 34:18–23; Deut. 16:16–17). Various types of sacrifice are involved in the statutory offerings – burnt offerings, cereal offerings, drink offerings and sin offerings – and there is also a daily offering of sweet incense (Exod. 30:1–9).

The establishment of the sanctuary and priesthood places considerable restrictions on sacrifice elsewhere, presented by laypeople. Leviticus 17 envisages such sacrifices coming to an end, and Deuteronomy 12 does the same, but with the recognition that this has not been possible while the difficulties of the wilderness wanderings have continued, during which time 'every man' has done 'whatever is right in his own eyes', because the Israelites have 'not as yet come to the rest and to the inheritance' of the Promised Land, when it will be possible for the Lord's sanctuary to be established 'in the place which the Lord will choose' (vv. 8–14). After the entry into the Promised Land, but before there was a regular succession of kings, every person continued doing 'what was right in his own eyes' (Judg. 17:6; 21:25), in ritual matters and more generally. The conquest of the land was gradual, and 'rest' was not fully achieved, as R. E. Averbeck points out, until the establishment of the dynasty of David and the capture of *Jerusalem (2 Sam. 7:1, 9–11; 1 Kgs. 5:3–4; 1 Chr. 22:9–10), which made possible the building of Solomon's temple there. Only then did the time for tolerating sacrifice outside the sanctuary, except in the most pressing circumstances, come to an end (1 Kgs. 3:2). The law of Exodus 20:24–26 had given authority for sacrifice 'in every place where I cause my name to be remembered', including not just the sanctuary but places like Mount Ebal, where the Lord specifically authorized sacrifice for a time (Deut. 27:5; Josh. 8:30–31). It is doubtful, however, whether this law applied to *all* places, and the idea that an altar of the kind described would not have stood in the sanctuary but only elsewhere is contrary to our definite knowledge of the second temple, where the brazen altar was accompanied by, or mounted upon, an altar of uncut stones (1 Macc. 4:47, 49; *Mishnah Middot* 1:6; 3:4), perhaps in continuation of an earlier practice. The great sacrifice offered away from the sanctuary belongs not to the old covenant but

to the new (Heb. 13:12).

The practice of sacrifice in the life of Israel came under intense criticism from the prophets, beginning with the anonymous prophet of 1 Samuel 2:27–36, who denounced the profane behaviour of the sons of Eli. As already noted, the prophets also denounced the nation's prevalent syncretism. Samuel told Saul that sacrifice, even when offered to the Lord, is far less important than *obedience, and is a mere formality without it (1 Sam. 15:22–23). The other prophets speak similarly (Jer. 7:21–23; Hos. 6:6; Amos 5:21–27; Mic. 6:6–8). Multitudes of sacrifices, combined with a wicked life, are an abomination to the Lord, says Isaiah (1:11–17). The wise man says the same thing (Prov. 15:8; 21:3, 27). It is not surprising, therefore, to see in the period of the monarchy the beginning of the reinterpretation of sacrificial language in terms of attitudes and acts of devotion. The psalmists speak of thanksgiving and contrition as acceptable sacrifices (Pss. 50:13–15; 51:16–17). Isaiah speaks of the returned exiles being brought back by their captors as an offering to the Lord (66:20). This use of sacrificial language continues in the intertestamental literature (Ecclus. 35:1–3; Gk. *Testament of Levi* 3:6; *Rule of the Community*, 8, 9; Philo, *De Somniis* 2:183) and it culminates in the NT. The attempt by some to refer at least the OT examples to literal sacrifices must be reckoned a failure.

The types of OT sacrifice

Burnt offerings, peace/fellowship offerings and the Passover sacrifice are the earliest types of OT animal sacrifice, all of them established before the erection of the tabernacle or the consecration of the priesthood, and they continue to be the most basic types in Israel's worship thereafter. They are the only animal sacrifices named in Deuteronomy (which is very concise in its references to ritual matters), and in the OT outside the Pentateuch they, along with the cereal offering, are the sacrifices most frequently mentioned. The drink offering, in contrast, is rarely mentioned (although it appears as early as Gen. 35:14); likewise the sin and guilt offerings. There are references to the sin offering in Psalm 40:6 and to the guilt offering in Isaiah 53:10, and both are prominent in Ezekiel's temple prophecy (Ezek. 40 – 48), but when David needs to atone for his sin in numbering the people, it is burnt offerings and peace/fellowship offerings that he presents (2 Sam. 24:25; 1 Chr. 21:26). It is possible that when, for whatever reason, sacrifice needed to be offered, and atonement made, away from the sanctuary, the sin offering, which atoned for sin in direct relationship to its defiling effect upon the sanctuary, was avoided, and the burnt offering, which also had an atoning function, was used instead. The only sin offering known to have been offered outside the sanctuary is that of Numbers 19:19, and even that is deliberately related to the sanctuary by the sprinkling of its blood (v. 4).

Four symbolic regulations which apply to all types of sacrifice in the Sinaitic legislation should be noted. First, salt is offered with all sacrifices (Lev. 2:13; *cf.* Ezek. 43:24). It is described as 'the salt of the covenant with your God'. A 'covenant of salt' (Num. 18:19; *cf.* 2 Chr. 13:5) is a permanent covenant, salt being a preservative. The sacrifices are offered under the terms of the Sinaitic covenant, and they maintain that covenant (Ps. 50:5).

Secondly, fat is to be eaten neither by priests nor by other worshippers, but is always to be burned on the altar, as part of the Lord's portion (Lev. 3:16–17; 7:22–25). This is probably because fat was reckoned the best part of the flesh. The law often mentions the fat on the kidneys in this connection, and the phrase 'the fat of wheat' or 'the kidney-fat of wheat' is used metaphorically to refer to the finest wheat (Deut. 32:14; Pss. 81:16; 147:14; author's translation).

Thirdly, the laying (lit. 'leaning') of the worshipper's hand upon the head of the sacrifice before it is killed (Lev. 1:4; 3:2; 4:4, *etc.*) probably indicates representation or substitution, the former perhaps with the burnt offering, the latter with the sin offering, and either or both with the peace/fellowship offering. In the case of the scapegoat (Lev. 16:21–22) it clearly implies the transference of sins, but here both hands are used, and the scapegoat is not killed but sent away.

A fourth regulation, which goes back to Genesis 9:4 and is much insisted on, is that blood must never be eaten. This is discussed below in the section on sin and guilt offerings, but applies more generally.

1. *The burnt offering.* The only type of animal sacrifice named in the patriarchal narratives is the burnt offering (*'ôlāh,* that

which goes up, Gen. 8:20; 22:2–13). It is also named in the book of Job (1:5; 42:8), which has a patriarchal setting, even if it was written somewhat later. The Mosaic ritual of the sacrifice is described in Leviticus 1:3–17; 6:8–13. The chief characteristic of the burnt offering is that the whole sacrifice is made over to God as a gift and consumed by fire. It is also called the 'whole' burnt offering (Deut. 33:10; Ps. 51:19), and its costliness to the worshipper is significant (2 Sam. 24:24). The burnt offering is a symbol of dedication, and the supreme expression of this dedication is the self-dedication to the will of God spoken of, in sacrificial terms, in Psalm 40:6–8 (*cf.* Rom. 12:1), and exemplified in Abraham's willingness even to offer his son Isaac as a burnt offering, if God wished it (Gen. 22; Heb. 11:17–19; Jas. 2:21–23). The ideas of costliness and dedication have entered, from biblical sources, into the common consciousness of humankind, and reflect what the word 'sacrifice' usually means to people today.

The references in Job show that the burnt offering is not without an atoning significance also, a fact recognized elsewhere (Lev. 1:4; 16:24; 2 Sam. 24:25). The 'pleasing odour' of the burning (Gen. 8:21) is a token of divine acceptance, and is used as a metaphor in the NT to mean that a sacrifice is acceptable to God (Eph. 5:2; Phil. 4:18).

2. *The peace/fellowship offering.* The only type of animal sacrifice other than the burnt offering that even begins to appear in the patriarchal period (though without the name) is the *peace offering. In the covenant sacrifice of Genesis 31:54, where Jacob makes a covenant with his relatives, the whole sacrifice is not consumed by fire, but concludes, as in the peace offering, with a meal. The name 'peace offering' (*šelem*) first occurs in Exodus 20:24; 24:5, and the Mosaic ritual is described in Leviticus 3:1–17; 7:11–34.

The peace/fellowship offering is, like the Passover, a sacrifice in which lay worshippers are allowed to share in the sacred meal, normally a priestly privilege. Nor do they just share the food of priests; they share the food of God. The tabernacle and temple symbolize the court of a king; indeed, the same word in Hebrew (*hêykal*) is used for a temple and a palace. The altar of burnt offering is the king's table (Mal. 1:7, 12), and the regular sacrifices there are accompanied by cereal offerings and drink offerings (Exod. 29:38–41; Num. 15:1–12) because the table of a king must have not only flesh on it but also bread and wine. The sacrifices are described as his bread or food (Lev. 3:11; 21:6, 8, 17, 21; 22:25; Num. 28:2; Ezek. 44:7), which his servants the priests are regularly allowed to eat (Lev. 21:22; *cf.* 1 Cor. 9:13), but this is a privilege which at Passover time and in the peace offering he bountifully extends to all his subjects. Such language is emphatically symbolic (Ps. 50:7–13), but the symbolism is significant. Paul points out that all who eat at the table of a god, after sacrifice, have fellowship with him, and this is a fellowship which Christians enjoy at the Lord's Supper, following the sacrifice of the cross (1 Cor. 10:14–22).

3. *The Passover sacrifice.* This sacrifice, the first to be explicitly instituted by God, dates from the eve of Israel's departure from Egypt. After the Lord had distinguished them from their captors in the great plagues which he brought upon the Egyptian nation, he commanded each household to sacrifice a *lamb or kid and to keep the Passover (*pesaḥ*). They were to mark the entrances of their houses with the blood of the sacrifice, so as to distinguish them in the last great plague which would complete their liberation (Exod. 12:7, 13, 22–23, 27). This is the first time that the blood of the sacrifice, symbolizing life laid down in death, receives special attention, and it underlines the atoning significance of the sacrifice (*cf.* Lev. 17:11). In later times, the blood of the Passover lambs, like that of other sacrifices, was sprinkled by the priests, as an atonement, on the altar of the temple court (2 Chr. 35:10–11).

A second development seen in this sacrifice, which is relatively innovative, is that after the lamb or kid has been killed, its flesh is roasted and forms the basis of a sacred meal (Exod. 12:8–9). In this respect the Passover resembles the peace/fellowship offering.

A third new development is that the Passover is instituted as an annual festival (Exod. 12:14–20, 24–27, 42; 13:3–10). Each year on the anniversary of the Exodus the Israelites are to repeat the sacrifice, in order that they may each year be reminded of their deliverance and may be thankful (Exod. 12:14, 42; 13:3, 9; Deut. 16:3). As an aid to their recollection, they are each year to eat

unleavened bread with the lamb, as they did on the first occasion, because they were leaving in haste before their dough could rise, and they are to continue eating unleavened bread for the next seven days (Exod. 12:8, 11, 14–20, 34, 39; 13:3, 6–9; Deut.16:3–4). The sacred meal which *Jesus afterwards instituted at the Passover season, on the eve of his death, was likewise a meal of remembrance, though in remembrance of a greater deliverance (Luke 22:19–20; 1 Cor. 11:24–26).

4. *The vegetable offerings.* Before the consecration of the sanctuary and priesthood, the vegetable offerings appear only in the drink offering (*neseḵ*, that which is poured out) offered by Jacob in Genesis 35:14. The cereal offering (*minḥâh*), with which the drink offering is afterwards frequently linked, first appears at the institution of the daily sacrifice in Exodus 29:41. The ritual of the cereal offering is described in Leviticus 2:1–16; 6:14–23, but the ritual of the drink offering is never described, possibly because of its simplicity, consisting just of the pouring upon the altar of a quantity (sometimes a prescribed quantity) of wine or strong drink.

Tithes and firstfruits are partly vegetable offerings, though not wholly, and the three Mosaic festivals linked with the annual harvest, the Sheaf (barley), Pentecost or Feast of Weeks (wheat) and Tabernacles or Ingathering (the rest of the harvest), centre on vegetable offerings. In the Holy Place of the sanctuary, which lay between the brazen altar of burnt offering and the Holy of Holies, only vegetable offerings were allowed: the incense of the golden altar; the oil of the lampstand; and the twelve loaves of the bread of the presence, the 'shewbread' (AV), symbolizing the twelve tribes of Israel; the one to whom they were 'shown' was the Lord (Exod. 25:30). Only in exceptional circumstances, of poverty or emergency, were vegetable offerings used for purposes of atonement (Lev. 5:11–13; Num. 16: 44–50).

5. *The sin and guilt offerings.* The sin or purification offering (*ḥaṭṭa't*) and the guilt or reparation offering (*'āšām*) were instituted at Sinai. The ritual is elaborate: that for ordinary occasions is described in Leviticus 4:1 – 6:7; 6:24 – 7:10; that for the Day of Atonement in Leviticus 16.

The primary characteristic of the sin and guilt offering is not, as with the burnt offering, the complete consumption of the sacrifice by fire, or, as with the peace/fellowship offering, the sacred meal that follows, but the application of the blood, which is used for atonement. Particular sins may be atoned for at any time in the year. If the sinner is a priest, or the whole nation (including the priests), the blood is taken to the Holy Place, where priests belong, and sprinkled before the veil and put on the horns of the incense altar. If the sinner is a ruler or commoner, the blood is put on the horns of the altar of burnt offering in the court, where laypeople belong. The residue of the blood is poured out at the base of the altar of burnt offering. In view of Leviticus 17:13 and Psalm 16:4, this pouring is probably not to be regarded as a drink offering, but either as a sanctifying ceremony (*cf.* Lev. 8:15) or just as reverent disposal, like the burning of the refuse of sacrifices outside the camp. On no account, however, must blood be eaten. Because blood symbolizes life laid down in death, and God has given it to make atonement, it must not be treated as a common thing (Lev. 17:10–12; Deut. 12:23–25).

No part of the sin offering may be eaten by the worshipper. However, part of it is reserved for the priests who present it to God (as also with the peace offering and cereal offering), the rest being burned on the altar; except in cases where the priests are involved in the transgression for which the sin offering is brought, in which case they forfeit their portion (Lev. 6:16–18, 29–30; 7:6–10, 14, 28–36; Num. 18:8–32).

Once a year, in addition to this atonement for particular sins, a general atonement for the sins of the whole nation, priests and people, is made. Beyond the Holy Place lies the Holy of Holies, separated by a further veil and in total darkness. Here, at the centre of Israel's worship, no image of God is permitted, but only a chest (the ark of the covenant) containing the stone tablets of his law. No-one may enter here, except once in the year, on the Day of Atonement, and then the high priest alone, who makes atonement with the blood of sin offerings for all his own sins and all those of Israel, sprinkling the blood upon and before the mercy seat that covers the tablets of the Ten Commandments, and making atonement also for the sanctuary, which dwells with Israel in the midst of their

uncleannesses and sins (Lev. 16:11–19). On this occasion an extra sin offering is provided, the scapegoat, for which atonement is made, and over which all the sins of Israel are confessed, after which it is sent away to carry them into the wilderness (vv. 10, 20–22; *cf.* 14:6–7). This is a clear indication that the sins of Israel, when atoned for, are removed.

Since the burnt offering also has an atoning function, the atoning roles of the sin and guilt offerings seem to be more specific. In Leviticus 4 – 7, they are mostly said to atone for unwitting sin, but Leviticus 6:2–5 is an exception to this rule, and the real contrast appears to be not with conscious sin but with arrogant and blasphemous sin, for which indeed there is no atonement (Num. 15:22–36; for the distinction *cf.* also Ps. 19:12–13) It is clear from Leviticus 5 – 6 that the guilt offering atones for those sins for which there is some possibility of reparation, and it is clear from many passages that the sin offering atones for sin as it affects the sanctuary, cleansing and sanctifying the sanctuary from sin's defilement (Exod. 29:36; 30:10; Lev. 8:14–15; 16:16–20; 2 Chr. 29:21; Ezek. 43:19–22; 45:18–20). These seem to be the more specific atoning roles that the guilt offering and sin offering fulfil.

The sacrifice of Christ

After the return from the Babylonian exile and the building of the second temple, the Mosaic law of sacrifice was once again put into practice in Jerusalem, and with less interference and fewer distractions, on the whole, than before. In the lifetime of Jesus this observance still continued. He had sacrifice offered for him, or offered it himself, at his presentation in the temple, at his last Passover, and presumably on those other occasions when he went up to Jerusalem for the feasts. After his death and resurrection, the apostles continued to frequent the temple, including even Paul, who went up to Jerusalem for the feast of Pentecost, and on that occasion offered the sacrifices, which included sin offerings, for the interruption of Nazirite vows (Acts 18:18; 21:23–26; see Num. 6:9–12).

Despite this outward continuity through the NT period, the teaching of the NT shows that everything had changed. The sacrifices on which it concentrates attention are not those of the temple but the atoning sacrifice of Christ and the spiritual sacrifices of Christians. In principle, the Mosaic sacrifices were now unnecessary. While the temple stood, Jewish Christians felt some duty to observe its ordinances, but when, in AD 70, the temple was destroyed by the Romans in suppressing the first Jewish revolt, and the offering of sacrifice there came to an end, Christians could see a certain appropriateness in the event. Ever since Jeremiah had announced a new covenant, and had thereby made the covenant of Sinai 'old', it had been 'obsolete and ... ready to vanish away' (Heb. 8:13), and now, through the coming and work of Christ, it had actually done so.

The fullest NT discussion of the OT sacrifices is found in the epistle to the Hebrews. The writer's teaching on those sacrifices has its positive side (11:4, 17–19, 28), but his great concern is to point out their inadequacy except as types foreshadowing the Christian realities. The fact that they cannot gain human beings entrance into the Holy of Holies proves that they cannot free the conscience from guilt, but are simply fleshly ordinances, imposed until a time of reformation (9:6–10). The rending of the veil came only with the death of Christ (Mark 15:37–38; Heb. 10:20). The inability of the sacrifices to atone is shown also by the fact that mere animals are offered (Heb. 10:4), and by the fact of their repetition (10:1–2). They are not so much remedies for sin as reminders of it (10:3).

The sacrifice of Christ is not only foreshadowed in the OT but also prophesied. The NT identifies Jesus with the suffering servant of Isaiah 52 – 53, who is to be a guilt offering for others (Is. 53:10), and since the prophecy distinguishes him both from the nation (Is. 53:8) and from the prophet himself (Is. 53:2–6), it is difficult to see who the suffering servant can be except an eschatological figure, such as the Messiah. In this prophecy, the ideas of atoning sacrifice and vicarious punishment are combined. In the law of Moses sacrifice and punishment are closely related concepts, as a comparison of Leviticus 16:16 with Numbers 35:33–34 clearly shows, and in Isaiah 52 – 53 the punishment sinners deserve is accepted by another, the one who offers himself as a guilt offering.

In Daniel 9 there is a prophecy of a Messiah or 'anointed one'. It is stated that he will be 'cut off', that is, killed (v. 26), and

that he will atone (*kipper*) for iniquity (v. 24).

Many of the NT references to Christ's sacrifice as a fulfilment of OT types represent him as a lamb, an animal used for various sacrifices (burnt offering, peace offering, and sin or guilt offering). He is represented as the slain lamb of God, whose precious blood takes away the sin of the world (John 1:29, 36; 1 Pet. 1:18–19; Rev. 5:6–10; 13:8). In a similarly general way, but again with the emphasis on atonement, the blood of his sacrifice is said to cleanse from sin (Heb. 9:13–14, 21–23; 10:19–22; 12:24; 1 Pet. 1:2; 1 John 1:7), and he is said to have been sent by God to be a propitiation for our sins (Rom. 3:25; 1 John 2:2; 4:10). More specifically, he is said to be our sacrificed Passover lamb (*pascha*, 1 Cor. 5:6–8); to have been 'made ... sin' (or a sin offering) for us (2 Cor. 5:21); to have been sent by God as a sin offering (*peri hamartias*, Rom. 8:3, *cf.* LXX Lev. 5:7, 11; 9:2, 3 *etc.*); and, in Hebrews 9 – 10, to be the fulfilment of the Day of Atonement offerings in Leviticus 16, of the red heifer sacrifice for corpse-uncleanness in Numbers 19, and of the covenant sacrifice in Exodus 24. His sacrifice has made true atonement; it cleanses the conscience and not just the flesh; and has introduced a new and eternal covenant.

In the epistle to the Hebrews, the sacrifice of Christ is expounded with great thoroughness, and is related also to his priesthood and sanctuary. His sanctuary is not an earthly one, but *heaven itself, the truly holy place (Heb. 8:1–5; 9:11–12, 23–24; 10:19–22). He entered there (9:24) when he passed through the heavens (4:14; *cf.* 7:26) at his ascension, following the rending of the veil in the temple at his death (10:19–20), and it is there, not on earth, that his priesthood rightly belongs (8:4–5). This does not alter the fact that his sacrifice belongs essentially on earth. The epistle lays repeated stress on the importance, in Christ's sacrifice, of his death (2:9, 14; 9:15–17, 22, 25–28; 13:12, 20). All that was costly in Christ's sacrifice, the part of the donor and the victim, took place on earth, at the cross. There remained, however, the truly priestly part, the acceptable presentation of the sacrifice to God in his sanctuary by a holy but sympathizing mediator, and this was performed by Christ when, in his glorified human nature, he returned to heaven. He is said to have offered something there (8:3), probably a reference to the sprinkling or offering of blood in the Holy of Holies by the high priest on the Day of Atonement, a typical action fulfilled by Jesus, the true High Priest (9:7, 21–26; *cf.* 12:24), and perhaps carried out by his simply 'appearing in the presence of God on our behalf' (9:24). Once he had appeared there, his sacrifice was complete, as is clear from many passages which speak of his sacrifice as once for all, past and finished, not only passages which speak of his sacrifice in general terms (1:3), but also · passages which speak of it specifically under its priestly aspect (7:27; 9:11–12, 25–28; 10:10–14, 18). The idea that Christ's sacrifice belongs wholly to heaven, because his priesthood does, or that it continues, like his priesthood, for ever, is quite contrary to the teaching of the epistle. Christ's continuing priestly work, like that of the priests in Psalm 99:6 and Joel 2:17, is not sacrificial but intercessory (Heb. 7:24–25). It is propitiatory (2:17) only in the same sense as his advocacy in 1 John 2:2, namely, that it is an intercession based on the once for all propitiation that he offered on the cross.

We referred earlier to the sacrificial act of self-dedication described by the psalmist in Psalm 40:6–8. In Hebrews 10:5–10, this passage is quoted and is stated to have been fulfilled in the sacrifice of Christ. It follows that his sacrifice was not a merely outward act, still less a merely ceremonial act, but was as much an act of inward devotion as the spiritual sacrifices of his followers, indeed more so, he being without sin (Heb. 4:15; 9:14). At the same time, it was unique among spiritual sacrifices in being an atoning act; the will of God to which the Son of God dedicated himself was that he should offer his body as a sacrifice, once for all, and by this act sinners are sanctified (10:8–14). As he said himself on the eve of his death, 'This is my blood of the covenant, which is poured out for many for the forgiveness of sins' (Matt. 26:28).

It is a mistake to think of Christ's sacrifice as no more than a figurative sacrifice. To do so is to take sacrifices of the OT sort as the norm whereas, according to the NT, they were simply types of the true sacrifice to come, which fulfilled them. Before one can have a house, one needs a plan, but what matters is not the plan but the house. The OT sacrifices provide providential categories for the interpretation of Christ's sacrifice, but it everywhere transcends those categories. For the blood of animals, we have the blood of the man Christ Jesus (Heb. 10:4). For spotlessness, we have sinlessness (Heb. 9:14; 1 Pet. 1:19). For a sweet smelling odour, we have true acceptability (Eph. 5:2). For the sprinkling of our bodies with blood, we have *forgiveness (Heb. 9:13–14, 19–22; 1 Pet. 1:2). For symbolic atonement, endlessly repeated, we have real atonement, once for all (Heb. 10:1–10).

The sacrifices of Christians

In the life of Israel, sacrificial language started to be reinterpreted in terms of attitudes and acts of devotion (see above). This view of sacrifice naturally commended itself to those separated from the temple, such as the Qumran community, and after the destruction of the temple it became prominent in the liturgy of rabbinical times. Its most far-reaching development, however, is in the NT. Here it is the sacrifice of Christ that has fulfilled atoning sacrifice and made ceremonial sacrifices obsolete. And it is through his atoning sacrifice that Christians also can offer acceptable sacrifices to God (Heb. 13:15; 1 Pet. 2:5), though not, of course, atoning sacrifices. His sacrifice has introduced the age of the *Holy Spirit, when all acceptable worship must be spiritual, that is, Spirit-inspired (John 4:23–24; Phil. 3:3), and the 'spiritual sacrifices' of Christians (1 Pet. 2:5; *cf.* Rom. 15:16) include acts of worship, such as praise and prayer (Heb. 13:15; Rev. 5:8; 8:3), but also acts of witness and service, such as evangelism, gifts to the ministry and gifts to the poor (Rom. 15:16–17; Phil. 4:18; Heb. 13:16), and comprehensive attitudes and expressions of devotion, such as faith (Phil. 2:17), the consecration of one's life to the will of God (Rom. 12:1) and the laying down of one's life for the sake of the gospel (Phil. 2:17; 2 Tim. 4:6; Rev. 6:9). The priests who present these sacrifices are those who give them, *i.e.* Christians (1 Pet. 2:5, 9; *cf.* also Is. 61:6; Rom. 15:17; Rev. 1:6; 5:10; 20:6), and the sanctuary where they present them is not the temple in Jerusalem, but heaven, to which after the rending of the veil, those who are in the Spirit already have access (John 4:21–24; Heb. 10:19–25).

See also: ATONEMENT; BLOOD.

Bibliography

R. E. Averbeck, in *NIDOTTE* 2, pp. 888–908; 4, pp. 996–1022; R. T. Beckwith and M. J. Selman (eds.), *Sacrifice in the Bible* (Carlisle and Grand Rapids, 1995); C. Eastwood, *The Royal Priesthood of the Faithful* (London, 1963); A. Edersheim, *The Temple: its Ministry and Services as they were at the time of Jesus Christ* (London, 1874); M. Haran, *Temples and Temple-Service in Ancient Israel* (Oxford, 1978); J. H. Kurtz, *Sacrificial Worship of the Old Testament* (ET, Edinburgh, 1863); H. H. Meeter, *The Heavenly High Priesthood of Christ* (Grand Rapids, 1916); J. Milgrom, *Leviticus 1–16*, AB (New York, 1991); L. Morris, *The Apostolic Preaching of the Cross* (London, 1955); J. B. Segal, *The Hebrew Passover from the earliest times to AD 70* (London, 1963).

R. T. BECKWITH

SAINTS, SANCTIFICATION, see HOLINESS

SALVATION

The nature of salvation

In essence salvation is the act or state of deliverance from harm or peril, whether that danger be physical or spiritual, temporal or eternal.

Terminology

The basic Hebrew root denoting salvation or deliverance is *yš'*, which is used 354 times in the OT. It is consistently rendered in the Septuagint by the Greek verb *sōzō* ('save') and its derivatives: *sōtēria* ('salvation'); *sōtēr* ('saviour'); *sōtērios* ('bringing salvation'); and compound verbs *anasōzō* ('rescue') and *diasōzō* ('preserve'). All these Greek words (except for *anasōzō*) are also used in the NT in reference to salvation. Other Old Testament terms that occupy the same general semantic field as the verb *yāša'* ('save', 'deliver', a form of the root *yš'*) are *'āzar* ('help'), *hiṣṣîl*, ('rescue'), *pālaṭ* ('bring to safety'), *millēṭ* ('deliver'), and the two forensic terms, *gā'al* ('redeem') and *pādâ* ('ransom', 'redeem'). Sometimes several of these terms are clustered. ' "I am with you to save [*hôšîa'*]

you and deliver [*hiṣṣîl*] you," declares the LORD. "I will deliver [*hiṣṣîl*] you from the hands of the wicked, and redeem [*pādâ*] you from the grasp of the cruel" ' (Jer. 15:20–21, author's translation). The name *Iēsous* ('Jesus') is the Greek form of the Hebrew name *yēšûa'*, a later form of *yᵉhôšûa'* ('Joshua'; 'Yahweh helps/is salvation'), which is formed from the root *yš'* (see Acts 7:45; Heb. 4:8 where *Iēsous* refers to Joshua, the successor of Moses; and Matt. 1:21, which links the name 'Jesus' with his role as 'Saviour').

Range of meaning

In biblical usage, salvation is a comprehensive term denoting all the benefits, physical or spiritual, that are graciously bestowed on humans by *God. The use of the Hebrew verb *hôšîa'* (the hiphil of *yš'*) and the Greek verb *sōzō* in reference to both physical and spiritual *healing reflects the Bible's holistic view of salvation, which can be summed up in the Hebrew term *šālôm* ('*peace') that refers to personal wholeness and well-being in every sphere. As preservation from danger, salvation may involve national deliverance (Neh. 9:27; Is. 45:17), relief from slavery (Deut. 24:18), recovery after illness (Ps. 69:29; Jas. 5:15) or the healing of disease (Acts 4:9), release from prison (Phil. 1:19), protection from danger (Matt. 8:25; Acts 27:20; Heb. 11:7), rescue from troubles (Ps. 34:6, 19) or from the wicked (Ps. 37:40), protection from *evil (Jas. 1:21) or from divine *judgment (1 Thess. 1:10) or from *death, whether physical (2 Cor. 1:10) or spiritual (Jas. 5:20). But salvation *from* some danger often also means salvation *for* some benefit (2 Tim. 4:17–18); the negative and the positive are intertwined. Deliverance from God's wrath (Rom. 5:9) comes about by the forgiveness of *sin (Luke 1:77; 24:47). Paul actually defines 'redemption' (*apolytrōsis*) as 'the forgiveness of sins' (Col. 1:14; *cf.* Ps. 130:4, 8).

Some commentators regard salvation as central to the NT. A. M. Hunter sees 'the theme of the New Testament as the consummation of God's saving purpose for his People declared in the Old Testament', comprising three main features: 'a message of salvation centring in a Saviour; a saved People; and the means of salvation' (*The Unity of the NT*, p. 107; *The Message of the*

NT, p. 118). J. Gnilka finds the centre in 'Jesus Christ, who acted in God's name and in whom God accomplished salvation' (*Neutestamentliche Theologie*, p. 7), while G. B. Caird organizes his *New Testament Theology* around the theme of salvation.

The provision of salvation

In both Testaments God is portrayed pre-eminently as 'a God who saves' (Ps. 68:20). His '*kingdom' is his eternal saving sovereignty (Ps. 145:13; Rev. 11:15), both his saving action as ruler and the realm where that salvific rule is exercised. The essence of each Testament is the announcement that salvation has been provided by God: in one case, at the *Exodus (Deut. 6:21–23), which brought about physical deliverance; in the other case, at the cross (Col. 1:19–20), which brought about spiritual emancipation.

In the OT

Various means were used to achieve salvation, some impersonal, such as the pillar of cloud and the wind at the Red Sea (Exod. 14:19–21), and some personal, such as Gideon (Judg. 6 – 8) and Esther (Est. 4 – 7). But whatever the means, it is God and God alone who brings salvation (2 Chr. 20:17; Hos. 1:7). 'I, even I, am the LORD, and apart from me there is no saviour' (Is. 43:11). When God's people were confronted by adversity, trust in military might or human artifice was misguided; the way of true wisdom was exclusive reliance on 'the God of (our) salvation' (Ps. 79:9; cf. Prov. 21:31). It was *God* who raised up *Moses (Ps. 105:26) and the judges (Judg. 2:18) to deliver his people.

The principal example of God's intervention to save, his salvation, was the Exodus, when 'the LORD saved Israel from the hands of the Egyptians' (Exod. 14:30; cf. 14:13; 15:2) and entered into *covenant relationship with the newly constituted nation (Exod. 19:1 – 20:17; Hos. 11:1), an event which marked their birth as a theocracy (Ps. 114:1–2). The covenant brought the two parties not merely into a contractual relationship but also into communion; God promised to be present with his people (Exod. 29:45–46; Lev. 26:12). From one viewpoint, the remainder of the OT is an account of Israelite deviations from the terms of the covenant (Neh. 9:9–31; Ps. 78:12–64; Jer. 7:21–26) and of prophetic exhortations to return to the LORD and his covenant (Jer. 11:1–8), exhortations that sometimes prompted covenantal renewal and religious reform.

One of the most distinctive OT descriptions of God is 'I am the LORD your God, who brought you out of Egypt, out of the land of slavery' (Exod. 20:2; Deut. 5:6; cf. Exod. 29:46; Lev. 26:13). Outside the Pentateuch similar descriptions are found in the historical books (Judg. 6:8; 2 Chr. 7:22), in the Psalms (Ps. 81:10), and in the prophets (Jer. 34:13; Dan. 9:15). This momentous act of salvation, this miraculous display of God's power (Neh. 9:10–11), became the pattern for the future deliverance of God's people. Accordingly, the return from *exile in Babylon, a second Egyptian captivity, was seen as another Exodus accomplished by God (Is. 43:14–21; 52:9; Jer. 16:14–15; Hos. 2:14–16).

In the NT

There are two crucially distinctive elements in the NT concept of salvation. First, whereas before it could be said that God 'bring(s) salvation upon the earth' (Ps. 74:12; cf. Exod. 14:13), now it can be said that 'salvation belongs to our God who is seated on the throne, *and to the Lamb*' (Rev. 7:10; cf. 1 Thess. 5:9; 2 Tim. 2:10). *Jesus Christ, the Lamb of God (John 1:29), appeared on earth to bring salvation (Titus 2:11), that is, 'to save sinners' (1 Tim. 1:15), 'to seek and to save the lost' (Luke 19:10). As 'the author of their salvation' (Heb. 2:10; cf. 7:25) he is the Saviour (Matt. 1:21; Luke 2:11) in whom people must believe if they are to be saved (John 14:6; Acts 4:12). The title 'our Saviour' is used in each chapter of Titus, first in reference to God (Titus 1:3; 2:10; 3:4), then, shortly after, in reference to Jesus (Titus 1:4; 2:13; 3:6), which is potent testimony to the deity of this Saviour.

Second, the benefits of the salvation procured by Christ are applied to individual believers by the *Holy Spirit, the *alter ego* of Jesus (John 14:16–18), the Spirit of God's Son (Gal. 4:6). In Jewish thought, the new age, the age to come, would be marked by the giving of the Spirit (Ezek. 11:19; 36:26–27). This 'promise of the Father' (Luke 24:49; Acts 1:4) was fulfilled on the day of Pentecost when God poured out his Spirit to reside permanently on all his people without distinction, young and old, male and female (Acts 2:17–21, citing Joel 2:28–32).

The scope of salvation

In the OT

Most of the recorded instances of God's saving intervention involve his chosen people, *Israel, and groups of people rather than isolated individuals. Although there are instances of individual salvation (*e.g.* 1 Sam. 1:16–20), especially in the Psalms (*e.g.* Pss. 43, 86), it is more often the community as a whole, whether small or large, that experiences God's deliverance. *Noah and his family are preserved from the flood (Gen. 7:1–7). The whole nation of Israel is rescued from Egypt (Exod. 14 – 15) and then from various surrounding peoples (*e.g.* Judg. 4 – 5; 2 Sam. 8:1–14).

But Israel is called to be both a saved nation and a saving nation. It is in Abraham's seed that all the peoples on earth will be blessed (Gen. 12:3; *cf.* Gal. 3:8, 14, 29). In the prophets the emphasis is less on salvation as deliverance from trouble and more on salvation as restoration to divine favour by penitence. Being seen less in national and political terms and more in spiritual terms, salvation becomes more universal. Gentiles will share its blessings (Is. 45:23–24; 49:8–12; 60:1–12). While there are many prophetic oracles of doom addressed to surrounding cities and *nations (*e.g.* Amos 1:3 – 2:3; Jer. 46 – 51), through the Servant of the LORD, whether regarded as an individual or as the whole nation, God will bring 'a light to the Gentiles, and salvation to the ends of the earth' (Is. 49:6; cited in Acts 13:47). At that time all the nations will stream into Zion, 'the city of the Lord' (Is. 2:2–3; 60:3, 14). In the last days 'everyone who calls on the name of the LORD will be saved, for on Mount Zion and in Jerusalem there will be deliverance' (Joel 2:32).

In the NT

Here the promise of salvation is not merely 'for you [Jews] and for your children' but also 'for all who are far off' (Acts 2:39; *cf.* 3:25; 28:28; Gal. 3:8), that is, Gentiles, who in Christ have been brought near to God through the blood of Christ (Eph. 2:13, 17). Salvation is universal in the sense that no-one is excluded from the invitation of Jesus for people to come to him and so find soul relief (Matt. 11:28–29) or from the gospel call to *repentance and *faith (Acts 20:21). 'There is no difference between Jew and Greek – the same Lord is Lord of all and bestows his riches on all who call on him, for "Everyone who calls on the name of the Lord will be saved"' (Rom. 10:12–13, citing Joel 2:32; LXX, 3:5). Salvation is not experienced by all without exception, but it is offered to all without distinction of race, status, or sex, so that for those in Christ Jesus 'there is neither Jew nor Greek, there is neither slave nor free, there is no "male and female" [Gen. 1:27]' (Gal. 3:28). God's desire is that all people be saved (1 Tim. 2:4).

It may be that when God is described as 'the Saviour of all people, especially (*malista*) of those who believe' (1 Tim. 4:10), he is depicted as the gracious benefactor and preserver of all humans (*cf.* Matt. 5:45) during this life (in which he dispenses what is often called 'common grace'), and of believers in the life to come (*cf.* W. Wagner, as cited by W. Foerster, in *TDNT* 7, p. 1017). However, it is possible that *malista* means 'namely' (thus T. C. Skeat), in which case 'all people' are 'those who believe'.

Throughout Scripture salvation is portrayed as both corporate and individual, but the OT tends to emphasize the former and the NT the latter. The common Pauline expression 'in Christ' combines both aspects. The believer is 'in (personal union with the risen) Christ' and also 'in (the body of) Christ', the *church.

The prerequisites of salvation

In the OT

God's intervention to help and deliver was always traced to his gracious compassion and initiative (Exod. 34:6–7; Neh. 9:27). It was God's prerogative to save, and to save when he chose and through what or whom he chose. Never was salvation regarded as a human right or desert or achievement.

Adherence to the prescribed *sacrifices of levitical legislation was required of the Israelite who trusted in God for protection and deliverance. But it was clear that God's pleasure was not in external animal sacrifice but in a 'steadfast spirit' and 'a broken and contrite heart' (Ps. 51:10, 16–17; *cf.* Joel 2:13). 'I desire steadfast love and not sacrifice, and acknowledgment of God rather than burnt offerings' (Hos. 6:6). God's action in saving was normally related to the spiritual state of the individual or the nation. For example, Psalm 32 makes it clear that the blessings of protection from trouble and forgiveness of sin are not given automatically but require repentance and confession, faith and *obedience (see esp. vv. 1, 5–7, 9–10). The book of Deuteronomy sets out *blessings for obedience and curses for disobedience (see esp. Deut. 11:26–28; 28).

In the NT

Here, too, salvation comes by God's free and *gracious choice (Eph. 2:5; 2 Thess. 2:13; Titus 2:11). On the timeless principle that 'without the shedding of blood there is no forgiveness [of sins]' (Heb. 9:22), it was through the shed *blood of Jesus, poured out voluntarily (Mark 14:24) and in accordance with God's set purpose (Acts 2:23), that full and final provision was made for the forgiveness of sins (Heb. 9:12, 14, 26–28; 10:10). Thus Jesus became 'the source of eternal salvation' (Heb. 5:9).

As in the OT, repentance, faith and obedience are the prerequisites on the human side for the experience of salvation. Repentance is that change of attitude towards God that prompts a change of conduct, particularly the confession and repudiation of sin (Matt. 3:6, 8; Acts 3:19; 17:30; 20:21). As for faith, the NT goes beyond the Old in requiring belief in Jesus the Messiah (John 20:31; Acts 17:3) alongside belief in God (John 14:1). Not that there are two competing personal objects of human faith: to believe in Jesus is to believe in God as well (John 12:44); it is in Christ that God brings the individual to salvation. This faith involves both an intellectual acceptance of the message of the *gospel (Rom. 10:9) and a commitment of oneself to the person of Christ (John 6:35; Acts 10:43). Just as repentance and faith once begun must be sustained, so too obedience. The initial 'obedience to the truth' (1 Pet. 1:22; cf. Rom. 6:17; 2 Thess. 1:8) must be followed by keeping Christ's commandments (John 14:15), especially his command to *love one another (1 John 3:23), if salvation is to be enjoyed as a present experience (see section below). So Paul can speak of 'the obedience that comes from faith' (Rom. 1:5; 16:26).

In NT times repentance and profession of faith in Christ were promptly followed by water *baptism in obedience to Christ's command (Matt. 28:19). In fact, baptism is so closely related to repentance and faith (see e.g., Acts 2:38; 16:30–33) that it may be seen as the natural and necessary concomitant of repentance and faith.

Salvation can never be achieved by human works (Rom. 3:20; Eph. 2:8–9; Titus 3:5). Even where human responsibility is stressed in the practical 'outworking' of salvation (Phil. 2:12), the emphasis is on assurance of the comprehensive divine 'inworking' (Phil. 2:13).

The three tenses of salvation

God's salvation encompasses the past, the present, and the future. Past deliverance points forward to present and future deliverance, which in turn look back to and are based on past deliverance.

In the OT

The Exodus was the pivotal point in the OT economy. The annual celebration of the Passover commemorated (and commemorates) God's deliverance of Israel from Egyptian bondage (Exod. 12:1 – 13:10). But Passover also reminded the Jews that God provides for and strengthens his people for their journey (Exod. 12:11, 35–36; Deut. 26:5–10), that their Saviour God daily bears their burdens (Ps. 68:19), and that 'the angel of the LORD encamps around those who fear him, and he delivers them' (Ps. 34:7; cf. Exod. 14:19). In addition, Passover pointed to the coming of the Messiah and anticipated the banquet to be celebrated in the messianic age (Is. 25:6; 65:13; cf. Matt. 8:11).

The messianic hope in Israel grew by stages, from its earliest adumbrations in the Pentateuch (Gen. 3:15; 49:10; Deut. 18:15, 18), through its classic expression in 2 Samuel 7:5–16 (cf. Pss. 89 and 132) and its appearance in the messianic psalms (Pss. 2, 45, 72, 110), to the more detailed intimations in the prophets, pre-exilic (Amos 9:11–15; Hos. 3:4–5; Mic. 5:2–4; Is. 9:2–7; 11:1–9; 32:1–8; Jer. 23:5–6; 33:14–18), exilic (Ezek. 34:22–24), and post-exilic (Hag. 2:21–23; Zech. 3:8; 4:1–7; 6:9–13; 9:9–10).

Belief in resurrection from the dead is expressed in at least eight passages (Job 19:26; Pss. 17:15; 49:15; 73:24; Is. 26:19; 53:10–12;

Dan. 12:2, 13). Also, resurrection terminology is used in two places (Ezek. 37:1–14; Hos. 6:2) to portray a future national and spiritual restoration brought about by a return from exile.

In the NT

The death and resurrection of Jesus are the focal point in the NT era. Once the benefits of the sacrifice of Christ have been personally appropriated, salvation can be spoken of as a past event (Titus 3:4–5; *cf.* Eph. 2:5–8). 'Being saved' comes about through calling on the name of the Lord Jesus (Rom. 10:9–13) and involves entrance into the kingdom of God (Mark 10:23–27) and into the church as the body of Christ (1 Cor. 12:13; Gal. 3:26–28). But salvation was actually achieved and made available before any human response to the message of salvation, as a result of the passion of Christ (1 Pet. 1:10–11).

But 'being saved' is also an ongoing process in the sense that when believers offer themselves to God as slaves of righteousness they experience release from the power and reign of sin (Rom. 6:6, 12–14, 19) and progress towards Christian maturity (Eph. 4:13; Col. 1:28). Thus Paul can describe Christians as 'those who are being saved' (*hoi sōzomenoi*, 2 Cor. 2:15; *cf.* 1 Cor. 1:18) and Peter can exhort his readers to grow up in their salvation (1 Pet. 2:2; *cf.* Heb. 6:9). Evidence of this present salvation is seen in good works (Eph. 2:10), also described as 'fruit in keeping with repentance' (Luke 3:8).

The consummation of salvation lies in the future (see *Eschatology, *Heaven). Christians were 'saved in hope' (Rom. 8:24): with the certain expectation of 'the redemption of the body' from its bondage to decay and sin, through its transformation (Rom. 8:23); with the *hope of the arrival of 'new heavens and a new earth in which righteousness has its home' (2 Pet. 3:13); and with the assurance of being delivered from God's coming wrath (Rom. 5:9; 1 Thess. 1:10). The final state of the saved may be characterized by six adjectives.

1. *Embodied.* The believer's 'spiritual body' (1 Cor. 15:44) is a body animated and guided by the perfected human spirit and revitalized by the divine Spirit, a body perfectly adapted to the ecology of heaven. It has a divine origin (1 Cor. 15:38), with God as its architect and builder (2 Cor. 5:1–2). It

is 'imperishable', free from any form of decay; 'glorious', of radiant and unsurpassed beauty; 'powerful', with limitless energy and perfect health (1 Cor. 15:42–43, 50, 52–54). It is 'angel-like', not because it is sexless (sexual identity, a crucial ingredient in personality, is retained in the resurrection) but because it is deathless (Luke 20:36) and without sexual passions or procreative powers (Matt. 22:30; Mark 12:25).

2. *Localized.* Although heaven is a condition, that of knowing and serving God, it is also and always a place, the locality where God's presence is most perfectly expressed and felt. The 'new heavens and new earth in which righteousness has its permanent home' (2 Pet. 3:13) correspond to the believer's resurrection body. Whether this 'newness' of creation comes about by annihilation or by transformation (both concepts find expression in Rev. 21:1, 5), the result will be that the whole material order will unswervingly serve the purposes of spirit.

3. *Personal.* Believers are not destined to be absorbed into the divine, but to bear the image of Christ without forfeiting their individuality (Rom. 8:29; 1 Cor. 15:49). Such a view leaves no room for a pantheistic immortality in which the many are absorbed into the one, or a racial immortality in which people survive solely in their posterity. From first to last God treats us as distinctive individuals.

4. *Corporate.* The life of the age to come is not marked by an exclusively individual enjoyment of the beatific vision of God so that myriads of individuals live in fellowship with God but in isolation from other worshippers. Although individual believers will enjoy unmediated interpersonal communion with the Lord, it is only in the corporate context of the City of God, the perfect society of the consummated kingdom (Rev. 21:1 – 22:5).

5. *Permanent.* Through their transformation, believers will assume an immortality that guarantees the permanency of their resurrection state (1 Cor. 15:53–55). 'They will reign for ever and ever' (Rev. 22:5).

6. *Active.* Redeemed believers will *worship and serve God and the Lamb enthusiastically and acceptably (Rev. 7:9–10; 14:1–4; 19:9; 22:3–4).

Romans 8:28–30 is the classic passage regarding the sequence of God's saving acts. First, *foreknowledge*, which is God's placing of his affectionate regard on people (his 'forelove'), equivalent or closely related to his *election (Eph. 1:4; 2 Thess. 2:13; 1 Pet. 1:1–2). Second, *predestination* (or 'fore-ordaining'), God's appointing of the elect to a special future destiny, conformity to the *image of Christ. Third, *calling*, God's effectual call into fellowship with his Son (1 Cor. 1:9) which leads to conversion and *regeneration. Fourth, *justification*, God's declaration granting sinners a new, right and permanent standing before him, a status that involves reconciliation and *adoption. Fifth, *glorification*, God's act of bringing the process of sanctification to a glorious climax by means of a resurrection that issues in immortality.

Conclusion

Various proposals have been made concerning the 'centre' of the OT, including covenant, promise, God as the Lord, the holiness of God, and God and Israel. The present writer's preference is 'God's salvation in Israel': 'In the LORD our God is the salvation of Israel' (Jer. 3:23). When I suggest that the 'centre' of the NT is 'God's salvation through Christ', I am proposing that the unifying theme, or dominant emphasis, or co-ordinating motif of the entire NT is God's provision, through the death and resurrection of Jesus, of a way for humans to become reconciled to himself and to lead lives that are pleasing to him. Two verses that encapsulate this main idea are 'God was in Christ, reconciling the world [of humans] to himself' (2 Cor. 5:19), and 'May God, the author of peace ... equip you with everything good for doing his will, producing in us what is pleasing in his sight, through Jesus Christ' (Heb. 13:20–21). Such an approach avoids the charge of Christomonism since it protects the theocentric nature of NT theology, where 'God' is normally the Father (*cf*. 1 Cor. 8:6; 15:28; Phil. 2:11).

See also: ATONEMENT; FORGIVENESS AND RECONCILIATION; RIGHTEOUSNESS, JUSTICE AND JUSTIFICATION.

Bibliography

G. B. Caird, *New Testament Theology* (Oxford, 1994); O. Cullmann, *Salvation in History* (ET, London, 1967); W. Eichrodt, *Theology of the Old Testament*, 2 vols. (ET, London, 1978); T. V. Farris, *Mighty to Save: A Study in Old Testament Soteriology* (Nashville, 1993); W. Foerster and G. Fohrer in *TDNT* 7, pp. 965–1024; J. Gnilka, *Neutestamentliche Theologie: Ein Überblick* (Wurzburg, 1989); E. M. B. Green, *The Meaning of Salvation* (London, 1965); G. W. Grogan, 'The experience of salvation in the Old and New Testaments', *VE* 5, 1967, pp. 4–26; D. Hill, *Greek Words and Hebrew Meanings: Studies in the Semantics of Soteriological Terms* (Cambridge, 1967); A. M. Hunter, *The Unity of the New Testament* (London, 1943) (= *The Message of the New Testament*, Philadelphia, 1944); L. Newbigin, *Sin and Salvation* (London, 1956); J. I. Packer, 'The way of salvation', *BibSac* 129, 1972, pp. 195–205, 291–306; C. R. Smith, *The Bible Doctrine of Salvation* (London, 1946).

M. J. HARRIS

SAMUEL, see Part 2

SARAH

Sarah, known initially as Sarai, is introduced in *Genesis as the wife of *Abraham. Immediately we are informed that she is barren and *childless (Gen. 11:29–30). Sarah's barrenness is in striking contrast to the blessing of human fertility described in the preceding genealogies of Genesis 1 – 11, and provides a significant context for reading the theologically programmatic divine blessings on Abraham in 12:1–3. God uttered his creative word at the beginning of the primeval history (1:3) in the context of a 'formless void' (1:2, NRSV); he speaks his redemptive word at the beginning of the ancestral history (12:1–3) in the context of barrenness (11:30).

Initially, Sarah's role in the story seems to be marginal. The divine promises of Genesis 12:1–3, including that of nationhood, are addressed to Abraham alone. Sarah's apparent unimportance is underlined when Abraham abandons her in Egypt in order to save his own life (12:10–20), and in contrast risks everything on the battlefield to rescue Lot (14:14–16).

The dramatic announcement that Abraham will father a son from whom the promised nation will come likewise makes no mention of Sarah (Gen. 15:4–5). Abraham believes that he will father a son, not that Sarah will bear a child (15:6). Thus, when Abraham fathers a child by *Hagar, his natural assumption is that Ishmael is the child of promise (16:15).

Genesis 17:15–16 is the pivotal statement in the narrative's presentation of Sarah: she will bear the child of promise. Abraham's reaction of falling flat on his face and laughing (17:17) indicates how unexpected and unbelievable this news is. The holding back of the announcement of Sarah's role until this point in the narrative emphasizes the radical grace inherent in God's promise. Sarah's apparently marginal status is now dramatically transformed: the least significant is actually the most significant. The fulfilment of the divine promise now rests with Abraham and *Sarah*. Sarah's change of name, unique among the women in the Bible, underlines this point (17:15).

The promise to Sarah is repeated in the context of the most impressive divine encounter in the ancestral narratives (Gen. 18:1–15). It is so extraordinary that neither Abraham (17:17) nor Sarah (18:12) can believe it. The subsequent charade in which Sarah is passed off once again as Abraham's sister (Gen. 20, cf. 12:10–20), when she is possibly pregnant with Isaac, underlines the difficulty of believing. Yet God's drastic action to rescue her emphasizes that without disregarded, barren Sarah the divine promises will not be fulfilled. At the climax of Isaac's birth, 'The Lord dealt *with Sarah* as he had said, and the Lord did *for Sarah* as he had promised' (Gen. 21:1).

Despite her significance within Genesis, Sarah is mentioned explicitly only once in the rest of the OT. Isaiah exhorts the righteous to 'Look to Abraham your father and to Sarah who bore you' (Is. 51:2a). The reversal of Sarah's barrenness is then applied typologically as the prophet foretells the reversal of Israel's calamities. Israel's 'waste places', 'wilderness' and 'desert' will become 'like Eden ... like the garden of the Lord' (Is. 51:3).

The barreness of Sarah is mentioned briefly in several NT passages (Rom. 4:19; 9:9; Heb. 11:11). The major passage dealing with Sarah however, is one in which she is not mentioned by name, and the focus of which is not her infertility (Gal. 4:21–31). It is now generally accepted that Paul's allegory concerning Hagar and Sarah is a rejoinder to an argument of his Judaizing opponents, who were appealing to the same scriptural examples. Their precise argument is unavailable to us, but apparently included an assertion that uncircumcised Gentile Christians were not true sons of Abraham. Paul counters that Gentile Galatian Christians are children of Sarah, the free woman, not of Hagar, the slave. Their contrasting roles are used by Paul to typify two contrasting attitudes to the law: the bondage demanded by the Judaizers, and the *freedom advocated by Paul. However, the manner in which Paul argues his case reflects midrashic traditions which his opponents have obviously been using (*e.g.* the radical contrast between Hagar and Sarah; Ishmael's persecution of Isaac; correlations between Is. 54:1 and Gen. 16), and which Paul utilizes in order to oppose them with their own logic.

In 1 Peter 3, Christian wives, in order to avoid anti-Christian sentiment, are exhorted not to antagonize their non-Christian husbands (1 Pet. 3:1–4), but like Sarah to accept their husbands' authority (1 Pet. 3:6). Peter may have chosen Sarah as an example because of analogies between the social setting of his Christian community and the setting outlined in the narratives of Genesis 12 and 20. Peter's fellow Christians are aliens (1 Pet. 1:1, 17; 2:11) who are treated unjustly (1 Pet. 2:18–20; 3:9, 17). So, he argues, just as Sarah was treated unjustly by her husband when they were in foreign parts (see Gen. 12:18; 20:9–10, 16b), so Christian wives living in the diaspora may be treated unjustly by their husbands. Thus, Sarah becomes a model for Christian perseverance in difficult circumstances.

Within Genesis Sarah moves, by the grace of God, from barrenness to fertility, from the margins to a position of significance. This transformation is the basis for her contribution to the theology of the rest of Scripture, in which she becomes a paradigm for divine intervention (Is. 51:2–3), Christian freedom (Gal. 4:21 – 5:1) and virtuous perseverance (1 Pet. 3:6).

Bibliography

M. Kiley, 'Like Sara: The tale of terror behind 1 Peter 3:6', *JBL* 106, 1987, pp. 689–692; R. N. Longenecker, 'Graphic illustrations of a believer's new life in Christ: Galatians 4:21–31', *RevExp* 91, 1994, pp. 183–199; L. A. Turner, *Announcements of Plot in Genesis* (Sheffield, 1990).

L. A. TURNER

SATAN, see SPIRITUAL POWERS
SCRIPTURE, see Part 1

SEED

Although in Scripture the term 'seed' often refers to plants, it is also frequently used of human beings. From a biblical-theological perspective, 'seed' is used of people in two important, and closely related, ways: 1. of Jesus Christ; 2. of Abraham's descendants.

Jesus Christ as the seed of promise

In writing to the churches in Galatia, the apostle Paul introduces the idea that the divine promises given to Abraham some two millennia earlier find their fulfilment in Jesus Christ. Focusing on the announcement that 'all nations will be blessed through you' (Gen. 12:3; 18:18; *cf.* 22:18; 26:4, NIV), Paul argues that Christ 'redeemed us in order that the blessing given to Abraham might come to the Gentiles through Christ Jesus, so that by faith we might receive the promise of the Spirit' (Gal. 3:14). The apostle then observes: 'The promises were spoken to Abraham and to his seed. The Scripture does not say "and to seeds", meaning many people, but "and to your seed", meaning one person, who is Christ' (Gal. 3:16).

Paul's affirmation that the divine promises to Abraham relate specifically to Jesus Christ is often considered to be an example of midrashic exegesis which distorts the true meaning of the relevant passages in *Genesis. However, Paul is not alone in considering Jesus Christ to be the seed through whom the *nations of the earth will be *blessed. Peter's observations in Acts 3:17–26, especially verses 25–26, include the same idea, as does, in a more subtle way, the genealogy in Matthew 1:1–17.

A careful analysis of Genesis, where the divine promises to Abraham are first recorded, suggests that Paul's exposition is well founded. Genesis traces a distinctive line of seed, which begins with *Adam, and then proceeds through his third-born son, Seth. Through the use of *tôlēdôt* formulae ('These are the generations of ...' [NRSV]; *cf.* Gen. 2:4; 5:1; 6:9; 11:10, 27; 25:12, 19; 36:1, 9; 37:2) this unique family line follows the lives of particular individuals and their immediate descendants. While Genesis acknowledges the existence of many peoples and nations, it concentrates on the lineage that descends from Adam to Noah (Gen. 5:1–32), and then from Noah to Terah (Gen. 11:10–26). After this the *tôlēdôt* heading in Genesis 11:27 focuses in upon the family of Terah, in particular his son Abraham. Further *tôlēdôt* headings in Genesis 25:19 and 37:2 centre attention on Abraham's son Isaac, his grandson Jacob (also known as Israel), and Jacob's twelve sons, the most prominent of these being *Joseph and Judah.

Associated with this family line are a number of important divine statements, the first of which comes in Genesis 3:15. Addressing the serpent, the Lord says, 'I will put enmity between you and the woman, and between your offspring [mg. seed] and hers [lit. her seed]; he will crush your head and you will strike his heel.' The use of the term 'seed' (Heb. *zera'*) is significant, for it is a key word in Genesis, occurring 59 times compared to 170 in the rest of the OT. Although the noun *zera'* does not have distinctive singular and plural forms, J. Collins argues on syntactical grounds that both occurrences in Genesis 3:15 are singular (*TynB* 48, pp. 139–148). This interpretation is strongly supported by the construction of the rest of Genesis around a single line of seed, descended from Eve. When Seth is born, Eve comments, 'God has granted me another child [lit. 'seed'] in place of Abel, since Cain killed him' (Gen. 4:25). There then follows a linear genealogy which traces Seth's descendants down to Noah. R. S. Hess (*Studies in the Personal Names of Genesis 1 – 11*, pp. 111–162) demonstrates how Seth's genealogy, by means of 'onomastic commentary' and brief narrative inserts, conveys a positive picture of hope for the future. This contrasts sharply with the genealogy of Cain which concludes by focusing on the murderous activity of Lamech (Gen. 4:17–24).

From Noah, who is described as being especially righteous (Gen. 6:9) and whose actions lead to the establishment of an eternal *covenant between God and all creatures

(Gen. 9:9–17), the line of seed is traced to Terah, the father of Abram (Gen. 11:10–26). Although Abram's wife Sarai (they are later renamed Abraham and *Sarah respectively) is barren, the Lord promises (Gen. 12:2), and later guarantees with a covenant (Gen. 15), that Abraham's descendants will become a great nation in the land of Canaan. The Lord also initially promises that 'all peoples on earth will be blessed' through Abraham (Gen. 12:3), a promise which stands in sharp contrast to the divine punishments that dominate the narrative in Genesis 3 – 11, stemming from the disobedience of Adam and Eve in Eden. The divine promise of world-wide blessing through Abraham, however, must be read in the light of the immediately preceding statement, 'I [the Lord] will bless those who bless you [Abram], and whoever curses you I will curse' (Gen. 12:3). Only those who are favourably inclined towards Abraham will experience God's blessing. Later, this promise of blessing is guaranteed by an eternal covenant, the details of which are set out in Genesis 17.

Two aspects of the covenant of *circumcision in Genesis 17 ought to be noted. First, this covenant is introduced by God to Abraham with the words, 'This is my covenant with you: You will be the father of many nations' (Gen. 17:4). This latter statement is then repeated in the next verse, where God announces that the name Abram is to be changed to Abraham. That Abraham will be the father of many nations is clearly a central feature of the covenant. Yet, if this is a promise referring to the biological descendants of Abraham, it is not fulfilled. Alternatively, however, the Hebrew term for father, 'ab, may have here a non-biological sense. It is sometimes 'used of a variety of social roles that carried authority or exercised a protective or caring function. It could be used of a prophet (2 Kgs. 6:21), priest (Judg. 18:19), king (1 Sam. 24:11), or governor (Is. 22:20–21)' (C. J. H. Wright, in *NIDOTTE* 1, p. 219). Indeed, much later in Genesis, Joseph tells his brothers that God has made him 'father to Pharaoh' (Gen. 45:8). The likelihood that Abraham's status as father is not viewed here as purely biological is supported by the observation that among those circumcised were some who were not his 'offspring/seed' (Gen. 17:12). Through this covenant, then, God confirms that Abraham

will be a source of blessing to others, including those who are not his physical descendants.

Secondly, although Genesis 17 records that all the males in Abraham's household were circumcised, God emphasizes that the covenant, which is described as 'eternal', will be established *only* with Isaac. Thus, Ishmael, the son born to Sarah's servant Hagar, is passed over in favour of a second son, Isaac, who has yet to be born. The establishment of the covenant with Isaac alone links it in a special way to the unique line of descendants traced in Genesis. After Isaac, the covenant is established with Jacob/Israel, but not with Esau, his older twin brother. While undoubtedly many were circumcised during the time of Abraham, Isaac and Jacob, Exodus 2:24 speaks of God's remembering 'his covenant with Abraham, with Isaac and with Jacob'. An important distinction is thus drawn between the special line of seed with whom the eternal covenant is established and those who participate in the benefits of this covenant through being circumcised. Circumcision, as the sign of this covenant, is a vivid reminder of the importance of Abraham's seed.

The promise of blessing being mediated through Abraham to others, which underlies the covenant of circumcision, is later linked to his seed in the oath sworn by God in Genesis 22:16–18. While the final part of this oath is often interpreted as referring to all of Abraham's descendants, syntactical considerations suggest that it refers to a single individual: 'Your seed will take possession of the cities of his enemies, and through your seed all nations on earth will be blessed' (see T. D. Alexander, 'Further observations on the term "Seed" in Genesis', *TynB* 48.2, 1997, pp. 363–367). This interpretation is reflected in Psalm 72:17 which echoes this passage in describing a future *king through whom justice and peace shall come to all the nations of the earth (*cf.* Gen. 17:6).

The story of Jacob provides further evidence that God's blessing will be mediated through a single line of seed descended from Abraham. Of central importance is Genesis 27 which describes how Jacob, prompted by his mother, deceived his elderly father Isaac into giving him the blessing traditionally pronounced upon the firstborn. While Jacob's deception of Isaac is hardly commendable,

Esau had previously despised his birthright by selling it to Jacob for the price of a meal (Gen. 25:29–34). When Esau learns that Isaac has made Jacob 'lord over' him (Gen. 27:37), Esau forces Jacob to flee for his life and live with his father's relatives in Paddan Aram. There, however, Jacob experiences God's blessing and years later, as a very wealthy man, returns to Canaan, seeking to be reconciled to Esau.

In the concluding chapters of Genesis, the line of seed appears to be continued through Jacob's son Joseph. Although he is the eleventh born of twelve sons, his father treats him as the firstborn (cf. 1 Chr. 5:1–2). Joseph's pre-eminence is underlined in two dreams (Gen. 37:5–11), but these cause his brothers, out of jealousy, to sell him into slavery in Egypt. Eventually, from being a prisoner in an Egyptian jail, Joseph is dramatically exalted to become prime minister of the whole land (Gen. 41:14–40). In this latter capacity he becomes a source of blessing to the people of Egypt and the surrounding nations during seven years of famine. Later, when Joseph brings his two sons to Jacob to be blessed, Jacob deliberately gives the blessing of the firstborn to Joseph's younger son, Ephraim, rather than Manasseh (Gen. 48:20). Thus the line of seed is continued through Ephraim.

When Jacob tells his sons what will become of them in the future, he comments that Joseph's descendants will be especially blessed by God (Gen. 49:22–26; cf. the comments of Moses in Deut. 33:13–17, esp. vv. 16–17). In the light of this, the rôle played later by Joshua takes on special significance. As an Ephraimite he leads the people of Israel into the Promised Land and establishes Shiloh as the cultic centre of the nation in territory allocated to the tribe of Ephraim (Josh. 18:1). However, as the book of Judges reveals, after Joshua the nation of Israel undergoes a process of spiritual and moral decline. When eventually a monarchy is created in Israel, the line of Ephraim, together with the priesthood in Shiloh, is rejected by God (cf. Ps. 78:56–72). While Saul, a Benjaminite, is anointed as the first king of Israel, he is soon rejected in favour of David, the son of Jesse, of the line of Judah.

Although Genesis records that the line of seed is initially traced through Joseph's son Ephraim, it anticipates future developments by drawing attention to the importance of Judah's seed. Thus, the Joseph story is interrupted by the account of Judah's relationship with Tamar, an episode which centres on 'seed' (Gen. 38:8–10; in these verses the NIV translates Hebrew zera' as 'offspring') and concludes with the birth of twins. Remarkably, the description of the birth tells how the younger son, Perez, breaks out before his brother Zerah, although Zerah's hand had come out first (Gen. 38:27–30). This extraordinary incident may have a special significance when viewed in the light of Ephraim's later rejection in favour of the line of Judah traced through Perez. Further evidence that Genesis anticipates a royal lineage from Judah comes in Jacob's very positive remarks about Judah's future (Gen. 49:8–12).

While Judges and the early chapters of Samuel highlight the demise of the Ephraimite line of seed after Joshua, the book of Ruth anticipates a new development involving the line of Judah. Set against the moral and spiritual decline portrayed in Judges, the story of Ruth focuses on the coming together of a God-fearing Moabitess and a righteous Israelite man. From their union, which has close parallels with the story of Tamar in Genesis, a son is born to the line of Perez. This is underlined by a linear genealogy, introduced by a tôlēdôt heading, which links Perez to 'Jesse the father of David' (Ruth 4:18–22).

Confirmation that the line of seed is transferred from Ephraim to Judah in the time of David comes through the successful transfer of the ark of the covenant to Jerusalem (2 Sam. 6) and the covenant which the Lord makes with David (2 Sam. 7; cf. Pss. 89:3–4, 19–37; 132:10–18). While 1 and 2 Kings chart the failure of the Davidic kings, with some exceptions, to remain fully obedient to the Lord, the expectation remains that God will not abandon his commitment to David (cf. 2 Kgs. 8:19).

The importance of the line of David is highlighted in other OT texts. During the reign of Ahaz, who builds an unauthorized altar in Jerusalem (2 Kgs. 16:10–18), the prophet Isaiah looks forward to the coming of a future, righteous king from the 'stump of Jesse' (Is. 11:1–13; cf. 9:1–7; Amos 9:11–15; Mic. 5:2–4). Immediately before and just after the downfall of the house of David at the time of the Babylonian exile, the prophets Jeremiah (Jer. 23:5–6; 33:14–18) and Ezekiel (Ezek. 34:22–24) also anticipate a future Davidic king through whom God will fulfil his purposes for Israel and the nations. Ultimately, as the writers of the NT affirm, this expectation finds its fulfilment in Jesus Christ, 'the son of David, the son of Abraham' (Matt. 1:1). With Christ's death, resurrection and exaltation, God's promise to bless all the nations of the earth through the seed of Abraham starts to be fully realized (cf., e.g., Matt. 28:18–20; Gal. 3:14; Rev. 5:9–10).

Abraham's descendants

God's promise to Abraham of a future 'seed' through whom the nations shall be blessed is closely associated in Genesis with the idea that Abraham's 'seed' will become a great nation (Gen. 12:2). This is necessary in order for a future royal line to be established. Thus, special attention is given to the extent of Abraham's seed in Genesis 15, where God covenants that they will become numerous and after four centuries take possession of the land of Canaan (Gen. 15:1–21).

Various images, which are not to be taken literally, are used to describe the extent of Abraham's descendants: they will be as numerous as the stars of heaven (Gen. 15:5; 22:17; 26:4), the dust of the earth (Gen. 13:16; 28:14), and the sand of the seashore (Gen. 22:17; 32:12). These images are repeated later to indicate the fulfilment of the covenant God made with Abraham in Genesis 15. Moses states, 'The LORD your God has increased your numbers so that today you are as many as the stars in the sky' (Deut. 1:10; cf. 10:22; 28:62; 1 Chr. 27:23; Neh. 9:23). During the reign of *Solomon, the people are as numerous as 'the sand on the seashore' (1 Kgs. 4:20) and 'the dust of the earth' (2 Chr. 1:9). Moreover, in Solomon's time the boundaries of the nation are extended to those promised to Abraham (1 Kgs. 4:21; cf. Gen. 15:18–21).

Yet, although Moses anticipated, prior to the Israelite invasion of Canaan, the fulfilment of God's covenant promise to Abraham, he also looked beyond this to a time when Abraham's descendants would be 'but few in number, because you did not obey the LORD your God' (Deut. 28:62). Furthermore, they will be 'uprooted from the land' (Deut.

28:63). Although God fulfils his promise to Abraham that his seed will take possession of Canaan after four hundred years, an important condition for continued occupation of the land is their *obedience to God (cf. Deut. 7:6–11). At the time of the Babylonian exile the prophet Ezekiel condemns the folly of those who lay claim to the land promised to Abraham while living in disobedience to the Lord (Ezek. 33:23–29). Centuries earlier the entire generation of adult Israelites who left Egypt with Moses, apart from Caleb and Joshua, perished in the wilderness without entering Canaan. In the light of this, it is clear that the divine promises to Abraham are only of advantage to those who, like Abraham, trust and obey God. The OT reveals clearly that the biological seed of Abraham must resemble him morally and spiritually in order to be blessed by God. Indeed, implicit in the Hebrew term zera' is a resemblance between progenitor and progeny (cf. Gen. 1:11–12).

This idea is picked up in the NT, where first John the Baptist (Matt. 3:9; Luke 3:8) and then Jesus (John 8:31–58) challenge those who see their descent from Abraham as a guarantee of being accepted by God. Indeed, Jesus states that the Pharisees are children of the devil, the hallmarks of their progenitor being their desire to kill him and their rejection of the truth (John 8:44; cf. 1 John 3:8–10). Likewise, Paul emphasizes that the true seed of Abraham are those who through *faith in Christ are made right with God: 'There is neither Jew nor Greek, slave nor free, male nor female, for you are all one in Christ Jesus. If you belong to Christ, then you are Abraham's seed, and heirs according to the promise' (Gal. 3:28–29; cf. Rom. 4:13–25).

The NT presents Jesus Christ as the one who brings to fulfilment the divine promises associated with the unique line of seed descended from Abraham. Through Christ God's blessing is mediated to the nations of the earth. Those who submit in faith and repentance to Jesus Christ as Lord and Saviour resemble Abraham and become his spiritual seed. This seed, produced through the activity of the Holy Spirit, is distinguished by its fruit from the seed which belongs to the evil one.

See also: ABRAHAM; DAVID; ENOCH; JACOB; JESUS CHRIST; JUDAH; NOAH; SERPENT.

Bibliography

T. D. Alexander, 'Royal expectations in Genesis to Kings: their importance for biblical theology', *TynB* 49, 1998, pp. 191–212; J. Collins, 'A syntactical note (Genesis 3:15): Is the woman's seed singular or plural?' *TynB* 48, 1997, pp. 139–148; R. S. Hess, *Studies in the Personal Names of Genesis 1 – 11* (Kevelaer and Neukirchen-Vluyn, 1993); P. E. Satterthwaite, 'Genealogy in the Old Testament', *NIDOTTE* 4, pp. 654–663; R. R. Wilson, *Genealogy and History in the Biblical World* (New Haven, 1977).

T. D. ALEXANDER

SERPENT

The serpent, with its crested head, glittering skin, fascinating, lidless, gazing eye, shameless lust, tortuous movement, venomous bite and grovelling posture, is well suited to be a type of Satan (see *Spiritual powers). Both use camouflage to deceive their prey (Gen. 3:1–4, 6, 13; John 8:44; Acts 13:10; 2 Cor. 4:4; 11:3; 2 Thess. 2:9–10; Rev. 2:9; 3:9). The fact that snakes haunted the same deserted ruins as demons and other threatening beasts (*e.g.* scorpions and jackels) strengthened their association with *evil (Is. 34:14–15; Matt. 12:43; Mark 1:13). Lying hidden in walls (Eccles. 10:8; Amos 5:19), snakes often struck with lightning speed, biting without warning (Gen. 49:17). This ever-present danger served as a metaphor of sudden *judgment (Is. 14:29; Amos 5:19). The association between snake bite and divine judgment was not a mere literary device, but a widely held belief (Acts 28:3–4; 1 Cor. 10:9). The names given to different types of snake were used to refer to those who do the devil's bidding (Matt. 3:7; 12:34; 23:33; Luke 3:7). The plots of the wicked are like snake's eggs, inevitably hatching greater evils (Is. 59:5); the wicked 'have sharpened their tongues' (Pss. 64:3; 140:3) in order to give a deadly wound, 'like a serpent' (Ps 58:4). By choosing the serpent to represent the religious leaders of his day (Matt. 12:34; 23:33), Jesus hints that they are to be abhorred and avoided just as one would avoid a nest of vipers.

The traditional interpretation of the place of the serpent in the fall of humanity

The identification of the serpent with the devil appears first in the Apocryphal literature: 'But by the envy of the devil death entered the world' (Wisdom of Solomon [written 100 BC – AD 40] 2:24). On logical and theological grounds the early church Fathers and the Reformers believed that Satan fell from grace, entered Eden, used the serpent as his tool, and was cursed (see *Blessing/curse) under the form of the serpent, to eternal punishment. It was recognized that there are elements in the judicial curse on the serpent that point beyond it to the figure of Satan; the curse was deliberately prophetic. This is how Paul read the text: 'The God of peace will soon crush [*syntripsei*, from *tribō*] Satan under your feet' (Rom. 16:20, NIV). The Hebrew word in Genesis 3:15 translated 'crush' occurs also in Job 9:17, where it is translated in the LXX as *ektripsē*, the same word used by Paul. It is best to view the post-Fall physionomy of the serpent as the result of deliberate divine alterations to its form, intended to reflect the place of God's enemy in the divine order. What the serpent represents in the physical world, Satan represents in the spiritual world. Genesis 3 is viewed as the original and prototypical Fall, the cause of all subsequent falls (Rom. 5:12–21; 1 Cor. 15:21–22). Because the human race fell with *Adam and Eve, no subsequent human fall is a fall from absolute innocence, but is instead only relative, a regression from an already corrupted state. The prophetic curse meant that both serpent and Satan shall eventually eat the dust (*i.e.* be utterly laid low in perpetual shame); the serpent's present eating of the dust as it takes food off the ground is the pledge of divine judgment on Satan (Is. 65:25; Mic. 7:17; Is. 49:23; Ps. 72:9).

The bronze serpent

Not all references in the Bible to serpents are negative. The staff of Moses was transformed into a snake which ate the snakes of the Egyptian magicians (Exod. 4:3; 7:10–12). During the wilderness wanderings 'fiery' serpents (probably so called because of the inflammation caused by their bite) killed many thousands because of the people's distrust of Yahweh, but *healing could be received by looking at Moses' bronze serpent. This serpent, lifted up, became a type of Jesus' crucifixion. The bronze serpent is an historical type rather than a prophetic one. 'Just as Moses lifted up the snake in the desert, so the Son of Man must be lifted up' (John 3:14), and just as those who looked upon the bronze serpent were healed, so those who look by faith to Christ crucified are saved (John 3:14–15). The bronze serpent typified the Son of Man, in that: 1. it had the form of the deadly serpent without the venom, just as Jesus was 'in the likeness of sinful flesh' yet without sin (Rom. 8:3), 'made … to be sin for us' though he 'had no sin' (2 Cor. 5:21); the bronze serpent seemed a most unlikely means of curing the serpents' bites, just as the condemned Christ seemed most unlikely to save the condemned; 2. the serpent was lifted up on a pole so as to be visible to all the Israelites, just as Jesus was 'clearly portrayed as crucified' (Gal. 3:1), so that all the 'ends of the earth' by looking to him may 'be saved' (Is. 45:22); he was 'lifted up from the earth', so drawing all people to him (John 12:32–34); 3. the cure of the body by physical looking corresponds to the cure of the soul by spiritual looking; faith is the eye of the soul turned to the Saviour (Heb. 12:2); a look will save, from no matter how far away (Heb. 7:25; Eph. 2:17; Acts 2:39), just as the Israelites were healed by a look from any distance.

Serpent worship

In Macalister's excavations at Gezer a bronze serpent was found; it was probably an object of *worship in pre-Israelite Palestine. Many snakes of bronze and terracotta have been found in Palestine, and snakes feature prominently in temple decorations; no doubt they were associated with the cults of various deities. Images of a serpent goddess were discovered by Rowe at Bethshan and by Albright at Kiriath-sepher. In Canaan, the dragon was the symbol for disruptive and destructive chaos. The serpent, as the personification of all evil, was worshipped out of fear, to avert the evil he might do. Figurines of Asherah, the fertility goddess, were often draped with representations of snakes, as were her altars. In various religions the serpent is used as a symbol of both beneficent and hostile supernatural power.

The worship of the serpent/snake is found in all ancient religions, even in India and further east. In Bel and the Dragon the Babylonians worship a serpent-like creature which Daniel destroys. The Phoenicians worshipped the serpent. Herodotus (Bk II.74) noted that the Egyptians worshipped serpents consecrated to Jupiter. These were small and had two horns. The church Fathers suggested that the devil, who tempted the first woman under the shape of a serpent, took pleasure in deifying it, as a sign of his victory over humankind. But for them, the conqueror's symbol of the impaled serpent symbolized the overcoming of temporal and spiritual evil.

Paradoxically, the serpent was also the symbol of *wisdom and healing, and Moses' serpent was an instrument of power against the magicians' serpents (Exod. 7:10–12). The bronze serpent was preserved for 730 years until Hezekiah (715–686 BC) broke it in pieces because the people were worshipping it (2 Kgs. 18:4). In contempt he gave it the name 'Nehushtan' (a play on the word naḥaš, 'serpent'), meaning a 'trifling thing' (2 Kgs. 18:4), because it had become an object of worship. (See G. W. Gilmore, 'Serpent in worship, mythology, and symbolism', in P. Schaff and J. J. Herzog [eds.], *The Encyclopedia of Religious Knowledge* [New York, 1908], vol. X, pp. 363–370.) There are some indications of serpent-worship in OT Israel (1 Kgs. 1:9, ['Zoheleth' = 'snake']; Neh. 2:13, NIV fn).

Serpents in Hebrew and Near Eastern mythology

In ancient mythology several deities are said to have benefited people by killing a serpent; these snakes include Cadmus, Apollo, the hydra of Lerna, the dragons of Colchis and the Hesperides. Such fables may be traditional echoes of the early promise: 'The seed of the woman shall bruise the head of the serpent'. The serpent was the emblem of Mercury and Aesculapius, the god of medicine; the symbol may derive from the scene recorded in Numbers 21. In the East, as among the Greeks and Romans, the snake, sometimes entwined around a rod, was the symbol of the gods of healing. Hindu mythology represents Krishna as first being bitten in the foot, then crushing the serpent's head beneath his feet; this tradition may stem from the promise recorded in Genesis 3:15. Many regard Genesis 3 as a myth, attributing it to the J source (2:4b – 3:24) and making a connection with the serpent in the Epic of Gilgamesh who robs Gilgamesh of a fragment of the sacred plant which may correspond to the Genesis tree of life, and so of immortality. In the ancient Babylonian *creation epic the negative aspect of the cosmos, *i.e.* chaos, the watery abyss, darkness, evil, *etc.*, is symbolized as a great dragon or serpent.

The dragon-monster of the great abyss, with whom Marduk, god of light, contended, is sometimes said to correspond to the Leviathan or *Rahab of exilic and post-exilic Hebrew literature. But whereas the Babylonian myths place the mythological dragons in the context of the creation of the heavens and the earth, no biblical passage refers to a creation-struggle between Yahweh and a monster. Isaiah (27:1), Amos (9:3) and Ezekiel (29:3; 32:2) announce God's judgment on his enemies in terms of the overcoming of massive animals: 'In that day, the LORD will punish with his sword, his fierce, great and powerful sword, Leviathan the gliding serpent, Leviathan the coiling serpent; he will slay the monster of the sea' (Is. 27:1; *cf.* Pss. 74:13–14; 104:26). 'Leviathan' may have been the inspiration for the great red dragon of Revelation 12:3–17.

Figurative and eschatological references

The serpent represented a real threat to human happiness. Its removal or extinction was a symbol of life in the new heavens and the new earth. The continuing power of Jesus on earth is seen in the ability of his disciples to handle serpents without using charms and without fear of being hurt (Mark 16:18). Immunity to serpents and poison symbolized for believers the waning influence of Satan and anticipated the age of the *Christus Victor* (Mark 16:18). Micah 7:17 prophesies that when the nations that have opposed God's purposes see the mighty deeds that he will perform, 'they will lick dust like a snake, like creatures that crawl on the ground'. The safety of godly people under Yahweh's protection is guaranteed by the promise that even if they stand on the cobra or the serpent no harm will come to them (Ps. 91:13). In the eschatological age, 'The infant will play near the hole of the cobra, and the young child put his hand into the viper's nest. They will neither harm nor destroy on all my holy mountain, for the earth will be full of the knowledge of the LORD as the waters cover the sea' (Is. 11:8).

Bibliography

J. D. Currid, *Ancient Egypt and the Old Testament* (Grand Rapids, 1997); A. Heidel, *The Babylonian Genesis* (Chicago, 1951), pp. 83–88; *idem, The Gilgamesh Epic and Old Testament Parallels* (Chicago, 1949), p. 92; K. R. Joines, *Serpent Symbolism in the Old Testament* (Haddonfield, 1974); G. E. Post, 'Serpent', in *HDB*, pp. 459–461.

L. McFALL

SERVANT OF THE LORD, see JESUS CHRIST
SICKNESS, see HEALING

SIGNS AND WONDERS

Introduction

All the workings of nature are part of the continuing activity of the self-existent *God, but the OT bears witness to events in which that activity especially impressed human consciousness, bringing fresh *revelation of God's *creative and saving energies (Exod. 34:10; Jer. 31:22) and arousing in people awe, amazement and submission. The Hebrew phrase 'signs and wonders' refers to miraculous events which are to be remembered (Deut. 7:19; 11:3; *cf.* Dan. 6:27).

Signs and wonders in Exodus

The miracles or plagues effected through Moses are called signs (Exod. 4:8–9, 17, 28, 30; 11:9–10). In the LXX the phrase 'signs and wonders' is generally associated with *Moses leading God's people to freedom (Exod. 7:3; 10:1–2), his miracles authenticate him as God's representative (Exod. 4:1–17) and demonstrate the divine origin of what he says. Exodus acknowledges that others could replicate some but not all of Moses' miracles 'by their secret arts' (Exod. 7:22; 8:7; *cf.* 8:18).

Signs and wonders in Deuteronomy

In Deuteronomy 26:8 the Exodus events are described as a series of miracles: 'The LORD brought us out of Egypt with … a terrifying display of power, and with signs and wonders' (NRSV). In the OT, the phrase 'signs and wonders' appears most often in Deuteronomy (Deut. 4:34; 6:22; 7:19; 11:3; 13:2; 26:8; 28:46; 29:3; 34:11). All but two of these references (which are in the singular, Deut 13:2; 28:46) are related to the Exodus. Moses' signs and wonders are evidence that God's saving power can be known in the present and expected in the immediate future, demonstrating 'that the LORD is God; there is no other besides him' (Deut. 4:35), an idea taken up in later OT traditions (1 Chr. 16:12; Neh. 9:10; Pss. 78:43–44; 105:26–45; Jer. 32:20–21). Also these signs and wonders are understood to validate the divine origin of an accompanying statement or revelation. But not all signs and wonders are pointers to God; false prophets, who can be distinguished by their false message, may offer validating signs and wonders (Deut. 13:1–3; cf. 5:7).

The miracles of Elijah and Elisha

The perspective of Deuteronomic history is reflected in the miracle stories of Elijah and Elisha. Elijah provides for a woman's needs and raises her son (1 Kgs. 17:8–24; cf. 2 Kgs. 4:1–7, 32–37 of Elisha), thus demonstrating that he is 'a man of God'. The calling down of fire on a drenched altar shows that the Lord is the God of Israel and that Elijah is his obedient servant (1 Kgs. 18:36–37, 40; cf. 2 Kgs. 1:9–17). Elisha's feeding of a large group of people with a small amount of food and his curing of leprosy shows that God's word is fulfilled through his prophet (2 Kgs. 4:42–44; 5:1–14).

These stories are echoed in the stories of *Jesus (e.g. Luke 7:15 / 1 Kgs. 17:23), and point to the function of Jesus' miracles, that is, to demonstrate who he is (cf. 1 Kgs. 17:24; Luke 7:16). For example, through the parallel between the raising of the boy from Nain and Elijah's raising of the widow's son, Jesus is portrayed as 'a man of God' with 'the word of the Lord' in his mouth (Luke 7:11–17; cf. 1 Kgs. 17:23–24). The parallel between Elisha's feeding of a hundred men with twenty loaves and Jesus' feeding of large numbers of people reveals Jesus as one greater than Elisha (2 Kgs. 4:42–44; Mark 6:32–44; 8:1–10, pars.; cf. John 6:1–15). In Luke Jesus' death is called his 'being taken up' (Luke 9:51); Elijah too is taken up to heaven (2 Kgs. 2:11), and is also expected to return (Mal. 4:5; cf. Mark 8:28).

Signs and wonders in Psalms

The psalmists consider all God's activities in creation and history to be wondrous deeds (Ps. 26:7), especially the awe-inspiring wonders of God (77:11) which Moses and Aaron performed in Egypt (78:43; 105:27; 135:9, the only occurrences of 'signs and wonders' in the psalms). Readers are encouraged to declare the marvellous works of God (96:3), which are reasons to remain faithful to God (78:11) who, out of his love (136:4), is able to do as he pleases (135:6–9), and to praise him (105:5) for his superiority over other gods (96:3–5).

Miracles in Matthew

Through the nine miracle stories of chapters 8 and 9, and the two-part panel which they form with the Sermon on the Mount, Matthew proposes not only that Jesus' ministry is one of word and deed, but also that teaching is more important than miracles. Of all the Gospel writers, Matthew attaches the least significance to miracles.

Matthew uses the miracle stories to develop his themes of Christology (8:2–17), discipleship (8:18 – 9:17) and especially *faith (8:10; 9:2, 18–31). In themselves miracles neither create faith nor dispel doubt but confirm a person's view of Jesus. Nevertheless, Jesus grants healing without any mention of faith (8:14–15), probably to show that his power is independent of it. Although the smallest imaginable amount of faith is all that is required to move mountains (17:20), the disciples need more than 'little faith' if they are to model the ministry of Jesus (8:26; 14:31; 16:8) in difficult circumstances, a lesson taught by the non-therapeutic or nature miracle stories.

The miracle stories reveal Jesus as the Son of David, the Son of God, the new Moses who not only teaches but fulfils the hopes of Isaiah 53 and is thus the Messiah in word and deed. So Jesus is more than a mighty miracle worker; he is the Messiah through whose miraculous deeds the reign of God, and God himself, are present (cf. Matt. 11:4–5). Yet Jesus is also a humble servant, acting out of compassion (15:32; 20:34), and associating with outsiders and outcasts (8:1–13).

Perhaps because of the difficulties caused by exorcists in the church (cf. 7:15–23), Matthew plays down the role of exorcism in the ministry of Jesus and the early church. However, like Luke, Matthew believes exorcisms reveal Jesus' true identity and are the first stage in the defeat of Satan (see *Spiritual powers); through them God fulfils his purpose to bring people the experience of God's reign. Jesus' miracles reveal the nature of *salvation and impart it to others.

More clearly than in the other Gospels Jesus performs his miracles in the shadow of the cross (12:13–14, 22–24). So for example, the feeding stories foreshadow the Last Supper (14:19; 15:36).

Miracles in Mark

Some think that Mark pours scorn on the miraculous and encourages faith in the powerless Jesus of the passion instead of the miracle-working Jesus of his earlier chapters. However, Mark uses miracles to interpret the passion (15:33, 38; 16:1–8) and to encapsulate (9:26–27) as well as adumbrate (6:41; 8:6) Jesus' self-giving death. Mark gives so much space to Jesus as a spectacularly powerful miracle worker whose clothes, touch and words bring healing or raise the dead (5:41–42) that he can hardly regard the miracles as less significant than, or separable from, the self-giving weakness described in the passion narrative. Further, in his portrait of the ministry of Jesus (1:21–32) Mark establishes the primacy of his miracles in relation to his teaching and other activities.

The primary function of the miracles in Mark is to be the principal means of revealing the identity of Jesus (cf. 1:21–28) as 'of God' (1:24), 'Son of God' (5:7), one empowered by the *Holy Spirit (3:22–30), the Messiah (8:22–30), one acting for God (2:1–12) and as God himself, uniquely present and active (6:47–52). Therefore the miracles, encapsulating the whole of Jesus' ministry, bring *eschatological salvation. In so far as the disciples are called to emulate the ministry of Jesus, the miracle stories also provide models for ministry (9:14–29).

However, the miracles are not unequivocal heavenly signs, but parabolic. They provoke hostility and criticism as well as acclamation. Faith is required in order to understand the miracle worker's identity and the purpose of the miracles. As 'parables', the miracles (especially the exorcisms) represent and are in themselves the destruction and plundering of Satan's kingdom and the realizing of God's

kingdom (3:27). Thus Mark indicates that Jesus' ministry involves a conflict, with Satan and the religious leaders; this reaches its climax in the passion.

Faith or *prayer (11:24), personal or vicarious, is so integral to Jesus' *healing of the sick that, apart from the exorcism narratives, there is no healing story that does not include some expression of trust in Jesus' willingness or ability to perform miracles either before, during or after the healing. The miracles are an encouragement, a summons or demand to *repentance and faith, to be with Jesus, to follow him, or to serve him, on the basis of the eschatological salvation they offer.

The virtual absence of miracle stories after Jesus arrives in Jerusalem allows full rein to the hints of the theme of Jesus' self-giving expressed in the earlier miracle stories. Jesus the powerful miracle worker chooses to offer himself, powerless, into the hands of the authorities in order to die 'for many' (10:45).

Some of Jesus' commands to his disciples to remain silent indicate that his true identity cannot be fully understood apart from his passion and death (1:11, 34; 3:12); the powerful miracle worker without the suffering Jesus is an incomplete and misunderstood Messiah. Other injunctions to silence underline the fact that Jesus' ministry cannot be hidden but spills out into Gentile territory; the Gentiles receive Jesus with acclaim equal to that accorded by the Jews.

Luke and Acts

The agenda Luke sets for Jesus (Luke 4:18–19), and the saying about Jesus casting out demons by the finger of God (which Luke would have understood as God's hand, arm or Spirit; 11:20), leave no doubt that Luke saw God's Spirit as the source of Jesus' ability to perform miracles. Another way in which Luke attributes the miracles of Jesus to God is through the use of the word 'power' (dynamis), which is to be understood primarily in the light of the Septuagint's association of power with God and the Spirit rather than in terms of the universal idea of magical miracles.

For Luke, Jesus' miracles do not illustrate or demonstrate the good news; they are themselves (with his teaching) the good news (11:20). Yet Luke's account of Jesus' miracles contains an ambiguity for which he offers no resolution. The 'power' of miracles is portrayed as an impersonal substance (5:17) which responds independently to those who seek healing (8:46). Yet the source of the miracles is also the Spirit (4:18), and it is assumed that anyone can perform miracles (11:14–23; Acts 8:9–11).

Nevertheless, not only do his miracles show Jesus to be the Messiah (Luke 4:18–21; 7:18–22; *cf.* Is. 61:1), a man of compassion (Luke 9:37–43a; *cf.* Mark 9:14–27), someone to be obeyed (Luke 4:35; *cf.* Mark 1:25–26), Master (particularly of his disciples, Luke 5:5; 17:13), and in control of the natural elements (8:22–25); they also identify Jesus as God at work in gracious salvation (8:25). Luke attributes no punitive miracles to the earthly Jesus, who offers *grace instead of divine punishment; he replaces the story of the cursing of the fig tree (Mark 11:12–14, 20–26) with the story of Jesus weeping for Jerusalem (Luke 19:41). Luke clearly distinguishes between the offer of saving grace in Jesus and the coming *judgment of God.

In Luke faith is the required preparation for and response to miracles; miracles are a ground of faith and discipleship (4:39; 5:8; 8:1–3). Luke equates a miracle of healing with salvation, and attributes it to faith in God (17:11–19; the literal translation of v. 19 is 'Your faith has saved you'). He gives no primacy to Jesus' words over his deeds (4:18–19; 7:22); his editorial adjustments to the stories in his tradition, and the arrangement of his material, reveal a balance of word and deed unique among the Gospel writers, which he carries through into Acts.

Luke sustains the importance of exorcism throughout Jesus' ministry. It is the first stage in the defeat of Satan, so that God can fulfil his purpose for his chosen people in bringing them the experience of God's reign (11:20).

Despite the significance of miracles Jesus performs no miracles during his ministry in Jerusalem (though see 22:50–51). At this stage miracles are no longer used to identify Jesus and to draw people to trust him; his identity has been established. Instead Jesus refers to dreadful portents (21:11) signalling the shaking of the universe (21:26), and to signs performed by deceivers (21:8). These miracles also foreshadow a great punitive act of God on Jerusalem.

In Acts God is the main character, through

his miracles (*cf.* P. H. Davids, in *DLNTD*). In the first major speech in Acts, Peter says that Jesus was 'a man attested to you by God with deeds of power, wonders, and signs (*terasi kai sēmeiois*) that God did through him' (Acts 2:22).

While the phrase 'wonders and signs' (sometimes 'signs and wonders' perhaps indicating different traditions) recalls the LXX, where miracles authenticate a message and cause people to believe (2:22; 8:6–7), and while it presents miracles as examples of God's saving power at work in the present (*cf.* Deut. 7:19), it was also used of marvels such as showers of stones, stars shining for seven days, an eclipse of the sun and monstrous births. Therefore by using the phrase for the miracles of Jesus only once in his two books (Acts 2:22), Luke is probably exercising caution in presenting Jesus as only a servant of God who performs mere marvels. The use of the phrase to refer to miracles performed by the followers of Jesus (*e.g.* 2:43; 4:30) may be intended to distinguish their miracles (for which they are dependent on Jesus) from those of Jesus himself.

Acts 10:38 summarizes Jesus' ministry as his going about 'doing good and healing all who were oppressed by the devil'. It is probable that 'doing good and healing' is a hendiadys: Luke has just mentioned Jesus' preaching, and sees the rest of Jesus' ministry as the performance of miracles. He also sees all Jesus' healing as deliverance from oppression by the devil (*cf.* Josephus, *Antiquities*, 6:211).

The ministry of Barnabas and Paul is summed up as 'signs and wonders' (15:12), and there are healing stories (*cf.* 3:1–10; 14:8–10; 16:16–18), as well as accounts of other miraculous events reminiscent of those found in the Gospel traditions (*cf.* Luke 9:28–36; Acts 2:1–4), so that miracle stories remain part of Luke's view that salvation through the power of the Spirit can include healing. The miracles in Acts also illustrate the intervention of God; this may explain the proportionally greater number of deliverance miracle stories in Acts as compared to the Gospel.

However, the miracles reported in Acts include types not associated with Jesus in Luke's Gospel, such as the miracles of judgment (5:1–11; 9:1–9), which reflect the OT tradition of warning against opposition to God (*cf.* Josh. 7:1–5) or his ways (Acts 13:6–

12; *cf.* 19:11–20). Thus one of the functions of the miracle stories in Acts is to distinguish the divine miracles of Jesus and his followers from others (*cf.* E. S. Fiorenza (ed.), *Aspects of Religious Propaganda* [Notre Dame, 1976], pp. 12–16).

John

Using only a few profound miracle stories in distinctive language, the Fourth Gospel makes Jesus' miracles the centrepiece of his ministry. The miracles do not illuminate the message of Jesus; they *are* the message, and his teaching is intended to explain them. They are *life-giving eschatological events.

Although the non-miraculous actions of Jesus also can be understood as 'symbolic actions', the miracles stand in a class of their own as 'signs' (*sēmeia*). John develops the theme of a new Exodus, characterized by miracles of *blessing, not miracles of judgment. In the OT the term 'signs' is linked to the Exodus; the 'I am' sayings recall God's self-revelation in the burning bush; the miracle of water into wine parallels the Exodus sign of water into blood; and great importance is attached to the festivals, especially the Passover.

Like the parables of the Synoptic Gospels, the signs in John point beyond themselves. They authenticate Jesus' filial relationship, even identity, with the Father. This may explain why John does not include the Synoptic idea of Jesus' miracles being inspired by the Spirit: in Jesus, the Father himself is encountered, not the Father's gift.

In John Jesus twice says, 'The hour comes and is now here' (John 4:23; 5:25; *cf.* 12:30–31). The *glory of Jesus is seen not only in his death but also in his signs. Therefore the miracles are not only signs of a glory to come; like the Synoptic miracles, they express God's present reign.

The signs increase in magnitude through the Gospel, and reach a climax in the raising of Lazarus, which both prefigures the great sign of Jesus' death and resurrection and is also the prism through which to look back at the other signs. Thus the ministry of miracle-signs, while no less significant than the great sign, also anticipates it.

In the great sign the glorification of Jesus is no longer focused in his relationship with the Father, evident in the miracles, but in his return to his Father. Thus the signs in the first half of the Gospel reveal the *identity* of Jesus, while the great sign in the second half reveals his *destiny* as the risen Lord ascended to his Father. This means that the miracle-signs are more than a preparation for the full revelation of God's glory in Jesus in the second half of the Gospel; they have a distinct if limited function in revealing the Jesus who will die and rise. So in John the signs are separated from the sign; the passion and resurrection narrative includes no other miracle stories. Yet in both the miracle-signs and the great sign of Jesus' death, resurrection and return to the Father, the glory of God in Jesus is being revealed.

But the Jesus of the signs is never fully disclosed; he is beyond what can be captured in even the most profound miracle. Parallels drawn between Jesus and (possibly) Dionysus (2:1–11), Moses (6:1–15) and Elijah (11:1–44) hint at his identity. It can also be discerned by looking through the prism of the signs to the passion and ascension in which his glory, as 'the Messiah, the Son of God' and the one who gives life (20:31), is fully revealed. However, even in the most spectacular miracle (the raising of a dead man) Jesus is presented not as a god or divine being but as an earthbound and perishable human being; he is the Word become flesh (1:14). Yet there is such a close identity between Father and Son that in Jesus' signs the Father is disclosed and encountered.

By using *ergon* ('work') to refer to the whole ministry of Jesus, as well as to individual miracles, the Fourth Gospel conveys the idea that God is the author of what is seen in Jesus' miracles (*cf.* G. H. Twelftree, *Jesus the Miracle Worker*, p. 225). While the miracles are a distinct 'work' of Jesus, John blurs the distinction between the miracles, the words and the total 'work' of Jesus, so that in the miracles as much as in the overall ministry of Jesus God is the agent of what is seen in Jesus.

This high view of Jesus is to be connected with him taking the initiative in performing miracles. Even when he is petitioned he maintains the initiative by responding in a different way from that expected by others (2:4; 11:6; 4:50).

In contrast to the Synoptic tradition, in John there are no references to exorcism. This is probably not because John is embarrassed by the techniques of exorcism; rather, commonplace exorcisms are insufficiently spectacular to convey the work of God in Jesus. In any case, highlighting the kingship of Jesus instead of the kingdom of God (closely associated with exorcism in the Synoptics) and tying the defeat of Satan to the cross necessitated John removing the exorcisms (*cf.* Mark 3:27).

The large catch of fish (John 21:4–8) is prol ably to be understood not so much as a sign as an allegory: the large number of fish may symbolize the resurrection and the expected success of the church in carrying out the great commission (20:21) through seemingly irrational obedience to Jesus; the church will be able to contain all who are brought into it, and will not be destroyed by division. In the recognition of Jesus in the taking and distributing of bread the miracle reveals that through his death his followers are fed.

Responses to Jesus and the signs include refusing to see the signs with faith, or seeing the signs as only the wonders of a miracle-worker, or believing in Jesus because of the miracles and so understanding his relationship with the Father. That some will believe in Jesus without seeing any signs seems to suggest that faith not based on miracles is a superior kind of faith. However, this is not a criticism of miracle-based faith in itself but a caution that such faith may involve a misunderstanding of who Jesus is. Miracles are not dispensable; nor will they cease or be replaced by the sacraments; some people will never believe without seeing miracles. Some see Jesus' signs without even knowing who he is, which shows that someone can experience a miracle without believing in Jesus before the event.

Miracles in the Pauline corpus

The evidence is strong that Paul performed miracles (Rom. 15:18–19; 1 Cor. 2:4; 2 Cor. 12:12; Gal. 3:5; 1 Thess. 1:5; *cf.* Acts 13:4–12; 14:8–18; 16:16–18; 19:11–12, 20; 20:7–12). Given the association between 'signs and wonders' and the miracle stories of the Exodus tradition, and the place of 'signs and wonders' in Paul's strategy for winning the Gentiles, the phrase 'signs and wonders' (only at Rom. 15:19; 2 Cor. 12:12; 2 Thess. 2:9) probably refers not only to Paul's sufferings but also to miracles performed by him as a means of revelation and a basis for faith.

Even though Paul was reluctant to draw attention to his miracles (1 Cor. 1:22; 2 Cor. 12:12) his *gospel work involved not only preaching but also miracles performed in the power of the Spirit (Rom. 15:18–19; 1 Thess. 1:5). Miracles functioned as a 'demonstration' (*apodeixis*, only in the NT at 1 Cor. 2:1–5) of his message. *Apodeixis* was a technical term for a compelling conclusion drawn from a reasoned argument; in Paul the argument was not verbal but 'of Spirit and of power'. That this is a reference not only to a transforming encounter with God but also to the miracles that formed part of Paul's presentation of the gospel (demonstrating its authenticity; *cf.* 2 Cor. 12:9–10; 1 Thess. 1:9) is probable on a number of counts. First, in 1 Corinthians 2 the demonstration of the gospel is something distinct from Paul's preaching. Secondly, in Romans 15:19 he draws a parallel between the power of the Spirit and the power of signs and wonders. Thirdly, when the Galatians received Paul's message they experienced miracles (*dynameis*, Gal. 3:5). Fourthly, in 1 Thessalonians 1:5, perhaps defending himself against a charge of not demonstrating the efficacy of his message, Paul says that it came not only in word but also in power and in the Holy Spirit and in full conviction (Rom. 4:21; *cf. 1 Clement* 42:3).

Yet, perhaps because his opponents seem to have performed miracles, and the lawless one of 2 Thessalonians 2:9 attempts to deceive through miracles empowered by Satan, Paul does not rely entirely on miracles as evidence for his apostleship or the truth of his message (*cf.* Rom. 15:19; 1 Cor. 2:4). He appeals to his holy life of dependence on God (2 Cor. 5:18–21; 2:17; 4:2; 7:2), his suffering and weakness which highlight the power of God (2 Cor. 4:7–15; 6:4–10; 11:21–33), and the reconciliation between God and the Corinthians (2 Cor. 3:1–6).

One of the manifestations of the Spirit's presence in a believer is the ability to work miracles: 'powers' (*dynameis*, 1 Cor. 12:28–29) or 'workings of powers' (*energēmata dynameōn*, 1 Cor. 12:10). The term 'powers' was commonly used to refer to miracles, including those performed by Paul (2 Cor. 12:12; Gal. 3:5; *cf.* Acts 19:11). Paul's 'powers' could be exorcisms, but more likely they are miracles involving nature; the word *energeia* was generally used to refer to God's miraculous intervention in the course of events (*e.g.* 2 Macc. 3:29; 3 Macc. 4:21;

5:28). Paul did not consider that everyone would have the ability to perform miracles (1 Cor. 12:9), and the varied lists of gifts (*cf*. 1 Cor. 12:8–10 and 12:28) may indicate that the gift of miracles was less closely associated with particular individuals than with the ministries of apostle, prophet and teacher. Paul indicates the importance he attaches to miracles by listing them immediately after these primary gifts.

Conclusion

The biblical theology of signs and wonders is dominated by Jesus. His ministry is reported to involve more miracles than that of any other figure of the period. His ministry is best understood in the light of OT conceptions of God's continuous creativity, in which some events reveal his nature and saving power more clearly than others.

The miracles of Jesus are more than the marvels of a prophet; the phrase 'signs and wonders' is scarcely used to refer to them. The miracles carry the signature of the one who performed them; God himself is revealed and is eschatologically at work in Jesus. The miracles not only authenticate Jesus' message but can also be the gospel. The revelation of God in miracles is ambiguous; it elicits a varied response. Notwithstanding, for Paul divine revelation is inconceivable apart from miracles, and the miracles demonstrate the truth of his message. In all the Gospels miracles can be the basis of faith in Jesus revealed to be God himself, uniquely present, at work saving and caring for his people.

See also: EXODUS (EVENT).

Bibliography

B. Blackburn, *Theios Anēr and the Markan Miracle Traditions* (Tübingen, 1991); P. H. Davids, 'Miracles in Acts', in *DLNTD*, pp. 746–752; J. D. G. Dunn, *Jesus and the Spirit* (London, 1975); J. A. Hardon, 'Miracle narratives in the Acts of the Apostles', *CBQ* 16, 1954, pp. 303–318; H. J. Held, 'Matthew as interpreter of the miracle stories', in G. Bornkamm, G. Barth and H. J. Held (eds.), *Tradition and Interpretation in Matthew* (London, 1982); J. Jervell, *The Unknown Paul* (Minneapolis, 1984), pp. 77–95; E. Käsemann, 'Die Legitimität des Apostels: Eine Untersuchung zu II Korinther 10 – 13', *ZNW* 41, 1942, pp. 33–71; H. Knight, 'The Old Testament concept of miracle', *SJT* 5, 1952, pp. 355–361; S. V. McCasland, 'Signs and Wonders', *JBL* 76, 1957, pp. 149–152; F. Neirynck, 'The miracle stories in the Acts of the Apostles: An introduction', *ETL* 48, 1979, pp. 169–213; H. E. Remus and Y. Zakovitch, 'Miracle', in *ABD* 4, pp. 845–869; M. M. B. Turner, 'The Spirit and the power of Jesus' miracles in the Lukan conception', *NovT* 33, 1991, pp. 124–152; G. H. Twelftree, 'Signs, wonders, miracles', in *DPL*, pp. 875–877; *idem, Jesus the Miracle Worker* (Downers Grove, 1999); H. Wheeler-Robinson, 'The nature-miracles of the Old Testament', *JTS* 45, 1944, pp. 1–12; M. Whittaker, 'Signs and Wonders: The pagan background', *SE* 5, 1968, pp. 155–158.

G. H. TWELFTREE

SIN

Introduction

Preoccupation with sin is one of the hallmarks of biblical religion. Denunciation of sin and the announcement of ensuing woes occupies more than half of the prophetic books (*cf*. Mic. 3:8); the psalms and wisdom writings include many confessions of and reflections on sin; the sacred history emphasizes the consequences of disobedience on the part of rulers and people; the focus is basically the same in the NT, which has a frightening finale in the book of Revelation.

The primary purpose of Christ's mission was to deal with sin. He 'appeared' in order to take sins away (1 John 3:5), just as the Baptist proclaimed (John 1:29); that was the reason he was named '*Jesus' (Matt. 1:21). He stated repeatedly that he had come for sinners and to shed his blood for the remission of sins (Matt. 9:13; 26:28). The gospel proclaims the *forgiveness of sins, made possible by his work (*cf*. Luke 1:77 and 24:47, a significant *inclusio*). The traditional core of the one saving faith affirms first 'that Christ died for our sins according to the Scriptures' (1 Cor. 15:3, NIV), and Paul underlines that 'he was delivered over to death for our sins' (Rom. 4:25). A host of other texts prove the same point; sin, not any metaphysical distance, creates the problem between God and *humankind (Is. 59:2). The purpose of the Son's saving ministry was therefore to deal with sin; not merely to dispel ignorance or to join humanity to the divine nature, but to do away with sin for ever (*cf.* also Heb. 9:26–28).

Vocabulary

Nowhere is the vocabulary of biblical Hebrew richer than in the semantic field of 'sin' (no fewer than fifty terms deserve consideration; E. Beaucamp *et al*, in *Supplément*, col. 407; R. C. Cover, in *ABD* 6, p. 31: 'The plethora of Hebrew terms and their ubiquitous presence in the Hebrew Bible testify to the fact that sin was a dominant concern'). Three of the most important words often appear together (*e.g.* Exod. 34:7; Ps. 32:1–2, 5; 51:1–3; Dan. 9:24). The one usually translated 'sin', and closely related terms of the same *ḥṭ'* root, occur about 600 times. Its original meaning is that of missing the target, failing, falling short of the norm or goal (Judg. 20:16; Job 5:24; Prov. 8:36). In cultic contexts, it is closely connected with uncleanness; sin must be washed away or *atonement made; the same word is also used metonymically for the sin-*offering*. The second main term, *'awôn* (translated 'iniquity' in older versions, and 'wickedness', 'perversity' or 'guilt' in modern versions), has a root meaning 'bending, twisting' (as in Is. 24:1; 'distorts its surface', NASV). It is a moot point whether the metaphor implies perversion, *i.e.* crooked behaviour, as opposed to straightness or rectitude, or the weight of guilt under which sinners bend their backs (Ps. 38:4, so Beaucamp *et al.*, col. 444); both images are consistent with the usage of the word. *Peša'*, usually rendered 'transgression', 'revolt' or 'rebellion', is used less frequently but is still important. Elihu's charge against Job, in Job 34:37, that 'to his sin he adds rebellion' (NIV) expresses both the distinctive meaning and the force of this third important word; in many instances, 'crime' may be the best equivalent. *Peša'* is sometimes an occasions for war (2 Kgs. 1:1).

Raša' (more than 260 occurrences) means 'wicked', or 'ungodly'; it is used to refer to someone who should be condemned in court (Deut. 25:1), branded as supremely infamous, a person of *b'liya'al* (traditionally rendered 'worthlessness', though there is now no scholarly consensus). *'Awen* is quite common and denotes 'falsehood', 'trouble', 'empti-ness'. It is used especially in the denunciation

of *idolatry; because of Jereboam's calf idol and syncretistic cult, Bethel, the 'house of God', is given the name of the nearby hamlet *bêt 'awen*, 'house of falsehood' (Hos. 4:15; 5:8; 10:5). Several verbs express the idea of defying *God's rule, of stepping over the lines he has drawn. Wisdom language associates sin with foolishness or folly (*'iwwelet*) and with stupidity or imperviousness to religion (*n'bālâ*; *cf.* Judg. 20:6), Mockers or scoffers (*lēṣîm*) deride both divine and human author-ity, until they learn that God has the last laugh (Ps. 2:4).

Metaphorical terms further enrich the OT concept of sin. To live is to walk or go on one's way (*derek*), and to obey is to follow the Lord. To sin, therefore, is to go astray (*sûr*), vainly to wander as a result of one's pretended autonomy (Is. 53:6), to slide down the road to ruin (Prov. 9:18) or to backslide, forsaking the Lord and following other gods. Jeremiah, especially, uses the symbolism of wounds and disease to great effect (Jer. 17:9; NIV's 'beyond cure' translates *'ānuš*, which denotes desperate sickness). The idea of ritual uncleanness resulting (for example) from leprosy (Lev. 13 and 14) unites the themes of sickness and impurity.

The vocabulary of the NT is less abundant and varied; the standard meaning of some Greek terms has been changed, through their LXX usage, so as more closely to reflect OT concepts. *Hamartia* and its cognates form the main word-group, and closely correspond to the *ḥṭ'* family; they even have a similar etymology, that of missing the mark. This word for 'sin' was not widely used among the Greeks; Aristotle prefers *adikia*, which denotes injustice or moral-spiritual evil. *Hamartia* refers to semi-voluntary error for which the agent should not be blamed too severely; it is half-way between injustice and mishap (W. Günther in *NIDNTT* 3, p. 577). *Adikia*, *anomia* (lawlessness) and *asebeia* (ungodliness, lack of due reverence for the deity) are also used frequently. *Parabasis* means 'trespass' or 'transgression', while *paraptōma* is a strong word evoking the image of a fall by the wayside (in Heb. 6:6 the verbal form refers to *apostasy); *parakoe* and *apeitheia* refer to disobedience. Paul uses *paraptōma* and *parakoe* in Romans 5:17–19 to denote the sin of *Adam.

In inter-testamental Judaism, the Aramaic *ḥôbâ* ('debt') became the most commonly used term for 'sin'; the phrase 'remission of debts' was used to denote the removal of guilt and the forgiveness of sin. The NT reflects this development. Jesus used the metaphor of debt in his parables (Matt. 18:21–35), and taught his disciples to pray: 'Forgive (remit) us our debts as we also have forgiven (remitted) our debtors' (Matt. 6:12; the parallel passage in Luke 11:4 replaces 'debts' with 'sins').

Thus the biblical vocabulary of sin conveys the ideas of failure to meet accepted standards and disruption of inter-personal relationships. Theological analysis, however, must move beyond purely linguistic considerations.

The concept of sin

Definition

Sin, according to the classical definition, is lack of conformity to the *law of God. The testimony of Scripture, as a whole, confirms this definition. Paraphrastic equivalents of 'sin' in prophetic indictments (*cf.* Ezek. 18) and penitent confessions (*cf.* Dan. 9:4–19) demonstrate its validity. The knowledge of sin comes through the law (Rom. 3:20; *cf.* 7:7): this must mean that the law defines sin, not that it convinces those with darkened minds that they are sinners and so corrects their defective self-understanding (see Eph. 4:18 and the Pharisees in the Gospels).

Appeal is often made to 1 John 3:4 in support of the definition, 'Everyone who sins breaks the law; in fact, sin is lawlessness' (NIV). However, *anomia* here probably does not mean simply the transgression of legal prescriptions. If it did, the statement would be more significant in reverse: every legal transgression is sin, not merely the breaking of a moral code but a rebellion against and insult to the Lord of lords. Sin is always *coram Deo*. Implied as early as Genesis 39:9, this principle is made explicit in 1 John 5:17a, 'All wrongdoing (*adikia*) is sin' (*cf.* Jas. 4:17). Ignace de la Potterie has argued that *anomia* in 1 John 3:4 has eschatological overtones (I. de la Potterie and S. Lyonnet, *La Vie selon l'Esprit, condition du chrétien*, [Paris, 1965], pp. 65–83); as already in 2 Thessalonians 2:3, 7, 9 and Matthew 24:12, *anomia* refers to the final revolt of humankind against God, the fullest expression of sinfulness in the spirit of Antichrist (*Psalm of Solomon* 17:11 calls Pompeius, a figure of Antichrist, the *anomos*).

John is saying to his readers that they should realize the horrendous seriousness of sin: 'Everyone who practices sin (*poiōn hamartian*) enters into the final rebellion against God: yes (*kai*), sin at its deepest level is nothing other than Antichrist's hatred of God.'

The law by which sin is defined is the law of God, not an impersonal and freestanding set of rules. The law reveals God's personal will; failure to obey his command entails personal opposition to him. Sin is mistrust (of God), betrayal, ingratitude and disloyalty; hence 'Everything that does not come from *faith is sin' (Rom. 14:23).

Essence

The foregoing definition is purely formal. Is it possible to identify a first principle of sin, its very essence? There have been many proposals: in the ancient church, sensuousness (concupiscence); later, pride, selfishness, unbelief, greed, *violence (especially in feminist theology) and inertia (neglect and laziness, if not cowardice). Advocates of each may point to some biblical evidence in its favour, but to none so conclusive that all other suggestions may be rejected. Some views can safely be discarded, such as those which lay the blame on the bodily nature of humankind (the Platonic verse in Wisdom of Solomon 9:15, 'A perishable body weighs down the soul, and its frame of clay burdens the mind' [NEB], has weighed down Christian theology for centuries) and those which explain sinful behaviour as the residue of past stages in evolutionary development. But several sins might plausibly be regarded as the fountainhead of all others. The issue is not settled by reference to the *love of God and neighbour, for what is the opposite of that love? Love of self? Love of material things? *Hatred of God?

The difficulty in identifying the 'essence' of sin is a reminder that sin, strictly speaking, has no 'essence'. Only a created being has an 'essence', a stable set of qualities which are constituted and held together by the divine Logos (John 1:3; Col. 1:16–17), and which our minds can understand. Sin is not a creature; it is not of God (Deut. 32:4; Jas. 1:13; 1 John 1:5).

Sin as corruption

Nevertheless, sin is 'real'; that is, it has

effects. This idea is expressed, in the metaphor of perversion or corruption, throughout the Bible, from Genesis 6:11-12 (*šāḥaṯ*) to Revelation 19:2 (*phtheirō*). Sin is always the corruption of something good. Its existence is parasitic; it borrows, or rather usurps, its reality from whatever it corrupts. Moreover, this does not happen independently of God's sovereign government. Though E. P. Sanders charges Paul with inconsistency, he rightly perceives that this was 'one of his basic theological views, a doctrine embraced in all the surviving Jewish literature of the period: God controls what happens, both in nature and in history' (in *ABD* 6, p. 46). The divine permission and ordering of *evil is a mystery. It does not lessen the enmity between God and sin, which is total, but it does explain the rhetoric of such passages as Ezekiel 14:9 or 2 Samuel 24:1.

Types of sin

One and many

The word 'sin' occurs in both singular and plural forms. Paul prefers the singular form (fifty-two out of sixty-four references; L. Ligier, *Péché*, vol. 2, p. 191) and goes so far as to personify sin (Rom. 7:8-11). Each form expresses an aspect of biblical truth. Sin consists in the transgression of commandments, and in this sense, there are many sins; yet sin is also a basic orientation of the whole person, a perversion of his or her whole life. Similarly, the law of God, which is broken by sin, is one, since the love it requires is an all-embracing, permanent commitment of the whole person; yet it is expressed in a variety of more specific precepts.

Jesus' reference to the Spirit's work of conviction in regard to sin, 'in regard to sin, because men do not believe in me' (John 16:9), does not nullify those definitions of sin which refer to the law. In the new stage of salvation history, the most heinous and damaging expression of sinfulness, through which sinners forfeit all chance of escaping condemnation, is unbelief vis-à-vis Jesus. John 15:22 may be taken in a comparative sense (*i.e.* they would not be *as* guilty), or it may mean that had Jesus not come, God would have broken his promises and denied his own character, resulting in the collapse of the whole moral universe.

Binary classifications

Jesus summed up the entire law in two commandments, and it has been customary to classify the first four of the Ten Commandments (supposedly those of the first 'table') as dealing with the love and service of God, and the last six (those of the second 'table') as dealing with love and service of other people. This may reflect a binary classification of sins; most commandments are prohibitions, directed against corresponding sins. Another traditional division, between sins of omission and sins of commission, is supported by James 4:17.

Another distinction is that between lighter and graver sins. It has clear support from Scripture (*e.g.* Ps 19:13; John 19:11) and corresponds to distinctions in the law (Matt. 23:23). Jesus' teaching in the Sermon on the Mount on the relationships between *anger and murder, and lust and *adultery (Matt. 5:22–28) does not simply equate the attitude of the heart and the outward act. The law of *sacrifices is said to provide atonement only for so-called 'unintentional' (*šāgag*, *šāgâ*) sins (Lev. 4:2, 13, 22, 27; 5:15, 18; Num. 15:28–29; Ps. 19:12; *š^egî'ôṯ*, 'errors' [NIV], is parallel to *nistārôṯ*, 'hidden [things]'; Lev. 4:13: 'The community is unaware of the matter'; 5:17: 'even though he does not know it'); Hebrews 9:7 thus uses the word *agnoēmata*, from the root 'to ignore' (the LXX uses the same root, although not the same word, in Lev. 4:13; 5:18, and in many verses it uses *akousiōs*, 'involuntarily'). In contrast, for sins done 'with a high hand' there is only punishment (Num. 15:30–31). The difference, however, must be relative, since the law stipulates that such intentional sins as stealing, swearing falsely in order to defraud one's neighbour, or seducing another man's (slave) fiancée may be atoned for by means of a *guilt-offering (Lev. 6:1–5; 19:20–22). It has been suggested that all sins were transmuted into *š^egāgoṯ* on the Day of Atonement (Ligier, *Péché*, vol. 1, p. 234), or in response to remorse and confession (J. H. Hayes, 'Atonement in the book of Leviticus', *Int* 52, 1998, p. 12).

This data probably implies that ignorance mitigates the seriousness of sin (se also Ps. 19:13; Luke 12:47–48; Rom. 2:12; 1 Tim. 1:13). There may be a difference between more and less important sins (Matt. 23:23), between sins resulting from mere weakness of will and more deeply 'unnatural' sins that pervert the basic order of God's creation (Rom. 1:26–27). Sinners' circumstances are another determinent of the gravity of their sins. *Judgment belongs to God alone; he can be unexpectedly lenient (Gen. 12:10) or severe (Num. 20:6–12).

The idea of 'venial' sins, that is, of sins so unimportant that they do not deserve punishment, has no basis in Scripture. The slightest infringement of a minor article of the law makes one guilty of the whole law (Jas. 2:10; Matt. 5:19); a few 'dead flies give perfume a bad smell' (Eccles. 10:1); even 'all our righteous acts are like filthy rags' in God's sight (Is. 64:6).

The distinction between 'sin that leads to death' and 'sin that does not' (1 John 5:16–17) is best understood, in the context of the epistle, as that between the sin of the 'antichrists', a radical perversion of the gospel, and such sins as Christians ('if any one sees his brother') may commit and from which they may be cleansed through *repentance and prayer (cf. 1 John 1:9; 2:1).

The unforgivable sin

1 John 5:16–17 and Hebrews 6:4–6 have often been linked to Jesus' words on the blasphemy against the Spirit that will not be forgiven (Matt. 12:31–32). The only common feature of the three passages, however, is the suggestion that forgiveness is not always available, which contrasts with the main message of Scripture, the free offer of salvation, open until Christ's return. The texts do not say explicitly that forgiveness is not always available. Hebrews 6 is best explained as a comment on apostasy and backsliding into Judaism (see R. R. Nicole, 'Some comments on Hebrews 6:4–6 and the doctrine of the perseverance of God with the saints', in G. F. Hawthorne [ed.], *Current Issues in Biblical and Patristic Interpretation* [Grand Rapids, 1975]). As for Jesus' logion, it exemplifies our Lord's taste for semi-enigmatic statements (after the manner of the sages), and calls for a brief explanation.

The first enigma of the passage is the sharp distinction drawn between the Son of Man and the *Holy Spirit. It is based on the partial incognito of the Christ before he fulfilled his mission and was glorified. As long as his glory was veiled by 'flesh', those who failed to recognize him were not as guilty as those who, faced with the wonderful acts of the Spirit, ascribed them to demonic power. But why is the sin against the Spirit unforgivable? It is commonly ascribed to extreme hardness of heart resulting from obstinate unbelief; thus those who have sinned against the Holy Spirit never fear having done so. A simpler answer, however, is that yielding to the Spirit's drawing power is the prerequisite of forgiveness, as it opens the only way to forgiveness; to oppose the Spirit, refusing to be convinced by his witness to the only way of salvation, it to deny oneself access to salvation (so G. C. Berkouwer, *Sin* [ET, Grand Rapids, 1971]).

Sin and human nature

'Like the rest, we were by nature objects of wrath' (Eph. 2:3): this phrase suggests that the whole person is tainted by sin from birth or even conception (cf. *phusei* in Gal. 2:15). Jesus stresses that the badness of the tree precedes that of the fruit, denouncing his hearers as a 'brood of vipers!' (Matt. 12:33–34; cf. 17:17; already Jer. 13:23). Paul's technical use of the word 'flesh' (translated 'sinful nature' by NIV in Eph. 2:3) forcefully expresses the same thought ('flesh' can refer to the human body or person, or to one's family). 'The mind of the flesh (*phronēma tēs sarkos*) is enmity towards God' (Rom. 8:7, author's translation). Does the choice of the word 'flesh' hint at some special role for the body in human sinfulness? Paul can speak of the 'body of sin' (Rom. 6:6) and 'of death' (Rom. 7:24), and of the law of sin which is in his 'members' (Rom. 7:23), and this could be interpreted as the effect of disorder among the components of the human personality (cf. 1 Cor. 9:27; Col. 2:11, 23). But Paul assumes the unity of that personality; thus for him 'fleshly' is synonymous with 'human' (1 Cor. 3:3–4, 'Are you not fleshly [*sarkikoi*]?' is parallel to 'Are you not human [*anthrōpoi*]?'; W. P. Dickson, *Saint Paul's Use of the Terms 'Flesh' and 'Spirit'* (Glasgow, 1883).

Sin is universal in a threefold sense. It is spread throughout the person's being, or members, or faculties, leaving nothing intact (Is. 59:3–11; Rom. 3:13–18; Titus 1:15). It affects human life from beginning to end (Gen. 8:21; Pss. 51:5; 58:3). No human, except Jesus only, can truly claim to be free from its stain (1 Kgs. 8:46; Ps. 14:3; Eccles. 7:20; Jer. 17:9; Prov. 20:9; Jas. 3:2; 1 John 1:8).

Yet, sin is not 'natural', *i.e.* intrinsic to created human nature; it is a matter of the will (*e.g.* Prov. 1:29; Is. 42:24; 65:12; Matt. 23:37; John 3:19; 5:40). Jesus taught that sin proceeds from the heart, the seat of thought and will (Matt. 15:18–20). The indictment of the heart is found in many places in Scripture, (from Genesis 6:5 onwards); the heart is said to be uncircumcised, or callous, or stony, or desperately sick. The 'stubbornness' of the sinful heart is a favourite theme, especially with Jeremiah (from 7:24 onwards; though according to Ligier, *Péché*, vol. 1, p. 106, *šᵉrirût* is rather the passionate impulse towards freedom). This term implies that sin is a foreign body in human nature 'as it was in the beginning' (to borrow Jesus' phrase in Matt. 19:8). Sinfulness must be distinguished from creatureliness (contra Cover, in *ABD*, p. 33, but he has to grant, p. 34, that it is doubtful whether the Hebrew poets 'ascribed the intrinsic human sinfulness to the handiwork of God').

The early chapters of Genesis contrast the inception of created things (which are all said to be very good) with the inception of *evil through the first sin. The doctrine of original sin has been framed to explain how sin spreads in a quasi-natural way throughout the human race and how human beings are none the less responsible for it. The doctrine highlights both the organic unity of the human family and its special structure, in which 'headship' is conferred upon Adam in a covenant made by God. Scripture provides both the basis and some hints as to the content of the doctrine.

The powers of sin

Through the infection of the 'flesh', sin makes the human person a slave. Jesus himself states this undeniable fact (John 8:34) and Paul further elaborates it (Rom. 6:6, 13–14, 16–23), using the verbs 'to reign' and 'to dominate' (vv. 12, 14). He says that 'the power of sin is the law' (1 Cor. 15:56), and that that power was broken when God 'condemned sin in the flesh' on the cross in the person of the sin-bearer (Rom. 8:3). Slavery to sin signals that sin is alienation, estrangement from the life of God (Eph. 4:18; *cf.* 2:12).

Two enslaving agencies are identified in addition to the flesh: the *world and the devil (see *Spiritual powers). All three are men-

tioned in Ephesians 2:2–3 and, more or less explicitly, in the parable of the sower (Matt. 13:19, 21, 22, the evil one; human nature in which the word does not take root; the concerns of this world). The word *kosmos* has a negative connotation throughout the Johannine corpus and in many other passages (*e.g.* 2 Cor. 7:10; Gal. 6:14; Col. 2:20; Jas. 4:4). It refers to the corporate dimension of sinfulness, but also to the emptiness of much human culture, its lust, and greed and pride (1 John 2:16). Customs, institutions, symbols and systems, dis-information and contagious passion, all make the world a tyrant. The use of the root *lmd*, to teach, in Jeremiah 13:23 (in the word *limmudê*, which denotes trained experts in evildoing) indicates that sin is also something one learns (*cf.* Deut. 18:9; Ligier, *Péché*, vol. 1, pp. 102f.).

The devil and his 'angels', who may be identified with demons, evil spirits, and hostile powers in the heavenlies, are represented as holding a universal sway through the universal reign of sin (see 1 John 5:19; Eph. 2:2 and the title 'prince of this world'; *cf.* Acts 10:38; Heb. 2:14–15). Although their origin is shrouded in mystery, they seem to be angels who 'sinned' (2 Pet. 2:4) and 'did not keep their *archē*', their principle or dignity or authority (Jude 6). In relation to human sin, the devil is preeminently the tempter (*ho peirazōn*, Matt. 4:3) and the accuser; his name 'Satan' (translated *diabolos* in Greek, from which the word 'devil' is derived) means 'accuser'. Satan's weapon is denunciation; he appeals to the demands of the law to shut sinners off from life-giving fellowship with God (the power of sin is the law). The full satisfaction of God's justice, the condemnation of sin in the flesh of Christ, the shed blood of the Lamb, deprive Satan of all power (Rev. 12:10–11). There may be collusion between spiritual powers and the structures of the 'world' (especially the political structures); the main biblical support for this view is found in Daniel 10. But they are not identical; references to the spirit-world may not be interpreted as mythological ways of denoting societal structures which cause alienation.

Sin and the right

Some 'sins' in the OT seem to have only ritual significance and they resemble taboo-regulations (*e.g.* Lev. 19:19). However, several wide-ranging pronouncements, including the second version of the law in Deuteronomy, relativize ritual actions and rules and suggest that inner attitudes and ethical conduct are what really matters to the Lord (1 Sam. 15:22–23; Ps. 15; Jer. 7:22–23, understanding 'al diḇrê to mean 'for the sake of'; Hos. 6:6; Amos 5:21–27; Mic. 6:6–8). Descriptions of the future imply a transition to a fully spiritual order (Jer. 3:16). Unlike that of heathen gods, the *holiness of the Lord is described in terms of *righteousness (Deut. 32:3–4); he 'abhors' (a strong word) even 'dishonest scales', i.e. inaccurate weights (Prov. 11:1).

This close relationship between holiness (the religious) and righteousness (the ethical) becomes even closer in the NT, which repudiates pagan notions of 'sacredness' (Acts 10:15): 'To the pure, all things are pure' (Titus 1:15; cf. Mark 7:19). OT regulations similar to those of pagan religions were temporary arrangements (Heb. 9:10; cf. Col. 2:16–17). Conversely, ethics is part of religion: 'All wrongdoing is sin' (1 John 5:17). David says to the Lord, concerning the sins of adultery and murder, 'Against you, you only, have I sinned' (Ps. 51:4); ultimately sin against other people is sin against God.

Sin is morally wrong and thus entails guilt. The main Hebrew words for 'guilt' are 'awôn (see above) and the corresponding verb; the guilt-offering is denoted by 'ašām (Is. 53:10). Indirect references include a description of inner oppression (Ps. 32:3–4), a picture of a multitude of sins pursuing and overtaking a harassed sinner (Ps. 40:12), and a metaphor of guilt being 'stored up' (Hos. 13:12). In the NT, the metaphor of debt is used to express the idea of guilt, and enochos may be a technical term for it (Matt. 5:21–22, four times; 1 Cor. 11:27).

Guilt has two components. The sinner's personal unworthiness is not transferable and remains even after sin has been remitted, i.e. forgiven, and the person 'justified'; so the apostle still considers himself the chief of sinners (1 Tim. 1:16) and the least of all the saints (Eph. 3:8). But guilt is also liability to punishment, the debt owed to retributive justice in the moral-spiritual order. To bear one's sin is to incur the punishment it deserves (Gen. 4:13; Exod. 28:43; Lev. 5:1, 17; 19:8; 22:9; 24:15; Num. 5:31; 9:13; 14:34; 18:22). To impute or reckon sin (Ps.

32:2; Rom. 5:13; 2 Cor. 5:19) is to apply the judicial rule and to exact the penalty, or to pay the (negative) wages the action deserves (Rom. 6:23). The wages of sin is *death, both as the logical consequence or harvest of behaviour which is secretly or overtly driven by a powerful death-wish (Gal. 6:7–8; Rom. 8:6), and as the requirement of justice (e.g. Rom. 1:32 – 2:12). The two components of guilt are often connected (Gen. 18:25; Deut. 24:16; Jer. 31:29–30; Ezek. 18), but the second may be transferred, as when a husband bears the sin of his wife (Num. 30:15).

The heart of the gospel proclamation is the good news that such a transfer was made on the cross of Jesus the Christ. He, the Bridegroom, to whom alone the bride belongs, gave himself up for her, the Head for the body, the King for his people, the Shepherd for his sheep, the Last Adam for the new creation humanity, the Master for his disciples and friends, our Lord for us. 'He himself bore our sins in his body on the tree' (1 Pet. 2:24). The exchange involved is explicated by the symmetry of Paul's sentence: 'God made him who had no sin to be sin for us, so that in him we might become the righteousness of God' (2 Cor. 5:21). The statement that Christ was 'made ... to be sin' may mean that he was made a sin-offering (the Hebrew word for 'sin' is also used for the corresponding sacrifice), but the antitheses make it more probable that 'made him ... to be sin' stands for 'reckoned sin to him' (the idea of imputation has already been introduced in v. 19); the guilt of human sin was reckoned to the account of the perfectly righteous Jesus Christ. Similar symmetry is found in Galatians 3:10–13; the curse that falls on all transgressors of the divine law was transferred to Christ the beloved, who was made a curse for us, so that we might be freed from the curse.

The legal debt of sin was thus cancelled (Col. 2:14) and all righteousness fulfilled. In particular, God demonstrated his justice, for while he now justifies the very wicked, he has perfectly satisfied the claims of his own holy justice, 'so as to be just and the one who justifies those who have faith in Jesus' (Rom. 3:25–26; cf. 4:5). This why there is no condemnation left for those who are in him, despite the sins they have committed (Rom. 8:1), and the devil, the Accuser, is defeated, having been deprived of his supreme weapon (Rev. 12:10–11). The day of the Lord shall reveal to all the efficacy of God's strange work; the redeemed will no longer be under any curse, and sin will be eradicated. (Rev. 22:3, 15).

See also: SALVATION.

Bibliography

S. Alsford, 'Sin and atonement in feminist perspective', in J. Goldingay (ed.), *Atonement Today* (London, 1995), pp. 148–165; E. Beaucamp, E. des Places and S. Lyonnet, 'Péché', in H. Cazelles and A. Feuillet (eds.), *Supplément au dictionnaire de la Bible 7*, fasc. 38-39 (Paris, 1962, 1963); H. A. G. Blocher, *Evil and the Cross: Christian Thought and the Problem of Evil* (ET, Leicester, 1994); *idem, Original Sin: Illuminating the Riddle* (Leicester and Grand Rapids, 1997); I. D. Campbell, *The Doctrine of Sin in Reformed and Neo-Orthodox Thought* (Fearn, 1999); R. C. Cover, 'Sin, sinners: Old Testament', in *ABD* 6, p. 31–34; T. Griffith, 'A non-polemical reading of 1 John: Sin, christology, and the limits of Johannine Christianity,' *TynB* 49, 1998, pp. 253-276; L. Ligier, *Péché d'Adam et péché du monde: Bible, Kippur, Eucharistie*, 2 vols. (Paris, 1960, 1961); T. Peters, *Sin: Radical Evil in Soul and Society* (Grand Rapids, 1994); D. L. Smith, *With Willful Intent: A Theology of Sin* (Wheaton, 1994).

H. A. G. BLOCHER

SINAI, see COVENANT
SLEEP, see DEATH AND RESURRECTION

SOLOMON

The two OT presentations of Solomon (in *Kings and *Chronicles) are somewhat different in emphasis. The authors of Kings present him as for the most part a wise king. However, his wisdom was not always used for honourable ends (1 Kgs. 2:13–46), and by the end of his reign it had largely degenerated into a self-indulgent playing of games with words (1 Kgs. 10:1–13). Similarly, he was for the most part a king committed to God. Yet even at the start of his reign his integrity was open to question (1 Kgs. 3:1–3 *etc.*); and

eventually his indiscretions turned to outright *apostasy (1 Kgs. 11:1–8). He was in many ways an ideal king ruling over an ideal kingdom, but ideal and reality were always in tension, and eventually the reality was much less than ideal. He was, most of all, a king *blessed by God, this blessing continuing even in the midst of *sin (1 Kgs. 11:9–13, 31–39). *God's* choice was thus in the end seen to be more important than *human* choices, even if mortals can never presume on grace in order to evade the demands of law. This hopeful ending to the Solomon story carries with it the implication that there could also be hope (the hope expressed in Solomon's own prayer in 1 Kgs. 8:22–53) at the end of Israel's story, when the as-yet-unfulfilled threats of 1 Kings 9:6–9 had finally become realities (2 Kgs. 24 – 25). For if David's son was always to sit on the throne (2 Sam. 7), God must forgive; a throne upon which he might sit must be restored; and a people over whom he could rule must be reconstituted.

The authors of 1–2 Chronicles pick up and develop this idea as they look ahead in the context of exile to the future *kingdom of God. Their portrayal of Solomon in fact reflects, even more strongly than that in Kings, a vision of the ideal Davidic ruler of the future as much as the reality of the Solomon of history, omitting as it does the more negative characteristics of Solomon as described in Kings. This vision is then further picked up and developed in the NT. Here Jesus is identified as *the* Son of David towards whom the Davidic promise ultimately points (Matt. 1:1–16; 21:1–11; 22:41–46), *the* king who sits upon David's throne (Luke 1:32–33; John 18:28–40; Acts 2:29–36). He is the one greater than Solomon, fulfilling the messianic promise of Isaiah 11:1–9 (with its backward glance at Solomon in vv. 2–3), to whose wisdom people should listen, as the Queen of Sheba listened to Solomon (Matt. 12:42; Luke 11:31; *cf.* also Matt. 13:54; Luke 2:40, 52). Like the wisdom teachers of the OT, indeed, Jesus often encourages his hearers to learn about God by observing how God's world works (*e.g.* Matt. 6:25–34; Luke 12:22–34). More than that, however, the NT presents him as the *incarnation* of wisdom, the very Wisdom of God (1 Cor. 1:24), present with the Father from the beginning of creation (John 1:1–18; Col. 1:15–20; *cf.* Prov. 3:19–20; 8:22–31). Jesus supersedes Solomon, not least in the fact that in Jesus wisdom and *obedience to law are perfectly integrated (Rom. 5:19; Heb. 5:8–10), whereas in Solomon they were always in tension and ultimately divorced; and Solomon points forward typologically to Jesus. Once this is realized, it is impossible to read the Solomon story without hearing echoes of the Jesus story (e.g. in the 'coronation' scene of 1 Kgs. 1:38–40; cf. Matt. 21:1–11).

Solomon is not simply a type of Christ, however, but also 'one of us', one of the people of God, and thus a warning and an example to the Christian believer. Given that a degree of ambivalence about Solomon's wealth is evident in Kings, it is interesting to note that the only reference to Solomon's 'splendour' in the NT occurs in a section of Jesus' teaching (recorded in slightly differing forms in Matt. 6:25–34 and Luke 12:22–31) which encourages believers not to allow concern about material needs to interfere with their seeking of God's kingdom. Both Gospels associate this with other teaching about 'not storing up treasures on earth', but rather in heaven, lest the heart go astray (Matt. 6:19–21; Luke 12:32–34), and Luke associates it also with the parable of the rich fool (Luke 12:13–21) and with the injunction to 'sell your possessions and give to the poor' (Luke 12:33). The emphasis in these texts on God's provision of the necessities of life and on the imperative to share wealth with others contrasts with the emphasis in 1 Kings 9:10 – 10:29 on Solomon's extravagance and apparent self-absorption. In Kings there is even a token pagan 'running after these things' (Matt. 6:32; Luke 12:30), that is, the Queen of Sheba.

The 'wisdom of Solomon' theme can also be developed with reference to Christian discipleship. The NT can be just as positive about wisdom as the Solomon story, and yet, like that story, it highlights the inadequacies of and dangers inherent in a wisdom which is simply 'from below'. The NT authors know that such wisdom can express itself in idle words and empty philosophy, if not in outright apostasy and 'freedom' from God's law (e.g. Rom. 1:21–25; Col. 2:8; Jas. 3:13–18), and throughout the NT the 'wise' are unable, of themselves, to receive the gospel (e.g. 1 Cor. 1:18–25). True wisdom must be revealed 'from above'; and it is characteristically revealed to 'children' (Luke 10:21), those who are not wise at all by worldly standards (e.g. 1 Cor. 1:26–31). Wisdom 'from above' is thus given the same central place in the NT as it is in the Solomon story (1 Kgs. 3); there too wisdom is revealed to 'a little child' who knows his need (3:7), and leads to wise judgment (cf. the expectation of 1 Cor. 6:5).

See also: DAVID; JESUS CHRIST; WISDOM.

Bibliography

I. W. Provan, 1 and 2 Kings, NIBC (Peabody, 1995); H. G. M. Williamson, 1 and 2 Chronicles, NCB (London, 1982).

I. W. PROVAN

SON OF DAVID, see JESUS CHRIST
SON OF GOD, see JESUS CHRIST
SON OF MAN, see JESUS CHRIST
SONG OF SONGS, see Part 2
SOUL, see HUMANITY
SPIRIT OF GOD, see HOLY SPIRIT
SPIRIT, see HUMANITY

SPIRITUAL GIFTS

This subject is much more complex and subtle than one might at first expect. The term 'spiritual gift/s' itself is very rare in the Bible (see below), being mainly a collective label that interpreters use to pigeonhole certain phenomena. But some use it very narrowly (limiting its meaning to the manifestations of the Spirit specifically named in 1 Cor. 12:8–10), while others use it much more broadly of almost any and every activity enabled by *God. And there is a spectrum of uses in between. Paul is perhaps the biblical writer who provides most theological help on the subject, so the section on Paul below is longer than the others. However, one of the key terms in Paul's discussion, the Greek word charisma/charismata, has also been subject to important misunderstandings that have skewed the contemporary debates.

Terminology and definition

The first problem is that of defining the subject matter. This is not an easy task, for two reasons.

First, there is no precise Hebrew/Greek equivalent to the English phrase 'spiritual gifts'. For example, the Greek *charismata pneumatika* appears nowhere in the LXX or NT, though the singular occurs, just once in Romans 1:11. Some of the English versions (*e.g.* NRSV and NIV) use 'spiritual gift(s)' in four other places, but in each case as a translation of some *other* Greek word. The phrase is used to translate the Greek noun *charisma* in 1 Corinthians 1:7; *pneumatika* (lit. 'spirituals' or 'spiritual things/workings') in 1 Corinthians 12:1 and 14:1; and *pneumata* (lit. 'spirits') in 1 Corinthians 14:12. These initial observations indicate that while 'spiritual gifts' is part of the English *reader's* conceptual scheme, it may not easily map onto that of the biblical writers.

Secondly, in practice there is little agreement amongst English speakers as to what the term 'spiritual gift(s)' should be used to denote. For some Pentecostal writers, there are just nine spiritual gifts, those listed in 1 Corinthians 12:8–10, and they are all fundamentally 'supernatural' in character. This definition of gifts is too restrictive (see below). At the other extreme, theologians such as Rahner and Moltmann use the expression to denote *any* kind of activity/enabling attributable to the Spirit. As Rahner and Moltmann understand the Spirit to be immanent in *all* life (*e.g.* on the basis of the OT texts discussed below), it follows for them that *any* existential experience of life/*grace, whether Christian or not, is a 'spiritual gift'. But this broad usage does not correspond to that of the NT, in which the Spirit's activity is largely restricted to believers.

A majority use the term as a rough equivalent for the English 'charism(s)', meaning a 'manifestation of the Spirit in an event or enabling for the service of God and/or his people'. But even this usage is not without its problems. While a prophecy or a healing might be a clear 'manifestation of the Spirit' (*cf.* 1 Cor. 12:6–10), it is less clear how (and to what degree) the Spirit is 'manifest' in relation to the various 'acts of service' and ministries listed in 1 Corinthians 12:28–30, Romans 12:3–8, Ephesians 4:7–13, *etc.* One reading of the majority view would suggest that all these are 'spiritual gifts' (and Eph: 4:7–8 *specifically* identifies the ministries of vv. 11–12 as Christ's 'gifts' [*domata*] to the church). But in practice many attempt to distinguish less supernatural 'ministries' from 'spiritual gifts' (or 'ministry gifts' from

'charismata'), while allowing that the Spirit may be active in both, albeit in different ways.

The safest way ahead will be to offer a provisional stereotype of 'spiritual gift', and explore the fuzzy areas through a survey of the biblical literature. We begin with the rough-and-ready 'majority' definition: a spiritual gift is a manifestation of the Spirit through an individual in an event or enabling for the service of God and/or his people.

Spiritual gifts in the OT

For a brief survey of the various kinds of manifestation of the Spirit, see *Holy Spirit. Two different types of tension are found in the material. First, the early narratives of Judges and 1 Samuel seem to suggest that the gift of the Spirit is an amoral and destructive power, even the 'Spirit of war', and are in tension with the later promises of the Spirit as the power of inner renewal, associated especially with obedient servant-liberator figures. However, in the Judges narratives, it is not said directly that the Spirit of God tore the lion apart (14:6), or wrought destruction on the Philistines (14:19; 15:14–15); nor is it even suggested that the Spirit prompted these actions. Rather, the impression is given that the man, made mighty by the Spirit, himself decides to do these things, in anger at his betrayal. And of course these narratives (and the similar, if more restrained ones in 3:7–11 [Othniel]; 6:34 – 7:23 [Gideon]; 11:29–40 [Jepthah], *etc.*), for all the ambiguity of their central characters, have to be understood in the context of Amalekite/Moabite/Philistine oppression/infiltration of *Israel, and of the cry of the nation for deliverance. The stories are part of a dialectic in which Israel learns what it means to be a holy nation, through separation from the surrounding nations and their idolatrous *worship (for a perceptive treatment, see M. Welker, *God the Spirit*, ch. 2).

Secondly, there is a tension between assertions that the Spirit is immanent in *all* *creation/*life (*e.g.* Gen. 1:2; 6:3, 17; 7:15; Ps. 33:6; Job 32:8; 33:4; 34:14–15; *etc.*) and the more particularist traditions which limit the Spirit to *Israel* (or even, restrict the Spirit's activity to different types of *leader). For Elihu, 'it is the S/spirit in a mortal, the breath of the Almighty, that makes for understanding' (Job 32:8, understood in the context of 33:1–7; 34:14–15). According to this pneumatology, *all* authentic *wisdom/ understanding, creative work, art and culture, can be understood as manifestations of the Spirit of life that glorify God (see esp. J. Moltmann, *The Spirit of Life*, and *cf.* M. Volf, *Work in the Spirit*). On this model, there is no radical dualism between nature and supernature, and any manifestations of human activity which enhance creation and society can be understood as 'spiritual gifts'. (This idea strains the provisional definition above in the case of gifts that are not consciously exercised in relation to God or for the benefit of God's *people.) A specific case in point might be that of Bezalel and his colleagues, of whom God says 'I have filled him with divine spirit (*rûaḥ 'elohîm*), with ability, intelligence, and knowledge in every kind of craft, to devise artistic designs, to work in gold ... [etc.]' (Exod. 31:3–4, NRSV). Readers of the NRSV could readily interpret this as the *immanent* God's sovereign moulding of human abilities, and use of them for his glory.

The other OT pneumatology presents the Spirit of God as a manifestation of his transcendence rather than of his immanence, that is, as the charismatic Spirit. On this model, the Spirit typically 'falls upon' or 'seizes' a person; 'fills' him or her, and enables immediate revelation, charismatic wisdom, inspired speech or acts of power, such as can be attributed only to *God's* direct work, not to ordinary human potential. (The Targumic and Rabbinic tradition actually takes Exod. 31:3–4 in this latter sense, attributing Bezalel's gifts to the charismatic 'Spirit of prophecy'.)

Passages asserting the immanence of the Spirit in *all* creation/life are in tension with those which portray the Spirit rather as a 'charismatic' endowment on only a few of Israel's leaders. This tension is undoubtedly an important and potentially creative one, but it makes decisions about what to label as a 'spiritual gift' problematic. Furthermore, there is a spectrum of other possibilities between these two models. This is perhaps seen most clearly in relation to 'wisdom'. It is unlikely that every instance of wisdom discerned in Bezalel, or in the seventy elders of Numbers 11:16–25, or in the messianic figure of Isaiah 11:1–4, would be so invasive in character that they would all be a clear

expression of 'charismatic Spirit'. Wisdom, in the sense of spiritual understanding and activity in conformity with it, will often be more like what Paul calls 'fruit' of the Spirit, and will involve reflection, meditation and application. Here the borders between 'natural' and 'supernatural' are distinctly fuzzy. When is the activity of the Spirit in providing wisdom appropriately designated a 'spiritual gift'? Similar problems will be found in the Pauline material.

In the Gospels and Acts

Cessationists who claim that the healings of *Jesus and the apostles were merely authenticating signs of their status as bearers of canonical *revelation misunderstand Jesus' own explanation of them. For Jesus, they are rather expressions of the liberating reign of God, bursting into history, and it is *as such* that they attest the message of the kingdom. Cessationists also claim that prophecy and revelations were given merely to provide the infallible soteriological subject matter of the NT scriptures (and to guide the church until the canon was complete). But they overlook the fact that the only prophecies reported in Acts have nothing to do with the provision of soteriological revelation, but with spontaneous praise to God (19:6; *cf.* 2:11; 10:46) or with particularistic guidance (11:28; 20:23; 21:4, 10–11). Similarly, the vast majority of revelations related in Acts concern, not general theological truths, but the sort of very specific guidance that the advent of the canon would not render unnecessary (see, *e.g.* Acts 8:29; 9:10–16; 10:19–20; 13:2; 16:6–7, 9; 18:9–10, *etc.*). More importantly, cessationists also overlook the fact that it is precisely what Judaism meant by the 'Spirit of prophecy', *i.e.* the gift promised in Joel 2:28–32, that Peter promises to *all* who repent and are *baptized (Acts 2:38–39, echoing Joel 2:32, and *cf.* Acts 2:16–18). Such a gift would *prototypically* include revelations, charismatic wisdom of various kinds, and invasive prophecy and praise. The most broad-ranging of these would be 'wisdom', which could include anything from understanding the proclamation of the gospel as *God's* good news (not merely human words) to the rejoicing response to the gospel (2:42–47; 8:39; 16:34, *etc.*); from the ability to handle contentious *church matters (6:3) to the ability to preach and teach arrestingly (2:14–

42; 4:31; 6:10; 11:23–24; 18:25, *etc.*) and to rejoice in *suffering (13:52). Indeed, for Luke most of Christian 'life' could be regarded as an expression of Spirit-enabled wisdom. (See also *Holy Spirit, *Signs and wonders, *Prophecy, Prophets, *Languages, *Healing and sickness.)

In the Pauline letters

Linguistic issues

In 1 Corinthians 12:4–7, opening a discussion mainly addressed to the use and misuse of tongues (chs. 12 – 14), Paul refers to a variety of what are often called 'spiritual gifts'. He characterizes these variously (and simultaneously) as *charismata* (v. 4, 8); 'acts of service' (*diakoniai*) given by the risen Lord (v. 5); 'workings' (*energēmata*) of God (v. 6); and 'manifestations (*phanerōseis*) of the Spirit' for the common good (v. 7). In 12:1 and 14:1 he refers to them as *pneumatika* ('Spirit-workings'[?]). It is frequently asserted that the first of these expressions is a technical term (though clearly the others are not), derived from the Greek *charis* ('grace'), and so characterizes the phenomena concerned as 'events of God's grace' (J. D. G. Dunn, *Jesus and the Spirit*, p. 254). From this supposed etymology, and from Paul's statement in verse 9 that 'to another' is given '*charismata* (plural) of healings' (suggesting that each event of healing is itself a *charisma*), it is deduced that the writer views *charismata* dynamically as short-term bursts of Spirit-given activity, rather than as people or long-term functions or abilities continuously available. A person has 'gifts' of healing (or prophecy, *etc.*), not 'the gift of healing'. For Dunn, Paul thought of 'ministry' simply as the regular exercise of such brief *charismata*, and for him it follows that the use of the word *charisma* to denote Timothy's (long-term) *office* (1 Tim. 4:14; 2 Tim. 1:6) represents a post-Pauline fading of the apostle's dynamic charismatic vision (Dunn, *Jesus*, pp. 345–50).

This etymology is, however, almost certainly incorrect (see M. Turner, in *Hearing the New Testament*, pp. 155–165). *Charisma* (like all -*sma* words) derives from a verb, not from another noun; from *charizomai* ('give generously'), not from *charis* ('grace'). And the -*(s)ma* ending denotes 'result of' not 'event of'. So the word simply means 'thing (generously) given', or more simply, 'gift'. Paul uses it interchangeably with three other words meaning 'gift' in Romans 5:15–17, where the gift is that of justification through Christ's death. Nor can anything safely be deduced concerning the duration of a *charisma* from its etymology. Indeed Paul uses the Greek word *charisma* to refer to eternal life (Rom. 6:23), his own celibacy (1 Cor. 7:7), and Israel's irrevocable covenant benefits (Rom. 11:29). An English speaker would not normally list *any* of these among the 'charismata'. (This point usefully illustrates the danger of confusing the sense of the Greek word *charisma(ta)* with that of the English words 'charism(s)'/'charisma(ta)'.)

In 1 Corinthians 12 Paul does indeed use the Greek *charisma* (amongst other expressions) to *refer* to what might in English be called 'spiritual gifts'. But this is not the *sense* of the word (Paul has to *add* the adjective *pneumatikon* to obtain this sense in Rom. 1:11). Here, as elsewhere, it simply means '(generous) gift'. And while Paul uses the word *charisma* only of gifts given by God, there is no reason to suppose that he could not also use it of gifts given by others. If the word *charisma* itself meant '*divine* gift', Paul would not have needed to add the words *ek theou* ('from God') to define the kind of *charisma* he is speaking about in 1 Corinthians 7.7 (*cf.* Rom. 11:29). In other words, we know the set of phenomena in 1 Corinthians 12:8–10 are '*spiritual* gifts' (in our definitional sense) only because the context asserts that they are workings of the Spirit, not because they are called *charismata*.

'Spiritual gifts' in 1 Corinthians 12 – 14

The Corinthians' over-valuation of glossolalia led them to misuse it (see *Languages). Paul begins his corrective, 1. by pointing to the functional nature of all spiritual gifts (they are given to enable believers to serve Christ and promote the common good) and 2. by relativizing tongues as one among many gracious gifts of God, rather than the supreme gift; hence the list in 12:8–10. This list is clearly ad hoc, rather than complete, and it probably reflects Corinthian interests more than Paul's broader understanding of gifts (which will emerge later). Thus it is the Corinthians who are most interested in 'messages of wisdom' (*cf.* the polemic in 1:17 – 2:13; 3:19) and 'messages of knowledge' (*cf.*

1:5; 8:1, 10–11; 13:2, 8; 'word of knowledge' in 12:8 is thus probably not what Pentecostals mean by the same term, namely supernatural insight into someone's personal condition). Probably their interest in the spectacular prompts Paul to include the next three items (charismatic expressions of 'faith', healings and working of other miracles). And the list closes with prophecy, discernment of 'spirits', tongues and interpretation, because these are the topics Paul intends to address. (In this context the 'spirits' discerned are manifestations of the Spirit [as at 14:12], particularly of prophecies [not detection of evil spirits; see G. D. Fee, *God's Empowering Presence*]). The absence from the list of the charismatic intercessory groan of Romans 8:26–27, the visions and revelations of 2 Corinthians 12 (*etc.*), and, above all, multiple forms of charismatic wisdom (other than 'words of wisdom'), indicate that it is not exhaustive.

From 1 Corinthians 12:12 to the end of the chapter, Paul critiques a primary interest in tongues by arguing that all have different gifts, so that they may be an interdependent unity, mutually co-operating parts of the 'body of Christ'. (What Paul says here and in 12:4–7 should not be taken to suggest that each has only one gift; nor that each person's gifts are fixed. He later bids the one who speaks in tongues in the assembly to seek the gift of interpretation too [14:13]; he suggests that all should seek prophecy [14:1; *cf.* 14:31]; and his own apostolate involved most of the gifts he mentions.) In 12:28 he recognizes among the gifts God has 'set' in the body various types of leadership function, as well as helpers and administrators. If he does not *explicitly* refer to these as *charismata*, it is implicit in the structure of the argument, and he does explicitly refer to such functions as *charismata* in Romans 12:6 in a parallel context. Whether or not he would call all such functions 'spiritual gifts' in the sense defined above is, however, much less clear. It is not obvious how helping, serving, teaching, alms-giving, performing acts of *mercy, *etc.*, can all be called 'manifestations of the Spirit' in the same direct sense, even though Paul may have expected them to be 'led by the Spirit' and to express the 'fruit of the Spirit' in a more general way.

Returning to the argument of 1 Corinthians 12 – 14, 12:31 exhorts the reader to seek the higher gifts (*charismata*), and the exhortation is resumed in 14:1 in terms of an injunction to seek above all the gift of prophecy. 1 Corinthians 13 sets these encouragements in the context of the need to exercise such gifts in love, which will endure into the eschaton, after the fragmentary phenomena of 'knowledge', tongues and prophecy have passed away. Chapter 14 then explains Paul's preference for prophecy (over the uninterpreted tongues the Corinthians are vaunting) on the basis of its ability to address the church comprehensibly and to console, encourage and build it up (1 Cor. 14:3; on the same grounds he also encourages them to seek the gift of interpretation, 14:13). For Paul, prophecy thus epitomizes the above definition of 'spiritual gifts'. The public use of tongues (*with* interpretation) takes second place to it, perhaps because Paul understands the gift primarily in terms of doxology to God rather than a direct address to the church (14:2). Without interpretation, tongues are to be limited to private worship and not used in the church.

1 Corinthians 14:26–33 gives a glimpse into the deeply charismatic life which Paul expects of the congregation, and largely matches the description of the spiritually gifted 'body' of 1 Corinthians 12, in which all participate. The first two items in this list ('hymn' and 'word of instruction') could be taken in a formal, liturgical sense, but in context they more probably refer to the kind of phenomena summarized by Ephesians 5:18–19 ('be filled with the Spirit, addressing one another in psalms and hymns and spiritual songs ...', RSV) and to instruction of the type denoted by 'word of wisdom/knowledge' in 12:8. The remaining items are all evidently 'spiritual gifts'. The 'revelation' of 14:26 may have been received before the meeting (contrast 14:30), but is expounded in a form of 'prophecy' which clearly involves some human contribution, not purely direct oracular speech (otherwise there would be no point in bidding the speaker give way to someone else who has just received a revelation: 14:30). And because of the mixed nature of the gift, the utterance needs to be carefully discerned (14:29; *cf.* 1 Thess. 5:19–21). Paul evidently expects several prophecies in any one meeting, even potentially that *all* might prophesy for the common good (14:31). Whatever the Corinthians may

earlier have thought, Paul insists that tongues and prophecy are not ecstatic phenomena; these expressions of the Spirit are subject to the speaker (14:32). If the gifts are to serve their edificatory purpose, rather than to create chaos, they need to be carefully regulated.

'Spiritual gifts' in Romans 12:3–8?

This passage too focuses on unity and diversity of gifts in the body of Christ, and 12:6 ('we have different gifts [charismata], according to the grace given us') could almost have been taken from 1 Corinthians. But of the list that follows, only the first item (prophecy), is clearly a 'spiritual gift' in the defined sense. The remainder – serving, teaching, encouraging (with NIV), contributing to the needs of others, caring for others (if that is the right sense of proistamenos here), and 'showing mercy' – are not self-evidently 'manifestations of the Spirit' in the 1 Corinthians 12:7 sense. Indeed, as Fee rightly notes, none of the other occurrences of the word charisma in Romans (1:11; 5:15–16; 6:23; 11:29) would lead the reader to think that the charismata of 12:6 means 'gifts of the Spirit' as such (1:11 so refers to these gifts, but only by the addition of the qualifying adjective pneumatikon). The items that follow prophecy in this list could be understood as God-given natural propensities, now dedicated to the service of Christ, and enhanced by the Spirit. Indeed the qualities described are closer to what Paul in Galatians calls 'fruit of the Spirit' than to the more 'immediate' actions ('manifestations') of the Spirit implied in 1 Corinthians 12:4–11.

Natural gifts, fruit of the Spirit and 'spiritual gifts'

The foregoing discussion has brought to light some of the ambiguities of the fuzzy term 'spiritual gifts' and of its relationship to the Greek term charisma. We need to recognize that, following the OT, Paul saw the whole of life as open to God. He can affirm of his pre-Christian days, 'God ... set me apart from the womb' (Gal. 1:15). How God is immanent and moulds the lives of people before they turn to Christ is not a matter he discusses. As with the rest of the NT writers, and unlike the OT, he does not attribute this presence and activity to God's Spirit. God's Spirit is now known only as the Spirit of Christ, and in

Paul's writing the realms of 'the flesh' (i.e. rebellious humanity before Christ) and of the Spirit/Christ are sharply antithetical. But when people turn to Christ, and receive the Spirit, their whole life becomes pneumatic. In the terms of Romans 8 and Galatians 5 – 6, all authentic Christian existence is 'led by the Spirit', bears the 'fruit of the Spirit', and is empowered by the Spirit. There is thus a sense in which all Christian life is the gift of the Spirit, the charisma of God expressed in a multitude of charismata. This is undoubtedly one of the reasons why it is difficult to provide from Paul a sharply defined class of 'spiritual gifts'.

It is easy enough, of course, to point to some gifts which appear to be almost entirely the work of God's Spirit, e.g. the gifts of healings and the working of miracles in the congregation (1 Cor. 12:9–10), and the signs and wonders of the apostle (Rom. 15:19). Other workings of the Spirit are clearly more 'mixed' in nature. Some events of preaching, teaching, serving or giving might seem so totally prompted by the Spirit, so powerful, and perhaps so contrary to the person's usual nature/ability, that they could be deemed 'manifestations of the Spirit'. At other times, however, these activities might appear as largely within the natural abilities and character of those performing them, and only their dedication to Christ's service and for the building up of the church makes them workings of the Spirit at all. And, of course, there is an infinite gradation between the two ends of the spectrum. So asking the question 'at what point does this or that activity of the Spirit become a "spiritual gift"?' is like asking how many hairs a man must lose before he becomes 'bald'.

'Wisdom/understanding' is clearly an example that potentially crosses all the definitional boundaries. For Jewish Christianity it is a prototypical gift of the Spirit of prophecy, and, in Paul's terms, only through the activity of the Spirit granting understanding of the gospel can one avoid the contrary wisdom of the world (which sees the cross as foolishness) and enter and sustain Christian existence at all (1 Cor. 1 – 3). Yet at the same time, a 'Spirit of wisdom and revelation' enables the deeper grasp of the gospel which liberates more fully (Eph. 1:17), and when by this Spirit one comes to understand something of the height, depth, length and breadth of the love of Christ, one is thereby filled with the fullness of God (Eph. 3:16–19). Here the gift of wisdom/understanding is most closely related to what is elsewhere called the 'fruit of the Spirit' (cf. Col. 4:5), but it depends on the Spirit's revelatory function (cf. Col. 1:9). The same gift of wisdom/understanding, however, can inform charismatic preaching/teaching (whether to God's people or to outsiders), and so bring it into the category of 'spiritual gift' (1 Cor. 12:8; cf. Col. 1:28; Acts 6:10, etc.). And for all Paul's criticism of the 'wisdom of this world' in 1 Corinthians 1 – 3, he must have recognized that it was not sheer coincidence that some of the most effective church leaders, administrators and teachers were converts whom the world would previously have deemed wise, and people of understanding. He was, of course, himself a case in point. Natural abilities, dedicated to Christ, and enhanced/empowered by the Spirit, play an important part in such functions.

'Spiritual gifts' and church office

The twentieth century saw vigorous debates about the relationship of charismatic gifts to church office. Dunn is not untypical in asserting (*Jesus*, pp. 259–350) that Paul recognized only charismatic *ministries*, not church *offices* (contrary to the view of him later presented by Luke in Acts 14:23; 20:17–35). Appointed offices (such as those of deacon, elder or overseer) were unnecessary and undesirable, because it was the Spirit's prerogative to gift people for the variety of ministry functions required by the church. All kinds of service in the church were provided as *charismata*, understood as dynamic 'events' of grace, sovereignly distributed by the Spirit. Ephesians 4:7–12 is seen as a watershed, because it speaks of the giving of *ministers* rather than leadership *functions*, and the Pastorals are well on their way to the (dreaded!) early catholicism of Ignatius and the sub-apostolic fathers, for *charisma* is now seen as something bestowed by the laying on of hands, and permanently resident in the one who receives it; it has become the power and authority of church office (1 Tim. 4:14; 2 Tim. 1:6).

The arguments for such views are far from convincing. They rest on the flawed idea of *charisma* as originally an 'event of grace',

rather than as a potentially enduring 'gift'. Even in Dunn's view, the Pauline church must have formally recognized, legitimated and remunerated some people who were exercising regular ministries on behalf of the church (Dunn acknowledges this with respect to the 'teachers' of Gal. 6.6 and the 'overseers' and 'servers/deacons' of Phil. 1:1). But such a practice would already reflect an elementary concept of 'office' (see B. Holmberg, *Paul and Power*, pp. 110–111); it would naturally be understood as a recognition of God's calling and regular gifting of the appointee, not as the bestowal of ecclesial powers where charismata were lacking. The event mentioned in 1 Timothy 4:14 and 2 Timothy 1:6 appears to have been a considerably 'charismatic' event, not merely the bestowal of an ecclesial power of office (of which there is no hint). The alleged antithesis between *charisma* and office has thus been seen by some commentators as a largely theologically-motivated reading strategy.

'Spiritual gifts' in the rest of the NT

The EVV use the language of '(spiritual) gift(s)' at only two further points: Hebrews 2:4 and 1 Peter 4:10. In the former, the writer reminds his readers that God attested his word through signs and wonders, and various miracles and 'gifts' (Gk *merismoi*, lit. 'distributions') of the Spirit. This assertion coheres entirely with similar statements in the Gospels and Acts. The Petrine reference is closer to Pauline teaching: 'Like good stewards of the manifold grace of God, serve one another with whatever gift [Gk *charisma*] each of you has received' (NRSV). The thought here is nearer to that of Romans 12 than to that of 1 Corinthians 12, the 'gifts' envisaged including both the ministry of 'speaking' God's *word and that of regular service to and on behalf of the church (1 Pet. 4:11).

Bibliography

J. D. G. Dunn, *Jesus and the Spirit* (London, 1975); G. D. Fee, *God's Empowering Presence: The Holy Spirit in the Letters of Paul* (Peabody, 1994); K. S. Hemphill, *Spiritual Gifts Empowering the New Testament Church* (Nashville, 1988); B. Holmberg, *Paul and Power* (Lund, 1978); J. Koenig, *Charismata: God's Gifts for God's People* (Philadelphia, 1978); J. Moltmann,

The Spirit of Life (London, 1992); K. Rahner, The Spirit in the Church (London, 1979); J. Ruthven, On the Cessation of the Charismata: The Protestant Polemic on Postbiblical Miracles (Sheffield, 1993); M. Turner, 'Modern linguistics and the New Testament', in J. B. Green (ed.), Hearing the New Testament: Strategies for Interpretation (Carlisle, 1995); idem, The Holy Spirit and Spiritual Gifts: Then and Now (Carlisle, 1996); G. H. Twelftree, Jesus the Miracle Worker (Downers Grove, 1999); M. Volf, Work in the Spirit: Towards a Theology of Work (New York, 1991); M. Welker, God the Spirit (Minneapolis, 1994).

M. TURNER

SPIRITUAL POWERS

The primary concern of this article is the spiritual powers which, to varying degrees, came to be portrayed as over against *God and his purposes. However, some reference is made to those which serve God. While the NT picture is more developed than that of the OT, there is significant continuity between the Testaments.

Spiritual powers in the OT

The earlier literature takes for granted the existence of an array of spiritual beings alongside Yahweh, and makes little differentiation between good and *evil powers. Although the earlier material is simpler and the latter more complex, it is not possible to plot a tidy development of the notion of spiritual powers in the OT.

The reality of other gods is frequently denied (Deut. 4:32–40). At other times their existence is acknowledged (Exod. 15:11), but only as subordinate to God; thus the OT writers preserve their strong monotheism, albeit with a hint of henotheism. By the turn of the eras these gods ('elōhîm) were regarded as God's angelic host; the LXX guards against polytheism by translating 'elōhîm as angeloi (cf. Pss. 8:5; 97:7; 138:1 with LXX).

The Council of Yahweh

Like the literature of other cultures, and from its earlier (Exod. 15:11) to its later material (Dan. 7:9–14), the Hebrew Bible depicts a heavenly council (Jer. 23:18) of spiritual beings, which is most clearly described in the vision of Micaiah (1 Kgs. 22:19–23). Over these, who have various names (Deut. 33:2–3; 1 Kgs. 22:19; Pss. 29:1; 82:6; 89:6), the incomparable Yahweh (Ps. 89:6–7), who *created them (Neh. 9:6), presides (Ps. 82:1), and is thus called 'the LORD of hosts' (Is. 47:4, NRSV). Before this council *prophets stand to hear God's word (Jer. 23:18, 22), and to his council God reveals his activities (Amos 3:7).

The members of the heavenly assembly can be sent to execute God's will (Num. 22:32; Josh. 5:14; 1 Kgs. 22:19–23; Job 1:6–12; 2:1–7; Dan. 10:13; 12:1), *worship him (Pss. 29:1–2; 148:2; Is. 6), execute his wrath (Ps. 78:49), and act as his heavenly armies (Is. 45:12).

Members of the council are sometimes ranked and depicted with specific roles: an adversary or satan; chief angels (perhaps derived from, e.g., Gen. 22:11–18; Exod. 23:20–21) such as Gabriel (Dan. 8:16) and Michael (Dan. 10:13–21). In Job 33:22–25 an angel acts as an advocate for the accused before the heavenly council (cf. Zech. 3:1–5).

The angel of Yahweh

Of all the spiritual powers with divine commissions, the most distinctive is the angel of Yahweh, who has various functions (Gen. 24:7, 40; Exod. 3:2; Num. 22:22; Josh. 5:13–15; 2 Sam. 24 [par. 1 Chr. 21]; 1 Kgs. 19:7; 2 Kgs. 19:35; Ps. 35:4–6; Is. 63:9), especially that of communicating God's message, notably to his prophets (Zech. 1:9 – 6:5).

In some accounts of divine interaction with human beings, Yahweh is not distinguished from his angel (e.g. Gen 16:7–14). This probably does not reflect an anthropomorphic view of God; rather, such passages provide a 'living portrayal of an encounter with God, which because of the dangers of an immediate theophany was also understood as having been mediated in some way' (D. N. Freedman et al., 'mal'aḵ', in TDOT 8, p. 321). In short, the angel of Yahweh, who appears throughout the OT, was understood as one of the means through which Yahweh acted in the human realm.

Leviathan

The parallels in other literature and between Isaiah 24:21 and 27:1 suggest that this mythical figure represents God's chief opponent among the spiritual powers. The name

'Leviathan' is mentioned only six times in the OT, and refers to a *serpent-like sea monster, probably identical to the '*Rahab' of Job 26:12 and the dragon of Isaiah 51:9.

In Job 3:8–9 Leviathan, associated with darkness, appears to stand in parallel to the rebellious seas that have been subjugated by God (cf. 26:12–13) but may be stirred by incantation. The most extensive description (Job 41:1, cf. 2–34) is of a fearless, single-headed crocodile-like creature who breathes fire, lives in the sea which boils as he passes through it, and cannot be defeated by humans. Leviathan is presented as God's most formidable and unequalled enemy, whom he holds in check (cf. Job 7:12). However, in Psalm 74:13–14 Leviathan the sea dragon is multi-headed (seven-headed in Ugaritic literature) and has already been defeated; probably he is understood to have been involved in the act of creation and thus as a supernatural power. In Psalm 104:26 he is merely one of Yahweh's playthings for whom he cares.

In Isaiah 27:1 the defeat of Leviathan represents Yahweh's defeat of evil, which is presented as an *eschatological event. The author of this (proto)-apocalyptic text borrows Leviathan from a much earlier Canaanite mythology in order to symbolize earthly power. But the striking Ugaritic parallels and the eschatological character of the prophecy suggest that the writer has in mind not only the earthly enemies of God's people but also the evil spiritual powers they represent (cf. Is. 24:21), powers that will be destroyed on the day of Yahweh.

Satan

Although not a prominent spiritual power, the satan (śāṭān, adversary) of the OT is important in providing the origins of the Satan more familiar from the NT. Sometimes humans perform the role of a satan (e.g. 1 Sam. 29:4; 1 Kgs. 5:4; Ps. 109:6). A celestial satan figure is mentioned in four OT passages: Numbers 22:22, 32; 1 Chronicles 21:1 (in these two passages the word appears without the definite article and could be a reference to an unspecified member of the heavenly assembly acting as an adversary); Job 1:6–12; 2:1 and Zechariah 3.1–2. The use of the definite article (14 times in Job 1 – 2) may indicate that a specific son of God (see Job 1:6, NIV fn.) is thought to hold the office

of accuser. However, more probably any member of the royal court was able to assume the role of accuser (cf. Ps 109:6), for neither in ancient Israel nor in the judicial terminology of Mesopotamia was there a legal office of accuser (H. J. Boecker, *Law and the Administration of Justice* [Minneapolis, 1980], p. 38). It is possible to interpret 1 Chronicles 21:1 to mean that, in his *anger, God permitted Satan to incite David; this suggests that Satan is not always viewed in a favourable light by God.

In the OT, Satan is a mere creature of God, acting at his command. The Satan (or satans) is portrayed both as a general adversary and as a legal accuser who tests the faithfulness of God's people. To him is ascribed responsibility for the supposedly evil acts that writers want to distance from God. By NT times direct responsibility for evil is ascribed to the archdemon or Satan.

The NT

The clearest statements about spiritual powers come from the Gospels, which portray the exorcisms of *Jesus as the first stage of their defeat, and from the Pauline corpus, which refers to 'powers'. The NT shows little interest in spiritual powers apart from their soteriological implications.

The Gospels

The Gospel writers use terms that reveal their belief in evil and good spiritual powers.

Angels. The term *angelos* ('angel') can be used of *humans, meaning 'messenger' (Luke 7:24; 9:52; cf. Mark 1:2), but it is generally used for spiritual powers or messengers which serve God and are associated with key events in the life of Jesus. The angel Gabriel, in announcing the birth of Jesus, brings a message from God (Luke 1:11–20). The angel that announces the birth to the shepherds (Luke 2:8–12) is accompanied by a multitude of heavenly hosts (Luke 2:13) who are presumably spiritual beings who attend God. In the temptation stories angels protect Jesus (Matt. 4:6; Luke 4:10) and serve him (Matt. 4:11; Mark 1:13), perhaps by feeding him (cf. 1 Kgs. 19:5–8) or strengthening him. In Luke 22:43–44 also Jesus is portrayed as being strengthened by angels (though this text is disputed). By saying that 'an angel of the Lord' (see above) rolled back the stone from Jesus' tomb, Matthew declares that God is involved in the resurrection (Matt. 28:2), which in the other Gospels the angels also announce (Matt. 28:5–6; *cf.* Mark 16:5; Luke 24:4; John 20:12–13). Finally, angels are portrayed as accompanying the Son of Man when he comes in glory to sit on his throne in *judgment (Matt. 25:31), and at the end of the age will separate the righteous from the evildoers (Matt. 13:39; Mark 13:27) whom they will throw into the fiery furnace (Matt. 13:42). So while in some texts angels are ontological entities, they are more often a periphrasis for God – especially in John's Gospel, in which they are rarely mentioned (John 1:51; [5:4;] 12:29; 20:12) – and for his glorious and powerful presence.

Demons. Portrayed as opposing Jesus and the inauguration of the *kingdom of God (Matt. 13:39) is an army of spiritual powers called 'spirits' (*pneumata*), a designation sometimes qualified by *ponēros* ('evil', Matt. 12:45 [par. Luke 11:26, *ponēroteros*] or *akathartos* ('unclean', Mark 6:7) words which imply idolatrous (*cf.* Ezek. 36:17; Jer. 32:34) connections or association with the dead (*cf.* Matt. 23:27; Mark 5:2); hence their contaminating effect and distinction from the *Holy Spirit. Jesus' exorcisms demonstrate his divine power and point to the continuing struggle between the holy God and that which contaminates his creation. The word *legiōn* ('legion', Mark 5:9) alludes to the multiform and infesting character of the spirits.

Satan. In line with the developing cosmology of the period (*Testament of Dan* 6:1; *Testament of Gad* 4:7) the evil spiritual powers appear to be led by a figure generally called the 'devil' (*diabolos*, Matt. 25:41; not used by Mark) or 'satan' (*satanas*), terms used interchangeably in the Gospels (*cf.* Matt. 4:1, 5, 8, 11 and 4:10; Mark 4:15 and Luke 8:12). By using the term 'Satan', which the LXX used to translate *šāṭān*, the Gospel writers maintain the devil's OT role as a *testing adversary (Matt. 4:1–11; Luke 22:31) and one who attempts to separate people from God (Mark 4:15).

Beelzeboul. This puzzling composite term (first attested in Mark 3:22) may have been coined during a debate between Jesus and his critics (Mark 3:22). The combination of *Ba'al* ('lord'), used mostly to refer to local manifestations of the Canaanite fertility and storm god, the chief adversary of the Israelite religion (1 Kgs. 18; 2 Kgs. 1:2–16; Hos. 2:8),

and *z'bul* ('exalted house' [1 Kgs. 8:13], 'temple' or 'heaven' [*War Scroll* 12:1–2]), meaning 'lord of heaven' (*cf.* Matt. 10:25), would have been readily understood as denoting Satan. Thus Satan and his angels are associated with God's enemies or pagan gods (*cf.* Ps 96:5 where the LXX substitutes 'demons' for 'idols').

Other titles. 'The enemy' and 'the evil one' (Matt. 13:19, 38–39) insinuate the inherent nature of the leader of the spiritual powers; 'the tempter' (only in NT at Matt. 4:3 and 1 Thess. 3:5) implies that the role of the evil spiritual powers is to divert God's people from the way of righteousness; 'the ruler of the demons' (Matt. 9:34; 12:24), implies that the devil is responsible for and represented by the activities of demons. John uses 'ruler of this world' (John 12:31; 14:30; 16:11) to highlight the role of Jesus' death in the defeat of the devil.

To equate 'the powers in the heavens' with the stars of heaven (Mark 13:25) is to imply that spiritual powers are identical with or related to the heavenly or cosmic bodies (*cf.* Col. 2:8). The context shows that in the eschatological catastrophe they will be deprived of their power.

Pauline corpus

The 'idea of sinister world powers and their subjugation by Christ is built into the very fabric of Paul's thought, and some mention of them is found in every epistle except Philemon' (G. B. Caird, *Principalities and Powers*, p. viii).

Satan. The Greek term for 'devil' (*diabolos*) occurs only in Ephesians, twice (4:27; 6:11) and in the Pastoral Epistles, six times (1 Tim. 3:6–7, 11; 2 Tim. 2:26; 3:3; Titus 2:3), sometimes referring to slanderers. Paul uses his preferred term 'Satan' (*satanas*) in 1 Corinthians 7:5, where Satan is portrayed in one of his traditional roles of inciting people to *sin, which in 2 Corinthians 2:11 is put in terms of his outwitting or taking advantage of people by his schemes, specifically by inspiring a lack of forgiveness and love in the *church.

Part of Paul's eschatological hope is that the hostile spiritual powers will be 'crushed under foot' (Rom. 16:20, alluding to Gen. 3:15; *cf.* Ps 91:13; *Testament of Simeon* 6:6) and he assumes that Satan stands behind false teachers who cause dissensions and put obstacles in the way of believers (*cf.* Rom 16:17). In 2 Corinthians 11:14 false apostles disguising themselves as apostles of Christ are said to parallel Satan's treacherous tactic of disguising himself as an angel of light. This deceitful activity is elaborated in 2 Thessalonians 2:9, where Satan is said to use 'all lying power, signs, and wonders' (*cf.* Acts 2:22). Nevertheless, in 1 Corinthians 5:5 (*cf.* 1 Tim. 1:20) it seems to be assumed that Satan is able to destroy the body (presumably through *death) but not the spirit, which is saved in the day of the Lord. Similarly, Satan's role as an agent of God's purposes (*cf.* Job 2:6–7) is seen in 2 Corinthians 12:7, where a thorn – perhaps a physical illness – is said to have been given (by God; *cf.* Gal. 3:21) to keep Paul humble. In 1 Timothy 1:20 (echoing Job 2:6–12 and 1 Cor. 5:5) the author depicts Satan as an instrument of correction.

In 1 Thessalonians 2:18 Satan is portrayed as an enemy of God's work. Paul says that his journey to the Thessalonians was blocked by Satan; perhaps he sees Satan behind the lawless (*cf.* 2 Thess. 2:9) rioting in Thessalonica which may have prevented his return (*cf.* Acts 17:5, 9). The adversarial role of Satan is also seen in 1 Timothy 5:15 (*cf.* v. 14) where those who have turned away to sin, either unchastity or heresy, are said to follow Satan.

Angeloi ('angels') in Paul may be either good or evil spiritual beings as distinct from human beings (1 Cor. 4:9; 13:1). They are represented as the authority behind the state (*cf.* Deut. 32:8; Dan. 10:13, 20) and behind human affairs and social order (*cf.* 1 Cor. 11:10). They are inferior in status to humans, even though they have knowledge of humans (1 Cor. 11:10; Gal 3:19; *cf.* Heb. 1:13–14). In some sense they are culpable, for they may separate believers from God (Rom. 8:38), and are to be judged by believers (1 Cor. 6:3). Not surprisingly, the writer of Colossians 2:18 censures the worship of angels as misplaced devotion.

The phrase *ta stoicheia tou kosmou* ('the elemental spirits of the world/universe', Gal. 4:3; Col. 2:8, 20; *cf.* Gal. 4:9) may refer to the rudiments of religious teaching associated with the immaturity of humanity prior to Christ, or to the physical elements (*cf.* Philo, *Quis Rerum Divinarum Heres Sit* 134; 2 Pet. 3:10, 12) of the universe. However, Paul speaks of them in connection with personal beings or forces (*cf.* Col. 2:10, 15). Most commentators therefore understand the phrase to denote spiritual beings or powers which are active within the physical and heavenly elements.

Even though in the LXX, in Josephus, and almost always in Philo, *archai* ('principalities' or 'rulers') denotes a human office (*cf.* Luke 20:20, 'jurisdiction'; Titus 3:1), in the Pauline letters (except in Rom. 8:38) the term is always associated with *exousia* ('authorities' or 'powers') in lists (1 Cor. 15:24; Col. 1:16; 2:10, 15; *cf.* Eph. 1:21; 3:10; 6:12), which shows that he takes these principalities to be spiritual powers. In 1 Corinthians 2:6, 8 *archontes* ('rulers') could refer to political figures. But the context suggests that the term embraces both human figures and spiritual powers operating through their offices (*cf.* Dan. 10:20–21; 12:1).

Included in the list of spiritual powers in Colossians 1:16 (*cf.* Eph. 1:21) are *kyriotēs* ('dominions'), and *thronoi* ('thrones'). It is possible that in the syncretistic teaching followed at Colossae these spiritual powers were thought to control the heavenly realm and access to the presence of God (Col. 2:8, 20). In order to obtain *salvation and access to the divine presence one would have not only to acknowledge Christ as one intermediary, but also to subdue the flesh, and thereby have a vision of heaven and participate in the angelic liturgy (A. T. Lincoln, *Ephesians* [Dallas, 1990], p. 63). However, Colossians asserts that, despite their idolatry, rebellion and hostility to God, the spiritual powers were created in, through and for Christ to serve him (W. Wink, *Naming the Powers*, p. 64). So, despite there being 'many gods and many lords', the believer recognizes only one God, the Father, and one Lord, Jesus Christ, through whom all things exist (1 Cor. 8:5–6).

At least the first stage of the defeat of the hostile spiritual powers is envisaged as having taken place in the cross (Col. 2:13–14), in which God 'disarmed the rulers and authorities and made a public example of them, triumphing over them in it' (Col. 2:15). As a result, believers have been rescued from the power of darkness and transferred into the kingdom of God's beloved Son (Col. 1:13). Therefore the spiritual powers are not to be feared, even though they retain some power (Rom. 8:37–39) until they are destroyed at the end (1 Cor. 15:24–25). (See *Atonement.)

More is said about (spiritual) powers in Ephesians than in any other book in the canon (Eph. 1:10, 21; 2:2; 3:10, 15; 4:8, 27; 6:11–12, 16). The powers in Ephesians have been understood as the general spirit or attitude of nations or localities, as revealed in their institutions (H. Schlier, *Principalities and Powers* [London, 1961]), or as both the state and spiritual powers (O. Cullman, *The State in the NT* [London, 1957]), or as a hierarchy of supernatural cosmic forces (P. T. O'Brien, in *Biblical Interpretation and the Church*), or as the angelic host surrounding the throne of God (W. Carr, *Angels and Principalities*), or as both heavenly and earthly, divine and human, good and evil powers (Wink, *Naming*). The evidence suggests that the language of Ephesians was commonly used in Jewish and Hellenistic circles to refer to evil spiritual beings that can be identified with heathen gods and that work in conjunction with the flesh and with sin to control human life (C. E. Arnold, *Ephesians*).

Ephesians speaks of an ultimate power of evil behind the other powers. He is the ruler of the air (Eph. 2:2; *cf.* Philo, *De Plantatione* 14) or heavenly realm (*cf.* Eph. 3:10; 6:12) who remains at work among the disobedient. In Ephesisans 4:27 he is the devil who may gain a foothold in the lives of believers through their anger; in 6:11 he is also the devil who subtly attacks believers; and in 6:16 he is the evil one firing flaming arrows.

The powers listed in Ephesians 1:21 are certainly spiritual and subordinate to Christ in his *exaltation, but they could be either good or evil. However, the powers mentioned in Ephesians 6:12 and 16 are clearly depicted as evil and as still retaining some power, for the believer is said to struggle against them (*cf.* Eph. 2:2; 4:8–10). This notion of *warfare with the spiritual powers is the distinctive element in Ephesians' treatment of the subject. But the spiritual powers are not to be feared; the readers are assured that they have access to armour supplied (or used, *cf.* Ps. 35:1–3) by God (Eph. 6:10–20) and that 'the "powers" can see that they have been devastatingly foiled by the emergence of the body of Christ, the church' (Eph. 3:10; Arnold, *Ephesians*, p. 64).

The rest of the NT

Hebrews mentions angels eleven times, giving rise to the speculation that the author is attacking excessive angel worship (*cf.* Col. 2:18). However, there is nothing to suggest that the recipients were enmeshed in such worship. Rather, the Son is portrayed as far superior to all heavenly beings who serve him. Hebrews also says that through his death Jesus destroyed (*katargeō*) the one who has the power of death, the devil (Heb. 2:14). This statement, probably based on Genesis 3 (*cf.* Wisdom of Solomon 2:23–24), implies that the devil is responsible for death and for introducing the *fear of it (Heb. 2:15; see H. Strack and P. Billerbeck, *Kommentar zum Neuen Testament aus Talmud und Midrash*, [Münich, 1922–61] 1:144–49). Hebrews 2:14 may also imply that the devil is defeated in two stages; *katargeō* is best translated as 'to condemn to inactivity' (G. Delling, 'argos ...', in *TDNT* 1, pp. 452–455), and points to both the devil's continued activity in the present and his future complete destruction. The traditional title 'Father of spirits' (*cf. 1 Enoch* 37:2; 2 Macc. 3:24) does not refer in Hebrews 12:9 to spiritual powers, but to the spiritual or heavenly Father (see v. 7).

In *1 Peter* 3:19 Jesus is said to have 'made a proclamation to the spirits in prison'. When the word is not qualified, 'spirit' in the NT always refers to spiritual beings, and usually to evil ones. Further, as there is a tradition that fallen angels were imprisoned by God (2 Pet. 2:4; Jude 6), and 1 Peter 3:20 refers to the days of Noah when these angels were thought to have been disobedient, the spirits mentioned here are probably fallen, malevolent angels (*cf.* Gen. 6:1–4; 1 Pet. 3:22). The prison for the evil spirits (2 Pet. 2:4; Rev. 18:2; 20:3, 7) is probably in heaven, for the verb 'to go' (*poreutheis*) is also used in 1 Peter 3:22 of Christ's ascension. Therefore the most natural reading of 1 Peter 3:18–22 is that in his risen state, during or in his ascension, Christ went and preached to these spiritual beings, perhaps announcing that their final destruction was imminent (1 Pet. 4:7). This is the same event as his subjection of the spiritual powers to himself in his exaltation (1 Pet. 3:22).

1 John 4:1 directs the reader to test the 'spirits', on the grounds that many false prophets have gone out into the world. As 'spirits' is unlikely here to refer to human beings (see above), and as it was commonly thought that spiritual beings inspired prophets (*cf. Rule of the Community* 4), the spirits mentioned are probably evil spiritual powers, children of the devil whose works the Son came to destroy (1 John 3:8). The activity of an evil spiritual power can be discerned; it inspires people to do what is not right or to be unloving towards other believers (1 John 3:10; 4:7–12).

Jude 6–7 probably reflects Genesis 6:1–4 in its reference to angels not keeping their proper position and being responsible for evil. Hence the Lord is said to have kept them in eternal chains until the day of judgment. In Jude 9 the 'archangel' (in the NT only here and in 1 Thess. 4:16) Michael (see above), the opponent of Satan (*cf.* Rev. 12:7), is said to have disputed with the devil's attempt, in his role as accuser, to condemn Moses and deny him an honourable burial. Michael respects the principle that no one is a law unto him/herself by asking the Lord to rebuke the devil.

Revelation uses the term 'angel' (*angelos*) seventy-seven times, mostly of spiritual beings who mediate between God and his creation (*e.g.* Rev 7:1–2; 8). Sometimes the term refers to 'the angels of the seven churches' (*e.g.* Rev 1:20), who have been understood as 1. human officials of the churches (*cf.* Mal. 2:7, but there is no clear evidence of episcopacy in Rev.); 2. human messengers (but these are unlikely to be symbolized by stars, Rev. 1:20); 3. personifications of the churches (an interpretation consistent with the texts but not with the symbolism of Rev. 1:20); or, 4. guardian angels of the churches (*cf.* Acts 12:15) (an interpretation consistent with biblical imagery but not with the fact that only a human may properly be held responsible for a church). This verse illustrates the difficulty of circumscribing the meaning of symbols.

Similarly, the 'seven spirits' (of Rev. 3:1) have been understood as the Holy Spirit in all his fullness (Is. 11:2–3 [LXX]; *1 Enoch* 61:11), as seven astral deities of ancient Near Eastern religion, or – more plausibly, as they are said to be before the throne of God (Rev. 1:4) – as angels (*cf. War Scroll* 12:8–9).

Satan or the devil is mentioned more often in Revelation than in any other book in the canon. He is also called an 'angel' (Rev. 9:11) – and his followers 'angels' (12:7, 9) – who,

by inspiring civil authorities (2:9; 13), emperor worship (2:13), immorality and idolatry (2:24), and some Jews (3:9), not only attacks the church (12:13–17), but also in his exercise of fearsome power attempts to thwart God's *redemptive plan, effected in Jesus (12:1–3). However, in a possible allusion to the victory of the cross, Satan is said to be thrown down to the earth (12:7–12; *cf.* John 12:31; see above on 'Leviathan'). Just as his army is consumed by fire, so also Satan is finally bound and thrown into the lake of fire (*cf.* 2 Kgs. 1:10) to be tormented for ever (Rev. 20:1–3, 7–10). Readers can take encouragement from knowing that the various attacks on them inspired by evil spiritual powers will eventually be defeated.

Conclusion

Perhaps because of increased contact with other cultures, though not because God was increasingly distant (*contra* W. Bousset, *Die Religion des Judentums* [Tübingen, ³1926]; *cf. 2 Baruch* 48:1–24; Tobit 3:1–6; 13:1–15), germinal ideas in the OT about spiritual powers came to full flower in the apocalyptic literature of Judaism from the middle of the second century BC, generally without compromising monotheism. The NT writers drew upon these ideas for their various references to spiritual powers in the heavenlies who stood behind human activity and institutions.

Some contemporaries of the biblical writers resigned themselves to fate in their contention with hostile spiritual powers; sometimes incantations were used, some people sought initiation into the mystery cults. The message of both Testaments is that God is sovereign over his creation, including those spiritual powers which are now his enemies. Although their power is to be respected, they are not to be feared. They will be defeated in two stages (*cf.* Is. 24:21–22). The second stage can be expected in the eschaton; the first takes place in the ministry of Jesus, either focused in his exorcisms (Matt. 12:28; par. Luke 11:20) or in the cross event (John 12:31), and is then played out in the ministry of his followers (Luke 10:17–18), and in the very existence of the church (Eph. 3:10).

See also: IDOLATRY.

Bibliography

C. E. Arnold, *Ephesians* (Cambridge,

1989); G. B. Caird, *Principalities and Powers* (Oxford, 1956); W. Carr, *Angels and Principalities* (Cambridge, 1981); D. J. A. Clines, 'The Significance of the "Sons of God" episode (Genesis 6:1–4) in the context of the "Primeval History" (Genesis 1–11)', *JSOT* 13, 1979, pp. 33–46; P. G. Davies, 'Divine Agents, Mediators, and New Testament Christology", *JTS* n.s. 45, 1994, pp. 479–503; J. Day, *God's Conflict with the Dragon and the Sea* (Cambridge, 1985); P. L. Day, *An Adversary in Heaven* (Atlanta, 1988); A. N. S. Lane (ed.), *The Unseen World* (Carlisle and Grand Rapids, 1996); C. H. T. Fletcher-Louis, *Luke-Acts: Angels, Christology and Soteriology* (Tübingen, 1997); E. T. Mullen, *The Assembly of the Gods* (Chico, 1980); R. North, 'Separated Spiritual Substances in the Old Testament', *CBQ* 29, 1967, pp. 419–449; P. T. O'Brien, 'Principalities and Powers: Opponents of the Church', in D. A. Carson (ed.), *Biblical Interpretation and the Church* (Exeter, 1984), pp. 110–150; S. H. T. Page, *Powers of Evil* (Grand Rapids and Leicester, 1995); E. Pagels, 'The Social History of Satan, The "Intimate Enemy": A Preliminary Sketch', *HTR* 84, 1991, pp. 105–128; K. van der Toorn, B. Becking and P. W. van der Horst (ed.), *Dictionary of Deities and Demons in the Bible* (Grand Rapids and Leiden, [2]1998); W. Wink, *Naming the Powers* (Minneapolis, 1992).

G. H. TWELFTREE

STATUTE, see LAW

SUFFERING

Introduction

Suffering is a common experience of humans, and arguably also of animals. Why it exists at all, and on such a scale, is by no means clear. Although suffering is a mystery to the secular mind, it poses a moral problem for the theist, and particularly for the theist who believes a god who is good, beneficent and omnipotent. It is difficult to see why such a deity should create a world in which suffering exists or within which suffering might arise.

Pain and suffering are, of course, related: pain is the physiological cause of many experiences of suffering. But emotional suffering may have no associated physiological pain; thus suffering is to be distinguished from pain. Further, both suffering and pain are to be distinguished from *evil. Evil is always evil, but both suffering and pain may be of strong positive value. And, as Emmanuel Kant said, evil is absolutely contrary to divine providence, whilst suffering and pain are only conditionally contrary to it.

Even if suffering were minimal it would still be a problem, and the thinking person would still question the reason for its presence in the world. But the sheer quantity of pain and suffering in the world intensifies the problem for the Christian. Moreover, some suffering brings no obvious benefits. For example, when a baby is born deformed and lives for only a short time, the event does not always evoke a compassionate response from those involved. Such experiences are sometimes called 'surd suffering'.

Suffering in the Bible

The Bible does not deal in any systematic way with the problem of suffering as a theological issue. It is, however, extremely significant that the Bible begins with an account of the source of the pains of childbirth and of the contrariness of nature (Gen. 3:1–19; Rom. 8:18–23) and ends with a picture of heaven in which there is no more pain, no crying, and in which nature gives abundantly of its fruits (Rev. 21:1–4; 22:1–5).

The book of *Job, often regarded as a treatise on suffering, is in fact primarily concerned with Job's commitment to God in the face of material deprivation and physical suffering. The various theories of suffering (paschologies) proposed by Job's friends are dismissed by Yahweh (Job 42:7–8), and even though the reader is shown the reason for Job's suffering, no explanation is given to Job himself.

The two Testaments address the issue of suffering in different but related ways. In the OT the emphasis is on the suffering of Israel as a nation although, in the *wisdom literature (especially in Ecclesiastes and Proverbs) and the Psalms, there is repeated acknowledgment of individual suffering. The suffering of those outside the people of God is rarely mentioned other than in the context of Yahweh's *judgment on the nations.

The NT writers are concerned first with the sufferings of *Jesus Christ, and then with the suffering of the church and of individual Christians. But again no consideration is given to the sufferings of the world at large.

To a degree this apparent indifference to the problem of human suffering reflects the attitude of the mass of humanity throughout history. Most people have seen human suffering as inevitable – a 'fact of life' – but not as a theological issue, still less as a possible barrier to faith in a beneficent God.

Suffering in the OT

As noted previously, the opening chapters of Genesis root some aspects of suffering in the *Adamic fall, but this theme is not developed systematically. Instead, the OT emphasis is on Israel's sufferings as a consequence of its own disobedience; this suffering is retributive and restorative. Leviticus 26 promises a life of plenty, lived in harmony with nature, as a reward for obedience to the covenant, but threatens illness, famine and calamity as a punishment for disobedience. However, this punishment is intended to bring Israel to repentance. Ezekiel expresses the righteous wrath of God directed against Israel, but balances this by the repeated 'they shall know' (*e.g.* Ezek. 2:5).

Ezekiel recognizes that humanity may not sin indefinitely without God's intervening judgment. Ammon, Moab, Edom, Philistia, Tyre and Egypt (chs. 25 – 29) are no less under the eye of Yahweh than is Israel, and his judgment will teach them that he is the Lord.

The account of the deliverance of Israel from Egypt (see *Exodus [event]) is paradigmatic for Israel's theology of *salvation. There are four stages in the Exodus narrative:

First, there is the suffering of the Israelites at the hands of the Egyptians. Both the suffering and the Egyptian oppression are real, but Yahweh is aware of both: 'I have observed the misery of my people who are in Egypt; I have heard their cry on account of their taskmasters. Indeed I know their sufferings' (Exod. 3:7, NRSV).

Secondly, there is the compassion (and indignation) of Yahweh: 'The cry of the Israelites has now come to me; I have also seen how the Egyptians oppress them' (3:9).

Thirdly, there is the preparation of a particular individual to deliver Israel: 'I will send you [Moses] to Pharaoh' (3:10).

Fourthly, there is the act of deliverance

from Egypt. The Egyptians suffer greatly through the successive plagues, the death of the firstborn, and the destruction of the pursuing Egyptian army at the Red Sea, but the author does not comment on their plight; nor (apparently) does it attract any compassionate response from Yahweh. The narrative is concerned only with the salvation of Israel and the corresponding punishment of the Egyptians. The accounts of other massacres exhibit the same apparent indifference to the sufferings of Israel's enemies: for example, the people of Jericho (Josh. 6), the Amalekites (1 Sam. 15) and the Moabites (2 Sam. 8:1–2). However, it is significant that David is not permitted to build the temple in Jerusalem precisely because of his many wars: 'You have shed much blood' (1 Chr. 22:6–10). There is at least a suggestion that the suffering of the surrounding nations resulting from the nationalistic aspirations of Israel and its need of salvation can be justified because of the good that flows from it. As Genesis 15:16 indicates, Israel's actions against these nations are viewed as a form of divine punishment.

But although the OT treatment of the theme of suffering is focused on that of Israel, some interest is shown in individual suffering, particularly in the wisdom literature. Proverbs draws attention to the problems of the righteous poor, whose reward is denied them by the oppression of the powerful (Prov. 13:23, 'The field of the poor may yield much food, but it is swept away through injustice.') In Ecclesiastes the Preacher comments bitterly, 'I saw all the oppressions that are practised under the sun. Look, the tears of the oppressed – with no one to comfort them!' (Eccles. 4:1). The Preacher can offer no hope except that of judgment beyond the grave. (Eccles. 3:17).

Individual suffering is also presented as one part of a wider divine purpose. For example, Joseph's brothers sell him as a slave, condemning him to imprisonment in Egypt. But Joseph later says to his brothers: 'Even though you intended to do harm to me, God intended it for good, in order to preserve a numerous people, as he is doing today' (Gen. 50:20).

Underlying some later thought is the concept of vicarious suffering. This is found in the servant songs of Isaiah, and especially in Isaiah 52:13 – 53:12. The prophet speaks of an unidentified figure who has suffered for his people, and of one who will suffer for all people. As Isaiah 52:13 – 53:5 expresses it, 'See, my servant ... He was despised and rejected by others, a man of suffering ... Surely he has born our infirmities and carried our diseases ... But he was wounded for our transgressions, crushed for our iniquities, upon him was the punishment that made us whole, and by his bruises we are healed.' A full understanding of the redemptive suffering foretold in the OT is accessible only after the inauguration of the new covenant.

Suffering in the NT

As stated above, the NT writers' treatment of this theme is focused on the suffering of Christ, especially his suffering on the cross. However, they are also concerned with the suffering of Christians. The Greek verb *paschein* and its related forms (including *pathein*) and compounds (such as *synkakopathein*, to sympathize; Heb. 4:15) are used to denote the various aspects of suffering. The theology of suffering is called 'paschology'. The noun *thlipsis* is frequently used to denote physical suffering.

In the synoptic Gospels *paschein* is used only for the sufferings of Christ. In Luke 9:22 (Mark 8:31), Jesus is recorded as saying: 'The Son of Man must undergo great suffering, and be rejected by the elders, chief priests and scribes, and be killed, and on the third day be raised.' The order of the statements here is significant. The 'great suffering' must include Jesus' sufferings before his crucifixion, and this means that the term 'to suffer' applies both to pain and to *death. When Jesus says to his disciples, 'I have eagerly desired to eat this Passover with you before I suffer' (Luke 22:15) he is referring to his imminent death. This statement is immediately followed by a call to his followers to take up the cross, to be prepared to lose their lives, and to accept present sufferings for the sake of a future share in the kingdom. Earlier, Jesus anticipates his suffering, death and resurrection as he and his disciples approach Jerusalem (Matt. 20:17–19). The Last Supper is explained in terms of a new covenant in which Jesus lays down his life 'for the forgiveness of sins' (Matt. 26:28), and in the account of his experience in Gethsemane, Jesus once again anticipates his sufferings (Mark 14:32–42).

There are comparatively few references to Christ's sufferings in John's Gospel because the evangelist interprets them as part of the process of Christ's glorification. However, he does describe the passion, in a graphic, if restrained, way.

We look to the cross not only as an act of redemption, but also as a revelation of God's identification with humanity. As Sobrino has put it in his Thesis Thirteen, 'On the cross of Jesus God Himself is crucified. The Father ... takes upon himself all the pain and suffering of history. In this ultimate solidarity with humanity he reveals himself as the God of love, who opens up a hope and a future through the most negative side of history' (J. Sobrino, *Christology at the Crossroads* [London, 1978], p. 224). Suffering may be the consequence of God's decision to create a universe of a particular kind, but he actively shares in the experience.

1 Peter emphasizes the *redemptive purpose of Christ's sufferings, which were not an accident, but foreordained (1 Pet. 1:11). His suffering on the cross was the result of his decision to bear the *sins of humanity (1 Pet. 2:24; 3:18), and is an example to his followers (1 Pet. 2:21). In Colossians 1:24 Paul refers to his suffering as serving to complete 'what is lacking in regard to Christ's afflictions [Gk. *thlipsis*] for the sake of his body, which is the church.' This suffering must be distinguished from Christ's redemptive sufferings, but it is clearly of value to the church. The NT description of the church as the body of Christ (1 Cor. 12:27; Eph. 4:12, Col. 1:18) is also relevant. We are not only incorporated into Christ; we are, at the same time, inducted into his sufferings.

Paul not infrequently associates Christian suffering with the suffering of Christ. To the Thessalonians he says, 'you suffered the same things from your own compatriots as they [the believers in Judea] did from the Jews, who killed both the Lord Jesus and the prophets, and drove us out' (1 Thess. 2:14–15). Suffering is a privilege for Christians (Phil. 1:29), and persecution is seen as the inevitable consequence of the holy lifestyle expected of them (2 Tim. 3:12). In Romans Paul acknowledges the universality of suffering: 'the whole creation has been groaning in labour pains until now' (Rom. 8:22). But he expects it to be freed from its futility (8:20–21).

Richard Hays bases his work on Christian ethics (*The Moral Vision of the New Testament*) on Philippians 3:10; chapter one of Part One is headed 'The *Koinonia* of His Sufferings'. Paul deliberately and forcefully associates Christian living with suffering: 'I want to know Christ and the power of his resurrection and the sharing of his sufferings by becoming like him in his death ...' As previously noted, these sufferings are not to be interpreted as redemptive, but are a consequence of identifying with Jesus as the one who proclaims the kingdom of God. The phrase used by Paul, 'the fellowship [*koinonia*] of his sufferings', is deeply significant. Christians do not merely tolerate suffering; rather, through it they share in each other's experience. In this respect the suffering of Christians differs from the redemptive sufferings of Christ, which he bore alone ('My God, my God, why have you forsaken me?', Mark 15:34). Peter also employs the concept of *koinonia* in suffering (1 Pet. 4:13). The word most often has a positive connotation: it denotes a sharing in good things. Here, however, Paul indicates that *koinonia* is also to do with sharing in suffering.

The structure of Philippians 3:10 is noteworthy. Firstly, Christ is given central place: 'I want to know Christ and the power of his resurrection and the sharing of his sufferings by becoming like him in his death.' Christ is the focus, not his power. Similarly, Christ's sufferings are the focus, not suffering in general. Secondly, 'the power of his resurrection' and 'the sharing of his sufferings' are directly linked by the shared definite article. It is impossible to know Christ and Christ's power without at the same time accepting his suffering. Thus the suffering of the Christian is twofold: suffering which is common to all humanity, and suffering which is a consequence of Christian rebirth, the new resurrection life. The reason for the first kind of suffering may be a mystery, but the reason for the second kind is clear. Just as Christ 'learned obedience through what he suffered' (Heb. 5:8) (and by this the writer cannot mean the redemptive sufferings of the cross, which were entirely vicarious), so the Christian learns obedience through suffering.

Philippians 3:10 concludes with reference to the death of Christ, and Paul creates a new verbal form: 'to have likeness-together-with'

(it occurs nowhere else in the NT). Paul reminds the Philippian Christians that the power which they seek can be gained only through weakness, that is, through the spiritual death to self which he describes in more detail in Romans 6:4–11.

Death is the greatest mystery of human existence. It is inescapable (Heb. 9:27), and comes in more or less painful ways through illness, accident or violence. It is terrifying because we have sinned (1 Cor. 15:56) and our sin warrants God's judgment. Death, at least as we know it today, was not originally ordained by God; it is the ultimate consequence of sin. However, through the obedience of the one man (Rom. 5:19), expressed in his redemptive sufferings, God has given eternal life to all those justified by grace.

In a sense the Christian is both dead and alive: dead to the sin that was the consequence of life without Christ, and alive in Christ, free from 'the law of sin and of death' (Rom. 8:2). All still face a natural death, but the fear of death is removed by the promise of resurrection and eternal life. Because of this, Paul could insist that for him 'death' was better than 'life' (2 Cor. 5:8). Christians can remain strong in the face of weakness and suffering in the hope that 'this slight momentary affliction is preparing us for an eternal weight of glory beyond all measure' (2 Cor. 4:17).

On at least two occasions Jesus is confronted with the broader issue of human suffering. In John 9 he meets a man born blind. Jesus' disciples see only two possible explanations for the man's condition: either he himself has sinned (in the womb) or his parents have sinned. The underlying assumption is that the cause of suffering is always sin. Jesus rejects both explanations, but provides no alternative valid for every experience of suffering. In Luke 13 he is told of the Galileans massacred in the temple precincts at the hands of Pilate, and of the eighteen people killed when part of an aqueduct fell on them. Such terrible tragedies were apparently considered, in contemporary Jewish theology, to be the consequence of terrible sins (Luke 13:2). Again Jesus rejects the theory without offering an alternative explanation.

Under the old covenant God required faithful obedience and trust from Job, even in the absence of a comprehensive explanation of human suffering. He requires the same from his people under the new covenant.

Bibliography

P. Cotterell, *Is God Helpless?* (London, 1996); P. Fiddes, *The Creative Suffering of God* (Oxford, 1988); R. Hays, *The Moral Vision of the New Testament* (Edinburgh, 1996); C. S. Lewis, *The Problem of Pain* (London, 1940); P. T. O'Brien, *The Epistle to the Philippians*, NIGTC (Grand Rapids and Carlisle, 1991); B. Reichenbach, *Evil and a Good God* (New York, 1982); B. Whitney, *What are They Saying About God and Evil?* (New York, 1989).

F. P. COTTERELL

SUFFERING SERVANT, see JESUS CHRIST
SYSTEMATIC THEOLOGY AND BIB-
LICAL THEOLOGY, see Part 1
TABERNACLE, see TEMPLE

TEMPLE

Introduction

Temples and holy places have long been an established feature of the world's religions. The Israelites, like their ancient Near Eastern neighbours, had their sanctuaries. Although the tabernacle, the early sanctuaries at Bethel and Shiloh and the temple of Jerusalem resembled other places of *worship in the ancient Near East in numerous ways they were conceived differently. In Israel the sanctuary was viewed not as part of the natural order of things but as *God's gracious gift. It was linked directly to the historic *covenant into which God had entered with his *people at Mt Sinai (Lev. 26:12). The desert sanctuary is called the 'tent' or 'tabernacle of the covenant' (Exod. 38:21; Num. 3:25; *etc.*). God was not seen as bound to his earthly dwelling. The temple and God's presence in it could not be taken for granted or as guaranteed (Jer. 7). As God had chosen to dwell there (1 Kgs. 8:27–30), so he could leave it if his people disobeyed him (Ezek. 10).

The idea of the divine indwelling is fundamental to the biblical tradition. Jewish *eschatology could thrive without the hope of a Messiah but never without the hope of God's dwelling with his people. When the temple was destroyed in 587 BC the hope of a new temple became central to eschatology. The early Christians worked out their understanding of their new faith in terms drawn from the temple and the hope of a new temple. The place which the temple holds in both history and eschatology is thus important for readers of the NT.

The tabernacle

The first sanctuary mentioned in the OT was a portable construction. 2 Samuel 7:6 appears to summarize the accounts of the tent-sanctuary. In his word to *David God said, 'I have not dwelt in a house since the day I brought up the people of Israel from Egypt to this day, but I have been moving about in a tent ['*ōhel mô'ēd*] for my dwelling [*miškān*]' (RSV). The story of the tabernacle begins at Mt Sinai, at the ratification of the covenant (Exod. 24). Directions for its construction follow in Exodus 25 – 31. It is an elaborate construction and serves several purposes. It is the place where God dwells in the midst of his people (25:8). It also serves as the place of the divine *revelation (25:22), and it is here that sacrifices are offered and atonement is made (29:38–43; 30:7–10). But before the tabernacle was built Israel had committed apostasy by making and worshipping a golden calf (ch. 32). In consequence God threatened to withdraw from Israel (33:1–3). At this point the text says that Moses 'used to take the tent and pitch it outside the camp, far off from the camp; and he called it the tent of meeting ('*ōhel mô'ēd*)' (33:7, NRSV). Moses would enter the tent and a cloud, symbol of the divine presence, would descend (from Mt Sinai) and stand outside the tent, and the Lord would speak with Moses (33:9). This tent, however, was replaced by the tabernacle following the latter's construction.

The tabernacle (*miškān*), in contrast, was erected in the midst of the camp (Exod. 40:33) and the cloud rested not outside but inside it (40:34–35). It comprised the holy place and the holy of holies; in the latter was the ark of the covenant and over it the mercy seat and the cherubim. The lampstand, table, incense altar, bronze altar and laver were also housed in the tabernacle (40:1–11). The tabernacle bears many similarities to the temple later built by *Solomon, reflecting the continuity of the divine indwelling through the ages. Nowhere is this more in evidence than in the story of the installation of the ark and the tent of meeting in the newly erected temple of Solomon and the descent of the cloud upon the temple (1 Kgs. 8:1–11). The entire ideology of the divine presence which runs throughout the Bible is thus already expressed in the tabernacle tradition. It is God's presence which is constitutive of the nation. From the place of his presence he reveals his will and pours out his *blessing upon his people.

The temple of Jerusalem

The unique position which the temple of *Jerusalem came to occupy for *Israel was due to a great extent to the centralization of worship there. This made it possible to fix the times at which the whole nation would assemble. The annual pilgrimages to the temple were occasions of great sentiment and the chief *joy of life (Is. 30:29; 35:10; Pss. 42:1–4; 43:3–4; 84:1–2; 122:1–9; 137:6). To go to Jerusalem is to go to the place where God is (Pss. 42:2; 63:2; 65:1–2; *etc.*). A single day spent in the sanctuary is better than a thousand elsewhere (Ps. 84:10).

The concentration of worship and sentiment at Jerusalem had the effect of creating a theology of Jerusalem. The city was included in the doctrine of *election: as God had chosen David, so he had chosen Zion (Ps. 132:11–14: 2 Sam. 7:12–17). Jerusalem and its temple were raised to a level of supra-historical importance. It was not enough that the temple had been built on the place indicated by David (1 Chr. 22:1; 2 Chr. 3:1). Its foundation belonged to creation itself and, lifted high above the vicissitudes of time, it would last for ever (Pss. 78:69; 125:1). Nor did it suffice to believe that the temple was the place where God revealed his will to Israel and blessed his people. The destinies of the *nations were decided there (Amos 1:1–15; Ps. 99:1–5); the wellbeing of the whole earth depended upon him who controlled the great deep from his throne in Zion (Pss. 29:10; 46:1–5; 93:1–4). Thus Jerusalem became the type of the final and universal *salvation of the eschatological age (Is. 2:2–4; Mic. 4:1–3; Zech. 14:16–19).

One can understand therefore the sense of distress and loss felt as a result of the destruction of the temple in 587 BC. This meant nothing less than the loss of God's presence (Ezek. 9:3; 10:4–5; 11:23). Particularly painful was the experience of the Jews who were uprooted and exiled in Babylon (Ps. 137:4–6). But God responded to their sense of deprivation. He promised to be a 'sanctuary' for them (Ezek. 11:16), and they discovered that his presence could be experienced in more places than they had thought (Ps. 139:7–12). They would return to their homeland and make a new beginning (Jer. 31:31–34; Ezek. 20:40–42; 34:1–16).

The new temple

Central to the hope of the restored nation was the new temple. This is described as in an architect's drawing in Ezekiel 40 – 48. In Isaiah it is the rendezvous not only of the exiles but also the nations, 'a house of prayer for all peoples' (Is. 56:7; *cf.* 60:4–7; 66:18–21). Haggai promises that 'the latter splendour of this house shall be greater than the former' (2:9), while Zechariah declares that Jerusalem will recover its *glory, and the nations will worship there (14:10, 16–21). Later Jewish writings continue the theme. Tobit describes the temple of the new age as lasting for ever (1:4). The *Psalms of Solomon* give the Messiah a significant role in relation to the eschatological temple (17:28–33), while the *Sibylline Oracles* make the new temple the centrepiece of the coming golden age (3:702–711, 772–776; *cf.* 5:423–434).

A development important for understanding the NT is the identification of the new temple with the heavenly temple. *1 Enoch* describes a magnificent building of crystal in which God is enthroned in majesty (14:15–20). The new temple, depicted in chapter 90 as 'greater and loftier than the first' (v. 29), is probably the heavenly temple set up upon earth. The heavenly temple and cult is described further in the *Testament of Levi* (3:4–6; 5:1–2), while the Jerusalem of the new age is the heavenly Jerusalem according to 2 Baruch 4:2–4. The same hope seems to have been entertained by the author of 4 Ezra 10:44, 48–54. Numerous texts in the rabbinic literature describe the heavenly Jerusalem and some predict that it will descend to earth (*Bet. ha-Midrash* 1.55, 23; 3.36, 29).

Another development significant for the NT is the spiritualizing of the temple. The Stoics frequently thought of the individual as the dwelling-place of the divine spirit (*e.g.* Seneca, *Epistles* 40.1–2; Epictetus, *Discourses* 1.14.13–14). Philo stands in the same tradition (*de Somniis* 1.21–34, 215; *de Opificio Mundi* 145–146). Although the idea of the individual as a temple appears in the NT (1 Cor. 6:19), it is nowhere nearly as prominent as the idea of the community of believers as a spiritual temple. Here the concept of the community as a temple in the Dead Sea Scrolls is particularly important (1 QS 5.5–6; 8.4–10; 9.3–6; *etc.*). It has to be said, however, that the spiritualizing of the temple and the cult undertaken at Qumran did not entail the permanent rejection of the material temple and its cult. The Jews of Qumran also looked for a new or restored temple at Jerusalem (*Damascus Document* 4.1–12; *War Scroll* 2.1–6; 12.12–18; 19.5–8; *Temple Scroll*).

Jesus and the temple

The Synoptic evangelists regard *Jesus' relations with the temple of Jerusalem as of crucial significance. They concentrate most of the relevant material into their accounts of his brief ministry in Jerusalem at the end of his life, to which they attach great importance, and ignore his earlier visits to the city. The entry of Jesus into Jerusalem is interpreted as the fulfilment of the eschatological hope of the coming of the Messiah to Zion (Matt. 21:9; Mark 11:9–10; Luke 19:38; John 12:14–15). Jesus' high-handed action in cleansing the temple is very likely understood by Mark as a Messianic action (Mal. 3:1–4; *Psalms of Solomon* 17:23–24). Mark's use of Isaiah 56:7 ('My house shall be called a house of prayer for all the nations') shows what he thought of those who had sacrificed Israel's calling to be a light to the Gentiles by commercializing their part of the temple, while the use of Jeremiah 7:11 points ahead to his teaching on the destruction of the temple (13:1–2; *cf.* 14:57–58; 15:37–38).

This radical view of the cleansing of the temple in Mark is supported by the account of the cursing and the withering of the barren fig tree, in which the story of the cleansing is embedded (11:11–25). A similar judgment on the order represented by the temple is probably intended by the prediction in Mark 11:23: the mountain of the Lord's house will not be elevated as expected (Is. 2:2 = Mic. 4:1), but cast down.

At Jesus' trial he was accused of saying, 'I will destroy this temple that is made with hands, and in three days I will build another, not made with hands' (Mark 14:58). According to John 2:19 Jesus uttered a saying like this (*cf.* Acts 6:14). Why Mark attributed it to false witness is therefore debated by scholars. Possibly the witness was false because it misrepresented what Jesus said. He had predicted that the temple would be destroyed (Mark 13:2) and he had said that he would be put to death (8:31; 9:31; 10:34), and these two things may have been unscrupulously combined. Support for this view can be found in John 2:19–20. There seems little doubt that Mark intended the reference to the temple 'not made with hands' to refer to the new temple. This is clearly the meaning intended by John who, significantly, places his saying about the new temple in the context of the cleansing of the temple (2:19–22).

The consequences of Jesus' rejection and death for the temple of Jerusalem are nowhere more in evidence than in Mark's statement that at the moment Jesus died the veil of the temple was torn apart (15:38). Coupled with this and immediately following it is the confession of faith by the Roman centurion (15:39). Whether the ruined veil was the one which hung in front of the holy place or the veil covering the entrance to the holy of holies, the meaning is not in doubt; the death of Jesus stands for the removal of the temple of Jerusalem and its replacement by a new means of *forgiveness, and the first person to avail himself of this is a representative of those who were denied a place in the part of the temple assigned for their use (1 Kgs. 8:41–43). Thus Mark ends his Gospel with Jesus leading the disciples away from Jerusalem and back to Galilee (14:28; 16:7).

The new temple in Luke-Acts

The temple of Jerusalem features prominently in Luke-Acts. In both writings the beginning of the new age is located in the temple of Jerusalem (Luke 2:25–32; Acts 1 – 7), but it is made clear that the gospel is for the nations (Luke 24:47), and that this will mean leaving Jerusalem and going to the ends of the earth (Acts 1:8; 28:23–31). But cutting the umbilical cord which joined the infant church to Jerusalem was not easy, or so it would appear from the story of Stephen (Acts

6 – 7). Stephen directs a frontal attack on the temple, or more precisely on the attitude of mind engendered by the temple. The charge brought against Stephen is attributed to false witnesses (6:13), but, since what Stephen says substantiates the charge to a great extent, it seems clear that, as in the case of the charge brought against Jesus at his trial, the falsity was very likely due more to misrepresentation than to perjury. The logical sequel is unsurprising; the martyrdom of Stephen is followed by the persecution of the church and the scattering of its members, first to Samaria (8:4–5) and then to Antioch (11:19–21). The way was thus prepared for Paul to take the gospel to the Gentile world (13:1–3) and for the book of Acts to end with the apostle not in Jerusalem but in Rome (28:30–31). Loyalty to the temple of Jerusalem was replaced by loyalty to the person of Jesus

The church as God's temple

There is one text in Paul's writings which depicts the individual as God's temple (1 Cor. 6:19–20). Parallels for this idea have frequently been sought in Philo and the Stoics. But it should be noted that Paul did not think of the divine indwelling as part of the natural order as the Stoics did. He saw it as a gift of the new age; it was part of his ecclesiology and eschatology.

In other texts the Christian community is identified as God's temple. The eschatological nuance of this imagery is prominent in 1 Corinthians 3:16–17, where Paul says that it is the Spirit who makes believers in Christ God's new temple. 'You are God's temple, since God's Spirit dwells in you' (author's translation). The *Holy Spirit is the divine gift of the new age (Ezek. 37:14; Joel 2:28–29; Acts 2:1–4).

The corporate character of the temple imagery is particularly clear in 1 Corinthians 3:16–17. 'You Corinthians – all of you – are God's dwelling-place' (author's translation). Over against the divisive tendencies at Corinth Paul sets the idea of the *church as God's temple. His Jewish Christian readers could not fail to see the point. God does not dwell in a multiplicity of temples. He is one and can inhabit only one shrine (cf. 1:13, 'is Christ divided?'). To cause disunity in the church is to desecrate the temple of God, and desecration of a holy place leads to its destruction.

Equal emphasis is laid on the sanctity of the new temple, a thought which would have strong resonance for both Jewish and Greek Christians. Paul thinks of the church in almost spatial terms. It is God's holy preserve. Schism amounts to profanation of a holy place and will bring its own fearful penalty.

Another text in which the temple image is used to address the practical needs of the church is 2 Corinthians 6:14 – 7:1. The key texts, Leviticus 26:12 and Ezekiel 37:27, used here in the string of testimonia, are already combined in a prediction of the new temple in *Jubilees* 1:17, and it is possible that Paul is using proof texts which were already in use in the early church or in Judaism (Qumran). Whatever the origin of the couplet, Paul gives it his own meaning. It is the Christian community that inherits the promises of God. The holiness which God's presence gives it must be preserved from defilement by unbelievers (6:17; 7:1). In this text, as in 1 Corinthians 3:16, it is the local congregation which is God's temple.

Ephesians 2:20–22, by contrast, uses the temple image for the church universal. Doctrinal instruction is the intention. The text forms a summarizing conclusion to a passage which describes the unity of Jews and Gentiles in the church (2:11–19). The terms 'far' and 'near' (vv. 13, 17) were used by the rabbis to describe Gentiles and Jews respectively (*Numbers Rabbah* 8:4), while the references to 'peace' (vv. 14, 17) denote the peace which was to prevail when Jews and Gentiles were united in the temple at Zion (Is. 2:2–4; Mic. 4:1–4; *1 Enoch* 90:29–33; *Sibylline Oracles* 3:755–776). This unity is further reflected in the idea of the removal of the wall dividing the races (v. 14), particularly if this is the wall in the temple of Jerusalem which separated Jews and Gentiles (Josephus, *Antiquities* 15.417; *Wars* 5.194–195). Thus Gentiles and Jews both have unhindered 'access' to the sanctuary of God's presence (v. 18).

The way is thus prepared for the architectural image of Jews and Gentiles forming the new temple (vv. 19–20). The passage is significant for its fusion of the temple (*naos*) and the building (*oikodomē*) and its specification of different parts of the building. The foundation is the apostles and prophets (NT prophets; *cf.* Rom. 12:6; 1 Thess. 5:20; Acts 11:27, *etc.*; Rev. 1:3, *etc.*).

In other words, Gentiles are assured that their membership of the church rests upon the bedrock of historic Christianity. Christ himself is the cornerstone or keystone, depending upon how one interprets *akrogōniaios*. Understood as a cornerstone, this particular stone was the first stone to be laid in the foundation, and all the others were lined up to it. This imagery gives Christ a determinative role in the church, and also explains how the building can be said to 'grow into a holy temple' (Eph. 2:21).

The rabbis viewed the cornerstone of Isaiah 28:16 physiologically, as the embryo from which the world grew (*Babylonian Talmud Yoma* 54a). The cornerstone unites the building because it is organically as well as structurally bound to it, and the building itself grows as further stones (Gentile converts) are added to it. The superstructure which arises from the foundation is described in parallel ways (Eph. 2:21–22), which are fused to create a double image. Viewed as a building, the church is still under construction; viewed as a temple, it is an inhabited dwelling. God deigns to dwell in his unfinished (and imperfect) church.

The crucial role which Christ has in the church is further explicated in 1 Peter 2:4–8. The reference to Christ as the cornerstone (v. 6) shows that the meaning of the verse is close to that of Ephesians 2:20; Christ is the source of the church's life and growth. It is for this reason that believers are exhorted to keep coming to him (v. 4). They are themselves 'living stones' and together with Christ they form a 'spiritual house' (v. 5). The strong Christological thrust of the text is indicated by the exhortation to 'offer spiritual sacrifices acceptable to God through Jesus Christ' (v. 5). That the edifice is understood to be a temple is shown by the mention of sacrifices and priesthood (v. 5). By reinterpreting priesthood as well as temple and sacrifice, the author has completed the circle of ideas represented by the temple image.

The heavenly temple

The sanctuary or temple in heaven is an important idea in the epistle to the Hebrews. Contrasting the old covenant and the new and better covenant, the writer says that Christ the high priest has entered into the heavenly shrine (9:11–12; *cf.* 6:19–20; 8:2). By referring to the heavenly sanctuary as 'true' (8:2; 9:24) and to its earthly counterpart as 'shadow' or 'copy' (8:5; 9:24) the author demonstrates the transcendence and superiority of Christianity over Judaism.

The heavenly temple is the setting for the drama which is played out in chapters 4 – 20 of the book of Revelation. John sees the throne of God (4:1–11). Nearby is the sea (possibly a reference to the laver which is next to the altar in 1 Kgs. 7:23–26) and the altar (6:9–11). Presently John sees the temple opened and the ark of the covenant revealed (11:19). Angels emerge from the temple (15:6) and God sends out his *judgments from it (16:1, 17). Beyond this, John is not interested in the heavenly temple as such; it is simply the stage for his *dramatis personae*. But the reader is alerted to expect the temple to play an important part in John's vision by his statement that the faithful will be made pillars in the temple of God (3:12).

It comes as a surprise, however, to be told that the new Jerusalem will not have a temple (21:22). The idea of Jerusalem without a temple runs counter to all the hopes of Judaism. It is taken by some commentators to mean that the whole city is a temple. It is noted that the city is cubiform (21:16; *cf.* 1 Kgs. 6:20). But John says that God and the *Lamb are the temple. This probably means that in the place where one would expect the temple one finds God and his Son. Such a conclusion seems to be what John intends when he says that the martyrs stand in the presence of God (7:15) and that the dwelling of God is God himself (21:3; note the play on the words *skēnē* and *skēnōsei*). Thus John finally says that the temple is the Lord God Almighty and the Lamb. One after another the barriers separating worshippers from God are removed until they enjoy uninterrupted communion with God. 'His servants will ... see his face' (22:3–4). This is the *summum bonum* John presents to his hard-pressed readers.

Conclusion

The temple is a central feature of the Bible. It is God's dwelling with his people that makes them the people of God, and when the temple of Jerusalem is destroyed the hope of a new temple became a central article of Jewish faith. The NT presents the church as the fulfilment of God's promise of a new temple. This spiritualizing of the temple, which had already begun in Judaism, resulted from the death and resurrection of Jesus Christ and the gift of the Spirit. For this reason full weight should be given to the adjective when speaking of the *new* temple.

As a metaphor of the church the temple is significant for its theocentric emphasis. The church is the temple of God, or of God's Spirit, and never the temple of Christ. The image thus serves ecclesiology by drawing attention to the fundamental concept of the church as the people of God. On the other hand, when the temple is viewed in architectural terms and seen as a building, Christ's place in the church and his relation to Christians and theirs to him is made clear. The fusion of sacral and architectural images may indicate a conscious and deliberate effort on the part of the NT writers to emphasize the position of Christ in the church. No greater significance could have been attached to Christ than by giving him pride of place as the chief stone in the new temple.

At the same time the close connection of Christians with their Lord is denoted by their being called 'stones' in the temple. Together Christ and Christians form God's dwelling. Christians are 'living stones' because they are united to Christ the living stone, *i.e.* the resurrected one. The merging of temple and building images introduces a dynamic element into NT ecclesiology; the church 'grows into a holy temple in the Lord' (Eph. 2:21).

The use of the temple image also serves to depict Christ's work in the eternal world. He secures forgiveness for his people and mediates their *prayers to God. Additionally, the heavenly temple image denotes the unhindered access to God which believers enjoy. Although still on earth, they join in the worship offered in heaven. This foretaste of the worship of the age to come is graphically portrayed in the book of Revelation which depicts God himself as the temple. God is directly and fully accessible to his people through his Son the Lamb.

See also: ATONEMENT; HOLINESS; PRIESTS; SACRIFICE.

Bibliography

R. E. Clements, *God and Temple* (Oxford, 1965); Y. M. J. Congar, *The Mystery of the Temple* (London, 1961); J. Coppens, 'The spiritual temple in the Pauline letters and its background', *SE* 6, 1973, pp. 53–66; M. Fraeyman, 'La spiritualisation de l'idée du Temple dans épîtres pauliniennes', *ETL* 23, 1947, pp. 378–412; B. Gärtner, *The Temple and the Community of Qumran and the New Testament* (Cambridge, 1965); M. Haran, *Temples and Temple Service in Ancient Israel* (Winona Lake, 1985); C. T. R. Hayward, *The Jewish Temple* (London and New York, 1991); D. Juel, *Messiah and Temple: The Trial of Jesus in the Gospel of Mark*, (Missoula, 1977); C. R. Koester, *The Dwelling of God: The Tabernacle in the Old Testament, Intertestamental Jewish Literature, and the New Testament* (Washington DC, 1989); R. J. McKelvey, *The New Temple: The Church in the New Testament* (Oxford, 1968); G. W. MacRae, 'Heavenly temple and eschatology in the letter to the Hebrews' *Semeia* 12, 1979, pp. 179–199; J. Maier, *The Temple Scroll* (Sheffield, 1985); W. von Meding, C. Brown and D. H. Madvig in *NIDNTT* 3, pp. 781–785; J. Patrich, 'Reconstructing the magnificent temple Herod built', *BR* 3, 1988, pp. 17–29; K. and L. Ritmeyer, 'Reconstructing Herod's temple mount in Jerusalem', *BASR* 15.6, 1989, pp. 23–53; E. P. Sanders, *Jesus and Judaism* (London, 1985); P. W. L. Walker, *Jesus and the Holy City* (Grand Rapids and Cambridge, 1990); H. Wenschkewitz, 'Die Spiritualisierung der Kultusbegriffe Tempel, Priester und Opfer im Neuen Testament', *Angelos* 4, 1932, pp. 77–230; M. O. Wise, in *DJG*, pp. 811–817.

R. J. MCKELVEY

TEMPTATION, see TESTING
TEN COMMANDMENTS, see LAW

TESTIMONY/WITNESS

The concepts and vocabulary of testimony are found throughout the canon of Scripture. Because of the cardinal role played by the *law in the formation and life of ancient Israel, the roots of testimony are juridical. But because that life was not divided into discrete legal and religious compartments, those juridical roots blossom throughout the biblical narrative into religious proclamation, confession and martyrdom. This intermingling of legal and religious testimony is entirely natural, for the law was given in order that *Israel, by obeying the law, might be a living testimony to its author, the Lord their God (Deut. 4:5–8; 26:16–19).

Giving testimony was not limited to God and people, but extended literally and metaphorically to an array of objects such as heaven and earth, altar and ark, song and stone, and to Scripture itself (Deut. 31:26; John 5:39; Rom. 3:21). Israel's jurisprudence relied heavily upon human witnesses, and treated the deposition of their testimony with the utmost gravity. The law obligates witnesses to testify, and requires that there be at least two or three witnesses in any given case (Lev. 5:1; Deut. 19:15). Significantly, the first reference to legal testimony appears in the Decalogue, which forbids perjury along with other serious transgressions such as idolatry, murder, adultery and theft (Exod. 20:16). Because the giving of false testimony was a grievous offence, perjurers were subject to the *lex talionis*, the 'eye for an eye' law, whereby the punishment for perjurers equalled that which their intended victims would have received (Deut. 19:16–21). A perjurer might therefore be put to death – the fate, for example, of the two men who testify falsely that Susanna has committed the capital offence of adultery (Susanna 61 – 62). Indeed, it became proverbial in Israel that 'a false witness will not go unpunished, and the liar will perish' (Prov. 19:9, NRSV).

The juridical foundation of Israel's testimony to God underlies the concept of the *rîb* (lawsuit). In Pentateuchal law the term refers to material lawsuits between persons (Exod. 23:2–3, 6), but in the era of the prophets it becomes a forensic metaphor for disputes in which God is pitted against Israel or the Gentiles. Central to these disputes is the sovereignty of God. Isaiah 40 – 55 provides an example of the use of *rîb* as a juridical metaphor: Isaiah proclaims that when the nations see the deliverance of Israel they will come to acknowledge the one true God (Is. 45:14). Here, in Isaiah's prophetic courtroom, God repeatedly declares of the people of Israel, 'You are my witnesses' (Is. 43:10, 12; 44:8). Testifying as the progeny of Abraham and David, Israel serves to advance God's promises of blessing and revelation to the nations (Gen. 12:2–3; 2 Sam. 7:23–26). Similarly, the Lord's servant fulfils his vocation as the witnessing instrument of

God's revelation to the Gentiles (Is. 42:6; 49:6).

Testimony to God's unfolding purpose to bless the nations is carried forward by *John the Baptist, *Jesus, the *Holy Spirit, the apostles (see *Mission) and the *church. The church's mission consists of worldwide witness to God's decisive act in Jesus; this witness is thus foundational for New Testament thought.

Although all four Evangelists show John preparing the way for Jesus, the Synoptic and Johannine portraits of John's ministry are distinct. Matthew, Mark and Luke depict him as messenger, prophet, preacher and baptizer, whereas John portrays him solely as a witness (John 1:6–8, 15, 19–34) (see *John, Gospel of). The Fourth Gospel's pronounced emphasis on testimony is unique in the NT. The Johannine Jesus testifies to himself, with corroborating evidence being supplied by the Father, Jesus' works and the Spirit (John 8:18; 5:36; 15:26). This panel of witnesses clearly reflects the Jewish legal mandate for multiple attestation, a mandate cited by Jesus when opponents challenge his testimony (John 8:12–18).

Testimony/witness vocabulary is comparatively scarce in the Synoptics. They do, however, include the idea of Jesus witnessing to himself. When, for example, John the Baptist enquires of Jesus if he is the one expected from God, Jesus responds by citing his works of healing as evidence of his identity (Matt. 11:1–6). The idea, if not the vocabulary, resembles the Johannine Jesus' appeal to his works as witnesses.

The Holy Spirit is vitally active in the testimony of the apostles and the church. Jesus anticipates this when promising his disciples that the Holy Spirit will testify through and with them (John 15:26–27; Luke 24:48–49). Although intimately connected in their witnessing, the Holy Spirit and the apostles maintain separate identities. When, for example, the apostles defend their proclamation of Jesus before the Sanhedrin, they say, 'We are witnesses to these things, and so is the Holy Spirit whom God has given to those who obey him' (Acts 5:32). The Spirit testifies not only through and with believers to others, but to believers themselves to confirm their status as God's children and their faith in Jesus Christ (Rom. 8:16; Heb. 10:15; 1 John 5:6).

At the end of each Gospel Jesus commissions his disciples as apostles to the world (Matt. 28:16–20; Mark 16:14–18 [almost certainly apocryphal]; Luke 24:48–49; John 20:19–23). In Luke's version, Jesus' words to his disciples echo those of God to Israel recorded by Isaiah (cited above), that they will be witnesses to the nations of God's redemptive action. Luke narrates the fulfilment of this commission in the second half of his chronicle, the book of *Acts, in which the apostles' identity is defined in these terms: 'You will be my witnesses in Jerusalem, in all Judea and Samaria, and to the ends of the earth' (Acts 1:8). The Pentecost event recounted in Acts 2, wherein people from 'every nation under heaven' hear the apostles' testimony to God's redemptive action in Jesus, presents in microcosm what will take place over many years and miles. By the end of Acts, the apostles' testimony has stretched out across the Roman empire.

What is true of the first apostles is true also of the apostle Paul. For all Paul's work as pastor and theologian, his primary task was that of a witness. His encounter with the risen Jesus and his resultant call to ministry are narrated three times in Acts. In these accounts the details of Paul's commission vary, but in each case (and also in a summary of his ministry given to the Ephesian elders) it is defined as a call to be a witness to Jesus (Acts 9:15; 22:15; 26:16; 20:24).

There is continuity and progression between Israel's testimony to the God of Israel as revealed in the OT and the church's testimony to the God of Israel as revealed in Jesus: 'Long ago God spoke to our ancestors in many and various ways by the prophets, but in these last days he has spoken to us by a Son' (Heb. 1:1–2). This is reflected, for example, in Paul's testimony to Jewish leaders in Rome, in which he tries to convince them about Jesus by using the law of Moses and the prophets (Acts 28:23). Such testimony is given both verbally and visually, as when Paul and Barnabas testify successfully in *words confirmed by their performance of miraculous deeds (see *Signs and wonders) (Acts 14:1–3). Indeed, words of testimony are no less a demonstration of God's activity than are miraculous deeds (1 Cor. 2:1–5; cf. Mark 13:9–11). This testimony to the evolving *revelation of God that climaxes in Jesus Christ is passed from him to the first apostles and to the whole church: '[The message] was declared at first through the Lord, and it was attested to us by those who heard him, while God added his testimony by signs and wonders and various miracles, and by the gifts of the Holy Spirit distributed according to his will' (Heb. 2:3–4).

Testimony is closely related to confession in the NT, where a confession is a public proclamation of one's beliefs about, and relationship with, the person of Jesus Christ. Whereas the Jewish confession, the Shema, declared, 'Hear, O Israel: the Lord is our God, the Lord alone' (Deut. 6:4), the earliest and most elementary forms of the Christian confession proclaimed, 'Jesus is the Christ' and 'Jesus is Lord'. These confessions were used within the church in teaching, worship and healing, and outside the church in evangelism.

A defining characteristic of witnesses is the willingness to confess Jesus Christ in the face of disbelief, opposition, persecution and even martyrdom. The exemplar for martyrdom is Jesus himself, the 'faithful witness' depicted as the slain lamb (Rev. 1:5; 5:6). The English word 'martyr' derives from the Greek word *martys*, a member of the family of NT Greek words used for testimony and witness. In the NT, therefore, a martyr is someone who dies not as an advocate for a cause, but as a witness for Jesus Christ. Paul recalls how the blood of God's witness (*martys*) Stephen was shed (Acts 22:20). Antipas of Pergamum was executed on account of his testimony to Jesus, and the call to church members to face martyrdom is a crucial theme of *Revelation (Rev. 2:13; cf. 6:9; 11:7; 12:11; 20:4).

When the Sanhedrin orders Peter and John to desist from preaching in the name of Jesus Christ, they reply, 'Judge for yourselves whether it is right in God's sight to obey you instead of God. For we cannot keep from proclaiming what we have heard and seen' (Acts 4:19–20, author's translation). From this it follows that testifying to the work of God in Jesus Christ is not an option but an obligation for his disciples. The task of bearing urgent witness passes from the NT church to succeeding generations of disciples, some of whom have performed it well, and some badly. But even where human witness falters, divine witness does not: 'If we are faithless, [Jesus] remains faithful – for he cannot deny himself' (2 Tim. 2:13). The risen

Jesus remains the faithful and true witness; the Holy Spirit abides as a witness through, and to, every generation of believers; the inspired Scripture stands as a written testimony to God's redemptive activity. The church is indeed endowed with a divine testimony that employs but surpasses human testimony (1 John 5:9).

The alpha and omega of biblical testimony resides in its narration of God's unfolding purpose to bring salvation to the ends of the earth, whereby every tongue will testify that there is but one true God, and that this one true God has made Jesus Christ Lord of all (Is. 45:20–25; Phil. 2:9–11).

Bibliography

D. Daube, *Witnesses in Bible and Talmud* (Oxford, 1986); R. G. Maccini, *Her Testimony Is True: Women as Witnesses according to John* (Sheffield, 1996); V. Neufeld, *The Earliest Christian Confessions* (Leiden, 1963); A. A. Trites, *The New Testament Concept of Witness* (Cambridge, 1977); *idem*, *New Testament Witness in Today's World* (Valley Forge, 1983).

R. G. MACCINI

TESTING

Introduction

Testing, or the temptation to be unfaithful to *God, arises from internal enticement to *sin and from external afflictions. While in some OT texts God alone does the testing, elsewhere in Scripture Satan (see *Spiritual powers) is a tool to provoke unfaithfulness while God tests in the hope of finding *faithfulness.

Testing in the OT

Although people are depicted as testing each other's reputation (1 Kgs. 10:1) and beliefs (Dan. 1:12) it is most often God who is seen testing the *obedience or faithfulness of his people (Gen. 22:1–19; Exod. 15:25; Deut. 8:2; 33:8; 1 Kgs. 22:21–23), sometimes even at their request (Ps. 26:2). In the call to sacrifice his son, Abraham is tested and presented as a model of obedience, *fear of God and trust in God to provide his needs (Gen. 22:1–14; *cf.* Heb. 11:17). Particularly in Deuteronomy the *Exodus signs and wilderness experiences of privation and supply are understood as tests of *love, *humility and acknowledgment of the uniqueness of God (Deut. 4:34; 8:2, 16; 13:3). In the Promised Land God tests his people with false *prophets (Deut. 13:3), through the presence of other *nations (Judg. 2:21–23) and also in the withholding of miracles (2 Chr. 32:31) so that faithfulness is tested by his absence.

Although the Lord is said to incite David to sin in 2 Samuel 24:1, 10, a later rewriting of the story introduces Satan as the one enticing to sin (1 Chr. 21:1). Under God's authority, Satan also tests Job to see if he fears God only for gain (Job 1:6–12) or for his health (Job 2:4). To pass the test is to remain faithful to God despite profound and incomprehensible *suffering.

There are also frequent references in the OT to God's being wrongfully put to the test by people. In Numbers 14:22–23 this testing is the reason for the Israelites' dying in the wilderness. Deuteronomy conveys the idea that the Israelites will test God in the Promised Land through the *worship of other gods and the ignoring of his demands (Deut. 6:10–25). In these ways, and in the questioning of his care (Exod. 17:1–7; Deut. 6:16), the refusal to recognize and remember his power (Num. 14:22), and the request that he should prove himself (Ps. 95:9), God's honour is violated.

Nevertheless, in response to the Israelites' testing of God by questioning his powerful presence among them he graciously provides water, demonstrating both his power and their lack of faith in his acts as displayed to them in Egypt (Exod. 17:2–7). Psalm 78 is a strong call not to forget or doubt what God has done in Egypt nor to become hardened in heart towards him and test him by demanding a miracle.

Testing in the Gospels

The OT theme of God's testing the faithfulness of his people, notably in the wilderness, is reflected pre-eminently in the temptation of *Jesus (*cf.* Deut. 8:2) in which he is conscious of the presence and direction of the *Holy Spirit (*cf.* Neh. 9:20; Is. 63:7–10). As Satan is the antagonist, Jesus is depicted in a spiritual and cosmic test of the highest order, a battle which continues as he faces human opposition.

In Matthew the immediate background to the temptations is the voice from heaven announcing Jesus' sonship (Matt. 3:17), which is successfully tested. Jesus proves his obedience by being prepared to find his sustenance, safety and sovereignty only in submission to his Father, who faithfully supplies his needs. Jesus' *victory over temptation is complete, although he will go on being tempted – always by Satan, who is the source of temptation (Matt. 6:13) – as when he later refuses to perform a *sign to engender faith (Matt. 16:1) or is tempted to be unfaithful to God as revealed in Scripture (Matt. 19:3; 22:18, 35). In all this Jesus is a model for his followers, who also are tempted and must pray for God's help (Matt. 6:13; 26:41).

For Mark the temptation story (Mark 1:12–13) is the first of an almost uninterrupted series of tests of Jesus' obedience and sonship. Mark is not explicit about the nature or outcome of the temptation. However, the association of the temptation story with the declaration of Jesus' sonship (Mark 1:11) and the reference to the ministering angels (Mark 1:13) recall the specific temptation, in the light of his being the Son of God, to throw himself off the temple and be saved by the angels (Matt. 4:5–7; Luke 4:9–12). Thus it may be that Jesus is being tempted to doubt his sonship. But as Satan's role in Mark is to deflect Jesus from his mission (Mark 3:23, 26; 4:15; 8:33), it is more likely that Mark's temptation story shows Satan's failing to thwart Jesus' mission, as Jesus emerges victorious and embarks on his mission (Mark 1:14–15). The mention of the angels also implies victory; in the OT angels ensured safe passage for God's people (Exod. 23:20, 23; 32:34; 33:2; 1 Kgs. 19:5–7). There is no suggestion that Satan is finally defeated, as is confirmed by Jesus continuing to be tempted (Mark 8:11; 10:2; 12:15).

Through a genealogy tracing Jesus back through *Adam to God (Luke 3:23–38), Luke also focuses on the sonship of Jesus in his temptation account. In echoing Deuteronomy 8:2 (Luke 4:2) God is portrayed as leading Jesus and testing his faithfulness. As a faithful son in the whole range of temptations (Luke 4:13), Jesus brings to an end the human disobedience typified in Adam and the Israelites during the Exodus. Yet Luke does not convey the idea that Satan was finally

defeated, for he anticipates further conflicts between Jesus and Satan (Luke 4:13; *cf.* 10:18; 11:18; 13:16).

Testing in the epistles

For the early Christians, ongoing trials or tests in the form of persecution, misfortune or suffering are like a transitory refining fire which reveals genuine faith (*cf.* 2 Cor. 13:5; 1 Pet. 4:12) and are to be considered nothing but joy because, even though they may come from the hand of Satan (Rev. 2:10), they produce endurance and, in turn, maturity resulting in praise (Rom. 5:2–3; Jas. 1:2–4; 1 Pet. 1:6–7). Thus it is not God who tempts the believer to failure (Jas. 1:13); God tests faithfulness desiring success (Rev. 3:10), while Satan seeks failure. Help for those tested is available not only from OT examples of faithfulness (Heb. 11:17, 37), but also from Jesus, whose faithfulness was tested in every way, including in his suffering (Heb. 2:18; 4:15). For Paul, Satan can use sexual desire to cause unfaithfulness (1 Cor. 7:5; *cf.* Jas. 1:14), but while there is a real possibility of failure on the part of the individual (1 Thess. 3:5), comfort can be taken in God's being faithful and not allowing believers to be tested beyond what they can endure (1 Cor. 10:13).

See also: GRUMBLING; WILDERNESS.

Bibliography

P. L. Day, *An Adversary in Heaven* (Atlanta, 1988); S. R. Garrett, *The Temptations of Jesus in Mark's Gospel* (Grand Rapids and Cambridge, 1998); J. Gibson, *The Temptations of Jesus in Early Christianity* (Sheffield, 1995); F. J. Helfmyer, 'nissâ', in *TDOT* 9, pp. 443–455; J. A. T. Robinson, 'The Temptations', in *Twelve New Testament Studies* (London, 1962); G. H. Twelftree, 'Temptation of Jesus', in *DJG*, pp. 821–827.

G. H. TWELFTREE

THANKSGIVING, see WORSHIP

THEOPHANY

What is a theophany?

Many times in biblical history God appeared in human form or revealed himself through the elements of nature. Sometimes he appeared to people when they were fully awake; at other times he revealed himself in a dream to someone asleep or in a trance. Such tangible instances of divine self-revelation are called theophanies.

Biblical poets often depict God coming in the storm in his role of warrior-king. These poetic descriptions are often purely literary, reflecting the poet's theological interpretation of an experience or event, not an actual divine appearance. But in other cases a poetic description *is* based on a literal divine appearance.

Divine appearances to individuals

The first biblical reference to a theophany is in Genesis 3:8, 'Then the man and his wife heard the sound of the LORD God as he was walking in the garden in the cool of the day' (NIV). The translation 'cool [literally, "wind"] of the day' may be inaccurate. Taking the Hebrew word *yôm* (normally 'day') as a rare homonym meaning 'storm', Niehaus translates the phrase 'in the wind of the storm'. If he is right, God appeared in a storm, as he frequently does in the Bible when he comes in judgment (J. J. Niehaus, *God at Sinai*, pp. 155–159) (see *Adam and Eve).

God revealed himself to *Abraham on several occasions. He appeared to him following his arrival in Canaan and promised to give the land to his offspring (Gen. 12:7). He later revealed his presence in symbolic fire as he confirmed this promise (Gen. 15:17). Prior to Isaac's birth, God appeared to Abraham to reassure the patriarch that Sarah would conceive and to warn him of his decision to judge Sodom and Gomorrah. On this occasion God appeared in human form. Genesis 18:1 observes, 'the LORD appeared to Abraham near the great trees of Mamre', while verse 2 explains that 'three men' visited him. The 'men' eventually departed for Sodom (v. 22), though the Lord continued to speak to Abraham. At this point in the story, the Lord seems to be distinct from the 'men'. However, Genesis 19:1 says that 'two angels' arrived in Sodom. If one identifies these angels (who are called 'men' in 19:5, 8, 10) with the 'men' mentioned earlier, then the missing third 'man' is probably the Lord himself, who stayed behind to talk with Abraham.

God later appeared to Isaac and *Jacob to assure them of his intention to bless them in fulfilment of his oath to Abraham (Gen. 26:24; 28:12–13; 35:1, 9; 48:3). In order to force Jacob to lay hold of the promised blessing, he even appeared in human form and engaged the patriarch in a wrestling match! The narrator, assuming Jacob's initial perspective, identifies God as 'a man' (Gen. 32:24), but by the story's end Jacob was certain he had encountered God 'face to face' (v. 30). However, a later tradition suggests Jacob wrestled with an angel (Hos. 12:4); the relationship between the two traditions is complex.

Other passages in the OT closely associate God with an angel (see *Spiritual powers), sometimes called the 'angel of the LORD/God' (Gen. 16:7–11; 22:11, 15; 31:11–13; Exod. 3:1–6; Judg. 6:11–23; 13:3–23). This angel sometimes speaks as if he were God (Gen. 31:11–13; Judg. 2:1–3) and those who encounter the angel sometimes react as if they have seen God (Gen. 16:11–13; Judg. 13:22). Therefore some argue that the angel is actually God himself assuming angelic form. Some even identify the angel as the preincarnate second person of the Trinity. However, in some cases the angel appears to be distinct from the Lord. For example, in Judges 6:11–23 the angel initiated the encounter with Gideon, speaking of the Lord in the third person (vv. 11–13). When Gideon baulked, the Lord himself spoke to Gideon, using the first person (vv. 14–17). When the angel left (v. 21), the Lord, who was apparently invisible, remained behind and assured Gideon he would not die (vv. 22–23). A close reading of several other passages also favours or at least allows for a distinction between God and his angel (*cf.* Gen. 21:17–19; 22:11–12, 15–17; Exod. 3:1–6). Where the angel is identified with the Lord, this is probably in a representational sense only, not in essence. The angel comes with full divine authority and can therefore speak for God (even in the first person!). Those who encounter the angel realize his authoritative status and treat him as if he were actually God. (The Ugaritic Baal myth contains an instructive parallel where the god Yam's messengers are addressed as 'Yam', as if they were actually the one who sent them. See J. C. L. Gibson, *Canaanite Myths and Legends* [Edinburgh, [2]1978], p. 42.)

Of all the people in the Bible, *Moses was the most well-acquainted with theophanies.

God initially appeared to Moses at Horeb in a fire within a bush (Exod. 3:1–6). When Moses realized he was looking at God, he hid his face (v. 6). Despite Moses' reluctance to look at God, he was to see him again. At Sinai the Lord invited Moses and several others to ascend the mountain and worship him (Exod. 24:1–2). They 'saw the God of Israel' (vv. 9–10) from a distance and God summoned Moses into his presence, where he remained for forty days (v. 18). Later Moses met with God at a special tent where they would speak 'face to face, as a man speaks with his friend' (Exod. 33:11; cf. Num. 14:14; Deut. 34:10). The idiomatic expression 'face to face' suggests intimacy. Moses saw some physical form of God (Num. 12:8) and communicated with God in a very personal way.

Though Moses enjoyed a special relationship with God, there were limits to God's self-*revelation. When Moses asked God to reveal his '*glory', God refused, replying, 'you cannot see my face, for no one may see me and live' (Exod. 33:20). God then passed by, but he covered Moses with his hand and allowed him to see only his back (vv. 21–23). This passage is difficult to harmonize with other texts in Exodus where God revealed his glory (16:10; 24:16–17), allowed himself to be seen (24:9–10) and spoke 'face to face' with Moses (33:11). Apparently God's 'glory' and 'face' refer in 33:18–23 to the full splendour of his majesty, which he was not willing to reveal.

Other leaders of God's covenant community also experienced theophanies at strategic points in their careers. After *Solomon became king, the Lord appeared to him in a dream and offered to give him whatever he desired (1 Kgs. 3:5). God appeared in the storm to the discouraged *Elijah, after the prophet fled for his life (1 Kgs. 19:11–18). The Lord's arrival was preceded by a strong wind, an earthquake and fire. Finally the Lord spoke in a thunderous, almost deafening voice, reaffirming to Elijah the power and sovereignty revealed earlier at Mt Carmel. The NIV translation of verse 12b ('And after the fire came a gentle whisper') reflects the traditional view of the passage (cf. AV, 'a 'still, small voice'). However, the Hebrew phrase is better translated 'a roaring, thunderous sound' (Niehaus, God at Sinai, pp. 247–249).

Several OT prophets received visions in which they saw God exalted as king. Micaiah saw God seated on his heavenly throne in the midst of the angelic host (1 Kgs. 22:19). In Isaiah's vision the Lord sat enthroned, surrounded by seraphim who declared his holiness (Is. 6:1–4). Ezekiel saw the 'glory of the LORD' in the form of a man seated on an exalted throne. He was fiery in appearance and surrounded by a rainbow-like aura (Ezek. 1:26–28; cf. 8:2–4). In one of Daniel's visions the 'Ancient of Days' was seated on a flaming throne surrounded by innumerable angels (Dan. 7:9–10). In each case a commissioning ceremony is a highlight of the theophanic vision. In Micaiah's vision the Lord commissions a spirit to deceive Ahab (1 Kgs. 22:20–22). Both Isaiah and Ezekiel are commissioned by God to confront their contemporaries and announce impending divine judgment (Is. 6:8–13; Ezek. 2:1–10). In Daniel's vision the 'Ancient of Days' commissions 'one like a son of man' to rule over the earth (Dan. 7:13–14).

God's theophanic self-revelation to Israel

As Israel left Egypt they were accompanied by a pillar of cloud and a pillar of fire, symbolizing God's protective presence (Exod. 13:21–22; 14:24; 33:9–10; 34:5). The Lord revealed his glory in the cloud (Exod. 16:10; 24:15), which covered the tent of meeting and filled the tabernacle (Exod. 40:34–38). Later, when the *temple was completed and the priests brought the ark into the holy place, the cloud of God's glory filled the temple, just as it had the tabernacle centuries before (1 Kgs. 8:10–12). In one of his prophetic visions of restored Jerusalem, Isaiah, in an obvious allusion to the Exodus tradition, envisaged Zion being covered by 'a cloud of smoke by day and a glow of flaming fire by night', symbolic of God's protective presence (Is. 4:5–6).

When the Israelites arrived at Sinai after leaving Egypt, the Lord descended on the mountain, revealing his presence through fire, thunder, lightning and a dense cloud. As smoke billowed up from the mountain, a trumpet-like blast sounded, causing the mountain to quake violently (Exod. 19:16–19). The Israelites heard God's voice, but saw no distinct form (Deut. 4:11–12). The Sinai theophany was God's declaration of kingship. He had defeated the Egyptian army and delivered his people from slavery; he now claimed their allegiance as he formed a covenantal relationship with them.

By demonstrating his authority over the elements of the storm, the Lord also asserted his superiority to Baal, the Canaanite storm god whom the Israelites would soon be tempted to worship. According to Canaanite myth, Baal defeated Yam, the god of the sea, and was proclaimed king over the gods. After his victory, Baal asserted his right to rule through a powerful storm theophany. But contrary to the claims of the Canaanites, it was the Lord who controlled the elements of the storm. He unleashed a thunderstorm against the Egyptians (Exod. 9:23–25) as one of his judgments on Pharaoh. At the Red Sea he demonstrated his authority over the waters of the sea (*cf.* Ps. 77:16–20), dividing them and then using them as his instrument of destruction. In response Moses declared, 'The LORD will reign for ever and ever' (Exod. 15:18). At Sinai the Lord revealed his power once more, making it clear that he, not Baal, was the true king and sovereign over the storm. As such, he possessed the power to protect Israel and to bless their crops with rain.

In Israel's early history the Lord continued to demonstrate his sovereignty over the elements of the storm and his superiority to Baal. He hurled hailstones down upon the Amorite kings at the battle of Gibeon (Josh. 10:11), used a flashflood to destroy the army of Sisera at the River Kishon (Judg. 5:20–21; *cf.* vv. 4–5) and thundered against the Philistines (1 Sam. 7:10). At Mt Carmel he defeated the prophets of Baal by hurling lightning from the sky (1 Kgs. 18:38–39). Before this God had sent a famine upon the land to punish Israel for their Baal worship. According to pagan mythology, Baal was subject to Mot, the god of death, during times of famine. At Mt Carmel the prophets of Baal were unable to resurrect their god by their frantic mourning rites, but the Lord proved that he controlled the storm and possessed the ability to bless Israel. The Lord completed his triumph by sending a torrential downpour (1 Kgs. 18:45).

Theophanic imagery in Hebrew poetry

Early Hebrew poetry depicted God as coming in the storm to conquer and judge his enemies and to deliver and protect his people. Moses pictured the Lord leading his angelic army from Sinai, the site of his theophany on the holy mountain, to superintend the blessing of Israel and lead his people to victory over their enemies (Deut. 33:2). Moses called him the one 'who rides on the heavens ... and on the clouds in his majesty' (Deut. 33:26). The Song of Deborah likewise depicts the Lord, 'the One of Sinai', as marching from the southeast in the storm to conquer Israel's enemies (Judg. 5:4–5; *cf.* Ps. 68:7–8). Hannah's song praises God for his justice and pictures him thundering against his enemies from heaven (1 Sam. 2:10). In an elaborate poetic theophany Psalm 18 depicts the Lord descending in clouds and fire as he thunders and hurls lightning bolts. Just in time, he pulls the sinking psalmist from the waters of death (Ps. 18:4–19; *cf.* 2 Sam. 22:5–20). Psalm 29 focuses on the powerful voice of the Lord which resounds in the heaven as he reveals himself through the storm. The revelation of God's power in the storm demonstrates his kingship and guarantees Israel's security and prosperity.

The OT prophets utilized theophanic imagery in describing the judgment of God. God appears in the storm and uses its elements as weapons. He marches from the southeast (Hab. 3:3, 7) in radiant splendour (Hab. 3:3–4), to do battle against his enemies. The earth and mountains shake before him (Is. 2:19, 21; 5:25; 13:13; 29:6; 63:19; 64:2; Joel 2:10; Amos 9:5; Mic. 1:3). Rain and thunder accompany his arrival (Is. 29:6; 30:30; Amos 9:6; Nah. 1:4). Habakkuk views the Lord's theophanic judgment as a 'revival' of his mighty acts in Israel's history (*cf.* 3:2), proving that the God of Sinai is alive and well and renewing the mighty deeds he performed in Israel's early history.

The incarnation as the culmination of theophanic revelation

God's theophanic self-revelation culminates in the *incarnation of Jesus Christ, God's Son. Jesus, the divine '*Word', became a man, lived among the human race and revealed God's glory (John 1:1–14; Heb. 1:3). Because he came in the role of a servant (Phil. 2:6–7), his divine majesty remained veiled for the most part, though he did allow his disciples to see his radiant splendour on one special occasion (Matt. 17:2; Mark 9:3; Luke 9:29, 32). His transfiguration was a foreshadowing of a future day when he will come in glorious, regal splendour to annihilate his enemies and establish his kingdom on earth (Matt. 24:27–30; Luke 21:27; 2 Thess. 1:7–10; Rev. 19:11–16).

Following his resurrection, Jesus appeared to his disciples on several occasions before ascending to heaven (Matt. 28:16–20; Mark 16:9–20; Luke 24:1–53; John 20:10 – 21:23; Acts 1:3–11). Even after his ascension, he continued to appear. When Stephen stood before his accusers, he 'saw the glory of God, and Jesus standing at the right hand of God' (Acts 7:55–56). Jesus revealed his presence to Saul of Tarsus through a blinding light (Acts 9:3–5).

The ascended and glorified Christ is the focal point of John's theophanic visions, recorded in the book of Revelation. Using language reminiscent of the theophanic visions of Ezekiel and Daniel, John describes Jesus as 'one like a son of man', who has a fiery appearance (Rev. 1:13–16). Like Isaiah and Ezekiel, John is given a prophetic commission (1:17–19). In a subsequent vision John sees God himself enthroned in his heavenly assembly (4:2 – 5:14; cf. 11:16). As so often in the Old Testament, elements of the storm are associated with the divine presence (4:19; cf. 11:19). Jesus, though called 'the Lion of the tribe of Judah' (5:5), appears in this vision as a lamb, whose redemptive work has given him the right to rule the earth (5:12–13). The theophanic elements of John's visions reach their climax in chapters 19 – 20, where Jesus rides forth from heaven on a white horse to do battle (19:11–16) and God, seated on a 'great white throne', decrees final judgment on anyone whose name is not found written in the book of life (20:11–15).

See also: GOD.

Bibliography

R. B. Chisholm, Jr, 'The Polemic against Baalism in Israel's Early History and Literature,' *BS* 150, 1994, pp. 267–283; J. Jeremias, *Theophanie* (Neukirchen-Vluyn, 1965); J. K. Kuntz, *The Self-Revelation of God* (Philadelphia, 1967); T. W. Mann, *Divine Presence and Guidance in Israelite Traditions* (Baltimore, 1977); J. J. Niehaus, *God at Sinai: Covenant and Theophany in the Bible and Ancient Near East* (Grand Rapids and Carlisle, 1995); M. Weinfeld, 'Divine Intervention in War in Ancient Israel and in the Ancient Near East', in H. Tadmor and M. Weinfeld (eds.), *History, Historiography and Interpretation* (Leiden, 1984), pp. 121–147.

R. B. CHISHOLM, JR

THESSALONIANS, see Part 2

TIME

Introduction

There are numerous references to time in the biblical writings, but only occasionally is there extended reflection on it. In what follows, the key biblical terms denoting time will be considered, and then the related ideas and practices. Three temptations are to be avoided: equating earlier cultural attitudes and practices with biblical teaching; overlooking the emphases of different writings in an overly systematic account; allowing present views of time to intrude on interpretation.

Key words

Theological conclusions should not be based only on the incidence of certain words. Not only is meaning more important than frequency; also the wider semantic field, not just particular terms, must be considered. However, an examination of some of the key terms associated with time may be a helpful point of departure.

Day, period

The most basic and common word for a division of time is 'day'. It can refer to the period of 'daylight' (Rom. 13:12), a twenty-four hour period (Gen. 7:4), or a period of indefinite duration, usually signified by the plural 'days' (Jer. 5:18). In combination with other terms, it can designate parts of the day, *e.g.* 'midday', or longer periods of time, *e.g.* a 'week', 'month', or even 'year'. Sometimes it specifies a date or period of time (Exod. 40:2); sometimes it designates the past (Deut. 4:32) or future (Mal. 3:17), whether immediate or distant. Apart from '*Sabbath' (Exod. 20:8–11), Hebrew does not give names to days of the week. In addition to these concrete uses of 'day', the plural sometimes designates time in general (Num. 9:22), reflecting a more abstract idea of time.

The word can also denote time defined not by its length but by the event, place or person associated with it. In this extended, metaphorical sense it is often (though not invariably) used with reference to sacred time. 'The day of the Lord' is used to signify a momentous event (Amos 5:18), *eschatological events (Zech. 12 – 14) and the return of Christ (1 Thess. 5:2–4). The expression 'the latter days' is first used of imminent personal (Job 42:12) or historical events (Num. 24:14), and is later associated with the messianic age. This age will be marked by tribulation for God's people (Dan. 10 – 11), their deliverance (Ezek. 38:14–23), the appearance of a divinely sent leader (Mic. 4:1–3), and the establishing of God's *kingdom (Is. 2:2–4). These end-time days are viewed first as a future *hope (Joel 2:28), but in the NT as partially fulfilled through the work of *Jesus (1 Pet. 1:19–21), the pouring out of the *Holy Spirit (Acts 2:17) and in the experience of the church (1 Cor. 10:11). The 'day' of Jerusalem (Ps. 137:7), of wrath (Rom. 2:5), and of Christ (Phil. 1:10) are also mentioned.

Specific, appointed time

Another group of words refers not to divisions of time but to a specified or appointed time associated with some activity. The length of time can be short (2 Chr. 29:17) or long (Ps. 71:8); sometimes the reference is to a set but unspecified duration (Neh. 2:6). The phrase 'at that time' can refer to past (Ezra 8:34) or future (Zeph. 1:12) events, or to the time at which events (such as a festival, Est. 9:27) normally (2 Sam. 11:1) or properly (Ezek. 4:10) occur. 'This day' can refer to the time of a divine appeal for action (Deut. 4:39–40). There are also references to 'seasons', both for regular events in life and occasional dramatic occurrences (Eccles. 3:1–8), including the rise and fall of kingdoms (Dan. 2:21). Occasionally a more general or abstract idea of time appears, as in the declaration that 'time and chance happen to all' (Eccles. 9:11, NIV).

The meaning of the Greek word kairos has been debated. J. Marsh and others have attempted to draw a clear distinction between kairos and chronos, the former referring to time as defined by its content, the latter to time as defined by its duration. As J. Barr demonstrates, however, while chronos often refers to a period of time (John 5:6), a considerable time (Acts 14:3), or the whole of a period of time (Acts 20:18), sometimes it denotes a point in time (Acts 7:17). Similarly, though kairos often signifies an opportune (Col. 4:5) or favourable (Acts 24:25) moment, it can also designate the present or a limited time (1 Cor. 7:5), or a period of longer duration (Eph. 2:12). So the distinction between a qualitative and a quantitative view of time cannot be established on purely linguistic grounds.

Long time, eternity

Other words mainly refer to prolonged periods of time. These may be past or future, within a person's lifetime (Exod. 21:6) or extending far beyond it (Exod. 15:18). The words can refer to God (Is. 40:28), to divine attributes (Ps. 25:6), to divine covenants with Abraham (Gen. 17:7) and David (2 Sam. 7:13), to various memorials (e.g. Josh. 4:7), to the temple (1 Kgs. 8:13), and to the priestly line of Melchizedek (Ps. 110:4). They carry the sense of an open-ended commitment, as distinct from one which may be abrogated (cf. Gen. 17:9–13). God's word (Ps. 119:152), love (Ps. 107:1) and rule (Jer. 10:10) are lasting.

Temporal terms are used also to refer to prolonged future time, to the coming messianic age (Eph. 2:7) and to eternal time (John 6:51). O. Cullmann contrasted kairos with aiōn, which is the most important Greek word referring to duration. But although aiōn never refers to a point in time, kairos sometimes designates duration (Heb. 9:9). Barr points out the danger of identifying such words with distinct theological ideas. The NT distinguishes between 'this present age' and 'the age to come' (Mark 10:30; Eph. 1:21). The *death and resurrection of Christ inaugurate a new creation, both human and cosmic. The *church lives in the tension between the two 'ages', continuing to live in the former even as, through the Spirit, it both experiences and anticipates the latter. Occasionally aiōn is used to refer to the whole of time (Ps. 90:2). Against Cullmann's argument that 'eternal' means 'endless time' rather than 'timelessness', Barr claims that the latter sense is implicit in plural (and some other) occurrences of the term.

Central ideas

God as Lord of time

*God is the author of time (Gen. 1:3–5). It is coterminous with *creation, and its instruments are servants of God (Gen. 1:16–18). In creating time, God sets in motion – and later reaffirms (Jer. 33:20–21) – a regular succession of days that will continue until the transformation of all things (Zech. 14:7). God also imprints a weekly pattern upon time, and the seventh day is 'made holy' (Gen. 2:2). There are monthly (Col. 2:16) and annual (Lev. 16:34) cycles, associated with the movement of the heavenly bodies and the remembrance of God's intervention respectively. There are also major historical-theological divisions of time, for example, from *Adam (Rom. 5:12–14), or *Abraham (Gal. 3:6–9, 17), to *Moses or the *law, from the law to Christ (Gal. 3:22–24), and from Christ's first to his second coming (1 Cor. 15:23–25). God does not reckon time only in terms of duration, but by the inner connections between events that anticipate and fulfil divine purposes. This is why to God a thousand years can seem like yesterday (Ps. 90:4) or one day (2 Pet. 3:8).

God's sovereignty over and in time extends to particular events in individuals' lives. This point is made strongly in the wisdom literature (Job 7:6; Ps. 31:15). People must not forget God and assume that they are in control of what will happen (Jas. 4:13–16); they should be aware that everything depends on God's will (1 Cor. 16:7). The prophets speak of divine acts of blessing and judgment upon nations, and of the promise (Is. 46:8–13) of salvation; in the 'fullness of time' this salvation appears (Gal. 4:4–5). It originates in what happened 'before all things' (Col. 1:15–18) but will be consummated only at the 'end of the ages' (Heb. 9:26). The time of this consummation, however, is determined by and known only to the Father (Acts 1:7).

Time as a gift

Everyday references to time are often overlooked in theological treatments of the subject, which usually focus on significant events or on eternity. Yet in the Bible theology is bound up with the ordinary. Everyday time is viewed as a gift from the Creator. The markers of time, such as the sun, moon and stars, are signs of God's goodness and generosity (Gen. 1:14–19). The cycles of time are ongoing and dependable (Gen. 8:22); through them people can revere God (Eccles. 3:14), and enjoy all aspects of life (Eccles. 3:2–8). For example, work is successful if it is done within the time parameters set by God, and sleep is a gift to those whom God loves (Ps. 127:1–2).

In the Bible time is often measured chronologically. Both the beginning and end of life are in God's hands (Job 1:21), as well as the destiny of individuals and peoples (Ps. 139:16). Compared to God's word, life is short; it is also difficult (Job 14:1–2). In the OT long life is generally regarded as a divine blessing, whereas in the NT being with Christ, whether on earth or in heaven, is more important (Phil. 1:21–24). The day will finally come when time as we know it will pass away with the cosmic bodies that mark its divisions (Is. 60:19). However, time will not end; rather it will be experienced in a different way (Rev. 21:23).

Everything has its season

Everything in life has its appropriate time: domestic (Gen. 29:7) and work (Is. 28:24–25) responsibilities; residing and travelling (Deut. 2:14); feasting and going hungry (Judg. 14:12; Ps. 37:19); menstruation (Lev. 15:25) and marriage (1 Sam. 18:19); youth (Ezek. 16:22) and old age (Job 5:26). There are times of temptation (Luke 8:13) and refreshment (Acts 3:19), distress (Nah. 1:7) and healing (Jer. 8:15), joy and adversity (Eccles. 7:14), affliction (Lam. 1:7) and salvation (Is. 49:8).

These ideas are most fully developed in the well-known statement in Ecclesiastes (Eccles. 3:2–8). For every person the major stages of life (which include experiences, responsibilities, relationships, and circumstances) have their appropriate times. But the outcome of human effort is questionable (3:9), and life is often burdensome (3:10) and enigmatic (3:11). The apostle Paul experiences the resurrection life of Christ in adversities and the perplexity that accompanies them (2 Cor. 4:7–12). Corporate worship also has its appropriate time. In the OT, certain days and festivals are set aside for weekly or seasonal acknowledgment of God by the community (Exod. 23:10–17). In the NT, it is predominantly, though not only (Acts 2:46), on 'the first day of the week' that members of the church gather to have fellowship with God and with one another (Acts 20:7).

Redeeming the time

Since the times are evil, people must reflect carefully on how to live. According to Paul, this entails *redeeming (*i.e.* buying back) time that would otherwise be spent unfruitfully. This is a call not to busyness but to a discerning use of time that gives priority to what God considers important (Eph. 5:15–17). Sometimes this will include ignoring the natural regularities God has established and giving a lower priority to family and social responsibilities (Matt. 14:23–25; Acts 20:31). It is important to understand the meaning of events, which the Jewish religious leaders failed to do when Jesus was among them (Luke 12:56), and when he was crucified (1 Cor. 2:7–8). Believers should be aware of what 'hour' it is and that their salvation is coming nearer (Rom. 13:11–12), even if they do not know at what time Jesus will return (Acts 1:6–7).

It is especially important to know the significance of 'today', for ignoring it can result in great loss (Ps. 95:7–11). Any time can be crucial to the fulfilment of God's purposes, and as Martha discovered, it is easy to miss its significance (Luke 10:38–42). 'Today' may be a historical moment (Deut. 32:48–49) in the life of an individual or group (2 Kgs. 7:9), or a daily experience (Matt. 6:11). In the context of corporate worship, the word 'today' can refer to a merging of past and present (Ps. 118:24), or present and future (Exod. 13:3–5; Matt. 26:26–29) horizons in the celebration of a divine action. Believers should exhort one another every day, as long as it is called 'today', lest they be drawn away from God and from one another (Heb. 3:13).

Conclusion

Attempts to distinguish between Hebrew and Greek views of time on the basis of the aspectual character of Hebrew tenses and the linear nature of biblical time are not defensible. Verbs can be aspectual in Greek too, and just as there are cyclical elements, *e.g.* festivals (see *Sacred meals) and other annual cycles, in the OT, so there are linear elements, *e.g.* the development of technology, among the Greeks. The Bible's approach to

time is dynamic and future-oriented, but its treatment of everyday time, with its regular responsibilities and unexpected variations, should not be overlooked.

Bibliography

R. Banks, *The Tyranny of Time* (Eugene, 1997); J. Barr, *Semantics of Biblical Language* (Oxford, 1961); *idem, Biblical Words for Time* (London, 1962); T. Boman, *Hebrew Thought Compared with Greek* (London, 1960); K. E. Brower and M. W. Elliott (eds.), *'The Reader Must Understand': Eschatology in Bible and Theology* (Leicester and Downers Grove, 1997); O. Cullmann, *Christ and Time: The Primitive Christian Conception of Time and History* (Philadelphia, 1964); S. J. De Vries, *Yesterday, Today and Tomorrow: Time and History in the Old Testament* (London, 1975); J. Marsh, *Fullness of Time* (London, 1952); J. Muilenberg, 'The biblical view of time', *HTR* 54, 1961, pp. 225–271; M. Sekine, 'Erwaegungen zur Hebraeischen Zeitauffassung', in *Congress Volume: Bonn 1962*, (Leiden 1963), pp. 66–80; N. Snaith, 'Time in the Old Testament,' in F. F. Bruce (ed.), *Promise and Fulfilment* (Edinburgh, 1963); G. Trompf, *The Idea of Historical Recurrence in Western Thought* (Berkeley, 1979); J. Wilch, *Time and Event: An Exegetical Study of 'eth in the Old Testament* (Leiden, 1969); H. W. Wolff, 'The Old Testament concept of time', in *Anthropology of the Old Testament* (London, 1974).

R. BANKS

TONGUES, see LANGUAGES

TRADITION

Definition: Scripture and tradition

The theological and technical uses of the term 'tradition' must be distinguished. Theologically, oral and written 'traditions' are distinct from a fixed canon of holy scriptures. Technically, holy scriptures also are traditions, since they are handed down by copying and translation. Some kind of tradition process is normally involved in the writing of holy scriptures; the study of this process is called 'tradition history'. The handing down of a tradition can be conservative (preserving the verbal contents) or creative (reshaping, interpreting and developing it).

Tradition in the OT

Since the concept of a closed canon of holy scriptures is found nowhere in the OT, the relationship between scripture and tradition is not discussed. There is not even a standard terminology for the handing down of tradition, but there are some indications of how traditions were passed on in OT times. Of Abraham it is said that he would 'command his sons and his house to preserve the way of the Lord' (Gen. 18:19, author's translation). In NT times it was believed that the tradition process began with *Moses; God revealed the *laws to him at Sinai and he 'passed them on' (*paredoken*) to the Israelites (Acts 6:14). According to the book of Deuteronomy Moses stressed the responsibility of fathers to instruct their sons (Deut. 32:7). The religious tradition that was passed on in families included salvation history (Exod. 10:2; 12:26-27; 13:8), the laws given through Moses (Deut. 11:18-19; Ps. 78:5-6), and general ethical teachings (*cf.* Prov. 4:3-27). The religious traditions of *Israel were developed also at the sanctuaries, at the royal courts and in prophetic circles.

The prophet-priest Samuel, residing at the sanctuary of Shiloh, 'wrote down the law of the king and placed the book before the LORD' (1 Sam. 10:25), apparently supplementing the received laws of Moses. Later, when the cult was centralized in Jerusalem, a temple-school was established, in which priests acted as scribes, preserving and interpreting the Torah, the law of Moses (*cf.* Jer. 8:8). Following the creation of a united monarchy under David and Solomon, another school was established at the royal court for the education of the princes, the royal servants and the sons of the upper classes (*cf.* 1 Kgs. 12:8). As at the Egyptian scribal schools, chronicles of kings were written (1 Kgs. 11:41; 14:29, *etc.*), and *wisdom sayings were taught, collected and written down (Prov. 25:1). The *prophets received messages from God by revelation and often delivered them to their hearers in short and memorable sayings (Heb. *meshalim*, sing. *mashal*). Jeremiah seems to have remembered his own sayings so well that he could dictate them much later to his secretary Baruch. Isaiah and other prophets gathered disciples around themselves (*cf.* Is. 8:16), and in these circles the prophetic books received their final redaction, in which written sources from the time of the prophets and the memories of their disciples were combined. Sometimes the disciples of a prophet may have creatively developed his message for a later situation under the direction of the *Holy Spirit.

Jesus and the 'traditions of the elders'

The NT has a standard term for 'tradition', *paradosis*. Jesus attacked some who kept the 'traditions of the elders' (*paradoseis tōn presbyterōn*)' for transgressing or rejecting the word of the Lord (Matt. 15:3, 6; Mark 7: 8–9, 13). Here 'tradition' is distinguished from the canon of holy scriptures. At the time of *Jesus the five books of Moses, the Torah or law of Moses, were accepted by all Jews, including Samaritans and Sadducees. These two groups did not include the prophets in their canons, but most Jews accepted the former prophets (from Joshua to Kings) and the latter prophets (from Isaiah to Malachi, excepting Daniel) as canonical (see the foreword to Ecclesiasticus, c. 180 AD) There was also a third collection of books, called 'the other Writings'; its content was still in dispute. Jesus accepted a threefold canon (Luke 24:44), including 'Moses and all the prophets' (Luke 24:27), but it is not easy to say which books he included among the 'writings'. In the early *church there was both a narrow OT canon and a wider one, which included some of the books later regarded as deuterocanonical (by the Catholic church) or apocryphal (in Protestant theology).

Jesus criticized some of his contemporaries for rejecting the commandments of the Lord in order to keep their own traditions (Mark 7:9). In 1st century Judaism, especially in Pharisaism, OT laws were adapted to new circumstances. The resulting case law was handed down, mainly in oral form. After some time the theory was formulated that Moses had received on Sinai the law in written form (the Pentateuch), but that oral commandments were passed on through the centuries by prophets, sages and rabbis. This oral law (Heb. *halakhah, i.e.* 'how one should walk') included all the case law developed from the written laws. Today in orthodox Judaism this traditional interpretation of the OT law, enshrined in the Talmudic literature, has almost the same authority as the OT itself. As in all casuistry, many of the rulings not only interpret the law, but also alter or abolish certain laws in the name of interpretation. In his hard words against Pharisees and scribes Jesus pointed out this danger. However, it is misleading to say simply that Jesus rejected 'Jewish tradition', since he created his own 'tradition', which included exegetical interpretations found in other Jewish literature.

The Jesus tradition

Jesus not only interpreted the OT in an authoritative way; he also went beyond it. This point is best illustrated by the so-called antitheses at the beginning of the Matthean Sermon on the Mount. There Jesus quotes the OT but adds his own authoritative word: 'You have heard that it was said to the men of old ... but, I say to you' (Matt. 5:21–22). When Jesus in his preaching sharpened (5:27–30) or suspended (5:31–32) OT precepts he did so in fulfilment of the law (5:17). He was entitled to do this because he was appointed by God as the Messiah whose teaching was to be heard (Mark 9:7 cf. Ps. 2:7; Is. 42:1; Deut 18:18); his heavenly Father had delivered everything (*panta moi paredothe*) to his Son, who could reveal (*apokalyptein*) it (Matt. 11:27; Luke 10:22). In this saying Jesus claimed that he had received God's ultimate revelation in the form of a 'tradition' which he could pass on to others. Jesus, full of 'wisdom and spirit' (Matt. 13:54; Luke 4:14; cf. Is. 11:1–4), proclaimed God's 'good news' (see *Gospel) at the end of the age (Luke 4:16–21; cf. Is. 61:1–2). For all those who believed in Jesus as the Messiah his sayings were of the highest authority even before his resurrection, since obedience to them would be the criterion of God's last judgment (Mark 8:38; Luke 9:26), and they would endure for eternity (Matt. 24:35).

Like the OT prophets, Jesus encapsulated his teaching in short, memorable sayings. These were characterized by their poetic form (parallelism, rhythm, rhyme, *etc.*), but also by certain introductory formulas such as 'Amen (truly), I say to you ...' Here Jesus created a new speech-form, thus hinting at the source of his authority. The Hebrew word *'amen* is normally the conclusion of a prayer. By beginning sayings with 'Amen' Jesus asserted the divine source of the message he was passing on to his hearers. When Jesus chose some disciples as messengers (Gk. *apostoloi*) to spread his message throughout Galilee, he repeated to them many of these sayings (*cf.* Matt. 10:27). As a result his apostles could instruct others (*cf.* Mark 6:30) in such a way that they heard not the opinions of the messengers, but the message of the sender (*cf.* Luke 10:16). Before his death Jesus gave special instructions to a selected group of his disciples, the twelve, who served as representatives of the new *people of God. He told them openly of what he had only implied in his preaching before the crowds, namely his Messianic identity and the atonement to be effected through his death on the cross (Mark 8:27–30). The Twelve were a living bridge of memory and tradition between the pre- and post-Easter periods.

The apostolic tradition

After Easter, when Jesus' claims were confirmed by God through his resurrection from the tomb, the words of Jesus became the foundation of a new 'tradition' which supplemented the OT. But the OT and the words of Jesus were not the only authority in the community of the new covenant (*cf.* Jer. 31:31–34). The Risen One chose some special messengers authoritatively to proclaim and to interpret his life and words. The nature of the apostles of Jesus Christ was clearly defined by Paul. Many of them had followed Jesus before Easter, but some had not, including Paul himself, who was chosen as the 'last of the apostles' (1 Cor. 15:3–8). They were specially endowed for their task by the Holy Spirit (1 Thess. 1:5–6; 1 Cor. 2:10; *cf.* John 16:13; Acts 1:8). The theological concept of apostolicity, elaborated in such passages as 1 John 1:1-4, was a logical consequence of the character of God's *revelation through the person and the history of Jesus. Jesus brought God's final revelation and authorized a number of witnesses to interpret it authoritatively. With these chosen apostles the time of revelation was finished; even some NT documents look back to it (Luke 1:1–4; Heb. 1:1–4). At the end of the apostolic period it became clear that Jesus was not only the bearer of God's ultimate revelation, but was God's last word in person, the pre-existent and eternal Son, of the same being as the Father (John 1:1–14). So it could be said: 'From his fullness we have received grace upon grace. For the law was given through Moses; grace and truth came through Jesus Christ. No one has ever seen God; the only Son, who is in the bosom of the Father, he has made him known' (John 1:16–18). Here a 'chain of tradition' is described; God gave the revelation of himself to his Son and Jesus made it known to his chosen disciples (*cf.* John 1:18 with 17:8; 19:35; 21:24).

The apostolic Jesus tradition included not only his words (1 Cor. 7:10; 9:14), but also the story of his life, interpreted in the light of OT prophecy and retold at the Lord's Supper (1 Cor. 11:23–25). Some of the apostles' basic ethical teaching was also recognized as authoritative tradition (1 Cor. 11:2; 2 Thess. 2:15; 3:6; *cf.* Acts 16:4). At an early stage salvation history was summarized in credal formulas (1 Cor. 15:3–5; Phil. 2:6–11; Rom. 1:3–4, *etc.*). Many of these developed traditions seem to be part of 'the teaching of the apostles' (Acts 2:42) from the Jerusalem church in the years between the resurrection of Jesus (30 AD) and the persecution under Agrippa I (41–44 AD). The basics of Christian belief and conduct were taught in connection with baptism (*cf.* Rom. 6:17), but also in other community gatherings (*cf.* 1 Cor. 4:14–17). Against the Corinthians, who thought they possesed higher divine wisdom through the Holy Spirit, Paul had to uphold the revelation of God in Christ by defending his apostolic authority and the received tradition of the community (1 Cor. 1 – 4; 11; 15; 2 Cor. 3 – 5). In 1 Corinthians 11:23 and 15:3 he used Jewish terminology for the 'delivering' (*paradidomai*) and 'receiving' (*paralambanein*) of a tradition, terminology found also in the Mishnah, the first official written collection of the rabbinic oral laws. This shows that with respect to their tradition the early Christians used common Jewish methods, as Jesus had done. The Pastoral Epistles stress the importance of the apostolic tradition, which they call 'a received good', Greek *parathēkē* (1 Tim. 6:20; 2 Tim. 2:12, 14), over against new teachings. According to the letter of Jude 'the faith delivered once for all to the saints' (Jude 3) is something complete and identifiable.

Tradition and canon

For Paul the ultimate revelation of God in Jesus Christ was the criterion for judging between genuine apostolic tradition and mere

human traditions, whether Jewish and religious (Gal. 1:14–16) or more philosophical (Col. 2:8). In Ephesians the church is said to be 'built upon the foundation of the apostles and prophets, Christ himself being the corner stone' (Eph. 2:20). The prophets here are either identical with the apostles or only second in rank to them (*cf.* 1 Cor. 12:28). It is impossible for the community to 'learn Christ' directly; rather they must 'hear and be taught' either through the apostles or through apostolic tradition (Eph. 4:20–21). As long as apostles were living, doctrines could be tested with reference to the apostolic consensus (*cf.* Gal. 2:2; Acts 15), but when the apostolic generation passed away, their traditions had to be put into written form (*cf.* Luke 1:1–4; John 21:20–24). In the second century the church debated where genuine apostolic tradition was to be found. They located it in two authoritative collections: thirteen letters of Paul, probably edited before the end of the first century, possibly by Luke, the companion of the apostle; and the four canonical Gospels, collected at Ephesus after the Gospel of John was edited there by his disciples. Disputes continued over some of the so-called catholic epistles and the book of Revelation, but by the end of the fourth century nearly all the churches accepted the present canon of twenty-seven NT books.

Since the Christian church has a fixed NT canon the relationship of Scripture and tradition is still a theological problem. In principle even the Catholic church accepts the canon of holy Scripture as the criterion for judging all other church traditions, but these traditions seem sometimes to override the message of the Bible. The Protestant position also has its problems, of which three may be mentioned here. 1. Is a distinction made even in Scripture between divine revelation and human tradition? Paul speaks of the unchangeable gospel (Gal. 1:6–9), but also of community customs (1 Cor. 11:16) and his personal opinion (1 Cor. 7:40). 2. Although in principle evangelicals set Scripture over all their own traditions, are not traditional interpretations of Scripture sometimes confused with its real meaning? Church history shows that Christian communities need credal formulas and basic ethical principles around which to unite, but these need a more secure biblical basis than a few proof texts quoted out of context. 3. Should some very old and widely accepted church traditions (*e.g.* the great confessions of the early ecumenical councils) be valued more highly than any individual's theological judgment, even though they are still open to evaluation against God's revelation in Christ, attested by Scripture?

See also: SCRIPTURE; THE CANON OF SCRIPTURE (both in part 1).

Bibliography

R. T. Beckwith, *The Old Testament Canon of the New Testament Church* (Grand Rapids, 1985); F. F. Bruce, *Tradition: Old and New* (Exeter, 1970); S. Byrskog, *Jesus the Only Teacher: Didactic Authority and Transmission in Ancient Israel, Ancient Judaism and the Matthean Community* (Stockholm, 1994); O. Cullmann, 'The Tradition' in A. J. B. Higgins (ed.), *The Early Church* (London, 1956), pp. 59–99; R. T. France, *Jesus and the Old Testament: His Application of Old Testament Passages to Himself and His Mission* (London, 1971); B. Gerhardsson and E. J. Sharpe, *Memory and Manuscript: Oral Tradition and Written Transmission in Rabbinic Judaism and Early Christianity* (Grand Rapids, ²1998); R. P. C. Hanson, *Tradition in the Early Church* (London, 1960); S. Kim, *The Origin of Paul's Gospel* (Tübingen and Grand Rapids, ²1984); *idem*, 'Sayings of Jesus', in *DPL*, pp. 474–492; D. A. Knight, 'Tradition history', in *ABD* 6, pp. 633–638; J. I. H. McDonald, *Kerygma and Didache: The Articulation and Structure of the Earliest Christian Message* (Cambridge, 1980); B. M. Metzger, *The Canon of the New Testament: Its Origin, Development, and Significance* (Oxford, 1988); R. Riesner, *Jesus als Lehrer: Eine Untersuchung zum Ursprung der Evangelien-Überlieferung* (Tübingen ³1988); *idem*, 'Jesus as Preacher and Teacher', in H. Wansbrough (ed.), *Jesus and the Oral Gospel Tradition*, pp. 185–210 (Sheffield, 1991); *idem*, 'Christology in the Early Jerusalem Community', *Mishkan* 24, 1996, pp. 6–17; K. Wegenast, 'Teach', in *NIDNTT* 3, pp. 759–775; D. Wenham, *Paul: Follower of Jesus or Founder of Christianity?* (Grand Rapids, 1995).

R. RIESNER

TRANSFIGURATION, see THEOPHANY
TRIALS, see TESTING
TRIBULATION, see SUFFERING

TRUTH

The English word 'truth' corresponds to *alētheia* in the NT and the LXX. This word is regularly used to translate the Hebrew *ʾemet*, a noun related to the verb *ʾāman*, meaning 'to sustain' or 'to establish'. In the English OT *ʾemet* is variously translated as 'firm', 'reliable', 'faithful', 'tested', 'true' and 'lasting'. Scholars often discuss whether there is a difference between Hebrew and Greek conceptions of truth in the Bible. However, it is probably more useful to consider the different contexts in which *ʾemet* and related words are used in the OT.

Two common translations of *ʾemet* are 'truth' and 'faithfulness'. This does not necessarily mean that each instance of the term encompasses both meanings (although faithfulness may be part of truth); rather that the term means 'truth' in some contexts and 'faithfulness' in others. Thus *God is described as consistent and trustworthy (Deut. 32:4; Ps. 31:5; Is. 65:16). He acts faithfully in accordance with his *word; he is known by the way he acts (*e.g.* Exod. 3:14), and truth is his very nature. His will cannot be altered, and his commandments are not arbitrary but have the quality of 'truth' (Neh. 9:13; Hos. 4:1).

Often God's truth is mentioned together with his *ḥesed*, his steadfast *love. In Genesis 24:27, when Eliezer meets Rebekah he praises God who, he says, 'has not forsaken his steadfast love and his faithfulness' (NRSV) to Abraham, thus implying that God has been loyal to his *covenant promises to Abraham. In Exodus 34:6, God renews his covenant with Abraham, assuring Moses that he is 'merciful and gracious, slow to anger and abounding in steadfast love and faithfulness'. This implies not only that he is worthy of complete trust but also that he is a God of integrity and uprightness; verse 7 juxtaposes the promise of loving *mercy and forgiveness for thousands and the warning of judgment and punishment for the guilty. The Psalms also draw together God's faithfulness and his steadfast love (*e.g.* 25:10; 57:3, 10; 69:13; 85:10).

God's truth and faithfulness are to be reflected in his *people's lives. So the king, who represents God as his ruler, must show faithfulness, be a champion of truth and be ready to expose whatever is unfair or false (Ps. 45:4; Zech. 7:9). He must carefully adhere to God's *law (*cf.* Prov. 29:14). Similarly, Israel must remain faithful and consistent in observing the law (1 Sam. 12:24; 1 Kgs. 2:4; 2 Kgs. 20:3).

Not only is Israel as a whole to be faithful; individuals also are to be true to God's ways and to live in accordance with his commandments. Thus in Psalm 43:3, the writer prays, 'Send out your light and your truth', which is a prayer that God will show him what is true in the face of the deceit and injustice of ungodly people (v. 1). The man of God realizes that the Lord requires 'truth in the inward being' (Ps. 51:6), which probably includes faithfulness as well as freedom from self-deception – 'may God reveal the truth of my condition'. Psalm 15:2 indicates that the person who is acceptable to God is the one who 'speaks truth from his heart', whose whole life (thoughts, words and deeds) is directed towards God's truth (vv. 3–5).

Thus truth is never merely theoretical in the OT. The God of truth reveals his ways in words and deeds, and this is also to be the practice of his people, particularly in their response to him and to their neighbours. God's law is to be delighted in (Ps. 119:142–143), but at the same time it is a lamp and a light (v. 105), it shows the true way in practice. God may be relied upon because of his faithfulness, and his word is truth in that it is real and has integrity: his sayings are consistent with his doings.

Many of these aspects of truth are taken up in the NT. Four words are used: *alētheia* (= truth, faithfulness); *alēthēs* (= true, sincere, correct, faithful, genuine); *alēthinos* (= genuine, valid, trustworthy); *alēthōs* (= truly, certainly). These words appear rarely in the Synoptic Gospels; only in Luke 4:25; 9:27; 12:44 and 21:3 are they attributed to Jesus. Elsewhere in the Synoptics they refer to Jesus' attitude to hypocrisy and inconsistency between word and deed (*e.g.* Matt. 23:2–3, 23–24; Luke 11:46). Jesus' words are consistent with his actions. For example, he proclaims the coming of the kingdom of God, and at the same time demonstrates its arrival by works of power; he proclaims God's love for the outcast, and eats with tax-collectors and sinners. Thus the concept of truthfulness

is present even when the words are absent.

But in the fourth Gospel the concept of truth is more prominent and its language more frequently used. John uses 'truth' to refer to genuineness, the opposite of falsehood, but also to the *revelation of God in *Jesus Christ, which can be understood only by disciples through faith. It is God who reveals Christ to an individual, and Christ is both the *gospel message itself and the messenger. Truth, when accepted, makes an impact on the believer's life and is never merely theoretical.

In the prologue to John's Gospel Christ is said to be 'full of grace and truth' (John 1:17). These terms are used together in the OT to speak of the way in which God relates to humankind, and refer to his favour and mercy. God's truth implies that he is trustworthy, faithful and reliable, and *gracious in dealing with his people; they can entrust themselves to him with confidence. Probably John is pointing his readers to Exodus 33 and 34 where, in response to Moses' request for God to show him his *glory, God causes his goodness to pass in front of him (33:19) and speaks of his graciousness and mercy, declaring that he 'abounds in steadfast love and faithfulness' (Exod. 34:6). The *incarnation of the Logos is compared with God's revelation to Moses on Sinai (John 1:17–18); in Christ, people can see God.

Thus for John, the Father is the truth. Jesus teaches only what the Father has given to him (John 3:33; 8:40; 18:37), and the Father is true (John 7:28; 8:26; 17:3). To understand his truth, it is necessary to have faith in Jesus as the one who has come down from heaven and is the way to God (John 14:6). To *worship the Father in truth, it is necessary to perceive him as he is revealed in Christ (John 4:23–24). To perceive truth as opposed to falsehood, *light as opposed to darkness, one need only look to God the Father (John 5:24; 8:31–32, 42–47).

Jesus himself can reveal truth because he has been commissioned and sent into the world by God (John 3:17; 5:30, 36; 6:29; 8:26). He has authority because God has sent him and told him what to speak. But John goes further. Jesus testifies to the Father, who in turn testifies to the Son (John 8:18–19), and they are one (John 10:30); indeed, to know one is to know the other (John 14:9).

So Jesus can say that he too is the truth (John 14:6), because of what he is and what he does (John 8:40). Jesus reveals divine truth in the world.

God's saving plan, foreshadowed in the history of Israel, has now been fulfilled in the coming of Christ. Thus he is the 'true light' (John 1:9), the 'true vine' (John 15:1, referring to Jer. 2:21) which bears fruit (unlike Israel which was like an unproductive vine), and the 'true bread from heaven' (John 6:32), which will not perish like the bread in the wilderness, but which will give eternal *life to those who partake of him (John 6:50–58).

The *Holy Spirit is called the 'Spirit of truth' (John 14:17; 15:26; 16:13; cf. 1 John 4:6; 5:6–7). He, like Jesus, is sent from the Father (John 15:26). He will continue the earthly work and mission of Jesus (14:16–17; 16:8–11, 14); he will lead the disciples into all the truth by speaking what he hears from the Father and the Son (John 16:13), and by acting as a Paraclete, an Advocate or Helper, who will be with them for ever, teach them everything and expose falsehood (John 14:16, 26). In effect, he will advance God's cause and undermine and judge all counterfeit claims to truth (16:5–11).

The Fourth Gospel also emphasizes 'doing the truth'. Jesus came into the world to testify to the truth and those who belong to the truth listen to him (John 18:37). They are sanctified by the truth (see *Holiness) and set apart from the world (17:15–19); they are in the light and stand in opposition to darkness and the father of lies (John 8:44). The fact that they have believed and come to the light means that they do what is true (John 3:21). They continue in Jesus' teaching, which is truth, and are set free by it (John 8:31–32). Truth is an indispensable part of both Christian faith and Christian living, leading disciples to obey all that Jesus has taught them (John 14:15, 23; 15:10, 14). 1 John 1:6–7 also brings together the ideas of walking in the light and truth as opposed to walking in darkness and falsehood. Profession and practice must cohere, otherwise 'we do not live according to the truth'.

Paul also draws on the OT view of truth, particularly when he speaks of God. In Romans 3:1–7, he seems to have the *meṯ of God in mind: he uses God's 'faithfulness' in v. 3 and his truthfulness in v. 7 almost as

synonyms, and he describes God as being 'true' (v. 4). In 1 Thessalonians 1:9 he contrasts the 'true' God with unreal idols. Romans 15:8 refers to Christ as the 'servant of the circumcised on behalf of the truth of God', thereby testifying to God's truthfulness and faithfulness.

The equation of 'truth' with the gospel is a usage distinctive to the Pauline corpus, and is particularly prominent in the Pastorals. In Galatians 2:5, Paul indicates that the key issue in his argument with those who oppose his message is 'the truth of the gospel'. For Paul, to weaken or undermine the gospel is to weaken or undermine the truth, and vice versa. To give in to his opponents is to deny the truth and compromise his converts' *salvation. Thus in Galatians 5:7, 'the truth' refers to the gospel: 'Who prevented you from obeying the truth?' Paul also speaks of 'the word of the truth, the gospel' (Col. 1:5) and 'the word of truth, the gospel of your salvation' (Eph. 1:13).

Similarly, in the Pastorals, to become a believer is 'to come to the knowledge of the truth' (1 Tim. 2:4; 2 Tim. 3:7), the revealed truth of the gospel message. But certain people will 'turn away from listening to the truth and wander away to myths' (2 Tim. 4:3–4); these are people who have a fixation for controversy, disputes about words 'and wrangling among those who are ... bereft of the truth' (1 Tim. 6:5). Thus truth in the Pastorals is the content of Christian revelation, a body of beliefs of which the church is the guardian. Timothy is to guard the truth, the 'good treasure', which the Holy Spirit has entrusted to him (2 Tim. 1:14). He is rightly to 'explain the word of truth' (2 Tim. 2:15), the content of the Christian message, which may be summarized in verses 11–13. Paul tells Titus that 'the knowledge of the truth' leads to godliness (Titus 1:1).

Paul uses 'truth' in a broader sense in Romans 1 and 2 to signify God's revelation of his will through the law and through *creation. Thus people 'by their wickedness suppress the truth' (Rom. 1:18) and exchange the truth about God for a lie (Rom. 1:25). There will be 'wrath and fury' for those who do not obey the truth (Rom. 2:8). However, the law is 'the embodiment of knowledge and truth' (Rom. 2:20). Truth here includes more than just the gospel. People will be judged because they reject the truth about God as creator and judge. Gentiles have deliberately suppressed the truth about God and his claims which is revealed in creation: 'his eternal power and divine nature ... have been understood and seen through the things he has made' (Rom. 1:20).

Paul believes that truth has the power to change people as they obey Christ's commands. God and his truth expose lies (Rom. 3:4). A commitment to and love for the truth can lead to salvation (2 Thess. 2:10). Speaking the truth in love leads to people's growing in Christ in all things (Eph. 4:15). Being taught the truth as it is in Jesus leads to their being created in God's likeness 'in true *righteousness and holiness' and turning away from deceitful desires (Eph. 4:21–24). Truth is demanded as part of the believer's new life in union with Christ (1 Cor. 5:8). Love and truth are inseparable; love rejoices at the truth (1 Cor. 13:6). The 'belt of truth' is part of the Christian's armour (Eph. 6:14). Thus for Paul truth has a number of facets, and he emphasizes God's truth in the transformation of people's lives through the gospel.

Outside Paul and John's Gospel, the term 'truth' appears infrequently, except in the Johannine epistles. Here the usage is similar to that in the fourth Gospel, with particular emphasis on the behaviour of the believer (see, e.g., 1 John 1:6, 8; 3:18; 4:6); 1 John 2:4 indicates the importance of behaviour's being rooted in divine revelation.

Throughout Scripture 'truth' refers to the character of God, his dealings with his people, and the way in which they are to deal with others. The NT focuses on the truth as it is found in Jesus Christ and his gospel, and on its transforming power in people's lives. The idea that knowledge of truth is possible only through divine revelation is central to the whole Bible.

Bibliography

R. Bultmann, 'aletheia' in TDNT 1, pp. 232–251; L. Morris, The Gospel according to John, NICNT (Grand Rapids, 1971); R. Nicole, 'The biblical concept of truth' in D. A. Carson and J. D. Woodbridge (eds.), Scripture and Truth, (Leicester, 1983), pp. 287–298; D. J. Theron, 'Alētheia in the Pauline Corpus', EvQ 26, 1954, pp. 3–18; A. Thiselton in NIDNTT 3, pp. 874–902.

P. D. WOODBRIDGE

UNCLEAN SPIRITS, see SPIRITUAL POWERS
UNCLEAN, see HOLINESS
UNDERSTANDING, see WISDOM
UNITY AND DIVERSITY OF SCRIPTURE, see Part 1

VANITY

Our English word 'vanity' embraces a wide semantic range; it may carry connotations of frustration, futility, unreality, insubstantiality, emptiness and vainglory. Such concepts are distributed far more widely throughout the Bible than a search for the equivalent Hebrew and Greek words might lead us to believe. The whole of biblical salvation history, from creation to the ultimate consummation of all things, illustrates the tension which arises between the wilful desires of human folly and the benevolent purposes of a loving God.

The earliest biblical example of this frustration is the divine curse (see *Blessing/curse) on the ground (Gen. 3:17–19), which resulted from the attempt of disobedient humanity to become autonomous, like God. The mutual harmony between God, humanity and the created order was disrupted, and working the land became toilsome and burdensome. Tension was experienced at the national as well as the individual level; the curses of Deuteronomy 28:15–68 show how the disobedient people of Israel would be frustrated by Yahweh in all their activities: 'You will build a house, but you will not live in it. You will plant a vineyard but you will not even begin to enjoy its fruit' (Deut. 28:30, NIV);. 'You who were as numerous as the stars of the sky will be left but few in number because you did not obey the LORD your God' (Deut. 28:62). Here again, we have the apparent frustration, due to the people's disobedience, of God's unconditional promises to Abraham. Partial fulfilment implies partial non-fulfilment; it generates expectations of a more profound fulfilment beyond the immediate future.

Part of Israel's disobedience was their refusal to trust their covenant God, Yahweh. Human initiatives to make the future secure always seemed an easier option than trusting the invisible yet living God. When Israel was under military pressure from hostile neighbours, they were tempted to form alliances to achieve some short-term advantage. Hezekiah was told that Egyptian help against the Assyrians was vanity (Heb. *hebel)* (Is. 30:7). In spite of prophetic assurances, the urge to trust the visible rather than the invisible led to disaster and futility.

Israel's desertion to the worship of lifeless idols and false gods is another example of futility, vanity and frustration. Pagan *idolatry was always manipulative and self-serving. The worshipper tended to become like the object of worship. 'They followed after *hebel,* and became *hebel* themselves' (Jer. 2:5, author's rendering). The futility/vanity of this is that much effort is spent for no result.

The pain of incomprehension, and the inconsolable longing for a vindication that seems an unattainable dream, is illustrated in Job's outcry: 'So I have been allotted months of futility, and nights of misery have been assigned to me' (Job 7:3). This incomprehension of life's injustices finds its *locus classicus* in the book of *Ecclesiastes. The phrase traditionally translated as 'Vanity of vanities' (AV) occurs in Ecclesiastes 1:2 and 12:8, and acts as an inclusio. The Hebrew word used here, *hebel,* occurs some thirty times in the book, and some twenty-four times in the rest of the OT. In its physical sense, it refers to a puff of air, or a vapour. Isaiah, referring to idols, says, 'The wind will carry all of them off, a mere breath will blow them away' (Is. 57:13). Job complains to his friends, 'Leave me alone for my days are but a *hebel'* (Job 7:16, author's rendering). In Ecclesiastes, we are faced with a number of difficulties in interpreting the *hebel* concept. Is the author orthodox or heterodox? Is he setting up a straw person only to knock it down again? Is he quoting popular sayings and then modifying them? Is he debating with himself? Is he a secular cynic, barely a believer? Disagreement over these matters leads to a wide variety of interpretative glosses for the *hebel* concept: vanity, meaningless, irrational, absurd, illogical, transitory, ephemeral, illusory, incomprehensible. But we should be careful not to import our 20th-century existentialism and nihilism into the biblical text. These were not options among the world views available to Qoheleth, the author of Ecclesiastes. Absurdity and meaninglessness at the heart of the universe are incompatible with biblical theism. Nevertheless, much of life is incomprehensible from our limited perspectives. But our inability to understand ought not to lead us to despair. Learning to live with ignorance and hiddenness is part of life in this temporal world order. Even in the light of the gospel, we still see as through puzzling reflections in a mirror (see 1 Cor. 13:12, JBP).

In the earliest days after the fall, the frustration of the *created order is typified in the proper name of Abel (Heb. *hebel),* who was murdered by his brother. The apostle Paul writes of the continuing frustration of the created order in Romans 8:20. (The Gk. word he uses is *matiotes,* the standard LXX translation of the Heb. *hebel.*) 'The creation was subjected to frustration, not by its own choice, but by the will of the one who subjected it in hope.' There is a divine *hope that looks beyond the divine curse. The bodily resurrection of Jesus is the firstfruits of a new world-order, new heavens and a new earth where death and decay have no place. Nevertheless, as Paul says, 'The whole creation has been groaning ... and we ourselves groan inwardly as we wait eagerly for our adoption as sons' (Rom. 8:22–23). The groaning of creation is not in vain; this is the Christian hope.

Bibliography

J. L. Crenshaw, *Ecclesiastes,* OTL (London, 1988); M. V. Fox, *A Time to Tear Down and a Time to Build Up: A Rereading of Ecclesiastes* (Grand Rapids and Cambridge, 1999); R. E. Murphy, *Ecclesiastes,* WBC (Waco, 1992); G. Ogden, *Qoheleth* (Sheffield, 1987); R. N. Whybray, *Ecclesiastes,* NCB (Grand Rapids and London, 1989).

T. D. GLEDHILL

VICTORY

Introduction

One simple assertion captures the entire range of biblical teaching on 'victory': victory ultimately belongs to the Lord, and is entirely within his gift. As the concept of 'victory' undergoes a significant shift in meaning as the message of the Bible unfolds, this central contention remains constant.

The victory of God in the OT

From the time of the *Exodus, Israel's

primary concern in facing military aggression was their attitude to Yahweh, rather than the threat of their enemies. When Israel sought Yahweh and obeyed, Yahweh engineered victory on their behalf (see *e.g.* Exod. 14:14; 1 Sam. 17:47, in contrast to Deut. 1:41–46; Josh. 7:1–12). Some of the high points of the national experience of pre-monarchical and early monarchical Israel are marked by the ascription of victory in battle to Yahweh alone (see the victory songs of Moses and Miriam in Exod. 15 and Deborah and Barak in Judg. 5). On the other hand, national failure is always preceded by an assumption that Israel's fate lies in its own hands (see *e.g.* Deut. 1:42–46). Israel sometimes praised its leaders rather than Yahweh for success in battle (see *e.g.* Judg. 8:22; even 1 Sam. 18:7; 21:12; 29:5); this praise played a major part in the supplanting of Yahweh's rule over his people by their longing for a human king (1 Sam. 8; 12).

As the OT progresses, however, it becomes clear that Israel is intrinsically disobedient. Victory in battle for God's people becomes an infrequent experience, and eventually both Israel and *Judah are crushed by powerful oppressors, leading to annihilation on the one hand and *exile on the other. This shift in national fortunes is matched by a shift in emphasis when speaking of the victory of Yahweh, particularly in the prophetic literature. National defeat may be a reality for Israel, but it is repeatedly asserted that the fate of the *nations is also settled on the basis of their guilt (Ezek. 25:15–17; Jer. 30:16; Nah. 3:11, 16). In addition, more appeals petition Yahweh to act, on account not of Israel's obedience, but of his own mercy, and in order to uphold the honour of his reputation (see *e.g.* Ps. 74; Is. 63:18; Ezek. 39:27).

Israel's naïve self-confidence may have been shattered, but confidence that victory still belonged to Yahweh was reflected also in two other strands of thought. The 'Zion theology' of some of the psalms claimed that Yahweh had conquered the cosmological forces of chaos (see *e.g.* Pss. 46; 74; 76). In the prophetic literature, the focus fell not on a decisive victory in the past, but on the coming decisive demonstration of the victory of God in the future. 'The day of Yahweh' plays an increasingly important role in prophetic literature, finding its fullest expression in the book of Joel (see Joel 1:15; 2:1, 11, 31; 3:14; and also Amos 5:18, 20; Zeph. 1:7; 2:2; 3:8, 14–16; Is. 13:6–13; 19:21; 22:12; 61:2; Jer. 25:33; 46:10; 50:31; Lam 1:12; Ezek. 13:5; 30:2–3; 39:8; Zech. 2:11; 9:16; 14:3, 7, 9, 20–21; Mal. 4: 1–3, 5). The vindication of (faithful) Israel in the future depends solely on the coming *eschatological demonstration of the ultimate victory of Yahweh.

The victory of God and the cross

In the NT, the victory of God is demonstrated supremely in the death and resurrection of *Jesus Christ. In Luke 11:14–22, Jesus describes his own ministry in terms of victory over the forces of *evil (*cf.* John 16:33, where Jesus overcomes 'the world'). In Matthew 12:20 an explicit link is made between the victory of God in the OT and the victory to be achieved by Jesus, in a quotation from the servant song of Isaiah 42. The NT language of *salvation (*sōzō, sōtēria*) draws heavily on the OT idea of the victory of Yahweh.

It is, however, supremely in the death, resurrection and ascension of Jesus Christ that this victory is achieved and demonstrated. In one sense this victory is achieved over God's personal adversary, the devil; in another the impersonal enemies of *sin and *death, resulting from human rebellion, are the defeated foes. Hence, in Colossians 2:13–15, Paul writes, 'He forgave us all our sins, having cancelled the written code, with its regulations, that was against us and that stood opposed to us; he took it away, nailing it to the cross. And having disarmed the powers and authorities, he made a public spectacle of them, triumphing over them by the cross' (NIV; see also Heb. 2:14–15). Similarly in 1 Corinthians 15:54–59, the victory achieved by Christ is said to free us from the power of the *law, sin and death. The function of the resurrection/ascension is to demonstrate this triumph (see *e.g.* Rom. 1:4; 4:25; 8:31–34; Eph. 1:20; Phil. 2:9–11; 2 Tim. 1:10).

The NT asserts on the one hand that God's victory has already been decisively achieved, and on the other, that the 'day of the Lord' has yet to come (see *e.g.* 1 Cor. 1:8; 5:5; Phil. 1:6, 10; 2:16; 2 Thess. 2:2). Eschatological victory has been accomplished, but has yet to celebrated or declared in a way which none can deny. The book of Revelation develops this idea in the most thoroughgoing way, making clear that whilst evil will have some temporary victories (see Rev. 6:2; 11:7; 13:7), the final victory has already been won by the *Lamb (3:21; 5:5; 12:11) and will be finally realized in the new heaven and earth (21:7, cf. Heb. 9:28). In the meantime those who are in Christ can participate in the victory that has already been won (see e.g. 1 John 2:13–14; 5:4–5). The final resolution may not yet have happened, but Paul can still affirm that we cannot ultimately lose, for we are 'more than conquerors' (Rom. 8:37).

Bibliography

B. Baloian 'Animosity', in NIDOTTE 4, pp. 385–391; O. Bauernfeind, 'nikaō', in TDNT 4, pp. 942–945; M. C. Lind, Yahweh Is a Warrior (Scottdale, 1980); J. A. Motyer in NBD, [3]1996, p. 1224; J. T. Strong, 'Zion Theology', in NIDOTTE 4, pp. 1314–1321.

J. G. MILLAR

VIOLENCE

The Bible begins with the foundational premise that the fallen world, and *humanity in particular, is violent. The primeval human history that unfolds east of Eden begins with fratricide and is characterized by the vengeful cry of Lamech, who boasts of committing retribution against those who commit violence against him. An entire episode of human history is sealed with the narrator's judgment that 'the earth was filled with violence' (Gen. 6:11, NRSV).

The biblical logic of *redemption, viewed through the canonical lens of the *incarnation and the cross (see *Atonement), allows no other course for its plot line than to run the gauntlet of human violence. But the outcome is a divine and dramatic resolution of violence, and the world-transforming power of the *gospel.

Violence and the story of Israel

Against the backdrop of the violence of peoples and nations, *Israel emerges as a finely articulated symbol of humanity enmeshed in a violent world. The story of Israel begins with the patriarch Abraham and his family as a fragile minority living at the mercy of a pharaoh of Egypt (Gen. 12:10–13) or an Abimelech of Gerar (Gen. 20:1–18). This vulnerable figure of Abraham is set in tension with an episode (foreshadowing Israel's conquest of the land) in which Abraham with his 318 trained men engages in violence as, with *God's aid (Gen. 14:20), he pursues and routs a coalition of Canaanite kings (Gen. 14).

But the status of Israel as the least and last among peoples is epitomized in their subjection to slavery in Egypt. God's conquest of the Egyptian army in the Exodus event shapes an archetypal image of *salvation in the Bible. It is a portrait of divine and redemptive violence in which God shows himself to be a divine warrior, superior to the powerful gods of Egypt (Exod. 15) and overthrowing the proud and mighty on behalf of the weak and the oppressed. Yet the Genesis story of Israel's descent into Egypt is fraught with violence within the patriarchal family (e.g. Gen. 37:12–36; cf. also Gen. 38; 49:5).

The law given at Sinai and expounded in Deuteronomy restrains the violence of murder or rape, but it also sanctions the violence of punishment for sins, the violence of Yahweh's wars and the substitutionary violence of animal *sacrifice. The law, however, cannot put an end to Israel's complicity in human violence. Murder and sexual violence, for example, do not cease in Israel but multiply. At times the text of the OT surges with violence, even including unspeakable violence within Israel (e.g. 2 Kgs. 6:28–29; Ezek. 5:10; Lam. 2:20; Judg. 19:22–30). These 'texts of terror' and the story of violence in Israel more generally are aptly summed up in the Pauline irony: 'When the law came, sin multiplied' (Rom. 5:20).

Perhaps the most obvious and enigmatic category of violence in the OT is the so-called holy warfare of Yahweh and Israel. In their ideal form these battles of conquest are Yahweh's battles by which he drives out the Canaanites from the land of Israel's inheritance (Deut. 7:1–2). Israel is to be the sanctified instrument of Yahweh's action. But Yahweh's command for Israel totally to annihilate the Canaanites (Deut. 7:2, 16; 20:16–17), killing not only male warriors but also women and children, presents an ethical dilemma. How can this command be reconciled with God's *love, *mercy and justice (see *Righteousness, justice and justification)? The issue is not easily resolved, but several considerations must be kept in view:

1. Yahweh is the creator and sovereign

God whose rule extends over all nations (*cf.* Deut. 7:6). Divine warfare is a work of violence by which he uncompromisingly enforces his sovereignty (see W. Brueggemann, *Theology of the Old Testament*, pp. 381–382) and ultimately brings about the redemption of his wayward creation.

2. In Genesis 15:12–21 God promises to give Abraham's descendants the land, but not until the fourth generation, 'for the sin of the Amorites has not yet reached its full measure' (Gen. 15:16, NIV). The conquest of the Canaanites is a divine *judgment upon their sin (Lev. 18:24–28), a sort of proleptic intrusion of the *eschatological judgment. Divine mercy is extended in the 'not yet' which gives time for them to repent. But ultimately these nations harden their hearts against the divine will and wage war against Israel (*cf.* Josh. 11:20).

3. Israel is God's chosen means of redeeming the nations, and it is God's design that when Israel has grown into a nation, it will be given a land, a 'garden' in the created order in which to fulfil its role as a 'new Adam'. The creator God allots territorial space to each nation (Deut. 32:8), including Israel, and in his sovereignty he displaces nations.

4. Israel must be delivered and preserved from *idolatry in order to serve the one living and true God (Exod. 20:3). The gods of Canaan are inextricably linked with the peoples of the land and with their violence; the putative claim of these peoples on the territory is longstanding. The Promised Land must be purified if God's holy people are to dwell within it, and idolatrous temptations must be removed (Deut. 20:18). Israel's temple and land are to be a sacred space at the centre of the world of nations.

5. These wars are primarily Yahweh's wars (Deut. 7:1–2), and the 'ban' (*ḥērem*) is, in a sense, an offering to him. It is sanctioned and redemptive violence to be carried out by sanctified warriors (Deut. 23:9–10; 1 Sam. 21:5). Unfortunately, the purity of the warfare is in certain memorable instances polluted by Israel's sinfulness, and it may be argued that a haze of ambiguity obscures all the battle stories. Israel's record in warfare is flawed (*e.g.* Num. 14:39–45; Josh. 7).

Yahweh's powerful hand delivers Israel from the oppressive violence of Egypt and gives the nation a land that, for the book of Joshua, symbolizes '*rest' from warfare (Josh.

1:13, 15; 11:23; 14:15; 21:44; 22:4; 23:1). But this deliverance from violence is short-lived. The book of Judges unfolds a violent serial epic. After the death of Joshua, Israel is still warring against the Canaanites (Judg. 1:1–3), and an assortment of battles and heroic engagements ensues. The judges of Israel enact a tangled story of obedience and disobedience, punctuated by shocking episodes of violence. The violence that increased east of Eden (Gen. 4 – 6) finds its corollary in an Israel in which there is no king, and 'everyone did as he saw fit' (Judg. 21:25, NIV).

The establishment of Israelite kingship is accompanied by new episodes of violence, some sanctioned and some not. The ideal ancient Near Eastern king was conceived as a great warrior who maintained sovereignty by the threat of the sword. Israel's ideal king was one who mirrored the heavenly kingship of Yahweh, shepherding his people and yet defending them against predatory enemies. But Saul's failed kingship includes violence not sanctioned by the covenant. And while David has slain his ten thousands to Saul's thousands (1 Sam. 18:7–8; 21:11; 29:5), David is generally observant of the covenantal restrictions on violence; he spares the life of Saul (1 Sam. 24, 26) and observes the purity regulations of warfare (1 Sam. 21:4–5; but *cf.* 2 Sam. 8:2; 1 Kgs. 2:8–9). The ensuing story of Israel's and Judah's kings is strewn with scenes of violence that defy the bounds of Yahweh's covenant, the most extreme instances being a product of pagan idolatry (*e.g.* that of Ahab and Jezebel). The story of unsanctioned violence in Israel under the kings is, by the logic of the Deuteronomic covenant, a contributing factor in the disaster of Israel's judgment and *exile.

The pre-exilic prophets warn of the dire consequences of violence. Amos declaims his oracles against nations, denouncing their violence, and then turns his attention to Israel and sketches vivid scenes of judgment on the inhabitants of Samaria who 'oppress the poor and crush the needy' (Amos 4:1, NIV). This prophetic theme makes its full impact in the metaphor of reversed holy warfare so aptly summed up in Jeremiah's warning to Zedekiah: Yahweh is about 'to turn against you the weapons of war that are in your hands, which you are using to fight the king of Babylon ... I myself will fight against you with an outstretched hand and a mighty arm in anger and fury and great wrath' (Jer. 21:4–5, NIV; *cf.* Lam. 2:5).

Isaiah articulates a new and powerful vision of redemption in which violence is absorbed and transformed. In Isaiah 52 – 53 the heralding of Israel's divine warrior returning to bring Zion's deliverance (Is. 52:7–12), suddenly gives way to a description of a suffering servant of Yahweh (Is. 52:13 – 53:12). This representative servant figure, who has 'done no violence' (Is. 53:9), suffers violence on behalf of Israel, even to the extent of being 'stricken by God, smitten by him, and afflicted' (Is. 53:4). His triumph and exaltation (framing the passage in Is. 52:13 and 53:12) is not a consequence of violent warfare but of his pouring out his life unto death (Is. 53:12).

The prophets also speak repeatedly of a 'day of the Lord' (or 'that day') in which Yahweh will act decisively to conquer *evil and to establish his redemptive purposes for Israel. From the prophets' perspective there will be many intermediate days of the Lord, whether against Babylon (Is. 13:1–8), Egypt (Jer. 46:1–10) or Edom (Obad. 8, 11, 15), for the term seems to be a future projection of the historical experience of Yahweh's wars, the divine warrior's day of conquest over his enemies. But there will be a decisive and cosmic 'day of the Lord' in which Yahweh will finally execute judgment against the nations of the earth and deliver his people (*e.g.* Is. 13:9–13). The biblical understanding of God's ultimate redemption of Israel and of the world assumes a violent divine action. But on the far side of the day of the Lord, the ultimate prophetic vision of the future is epitomized as a *peaceable *kingdom in which families, nations and creation are at rest, evil is vanquished and violence is no more (*e.g.* Is. 2:4; 11:6–9; 41:18–19; 51:3; 65:25; Mic. 4:3–4).

In the Psalms the voice of Israel speaks, reflecting the nation's historical experience and protesting against injustice and violence. The strong language of imprecation against Babylon in Psalm 137:8–9 ('happy is he who repays you ... who seizes your infants and dashes them against the rocks', NIV) is the cry of Israel in the despair of exile, committing to Yahweh its strongest desire for revenge and trusting him to do what is right. Psalms such as this speak the language of Israel's heart,

passionate for God's honour and glory, immersed in the pain, ambiguities and turmoil of history, and offering them all to God.

Violence in NT perspective

The NT introduces a new and transforming perspective on violence. It is most pointedly expressed in Jesus' words: 'You have heard that it was said, "Love your neighbour and hate your enemy." But I tell you: Love your enemies and pray for those who persecute you' (Matt. 5:43–44, NIV). The commandment to love one's neighbour is found in Leviticus 19:18, but the commandment to hate one's enemy is not expressed in so many words within the OT. It may be a summary statement of passages such as Psalm 139:21–22 and the Deuteronomic instructions regarding warfare, or simply a reference to conventional thinking. But in loving their enemies, Jesus' disciples will show themselves to be children of their Father in heaven (Matt. 5:45). Jesus refers to the same God who ordered Israel to annihilate the nations of Canaan, but now God and his true 'Israel' are to be identified by love for the enemy. We must conclude that Jesus does not see the OT record as standing in irreconcilable contradiction to his command. Even the most clearly expressed OT instances of divinely ordained violence against enemies are to be viewed from the vantage point of Jesus' expression of the divine will.

Jesus' submission to the violence of the cross demonstrates God's will to absorb in the Son the wrath (see *Anger) that is due to Israel and the world. Jesus' prayer to the Father from the cross, 'forgive them, for they do not know what they are doing' (Luke 23:34; *cf.* Acts 7:60), though not found in all manuscripts, memorably expresses the commandment to love one's enemies even as they perpetrate their violence. The cross embodies Jesus' *victory over violence and is the climax of the biblical story of violence.

The theme of loving one's enemy is reiterated by Paul in Romans 12:17–21. Revenge is strictly ruled out, and believers are to 'leave room for God's wrath, for it is written: "It is mine to avenge; I will repay," says the Lord' (Rom. 12:19). God's love demands human imitation; it is the foundation of the 'law of Christ' (Gal. 6:2; *cf.* 5:6, 14; Jas. 2:8). But God's wrath does not demand imitation, which is fraught with pitfalls and failure. As Paul points out, God's own action towards us, 'when we were God's enemies', was not wrathful vengeance but reconciliation 'through the death of his Son' (Rom. 5:10). And Paul habitually transposes the imagery of warfare into the context of spiritual warfare (*e.g.* Rom. 6:13; 2 Cor. 10:3–6; Eph. 6:10–17). James warns those who would take the course of violence: 'the anger of man does not work the righteousness of God' (Jas. 1:20, RSV; *cf.* 2:11–13). And Hebrews commends those who, without anger or retaliation, have suffered violence for the sake of the gospel (Heb. 10:32–34).

The righteousness of God will be expressed further in eschatological judgment. Jesus employs imagery of violent judgment (*e.g.* Hades, fire of hell, eternal punishment) to speak of the end of those who ultimately resist God's will. Paul and other apostles follow this pattern in speaking of the violent destruction that will accompany the 'coming wrath' (1 Thess. 1:10) when Jesus the divine warrior will come in 'blazing fire' and punish his enemies with 'everlasting destruction' (2 Thess. 1:6–10; 2:1–12). 2 Peter 3:10–13 speaks of a violent, fiery judgment that will envelop the cosmos as a precursor to the emergence of a new heaven and earth. And the book of Revelation depicts manifold violent judgments and scenes of divine warfare (Rev. 19:11–21; 20:7–10) that precede the advent of the new creation (Rev. 21). But this apocalyptic violence takes place according to the sovereign will of God, the all-wise creator and redeemer. The people of God are followers of the slain Lamb (Rev. 5:5–6, 9–10), a veritable army 144,000 strong, sanctified for holy warfare like Israel's warriors of old (Rev. 14:4). Their strategy is not violence but faithful witness to the Lamb, even to the point of *suffering the violence of martyrdom.

The twentieth century was probably the most violent in human history. All too frequently and sadly, violence in the West has been undergirded by an appeal to biblical texts. Consequently serious charges have been laid against the Bible, its interpreters and Christianity. The irony, however, is that this moral aversion to violence and concern for its victims owes much if not all of its impetus to the influence of the Bible, and particularly the cross of Christ. As René Girard has argued, it is the gospel of Christ crucified that subverts the world's ideologies of violence. Any consideration of the question of divine and human violence in the Bible must begin by admitting that the issue resists easy resolution, for violence (in its many dimensions) involves a seemingly impenetrable mystery. But extracting biblical texts of violence from their canonical context, particularly from their climactic resolution in the NT, leads to a serious misreading of these texts and of the biblical story as a whole.

See also: SIN; WARFARE.

Bibliography

G. Bailie, *Violence Unveiled: Humanity at the Crossroads* (New York, 1995); W. Brueggemann, *Revelation and Violence: A Study in Contextualization* (Milwaukee, 1986); *idem, Theology of the Old Testament: Testimony, Dispute, Advocacy* (Minneapolis, 1997); P. C. Craigie, *The Problem of War in the Old Testament* (Grand Rapids, 1978); R. Girard, *The Girard Reader*, ed. J. G. Williams (New York, 1996); R. B. Hays, *The Moral Vision of the New Testament* (San Francisco and Edinburgh, 1996, 1997); T. Longman III and D. G. Reid, *God Is a Warrior* (Grand Rapids and Carlisle, 1995); S. Niditch, *War in the Hebrew Bible: A Study in the Ethics of Violence* (New York, 1993); P. Trible, *Texts of Terror: Literary-Feminist Readings of Biblical Narratives* (Minneapolis, 1984); R. Weems, *Battered Love: Marriage, Sex, and Violence in the Hebrew Prophets* (Minneapolis, 1995); J. H. Yoder, *The Politics of Jesus* (Grand Rapids and Carlisle, [2]1994).

D. G. REID

WAGES, see REWARD

WARFARE

Introduction

*Violence, conflict and warfare are found throughout the Bible. From Genesis 3 (the story of the fall) to Revelation 20, we read of strife and fighting. Only the first two chapters of the Bible (creation) and the last two (re-creation) fall outside the long period of human conflict.

But the conflict is more than human. *God

himself enters history and takes the role of a warrior, fighting both human and spiritual enemies.

Warfare in the Bible is more than a sociological category, describing historical events; it is an important and pervasive theological theme. Furthermore, as we will see, the wars of the Bible are more than isolated events; they provide a unified but varied story as we proceed from Genesis to Revelation. However, rather than moving book by book through the Bible, we will explore this important theme first by describing the theology of OT war, and then by tracing the development of the theme of divine warfare through five phases from the beginning to the end of the biblical revelation.

Divine warfare has sometimes been called 'holy war'. While this term is never used in the Bible, it correctly emphasizes the sacral nature of divine warfare. However, due to the term's undesirable associations today, it is more usual to refer to sacral warfare in the Bible as 'Yahweh war', since Yahweh is at the centre of the battle.

The theology of Yahweh war

We garner the evidence for the following description from two major sources: 1. the laws for the waging of warfare in *Deuteronomy 7 and 20, and 2. the descriptions of Yahweh war in the historical books. We will synthesize this material and present it under three headings: 1. before a war; 2. during a war; 3. after a war.

Before a war

The *Israelites did not decide on the appropriate time to initiate war. God revealed to them, in a variety of ways, when and whom they were to fight. *Joshua 5:13–15 narrates a theophany in which God, the warrior, appears to Joshua and gives him the battle strategy for the defeat of Jericho. In 1 Samuel 23:1–5, God does not initially reveal his desire that *David lead his army against the Philistines at Keilah. David hears that the enemy has attacked the Israelites there, and responds by asking the LORD, through the priest Abiathar and presumably with the oracular ephod, if he should attack. He proceeds only after the oracle replies in the affirmative. In Joshua 9, without consulting the LORD, Joshua decides not to wage war against the Gibeonites, and thus incurs God's displeasure.

The sacred nature of warfare in the Bible is revealed by the rituals which surround it. Many of these were performed before the battle: Israelite soldiers had to make ritual preparations to fight in a Yahweh war. In the unusual circumstances preceding the battle of Jericho, the Israelite men underwent circumcision, which was not *militarily* wise (Josh. 5; cf. Gen. 34). From reports like that of 1 Samuel 13:1–15, it seems that every act of Yahweh war was preceded by *sacrifice.

During a war

The sacred nature of warfare in ancient Israel is revealed also in the people's march into battle. The ark of the covenant was the Israelites' most potent symbol of God's presence. During times of peace it was lodged in the most holy place in the tabernacle (or, later, the temple). At times of war, however, the army took it with them.

The ark, representing God's presence as divine warrior, took the lead as the nation marched to war. During the wilderness wanderings, the ark led Israel during its slow march towards the battles of the conquest. That the wanderings were understood to be the march of an army into battle is shown by the words of Moses at the beginning of a day's march as the ark set out:

> Rise up, O LORD!
> May your enemies be scattered;
> may your foes flee before you.
> (Num. 10:35, NIV)

The location of the ark in the Israelites' camp is a further indication of its role as the symbol of God's presence as warrior. The ark was situated at the centre of the camp, the place where the tent of the human war leader would normally be found (Num. 2).

Psalm 24 is a liturgy recited at the conclusion of a successful Yahweh war. As the army, led by the priests bearing the ark, approaches the gates of Jerusalem, there is a ritual interchange between the doorkeeper and the army:

> Lift up your heads, O you gates;
> be lifted up, you ancient doors,
> that the King of glory may come in.
> Who is this King of glory?
> The LORD strong and mighty,
> the LORD mighty in battle.
> Lift up your heads, O you gates;
> lift them up, you ancient doors,
> that the King of glory may come in.

Who is he, this King of glory?
  The LORD Almighty—
  he is the King of glory.
    (Ps. 24:7–10)

Perhaps the best known characteristic of OT sacral war is that Israel does not rely on a large army or powerful weapons. In fact, the nation is not expected to have many troops. As Gideon assembles an army for an assault on the Midianites, God informs him that he has 'too many men for me to deliver Midian into their hands' (Judg. 7:2). He directs Gideon to reduce the size of his army, first by allowing all who are afraid to go home and then by making the remaining soldiers drink water from the wadi Harod. No special skill is involved in this 'test'; its only purpose is to get rid of the vast majority of the troops. Further, the Israelite army does not use powerful weapons. Joshua hamstrings horses and burns chariots (Josh. 11:6–9) captured in battle. David does not wear armour in the fight with Goliath and is equipped only with a sling (1 Sam. 17).

This strategy is at the heart of Yahweh war. Why fight with fewer soldiers and with less effective weapons than one's opponents have? To do so is to acknowledge that *victory results not from human skill or resources, but only from God's power and will. As the psalmist expressed it:

Some trust in chariots and some in
    horses,
  but we trust in the name of the LORD
    our God.
They are brought to their knees and
    fall,
  but we rise up and stand firm.
    (Ps. 20:7)

Of course, this is not to say that the people of God stand idly by while God wins the victory. On each occasion God calls on his people to act in some way. Even in Jericho, where the walls fall down (Josh. 6), Israel must march and shout. God wins the victory, but the people participate actively.

After a battle

Yahweh fights for Israel in their sacral wars against their enemies. Thus Israel, when obedient, always wins. The praise, however, goes only to God, without whom Israel would have been defeated. The OT includes many songs celebrating the victories that God won for Israel. One of the most notable is the Song of the Sea, associated with the crossing of the Red Sea:

I will sing to the LORD,
  for he is highly exalted.
The horse and its rider
  he has hurled into the sea.
The LORD is my strength and my
    song;
  he has become my salvation.
He is my God, and I will praise him,
  my father's God, and I will exalt
    him.
The LORD is a warrior;
  the LORD is his name.
    (Exod. 15:1–3)

Many psalms were written in order to celebrate God's victory in battle (cf. Ps. 68).

Perhaps the most difficult aspect of Yahweh war for modern readers to understand is the ḥērem. This is a difficult word to translate, but it expresses the idea that all the booty and the prisoners of war are the property of Yahweh. After all, Yahweh is responsible for the victory; he deserves the spoils. This means, on the one hand, that all the spoils (the precious metals and other treasures) are placed in the temple treasuries. On the other hand, it means that all the prisoners of war – men, women, and children – are executed. Sinful people who do not atone for their sin by sacrifice are destroyed because of their wrongdoing.

The five phases of Yahweh war

Having synthesized the material on Yahweh war in the OT, we will now describe the development of the theme through five phases from Genesis to Revelation.

God fights the flesh-and-blood enemies of his people

In the OT, God frequently appears to fight on behalf of his people. He fights against the Egyptians at the Red Sea, the Canaanites during the wars of conquest, the encroaching foreign nations during the period of the judges, and so on until the eve of the exile. The prophet *Nahum utilizes the divine warrior theme as he looks forward to the destruction in the near future of Nineveh, capital city of Israel's oppressor Assyria. The prophet spoke some time between 664 BC, when the city of Thebes (whose defeat is remembered in 3:8) fell, and 612 BC, the date of the fall of Nineveh. God fights for his people when they are obedient to his law in fulfilment of the *covenant/treaty blessing recorded in (e.g.) Deuteronomy 28:7: 'The LORD will grant that the enemies who rise up against you will be defeated before you. They will come at you from one direction but flee from you in seven.'

God fights against Israel

However, Israel is not consistently faithful to the Lord. In the covenant/treaty between God and Israel, there are not only blessings for obedience but also curses upon disobedience (Deut. 28:49–52).

This second 'phase' overlaps historically with the first. After Jericho comes Ai (Josh. 7). With God's help Israel defeats the impressive walled city of Jericho, but is then easily defeated by the inhabitants of Ai (which means 'ruin') because one individual, Achan, breaks the *herem* (Josh. 7:24–25). Later Israel is defeated despite the presence of the ark of the covenant, since it is regarded by the war leaders, Hophni and Phinehas, more as a magic charm than as a symbol of God's presence (1 Sam. 4:1–11). That Israel loses this battle as a result not of God's inability to rescue them but of his unwillingness to do so is evident from the account of his power put forth in the temple of Dagon (1 Sam. 5:1–12).

The most horrific display of God's power against his people is the destruction of Jerusalem in 586 BC. The book of Lamentations records the terror felt by the faithful as they see the holy city in chaos. They knew that God was the author of the destruction:

> Like an enemy he [God] has strung his
> bow;
> his right hand is ready.
> Like a foe he has slain
> all who were pleasing to the eye;
> he has poured out his wrath like fire
> on the tent of the Daughter of Zion.
> The Lord is like an enemy;
> he has swallowed up Israel.
> He has swallowed up all her palaces
> and destroyed her strongholds.
> He has multiplied mourning and
> lamentation
> for the Daughter of Judah.
> (Lam. 2:4–5)

God, the future warrior

But the OT does not conclude on this negative note. The exilic and post-exilic prophets speak about the future with hope. Daniel 7, for instance, speaks of 'one like a son of man' who appears on the clouds of heaven, the chariot of God the warrior (cf. Pss. 18:7–15; 68:4, 33; 104:1–3; Nah. 1:3, also antecedents in Ugarit literature with Baal the 'rider on the clouds'). Zechariah 14 also looks into the future and announces the coming day of the Lord (see *Eschatology), when the Lord 'will go out and fight against those nations, as he fights in the day of battle' (Zech. 14:3). It is with this expectation of coming liberation that the OT ends.

Jesus Christ, the divine warrior

The hope expressed at the conclusion of the OT is affirmed at the beginning of the NT. John the Baptist, in the wilderness, announces the coming crisis: 'I baptize you with water for repentance. But after me will come one who is more powerful than I, whose sandals I am not fit to carry. He will baptize you with the Holy Spirit and with fire. His winnowing fork is in his hand, and he will clear his threshing floor, gathering his wheat into the barn and burning up the chaff with unquenchable fire' (Matt. 3:11–12).

*Jesus appears in the wilderness at the Jordan, and John recognizes him as the coming one. Soon after Jesus' baptism, John is imprisoned and Jesus' ministry begins. However, while he is in prison, John hears reports that disturb him: that Jesus is healing the sick, exorcising demons and preaching the good news. John is worried. Where is the burning, the *judgment and the warrior?

His concern leads him to send his disciples to ask Jesus, 'Are you the one who was to come, or should we expect someone else?' (Matt. 11:3). Jesus responds to them, not with words, but with more of the same actions. His message to John is, 'Yes, I am the divine warrior, but I have intensified the battle. I focus my attention not on mere human evil, but on the *spiritual powers and principalities.'

This is why Jesus fights the battle with spiritual weapons, not with physical. Indeed, when Peter tries to use the sword to protect his Lord, Jesus rebukes him and chooses instead the cross (Matt. 26:50–56). Paul understands Christ's death on the cross in terms of warfare; he describes the death of Christ as disarming the powers and authorities (Col. 2:15), and the ascension of Christ (see *Exaltation) as a victory parade with the prisoners of war in the victor's train (Eph. 4:7–8, with a quotation from Ps. 68, a divine warrior hymn).

Jesus won the greatest battle of all, not by killing but by dying. Thus he set an example for his people living in the NT age. They too fight not by killing, but by laying down their lives when necessary. They fight not with sword, spear and shield, but with spiritual weapons like *faith, *righteousness and the *word of God (Eph. 6:10–18). Indeed, the battle is not only outward; it is also in the heart, as indicated by a number of passages which describe believers' struggles against evil remaining within (Rom. 7:7–25; 2 Cor. 10:1–6).

Jesus, the future warrior

But according to the apocalyptic portions of the NT, there is more divine warfare to come. Jesus looked forward to the day when 'the Son of Man' would come on the clouds of heaven (Mark 13:26). This language obviously echoes Daniel 7:13, and shows that John the Baptist was not wrong in his anticipation of a coming violent judgment; he simply saw a two-act drama as one event. A second coming of Christ is anticipated and is most fully described in the book of Revelation, in which divine warrior language abounds. Revelation 19:11–16 describes the coming of Christ on a white horse with a sword coming from his mouth. He is followed by the armies of heaven as he 'judges and makes war' (v. 11). The Bible concludes with a dramatic picture of the final battle, which symbolizes the final judgment and just punishment of all God's human and spiritual enemies. Thus ends the conflict that began at the Fall with the curse upon the serpent, who is understood by later writers (Rom. 16:20; Rev. 12:9) to represent the worst extreme of spiritual *evil:

'Cursed are you above all the livestock
  and all the wild animals!
You will crawl on your belly
  and you will eat dust
  all the days of your life.
And I will put enmity
  between you and the woman,

and between your offspring and hers;
he will crush your head,
  and you will strike his heel.'
(Gen. 3:14–15)

Conclusion

The theme of divine warfare is a pervasive and important one in biblical theology. It is found throughout the biblical narrative. However, the Bible never glorifies warfare or violence in themsleves. Indeed, the ideal state is one of perfect *peace. Micah looks forward to a day when:

'They will beat their swords into
    ploughshares
  and their spears into pruning hooks.
Nation will not take up sword against
    nation,
  nor will they train for war any more.'
(Mic. 4:3)

Warfare is God's 'strange' work (Is. 28:21) in which he judges evil. The purpose of Yahweh war is the eradication of evil and the punishment of *sin. Its climax is the final judgment.

The purpose and dynamic of sacred warfare in the Bible indicate that this theme cannot be used to justify war between nations today (although many Christians believe that war can sometimes be justified on other grounds). For God's people spiritual warfare has replaced physical, and they are no longer a single nation; thus a modern war cannot be called Yahweh war.

The NT places God's people today in the period between the fourth and the fifth phases. We fight a spiritual war against the powers and principalities (Eph. 6:10–18), while knowing that victory has been won on the cross. We look forward to the culmination of the conflict when Christ comes again 'with the clouds' (Rev. 1:7).

Bibliography

T. Longman III and D. G. Reid, *God is a Warrior* (Grand Rapids and Carlisle, 1995); P. D. Miller, Jr, *The Divine Warrior in Early Israel* (Cambridge, 1973); G. von Rad, *Holy War in Ancient Israel* (Grand Rapids and Leominster, 1991).

T. LONGMAN III

WATER

Water has both positive and negative aspects; it can give *life or cause destruction.

Creation

Water is created by Yahweh, the Creator of the whole cosmos, both heavens and earth (Gen. 1:1). Of itself water creates nothing, though the earth comes out of it (Gen. 1:9–10). In contrast, in the Babylonian *creation myth *Enuma Elish* all things emanate from two pre-existent primordial waters, Apsu and Tiamat.

Some claim that the *tĕhôm* of Genesis 1:2 is uncreated and, like Tiamat, is a chaos-water out of which the cosmos comes. But the verse does not refer to a watery chaos; it indicates that the earth is unproductive and uninhabited, totally under water (see vv. 9–10 and D. T. Tsumura, *The Earth and the Waters in Genesis 1 and 2*).

In Genesis 2:5–6 the underground water (*'ēd*) supplies the arable land (*'ǎḏāmâ*), which is only one part of the earth (*'ereṣ*), but no rain has yet descended from heaven. Both the subterranean water and the rain are controlled by God. This environment is not a waterless desert or a dry chaos (so Gunkel, von Rad, *etc.*); rather, water is controlled in order to make a garden for humankind in Eden, where there is an abundant water supply (*cf.* Gen. 13:10). As long as humans keep God's command, they can stay in the garden, but because of their rebellion, they die spiritually and are driven out. Thereafter they suffer frequently from having too little or too much water.

Fertility and drought

Water is essential to the fertility of the *land and is provided for all creatures by the compassionate God even after the fall (Ps. 104:10–12). In the desert the Lord makes water flow from the rock for the people of Israel (Exod. 17:1–6; Is. 48:21). He brings the Israelites 'into a good land – a land with streams and pools of water, with springs flowing in the valleys and hills' (Deut. 8:7, NIV). He provides rain and dew to enrich the land abundantly (Ps. 65:9–10), or withholds them (1 Kgs. 17:1). In the days to come, he will lead his people beside springs of water (Is. 49:10) and they will never again thirst (Rev. 7:16; Is. 49:10).

Destruction

The flood destroyed almost all earth-dwelling creatures. Through it God fulfilled his holy decree against human injustice (Gen. 6:11–13). The flood (Heb. *mabbûl*; Akk. *abubum*) is clearly distinguished from the annual high water inundation (Akk. *mîlu*), and the expression 'all the springs of the great deep burst forth, and the floodgates of the heavens were opened' (Gen. 7:11b) does not refer to 'the near return of the earth to pre-creation chaos' (B. W. Anderson in *IDB*, p. 808; see P. J. Harland, *The Value of Human Life*).

God is often described as fighting or subduing destructive waters such as the 'sea' and the 'mighty waters' (Hab. 3:15), which are often personified as *Rahab (Ps. 89:10; Is. 51:9), Leviathan (Ps. 74:14; Is. 27:1), a monster (Ps. 74:13), *etc.* Some identify these enemies as uncreated chaos water, the enemy of the Creator in primordial times. But in the Bible there is no battle at the creation of the universe. Rather the water motif is used to indicate that God's enemies are destined to be destroyed by him, whether they are the historical enemies of Israel (as in Exod. 15:8–10) or spiritual enemies (as in Is. 27). (See Tsumura, *TynB* 40.)

Cultic significance

Ceremonial cleansing is important when approaching the holy God. Sometimes it is carried out by sprinkling with 'the water of cleansing' (Num. 8:7; 31:23). Also 'a bronze basin for washing' is placed between the altar and the tent of meeting (Exod. 30:18) or the temple (2 Chr. 4:6). This washing is observed strictly by the Pharisees during the time of Jesus (Mark 7:3–4; John 2:6; 3:25).

In the days to come, Yahweh himself 'will sprinkle clean water' on the house of Israel (Ezek. 36:25). Paul writes that Christ loved the church enough 'to make her holy, cleansing her by the washing with water through the word' (Eph. 5:26). 'He saved us through the washing of rebirth and renewal by the Holy Spirit' (Titus 3:5). (See *Holiness.)

Water's purificatory function prefigures *baptism; John baptizes with water for repentance. However, Jesus baptizes with the Holy Spirit and with fire (Matt. 3:11; Mark 1:8; Luke 3:16; *cf.* John 1:33; Acts 1:5).

Peter interprets the water of the flood as a symbol of the baptism that now saves believers (1 Pet. 3:20b–21a), and Paul associates baptism with the crossing of the Red Sea (1 Cor. 10:1–2).

Wisdom and Spirit

Water is associated with *wisdom in the ancient Near East. According to Proverbs 18:4, 'The words of a man's mouth are deep waters, but the fountain of wisdom is a bubbling brook'. In Mesopotamia, the water god Ea (= Enki) is a god of wisdom, and hence of magic. In the Bible the Lord is 'the only wise God' (Rom. 16:27).

Water and Spirit are associated from the time of creation (Gen. 1:2b): 'and the Spirit of God was hovering over the waters'. Sometimes this 'Spirit' is interpreted as a wind, but more probably the verse indicates that by his Spirit God was deeply involved with his creation, water.

Throughout the Bible, 'water' or 'living water' is a metaphor for the Spirit. In Isaiah 44:3, pouring water is compared with the pouring out of God's Spirit. John 1:33 and Acts 1:5 contrast baptism in water with the baptism in the *Holy Spirit. Jesus says that one must be born of water and the Spirit (John 3:5) and that 'streams of living water' (i.e. of the Spirit), will flow from within anyone who believes in him (7:37–39; also 4:14).

The Lord is the spring from which living water flows (Jer. 17:13; also 2:13). 'On that day living water will flow out from Jerusalem' (Zech. 14:8). Jesus refers to himself as the giver of 'living water' (John 4:10–14). In Revelation, John refers to the Lamb who will lead his people to springs of living water (Rev. 7:17) and to the enthroned one who 'will give to drink without cost from the spring of the water of life' (Rev. 21:6; also 22:1), which flows 'from the throne of God and of the Lamb' (Rev. 22:1).

Bibliography

B. W. Anderson, in *IDB* R–Z, pp. 806–810; O. Böcher, in *NIDNTT* 3, pp. 982–991; P. J. Harland, *The Value of Human Life: A Study of the Story of the Flood (Genesis 6 – 9)* (Leiden, 1996); D. T. Tsumura, *The Earth and the Waters in Genesis 1 and 2: A Linguistic Analysis* (Sheffield, 1989); idem, 'Ugaritic poetry and Habakkuk 3', *TynB* 40, 1989, pp. 24–48.

D. T. TSUMURA

WEALTH, see POOR/POVERTY

WILDERNESS

Introduction

Numerous Hebrew terms are used in the OT, often interchangeably, for anything from semi-arid pasture to utter desolation. Generally, however, they denote a *waterless area (Ps. 107:4–5), without trees or vegetation (Num. 20:5), and inhospitable to husbanded animals and humans (Jer. 2:6). Only snakes and scorpions (Num. 21:6; Deut. 8:15), wild animals (Mal. 1:3; Ps. 102:6; Job 24:5; Jer. 5:6; Lam. 4:3; Ezek. 34:5, 25) and terrifying creatures (Is. 13:21; 34:14) live in this dark (Jer. 2:6, 31), 'uncreated' place (Deut. 32:10; Is. 45:18–19). Two fundamental wilderness typologies emerge, the first related to *creation, and the second arising out of Israel's *Exodus experience, both of which are taken up in the NT.

Creation and wilderness

The earth's 'formless and void' condition (Gen. 1:2) is reminiscent of uncultivated wilderness (2:5; cf. Deut. 32:10; Jer. 4:23–26; Is. 27:10; 45:18–19; Ps. 107:40; Job 6:18; 12:24). In contrast, Eden ('delight'), with its subdued animals, contains trees and is well watered (Gen. 2:8–20), but humanity's occupation of it depends on their loyalty to Yahweh. After the fall, Cain's exile in the land of wandering (Nod, Gen. 4:14; cf. 1 Kgs. 14:15; 2 Kgs. 21:8; Dan. 4:14) heightens humanity's alienation and exacerbates the loss of Eden's settled fertility. The wilderness thus becomes a place of *exclusion, deprivation and wandering (e.g. Gen. 16:7; 21:14; 37:15, 22). Cain's building of a city is an attempt to mitigate his circumstances (4:17). Such settlements quickly reflect their origins, leading to the hubris of Babel whose inhabitants too become wanderers (Gen. 11:4–9). Abram's story is a repudiation of these makeshift and degenerate 'Cainite' cities, as he embarks on a 'wandering' journey (Gen. 20:13) to a restored Eden, a new city whose ruler and maker is God (cf. Heb. 11:10).

The Exodus

Israel's Exodus ironically reverses Cain's 'expulsion'. Not only does the fugitive *Moses flee to the wilderness (Exod. 2:11–

15), but Pharaoh expels Israel from his anti-Eden city (Exod. 6:1; 11:1; 12:39) and they journey through the wilderness, arriving in an edenic Canaan (Exod. 15:1–21; Pss. 74:13–14; 78:54; cf. Exod. 3:8, 17). In the wilderness accounts (Exod. 15:22 – 19:2; Num. 10:33 – 22:1; 33:1–49), Israel's acceptance of the law and covenant is an implicit rejection of humanity's rebellious autonomy (Gen. 3), and an affirmation that knowledge and life belong to Yahweh (Deut. 11:26; 30:11–20) who provides *leadership (Num. 10; Deut. 1:29–33) and food, water and other necessities (Deut. 8:4; 32:10). Even the desert hardships are part of his fatherly formation of his 'son' (Deut. 8:2–5).

Israel responds, however, with *grumbling (Exod. 14 – 17; Num. 11) and *idolatry (Exod. 32; Num. 25; Deut. 9:7). Having tested Yahweh 'ten times' (e.g. Num. 14:22; cf. the ten plagues?), the people refuse to enter Canaan (Num. 13 – 14). God grants their prayer (Num. 14:2b), and the wilderness becomes a place of 'wandering' *death for that generation (Num. 14:22–23, 35; 32:13; Deut. 2:1–3; cf. Moses in Num. 20:2–13; 27:12–14). In the Azazel rite the *sin-bearer is 'expelled' into the wilderness (Lev. 16:10–26), the proper abode of the unclean (Num. 5:1–3), which stands in opposition to the Holy of Holies to which the blood of the second goat is brought (Lev. 16:2, 14–15).

The prophets and writings

Under God's *judgment, the land inhabited by a nation may become a wilderness (Pss. 11:6b; 68:6b). This principle is applied most often to Israel (Is. 32:12–14; 64:10; Jer. 4:23–26; 9:10–11; 22:6; Ezek. 19:10–14; Hos. 2:3; Joel 2:3), but also to *Babylon (Is. 13:20–22; Jer. 50:12), Egypt (Ezek. 29:5; Joel 3:19), Edom (Is. 34:11; Jer. 49:17–18), Assyria, Moab, Ammon (Zeph. 2:9–13) and the '*world city' (Is. 24:10).

Cain-like wandering is seen as a judgment from which individuals need to be rescued (Job 12:24; Ps. 107:40), as is Israel's *exile (1 Kgs. 14:15; cf. 2 Kgs. 21:8), while the restoration sees the land, previously a wilderness, re-created as a new Eden (Is. 35:1–7; 41:18–20; 51:3; Ezek. 36:35; 47) by Yahweh's Spirit (Is. 32:15–16; cf. Gen. 1:2; Ps. 104:30). Israel itself is a wilderness, whom Yahweh 're-creates' through his Spirit (Is. 44:3; 63:10–14; cf. Ezek. 37).

Like Moses, David, who also tended sheep in the wilderness (1 Sam. 17:28), escapes there from his enemy (1 Sam. 23; 26:3).

The imagery of wilderness wandering evokes Yahweh's presence at Sinai (Judg. 5:4; Hab. 3:3; Pss. 18:7–15; 68:7–9), and his provision and leadership (Hos. 13:5; Amos 2:10; Pss. 78:14–29; 105:39–41; 114:8; 136:16; Neh. 9:19–21). Yahweh promises to take his people on a new wilderness journey from the 'world city', Babylon (Is. 40:3, 11; 43:19; 49:9–11; 52:11–12; Hos. 12:9).

The wilderness recalls Israel's youthful devotion, in contrast to their present *apostasy (Jer. 2:2–6; Hos. 9:10). Yahweh will return them there to allure them, making a new creation covenant with the animals (Hos. 2:14–20; Jer. 31:2). The wilderness also connotes Israel's apostasy, in which they persist in spite of Yahweh's forbearance (Ezek. 20:13–21; Pss. 78; 106; cf. 95:7b–11). Their sins in the wilderness brought about the exile (Ezek. 20:23–24; Ps. 106:25–27) which, like the wilderness wandering, is an occasion for Yahweh to purge the rebels from Israel (Ezek. 20:36–38; cf. Ps. 81:7).

The NT

While Jesus sometimes seeks solitude in the wilderness (Mark 1:35, 45, par.; Matt. 14:13; Luke 5:16; John 11:54), as the setting for *John the Baptist's preaching (Matt. 3:1; Luke 7:24, par.) it is the place of eschatological expectation, specifically of a new Exodus (Mark 1:3, par.; Is. 40:3; Exod. 23:20; cf. Matt. 24:26; John 6:15; Acts 21:38). Jesus' wilderness temptation recapitulates Israel's experience, though he succeeds where they failed (Matt. 4:1–11 par.), as do his wilderness feedings (Mark 6:31–44 par.) and even his being 'lifted up' (John 3:14). Wilderness traditions evoke Israel's rebellion against Moses and Yahweh (Acts 7:30–43; cf. 13:18; Heb. 3:7–19) and serve as a warning to Christians not to follow their example (1 Cor. 10:1–11). On the other hand, in Revelation the wilderness provides a refuge from the dragon for the fleeing woman (12:6).

Again, the wilderness is the habitation of demons (Matt. 12:43, par.) and a place of alienation and wandering (Luke 8:29; 15:4). Symbolizing God's judgment (Matt. 12:25; 23:38; 24:15, par.; of Judas, Acts 1:20; Rev. 8:7; 11:6; cf. Gal. 4:27), it is a fitting location for the world's great city (Rev. 17:3), which is itself made desolate (Rev. 18:17–19), while Yahweh's people enter the restored Eden, the city of God's new creation (Rev. 21 – 22).

Bibliography

U. Mauser, *Christ in the Wilderness* (London, 1963); W. Swartley, *Israel's Scripture Traditions and the Synoptic Gospels* (Peabody, 1994); S. Talmon, 'The "desert motif" in the Bible and in Qumran literature', in A. Altmann (ed.), *Biblical Motifs* (Cambridge, 1963).

R. E. WATTS

WISDOM

Introduction

Wisdom can be defined as the 'capacity of judging rightly in matters relating to *life and conduct', as 'the ability to cope', as 'experiential knowledge', as 'intellectual activity', as 'the legacy of parents to their children', or as 'the quest for self-understanding and for mastery of the *world'. The difficulty of defining wisdom is due to a. the large number of Hebrew and Greek terms denoting wisdom; b. the large number of additional concepts in close syntactical relationship with those terms, such as prudence, perception, teaching, plan, advice and success; c. the difficulty in establishing precise definitions in the area of knowledge relating to praxis. In biblical studies the term 'wisdom' is variously used as a literary category for classifying certain books (*Prov., *Eccles., *Job), as a theological category for describing an approach to reality which focuses on *creation, and as a sociological category for evaluating the activity of parents, elders and teachers.

Categories of Israelite wisdom

Perceiving wisdom focuses on comprehension of the world in which *humanity lives. The OT includes numerous observations on attitudes and frames of mind, on human relations and on social affairs (Prov. 15:17; 16:11, 20, 26; 21:9), on legal and economic matters (Prov. 17:26; 18:17; 20:14, 23), on other nations and animate and inanimate nature, and on *death and the meaning of life. Proper knowledge and the instruction which results from it are valued more highly than gold (Prov. 8:10). The sages ask the hard questions of life, questions about the *suffering of the righteous who do not deserve their trials (Job) and basic questions about the meaning of human existence (Eccles.).

Action-related wisdom focuses on conduct as a consequence of right perception, on proper behaviour in everyday life. The sages emphasize, among other themes, the mastering of the tongue and the ability to remain silent at the proper time (Prov. 17:27–28), self-control, *e.g.* with regard to drinking (Prov. 23:29–35) or sex (Prov. 6:20–35), prudence, *e.g.* in terms of industry (Prov. 10:4), and avoidance of evil (Prov. 14:16). The ability to control one's passions is highly praised: 'One who is slow to anger is better than the mighty, and one whose temper is controlled than one who captures a city' (Prov. 16:32, NRSV). Prototypes of wisdom are Joseph (Gen. 41; 47), David and Solomon (1 Kgs. 3:9–14).

Communicating wisdom focuses on teaching, on exhortation and on evaluating people's conduct. Teaching and education are the major means of acquiring wisdom (Prov. 1:1–6). Most proverbs convey values and are therefore explicitly didactic, seeking to influence action. The origins of Israelite wisdom both in family and tribal wisdom and in schools in Jerusalem reflect this interest, the former being focused as much on instruction as on purely aesthetic appreciation. The personification of wisdom in Job 28 and Proverbs 8 highlights *God's summons to his creatures to accept his promise of life, through the wisdom which is revealed in his creation.

The faith of the Israelite sages

The focus on creation. Wisdom texts find their theological centre in creation, with regard to both human life (anthropology) and to nature (cosmology; *cf.* L. G. Perdue, *Wisdom and Creation*). Proverbs portrays the cosmos as the creation of God who established and who now sustains and guides life. God's divine wisdom was active in the process of creation (Job 28:25–27; Prov. 3:19; 8:22–31; Ps. 104). As a result, sapiential observation and reflection attempts to understand the entire animate and inanimate world. Solomon was known for having described, in thousands of proverbs and songs, 'trees, from the cedar that is in the Lebanon to the hyssop that grows in the wall … animals, and birds, and reptiles, and fish' (1 Kgs. 4:32–33). Proverbs contains numerous observations concerning animal behaviour (cf. Prov. 1:17; 6:5–6; 7:22–23; 30:15, 17–19, 24–31) and reflections on the physical world (cf. Prov. 10:25; 16:25; 25:13; 30:4).

The search for order. Most scholars assert that the search for and maintenance of order is a fundamental aspect of wisdom. Israel's sages believed that both nature and the world of human beings were determined by a fundamental order. To act in harmony with the universal order which sustained creation was their supreme goal: human behaviour either strengthened the existing order or contributed to the forces of chaos which threatened life (J. L. Crenshaw, *Old Testament Wisdom*, p. 66). In this context some statements of the sages are in a rather dogmatic form, such as sayings which seem to relate deed and result in a mechanical way, expressing the view that a good deed produces a good result and an evil deed produces an evil result. Yet at the same time the sages are aware of mystery and uncertainty: the events of our lives are not always simply the results of our actions, *reward and punishment being determined by some objective order, but are also the result of the Lord's being active in all that happens (Job 11:7–8; 36:22–26). The sages were aware of their limitations: 'No wisdom, no understanding, no counsel can avail against the Lord' (Prov. 21:30). But they were convinced that their advice on how to live a successful life was valid, and that planning for future actions was necessary, even though certainty was not always possible: 'The human mind plans the way, but the Lord directs the steps' (Prov. 16:9). Possession of purely human 'wisdom' can blind a person to reality; the *fear of the Lord is the most important attitude (Prov. 3:5). The sages allowed for a margin of error 'because they had experienced mystery as well as certainty' (R. E. Murphy, in *ABD* 6, p. 923). Wisdom is always a gift of God, not a virtue manufactured by human beings (Prov. 2:6).

The concern for righteousness. Some proverbs appear to teach a strictly pragmatic wisdom ('A bribe is like a magic stone in the eyes of those who give it; wherever they turn they prosper', Prov. 17:8). However, in many proverbs folly is not simply ignorance but also wickedness, and wisdom is synonymous with *righteousness: 'Crooked minds are an abomination to the Lord, but those of blameless ways are his delight' (Prov. 11:20; cf. 10:2, 16; 17:23). The wisdom teachers' goal is to promote a life of righteous wisdom which is pleasing to God. They know that wise living does not guarantee a life free from *poverty or suffering: 'Better is a little with righteousness than large income with injustice' (Prov. 16:8; cf. 15:16; 28:6; Eccles. 4:13; 9:15). But the book of Job teaches that a righteous and wise life is worth living even when one has lost everything.

The integrity of honest enquiry. The sages are not only prepared to admit their ignorance (as does Agur, Prov. 30:1–6), but also have the courage to raise questions which have no easy or reasonable answer. The book of Job shows that the application of human standards of justice to God does not work in all circumstances. This does not necessarily represent a 'crisis' for wisdom, as some scholars believe; rather it proves the resilience of the wisdom movement, which does not evade problems (Murphy, in *ABD*, p. 926). Because the sages wanted to investigate and understand the order of the world and the workings out of God's purpose, they were prepared to acknowledge pain: that it existed and that it could not always be explained. They could praise the beauty of creation and the goodness of God with awe and wonder, and they could comment on central issues concerning the divine purpose and the meaning of human existence in cynical or pessimistic terms. These diverse voices were allowed to stand alongside each other in canonical Scripture, as each was considered to be a true reflection of human experience in the world which is God's fallen creation. They are to be read 'as complementary statements marking out the parameters of faith' (G. H. Wilson, in *NIDOTTE* 4, p. 1282).

The importance of learning. The frequent exhortation of the sages to seek wisdom and understanding through their teachings (Prov. 2:1–5) presupposes the conviction that wisdom is available to all who seek to acquire it. Association with wise people increases wisdom.

The metaphor of the way. An important image in Proverbs is the path or way to life

(Prov. 1:15; 2:8–9; 10:8, 21–22, 27, *etc*.). At birth everybody embarks on a journey which leads either to a full life or to doom. The foolish are those who rely on their own ingenuity, who think they do not need instruction and advice; they walk towards destruction and death. The journey of life will be successful if one heeds the instructions of the sages, which are like a road map; following the path which they describe constitutes wisdom. Still, God may overrule wise planning and a prudent lifestyle: 'All our steps are ordered by the Lord; how then can we understand our own way?' (Prov. 20:24).

Wisdom, covenant and law. The presence of wisdom literature and its concerns in the OT canon warns readers not entirely to subsume the OT under categories of *salvation history such as covenant and law, and point to the fact that salvation history cannot be properly understood unless wisdom theology with its focus on creation is taken into account. God's activity cannot be limited to Israel's history; it is also related to the world as the creation of God, who providentially rules over cosmos and history (Perdue, *Wisdom and Creation*, p. 341). This idea is evident in the personification of wisdom as a divine figure.

Divine wisdom

Wisdom as divine communication. Personified wisdom focuses on God's involvement with the world: wisdom is involved with the divine creative activity (Job 28:24–27); wisdom is the firstborn of creation (Prov. 8:22–31); wisdom was present when God made the world (Prov. 8:27–30); God founded the earth by wisdom (Prov. 3:19; 8:30). This divine wisdom, sometimes called 'Lady Wisdom', is not to be understood as a hypostasis, that is, an intermediary being between God and creation (H. Ringgren, *Word and Wisdom*), since wisdom is not given the status of an independent entity – the figure of wisdom is a vivid poetic personification. And wisdom is not simply an attribute of the world, the mysterious order of the world which beckons to human beings (G. von Rad, *Wisdom in Israel*, pp. 156–157), since Proverbs 8 stresses (six times) her existence before creation and thus points to her divine origins. The figure of wisdom is the Lord himself, who cares for his creation and who summons human beings to observe the

nearness, the acts, and the personal call of God. Intimacy with wisdom is not distinguished from intimacy with God. Divine wisdom is a communication of God showing the path to life.

God's gracious sovereignty. The description of divine wisdom which was present at and active in creation is misunderstood when theologians conclude that, as a result of humanity's being part of creation, we are able to grasp wisdom, to gain understanding of the world and thus perhaps to perceive the nature of God. The wisdom tradition of the OT does not promulgate any kind of natural theology, not even in Proverbs 8, and Job 28:1–14 affirms that even if humans dig as deep as the miners dig, they cannot find wisdom by themselves.

True wisdom. The figure of wisdom underlines the conviction of the sages that true wisdom comes from God. It is God who gives to humans a heart capable of discerning good from evil (1 Kgs. 3:9). The original sin of humankind was the belief that it was possible to acquire wisdom by human powers alone, disregarding the will of God (Gen 3:5–6). The beginning of true wisdom is the fear of the Lord (Prov. 1:7; 9:10; Job 28:28) which is the source of all life (Prov. 14:27). The prophets repeatedly speak out against counsellors who devise human policies in a self-sufficient spirit, ignoring God and his power in their deliberations (Is. 5:21; 29:14). Isaiah anticipates a future Davidic king who will possess perfect wisdom, but who will receive it from the spirit of the Lord (Is. 11:2).

Wisdom as law. The divine wisdom in Job 28 and Proverbs 8 is a complex figure, a fact which provided later sages with the opportunity to personify other concepts. The priestly scribe Ben Sira, writing around 200–180 BC in Jerusalem, identified divine wisdom with divine Torah (Ecclus. 24:23). He taught his own generation, which was increasingly exposed to Hellenistic wisdom and culture that true wisdom was not found in Athens or in Alexandria but in Jerusalem (Ecclus. 24:11); she had taken root in Jacob and made Israel, the glorious people, her inheritance (Ecclus. 24:8, 12).

Jesus, the wisdom of God

Jesus as wisdom teacher. The Gospels portray *Jesus as a (prophetic) wisdom teacher who used aphorisms, riddles and parables to convey his message (according to some scholars over 70% of the Jesus tradition is in the form of some sort of sapiential utterance). Most recently B. Witherington has drawn attention to this fact (*Jesus the Sage*). Indeed, Jesus himself describes his mission, and even his person, in terms of divine wisdom. He uses the figure of personified wisdom in Matthew 11:16–19 (par. Luke 7:31–35) to assert that all previous messengers of wisdom culminate in himself and John the Baptist. He claims that his message is greater than the preaching of Jonah and the wisdom of Solomon; he is a messenger who proclaims God's wisdom with eschatological urgency (Matt. 12:42; Luke 11:31).

Jesus as wisdom *incarnate. In the context of Matthew 11:2–4. Jesus virtually identifies himself as the embodiment of divine wisdom. In Matthew 11:25–27 (par. Luke 10:21–22) he emphasizes the unique character of his filial relationship with God, and asserts that the wisdom which only God knows fully is revealed by him to those who are prepared to accept it as a gift from him. His teaching is the final expression of God's *revelation; his followers receive his words as divine revelation (Matt. 5:18). Jesus not merely announced the dawn of God's rule on earth; he believed that he brought it and that he in some sense embodied it. Neither in the OT nor in early Jewish tradition had any king, prophet, priest, or teacher dared to suggest that he was a human embodiment of an attribute of God (*e.g.* God's wisdom; Witherington, *Jesus the Sage*, p. 204).

Jesus as God's wisdom. Paul articulated the significance of the person and mission of Jesus Christ in terms of wisdom. He may have arrived at the identification of divine wisdom and Jesus Christ as a result of the Damascus revelation: he saw Jesus as the Lord exalted by God, sitting at his right hand, and he came to believe that Jesus was the Son of God not only in the messianic sense, but also in the sense of standing in a unique relationship with God from the beginning, being the *image of God and his agent in creation and now in salvation (S. Kim, *The Origins of Paul's Gospel*). Thus he calls Jesus explicitly 'the wisdom of God' (1 Cor. 1:24, 30). God cannot be grasped through human wisdom (1 Cor. 1:21); he is not a God only for the elite and the deserving. The wisdom of God has become personified in Christ who had died on

a cross: that this should be the climactic expression of God's wisdom and power cannot be grasped by human wisdom. Therefore, the message of the gospel is 'God's wisdom' (1 Cor. 2:7), divine wisdom derived from the Creator whose previously hidden plan of salvation has become reality through Jesus' death on the cross (2:8).

The deity of Jesus Christ. The followers of Jesus soon came to believe that their master was more than a gifted wisdom teacher, and more than a powerful prophet preaching the arrival of God's new world. As the resurrection gave meaning to Jesus' death, it also pointed his followers to his true identity. It appears that terms and concepts of the Hebrew wisdom tradition, particularly the figure of personified divine wisdom, were used by the early Jewish Christians to describe who Jesus was. This is very obvious in Paul's writings. As he designates Jesus as the personified wisdom of God, he transfers traditional attributes of wisdom to Christ. The christological passages in Philippians 2:6–11 and Colossians 1:15–20 are believed by scholars to include Jewish wisdom theology as part of their hermeneutical context (*cf.* Prov. 8:22–25; Ecclus. 1:4; 24:9; Wisdom of Solomon 7:26; 9:4, 9–10). The designation of Christ as being 'in the form of God' and 'equal to God' (Phil. 2:6) recalls the figure of wisdom who is near to God, shares in God's nature and exists before creation. The description of Christ as 'the image of the invisible God', 'the firstborn of all creation', 'the beginning' and dwelling place of 'all the fullness of God' (Col. 1:15, 18, 19) also takes over attributes of the wisdom figure: Jesus the Son of God is the manifestation of God in creation; he enjoys precedence in both rank and existence over creation, he is the effective presence of the divine creative power, and he is the perfect manifestation of the attributes and activities of God. With the confession that Jesus Christ is Lord 'through whom are all things and through whom we exist' (1 Cor. 8:6) Paul stresses his conviction that Christ is the mediator of both creation and salvation (*cf.* Col. 1:16). In Ephesians 1:10 Paul emphasizes, again using wisdom language, that Christ is the goal of creation and therefore of history. (See also John 1:1–18; Heb. 1:2–4.) Wisdom Christology is a very high Christology, referring to the protological identity of Jesus of Nazareth who had died and been raised from the dead, who existed before his coming into the world, who was the visible manifestation of God, who was God in the flesh. The language of the Hebrew wisdom tradition, particularly the figure of personified divine wisdom, enabled the first Christians to assert the divine nature of Jesus Christ without denying their Jewish conviction that there is only one God.

The life of Christians

Proper behaviour. As the Hebrew wisdom tradition sought to interpret life and the world, by means of exhortation and proper behaviour, it is not surprising that the wisdom tradition influenced early Christian ethics. Lists of virtues and vices (1 Cor. 5:9–11; 6:9–10; Gal. 5:19–21, 22–23; Eph. 5:5; Phil. 4:8; Col. 3:5, 8, 12) and household codes (Eph. 5:21 – 6:9; Col. 3:18 – 4:1; 1 Tim. 2:8–15; 6:1–2; Titus 2:1–10) can be compared with similar forms and concepts in the OT and early Jewish wisdom tradition (*cf.* Prov. 6:17–18; Ecclus. 7:18–28; Wisdom of Solomon 14:23–26). Like the Israelite sages, Paul refers to what is generally accepted, necessary and fitting (1 Thess. 5:15; 1 Cor. 11:13; Rom. 12:2, 9; 13:3; 14:16; 15:2; Eph. 6:1; Phil 1:10; 4:8; Col. 3:18, 20; 1 Tim. 2:10; Titus 3:8, 14). He wants Christians to make (their own) right decisions as to the proper behaviour in specific circumstances, with the Spirit as their guide (Col. 1:9–10). There is no contradiction between this sapiential emphasis on personal responsibility for ethical decisions and the simultaneous stress on binding norms to which Christians are meant to adhere (*cf.* Rom. 3:31; 8:3–4; 1 Cor. 7:19). The structure of Paul's ethics, comprising both cognitive (wisdom) and authoritative (law) elements, can be understood in terms of the early Jewish correlation of law and wisdom, fused with God's revelation in Jesus Christ. Christians are called and enabled to submit to God's will as revealed in the law, in the words of Jesus Christ and in the pronouncements of the apostles, and at the same time they have the responsibility to work out what God's will is in the diverse circumstances of everyday life (E. J. Schnabel, *Law and Wisdom*, pp. 227–349).

Appeal to cognitive faculties. The apostle Paul appeals to reason (Gk. *nous*) by which people perceive what is good and right in specific situations (2 Cor. 10:5; Rom. 12:2; 14:5; *cf.* the verb *nouthetein*, 'to put in the right mind, encourage', in 1 Thess. 5:12, 14; 1 Cor. 4:14; Rom. 15:14). He calls for discernment and responsible choice (1 Thess. 5:21; Gal. 6:2–5; Rom. 12:2; 14:22–23; Phil. 1:9–11). He appeals to the conscience which is, in part, rooted in God's universally revealed law and wisdom (Rom. 2:15) and which provides evaluation of one's own moral conduct (*cf.* 1 Cor. 4:4; 2 Cor. 1:12; Rom. 13:5). Paul does not look for blind obedience but calls for understanding, so linking his ethics with the wisdom tradition (*cf.* Col. 1:28; 3:16).

Wisdom from above. *James reminds his readers that genuine wisdom is a gift of God to believers and leads to practical wisdom, manifesting itself in good and godly character and behaviour (Jas. 1:5–8; 3:13–18; the letter of James is heavily indebted to the Hebrew wisdom traditions).

Conclusion

Throughout the biblical tradition wisdom is linked with God, the creator of the world and of humankind. Israelite sages sought to understand how life and the world worked, asking questions which today are part of scientific enquiry and philosophical reflection: enquiry into the animate and inanimate world; reflection on the meaning of existence and the justice of God. The entire biblical wisdom tradition acknowledges, however, that wisdom is a divine gift. Wisdom is never an independent human enterprise. A second important emphasis is the inscrutability of God's ways, which sometimes defy explanation from a rational, human point of view, as in the suffering of the righteous in the OT, and the death of Jesus the Messiah on the cross as the climactic realization of salvation in the NT. A third emphasis of biblical wisdom is the conviction that genuine wisdom manifests itself in proper behaviour which pleases God. Old and young, men and women, are exhorted to make wise decisions in their everyday lives. A fourth emphasis is the importance of teaching: proper behaviour does not come automatically, but has to be learnt and must be passed on from one generation to the next. An emphasis unique to the NT is the conviction that God's wisdom is now embodied in a climactic and final way in Jesus the Messiah, Son of Man and Son of

God. Referring to OT passages in which wisdom, God's communication with his creation was personified, the early Christians asserted that God in his wisdom became incarnate in Jesus Christ, who is the source of life.

See also: SOLOMON.

Bibliography

J. J. Collins, *Jewish Wisdom in the Hellenistic Age* (Louisville and Edinburgh, 1997, 1998); J. L. Crenshaw, *Old Testament Wisdom: An Introduction* (London, 1981); J. G. Gammie and L. G. Perdue, *The Sage in Israel and the Ancient Near East* (Winona Lake, 1990); S. Kim, *The Origin of Paul's Gospel* (Tübingen, 1984); H. von Lips, *Weisheitliche Traditionen im Neuen Testament* (Neukirchen-Vluyn, 1990); R. E. Murphy, *Wisdom Literature* (Grand Rapids, 1981); *idem*, 'Wisdom in the OT', in *ABD* 6, pp. 920–931; L. G. Perdue, *Wisdom and Creation: The Theology of Wisdom Literature* (Nashville, 1994); H. D. Preuss, *Einführung in die alttestamentliche Weisheitsliteratur* (Stuttgart, 1987); G. von Rad, *Wisdom in Israel* (ET, London and Nashville, 1972); H. Ringgren, *Word and Wisdom* (Lund, 1947); E. J. Schnabel, *Law and Wisdom from Ben Sira to Paul* (Tübingen, 1985); G. H. Wilson, 'Wisdom', in *NIDOTTE* 4, pp. 1276–1285; B. Witherington, *Jesus the Sage: The Pilgrimage of Wisdom* (Edinburgh, 1994).

E. J. SCHNABEL

WITNESS, see TESTIMONY/WITNESS
WONDERS, see SIGNS AND WONDERS

WORD

Foundational to biblical theology and religion is the conviction that *God has spoken. Through his word, God has revealed himself, his will and his actions on behalf of his *people and the world. God's word has always come to his people in the context of his personal relationship with them, as an expression of his *grace and power in their historical circumstances. In biblical theology, 'word' refers primarily to God's word, which is the focus of this article.

Few topics are mentioned more frequently in the Bible than that of 'word' or 'speech'. Even with reference only to God's word, the range of usage is extensive. God's word in the Bible incorporates various modes of speaking (direct address, words in a dream or vision, speech through a messenger, written communication), different types of content (command, instruction, *blessing, *forgiveness, promise, reproof, warning, declaration of the divine will, *etc.*), and different intentions (locutionary vs. illocutionary acts; see below). The terms most commonly used for 'word' or 'speech' are *dābār* and *'ēmer* and their cognates in Hebrew, and *legō/logos* and *rhēma* in Greek, but a wide variety of other terms and phrases are used for more specialized modes or types of speaking (*e.g.* terms for command, answer, promise) or figuratively to refer to speech (*e.g.* 'voice', 'mouth', 'lips').

God's word in the OT

Word and deed

It is common in the literature on this topic to find, even in the standard works, some degree of confusion about the supposed Hebrew concept of the 'word' and its relationship to reality. It is often said that the Hebrew way of thinking, and thus the OT, made no distinction between word and thing (*i.e.* an utterance and the reality to which it refers) or between word and deed or effect (*i.e.* an utterance and what it produces). Similarly it is said that words possess an inherent power and so once uttered they exert a mysterious force which leads to the fulfilment of what is spoken. This confusion is due to a cluster of linguistic and theological misunderstandings that are well-discussed elsewhere (see J. Barr, *The Semantics of Biblical Language*, pp. 131–140; *idem*, in *JSS*; A. Thiselton, in *JTS*; P. Cotterell and M. Turner, *Linguistics and Biblical Interpretation*, pp. 175–178).

In fact, in the OT speech is often connected with action by metonymy or other figurative extension. Also utterances are personified as a figurative way of expressing personal involvement. In the case of the faithful, sovereign God of the OT, what he says will occur and what he does to accomplish it can easily be conceptually conjoined. This does not indicate, however, that ancient Hebrews understood words to possess a magical power or concrete existence in themselves. The identity and reliability of the speaker and his or her authority and power to act in accordance with his/her word is all-important.

On the other hand, numerous statements can be found in the OT showing that ancient Hebrews could distinguish words from deeds or words from their effects. In a number of texts the Lord is quoted as saying that he has spoken and will accomplish it, indicating a distinction between utterance and action, yet assuring the reader that what God says, he will do (Num. 14:35; Is. 46:11; Ezek. 12:25, 28; 17:24; 22:14; 24:14; 36:36; 37:14). The OT writers are well aware that words can be superficial, that mere speech is no substitute for action, and that statements may not correspond to reality (*e.g.* 2 Kgs. 18:20; Job 21:34; 35:16; Ps. 41:6; Prov. 14:23; 26:23; 29:19; Is. 59:4; Hos. 10:4).

God's word as revelation

The OT is clear that Yahweh is a God who speaks and that *Israel is remarkably privileged in having him speak to them: 'Did any people ever hear the voice of a god speaking out of the midst of the fire, as you have heard, and still live?... From heaven he let you hear his voice' (Deut. 4:33, 36, RSV; Exod. 20:22). One of the marks of a false god is that it cannot speak (Ps. 115:5; Is. 41:26; Jer. 10:5). The true God is a God who speaks to reveal himself and his will.

The OT is filled with references to Yahweh's speaking. Phrases like 'the word(s) of the LORD', 'thus says the LORD', 'the LORD says/said', 'the word(s) of God', and related expressions ('his word'; 'he says/said'; references to God's voice, mouth, lips, *etc.*) occur hundreds of times and in every part of the OT. God speaks in *theophanies (Gen. 18:1–33; Judg. 6:11–18), in dreams and visions (Gen. 15:1; 1 Kgs. 3:5), through his messengers (2 Kgs. 7:1; Is. 39:5–7), and in written form (Exod. 24:1–7; Jer. 36:1–7).

God's word is the primary means of revelation in the OT. God reveals himself and his ways in the created world and in his deeds in history, but his word is essential for a proper understanding of what *creation and history reveal. Through his word God reveals what he is like, what he has done and will do in the outworking of his purposes, and how *humankind should respond to him. His word takes the form of self-disclosure,

command, *law, promise, warning, *judgment, blessing, forgiveness, reassurance, commissioning, announcement of divine intention, *etc.* (*e.g.* Gen. 15:1; 21:1; 22:2; Exod. 20:1–17; Jer. 31:31–34). Some of these forms of speech are also acts of pronouncing, appointing, *etc.* (*i.e.* performative speech; *e.g.* Exod. 3:17; Jer. 21:8; Hos. 4:6).

God's word, whatever form it takes, is thus a communication from him. It is intelligible and articulate, addressed to people in human language so that they may understand and act on it. The OT contains little reflection on how it is possible for an infinite God to address finite humans in an understandable way, though it regularly expresses awe and gratitude for such condescension. Human language is assumed to be a sufficient and effective means, if not a perfect one, of communication from God to people.

God's word and God's people

In the OT God speaks always in a context of initiating and pursuing a relationship with people. From the first interaction in Eden (Gen. 2:16–17; 3:9–19), through the establishing of the *covenants with Abraham (Gen. 12:1–3; 15:1–21; 17:1–27), the giving of the Torah through *Moses (*e.g.* Exod. 19 – 23; *cf.* 34:28, in which the Ten Commandments are called 'the ten words' [RSV mg]) and God's promise to David (2 Sam. 7:4–17), to the announcement of judgment and *hope through the *prophets (*e.g.* Is. 40; Jer. 30 – 31; Ezek. 37), God is active by his word to establish, guide, judge and deliver his people. Since God through his word reveals his character and declares his will, it is part of his relationship with his people. His calling them to live by his commands, promising blessing, and announcing judgment on disobedience are rooted in his grace in calling Israel to be his people. Through the word God reaches out to his people and expresses his emotions towards them (*e.g.* Num. 14:10–11; Is. 65:1–2; Jer. 31:20; Hos. 11:8), and through the word his people are enabled to know him more fully (*e.g.* Num. 12:6–8; Deut. 31:11–13). The word of the Lord is thus an extension of his grace and power towards the people he has chosen and through them towards the *nations of the world (*e.g.* Exod. 9:16; Pss. 96:3, 10; 138:4). In response his people must make his word their meditation, their delight, and their sustenance (*e.g.* Deut. 8:3; 32:46–47; Pss. 1:1–2; 119:11, 16, 97, 162; Jer. 15:16).

The authority of God's word

The formulas used so frequently to introduce God's word in the OT emphasize that God is its source. Even when the message is delivered through a prophet or *leader of God's people, the expressions 'thus says the LORD', 'hear the word of the LORD', 'the word of the LORD came to ...' *etc.* deflect attention away from the human instrument to the divine source of the utterance. Thus the message is invested with the authority and trustworthiness of the sovereign, faithful God. His word is completely pure, flawless and does not lie (Num. 23:19; Pss. 12:6; 18:30; Prov. 30:5). Because the word expresses God's will and possesses God's authority, it has eternal validity (Ps. 119:89; Is. 40:7–8). Even the passages in which God is said to 'repent' or change his mind concerning something he has said (Exod. 32:9–14; Is. 38:1–6; Jonah 3:4–10) do not afford exceptions to this rule. They refer to pronouncements of judgment that serve not as expressions of God's inexorable will but as warnings to turn from wickedness. It is clear that judgment can be averted by a righteous response (*cf.* Jer. 18:7–10; 26:3–6, 19).

Two implications follow from the supreme authority of God's word. The first is that all who hear God's word are expected to respond with full *obedience and *faith. Though the word possesses only a derived authority (it is not divine), it must be treated as the expression of the sovereign God, and any disobedience or unbelief is an offence against his authority. To doubt or reject his word is to doubt or reject God himself. This is true regardless of whether the word comes by God's direct address (Gen. 2:16–17) or through his human messenger (1 Sam. 15:1–26). What God says to Moses about prophets is paradigmatic for God's word: 'I will raise up for them a prophet like you from among their brethren; and I will put my words in his mouth, and he shall speak to them all that I command him. And whoever will not give heed to my words which he shall speak in my name, I myself will require it of him' (Deut. 18:18–19).

The second implication is that since the word comes from the almighty God, his command and his action to accomplish what he desires are sometimes identical: the first implies the second; God's word accomplishes his will. For example, when God speaks his creative word (Gen. 1:3, 9, 11), he speaks and the work is done, seemingly without any accompanying act of creating (*cf.* Pss. 33:6, 9; 104:5–7). But the OT shows in several places that God's creative acts do accompany his commands; for example, in Genesis 1:6–7: 'God said, "Let there be a firmament" ... And God made the firmament ...' (*cf.* vv. 14–18, 20–21, 24–25; Is. 45:12; 48:3, 13). The references to God creating by his word (*e.g.* Gen. 1:3, 9, 11; Pss. 33:6, 9; 104:5–7) are shorthand references to both his words and his deeds, emphasizing his sovereignty and power, the 'absolute effortlessness of the divine creative action' (G. von Rad, *Old Testament Theology*, p. 142).

God's word in the NT

The NT writers share with the OT writers the conviction that God has spoken as a cardinal means of bringing his grace and power to bear on this world. But God's mode of speaking changes (the OT prophetic introductory formulas are hardly ever used in the NT). Instead the focus of God's speaking becomes the word of God through *Jesus (Jesus' authoritative teaching) and the word of God about Jesus (the *gospel message about God's work of *salvation through Christ). In his person and work Jesus becomes the ultimate form of God's communication, as Hebrews 1:1–2a declares: 'God spoke long ago in various portions and in various ways to the fathers through the prophets, but in these last days he has spoken to us in a Son' (author's translation).

Jesus' teaching

While Jesus' words are never introduced by the OT prophetic formulas like 'thus says the LORD', 'hear the word of the LORD', or 'the word of the LORD came to...', his teaching and preaching are clearly understood to originate in God and to be invested with supreme authority. He proclaims the gospel of the *kingdom of God (Matt. 4:17, 23; 9:35; Mark 1:15; Luke 4:43; 8:1). To hear Jesus' teaching is to hear the word of God (Luke 5:1; 8:11, 21; 11:28). His unique relationship with God his Father sets him apart from every mere prophet: 'All things have been delivered to me by my Father; and no one knows the Son except the Father, and no one knows the Father except the Son and any one to whom the Son chooses to reveal him' (Matt. 11:27; *cf.* John 7:29; 10:15; 13:3; 17:25). John is especially emphatic that Jesus, as God's unique Son, speaks the words of God: 'I am in the Father and the Father is in me. The words that I say to you I do not speak on my own authority' (14:10b); 'The word which you hear is not mine but the Father's who sent me' (14:24b); 'I have given them the words which you gave to me' (17:8; *cf.* 3:34–35; 5:38; 6:63, 68; 8:42–47; 17:14).

So Jesus' words have paramount authority. His teaching is acknowledged as superior in authority to that of the Jewish scribes, and his miracles of healing and exorcism confirm it (Matt. 7:28–29; Mark 1:22, 27; Luke 4:32, 36). In the so-called 'antitheses' ('[you have heard that] it was said [regarding some regulation of the Law] ... But I say to you' [Matt. 5:21–48; *cf.* 19:8–9]), he takes it upon himself to declare the true meaning of the Law and the Prophets. These statements are followed, at the end of the Sermon on the Mount, by his claim that personal security or destruction depends entirely on how one responds to his words (Matt. 7:24–27; *cf.* Luke 6:46–49).

Jesus' awareness of the supreme authority of his teaching is reflected also in his frequent use of the formula 'truly I say to you' (50 times in the Synoptics; 25 times in John, always with the double affirmation 'truly, truly'). In the sayings which follow this formula Jesus presumes to give instruction on future judgment and *reward, qualifications for entering the kingdom, and other future events of this life and the eschaton. Being ashamed of Jesus and his words will bring dire consequences in the coming judgment (Mark 8:38; John 12:48), but whoever keeps his word will never see *death (John 8:51). His teaching has lasting validity; *heaven and earth will pass away, but his words will not (Matt. 24:35; Mark 13:31; Luke 21:33; *cf.* Matt. 5:18).

The gospel message

In Acts and the epistles the emphasis moves away from the word of God through Jesus to the word of God about Jesus. The phrases 'word of God', 'word of the Lord', and simply 'the word' are used mostly to denote the gospel, the message about God's work of salvation through the death and resurrection of Jesus Christ. This is the word preached by the apostles and the early church as they went out as Spirit-empowered witnesses to Jesus (Acts 1:8; see Peter's witness in Acts 2 – 4).

That this is the meaning of 'the word' and related phrases is most clearly seen where they occur in contexts that define the nature of the message. Acts 8:14, for example, speaks of the apostles in Jerusalem hearing that 'Samaria had received the word of God'. Samaria had responded to Philip preaching Christ (v. 5) and proclaiming 'good news about the kingdom of God and the name of Jesus Christ' (v. 12). Similarly in Acts 11:1 the report comes to Jerusalem of the Gentiles having received the word of God. The message to which Cornelius and others responded was Peter's proclamation about God's forgiveness offered in the life, death and resurrection of Jesus of Nazareth, summarized in 10:34–43 (see also 13:44–49, following the account of Paul's message in vv. 16–41). Another indication that 'the word' refers to the gospel is the common occurrence of explanatory genitives like 'the message [lit. 'word'] of this salvation' (Acts 13:26), 'the word of the gospel' (Acts 15:7), 'the word of his grace' (Acts 14:3; 20:32), 'the word of faith which we preach' (Rom. 10:8; *cf.* vv. 9–17), 'the word of the cross' (1 Cor. 1:18; *cf.* 2:2), 'the word of truth, the gospel of your salvation' (Eph. 1:13; *cf.* Col. 1:5), 'the word of life' (Phil. 2:16). 'The word' is identified with the gospel also in James 1:18, 21 and 1 Peter 1:23–25.

It is only right that this gospel which the early Christians proclaimed should be called 'God's word'. It is a message that comes from God and carries his authority and pledge, as though God himself were speaking through his messengers. It is also a message about God's work of salvation, a work planned, put into action, and ultimately accomplished by God himself. So at two levels this message or gospel comes from God; the proclamation and the reality it describes are both from God. Paul makes this point in 2 Corinthians 5:18–21: 'God was in Christ reconciling the world to himself... and he has committed to us the message [lit. 'word'] of reconciliation. So we are ambassadors for Christ, God making his appeal through us ...' (vv. 19–20a; *cf.* Rom. 1:1–4; Titus 1:1–3).

Because the gospel is from God, it is powerful and effective as an extension of his saving work in the world (Rom. 1:16; 1 Cor. 1:18; 1 Thess. 2:13). 'The word of God is living and active' not in itself, but because God is at work through it (Heb. 4:12–13).

God's word and false teaching

God's word of salvation in the gospel is so important that its pure message must be guarded against distortion, corruption or adulteration. This is the point Paul makes in 2 Corinthians 2:17 and 4:2, emphasizing that God's word is a matter of life or death with respect to the destiny of individuals (*cf.* 2:14–16; 4:3–7). Jesus himself warns against false teachers who will come in like wolves to lead the flock of God's people astray (Matt. 7:15; 24:11, 24). Paul uses the same imagery in Acts 20:26–32. He warns the Ephesian elders against those who would savage the flock by 'speaking perverse things [lit. 'words']' to lure people into following them, and he commends them instead 'to God and to the word of his grace' that is able to keep them sound. In 1 Corinthians 15, Paul combines references to the gospel and to the word that he preached (vv. 1–2), as he corrects the distorted teaching of some of the Corinthians regarding the resurrection (v. 12). The death and resurrection of Christ is central to Paul's gospel (vv. 3–11), and the Corinthians' teaching is incompatible with this message (vv. 12–28). In more vehement terms Paul warns the Galatians about the difference between a distorted gospel (Gal. 1:7) and the one he received through revelation (vv. 12, 16).

However, Paul acknowledges also that the gospel of Christ that he preached is not his alone; he received it by *tradition from others who were in the faith before him (1 Cor. 15:3). The ideas of handing over, entrusting and receiving Christian teaching are common in the NT, in early and late books (Acts 16:4; Rom. 6:17; 1 Cor. 11:2, 23; 15:1–3; 1 Thess. 4:1–2; 2 Thess. 2:15; 3:6; 1 Tim. 6:20; 2 Tim. 1:13–14; 2:2; 2 Pet. 2:21; Jude 3). God is viewed as the ultimate source of this teaching, and so Christians are expected to hold firmly to it (Rom. 16:17; 1 Cor. 14:37; 2 John 9–11). In some later NT books (*e.g.* Pastorals, 2 Peter and Jude, Johannine letters) the need to maintain the purity of the message receives more attention because false teaching is more threatening. But, as shown above, this concern is not limited to later books.

Jesus as the Word

We have indicated that in the NT the 'word of God' is usually the message given by Jesus and about Jesus. In a few places 'the Word' (Gk. *Logos*) or 'the Word of God' is used as a title for Jesus personally (John 1:1, 14; Rev. 19:13). Much has been written about the background of this usage; the most plausible view is that John draws primarily from OT and Jewish ideas rather than from Hellenistic ones (see R. E. Brown, *The Gospel According to John*, pp. 519–524 for details).

As to what this title signifies, three points should be noted. First and most importantly, it defines Jesus' relationship with God. John 1:1b presents Jesus as distinct from God (the Father) yet in close communion with him ('the Word was with God'). The next statement declares the full deity of Jesus as the Word (v. 1c, 'the Word was God'). This idea is developed through the Gospel in a number of themes that emphasize Jesus' unique Sonship (1:14, 18; 3:16, 18), his oneness with God in person and action (5:17–21; 10:30; 14:11, 20; 17:11), his sharing the divine glory before the world began (17:5, 24), *etc.* The account of Thomas's climactic experience indicates that John intends to bring all his readers to confess that Jesus is 'Lord and God' (20:28) and to believe in him as 'the Christ, the Son of God' (20:30–31). Because of his relationship and identity with God, no better revealer of the Father could be found, as the Prologue states in its conclusion: 'No one has ever seen God. The unique Son, God, who is in the bosom of the Father, he has made him known' (1:18, author's translation; *cf.* 14:7–9). Hebrews 1:1–4 presents a similar idea; God's ultimate way of speaking is in his Son, the one who shares his divine glory and nature.

Secondly, the title defines Jesus' relationship to creation. John indicates that Jesus existed before creation. 'In the beginning was the Word ... He was in the beginning with God' (John 1:1–2, an allusion to Gen. 1:1, which describes the beginning of God's creative work). Also he was separate from and an agent in God's creative work; 'all things were made through him, and apart from him not anything was made that was made' (1:3). This statement clearly draws upon the OT ideas of God's creative word (Gen. 1:3, 9, 11; Pss. 33:6, 9; 104:5–7) and the personification of *Wisdom as God's companion in creating and sustaining the world (*e.g.* Prov. 8:22–31; *cf.* Ecclus. 24:1–9; Wisdom of Solomon 7:22–28), but it also develops them.

Finally, John uses the title to define Jesus' relationship to humanity. 'In him was life, and the life was the light of men ... The Word became flesh and dwelt among us ... we have beheld his glory' (1:4, 14). The Word who was God became truly human in order to bring the life of God to his fallen creatures. These statements incorporate OT ideas of God's word sent by him as a *life-giving force (Deut. 32:46–47; Ps. 107:20; Is. 55:11), but with profound differences; this Word is not just personified, but enters human existence in order to bring God's eternal life to humankind. So it is fitting for the exalted Christ to be presented as 'the Word of God' in the account of his return in power and great glory at the consummation of history (Rev. 19:13). In 1 John 1:1–2 'the word of life' is probably one step removed from a reference to Jesus personally, but it refers to the message about him and the life he brings, to which John can testify from direct personal experience.

God's word and Scripture

This article has focused on God's word as spoken or oral communication. But the OT and NT both make clear that the word of God may exist in written form as well. Just as God's spoken word is fully authoritative whether it comes through direct address or through a human messenger, so according to both the OT and the NT God's written word commands full obedience and faith. In Exodus 24 Moses recounts the Lord's commands orally and the people pledge their obedience (v. 3); then Moses writes down 'all the words of the LORD' (v. 4) and subsequently reads from this book in inaugurating the covenant: 'Then he took the book of the covenant, and read it in the hearing of the people; and they said, "All that the LORD has spoken we will do, and we will be obedient"' (v. 7). The same reverence for God's word, spoken and written, is found throughout the OT (Deut. 28:58–61; 31:24–29; Josh. 8:34; 2 Chr. 34:21; Neh. 8:13; Is. 30:8; Jer. 30:1–3; 36:1–7, 27–32). The NT also understands the OT to be God's word in written form,

because God speaks through its writers (Matt. 1:22; 2:15; 19:4–5; Mark 12:26, 36; John 10:34–36; Acts 1:16; 3:18; 4:25–26; 28:25; Rom. 12:19; 1 Cor. 14:21; 2 Cor. 6:17–18; 2 Tim. 3:16–17; Heb. 3:7; 9:8; 10:15; 2 Pet. 1:19–21). Given the early Christian's view of the OT, it was only natural that the growing collection of Paul's letters and Jesus' teachings in written form came eventually to be regarded as Scripture as well (since, as shown above, they also were regarded as God's word), and the beginnings of this process can be seen even in some NT writings (1 Tim. 5:18; 2 Pet. 3:15–16; *cf.* 1 Cor. 7:25, 40; 14:37; 1 Thess. 4:2, 8).

See also: REVELATION (concept).

Bibliography

F. R. Ames in *NIDOTTE* 1, pp. 912–915; J. Barr, *The Semantics of Biblical Language* (London, 1961); *idem*, 'Hypostatization of linguistic phenomena in modern theological interpretation', *JSS* 7, 1962, pp. 85–94; J. Bergman *et al.* in *TDOT* 3, pp. 84–125; R. E. Brown, *The Gospel According to John* (Garden City and London, 1966, 1971); P. Cotterell and M. Turner, *Linguistics and Biblical Interpretation* (Downers Grove and London, 1989); A. Debrunner *et al.* in *TDNT* 4, pp. 69–136; T. E. Fretheim in *ABD* 6, pp. 961–968; H. Haarbeck *et al.* in *NIDNTT* 3, pp. 1078–1146; H. Hübner in *EDNT* 2, pp. 346–347; D. H. Johnson in *DJG*, pp. 481–484; J. A. Lund in *NIDOTTE* 1, pp. 443–449; G. von Rad, *Old Testament Theology*, vol. 2 (ET, New York and Edinburgh, 1965); H. Ritt in *EDNT* 2, pp. 356–359; A. C. Thiselton, 'The supposed power of words in the biblical writings', *JTS* n.s. 25, 1974, pp. 283–299; S. Wagner *et al.* in *TDOT* 1, pp. 328–345.

B. M. FANNING

WORK, see REST

WORLD

Introduction

The biblical relationship between *God and the world, and that between the *people of God and the world, are ambiguous. On the one hand, the whole world belongs to God (Ps. 24:1; *cf.* 89:11); on the other, while the heavens belong to Yahweh, *humanity is responsible for the world (Ps. 115:16). Whereas John's gospel declares God's *love for the world (John 3:16), John also warns Christians not to love the world (1 John 2:15). The reason for these ambiguities lies in the fact that human beings are charged with taking care of the world as God's representatives, but have failed to represent God faithfully. In consequence the world is shaped not only by God's design in *creation, but also by human rebellion (see *Sin) against God. As God's creation the whole world is the focus of God's love and should therefore be the focus of human love and attention as well. As the place of human rebellion against God, it stands in contrast to God's *kingdom, and as an alternative focus of trust and commitment it can come to stand over against God himself.

The world in God's plan

The book of Genesis tells us that the whole universe ('heaven and earth') was created by one God who ordered it and filled it with living things (Gen. 1:1 – 2:3). God's creation of the world establishes his sovereignty (see *Providence) over it (celebrated, *e.g.,* in Pss. 24:1–2; 104; *cf.* Is. 44:24; Acts 4:24; 14:15; 17:24). On the basis of this sovereignty, God can use the world to *bless or curse his people (see *e.g.* Deut. 28). The world is created good and is designed to develop further ('each according to its kind') under the guidance of human beings (*cf.* Gen. 2:15), who are created in the *image of God; that is, they are able to relate to him and to act as his representatives on earth ruling over the other creatures (Gen. 1:28; *cf.* Ps. 8:5–8). But the first human couple subvert this order by listening to a creature and disobeying the command of the creator (Gen. 2:4 – 3:24), with the result that not only humanity's relationship with God but also its relationship with the world becomes distorted (Gen. 3:17–19; *cf.* 4:11). Instead of guarding and watching over creation, humanity corrupts the world. God's first response to humanity's destruction of the world is to destroy 'all flesh' (Gen. 6:11–13). A new beginning is made with the renewal of God's blessing on humankind, which includes his intention that they should 'be fruitful and multiply and fill

the earth' (Gen. 9:1; *cf.* v. 7). God's blessing allows humanity to expand over time (as shown in the genealogies) and to develop into many ethnic and cultural groups (Gen. 10). This diversity is achieved, however, only after God intervenes to prevent humanity from collectively disregarding his intention in an attempt to preserve a self-centred unity (Gen. 11:1–9). God's interest in the whole human race is preserved in the call of Abram in whom 'all the families of the earth shall find blessing' (12:3; my translation). God's special purpose for his people is part of a universal plan.

Israel and the nations

*Israel is called to mediate God's blessing to the world, revealing the nature of God's kingdom in every area of human life, including politics and culture (*cf.* Exod. 19:5–6). The ultimate goal is for the nations to come to Zion to serve and learn from Yahweh, who will mediate between them and abolish war (Is. 2:2–4; Mic. 4:1–4). The relationship between Israel and the rest of the world is to be governed by Israel's relationship with God. Consequently, Israel is expressly forbidden to tolerate in its midst *nations that God had rejected (Deut. 20:16–18) and to imitate those practices of other nations that are abhorrent to Yahweh (Deut. 12:30–31; 18:9–14), and the prophets continually warn Israel against trusting in alliances with foreign nations rather than in God. While the prophets deal mostly with Israel and Judah, they apply God's norm to other nations as well, and thereby affirm that Yahweh's sovereignty extends over all nations and that the whole world is accountable to him (*e.g.* Is. 13 – 24; Jer. 46 – 51; Ezek. 25 – 32). Some of the last books of the OT to be written also underline the unity of humankind (1 Chr. 1) and the vision that the Lord will become king over all the earth (Zech. 14:9).

Jesus and the world

John's Gospel frequently describes *Jesus as the one who was coming (1:9; 6:14; 11:27) or has come (12:46; 16:28; 18:37) into the world (*cf.* 3:16–17). Jesus is the one through whom the world came into being (*cf.* Col. 1:16), but who was not recognized by the world (John 1:10). Nevertheless, God's sending of Jesus into the world demonstrates his love and saving purpose for the world (3:16–

17; *cf.* 12:47). When they recognize that Jesus is the one who was to come into the world, the people want to make him king (6:14–15); but the kingship of Jesus is of an altogether different kind, in that he comes into the world to testify to the truth (18:37). This kind of kingship involves submission to the one God and Jesus therefore rejects the tempter's offer of 'all the kingdoms of the world' (Matt. 4:8–10; *cf.* Luke 4:5–8). His authority on earth is to forgive sins (Matt. 9:6; *cf.* Mark 2:10; Luke 5:24), and he delegates this authority to his disciples (Matt. 16:19; 18:18). The good news of the kingdom will be proclaimed throughout the world (Matt. 24:14), on the basis of the authority in heaven and on earth which is given to Jesus (Matt. 28:18–20).

The glorification of God through Jesus brings *judgment on 'the ruler of this world', who has no hold on Jesus (John 12:31; 14:30; 16:33; see *Spiritual powers). Those who accept the word of Jesus are said no longer to belong to this world (15:18–19; 17:14, 16), because they do not identify with the ruler of this world, but with the one who came from heaven. This world cannot receive the Spirit of truth (14:17), but the Spirit sent by Jesus will prove the world wrong (16:7–11). The contrast between those who accept the light and those who prefer the darkness (3:19–21) makes the world a hostile environment for those who receive Jesus (15:18–19; *cf.* 7:7). Yet Jesus' disciples are not taken out of the world, but are to continue Jesus' *mission to the world under God's protection (17:15, 18).

In the end, the contrast between heaven as the place where God rules and earth as the place where God's rule is challenged is overcome in Jesus, who reconciles the creation with the Creator by his death on the cross (1 Cor. 8:5–6; Eph. 1:10; Col. 1:15–17, 20).

The people of God from all nations sent to all nations

While people from other nations can be incorporated into the people of God throughout the OT period, it is only through the breaking down of the wall between Jews and Gentiles in the work of Jesus Christ (Gal. 3; *cf.* Rom. 3) that the people of God becomes truly international. Now the call to believe in the God of Israel goes out to the whole world, as described in Luke-Acts (see Acts 1:8). The *Holy Spirit plays a crucial role in widening the circle of people addressed by the word of God (see Acts 2, 8 and 10).

The Holy Spirit also reveals the difference between a 'spiritual' and a 'wordly' way of life, developing the command to Israel to be *holy (Lev. 19). The difference is not between two compartments of life, one religious and one secular, but between life ordered under the rule of God and life in conformity to the human tradition of rebellion against God. In this sense, the Christian is not to love the world (*e.g.* 1 John 2:15–17; *cf.* Rom. 12:2). The NT therefore challenges its readers to decide between allegiance to the values of God's kingdom, the new world that has already come into being (2 Cor. 5:16–17), and the wisdom and values of unbelievers who are still under the spell of 'the god of this world' (2 Cor. 4:4), a world that (generally speaking) does not yet submit to God (*cf.* Gal. 6:14; Col. 2:8, 20).

The consummation of God's plan for the world

The present world order will pass away to be replaced by the kingdom of God, which will extend over all creation (*e.g.* Mark 13:31; 2 Pet. 3; Rev. 21; see *Eschatology). The logical and appropriate consequence of *one* God's provision of *salvation through *one* human is *one* world confessing this God to be Lord (Phil. 2:10–11; *cf.* Is. 45:23). Then the three parts of creation, that is, heaven, earth and netherworld, will again fully belong to the one from whom they came (Phil. 2:10 *cf.* Eph. 1:10; Col. 1:20). This will truly be a new creation. In Christ, we already participate to some extent in this new creation and are challenged to live according to the values of this new world (*e.g.* in Col. 3:1–5).

Bibliography

J. Painter in *DJG*, pp. 887–891; *idem* in *DPL*, pp. 979–982; C. H. H. Scobie, 'Israel and the nations: An essay in biblical theology', *TynB* 43, 1992, pp. 283–305.

T. RENZ

WORSHIP

Nowhere in Scripture is worship actually defined. But when key biblical terms for worship are examined in a variety of contexts it is clear that the central concepts are homage, service and reverence. In the OT, ideally worship is focused at the sanctuary appointed by *God. It follows the rituals laid down by God and is facilitated by the *priesthood he has ordained. But this cultic activity is not honouring to the LORD unless it leads to *obedience and praise in every sphere of life. In the NT, the same terminology of worship is used in a transformed way to portray the work of Christ and the response that pleases God. *Jesus as Son of God and high priest of the new *covenant fulfils and replaces the whole system of approach to God that was at the heart of the old covenant. His incarnation, death, resurrection and ascension make possible an engagement with God 'in spirit and truth', which culminates in the unceasing worship of the new creation.

Biblical terms for worship

Worship as homage or grateful submission to God

The Hebrew verb most commonly translated 'to worship' (hištaḥ'wâ) literally means 'bend oneself over at the waist'. It is regularly translated by proskynein in the Greek Bible. From earliest times, this term expressed the oriental custom of bowing down or casting oneself on the ground, kissing the feet, the hem of a garment or the ground, as a total bodily gesture of respect before a great one (e.g. Gen. 18:2; Exod. 18:7; 2 Sam. 14:4). Applied to the gods of paganism, it meant bending over or falling down before an image or making some literal gesture of homage to the god. At an early stage, it also came to be used for the inward attitude of homage or respect which the outward gesture represented.

In the OT, this gesture expressed surrender or submission to the living and true God. Sometimes it was an immediate and spontaneous reaction to a divine action or revelation, specifically motivated by awe and gratitude (e.g. Gen. 24:26–27, 52; Exod. 4:31; 34:8; Judg. 7:15). Bending over before the LORD, as a gesture of homage or grateful submission, also became associated with *sacrifice and public praise in Israel. In such contexts, it could be a formal way of expressing devotion to or dependence on God (e.g. Deut. 26:1–11; Ps. 95:1–7; 1 Chr. 29:20–21; 2 Chr. 7:3–4; 29:28–30; Neh. 8:6). But the gesture was meaningful only if it

expressed a recognition of God's majesty and holiness and a desire to acknowledge him as king.

Worship as service to God

Another biblical term often translated 'to worship' is the Hebrew 'aḇad, which literally means 'to serve'. When this verb refers specifically to the service offered to God, it is often rendered by latreuein in the LXX. The purpose of *Israel's redemption from slavery in Egypt was to release the *people for exclusive service to the LORD (e.g. Exod. 3:12; 4:23; 8:1). When the parallel expressions 'to sacrifice to the LORD' (3:18; 5:3, 8, 17; 8:8, 25–29) and 'to hold a festival' (5:1) are used, it is clear that some form of ritual service is in view.

A complex system of sacrifices and rituals was instituted by God so that Israel could serve him appropriately at his chosen sanctuary. For example, the Passover was a 'service' to be observed in remembrance of the LORD's saving work at the time of the Exodus (12:25–27; 13:5). The ministry of priests and Levites was a specialized form of service to God and this is generally indicated in the LXX by the use of the verb leitourgein and related terms (usually translating the Heb. šārēṯ). But some passages set Israel's service within the broader framework of *fearing God, walking in all his ways, and observing all his commands and decrees. A total lifestyle of allegiance to God was clearly required of God's people (e.g. Deut. 10:12–13; Josh. 22:5; 24:14–24). Consequently, bowing down and serving created things or other gods was strictly forbidden (e.g. Deut. 4:19, 28; 5:9; 7:4, 16) and provisions were made for removing every temptation to *idolatry.

Worship as reverence or respect for God

A final group of terms was used to indicate the fear, reverence or respect due to God. In Greek, these were words based on the seb-stem or words in the phoboun group, generally translating the Hebrew yārē' and its cognates. Such fear involved keeping his commandments (e.g. Deut. 5:29; 6:2, 24; Eccles. 12:13), obeying his voice (e.g. 1 Sam. 12:14; Hag. 1:12), walking in his ways (e.g. Deut. 8:6; 10:12; 2 Chr. 6:31), turning away from evil (e.g. Job. 1:1, 8; 2:3; 28:28; Prov. 3:7), and serving him (e.g. Deut. 6:13; 10:20;

Josh. 24:14; Jonah 1:9). Sacrifice and other rituals were clearly a way of expressing reverence for God, but *faithfulness and obedience to the covenant demands of God in every sphere of life were also the distinguishing marks of true religion (e.g. Exod. 18:21; Ps. 25:14; Mal. 3:16; 4:2).

Revelation and redemption: the means of acceptable worship

In various ways the Bible makes it plain that worship is acceptable to God only if it is based on a true knowledge of God and of his will. Worship outside this framework is idolatrous. Thus, in the traditions associated with Mt Sinai, the terms of the relationship between the LORD and his people were set out in great detail and the pattern for acceptable worship was laid down. These regulations were God's special provision for those whom he had redeemed and brought to himself (Exod. 19:3–4). The Israelites were shown how to express their special status as 'a kingdom of priests and a holy nation' (Exod. 19:5–6) in every area of their lives.

Israel's relationship with God was not to be at the level of the mysterious and the irrational. They were to enjoy a personal and moral fellowship with the one who gave his ten 'words' to them (Exod. 20:1–17). These state the fundamental principles of living in a relationship with the God who had graciously brought them 'out of the land of slavery' and consecrated them to himself. The call for exclusive devotion to the God who had redeemed them involved not only the commands to avoid idolatry, sanctify God's name and observe the sabbath (vv. 1–11), but also the demand for obedience to God in the everyday relationships of family and nation (vv. 12–17). The material in Exodus 20:22 – 23:33 functioned as an application of those principles to various aspects of life in the Promised Land. A similar mix of moral, social and ritual laws is found throughout Leviticus, Numbers and Deuteronomy, indicating what it meant for Israel to serve the LORD.

Cultic worship in Israel

Like other nations in the ancient world, Israel expressed its relationship with God through sacrifice and ritual, using sacred enclosures, and depending upon the mediation of priests. In contrast with the many cults of paganism, one national cult, with a single sanctuary, is contemplated in the Mosaic *law (e.g. Deut. 12). The prophets later condemned any departure from this ideal (e.g. 1 Kgs. 12:26 – 14:20).

The significance of the tabernacle

In Exodus 25 – 31 great importance is given to the setting up of a sanctuary or 'holy place' (25:8). The Israelites were to make a tabernacle (Heb. mišᵉkān, 'dwelling', 25:9), with furnishings exactly as God would show them, so that the LORD himself might dwell among them. The divine presence in Israel was not to be linked to any kind of image, since they saw 'no form' of any kind when the LORD spoke to them at Sinai out of the fire (Deut. 4:15–20). Nevertheless, God's continuing presence with them was to be proclaimed and expressed by this tent-sanctuary.

The focal-point of the tabernacle was the ark (Exod. 25:10–22), which was a chest containing the tables of the covenant. This was to remind the Israelites of God's fundamental will for them as his covenant people. But the LORD also promised to meet with Moses and give further instruction for the Israelites, 'above the cover between the cherubim that are over the ark of God' (v. 22, NIV). God's presence and God's rule were jointly expressed by the tabernacle, which was symbolically the throne-room of God in the midst of his people. It was to be located at the very centre of Israel's life on the march from Sinai to the Promised Land (cf. Exod. 40:36–38; Num. 2). The covenant relationship graciously established by the LORD contained at its heart the assurance that he would be their God and they would be his people (e.g. Gen. 17:7–8; Exod. 6:7). Consequently, he would be uniquely with them, to fulfil his purposes and bring blessing to them (e.g. Gen. 28:13–15; Exod. 3:7–8).

With its outer court, inner court, and 'holy of holies' (which only the high priest could enter on the annual Day of Atonement), the tabernacle also reflected the holiness of the God who dwelt in Israel's midst. In concrete form it expressed the truth that human beings could not come into his presence on their own terms. The complex provisions for sacrifice in connection with the tabernacle were the cultic means for acknowledging God's kingship over their lives. The whole system was designed to keep a sinful people in relationship with the Holy One.

The role of the priests

The ordinary Israelite was forbidden to enter the holy place, but could meet with the LORD at the entrance curtain of the tabernacle (Exod. 29:42–46). Only if the sacrificial ordinances of God were carried out according to his decrees would he manifest himself in grace, allowing his glory and his word to dwell among them, to bless them. God consecrated a special priesthood to himself from amongst the Israelites to enable them to relate to him through the cult. The priests did not derive their authority and function from the community but from God, who set them apart to be his servants, attending to the maintenance of his 'house'. The LORD consecrated the sanctuary in which the priests would operate by allowing his glory to dwell there in the first place, and all this was so that he could continue to reveal himself to his people in glory. In making his presence known among them through his word, he would be fulfilling his covenant promise to be 'their God' and his purpose in saving them 'out of Egypt'.

Sacred festivals

Annual festivals were prescribed to enable God's people to acknowledge his hand in the fruitfulness of the earth and to celebrate his goodness with sacrifices and feasting. The Passover, followed by the seven days of unleavened bread, was connected with the barley harvest (Exod. 12:6; 23:15; Lev. 23:5–8; Num. 28:16–25; Deut. 16:1–8); Pentecost, the Feast of Weeks, celebrated the wheat harvest (Exod. 34:22; Lev. 23:10–14; Num. 28:26–31); and Tabernacles (Booths) was at the same time the Feast of Ingathering, the general harvest festival (Exod. 23:16; Lev. 23:33–36, 39–43; Deut. 16:13–15). These occasions were also related to the saving acts of God by which he brought Israel to himself. The Israelites were regularly reminded that the God of creation is the LORD who had revealed himself uniquely to Israel in the great events of her history. The Sabbath, which was a weekly festival, was meant to be another sign of the special relationship between God as creator and redeemer and Israel as his holy people (Exod. 31:13–17).

The fact that the year was marked by a whole series of festivals is a reminder of the extent to which celebration, praise and thanksgiving were at the heart of Israelite religion. It would be wrong to think that people in OT times were wholly occupied with the business of atonement for sins and to regard their worship as a sombre and dreary necessity. The Psalms especially testify to the joy of the pilgrims journeying to Jerusalem and the longing of the godly to meet with God and his people in the courts of his *temple (e.g. Pss. 122; 42; 43; 48; 118:19–29). Indeed, praise and thanksgiving belonged to the whole life of God's people. (See *Sacred meals.)

Temple and sacrifice in prophetic perspectives

The temple as God's earthly dwelling-place

Apart from obvious differences in size and magnificence, the design of the temple reflected to a large extent the pattern provided for the tabernacle. Like the tabernacle, the temple was to represent God's rule over Israel and to be a reminder of his special presence among them, to bless them and make them a source of blessing to the nations. This was made very clear at the dedication ceremony (1 Kgs. 8:1–21). Solomon's prayer questions whether God can really dwell on earth (8:27). Nevertheless, he is conscious of being in God's presence (literally 'before your face', 8:28) and requests that *prayers directed towards 'this place' might be answered by God from heaven, his dwelling-place (8:30). In particular, the temple signified that there was a future for Israel as the people of God because the building itself expressed the continuation of God's covenant promise to be with them and bless them (8:56–61). Even when national sin reached its ultimate end in exile, prayer directed to the place where God had set his name would bring restoration and forgiveness (8:46–51).

Prophetic criticisms of sacrifice and the temple

Numerous passages in the prophetic writings condemn priests and people for their corruption of the sacrificial system (e.g. Amos 4:4–13; Hos. 8:11–13; Jer. 7:21–26; Ezek. 16:15–21; 20:25–31). Sometimes these deal with the introduction of pagan ideas and practices into Israelite worship, or the attempt to worship other gods whilst still claiming to serve the LORD. Often they attack the hypocrisy of engaging in the sacrificial ritual without genuine *repentance or a desire to live in obedience to God's moral law. Sometimes, in order to clarify the sort of response the cult was meant to inculcate in God's people, prophecies are worded in ways that appear to reject the cult categorically (e.g. Amos 5:21–27; Hos. 6:6; Is. 1:10–17; 66:1–4; Mic. 6:6–8). However, there are also texts which speak with approval of future sacrificial activity, portraying a time when God would renew his people and their worship (e.g. Is. 19:19–21; 56:6–7; 60:7; Jer. 17:24–27; 33:10–11, 17–18; Ezek. 20:40–41). In other words, it is not correct to say that the prophets condemned sacrifice absolutely or that they envisaged the survival of Israel apart from the provision of some form of sacrifice.

Although the prophets could argue that the LORD's presence with his people in his sanctuary on Mt Zion meant that he would defend them against their enemies and bless them (e.g. Is. 8:9–10; 31:4–5; 37:33–35), they made it clear that God's protection was not to be regarded as unconditional (e.g. Is. 29:1–4; Jer. 7:1–15). If Israel remained disobedient to the covenant and neglectful of the worship that was truly honouring to him, terrible judgment would come from the hand of the LORD himself (e.g. Is. 1; Mic. 3). If his holiness continued to be desecrated by their corrupt practices, then the temple would have to be destroyed (e.g. Jer. 7:1–15; Ezek. 7 – 9).

Sacrifice and temple in the prophetic hope

Although the prophets saw God as acting in judgment at the time of the exile, they proclaimed that in due time he would act in forgiveness and restoration, allowing a remnant to return to their homeland (Is. 40:1–11; Jer. 31:31–34; Ezek. 20:39–44). Some indicated that the temple would be restored and become the spiritual centre not only of Israel but also of the *nations (e.g. Is. 2:2–3; 44:28; cf. Mic. 4:1–3; Jer. 3:17–18). The coming of the Gentiles, with all their offerings, to God would be the means by which he would adorn his glorious house in the coming age and glorify himself in their midst (Is. 60). Ezekiel's prophecy of the restoration actually included a plan for a new temple (Ezek. 40 – 48). The purifying and sanctifying influence of the new temple upon the *land would restore it to a paradise for God's people (47:1–12; cf. Ps. 36:7–9), for God himself would be there (cf. 48:35). This temple plan, with all its symbolism, combines a number of biblical ideals and points to their ultimate fulfilment, not by some human building programme, but by the sovereign and gracious act of God (cf. Ezek. 20:40–44).

Worship under the new covenant

The replacement of the temple

The Gospels give various indications of the way in which Jesus replaces the Jerusalem temple in the plan and purpose of God. For example, Matthew records his claim that 'one greater than the temple is here' (12:6). As the incarnate Son of God, Jesus represented God's royal presence and authority more fully than did the temple. Moreover, his cleansing of the temple expressed God's imminent judgment against those who abused it (cf. particularly Mark 11:12–21). At the end of the Gospels, the resurrected Jesus indicates that he will continue to draw many into relationship with himself through the witness and teaching of his disciples, thus becoming the centre of salvation and blessing for the nations (Matt. 28:18–20; Luke. 24:46–49; cf. John 12:20–33). The prophetic hope of the nations' uniting with the faithful in Israel to acknowledge and serve the LORD is being fulfilled in Christ. The tearing of the curtain of the temple from top to bottom at the moment of his death (e.g. Matt. 27:51) further suggests the opening of a new way of access to God.

Jesus' cleansing of the temple in John 2:12–22 more explicitly reveals him as the one sent to replace the institutions of the Mosaic covenant. 'Destroy this temple' he claims, 'and I will raise it again in three days' (v. 19). The insight that this saying referred to his resurrection body came only after he had been raised and the disciples 'believed the Scripture and the words that Jesus had spoken' (v. 22). John indicates that Jesus' concern to establish the purpose of God for Israel, *Jerusalem, and the temple will destroy him. Because of this zeal, the Jewish leaders will bring about his death, but Jesus will take up his life again. The temple is fulfilled and replaced in John's perspective by the *death and resurrection of the incarnate Son of God,

859

which secure the ultimate liberation from sin and bring believers to eternal life. The apostle Paul later extends this image to include the community of those who are united to Christ by faith and who are indwelt by his Spirit (*e.g.* 1 Cor. 3:16–17; 2 Cor. 6:16–18; Eph. 2:20–22).

Worship 'in spirit and truth'

In John 4:20–24, a Samaritan woman inquires about the appropriate place to worship God, leading Jesus to speak more fundamentally about *how* to worship God acceptably. In contrast with Samaritan worship, Jewish worship was truly based on divine revelation and was therefore honouring to God (v. 22). However, 'the hour is coming and now is' (RSV), when the OT method of approaching God is to be fulfilled and replaced (vv. 21, 23). The coming 'hour' is the time of Jesus' return to the Father (*e.g.* John 2:4; 7:30; 12:23; 13:1; 17:1). Through his cross and resurrection the new temple is raised up (2:19–22) and the Spirit is given (7:37–39). Thus, Jesus becomes the means by which the Father obtains 'true worshippers' (Greek, *alēthinoi proskynētai*) from every nation (4:23; *cf.* 12:32). This expression suggests that the OT pattern of worship prepared for the reality which was to come in Jesus.

Worship 'in spirit and truth' (4:23) involves acknowledging Jesus as the truth (14:6), who uniquely reveals the Father and his purposes (8:45; 18:37). It also means receiving from him the Spirit who is available for all who believe in him (7:37–39). Jesus is not the object of worship in John 4 but the means to a God-honouring worship under the new covenant. True homage and devotion to God is possible only for those who recognize the significance of Christ and yield him their allegiance. Furthermore, the relationship with God that Jesus makes possible is not tied to any earthly 'place' (4:20) or cult, for the prophetic hope of the temple as the centre for the universal worship of God in the End time (*e.g.* Is. 2:1–4) has been fulfilled in the person and work of the Messiah. The exalted Christ is now the 'place' where God is to be acknowledged and honoured. The Father cannot be honoured unless Jesus is given all the honour due to him as the Son (*cf.* John 5:22–23; 8:49).

The Greek verb *proskynein* is used elsewhere in the NT to show that the Son of God himself is to be accorded the homage and devotion due to the LORD God of Israel (*e.g.* Matt. 14:33; 28:9, 17; Luke 24:52; John 9:38; Heb. 1:6; Rev. 5:9–14; *cf.* Phil. 1:9–11; Rev. 1:12–18). Even where the terminology is not employed, it could be argued that apostolic preaching aimed to bring people to worship Christ in the sense of yielding their allegiance to him as Saviour and Lord (*e.g.* Acts 2:36–39; 10:36–43; *cf.* Rom. 10:9–13). 'Bending over to the Lord' in NT terms means responding with repentance and faith to the person and work of the Lord Jesus Christ. Those who are concerned about God-honouring worship will be pre-occupied with bringing people to Christ. Such worship also involves praying to him (*e.g.* Acts 7:59–60; 1 Cor. 16:22b; 1 Thess. 3:11), calling upon his name as Lord (*e.g.* 1 Cor. 1:2), and obeying him in all the affairs of life.

Pauline perspectives on new covenant worship

The worship that Jesus' sacrifice makes possible

The apostle Paul describes Jesus' death as 'a sacrifice of atonement through faith in his blood' (Rom. 3:25, NIV; *cf.* Eph. 5:2). Only by his sacrifice can the wrath of God be averted (*cf.* Rom. 1:18–28; 2:5). Paradoxically, as in OT teaching about the sacrificial system, it is God who provides the means of forgiveness, cleansing and restoration. In Romans 5:8–9 Jesus' *blood/death is again identified as the means by which sinners are justified and saved from the wrath of God. It is the sacrifice which secures for believers all the blessings of the new covenant and the kingdom of God.

In response to what God has done for believers in Jesus Christ, they are to present themselves to him as 'living sacrifices, holy and pleasing to God' (Rom. 12:1). The sacrifice in question is their 'bodies', meaning themselves as a totality, not just skin and bones (*cf.* 6:13, 16, 'offer yourselves'). Christ's obedience makes possible a new obedience for the people of God. As those who have been brought from death to life, through Jesus' death and resurrection (*cf.* Rom. 6:4–11), they belong to God as a 'living sacrifice'. This is further described as their (literally) 'understanding service' (Gk. *logikēn* *latreian*), suggesting that the presentation of themselves to God in Christ is the essence of Christian worship. The mind is certainly central to Paul's teaching here, but his focus is not simply on rationality. The service for which he calls is obedience motivated by faith in Jesus Christ and what he has done for believers. The lifestyle of those whose minds are being transformed and renewed by God will no longer be conformed to the values, attitudes and behaviour of 'this age' (Rom. 12:2; *cf.* Col. 3:9–10; Eph. 4:22–24). Acceptable worship is the service rendered by those who truly understand the *gospel and want to live out its implications in every sphere of life. In common parlance the word 'service' is so linked to Christian gatherings that the Bible's teaching on the whole of life as the context in which to offer 'divine service' is easily forgotten.

Worship and Christian ministry

The link between ministry to others and service to God is particularly obvious in what Paul says about himself. In Romans 1:9 he indicates that his service takes place specifically in the sphere of gospel ministry. Intercessory prayer is part of it (1:8–10), but gospel preaching is the focus and goal of all his activity (1:11–15). In Romans 15:16, Paul again describes his work using transformed worship terminology. As 'a minister of Christ Jesus to the Gentiles', he is God's designated servant, bestowing benefits on the Gentiles with the gospel. Indeed, he is engaged on Christ's behalf in discharging a 'priestly' ministry. Sacral terminology is used in a transformed way to portray the work of preaching by which he enables the Gentiles to offer themselves to God as an acceptable sacrifice, 'sanctified by the *Holy Spirit'. Gospel preaching brings about the obedience of faith through Jesus Christ, which is the 'understanding worship' that pleases God. Since preaching was not regarded as a ritual activity in Paul's world, he clearly gives that ministry a novel significance when he describes it as the means by which he worships or serves God.

The apostle uses another verb (Gk. *leitourgein*) in Romans 15:27 to describe the service offered by certain Gentile churches to 'the poor among the saints at Jerusalem'. The service to which he refers is financial support. The Gentiles have shared in the Jews' spiritual blessings and owe it to them literally 'to benefit them in material things'. Here, and in 2 Corinthians 9:12 ('this service that you perform'), the terminology refers to the bestowal of public benefits on those in need by those with means (*cf.* also Phil. 2:25, 30). However, this is clearly a ministry that will glorify God (2 Cor. 9:13) and such gifts are 'a fragrant offering, a sacrifice acceptable and pleasing to God' (Phil. 4:18, NRSV). The notion of worshipping or serving God *by means of serving one another* is thus implied.

Worship and edification

Paul regularly uses the terminology of up-building or edification, rather than the language of worship, to indicate the purpose and function of Christian gatherings (*e.g.* 1 Cor. 14:3–5, 12, 17, 26; 1 Thess. 5:11; Eph. 4:11–16). This imagery portrays the founding, maintaining and advancing of the *church as God's eschatological 'building'. While all ministry must be understood as a response to God's grace, and not in any sense as a cultivation of his favour, ministry to others is an aspect of our service or self-giving to God. Moreover, edification is really the exalted Christ's work in our midst, through the gifts and ministries that he empowers and directs by his Spirit (Eph. 2:20–22; 4:7–16; see *Spiritual gifts). When Christians gather together to minister the *truth of God to one another in love, the church is manifested, maintained and advanced in God's way.

It may be best to speak of congregational worship as a particular expression of the total life-response that is the worship of the new covenant. In the giving and receiving of various ministries, Christians may encounter God and submit themselves to him afresh in praise and obedience, repentance and faith (*cf.* Col. 3:16; 1 Cor. 14:24–25). Worship and edification can be two different ways of describing the same activity. Ministry exercised for the building up of the body of Christ is a significant way of worshipping and glorifying God.

Drawing near to God through Jesus as high priest

Jesus' high priestly ministry

Hebrews says much about how the ministry of Christ fulfils and replaces the priesthood and cult associated with the old covenant. 'Sacrifices and offerings, burnt offerings and sin offerings' are all set aside by 'the sacrifice of the body of Jesus Christ once for all' (10:5–14, NIV). As the high priest of the new covenant, he has entered once for all into the heavenly sanctuary, 'having obtained eternal redemption' (9:11–12, 24–28). The writer several times insists on the unique and unrepeatable character of Jesus' sacrifice, in contrast with the numerous and repeated offerings prescribed in the OT (e.g. 7:27; 9:24–28; 10:10, 12, 14). The priestly ministry of Jesus is superior because it involved the offering of *himself* as a pure and unblemished sacrifice to God (7:26–27), securing all the benefits promised in Jeremiah 31:31–34 (cf. Heb. 8:6–13). As a heavenly high priest, 'he is able to save completely those who come to God though him, because he always lives to intercede for them' (7:25). He is willing and able to go on applying the benefits of his once-for-all sacrifice to believers, in the midst of all their trials and temptations (cf. 4:14–16; Rom. 8:34; 1 John 2:1–2). In the argument of Hebrews, the sacrifices, altar and priesthood of the OT all find their fulfilment in the saving work of Jesus Christ, not in some ongoing activity in the Christian congregation.

Experiencing the benefits of Christ's saving work

In two key passages of exhortation, Hebrews challenges Christians to hold fast to their confession and to keep on 'drawing near' to God with confidence (4:14–16; 10:19–23). This is another important worship term adapted from the LXX (Gk. *proserchesthai*, e.g. Exod. 16:9; Lev. 9:5; Num. 16:40). In both cases, the appeal is based on the fact that Christ is the perfected and enthroned high priest, who has entered the heavenly sanctuary by means of his death and heavenly *exaltation and opened up 'a new and living way' into that sanctuary for us. Christians can approach God without the aid of human priesthood, because they rely on the priestly mediation of Jesus Christ. 'Drawing near to God with confidence' is at the heart of what it means to be a Christian. It is the expression of an ongoing relationship of trust and dependence (10:22, 'with a true heart in full assurance of faith'). In 4:16 it means specifically seeking mercy for past failures and 'grace to help us in our time of need'.

Although believers must draw near to God individually, it is also true that those who turn to Christ come *together* into the heavenly presence, to join by faith in the celebration of the heavenly assembly (cf. 12:22–24). The notion of collectively drawing near to God is similarly suggested by the context of Hebrews 10:22. Gathering together is an important means of encouraging one another to persevere in *love and obedience (10:24–25; cf. 3:12–14). As Christians expose themselves to the ministries of others and to the word of God, they engage with God as the *family of God together.

Serving God in the perspective of Hebrews

As in Romans 12:1, in Hebrews Christian worship is also the service rendered in everyday life (Heb. 9:14; 12:28, where *latreuein* is used). The motivation and power for such service is specifically the cleansing that comes from the finished work of Christ (9:28) and the *hope which that work sets before believers (12:28). Gratitude expressed in service is the sign that the grace of God has been grasped and appreciated. However, the writer introduces a more serious note when he asserts that acceptable worship is characterized by 'reverence and awe', and supports his challenge with an allusion to the coming judgment of God ('for our God is a consuming fire'). Hebrews 13:1–7 shows what this means in terms of practical lifestyle.

In 13:8–16 there is a restatement of the theme that the OT system of worship finds its fulfilment in the work of Christ, concluding with another reference to the worship that is 'pleasing to God' (vv. 15–16). The 'sacrifice of praise' Christians are to offer to God through Jesus is 'the fruit of lips that confess his name'. This could involve the celebration of Christ as Saviour and Lord in personal or corporate acts of praise. However, the writer's meaning here cannot simply be restricted to what might be called 'church activities'. His concern in the immediate context is to exhort believers to acknowledge Christ *in the world,* in the face of opposition and suffering (vv. 12–14). In its widest sense, this sacrifice of praise will be rendered by those who confess Jesus 'outside the camp', in various forms of public testimony or evangelism. The offering up of praise to God is certainly not just a matter of singing hymns or giving thanks in a congregational context, though these activities can be a stimulus to effective proclamation elsewhere (cf. Eph. 5:18–20; Col. 3:16–17).

The heavenly locus of new covenant worship

Like Hebrews, the Revelation of John focuses on the realm where Jesus the crucified Messiah reigns in glory. The whole of life is to be lived in relation to the new Jerusalem and the victory of 'the Lamb who was slain' (5:12). Visions of heaven portray the offering of adoration and praise to God and the Lamb, and the language of worship pervades the whole document. Most significantly, the Greek worship term *proskynein* is used twenty-four times, in ways that indicate the centrality of this theme to the author's message. In most passages the word describes some form of homage to the living and true God by heavenly beings or by those redeemed from earth (Rev. 4:10; 5:14; 7:11; 11:1, 16; 14:7; 15:4; 19:4, 10; 22:9). Such homage is offered by gesture and by words of acclamation and praise.

However, despite this interest in the worship of the heavenly host, John's apocalypse also concentrates on the earthly scene. Various forms of idolatry are portrayed (9:20; 13:4, 8, 12), together with prophecies of the aweful judgment coming upon those who bow to false gods and refuse to acknowledge the living and true God. John effectively divides humanity into two categories, the worshippers of the dragon and the beast, and the worshippers of God and the *Lamb (e.g. 14:1–11). The vision of the new creation (21:9 – 22:5) portrays the future of the faithful in terms of a city where God himself dwells (21:22) and where his servants serve him unceasingly (22:3; Gk. *latreuein*, cf. 7:15). This fulfils the ideal of the OT, which was only partially realized for Israel in the prescriptions of the Mosaic law. Meanwhile, faithful service to God as 'a kingdom and priests' on earth is commanded (1:4–6; 2:1 – 3:22; 14:12; cf. Exod. 19:6; 1 Pet. 2:5, 9).

More than any other NT book, Revelation stresses the importance of praise and acclamation as a means of honouring God and encouraging his people to trust and obey him. The pattern of the heavenly assembly suggests that singing the praises of God and the Lamb is a way of affirming fundamental gospel truths and of acknowledging God's powerful but gracious rule over nature and history. Together with teaching and various forms of exhortation, it can strengthen Christians to maintain their confidence in God and in the outworking of his purposes in a world devoted to idolatry and every kind of God-rejecting activity. Testifying to the goodness and power of God in the congregation of his people can be a means of encouraging faithful testimony before unbelievers in everyday life.

Bibliography

R. T. Beckwith and M. J. Selman (eds.), *Sacrifice in the Bible* (Carlisle and Grand Rapids, 1995); D. A. Carson (ed.), *Worship: Adoration and Action* (Carlisle and Grand Rapids, 1993); R. P. Martin, *The Worship of God: Some Theological, Pastoral and Practical Reflections* (Grand Rapids, 1982); C. F. D. Moule, *Worship in the New Testament* (Bramcote, [2]1977–78); D. G. Peterson, *Engaging with God: A Biblical Theology of Worship* (Leicester and Grand Rapids, 1992).

D. G. PETERSON

WRATH, see ANGER
ZEAL, see ASSURANCE
ZECHARIAH, see Part 2
ZEPHANIAH, see Part 2
ZION, see JERUSALEM

Index of Articles